NIV
Compact Nave's Topical Bible

John R. Kohlenberger III

ZondervanPublishingHouse
Academic and Professional Books
Grand Rapids, Michigan

A Division of HarperCollins*Publishers*

The NIV Compact Nave's Topical Bible
Copyright © 1993 by John R. Kohlenberger III

Requests for information should be addressed to:
Zondervan Publishing House
Grand Rapids, Michigan 49530

ISBN 0-310-22869-7 (softcover)

NIV™ IS A REGISTERED TRADEMARK OF THE INTERNATIONAL BIBLE SOCIETY.

All Scripture quotations, unless otherwise indicated, are taken from the Holy Bible, New International Version (North American Edition). Copyright © 1973, 1978, 1984 by International Bible Society. Used by permission of Zondervan Bible Publishers.

"NIV" and "New International Version" are registered in the United States Patent and Trademark Office by the International Bible Society.

Printed in the United States of America

99 00 01 02 03 04 /DC/ 7 6 5 4

Contents

Acknowledgments iv

Introduction v

Abbreviations and Symbols xii

The NIV Compact Nave's Topical Bible . . . . 1 — 521

Index of Goodrick/Kohlenberger to Strong's Numbers   523 — 561

Acknowledgments

Special thanks are due to Paul Hillman, former President of Zondervan Publishing House, who first gave me the commission to revise the classic *Nave's Topical Bible*. Thanks to Stan Gundry, Vice President and Publisher/Academic Books and Electronic Publishing and Bruce Ryskamp, Corporate Vice President/Book, Bible, and Electronic Group Executive, for their patience and support over the years.

Imprint Editor Ed van der Maas has been involved in all aspects of design and production and has been a special friend to me and my family. Verlyn D. Verbrugge provided many valuable suggestions that helped improve the full-sized edition of *The NIV Nave's Topical Bible*. Rachel Berens offered much-needed editorial assistance. Cathy Morton did a fine job of proofreading.

Special thanks to Doris Rikkers, Bible Editor of Zondervan Bible Publishers, for allowing us to use the excellent book outlines and several essays from the outstanding *NIV Study Bible*.

David J. Jirak, Associate Editor of this project, spent many years and endless hours of data input, evaluation, and editing. This book would not be the same without him. Kathy Jirak and Brian Wheeler also had a part in the data input.

James A. Swanson provided the definitions of proper names, checked KJV-specific headings against NIV vocabulary, and supplemented many articles.

Roger Green and Don Wills of Telios Systems in Portland, Oregon developed special programming to create a printout that assisted David J. Jirak in evaluating Nave's biblical citations against the NIV.

Mike Petersen and the rest of the staff of Multnomah Graphics permitted me 24-hour access to their equipment. Art director Bruce DeRoos offered useful insights on the page design.

Special thanks to my wife, Carolyn, and to my children, Sarah and Joshua, for their encouragement and their patience.

Through the talents of these individuals, *The NIV Compact Nave's Topical Bible* is a far better book than the general editor alone could have made it. However, the editor does accept full responsiblity for any shortcomings or errors found in the book.

Introduction

What is a Topical Bible?

The NIV Compact Nave's Topical Bible combines the most useful features of a Bible Handbook, a Bible Dictionary, and a Bible Concordance. Like a Bible Handbook, this Topical Bible introduces the reader to each book of the Bible and surveys its contents. Like a Bible Dictionary, this Topical Bible is an alphabetically organized presentation of biblical and extrabiblical information on Bible people, places, events, and objects. Like a Concordance, this Topical Bible indexes the Scriptures with thousands of biblical references, but without contexts.

The NIV Nave's Topical Bible is also much more than these other general reference works. A Bible Handbook offers only selected comments on the biblical text; this Topical Bible offers a thorough survey of most biblical topics, people, places, and events. A Bible Dictionary cites a handful of biblical texts to document its articles; this Topical Bible cites more than 100,000 verses. A Bible Concordance indexes only exact forms of words; this Topical Bible indexes words, phrases, synonymns and examples.

A Concise History of *Nave's Topical Bible*

Orville James Nave (1841-1917) was an army chaplain who assembled the original *Nave's Topical Bible* while stationed at Fort McPherson in Georgia. With the assistance of his wife Anna Semans Nave, over a fourteen-year period Nave attempted to "classify everything found in the Scriptures." Nave covered thousands more topics than the earlier analyses of Matthew Talbot and Roswell D. Hitchcock. In fact, he believed it to be an "approximately exhaustive" digest of the King James Version.

Nave's Topical Bible was first published in 1896. Nave saw it through seven editions over the next twenty years, including its reorganization into *Nave's Topical Study Bible* in 1907. It inspired several similar works. Notable among these were Thomas David Williams *A Textual Concordance of the Holy Scriptures* (1908) based on the Douay-Rheims translation and from a Catholic perspective. Harold E. Monser and twelve contributors created *The Cross-Reference Bible* to the American Standard Version (1910) and its spin-off, *Cross Reference Dictionary of Bible References* (1914), sometimes reprinted as *Topical Index and Digest of the Bible*. Walter A.

Elwell revised *Hitchcock's New and Complete Analysis of the Holy Bible* of 1873, which was released as the *Topical Analysis of the Bible* using the New International Version (Baker, 1991).

Moody Press also issued a modestly revised and abridged edition in 1974, edited by S. Maxwell Coder. Their *Nave's Compact Topical Bible* (n.d.) presents 1,000 key topics in 255 pages. Tyndale House published *Nave's Topical Living Bible* in 1982.

Seventy-three years after the publication of the original, Zondervan commissioned an update and expansion of the best-selling *Nave's*. Edward Viening added new articles and supplemented many of the existing articles to create the *Zondervan Topical Bible* in 1969. Currently reprinted as *Nave's Topical Bible: Revised and Enlarged*, this was the most thorough revision of *Nave's* to appear until *The NIV Nave's Topical Bible* was issued in 1992.

In 1972 Zondervan released *The New Compact Topical Bible*, now *The Nave's Compact Topical Bible*, another revised and restructured edition of *Nave's*. Editor Gary Wharton added more than one hundred new articles and classified many of the descriptive texts Nave simply listed under the heading "Unclassified Scriptures." *The Nave's Compact* is not compact because it abridges Nave's content, but because it does not print out the text of the Scriptures it indexes.

A Concise History of
The NIV Nave's Topical Bibles

The continuing popularity of *Nave's* and the growing acceptance of the New International Version suggested a marriage of the two standards. General editor John R. Kohlenberger III designed the project and assigned most of the early responsibilites to associate editor David J. Jirak. David and his wife Kathy created an electronic database from *The Nave's Compact Topical Bible*. David then compared these data to Zondervan's enlarged edition of *Nave's* to note which verses had been printed out in full. Roger Green of Telios Systems created a computer program to generate a massive printout to assist David in evaluating every verse in *Nave's* against the NIV to be certain the translation appropriately represented each topic.

After this database had been settled, John evaluated each entry heading against the vocabulary of the NIV to create new headings, new cross-references, and new articles. John also created exhaustive lists indexing NIV vocabulary to the original Hebrew, Aramaic, and Greek, based on the materials he and Edward W. Goodrick developed for the *NIV Exhaustive Concordance*. James A. Swanson offered definitions for proper names, additional KJV to NIV referencing, and supplemented many articles. The restructured and redesigned materials were then proofed by Verlyn D. Verbrugge, Laura Weller, and David Jirak.

As a result, *The NIV Nave's Topical Bible* preserves the essence of the time-tested original, while adding more than 500 headings, 2000 subtopics, 1300 cross-references, and exhaustive referencing to the NIV and to the original biblical languages. The articles continue to represent Nave's conservative Christianity, while attempting to acknowledge a variety of interpretive perspectives on controversial subjects. New articles, such as Abuse, Ecology, and Homosexual, and revised articles, such as Abortion, Discipleship, Wine, and Women help make *The NIV Nave's Topical Bible* the new standard for the current generation.

The NIV Compact Nave's Topical Bible is a compact edition of *The NIV Nave's Topical Bible* on the model of the original *Nave's Compact Topical Bible*. Every article appears in full (with some slight modifications), Only the text of the NIV and "NIV+" cross-references have been eliminated from the full-sized edition.

How to Use *The NIV Compact Nave's Topical Bible*

The NIV Compact Nave's Topical Bible offers quick and easy access to more than 7000 biblical topics. Simply look up any subject, person, place, or book of the Bible in alphabetical order. There you will find a concise summary of biblical insights, well documented with Scripture references.

Entry Headings

The following shows the three elements that can appear in an entry heading:

ABEDNEGO [6284, 10524] (*servant of Nego* or *Nebo*).

Proper and place names are indexed according to NIV spelling. In brackets are the Goodrick-Kohlenberger (G/K) numbers of the *NIV Exhaustive Concordance*. These indicate every Hebrew, Aramaic, and Greek word translated by the entry word. If the list is preceded by an asterisk (*), it only represents the most frequent words; otherwise the list is exhaustive. (See below, pages x-xi.) The definition of the name follows in parentheses and italics. When sources disagree on the definitions, these differences are listed and documented:

ASA [654, 809] (possibly *healer* BDB; *myrtle* KB).

The abbreviations are explained in the tables following the introduction on page xii.

Sometimes an entry heading contains only a cross-reference to another article. This is often the case of KJV terms, such as:

ABEZ *See Ebez.*

WINEBIBBER *See Drunkard; Drunkenness; Wine.*

The Entry Proper

An entry can be as simple as:

JAGUR [3327]. A town of Judah (Jos 15:21).

or as complex as JESUS THE CHRIST, which fills 13 pages with 454 paragraphs of information including 84 primary subdivisions, 20 secondary subdivisions, 43 cross-references to 68 topics, and more than 4,100 biblical references.

Subdivisions

Short articles appear as single paragraphs. Longer articles are usually subdivided to one or two levels.

Proper names that refer to more than one person or place are subdivided by numbered paragraphs. For example, there are three listings for Abel; thirty-one for Zechariah. More than 3000 proper name subdivisions are identified.

Primary subdivisions are set flush left in bold print. Secondary subdivisions are indented, italicized, and followed by a dash:

JESUS THE CHRIST

. . .

Death of:
Purpose of His Death—

Biblical References

More than 100,000 biblical references are indexed in the entries, but no biblical text is printed out. This is the main difference between the full-sized and compact editions of the *NIV Nave's Topical Bibles*.

The ampersand symbol (&) and "w" (with) are used to indicate closely related texts, often New Testament citations of the Old and parallel passages:

> Jesus as Head of the Church (Ps 118:22-23 w Mt 21:42-43 & Mk 12:10)

The biblical citations index and illustrate the information of the entries. *The NIV Compact Nave's* is an index to the Bible, not a substitute for the Bible. Always look up each reference in the Bible itself. Read the whole context in order to see how the text functions in the NIV or in any other translation. The easiest way to misinterpret the Bible is to study its texts out of their contexts. The editors have taken great care to select only relevant texts, but we strongly encourage users not only to double-check our work, but to double-check your own insights.

Cross-References

More than 3,700 cross-references to 6,100 entries are set in italics:

> *See Jesus the Christ, Second Coming; Millennium.*

Entry headings are separated by semicolons; entry subdivisions follow commas.

How to Use *The NIV Compact Nave's Topical Bible* With *The NIV Exhaustive Concordance*

The NIV Compact Nave's Topical Bible and the *NIV Exhaustive Concordance* are made for each other. The *Concordance* provides an exhaustive index of every word in the NIV, listed in biblical order from Genesis to Revelation, and an exhaustive index of the relationship of the NIV to the original biblical languages. The *NIV Compact Nave's* provides a biblical index that is organized by subjects, that is not limited to NIV vocabulary, and is arranged by thematic development rather than by biblical order. Together these works provide endless access to the riches of God's Word.

Exhaustive NIV Word Studies _____

The *Concordance* indexes every reference to every NIV word. The *NIV Compact Nave's,* while not exhaustive in its treatment of NIV vocabulary, does list every person and place in the NIV.

When you want to study any NIV word in full, begin with the *Concordance.* Look up the word exactly as it is spelled in the NIV. The *Concordance* also gives you a complete listing of related NIV words you can work through as well. Then check the *NIV Compact Nave's* for insights from its analysis and cross-references.

Thorough Synonym Studies: Suggested by the NIV Compact Nave's _____

While working through any entry in the *NIV Compact Nave's*, you will notice that the verses cited regularly contain key words that are synonymns of the entry heading. This is one major advantage of the Topical Bible over the Concordance. For example, the entry on Truth contains the synonymns "faithful," "faithfulness," "just," "love," and "right." The *Concordance* indexes 224 verses on "truth" and another 142 on its related words. When you add the five synonymns identified in the *NIV Nave's*, you get another 1,546 references—and that does not even count their related words!

Thorough Synonym Studies:
Suggested by the Original Languages

The NIV is an English translation of the original biblical languages: Hebrew, Aramaic, and Greek. The *NIV Exhaustive Concordance* identifies the relationship of the NIV to the original languages by means of a numbering system that is used in the *Concordance* and in the *NIV Compact Nave's Topical Bible*. Hebrew words have a one- to four-digit number in normal type. Aramaic words have a five-digit number. Greek word numbers are in italics.

The biblical language indexes of the *Concordance* offer another source of words for synonym study. There are eighteen G/K numbers listed in the *NIV Nave's* entry on Love. (The asterisk indicates this is a selective list of only the most frequent words in the original languages.) If you looked up the first italicized number (*26*) in the Greek-English Index on page 1673 of the *Concordance*, you would find that every NIV word in the list is related to "love," except for "longed for." However, the first Hebrew word (170), indexed on page 1362 of the *Concordance*, lists the synonyms "adore," "allies," "ally," "attracted to," "desires," "friend," "friends," "like," "liked," and "value" in addition to related words to "love." Again, all these synonyms can be studied with the *Concordance* and many will appear in the *NIV Compact Nave's*.

Thorough Study of the Original Languages

The *NIV Compact Nave's* and the *Concordance* are based on the English of the NIV and are indexed to the original biblical languages. You may wish at times to study a word or topic as indexed in the original languages and not only in the NIV.

The G/K numbers identify the relationship of the NIV to the original lanuages. The *Concordance* offers an index to the majority of occurrences of Hebrew, Aramaic, and Greek words by combining the information of its indexes and the main concordance.

Using the example of "Love" from the previous section, let's say you wanted to study through the words represented by the eighteen numbers listed in the *NIV Nave's*:

1. First you must locate the number in its proper index: Hebrew, Aramaic, or Greek.

2. Next make a list of all unique NIV words in the number's index. For example, Greek word *26* has eight lines in its index, but only five unique words. (The word "love" appears in the phrases "truly love" and "showed love.")

3. Look up each of these unique NIV spellings in the main concordance. At the end of each context line is a G/K number or an abbreviation. By locating all of the G/K numbers that match the number you are working with, you can make a thorough word study of any Hebrew, Aramaic, or Greek term—and study it in an English translation.

We have used the word "thorough" instead of "exhaustive" because the NIV does not always translate every word of the original languages in a way you can locate with the *NIV Exhaustive Concordance*. For example, the index to Hebrew word 170 notes that the word is "untranslated" two times. The index to Greek word *27* notes that the NIV uses the pronoun "it" to translate *agape* in one verse. Because "it" is not indexed with contexts in the *Concordance*, you cannot locate that one occurrence. Exhaustive NIV-based concordances to the Greek New Testament and the Hebrew-Aramaic Old Testament are scheduled for release in 1993 and 1995 respectively. With these concordances you will be able to locate those rare occurrences of untranslated or unindexed words for exhaustive study.

A 37-page Index of G/K to Strong's Numbers (525-561) shows the relationship of this new numbering system to the old system developed by James A. Strong, which is still used in many reference books.

Selected Resources for Additional Studies

The NIV Compact Nave's Topical Bible combines the best features of the most essential biblical reference books. But as useful as that combination is, it is not exhaustive. The following list suggests dozens of additional tools for further research. All works represent an evangelical approach to the Bible, unless otherwise noted.

Study Bibles

The most essential companion to *The NIV Compact Nave's Topical Bible* is a full-text Study Bible. *The NIV Study Bible* (Zondervan, 1985) is the finest academic evangelical Study Bible yet produced. For additional topical insights, the classic *Thompson Chain-Reference Bible* (Kirkbride, Revised NIV edition 1991) and the *NIV Topical Study Bible* (Zondervan, 1989) are most useful. The latter work, edited by Verlyn D. Verbrugge, is especially useful in identifying topics that are key to each book of the Bible and in noting prophecies and their fulfillments.

Bible Dictionaries and Encyclopedias

Bible dictionaries and encyclopedias provide biblical and historical information on people, places, customs, events, objects, and books of the Bible. On a basic level *The NIV Compact Bible Dictionary* (Zondervan, 1989) and *Young's Compact Dictionary of the Bible* (Tyndale, 1989) stand out. On an intermediate level, *The New International Dictionary of the Bible* (Zondervan, 1987) and *The New Unger's Bible Dictionary* (Moody, 1988) are standards. The five-volume *Zondervan Pictorial Encyclopedia of the Bible* (Zondervan, 1976) is accessible to all readers while the four-volume *International Standard Bible Encyclopedia* (Eerdmans, 1979-88) is written on a more technical level.

Bible Commentaries

Commentaries provide insights on the biblical text. They offer additional information on interpretation, history and culture, biblical languages, and even spiritual and devotional insights. A companion to this volume, *The NIV Compact Bible Commentary* is scheduled for release in 1994. Among the best one-volume commentaries on the whole Bible is the *International Bible Commentary* (Zondervan, 1986). The twelve-volume *Expositor's Bible Commentary* (Zondervan, 1976-92) is among the best series for the general reader. The technical and as yet incomplete *Word Biblical Commentary* (Word, 1982-) is highly regarded for the serious researcher. Thousands of additional titles and series are recommended in Douglas Stuart's *A Guide to Selecting and Using Bible Commentaries* (Word, 1990), Tremper Longman's *Old Testament Commentary Survey* (Baker, 1991), and D. A. Carson's *New Testament Commentary Survey* (Fourth edition, Baker, 1993).

Bible History and Archaeology

In addition to dictionaries and commentaries, several kinds of reference works offer additional information on Bible backgrounds. *Chronological and Background Charts of the Old Testament* (Zondervan, 1978) and *Chronological and Background Charts of the New Testament* (Zondervan, 1981) offer much historical information in chart form. *A Survey of Israel's History* (Zondervan, Revised 1986) and *New Testament History* (Doubleday, 1969) are standard textbooks. *The New International Dictionary of Biblical Archaeology* (Zondervan, 1983) is a specialized Bible dictionary of archaeological insights on biblical people, places, and events.

Theology and Ethics

The implications of biblical texts for theology and ethics are often covered in Bible dictionaries and commentaries. More thorough coverage is found in theological textbooks, such as Ericksen's *Christian Theology* (Baker, 1985). The *Evangelical Dictionary of Theology* (Baker, 1984) is one of the finest theological dictionaries, offering concise overviews and bibliographies on thousands of theological and ethical topics. The *Topical Analysis of the Bible* (Baker, 1991) offers 35,000 biblical citations to illustrate twenty-seven major theological topics, divided into over 6000 subdivisions. *The Dictionary of the Ecumenical Movement* discusses many theological and ethical issues from a historical and modern ecumenical perspective. The *Dictionary of Charismatic and Pentecostal Movements* (Zondervan, 1988) offers a unique perspective on biography and theology.

Abbreviations and Symbols

Books of the Bible

1Ch	1 Chronicles
1Co	1 Corinthians
1Jn	1 John
1Ki	1 Kings
1Pe	1 Peter
1Sa	1 Samuel
1Th	1 Thessalonians
1Ti	1 Timothy
2Ch	2 Chronicles
2Co	2 Corinthians
2Jn	2 John
2Ki	2 Kings
2Pe	2 Peter
2Sa	2 Samuel
2Th	2 Thessalonians
2Ti	2 Timothy
3Jn	3 John
Ac	Acts
Am	Amos
Col	Colossians
Da	Daniel
Dt	Deuteronomy
Ecc	Ecclesiastes
Eph	Ephesians
Est	Esther
Ex	Exodus
Eze	Ezekiel
Ezr	Ezra
Gal	Galatians
Ge	Genesis
Hab	Habakkuk
Hag	Haggai
Heb	Hebrews
Hos	Hosea
Isa	Isaiah
Jas	James
Jdg	Judges
Jer	Jeremiah
Jn	John
Jnh	Jonah
Job	Job
Joel	Joel
Jos	Joshua
Jude	Jude
La	Lamentations
Lev	Leviticus
Lk	Luke
Mal	Malachi
Mic	Micah
Mk	Mark
Mt	Matthew
Na	Nahum
Ne	Nehemiah
Nu	Numbers
Ob	Obadiah
Phm	Philemon
Php	Philippians
Pr	Proverbs
Ps	Psalms
Rev	Revelation
Ro	Romans
Ru	Ruth
SS	Song of Songs
Tit	Titus
Zec	Zechariah
Zep	Zephaniah

Books of the Apocrypha

1Es	1 Esdras
1Mc	1 Maccabees
2Es	2 Esdras
2Mc	2 Maccabees
3Mc	3 Maccabees
4Mc	4 Maccabees
Bar	Baruch
Bel	Bel and the Dragon
Sir	Sirach
Tob	Tobit
Wis	Wisdom

Other

&	"and"; read this biblical text with the preceding
Antiq	Josephus, *Antiquities of the Jews*.
BDB	Brown, Driver and Briggs *Hebrew and English Lexicon* (Oxford, 1907).
ISBE	*International Standard Bible Encyclopedia* (Eerdmans, 1979-88).
KB	Koehler and Baumgartner *Lexicon in Veteris Testamenti Libros* (Eerdmans, 1951-53).
JB	Jerusalem Bible
KJV	King James Version
NIV	New International Version
NRSV	New Revised Standard Version
w	"with"; read this biblical text with the preceding
ZPBE	*Zondervan Pictorial Bible Encyclopedia* (Zondervan, 1976).

The NIV
Compact Nave's
Topical Bible

AARON [195, 2].

Personal History:

Lineage of: a son of Amram of the Kohathites, and brother of Moses and Miriam (Ex 6:16-20; Nu 26:59-60; Jos 21:4, 10; 1Ch 6:2-3). His marriage to Elisheba, daughter of Amminadab (Ex 6:23). The children of: Nadab, Abihu, Eleazar and Ithamar (Ex 6:23, 25; 1Ch 6:3-4; 24:1-2). Descendants of (1Ch 6:3-15, 50-53; 24).

Character of (Ps 106:16).

As a Leader Ordained by God:

Meets Moses in the wilderness and is made spokesman for Moses (Ex 4:14-16, 27-31; 7:1-2, 6-7). Commissioned as a deliverer of Israel (Ex 6:13, 26-27; Jos 24:5; 1Sa 12:8; Ps 77:20; 105:26; Mic 6:4). Inspiration of (Ex 12:1; Lev 10:8; 11:1; 13:1; 15:1; Nu 2:1; 4:1, 17; 18:1; 19:1; 20:12). Summoned to Sinai with Nadab, Abihu, and seventy elders (Ex 19:24; 24:1, 9-10).

Events in the Life of:

Murmured against by the people (Ex 5:20-21; 16:2-12; Nu 14:2-5, 10; 16:3-11, 41; 20:2; Ps 106:16). Places pot of manna in the ark (Ex 16:34). With Hur supports the hands of Moses during battle (Ex 17:10-13). Judges Israel in the absence of Moses (Ex 24:13-14). Makes the golden calf (Ex 32; Dt 9:7-21; Ac 7:40-41).

His benedictions upon the people (Lev 9:22; Nu 6:23-26). Forbidden to mourn the death of his sons Nadab and Abihu (Lev 10:6, 19).

Gossips with Miriam about Moses because of jealousy (Nu 12:1). Intercedes for Miriam (Nu 12:11-12). Stops the plague started by Korah's rebellion, by priestly intercession (Nu 16:46-48). Rod of buds (Nu 17; Heb 9:4), preserved in the ark of the covenant (Nu 17; Heb 9:4).

He and Moses dishonor God in the presence of the Israelites when the rock is struck (Nu 20:12, 23-29). Moses and Aaron are not allowed to enter the land of Canaan because of this lack of faith at the waters of Meribah Kadesh in the Desert of Zin (Dt 32:51-52).

Dies at 123 years of age on Mt. Hor (Nu 33:38-39). Death and burial of (Nu 20:27-28; Dt 10:6; 32:50).

As a Priest:

Priesthood of (Ex 28:1; 29:9; Nu 17; 18:1; Ps 99:6; Heb 5:4). Consecration of, to the priesthood (Ex 28; 29; Lev 8). Enters the priestly office (Lev 9).

Descendants of, ordained priests forever (Ex 28:40-43; 29:9; Nu 3:3; 18:1; 1Ch 23:13; 2Ch 26:18). See *Priest, High Priest.*

AARONITES Descendants of Aaron who were priests, numbering 3700 fighting men under Jehoiada who joined David at Hebron (1Ch 12:27). Their leader was Zadok (1Ch 27:17).

AB The Babylonian name of the fifth month in sacred sequence, month eleven in civil sequence. In the Bible it is referred to only as "the fifth month" (Nu 33:38; Ezr 7:8; Jer 1:3). The dry season (July-August); ripening season for grapes, figs, and olives. See *Month, 5*.

ABADDON [3] (*destruction*). A Hebrew word for the underworld, meaning the place of destruction (Job 31:12, ftn), and in the OT is a synonym of death (Hell) and Sheol. The abode of the dead (Job 26:6, ftn; Pr 15:11, ftn; 27:20, ftn).

The name of the angel of the bottomless pit (Rev 9:11, ftn), whose Greek name is Apollyon which means destroyer.

ABAGTHA [5]. One of seven eunuchs that served King Xerxes (Est 1:10).

ABANA [76]. A river of Damascus mentioned by the leprous Naaman (2Ki 5:12).

ABARIM [6305] (*geographic regions beyond*). Either a region E of the Jordan and SE of the Dead Sea, or a mountain range NW of Moab (Nu 27:12; 33:47-48; Dt 32:49; Jer 22:20). See *Nebo, 2*.

ABBA [5]. An Aramaic word meaning *father*, which is a customary title of God in prayer. It is found in the Babylonian Talmud where it is used, of a child to his father, and also as a type of address to rabbis. It is equivalent to *papa*. This term conveys a sense of warm intimacy and also respect for the father. The Jews found it too presumptuous and nearly blasphemous; they would therefore never address God in this manner.

Jesus called God "Father" and gave that same right to his disciples (Mt 6:5-15). Paul sees this as symbolic of the Christian's adoption as a child of God and of possession of the Spirit (Mk 14:36; Ro 8:15; Gal 4:6).

ABDA [6272] (*servant of Yahweh*).
1. Father of Adoniram (1Ki 4:6).
2. A Levite of the family of Jeduthun, the son of Shammua (Ne 11:17).

ABDEEL [6274] (*servant of God [El]*). Father of Shelemiah, who was appointed by Jehoiakim, the king of Judah, "to arrest Baruch the scribe and Jeremiah the prophet" (Jer 36:26).

ABDI [6279] (*servant of Yahweh* or *my servant*).
1. A Levite in the reign of Hezekiah, the father of Kishi and grandfather of Ethan (1Ch 6:44; 2Ch 29:12).
2. A son of Elam (Ezr 10:26).

ABDIEL [6280] (*servant of God [El]*). A Gadite chief, the father of Ahi (1Ch 5:15).

ABDON [6277, 6278] (*servant*).

1. A Levitical city given to the tribe of Asher (Jos 19:28, ftn; 21:30; 1Ch 6:74).

2. A son of Hillel, from Pirathon in Ephraim, the hill country of the Amalekites; a judge of Israel for eight years (Jdg 12:13-15).

3. A son of Shashak (1Ch 8:23, 25, 28).

4. Firstborn son of Jeiel of Gibeon (1Ch 8:30; 9:35-36).

5. The son of Micah, an official of King Josiah (2Ch 34:20). Also called Acbor, son of Micaiah (2Ki 22:12).

ABEDNEGO [6284, 10524] (*servant of Nego* or *Nebo*). His Hebrew name was Azariah. He was taken as a captive to Babylon with Daniel, Hananiah, and Mishael, where each was given a Babylonian name (Da 1:6-20; 2:17, 49; 3:12-30). Azariah was given the Akkadian name Abednego, which was the Babylonian god of wisdom, connected with the planet Mercury.

Shadrach, Meshach, and Abednego were chosen to learn the language and the ways of the Chaldeans (Babylonians) so that they could enter the king's service (Da 1:3-5, 17-20). These three were eventually thrown into the king's furnace because they refused to bow down and worship Nebuchadnezzar's golden image (Da 3:1, 4-6, 8-30).

ABEL [64, 2040, 6] (proper name *morning mist*; place name *meadow* or *stream*).

1. The second son of Adam and Eve (Ge 4:1-2). The history of (Ge 4:1-15, 25). NT references to the death of (Mt 23:35; Lk 11:51; Heb 11:4; 12:24; 1Jn 3:12).

2. A city in Naphtali (2Sa 20:14, ftn; 20:18).

3. An element of certain place names. *See seven place names following.*

ABEL, GREAT STONE OF. KJV "the great *stone of* Abel" (1Sa 6:18) is "the large rock" in the NIV text; "Greater Abel" in the note.

ABEL BETH MAACAH [68] (*meadow of the house of Maacah [oppression]*). Sheba son of Bicri fled there from King David (2Sa 20:14-22). A town in Naphtali (2Sa 20:15). Ben-Hadad later seized it (1Ki 15:20). Tiglath-Pileser, king of Assyria captured it (2Ki 15:29).

ABEL-CHERAMIM *See Abel Keramim.*

ABEL KERAMIM [70] (*meadow of vineyards*). A place in Ammon, east of the Jordan, to which Jephthah pursued the Ammonites (Jdg 11:33).

ABEL MAIM [72] (*meadow of waters*). A city conquered by Ben-Hadad (2Ch 16:4). Also known as Abel Beth Maacah (2Ch 16:4, ftn).

ABEL MEHOLAH [71] (*meadow of the round dance*). A town probably in the Jordan Valley, named in conjunction with the retreat of the Midianites from Gideon (Jdg 7:22; 1Ki 4:12). Probably Elisha's birthplace (1Ki 19:16).

ABEL MIZRAIM [73] (*meadow of Egypt*, or *mourning of Egypt*). The place was the threshing floor of Atad where the Israelites and all Pharaoh's officials mourned for Jacob (Ge 50:11).

ABEL SHITTIM [69] (*meadow of the acacia trees*). A place where the Israelites made their final camp before crossing the Jordan into Canaan (Nu 33:49). *See Shittim.*

ABETTING *See Complicity.*

ABEZ *See Ebez.*

ABI *See Abijah, 7.*

ABIA, ABIAH *See Abijah, 1 & 3.*

ABI-ALBON [50] (*[my] father is Albon*). Also called Abiel (1Ch 11:32). *See Abiel.* One of David's mighty men (2Sa 23:31).

ABIASAPH [25] (*[my] father has gathered*). A Levite, and the last son of Korah (Ex 6:24). He is also identified as Ebiasaph (1Ch 6:23, 37; 9:19). *See Ebiasaph.*

ABIATHAR [59, 8] (*[my] father gives abundance* or *the father is preeminent*).

1. High priest under David.

He is the son of Ahimelech and, like his father, a high priest at Nob; he alone escaped from the massacre of his family and all the priests at Nob by Saul to join with David at Keilah, bringing an ephod with him (1Sa 22:6-23). Consults the ephod for David (1Sa 23:9; 30:7). David did not depose Zadok whom Saul had appointed to the priesthood; instead, the two constituted a double high priesthood (2Sa 15:35; 20:25; 1Ki 4:4; 1Ch 15:11). Abiathar was loyal to David when Absalom rebelled; leaves Jerusalem with the ark of the covenant, but is directed by David to return with the ark (2Sa 15:24-29). Helps David by sending his son Jonathan from Jerusalem to David with secret information concerning the counsel of Ahithophel (2Sa 15:35-36; 17:15-22; 1Ki 2:26).

Later he supports Adonijah's attempt to succeed David to the royal throne at David's death (1Ki 1:7). Because of this he is forced out of office by Solomon and is banished to Anathoth (1Ki 2:26-27). With this, the priestly line was confined to Zadok, an Aaronite, and the rule of Eli's house ended in fulfillment of prophecy (1Sa 2:31-35).

The reference to "Ahimelech son of Abiathar" as priest with Zadok is confusing because in other places "Abiathar son of Ahimelech" is known as the high priest. This problem is sometimes solved by saying that the names were transposed by a copyist error; many find this to be an improbable solution since the reference to Ahimelech, the son of Abiathar, as priest is too clear to make a mistake (2Sa 8:17; 1Ch 18:16; 24:3, 6, 31). One of the best explanations is that as the aged Abiathar came near to the end of David's reign, and his life, the responsibilities of office became heavy enough for him to shift many of those duties over to his oldest son Ahimelech; Ahimelech therefore became the functioning high priest.

When Jesus refers to "Abiathar as high priest" at Nob (instead of his father Ahimelech), it is perhaps best understood as Jesus referring to the "passage concerning Abiathar as high priest," by analogy with the way he refers to the burning bush (Mk 12:26).

2. See Ahimelech, 3.

ABIB [26] (*heads or spikes of grain*). Hebrew name of the first month in sacred sequence, month seven in civil sequence (Ex 12:2). The name was changed to Nisan after the Exile (Ne 2:1; Est 3:7). The season of later rains (March-April); beginning of the barley and flax harvest.

The Passover and the Feast of Unleavened Bread were instituted, and the Israelites departed from Egypt in (Ex 13:4; 23:15; 34:18; Dt 16:1). It was to become a memorial month to the deliverance of the Israelites from Egypt (Ex 12, w 13:3-4; Dt 16:1-8, 16).

The order of events during the celebration month:

1. On the tenth day the Passover lamb was chosen.

2. On the fourteenth day the lamb was slain and eaten.

3. On the fifteenth day they began harvesting by gathering sheaves of the barley firstfruits.

4. On the sixteenth day they offered the sheaves. The tabernacle, the Tent of Meeting, was set up in (Ex 40:2, 17). The Israelites arrived at the Desert of Zin, staying at Kadesh (Nu 20:1). Canaan entered in (Jos 4:19). Jordan's overflow in (1Ch 12:15).

See Month, 1; Nisan.

ABIDA [30] (*[my] father knows*). Fourth of five sons of Midian, and the grandson of Abraham and Keturah (Ge 25:4; 1Ch 1:33).

ABIDAN [29] (*[my] father is judge*). A son of Gideoni, and a prince of the tribe of Benjamin chosen to represent his tribe in the wilderness of Sinai (Nu 1:11; 2:22; 10:24). He was present at the dedication of the tabernacle (Nu 7:60, 65).

ABIEL [24] (*[my] father is God [El]*).

1. The grandfather of Saul and Abner (1Sa 9:1; 14:51).

2. One of David's mighty men (1Ch 11:32), also called Abi-Albon (2Sa 23:31). Albon is a copyist's transference from the following verse; some mss of the LXX have Abiel here.

ABIEZER, ABIEZRITES [48, 49] (*[my] father is help*).

1. Founder of a clan of Manasseh (Jos 17:2; Jdg 6:34; 8:2). He was the second son of Ham-

molkeketh, sister of Gilead and granddaughter of Manasseh (1Ch 7:17-18).

Also called Iezer, a shortened form, the progenitor of the Iezerites (Nu 26:30). *See Iezer, Iezerites.*

2. One of David's mighty men (2Sa 23:27; 1Ch 11:28; 27:12).

ABIGAIL [28] (*[my] father rejoices* or *father [cause] of joy*).

1. The wife of Nabal of Carmel, a Calebite, and, after Nabal's death, of David (1Sa 25:3, 14-44; 27:3; 30:5; 2Sa 2:2), to whom she bore his second son, Kileab (2Sa 3:3), or Daniel (1Ch 3:1).

2. A sister of David, daughter of Nahash (Jesse), wife of Jether (Ithra, KJV) an Israelite (some Hebrew mss have Ishmaelite), and mother of Amasa, commander of David's army (2Sa 17:25; 1Ch 2:16-17).

ABIHAIL [35, 38] (*[my] father has strength/wealth* or *cause of strength/wealth*).

1. A Levite, the father of Zuriel, leader of the Merarite clans (Nu 3:35).

2. The wife of Abishur (1Ch 2:29).

3. A Gadite who lived in Gilead of Bashan and on the pasturelands of Sharon (1Ch 5:14).

4. The wife of Rehoboam, king of Judah. A daughter of Eliab, David's oldest brother (2Ch 11:18).

5. The father of Queen Esther (Est 2:15; 9:29).

ABIHU [33] (*he is [my] father*). Son of Aaron (Ex 6:23; Nu 3:2). Summoned by God to Sinai (Ex 24:1, 9). Called to the priesthood (Ex 28:1). Died because he and Nadab offered unauthorized fire to the Lord (Lev 10:1-2; Nu 26:61). Died childless (Nu 3:4).

ABIHUD [34] (*[my] father has majesty*). A son of Bela, the oldest son of Benjamin (1Ch 8:3).

ABIJAH [23, 31, 32, 7] (*[my] father is Yahweh*).

1. The second son of Samuel; appointed, with his brother Joel, as judges but did not follow in Samuel's ways. They followed after dishonest gains, bribes, and perverted justice. Because of this the Israelites demanded a king to lead them (1Sa 8:1-5; 1Ch 6:28).

2. A son of Jeroboam I of Israel (1Ki 14:1-18). He died of illness when still a child, in fulfillment of a prediction by the prophet Ahijah.

3. The wife of Judah's grandson Hezron and mother of Ashhur the father of Tekoa (1Ch 2:24).

4. The seventh son of Beker, the son of Benjamin (1Ch 7:8).

5. The second king of Judah, the son and successor of Rehoboam, and the grandson of Solomon (1Ch 3:10). Name is spelled "Abijam" in 1 Kings 14 and 15 (See NIV ftn). He reigned three years (2Ch 12:16). Prosperity tempted him to follow the evil ways of his father (1Ki 15:3). He had fourteen wives by whom he had twenty-two sons and sixteen daughters (2Ch 13:21).

He made war on Jeroboam I, the king of Israel, in an effort to recover the ten tribes of Israel (2Ch 13). Before the battle, Abijah condemns the apostasy of the Northern kingdom and at the same time affirms a theocratic institution; he shows the folly of opposing Yahweh's kingdom and concludes by urging Israel not to fight against Yahweh. Jeroboam I, with a numerically stronger army, was routed by Yahweh; the two nations were not allied as they once were, but Jeroboam never made war with Abijah again (1Ki 15:1-8; 2Ch 11:22; 13). He was succeeded by Asa his son (1Ki 15:8; 2Ch 14:1).

6. A descendant of Aaron. The ancestral head of the eighth of the 24 groups into which David had divided the priests (1Ch 24:10).

7. The daughter of Zechariah, and mother of king Hezekiah (2Ch 29:1). Also called Abi (2Ki 18:2, ftn).

8. A priest of Nehemiah's time (Ne 10:7).

9. A chief of the priests who returned from Babylon with Zerubbabel (Ne 12:4, 17). Probably the same as 8.

ABIJAM [*my father is the sea* or *father of the West*]. See Abijah, 5.

ABILENE [9] (probably *meadow*). A territory surrounding the city of Abila NW of Damascus (Lk 3:1).

ABIMAEL [42] ([*my*] *father is God [El]*). The ninth of the thirteen sons or descendants of Joktan, who was descended from Shem (Ge 10:28; 1Ch 1:22).

ABIMELECH [43] ([*my*] *father is a king* or [*my*] *father is Molech*).

1. A Philistine king of Gerar, S of Gaza in the foothills of the Judean mountains (Ge 20:1-18).

2. A second king of Gerar, probably the son of the one mentioned in 1, at whose court Isaac tried to pass off his wife Rebekah as his sister (Ge 26:1-11).

3. The son of Gideon by a concubine (Jdg 8:31; 9:1-57, w 6:32 & 7:1).

4. A Philistine king mentioned in the title of Psalm 34, who very likely is the same as Achish, king of Gath (1Sa 21:10-22:1), with whom David sought refuge when he fled from Saul.

5. A priest in the days of David. A son of Abiathar (2Sa 8:17; 1Ch 18:16). Also called Ahimelech in the LXX and in the Chronicles (1Ch 24:6).

6. See Achish; Ahimelech.

ABINADAB [44] ([*my*] *father is generous* or [*my*] *father is Nadab*).

1. A Levite, in whose house the ark of God rested twenty years (1Sa 7:1-2; 2Sa 6:3-4; 1Ch 13:7).

2. The second son of Jesse (1Sa 16:8; 17:13).

3. Son of Saul (1Sa 31:2), also called Ishvi (1Sa 14:49).

4. Father of one of Solomon's governors who supplied provisions for the king and the royal household. Also called Ben-Abinadab (1Ki 4:11).

ABINOAM [45] ([*my*] *father is graciousness*). The father of Barak (Jdg 4:6, 12; 5:1, 12).

ABIRAM [53] ([*my*] *father is exalted*).

1. One of the sons of Eliab, a Reubenite, who conspired with Dathan and with On against Moses and Aaron; the earth opened and swallowed them (Nu 16; 26:9-10; Dt 11:6; Ps 106:17).

2. The son of Hiel of Bethel; in rebuilding Jericho, Hiel's firstborn, Abiram, died, as well as his youngest son, Segub, in accordance with the word of the Lord spoken to Joshua (1Ki 16:34, w Jos 6:26).

ABISHAG [54] ([*my*] *father strays*). The Shunammite who looked after David in his old age (1Ki 1:3-4, 15). After David died, Adonijah, his oldest son, wished to marry Abishag. He tried using Bathsheba as leverage to gain Abishag as his wife. Solomon saw this as an attempt to gain the throne by controlling and possessing the king's harem which was a royal right. Solomon had him killed (1Ki 2:13-25).

ABISHAI [57, 93] ([*my*] *father is Jesse* or *father exists*). The son of Zeruiah, David's sister (1Sa 26:6; 1Ch 2:16). Became the chief of the Three, David's chief men, because he killed 300 men with his spear (2Sa 23:18-19).

Goes into Saul's camp with David; they find Saul asleep with his spear planted in the ground near his head; Abishai tells David that he will pin Saul to the ground with one thrust of the spear, which David does not allow (1Sa 26:6-8). Abishai and his brother Joab pursue Abner all day until they reach the hill of Ammah near Giah; later they murder Joab (2Sa 2:24; 3:30). Defeats the Ammonites (2Sa 10:10, 14). Defeats 18,000 Edomites in the Valley of Salt (1Ch 18:12).

Seeks the life of Shimei son of Gera (2Sa 16:5-9; 19:18-23). Leads a division of David's army against Absalom (2Sa 18:2, 5). Overthrows Sheba (2Sa 20:1-22). Saves David from being killed by Ishbi-Benob, one of the descendants of Rapha, a Philistine (2Sa 21:16-17). Obtains water from the well of Bethlehem for David (1Ch 11:15-20).

ABISHALOM [58] ([*my*] *father is peace*). A longer form of Absalom (1Ki 15:2, 10). See Absalom.

ABISHUA [55] ([*my*] *father is salvation*).

1. The son of Phinehas the priest (1Ch 6:4-5, 50; Ezr 7:5).

2. A Benjamite of the family of Bela (1Ch 8:4).

ABISHUR [56] ([*my*] *father is a wall*). A man of Judah, the son of Shammai (1Ch 2:28-29).

ABITAL [40] ([*my*] *father is [the] night dew*). The fifth wife of David and mother of Shephatiah (2Sa 3:4; 1Ch 3:3).

ABITUB [39] (*[my] father is good*). A Benjamite, son of Shaharaim and Hushim (1Ch 8:8-11).

ABIUD [10] (*[my] father has majesty*). The son of Zerubbabel (Mt 1:13).

ABLUTION *See Washings.*

ABNER [46, 79] (*[my] father is Ner [lamp]*). Son of Ner. Cousin of Saul (1Sa 14:50-51). Commander of the army of Saul (1Sa 14:50; 17:55; 26:5, 14). Abner breaks with Ish-Bosheth and the house of Saul (2Sa 3:6-11) and transfers his loyalty to the house of David (2Sa 3:12-21). Murdered by Joab; David's sorrow for (2Sa 3:22-39). Dedicated spoils of war to the tabernacle (1Ch 26:27-28).

ABOMINATION [9199, 9359, 1007]. Activities that are offensive in a moral, religious, or even a natural sense of repulsion.

God's Law Regarding:
Sexual relations: incest (Lev 18:6-18; Dt 27:20), lying with a woman in her monthly period (Lev 18:19; 20:18), adultery (Lev 18:20), homosexuality (Lev 18:22; 20:13), bestiality (Lev 18:23; 20:15-16). Idolatry (Dt 7:25-26; 27:15; 32:16-42), divination, sorcery, interpreting omens, witchcraft, casting spells, mediums or spiritists, those who consult the dead (Dt 18:9-15), offering children in sacrifice by fire to Molech (Dt 18:10, w Lev 18:21). Wearing clothes of opposite sex (Dt 22:5), the earnings of a female or a male prostitute to pay a vow (Dt 23:18), remarriage of defiled wife (Dt 24:1-4). Unjust weights and measures (Dt 25:13-16; Pr 11:1; 20:10, 23).
See Law.

Idols:
(Dt 7:25-26; 27:15; 29:17-18; Eze 7:20-21). Solomon, in his old age, followed other gods and was punished (1Ki 11:1-12), Ashtoreth of the Sidonians, Molech of the Ammonites, Chemosh of the Moabites (1Ki 11:5-8; 11:33; 2Ki 23:13).
There are no gods apart from God (Dt 6:4; 1Ch 17:20; Isa 43:10-13; 44:6-28). Conditions for blessing: Return to God and turn from worthless gods (Jer 4:1-2), or receive disaster (Eze 5:5ff).
Idols, the worship of, and related practices: (Eze 16:1-63; Hos 9:10).
See Idol; Idolatry.

Actions and Attitudes:
A false witness who pours out lies (Dt 19:15-21; Pr 6:19; 21:28), perverseness (Pr 3:32; 11:20), false pride (Pr 6:17; 16:5), murder (Pr 6:17), lying (Pr 6:17, 19; 12:22), one who devises wicked schemes (Pr 6:18), wicked imaginations, *i.e.,* the thoughts of the wicked (Pr 6:18; 15:26; 21:27), wickedness (Pr 8:7).
See Falsehood.

People, Types:
False witness (Pr 6:19; 17:15), trouble maker (Pr 6:19), mocker (Pr 24:9), dishonest (Pr 29:27).

Of Wicked:
Sacrifice (Pr 15:8; 21:27; Isa 1:13), ways (Pr 15:9), thoughts (Pr 15:26), prayer (Pr 28:9).
See Wicked.

ABOMINATION THAT CAUSES DESOLATION
[9037+9199, 1007+2247]. An utterly abhorrent abomination (Da 9:27; 11:31; 12:11). Daniel's prophecies may refer to one or all of three events: to Antiochus' desecration of the temple in 167-169 B.C. (1Mc 1:21-61), to the destruction of Jerusalem in A.D. 70 (Mt 24:15; Mk 13:14), and to the setting up of the image of the beast (Rev 13:14-15). *See Antiochus, 4.*

ABORTION Induced termination of pregnancy by killing the fetus. Clinical abortions are not addressed in the Bible. But the value of the unborn is clearly seen in texts that speak of their value and of judgments on those who kill them.
The value of the unborn (Job 31:15; Ps 139:13-16; Ecc 11:5; Isa 44:2, 24; 49:1, 5; Jer 1:4; Lk 1:41-45).
Punishment for injury to a pregnant mother and her unborn child (Ex 21:22-25). Punishment for the atrocity of ripping open pregnant women (2Ki 8:12; 15:16; Hos 13:16; Am 1:13-15).
See Miscarry.

ABRAHAM, ABRAM [90, 92, 11] (*father of many* or *exalted father*).

Events in the Life of:
Called Abram, son of Terah (Ge 11:26-27). Abram marries Sarai (Ge 11:29). Dwells in Ur of the Chaldeans, but moves. Terah, his father, took Abram and the rest of the family, intending to move to Canaan. On the way they stop and settle in Haran in NW Mesopotamia, where Terah dies (Ge 11:31; Ne 9:7; Ac 7:4). Eventually Abram, at seventy-five, sets out from Haran for the land of Canaan (Ge 12:1-6; Ac 7:4).
The divine call of (Ge 12:1-3; Jos 24:3; Ne 9:7-8; Isa 51:2; Ac 7:2-4; Heb 11:8). *See Call.*
Canaan given to (Ge 12:1, 6-7; 15:7-21; Eze 33:24). Dwells in the hills of Bethel and W of Ai (Ge 12:8). Relocates to Egypt because of a famine in Canaan (Ge 12:10-20; 26:1). Upon leaving Egypt, they travel to the Negev and on to Bethel; since there is not enough land in one place to support their large herds of sheep, Abram gives Lot his choice of land; Lot chooses the plain of Jordan, leaving Abram to live at the great trees of Mamre the Amorite at Hebron (Ge 13; 14:13; 35:27). Dwells in Gerar and Beersheba (Ge 20; 21:22-34).
Defeats Kedorlaomer king of Elam (Ge 14:5-16; Heb 7:1). Is blessed by Melchizedek (Ge 14:18-20; Heb 7:1-10). *See Melchizedek.*
God's covenant with (Ge 15; 17:1-22; Mic 7:20; Lk 1:73; Ro 4:13; 15:8; Heb 6:13-15; Gal 3:6-29; 4:22-31). *See Covenants, Major in the Old Testament.*
Ishmael born to (Ge 16:3, 7-16). Renamed

Abraham by the Lord (Ge 17:5; Ne 9:7). Circumcision of (Ge 17:10-14, 23-27). *See Circumcision.* Angels appear to (Ge 18:1-16; 22:11-12, 15; 24:7). His questions and intercession concerning the destruction of the righteous and wicked in Sodom (Ge 18:23-32). Witnesses the destruction of Sodom (Ge 19:27-29). Dwells in Gerar; deceives Abimelech concerning Sarah, his wife (Ge 20). Isaac born to Abraham when he is 100 years old according to the promise of Yahweh (Ge 21:1-5; Gal 4:22-30). Sends Hagar and Ishmael away (Ge 21:10-14; Gal 4:22-30).

Trial of his faith in the offering of Isaac (Ge 22:1-19; Heb 11:17-19; Jas 2:21). *See Faith, Instances of trial of.* Sarah, his wife, dies (Ge 23:1-2). He purchases a place for her burial and buries her in a cave (Ge 23:3-20). *See Burial; Burying Places.* Provides a wife for Isaac (Ge 24). Marries Keturah (Ge 25:1). Death (Ge 15:15; 25:8-10). In Paradise (Mt 8:11; Lk 13:28; 16:22-31).

Wealth of (Ge 13:2; 24:35). Children of (Ge 16:15; 21:2-3; 25:1-4; 1Ch 1:32-34). Inheritance of (Ge 25:5-6). *See Inheritance.* Age of at different periods (Ge 12:4; 16:16; 21:5; 25:7).

Character Qualities of:

Personal piety of and promises to (Ge 12:7-8; 13:4, 18; 18:18-33; 20:7; 21:33; 22:3-13; 26:5; Ne 9:7-8; 2Ch 20:7; Isa 41:8; Ro 4:16-18; Jas 2:23). *See Worship.* Unselfishness of (Ge 13:9; 21:25-30). Independence of, in character (Ge 14:23; 23:6-16). Faith of (Ge 15:6; Ro 4:1-22; Gal 3:6-9; Heb 11:8-19; Jas 2:21-24). *See Faith, Instances of.* A prophet (Ge 20:7). Friend of God (2Ch 20:7; Isa 41:8; Jas 2:23).

How regarded by his descendants (Mt 3:9; Lk 13:16, 28; 19:9; Jn 8:33-40, 52-59).

ABRAHAM'S SIDE
In the Lukan account of the rich man and Lazarus, Lazarus is being comforted at Abraham's side [KJV "bosom"] while the rich man is being tormented in the fires of hell (Lk 16:22-23). *See Lazarus.*

In the Talmudic language, to sit in Abraham's side is to enter Paradise (compare 4Mc 13:17). It is the place where the righteous go at the moment of death and where judgment is enacted as preliminary and perhaps probationary, to the Final Judgment at the end of the age.

See Hades; Hell; Immortality; Paradise; Righteous, Promises to; Sheol; Spirit; Wicked, Punishment of.

ABRAM
See Abraham, Abram.

ABRECH, ABREK
Transliteration of a term, perhaps of Egyptian origin, translated "make way" or "bow down" in the NIV (Ge 41:43; see NRSV ftn).

ABRONAH
[6307]. A place where the Israelites camped (Nu 33:34-35).

ABSALOM
[94] (*father is peace*).

1. The third son of David by Maacah, daughter of Talmai, king of Geshur (2Sa 3:3; 1Ch 3:2), also known as Abishalom (1Ki 15:2, 10, w 1Ch 11:20-21).

Absalom hates Amnon, one of his stepbrothers and David's first son, because Amnon had raped his sister Tamar; after two years, Absalom avenges Tamar (2Sa 13:1-29). He flees to Geshur and stays there three years (2Sa 13:37-38). He is permitted by David to return to Jerusalem (2Sa 14:1-24). He is more handsome than anyone in all Israel (2Sa 14:25). Children of (2Sa 14:27; 1Ki 15:2, 10; 2Ch 11:20). He is not allowed to see David for two years after his return from exile in Geshur (2Sa 14:28), at which time he forces Joab to get him an audience with the king (2Sa 14:31-33).

His popularity (2Sa 15:2-6, 13). Conspiracy (2Sa 15-17). Death and burial (2Sa 18:9-17). Pillar of (2Sa 18:18). David's mourning for (2Sa 18:33; 19:1-8).

2. Rehoboam's father-in-law (2Ch 11:20-21).

3. In the Apocrypha, an ambassador of Judas Maccabaeus, the father of Mattathias and Jonathan (1Mc 11:70; 13:11; 2Mc 11:17).

ABSTEMIOUSNESS
See Abstinence; Temperance.

ABSTINENCE

From Intoxicating Beverages:

Abuse of alcohol condemned (Pr 23:20, 31-35; Lk 21:34). Exemplified by Aaron and the Levitical priesthood, while on duty (Lev 10:8-11; Eze 44:21); Nazirites, while taking a special vow (Nu 6:2-4, 20); Manoah's wife, Samson's mother, during pregnancy (Jdg 13:2-5, 13-14); Kings and princes (Pr 31:4-5); John the Baptist (Lk 1:15).

Instances of:

Israelites in the wilderness (Dt 29:6). Samson (Jdg 16:17, w 13:3-5, 13-14 & Nu 6:3-4). Recabites, honoring an ancestral commitment (Jer 35:1-14). Daniel (Da 1:8, 12). John the Baptist (Mt 11:18; Lk 1:15; 7:33). *See Temperance.*

Other Things Abstained From:

Food, in fasting (Lev 16:29; 23:27; 1Sa 7:6; Ne 9:1; Joel 2:12; Mt 6:16-18). *See Fasting.* Sexual contact within marriage, temporarily (Ex 19:15; 1Co 7:1-5).

In Israel—

The use of blood or fat (Ge 9:4; Lev 3:17). The tendon of the hip (Ge 32:32). Meat not properly bled and prepared (Ex 22:31; Dt 14:21). Whole groups of animals (Lev 11). Contact with unclean person (Lev 15). *See Unclean.*

Christians—

From evil and immorality (Ac 15:20, 29; Eph 4:17-5:21; Col 3:1-11; 1Pe 2:11-12). For the sake of a weaker brother (Ro 14; 1Co 8). Wrongly used as a form of self-righteousness (Col 2:20-23; 1Ti 4:1-3). From an appearance of evil (1Th 5:22).

ABUNDANCE
[*8041, 8044, 8425, 10678].

General:

(Ecc 5:9-20; Isa 15:7; Mt 13:12; 25:29; Mk

12:42-44; Lk 21:1-4; 2Co 8:12-15). Steadfast love (Ex 34:6-7; Ps 69:13; 103; Jnh 4:2). Peace (Lev 26:3, 6; Ps 37:10-11; Jer 33:6-9). Pardon (Nu 14:17-19; 2Ch 30:18-20; Isa 1:18; 55:7; Joel 3:20-21; Mic 7:18-20). Prosperity (Dt 28:47). Anguish (1Sa 1:16). Wealth (2Ch 17:3-6; 18:1; 20:25-27; 24:8-14; Ps 37:16; 52:6-7; Jer 48:36-38; 51:12-13). Honor (2Ch 17:5; 18:1; 1Co 12:23-24). Glory of Zion (Isa 66:11). Overflow of the heart (Mt 12:34; Lk 6:45). Life (Jn 5:39-40; 10:10; 20:30-31), is not in the abundance of possessions (Lk 12:15). Grace (Ro 5; 2Co 4:15), of giving (2Co 8:1-15), through the knowledge of our God and Savior Jesus Christ (2Pe 1:2). Affection, brotherly (2Co 7:15). Plunder (2Ch 20:25). Immeasurably more than we ask (Eph 3:20). Holy Spirit (Tit 3:5-6).

From God:
Provisions, *i.e.* needs (Lev 26:3-5; Dt 30:9-10; Ps 132:13-15; Pr 3:9-10; Isa 30:23; Eze 36:29-30; Am 9:13; Zec 8:12; Php 4:19), grace (2Co 9:8), joys (Ps 36:8), life (Jn 10:10), power (Eph 3:20), participation in the divine nature and a rich welcome into the eternal kingdom (2Pe 1:3-11).

ABUSE

Substance Abuse: (1Co 6:12-13).
Of alcohol: Biblical condemnation of alcohol abuse may be generalized to apply to abuse of any mind- or behavior-altering substance. Condemned (Pr 20:1; 21:17; 23:20, 30-35; Isa 5:22; Eph 5:18; 1Ti 3:8; Tit 2:3). Examples of (Ge 9:20-24; 19:30-36; Isa 28:7-8; 1Co 11:20-22). *See Abstinence; Temperance.*
Of food (Pr 23:1-3, 20-21; 25:16; 30:22; Isa 56:10-11; Am 6:4-7; 1Co 6:12-13; 1Co 11:20-22; Php 3:18-19).

Sexual Abuse:
Rape punished by death (Dt 22:25-27). Examples of: rape (Ge 34:1-7; Jdg 19:25-20:13; 2Sa 13:1-20; Zec 14:2), attempted homosexual rape (Ge 19:4-9; Jdg 19:22-24).

Abuse of Persons:
Physical injury: Punished in like kind (Ex 21:22-25; Lev 24:19-20).
Servants and slaves: Set free if physically abused (Ex 21:26-27).
Family: Under the law, an unfavored wife still had to be cared for (Ex 21:10-11; Dt 21:15-17). A child could be put to death for abuse of parents (Ex 21:15, 17; Dt 21:18-21). Corporal punishment, if done out of the motivation of love, is not abuse (Pr 3:11-12; 13:24; 29:15; Heb 12:7-11).

ABYSS [12, 5853] (*unfathomable depth*).
The abode of demons (Lk 8:31) and the place of the dead (Ro 10:7). The bottomless pit; a place of torment and of imprisoned demons (Rev 9:1-2, 11; 11:7; 17:8; 20:1-3).

ACACIA [8847]. A tree (Isa 41:19). The ark of the covenant made of its wood (Ex 25:10), poles of the ark (Ex 25:13; 38:6), boards in the

tabernacle (Ex 26:15-37), the altar of burnt offerings (Ex 38:1, 6).

ACBOR [6570] (*mouse* or *jerboa*).
1. The father of Baal-Hanan, a king of Edom (Ge 36:38-39; 1Ch 1:49).
2. The son of Micaiah, a messenger of King Josiah (2Ki 22:12-14). Also called Abdon the son of Micah (2Ch 34:20). *See Abdon, 5.*
3. The father of Elnathan (Jer 26:22; 36:12).

ACCAD See Akkad.

ACCEPTED BY GOD Lot's prayers (Ge 19:19-21), Job's prayers (Job 42:9), willing praise (Ps 119:108).

Israelites:
(Ex 28:38; Eze 20:40-41; 43:27). The OT prophets continually affirmed that offerings were only acceptable when the person was acceptable; the offerer never became acceptable to God by giving him gifts (Hos 8:13; Mal 1:6-14).

NT Believers:
People from every nation who fear God and do what is right (Ac 10:34-35). The believer's goal is to please God (2Co 5:9). Through Christ (Eph 1:4-6).

ACCEPTED TIME The time favorable for seeking God. When forgiven (Ps 32:5-6). When in trouble (Ps 69:13). Today, *i.e., now* (Ps 95:7-8; Isa 49:8; 2Co 6:2).

ACCESS TO GOD Exemplified (Ex 24:2; 34:4-7). Typified (Lev 16:12-15, w Heb 10:19-22). In prayer (Dt 4:7; 2Ki 4:33; Mt 6:6; 1Pe 1:17). *See Prayer.* A privilege of believers (Dt 4:7; Ps 15; 23:6; 24:3-5). In his temple (Ps 15:1; 27:4-5; 43:3; 65:4). Blessedness of (Ps 16:11; 65:4; 73:28). Believers earnestly seek (Ps 27:4; 42:1-2; 43:3-4; 84:1-2). Is of God (Ps 65:4). Promises connected with (Ps 145:18-20; Isa 55:1-5; Mt 6:6; Jas 4:8). Urge others to seek (Isa 2:3; Jer 31:6). The wicked commanded to seek (Isa 55:6; Jas 4:8). Promised to repenting sinners (Hos 14:2; Joel 2:14). *See Repentance.* Is by Christ (Jn 10:7-10; 14:6-7; Ro 5:1-2; Eph 2:13; 3:12; Heb 7:18-19; 10:1-25; 1Pe 3:18). Obtained through faith (Ac 14:27; Ro 5:1-2; Eph 3:12; Heb 11:6). Is by the Holy Spirit (Eph 2:18). Believers have with confidence (Eph 3:12; Heb 4:16; 10:19-22). Follows upon reconciliation to God (Col 1:21-22). To obtain mercy and grace (Heb 4:16).

ACCESSORY See Complicity.

ACCO [6573]. A town on the Mediterranean coast c. thirty miles south of Tyre, and ten from Mt. Carmel (Jdg 1:31, NIV). Also called Ptolemais by the ancient Greeks and Romans because Ptolemy, the Egyptian king, rebuilt the city in c. 100 B.C.; a town of Phoenicia (Ac 21:7, NIV, Ptolemais). *See Ptolemais.*

ACCOMPLICE See Complicity.

ACCOUNTABILITY See
Responsibility.

ACCURSED [460, 2404, 7837, 7839, 2932]. People that are cursed (Dt 21:23; Jos 6:18; 7:1, 11, 13, 15; 1Ch 2:7; Isa 65:20; Ro 9:3; 1Co 12:3; Gal 1:8).
Things that are cursed (Jos 6:17-18; 7:12).
See Abomination; Anathema; Idolatry.

ACCUSATION, FALSE [8189, 8357, 8476, *1592, 2989, 2991*].
Forbidden
(Ex 23:1, 7; Lev 19:16; Lk 3:14; Tit 2:3).
Consolation for falsely accused (Mt 5:11; Jn 15:19-21; 1Pe 4:14).
Instances of False Accusation:
Joseph by Potiphar's wife (Ge 39:7-20); Joseph's brothers by Joseph (Ge 42:6-14); Moses by Korah (Nu 16:1-3, 13); the prophet Ahimelech by Saul (1Sa 22:11-16); Abner by Joab (2Sa 3:24-27); Elijah by Ahab (1Ki 18:17-18); Naboth by Jezebel (1Ki 21:1-14); the Jews who returned under Ezra, accused by the men of Trans-Euphrates (Ezr 4:6-16; Ne 6:5-9); Job by Satan (Job 1:9-10; 2:4-5). David (Ps 41:5-9), by the princes of Ammon (2Sa 10:1-4; 1Ch 19:1-4), Jeremiah (Jer 26:8-15; 37:12-15; 43:1-4), Amos (Am 7:10-11), Mary (Mt 1:19), Jesus (Mt 9:34; 10:25; 12:2-14; 26:59-61; Mk 3:22; 14:53-65; Lk 23:2; Jn 18:30), Stephen (Ac 6:11-14), Paul (Ac 17:6-7; 21:27-29; 24:1-9, 12-13; 25:1-2, 7; Ro 3:8), Paul and Silas (Ac 16:19-21).
In last days, people will be slanderous (2Ti 3:3).
See Conspiracy; Evidence; False Witness; Persecution; Speaking; Evil; Talebearer.

ACELDAMA See *Akeldama.*

ACHAIA [*938*]. A region of Greece, on the S coast of the gulf of Corinth. Paul visits (Ac 18; 19:21; 1Co 16:15; 2Co 1:1). Generosity of the Christians in (Ro 15:26; 2Co 9:2; 11:10).

ACHAICUS [*939*] (*belonging to Achaia*). A Corinthian Christian who helped Paul, visited him at Ephesus and was commended for his good will toward Paul (1Co 16:17-19).

ACHAN [6575] (*a word play from Achar: troubler*). The son of Carmi and a Judahite of Zerah's clan who participated in the assault upon Jericho; he also violated the sacrificial ban by stealing gold, silver, and a beautiful robe from the spoil taken. After Israel failed to take Ai, inquiry was made by lot, and Achan was found to be guilty. Sin and punishment of (Jos 7; 22:20; 1Ch 2:7).

ACHAR [6580] (*trouble*). A variant spelling of Achan (1Ch 2:7).

ACHAZ See *Ahaz.*

ACHBOR See *Acbor.*

ACHIM See *Akim.*

ACHISH [429] (*the king gives*). King of the Philistines, also called Abimelech (Ps 34, title). David escapes to (1Sa 21:10-15; 27; 28:1-2; 29). Achish continues as king of Gath during the reign of Solomon (1Ki 2:39-40).

ACHMETHA See *Ecbatana.*

ACHOR [6574] (*trouble*). A valley near Jericho in which Achan was stoned (Jos 7:24-26; 15:7; Isa 65:10; Hos 2:15).

ACHSA, ACHSAH See *Acsah.*

ACHSHAPH See *Acshaph.*

ACHZIB See *Aczib.*

ACKNOWLEDGE [*1981, 3359, 5795, 10313, *3933*].
General (Isa 61:9; 63:16; 1Co 14:37-38).
Acknowledging, in an imperative sense, that the Lord is God and that there is no other (Dt 4:39; Pr 3:5-6), in an imprecatory sense (Ps 79:6-7; Jer 10:23-25).
We acknowledge our sins (Ps 32:5; 51:1-6; Isa 59:12-13), our rebellion, idolatry, and wickedness (Jer 3:13; 14:20).
Recognition (1Co 16:17-18).

ACRE [5103+7538]. The amount of land a pair of oxen could plow in a day (1Sa 14:14; Isa 5:10).

ACROPOLIS (*crest of city, high ground of city*). The upper or higher city, citadel, or castle of a Greek city. Especially the high rocky promontory in Athens where the treasury of the city and its finest temples were located.

ACROSTIC A literary device by which the first letter of each line of poetry forms either a word or the successive letters of the alphabet. An outstanding example is Psalm 119, in which each successive set of eight verses begins with a different letter of the Hebrew alphabet. The effect is not apparent in the English translation, but the Hebrew letters are given between the lines in order to show the construction. NIV notes identify other acrostic poems (Ps. 9-10; 24; 34; 37; 111; 112; 145; Pr 31:10-31; La 1; 2; 3; 4).

ACROSTIC POETRY See *Poetry.*

ACSAH [6578] (*decorative anklet*). Caleb's daughter (1Ch 2:49). Caleb offered her as a reward, to be married, to the man who would capture the city of Debir, which was formerly called Kiriath Sepher. Caleb's nephew, Othniel, took the city and won the prize (Jos 15:16-19; Jdg 1:9-15).

ACSHAPH [439] (*fascination*). An important Canaanite city which Joshua captured with its king (Jos 11:1; 12:7, 20). It is named as being on

the border of the lot assigned to Asher (Jos 19:24-25).

ACTIONS AT LAW Duty of defendant (Mt 5:40; 1Co 6:7). *See Adjudication at Law; Arbitration.*

ACTIVITY, EVIL Of sinners in general (Pr 1:10-16; 4:14-17; 6:18; Isa 59:7; Mic 2:1-2; 7:3; Ro 3:15-18). Of Pharisees (Mt 23:15). Of Paul in persecuting the church (Ac 9:2; 26:11; Gal 1:13; Php 3:6). Of busybodies in the church, stirring up strife (2Th 3:10-12; 1Ti 5:13; 1Pe 4:15). Of Satan (1Pe 5:8).

ACTS OF THE APOSTLES

Author: Anonymous; traditionally Luke, the companion of Paul

Date: Probably between A.D. 63 and 67

Outline:

I. Peter and the Beginnings of the Church in Israel (chs. 1-12).
  A. "Throughout Judea, Galilee and Samaria" (1:1-9:31; see 9:31).
    1. Introduction (1:1-2).
    2. Christ's post-resurrection ministry (1:3-11).
    3. The period of waiting for the Holy Spirit (1:12-26).
    4. The filling with the Spirit (ch. 2).
    5. The healing of the lame man and the resultant arrest of Peter and John (3:1-4:31).
    6. The community of goods (4:32-5:11).
    7. The arrest of the twelve apostles (5:12-42).
    8. The choice of the Seven (6:1-7).
    9. Stephen's arrest and martyrdom (6:8-7:60).
    10. The scattering of the Jerusalem believers (8:1-4).
    11. Philip's ministry (8:5-40).
      a. In Samaria (8:5-25).
      b. To the Ethiopian eunuch (8:26-40).
    12. Saul's conversion (9:1-31).
  B. "As far as Phoenicia, Cyprus and Antioch" (9:32-12:25; see 11:19).
    1. Peter's ministry on the Mediterranean coast (9:32-11:18).
      a. To Aeneas and Dorcas (9:32-43).
      b. To Cornelius (10:1-11:18).
    2. The new Gentile church in Antioch (11:19-30).
    3. Herod's persecution of the church and his subsequent death (ch. 12).
II. Paul and the Expansion of the Church From Antioch to Rome (chs. 13-28).
  A. "Throughout the region of Phrygia and Galatia" (13:1-15:35; see 16:6).
    1. Paul's first missionary journey (chs. 13-14).
    2. The Jerusalem conference (15:1-35).
  B. "Over to Macedonia" (15:36-21; see 16:9).
    1. Paul's second missionary journey (15:36-18:22).
    2. Paul's third missionary journey (18:23-21:16).
  C. "To Rome" (21:17-28:31; see 28:14).
    1. Paul's imprisonment in Jerusalem (21:17-23:35).
      a. Arrest (21:17-22:29).
      b. Trial before the Sanhedrin (22:30-23:11).
      c. Transfer to Caesarea (23:12-35).
    2. Paul's imprisonment in Caesarea (chs. 24-26).
      a. Trial before Felix (ch. 24).
      b. Trial before Festus (25:1-12).
      c. Hearing before Festus and Agrippa (25:13-26:32).
    3. Voyage to Rome (27:1-28:15).
    4. Two years under house arrest in Rome (28:16-31).

See Missionary Journeys of Paul.

ACZIB [424] (*deceit*).

1. A city of Judah in the Shephelah (Jos 15:44; Mic 1:14) perhaps the same as modern Tell el-Beida, which is SW of Adullam. Taken by Sennacherib, c. 701 B.C. Also called Kezib (Ge 38:5) and Cozeba (1Ch 4:22).

2. A town in Asher on the coast N of Acco (Jos 19:29; Jdg 1:31).

ADADAH [6368]. A city in Judah (Jos 15:22).

ADAH [6336] (*adornment*).

1. The wife of Lamech and mother of Jabal (Ge 4:19-20, 23).

2. The daughter of Elon the Hittite, and the first of three wives of Esau; she was the mother of Eliphaz (Ge 36:2, 4, 10, 12, 16).

ADAIAH [6347, 6348] (*adornment of Yahweh*).

1. A native of Bozkath; the father of Jedidah, the mother of Josiah, the king of Judah (2Ki 22:1).

2. A Levite of the family of Gershom; the son of Ethni and father of Zerah, in the ancestry of Asaph (1Ch 6:41-43).

3. The son of Shimei and one of the chief Benjamites in pre-exilic Jerusalem (1Ch 8:1, 21).

4. A priest and a Levite; the son of Jeroham (1Ch 9:10-12), also in the parallel list in Nehemiah, although the genealogies do not agree in all details (Ne 11:12).

5. The father of Maaseiah, an army officer who helped make Joash king in the overthrow of Athaliah (2Ch 23:1).

6. A man who married a foreign wife during the Exile and divorced her after the Captivity (Ezr 10:29).

7. Another man who did the same (Ezr 10:39).

8. A descendant of Judah whose posterity lived in Jerusalem after the captivity (Ne 11:5).

ADALIA [130] (possibly *honorable*). The fifth son of Haman (Est 9:8).

ADAM [134, 136, 77] (*[red] earth,* or *[ruddy] skin color*).

1. The first man. His creation (Ge 1:26-28; 2:7; 1Co 15:45; 1Ti 2:13). The history of, before he sinned (Ge 1:26-30; 2:16-25). His temptation and sin (Ge 3; Job 31:33, ftn; Isa 43:27; Hos 6:7; Ro 5:14-21; 1Ti 2:14). The subsequent history of (Ge 3:20-24; 4:1-2, 25; 5:1-5). His death (Ge 5:5). Progenitor of the human race (Dt 32:8; Mal 2:10). A type of Christ (Ro 5:14). Brought sin and death into the world (1Co 15:22, 45).

2. Christ: the last Adam (1Co 15:45).

3. A city in the Jordan Valley where the Israelites entered the promised land (Jos 3:16).

ADAMAH [142] (*[red] earth*). A city of Naphtali (Jos 19:36). The location is disputed, yet it may be the modern city of Tell ed-Damiyeh.

ADAMANT NIV "hardest stone" (Eze 3:9; Zec 7:12). *See Diamond; Flint, 2; Hardest Stone; Minerals of the Bible, 1; Stones.*

ADAMI NEKEB [146] (*the ground of piercing*). A place on the border of Naphtali (Jos 19:33).

ADAR [160, 10009] (possibly *dark, clouded*). Month twelve in sacred sequence, six in civil sequence (Ezr 6:15; Est 3:7; 8:12; 9:1, 15-21). The rainy season (February-March); the season for harvesting citrus fruit. *See Month, 12.*

ADAR SHENI (*Second Adar*). This inter-calary month (not in Bible) was added about every three years so the lunar calendar would correspond to the solar year. *See Month, 13.*

ADBEEL [118] (*[the] grief of God [El]*). The third son of Ishmael (Ge 25:13; 1Ch 1:29).

ADDAN *See Addon.*

ADDAR [161, 162] (*glorious*).

1. Also called Ard (Ge 46:21; Nu 26:40). A son of Bela, and grandson of Benjamin (1Ch 8:3). Counted as a son of Benjamin and head of a family in the tribe.

2. A place on the S border of Judah (Jos 15:3). *See Hazar Addar; Ataroth Addar.*

ADDER [704]. A poisonous snake (Job 20:16; Isa 30:6; 59:5). *See Cobra; Serpent.*

ADDI [79] (*my witness,* or *adorned*). An ancestor of Joseph, the husband of Mary (Lk 3:28).

ADDICTION (1Co 6:12-13; 2Pe 2:19; Ro 6:16-21). *See Abuse.*

ADDON [124, 150]. The inhabitants of Addon came up after the Babylonian captivity, but were unable to prove their lineage as descendants of Israel (Ezr 2:59; Ne 7:61).

ADER *See Eder.*

ADIEL [6346] (*adornment of God [El]*).

1. A descendant of Simeon who gained more pastoral land for himself in the region of Gedor in the time of Hezekiah (1Ch 4:36).

2. A priest, son of Jahzerah and the father of Maasai; Maasai returned after the Babylonian captivity and was very active in reconstructing the temple (1Ch 9:12).

3. Father of Azmaveth, who was supervisor of David's treasuries (1Ch 27:25).

ADIN [6350] (*voluptuous, luxurious*).

1. One whose family returned from exile with Zerubbabel (Ezr 2:15; Ne 7:20).

2. One whose posterity came back with Ezra (Ezr 8:6).

3. The name of a family sealing the covenant (Ne 10:16).

ADINA [6351] (*adorned*). The son of Shiza, a Reubenite; one of David's mighty men (1Ch 11:42).

ADINO (*his adorned one*). KJV "Adino the Eznite" is a variant reading in the NIV (2Sa 23:8, ftn). *See Josheb-Basshebeth.*

ADITHAIM [6353] (*double [row] of adornments*). A city of Judah in the Shephelah (Jos 15:36).

ADJUDICATION AT LAW To be avoided (Pr 17:14; 20:3; 25:8-10; Mt 5:25, 40; Lk 12:58). *See Actions at Law; Arbitration; Compromise; Court, of Law; Justice; Litigation.*

ADJURATION KJV "adjure" is in the NIV to "pronounce" or "bind under oath," to "make someone swear an oath." It is an act or appeal in which a person in authority imposes some obligation upon another with the strength and solemnity of an oath (Jos 6:26; 1Sa 14:24; 1Ki 22:16; 2Ch 18:15). In the NT the high priest calls upon Jesus to acknowledge that he was the Messiah (Mk 5:7). The oath was binding and required a reply. *See Oath.*

It is also used to exorcise demons (Ac 19:13).

ADLAI [6354] (*be just*). The father of Shaphat, who was David's chief herdsman (1Ch 27:29).

ADMAH [144] (*[red] earth*). A city near Gomorrah and Zeboiim (Ge 10:19). The king was Shinab (Ge 14:2, 8). Admah was destroyed along with Sodom and Gomorrah (Dt 29:23, w Ge 19:24-28; Hos 11:8).

ADMATHA [148] (*unrestrained*). The third named prince of Persia and Media (Est 1:14).

ADMINISTRATORS [*6913, 10518,

1354, 3873]. Officers who ruled in Darius's king-dom; satraps report to (Da 6:2-7).

ADMONITION [5184, 6386, *3805*]. See Wicked, Warned.

ADNA [6363] (*delight*).
1. A son of Pahath-Moab who had married a foreign wife during the Exile (Ezr 10:30).
2. A chief priest, and the head of his father's house in the days of Joiakim (Ne 12:12-15).

ADNAH [6365, 6367] (*delight*).
1. One of the captains of the tribe of Manasseh who joined David at Ziklag (1Ch 12:20).
2. A man of Judah who held high military rank under Jehoshaphat (2Ch 17:14).

ADONI-BEZEK [152] (*lord of Bezek*).
The king of Bezek, who had the thumbs and big toes of 70 kings cut off: when the Israelites routed the Canaanites and Perizzites and captured Adoni-Bezek, they had his thumbs and big toes cut off (Jdg 1:4-7). See Bezek.

ADONIJAH [153, 154] (*[my] lord is Yahweh*).
1. The fourth son of David by his wife Haggith (2Sa 3:4; 1Ki 1:5-6; 1Ch 3:2). Usurpation of, and downfall (1Ki 1). Executed by Solomon (1Ki 2:13, 25).
2. A Levite whom Jehoshaphat sent to assist in teaching the law to the people of Judah (2Ch 17:8).
3. A leader who with Nehemiah sealed the covenant (Ne 10:16). See Adonikam.

ADONIKAM [156] (*[my] lord arises*). One of the Jews who returned with Ezra from Babylon with Zerubbabel (Ezr 2:13). Later three of his descendants came with Ezra (Ne 7:18). Probably the same as Adonijah, 3 (Ne 10:16).

ADONIRAM [157, 2067] (*[my] Lord is exalted*). A man in charge of forced labor during the reigns of David (2Sa 20:24), and later under Solomon (1Ki 4:6; 5:14), and then Solomon's son, Rehoboam (1Ki 12:18; 2Ch 10:18). He was stoned to death by the people of Israel as their first act of rebellion and revolt, which was lead by Jeroboam, son of Nebat, during the division of the monarchy. Also spelled Adoram (1Ki 12:18; 2Sa 20:24) and Hadoram (2Ch 10:18, ftn).

ADONI-ZEDEK [155] (*[my] lord is right-eousness*). The Amorite king of Jerusalem who with four other kings was defeated in battle and slain by Joshua at Gibeon (Jos 10:1-27).

ADOPTION [*1047, 4340, *5625*].
Explained: (2Co 6:18).

Of Children:
Instances of: Of one born in Abram's house (Ge 15:3), of Joseph's sons (Ge 48:5, 14, 16, 22), of

Moses (Ex 2:5-10; Ac 7:20-21; Heb 11:24), of Esther (Est 2:7).

Spiritual Adoption:
Of Israel (Ex 4:22-23; Nu 6:27; Dt 14:1-2; 26:18-19; 27:9; 28:9-10; 32:5-6; 2Ch 7:14; Isa 63:8, 16; Jer 3:19; 31:9, 20; Hos 1:9-10; 11:1; Ro 9:4); of Solomon (2Sa 7:14; 1Ch 22:10; 28:6).
Of the righteous (Pr 14:26; Isa 43:1-6; 63:8, 16; Mt 5:9, 44-45; 12:50; 13:43; Lk 6:35; Jn 11:52; Ro 9:8, 26; 2Co 6:17-18; Eph 2:19; Php 2:15; Heb 12:6-7, 9; 1Jn 3:1-2, 10; 4:4).
Of the Gentiles promised (Hos 2:23; Ro 9:24-26; Eph 3:6, 14-15; Heb 2:10-11, 13); testified to by the Holy Spirit (Ro 8:14-17, 19, 21, 29; Gal 4:5-7); through the gospel (Eph 3:6).

The Means of Adoption:
By God's grace (Eze 16:3-6; Ro 4:16-17; Eph 1:5-6, 11); by faith (Jn 1:12-13; Gal 3:7, 26, 29; Eph 1:5); through Christ (Jn 1:12-13; Gal 3:26; 4:4-5; Eph 1:5; Heb 2:10-11, 13); according to promise (Ro 9:8; Gal 3:29; Eph 3:6); through the gospel (Eph 3:6).

Role of the Holy Spirit:
Witnessed to by the Spirit (Ro 8:16); led by the Spirit as evidence of (Ro 8:14); the Spirit of sonship received (Ro 8:15; Gal 4:6).

Results:
A new name (Nu 6:27; Isa 62:2; Ac 15:17); disciplined by the Father (Dt 8:5; 2Sa 7:14; Pr 3:11-12; Heb 12:5-11); safety (Pr 14:26); God is Father-Redeemer (Isa 63:16); recipient of God's long-suffering mercy (Jer 31:1, 19-20); a new inheritance (Mt 13:43; Ro 8:17); the new birth (Jn 1:12-13); will become brothers and sisters of Christ (Jn 20:17; Heb 2:11-12).
A new lifestyle: A love of peace (Mt 5:9); desire for God's glory (Mt 5:16); likeness to God (Mt 5:44-45, 48); avoidance of pretense (Mt 6:1-4); a forgiving spirit (Mt 6:14); confidence in God (Mt 6:25-34); a spirit of prayer (Mt 7:7-11); a merciful spirit (Lk 6:35-36); holiness (2Co 6:17-18; 7:1; Php 2:15); following God (Eph 5:1).
A new future: Gathered as one by Christ (Jn 11:52); final consummation (Ro 8:19, 23; 1Jn 3:2).

ADORAIM [126] (possibly *pair of knolls*).
A fortified city in SW Judah, five miles SW of Hebron, fortified by Rehoboam, son of Solomon (2Ch 11:9).

ADORAM See Adoniram.

ADORNING [*3636, 6335, 6995, *3175, 3180*].

Physical:
Bracelets (Ge 24:22; Nu 31:50; 2Sa 1:10). Earrings (Ge 35:4; Ex 32:2; 35:22; Nu 31:50; Jdg 8:24; Pr 25:12; Eze 16:12). Chains, used as ornaments (Ge 41:42; Pr 1:9; Eze 16:11; Da 5:29). Rings, for the fingers (Ge 41:42; Ex 35:22; Est 3:10; 8:8; Job 42:11; Isa 3:21; Hos 2:13; Lk

15:22). Ornaments, wearing of (Ex 33:4; Isa 3:18; Jer 2:32; 4:30; Eze 16:11; 23:40).

Jewels:

General references to (Ex 35:22; Nu 31:50). Discarded or refusal to wear (Ge 35:4; Ex 33:4; 1Pe 3:3). Brought as offerings to God (Ex 35:22; Nu 31:50; Mt 2:1-2, 9-11).

Spiritual:

Clothed in righteousness, salvation, strength (Job 29:14; Ps 132:16; Isa 52:1; 61:10; Zec 3:4; Mt 22:11). General references to (Ps 45:13; Pr 1:9; 4:9; SS 1:10; Isa 61:10; 1Pe 3:3-4; Rev 21:2). White clothing, the heavenly garment (Mt 17:2; Rev 3:5; 3:18; 4:4; 7:9; 19:8).

ADRAMMELECH [165, 166] *(nobility of Molech [king])*.

1. The name given to Adar, the god brought to Samaria from Assyria by the Sepharvites (2Ki 17:31).

2. One of the sons of Sennacherib, who along with his brother Sharezer, killed their father while he was worshiping in the temple of his god Nisroch (2Ki 19:37; Isa 37:38).

ADRAMYTTIUM [101] *(the mansion of death)*. A port city of Mysia, in the NW part of the Roman province of Asia (Ac 27:2).

ADRIATIC [102]. The Adriatic Sea, a body of water between Italy on the W and Dalmatia, Macedonia, and Achaia on the E (Ac 27:27).

ADRIEL [6377] ([my] help is God [El]). The son of Barzillai the Meholathite; Saul's son-in-law (1Sa 18:19; 2Sa 21:8-9).

ADULLAM, ADULLAMITE [6355, 6356] *(retreat or refuge; possibly [they are] just)*.

1. A cave near the Dead Sea. David takes refuge in (1Sa 22:1; 2Sa 23:13; 1Ch 11:15). *See also the titles of Pss 57 and 142.*

2. An ancient city of Canaan (Ge 38:1; Jos 12:15; 15:35), fortified by Rehoboam (2Ch 11:5-7), inhabited after the Exile (Ne 11:25-30), referred to by Micah (Mic 1:15).

3. The people of Adullam, used of Hirah, Judah's friend (Ge 38:1, 12, 20).

ADULLAMITE See Adullam, 3.

ADULTERY [*2388, 2393, 2424, 5537, 3655, 3656, 3657, 3658, 3659, 4518, 4519, 4521].

Defined:

(Mt 5:28, 32; 19:9; Mk 10:11-12; Lk 16:18; Ro 7:1-3). Laws concerning (Nu 5:11-31; Dt 22:13-29).

Repulsive to the righteous (Job 31:1-12; Eze 18:5-6, 9). Fatal consequences of (Pr 2:16-19; 5:3-4, 5-23; 6:23-35; 7:1-27; 9:13-18; 22:14; 23:26-28). Moral and spiritual corruption by (Jer 3:1-2; 5:7-8; Hos 4:1-2, 9-19). Source of: the heart (Mt 15:19; Mk 7:21-23), the sinful nature (Gal 5:19-21).

Figurative:

(Jer 3:1-2; 9:2; 23:10; Eze 16:15-16; Hos 1; 2:1-2; 3:1; 7:1-4; Ro 7:1-6).

Forbidden:

(Ex 20:14; Lev 18:20; 19:29; Dt 5:18; 23:17; Pr 31:3; Mt 5:27-28; 19:16-19; Mk 10:17-19; Lk 18:18-20; Ac 15:20, 29; Ro 13:9, 13; 1Co 5:9-11; 6:13-16-18; 10:7-8; Eph 4:17-19; 5:3; Col 3:5; 1Th 4:3-7; 1Ti 1:9-10; Jas 2:10-11).

Forgiveness of:

(Jdg 19:1-4; Jn 4:16-26, 39-42; 8:10-11).

Lack of Repentance in:

(Pr 30:20; Isa 57:3-4; Jer 7:9-15; Ro 1:28-32; 2Co 12:21; 1Pe 4:3-4; Rev 9:20-21).

Instances of:

The Sodomites (Ge 19:4-8; Jude 7). Lot and his two daughters (Ge 19:31-38). Shechem (Ge 34:1-2). Reuben (Ge 35:22). Judah (Ge 38:1-26). Potiphar's wife (Ge 39:6-12). Israelites (Ex 32:6; Jer 23:10-11; 29:23; Eze 22:9-11; 33:26; Hos 7:4). Gilead, the father of Jephthah (Jdg 11:1). Samson (Jdg 16:1). The Levite's concubine (Jdg 19:1-2). The men of Gibeah (Jdg 19:22-25). The sons of Eli (1Sa 2:22). David (2Sa 11:1-5). Amnon, David's oldest son by Ahinoam (2Sa 13:1-20). Absalom, David's third son by Maacah (2Sa 16:22). Herod (Mt 14:3-4; Mk 6:17-18; Lk 3:19). The Samaritan woman (Jn 4:17-18). The woman brought to Jesus in the temple (Jn 8:3-11). The Corinthians (1Co 5:1-5). Gentiles (Eph 4:17-20; 1Pe 4:3-4). Those living in the last days (2Ti 3:6).

Penalties for:

Curses (Nu 5:11-31; Dt 27:20-23; Job 24:15-18). Death (Ge 20:3, 7; 26:11; 38:24; Lev 20:10-12; 21:9; Dt 22:13-27; 2Sa 12:7-14; Eze 23:45-48; Jn 8:4-5). Fines (Ex 22:16-17; Dt 22:19, 28-29). Make a guilt offering (Lev 19:20-22). Divine judgments (2Sa 12:10-12; Jer 29:22-23; Eze 16:38-41; Mal 3:5; 1Co 10:8; Heb 13:4; 2Pe 2:9-10, 14; Rev 2:20-22; 18:9-10). Excommunication (1Co 5:1-13; Eph 5:11-12). Exclusion from the kingdom of God (1Co 6:9-10; Gal 5:19, 21; Eph 5:5-6; Jude 7; Rev 21:8; 22:14-15).

See Fornication; Idolatry; Lasciviousness; Prostitute; Rape; Sensuality; Homosexual; Prostitute.

ADUMMIM [147] *(red [streaks])*. A pass on the road between Jerusalem and Jericho (Jos 15:7; 18:17), on the north border of Judah and the south border of Benjamin. Held to be the scene of Jesus' parable of the Good Samaritan (Lk 10:30-35).

ADVENT See Jesus the Christ, Second Coming; Millennium.

ADVERSARY [*7640, 7756, 8477, 8533, 508]. In general, an enemy, personal, national, or supernatural (Ex 23:22; 1Sa 2:10; Na 1:2; Mt 5:25). Specifically, Satan is the enemy of all mankind (1Pe 5:8).

ADVERSITY See Afflictions.

ADVICE *See Counsel.*

ADVOCATE [8446, *2858*, *2859*] (*helper, Paraclete*). An advocate is one who pleads the case or the cause of another. The Holy Spirit or Counselor (Jn 14:16-17, 26; 15:26; 16:7), Jesus Christ himself (1Jn 2:1).

AENEAS [*138*] (possibly *praise*). A paralytic, healed at Lydda by Peter (Ac 9:32-35).

AENON [*143*] (*spring*). A place probably N of Jerusalem to the W of the Jordan Valley because the Johannine account indicates that there was "plenty of water." Some scholars identify ancient Salim with present-day Salim, which is about three to four miles E of Nablus (Shechem). A place near Salim, W of the Jordan, where John the Baptist baptized (Jn 3:22-23).

AEON [*172*] (*a segment of time, eternity*). A Greek word indicating a period of time, usually translated ever or forever (Eph 3:21; Jn 6:51, 58), age or ages (Eph 1:21; Col 1:26), world (Ro 12:2; 2Ti 4:10).

AFFECTIONS [3137, 5883, *5073*].

Of Believers:
Supremely set on God (Dt 6:5; Ps 42:1; 73:23-26; 119:9-20; Mk 12:30). Should be zealous for God (Ps 69:9; 119:139; Gal 4:18). Should not grow cold (Ps 106:12-13; Mt 24:12; Gal 4:14-16; Rev 2:4). Should be set upon the house and worship of God (1Ch 29:3; Ps 26:8; 27:4; 84:1-2), the people of God (Ps 16:3; Ro 12:10; 2Co 7:13-16; 1Th 2:8), the commandments and statutes of God (Ps 19:8-10; 119), heavenly things (Col 3:1-2).
Blessedness of making God the object of our affections (Ps 91:14). Christ claims the first place in (Mt 10:37; Lk 14:26). Stirred up by communion with Christ (Lk 24:32).

Of the Wicked:
Not sincerely set on God (Isa 58:1-2; Eze 33:31-32; Lk 8:13), are unnatural and perverted (Ro 1:18-32; 2Ti 3:1-9; 2Pe 2:10-22). Desires of the flesh, crucified in believers (Ro 6:5-7; Gal 5:24), should be put to death by the Spirit (Ro 8:12-13; 13:14; 1Co 9:27; Col 3:5-6; 1Th 4:3-7). False teachers seek to captivate (Gal 1:9-10; 4:17; 2Ti 3:6; 2Pe 2:3, 18; Rev 2:14, 20).

AFFLICTED [1868, 1895, 2688, 2703, 5595, 5597, 5782, 6700, 6705, 6714].

In General:
Sympathy with (Job 6:14; Mt 25:34-40). Help for (Job 22:29; Isa 58:6-7; Lk 10:30-37; 1Ti 5:9-10). Rewards of service to (Isa 53:10; Mt 25:34-45). Exhorted to pray (Jas 5:13). Prayer for healing (Jas 5:14-15).

Duty to:
Pity (Job 6:14), comfort (Job 16:5; 29:25; 2Co 1:3-5; 1Th 4:18), relieve (Job 31:19-20; Isa 58:9-12; Php 4:14; 1Ti 5:10), protect the poor (Ps 82:3; Pr 22:22; 31:5), pray (Ac 12:5; Php 1:19; Jas 5:14-16), sympathize (Ro 12:15; Gal 6:2), remember those in prison and those who are mistreated (Heb 13:3).

AFFLICTED BELIEVERS

God's Relation to:
God is a refuge and strength to (Ps 27:5-6; Isa 25:4; Jer 16:19; Na 1:7), delivers (Ps 34:4, 19; Pr 12:13; Jer 39:17-18), protects (Ps 34:20), is with (Ps 46:5, 7; Isa 43:2-3), comforts (Isa 49:13; Jer 31:13; Mt 5:4; 2Co 1:3-5; 7:6).
Christ comforts (Isa 61:2, w Lk 4:18-19; Mt 11:28-30; Lk 7:13; Jn 14:1; 16:33), preserves (Isa 63:9; Lk 21:18), is with (Jn 14:18), supports (2Ti 4:17; Heb 2:18), delivers (Rev 3:10).

Attitudes and Actions of:
Should be resigned (1Sa 3:18; 2Ki 20:19; Job 1:21; Ps 39:9), acknowledge the justice of their discipline (Ne 9:33; Job 2:10; Isa 64:5-7; La 3:39; Mic 7:9), not despise discipline (Job 5:17-18; Pr 3:11-12; Heb 12:5-6), trust in the goodness of God (Job 13:15; Ps 71:20; 2Co 1:9), avoid sin (Job 34:31-32; Jn 5:14; 1Pe 2:12), praise God (Ps 13:5-6; 56:8-11; 57:6-7; 71:20-23), take encouragement from former mercy (Ps 27:9; 2Co 1:10), call upon God in the day of trouble (Ps 50:15; 55:16-17). *See Affliction, Prayer under.* Turn and devote themselves to God (Ps 116:7-9; Jer 50:3-5; Hos 6:1), be patient (Lk 21:19; Ro 12:12; 2Th 1:4-7; Jas 1:4; 1Pe 2:20), imitate Christ (Heb 12:1-3; 1Pe 2:21-23), imitate the prophets (Jas 5:10).

Examples of:
Joseph (Ge 39:20-23; Ps 105:17-19), Eli (1Sa 3:11-18), David (2Sa 12:15-23), Nehemiah (Ne 1:3-4), Job (Job 1:20-22), Paul (Ac 20:22-24; 21:13), the apostles (1Co 4:13; 2Co 6:4-10), Moses (Heb 11:24-29).

AFFLICTION [2716, 4316, 6411, 6700, 6715, *2568*].

Consolation Under:
God is the Author and Giver of (Ps 23:4; Ro 15:5; 2Co 1:3-4; 7:6-7; Col 1:11; 2Th 2:16-17). Christ is the Author and Giver of (Isa 61:1-3; Jn 14:18; 2Co 1:5). The Holy Spirit is the Author and Giver of (Jn 14:16-17; 15:26; 16:7; Ac 9:31).
In the prospect of death (Job 19:25-27; Ps 23:4; Jn 14:1-3; 2Co 5:1; 1Th 4:12-13; Heb 4:9-10; Rev 7:14-17; 14:13). Through the Holy Scriptures (Ps 119:50, 76; Ro 15:4). Pray for (Ps 119:81-83). By ministers of the gospel (Isa 40:1-2; 1Co 14:3; 2Co 1:4, 6). Promised (Ps 119:76; Isa 51:3, 12; 66:13; Eze 14:22-23; Hos 2:14; Zec 1:17). Believers should administer to each other (1Th 4:18; 5:11, 14). Under the infirmities of age (Ps 71:9, 18).
Is sought in vain from the world (Ps 69:20; Ecc 4:1; La 1:2), abundant (Ps 71:21; Isa 66:10-11), a cause of praise (Isa 12:1; 49:13), everlasting (2Th 2:16-17), firm and secure (Heb 6:17-20).
To the persecuted (Dt 33:27), the poor (Ps 10:14; 34:6, 9-10), those deserted by friends or family (Ps 27:10; 41:9-12; Jn 14:18; 15:18-19), the sick (Ps 41:3), the troubled in mind (Ps 42; 94:19; Jn

14:1, 27; 16:20-22), those who mourn for sin (Ps 51:17; Isa 1:18; 40:1-2; 61:1-3; Mic 7:18-19; Lk 4:18-19), the tempted (Ro 16:17-20; 1Co 10:13; 2Co 12:9; Jas 1:12; 4:7-10; 2Pe 2:9; Rev 2:10).

Prayer Under:

For the presence and support of God (Ps 10:1; 102:2). Exhortation to (Jas 5:13). That, God would consider our trouble (2Ki 19:16; Ne 9:32; Ps 9:13; La 5), we may be taught the uncertainty of life (Ps 39:4), the Holy Spirit may not be withdrawn (Ps 51:11), we may be turned to God (Ps 51:12-15; 80:7; 85:4-7; Jer 31:18).

For, protection and preservation from enemies (2Ki 19:19; 2Ch 20:12; Ps 17:8-9; 143:11-12), divine teaching and direction (Job 34:32; Ps 27:11; 143:10), divine comfort (Ps 4:6; 119:76-77), mercy (Ps 6:2; Hab 3:2), deliverance from troubles (Ps 25:17, 22; 39:10; Isa 64:9-12; Jer 17:14), pardon and deliverance from sin (Ps 39:8; 51:1-17; 79:8-9), relief from troubles (Ps 39:12-13), restoration of joy (Ps 51:8, 12; 69:29; 90:14-15), increase of faith (Mk 9:24).

AFFLICTIONS [4804, 5596, *2568*].

In General:

God, determines the continuance of (Ge 15:13-14; Nu 14:33; Isa 10:25; Jer 29:10), appoints (2Ki 6:33; Job 5:6, 17; Ps 66:10-11; Am 3:6; Mic 6:9), dispenses as he will (Job 11:10; Isa 10:15-16; 45:7), regulates the measure of (Ps 80:5; Isa 9:1; Jer 46:28), does not willingly send (La 3:33).

Consequent upon the Fall (Ge 3:16-19). Frequently end in good (Ge 50:20; Ex 1:11-12; Dt 8:15-18; Jer 24:5-7; Eze 20:37). Sin visited with (2Sa 12:14; Ps 89:30-32; Isa 57:17; Ac 13:10-11). Sin produces (Job 4:8; 20:11; Pr 1:31).

Always less than we deserve (Ezr 9:13; Ps 103:10).Man is born to (Job 5:6-7; 14:1). Often severe (Job 16:7-16; Ps 42:7; 66:12; Rev 7:14). Tempered with mercy (Ps 78:38-39; 106:43-46; Isa 30:18-21; La 3:32; Mic 7:7-9; Na 1:12). Believers are to expect (Jn 16:33; Ac 14:22). Believers appointed to (1Th 3:3).

Of Believers:

Exhibit the love and faithfulness of God (Dt 8:5; Ps 119:75; Pr 3:11-12; 1Co 11:32; Heb 12:6-11; Rev 3:19-22). Believers have joy under (Job 5:17-18; Jas 5:11). Are but temporary (Ps 30:5; 103:9-10; Isa 54:7-8; Jn 16:20; 1Pe 1:6; 5:10). End in joy and blessedness (Ps 126:5-6; Isa 61:2-3; Mt 5:4; 1Pe 4:13-14). Often comes from the profession of the gospel (Mt 24:9; Jn 15:21; 2Ti 3:11-12). Are comparatively light (Ac 20:23-24; Ro 8:18; 2Co 4:17-18).

Benefits to Believers:

In, trying our faith and obedience (Ge 22:1-2, w Heb 11:17-18; Ex 15:23-25; Dt 8:2-3, 16; 1Pe 1:7; Rev 2:10), humbling us (Dt 8:3, 16; 2Ch 7:13-14; La 3:19-24; 2Co 12:7), leading us to confession of sin (Nu 21:7; Ps 32:4-5; 51:3-6), turning us to God (Dt 4:30-31; Ne 1:8-9; Ps 78:34-38; Isa 10:20-21; Hos 2:6-7), leading us to seek God in prayer (Jdg 4:3; Jer 31:18; La 2:17-19; Hos 5:14-

15; Jnh 2:1), testing and exhibiting our sincerity (Job 23:10; Ps 66:10; Pr 17:3), keeping us from again departing from God (Job 34:31-32; Isa 10:20; Eze 14:10-11), convincing us of sin (Job 36:8-10; Ps 119:67; Lk 15:16, 18), exhibiting the power and faithfulness of God (Ps 34:19-20; 2Co 4:8-11), exercising our patience (Ps 40:1; Ro 5:3; Jas 1:3; 1Pe 2:20), teaching us the will of God (Ps 119:71; Isa 26:9), purifying us (Ecc 7:2-3; Isa 1:25-26; 48:10; Jer 9:6-7; Zec 13:9; Mal 3:2-3), promoting the glory of God (Jn 9:1-3; 11:3-4; 21:18-19), rendering us fruitful in good works (Jn 15:2; Heb 12:10-11), furthering the gospel (Ac 8:3-4; 11:19-21; Php 1:12-13; 2Ti 2:8-10; 4:16-18).

Examples of Benefits to Believers—

Joseph's brothers (Ge 42:21), Joseph (Ge 45:5-8), Israel (Dt 8:3-5), Josiah (2Ki 22:19), Hezekiah (2Ch 32:25-26), Manasseh (2Ch 33:12), Jonah (Jnh 2:7), Prodigal son (Lk 15:21).

Of the Wicked:

Are ineffective of themselves, for their conversion (Ex 9:30; Isa 9:13; Jer 2:30; Hag 2:17). God is glorified in (Ex 14:4; Eze 38:22-23). Their persecution of believers, a cause of (Dt 30:7; Ps 55:19; Zec 2:9; 2Th 1:6). Are multiplied (Dt 31:17; Job 20:12-18; Ps 32:10). Sometimes humble them (1Ki 21:27). Frequently harden (Ne 9:28-31; Jer 5:3). Are continual (Job 15:20; Ecc 2:23; Isa 32:10). Produce slavish fear (Job 15:24; Ps 73:19; Jer 49:3, 5). Are often judicially sent (Job 21:17; Ps 107:17; Jer 30:15). God holds in derision (Ps 37:13; Pr 1:26-27). Are for examples to others (Ps 64:7-9; Zep 3:6-7; 1Co 10:5-13; 2Pe 2:6). Are often sudden (Ps 73:19; Pr 6:15; Isa 30:12-13; Rev 18:10). Failure to repent is a cause of (Pr 1:30-31; Eze 24:13; Am 4:6-12; Zec 7:11-12; Rev 2:21-22). Believers should not be alarmed at (Pr 3:25-26).

Examples of Afflictions of the Wicked—

Pharaoh and the Egyptians (Ex 9:14-15; 14:24-25), Ahaziah (2Ki 1:1-4), Gehazi (2Ki 5:27), Jehoram (2Ch 21:12-16), Uzziah (2Ch 26:19-21), Ahaz (2Ch 28:5-8, 22).

AFTERWARD [*339, 928, 2256, 3869, 4200, 4946, *2779, 3552, 3958*]. (Ps 73:24; Pr 20:17; Mt 25:11; Jn 13:36; 1Co 15:46; Gal 3:23; Heb 12:11, 17).

AGABUS [*13*]. A prophet living in Jerusalem who prophesied a world-wide famine which was fulfilled during the reign of Claudius (Ac 11:27-30). He also met Paul in Caesarea and warned him that he would be arrested in Jerusalem (Ac 21:10-11).

AGAG [97] (possibly *violent*).

1. The king of Amalek, referred to by Balaam (Nu 24:2-3, 7).

2. Another king of Amalek. Saul spared Agag when he should have killed him. When Samuel came into the camp, he rebuked Saul and ordered that Agag be brought to him. Samuel killed Agag

as Saul should have according to God's command (1Sa 15:8-33).

AGAGITE [98] (possibly *violent*). A description of Haman (Est 3:1, 10; 8:3, 5; 9:24). The LXX understood the term to mean "enemy." Josephus explains it as a synonym of Amalek, a descendant of Agag (Ant. xi, 6, 5). *See Agag, 2.*

AGAPE [26, 27] (*love; volitional and self-sacrificial love*). A Greek word meaning "love" and "love feasts." *See Love; Love Feast.*

AGAR *See Hagar.*

AGATE [8648]. A precious stone used in the high priest's breastpiece (Ex 28:19; 39:12). KJV "agates" is also translated "rubies" in the NIV (Isa 54:12; Eze 27:16). *See Minerals of the Bible, 1; Ruby; Stones.*

AGE *See Aeon.*

AGE (OLD), AGED *See Old Age.*

AGEE [96] (possibly *fugitive*). A Hararite and the father of Shammah (2Sa 23:11).

AGENCY Duties entrusted to God's servants.
In salvation of people (Job 33:14-30; Ps 8:2; Mt 4:19; 5:13-16; Lk 1:17; 5:10; 10:17; 1Co 1:26-29; 1Th 2:4; 1Ti 1:11; 6:20; Jas 5:20).
In executing judgments (Ge 3:15; 1Sa 15:18; 2Sa 7:14; 2Ki 9:6-9; 19:25-26; 2Ch 22:7; Ps 17:13-14; Isa 10:5-6; 13:5; 41:15; Jer 27:8; 51:20-23).

AGONY [987, 1631, 2655, 7815, 8358, *990, 3849, 4506, 6047*]. Under judgment of God (Eze 30:16; Mic 4:10; Rev 9:5; 16:10). Of the rich man (Lk 16:24-25). Of Jesus (Ac 2:24).

AGORA [59] (*marketplace*). In ancient cities the town meeting place was the market where the public met for the exchange of merchandise, information, and ideas (Mk 6:56; Ac 17:17).

AGRAPHA (*unwritten things*). Sayings ascribed to Jesus transmitted to us outside of the canonical Gospels. The number is not large, and most are obviously apocryphal or spurious. They are found in the NT outside of the Gospels (Ac 1:4ff; 11:16; 20:35; 1Co 7:10), ancient manuscripts of the NT, patristic literature, papyri, and apocryphal gospels.

AGRICULTURE The occupation of man before the Fall (Ge 2:15). Rendered laborious by the curse on the earth (Ge 3:17-19). Man condemned to labor in, after the Fall (Ge 3:23). Contributes to the support of all (Ecc 5:9). The providence of God to be acknowledged in the produce of (Jer 5:24; Hos 2:8).

Requires:
Hard work will be abundantly recompensed (Pr 12:11; 13:23; 28:19; Heb 6:7). Diligence (Pr

27:23-27; Ecc 11:6). Wisdom (Isa 28:26). Hard work (2Ti 2:6). Patience in waiting (Jas 5:7).

Persons Engaged in, Called:
Workers of the ground (Ge 4:2). Workers or hired men (Mt 9:37; 20:1).

In General:
Patriarchs engaged in (Ge 4:2; 9:20). The labor of, supposed to be lessened by Noah (Ge 5:29, w Ge 9:20). Soil of Canaan suited to (Ge 13:10; Dt 8:7-10). Climate of Canaan favorable to (Dt 11:10-12). The Israelites loved and followed (2Ch 26:10). Peace favorable to (Jer 31:24). War destructive to (Jer 5:16-17; 51:23).

Was Promoted Among the Israelites by:
The prohibition against usury (Ex 22:25). The right of redemption (Lev 25:23-28). The promises of God's blessing on (Lev 26:4; Dt 7:13; 11:14-15). Allotments to each family (Nu 36:7-9).

Enactments to Protect:
Against, the trespass of cattle (Ex 22:5), injuring the produce of (Ex 22:6). Not to, be engaged in during the Sabbatical year (Ex 23:10-11), move the fields of another (Dt 5:21), covet landmarks (Dt 19:14; Pr 22:28), cut down crops of another (Dt 23:25). Produce of, exported (1Ki 5:11; Eze 27:17). Often performed by hired help (1Ch 27:26; 2Ch 26:10; Mt 20:8; Lk 17:7). Produce of, often reduced in yield because of sin (Isa 5:10; 7:23; Jer 12:13; Joel 1:10-12). Grief resulted from the failure of the fruits of (Joel 1:11; Am 5:16-17).

Activities in:
Binding sheaves of grain or weeds into bundles (Ge 37:7; Mt 13:30). Stacking (Ex 22:6). Gleaning (Lev 19:9; Ru 2:3). Pruning (Isa 5:6; Jn 15:2). Watering (Dt 11:10; 1Co 3:6-8). Threshing (Dt 25:4; Jdg 6:11). Winnowing (Ru 3:2; Job 39:12; Mt 3:12). Plowing (Job 1:14). Harrowing (Job 39:10; Isa 28:24). Mowing (Ps 72:6; Am 7:1; Jas 5:4). Planting (Pr 31:16; Isa 44:14; Jer 31:5). Sowing (Ecc 11:4; Isa 32:20; Mt 13:3). Clearing out the stones (Isa 5:2). Hedging (Isa 5:2, 5; Hos 2:6). Digging (Lk 13:8; 16:3). Reaping (Isa 17:5). Fertilizing (Isa 25:10; Lk 14:34-35). Storing in barns (Mt 6:26; 13:30). Weeding (Mt 13:28). Grafting (Ro 11:17-19, 24).

Animals Used in:
The donkey (Dt 22:10), ox (Dt 22:10; 25:4), horse (Isa 28:28).

Tools of:
The sickle (Dt 16:9; 23:25), cart (1Sa 6:7; Isa 28:27-28), mattock (1Sa 13:20), ax (1Sa 13:20), plow (1Sa 13:20), fork (1Sa 13:21), iron pick (2Sa 12:31), hoe (Isa 7:25), pruning knives (Isa 18:5; Joel 3:10), rod (Isa 28:27), winnowing fork (Jer 15:7; Mt 3:12; Lk 3:17), shovel (Isa 30:24), threshing sledge (Isa 41:15), sieve (Am 9:9).

Illustrative of:
Cultivating the heart (Jer 4:3; Hos 10:12). Cultivating the church (1Co 3:9).

AGRIPPA I [68]. Known in history as King Herod Agrippa I or Herod Agrippa, and in the NT

as Herod, 10 B.C. to A.D. 44 He was the grandson of Herod the Great and ruled over the whole of Judea from A.D. 41 to 44. He killed James to please the Jews and intended to do the same to Peter (Ac 12:1-5). He died suddenly in Caesarea (Ac 12:19-23; Jos. Antiq. XIX.viii.2), A.D. 44.

AGRIPPA II [68]. Known in history as King Herod Agrippa II, Marcus Julius Agrippa, and in the NT as Agrippa, A.D. 28 to after A.D. 93, probably c. A.D. 100. He was the son of Agrippa I, and ruled over only a small part of his father's territory. Paul appeared before the tribunal of Agrippa and Festus (Ac 25:23-26). Died in c. A.D. 100.

AGUE NIV "fever"; a disease "that will destroy your sight and drain away your life" (Lev 26:16). *See Fever.*

AGUR [101] (*gatherer,* possibly *wage earner*). The son of Jakeh; author or collector of the wise sayings of the Proverbs 30:1.

AHA [177, 208, 2027, 2098, 8011]. A term of derision (Ps 35:21; 40:15; 70:3; Eze 25:3; 26:2).

AHAB [281, 282] (*brother of father*).
1. King of Israel for twenty-two years, reigning in Samaria (1Ki 16:29). Idolatry of (1Ki 16:30-33; 18:18-20; 21:25-26). Marries Jezebel (1Ki 16:31). Reproved by Elijah; assembles the prophets of Baal (1Ki 18:15-46). Defeats Ben-Hadad (1Ki 20). Illegally confiscates Naboth's vineyard (1Ki 21). Closing history and death of (1Ki 22:1-41; 2Ch 18). Succeeded by his son, Ahaziah (1Ki 22:40). Prophecies against (1Ki 20:42; 21:19-24; 22:19-28; 2Ki 9:8, 25-26). Other wickedness of (2Ki 3:2; 2Ch 21:6; 22:3-4; Mic 6:16). The seventy sons of, all his chief men, his close friends, and his priest were murdered (2Ki 10:1-11).
2. A false prophet (Jer 29:21-22).

AHARAH [341] (*brother of Rah*). Also called Ashbel, Ahiram, and Aher, the third son of Benjamin (Ge 46:21; Nu 26:38; 1Ch 7:12; 8:1).

AHARHEL [342] (*brother of Rachel*). A son of Harum, and the founder of a family enrolled in the tribe of Judah (1Ch 4:8).

AHASAI *See Ahzai.*

AHASBAI [335] (*I seek refuge in Yahweh*). A Maacathite and the father of Eliphelet, one of David's heroes (2Sa 23:34). Possibly the same as Ur (1Ch 11:35). *See Ur.*

AHASUERUS Hebrew transliteration of the name of the Persian king Xerxes. *See Xerxes.*

AHAVA [178]. A Babylonian town on the Ahava Canal (Ezr 8:15, 21, 31).

AHAZ [298, 937] (*he has grasped*).
1. King of Judah, son and successor of Jotham (2Ki 15:38; 16:1; 2Ch 27:9; 28:1). Idolatrous

abominations of (2Ki 16:3-4; 2Ch 28:2-4, 22-25). Kingdom of, invaded by the kings of Syria and Samaria (2Ki 16:5-6; 2Ch 28:5-8). Robs the temple to purchase aid from the king of Assyria (2Ki 16:7-9, 17-18; 2Ch 28:21). Visits Damascus, obtains a unique pattern of an altar, which he substitutes for the altar in the temple in Jerusalem and otherwise perverts the forms of worship (2Ki 16:10-16). Stairway of (2Ki 20:11; Isa 38:8). Prophets in the reign of (Isa 1:1; Hos 1:1; Mic 1:1). Prophecies concerning (Isa 7:13-25). Succeeded by Hezekiah (2Ki 16:20).
2. Son of Micah and great-grandson of Jonathan (1Ch 8:35; 9:41-42).

AHAZIAH [301, 302, 3370] (*Yahweh has upheld*).
1. King of Judah. Also called Azariah (2Ch 22:6, ftn) and Jehoahaz (2Ch 21:17, ftn). History of (2Ki 8:25-29; 9:16-29). Gifts of, to the temple (2Ki 12:18). Brothers of, slain (2Ki 10:13-14). Succeeded by Athaliah (2Ch 22:10-12).
2. King of Israel. History of (1Ki 22:40, 49, 51-53; 2Ch 20:35-37; 2Ki 1). Succeeded by Jehoram (2Ki 3:1).

AHBAN [283] (*brother of intelligent one*). A Judahite, of the house of Jerahmeel (1Ch 2:29).

AHER [338] (*another, a substitute*). A Benjamite (1Ch 7:12). *See Aharah.*

AHI [306] (*my brother,* possibly *Yahweh is [my] brother*).
1. Chief of the Gadites in Gilead (1Ch 5:15).
2. A man of Asher, son of Shomer (1Ch 7:34).

AHIAH [308] (*brother of Yahweh*).
1. A leader of Israel who agreed to the covenant of Nehemiah (Ne 10:26).
2. *See Ahijah.*

AHIAM [307] (*brother of mother*). One of David's heroes (2Sa 23:33). The son of Sacar (1Ch 11:35).

AHIAN [319] (*little brother*). Son of Shemida (1Ch 7:19).

AHIEZER [323] (*[my] brother is a help*).
1. Captain of the tribe of Dan (Nu 1:12; 2:25-26). Contributes to the tabernacle (Nu 7:66-71).
2. One of David's valiant men (1Ch 12:3).

AHIHUD [310, 312] (*[my] brother has majesty*).
1. A prince of Asher, assists in allotting the land of Canaan among the tribes (Nu 34:27).
2. A son of Bela (1Ch 8:7).

AHIJAH [308, 309] (*[my] brother is Yahweh*).
1. Son of Bela (1Ch 8:7).
2. Son of Jerahmeel (1Ch 2:25).
3. A priest in Shiloh, probably identified with Ahimelech (1Sa 22:11). Was priest in Saul's reign (1Sa 14:3, 18). Killed (1Sa 22:11-19).

4. One of David's heroes (1Ch 11:36). Also called Eliam (2Sa 23:34).

5. A Levite who was treasurer in the tabernacle (1Ch 26:20).

6. Son of Shisha, secretary of Solomon (1Ki 4:3).

7. A prophet in Shiloh (1Ki 11:29-39; 12:15).

8. Father of Baasha (1Ki 15:27, 33; 2Ki 9:9). *See Ahiah.*

AHIKAM [324] (*[my] brother stands*). Son of Shaphan (2Ki 22:12-14; 25:22; 2Ch 34:20; Jer 26:24; 39:14; 40:5-16; 41:1-18; 43:6).

AHILUD [314] (*[my] brother is born*). Father of: Baana (1Ki 4:12), Jehoshaphat (2Sa 8:16; 20:24; 1Ki 4:3; 1Ch 18:15).

AHIMAAZ [318] (*[my] brother is fury*).

1. Father-in-law of king Saul (1Sa 14:50).

2. Son of Zadok, the high priest. Loyal to David (2Sa 15:36; 17:17-20; 18:19-33; 1Ch 6:8-9, 53).

3. One of Solomon's twelve district governors (1Ki 4:15). He married Basemath, the daughter of Solomon. Some suggest that he should be identified with the son of Zadok.

AHIMAN [317] (possibly *[my] brother is a gift*).

1. One of the three giant sons of Anak seen in Mt. Hebron by the spies (Nu 13:22). Sheshai, Ahiman, and Talmai, were driven by Caleb from Hebron (Jos 15:14) and killed (Jdg 1:10).

2. A Levite gatekeeper (1Ch 9:17).

AHIMELECH [316] (*[my] brother is king*).

1. Saul's high priest who helped David by giving him the bread of the Presence and Goliath's sword. Upon hearing this, Saul ordered the death of Ahimelech and the other priests with him (1Sa 21-22). Abiathar, son of Ahimelech, escaped.

2. A Hittite who, with Abishai, was asked to accompany David to Saul's camp (1Sa 26:6).

3. Son of Abiathar, and grandson of Ahimelech (2Sa 8:17; 1Ch 18:16; 24:6). *See Abiathar.*

AHIMOTH [315] (*[my] brother is my support* possibly *my brother is Mot*). Son of Elkanah (1Ch 6:25), descendant of Kohath and a Levite.

AHINADAB [320] (*[my] brother is willing*). Son of Iddo (1Ki 4:14).

AHINOAM [321] (*[my] brother is pleasant*).

1. Wife of King Saul (1Sa 14:50).

2. One of David's wives, a Jezreelitess (1Sa 25:43), who lived with him at Gath (1Sa 27:3). Captured by the Amalekites at Ziklag (1Sa 30:5) but rescued by David (1Sa 30:18). Ahinoam bore Amnon, David's first son (2Sa 3:2).

AHIO [311] (*[my] brother is Yahweh*).

1. A Levite who drove the cart bearing the ark (2Sa 6:3-4; 1Ch 13:7).

2. A Benjamite (1Ch 8:14).

3. Son of Jeiel (1Ch 8:31; 9:37).

AHIRA [327] (*[my] brother is my friend,* or *[my] brother is evil*). Prince captain of the tribe of Naphtali (Nu 1:15; 2:29; 7:78, 83; 10:27).

AHIRAM, AHIRAMITE [325, 326] (*[my] brother is exalted*). Son of Benjamin (Nu 26:38). *See Aharah.*

AHISAMACH [322] (*[my] brother is a support*). A Danite, the father of Oholiab (Ex 31:6; 35:34; 38:23).

AHISHAHAR [328] (*[my] brother was born at early dawn*). A descendant of Benjamin through Jediael and Bilhan (1Ch 7:10).

AHISHAR [329] (*[my] brother is upright,* or *[my] brother has sung*). An official over Solomon's household (1Ki 4:6).

AHITHOPHEL [330] (possibly *[my] brother is in the desert* or *[my] brother is foolishness*). One of David's counselors (2Sa 15:12; 1Ch 27:33). Joins Absalom (2Sa 15:31, 34; 16:15, 20-23; 17:1-23). Possibly referred to by David in Ps 55:12-14. Suicide of (2Sa 17:1-14, 23).

AHITUB [313] (*[my] brother is goodness*).

1. High Priest, father of Ahiah (1Sa 14:3; 22:9, 11-12, 20).

2. Father of Zadok (2Sa 8:17; 1Ch 18:16).

3. Ruler of the house of God (1Ch 9:11; Ne 11:11).

4. The Ahitub mentioned (1Ch 6:8, 11-12) is probably identical with the last described above, or else he is confused with Azariah (2Ch 31:10).

AHLAB [331] (*fat, fruitful, healthy*). A town of Asher from which the Israelites were not able to drive the inhabitants (Jdg 1:31).

AHLAI [333] (*Alas! I wish that!*).

1. The father of Zabad, one of David's soldiers (1Ch 11:41).

2. A daughter of Sheshan who married her father's Egyptian slave Jarha. They had a son Attai (1Ch 2:31-35).

AHOAH [291] (*brotherly*). A son of Bela (1Ch 8:4) and his descendants (2Sa 23:9, 28; 1Ch 11:12). *See Ahohite.* Also called Ahijah (1Ch 8:7) and Iri (1Ch 7:7).

AHOHITE [292]. A name given to the descendants of Ahoah, Dodo (2Sa 23:9), Zalmon (2Sa 23:28), Ilai (1Ch 11:29).

AHOLAH, AHOLA *See Oholah.*

AHOLIAB *See Oholiab.*

AHOLIBAH *See Oholah; Oholibah.*

AHOLIBAMAH *See Oholibamah.*

AHUMAI [293]. Son of Jahath (1Ch 4:2).

AHUZZAM [303] (*possessor*). Son of Ashhur (1Ch 4:6).

AHUZZATH [304] (*possession*). A "friend" of Abimelech, who made a peace treaty with Isaac at Beersheba after they saw that the Lord had blessed him (Ge 26:23-33).

AHZAI [300] (*Yahweh has grasped*). A priest who lived in Jerusalem (Ne 11:13).

AI [6504] (*the ruin, the heap*).
1. A royal city of the Canaanites. Conquest and destruction of (Jos 7; 8). Population of (Jos 8:25). Rebuilt (Ezr 2:28).
Also called Aija (Ne 11:31) and Aiath (Isa 10:28).
2. A city of the Ammonites (Jer 49:3).

AIAH [371] (*black kite [a type of hawk]*).
1. A Horite (Ge 36:24; 1Ch 1:40).
2. The father of Rizpah, Saul's concubine (2Sa 3:7; 21:8).

AIATH [6569] (possibly *ruin, heap*). Feminine form of the city Ai (Isa 10:28).

AIJA [6509] (*ruin, heap*). Another spelling of Ai (Ne 11:31). *See Ai, 1.*

AIJALON [389] (*[the] place of the deer*).
1. A city of Dan (Jos 19:42). Assigned to the Levites (Jos 21:24; 1Sa 14:31; 1Ch 6:69). Amorites of, not exterminated (Jdg 1:35).
2. A city of Zebulun (Jdg 12:12).
3. A city of Judah (2Ch 28:18; 11:10).
4. A valley (Jos 10:12).

AIJELETH SHAHAR KJV title of Ps 22; NIV "The Doe of the Morning." A musical term which probably indicated the tune to which the psalm was sung. *See Music, Symbols Used in.*

AIN [6526] (*an eye[ball]* or *spring [of water]*).
1. A city of Simeon (Jos 19:7; 15:32; 21:16; 1Ch 4:32). Also called Ashan (1Ch 6:59). Possibly identical with En Rimmon (Ne 11:29).
2. A landmark on the northern boundary of Israel (Nu 34:11).

AIN FESHKA (*spring of Feshka*). Oasis on the W side of the Dead Sea, S of Khirbet Qumran. Used for farming by the community that produced the Dead Sea Scrolls.

AJAH *See Aiah.*

AJALON *See Aijalon.*

AKAN [6826]. A Horite (Ge 36:27; 1Ch 1:42). Also spelled Jaakan (1Ch 1:42, ftn).

AKELDAMA [192] (*field of blood*). The "Field of Blood" (Mt 27:8) purchased with money which Judas received for betraying Jesus (Ac 1:18-19).

AKHENATEN (*blessed spirit of [the god] Aten*). The name chosen by Amenhotep IV (1379-1362 B.C.), ruler in the Eighteenth Dynasty of Egypt, during the biblical era of the judges. He was a monotheist, demanding that all worship only the sun god under the name Aten. The Amarna Letters date from his era. *See Amarna, Tell El.*

AKIM [943] (*Yahweh is my brother*). A descendant of Zerubbabel (Mt 1:14). Ancestor of Christ.

AKKAD [422]. An ancient center of Hamitic imperial power conquered by Nimrod (Ge 10:10). The city is evidently Agade which Sargon I brought into prominence as the capital of his Semitic empire, c. 2360-2180 B.C..

AKKUB [6822] (*guard*).
1. Son of Elioenai (1Ch 3:24).
2. A Levite who founded a family of temple gatekeepers (1Ch 9:17).
3. The head of a family of the temple servants (Ezr 2:45).
4. A Levite who helped expound the Law (Ne 8:7).

AKRABBIM (*scorpions*). *See Scorpion Pass.*

ALABASTER [223]. A white stone. Jars made of (Mt 26:7; Mk 14:3; Lk 7:37).

ALAMETH *See Alemeth.*

ALAMMELECH *See Allammelech.*

ALAMOTH [6628]. A musical term (1Ch 15:20). In the title to Ps 46. *See Music, Symbols Used in.*

ALCOHOL *See Abstinence; Abuse, Substance Abuse; Beer; Drunkenness; Fermented Drink; Wine.*

ALEMETH [6630, 6631] (*concealment*).
1. A son of Beker and grandson of Benjamin (1Ch 7:8).
2. Son of Jehoaddah or Jadah (1Ch 8:36; 9:42).
3. A Levitical city (1Ch 6:60).
See Almon.

ALEXANDER [235] (*man's defender*).
1. Son of Simon who carried the cross of Jesus (Mk 15:21).
2. A relative of the high priest, present at the defense of Peter and John (Ac 4:6).
3. A Jew of Ephesus (Ac 19:33).
4. A metalworker (1Ti 1:20; 2Ti 4:14).

ALEXANDER THE GREAT (*man's defender*). Son of Philip, King of Macedon. Lived from 356-323 B.C. He conquered the civilized world from Greece eastward to India. He is the "shaggy goat" of Da 8:5-8, 21. His hellenization of the world changed the trade language from

Aramaic to Greek, the language of the NT. *See Testaments, Time Between.*

ALEXANDRA Wife of Aristobulus, King of the Jews (104-103 B.C.).

ALEXANDRIA [233]. A city of Egypt (Ac 6:9). Ships of (Ac 27:6; 28:11). Apollos born in (Ac 18:24).

ALGUM, ALGUMWOOD [454].
Probably a variant of almugwood (1Ki 10:11-12, ftn; 2Ch 2:8; 9:10-11). *See Almug, Almugwood.*

ALIAH *See Alvah.*

ALIAN *See Alvan.*

ALIENS [1591, 1731, 2424, 4472, 5797, 5799, *3828, 4230*] (*sojourner, stranger, foreigner*). To be treated with justice (Ex 22:21; 23:9; Lev 19:33-34; Dt 1:16; 10:19 24:14, 17; 27:19; Jer 7:6; 22:3; Eze 22:29; Mal 3:5). Religious privileges of (Ex 12:48-49; Nu 9:14; 15:14-15). Kindness to Edomites, commanded (Dt 23:7).

Israelites Authorized:
To purchase, as slaves (Lev 25:44-45). To take usury from (Dt 15:3; 23:20). Not permitted to make kings of (Dt 17:15).

Forbidden to eat the passover (Ex 12:45). Partially exempt from the law (Dt 14:21). Numerous in times of David and Solomon (2Sa 22:45-46; 2Ch 2:17; 15:9). Oppressed (Eze 22:29). Rights of (Nu 35:15; Jos 20:9; Eze 47:22-23). David's kindness to (2Sa 15:19-20). Hospitality to, required by Jesus (Mt 25:35, 38, 43).

See   Glean;   Heathen;   Hospitality; Inhospitableness; Proselyte; Strangers.

ALL THINGS [*3972, 6017, 10353, *570, 3910, 4246*]. The whole created order. God created and rules over (1Ch 29:12; Ps 119:91; Ecc 11:5; Isa 44:24; Jer 10:16; 51:19; Jn 1:3; Ro 8:28; 1Co 8:6; Rev 4:11). Under Jesus' authority (Mt 11:27; 28:20; Lk 10:22; Jn 13:3; Eph 1:10, 22; Col 1:16, 17, 20; Heb 1:2, 3). All things are possible with God (Mt 19:26; Mk 10:27).

ALLAMMELECH [526] (*oak of the king* or *oak of [the god] Molech*). A town of Asher (Jos 19:26).

ALLEGORY [2648].
Explained:
Allegory is a literary genre that attempts to explain spiritual truths in pictorial forms. Some parables, for example, are a type of allegory. Allegory is also a method of interpretation that searches for a mysterious, hidden meaning beyond the literal understanding of the text.

In the OT:
Of the trees seeking a king (Jdg 9:8-15). Israel is a vine brought from Egypt (Ps 80). Wisdom is pictured as a noble woman (Pr 1:2-33); folly as a harlot (Pr 9:13-18). Messiah's kingdom repre-

sented by the wolf and the lamb dwelling together (Isa 11:6-8).

In the NT:
Jesus used allegory, as in the interpretation of his parable of the sower (Mt 13:18-23; Mk 4:14-20; Lk 8:11-15). Paul used allegory in using Hagar and Sarah to represent the differences between the Old and New Covenants (Gal 4:21-31). Many events and characters in the book of Revelation are used allegorically; most are clear or explained in context. For example, the Lamb and the Lion of Judah are both Jesus (Rev 5:5-14); the dragon is Satan (Rev 12:9).

Allegory in Interpretation:
Allegory is used as a literary device in the Bible. But, with the exception of Gal 4:21-31, allegory is not used in the NT to interpret the OT. However, allegory became increasingly important during the Apostolic period and into the Ante-Nicene period. The Alexandrian Jews of this period wished to reconcile Christianity with Greek thought. Origen taught a threefold sense of Scripture, corresponding to the body, soul, and the spirit.

In the Middle Ages four senses were found: historical, allegorical, moral, and anagogical (mystical). Jerusalem is *literally* a city in Israel, *allegorically* the church, *morally* the believing soul, *anagogically* the heavenly Jerusalem. The conquests of Joshua have been understood to be an allegory of the soul's victory over sin and self. Many Jewish scholars understand the Song of Songs to be allegorical, depicting God's love for Israel. On the other hand, many Christian scholars understand this as Christ's love for his church.

See Fable; Parable; Symbols and Similitudes.

ALLELUIA *See Hallelujah.*

ALLIANCES [*170, 907, 2489, 6468].
Forbidden:
(Ex 23:32; 34:12; Dt 7:2-3; 13:6, 8; Jos 23:6-7; Jdg 2:2; Ezr 9:12; Pr 1:10, 15; 2Co 6:14-17; Eph 5:11). Lead to idolatry (Ex 34:15-16; Nu 25:1-8; Dt 7:4; Jdg 3:5-7; Rev 2:20). Have led to murder and human sacrifice (Ps 106:37-38). Provoke the anger of God (Dt 7:4; 31:16-17; 2Ch 19:2; Ezr 9:13-14; Ps 106:29, 40; Isa 2:6). Provoke God to leave people to reap the fruits of them (Jos 23:12-13; Jdg 2:1-3).

Are ensnaring (Ex 23:33; Nu 25:18; Dt 12:30; 13:6; Ps 106:36). Are enslaving (2Pe 2:18-19). Are defiling (Ezr 9:1-2). Are degrading (Isa 1:23). Are ruinous to spiritual interests (Pr 29:24; Heb 12:14-15; 2Pe 3:17). Are ruinous to moral character (1Co 15:33). Are a proof of folly (Pr 12:11).

Children who enter into, bring shame upon their parents (Pr 28:7). Evil consequences of (Pr 28:19; Jer 51:7). The wicked are prone to (Ps 50:18; Jer 2:25). The wicked tempt believers to (Ne 6:2-4). Sin of, to be confessed, deeply repented of, and forsaken (Ezr 10).

Involve Believers:
In their guiltiness (2Jn 9-11; Rev 18:4). In their

punishment (Nu 16:26; Jer 51:6; Rev 18:4). Unbecoming in those called believers (2Ch 19:2; 2Co 6:14, 16; Php 2:15). Exhortations to shun all inducements to (Pr 1:10-15; 4:14-15; 2Pe 3:17). Exhortations to hate and avoid (Pr 14:7; Ro 16:17; 1Co 5:9-11; Eph 5:6-7; 1Ti 6:5; 2Ti 3:5). A call to come out from (Nu 16:26; Ezr 10:11; Jer 51:6, 45; 2Co 6:17; 2Th 3:6; Rev 18:4). Means of preservation from (Pr 2:10-20; 19:27).

Blessedness of avoiding (Ps 1:1). Blessedness of forsaking (Ezr 9:12; Pr 9:6; 2Co 6:17-18). Believers grieve to meet with, in their dealings with the world (Ps 57:4; 120:5-6; 2Pe 2:7-8). Believers grieve to witness in their brothers (Ge 26:35; Ezr 9:3; 10:6). Believers hate and avoid (Ps 26:4-5; 31:6; 101:7; Rev 2:2). Believers deprecate (Ge 49:6; Ps 6:8; 15:4; 101:4, 7; 119:115; 139:19). Believers are separate from (Ex 33:16; Ezr 6:21). Believers should be careful when accidentally thrown into (Mt 10:16; Col 4:5; 1Pe 2:12). Pious parents prohibit, to their children (Ge 28:1). Persons in authority should denounce (Ezr 10:9-11; Ne 13:23-27). Punishment of (Nu 33:56; Dt 7:4; Jos 23:13; Jdg 2:3; 3:5-8; Ezr 9:7, 14; Ps 106:41-42; Rev 2:16, 22-23).

Exemplified:
Solomon (1Ki 11:1-8). Rehoboam (1Ki 12:8-9). Jehoshaphat (2Ch 18:3; 19:2; 20:35-38). Jehoram (2Ch 21:6). Ahaziah (2Ch 22:3-5). Israelites (Ezr 9:1-2). Israel (Eze 44:7). Judas Iscariot (Mt 26:14-16).

Examples of Avoiding—
Man of God (1Ki 13:7-10). Nehemiah (Ne 6:2-4; 10:29-31). David (Ps 101:4-7; 119:115). Jeremiah (Jer 15:17). Joseph of Arimathea (Lk 23:51). Church of Ephesus (Rev 2:6).

Examples of Forsaking—
Israelites (Nu 16:27; Ezr 6:21-22; 10:3-4, 16-17). Sons of the priests (Ezr 10:18-19).

Examples of God's Judgments Against—
Korah (Nu 16:32). Ahaziah (2Ch 22:7-8). Judas Iscariot (Ac 1:18).

ALLON [474] (*oak*).
1. Son of Jedaiah (1Ch 4:37).
2. KJV Allon, a city of Naphtali (Jos 19:33), is "the large tree" in the NIV.

ALLON BACUTH [475] (*oak of weeping*). Place where Rebekah was buried (Ge 35:8).

ALLOY See *Refining.*

ALMIGHTY [7372, 8724, *4120, 4877*] (NIV rendering of *Shaddai* in the OT, *Pantokrator* in the NT). Used 56 times for: Identification (Ge 17:1). Invocation (Ge 28:3). Description (Eze 10:5). Praise (Rev 4:8). *See God, Names of.*

ALMODAD [525] (*God [El] is loved*). First mentioned of Joktan's thirteen sons (Ge 10:26; 1Ch 1:20).

ALMON [6626]. Levitical city of Benjamin (Jos 21:18). Called Alemeth (1Ch 6:60).

ALMON DIBLATHAIM [6627] (*way of the double fig cakes*). A stopping place in the wilderness journeys of the Israelites in Moab (Nu 33:46-47). Probably the same as Beth Diblathaim (Jer 48:22), and Diblah (Eze 6:14). *See Beth Diblathaim.*

ALMOND [4280, 5481, 9196]. A tree (Ge 30:37). Fruit of (Ge 43:11). Aaron's rod of the (Nu 17:8). Bowls of lampstand in the tabernacle fashioned after the flowers of the (Ex 25:33-34; 37:19-20).

Figurative: Of old age (Ecc 12:5), of God's watching (Jer 1:11-12).

ALMS KJV "alms" is rendered "give (to the poor)" and "acts of righteousness" in the NIV.

To be Given:
Without public show (Mt 6:1-4; Ro 12:8). Freely (2Co 9:6-7). Commanded (Dt 15:7-11; Mt 5:42; 19:21; Lk 12:33; 2Co 9:5-7; Gal 2:10; 1Ti 6:18; Heb 13:16). Asked by the unfortunate (Jn 9:8; Ac 3:2). Withholding, not of love (1Jn 3:17).

Instances of Giving:
Zacchaeus (Lk 19:8). Dorcas (Ac 9:36). Cornelius (Ac 10:2). The early Christians (Ac 2:44-45; 4:34-37; 6:1-3; 11:29-30; 24:17; Ro 15:25-28; 1Co 16:1-4; 2Co 8:1-4; 9:1; Heb 6:10).

See Beneficence; Charitableness; Gifts From God; Giving; Liberality; Neighbor; Poor; Works, Good.

ALMUG, ALMUGWOOD [523].
Probably a variant of algum and algumwood (1Ki 10:11-12; 2Ch 2:8; 9:10-11, ftn). Trees of Ophir and Lebanon used in building the temple and musical instruments. *See Algum, Algumwood.*

ALOES [189, 193, *264*]. Used as perfume (Ps 45:8; Pr 7:17; SS 4:14). In embalming the dead (Jn 19:39). Descriptive of the camping places of the Israelites (Nu 24:6).

ALOTH [6599]. One of the districts in Israel during the reign of Solomon that shared the responsibility of supplying provisions for the king and the royal household for one month in the year (1Ki 4:16).

ALPHA AND OMEGA [270+6042]. A title of Christ, meaning "First and Last" and "Beginning and End" (Rev 1:8, cf. 17; 21:6; 22:13; cf. Isa 41:4; 44:6; 48:12).

ALPHAEUS [271].
1. Father of James (Mt 10:3; Mk 3:18).
2. Father of Levi (Mk 2:14).
3. Possibly Clopas, husband of the Mary at the cross (Jn 19:25; also Mk 15:40), as Clopas and Alphaeus are of Semitic derivation. Unlikely the Cleopas on the Emmaus road (Lk 24:18) since Clopas was a common Greek name.

ALTAR OF BURNT OFFERING

Dimensions of (Ex 27:1; 38:1). Horns on the corners of (Ex 27:2; 38:2). Covered with bronze (Ex 27:2). All its vessels of bronze (Ex 27:3; 38:3). A network grating of bronze placed in (Ex 27:4-5; 38:4). Furnished with rings and poles (Ex 27:6-7; 38:5-7). Made after a divine pattern (Ex 27:8).

Called:

The bronze altar (Ex 39:39; 1Ki 8:64). The altar of God (Ps 43:4). The altar of the Lord (Mal 2:13). Placed in the court before the door of the tabernacle (Ex 40:6, 29). Sanctified by God (Ex 29:44). Anointed and sanctified with holy oil (Ex 40:10; Lev 8:10-11). Cleansed and purified with blood (Ex 29:36-37). Was most holy (Ex 40:10). Sanctified whatever touched it (Ex 29:37). All sacrifices to be offered on (Ex 29:38-42; Isa 56:7). All gifts to be presented at (Mt 5:23-24). Nothing polluted or defective to be offered on (Lev 22:22; Mal 1:7-8). Offering at the dedication of (Nu 7).

The Fire Upon:

Came from before the Lord (Lev 9:24). Was continually burning (Lev 6:13). Consumed the sacrifices (Lev 1:8-9). Sacrifices bound to the horns of (Ps 118:27, ftn). The blood of sacrifices put on the horns and poured at the foot of (Ex 29:12; Lev 4:7, 18, 25; 8:15).

The Priests:

Alone to serve (Nu 18:3, 7). Derived support from (1Co 9:13). Ahaz removed and profaned (2Ki 16:10-16). The Jews were condemned for swearing lightly by (Mt 23:18-19). A type of Christ (Heb 13:10).

ALTAR OF INCENSE

Dimensions of (Ex 30:1-2; 37:25). Covered with gold (Ex 30:3; 37:26). Top of, surrounded with a crown of gold (Ex 30:3; 37:26). Had four rings of gold under the crown for the poles (Ex 30:4; 37:27). Poles of, covered with gold (Ex 30:5). Called the golden altar (Ex 39:38). Placed before the veil in the outer sanctuary (Ex 30:6; 40:5, 26). Said to be before the Lord (Lev 4:7; 1Ki 9:25). Anointed with holy oil (Ex 30:25-27). The priest burned incense on, every morning and evening (Ex 30:7-8). No strange incense nor any sacrifice to be offered on (Ex 30:9). Atonement made by the high priest once every year (Ex 30:10; Lev 16:18-19). The blood of all sin offerings put on the horns of (Lev 4:7, 18). Covered by the priests before removal from the sanctuary (Nu 4:11). A type of Christ (Rev 8:3; 9:3).

Punishment for: Offering unauthorized fire on (Lev 10:1-2). Unauthorized offering on (2Ch 26:16-19).

ALTARS

[789, 2219, 2802, 4246, 4640, 5232, 10401, *1117*, *2593*, *2603*].

Designed for sacrifice (Ex 20:24). To be made of earth or uncut stone (Ex 20:24-25; Dt 27:5-6). Of brick, detestable to God (Isa 65:3). Natural rocks sometimes used as (Jdg 6:19-21; 13:19-20). Were

not to have steps up to them (Ex 20:26). For idolatrous worship, often built on roofs of houses (2Ki 23:12; Jer 19:13; 32:29). Idolaters raised Asherah poles near (Jdg 6:30; 1Ki 16:32-33; 2Ki 21:3). The Israelites not to raise Asherah poles (Dt 16:21). For idolatrous worship, to be destroyed (Ex 34:13; Dt 7:5). Probable origin of inscriptions on (Dt 27:8).

Mentioned in Scripture:

Of Noah (Ge 8:20). Of Abraham (Ge 12:7-8; 13:18; 22:9). Of Isaac (Ge 26:25). Of Jacob (Ge 33:20; 35:1, 3, 7). Of Moses (Ex 17:15; 24:4). Of Balaam (Nu 23:1, 14, 29). Of Joshua (Jos 8:30-31). Of the temple of Solomon (2Ch 4:1, 19). Of the second temple (Ezr 3:2-3). Of Reubenites, E of Jordan (Jos 22:10). Of Gideon (Jdg 6:26-27). Of the people of Israel (Jdg 21:4). Of Samuel (1Sa 7:17). Of David (2Sa 24:21, 25). Of Jeroboam at Bethel (1Ki 12:33). Of Ahaz (2Ki 16:10-12). Of the Athenians (Ac 17:23). For burnt offering (Ex 27:1-8). For incense (Ex 30:1-6). Protection afforded by (1Ki 1:50-51). Afforded no protection to murderers (Ex 21:14; 1Ki 2:18-34).

AL-TASCHITH

[*do] not destroy*]. In KJV titles of Pss 57-59; 75; NIV "Do Not Destroy." Probably the tune to which these psalms were sung. The phrase occurs in Isa 65:8, leading some to deduce it is the name of a vintage or wine-making song. *See Music, Symbols Used in.*

ALTRUISM

(*concern and actions for the welfare of others*).

Jesus Commends:

By teaching (Mt 20:26-27; 23:11; Mk 9:35; 10:43-45; Lk 22:26-27; Jn 13:4-17; Ac 20:35). By example (Jn 13:4-17), came to serve (Mt 20:28; Php 2:7), went about doing good works (Ac 10:38), pleased not himself (Ro 15:3), became poor for others (2Co 8:9).

Paul Commends:

By teaching, to help the weak (Ac 20:33-35; Ro 15:1-2), to promote the welfare of others (1Co 10:24, 31-33; Gal 6:1-2, 10; Php 2:4-9). By example, became servant of all (1Co 9:18-22; 2Co 4:5), made many rich (2Co 6:10).

Motives Inspiring to:

Love of neighbor (Lk 10:25-37). To save people (1Co 9:22). For Jesus' sake (2Co 4:5). Example of Jesus (2Co 8:9; Php 2:3-8).

See Alms; Beneficence; Charitableness; Duty of People to People; Liberality; Love.

ALUSH

[478]. Camping place of the Israelites (Nu 33:13).

ALVAH

[6595]. Chief of Edom, descended from Esau (Ge 36:40; 1Ch 1:51).

ALVAN

[6597] (possibly *ascending one*, or *tall*). Son of Shobal, a descendant of Seir (Ge 36:23). Also spelled Alian (1Ch 1:40, ftn).

AMAD

[6675]. A town of Asher (Jos 19:26).

AMAL [6663] (*laborer, troubler*). Son of Helem (1Ch 7:35).

AMALEK [6667]. Son of Eliphaz (Ge 36:12; 1Ch 1:36). Probably not the ancestor of the Amalekites mentioned in the time of Abraham (Ge 14:7).

AMALEKITE(S) [6667, 6668]. Descent of (Ge 36:12, 16).

Character of:
Wicked (1Sa 15:18). Oppressive (Jdg 10:12). Warlike and cruel (1Sa 15:33). Governed by kings (1Sa 15:20, 32). A powerful and influential nation (Nu 24:7). Possessed cities (1Sa 15:5).

Country of:
In the south of Canaan (Nu 13:29; 1Sa 27:8). Extended from Havilah to Shur (1Sa 15:7). Was the scene of ancient warfare (Ge 14:7). Part of the Kenites dwelt among (1Sa 15:6).

Conflict With Israel:
Were the first to oppose Israel (Ex 17:8). Beaten at Rephidim, through the intercession of Moses (Ex 17:9-13). Doomed to utter destruction foretold (Nu 24:20). Presumption of Israel punished by (Nu 14:45). United with Eglon against Israel (Jdg 3:13). Part of their possessions taken by Ephraim (Jdg 5:14, w Jdg 12:15). With Midian, oppressed Israel (Jdg 6:3-5). Saul overcame, and delivered Israel (1Sa 14:48), commissioned to destroy (1Sa 15:1-3), massacred (1Sa 15:4-8), condemned for not utterly destroying (1Sa 15:9-26; 28:18). Agag, king of, slain by Samuel (1Sa 15:32-33). Invaded by David (1Sa 27:8-9). Pillaged and burned Ziklag (1Sa 30:1-2). Pursued and slain by David (1Sa 30:10-20). Spoil taken from, consecrated (2Sa 8:11-12). Confederated against Israel (Ps 83:5-7). Remnant of, completely destroyed during the reign of Hezekiah (1Ch 4:41-43).

AMAM [585]. A city of Judah (Jos 15:26). Probably within the district later assigned to Simeon (Jos 19:1-9).

AMANA [592] (*constant*). A mountain near Lebanon (SS 4:8), from which flows the Abana River (2Ki 5:12). *See Abana.*

AMANUENSIS A secretary employed to write from dictation or to copy manuscripts.
Examples: Baruch (Jer 36:4; 45:1), Tertius (Ro 16:22), perhaps Silas (1Th 1:1; 2Th 1:1; 1Pe 5:12) and Timothy (2Co 1:1; Php 1:1; Col 1:1; 1Th 1:1; 2Th 1:1; Phm 1:1).

AMARANTHINE A type of straw flower that does not shrivel when picked. NIV "can never fade" (1Pe 1:4; 5:4).

AMARIAH [618, 619] (*Yahweh has said*).
1. Two Levites (1Ch 6:7, 52; 23:19; 24:23).
2. Chief priest in the reign of Jehoshaphat (2Ch 19:11).

3. A high priest, father of Ahitub (1Ch 6:11; Ezr 7:3).
4. A Levite, who assisted in distributing temple gifts (2Ch 31:15-19).
5. Son of Hezekiah (Zep 1:1).
6. Father of Zechariah (Ne 11:4).
7. A priest, returned from exile (Ne 10:3; 12:2). Probably also in Ne 12:13.
8. A returned exile. Divorces his idolatrous wife (Ezr 10:42).

AMARNA, TELL EL (*the hill Amarna*). The modern name for the ancient capital of Amenhotep IV (c. 1379-1362 B.C.), where in 1887 a large number of clay tablets containing the private correspondence between the ruling Egyptian pharaohs and the political leaders in Canaan were discovered. *See Akhenaten; Texts, Ancient Near Eastern Non-Biblical Texts Relating to the Old Testament.*.

AMASA [6690] (*[my] people are from Jesse*).
1. Nephew of David (2Sa 17:25; 1Ch 2:17). Joins Absalom (2Sa 17:25). Returns to David and is made captain of the host (2Sa 19:13). Slain (2Sa 20:8-12; 1Ki 2:5, 32).
2. Son of Hadlai (2Ch 28:12).

AMASAI [6691] (*[my] people are from Jesse*).
1. A Levite and ancestor of Samuel (1Ch 6:25, 35).
2. Leader of a body of men unhappy with Saul, who joined David (1Ch 12:18).
3. A priest and trumpeter (1Ch 15:24).
4. A Levite of the Kohathites (2Ch 29:12).

AMASHSAI [6692]. Priest in Nehemiah's time (Ne 11:13).

AMASIAH [6674] (*Yahweh carries a load*). A captain under Jehoshaphat (2Ch 17:16).

AMAZIAH [604, 605] (*Yahweh is powerful*).
1. A Levite (1Ch 6:45).
2. King of Judah. History of (2Ki 14; 2Ch 25).
3. An idolatrous priest at Bethel (Am 7:10-17).
4. Father of Joshah (1Ch 4:34).

AMBASSADORS [7495, 4563].
Sent by:
Moses to Edom (Nu 20:14), to the Amorites (Nu 21:21), by Gibeonites to the Israelites (Jos 9:4), Israelites to various nations (Jdg 11:12-28).
Hiram to David (2Sa 5:11), Solomon (1Ki 5:1).
Ben-Hadad to Ahab (1Ki 20:2-6), Amaziah to Jehoash (2Ki 14:8), Ahaz to Tiglath-Pileser (2Ki 16:7), Hoshea to So, king of Egypt (2Ki 17:4), Sennacherib through the field commander, to Hezekiah (2Ki 19:9), Merodach-Baladan to Hezekiah (2Ki 20:12; 2Ch 32:31), Zedekiah to Egypt (Eze 17:15).
Other references to (Pr 13:17; Isa 18:2; 30:4; 33:7; 36:11; 39:1-2; Lk 14:32).

Figurative (Job 33:23; Ob 1; 2Co 5:20; Eph 6:20).

AMBER NIV "glowing metal" (Eze 1:4, 27; 8:2). *See Glowing Metal; Minerals of the Bible, 1; Stones.*

AMBITION [*2249, 5818*].

Worthy: (1Ti 3:1).

Worldly: (Jas 4:1-2; 1Jn 2:16).

Cursed (Isa 5:8; Heb 2:9). Insatiable (Hab 2:5-6, 9). Perishable (Job 20:6-7; Ps 49:11-13). False accusation against Moses (Nu 16:13). Parable illustrating (2Ki 14:9). Rebuked by Jesus (Mt 16:26; 18:1-3; 20:20-28; 23:5-7, 12; Mk 9:33-37; 10:35-45; 12:38-39; Lk 9:25, 46-48; 11:43; 22:24-30; Jn 5:44). Temptation by Satan (Mt 4:8-10; Lk 4:5-8).

Instances of:

King of Babylon (Isa 14:12-15). Eve (Ge 3:5-6). Korah and his followers (Nu 16:3-35). Abimelech (Jdg 9:1-6). Absalom (2Sa 15:1-13; 18:18). Haman (Est 5:9-13). Disciples of Jesus (Mt 18:1-3; 20:20-24; Mk 9:33-37; 10:35-45; Lk 9:46-48; 22:24-30). Diotrephes (3Jn 9-10).

Disappointed: Ahithophel (2Sa 17:23), Adonijah (1Ki 1:5), Haman (Est 6:6-9).

AMBUSH [*741, 2675, 4422, 5041, 6811, 1909, 1910*].

Instances of: At Ai (Jos 8:2-22), Shechem (Jdg 9:25, 34), Gibeah (Jdg 20:29-41), near Zemaraim (2Ch 13:13). By Jehoshaphat (2Ch 20:21-22).

See Armies.

Figurative (Jer 51:12).

AMEN [*589, 297*] (*so be it*). A word used to reinforce a statement (Nu 5:22; Dt 27:12-26; Ne 5:13; 2Co 1:20; Rev 5:14; 22:20).

Used in prayer (1Ki 1:36; 1Ch 16:36; Ne 8:6; Ps 41:13; 72:19; 89:52; 106:48; Jer 28:6; Mt 6:13; 1Co 14:16; Rev 5:14; 19:4).

A title of Christ (Rev 3:14).

AMETHYST [*334, 287*]. A precious stone (Ex 28:19; 39:12; Rev 21:20). *See Minerals of the Bible, 1; Stones.*

AMI [*577*] (*trustworthy, reliable, faithful*). A servant of Solomon (Ezr 2:57). Also called Amon (Ne 7:59). *See Amon.*

AMINADAB *See Amminadab.*

AMITTAI [*624*] (*true*). Father of Jonah (2Ki 14:25; Jnh 1:1).

AMMAH [*565*] (*cubit*). A hill around Gibeon where Joab and Abishai halted in their pursuit of Abner and his forces after they defeated him in the battle of Gibeon (2Sa 2:24-32).

AMMI (*my people*). Name given to Israel symbolizing acceptance (Hos 2:1, KJV); opposite of Lo-Ammi, "not my people" (Hos 1:9).

AMMIEL [*6653*] (*God [El] is my kinsman*).

1. The son of Gemalli and spy sent out by Moses (Nu 13:12).

2. The father of Makir of Lo Debar (2Sa 9:4-5; 17:27).

3. The father of Bathsheba, one of David's wives (1Ch 3:5). Called also Eliam (2Sa 11:3).

4. The sixth son of Obed-Edom, who, with his family, was associated with the temple gatekeepers (1Ch 26:5).

AMMIHUD [*6654*] (*[my] people have majesty*).

1. The father of Elishama, chief of Ephraim (Nu 1:10; 2:18; 7:48, 53), and the son of Ladan (1Ch 7:26).

2. A man of Simeon and father of Shemuel (Nu 34:20).

3. A Naphtalite whose son, Pedahel, also assisted in the division of the land (Nu 34:28).

4. Father of Talmai and king of Geshur. Absalom fled to Talmai after he killed his brother Amnon (2Sa 13:37).

5. Son of Omri, father of Uthai (1Ch 9:4).

AMMIHUR *See Ammihud.*

AMMINADAB [*6657, 300*] (*my people are generous*).

1. A Levite. Aaron's father-in-law (Ex 6:23).

2. A prince of Judah (Nu 1:7; 2:3; 7:12, 17; 10:14; Ru 4:19-20; 1Ch 2:10; Mt 1:4; Lk 3:33).

3. A son of Kohath, son of Levi (1Ch 6:22). Perhaps the same as 1.

4. A Kohathite who assisted in the return of the ark from the house of Obed-Edom (1Ch 15:10-11).

AMMINADIB KJV "chariots of Amminadib" are "royal chariots of my people" in the NIV (SS 6:12, see also ftn). *See Amminadab.*

AMMISHADDAI [*6659*] (*Shaddai is [my] kinsman*). Father of Abiezer, captain of the tribe of Dan in Moses' time (Nu 1:12; 2:25; 7:66, 71; 10:25).

AMMIZABAD [*6655*] (*[my] people have given a gift*). Son of Benaiah, third of David's captains (1Ch 27:6).

AMMON [*6648, 6649*] (*people*). Ammon or Ben-Ammi is the name of one of the sons of Lot born to him by his youngest daughter in Zoar (Ge 19:38). *See Ammonite(s).*

AMMONI *See Kephar Ammoni.*

AMMONITE(S) [*1201+6648, 6648, 6649*].

History of:

Descendants of Ben-Ammi, one of the sons of Lot (Ge 19:38). Character of (Jdg 10:6; 2Ki 23:13; 2Ch 20:22-23; Jer 27:3, 9; Eze 25:1-7; Am 1:13; Zep 2:10). Territory of (Nu 21:24; Dt 2:19; Jos 12:2; 13:10, 25; Jdg 11:13).

Israelites forbidden to disturb (Dt 2:19, 37). Excluded from the congregation of Israel (Dt 23:3-6). Confederated with Moabites and Amalekites against Israel (Jdg 3:12-13). Defeated by the Israelites (Jdg 10:7-18; 11:32-33; 12:1-3; 1Sa 11; 2Sa 8:12; 10; 11:1; 12:26-31; 17:27; 1Ch 18:11; 20:1-3; 2Ch 20; 26:7-8; 27:5). Conspired against the Jews (Ne 4:7-8).

Solomon took wives from (1Ki 11:1; Ne 13:26). Rehoboam took wives from (2Ch 12:13). Jews intermarried with (Ezr 9:1, 10-12; 10:10-44; Ne 13:23).

Kings of: Baalis (Jer 40:14; 41:10).

Idols of: Molech (2Ki 23:13). *See Molech.*

Prophecies Concerning:
(Isa 11:14; Jer 9:25-26; 25:15-21; 27:1-11; 49:1-6; Eze 21:20, 28-32; 25:1-11; Da 11:41; Am 1:13-15; Zep 2:8-11).

AMNESTY For political offenses: Shimei (2Sa 19:16-23). Amasa (2Sa 19:13, w 17:25).

AMNON [578, 596] (*trustworthy*).
1. Son of David (2Sa 3:2; 1Ch 3:1). Incest of, and death (2Sa 13).
2. Son of Shimon (1Ch 4:20).

AMOK [6651] (*capable* KB). Priest who returned with Zerubbabel from exile (Ne 12:7, 20).

AMON [571, 572, *321*] (*trustworthy*).
1. Governor of the city of Samaria (1Ki 22:26; 2Ch 18:25).
2. King of Judah (2Ki 21:18-26; 2Ch 33:21-25; Zep 1:1; Mt 1:10).
3. Ancestor of one of the families of the temple servants (Ne 7:59). Called Ami (Ezr 2:57). *See Ami.*
4. A city thought by most scholars to be the same as the city of No (Hebrew) (Jer 46:25). It was the capital of Egypt. Thebes is the Greek name.

AMORITE(S) [616] (possibly *hill dwellers* BDB; *westerners* KB). Descendants of Canaan (Ge 10:15-6; 1Ch 1:13-14). Were giants (Am 2:9). Conquered by Kedorlaomer and rescued by Abraham (Ge 14).

Territory of (Ge 14:7; Nu 13:29; 21:13; Dt 1:4, 7, 19; 3:8-9; Jos 5:1; 10:5; 12:2-3; Jdg 1:35-36; 11:22), given to descendants of Abraham (Ge 15:21; 48:22; Dt 1:20; 2:26-36; 7:1; Jos 3:10; Jdg 11:23; Am 2:10), allotted to Reuben, Gad, and Manasseh (Nu 32:33-42; Jos 13:15-21), conquest of (Nu 21:21-30; Jos 10:11; Jdg 1:34-36).

Chiefs of (Jos 13:21). Wickedness of (Ge 15:16; 2Ki 21:11; Ezr 9:1). Idolatry of (Jdg 6:10; 1Ki 21:26). Judgments denounced against (Ex 23:23-24; 33:2; 34:10-11; Dt 20:17-18). Hornets sent among (Jos 24:12). Not exterminated (Jdg 1:34-36; 3:1-3, 5-8; 1Sa 7:14; 2Sa 2:2; 1Ki 9:20-21; 2Ch 8:7). Intermarry with Jews (Ezr 9:1-2; 10:18-44). Kings of (Jos 10:3-26).

AMOS [6650, *322*] (*burden bearer*). A prophet (Am 1:1). Forbidden to prophesy in Israel (Am 7:10-17). Vision of (Am 8:2).

AMOS, BOOK OF

Author: Amos of Tekoa

Date: Probably between 760-750 B.C.

Outline:
I. Superscription (1:1).
II. Introduction to Amos's Message (1:2).
III. Judgments on the Nations (1:3-2:16).
  A. Judgment on Aram (1:3-5).
  B. Judgment on Philistia (1:6-8).
  C. Judgment on Phoenicia (1:9-10).
  D. Judgment on Edom (1:11-12).
  E. Judgment on Ammon (1:13-15).
  F. Judgment on Moab (2:1-3).
  G. Judgment on Judah (2:4-5).
  H. Judgment on Israel (2:6-16).
    1. Ruthless oppression of the poor (2:6-7a).
    2. Unbridled profanation of religion (2:7b-8).
    3. Contrasted position of the Israelites (2:9-12).
    4. The oppressive system will perish (2:13-16).
IV. Oracles Against Israel (3:1-5:17).
  A. Judgment on the Chosen People (ch. 3).
    1. God's punishment announced (3:1-2).
    2. The announcement vindicated (3:3-8).
    3. The punishment vindicated (3:9-15).
  B. Judgment on an Unrepentant People (ch. 4).
    1. Judgment on the socialites (4:1-3).
    2. Perversion of religious life (4:4-5).
    3. Past calamities brought no repentance (4:6-11).
    4. No hope for a hardened people (4:12-13).
  C. Judgment on an Unjust People (5:1-17).
    1. The death dirge (5:1-3).
    2. Exhortation to life (5:4-6).
    3. Indictment of injustices (5:7-13).
    4. Exhortation to life (5:14-15).
    5. Prosperity will turn to grief (5:16-17).
V. Announcements of Exile (5:18-6:14).
  A. A Message of Woe Against Israel's Perverted Religion (5:18-27).
  B. A Message of Woe Against Israel's Complacent Pride (6:1-7).
  C. A Sworn Judgment on the Proud and Unjust Nation (6:8-14).
VI. Visions of Divine Retribution (7:1-9:10).
  A. Judgment Relented (7:1-6).
    1. A swarm of locusts (7:1-3).
    2. A consuming fire (7:4-6).
  B. Judgment Unrelented (7:7-9:10).
    1. The plumb line (7:7-17).
    a. The vision (7:7-9).
    b. Challenged and vindicated (7:10-17).
    2. The basket of ripe fruit (ch. 8).
    a. The vision (8:1-3).
    b. The exposition (8:4-14).
    3. The Lord by the altar (9:1-10).

a. The vision (9:1-4).

b. The exposition (9:5-10).

VII. Restored Israel's Blessed Future (9:11-15).

A. Revival of the House of David (9:11-12).

B. Restoration of Israel to an Edenic Promised Land (9:13-15).

See Prophets, The Minor.

AMOZ [576] (*strong*). Father of Isaiah (2Ki 19:2, 20; 20:1; Isa 1:1; 13:1).

AMPHIPOLIS [315] (*a city surrounded* or *a city conspicuous*). City of Macedonia not far from Philippi. Paul passed through it (Ac 17:1).

AMPLIATUS [309]. A Christian to whom Paul sent a greeting (Ro 16:8).

AMRAM, AMRAMITES [6688, 6689] (*exalted people*).

1. Father of Moses (Ex 6:18, 20; Nu 26:58-59; 1Ch 6:3, 18; 23:12-13). Head of one of the branches of Levites (Nu 3:19, 27; 1Ch 26:23). Age of, at death (Ex 6:20).

2. Son of Bani (Ezr 10:34).

3. *See Hemdan.*

AMRAPHEL [620]. King of Shinar (Ge 14:1, 9).

AMULET *See Charmers and Charming.*

AMUN *See Amon.*

AMUSEMENTS AND WORLDLY PLEASURES Belong to

the works of the flesh (Gal 5:19, 21). Are transitory (Job 21:12-13; Heb 11:25), meaningless (Ecc 2:11), choke the Word of God in the heart (Lk 8:14), formed a part of idolatrous worship (Ex 32:4, 6, 19, w 1Co 10:7; Jdg 16:23-25).

Lead to:

Rejection of God (Job 21:12-15), poverty (Pr 21:17), disregard of the judgments and works of God (Isa 5:12; Am 6:1-6), sorrow (Pr 14:13), greater evil (Job 1:5; Mt 14:6-8), attempting to find fulfillment in (Ecc 2:1-8).

Indulgence in:

A proof of folly (Ecc 7:4), a characteristic of the wicked (Isa 47:8; Eph 4:17, 19; 2Ti 3:4; Tit 3:3; 1Pe 4:3), a proof of spiritual death (1Ti 5:6), an abuse of riches (Jas 5:1, 5), wisdom of abstaining from (Ecc 7:2-3), shunned by the early believers (1Pe 4:3).

Abstinence From:

Seems strange to the wicked (1Pe 4:4), denounced by God (Isa 5:11-12), exclude from the kingdom of God (Gal 5:21), punishment of (Ecc 11:9; 2Pe 2:13), renunciation of, exemplified by Moses (Heb 11:25).

See Dancing; Games; Pleasure, Worldly; Worldliness.

AMZI [603] (possibly *Yahweh is my strength*).

1. A descendant of Merari and of Levi, and

progenitor of Ethan, whom David set over the service of song (1Ch 6:44-46).

2. An ancestor of Adaiah, a priest in the second temple (Ne 11:12).

ANAB [6693] (*grape*). A city of the Anakites taken by Joshua (Jos 11:21). It fell to Judah (Jos 15:50). SE of Debir, SW of Hebron. It retains its ancient name.

ANAH [6704].

1. Daughter of Zibeon and mother of Oholibamah, Esau's wife (Ge 36:2, 14, 25).

2. Son of Seir, chief of Edom (Ge 36:20, 29; 1Ch 1:38).

3. Son Zibeon (Ge 36:24; 1Ch 1:40-41). Also called Beeri (Ge 26:34).

ANAHARATH [637]. City on the border of Issachar (Jos 19:19). Modern en-Naura.

ANAIAH [6717] (*Yahweh responds*).

1. A leader or priest who assisted in the reading of the law to the people (Ne 8:4).

2. A returned exile who, with Nehemiah, sealed the covenant (Ne 10:22). Possibly the same as 1.

ANAK [6710, 6737] (*[long] necked, tall*). Descendant of Arba (Jos 15:13), and the ancestor of the Anakites (Nu 13:22, 28, 33). *See Anakites.*

ANAKITES [1201+6737, 6737] (*[long-] necked, tall*). Descent of (Nu 13:22; Jos 15:13). Called the descendants of Anak (Nu 13:33), Anakites (Dt 1:28; 9:2).

Divided into three tribes (Jos 15:14). Inhabited the mountains of Judah (Jos 11:21). Hebron, chief city of (Jos 14:15, w 21:11). Of gigantic strength and stature (Dt 2:10-11, 21). Israel terrified by (Nu 14:1, w 13:33). Hebron a possession of, given to Caleb for his faithfulness (Jos 14:6-14). Driven from Hebron by Caleb (Jos 15:13-14). Driven from Kiriath Sepher or Debir by Othniel (Jos 15:15-17; Jdg 1:12-13). Almost annihilated (Jos 11:21-22).

ANAMITES [6723]. A tribe descended from Mizraim (Ge 10:13; 1Ch 1:11).

ANAMMELECH [6724] (*Anath is king*). An Assyrian idol (2Ki 17:31).

ANAN [6728] (*cloud*). A Jew, returned from Babylonian captivity (Ne 10:26).

ANANI [6730] (*Yahweh is a covering*). A descendant of David (1Ch 3:24).

ANANIAH [6731, 6732] (*Yahweh is a covering*).

1. Son of Maaseiah (Ne 3:23).

2. Town of Benjamin (Ne 11:32).

ANANIAS [393] (*Yahweh is gracious*).

1. High priest, before whom Paul was tried (Ac 23:2-5; 24:1; 25:2).

2. A covetous member of church at Jerusalem. Falsehood and death of (Ac 5:1-11).

3. A Christian in Damascus (Ac 9:10-18; 22:12-16).

ANARCHY

In Israel: (Jdg 17:6; 18:1; 19:1; 21:25; Isa 3:5-8).

In the Early Church: Warned against (Gal 5:13-14). Insubordinate members hostile to authority (2Pe 2:10-19; Jude 8-13).

ANATH [6742] (a Semitic goddess).

1. Father of the judge Shamgar (Jdg 3:31; 5:6).

2. A Canaanite goddess of war and of love, sometimes identified with Astarte, Asherah, and Ashtoreth. She was the sister and consort of Baal. The name is reflected in the city Beth Anath (Jos 19:38; Jdg 1:33). See Asherah; Ashtoreth; Beth Anath.

ANATHEMA [353] (devoted to destruction).

A thing devoted to God becomes his and is therefore irrevocably withdrawn from common use (Lev 27:28-29; Ro 9:3; 1Co 12:3; 16:22; Gal 1:9).

ANATHEMA MARANATHA These
words from 1Co 16:22 were formerly interpreted as a double curse. Anathema does mean cursed (1Co 12:3). Marana tha is Aramaic for "Come, O Lord!" (cf. Rev 22:20).

See Blasphemy; Cursing; God, Name of; Oath.

ANATHOTH, ANATHOTHITE
[6743, 6744, 6745] (plural of Anath).

1. A Levitical city in Benjamin (Jos 21:18; 1Ch 6:60). Abiathar confined in (1Ki 2:26).

Birthplace of Jeremiah (Jer 1:1; 32:7-12), of Abiezer (2Sa 23:27), of Jehu (1Ch 12:3). Prophecies against (Jer 11:21-23). Inhabitants of, after Babylonian captivity (Ezr 2:23; Ne 7:27).

2. Son of Beker (1Ch 7:8).

3. A Jew, who returned from Babylon (Ne 10:19).

ANCHOR [46, 149, 4694, 5007]. Literal (Ac 27:17, 29, 30, 40). Figurative (Heb 6:19).

ANCIENT OF DAYS A title of Yahweh (Da 7:9, 13, 22).

ANCIENT TEXTS RELATING TO THE OLD TESTAMENT See
Texts, Ancient Near Eastern Non-Biblical Texts Relating to the Old Testament.

ANCIENTS Those of the past (1Sa 24:13). See Elders.

ANDREW [436] (manly). An apostle. A
fisherman (Mt 4:18). Of Bethsaida (Jn 1:44). A disciple of John (Jn 1:40). Finds Peter, his brother, and brings him to Jesus (Jn 1:40-42). Call of (Mt 4:18; Mk 1:16). His name appears in the list of the apostles (Mt 10:2; Mk 3:18; Lk 6:14). Asks the Master privately about the destruction of the temple (Mk 13:3-4). Tells Jesus of the Greeks who wanted to see him (Jn 12:20-22). Reports the number of loaves at the feeding of the five thousand (Jn 6:8). Meets with the disciples after the Lord's ascension (Ac 1:13).

ANDRONICUS [438] (victor [over] man).
Relative of Paul; an apostle (Ro 16:7).

ANEM [6722] (springs). A Levitical city (1Ch 6:73).

ANER [6738, 6739].

1. A Canaanite chief and brother of Mamre (Ge 14:13, 24).

2. A Levitical city of Manasseh (1Ch 6:70).

ANGEL [OF THE LORD] [4855,
10417, 34] (messenger). In addition to 54 occurrences of "the angel of the Lord" (Ex 3:2; Jdg 2:1), many uses of "angel" indicate a manifestation of God himself. These include: angel (Ac 7:30, 35 w Ex 3:2), my angel (Ex 23:20-23; 32:34), angel of God (Ex 14:19; Jdg 13:6; 2Sa 14:17, 20), angel of his Presence (Isa 63:9). See Angels.

ANGEL OF THE CHURCHES
Heavenly messengers and guardians or earthly messengers and pastors (Rev 1:20; 2:1, 8, 18; 3:1, 7, 14).

ANGELS [52, 466+1201, 466+1201+2021,
4855, 34, 2694].

Elect:

Created by God and Christ (Ne 9:6; Col 1:16). Worship God and Christ (Ne 9:6; Php 2:9-11; Heb 1:6). Are ministering spirits (1Ki 19:5; Ps 68:17; 104:4; Lk 16:22; Ac 12:7-11; 27:23; Heb 1:7, 14). Communicate the will of God and Christ (Da 8:16-17; 9:21-23; 10:11; 12:6-7; Mt 2:13, 20; Lk 1:19, 28; Ac 5:20; 8:26; 10:5; 27:23; Rev 1:1). Obey the will of God (Ps 103:20; Mt 6:10). Execute the purposes of God (Nu 22:22; Ps 103:21; Mt 13:39-42; 28:2; Jn 5:4; Rev 5:2). Execute the judgments of God (2Sa 24:16; 2Ki 19:35; Ps 35:5-6; Ac 12:23; Rev 16:1). Celebrate the praises of God (Job 38:7; Ps 148:2; Isa 6:3; Lk 2:13-14; Rev 5:11-12; 7:11-12). The law given by the mediation of (Ps 68:17; Ac 7:53; Heb 2:2).

Announced: The conception of Christ (Mt 1:20-21; Lk 1:31). The birth of Christ (Lk 2:10-12). The resurrection of Christ (Mt 28:5-7; Lk 24:23). The ascension and second coming of Christ (Ac 1:11). The conception of John the Baptist (Lk 1:13, 36).

Minister to Christ (Mt 4:11; Lk 22:43; Jn 1:51). Are subject to Christ (Eph 1:21; Col 1:16; 2:10; 1Pe 3:22). Shall execute the purposes of Christ (Mt 13:41; 24:31). Shall attend Christ at his second coming (Mt 16:27; 25:31; Mk 8:38; 2Th 1:7). Know and delight in the gospel of Christ (Eph 3:9-10; 1Ti 3:16; 1Pe 1:12). Mediation of, in response to prayer (Mt 26:53; Ac 12:5, 7). Rejoice over every repentant sinner (Lk 15:7, 10). Have charge over the children of God (Ps 34:7; 91:11-12; Da 6:22; Mt 18:10). Are of different orders (Isa 6:2; 1Th 4:16; 1Pe 3:22; Jude 9; Rev 12:7). Not to be worshiped (Col 2:18; Rev 19:10; 22:9). Are examples of meekness (2Pe 2:11; Jude 9). Are wise (2Sa 14:20). Are mighty (Ps 103:20). Are holy (Mt 25:31). Are elect (1Ti 5:21). Are innumerable (Job 25:3; Heb 12:22).

Fallen: (Job 4:18; Mt 25:41; 2Pe 2:4; Jude 6; Rev 2:9). *See Demons.*

ANGER [678, 2405, 2779, 3019, 4087, 4088, 4089, 5757, 6301, 6939, 7287, 7861, 7863, 7911, 7912, 8074, 8120, *2596, 3973, 3974*].

Forbidden (Mt 5:22; Ro 12:19). A work of the flesh (Gal 5:20). A characteristic of fools (Pr 12:16; 14:29; 27:3; Ecc 7:9).

Connected With:
Pride (Pr 21:24). Cruelty (Ge 49:7; Pr 27:3-4). Clamor and evil-speaking (Eph 4:31). Malice and blasphemy (Col 3:8). Strife and contention (Pr 21:19; 29:22; 30:33). Brings its own punishment (Job 5:2; Pr 19:19; 25:28). Grievous words stir up (Jdg 12:4; 2Sa 19:43; Pr 15:1). Should not betray us into sin (Ps 37:8; Eph 4:26). In prayer be free from (1Ti 2:8). May be averted by wisdom (Pr 29:8). Meekness pacifies (Pr 15:1; Ecc 10:4). Children should not be provoked to (Eph 6:4; Col 3:21). Be slow to (Pr 15:18; 16:32; 19:11; Tit 1:7; Jas 1:19). Avoid those given to (Ge 49:6; Pr 22:24).

Justifiable, Exemplified:
Our Lord (Mk 3:5). Jacob (Ge 31:36). Moses (Ex 11:8; 32:19; Lev 10:16; Nu 16:15). Nehemiah (Ne 5:6; 13:17, 25).

Sinful, Exemplified:
Cain (Ge 4:5-6). Esau (Ge 27:45). Simeon and Levi (Ge 49:5-7). Moses (Nu 20:10-11). Balaam (Nu 22:27). Saul (1Sa 20:30). Ahab (1Ki 21:4). Naaman (2Ki 5:11). Asa (2Ch 16:10). Uzziah (2Ch 26:19). Haman (Est 3:5). Nebuchadnezzar (Da 3:13). Jonah (Jnh 4:4). Herod (Mt 2:16). Jews (Lk 4:28). High Priest (Ac 5:17; 7:54).

ANGER OF GOD

Turned away by Christ (Lk 2:11, 14; Ro 5:9; 2Co 5:18-19; Eph 2:14, 17; Col 1:20; 1Th 1:10). Is turned away from them that believe (Jn 3:14-18; Ro 3:25; 5:1). Is turned away upon confession of sin and repentance (Job 33:27-28; Ps 106:43-45; Jer 3:12-13; 18:7-8; 31:18-20; Joel 2:12-14; Lk 15:18-20). Is slow (Ps 103:8; Isa 48:9; Jnh 4:2; Na 1:3). Is righteous (Ps 58:10-11; La 1:18; Ro 2:6, 8; 3:5-6; Rev 16:6-7). The justice of, not to be questioned (Ro 9:18, 20, 22). Manifested in terrors (Ex 14:24; Ps 76:6-8; Jer 10:10; La 2:20-22). Manifested in judgments and afflictions (Job 21:17; Ps 78:49-51; 90:7; Isa 9:19; Jer 7:20; Eze 7:19; Heb 3:17). Cannot be resisted (Job 9:13; Na 1:6). Aggravated by continual provocation (Nu 32:14). Specially reserved for the

day of wrath (Zep 1:14-18; Mt 25:41; Ro 2:5, 8; 2Th 1:8; Rev 6:17; 11:18; 19:15).

Against:
The wicked (Ps 7:11; 21:8-9; Isa 3:8; 13:9; Na 1:2-3; Ro 1:18; 2:8; Eph 5:6; Col 3:6). Those who forsake him (Ezr 8:22; Isa 1:4). Unbelief (Ps 78:21-22; Jn 3:36; Heb 3:18-19). Impenitence (Ps 7:12; Pr 1:30-31; Isa 9:13-14; Ro 2:5). Apostasy (Heb 10:26-27). Idolatry (Dt 29:20, 27-28; 32:19-20, 22; Jos 23:16; 2Ki 22:17; Ps 78:58-59; Jer 44:3). Sin, in believers (Ps 89:30-32; 90:7-9; 99:8; 102:9-10; Isa 47:6). Extreme, against those who oppose the gospel (Ps 2:2-3, 5; 1Th 2:16). Folly of provoking (Jer 7:19; 1Co 10:22). To be dreaded (Ps 2:12; 76:7; 90:11; Mt 10:28). To be deprecated (Ex 32:11; Ps 6:1; 38:1; 74:1-2; Isa 64:9). Removal of, should be prayed for (Ps 39:10; 79:5; 80:4; Da 9:16; Hab 3:2). Tempered with mercy to believers (Ps 30:5; Isa 26:20; 54:8; 57:15-16; Jer 30:11; Mic 7:11). To be borne with submission (2Sa 24:17; La 3:39, 43; Mic 7:9). Should lead to repentance (Isa 42:24-25; Jer 4:8).

Exemplified Against:
The old world (Ge 7:21-23). Builders of Babel (Ge 11:8). Cities of the plain (Ge 19:24-25). Egyptians (Ex 7:20; 8:6, 16, 24; 9:3, 9, 23; 10:13, 22; 12:29; 14:27). Israelites (Ex 32:35; Nu 11:1, 33; 14:40-45; 21:6; 25:9; 2Sa 24:1, 15). Enemies of Israel (1Sa 5:6; 7:10). Nadab (Lev 10:2). The Spies (Nu 14:37). Korah (Nu 16:31, 35). Aaron and Miriam (Nu 12:9-10). Five Kings (Jos 10:25). Abimelech (Jdg 9:56). Men of Beth Shemesh (1Sa 6:19). Saul (1Sa 31:6). Uzzah (2Sa 6:7). Saul's family (2Sa 21:1). Sennacherib (2Ki 19:28, 35, 37).

ANIAM [642] (*I am kinsman*). A son of Shemida, a Manassehite (1Ch 7:19).

ANIM [6719] (*springs*). A city of Judah (Jos 15:50).

ANIMALS [*989, 2651, 3274, 7366, 8802, 10263, *4465, 5488*].

Creation of:
(Ge 1:24-25; 2:19; Jer 27:5). Food of (Ge 1:30). Named (Ge 2:20). Ordained as food for man (Ge 9:2-3; Lev 11:3, 9, 21-22; Dt 14:4-6, 9, 11, 20). God's care of (Ge 9:9-10; Dt 25:4; Job 38:41; Ps 36:6; 104:11, 21; 145:15-16; 147:9; Jn 4:11; Mt 6:26; 10:29; Lk 12:6, 24; 1Co 9:9). Under the curse (Ge 3:14; 6:7, 17). Suffer under divine judgments sent upon man (Jer 7:20; 14:4; 21:6; Eze 14:13, 17, 19-21; Joel 1:18-20). Two of every kind preserved in the ark (Ge 6:19-20; 7:2, 9, 14-15; 8:19). Seven clean of every kind preserved in the ark (Ge 7:2-3). Suffered the plagues of Egypt (Ex 8:17; 9:9-10, 19; 11:5). Perish at death (Ecc 3:21). Possessed by demons (Mt 8:31-32; Mk 5:13; Lk 8:33). Clean and unclean (Ge 7:2, 8; 8:20; Lev 7:21; 11; 20:25; Dt 14:3-20; Ac 10:11-15; 1Ti 4:3-5).

God's Control of:

(Ps 91:13; Lk 10:19). Instruments of God's will (Ex 8; 10:4-15, 19; Nu 21:6; 22:28; Jos 24:12; Joel 1:4). Belong to God (Ps 50:10-12). Sent in judgment (Lev 26:22; Nu 21:6-7; Dt 8:15; Eze 5:17; 14:15; Rev 6:8).

Nature of:

(Job 41; Ps 32:9; Jas 3:7). Habits of (Job 12:7-8; 37:8; 39; 40:20-21; Ps 104:20-25; Isa 13:21-22; 34:14). Breeding of (Ge 30:35-43; 31:8-9). Instincts of (Dt 32:11; Job 35:11; 39; 40:15-24; Ps 104:11-30; Pr 6:5-8; 30:25-28; Isa 1:3; Jer 2:24; 8:7; La 4:3; Mt 24:28). Abodes of (Job 24:5; 37:8; 39:5-10, 27-29; Ps 104:20, 22, 25; Isa 34:14-15; Jer 2:24; 50:39; Mk 1:13).

Cruelty to:

Of Balaam to his donkey (Nu 22:22-33). Hamstringing horses (2Sa 8:4; 1Ch 18:4).

Kindness to:

By the righteous (Pr 12:10). In not muzzling an ox while threshing (Dt 25:4; 1Ti 5:18). In relieving the overburdened (Ex 23:5; Dt 22:4). In rescuing from pits (Mt 12:11; Lk 13:15; 14:5). In feeding (Ge 24:32; 43:24; Jdg 19:21).

Instances of: Jacob in making shelters for his cattle (Ge 33:17). People of Gerar in providing tents for cattle (2Ch 14:15).

Laws Concerning:

Sabbath rest for (Ex 20:10; Dt 5:14).

Treatment of vicious (Ex 21:28-32, 35-36). Penalty for injury of (Ex 21:33-34). Hybridizing of, forbidden (Lev 19:19). Working of (Dt 22:10). Mother birds and their young (Dt 22:6-7).

Names of:

Antelopes (Dt 14:5; Isa 51:20). Apes (1Ki 10:22). Baboons (1Ki 10:22; 2Ch 9:21). Donkeys, beasts of burden (Ge 22:3; Nu 22:28; Dt 22:10; Jdg 5:10; 10:4 1Sa 9:3; Mt 21:2). Bears (1Sa 17:34; 2Sa 17:8; 2Ki 2:24; Pr 17:12; 28:15; Isa 11:7). Behemoth (Job 40:15-24). Boars (Ps 80:13). Bull, as offerings (Ex 29:10-11, 36; Lev 4:4; Nu 15:8; 1Ki 18:33; 2Ch 13:9; Ezr 6:17; Ps 66:15). Calves (Ge 18:7; 1Sa 28:24; Am 6:4; Lk 15:23). Camels (Ge 12:16; 30:43; Lev 11:4; Jdg 6:5; 1Sa 30:17; 1Ch 5:21; Job 1:3; Mt 19:24; 23:24). Cattle, livestock (Ge 1:25; 31:18; Ex 9:4; 20:10; Nu 32:1; Jos 14:4; Eze 39:18; Am 4:1). Coneys, rock badgers (Lev 11:5; Ps 104:18; Pr 30:26). Cows (Ge 32:15; Dt 7:13; 1Sa 6:7). Deer (Dt 14:5; 2Sa 2:18; 22:34; 1Ch 12:8; Ps 42:1; Pr 5:19; 6:5; 1Sa 35:6; Jer 14:5). Dogs (1Ki 14:11; 22:38; Ps 59:6; Pr 26:17; Ecc 9:4; Lk 16:21). Dragons (Rev 12:3-17). Elephants (Job 40:15, ftn). Foxes (Jdg 15:4; Ne 4:3; Ps 63:10; SS 2:15; Mt 8:20). Gecko (Lev 11:30). Goats, as offerings (Ge 15:9; Lev 4:24; 16:15; Jdg 13:19; 2Ch 29:23). Heifers, offered as sacrifices (Ge 15:9; Nu 19:2; Dt 21:3; Heb 9:13). Horses (Dt 17:16; 2Ki 23:11; Job 39:19; Ps 32:9; 33:17; Isa 31:1). Lambs, for offerings (Ex 29:38-39; Lev 3:7; 4:32; 5:6; Nu 6:12). Leopards (SS 4:8; Isa 11:6; Jer 5:6; 13:23; Hos 13:7; Hab 1:8). Lions, general references to

(Jdg 14:5; 1Sa 17:34; 1Ki 13:24; Da 6:19), characteristics of (Dt 33:22; Jdg 14:18; 2Sa 17:10; Job 10:16; Ps 17:12; Pr 30:30; Isa 31:4; Na 2:12). Lizards (Lev 11:30). Mountain sheep (Dt 14:5). Mules (2Sa 13:29; 18:9; 1Ki 1:33; Ps 32:9; Zec 14:15). Oxen, laws concerning (Ex 21:28; 22:1; 23:4; Lev 17:3; Dt 5:14; 22:1; 25:4; Lk 13:15; 1Co 9:9; 1Ti 5:18). Pigs (Lev 11:7; Isa 65:4; 66:17; Mt 7:6; 8:30; Lk 15:15; 2Pe 2:22). Rabbit (Lev 11:6). Rams, used in sacrifices (Ge 15:9; 22:13; Ex 29:15; Lev 5:15; Nu 5:8). Rats (Lev 11:29; 1Sa 6:4; Isa 66:17). Rooster (Pr 30:31). Sheep (Ge 4:4; 30:32; Dt 18:4; 32:14; 2Ch 7:5; 15:11; Job 1:3; 42:12; Mt 12:11). Wild oxen (Nu 23:22; Dt 33:17; Job 39:9; Ps 29:6; Isa 34:7). Vipers, poisonous serpents (Job 20:16; Isa 30:6; 59:5). Weasel (Lev 11:29). Wolves, illustrative of the wicked (Mt 7:15; 10:16; Jn 10:12; Ac 20:29).

See Birds; Insects.

ANISE *See Dill.*

ANKLET An ornament worn by women on the ankles (Isa 3:16, 20). *See Jewel, Jewelry.*

ANNA [483] *(grace).* A widow and prophetess who at the age of 84 recognized Jesus as the Messiah when He was brought into the Temple (Lk 2:36-38).

ANNAS [483, 484] *(grace).* Associate high priest with Caiaphas (Lk 3:2; Jn 18:13, 19, 24; Ac 4:6).

ANNIHILATION The belief that there is no existence after death or that there is no existence for the wicked after death.

Some texts seem to imply death as final (Job 14:12, 18-22; Ps 6:5; 88:10; Isa 26:14). The resurrection is the hope of all believers (Ps 16:9-11; Isa 53:11; Da 12:1-3). In the teaching of Jesus (Mt 22:33-32; Lk 14:14; Jn 11:24-26), of the apostles (Ac 4:1-4, 33; 23:6-8; 24:10-21; 1Co 15). *See Resurrection.*

Eternal punishment of the wicked is also clearly taught (Da 12:2; Mt 18:8-9; Jn 3:36; 2Th 1:9; Rev 14:11; 20:4-15). *See Wicked, Punishment of.*

ANNUAL FEASTS All but Purim and Dedication instituted by Moses.

Designated as:

Solemn feasts (Nu 15:3; 2Ch 8:13; La 2:6; Eze 46:9). Set feasts (Nu 29:39; Ezr 3:5). Appointed feasts (Isa 1:14). Holy convocations (Lev 23:4). First and last days were Sabbatic (Lev 23:39-40; Nu 28:18-25; 29:12, 35; Ne 8:1-18). Kept with rejoicing (Lev 23:40; Dt 16:11-14; 2Ch 30:21-26; Ezr 6:22; Ne 8:9-12, 17; Ps 122:4; Isa 30:29; Zec 8:19). Divine protection given during (Ex 34:24).

All males were required to attend (Ex 23:17; 34:23; Dt 16:16; Eze 36:38; Lk 2:41-42; Jn 4:45; 7). Aliens permitted to attend (Jn 12:20; Ac 2:1-11). Attended by women (1Sa 1:3, 9; Lk 2:41).

Observed:

By Jesus (Mt 26:17-20; Lk 2:41-42; 22:15; Jn

2:13, 23; 5:1; 7:10; 10:22). By Paul (Ac 20:6, 16; 24:11, 17).

New Moon:
(Nu 10:10; 28:11-15; 1Ch 23:31; 2Ch 31:3; Ezr 3:5). Buying and selling at time of, suspended (Am 8:5).

The Passover:
Institution of (Ex 12:3-49; 23:15-18; 34:18; Lev 23:4-8; Nu 9:2-5, 13-14; 28:16-25; Dt 16:1-8, 16; Ps 81:3, 5). Design of (Ex 12:21-28).

Special Passover, for those who were unclean, or on journey to be held in second month (Nu 9:6-12; 2Ch 30:2-4). Lamb killed by Levites, for those who were ceremonially unclean (2Ch 30:17; 35:3-11; Ezr 6:20). Strangers authorized to celebrate (Ex 12:48-49; Nu 9:14).

Observed at place designated by God (Dt 16:5-7). With unleavened bread (Ex 12:8, 15-20; 13:3, 6; 23:15; Lev 23:6; Nu 9:11; 28:17; Dt 16:3-4; Mk 14:12; Lk 22:7; Ac 12:3; 1Co 5:8). Penalty for neglecting to observe (Nu 9:13).

Reinstituted by Ezekiel (Eze 45:21-24).

Observation of—
Renewed, by the Israelites on entering Canaan (Jos 5:10-11). By Hezekiah (2Ch 30:1). By Josiah (2Ki 23:22-23; 2Ch 35:1, 18). After return from captivity (Ezr 6:19-20). Observed by Jesus (Mt 26:17-20; Lk 22:15; Jn 2:13, 23; 13). Jesus when twelve years old, in the temple at time of (Lk 2:41-50). Jesus crucified at time of (Mt 26:2; Mk 14:1-2; Jn 18:28). Lord's Supper ordained at (Mt 26:26-28; Mk 14:12-25; Lk 22:7-20). The lamb of, a type of Christ (1Co 5:7).
Prisoners released at, by the Romans (Mt 27:15; Mk 15:6; Lk 23:16-17; Jn 18:39). Peter imprisoned at time of (Ac 12:3).

Christ Called—
Our Passover lamb (1Co 5:7; see also Jn 1:36; Rev 5:6-14).

Pentecost:
Called Feast of Weeks (Ex 34:22; Dt 16:10). Feast of Harvest (Ex 23:16). Day of First Fruits (Nu 28:26). Day of Pentecost (Ac 2:1; 20:16; 1Co 16:8).
Institution of (Ex 23:16; 34:22; Lev 23:15-21; Nu 28:26-31; Dt 16:9-12, 16).
Holy Spirit given to the apostles on the day of (Ac 2).

Purim:
Instituted by Esther and Mordecai to commemorate the deliverance of the Jews from the plot of Haman (Est 9:20-32).

Tabernacles:
Also called Feast of Ingathering. Instituted (Ex 23:16; 34:22; Lev 23:34-43; Nu 29:12-40; Dt 16:13-16). Design of (Lev 23:42-43). The law read in connection with, every seventh year (Dt 31:10-12; Ne 8:18).

Observance of—
After the captivity (Ezr 3:4; Ne 8:14-18). By Jesus (Jn 7:2, 14). Observance of, omitted (Ne 8:17). Penalty for not observing (Zec 14:16-19).

Jeroboam institutes an idolatrous feast parallel to, in the eighth month (1Ki 12:32-33).

Trumpets:
When and how observed (Lev 23:24-25; Nu 29:1-6). Celebrated after the captivity with joy (Ne 8:2, 9-12).

Dedication or Hanukkah:
Instituted in the Intertestamental era, commemorating the dedication of the temple by Judas Maccabeus (1Mc 4:59). Observed by Jesus (Jn 10:22-39).

See Feasts; see also each feast by name.

ANOINTING [*5417, 5418, 5431, *230, 5987, 5984*].

Of the body (Dt 28:40; Ru 3:3; Est 2:12; Ps 92:10; 104:15; 141:5; Pr 27:9, 16; Ecc 9:8; SS 1:3; 4:10; Isa 57:9; Am 6:6; Mic 6:15). Of guests (2Ch 28:15; Lk 7:46). The sick (Isa 1:6; Mk 6:13; Lk 10:34; Jas 5:14; Rev 3:18). The dead (Mt 26:12; Mk 14:8; 16:1; Lk 23:56). Of Jesus, as a token of love (Lk 7:37-38, 46; Jn 11:2; 12:3). Omitted in mourning (2Sa 12:20; 14:2; Isa 61:3; Da 10:3). God preserves those who receive (Ps 18:50; 20:6; 89:20-23). Believers receive (Isa 61:3; 1Jn 2:20).

In Consecration:
Of high priests (Ex 29:7, 29; 40:13; Lev 6:20; 8:12; 16:32; Nu 35:25; Ps 133:2).
Of priests (Ex 28:41; 30:30; 40:15; Lev 4:3; 8:30; Nu 3:3).
Of kings (Jdg 9:8, 15), Saul (1Sa 9:16; 10:1; 15:1), David (1Sa 16:3, 12-13; 2Sa 2:4; 5:3; 12:7; 9:21; 1Ch 11:3). Solomon (1Ki 1:39; 1Ch 29:22), Jehu (1Ki 19:16; 2Ki 9:1-3, 6, 12). Hazael (1Ki 19:15), Joash (2Ki 11:12; 2Ch 23:11), Jehoahaz (2Ki 23:30), Cyrus (Isa 45:1).
Of prophets (1Ki 19:16).
Of the tabernacle (Ex 30:26; 40:9; Lev 8:10; Nu 7:1), altars of (Ex 30:26-28; 40:10; Lev 8:11; Nu 7:1), vessels of (Ex 30:27-28; 40:9-10; Lev 8:10-11; Nu 7:1).
Jacob's pillar at Bethel (Ge 28:18; 31:13; 35:14).
See Dedication.

Figurative:
Of Christ's kingly and priestly office (Ps 45:7; 89:20; Isa 61:1; Da 9:24; Lk 4:18; Ac 4:27; 10:38; Heb 1:9). Of spiritual gifts (2Co 1:21; 1Jn 2:20, 27). Of God's choice and enabling of leaders (Ex 40:13-15; Lev 8:12; 1Sa 16:13; 1Ki 19:16).
Symbolic of Jesus' death (Mt 26:7-12; Jn 12:3-7).

ANOINTING OIL Formula of, given by Moses (Ex 30:22-25, 31-33). *See Oil; Ointment.*

ANOTH See Beth Anoth.

ANT [5805]. Illustrate work ethic (Pr 6:6-8; 30:25).

ANTEDILUVIANS (*those who lived before the flood*). Worship God (Ge 4:3-4, 26). Occupations of (Ge 4:2-3, 20-22). Arts of (Ge 4:2-3, 20-22; 6:14-22). Enoch prophesies to (Jude

14-15). Noah preaches to (2Pe 2:5). Wickedness of (Ge 6:5-7). Destruction of (Ge 7:1, 21-23; Job 22:15-17; Mt 24:37-39; Lk 17:26-27; 2Pe 2:5). *See Flood.*

Longevity of. *See Longevity.*
Giants among. *See Giants.*

ANTELOPE [9293]. (Dt 14:5; Isa 51:20). *See Deer.*

ANTHOTHIJAH [6746]. Son of Shashak, a Benjamite (1Ch 8:24-25).

ANTHROPOMORPHISMS Figures of speech that attribute human anatomy, acts, and affections to God.

Anatomy:
Arm (Ps 89:13), body or form (Nu 11:25), ear (Ps 34:15), eye (2Ch 16:9; Isa 1:15), mouth (Ps 33:6), voice (Eze 1:24, 28), wings (Ps 36:7; 57:1).
See terms for body parts, e.g., Arm, Eye, Hand.

Intellectual Facilities:
Knowing (Ge 18:17-19), reason (Isa 1:18), remembering (Ge 9:16; 19:29; Ex 2:24; Isa 43:26; 63:11), understanding (Ps 147:5), will (Ro 9:19).

Actions:
Breathing (Ps 33:6), grasping, with hand (Ps 35:2), hearing (Ps 94:9), laughing (Ps 2:4; 37:13; 59:8; Pr 1:26), not tiring (Isa 40:28), resting (Ge 2:2-3, 19; Ex 20:11; 31:17; Dt 5:14; Heb 4:4, 10), seeing (Ge 18:21; Ex 14:24; Ps 94:9), sleeping (Ps 44:23; 78:65; 121:4), speaking (Ge 18:33; Nu 11:25; Ps 33:6), standing (Ps 35:2), walking (Ge 3:8; Lev 26:12; Dt 23:14; Job 22:14; Hab 3:15).

Affections and Emotions:
Amazement (Isa 59:16; 63:5; Mk 6:6), grief (Ge 6:6; Jdg 10:16; Ps 95:10; Heb 3:10, 17), jealousy (Ex 20:5; 34:13-14; Nu 25:11; Dt 29:20; 32:16, 21; 1Ki 14:22; Ps 78:58; 79:5; Isa 30:1-2; 31:1, 3; Eze 16:42; 23:25; 36:5-6; 38:19; Zep 1:18; 3:8; Zec 1:14; 8:2; 1Co 10:22), swearing an oath (Isa 62:8; Heb 6:16-17; 7:21, 28). *See Anger of God; Oath.*

ANTICHRIST(S) [532] (*against* or *substitute Christ*). (Mt 24:5, 23-24, 26; Mk 13:6, 21-22; Lk 21:8; 2Th 2:3-12; 1Jn 2:18, 22; 4:3; 2Jn 7). To be destroyed (Rev 19:20; 20:10, 15).

ANTI-LEBANON *See Lebanon.*

ANTIOCH [522, 523].
1. A city of Syria. Disciples first called Christians in (Ac 11:19-30). Church in (Ac 13:1; 14:26-27). Barnabas and Paul make second visit to (Ac 14:26-28). Dissension in church of (Ac 15:22, w 15:1-35). Paul and Peter's controversy at (Gal 2:11-15).
2. A city of Pisidia. Persecutes Paul (Ac 13:14-52; Ac 14:19-22; 18:22; 2Ti 3:11).

ANTIOCHUS (*opposer*). A favorite name of the Seleucid kings of Syria, referred to as the kings of the North in Da 11.

1. Antiochus II Theos (286-246 B.C.) married Berenice, daughter of Ptolemy II, the "king of the South" (Da 11:6).
2. Antiochus III, the Great (242-187 B.C.) gained control of Israel in 198 B.C. (Da 11:10-19).
3. Antiochus IV (Epiphanes), son of III (215-163 B.C.); his attempt to hellenize the Jews led to the Maccabean revolt (Da 8:9-12, 23-25; 11:21-35; see also 1 and 2Mc). *See Abomination That Causes Desolation; Testaments, Time Between.*

ANTIPAS [525] (possibly a contraction of *Antipater*).
1. A Christian martyr of Pergamum (Rev 2:13).
2. Herod Antipas, son of Herod the Great; ruled Galilee and Perea from 4 B.C. to A.D. 39. *See Herod.*

ANTIPATER *See Herod.*

ANTIPATRIS [526]. A city in Samaria (Ac 23:31).

ANTITYPE *See Types.*

ANTONIA, TOWER OF A fortress connected with the temple at Jerusalem, built by Herod the Great. It was garrisoned by Roman soldiers who watched the temple area (Ac 21:30ff).

ANTOTHIJAH *See Anthothijah.*

ANTOTHITE *See Anathoth, Anathothite.*

ANUB [6707] (*fruitful*). Son of Koz of the tribe of Judah (1Ch 4:8).

ANVIL [7193]. (Isa 41:7).

ANXIETY [1796, 4088, 8595, *267, 3533, 3849*]. Forbidden (Mt 6:25-34; Lk 12:11-12, 22-28; 1Co 7:32; Php 4:6; 1Pe 5:7).
Unavailing (Ps 39:6; Mt 6:27; Lk 12:25-26). Proceeds from unbelief (Mt 6:26, 28-30; Lk 12:24, 27-28). Martha rebuked for (Lk 10:40-41).
Remedy for (Ps 37:5; 55:22; Heb 13:5; 1Pe 5:6-7). *See Care, Worldly.*

APARTMENT [1074]. (Jer 36:22). *See Winter Apartment, Winter House.*

APES [7761]. In Solomon's zoological collections (1Ki 10:22; 2Ch 9:21).

APELLES [593]. A disciple in Rome (Ro 16:10).

APHARSACHITES, APHARSATHCHITES, APHARSITES Aramaic terms transliterated as proper names in the KJV are translated "officials" in the NIV (Ezr 5:6; 6:6).

APHEK [707] (*stronghold*).
1. A city of the tribe of Asher (Jos 19:30). A city

whose inhabitants were not driven out by Asher (Jdg 1:31).

2. A city of the tribe of Issachar. Philistines defeat Israelites at (1Sa 4:1-11). Saul slain at (1Sa 29:1, w 1Sa 31). Probably the same as the royal city of the Canaanites (Jos 12:18).

3. A city between Damascus and Israel. Ben-Hadad defeated at (1Ki 20:26-30).

APHEKAH [708] (the fortress). A city in the mountains of Judah (Jos 15:53).

APHIAH [688]. Ancestor of Saul (1Sa 9:1).

APHIK See Aphek.

APHRAH See Beth Ophrah; Ophrah.

APHSES See Happizzez.

APOCALYPSE (disclosure). Greek title of the book of Revelation. See Apocalyptic Literature; Revelation, Book of.

APOCALYPTIC LITERATURE A type of prophetic literature that communicates the ultimate triumph of God over evil through dreams, visions, and symbols. Daniel and Revelation and parts of Ezekiel and Zechariah are canonical apocalypses. Many non-canonical apocalypses appeared between c. 200 B.C. and A.D. 200 in the style of Daniel, also claiming to have been written by a famous OT character. Major examples are 1 and 2 Enoch, Jubilees, Assumption of Moses, 2 Esdras, Apocalypse of Baruch, The Testaments of the Twelve Prophets, and the Psalms of Solomon.

APOCRYPHA (hidden, obscure). Books and chapters interspersed among the canonical books of the OT in the LXX and Vulgate, but not found in the Hebrew OT. The Jewish people, who produced them, and Protestants do not consider them canonical. The Roman Catholic Church received the following as deuterocanonical at the Council of Trent (1546): Tobit, Judith, Additions to Esther, Wisdom of Solomon, Ecclesiasticus, Baruch, Letter of Jeremiah, The Prayer of Azariah and the Song of the Three Young Men, Susanna, Bel and the Dragon, and 1 and 2 Maccabees. Other works are considered deuterocanonical by the Orthodox Church: 1 and 2 Esdras, The Prayer of Manasseh, Psalm 151, 3 and 4 Maccabees. See Testaments, Time Between.

APOLLONIA [662]. A city of Macedonia (Ac 17:1).

APOLLOS [663]. An eloquent Christian convert at Corinth (Ac 18:24-28; 19:1; 1Co 1:12; 3:4-7). Refuses to return to Rome (1Co 16:12). Paul writes Titus about (Tit 3:13). Born in Alexandria (Ac 18:24).

APOLLYON [661] (destroyer). Angel of the bottomless pit (Rev 9:11).

APOSTASY (abandoning God).

Described:
(Dt 13:13, 32; 32:15; Isa 65:11-12; Mt 12:45; Lk 11:24-26; Ac 7:39-43; 1Ti 4:1-3; 2Ti 3:6-9; 4:3-4; Heb 3:12; 2Pe 2:15-22; Jude 8). Foretold (Mt 24:12; 2Th 2:3; 1Ti 4:1-3; 2Ti 3:1-9; 4:3-4; 2Pe 2:1).

Admonitions against (Mt 24:4-5; Mk 13:5-6; Heb 3:12; 2Pe 3:17; 2Jn 8; Jude 4-6). No remedy for (Heb 6:4-8; 10:26-29).

Punishment (1Ch 28:9; Isa 1:28; 65:12-15; Jer 17:5-6; Eze 3:20; 18:24, 26; 33:12-13, 18; Zep 1:4-6; Jn 15:6; 2Th 2:11-12; Heb 10:25-31, 38-39; 2Pe 2:17-22; Jude 6).

Caused by:
Persecution (Mt 13:20-21; 24:9-12; Mk 4:5-17; Lk 8:13). Worldliness (2Ti 4:10).

Instances of:
Israelites (Ex 32; Nu 14; Ac 7:39-43), Saul (1Sa 15:26-29; 18:12; 28:15, 18), Amaziah (2Ch 25:14, 27), disciples (Jn 6:66), Judas (Mt 26:14-16; 27:3-5; Mk 14:10-11; Lk 22:3-6, 47-48; Ac 1:16-18), Hymenaeus and Alexander (1Ti 1:19-20), Phygelus and Hermogenes (2Ti 1:15).

See Antichrist(s); Apostates; Backsliding; Instances of Israel's Backsliding; Backsliders; Reprobacy; Reprobates.

APOSTATES

Described:
(Dt 13:13; Heb 3:12). Persecution tends to make (Mt 24:9-10; Lk 8:13). A worldly spirit tends to make (2Ti 4:10). Never belonged to Christ (1Jn 2:19). Believers do not become (Ps 44:18-19; Heb 6:9; 10:39). It is impossible to restore (Heb 6:4-6). Guilt and punishment of (Zep 1:4-6; Heb 10:25-31, 39; 2Pe 2:17, 20-22). Cautions against becoming (Heb 3:12; 2Pe 3:17). Shall abound in the latter days (Mt 24:12; 2Th 2:3; 1Ti 4:1-3).

Examples of:
Amaziah (2Ch 25:14, 27). Professed disciples (Jn 6:66). Hymenaeus and Alexander (1Ti 1:19-20). See Apostasy.

APOSTLE [692, 693] (to send off or out). A title of Jesus (Heb 3:1). See Apostles.

APOSTLES [693, 6013] (to send off or out).

The Twelve:
In the Gospels, a title distinguishing the twelve disciples, whom Jesus selected to be intimately associated with himself (Lk 6:13). Names of the twelve (Mt 10:2-4; Mk 3:16-19; Lk 6:13-16; Ac 1:13, 26).

Selection of (Mt 4:18, 22; 9:9-10; 10:2-4; Mk 3:13-19; Lk 6:13-16; Jn 1:43).

Commission of (Mt 10; 28:19-20; Mk 3:14-15; 6:7-11; 16:15; Lk 9:1-5; 22:28-30; Jn 20:23; 21:15-19; Ac 1; 2; 10:42). Uneducated (Mt 11:25; Ac 4:13). Miraculous power given to (Mt 10:1; Mk 3:15; 6:7; 16:17; Lk 9:1-2; 10:9, 17; Ac 2:4,

43; 5:12-16; 1Co 14:18; 2Co 12:12). Authority of (Mt 16:19; 18:18; 19:28).

Inspiration of (Mt 10:27; 16:17-19; Lk 24:45; Ac 1:2; 13:9). Duties of. *See above, Commission of.* For more information see Lk 24:48; Jn 15:27; Ac 1:8, 21-22; 2:32; 3:15; 4:33; 5:32; 10:39-41; 13:31; 2Pe 1:16, 18; 1Jn 1:1-3. *See Minister.*

Moral state of, before Pentecost (Mt 17:17; 18:3; 20:20-22; Lk 9:54-55). Slow to receive Jesus as Messiah (Mt 14:33). Forsake Jesus (Mk 14:50).

Fail to comprehend the nature and mission of Jesus, and the nature of the kingdom he came to establish (Mt 8:25-27; 15:23; 16:8-12, 21-22; 19:25; Mk 4:13; 6:51-52; 8:17-18; 9:9-10, 31-32; 10:13-14; Lk 9:44-45; 18:34; 24:19, 21; Jn 4:32-33; 10:6; 11:12-13; 12:16; 13:6-8; 14:5-9, 22; 16:6, 17-18, 32; 20:9; 21:12; Ac 1:6).

Other Than the Twelve:

Matthaias (Ac 1:26), Paul and Barnabas (Ac 14:1-4, 14), Paul (Ro 1:1), Andronicus and Junias (Ro 16:7). A spiritual gift (1Co 12:28-31; Eph 4:11-13).

See Andronicus; Barnabas; Junias; Matthias; Minister; Paul.

False: (2Co 11:13; Rev 2:2).

See Teachers, False.

APOTHECARY   *See Perfume, Perfumer.*

APPAIM   [691] (*[a pair of] nostrils*). Son of Nadab (1Ch 2:30-31).

APPAREL   *See Dress.*

APPEAL   [2011, 2704, 7924, *2126, 4151, 4155*]. Paul makes, to Caesar (Ac 25:10-11, 21-27; 26:32; 28:19). *See Change of Venue; Court, of Law.*

APPEAL TO GOD   To witness (Ge 31:50; Dt 30:19; Jdg 11:10; 1Sa 12:5; Job 16:19; Ro 1:9; 2Co 1:23; Php 1:8; 1Th 2:5).

APPEARANCES   [*2118, 2180, 5260, 8011, *1586, 1872, 2210, 2211, 3972, 4134, 5743, 5746*]. Of God to people (Ge 12:7; 17:1; 18:1; 26:2; 35:9; Ex 3:16; 1Ki 3:5; 9:2; 2Ch 3:1).

APPEARING   *See Eschatology.*

APPELLATIO   The judicial process of appealing to a higher magistrate (Ac 25:1-12).

APPETITE   [5883, *3120*]. Kept in subjection (Pr 23:1-2; Da 1:8-16; 1Co 9:27). *See Temperance.*

APPHIA   [*722*]. Christian at Colosse (Phm 2).

APPIAN WAY   An ancient Roman road on which Paul traveled (Ac 28:13-16).

APPIUS, FORUM OF   [*716*]. A market town forty-three miles from Rome, where Paul met a delegation of Roman Christians (Ac 28:15).

APPLE   [413, 949, 9515]. A fruit (Pr 25:11; SS 2:3, 5; 7:8; 8:5; Joel 1:12).

APPLE OF THE EYE   The eyeball; symbolizing that which is precious and protected (Dt 32:10; Ps 17:8; Pr 7:2; Zec 2:8).

APRON   *See Dress.*

AQABAH, GULF OF   The eastern arm of the Red Sea, where Solomon's seaport was located (1Ki 9:26). *See Ezion Geber.*

AQUEDUCT   [9498] (*water channel*). A channel made of stone to convey water to places where the water is to be used (2Ki 18:17; Isa 7:3; 36:1). Many fine Roman aqueducts survive.

AQUILA   [*217*] (*eagle*). A Jewish Christian, a tentmaker by trade, who with his wife Priscilla labored with Paul at Corinth and was of help to Apollos and many others (Ac 18:2, 18, 26; Ro 16:3-4; 1Co 16:19; 2Ti 4:19).

AR   [6840] (possibly *city*). A city of Moab (Nu 21:15; Dt 2:9, 18, 24, 29). Destruction of (Nu 21:26-30; Isa 15:1).

ARA   [736]. Son of Jether (1Ch 7:38).

ARAB   [742, 6861, 6862] (*desert* or *steppe*).
1. A city of Judah (Jos 15:52).
2. *See Arabia; Arabians.*

ARABAH   [6858] (*desert*). A name applying to the rift running from Mt. Hermon to the Gulf of Aqabah. It is a narrow valley of varying breadth and productivity. The Israelites made stops there in their wilderness wanderings, and Solomon got iron and copper from its mines (Dt 1:1, 7; 11:30; Jos 3:16; 1Sa 23:24; Jer 39:4).

ARABIA   [6851, *728*] (*desert* or *steppe*). Paid tribute to Solomon (2Ch 9:14) and Jehoshaphat (2Ch 17:11). Exports of (Eze 27:21). Prophecies against (Isa 21:13; Jer 25:24). Paul visits (Gal 1:17).

ARABIANS, ARABS   [6861,   *732*] (*desert plateau dwellers*). Paid tribute to Solomon (2Ch 9:14) and Jehoshaphat (2Ch 17:11). Invade and defeat Judah (2Ch 21:16-17; 22:1). Defeated by Uzziah (2Ch 26:7). Oppose Nehemiah's rebuilding the walls of Jerusalem (Ne 2:19; 4:7). Commerce of (Eze 27:21). Gospel preached to (Ac 2:11; Gal 1:17). Prophecies concerning (Isa 21:13-17; 42:11; 60:7; Jer 25:24).

ARAD   [6865, 6866] (*wild donkey*).
1. A city on the S of Canaan (Nu 21:1; 33:40). Subdued by Joshua (Jos 12:14; Jdg 1:16).
2. Son of Beriah (1Ch 8:15).

ARAH   [783, 6869] (*he wanders*).
1. An Asherite (1Ch 7:39).

2. Father of a family that returned from exile (Ezr 2:5; Ne 7:10).

3. Jew whose granddaughter became the wife of Tobiah the Ammonite (Ne 6:18).

4. Town in NE Palestine belonging to Sidonians (Jos 13:4).

ARAM [806].

1. Son of Shem (Ge 10:22-23).

2. Son of Kemuel, Abraham's nephew (Ge 22:21).

3. An Asherite (1Ch 7:34).

4. Ancestor of Jesus (Mt 1:3-4; Lk 3:33). *See Ram, 1.*

5. Place in Gilead (1Ch 2:23).

6. Region corresponding to modern Syria (Nu 23:7; 2Sa 8:5; 1Ki 20:20; Am 1:5). The Aramean people spread from Phoenicia to the Fertile Crescent and were closely related to Israel, with whom their history was intertwined. *See Syria.*

ARAM MAACAH [807]. Also called Maacah. A small kingdom in Northwest Mesopotamia (1Ch 19:6, ftn). The states of Aram Maacah, Aram Naharaim, and Zobah were N and NE of Israel and formed a solid block from the region of Lake Huleh through the Anti-Lebanons to beyond the Euphrates.

See Aram Naharaim; Aram Zobah; Zobah.

ARAM NAHARAIM [808]. A region in NW Mesopotamia (Ge 24:10; Dt 23:4; Jdg 3:8; 1Ch 19:6 and notes). *See Aram Maacah.*

ARAM ZOBAH [809]. Only in the Title of Ps 60 (Ps 60, ftn). *See Aram Maacah; Zobah.*

ARAMAIC [811, *1365+1579, 1580*]. A Semitic language closely related to Hebrew, which developed various dialects and spread to all of SW Asia. Aramaic portions in the OT are Da 2:4-7:28; Ezr 4:8-6:18; 7:12-26; Jer 10:11. Aramaic words occur in the NT (Mk 5:41; 15:34; Mt 27:46; Ro 8:15; Gal 4:6; 1Co 16:22). Aramaic was the colloquial language of Israel from the time of the return from the Exile.

ARAN [814] (*wild goat*). Son of Dishan (Ge 36:28; 1Ch 1:42).

ARARAT [827]. Modern Armenia (2Ki 19:37; Isa 37:38, KJV) and to its mountain range (Ge 8:4), the resting place of Noah's ark. The region is now part of Turkey.

ARATUS A Cilician poet (315-240 B.C.). Paul quotes from his *Phaenomena* (Ac 17:28). *See Asceticism; Cleanthes; Stoicism; Stoics.*

ARAUNAH [779, 821] (*strong*). A Jebusite from whom David bought a site for an altar (2Sa 24:16-24). Also spelled Ornan (1Ch 21:15 ftn, 18-28).

ARBA (*four*). Giant ancestor of Anak (Jos 14:15; 15:13; 21:11).

ARBATHITE [6863] (*person from Arabah*). A native of Beth Arabah (2Sa 23:31; 1Ch 11:32).

ARBEL *See Beth Arbel.*

ARBITE [750]. Paarai, one of David's mighty men (2Sa 23:35).

ARBITRATION [3519, *3537*]. The two prostitutes before Solomon (1Ki 3:16-28). Urged by Paul as a mode of action for Christians (1Co 6:1-8). *See Court, of Law.*

ARCH *See Architecture.*

ARCHAEOLOGY (*study of ancient things*). Study of the material remains of the past by excavating ancient buried cities and examining their remains; deciphering inscriptions; and evaluating the language, literature, art, architecture, monuments, and other aspects of human life and achievement. Biblical archaeology is concerned with Israel and the countries with which the Hebrews and early Christians came into contact. Modern archaeology began with Napoleon's expedition to Egypt, on which many scholars accompanied him to study Egyptian monuments (1798), and with the work of Edward Robinson in Palestine (1838, 1852). Discoveries of great importance which throw much light upon the patriarchal period are the Mari Tablets, the Nuzi Tablets, the Tell-el Amarna Tablets, and the Ras Shamra Tablets. The discovery of the Dead Sea Scrolls and the excavation of Qumran are among the more recent archaeological finds of importance. Archaeology is of great help in better understanding the Bible, in dealing with critical questions regarding the Bible, and in gaining an appreciation of the ancient world.

ARCHANGEL [791] (*ruling angel*). A high order of angels (1Th 4:16). Michael called a "prince" (Da 10:13, 21; 12:1; Jude 9; Rev 12:7). *See Angels.*

ARCHELAUS [793] (*ruler of people*). The son of Herod the Great. He ruled over Judea, Samaria, and Idumea from 4 B.C. to A.D. 6 (Mt 2:22).

ARCHERS [1251+2932, 2005, 3452, 4619, 8008+, 8043]. Hunters or warriors with bow and arrow, weapons universally used in ancient times (Ge 21:20; 1Sa 20:17-42; Isa 21:17). "Arrow" is often used figuratively (Job 6:4; Jer 9:8), as is also "bow" (Ps 7:12). *See Archery.*

ARCHERY Practiced by Ishmael (Ge 21:20), Esau (Ge 27:3), Jonathan (1Sa 20:20, 36-37), Sons of Ulam (1Ch 8:40), Philistines (1Sa 31:1-3; 1Ch 10:3), Persians (Isa 13:17-18), people of Kedar (Isa 21:17), Syrians (1Ki 22:31-34), Israelites (2Sa 1:18; 1Ch 5:18; 12:2; 2Ch 14:8; 26:14; Ne 4:13; Zec 9:13), Lydians (Jer 46:9).

In war (Ge 49:23; Jdg 5:11; 1Sa 31:3; Isa 22:3; Jer 4:29; Zec 10:4).

See Archers; Armies; Arrows; Bow; War.

ARCHEVITES *See Erech, 2.*

ARCHI, ARCHITES *See Arkite(s).*

ARCHIPPUS [800] (*master of the horse*).
An office bearer in the church at Colosse (Col 4:17; Phm 2).

ARCHITECTURE The materials of architecture in antiquity were wood, clay, brick (formed of clay, whether sun-baked or kiln-fired), and stone. The determining factor in the choice of material used was local availability. The homes of the poor had no artistic distinction. The wealthy and the nobility, however, adorned their palatial homes ornately with gold and ivory. Architectural remains—temples, city gates, arches, ziggurats, pyramids—survive intact in great abundance, and archaeology has uncovered the foundations of countless buildings. Each country had its own distinctive style of architecture. No architecture has surpassed that of Greece, although the temple of Solomon and the one rebuilt by Herod were universally admired.

ARCHIVES [10103+10148; 10103+10515].
Storage place for royal documents (Ezr 4:15; 5:17; 6:1).

ARCTURUS Constellation: the Bear (Job 9:9; 38:32). *See Astronomy; Bear, Illustrative of.*

ARD, ARDITE [764, 766] (*hunchbacked*).
1. Son of Benjamin (Ge 46:21).
2. Son of Bela and his clan (Nu 26:40).

ARDON [765] (*hunchbacked*). Son of Caleb (1Ch 2:18).

ARELI, ARELITE [739, 740]. Son of Gad (Ge 46:16) and his clan (Nu 26:17).

AREOPAGITE A member of the Areopagus (Ac 17:34).

AREOPAGUS [740, 741] (*hill of the Greek god, Ares*).
1. The rocky hill of the Greek god of war Ares (Mars) on the Acropolis at Athens.
2. The name of a council which met on Mars Hill. In NT times it was primarily concerned with morals and education. Paul was brought before it (Ac 17:19-34).

ARETAS [745] (*virtuous*). A Nabataean king, father-in-law of Herod Antipas (2Co 11:32).

ARGOB [758, 759] (*mound*).
1. A region in Bashan taken by the Israelites under Moses (Dt 3:4) and given to the half-tribe of Manasseh (Dt 3:13).
2. Could also be a place or a person (2Ki 15:25). The Hebrew text is uncertain.

ARIDAI [767] (perhaps *delight of Hari*). Son of Haman killed by the Jews (Est 9:9).

ARIDATHA [792] (perhaps *given by Hari*). A son of Haman killed by the Jews (Est 9:8).

ARIEH [794] (*lion*). Either a person or a place. The text is uncertain (2Ki 15:25).

ARIEL [790, 791] (*lioness of God [El]*).
1. Leader under Ezra (Ezr 8:16-17).
2. Figurative name for Jerusalem (Isa 29:1-2, 7).
3. In 2Sa 23:20 and 1Ch 11:22 "best men" (KJV "lionlike men") translates a word similar to Ariel.

ARIMATHEA [751]. Home of Joseph who buried Jesus in his own tomb (Mt 27:57; Mk 15:43; Lk 23:51; Jn 19:38). Its location is in doubt, but it is conjectured to be Ramathaim-Zophim, c. twenty miles NW of Jerusalem.

ARIOCH [796, 10070].
1. King of Ellasar (Ge 14:1, 9).
2. Captain of Nebuchadnezzar's guard (Da 2:14-15, 24-25).

ARISAI [798]. Son of Haman (Est 9:9).

ARISTARCHUS [752] (*best ruler*). A Thessalonian traveling companion of Paul (Ac 19:29; 20:4; 27:2; Col 4:10; Phm 24).

ARISTOBULUS [755] (*best adviser*). A Roman Christian greeted by Paul (Ro 16:10).

ARK [778, 9310, *3066*] (*box*).
1. A boat. Directions for building of (Ge 6:14-16). Noah and family preserved in (Ge 6:18; 7:8; Mt 24:38; Heb 11:7; 1Pe 3:20). Animals saved in (Ge 6:19-20; 7:1-16).
2. A box or chest. *See Ark of the Covenant.*

ARK OF THE COVENANT
Description of:
Dimensions of (Ex 25:10; 37:1). Entirely covered with gold (Ex 25:11; 37:2). Surrounded with a crown of gold (Ex 25:11). Furnished with rings and poles (Ex 25:12-15; 37:3-5). Tables of testimony alone placed in (Ex 25:16, 21; 1Ki 8:9, 21; 2Ch 5:10; Heb 9:4). Atonement cover laid upon (Ex 25:21; 26:34). Placed in the Most Holy Place (Ex 26:33; 40:21; Heb 9:3-4). The pot of manna and Aaron's rod laid up before (Heb 9:4, w Ex 16:33-34; Nu 17:10). A copy of the law laid in the side of (Dt 31:26). Anointed with sacred oil (Ex 30:26). Covered with the veil by the priests before removal (Nu 4:5-6).

A symbol of the presence and glory of God (Nu 14:43-44; Jos 7:6; 1Sa 14:18-19; Ps 132:8). Considered the glory of Israel (1Sa 4:21-22). Was holy (2Ch 35:3). Sanctified its resting place (2Ch 8:11). The Israelites inquired of the Lord before (Jos 7:6-9; Jdg 20:27; 1Ch 13:3). Profanation of, punished (Nu 4:5, 15; 1Sa 6:19; 1Ch 15:13). Protecting of, rewarded (1Ch 13:14).

Was Called the:

Ark of God (1Sa 3:3). Ark of God's might (2Ch 6:41; Ps 132:8). Ark of the covenant of the Lord (Nu 10:33). Ark of the testimony (Ex 30:6; Nu 7:89).

Was Carried:

By priests or Levites alone (Dt 10:8; Jos 3:14; 2Sa 15:24; 1Ch 15:2). Before the Israelites in their journeys (Nu 10:33; Jos 3:6). Sometimes to the camp in war (1Sa 4:4-5).

History and Miracles Connected With:

Jordan divided (Jos 4:7). Fall of the walls of Jericho (Jos 6:6-20). Captured by the Philistines (1Sa 4:11). Fall of Dagon (1Sa 5:1-4). Philistines plagued (1Sa 5:6-12). Manner of its restoration (1Sa 6:1-18). At Kiriath Jearim twenty years (1Sa 7:1-2). Removed from Kiriath Jearim to the house of Obed-Edom (2Sa 6:1-11). David made a tent for (2Sa 6:17; 1Ch 15:1). Brought into the city of David (2Sa 6:12-15; 1Ch 15:25-28). Brought by Solomon into the temple with great solemnity (1Ki 8:1-6; 2Ch 5:2-9). A type of Christ (Ps 40:8; Rev 11:19).

ARKITE(S) [805, 6909]. Descendants of Canaan (Ge 10:17; 1Ch 1:15). Member of a clan in Ephraim (Jos 16:2; 1Ch 27:33).

ARM [274, 2432, 2741, 3338, 4190, 7396, *1098, 3959*]. Figurative of divine providence and salvation (Ex 6:6; 15:16; Dt 4:34; 5:15; 7:19; 9:29; 11:2; 26:8; 33:27; 1Ki 8:42; 2Ki 17:36; 2Ch 6:32; Ps 77:15; 89:10, 13, 21; 98:1; 136:12; SS 2:6; Isa 33:2; 40:10-11; 51:5, 9; 52:10; 53:1; 59:16; 62:8; 63:5, 12; Jer 21:5; 27:5; 32:17; Eze 20:33; Lk 1:51; Ac 13:17). *See Anthropomorphisms.*

ARMAGEDDON [762] (*Mount of Megiddo*). Found only in Rev 16:16; the final battlefield between the forces of good and evil. Located on the S rim of Esdraelon, the scene of many decisive battles in the history of Israel (Jdg 5:19-20; 6:33; 1Sa 31; 2Ki 23:29-30). *See Megiddo.*

ARMENIA *See Ararat.*

ARMIES [2657, 4722, 5120, 7372, *4213, 5128, 5136*]. Those of the Israelites who were subject to service in (Nu 1:2-3; 26:2; 2Ch 25:5), who were exempt from service in (Nu 1:47-50; 2:33; Dt 20:5-9; Jdg 7:3). Numbering of Israel's military forces (Nu 1:2-3; 26:2; 1Sa 11:8; 2Sa 18:1-2; 24:1, 9; 1Ki 20:15; 2Ch 25:5). Levies for (Nu 31:4; Jdg 20:10). Compulsory service in (1Sa 14:52).

See Cowardice.

How Commanded:

Commander-in-chief (1Sa 14:50; 2Sa 2:8; 8:16; 17:25; 19:13; 20:23), Generals of corps and divisions (Nu 2:3-31; 1Ch 27:1-22; 2Ch 17:12-19), Captains of thousands (Nu 31:14, 48; 1Sa 17:18; 1Ch 28:1; 2Ch 25:5), of hundreds (Nu

31:14, 48; 2Ki 11:15; 1Ch 28:1; 2Ch 25:5), of fifties (2Ki 1:9; Isa 3:3). *See Cavalry; Chariot.*

Mustering of:

Methods employed in mustering: Sounding a trumpet (Nu 10:9; Jdg 3:27; 6:34; 1Sa 13:3-4), Cutting oxen in pieces, and sending the pieces throughout Israel (1Sa 11:7). Refusal to obey the summons, instance of (Jdg 21:5-11, w Jdg 20).

Tactics:

Camp and march (Nu 2). March in ranks (Joel 2:7). Move in attack in three divisions (Jdg 7:16; 9:43; 1Sa 11:11; 13:17, 18; 2Sa 18:2; Job 1:17). Flanks called wings (Isa 8:8). Orders delivered with trumpets (2Sa 2:28; 18:16; 20:1, 22; Ne 4:18, 20). *See Strategy.*

Strategies:

Ambushes at: Ai (Jos 8:2-22), Shechem (Jdg 9:25, 34), Gibeah (Jdg 20:29-43), Zemaraim (2Ch 13:4, 13). By Jehoshaphat (2Ch 20:20-22).

Reconnaissances:

Of Jericho (Jos 2:1-24), Ai (Jos 7:2-3), Bethel (Jdg 1:23-24), Laish (Jdg 18:2-10). Night attacks (Ge 14:15; Jdg 7:16-22). Decoy (Jos 8:4-22; Jdg 20:29-43; Ne 6). Delay (2Sa 17:7-14).

Speed of Action:

Abraham, in pursuit of Kedorlaomer (Ge 14:14-15). Joshua, against the Amorites (Jos 10:6, 9), the confederated kings (Jos 11:7). David's attack upon the Philistines (2Sa 5:23-25). Forced marches (Isa 5:26-27). Sieges (Jer 39:1), of Jericho (Jos 6), Samaria (2Ki 6:24-33:7), Jerusalem (2Ki 25:1-3).

Machines used (2Ch 26:15; Jer 6:6; Eze 26:9). Fortifications (Jdg 9:31; 2Sa 5:9; 2Ki 25:1; 2Ch 11:11; 26:9; Ne 3:8; 4:2; Isa 22:10; 25:12; 29:3; 32:14; Jer 6:6; 32:24; 33:4; 51:53; Eze 4:2; 17:17; 21:22; 26:8; 33:27; Da 11:15, 19; Na 2:1; 3:14). Standards (Nu 2:2-3, 10, 17-18, 25, 31, 34; 10:14, 18, 22, 25). Uniforms of (Eze 23:6, 12; Na 2:3). Standing armies (1Sa 13:2; 1Ch 27; 2Ch 1:14; 17:12-19; 26:11-15).

Religious Ceremonies Attending:

Seeking counsel from God before battle (Nu 27:21; Jdg 1:1; 1Sa 14:19, 37-41; 23:2-12; 30:8; 2Sa 2:1; 5:19, 23; 1Ki 22:7-28; 2Ki 3:11-19; 1Ch 14:10, 14; Jer 37:7-10). Sacrifices (1Sa 13:11-12). Purifications (Nu 31:19-24). Prophets prophesy before (2Ch 20:14-17). Holiness required (Dt 23:9). Officers consecrate themselves to God (2Ch 17:16). Army choir and songs (2Ch 20:21-22). Ark taken to battle (Jos 6:6-7, 13; 1Sa 4:4-11).

Divine Assistance to:

When Aaron and Hur held up Moses' hands (Ex 17:11-12). In siege of Jericho (Jos 6). Sun stands still (Jos 10:11-14). Gideon's victory (Jdg 7). Samaria's deliverances (1Ki 20; 2Ki 7). Jehoshaphat's victories (2Ki 3; 2Ch 20). Angel of the Lord puts to death the Assyrians (2Ki 19:35).

Determine royal succession (2Sa 2:8-10; 1Ki 16:16; 2Ki 11:4-12).

Composed of insurgents (1Sa 22:1-2). Mercenaries (2Sa 10:6; 1Ch 19:6-7; 2Ch 25:5-6). Confederated (Jos 10:1-5; 11:1-5; Jdg 1:3; 2Sa 10:6, 15-16, 19; 1Ki 15:20; 22:1-4; 2Ki 16:9; 18:19-21; 1Ch 19:6-7; 2Ch 16:2-9; 18:1, 3; 20:1; 22:5; 28:16, 20; Ps 83:1-12; Isa 7:1-9; 8:9-12; 54:15). Exhorted before battle (Dt 20:1-9). Battle shouts (Jdg 7:18; 1Sa 17:20, 52).

Triumphs of, Celebrated:
With songs (Jdg 5; 1Sa 18:6-7), music (2Ch 20:28), dancing (1Sa 18:6-7).

Rewards for Meritorious Conduct:
The general offers his daughter in marriage (Jos 15:16-17). King offers his daughter (1Sa 17:25; 18:17-28). Promotion (2Sa 23:8-39; 1Ch 11:6, 10-47). Share the spoils (Nu 31:25-47).

Insubordination in, punished, Achan (Jos 7). Check roll call (1Sa 14:17; Nu 31:48-49).

Panics (Isa 30:17): Among the Midianites (Jdg 7:21), Philistines (1Sa 14:15-19), Syrians (2Ki 7:7-15). Soldiers destroy each other to escape captivity (1Sa 14:20; 31:4-6).

Champions fight instead of (1Sa 17:8-53; 2Sa 2:14-17; 21:15-22). Confidence in vain (Ps 33:16; 44:6). Escort duty performed by (2Ki 1:9; Ac 23:23-24, 31-33).

Roman Army:
Commanders of (Ac 22:24-29). Centurions (Mt 8:5, 8; 27:54; Lk 7:2; 23:47; Ac 10:1, 7, 22; 21:32; 22:26; 23:17, 23; 24:23; 27:1, 11, 43; 28:16). Divided into regiments (Ac 10:1; 27:1).

For other than armies of the Israelites and Romans: *See Amalekite(s); Assyria; Babylon; Egyptians; Midianite(s); Persia; Syria.*

For commissaries of: *See Commissary.*

For weapons used: *See Armor.*

See Ambush; Cavalry; Fort; Garrison; Herald; Hostage; Navy; Reconnaissance; Siege; Soldiers; Spies; Standard; Strategy; Truce; War.

Figurative: (Dt 33:2; 2Ki 6:17; Ps 34:7; 68:17; Rev 9:16).

See Army.

ARMLET, BRACELET [731]. An ornament usually for the upper arm, worn by both men and women (Ex 35:22; Nu 31:50; 2Sa 1:10; Isa 3:20). *See Bracelet.*

ARMONI [813] (*[one] born in the dwelling tower, the palace*). A son of Saul by his concubine Rizpah, slain by the Gibeonites to satisfy justice (2Sa 21:8-11).

ARMOR [2520, 3998, 5516, 6246, 7989+9234, 9234, *3960*, *4110*]. The equipment of a soldier (1Sa 13:22; Jer 46:3-4; Eph 6:14-17).

Defensive:
Helmet (1Sa 17:5, 38; 2Ch 17:17; 26:14; Jer 46:4; Eze 23:24). Breastplate (Rev 9:9-17). Coat of armor (1Sa 17:5, 38; 1Ki 22:34; 2Ch 18:33). Greaves, protection for the leg (1Sa 17:6). Shield (2Sa 1:21; 8:7; 1Ki 10:16, 17; 14:27; 2Ch 9:16; 26:14; Ne 2:3).

Offensive:
Bows (Ge 21:16, 20). Made of bronze (2Sa 22:35; Job 20; Ps 18:34). Of wood (Eze 39:9). David instructed the Israelites in the use of, by writing war song (2Sa 1:18). Arrows (1Sa 31:3; 2Sa 22:15; 1Ki 22:34; 2Ki 19:32; 2Ch 17:17; Ps 7:13; Isa 22:3; Jer 51:3).

War club (Job 41:29; Jer 51:20). Spear (Nu 25:7; 1Sa 18:10; 2Sa 18:14). Javelin, a heavy lance (Eze 39:9). Used by Goliath (1Sa 17:6). By Saul (1Sa 18:11; 19:9-10).

Sling, used for throwing stones (Pr 26:8). David slays Goliath with (1Sa 17:40-50). Skilled use of (Jdg 20:16). Used in war (Jdg 20:16; 2Ki 3:25; 2Ch 26:14).

Sword, used by Gibeon (Jdg 7:20). By Peter (Mt 26:51; Jn 18:10). David's army equipped with (1Ch 21:5).

Figurative: (Ro 13:12; 2Co 6:7; 10:4; Eph 6:11-17; 1Th 5:8).

ARMOR-BEARER [3998+5951]. An attendant who carried a soldier's equipment.

Of Abimelech (Jdg 9:54), Jonathan (1Sa 14:6-7, 12, 14, 17), Saul (1Sa 16:21; 31:6), Goliath (1Sa 17:7), Joab (2Sa 18:15).

ARMORY [1074+3998, 5977]. A place for the storage of armor (Ne 3:19; SS 4:4; Isa 22:8; 39:2). In different parts of the kingdom (1Ki 10:17; 2Ch 11:12). *See Jerusalem.*

Figurative: (Jer 50:25).

ARMY [408, 408+4878, 554, 824, 1201, 2162+, 2432, 2657+, 2741, 4595, 4713, 4722, 6639+, 7372, 7736+, 10264, *5128*].

In Israel males (except Levites) were subject to military duty at the age of twenty (Nu 1:3, 17). Army divisions were subdivided into thousands and hundreds, with respective officers (Nu 31:14). Until Israel got its first king it had no standing army, but whenever there was need, God raised up men of special ability to save the country from its enemies. Down to the time of Solomon, Israel's armies were composed mostly of footmen (1Sa 4:10); later horsemen and chariots were added (2Sa 8:4; 1Ki 10:26, 28-29). The Roman army was composed of legions divided into cohorts, maniples, and centuries (Ac 10:1; 21:31).

See Armies.

ARNAN [820]. Name of a family descended from David (1Ch 3:21).

ARNON [818]. A river emptying into the Dead Sea from the east. Boundary between Moabites and Amorites (Nu 21:13-14, 26; Dt 2:24, 36; 3:8, 16; Jos 12:1). Fords of (Isa 16:2). Miracles at (Nu 21:14).

ARODI, ARODITE [771, 772] (*hunchbacked*). The sixth son of Gad (Ge 46:16) and his clan (Nu 26:17).

AROER, AROERITE [6876, 6901]
(*juniper*).

1. A city of the Amorites in the valley of the Arnon River (Dt 4:48). Conquered by Israelites (Dt 2:36; 3:12; Jdg 11:26). Taken by Hazael (2Ki 10:33).

2. A city built, or, probably more correctly, rebuilt, by the Gadites (Nu 32:34; Jos 13:25). Jephthah kills the Ammonites at (Jdg 11:33).

3. A city in Judah (1Sa 30:28). Birthplace of two of David's heroes (1Ch 11:44).

AROMATIC RESIN [978]. Fragrant
gum or resin listed with precious stones (Ge 2:12; Nu 11:7). *See Minerals of the Bible, 1; Resin.*

ARPAD [822]. A fortified city of Syria, per-
haps identical with Arvad (2Ki 18:34; 19:13). Idols of (Isa 36:19).

ARPHAXAD [823, 790]. Son of Shem (Ge
10:22; 11:10-13; 1Ch 1:17-18, 24; Lk 3:36).

ARREST [*9530, 2095+3836+5931, 3195,
4140, 4389, 5197]. Of Jesus (Mt 26:57; Mk 14:46; Lk 22:54; Jn 18:12), apostles (Ac 5:17-18; 6:12), Paul and Silas (Ac 16:19), Paul (Ac 21:30). Paul authorized to arrest Christians (Ac 9:2).

See Extradition; Prison; Prisoners.

ARROGANCE [*1454, 1452, 2147, 2294,
2295, 2326, 3400, 5881]. (1Sa 2:3; Pr 8:13; Isa 13:11). *See Pride.*

ARROWS [2932, 2943, 3721, 4751, 8008,
1018].
Described:
Deadly and destructive weapons (Pr 26:18). Sharp (Ps 120:4; Isa 5:28). Bright and polished (Isa 49:2; Jer 51:11). Sometimes poisoned (Job 6:4). Carried in a quiver (Ge 27:3; Isa 49:2; Jer 5:16; La 3:13). Swiftness of, alluded to (Zec 9:14). The ancients divined by (Eze 21:21).
Discharged:
From a bow (Ps 11:2; Isa 7:24). From machines (2Ch 26:15). At a mark for amusement (1Sa 20:20-22). At the beasts of the earth (Ge 27:3). Against enemies (2Ki 19:32; Jer 50:14). With great force (Nu 24:8; 2Ki 9:24).
Figurative:
Of Christ (Isa 49:2). Of the word of Christ (Ps 45:5). Of God's judgment (Dt 32:23-42; Ps 7:13; 21:12; 64:7; Eze 5:16). Of severe afflictions (Job 6:4; Ps 38:2). Of bitter words (Ps 64:3). Of slanderous tongues (Jer 9:8). Of false witnesses (Pr 25:18). Of devices of the wicked (Ps 11:2). Of young children (Ps 127:4). Of lightning (Ps 77:17-18; Hab 3:11). Broken, of destruction of power (Ps 76:3). Falling from the hand, of the paralyzing power (Eze 39:3).

ARSON (Ps 74:7-8). Law concerning (Ex
22:6). Instances of: Samson (Jdg 15:4-5), Absalom (2Sa 14:30), Zimri (1Ki 16:18).

ART Seen in the gifting of Bezalel and Oholiab
to build the tabernacle and its furnishings (Ex 31:1-12; 35:30-39:43); of Huram(-abi) and his work on the temple of Solomon (1Ki 7:13-45; 2Ch 2:13-4:16).

Israel was not to apply artistic talents to create idols (Ex 20:4, 23; 32:1-24; 34:17; Lev 26:1). *See Arts and Crafts; Bezalel; Huram; Tabernacle; Temple.*

ARTAXERXES [831, 10078] (*kingdom of
righteousness*). There are three kings with the name of Artaxerxes.

1. Artaxerxes I (465-425 B.C.), son of Xerxes I; known as Macrocheir or Longimanus. He overcame revolts in Egypt, where, with Athenian support, unrest started in 460 and lasted until 454, and in other parts of the Persian Empire. During that time some of the eastern possessions were lost. By the peace treaty of Callias (449), signed at Susa, the relations between Athens and Persia were stabilized on a *status quo ante bellum* basis. Artaxerxes was buried at Naqsi Rustam next to the tombs of his father and grandfather.

Artaxerxes I authorized Ezra's mission to Jerusalem in 458 (Ezr 7:8, 11-26). He temporarily halted the reconstruction of Jerusalem (4:7-23). Nehemiah's two missions were under his reign and with his permission, the first in 445 (Ne 2:1ff; 13:6).

2. Artaxerxes II (404-359 B.C.), son of Darius II and grandson of Artaxerxes I; known as Mnemon. He crushed the rebellion of his brother Cyrus (Battle of Cunaxa, 401), as related by Xenophon in his *Anabasis*. He lost Egypt during 402 or 401, repelled the meddling of Sparta in the affairs of Asia Minor (Peace of Antalcidas, 386), and suppressed other rebellious movements led by local satraps. Several of his inscriptions refer to his building activities. The palace he built at Susa is considered by some authorities to be identical with the palace described in Esther (Est 1:5-6).

3. Artaxerxes III (359-338 B.C.), son of Artaxerxes II; known as Ochus. By the use of skillful diplomacy and military force he succeeded in maintaining a superficially strong empire, until the time when he was murdered as the result of a conspiracy led by Bagoas (338).

ARTEMAS [782] (*[given by] Artemis*). A
companion of Paul (Tit 3:12).

ARTEMIS [783]. The Greek goddess of
hunting, corresponding to the Roman Diana. Her largest and most famous temple was at Ephesus; it was regarded as one of the wonders of the ancient world (Ac 19:23-41).

ARTIFICER See Arts and Crafts; Occupa-
tions and Professions.

ARTILLERY See Armory.

ARTISANS [4994]. See Occupations.

ARTS AND CRAFTS
Armorer (1Sa 8:12). Baker (Ge 40:1; 1Sa 8:13). Brickmaker (Ge 11:3; Ex 5:7-8, 18). Blacksmith (Ge 4:22; 1Sa 13:19). Carver (Ex 31:5; 1Ki 6:18). Carpenter (2Sa 5:11; Mk 6:3). Caulker (Eze 27:9, 27). Dyer (Ex 25:5). Embroiderer (Ex 35:35; 38:23). Embalmer (Ge 50:2-3, 26). Engraver (Ex 28:11; Isa 49:16; 2Co 3:7). Gardener (Ge 4:2; 9:20; Jer 29:5; Jn 20:15). Goldsmith (Isa 40:19; Jer 10:9). Launderer (2Ki 18:17; Mk 9:3). Mariner (Eze 27:8-9). Mason (2Sa 5:11; 2Ch 24:12). Musician (1Sa 18:6; 1Ch 15:16). Perfumer (Ex 30:25, 35; 1Sa 8:13). Potter (Isa 64:8; Jer 18:3; La 4:2; Zec 11:13). Refiner of metals (1Ch 28:18; Mal 3:2-3). Rope-maker (Jdg 16:11). Silversmith (Jdg 17:4; Ac 19:24). Stonecutter (Ex 20:25; 1Ch 22:15). Shipbuilder (1Ki 9:26). Smelter of metals (Job 28:2). Spinner (Ex 35:25; Pr 31:19). Tailor (Ex 28:3). Tanner (Ac 9:43; 10:6). Tent maker (Ge 4:20; Ac 18:3). Tool maker (Ge 4:22; 2Ti 4:14). Weaver (Ex 35:35; Jn 19:23). Wine maker (Ne 13:15; Isa 63:3).

ARUBBOTH
[749]. A district laid under tribute to Solomon's governor (1Ki 4:10).

ARUMAH
[777] (*lofty*). Place near Shechem where Abimelech lived (Jdg 9:41).

ARVAD, ARVADITES
[770, 773]. Island off the coast of Phoenicia (Eze 27:8, 11). Its people were descendants of Ham (Ge 10:18; 1Ch 1:16; Eze 27:8, 11).

ARZA
[825] (perhaps *gracious*). A steward of Elah (1Ki 16:9).

ASA
[654, 809] (possibly *healer* BDB; *myrtle* KB).

1. King of Judah (1Ki 15:8-24; 1Ch 3:10; 2Ch 14; 15; 16; Mt 1:7).
2. A Levite (1Ch 9:16).

ASAHEL
[6915] (*God [El] has made*).

1. Nephew of David and one of his captains (2Sa 2:18-24, 32; 3:27; 23:24; 1Ch 2:16; 11:26; 27:7).
2. A Levite commissioned by Jehoshaphat to teach the law to Judah (2Ch 17:8).
3. A Levite who had charge of tithes (2Ch 31:13).
4. Father of Jonathan (Ezr 10:15).

ASAIAH
[6919] (*Yahweh has made*).

1. An officer of King Josiah (2Ki 22:12-20; 2Ch 34:20-28).
2. A Simeonite (1Ch 4:36).
3. Levite in the time of David (1Ch 6:30).
4. A Shilonite (1Ch 9:5).
5. Chief Levite in David's day who helped bring the ark to Jerusalem (1Ch 15:6, 11).

ASAPH
[666] (*gatherer*).

1. Father of Joah (2Ki 18:18; Isa 36:3, 22).
2. Son of Berekiah. One of the three leaders of music in David's organization of the tabernacle

service (1Ch 15:16-19; 16:5-7; 25:1-9; 2Ch 5:12; 35:15; Ne 12:46). Appointed to sound the cymbals in the temple choir (1Ch 15:17, 19; 16:5, 7). A composer of sacred lyrics (2Ch 29:13-30). See *titles of Pss 50; 73-83*. Descendants of, in the temple choir (1Ch 25:1-9; 2Ch 20:14; 29:13; Ezr 2:41; 3:10; Ne 7:44; 11:22).

3. A Levite whose descendants lived in Jerusalem after the exile (1Ch 9:15).
4. A Kohath Levite (1Ch 26:1).
5. Keeper of forests (Ne 2:8).

ASAREL
[832]. Son of Jehallelel (1Ch 4:16).

ASARELAH
[833]. One of the temple choir (1Ch 25:2, 14). Probably identical with Azarel.

ASCENSION OF CHRIST
Prophecies respecting (Ps 24:7; 68:18, w Eph 4:7-8). Foretold by himself (Jn 6:62; 7:33; 14:28; 16:5; 20:17). Forty days after his resurrection (Ac 1:3). Described (Ac 1:9). From Mount of Olives (Lk 24:50; w Mk 11:1; Ac 1:12). While blessing his disciples (Lk 24:50). When he had atoned for sin (Heb 9:12; 10:12). Was triumphant (Ps 68:18). Was to supreme power and dignity (Lk 24:26; Eph 1:20-21; 1Pe 3:22). As the Forerunner of His people (Heb 6:20). To intercede (Ro 8:34; Heb 9:24). To send the Holy Spirit (Jn 16:7; Ac 2:33). To receive gifts for people (Ps 68:18, w Eph 4:8-11). To prepare a place for his people (Jn 14:2). His second coming shall be in like manner as (Ac 1:10-11).

Typified (Lev 16:15, w Heb 6:20; 9:7, 9, 12).

ASCENTS, SONGS OF
Title given Psalms 120 to 134. These psalms were, with 135 and 136, part of the liturgical collection "The Great Hallel." They were probably sung during the pilgrimage or "ascent" to Jerusalem required by the annual feasts.

ASCETICISM
A philosophy that leads to severe self-discipline in subordinating the body to the control of the moral attributes of the mind. Extreme application of, rebuked by Jesus (Mt 11:19; Lk 7:34), by Paul (Col 2:20-23; 1Ti 4:1-4, 8). See *Stoicism; Stoics*.

Instances of the practice of: John the Baptist (Mt 11:18; Lk 7:33). Those who practiced celibacy for the kingdom of heaven (Mt 19:12).

ASENATH
[664] (*belonging to] the goddess Neith*). Wife of Joseph and mother of Manasseh and Ephraim (Ge 41:45, 50; 46:20).

ASER
See Asher.

ASH
See Pine.

ASHAN
[6941] (*smoke*). A Levitical city of Judah, later of Simeon (Jos 15:42; 19:7; 1Ch 4:32; 6:59). See *Ain, 1*.

ASHBEA
See Beth Ashbea.

ASHBEL, ASHBELITE [839, 840]
(possibly a form of *man of Baal* BDB; *having a long upper lip* KB). Son of Benjamin (Ge 46:21; 1Ch 8:1) and his clan (Nu 26:38).

ASHCHENAZ See Ashkenaz.

ASHDOD [846, 847, 848] (perhaps *fortress*).
A city of the Philistines (Jos 13:3; 1Sa 6:17; Am 3:9). Anakites inhabit (Jos 11:22). Assigned to Judah (Jos 15:47). Dagon's temple in, in which was deposited the ark (1Sa 5).

Conquest of: by Uzziah (2Ch 26:6), by Assyrian supreme commander (Isa 20:1).

People of, conspire against the Jews (Ne 4:7-8). Jews intermarry with (Ne 13:23-24). Prophecies concerning (Jer 25:20; Am 1:8; 3; Zep 2:4; Zec 9:6). Called Azotus in NT times (Ac 8:40).

ASHDOTH-PISGAH (*slopes of Pisgah*). See Pisgah.

ASHER [888, 888+1201, 896, *818*] (*Happy One!*).
1. Son of Jacob, by Zilpah (Ge 30:13; 35:26; 49:20; Ex 1:4; 1Ch 2:2). Descendants of (Ge 46:17; Nu 26:44-47; Lk 2:36).

2. Tribe of.
Census of, by families (Nu 1:40-41; 26:44-47; 1Ch 7:40; 12:36). Station of, in camp (Nu 2:25, 27). Prophecies concerning Moses (Dt 33:24-25), by John (Rev 7:6). Allotment to, of land in Canaan (Jos 19:24-31; Eze 48:2). Criticized by Deborah (Jdg 5:17). Summoned by Gideon (Jdg 6:35; 7:23). Join Hezekiah (2Ch 30:11).

3. A city of Shechem (Jos 17:7; 1Ki 4:16).

ASHERAH [895].
1. Canaanite goddess, sometimes identified with Anath and Ashtoreth. See Anath; Ashtoreth.

2. Asherah poles: images of or trees planted to the goddess Asherah. Forbidden to be established (Ex 34:13; Dt 7:5; 16:21; Isa 1:29; 17:8; 27:9; Mic 5:14). Worshiped by Israelites (Jdg 3:7; 1Ki 14:15, 23; 15:13; 2Ki 13:6; 17:10, 16; 21:3-7; 2Ch 24:18; Jer 17:2). Destroyed by Gideon (Jdg 6:28), Hezekiah (2Ki 18:4), Josiah (2Ki 23:14; 2Ch 34:3-4), Asa (2Ch 14:3), Jehoshaphat (2Ch 17:6; 19:3). See High Places; Idolatry.

ASHES [709, 2014, 2016, 6760, *5075*, *5491*].
Uses of, in purification (Nu 19:9-10, 17; Heb 9:13). A symbol of mourning (2Sa 13:19; Est 4:1, 3). Sitting in (Job 2:8; Isa 58:5; Jer 6:26; Eze 27:30; Jnh 3:6; Lk 10:13). Repenting in (Job 42:6; Da 9:3; Jnh 3:6; Mt 11:21; Lk 10:13). Disguises of (1Ki 20:38, 41).

ASHHUR [858] (possibly *darkness, dawn* BDB; *a Babylonian goddess* KB). Son of Hezron (1Ch 2:24; 4:5).

ASHIMA [860]. An idol (2Ki 17:30).

ASHKELON [884, 885]. One of the five

chief cities of the Philistines (Jos 13:3). Captured by the people of Judah (Jdg 1:18). Samson slays thirty men of (Jdg 14:19). Tumors of (1Sa 6:17). Prophecies concerning (Jer 25:20; 47:5, 7; Am 1:8; Zep 2:4, 7; Zec 9:5).

ASHKENAZ [867]. Son of Gomer (Ge 10:3; 1Ch 1:6). Descendants of (Jer 51:27).

ASHNAH [877]. A name of two towns in Judah (Jos 15:33, 43).

ASHPENAZ [881] (*guest*). A prince in Nebuchadnezzar's court (Da 1:3).

ASHRIEL See Asriel.

ASHTAROTH [6958].
1. Plural form of Ashtoreth. See Ashtoreth.

2. The capital city of Bashan (Dt 1:4; Jos 9:10). Giants dwell at (Jos 12:4). Allotted to Manasseh (Jos 13:31; 1Ch 6:71). Possibly identical with Ashteroth Karnaim (Ge 14:5).

ASHTERATHITE [6960]. A native of Ashtaroth (1Ch 11:44).

ASHTEROTH KARNAIM [6959]
(*Ashteroth of the pair of horns, [two peaks?]*). An ancient city of Palestine taken by Kedorlaomer (Ge 14:5).

ASHTORETH [6956]. An idol of the Philistines, Sidonians, and Phoenicians, sometimes identified with Anath and Asherah. See Anath; Asherah. Probably identical with queen of heaven (Jer 7:18). Worshiped by Israelites (Jdg 2:13; 10:6; 1Sa 7:3-4; 12:10; 1Ki 11:5, 33; 2Ki 23:13). Temple of (1Sa 31:10). High places of, at Jerusalem, destroyed (2Ki 23:13).

ASHUR See Ashhur.

ASHURBANIPAL [10055] (*Ashur creates a son*). King of Assyria who colonized the cities of Samaria after the Israelites were taken captive to Assyria (Ezr 4:10). Reigned from 688-626 B.C. He was a great lover of learning—his library (over 22,000 tablets) survives.

ASHURI [856]. A tribal region, possibly Asher (2Sa 2:9).

ASHURNASIRPAL II Ruthless king of Assyria, reigned early in ninth century B.C.

ASHVATH [6937] (possibly *wrought iron*). Son of Japhlet (1Ch 7:33).

ASIA [*823*, *824*]. Inhabitants of, in Jerusalem, at Pentecost (Ac 2:9; 21:27; 24:19). Paul and Silas forbidden by the Holy Spirit to preach in (Ac 16:6). Gospel preached in, by Paul (Ac 19; 20:4). Paul leaves (Ac 20:16). Churches of (1Co 16:19; Rev 1:4, 11). High officials of Asia were friends of Paul (Ac 19:31).

ASIARCHS High officials of Asia. *See Asia.*

ASIEL [6918] (*God [El] has made*). Grandfather of Jehu (1Ch 4:35).

ASKELON *See Ashkelon.*

ASNAH [663] (possibly *thornbush* BDB; *he who belongs to [the god] Nah* IDB). Descendants of, return to Jerusalem (Ezr 2:50).

ASNAPPER *See Ashurbanipal; Samaria.*

ASP *See Cobra; Serpent; Viper.*

ASPATHA [672] (possibly *given from a sacred horse*). Son of Haman (Est 9:7).

ASPHALTUM *See Caulkers; Pitch; Tar.*

ASRIEL [835] (either *God has filled with joy*, or *[the object of] joy is God*).
1. Descendant of Manasseh (Nu 26:31; Jos 17:2).
2. Son of Manasseh, Asriel (1Ch 7:14).

ASS *See Donkey, Domestic; Donkey, Wild.*

ASSAR *See Tel Assar.*

ASSASSINATION [4637, 5782]. David's abhorrence of (2Sa 4:9-12). Laws prohibiting (Dt 27:24).

Instances of:
Of Eglon, by Ehud (Jdg 3:15-22), Abner, by Joab (2Sa 3:27), Ish-Bosheth, by the sons of Rimmon (2Sa 4:5-7), Amnon, by Absalom (2Sa 13:28-29), Amasa, by Joab (2Sa 20:9-10), Joash, by his servants (2Ki 12:19-20), Sennacherib, by his sons (2Ki 19:37; Isa 37:38).

ASSAULT AND BATTERY

Laws Concerning:
(Ex 21:15, 18-19, 22-27; Dt 17:8-12; Mt 5:39; Lk 6:29). Damages and compensation for (Ex 21:18-19, 22).
See Abuse; Bruise(s); Flog, Flogging; Scourging; Stripes, 1-3; Stoning.

The Beating of Jesus:
Prophecies of (Isa 50:6; La 3:30). The attacks upon (Mt 26:67; 27:30; Mk 14:65; Lk 22:63; Jn 19:3).

ASSHUR [855]. Son of Shem, and ancestor of the Assyrians (Ge 10:11, 22; 1Ch 1:17; Eze 32:22). *See Assyria.*

ASSHURITES [857]. Descendants of Dedan (Ge 25:3).

ASSIR [661] (*prisoner*).
1. Son of Korah (Ex 6:24; 1Ch 6:22).
2. Son of Ebiasaph (1Ch 6:23, 37).
3. Son of Jehoiachin (1Ch 3:17).

ASSOCIATION-SEPARATION

Evil associations:
Warnings concerning (Ex 23:2; 34:12; Ps 1:1; Pr 4:14; 24:1; 1Co 5:11; 2Co 6:14). Results of (Nu 33:55; 1Ki 11:2; 2Ch 19:2; Pr 28:7; Jn 18:18; 18:25; 1Co 15:33).

Contact with impurity (Lev 5:2; 15:11; Nu 19:13; Isa 52:11; 2Co 6:17; Col 2:21).

Separation from unclean (Lev 13:5, 21, 33, 46; Nu 5:3). Israel from nations (Lev 20:26; Nu 23:9; Dt 7:2; Jos 23:7; Jdg 2:2; Ezr 9:12; 10:11; Isa 52:11; Jer 15:19). Believers from evil associations (Jn 15:19; Ac 2:40; Eph 5:11; 2Th 3:6). Final separation of evil from good (Mt 13:30, 49; 25:32; Lk 16:26; 17:34).

Good associations:
Companionship (Ps 119:63; Pr 2:20; 13:20; 2Th 3:14). Personal contact with Jesus (Mt 9:20, 25; 14:34-36; Mk 3:10; 9:27; Lk 6:19), Peter (Ac 3:7; 9:41).

ASSOS [840]. A seaport in Mysia (Ac 20:13-14).

ASSURANCE [586, 622, 6859, 4244, 4443].
Produced by faith (Eph 3:12; 2Ti 1:12; Heb 10:22). Made full by hope (Heb 6:11, 19). Confirmed by love (1Jn 3:14, 19; 4:18). Is the effect of righteousness (Isa 32:17). Is abundant in the understanding of the gospel (Col 2:2; 1Th 1:5).

Believers Privileged to Have:
Their election (Ps 4:3; 1Th 1:4). Their redemption (Job 19:25). Their adoption (Ro 8:16; 1Jn 3:2). Their salvation (Isa 12:2). Eternal life (1Jn 5:13). The unalienable love of God (Ro 8:38-39). Union with God and Christ (1Co 6:15; 2Co 13:5; Eph 5:30; 1Jn 2:5; 4:13). Peace with God by Christ (Ro 5:1). Preservation (Ps 3:6, 8; 27:3-5; 46:3). Answers to prayer (1Jn 3:22; 5:14-15). Continuance in grace (Php 1:6). Comfort in affliction (Ps 73:26; Lk 4:18-19; 2Co 4:8-10, 16-18). Support in death (Ps 23:4). A glorious resurrection (Job 19:26; Ps 17:15; Php 3:21; 1Jn 3:2). A kingdom (Heb 12:28; Rev 5:10). A crown (2Ti 4:7-8; Jas 1:12). Give diligence to attain to (2Pe 1:10-11). Strive to maintain (Heb 3:14, 18). Confident hope in God restores (Ps 42:11).

Exemplified:
David (Ps 23:4; 73:24-26). Paul (2Ti 1:12; 4:18).

ASSYRIA [824+855, 855]. Antiquity and origin of (Ge 10:8-11). Situated beyond the Euphrates (Isa 7:20). Watered by the Tigris River (Ge 2:14).

Called:
The land of Nimrod (Mic 5:6). Shinar (Ge 11:2; 14:1). Asshur (Nu 24:22, 24). Nineveh, chief city of (Ge 10:11; 2Ki 19:36). Governed by kings (2Ki 15:19, 29).

Celebrated for:
Fertility (2Ki 18:32; Isa 36:17). Extent of con-

quests (2Ki 18:33-35; 19:11-13; Isa 10:9-14). Extensive commerce (Eze 27:23-24). Idolatry, the religion of (2Ki 19:37).

Described:
Most formidable (Isa 28:2). Intolerant and oppressive (Na 3:19). Cruel and destructive (Isa 10:7). Selfish and reserved (Hos 8:9). Unfaithful (2Ch 28:20-21). Proud and haughty (2Ki 19:22-24; Isa 10:8). An instrument of God's vengeance (Isa 7:18-19; 10:5-6). Chief men of, described (Eze 23:6, 12, 23). Armies of, described (Isa 5:26-29).

Invaded Israel (2Ki 15:19). Bought off by Menahem (2Ki 15:19-20).

Tiglath-Pileser, King of:
Ravaged Israel (2Ki 15:29). Asked to aid Ahaz against Syria (2Ki 16:7-8). Took money from Ahaz, but did not strengthen him (2Ch 28:20-21). Conquered Syria (2Ki 16:9).

Shalmaneser, King of:
Reduced Israel to tribute (2Ki 17:3). Was conspired against by Hoshea (2Ki 17:4). Imprisoned Hoshea (2Ki 17:4). Carried Israel captive (2Ki 17:5-6). Assassinated by his sons (2Ki 19:37). Repopulated Samaria from Assyria (2Ki 17:24).

Sennacherib, King of:
Invaded Judah (2Ki 18:13). Bought off by Hezekiah (2Ki 18:14-16). Insulted and threatened Judah (2Ki 18:17-32; 19:10-13). Blasphemed the Lord (2Ki 18:33-35). Prayed against by Hezekiah (2Ki 19:14-19). Reproved for pride and blasphemy (2Ki 19:20-34; Isa 37:21-29). His army destroyed by God (2Ki 19:35). Assassinated by his sons (2Ki 19:37). Condemned for oppressing God's people (Isa 52:4). Manasseh taken captive to (2Ch 33:11). The repopulating of Samaria from, completed by Ashurbanipal (Ezr 4:10). Idolatry of, brought into Samaria (2Ki 17:29). Judah condemned for trusting (Jer 2:18, 36). Israel condemned for trusting (Hos 5:13; 7:11; 8:9). The Jews condemned for following the idolatries of (Eze 16:28; 23:5, 7). The greatness, extent, duration, and fall of, illustrated (Eze 31:3-17).

Predictions Respecting:
Conquest of the Kenites by (Nu 24:22). Conquest of Syria by (Isa 8:4). Conquest and captivity of Israel by (Isa 8:4; Hos 9:3; 10:6; 11:5). Invasion of Judah by (Isa 5:26; 7:17-20; 8:8; 10:5-6, 12). Restoration of Israel from (Isa 27:12-13; Hos 11:11; Zec 10:10). Destruction of (Isa 10:12-19; 14:24-25; 30:31-33; 31:8-9; Zec 10:11). Participation in the blessings of the gospel (Isa 19:23-25; Mic 7:12).

ASTARTE *See Anath; Ashtaroth, 1; Ashtoreth.*

ASTONISHMENT [*7099, 9449, *1742, 2014, 2513]. Christ causes (Mt 13:54; 15:31; 22:22, 33; Mk 2:12; 4:41; 7:37; 10:24; Lk 2:48; 4:22, 26; 8:25).

ASTROLOGER, ASTROLOGY
[2042+9028, 4169, 10373]. One who tries to find out the influence of the stars upon human affairs or to foretell events by their positions and aspects (Isa 47:13; Jer 10:1-2; Da 1:20; 2:27; 4:7; 5:7, 11; Isa 47:12-13). *See Astronomy; Sorcery.*

ASTRONOMY
Phenomena Concerning the Universe:
God the creator of (Job 9:6-9; 26:7, 13; 37:18; Ps 8:3; 136:5-9; Isa 40:22, 26). God the ruler of (Job 38:31-33; Ps 68:33; Eze 32:7-8; Am 5:8). Immeasurable (Jer 31:37; 33:22). Laws of, permanent (Ecc 1:5; Jer 31:35-36). Declares God's glory (Ps 19:1-6). Destruction of (Mt 24:35; 2Pe 3:10; Rev 6:12-14; 21:1).

Celestial Phenomena:
Fire from heaven, on the cities of the plain (Ge 19:24-25), on the two captains and their fifties (2Ki 1:10-14), on the flocks and servants of Job (Job 1:16).

Thunder and lightning on Mt. Sinai (Ex 19:16, 18; 20:18). Pillar of cloud and fire (Ex 13:21-22; 14:19, 24; 40:38; Nu 9:15-23; Ps 78:14). The sun and moon standing still (Jos 10:12-14). Hail on the Egyptians (Ex 9:22-34).

Darkness on the Egyptians (Ex 10:21-23), at the crucifixion of Christ (Mt 27:45; Lk 23:44-45).

Sun seemingly rotating (Ecc 1:5). Wandering stars (Jude 13).

Signs in the Sun, Moon and Stars:
(Joel 2:30-31; Isa 13:10). Foretold by Jesus as part of his second coming (Mt 24:29, 35; Mk 13:24-25; Lk 21:25; Ac 2:19-20). In the final judgments (Rev 8:10-12; 9:1-2; 10:1-2; 12:3-4; 13:13; 16:8-9; 19:11-14).

Constellations:
Glory of (1Co 15:41). Darkened (Isa 13:10). The serpent (Job 26:13), Bear, Orion and Pleiades (Job 9:9; 38:31; Am 5:8).

See Constellations; Eclipse; Heaven; Meteorology; Moon; Stars; Sun.

ASUPPIM NIV "storehouses" at the S gate of the temple (1Ch 26:15, 17; Ne 12:25).

ASWAN [6059]. Egyptian town on border of Egypt and Ethiopia (Isa 49:12; Eze 29:10; 30:6).

ASYNCRITUS [*850*] (*incomparable*). A disciple at Rome (Ro 16:14).

ATAD [354] (*thornbush*). The place where the sons of Jacob mourned for their father (Ge 50:10-11).

ATARAH [6499] (*circlet, wreath*). Wife of Jerahmeel (1Ch 2:26).

ATAROTH [6500] (*circlets, wreaths*). Also called Atroth.
1. A city E of Jordan (Nu 32:3, 34).
2. A city, or possibly two different cities, of Ephraim (Jos 16:2, 5, 7; 18:13).

3. A city of Judah (1Ch 2:54). Called Atroth Beth Joab. *See Atroth Beth Joab; Joab, 4.*

4. A city of Gad (Nu 32:35).

ATAROTH ADDAR [6501] (*wreaths of majesty*). *See Ataroth, 2.*

ATER [359] (possibly *crippled one, left-handed one*, or *the proper name Etir*).

1. A descendant of Hezekiah who returned from Babylon (Ezr 2:16; Ne 7:21; 10:17).

2. A gatekeeper (Ezr 2:42; Ne 7:45).

3. An Israelite who agreed to Nehemiah's covenant (Ne 10:17).

ATHACH [6973]. A city of Judah (1Sa 30:30).

ATHAIAH [6970] (possibly *[the] superiority of Yahweh*). Son of Uzziah (Ne 11:4).

ATHALIAH [6975, 6976] (possibly *Yahweh is exalted* BDB; *oldest of Yahweh* KB).

1. Wife of Jehoram, king of Judah (2Ki 8:18, 26; 11:1-3, 12-16, 20; 2Ch 22:10-12; 23:12-15, 21).

2. Son of Jehoram (1Ch 8:26).

3. Father of Jeshaiah (Ezr 8:7).

ATHARIM [926] (traditionally *way of the spies*). The Israelites, under Moses, were attacked by the king of Arad, and some were taken captive (Nu 21:1ff).

ATHEISM Instances of (Ps 10:4; 14:1; 53:1). Arguments against (Job 12:7-25; Ro 1:19-20).
See God; Faith; Unbelief.

ATHENS, ATHENIANS [121, 122]. A leading city of Greece and its inhabitants (Ac 17:15-34; 1Th 3:1).

ATHLAI [6974] (possibly *Yahweh is exalted* BDB; *oldest of Yahweh* KB). A son of Bebai (Ezr 10:28).

ATHLETE, ATHLETICS *See Games.*

ATOMS OF MATTER NIV "dust of the world" (Pr 8:26).

ATONEMENT [4105, 4113, 4114, *2661, 2662, 2663*].
The divine act of grace in which God accepts an offering as a substitute for the punishment for sin. In the OT, the shed blood of sacrificial offerings effected atonement. The blood shed in the sacrifices was sacred. It epitomized the life of the sacrificial victim. Since life was sacred, blood (a symbol of life) had to be treated with respect (Ge 9:5-6). Eating blood was therefore strictly forbidden (Lev 7:26-27; Dt 12:16, 23-25; 15:23; 1Sa 14:32-34). Lev 17:14 stresses the intimate relationship between blood and life by twice declaring that "the life of every creature is its blood." Life is the precious and mysterious gift of God, and people are not to seek to preserve it or increase their life-force by eating "life" that is "in

the blood" (Lev 17:11)—as many pagan peoples throughout history have thought they could do (Ge 9:4).

Practically every sacrifice included the sprinkling or smearing of blood on the altar or within the tabernacle (Lev 1:5; 3:2; 4:6, 25; 7:2; 17:6), thus teaching that atonement involves the substitution of life for life. The blood of the OT sacrifice pointed forward to the blood of the Lamb of God, who obtained for his people "eternal redemption" (Heb 9:12). "Without the shedding of blood there is no forgiveness" (Heb 9:22).

For tabernacle and furniture (Lev 16:15-20, 33). In consecration of the Levites (Nu 8:21). For those defiled by the dead (Nu 6:11). Made for houses (Lev 14:53). Sin. *See below, Sin.*

By:
Meat offerings (Lev 5:11-13), jewels (Nu 31:50), money (Ex 30:12-16; Lev 5:15-16; 2Ki 12:16), incense (Nu 16:46-50). By animals. *See below, Made by Animal Sacrifices.* By Jesus. *See below, Made by Jesus.*

Day of:
Time of (Ex 30:10; Lev 23:27; 25:9; Nu 29:7). How observed (Ex 30:10; Lev 16:2-34; 23:27-32; Nu 29:7-11; Heb 5:3; 9:7).

Made by Animal Sacrifices:
In the blood shed (Lev 17:11). In burnt offerings (Lev 1:4). For unintentional sin (Lev 4:13-21; Nu 15:22-28; 28:27-31; 29), for purification after childbirth (Lev 12:6-8).

In guilt offerings for sin (Lev 5:6-10; 6:7), for cleansing from a skin disease (Lev 14:12-32).

In sin offerings (Ex 29:36; Lev 4:20) for unintentional sins of a leader (Lev 4:22-35), of the descendants of Aaron (Lev 9:7; 10:17; 16:6-9). The scapegoat (Lev 16:10-34). On festival days (Nu 28:22; 29).

Forgiveness of sins through (Lev 5:10; 19:22).

Made by Jesus:
Through his blood shed (Lk 22:20; 1Co 1:23; Eph 2:13-15; Heb 9:12-15, 25-26; 12:24; 13:12, 20-21; 1Jn 5:6; Rev 1:5; 5:9; 7:14; 12:11), his death (Ro 3:24-26; 5:11-15; 1Th 1:10; Heb 13:12; 1Jn 2:2; 3:5; 4:10; Rev 5:6, 9; 13:8).

Typified in Passover lamb (Ex 12:5, 11, 14; 1Co 5:7), in sacrifices (Ex 24:8; Lev 16:30, 34; 17:11; 19:22; Heb 9:11-28). Compare Ge 4:4, w Heb 11:4; Ge 22:2, w Heb 11:17, 19; Ex 12:5, 11, 14, w 1Co 5:7; Ex 24:8, w Heb 9:10; Lev 16:30, 34, w Heb 9:7, 12, 28; Lev 17:11, w Heb 9:22.

Divinely inspired (Lk 2:30-31; Gal 4:4-5; Eph 1:3-12, 17-22; 2:4-10; Col 1:19-20; 1Pe 1:20; Rev 13:8). A mystery (1Co 2:7; 1Pe 1:8-12). Once for all (Heb 7:27; 9:24-28; 10:10, 12, 14; 1Pe 3:18). Made on our behalf (Isa 53:4-12; Mt 20:28; Jn 6:51; 11:49-51; Gal 3:13; Eph 5:2; 1Th 5:9-10; Heb 2:9; 1Pe 2:24).

For reconciliation (Da 9:24-27; Ro 5:1-21; 2Co 5:18-21; Eph 2:16-17; Col 1:20-22; Heb 2:17). For remission of sins (Zec 13:1; Mt 26:28; Lk 22:20; 24:46-47; Jn 1:29; Ro 4:25; 1Co 15:3; Gal 1:3-4; Eph 1:7; Col 1:14; Heb 1:3; 10:1-20; 1Jn

1:7; 3:5). For redemption (Mt 20:28; Ac 20:28; Gal 3:13; 1Ti 2:6; Heb 9:12; Rev 5:9).

See Blood; Jesus the Christ, Death of, Mission of, Sufferings of; Redemption; Salvation.

ATONEMENT COVER [4114, *2663*].
KJV "mercy seat." Description of (Ex 25:17-22). Placed on the ark of the testimony (Ex 26:34; 30:6; 31:7; 40:20; Heb 9:5). Materials of, to be a freewill offering (Ex 35:4-12). Made by Bezalel (Ex 37:1, 6-9).

Sprinkled with blood (Lev 16:14-15). There God met with his people (Ex 25:22; 30:6, 36; Lev 16:2; Nu 7:89; 17:4; 1Sa 4:4; 2Sa 6:2; 2Ki 19:15; 1Ch 13:6; Ps 80:1; Ps 99:1; Isa 37:16; Heb 4:16).

In Solomon's temple (1Ch 28:11).

See Tabernacle.

ATONEMENT, DAY OF *See Day of Atonement.*

ATONING SACRIFICE [2662]. *See Propitiation.*

ATROPHY *See Disease; Shriveled Hand.*

ATROTH BETH JOAB [6502]
(*circlets, folds of the house of Joab*). Descendants of Salma; the house of Joab, occurs in the genealogy of Judah (1Ch 2:54).

ATROTH SHOPHAN [6503] (*circlets, folds of Shophan*). Town built by Gadites E of Jordan (Nu 32:35).

ATTAI [6968] (*timely, or perhaps an abbreviation of Athaiah*).
1. A Gadite warrior (1Ch 12:11).
2. Son of Rehoboam (2Ch 11:20).
3. Grandson of Sheshan (1Ch 2:35-36).

ATTALIA [*877*]. A seaport of Pamphylia (Ac 14:25).

ATTORNEY *See Lawyer.*

ATTRIBUTES OF GOD *See God.*

AUGUSTUS [*880*] (*reverent, holy*). A title of Roman emperors (Lk 2:1). "Emperor" and "Imperial" [*4935*] in Ac 25:21, 25; 27:1 are rendered Augustus in the KJV.

AUL *See Awl.*

AVA *See Avva.*

AVARICE Love of money: a root of evil (1Ti 6:10). Insatiable (Ecc 4:7-8; 5:10-11). Forbidden in overseer (1Ti 3:2-3; Tit 1:7).

Instances of: Descendants of Joseph (Jos 17:14-18). *See Covetousness; Greed; Rich, The; Riches.*

AVEN [*225*] (*evil power, wickedness*).
1. Valley of Aven (Am 1:5, ftn).
2. Bethel (Am 5:5, ftn).
3. Beth Aven (Hos 10:8, ftn). *See Beth Aven.*

4. A possible spelling for On or Heliopolis (Eze 30:17, ftn).

AVENGER OF BLOOD [1457].
Premosaic:
Cain fears (Ge 4:14-15), Lamech fears (Ge 4:24). Edict of God (Ge 9:5-6).

Mosaic Law Concerning:
Cities of refuge from (Nu 35:6-34; Dt 19:1-13; Jos 20:1-9; 21:13, 21, 27, 32, 38; 1Ch 6:57, 67). Set aside by David (2Sa 14:4-11).

Figurative: (Ps 8:2; 44:16; Ro 13:4; 1Th 4:6). *See Homicide.*

AVITH [6400]. Capital city of the Edomites (Ge 36:35; 1Ch 1:46).

AVVA [6379]. Also called Ivvah. A district near Babylon (2Ki 17:24; 18:34; 19:13; Isa 37:13).

AVVIM [6399].
1. A city of Benjamin (Jos 18:23).
2. A tribe in southern Palestine. *See Avvites.*

AVVITES [6398].
1. A people driven out of Canaan by the Philistines (Dt 2:23; Jos 13:3).
2. Colonists of Samaria (2Ki 17:31).

AWAKENINGS, REFORMS
General references (1Ki 18:39; 2Ch 30:11; Ezr 10:1; Lk 3:7-10; Jn 4:39; Ac 2:40-41; 8:6; 9:35; 11:21; 13:48; 18:8; 19:18).

Instances: Asa (1Ki 15:12). Jehu (1Ki 10:27). Jehoiada (2Ki 11:18). Josiah (2Ki 23:4). Jehoshaphat (2Ch 19:3). Hezekiah (2Ch 31:1). Manasseh (2Ch 33:15). Ezra (Ezr 10:3). Nehemiah (Ne 13:19).

AWL [5345]. A sharp piercing tool (Ex 21:6; Dt 15:17).

AX, AXHEAD [1366, 1749, 4172, 4477, 4490, 7935, *544*]. A tool for cutting wood (Dt 19:5; 20:19; 1Sa 13:20-21; 2Sa 12:31; Ps 74:5-6). A weapon of war (Jer 46:22). Elisha causes an axhead to float (2Ki 6:5-6).

Figurative of judgment (Jer 46:22; Mt 3:10).

AXLES [3338, 6248]. Part of a wheeled vehicle, like the movable stands (1Ki 7:30-33).

AYYAH [6509]. A city in Ephraim (1Ch 7:28).

AZAL *See Azel, 1.*

AZALIAH [729] (*Yahweh is keeping in reserve*). Father of Shaphan (2Ki 22:3; 2Ch 34:8).

AZANIAH [271] (*Yahweh has listened*). Father of Jeshua (Ne 10:9).

AZAREL [6475] (*God [El] has helped*).
1. Aaronite of the family of Korah (1Ch 12:6).
2. A musician in the temple (1Ch 25:18), also called Uzziel. *See Uzziel 4.*

3. A Danite prince (1Ch 27:22).
4. A son of Bani (Ezr 10:41).
5. A priest (Ne 11:13; 12:36).

AZARIAH [6481, 6482, 10538] (*Yahweh has helped*).
1. Man of Judah (1Ch 2:8).
2. King of Judah. See *Uzziah, 1*.
3. Son of Jehu (1Ch 2:38).
4. Son of Ahimaaz (1Ch 6:9).
5. Levite (1Ch 6:36).
6. Son of Zadok (1Ki 4:2).
7. High priest (1Ch 6:10).
8. Son of Nathan (1Ki 4:5).
9. Prophet (2Ch 15:1-8).
10. Son of King Jehoshaphat (2Ch 21:2).
11. Son of Jehoram (2Ch 22:6, ftn). See *Ahaziah*.
12. Son of Jehoram (2Ch 23:1).
13. Son of Johanan (2Ch 28:12).
14. Levite (2Ch 29:12).
15. High priest (2Ch 26:16-20).
16. Son of Hilkiah (1Ch 6:13-14).
17. Opponent of Jeremiah (Jer 43:2).
18. Jewish captive of Babylon (Da 1:7). See *Abednego*.
19. Son of Maaseiah (Ne 3:23).
20. Levite (Ne 8:7).
21. Priest (Ne 10:2).
22. Prince of Judah (Ne 12:32-33).

AZARIAHU [6482]. A son of Jehoshaphat (2Ch 21:2).

AZAZ [6452] (*strong*). Father of Bela (1Ch 5:8).

AZAZEL [6439]. NIV "scapegoat," one of the goats chosen for the service of the Day of Atonement (Lev 16:8, 10, 26). It has been interpreted both personally and impersonally as meaning: 1. remission of sin, 2. a place name, 3. an evil spirit, 4. the devil. See *Scapegoat*.

AZAZIAH [6453] (*Yahweh is strong*).
1. A harpist in the temple (1Ch 15:21).
2. Father of Hoshea (1Ch 27:20).
3. An overseer in the temple (2Ch 31:13).

AZBUK [6443]. The father of Nehemiah (Ne 3:16).

AZEKAH [6467] (possibly *hoe [the ground]*). A town of Judah (Jos 10:10-11; 15:35; 1Sa 17:1; 2Ch 11:9; Ne 11:30; Jer 34:7).

AZEL [727, 728] (*noble*).
1. A place near Jerusalem (Zec 14:5).
2. A Benjamite (1Ch 8:37-38; 9:43-44).

AZEM See *Ezem*.

AZGAD [6444] (*strong is Gad*).
1. Ancestor of certain captives who returned from Babylon (Ezr 2:12; Ne 7:17).

2. A returned exile (Ezr 8:12).
3. A leader who signed Nehemiah's covenant (Ne 10:15).

AZIEL [6456] (*God is my strength*). A temple musician (1Ch 15:20).

AZIZA [6461] (*powerful*). Son of Zattu (Ezr 10:27).

AZMAVETH [6462, 6463] (*strong one of death* ISBE; *camel fodder, a plant of the plumose family* KB).
1. One of David's heroes (2Sa 23:31).
2. Benjamite (1Ch 12:3).
3. David's treasurer (1Ch 27:25).
4. Descendant of Jonathan (1Ch 8:36).
5. Place N of Anathoth (Ezr 2:24; Ne 12:29).

AZMON [6801] (*strongly [built body]*). A place on the S of Canaan (Nu 34:4, 5; Jos 15:4).

AZNOTH TABOR [268] (possibly *peaks of Tabor*). A town in Naphtali (Jos 19:34).

AZOR [110] (*help*). Ancestor of Jesus (Mt 1:13-14). Perhaps identical with Azrikam (1Ch 3:23).

AZOTUS [111]. The name of Ashdod in NT times (Ac 8:40). See *Ashdod*.

AZRIEL [6480] (*God [El] is [my] help*).
1. A chief of Manasseh (1Ch 5:24).
2. Father of Jerimoth (1Ch 27:19).
3. Father of Seraiah (Jer 36:26).

AZRIKAM [6483] (*[my] help arises*).
1. Son of Neariah (1Ch 3:23).
2. Son of Azel (1Ch 8:38; 9:44).
3. A Levite (1Ch 9:14; Ne 11:15).
4. Governor of the house of Ahaz (2Ch 28:7).

AZUBAH [6448] (*abandonment*).
1. Mother of Jehoshaphat (1Ki 22:42; 2Ch 20:31).
2. Wife of Caleb (1Ch 2:18-19).

AZUR See *Azzur*.

AZZAH See *Gaza, 1*.

AZZAN [6464] (*strong*). Father of Paltiel of the tribe of Issachar; chosen to help distribute the territory W of the Jordan among the various tribes who settled there (Nu 34:26).

AZZUR [6473] (*help*).
1. A leader who sealed Nehemiah's covenant (Ne 10:17).
2. A Gibeonite, the father of Hananiah, a false prophet in the days of King Zedekiah (Jer 28:1).
3. Father of Jaazaniah, an Israelite prince (Eze 11:1).

BAAL [1251, 1252, 955] (*master, owner, lord*).
1. A god worshiped by the Canaanites and the Phoenicians; a god of storms and fertility. Often in the plural (Jdg 2:11; 3:7).

Wickedly worshiped by the Israelites in the time of the judges (Jdg 2:10-23; 1Sa 7:3-4), by the kingdom of Israel (2Ki 17:16; Jer 23:13; Hos 11:2; 13:1), under Ahab (1Ki 16:31-33; 18:18; 19:18), Jehoram (2Ki 3:2), by the Israelites (2Ki 21:3; 2Ch 22:2-4; 24:7; 28:2; 33:3). Jeremiah preaches against the worship of (Jer 2:8, 23; 7:9).

Altars of, destroyed by Gideon (Jdg 6:25-32), by Jehoiada (2Ki 11:18), by Josiah (2Ki 23:4-5).

Prophets of, slain by Elijah (2Ki 18:4). All worshipers of, destroyed by Jehu (2Ki 10:18-25).

2. A Benjamite (1Ch 8:30; 9:36).

3. A Reubenite (1Ch 5:5).

4. A city in the tribe of Simeon (1Ch 4:33). Called Baalath Beer (Jos 19:8).

BAAL-BERITH [1253] (*lord [Baal] of a covenant*). A god of the Shechemites (Jdg 9:4). Worshiped by Israelites (Jdg 8:33). Also called El-Berith (Jdg 9:46). *See El-Berith.*

BAAL GAD [1254] (*lord [Baal] of good luck*). A city of the Canaanites (Jos 11:17; 12:7; 13:5). Probably Baal Hermon (Jdg 3:3; 1Ch 5:23).

BAAL-GUR *See Gur Baal.*

BAAL HAMON [1255] (*lord [Baal] of Hamon,* or *possessor of abundance*). A place where Solomon had a vineyard (SS 8:11). Its location is unknown. Called Hammon (Jos 19:28).

BAAL-HANAN [1257] (*lord [Baal] is gracious*).
1. The son of Acbor and king of Edom (Ge 36:38; 1Ch 1:49).

2. An official under David (1Ch 27:28).

BAAL HAZOR [1258] (*lord [Baal] of Hazor*). Where Absalom had a sheep-range and where he brought about the death of Amnon in revenge for the rape of his sister (2Sa 13:23).

BAAL HERMON [1259] (*lord [Baal] of Hermon*).
1. A city near Mt. Hermon (1Ch 5:23). Probably identical with Baal Gad. *See Baal Gad.*

2. A mountain of Lebanon (Jdg 3:3).

BAAL MEON [1260]. A city of the Reubenites (Nu 32:38; 1Ch 5:8; Eze 25:9). Also called: Beth Meon (Jer 48:23), Beth Baal Meon (Jos 13:17), Beon (Nu 32:3).

BAAL PEOR [1261] (*lord [Baal] of Peor*).

An idol of Moab (Nu 25:3, 5; Dt 4:3; Ps 106:28; Hos 9:10).

BAAL PERAZIM [1262] (*lord [Baal] of making a breach, breaking through*). A place in the valley of Rephaim (2Sa 5:20; 1Ch 14:11). Called Mt. Perazim (Isa 28:21).

BAAL SHALISHAH [1264] (*lord [Baal] of Shalisha*). A place near Gilgal (1Sa 9:4; 2Ki 4:42).

BAAL TAMAR [1265] (*lord [Baal] of the palm tree*). A place near Gibeah (Jdg 20:33).

BAAL-ZEBUB [1256] (*lord [Baal] of the flies*). Name under which Baal was worshiped by the Philistines of Ekron (2Ki 1:2-3, 6). An intentional biblical corruption of the original name Baal-Zebul, "Baal the prince." *See Beelzebub.*

BAAL ZEPHON [1263] (*lord [Baal] of the North*). A place near which the Israelites encamped just before they crossed the Red Sea (Ex 14:2, 9; Nu 33:7). The site is unknown.

BAALAH [1267] ([feminine of Baal] *lady*).
1. A city in the S of Judah (Jos 15:29). Apparently identical with Balah (Jos 19:3) and Bilhah (1Ch 4:29).

2. A city in the N of Judah called also Kiriath Jearim. *See Kiriath Jearim.*

3. A mountain in Judah (Jos 15:11). Probably identical with Mt. Jearim.

BAALAH OF JUDAH (*lords [Baals] of Judah*). Town on N border of Judah; the same as Baalah and Kiriath Baal and Kiriath Jearim (2Sa 6:2; 1Ch 13:6).

BAALATH [1272] (feminine of Baal "lord" *lady*). A city of Dan (Jos 19:44; 1Ki 9:18; 2Ch 8:6).

BAALATH BEER [1273] (*lord [Baal] of the well*). A city in the tribe of Simeon (Jos 19:8). *See Baal, 4.*

BAALBEK (*city of Baal*). City of Coele-Syria, c. forty miles NW of Damascus, famous for its ruins.

BAALI (*my lord* or *my husband*). Name often given to Yahweh by Israel, no longer to be used when Baal worship is eradicated (Hos 2:16, ftn).

BAALIM Plural form of Baal in KJV (Jdg 2:11; 1Sa 7:4; Hos 2:13, 17; 11:2). *See Baal.*

BAALIS [1271] (possibly *son of delight,* or *Baals*). King of the Ammonites (Jer 40:14).

BAANA [1275] (son of affliction).
1. Son of Ahilud (1Ki 4:12).
2. Father of Zadok (Ne 3:4).
3. A son of Hushai (1Ki 4:16).

BAANAH [1276] (son of affliction).
1. A captain of Ish-Bosheth's army (2Sa 4:2, 5-6, 9).
2. Father of Heled (also Heleb) (2Sa 23:29, ftn; 1Ch 11:30).
3. Jewish leader of the Exile (Ezr 2:2; Ne 7:7; 10:27).
4. See Baana, 3.

BAARA [1281] (passionate [burning] one).
Wife of Shaharaim (1Ch 8:8). Called Hodesh.

BAASEIAH [1283] (the Lord is bold). An ancestor of Asaph, the musician (1Ch 6:40).

BAASHA [1284] (boldness). King of Israel (1Ki 15:16-22, 27-34; 16:1-7; 21:22; 2Ki 9:9; 2Ch 16:1-6; Jer 41:9).

BABBLER [5066]. A sarcastic title applied to Paul (Ac 17:18).

BABBLING [1006]. Condemned (Mt 6:7; 1Ti 6:20; 2Ti 2:16).

BABEL [951] (gate of god[s]; Ge 11:9 confused). A city in the plain of Shinar. Tower built and tongues confused at (Ge 11:1-9). See Babylon.

BABIES [1201, 3528, 3529, 6403, 1100, 4086, 5503]. In the mouths of, praise is ordained (Mt 21:16).
Symbolize: Those without guile (Ps 8:2; Mt 11:25; Lk 10:21), the children of the kingdom of heaven (Mt 18:2-6; Mk 10:15; Lk 18:17), weak Christians (Ro 2:20; 1Co 3:1; Heb 5:13; 1Pe 2:2).
See Children; Parents.

BABOONS [9415]. Imported by Solomon (1Ki 10:22; 2Ch 9:21).

BABYLON, BABYLONIA
[824+951, 824+4169, 951, 9114, 10093, 10094, 10373, 956] (gate of god[s]).

Described:
Origin of (Ge 10:8, 10). Origin of the name (Ge 11:8-9). Land of the Chaldeans (Eze 12:13). Land of Shinar (Da 1:2; Zec 5:11, ftn). Land of Merathaim (Jer 50:21). Desert of the sea (Isa 21:1, 9). Sheshach, a cryptic term for Babylon (Jer 25:12, 26, ftn). Lady of kingdoms (Isa 47:5). Situated beyond the Euphrates (Ge 11:31, w Jos 24:2-3). Formerly a part of Mesopotamia (Ac 7:2). Conquered by the Assyrians and a part of their empire (2Ki 17:24, w Isa 23:13). Watered by the rivers Euphrates and Tigris (Ps 137:1; Jer 51:13). Composed of many nations (Da 3:4, 29). Governed by Kings (2Ki 20:12; Da 5:1). Languages spoken in (Da 1:4; 2:4). With Media and Persia divided by Darius into 120 provinces (Da 6:1). Ad-

ministrators placed over (Da 2:48; 6:2). Babylon the chief province of (Da 3:1).

Babylon the Capital of:
Its antiquity (Ge 11:4, 9). Enlarged by Nebuchadnezzar (Da 4:30). Surrounded with a great wall and fortified (Jer 51:53, 58). Called the jewel of kingdoms and the glory of Babylonians' pride (Isa 13:19), the golden city (Isa 14:4, KJV), the city of merchants (Eze 17:4), Babylon the great (Da 4:30).

Remarkable for:
Antiquity (Jer 5:15). Naval power (Isa 43:14). Military power (Jer 5:16; 50:23). National greatness (Isa 13:19; Jer 51:41). Wealth (Jer 50:37; 51:13). Commerce (Eze 17:4). Manufacture of garments (Jos 7:21). Wisdom of officials (Isa 47:10; Jer 50:35).

Inhabitants of:
Idolatrous (Jer 50:38; Da 3:18). Addicted to magic (Isa 47:9, 12-13; Da 2:1-2). Profane and sacrilegious (Da 5:1-3). Wicked (Isa 47:10).

As a Power Was:
Arrogant (Isa 14:13-14; Jer 50:29, 31-32). Secure and self-confident (Isa 47:7-8). Grand and stately (Isa 47:1, 5). Covetous (Jer 51:13). Oppressive (Isa 14:4). Cruel and destructive (Isa 14:17; 47:6; Jer 51:25; Hab 1:6-7). An instrument of God's vengeance on other nations (Jer 51:7; Isa 47:6). Armies of, described (Hab 1:7-9).

Represented by:
A great eagle (Eze 17:3). A head of gold (Da 2:32, 37-38). A lion with eagle's wings (Da 7:4). Ambassadors of, sent to Hezekiah (2Ki 20:12). Figure of a woman (Rev 17).

Nebuchadnezzar, King of:
Made Jehoiakim vassal (2Ki 24:1). Besieged Jerusalem (2Ki 24:10-11). Took Jehoiachin captive to Babylon (2Ki 24:12, 14-16; 2Ch 36:10). Sacked the temple (2Ki 24:13). Made Zedekiah king (2Ki 24:17). Besieged and took Jerusalem (2Ki 24:20; 25:1-4). Burned Jerusalem (2Ki 25:9-10). Took Zedekiah captive to Babylon (2Ki 25:7, 11, 18-21; 2Ch 36:20). Sacked and burned the temple (2Ki 25:9, 13-17; 2Ch 36:18-19). Revolt of the Israelites from, and their punishment illustrated (Eze 17). The Israelites exhorted to be subject to, and settle in (Jer 27:17; 29:1-7). Treatment of the Israelites in (2Ki 25:27-30; Da 1:3-7). Grief of the Israelites in (Ps 137:1-6). Destroyed by the Medes (Da 5:30-31). Restoration of the Israelites from (2Ch 36:23; Ezr 1; 2:1-67). The gospel preached in (1Pe 5:13). A type of Antichrist (Rev 16:19; 17:5).

Predictions Respecting:
Conquests by (Jer 21:3-10; 27:2-6; 49:28-33; Eze 21:19-32; 29:18-20). Captivity of the Israelites by (Jer 20:4-6; 22:20-26; 25:9-11; Mic 4:10). Restoration of the Israelites from (Isa 14:1-4; 44:28; 48:20; Jer 29:10; 50:4, 8, 19). Destruction of (Isa 13; 14:4-22; 21:1-10; 47; Jer 25:12; 50; 51). Perpetual desolation of (Isa 13:19-22;

14:22-23; Jer 50:13, 39; 51:37). Acknowledgment of Yahweh (Ps 87:4).

BACA [1133] (*balsam tree*, or *weeping*). An unknown valley of Israel (Ps 84:6), figurative of an experience of sorrow turned into joy.

BACHRITES See *Beker, Bekerite.*

BACKBITING Evil of (Ps 15:1-3; Pr 25:23; Ro 1:29-30; 2Co 12:20).

See *Accusation, False; Slander; Speaking, Evil.*

BACKSLIDERS

Described as:
Blind (2Pe 1:9; Rev 3:17), godless (2Jn 9), idolaters (1Co 10:7), lukewarm (Rev 3:15-16), grumblers (Ex 17:7; 1Co 10:10), forsaking God (Jer 17:13), tempting Christ (1Co 10:9), forsaking God's covenant (Ps 78:10-11; Pr 2:17), turned aside to evil (Ps 125:5; 1Ti 5:15), unfit for God's kingdom (Lk 9:62).

God's Forbearance With:
(Dt 32:5-6, 26-27; Ezr 9:10, 14; Isa 42:3).
God's concern for (Dt 32:28-29; Ps 81:13-14; Isa 1:4-9, 21-22; 65:2-3; Jer 2:5, 11-13, 17, 31-32; 18:13-15; 50:6; Hos 6:4-11; 11:1-4; 11:7-9; Mt 23:37).
Called to repentance (Isa 30:9, 15; 31:6; Jer 3:4-7, 12-14, 21-22; 4:14; 6:16; Hos 14:1; Mal 3:7; Rev 2:4-5, 20-22; 3:2-3, 18-19).
Promises to penitent: Of finding the Lord (Dt 4:29-31; 2Ch 15:2-4). Of spiritual enlightenment (Isa 29:24; Jer 3:14-19; Hos 6:3). Of restoration (Dt 30:1-10; Pr 24:16; Isa 57:18-19; Hos 14:4; Zec 10:6). Of temporal prosperity (Lev 26:40-42; Dt 30:1-5, 7-10; Job 22:23-30). Return of (Jer 31:18-19; 50:4-5; Hos 3:5; Jnh 2:4).

Judgment of:
Warnings to (Dt 4:25-28; 28:58-59; 29:18; 31:16-18; 1Ki 9:6-9; 2Ch 7:19-22; Jer 7:13-34; 11:9-17; Mk 9:50).
Corrective judgments upon (Dt 32:16-25; 1Ki 8:33; 2Ch 7:19-22; Ne 9:26-30; Job 34:26-27; Isa 50:1; Jer 8:1-15; 16:22; Eze 22:18-22; Hos 8:14; 9:1-17).
Punishment of: By temporal loss (Dt 28:15-68; Ezr 8:22; Jer 13:24-25; Eze 15; Am 2:4-6). By being overthrown by enemies (Nu 14:43; Dt 4:27-28; Jdg 2:12-15; 2Ki 18:11-12; 2Ch 29:6-8; Ps 78:40-43, 56-64). By being forsaken of God (2Ch 24:20; Isa 2:6; Jer 6:30; 12:7; 14:7, 10; 15:1; Hos 4:6, 10). By bearing the fruits of their sin (Pr 14:14; Eze 11:21; 16:43; 23:35).

Instances of:
Saul (1Sa 15:11, 26-28). Solomon (1Ki 11:4-40; Ne 13:26). Amon (2Ki 21:22-23). Rehoboam (2Ch 12:1-2). Joash (2Ch 24:24). Amaziah (2Ch 25:27). Jonah (Jnh 1:3). Disciples of Jesus (Jn 6:66). Peter (Mt 26:69-75). Corinthian Christians (1Co 5:1-8). Galatians (Gal 3:1; 4:9-11; 5:6-7). Hymenaeus and Alexander (1Ti 1:20). Phygelus and Hermogenes (2Ti 1:15). Demas (2Ti

4:10). Churches of Asia (2Ti 1:15; Rev 2:4; 3:2-3, 15-18).
See *Apostasy; Backsliding; Church, The Body of Believers, Evil Conditions of; Reprobacy.*

BACKSLIDING [294, 5412] Turning from God (1Ki 11:9). Leaving the first love (Rev 2:4). Departing from the simplicity of the gospel (2Co 11:3; Gal 3:1-3; 5:4, 7).
God is displeased at (Ps 78:57, 59). Despised by believers (Ps 101:3). Warnings against (Ps 85:8; 1Co 10:12). Guilt and consequences of (Nu 14:43; Ps 125:5; Isa 59:2, 9-11; Jer 5:6; 8:5, 13; 15:6; Lk 9:62). Brings its own punishment (Pr 14:14; Jer 2:19). A haughty spirit leads to (Pr 16:18). Leaning to (Pr 24:16; Hos 11:7). Liable to continue and increase (Jer 8:5; 14:7). Exhortations to return from (2Ch 30:6; Isa 31:6; Jer 3:12, 14, 22; Hos 6:1). Pray to be restored from (Ps 80:3; 85:4; La 5:21). Punishment of tempting others to the sin of (Pr 28:10; Mt 18:6). Not hopeless (Ps 37:24; Pr 24:16).
Attempt to bring back those guilty of (Gal 6:1; Jas 5:10, 20). Sin of, to be confessed (Isa 59:12-14; Jer 3:13, 14; 14:7-9). Pardon of, promised (2Ch 7:14; Jer 3:12; 31:20; 36:3). Healing of, promised (Jer 3:22; Hos 14:4). Afflictions sent to heal (Hos 5:15). Blessedness of those who keep from (Pr 28:15; Isa 26:3-4; Col 1:21-23).

Instances of Israel's Backsliding:
At Meribah (Ex 17:1-7), when Aaron made the golden calf (Ex 32), after Joshua's death (Jdg 2), during Asa's reign (2Ch 15), Hezekiah's reign (2Ch 30:2-12).
See *Apostasy; Backsliders.*

BACUTH See *Allon Bacuth.*

BAD COMPANY See *Company, Evil.*

BADGER See *Sea Cow.*

BAG [3038, 3967, 3998, 7655, *1186+2400, 4385*]. Sack or pouch made for holding anything. Many kinds are mentioned in Scripture (Dt 25:13; 2Ki 5:23; Mt 10:10).

BAGPIPE (RSV); NIV "pipes." A musical instrument (Da 3:5, 7, 10, 15). See *Music, Instruments of.*

BAHURIM, BAHARUMITE [1038, 1049] (*young men*). A village between Jericho and Jerusalem, on the eastern slope of the Mount of Olives; modern Ras et-Tmim (2Sa 3:16; 16:5; 17:18; 19:16; 1Ki 2:8).

BAIL See *Creditor; Debt; Debtor; Security, For Debt.*

BAJITH NIV "temple"; a place of idolatrous worship in Moab (Isa 15:2). See *Idolatry; Sanctuary, 4; Shrine.*

BAKBAKKAR [1320] (*investigator*). A Levite (1Ch 9:15).

BAKBUK [1317] (*gurgling [sound coming out of a bottle]*). The founder of a family of temple servants who returned from the Captivity with Zerubbabel (Ezr 2:51; Ne 7:53).

BAKBUKIAH [1319] (*Yahweh pours out*). A name occurring three times in Nehemiah (Ne 11:17; 12:9, 25), a Levite in high office in Jerusalem right after the Exile.

BAKER [685]. (1Sa 8:13; Jer 37:21; Hos 7:4, 6). Pharaoh's chief baker (Ge 40). *See Bread.*

BALAAM [1189, 962] (possibly *Baal [lord] of the people* BDB; possibly *the clan brings forth* IDB; *devourer, glutton* KB). Son of Beor. From Mesopotamia (Dt 23:4). A soothsayer (Jos 13:22). A prophet (Nu 24:2-9; 2Pe 2:15-16). Balak sends for, to curse Israel (Nu 22:5-7; Jos 24:9; Ne 13:2; Mic 6:5). Anger of, rebuked by his donkey (Nu 22:22-35; 2Pe 2:16). Counsel of, an occasion of Israel's corruption with the Midianites (Nu 31:16; Rev 2:14-15). Greed of (2Pe 2:15; Jude 11). Death of (Nu 31:8; Jos 13:22).

BALAC *See Balak.*

BALADAN [1156] Father of Merodach-Baladan (2Ki 20:12; Isa 39:1).

BALAH [1163] (*old, worn out*). A city of Simeon (Jos 19:3). Called Bilhah (1Ch 4:29).

BALAK [1192, 963] (*devastator*). King of Moab (Nu 22:4; Jos 24:9; Jdg 11:25; Mic 6:5). Tried to bribe Balaam to curse Israel (Nu 22:5-7, 15-17). *See Balaam.*

BALANCES [4404, 6369, 7144]. Used for weighing (Job 31:6; Isa 40:12, 15; Eze 5:1). Money weighed with (Isa 46:6; Jer 32:10). Must be just (Lev 19:36; Pr 16:11; Eze 45:10).
    False balance: Used (Hos 12:7; Am 8:5; Mic 6:11), an abomination (Pr 11:1; 20:23).
    Figurative (Job 6:2; 31:6; Ps 62:9; Isa 40:12; Da 5:27; Rev 6:5).

BALD LOCUST *See Insects.*

BALDNESS [1477, 6867, 7944, 7947+, 7949]. (Lev 13:40, 41). A judgment (Isa 3:24; Jer 47:5; 48:37; Eze 7:18). Artificial, a sign of mourning (Isa 22:12; Jer 16:6; Eze 27:31; 29:18; Am 8:10; Mic 1:16). Artificial as an idolatrous practice, forbidden (Lev 21:5; Dt 14:1).
    Instance of: Elisha (2Ki 2:23).

BALL [1885]. Playing at (Isa 22:18).

BALM [6057, 7661]. A medicinal balsam (Ge 37:25; 43:11; Jer 8:22; 46:11; 51:8; Eze 27:17).

BALSAM TREES *See Tree.*

BAMAH [1196] (*high location [for cultic worship]*). A high place (Eze 20:29).

BAMOTH [1199] (*high locations [for cultic worship]*). A camping place of the Israelites (Nu 21:19-20).

BAMOTH BAAL [1200] (*high places for Baal [worship]*). A city assigned to Reuben as part of his inheritance (Jos 13:17).

BANI [1220] (*descendant*).
    1. KJV a Gadite, "son of" (2Sa 23:36).
    2. Levite (1Ch 6:46).
    3. Descendant of Judah (1Ch 9:4).
    4. Levite (Ne 3:17).
    5. Levite (Ne 9:4).
    6. Levite (Ne 11:22).
    7. Levite (Ne 10:13).
    8. Man who signed covenant (Ne 10:14).
    9. Ancestor of Jews who returned from the Captivity (Ezr 10:29).
    10. KJV Bani; NIV "descendants of" (Ezr 10:38).

BANISHMENT [*1763, 5610, 5927, 5615]. (Ezr 7:26). Of Adam and Eve, from Eden (Ge 3:22-24). Of Cain, to be "a restless wanderer" (Ge 4:14). Of Jews, from Rome (Ac 18:2). Of John, to Patmos (Rev 1:9). *See Exile.*

BANK [1473, 1536, 3338, 8557, *3204]. A primitive kind of banking was known in ancient times. Israelites could not charge each other interest (Ex 22:25) but could charge Gentiles (Dt 23:20). The concept of a bank as a savings institution was unknown. *See Borrowing; Interest; Lending.*

BANNER [253, 1839, 1840, 5812]. Banners, ensigns, or standards (not flags) were used in ancient times for military, national, and ecclesiastical purposes very much as they are today (Nu 2:2; Isa 5:26; 11:10; Jer 4:21).

BANQUET [3516+, 5492, 10389, 10447, 804, 1141, 1270, 1531]. Social feasting was common among the Hebrews. There were feasts on birthdays (Ge 40:20), marriages (Ge 29:22), funerals (2Sa 3:35), grape-gatherings (Jdg 9:27), sheep-shearing (1Sa 25:2, 36), sacrifices (Ex 34:15), and on other occasions. Often a second invitation was sent on the day of the feast (Lk 7:45), and their feet were washed (Lk 7:44). Banquets were often invigorated with music, singing, and dancing (Lk 15:23-25).

BAPTISM [966+, 967, 968] (*dip, or immerse*).
    As administered by John (Mt 3:5-12; Jn 3:23; Ac 13:24; 19:4). Sanctioned by Christ's submission to it (Mt 3:13-15; Lk 3:21). Adopted by Christ (Jn 3:22; 4:1-2). Appointed an ordinance of the Christian church (Mt 28:19-20; Mk 16:15-16). To be administered in the name of the Father, the Son, and the Holy Spirit (Mt 28:19). Water, the outward and visible sign in (Ac 8:36; 10:47). Regeneration, the inward and spiritual grace of (Jn

3:3, 5-6; Ro 6:3-4, 11). Remission of sins, signified by (Ac 2:38; 22:16). Unity of the church effected by (1Co 12:13; Gal 3:27-28). Confession of sin necessary to (Mt 3:6). Repentance necessary to (Ac 2:38). Faith necessary to (Ac 8:37; 18:8). There is but one (Eph 4:5).

Administered to: Individuals (Ac 8:38; 9:18). Households (Ac 16:15; 1Co 1:16). Emblematic of the influences of the Holy Spirit (Mt 3:11; Tit 3:5). Typified (1Co 10:2; 1Pe 3:20-21).

BAR An Aramaic word meaning "son"; in the NT used as a prefix (Mt 16:17, KJV). *See Barabbas; Barnabas; Barsabbas; Bartholomew; Bar-Jesus; Bar-Jona.*

BARABBAS [972] (*son of a father*, possibly *son of a rabbi [teacher]*). A prisoner released by Pilate (Mt 27:16-26; Mk 15:7-15; Lk 23:18-25; Jn 18:40; Ac 3:14).

BARACHEL *See Barakel.*

BARACHIAH, BARAKIAH *See Berekiah, 5.*

BARAH *See Beth Barah.*

BARAK [1399, 973] (*lightning*). Israelite who defeated Sisera at the command of Deborah the judge (Jdg 4-5; 1Sa 12:11; Heb 11:32).

BARAKEL [1387] (*God [El] blesses*). A Buzite, whose son Elihu was the last of Job's friends to reason with him (Job 32:2, 6).

BARBARIAN [975]. A foreigner (Ac 28:2-4; Ro 1:14; 1Co 14:11; Col 3:11). *See Strangers.*

BARBER [1647]. A barber's razor (Eze 5:1).

BARHUMITE [1372]. Azmaveth the Barhumite, one of the Thirty (2Sa 23:31).

BARIAH [1377] (possibly *board, bar; fugitive* ISBE; *descendant* KB). Son of Shecaniah (1Ch 3:22).

BAR-JESUS [979] (*son of Joshua*). A false prophet (Ac 13:6).

BAR-JONA NIV "Simon son of Jonah," surname of Peter (Mt 16:17).

BARKOS [1401] (*son of [pagan god] Kos*). A Jew whose descendants returned from the Exile (Ezr 2:53; Ne 7:55).

BARLEY [8555, 3208, 3209]. A product of: Egypt (Ex 9:31), Israel (Dt 8:8; 1Ch 11:13; Jer 41:8).

Fed to horses (1Ki 4:28). Used in offerings (Nu 5:15; Eze 45:15). Selling of (2Ch 2:10; Hos 3:2). Tribute in (2Ch 27:5). Priests estimated value of (Lev 27:16; 2Ki 7:1; Rev 6:6). Absalom burns Joab's field of (2Sa 14:30).

Loaves of (Jn 6:9, 13).

BARN [662, 4476, *630*]. A storehouse for crops (Dt 28:8; Ps 144:13; Pr 3:10; Hag 2:19; Mt 3:12; 6:26; 13:30; Lk 12:18, 24).

See Granary; Storehouse.

BARNABAS [982] (*son of comfort*). Also called Joseph (Ac 4:36). A prophet (Ac 13:1). An apostle (Ac 14:14). A Levite who gave his possessions to be owned in common with other disciples (Ac 4:36-37). Goes to Tarsus to find Paul, brings him to Antioch (Ac 11:25-26). Accompanies Paul to Jerusalem (Ac 11:30). Returns with Paul to Antioch (Ac 12:25).

Goes With Paul to Seleucia (Ac 13), Iconium (Ac 14:1-7).

Called Jupiter (Ac 14:12-18). Goes to Derbe (Ac 14:20). Is sent as delegate to Jerusalem (Ac 15; Gal 2:1-9). Estranged from Paul (Ac 15:36-39). Is reconciled to Paul (1Co 9:6). Piety of (Ac 11:22-24). Devotion of, to Jesus (Ac 15:25-26).

BARNEA *See Kadesh Barnea.*

BARREL A clay jar (1Ki 17:12, 14, 16; 18:33). *See Jar(s); Pottery.*

BARRENNESS [1678, 4497, 6808, 6829, 9039, 9155, 9332, *5096*]. Inability of women to bear children. A reproach (Ge 30:22-23; 1Sa 1:6, 7; 2:1-11; Isa 4:1; Lk 1:25). Sent as a judgment (Ge 20:17-18). *See Childlessness.*

Barrenness miraculously removed: Sarai (Ge 17:15-21), Rebekah (Ge 25:21), Manoah's wife (Jdg 13), Hannah (1Sa 1:6-20), Elizabeth (Lk 1:5-25).

BARSABBAS [984] (*son of the Sabbath* or *son of Saba*).
1. Surname of Joseph (Ac 1:23).
2. Judas (Ac 15:22).

BARTER [4126, 5989]. (Job 6:27; 41:6; La 1:11). *See Commerce.*

BARTHOLOMEW [978] (*son of Talmai*). One of the apostles (Mt 10:3; Mk 3:18; Lk 6:14; Ac 1:13).

BARTIMAEUS [985] (*son of Timai*, or *son of uncleanness*). A blind man (Mt 20:29-34; Mk 10:46-52; Lk 18:35-43).

BARUCH [1358] (*be blessed*).
1. An amanuensis of Jeremiah (Jer 32:12-16; 36:4-32; 43:3-6; 45:1-2).
2. Son of Zabbai (Ne 3:20; 10:6).
3. A descendant of Perez (Ne 11:5).

BARUCH, BOOK OF Jewish pseudepigraphal book found in the Apocrypha; alleging to be a treatise by Jeremiah's scribe Baruch to Jewish exiles in Babylon.

BARZILLAI [1367] (*[made] of iron*).
1. A friend of David (2Sa 17:27-29; 19:31-39; 1Ki 2:7; Ezr 2:61; Ne 7:63).

2. Father of Adriel (2Sa 21:8).

3. A priest (Ezr 2:61; Ne 7:63).

BASE FELLOWS Derogatory term "sons of Belial"; NIV "evil" or "wicked men" (Dt 13:13; 1Sa 2:12; 10:27; 25:17; 30:22; 1Ki 21:10; 2Ch 13:7). *See Wicked.*

BASEMATH [1412] (*fragrant*).

1. Wife of Esau (Ge 26:34).

2. Ishmael's daughter (Ge 36:3-4, 13, 17). Also called Mahalath (Ge 28:9).

3. Solomon's daughter (1Ki 4:15).

BASHAN [824+1421, 1421] (*fertile stoneless plain*). A region E of the Jordan and N of Arnon (Ge 14:5); modern Golan Heights. Og, king of (Jos 13:12). Allotted to the two and one half tribes, which had their possession E of the Jordan (Nu 32:33; Dt 3:10-14; Jos 12:4-6; 13:29-31; 17:1). Invaded and taken by Hazael, king of Syria (2Ki 10:32-33). Retaken by Jehoash (2Ki 13:25). Fertility and productivity of (Isa 33:9; Jer 50:19; Na 1:4). Forests of famous (Isa 2:13; Eze 27:6; Zec 11:2). Distinguished for its fine cattle (Dt 32:14; Ps 22:12; Eze 39:18; Am 4:1; Mic 7:14).

See Argob; Ashtoreth; Edrei; Jair.

BASHAN-HAVOTH-JAIR *See Havoth Jair.*

BASHEMATH, BASMATH *See Basemath.*

BASIC PRINCIPLES OF THIS WORLD [5122+3180]. Legalism and human traditions opposed to faith in Christ (Gal 4:3; Col 2:8, 20). *See Commandments and Statutes, of Men; Legalism.*

BASIN [3963, 6195, 3781]. Made of gold (1Ki 7:50; 1Ch 28:17; 2Ch 4:8, 22; Ezr 1:10; 8:27), bronze (Ex 27:3; 38:3; 1Ki 7:45).

See Bronze Basin; Bronze Sea; Tabernacle.

BASKET [406, 1857, 3244, 3990, 3998, 6130, 8955, 9310, 4914, 5083]. (Ge 40:16-17; Ex 29:3, 23, 32; Lev 8:2; Nu 6:15; Dt 26:2; 28:5, 17; 2Ki 10:7). Received the fragments after the miracles of the loaves (Mt 14:20; 15:37; 16:9-10). Paul let down from the wall (Ac 9:25; 2Co 11:33).

BASON *See Basin.*

BASTARD *See Illegitimate.*

BAT [6491]. Unclean for food (Lev 11:19; Dt 14:18; Isa 2:20).

BATH [1427, 3374, 8175, 10126].

1. Bathing for physical cleanliness or refreshment is not often mentioned in the Bible, where most references to bathing are to partial washing. Bathing in the Bible stands primarily for ritual acts—purification of ceremonial defilement (Ex 30:19-21; Lev 16:4, 24; Mk 7:3-4).

2. A Hebrew measure for liquids, containing about six gallons or twenty-two liters (1Ki 7:26, 38; Ezr 7:22; Isa 5:10; Eze 45:10-11, 14). *See Measure.*

BATH RABBIM [1442] (*daughter of a multitude*). A gate in the city of Heshbon (SS 7:4).

BATHSHEBA [1444] (*seventh daughter* or *daughter of an oath*). Wife of Uriah and later wife of David. Also spelled Bathshua (1Ch 3:5, ftn). Adultery of (2Sa 11:2-5). Solomon's mother (1Ki 1:11-31; 2:13-21; 1Ch 3:5).

BATHSHUA (possibly *daughter of opulence* BDB).

1. The daughter of Shua (Ge 38:2; 1Ch 2:3).

2. *See Bathsheba.*

BATTERING RAM [4119, 7692]. (2Sa 20:15; Eze 4:2; 21:22).

BATTERY *See Assault and Battery.*

BATTLE [*4309, 4878, 5120, 7372, 7930, 8131, 9558, 4483]. Shouting in (Jdg 7:20; 1Sa 17:20). Priests in (2Ch 13:12). Prayer before: by Asa (2Ch 14:11), Jehoshaphat (2Ch 20:3-12). *See Armies; War.*

BATTLE OF LIFE

Ancient Heroes:
Joshua (Jos 11:23). Gideon (Jdg 7:14). Jonathan (1Sa 14:6). David (1Sa 17:45). Elisha (2Ki 6:17). Jehoshaphat (2Ch 20:20).

The Spiritual Conflict:
An inward battle (Ro 7:23). Spiritual weapons (2Co 10:4). Invisible foes (Eph 6:12). Young soldiers enlisted (1Ti 1:18). A fight of faith (1Ti 6:12). Demands entire consecration (2Ti 2:4).

The Soul's Enemies:
(Ps 86:14; Jer 2:34; 18:20; Eze 13:18; 22:25; Lk 22:31; Eph 6:12; 1Pe 5:8).

Weapons and Armor:
(1Sa 17:45; 2Co 10:4; Eph 6:17; Heb 4:12; Rev 12:11).

Divine Protection:
Promised to believers (2Ch 16:9; Ps 34:7; 91:4; 125:2; Zec 2:5; Lk 21:18).

Examples of:
(Ge 35:5; Ex 14:20; 2Ki 6:17; Ezr 8:31; Da 6:22; Rev 7:3).

The Victory:
(Isa 53:12; Mt 12:20; Jn 16:33; 1Co 15:24; Rev 3:21; 6:2; 17:14).

BATTLE-AX *See Club.*

BATTLEMENTS [9087]. Parapets on the tops of walls (Isa 54:11).

BAVAI *See Binnui, 1.*

BAY TREE NIV "tree" (Ps 37:35). *See Tree.*

BAZLUTH [1296]. One of the temple servants (Ezr 2:52; Ne 7:54).

BDELLIUM *See Aromatic Resin; Minerals of the Bible.*

BE ESHTARAH [1285]. A Levitical city (Jos 21:27). Called Ashtaroth (1Ch 6:71).

BEACON NIV "flagstaff" (Isa 30:17). *See Ensign; Standard.*

BEALIAH [1270] (*Yahweh is Lord*). A Benjamite soldier who joined David at Ziklag (1Ch 12:5).

BEALOTH [1268] (*feminine plural of Baal "lord" lady*). A town in Judah (Jos 15:24).

BEAM [781, 1464, 4096, 4164, 6770, 7521, 7771, 7936, 10058]. Large long piece of timber for use in houses (1Ki 6:9-10; 7:3). Used for impaling (Ezr 6:11). Used in figurative sense by Jesus; NIV "plank" (Mt 7:3; Lk 6:41).

BEANS [7038]. Part of a simple diet (2Sa 17:28; Eze 4:9).

BEAR, THE [1800, 10155].

Described as:
Voracious (Da 7:5). Cunning (La 3:10). Cruel (Am 5:19). Often attacks men (2Ki 2:24; Am 5:19). Attacks the flock in the presence of the shepherd (1Sa 17:34). Particularly fierce when deprived of its young (2Sa 17:8; Pr 17:12). Growls when annoyed (Isa 59:11). Miraculously killed by David (1Sa 17:36-37).

Illustrative of:
God in his judgments (La 3:10; Hos 13:8). Peace in the Messianic era (Isa 11:7). Wicked rulers (Pr 28:15). The kingdom of the Medes (Da 7:5). The kingdom of Antichrist (Rev 13:2).
A constellation (Job 9:9; 38:32).

BEARD [2417, 5307]. Worn long by Aaron (Ps 133:2), Samson (Jdg 16:17), David (1Sa 21:13; Eze 5:1).
Shaven by Egyptians (Ge 41:14). Untrimmed in mourning (2Sa 19:24). Plucked (Ezr 9:3). Cut (Isa 7:20; 15:2; Jer 41:5; 48:37). Lepers required to shave (Lev 13:29-33; 14:9). Idolatrous practice of marring forbidden (Lev 19:27; 21:5). Beards of David's ambassadors half shaven by the king of the Amorites (2Sa 10:4).

BEAST [*989, 2651, 3274, 10263, 2563].
1. A mammal, not man, distinguished from birds and fish (Ge 1:29-30).
2. A wild, as distinguished from a domesticated animal (Lev 26:22; Isa 13:21-22).
3. Any of the inferior animals, as distinguished from man (Ps 147:9; Ecc 3:19).

4. Apocalyptic symbol of brute force—sensual, lawless, and God-opposing (Da 7; Rev 13:11-18).

BEATEN WORK Of metals (Ex 25:18; 37:17, 22; Nu 8:4).

BEATING [4547, 4804, 5782, *1296, 2710, 3139, 4435, 5597*]. As a punishment (Ex 5:14; Dt 25:3; Mk 13:9; Ac 5:40; 16:22, 37; 18:17; 21:32; 22:19).
See Assault and Battery; Punishment; Scourging.

BEATITUDES [*897, 1385, 2328, 3421*] (*divine favor*). A word not found in the English Bible, but meaning either:
1. The joys of heaven.
2. A declaration of blessedness. Beatitudes occur frequently in the OT (Ps 32:1-2; 41:1). The Gospels contain isolated beatitudes by Christ (Mt 11:6; 13:16; Jn 20:29), but the word is most commonly used of those in Mt 5:3-11 and Lk 6:20-22, which set forth the qualities that should characterize his disciples. *See Graces; Sermon on the Mount.*

BEAUTY [*3202+, 3636, 3642, 3637+, 7382, 2819, 6053*]. Vanity of (Ps 39:11; Pr 6:25; 31:30; Isa 3:24; Eze 16:14; 28:17). Consume away (Ps 39:11; 49:14).

Instances of:
Sarah (Ge 12:11). Rebekah (Ge 24:16). Rachel (Ge 29:17). Joseph (Ge 39:6). Moses (Ex 2:2; Heb 11:23). David (1Sa 16:12, 18). Bathsheba (2Sa 11:2). Tamar (2Sa 13:1). Absalom (2Sa 14:25). Abishag (1Ki 1:4). Vashti (Est 1:11). Esther (Est 2:7).

Spiritual:
(1Ch 16:29; Ps 27:4; 29:2; 45:11; 90:17; 110:3; Eze 16:14; Zec 9:17).

BEAUTY AND BANDS NIV "Favor" and "Union"; staffs representing God's favor and the union of Israel and Judah; broken (Zec 11:7-14).

BEBAI [950] (*child*). The name of three Jews whose descendants came from exile (Ezr 2:11; 8:11; 10:28; Ne 7:16; 10:15).

BECHER *See Beker, Bekerite.*

BECORATH [1138] (*firstborn*). Son of Aphiah (1Sa 9:1).

BED [1655+, 3661, 3667, 4753, 5201, 5267, 5435, 6911+, 8886+, 10444, 2879, 3109, 3130]. Made of: iron (Dt 3:11), ivory (Am 6:4), gold and silver (Est 1:6). Used at meals (Am 6:4). Exempt from execution for debt (Pr 22:27). Perfumed (Pr 7:17).
Figurative (Ps 139:8).

BEDAD [971] (*solitary*). Father of Hadad (Ge 36:35).

BEDAN [979] (*son of judgment*).
1. In 1Sa 12:11 *See* Barak.
2. Son of Ulam (1Ch 7:17).

BEDEIAH [973] (*servant of Yahweh*). A son of Bani who had taken a foreign wife (Ezr 10:35).

BEE [1805]. In Israel (Dt 1:44; Jdg 14:8; Ps 118:12; Isa 7:18). Figurative of the Assyrians summoned for judgment (Isa 7:18). *See* Honey.

BEELIADA [1269] (*the lord [Baal] knows*). Son of David (1Ch 14:7). Called Eliada (2Sa 5:16; 1Ch 3:8).

BEELZEBUB [1015] (*lord of the flies*). The prince of demons (Mt 10:25; 12:24, 27; Mk 3:22; Lk 11:15, 18-19). *See* Baal-Zebub.

BEELZEBUL *See* Baal-Zebub.

BEER [932, 8911] (as a place name *cistern, well*).
1. A stopping place of the Israelites (Nu 21:16-18).
2. A town in the tribe of Judah (Jdg 9:21).
3. A fermented, intoxicating beverage; its abuse condemned (1Sa 1:15; Pr 20:1; 31:4-6; Isa 28:7; 56:12; Mic 2:11). *See* Abuse, Substance Abuse; Drunkenness; Fermented Drink; Wine.

BEER ELIM [935] (*cistern, well of Elim*). A city of Moab (Isa 15:8).

BEER LAHAI ROI [936] (*well that belongs to the Living One seeing me*).
A well, probably near Kadesh, where the Lord appeared to Hagar (Ge 16:7, 14) and where Isaac lived for some time (Ge 24:62; 25:11).

BEERA [938] (*cistern, well*). Son of Zophah (1Ch 7:37).

BEERAH [939] (*cistern, well*). A Reubenite (1Ch 5:6).

BEERI [941] (*[my] cistern, well*).
1. A Hittite (Ge 26:34). *See* Anah.
2. Father of Hosea (Hos 1:1).

BEEROTH, BEEROTHITE [940, 943] (*cisterns, wells*).
1. NIV "wells" (Dt 10:6). *See* Bene Jaakan.
2. A city of the Hivites (Jos 9:17; 18:25; 2Sa 4:2; Ezr 2:25; Ne 7:29).
3. Inhabitants of Beeroth (2Sa 4:2, 5, 9; 23:37).

BEERSHEBA [937] (*the seventh well*).
1. The most southern city of Israel (Jdg 20:1). Named by Abraham, who dwelt there (Ge 21:31-33; 22:19). The dwelling place of Isaac (Ge 26:23). Jacob went out from, toward Haran (Ge 28:10). Sacrifices offered at, by Jacob when traveling to Egypt (Ge 46:1). In the inheritance of Judah (Jos 15:20, 28; 2Sa 24:7). Afterward assigned to Simeon (Jos 19:2, 9; 1Ch 4:28). Two

sons of Samuel were judges at (1Sa 8:2). Became a seat of idolatrous worship (Am 5:5; 8:14).
2. Well of, belonged to Abraham and Isaac (Ge 21:25-26).
3. Wilderness of, Hagar miraculously sees a well in (Ge 21:14-19). An angel fed Elijah in (1Ki 19:5, 7).

BEETLE NIV "cricket" (Lev 11:22). *See* Insects.

BEGGAR [8626, 4777]. Set among princes (1Sa 2:8). Not the seed of the righteous (Ps 37:25). The children of the wicked (Ps 109:10; Pr 20:4; Lk 16:3).
Instances of: Bartimaeus (Mk 10:46), Lazarus (Lk 16:20-22), the blind man (Jn 9:8), the lame man (Ac 3:2-5).
See Poor.

BEHEADING [642, 4284]. Execution by: John the Baptist (Mt 14:10; Mk 6:27), James (Ac 12:2), martyrs (Rev 20:4). *See* Punishment.

BEHEMOTH [990]. The word is a Hebrew plural and means "beast par excellence," referring to a large land animal, possibly the hippopotamus or the elephant (Job 40:15, ftn). Much of the language used to describe it in vv. 16-24 is highly poetic and hyperbolic (Job 40:15-24).

BEKA [1325]. A half shekel (Ex 38:26). *See* Measure.

BEKER, BEKERITE [1146, 1151] (*young male camel*).
1. Son of Benjamin (Ge 46:21; 1Ch 7:6, 8).
2. A family of Ephraim (Nu 26:35). Called Bered (1Ch 7:20).

BEL [1155] (Babylonian deity *Bel*). A Babylonian god (Isa 46:1; Jer 50:2; 51:44).

BELA, BELAITE [1185, 1186, 1188] (*swallower, devourer*).
1. A city called also Zoar (Ge 14:2, 8).
2. King of Edom (Ge 36:32-33; 1Ch 1:43-44).
3. Son of Benjamin (Ge 46:21; Nu 26:38, 40; 1Ch 7:6-7; 8:1, 3).
4. Son of Azaz (1Ch 5:8).

BELIAL [1016] (*wicked, without use*). A word meaning "worthlessness," "wickedness," "lawlessness" translated as a proper noun in the KJV (Dt 13:13; Jdg 19:22; 1Sa 25:25). Personified (2Co 6:15). *See* Base Fellows; Wicked.

BELIEVER *See* Righteous.

BELIEVING *See* Faith.

BELLOWS [5135]. Used with the refiner's furnace (Jer 6:29).

BELLS [5197, 7194]. Attached to the hem of the priest's robe (Ex 28:33-34; 39:25-26). On horses (Zec 14:20).

BELLY [1061, 1623, 2824, 10435, *3120*]. Used figuratively for the seat of the affections (Job 15:2, 35; 20:20; Ps 44:25; Pr 18:20; 20:27, 30; Hab 3:16; Jn 7:38; Tit 1:12).

BELOVED DISCIPLE [26, *5797*]. Probably the apostle John (Jn 13:23; 19:26; 20:2; 21:7, 20).

BELSHAZZAR [1157, 10105, 10109] (*Bel protect the king*). King of Babylon (Da 5:1-30).

BELT [*258, 2512, 2513, 2514, 2520, *2438*]. Made of leather (2Ki 1:8; Mt 3:4), linen (Jer 13:1), gold (Da 10:5). Warrior's belt, used to bear arms (2Sa 18:11; 20:8), Jonathan gives his to David (1Sa 18:4).
  Figurative (Isa 11:5; Eph 6:14).
  Symbolic (Jer 13:1-11; Ac 21:11; Rev 15:6). *See Dress; Sash.*

BELTESHAZZAR [1171, 10108] (*protect his life*). His Hebrew name was Daniel. He was taken as a captive to Babylon with Hananiah, Mishael, and Azariah, where each one was given a Babylonian name (Da 1:6-20; 2:17, 49; 3:12-30). Daniel was given the name Belteshazzar. *See Daniel.*

BEMA *See Judgment Seat.*

BEN Hebrew word meaning "son" or "descendant"; possibly the name of a Levite (1Ch 15:18, ftn).

BEN-ABINADAB [1203] (*son of Abinadab*). *See Abinadab.*

BEN-AMMI [1214] (*son of my people*). Son of one of Lot's daughters; progenitor of Ammonites (Ge 19:38).

BEN-DEKER [1206] (*son of Deker [pierces]*). The father of one of Solomon's suppliers (1Ki 4:9).

BEN-GEBER [1205] (*son of strength*). *See Geber.*

BEN-HADAD [1207] (*son of Hadad*).
  1. King of Syria (1Ki 15:18-20; 2Ch 16:2-4).
  2. A king of Syria, who reigned in the time of Ahab, son of Ben-Hadad I (1Ki 20; 2Ki 5-7; 8:7-15).
  3. Son of Hazael and king of Syria (2Ki 13:3, 24-25; Am 1:4).

BEN-HAIL [1211] (*son of strength*). A prince of Judah (2Ch 17:7).

BEN-HANAN [1212] (*son of grace*). A son of Shimon (1Ch 4:20).

BEN-HESED [1213] (*loyal love*). Father of one of Solomon's officers (1Ki 4:10).

BEN HINNOM [1208] (*valley of the son [or sons] of Hinnom*). A valley on the W and SW of Jerusalem which formed part of the border between Judah and Benjamin (Jos 15:8; 18:16; Ne 11:30-31). It later became the place of pagan sacrifice (2Ch 28:3; 33:6; Jer 32:35). Josiah defiled it by making it the city dump, where fires were kept constantly burning to consume the refuse (2Ki 23:10). Jewish apocalyptic writers called it the entrance to hell, and it became a figure of hell itself. Jesus used the term *gehenna* (NIV "hell") in this sense (Mt 5:22; 18:9; 23:15).
  See Hades; Hell; Hinnom, Valley of; Topheth, Tophet.

BEN-HUR [1210] (*son of Hur*). *See Hur, 4.*

BEN-ONI [1204] (*son of my sorrow*). Name given Benjamin by Rachel (Ge 35:18). *See Benjamin.*

BEN-ZOHETH [1209] (*son of Zoheth*). Son of Ishi (1Ch 4:20).

BENAIAH [1225, 1226] (*Yahweh has built*).
  1. Son of Jehoiada, commander of the Kerethites and Pelethites (2Sa 8:18; 1Ki 1:38). A distinguished warrior (2Sa 23:20-23; 1Ch 11:22-25; 27:5-6). Loyal to Solomon (1Ki 1:8, 10; 4:4).
  2. An Ephraimite and distinguished warrior (2Sa 23:30; 1Ch 11:31; 27:14).
  3. A Levitical musician (1Ch 15:18, 20; 16:5).
  4. A priest (1Ch 15:24; 16:6).
  5. Son of Jeiel (2Ch 20:14).
  6. A Levite in time of Hezekiah (2Ch 31:13).
  7. A chief of the Simeonites (1Ch 4:36).
  8. Son of Parosh (Ezr 10:25).
  9. Son of Pahath-Moab (Ezr 10:30).
  10. Son of Bani (Ezr 10:35).
  11. Son of Nebo (Ezr 10:43).
  12. Father of Pelatiah (Eze 11:1, 13).

BENCHES [2756]. Of those selling doves in the temple (Mt 21:12; Mk 11:15).

BENE BERAK [1222] (*sons of Barak [lightning]*). A city of Dan (Jos 19:45).

BENE JAAKAN [1223] (possibly *son of Jaakan*). A tribe that gave its name to certain wells in the wilderness (Nu 33:31-32; Dt 10:6). *See Jaakan, Jaakanites.*

BENEDICTIONS (*pronouncements of blessing*). Divinely appointed (Dt 10:8; 21:5; Nu 6:23-26).

By God:
  Upon creatures he had made (Ge 1:22), mankind (Ge 1:28), Noah (Ge 9:1-2).

Instances of:
  By Melchizedek upon Abraham (Ge 14:19-20; Heb 7:7). By Bethuel's household upon Rebekah (Ge 24:60). By Isaac upon Jacob (Ge 27:23-29, 37; 28:1-4), Esau (Ge 27:39-40). By Jacob upon Pharaoh (Ge 47:7-10), Joseph's sons (Ge 48), his own sons (Ge 49). By Moses upon the tribes of

Israel (Dt 33). By Aaron (Lev 9:22-23), half the tribes who stood on Mt. Gerizim (Dt 11:29-30; 27:11-13; Jos 8:33). By Joshua upon Caleb (Jos 14:13), the Reubenites and Gadites, and the half tribe of Manasseh (Jos 22:6-7). By Naomi upon Ruth and Orpah (Ru 1:8-9). By the elders and people upon Ruth (Ru 4:11-12). By Eli upon Ruth (1Sa 1:17), upon Elkanah (1Sa 2:20). By David upon the people (2Sa 6:18), upon Barzillai (2Sa 19:39). By Araunah upon David (2Sa 24:23). By Solomon upon the people (1Ki 8:14, 55-58; 2Ch 6:3).

By Simeon upon Jesus (Lk 2:34). By Jesus (Lk 24:50).

Levitical: (Nu 6:23-26).

Apostolic: (Ro 1:7; 15:5, 13, 33; 16:20; 1Co 1:3; 16:23; 2Co 1:2; 13:14; Gal 1:3; 6:16, 18; Eph 1:2; 6:23-24; Php 1:2; 4:23; Col 1:2; 1Th 1:1; 5:23; 2Th 1:2; 3:16, 18; 1Ti 1:2; 6:21; 2Ti 1:2; 4:22; Tit 3:15; Phm 3, 25; Heb 13:20-21, 25; 1Pe 1:2; 5:10-11, 14; 2Pe 1:2-4; 2Jn 3; Jude 2; Rev 22:21).

BENEFACTOR [2309]. A title of honor bestowed by ancient states upon those famous for notable deeds of benevolence (Lk 22:25).

BENEFICENCE (goodness, kindness).
Commanded:
(Lev 25:35-43; Dt 15:7-15, 18; Pr 3:27-28; 25:21-22; Mt 5:42; 19:21; 25:35-45; Mk 10:21; Lk 3:11; Ro 15:27; 1Co 13:3; 16:1-3; 2Co 8:7-15, 24; 9:1-15; Gal 2:10; 1Ti 5:8, 16; Heb 13:16; Jas 2:15-16; 1Jn 3:17).

Results:
Blessed (Ps 41:1; Pr 22:9). Rewarded (Ps 112:9; Pr 11:25; 28:27; Isa 58:6-11; Eze 18:5-9; Mt 19:21; Mk 9:41; 10:21; Heb 6:10).

Examples:
(Mt 25:35-45; Ac 11:29-30; Ro 15:25-27; 2Co 8:1-15; Php 4:10-18; 1Ti 6:18).
See Alms; Liberality; Poor, Duty to; Rich, The; Riches.

Instances of:
The old man of Gibeah (Jdg 19:16-21). Boaz (Ru 2). The Jews returned from Exile (Ne 5:8-12; 8:10-11). Job (Job 29:11-17; 31:16-23). The Temanites (Isa 21:14). The good Samaritan (Lk 10:33-35). Zacchaeus (Lk 19:8). The first Christians (Ac 2:44-46; 4:32-37). Cornelius (Ac 10:2, 4). Onesiphorus (2Ti 1:16-18).
See Alms; Poor, Duties to.

BENEVOLENCE *See Alms; Beneficence; Charitableness; Liberality; Love.*

BENINU [1231] (our son). A Levite (Ne 10:13).

BENJAMIN, BENJAMITE(S)
[278+2157, 408+, 1228+, 1229, 3549, 1021] (son of [the] right hand BDB; southerner KB).
1. Son of Jacob by Rachel (Ge 35:18, 24; 46:19). Taken into Egypt (Ge 42-45). Prophecy concern-

ing (Ge 49:27). Descendants of (Ge 46:21; Nu 26:38-41).

2. Tribe of. Census of, at Sinai (Nu 1:37), in the plain of Moab (Nu 26:41). Clans of (Nu 26:38-40; 1Ch 7:6-12; 8). Position of, in camp and march (Nu 2:18, 22). Moses' benediction upon (Dt 33:12). Allotment in the land of Canaan (Jos 18:11-28). Reallotment (Eze 48:23). Did not exterminate the Jebusites (Jdg 1:21). Join Deborah in the war against Sisera (Jdg 5:14). Territory of, invaded by the Ammonites (Jdg 10:9). Did not avenge the crime of the Gibeonites against the Levite's concubine, the war that followed (Jdg 19-20). Saul, the first king of Israel, from (1Sa 9:1, 17; 10:20-21). Its rank in the time of Samuel (1Sa 9:21). Jerusalem within the territory of (Jer 6:1). A company of, joins David at Ziklag (1Ch 12:1-2, 16). Not enrolled by Joab when he took a census of the military forces of Israel (1Ch 21:6). Loyal to Ish-Bosheth, the son of Saul (2Sa 2:9, 15, 31; 1Ch 12:29). Subsequently joins David (2Sa 3:19; 19:16-17). Loyal to Rehoboam (1Ki 12:21; 2Ch 11:1). Military forces of, in the reign of Asa (2Ch 14:8), of Jehoshaphat (2Ch 17:17). Skill in archery and as slingers of stones (Jdg 3:15; 20:16; 1Ch 8:40; 12:2). Return to Israel from the Exile in Babylon (Ezr 1:5). Saints of, seen in John's vision (Rev 7:8). Paul, of the tribe of (Ro 11:1; Php 3:5).
See Israel.

3. Grandson of Benjamin (1Ch 7:10).

4. A son of Harim (Ezr 10:32). Probably identical with the man mentioned in Ne 3:23.

5. A Jew who assisted in purifying the wall of Jerusalem (Ne 12:34).

6. A gate of Jerusalem (Jer 20:2; 37:13; 38:7; Zec 14:10).

BENO [1217] (his son). A descendant of Merari (1Ch 24:26-27).

BENOTH *See Succoth Benoth.*

BEON [1274]. A place E of Jordan, probably the same as Baal Meon (Nu 32:3, 38). *See Baal Meon.*

BEOR [1242, 1027] (perhaps a burning).
1. Father of Bela (Ge 36:32; 1Ch 1:43).
2. Father of Balaam (Nu 22:5; 24:3, 15; 31:8; Dt 23:4; Jos 13:22; 24:9; Mic 6:5; 2Pe 2:15).

BERA [1396] (gift). King of Sodom, defeated by Kedorlaomer in the days of Abraham (Ge 14:2, 8).

BERACAH [1389, 1390] (blessing).
1. An Israelite, who joined David at Ziklag (1Ch 12:3).
2. A valley in the S of Judah, where Jehoshaphat assembled the Israelites to offer praise to God for victory over the Ammonites and Moabites (2Ch 20:26). Between Bethlehem and Hebron.

BERACHIAH, BERECHIAH *See Berekiah.*

BERAIAH [1349] (*Yahweh creates*). Son of Shimei (1Ch 8:21).

BERAK *See Bene Berak.*

BEREA, BEREANS [*1023, 1024*]. A city in the S of Macedonia (Ac 17:10, 13; 20:4). Its inhabitants are important as an example of comparing new teaching to the received Scriptures.

BEREAVEMENT [8892, 8897, 8898]. From God (Hos 9:12). Mourning in, forbidden to Aaron, on account of his son's wickedness (Lev 10:6). To Ezekiel, for his wife (Eze 24:16-18).

Instances of:
Abraham, of Sarah (Ge 23:2). Jacob, of Joseph (Ge 37:34-35). Joseph, of his father (Ge 50:1, 4). The Egyptians, of their firstborn (Ex 12:29-33). Naomi, of her husband (Ru 1:3, 5, 20-21). David, of his child by Bathsheba (2Sa 12:15-23), of Absalom (2Sa 18:33; 19:4).

Resignation in:
Job (Job 1:18-21). David (2Sa 12:22, 30). Solomon (Ecc 7:2-4). Christians (1Th 4:13-18).
See Affliction, Consolation Under; Prayer Under; Resignation.

BERED [1354, 1355] (possibly *freezing rain*).
1. A town in the S of Israel (Ge 16:14).
2. A son of Shuthelah (1Ch 7:20). Probably the same as Beker (Nu 26:35).

BEREKIAH [1392, 1393, *974*] (*Yahweh blesses*).
1. Father of Asaph (1Ch 6:39; 15:17, 23).
2. A warrior of Ephraim (2Ch 28:12).
3. A brother of Zerubbabel (1Ch 3:20).
4. Son of Asa (1Ch 9:16).
5. Son of Iddo, father of Zechariah (Zec 1:1, 7; Mt 23:35).
6. Son of Meshullam (Ne 3:4, 30; 6:18).

BERI [1373] (*wisdom*). Son of Zophah (1Ch 7:36).

BERIAH, BERIITE [1380, 1381] (*prominent, excellent*).
1. Son of Asher (Ge 46:17; 1Ch 7:30) and his clan (Nu 26:44-45).
2. Son of Ephraim (1Ch 7:20-23).
3. A Benjamite (1Ch 8:13).
4. Son of Shimei (1Ch 23:10-11).

BERITES [1379] (*choice young men*). Followed Sheba in his rebellion against David (2Sa 20:14).

BERITH *See Baal-Berith.*

BERNICE [*1022*] (*victorious*). Daughter of Agrippa (Ac 25:13, 23; 26:30).

BERODACH-BALADAN *See Merodach-Baladan.*

BEROTHAH [1363] (*well*). Part of the northern boundary of Canaan (Eze 47:16).

BEROTHAI, BEROTHITE [1408]. A city of Zobah (2Sa 8:8) and its inhabitants (1Ch 11:39).

BERYL [1403, 1404, *1039*] (*yellow jasper*).
1. Set in the priestly breastplate (Ex 28:17; 39:10).
2. A precious stone (Eze 28:13).
3. John saw, in the foundation of the new Jerusalem (Rev 21:20).
See Minerals of the Bible, 1; Stones.

BESAI [1234] (*in secret council of Yahweh* KB). One of the temple servants (Ezr 2:49; Ne 7:52).

BESODEIAH [1233] (*in secret council of Yahweh*). Father of Meshullam (Ne 3:6).

BESOM *See Broom.*

BESOR [1410]. A brook near Gaza (1Sa 30:9-10, 21).

BESTIALITY (*Sexual relations between a human and an animal*). (Ex 22:19; Lev 18:23; 20:16).

BETAH *See Tebah, 2.*

BETEN [1062] (*womb, bowels*). A city of Asher (Jos 19:25).

BETH The most common OT word for house, family or dynasty. Used in the more than fifty place names that follow.

BETH ANATH [1117] (*house of Anath*). A fortified city of Naphtali (Jos 19:38; Jdg 1:33).

BETH ANOTH [1116] (*house of Anath [plural]*). A city in Judah (Jos 15:59).

BETH ARABAH [1098] (*house of Arabah [desert plain]*). A city in the valley of the Dead Sea (Jos 15:6, 61; 18:22). Called Arabah (Jos 18:18).

BETH-ARAM *See Beth Haram.*

BETH ARBEL [1079] (*house of Arbel*). A city devastated by Shalman (Hos 10:14).

BETH ASHBEA [1080] (*house of Ashbea*). A descendant of Shelah (1Ch 4:21).

BETH AVEN [1077] (*house of idolatry*). A place on the mountains of Benjamin (Jos 7:2; 18:12; 1Sa 13:5; 14:23; Hos 4:15; 5:8; 10:5).

BETH AZMAVETH [1115] (*strong of death* ISBE; *house of Azmaveth [camel fodder, a plant of the plumose family]* KB). A town of

Benjamin (Ne 7:28). Called Azmaveth (Ne 12:29; Ezr 2:24).

BETH BAAL MEON [1081] (*house of Baal Meon*). A place in the tribe of Reuben (Jos 13:17).

Called Baal Meon (Nu 32:38; Eze 25:9), Beon (Nu 32:3), Beth Meon (Jer 48:23).

Subdued by the Israelites (Nu 32:3-4). Assigned to the Reubenites (Jos 13:17).

BETH BARAH [1083] (*house of Barah [the river ford]*). A city E of the Jordan (Jdg 7:24).

BETH BIRI [1082] (*house of Biri or den of a lioness*). A town of Simeon S of Judah (1Ch 4:31). *See Beth Lebaoth.*

BETH CAR [1105] (*site [house] of a lamb*). A place W of Mizpah (1Sa 7:11).

BETH DAGON [1087] (*temple [house] of Dagon*).
1. A city of Judah (Jos 15:41).
2. A city of Asher (Jos 19:27).

BETH DIBLATHAIM [1086] (*house of Diblathaim*). A city of Moab (Jer 48:22). *See Almon Diblathaim.*

BETH EDEN [1114] (*house of Eden; garden place*). Probably another name for Damascus (Am 1:5). *See Damascus.*

BETH EKED [1118]. Forty-two relatives of Ahaziah slaughtered there (2Ki 10:12-14).

BETH EMEK [1097] (*house of Emek or site of the valley*). A city of Asher (Jos 19:27).

BETH EZEL [1089] (*house of Ezel or site nearby*). A town of Judah (Mic 1:11).

BETH GADER [1084] (*house of Gader or site of a stone hedge*). A place in Judah (1Ch 2:51). Probably identical with Geder (Jos 12:13); and with Gedor (Jos 15:58).

BETH GAMUL [1085] (*house of recompense*). A city of Moab (Jer 48:23).

BETH GILGAL [1090]. Perhaps an alternate name for Gilgal (Ne 12:29). *See Gilgal.*

BETH-HACCEREM See Beth Hakkerem.

BETH HAGGAN [1091] (*house of Haggan or site of the garden*). A garden house (2Ki 9:27). Probably identical with En Gannim (Jos 19:21).

BETH HAKKEREM [1094] (*house of Hakkerem or site of the vineyard*). A mountain in Judah (Ne 3:14; Jer 6:1).

BETH HARAM [1099]. A fortified city of Gad, E of the Jordan (Jos 13:27).

BETH HARAN [1100] (*house of the mountaineer*). A fortified city E of Jordan (Nu 32:36).

BETH HOGLAH [1102] (*house of Hoglah or site of the partridge*). A place on the border of Judah (Jos 15:6; 18:19, 21).

BETH HORON [1103] (*house of Horon or site of a ravine*). Two ancient cities of Canaan, near which Joshua defeated the Amorites (Jos 10:10-11; 16:3, 5; 18:13-14; 1Sa 13:18; 1Ch 7:24). Solomon builds (1Ki 9:17; 2Ch 8:5). Taken from Judah by the ten tribes (2Ch 25:13).

BETH JESHIMOTH [1093] (*house of Jeshimoth or site of desolation*). A place in the plains of Moab, the S limit of Israel's encampment (Nu 33:49). It was assigned to the Reubenites (Jos 13:20), but was later in Moabite possession (Eze 25:9). Modern Tell el-Azeimeh, about twelve miles SE of Jericho (Jos 12:3).

BETH JOAB See Atroth Beth Joab.

BETH LEBAOTH [1106] (*house of Lebaoth or den of the lioness*). A town of Simeon in the S part of Judah (Jos 19:6). Called Lebaoth (Jos 15:32), and the same as Beth Biri (1Ch 4:31).

BETH-LEHEM-JUDAH See Bethlehem; Judah.

BETH-MAACHAH (*house of Maacah*). See Abel Beth Maacah.

BETH MARCABOTH [1096, 1112] (*site [house] of Marcaboth [chariots]*). A town of Simeon (Jos 19:5; 1Ch 4:31). Probably identical with Madmannah, which may have been its older name (Jos 15:31).

BETH MEON [1110] (*house of habitation*). A city of Moab (Jer 48:23); the same as Beth Baal Meon (Jos 13:17).

BETH MILLO [1109] (*house of Millo or site of earth fill*).
1. Beth Millo probably refers to the earthen fill used to erect a platform on which walls and other large structures were built (Jdg 9:6, 20). It may be identical to the "stronghold" of v. 46 (Jdg 9:46).
2. A name given to part of the citadel of Jerusalem, NIV "supporting terraces" (2Sa 5:9, ftn; 1Ch 11:8, ftn). King Solomon raised a levy to repair (1Ki 9:15, 24, ftn; 11:27, ftn). King Joash murdered at (2Ki 12:20). Repaired by King Hezekiah (2Ch 32:5, ftn).

BETH NIMRAH [1113] (*house of Nimrah [spotted leopard] BDB; house of a basin of clear, limpid water KB*). A fortified city E of Jordan (Nu 32:36; Jos 13:27).

BETH OPHRAH [1108] (*house of*

Ophrah or *house of dust*). A city found in the Shephelah (Mic 1:10, ftn).

BETH-PALET See *Beth Pelet.*

BETH PAZZEZ [1122]. A city in Issachar (Jos 19:21).

BETH PELET [1120] (*house of Pelet [escape]*). A city in Judah (Jos 15:27; Ne 11:26).

BETH PEOR [1121] (*house of Peor*). A place in the tribe of Reuben (Dt 3:29; 4:46; 34:6). Near the burial place of Moses (Jos 13:20).

BETH RAPHA [1125] (*house of Rapha [healing]*). Son of Eshton (1Ch 4:12).

BETH REHOB [1124] (*house of Rehob [main street, market]*). A place in Dan (Jdg 18:28; 2Sa 10:6). Called Rehob.

BETH SHAN [1126] (*site [house] of Shan [repose]*). A city of Manasseh (Jos 17:11; 1Ch 7:29). Not subdued (Jdg 1:27). Bodies of Saul and his sons exposed in (1Sa 31:10, 12). District of, under tribute to Solomon's governor (1Ki 4:12).

BETH-SHEAN See *Beth Shan.*

BETH SHEMESH [1127, 1128] (*temple [house] of Shemesh [pagan sun god]*).
1. A priestly city of Dan (Jos 21:16; 1Sa 6:15; 1Ch 6:59). On the northern border of Judah (Jos 15:10; 1Sa 6:9, 12). In later times transferred to Judah (2Ki 14:11). Mentioned in Solomon's governed districts (1Ki 4:9). Amaziah taken prisoner at (2Ki 14:11-13; 2Ch 25:21-23). Retaken by the Philistines (2Ch 28:18). Called Ir Shemesh (Jos 19:41).
2. A city near Jerusalem (Jos 19:22).
3. A fortified city of Naphtali (Jos 19:38; Jdg 1:33).
4. Literally "Beth Shemesh in Egypt," with the qualifying phrase being used to distinguish it from "Beth Shemesh in Judah" (2Ki 14:11). Called On (in Hebrew) in Egypt; also known as Heliopolis, about five miles NE of Cairo, where there was a temple of Ra (Jer 43:13, ftn).

BETH SHITTAH [1101] (*house of Shittah [acacias]*). A place near the Jordan (Jdg 7:22).

BETH TAPPUAH [1130] (*house of Tappuah [apricot;apple tree]*). A town of Judah (Jos 15:53).

BETH TOGARMAH [1129]. A city in E Asia Minor (Eze 27:14; 38:6). See *Togarmah.*

BETH ZUR [1123] (*cliff house*). A town in Judah (Jos 15:58; 1Ch 2:45; 2Ch 11:7; Ne 3:16).

BETHANY [1029] (*house of Ananiah* or *poor ones* or *unripe figs*). A village on the eastern slope of the Mount of Olives (Jn 11:18). Mary, Martha, and Lazarus dwell at (Lk 10:38-41).

Lazarus dies and is raised to life at (Jn 11). Jesus attends a feast in (Mt 26:6-13; Jn 12:1-9). The colt on which Jesus made his triumphal entry into Jerusalem obtained at (Mk 11:1-11). Jesus stays at (Mt 21:17; Mk 11:11-12, 19).

BETHEL [1078, 1088] (*temple [house] of God [El]*).
1. A city N of Jerusalem. The ancient city next to, and finally embraced in, was called Luz (Jos 18:13; Jdg 1:23-26). Abraham establishes an altar at (Ge 12:8; 13:3-4). The place where Jacob saw the vision of the stairway (Ge 28:10-22; 31:13; Hos 12:4), and builds an altar at (Ge 35:1-15). Deborah dies at (Ge 35:8). Conquered by Joshua (Jos 8:17, w 12:16), by the house of Joseph (Jdg 1:22-26). Allotted to Benjamin (Jos 18:13, 22). Court of justice held at, by Deborah (Jdg 4:5), by Samuel (1Sa 7:16).
Tabernacle at, and called House of God (Jdg 20:18, 31; 21:2). Jeroboam institutes idolatrous worship at (1Ki 12:25-33; 2Ki 10:29). Idolatry at (Jer 48:13; Am 4:4). Shalmaneser sends a priest to (2Ki 17:27-28). Prophecies against the idolatrous altars at (1Ki 13:1-6, 32; 2Ki 23:4, 15-20; Am 3:14). The company of prophets at (2Ki 2:3). Children of, mock Elisha (2Ki 2:23-24). People of, return from Babylon (Ezr 2:28; Ne 7:32). Prophecies against (Am 5:5).
2. A city in the S of Judah (1Sa 30:27).
3. A mountain (1Sa 13:2).

BETHER (perhaps *house [shrine] of the mountain*). Mountains of (SS 2:17, ftn, text "rugged hills").

BETHESDA [1031] (*site [house] of mercy*). A spring-fed pool in Jerusalem (Jn 5:1-16) into which the sick went for healing.

BETHHANAN See *Elon Bethhanan.*

BETHLEHEM [1095, 1107, 1033] (*house of bread;* possibly *temple [house] of Lakhmu [pagan deity]*).
1. A city SW of Jerusalem (Jdg 17:7; 19:18). Called Ephrathah and Ephrath (Ge 48:7; Ps 132:6; Mic 5:2), and Bethlehem in Judah (Jdg 17:7-9; 19:1, 18; Ru 1:1; 1Sa 17:12). Rachel dies and is buried at (Ge 35:16, 19; 48:7). The city of Boaz (Ru 1:1, 19; 2:4; 4). Taken and held by the Philistines (2Sa 23:14-16). Jeroboam converts it into a military stronghold (2Ch 11:6). The city of Joseph (Mt 2:5-6; Lk 2:4). Birthplace of Jesus (Mic 5:2; Mt 2; Lk 2:4, 15). Herod slays the children of (Mt 2:16-18).
2. A town of Zebulun, six miles W of Nazareth (Jos 19:15). Israel judged at (Jdg 12:10).

BETHPHAGE [1036] (*house of unripe figs*). A village on the Mount of Olives (Mt 21:1; Mk 11:1; Lk 19:29).

BETHSAIDA [1034] (*house of fishing*).
1. A city of Galilee. The city of Philip, Andrew,

and Peter (Jn 1:44; 12:21). Jesus visits (Mk 6:45), cures a blind man in (Mk 8:22), prophesies against (Mt 11:21; Lk 10:13).

2. Secluded area E of the sea of Galilee; Jesus feeds five thousand people in (Mt 14:13; Mk 6:32; Lk 9:10).

BETHUEL [1432, 1433] (*man of God [El]*). Son of Nahor, father of Rebekah (Ge 22:22-23; 24:15, 24; 25:20; 28:2, 5).

BETHUL [1434]. A city of Simeon (Jos 19:4). Called Kesil (Jos 15:30) and Bethuel (1Ch 4:30).

BETONIM [1064] (*pistachio nuts*). A town of Gad (Jos 13:26).

BETRAYAL [953, 1655, 5085, 8228, 9213, *4140*+]. Of Jesus (Mt 26:14-16, 45-50; Mk 14:10-11; Lk 22:3-6; 22:47-48; Jn 13:21). Of others, foretold (Mt 20:18; 24:10). Of David, by Doeg (1Sa 22:9-10, w 1Sa 21:1-10). Of cities (Jdg 1:24-25). *See Confidence, Betrayed.*

BETROTHAL [829]. Of Jacob (Ge 29:18-30). Exempts from military duty (Dt 20:7). A quasi-marriage (Mt 1:18; Lk 1:27).
Figurative (Isa 62:4; Hos 2:19-20; 2Co 11:2).
See Marriage.

BETTING By Samson (Jdg 14:12-19).

BEULAH [1241] (*married*). Poetic name for restored Israel (Isa 62:4).

BEZAI [1291].
1. Head of a Jewish family that returned from Babylon (Ezr 2:17; Ne 7:23).
2. A family that sealed the covenant with Nehemiah (Ne 10:18).

BEZALEL [1295] (*in the shadow of God [El]*).
1. A divinely inspired architect and master craftsman who built the tabernacle (Ex 31:2; 35:30-35; 36:1; 37:1; 38:1-7, 22).
2. Son of Pahath-Moab (Ezr 10:30).

BEZEK [1028] (*scattering, sowing*).
1. Residence of Adoni-Bezek (Jdg 1:5). *See Adoni-Bezek.*
2. A rendezvous of Israel under Saul (1Sa 11:8).

BEZER [1310, 1311] (*[metallic] ore,* or *place of refuge*).
1. A city of refuge, E of the Jordan (Dt 4:43; Jos 20:8; 21:36; 1Ch 6:78).
2. Son of Zophah (1Ch 7:37).

BIBLE, THE General references to (2Sa 22:31; Ps 12:6; 119:9, 50; 147:15; Mk 12:24; Lk 8:11; Eph 6:17). The Book of the ages (Ps 119:89; Mt 5:18; 24:35; 1Pe 1:25). Food for the soul (Dt 8:3; Job 23:12; Ps 119:103; Jer 15:16; 1Pe 2:2). Divinely inspired (Jer 36:2; Eze 1:3; Ac 1:16; 2Ti 3:16; 2Pe 1:21; Rev 14:13). Precepts written in the heart (Dt 6:6; 11:18; Ps 119:11; Lk 2:51; Ro 10:8; Col 3:16). Furnishes a light (Ps 19:8; 119:105, 130; Pr 6:23; 2Pe 1:19). Loved by the believers (Ps 119:47, 72, 82, 97, 140; Jer 15:16).

Mighty in its influence: a devouring flame (Jer 5:14), a crushing hammer (Jer 23:29), a life-giving force (Eze 37:7), a saving power (Ro 1:16), a penetrating sword (Eph 6:17; Heb 4:12).

Blessings to those who reverence it (Jos 1:8; Ps 19:11; Mt 7:24; Lk 11:28; Jn 5:24; 8:31; Rev 1:3). Purifies the life (Ps 119:9; Jn 15:3; 17:17; Eph 5:26; 1Pe 1:22). Written with a purpose (Jn 20:31; Ro 15:4; 1Co 10:11; 1Jn 5:13). The standard of faith (Pr 29:18; Isa 8:20; Jn 12:48; Gal 1:8; 1Th 2:13). Its words sacred (Dt 4:2; 12:32; Pr 30:6; Rev 22:19). The study of it commanded (Dt 17:19; Isa 34:16; Jn 5:39; Ac 17:11; Ro 15:4). Contains seed for the sower (Ps 126:6; Mk 4:14-15; 2Co 9:10). Absolutely trustworthy (1Ki 8:56; Ps 111:7; Eze 12:25; Mt 5:18; Lk 21:33). Profitable for instruction (Dt 4:10; 11:19; 2Ch 17:9; Ne 8:13; Isa 2:3). Ignorance of, dangerous (Mt 22:29; Jn 20:9; Ac 13:27; 2Co 3:15).
See Word of God.

BICRI [1152] (*first born*). Father of Sheba (2Sa 20:1).

BIDKAR [982] (*son of Deker [piercing]*). Jehu's captain (2Ki 9:25).

BIER [4753, 5435]. (2Sa 3:31; Lk 7:14).

BIGAMY *See Polygamy.*

BIGOTRY

Condemned:
Exhibited: In self-righteousness (Isa 65:5; Mk 2:16; Lk 15:2; 18:9-14). In intolerance (Lk 9:49-50; Ac 18:12-13).
Rebuked (Ac 10:28, 45). Paul's argument against (Ro 3:1-23; 4:1-25).

Instances of:
Joshua (Nu 11:27-29). The Jews with the Samaritans (Jn 4:9, 27), Jesus (Lk 4:28; 7:39; 11:38-39; 15:22; 19:5-7; Jn 5:18), the blind man (Jn 9:29-34), Paul (Ac 21:28-29; 22:22). John (Mk 9:38-40; Lk 9:49-50). James and John (Lk 9:51-56). The early Christians (Ac 10:45; 11:2-3; 15:1-10, w Gal 2:3-5). Paul (Ac 9:1-2; 22:3-4; 26:9-11; Gal 1:13-14; Php 3:6).
See Intolerance; Religious; Persecution; Respect of Persons; Uncharitableness.

BIGTHA [960] (*gift of God*). Eunuch and servant of Xerxes (Est 1:10).

BIGTHANA [961, 962] (*gift of God*). A conspiring Persian officer (Est 2:21-23; 6:2).

BIGVAI [958] (*fortunate*).
1. Man who returned from the Captivity (Ezr 2:2; Ne 7:19).
2. Ancestor of family that returned from the Captivity (Ezr 2:14; Ne 7:19).

3. Probably the same as 2 above (Ezr 8:14).

BILDAD [1161] (*Bel has loved*). One of Job's friends (Job 2:11; 8:1; 18:1; 25:1).

BILEAM [1190] (*[a gift] brought to the people*). A town of Manasseh (1Ch 6:70). Called Ibleam (Jos 17:11) and Gath Rimmon (Jos 21:25).

BILGAH [1159] (*gleam, smile*).
1. One of the chiefs of the priestly courses in the temple (1Ch 24:14).
2. A priest (Ne 12:5, 18), perhaps identical with Bilgai (Ne 10:8).

BILGAI [1160] (*gleam, smile*). A priest (Ne 10:8).

BILHAH [1167, 1168] (perhaps *simplicity*, or *modesty*, or *to be without concern*).
1. Rachel's servant, bears children by Jacob (Ge 29:29; 30:3-4; 37:2). Mother of Dan and Naphtali (Ge 30:1-8; 35:25; 46:23, 25). Reuben's incest with (Ge 35:22; 49:4).
2. A place in the land of Simeon (1Ch 4:29). Called Balah (Jos 19:3) and Baalah (Jos 15:29).

BILHAN [1169] (*foolish*).
1. A Horite chief (Ge 36:27; 1Ch 1:42).
2. A Benjamite (1Ch 7:10).

BILL OF DIVORCE See *Divorce*.

BILSHAN [1193] (*their Bel [lord]*). A Jew of the Captivity (Ezr 2:2; Ne 7:7).

BIMHAL [1197] (*son of circumcision*). Son of Japhlet (1Ch 7:33).

BINDING AND LOOSING [*1313, 3395]. The carrying of a key or keys was a symbol of the delegated power of opening and closing (Mt 16:19; Rev 1:18). See *Key*.
The apostles were given power to bind and to loose (Mt 16:19; 18:18). Peter loosed the feet of the lame man at the temple gate (Ac 3:1-10), and Paul bound the sight of Elymas (Ac 13:8-11). Peter was present when the Holy Spirit was poured out on the Jews (Ac 2), Samaritans (Ac 8:14-17), and Gentiles (Ac 10:34-48).

BINEA [1232]. A descendant of King Saul (1Ch 8:37; 9:43).

BINNUI [1218] (*a son*).
1. Man who helped rebuild walls of Jerusalem (Ne 3:18, ftn).
2. A Jew of the Captivity (Ne 7:15). Called Bani (Ezr 2:10).
3. A Levite of the Captivity (Ne 3:24; 12:8; 10:9).
4. Father of Noadiah (Ezr 8:33).
5. Descendant of Pahath-Moab who married a foreign wife (Ezr 10:30).
6. KJV; NIV "descendants of" (Ezr 10:38).

BIRDS [1251+4053, 3687, 4053+7606, 6416,

6514, 7256, 7606, 10533, 10616, *3997, 4374, 4764*]. Creation of, on the fifth creative day (Ge 1:20-30). Mankind's rule over (Ge 1:26, 28; 9:2-3; Ps 8:5-8; Jer 27:6; Da 2:38; Jas 3:7). Given for food (Ge 9:2-3; Dt 14:11-20). What species were unclean (Lev 11:13-20; Dt 14:12-19).
Used for sacrifice. See *Dove; Pigeon*. Divine care of (Job 38:41; Ps 147:9; Mt 10:29; Lk 12:6, 24). Songs of, at the break of day (Ps 104:12; Ecc 12:4; SS 2:12). Domesticated (Job 41:5; Jas 3:7). Solomon's proverbs of (1Ki 4:33). Nests of (Ps 104:17; Mt 8:20; 13:32). Instincts of (Pr 1:17). Habits of (Job 39:13-18, 26-30). Migrate (Jer 8:7).
Mosaic law protected the mother from being taken with the young (Dt 22:6-7). Cages of (Jer 5:27; Rev 18:2). See *Snare*.
Figurative (Isa 16:2; 46:11; Jer 12:9; Eze 39:4).
Symbolic (Da 7:6).
See *Cormorant; Dove; Eagle; Falcon; Gull; Hawk; Hen, 2; Heron; Hoopoe; Kite; Osprey; Ostrich; Owl; Partridge; Pigeon; Quail; Raven; Red Kite; Screech Owl; Sparrow; Stork; Swallow; Swift; Thrush; Vulture; White Owl*.

BIRSHA [1407] (*disagreeable in taste*). A king of Gomorrah (Ge 14:2-10).

BIRTH [*1061, 1800, 2655, 3528, 3533, 3535, 5951, 6584+7924, 6913, 8167, *1002, 1164, 1181, 2844, 3120+3613, 4472, 5503, 5770*]. Pangs in giving (Ps 48:6; Isa 13:8; 21:3; Jer 4:31; 6:24; 30:6; 31:8). Giving, ordained to be in sorrow (Ge 3:16).
Famous births: Cain (Ge 4:1), Abel (Ge 4:2), Noah (Ge 5:28-29), Isaac (Ge 21:1-5), Esau and Jacob (Ge 25:24-26), the children of Jacob (Ge 29:31-30:24; 35:16-18), Moses (Ex 2:1-4), John the Baptist (Lk 1:5-25, 57), Jesus (Mt 1:18-25; Lk 1:26-38; 2:1-20).
See *Abortion; Children*.

BIRTHDAY [3427+3528, *1160*]. Celebrated by feasts (Ge 40:20; Mt 14:6). Cursed (Job 3; Jer 20:14, 18).

BIRTHRIGHT [1148].
Described:
Belonged to the firstborn (Dt 21:15-16). Entitled the firstborn to a double portion of inheritance (Dt 21:15-17), a royal succession (2Ch 21:3). An honorable title (Ex 4:22; Ps 89:27; Jer 31:9; Ro 8:29; Col 1:15; Heb 1:6; 12:23; Rev 1:5).
Lost by Firstborn:
Sold by Esau (Ge 25:29-34; 27:36, w 25:33; Heb 12:16; Ro 9:12-13). Forfeited by Reuben (1Ch 5:1-2). Set aside: that of Manasseh (Ge 48:15-20), Adonijah (1Ki 2:15), Hosah's son (1Ch 26:10).
See *Firstborn*.

BIRZAITH [1365] (*well of olive oil*). A descendant of Asher (1Ch 7:31).

BISHLAM [1420] (*son of Shalom [peace]*). A Samaritan who obstructed the rebuilding of the temple at Jerusalem (Ezr 4:7-24).

BISHOP The same as elder or overseer (Ac 20:28; Php 1:1; 1Ti 3:1; Tit 1:7, ftns). *See Elders; Overseer.*

BIT [1323, 5496, 8270, *5903*]. Part of a bridle (Ps 32:9; Jas 3:3).

BITHIAH [1437] (possibly *worshiper of Yahweh* BDB; *[female pagan god] queen* KB). Daughter of Pharaoh; wife of Mered of Judah (1Ch 4:18).

BITHRON [1443] (*gully*). A district bordering on the Jordan (2Sa 2:29).

BITHYNIA [*1049*]. A Roman province in Asia Minor (Ac 16:7; 1Pe 1:1).

BITTER HERBS Eaten symbolically with the Passover (Ex 12:8; Nu 9:11).

BITTER WATER At Marah (Ex 15:23). A ceremonial water used by the priest to determine marital faithfulness (Nu 5:18-27).

BITTERN *See Owl.*

BITTERNESS [4360, 4933, 5253, 5289, 5352, 5353, 8032, *4394*]. A poisonous and bitter plant (Hos 10:4; Am 6:12). *See Gall, 3.*

Of spirit (Dt 32:32; Jer 4:18; Ac 8:23; Ro 3:14; Eph 4:31; Heb 12:5; Jas 3:14).

BITUMEN *See Tar.*

BIZIOTHIAH [1026] (*contempt of Yahweh*). A town in Judah (Jos 15:28). Baalath Beer (Jos 19:8), and Balah (Jos 19:3).

BIZTHA [1030] (perhaps *eunuch*, or *bound*). A eunuch and servant of the Persian king Xerxes (Est 1:10).

BLACK VULTURE An unclean bird, not to be eaten under the law (Lev 11:13; Dt 14:13). *See Vulture.*

BLACKNESS [370, 3124, 3125, 4025, 6465, 6906, 7516, 7722, 8837, 8839, *3506*]. Overcoming the day (Job 3:5). On the day of the LORD (Joel 2:6; Zep 1:15). God turning to dawn (Am 5:8).

See Colors, Figurative and Symbolic.

BLACKSMITH [3093]. *See Smith.*

BLAIN *See Boil.*

BLASPHEMY [*1552, 5542, 5919, 7837, 1059, 1060, 1061*] (*speak against, revile*).

Described:
Reproaching God (2Ki 19:22; 2Ch 32:19; Ps 73:9, 11; 74:18; 139:20; Pr 30:9; Isa 5:19; 8:21-22; 37:23; 45:9; 52:5; Eze 35:12-13; Da 7:25; Mt 10:25). Defying God (Isa 29:15-16; 36:15-21; 37:10; Eze 8:12; 9:9; Mal 3:13-14). Denying God's word (Jer 17:15). Speaking lies against God

(Hos 7:13). Attributing ignorance to God (Ps 10:11, 13; Isa 40:27). Exalting oneself above God (Da 11:36-37; 2Th 2:4). Calling Jesus accursed (1Co 12:3; Jas 2:7). Against the Holy Spirit (Mt 12:31-32; Mk 3:29-30; Lk 12:10). Occasioned by sins of believers (2Sa 12:14; Ro 2:24).

Foretold by Peter (2Pe 3:3-4). Foretold by John (Rev 13:1, 5-6; 16:9, 11, 21; 17:3).

Forbidden (Ex 20:7; 22:28; Lev 19:12; 22:32; Jas 3:10; 5:12).

Punishment for (Lev 24:10-16; Isa 65:7; Heb 10:29).

Instances of:
The depraved son of Shelomith, who, in a fight with an Israelite, cursed God (Lev 24:10-16). Of the Israelites, in grumbling against God (Nu 21:5-6). Infidels who used the adultery of David as an occasion to blaspheme (2Sa 12:14). Shimei, in his malice toward David (2Sa 16:5). One of Sennacherib's field commanders, in the siege of Jerusalem (2Ki 18:22; 19; Isa 36:15-20; 37:10-33). Job's wife, when she exhorted Job to curse God and die (Job 2:9). Israel (Eze 20:27-28). Peter, when accused of being a disciple of Jesus (Mt 26:74; Mk 14:71). The revilers of Jesus, when He was crucified (Mt 27:40-44, 63). The early Christians, persecuted by Saul of Tarsus compelled to blaspheme the name of Jesus (Ac 26:11; 1Ti 1:13). Two disciples, Hymenaeus and Alexander, who were delivered to Satan that they might learn not to blaspheme (1Ti 1:20). Man of sin (2Th 2:3-4). Backslidden Ephesians (Rev 2:9).

False Accusations of:
Against Naboth (1Ki 21:13). Against Jesus (Mt 9:3; 26:65; Mk 2:7; 14:58; Lk 5:21; 22:70-71; Jn 5:18; 10:33; 19:7). Against Stephen (Ac 6:11, 13).

BLAST [*5870, 5972, 7754, 7938, 8120*].
1. From God's nostrils, figurative of judgment (Ex 15:8; 2Sa 22:16; Job 4:9; Ps 18:15).
2. From a horn, a call to assemble (Ex 19:13, 16; Lev 23:24) or to battle (Jos 6:5, 16; Job 39:25).

BLASTUS [*1058*] (*sprout [of a vine, branch]*). One of Herod's officers (Ac 12:20).

BLEEDING, SUBJECT TO
A woman who had been bleeding for twelve years could not be healed by physicians (Mt 9:20; Mk 5:25; Lk 8:43, ftn). The precise nature of the woman's problem is not known. Her existence was wretched because she was shunned by people generally, since anyone having contact with her was made ceremonially unclean (Lev 15:25-33). Jesus healed her (both physically, "be freed from your suffering," and spiritually, "go in peace"; Mk 5:34) as a result of her simple act of faith.

BLEMISH [4583, 8845, *320, 3700, 5069*]. A physical deformity. Barred sons of Aaron from exercise of priestly offices (Lev 21:17-23). Animals with, forbidden to be used for sacrifice (Lev 22:19-25).

Figurative (Eph 5:27; 1Pe 1:19).

BLESSING [*887, 897, 1385, 1388, *1922, 2328, *2330, 3421]. For blessing before eating, *See Benedictions; Prayer, Thanksgiving, and Before Taking Food.*

BLESSINGS, SPIRITUAL

From God:

(Dt 33:25, 27; Ps 18:28-36; 29:11; 37:6, 17, 24, 39; 63:8; 66:8-9; 68:18, 28, 35; 84:5, 11; Isa 40:11, 29, 31; 41:10, 13, 16; Ac 3:19; 1Co 2:9; Php 4:13; Jas 1:17; Jude 24).

Guidance (Ex 33:16; Ps 23:2-3; 119:102; Isa 40:11; 58:11).

Sanctification (Ex 31:13; Lev 21:8; Isa 1:25; 4:3-4; 6:6-7; 1Jn 1:9; Jude 1).

The perfecting of salvation (2Co 1:21; Php 1:6; 2:13; 4:19; Col 1:11-12; 1Th 5:24; Heb 13:20-21; 1Pe 1:5; 2Pe 1:2-4).

The deposit of the Spirit, guaranteeing what is to come (2Co 1:22; 5:5).

Peace (Isa 26:12; 57:19; Mal 4:2; Php 4:7).

From Christ:

(Jn 1:16; Ro 1:7; 16:20; 1Co 1:3; 16:23; 2Co 1:2; 13:14; Gal 1:3; 6:16, 18; Eph 1:2; 6:23-24; Php 1:2; 4:23; 1Th 5:28; 2Th 1:2; 3:16, 18; 1Ti 1:2; 2Ti 1:2; Phm 3, 25; 2Pe 1:1; 2Jn 3).

Contingent Upon Obedience; Resulting in:

Divine favor (Ex 19:5; Jer 7:23), mercy (Ex 20:6; Dt 5:10, 16; 7:9; 1Ki 8:23; 2Ch 30:9), holiness (Dt 28:9; 30:1-3, 6; Col 1:22-23), eternal salvation (Mt 10:22; 24:13; Mk 13:13; Heb 3:6, 14; 10:36; Rev 2:10).

See Contingencies; Faithfulness; Regeneration; Salvation.

BLESSINGS, TEMPORAL

From God: (Ps 136:25).

Rain (Dt 11:14; 28:12; Job 37:6; 38:25-27; Ps 68:9; 135:7; 147:8; Jer 10:13; 14:22; 51:16; Joel 2:23; Am 4:7; Zec 10:1, 12; Mt 5:45; Ac 14:17).

Seedtime and harvest (Ge 8:22; Lev 25:20-22; 26:4-5; Ps 107:35-38; Isa 55:10; Jer 5:24; Eze 36:30; Mal 3:11; Ac 14:17).

Food and clothing (Ge 9:1-3; 28:20-21; Dt 8:3-4; 10:18; 29:5; Ru 1:6; 2Ch 31:10; Ps 65:9; 68:1-10; 81:16; 104:14-15, 27-28; 111:5; 132:15; 145:15-16; 146:7; Ecc 2:24; 3:13; Isa 33:15-16; Joel 2:26; Mt 6:26, 30-33; Lk 12:22-31; Jn 6:31).

Preservation of life (Dt 4:1, 40; 5:33; 7:15; Ps 21:4; 23:6; 91:16; 103:2-5; Da 6:20, 22).

Children (Ps 113:9; Ps 127:3-5).

Prosperity (Ge 24:56; 26:24; 49:24-25; Nu 10:29; Dt 8:7-10, 18; 1Sa 2:7-8; 1Ch 29:12, 14, 16; 2Ch 1:12; Ezr 8:22; Ps 147:13-14; Ecc 5:19; Isa 30:23; Hos 2:8).

National greatness (Ge 22:17; 26:3-4; Dt 1:10; 7:13-14; 15:4, 6; 26:18-19; 32:13-14; Job 12:23; Ps 69:35-36; Isa 51:2; Jer 30:19; Eze 36:36-38; Da 5:18), social peace (Lev 26:6; 1Ch 22:9), victory over enemies (Ex 23:22; Lev 26:6-9; Dt 28:7; Ps 44:3), worldly honors (2Sa 7:8-9; 1Ch 17:7-8).

Exemplified to:

Noah at the time of the Flood (Ge 7:1). Abraham (Ge 24:1). Isaac (Ge 26:12-24, 28). Jacob (Ge 35:9-15). Israelites in Egypt (Ex 11:3), in the wilderness, supplying water (Ex 17:1-7; Nu 20:10-11; Ps 78:15-20; 105:4), manna (Ex 16:14, 31; Nu 11:7-9; Ne 9:15; Ps 78:23-24), quail (Nu 11:31-33; Ps 78:23-30; 105:40). David (2Sa 5:10; 1Ch 14:17). Obed-Edom (2Sa 6:11). Solomon (1Ki 3:13; 1Ch 29:25; 2Ch 1:1). Elijah, fed by ravens (1Ki 17:2-7), by an angel (1Ki 19:5-8). The widow of Zarephath (1Ki 17:12-16). Hezekiah prospered (2Ki 18:6-7; 2Ch 32:29), restored to health (2Ki 20:1-7). Asa (2Ch 14:6-7). Jehoshaphat (2Ch 17:3-5; 20:30). Uzziah (2Ch 26:5-15). Jotham (2Ch 27:6). Job (Job 1:10; 42:10, 12). Daniel (Da 1:9).

Prayer for:

Rain (1Ki 8:36; 2Ch 6:27). Plentiful harvests (Ge 27:28; Dt 26:15; Dt 33:13-16). Daily bread (Mt 6:11; Lk 11:3), prosperity (Ge 28:3-4; 1Ch 4:10; Ne 1:11; 3Jn 2), providential guidance (Ge 24:12-14, 42-44; Ro 1:10; 1Th 3:11).

Instances of Prayer for:

Abraham (Ge 15:2-4). Abraham's servant (Ge 24:12). Laban (Ge 24:60). Isaac (Ge 25:21). Hannah (1Sa 1:11). Elijah (1Ki 17:20-21; 18:42, 44; Jas 5:17-18). Ezra (Ezr 8:21-23). Nehemiah (Ne 1:11; 2:4; 6:9).

Contingent Upon Obedience; Resulting in:

Longevity (Ex 20:12; Dt 4:40; 5:16; 1Ki 3:14; Pr 3:1-2). Deliverance from enemies (Ex 23:22; Lev 26:6-8; Dt 28:7; 30:1-4; Pr 16:7; Jer 15:19-21). Prosperity (Lev 26:3-5; Dt 7:12-14; 15:4-5; 28:2-12; 29:9; 30:1-5, 9-20; Jos 1:8; 1Ki 2:3-4; 9:3-9; 1Ch 22:13; 28:7-8; 2Ch 7:17-22; 26:5; 27:6; 31:10; Job 36:11; Isa 1:19; Jer 7:3-7; 11:1-5; 12:16; 17:24-27; 22:4-5, 15-16; Mal 3:10-12). Favors to children (Dt 4:1, 40; 5:29; 7:9; 12:25, 28). Preeminent honors (Dt 28:1, 13; Zec 3:7). Averted judgments (Ex 15:26; Dt 7:15).

See God, Goodness of; Providence of; Prosperity.

BLIGHT [5782, 8730]. Destructive plant disease, sent as a judgment (Dt 28:22; 1Ki 8:37; Am 4:9; Hag 2:17).

BLIND [*6177, 6422, 6426, *5603, *5604]. Cruelty to, forbidden (Lev 19:14; Dt 27:18). Hated by David (2Sa 5:8). *See Blindness.*

BLINDNESS [6177, 6427]. Disqualified for priestly office (Lev 21:18). Of animals, disqualified for a sacrifice (Lev 22:22; Dt 15:21; Mal 1:8). Miraculously inflicted upon the Sodomites (Ge 19:11), Syrians (2Ki 6:18-23), Saul of Tarsus (Ac 9:8-9), Elymas (Ac 13:11). Sent as a judgment (Dt 28:28).

Miraculous healing of (Mt 9:27-30; 11:5; 12:22; 21:14), Bartimaeus (Mt 20:30-34; Mk 10:46-52), a man of Bethsaida (Mk 8:22-25), a man born blind (Jn 9:1-7).

Instances of:
Isaac (Ge 27:1). Jacob (Ge 48:10). Eli (1Sa 4:14-15). Ahijah (1Ki 14:4).

Spiritual:
Instances of (Dt 29:4; Job 5:14; Isa 29:10-12; 56:10; 59:10; Jer 2:8; 5:21; 9:3; Eze 12:2; Ro 11:8). Foretold (Isa 60:2; Ro 2:4; 11:10).

Manifested:
In ignorance of God (Ex 5:2; Isa 1:3; Jer 4:22; Hos 4:1, 6; Jn 7:28; 15:21; 16:2-3; 17:25; Ac 17:23; 1Co 1:18-21; 2:8, 14-15; 15:34; Gal 4:8; Eph 4:17-19; 1Th 4:4-5; 1Jn 4:8; 3Jn 11), of Christ (Mt 16:3, 9; Lk 23:34; Jn 1:5, 10; 4:10-11, 15, 22; 8:15, 19, 27, 33, 42-43, 52-57; 9:29-39; Ac 3:14, 17; Ro 11:7-8, 25; 1Pe 1:14; 1Jn 3:1, 6), the Holy Spirit (Jn 14:17; Ac 19:2), of the Scriptures (Mt 22:29; Mk 12:24; Ac 13:27; 2Co 3:14-15; Heb 5:11-12; 2Pe 3:16).
In ignorance of moral truth (Dt 32:28; Pr 4:19; 28:5; Isa 5:13; Da 12:10; Mt 15:14, 16; 16:3, 9; 23:19, 24, 26; Mk 7:18; Lk 6:39; 12:48, 57; 2Ti 3:7; Jude 10), of the way of salvation (Lk 19:42; Jn 3:4; 6:52, 60; 2Pe 1:9; 1Jn 1:6, 8; 2:4, 9, 11; Rev 3:17), of God's ways (Ps 95:10; Jer 5:4; 8:7-9; Mic 4:12).
In unbelief (Ps 14:1, 4; Isa 15:1; Mk 16:14; Jn 12:35, 38; Ac 28:25, 27; 2Co 4:3-4, 6; 2Th 2:11-12). In insensibility (Dt 29:4; Jdg 16:20; Pr 7:7-23; 17:16; Isa 6:9-10; 42:18-20; 44:18-20; 48:8; Jer 16:10; Hos 7:11; Mt 6:23; 13:13-15; Mk 4:11-12; 6:52; 8:18; Lk 8:10; Jn 12:40; Ac 28:25-27). In presumption (Ps 10:5-6; 94:7-8; Isa 28:10-15; 40:21, 27-28; Jer 8:8-9; Am 9:10). In perversity (Job 21:14-15; Pr 1:7, 22, 29-30; 13:18; 19:2-3; Isa 5:20; 26:10-11; Jer 9:3, 6; Eze 12:2-3; Hos 5:4; Mt 21:32; Mk 3:5; Lk 11:52; Jn 3:19; Ro 1:19-23, 28-31). In hypocrisy (Tit 1:15-16).

Consequences of: (Pr 10:21; 14:12; Isa 27:11; Hos 4:6, 14; 2Th 1:8).

Remedy for: (Isa 9:2; 25:7; 35:5; 42:6-7; Lk 4:18; Jn 8:12; Ac 26:18; 2Co 4:6; Eph 5:8; Col 1:13; 1Pe 2:9).
See Affliction, Prayer Under; God, Providence of, Mysterious and Misinterpreted.

BLOOD [408+1460, 1414+8638, 1414, 1947, 2446, 2743+3655+4946, 3655+3870+4946, 5906, 6795, *135+*, *136*]. Is the life (Ge 9:4; Lev 17:11, 14; 19:16; Dt 12:23; Mt 27:4, 24). Forbidden to be used as food (Ge 9:4; Lev 3:17; 7:26-27; 17:10-14; 19:26; Dt 12:16, 23; 15:23; Eze 33:25; Ac 15:20, 29; 21:25). Plague of (Ex 7:17-25; Ps 78:44; 105:29).

Sacrificial:
Sprinkled on altar and people (Ex 24:6-8; Eze 43:18, 20). Sprinkled on door posts (Ex 12:7-23; Heb 11:28). Without shedding of, no remission (Heb 9:22).

Of Sin Offering:
Sprinkled seven times before the veil (Lev 4;5-6, 17), on horns of the altar of sweet incense, and at the bottom of the altar of burnt offering (Ex 30:10;

Lev 4:7, 18, 25, 30; 5:9; 9:9, 12). Of bull of sin offering, put on the horns of the altar (Ex 29:12; Lev 8:15), poured at the bottom of the altar (Ex 29:12; Lev 8:15). *See Offerings.*

Of Trespass Offering:
Sprinkled on the altar (Lev 7:2). *See Offerings.*

Of Burnt Offering:
Sprinkled round about, and upon the altar (Ex 29:16; Lev 1:5, 11, 15; 8:19; Dt 12:27). *See Offerings.* Used for cleansing of leprosy (Lev 14:6-7, 17, 28, 51-52). *See Offerings.*

Of Peace Offering:
Sprinkled about the altar (Lev 3:2, 8, 13; 9:19). Blood of the ram of consecration put on tip of right ear, thumb, and large toe of, and sprinkled upon, Aaron and his sons (Ex 29:20-21; Lev 8:23-24, 30). *See Offerings.*

Blood of the Covenant: (Ex 24:5-8; Zec 9:11; Mt 26:28; Heb 9:18-19, 22; 10:29; 13:20).
See Offerings.

Of Atonement:
Sprinkled on atonement cover (Lev 16:14-15, 18-19, 27; 17:11).

Figurative:
Of victories (Ps 58:10), oppression and cruelty (Hab 2:12), destruction (Eze 35:6), guilt (Lev 20:9; 2Sa 1:16; Eze 18:13), judgments (Eze 16:38; Rev 16:6).

Of Jesus:
Shed on the Cross (Jn 19:18, 34). Atoning (Mt 26:28; Mk 14:24; Lk 22:20; Ro 3:24-25; 5:9; Eph 2:13, 16; Heb 10:19-20; 12:24; 13:20; 1Jn 5:6, 8). Redeeming (Ac 20:28; Eph 1:7; Col 1:14, 20; Heb 9:12-14; 1Pe 1:18-19; Rev 1:5; 5:9; 7:14). Sanctifying (Heb 10:29; 13:12). Justification through (Ro 3:24-25; 5:9). Victory through (Rev 12:11). Eternal life by (Jn 6:53-56). Typified by the blood of sacrifices (Heb 9:6-28). Symbolized by the wine of the Lord's Supper (1Co 10:16; 11:25).
See Atonement; Jesus the Christ, Mission of, Sufferings of.

BLOOD, AVENGER One who took it upon himself to avenge the blood of a slain relative (Ge 9:6; Nu 35:6). *See Avenger of Blood.*

BLOOD, ISSUE OF *See Bleeding, Subject to; Disease.*

BLOOD MONEY [*135+5507*]. Paid to Judas for betraying Jesus (Mt 27:6). *See Conscience Money.*

BLOODY SWEAT *See Disease; Sweat, Bloody.*

BLUE [9418, *5610*]. *See Colors, Figurative and Symbolic.*

BLUSHING [4007]. With shame (Ezr 9:6; Jer 6:15; 8:12).

BOANERGES [*1065*] (*sons of thunder*). Surname of the sons of Zebedee (Mk 3:17).

BOARS, WILD [2614]. (Ps 80:13). *See Pig.*

BOASTING [*606, 607, 966, 2146, 9514, 10647, *225, 2878, 3016, 3017, 3018, 3306*]. Folly of (Ps 49:6-9; Pr 27:1; Isa 10:15; Jas 4:16). Deceitful (Pr 20:14; 25:14). Of the wicked (Ps 52:1; 94:4; Ro 1:30). Of the tongue (Jas 3:5). Forbidden (Jer 9:23).
   Spiritual (Ps 52:1; 94:4; Ro 3:27; 11:17-21; 1Co 1:29; 4:6-7; 2Co 10:12-18; Eph 2:8-10).

Instances of:
   Goliath (1Sa 17). Ben-Hadad (1Ki 20:10). Amaziah (2Ch 25:17-20). Sennacherib (2Ki 18:19, 28-35; 19:8-13; Isa 10:8-15). The disciples (Lk 10:17, 20).
   See Ostentation.

BOAT [641, 3998, *4449, 4450*]. *See Ship.*

BOAZ [1244, 1245, *1067, 1078*] (perhaps *in him is strength*).
   1. An ancestor of Jesus (Mt 1:5; Lk 3:32). History of, Ruth (Ru 2-4).
   2. One of Solomon's bronze pillars erected at the temple. It stood on the left (north) side of the porch (1Ki 7:21; 2Ch 3:17).

BOAZ AND JAKIN *See Boaz, 2; Jakin, 2; Temple, Solomon's.*

BOCHERU *See Bokeru.*

BOCHIM *See Bokim.*

BODY [*1061, 1414, 1581, 2728, 5055, 5516, 5577, 5883, 6795, 7007, 10151, *3517, 4773, 4922, 5393*].
   Called: house (2Co 5:1), house of clay (Job 4:19), golden bowl (Ecc 12:6), earthen vessel (2Co 4:7), tabernacle (2Pe 1:13), temple of God (1Co 3:16-17; 6:19), member of Christ (1Co 6:15).
   Perishable (Job 17:14; 1Co 15:53-54). To be consecrated to God (Ro 12:1). To be kept unto holiness (1Co 6:13-20).
   Resurrection of, to a spiritual body (1Co 15:19-54; 2Co 5:14; Php 3:21). *See Resurrection.*

BOHAN [992] (*thumb, big toe*). A Reubenite (Jos 15:6; 18:17).

BOIL [1240, 1418, 1419, 5870, 8409+8410, 8825]. A tumor or running sore. Plague of Egyptians (Ex 9:9-10; Dt 28:27, 35), of the Philistines, (1Sa 5:6, 9; 1Sa 6:5). Of Hezekiah, healed (2Ki 20:7; Isa 38:21). Of Job (Job 2:7-8). Levitical ceremonies prescribed for (Lev 13:18-23).

BOILING POT Parable of (Eze 24:3-5).

BOKERU [1150] (*his first born*). Son of Azel (1Ch 8:38; 9:44).

BOKIM [1141] (*weepings*). A place W of Jordan, near Gilgal (Jdg 2:1, 5).

BOLDNESS OF THE RIGHTEOUS [*3283, *2509, 4244, 4245*].
   Exemplified (Pr 28:1; Ac 18:26; 19:8; Heb 13:6). In prayer (Heb 4:16; 10:19; 1Jn 3:21-22; 5:14-15). Inspired by, fear of the Lord (Pr 14:26). Faith in Christ (Eph 3:12).
   Instances of boldness in prayer: Abraham (Ge 18:23-32). Moses (Ex 33:12-18). In the day of judgment (1Jn 2:28; 4:17). Its effect on others (Ac 4:13).
   See Courage.

BOLSTER *See Pillow.*

BOLT, FIERY (Hab 3:5).

BOND [673, 4593, 5037, *2653, 5278*]. Of the covenant (Eze 20:37), of peace (Eph 4:3). Posting bond (Ac 17:9).

BONDAGE [6268, 6269, 6275, 6285, *1525*]. Of Israelites, in Egypt (Ex 1:14; 2:23; 6:6), in Persia (Ezr 9:9). *See Emancipation; Servant.*

BONDMAN *See Servant.*

BONES [1752, 4157, 6793, 6795, 10150, *4014*]. Vision of the dry (Eze 37:1-14). None of Christ's broken (Ps 34:20; Jn 19:36).

BONNET *See Dress; Turban.*

BOOK [4181, 6219, 10515, *1046, 1047, 3364*]. Genealogies kept in (Ge 5:1). Law of Moses written in (Nu 5:23; Dt 17:18; 31:9, 24, 26; 2Ki 22:8). Topography of Israel, recorded in (Jos 18:9).

Non-biblical books cited in the Bible:
   Book of Jashar (Jos 10:13; 2Sa 1:18), records of Samuel, Nathan, and Gad (1Sa 10:25; 1Ch 29:29), Iddo (2Ch 12:15; 13:22), Isaiah (2Ch 26:22; 32:32; Isa 8:1).

Annals of the Kings of Judah and Israel:
   Of David (1Ch 27:24), Solomon (1Ki 11:41), Jehu (2Ch 20:34), other kings (2Ch 24:27; 16:11; 25:26; 27:7; 28:26; 35:27; 36:8), the kings of Israel (1Ki 14:19; 2Ch 20:34; 33:18).
   Other records kept in (Ezr 4:15; 6:1-2; Est 6:1; 9:32; Jer 32:12; Ac 19:19). Prophecies written in, by Jeremiah (Jer 25:13; 30:2; 45:1; 51:60, 63; Da 9:2). Other prophecies written in (2Ch 33:18-19). Lamentations written in (2Ch 35:25). Numerous (Ecc 12:12). Eating of (Jer 15:16; Eze 2:8-10; 3:1-3; Rev 10:2-10). Of magic (Ac 19:19). Paul's left at Troas (2Ti 4:13).
   Made in a roll (Jer 36:4; Zec 5:1). Sealed (Isa 29:11; Da 12:4; Rev 5:1-5).
   Kiriath Jearim was called Kiriath Sepher, which signifies a city of books (Jos 15:15-16; Jdg 1:11-12).

Figurative:

Of Life: righteous written in (Ex 32:32; Da 12:1; Lk 10:20; Php 4:3; Heb 12:23; Rev 3:5; 21:27), wicked blotted out of (Ex 32:33; Rev 22:18-19), wicked not written in (Rev 13:8; 17:8; 20:15).

Of remembrance (Ps 56:8; 139:16; Mal 3:16; Rev 20:12).

BOOTH [6109, 5468]. Made for shelter (Jnh 4:5), for cattle (Ge 33:17), watchmen (Job 27:18; Isa 1:8; 24:20). Prescribed for the Israelites to dwell in during the Feast of Tabernacles to remember their wanderings in the wilderness (Lev 23:40-43; Ne 8:15-16).

BOOTY [1023, 8965]. Spoils of war. Property and persons were sometimes preserved and sometimes completely destroyed (Jos 6:18-21; Dt 20:14, 16-18). Abraham gave a tenth (Ge 14:20), David ordered that booty be shared with baggage guards (1Sa 30:21-25).

BOOZ See Boaz, 1.

BOR ASHAN [1016] (*pit of smoke*). A town in Judah (1Sa 30:30). Perhaps identical with Ashan (Jos 15:42). See Ain, 1; Ashan.

BORING THE EAR See Piercing the Ear.

BORN AGAIN See New Birth.

BORROWING [4278, 928+5957, 6292, 8626, 1247]. Dishonesty in (Ps 37:21). Obligations in (Ex 22:14-15). Distress from (Ne 5:1-5; Pr 22:7). Compassion toward debtors commanded (Ne 5:6-13). Christ's rule concerning (Mt 5:42).
See Lending; Interest.

Instances of: Israelites from the Egyptians (Ex 3:22; 11:2; 12:35); iron axhead (2Ki 6:5); returned exiles from each other (Ne 5:1-13).

Borrowing trouble. See Security, For Debt.

BOSCATH See Bozkath.

BOSOM [1843, 2668]. Used in the sense of sexual intimacy (Pr 5:20; Eze 23:8, 21). KJV "bosom" is NIV "arms" (Ge 16:5; Nu 11:12; 2Sa 12:3), "side" (Jn 1:18), "next to" (Jn 13:23).

BOSOR See Beor; Bozrah.

BOSS See Shield.

BOTANICAL GARDENS Garden of Eden (Ge 2:8-3:24), of Uzza (2Ki 21:18, 25), king's garden (2Ki 25:4; Ne 3:15 w Ecc 2:5), of Susa (Est 1:5-6;7:7-8).

BOTANY Laws of nature in the vegetable kingdom uniform in action (Mt 7:16-18, 20; Lk 6:43-44; 1Co 15:36-38; Gal 6:7). Lily, beauty of (Mt 6:28-29). The size of the harvest is related to the amount of seed sown (2Co 9:6).
See Algum; Almond; Aloes; Apple; Balm; Barley; Bay Tree; Beans; Bramble; Broom Tree;

Bush; Cane; Caraway; Cassia; Cedar; Cinnamon; Citron Wood; Coriander; Cucumbers; Cummin; Cypress Wood; Date; Ebony; Fig Tree; Fir Tree; Flax; Frankincense; Galbanum; Gall, 3; Garlic; Gourd; Grain; Grass; Gum Resin; Hemlock; Henna Blossoms; Husk; Hyssop; Leek; Lentil(s); Lily; Mandrake; Melon; Millet; Mint; Mulberry Tree; Mustard Seed; Myrrh; Myrtle; Nard; Nettles; Nut; Oak; Olive; Onion; Palm Tree; Perfume; Pine; Plants of the Bible; Pomegranate; Poplar; Reed; Rose; Rue; Salt Herbs; Shittim; Spelt; Sycamore-Fig; Terebinth; Thistle; Thorn; Tree; Vine; Weeds; Wheat; Willow; Wormwood.

BOTCH See Boil.

BOTTLE [1074, 4202+7337]. Perfume bottles (Isa 3:20). See Wine; Wineskin.

BOTTOMLESS PIT See Abyss.

BOUNDARY STONES [1473, 1474]. Stones used, to mark the boundary of property (Jos 13:21), to remove them was forbidden (Dt 27:17).

BOW [995, 2005, 2556, 3857, 4104, 4156, 4798, 5989, 6032, 8000, 8008, 8820, 9413, 2828, 4406, 4749, 5534].

A Weapon:

(Ge 21:16, 20). Made of, bronze (2Sa 22:35; Job 20:24; Ps 18:34), wood (Eze 39:9). Used in war (Isa 13:18; La 2:4; Eze 39:3) and in hunting (Ge 27:3). David's lament of the bow (2Sa 1:18-27). Used by the Elamites (Jer 49:35). See Archery; Arrows.

Figurative:

(Ge 49:24; Job 16:13; 29:20; Ps 78:57; La 3:12; Hos 1:5; Hab 3:9; Rev 6:2).

Rainbow:

A sign from God (Ge 9:8-16). A likeness of God's glory (Eze 1:28; Rev 4:3; 10:1).

BOWELS [5055]. Diseased (2Ch 21:15-20). Judas's gushed out (Ac 1:18).

Figurative: Of the sensibilities (Ge 43:30; 1Ki 3:26; Job 30:27; Ps 22:14; SS 5:4; Jer 4:19; 31:20; La 1:20; Php 1:8; 2:1; Col 3:12; 1Jn 3:17).
See Heart.

BOWING [2556, 4104, 8820]. In worship (2Ch 7:3). See Obeisance; Worship, Attitudes in.

BOWL [*110, 1657, 4094, 4670, 4932, 4984, 3654, 5581, 5786]. Made of gold: for the tabernacle (Ex 25:29; 37:16), temple (1Ki 7:50; 1Ch 28:17; 2Ch 4:8). Of silver (Nu 4:7; 7:13, 19, 25, 31, 37, 43, 49, 55, 61, 67, 73, 79, 84). Stamped "HOLY TO THE LORD" (Zec 14:20-21). See Basin.

Figurative of fragile life (Ecc 12:6).

Symbolic: Of prayer (Rev 5:8). Seven bowls of judgment (Rev 15:7-16:17).

BOX Containing portions of Scripture (Mt 23:5, ftn). See *Jar(s)*.

BOX TREE See *Cypress Wood*.

BOXING Figurative of personal discipline (1Co 9:26-27). See *Games*.

BOZEZ [1010] (*oozing place*). A rock near Gibeah (1Sa 14:4).

BOZKATH [1304] (*[swollen,] elevated spot*). A city of Judah (Jos 15:39; 2Ki 22:1).

BOZRAH [1313] (*enclosure [for sheep], fortress*).
1. A city of Edom (Ge 36:33). Prophecies concerning (Isa 34:6; 63:1; Jer 49:13, 22; Am 1:12).
2. A town of Moab (Jer 48:24).

BRACELET [7543, 9217]. Present of (Ge 24:22). Worn by women (Ge 24:30; Isa 3:19); men, NIV "cord" (Ge 38:18, 25). Dedicated to the tabernacle (Ex 35:22; Nu 31:50). Taken as spoils (Nu 31:50; 2Sa 1:10).
Figurative of God's care for Israel (Eze 16:11).

BRAMBLE [2560]. (Isa 34:13; Lk 6:44). Allegory of (Jdg 9:14-15).

BRANCH [*1936, 2367, 4093, 4751, 5234, 5746, 5916, 6733, 6997, 7542, 7866, 7908, 8585, 10561, *3080, *3097*].

Of Trees:
(Ge 30:37-43). Used in the Feast of Tabernacles (Lev 23:39-43; Ne 8:16-17). At the Triumphal Entry (Mt 21:6-9).

Figurative:
(Pr 11:28; Hos 14:6; Isa 60:21; Jn 15:2-5). Pruning of (Isa 18:5; Da 4:14; Jn 15:6; Ro 11:17, 21). Fruitless, cut off (Jn 15:2, 6). A title of Christ (Ps 80:15; Isa 4:2; 11:1; Jer 23:5; 33:15; Zec 3:8; 6:12). Symbolic name of Joshua (Zec 6:12).
See *Graft*.

BRASS See *Bronze*.

BRAVERY See *Boldness of the Righteous; Courage*.

BRAY [5640]. The sound of a hungry donkey; a metaphor of humans crying out in need (Job 6:5; 30:7).

BRAZEN SEA See *Bronze Basin*.

BRAZEN SERPENT See *Bronze Snake*.

BRAZIER See *Coppersmith; Craftsman; Occupations and Professions*.

BREAD [*4312, 5121, 5174, 6314, *109, *788, *6040*].
Kinds of:
Bread of affliction (1Ki 22:27; Ps 127:2; Hos

9:4; Isa 30:20), leavened (Lev 7:13; 23:17; Hos 7:4; Am 4:5; Mt 13:33), unleavened (Ge 19:3; Ex 29:2; Jdg 6:19; 1Sa 28:24).
Made of wheat flour (Ex 29:2; 1Ki 4:22; 5:11; Ps 81:16), manna (Nu 11:8), meal (1Ki 17:12), barley (Jdg 7:13).

How Prepared:
Mixed with oil (Ex 29:2, 23), honey (Ex 16:31), with yeast. See *Yeast; see above, Kinds of*.
Kneaded (Ge 18:6; Ex 8:3; 12:34; 1Sa 28:24; 2Sa 13:8; Jer 7:18; Hos 7:4).
Made into loaves (1Sa 10:3; 17:17; 25:18; 1Ki 14:3; Mk 8:14), cakes (2Sa 6:19; 1Ki 14:3; 17:12), wafers (Ex 16:21; 29:23).
Baked in ovens (Ex 8:3; Lev 2:4; 7:9; 11:35; 26:26; Hos 7:4), in pans (Lev 2:5, 7; 2Sa 13:6-9), on hearths (Ge 18:6), on coals (1Ki 19:6; Isa 44:19; Jn 21:9).
Made by men (Ge 40:2), women (Lev 26:26; 1Sa 8:13; Jer 7:18). Trade in (Jer 37:21; Mk 6:35-37). Offered in sacrifice (Lev 21:6, 8, 17, 21-22; 22:25; 1Sa 2:36; 2Ki 23:9). By idolaters (Jer 7:18; 44:19).
See *Bread, Consecrated; Offerings*.

Figurative:
(Isa 55:2; 1Co 10:17; 2Co 9:10). Christ: the bread of life (Jn 6:32-59).

Symbolic:
Of the body of Christ (Mt 26:26; Ac 20:7; 1Co 11:23-24).

BREAD, CONSECRATED (1Sa 21:4, 6; 1Ch 28:16; 2Ch 2:4; 29:18; Mt 12:4; Mk 2:26; Lk 6:4; Heb 9:2).
Required to be kept before the LORD continually (Ex 25:30; 2Ch 2:4). Placed on the table "in the Tent of Meeting" (Ex 40:22-23). See *Table of, below*. Ordinance concerning (Lev 24:5-9). Unlawfully eaten by David (1Sa 21:6; Mt 12:3-4; Mk 2:25-26; Lk 6:3-4). Prepared by the Levites (1Ch 9:32; 23:29). Provided by a yearly per capita tax (Ne 10:32-33).

Table of:
(Heb 9:2). Ordinances concerning (Ex 25:23-28; 37:10-15). Its situation in the tabernacle (Ex 26:35; 40:22). Furniture of (Ex 25:29-30; 37:16; Nu 4:7). Consecration of (Ex 30:26-27, 29). How removed (Nu 4:7, 15). For the temple (1Ki 7:48, 50; 2Ch 4:19, 22).

BREAST [1843, 2601, 3751, 4422, 6403, 8716, 8718, *3466, *5111*]. Breast in the Bible can simply refer to the chest area of the body (Lk 18:13). It can also refer to the female mammary glands (Ge 49:25; La 4:3; Lk 23:29), both in nurturing (Ps 22:9; Joel 2:16; Isa 60:16) and erotic contexts (SS 4:5; 7:7; Eze 23:3, 21). To beat one's breast with a fist was a sign of sorrow or repentence (Eze 21:12; Lk 18:13; 23:48). See *Bosom*.

BREASTPLATE [3136, 9234, *2606*].
1. For high priest (Ex 25:7). Directions for the making of (Ex 28:15-30). Made by Bezalel (Ex

31:2-5; 39:8, 21). Freewill offering of materials for (Ex 35:9, 27). Worn by Aaron (Ex 29:5; Lev 8:8).

2. Armor for soldiers (Rev 9:9, 17).
Figurative (Isa 59:17; Eph 6:14; 1Th 5:8).

BREATH
[678, 2039, 3640, 5883, 5972, 8120, *4460, 4466*]. Of life (Ge 2:7; 7:22; Ac 17:25). Of God (2Sa 22:16; Job 4:9; 15:30; 33:4; 37:10; Ps 18:15; 33:6; Isa 30:33).
Figurative (Eze 37:9).

BREECHES
See Dress; Undergarments.

BRETHREN
See Brother; Brothers of Our Lord.

BRIBERY
[4111, 5510, 8815, 8816, 8936, 9556, *5975*]. (Ps 26:9-10; Pr 15:27; Isa 33:15-16). Corrupts conscience (Ge 23:8; Dt 16:18-19; Ecc 7:7). Perverts justice (1Sa 8:1-3; 12:3; Pr 17:23; 28:21; Isa 1:23; 5:22-23; Eze 22:12; Am 5:12; Mic 7:3). Destroys national welfare (Pr 29:4). Profanes God (Eze 13:19). Condemnation of (Job 15:34; Eze 22:12-13). Punishment for (Dt 27:25; Am 2:6).

Instances of:
Delilah (Jdg 16:4-5). Samuel's sons (1Sa 8:1-3). The false prophet, Shemaiah (Ne 6:10-13). Ben-Hadad (1Ki 15:18-19). Haman bribes Xerxes to destroy the Jews (Est 3:8-9). Chief priests bribe Judas (Mt 26:15; 27:3-9; Mk 14:11; Lk 22:5). Soldiers bribed to declare that the disciples stole the body of Jesus (Mt 28:12-15). Felix seeks a bribe from Paul (Ac 24:26).

BRICK
[4236, 4246, 4861]. Used in building: Babel (Ge 11:3), cities in Egypt (Ex 1:11, 14), houses (Isa 9:10), altars (Isa 65:3). Made by Israelites (Ex 5:7-19), slave labor (2Sa 12:31), Ninevites (Na 3:14).

BRICKKILN
See Brick.

BRIDE
[3987, 3994, 4558, 8712, *1222, 3811*]. Presents to (Ge 24:53). Maids of (Ge 24:59, 61; 29:24, 29). Ornaments of (Isa 49:18; 61:10; Jer 2:32; Rev 21:2).
Figurative (Ps 45:10-17; Eze 16:8-14; Rev 19:7-8; 21:2, 9; 22:17).

BRIDECHAMBER
See Bridegroom; Wedding.

BRIDEGROOM
[1033, 3163, *3812, 3813*]. Ornaments of (Isa 61:10). Exempt from military duty (Dt 24:5). Companions of (Jdg 14:11). Joy with (Mt 9:15; Mk 2:19-20; Lk 5:34-35).
Parable of (Mt 25:1-13; SS 4:7-16).
Figurative (Eze 16:8-14).

BRIDGE
"River crossings" (Jer 51:32) may have included bridges or ferries. The Israelites generally crossed streams at a ford (Ge 32:22; 2Sa 19:18).

BRIDLE
[8270+, *5903*]. To control an animal (Ps 32:9; Pr 26:3; Rev 14:20). *See Bit.*
Figurative (2Ki 19:28; Ps 39:1; Jas 1:26).

BRIER
[1402, 2537, 2560, 6141, 6235, 6252, 7853, 9031, *1003*]. Figurative (Isa 5:6; 55:13; Eze 2:6; 28:24).

BRIGANDINE
See Armor.

BRIMSTONE
See Sulfur.

BRONZE
[4607, 5702, 5703, 5733, 10473, *5905, 5909, 5910*]. An alloy of copper and tin. Smelted (Eze 22:20; Job 28:2). Found in Canaan (Dt 8:9; Jos 22:8), Syria (2Sa 8:8). Tyrians traded in (Eze 27:13). Abundance of, for the temple (1Ki 7:47; 1Ch 22:14).

Articles made of:
Altar, vessels, and other articles of the tabernacle and temple (Ex 38:28-31; 1Ki 7:14-47; Ezr 8:27), cymbals (1Ch 15:19), trumpets (1Co 13:1), armor (1Sa 17:5-6; 2Ch 12:10), bows *See Bow*, fetters (Jdg 16:21; 2Ki 25:7), gates (Ps 107:16; Isa 45:2), bars (1Ki 4:13), idols (Da 5:4; Rev 9:20), mirrors (Ex 38:8), household vessels (Mk 7:4).

Workers in: Tubal-Cain (Ge 4:22), Hiram (1Ki 7:13-14), Alexander (2Ti 4:14).

See Bronze Basin; Bronze Sea; Copper; Molding.

Figurative:
(Lev 26:19; Dt 33:25; Isa 48:4; Jer 1:18; Eze 1:7; Da 2:32, 39; 7:19; 10:6; Zec 6:1; Rev 1:15).

BRONZE BASIN
[3963]. Directions for making (Ex 30:18-20). Situation of, in the tabernacle, tent of the congregation, and the altar (Ex 40:7). Sanctified (Ex 30:28; 40:11; Lev 8:11). Used for washing (Ex 40:30-32).
Figurative (Rev 4:6; 15:2, w Ex 38:8).
See Bronze Sea; Tabernacle.

BRONZE SEA
[3542]. Made by Solomon for the temple (1Ki 7:23-26, 30, 38-39; 2Ch 4:2-14). Altered by Ahaz (2Ki 16:17). Broken and carried to Babylon by the Chaldeans (2Ki 25:13, 16; Jer 52:17, 20).
Figurative (Rev 4:6; 15:2, w 1Ki 7:23).
See Bronze Basin; Temple.

BRONZE SNAKE
Made by Moses for the healing of the Israelites (Nu 21:8-9). Worshiped by Israelites (2Ki 18:4). A symbol of Christ's crucifixion (Jn 3:14-15).

BROOK
[4782+4784, 5707]. *See River; River of Egypt.*

BROOM
[4748]. A metaphor of Babylon swept away in judgment (Isa 14:23).

BROOM TREE
[8413]. A desert shrub (1Ki 19:4-5; Job 30:4; Ps 120:4).

BROTH [5348]. (Jdg 6:19-20; 2Ki 4:38; Isa 65:4). Symbolic (Eze 24:5).

BROTHEL See Groves; High Places; Idolatry; Prostitute.

BROTHER [278+, 288, 408, 3303, 3304, 10017, *81, 82, 5789, 5790, 6012*].

Signifies a relative (Ge 14:16; 29:12), a neighbor (Dt 23:7; Jdg 21:6; Ne 5:7), any Israelite (Jer 34:9; Ob 10), an inclusive term for all mankind (Ge 9:5; Mt 18:35; 1Jn 3:15), a companion (2Sa 1:26; 1Ki 13:30; 20:33).

Love of (Pr 17:17; 18:24; SS 8:1). Unfaithful (Pr 27:10). Reuben's love for Joseph (Ge 37:21-22). Joseph's, for his brothers (Ge 43:30-34; 45:1-5; 50:19-25).

A fraternal title, especially among Christians. Instituted by Christ (Mt 12:50; 25:40; Heb 2:11-12). Used by disciples (Ac 9:17; 21:20; Ro 16:23; 1Co 7:12; 2Co 2:13), Peter (1Pe 1:22). Used among the Israelites (Lev 19:17; Dt 22:1-4).

Brother's widow, law concerning Levirate marriage of (Dt 25:5-10; Mt 22:24; Mk 12:19; Lk 20:28).

See Fraternity.

BROTHERLY KINDNESS See Brother; Charitableness; Fellowship; Fraternity; Friendship; Love.

BROTHERS OF OUR LORD

James, Joseph, Simon, and Judas are called the Lord's brothers (Mt 13:55). He also had sisters (Mt 13:56). John records that his brothers did not believe in him (Jn 7:1-10). There are differences of opinion as to whether the "brothers" were full brothers, cousins, or children of Joseph by a former marriage.

BRUISE(S) [2467, 5080, 6700, 7205, 7206, 8368, 8691, *5341*].

1. The so-called law of retaliation was meant to limit the punishment to fit the crime (Ex 21:25). By invoking the law of love, Jesus corrected the popular misunderstanding of the law of retaliation (Mt 5:38-42).

2. Castrated animals were not acceptable sacrifices (Lev 22:24).

3. Wounds inflicted, by shackles (Ps 105:18), because of drunkenness (physical and psychological effects) (Pr 29:35), by God upon Israel, because of the sins of the people, will be healed by the Lord (Isa 30:26). See Bruised Reed, 1.

BRUISED REED

1. Descriptive of someone who is weak; the "servant of the Lord" will mend broken lives (Isa 42:3; Mt 12:20).

2. NIV "splintered reed"; descriptive of depending on weak political alliances rather than relying on the Lord (2Ki 18:21; cf Isa 30:1-5; 31:1-3).

See Bruise(s).

BUBASTIS [7083] (*house of the cat goddess Basht*). One time capital of Lower Egypt; about forty miles NE of Cairo; modern Tel Basta. Prophesied against by Ezekiel (Eze 30:17, ftn). KJV Phi-Beseth.

BUCKET [1932]. For water (Ex 7:19; Nu 24:7; Isa 40:15).

BUCKLER [7558]. See Shield.

BUILDER [*802, 1321, 2941*]. Of the tabernacle. See Bezalel; Master Craftsman. Of the temple (2Ki 12:11; 22:6; Ezr 3:10). Of the wall of Jerusalem (Ne 4:18). Of the church (1Co 3:10). God (Heb 3:4; 11:10). Who rejected the capstone (Ps 118:22; Mt 21:42; Ac 4:11; 1Pe 2:7). See Carpentry; Foundation.

BUILDING [1074, 1215, 1224, 1230, 4445, 4856, 5016, 6590, 10111, 10112, 2224, 3868, 3871, 3869]. The church as God's building (1Co 3:9; Eph 2:21). The eternal body compared to the earthly tent (2Co 5:1).

BUKKI [1321] (*proved of Yahweh* BDB; *mouth [gurgle sounds] of Yahweh* ISBE).

1. Son of Abishua (1Ch 6:5, 51; Ezr 7:4).

2. A prince of Dan (Nu 34:22).

BUKKIAH [1322] (*proved of Yahweh*). A Levite (1Ch 25:4, 13).

BUL [1004]. Month eight in sacred sequence, month two in civil sequence. Also called Marcheshvan (not in Bible). The temple completed in (1Ki 6:38). Jeroboam institutes an idolatrous feast in, to correspond with the Feast of Tabernacles (1Ki 12:32-33). Time for planting wheat and barley (October-November). See Month, 8.

BULL [52, 1330+, 7228, 8802, 10756, *5436*].

Uses of: For sacrifice (Ex 29:3, 10-14, 36; Lev 4:8, 16; Nu 7:87-88; 28:11-31; 29; Heb 9:13; 10:4), plowing (1Sa 14:14; 1Ki 19:19; Pr 14:4; Isa 32:20; Jer 31:18), treading out grain (Dt 25:4), with wagons (Nu 7:3-8; 2Sa 6:3-6).

Laws concerning: trespass by (Ex 21:28-36), theft of (Ex 22:1-10), rest for (Ex 23:12), not to be muzzled when treading grain (Dt 25:4; 1Co 9:9; 1Ti 5:18), not to be yoked with a donkey (Dt 22:10).

Twelve bronze, under the cast metal Sea in Solomon's temple (1Ki 7:25; 2Ch 4:4; Jer 52:20). See Cattle; Offerings.

Symbolic (Eze 1:10; Rev 4:7).

BULRUSH See Papyrus; Reed.

BULWARK (Dt 20:20; 2Ch 26:15; Ecc 9:14). Figurative (Ps 48:13; Isa 26:1).

BUNAH [1007]. Son of Jerahmeel (1Ch 2:25).

BUNNI [1221].

1. A Levite, a teacher with Ezra (Ne 9:4).

2. Ancestor of Shemaiah (Ne 11:15).

3. A family of Jews (Ne 10:15).

BURDEN [*3877, 5362, 6024, 6268, 6673, 6701+6721, 976, 983, 2096, 2915, 5845]. Figurative: Of oppressions (Isa 58:6; Mt 23:4; Lk 11:46; Gal 6:2). Of the prophetic message (Isa 13:1; 15:1; 17:1; 19:1).

BURGLARY See Theft.

BURIAL [*3243, 7690, 7699, 7700, 1946, 1947, 2507, 5313]. Rites of (Jer 34:5). Soon after death (Dt 21:23; Jos 8:29; Jn 19:38-42; Ac 5:9-10). With spices (2Ch 16:14; Mk 16:1; Lk 23:56). Bier used at (2Sa 3:31; Lk 7:14).

Attended by relatives and friends: Of Jacob (Ge 50:5-9), Abner (2Sa 3:31), child of Jeroboam (1Ki 14:13), the son of the widow of Nain (Lk 7:12-13), Stephen (Ac 8:2).

Lack of, a disgrace (2Ki 9:10; Pr 30:17; Jer 16:4; 22:19; Eze 39:15). Directions given about, before death, by Jacob (Ge 49:29-30), Joseph (Ge 50:25). Burial of Gog (multitude) requiring 7 months (Eze 39:12-13).

BURNING [*202, 430, 836+, 1277, 1624, 1730, 2779, 3013, 3019, 3081, 3675, 3678, 3918, 4003, 4805, 6590, 6592, 7787, 8596, 8599, 9462, 2794, 2876, 3906, 4786, 4792, 4796]. As a punishment (Ge 19:28; Jos 6:24; 8:20; 11:13; Jdg 18:27; 1Sa 30:1; 1Ki 9:16; 2Ch 36:19; Job 1:16). See Punishment.

BURNING BUSH The LORD appears to Moses (Ex 3:2-5; Ac 7:30).

BURNT OFFERING See Offerings, Burnt.

BURYING PLACES Bought by Abraham (Ge 23; 25:9). Prepared by Jacob (Ge 50:5), Asa (2Ch 16:14), Joseph (Mt 27:60). On hills (2Ki 23:16; Jos 24:33). In valleys (Jer 7:32).

Family (Ge 47:30; 49:29; Ac 7:16). Of kings (1Ki 2:10; 2Ch 32:33), a place of honor (2Ch 24:16, 25; 21:20). For poor and strangers (Jer 26:23; Mt 27:7).

Tombs: In houses (1Sa 25:1; 1Ki 2:34), gardens (2Ki 21:18, 26; Jn 19:41), caves (Ge 23:9), under trees. Deborah's (Ge 35:8), King Saul's (1Sa 31:13).

Closed with stones (Mt 27:60, 66; Jn 11:38; 20:1). Sealed (Mt 27:66). Marked with pillars: Rachel's (Ge 35:20). Inscriptions (2Ki 23:17). Painted and decorated (Mt 23:27, 29).

Demon-possessed lived in (Mt 8:28). Any who

touched were unclean (Nu 19:16, 18; Isa 65:4). Refused to the dead (Rev 11:9). Robbed (Jer 8:1).

See Cremation; Dead; Death, Physical; Elegy; Grave; Mourning.

Figurative (Isa 22:16; Ro 6:4; Col 2:12).

BUSH [6174, 6899, 8489, 1003+]. Desert shrubs (Ge 21:15; Jer 17:6). See Burning Bush.

BUSHELS [1669+3174]. (Lk 16:7). See Measure.

BUSINESS LIFE

Virtues Found in:

Diligence (Pr 10:4; 13:4; 22:29; 2Pe 3:14). Fidelity (Ge 39:6; 2Ch 34:11-12; Ne 13:13; Da 6:4; 1Co 4:2; Heb 3:5). Honesty (Lev 19:35-36; Dt 25:15; Pr 11:1; Ro 12:17; 13:8). Industry (Ge 2:15; Pr 6:6; 10:5; 12:11; 13:11; 20:13; Ro 12:11). Giving of just weights (Lev 19:36; Dt 25:13; Pr 11:1; 16:11; 20:10; Eze 45:10; Mic 6:11). Integrity (Ps 41:12; Pr 11:3; 19:1; 20:7).

Vices Found in:

Breach of trust (Lev 6:2; SS 1:6; Eze 16:17; Lk 16:12). Dishonesty (Dt 25:13; Pr 11:1; 20:14; 21:6; Hos 12:7). Extortion (Isa 10:2; Eze 22:12; Am 5:11; Mt 18:28; 23:25; Lk 3:13). Fraud (Lev 19:13; Mk 10:19; 1Co 6:8). Unjust gain (Pr 16:8; 21:6; 22:16; Jer 17:11; 22:13; Eze 22:13; Jas 5:4). Slothfulness (Pr 18:9; 24:30-31; Ecc 10:18; 2Th 3:11; Heb 6:12).

BUSYBODY [4318, 4319]. Meddlers denounced (Pr 26:17; 1Ti 5:13; 2Th 3:11-12). Command against (Lev 19:16; 1Pe 4:15).

See Backbiting; Talebearer; Speaking, Evil.

BUTLER (1Ki 10:5; 2Ch 9:4; Ne 1:11; 2:1). Pharaoh's, imprisoned and released (Ge 40). *See Cupbearer.*

BUTTER [2772, 4717]. (Ge 18:8; Dt 32:14; Jdg 5:25; 2Sa 17:29; Job 20:17; Isa 7:15, 22). Made by churning (Pr 30:33).

BUZ [998] (contempt).
1. Son of Nahor (Ge 22:21).
2. Father of Jahdo (1Ch 5:14).

BUZI [1001] (contempt). The father of Ezekiel (Eze 1:3).

BYBLOS See Gebal.

BYWAYS NIV "winding paths," traveled to avoid danger (Jdg 5:6).

C

CAB [7685]. A dry measure containing about two quarts (2Ki 6:25). *See Measure.*

CABBON [3887]. A place in Judah (Jos 15:40).

CABINET Heads of departments in government. David's (2Sa 8:15-18; 15:12; 20:23-26; 1Ch 27:32-34), Solomon's (1Ki 4:1-7), Hezekiah's (Isa 36:3), Artaxerxes' (Ezr 7:14). *See Counselor.*

CABUL [3886] (*good for nothing*).
1. A city in the N of Israel (Jos 19:27).
2. Name given by Hiram to certain cities in Galilee (1Ki 9:13).

CAESAR [2790].
1. Augustus (Lk 2:1).
2. Tiberius (Lk 3:1; 20:22).
3. Claudius (Ac 11:28).
4. Nero (Php 4:22).

CAESAREA [2791]. A seaport in Israel.
Home of Philip (Ac 8:40; 21:8), Cornelius, the centurion (Ac 10:1, 24), Herod (Ac 12:19-23), Felix (Ac 23:23-24).
Paul taken to, by the disciples to save him from his enemies (Ac 9:30), by Roman soldiers to be tried by Felix (Ac 23:23-35).

CAESAREA PHILIPPI [2791+5805]. A city in the N of Israel, visited by Jesus (Mt 16:13; Mk 8:27).

CAGE [3990, 6050]. For birds (Jer 5:27; Rev 18:2).

CAIAPHAS [2780]. High priest (Lk 3:2), son-in-law of Annas (Jn 18:13). Prophesies concerning Jesus (Jn 11:49-51; 18:14). Jesus tried before (Mt 26:2-3, 57, 63-65; Jn 18:24, 28). Peter and other disciples accused before (Ac 4:1-22).

CAIN [7803, 2782] (*metal worker* BDB KB; *brought forth, acquired* Ge. 4:1).
1. Son of Adam (Ge 4:1). Jealousy and crime of (Ge 4:3-15; Heb 11:4; 1Jn 3:12; Jude 11). Settles in the land of Nod (Ge 4:16). Children and descendants of (Ge 4:17-18).
2. *See Kain, 1.*

CAINAN [2783] (*worker in iron, metal worker*).
1. Also called Kenan. Son of Enos (Ge 5:9-15; 1Ch 1:2; Lk 3:37).
2. Son of Arphaxad (Lk 3:36).

CAKES [862, 882, 1811, 2705+, 3924, 5926, 6314, 7540, 7811]. Of unleavened bread (Ex 12:39), mixed with oil for offerings (Ex 29:2), offered to the Queen of Heaven (Jer 7:18); of raisins and figs (1Sa 25:18); of dates (2Sa 6:19); of barley (Eze 4:12).

CALAH [3996] (*strength, vigor*). An ancient city of Assyria (Ge 10:11-12).

CALAMUS [7866]. A sweet cane (SS 4:14; Eze 27:19). An ingredient of the holy ointment (Isa 43:24). Imported (Jer 6:20; Eze 27:19).

CALCOL [4004]. Son of Mahol (1Ki 4:31). Son of Zerah (1Ch 2:6).

CALDRON [1857, 6105, 7831]. In the tabernacle (1Sa 2:14), the temple (2Ch 35:13; Jer 52:18-19). Figurative of judgment (Eze 11:3-11).

CALEB [3979, 3992] (*dog* BDB; *snappish, warding off* KB).
1. Son of Jephunneh. Also spelled Kelubai (1Ch 2:9, ftn). One of the two survivors of the Israelites permitted to enter the land of promise (Nu 14:30, 38; 26:63-65; 32:11-13; Dt 1:34-36; Jos 14:6-15). Sent to Canaan as a spy (Nu 13:6). Brings favorable report (Nu 13:26-30; 14:6-9). Assists in dividing Canaan (Nu 34:19). Life of, miraculously saved (Nu 14:10-12). Leader of the Israelites after Joshua's death (Jdg 1:11-12). Age of (Jos 14:7-10). Inheritance of (Jos 14:6-15; 15:13-16). Descendants of (1Ch 4:15).
2. Third son of Hezron (1Ch 2:9). Ancestor of Bezalel the craftsman who built the tabernacle (1Ch 2:18-20).
3. Brother of Jerahmeel (1Ch 2:42, 50), possibly the same as 1.

CALEB EPHRATHAH [3980]. A place near Bethlehem (1Ch 2:24).

CALENDAR In the biblical era, time was reckoned solely on astronomical observations. Days, months, and years were determined by the sun and moon.
1. Days of the week were not named by the Israelites, but were designated by ordinal numbers. Jewish day began in the evening with the appearance of the first stars. Days were subdivided into hours and watches. Israelites divided nights into three watches (Ex 14:24; Jdg 7:19; Isa 2:19), the Romans four (Mt 14:25).
2. Egyptians had a week of ten days. The seven-day week is of Semitic origin (the Creation account), and ran consecutively irrespective of lunar or solar cycles. This was done for man's physical and spiritual welfare. The biblical records are silent regarding the observance of the Sabbath day from creation to the time of Moses. Sabbath observance was either revived or given special emphasis by Moses (Ex 16:23; 20:8).
3. The Hebrew month began with the new moon.

Before the Exile months were designated by numbers. After the Exile names adopted from the Babylonians were used.

4. The Jewish calendar had two concurrent years, the sacred year, beginning in the spring with the month Nisan, and the civic year, beginning with Tishri (see chart below). The sacred year was instituted by Moses and consisted of lunar months of twenty-nine or thirty days each, with an intercalary month called Adar Sheni added about every three years. Every seventh year was a sabbatical year for the Israelites—a year of solemn rest for landlords, slaves, beasts of burden, and land, and freedom for Hebrew slaves. Every fiftieth year was a Jubilee year, observed by family reunions, canceled mortgages, and return of lands to original owners (Lev 25:8-17).

Synchronized Jewish Sacred Calendar			
Sacred	Name	Modern Equivalent	Civic
1	Nisan	March-April	7
2	Iyyar	April-May	8
3	Sivan	May-June	9
4	Tammuz	June-July	10
5	Ab	July-August	11
6	Elul	August-September	12
7	Tishri	September-October	1
8	Bul	October-November	2
9	Kislev	November-December	3
10	Tebeth	December-January	4
11	Shebat	January-February	5
12	Adar	February-March	6

See Month; Time; also see each month under its respective topic heading.

CALF [1201+1330, 5309, 6319, 8802, *3674, 3675*]. Offered in sacrifice (Mic 6:6). Golden idol, made by Aaron (Ex 32; Dt 9:16; Ne 9:18; Ps 106:19; Ac 7:41).

Images of, set up in Bethel and Dan by Jeroboam (1Ki 12:28-33; 2Ki 10:29). Worshiped by Jehu (2Ki 10:29). Prophecies against the golden calves at Bethel (1Ki 13:1-5, 32; Jer 48:13; Hos 8:5-6; 10:5-6, 15; 13:2; Am 3:14; 4:4; 8:14). Altars of, destroyed (2Ki 23:4, 15-20).

CALKERS *See Caulkers.*

CALL [*606, 887, 2011, 2410, 6386, 7590, 7695, 7837, 7924, 8775, 9005, 10637, 10721, 1639, 3306, 3104, 3189, 1066, 5157, 2126, 2126, 3105, 5888, 4673, 3306, 2813*].

Personal:

By Christ (Isa 55:5; Ro 1:6), his Spirit (Rev 22:17), his works (Ps 19:2-3; Ro 1:20), his ministers (Jer 35:15; 2Co 5:20), his gospel (2Th 2:14).

Is from darkness to light (1Pe 2:9). Addressed to all (Isa 45:22; Mt 20:16). Most reject (Pr 1:24; Mt 20:16). Effective to believers (Ps 110:3; Ac 13:48; 1Co 1:24). Not to many wise by human standards (1Co 1:26). To repentance (Isa 55:1).

To believers is of grace (Gal 1:6; 2Ti 1:9), according to the purpose of God (Ro 8:28; 9:11, 23-24), without repentance (Ro 11:29), high (Php 3:14), holy (2Ti 1:9), heavenly (Heb 3:1), to fellowship with Christ (1Co 1:9), to holiness (1Th 4:7), to a prize (Php 3:14), to liberty (Gal 5:13), to peace (1Co 7:15; Col 3:15), to glory and virtue (2Pe 1:3), to the eternal glory of Christ (2Th 2:14; 1Pe 5:10), to eternal life (1Ti 6:12).

Partakers of justified (Ro 8:30), walk worthy of (Eph 4:1; 2Th 1:11), blessedness of receiving (Rev 19:9), is to be made sure (2Pe 1:10), praise God for (1Pe 2:9), illustrated (Pr 8:3-4; Mt 23:3-9).

Rejected (Jer 6:16; Mt 22:3-7).

Rejection of leads to judicial blindness (Isa 6:9, w Ac 28:24-27; Ro 11:8-10), delusion (Isa 66:4; 2Th 2:10-11), withdrawal of the means of grace (Jer 26:4-6; Ac 13:46; 18:6; Rev 2:5), temporal judgments (Isa 28:12; Jer 6:16, 19; 35:17; Zec 7:12-14), rejection by God (Pr 1:24-32; Jer 6:19, 30), condemnation (Jn 12:48; Heb 2:1-3; 12:25), destruction (Pr 29:1; Mt 22:3-7).

To Special Religious Duty:

Abraham (Ge 12:1-3; Isa 51:2; Heb 11:8). Moses (Ex 3:2, 4, 10; 4:1-16; Ps 105:26; Ac 7:34-35). Aaron and his sons (Ex 4:14-16; 28:1; Ps 105:26; Heb 5:4). Joshua (Nu 27:18-19, 22-23; Dt 31:14, 23; Jos 1:1-9). Gideon (Jdg 6:11-16). Samuel (1Sa 3:4-10). Solomon (1Ch 28:6, 10). Jehu (2Ki 9:6-7; 2Ch 22:7). Cyrus (Isa 45:1-4). Amos (Am 7:14-15). Apostles (Mt 4:18-22; 9:9; Mk 1:16-17; 2:14; 3:13-19; Lk 5:27; 6:13-16; Jn 15:16). The rich young ruler (Mk 10:21-22). Paul (Ac 9:4-6, 15-16; 13:2-3; Ro 1:1; 1Co 1:1; 2Co 1:1; Gal 1:1, 15-16; Eph 1:1; Col 1:1; 1Ti 1:1; 2Ti 1:1).

To All Believers:

(Ro 8:30; 1Co 1:2, 9, 24; 1Th 2:11-12; 2Th 2:13-14; 2Ti 1:9; Heb 3:1-2, 3:7-8; 1Pe 5:10; 2Pe 1:3, 10; Jude 1; Rev 17:14).

See Minister, Call of; Backsliders; Seekers.

CALLING, THE CHRISTIAN (1Co 1:26; Eph 1:18; 4:1; Php 3:14; 1Th 2:12; 2Th 2:14; 2Ti 1:9; Heb 3:1; 1Pe 5:10; 2Pe 1:10). *See Call.*

CALNEH [4011] (*all of them*). Also called Canneh and Calno, a city of Assyria (Ge 10:10; Isa 10:9; Eze 27:23; Am 6:2).

CALNO [4012] (*all of them*). City which tried to resist the Assyrians (Isa 10:9).

CALVARY *See Golgotha.*

CAMEL [1145, 1695, 4140, *2823*]. Herds of (Ge 12:16; 24:35; 30:43; 1Sa 30:17; 1Ch 27:30; Job 1:3, 17; Isa 60:6). Docility of (Ge 24:11).

Uses of: For riding (Ge 24:10, 61, 64; 31:17), posts (Est 8:10, 14; Jer 2:23), drawing chariots (Isa 21:7), for carrying burdens (Ge 24:10; 37:25; 1Ki 10:2; 2Ki 8:9; 1Ch 12:40; Isa 30:6), for cavalry (1Sa 30:17), for milk (Ge 32:15). Forbidden as food (Lev 11:4). Hair of, made into cloth (Mt 3:4;

Mk 1:6). Ornaments of (Jdg 8:21, 26). Stables for (Eze 25:5).

CAMEL'S HAIR [2823]. John the Baptist wore a garment made of camel's hair (Mt 3:4; Mk 1:6). Such garments are still used in the Near East.

CAMON See Kamon.

CAMP [2837, 4328, 4722, 4869, 5046, 5825+, 7155, 8905, 9381, 4213]. Of the Israelites around the tabernacle (Nu 2; 3). See Itinerary.

CAMPHIRE See Henna Blossoms.

CANA [2830] (reed). Marriage at (Jn 2:1-11). Nobleman's son healed at (Jn 4:46-47). Nathanael's home at (Jn 21:2).

CANAAN [4046, 4050, 5913] (land of purple hence merchant, trader).

1. Son of Ham (Ge 9:18, 22, 25-27). Descendants of (Ge 10:6, 15; 1Ch 1:8, 13).

2. Land of (Ge 11:31; 17:8; 23:2). Called Israel (Ex 15:14), the land of Israel (1Sa 13:19), of the Hebrews (Ge 40:15), of the Jews (Ac 10:39), of promise (Heb 11:9), the Beautiful Land (Da 8:9), the holy land (Zec 2:12), the Lord's land (Hos 9:3), Immanuel's land (Isa 8:8), Beulah (Isa 62:4).

Promised to Abraham and his seed (Ge 12:1-7; 13:14-17; 15:18-21; 17:8; Dt 12:9-10; Ps 105:11) and the promise renewed to Isaac (Ge 26:3). Extent of: According to the promise (Ge 15:18; Ex 23:31; Dt 11:24; Jos 1:4; 15:1), after the Conquest by Joshua (Jos 12:1-8), in Solomon's time (1Ki 4:21, 24; 2Ch 7:8; 9:26). Prophecy concerning, after the restoration of Israel (Eze 47:13-20).

Fertility of (Dt 8:7-9; 11:10-13). Fruitfulness of (Nu 13:27; 14:7-8; Jer 2:7; 32:22). Products of: Fruits (Dt 8:8; Jer 40:10, 12), minerals (Dt 8:9). Exports of (Eze 27:17).

Famines in (Ge 12:10; 26:1; 47:13; Ru 1:1; 2Sa 21:1; 1Ki 17). See Famine.

Spies sent into, by Moses (Nu 13:17-29). Conquest of, by the Israelites (Nu 21:21-35; Dt 3:3-6; Jos 6-12; Ps 44:1-3). Divided by lot among the twelve tribes and families (Nu 26:55-56; 33:54; 34:13), by Joshua, Eleazar, and a prince from each tribe (Nu 34:16-29; 35:1-8; Jos 14-19). Divided into twelve provinces by Solomon (1Ki 4:7-19). Into two kingdoms, Judah and Israel (1Ki 11:29-36; 12:16-21). Roman provinces of (Lk 3:1; Jn 4:3-4). See Canaanite(s).

CANAANITE, SIMON THE See Simon, 2; Zealot, Simon the.

CANAANITE(S) [4046, 4050, 5914] (land of purple hence merchant, trader).

Eleven nations descended from Canaan (Ge 10:15-19; Dt 7:1; 1Ch 1:13-16). Territory of (Ge 10:19; 12:6; 15:18; Ex 23:31; Nu 13:29; 34:1-12; Jos 1:4; 5:1), given to the Israelites (Ge 12:6-7; 15:18; 17:8; Ex 23:23; Dt 7:1-3; 32:49; Ps 135:11-12).

Wickedness of (Ge 13:13; Lev 18:25, 27-28;

20:23). To be expelled from the land (Ex 33:2; 34:11). To be destroyed (Ex 23:23-24; Dt 19:1; 31:3-5). Not expelled (Jos 17:12-18; Jdg 1:1-33; 3:1-3). Defeat the Israelites (Nu 14:45; Jdg 4:1-3). Defeated by the Israelites (Nu 21:1-3; Jos 11:1-16; Jdg 4:4-24), by the Egyptians (1Ki 9:16). Chariots of (Jos 17:18).

Isaac forbidden by Abraham to take a wife from (Ge 28:1). Judah marries a woman of (Ge 38:2; 1Ch 2:3). The Jews intermarry with after the Exile (Ezr 9:2).

Prophecy concerning (Ge 9:25-27).

CANANAEAN See Zealot, Simon the.

CANDACE [2833] (roughly queen). Queen of Ethiopia (Ac 8:27).

CANDIDATE Instance of Absalom, campaigning for popular favor (2Sa 15:1-6).

CANDLE See Lamp.

CANDLESTICK See Lampstand.

CANE [5475, 7866]. Probably the sweet calamus (Isa 43:24; Jer 6:20).

CANKER See Gangrene.

CANKERWORM See Locust.

CANNEH [4034]. An alternate form of Calneh. A city of Assyria (Eze 27:23). See Calneh.

CANNIBALISM (Lev 26:29; Dt 28:53-57; 2Ki 6:28-29; Jer 19:9; La 2:20; 4:10; Eze 5:10).

CANONICITY By the canon is meant the list of the books of the Bible recognized by the Christian church as genuine and inspired. The Protestant canon includes thirty-nine books in the OT and twenty-seven in the New. The Roman Catholic canon has fourteen more books and additions to the OT; the Orthodox as many as eighteen. See Apocrypha. The Jewish canon is the same as the Protestant OT. The OT canon was formed before the time of Christ, as is evident from Josephus (Against Apion 1:8), who wrote c. A.D. 90. We know very little of the history of the acceptance of the OT books as canonical. There is much more documentary evidence regarding the formation of the NT canon. The Muratorian Canon (c. A.D. 170), which survives only as a fragment, lists most of the NT books. Some of the books were questioned for a time for various reasons, usually uncertainty of authorship, but by the end of the fourth century our present canon was almost universally accepted, and this was done not by arbitrary decree of bishops, but by the general consensus of the church.

CANTICLES See Song of Solomon.

CAPERNAUM [3019] (village of Nahum). A city on the shore of the Sea of Galilee. Jesus chose, as the place of his abode (Mt 4:13; Lk

4:31). Miracles of Jesus performed at (Mt 9:1-26; 17:24-27; Mk 1:21-45; 2; 3:1-6; Lk 7:1-10; Jn 4:46-53; 6:17-25, 59).

Jesus' prophecy against (Mt 11:23; Lk 10:15).

CAPHTOR [4116]. Place from which the Philistines originally came (Am 9:7), probably from the island of Crete (Jer 47:4; Am 9:7).

CAPHTORITES [4118]. People of Caphtor (Ge 10:14; Dt 2:23; 1Ch 1:12).

CAPITAL [4196, 4638+5477, 7633]. The uppermost member of a column or pilaster crowning the shaft and taking the weight of the entablature (Ex 36:38; 1Ki 7:16-42; 2Ki 25:17; 2Ch 4:12-13; Jer 52:22).

CAPITAL AND LABOR Strife between (Mt 21:33-41; Mk 12:1-9; Lk 20:9-10). See Employee; Employer; Master; Rich, The; Servant.

CAPITAL PUNISHMENT See Punishment.

CAPPADOCIA [2838]. Easternmost Roman province of Asia Minor (Ac 2:9; 1Pe 1:1).

CAPSTONE [7157+8031, 74+8036, 1224+3051]. The keystone of an arch or the last stone put in place to complete a building. Figurative of Jesus: first rejected; finally taking his rightful place of supremacy (Ps 118:22; Zec 4:7; Mt 21:42; Mk 12:10; Lk 20:17; Ac 4:11; 1Pe 2:7). See Cornerstone.

CAPTAIN [1251, 2021+2480+8042, 2980, 6233, 8569+, 8957, 3237, 5130]. Commander-in-chief of an army (Dt 20:9; Jdg 4:2; 1Sa 14:50; 1Ki 2:35; 16:16; 1Ch 27:34). Of the tribes (Nu 2). Of thousands (Nu 31:48; 1Sa 17:18; 1Ch 28:1). Of hundreds (2Ki 11:15). See Centurion. Of fifties (2Ki 1:9; Isa 3:3). Of the guard (Ge 37:36; 2Ki 25:8). Of the ward (Jer 37:13).

Signifying any commander (1Sa 9:16; 22:2; 2Ki 20:5), leader (1Ch 11:21; 12:34; 2Ch 17:14-19; Jn 18:12).

David's captains or chief heroes (2Sa 23; 1Ch 11; 12). King appoints (1Sa 18:13; 2Sa 17:25; 18:1).

Angel of the Lord called (Jos 5:14; 2Ch 13:12). See Armies.

CAPTIVE [*659, 660, 673, 1655, 4334, 4374, 8647, 8660, 8664, 9530, 168, 5197]. Prisoner of war (Ge 14:12; 1Sa 30:1-2).

Cruelty to: Putting to death (Nu 31:9-20; Dt 20:13; 21:10; Jos 8:29; 10:15-40; 11:11; Jdg 7:25; 8:21; 21:11; 1Sa 15:32-33; 2Sa 8:2; 2Ki 8:12; Jer 39:6), 20,000 by Amaziah (2Ch 25:11-12), ripping open pregnant women (2Ki 8:12; 15:16; Am 1:13), enslaved or tortured with picks and axes (2Sa 12:31; 1Ch 20:3), blinded (Jdg 16:21; Jer 39:7), maimed (Jdg 1:6-7), ravished (La 5:11-13; Zec 14:2), enslaved (Dt 20:14; 2Ki 5:2; Ps 44:12;

Joel 3:6), robbed (Eze 23:25-26), confined in pits (Isa 51:14). Other indignities to (Isa 20:4).

Kindness to (2Ki 25:27-30; Ps 106:46). Advanced to positions in state (Ge 41:39-45; Est 2:8; Da 1).

CAPTIVITY [1655, 3448, 8654, 8660, 8664, 168]. Of the, Israelites foretold (Lev 26:33; Dt 28:36), ten tribes (2Ki 17:6, 23-24; 18:9-12).

Of Judah in Babylon, prophecy of (Isa 39:6; Jer 13:19; 20:4; 25:2-11; 32:28), fulfilled (2Ki 24:11-16; 25; 2Ch 36; Jer 52:28-30). Israelites in, promises to (Ne 1:9). Jews return from (Ezr 2; 3; 8).

As a judgment (Ezr 5:12; 9:7; Isa 5:13; Jer 29:17-19; La 1:3-5; Eze 39:23-24).

Figurative:
(Isa 61:1; Ro 7:23; 1Co 9:27; 2Co 10:5; 2Ti 2:26; 3:6). "Take captive your captives" (Jdg 5:12), "led captives in your train" (Ps 68:18; Eph 4:8).

CAR See Beth Car.

CARAVAN [785, 2657]. Company of travelers united together for a common purpose or for mutual protection and generally equipped for a long journey, especially in desert country or through foreign and presumably hostile territory (Ge 32-33; 1Sa 30:1-20).

CARAWAY [7902]. (Isa 28:25-27).

CARBUNCLE NIV "sparkling jewels," (Isa 54:12), "beryl," and "chrysolite." See Beryl; Chrysolite, 1; Minerals of the Bible, 1; Stones.

CARCAS [4139] (perhaps vulture). A eunuch and servant of the Persian king Xerxes (Est 1:10).

CARCASS [1581, 5147, 5577, 7007, 4773]. The dead body of a human or animal. Israelites were ceremonially unclean if they touched a carcass (Lev 11:8-40; Nu 6:6-7; 9:10; Dt 14:8).

CARCHEMISH [4138]. A Babylonian city on the Euphrates, against which the king of Egypt made war (2Ch 35:20; Isa 10:9; Jer 46:2).

CARE [*2011, 3338, 3359, 5466, 7212, 8286, 9068, 2150, 2499, 3508, 5555]. Worldly (Ecc 4:8; Mt 6:25-34; 13:22; Mk 4:19; Lk 8:14; 12:27; 14:18-19; 21:34; 1Co 7:32-33; Php 4:6; 2Ti 2:4). In vain (Ps 39:6; 127:2; Mt 6:27; Lk 12:25-26). Proceeds from unbelief (Mt 6:26, 28-30; Lk 12:24, 27-28), Martha rebuked for (Lk 10:40-41).

Remedy for (Ps 37:5; 55:22; Pr 16:3; Jer 17:7-8; Mt 6:26-34; Lk 12:22-32; Php 4:6-7; Heb 13:5; 1Pe 5:6-7).

Instances of: Martha (Lk 10:40-41). Certain ones who desired to follow Jesus (Mt 8:19-22; Lk 9:57-62).

See Anxiety; Carnal Mindedness; Rich, The; Riches; Worldliness.

CAREAH *See Kareah.*

CARITES [4133]. Mercenary soldiers from Caria in SW Asia Minor (2Ki 11:4, 19).

CARMEL [4150, 4151, 4153] (*orchard planted with vine and fruit trees*).
1. A fertile and lovely mountain in Israel (SS 7:5; Isa 33:9; 35:2; Jer 46:18; 50:19; Am 1:2). Forests of (2Ki 19:23). Caves of (Am 9:3). An idolatrous high place upon; Elijah builds an altar upon, and confronts the worshipers of Baal, putting to death 450 of its prophets (1Ki 18:17-46). Elisha's abode in (2Ki 2:25; 4:25).
2. A city of Judah (Jos 15:55). Saul erects a memorial at (1Sa 15:12). Nabal's possessions at (1Sa 25:2). King Uzziah, who delighted in agriculture, had vineyards at (2Ch 26:10).

CARMELITE [4153]. Hezro, one of David's mighty men, a native of Judean Carmel (1Sa 27:3; 1Ch 11:37).

CARMI, CARMITE [4145, 4146] (possibly *[fruitful] vine, vineyard owner* IDB).
1. Son of Reuben (Ge 46:9; Ex 6:14).
2. Son of Hezron (1Ch 4:1).
3. Father of Achan (Jos 7:1, 18; 1Ch 2:7) and his clan (Nu 26:6).

CARNAL MINDEDNESS Is in conflict with, the inner being (Ro 7:14-22), the Holy Spirit (Gal 5:17). Is at enmity with God (Ro 8:6-8; Jas 4:4). In the children of wrath (Eph 2:3). To be crucified (Ro 8:13; Gal 5:24). Excludes from kingdom of God (Gal 5:19-21). Reaps corruption (Gal 6:8).
See Care, Worldly; Flesh; Riches; Sin, Fruits of; Worldliness.

CARNELIAN [4917]. Seen in John's vision of the glory of God (Rev 4:3) and the foundation of the New Jerusalem (Rev 21:20).
See Minerals of the Bible, 1; Stones.

CARPENTRY [3093, 6770, 5454]. Building the ark (Ge 6:14-16). Tabernacle and furniture of (Ex 31:2-9). *See Tabernacle.* David's palace (2Sa 5:11). Temple (2Ki 12:11; 22:6). *See Temple.* Making idols (Isa 41:7; 44:13). Carpenters (Jer 24:1; Zec 1:20), Joseph (Mt 13:55), Jesus (Mk 6:3).
See Carving; Master Craftsman.

CARPET *See Tapestry.*

CARPUS [2842] (*fruit(ful)*). A Christian at Troas (2Ti 4:13).

CARRIAGE [712, 4753, 4832]. A richly adorned royal means of transportation, a palanquin (SS 3:7, 9-10). In the description of fallen Babylon (Rev 18:13).

CARSHENA [4161] (possibly *black*). A Persian prince (Est 1:14).

CART(S) [5047, 6322]. Vehicle(s) with wheels for carrying goods as well as persons (Ge 45:19, 21; 46:5; 1Sa 6:7-14; 2Sa 6:3; Isa 28:27-28).

CARVING [2977, 2634, 5237, 5381, 6913, 7178, 7180, 7181, 7334, 7338, 7844]. Woodwork of the temple was decorated with carvings of flowers, cherubim, and palm trees (1Ki 6:18, 29, 32, 35; Ps 74:6). Beds decorated with (Pr 7:16). Idols manufactured by (Dt 7:5; Isa 44:9-17; 45:20; Hab 2:18-19).
Persons skilled in: Bezalel (Ex 31:1-5), Huram (1Ki 7:13-51; 2Ch 2:13-14).

CASIPHIA [4085]. A place in the Persian Empire (Ezr 8:17).

CASLUHITES [4078]. A people whose progenitor was a son of Mizraim (Ge 10:14; 1Ch 1:12).

CASSIA [7703, 7904]. An aromatic plant, probably cinnamon (Ps 45:8; Eze 27:19). An ingredient of the sacred oil (Ex 30:24).

CASTING *See Molding.*

CASTING LOTS [*3214, 3721, 5877, 5989, 8959, 965, 1443]. To get a decision from God (Lev 16:8; Jos 18:6-10; 1Sa 14:42; 1Ch 24:31; 26:13-14; Jnh 1:7; Ac 1:26). To set a date (Est 3:7). To settle disputes (Pr 18:18). In divination (Eze 21:21). In gambling (Job 6:27; Ps 22:18; Mt 27:35). The decision is from the LORD (Pr 16:33). *See Lot, The.*

CASTLE *See Fort; Tower.* For the concept "My house is my castle" see Dt 24:10-11.

CASTOR AND POLLUX [1483]. Twin sons of Zeus, Greek gods thought to have power over wind and wave (Ac 28:11).

CATACOMBS Subterranean burial places used by the early church. Most are in Rome, where they extend for 600 miles.

CATERPILLAR(S) *See Grasshopper; Locust.*

CATHOLIC EPISTLES *See General Letters.*

CATHOLICITY (liberality of religious sentiment, inclusiveness).
Taught:
In Christ's reproof of John (Mk 9:38-41; Lk 9:49-50). In Peter's vision of the sheet and visit to Cornelius (Ac 10:1-48). In Paul's commission (Ro 1:1-7, 14-16). In Paul's rebuke of Jewish exclusiveness (Ro 3:20-31; 4:1-25). In the judgment of apostolic church (Ac 15:1-31). In the unity of believers (Ro 5:1-2; Gal 3:27-28; Eph 2:14-17; Col 3:11-15). In the gifts of Holy Spirit to Gentiles as well as to Jews (Ac 10:44-48; 11:17-18).

See Heathen; Strangers.

Instances of:

Solomon, in his prayer (1Ki 8:41-43). Paul, in recognizing devout Gentiles (Ac 13:16, 26, 42-43). Peter (Ac 10:34-35). Rulers of the synagogue at Salamis, permitting the apostles to preach (Ac 13:5).

CATTLE [989+, 1248, 1330, 5238, 8802, 10756, *1091, 3229, 4990*]. Of the bovine species. Used for sacrifice (1Ki 8:63). *See Heifer; Offerings.* Sheltered (Ge 33:17). Pharaoh's dream of (Ge 41:2-7, 26-30). Stall-fed (Pr 15:17).

Gilead adapted to the raising of (Nu 32:1-4), and Bashan (Ps 22:12; Eze 39:18; Am 4:1).

See Animals; Bull; Cow; Heifer; Offerings.

CAUDA [3007]. An island near Crete (Ac 27:16).

CAULKERS [2616]. Those who drive some suitable substance into the seams of a ship's planking to render them watertight (Eze 27:9). *See Pitch; Tar.*

CAUL(S)

1. NIV "covering" of the liver. Burnt with sacrifice (Ex 29:13, 22; Lev 3:4, 10, 15; 4:9; 7:4; 8:16, 25; 9:10, 19).

2. NIV "headbands" (Isa 3:18). *See Headbands.*

CAUSE *See Actions at Law.*

CAUTION [9365, *4133*]. *See Expediency; Prudence.*

CAVALRY [7305, *2689*]. Mounted on, horses (Ex 14:23; 1Sa 13:5; 2Sa 8:4; 1Ki 4:26; 2Ch 8:6; 9:25; 12:3; Isa 30:16; 31:1; Jer 4:29; Zec 10:5; Rev 9:16-18), camels (1Sa 30:17).

See Armies.

CAVE [5117, 5942, 6186, 7074, *5068*]. Used as a dwelling: By Lot (Ge 19:30), Elijah (1Ki 19:9), Israelites (Eze 33:27), believers (Heb 11:38). Place of refuge (Jos 10:16-27; Jdg 6:2; 1Sa 13:6; 1Ki 18:4, 13; 19:9, 13). Burial place (Ge 23:9-20; 25:9; 49:29-32; 50:13; Jn 11:38).

Of Adullam (1Sa 22:1; 2Sa 23:13; 1Ch 11:15). En Gedi (1Sa 24:3-8).

CEDAR [780, 781, 4248]. Valuable for building purposes (Isa 9:10). David's ample provision of, in Jerusalem, for the temple (2Ch 1:15; 22:4). Furnished by Hiram, king of Tyre, for Solomon's temple (1Ki 5:6-10; 9:11; 2Ch 2:16).

Used in rebuilding, the temple (Ezr 3:7), David's palace (2Sa 5:11; 1Ch 17:1), Solomon's palace (1Ki 7:2), masts of ships (Eze 27:5). Used in purifications (Lev 14:4, 6, 49-52; Nu 19:6).

Figurative (Ps 72:16; 92:12; Isa 2:13; 14:8; Jer 22:7; Eze 31:3; Zec 11:2).

CEDRON *See Kidron.*

CEILING [6212, 7771, 7815]. A reference is to the walls of the temple (1Ki 6:15).

CELESTIAL PHENOMENA Fire from heaven, on the cities of the plain (Ge 19:24-25), on the two captains and their fifties (2Ki 1:10-14), on the flocks and servants of Job (Job 1:16). Hail, on the Egyptians (Ex 9:22-34).

Darkness, on the Egyptians (Ex 10:22-23), at the crucifixion of Jesus (Mt 27:45; Lk 23:44-45). Pillar of cloud and fire (Ex 13:21-22; 14:19, 24; 40:38; Nu 9:15-23; Ps 78:14). Thunder and lightning on Mt. Sinai (Ex 19:16, 18; 20:18). Sun stood still (Jos 10:12-13).

Prophecy of darkening of sun, moon, and stars (Joel 2:30, 32; Mt 24:29; Lk 21:25; Ac 2:19-20).

See Astronomy.

CELIBACY (*Abstaining from marriage and sexual activity*). Lamented by Jephthah's daughter (Jdg 11:38-39). Not obligatory (1Co 7:1-9, 25-26; 9:5; 1Ti 4:1-3). Practiced for kingdom of heaven's sake (Mt 19:10-12; 1Co 7:32-40). The 144,000 (Rev 14:1-4).

CELLAR *See Storehouse.*

CENCHREA [3020]. A seaport near Corinth (Ac 18:18; Ro 16:1).

CENSER [4746, 5233, *3338*]. Used for offering incense (Lev 16:12; Nu 16:6-7, 16-18, 46; Rev 8:3). For the temple, made of gold (1Ki 7:50; 2Ch 4:22; Heb 9:4). Those which Korah used were converted into plates (Nu 16:37-39). Used in idolatrous rites (Eze 8:11).

Symbolic: (Rev 8:3, 5).

CENSORIOUSNESS *See Charitableness; Speaking, Evil; Uncharitableness.*

CENSUS [408+6296, 4948, 5031, 5951+8031, 6218+, 7212, *615, 616*]. Numbering of Israel by Moses (Ex 38:26; Nu 1; 3:14-43; 26), David (2Sa 24:1-9; 1Ch 21:1-8; 27:24).

A poll tax to be levied at each (Ex 30:12-16; 38:26).

Of the Roman Empire, by Caesar (Lk 2:1-3).

CENTURION [1672, *3035*] (*ruler over 100*). A commander of 100 soldiers in the Roman army (Mk 15:44-45; Ac 21:32; 22:25-26; 23:17, 23; 24:23). Of Capernaum, comes to Jesus in behalf of his servant (Mt 8:5-13; Lk 7:1-10). In charge of the soldiers who crucified Jesus, testifies, "Truly this was the Son of God" (Mt 27:54; Mk 15:39; Lk 23:47).

See Cornelius; Julius.

CEPHAS [3064] (*rock*). *See Peter, Simon.*

CEREMONIAL WASHING [3200, *49, 968, 2752, 4778*]. The Mosaic Law, relative to cleansing, stresses that sin defiles. To keep this great truth constantly before the Israelites, specific ordinances concerning washings were given to

Moses. The purpose was to teach, by this object lesson, that sin pollutes the soul, and that only those who were cleansed from their sins could be pure in the sight of the Lord (Heb 9:10; 10:22).

Of Garments (Ex 19:10, 14). Of priests (Ex 29:4; 30:18-21; 40:12, 31-32; Lev 8:6; 16:4, 24, 26, 28; Nu 19:7-10, 19; 2Ch 4:6). Of burnt offerings (Lev 1:9, 13; 9:14; 2Ch 4:6). Of the hands (Mt 15:2; Mk 7:2-5; Lk 11:38). Of the feet (1Ti 5:10).

For defilement (Lev 11:24-40). Of lepers (Lev 13:6; 14:9). Of those having bodily discharge (Lev 15:5-13). Of those having eaten or touched that which died (Lev 11:25, 40; 17:15-16).

Traditional forms of, not observed by Jesus (Lk 11:38-39).

See Defilement; Purification; Washings.

CERTIFICATE OF DIVORCE
[6219, 687, 1046]. Given by the husband to his wife upon divorce (Dt 24:1-4; Mt 5:31; 19:7; Mk 10:4). Figurative of God's judgment on Israel (Isa 50:1; Jer 3:8). *See Divorce.*

CESAR *See Caesar.*

CESAREA *See Caesarea.*

CESAREA PHILIPPI *See Caesarea Philippi.*

CHAFF
[3143, 5161, 7990, 10534, 949]. Winnowing of figurative of judgment (Job 21:18; Ps 1:4; 35:5; Isa 17:13; Da 2:35; Hos 13:3; Mt 3:12; Lk 3:17).

CHAINS
[*272, 2414, 4591, 4593, 6310, 9249, 10212, 268, 1301, 1313]. Used as ornaments. Worn by princes (Ge 41:42; Da 5:7, 29), on ankles (Nu 31:50; Isa 3:19), on the breastplate of high priest (Ex 28:14; 39:15). As ornaments on camels (Jdg 8:26). A partition of, in the temple (1Ki 6:21; 7:17).

Used to confine prisoners (Ps 68:6; 149:8; Jer 40:4; Ac 12:6-7; 21:33; 28:20; 2Ti 1:16). *See Fetters.*

Figurative (Ps 73:6; Pr 1:9; La 3:7; Eze 7:23-27; Jude 6; 2Pe 2:4; Rev 20:1).

CHALCEDONY
[5907]. A precious stone (Rev 21:19). *See Minerals of the Bible, 1; Stones.*

CHALCOL *See Calcol.*

CHALDEA
[4169]. The southern portion of Babylonia. Often used interchangeably with Babylon as the name of the empire founded in the valley of the Euphrates. Abraham a native of (Ge 11:28, 31; 15:7). Founded by the Assyrians (Isa 23:13). Character of its people (Hab 1:6).

See Babylon; Chaldeans.

CHALDEAN ASTROLOGERS
See Wise Men.

CHALDEANS
[4169, 5900, 10373].

1. Virtually synonymous with the Babylonians

(2Ki 25:4; 2Ch 36:17; Isa 13:19, ftns). *See Babylon; Chaldea.*

2. Learned and wise men of the east, NIV "astrologers" (Da 2:2, 4, 5, 10; 3:8; 4:7; 5:7).

CHALDEES *See Chaldeans; Ur.*

CHALK [1732]. (Isa 27:9).

CHAMBERING *See Adultery; Fornication.*

CHAMBERLAIN *See Eunuch.*

CHAMBERS OF IMAGERY NIV
"shrine of his own idol." Rooms in the temple where seventy elders of Israel worshiped idols (Eze 8:12).

CHAMELEON
[9491]. Forbidden as food (Lev 11:30).

CHAMOIS NIV "mountain sheep"; permitted as food (Dt 14:5). *See Animals.*

CHAMPAIGN Dt 11:30, KJV. *See Arabah.*

CHAMPIONSHIP
[408+1227+2021, 408+2657, 1475]. Instances of battles decided by: Goliath and David (1Sa 17:8-53). Young men of David's and Abner's armies (2Sa 2:14-17). Representatives of the Philistines' and David's armies (2Sa 21:15-22).

CHANAAN *See Canaan.*

CHANCELLOR A state officer (Ezr 4:8-9, 17). *See Cabinet; Officer.*

CHANGE OF VENUE Granted Paul (Ac 23:17-35). Declined by Paul (Ac 25:9, 11).

CHANGERS OF MONEY See Money Changers.

CHAPITER *See Capital.*

CHAPMAN NIV "merchants" (2Ch 9:14). *See Merchant; Trade and Travel.*

CHARACTER
[2657, 467, 1509, 2302, 2456].

Of Believers:
Attentive to Christ's voice (Jn 10:3-4), blameless and harmless (Php 2:15), bold (Pr 28:1), contrite (Isa 57:15; 66:2), devout (Ac 8:2; 22:13), faithful (Rev 17:14), fearing God (Mal 3:16; Ac 10:2), following Christ (Jn 10:4, 27), godly (Ps 4:3; 2Pe 2:9), without falsehood (Jn 1:47), holy (Dt 7:6; 14:2; Col 3:12), humble (Ps 34:2; 1Pe 5:5), hungering for righteousness (Mt 5:6), just (Ge 6:9; Hab 2:4; Lk 2:25), led by the Spirit (Ro 8:14), generous (Isa 32:8; 2Co 9:13), loathing themselves (Eze 20:43), loving (Col 1:4; 1Th 4:9), lowly (Pr 16:19), meek (Isa 29:19; Mt 5:5), merciful (Ps 37:26; Mt 5:7), new creatures (2Co 5:17; Eph 2:10), obedient (Ro 16:19; 1Pe 1:14), poor in

spirit (Mt 5:3), prudent (Pr 16:21), pure in heart (Mt 5:8; 1Jn 3:3), righteous (Isa 60:21; Lk 1:6), sincere (2Co 1:12; 2:17), steadfast (Ac 2:42; Col 2:5), taught of God (Isa 54:13; 1Jn 2:27), true (2Co 6:8), undefiled (Ps 119:1), upright (1Ki 3:6; Ps 15:2), watchful (Lk 12:37), zealous of good works (Tit 2:14). *See Righteous, Described.*

Of the Wicked:

Abominable (Rev 21:8), alienated from God (Eph 4:18; Col 1:21), blasphemous (Lk 22:65; Rev 16:9), blinded (2Co 4:4; Eph 4:18), boastful (Ps 10:3; 49:6), conspiring against believers (Ne 4:8; 6:2; Ps 38:12), corrupt (Mt 7:17; Eph 4:22), covetous (Mic 2:2; Ro 1:29), deceitful (Ps 5:6; Ro 3:13), delighting in the iniquity of others (Pr 2:14; Ro 1:32), despising believers (Ne 2:19; 4:2; 2Ti 3:3-4), destructive (Isa 59:7), disobedient (Ne 9:26; Tit 3:3; 1Pe 2:7), enticing to evil (Pr 1:10-14; 2Ti 3:6), envious (Ne 2:10; Tit 3:3), evildoers (Jer 13:23; Mic 7:3), fearful (Pr 28:1; Rev 21:8), fierce (Pr 16:29; 2Ti 3:3), foolish (Dt 32:6; Ps 5:5), forgetting God (Job 8:13), fraudulent (Pr 21:8; Isa 57:17), glorying in their shame (Php 3:19), hardhearted (Eze 3:7), hating the light (Job 24:13; Jn 3:20), heady and conceited (2Ti 3:4), hostile to God (Ro 8:7; Col 1:21), hypocritical (Isa 29:13; 2Ti 3:5), ignorant of God (Hos 4:1; 2Th 1:8), impudent (Eze 2:4), infidel (Ps 10:4; 14:1), loathsome (Pr 13:5), lovers of pleasure, not of God (2Ti 3:4), lying (Ps 58:3; 62:4; Isa 59:4), mischievous (Pr 24:8; Mic 7:3), murderous (Ps 10:8; 94:6; Ro 1:29), persecuting (Ps 69:26; 109:16), perverse (Dt 32:5), prayerless (Job 21:15; Ps 53:4), proud (Ps 59:12; Ob 3; 2Ti 3:2), rebellious (Isa 1:2; 30:9), rejoicing in the affliction of believers (Ps 35:15), reprobate (2Co 13:5; 2Ti 3:8; Tit 1:16), selfish (2Ti 3:2), sensual (Php 3:19; Jude 19), sold under sin (1Ki 21:20; 2Ki 17:17), stiff-hearted (Eze 2:4), stiff-necked (Ex 33:5; Ac 7:51), uncircumcised in heart (Jer 9:26), unclean (Isa 64:6; Eph 4:19), unjust (Pr 11:7; Isa 26:18), ungodly (Pr 16:27), unholy (2Ti 3:2), unmerciful (Ro 1:31), unprofitable (Mt 25:30; Ro 3:12), unruly (Tit 1:10), unthankful (Lk 6:35; 2Ti 3:2), unwise (Dt 32:6), without self-control (2Ti 3:3). *See Wicked, Described as.*

Good:

(Pr 22:1; Ecc 7:1). Defamation of, punished (Dt 22:13-19). Revealed in countenance (Isa 3:9).

Steadfastness of:

(Ps 57:7; 108:1; 112:7; Mk 4:20; 2Th 3:3). Exhortations to steadfastness (1Co 7:20; 15:58; 16:13; Eph 4:14-15; Php 1:27; 4:1; Col 1:23; 1Th 3:8; 2Th 2:15; Heb 3:6, 14; 10:23; 13:9; 1Pe 5:9; 2Pe 3:17; Rev 3:11). Reward of steadfastness (Mt 10:22; Jas 1:25). Continuing of (Rev 22:11).

Instances of Steadfastness:

Joseph (Ge 39:12). Moses (Heb 11:24-26). Joshua (Jos 24:15). Daniel (Da 1:8; 6:10). Three Hebrews (Da 3:16-18). Pilate (Jn 19:22). Peter and John (Ac 4:19-20). Paul (Ac 20:22-24; 21:13-14). *See Decision; Stability.*

Instability of:

(Pr 27:8; Jer 2:36; Hos 6:4; 7:8; 10:2; Mt 13:19-22; Mk 4:15-19; Lk 8:5-15; 2Pe 2:14; Rev 2:4). Warnings against (Pr 24:21-22; Lk 9:59-62; Eph 4:14; Heb 6:4-6; 13:9; Jas 1:6-8; 4:8; 2Pe 2:14).

Instances of Instability:

Reuben (Ge 49:3-4). Pharaoh (Ex 8:15, 32; 9:34; 14:5). Israelites (Ex 32:8; Jdg 2:17-19; 2Ch 11:17). Saul (1Sa 18:19). Solomon (1Ki 11:4-8). Rehoboam (2Ch 12:1). Pilate (Jn 18:37-40; 19:1-6). Demas (2Ti 4:10).

CHARASHIM *See Craftsman; Ge Harashim.*

CHARGE Delivered to ministers: *See Ministers.*

CHARGER *See Plate, Platter.*

CHARIOT [1649, 5323, 5324, 8206, 8207, 8208, 8213, 8224, 8957, 761]. For war (Ex 14:7, 9, 25; Jos 11:4; 1Sa 13:5; 1Ki 20:1, 25; 2Ki 6:14; 2Ch 12:2-3; Ps 20:7; Jer 46:9; 47:3; 51:21; Joel 2:5; Na 2:3-4; 3:2). Wheels of Pharaoh's, providentially taken off (Ex 14:25).

Commanded by captains (Ex 14:7; 1Ki 9:22; 22:31-33; 2Ki 8:21). Made of iron (Jos 17:18; Jdg 1:19). Introduced among Israelites by David (2Sa 8:4). Imported from Egypt by Solomon (1Ki 10:26-29). Cities for (1Ki 9:19; 2Ch 1:14; 8:6; 9:25). Royal (Ge 41:43; 46:29; 2Ki 5:9; 2Ch 35:24; Jer 17:25; Ac 8:29). Drawn by camels (Isa 21:7; Mic 1:13).

Kings ride in (2Ch 35:24; Jer 17:25; 22:4). Cherubim in Solomon's temple mounted on (1Ch 28:18).

Figurative:

Chariots of God (Ps 68:17; 104:3; 2Ki 6:17; Isa 66:15; Hab 3:8; Rev 9:9).

Symbolic: (Zec 6:1-8; 2Ki 2:11-12).

CHARISM, CHARISMA, CHARISMATA [5922]. An inspired gift, bestowed on the apostles and early Christians without any claim of merit on the individual's part, for the good of the church (Mt 10:1, 8; Mk 16:17-18; Lk 10:1, 9, 17, 19; Ac 2:4; 10:44-46; 19:6; 1Co 12).

See Gifts From God; Miracles; Spiritual Gifts; Tongues, Gift of.

CHARITABLENESS Encouraged (Pr 10:12; 17:9). Commanded (Mt 5:23-24; 7:1-5; 18:21-22; Lk 6:36-42; 17:3-4; Jn 7:24; Ro 14:1-23; 15:1-2; 1Co 10:28-33; 16:14; 2Co 2:7; Gal 6:1; Eph 4:32; Col 3:13-14; 1Ti 1:5; 4:12; 2Ti 2:22; Jas 2:13; 4:11-12; 1Pe 3:9). Described (1Co 13:1-13). Covers sins (Pr 10:12; 17:9; 19:11; 1Pe 4:8). Pleases God (Mt 6:14-15; 18:23-35).

See Love; Uncharitableness.

CHARITY *See Alms; Beneficence; Liberality; Love.*

CHARMERS AND CHARMING
[1251+4383, 2834, 2858, 4086, 4317, 4318, 4318, 5833]. Prohibited (Dt 18:11). Of serpents (Ps 58:4-5; Jer 8:17). Magic charms and amulets (Pr 17:8; Isa 3:20; Eze 13:18, 20). *See Sorcery.*

CHARRAN *See Haran, 4.*

CHASTISEMENT, FROM GOD
[3519, 3579]. A blessing (Job 5:17; Ps 94:12-13; Heb 12:11). Corrective (Dt 11:2-9; 2Sa 7:14-15; 2Ch 6:24-31; 7:13-14; Job 33:19; 34:31; Ps 73:14; 118:67, 75; Isa 57:16-18; Jer 24:5-6; 46:28; 1Co 11:32).

Inflicted for sins (Lev 26:28; Ps 89:32; 107:10-12, 17; Isa 40:2; Jer 30:14; La 1:5; Hos 7:12; 10:10; Am 4:6). Administered in love (Dt 8:5; Pr 3:11-12; Heb 12:5-10; Rev 3:19).

Repentance under (Ps 106:43-44; 107:10-13, 17-19; Isa 26:16; Jer 31:18-19). Failure to repent under (Isa 42:25; Jer 2:30; Hag 2:17).

Prayer to be spared from (Ps 6:1; 38:1; 107:23-31). Vicariously borne by Jesus (Isa 53:4-5).

See Afflictions; Judgments; Punishment; Wicked, Punishment of.

CHASTITY
Commanded:
(Ex 20:14; Pr 2:10-11, 16-22; 5:3—21; 6:24-25; 7:1-5; 31:3; Mt 5:27-32; Ac 15:20; Ro 13:13; 1Co 6:13-19; 7:1-2, 7-9, 25-26, 36-37; Eph 5:3; Col 3:5; 1Th 4:3, 7).

Instances of:
Joseph (Ge 39:7-20). Boaz (Ru 3:6-13). Job (Job 31:1, 9-12). Paul (1Co 7). The 144,000 (Rev 14:1-5).

See Celibacy; Self-Control.

CHEATING
[5792, 6430, 6943, 9438, *691, 5193*]. *See Dishonesty.*

CHEBAR *See Kebar.*

CHEDORLAOMER *See Kedorlaomer.*

CHEERFULNESS
[3202, 3512, 4401, 8524, *1877+ 2660, 2510, 2659*]. *See Contentment.*

CHEESE
[1482, 2692+3043, 9147] (1Sa 17:18; 2Sa 17:29; Job 10:10).

CHELAL *See Kelal.*

CHELLUH *See Keluhi.*

CHELUB *See Kelub.*

CHELUBAI *See Caleb, 1.*

CHEMARIM
NIV "pagan [priests]" (Zep 1:4). *See Groves; High Places; Idol; Idolatry; Priest, Corrupt.*

CHEMOSH
[4019]. An idol of the Moabites and Ammonites (1Ki 11:7, 33; 2Ki 23:13; Jer 48:7, 13, 46), and Amorites (Jdg 11:24).

CHENAANAH *See Kenaanah.*

CHENANI *See Kenani.*

CHENANIAH *See Kenaniah.*

CHEPHAR-HAAMMONAI *See Kephar Ammoni.*

CHEPHIRAH *See Kephirah.*

CHERAN *See Keran.*

CHERETHIMS, CHERETHITES
See Kerethite(s).

CHERITH *See Kerith.*

CHERUB *See Kerub.*

CHERUBIM
[4131, *5938*]. A classification or order of heavenly beings.

Eastward of the garden of Eden (Ge 3:24).

In the tabernacle (Ex 25:18-20; 37:7-9). Ark rested beneath the wings of (1Ki 8:6-7; 2Ch 5:7-8; Heb 9:5). Figures of, embroidered on walls of tabernacle (Ex 26:1; 36:8), and on the veil (Ex 26:31; 36:35).

In the temple (1Ki 6:23-29; 2Ch 3:10-13). Figures of, on the veil (2Ch 3:14), walls (1Ki 6:29-35; 2Ch 3:7), movable stands (1Ki 7:29, 36).

In Ezekiel's vision of the temple (Eze 41:18-20, 25).

Figurative (Eze 28:14, 16).

Symbolic (Eze 1; 10).

CHESALON *See Kesalon.*

CHESED *See Kesed.*

CHESIL *See Kesil.*

CHEST
[761, 778, 4213, 10249, *3466, 5111*].
1. The ark of the covenant (Ex 25:10-14; Dt 10:1-2).
2. For money (2Ki 12:9-10; 2Ch 24:8-11).
3. The torso (Job 41:24; Da 2:32; Rev 1:13).

CHESTNUT TREE *See Plane Tree.*

CHESULLOTH *See Kesulloth.*

CHEZIB *See Kezib.*

CHICKEN *See Hen, 2.*

CHIDING *See Rebuke.*

CHIDON *See Kidon.*

CHILDBEARING
[2228, 3528, *5349, 5450, 6048*]. Pain of increased as part of the curse (Ge 3:16). Salvation through (1Ti 2:15), a verse of uncertain meaning.

CHILDLESSNESS
[3528+4202, 6829, 6884, 8891, 8897, *866*]. A reproach (Ge 16:2;

29:32; 30:1-3, 13; 1Sa 1:6; Isa 4:1; Lk 1:25). *See Barrenness.*

CHILDREN [*1201, 2446, 3251, 3528, 3528, 3529, 5830, 5853, 6407, 6408, 6884, 8890, 8897, *3758, 4086, 5065, 5448, 5451, 5451, 5626*].

A Blessing:

[Ge 5:29; 30:1; Ps 127:3-5; Pr 17:6). The gift of God (Ge 4:1, 25; 17:16, 20; 22:17; 28:3; 29:32-35; 30:2, 5-6, 17-20, 22-24; 48:9, 16; Ru 4:13; Job 1:21; Ps 107:38, 41; 113:9; 127:3). Promised to the righteous (Dt 7:12, 14; Job 5:25; Ps 128:2-4, 6). Given in answer to prayer to, Abraham (Ge 15:2-5; 21:1-2), Isaac (Ge 25:21), Leah (Ge 30:17-22), Rachel (Ge 30:22-24), Hannah (1Sa 1:9-20), Zechariah (Lk 1:13).

In Infancy:

Circumcision of. *See Circumcision.* Dedicated to God, Samson (Jdg 13:5, 7), Samuel (1Sa 1:24-28), Jesus (Lk 2:22). Nurses for (Ex 2:7-9; Ru 4:16; 2Sa 4:4; 2Ki 11:2; Ac 7:20). Treatment of (Eze 16:4-6; Lk 2:7, 12). Weaning of (Ge 21:8; 1Sa 1:22; 1Ki 11:20; Ps 131:2; Isa 28:9).

In Early Childhood:

Amusements of (Job 21:11; Zec 8:5; Mt 11:16-17; Lk 7:31-32). Early piety of, Samuel (1Sa 2:18; 3), Jeremiah (Jer 1:5-7), John the Baptist (Lk 1:15, 80), Jesus (Lk 2:40, 46-47, 52). Taught to walk (Hos 11:3). Tutored (2Ki 10:1; Ac 22:3; Gal 3:24; 4:1-2). *See Tutor.*

God's Care Of:

(Ex 22:22-24; Dt 10:18; 14:29; Job 29:12; Ps 10:14, 17-18; 27:10; 68:5; 146:9; Jer 49:11; Hos 14:3; Mal 3:5). Blessed by Jesus (Mt 19:13-15; Mk 10:13-16; Lk 18:15-17). Intercessional sacrifices in behalf of (Job 1:5).

Commandments to—

To honor and obey parents (Ex 20:12; Lev 19:3, 32; Dt 5:16; Pr 1:8-9; 6:20-23; 23:22; Mt 15:4; Mk 10:19; Lk 18:20; Eph 6:1, 2-3; Col 3:20; 1Ti 3:4). To seek wisdom (Pr 4:1-11, 20-22; 5:1-2; 8:21-33; 27:11). To praise the Lord (Ps 148:12-13). To remember their Creator (Pr 23:26; Ecc 12:1). To obey (Ps 119:9; Pr 3:1-3; 6:20-25). To be pure (Ecc 11:9-10; La 3:27; 1Ti 4:12; 2Ti 2:22; Tit 2:6). *See Young Men.*

Miracles on behalf of—

Raised from the dead, by Elijah (1Ki 17:17-23), Elisha (2Ki 4:17-36), Jesus (Mt 9:18, 24-26; Mk 5:35-42; Lk 7:13-15; 8:49-56). Healing of (Mt 15:28; 17:18; Mk 7:29-30; 9:23-27; Lk 8:42-56; 9:38-42; Jn 4:46-54).

Prayer in behalf of—

For healing (2Sa 12:16). For divine favor (Ge 17:18). For spiritual wisdom (1Ch 22:12; 29:19). For sins (Job 1:5).

Promises and assurances to—

Promise of divine instruction (Isa 54:13). Long life to the obedient (Ex 20:12; Dt 5:16; Pr 3:1-10; Eph 6:2-3). Love and peace (Pr 8:17, 32; Isa 40:11; 54:13). Acceptance by Jesus (Mt 18:4-5, 10; 19:14-15; Mk 9:37; 10:16; Lk 9:48; 18:15-16).

Joy to parents of wise children (Pr 23:15-16, 24-25; 29:3). Forgiven sins (1Jn 2:12-13).

The righteous, blessed by God—

In escaping judgments (Ge 6:18; 7:1; 19:12, 15-16; Lev 26:44-45; 1Ki 11:13; 2Ki 8:19; Pr 11:21; 12:7). In temporal prosperity (Ge 12:7; 13:15; 17:7-8; 21:13; 26:3-4, 24; Dt 4:37; 10:15; 12:28; 1Ki 15:4; Ps 37:26; 102:28; 112:2-3; Pr 13:22). In divine mercy (Ps 103:17-18; Pr 3:33; 20:7; Isa 44:3-5; 65:23; Jer 32:39; Ac 2:39; 1Co 7:14).

Parental Relationships:

Love of, for parents: Ruth (Ru 1:16-18), Jesus (Jn 19:26-27). Counsel of parents to (1Ki 2:1-4; 1Ch 22:6-13; 28:9-10, 20). Of ministers (1Ti 3:4; Tit 1:6).

Instruction of—

The law (Dt 6:6-9; 11:19-20; 31:12-13; Jos 8:35; Ps 78:1-8). The fear of the Lord (Ps 34:11). The providence of God (Ex 10:2; 12:26-27; 13:8-10, 14-16; Dt 4:9-10; Joel 1:3). Righteousness (Pr 1:1, 4; 22:6; Isa 28:9-10; 38:19). The Scriptures (Ac 22:3; Eph 6:4; 2Ti 3:15).

See Instruction; Tutor; Young Men.

Correction and punishment—

By discipline (Pr 19:18; 23:13; 29:15; Eph 6:4; Col 3:2). By the rod (Pr 13:24; 22:15; 23:13-14; 29:15). By death (Ex 21:15; 21:17; Lev 20:9; Dt 21:21; 27:16; Pr 20:20; 22:15; 30:17; Mt 15:4; Mk 7:10).

Differences and partiality—

Differences made between male and female (Lev 12). Partiality of parents, Rebekah for Jacob (Ge 27:6-17), Jacob for Joseph (Ge 37:3-4). Partiality among, forbidden (Dt 21:15-17).

Death and Mistreatment—

Death, as a judgment upon parents: Firstborn of Egypt (Ex 12:29; Nu 8:17; Ps 78:5), sons of Eli (1Sa 3:13-14), sons of Saul (1Sa 28:18-19), David's child by Uriah's wife (2Sa 12:14-19). Eaten. *See Cannibalism.* Edict to murder: Of Pharaoh (Ex 1:22), Jehu (2Ki 10:1-8), Herod (Mt 2:16-18). Caused to pass through fire (2Ki 16:3; 17:7; Jer 32:35; Eze 16:21). Sacrificed (2Ki 17:31; Eze 16:20-21). Sold for debt (2Ki 4:1; Ne 5:5; Job 24:9; Mt 18:25). Sold in marriage, law concerning (Ex 21:7-11). Instance of Leah and Rachel (Ge 29:15-30).

Religious Involvement:

Attend divine worship (Ex 34:23; Jos 8:35; 2Ch 20:13; 31:16; Ezr 8:21; Ne 8:2-3; 12:43; Mt 21:15; Lk 2:46). Entitled to enjoy religious privileges (Dt 12:12-13). Illegitimate excluded from privilege of congregation (Dt 23:2; Heb 12:8).

Covenant involvement—

Bound by covenants of parents (Ge 17:9-14). Share benefits of parents' covenant privileges (Ge 6:18; 12:7; 13:15; 17:7-8; 19:12; 21:23; 26:3-5, 24; Lev 26:44-45; Isa 65:23; 1Co 7:14). Involved in guilt of parents (Ex 20:5; 34:7; Lev 20:5; 26:39-42; Nu 14:18, 33; 1Ki 16:12; 21:29; Job 21:19; Ps 37:28; Isa 14:20-21; 65:6-7; Jer 32:18; Da 6:24). Not punished for parent's sake (2Ki 14:6; Jer 31:29-30; Eze 18:1-30).

Character of:

Known by conduct (Pr 20:11). Future state (Mt 18:10; 19:14). Status of minors (Gal 4:1-2). Alienated: Ishmael, to gratify Sarah (Ge 21:9-15). Adopted. *See Adoption; Parents.*

Good—

Have Lord's presence (1Sa 3:19). Blessed of God (Pr 3:1-4; Eph 6:2-3). Honor the aged (Job 32:6-7). Honor father (Mal 1:6). A joy to parents (Pr 10:1; 15:20; 23:24; 29:3; 29:17). Keep the law (Pr 28:7). Know the scriptures (2Ti 3:15). Love parents (Ge 46:29). Obey parents (Ge 28:7; 47:30; Pr 13:1), which pleases God (Col 3:20). Attend to parental teaching (Pr 13:1). Partake of God's promises (Ac 2:39). Extol the Savior (Mt 21:15-16; Ps 8:2). Take care of parents (Ge 45:9-11; 47:12; Mt 15:5). Wise (Ecc 4:13).

Illustrative of conversion (Mt 18:3), of a teachable spirit (Mt 18:4). Symbolic of regeneration (Mt 18:2-6, 10; 19:14-15; Mk 9:36-37; 10:13-15; Mk 10:16; Lk 9:46-48; 18:15, 17).

Good, Instances of—

Shem and Japheth (Ge 9:23). Isaac (Ge 22:6-12). Esau (Ge 28:6-9). Jacob (Ge 28:7). Judah (Ge 44:18-34). Joseph (Ge 45:9-13; 46:29; 47:11-12, 29-30; 48:12; 50:1-13). Moses (Ex 15:2; 18:7). Jephthah's daughter (Jdg 11:36-39). Ruth (Ru 1:15-17). Samuel (1Sa 2:26; 3:10). David (1Sa 22:3-4; Ps 71:5, 17). Solomon (1Ki 2:19-20; 3:3-13). Abijah (1Ki 14:13). Obadiah (1Ki 18:12). Jehoshaphat (1Ki 22:43; 2Ch 17:3). The captive maid (2Ki 5:2-4). Jewish children (2Ch 20:13; Ne 8:3; 12:43). Josiah (2Ch 34:1-3). Job (Job 29:4). Elihu (Job 32:4-7). Jeremiah (Jer 1:5-7). The Recabites (Jer 35:18-19). Daniel and the three Hebrews (Da 1:8-20). Children in the temple (Mt 21:15). John (Lk 1:80). Jesus (Lk 2:51-52). Timothy (1Ti 1:5; 3:15).

Wicked—

Disrespectful, to parents (Dt 27:16; Pr 15:20; 30:11; Eze 22:7; Mic 7:6; Job 19:18; 2Ki 2:23). Disobedient to parents (Dt 21:18-21; Pr 13:1; 15:5; 30:13; Ro 1:30; 2Ti 3:2). Defraud parents (Pr 28:7, 24; Mk 7:9-13). Disgrace parents (Pr 10:1; 17:2, 21, 25; 19:13, 26; 23:22). Betray parents (Mk 13:12).

Wicked, Instances of—

Canaan (Ge 4:25). Lot's daughters (Ge 19:14, 30-38). Ishmael (Ge 21:9). Eli's sons (1Sa 2:12, 22-25). Samuel's sons (1Sa 8:3). Absalom (2Sa 15). Adonijah (1Ki 1:5). Abijah (1Ki 15:3). Ahaziah (1Ki 22:52). Children at Bethel (2Ki 2:23-24). Samaritan's descendants (2Ki 17:41). Adrammelech and Sharezer (2Ki 19:37; 2Ch 32:31). Amon (2Ki 21:21).

See Babies; Young Men.

CHILDREN OF GOD *See Righteous.*

CHILEAB *See Kileab.*

CHILION *See Kilion.*

CHILMAD *See Kilmad.*

CHIMHAM *See Kimham.*

CHIMNEY NIV "window" (Hos 13:3). *See Window.*

CHINESE KJV "Sinim" is believed by some to be a reference to the Chinese; NIV has "Aswan" (Isa 49:12). *See Aswan.*

CHINNERETH, CHINNEROTH *See Kinnereth.*

CHIOS *See Kios.*

CHISLEU *See Kislev.*

CHISLON *See Kislon.*

CHISLOTH-TABOR *See Kisloth Tabor.*

CHITTIM *See Kittim.*

CHIUN NIV "pedestal"; perhaps the proper name "Kaiwan" (Am 5:26, ftn). *See Rephan.*

CHLOE [*5951*] (*tender shoot*). A Christian of Corinth (1Co 1:11).

CHOICE [*1040, 1047, 1374, 1405, 2773, 3202, 3359, 3519, 4269, 4334, 4374, 4436, 4458, 8011, 8040, 8603, 145, 1089, 1721, 1723, 1724, 2527*].

Between life and death (Dt 30:19-20). God and false gods (Jos 24:15-18). Judgments by David (2Sa 24:12-14; 1Ch 21:11-13). Between God and Baal (1Ki 18:21, 39-40). Of Moses (Heb 11:24-25).

See Contingencies; Blessings, Spiritual Contingent Upon Obedience.

CHOIR [8876, 9343]. Leaders of (1Ch 25:2-6; Ne 12:42). Presided over by chief musician (Ps 4; Hab 3:19). Instructed by teachers (1Ch 15:22, 27; 25:7-8).

In the tabernacle (1Ch 6:31-47). Composed of singers and instrumentalists (1Ch 15:16-21; 25:1-7; 2Ch 5:12-13; 23:13; Isa 38:20). Mixed choirs (2Ch 35:15, 25; Ezr 2:64-65). Sang every morning and evening (1Ch 9:33; 23:5, 30), during offering of sacrifices (1Ch 16:41-42; 2Ch 29:27-28), at restoration of the temple (Ezr 2:41; 3:10-11), at the dedication of the wall of Jerusalem (Ne 12:27-30). Appointed from the army to sing praises to God as a military strategy (2Ch 20:21).

See Music.

CHOOSING *See Choice.*

CHOR-ASHAN *See Bor Ashan.*

CHORAZIN *See Korazin.*

CHORUSES *See Music.*

CHOSEN [*1405, 3519, 3359, 4334, 1721, 1723, 1724*]. Also referred to as elect (Mt 24:22,

24, 31). Few (Mt 20:16). Called (1Pe 2:9; Rev 17:14).
See Elect; Election; Foreknowledge of God; Predestination.

CHOZEBA *See Cozeba.*

CHRIST [5986] *(the Anointed One). See Jesus the Christ.*

CHRISTIAN [5985] *(follower of Christ).*
Believers called (Ac 11:26; 26:28; 1Pe 4:16). *See Righteous.*

CHRISTIANITY
The word does not occur in the Bible. It was first used by Ignatius, in the first half of the second century. It designates all that which Jesus Christ brings to people of faith, life, and salvation.

CHRISTMAS
The anniversary of the birth of Christ and its observance. The date of the birth of Christ is not known. Celebrated by most Protestants and by Roman Catholics on December 25, by Eastern Orthodox churches on January 6, and by the Armenian church on January 19. The first mention of its observance on December 25 is in the time of Constantine, c. A.D. 325. The word *Christmas* is formed of *Christ* plus *Mass*, meaning a religious service in commemoration of the birth of Christ. It is not clear whether the early Christians thought of or observed Christmas, but once introduced, the observance spread throughout Christendom. Some Christian groups disapprove of the festival.

CHRONICLES, 1 and 2

Author: Anonymous; according to ancient Jewish tradition, Ezra

Date: Latter half of the fifth century B.C.

Outline:

I. Genealogies: Creation to Restoration (1Ch 1-9).
  A. The Patriarchs (ch. 1).
  B. The 12 Sons of Jacob/Israel (2:1-2).
  C. The Family of Judah (2:3-4:23).
  D. The Sons of Simeon (4:24-43).
  E. Reuben, Gad and the Half-Tribe of Manasseh (ch. 5).
  F. Levi and Families (ch. 6).
  G. Issachar, Benjamin, Naphtali, Manasseh, Ephraim and Asher (chs. 7-9).
II. The Reign of David (1Ch 10-29).
  A. Death of Saul (ch. 10).
  B. Capture of Jerusalem; David's Power Base (chs. 11-12).
  C. Return of the Ark; Establishment of David's Kingdom (chs. 13-16).
  D. Dynastic Promise (ch. 17).
  E. David's Conquest (chs. 18-20).
  F. The Census (ch. 21).
  G. Preparations for the Temple (ch. 22).
  H. Organization of the Temple Service (chs. 23-26).
  I. Administrative Structures of the Kingdom (ch. 27).
  J. David's Final Preparations for Succession and the Temple (28:1-29:20).
III. The Reign of Solomon (2Ch 1-9).
  A. The Gift of Wisdom (ch. 1).
  B. Building the Temple (2:1-5:1).
  C. Dedication of the Temple (5:2-7:22).
  D. Solomon's Other Activities (ch. 8).
  E. Solomon's Wisdom, Splendor and Death (ch. 9).
IV. The Schism, and the History of the Kings of Judah (2Ch 10-36).
  A. Rehoboam (chs. 10-12).
  B. Abijah (13:1-14:1).
  C. Asa (14:2-16:14).
  D. Jehoshaphat (17:1-21:3).
  E. Jehoram and Ahaziah (21:4-22:9).
  F. Joash (22:10-24:27).
  G. Amaziah (ch. 25).
  H. Uzziah (ch. 26).
  I. Jotham (ch. 27).
  J. Ahaz (ch. 28).
  K. Hezekiah (chs. 29-32).
  L. Manasseh (33:1-20).
  M. Amon (33:21-25).
  N. Josiah (34:1-36:1).
  O. Josiah's Successors (36:2-14).
  P. Exile and Restoration (36:15-23).

CHRONOLOGY, NEW TESTAMENT

In ancient times historians were not accustomed to recording history under exact dates, but were satisfied when some specific event was related to the reign of a noted ruler or a famous contemporary. Our method of dating events in reference to the birth of Christ was started by Dionysius Exiguus, a monk who lived in the sixth century, but who wrongly calculated Jesus' birth year. The birth of Christ must be dated in or before 5 B.C., as it is known that Herod the Great died in 4 B.C., and according to the Gospels Jesus was born some time before the death of the king. Luke gives the age of Jesus at his baptism as "about thirty years" (Lk 3:23). This would bring the baptism at c. A.D. 26 or 27. Since Herod began the reconstruction of the temple in 20 B.C., the "forty-six years" mentioned by the Jews during the first Passover of Jesus' public ministry (Jn 2:13-22), brings us to A.D. 27 for this first Passover. The ministry of John the Baptist began about the middle of A.D. 26. The time of the Crucifixion is determined by the length of the ministry of Jesus. Mark's Gospel seems to require at least two years. John's Gospel explicitly mentions three Passovers (Jn 2:23; 6:4; 11:55). If the feast (Jn 5:1) is also a Passover, as seems probable, then the length of the ministry of Jesus was a full three years and a little over. This places the Crucifixion at the Passover of A.D. 30.

As for the Apostolic Age the chronological data are very limited and uncertain. The death of Herod Agrippa I in A.D. 44 is one of the fixed dates of the NT. This was the year of Peter's arrest and miraculous escape from prison. The proconsulship of Gallio was between 51 and 53, and this would bring the beginning of Paul's ministry at Corinth to c. A.D. 50. The accession of Festus as governor, under whom Paul was sent to Rome, probably took place c. 59/60.

New Testament Chronology	
Birth of Jesus	7-5 B.C.
Baptism of Jesus	A.D. 26
Crucifixion of Jesus	30
Conversion of Saul	34/35
Death of Herod Agrippa I	44
James written	before 50 (?)
First Missionary Journey	46-48
Galatians written	48/49
Jerusalem Conference	49/50
Second Missionary Journey	50-52
Paul at Corinth	50-52
1 and 2 Thessalonians written	51
Arrival of Gallio as Proconsul	52
Third Missionary Journey	53-57
Paul at Ephesus	54-57
1 and 2 Corinthians written	55
Romans written	57
Paul's Arrest in Jerusalem	57
Imprisonment at Caesarea	57-59
On Island of Malta	59
Arrival at Rome	59
Roman Imprisonment	59-61/62
Colossians, Philemon, Ephesians written	60
Philippians written	61
Paul's Release and Further Work	62-67
1 Timothy and Titus written	63-65
Synoptic Gospels and Acts written	before 67
1 and 2 Peter written	67/68
Peter's Death at Rome	67/68
Paul's Second Roman Imprisonment	67/68
2 Timothy written	67/68
Paul's Death at Rome	67/68
Jude written	c. 65-80
Writings of John	c. 90-100
Death of John	c. 100

CHRONOLOGY, OLD TESTAMENT

For the period from the Creation to the Flood the only Biblical data are the ages of the patriarchs in the genealogical tables of Genesis 5, 7, and 11. Extrabiblical sources for this period are almost completely lacking. For the period from the Flood to Abraham we are again dependent upon the genealogical data in the Bible. The numbers vary in the Masoretic text, the LXX, and the Samaritan Pentateuch. The construction of an absolute chronology from Adam to Abraham is not now possible on the basis of the available data.

The following chart is based on the early date of the Exodus. The later date (c. 1230 B.C.) only affects the dating of the patriarchs and judges.

Old Testament Chronology (From Abraham)	
Abram born	2166 B.C.
Abraham dies	1991
Jacob and family in Egypt	1876
Moses born	1526
The Exodus	1446
Moses dies; Israelites enter Canaan	1406
The Judges	1375-1050
Saul as king	10501010
David as king	1010-970
Solomon as king	970-930
Northern kingdom of Israel	930-722
Southern kingdom of Judah	930-586
Exile	586-538
First return under Zerubbabel	538
Temple rebuilt	536-516
Second return under Ezra	458
Wall of Jerusalem rebuilt	445
Third return under Nehemiah	432
Close of OT history and prophecy	c. 400

For the chronology of the kings, See Kings. For the approximate dates of OT books, see each by name.

CHRYSOLITE [9577, 5994].
1. One of the precious stones set in the priestly breastpiece (Ex 28:17; 39:10).
2. A precious stone used in poetic, prophetic, and apocalyptic literature (SS 5:14; Eze 1:16; 10:9; 28:13; Da 10:6; Rev 21:20).
See Minerals of the Bible, 1; Stones.

CHRYSOPRASE [5995]. A precious
stone (Rev 21:20).
See Minerals of the Bible, 1; Stones.

CHUB *See Libya.*

CHUN *See Cun.*

CHURCH, PLACE OF WORSHIP [1711, 4436].
Note: Nowhere in scripture does the word "church" identify a place of worship, but rather a group (or body) of believers, and only in the NT.

The Place Where God Was Worshiped:

Courts (Ps 65:4; 84:2, 10; 92:13; 96:8; 100:4; 116:19; Isa 1:12; 62:9; Zec 3:7). Holy Oracle (Ps 28:2). Holy place (Ex 28:29; 38:24; Lev 6:16; 10:17; 14:13; 16:2-24; Jos 5:15; 1Ki 8:8; 1Ch 23:32; 2Ch 29:5; 30:27; 35:5; Ezr 9:8; Ps 24:3; 46:4; 68:17; Ecc 8:10; Isa 57:15; Eze 41:4; 42:13; 45:4; Mt 24:15; Ac 6:13; 21:28; Heb 9:12, 25). Holy temple (Ps 5:7; 11:4; 65:4; 79:1; 138:2; Jnh 2:4, 7; Mic 1:2; Hab 2:20; Eph 2:21; 3:17). House of God (Ge 28:17, 22; Jos 9:23; Jdg 18:31; 20:18, 26; 21:2; 1Ch 9:11; 24:5; 2Ch 5:14; 22:12; 24:13; 33:7; 36:19; Ezr 5:8, 15; 7:20, 23;

Ne 6:10; 11:11; 13:11; Ps 42:4; 52:8; 55:14; 84:10; Ecc 5:1; Isa 2:3; Hos 9:8; Joel 1:16; Mic 4:2; Zec 7:2; Mt 12:4; 1Ti 3:15; Heb 10:21; 1Pe 4:17). House of the Lord (Ex 23:19; 34:26; Dt 23:18; Jos 6:24; Jdg 19:18; 1Sa 1:7, 24; 2Sa 12:20; 1Ki 3:1; 6:37; 7:40; 8:10, 63; 10:5; 2Ki 11:3-4, 15, 18-19; 12:4, 9-10, 13, 16; 16:18; 20:8; 23:2, 7, 11; 25:9; 1Ch 6:31; 22:1, 11, 14; 23:4; 26:12; 2Ch 8:16; 26:21; 29:5, 15; 33:15; 34:15; 36:14; Ezr 7:27; Ps 23:6; 27:4; 92:13; 116:19; 118:26; 122:1, 9; 134:1; Isa 2:2; 37:14; Jer 17:26; 20:1-2; 26:2, 7; 28:1, 5; 29:26; 35:2; 36:5-6; 38:14; 41:5; 51:51; La 2:7; Eze 44:4; Hag 1:2; Zec 8:9). House of Prayer (Isa 56:7; Mt 21:13; Mk 11:17; Lk 19:46). My Father's House (Jn 2:16; 14:2).

Sanctuary (Ex 25:8; Lev 19:30; 21:12; Nu 3:28; 4:12; 7:9; 8:19; 10:21; 18:1, 5; 19:20; 1Ch 9:29; 22:19; 24:5; 28:10; 2Ch 20:8; 26:18; 29:21; 30:8, 19; Ne 10:39; Ps 20:2; 28:2; 63:2; 68:24; 73:17; 74:3, 7; 77:13; 78:69; 150:1; Isa 16:12; 63:18; La 2:7, 20; 4:1; Eze 5:11; 42:20; 44:5, 27; 45:3; 48:8, 21; Da 8:11, 13-14; 9:17, 26; 11:31; Heb 8:2; 9:1-2). Tabernacle (Ex 26:1; Lev 26:11; Jos 22:19; Ps 15:1; 61:4; 76:2; Heb 8:2, 5; 9:2, 11; Rev 13:6; 21:3). Temple (1Sa 1:9; 3:3; 2Ki 11:10, 13; Ezr 4:1; Ps 5:7; 11:4; 27:4; 29:9; 48:9; 68:29; Isa 6:1; Mal 3:1; Mt 4:5; 23:16; Lk 18:10; 24:53). Zion (Ps 9:11; 48:11; 74:2; 132:13; 137:1; Isa 35:10; Jer 31:6; 50:5; Joel 2:1, 15).

Buildings: *See Synagogue; Tabernacle; Temple.*

Nature:

Instituted by divine authority (Ex 25:8-9; Dt 12:11-14). Holy (Ex 30:26-29; 40:9; Lev 8:10-11; 16:33; 19:30; 21:12; 26:2; Nu 7:1; 8:19; 1Ki 9:3; 1Ch 29:3; 2Ch 3:8; Isa 64:11; Eze 23:39; 43:12). Should be shown reverence (Lev 19:30; 26:2). Figurative (1Co 3:17).

CHURCH, THE BODY OF
BELIEVERS [1711, 4436] (assembly).

"Church" in this entry encompasses organized bodies of believers in both testaments. In the OT, the church was a group of "gathered together" Hebrew believers, a congregation. In the NT, the church (technically) was a group of "called out" Christian believers.

Called:

In the OT, the congregation, congregation of Israel, or community of Israel (Ex 12:3, 6, 19, 47; 16:1, 2, 9-10, 22; Lev 4:13, 15; 10:17; 24:14). Zion (2Ki 19:21, 31; Ps 9:11; 48:2, 11-12; 74:2; 132:13; 137:1; Isa 35:10; Isa 40:9; 49:14; 51:16; 52:1-2, 7-8; 60:14; 62:1, 11; Jer 31:6; 50:5; La 1:4; Joel 2:1, 15). Also (Ro 9:33; 11:26; 1Pe 2:16). Daughter of Zion (Isa 62:11; Zec 9:9). Also (Mt 21:5; Jn 12:15). In the NT, church (Mt 16:18; 18:17; Ac 2:47; 7:38; 20:28; 1Co 11:18; 14:19, 23, 28, 33-34; 15:9; Gal 1:13; Eph 1:22; 1Ti 3:15).

Described as:

Assembly of believers (Ps 89:7). The upright (Ps 111:1). Body of Christ (1Co 12:27; Eph 1:22-23;

4:12; Col 1:24). Branch of God's planting (Isa 60:21). Bride (Gal 6:16). Bride of Christ (Rev 21:9). Christ's body (Ro 12:5; 1Co 12:12, 27; Eph 1:22-23; 4:12; Col 1:24). Church of God (Ac 20:28). Church of the living God (1Ti 3:15). Church of the firstborn (Heb 12:23). Congregation of Believers (Ps 149:1). Congregation of the Lord's Poor (Ps 74:19). Dove (SS 2:14; 5:2). Family in heaven and earth (Eph 3:15). Flock of God (Eze 34:15; 1Pe 5:2). Fold of Christ (Jn 10:16). General Assembly of the Firstborn (Heb 12:23). The God of Jacob (Isa 2:3). Golden lampstand (Rev 1:20). God's building (1Co 3:9). God's field (1Co 3:9). God's heritage (Joel 3:2; 1Pe 5:3). Habitation of God (Eph 2:22). Heavenly Jerusalem (Gal 4:26; Heb 12:22). Holy City (Rev 21:2). Holy Mountain (Zec 8:3). Holy hill (Ps 2:6; 15:1). House (Heb 3:6). House of God (1Ti 3:15; Heb 10:21). House of Christ (Heb 3:6). Household of God (Eph 2:19). Inheritance (Ps 28:9; Isa 19:25). Israel of God (Gal 6:16). Joy of the whole earth (Ps 48:1-2, 11-13). Kingdom of God (Mt 6:33; 12:28; 19:24; 21:31). Kingdom of heaven (Mt 3:2; 4:17; 5:3, 10, 19-20; 10:7). His kingdom (Ps 103:19; 145:12; Mt 16:28; Lk 1:33). My kingdom (Jn 18:36). Your kingdom (Ps 45:6; 145:11, 13; Mt 6:10; Lk 23:42). Lamb's bride (Eph 5:22-32; Rev 22:17). Lamb's wife (Rev 19:7-9; 21:9). The Lord's portion (Dt 32:9). Lot of God's inheritance (Dt 32:9). Mount Zion (Heb 12:22). Mountain of the Lord's house (Isa 2:2). New Jerusalem (Rev 21:2). Pillar and ground of the truth (1Ti 3:15). Place of God's throne (Eze 43:7). Pleasant portion (Jer 12:10). River of gladness (Ps 46:4-5). Sanctuary of God (Ps 114:2). Sought out, a city not forsaken (Isa 62:12). Spiritual house (1Pe 2:5). Strength and Glory of God (Ps 78:61). Temple of God (1Co 3:16-17). Temple of the Living God (2Co 6:16). Vineyard (Jer 12:10; Mt 21:41).

Discipline:

In the Mosaic Institution—
(Ge 17:14; Ex 12:15; 30:33, 37-38; Lev 7:27; 17:8-9; 19:5-8; 20:18; 22:3; Nu 9:13; 15:31; 19:13, 20; Dt 13:12-18; 17:2—13; 19:16-21; 21:1-9, 18-21; 22:13-29; Ezr 10:7-8).

In the Christian Church—
Designed to save the sinner (Mt 18:15; 1Co 5:1-13; 2Th 3:14). Designed to warn others (1Ti 5:20). Designed to preserve sound doctrine (Ro 16:17; Gal 5:10; 1Ti 1:19-20; Tit 1:13). Exercised with kindness (2Co 2:6-11; Gal 6:1; Jude 22-23). Exercised with forbearance (Ro 15:1-3). Reasons for discipline: Heresy (1Ti 6:3-5; Tit 3:10-11; 2Jn 10-11). Reasons for discipline: Immorality (Mt 18:17-18; 1Co 5:1-7, 11-13; 2Th 3:6). For schism (Ro 16:17). Discipline by reproof (2Co 7:8; 10:1-11; 13:2, 10; 1Th 5:14; 2Th 3:15; 1Ti 5:1-2; 2Ti 4:2; Tit 2:15). Witnesses required in (Mt 18:16; 2Co 13:1; 1Ti 5:19).

Evil Conditions of:

Backslidden (Rev 2:1-5, 12-25; 3:1-4, 14-20). *See Backsliders; Backsliding.* Barren (Mt 21:19-20; Mk 11:13-14; Lk 13:6-9). Corrupt (Isa 5:1-7;

Mt 21:33-46; Mk 12:1-12; Lk 20:9-19). Corruption in (Hos 4:9; Mic 3:1-4, 9, 11; Mt 21:33-41; 23:2-7, 13, 15-33; 26:14-16, 59-68; Mk 12:1-12; 14:10-11; Lk 22:3-6). Dissensions in (1Co 1:11-13; 3:3-4; 11:18-19; 2Co 12:20-21). Divisions in, to be shunned (Ro 16:17; 1Co 1:10; 3:3). Persecution of (Ac 8:1-3; 1Co 15:9; 1Th 2:14-15). See *Persecution.*

God's Care for:

Clothed in righteousness (Rev 19:8). Defended by God (Ps 89:18; Isa 4:5; 49:25; Mt 16:18). Edified by the Word (Ro 12:6; 1Co 14:4, 13; Eph 4:15-16; Col 3:16). Is glorious (Ps 45:13; Eph 5:27). Growth of continuous (Ac 2:47; 5:14; 11:24). Harmonious fellowship (Ps 133:1-3; Jn 13:34; Ac 4:32; Php 1:4; 2:1; 1Jn 3:4). Indwelt by God (Ps 132:14). Loved. See below, *Loved.* Not to be Despised (1Co 11:22). Privileges of (Ps 36:8; 87:5). Provides leaders (Jer 3:15; Eph 4:11-12). Punishment for defiling (1Co 3:17). Safe under God's care (Ps 46:1-2, 5). Triumphant (Gal 4:26; Heb 12:22-23; Rev 3:12; 21:3, 10).

Qualifications for Elders/Overseers and Deacons:		
Self-controlled	Elder	1Ti 3:2; Tit 1:8
Hospitable	Elder	1Ti 3:2; Tit 1:8
Able to teach	Elder	1Ti 3:2; 5:17; Tit 1:9
Not violent but gentle	Elder	1Ti 3:3; Tit 1:7
Not quarrelsome	Elder	1Ti 3:3
Not a lover of money	Elder	1Ti 3:3
Not a recent convert	Elder	1Ti 3:6
Good reputation with outsiders	Elder	1Ti 3:7
Not overbearing	Elder	Tit 1:7
Not quick-tempered	Elder	Tit 1:7
Loves what is good	Elder	Tit 1:8
Upright, holy	Elder	Tit 1:8
Disciplined	Elder	Tit 1:8
Above reproach (blameless)	Elder / *Deacon*	1Ti 3:2; Tit 1:6 / *1Ti 3:9*
Husband of one wife	Elder / *Deacon*	1Ti 3:2; Tit 1:6 / *1Ti 3:12*
Temperate	Elder / *Deacon*	1Ti 3:2; Tit 1:7 / *1Ti 3:8*
Respectable	Elder / *Deacon*	1Ti 3:2 / *1Ti 3:8*
Not given to drunkenness	Elder / *Deacon*	1Ti 3:2; Tit 1:7 / *1Ti 3:8*
Manages his own family well	Elder / *Deacon*	1Ti 3:4 / *1Ti 3:12*
Sees that his children obey him	Elder / *Deacon*	1Ti 3:4-5; Tit 1:6 / *1Ti 3:12*
Does not pursue dishonest gain	Elder / *Deacon*	Tit 1:7 / *1Ti 3:8*
Keeps hold of the deep truths	Elder / *Deacon*	Tit 1:9 / *1Ti 3:9*
Sincere	*Deacon*	*1Ti 3:8*
Tested	*Deacon*	*1Ti 3:10*

Government:

Of the Mosaic Institution: (Dt 17:8-13).

Of the Christian Church:
Authority of apostles (Mt 16:19; Jn 20:23; Ac 1:15, 23-26; 5:1-11; 1Co 7:17; 11:2, 33-34; Gal 2:9). Authority of apostolic council (Ac 15:1-31; 16:4-5). Authority of congregation (1Co 16:3, 16; Jude 22-23). Leadership by apostles. See above, *Authority of apostles.* Leadership by deacons (Ac 6:2-6; 1Ti 3:8-13). Leadership by elders (Ac 14:23; 20:17, 28; 1Ti 5:1, 17, 22; Tit 1:5; Jas 5:14-15; 1Pe 5:1-3). Leadership by overseers (1Ti 3:1-5). *See chart above: Qualifications for Elders/ Overseers and Deacons.* Leadership by prophets and teachers (Ac 13:1, 3, 5; 1Ti 4:14; 2Ti 1:6). Obedience to rulers (Heb 13:17, 24).

Responsibilities of Believers to Leaders—
To encourage (1Co 16:10-11). To esteem (Php 2:29; 1Th 5:12-13; 1Ti 5:17). To imitate the example of (1Co 11:1; Php 3:17; 2Th 3:7; Heb 13:7; 1Pe 5:3). To obey (Heb 13:17). To receive (Php 2:29). To reimburse (1Co 9:7-23; 2Co 12:13; Gal 6:6; Php 4:10-18; 2Th 3:7-9; 1Ti 5:17-18). To seek instruction from (Mal 2:7). Of leaders, to shepherd believers (Ac 20:28).

Loved:

By God (Isa 27:2-3; 43:1-7; 49:14-17; Jer 3:14-15; 13:11). By Christ (Jn 10:8, 11, 14; Eph 5:25-32; Rev 3:9). By believers (Ps 84:1-2; 87:7; 102:14; 137:5; 1Co 12:25; 1Th 4:9). Manifested, by prayer for (Ps 122:6; Isa 62:6). Manifested, by distress at misfortunes of (Ps 137:1-6; Isa 22:4; Jer 9:1; 14:17; 51:50-51; La 2:11; 3:48-51). Manifested, by joy at prosperity of (Isa 66:10, 13-14). Manifested, by zeal for (Isa 58:12; 62:1, 6-7).

New Testament Church:

List of NT Churches—
Antioch (Ac 13:1). Asia (1Co 16:19; Rev 1:4). Babylon (1Pe 5:13). Cenchrea (Ro 16:1). Caesarea (Ac 18:22). Cilicia (Ac 15:41). Corinth (1Co 1:2). Ephesus (Eph 1:22; Rev 2:1). Galatia (Gal 1:2). Galilee (Ac 9:31). Jerusalem (Ac 15:4). Joppa (Ac 9:42). Judea (Ac 9:31). Laodicea (Rev 3:14). Pergamum (Rev 2:12). Philadelphia (Rev 3:7). Samaria (Ac 9:31). Sardis (Rev 3:1). Smyrna (Rev 2:8). Syria (Ac 15:41). Thessalonica (1Th 1:1). Thyatira (Rev 2:18).

Described—
Beneficence of. See *Beneficence; Giving; Liberality.* Christ, the head of (Ps 118:22-23; Isa 28:16; 33:22; 55:4; Mt 12:6, 8; 21:42-43; 23:8, 10; Mk 2:28; 12:10; Lk 6:5; 20:17-18; Jn 13:13; 15:1-8; Ac 2:36; Ro 8:29; 9:5; 1Co 3:11; 11:3; 12:5; Eph 1:10, 22-23; 2:20-22; 4:15; 5:23-32; Col 1:13, 18; 2:10, 19; 3:11; Heb 3:3, 6; 1Pe 2:7; Rev 1:13; 2:1-28; 3:1, 7; 5:6; 21:22-23; 22:16). See *Jesus, Kingdom of.* Community in (Ac 4:32). Decrees of (Ac 15:28-29; 16:4). Design of (Ro 3:2; 9:4; Eph 2:20-22; 1Ti 3:15). Discipline. See above, *Discipline.* Diversity of callings in (1Co 12:5, 28; Eph 4:11-12). Divinely established or instituted (Mt 16:15-18; Eph 2:20-

22; 1Th 1:1; 2Th 1:1; 1Ti 3:15). Founded on the lordship of Christ (Mt 16:18). Duty. *See Responsibilities below.* Edification, by teachers (Eph 4:11-12). By public worship (Col 3:16; Heb 10:25). Government. *See above, Government.* Growth of, rapid (Ac 2:41, 47; 4:4; 5:14; 6:7; 9:35; 11:21, 24; 14:1; 19:17-20). Growth of, cut back (Isa 2:2; Eze 17:22-24; Da 4:35). Holiness of (2Co 11:2; Eph 5:27; 2Pe 3:14; Rev 19:8). Loved. *See above, Loved.* Membership in (Mt 12:50; 19:14; Mk 10:14; Lk 18:16; Jn 15:5-6; Ac 2:41, 47; 4:4; 5:14; 9:35, 42; 11:21; Ro 12:4-5; 1Co 3:11-15; 12:12-28; Eph 4:25; 5:30; Php 4:3; Rev 21:27). Militancy of (SS 6:10; Php 2:25; 2Ti 2:3; 4:7; Phm 2). Mission of. *See below, Mission.* Pastoral care of (Ac 20:28). Responsibilities. *See below, Responsibilities.* Unity of (Ps 133:1; Jn 10:16; 17:11, 21-23; Ro 12:4-5; 1Co 10:17; 12:5, 12-27; Gal 3:26-28; Eph 1:10; 2:14-21; 3:6, 15; 4:4-6, 12-16, 25; Col 3:11, 15). Union of, with Christ (Jn 15:1-7; Ro 11:17; 2Co 11:2; Eph 5:30, 32; Rev 19:7; 21:9). Worship, to be attended (Heb 10:25). To be conducted with order (Ecc 5:1, 3; 1Co 11:4-5, 33; 14:26, 33, 40; 1Ti 3:15).

Mission of—
To be entrusted with the oracles of God (Ro 3:2; 9:4). To bring peace (Ps 22:27-31; Isa 2:2-5; 11:6-9; 52:1, 2, 7-8; 61:1-3; 65:25). To bring spiritual enlightenment (Isa 2:3; 29:18-19; Joel 2:26-32; Hab 2:14; Ac 2:16-21). To bring moral transformation (Isa 4:2-6; 32:3-4, 15-17; 35:1-2, 5-7; 44:3-5; 55:10-13; Zep 3:9). To be the salt and light of the world (Mt 5:13).

Prophecies Concerning—
Its universality (Ge 12:3; Isa 2:2; 40:5; 42:3-4; 45:23; 52:10, 15; 54:1-5; 56:7-8; 59:19; 60:1-9; 66:12, 19, 23; Jer 3:17; 4:2; 16:19; 31:7-9, 34; 33:22; Da 2:35, 44; 7:13-14, 18, 22, 27; Am 9:11-12; Zep 2:11; Zec 9:1, 10; 14:6-9, 16; Mal 1:11; Mt 8:11; Jn 10:16; Rev 11:15; 15:4).

Its prosperity (Ps 72:7-11, 16, 19; 86:9; 102:15-16, 18; 132:15-18; Isa 4:2-6; 25:6-8; 33:20-21; 49:6-12, 13-18; 51:3-8; 52:1-8, 10, 15; 54:1-5, 11-14; 55:5, 10-13; 60:1-9, 19-20; 61:1-11; 62:2-3, 12; 65:18-19, 23-25; 66:12, 19, 23; Jer 31:34; Eze 17:22-24; 34:26, 29-31; 47:3-12; Joel 2:26-32; Am 9:11-12; Mic 4:3-4; 5:2, 4, 7; Hab 2:14; Zep 3:9; Hag 2:7-9; Zec 2:10-11; 6:15; 8:20-23).

Its lasting (Isa 9:7; 33:20; Da 7:14, 27; Mt 16:18; Eph 1:10; Heb 12:23-24, 27-28; Rev 5:10, 13-14; 11:15; 12:10; 15:4; 20:4-6; 21:9-27; 22:1-5). *See Jesus the Christ, Kingdom of.*

State: Relationship of Church and State:

Ecclesiastical Power Superior to Civil—
Appoints kings (1Sa 10:1). Directs administration (1Sa 15:1-4). Reproves rulers (1Sa 15:14-35), withdraws support and anoints a successor (1Sa 16:1-13; 2Ki 9:1-26; 11:4-12). Attempted usurpation of ecclesiastical functions by civil authorities reproved (1Sa 13:8-14; 2Ch 26:16-21).

State Superior to Church—
Evident, in David's appointments (1Ch 23-25; 2Ch 35:4). In Solomon's power (1Ki 2:26-27; 5-

8). In Hezekiah reorganizing temple service (2Ch 31:2-19). In Jeroboam subverting the Jewish religion (1Ki 12:26-33). In Manasseh subverting and restoring the true religion (2Ch 33:2-9, 15-17). In Joash supervising the repairs of the temple (2Ki 12:14-18). In Ahaz transforming the altars (2Ki 16:10-16). In Josiah exercising the function of a priest (2Ch 34:29-33).

State Favorable to the Church—
Cyrus, in proclamation to restore the temple (2Ch 36:22-23; Ezr 1:1-11). Darius, in edict to further restoration of the temple (Ezr 6:1-14). Artaxerxes, in exempting religious institution from taxes (Ezr 7:24).

See Ecclesiasticism; Jesus the Christ, Kingdom of; Ministers; Usurpation, in Ecclesiastical Affairs.

CHURNING [1931, 2816, 4790, 8409, 8088, 10137]. (Pr 30:33). *See Butter.*

CHUSHAN-RISHATHAIM *See Cushan-Rishathaim.*

CHUZA *See Cuza.*

CILICIA [3070]. Maritime province of Asia Minor. Jews dwell in (Ac 6:9). Churches of (Ac 15:23, 41; Gal 1:21). Sea of (Ac 27:5).

CINNAMON [7872, 3077]. A spice (Pr 7:17; SS 4:14; Rev 18:13). An ingredient of the sacred oil (Ex 30:23).

CINNERETH, CINNEROTH *See Kinnereth; Galilee, Sea of.*

CIRCUMCISION [*4576, 213, 4362, 4364].

Institution of (Ge 17:10-14; Lev 12:3; Jn 7:22; Ac 7:8; Ro 4:11). A seal of righteousness (Ro 2:25-29; 4:11). Performed on all males on the eighth day (Ge 17:12-13; Lev 12:3; Php 3:5). Rite of, observed on the Sabbath (Jn 7:23). A prerequisite of the privileges of the Passover (Ex 12:48). Child named at the time of (Ge 21:3-4; Lk 1:59; 2:21). Neglected (Jos 5:7). Covenant promises of (Ge 17:4, 14; Ac 7:8; Ro 3:1; 4:11; 9:7-13; Gal 5:3). Necessity of, falsely taught by Judaizing Christians (Ac 15:1). Paul's argument against the continuance of (Ro 2:25, 28; Gal 6:13). Characterized by Paul as a yoke (Ac 15:10). Abrogated (Ac 15:5-29; Ro 3:30; 4:9-11; 1Co 7:18-19; Gal 2:3-4; 5:2-11; 6:12; Eph 2:11, 15; Col 2:11; 3:11).

Instances of:
Abraham (Ge 17:23-27; 21:3-4). Shechemites (Ge 34:24). Moses (Ex 4:25). Israelites at Gilgal (Jos 5:2-9). John the Baptist (Lk 1:59). Jesus (Lk 2:21). Paul (Php 3:5). Timothy (Ac 16:3).

Figurative:
(Ex 6:12, ftn; Dt 10:16; 30:6; Jer 4:4; 6:10, ftn; 9:26; Ro 2:28-29; 15:8, ftn; Php 3:3; Col 2:11; 3:11).

A designation of the Jews (Ac 10:45; 11:2; Ro

15:8, ftn; Eph 2:11; Col 4:11; Tit 1:10), of Christians (Php 3:3).

CIS *See Kish.*

CISTERN [1014, 1463, 1465]. An artificial reservoir dug in the earth or rock for the collection and storage of water from rain or spring (Pr 5:15; Ecc 12:6; Isa 36:16; Jer 2:13). Cisterns were a necessity in Israel with its long, dry summers. Empty cisterns were sometimes used as prisons (Ge 37:22; Jer 38:6; Zec 9:11). *See Wells.*

Figurative: (2Ki 18:31; Pr 5:15; Ecc 12:6).

CITIES [4448, 6551, 7953, 9133, *4484*]. Ancient (Ge 4:17; 10:10-12). Fortified (Nu 32:36; Dt 9:1; Jos 10:20; 14:12; 2Ch 8:5; 11:10-12; 17:2, 19; 21:3; Isa 23:11). Gates of. *See Gates.*

Designated as:
Royal (Jos 10:2; 1Sa 27:5; 2Sa 12:26; 1Ch 11:7), treasure (Ge 41:48; Ex 1:11; 1Ki 9:19; 2Ch 8:4; 16:4; 17:12), chariot (2Ch 1:14; 8:6; 9:25), merchant (Isa 23:11; Eze 17:4; 27:3).

Town clerk of (Ac 19:35). Government of, by rulers (Ne 3:9, 12, 17-18; 7:2). *See Government.*

Suburbs of (Nu 35:3-5; Jos 14:4).

Watchmen of. *See Watchman.*

Figurative:
(Heb 11:10, 16; 12:22; 13:14).

CITIES OF REFUGE Six cities set apart by Moses and Joshua as places of asylum for those who had accidentally committed manslaughter: Bezer (Benjamin), Ramoth Gilead (Gad), Golan (Manasseh), Hebron (Judah), Shechem (Ephraim), Kedesh (Naphtali). There they remained until a fair trial could be held. If proved innocent of willful murder, they had to remain in the city of refuge until the death of the high priest (Nu 35; Dt 4:43; 9:1-13; Jos 20).

CITIES OF THE PLAIN Cities near the Dead Sea, including Sodom, Gomorrah, Admah, Zeboiim, and Zoar. Lot lived in Sodom (Ge 13:10-12). They were destroyed because of their wickedness (Ge 19). Josephus (Wars, 4.8.4) identified the area of the five cities at the "Lake Asphaltitus" (the Dead Sea) and said traces of the five cities were still visible. No archaeological evidence, however, backs up that siting and so the sites remain unidentified.

CITIZENS [275, 1251, 3782, *4486, 4487, 4871+, 4889, 5232*].

Duties of:
Honors rulers (Ex 22:28; Nu 27:20; Job 34:18; Pr 16:14-15; 24:21; 25:6-7a, 15; Ecc 10:4, 20; Ac 23:5; 1Pe 2:17). Pray for rulers (Ezr 6:10; 1Ti 2:1-2). Promote peace (Jer 29:7). Obey the law (Ezr 7:26; 10:8; Ecc 4). Pay taxes (Mt 17:24-27; 22:17-21; Mk 12:14-17; Lk 20:22-25; Ro 13:5-7).

Rights of:
Public vindication when falsely accused (Ac 16:37). Protection from mob violence (Ac 19:36-41). Fair trial (Ac 22:25-29; 24:18-19; 25:5, 10-11, 16).

Loyal, Instances of:
Israelites (Jos 1:16-18; 2Sa 3:36-37; 15:23, 30; 18:3; 21:17; 1Ch 12:38). David (1Sa 24:6-11; 26:6-16; 2Sa 1:14). Hushai (2Sa 17:15-16). David's soldiers (2Sa 18:12-13; 23:15-16). Joab (2Sa 19:5-6). Barzillai (2Sa 19:32). Jehoiada (2Ki 11:4-12). Isaiah (Isa 22:4). Jeremiah (La 1-5). Mordecai (Est 2:21-23).

Wicked and Treacherous: (Pr 17:11; Pr 19:10, 12; 20:2; 2Ti 3:1-4; 2Pe 2:10; Jude 8).

Instances of—
Miriam and Aaron (Nu 12:1-11). Korah, Dathan, and Abiram (Nu 16:1-35; 26:9). Shechemites (Jdg 9:1-6, 22-25, 46-49). Ephraimites (Jdg 12:1-4). Israelites (1Sa 10:27; 1Ki 12:16-19). Absalom (2Sa 15:10-13). Ahithophel (2Sa 15:12; 17:1-4). Sheba (2Sa 20:1-2). Adonijah (1Ki 1:5-7). Jeroboam (1Ki 11:14-26; 12:20; 2Ch 13:5-9). Baasha (1Ki 15:27). Zimri (1Ki 16:9-10). Jozabad the son of Shimeath and Jehozabad son of Shomer (2Ki 12:19-21; 14:5). Shallum (2Ki 15:10). Menahem (2Ki 15:14). Pekah (2Ki 15:25). Hoshea (2Ki 15:30). Sons of Sennacherib (2Ki 19:37; 2Ch 32:21). Ishmael (Jer 40:14-16; 41). Bigthana and Teresh (Est 2:21). Jews (Eze 17:12-20). Barabbas (Mk 15:7). Theudas and 400 (Ac 5:36-37). An Egyptian (Ac 21:38).

Figurative:
Citizenship in heaven (Eph 2:12, 19; Php 3:20; 1Pe 2:11).

CITRON WOOD [*2591*]. An aromatic wood; KJV "thyine" (Rev 18:12).

CITY CLERK [*1208*]. An official in Greco-Roman cities of the first century, as at Ephesus (Ac 19:35-41).

CITY OF DAVID
1. Jebusite stronghold of Zion captured by David and made by him his royal residence (2Sa 5:6-9).
2. Bethlehem, the home of David (Lk 2:4).

CITY OF DESTRUCTION A city of Egypt; exact location unknown (Isa 19:18, ftn). Some mss of the Massoretic Text, Dead Sea Scrolls, and the Vulgate have "City of the Sun" (Heliopolis). *See Heliopolis.*

CIVIL DAMAGES *See Damages and Compensations.*

CIVIL ENGINEERING (Jos 18:9; Job 28:9-11).

CIVIL SERVICE School for (Da 1:3-21). Appointment in, on account of merit (Ge 39:1-6, 17-21; 41:38-44; 1Ki 11:28; Est 6:1-11; Da 1:7, 17-21; 6:1-3; Mt 25:14-15, 23-30; Lk 19:12-27). Corruption in (Ne 5:15; Da 6:4-17; Mk 15:15; Ac 24:26). Reform in (Ne 4:14-15). Influence in (1Ki 1:5-40; 2Ki 4:13; Mt 20:20-23; Mk 10:35).

CLAIRVOYANCE See Sorcery.

CLAP [4673, 5782, 6215, 8492, 8562, 9546].
Clapping in joy (2Ki 11:12), in praise (Ps 47:1), in astonishment (Job 21:5), in scorn (Job 27:23; 34:37), in praise (Ps 98:8; Isa 55:12).

CLASP [7971, 8562, 3195].
1. Used to fasten the curtains on the tabernacle (Ex 26:6, 11, 33; 35:11, 13, 18, 33).
2. To shake hands in agreement and pledge for some obligation (Isa 2:6 w Pr 6:1).
3. Worshipers clasped Jesus' feet (Mt 28:9).

CLAUDA See Cauda.

CLAUDIA [3086] (possibly lame). A female disciple (2Ti 4:21).

CLAUDIUS [3087]. The fourth Roman emperor (c. A.D. 41-54). The famine foretold by Agabus took place in his reign (Ac 11:28). He banished all Jews from Rome (Ac 18:2).

CLAUDIUS LYSIAS [3087, 3385]. A Roman military officer (Ac 21:31-40; 22:23-30). Had Paul transferred from Jerusalem to Caesarea and wrote a letter to Governor Felix in order to protect him from an assassination plot (Ac 23:10-35; 24:7, ftn; 24:22).

CLAY [141, 824, 2817, 3084, 3226, 4246, 4879, 6760, 10279, 4017, 5878]. Man formed from (Job 33:6). Seals made of (Job 38:14). Used by a potter (Isa 29:16; 41:25; 45:9). Blind man's eyes anointed with (Jn 9:6).
Figurative (Job 4:19; Ps 40:2; Isa 45:9; 64:8; Jer 18:6; Ro 9:21).
Symbolic (Da 2:33-41).

CLAY TABLETS Made of clay which, while still wet, had wedge-shaped letters imprinted on them with a stylus, and then were kiln-fired or sun-dried. They were made of various shapes, and were often placed in a clay envelope. Vast quantities have been excavated in the Near East. The earliest examples date to 3000 B.C.

CLEAN AND UNCLEAN ANIMALS See Animals; Birds; Fish; Insects.

CLEANLINESS [430, 2342, 2899, 3196, 3197, 3198, 3200, 5470, 5929, 5931, 49, 2751, 2754, 2755, 4924].Taught by frequent washings. See Purification; Washing. Regulation relating to, in camp (Dt 23:12-14).
Figurative (Ps 51:7, 10; 73:1; Pr 20:9; Isa 1:16; Eze 36:25; 1Jn 1:7, 9; Rev 1:5).
See Sanitation and Hygiene

CLEANSING See Washing.

CLEANTHES The son of Phanius of Assos and head of the Stoic school in Athens from 263-232 B.C. His poem, Hymn to Zeus, is quoted by Paul before the Areopagus Court (Ac 17:28). He made Stoicism more religious in its orientation by teaching that the universe was a living being, that God was its soul, and that the sun was its heart. He taught detachment from moral concerns. Doing good for gain was like feeding cattle for meat. He also maintained that evil thoughts were worse than evil deeds, just as a tumor which does not break open is more dangerous than one which does.
See Aratus; Asceticism; Stoicism; Stoics.

CLEMENCY Of David toward disloyal subjects: Shimei (2Sa 16:5-13; 19:16-23), Amasa (2Sa 19:13, w 2Sa 17:25).
Divine. See God, Longsuffering of, and Mercy of; Kindness.

CLEMENT [3098] (mild). A disciple at Philippi (Php 4:3).

CLEOPAS [3093] (renowned father). A disciple to whom Jesus appeared after his resurrection (Lk 24:18).

CLEOPHAS See Clopas.

CLERGYMAN See Deacon; Elders; Minister; Pastor; Overseer.

CLERK [1208]. Town (Ac 19:35).

CLOAK [168, 955, 2668, 4064, 4762, 5077, 5516+, 8100, 8515, 8529, 2668, 5742]. Outer garment, not to be taken in pledge for a loan (Ex 22:26-27). Elijah's (1Ki 18:46; 19:13); used in calling Elisha (1Ki 19:19); parting the Jordan (2Ki 2:8; 2Ki 2:14); passes to Elisha (2Ki 2:13). Jesus' touched by the woman; her bleeding healed (Mt 9:20-21). Paul's left at Troas (2Ti 4:13).
Figurative of a curse (Ps 109:19).

CLOPAS [3116]. Husband of Mary (Jn 19:25). See Mary, 2.

CLOSET See Room.

CLOTH [955, 1865, 3156, 4802, 8391, 8529, 9271, 9418, 4527, 4820, 4984, 5051, 5058]. Parable of old and new (Mt 9:16). Burial (Mt 27:59; Mk 15:46).

CLOTHING [*955, 4229, 4252, 4860, 8515, 8529, 10382, 10383, 1218, 1903, 1907, 2264, 2668, 2669, 4314]. Of the Israelites, did not wear out (Dt 8:4; 29:5; Ne 9:21). See Dress.

CLOUD [2613, 5366, 5368, 5955, 6265, 6380, 6727, 6729, 6882, 6906, 6940, 7798, 8836, 10560, 3749, 3751].

Pillar of, With Fire:
Symbolic of the Lord's presence (Ex 13:21-22; 16:10; 19:9, 16; 24:16-18; 33:9-10; 34:5; Lev 16:2; Nu 11:25; 12:5, 10; 14:10; 16:19, 42; Dt 31:15; 1Ki 8:10-11; 2Ch 7:1-3; Isa 6:1, 4; Mt 17:5; Lk 9:34-35; 1Co 10:1). A guide to Israel (Ex 14:19, 24; 40:36-38; Nu 9:15-23; 10:11-12, 33-

36; Dt 1:33; Ne 9:12, 19; Ps 78:14; 105:39; Isa 4:5). In Isaiah's prophecy (Isa 4:5). In Ezekiel's vision (Eze 10:3-4, 18-19; 11:22-23).
Figurative (Jer 4:13; Hos 6:4; 13:3).
Symbolic (Rev 14:14).
See Celestial Phenomena.

CLOUT See Dress.

CLUB [4751, 5138, 5151, 8657, 9371, 3833].
War club or club used by shepherds (2Sa 23:21; Job 41:29; Pr 25:18; Jer 51:20; Eze 39:9).

CNIDUS [3118] (age). A city in Asia Minor (Ac 27:7).

CO-HEIRS [5169]. As God's children, Christians share in Christ's glory (Ro 8:17). See Inheritance.

COAL [836, 1624, 1625, 7073, 8363, 471, 472]. The Bible never refers to true mineral coal, which has not been found in Israel proper. The references are always either to charcoal or to live embers of any kind. Hebrews usually used charcoal for warmth or cooking (Isa 47:14; Jn 18:18; 21:9).
Figurative (Pr 25:22).
Symbolic (Isa 6:6-7; 2Sa 14:7).

COAL OIL See Oil.

COAT OF ARMOR (1Sa 17:5, 38; 1Ki 22:34; 2Ch 18:33). See Armor.

COBRA [7352]. A poisonous snake (Dt 32:33; Pr 23:32). Venom of, illustrates the speech of the wicked (Ps 58:4). Child playing with illustrates Messianic age (Isa 11:8-9).
See Serpent; Viper.

COCK See Birds; Rooster.

COCK CROWING See Rooster.

COCKATRICE See Viper.

COCKLE See Weeds.

COELE-SYRIA (hollow Syria). A name for that part of Syria that lay between the Lebanon and Anti-Lebanon Mountains.

COERCION Religious: Penalty for (Ex 22:20). Oath against (2Ch 15:12-15).
Instances of (Da 3:2-6, 29; 6:26-27).
See Bigotry; Intolerance.

COFFER See Chest, 2; Treasury.

COFFIN [778, 5049]. Joseph placed in for burial (Ge 50:26). See Burial.

COIN [736, 1324, 1534, 3047, 3321, 3790, 5088]. See Money.

COL-HOZEH [3997] (every seer). Father of Baruch (Ne 11:5).

COLLAR [7023, 9389]. See Dress.

COLLECTION [7689, 3356]. Of money for the poor.
See Alms; Beneficence; Giving; Liberality.

COLLEGE NIV "Second District" of the city of Jerusalem (2Ki 22:14; 2Ch 34:22). See School.

COLLOP NIV "bulges" of fat (Job 15:27).

COLLUSION In Sin (Lev 20:4-5). See Complicity; Connivance.

COLONIZATION Of conquered countries and people (2Ki 17:6, 24; Ezr 4:9-10).

COLORS, FIGURATIVE AND SYMBOLIC [2635, 7389, 8391].
Black:
Of affliction (Job 3:5; Ps 107:10-11; 143:3; Isa 9:19; 24:11). Of calamity (Isa 5:30; 8:22; 50:3; Joel 2:6, 10; 3:14-15; Na 2:10). Of the day of wrath (Zep 1:14-15). Of death (Job 10:20-22; Am 5:8). Of the abode of the lost (Mt 8:12; 22:13; 25:30; 2Pe 2:4; Jude 13; Rev 16:10).
Blue:
Of deity (Ex 25:3-4; 26:1; 28:28, 37; 38:18; 39:1-5, 21, 24, 29, 31; Nu 4:5-12; 15:38-40; 2Ch 2:7, 14; 3:14). Of royalty (Est 8:15; Eze 23:6). Predominant color in drapery and furnishings of the tabernacle, and in clothing of the priests (Ex 24:10; Jer 10:9; Eze 1:26; 10:1).
Crimson, Red, Purple, and Scarlet:
Of iniquity (Isa 1:18; Rev 17:3-4; 18:12, 16). Of prosperity (2Sa 1:24; Pr 31:21; La 4:5). Of conquest (Isa 63:2; Na 2:3; Rev 12:3). Of royalty (Jdg 8:26; Da 5:7, 16, 29; Mt 27:28). Types and shadows of the Atonement (Ex 25:3-5; 26:1, 14, 31, 36; 27:16; 28:4-6, 8, 15, 31, 33, 37; 35:5-7, 23-25, 35; 36:8, 19, 35, 37; 38:23; 39:1-43; Lev 14:4, 6, 49-52; Nu 4:7-8 13; 19:2, 5-6; Isa 63:1-3; Heb 9:19-23).
White:
Of Holiness (Lev 16:4, 32; Ps 51:7; Ecc 9:8; Isa 1:18; Da 7:9; 11:35; 12:10; Mt 17:1-2; 28:2-3; Mk 9:3; Rev 1:13-14; 2:17; 3:4-5, 18; 4:4; 6:2, 11; 7:9, 13-14; 15:6; 19:8, 11, 14; 20:11). Choir singers arrayed in white (2Ch 5:12).

COLOSSE [3145] (punishment). A city of Phrygia (Col 1:2, 7-8).

COLOSSIANS, BOOK OF
Author: The apostle Paul
Date: c. A.D. 60
Outline:
I. Introduction (1:1-14).
   A. Greetings (1:1-2).
   B. Thanksgiving (1:3-8).
   C. Prayer (1:9-14).
II. The Supremacy of Christ (1:15-23).

III. Paul's Labor for the Church (1:24-2:7).
   A. A Ministry for the Sake of the Church (1:24-29).
   B. A Concern for the Spiritual Welfare of His Readers (2:1-7).
IV. Freedom From Human Regulations Through Life With Christ (2:8-23).
   A. Warning to Guard Against the False Teachers (2:8-15).
   B. Pleas to Reject the False Teachers (2:16-19).
   C. An Analysis of the Heresy (2:20-23).
V. Rules for Holy Living (3:1-4:6).
   A. The Old Self and the New Self (3:1-17).
   B. Rules for Christian Households (3:18-4:1).
   C. Further Instructions (4:2-6).
VI. Final Greetings (4:7-18).

COLT [912+1201, 6555, *4798*]. Ridden by Jesus (Mt 21:2, 5, 7; Mk 11:2; Jn 12:15).

COMFORT [5653, 5714, 5717, 5719, 5739, 5764, *4151, 4155, 4170, 4171, 4172, 4219*]. *See Affliction, Consolation Under; Righteous, Promises to.*

COMFORTER *See God, Grace of; Holy Spirit.*

COMMANDMENT [1821, 5184, *1953*]. Used in the English Bible to translate a number of Hebrew and Greek words meaning law, ordinance, statute, word, judgment, precept, saying, charge, etc.

COMMANDMENTS AND STATUTES, OF GOD

Admonishing Against:

Backsliding (Dt 8:11-17; 28:18; Eze 33:12-13, 18; Lk 9:62; 1Co 10:12; Heb 3:12-13; 12:15; 2Pe 2:20-21). Conspiracy (Ex 23:1-2). Hypocrisy (Mt 6:1-5, 16; Lk 20:46-47; 1Pe 2:1). Lusts (Pr 31:3; Ro 13:13-14; Gal 5:16; 1Pe 2:11). Oppression of foreigners (Ex 22:21; 23:9; Dt 24:14; Zec 7:10). Popular corruption (Ex 23:2). Reviling rulers (Ex 22:28; Ac 23:5).

Concerning:

Children, commanding obedience to parents (Pr 6:20; Eph 6:1-3; Col 3:20). *See below, Commanding Reverence for Parents.* Debtors' protection (Dt 24:10, 12-13). Father's concern for children (Eph 6:4; Col 3:21). A husband's love for his wife (Eph 5:23; Col 3:19), honor for his wife (1Pe 3:7). Permanence of marriage (Ge 2:24; Mt 19:6; Mk 10:9; 1Co 7:1-16). Lost property (Ex 23:4; Dt 22:1-3). Man's supremacy over animals (Ge 9:2). Masters', equity (Col 4:1), humane treatment of servants (Eph 6:9). Ministers (Ac 20:31; 1Ti 1:4; 3:2-13; 4:12-16; 5:20-22; 2Ti 2:1-3, 14-16, 22-24; Tit 1:5-9; 2:1-10, 15; 1Pe 5:2-3). Faithfulness (Col 4:17; 1Ti 6:11-12, 14; 2Ti 1:8, 13). Fortitude (2Ti 2:3). Foolish questions (2Ti 2:23). Sanctification (1Th 4:3). Strife (2Ti 2:24). Places of public worship

(Dt 12:11). Restitution (Ex 21:30-36; 22:1-15; Lev 6:4-5; 24:18; Nu 5:7). Servants' obedience (Eph 6:5-8; Col 3:22-25; Tit 2:9-10; 1Pe 2:18-19). Vicious animals (Ex 21:28-32, 35-36). Wives' obedience (Eph 5:22; Col 3:18; 1Pe 3:1-4). Women (Eph 5:22, 24; Tit 2:3-5; 1Pe 3:1-3). Young men's parental obedience (Pr 6:20; 23:22).

The Decalogue: (Ex 20:3-17; Dt 5:6-21). *See Decalogue; Tablets of the Law.*

Commanding:

Hate, of the abominations of the wicked (Dt 7:25-26). Hatred of evil (Ro 12:9-21). Abiding in Christ (Jn 15:4, 9; 1Jn 2:28). Abstinence from evil (1Th 5:22). Accord with Christ, and concord with one another (Php 2:2-5). Admonition and encouragement (1Th 5:14). Altruistic service (Mt 20:26; Mk 9:35; 10:42-45; Lk 22:26; Jn 13:14; Ro 15:1-2; 1Co 10:24; Gal 6:10; Php 2:3-4). Assistance to the distressed (Ps 82:4; Pr 24:11).

Building a sanctuary (Ex 25:8). Casting anxiety upon the Lord (1Pe 5:7). Charitableness (Mt 18:10; Lk 6:37-38; Ro 14:1-3, 13, 19). Chastity (Pr 5:15-19; Mt 5:27-28). Cheerfulness (Ecc 9:7-9). Choice of wise men for rulers (Ex 18:21; Dt 1:13). Christian graces (2Co 13:11; Col 3:12-17; 2Ti 2:22). Christian tolerance toward the weak (Ro 15:1). Confession of sin (Nu 8:12; Jas 5:16). Contentment (Lk 3:14; Heb 13:5). Courage (Dt 31:6-7; Jos 1:6-7, 9; 1Ki 2:2-3; 1Ch 28:20; Ne 4:14; Jer 1:8; Eze 2:6). Cross bearing (Mt 16:24; Mk 8:34).

Destruction of idols (Ex 23:24; 34:13; Nu 33:52; Dt 7:25; 12:13). Diligence (Ecc 9:10; 11:6), in business (Pr 27:23). Discipleship (Mt 19:21; Mk 10:21; Lk 18:22). Discipline of, disorderly church members (2Th 3:6). Of Children (Mt 19:14; Mk 10:14; Lk 18:16-17). Discreet conduct (Ro 12:17; Eph 4:1-3; 5:15-16; Php 1:27, 5; 1Pe 2:11-12). Doing all to the glory of God (1Co 10:31; Col 3:17, 23).

Equity of servants (Col 4:1). Establishing and providing for the ordination of a holy ministry (Ex 28:1-3; 40:12-15; Lev 8:1-13). Esteem for pastors (1Th 5:12-13; 1Ti 5:17; Heb 13:7). Evangelism (Mt 28:19).

Faith (Ex 14:13; 2Ch 20:20; Ps 37:3, 5; 62:8; 115:9, 11; Pr 3:5; Isa 26:4; 50:10; Jer 49:11; Mk 1:15; 5:36; 11:22; Jn 6:29; 12:36; 14:1, 11; 20:27), in Christ (1Jn 3:23). Faithfulness to ministers (Col 4:17; 1Ti 6:11-12, 14; 2Ti 1:8, 13), to friends (Pr 27:10). Family support (1Ti 5:8). Fear of God (Lev 19:14, 32; 25:17; Dt 6:13; 10:12, 20; 13:4; Jos 24:14; 1Sa 12:24; 2Ki 17:39; Pr 3:7; 23:17; 24:21; Ecc 12:13; Isa 8:13; 1Pe 2:17). Fidelity in marriage (Ge 2:24; Mt 19:6; Mk 10:8; 1Co 7:10-11), to God (1Sa 12:20; Mt 22:21), to God and government (Mt 22:21; Mk 12:17; Lk 20:25), to vows (Nu 30:2; Dt 23:21-23; Ps 50:14; Ecc 5:4). Forbearance (Eph 4:2; Col 3:13). Forgiveness (Mt 18:22; Mk 11:25; Lk 17:3-4; Ro 12:14; Eph 4:32; Col 3:13). Fortitude under persecution (Mt 10:26-28; Mk 13:9, 11-13; 2Ti 2:3; Rev 2:10). Fraternal reproof (Mt 18:15-17; Lk 17:3-4). Fruits of righteousness (Lk 3:11, 14).

Gentleness (Tit 3:2). Godliness (Eph 5:1). Golden Rule, in conduct (Mt 7:12; Lk 6:31). Good works (1Pe 3:21). Growth in grace (Heb 6:1; 2Pe 1:5-8; 3:18; Jude 20-21).

Heed to instruction (Pr 4:10; 19:20; 22:17), to parental instruction (Pr 1:8; 23:22), to the truth (Mt 11:15; Mk 4:9; Rev 2:7). Helpfulness (1Co 10:24; Gal 6:1-2; Php 2:4; 1Th 5:11). Holiness (Ex 22:31; 30:29; Lev 11:44; 20:7, 25-26; 21:7; Nu 15:40; Dt 18:13; Jos 7:13; Isa 1:16-17; Jer 6:16; Am 5:14-15; 1Co 5:7; 2Co 7:1; Eph 4:22-32; Col 3:5, 8-9; 1Th 4:3-7; 2Ti 2:19, 22; Heb 12:14; Jas 1:21; 4:8; 1Pe 1:13-16; 2:11-12; 3:15; 3Jn 11). Holiness in ministers (Lev 21:6; Nu 8:14-15). Honesty (Lev 19:35-36; Dt 25:13-16; 1Th 4:12), in service (1Co 4:2; Eph 6:5-7; Col 3:22-23; Tit 2:9-10), in office (Lk 3:13). Honor, to civil rulers (1Pe 2:17), to wife (1Pe 3:7). Hospitality (Ro 12:13; Heb 13:2; 1Pe 4:9). Humane treatment of servants (Eph 6:9). Humility (Ro 12:16; Php 2:3; Jas 4:10; 1Pe 3:8; 5:6-7).

Imitation of Christ (Ro 13:14; Col 2:6-7). Industry (Pr 6:6; Eph 4:28; 1Th 4:11; 2Th 3:12). Influence for righteousness (Mt 5:16; Php 2:15). Joyfulness (Ro 12:12; Php 3:1; 4:4; 1Th 5:16). Justice (Lev 19:15; Isa 56:1; Zec 7:9-10; Jn 7:24), in courts (Dt 1:17; 25:1-2), to foreigners (Lev 19:33-34; 24:22).

Keeping the Sabbath holy (Ex 16:29; 20:8; 31:12-16; 35:2-3; Lev 19:3, 30; 26:2; Dt 5:12). Kindness (Pr 3:27-28; Eph 4:32; Col 3:12; 1Th 5:15). Kindness to animals (Dt 25:4). To enemies (Ex 23:4-5; Pr 25:21; Ro 12:20).

Labor (Ex 20:9; 35:2; Dt 5:13). Laying up treasure in heaven (Mt 6:20). Liberality (Pr 3:9; Ecc 11:1; Mt 5:42; Lk 6:30; 12:33; 2Co 8:7; Heb 13:16). Liberality in God's service (Mal 3:10), in support of religion (Dt 15:19; 16:17), toward the house of God (Ex 22:29; 30:12-16; 34:26; 35:4-9), to the poor (Lev 19:9-10; 23:22; Dt 15:7-15; 24:19-21; Ro 12:13; Heb 13:16; 1Jn 3:17). Love, for enemies (Mt 5:44; Lk 6:27-29; Ro 12:14-15), for foreigners (Lev 19:34; Dt 10:19). Love for God (Dt 6:5; 10:12; 11:1, 8, 13; 30:16; Jos 22:5; 23:11; Mt 22:37; Mk 12:30; Lk 10:27). Love for other people (Lev 19:18, 33-34; Mt 19:19; 22:39; Mk 12:31; Lk 10:27; Jn 13:34; 15:12, 17; Ro 12:9-10; 13:8-10; 1Co 16:14; Gal 5:14; Eph 5:2; Col 3:14; 1Th 3:12; 4:9; Heb 13:1; Jas 2:8; 1Pe 2:17; 3:8; 4:8; 1Jn 3:11, 18, 23; 1Jn 4:7, 21; 2Jn 5). Love for wife (Eph 5:23; Col 3:19). Loving truth and peace (Zec 8:19).

Maturity (1Co 16:13-14). Mature thinking (1Co 14:20; Tit 2:2). Meekness (Mt 5:39-40; Lk 6:29; Eph 4:2; Col 3:12; Tit 3:2). Mercy (Pr 3:3; Zec 7:9-10; Lk 6:36). Mercy to debtors (Dt 24:6).

Oaths in God's name (Dt 6:13; 10:20). Obedience (Pr 7:1-4; Lev 18:4-5, 26, 30; 19:19, 37; 20:8, 22; 22:31; 25:18; Nu 15:40; Dt 4:1, 6, 23, 30; 5:32-33; 6:17-18; 7:11; 8:1, 6; 10:12-13; 11:1, 8, 13, 32; 12:28, 32; 13:4; 27:1, 10; 29:9; 30:2, 8, 16; 1Sa 15:1; 1Ki 2:2-3; 2Ki 17:37-38;

1Ch 28:20; Pr 3:6; 4:20-21; 5:7; 7:5-14; Ecc 12:13; Jn 13:15). Obedience of children (Pr 6:20; Eph 6:1-3; Col 3:20), of servants (Eph 6:5-8; Col 3:22-25; Tit 2:9-10; 1Pe 2:18-19), of soldiers (Dt 20:3; Lk 3:14), of wives (Eph 5:22; Col 3:18; 1Pe 3:1-4), of young men (Pr 6:20; 23:22). Obedience to Christ as Lord (1Pe 3:15), to civil government (Ecc 8:2; Mk 12:17; Lk 20:25; Ro 13:1, 7; Tit 3:1; 1Pe 2:13), to God's law (Dt 11:8, 13, 32; 30:16; Jos 22:5; 2Ki 17:37-38; 1Ch 28:8), to parents (Pr 6:20; Eph 6:1-3; Col 3:20). Orderly conduct of divine worship (1Co 14:26-33).

Patience (Jas 1:4; 5:7-9). Patience under afflictions (Pr 3:11), under tribulations (Ro 12:12; Jas 1:2-4; 1Pe 4:1). Peaceableness (Ro 12:18; Col 3:15; 1Th 4:11; Heb 12:14). Perfection (Pr 17:1; Mt 5:48). Praise (Ps 146-150). See Praise. Prayer (Jer 33:3; Mt 7:7-11; Lk 11:9-13; Php 4:6; Col 4:2; 1Th 5:17-18; 1Ti 2:8), for more laborers in the Lord's vineyard (Mt 9:38), for rulers (1Ti 2:1-2). Prayerfulness (Lk 22:40; Ro 12:12; 1Th 5:17). Preparation for the Sabbath (Ex 16:23). Preparedness (Mt 24:44; 25:13, 1-12; 1Th 5:8). Propagation of children (Ge 9:1, 7). Propriety in worship (1Co 14:26-33, 40). Prudence (Col 4:5), in guests (Pr 23:1-2), in speech (Ecc 5:2, 6; 7:21; 10:20). Public instruction in the word of God (Dt 31:10-13). Worship (Ex 34:23; Dt 12:5-7, 11-14, 17-18, 26-27; 16:16). Pure conversation (Eph 4:29; 1Pe 3:10). Purity (2Co 7:1; Eph 5:1-4; 1Ti 5:22; Heb 13:4), in the family of a minister (Lev 21:9), of thought (Php 4:8). Quietness (1Th 4:11).

Rebuke of sin (Lev 19:17; Eph 5:11). Reconciliation between Christian brothers (Mt 5:23-25). Regard for consciences of others (1Co 10:28). Regulated enjoyments (Ecc 11:9-10). Religious instruction of children (Dt 4:9; 6:7-9; 11:19-20; 32:46; Eph 6:4). Remembrance, of God in youth (Ecc 12:1), of God's mercies (Dt 5:15; 8:2). Of the law (Dt 6:6-9; 11:18; 32:46; 1Ch 16:15). Renunciation of sources of temptation (Mt 5:29-30; 18:8-9; Mk 9:43-48). Repentance (Pr 1:23; Eze 33:11; Mal 3:7; Mt 3:2; 7:13-14; Mk 1:15; Ac 2:38; 17:30; Rev 3:19). Reproof of the erring (1Ti 5:20). Resistance of evil (Jas 4:7). Respect for religious instruction (1Th 5:20). Rest on the Sabbath (Ex 20:10; 23:12; 32:21; 35:2-3; Lev 23:3, 24; Dt 5:14). Restraint of temper (Ecc 7:9; Eph 4:26, 31; Jas 1:19). Returning good for evil (Mt 5:4; 1Co 6:7; 1Pe 3:9). Reverence, for God's house (Lev 19:30; 26:2; Ecc 5:1), for holy places (Ex 3:5; Jos 5:15; Ac 7:33), for parents (Ex 20:12; Lev 19:3; 20:9; Dt 5:16; Pr 23:22; Mt 15:4; 19:19; Lk 18:20; Eph 6:1-2), for the aged (Lev 19:32). Right conduct (Pr 6:18; Pr 4:26-27; Php 1:27; Jas 1:19). Righteousness (Ex 23:7; Eze 45:9; Hos 12:6; Lk 13:24; Ro 13:7-8). Rulers to study God's law (Dt 17:18-20).

Secrecy in giving alms (Mt 6:3). Seeking, the Lord (1Ch 16:11; Isa 55:6; Am 5:4, 6), the kingdom of God (Mt 16:24; Mk 8:34; 10:21; Lk 9:23; 18:22; Ro 15:2). Self-discipline (Mt 5:29-30; Mk 9:45-48). Self-examination (2Co 13:5). Service for God (Ex 23:25; Dt 6:13; 10:12, 20). Simplicity in worship (Mt 6:7). Six days of labor, and one day of rest (Ex 20:9-11; 35:2). Sobermindedness (Tit 2:6). Sobriety (1Th 5:8; 1Pe 1:13; 4:7; 5:8-9). Social peace (1Th 5:13). Spiritual diligence (Ro 12:11; 13:12; Heb 4:11; 2Pe 1:10; 3:14). Spirituality (Gal 5:16). Steadfastness (Dt 13:8, 10; Ro 12:21; 1Co 15:58; 16:13; Gal 5:1; Eph 6:11, 13-14, 18; Php 1:27; 4:1; 1Th 5:21; 2Th 2:15; 2Ti 1:13; 1Pe 1:13; Jude; Rev 3:11). Steadfastness in prayer (Ro 12:12; Eph 6:18; 1Th 5:17). Submission to God (2Ch 30:8; Pr 3:11; Jas 4:7), to fraternal counsel (Eph 5:21). Suffering, one for another (1Jn 3:16-17). Sympathy (Ro 12:15; Heb 13:3; 1Pe 3:8). Support of ministers (Dt 12:19; Gal 6:6; 1Ti 5:17-18).

Thankfulness (Dt 8:10; Col 2:6-7; 3:15). Thanksgiving (Eph 5:4, 20; Php 4:6; Col 3:17; 1Th 5:17-18; 1Ti 2:1; Heb 13:15). Tithing (Dt 12:6; 14:22). Truthfulness (Pr 3:3; Zec 8:16-17, 19; Eph 4:25).

Various Christian duties (Ro 12:6-8; Eph 6:10-20; Jas 4:8-11; 5:7-9, 12, 14; 1Pe 1:13-17; 2:11-25; 3:8-9, 15; 4:7-15; 5:5-8; 2Pe 1:5-7).

Watchfulness (Pr 4:23; Mt 24:42, 44; 25:13; Mk 13:35-37; Lk 12:35-40; 21:36; 1Co 16:13-14; Eph 5:15; Php 3:2; Col 4:2; 1Th 5:6; 1Pe 5:8-9; Rev 3:2). Watchfulness against backsliding (Dt 4:9; 8:11; 11:16, 28; 2Pe 3:17), against covetousness (Dt 15:9; Lk 12:15), against false Christs (Mt 24:23-26; Mk 13:21-23; Lk 17:23). Wholehearted service (Jos 22:5; 24:14; 1Sa 12:24; 1Ch 28:9; Ecc 9:10). Wisdom (Pr 3:21; 4:5, 13; 5:1; 8:5-6, 32-33; 23:12, 23), in speech (Pr 23:9; 26:4-5; Col 4:6). Wise self-restraint (Ecc 7:16-18, 21). Witnessing for Christ (Mk 5:19; 1Pe 3:15). Worship (Ge 35:1; Ex 20:24; Rev 19:10; 22:9; Eph 5:19; Col 3:16).

Zeal for righteousness (Jn 6:27; 1Co 15:58), for the faith (Jude 3), in one's calling (Ro 12:6-8).

Fixing Penalty for:

Adultery (Lev 20:10; 21:9; 1Co 6:9-10; Gal 5:19, 21). Arson (Ex 22:6).

Bestiality (Ex 22:19; Lev 20:13, 15-16). Blasphemy (Lev 24:16).

Carnality (Lev 19:20). Contempt of authority (Dt 17:12). Criminal neglect to safeguard life (Ex 21:28-36). Cursing parents (Ex 21:17; Lev 20:9).

Destruction of neighbor's property (Lev 24:18). Disobedience (Nu 15:30-31).

False Witness (Dt 19:18-19). Fornication (Ac 15:20; 1Co 6:18; 10:8).

Idolatry (Lev 20:2-5; Dt 17:2-5), enticement to idolatry (Dt 13:5, 9-10, 15). Impenitence (Lev 23:29). Incest (Lev 20:11-12, 14, 17, 19-21).

Kidnapping (Ex 21:16; Dt 24:7). Murder (Ex 21:12; Lev 24:17; Nu 35:31; Dt 19:11-13).

Laziness (2Th 3:10). Loss of borrowed property (Ex 22:14-15), of property held in trust (Ex 22:7, 13).

Personal injury (Ex 21:18-27; Lev 24:19-20).

Sabbath breaking (Ex 31:14; 35:2). Seduction (Ex 22:16).

Theft (Ex 22:1-4). Trespass (Ex 22:5).

Untimely cohabitation (Lev 20:18).

Witchcraft (Ex 22:18; Lev 20:27).

Forbidding:

Adultery (Ex 20:14; Lev 18:20; Dt 5:18; Mt 5:27; 19:18; Lk 18:20; Ro 13:9; 1Co 10:8). Anxiety (Mt 6:25-34; 10:19-23; Lk 12:11, 22-32; Jn 14:27; Php 4:6). Association with evil company (Pr 1:10-19), with harlots (Pr 2:16; 5:3-21; 6:20, 24-26; 7:1-27; 23:26-28).

Bestiality (Lev 18:23; 20:13, 15-16). Boasting (Dt 9:4). Bribe taking (Ex 23:8; Dt 16:19; 27:25).

Causeless strife (Pr 3:30). Change in God's law (Dt 4:2; 12:32). Class distinction (Ex 23:3; Lev 19:15; Nu 15:29; Dt 16:19), legislation (Lev 24:22). Company with drunkards (Pr 23:20). Conformity to the world (Lev 20:23). Contention (Ro 13:13; Php 2:14; 2Ti 2:14; Tit 3:2). Corrupt conversation (Eph 4:29; 5:4; Col 3:8). Covetousness (Ex 20:17; Dt 5:21; 7:25-26; Lk 12:15; Ro 13:9; Eph 5:3; Col 3:5; 1Ti 6:10-11; Heb 13:5).

Dishonesty in business (Lev 19:13, 35; 25:14; Dt 25:13-15; Mk 10:19). Divorce (1Co 7:10-11, w Mt 5:32; 19:9; Mk 10:11-12; Lk 16:18). Drunkenness (Ro 13:13; Eph 5:18).

Envy (Pr 3:31; 23:17; 24:1, 19; Ro 13:13; 1Pe 2:1). Evil speech (Ps 34:13; Pr 4:24; 30:10; Tit 3:2; 1Pe 3:10). Evil, to a neighbor (Ex 20:16; Lev 19:13, 16; Pr 3:29).

False, dealing (Lev 6:1-5; 19:11), swearing (Lev 19:12), witness (Ex 20:16; 23:1; Lev 19:16; Dt 5:20; Pr 24:28; Mt 19:18; Lk 18:20). Falsehood (Lev 19:11; Eph 4:25; Col 3:9). Fellowship with the wicked (Pr 1:10-15; 4:14-15; Ro 16:17; 1Co 5:9-11; 2Co 6:14, 17; Eph 5:11; 2Th 3:6; 2Ti 3:5). Foolish, unlearned questions (2Ti 2:23). Fraud (Lev 19:11, 13, 35; 1Th 4:6).

Giving cause for stumbling (1Co 8:9; 10:32). Grudges (Lev 19:18). Haste for riches (Pr 23:4), in litigation (Pr 25:8-9). Hatred (Lev 19:17; Eph 4:31; Col 3:8). Heed to false teachers (Dt 13:1-18).

Idolatry (Ex 20:3-5, 23; Lev 18:21; 20:2-5; 26:1; Dt 4:16-19, 23; 5:7-9; 6:14; 13:2-3; 16:21-22; Jos 24:14; 2Ki 17:35; Eze 20:18; 1Co 10:7; 1Jn 5:21). Impure marriages (Lev 21:7). Incest (Lev 18:6; 20:11-12, 13, 17, 19-21; Dt 22:30). Indulgence in wine (Pr 23:31; Eph 5:18; Tit 2:3). Injustice (Ex 23:2-3; Lev 19:15; 25:17; Dt 16:19), to foreigners (Ex 12:49; 22:21; Lev 19:33-34; Dt 1:16; 24:14, 17), to the poor (Ex 23:6). Intolerance (Mk 9:39; Lk 9:49-50). Improper respect of persons (Jas 2:1-9).

Labor on the Sabbath (Ex 20:10; 23:12; 34:21; 35:2-3; Lev 23:3; Dt 5:14). Lewdness (Pr 31:3; Ro 13:13; Eph 4:17-32; 5:3; 1Th 4:2-6; 2Ti 2:22). Lawlessness (Dt 12:8). Laziness (2Th 3:10). Love of the world (1Jn 2:15).

Malice (Lev 19:17-18; Eph 4:31; Col 3:8; 1Pe 2:1). Malicious mischief (Lev 19:14). Meddling (1Pe 4:15). Murder (Ex 20:13; Dt 5:17; Mt 5:21; 19:18; Ro 13:9; Jas 2:11; 1Pe 4:15). Murmuring (1Co 10:10; Php 2:14; Jas 5:9).

Offerings with blemish implying insincere or imperfect service of God (Lev 1:3, 10; 3:1, 6; 4:3, 23,

28, 32; 5:15, 18; 6:6; 9:2-3; 22:18-22; Dt 15:21; 17:1). Oppression (Lev 19:13; Pr 22:22), of the poor (Dt 24:14), of the widows and orphans (Ex 22:22-24; Jer 22:3; Zec 7:10). Ostentation in giving, in fasting, and in prayer (Mt 6:1, 5-6, 17-18).

Perjury (Lev 19:12). Perversion of justice (Dt 16:19-20; 24:17). Prejudice (Ex 23:3). Profane swearing (Mt 5:34-36; Jas 5:12). Profaning God's name (Ex 20:7; Lev 18:21; 19:12; 21:6; 22:32; Dt 5:11). Prostitution of a daughter (Lev 19:29). Putting a neighbor's life in peril by false witness (Lev 19:16).

Removal of landmarks (Dt 19:14; Pr 22:28; 23:10). Resistance (Mt 5:39). Retaliation (Lev 19:18; Pr 24:29; Mt 5:38-42; Ro 12:17; 1Th 5:15; 1Pe 3:9). Robbery (Lev 19:13; Pr 22:22).

Sabbath breaking (Ex 31:14; Jer 17:21-22). Self-confidence (Pr 3:5, 7). Self-pride (Ro 12:3). Self-praise (Pr 27:2). Selfishness (1Co 10:24; Php 2:4). Strife (2Ti 2:24). Homosexuality (Lev 18:22; 20:13).

Taking of interest (Ex 22:25; Lev 25:35, 37). Talebearing (Lev 19:16). Theft (Ex 20:15; Lev 19:11; Dt 5:19; Mt 19:18; Lk 18:20; Ro 13:9; Eph 4:28; 1Pe 4:15).

Uncharitable judgments (Mt 7:1-5; Lk 6:37, 42; Ro 14:1-3, 13). Uncharitableness (Pr 24:17; Mt 18:10). Unholy ambition (Php 2:3). Unrighteous anger (Mt 5:22). Unrighteous judgments (Lev 19:15). Use of alcohol by priests on duty (Lev 10:9).

Vain repetitions in prayer (Mt 6:7-8). Various vices (Ro 13:12-13; Gal 5:19-21; Eph 4:28-31; 5:3-6, 11, 18; Col 3:5, 8-9; 1Th 4:3-6; 5:15, 22; 1Ti 3:3, 8; 6:17; 2Ti 3:2-5; Tit 2:3, 10; Heb 13:5; Jas 1:21; 2:11; 4:11; 5:9, 12; 1Pe 2:11; 3:9; 4:3).

Witchcraft (Lev 19:26, 31; 20:6). Withholding a servant's wages (Lev 19:13). Worldliness (Mt 6:19; Ro 12:2; 1Jn 2:15). Worldliness of ministers (2Ti 2:4-5).

Implied:
Commanding an exact conscience (Mt 6:22-24). Against self-righteousness (Mt 7:3).

Precepts of Jesus:
Stated or implied (Mt 5:16, 22-24, 27-48; 6:1-4, 6-8, 16-25, 31-34; 7:1-29; 10:5-42; 16:24; 18:8-10, 15-17; 18:21-22; 19:16-19; 20:25-28; 22:21, 34-40; 24:42-51; 25:34-46; Mk 6:7-11; 8:34; 9:35-50; 10:9-12, 17, 22; 11:22; 12:17; 13:33-37; Lk 6:27-42; 10:28-37; 12:12-31; 13:24; Jn 7:24; 13:34-35; 14:11, 15, 23-24; 15:2-12, 17, 20-22).

Prescribing:
Law of evidence (Dt 17:6; 19:15). Number of stripes in punishment (Dt 25:3). Priestly benedictions (Nu 6:23-26). Stimulants for the perishing (Pr 31:6).

Warning: The rich (1Ti 6:17-19).

Warning against:
Covetousness (Lk 12:15). False teachers (Mt 7:15; Eph 5:6-7; Col 2:8). Love of money (Heb 13:5). Quenching the Spirit (1Th 5:19). Sensuality

(Pr 6:24-25). Sinful indulgence (Lk 21:34). Sinning against the Holy Spirit (Eph 4:30; 1Th 5:19). Temptations (Pr 1:10-15; 19:27).

See Adultery; Children; Citizens; Homicide; Instruction; Ministers; Obedience, Commanded; Servant; Theft; Wife; Women.

COMMANDMENTS AND STATUTES, OF MEN

Traditions (Isa 29:13; Ro 14:1-6, 10-21; Gal 1:14; Col 2:8; 1Ti 4:1-3). Rejected by Jesus (Mt 15:2-20; Mk 7:2-23).

COMMERCE

Laws concerning (Lev 19:36-37; 25:14, 17). Carried on by means of caravans (Ge 37:25, 27; Isa 60:6), ships (1Ki 9:27-28; 10:11; 22:48; Ps 107:23-30; Pr 31:14; Rev 18:19). Conducted in fairs (Eze 27:12, 19; Mt 11:16). Of the Arabs (Isa 60:6; Jer 6:20; Eze 27:21-24), Egyptians (Ge 42:2-34), Ethiopians (Isa 45:14), Ishmaelites (Ge 37:27-28), Israelites (1Ki 9:26-28; Ne 3:31-32; Eze 27:17), Ninevites (Na 3:16), Syrians (Eze 27:16, 18), Tyrians (2Sa 5:11; 1Ki 5:6; Isa 23:8; Eze 27; 28:5), Sidonians (Isa 23:2; Eze 27:8), Babylonians (Rev 18:3, 11-13), Israelites (Eze 27:17). From Tarshish (Jer 10:9; Eze 27:25).

Evil practices connected with (Pr 29:14; Eze 22:13; Hos 12:7).

Articles of:
Apes and baboons (1Ki 10:22), balm (Ge 37:25), blue cloth (Eze 27:24), bronze (Eze 27:13; Rev 18:12), cinnamon (Rev 18:13), cattle (Eze 27:21), chest of rich apparel (Eze 27:24), citron wood (Rev 18:12), clothes for chariots (Eze 27:20), embroidery (Eze 27:16, 24), frankincense (Jer 6:20; Rev 18:13), gold (1Ki 9:28; 10:22; 2Ch 8:18; Isa 60:6; Rev 18:12), honey (Eze 27:17), horses (1Ki 10:29; Eze 27:14; Rev 18:13), ivory (1Ki 10:22; 2Ch 9:21; Eze 27:15; Rev 18:12), iron (Eze 27:12, 19), land (Ge 23:13-16; Ru 4:3), lead (Eze 27:12), linen (Rev 18:12), oil (1Ki 5:11; Eze 27:17), pearls (Rev 18:12), perfumes (SS 3:6), precious stones (Eze 27:16, 22; 28:13, 16; Rev 18:12), purple (Eze 27:16; Rev 18:12), sheep (Rev 18:13), slaves (Ge 37:28, 36; Dt 24:7), silk (Rev 18:12), silver (1Ki 10:22; 2Ch 9:21; Rev 18:12), sweet cane (Jer 6:20), timber (1Ki 5:6, 8), tin (Eze 27:12), wheat (1Ki 5:11; Eze 27:17; Rev 18:13), white wool (Eze 27:18), wine (2Ch 2:15; Eze 27:18; Rev 18:13), human bodies and souls (Rev 18:13).

Transportation of passengers (Jnh 1:3; Ac 21:2; 27:2, 6, 37).

See Merchant; Tarshish, 2, 3; Trade and Travel; Traffic.

COMMISSARY

For armies, cattle driven with (2Ki 3:9). *See Armies.* For royal households (2Ki 4:7-19, 27-28).

COMMITMENT

Through the word of truth (Jn 17:17). To the Lord (Pr 16:3; 1Co 1:2; 2Co 7:1; 1Pe 1:15-16).

COMMONWEALTH See Citizens.

COMMUNION With God (Ps 16:7; Jn 14:23; 2Co 6:16; 1Jn 1:3). With Christ (Jn 14:23; 1Jn 1:3; Rev 3:20). With the Spirit (Jn 14:16-18; 2Co 13:14; Gal 4:6; Php 2:1-2). See Fellowship.

Instances of:
Enoch (Ge 5:22, 24). Noah (Ge 6:9, 13-22; 8:15-17). Abraham (Ge 12:1-3, 7; 17:1-2; 18:1-33; 22:1-2, 11-12, 16-18). Hagar (Ge 16:8-12). Isaac (Ge 26:2, 24), in dreams (Ge 28:13, 15; 31:3; 35:1, 7; 46:2-4). Moses (Ex 3; 4:1-17; 33:9, 11; 34:28-35; Nu 12:8). Joshua (Jos 6:11-24; 7:10-15). Gideon (Jdg 6:11-24). Solomon (1Ki 3:5-14; 2Ch 1:7-12).

Of Believers:
Unity (Ps 119:63; 133:1-3; Am 3:3; Jn 17:20-21; 1Co 10:16-17; 12:12-13). Commanded (Ro 12:15; 2Co 6:14-18; Eph 4:1-3; 5:11; Col 3:16; 1Th 4:18; 5:11, 14; Heb 3:13; 10:24-25; Jas 5:16). Exemplified (1Sa 23:16; Ps 55:14; Mal 3:16; Lk 22:32; 24:17, 32; Ac 2:42; 1Jn 1:3, 7). See Eucharist; Fellowship.

COMMUNITY [824, 6337, 7736, 2681+4436]. Christian (Ac 2:44-45; 4:32-37; 5:1-10).

COMPANY [782+2495+4200, 907+2118, 1201, 1887, 2657, 4722, 6051, 6337, 6640, 7233, 7372, 7736, 8031, 253+608+714, 1855, 3918, 4436, 5061, 5322].

Evil:
Perils of (Ge 19:14-15; Nu 16:21-26; 33:55; Jdg 2:1-3; 2Ch 19:2; Ezr 9:14; Ps 50:18; 106:35-36; Pr 13:20; Hos 7:5, 8-9; Mic 6:16). Seductive (Pr 12:11, 26; 16:29; Ecc 9:18; Mt 24:12; 1Co 15:33; 2Pe 2:7-8, 18). Shunned by the righteous (Ps 6:8; 26:4-5, 9; 28:3; 31:6; 84:10; 101:4, 7; 119:115; 120:5-7; 139:19-22; 141:4; Pr 14:7; 17:12; Jer 9:2; 15:17; Hos 4:17; Rev 2:2).
Warnings against (Ge 49:6; 2Sa 23:6-7; Pr 2:11-12, 16, 19; 4:14-15; 5:8; 20:19; 22:5, 10; 22:24-25; 23:6, 20; 24:1; 28:7, 19; 29:24; 1Ti 6:5). Forbidden (Ex 23:2, 32-33; 34:12-15; Lev 18:3; 20:23; Dt 7:2-4; 12:30; Jos 23:6-13; Pr 1:10-15; Isa 8:11-12; Jer 51:6, 45; Ro 16:17-18; 1Co 5:6, 9-11; 2Co 6:14-17; Gal 5:9; Eph 5:6-7, 11; 2Th 3:6; 1Ti 5:22; 2Ti 3:4-5; 2Jn 10-11; Rev 18:4).
See Example; Influence, Evil.

Good: (Ps 1:1; 15:1-5; Pr 13:20).

See Communion, Of Believers; Example; Fellowship; Influence, Good.

COMPASSES [4684]. Carpenter's (Isa 44:13).

COMPASSION [2571+6524, 2843, 2798, 5714, 5716, 5719, 6524+8317, 8163, 8171, 2359, 3880, 3882, 4499, 5072].

Of God: See God, Mercy of.

Of Christ: See Jesus the Christ, Compassion of.

COMPEL [706, 928, 7439, 10264, 337,

340+2130, 1313, 5309]. By God (Ex 3:19; Ac 20:22; 1Co 9:16; 2Co 5:14). By people (Ezr 4:23; Gal 2:3; 6:12). By circumstances (1Sa 13:12; Ac 28:19).

COMPLACENCY [1055, 7884, 8633, 8932]. Indifference to God is judged (Pr 1:32-33; Isa 32:9, 11; Am 6:1; Zep 1:12; Lk 11:23). See Lukewarmness.

COMPLAINT [606, 645, 1819, 8087, 8189, 8190, 8488, 8490, 9350, 9442]. See Murmuring.

COMPLICITY

Warnings Against: (Ps 50:18; Pr 29:24; Ro 1:32; 2Jn 10-11).

Instances of:
Sarah, in deceiving Pharaoh (Ge 12:11-19), Abimelech (Ge 20:2-5, 11-14). Rebekah, in deceiving Isaac (Ge 27:5-17). The elders and nobles of Jezreel, in stoning Naboth (1Ki 21:7-14). Jews who opposed building the temple (Ne 6:10-19). Daughter of Herodias, in death of John the Baptist (Mt 14:8; Mk 6:25). Pilate, in the death of Christ (Mt 27:17-26; Mk 15:9-15; Lk 23:13-25; Jn 19:13-16). Paul, in death of Stephen (Ac 7:58).
See Collusion; Connivance; Conspiracy.

COMPROMISE Before litigation, commanded by Solomon (Pr 25:8-10), by Christ (Mt 5:25-26; Lk 12:58-59). See Adjudication at Law; Arbitration; Court, Of Law; Justice.

CONANIAH [4042] (Yahweh sustains).
1. A Levite (2Ch 31:12-13).
2. Another Levite (2Ch 35:9).

CONCEALMENT, EXPOSURE [*4059, 7621, 636, 649, 2821, 5158, 5745, 5746].

Concealment of Sin:
(Ge 3:8; Jos 7:21; Pr 28:13; Isa 29:15; 30:1).

Secret Sins:
Warning against (2Ki 17:9; Job 24:16; Ps 19:12; 90:8; Eze 8:12; Eph 5:12). Called works of darkness (Job 24:14; Pr 7:8-9; Jn 3:20; Ro 13:12; Eph 5:11; 1Th 5:7).

Exposure of Sin:
Inevitable (Nu 32:23; Job 20:27; Pr 26:26; Ecc 12:14; Lk 12:2; 1Co 4:5). Rendered doubly certain (Job 10:14; 14:16; Jer 16:17; Eze 11:5; Hos 7:2; Am 5:12).

CONCEIT [1452, 1470, 2295, 3029, 3030, 5605, 5643, 5861]. Of the foolish (Pr 12:15; 26:5, 12, 16; 28:26; Ro 1:22). Of the rich (Pr 28:11). Of the self-righteous (Ps 36:2; Lk 18:11-12). Warnings against (Pr 3:5, 7; 23:4; Isa 5:21; Jer 9:23; Ro 11:25; 12:16; 1Co 3:18; Gal 6:3).
See Hypocrisy; Pride; Self-Exaltation.

CONCEPTION [1061, 2225, 2231, 2473, 3501, 326, 1164, 1877+3120+8197, 5197]. Miraculous: By Sarah (Ge 21:1-2), Rebekah (Ge 25:21), Rachel (Ge 30:22), Manoah's wife (Jdg

13:3-24), Hannah (1Sa 1:19-20), Elizabeth (Lk 1:24-25, 36-37, 58), Mary (Mt 1:18, 20; Lk 1:31-35).

CONCISION *See Circumcision; Mutilators.*

CONCUBINAGE [7108, 10390]. Laws concerning (Ex 21:7-11; Lev 19:20-22; Dt 21:10-14). Concubines might be dismissed (Ge 21:9-14). Called wives (Ge 37:2; Jdg 19:3-5). Children of, not heirs (Ge 15:4; 21:10).

Practiced by Abraham (Ge 16:3; 25:6; 1Ch 1:32). Nahor (Ge 22:23-24), Jacob (Ge 30:4), Eliphaz (Ge 36:12), Gideon (Jdg 8:31), a Levite (Jdg 19:1), Caleb (1Ch 2:46-48), Manasseh (1Ch 7:14), Saul (2Sa 3:7), David (2Sa 5:13; 15:16), Solomon (1Ki 11:3), Rehoboam (2Ch 11:21), Abijah (2Ch 13:21), Belshazzar (Da 5:2).

See Marriage; Polygamy.

CONCUPISCENCE Intense longing for what God would not have us to have (Ro 7:8; Col 3:5; 1Th 4:5). *See Covetousness.*

CONDEMNATION, SELF *See Self-Condemnation.*

CONDESCENSION

Of God:

In Reasoning With His Creatures—

Sets forth his reasons for sending the flood (Ge 6:11-13). Enters into covenant with Abraham (Ge 15:1-21; 18:1-22). Indulges Abraham's intercession for Sodom (Ge 18:23-33). Warns Abimelech in a dream (Ge 20:3-7). Reasons with Moses (Ex 4:2-17). Sends quail to the Israelites in response to their murmuring (Ex 16:12). Indulges Moses' prayer to see his glory (Ex 33:18-23). Indulges Gideon's tests (Jdg 6:36-40). Reasons with Job (Job 38; 39; 40; 41). Invites sinners, "Come now, let us reason together" (Isa 1:18-20). Expostulates with backsliding Israel (Isa 41:21-24; 43:1-19; 65:1-16; Jer 3:1-15; 4:1-31; 7:1-34; Eze 18:25-32; 33:10-20; Hos 2; Mic 6:1-9; Mal 3:7-15).

In His Care—

For mankind (Ps 8:4-6; 144:3). For the world (Ps 113:5-6). In redemption (Isa 45:11; Jn 3:16; Ro 5:8; Heb 2:11; 6:17-18; 1Jn 4:10, 19).

Of Christ: (Lk 22:27; Jn 13:5; 14; 2Co 8:9; Php 2:7-8; Heb 2:11).

CONDOLENCE Instances of: David, to Hanun (2Sa 10:2). King of Babylon, to Hezekiah (2Ki 20:12-13). The three friends of, to Job (Job 2:11). Jesus, to Mary and Martha (Jn 11:23-35).

See Affliction, Consolation Under; Sympathy.

CONDUCT, CHRISTIAN [784, 1821, 2006, 2143, 6913, 7189, *418*, *4488*]. Believing God (Mk 11:22; Jn 14:11-12). Fearing God (Ecc 12:13; 1Pe 2:17). Loving God (Dt 6:5; Mt 22:37). Following God (Eph 5:1; 1Pe 1:15-16). Obeying God (Lk 1:6; 1Jn 5:3). Rejoicing in God (Ps 33:1; Hab 3:18). Believing in Christ (Jn 6:29; 1Jn 3:23).

Loving Christ (Jn 21:15; 1Pe 1:7-8). Following the example of Christ (Jn 13:15; 1Pe 2:21-24). Obeying Christ (Jn 14:21; 15:14).

Living:

To Christ (Ro 14:8; 2Co 5:15). To righteousness (Mic 6:8; Ro 6:18; 1Pe 2:24). Soberly, righteously, and godly (Tit 2:12).

Walking:

Honestly (1Th 4:12). Worthy of God (1Th 2:12). Worthy of the Lord (Col 1:10). In the Spirit (Gal 5:25). After the Spirit (Ro 8:1). In newness of life (Ro 6:4). Worthy of our vocation (Eph 4:1). As children of light (Eph 5:8). Rejoicing in Christ (Php 3:1; 4:4). Loving one another (Jn 15:12; Ro 12:10; 1Co 13; Eph 5:2; Heb 13:1). Striving for the faith (Php 1:27; Jude 3). Putting away all sin (1Co 5:7; Heb 12:1). Abstaining from all appearance of evil (1Th 5:22). Perfecting holiness (Mt 5:48; 2Co 7:1; 2Ti 3:17). Hating defilement (Jude 23). Following after that which is good (Php 4:8; 1Th 5:15; 1Ti 6:11). Overcoming the world (1Jn 5:4-5). Adorning the gospel (Mt 5:16; Tit 2:10). Showing a good example (1Ti 4:12; Tit 2:7; 1Pe 2:12). Abounding in the work of the Lord (1Co 15:58; 2Co 8:7; 1Th 4:1). Shunning the wicked (Ps 1:1; 2Th 3:6). Controlling the body (1Co 9:27; Col 3:5). Subduing the temper (Eph 4:26; Jas 1:19). Submitting to injuries (Mt 5:39-41; 1Co 6:7). Forgiving injuries (Mt 6:14; Ro 12:20). Living peaceably with all (Ro 12:18; Heb 12:14). Visiting the afflicted (Mt 25:36; Jas 1:27). Doing as we would be done by (Mt 7:12; Lk 6:31). Sympathizing with others (Gal 6:2; 1Th 5:14). Honoring others (Ps 15:4; Ro 12:10). Fulfilling domestic duties (Eph 6:1-8; 1Pe 3:1-7). Submitting to authorities (Ro 13:1-7). Being liberal to others (Ac 20:35; Ro 12:13). Being contented (Php 4:11; Heb 13:4). Blessedness of maintaining (Ps 1:1-3; 19:9-11; 50:23; Mt 5:3-12; Jn 7:17; 15:10).

CONDUIT *See Aqueduct.*

CONEY [9176]. Rock badger; unclean for food (Lev 11:5, ftn; Dt 14:7; Ps 104:18; Pr 30:26).

CONFECTION [7154]. A blend of incense or perfume (Ex 30:35; 1Sa 8:12). Difficult term transliterated "Pannag" in KJV (Eze 27:17). *See Perfume.*

CONFECTIONARY A perfumer (1Sa 8:13). *See Perfume.*

CONFEDERACIES Of kings (Ge 14:1-2; Jos 10:1-5; 11:1-5; 1Ki 20:1). *See Alliances.*

CONFESSION [606, 3344, 5583, 9343, *2018, 3933, 3934, 3951*]. To acknowledge one's faith in anything, as in the existence and authority of God, or the sins of which one has been guilty (Mt 10:32; Lev 5:5; Ps 32:5), to concede or allow (Jn 1:20; Ac 24:14; Heb 11:13), to praise God by thankfully acknowledging him (Ro 14:11; Heb 13:15).

Of Christ:

In baptism (Ac 19:4-5; Gal 3:27). To salvation (Mt 10:32; Lk 12:8; Ro 10:9-11). Inspired by the Holy Spirit (1Co 12:3; 1Jn 4:2-3). Fellowship with the Father through (1Jn 2:23; 4:15). Timid believers deterred from (Jn 12:42-43). Those refusing to make, rejected (Mt 10:33; Mk 8:38; Lk 12:9; 2Ti 2:12). Hypocritical (Mt 7:21-23; Lk 13:26; 1Jn 1:6; 2:4). Commanded (2Ti 1:8). Exemplified (Mt 3:11; 14:23; 16:16; Jn 1:15-18; 6:29; 9:22-38; 11:27; Ac 8:35-37; 9:20; 18:5; Ro 1:16).

Of Sin: *See Sin, Confession of.*

CONFIDENCE [1053, 1055, 1059, 4073, 4074, 4440, 6051, 6164, *2509, 4244, 4275, 4301, 5712*].

In People:

Warned against (Jer 9:4; 12:6; Mic 7:5).

Betrayed—

Joshua, by the Gibeonites (Jos 9:3-15). Eglon, by Ehud (Jdg 3:15-23). Sisera, by Jael (Jdg 4:17-22). Samson, by Delilah (Jdg 16:17-20). Ahimelech, by David (1Sa 21:1-9). Abner, by Joab (2Sa 3:27). Amasa, by Joab (2Sa 20:9-10). Worshipers of Baal, by Jehu (2Ki 10:18-28). *See Betrayal.*

False: *See False Confidence.*

In God:

(Ps 118:8; Pr 3:26; 14:26; Ac 28:31; Eph 3:12; Heb 3:16; 10:35; 1Jn 2:28; 3:21; 5:14). *See Faith.*

CONFISCATION [10562, *771*]. Of property: By David, that of Mephibosheth (2Sa 16:4). By Ahab, of Naboth's vineyard (1Ki 21:7-16). By Xerxes, of Haman's house (Est 8:1). As a penalty (Ezr 10:8).

CONFLAGRATIONS *See Burning.*

CONFORMITY [3869+6913, *2848, 5372*].

Conformity to the world, condemned (Ro 12:1-2; Eze 5:7; 11:12; 1Pe 1:14-16).

Conformity to Christ, commanded (Ro 8:29; Eph 5:1-2; 1Co 4:16; 1Th 1:6; 2:14; Heb 6:12; 13:7; 3Jn 11).

CONFUSION [1003, 1176, 1182, 2162, 2169, 2917, 4428, 4539, 9332, 9337, 9451, *5177, 5429*]. Of languages (Ge 11:1-9). Of Israel's enemies in battle (Ex 14:24; 23:27; Jos 10:10). Of Israel in judgment (Dt 28:20, 28; Jer 51:34). Of believers by false teachers (Gal 1:7; 5:10).

CONGESTION NIV "swelling" (Lev 13:28) or "inflamation" (Dt 28:22). *See Disease.*

CONGREGATION, OF ISRAEL [5220, 7736, *1711, 5252*]. Collective term for God's chosen in the OT, or an assembly of the people summoned for a definite purpose (1Ki 8:65), either the whole assembly, or a part (Nu 16:3; Ex 12:6; 35:1; Lev 4:13).

Often considered in a non-technical sense, as a gathering of believers or chosen, the church of the

OT. For that purpose. *See Church, The Body of Believers.*

CONIAH (*Yahweh sustains*). A name given to Jehoiachin, king of Judah, who was carried captive by Nebuchadnezzar (Jer 22:24, ftn; 22:28; 37:1, ftn), c. 597 B.C. *See Jehoiachin.*

CONNIVANCE Judged (Lev 20:4; 1Sa 3:11-13). Result (Pr 10:10).

CONONIAH *See Conaniah.*

CONQUESTS [*3769, 3771, 5782, 8647, 3771*]. Of the Gentiles by Israel (Jos 6:20; 8:24; 10:28-29; 11:8, 23; 12:7; Jdg 1:8; 3:30; 4:16; 8:28; 9:45; 11:33).

CONSCIENCE [4213, 4222, *4029+5323, 5287*]. Guide (Ps 51:3; Pr 20:12; Mt 6:22-23; Lk 11:33-36; Ro 2:14-15; 7:18, 22; 2Co 5:11). Approves (Job 27:6; Pr 21:2; Ac 23:1; 24:16; Ro 9:1; 1Co 4:4; 2Co 1:12; 1Ti 1:5, 19; 3:9; 2Ti 1:3; Heb 13:18; 1Pe 2:19; 3:16, 21; 1Jn 3:20-21). Struggle with (Job 15:21, 24; Ps 51:3; Mt 6:22-23; Lk 11:33-36; Ro 7:15-23). Purged (Heb 9:14; 10:22). *See Honesty; Integrity.* Of another, to be respected (Ro 14:2-20; 1Co 8:7-13; 10:27-32; 2Co 4:2).

Instances of Faithful:

Pharaoh, when he took Sarah into his harem (Ge 12:18-19). Abimelech, when he took Sarah for a concubine (Ge 26:9-11). Jacob, in his care of Laban's property (Ge 31:39), in his greeting of Esau (Ge 33:1-12). Joseph, with Potiphar's wife (Ge 39:7-12). Nehemiah, with taxes (Ne 5:15). Daniel, with the king's meat (Da 1:8). Peter, in his preaching (Ac 4:19-20; 5:29).

Unfaithful Conscience:

Corrupt (Mt 6:23; Lk 11:34; Jn 16:2-3). Dead (Pr 16:25; 30:20; Jer 6:15; Am 6:1-6; Ro 1:21-25; Eph 4:17-29). Defiled (Tit 1:15). Seared (1Ti 4:2). Guilty (Job 15:21, 24; Ps 51:1-14; 73:21; Pr 28:1 ; Isa 59:9-14; Mt 14:1-2; 27:3-5; Mk 6:14, 16; Jn 8:9; Ac 2:37; 1Ti 4:2; Tit 1:15; Heb 9:14; 10:26-27). *See Blindness, Spiritual.*

Instances of Guilty—

Adam and Eve, after they sinned (Ge 3:7-8). Jacob, after defrauding Esau (Ge 33:1-12). Joseph's brothers (Ge 42:21; 44:16). Pharaoh, after the plagues (Ex 9:27). Micah, after stealing (Jdg 17:2). David, for his indignity to Saul (1Sa 24:5), for his adultery and for his murder of Uriah (Ps 32; 38; 40:11-12; 51), for numbering Israel (2Sa 24:10; 1Ch 21:1-8). The old prophet of Bethel (1Ki 13:18, 29-32). The lepers of Samaria (2Ki 7:8-10). Jonah (Jnh 1:12). Herod, for beheading John the Baptist (Mt 14:2; Lk 9:7). Peter, after denying the Lord (Mt 26:75; Mk 14:72; Lk 22:62). Judas (Mt 27:3-5). The accusers of the women taken in adultery (Jn 8:9).

CONSCIENCE MONEY *See Money.*

CONSCIENTIOUSNESS *See Integrity.*

CONSCRIPTION [6218, 6590, 7371]. Of soldiers (1Sa 14:52). Of forced labor (1Ki 5:13-18; 19:15-23; 2Ki 25:19).

CONSECRATED THINGS [3338+ 4848, 2883, 5121, 5692, 7705, 7727, 7731, 39, 41+2813, 4606]. Laws regarding (Lev 27; Nu 18:8-32). See Firstborn; Firstfruits.

CONSECRATION [7727]. Of Aaron. See Aaron. Of Priests. See Priest. Of the altar. See Altar. Of the temple. See Temple, Solomon's; Offerings.

Commanded (Ex 32:29). Personal (Ps 51:17; Mt 13:44-46; Ro 6:13, 16, 19; 12:1; 2Co 8:5). Conditional (Ge 28:20-22; 2Sa 15:7-8).

Instances of: Cain and Abel (Ge 4:4-7). Abraham, of Isaac (Ge 22:9-12). Jephthah, of his daughter (Jdg 11:30-40). Hannah, of Samuel (1Sa 1:11, 24-28). David consecrates the water (2Sa 23:16; 1Ch 11:18). Zicri, of himself (2Ch 17:16).

See Dedication; Offerings.

CONSERVATION See Ecology.

CONSISTENCY Encouraged (Ne 5:9; Mt 6:24; Lk 16:13; Ro 14:22; 1Co 10:21).

See Deceit; Expediency; Hypocrisy; Inconsistency; Obduracy; Prudence.

CONSOLATION [5714, 5717, 9487, 9488, 4155]. See Affliction, Consolation Under; Holy Spirit.

CONSPIRACY [6051, 8003, 8004, 5371]. Law against (Ex 23:1-2).

Instances of:
Joseph's brothers, against Joseph (Ge 37:18-20). Miriam and Aaron, against Moses (Nu 12; 14:4; 16:1-35). Abimelech, against Gideon's sons (Jdg 9:1-6). Gaal, against Abimelech (Jdg 9:23-41). Delilah, against Samson (Jdg 16:4-21). Abner, against Ish-Bosheth (2Sa 3:7-21). Of Absalom (2Sa 15:10-13). Of Jeroboam (1Ki 14:2). Of Baasha (1Ki 15:27). Of Zimri (1Ki 16:9). Of Jezebel, against Naboth (1Ki 21:8-13). Of Jehu (2Ki 9:14-26). Of Jehoiada (2Ki 11:4-16). Of servants, against Joash (2Ki 12:20).

People in Jerusalem, against Amaziah (2Ki 14:19). Shallum, against Zechariah (2Ki 15:10). Pekahiah (2Ki 15:23-25). Pekah (2Ki 15:30). Amon (2Ki 21:23). Sennacherib (2Ki 19:37). Amaziah (2Ch 25:27). Xerxes (Est 2:21-23). Jeremiah (Jer 18:18). Daniel (Da 6:4-17). Shadrach, Meshach, and Abednego (Da 3:8-18).

Against Jeremiah (Jer 11:9, 19). Jesus (Mt 12:14; 21:38-41; 26:3-4; 27:1-2; Mk 3:6). Paul (Ac 18:12; 23:12-15).

Falsely accused of: Jonathan (1Sa 22:8).

CONSTANCY [419, 1942+3265, 3429, 4296+9442, 4946+5584, 9458, 1384]. In obedience (Ps 119:31, 33). In friendship (Pr 27:10). Under suffering (Mt 5:12; Heb 12:5; 1Pe

4:12-16). In prayer (Lk 18:1; Ro 12:12; Eph 6:18; Col 4:2; 1Th 5:17). In beneficence (Gal 6:9). In profession (Heb 10:23).

Instances of: Ruth (Ru 1:14). Jonathan (1Sa 18:1; 20:16), Priscilla and Aquila (Ro 16:3-4).

See Character; Stability.

CONSTELLATIONS [2540, 4068, 4655, 4666]. (2Ki 23:5; Job 9:9; 38:32; Isa 13:10). The serpent (Job 26:13). Orion (Job 9:9; Am 5:8).

See Astronomy.

CONSTITUTION Agreement between the ruler and the people. King commanded to study and obey the Mosaic Law (Dt 17:18-20). Made by David (2Sa 5:3; 1Ch 11:3). Made for Joash (2Ch 23:2-3, 11). Made by Zedekiah, proclaiming liberty (Jer 34:8-11). King of Medes and Persians bound by (Da 6:12-15). See Covenant.

CONSUMPTION NIV "wasting diseases" (Lev 26:16; Dt 28:22). See Disease.

CONTEMPT [997, 1022, 1994, 2295, 2725, 3070, 3075, 5540, 5542, 5571, 7837, 2024, 2969]. Sin of (Job 31:13-14; Pr 14:21). Folly of (Pr 11:12). A characteristic of the wicked (Pr 18:3; Isa 5:24; 2Ti 3:3).

Forbidden Toward:
Parents (Pr 23:22). Christ's little ones (Mt 18:10). Weak brothers (Ro 14:3). Young ministers (1Co 16:11). Believing masters (1Ti 6:2). The poor (Jas 2:1-3). Self-righteousness prompts to (Isa 65:5; Lk 18:9, 11). Pride and prosperity prompt to (Ps 123:4). Ministers should give no occasion for (1Ti 4:12). Of ministers, is a despising of God (Lk 10:16; 1Th 4:8).

Toward the Church:
Often turned into respect (Isa 60:14). Often punished (Eze 28:26). Causes believers to cry to God (Ne 4:4; Ps 123:3).

The Wicked Exhibit Toward:
Christ (Ps 22:6; Isa 53:3; Mt 27:29). Believers (Ps 119:141). Authorities (2Pe 2:10; Jude 8). Parents (Pr 15:5, 20). The afflicted (Job 19:18). The poor (Ps 14:6; Ecc 9:16). Believers sometimes guilty of (Jas 2:6).

Exemplified:
Hagar (Ge 16:4). Troublemakers (1Sa 10:27). Nabal (1Sa 25:10-11). Michal (2Sa 6:16). Sanballat (Ne 2:19; 4:2-3). False teachers (2Co 10:10).

CONTENTION [4506, 5809]. See Strife.

CONTENTMENT [5833, 8934, 10710, 894]. Desirable (Pr 14:14; 15:13, 15, 30; 16:8; 17:1, 22; 30:8; Ecc 2:24; 4:6; 5:12; 6:9). Commanded (Ps 37:7; Ecc 9:7-9; Lk 3:14; 1Co 7:17, 20-24; Gal 5:26; 1Ti 6:6-8; Heb 13:5).

Instances of: Esau (Ge 33:9). Barzillai (2Sa 19:33-37). The Shunammite (2Ki 4:13). David (Ps 16:6). Paul (Php 4:11-12).

See Affliction, Consolation Under; Resignation.

CONTINENCE *See Chastity; Self-Control.*

CONTINENTS (Ge 1:9-10; Job 26:7, 10; 28:8-11; 38:4-18; Ps 95:5; 104:5-9; 136:6; Pr 8:29; 30:4). *See Geology.*

CONTINGENCIES

In Divine Government of Mankind:

Conditional Rewards (Ge 4:7; 18:19; Ex 19:5; Lev 26:3-4; Dt 7:12; 11:26-27; 30:15-16, 19; 1Ki 3:14; 1Ch 28:7; 2Ch 26:5; Job 36:11; Jer 11:4; 18:9-10; 22:4-5; Mt 19:17; 23:37; Jn 14:23; 15:7; Col 1:22-23; Heb 3:14; Rev 22:17). Conditional Punishment (Ge 2:16-17; 3:3; Lev 26:14-16; Dt 11:28; 30:15, 19; 1Ki 3:14; 20:42; Job 36:12; Jer 12:17; 18:8; Eze 33:14-16; Jnh 3:10; Mt 6:15; Jn 9:41; 15:6; 2Th 2:8-11; Rev 2:22; 3:3).

Instances of choice:

Joshua (Jos 24:15). David (2Sa 24:12-14). Jesus (Mt 26:39).

See Blessings, Spiritual, Contingent Upon Obedience; Predestination; Will.

CONTRACTS Binding force of (Jos 9:19; Pr 6:1-5; Mt 20:1-16; Gal 3:15). Penalty for breach of (Lev 6:1-7).

Dissolved:

By mutual consent (Ex 4:18), by blotting out (Col 2:14).

Ratified:

By giving presents (Ge 21:25-30; 1Sa 18:4), by consummating in the presence of the public at the gates of the city (Ge 23:17-18; Ru 4:1-11), by erecting a heap of stones (Ge 31:44-54), by oaths (Ge 26:3, 28, 31; Jos 9:15, 20; 1Ch 16:16; Heb 6:16-17), by joining hands (Pr 6:1; 17:18; 22:26), with salt (Nu 18:19), by taking off the sandal (Ru 4:6-8), by written instrument (Jer 32:10-15). By piercing the servant's ear (Ex 21:2-6).

Instances of:

Between Abraham and Abimelech, concerning wells of water (Ge 21:25-32), violated (Ge 26:15). Between Laban and Jacob, for Laban's daughter (Ge 29:15-20, 27-30), violated (Ge 29:23-27); regarding sharing flocks and herds (Ge 30:28-34), violated (Ge 30:27-43; 31:7). Between Joshua and Gibeonites (Jos 9:3-9, 15-19). Between Solomon and Hiram (1Ki 5:8-12; 9:11).

See Covenant; Land; Vows.

CONTRITION [1917, 1918, 1920, 5783]. *See Repentance; Sin, Confession of.*

CONVENTION For counsel (Pr 15:22). *See Counsel.*

CONVERSATION [1821, 3364]. Profane, forbidden (Mt 5:37; Jas 5:12). Corrupt, forbidden (Eph 4:29; Col 3:8). Edifying, commanded (Eph 4:29; Col 4:6). People judged by (Mt 12:36-37). *See Speaking.*

For KJV "conversation" *See Conduct, Christian.*

CONVERSION A turning, which may be literal or figurative, ethical or religious, either from God, or, more frequently, to God. It implies a turning and a turning to something, and is therefore associated with repentance (Ac 3:19; 26:20), and faith (Ac 11:21). On its negative side it is turning from sin, and on its positive side it is faith in Christ (Ac 20:21). Although it is an act of man, it is done by the power of God (Ac 3:26). In the process of salvation, it is the first step in the transition from sin to God. *See Converts.*

CONVERTS [569, 2189+3836, 3745, 4670]. Parable illustrating four levels of receiving the Word: "Along the path" (Mt 13:4, 19). "Rocky places" (Mt 13:5, 20-21). "Choked" (Mt 13:7, 22). "Good soil" (Mt 13:8, 23; Lk 8:4-15).

See Backsliders; Conversion; Proselyte; Revivals.

Instances of:

Ruth (Ru 1:16). Nebuchadnezzar (Da 4). The mariners with Jonah (Jnh 1:5-6, 14, 16). Ninevites (Jnh 3). Gerasenes (Lk 8:35-39). The Samaritans (Jn 4:28-42). The thief on the cross (Lk 23:39-43). At Pentecost, three thousand (Ac 2:41). Post-Pentecostal (Ac 4:4). The eunuch (Ac 8:35-38). Saul of Tarsus (Ac 9:3-18). Sergius Paulus (Ac 13:7, 12; 26:12-23). Cornelius (Ac 10). Jews and Greeks at Antioch (Ac 13:43). Lydia (Ac 16:14-15). Jailer (Ac 16:27-34). Greeks (Ac 17:4, 12).

Zealous:

Instances of: Nebuchadnezzar (Da 3:29; 4:1-37). Andrew (Jn 1:40-41). Philip (Jn 1:43-45). The woman of Samaria (Jn 4:28-29). The man possessed of demons (Lk 8:39). The blind men (Mt 9:31; Jn 9:8-38). The mute man (Mk 7:36).

CONVEYANCE Of land: *See Land.*

CONVICTION, OF SIN [872, 3519, 7756, 1794, 4443]. To convince or prove guilty. The first stage of repentance.

Produced:

By dreams (Job 33:14-17). By visions (Ac 9:3-9). By adversity (Job 33:18-30; La 1:20; Lk 15:17-21). By the gospel (Ac 2:37; 1Co 14:24-25). By conscience (Jn 8:9; Ro 2:15). By the Holy Spirit (Jn 16:7-11). By God (Dt 28:65-67; Ps 38:1-22; 51:1-4, 7-17).

Instances of:

Adam and Eve, after their disobedience (Ge 3:8-10). Cain, after he killed Abel (Ge 4:13). Joseph's brothers, because of their cruelty to him (Ge 42:21-22; 44:16; 45:3; 50:15-21). Pharaoh, after the plague of hail (Ex 9:27-28), of locusts (Ex 10:16-17), after the death of the firstborn (Ex 12:31).

The Israelites, after worshiping the golden calf and being rebuked (Ex 33:4), after the death of ten spies and their sentence (Nu 14:39-40), after murmuring against God and being bitten by the serpents (Nu 21:7). After being judged for disobedience (Dt 28:65-67; Eze 33:10). In the last days (Eze 7:16-18, 25-26).

Saul, after sparing Agag and the best of the spoils (1Sa 15:24). David, after the pestilence sent because he numbered the people (1Ch 21:8, 30). After his sin with Bathsheba (2Sa 9:12-13; Ps 51:1-17). In penitential Psalms (Ps 31:10; 38:1-22). *See Psalms.* Widow of Zarephath, when her son died (1Ki 17:18). Job, in his distress (Job 40:4-5).

Isaiah, after his vision of God's throne (Isa 6:5). Belshazzar, after the handwriting on the wall (Da 5:6). Darius, when Daniel was in the lions' den (Da 6:18). Mariners, after casting Jonah into the sea (Jnh 1:16). Ninevites, at the preaching of Jonah (Jnh 3; Mt 12:41; Lk 11:32). Jonah, in the fish's belly (Jnh 2).

Herod, when he heard of the fame of Jesus (Mt 14:2; Mk 6:14; Lk 9:7). Jews, who condemned the woman taken in adultery (Jn 8:9). Judas, after his betrayal of Jesus (Mt 27:3-5). Peter, after the large catch of fish (Lk 5:8). Paul, on the way to Damascus (Ac 9:4-18). Felix, under the preaching of Paul (Ac 24:25). Philippian jailer, after the earthquake (Ac 16:29-30).

See Penitent; Remorse; Repentance; Sin, Confession of; Wicked.

CONVOCATION [5246+7924]. NIV "assembly"; a religious festival during which no work could be done (Ex 12:16; Lev 23:2-37; Isa 1:13).

COOKING [1418, 2326, 3184, 3185, 3968, 6105, 6913, 9462]. Of the Passover lamb (Ex 12:9). A young goat might not be cooked in the mother's milk (Ex 23:19; Dt 14:21). Spice used in (Eze 24:10). Ephraim, a cake unturned (Hos 7:8). In the temple (Eze 46:19-24).

See Bread; Oven.

COOS *See Cos.*

COPING NIV "eaves"; a parapet on the temple roof (1Ki 7:9).

COPPER [5703, 5733, *3321*, *5910*]. A mineral resource of Israel (Dt 8:9; Job 28:2). Refining, figurative of judgment (Eze 22:20; 24:11). Used as money (Mt 10:9; Mk 12:42). Alloyed with tin to make bronze. *See Bronze; Money.*

COPPERSMITH NIV Alexander the "metalworker" (2Ti 4:14).

COPULATION Forbidden between persons near of kin (Lev 18:6-16). During menses (Lev 15:19; 18:19), with animals (Ex 22:19).

See Adultery; Bestiality; Homosexual; Lasciviousness.

COR [4123, 10367]. A measure of dry capacity, equal to the homer, containing ten ephahs or baths (1Ki 4:22; 5:11; 2Ch 2:10; 27:5; Ezr 7:22; Eze 45:14). *See Measure.*

CORAL [8029]. Ranked by Hebrews with precious stones (Job 28:18; Eze 27:16).

See Minerals of the Bible, 1; Stones.

CORBAN [*3167*] (*gift*). An offering dedicated to God (Lev 1:2-3; 2:1; 3:1; Nu 7:12-17; Mk 7:11).

CORD [99, 109, 2475, 2562, 3857, 4798, 5436, 6310, 7348, 9219, 9535, *5389*].

Ancient Uses of:

In casting lots (Mic 2:5), fastening tents (Ex 35:18; 39:40; Isa 54:2), leading or binding animals (Ps 118:27, ftn; Hos 11:4), hitching to a cast or plow (Job 39:10), binding prisoners (Jdg 15:13), measuring ground (2Sa 8:2; Jos 17:14; Ps 78:55; Am 7:17; Zec 2:1), worn on the head as a sign of submission (1Ki 20:31).

Figurative:

Of spiritual blessings (Ps 16:6). Of sin (Pr 5:22). Of life (Ecc 12:6). Of friendship (Ecc 4:12; Hos 11:4).

Symbolic Uses of:

Tassels of thread on the corners of garments served as a reminder to obey God's commands (Nu 15:38; cf Dt 6:4-9). Token in mourning (Jos 17:14). Token in mourning (1Ki 20:31-33; Job 36:8). Ribbon used in poetic imagery (SS 4:3).

CORIANDER [1512]. A spice (Ex 16:31; Nu 11:7).

CORINTH [*3172*] (*decoration*). A city of Achaia.

Visited:

By Paul (Ac 18; 2Co 12:14; 13:1, w 1Co 16:5-7 & 2Co 1:16). Apollos (Ac 19:1), Titus (2Co 8:16-17; 12:18). Erastus, a Christian of (Ro 16:23; 2Ti 4:20).

Church of:

Schism in (1Co 1:12; 3:4). Immoralities in (1Co 5; 11). Writes to Paul (1Co 7:1). Alienation of, from Paul (2Co 10). Abuse of ordinances in (1Co 11:22; 14). Heresies in (1Co 15:12; 2Co 11). Lawsuits in (1Co 6). Liberality of (2Co 9). Paul's letters to (1Co 1:2; 16:21-24; 2Co 1:1, 13).

CORINTHIANS, 1 and 2

1 Corinthians:

Author: The apostle Paul

Date: c. Spring A.D. 55

Outline:

I. Introduction (1:1-9).
II. Divisions in the Church (1:10-4:21).
    A. The Fact of the Divisions (1:10-17).
    B. The Causes of the Divisions (1:18-4:13).
        1. A wrong conception of the Christian message (1:18-3:4).
        2. A wrong conception of Christian ministry and ministers (3:5-4:5).
        3. A wrong conception of the Christian (4:6-13).

C. The Exhortation to End the Divisions (4:14-21).

III. Moral and Ethical Disorders in the Life of the Church (chs. 5-6).
   A. Laxity in Church Discipline (ch. 5).
   B. Lawsuits Before Non-Christian Judges (6:1-11).
   C. Sexual Immorality (6:12-20).

IV. Instruction on Marriage (ch. 7).
   A. The Prologue: General Principles (7:1-7).
   B. The Problems of the Married (7:8-24).
   C. The Problems of the Unmarried (7:25-40).

V. Instruction on the Questionable Practices (8:1-11:1).
   A. The Principles Involved (ch. 8).
   B. The Principles Illustrated (ch. 9).
   C. A Warning From the History of Israel (10:1-22).
   D. The Principles Applied (10:23-11:1).

VI. Instruction on Public Worship (11:2-14:40).
   A. Propriety in Worship (11:2-16).
   B. The Lord's Supper (11:17-34).
   C. Spiritual Gifts (chs. 12-14).
      1. The test of the gifts (12:1-3).
      2. The unity of the gifts (12:4-11).
      3. The diversity of the gifts (12:12-31a).
      4. The necessity of exercising the gifts in love (12:31b-13:13).
      5. The superiority of prophecy over tongues (14:1-25).
      6. Rules governing public worship (14:26-40).

VII. Instruction on the Resurrection (ch. 15).
   A. The Certainty of the Resurrection (15:1-34).
   B. The Consideration of Certain Objections (15:35-37).
   C. The Concluding Appeal (15:58).

VIII. Conclusion: Practical and Personal Matters (ch. 16).

2 Corinthians:

Author: The apostle Paul

Date: c. Fall A.D. 55

Outline:

I. Primarily Apologetic: Paul's Explanation of His Conduct and Apostolic Ministry (chs. 1-7).
   A. Salutation (1:1-2).
   B. Thanksgiving for Divine Comfort in Affliction (1:3-11).
   C. The Integrity of Paul's Motives and Conduct (1:12-2:4).
   D. Forgiving the Offender at Corinth (2:5-11).
   E. God's Direction in the Ministry (2:12-17).
   F. The Corinthian Believers—a Letter from Christ (3:1-11).
   G. Seeing the Glory of God With Unveiled Faces (3:12-4:6).
   H. Treasure in Clay Jars (4:7-16a).
   I. The Prospect of Death and What It Means for the Christian (14:16b-5:10).
   J. The Ministry of Reconciliation (5:11-6:10).
   K. A Spiritual Father's Appeal to His Children (6:11-7:4).
   L. The Meeting With Titus (7:5-16).

II. Hortatory: The Collection for the Christians at Jerusalem (chs. 8-9).
   A. Generosity Encouraged (8:1-15).
   B. Titus and His Companions Sent to Corinth (8:16-9:5).
   C. Results of Generous Giving (9:6-15).

III. Polemical: Paul's Vindication of His Apostolic Authority (chs. 10-13).
   A. Paul's Defense of His Apostolic Authority and the Area of His Mission (ch. 10).
   B. Paul Forced Into Foolish Boasting (chs. 11-12).
   C. Final Warnings (13:1-10).
   D. Conclusion (13:11-14).

CORMORANT [8960]. A bird forbidden as food (Lev 11:17; Dt 14:17). *See Birds.*

CORN *See Grain.*

CORNELIUS [3173] (*of a horn*). Roman centurion stationed at Caesarea, and the first Gentile convert (Ac 10:1).

CORNERSTONE [74+7157, 7157, *214, 214+1639*]. Determined the design and structure of a building; the most important stone in the foundation (Isa 28:16). Figurative of Creation (Job 38:6). Of Christ (Isa 28:16; Zec 10:4; Eph 2:20; 1Pe 2:6).
See Capstone; Stones.

CORNET *See Music, Instruments of; Horn; Sistrums.*

CORPORAL PUNISHMENT *See Punishment.*

CORPULENCY Instances of: Eglon (Jdg 3:17), Eli (1Sa 4:18).

CORRECTION [3519, 3574, 3579, 4592, 9350, *1794, 2061*]. *See Afflictions, Of Believers; Chastisement, From God; Children, Correction of; Parents; Punishment; Reproof; Rod of Correction; Scourging.*

CORRUPTION [480, 1175, 2095, 2866, 3237, 4299, 5422, 5614, 6074, 6838, 8845, 10705, *1425, 3620, 3621, 3622, 4922, 5021, 5780, 5785*].

Physical Decomposition:
After death (Ge 3:19; Job 17:14; 21:26; 34:15; Ps 16:10; 49:9; 104:29; Ecc 3:20; 12:7; Jnh 2:6; Ac 2:27, 31; 13:34-37; 1Co 15:42, 50).

Figurative:
Of sin (Isa 38:17; Ro 8:21; Gal 6:8; 2Pe 1:4; 2:12, 19). Hill of (2Ki 23:13).

Judicial: *See Court, Of Law; Government; Judge.*

Ecclesiastical: *See Church, The Body of Believers, Corrupt; Ministers.*

Political: *See Bribery; Civil Service; Government; Politics.*

COS [*3271*] (*summit*). Island off the SW coast of Asia Minor (Ac 21:1).

COSAM [*3272*] (*diviner*). An ancestor of Christ (Lk 3:28).

COSMETICS [9043, 9475]. Any of the various preparations used for beautifying the hair and skin (2Ki 9:30; Jer 4:30; Eze 23:40).

COTTON *See Linen.*

COUCH [3661, 4753, 5435, 6911]. A piece of furniture for reclining, but sometimes only a rolled up mat (Am 6:4; Mt 9:6).

COULTER *See Plowshare.*

COUNCIL [4595, 4632, 6051, *1085, 4564, 5206, 5284*].
1. Group of people gathered for deliberation (Ge 49:6; 2Ki 9:5).
2. The Jewish Sanhedrin (Mt 26:59; Ac 5:34) and lesser courts (Mt 10:17; Mk 13:9).

COUNSEL [1821, 3446, 3619, 4600, 6051, 6783, *1089, 5205*]. Wisdom in (Ex 18:14-23; Pr 1:5; 11:14; 15:22; 19:20; 20:18; 24:6). The wise profit by (Pr 1:5; 9:9; 12:15; 27:9). Rejected, by Rehoboam (1Ki 12:8-16), by rich young ruler (Mt 19:22). Consequences of rejecting divine (Pr 1:24-32).
See Prudence.

COUNSELOR [408+6783, 3446, *4156, 5207*]. A wise man, versed in law and diplomacy (1Ch 27:32-33). Ahithophel was, to David (2Sa 16:23; 1Ch 27:33), to Absalom (2Sa 16:23). A title of Christ (Isa 9:6). A title of the Holy Spirit (Jn 14:16, 26; 15:26; 16:7).

COUNTENANCE [7156]. Angry (Pr 25:23). Cheerful (Job 29:24; Ps 4:6; 21:6; 44:3; Pr 15:13; 27:17). Fierce (Dt 28:50; Da 8:23). Guilty (Ge 4:5; Isa 3:9). Health indicated in (Ps 42:11; 43:5). Pride in (2Ki 5:1; Ps 10:4). Reading of (Ge 31:2, 5). Sad (1Sa 1:18; Ne 2:2-3; Ecc 7:3; Eze 27:35; Da 1:15; 5:6). Transfigured (Ex 34:29-35; Lk 9:29; 2Co 3:7, 13).
See Face.

COUNTRY [*141, 278, 824, 1473, 2215, 8276, 8441, 69, 1178, 3978, 4258, 4369, 6001*]. Loved by Israelites in Exile (Ne 1; 2; 5; Ps 137:1-6). *See Church, The Body of Believers; Congregation, Of Israel; Patriotism.*

COURAGE [599, 1201+2657, 2616, 3338+ 8332, 4213, 4222, 5162, 5883, 8120, *437, 2313, 2510, 4244*]. Of the righteous (Pr 28:1; 2Ti 1:7). Exhortations to (Ps 31:24; Isa 51:7, 12-16; Eze 2:6; 3:9; Mt 10:28; Lk 12:4; 1Co 16:13; Php 1:27-28).

Commanded:
Upon Joshua (Dt 31:7-8, 22-23; Jos 1:1-9), the Israelites (Lev 26:6-8; Jos 23:6; 1Ch 19:13; 2Ch

32:7-8; Isa 41:10; 51:7, 12-16), Solomon (1Ch 22:13; 28:20), Asa (2Ch 15:1-7), the disciples (Mt 10:26, 28; Lk 12:4), Paul (Ac 18:9-10), other Christians (1Co 16:13; Php 1:27-28). By Jehoshaphat, upon judicial and executive officers (2Ch 19:11).

Instances of the Courage of Conviction:
Abraham, in leaving his fatherland (Ge 12:1-9), in offering Isaac (Ge 22:1-14). Gideon, in destroying the altar of Baal (Jdg 6:25-31). Ezra, in undertaking the perilous journey from Babylon to Israel without a guard (Ezr 8:22-23). The Jews, in returning answer to Tattenai (Ezr 5:11). The three Hebrews who refused to bow down to the image of Nebuchadnezzar (Da 3:16-18). Daniel, in persisting in prayer, regardless of the edict against praying (Da 6:10).
Peter and John, in refusing to obey men rather than God (Ac 4:19; 5:29).

Instances of Personal Bravery:
Joshua and Caleb, in advising that Israel go at once and possess the land (Nu 13:30; 14:6-12). Othniel, in killing Kiriath Sepher (Jos 15:16-17). Gideon, in attacking the confederate armies of the Midianites and Amalekites with 300 men (Jdg 7:7-23). Deborah, in leading Israel's armies (Jdg 4). Jael, in killing Sisera (Jdg 4:18-22). Agag, in the indifference with which he faced death (1Sa 15:32-33). David, in killing Goliath (1Sa 17:32-50), in entering the tent of Saul and carrying away Saul's spear (1Sa 26:7-12). David's captains (2Sa 23). Joab, in reproving King David (2Sa 19:5-7). Nehemiah, in refusing to take refuge in the temple (Ne 6:10-13). Esther, in going to the king to save her people (Est 4:8, 16; 5:7).
Joseph of Arimathea, in caring for the body of Jesus (Mk 15:43). Thomas, in being willing to die with Jesus (Jn 11:16). Peter and other disciples (Ac 3:12-26; 4:9-13, 19-20, 31). The apostles, under persecution (Ac 5:21, 29-32). Paul, in going to Jerusalem, despite his impressions that bonds and imprisonments awaited him (Ac 20:22-24; 24:14, 25).
See Boldness of the Righteous; Ministers; Reproof, Faithfulness in; Cowardice.

COURSE OF PRIESTS AND LEVITES
David divided the priests and Levites into 24 groups, called courses (Lk 1:8), each with its own head (1Ch 24:1ff). Each course officiated a week at a time.

COURT, OF BUILDINGS
[*1074, 2958, 5477, 6247, 6478, 7232, 9133, 10170, 1037, 2639*].

Of the Tabernacle:
(Ex 27:9, 12, 16-19; 35:17-18; 38:9, 15-20, 31; 39:40; 40:8, 33; Lev 6:16, 26; Nu 3:26, 37; 4:26).

Of the Temple:
(1Ch 28:12; 2Ch 4:9; 6:13; 23:5; 33:5). The inner court (1Ki 6:36; 7:12). The middle court (1Ki 8:64; 2Ch 7:7).

COURT, OF LAW [*1074, 2958, 5477, 6247, 6478, 7232, 9133, 10170, *1037, *2639*].

Ecclesiastical: (1Ch 26:29-32; 2Ch 19:8-11; Mt 18:15-18; Jn 20:23).

See Church, The Body of Believers, Discipline.

Civil:

Held, outside the camp (Lev 24:14), at the tabernacle (Nu 27:2), at the gates of the city (Dt 21:19; 22:15; 25:7; Jos 20:4; Ru 4:1; Zec 8:16), under a palm tree (Jdg 4:5). Circuit (1Sa 7:15-17).

Composition of, and mode of procedure (Ex 18:25-26; Dt 1:15-17; 17:9; Ru 4:2-5; 1Ch 26:29; 2Ch 19:8-11; Mt 26:54-71; Mk 14:53, 55-65; 15:1; Lk 22:50-71; Jn 18:13-28; Ac 5:17-21, 25-28, 34, 38-41). Accused spoke in his own defense (Jer 26:11-16; Mk 15:3-5; Ac 4:8-12, 18-20, 29-32). Stephen before the Sanhedrin (Ac 7:1-60). Paul before the Sanhedrin (Ac 23:1-7), before Agrippa (Ac 26:1-32). *See Appeal; Punishment; Witness.* Superior and inferior (Ex 18:21-26; 24:14; Dt 1:15-17; 17:8-13; 2Ch 19:5-10).

Justice required of (Ex 23:2-3, 6-8; Dt 1:15-17; 25:1; 27:19; 2Ch 19:5-10; Ac 25:16). Sentence of, final and obligatory (Dt 17:8-12). Contempt of (Dt 17:8-13; Mic 5:1; Ac 23:1-5). *See Judge; Justice.*

Corrupt (Pr 17:15; 29:26; Isa 1:23; 5:23; 10:1-2; Mic 3:11; 7:3; Zep 3:3; Mt 26:59-62; 27:18-26; Mk 14:53-65; 15:10; Ac 4:15-18; 6:11-14; 24:26-27). *See Bribery.*

See Judge; Justice; Priest.

COURTESY *See Manners.*

COURTSHIP Ancient customs of: Suitor visited the woman (Jdg 14:7), women proposed marriage (Ru 3:9-13). *See Marriage.*

COVENANT [1382, 4162, 6343, *1347*] (*agreement, contract*).

Of God With People:

See Covenants, Major in the Old Testament. Salt is an emblem of (Lev 2:13; Nu 18:19; 2Ch 13:5). Confirmed with an oath (Ge 22:16; 26:3; 50:24; Ex 34:27-28; Nu 32:11; Ps 89:35; 105:9; Lk 1:73; Heb 6:13, 17-18). Binding (Lev 26; Jer 11:2-3; Gal 3:15). Everlasting (Ge 8:20-22; 9:1-17; Ps 105:8, 10; Isa 54:10; 61:8). God faithful to (Lev 26:44-45; Dt 4:31; 7:8-9; Jdg 2:1; 1Ki 8:23; Ps 105:8-11; 106:45; 111:5; Mic 7:20).

Instances of, With Individuals and Groups—

With Adam (Ge 2:16-17), Noah (Ge 6:18; 8:16; 9:8-17), Abraham (Ge 12:1-3; 15; 17:1-22; Ex 6:4-8; Ps 105:8-11; Ro 9:7-13; Gal 3). *See Circumcision.* Isaac (Ge 17:19), Jacob (Ge 28:13-15). Israel, to deliver them from Egypt (Ex 6:4-8), to destroy Amalek (Ex 17:14-16). Phinehas (Nu 25:12-13). Levites (Ne 13:29; Mal 2:4-5).

Instances of, with Israel at Sinai—

At Horeb (Ex 34:27; Dt 5:2-3), in Moab (Dt 29:1-15). Blood of (Ex 24:8). *See Blood, Blood of the Covenant.* Book of (Ex 24:7). The Sabbath (Ex 31:16). The Ten Commandments (Ex 34:28; Dt 5:2-3; 9:9).

Major Social Concerns in the Covenant—

1. Personhood. Everyone's person is to be secure (Ex 20:13; 21:16-21, 26-31; Lev 19:14; Dt 5:17; 24:7; 27:18).

2. False Accusation. Everyone is to be secure against slander and false accusation (Ex 20:16; 23:1-3; Lev 19:16; Dt 5:20; 19:15-21).

3. Woman. No woman is to be taken advantage of within her subordinate status in society (Ex 21:7-11, 20, 26-32; 22:16-17; Dt 21:10-14; 22:13-30; 24:1-5).

4. Punishment. Punishment for wrongdoing shall not be excessive so that the culprit is dehumanized (Dt 25:1-5).

5. Dignity. Every Israelite's dignity and right to be God's freedman and servant are to be honored and safeguarded (Ex 21:2, 5-6; Lev 25; Dt 15:12-18).

6. Inheritance. Every Israelite's inheritance in the promised land is to be secure (Lev 25; Nu 27:5-7; 36:1-9; Dt 25:5-10).

7. Property. Everyone's property is to be secure (Ex 20:15; 21:33-36; 22:1-15; 23:4-5; Lev 19:35-36; Dt 5:19; 22:1-4; 25:13-15).

8. Fruit of Labor. Everyone is to receive the fruit of his labors (Lev 19:13; Dt 24:14; 25:4).

9. Fruit of the Ground. Everyone is to share the fruit of the ground (Ex 23:10-11; Lev 19:9-10; 23:22; 25:3-55; Dt 14:28-29; 24:19-21).

10. Rest on Sabbath. Everyone, down to the humblest servant and the resident alien, is to share in the weekly rest of God's Sabbath (Ex 20:8-11; 23:12; Dt 5:12-15).

11. Marriage. The marriage relationship is to be kept inviolate (Ex 20:14; Dt 5:18; see also Lev 18:6-23; 20:10-21; Dt 22:13-30).

12. Exploitation. No one, however disabled, impoverished or powerless, is to be oppressed or exploited (Ex 22:21-27; Lev 19:14, 33-34; 25:35-36; Dt 23:19; 24:6, 12-15, 17; 27:18).

13. Fair Trial. Everyone is to have free access to the courts and is to be afforded a fair trial (Ex 23:6, 8; Lev 19:15; Dt 1:17; 10:17-18; 16:18-20; 17:8-13; 19:15-21).

14. Social Order. Every person's God-given place in the social order is to be honored (Ex 20:12; 21:15, 17; 22:28; Lev 19:3, 32; 20:9; Dt 5:16; 17:8-13; 21:15-21; 27:16).

15. Law. No one shall be above the law, not even the king (Dt 17:18-20).

16. Animals. Concern for the welfare of other creatures is to be extended to the animal world (Ex 23:5, 11; Lev 25:7; Dt 22:4, 6-7; 25:4).

Repudiated by God on account of Israelite's idolatry (Jer 44:26-27; Heb 8:9). Broken by the Israelites (Jer 22:9; Eze 16:59; Heb 8:9). Punishment for breaking (Lev 26:25-46).David (2Sa 7:12-16; 1Ch 17:11-14; 2Ch 6:16), David and his house (2Sa 23:5; Ps 89:20-37; Jer 33:21), God's people (Isa 55:3; 59:21).

Of People With God:

Jacob (Ge 28:20-22). Joshua (Jos 24:25). Absalom (2Sa 15:7-8). Jehoiada and Joash (2Ki

11:17). Josiah (2Ki 23:3). Asa (2Ch 15:12-15). Nehemiah (Ne 9:38; 10). Israelites (Ex 24:3, 7; 19:8; Dt 5:27; 26:17; Jer 50:5). *See Vows.*

Of People With People:

Sacred (Jos 9:18-21; Gal 3:15). Binding (Jos 9:18-20; Jer 34:8-21; Eze 17:14-18; Gal 3:15), on those represented as well (Dt 29:14-15). Breach of, punished (2Sa 21:1-6; Jer 34:8-22; Eze 17:13-19). National. *See Alliances.*

Ratified:

By giving the hand (Ezr 10:18; La 5:6; Eze 17:18), loosing the sandal (Ru 4:7-11), writing and sealing (Ne 9:38; Jer 32:10-12), giving presents (Ge 21:27-30; 1Sa 18:3-4), making a feast (Ge 26:30), erecting a monument (Ge 31:45-46, 49-53), offering a sacrifice (Ge 15:9-17; Jer 34:18-19), salting (Lev 2:13; Nu 18:19; 2Ch 13:5), taking an oath (Ge 21:23-24; 25:33; 26:28-31; 31:53; Jos 2:12-14; 14:9). *See Oath.*

See Contracts; Vows.

Instances of:

Abraham and Abimelech (Ge 21:22-32). Abimelech and Isaac (Ge 26:26-31). Jacob and Laban (Ge 31:44-54). Jonathan and David (1Sa 18:3-4; 20:16, 42; 2Sa 21:7). Jews with each other, to serve God (2Ch 15:12-15; Ne 10:28-32). King Zedekiah and his subjects (Jer 34:8). Ahab with Ben-Hadad (1Ki 20:34). Subjects with sovereign (2Ch 23:1-3, 16).

New Covenant:

Prophecy concerning (Jer 31:31-34; Isa 59:21; 61:8-9; Eze 16:59-63; 34:25-31; 37:24-28; Heb 8:4-13). Characterized by the Spirit rather than the letter (2Co 3:6-17). Purchased or ratified by the blood of Jesus (Mt 26:28; Mk 14:24; Lk 22:20; 1Co 11:25). Jesus the mediator (Heb 12:18-24). Everlasting (Heb 13:20).

See Covenants, Major in the Old Testament.

COVENANTS, MAJOR IN THE OLD TESTAMENT

Major Types:

Royal Grant (unconditional)—

A king's grant (of land or some other benefit) to a loyal servant for faithful or exceptional service. The grant was normally perpetual and unconditional, but the servant's heirs benefited from it only as they continued their father's loyalty and service (1Sa 8:14; 22:7; 27:6; Est 8:1).

Parity (conditional)—

A covenant between equals, binding them to mutual friendship or at least to mutual respect for each other's spheres and interests. Participants called each other "brothers" (Ge 21:27; 26:31; 31:44-54; 1Ki 5:12; 15:19; 20:32-34; Am 1:9).

Suzerain-vassal (unconditional)—

A covenant regulating the relationship between a great king and one of his subject kings. The great king claimed absolute right of sovereignty, demanded total loyalty and service (the vassal must "love" his suzerain) and pledged protection of the subject's realm and dynasty, conditional on the vassal's faithfulness and loyalty to him. The vassal pledged absolute loyalty to his suzerain—whatever service his suzerain demanded—and exclusive reliance on the suzerain's protection. Participants called each other "lord" and "servant" or "father" and "son" (Jos 9:6, 8; Eze 17:13-18; Hos 12:1).

Major Instances:

1. Noahic—Ge 9:8-17.

Type: Royal Grant.

Participant: Made with "righteous" (Ge 6:9) Noah (and his descendants and every living thing on earth—all life that is subject to man's jurisdiction).

Description: An unconditional divine promise never to destroy all earthly life with some natural catastrophe; the covenant "sign" being the rainbow in the storm cloud.

2. Abrahamic A—Ge 15:9-21.

Type: Royal (land) Grant.

Participant: Made with "righteous" (his faith was "credited to him as righteousness," v. 6) Abram (and his descendants, v. 16).

Description: An unconditional divine promise to fulfill the grant of the land; a self-maledictory oath symbolically enacted it (v. 17).

3. Abrahamic B—Ge 17.

Type: Suzerain-vassal.

Participant: Made with Abraham as patriarchal head of his household.

Description: A conditional divine pledge to be Abraham's God and the God of his descendants (cf. "As for me," v. 4; "As for you," v. 9); the condition: total consecration to the Lord as symbolized by circumcision.

4. Sinaitic—Ex 19-24.

Type: Suzerain-vassal.

Participant: Made with Israel as the descendants of Abraham, Isaac and Jacob and as the people the Lord has redeemed from bondage to an earthly power.

Description: A conditional divine pledge to be Israel's God (as her Protector and the Guarantor of her blessed destiny); the condition: Israel's total consecration to the Lord as his people (his kingdom) who live by his rule and serve his purposes in history.

5. Phinehas—Nu 25:10-13.

Type: Royal Grant.

Participant: Made with the zealous priest Phinehas.

Description: An unconditionally divine promise to maintain the family of Phinehas in a "lasting priesthood" (implicitly a pledge to Israel to provide her forever with a faithful priesthood).

6. Davidic—2Sa 7:5-16.

Type: Royal Grant.

Participant: Made with faithful King David after his devotion to God as Israel's king and the Lord's vassal had come to special expression (v. 2).

Description: An unconditional divine promise to establish and maintain the Davidic dynasty on the throne of Israel (implicitly a pledge to Israel) to provide her forever with a godly king like David and through that dynasty to do for her what he had done through David—bring her into rest in the promised land (1Ki 4:20-21; 5:3-4).

7. *New—Jer 31:31-34.*

Type: Royal Grant.

Participant: Promised to rebellious Israel as she is about to be expelled from the promised land in actualization of the most severe covenant curse (Lev 26:27-39; Dt 28:36-37, 45-68).

Description: An unconditional divine promise to unfaithful Israel to forgive her sins and establish his relationship with her on a new basis by writing his law "on their hearts"—a covenant of pure grace.

See Covenant.

COVERING THE HEAD
A symbol of sorrow and/or shame (2Sa 15:30; Est 6:12; Jer 14:3-4).

A symbol of authority (1Co 11:10). In Corinth men are commanded to pray and prophesy only with uncovered heads; women with heads covered with a veil or long hair (1Co 11:3-16).

COVETOUSNESS
[2773, 2121, 2123, 2420]. The Tenth Commandment against (Ex 20:17; Dt 5:21; Ro 13:9).

See Avarice; Bribery; Greed; Rich, The; Riches.

COW
[1330, 7239, 8802, 9391]. Used for pulling carts (1Sa 6:7-12; Hos 10:11). Milk of, used for food. *See Milk; Cattle.*

Figurative (Am 4:1).

COWARDICE
[3950, 7579, 8820, *1264*]. Described (Pr 28:1). Disqualified for military service (Dt 20:8; Jdg 7:3). God inflicted on enemies (Jos 23:10). Inflicted as judgment (Lev 26:36-37; Dt 32:30). Rebuke for (Isa 51:12-13). Cause of adversity (Pr 29:25). Caused by adversity (Job 15:24; 18:11). Caused by wickedness (Pr 28:1).

Instances of:

Adam, in attempting to shift responsibility for his sin upon Eve (Ge 3:12). Abraham, in calling his wife his sister (Ge 26:7-9). Jacob, in flying from Laban (Ge 31:31). Aaron, in yielding to the Israelites when they demanded an idol (Ex 32:22-24). The ten spies (Nu 13:28, 31-33). Israelites, in fearing to undertake the conquest of Canaan (Nu 14:1-5; Dt 1:26-28), in the battle with the people of Ai (Jos 7:5), to meet Goliath (1Sa 17:24), to fight with the Philistines (1Sa 13:6-7). Twenty thousand of Gideon's army (Jdg 7:3). Ephraimites (Ps 78:9). Ephraimites and Manassites (Jos 17:14-18). Amorite kings (Jos 10:16). Canaanites (Jos 2:11; 5:1). Samuel, fearing to obey God's command to anoint a king in Saul's place (1Sa 16:2). David, in fleeing from Absalom (2Sa 15:13-17).

Nicodemus, in coming to Jesus by night (Jn 3:1-2). Joseph of Arimathea, secretly a disciple (Jn 19:38). Parents of the blind man, who was restored to sight (Jn 9:22). Early converts among the rulers (Jn 12:42-43). Disciples, in the storm at sea (Mt 8:26; Mk 4:38; Lk 8:25), when they saw Jesus walking on the water (Mt 14:25; Mk 6:50; Jn 6:19), when Jesus was apprehended (Mt 26:56). Peter, in denying the Lord (Mt 26:69-74; Mk 14:66-72; Lk 22:54-60; Jn 18:16-17, 25, 27). Pilate, in condemning Jesus, through fear of the people (Jn 19:12-16). Guards of the tomb of Jesus (Mt 28:4). The Philippian jailer (Ac 16:27). Peter and other Christians, at Antioch (Gal 2:11-14). False teachers (Gal 6:12). Companions of Paul (2Ti 4:16).

COZ
See Koz.

COZBI
[3944] (*deceitful* ISBE; *the luxurient* KB). Daughter of Zur (Nu 25:15, 18).

COZEBA
[3943] (*liar*). A city of Judah (1Ch 4:22). *See Kezib; Aczib.*

CRACKNEL
See Cakes.

CRAFTINESS
[4659, 5915, 6874, 6891, *4111, 4112*].

Instances of: Satan, in the temptation of Eve (Ge 3:1-5). Jacob, in the purchase of Esau's birthright (Ge 25:31-33), obtaining Isaac's blessing (Ge 27:6-29), in management of Laban's flocks and herds (Ge 30:31-43). Gibeonites, in deceiving Joshua and the Israelites into a treaty (Jos 9:3-15). Sanballat, in trying to deceive Nehemiah into a conference (Ne 6). Jews, in seeking to entangle the Master (Mt 22:15-17, 24-28; Mk 12:13-14, 18-23; Lk 20:19-26), in seeking to slay Jesus (Mt 26:4; Mk 14:1).

CRAFTSMAN
[570, 588, 1215, 2682, 3086, 3093, 3110, *5493*]. Valley of (1Ch 4:14, ftn; Ne 11:35).

See Art; Ge Harashim; Master Craftsman.

CRANE
See Swift.

CREATION
[*1343, 7865, 2856, 3231, 3232, 3233*]. The Bible clearly teaches that the universe, "all things," came into existence through the will of the eternal God (Ge 1; 2; Jn 1:1-3; Heb 11:3; Rev 4:11). The Bible gives no information as to how long ago the original creation of matter occurred, or when the first day of creation began, or the sixth day ended. The two Creation accounts supplement each other (Ge 1; 2). Genesis 1 describes the creation of the universe as a whole, while Genesis 2 gives a more detailed account of the creation of man and says nothing about the creation of matter, light, heavenly bodies, plants, and animals, except to refer to the creation of animals as having taken place at an earlier time.

CREATOR
[1343, 3670, 7865, *3231, 3234*]. Creator of the universe, God as (Ge 1:1; Ne 9:6; Job 26:7; Ps 102:25; Ac 14:15; Heb 11:3). The Word (Jesus) as (Jn 1:1-3). Holy Spirit as (Ge 1:2; Job 26:13; 33:4; Ps 104:30). Creator of mankind, God as (Ge 1:26; 2:7; 5:2; Dt 4:32; Job 33:4; Ps 8:5; 100:3; Isa 51:13; Mal 2:10; Ac 17:28).

CREATURE [*1414, 2651, 5883, 7470, 8254, 9238, *2442*]. That which has been created (Ro 1:25; 8:39; Heb 4:13).

CREATURES, LIVING Heavenly beings with four faces and four or six wings (Eze 1:5-24; 3:13; 10:15-22; Rev 4:6-9; 5:6-14; 6:1-7; 7:11; 14:3; 15:7; 19:4). Identified as cherubim (Eze 10:15). *See Cherubim.*

CREDIT *See Borrowing; Creditor; Debt; Lending; Security, For Debt.*

CREDITOR [5957].

Mosaic laws concerning:
Release of debtor-servants (Ex 21:2-6). Must return cloak left as a pledge (Ex 22:25-27; Dt 24:10-13). Must not take, widows' cloak for pledge (Dt 24:17). Nor millstones (Dt 24:6). Must not extort interest of the poor (Lev 25:35-37; Dt 15:2-3; 23:19-20). Must not oppress neighbor (Lev 25:14-17).

Christ's injunctions to: (Mt 5:42; Lk 6:34).

Oppression by:
Seizing debtor's personal property (Job 22:6; 24:3, 10; Pr 22:26-27). Seizing debtor's houses (Job 20:18-20). Imprisoning debtor (Mt 5:25-26; 18:28-35; Lk 12:58-59). Enslaving debtor's children (2Ki 4:1; Ne 5:1-13; Job 24:9).

Merciful: (Ps 112:5; Mt 18:23-27; Lk 7:41-43).

See Debt; Debtor; Jubilee; Security, For Debt.

CREDULITY Willingness to trust too easily (Ge 3:6; Jos 9:14; Pr 14:15).

CREED A succinct statement of faith epitomizing the basic tenets of religious faith (Dt 4:4-6; 26:5-9). Various NT passages give the biblical foundation for the Christian creeds: the Apostles' Creed, the Nicene Creed, and the Athanasian Creed (Mt 16:16; 1Ti 3:16).

CREEK NIV "bay" (Ac 27:39). Identified as St. Paul's Bay, c. eight miles NW of the town of Zaletta on the island of Malta.

CREEPING THINGS NIV "creatures that move along the ground." A general term for animals (Ge 1:26; Lev 11:20-23, 29-31, 42; Ps 104:20, 25; Ro 1:23). Unclean (Lev 5:2; 11:20, 29-44; Dt 14:19). Clean (Lev 11:21-22). Used in idolatrous worship (Eze 8:10).

CREMATION (Jos 7:25; 1Sa 31:12; 2Ki 23:20; Am 2:1; 6:10).
See Burial.

CRESCENS [*3206*] (*increasing*). A disciple with Paul at Rome (2Ti 4:10).

CRETE, CRETAN [*3205, 3207*]. An island in the Mediterranean, 165 miles long, 6 to 35 miles wide, forming a natural bridge between Europe and Asia Minor. It was the legendary birthplace of Zeus. Paul and Titus founded a church there (Tit 1:5-14). The Cretans in the OT are called Kerethites (1Sa 30:14; Eze 25:16). Cretans were in Jerusalem on the Day of Pentecost (Ac 2:11). According to Paul they were not of a high moral character (Tit 1:12).

CRIB *See Manger.*

CRICKET [3005]. Permitted as food (Lev 11:22). *See Insects.*

CRIME [2365, 2627, 2805, 6240, 6406, 6411, 7322, 8288, 8402, *93, 162, 2805, 4815*]. Some lists (Eze 22:8-12, 27-30; Hos 4:1-2; Mt 15:19; Mk 7:21-22; Ro 1:24, 29-32; 3:14-18; 13:9; 1Co 5:11; Gal 5:19-21).
See various crimes or sins, such as Adultery, Arson, Homicide. See also, Punishment.

CRIMINALS [2629, *2804, 2805+4472, 2806*]. Released at feasts (Mt 27:15, 21; Mk 15:6; Lk 23:17). Confined in prisons (Ge 39:20-23; Ezr 7:26; Ac 4:3; 12:4-5; 16:19-40), in dungeons (Ge 40:15; 41:14; Ex 12:29; Isa 24:22; Jer 37:16; 38:10; La 3:53, 55). Crucified with Jesus (Mt 27:38-44; Lk 23:32-39).
Cruelty to. *See Scourging; Stoning; Mocking.*
Punishment of. *See various crimes, such as Adultery, Arson, Homicide. See also, Punishments.*

CRIMINATION *See Self-Incrimination.*

CRIMSON [2808, 4147, 9355]. Brilliant red dye obtained from an insect (2Ch 2:7, 14; Jer 4:30; Isa 1:18).

CRISPING PIN NIV "purses" (Isa 3:22). *See Purse.*

CRISPUS [*3214*] (*curled*). Former ruler of the Jewish synagogue at Corinth, converted by Paul (Ac 18:8; 1Co 1:14).

CRITICISM [4394, 7639, 8189, *1359, 3699*]. Unjust. *See Uncharitableness.*

CROCODILE *See Leviathan.*

CROCUS [2483]. A flower (Isa 35:1). *See Plants of the Bible.*

CROP [*3292, 5263, 6913, 9311, *2843, 2844*].
1. Pouch-like enlargement in the gullet of many birds in which food is partially prepared for digestion (Lev 1:16).
2. Produce of the land (Ge 26:12; Ex 23:10). Cursed (Ge 4:12). In the New Jerusalem (Rev 22:2).

CROSS [2005, 6015, 6296, *599, 1385, 4699, 5089*]. Jesus crucified on (Mt 27:32; Mk 15:21; Lk 23:26; Ac 2:23, 36; 4:10; 1Co 1:23; 2:2, 8; Eph 2:16; Php 2:8; Col 1:20; 2:14; Heb 12:2). Borne by Simon (Mt 27:32; Mk 15:21; Lk 23:26), by Jesus (Jn 19:17). Death on, a disgrace (Gal 3:13).

Figurative:
Of duty (Mt 10:38; 16:24; Mk 8:34; 10:21; Lk 9:23; 14:27). Of Christ's vicarious death (1Co 1:17-18; Gal 5:11; 6:14; Php 3:18).
See Crucifixion; Self-Denial.

CROSS-EXAMINED [373]. Skill in cross-examining (Pr 20:5). Instance of (Ac 12:19).
See Witness.

CROW [231, 5888]. *See Birds; Rooster.*

CROWN [4194, 4195, 4200, 4887, 5694, 6497, 6498, 6584, 6996, 7619, 7721, 5109, 5110]. Prescribed for priests (Ex 29:6; 39:30; Lev 8:9). Worn by kings (2Sa 1:10; 12:30; 2Ki 11:12; Est 6:8; SS 3:11; Rev 6:2), by queens (Est 1:11; 2:17; 8:15). Made of gold (Ps 21:3; Zec 6:11). An ornament (Eze 16:12; 23:42). Set with gems (2Sa 12:30; 1Ch 20:2; Zec 9:16; Isa 62:3). Given victor in games (1Co 9:25; 2Ti 2:5). Of thorns (Mt 27:29; Mk 15:17; Jn 19:5).

Figurative:
Of gracious visitation (Isa 28:5). Of heavenly reward (1Co 9:25; 2Ti 4:8; Jas 1:12; 1Pe 5:4; Rev 2:10; 3:11).

Symbolic: (Rev 4:4, 10; 6:2; 9:7; 12:1, 3; 13:1; 14:14; 19:12).

CRUCIBLE [5214]. The crucible in which ore is melted to be purified and separated from dross (Pr 17:3; 27:21).

CRUCIFIXION [416, 5090, 5365]. The reproach of (Gal 3:13; 5:11). Of Jesus. *See Jesus the Christ, History of.* Of two criminals (Mt 27:38). Of disciples, foretold (Mt 23:34).

Figurative:
Of old nature (Ro 6:6; Gal 5:24). Of self-centered life (Gal 2:20; 6:14).
See Cross, Figurative.

CRUELTY [426, 427, 2807, 6883, 7996, 7997, 8273, 8288, 8368].
Instances of: Of Sarah to Hagar (Ge 16:6; 21:9-14). Egyptians to the Israelites (Ex 5:6-18). Peninnah to Hannah (1Sa 1:4-7; 2:3). Of Jews to Jesus (Mt 26:67; 27:28-31), soldiers to Jesus (Lk 22:64; Jn 19:3). In war (Isa 13:16, 18).
See Animals, Cruelty to; Kindness; Love; Malice; Prisoners, Of War.

CRUSE *See Jar(s).*

CRYING *See Mourning; Praise; Prayer; Weeping.*

CRYSTAL [2343, 3222, 3223]. A precious stone (Job 28:17 Rev 4:6; 21:11; 22:1).
See Minerals of the Bible, 1; Stones.

CUB [*1594, 1596, 8891]. The young of a dog or a beast of prey; a cub (Ge 49:9; Dt 33:22; Jer 51:38; Na 2:11-12).

CUBIT [564, 4388]. A measure of distance, c. eighteen inches (Ge 6:16; Dt 3:11; Eze 40:5; 43:13; Rev 21:17). No one by worrying can add to his height (Mt 6:27; Lk 12:25 notes).

CUCKOO *See Gull.*

CUCUMBERS [7991]. Vegetables enjoyed by Israel in Egypt (Nu 11:5).

CUD [1742]. Chewing of, was one of the facts by which clean and unclean animals were distinguished (Lev 11:3-8; Dt 14:3-8).

CUMMIN [4021, 3248]. A plant bearing a small aromatic seed (Isa 28:25, 27; Mt 23:23).

CUN [3923] (*chosen*). A Syrian city (1Ch 18:8).
See Tebah, 2; Berothai.

CUNEIFORM A system of writing by symbolic wedge-shaped characters upon clay tablets used primarily in Mesopotamia in ancient times. More than half a million such clay tablets have been found.

CUP [1483, 3926, 6195, 4539]. (Ge 40:11; 2Sa 12:3; 1Ki 7:26; Mt 23:25). Made of silver (Ge 44:2), gold (1Ch 28:17; Jer 52:19). Used in the institution of the Lord's Supper (Mt 26:27; Mk 14:23; Lk 22:20; 1Co 10:21). Of the table of demons (1Co 10:21).

Figurative:
Of sorrow (Ps 11:6; 73:10; 75:8; Isa 51:17, 22; Jer 25:15-28; Eze 23:31-34; Mt 20:22-23; 26:39; Mk 14:36; Lk 22:42; Jn 18:11; Rev 14:10). Of consolation (Jer 16:7). Of joy (Ps 23:5). Of salvation (Ps 116:13).

CUPBEARER [5482]. A palace official who served wine at a king's table (Ge 40:11; 1Ki 10:5; 2Ch 9:4; Ne 1:11).

CUPIDITY *See Avarice; Covetousness; Lust.*

CURES [665, 8324, 557, 2543, 2751, 5392, 5618]. Miraculous. *See Miracles; Disease; Physician.*

CURIOSITY Insatiable (Pr 27:20). Advised against (Ecc 7:21).

Instances of:
Of Eve (Ge 3:6). Of Abraham, to know whether God would destroy the righteous in Sodom (Ge 18:23-32). Of Jacob, to know the name of the angel (Ge 32:29). Of the Israelites, to see God (Ex 19:21, 24), to witness the offering in the Most Holy Place (Nu 4:19-20). Of Manoah, to know the name of an angel (Jdg 13:17-18). Of the people of Beth Shemesh, to see inside the ark (1Sa 6:19). Of the Babylonians, to see Hezekiah's treasures (2Ki 20:13). Of Daniel, to know a vision (Da 8:9).

Of Peter, to know what was being done with Jesus (Mt 26:58), to know what John would be appointed to do (Jn 21:21-22). A disciple, to know if there be few that be saved (Lk 13:23). Of Herod, to see Jesus (Lk 9:9; 23:8). Of the Jews, to see Lazarus, after he was raised from the dead (Jn 12:9), and to see Jesus (Jn 12:20-21). Of the disciples, to know whether Jesus would restore the kingdom of the Jews (Ac 1:6-7). Of the Athenians, to hear some new thing (Ac 17:19-21). Of angels, to look into the mysteries of salvation (1Pe 1:12).

CURSE [*457, 460, 826, 1385, 4423, 7686, 7837, 7839, *353, *1059, *2129, *2800, *2932, *2933*].
Pronounced upon, the serpent (Ge 3:14-15), Adam and Eve (Ge 3:15-19), the ground (Ge 3:17-18), Cain (Ge 4:11-16), Canaan, Ham's son (Ge 9:24-27), the disobedient (Dt 28:15-68; Jer 11:3-17), Meroz (Jdg 5:23), Gehazi (2Ki 5:27). Barak commands Balaam to curse Israel (Nu 22:6; 23:11). Paternal (Ge 27:12-13; 49:5-7).

In the covenant with Abraham (Ge 12:3). Of the Mosaic law, enforcing the covenant (Dt 11:26-32; 27:12-26; 28:15-68; Jos 8:30-34).

Assumed for others (Mt 27:25). Rebekah for Jacob (Ge 27:13). Paul wishes he could assume for Israel (Ro 9:3). *See Blessings.* Christ assumed the curse of the Mosaic law for us (Gal 3:13). *See Jesus the Christ, Vicarious Death of.*

CURSING [457, 460, 7837, 7839, *725, *2932*]. Of God (Lev 24:11-16; Isa 8:21). Of parents (Ex 21:17; Mt 15:4; Mk 7:10). Shimei curses David (2Sa 16:5-8). The precepts of Jesus concerning (Mt 5:44; Lk 6:28). Apostolic (Ro 12:14).

See Anathema Maranatha; Blasphemy; God, Name of; Oath.

CURTAINS [3749, 5009, 7267, *2925*].

Of the tabernacle:
Ten curtains formed the inner lining of the tabernacle, of embroidered linen (Ex 26:1-6). Eleven curtains of goat hair formed the tent over it (Ex 26:7-13). A single linen curtain covered the entrance (Ex 26:36-37). The courtyard was fenced by curtains (Ex 27:9-18). Made by Bezalel and Oholiab (Ex 36:8-38).

A single linen curtain divided the Most Holy Place from the Holy Place (Ex 26:31-33; 35:12; 39:34; 40:21), also in the temple (2Ch 3:14); called the second curtain (Heb 9:3); used to cover the ark (Nu 4:5). A type of the humanity or body of Christ (Heb 10:20). Figurative of the believer's access to God (Heb 6:19).

Of the temple:
Divided the Most Holy Place from the Holy Place (2Ch 3:14). Torn at the time of the crucifixion of Christ (Mt 27:51; Mk 15:38; Lk 23:45).

See Tabernacle; Tapestry.

CUSH [3932, 3933].
1. Son of Ham (Ge 10:6-8; 1Ch 1:8-10).
2. A Benjamite, the title of the Psalm (Ps 7).

3. Land of (Ge 2:13; Ps 68:31; Isa 18:1). *See Cushite; Ethiopia.*

CUSHAN [3936]. Poetic form of Cush (Hab 3:7). *See Ethiopia.*

CUSHAN-RISHATHAIM [3937]
(*man of Cush, doubly guilty*). King of Aram Naharaim; that is, NW Mesopotamia (Jdg 3:8-10).

CUSHI [3935].
1. *See Cushite, 2.*
2. Father of Shelemiah (Jer 36:14).
3. Father of Zephaniah (Zep 1:1).

CUSHITE [3932, 3934].
1. Moses' wife (Nu 12:1).
2. A messenger who brought news to David (2Sa 18:21-32).
3. Tirhakah, king of Egypt. *See Tirhakah.*
4. Zerah, perhaps Pharaoh Oskoron I. *See Zerah, 7.*
5. Ebed-Melech, who pulled Jeremiah from the cistern (Jer 38:7-13). *See Ebed-Melech.*
6. A people, probably Ethiopians (2Ch 12:3; 14:12-13). *See Ethiopia.*

CUSTOM [*2978, 5477, 6913, *1621, *1665*].
When not referring to a tax, usually means "manner," "way," or "statute" (Ge 31:35; Jdg 11:39; Jer 32:11). In the NT means "manner," "usage" (Lk 1:9; Ac 6:14), and "religious practices."

CUSTOM, RECEIPT OF *See Tax.*

CUTHAH [3939, 3940]. A district of Asia, from which colonists were transported to Samaria (2Ki 17:24-30; Ezr 4:10).

CUTTINGS [1548, 3093, 4156, 4162, 5877, 7103, 7287, 7894, *149, *644, *904, *4311*]. A heathen practice, including tattooings, gashes, castrations, usually done in mourning for the dead and to propitiate deities. Forbidden to the Israelites (Lev 19:28; 21:5; Dt 14:1; Jer 16:6).

CUZA [*5966] (*little judge*). Herod's steward (Lk 8:3).

CYLINDER SEALS *See Seal.*

CYMBAL [5199, 7529, *3247*]. A musical instrument. Of bronze (1Ch 15:19, 28; 1Co 13:1).
Used in the tabernacle service (2Sa 6:5; 1Ch 13:8; 15:16, 19, 28), in the temple service (2Ch 5:12-13; 1Ch 16:5, 42; 25:1, 6; Ps 150:5).
Used on special occasions: the Day of Atonement (2Ch 29:25), laying of the foundation of the second temple (Ezr 3:10-11), dedication of the wall (Ne 12:27, 36).

CYPRESS WOOD [1729, 9309, 9560].
(Isa 44:14; SS 1:14; 4:13). Probably the wood from which Noah's ark was made; KJV "gopher wood" (Ge 6:14). Used in making idols (Isa 44:12-17).

CYPRUS [4183, *3250, 3251*] (*copper*). An island (Ac 21:3; 27:4). Barnabas born in (Ac 4:36). Persecuted Jews preached the gospel at (Ac 11:19-20). Visited by Barnabas and Saul (Ac 13:4-12). Barnabas and Mark visit (Ac 15:39). Mnason, a disciple of (Ac 21:16).

CYRENE, CYRENIAN [*3254, 3255*] (*wall*). A city in N Africa, W of Egypt, c. ten miles from the coast. Originally a Greek city, it passed into the hands of the Romans. Simon, who helped Jesus carry his cross, came from there (Lk 23:26).

People from Cyrene were in Jerusalem on the Day of Pentecost (Ac 2:10). Jews from the synagogue of the Cyrenians disputed with Stephen (Ac 6:9).

CYRENIUS *See Quirinius.*

CYRUS [3931, 10350]. King of Persia. Issued a decree for the emancipation of the Jews and rebuilding the temple (2Ch 36:22-23; Ezr 1; 3:7; 4:3; 5:13-14; 6:3). Prophecies concerning (Isa 13:17-22; 21:2; 41:2; 44:28; 45:1-4, 13; 46:11; 48:14-15).

DABAREH *See Daberath.*

DABBESHETH [1833] (*hump*). A place on the boundary line of Zebulun (Jos 19:11).

DABERATH [1829] (*pasture*). A town of Issachar (Jos 19:12; 21:28). Assigned to the Levites (1Ch 6:72).

DAGGER [2995]. A short sword (Jdg 3:16-22).

DAGON [1837] (*[god of] grain* IDB; *fish* ISBE). A pagan deity with the body of a fish, head and hands of a man. Probably the god of agriculture. Worshiped in Mesopotamia and Canaan, with temples in Ashdod (1Sa 5:1-7), Gaza (Jdg 16:21-30), and in Israel (1Ch 10:10). Samson destroyed the temple in Gaza (Jdg 16:30).

DAILY SACRIFICE Ordained in Mt. Sinai (Nu 28:6). A lamb as a burnt offering, morning and evening (Ex 29:38-39; Nu 28:3-4). Doubled on the Sabbath (Nu 28:9-10). Required to be with a meat and drink offering (Ex 29:40-41; Nu 28:5-8). Slowly and entirely consumed (Lev 6:9-12). Perpetually observed (Ex 29:42; Nu 28:3, 6). Pleasing (Nu 28:8; Ps 141:2). Secured God's presence and favor (Ex 29:43-44). Times of offering, were seasons of prayer (Ezr 9:5; Da 9:20-21, w Ac 3:1). Restored after the Captivity (Ezr 3:3). The abolition of, foretold (Da 9:26-27; 11:31).

Illustrative of:
Christ (Jn 1:29, 36; 1Pe 1:19). Acceptable prayer (Ps 141:2).
See Sacrifices.

DALAIAH *See Delaiah.*

DALE, THE KING'S *See Valley, Vale.*

DALMANUTHA [1236]. South of the Plain of Gennesaret a cave has been found bearing the name "Talmanutha," perhaps the spot where Jesus landed. Matthew says Jesus went to the vicinity of Magadan (Mt 15:39). Dalmanutha and Magadan (of Magdala), located on the western shore of the Sea of Galilee, may be names for the same place or for two places located close to each other (Mk 8:10). *See Magadan.*

DALMATIA [1237] (*deceitful*). Province on the NE shore of the Adriatic Sea also called Illyricum (Ro 15:19; 2Ti 4:10).

DALPHON [1943] (*crafty* ISBE; *sleepless* KB). The son of Haman (Est 9:7).

DAMAGES AND COMPENSATIONS Listed (Nu 5:5-8).

For assault (Ex 21:18-19, 22). For personal injury (Ex 21:28-34). For deception (Lev 6:1-5). For slander (Dt 22:13-19). For seduction (Dt 22:28-29). *See Fine.*

DAMARIS [1240]. A female convert of Athens (Ac 17:34).

DAMASCUS, DAMASCENES [1877, 1966, 2008, *1241, 1242*]. An ancient city (Ge 14:15; 15:2). The capital of Syria (1Ki 20:34; Isa 7:8; Jer 49:23-29; Eze 47:16-17). Laid under tribute to David (2Sa 8:5-6). Besieged by Rezon (1Ki 11:23-24). Recovered by Jeroboam (2Ki 14:28). Taken by the king of Assyria (2Ki 16:9). Walled (Jer 49:27; 2Co 11:33). Garrisoned (2Co 11:32). Luxury in (Am 3:12). Paul's experiences in (Ac 9; 22:5-16; 26:12-20; 2Co 11:32; Gal 1:17). Prophecies concerning (Isa 8:4; 17:1-2; Jer 49:23-29; Am 1:3, 5; Zec 9:1).
Wilderness of (1Ki 19:15).
See Syria.

DAMMIM *See Ephes Dammim, Pas Dammim.*

DAMNATION When referring to the future it means primarily eternal separation from God with accompanying punishments (Mt 5:29; 10:28; 23:33; 24:51). The severity of the punishment is determined by the degree of sin (Lk 12:36-48), and is eternal (Isa 66:24; Mk 3:29; 2Th 1:9; Jude 6-7). *See Punishment; Wicked, Punishment of.*

DAN, DANITE(S) [1201+1968, 1968, 1969, 1974] (*judge*).
1. The fifth son of Jacob and Bilhah (Ge 30:6; 35:25). Descendants of (Ge 46:23; Nu 26:42-43). *See below, Tribe of.* Blessed of Jacob (Ge 49:16-17).
2. Tribe of: Census of (Nu 1:39; 26:42-43). Inheritance of, according to the allotment of Joshua (Jos 19:40-47), of Ezekiel (Eze 48:1). Position of, in journey and camp, during the exodus out of Egypt (Nu 2:25, 31; 10:25). Blessed by Moses (Dt 33:22). Fail to conquer the Amorites (Jdg 1:34-35). Conquests by (Jos 19:47; Jdg 18:27-29). Deborah rebukes, for cowardice (Jdg 5:17). Idolatry of (Jdg 18). Commerce of (Jdg 5:17; Eze 27:19).
See Israel, Israelites.
3. A city of the tribe of Dan. Called Laish (Jdg 18:7, 13, 27, 29) and Leshem (Jos 19:47) and later known as Dan. *See Laish; Leshem.* Captured by the people of Dan (Jdg 18:7). Idolatry established at (Jdg 18; 1Ki 12:28-29; Am 8:14). Captured by Ben-Hadad (1Ki 15:20; 2Ch 16:4).

DAN JAAN [1970]. A place, probably in Dan, covered by David's census (2Sa 24:6).

DANCING [2565, 4159, 4688, 4703, 7174, 8376, 8471, *4004*, *5962*]. Of children (Job 21:11). Of women (Ex 15:20; Jdg 11:34; 21:19-21; 1Sa 18:6; 21:11). Of David (2Sa 6:14-16; 1Ch 15:29). In the marketplace (Mt 11:16-17). At feasts (Jdg 21:19-21; Mt 14:6; Mk 6:22; Lk 15:23-25). As a religious ceremony (Ps 149:3; 150:4). Idolatrous (Ex 32:19; 32:25).

Figurative: Of joy (Ps 30:11; Ecc 3:4; Jer 31:4; 31:13; La 5:15).

DANIEL [1975, 10181, *1248*] (*God [El] is my judge*).

1. An Israelite captive, also called Belteshazzar. *See Belteshazzar.* Educated at king's court (Da 1). Interprets visions (Da 2; 4; 5). Promotion and executive authority of (Da 2:48-49; 5:11, 29; 6:2). Conspiracy against, cast into the lions' den (Da 6). Prophecies of (Da 4:8-9; 7-12; Mt 24:15).

Special diet of (Da 1:8-16). Wisdom of (Da 1:17; Eze 28:3). Devoutness of (Da 2:18; 6; 9; 10; 12; Eze 14:14). Courage and fidelity of (Da 4:27; 5:17-23; 6:10-23). Worshiped by Nebuchadnezzar (Da 2:6).

2. David's son. Also called Kileab (2Sa 3:3; 1Ch 3:1).

3. A descendant of Ithamar, and a companion of Ezra (Ezr 8:2; Ne 10:6).

DANIEL, BOOK OF

Author: Daniel

Date: c. 530 B.C.

Outline:

I. Prologue: The Setting (ch. 1; in Hebrew).
   A. Historical Introduction (1:1-2).
   B. Daniel and His Friends Are Taken Captive (1:3-7).
   C. The Young Men Are Faithful (1:8-16).
   D. The Young Men Are Elevated to High Positions (1:17-21).
II. The Destinies of the Nations of the World (chs. 2-7, in Aramaic, beginning at 2:4b).
   A. Nebuchadnezzar's Dream of a Large Statue (ch. 2).
   B. Nebuchadnezzar's Making of a Gold Image and His Decree That It Be Worshiped (ch. 3).
   C. Nebuchadnezzar's Dream of an Enormous Tree (ch. 4).
   D. Belshazzar's and Babylon's Downfall (ch. 5).
   E. Daniel's Deliverance (ch. 6).
   F. Daniel's Dream of Four Beasts (ch. 7).
III. The Destiny of the Nation of Israel (chs. 8-12; in Hebrew).
   A. Daniel's Vision of a Ram and a Goat (ch. 8).
   B. Daniel's Prayer and His Vision of the 70 "Sevens" (ch. 9).
   C. Daniel's Vision of Israel's Future (chs. 10-12).
      1. Revelation of things to come (10:1-3).

2. Revelation from the angelic messenger (10:4-11:1).
3. Prophecies concerning Persia and Greece (11:2-4).
4. Prophecies concerning Egypt and Syria (11:5-35).
5. Prophecies concerning the antichrist (11:36-45).
6. Distress and deliverance (12:1).
7. Two Resurrections (12:2-3).
8. Instruction to Daniel (12:4).
9. Conclusion (12:5-13).

DANNAH [1972] (*stronghold*). A city in the mountains of Judah (Jos 15:49).

DARA *See Darda.*

DARDA [1997]. Also called Dara. A famous wise man (1Ki 4:31; 1Ch 2:6).

DARIC [163]. Persian gold coin used in Israel after the return from the Captivity; said to have been named from the first Darius (1Ch 29:7; Ezr 8:27). Although the NIV has "drachmas" for the following references, some believe that the coin intended was the daric (Ezr 2:69; Ne 7:70-72). *See Drachma.*

DARIUS [2003, 10184] (*Old Persian he who upholds the good*). A common name for Medo-Persian rulers.

1. Darius the Mede (Gubaru), the son of Xerxes (Da 5:31; 9:1), made governor of Babylon by Cyrus, but he seems to have ruled for only a brief time (Da 10:1; 11:1), prominent in the book of Daniel (Da 6:1, 6, 9, 25, 28; 11:1).

2. Darius I called the Great (spelled variously Hystaspos, Hystaspis, or Hystaspes), fourth and greatest of the Persian rulers (522-486 B.C.); reorganized the government into satraps and extended boundaries of the empire; a great builder; he was defeated by the Greeks at Marathon in 490 B.C.; renewed the edict of Cyrus and helped to rebuild the temple (Ezr 4:5, 24; 5:5-7; 6:1-12; Hag 1:1; 2:1, 10, 18; Zec 1:1, 7; 7:1). Died in 486 B.C. and was succeeded by Xerxes, the grandson of Cyrus the Great.

3. Darius, the Persian (spelled variously Codomanus or Codomannus), the last king of Persia (336-330 B.C.); defeated by Alexander the Great (330 B.C.) (Ne 12:22). Some scholars identify him with Darius II (Nothus), who ruled Persia and Babylon (423-404 B.C.).

DARKNESS [694, 696, 3124, 3125, 3127, 3128, 4419, 4420, 4743, 6547, 6602, 6906, 7223, 7516, 7725, 9507, 10286, *1190*, *2432*, *5027*, *5028*, *5030*, *5031*]. Over the face of the earth (Ge 1:2; Job 38:9; Jer 4:23). Called "night" (Ge 1:5). God created (Isa 45:7). The NIV uses "[deep] darkness" to translate a word formerly translated "shadow of death," usually in a context of deep emotional despair or grief (Job 3:5; 10:21, 22; 12:22; 16:16; 24:17, 17; 28:3; 34:22; 38:17; Ps

23:4; 44:19; 107:10, 14; Isa 9:2; Jer 2:6; 13:16; Am 5:8).

Miraculous:

In Egypt (Ex 10:21-22; Ps 105:28), at Sinai (Ex 20:21; Heb 12:18), at the Crucifixion (Mt 27:45; Mk 15:33).

Figurative:

Of judgments (Pr 20:20; Isa 8:22; 13:10; Jer 4:28; 13:16; La 3:2; Eze 32:7-8; Joel 2:2, 10; Am 4:13; 5:18, 20; 8:9; Mic 7:8; Mt 24:29; Mk 13:24; Lk 23:45; Rev 8:12; 9:2). Of powers of evil (Lk 22:53; Eph 6:12; Col 1:13; 1Th 5:5; Rev 16:10).

Of the abode of the lost (Mt 8:12; 22:13; 25:30).

Of spiritual blindness (Isa 9:2; 42:16; 50:10; Mt 4:16; 6:22-23; Lk 1:79; 11:34; Jn 1:5; 3:19-21; 8:12; 11:9-10; Ac 26:18; Ro 1:21; 13:12-13; 1Co 4:5; 2Co 4:6; 6:14; Eph 5:8, 11; 1Th 5:4-5; 1Pe 2:9; 1Jn 1:5-7; 2:8-11). *See Blindness, Spiritual.*

Symbolic:

Of divine inscrutability (2Sa 22:10-12; Ps 18:11; 97:2). On Mt. Sinai (Ex 19:16; 20:21; Dt 4:11; 5:22; Heb 12:18). In the Sanctuary (1Ki 8:12; 2Ch 6:1).

See Tabernacle.

DARKON [2010] (perhaps *rough,* or *stern*). A descendant of Solomon's servant, Jaala, who returned with Zerubbabel from Exile (Ezr 2:56; Ne 7:58).

DART [5025]. A weapon (Job 41:26). *See Armor; Arrows.*

DATE [882, 3427, *2789*]. A fruit (2Ch 31:5).

DATHAN [2018] (*strong*). A conspirator against Moses (Nu 16:1-35; 26:9; Dt 11:6; Ps 106:17).

DAUGHTER [1426, 1435, 3528, 5922, *2588, 2589, 5451*]. Daughter can refer to both persons and things, often without regard to relationship or gender.

1. Daughter (Ge 11:29) or other female descendant (Ge 24:48).

2. Women in general (Ge 28:6; Nu 25:1).

3. Worshipers of the true God (Ps 45:10; Isa 62:11; Mt 21:5; Jn 12:15).

4. City (Isa 37:22).

5. Citizens (Zec 2:10).

DAUGHTER-IN-LAW [3987, *3811*].

Filial: Instance of, Ruth (Ru 1:11-18; 4:15).

Unfilial: Prophecy of (Mic 7:6; Mt 10:35).

DAVID [1858, *1253*] (*beloved one*).

1. King of Israel. Genealogy of (Ru 4:18-22; 1Sa 16:11; 17:12; 1Ch 2:3-15; Mt 1:1-6; Lk 3:31-38). A shepherd (1Sa 16:11). Kills a lion and a bear (1Sa 17:34-36). Anointed king, while a youth, by the prophet Samuel, and inspired (1Sa 16:1, 13; Ps 89:19-37). Chosen of God (Ps 78:70).

Described to Saul (1Sa 16:18). Detailed as armor-bearer and musician at Saul's court (1Sa

16:21-23). Slays Goliath (1Sa 17). Love of Jonathan for (1Sa 18:1-4). Popularity and discretion of (1Sa 18). Saul's jealousy of (1Sa 18:8-30). Is defrauded of Merab and given Michal for his wife (1Sa 18:17-27). Jonathan intercedes for (1Sa 19:1-7). Probably writes Ps 11 at this period of his life.

Conducts a campaign against, and defeats, the Philistines (1Sa 19:8). Saul attempts to slay him; he escapes to Ramah and dwells at Naioth, where Saul pursues him (1Sa 19:9-24). About this time he writes Ps 59. He returns, and Jonathan makes a covenant with him (1Sa 20). He escapes by way of Nob, where he obtains some consecrated bread and Goliath's sword from Abimelech (1Sa 21:1-6; Mt 12:3-4), to Gath (1Sa 21:10-15). At this time he probably writes Pss 34, 35, 52, 56, and 120. He recruits an army of insurgents, goes to Moab, returning to Hereth (1Sa 22). Probably writes Pss 17, 58, 64, 109, and 142. He saves Keilah (1Sa 23:1-13). He makes a second covenant with Jonathan (1Sa 23:16-18). He goes to the wilderness of Ziph, and is betrayed to Saul (1Sa 23:13-26). He writes Ps 54 about the betrayal and probably Pss 22, 31, and 140. Saul is diverted from pursuit of (1Sa 23:27-28). At this time he probably writes Ps 12. Goes to En Gedi (1Sa 23:29). Writes Ps 57. Covenants with Saul (1Sa 26). Marries Nabal's widow, Abigail, and Ahinoam (1Sa 25). Dwells in the wilderness of Ziph, has the opportunity to kill Saul but takes his spear only, Saul is contrite (1Sa 26). Flees to Achish and dwells in Ziklag (1Sa 27). List of men who join him (1Ch 12:1-22). Conducts an expedition against Amalekites, misinforms Achish (1Sa 27:8-12). At this time probably writes Ps 141. Is refused permission to accompany the Philistines to battle against the Israelites (1Sa 28:1-2; 29). Rescues the people of Ziklag, who had been captured by the Amalekites (1Sa 30). Probably writes Ps 13. Death and burial of Saul and his sons (1Sa 31; 2Sa 21:1-14). Slays the murderer of Saul (2Sa 1:1-16). Lamentation over Saul (2Sa 1:17-27).

After dwelling one year and four months at Ziklag (1Sa 27:7), goes to Hebron, and is anointed king by Judah (2Sa 2:1-4, 11; 5:5; 1Ki 2:11; 1Ch 3:4; 11:1-3). List of those who join him at Hebron (1Ch 12:23-40). Ish-Bosheth, the son of Saul, crowned (2Sa 2-4). David wages war against, and defeats, Ish-Bosheth (2Sa 2:13-32; 3:4). Demands the restoration of Michal, his wife (2Sa 3:14-16). Abner revolts from Ish-Bosheth, and joins David, but is slain by Joab (2Sa 3). David punishes Ish-Bosheth's murderers (2Sa 4).

Anointed king over all Israel, after reigning over Judah at Hebron seven years and six months, and reigns thirty-three years (2Sa 2:11; 5:5; 1Ch 3:4; 11:1-3; 12:23-40; 29:27). Makes a conquest of Jerusalem (2Sa 5:6; 1Ch 11:4-8; Isa 29:1). Builds a palace (2Sa 5:11; 2Ch 2:3). Friendship of, with Hiram, king of Tyre (2Sa 5:11; 1Ki 5:1). Prospered of God (2Sa 5:10, 12; 1Ch 11:9). Fame of (1Ch 14:17). Philistines make war against, and are defeated by him (2Sa 5:17, 25).

Assembles 30, 000 men to escort the ark to Jerusalem with music and thanksgiving (2Sa 6:1-5). Uzzah is stricken when he attempts to steady the ark (2Sa 6:6-11). David is terrified and leaves the ark at the house of Obed-Edom (2Sa 6:9-11). After three months brings the ark to Jerusalem with dancing and great joy (2Sa 6:12-16; 1Ch 13). Organized the tabernacle service (1Ch 9:22; 15:16-24; 16:4-6, 37-43). Offers sacrifice, distributes gifts, and blesses the people (2Sa 6:17-19). Michal rebukes him for his religious enthusiasm (2Sa 6:20-23). Desires to build a temple, is forbidden, but receives promise that his seed should reign forever (2Sa 7:12-16; 23:5; 1Ch 17:11-14; 2Ch 6:16; Ps 89:3-4; 132:11-12; Ac 15:16; Ro 15:12). *See Covenants, Major in the Old Testament.* Interpretation and fulfillment of this prophecy (Ac 13:22-23). At this time, probably writes Pss 15, 16, 24, 101, and 138. Conquers the Philistines, Moabites, and Syria (2Sa 8).

Treats Mephibosheth, the lame son of Jonathan, with great kindness (2Sa 9:6; 19:24-30). Sends commissioners with a message of sympathy to Hanun, son of the king of Ammon; the message is misinterpreted and commissioners treated with indignity; David retaliates by invading his kingdom and defeating the combined armies of the Ammonites and Syrians (2Sa 10; 1Ch 19). Probably writes Pss 18, 20, and 21.

Commits adultery with Bathsheba (2Sa 11:2-5). Wickedly causes the death of Uriah (2Sa 11:6-25). Takes Bathsheba to be his wife (2Sa 11:26-27). Is rebuked by the prophet Nathan (2Sa 12:1-14). Repents of his crime and confesses his guilt (Pss 6; 32; 38; 39; 40; 51). Is disciplined on account of his crime (Ps 38; 41; 69). His infant son by Bathsheba dies (2Sa 12:15-23). Solomon is born (2Sa 12:24-25).

Ammonites defeated and tortured (2Sa 12:26-31). Amnon's crime, his murder by Absalom, and Absalom's flight (2Sa 13). Absalom's return (2Sa 14:1-24). Absalom's usurpation (2Sa 14-15). David's flight from Jerusalem (2Sa 15:13-37). He probably writes, at this time Pss 5, 7, 26, 61, 69, 70, 86, and 143. Shimei curses him (2Sa 16). Crosses the Jordan (2Sa 17:21-29). Absalom's defeat and death (2Sa 18). Laments the death of Absalom (2Sa 18:33; 19:1-4). Reprimanded by Joab (2Sa 19:5-7). David reprimands the priests for not showing loyalty amid the murmurings of the people against him (2Sa 19:9-15). Shimei sues for clemency (2Sa 19:16-23). Mephibosheth sues for the king's favor (2Sa 19:24-30). Barzillai rewarded (2Sa 19:31-40). Judah accused by the ten tribes of stealing him away (2Sa 19:41-43). Returns to Jerusalem (2Sa 20:1-3). At this time, probably composes Pss 27, 66, 122, and 144.

Sheba's conspiracy against David, and his death (2Sa 20). Makes Amasa general (2Sa 19:13). Amasa is slain (2Sa 20:4-10). Consigns seven sons of Saul to the Gibeonites to be slain to atone for Saul's persecution of the Gibeonites (2Sa 21:1-14). Buries the bones of Saul and his sons (2Sa 21:12-14).

Defeats the Philistines (2Sa 21:15-22; 1Ch 20:4-8). Takes the military strength of Israel without divine authority, and is reproved (2Sa 24; 1Ch 21; 27:24). Probably composes Pss 20, 131. Marries Abishag (1Ki 1:1-4). Probably composes Pss 19 and 111.

Reorganizes the tabernacle service (1Ch 22-26; 2Ch 7:6; 8:14; 23:18; 29:27-30; 35:15; Ezr 3:10; 8:20).

Adonijah usurps the scepter. Solomon is appointed to the throne (1Ki 1; 1Ch 23:1). Delivers his charge to Solomon (1Ki 2:1-11; 1Ch 22:6-19; 28: 29). Probably composes Pss 23 and 145.

Last words of (2Sa 23:1-7). Death probably (1Ki 2:10; 1Ch 29:28; Ac 2:29-30). Tomb of (Ac 2:29). Age of, at death (2Sa 5:4-5; 1Ch 29:28). Length of reign, forty years (1Ki 2:11; 1Ch 29:27-28).

Wives of (2Sa 3:2-5; 11:3, 27; 1Ch 3:5). Children born at Hebron (2Sa 3:2-5; 1Ch 3:4), at Jerusalem (2Sa 5:14-16; 1Ch 3:5-8; 14:4-7). Descendants of (1Ch 3).

Civil and military officers of (2Sa 8:16-18). *See Cabinet.*

List of his heroes and of their exploits (2Sa 23; 1Ch 11; 12:23-40).

Devoutness of (1Sa 13:14; 2Sa 6:5, 14-18; 7:18-29; 8:11; 24:25; 1Ki 3:14; 1Ch 17:16-27; 29:10; 2Ch 7:17; Zec 12:8; Ps 6; 7; 11; 13; 17; 22; 26; 27:7-14; 28; 31; 35; 37; 38; 39; 40:11-17; 42; 43; 51; 54; 55; 56; 57; 59; 60; 61; 62; 64:1-6; 66; 69; 70; 71; 86; 101; 108; 120:1-2; 140; 141; 142; 143; 144; Ac 13:22).

Justice in the administration of (2Sa 8:15; 1Ch 18:14). Discretion of (1Sa 18:14, 30). Meekness of (1Sa 24:7; 26:11; 2Sa 16:11; 19:22-23). Merciful (2Sa 19:23).

David as a musician (1Sa 16:21-23; 1Ch 15:16; 23:5; 2Ch 7:6; 29:26; Ne 12:36; Am 6:5), poet (2Sa 22). *See Psalms.* David as a prophet (2Sa 23:2-7; 1Ch 28:19; Mt 22:41-46; Ac 2:25-38; 4:25).

Type of Christ (Ps 2; 16; 18:43; 69:7-9, 20-21, 26, 29; 89:19-37). Jesus called son of (Mt 9:27; 12:23; 15:22; 20:30-31; 21:9; 22:42; Mk 10:47-48; Lk 18:37, 39).

Prophecies concerning him and his kingdom (Nu 24:17, 19; 2Sa 7:11-16; 1Ch 17:9-14; 22; 2Ch 6:5-17; 13:5; 21:7; Ps 89:19-37; Isa 9:7; 16:5; 22:20-25; Jer 23:5; 33:15-26; Lk 1:32-33).

Chronicles of, written by Samuel, Nathan, and Gad (1Ch 29:29-30).

2. A prophetic name for Christ (Jer 30:9; Eze 34:23-24; 37:24-25; Hos 3:5).

DAVID, CITY OF

1. Portion of Jerusalem occupied by David in c. 1003 B.C.; 2500 feet above sea level. Originally a Canaanite city (Eze 16:3), it dates back to the third millennium. Solomon enlarged the City of David for the temple and other buildings, and later kings enlarged the city still more (2Ch 32:4-5, 30; 2Ki 20:20; Isa 22:9-11).

2. Bethlehem (Lk 2:11).

DAY [*2256, 3427, 3429, 4740, 8702, 8840, 10317, *892, 2069, 2465, 4187, 4879, 4958*]. A creative period (Ge 1:5, 8, 13, 19, 23, 31; 2:2). Divided into twelve hours (Jn 11:9). Prophetic (Da 8:14, 26; 12:11-12; Rev 9:15; 11:3; 12:6). Six working days ordained (Ex 20:9; Eze 46:1). Sixth day of the week called preparation day (Mk 15:42; Jn 19:14, 31, 42). First day of the week called the Lord's Day (Rev 1:10). With the Lord as a thousand years (2Pe 3:8).

Day's journey, eighteen or twenty miles (Ex 3:18; 1Ki 19:4; Jnh 3:4). Sabbath day's journey, about two thousand paces (Ac 1:12). The seventh of the week ordained as a day of rest. *See Sabbath.*

DAY OF ATONEMENT An annual Hebrew feast when the high priest offered sacrifices for the sins of the nation (Lev 23:27; 25:9). It was the only fast period required by Mosaic law (Lev 16:29; 23:31). The day marked the only entry of the high priest into the Most Holy Place (Lev 16). It was observed on the tenth day of the seventh month; a day of great solemnity and strictest conformity to the law.

DAY OF CHRIST The period connected with reward and blessing at the coming of Christ for believers (1Co 1:8; Php 1:6, 10; 2:16). *See below, Day of the Lord.*

DAY OF THE LORD
1. A "day" of God's judgment on the nations (Isa 13:6-9; Eze 30:3; Joel 3:14; Ob 1:15), on Israel (Joel 1:15; 2:1, 11, 31; Am 5:18-20).
2. The period commencing with the second advent of Christ and terminating with the making of a new heaven and a new earth (Isa 65:17-19; 66:22; 2Th 2:2; 2Pe 3:13; Rev 21:1). Preceded and introduced by apocalyptic judgments (Rev 4:1–19:6).

DAY'S JOURNEY Eighteen or twenty miles (Ex 3:18; 1Ki 19:4; Jnh 3:4). Sabbath day's journey, about two thousand paces (Ac 1:12).

DAYSMAN NIV "someone to arbitrate" (Job 9:33). *See Mediation.*

DAYSPRING NIV "dawn" (Job 38:12) and "rising sun" (Lk 1:78).

DAYSTAR *See Morning Star.*

DEACON [*1354, 1356*] (*serve*). An officer charged with the temporal affairs of the church. The seven men chosen to help the apostles are often considered deacons (Ac 6:1-6). Qualifications of (1Ti 3:8-13). The Greek word translated deacon signifies servant, and is so translated (Mt 23:11; Jn 12:26). Also translated minister (Mk 10:43; 1Co 3:5; 1Th 3:2).

DEACONESS [*1354, 1356*] (*serve*). Phoebe is called a "servant of the church," which could be translated a "deaconess" (Ro 16:1, ftn).

1Ti 3:1-13 lists character qualities of deacons. V. 11 refers either to deacons' wives or to special qualities required of deaconesses (see ftn). *See Women, In Leadership.*

DEAD [*6, 1588, *1775*, 2222, 2728, 4637, 4638, 5577, 5782, 5877, 5883, 7007, 7516, 8327, 8619, 10625, *633, 650, 1586, 2505, 2506, 2569, 3121, 3156, 3738, 5271, 5462*]:

Raised to life, instances of:
Son of the widow of Zarephath (1Ki 17:17-23), Shunammite's son (2Ki 4:32-37), young man laid in Elisha's tomb (2Ki 13:21), widow's son (Lk 7:12-15), Jairus' daughter (Lk 8:49-55), Lazarus (Jn 11:43-44), Dorcas (Ac 9:37-40), Eutychus (Ac 20:9-12, w Heb 11:35).

Prepared for burial by washing (Ac 9:37), anointing (Mt 26:12), wrapping in linen (Mt 27:59). Burned. *See Cremation.* Burnings of incense made for (2Ch 16:14; 21:19; Jer 34:5).
See Burial; Cremation; Embalming.

Pictured as:
Rest (Job 3:13-19). Sleep (Job 14:11-15, 21; Da 12:12). Hopelessness (Job 17:13-15; Ecc 9:5-6; Eze 32:27, 30). Separation from God (Ps 6:5; 30:9; 88:10-12; 115:17).
Life after (Job 14:12-15; Ps 49:15; Da 12:2; Lk 20:35-36; Jn 11:25). Understanding after (Eze 32:31; Lk 16:19-31).

Abode of:
The pit (Job 17:13-15). Abraham's side (Lk 16:22), hell (Lk 16:23). *See Hades; Hell; Grave; Sheol.* Paradise (Lk 23:43).
See Burial; Death, Physical; Mourning; Resurrection; Righteous, Promises to; Wicked, Punishment of.

DEAD SEA Lies SE of Jerusalem. Called the Salt Sea (Ge 14:3; Nu 34:12), Sea of the Plain (Dt 3:17; 4:49; Jos 3:16), eastern sea (Joel 2:20; Zec 14:8). Prophecy concerning (Eze 47:7-10, 18).

DEAD SEA SCROLLS Discovered in 1947 by a Bedouin in caves a mile or so W of the NW corner of the Dead Sea, at Qumran. So far mss have been found in 11 caves, and they are mostly dated as coming from the last two centuries B.C. and the first century A.D. At least 382 mss are represented by the fragments of Cave Four alone, c. 100 of which are biblical mss. These include fragments of every book of the Hebrew Bible except Esther. Some of the books are represented in many copies. Not all the mss are in fragments; some are complete or nearly complete. In addition to biblical books, fragments of apocryphal and apocalyptic books, commentaries, psalms, and sectarian literature have been found. Near the caves are the remains of a monastery of huge size, possibly the headquarters of a monastic sect of Jews called the Essenes. The discoveries at Qumran are important for biblical studies in general. They are of great importance for a study of the OT text, both Hebrew and the LXX. They are also of importance in relation to the NT, as they furnish the background to the preaching of John the Baptist and Jesus. There is no evidence that either John the Baptist or Jesus was a member of the group. *See Testaments, Time Between.*

DEAFNESS [263+4202, 3087, 3094, 4946+9048, *3273*]. Law concerning (Lev 19:14). Inflicted by God (Ex 4:11). Miraculous cure of (Mt 11:5; Mk 7:32; 9:25).

Figurative of moral insensitivity (Isa 6:10; 29:18; 35:5; Eze 12:2; Mt 13:15; Jn 12:40; Ac 28:26-27).

See Blindness, Spiritual; Conscience, Dead; Impenitence; Obduracy.

DEATH, PHYSICAL [*See DEAD]. Universal to mankind (Ecc 3:2, 19-21; Ro 5:12, 14; 1Pe 1:24). Time of, unknown (Ge 27:2; Ps 39:4, 13). Nearness to (Jos 23:14; 1Sa 20:3). Separates spirit and body (Ecc 12:5, 7).

Does not end conscious existence (Lk 20:34-38; 23:39-43; Rev 20:12-13). Exemplified in the appearance of Moses and Elijah at the transfiguration of Jesus (Mt 17:2-3; Mk 9:4-5; Lk 9:30-33).

Not to be feared by the righteous (Mt 10:28). Brings rest to the righteous (Job 3:13, 17-19). Dispossesses of earthly goods (Job 1:21; Ps 49:17; Lk 12:16-20; 1Ti 6:7).

A judgment (Ge 2:17; 3:19; 6:7, 11-13; 19:12-13, 24-25; Jos 5:4-6; 1Ch 10:13-14). God's power over (Dt 32:39; 1Sa 2:6; Ps 68:20; 2Ti 1:10). Christ's power over (Heb 2:14-15; Rev 1:18). To be destroyed (Isa 25:8; Hos 13:14; 1Co 15:21-22, 26, 55-57; Rev 20:14; 21:4).

Preparation for (2Ki 20:1; Lk 12:35-37). By Moses (Nu 27:12-23), by David (1Ki 2:1-10), by Ahithophel (2Sa 17:23). Apostrophe to (Hos 13:14; 1Co 15:55).

Described as:

Sleep (Dt 31:16; 1Ki 14:31; 15:8, 24; 16:6, 28; Job 7:21; 14:12; Ps 76:5-6; Jer 51:39; Da 12:2; Jn 11:11; Ac 7:60; 13:36; 1Co 15:6, 18, 51; 1Th 4:13-15). "Breathing one's last" or "giving up one's spirit" (Ge 25:8; 35:29; La 1:19; Ac 5:10). King of terrors (Job 18:14). A change (Job 14:14). Going to your fathers (Ge 15:15; 25:8; 35:29). Putting off this tabernacle (2Pe 1:14). Requiring the soul (Lk 12:20). Going the way from which there is no return (Job 16:22). Being gathered to our people (Ge 49:33). In silence (Ps 94:17; 115:17). Returning to dust (Ge 3:19). Being cut down (Job 14:2). Fleeing as a shadow (Job 14:2). Departing (Php 1:23).

Desired:

(Jer 8:3; Rev 9:6). By Moses (Nu 11:15). By Elijah (1Ki 19:4). By Job (Job 3; 6:8-11; Job 7:1-3, 15-16; 10:1). By Jonah (Jnh 4:8). By Simeon (Lk 2:29). By Paul (2Co 5:2, 8; Php 1:20-23).

Exemption from:

Enoch (Ge 5:24; Heb 11:5). Elijah (2Ki 2). Promised to saints, when Christ returns for

believers (1Co 15:51; 1Th 4:15, 17). No death in heaven (Lk 20:36; Rev 21:4).

Inevitable:

(2Sa 14:14; Job 7:1, 8-10, 21; 10:21-22; 14:2, 5, 7-12, 14, 19-21; 16:22; 21:23, 25-26, 32-33; 30:23; 34:15, 19; Ps 49:7-10; 82:7; 89:48; 144:4; Ecc 2:14-18; 5:15; 8:8; 9:5, 10; Isa 51:12; Jn 9:21; Zec 1:5; Jn 9:4; Heb 9:27; 13:14; Jas 1:10-11).

Of the Righteous:

A transition (Lk 16:22; 23:43). Balaam extols (Nu 23:10). Peaceful (Ps 37:37). Precious in the sight of the Lord (Ps 116:15). A merciful providence in (Isa 57:1-2). Anticipated with confidence (Pr 14:32; Lk 2:29; Ac 7:59; Ro 14:7-8; 1Co 3:21-23; 2Co 5:1, 4, 8; 1Th 5:9-10; 2Ti 4:6-8; Heb 11:13). Hope in (Da 12:13; 1Co 15:51-57; 2Co 1:9-10; 1Th 4:13-14; 2Pe 1:11, 14; Rev 14:13).

Of the Wicked:

(Job 18:14, 18; 20:4-5, 8, 11; 21:13, 17-18, 23-26; 24:20, 24; 27:8, 19-23; Ps 37:1-2, 9-10, 35-36; 49:7, 9-10, 14, 17, 19-20; Pr 5:22-23; 11:7, 10; 21:16; Ecc 8:10; Isa 14:11, 15). Sudden (Nu 16:32; Pr 10:25, 27; Isa 17:14; Ac 5:3-10). A judgment (Nu 16:29-30; 1Sa 25:38; Job 36:12, 14, 18, 20; Ps 55:23; 58:9; 78:50; 92:7; Pr 2:22; 14:32; Isa 26:14; Jer 16:3-4; Eze 28:8, 10; Am 9:10; Lk 12:20).

Scenes of:

Jacob blessing his sons (Ge 49:1-33; Heb 11:21). Moses (Dt 34:1-7). Samson (Jdg 16:25-30). Eli (1Sa 4:12-18). The wife of Phinehas (1Sa 4:19-21). Zechariah (2Ch 24:22). Jesus (Mt 27:34-53; Mk 15:23-38; Lk 23:27-49; Jn 19:16-30). Stephen (Ac 7:59-60).

Death Penalty:

Shall not be remitted (Nu 35:31). In the Mosaic law the death penalty was inflicted for murder (Ge 9:5-6; Nu 35:16-21, 30-33; Dt 17:6), adultery (Lev 20:10; Dt 22:24), incest (Lev 20:11-12, 14), bestiality (Ex 22:19; Lev 20:15-16), sodomy (Lev 18:22; 20:13), rape of a betrothed virgin (Dt 22:25), perjury (Zec 5:4), kidnapping (Ex 21:16; Dt 24:7), upon a priest's daughter, who committed immorality (Lev 21:9), witchcraft (Ex 22:18), offering human sacrifice (Lev 20:2-5), striking or cursing father or mother (Ex 21:15, 17; Lev 20:9), disobedience to parents (Dt 21:18-21), theft (Zec 5:3-4), blasphemy (Lev 24:23), Sabbath desecration (Ex 35:2; Nu 15:32-36), prophesying falsely or propagating false doctrines (Dt 13:10), sacrificing to false gods (Ex 22:20), refusing to abide by the decision of the court (Dt 17:12), treason (1Ki 2:25; Est 2:23), sedition (Ac 5:36-37).

Not inflicted on the testimony of less than two witnesses (Nu 35:30; Dt 17:6; 19:15).

Modes of Execution of the Death Penalty—
Burning (Ge 38:24; Lev 20:14; 21:9; Jer 29:22; Eze 23:25; Da 3:19-23). Stoning (Lev 20:2, 27; Nu 14:10; 15:33-36; Dt 13:10; 17:5; 22:21, 24; Jos 7:25; 1Ki 21:10; Eze 16:40). Hanging (Ge 40:22;

Dt 21:22-23; Jos 8:29; Est 7:10). Beheading (Mt 14:10; Mk 6:16, 27-28). Crucifixion (Mt 27:35, 38; Mk 15:24, 27; Lk 23:33). The sword (Ex 32:27-28; 1Ki 2:25, 34, 46; Ac 12:2).

Executed By—
The witnesses (Dt 13:9; 17:7; Ac 7:58). The congregation (Nu 15:35-36; Dt 13:9).

Figurative:
(Ro 6:2-11; 7:1-11; 8:10-11; Col 2:20; 2Ti 2:11). Symbolized by the pale horse (Rev 6:8).
See Dead; Regeneration; Second Death; Spiritual Death.

DEBAR *See Lo Debar.*

DEBIR [1809, 1810] (*back room [of a shrine temple for oracle pronouncement]*).
1. King of Eglon (Jos 10:3-27).
2. A town in the mountains of Judah. Also called Kiriath Sepher which signifies a city of books (Jos 15:15-16). Anakites expelled from, by Joshua (Jos 11:21). Taken by Othniel (Jos 15:15-17, 49; Jdg 1:12-13). Allotted to the Aaronites (Jos 21:15).
3. A place near the Valley of Achor (Jos 15:7).

DEBORAH [1806] (*hornet, wasp, wild honey bee*).
1. A nurse to Rebekah (Ge 24:59). Buried beneath an oak under Bethel (Ge 35:8).
2. The prophetess, a judge of Israel (Jdg 4:4-5; 5:7). Inspires Barak to defeat Sisera (Jdg 4:6-16). Triumphant song of (Jdg 5).

DEBT [2471, 4200+5957, 5391, 5963, 9024, 9023, *625*, *1245*, *4051*, *4052*, *4053*]. Teaching against (Ro 13:8).

Security for: Warnings against becoming a guarantor for others (Pr 11:15; 22:26). Clothing taken as, must be returned by sundown (Ex 22:25-27; Dt 24:10-13; Job 22:6; Am 2:8). Houses and property (Ne 5:3-4). Children (Job 24:9). Millstones forbidden (Dt 24:6).
See Debtor; Creditor; Security, For Debt.

DEBTOR [5967, *4050*, *5971*]. Laws concerning (Ex 21:2-6; 22:10-15; Lev 25:14-17, 25-41, 47-55; Dt 24:10-13; Ne 10:31; Mt 5:25-26, 40; 18:25). Sold for debt (2Ki 4:1-7; Ne 5:3-5; Mt 18:25). Imprisoned for debt (Mt 18:30). Oppressed (2Ki 4:1-7; Ne 5:3-5; Job 20:18-19; Mt 18:28-30). Mercy toward, commanded (Mt 18:23-27). Wicked (Lk 20:9-16).
See Creditor; Debt; Security, For Debt.

DECALOGUE (*ten words*). Written by God (Ex 24:12; 31:18; 32:16; Dt 5:22; 9:10; Hos 8:12). Divine authority of (Ex 20:1; 34:27-28; Dt 5:4-22). Called the Words of the Covenant (Ex 34:28; Dt 4:13). Tables of Testimony (Ex 31:18; 34:29; 40:20).
Listed (Ex 20:1-17; Dt 5:6-21). Confirmed, by Jesus (Mt 19:18-19; 22:34-40; Lk 10:25-28), by Paul (Ro 13:8-10).
See Commandments and Statutes, of God.

DECAPOLIS [*1279*] (*[league of] ten cities*). Ten cities situated in one district on the east of the Sea of Galilee (Mt 4:25; Mk 5:20; 7:31).

DECEIT [*423, 1704, 2744, 3950, 5327, 5958, 6810, 7331, 8228, 8245, 8736, 9214, 9438, 9567, *572*, *573*, *1515*, *1987*, *4165*, *4414*, *4415*, *4418*, *5854*, *5855*, *6022*]. Is falsehood (Ps 119:118). The tongue is an instrument of (Ro 3:13). Comes from the heart (Mk 7:22). Characteristic of the heart (Jer 17:9). God abhors (Ps 5:6). Forbidden (Pr 24:28; 1Pe 3:10). Christ was perfectly free from (Isa 53:9, w 1Pe 2:22).
Saints free from (Ps 24:4; Zep 3:13; Rev 14:5), purpose against (Job 27:4), avoid (Job 31:5), shun those addicted to (Ps 101:7), pray for deliverance from those who use (Ps 43:1; 120:2), delivered from those who use (Ps 72:14), should beware of those who teach (Eph 5:6; Col 2:8), should lay aside, in seeking truth (1Pe 2:1). Ministers should lay aside (2Co 4:2; 1Th 2:3).
The wicked are full of (Ro 1:29), devise (Ps 35:20; 38:12; Pr 12:5), utter (Ps 10:7; 36:3), work (Pr 11:18), increase in (2Ti 3:13), use, to themselves (Jer 37:9; Ob 7), delight in (Pr 20:17).
False teachers are workers of (2Co 11:13), preach (Jer 14:14; 23:26), impose on others by (Ro 16:18; Eph 4:14), sport themselves with (2Pe 2:13). Hypocrites practice (Hos 11:12). False witnesses use (Pr 12:17). A characteristic of Antichrist (2Jn 7). Characteristic of apostasy (2Th 2:10).
Evil of: Hinders knowledge of God (Jer 9:6). Keeps from turning to God (Jer 8:5). Leads to pride and oppression (Jer 5:27-28), to lying (Pr 14:25). Often accompanied by fraud and injustice (Ps 10:7; 43:1). Hatred often concealed by (Pr 26:24-26). The folly of fools is (Pr 14:8). The kisses of an enemy are (Pr 27:6). Punishment of (Ps 55:23; Jer 9:7-9).
Blessedness of being free from (Ps 24:4-5; 32:2).
See Confidence, False; Deception; Falsehood; Flattery; Hypocrisy.

DECEPTION [See DECEIT].
Instances of:
By Satan (Ge 3:4). Abraham, in saying that Sarah was his sister (Ge 12:13; 20:2). Isaac, in saying that his wife was his sister (Ge 26:7). Jacob and Rebekah, in imposing Jacob on his father, and Jacob's impersonating Esau (Ge 27:6-23). Jacob's sons, in entrapping the Shechemites (Ge 34:13-31), in representing to their father that Joseph had been destroyed by wild beasts (Ge 37:29-35). Joseph, in his ruse with his brothers (Ge 42-44). The Gibeonites, in misrepresenting their habitat (Jos 9:3-15). Ehud deceives Eglon, and slays him (Jdg 3:15-30). Delilah deceives Samson (Jdg 16:4-20). David feigns insanity (1Sa 21:10-15). Amnon deceives Tamar by feigning sickness (2Sa 13:6-14). Hushai deceives Absalom (2Sa 16:15-19). Sanballat tries to deceive Nehemiah (Ne 6). By Absalom, when he avenged his sister (2Sa

13:24-28), when he began his conspiracy (2Sa 15:7). The old prophet (1Ki 13:18). Gehazi (2Ki 5:20). Job's friends (Job 6:15). Doeg (Ps 52:2).

Herod (Mt 2:8). Pharisees (Mt 22:16). Chief priests (Mk 14:1). Lawyer (Lk 10:25). Ananias and Sapphira (Ac 5:1).

See Deceit; Hypocrisy; Falsehood; False Witness.

Self Deception: *See False Confidence; Flattery.*

DECISION [*3025, 3519, 5477, 9149, 10418, *3212*].

Teaching Concerning:
Choosing life (Dt 30:19). Committing to the Lord (Jos 24:15; 1Sa 12:20; 1Ki 18:21; Isa 50:7; Mt 6:24; 8:21-22; Lk 9:59-62; 1Co 15:58). Walking righteously (Jos 1:7; 2Ch 19:11; Pr 4:25-27; Mt 4:17; 2Th 3:13; 1Ti 6:11-14; Heb 12:1; 1Pe 1:13; 2Pe 1:10). Remaining in Christ (Jn 15:4-5, 7, 9; 1Jn 2:24, 28).

Endurance in:
Obedience (Jn 8:31; 1Co 15:58; Col 2:6-7; 2Th 2:15, 17; 2Pe 3:17-18; 2Jn 8), grace (Ac 13:43; 2Ti 2:1, 3), faith (Ac 14:22; 1Co 16:13; Php 1:27; Col 1:23; Heb 3:6-8, 14; 4:14; 10:23, 35; 1Pe 5:8-9; Jude 20-21), Christian liberty (Gal 5:1-26), the Lord (Php 4:1), holiness (1Th 3:8, 13), sound doctrine (Eph 4:12; 2Ti 1:13-14; Tit 1:7, 9; Heb 2:1; 13:9, 13).

Instances of:
Abel (Heb 11:4). Enoch (Heb 11:5-6). Noah (Heb 11:7). Abraham (Heb 11:8, 17-19). Jacob (Ge 28:20-22). Joseph (Ge 39:9). Moses (Nu 12:7; Heb 3:5; 11:24-26, 27). Israelites (Ex 19:7-8; 24:3, 7; Dt 4:4; 5:27; 26:17; Jos 22:34; 24:21-25; 1Ki 19:18; 2Ki 11:17; 2Ch 11:16; 13:10-11; 15:12, 15; 23:16; 29:10; Ezr 10:3-44; Ne 9:38; 10:28-31; Jer 34:15; 42:5-6; 50:5; Hos 11:12). Levites (Ex 32:26). Caleb (Nu 14:6-10, 24; Dt 1:36; Jos 14:14). Balaam (Nu 22:15-18; 24:13). Phinehas (Nu 25:7-13). Joshua (Jos 24:15). Gideon (Jdg 6:25-28). Ruth (Ru 1:16).

Saul (1Sa 11:4-7). David (1Sa 17:32-37; 2Sa 22:22-24). Psalmist (Ps 17:3; 26:6, 11; 27:3-8; 40:9-10; 56:12; 57:7-8; 71:17; 86:11; 101:2-3; 108:1; 116:9, 13-14, 16; 119:8, 30-31, 33-36, 57, 94, 106, 115, 125, 145-146). A prophet of Judah (1Ki 13:8-10). Elijah (1Ki 18:22). Jehoshaphat (1Ki 22:7-8; 2Ch 18:6-7). Micaiah (1Ki 22:13-14; 2Ch 18:6-7). Naaman (2Ki 5:13-17). Hezekiah (2Ki 18:6; 2Ch 15:17). Josiah (2Ki 22:2-3; 23:25; 2Ch 34:31). Nehemiah (Ne 2; 4:6; 6:11). Esther (Est 4:16). Job (Job 2:9-10). Daniel (Da 1:8). The three Hebrews (Da 3:11-12, 16-18).

Matthew (Mt 9:9). Joseph (Mk 15:43). Nathanael (Jn 1:49). Martha (Jn 11:27). Disciples (Lk 18:28; Jn 6:68-69; Ac 2:42). Paul (Ac 9:29; Ro 1:16; 8:38-39; Php 1:20-21; 2Ti 4:7-8). Church, of Ephesus (Rev 2:2-3). Of Sardis (Rev 3:4, 8, 10). Saints (Rev 14:4).

See Character.

DECISION, VALLEY OF [3025].
See Jehoshaphat, Valley of.

DECREE [*1819, 1821, 2976, 2978, 3076, 4180, 7422, 7756, 10057, 10186, 10302, *1504*].
An official ruling or law (Da 2:9; Est 1:20; Jnh 3:7; Ac 16:4; Rev 13:8).

DEDAN [1847].
1. A son of Raamah (Ge 10:7; 1Ch 1:9).
2. A son of Jokshan (Ge 25:3; 1Ch 1:32).
3. A country, probably bordering on Edom (Jer 49:8; Eze 25:13; 27:15, 20; 38:13).

DEDANITES [1848]. Descendants of Dedan (Isa 21:13).

DEDICATION [2853, 5694, 10273, *1589, 2952*]. Law concerning dedicated things (Lev 27; Nu 18:14; 1Ch 26:26-27). Must be without blemish (Lev 22:18-23; Mal 1:14). Not redeemable (Lev 27:28-29). Offering must be voluntary (Lev 1:3; 22:19). *See Offerings; Vows.* Of the tabernacle (Nu 7). Solomon's temple (1Ki 8; 2Ch 7:5). Second temple (Ezr 6:16-17). Of the wall of Jerusalem (Ne 12:27-43). Of houses (Dt 20:5). Of Samuel by his mother (1Sa 1:11, 22).

Of Self. *See Consecration.*

For instances of liberality in dedicated things. *See Liberality.*

DEDICATION, FEAST OF Annual Jewish feast celebrating the restoration of the temple following its desecration by Antiochus Epiphanes. Jesus delivered a discourse at this feast (Jn 10:22ff).

See Feasts; Hanukkah; Kislev; Maccabees; Month, 9.

DEED [1524, 1525, 1691, 1821, 3208, 3707, 4616, 4856, 5042, 5095, 5126, 5148, 6219, 6411, 6613, 6614, 6913, 7189, 7190, 7407, 8288, 8400, 9335, *2240, *3197, 4552, 4556*]. To the land (Jer 32:12, 14, 44). *See Land.* For works. *See Works, Good.*

DEEP [*696, 1524, 4394, 5099, 5185, 6676, 6678, 6906, 7516, 8041, 8101, 8145, 9166, 9333, 9554, *958, 960*]. The ocean (Ne 9:11), chaos (Ge 1:2), the deepest part of the sea (Ge 49:25), Abyss (Lk 8:31; Rev 9:1; 11:7).

DEER [385, 387, 3502, 3607]. Also called doe, roe deer. Designated among the clean animals, to be eaten (Dt 12:15; 14:5). Provided for Solomon's household (1Ki 4:23). Swiftness of (2Sa 2:18; 1Ch 12:8; Pr 6:5; SS 8:14; Isa 35:6). Surefootedness of (2Sa 22:34). Gentleness of (Pr 5:19).

DEFENSE [*1462, 1713, 1906, 3519, 5911, 8189, 9149, *664, 665*]. An argument made before a court. Of Jeremiah (Jer 26:12-16), Peter (Ac 4:8-13; 5:23-29), Stephen (Ac 7), Paul (Ac 22; 23:1-6; 24:10-21; 26:1-23). Military defenses. *See Fort; Armies.*

DEFILEMENT [*1458, 2725, 2729, 2866, 3237, 3238, 9210, *3662*]. Laws relating to (Lev 7:18-21; 11:43; 22:2-7). Caused by, leprosy (Lev 13:3, 44-46; 14; 22:4-7), copulation (Lev 15:17), discharges (Lev 15:1-17), childbirth (Lev 12:2-8; Lk 2:22), menses (Lev 15:19-33; 2Sa 11:4), touching the dead (Nu 19:11-22; 31:19-20), touching carcass of any unclean animal (Lev 11:39-40; 17:15-16; 22:8), touching carcass of any unclean thing (Lev 5:2-13; 11:8, 24-28, 31-38; 14:46-57; 15:5-11; Dt 23:10-11), slaying in battle (Nu 31:19-20). Contact with sinners falsely supposed to cause (Jn 18:28). Of priests (Lev 16:26, 28; Nu 19:7-10; Eze 44:25-26).

Egyptian perspective (Ge 43:32).

See Purification; Unclean, Uncleanness; Washings.

DEFORMITY [5426, 8594]. *See Blemish.*

DEGRADATION [2725, 7829, 9493, *869*]. Of God's people (Ex 32:25; Eze 16:6; 20:31; 2Pe 2:22).

DEGREES NIV "steps" on the stairway of Ahaz (2Ki 20:9-11).

DEGREES, SONGS OF Title of Pss 120 to 134 in the KJV. *See Ascents, Songs of.*

DEHAVITES At the end of Ezra 4:9 the KJV lists three peoples: "the Susanchites, the Dehavites, *and* the Elamites," while the NIV reads "the Elamites of Susa." The KJV transliterated "the Dehavites" from a difficult Aramaic term, rightly rendered "of" in the NIV.

DEITY OF JESUS *See Jesus the Christ, Deity of.*

DEKAR *See Ben-Deker, Ben-Dekar.*

DELAIAH [1933, 1934] (*Yahweh draws up [like water in a bucket]*).
1. Descendant of David (1Ch 3:1-24).
2. Head of the twenty-third course of priests (1Ch 24:18).
3. Prince who tried to save Jeremiah's roll from destruction (Jer 36:12, 25).
4. An ancestor of the tribe that returned under Zerubbabel (Ezr 2:60; Ne 7:62).
5. The father of Shemaiah (Ne 6:10).

DELIGHTING IN GOD [*9503, 2773, 2911, 2913, 2914, 4718, 5375, 6695, 8193, 8354, 8356, 8464, 8523, 8524, 9130, 9141, *2305, 5897*]. Commanded (Ps 37:4). Reconciliation leads to (Job 22:21, 26). Observing the Sabbath leads to (Isa 58:13-14).

Saints' Experience in:
Communion with God (SS 2:3). The law of God (Ps 1:2; 119:24, 35). The goodness of God (Ne 9:25). The comforts of God (Ps 94:19). Promises to (Ps 37:4). Blessedness of (Ps 112:1).

Hypocrites:
Pretend to (Isa 58:2). In heart despise (Job 27:10; Jer 6:10).

DELILAH [1935] (*tease*). Philistine woman who lured Samson to his ruin (Jdg 16:4-20).

DELIVERANCE [2208, 3802, 3828, 5911, 7119, 7129, 9591, *5401*]. *See Affliction; God, Providence of; Prayer, Answer to.*

DELIVERER [3802, 4635, 7117, *3392, 4861*]. A title of Jesus (Ro 11:26). *See Titles and Names.*

DELUGE *See Flood.*

DELUSION, SELF *See Self-Delusion.*

DEMAGOGISM Instances of: Absalom (2Sa 15:2-6). Pilate (Mt 27:17-26; Mk 15:15; Lk 23:13-24; Jn 18:38-40; 19:6-13). Felix (Ac 24:27). Herod (Ac 12:3).

DEMAS [*1318*] (*[common] folks*). Fellow laborer with Paul (Col 4:14; Phm 24), who later deserted him (2Ti 4:10).

DEMETRIUS [*1320*] (*of Demeter*).
1. A disciple praised by John (3Jn 12).
2. A silversmith at Ephesus who made trouble for Paul (Ac 19:23-27).

DEMONS [8717, *794, 1227, 1228, 1230*].
General:
Worship of (Lev 17:7; Dt 32:17; 2Ch 11:15; Ps 106:37; Mt 4:9; Lk 4:7; 1Co 10:20-21; 1Ti 4:1; Rev 13:4). Worship of, forbidden (Lev 17:7; Zec 13:2; Rev 9:20).

Testify to the deity of Jesus (Mt 8:29; Mk 1:23-24; 3:11; 5:7; Lk 8:28; Ac 19:15).

Adversaries of men (Mt 12:45). Sent to cause trouble between Abimelech and the Shechemites (Jdg 9:23). Messages given false prophets by (1Ki 22:21-23).

Believe and tremble (Jas 2:19). To be judged at the general judgment (Mt 8:29, w 2Pe 2:4; Jude 6). Punishment of (Mt 8:29; 25:41; Lk 8:28; 2Pe 2:4; Jude 6; Rev 12:7-9).

Possession By:
instances of—
Saul (1Sa 16:14-23; 18:10-11; 19:9-10). Two men of the Gadarenes (Mt 8:28-34; Mk 5:2-20). The mute man (Mt 9:32-33). The blind and mute man (Mt 12:22; Lk 11:14). The daughter of the Syrian Phoenician (Mt 15:22-29; Mk 7:25-30). The child with seizures (Mt 17:14-18; Mk 9:17-27; Lk 9:37-42). The man in the synagogue (Mk 1:23-26; Lk 4:33-35). Mary Magdalene (Mk 16:9; Lk 8:2-3). The herd of pigs (Mt 8:30-32).

Jesus falsely accused of being possessed of (Mk 3:22-30; Jn 7:20; 8:48; 10:20).

Exorcised—
Cast out by Jesus (Mt 4:24; 8:16; Mk 3:22; Lk 4:41).

Power over, given the disciples (Mt 10:1; Mk 6:7; 16:17). Cast out by the disciples (Mk 9:38; Lk 10:17), by Peter (Ac 5:16), by Paul (Ac 16:16-18; 19:12), by Philip (Ac 8:7). The disciples could not expel (Mk 9:18, 28-29). Sceva's sons exorcise (Ac 19:13-16). The parable of the man repossessed (Mt 12:43-45).

See Devil; Satan.

DENARIUS *[1324]. See Money.*

DENS [4995, 5104, 10129, *5068*]. Used as places of refuge (Jdg 6:2; Heb 11:38; Rev 6:15).

DENYING JESUS [4202, 5742, 6073, 6700, *237+2848+6017, 565, 766*]. *See Jesus the Christ, Rejected.*

DEPRAVITY [8845, *99, 1406, 2967, 2798, 5785*].

In the Nature of Humanity: (Ge 6:5-8; 8:21; Job 4:17-19; 9:2-3, 20, 29-31; 11:12; 14:4; 15:14-16; 25:4-6; Ps 5:9; 51:5; 58:1-5; 94:11; 130:3; Pr 10:20; 20:6, 9; 21:8; Isa 1:5-6; 51:1; Jer 13:23; 16:12; 17:9; Hos 6:7; Mic 7:2-4; Mt 7:17; 12:34-35; 15:19; Mk 7:21-23; Jn 3:19; 8:23; 14:17; Ro 1:21-32; Ro 2:1; 6:6, 19-20; 7:5, 11-15, 18-25; 8:5-8, 13; 1Co 2:14; 3:3; 5:9-10; 2Co 5:14; Gal 5:17, 19-21; Eph 2:1-3, 12; 4:17-19, 22; Jas 4:5; 1Pe 1:18; 2:25; 1Jn 1:8, 10; 2:16).

Universal: (Ge 6:11-13; 2Ch 6:36; Ps 14:1-3; 53:1-3; 143:2; Ecc 7:20; Isa 53:6; 64:6; Mic 7:2-4; Ro 3:9-19, 23; 5:6, 12-14; 11:32; Gal 3:10-11, 22; Jas 3:2; 1Jn 5:19).

See Fall of Mankind, The; Sin.

DEPRESSION *See Despondency.*

DEPUTY [5893, 7224]. An officer who administers the functions of a superior in his absence (1Ki 22:47; 2Ki 15:5; Ac 13:7-8; 18:12; 19:38).

DERBE [*1291, 1292*]. A city of Lycaonia. Paul fled to (Ac 14:6, 20). Visited by Paul and Silas (Ac 16:1). Gaius born in (Ac 20:4).

DERISION [996, 4353, 7840, 7841, 8562, 9240]. The wicked held in, by God (Ps 2:4; Pr 1:26).

Instances of: Sarah, when the angels gave her the promise of a child (Ge 18:12). The evil children of Bethel deride Elisha (2Ki 2:23). The people of Israel scoff at Hezekiah (2Ch 30:1-10).

See Irony; Sarcasm; Scoffing.

DESERTS [2999, 4497, 5877, 6440, 6858, 7233, 7470, 7480, 7481, 7684, 7708, 9220, *2244, 2245*]. Vast barren plains (Ex 5:3; Jn 6:13). Uninhabited places (Mt 14:15; Mk 6:31).

Described as:

Uninhabited and lonesome (Jer 2:6). Uncultivated (Nu 20:5; Jer 2:2). Desolate (Eze 6:14). Dry and without water (Ex 17:1; Dt 8:15). Trackless (Isa 43:19). Great and terrible (Dt 1:19). Waste and howling (Dt 32:10). Infested with wild beasts (Isa 13:21; Mk 1:13). Infested with serpents (Dt 8:15). Infested with robbers (Jer 3:2; La 4:19). Danger of traveling in (Ex 14:3; 2Co 11:26). Guides required in (Nu 10:31; Dt 32:10).

Phenomena of, Alluded to:

Mirage or deceptive appearance of water (Jer 15:18). Scorching wind (Jer 4:11). Tornadoes or whirlwinds (Isa 21:1). Clouds of sand and dust (Dt 28:24; Jer 4:12-13).

Mentioned in Scripture:

Arabian or great desert (Ex 23:31). Beth Aven (Jos 18:12). Beersheba (Ge 21:14; 1Ki 19:3-4). Damascus (1Ki 19:15). Edom (2Ki 3:8). En Gedi (1Sa 24:1). Gibeon (2Sa 2:24). Judea (Mt 3:1). Jeruel (2Ch 20:16). Kedemoth (Dt 2:26). Kadesh (Ps 29:8). Maon (1Sa 23:24-25). Paran (Ge 21:21; Nu 10:12). Shur (Ge 16:7; Ex 15:22). Sin (Ex 16:1). Sinai (Ex 19:1-2; Nu 33:16). Ziph (1Sa 23:14-15). Zin (Nu 20:1; 27:14). Of the Red Sea (Ex 13:18). Near Gaza (Ac 8:26). Wastelands often found in (Jer 17:6). Parts of, afforded pasture (Ge 36:24; Ex 3:1). Inhabited by wandering tribes (Ge 21:20-21; Ps 72:9; Jer 25:24). The persecuted fled to (1Sa 23:14; Heb 11:38). The disaffected fled to (1Sa 22:2; Ac 21:38).

Illustrative of:

Barrenness (Ps 106:9; 107:33, 35). Those deprived of all blessings (Hos 2:3). The world (SS 3:6; 8:5). The Gentiles (Isa 35:1, 6; 41:19). What offers no support (Jer 2:31). Desolation by armies (Jer 12:10-13; 50:12).

DESIGN [3110, 4742, 5126, 5504, 7451, *1927*]. In nature, evidence of (Job 12:7-11; Pr 16:4).

DESIRED OF ALL NATIONS

Some see as a title of Jesus (Hag 2:7). Others deny a messianic application and hold that it means the precious gifts of all nations (Hag 2:8 w Isa 60:5).

DESIRE, SPIRITUAL

[*203, 2094, 2773, 2775, 2911, 2913, 2914, 5883, 8356, 9294, 9592, 2121, 2123, 2420, 2527*]. For divine piety (Ps 17:11; 51:1-4, 7-13; 119:82; Hab 3:2). For divine fellowship (Ps 62:1; 63:1, 8). For divine help (Ps 25:5, 15; 68:28; 119:77, 116-117).

Exhortations concerning (Ps 70:4; 105:4; Isa 55:1-2; 55:3, 6; Hos 10:12).

For God (Ps 24:6; 27:8; 33:20; 40:1; 42:1-11; 69:3; 73:26; 119:10, 12, 19-20, 25, 40, 81, 88, 123, 131-132, 135-136, 149, 156, 174; 123:1-2; 130:5-6; 143:6-12; Isa 8:17, 19; 26:8-9; Mt 13:17; Lk 10:42; Php 3:12-14; 1Pe 1:10). For his holy courts (Ps 84:2).

Reward of (Dt 4:29; Ps 34:10; 37:4, 9, 34; 107:9; 119:2; Pr 2:3-5; Isa 40:31; Jer 29:13; Mt 5:6; Lk 1:53; 6:21; Jn 6:35; Heb 11:6).

See Hunger, Figurative; Thirst.
Evil desire: *See Imagination; Lust.*

DESOLATION, ABOMINATION OF
See Abomination That Causes Desolation.

DESPAIR [631, 1017, 3286, 3707, 3910, 5000, 7041, 9039, 9041, *1989*]. *See Despondency.*

DESPISERS [*996, 1022, 1718, 2361, 4415, 5540, 9493, *2969*]. General references to (Pr 1:30; 9:8; Mt 7:6; Ac 13:41; Ro 2:4; 2Ti 3:3; Heb 10:28; 2Pe 2:10).

DESPONDENCY (Isa 35:3-4; Heb 12:12-13). Caused by corrective judgments (Nu 17:12-13; Dt 28:65-67; Isa 2:19; Hos 10:8; Mt 24:30; Lk 23:29-30; Rev 6:14-17; 9:5-6), deferred hope (Pr 13:12), adversity (Job 4:5; 9:16-35; 17:7-16).

Lament in (Job 3:1-26; 17:13-16; Ps 6:6; 22:1-2; 55:4-7; 77:7-9; 88:3-17; Ecc 2:20; Jer 8:20; La 3:1-20; 5:15-22; Mic 7:1-7).

Instances of:

Cain, when God pronounced judgment upon him (Ge 4:13-14). Hagar, when cast out of the household of Abraham (Ge 21:15-16). Moses, when sent on his mission to the Israelites (Ex 4:1, 10, 13; 6:12), at the Red Sea (Ex 14:15), when the people lusted for flesh (Nu 11:15). The Israelites, on account of the cruel oppressions of the Egyptians (Ex 6:9). Joshua, over the defeat at Ai (Jos 7:7-9). Elijah, when he fled from Jezebel to the wilderness and sat under the broom tree and wished to die (1Ki 19:4). Jonah, after he had preached to the Ninevites (Jnh 4:3, 8). The mariners with Paul (Ac 27:20).

See Affliction, Consolation Under; Righteous, Promises to.

DESPOTISM *See Government, Monarchical.*

DESTINY [344, 784, 4200, 4948, 4972, 5247, 6067, 9286, *641, 3023, 4633, 5465, 5502*].
1. Final determined end. Of all people (Ecc 7:2; 9:2-3; Heb 9:27). Of the wicked (Ps 73:17; Jer 15:2; 43:11). Of believers (1Co 2:7).
2. The pagan god of fate (Isa 65:11).

DETECTIVES *See Spies.*

DEUEL [1979] (*known of God [El]*). Also called Reuel (Nu 2:14, ftn). Captain of the tribe of Dan (Nu 1:14; 2:14; 7:42; 10:20).

DEUTERONOMY (*second [giving] of the law*).

Author: Moses, though the preamble (1:1-5) and ftn of Moses' death (ch. 34) were written by someone else.

Date: c. 1406 B.C.

Outline:
I. The Preamble (1:1-5).
II. The Historical Prologue (1:6-4:43).
III. The Stipulations of the Covenant (4:44-26:19).
  A. The Great Commandment: The Demand for Absolute Allegiance (4:44-11:32).
  B. Supplementary Requirements (chs. 12-26).

1. Ceremonial consecration (12:1-16:17).
2. Governmental leaders and a righteous nation (16:18-21:21).
3. Sanctity of God's kingdom (21:22-25:19).
4. Confession of God as Redeemer-King (ch. 26).
IV. Ratification; Curses and Blessings (chs. 27-30).
V. Covenant Leadership Succession (chs. 31-34).
  A. Change of Leadership (31:1-29).
  B. Song of Moses (31:30-32:47).
  C. Moses' Testamental Blessing on the Tribes (32:48-33:29).
  D. Death of Moses and Succession of Joshua (ch. 34).

Alternate Outline:
I. First Address (1:1-4:43).
II. Second Address (4:44-28:68).
III. Third Address (chs. 29-33).
IV. Moses' Death (ch. 34).

DEVIL [*1229, 1333*] (*slanderer* or *liar*). One of the principal titles of Satan, the archenemy of God and of mankind. It is not known how he originated, unless Isaiah and Ezekiel give us a clue (Isa 14:12-20; Eze 28:12-19), but it is certain that he was not created evil. He rebelled against God when in a state of holiness and apparently led other angels into rebellion with him (Jude 6; 2Pe 2:4). He is a being of superhuman power and wisdom but is not omnipotent or omniscient. He tries to frustrate God's plans and purposes for human beings. His principal method of attack is by temptation. His power is limited, and he can go only as far as God permits. On the Judgment Day he will be cast into hell to remain there forever.
See Satan.

DEVOTED THING [1467, 2143, 2616, 2883, 3049, 3051, 3922, 5989, 8969, *41, 504, 1565, 1639+4674, 5082, 5309, 5435, 5816, 6067*]. That which is set apart to the Lord and therefore no longer belongs to the former owner (Lev 27:29, and ftn; Jos 7:1-15). *See Corban.*

DEVOTION [2876, 6313, 8354, 8491, 8969+, *605, 2339*].

To God: *See Religion.*
For conspicuous instances of, study Enoch, Noah, Abraham, Moses, David, Solomon's early life, Josiah, Asa, Isaiah, Elijah, Jeremiah, Daniel, Shadrach, Meshach, and Abednego.

To Jesus: *See Peter, Simon; John; Paul; Mary.*
For elaborated topics covering the subject, *See Love, Of People for God; Consecration; Zeal.*

DEW [3228, 10299]. A merciful providence (Dt 33:13). Forms imperceptibly (2Sa 17:12), in the night (Job 29:19). From the clouds (Pr 3:20). Called the dew of heaven (Da 4:15). Absence of (1Ki 17:1). Miraculous profusion and absence of (Jdg 6:36-40). *See Meteorology.*
Figurative (Ps 110:3; Isa 26:19; Hos 6:4; 13:3; 14:5).

DIADEM [5694, 7565]. A golden plate worn on the turban of the high priest (Ex 29:6; 39:30; Lev 8:9). A royal crown (Isa 62:3). *See Crown.*

DIAL NIV "stairway" (2Ki 20:11; Isa 38:8). *See Stairs.*

DIAMOND *See Emerald; Flint; Minerals of the Bible, 1; Stones.*

DIANA Goddess of the Ephesians (Ac 19:24, 27-28, 35). *See Artemis.*

DIASPORA (*scattered [like] seed*). The name applied to the Jews living outside of Israel and maintaining their religious faith among the Gentiles (Jas 1:1; 1Pe 1:1). By the time of Christ the diaspora must have been several times the population of Israel. *See Dispersion; Testaments, Time Between.*

DIBLAH [1812]. Probably an early copyist's error for Riblah, a town c. fifty miles S of Hamath (Eze 6:14).

DIBLAIM [1813] (*lump of [two dried fig] cakes*). Father of Hosea's wife (Hos 1:3).

DIBLATHAIM *See Almon Diblathaim; Beth Diblathaim.*

DIBON, DIBON GAD [1897, 1898].
1. Also called Dibon Gad and Dimon. A city on the northern banks of the Arnon (Nu 21:30). Israelites encamp at (Nu 33:45). Allotted to Gad and Reuben (Nu 32:3, 34; Jos 13:9, 17). Taken by Moab (Isa 15:2; Jer 48:18, 22).
2. A city in the tribe of Judah (Ne 11:25), probably identical with Dimonah (Jos 15:22).

DIBRI [1828] (possibly *speak*). The father of Shelomith (Lev 24:11).

DIDRACHMA (*two drachma*). The annual temple tax was two drachmas (Mt 17:24). *See Drachma; Money.*

DIDYMUS [1441] (*twin*). The surname of Thomas (Jn 11:16; 20:24; 21:2).

DIKLAH [1989] (*[place of] date palms*). The son of Joktan, and the name of a district inhabited by his descendants (Ge 10:27; 1Ch 1:21).

DILEAN [1939] (*cucumber* ISBE; *protrude* KB). A city of Judah (Jos 15:38).

DILIGENCE [3026, 6913, 10012, 10056, 5082, 1639]. Jesus as an example of (Mk 1:35; Lk 2:49).

Required:
By God in seeking him (1Ch 22:19; Heb 11:6), obeying him (Dt 6:17; 11:13), listening to him (Isa 55:2), striving after perfection (Php 3:13-14), developing Christian qualities (2Pe 1:5), keeping the soul (Dt 4:9), keeping the heart (Pr 4:23),

labors of love (Heb 6:10-12), following every good work (1Ti 3:10), guarding against defilement (Heb 12:15), seeking to be found spotless (2Pe 3:14), making our calling sure (2Pe 1:10), self-examination (Ps 77:6), lawful business (Pr 27:23; Ecc 9:10), teaching religion (2Ti 4:2; Jude 3), instructing children (Dt 6:7; 11:19), discharging official duties (Dt 19:18), saints should abound in (2Co 8:7).

Required in the service of God (Jn 9:4; Gal 6:9). Is not in vain (1Co 15:58). Preserves from evil (Ex 15:26). Leads to assured hope (Heb 6:11). God rewards (Dt 11:14; Heb 11:6).

In temporal matters leads to favor (Pr 11:27), prosperity (Pr 10:4; 13:4), honor (Pr 12:24; 22:29).

Figurative: (Pr 6:6-8).

Exemplified:
Ruth (Ru 2:17). Hezekiah (2Ch 31:21). Nehemiah and his helpers (Ne 4:6). Psalmist (Ps 119:60). Apostles (Ac 5:42). Apollos (Ac 18:25). Titus (2Co 8:22). Paul (1Th 2:9). Onesiphorus (2Ti 1:17).

See Industry; Zeal; Idleness; Slothfulness.

DILL [464]. A plant whose aromatic seeds are used in cooking (Mt 23:23).

DIMNAH [1962] (*manure*). A Levite town in Zebulun (Jos 21:35). May be the same as Rimmono (1Ch 6:77).

DIMON [1904]. A town in Moab, generally called "Dibon," but it is called Dimon two times (Isa 15:9, ftn), c. four miles N of Aroer.

DIMONAH [1905]. A town in the S of Judah (Jos 15:22), probably the same as the "Dibon" of Nehemiah (Ne 11:25).

DINAH [1909] (*female judge*). The daughter of Jacob and Leah (Ge 30:21). Rape of (Ge 34).

DINAITES NIV "judges" (Ezr 4:9).

DINHABAH [1973]. A city of Edom (Ge 36:32; 1Ch 1:43).

DINNER [5492, 367, 756, 1270, 2266, 2879, 5263]. Eaten at noon (Ge 43:16). *See Feasts.*

DIONYSIUS, THE AREOPAGITE [1477] (*belonging to Dionysus*). A member of the Areopagus, Athenian supreme court; converted by Paul (Ac 17:34).

DIOSCURI *See Castor and Pollux.*

DIOTREPHES [1485] (*nurtured by Zeus*). A domineering Christian leader condemned by John (3Jn 9-10).

DIPLOMACY
Ecclesiastical:
Paul, in winning souls to Christ (1Co 9:20-23), in

circumcising Timothy (Ac 16:3), in performing certain temple services to placate the Jews (Ac 21:20-25, w Gal 6:12).

Corrupt practices in:

The officers of Nebuchadnezzar's court to secure the destruction of Daniel (Da 6:4-15).

Instances of:

Abimelech (Ge 21:22-23; 26:26-31). The Gibeonites, in securing a league with the Israelites through deception (Jos 9:3-16). Of Jephthah, with the king of Moab, unsuccessful (Jdg 11:12-28). Of Abigail (1Sa 25:23-31). Of Hiram, to secure the goodwill of David (2Sa 5:11). Of Tou, to promote the friendship of David (2Sa 8:10). David, in sending Hushai to Absalom's court (2Sa 15:32-37; 16:15-19; 17:1-14). The wise woman of Abel (2Sa 20:16-22). Absalom winning the people (2Sa 15:2-6). Solomon, in his alliance with Hiram (1Ki 5:1-12; 9:10-14, 26-27; 10:11), by intermarriage with other nations (1Ki 1:1-5). Ambassadors from Ben-Hadad to Ahab (1Ki 20:31-34). Jehoash purchases peace from Hazael (2Ki 12:18). Ahaz purchases aid from the king of Assyria (2Ki 16:7-9). The king of Assyria's field commander, in trying to entice Jerusalem to surrender by bombastic harangue (2Ki 18:17-37; 19:1-13; Isa 36:11-22). Sanballat, in an attempt to prevent the rebuilding of Jerusalem by Nehemiah (Ne 6).

The people of Tyre and Sidon, in securing the favor of Herod (Ac 12:20-22). Paul, in turning the Pharisees and Sadducees against each other at his trial (Ac 23:6-10).

See Prudence; Tact.

DISASTERS *See Burning.*

DISBELIEF *See Unbelief.*

DISCERNING OF SPIRITS The ability to discern between those who spoke by the Spirit of God and those who were moved by false spirits (1Co 12:10).

DISCHARGE, BODILY [2307, 2308]. Caused ceremonial uncleanness. Of a male (Lev 15:2-15, 32). Of a female (Lev 15:25-33). Of a priest (Lev 22:3). *See Disease.*

DISCIPLE [1201, 4341, 899, 3411, 3412, 3413, 5209] (*student*). A name given to the followers of any teacher. Of John the Baptist (Mt 9:14). Of the Pharisees (Lk 5:33). Of Jesus (Mt 10:1; 20:17; Ac 9:26; 14:20; 21:4). The seventy sent forth (Lk 10:1). First called Christians at Antioch (Ac 11:26).

See Apostles; Righteous.

DISCIPLESHIP Following Jesus.

Evangelism—Making Disciples: (Mt 28:18-20; Ac 6:7).

Personal Growth—Being a Disciple:

Characterized by putting Jesus first in all things (Mt 10:32-39; Mk 8:34-38; Lk 14:26-27, 33; Jn 21:15-19), by following Jesus' teaching (Jn 8:31-

32), by fruitfulness (Jn 15:5-8), by love for other disciples (Jn 13:34-35).

See Commandments and Statutes, of God; Identification.

DISCIPLINE [3519, 3579, 4592, *4082, 4084*]. Of armies, for disobedience of orders (Jos 7:10-26; Jdg 21:5-12). *See Armies.*

Church Discipline: See Church, The Body of Believers, Discipline.

See Chastisement, From God; Graces; Self-Control; Self-Discipline.

DISCONTENTMENT *See Contentment; Murmuring.*

DISCOURAGEMENT [3169, 4206, 4213+5648, 7919+8120, 8368, *126, 1591*]. *See Despondency.*

DISEASE [1821, 2688, 2716, 4700, 4701, 5710, 7665, 7669, 8137, 8831, *3798*]. Sent from God (Lev 14:34). As judgments (Ps 107:17; Isa 3:17).

Instances of:

Upon the Egyptians. *See Plague.* Upon Nabal (1Sa 25:38), David's child (2Sa 12:15), Gehazi (2Ki 5:27), Jeroboam (2Ch 13:20), Jehoram (2Ch 21:12-19), Uzziah (2Ch 26:17-20).

Threatened as judgments (Lev 26:16; Dt 7:15; 28:22, 27-28, 35; 29:22).

Healing of, from God (Ex 15:26; 23:25; Dt 7:15; 2Ch 16:12; Ps 103:3; 107:20).

In answer to prayer:

Of Hezekiah (2Ki 20:1-11; Isa 38:1-8), David (Ps 21:4; 116:3-8).

Miraculous healing *See Miracles.*

Physicians employed for (2Ch 16:12; Jer 8:22; Mt 9:12; Mk 5:26; Lk 4:23). Remedies used (Pr 17:22; 20:30; Isa 38:21; Jer 30:13; 46:11), medicinal compress (2Ki 20:7), ointments (Isa 1:6; Jer 8:22), wine and oil (Lk 10:34).

Of the sexual organs (Lev 15; 22:4; Nu 5:2; Dt 23:10). *See Bleeding, Subject to; Circumcision; Menstruation.* Treatment of fractures (Eze 30:21).

See Affliction.

Figurative: (Ps 38:7; Isa 1:6; Jer 30:12). Various kinds of: *See Bleeding, Subject to; Blindness; Boil; Congestion; Consumption; Deafness; Demons; Discharge, Bodily; Dropsy; Dysentery; Fever; Gout; Hemorrhage; Hemorrhoids; Indigestion; Inflammation; Insanity; Itch; Lameness; Leprosy; Paralysis; Pestilence; Seizures; Sore; Stammering; Sunstroke; Tumor; Worm.*

Of the bowels. *See Bowels.*

DISFELLOWSHIP

From God and People:

Of the uncircumcised (Ge 17:14). Of violators of the law, of unleavened bread (Ex 12:15), of sacrifices (Lev 17:9; 19:5-7), of purification (Nu 19:20). Of those defiled, by eating prohibited food (Lev 7:25, 27; 17:10; 19:8), by touching the dead

(Nu 19:13), by committing abominations (Lev 18:29; 20:3-6).

Commanded:

For blasphemy (Nu 15:31). For schism (Ro 16:17). For heresy (1Ti 6:3-5; Tit 3:10-11; 2Jn 10-11). For immorality (Mt 18:17-18; 1Co 5:1-7, 11, 13; 2Th 3:6).

See Excommunication.

DISGUISES [2924, 5795, 6634, 9101]. Examples of (Ge 38:14; 1Sa 28:8; 1Ki 14:2; 20:38; 22:30; 2Ch 35:22).

DISH [113, 3998, 4090, 4094, 7505, *4243, 4402*]. Usually made either of baked clay or of metal. Orientals ate from a central platter or dish (Mt 26:23). Dishes used in the tabernacle and temple were made of gold (Ex 37:16; Nu 7:14ff; 2Ch 4:22, 24:14) or bronze (1Ki 7:38-40; 2Ki 25:14).

DISHAN [1914, 1915] (*ibex [?]*). The son of Seir (Ge 36:21, 30; 1Ch 1:38).

DISHON [1914] (*ibex [?]*).

1. The son of Seir (Ge 36:21, 30; 1Ch 1:38).

2. The grandson of Seir (Ge 36:25; 1Ch 1:41).

DISHONESTY [1299, 2039, 5327, 6404, 8400, *94, 96, 153, 156*]. In not paying debts (Ps 37:12, 21; Jas 5:4). In collusion with thieves (Ps 50:18). In wicked devices for gain (Job 24:2-11; Pr 1:10-14; 20:14; Isa 32:7; Jer 22:13; Eze 22:29; Hos 12:7; Am 3:10; 8:5; Mic 6:10-11).

Denounced (Jer 7:8-10; 9:4-6; 9:8; Hos 4:1-2; Na 3:1). Forbidden (Lev 19:13, 35-36; Dt 25:13-16; Ps 62:10; Pr 3:27-28; 11:1; 20:10, 23; 1Th 4:6). Penalties for (Lev 6:2-7; Pr 20:17; Zep 1:9; Zec 5:3-4). Parable concerning (Lk 16:1-8).

Instances of:

Abimelech's servants usurp a well of water (Ge 21:25; 26:15-22). Jacob obtains his brother's birthright by unjust advantage (Ge 25:29-33), steals his father's blessing (Ge 27:6-29), Laban's flocks by skillful manipulation (Ge 30:31-43). Rebekah's guile in Jacob's behalf (Ge 27:6-17). Laban's treatment of Jacob (Ge 29:21-30; 31:36-42). Rachel steals the household gods (Ge 31:19). Simeon and Levi deceive the Shechemites (Ge 34:15-31). Achan hides the wedge of gold and the Babylonian garment (Jos 7:11-26). Micah steals eleven hundred pieces of silver (Jdg 17:2). Micah's priest steals his images (Jdg 18:14-21). Joab's guile in securing Absalom's return (2Sa 14:2-20). Ahab usurps Naboth's vineyard (1Ki 21:2-16). Judas's hypocritical sympathy for the poor (Jn 12:6).

See Diplomacy; Hypocrisy; Injustice; Treason.

DISOBEDIENCE TO GOD

[*4202+9048, 5286, 6296, 577, 578, 579, 4157*]. Originated in Adam (Ro 5:19). Characteristic of all (Ro 1:32; Eph 2:2; 5:6; Col 3:6; Tit 1:16; 3:3; Heb 2:2; 1Pe 2:8). Temptation to (Ge 3:1-5).

Denunciations against (Nu 14:11-12, 22-23; 32:8-13; Dt 18:19).

Punishment of:

Of the Israelites by covenant curses (Lev 26:14-46; Dt 28:15-68). *See Wicked.* Of the Egyptians by plagues. *See Plague; Sin, Punishment of.*

Instances of:

Of Adam and Eve, eating the forbidden fruit (Ge 3:6-11). Of Lot, in refusing to go to the mountain, as commanded by the angels (Ge 19:19-20). Of Lot's wife, in looking back upon Sodom (Ge 19:26). Of Moses, in making excuses when commissioned to deliver Israel (Ex 4:13-14), when he struck the rock (Nu 20:11, 23-24). Of Aaron, at the striking of the rock by Moses (Nu 20:23-24). Of Pharaoh, in refusing to let the Israelites go (Ex 5:2; 7:13, 22-23; 8:15, 19, 32; 9:12, 34; 10:20, 27; 11:10; 14:8). Of the Israelites, in gathering excessive quantities of manna (Ex 16:19-20), in refusing to enter the promised land (Dt 1:26, w Nu 14:1-10; Jos 5:6; Ps 106:24-25). Of Nadab and Abihu, in offering unauthorized fire (Lev 10:1-2). Of Balaam, in accompanying the messengers from Balak (Nu 22:22). Of Achan, in hiding the wedge of gold and the Babylonian garment (Jos 7:15-26). Of Saul, in offering a sacrifice (1Sa 13:13), in sparing Agag and the spoils of the Amalekites (1Sa 15; 28:18). Of David, in his adultery, and in the killing of Uriah (2Sa 12:9). Of Solomon, in building places for idolatrous worship (1Ki 11:7-10). Of the prophet of Judah, in not keeping the commandment to deliver his message to Jeroboam without delay (1Ki 13). Of a man of Israel, who refused to smite the prophet (1Ki 20:35-36). Of *ʾ*hab, in suffering the king of Assyria to escape out of his hands (1Ki 20:42). Of priests, in not performing their functions after the due order (1Ch 15:13). Of the people of Judah (Jer 43:7), in going to dwell in Egypt contrary to divine command (Jer 44:12-14). Of Jonah, in refusing to deliver the message to the Ninevites (Jnh 1).

Of the blind men Jesus healed, and commanded not to tell of their healing (Mt 9:30-31). Of the leper whom Jesus healed, and commanded not to tell of the fact (Mk 1:45). Of Paul, in going to Jerusalem contrary to repeated admonitions (Ac 21:4, 10-14).

Of the righteous. *See Commandments and Statutes, of God.*

Of children. *See Children, Commandments to.*

DISPENSATION (*law or arrangement of a house*). The Greek word *oikonomia* means management or administration of a job or trust (Lk 16:2-4; 1Co 9:17; Eph 1:10; 3:2, 9; Col 1:25; 1Ti 1:4).

DISPENSATIONS An era of time during which mankind's obedience to God is tested according to the revelation of God available to him. From two dispensations (or covenants) to seven (innocence, conscience, human government, promise, law, grace, the kingdom) are held by various schools of interpretation.

DISPERSION Of the descendants of Noah (Ge 10). After building the tower of Babel (Ge 11:1-9; Dt 32:8). Of the Jews, foretold (Jer 16:15; 24:9; Jn 7:35). See Diaspora.

DISPLAY [2555, 3359, 3723, 5989, 6995, 7098, 7298, 8011, *617, 1892*]. General references to (Est 1:4; 5:11; Isa 39:2; Lk 20:46; Ac 25:23).
   In religious service (2Ki 10:16; Mt 6:2, 5, 16; 23:5).

DISPUTE [1821, 3519, 4506, 5477, 6699, 8189, 8190, 9149, *1359, 2427, 3215, 4547, 5087, 5202, 5808*]. About property. See Property.

DISSEMBLING See Deception; Hypocrisy.

DISSENSION [4506, *1496, 2251*]. In churches (1Co 1:10-13; 3:3-4; 11:18-19).

DISSIPATION [*861, 3190*]. Dangers of (Job 1:5). See Drunkenness.

DISTAFF [3969]. Used in spinning thread (Pr 31:19).

DITCH [1463]. See Pit.

DIVES (rich). In the Vulgate, the name given to the rich man in the parable of the rich man and Lazarus (Lk 16:19-31).

DIVIDING WALL [3546]. The barrier between the Court of the Gentiles and the Court of the Jews in the temple in Jerusalem. For a Gentile to go beyond it meant death (Josephus, Antiq. 15.11.5). Figurative of Christ bringing Jews and Gentiles together as one in the church (Eph 2:14).

DIVINATION [5241, 5727, 6726, 7876, 7877, 10140]. The practice of foreseeing or foretelling future events or discovering hidden knowledge; forbidden to Jews (Lev 19:26; Dt 18:10; Isa 19:3; Ac 16:16). Various means were used: reading omens, dreams, the use of the lot, astrology, necromancy, and others.

DIVINITY OF CHRIST See Jesus the Christ, Deity of.

DIVISIONS [477, 1074, 1522, 2745, 4713, 7372, 8031, 10585, *1375, 1496, 5388*]. Forbidden in the church (1Co 1:10). Condemned in the church (1Co 1:11-13; 11:18). Improper in the church (1Co 12:24-25).
   Are contrary to: the Unity of Christ (1Co 1:13; 12:13). Desire of Christ (Jn 17:21-23). Purpose of Christ (Jn 10:16). Spirit of the primitive church (1Co 11:16). Are a proof of a sinful spirit (1Co 3:3). Avoid those who cause (Ro 16:17). Evil of, illustrated (Mt 12:25).

DIVORCE [1763, 4135, 8938, *668, 687, 918, 3386*]. Mosaic laws concerning (Ex 21:7-11; Dt 21:10-14; 24:1-4). Authorized for marital unfaith-

fulness (Mt 5:31-32; 19:3-11). Unjust reproved (Mal 2:14-16). From Gentile wives, required by Ezra (Ezr 10:1-16). Disobedience, a cause for, among the Persians (Est 1:10-22). Final, after remarriage of either party (Jer 3:1). Christ's injunctions concerning (Mk 10:2-12; Lk 16:18). Paul's injunctions concerning (1Co 7:10-17).
   Figurative of God's judgment of Israel (Isa 50:1; 54:4-8; Jer 3:8).
   See Certificate of Divorce; Marriage.

DIZAHAB [1903] (that which has gold). A place in the region of Sinai where Moses gave a farewell address (Dt 1:1).

DOCTOR [2620]. A physician (Mt 9:12; Mk 2:17; 5:26; Lk 5:31). Luke (Col 4:14).
   See Physician; Disease.

DOCTRINES [*1436, 2281*].

Origin in God:
(Jn 7:16-17). Set forth by church councils (Ac 15:6-29).

False:
Jesus accuses scribes and Pharisees of false teaching (Mt 5:19-20; 15:9).
   False teachers, to be avoided (Ro 16:17-18; 1Co 3:11, 21; 1Ti 1:3-7; 6:3-5, 20-21), accursed (Gal 1:6-8; Jude 4, 11), rejected (Tit 1:10-11, 14; 3:10-11; 2Jn 9-11). Admonitions against (Ro 16:17-18; Eph 4:14; Col 2:4, 8, 18-23; 1Ti 1:3-7; 4:7; 6:20-21; 2Ti 2:16; Tit 3:10-11; Heb 13:9).
   False doctrine called: heresies (1Co 11:18-19; 2Pe 2:1-2), corruption (2Co 2:17; 11:3-4; Gal 1:6-8; 2Ti 2:14-18; 3:6-9; 2Pe 2:14-19).
   Origin of false doctrine: people (Mt 15:9; Ro 16:17-18; 1Co 3:11, 21; 2Co 2:17; Eph 4:14; Col 2:4, 8, 18-23; 2Ti 3:6-9, 13; Tit 1:10-11, 14; 2Pe 2:1-3), Satan (2Co 11:3-4; 1Ti 4:1-3), Antichrist (1Jn 4:3; 2Jn 7, 9-11).
   See Minister, False and Corrupt; Schism; Teachers, False.

DODAI [1862] (beloved). An officer in David's army (1Ch 27:4).

DODANIM See Rodanim.

DODAVAHU [1845] (beloved of Yahweh). Eliezer's father (2Ch 20:37).

DODO [1861] (beloved).
   1. The grandfather of Tola (Jdg 10:1).
   2. The son of Ahohite (2Sa 23:9).
   3. The father of one of David's mighty men (2Sa 23:24).

DOEG [1795] (anxious). An Edomite, present when Ahimelech helped David (1Sa 21:7; 22:9, 22; Ps 52:T). Killed eighty-five priests (1Sa 22:18-19).

DOER OF THE WORD Example of belief (Mt 7:21; 12:50; Lk 11:28; Ro 2:13-15; 2Co 8:11; Jas 1:22-27; 4:11). See Hearers.

DOG [3978, 7046, *3249, 3264*]. Among the Israelites (Ex 11:7; 22:31). Shepherd dogs (Job 30:1).

Habits of:
Licking blood (1Ki 21:19; 22:38), licking sores (Lk 16:21), returns to his vomit (Pr 26:11; 2Pe 2:22), lapping of (Jdg 7:5). Mute and sleeping (Isa 56:10-11).
Title of contempt (1Sa 17:43; 24:14; 2Sa 3:8; 9:8; 16:9; 2Ki 8:13; Isa 56:10-11; Mt 15:26).

Figurative:
Of sinners (Php 3:2; Rev 22:15). Of male prostitutes (Dt 23:18).

DOGMATISM *See Commandments and Statutes, of Men.*

DOMICILE Rights of (Dt 24:10-11).

DOMINION, OF MANKIND [4867, 4939, 5428, 5440, 10424, 10717, *794, 2026, 3262*]. *See Mankind, Design of.*

DONATIONS *See Liberality.*

DONKEY, DOMESTIC [912, 2789, 6554, 6555, 7230, 7241, *3229, 3942, 3952, 5689*]. Unclean for food (Lev 11:2-3, 26; Ex 13:13).

Described as:
Knowing its master (Isa 1:3). Strong (Ge 49:14). Fond of ease (Ge 49:14-15). Formed a part of patriarchal wealth (Ge 12:16; 30:43; Job 1:3; 42:12).

Was Used:
In agriculture (Isa 30:6, 24). For bearing burdens (Ge 42:26; 1Sa 25:18). For riding (Ge 22:3; Nu 22:21-23). In harness (Isa 21:7). In war (2Ki 7:7, 10). Governed by a bridle (Pr 26:3). Urged on with a staff (Nu 22:23, 27). Women often rode on (Jos 15:18; 1Sa 25:20). Persons of rank rode on (Jdg 10:3-4; 2Sa 16:2). Judges of Israel rode on white (Jdg 5:10). Young, most valued for labor (Isa 30:6, 24). Trustworthy persons appointed to take care of (Ge 36:24; 1Sa 9:3; 1Ch 27:30). Often taken unlawfully by corrupt rulers (Nu 16:15; 1Sa 8:16; 12:3). Sometimes counted an ignoble creature (Jer 22:19).

Laws Respecting:
Not to be coveted (Ex 20:17). Fall under a burden, to be assisted (Ex 23:5). Astray, to be brought back to its owner (Ex 23:4; Dt 22:1). Astray, to be taken care of till its owner appeared (Dt 22:2-3). Not to be yoked with an ox (Dt 22:10). To enjoy the Sabbath rest (Dt 5:14). Firstborn of, if not redeemed, to have its neck broken (Ex 13:13; 34:20). Christ entered Jerusalem on (Zec 9:9; Jn 12:14).

Miracles Connected With:
Mouth of Balaam's opened to speak (Nu 22:28; 2Pe 2:16). A thousand men slain by Samson with a jawbone of (Jdg 15:15-17). Not torn by a lion (1Ki 13:28). Eaten during famine in Samaria (2Ki 6:25).

DONKEY, WILD
Inhabits wild and solitary places (Job 39:6; Isa 32:14; Da 5:21). Ranges the mountains for food (Job 39:8). Brays when hungry (Job 6:5). Suffers in time of scarcity (Jer 14:6).

Described as:
Fond of liberty (Job 39:5). Intractable (Job 11:12). Unsocial (Hos 8:9). Despises his pursuers (Job 39:5-7). Supported by God (Ps 104:10-11).

Illustrative of:
Intractableness of natural man (Job 11:12). The wicked in their pursuit of sin (Job 24:5). Israel in their love of idols (Jer 2:23-24). The Assyrian power (Hos 8:9). The Ishmaelites (Ge 16:12).

DOOR [1923, 1946, 6197, 7339, *2598, 2601, 4784, 5327*]. Posts of, sprinkled with the blood of the Passover lamb (Ex 12:22), the law to be written on (Dt 11:20). Hinges of (Pr 26:14), made of gold (1Ki 7:5). Doors of the temple made of two leaves, cherubim and flowers carved upon, covered with gold (1Ki 6:31-35).

Figurative:
Door of hope (Hos 2:15), of opportunity (1Co 16:9; Rev 3:8), closed (Mt 25:10; Lk 13:25; Rev 3:7).

DOORKEEPER [6197+9068, 6214, 8788]. Keeper of doors and gates in public buildings, temples, walled cities, etc., often called "gatekeepers" (2Ki 7:10; 1Ch 23:5; Ps 84:10; Ezr 7:24; Mk 13:34). *See Gatekeepers.*

DOPHKAH [1986] (*drive [sheep]*). The first stopping place of the Israelites after they left the wilderness of Sin. It is usually identified with the Egyptian mining center at Serabit el-Khadim in Sinai (Nu 33:12).

DOR [1799, 1888]. A town and district of Israel (Jos 11:2). Conquered by Joshua (Jos 12:23; 1Ki 4:11). Allotted to Manasseh, although situated in the territory of Asher (Jos 17:11; Jdg 1:27).

DORCAS [*1520*] (*gazelle*). A Christian woman living at Joppa whom Peter raised from the dead (Ac 9:36-43).

DOTHAN [2019] (*two wells*). A place c. thirteen miles N of Shechem near where Joseph was sold (Ge 37:17) and where Elisha saw a vision of angels (2Ki 6:13-23).

DOUBLE-MINDED [6189, *1500*]. One who is a doubter, unstable (Ps 119:113; Jas 1:8; 4:8).

DOUBTING [242, 517, 603+1181, 1359, 1369, 1491]. In prayer (Mt 21:21; Jas 1:6-8). Admonishings against (Pr 24:10; Mt 8:26; 14:31; 17:17; Mk 4:40; 9:19; Lk 8:25; 9:40).

Instances of:
Job (Job 3; 4:3-6; 9:16-23; 30:20-21). Abraham (Ge 12:12-13; 15:8). Sarah (Ge 18:12-14). Lot

(Ge 19:30). Moses (Ex 3:11; 4:1, 10, 13; 5:22-23; 6:12; Nu 11:21-22). Israelites (Ex 14:10-12, 15; 1Sa 17:11, 24; Isa 40:27-28; 49:14-15). Gideon (Jdg 6:13, 15). Samuel (1Sa 16:1-2). Psalmists (Ps 22:2; 31:22; 42:5-6; 49:5; 73:13-17; 77:3, 7-9). Obadiah (1Ki 18:7-14). Elijah (1Ki 19:13-18). Jeremiah (Jer 1:6; 8:18; 32:24-25; 45:3; La 3:8, 17-18; 5:20).

Christ's disciples (Mt 8:23-27; 14:29-31; 17:14-21; 28:17; Mk 4:38, 40; 9:14-29; 16:10-11; Lk 8:25; 9:40-41; Jn 14:8-11; 20:24-27). John the Baptist (Mt 11:2-3). Ananias (Ac 9:13-14). Peter (Mt 14:30-31). Thomas (Jn 20:25). Early believers (1Pe 1:6).

See Cowardice; Murmuring.

DOUGH [1302, *2435, 5878*]. First of, offered to God (Nu 15:19-21; Ne 10:37). Kneaded (Jer 7:18; Hos 7:4). Part of, for priest (Eze 44:30). *See Bread; Oven.*

DOVE [3433, 9367, *4361, 5583*]. Sent out from the ark by Noah (Ge 8:8-11). Mourning of (Isa 38:14; 59:11; Na 2:7). Domesticated (Isa 60:8). Nests of (Jer 48:28). Harmlessness of, typical of Christ's gentleness (Mt 10:16). Sacrificial uses of (Ge 15:9). Prescribed for purification, of women (Lev 12:6, 8; Lk 2:24), of Nazirites (Nu 6:10), of lepers (Lev 14:22). Burnt offering of (Lev 1:14-17). Trespass offering of, for the poor (Lev 5:7-10; 12:8). Sin offering, for those who touched any dead body (Nu 6:10). Market for, in the temple (Mt 21:12; Jn 2:14).

Symbolic of the Holy Spirit (Mt 3:16; Lk 3:22; Jn 1:32).

See Pigeon.

DOVE'S DUNG NIV "seed pods" (2Ki 6:25 and ftn). *See Plants of the Bible.*

DOWRY Sum paid to parents for a daughter taken as wife (Ex 22:16-17), by Shechem for Dinah (Ge 34:12), by Boaz for Ruth (Ru 4:3-9), by David to Saul for Michal (1Sa 18:25).

DOXOLOGY *See Praise.*

DRACHMA [2007, *736*]. A Greek silver coin worth about a day's wages (Lk 15:8; Ac 19:19). The temple tax was two drachmas (Mt 17:24). In Ezr 2:69 and Ne 7:70-72 the term may refer to the Persian daric. *See Daric; Money.*

DRAGON [*1532*]. Any terrible creature, as a venomous serpent (Dt 32:33; Ps 91:13), a sea monster (Ps 74:13; 148:7; Isa 27:1; Eze 29:3; 32:2). Figurative of forces opposed to God: Egypt (Isa 51:9), Satan (Rev 12; 13; 16:13; 20:2). *See Serpent.*

DRAM *See Daric.*

DRAMA *See Pantomime.*

DRAUGHT HOUSE *See Latrine.*

DRAWER OF WATER One who brought water from a well or a spring to a house (Dt 29:11; Jos 9:23-27).

DRAWING [*2980*]. Of pictures on tile (Eze 4:1).

DREAM [2111, 2612, 2706, 2731, 10267, *1965, 1966, 3941*]. Transitory (Job 20:8). Vanity of (Ecc 5:3, 7).

Revelations by (Nu 12:6; Job 33:15-17; Jer 23:28; Joel 2:28; Ac 2:17). The dreams of the cupbearer and baker (Ge 40:8-23), of Pharaoh (Ge 41:1-36).

Interpreted by Joseph (Ge 40:12-13, 18-19; 41:25-32), by Daniel (Da 2:16-23, 28-30; 4). Delusive (Isa 29:7-8).

False prophets pretended to receive revelations through (Dt 13:1-5; Jer 23:25-32; 27:9; 29:8; Zec 10:2). *See Vision.*

Instances of:
Of Abimelech, concerning Sarah (Ge 20:3). Of Jacob, concerning the stairway (Ge 28:12), the speckled goats (Ge 31:10-13), concerning his going down into Egypt (Ge 46:2). Of Laban, concerning Jacob (Ge 31:24). Of Joseph, concerning the sheaves (Ge 37:5-10). Of the Midianite, concerning the cake of barley (Jdg 7:13). Of Solomon, concerning his choice of wisdom (1Ki 3:3-15). Of Eliphaz, of a spirit speaking to him (Job 4:12-21). Of Daniel, concerning the four beasts (Da 7). Of Joseph, concerning Mary's innocence (Mt 1:20-21), concerning the flight into Egypt (Mt 2:13), concerning the return into Israel (Mt 2:18-22). Of Pilate's wife, concerning Jesus (Mt 27:19). Cornelius's vision, concerning Peter (Ac 10:3-6). Peter's vision of the unclean beasts (Ac 10:10-16). Paul's vision of the man in Macedonia, crying, "Come over to Macedonia and help us" (Ac 16:9), relating to his going to Rome (Ac 23:11), concerning the shipwreck and the safety of all on board (Ac 27:23-24).

DRESS [*1607, 4229, 4252, 4732, 8324, *314, 1907, 2439, 2667, 4314*]. Of fig leaves (Ge 3:7). Of skins (Ge 3:21). Of other materials. *See Hair; Goats' Hair; Leather; Linen; Sackcloth; Silk; Wool.* Mixed materials in, forbidden (Dt 22:11). Men forbidden to wear women's, and women forbidden to wear men's (Dt 22:5). Rules with respect to women's (1Ti 2:9-10; 1Pe 3:3). Not to be held over night as a pledge for debt (Ex 22:26). Ceremonial purification of (Lev 11:32; 13:47-59; Nu 31:20). Tearing of. *See Mourning.*

Of the head:
Turbans prescribed by Moses, for the priests (Ex 28:40; 29:9; 39:28), by Ezekiel (Eze 44:18). Turbans and headdresses worn by men (Da 3:21) and by women (Isa 3:20; Eze 24:17, 23). Shawls (Isa 3:23). Veils (Eze 13:18, 21).

Various articles of:
Mantle, robe, or cloak (Ezr 9:3; 1Ki 19:13; 1Ch 15:27; Job 1:20), richly ornamented (2Sa 13:18),

purple (Jn 19:2, 5). Robe (Ex 28:4; 1Sa 18:4). Capes (Isa 3:22). Embroidered coat (Ex 28:4, 40; 1Sa 2:19; Da 3:21). Sleeveless shirt, called coat (Mt 5:40; Lk 6:29; Jn 19:23; Ac 9:39). Cloak (2Ti 4:13; Jn 19:2, 5). Trousers (Da 3:21). Skirts (Eze 5:3). Sashes (Isa 3:20). *See Veil.*

Changes of clothing, the folly of excessive (Job 27:16). Uniform vestments kept in store for worshipers of Baal (2Ki 10:22-23; Zep 1:8), for wedding feast (Mt 22:11). Presents made of changes of clothing (Ge 45:22; 1Sa 18:4; 2Ki 5:5; Est 6:8; Da 5:7). Garments of priests. *See Priest.* Dress in mourning. *See Mourning.*

Symbolic:
Filthy, of unrighteousness and judgment (Isa 64:6; Zec 3:3-4). Clean, of acceptance (Zec 3:4-7).

See Colors, Figurative and Symbolic.

DRINK [*5172, 5492, 5821, 6010, 6011, 8115, 8893, 8910, 8911, 8912, 8913, 9197, 9198, 9272, 9275, 9276, 10302, 10483, 10748, 3494, 3499, 3500, 3501, 3884, 3886, 4232, 4403, 4503, 4530, 4540, 4975, 5064, 5228, 5621].
Beverages of the Israelites were water (Nu 24:11-18), wine (Ge 14:18; Jn 2:3), and milk (Jdg 4:19).

DRINK OFFERING *See Offerings, Drink; Libation.*

DRIVING [*5627]. Rapid, by Jehu (2Ki 9:20).

DROMEDARY *See Camel.*

DROPSY [5622]. (Lk 14:2).

DROSS [6092]. Refuse separated from molten ore or metal. Figurative of divine judgment (Ps 119:119; Pr 25:4; 26:23; Isa 1:22; Eze 22:18-19).

DROUGHT [1314, 1316, 2996, 3312, 7480]. (Ge 31:40; 1Ki 17; 18; Jer 14:1-6). Sent by God as a judgment (Dt 28:23-24; 1Ki 8:35; 2Ch 6:26; 7:13; Hos 13:15).

See Famine; Meteorology; Rain.
Figurative: (Ps 32:4; Isa 44:3).

DRUG ABUSE Not mentioned in the Bible, but the principles derived from alcohol abuse would apply to drugs. *See Abuse, Substance Abuse; Drunkenness.*

DRUNKARD [6010, 8893, 3500, 3501, 3884].
Described:
(Pr 23:29-35). The psalmist mocked by (Ps 69:12). Fellowship with, forbidden (1Co 5:11).

End Result:
Poverty (Pr 23:21; Isa 28:1, 3), cut off (Joel 1:5), destroyed (Na 1:10), trodden under feet (Isa 28:1, 3), shame (Hab 2:16), death (Dt 21:20-21). Insatiable appetite of (Hab 2:5-6). Excluded from the kingdom (1Co 6:9-10). Punishment of (Dt 21:20-21).

See Drunkenness; Wine; Temperance; Abstinence.

DRUNKENNESS [8893, 8913, 9275, 3494, 3886, 4232].
Condemned:
Repugnancy of (Isa 28:7-8; 56:12; Hos 7:5, 14; Joel 1:5; 3:3; Am 2:8, 12; Mt 24:49; Lk 12:45). Mockery of (Ps 69:12; Pr 20:1).

Consequences of (Pr 21:17; 23:21, 29-35; Isa 19:14; 24:9-11; 28:7; Hos 4:11). Death penalty for (Dt 21:20-21; 29:19-20; Jer 25:27). Excludes from the kingdom of God (1Co 6:9-10; Gal 5:19-21).

Forbidden (1Sa 1:13-14; Pr 23:20, 31-32; 31:4-7; Lk 21:34; Ro 13:13; 1Co 11:21-30; Eph 5:18; 1Th 5:7-8; 1Pe 4:3). Woes denounced against (Isa 5:11-12, 22; 28:1, 3, 7-8; Am 6:1, 6; Na 1:10; Hab 2:15-16).

Figurative:
(Isa 28:8; 51:17, 21-23; 63:6; Jer 25:15-16, 27-28; 51:7-9; La 3:15; Eze 23:31-34; Hab 2:15-16).

See Abstinence; Drunkard; Sobriety; Wine.

Instances of:
Noah (Ge 9:21). Lot (Ge 19:33). Nabal (1Sa 25:36). Uriah (2Sa 11:13). Amnon (2Sa 13:28). Elah (1Ki 16:9). Ben-Hadad and his thirty-two confederate kings (1Ki 20:16). Xerxes (Est 1:10-11). Belshazzar (Da 5:1-6). Believers (1Co 11:21).

Falsely Accused of:
Hannah (1Sa 1:12-16). Jesus (Mt 11:19). The apostles (Ac 2:13-15).

DRUSILLA [*1537*]. Daughter of Herod Agrippa I; married first to Azizus, king of Emesa; later to Felix, procurator of Judea (Ac 24:24-25).

DRY PLACES [62, 2427, 2893, 2990, 2992, 2996, 3000, 3019, 3143, 3312, 3313, 3317, 3318, 4908, 5172, 5980, 6877, 7480, 7534, 7535, 7546, 3831]. (Nu 20:2; 2Ki 3:9; Ps 68:6; Isa 1:30; Jer 14:3; 17:6).

DUKE NIV "chief." Of Edom (Ge 36:15-43; Ex 15:15; 1Ch 1:51-54). Of the Midianites (Jos 13:21).

DULCIMER NIV "pipes" (Da 3:5, 10, 15). *See Music, Instruments of.*

DUMAH [1873, 1874] (*silence, name of underworld*).
1. Son of Ishmael (Ge 25:14; 1Ch 1:30; Isa 21:11-12).
2. A city of Canaan assigned to Judah (Jos 15:52).

DUMB *See Mute.*

DUNG [883, 1645, 1672]. Laws were made regarding excrement of human beings and animals used in sacrifice (Dt 23:12-14; Ex 29:14; Lev 8:17). Dry dung was often used as fuel (Eze 4:12-15), also fertilizer (Isa 25:10; Lk 13:8).

DUNG GATE A gate in the Jerusalem wall that led out to the Valley of Hinnom where rubbish was dumped (Ne 3:14).

DUNGEON [1014, 1074+3975, 8846, 4987]. In prisons (Jer 38:6; La 3:53). *See Prison.*

DURA [10164]. A plain of Babylon where Nebuchadnezzar set up his image (Da 3:1).

DUST [85, 141, 709, 824, 1919, 6760, 8836, 3155, 5954, 5967]. Man made from (Ge 2:7; 3:19, 23; Ecc 3:20). Casting of, in anger (2Sa 16:13). Shaking from feet (Mt 10:14; Ac 13:51). Put on the head in mourning (Jos 7:6; 1Sa 4:12; 2Sa 1:2; 15:30; Job 2:12; 42:6).

DUTY [995, 1460, 1821, 3302, 3655, 5096, 5466, 6584, 6641, 9068, 9250, 10208, 2601, 2646, 4051, 4488, 5465].
1. Tribute levied on foreign commerce by Solomon (1Ki 10:15).
2. Escape from, sought by Moses (Ex 3:11; 4:1, 10, 13; 6:12, 30), by Jonah (Jnh 1:1-15), by Ananias (Ac 9:13-14).

Of People to God:
To love (Dt 6:5; 11:1; 30:15-20; Jos 23:11; Ps 31:23; Mt 22:37; Lk 12:27). To obey (Dt 10:12-13; 30:15-20; Jos 22:5; Pr 23:26; Mt 12:50; 22:21; 23:23; Lk 17:10; Jn 14:15, 21; 15:14; Ac 4:19-20; 5:29).

Of People to People:
To love (Lev 19:18; Mt 19:19; 22:39; Mk 12:31; Jn 13:34; Ro 13:8-10; Gal 5:14; Jas 2:8). To help (Isa 58:6-7; Mt 25:34-46; Lk 10:23-36). To forgive (Mt 18:21-35; Lk 17:3-4; Eph 4:32; Col 3:13). To practice "the golden rule" toward (Mt 7:12). To respect a brother's conscience (Ro 14:1-23; 1Co 8:1-13). To restore a sinning brother (Gal 6:1-2).

See Commandments and Statutes, of God; Children; Husband; Minister, Duties of; Parents; Wife.

DWARFED [1987]. Could not officiate at the altar (Lev 21:20).

DYEING [131]. Of fabric (Ex 25:5; 26:14; Isa 63:1; Eze 23:15).

DYING *See Death, Physical.*

DYSENTERY [1548]. (Ac 28:8).

DYSPEPSIA *See Indigestion.*

EAGLE [5979, 10495, *108*].

General:

As food: Forbidden as food, classified as detestable (Lev 11:13; Dt 14:12). *See Birds.*

Species of: Osprey (Lev 11:18; Dt 14:17). Vulture (Job 15:23; Pr 30:17; Mic 1:16; Mt 24:28; Lk 17:37).

Flight of: The swift flight of, as an analogy of the swiftness of destruction to come (Dt 28:49; Jer 4:13; 48:40; 49:22; La 4:19). Its soaring capability (Job 39:27; Isa 40:31; Jer 49:22; Ob 4). Their graceful flight as a simile for various themes (Pr 23:5; Isa 40:31; Ob 4).

Care of young: Nest of (Dt 32:11; Job 39:27-30; Jer 49:16). Bears young on her wings (Dt 32:11). Life is renewed like an eagle's (Ps 103:5; Isa 40:31).

Figurative:

Of God's care (Ex 19:4; Dt 32:11). Of warriors (2Sa 1:23; Jer 4:13; 48:40; Hos 8:1). Of the swiftness of life (Job 9:26). Of renewed life (Isa 40:31).

Symbolic:

Of the glory of God (Eze 1:10; 10:14). An allegory, the "seed of the land" (Zedekiah) is planted by a "great eagle" (Nebuchadnezzar) and grows up to be a "spreading vine"; this spreading vine is then transplanted by another eagle (Hophra) (Eze 17:1-8). A lion with wings of an eagle representing the majesty and strength of Babylon (Da 7:4). Of redeemed man (Rev 4:7). Of the church (Rev 12:14).

EAR [263, 265+, 3087, *198*, 4044, 6064, 6065].

Attentiveness:

To what God says, to what is right, to his voice, to his commands, and to keep all his decrees (Ex 15:26; 23:22; Dt 11:13; 15:5; 28:1; Jer 11:6; Mt 13:23; Lk 8:15; Ac 17:11). To a truth worthy of attention (Mt 11:15; 13:9, 43; Mk 4:23; Lk 14:35). To Jesus' words (Lk 19:48). A stringent demand for attention to the utterances of prophets who were inspired by the Spirit (Rev 2:7, 11, 29; 3:6, 13, 22; 13:9).

Blocked:

God will listen to the righteous, not to sinners (Ge 18:23-32; 1Sa 8; Ps 34:15-16; 145:18-19; Pr 15:29; Isa 59:1-2; Jn 9:31; 15:7; Jas 5:16-18; 1Jn 5:14-15). *See God, Access to; Righteous, Promises to; Wicked, Prayers of.*

The result of ignoring, the law (Nu 15:30-31; Dt 1:43-46; Pr 28:9; Isa 1:10-15; 24:4-13). Ignoring the Lord (1Sa 2:27-33; 8; Isa 65:12-15; 66:4; Zec 7:11-14; Lk 9:26; 2Ti 2:11-13; Heb 6:4-6; 2Pe 2:1). *See God, Rejected; Jesus the Christ, Rejected.* The result of ignoring the plight of the poor (Dt 15:7-11; Pr 21:13; 22:16, 22-23; 28:8; Isa 10:1-4; Eze 16:49-50; Zec 7:9-14; Jas 2:1-13). Hearing blocked by life's troubles (Mt 13:18-23, esp. 22). *See Sower.*

See Poor, Warning Against Neglect; Poor, Oppression of.

The inability of idols to hear (1Ki 18:22-39; Ps 115:4-8; 135:15-18; Isa 46:7; Jer 10:2-5; 1Co 8:4-6; 12:2). *See Idol; Idolatry, Folly of.*

Ceremonies:

Pierced as a sign of servitude (Ex 21:5-6; Dt 15:16-17). Blood put upon, in consecration of priests (Ex 29:20; Lev 8:23), in cleansing lepers (Lev 14:14, 25). *See Leprosy.* Anointed with oil in purifications (Lev 14:17, 28).

Deaf:

Hearing closed to prevent obedience and subsequent salvation (Jos 11:20; Isa 6:10; 63:17; Jn 12:37-41; Ro 9:10-18; 11:25). *See Deafness.* The Lord, in refusing to listen to a petition (Dt 1:45), is petitioned to hear and to not refuse to answer (1Ki 8:28-53, esp. vv. 28-30, 32, 34, 36, 39, 43, 45, 49, 52; 2Ki 19:16; Ne 1:6).

Fearful:

The nations, because of reports of what God had accomplished (Ex 15:13-16; Dt 2:24-25; Jos 2:8-9; 1Sa 4:6-9; Est 8:15-17; Ps 48:4-7), from the knowledge of God's majesty (Ps 99:1-3; 114:7-8; Eze 38:20). *See Fear of God.* Of hearing God speak (Ex 20:19; Dt 5:25; Heb 12:18-21). *See Voice, of God; Anthropomorphisms, Acts.* Israel, from reports of punishment (Dt 13:11; 17:12-13; 19:18-21; 1Ti 5:20). *See Punishment.*

Figurative:

Anthropomorphic uses of: (Ps 17:6; 39:12; 77:1; 80:1; 84:8).

Misguided:

The value of listening to instruction (Pr 1:8-9; 2:1-22; 3:1-2; 4; 5:1-6; 6:20-29; 7:1-5; 19:27; 22:17-19). *See Counsel; Instruction; Knowledge; Wisdom.*

Listening to the advice of fools (Pr 13:20; Ecc 7:5-6). *See Speaking, Speech, Foolish.*

Misunderstood:

Taking the words of others too seriously (Ecc 7:21-22). Those listening to Jesus' words from the cross (Mt 27:46-47; Mk 15:34-35). Those who heard the voice of God (Jn 12:29).

Quick to hear:

Listening carefully to what others say (Jas 1:19).

Rational:

Words are tested by hearing (Job 12:11; 34:3). Powerful presentation (Job 29:21-25; 32:11-12). God will teach men (Isa 54:13; Jer 31:33-34; Jn 6:45; 1Co 2:13; 1Th 4:9; 1Jn 2:26-27).

Refusal to listen:

A rebellious people (Eze 12:2; Zec 7:11-14). The

Jews (Jn 8:43; 10:20; Ac 13:44-50). The Sanhedrin (Ac 7:57). Men will reject the truth and accept a lie (2Ti 4:2-4).

Unconcerned:

People are not concerned with the pleading of God by his Spirit or by his prophets (Ne 9:29-30; Zec 7:11-12). *See Holy Spirit, Sin Against; Holy Spirit, Withdrawn From Unrepentant Sinners.* Idols, are absolutely indifferent to the prayers of people (Ps 115:6).

Israel, with ears which are open yet unable to hear (Isa 6:9-10; 42:18-20; 43:8). Those not concerned to take Jesus' words seriously (Mt 7:26-27). The reason Jesus speaks in parables (Mt 13:13). Those who hear the word but do not do what it says (Jas 1:22-25).

Worthless:

The parable of the sower (Mt 13:20-22; Mk 4:16-19; Lk 8:13-14). John the Baptist and Herod (Mk 6:20). Paul, in Athens at the Areopagus (Ac 17:19, 32), before Felix (Ac 24:24-26), before Agrippa and Festus (Ac 26:1-29).

EAR OF GRAIN   *See Grain.*

EARLY RAIN   *See Rain.*

EARLY RISING

General references to:

To rise early (Ge 19:27; 26:31; Ex 8:20; 34:4; Jos 3:1; Jdg 6:38; 1Sa 5:4; 15:12; 17:20; 2Ch 20:20). Daybreak (Jos 6:15; 1Sa 9:26; Ps 46:5; 57:8; Da 6:19; Mk 16:2; Lk 24:22). Prior to daybreak (Ru 3:14; Pr 31:15). Morning (Ps 90:14; 101:8). *See Morning.*

To do evil: (Ex 32:6; Nu 14:40; Job 24:14; Isa 5:11).

EARNEST   A pledge or token (Ps 86:17). The Spirit, as a guarantee of the future redemption of our bodies (Ro 8:23), of our inheritance (Ro 8:23; Eph 1:13-14), of the promise to come (2Co 1:22). *See Inheritance; Token, 1.*

EARNESTNESS   [5883, 8626, 8838, *1699, 1755+ 1877, 1757, 2118, 2418, 4498, 4666+4667, 5081, 5082, 5655*].   An intense desire which results in repentance, produced by godly sorrow (2Co 7:11). Sincerity in your love (2Co 8:7-8). *See Sincerity; Zeal.*

EARRING   [5690, 5755, 6316, 9366].

As an offering:

Offering of, for the golden calf (Ex 32:2-3). As a wave offering for the tabernacle (Ex 35:22). As an offering to the Lord to make atonement (Nu 31:50).

Types of:

Gold (Ex 32:2-3; Jdg 8:24; Pr 25:12). Gold studded with silver (SS 1:11).

Worn:

By the Israelites (Ex 32:2-3; Jdg 8:24). By Ishmaelites, as a cultural habit (Jdg 8:24). For idolatrous purposes (Ge 35:4; Isa 3:19).

EARTH   [141, 824, 6760, 8073, 9315, 10075, 10077, 10309, *1178, 2103, 2973, 3180, 4922, 5954*].

Creation of:

By God (Ge 1:1; Ex 20:11; 31:17; 2Ki 19:15; 2Ch 2:12; Ne 9:6; Job 38:4; Ps 90:2; 102:25; 104:5; 115:15; 124:8; 146:5-6; Pr 8:22-26; Isa 37:16; 45:18; 66:1-2; Jer 10:12; 27:5; 32:17; 51:15; Ac 14:15; Heb 11:3; 2Pe 3:5; Rev 10:6; 14:7). By Christ (Jn 1:3, 10; Heb 1:10). Primitive condition of (Ge 1:2, 6-7; Job 26:7; 38:4-7; Ps 104:5-9; Pr 3:19-20; Isa 40:22; Jer 4:23-26). *See Creation; God, Creator.* Created to be inhabited (Isa 45:18). By design (Isa 45:18).

Early divisions of (Ge 10-11; Dt 32:8; Ps 74:17).

Belongs to:

The Lord (Ex 9:29; 19:5; Dt 10:14; 1Sa 2:8; Ps 24:1; 50:12; Isa 66:1; 1Co 10:26). God controls (Job 9:6; Rev 7:1). God's footstool (Isa 66:1; La 2:1; Mt 5:35; Ac 7:49).

Cursed:

Cursed by God (Ge 3:17-19; 5:29; Ro 8:19-22).

Future of:

Perpetuity of (Ge 49:26; Dt 33:15; Ps 78:69; 104:5; Ecc 1:4; Hab 3:6). Will be judged (1Sa 2:10; Ps 96:13; 98:9). Destruction of, foretold (Ps 102:25-27; Isa 24:19-20; 51:6; 1Jn 2:17; Mt 24:35; 2Pe 3:10-13; Rev 20:11; 21:1). A new earth (Isa 65:17; 66:22; 2Pe 3:13; Rev 21:1).

Residence of mankind: (Ps 115:16).

EARTHENWARE   [3084]. *See Pottery.*

EARTHQUAKES   [8323, *4939*] (*shaking, trembling*).   (Job 9:6; Ps 18:7; 46:2-3; 104:32; Jer 4:24). *See Mountain.* As judgments (Ps 18:15; 60:2; Isa 13:13; 24:18-20; 29:6; Na 1:5; Rev 6:12-14; 11:13; 16:18, 20). *See Judgment.* Prophecies of (Eze 38:19-20; Zec 14:4; Mt 24:7; Mk 13:8; Lk 21:11; Rev 11:19).

Instances of:

At Sinai (Ex 19:18; Ps 68:8; 77:18; 114:4-7; Heb 12:26). When Korah, Dathan, and Abiram were swallowed up (Nu 16:31-34). When Jonathan and his armor-bearer attacked the garrison at Gibeah (1Sa 14:15). When the Lord revealed himself to Elijah in the still small voice (1Ki 19:11). In Canaan, in the days of Uzziah, king of Judah (Am 1:1; Zec 14:5). At the crucifixion of Jesus (Mt 27:51). At the resurrection of Jesus (Mt 28:2). When Paul and Silas were in prison at Philippi (Ac 16:26).

EAST   [*4667, 6298, 7156, 7708, 7710, 7711, 7713, 7719, 424*].

An Important Direction for God:

Glory of God from (Eze 43:2). Angel from (Rev 7:2).

An Important Direction for People:

The Garden of Eden (Ge 2:8; 3:24). *See Garden.* An east wind (Ge 41:6, 23, 27; Ex 10:13; 14:21; Job 15:2; 27:21; 38:24; Ps 48:7; 78:26; Isa 27:8; Jer 18:17; Eze 17:10; 19:12; 27:26; Hos 12:1; 13:15; Hab 1:9). *See Wind.* A significant direction for the Hebrews (Ex 38:13; Nu 3:38; 10:5; Eze 10:19; 11:23; 43:2, 4). God has removed our transgressions (Ps 103:12). Faces toward in worship (Eze 8:16).

People of:

Eastern people (Ge 29:1; Jdg 6:3, 33). Eastern people had a special reputation for wisdom (1Ki 4:30; Mt 2:1-12). "People of the east" denotes Arab groups who accompanied the Midianites and the Amalekites in attacking Israel (Job 1:3; Jer 49:28; Eze 25:4, 10). Kings of (Rev 16:12).

EAST WIND Hot, dry wind coming from the S and SE of Israel (Jer 4:11; Hos 13:15), destructive (Ge 41:6; Ps 48:7; Eze 17:10; 27:26), used as a means of salvation for Israel by God (Ex 14:21), used as a means of judgment by God (Isa 27:8; Jer 18:17; Jnh 4:8).

EASTER The day on which the church celebrates the resurrection of Jesus Christ. KJV "Easter" should be "Passover" as in NIV (Ac 12:4). *See Feasts; Passover.*

EASTERN SEA *See Dead Sea.*

EATING [*430, 433, 1356, 4312, 4310, 8286, 8425, 10030, 10301, 753, 1109, 1111, 1174, 2266, 2879, 2983, 4689, 5263, 5303, 5592, 5963]. The host acting as waiter (Ge 18:8). Favored guests served an extra portion (Ge 43:34). *See Hospitality.* Sitting at table (Ex 32:6). *See Table.* Table used in (Jdg 1:7). Reclining on couches (Am 6:4, 7; Mt 26:7, 20; Mk 14:3, 18; Jn 12:2; 13:23). *See Couch.* Washing before (Mt 15:2).

See Feasts; Food; Gluttony.

EBAL [6506, 6507].

1. A Horite (Ge 36:23; 1Ch 1:40).

2. A mountain of Ephraim lying N and directly opposite Mt. Gerizim. These two mountains form the two sides of an important E-W pass. Upon entering the land of Canaan, after the time of Moses, the Hebrews were to confirm their covenant with Yahweh. This required that half of the tribes were to be on Mt. Gerizim to proclaim the blessings, the other half of the tribes were to stand on Mt. Ebal to proclaim the curses of the covenant with the ark of the covenant between them (Dt 11:29; 27:12-13; Jos 8:33). Altar built on (Dt 27:4-6; Jos 8:30). They were to sacrifice a fellowship offering there, eating and rejoicing in the presence of the Lord (Dt 27:7). Traditionally these were called peace offerings (Dt 27:7, ftn). All the words of this covenant were to be written very clearly on the stones of the altar that they set up (Dt 27:8). *See Gerizim.*

3. Son of Joktan (1Ch 1:22). *See Obal.*

EBED [6270] (*servant*).

1. Father of Gaal, who led the rebellion against Abimelech at Shechem (Jdg 9:26-45).

2. The son of Jonathan, one of those who returned to Israel with Ezra (Ezr 8:6).

3. The title *Ebed* was adopted, apparently by David, from an Akkadian practice, which was also used in Edom and Ammon. It was a designation of the class of court officials as distinguished from the older institution of tribal elders. In Ebed-Melech it becomes a proper name.

EBED-MELECH [6283] (*servant of Melek [king]*). An Ethiopian eunuch in Zedekiah's court who interceded on Jeremiah's behalf before King Zedekiah to have Jeremiah pulled out of a mud filled cistern (Jer 38:1-13). The prophecy concerning Ebed-Melech promised that he would survive the destruction of the kingdom as a reward for his efforts (Jer 39:16-18).

EBENEZER [75] (*stone of help*). A town near Aphek where the Israelites fought two battles with the Philistines and were defeated, losing the ark in the second battle (1Sa 4:1-11; 5:1). Later, after defeating the Philistines, the Israelites erected a memorial stone, naming it Ebenezer (1Sa 7:12).

EBER [6299, 1576] (*[regions] beyond [the river]*, or source of the word *Hebrew*).

1. The probable founder of the Hebrew race (Ge 10:21-25; 11:14-17; 1Ch 1:18-19, 25; Lk 3:35). Prophecy concerning (Nu 24:24). Perhaps Eber in this passage should be understood not as a proper name but as the word for "region beyond" (here, beyond the Euphrates), which is the same as the name Eber in Hebrew.

2. A Gadite (1Ch 5:13).

3. A Benjamite (1Ch 8:12).

4. Another family of the tribe of Benjamin (1Ch 8:22).

5. A postexilic priest (Ne 12:20).

6. Father of Peleg and Joktan (Lk 3:35).

EBEZ [82]. A town given by lot to Issachar (Jos 19:20).

EBIASAPH [47] (*[my] father has gathered*). A son of Korah (1Ch 6:23, 37; 9:19; 26:1). *See Korah, 4.* Abiasaph is an alternate form (Ex 6:24). *See Abiasaph.* Called also Asaph (1Ch 26:1). *See Asaph.*

EBONY [2041]. A highly prized core wood of a tree imported from S India, Ceylon, and perhaps Ethiopia. It was valued by the Egyptians, Phoenicians, Babylonians, Greeks, and Romans for its use, along with ivory, in fine furniture, vessels, and turned objects. It was also used in the Near East for idols. *See Image; Idol; Idolatry; Temple, Idolatrous.* Merchandise in (Eze 27:15).

EBRONAH *See Abronah.*

ECBATANA [10020] (perhaps *place of gathering*). A city located at the foot of the Alvand Mountain which is now Hamadan. The capital of Media, during the reign of Darius I, a copy of Cyrus's decree was found which authorized the rebuilding of the temple in Jerusalem (Ezr 6:2, 3-12). *See Cyrus; Darius; Medes; Persia; Temple, The Second.*

ECCLESIASTES

Author and Date:
Several passages strongly suggest that King Solomon is the author (1:1, 12, 16; 2:4-9; 7:26-29; 12:9; cf. 1Ki 2:9; 3:12; 4:29-34; 5:12; 10:1-8). On the other hand, the writer's title ("Teacher," Hebrew *Qoheleth*), his unique style of Hebrew and his attitude toward rulers (suggesting that of a subject rather than a monarch—see, e.g., 4:1-2; 5:8-9; 8:2-4; 10:20) may point to another person and a later period.

Outline:
I. Author (1:1).
II. Theme: The Meaninglessness of Man's Efforts on Earth Apart From God (1:2).
III. Introduction: The Profitlessness of Working to Accumulate Things to Achieve Happiness (1:3-11).
IV. Discourse, Part 1: In Spite of Life's Apparent Enigmas and Meaninglessness, It is to be Enjoyed as a Gift From God (1:12-11:6).
V. Discourse, Part 2: Since Old Age and Death Will Soon Come, Man Should Enjoy Life in His Youth, Remembering That God Will Judge (11:7-12:7).
VI. Theme Repeated (12:8).
VII. Conclusion: Reverently Trust in and Obey God (12:9-14).

ECCLESIASTICISM Jewish, rebuked by Jesus (Mt 9:10-13; 23:2-35), to be overthrown (Mt 21:19-20, 28-44). Arrogance of (Mt 12:2-8; 23:4). Traditional rules of the Jewish (Mt 15:1-20; Mk 7:2-23). *See Church, The Body of Believers; Commandments and Statutes, of Men; Minister, False and Corrupt; Usurpation, in Ecclesiastical Affairs.*

ECLIPSE Of the sun and moon (Isa 13:10; 60:19; Eze 32:7-8; Joel 2:10, 31; 3:15; Am 8:9; Mic 3:6; Mt 24:29; Mk 13:24; Ac 2:20; Rev 6:12; 8:12). *See Sun; Moon.*

ECOLOGY Mankind created to care for the earth (Ge 1:28; 2:15; Ps 8:6-8; 115:16). The land was to enjoy rest every seven years (Lev 25:1-7); the land enjoyed its rest during Israel's exile (2Ch 36:20-21). Animals were to rest on the Sabbath (Ex 20:10). Fruit trees were not to be cut down in war time (Dt 20:19-20). A bird and its young were not to be caught together (Dt 22:6-7). Babylon judged for violence to the forests of Lebanon and its animals (Hab 2:17 w Isa 14:8).

ECONOMICS Political (Ge 41:33-57).

Household (Pr 24:27; 31:10-31; Ecc 11:4-6; Jn 6:12-13). *See Family; Frugality; Industry.*

ECONOMY *See Economics; Government.*

ECUMENICISM (*the inhabited earth*). A movement among Christian religious groups—Protestant, Eastern Orthodox, Roman Catholic—to bring about a closer unity in work and organization. The word is not found in the NIV, but backing for the movement may be found in John 17 where Jesus prays for the unity of his church.

ED KJV transliterates the name of the altar erected by the tribes Reuben, Gad, and Manasseh at the fords of the Jordan (Jos 22:34); NIV "Witness."

EDAR *See Eder.*

EDEN [6359, 6360, 6361] (*paradise, delight, possibly flat land*).
1. The Garden of Eden (Ge 2:8-17; 3:23-24; 4:16; Isa 51:3; Eze 28:13; 31:9, 16, 18; 36:35; Joel 2:3).
2. Gods of (2Ki 19:12; Isa 37:12; Am 1:5).
3. A Gershonite (2Ch 29:12).
4. A Levite (2Ch 31:15).
5. A marketplace of costly merchandise (Eze 27:23-24).

EDER [6374, 6375, 6376] (*flock*).
1. A tower near Ephrath where Jacob encamped on the way back to Canaan (Ge 35:21).
2. A city of Judah (Jos 15:21).
3. A son of Beriah, grandson of Shaharaim, a Benjamite (1Ch 8:15).
4. A grandson of Merari (1Ch 23:23; 24:30).

EDICT [1821, 2017, 7330, 10601, 10628, *1409*]. A public proclamation, written and sealed with the king's signet and publicly read (Ezr 6:11-12; Est 2:8; 8:8-13; 9:1, 13). Penalties were severe for violating a Persian edict (Ezr 6:11). Moses' parents are listed as an example of those who were not afraid to transgress the royal edict (Heb 11:23).

EDIFICATION, EDIFY, EDIFYING

[3868, 3869] (Latin *to build up*). The root of this Greek word is found in various words and compound words in the NT, i.e., build (Mt 23:29; 26:61), building (Jn 2:20), builder (1Co 3:10; Heb 3:3-4), builds up (1Co 8:1), strengthen (1Co 8:10), edified (1Co 14:5, 17), edification (Ro 14:19).

Paul uses the word group frequently but never in the literal sense of "building" a building. He uses it often in the metaphorical sense of "building" or "building up" the church, and of "building up" fellow believers. Paul refers to the church as a building (1Co 3:9; Eph 2:21), and of building the church upon the foundation that he and the apostles and the prophets laid (1Co 3:10, 12, 14; Eph 2:20).

Paul uses the words more frequently in the sense of "strengthening, unifying, making for peace." Christians are to build up each other in this sense (1Th 5:11). It is primarily love that "builds up" (1Co 8:1).

EDOM [121+824, 121] (red).

1. A name of Esau, possibly on account of his being covered with red hair (Ge 25:25, 30; 36:1, 8, 19).

2. A name of the land occupied by the descendants of Esau. It extended from the Gulf of Aqabah to the Red Sea, and was also called Idumea (Ge 32:3; 36:16-17, 21; Jer 40:11).

Prophecies concerning (Jer 25:21-23; 27:1-11; Da 11:41). Noted for its wise men (Ob 8). Sins of (Ob 10-14). Wilderness of (2Ki 3:8).

See Edomite(s).

Figurative of the foes of Zion (Isa 63:1).

EDOMITE(S) [121+1201, 121, 122] (red).

Called also Edom. Land of (Ge 32:3; Dt 2:4-5, 12). Descendants of Esau (Ge 36). Rulers of (Ge 36:9-43; Ex 15:15; 1Ch 1:51-54). Kings of (Ge 36:31-39; Nu 20:14; 1Ch 1:43-50; Eze 32:29; Am 2:1).

Prophecies concerning (Ge 25:23; 27:29, 37-40; Nu 24:18; Isa 11:14; 21:11-12; 34; 63:1-6; Jer 9:25-26; 27:1-11; 49:7-22; La 4:21-22; Eze 25:12-14; 32:29-30; 36:5; Joel 3:19; Am 1:11-12; 9:12; Ob 1-21; Mal 1:2-5).

Protected by divine command from desolation by the Israelites (Dt 2:4-6), from being held in abhorrence by the Israelites (Dt 23:7). Children of the third generation might be received into the congregation of Israel (Dt 23:8). Refuse the Israelites passage through their country (Nu 20:18-21). Saul makes war against (1Sa 14:47). Garrisons of (2Sa 8:14). David conquers (1Ki 11:14-16; 1Ch 18:11-13), writes battle songs concerning his conquest of (Ps 60:8-9; 108:9-10). Ruled by a deputy king (1Ki 22:47). Become confederates of Jehoshaphat (1Ki 3:9, 26). Revolt in the days of Jehoram (2Ki 8:20-22; 2Ch 21:8-10). Amaziah, king of Judah, invades the territory of Edom, defeating ten thousand Edomites (2Ki 14:7, 10; 2Ch 25:11-12; 28:17). The Lord delivers the army of, into the hands of Jehoshaphat (2Ch 20:20, 23). A Jewish prophet in Babylon denounces (Ps 137:7; Eze 25:12-14; 35). Join Babylon in the war against the Israelites (Eze 35:5; Am 1:9-11; Ob 11-16).

EDREI [167] (strong).

1. A chief city of Og, king of Bashan (Dt 1:4; Jos 12:4). Assigned to Manasseh (Jos 13:12, 31). Located c. ten miles NE of Ramoth-Gilead.

2. A city of Naphtali, the location is unknown (Jos 19:37).

EDUCATION See Instruction; Teachers; School.

EGG [1070, 1842, 2733, 4880, 6051] (whiteness). (Job 6:6; Lk 11:12). Appears also in the plural (Dt 22:6; Job 39:14; Isa 10:14).

EGLAH [6321] (heifer). The wife of David (2Sa 3:5; 1Ch 3:3).

EGLAIM [104]. A city on the border of Moab (Isa 15:8).

EGLATH SHELISHIYAH [6326] (possibly the third Eglath). A town near Zoar mentioned in prophetic oracles of judgment on Moab (Isa 15:5; Jer 48:34).

EGLON [6323, 6324] (circle ISBE; young bull KB).

1. A city of Canaan located between Gaza and Lachish (Jos 10:3, 5, 23), captured by Joshua (Jos 10:36-37; 12:12), assigned to Judah (Jos 15:39).

2. The king of Moab who captured Jericho (the City of Palms) from the Israelites as a judgment against them, controlling it for eighteen years (Jdg 3:12-14). Eglon was assassinated by Ehud, a judge, because the Israelites cried out to the Lord (Jdg 3:15-23).

EGOTISM See Conceit.

EGYPT [5191, 5213+, 7356+, 131+, 2016].

The Country of:

Fertility of (Ge 13:10). Imports of (Ge 37:25, 36). Productions of (Nu 11:5; Ps 78:47; Pr 7:16; Isa 19:5-10). Irrigation employed in (Dt 11:10). Called, Rahab which is the poetic name for Egypt (Ps 87:4; 89:10), the land of Ham (Ps 105:23; 106:21-22). Exports of (Pr 7:16; Eze 27:7), and of horses (1Ki 10:28-29). Limits of (Eze 29:10).

Abraham dwells in (Ge 12:10-20; 13:1). The king acquires title to land of (Ge 47:18-26). Joseph's captivity in and subsequent rule over. See Joseph, 1. Israelites in bondage in. See Israel, Israelites. Plagues in. See Plague. Civil war in (Isa 19:2). Overflowed by the Nile (Am 8:8; 9:5). Joseph takes Jesus to (Mt 2:13-20).

Prophecies against (Ge 15:13-14; Isa 19; 20:2-6; 45:14; Jer 9:25-26; 43:8-13; 44:30; 46; Eze 29-32; Hos 8:13; Joel 3:19; Zec 10:11).

See Egyptians.

Famine in (Ge 41; Ac 7:11). See Famine. Magi of (Ge 41:8; Ex 7:11; 1Ki 4:30; Ac 7:22). See Magi. Priests of (Ge 41:45; 47:22). Army of, destroyed in the Red Sea (Ex 14:5-31; Isa 43:17). See Army. Armies of (Ex 14:7; Isa 31:1). Idols of (Eze 20:7-8).

River, or Brook of:

Perhaps identical with Shihor. See River of Egypt; Shihor. A small stream flowing into the Mediterranean Sea, the western boundary of the land promised to the Israelites (Ge 15:18; Nu 34:5; Jos 13:3; 15:4, 47; 1Ki 8:65; 2Ki 24:7; Isa 27:12; Eze 47:19; 48:28).

Symbolic: (Rev 11:8).

EGYPTIANS [5212, 5213, *130*]. Descendants of the Mizraim (Ge 10:6, 13-14, ftn). Hospitality of, to Abraham (Ge 12:10-20). Slaves bought by (Ge 37:36). The art of embalming the dead practiced by (Ge 50:2-3, 26). Oppressed the Israelites (Ex 1-2). Refuse to release the Israelites (Ex 5-10). Judged by plagues (Ex 7-12; Ps 78:43-51), firstborn of destroyed (Ex 12:29; Ps 78:51; 105:36; 136:10). Sent the Israelites away (Ex 12:31-42). Army pursued the Israelites, and was destroyed (Ex 14:5-31; Ps 106:7; Heb 11:29). Wisdom of (1Ki 4:30).

Refused to eat with the Hebrews (Ge 43:32). Abhorred shepherds (Ge 46:34). Eligible to membership in Israelite congregation in the third generation (Dt 23:7-8). Alliances with, without first consulting God, forbidden to the Israelites (Isa 30:1-5; 31:1-3; 36:6; Eze 17:15). Intermarry with the Israelites (1Ki 3:1).

Invasions of Israel: Under Shishak (1Ki 14:25-26; 2Ch 12:2-9), Pharaoh Neco (2Ki 23:29-35; 2Ch 35:20-24; 36:2-4). Aid the Israelites against the Chaldeans (Jer 37:5-11). An enthusiastic Egyptian instigated a rebellion against the Roman government (Ac 21:38).

Conversion of, foretold (Isa 19:18). Prophecies of dispersion and restoration of (Eze 29:12-16; 30:23-26).

See Egypt.

EHI [305] (*my brother [is exalted]*). A son of Benjamin (Ge 46:21).

EHUD [179, 287] (*united*).
1. A Benjamite judge, the assassin of Eglon (Jdg 3:15-30; 1Ch 8:6). *See Eglon, 2.*
2. Son of Bilhan (1Ch 7:10).

EKED *See Beth Eked.*

EKER [6831] (possibly *offspring*). The son of Ram, part of the postexilic clan of Jerahmeel (1Ch 2:27).

EKRON, EKRONITES [6833, 6834] (perhaps *barren place* or *fertile place*). One of the five chief cities of the Philistines (Jos 13:3). Conquered and allotted to Judah (Jos 15:11, 45; Jdg 1:18). Allotted to Dan (Jos 19:43). The ark of God taken to (1Sa 5:10). Temple of Baal-Zebub, the god of Ekron, at (2Ki 1:2). Prophecies against (Jer 25:20; Am 1:8; Zep 2:4; Zec 9:5).

EL (*God; Mighty One*). A generic word for God in the Semitic languages. The chief Canaanite god was El. The God of Israel is usually referred to in the plural form, *Elohim,* or in compound names, as in the following articles. *See Elohim.*

EL-BERITH [451] (*a god of a covenant*). An alternate name for the god worshiped at Shechem, in whose temple some of the people of Shechem took refuge when Abimelech destroyed the city (Jdg 9:46). *See Baal-Berith.*

EL BETHEL [450] (*God [El] of Bethel*). A name given by Jacob to Luz because God there revealed Himself to him (Ge 35:7).

EL ELOHE ISRAEL [449] (*God, the God of Israel*). Name of an altar erected by Jacob near Shechem (Ge 33:20).

EL PARAN [386] (*tree of Paran*). A place in the wilderness of Paran (Ge 14:6).

EL SHADDAI (*God of mountains* or *God who is self-sufficient* KB or in older etymology *God of breasts*). Translated "God Almighty" in the NIV following the NT rendering of *Shaddai* by *pantokrator.* The name by which God appeared to Abraham, Isaac, and Jacob (Ex 6:3).
See God, Names of; Shaddai.

ELA [452]. The father of Shimei, one of Solomon's district governors (1Ki 4:18).

ELAH [462, 463] (*a species of a mighty tree*).
1. A chief of Edom (Ge 36:41).
2. The valley (valley of the terebinth), in which David killed Goliath (1Sa 17:2, 19; 21:9).
3. The king of Israel, son of Baasha; killed by Zimri (1Ki 16:8-10).
4. The father of Hoshea, the last king of Israel (2Ki 15:30; 17:1; 18:1, 9).
5. The son of Caleb (1Ch 4:15).
6. The Benjamite, son of Uzzi (1Ch 9:8).
7. *See Ela.*

ELAM [6520, 6521] (*highland*).
1. The son of Shem (Ge 10:22; 1Ch 1:17).
2. The son of Shashak (1Ch 8:24).
3. The son of Meshelemiah (1Ch 26:3).
4. The ancestor of a family which returned from the Exile (Ezr 2:7; Ne 7:12).
5. Another ancestor of a returned family (Ezr 2:31; Ne 7:34).
6. The father of two sons returned from the Exile (Ezr 8:7).
7. The ancestor of a man who married a foreign woman (Ezr 10:2, 26).
8. A chief who sealed a covenant with Nehemiah (Ne 10:14).
9. A priest who took part in the dedication of the wall (Ne 12:42).
10. A country situated on the E side of the Tigris opposite Babylonia; was one of the earliest civilizations; figures prominently in Babylonian and Assyrian history. Some of its people were brought to Samaria by the Assyrians (Ezr 4:9-10). Elamites at Jerusalem on the Day of Pentecost (Ac 2:9).

ELAMITES [10551, *1780*] (*highland*). Descendants of Shem (Ge 10:22). They were present at Pentecost (Ac 2:9).

ELASAH [543] (*God has fashioned*).
1. The son of Pashhur the priest, and one of those with foreign wives (Ezr 10:22).

2. The son of Shaphan and one of Zedekiah's emissaries to Nebuchadnezzar who took a letter to the exiles in Babylon for Jeremiah (Jer 29:3).

ELATH [393, 397] (*grove of large trees*). A city on the coast of Edom situated at the head of the Gulf of Arabah (Dt 2:8; 1Ki 9:26; 2Ch 8:17). The conquest of, by the Edomites (2Ki 16:6), by Uzziah (2Ch 26:1-2).

ELDAAH [456] (*God [El] is [my] desire*). A descendant of Abraham (Ge 25:4; 1Ch 1:33).

ELDAD [455] (*beloved of God [El]*; possibly *Dadi [pagan god] is god*). One of Moses' 70 elders (Nu 11:24-29).

ELDERS [2418, 10675, 1172, 4564, 4565, 5236].

In the Mosaic System: *See Elders, Council of; Government, Mosaic.*

In the NT Church:

Received gifts on behalf of church (Ac 11:29-30). Ordained (Ac 14:23; Tit 1:5-9). Overseers of the church (Ac 15:1-29; 16:4-5; 20:17, 28-32; 21:18; 1Ti 5:17-19; 1Pe 5:1-5). Performed ecclesiastical duties (1Ti 4:14; Jas 5:14-15).

John's Vision of the Twenty-four Elders:

(Rev 4:4, 10; 5:5-6, 8, 11, 14; 7:11, 13; 11:16; 14:3; 19:4).

See Bishop; Church, Government of the Christian Church; Deacon; Overseer.

ELDERS, COUNCIL OF

Described:

Chosen elders of the nation, vested with representative, judicial, and executive authority (Ex 4:29; 5:15, 19; 6:14-25; 12:21; Nu 11:16-30). Called the council (Nu 16:2; Mk 15:43); council of the elders (Ps 107:32; Lk 22:66); elders of Israel (Ex 3:16, 18), of Judah (1Sa 30:26), of the people (Ex 19:7), of the community (Lev 4:15), of the Jews (Ezr 5:5); Sanhedrin (Mt 5:22; 26:59; Ac 4:15; 5:21-41).

Closely associated with Moses and subsequent leaders (Ex 3:16-18; 4:29; 12:21; 17:5-6; 18:12; 19:7; 24:1, 14; Nu 16:25; Dt 5:23; 27:1; 29:10; 31:9, 28; Jos 7:6; 8:10, 33; 23:2; 24:1; Jdg 11:5-11; Ac 5:17-18, 21). Made confession of sin in behalf of the nation (Lev 4:15; 9:1).

A similar council existed among the Egyptians (Ge 50:7), the Midianites and Moabites (Nu 22:4, 7-8), the Gibeonites (Jos 9:11).

Events Relating to:

Demands a king (1Sa 8:4-10, 19-22). Saul pleads to be honored before (1Sa 15:30). Chooses David as king (2Sa 3:17-21; 5:3; 1Ch 11:3). Closely associated with David (2Sa 12:17; 1Ch 15:25; 21:16). Joins Absalom in his usurpation (2Sa 17:4). David rebukes (2Sa 19:11). Assists Solomon at the dedication of the temple (1Ki 8:1-3; 2Ch 5:2-4). Counsels King Rehoboam (1Ki 12:6-8, 13). Counsels King Ahab (1Ki 20:7-8).

Josiah assembles, to hear the law of the Lord (2Ki 23:1; 2Ch 34:29, 31).

Legislates with Ezra in reforming certain marriages with the Gentiles (Ezr 10:8-14). Legislates in later times (Mt 15:2, 7-9; Mk 7:1-13). Sits as a court (Jer 26:10-24). Constitutes, with priests and scribes, a court for the trial of both civil and ecclesiastical causes (Mt 21:23; 26:3-5, 57-68; 27:1-2; Mk 8:31; 14:53-65; 15:1; Lk 22:52-71; Ac 4:1-21; 6:12-15). Seeks counsel from prophets (Eze 8:1; 14:1; 20:1, 3). Corrupt (1Ki 21:8-14; Eze 8:11-12; Mt 26:14-15; 27:3-4).

ELEAD [537] (*God [El] has testified*). A descendant of Ephraim (1Ch 7:21).

ELEADAH [538] (*God [El] has adorned*). The son of Ephraim (1Ch 7:20).

ELEALEH [541, 542] (*God [El] is high*). A city in Transjordan, rebuilt by the tribe of Reuben (Nu 32:3, 37). Repossessed by the Moabites (Isa 15:4; 16:9; Jer 48:34).

ELEASAH [543] (*God [El] has fashioned*).
1. A person or family of the clan of Jerahmeel of the tribe of Judah (1Ch 2:39-40).
2. A member of the tribe of Benjamin, descended from Saul (1Ch 8:37; 9:43).

ELEAZAR [540, 1789] (*God [El] is a help*).
1. The son of Aaron (Ex 6:23; 28:1). He married a daughter of Putiel, who bore him Phinehas (Ex 6:25). After the death of Nadab and Abihu he is made the chief of the tribe of Levi (Nu 3:32). The duties of (Nu 4:16).

He succeeds Aaron as the high priest (Nu 20:26, 28; Dt 10:6). Assists Moses in the census (Nu 26:63). With Joshua, divides Israel (Nu 34:17). Death and burial of (Jos 24:33). Descendants of (1Ch 24:1-19).
2. An inhabitant of Kiriath Jearim who attended the ark (1Sa 7:1-2).
3. Son of Dodai the Ahohite, and one of David's three mighty men (2Sa 23:9-10, 13; 1Ch 11:12).
4. A Merarite Levite (1Ch 23:21-22; 24:28).
5. The son of Phinehas (Ezr 8:33; Ne 12:42).
6. A returned Israelite exile (Ezr 10:25).
7. The great-grandfather of Joseph, the husband of Mary (Mt 1:15).

ELECT [1723, 1724] (*chosen*). Those chosen by God for some special purpose (Ps 106:23; Isa 43:10; 45:4). Among the elect mentioned in Scripture are Moses, the Israelites, Christ, the angels, Christ's disciples.

ELECTION [1724]. By grace (Mt 22:14; Jn 15:16; 17:6; Ro 11:5; Eph 1:4; 2:10; 2Th 2:13; 1Pe 2:9).

Of Israel (Dt 7:6; Isa 45:4). Of rulers (Ne 11:1). Of Christ as Messiah (Isa 42:1; 1Pe 2:6). Of ministers (Lk 6:13; Ac 9:15). Of good angels (1Ti 5:21). Of churches (1Pe 5:13).

See Chosen; Elect; Predestination.

ELECTIONEERING
By Absalom (2Sa 15:1-6). Adonijah (1Ki 1:7). *See Candidate.*

ELEGY
A song of sorrow. By David, on Saul and Jonathan (2Sa 1:17, 19-27), on Abner (2Sa 3:33-34).

See Lamentations, Book of; Poetry.

ELEMENTS
[5122] (*rows, series, alphabet, first principles of a science, physical elements, heavenly bodies, planets, personal cosmic powers*). Heathen deities and practices (Gal 4:3, 9), rudiments (Col 2:8, 20), first principles (Heb 5:12). *See Basic Principles of this World.*

ELEPH
See Haeleph.

ELEPHANT
The Hebrew *behemoth* may be the elephant or hippopotamus (Job 40:15, ftn). *See Ivory.*

ELEVEN, THE
[1894]. The eleven apostles who remained after the defection of Judas (Mk 16:14; Lk 24:9, 33; Ac 2:14).

ELHANAN
[481] (*God [El] is gracious*).
1. The son of Dodo, one of David's heroes (2Sa 23:24; 1Ch 11:26).
2. A distinguished warrior in the time of David who killed Lahmi the brother of Goliath the Gittite (1Ch 20:5), or the Bethlehemite who killed Goliath (2Sa 21:19). The two accounts may be harmonized if an early copyist of Samuel misread "Lahmi the brother of" as "the Bethlehemite."

ELI
[6603] (*Yahweh is exalted* IDB; *[God [El]] is exalted* KB). Misjudges and rebukes Hannah (1Sa 1:13-14). His benediction upon Hannah (1Sa 1:17-18; 2:20). Officiates when Samuel is presented at the tabernacle (1Sa 1:24-28). High priest (1Sa 1:25; 2:11; 1Ki 2:27). Judge of Israel (1Sa 4:18, ftn). Indulgent of his corrupt sons (1Sa 2:22-25, 29; 3:11-14). His concern for the ark (1Sa 4:11-18). Death of (1Sa 4:18).
Prophecies of judgments upon his house (1Sa 2:27-36; 3:11-14, w 1Ki 2:27).

ELI, ELI, LAMA SABACHTHANI
See Eloi, Eloi, Lama Sabachthani.

ELIAB
[482] (*God [El] is [my] father*).
1. Son of Helon (Nu 1:9; 2:7; 7:24, 29; 10:16).
2. A Reubenite, progenitor of Dathan and Abiram (Nu 16:1, 12; 26:8-9; Dt 11:6).
3. The son of Jesse, and eldest brother of David (1Sa 16:6; 17:13, 28; 1Ch 2:13). Elihu, an officer over the tribe of Judah (1Ch 27:18).
4. An ancestor of Samuel (1Ch 6:27). Called also Elihu in the parallel genealogies (1Sa 1:1), and Eliel (1Ch 6:34).
5. A hero of the tribe of Gad (1Ch 12:9).
6. A Levite, a gatekeeper and musician (1Ch 15:18, 20; 16:5).

ELIADA
[486] (*God [El] knows*).
1. The son of David (2Sa 5:16; 1Ch 3:8).
2. Father of Rezon (1Ki 11:23).
3. Benjamite general (2Ch 17:17).

ELIAHBA
[494] (*God [El] hides*). The Shaalbonite, one of David's heroes (2Sa 23:32; 1Ch 11:33).

ELIAKIM
[509, 1806] (*God [El] establishes*).
1. The master of Hezekiah's household; sent by the king to negotiate with invading Assyrians (2Ki 18:17-37; Isa 36:1-22), and then to seek help of Isaiah the prophet (2Ki 19:2; Isa 37:2).
2. The original name of King Jehoiakim (2Ki 23:34; 2Ch 36:4). *See Jehoiakim.*
3. Priest (Ne 12:41).
4. The ancestor of Jesus (Mt 1:13).
5. Another and earlier ancestor of Jesus (Lk 3:30).

ELIAM
[500] (*God [El] is [my] kinsman*).
1. The father of Bathsheba (2Sa 11:3). Called Ammiel (1Ch 3:5).
2. One of David's mighty men known as the "Thirty" (2Sa 23:34). Called Ahijah (1Ch 11:36).

ELIAS
See Elijah.

ELIASAPH
[498] (*God [El] has added*).
1. The son of Deuel, a leader of the tribe of Gad (Nu 1:14; 2:14; 7:42, 47; 10:20).
2. The son of Lael, a leader of the families of the Gershonites (Nu 3:24).

ELIASHIB
[513] (*God [El] restores*).
1. A descendant of Zerubbabel and remotely related to David (1Ch 3:24).
2. A priest in the time of David (1Ch 24:12).
3. An ancestor of a man who helped Ezra (Ezr 10:6; Ne 12:10, 22-23).
4. A Levite who put away his foreign wife (Ezr 10:24).
5. A man who married a foreign woman (Ezr 10:27).
6. Another man who married a foreign woman (Ezr 10:36).
7. A high priest in the time of Nehemiah (Ne 3:1, 20-21; 13:4, 7, 28).

ELIATHAH
[484, 517] (*God [El] comes*). A temple musician, the son of Heman (1Ch 25:4, 27).

ELIDAD
[485] (*God [El] is [my] beloved*). A Benjamite, the son of Kislon (Nu 34:21). Eleazar the priest and Joshua were appointed to assign the land west of the Jordan to the tribes who were to settle there. God also appointed one man from each of the tribes to help Eleazar and Joshua, Elidad being the leader from the tribe of Benjamin.

ELIEHOENAI
[492] (*my eyes [look] to Yahweh*).

1. A Korahite gatekeeper of the tabernacle (1Ch 26:3).

2. One of the family heads who returned with Ezra; the son of Zerahiah (Ezr 8:4). *See Elioenai.*

ELIEL [483] (*God [El] is [my] God*).

1. The chief of Manasseh (1Ch 5:24).

2. The ancestor of Samuel (1Ch 6:34). Called Eliab (1Ch 6:27).

3. The son of Shimei (1Ch 8:20).

4. The son of Shashak (1Ch 8:22).

5. A Mahavite and a captain in David's army (1Ch 11:46).

6. One of David's heroes (1Ch 11:47).

7. A Gadite; perhaps the same as 5 or 6 (1Ch 12:11).

8. A chief Levite (1Ch 15:11).

9. A chief of Judah; perhaps the same as 5 (1Ch 15:9).

10. A Levite overseer (2Ch 31:13).

ELIENAI [501] (*my eyes [look] to Yahweh*).
A Benjamite citizen of Jerusalem (1Ch 8:20).

ELIEZER [499, 1808] (*God [El] is [my] help*).

1. Steward of Abraham, who in place of a son, would have become Abraham's heir (Ge 15:2). Perhaps the same as the servant mentioned in (Ge 24).

2. The son of Moses and Zipporah (Ex 18:4; 1Ch 23:15, 17; 26:25).

3. The grandson of Benjamin (1Ch 7:8).

4. A priest (1Ch 15:24).

5. A Reubenite chief (1Ch 27:16).

6. A prophet who rebuked Jehoshaphat (2Ch 20:37).

7. A chieftain sent to induce the Israelites to return to Jerusalem (Ezr 8:16).

8. A priest who put away his foreign wife (Ezr 10:18).

9. A Levite who put away his foreign wife (Ezr 10:23).

10. A son of Harim who put away his foreign wife (Ezr 10:31).

11. An ancestor of Jesus (Lk 3:29).

ELIHOREPH [495]. A son of Shisha (1Ki 4:3).

ELIHU [490, 491] (*Yahweh is [my] God*).

1. A son of Tohu, an Ephraimite, an ancestor of Samuel (1Sa 1:1). Probably identical with Eliab (1Ch 6:27), and Eliel (1Ch 6:34).

2. A Manassite warrior, who joined David at Ziklag (1Ch 12:20).

3. A Korahite gatekeeper of the tabernacle (1Ch 26:7).

4. A chief of the tribe of Judah and one of David's brothers (1Ch 27:18). Possibly Eliab, the oldest brother of David (1Sa 16:6).

5. A son of Barakel the Buzite who speaks to Job when his three friends have failed to silence him (Job 32-37).

ELIJAH [488, 489, 2460] (*Yahweh is [my] God*).

1. The Tishbite, a Gileadite and prophet. Announces to Ahab the coming of a disastrous drought (1Ki 17:2-7). The severity of Ahab, which is noted in secular literature as well, i.e., Jos. *Antiq.* VIII.xiii.2, prompts Elijah to escape into the wilderness, where he is miraculously fed by ravens (1Ki 17:1-6). By divine direction, he goes to Zarephath of Sidon where he is sustained in the household of a widow (1Ki 17:8-16). The widow's son becomes fatally ill; Elijah prays over him with the result that his life is restored (1Ki 17:16-24). Paul has a similar experience with a young man named Eutychus (Ac 20:7-12). He returns and sends a message to Ahab through Obadiah, a devout believer in the Lord, who was in charge of Ahab's palace (1Ki 18:1-16). Meets Ahab and directs him to assemble the prophets of Baal (1Ki 18:17-20). Derisively challenges the priests of Baal to offer sacrifices (1Ki 18:25-29). Slays the prophets from Baal (1Ki 18:40). Escapes to the wilderness from the fierceness of Jezebel (1Ki 19:1-18). Fasts forty days (1Ki 19:8). Despondency and murmuring of (1Ki 19:10, 14). Consolation given to (1Ki 19:11-18). Flees to the wilderness of Damascus; directed to anoint Hazael as king over Aram, Jehu son of Nimshi king over Israel, and Elisha to be a prophet in his own place (1Ki 19:9-21). Personal aspect of (2Ki 1:8).

Piety of (1Ki 19:10, 14; Lk 1:17; Ro 11:2; Jas 5:17). His translation to heaven in a whirlwind (2Ki 2:11). Antitype of John the Baptist (Mt 11:14; 17:10-13; Mk 9:11-13; Lk 1:17; Jn 1:21-25). Appears to Jesus at his transfiguration (Mt 17:1-4; Mk 9:2-5; Lk 9:28-33).

Miracles of:

Increases the oil of the widow of Zarephath (1Ki 17:14-16). Raises from the dead the son of the woman of Zarephath (1Ki 17:17-24). Causes fire to consume the sacrifice (1Ki 18:24, 36-38). Causes rain after a drought of three and a half years (1Ki 18:41-45; Jas 5:17-18). Calls fire down upon the soldiers of Ahaziah (2Ki 1:10-14; Lk 9:54, ftn).

Prophecies of:

Foretells, a drought (1Ki 17:1), the destruction of Ahab and his house (1Ki 21:17-29; 2Ki 9:25-37), the death of Ahaziah (2Ki 1:2-17), the plague sent as a judgment upon the people in the time of Jehoram, king of Israel (2Ch 21:12-15).

2. A Benjamite chief, the son of Jeroham (1Ch 8:27).

3. A postexilic Jew who divorced his foreign wife; a descendant of Harim (Ezr 10:21).

4. A postexilic Jew who divorced his foreign wife; a descendant of Elam (Ezr 10:26).

ELIKA [508]. A Harodite, one of David's mighty men known as the "Thirty" (2Sa 23:25).

ELIM [396] (*big trees*). The fourth stopping place of the Israelites after they crossed the Red

Sea; they found twelve springs and seventy palm trees (Ex 15:27; 16:1; Nu 33:9-10).

ELIMELECH [497] (*God [El] is [my] king*). An Ephrathite from Bethlehem of Judah who, with his wife, Naomi and his two sons, immigrated from Judah to Moab in the days of the judges to escape a famine in the land (Ru 1:2, 3; 2:1, 3; 4:3, 9).

ELIOENAI [493] (*my eyes [look] to Yahweh*).
1. The son of Neariah (1Ch 3:23-24).
2. A Simeonite leader (1Ch 4:36).
3. A Benjamite (1Ch 7:8).
4. A man who divorced his foreign wife (Ezr 10:22).
5. A man who divorced his foreign wife (Ezr 10:27).
6. A priest, perhaps the same as 4 (Ne 12:41).

ELIPHAL [503] (*[my] God [El] sit in judgment*). Perhaps the same as Eliphelet (2Sa 23:34). One of David's mighty men known as the "Thirty" (1Ch 11:35).

ELIPHAZ [502] (*God [El] is fine gold or God crushes*).
1. The oldest son of Esau by his Hittite wife Adah (Ge 36:4, 10-12, 15-16; 1Ch 1:35-36).
2. One of Job's three friends; wise, rich, and a ruler of men. He was probably the leader of this trio (Job 42:7), and also the oldest. He took for granted that Job must have committed some major sin as the only explanation for his tremendous suffering. He tries to make it as easy as possible for Job to repent because of the powerful impact of the dream he had had concerning man's sinful condition in the presence of God (Job 4:12-21). In his second address, Eliphaz's point of view is that Job's problems stem from his strong sense of personal righteousness; that Job believes that he has all the wisdom that he needs, therefore, he has no need of input from God or wise men (Job 15). In his third address, Eliphaz condemns Job of many sins, calling him back to right relationship and the resultant blessing of God (Job 22).

ELIPHELEHU [504] (*God [El], distinguish him!*). A Levite musician (1Ch 15:18, 21).

ELIPHELET [505] (*God [El] is [my] deliverance*).
1. A son of David, probably identical with #2 (2Sa 5:16; 1Ch 3:8; 14:7).
2. One of David's mighty men known as the "Thirty" (2Sa 23:34).
3. A son of David (1Ch 3:6; 14:7). Called Elpelet (1Ch 14:5).
4. A descendant of Saul (1Ch 8:39).
5. A companion of Ezra (Ezr 8:13).
6. A priest from among the Israelites who had married a foreign woman and had pledged to divorce his wife (Ezr 10:33).

ELISABETH *See Elizabeth.*

ELISHA [515, *1811*] (*God [El] is [my] salvation*). The successor to Elijah the prophet . Elijah is instructed to anoint (1Ki 19:16). Called by Elijah (1Ki 19:19). Ministers to Elijah (1Ki 19:21). Witnesses Elijah's translation, receives a double portion of his spirit (2Ki 2:1-15; 3:11). Mocked by the children of Bethel (2Ki 2:23-24). Causes the king to restore the property of the hospitable Shunammite (2Ki 8:1-6). Instructs that Jehu be anointed the king of Israel (2Ki 9:1-3). Life of, sought by Jehoram (2Ki 6:31-33). The death of (2Ki 13:14-20). Bones of, restore a dead man to life (2Ki 13:21).

Miracles of:
Divides the Jordan (2Ki 2:14). Purifies the waters of Jericho by casting salt into the fountain (2Ki 2:19-22). Increases the oil of the woman whose sons were to be sold for debt (2Ki 4:1-7). Raises from the dead the son of the Shunammite (2Ki 4:18-37). Neutralizes the poison of the stew (2Ki 4:38-41). Increases the bread to feed one hundred men (2Ki 4:42-44). Heals Naaman the leper (2Ki 5:1-19; Lk 4:27). Sends leprosy as a judgment upon Gehazi (2Ki 5:26-27). Recovers the axhead that had fallen into a stream by causing it to float (2Ki 6:6). Reveals the counsel of the king of Syria (2Ki 6:12). Opens the eyes of his servant to see the hosts of the Lord (2Ki 6:17). Brings blindness upon the army of Syria (2Ki 6:18).

Prophecies of:
Foretells a son to the Shunammite woman (2Ki 4:16); plenty to the starving in Samaria (2Ki 7:1); death of the unbelieving prince (2Ki 7:2); seven years' famine in the land of Canaan (2Ki 8:1-3); death of Ben-Hadad, king of Syria (2Ki 8:7-10); elevation of Hazael to the throne (2Ki 8:11-15); the victory of Jehoash over Syria (2Ki 13:14-19). Elisha is referred to once in the NT (Lk 4:27).

ELISHAH [511] (*God [El] saves*). The son of Javan, whose name was given to an ancient land and its people, not identified (Ge 10:4; 1Ch 1:7; Eze 27:7).

ELISHAMA [514] (*God [El] has heard*).
1. A leader of the tribe of Ephraim during the census in the wilderness. The grandfather of Joshua (Nu 1:10; 2:18; 7:48, 53; 10:22; 1Ch 7:26).
2. A son of David (2Sa 5:16; 1Ch 3:8; 14:7).
3. KJV Elishama, another son of David, is NIV Elishua (1Ch 3:6, ftn). *See Elishua.*
4. The grandfather of the Ishmael who killed Gedaliah the governor of Israel appointed by Nebuchadnezzar (2Ki 25:25; Jer 41:1).
5. Of the tribe of Judah, descended from Sheshan (1Ch 2:41).
6. A priest sent by Jehoshaphat to teach the law in Judah (2Ch 17:8).
7. A secretary to Jehoiakim (Jer 36:12, 20-21).

ELISHAPHAT [516] (*God [El] is [my]*

judge). One of five Judean commanders who helped Jehoiada the priest in the overthrow of Athaliah to make Joash king (2Ch 23:1).

ELISHEBA [510] (*God [El] is an oath* BDB; *God [El] is [my] fill* KB). The daughter of Amminadab and wife of Aaron (Ex 6:23).

ELISHUA [512] (*God [El] is [my] salvation*). A son of David (2Sa 5:15; 1Ch 14:5). Elishama (1Ch 3:6, ftn) is probably a scribal error in Hebrew mss.

ELIUD [1809] (*God [El] is [my] grandeur*). An ancestor of Jesus; in the fifth generation before Jesus, he was the son of Akim and the father of Eleazar (Mt 1:14-15).

ELIZABETH (God is [my] oath).[*1810*]. The wife of Zechariah and mother of John the Baptist (Lk 1:5-60).

ELIZAPHAN [507] (*God [El] is [my] hiding*).
1. A Levite (Ex 6:22; Lev 10:4). The son of Uzziel, the leader of the families of the Kohathite clans who had the responsibility to take care of the ark, the table, the lampstand, and the vessels of the sanctuary (Nu 3:30; 1Ch 15:8; 2Ch 29:13).
2. A leader of Zebulun (Nu 34:25).

ELIZUR [506] (*God [El] is [my] rock*). A leader of Reuben, the son of Shedeur; one of the leaders who helped Moses take the census in the wilderness (Nu 1:5; 2:10; 7:30, 35; 10:18).

ELKANAH [555] (*God [El] has possessed*).
1. The grandson of Korah (Ex 6:24; 1Ch 6:23).
2. The father of Samuel (1Sa 1:1, 4, 8, 19, 21, 23; 2:11, 20; 1Ch 6:27, 34).
3. A Levite (1Ch 6:25, 36).
4. Possibly identical with 3 (1Ch 6:26, 35).
5. A Levite (1Ch 9:16).
6. A Levite who joined David at Ziklag (1Ch 12:6).
7. A doorkeeper for the ark, perhaps identical with 6 (1Ch 15:23).
8. A prince of Ahaz (2Ch 28:7).

ELKOSH [556]. The birthplace of Nahum the prophet (Na 1:1).

ELLASAR [536]. A city-state in Babylonia in the time of Abraham (Ge 14:1, 9).

ELM See Terebinth.

ELMADAM [*1825*]. An ancestor of Jesus (Lk 3:28).

ELNAAM [534] (*God [El] is pleasantness*). The father of two of David's mighty men known as the "Thirty" (1Ch 11:46).

ELNATHAN [535] (*God [El] has given*).
1. The grandfather of Jehoiachin (2Ki 24:8).
2. Levites who helped Ezra (Ezr 8:16).

3. The son of Acbor and a high official of King Jehoiakim (Jer 26:22; 36:12, 25).

ELOHE See El Elohe Israel.

ELOHIM (*a god, the God; Mighty One*).

Used of the God of Israel:
The most frequent Hebrew word for God, gods, angels, or magistrates. The plural *Elohim* when used for God in the OT is singular in meaning, and is often called "plural of majesty." See God, Names of, Elohim; El.

Used of Pagan Gods:
The Philistine god Dagon (Jdg 16:23-24), the Sidonian goddess Ashtoreth (1Ki 11:5, 33), the Moabite god Chemosh (1Ki 11:33), the Ammonite god Chemosh (1Ki 11:33), and Baal-Zebub of Ekron (2Ki 1:2, 3, 6) are also referred to in the plural.

Used of Other Groups:
Judges (Ex 21:6; 22:8-9), heavenly beings (Ps 8:5), those high among people (Ps 36:7).

ELOI, ELOI, LAMA SABACHTHANI [*1830+3316+4876*] (*My God, my God, why have you forsaken me?*). One of the seven cries of Jesus from the cross (Mt 27:46; Mk 15:34 w Ps 22:1).

ELON, ELONITE [390, 391, 472, 533] (*a species of a mighty tree*).
1. The father-in-law of Esau (Ge 26:34; 36:2).
2. A son of Zebulun (Ge 46:14) and his clan (Nu 26:26).
3. A town of Dan (Jos 19:43).
4. A Hebrew judge (Jdg 12:11-12).

ELON BETHHANAN [392] (*tree of Bethhanan*). A town of Dan (1Ki 4:9). Perhaps identical with Elon (Jos 19:43).

ELOTH See Elath.

ELPAAL [551] (*God [El] creates*). A Benjamite (1Ch 8:11-12, 18).

ELPELET [550] (*God [El] is deliverance*). A son of David (1Ch 14:5). Called Eliphelet (1Ch 3:6).

ELTEKEH [558, 559] (*meeting place*). A city of Dan (Jos 19:44; 21:23).

ELTEKON [560] (*God [El] has arranged*). A city of Judah (Jos 15:59).

ELTOLAD [557] (*generation* IDB; *kindred of God [El]* ISBE; *God [El] + place where children could be obtained* KB). A city of Judah (Jos 15:30; 19:4). Called Tolad (1Ch 4:29).

ELUL [469]. The sixth month in sacred sequence, month twelve in civil sequence. The returned Jews finish the wall of Jerusalem in (Ne

6:15). Zerubbabel builds the temple in (Hag 1:14-15).

A transitional season from dry to rainy (August-September). The season for processing grapes, figs, and olives. See Month, 6.

ELUZAI [539] (*God [El] is my strength*). A Benjamite warrior who joined David while he was in exile from Saul at the Philistine city of Ziklag (1Ch 12:5). He was able to use a bow or sling with either hand.

ELYMAS [1829] (possibly *wise one* hence *magician*). A Jewish magician and false prophet associated with Proconsul Sergius Paulus at Paphos on Cyprus. He was punished with blindness when he opposed Paul and Barnabas and tried to turn the proconsul from the faith (Ac 13:8-11).

ELZABAD [479] (*God [El] has given*).
1. A Gadite warrior who joined David at Ziklag (1Ch 12:12).
2. A Korahite gatekeeper (1Ch 26:7).

ELZAPHAN See Elizaphan.

EMANCIPATION Of all Hebrew servants (Ex 21:2; Lev 25:8-17, 39-41; Dt 15:12).
Proclamation of: By Cyrus (2Ch 36:23; Ezr 1:1-4), by Zedekiah (Jer 34:8-11). See Exodus; Jubilee.

EMBALMING [2846, 2847]. Of Jacob (Ge 50:2-3), of Joseph (Ge 50:26), of Asa (2Ch 16:14), of Jesus (Mk 15:46; 16:1; Jn 19:39-40).

EMBEZZLEMENT (Lk 16:1-7). See Dishonesty.

EMBLEMS OF THE HOLY SPIRIT See Holy Spirit, Emblems of.

EMBROIDERY [8387, 8391]. In blue, purple, and scarlet, on the curtains of the tabernacle (Ex 26:1, 36; 27:16), on the ephod and coat of the high priest, mingled with gold (Ex 28:4-5, 39). Bezalel and Oholiab divinely inspired for in the work of the tabernacle (Ex 35:30-35; 38:22-23). On the garments of Sisera (Jdg 5:30). On the garments of women (Ps 45:14; Eze 16:10, 13, 18). On the garments of princes (Eze 26:16).
See Tapestry.

EMEK See Beth Emek; Emek Keziz.

EMEK KEZIZ [6681] (*valley of Keziz*). A valley and city of Benjamin (Jos 18:21).

EMERALD [3402, 5039, 5040]. One of the jewels in the priestly breastplate (Ex 28:18; 39:11; Jer 17:1).
Figurative:
Ezekiel uses imagery of the Creation and the Fall to picture the career of the king of Tyre; unlike Adam, who was naked, the king is pictured as a fully clothed priest, ordained to guard God's holy place; the nine stones listed are among the twelve worn by the priest (Eze 28:13).
Since God dwells in "unapproachable light" and is one "whom no one has seen or can see" (1Ti 6:16), he is described in terms of the reflected brilliance of precious stones—an emerald rainbow around the throne (Rev 4:3).
Symbolic:
In the foundation of the holy city (Rev 21:19).
See Minerals of the Bible, 1; Stones.

EMERGENCY See Decision.

EMERODS See Hemorrhoids.

EMITES [400] (*frightening beings*). Early inhabitants of the area around Kiriathaim which is E of the Dead Sea. They were defeated in the time of Abraham by the four invading kings (Ge 14:5). A race of giants who were "strong and numerous, and as tall as the Anakites" (Dt 2:10-11). See Rephaites.

EMMANUEL See Immanuel.

EMMAUS [1843] (*hot springs*). A village seven miles from Jerusalem (Lk 24:7-35).

EMPLOYEE
Rights of an Employee:
Prompt payment (Lev 19:13). Participation of produce (Lev 25:6). Just compensation (Mt 10:10; Lk 10:7; Ro 4:4; Col 4:1; 1Ti 5:18). Oppression of (Dt 24:14-15; Pr 22:16; Mal 3:5; Lk 15:15-17; Jas 5:4). Kindness to exemplified (Ru 2:4; Lk 15:17, 19).
Character of Unrighteous: (Job 7:1-3; 14:1, 6; Mt 20:1-16; 21:33-41; Jn 10:12-13).
See Employer; Master; Servant; Slave.

EMPLOYER Required: To grant a Sabbath rest (Ex 20:10; Dt 5:14). To make prompt payment (Lev 19:13; Dt 24:15; Jas 5:4-5). To be kind (Lev 25:39-43; Job 31:13-15; Eph 6:9; Phm 15-16). Not to oppress (Dt 24:14-15; Pr 22:16; Mal 3:5). To accord just compensation (Jer 22:13; Mt 10:10; 20:1-15; Lk 10:7; Ro 4:4; Col 4:1; 1Ti 5:18).
See Employee; Labor; Master; Servant.

EMULATION To create a desire for salvation (Ro 11:11, 14). To generosity in giving to aid others (2Co 8:1-8; 9:1-5). To love and good works (Heb 10:24).
Illustrated: In Esau's marriages (Ge 28:6-9). In Jacob's household (Ge 30:1-24).

EN EGLAIM [6536] (*spring of two calves*). Possibly modern Ain Feshka at the NW corner of the Dead Sea (Eze 47:10).

EN GANNIM [6528] (*spring of gardens*).
1. A city of Judah (Jos 15:34).
2. A city of Issachar (Jos 19:21; 21:29).

EN GEDI [6527] (*spring of young goat*). Called Hazazon Tamar. Built by the Amorites (Ge 14:7; 2Ch 20:2). A city allotted to Judah (Jos 15:62). Famous for its vineyards (SS 1:14).

Wilderness of, near the Dead Sea. David uses as a stronghold (1Sa 23:29; 24). Cave of (1Sa 24:3).

EN HADDAH [6532] (*spring of gladness*). A city of Issachar probably located c. six miles E of Mount Tabor (Jos 19:21).

EN HAKKORE [6530] (*spring of the partridge* or *spring of the caller*). A spring at Lehi from which Samson drank after slaughtering the Philistines (Jdg 15:19).

EN HAZOR [6533] (*spring of Hazor*). En Hazor was a fortified city assigned to Naphtali (Jos 19:37).

EN MISHPAT [6535] (*spring of judgment*). The ancient name of Kadesh (Ge 14:7). *See Kadesh.*

EN RIMMON [6538] (*spring of Rimmon*). A city of Judah in the Negev, later assigned to Simeon (Jos 19:7; 1Ch 4:32). Probably identical with Ain and Rimmon (Jos 15:32; 1Ch 4:32). Those returning from the Exile resettled at En Rimmon (Ne 11:29).

EN ROGEL [6537] (*spring of the fuller*, or *wanderer,* or *spy*). A spring near Jerusalem (Jos 15:7; 18:16; 2Sa 17:17), possibly the Jackal Well (Ne 2:13). A rebellious feast at (1Ki 1:9).

EN SHEMESH [6539] (*spring of Shemesh,* [sun or pagan god]). A place on the N boundary of Judah and the S boundary of Benjamin (Jos 15:7; 18:17). The last spring on the road between Jerusalem and the Jordan Valley was found there. En Shemesh has been called the "Spring of the Apostles" since the fifteenth century.

EN TAPPUAH [6540] (*spring of apple*). A spring of uncertain location at the S border of Manasseh (Jos 17:7); usually identified with modern Sheikh Abu Zarad c. eight miles S of Shechem. The town was a Canaanite stronghold that held out against the Israelites for a period of time during the conquest of the land by the Israelites.

ENAIM [6542] (*two springs*). It is most likely located in the high hill country SE of Jerusalem between Adullam and Timnah; KJV "open place" (Ge 38:14, 21).

ENAM [6543]. A town in the western foothills of Judah (Jos 15:34).

ENAN [6544] (*spring*). The father of Ahira who was a military leader of the tribe of Naphtali and one who assisted in the Sinai census (Nu 1:15; 2:29; 7:78, 83; 10:27).

ENCAMPMENT [2837, 3655+4722, 8905]. Places where the Israelites encamped on the way from Egypt to Canaan (Nu 33). Also headquarters of armies (1Sa 13:16; 2Ch 32:1). *See Camp.*

ENCHANTMENT [879, 2489+2490, 4318, 10081]. The use of any form of magic, including divination; forbidden to God's people (Dt 18:10; Ac 8:9, 11; 13:8, 10; 19:19). *See Divination; Magic; Sorcery.*

END OF THE WORLD

Consummation of the age (Mt 13:39, 49; 24:3; 28:20; Heb 9:26). *See Eschatology.*

ENDOR [6529] (*spring of Dor*). A city of Issachar allotted to Manasseh (Jos 17:11). Deborah triumphs at, over Sisera (Jdg 4; Ps 83:10). The medium of, consulted by Saul (1Sa 28:7-25).

ENDURANCE [*586, 2118, 3920, 5951, 6641, 7756, 8425, *3531*, *5702*, *5705*]. *See Perseverance.*

ENEAS *See Aeneas.*

ENEMY [*367, 7640, 7675, 7756, 8533, 2398].

Kindness to:
Commanded (Ex 23:4-5; Pr 25:21-22; Mt 5:43-48; Lk 6:27-36; Ro 12:14, 20).

Forgiveness of:
Commanded (Mt 6:12-15; 18:21-35; Mk 11:25; Lk 17:3-4; Eph 4:31-32; Col 3:13; 1Pe 3:9).

Instances of Forgiveness—
Esau, of Jacob (Ge 33:4, 11). Joseph, of his brothers (Ge 45:5-15; 50:19-21). Moses, of Miriam and Aaron (Nu 12:1-13). David, of Saul (1Sa 24:10-12; 26:9, 23; 2Sa 1:14-17), of Shimei (2Sa 16:9-13; 19:23; 1Ki 2:8-9), of Absalom and his co-conspirators (2Sa 18:5, 12, 32-33; 19:6, 12-13). The prophet of Judah by Jeroboam (1Ki 13:3-6). Jesus, of his persecutors (Lk 23:34). Stephen, of his murderers (Ac 7:60).

Destruction of:
Requested by David (Ps 35:1-7). The wickedness of David's enemies (Ps 56:2, 5-6; 57:4, 6; 62:4; 69:4; 71:10; 102:8; 109:2-5; 129:1-3). *See Prayer, Imprecatory.*

Rejoicing at the destruction of, forbidden (Pr 24:17-18). Rejoicing at the destruction of, not practiced by Job (Job 31:29-30).

Figurative:
Of the devil (Mt 13:25, 28, 39).

ENGAGEMENT *See Betrothal.*

ENGINE NIV "machines" of war (2Ch 26:15) or "battering rams" (Eze 26:9). *See Armies; Fort.*

ENGRAFTING *See Graft.*

ENGRAVING [2933, 2980, 3100, 4180,

5237, 7334, 7338, *1963*]. On the stones set in the priest's breastplate (Ex 28:9-11, 21, 36; 39:8-14). In making idols (Ex 32:4), in the priest's ephod (Ex 39:6), in the priest's crown (Ex 39:30).

ENOCH [2840, *1970*] (*initiated* ISBE; *follower* KB).

1. Cain's eldest son (Ge 4:17).

2. A city built by Cain (Ge 4:17).

3. The father of Methuselah (Ge 5:21-22). Walked with God and then was translated to heaven by God (Ge 5:24; Heb 11:5).

ENOCH, BOOKS OF   Apocalyptic
literature written by various authors and circulated under the name of Enoch; written c. 163 B.C. to A.D. 50. Possibly quoted in Jude 14-15.

ENON See Aenon.

ENOSH [633, *1968*] (*[mortal] man*). The son of Seth (Ge 4:26; 5:6-11; 1Ch 1:1; Lk 3:38).

ENQUIRING OF GOD See *Affliction, Prayer Under; Prayer.*

ENSIGN A standard or banner (Ps 74:4; Isa 5:26; 11:10, 12; 18:3; 30:17; 31:9; Zec 9:16). See *Banner; Standard.*

ENTERTAINMENTS [8471, 10166, *1926, 3826, 4138, 5810*]. Often great (Ge 21:8; Da 5:1; Lk 5:29). Preparations made for (Ge 18:6-7; Mt 22:4; Lk 15:23).

Given on Occasions of:
Weaning children (Ge 21:8). Ratifying covenants (Ge 26:30; 31:54). Offering voluntary sacrifice (Ge 31:54; Dt 12:6-7; 1Sa 1:4-5). After wine was trodden (Jdg 9:27). Harvest home (Ru 3:2-7; Isa 9:3). Festivals (1Sa 20:5, 24-26). Sheepshearing (1Sa 25:2, 36; 2Sa 13:23). Return of friends (2Sa 12:4; Lk 15:23). Coronation of kings (1Ki 1:9, 18-19; 1Ch 12:39-40; Hos 7:5). Taking leave of friends (1Ki 19:21). National deliverance (Est 8:17; 9:17-19). Marriage (Mt 22:2). Birth days (Mk 6:21).

Kinds of, Mentioned in Scripture:
Dinner (Ge 43:16; Mt 22:4; Lk 14:12). Banquet (Est 5:4-6). Served often by hired servants (Mt 22:3; Jn 2:5). Served often by members of the family (Lk 10:40; Jn 12:2). Supper (Lk 14:12; Jn 12:2). Under the direction of a master of the feast (Jn 2:8-9).

Invitations to:
Should be sent to the poor (Dt 14:29, w Lk 14:13). Often by the master in person (2Sa 13:24; Est 5:4; Zep 1:7; Lk 7:36). Often only to relatives and friends (1Ki 1:9; Lk 14:12). Often addressed to many (Lk 14:16). Repeated through servants when all things were ready (Lk 14:17).

Often Given in:
The house (Lk 5:29). Near landmarks (1Ki 1:9). The court of the house (Est 1:5-6; Lk 7:36-37).

The upper room or guest chamber (Mk 14:14-15). The house (Lk 5:29).

Guests at:
Had their feet washed when they came a distance (Ge 18:4; 43:24; Lk 7:38, 44). Arranged according to rank (Ge 43:33; 1Sa 9:22; Lk 14:10). Often had separate dishes (Ge 43:34; 1Sa 1:4). A choice portion reserved for principal guests (Ge 43:34; 1Sa 1:5; 9:23-24). Began with thanksgiving (1Sa 9:13; Mk 8:6). Often scenes of great intemperance (1Sa 25:36; Da 5:3-4; Hos 7:5). Portions often sent to the absent (Ne 8:10; Est 9:19). None asked to eat more than he liked at (Est 1:8). Men and women did not usually meet at (Est 1:8-9; Mk 6:21, w Mt 14:11). Given by the guests in return (Job 1:4; Lk 14:12). Usually anointed (Ps 23:5; Lk 7:46). Music and dancing often introduced at (Am 6:5; Mk 6:22; Lk 15:25). Eager to take chief seats at, condemned (Mt 23:6; Lk 14:7-8). Often ate from the same dish (Mt 26:23). Concluded with a hymn (Mk 14:26). None admitted after the master had risen and shut the door (Lk 13:24-25). Offense given by refusing to go to (Lk 14:18, 24). Anxiety to have many guests at, alluded to (Lk 14:22-23). See *Feasts.*

ENTHUSIASM [2419, 5080]. Instances of: Gideon (Jdg 6-7), Jehu (2Ki 9:1-14; 10:1-28). See *Zeal.*

ENUMERATION See *Census.*

ENVY [7861, 7863, 8353, *2419, 2420, 4057+4505, 4143, 5784*].

Characteristic of:
Depravity (Ro 1:29; Tit 3:3). Worldliness (Ro 13:13; 1Co 3:3; 12:20; Gal 5:19-21; 1Ti 6:4; Jas 3:14, 16; 4:5).

Not characteristic of love (1Co 13:4).

Described as:
Destructive (Job 5:2). The cause of rotting bones (Pr 14:30). All consuming (Pr 27:4; SS 8:6). Drives people to achievement (Ecc 4:4). As unyielding as the grave (SS 8:6). Where envy and selfish ambition are found, disorder and every evil practice are found (Jas 3:16).

Forbidden: (Ps 37:1, 7; 49:16-20; Pr 3:31-32; 23:17-18; 24:1-2, 19-20; Ro 13:13; Gal 5:25-26; Jas 5:8-9; 1Pe 2:1-2).

Punishment for: (Eze 35:11).

Instances of:
Cain, of Abel (Ge 4:4-8). Sarah, of Hagar (Ge 16:5-6; 21:9-10). Philistines, of Isaac because of the large number of flocks and herds he owned (Ge 26:14). Rachel, of Leah (Ge 30:1). Leah, of Rachel (Ge 30:15). Laban's sons, of Jacob (Ge 31:1). Joseph's brothers, of Joseph (Ge 37:4-11, 18-20; Ac 7:9). Joshua, of Eldad and Medad (Nu 11:28-30). Miriam and Aaron, of Moses (Nu 12:1-10). Korah, Dathan, and Abiram, of Moses (Nu 16:3; Ps 106:16-18). Saul, of David (1Sa 18:8-9, 29; 1Sa 20:31). Haman, of Mordecai (Est 5:13). Asaph, at prosperity of wicked (Ps 73:2-3). The

wicked, at the prosperity of the righteous (Ps 112:10; Isa 26:11). The princes of Babylon, of Daniel (Da 6:3-4).

Priests, of Jesus (Mt 27:18; Mk 15:10; Jn 11:47-48). Jews, of Paul and Barnabas (Ac 13:45; 17:5). *See Jealousy.*

EPAENETUS *See Epenetus.*

EPAPHRAS [*2071*] (*handsome*). A co-worker with Paul (Col 1:7; 4:12; Phm 23).

EPAPHRODITUS [*2073*] (*handsome*). A messenger of Paul (Php 2:25; 4:18). Sick at Rome (Php 2:26-27, 30).

EPENETUS [*2045*] (*praised*). A convert to Christ in the province of Asia (Ro 16:5).

EPHAH [406, 6548, 6549] (*darkness*).
1. A son of Midian (Ge 25:4; 1Ch 1:33; Isa 60:6).
2. Caleb's concubine (1Ch 2:46).
3. A son of Jahdai (1Ch 2:47).
4. A measure of about 3/5 bushel. *See Measure, Dry Capacity.*

EPHAI [6550] (*my bird*). A Netophathite (Jer 40:8). Sons warned Gedaliah (Jer 40:8-16; 41:3).

EPHER [6761] (*[small] gazelle*).
1. A son of Midian (Ge 25:4; 1Ch 1:33).
2. A son of Ezra (1Ch 4:17).
3. A chief of Manasseh (1Ch 5:24).

EPHES DAMMIM [702] (*border of Dammim [blood]*). A place between Socoh and Azekah in Judah, where David killed Goliath (1Sa 17:1). Called Pas Dammim (1Ch 11:13).

EPHESIANS, EPISTLE TO THE

Author: The apostle Paul

Date: c. A.D. 60

Outline:
I. Greetings (1:1-2).
II. The Divine Purpose: The Glory and Headship of Christ (1:3-14).
III. Prayer That Christians May Realize God's Purpose and Power (1:15-23).
IV. Steps Toward the Fulfillment of God's Purpose (chs. 2-3).
  A. Salvation of Individuals by Grace (2:1-10).
  B. Reconciliation of Jew and Gentile Through the Cross (2:11-18).
  C. Uniting of Jew and Gentile in One Household (2:19-22).
  D. Revelation of God's Wisdom Through the Church (3:1-13).
  E. Prayer for Deeper Experience of God's Fullness (3:14-21).
V. Practical Ways to Fulfill God's Purpose in the Church (4:1-6:20).
  A. Unity (4:1-6).
  B. Maturity (4:7-16).
  C. Renewal of Personal Life (4:17-5:20).

D. Deference in Personal Relationships (5:21-6:9).
  1. Principle (5:21).
  2. Husbands and wives (5:22-33).
  3. Children and parents (6:1-4).
  4. Slaves and masters (6:5-9).
  E. Strength in the Spiritual Conflict (6:10-20).
VI. Conclusion, Final Greetings and Benediction (6:21-24).

EPHESUS [*1650, 2386, 2387*]. Paul visits and preaches in (Ac 18:19-21; 19; 20:16-38). Apollos visits and preaches in (Ac 18:18-28). Sceva's sons attempt to expel a demon in (Ac 19:13-16). Timothy directed by Paul to remain at (1Ti 1:3). Onesiphorus lives at (2Ti 1:18). Paul sends Tychicus to (2Ti 4:12). Church at (Rev 1:11). Apocalyptic message to (Rev 2:1-7).
See Ephesians, Epistle to the.

EPHLAL [697] (*judgment, arbitration*). A descendant of Judah through Perez and the family of Jerahmeel (1Ch 2:37).

EPHOD [680, 681].
1. A sacred vestment worn by the high priest. Described (Ex 25:7; 28:6-14, 31-35). Breastplate attached to (Ex 28:22-30). Making of (Ex 39:2-26). Worn by Aaron (Ex 39:5).
An ephod made by his mother was worn by Samuel as a young boy ministering before the Lord (1Sa 2:18), by the common priests (1Sa 22:18), by David (2Sa 6:14). Used as an oracle (1Sa 23:9, 12; 30:7-8).
As an idol—
Gideon made an ephod out of gold, placing it in his hometown of Ophrah, the ephod subsequently becoming an idol to Israel (Jdg 8:27). Micah from the hill country of Ephraim made one of gold (Jdg 17:5; 18:14). Prophecy concerning the absence of an ephod from Israel (Hos 3:4).
2. A man of Manasseh (Nu 34:23).

EPHPHATHA [*2395*] (*to open*). An Aramaic passive imperative transliterated into the Greek (Mk 7:34).

EPHRAIM [713+, *2394*] (*doubly fruitful*).
1. The second son of Joseph (Ge 41:52). Adopted by Jacob (Ge 48:5). Blessed before Manasseh; prophecies concerning (Ge 48:14-20). Descendants of (Nu 26:35-37; 1Ch 7:20-27). Mourns for his sons (1Ch 7:21-22).
2. A tribe of Israel. Prophecy concerning (Ge 49:25-26; Isa 7; 9:18-21; 11:13; 28:1-6; Jer 31; Hos 5:13-14; Zec 9:10-13; 10:7-12). Numbered at Sinai and in the plains of Moab (Nu 1:33; 26:37). Place in camp and march (Nu 2:18, 24; 10:22). Blessed by Moses (Dt 33:13-17).
Territory allotted to, after the conquest of Canaan (Jos 16:5-9; 17:9-10, 15-18; 1Ch 7:28-29). Fail to expel the Canaanites (Jos 16:10). Take Bethel in battle (Jdg 1:22-25). Join Gideon against the Midianites (Jdg 7:24-25). Rebuke Gideon for not summoning them to join the war against the

Midianites (Jdg 8:1). Their jealousy of Jephthah (Jdg 12:1). Defeated by him (Jdg 12:4-6). Receive Ish-Bosheth as king (2Sa 2:8-9). Revolt from the house of David (1Ki 12:25; 2Ch 10:16). Jeroboam set up a golden calf in Bethel (1Ki 12:29). Some of the tribe join Judah under Asa (2Ch 15:9). Chastise Ahaz and Judah (2Ch 28:7). Join Hezekiah in reinstituting the Passover (2Ch 30:18). Join in the destruction of idols in Jerusalem (2Ch 31:1). Submit to the scepter of Josiah (2Ch 34:1-6). Envied other tribes (Isa 11:13). Exalted by other tribes (Hos 13:1). Real-lotment of territory to, by Ezekiel (Eze 48:5). Worshiped Baal (Hos 13:1). Sin of, remembered by God (Hos 13:12).

Name, applied to the ten tribes (2Ch 17:2; 25:6-7; Isa 7:8-9; 11:12-13; 17:3; Jer 31:18, 20; Hos 4:17; 5:3, 5; 6:4, 10; 8:11; 12:14). Tribe of, called Joseph (Rev 7:8).

3. Mount of. A range of low mountains (Jos 17:15-18). Joshua has his inheritance in (Jdg 2:9). Residence of Micah (Jdg 17:8). A place of hiding for the Israelites (1Sa 14:22). Sheba resides in (2Sa 20:21). Prophecy concerning its conversion (Jer 31:6). Noted for rich pastures (Jer 50:19).

4. A wood E of the Jordan. Absalom killed in (2Sa 18:6-17).

5. A gate of Jerusalem (2Ki 14:13; 2Ch 25:23; Ne 8:16; 12:39).

6. A city in the territory of Ephraim to which Jesus escapes to evade the persecution of Caiaphas (Jn 11:54).

EPHRAIMITE [713+, 718] (doubly fruit-ful). A member of the tribe of Ephraim (Jos 16:5-10; Jdg 12).

EPHRATH, EPHRATHAH [714, 715, 716, 717, 718] (fruitful land).

1. A place near Bethel where Rachel died and was buried (Ge 35:16, 19; 48:7).

2. A name of Bethlehem (Ru 4:11; Mic 5:2).

3. The second wife of Caleb, mother of Hur (1Ch 2:19, 50; 4:4).

4. An area associated with Kiriath Jearim (Ps 132:6, ftn).

EPHRON [6766, 6767] (gazelle).

1. The son of Zohar; the Hittite from whom Abraham purchased the field containing the cave of Machpelah, to the E of Mamre (Ge 23:8-17; 25:9; 49:29-30; 50:13).

2. Mount Ephron, a district whose cities were on the border of Judah (Jos 15:9).

3. A city near Bethel from which Abijah took Jeroboam I (2Ch 13:19).

4. A strongly fortified city between Karnaim and Beth Shan (Scythopolis) in the Maccabean period. It tried to prevent the passage of Judas and the Israelites with him, but Judas took the city, plundered it, and killed all its male inhabitants (1Mc 5:46-52; 2Mc 12:27-29).

EPIC Heroic poetry. Miriam's song (Ex 15:1-19, 21). Deborah's song (Jdg 5). See Poetry.

EPICUREANS [2134]. A style of life familiar to Solomon long before Epicurus (341-270 B.C.) defined the doctrine through his school of philosophy in Athens (Ecc 2:1-10). Paul con-fronts a group of Epicurean and Stoic philosophers at a meeting of the Court of the Areopagus (Mars Hill) which is NW of the Acropolis and connected to it (Ac 17:16-34). See Aratus; Cleanthes; Stoicism; Stoics. It is suspected that by the Christian era the respon-sibility of the Court of the Areopagus was to cen-sor the religious life of the community, and because of Paul's teaching concerning Jesus and the Resurrection they were exercising that right of censor.

See Sensuality.

EPILEPSY See Seizures.

EPISTLE (letter). Formal letters containing Christian doctrine and exhortation, referring par-ticularly to the twenty-one epistles of the NT, divided into Pauline and General epistles. Not all the letters of the apostles have survived (1Co 5:9; Col 4:16).

EPISTLES, GENERAL See General Letters.

EPISTLES, PASTORAL See Pastoral Epistles.

EQUALITY See Mankind, Equality of All People.

EQUITY [4797]. See Justice.

ER [6841, 2474] (watcher, watchful).

1. The eldest son of Judah (Ge 38:3, 6-7; 46:12; Nu 26:19; 1Ch 2:3).

2. A son of Judah's son Shelah (1Ch 4:21).

3. An ancestor of Jesus (Lk 3:28).

ERAN, ERANITE [6896, 6897] (watcher, watchful). A grandson of Ephraim and his clan (Nu 26:36).

ERASTUS [2235] (beloved).

1. A convert of Paul sent with Timothy from Ephesus into Macedonia on an errand (Ac 19:22).

2. The "city treasurer" or the "city director of public works" of Corinth; a Christian (Ro 16:23).

3. A companion of Paul who remained in Corinth (2Ti 4:20). Possibly the same as 1 above.

ERECH [804, 10074].

1. A Babylonian city founded by Nimrod (Ge 10:10), located forty miles NW of Ur toward Bab-ylon.

2. The men of Erech along with the men of Tripolis, Persia, and Babylon were settled in the cities of Samaria and elsewhere in Trans-Euphrates by Ashurbanipal (Ezr 4:9-10).

ERI, ERITE [6878, 6879] (watcher). The

fifth son of Gad, the grandson of Jacob (Ge 46:16) and his clan (Nu 26:16).

ERRORS [2628, 5413, 8704, 8705, 8706, 8709, 9334, 9360, 9494, *4414*, *4415*]. In teachers and doctrines. *See Teachers, False.*

ESAIAS *See Isaiah.*

ESARHADDON [675] (*Ashur has given a brother [for a lost son]*). The son and successor of Sennacherib after Sennacherib was murdered by his sons Adrammelech and Sharezer in 681 B.C.; ruled Assyria 681-669 B.C. (2Ki 19:37; 2Ch 32:21; Isa 37:38); restored the city of Babylon; conquered Egypt; brought deportees into Samaria (Ezr 4:2); took Manasseh captive (2Ch 33:11).

ESAU [6916, *2481*] (*hairy*). The eldest of twin sons born to Isaac and Rebekah. Birth of (Ge 25:19-26; 1Ch 1:34). A hunter (Ge 25:27-28). Beloved by Isaac (Ge 25:27-28). Sold his birthright for a single meal of stew (Ge 25:29-34; 27:36; Heb 12:16). He was alternately called Edom because he had red coloring; Edom means red (Ge 25:25, 30). Married two Hittite women (Ge 26:34). Polygamy of (Ge 26:34; 28:9; 36:2-3). His marriages a grief to Isaac and Rebekah (Ge 26:35). Was defrauded of his father's blessing by Jacob (Ge 27; Heb 11:20). Met Jacob after the return of the latter from Haran (Ge 33:1). With Jacob, buried his father (Ge 35:29).

Descendants of (Ge 36; 1Ch 1:35-57). Called Edom (Ge 25:30; 36:1, 8). His name used to denote his descendants and their country (Dt 2:5; Jer 49:8, 10; Ob 6). Ancestor of Edomites (Jer 49:8). Enmity of descendants of, toward descendants of Jacob (Ob 10-14). Prophecies concerning (Ob 18).

ESCAPE [*3655, 4200+8965, 4880, 4946+, 5674, 5911, 7127, 7129, *709*, *1767*, *5771*].

God Provides for the Righteous:
Noah and his family (Ge 7:7). The infant Jesus (Mt 2:13). By salvation (Ps 68:20). From temptation (Ecc 7:26; 1Co 10:13; 2Ti 2:26; 2Pe 1:4).

No Escape From the Judgment of God:
Adam and Eve (Ge 3:7-11). Cain (Ge 4:9-12). Mankind (Job 34:21-30; Ps 56:7; Isa 10:1-3; Mt 23:33; Ro 2:3; 1Th 5:2-3; Heb 2:2-3; 12:25-26; Rev 6:15-17).
See Sin, Fruits of; Punishment of; Judgment; Judgments.

ESCHATOLOGY (*study of last events*). Division of systematic theology dealing with the doctrine of last things such as death, resurrection, second coming of Christ, end of the age, divine judgment, and the future state. The OT teaches a future resurrection and judgment day (Job 19:25-27; Isa 25:6-9; 26:19-21; Da 12:2-3).

The NT interprets, enlarges, and completes the OT eschatology. It stresses the Resurrection (Ro 8:11; 1Co 15), the second coming of Christ (Mt 16:27; Lk 17:30; 1Co 1:7; 4:5; 1Th 2:19; 3:13;

4:13-18; 2Th 1:7-10; 2:1-6; 1Pe 1:7; 1Jn 2:28), the final judgment when the unsaved are cast into hell (Rev 20), and the righteous enter heaven (Mt 25:31-46). Christians differ on how the Millennium is to be interpreted, dividing themselves into amillennialists, postmillennialists, and premillennialists (Rev 20:1-6). *See Millennium.*

ESCHEAT *See Confiscation.*

ESDRAELON (*the valley of God's sowing* or *God will sow*). Mentioned as "Esdraelon" only in the Apocrypha. The Valley of Jezreel which lies between Galilee on the N and Samaria on the S (Jos 17:16; Jdg 6:33). Assigned to Issachar (Jos 15:56). Known as the "fertile valley."

ESDRAS, BOOKS OF *See Apocrypha.*

ESEK [6922] (*dispute*). A well dug by Isaac's servants in the valley near Gerar. A dispute arose between Isaac's herdsmen and the herdsmen of Gerar over rights to the water, so he named it Esek which means *dispute.* Isaac's men moved to another place and found the same problem, so he named it Sitnah which means *opposition.* Finally they dug a third well that no one quarreled over, so he named Rehoboth, which means *room* (Ge 26:19-22).

ESHAN [878] (*support*). A city in Judah (Jos 15:52).

ESH-BAAL [843] (*man of Baal*). Ish-Bosheth, the youngest son of Saul; he was made king over Israel by Abner to repudiate David's claim to the throne; he ruled two years and then was murdered by David's men (2Sa 2:8-10; 4:5-12). He was originally called Esh-baal (1Ch 8:33; 9:39).

ESHBAN [841] (*man of understanding*). A son of Dishon, a Horite chief from the region of Mt. Seir (Ge 36:26; 1Ch 1:41).

ESHCOL [865, 866] (*[grape] cluster*).
1. An Amorite, and ally of Abraham (Ge 14:13, 24).
2. A valley or brook near Hebron (Nu 13:23-24; 32:9; Dt 1:24).

ESHEK [6944] (*oppressor*). A descendant of Jonathan (1Ch 8:38-40).

ESHTAOL, ESHTAOLITES [900, 901] (*[place of oracles] inquiry*). A town of Judah (Jos 15:33). Allotted to Dan (Jos 19:41; Jdg 18:2, 8, 11). Samson moved by the Spirit of the Lord near (Jdg 13:25). Samson buried near (Jdg 16:31).

ESHTEMOA, ESHTEMOH [903, 904] (*[place where oracle is] heard*).
1. A town of Canaan assigned to Judah (Jos 15:50). Allotted to the Aaronites (Jos 21:14; 1Ch 6:57). David shared the spoil with (1Sa 30:28).

2. A descendant of Ezra (1Ch 4:17, 19).

ESHTON [902] (possibly *hen-pecked [husband]* or *effeminate*). A son of Mehir, the son of Kelub (1Ch 4:11-12).

ESLI [2268] (*Yahweh sets apart*). An ancestor of Jesus (Lk 3:25).

ESROM See *Hezron*.

ESSENES An important Jewish community which was flourishing in Israel during the lifetime of Jesus. They were not mentioned in the Bible, but are presumed to be the inhabitants of Josephus and Philo, since Dead Sea Scrolls were discovered. Most lived communal, celibate lives. They observed the law strictly; they practiced ceremonial baptisms; they were apocalyptic; they opposed the temple priesthood. See *Testaments, Time Between*.

ESTATE [1074, 5709, 9165, *4045, 6005*]. See *Land*.

ESTHER [676] (Persian *star,* possibly *[Babylonian goddess] Ishtar*). Called also Hadassah (Est 2:7). The cousin of Mordecai (Est 2:7, 15). Chosen to be queen (Est 2:17). Tells the king of the plot against his life (Est 2:22). Fasts on account of the decree to destroy the Israelites; accuses Haman to the king; intercedes for her people (Est 4-9).

ESTHER, BOOK OF

Author: Anonymous

Date: Shortly after the events narrated, c. 460 B.C.

Outline:
I. The Feasts of Xerxes (1:1-2:18).
   A. Vashti Deposed (ch. 1).
   B. Esther Made Queen (2:1-18).
II. The Feasts of Esther (2:19-7:10).
   A. Mordecai Uncovers a Plot (2:19-23).
   B. Haman's Plot (ch. 3).
   C. Mordecai Persuades Esther to Help (ch. 4).
   D. Esther's Request to the King: First Banquet (5:1-8).
   E. A Sleepless Night (5:9-6:14).
   F. Haman Hanged: The Second Banquet (ch. 7).
III. The Feasts of Purim (chs. 8-10).
   A. The King's Edict in Behalf of the Jews (ch. 8).
   B. The Institution of Purim (ch. 9).
   C. The Promotion of Mordecai (ch. 10).

ETAM [6515] (possibly *place of birds of prey*).
1. A rock where Samson was bound and delivered to the Philistines (Jdg 15:8, 11-13).
2. A name in the list of Judah's descendants, but probably referring to 4 (1Ch 4:3).
3. A village of Simeon (1Ch 4:32).
4. A city in Judah (2Ch 11:6).

ETERNAL LIFE [5905, 6329, 6409, 7710, 10550, *132, 172, 173*]. Participation in the life of Jesus Christ, the eternal Son of God (Jn 1:4; 10:10; 17:3; Ro 6:23), which reaches its fruition in the life to come (Mt 25:46; Jn 6:54; Ro 2:7; Tit 3:7). It is endless in its duration and divine in quality. See *Immortality; Life, Everlasting*.

ETERNAL PUNISHMENT See *Punishment, Eternal*.

ETERNITY [5905, 6329, 6409, 7710, 10550, *132, 172, 173, 353*]. God inhabits (Isa 57:15; Mic 5:2), rules (Jer 10:10).
   God, adoration for (Ps 30:12; 41:13), steadfastness of (Ps 72:17; 90:2; Mt 6:13), righteousness of (Ps 119:142; 2Co 9:9). See *God, Eternity of*.
   Priestly order of Melchizedek (Ps 110:4). See *Christ, Eternity of*.
   Angels (Jude 6). See *Life, Everlasting; Punishment, Eternal*.

ETH KAZIN [6962]. A landmark in the boundary line of Zebulun (Jos 19:13).

ETHAM [918] (possibly *fort*). The second camping place of Israel (Ex 13:20; Nu 33:6-8).

ETHAN [420] (*long lived, ever-flowing [streams]*).
1. An exceptionally wise man in Solomon's time; an Ezrahite (1Ki 4:31; Ps 89:T).
2. A son of Zerah (1Ch 2:6, 8).
3. A descendant of Gershon (1Ch 6:42-43).
4. A Levite singer (1Ch 6:44; 15:17, 19).

ETHANIM [923] (*ever-flowing [streams]*). Seventh month in sacred sequence, First in civil sequence. The Feast of Trumpets in (Lev 23:23-25). The Day of Atonement, on the tenth day of (Lev 23:26-32). The Feast of Tabernacles, beginning on the fifteenth day of (Lev 23:33-43). The Jubilee proclaimed on the tenth day of the fiftieth year (Lev 25:9). The temple dedicated in and the ark restored (1Ki 8:2). The altar restored in, after the Captivity (Ezr 3:1, 6). Called Tishri in current Jewish calendar.
   Beginning of the early rains (September-October), the time of plowing. See *Month, 7*.

ETHBAAL [909] (*with [him is] Baal*). The king of Sidon; the father of Jezebel (1Ki 16:31).

ETHER [6987] (perhaps *perfume*). A city of Canaan. Assigned to Judah (Jos 15:42). Subsequently allotted to Simeon (Jos 19:7). Called Token in the parallel passage (1Ch 4:32).

ETHIOPIA [3934, *134*]. A region in Africa, inhabited by the descendants of Ham, S of Egypt. Was called the land of Cush (Ge 10:6; 1Ch 1:9; Isa 11:11). Rivers of (Ge 10:6; Isa 18:1). Moses marries a Cushite woman (Nu 12:1). Tirhakah, the king of Ethiopia, attempted to stop Sennacherib's invasion of Israel in the time of Hezekiah (2Ki

19:9). Zerah was defeated by Asa in the Valley of Zephathah near Mareshah (2Ch 14:9-15; 16:8). Was ruled by Xerxes as a part of the Babylonian Empire (Est 1:1). Prophecies concerning the submission of (Ps 68:31; 87:4; Isa 45:14; Da 11:43). Desolation of (Isa 20:2-6; 43:3; Eze 30:4-9; Hab 3:7; Zep 2:12). Merchandise of (Isa 45:14). Ebed-Melech, an official in the royal palace, probably a eunuch and keeper of the royal harem, a native of; treats Jeremiah with kindness by interceding on his behalf before Zedekiah (Jer 38:7-13; 39:15-18). Warriors of (2Ch 12:3; 16:8; Jer 46:9; Eze 38:5). Bordered Egypt on the S (Eze 29:10). Candace, queen of (Ac 8:27). A eunuch from, becomes a disciple under the preaching of Philip (Ac 8:27-39).

ETHIOPIAN EUNUCH Treasurer of Candace, queen of the Ethiopians (Ac 8:26-39), became a Christian through Philip.

ETHNAN [925] (*gift* or *hire*). One of the sons of Helah, of the tribe of Judah (1Ch 4:7); some identify him with Ithnan, a town in S Judah in the Negev (Jos 15:23).

ETHNI [922] (*gift* or *hire*). An ancestor of Asaph, a musician (1Ch 6:41).

ETIQUETTE *See Manners.*

EUBULUS [2300] (*good counsel*). A Roman Christian who was a friend of Paul's during his second Roman imprisonment; he sent greetings with Paul's letter to Timothy (2Ti 4:21). His name is common in papyri and inscriptions.

EUCHARIST (*thanksgiving*). One name for the Lord's Supper, meaning "giving of thanks." *See Lord's Supper.*

Instituted (Mt 26:17-29; Mk 14:22-25; Lk 22:19-20; Jn 13:1-4). Celebrated by the early Church (Ac 2:42, 46; 20:7; 1Co 11:26). Bread and cup of, symbols of the body and blood of Christ (Mt 26:26-28; 1Co 10:16-17, 21-22; 11:23-25). Profanation of, forbidden (1Co 11:20-22, 33-34). Self-examination before taking, commanded (1Co 11:27-32).

EUNICE [2332] (*good victory*). The daughter of Lois, Timothy's mother, and the wife of a Gentile (Ac 16:1; 2Ti 1:5).

EUNUCH [6247, 2336] (*one emasculated*). Castrated males, used as custodians of royal harems and court officials (2Ki 20:18; Est 1:10-15; 2:21; Jer 41:16; Da 1:3; Ac 8:27). Not practiced by Israelites; eunuchs not allowed to enter the assembly of the Lord (Dt 23:1). *See Ethiopian Eunuch.*

Figurative of those who stay unmarried for the sake of the kingdom (Mt 19:10-12).

EUODIA [2337] (*good fragrance*). A Christian woman at Philippi (Php 4:2).

EUPHRATES [7310, 2371] (*to break forth*). A river in the Garden of Eden (Ge 2:14). The eastern limit of the kingdom of Israel (Ge 15:18; Ex 23:31; Dt 1:7; 11:24; Jos 1:4; 2Sa 8:3; 1Ki 4:21; 1Ch 5:9; 18:3). Pharaoh Neco, king of Egypt, made conquest to (2Ki 24:7; Jer 46:2-10). On the banks of, Jeremiah symbolically buries his belt (Jer 13:1-7; see v.4, ftn). Jeremiah instructs staff officer Seraiah son of Neriah to cast the roll containing prophecies against Babylon into the Euphrates (Jer 51:59-64).

Symbolic: Of the extension of the empire of Assyria (Isa 8:6-8). In the Apocalypse (Rev 9:14; 16:12).

EUROCLYDON, EURAQUILO
See Northeaster.

EUTYCHUS [2366] (*fortunate*). A youth who fell asleep and fell out of the window to his death while Paul preached; was restored to life by Paul (Ac 20:9-10).

EVANGELISM *See Minister, Duties of; Zeal.*

EVANGELIST [2296] (*[a bringer of] good news*).

1. A Church leader (Eph 4:11). One who preached the good news of Jesus Christ from place to place (Ac 8:12, 26-39; 14:7; 1Co 1:17; 3:6). Philip is a typical example (Ac 21:8). Timothy was encouraged by Paul to do the work of an evangelist (2Ti 4:5).

2. In biblical studies: the author of a Gospel.

EVAPORATION (Ps 135:7; Jer 10:13; 51:16; Am 5:8; 9:6).

EVE [2558, 2293] (*life*). Creation of (Ge 1:26-28; 2:21-24; 1Ti 2:13). Named by Adam (Ge 2:23; 3:20). Deceived by Satan (Ge 3; 2Co 11:3; 1Ti 2:14). Clothed with fig leaves (Ge 3:7), with skins (Ge 3:21). Messiah promised to (Ge 3:15). Curse denounced against (Ge 3:16). Children of (Ge 4:1-2, 25; 5:3-4).

EVENING SACRIFICE One of two daily offerings prescribed in the Mosaic ritual (Ex 29:38-42; Nu 28:3-8).

EVENING, THE [*5742, 6845, 6847, 2270, 4067, 4070]. The day originally began with (Ge 1:5). Divided into two, commencing at 3 o'clock, and sunset (Ex 12:6; Nu 9:3).

Called the cool of the day (Ge 3:8). People cease from labor in (Ru 2:17; Ps 104:23). Wild beasts come forth in (Ps 59:6, 14). Where morning dawns and evening fades God calls forth songs of joy (Ps 65:8). The enemies of Jerusalem were so zealous to attack and defeat her that the soldiers encouraged each other to do battle at times of the day when attacks were rarely made, i.e., noon and evening (Jer 6:4-5).

A Time For:
Custom of sitting at the gates in (Ge 19:1). Meditation (Ge 24:63). Passover lamb killed in (Ex 12:6, 18). The golden lampstand lighted in (Ex 27:21, w Ex 30:8). Part of the daily sacrifice offered in (Ex 29:41; Ps 141:2; Da 9:21). All defiled persons unclean until (Lev 11:24-28; 15:5-7; 17:15; Nu 19:19). Humiliation often continued until (Jos 7:6; Jdg 20:23, 26; 21:2; Ezr 9:4-5). Exercise (2Sa 11:2). Prayer (Ps 55:17; Mt 14:15, 23). Taking food (Mk 14:17-18; Lk 24:29-30). The sky red in, a token of fair weather (Mt 16:2).

EVERLASTING ARMS (Dt 33:27).

EVERLASTING FIRE See Fire, Figurative.

EVERLASTING LIFE See Life, Everlasting.

EVERLASTING PUNISHMENT
See Punishment, Eternal.

EVI [209] (desire). One of five Midianite kings killed by the Israelites under Moses (Nu 31:8; Jos 13:21).

EVICTION Of tenants (Mt 21:41; Mk 12:9).

EVIDENCE [6332, 9149, 1182, 1328, 1891, 3456, 6019]. False, forbidden (Ex 20:16; 23:1, 7; Pr 24:28; Mt 19:18). Concealment of, punished (Lev 5:1). The entire community involved in (Lev 24:14). Two or more witnesses required in to sustain an allegation (Nu 35:30; Dt 17:6-7; 19:15; Mt 18:16; Heb 10:28). Punishment for falsehood in (Dt 19:16-21). Self-incriminating, demanded (Jos 7:19-21).
See Witness; False Witness; Accusation, False; Self-Incrimination.

EVIL [*2365, 4659, 6401, 6404, 6406, 8273, 8278, 8288, 8317, 8399, 8400, 8401, 94, 176, 2123, 2798, 2803, 2805, 4504, 4505, 5765]. Tree of the knowledge of good and evil (Ge 2:9, 17). Knowledge of (Ge 3:5, 22). In the heart (Ge 6:5; 8:21; Lk 6:45).
To be forsaken (Ps 34:14; 37:27; Pr 3:7; 1Pe 3:11). To be abhorred (Ps 97:10; Am 5:15; Ro 12:9). You are not to repay evil for evil done to you (Ro 12:17; 1Th 5:15; 1Pe 3:9).
Appearance of to be avoided (Ro 14:1-23; 1Co 8:7-13; 10:28-33; 1Th 4:11-12; 5:22), exemplified by Paul, refusing to eat that which was offered to idols (1Co 8:13), in supporting himself (1Co 9:7-23).
See Company, Evil; Imagination, Of Mankind, Evil; Nonresistance.

EVIL-MERODACH [213] (worshiper of Marduk[s] changed in textual transmission to read fool of [blessing]). Son and successor of Nebuchadnezzar. Released Jehoiachin from prison (2Ki 25:27-30; Jer 52:31-34).

EVIL FOR EVIL See Retaliation.

EVIL FOR GOOD (Ps 7:4-5; 35:12; 109:5; Pr 17:13).
Instances of:
Joseph accuses his brothers of rendering (Ge 44:4). Israelites, to Moses (Ex 5:21; 14:11; 15:24; 16:2-3; 17:3-4). Saul returns, to David (1Sa 19:1, 4-5, 10). Nabal returns, to David (1Sa 25:21), David, to Uriah (2Sa 11), to Joab (1Ki 2:4-6).
See Enemy; Good for Evil.

EVIL PUT AWAY (Dt 13:5; 17:7; 19:19; 21:21; 22:21; 24:7; Job 22:23; 1Co 5:13).

EVIL SPEAKING See Speaking, Evil.

EVIL SPIRITS See Demons.

EVILDOERS [224+7188, 1201+6594, 6913+8402, 8288, 8317, 8401, 94+2239, 96, 490+2237+3836]. Warnings to (Ps 34:16; 37:9; 94:16; 119:115; Isa 9:17; 14:20; 31:2). Examples of (Jdg 2:11; 3:7; 4:1; 6:1; 10:6; 13:1; 1Ki 14:22; 15:26; 16:7; 2Ki 8:27; 13:2; 14:24; 15:9, 28; 17:2; 21:2; 23:32; 24:9; Ne 9:28; Isa 65:12; 2Ti 4:14).

EWE [3898, 7366, 8161]. Female sheep.

EXALTATION [*1467, 1540, 5294, 5951, 6590, 8123, 8435, 5738].
Of Christ See Jesus the Christ, Exaltation of.
Of Self See Self-Exaltation.

EXAMPLE [*5596, 5682].
Bad:
Admonitions against (Lev 18:2-3; 20:23; Dt 18:9; 2Ch 30:7; Isa 8:11; Hos 4:9, 15; Zec 1:4; Mt 23:1-3; 1Co 8:9-13; 10:6; Eph 4:17; 3Jn 11). Corrupting (Pr 22:24-25; Jer 16:12; 17:1-2; Eze 20:18; Hos 4:9; 5:5).
Good:
Commanded (1Ti 4:12; Tit 2:7-8; 1Pe 5:3). Inspiring (Ne 5:8-19; 1Th 1:6-8; 1Pe 2:11-25). To be imitated (Heb 13:7; Jas 5:10-11). Illustrated (Ps 101:2; 1Pe 3:5-6).
God, our:
In holiness (Lev 11:44; 19:2). In perfection (Mt 5:48). In mercy (Lk 6:36). In not discriminating (Eph 6:9).
Christ, our:
In service (Mt 20:28; Mk 10:43-45; Lk 22:27; Jn 13:13-17, 34; Php 2:5-8). In meekness (2Co 10:1; 1Pe 2:20-25). In self-renunciation (Ro 15:2-7; 2Co 8:7; Eph 5:1-2; 1Jn 3:16). In enduring persecution (1Pe 3:17-18; 4:1). In forgiving (Col 3:13). In obedience (1Jn 2:6). In steadfastness (Heb 12:2-3). In perseverance (Rev 3:21). See Jesus the Christ, Our Example.
Paul, our:
Commanded (1Co 4:16; 11:1; Php 3:17; 4:9; 1Ti 1:16; 2Ti 1:13). In self-control (1Co 7:7-8). In

self-maintenance (1Th 3:7-10). In beneficence (Ac 20:35).

See Influence.

EXCHANGERS *See Money Changers.*

EXCOMMUNICATION
Disciplinary exclusion from church fellowship. Jews had temporary and permanent excommunication (Jn 9:22; 12:42; 16:2). Early church practiced it (1Co 5:5; 1Ti 1:20). *See Disfellowship.*

EXCUSES
[8200, *406, 2400+4148, 4733*]. For disobedience (Ge 3:12-13; Ex 32:22-24; Dt 30:11-14). For rejecting salvation (Lk 14:18-20; Jn 15:22; Ac 24:25; Ro 1:20-21; 3:19). Inexcusable (Ro 2:1).

Examples:
For release from duty: By Moses, when commissioned to deliver Israel (Ex 3:11; 4:1, 10-14), by Gideon (Jdg 6:12-17), by Jesus' disciples (Mt 8:21; Lk 9:59-62).

When called to be a prophet: Elisha (1Ki 19:19-21), Isaiah (Isa 6:5-8), Jeremiah (Jer 1:5-10).

For physical healing: Naaman, the leper (2Ki 5:10-14).

EXECUTION *See Death, Death Penalty.*

EXECUTIONER
[*5063*] (*punishment*). (Ge 37:36; Pr 16:14; Jer 39:9; Da 2:14; Mt 14:10). *See Punishment.*

EXHORTATIONS, SPECIAL
[*4151, 4155*]. To avoid various forms (Pr 4:15; Ro 16:17; 1Ti 6:20; 2Ti 2:16, 23; Tit 3:9). To choose between good and evil (Ex 32:26; Dt 30:19; Jos 24:15; 1Ki 18:21).

EXILE
[*1583, 1655, 1661, 2143, 5615, 8654, 8660, 8938, 10120+10145, 3578, 3579*]. Usually refers to the period of time during which the Southern Kingdom (Judah) was forcibly detained in Babylon. Began in the reign of Jehoiakim (609-598 B.C.), culminating in the fall of Jerusalem (c. 586 B.C.). It ended with the decree of Cyrus permitting Jews to return to Israel c. 536 B.C. *See Diaspora; Outcasts.*

EXODUS
[*2016*] (*a going out*). Departure of Israel from Egypt under Moses (Heb 11:22). *See Exodus, Book of.*

EXODUS, BOOK OF

Author: Moses

Date: c. 1445-1406 B.C.

Outline:

I. Divine Redemption (chs. 1-18).
  A. Fulfilled Multiplication (ch. 1).
    1. The promised increase (1:1-7).
    2. The first pogrom (1:8-14).
    3. The second pogrom (1:15-21).
    4. The third pogrom (1:22).
  B. Preparations for Deliverance (2:1-4:26).
    1. Preparing a leader (2:1-10).
    2. Extending the time of preparation (2:11-22).
    3. Preparing the people (2:23-25).
    4. Calling a deliverer (3:1-10).
    5. Answering inadequate objections (3:11-4:17).
    6. Preparing a leader's family (4:18-26).
  C. First Steps in Leadership (4:27-7:5).
    1. Reinforced by brothers (4:27-31).
    2. Rebuffed by the enemy (5:1-14).
    3. Rebuffed by the enslaved (5:15-21).
    4. Revisited by old objections (5:22-23).
    5. Reinforced by the name of God (6:1-8).
    6. Reminded of one's lowly origins (6:9-7:5).
  D. Judgment and Salvation Through the Plagues (7:6-11:10).
    1. Presenting the signs of divine authority (7:6-13).
    2. First plague: water turned to blood (7:14-24).
    3. Second plague: frogs (7:25-8:15).
    4. Third plague: gnats (8:16-19).
    5. Fourth plague: flies (8:20-32).
    6. Fifth plague: against livestock (9:1-7).
    7. Sixth plague: boils (9:8-12).
    8. Seventh plague: hail (9:13-35).
    9. Eighth plague: locusts (10:1-20).
    10. Ninth plague: darkness (10:21-29).
    11. Tenth plague announced: death of the firstborn (ch. 11).
  E. The Passover (12:1-28).
    1. Preparations for the Passover (12:1-13).
    2. Preparations for Unleavened Bread (12:14-20).
    3. Celebration of the Passover (12:21-28).
  F. The Exodus From Egypt (12:29-51).
    1. Death at midnight (12:29-32).
    2. Expulsion from Egypt (12:33-42).
    3. Regulations for the Passover (12:43-51).
  G. The Consecration of the Firstborn (13:1-16).
  H. Crossing the "Red Sea" (13:17-15:21).
    1. Into the wilderness (13:17-22).
    2. At the "Red Sea" (14:1-14).
    3. Across the "Red Sea" (14:15-31).
    4. Song at the sea (15:1-21).
  I. Journey to Sinai (15:22-18:27).
    1. The waters of Marah (15:22-27).
    2. The manna and the quail (ch. 16).
    3. The waters of Meribah (17:1-7).
    4. The war with Amalek (17:8-16).
    5. The wisdom of Jethro (ch. 18).
II. Covenant at Sinai (chs. 19-24).
  A. The Covenant Proposed (ch. 19).
  B. The Decalogue (20:1-17).
  C. The Reaction of the People to God's Fiery Presence (20:18-21).
  D. The Book of the Covenant (20:22-23:33).
    1. Prologue (20:22-26).
    2. Laws on slaves (21:1-11).
    3. Laws on homicide (21:12-17).
    4. Laws on bodily injuries (21:18-32).
    5. Laws on property damage (21:33-22:15).

6. Laws on society (22:16-31).
7. Laws on justice and neighborliness (23:1-9).
8. Laws on sacred seasons (23:10-19).
9. Epilogue (23:20-33).
E. Ratification of the Covenant (ch. 24).
III. Divine Worship (chs. 25-40).
A. Instructions Concerning the Tabernacle (chs. 25-31).
1. Collection of the materials (25:1-9).
2. Ark and atonement cover (25:10-22).
3. Table of the bread of the Presence (25:23-30).
4. Gold lampstand (25:31-40).
5. Curtains and frames (ch. 26).
6. Altar of burnt offering (27:1-8).
7. Courtyard (27:9-19).
8. Priesthood (27:20-28:5).
9. Garments of the priests (28:6-43).
10. Ordination of the priests (ch. 29).
11. Altar of incense (30:1-10).
12. Census tax (30:11-16).
13. Bronze basin (30:17-21).
14. Anointing oil and incense (30:22-38).
15. Appointment of craftsmen (31:1-11).
16. Sabbath rest (31:12-18).
B. False Worship (chs. 32-34).
1. The golden calf (32:1-29).
2. Moses' mediation (32:30-35).
3. Threatened separation and Moses' prayer (ch. 33).
4. Renewal of the covenant (ch. 34).
C. The Building of the Tabernacle (chs. 35-40).
1. Summons to build (35:1-19).
2. Voluntary gifts (35:20-29).
3. Bezalel and his craftsmen (35:30-36:7).
4. Progress of the work (36:8-39:31).
5. Moses' blessing (39:32-43).
6. Erection of the tabernacle (40:34-38).
7. Dedication of the tabernacle (40:34-38).

EXORCISM (*to bind with an oath, to conjure*). The casting out of demons by means of magical formulas and ceremonies (Mt 12:27; Mk 9:38; Ac 19:13). *See Demons.*

EXPANSE [8385]. The heavens above the earth (Ge 1:6-8, 14-17, 20).

EXPECTATION [7595, 9536, *638, 1693*]. Of the righteous (Ps 62:5; Pr 24:14; Php 1:20). Of the wicked (Pr 10:28; 11:7, 23; Zec 9:5; Ac 12:11).

EXPEDIENCY To avoid offending others weaker (Ro 14:1-2, 14-22; 1Co 6:12; 8:8-13; 9:22-23; 10:23-29, 32-33). To save people (1Co 9:19-23). Rule governing (1Co 10:30-31). Exemplified by Paul, in circumcising Timothy (Ac 16:3), in purifying himself at the temple (Ac 21:23-27).
See Evil; Prudence.

EXPERIENCE [3359, 7212, *3972*].

Solomon's (Ecc 1:2). Religious, relating of. *See Testimony, Religious.*

EXPERIMENT In worldly pleasure, Solomon's (Ecc 1; 2).

EXPIATION The act or means of making amends or reparation for sin. *See Atonement.*

EXPORTS [3655]. From Egypt: horses and chariots, and linen yarn (1Ki 10:28-29; 2Ch 1:16-17), grain (Ge 42; 43).
From Gilead: spices (Ge 37:25).
From Ophir: gold (1Ki 10:11; 22:48; 1Ch 29:4).
From Tarshish: gold (1Ki 10:22), ivory, apes, and baboons (1Ki 10:22), silver, iron, tin, lead, bronze, slaves (Eze 27:12-13).
From Arabia: sheep and goats (Eze 27:21).
From Israel: honey (Eze 27:17).
See Imports; Commerce.

EXPOSTULATION *See Reproof.*

EXTERMINATION [6, 3049, 9012]. *See War.*

EXTORTION [5131, 5298, 6294, 6943+ 6945, 6945, *1398*]. Prayed upon the wicked by David (Ps 109:11). Warning against (Pr 22:16). Purged out of the land (Isa 16:4). Judged by God (Eze 22:12). Cruel (Mic 2:3).
Scribes and Pharisees accused of by Christ (Mt 23:25). Pharisee judges himself not guilty of (Lk 18:11).
Forbidden (Lk 3:13-14). Cause for disfellowship (1Co 5:10-11). Excludes from the kingdom of God (1Co 6:10).
Instances of:
Jacob, in demanding Esau's birthright for a bowl of stew (Ge 25:31). Pharaoh in exacting of the Egyptians lands and persons for grain (Ge 47:13-26); The Jews after the Captivity (Ne 5:1-13).
See Interest; Usury.

EXTRADITION Instances of: Elijah from hiding to Ahab by Obadiah (1Ki 18:7, 10). Uriah from Egypt to Jehoiakim by Elnathan and company (Jer 26:21-23). Early believers from Damascus chief priests, in Jerusalem by Paul (Ac 9:2, 14; 22:5).

EXTRAVAGANCE Not to be pursued (Pr 21:17, 20; Lk 16:19). *See Gluttony.*

EYE [5260, 6523, 6524, 9193, 10540, *3669, 4056, 4057, 5557, 5584, 5585*]. Anthropomorphisms, figurative of God's omniscience (Ps 11:4; Pr 15:3), justice (Am 9:8), holiness (Hab 1:13), care (Ps 33:18-19; 34:15; 121:3-5; Isa 1:15; 1Pe 3:12), glory (Isa 3:8). *See Anthropomorphisms.*

Figurative:
Of the moral state (Mt 7:3-5; 13:15-16; Mk 7:22). Of moral perception (Mt 6:22-23; Mk 8:18; Lk 10:23; Ac 26:18).
Of insatiable desire (Pr 27:20; Ecc 1:18; 2Pe

2:14; Hos 2:16). Of evil pleasure (Mt 5:29; 18:9; Mk 9:27).

EYE FOR EYE *See Retaliation.*

EYES, OPENED (Ge 21:19; Nu 22:31; 2Ki 6:17; Lk 24:31).

EYES, PAINTING OF *See Cosmetics.*

EYESALVE Used figuratively for restoration of spiritual vision (Rev 3:18).

EZBAI [256]. Father of Naarai (1Ch 11:37). Possibly identical with Paarai (2Sa 23:35).

EZBON [719].
1. A son of Gad (Ge 46:16). Called Ozni (Nu 26:16).
2. A son of Bela (1Ch 7:7).

EZEKIAS *See Hezekiah.*

EZEKIEL [3489] (*God [El] strengthens*). A priest. The time of his prophecy (Eze 1:1-3). Persecution of (Eze 3:25). Visions of: Of God's glory (Eze 1; 8; 10; 11:22), of Israelites' abominations (Eze 8:5-6), of their punishment (Eze 9:10), of the valley of dry bones (Eze 37:1-14), of a man with a measuring line (Eze 40-48), of the river (Eze 47:1-5).

Teaches by pantomime: Feigns muteness (Eze 3:26; 24:27; 33:22), symbolizes the siege of Jerusalem by drawings on a tile (Eze 4), shaves himself (Eze 5:1-4), removes his belongings to illustrate the approaching Israelite captivity (Eze 12:3-7), sighs (Eze 21:6-7), employs a boiling pot to symbolize the destruction of Jerusalem (Eze 24:1-14), omits mourning at the death of his wife (Eze 24:16-27), prophesies by parable of an eagle (Eze 17:2-10). Other parables (Eze 15; 16; 19; 23).

Prophecies of concerning various nations (Eze 25-29). His popularity (Eze 33:31-32).

EZEKIEL, BOOK OF

Author: Ezekiel

Date: See chart below

Outline:

I. Oracles of Judgment Against Israel (chs. 1-24).
  A. Ezekiel's Inaugural Vision (chs. 1-3).
    1. The divine overwhelming (ch. 1).
    2. The equipping and commissioning (2:1-3:15).
    3. The watchman 3:16-21).
    4. Further stipulations (3:22-27).
  B. Symbolic Acts Portraying the Siege of Jerusalem (chs. 4-5).
    1. The city of Jerusalem on a clay tablet (4:1-3).
    2. Prophetic immobility (4:4-8).
    3. Diet for the siege and exile (4:9-17).
    4. The divine razor and its consequences (ch. 5).

C. Oracles Explaining Divine Judgment (chs. 6-7).
    1. Doom for the mountains of Israel (ch. 6).
    2. The end (ch. 7).
  D. Vision of the Corrupted Temple (chs. 8-11).
    1. Four abominations (ch. 8).
    2. Destruction of the city (ch. 9).
    3. God's glory leaves Jerusalem (ch. 10).
    4. Conclusion of the vision (ch. 11).
  E. Symbolic Acts Portraying Jerusalem's Exile (ch. 12).
    1. An exile's baggage (12:1-16).
    2. Anxious eating (12:17-20).
    3. The nearness of judgment (12:21-28).
  F. Oracles Explaining Divine Judgment (chs. 13-24).
    1. False prophets and magic charms (ch. 13).
    2. The penalty for idolatry (14:1-11).
    3. Noah, Daniel and Job (14:12-23).
    4. Jerusalem as a burnt vine branch (ch. 15).
    5. Jerusalem as a wayward founding (16:1-43).
    6. Jerusalem compared to other cities (16:44-63).
    7. Jerusalem's kings allegorized (17:1-21).
    8. The new tree (17:22-24).
    9. The lesson of three generations (ch. 18).
    10. The twofold lament (ch. 19).
    11. Israel is a hardened repeater (ch. 20).
    12. The sword of the Lord (ch. 21).
    13. Jerusalem the city of blood (ch. 22).
    14. Oholah and Oholibah (ch. 23).
    15. The final fire: Jerusalem's end (24:1-14).
    16. The death of Ezekiel's wife and the destruction of the temple (24:15-27).
II. Oracles of Judgment Against the Nations (chs. 25-32).
  A. Against Ammon (25:1-7).
  B. Against Moab (25:8-11).
  C. Against Edom (25:12-14).
  D. Against Philistia (25:15-17).
  E. Against Tyre (26:1-28:19).
    1. The end of the city (ch. 26).
    2. A lament for Tyre (ch. 27).
    3. Against the king of Tyre (28:1-19).
  F. Against Sidon (28:20-24).
  G. A Note of Promise for Israel (28:25-26).
  H. Against Egypt (chs. 29-32).
    1. As a doomed monster (29:1-16).
    2. As a payment to Nebuchadnezzar (29:17-21).
    3. The approaching day (30:1-19).
    4. Pharaoh's arms are broken (30:20-26).
    5. As a felled cedar (ch. 31).
    6. A lament over Pharaoh (32:1-16).
    7. As consigned to the pit among the uncircumcised (32:17-32).
III. Oracles of Consolation for Israel (chs. 33-48).
  A. The Watchman (33:1-20).
  B. Jerusalem's Fall Reported and Explained (33:21-33).
  C. The Lord as the Good Shepherd (ch. 34).
  D. Oracles Against Edom (ch. 35).

E. Consolations for the Mountains of Israel (36:1-15).

F. Summary of Ezekiel's Theology (36:16-38).

G. Vision of National Restoration (ch. 37).
1. National resurrection (37:1-14).
2. National reunification (37:15-28).

H. The Final Battle (chs. 38-39).

I. Vision of Renewed Worship (chs. 40-48).
1. Wall around the temple (40:1-47).
2. Temple exterior (40:48-41:26).
3. Temple interior (ch. 42).
4. The return of God's glory (ch. 43).
5. The priesthood (ch. 44).
6. Land allotment (ch. 45).
7. The duties of the prince (ch. 46).
8. Life-giving water (47:1-12).
9. Land allotment (47:13-48:35).

EZEL *See Beth Ezel.*

EZEM [6796] (*bone [strength]*). A city in the S of Judah (Jos 15:29; 19:3; 1Ch 4:29).

EZER [733, 6470, 6472] (*help*).
1. The sixth son of Seir; a clan chief of the native Horite inhabitants of Edom (Ge 36:21, 27, 30; 1Ch 1:38, 42).
2. A Judahite, father of Hushah (1Ch 4:4).
3. An Ephraimite slain by the men of Gath (1Ch 7:21).
4. A Gadite warrior who went over to David (1Ch 12:9).
5. A Levite, son of Jeshua, who repaired a section of the wall of Jerusalem under Nehemiah's direction (Ne 3:19).
6. A priest who participated in the dedication of the wall (Ne 12:42).

EZION GEBER [6787] (*giant, the giant backbone*). The last encampment of Israel before coming to the wilderness of Zin (Nu 33:35-36; Dt 2:8). Solomon, built a navy at (1Ki 9:26), visited (2Ch 8:17). Jehoshaphat's ships built at (2Ch 20:36), wrecked at (1Ki 22:48).

EZRA [6474, 10537] (*help*). A famous scribe and priest (Ezr 7:1-6, 10-12, 21; Ne 12:36). Appoints a fast (Ezr 8:21). Commissioned by Artaxerxes to rebuild the temple in Jerusalem which he directs (Ezr 7:8). Persecuted by Tattenai the governor (Ezr 6:3-17). Darius renews the decree of Cyrus for rebuilding the temple which he directs to completion (Ezr 6:1-15). His charge to the priests (Ezr 8:29). Exhorts people to put away heathen wives (Ezr 10:1-17). Reads the law (Ne 8). Reforms corruption (Ezr 10; Ne 13). Participates in the dedication of the wall of Jerusalem (Ne 12:27-43).

EZRA, BOOK OF

Author: According to Jewish tradition Ezra wrote Ezra and Nehemiah and also 1 and 2 Chronicles.

Date: c. 440 B.C.

Outline:
I. First Return From Exile and Rebuilding of the Temple (chs. 1-6).
A. First Return of the Exiles (ch. 1).
1. The edict of Cyrus (1:1-4).
2. The return under Sheshbazzar (1:5-11).
B. List of Returning Exiles (ch. 2).
C. Revival of Temple Worship (ch. 3).
1. The rebuilding of the altar (3:1-3).
2. The Feast of Tabernacles (3:4-6).
3. The beginning of temple reconstruction (3:7-13).
D. Opposition to Rebuilding (4:1-23).
1. Opposition during the reign of Cyrus (4:1-5).
2. Opposition during the reign of Xerxes (4:6).
3. Opposition during the reign of Artaxerxes (4:7-23).
E. Completion of the Temple (4:24-6:22).
1. Resumption of work under Darius (4:24).
2. A new beginning inspired by Haggai and Zechariah (5:1-2).
3. Intervention of Tattenai (5:3-5).
4. Report to Darius (5:6-17).
5. Search for the decree of Cyrus (6:1-5).
6. Darius's order for the rebuilding of the temple (6:6-12).
7. Completion of the temple (6:13-15).
8. Dedication of the temple (6:16-18).
9. Celebration of Passover (6:19-22).
II. Ezra's Return and Reforms (chs. 7-10).
A. Ezra's Return to Jerusalem (chs. 7-8).
1. Introduction (7:1-10).
2. The authorization by Artaxerxes (7:11-26).
3. Ezra's doxology (7:27-28).
4. List of those returning with Ezra (8:1-14).
5. The search for Levites (8:15-20).
6. Prayer and fasting (8:21-23).
7. The assignment of the sacred articles (8:24-30).
8. The journey and arrival in Jerusalem (8:31-36).
B. Ezra's Reforms (chs. 9-10).
1. The offense of mixed marriages (9:1-5).
2. Ezra's confession and prayer (9:6-15).
3. The people's response (10:1-4).
4. The public assembly (10:5-15).
5. Investigation of the offenders (10:16-17).
6. The list of offenders (10:18-43).
7. Dissolution of mixed marriages (10:44).

EZRAH [6477]. A Judahite (1Ch 4:17).

EZRAHITES [276]. The family or clan of Ethan and Heman, legendary wise men and poets (1Ki 4:31; Ps 88:T; 89:T). The word is probably a gentilic form of "Zerah," since 1Ch 2:6 designates Ethan and Heman as sons of Zerah.

EZRI [6479] (*my help*). Son of Kelub; the steward in charge of the agriculture of the crown lands in the time of David (1Ch 27:26).

FABLE (*talk, tale, legend, myth*). A type of literary genre in which animals and inanimate objects are used as persons or actors, speaking and using human behavior as if they actually were human beings. The fable is akin to the *allegory* and the *parable*. The fable is distinguished from the others in that there is a moral to the story; while the primary point of the allegory and the parable is to teach spiritual virtues.

There are two fables in the OT. In the first, the people of Shechem are warned by Jotham, the sole survivor of Abimelech's coup, that Abimelech is treacherous and will provide certain tyranny (Jdg 9:7-15). In the second, Jehoash, king of Israel, snubs Amaziah, king of Judah, with an insult, warning that he is courting disaster (2Ki 14:9).

In the NT, the debate among the parts of the body may be considered a fable (1Co 12:14-26). For KJV "fable" (1Ti 1:4; 4:7; 2Ti 4:4; Tit 1:14; 2Pe 1:16). *See Myths.*

See Allegory; Parable.

FACE [*678, 5260, 5790, 6524, 7155, 7156, 8011, 8559, 10228, *4725, 5125*].

General References to:
Refers to the face of, the waters (Ge 1:2), the earth (Ge 1:29), a man (Ge 3:19; Jas 1:23), flocks (Ge 30:40), God (Nu 6:25), the moon (Job 26:9), the seraphs (Isa 6:2), and the sky (Mt 16:3), Christ (2Co 4:6), the living creatures around the throne (Rev 4:7). The man himself may be meant (Dt 7:10), as in the Oriental circumlocution for "I." Character revealed in (Isa 3:9). Disfiguring of, in fasting (Mt 6:16).

Reflects Feelings:
(Ge 4:5; Pr 15:13). Moses in the presence of God (Ex 3:6). Favors are granted when the face is lifted up (Nu 6:25). Ruth bowed with her face to the ground in humility (Ru 2:10). Mourning (2Sa 19:4). To turn away or to hide the face is rejection (Pr 13:1). To seek the face is a desire for an audience (Ps 105:4). To harden the face is to promise no appeal (Pr 21:29). To spit on the face is a serious insult (Mt 26:67). Determination was evident when Jesus set his face to go to Jerusalem (Lk 9:51).

Covered:
By a harlot (Ge 38:15). Moses, when talking to the people after he was in the presence of God (Ex 34:29-35; 2Co 3:13-18). David (2Sa 19:4). In the doom of Haman (Est 7:8).

Of God:
Applied to God, it denotes his presence. Jacob struggles with God until daybreak and lives; he names the place where he fought, Peniel, which means "face of God," because "I saw God face to face, and yet my life was spared" (Ge 32:30). God himself or his glory which could not be seen by

Moses (or by any man) or he would die (Ex 33:20). God hides his face when angry (Job 13:24). God also hides his face from sin to show his displeasure (Pr 27:9) and to show that he has forgiven sin (Ps 51:9). John says that the Son of God alone has ever seen God face to face (Jn 1:18). The literal translation for the "bread of the Presence" would be the "bread of the face" (Ex 25:30).

Transfigured:
Moses (Ex 34:29-35), Jesus (Mt 17:2; Lk 9:29). *See Countenance.*

FAIR [622, 3206, 3208, 3637, 4797, 9185, *2304, 2699*]. Has the meaning of, just (Jdg 16:9; Pr 1:3; 2:9; 2Co 6:13; Col 4:1), clear skies (Job 26:13; Mt 16:2), persuasive (Pr 7:21), clean (Zec 3:5), beautiful (Hos 10:11; Ac 7:20).

It is not used to describe complexion.

FAIR HAVENS [*2816*]. A small bay near Lasea on the S coast of Crete, about five miles E of Cape Matala. Paul stayed here for a short time on his way to Rome (Ac 27:8-12).

FAITH [574, 575, 586, 953, 5085+5086, 5085, 9459, *601, 602, 1650+4411+4411, 1666+4411, 3898, 3899, 4409, 4411, 4412*].

General Explanation of:
Faith has both an active and a passive sense in the Bible. The former meaning relates to one's loyalty to a person or fidelity to a promise; the latter confidence in the word or assurance of another. Faith is not merely *what* a person believes, i.e., accurate doctrine or creed, but also and more importantly, that the object of his faith is valid. A man's life is governed by his thoughts; he will ultimately become that which he dwells most upon in his mind. This is the reason for Paul's instruction to the Romans, "Do not conform any longer to the pattern of this world, but be transformed by the renewing of your mind" (Ro 12:2). He wrote similar instruction to the Philippians, "Finally, brothers, whatever is true, whatever is noble, whatever is right, whatever is pure, whatever is lovely, whatever is admirable—if anything is excellent or praiseworthy—think about such things" (Php 4:8).

The Value of:
People are kept secure by (2Ch 20:20; Ro 11:20; 2Co 1:24; 1Jn 5:4), are established by (Isa 7:9), are saved by (Jn 3:15; Ac 16:31; Ro 9:30-32; Gal 2:16; Eph 2:8-9; Php 3:9), healed by (Ac 14:9; Jas 5:15), are sanctified by (Ac 26:18), receive the Holy Spirit by (Gal 3:5, 14), live by (2Co 5:7). Causes men to be a blessing to others (Jn 7:38). Disbelieving God is a great sin (Jn 16:9; Ro 14:23). Faith is necessary to please God (Heb 11:6).

The Gift of God:
The apostles ask Jesus to increase (Lk 17:5). God gives a certain measure of (Ro 12:3; 1Co 2:4-5). Given by the Spirit (1Co 12:8-9).

The Purpose of:
To gain understanding and to grow in the truth (Ps 119:97-105, 129-131; Jn 8:31-32; 2Ti 2:15; 1Jn 2:5, 14). To grow in the grace of God (Ac 2:42-47; Ro 4:4-5; 5:2; 1Co 15:10; Eph 4:15; Heb 4:16). To help us to rejoice through our faith (Ro 5:2-5, 11; 15:13; Php 1:18-19; 2:17-18). To strengthen the man of faith (Ro 6:12-14; 11:20; 1Co 9:27; Php 4:6-7; 2Th 3:3; 2Ti 4:7-8; 1Pe 1:3-5). To be transformed into the image of Christ (Ro 8:29; 1Co 15:49; 2Co 3:18; 4:3-6). To become strong people of faith (Eph 4:1-3, 11-13, 15-16).

The Effect of:
Faith not works (Gal 5:5-6). Produces good works (1Th 1:3; 2Th 1:11), internal changes (1Th 2:13), perseverance (Jas 1:3).

The Righteousness of:
The true righteousness of God comes from (Ro 1:17; 3:21-30; 4:3, 11; 9:31-33; 10:4-11; Gal 2:16; Php 3:9; Heb 11:7).

The Biblical Position Concerning:
Credited as righteousness (Ge 15:6; Ro 4:3; Gal 3:6; Jas 2:23). Inspired by God's goodness (Ps 36:7, 9). Inspired by the Holy Spirit (1Co 12:8-9). Explained (Ps 118:8-9; Lk 17:6; 18:8; 1Ti 4:12; Heb 11:1-3, 6). Worry, doubt, and the lack of faith (Mt 6:25-34; 14:31; Lk 9:40; 17:5). Prayer for increase of faith (Mk 9:24; Lk 17:5). The gift of God (Ro 12:3). The righteous live by (Hab 2:4; Ro 1:17; Gal 3:11; Heb 10:38). Miracles accomplished by (Mt 17:18-20; 21:21-22; Mk 9:23; 11:23-24). Secures salvation (Col 2:12; 2Th 2:13; Heb 4:1-11; 6:1, 12, 18).

The Old Testament Use:
In the OT, the word "faith" in the sense of belief occurs only five times (2Ch 20:20; Isa 7:9; 26:2; Hab 2:4). Faith is also communicated by words such as "believe," "fear," "hope," "love," and "trust." Faith is seen in the examples of the servants of God who committed their lives to him in unwavering trust and obedience. OT faith is never mere assent to a set of doctrines or outward acceptance of the Law, but absolute confidence in the faithfulness of God and a loving obedience to his will.

The New Testament Use:
In the NT "faith" and "believe" occur almost 500 times. The NT makes the claim that the promised Messiah had come and that Jesus of Nazareth was this promised Messiah. To believe on him meant to become a Christian, and was pivotal in the experience of the individual. Jesus offered himself as the object of faith and made plain that faith in him was necessary for eternal life.

The first Christians called themselves believers (Ac 2:44) and endeavored to persuade others to believe in Jesus (Ac 6:7; 28:24). In the epistles of Paul, faith is contrasted with works as a means of salvation (Ro 3:20-22). Faith is trust in the person of Jesus, the truth of his teaching, and the redemptive work which he accomplished at Calvary.

Faith may also refer to the body of truth which constitutes the whole of the Christian message (Jude 3).

Examples in the NT: In God (Lk 1:38-55; Ac 27:25; Ro 4:24; Heb 6:1; 1Pe 1:21; 4:19; 1Jn 3:21).

Strengthened by Miracles:
Of Abraham (Ge 15:8-18), of Gideon (Jdg 6:17, 36-40), of Hezekiah (2Ki 20:8-11), of Zechariah (Lk 1:18-20, 64).

In Affliction:
Exemplified by Job (Job 13:15-16; 14:15; 16:19; 19:25-27).

In Adversity:
Exemplified by, Hagar (Ge 16:15), Moses (Nu 14:8-9), Asa (2Ch 14:11), Jehoshaphat (2Ch 20:12), Hezekiah (2Ch 32:7-8), Nehemiah (Ne 1:10; 2:20), the psalmist (Ps 3:3, 5-6; 4:3, 8; 6:8-9; Ps 7:1, 10; 9:3-4; 11:1; 13:5; 17:6; 20:5-7; 31:1, 3-6, 14-15; 32:7; 33:20-22; 35:10; 38:9, 15; 42:5-6, 8; 43:5; 44:5, 8; 46:1-3, 5, 7; 54:4; 55:16-17, 23; 56:3-4, 8-9; 57:1-3; 59:9, 17; 60:9-10, 12; 61:2, 4, 6-7; 62:1, 5-7; 63:6-7; 69:19, 35-36; 70:5; 71:1, 3, 5-7, 14, 16, 20-21; 73:23-24, 26, 28; 86:2, 7; 89:18, 26; 91:1-2, 9-10; 92:10, 15; 94:14-15, 17-18, 22; 102:13; 108:10-13; 118:6-7, 10, 14, 17; 119:42, 57, 74, 81, 114, 166; 121:2; 138:7-8; 140:6-7, 12; 142:3, 5; 143:8-9), Jeremiah (La 3:24), Daniel (Da 3:16-17), Jonah (Jnh 2:2), Micah (Mic 7:7-9, 20), Paul (Ac 27:25; 2Co 1:10; 4:8-9, 13, 16-18; Php 1:19-21; 1Ti 4:10; 2Ti 1:12-13; 4:7-8, 18), the author of the letter to the Hebrews (Heb 10:34).

Commanded:
(Ps 4:5; 115:9, 11; Ecc 11:1; Isa 26:4; Mt 6:25-34; Mk 1:15; 11:22; Lk 12:32; 1Ti 6:11-12, 17; Jas 1:6). In time of public danger (Ex 14:13; Nu 21:34; Dt 1:21, 29-30; 3:2, 22; 7:17-21; 20:1; 31:8, 23; Jos 10:25; Jdg 6:14-16; 2Ki 19:6-7; 2Ch 20:15, 17, 20; 32:7-8; Ne 4:14; Isa 37:6; Jer 42:11). In time of adversity (Ps 37:3, 5, 7; 55:22; 62:8; Isa 43:1-2, 5, 10; 44:2, 8).

Commanded upon public leaders (Jos 1:5-9; 2Ch 15:7). Upon the young (Pr 3:5-6, 24-26). Upon the discouraged (Isa 35:3-4; 41:10, 13-14; 50:10). Upon widows (Jer 49:11).

Exemplified:
By Asa (2Ch 14:11). By Jehoshaphat (2Ch 20:12). By Hezekiah (2Ch 32:8). By Job (Job 1:21-22; 2:10; 5:8-9; 19:25-27). By the psalmists, setting forth supreme confidence in God (Ps 4:3, 8; 11:1; 13:5-6; 16:1-2, 5, 8-11; 18:1-3, 30-50; 20:5-8; 23:1-6; 25:1-15; 27:1-14; 31:1-5, 22-23, 24; 40:1-11; 46:1-11; 56:10-13; 57:1-11; 60:6-12; 61:1-8; 62:5-12; 63:1-8). By the following Psalms in their entirety (Ps 91; 95; 105-108; 115-118; 121; 123-126; 130; 135-136; 138-140; 145-150). By Isaiah (Isa 8:10, 17; 12:2; 17:13-14; 25:9;

26:1, 8; 33:1, 22; 50:7-9; 63:16; 64:8). By Jeremiah (Jer 14:9, 22; 16:19; 17:17; 20:11).

Instances of:

Abel (Heb 11:4). Noah, in building the ark (Ge 6:14-22; Heb 11:7). Abraham, in forsaking the land of his birth at the command of God (Ge 12:1-4; Heb 11:8), in believing the promise of many descendants (Ge 12:7; 15:4-6; Ro 4:18-21; Heb 11:11-12), in the offering up of Isaac (Ge 22:1-10; Heb 11:17-19). Jacob, in blessing Joseph's sons (Ge 48:8-21; Heb 11:21). Joseph, concerning God's providence in his being sold into Egypt, and the final deliverance of Israel (Ge 50:20, 24; Heb 11:22). Job (Job 1:21-22; 2:10). Eliphaz, in the overruling providence of God, that afflictions are for the good of the righteous (Job 5:6-27).

Jochebed, in caring for Moses (Ex 2:2-3; Heb 11:23). Pharaoh's servants, who obeyed the Lord (Ex 9:20). Moses, in espousing the cause of his people (Heb 11:24-28), at the death of Korah (Nu 16:28-29). Israelites (Ps 22:4-5), when Aaron declared the mission of himself and Moses (Ex 4:31), for forty years wanderings (Dt 8:2), in the battle with the Canaanites (1Ch 5:20), and other conquests (2Ch 13:8-18), by the waters of Meribah (Ps 81:7). Caleb, in advising to take the land of promise (Nu 13:30; 14:6-9), when he asked for Hebron (Jos 14:12). Rahab, in hospitality to the spies (Jos 2:9, 11; Heb 11:31). The spies sent to look over Jericho (Jos 2:24). Conquest of Jericho (Jos 6; Heb 11:30). Manoah's wife (Jdg 13:23). Hannah (1Sa 1). Jonathan, in killing the Philistines (1Sa 14:6).

David, in killing Goliath, the hero of the Philistines (1Sa 17:37, 45-47), in choosing to fall into the hands of the Almighty in his punishment for numbering Israel (2Sa 24:14), in believing God's promise that his kingdom would be a perpetual kingdom (Ac 2:30). The widow of Zarephath, in feeding Elijah (1Ki 17:13-15). Elijah, in his controversy with the priests of Baal (1Ki 18:32-38). Hezekiah (2Ki 18:5, 19). Amaziah, in dismissing the Ephraimites in obedience to the command of God, and going alone to battle against the Edomites (2Ch 25:7-10).

The three Hebrews who refused to worship Nebuchadnezzar's idol (Da 3:13-27). Daniel, in the lions' den (Da 6). Nebuchadnezzar (Da 6:16). The Ninevites, in obeying Jonah (Jnh 3:5). Habakkuk (Hab 3:17-19). Ezra, in making the journey from Babylon to Jerusalem without a military escort (Ezr 8:22). Mordecai, in the deliverance of the Jews (Est 4:14). Esther, in going before the king (Est 4:9-5:4).

Joseph, in obeying the vision about Mary and to flee into Egypt (Mt 1:18-24; 2:13-14). Mary, in believing the angel of the Lord, and in submitting to the Lord's will (Lk 1:38). Simeon, when he saw Jesus in the temple (Lk 2:25-35). Paul (Ro 8:18, 28, 38-39; 1Co 9:24-27; 2Co 5:7; Gal 5:5). The great people of faith (Heb 11:32-34).

The Trial of:

To prove depth of faith (Dt 8:2; 1Ch 29:17; Ps 26:2). To test spirituality (Mt 13:9-22; Lk 8:13-14). By tribulations (Mt 24:21-25; 2Th 1:3-5). By deferred hope (Heb 6:13-15). By trials (Jas 1:3, 12). Is precious (1Pe 1:7).

Instances of—

Noah (Ge 6:14-22; Heb 11:7). Abraham, when commanded to leave his native land (Ge 12:1-4; Heb 11:8), when commanded to offer Isaac (Ge 22:1-19; Heb 11:17-19). Moses, when sent to Pharaoh (Ex 3:11-12; 4:10-17; Heb 11:25-29), at the Red Sea, by the murmurings of the people (Ex 14:15; Heb 11:29). Joshua and the Israelites, in the method of taking Jericho (Jos 6; Heb 11:30). Gideon, when commanded to deliver Israel (Jdg 6:36-40; Heb 11:32). Ezra, in leaving Babylon without a military escort (Ezr 8:22). Job, by affliction and adversity (Job 1; 2). The three Hebrews, when commanded to worship Nebuchadnezzar's image (Da 3:8-30; Heb 11:32-34). Daniel, when forbidden by decree to pray to Yahweh (Da 6:4-23; Heb 11:32-33).

The two blind men who appealed to Jesus for sight (Mt 9:28). The Syrian Phoenician woman (Mt 15:21-28; Mk 7:24-30). The disciples, by the question of Jesus, in the storm at sea (Mt 8:23-27; Mk 4:36-41; Lk 8:22-26), as to who he was (Mt 16:15-20; Lk 9:20-21), by their inability to cast out the evil spirit from the boy (Mt 17:14-21; Mk 9:14-29; Lk 9:37-42) Of Philip, when questioned by Jesus as to how the multitude would be fed (Jn 6:5-6). Of Peter, when asked whether he loved Jesus (Jn 21:15-17).

See Tribulation.

Rewards of:

Protection (2Sa 22:31; Ps 5:11; 9:9-10; 18:30; 33:18-20; Pr 29:25; 30:5; Jer 39:18; Na 1:7; Heb 13:5-6). Spiritual peace (Ps 2:12; 32:10; 40:4; 84:5, 12; Isa 26:3; Ro 15:13). Prosperity (Pr 28:25; Isa 57:13; Jer 17:7-8). Eternal life (2Ti 1:1, 8).

See Faith in Christ.

FAITH, TEACHINGS OF JESUS Beliefs held in common by apostles and early believers (Ac 6:7; 16:5; 1Co 16:13; Gal 1:23; 3:23, 25; 6:10; Php 1:27; 1Ti 3:9; 4:1; 5:8; 6:10, 21; 2Ti 3:8; 4:7; Tit 1:1, 4, 13; 3:15; Jude 3; Rev 2:13).

FAITH IN CHRIST

General References Concerning:

Commanded (Mt 17:7; Jn 6:20; 20:27, 29; 1Jn 3:23). All things possible by (Mt 21:22; Mk 9:23; Lk 17:6). Prayer for increase of (Mk 9:24).

Leads to salvation (Jn 1:12; 3:14-18, 36; 5:24; 6:40, 47; 7:38; 12:36, 46; 20:31; Ac 10:43; 13:48; 15:9, 11; 16:31; 20:21; 26:18; Ro 1:16-17; 3:22-28; 4:1-25; 5:1-2; 9:31-33; 10:4-10; 11:20; 1Co 1:21; 2:5; Gal 2:16; Gal 3:1-29; 5:5-6; Eph 1:12-14; 2:8; 3:12, 17; 1Ti 1:16; 2Ti 1:13; 3:15; 1Pe

1:9; 2:6-7; 2Pe 1:1; Rev 3:20). Will result in good works (Jn 14:12; Jas 2:1-26).

Christ, the focus of faith (Ps 2:12; Heb 12:2). The Christian triumphs by (Ro 8:35, 37; 2Co 1:24; Eph 4:13; 6:16; Php 3:9; Col 1:23; 2:7; Heb 10:22, 38-39; 13:7; 1Pe 1:5, 7-9; 1Jn 5:4-5, 10, 14).

Exemplified by:

The wise men of the East as they worship the infant King Jesus (Mt 2:1-2, 11). The disciples in response to the call of Jesus (Mt 4:18-22; Mk 1:16-20; Lk 5:4; Lk 5:5-11; Jn 1:35-49; 6:68-69; 16:27, 30, 33). Peter (Mt 4:18-22; 16:16; Mk 1:16-20; Lk 5:4-5; Jn 6:68-69). Andrew (Mt 4:18-22; Mk 1:16-20; Jn 1:41). James and John (Mt 4:21-22; Mk 1:19-20). Philip (Jn 1:43-46). Nathanael (Jn 1:46-49). The disciples, through the miracle at Cana of Galilee (Jn 2:11). Jews at Jerusalem (Jn 2:23; 8:30; 11:45; 12:11). The Samaritans, who believed through the preaching of Jesus (Jn 4:39-42), of Philip (Ac 8:9-12).

Those who were healed by Jesus: the leper (Mt 8:2; Mk 1:40; Lk 5:12-13). The centurion, for the healing of his servant (Mt 8:5-10, 13; Lk 7:3-9). Those who brought the paralytic to Jesus (Mt 9:1-2; Mk 2:1-5; Lk 5:18-20). Jairus, for the healing of his daughter (Mt 9:18, 23-25; Mk 5:22-43; Lk 8:41-56). The woman subject to bleeding (Mt 9:20-22; Mk 5:25-34; Lk 8:43-48). Two blind men (Mt 9:27-30). The disciples in the storm (Mt 14:33). The sick of Gennesaret (Mt 14:36; Mk 3:10; 6:54-56). The Syrian Phoenician woman (Mt 15:22-28; Mk 7:25-30). The people of Decapolis (Mt 15:30). The father of the demon-possessed child (Mt 17:14-15; Mk 9:24; Lk 9:38, 42). Blind Bartimaeus, and a fellow blind man (Mt 20:30-34; Mk 10:46-52; Lk 18:35-43). Those who brought the deaf and mute man to Jesus (Mk 7:32). The woman who was a sinner (Lk 7:38, 44-48, 50). Mary, the sister of Martha (Lk 10:38-42; Jn 11:32). The Samaritan leper (Lk 17:11-19).

The nobleman, for the healing of his son (Jn 4:46-47, 50). The people who saw the feeding of the five thousand (Jn 6:14). The blind man whom Jesus healed on the Sabbath (Jn 9:13-38). The people in Bethany beyond the Jordan (Jn 10:41-42). Zacchaeus (Lk 19:1-6). The thief, on the cross (Lk 23:42). John, the disciple, after the resurrection (Jn 20:8). Thomas, after the resurrection (Jn 20:28).

Those in the early church. By three thousand, at Pentecost (Ac 2:41). By five thousand (Ac 4:4). By multitudes (Ac 5:14). By Stephen (Ac 6:8; 7:55-56). By the Ethiopian eunuch (Ac 8:36, 38). By the cripple at Lystra (Ac 14:8-10). Paul (Ro 7:24-25; 2Co 12:9-10; Gal 2:20; Php 4:13; 2Ti 1:12; 4:18). Expressed as a response to the preaching of the gospel. Of Lydda and Sharon (Ac 9:35), of Joppa (Ac 9:42), of Antioch (Ac 11:21-24). Barnabas (Ac 11:24). Eunice, Lois, and Timothy (Ac 16:1; 2Ti 1:5). Lydia (Ac 16:14). Philippian jailer (Ac 16:31-34). Crispus (Ac 18:8). The Corinthians (Ac 18:8; 1Co 15:11). Jews at Rome (Ac 28:24). Ephesians (Eph 1:13, 15). Colossians

(Col 1:2, 4). Thessalonians (1Th 1:6; 3:6-8; 2Th 1:3-4). Philemon (Phm 5). Church at Thyatira (Rev 2:19).

FAITHFUL SAYINGS
These are trust-worthy statements; words that you may depend upon as truthful and everlasting (1Ti 1:15; 3:1; 4:9; 2Ti 2:11; Tit 3:8).

FAITHFULNESS
[*573, 574, 575, 586, 622, 2874, 2876, 2883, 9068, *4411, *4412*].

Described:

Scarce (Ps 12:1; Pr 20:6). Tested (Lk 16:10-12). A fruit of the Spirit (Gal 5:22). Rewards of (Ps 31:23; Pr 28:20; Mt 10:22; 13:12; 25:29; Mk 13:13; Heb 10:34; Rev 2:10).

Required:

(Mt 24:45-51, w Lk 12:36-48; Mt 25:14-30, w Lk 19:12-27). Of those who are trusted (1Co 4:2). Of servants (Eph 6:5-9; Col 3:22).

Instances of:

Abraham's servant (Ge 24:33). Moses (Nu 12:7; Heb 3:3, 5). Ruth (Ru 1:15-18). Ittai the Gittite (2Sa 15:19-22). David (2Sa 22:22-25). Elijah (1Ki 19:10, 14). Workmen in temple repairs (2Ki 12:15; 2Ch 34:12). Josiah (2Ki 22:2). Abijah (2Ch 13:10-12). Jehoshaphat (2Ch 20:1-30). Hanani and Hananiah (Ne 7:2). Abraham (Ne 9:7-8; Gal 3:9). Nehemiah's treasurer (Ne 13:13). Job (Job 1:21-22; 2:9-10). The three Hebrew captives (Da 3:16-18). Daniel (Da 6:10). Jesus (Jn 4:34; Heb 3:2). Abraham (Gal 3:9). Paul (1Ti 1:12; 2Ti 4:7).

See Reward, A Motive, To Faithfulness.

See also, Jesus the Christ, Faithfulness of; God, Faithfulness of; Minister, Faithful.

FALCON
[370, 1901]. A bird of prey (Job 28:7; Isa 34:15), unclean for food (Dt 14:13). *See Birds.*

FALL OF MANKIND, THE
The fall of mankind as related in Genesis 3 is the historical choice by which Adam and Eve sinned voluntarily, and consequently involved all the human race in evil. Since the Fall, there is no person who continually does what is right and never sins (1Ki 8:46; Ps 130:3; 143:2; Pr 20:9; Ecc 7:20; Ro 3:8-10; 5:12; 1Co 15:22; 1Jn 1:8). By the Fall mankind was alienated from God. Mankind was created in God's own image, with a rational and moral nature like God's, with no inner impulse to sin, and with a will free to choose the will of God. Yielding to the outward temptation turned mankind from God and created an environment in which sin became a potent factor. Redemption from the Fall is accomplished through the second Adam, Jesus Christ (Ro 5:12-21; 1Co 15:21-22, 45-49).

Consequences of:

Knowledge of, nakedness (Ge 3:7). Guilt (Ge 3:8-10). Cursing of, the serpent (Ge 3:14-15). Cursing of the ground (Ge 3:17-18). Multiplying of sorrows (Ge 3:16-19). Death, physical (Ge

3:19; Ro 5:12, 14; 1Co 15:21-22). Spiritual (Ro 5:12, 14, 18-19, 21).

Means of:
By transgression of commandments (Ge 2:16-17; 3:1-3, 6, 11-12; Job 31:33; Isa 43:27; Hos 6:7). Through deception of Satan (Ge 3:4-5, 13; 2Co 11:3; 1Ti 2:14). Through evil desire (Ge 3:6; Ecc 7:29).
See Depravity.

FALLOW DEER *See Animals; Deer.*

FALLOW GROUND Land that is left idle for a growing season, after plowing and harrowing, so that weeds and insects are killed while the soil regains its fertility. *See Agriculture.*

Practical Application:
Israel is instructed to follow this practice every seventh year (Ex 23:11), but through much of its history, they failed to allow their land a sabbath rest (Lev 26:34-35).

Spiritual Application:
Israel is encouraged to seek God and to become spiritually active (Jer 4:3; Hos 10:12).

FALSE ACCUSATION *See Accusation, False.*

FALSE APOSTLES [6013]. Paul speaks of false apostles in 2 Corinthians only. These people "masquerade as apostles of Christ" (2Co 11:13). Paul denounces them as servants of Satan (2Co 11:14), "masquerading as servants of righteousness," which is not surprising, since their master "masquerades as an angel of light" (2Co 11:14-15). Yet they claim to be servants of Christ (2Co 11:23). Apparently they boasted of their Jewish heritage, using this to help justify their self-proclaimed position as "apostle of Christ" (2Co 11:22).

FALSE CHRISTS [6023]. These are people who make a false claim to be the Messiah. Jesus warned his disciples that imitators and pretenders would follow him who would try to deceive his followers (Mt 24:5-11, 23-25; Mk 13:6, 21, 23; Lk 21:8). False Christs are to be distinguished from the Antichrist. The false Christ is an impostor while the latter is one who opposes Christ. His opposition is mainly through the doctrines about Jesus' person and work which are contrary to the truth.

FALSE CONFIDENCE

Described:
In self (Dt 29:19; 1Ki 20:11; Pr 3:5, 7; 26:5, 12; 28:26; Isa 5:21; Ro 12:16; 2Co 1:9). In outward resources (Ps 20:7; 33:17; 44:6; 49:6; Pr 11:28; Isa 22:9-11; 31:1-3; Jer 48:7; Zec 4:6; Mk 10:24, ftn). In man (Ps 33:16; 62:9; 118:8; 146:3-4; Isa 2:22; Jer 17:5; Hos 5:13; 7:11).

Instances of:
At the tower of Babel (Ge 11:4). Sennacherib, in the siege of Jerusalem (2Ki 19:23). Asa, in relying on Syria rather than on God (2Ch 16:7-9). Hezekiah, in the defenses of Jerusalem (Isa 22:11). Peter, in asserting his devotion to Jesus (Mt 26:35; Lk 22:33-34; Jn 13:37-38).
See Confidence.

FALSE PROPHET [967, 6021]. Any person pretending to possess a message from God, but not possessing a divine commission (Jer 29:9). Test for (Dt 13:1-5; 18:20-22).

The False Prophet of the Apocalypse:
The false prophet is mentioned in the book of Revelation (Rev 19:20) and is usually identified with the two-horned beast of Revelation (Rev 13:11-18).

FALSE TEACHERS *See Teachers, False.*

FALSE WITNESS [8736, 9214, 6018, 6019, 6020].

Described:
Punishment for (Dt 19:16-20; Pr 19:5, 9; 21:28; Zec 5:3-4). Innocent suffer from (Ps 27:12; 35:11). Proverbs concerning (Pr 6:16-19; 12:17; 14:5, 8, 25; 19:5, 9; 21:28; 24:28; 25:18). God hates (Pr 6:16-19). Results from a corrupt heart (Mt 15:19).
See Evidence; Falsehood; Perjury; Witness.

Forbidden:
(Ex 20:16; 23:1-3; Lev 6:1-5; 19:11-12, 16; Dt 5:20; Pr 24:28; Mt 19:18; Lk 3:14; 18:20; 1Ti 1:9-10).

Instances of:
Witnesses against, Naboth (1Ki 21:13), Jesus (Mt 26:59-61; Mk 14:54-59), Stephen (Ac 6:11-13), Paul (Ac 16:20-21; 17:5-7; 24:5; 25:7-8).

FALSEHOOD [5086, 8736, 9214, 4415, 6022, 6025].

Described:
Atonement for (Lev 6:2-7). Punishment for (Ps 12:2-4; 52:4-5; 55:23; 63:11; Pr 10:10, 31; 12:19; 14:5, 25; 19:5, 9; Rev 21:8, 27; 22:15). Falsehood will be found out (Pr 10:9; 28:18). Destructive (Pr 11:9; 26:18-19, 24-26, 28; Isa 32:7).
See Accusation, False; Conspiracy; Deceit; Deception; False Witness; Flattery; Hypocrisy; Perjury; Teachers, False.
All guilty of (Job 13:4; Ps 116:11; Jer 9:3-5; Hos 7:13; Mic 6:12; Ro 3:4). Refrained from by the righteous (Job 27:4; 31:5-6, 33; 36:4; Pr 14:5, 25; Isa 63:8). Practiced by the wicked (Ps 10:7; 28:3; 36:3; 50:19-20; 52:2-4; 58:3; 62:4; 109:2; Pr 2:12-15; 12:17, 20; 21:6; Isa 28:15; 57:11; 59:3-4, 12-13; Jer 7:8, 28; 9:3, 5-6, 8; 12:6; Hos 4:1-2; Ob 7; Mic 6:12; Na 3:1; Jn 8:44-45; 1Ti 4:2; 1Pe 3:16). Wicked easily misled by (Pr 14:8; 17:4). An abomination to the Lord (Ps 5:6, 9; Pr 6:12-13, 16-19; 12:22). Abhorred by the righteous (Ps 31:18; 59:12; 101:5, 7; 119:29, 69, 163; 120:2-4; 144:8, 11; Pr 10:18; 13:5; 20:17).

Forbidden:

(Ex 20:16; 23:1; Lev 19:11-12, 16; Ps 34:13, w 1Pe 3:10; Pr 17:7; Ecc 5:6; Zep 3:13; Eph 4:25, 29; Col 3:9; 1Ti 1:9-10).

Instances of:

Satan, in deceiving Eve (Ge 3:4-5), in impugning Job's motives for being righteous (Job 1:9-10; 2:4-5), in his tempting of Jesus (Mt 4:8-9; Lk 4:6-7). Adam and Eve, in attempting to avoid responsibility (Ge 3:12-13). Cain, in denying knowledge of his brother (Ge 4:9). Abraham, in denying that Sarah was his wife (Ge 12:11-19; 20:2). Sarah, to the angels, denying her laugh of unbelief (Ge 18:15), in denying to the king of Gerar, that she was Abraham's wife (Ge 20:5, 16). Isaac, denying that Rebekah was his wife (Ge 26:7-10). Rebekah and Isaac, in the conspiracy against Esau (Ge 27:6-24, 46). Jacob's sons, in the scheme to destroy the Shechemites by first having them circumcised (Ge 34). Joseph's brothers in deceiving their father into a belief that Joseph was killed by wild beasts (Ge 37:29-35). Potiphar's wife, in falsely accusing Joseph (Ge 39:14-17). Joseph, in the deception he carried on with his brothers (Ge 42-44).

Pharaoh, in dealing deceitfully with the Israelites (Ex 7-12). Aaron, in attempting to shift responsibility for the making of the golden calf (Ex 32:1-24). Rahab, in denying that the spies were in her house (Jos 2:4-6). The Gibeonites' ambassadors, in the deception they perpetrated upon Joshua and the elders of Israel in leading them to believe that they came from a distant region, when in fact they dwelt in the immediate vicinity (Jos 9). Ehud, in pretending to bear secret messages to Eglon, king of Moab, while his object was to assassinate him (Jdg 3:16-22). Sisera, who instructed Jael to mislead his pursuers (Jdg 4:20).

Saul, in professing to Samuel to have obeyed the commandment to destroy all spoils of the Amalekites, when in fact he had not obeyed (1Sa 15:1-20), in accusing Ahimelech of conspiring with David against himself (1Sa 22:11-16), in deceiving the medium of Endor as to his identity (1Sa 28:7-12). Michal, in the false statement that David was sick, in order to save him from Saul's violence (1Sa 19:12-17).

David, who lied to Ahimelech, professing to have a mission from the king, in order that he might obtain provisions and armor (1Sa 21), in feigning madness (1Sa 21:13-15), and other deceits with the Philistines (1Sa 27:8-12), the falsehood he put in the mouth of Hushai, of friendship to Absalom (2Sa 15:34-37). The Amalekite who claimed to have slain Saul (2Sa 1:10-12). Hushai, in false professions to Absalom (2Sa 16:16-19), in his deceitful counsel to Absalom (2Sa 17:7-14). The wife of the Baharumite who saved the lives of Hushai's messengers, sent not to inform David of the movements of Absalom's army (2Sa 17:15-22).

The old prophet of Bethel who misguided the prophet of Judah (1Ki 13:11-22), Jeroboam's

wife, pretending to be another woman (1Ki 14:1-6). Jezebel, Ahab, and the conspirators against Naboth (1Ki 21:7-13). Gehazi, when he ran after Naaman and misrepresented that Elisha wanted a talent of silver and two changes of clothing (2Ki 5:20-24). Hazael, servant of the king of Syria, lied to the king in misrepresenting the prophet Elisha's message in regard to the king's recovery (2Ki 8:7-15). Jehu lied to the worshipers of Baal in order to gain advantage over them and destroy them (2Ki 10:18-28). Zedekiah, in violating his oath of allegiance to Nebuchadnezzar (2Ch 36:13; Eze 16:59; 17:13-20).

Samaritans, in their efforts to hinder the rebuilding of the temple at Jerusalem (Ezr 4). Sanballat, in trying to obstruct the rebuilding of Jerusalem (Ne 6). Haman, in his conspiracy against the Jews (Est 3:8). In the answers of Job's friends (Job 21:34). Jeremiah's adversaries in accusing him of joining the Chaldeans (Jer 37:13-15). Princes of Israel, when they went to Jeremiah for a vision from the Lord (Jer 42:20).

Herod, to the wise men, in professing to desire to worship Jesus (Mt 2:8). Jews, in falsely accusing Jesus of blasphemy, when he forgave sin (Mt 9:2-8; Mk 2:5-12; Lk 5:21-26), in falsely accusing Jesus of being a glutton and a drunkard (Mt 11:19), in refusing to bear truthful testimony concerning John the Baptist (Mt 21:24-27), when he announced that he was the Son of God (Mt 26:65; Mk 14:64; Jn 10:33-38). The disobedient son who promised to work in the vineyard but did not (Mt 21:30). Peter, in denying Jesus (Mt 26:69-75; Mk 14:66-72; Jn 18:16-18, 25-27). The Roman soldiers, who said the disciples stole the body of Jesus (Mt 28:13, 15).

Ananias and Sapphira falsely state that they had sold their land for a given sum (Ac 5:1-10). Stephen's accusers, who falsely accused him of blaspheming Moses and God (Ac 6:11-14). Paul's opponents, falsely accusing him of treason to Caesar (Ac 16:20-21; 17:5-7; 24:5; 25:7-8). The Cretans, who are always liars, evil brutes, lazy gluttons (Tit 1:12).

See Accusation, False; Conspiracy; False Witness; Hypocrisy; Perjury; Teachers, False.

FAME OF JESUS (Mt 4:24-25; 9:26, 31; 14:1; Mk 1:28, 45; Lk 4:14, 37; 5:15; 7:17).

FAMILIAR SPIRITS *See Spiritists.*

FAMILY [*3, 3+1074, 278, 1074, 1215, 2446, 3509, 4580, 5476, 5476, 9352, *1169*, *3836+*, *3858*, *3875*]. The concept of the family in the Bible differs from the modern institution. The Hebrew family was larger than families today, including the father of the household, his parents, if living, his wife or wives and children, his daughters and sons-in-law, slaves, guests, and foreigners under his protection. Marriage was arranged by the father of the groom, and the family of the bride, for whom a dowry or purchase money was paid to her father (Ge 24). Polygamy and concubinage

were practiced, though not favored by God. A husband could divorce his wife, but she could not divorce him.

The father of a family had the power of life and death over his children. To dishonor a parent was punishable by death (Ex 21:15, 17).

The NT concept followed that of the OT. Parents and children, husbands and wives, masters and slaves were commanded to live together in harmony and love (Eph 5:22-6:9; Col 3:18-4:1).

Good, Exemplified:
Abraham (Ge 18:19). Jacob (Ge 35:2). Joshua (Jos 24:15). David (2Sa 6:20). Job (Job 1:5). Lazarus of Bethany (Jn 11:1-5). Cornelius (Ac 10:2, 33). Lydia (Ac 16:15). The Philippian jailer (Ac 16:31-34). Crispus (Ac 18:8). Lois (2Ti 1:5).

Unhappiness in:
Caused, by indiscreetness (Pr 11:22; 12:4; 14:1; 30:21, 23). By hatred (Pr 15:17). By contention (Pr 18:19; 19:13; 21:9, 19; 25:24; 27:15-16).

Instances of —
Of Abraham, on account of Hagar (Ge 16:5; 21:10-11). Of Isaac, on account of disagreement between Jacob and Esau (Ge 27:4-46). Of Jacob, polygamous jealousy between Leah and Rachel (Ge 29:30-34; 30:1-25). Moses and Zipporah (Ex 4:25-26). Elkanah, on account of feuds (1Sa 1:4-7). David and Michal (2Sa 6:16, 20-23). Xerxes, on account of Vashti's refusing to appear before his drunken officials (Est 1:10-22).

Instituted:
(Ge 2:23-24). Government of (Ge 3:16; 18:19; Est 1:20, 22; 1Co 7:10; 11:3, 7-9; Eph 5:22-24; Col 3:18; 1Ti 3:2, 4-5, 12; 1Pe 3:1, 6). Husband should provide for (Ge 30:30; 1Ti 5:8). Duty to (Isa 58:7). Idolatrous (Jer 7:18).

Persian customs in (Est 1:10-22). *See Harem.*

See Children; Husband; Orphan; Widow; Wife.

Of Saints:
Live in unity (Ge 45:24; Ps 133:1). Live in mutual forbearance (Ge 50:17-21; Mt 18:21-22). Should be taught God's Word (Dt 4:9-10). Rejoice together before God (Dt 14:26). Warned against departing from God (Dt 29:18). Deceivers and liars should be removed from (Ps 101:7). Blessed (Ps 128:3, 6). Should be managed wisely (Pr 31:27; 1Ti 3:4-5, 12). Punishment of irreligious (Jer 10:25). Worship God together (1Co 16:19).

Religion in:
Purpose: To keep the way of the Lord (Ge 18:19), to keep children from sinning (Job 1:5), to be an example to the household (Ps 101:2).

Observed by: Abraham (Ge 12:7-8; 13:3-4; 18:19), Joshua (Jos 24:15), Job (Job 1:5), David (Ps 101:2).

Manifested in observance of religious rites (Ge 17:12-14; 35:2-4, 7; Lk 2:21; Ac 10:2, 47-48; 16:15; 16:25-34; 1Co 1:16), in religious instruction of children (Dt 4:9-10; 11:19-20), in household consecration (Dt 12:5-12; Jos 24:15; Ac 10:1-2; 18:8).

FAMINE [4103, 8279, 8280, 8282, *3350*].
Described:
Pharaoh forewarned of, in dreams (Ge 41). Sent as a judgment (Lev 26:19-29; Dt 28:23-24, 38-42; 1Ki 17:1; 2Ki 8:1; 1Ch 21:12; Ps 105:16; 107:33-34; Isa 3:1-8; 14:30; Jer 14:15-22; 19:9; 29:17, 19; La 5:4-5, 10; Eze 4:16-17; 5:16-17; 14:13-14; Joel 1:15-16; Am 4:6-9; 5:16-17; Hag 1:10-11; Mt 24:7; Lk 21:11; Rev 6:5-8). Description of (Dt 28:53-57; Isa 5:13; 9:18-21; 17:11; Jer 5:17; 14:1-6; 48:33; La 1:11, 19; 2:11-22; 4:4-10; Joel 1:17-20). Righteous delivered from (Job 5:20; Ps 33:19; 37:19).

Cannibalism in (Dt 28:53; 2Ki 6:28).

Instances of:
In Canaan (Ge 12:10; 26:1; 2Sa 21:1; 1Ki 17; 18:1; 2Ki 6:25-29; 7:4). In Egypt (Ge 41:53-57). In Jerusalem, from siege (2Ki 25:3; Jer 52:6). Universal (Ac 11:28).

Figurative:
God will withdraw from those who will not listen to the words of his prophets in the same way that food and water is scarce during famine (Am 8:11).

FAN *See Winnow; Winnowing.*

FANATICISM
Absolute and aggressive devotion to religion. The prophets of Baal (1Ki 18:28). The Jews against Christ (Jn 19:15). The Jews in stoning Stephen (Ac 7:57). Saul in persecuting the church (Ac 9:1). The Jews in their rage against Paul (Ac 21:36; 22:23).

FAREWELLS
Allusions to (Ru 1:14; Lk 9:61; Ac 18:21; 20:38; 21:6; 2Co 13:11).

FARMER [*438, 3086, 5749, *1177*, *5062*].
An agriculturalist (Isa 28:24; Jer 14:4; Mt 21:33-46; Mk 12:1-9; Jn 15:1; 1Co 3:9).

Parables of, describing the spread of the gospel (Mt 13:3-23); describing the unfaithful Jews, given over to corruption and hypocrisy (Mt 21:33-46; Mk 12:1-12; Lk 20:9-19).

Figurative:
Of God as the master gardener (Jn 15:1). Of the spread of the gospel (Mt 13:3-23); of Paul and Apollos 1Co 3:5-9). *See Agriculture; Farming.*

FARMING [438, 3086, 4494, 6268, 6275, *1175*, *1177*, *5062*]. Was the chief occupation of the people of Israel after the conquest of Canaan. Each family received a piece of ground marked by boundaries that could not be removed (Dt 19:14). Plowing took place in the autumn when the ground was softened by the rain. Grain was sown during the month of February; harvest began in the spring and usually lasted from Passover to Pentecost. The grain was cut with a sickle, and gleanings were for the poor (Ru 2:2). The grain was threshed out on the threshing floor, a saucer-shaped area of beaten clay 25 or more feet in diameter, on which animals dragged over a sledge over the sheaves to beat out the grain. The grain was

winnowed by tossing it into the air to let the chaff blow away and was then sifted to remove impurities (Ps 1:4). Wheat and barley were the most important crops, but other grains and vegetables were cultivated as well. *See Agriculture; Fallow Ground.*

FARTHING NIV "penny." *See Money.*

FASTING [7426, 7427, *3763*, *3764*].

Described:

Accompanied by self-denial (Dt 9:18; Ne 9:1), confession of sin (1Sa 7:6; Ne 9:1-2), reading of the Scriptures (Jer 36:6), prayer (Da 9:3; Mt 17:21).

Commanded (Joel 1:14; 2:12-13). Precepts concerning (Mt 6:16-18).

Of the disobedient, unacceptable (Isa 58:3-7; Jer 14:12; Zec 7:5; Mt 6:16).

Observed:

In times of bereavement, of the people of Jabesh Gilead, for Saul and his sons (1Sa 31:13; 1Ch 10:12), of David, at the time of Saul's death (2Sa 1:12), of Abner's death (2Sa 3:35), of his child's sickness (2Sa 12:16, 21-23).

On occasions of, public calamities (2Sa 1:12; Ac 27:33), private afflictions (2Sa 12:16), approaching danger (Est 4:16; Ac 27:9, 33-34), afflictions (Ps 35:13; Da 6:18), religious observances (Zec 8:19), ordination of ministers (Ac 13:3; 14:23).

Habitual, of the Israelites (Zec 8:19), by John's disciples (Mt 9:14), by Pharisees (Mt 9:14; Mk 2:18; Lk 18:12), by Anna (Lk 2:37), by Cornelius (Ac 10:30), by Paul (2Co 6:5; 11:27).

Prolonged, forty days and nights, by Moses (Ex 24:18; 34:28; Dt 9:9, 18), forty days and nights, by Elijah (1Ki 19:8), three weeks, by Daniel (Da 10:2-3), forty days and nights, by Jesus (Mt 4:2; Mk 1:12-13; Lk 4:1-2).

See Humiliation and Self-Affliction; Humility.

Instances of:

Of the Israelites, in the conflict between the other tribes with the tribe of Benjamin, on account of the wrong suffered by a Levite's concubine (Jdg 20:26), when they went to Mizpah for the ark (1Sa 7:6).

Of David, at the death of Saul (2Sa 1:12), during the sickness of the child born to him by Bathsheba (2Sa 12:16-22), while interceding in prayer for his friends (Ps 35:13), in his zeal for Zion (Ps 69:10), in prayer for himself and his adversaries (Ps 109:4, 24). Of Ahab, when Elijah prophesied the destruction of himself and his house (1Ki 21:27, w 21:20-29). Of Jehoshaphat, at the time of the invasion of the confederated armies of the Canaanites and Syrians (2Ch 20:3).

Of the Jews, in Babylon, with prayer for divine deliverance and guidance (Ezr 8:21, 23), when Jeremiah prophesied against Judea and Jerusalem (Jer 36:9). Of Ezra, on account of the idolatrous marriages of the Jews (Ezr 10:6). Of Nehemiah, on account of the desolation of Jerusalem and the temple (Ne 1:4). Of Darius, when he put Daniel in

the lions' den (Da 6:18). Of Daniel, on account of the captivity of the people, with prayer for their deliverance (Da 9:3), at the time of his vision (Da 10:1-3). Of the Ninevites, when Jonah preached to them (Jnh 3:5-10).

Of Paul, at the time of his conversion (Ac 9:9). Of the disciples, at the time of the consecration of Barnabas and Saul (Ac 13:2-3). Of the consecration of the elders (Ac 14:23).

FAT [487, 1374, 2693, 4671, 4833, 5458, 7022, 9042, 9043].

Offered in Sacrifices:

The layer of fat around the kidneys and other viscera of sacrificial animals which was forbidden for food, but which was burned as an offering to Yahweh (Lev 4:31). Offered in sacrifice (Ex 23:18; 29:13, 22; Lev 1:8; 3:3-5, 9-11, 14-17; 4:8-10; 7:3-5; 8:16, 25-26; 10:15; 17:6; 1Sa 2:15-16; Isa 43:24). Belonged to the Lord (Lev 3:16). Forbidden as food (Lev 3:16-17; 7:23). Idolatrous sacrifices of (Dt 32:38).

Instances of Fat People:

Eglon king of Moab (Jdg 3:17, 22). Eli the priest (1Sa 4:18). *See Corpulency.*

FATHER [3, 408, 587, 3528, 8037, 10003, *574*, *1164*, *4252*, *4257*, *4260*, *4262*].

Described:

Has various meanings in the Bible:

1. The originator of a way of life (Ge 4:20).

2. A male ancestor, immediate or remote, the father of nations or peoples (Ge 17:4; Ro 9:5).

3. An immediate male progenitor (Ge 42:13).

4. An adviser (Jdg 17:10), or a source (Job 38:28).

5. A spiritual ancestor (Jn 8:44; Ro 4:11).

God is the Creator of the human race (Mal 2:10) and is called the Father of the universe (Jas 1:17).

FATHERHOOD, OF GOD *See God, Fatherhood of.*

FATHER-IN-LAW [2767, 3162, *4290*].

Unjust, Laban to Jacob (Ge 29:21-23; 31:7, 39-42). Hospitable to son-in-law, a man of Bethlehem in Judah (Jdg 19:3-9).

FATHERLESS [3+401, 3846]. *See Orphan.*

FATHERS' GOD (Ex 3:13; Dt 1:11; 4:1; Jos 18:3; 2Ch 28:9; 29:5). *See God.*

FATHOM *See Sounding.*

FATTENED CALF [80, 2693, 5272, 5309, *4988*, *4990*, *5555*]. A clean animal fattened for offering to God (1Sa 28:24; 2Sa 6:13; Lk 15:23).

FAULT FINDING [*3523*]. (Jude 16). *See Murmuring; Rebuke; Uncharitableness.*

FAVOR [*1388*, 2704+7156, 2834, 2858,

2876, 3202, 5840, 7155, 8354, 8356, 9120, 9373, *473, 1283, 5921*]. *See God, Grace of.*

FAVORITISM [2075+, *1639+4720, 2848+ 4680, 4719, 4721+*]. Instances of: Rebekah, for her son Jacob (Ge 27:6-17). Jacob, for Rachel (Ge 29:30, 34). Israel (Jacob), for Joseph (Ge 37:3-4). Joseph, for Benjamin (Ge 43:34). Forbidden in parents (Dt 21:15-17). Elkanah, for Hannah (1Sa 1:4-5).

See Partiality.

FEAR [*399, 1593, 1796, 3006, 3010, 3328, 3707, 3710, 3711, 4570, 4616, 5022, 6907, 7064, 7065, *925, 5828, 5832*]. *See Cowardice; Fear of God.*

FEAR OF GOD

Described:

As, wisdom (Job 28:28; Pr 15:33), pure (Ps 19:9), the beginning of wisdom (Ps 111:10; Pr 9:10; 15:33), the beginning of knowledge (Pr 1:7), hating evil (Pr 8:13), adding length to life (Pr 10:27), a fountain of life (Pr 14:27), leading to life (Pr 19:23).

Commanded (Lev 19:14, 32; 25:36, 43; Dt 6:13; 10:20; 13:4; 2os 24:14; 1Sa 12:24; 2Ki 17:36; 1Ch 16:30; 2Ch 19:7, 9; Ne 5:9; Ps 2:11; 22:23; 34:9; 96:4; Pr 3:7; 23:17; 24:21; Ecc 5:7; 12:13; Isa 8:13; 29:23; Ro 11:20-21; Col 3:22; 1Pe 2:17; Rev 14:7). Cultivated by God (Ex 3:5; 19:12-13; Heb 12:18-24).

Deters from sin (Ex 20:18-20; Pr 16:6; Jer 32:39-40). Averts temporal calamity (Dt 28:47-49; 28:58-68; 2Ki 17:36-39). Secures divine blessing (Dt 5:29; Ps 25:12-14; 31:19-20; 33:18-19; 34:7, 9; 85:8-9; 103:11, 13, 17; 111:5; 112:1; 115:11, 13; 128:1-4; 145:18-19; Pr 22:4; Ecc 7:18; 8:12-13; Mal 4:2; Lk 1:50; Ac 10:34-35).

Universality of, foretold (Ps 76:11-12; 102:15). A bond of fellowship among righteous (Mal 3:16-18).

Instances of Guilty Fear:

Adam and Eve (Ge 3:8-13). The wicked (Job 15:20-25; 18:11; Pr 10:24). Those without moral direction (Pr 1:24-27). Those without God in general (Isa 2:19-21; 33:14). King Belshazzar (Da 5:6). The nations (Mic 7:17). Judas (Mt 27:3-5). The guards at Jesus' tomb (Mt 28:4). Christians no longer fear (Ro 8:15; 2Ti 1:7). Demons (Jas 2:19). The nations in the day of wrath (Rev 6:16).

Instances of Godly Fear:

Noah, in preparing the ark (Heb 11:7). Abraham, tested in the offering of his son Isaac (Ge 22:12). Jacob, in the vision of the stairway, and the covenant of God (Ge 28:16-17; 42:18). The midwives of Egypt, in refusing to take the lives of the Hebrew children (Ex 1:17, 21). The Egyptians, at the time of the plague of thunder and hail and fire (Ex 9:20).

Phinehas, in turning away the anger of God at the time of the plague (Nu 25:11, w 25:6-15). The nine-and-one-half tribes of Israel west of the Jordan (Jos 22:15-20). Obadiah, in his devotion to God, sheltered one hundred prophets against Jezebel because he feared God more than he feared the wrath of Jezebel (1Ki 18:3-4). Jehoshaphat, in proclaiming a fast when the land was about to be invaded by the armies of the Ammonites and Moabites (2Ch 20:3).

Nehemiah, in his reform of the public administration which had heavily taxed the people and lorded their rule over the people (Ne 5:15). Hanani who qualified him to be ruler over Jerusalem (Ne 7:2). Job, according to the testimony of Satan (Job 1:8). David (Ps 119:38). Hezekiah, in his treatment of the prophet Micah, who prophesied evil against Jerusalem (Jer 26:19). The Israelites, in obeying the voice of the Lord (Hag 1:12).

The women at the tomb (Mt 28:8). Cornelius, who feared God with all his house (Ac 10:2).

Motivates God's:

Power (Jos 4:24; Ps 99:1; Jer 5:22; Mt 10:28; Lk 12:5), providence (1Sa 12:2-4), power and justice (Job 37:19-24), wrath (Ps 90:11), forgiveness (Ps 130:4), majesty (Jer 10:7).

See Conviction, of Sin; Faith.

Motivates People:

To respect others (Lev 19:14, 30; 25:17, 36, 43). To obedience (Nu 32:15; Dt 6:13-15; 7:1-4; 8:5-6; 10:12-13, 20; 13:4, 6-11; 17:11-13; 21:18-21; 28:14-68; 31:11-13; 1Sa 12:24-25; Job 13:21; 31:1-4, 13-23; Isa 1:20; Jer 4:4; 22:5; Mt 10:28; Lk 12:4-5; 2Co 5:10-11; 2Ti 4:1-2; 2Pe 3:10-12; Rev 14:9-10). To truthfulness (Dt 15:9; 19:16-20). To filial obedience (Dt 21:21).

Reverence:

Expressed in the Old Testament (Ge 35:5; Ex 18:21; 20:18-26; Lev 22:32; Dt 4:10; 5:29; 6:2; 10:12-13, 20-21; 14:23; 17:13; 28:58; 2os 24:14-15; 1Sa 12:14-15, 23-25; 2Sa 23:3-4; 1Ki 8:40; 2Ki 17:36-39; 1Ch 16:30; 2Ch 19:7, 9-10; Ezr 10:3; Job 28:28; 37:24; Ps 2:11; 15:4; 19:9; 22:23, 25; 31:19; 33:8, 18; 34:11; 37:7, 9, 11; 46:10; 52:6; 60:4; 64:9; 67:7; 72:5; 76:7, 11; 85:9; 86:11; 89:7; 90:11; 96:4, 9; 99:1; 102:15; 103:11, 13, 17; 111:5, 10; 112:1; 115:11, 13; 118:4; 119:63, 74, 79; 128:1, 4; 130:4; 135:20; 145:19; 147:11; Pr 1:7; 2:5; 3:7; 8:13; 9:10; 10:27; 14:2, 16, 26-27; 15:16, 33; 16:6; 19:23; 22:4; 23:17; 24:21; 28:14; 31:30; Ecc 3:14; 7:18; 8:12-13; 12:13; Isa 2:10, 19-21; 25:3; 33:6, 13; 50:10-11; 59:19; 60:5; Jer 5:22; 10:7; 32:39, 40; 33:9; Hos 3:5; Mic 7:16-20; Zep 3:7; Zec 2:13; Mal 3:16; 4:2).

Expressed in the New Testament (Mt 10:28; Lk 1:50; 12:5; 23:40; Ac 10:34-35; 13:26; Ro 11:20; 2Co 5:10-11; 7:1; Eph 5:21; 6:5; Php 2:12-13; Col 3:22; Heb 5:7; 12:28-29; Jas 2:19; 1Pe 1:17; 3:1-2; 1Jn 4:16-18; Rev 11:18; 14:7; 19:5).

See Punishment, Design of, to Secure Obedience; Reward, A Motive, To Faithfulness.

FEASTS [*430, 2504, 4595, 5492, *109, 369, 2038*].

Described:

The host serves his guests (Ge 18:8). Men alone

present at (Ge 40:20; 43:32, 34; 1Sa 9:22; Est 1:8; Mk 6:21; Lk 14:24), women alone (Est 1:9). Guests arranged according to age (Ge 43:33), rank (1Sa 9:22; Lk 14:8-10). Men and women attend (Ex 32:6, w 2-3; Da 5:1-4). Marriage feasts provided by the bridegroom (Jdg 14:10, 17). Given by kings (1Sa 20:5; 25:36; 2Sa 9:10; 1Ki 2:7; Est 1:3-8; Da 5:1-4). Drunkenness at (1Sa 25:36; Est 1:10; Da 5:1-4). Wine served at (Est 5:6; 7:7; Isa 5:12). Music at (Isa 5:12; Am 6:4-5; Lk 15:25). Reclined on couches (Am 6:4, 7; Jn 13:23, 25). Dancing at (Mt 14:6; Lk 15:25). Served in one dish (Mt 26:23). Were presided over by a master of the banquet (Jn 2:8-9). *See Entertainments.*

Covenants ratified by (Ge 26:28-31).

Annual Festivals:

Instituted by Moses: Divine protection given during (Ex 34:24). Designated as, sacred assemblies (Lev 23:4). First and last days were sabbatic (Lev 23:39-40; Nu 28:18-25; 29:12, 35; Ne 8:1-18). Kept with rejoicing (Lev 23:40; Dt 16:11-14; 2Ch 30:21-26; Ezr 6:22; Ne 8:9-12, 17; Ps 42:4; Isa 30:29; Zec 8:19). Solemn feasts (Nu 15:3; 2Ch 8:13; La 2:6; Eze 46:9), Appointed feasts (Nu 29:39; Ezr 3:5; Isa 1:14).

The three principal festivals were Passover, Pentecost, and Tabernacles. All males were required to attend (Ex 23:17; 34:23; Dt 16:16; Ps 42:4; 122:4; Eze 36:38; Lk 2:41; Jn 4:45; 7). Attended by women (1Sa 1:3, 9; Lk 2:41). Aliens permitted to attend (Jn 12:20; Ac 2:1-11).

Celebrations for:

Birthdays (Ge 40:20; Mk 6:21), coronations (1Ki 1:25; 1Ch 12:38-40), national deliverances (Est 8:17; 9:17-19).

Figurative:

(Mt 22:1-14; Lk 14:16-24; Rev 19:9, 17).

Observed:

By Jesus (Mt 26:17-20; Lk 2:41-42; 22:15; Jn 2:13, 23; 5:1; 7:10; 10:22-23), by Paul (Ac 20:6, 16; 24:11, 17).

See for full treatment of annual feasts: Dedication; Hanukkah; Kislev; Passover; Pentecost; Purim; Tabernacles, Feast of; Trumpets, Feast of.

FEET [*564+, 892, 5274, 7193, 7895, 8079, 8081, 10039+, 10655, *4267, 4270, 4546*]. Sitting at (Lk 8:35; 10:39; Jas 2:3). Washing of, as an example, by Jesus (Jn 13:4-14). *See Washings.*

FELIX [*5772*] (*fortunate, lucky*). Governor of Judea. Paul tried before (Ac 23:24-35; 24). Trembles under Paul's preaching (Ac 24:25). Leaves Paul in bonds (Ac 24:26-27; 25:14).

FELLOES *See Rim.*

FELLOW [*278, 408, 8276, *476, 5257, 5281, 5301, 5369*]. A term of reproach (Ge 19:9; 1Sa 21:15; Mt 12:24; 26:61).

FELLOWSHIP [6051, 8968, *3126, 3545*]. Defined (Ecc 4:9, 12; Am 3:3).

Of the Righteous:

In brotherhood (Lev 18:19; 1Sa 23:16-18; Mt 23:8; Jn 13:34-35; 15:17; Ro 14:1-4, 10, 13-21; 1Co 1:10; 12:13; 16:19-20; Gal 6:10; Eph 2:14-21; 5:30; 1Th 4:9-10; Heb 13:1; 1Pe 1:22-23). In worship (Ps 55:13-14; 1Co 10:16-17; Eph 5:19; Col 3:16). In unity of purpose (Ps 119:63; 133:1-3; Am 3:3; Mal 3:16; Jn 17:11, 21-23; Ac 1:14; 2:1, 42, 44-47; Ro 15:6-7; 1Co 1:10; Php 1:3-6, 27-30; 2:1-4; Col 2:2; 1Pe 3:8-9). In ministry (Mt 20:25-28; Mk 10:42-45; Lk 22:32; Ac 20:34-35; Ro 1:12; 15:1-7; Gal 6:2, 10; 1Th 4:18; 5:11, 14; Heb 3:13; 10:24-25; 1Pe 2:17; 1Jn 3:14; 4:7-8, 11-13). Exemplified (Gal 2:9).

With God:

Signified in people walking with God (Ge 5:22, 24; 6:9). Signified in God dwelling with people (Ex 29:45; Ps 101:6; Isa 57:15; Zec 2:10; Jn 14:23; 2Co 6:16; 1Jn 3:24; 4:13; Rev 21:3-4). General (Ex 33:11, 14-17; Lev 26:12; Am 3:3; 2Co 13:11; 1Jn 1:3, 5-7). Possible only through Christ (Mk 9:37; Jn 17:21, 23). *See Communion, With God.*

With Christ:

Attained, by receiving Christ (Mk 9:37; Rev 3:20). By doing God's will (Mt 12:48-50; Lk 8:21). Through a gathering of believers (Mt 18:20; 28:20), commemorating Christ's death (1Co 10:16-17), by walking in the light (1Jn 1:3, 5-7). By abiding in Christ (1Jn 2:6, 24, 28; 3:6, 24). By keeping God's commandments (1Jn 3:6, 24). By continuing in his teaching (2Jn 9). General (Mt 18:20; Lk 24:32; 1Co 1:9; 10:16-17; 1Jn 1:3, 5-7; Rev 3:20). Signified in Christ dwelling with people (Jn 6:56; 14:23; Eph 3:17; Col 1:27; 1Jn 3:24; 4:13). Signified in our union with Christ (Jn 15:1-8; 17:21-23, 26; Ro 7:4; 8:1, 10, 17; 11:17; 12:5; 1Co 6:13-15, 17; 12:12, 27; 2Co 11:2; 13:5; Eph 5:30; Col 3:3; 1Th 5:9-10; Heb 2:11; 1Jn 5:12, 20). Through the Spirit (Jn 14:16; 1Jn 3:6, 24; 4:13). *See Communion, With the Spirit.*

With the Holy Spirit:

General (Jn 14:16-17; Ro 8:9; 1Co 3:16; 2Co 13:14; Gal 4:6; Php 2:1). *See Communion, With the Spirit.*

With the Wicked:

Abhorred by the righteous (Ge 49:6; Ex 33:15-16; Ezr 6:21-22; 9:14; Ps 6:8; 26:4-5). Implicating (Ps 50:18). Revelry (Ps 50:18; Pr 12:11; 29:24; 1Co 15:33; 2Pe 2:18-19). Impoverishing (Pr 28:19). Forbidden with those who provide the wrong type of influence (Ex 23:32-33; 34:12-16; Nu 16:26; Dt 7:2-3; 12:30; 13:6-11; Jos 23:6-8, 13; Ezr 9:12; 10:11; Ps 1:1; Pr 1:10-16; 4:14-17; 14:7; Mt 18:17; Ro 16:17; 1Co 5:9-13; 2Co 6:14-17; Eph 5:11; 2Th 3:6, 14-15; 1Ti 6:3-5; 2Ti 3:2-9; 2Pe 3:17-18; 2Jn 9-11; Rev 18:1-4). Punishment for fellowship with the wicked (Nu 25:1-8; 33:55-56; Dt 31:16-17; Jos 23:12-13; Jdg

3:5-8; Ezr 9:7, 14; Ps 106:34-35, 41-42; Rev 2:16, 22-23).

Instances of Evil Fellowship With the Wicked—
By Solomon (1Ki 11:1-8), Rehoboam (1Ki 12:8-9), Jehoshaphat (2Ch 18:3; 19:2; 20:35-37), Jehoram (2Ch 21:6), Ahaziah (2Ch 22:3-5), Israelites (Ezr 9:1-2), Israel (Eze 44:7), Judas Iscariot (Mt 26:14-16).

Instances of Avoiding Fellowship With the Wicked—
The man of God (1Ki 13:7-10). Nehemiah (Ne 6:2-4; 10:29-31). David (Ps 101:4-7; 119:115). Jeremiah (Jer 15:17). Joseph of Arimathea (Lk 23:51). Church of Ephesus (Rev 2:6).
See Company, Evil; Influence, Evil.

FELLOWSHIP OFFERINGS
[8968]. Traditionally "peace" offerings (Ex 20:24; 24:5; Lev 3:6; 7:11; 19:5). Offered by the leaders (Nu 7:17), by Joshua (Jos 8:31), by David (2Sa 6:17; 24:25). *See Offerings.*

FENCE
[1555]. Walls made of stone enclosing a field, town, etc. (Nu 22:24; Ps 62:3; Pr 24:30-31; Isa 5:2; Mic 7:11). Hedge (Job 1:10; Isa 5:5; Mic 7:4; Hos 2:6).
Figurative (Eze 22:30).

FENCED CITY *See Walled Cities.*

FERMENTED DRINK
[8911, 4975]. Intoxicating beverages, usually other than grape wine (Dt 14:26). Used in drink offerings (Nu 28:7). Forbidden to priests on duty (Lev 10:9); to Nazirites while under a vow (Nu 6:3; cf. Jdg 13:4, 7, 14; Lk 1:15). *See Abstinence; Beer; Drunkenness; Wine.*

FERRET *See Gecko.*

FERTILE CRESCENT
A modern description of the territory from the Persian Gulf to Egypt, which is watered by the Euphrates, Tigris, Orontes, Jordan, and Nile rivers. *See Canaan; Mesopotamia; Palestine.*

FESTIVALS
[2136, 2504, 2510, 2544, 4595, *2037, 2038*]. *See Feasts.*

FESTUS, PORCIUS
[5776] (*festal, joyful*). Was the Roman governor who succeeded Felix in the province of Judea (Ac 24:27). He presided at the hearing of the apostle Paul when he made his defense before Herod Agrippa II (Ac 24:27; 26:32). When Paul appealed to Caesar, Festus sent him to Rome. The date of Festus's accession is uncertain, probably A.D. 59/60. He died in office in A.D. 62.

FETTERS
[673, 2414, 6310]. A translation of words which have the general meaning "anything that restricts or restrains" as well as those which bear the specific definition "shackle for the foot." Fetters were made from wood, bronze, or iron. The prisoner would have manacles on his wrists which were suspended from his neck by a rope. His feet would have been shackled and connected by a short piece of rope or chain so that the hobbled prisoner could take only short steps (2Sa 3:34; Job 36:13; Ps 2:3; 105:18; 149:8). Used for securing prisoners (2Ch 33:11; 36:6; Mk 5:4). *See Chains; Shackles.*

FEVER
[2363, 2996, 7707, *4789, 4790*]. (Lev 26:16; Dt 28:22; Job 30:30; Mt 8:14; Ac 28:8).

FEW SAVED
The number saved spoken of as few (Mt 7:14; 22:14; Lk 13:24; 1Pe 3:20; Rev 3:4).

FICKLENESS *See Instability.*

FIELD
[*141, 824, 2575, 2754, 3320, 4149, 8072, 8441, 8442, 8727, 10119, 69, *2546, 6001, 6005*]. The biblical field was generally not enclosed, but was marked off from its neighbors by boundary markers (Dt 19:14; 27:17; Job 24:2; Pr 22:28; 23:10; Hos 5:10). A cultivated area where crops are grown (Ru 2:2; Ps 107:37), a place where herds could graze (Ge 34:5; Ex 9:21; Nu 22:24).

FIG
[1136, 1811, 7811, 9204, 9300, *5190, 5192*]. Aprons made of fig leaves, by Adam and Eve (Ge 3:7). Common to Palestine (Nu 13:23; Dt 8:8), to Egypt (Ps 105:33). Two hundred cakes of, sent by Abigail to David (1Sa 25:18, 19-35). Dried and preserved (1Sa 30:12). Employed as a remedy (2Ki 20:7; Isa 38:21). Trade in (Ne 13:15).

FIG TREE
In an allegory (Jdg 9:11). Jeremiah's parable of (Jer 24:1-10). Jesus' cursing of (Mt 21:18-22; Mk 11:12-14, 20-26). Barren, parable of (Lk 13:6-9; 21:29-31).
Figurative of signs of the end times (Mt 24:32; Rev 6:13).

FIGHT OF FAITH
(1Ti 6:12; 2Ti 4:7; Heb 10:32; 11:32-34).

FIGURE
See "Figurative" under principal topics throughout the work. *See also, Allegory; Pantomime; Parable; Symbols and Similitudes; Types.*

FILIGREE
[5401, 8687]. Ornate gold settings for the jewels of the ephod and breastpiece (Ex 28:13, 20; 39:6, 13, 16).

FINANCES
Methods of raising money. *See Money; Temple; Tribute.*

FINE
[*6740, 6741*]. For personal injury (Ex 21:22, 30). For theft (Ex 22:4, 7-9; Pr 6:30-31). When sinning unknowingly (Lev 5:15-16; 22:14). For deception (Lev 6:2-6). Restitution for any wrongdoing (Nu 5:5-8).
See Damages and Compensations.

FINGER
[720, 3338, 4090, 7782, 10064, *1235, 5931*]. Used in priestly service (Ex 29:12; Lev 4:6, 17, 25, 30, 34). Six on one hand (2Sa 21:20; 1Ch 20:6).

FINGER OF GOD Anthropomorphism, indicating God's interaction with his creation. Creation (Ps 8:3). Miracles (Ex 8:19). Writing the tablets of the law (Ex 31:18; Dt 9:10). Exorcism (Lk 11:20). *See Anthropomorphisms.*

FINGERS, FINGERBREADTH A unit of measurement. The two bronze pillars of Solomon's temple were four fingers thick and hollow in the center (Jer 52:21). *See Measure.*

FINING POT *See Crucible.*

FIR TREE [1361, 9329]. Wood of, used for building (SS 1:17).

FIRE [*239, 241, 836, 852, 1277, 8596, 8599, 10471, *471, *3106, *4786, *4787, *5824*]. Children sacrificed in (2Ki 16:3; 17:17). Used as a signal in war (Jer 6:1). Men were burned in a furnace (Jer 29:22; Heb 11:34). The threat of being thrown into a furnace is used by Nebuchadnezzar for all those who would not fall down and worship the image that he set up of (Da 3:6, 11, 15, 21).

Figurative:
Of judgments (Dt 4:24; 32:22; Isa 33:14; Jer 23:29; Am 1:4, 7, 10, 12, 14; 2:2; Mal 3:2; Lk 12:49; Rev 20:9), spiritual power (Ps 104:4; Jer 20:9; Mt 3:11; Lk 3:16), cleansing (Isa 6:6-7), of the destruction of the wicked (Mt 13:42, 50; 25:41; Mk 9:48; Rev 9:2; 21:8).
Everlasting fire (Isa 33:14; Mt 18:8; 25:41; Mk 9:48).

Miracles Connected With:
Miraculously descends upon and consumes Abraham's sacrifice (Ge 15:17), Elijah's (1Ki 18:38), David's (1Ch 21:26), Solomon's, at dedication of the temple (2Ch 7:1-3). Pillar of fire (Ex 13:21-22; 14:19, 24; 40:38; Nu 9:15-23).
Display of, at Elijah's translation (2Ki 2:11). Consumes the conspirators with Korah, Dathan, and Abiram (Nu 16:35), the captains and their fifties (2Ki 1:9-15).
Torture by (Jer 29:22; Eze 23:25, 47; Da 3).
See Celestial Phenomena; Cloud, Pillar of.

Symbolic:
Of God's presence, with Abram in the covenant (Ge 15:17), in the burning bush (Ex 3:2), on Sinai (Ex 19:18).
Tongues of, on the disciples (Ac 2:3).
See Arson.

FIREBRAND [2415, 4365]. Burning wood used for light (Jdg 7:16), torches used as weapons (Pr 26:18), a remnant of a burnt stick (Am 4:11). *See Torches.*

FIREPAN [279, 836+3963, 4746, 9486] (*to rake together*). A vessel for carrying live coals (Ex 27:3; 38:3).

FIRKIN *See Gallon.*

FIRMAMENT *See Expanse.*

FIRST BEGOTTEN *See Firstborn.*

FIRST DAY OF THE WEEK *See Sunday.*

FIRSTBORN [1144, 1147, 1148, 7081+, 7082, *1380+3616, *4758*]. The first male born, whether man or animal, was reserved by God for himself (Ex 13:2, 12-16; 22:29-30; 34:19-20; Lev 27:26; Nu 3:13; 8:17-18; Dt 15:19-23; Ne 10:36).
Redemption of (Ex 13:13; 34:20; Lev 27:26-27; Nu 3:40-51; 18:15-17). Levites taken instead of firstborn of the families of Israel (Nu 3:12, 40-45; 8:16-18).

Birthright of:
Had precedence over other sons of the family (Ge 4:1, 5-7; Dt 21:15-17), a double portion of inheritance (Dt 21:15-17), royal succession (2Ch 21:3). Sold by Esau (Ge 25:29-34; 27:36; Ro 9:12-13; Heb 12:16). Set aside, that of Manasseh (Ge 48:15-20; 1Ch 5:1), Adonijah (1Ki 2:13-15), Hosah's son (1Ch 26:10). Forfeited by Reuben (Ge 49:3-4; 1Ch 5:1-2). Honorable distinction of (Ex 4:22; Ps 89:27; Jer 31:9; Ro 8:29; Col 1:15; Heb 1:6; 12:23; Rev 1:5).
See Birthright.

Jesus as Firstborn:
Among many brothers (Ro 8:29), over all creation (Col 1:15), from the dead (Col 1:18; Rev 1:5), God's firstborn (Heb 1:6).

FIRSTFRUITS [1137, 7262+8040, 8040, 569].

Offerings of:
First ripe of fruits, grain, oil, wine, and first of the fleece, required as an offering (Ex 22:29; Lev 2:12-16; Nu 18:12; Dt 18:4; 2Ch 31:5; Ne 10:35, 37, 39; Pr 3:9; Jer 2:3; Ro 11:16).
Offerings of, presented at the tabernacle (Ex 22:29; 23:19; 34:26; Dt 26:3-10), belonged to the priests (Lev 23:20; Nu 18:12-13; Dt 18:3-5), must be free from blemish (Lev 22:21; Nu 18:12). Freewill offerings of, given to the prophets (2Ki 4:42).

Offerings described:
Drink (Ge 35:14; Ex 29:40-41; 30:9; 37:16; Lev 23:13, 18, 37; Nu 4:7; Nu 6:15, 17; 15:5, 7, 10, 24; 28:7-31; 29:6, 11, 16, 18-39; Dt 32:38; 2Ki 16:13-15; 1Ch 29:21; 2Ch 29:35; Ezr 7:17; Isa 57:6; Jer 7:18; 19:13; 32:29; 44:17-25; 52:19; Eze 20:28; 45:17; Joel 1:9, 13; 2:14; Php 2:17; 2Ti 4:6). Freewill (Ex 35:29; 36:3; Lev 7:16; 22:18, 21, 23; 23:37-38; Nu 15:3; 29:39; Dt 12:6, 17; 16:10; 2Ch 31:14; Ezr 1:4, 6; 2:68; 3:5; 7:16; 8:28; Ps 54:6; Eze 46:12; Am 4:5). Burnt (Lev 1; 6:8-13). Grain (Lev 2; 6:14-23). Fellowship (Lev 3; 7:11-21). Sin (Lev 4; 5:13; 6:24-30). Guilt (Lev 5:14-6:7; 7:1-10). Wave offering (Ex 29:22-26; 35:22; Lev 7:30; 23:10-14, 17).
To be offered as a thank offering upon entrance into the Land of Promise (Dt 26:3-10; 2Ch 29:31; 33:16; Ps 50:14, 23; 56:12; 107:22; 116:17; Jer 17:26; 33:11; Am 4:5).

Figurative: (Ro 8:23; 11:16; 1Co 15:20, 23; Jas 1:18).

See Offerings.

FIRSTLING *See Firstborn.*

FISH [1794, 1834, 1836, *244, 2715, 2716, 3063, 4066, 4709*]. Creation of (Ge 1:20-22). Appointed for food (Ge 9:2-3). Clean and unclean (Lev 11:9-12; Dt 14:9-10). Broiled (Jn 21:9-13; Lk 24:42).

Caught with, spears (Job 41:7), nets (Ecc 9:12; Hab 1:14-17; Lk 5:2-6; Jn 21:6-8), hooks (Isa 19:8; Am 4:2; Hab 1:15; Mt 17:27). Sold by men from Tyre living in Jerusalem (Ne 13:16).

Figurative: (Eze 47:9-10).

Miracles Connected With:

Jonah swallowed by (Jnh 1:17; 2; Mt 12:40). The loaves and fishes (Mt 14:19; 15:36-38; Lk 9:13-17). Coin obtained from mouth of (Mt 17:27). Overflowing nets (Lk 5:6-7; Jn 21:6, 8, 11). Furnished for the disciples by Jesus after his resurrection (Lk 24:42; Jn 21:9-13).

FISH GATE An ancient gate on the E side of Jerusalem near Gihon where Tyrians held a fish market (2Ch 33:14; Ne 3:3; 12:39; 13:16; Zep 1:10).

FISH POOL *See Pool.*

FISH SPEAR *See Spear.*

FISHERMEN [1854, 1900, *243*]. Certain apostles (Mt 4:18-21; Mk 1:16-20; Jn 21:2-3).

Figurative (Jer 16:16; Mt 4:19).

FISHHOOK [1855+6106, 2676]. *See Hooks.*

FITCH *See Caraway.*

FLAG *See Ensign; Reed.*

FLAGON *See Wine.*

FLATTERY [2728, 2744, 2747, 4033, 7331, *2330, 2513+4725, 3135*]. Condemned and rebuked (Job 32:21-22; Ps 12:2-4; Pr 28:23; Lk 6:26). Deceives, self (Pr 36:2). The simple (Ro 16:18).

Practiced by enemies (Ps 12:2; Pr 26:28; 29:5; Jude 16). Against God (Ps 78:36). By seducing women (Pr 5:3; 6:24; 7:5, 21). Not practiced by Paul (1Th 2:4-6).

Instances of:

Jacob (Ge 33:10). Gideon (Jdg 8:1-3). Mephibosheth (2Sa 9:8). Woman of Tekoa (2Sa 14:17-20). Absalom (2Sa 15:2-6). Israel and Judah (2Sa 19:41-43). Adonijah (1Ki 1:42). Ahab (1Ki 20:4). False prophets (1Ki 22:1-13). Darius's officials (Da 6:1-9). Herodians (Lk 20:21). Tyrians (Ac 12:22). Tertullus flatters Felix (Ac 24:2-4). Paul flatters Felix (Ac 24:10). Agrippa (Ac 26:2-3).

FLAX [7324, 7325]. In Egypt (Ex 9:31). In Palestine (Jos 2:6). Linen made from (Pr 31:13; Isa 19:9). *See Linen.*

FLEA [7282] (*mosquito*). (1Sa 24:14; 26:20).

FLEECE [1600, 1603]. *See Prayer; Token, 1; Wool.*

FLESH [1414, 2693, 2743+3655+4946, 3655+3870+4946, 4695, 5055, 6425, 6889, 6913+7089, 8638, 10125, *4922*].

1. The physical part of the body of people or animals (Ge 17:13-14; 1Co 15:39).

2. Human nature, deprived of the Holy Spirit, and dominated by sin (Ro 7:5, ftn); usually "sinful [nature]" in the NIV.

See Body; Carnal Mindedness.

FLESHHOOK *See Meat Forks.*

FLIES [2279, 4031, 6414, 6856]. Plague of (Ex 8:21-31; Ps 78:45; 105:31). Common sense analogy (Ecc 10:1). Figurative (Isa 7:18).

FLINT [2734, 7641, 7644, 9032].

1. Knives of flint used for circumcision (Ex 4:25; Jos 5:2-3).

2. Judah's heart had been inscribed with the point of a flint (Jer 17:1). The Israelites make their hearts harder than flint (Zec 7:12).

Figurative (Isa 5:28; 50:7; Jer 17:1; Eze 3:9; Zec 7:12).

See Hardest Stone; Minerals of the Bible, 1; Stones.

FLOCK [3105, 4166, 5238, 5338, 6337, 6373, 7366, 8286, 8445, *2576, 4479, 4480*]. A collection of sheep under the care of a shepherd, sometimes including goats as well (Ge 27:9; 30:32). Used figuratively of Christ's disciples (Lk 12:32; 1Pe 5:2-3).

FLOG, FLOGGING [5596, 5782, *2666, 3463, 3464, 3465*].

Described:

The practice or system of punishment by repeated lashes or blows, usually with a rod or whip; or an instance of such punishment.

1. Beating is recognized as a legitimate form of punishment (Dt 25:1-3). According to Proverbs, hasty and poor judgments, like careless talk, often lead to strife; the settling of strife involves punishment for those who have been wrong, and it should be recognized that flogging (beating) is "for the back of fools" (Pr 19:29, w 18:6; 20:3).

It is permissible to discipline a child, and parents are encouraged to apply the rod of punishment to drive out folly (Pr 22:15) so that the child will not follow a path of destruction (Pr 19:18; 23:13-14).

The rod "imparts wisdom" (Pr 29:15) and promotes a healthy and happy family (Pr 29:17). Discipline is rooted in love not anger (Pr 3:11-12). *See Abuse.*

2. Elsewhere in the OT it is recognized that even

the innocent may sometimes be scourged and crushed by evil individuals (Isa 52:13-53:12, esp 53:5). The suffering of the innocent, often at the hands of evildoers, is a common theme in the Psalms (13; 22; 28; 31:9-24; 35; 38; 41; 69; 71; 86; 102; 109).

3. Jesus warned certain of his disciples that they would be beaten in the synagogues if they continued to preach the gospel (Mk 13:9). According to Ac 5:40, the apostles were beaten by representatives of the Sanhedrin and ordered not to speak in the name of Jesus, but only after Gamaliel had pleaded with his fellow members not to put the defendants to death (Ac 5:33-39). Paul, who himself had beaten and imprisoned many Christians (Ac 22:19-20), was flogged with rods three times (2Co 11:25). In Ac 16:11-24, both Paul and Silas were involved.

Flogging of Jesus:

Prophesied (Isa 50:6). Described (Mt 20:19; 26:67-68; 27:26, 30; Mk 10:34; 15:15, 19; Lk 22:63-64; 23:16; Jn 18:22; 19:1).

See Assault and Battery; Bruise(s); Lashes; Scourging; Stoning; Stripes.

FLOOD [4059, 4429, 4784, 5643, 8466, 8851, 8852, 9180, *431, 2886, 4439*]. Foretold (Ge 6:13, 17). History of (Ge 6-8). The promise that it should not recur (Ge 8:20-22; Isa 54:9). References to (Job 22:16; Mt 24:38-39; Lk 17:26-27; Heb 11:7; 1Pe 3:20; 2Pe 2:5).

See Meteorology.

FLOUR [6159, 7854, *236, 4947*]. Finely crushed and sifted grain, generally wheat, rye, or barley (Jdg 6:19).

FLOWER [5481, 5890, 7258, 5900, 7488, 7491, *470*]. *See Plants of the Bible.*

FLUTE [2720, 5704, 6385, 10446, *884, 886, 888*]. A wind instrument (Da 3:5, 7, 10, 15). *See Music, Instruments of.*

FOAL [1201, *5626*]. *See Animals.*

FODDER [1173, 5028] (*mix, mingle*). Food for animals consisting of a mixture of grains (Ge 24:25, 32; 43:24; Jdg 19:19; Job 6:5; 24:6; Isa 30:24).

FOLLY [222, 4070, 4074, 5576, 6121, 8508, *486, 932*]. *See Fool.*

FOOD [*431, 430, 433, 1376, 3272, 4312, 4407, 4761, 4950, 7329, 7474, 7476, 10410, *788, 1109, 1111, 1628, 2266, 5575*].

Articles of:

Bread (Ge 18:5-6; 1Sa 17:17), milk (Ge 49:12; Pr 27:27), vinegar (Nu 6:3; Ru 2:14), oil (Dt 12:17; Pr 21:17, 20; Eze 16:13, 18-19), butter (Ps 55:21; Pr 30:33), roasted grain (Ru 2:14; 1Sa 17:17; 25:18), cheese (1Sa 17:18; Job 10:10), dried fruit (1Sa 25:18; 30:12), meat (Pr 9:2), wine (Jn 2:3-10), fruit (2Sa 16:2), herbs (Ex 12:8; Nu

9:11; 2Ki 4:39; Job 30:4; La 3:15; Lk 11:42), honey (SS 5:1; Isa 7:15), fish (Mt 7:10; Lk 24:42).

From God (Ge 1:29-30; 9:3; Job 36:31; Ps 23:5; 104:14-15; 111:5; 136:25; 145:15; 147:9; Pr 30:8; Isa 3:1; Mt 6:11; Ac 14:17; Ro 14:14, 21; 1Ti 4:3-5).

Practices Concerning:

Men and women did not partake together (Ge 18:8-9; Est 1:3, 9). Prepared by females (Ge 27:9; 1Sa 8:13; Pr 31:15). A hymn sung after (Mt 26:30). Thanks given before (Mk 8:6; Ac 27:35).

Things prohibited as (Ex 22:31; Lev 11:4-8, 10-20, 41-42; 17:13-15). Peter's vision concerning (Ac 10:10-16). Paul's teaching concerning the eating of food offered to idols (Ro 14:2-23; 1Co 8:4-13; 10:18-32). Flesh unwarrantedly forbidden as (1Ti 4:3-4).

See Bread; Eating; Oven.

FOOL [211, 2147, 4067, 5571, 5572, 6118, 6119, 6618, 9438, *932, 933, 3704*]. In Scripture connotes conceit and pride, or deficiency in judgment rather than mental inferiority.

Described as:

Arrogant (Ps 5:5). Iniquitous (Ps 107:17; Tit 3:3). Atheistic (Ps 14:1; 53:1). A reproach (Ps 74:18, 22). Despising wisdom (Pr 1:7, 22; 18:2). Deceitful (Pr 1:14, 18). Contentious (Pr 1:18; 18:6-7; 29:9). Clamorous (Pr 9:13). An embarrassment to his father (Pr 10:1; 15:20; 17:25; 19:13). Excessively talkative (Pr 10:8, 10; 29:11; Ecc 10:12-14). A mocker (Pr 14:9). A dreamer (Pr 17:24). Quarrelsome (Pr 20:3). Wasteful (Pr 21:20). Idle (Ecc 4:5). Willful (Pr 1:7; 27:22). Lacking in understanding (Pr 9:13; 10:13; 15:21; 26:1, 3-12; Ecc 7:4-6). Deficient in conscience (Pr 10:23). Practice deception (Pr 14:8). Gullible (Pr 14:15). Unknowledgeable (Pr 15:7). Angry (Ecc 7:9). Unperceptive (Mt 7:26-27).

General:

Causes sorrow (Pr 10:1; 17:25; 19:13). To be forsaken (Pr 9:6). To be avoided (Pr 14:8). Some suffer affliction because of (Ps 107:17).

Parables of:

The foolish virgins (Mt 25:1-13). The rich fool (Lk 12:16-20).

FOOT [*564+, 892, 5274, 7193, 7895, 8079, 8081, 10039+, 10655, *4267, 4270, 4546*]. Washing the feet, of the disciples by Jesus (Jn 13:4-16), by disciples (1Ti 5:10). *See Purification; Washing.*

Figurative (Mt 18:8).

For footwear: *See Sandal.*

FOOTMAN *See Runner.*

FOOTSTOOL [2071, 3900, *5711*]. A literal support for the feet (2Ch 9:18), a figure of subjection (Ps 110:1; Isa 66:1; Mt 5:35).

FORD [5044, 5045, 6296, 6302] (*pass over, through*). A shallow place in a stream where people and animals could cross on foot (Ge 32:22; Isa 16:2).

FOREHEAD [1068+6524, 1477, 1478, 5195, 6991, *3587*]. The part of the face above the eyes. Often revealing the character of the person— Shamelessness (Jer 3:3), courage (Eze 3:9), or godliness (Rev 7:3).

FOREIGNER [1201+5797, 1201+2021+ 5797, 2424, 4927, 5799, 6850, *254, 975, 2283, 3828, 4230*]. Among the Jewish people, anyone outside the nation was regarded as inferior (Ge 31:15) and possessed restricted rights.

He could not eat the Passover (Ex 12:43), intermarry on equal terms (Ex 34:12-16), become king (Dt 17:15), enter the sanctuary (Eze 44:9; Ac 21:28-29). They could be included in the nation by accepting the law and its requirements.

In the NT the word is applied to those who are not members of God's kingdom (Eph 2:19).

FOREKNOWLEDGE OF GOD [*4589, 4590*]. See God, Foreknowledge of, Wisdom of.

FOREMAN [5893+, 5904, 8853, *2208*]. See Master Craftsman.

FOREORDINATION See Predestination.

FORERUNNER Figurative of Christ, "who went before us" (Heb 4:14; 6:20).

FORESKIN [6889]. The fold of skin cut off in the process of circumcision (Ge 17:11, 14; Ex 4:25; 1Sa 18:25, 27; 2Sa 3:14). See Circumcision.

FORESTS [3091, 3623, 7236, *5627*].
Described:
Abounded with wild honey (1Sa 14:25-26). Populated by wild beasts (Ps 50:10; 104:20; Isa 56:9; Jer 5:6; Mic 5:8). Undergrowth often in (Isa 9:18). Tracts of land covered with trees (Isa 44:14). Often afforded pasture (Mic 7:14).

Were places of refuge (1Sa 22:5; 23:16). Hereth (1Sa 22:5). Ephraim (2Sa 18:6, 8). Supplied timber for building (1Ki 5:6-8). Lebanon (1Ki 7:2; 10:17). Carmel (Isa 33:9; 35:1-2; Na 1:4). Often destroyed by enemies (2Ki 19:23; Isa 37:24; Jer 46:23). Jotham built towers in (2Ch 27:4). Owned by King Artaxerxes and kept by Asaph (Ne 2:8). The power of God extends over (Ps 29:9). The oaks of Bashan (Isa 2:13; Eze 27:6; Zec 11:2). Arabia (Isa 21:13). Called on to rejoice at God's mercy (Isa 44:23).

Illustrative:
Prophecies concerning the coming invasion of Jerusalem by Sennacherib, its failure to withstand the invasion, and the unbelief of the Jews. The moral change in the Jewish nation shall be as great as if the wooded Lebanon were to become a fruitful field and vice versa (Isa 29:17). These prophecies are illustrative of those accustomed to

a life of self-indulgence, who because of the devastations of the enemy would now go without (Isa 32:15, 19). Illustrative of the southern kingdom (Eze 20:46-47).

Destruction of illustrates the destruction of the wicked (Isa 9:18; 10:17-18; Jer 21:14).

FORGERY See Seal.

FORGETTING GOD [*4213+4946+8894, 5960, 8894, 8895, *2140, 1720, 2144, 3284+3330, 3291, 3648+4033*]. A characteristic of the wicked (Pr 2:17; Isa 65:11). Backsliders guilty of (Jer 2:32; 3:21).

Is forgetting his covenant (Dt 4:23; 2Ki 17:38), past deliverances (Jdg 8:34; Ps 78:42-43), what he has done (Ps 78:7, 11; 106:13), benefits (Ps 103:2), kindnesses (Ps 106:7), law (Ps 119:153, 176; Hos 4:6), Jerusalem (Ps 137:5), power to deliver (Isa 51:13-15), word of encouragement (Heb 12:5), Word of God (Jas 1:22-25).

Cautions against (Dt 6:12; 8:11). Prosperity leads to (Dt 8:11-20; Hos 13:6). Trials should not lead to (Ps 44:17-22). Exhortation to those guilty of (Ps 50:22). Resolve against (Ps 119:16, 93). Encouraged by false teachers (Jer 23:27).

Punishment of (Job 8:12-13; Ps 9:17; Isa 17:10-11; Eze 23:35; Hos 8:11-14), threatened (Ps 50:22).

See Apostasy; Backsliders; Forsaking God.

FORGIVENESS [*4105, 5951, 6142, 6145, 6296, *912, 668, 918, 3195, 5919*].
Of Enemies:
By showing kindness to enemy's animal (Ex 23:4-5). By giving (Pr 25:21-22; Mt 5:39-41; Ro 12:20). Commanded (Pr 24:17; Mt 5:38-48; 18:21-35; Mk 11:25; Lk 6:27-37).

See Enemy.

Each Other:
(Lk 17:3-4; Eph 4:32; Col 3:13; Phm 10, 18). A condition of divine forgiveness (Mt 6:12-15; 18:21-35; Mk 11:25; Lk 11:4).

Spirit of, disallows rejoicing (Pr 24:17-18). Disallows retaliation (Pr 24:29; Ro 12:17, 19). Blesses (Ro 12:14; 1Co 4:12-13; 1Pe 3:9).

FORM [1215, 1952, 3670, 3922, 4162, 6886, 9307, 9322, 9454, *1626, 1639, 3671, 3673, 3674, 3929, 5386, 5395, 5596*]. In religious service (1Ch 15:13-14; 2Ch 29:34). Irregularity in (2Ch 30:2-5, 17, 20; Mt 12:3-4).

See Church, The Body of Believers, State.

FORMALISM Despised by God (Isa 1:11-15; 29:13-16; Ps 50:8-15; Jer 6:20; 14:12; Am 5:21-23; Mal 1:6-14; Lk 13:24-27; 2Ti 3:1-5). Empty (Mt 15:8-9; Ro 2:17-29; 1Co 7:19; Php 3:4-7).

Rejected by God for presenting sacrifices rather than, obedience (1Sa 15:22-23; Ecc 5:1; 1Co 7:19; 1Jn 2:3-11), thanksgiving (Ps 50:8-15; 69:30-31), repentance (Ps 51:16-17), mercy (Hos 6:6; Mic

6:6-8; Mt 9:13; 12:7), justice, mercy, and humility (Mic 6:6-8), a pure heart (Mt 15:8-9; Ro 2:17-29).

FORNICATION Instructions concerning illicit sexual intercourse (Ac 15:20, 29; 21:25; 1Co 5:1; 6:13, 18; 7:2). More specifically and primarily unlawful intercourse of an unwed person (Mt 15:19; Mk 7:21; 1Co 6:9, 18; Gal 5:19). It was commonly associated with heathen worship (Jer 2:20; 3:6) and was used as a figure of disloyalty to God (Eze 16:3-22).

See Adultery; Prostitute.

FORSAKING GOD [*5759, 6440, 1593].

Exemplified:

The wicked guilty of (Dt 28:20). Idolaters guilty of (1Sa 8:8; 1Ki 11:33). Backsliders guilty of (Jer 15:6).

Israelites (1Sa 12:10). Saul (1Sa 15:11). Ahab (1Ki 18:18). Amon (2Ki 21:22). Kingdom of Judah (2Ch 12:1, 5; 21:10; Isa 1:4; Jer 15:6). Kingdom of Israel (2Ch 13:11, w 2Ki 17:7-18). Many disciples (Jn 6:66). Phygelus and Hermogenes (2Ti 1:15). Balaam son of Beor (2Pe 2:15).

Condemned:

Forsaking the covenant (Dt 29:25; 1Ki 19:10; Jer 22:9; Da 11:30). Prosperity tempts to (Dt 31:20; 32:15). Provokes God to forsake people (Jdg 10:13; 2Ch 15:2; 24:20, 24). Resolve against (Jos 24:16; Ne 10:29-39).

Warnings against (Jos 24:20; 1Ch 28:9). His house (2Ch 29:6). His commandments (Ezr 9:10). Sin of, to be confessed (Ezr 9:10). Unreasonableness and ingratitude of (Jer 2:5-6). Leads men to follow their own devices (Jer 2:13). Wickedness of (Jer 2:13; 5:7). Trusting in man is sin (Jer 17:5). Curse pronounced upon (Jer 17:5). Brings confusion (Jer 17:13). Brings down his wrath (Ezr 3:12). Followed by remorse (Eze 6:9). The right way (2Pe 2:15).

See Forgetting God; Apostasy.

FORT, FORTIFICATION [810, 1072, 1215, 1290, 1315, 2616, 2658, 4448, 5057, 5058, 5171, 5181, 5190, 5193, 6434, 6437].

A Military Defense:

Caves used for (Jdg 6:2; 1Sa 23:26). Field-made during military operations (Dt 20:19-20; 2Ki 25:1; Jer 6:6; 32:24; 33:4; Eze 4:2; 17:17; 26:8; Da 11:15). Defenses of cities (2Sa 5:9; 2Ch 11:10-11; 26:9, 15; Ne 3:8; 4:2; Isa 22:10; 25:12; 29:3; Jer 51:53; Na 3:14). Erected in, vineyards and herding grounds (Isa 5:2; Mt 21:33; Mk 12:1), the desert (2Ch 26:10).

Figurative:

Of God's care (2Sa 22:2-3, 47; Ps 18:2; 31:3; 71:3; 91:2; 144:2; Pr 18:10; Na 1:7).

FORTITUDE *See Courage.*

FORTUNATUS [5847] (*fortunate*). A Corinthian Christian, a friend of Paul (1Co 16:17).

FORTUNE [238, 1513, 3888, 7876, 8654, 8669].

1. Changes of. See illustrated in lives of Joseph, from slave to prime minister. *See Joseph, 1.* Pharaoh's butler and baker (Ge 40). David, from shepherd boy to king, noting the changes (1Sa 15:3, 7-16:13; 2Sa 2:1-7). *See David; also Jeroboam; Haman; Mordecai; Esther; Job; Daniel.*

2. A pagan god (Isa 65:11).

FORTUNE-TELLING [3446]. *See Sorcery.*

FORTY [752, 5477, 5478]. A significant number.

Days:

Of rain, at the time of the flood (Ge 7:17), of flood, before sending forth the raven (Ge 8:6). For embalming (Ge 50:3). Jesus in the desert (Mt 4:2; Mk 1:15; Lk 4:2), compare to Israel's forty years in the desert. Spies in the land of promise (Nu 13:25). Goliath challenged Israel (1Sa 17:16). Symbolic (Eze 4:6). Of probation, given to the Ninevites (Jn 3:4). Christ's stay after the Resurrection (Ac 1:3).

Days of fasting:

By Moses (Ex 24:18; 34:28; Dt 9:9, 25), Elijah (1Ki 19:8), Jesus (Mt 4:2).

Years:

Isaac's and Esau's age at time of marriages (Ge 25:20; 26:34). Wandering of the Israelites in the desert (Ex 16:35; Nu 14:34). Caleb's age when he spied out the land (Jos 14:7). Peace in Israel (Jdg 3:11; 5:31; 8:28). Eli as judge (1Sa 4:17), Saul as king (Ac 31:21), David as king (2Sa 5:4), Solomon (1Ki 11:42), Joash (2Ki 12:1). Egypt, to be desolated (Eze 29:11), to be restored after (Eze 29:13).

Lashes:

Administered as punishment for criminals (Dt 25:3; 2Co 11:24).

FORUM OF APPIUS [5842]. A place forty-three miles SE of Rome, where Paul was met by friends (Ac 28:15).

FOUNDATION [99, 575, 3569, 3572, 3573, 4586, 4587, 4588, 4589, 4806, 4807, 4996, 10079, 1613, 2528, 2529, 2530]. The lowest part of a building, and on which it rests (Lk 14:29; Ac 16:26).

Described:

Of stone (1Ki 5:17). Joined together by cornerstones (Ezr 4:12, w 1Pe 2:6, & Eph 2:20). Strongly laid (Ezr 6:3). Security afforded by (Mt 7:25; Lk 6:48). Deep laid (Lk 6:48).

Figuratively Applied to:

Kingdoms (Ex 9:18). The mountains (Dt 32:22). The heavens (2Sa 22:8). The earth (Job 38:4; Ps 104:5). The world (Mt 13:35). The ocean (Ps 104:8).

Illustrative of:

Hope of saints (Ps 87:1). The righteous (Pr 10:25). Christ (Isa 28:16; 1Co 3:11). Doctrines of the apostles (Eph 2:20). Decrees and purposes of God (2Ti 2:19). First principles of the gospel (Heb 6:1-2). Security of saints' inheritance (Heb 11:10).

Laid for:

Cities (Jos 6:26; 1Ki 16:34). Temples (1Ki 6:37; Ezr 3:10). Walls (Ezr 4:12; Rev 21:14). Houses (Lk 6:48). Towers (Lk 14:28-29).

FOUNDING See Molding.

FOUNTAIN [1644, 5078, 5227, 6524].
Fountain of life (Ps 36:9; Pr 10:11; 13:14; 14:27; 16:22). Figurative of faithful wife (Pr 5:18; SS 4:12, 15).

Prophetic life-giving and cleansing fountain from the temple (Joel 3:18; Zec 13:1, w Rev 22:1-2).

See Fountain of Life; Spring; Wells.

FOUNTAIN GATE A gate in the walls of Jerusalem (Ne 2:14; 3:15; 12:37).

FOUNTAIN OF LIFE (Ps 36:9; Pr 13:14; 14:27; Jer 2:13; 17:13; Zec 13:1; Rev 7:17).

FOWL See Birds.

FOWLER, FOWLER'S SNARE
[3687, 3704]. A bird-catcher (Ps 91:3; 124:7).

Figurative:

1. Of the calamities and plots which await (Job 22:10; Ps 91:3; 124:7; Pr 22:5; Isa 24:17; Jer 48:43; Hos 9:8).

2. As the source or agent of calamity (Jos 23:13; Ps 69:22; Isa 8:14; Hos 5:1).

FOX [8785, 273]. Samson uses, to burn the field of the Philistines (Jdg 15:4-5). Depreciations of (SS 2:15). Dens of (Mt 8:20; Lk 9:58).

Figurative: Of heretics (SS 2:15). Of unfaithful prophets (Eze 13:1-7). Of craftiness (Lk 13:32).

See Jackal.

FRACTURES [8691]. Treatment of (Eze 30:21).

Figurative: David calling for God to break the arm of the wicked man (Ps 10:15). David claiming that the power of the wicked will be broken (Ps 37:17). The strength of Moab is broken (Jer 48:25).

FRAGRANCE [1411, 5351, 5767, 6160, 6986, 8193, 8194, 4011]. Fragrant offerings (Lev 4:7; Nu 4:16). Metaphorical of acceptable service to God (2Co 2:14, 16; Eph 5:2; Php 4:18).

FRANKINCENSE [4247, 3337]. A fragrant gum resin consisting of small, white chunks and beads which are easily ground into a powder; this powder emits a sweet odor when burned. An ingredient of the sacred oil (Ex 30:34). Commerce in (Rev 18:11-13).

FRATERNITY (*mutual, familial love*).

Commanded by:

Moses to the Israelites (Dt 15:7-15; Jos 1:14-15). David (Ps 22:22; 133:1-3). Malachi (Mal 2:10). Jesus (Ps 22:22; Mt 5:22-26; 18:15-18, 21-22, 35; 23:8; 25:40; Jn 13:34-35; 15:12-14; 21:17). Paul (Ro 12:10; 1Co 6:1-8; Gal 6:1-5; 1Th 4:9; 2Th 3:14-15). In Hebrews (Heb 13:1). Peter (1Pe 1:12; 2:17; 3:8; 2Pe 1:5, 7). John (1Jn 2:9-11).

Nazirites, vows of (Nu 6:1-21; La 4:7; Am 2:11-12; Ac 21:24-31). *See Nazirite(s), Nazarite(s).*

Unity (Ps 133:1-3). Broken (Zec 11:14). Incompatible with, pride of title (Mt 23:8). Indifference to another's conscience (1Co 8:1-13; 10:28-29). Selfishness (1Jn 3:17).

Exemplified:

By Abraham and Lot (Ge 13:8). By Jonathan and David (1Sa 18:1; 19:2-7; 20:17, 41-42; 23:16-18). By early Christians (Ac 2:42-47). By Paul (Ro 9:2-3; 10:1-4; 1Co 9:20-23). By James, Peter, and John (Gal 2:9). By Epaphroditus (Php 2:25-26). By the Thessalonian church (2Th 1:3).

See Brother; Church, The Body of Believers; Fellowship; Friendship; Love.

FRATRICIDE One who kills or murders his own brother or sister. Instances of: Cain (Ge 4:8). Abimelech (Jdg 9:5). Absalom (2Sa 13:28-29). Solomon (1Ki 2:23-25). Jehoram (2Ch 21:4). *See Homicide; Murder.*

FRAUD [9214]. *See Dishonesty.*

FREEDMAN [592]. A slave who has been granted his freedom (1Co 7:22), or a free man as contrasted with a slave (Gal 4:22-23), among Christians (Col 3:11).

FREEDMEN [3339]. One of a number of synagogues at Jerusalem, conducted for Jews who spoke Greek rather than Aramaic, the latter being the native language of Palestinian Jews (Ac 6:9).

See Emancipation.

FREEDOM [2002, 2928, 8146, 457, 912, 1181+1801, 1800, 2026, 4244]. From servitude. *See Emancipation; Jubilee.*

FREEWILL [5605, 5607, 10461]. *See Blessings, Spiritual, Contingent Upon Obedience.*

FREEWILL OFFERINGS [5605, 5607, 10461]. In the category of gifts, freewill offerings were voluntary offerings prompted solely by the impulse of the donor (Lev 22:21, 23; 23:38; Nu 29:39; Dt 12:6, 17; 2Ch 31:14; Ezr 3:5; 7:16; 8:28; Ps 119:108; 2Co 8:1-15).

See Beneficence; Gift; Giving; Liberality; Offerings.

FRET [3013]. The verb means to be irritated, angry, or nervous (Ps 37:1, 7-8; Pr 24:19).

FRIENDS [*170, 173, 278, 476, 2492, 3359, 5335, 8276, 8291, 8934, 10245, *28, *2279, *5813*].

General:

Affectionate (Dt 13:6; 1Sa 18:1; 20:17; Jn 15:9-17). Sympathetic (Job 2:11; 6:14; Ps 35:14). Mercenary (Pr 14:20; 19:4, 6). Forsaken (Pr 19:7; 27:14). Faithful (Pr 17:17; 18:24; 27:6). Of mutual help (Pr 27:9, 19). Cause rejoicing (Pr 27:9). Not to forsake (Pr 27:10). *See Friendship.*

Jesus calls his disciples (Lk 12:4; Jn 15:14-15).

False: (Ps 41:9; 88:18; Zec 13:6).

Instances of: Pharaoh's chief cupbearer to Joseph (Ge 40:23). Delilah to Samson (Jdg 16:4-21). The wife of a Levite living in the hill country of Ephraim (Jdg 19:1-2). David, to Uriah (2Sa 11), to Joab (1Ki 2:5-6). Ahithophel to David (2Sa 15:12). Job's friends (Job 6:14-30; 19:13-22). David's friends to David (Ps 31:11-12; 35:11-16; 41:9; 55:12-14, 20-21; 88:8). Judas (Mt 26:48-49; Mk 14:43-50; Lk 22:47-48; Ac 1:16-17). Jesus' disciples (Mt 26:56, 58). Paul's friends (2Ti 4:16).

See Hypocrisy.

FRIENDSHIP [173, 2256+3208+8934, 6051, 8276, *5802*].

General:

Value of (Ecc 4:9-12). Faithfulness in (Ps 35:13-14; Pr 17:9, 17; 27:6, 9-10, 14, 17, 19). Trials growing out of (Dt 13:6-9; Pr 22:24-25).

Promoted by, sympathy (Job 6:14-15). Fidelity (Pr 11:13). Not wearing out one's welcome (Pr 25:17). Mutual understanding (Am 3:3).

See Friends.

Instances of:

Abraham and Lot (Ge 14:14-16). Ruth and Naomi (Ru 1:16-17). David and Jonathan (1Sa 18:1-4; 20; 23:16-18; 2Sa 1:17-27; 9:1-13). David and Abiathar (1Sa 22:23). David and Mephibosheth (2Sa 9). David and Nahash (2Sa 10:2). David and Ittai (2Sa 15:19-22). David and Hushai (2Sa 15:32-37; 16; 17:1-22). David and Hiram (1Ki 5:1). Joram and Ahaziah (2Ki 8:28-29; 9:16). Jehu and Jehonadab (2Ki 10:15-27). Job and his three friends (Job 2:11-13). Daniel and his three companions (Da 2:49).

The Marys, and Joseph of Arimathea, for Jesus (Mt 27:55-61; 28:1-8; Lk 24:10; Jn 20:11-18). Mary, Martha, and Lazarus, and Jesus (Lk 10:38-42; Jn 11:1-46). Luke and Theophilus (Ac 1:1). Paul and his nephew (Ac 23:16). Paul, Priscilla, and Aquila (Ro 16:3-4). Paul, Timothy, and Epaphroditus (Php 2:19-20, 22, 25).

FRINGES *See Tassel(s).*

FROGS [7630, *1005*]. Plague of (Ex 8:2-14; Ps 78:45; 105:30).

Symbolic (Rev 16:13).

FRONTLETS A leather band worn on the forehead (Ex 13:6-16; Dt 6:1-8; 11:18). *See Phylactery.*

FROST [4095, 7885, 7943]. Appeared in winter on the high elevations in Bible lands (Job 37:10; 38:29).

FROWARDNESS *See Disobedience to God.*

FRUGALITY

General:

Diligent (Pr 12:27). Good (Pr 13:22). Wise (Pr 21:17; 21:20). Prudent (Pr 22:3). Industrious (Eph 4:28). The mark of a virtuous woman (Pr 31:27).

Admonition regarding (Pr 23:20-21). Commanded by Jesus (Jn 6:12).

Pretense to cover greed (Mk 14:4-5).

Instances of:

The provisions made by the Egyptians against famine (Ge 41:48-54), the gathering of manna (Ex 16:17-18, 22-24). The gathering of bread and fish after the feeding of the multitudes (Mt 14:20; 15:37).

See Extravagance; Industry.

FRUIT TREES Planting and first harvest (Lev 19:23-25). Care for (Dt 20:19-20). In Ezekiel's vision, evergreen and with healing properties (Eze 47:12). *See Tree.*

FRUITS [*3330, 7238, 7262, 7811, 9482, 10004, *1163, *2843, *2844*].

Natural: Created (Ge 1:11-12, 27-29).

See the list of various fruit-producing trees at Tree.

Spiritual: (Gal 5:22-23). *See Righteousness, Fruits of; Sin, Fruits of; Holy Spirit, Fruit of.*

FRYING PAN *See Pan(s).*

FUEL [433, 836+928+1896, 836+1198+8596, 836+ 1277, 1277, 4409]. Wood, charcoal, dried grass, and even the dung of animals and humans was used for fuel (Eze 4:12, 15; Mt 6:30; Jn 18:18).

FUGITIVES [1371, 5610, 5615, 5674, 7127, 7128, 7129].

From Servitude:

Not to be returned (Dt 23:15-16).

From Justice:

Moses (Ex 2:15), Absalom (2Sa 13:34-38).

From the Avenger of Blood:

See Avenger of Blood; Cities of Refuge.

From the Wrath of the King:

David (1Sa 21:10), Jeroboam (1Ki 11:40), Joseph, to Egypt (Mt 2:13-15).

Instances of:

From slavery, Shimei's servants (1Ki 2:39), Onesimus (Phm 10).

See Exodus.

FULLER NIV "launderer"; one who cleans or dyes cloth or garments. The word is also used at times for one who thickens and shrinks newly

shorn wool and newly woven cloth after cleansing it of natural oils. He may also have traded in textiles (Mal 3:2; Mk 9:3). *See Soap.*

FULLER'S FIELD *See Washerman's Field.*

FULLNESS OF TIME
The time appointed when God's purposes for mankind and history for a particular event have been fulfilled (Mk 1:15; Gal 4:4; Eph 1:10; 1Ti 2:6; Tit 1:3; Heb 9:26).

FUNERAL
[5301, 5386]. The ceremonies used in disposing of a dead human body. In Palestine the body was buried within a few hours after death in a tomb or cave. The body was washed, anointed when spices, and wrapped in cloths (Jn 12:7; 19:39-40). Refusal of proper burial was utter disgrace (Jer 22:19).

FURLONG *See Stadia.*

FURNACE
[3901, 3929, 6612, 9486, 10086, 2825]. Furnaces of the biblical period were made of brick or stone and were designed for different purposes, from small domestic types to large commercial smelters as those at Ezion Geber.

Figurative:
Of affliction (Dt 4:20; 1Ki 8:51; Ps 12:6; Isa 48:10; Jer 11:4). Of the Lord who refines the heart (Pr 17:3). Of lust (Hos 7:4). Of hell (Mal 4:1; Mt 13:42, 50; Rev 9:2).

Uses of:
For refining gold (Pr 17:3), silver (Eze 22:22; Mal 3:3). For melting lead and tin (Eze 22:20). For capital punishment, Shadrach, Meshach, and Abednego cast into by Nebuchadnezzar (Da 3:6-26).

FURNITURE
The principle reference to furniture in the Bible concerns the articles in the tabernacle and temple. Common people had little furniture; kings had beds (Dt 3:11) and tables (Jdg 1:7).

FUTURE
[294, 339, 340, 344, 344+3427, 995, 2118+ 4537+8611, 3427+4737, 3427+8041, 4737, 4946+8158, 6961, 10021+10180, *608+785, 3516, 4460+4780*]. *See Immortality; Eschatology.*

FUTURE PUNISHMENT *See Punishment, Eternal.*

GAAL [1720] (*loathing*). Son of Ebed, who led the men of Shechem in a revolt against Abimelech, the son of Gideon (Jdg 9:26-41).

GAASH [1724] (*rumble, quake*). A foothill of Mt. Ephraim. Joshua's inheritance embraced (Jos 24:30). Joshua buried on the north side of (Jos 24:30; Jdg 2:9). Brooks of (2Sa 23:30).

GABA See *Geba.*

GABBAI [1480] (*collector*). A chief of Benjamin (Ne 11:8).

GABBATHA [1119] (possibly *height, ridge*). The place called "the Stone Pavement" (Jn 19:13), where Jesus was tried before Pilate.

GABRIEL [1508, 1120] (*[strong] man of God [El]*). A messenger of God. Appeared to Daniel (Da 8:16; 9:21), to Zechariah (Lk 1:11-19), to Mary (Lk 1:26-29).

GAD, GADITES [1201+1532, 1201+1514, 1514, 1532, 1122] (*fortune*).

1. Jacob's seventh son (Ge 30:11; 35:26; Ex 1:4). Children of (Ge 46:16; Nu 26:15-18; 1Ch 5:11). Prophecy concerning (Ge 49:19).

2. A tribe of Israel. Blessed by Moses (Dt 33:20). Enumeration of, at Sinai (Nu 1:14, 24-25), in the plains of Moab (Nu 26:15-18), in the reign of Jotham (1Ch 5:11-17). Place of, in camp and march (Nu 2:10, 14, 16). Wealth of, in cattle, and spoils (Nu 32:1; Jos 22:8). Petition for their portion of land E of the Jordan (Nu 32:1-5; Dt 3:12, 16-17; 29:8). Boundaries of territory (Jos 13:24-28; 1Ch 5:11). Aid in the conquest of the region W of the Jordan (Nu 32:16-32; Jos 4:12-13; 22:1-8). Erect a monument to signify the unity of the tribes E of the Jordan with the tribes W of the river (Jos 22:10-14).

Disaffected toward Saul as king and joined the faction under David in the wilderness of Hebron (1Ch 12:8-15, 37-38). Join the Reubenites in the war against the Hagrites (1Ch 5:10, 18-22). Smitten by the king of Syria (2Ki 10:32-33). Carried into captivity to Assyria (1Ch 5:26). Land of, occupied by the Ammonites, after the tribe is carried into captivity (Jer 49:1). Reallotment of territory to, by Ezekiel (Eze 48:27, 29).

3. A prophet of David (2Sa 24:11). Requests David leave Adullam (1Sa 22:5). Bears the divine message to David offering choice between three evils, for his presumption in numbering Israel (2Sa 24:11-14; 1Ch 21:9-13). Requests David build an altar on threshing floor of Araunah (2Sa 24:18-19; 1Ch 21:18-19). Assists David in organizing temple service (2Ch 29:25). Writings of (1Ch 29:29).

GADARENES [1123]. The region around the city of Gadara is six miles SE of the S end of the Sea of Galilee (Mt 8:28). Mark and Luke identify the region by the capital city Gerasa, located about thirty-five miles southeast of the Sea (Mk 5:1; Lk 8:26 and ftns). See *Gerasenes.*

GADDAH See *Hazar Gaddah.*

GADDI [1534] (*my fortune*). A chief of Manasseh. One of the twelve spies who explored Canaan (Nu 13:11).

GADDIEL [1535] (*God [El] is my fortune* BDB; *[pagan god] Gad is [my] god* KB). A chief of Zebulun. One of the twelve spies (Nu 13:10).

GADER See *Beth Gader.*

GADI [1533] (*my fortune*). Father of Menahem, a king of Israel (2Ki 15:14-20).

GAHAM [1626] (*burning brightly*). A son of Nahor by his concubine Reumah (Ge 22:24).

GAHAR [1627] (*[born in the] year of little rain*). One of the temple servants (Ezr 2:47; Ne 7:49).

GAIUS [1127].

1. A Macedonian and companion of Paul. Seized at Ephesus (Ac 19:29).

2. A man of Derbe. Accompanied Paul from Macedonia (Ac 20:4).

3. A Corinthian, whom Paul baptized (Ro 16:23; 1Co 1:14).

4. Man to whom 3 John was addressed (3Jn 1).

GALAL [1674] (possibly *tortoise* IDB; *roll away* KB).

1. A Levite (1Ch 9:15).

2. Son of Jeduthun (1Ch 9:16; Ne 11:17).

GALATIA [1130, 1131]. A province of Asia Minor. Its churches visited by Paul (Ac 16:6; 18:23). Collection taken in, for Christians at Jerusalem (1Co 16:1). Peter's address to (1Pe 1:1). Churches in (Gal 1:1-2). See *Galatians, Epistle to the.*

GALATIANS, EPISTLE TO THE

Author: The apostle Paul

Date:

If the letter was addressed to churches located in north-central Asia Minor (Pessinus, Ancyra and Tavium), Galatians was written between A.D. 53 and 57.

If the letter was addressed to churches in the southern area of the Roman province of Galatia

(Antioch, Iconium, Lystra and Derbe), Galatians was written A.D. 48 or 49.

Outline:

I. Introduction (1:1-9).
  A. Salutation (1:1-5).
  B. Denunciation (1:6-9).
II. Personal: Authentication of the Apostle of Liberty and Faith (1:10-2:10).
  A. Paul's Gospel Was Received by Special Revelation (1:10-12).
  B. Paul's Gospel Was Independent of the Jerusalem Apostles and the Judean Churches (1:13-2:21).
    1. Evidenced by his early activities as a Christian (1:13-17).
    2. Evidenced by his first post-Christian visit to Jerusalem (1:18-24).
    3. Evidenced by his visit to Jerusalem fourteen years later (2:1-10).
    4. Evidenced by his rebuke of Peter at Antioch (2:11-21).
III. Doctrinal: Justification of the Doctrine of Liberty and Faith (chs. 3-4).
  A. The Galatians' Experience of the Gospel (3:1-5).
  B. The Experience of Abraham (3:6-9).
  C. The Curse of the Law (3:10-14).
  D. The Priority of the Promise (3:15-18).
  E. The Purpose of the Law (3:19-25).
  F. Sons, Not Slaves (3:26-4:11).
  G. Appeal to Enter Into Freedom From Law (4:12-20).
  H. The Allegory of Hagar and Sarah (4:21-31).
IV. Practical: Practice of the Life of Liberty and Faith (5:1-6:10).
  A. Exhortation to Freedom (5:1-12).
  B. Life by the Spirit, Not by the Flesh (5:13-26).
  C. Call for Mutual Help (6:1-10).
V. Conclusion (6:11-18).

GALBANUM [2697]. A fragrant gum used in the sacred oil (Ex 30:34).

GALEED [1681] (*heap of [stones that are a] witness*). The name given by Jacob to the heap of stones which he and Laban raised as a memorial of their compact (Ge 31:47-48).

GALILEAN [*1134*]. A native of Galilee (Mt 26:69; Jn 4:45; Lk 5:37).

GALILEE [824+1665, 1665, *1133, 1134*] (*ring, circle,* hence *region*). The northern district of Israel. A city of refuge in (Jos 20:7; 21:32; 1Ch 6:76). Cities in, given to Hiram (1Ki 9:11-12). Taken by king of Assyria (2Ki 15:29). Prophecy concerning (Isa 9:1; Mt 4:15). Called Galilee of the nations (Isa 9:1). Herod, tetrarch of (Mk 6:21; Lk 3:1; 23:6-7). Jesus resides in (Mt 17:22; 19:1; Jn 7:1, 9). Teaching and miracles of Jesus in (Mt 4:23, 25; 15:29-31; Mk 1:14, 28, 39; 3:7; Lk 4:14, 44; 5:17; 23:5; Jn 1:43; 4:3, 43-45; Ac 10:37). People of, receive Jesus (Jn 4:45, 53). Disciples were chiefly from (Ac 1:11; 2:7). Women from, ministered to Jesus (Mt 27:55-56; Mk 15:41; Lk 23:49, 55). Jesus appeared to his disciples in, after his resurrection (Mt 26:32; 28:7, 10, 16-17; Mk 14:28; 16:7; Jn 21).

Routes from, to Judea (Jdg 21:19; Jn 4:3-5). Dialect of (Mk 14:70). Called Gennesaret (Mt 14:34; Mk 6:53). Churches in (Ac 9:31).

GALILEE, SEA OF Also called the Lake of Gennesaret (Lk 5:1), the Sea of Kinnereth (Nu 34:11, ftn; Dt 3:17), and the Sea of Tiberias, because Herod's capital was on its shores (Jn 6:1; 21:1). The lake is thirteen miles long and eight miles wide, filled with fresh and clear water, and full of fish. Because it was located in a pocket in the hills, it was subject to sudden violent storms. *See Gennesaret, 2; Kinnereth, 3; Tiberias.*

GALL [4360, 5354, 8032, *5958*].
1. The secretion of the human gall bladder (Job 16:13).
2. The poison of serpents (Job 20:14).
3. A bitter and poisonous herb (Jer 9:15; Hos 10:4; Am 6:12), perhaps used to deaden pain (Mt 27:34).

Figurative of the bitter end of immorality (Pr 5:4).

GALLERY [916]. A balcony of the temple in Ezekiel's vision (Eze 41:16; 42:3, 5-6).

GALLEY [639]. *See Ship.*

GALLIM [1668] (*heaps*). A town of Benjamin (Isa 10:30; 1Sa 25:44).

GALLIO [*1136*]. Proconsul of Achaia. Dismisses complaint of Jews against Paul (Ac 18:12-17).

GALLON A unit of liquid measure. Six gallons is equal to the biblical measure known as a bath. Four quarts (one gallon), which is one sixth of a bath, is known as a hin. John records that the water jars used to hold water for ceremonial washing would hold twenty to thirty gallons of water; Jesus used this water to replenish the wine supply at the marriage celebration at Cana in Galilee (Jn 2:6).

GALLOWS [6770]. Used for execution of criminals (Est 2:23; 5:14; 6:4; 7:9-10; 9:13, 25). Reproach of being hanged upon (Gal 3:13). *See Punishment.*

GAMALIEL [1697, *1137*] (*recompense of God [El]*).
1. Chief of tribe of Manasseh (Nu 1:10; 2:20; 10:23).
2. An eminent Pharisee and teacher of the law, the teacher of Paul (Ac 22:3). He was broad-minded and tolerant toward early Christians (Ac 5:34-39).

GAMBLING *See Betting; Lot, The.*

GAMES [76]. Footraces (1Co 9:24, 26; Gal 2:2; Php 2:16; Heb 12:1). Gladiatorial (1Co 4:9; 9:26; 15:32; 2Ti 4:7).

Figurative:
Of the Christian life (1Co 9:24, 26; Gal 5:7; Php 2:16; 3:14; Heb 12:1). Of a successful ministry (Gal 2:2; Php 2:16). Fighting wild beasts, of spiritual conflict (1Co 4:9; 9:26; 15:32; 2Ti 4:7).

GAMMAD [1689] (probably *valiant men*). Men of in the watchtowers of Tyre (Eze 27:11).

GAMUL [1690] (*weaned*). The head of the twenty-second course of priests (1Ch 24:17).

GANGRENE [*1121*]. Perhaps in a running or festering sore (Ex 9:9-10; Lev 21:20, 22:22; Dt 28:27; Job 7:5). False teaching spreads like gangrene (2Ti 2:17).

GANNIM See En Gannim.

GARDEN [1703, 1708, 5750, *3057, 3303*]. A cultivated piece of ground planted with flowers, vegetables, shrubs, or trees, fenced with a mud or stone wall (Pr 24:31) or with thorny hedges (Isa 5:5). Gardens were sometimes used for burial places (Ge 23:17; 2Ki 21:18, 26; Jn 19:41). The future state of the saved is figuratively represented by a garden (Rev 22:1-5).

GARDENER [*1177, 3058*]. See Occupations and Professions.

GAREB [1735, 1736] (*scabby*).
1. One of David's warriors (2Sa 23:38; 1Ch 11:40).
2. A hill near Jerusalem (Jer 31:39).

GARLAND [4292]. A crown or wreath for the head; figurative of the rewards of wisdom (Pr 1:9; 4:9). See Crown.

GARLIC [8770]. (Nu 11:5).

GARMENT [*168, 955, 4053, 4189, 4230, 4503, 6041, 7389, 8515, 8529, *2668, 4984*]. Of righteousness (Isa 61:10; Mt 22:11; 2Co 5:3; Rev 3:18; 7:14; 16:15; 19:8). See Dress; Robe.

GARMITE [1753] (*bone, bony*). A title applied to Keilah (1Ch 4:19).

GARNER See Barn; Granary; Storehouse.

GARRISON [5163, 5907]. A fortress manned by soldiers, used chiefly for the occupation of a conquered country (1Sa 10:5; 13:3; 14:1, 6; 2Sa 8:6, 14). See Fort.

GASHMU See Geshem.

GATAM [1725]. Grandson of Esau (Ge 36:11, 16; 1Ch 1:36).

GATE, INSPECTION Name of one of the gates of Jerusalem (Ne 3:31).

GATEKEEPERS [8788, 10777]. Guards at the city gates, the doors of the king's palace, and doors of the temple (1Ch 9:17-32; 2Ch 34:13; 35:15). Lodged round about the temple in order to be present for opening the doors (1Ch 9:27). One-third were gatekeepers of the temple (2Ch 23:4), one-third were gatekeepers of the king's house (2Ch 23:5), one-third were gatekeepers of the gate of the foundation (2Ch 23:5). They served, also, as gatekeepers of the gates of the walls (Ne 12:25). They served in twenty-four courses (1Ch 26:13-19). Their posts were determined by lot (1Ch 24:31; 26:13-19).

GATES [964, 1378, 1946, 4981, 7339, 9133, *2598, 4783, 4784*]. Of cities (Dt 3:5; Jos 6:26; 1Sa 4:18; Ps 69:12; Pr 1:21; Jer 17:19-20). Of wood (Ne 1:3); bronze (Ps 107:16; Isa 45:2). Double doors (Isa 45:1; Eze 41:24).

The open square of, a place for idlers (Ge 19:1; 1Sa 4:18; Ps 69:12; Pr 1:21; Jer 17:19-20). Religious services held at (Ac 14:13). The law read at (Ne 8). Place for the transaction of public business, announcement of legal transactions (Ge 23:10, 16), conferences on public affairs (Ge 34:20), holding courts of justice (Dt 16:18; 21:19; 22:15; Jos 20:4; Ru 4:1; 2Sa 15:2; Pr 22:22; Zec 8:16). Place for public concourse (Ge 23:10; Pr 1:21; 8:3; Jer 14:2; 22:2). Thrones of kings at (1Ki 22:10; 2Ch 18:9; Jer 38:7; 39:3). Punishment of criminals outside of (Dt 17:5; Jer 20:2; Ac 7:58; Heb 13:12). Closed at night (Jos 2:5, 7), on the Sabbath (Ne 13:19). Guards at (2Ki 7:17; Ne 13:19, 22). Jails made in the towers of (Jer 20:2). Bodies of criminals exposed to view at (Jos 8:2-9; 2Ki 10:8).

Figurative:
Of the people of a city (Isa 3:26). Of the gospel (Isa 60:11). Of the powers of hell (Mt 16:18). Of death (Job 38:17; Ps 9:13; Isa 38:10). Of the grave (Isa 38:10). Of righteousness (Ps 118:19). Of salvation (Ge 28:17; Ps 24:7; 118:19-20; Isa 26:2). Narrow gate, of the way to life (Mt 7:13-14).

Symbolic: (Rev 21:12-13, 21, 25).

See Jerusalem, Gates of.

GATH [1781, 1785] (*winepress*). One of the five chief cities of the Philistines (Jos 13:3; 1Sa 6:17; Am 6:2; Mic 1:10). Anakites, a race of giants, inhabitants of (Jos 11:22). Goliath dwelt in (1Sa 17:4; 1Ch 20:5-8). The ark taken to (1Sa 5:8). Inhabitants of, called Gittites (Jos 13:3). David takes refuge at (1Sa 21:10-15; 27:2-7). Band of Gittites, attached to David (2Sa 15:18-22). Taken by David (1Ch 18:1). Shimei's servants escape to (1Ki 2:39-41). Fortified by Rehoboam (2Ch 11:8). Taken by Hazael (2Ki 12:17). Recovered by Jehoash (2Ki 13:25). Besieged by Uzziah (2Ch 26:6). Called Metheg Ammah (2Sa 8:1).

GATH HEPHER [1783] (*winepress water pit*). A town on the border of Zebulun (Jos 19:12-

13) and birthplace of Jonah the prophet (2Ki 14:25).

GATH RIMMON [1784] (*winepress of pomegranate*).

1. A city of Dan on the Philistine plain (Jos 19:45).

2. A town of Manasseh, W of Jordan, assigned to Levites (Jos 21:25).

GAULANITIS A province NE of the Sea of Galilee, ruled by Herod Antipas. It encompassed the region of OT Golan. *See Golan.*

GAZA [6445, 6484, *1124*] (*strong*).

1. A city of the Philistines (Jos 13:3; Jer 25:20). One of the border cities of the Canaanites (Ge 10:19). A city of the Avvim and Anakim (Dt 2:23; Jos 11:22). Allotted to Judah (Jos 15:47; Jdg 1:18). A temple of Dagon, situated at (Jdg 16:23). Samson dies at (Jdg 16:21-31). On the western boundary of the kingdom of Israel in the time of Solomon (1Ki 4:24). Smitten by Pharaoh (Jer 47:1). Prophecies relating to (Am 1:6-7; Zep 2:4; Zec 9:5). Desert of (Ac 8:26-39).

2. A city of Ephraim (Jdg 6:4; 1Ch 7:28).

GAZATHITES, GAZITES

NIV "[people of] Gaza" (Jos 13:3; Jdg 16:2). *See Gaza, 1.*

GAZELLE [7373, 7374, 7383, 7386]. *See Animals.*

GAZER *See Gezer.*

GAZEZ [1606] (possibly *sheep shearer* IDB; possibly *one born at the time of shearing* KB). The name of the son and of the grandson of Ephah (1Ch 2:46).

GAZZAM [1613] (*some kind of bird or insect*). One of the temple servants (Ezr 2:48; Ne 7:51).

GE HARASHIM [1629]. It may be the broad valley between Lod and Ono (1Ch 4:14, ftn; Ne 11:35).

GEBA [1494] (*hill*). A town in the territory of Benjamin (Jos 18:24; Ezr 2:26; Ne 7:30), assigned to the Levites (Jos 21:17). Jonathan defeated the Philistines at Geba (1Sa 13:3). Asa fortified the city (1Ki 15:22), and in Hezekiah's time it was the northern most city of Judah (2Ki 23:8). Men from Geba returned after the Exile (Ezr 2:26).

GEBAL [1488, 1489, 1490] (possibly *border* BDB; *hill* KB).

1. A seaport of Phoenicia N of Sidon, also known as Byblos. Modern Jebeil, twenty-five miles N of Beirut. The land of the Gebalites is mentioned (Jos 13:5-6). The town was renowned for its expert stonemasons (1Ki 5:17-18) and for shipbuilding (Eze 27:9).

2. A land between the Dead Sea and Petra (Ps 83:6-8).

GEBALITES [1490]. The inhabitants of Gebal or Byblos (Jos 13:5). *See Gebal.*

GEBER [1506] (*[strong young] man*).

1. One of Solomon's suppliers in Ramoth Gilead (1Ki 4:13). Called Ben-Geber.

2. The son of Uri (1Ki 4:19).

GEBIM [1481] (*ditches*). A place near Anathoth (Isa 10:31).

GECKO [652]. (Lev 11:30). *See Animals, Names of.*

GEDALIAH [1545, 1546] (*great is Yahweh*).

1. Governor appointed by Nebuchadnezzar after carrying the Israelites into captivity (2Ki 25:22-24). Jeremiah committed to the care of (Jer 39:14; 40:5-6). Warned of the conspiracy of Ishmael by Johanan and the captains of his army (Jer 40:13-16). Slain by Ishmael (2Ki 25:25-26; Jer 41:1-10).

2. A musician (1Ch 25:3, 9).

3. A priest, who divorced his Gentile wife after the Exile (Ezr 10:18).

4. Ancestor of Zephaniah (Zep 1:1).

5. A prince who caused imprisonment of Jeremiah (Jer 38:1).

GEDEON *See Gideon.*

GEDER [1554] (*wall [of stones]*). An ancient city of Canaan (Jos 12:13). Possibly identical with Gedor, 2 or 3.

GEDERAH [1557] (*stone pen, sheep corral*). Located between the valleys of Sorek and Aijalon in the hills of Judah (Jos 15:36). Often identified as modern Jedirah, though others identify it with Khirbet Judraya.

GEDEROTH [1558] (*stone pens, sheep corrals*). A city in the plain of Judah (Jos 15:41; 2Ch 28:18).

GEDEROTHAIM [1562] (*two stone pens, two sheep corrals*). A city in the plain of Judah (Jos 15:36).

GEDI *See En Gedi.*

GEDOR [1529, 1530] (*wall* BDB; *pockmarked* KB).

1. A city in mountains of Judah (Jos 15:58).

2. The town of Jeroham (1Ch 12:7). Possibly identical with Geder. *See Geder.*

3. Valley of, taken by Simeonites (1Ch 4:39). *See Geder.*

4. An ancestor of Saul (1Ch 8:31; 9:37).

5. Either a place or a person, authorities disagree (1Ch 4:4, 18).

GEHAZI [1634] (possibly *valley of vision*). The servant of Elisha (2Ki 4:8-37; 5:1-27; 8:4-6). He was punished for greed by becoming a leper.

GEHENNA (*valley of Hinnom*). See Ben Hinnom; Hell.

GELILOTH [1667] (*region*). A place mentioned (Jos 18:17), as marking the boundary of Benjamin. Gilgal is substituted (Jos 15:7).

GEMALLI [1696] (*my reward* KB). Father of Ammiel, and one of the twelve spies (Nu 13:12).

GEMARIAH [1701, 1702] (*Yahweh has accomplished*).
1. Son of Shaphan the scribe and friend of Jeremiah (Jer 36:10-25).
2. A son of Hilkiah, sent as ambassador to Nebuchadnezzar (Jer 29:3).

GENEALOGY [3509, 3510, 9352, *37, 1157, 1161*] (*account of one's descent*). (Nu 1:18; 2Ch 12:15; Ezr 2:59; Ne 7:5; Heb 7:3). Of no spiritual significance (Mt 3:9; 1Ti 1:4; Tit 3:9).

From Adam to Noah (Ge 4:16-22; 5; 1Ch 1:1-4; Lk 3:36-38), to Abraham (Ge 11:10-32; 1Ch 1:4-27; Lk 3:34-38), to Jesus (Mt 1:1-16; Lk 3:23-38). Of the descendants of Noah (Ge 10), of Nahor (Ge 22:20-24), of Abraham, by his wife Keturah (Ge 25:1-4; 1Ch 1:32-33), of Ishmael (Ge 25:12-16; 1Ch 1:28-31), of Esau (Ge 36; 1Ch 1:35-54), of Jacob (Ge 35:23-26; Ex 1:5; 6:14-27; Nu 26; 1Ch 2-9), of Perez to David (Ru 4:18-22). Of the Jews who returned from the Captivity (Ezr 7:1-5; 8:1-15; Ne 7; 11:12). Of Joseph (Mt 1; Lk 3:23-38).

GENEALOGY OF JESUS
CHRIST Two genealogies are given in the NT (Mt 1:1-17; Lk 3:23-28). Matthew traces the descent of Jesus from Abraham and David, and divides it into three sets of fourteen generations. He omits three generations after Joram, namely Ahaziah, Joash, and Amaziah (1Ch 3:11-12). Contrary to Hebrew practice, he names five women: Tamar, Rahab, Ruth, Bathsheba, and Mary. The sense of "became the father of" in Hebrew genealogies is not exact; it indicated immediate or remote descent, an adoptive relation, or legal heirship. Luke's genealogy moves from Jesus to Adam, agreeing with the accounts in 1 Chronicles between Abraham and Adam (1Ch 1:1-7, 24-28). From David to Abraham he agrees with Matthew; from Jesus to David he differs from Matthew. Perhaps Matthew gives the line of legal heirship, while Luke gives the line of physical descent.

GENERAL LETTERS The seven letters following Hebrews; 1 and 2 Peter; 1, 2, and 3 John and Jude—have often been designated as the General Letters. This term goes back to the early church historian Eusebius (c. A.D. 265-340), who in his *Ecclesiastical History* (2.23-25) first referred to these seven letters as Catholic Letters, using the word "catholic" to mean "universal."

The letters so designated may be said to be, for the most part, addressed to general audiences rather than to specific persons or localized groups. 2 and 3 John, the two letters that seem most obviously addressed to individuals, have long been viewed as appendages of 1 John, which is clearly general in its address. However, when compared with Paul's letters, all these letters except 3 John are clearly general in nature. By contrast, Paul addresses his letters to such recipients as the saints at Philippi, or the churches of Galatia, or Timothy or Titus.

As Eusebius noted long ago, one interesting fact connected with the General Letters is that most of them were at one time among the disputed books of the NT. James, 2 Peter, 2 John, 3 John, and Jude were all questioned extensively before being admitted to the canon of Scripture.

GENERALS [*5941*]. Roman military leaders (Rev 6:15; 19:18). *See* Captain.

GENERATION [1887, 8055, 8067, 9000, 10183, *1155*]. A period of time (Ex 3:15; Da 4:3; Lk 1:50), or all the people living in a given period (Jdg 2:10; Mt 11:16), or a class of people having a certain quality (Dt 32:5, 20; Mt 8:38), or a company gathered together (Ps 49:19).

GENERATION, EVIL (Dt 32:5; Pr 30:12; Mt 3:7; 12:39, 45; Lk 9:41; Ac 2:40).

GENEROSITY [*2858, *605, *2330, *2331*]. *See* Beneficence; Giving; Liberality.

GENESIS [1414] (*beginning*).
Author: Historically, Jews and Christians alike have held that Moses was the author/compiler of the first five books of the OT.
Date: c. 1446 to 1406
Outlines:
Literary Outline:
I. Introduction (1:1-2:3).
II. Body (2:4-50:26).
  A. "The account of the heavens and the earth" (2:4-4:26).
  B. "The written account of Adam's line" (5:1-6:8).
  C. "The account of Noah" (6:9-9:29).
  D. "The account of Shem, Ham and Japheth" (10:1-11:9).
  E. "The account of Shem" (1:10-26).
  F. "The account of Terah" (11:217-25:11).
  G. "The account of Abraham's son Ishmael" (25:12-18).
  H. "The account of Abraham's son Isaac" (25:19-35:29).
  I. "The account of Esau" (36:1-37:1).
  J. "The account of Jacob" (37:2-50:26).
Thematic Outline:
I. Primeval History (1:1-11:26).
  A. Creation (1:1-2:3).
    1. Introduction (1:1-2).
    2. Body (1:3-31).
    3. Conclusion (2:1-3).

B. Adam and Eve in Eden (2:4-25).
C. The Fall and Its Consequences (3:1-24).
D. The Rapid "Progress" of Sin (4:1-16).
E. Two Genealogies (4:17-5:32).
1. The genealogy of pride (4:17-24).
2. The genealogy of death (4:25-5:32).
F. The Extent of Sin Before the Flood (6:1-8).
G. The Great Flood (6:9-9:29).
1. Preparing for the Flood (6:9-7:10).
2. Judgment and redemption (7:11-8:19).
a. The rising of the waters (7:11-24).
b. The receding of the waters (8:1-19).
3. The flood's aftermath (8:20-9:29).
a. A new promise (8:20-22).
b. New ordinances (9:1-7).
c. A new relationship (9:8-17).
d. A new temptation (9:18-23).
e. A final word (9:24-29).
H. The Spread of the Nations (10:1-11:26).
1. The diffusion of nations (10:1-32).
2. The confusion of tongues (11:1-9).
3. The first Semitic genealogy (11:10-26).
II. Patriarchal History (11:27-50:26).
A. The Life of Abraham (11:27-25:11).
1. Abraham's background (11:27-32).
2. Abraham's land (12:1-14:24).
3. Abraham's people (15:1-24:67).
4. Abraham's last days (25:1-11).
B. The Descendants of Ishmael (25:2-18).
C. The Life of Jacob (25:19-35:29).
1. Jacob at home (25:19-27:46).
2. Jacob abroad (28:1-30:43).
3. Jacob at home again (31:1-35:29).
D. The Descendants of Esau (36:1-37:1).
E. The Life of Joseph (37:2-50:26).
1. Joseph's career (37:2-41:57).
2. Jacob's migration (42:1-47:31).
3. Jacob's last days (48:1-50:14).
4. Joseph's last days (50:15-26).

GENIUS Mechanical, a divine inspiration (Ex 28:3; 31:2-11; 35:30-35; 36:1). *See Inspiration.*

GENNESARET [1166].

1. "The land of Gennesaret" is a plain on the NW shore of the Sea of Galilee (Mt 14:34; Mk 6:53).
2. "The Lake of Gennesaret" is the same as the Sea of Galilee (Lk 5:1). *See Galilee, Sea of.*

GENTILES [1580, 260, 1619, 1620, 1818] (*nation, people*). Usually meaning non-Israelite people. *See Heathen.*

General:
Ways of, condemned (Jer 10:2-3; Eph 4:17-19). God's forbearance toward (Ac 14:16). Impartiality toward (Ro 2:9-11). Ignorant worship practices of (Mt 6:7-8, 31-32; Ac 17:4, 16, 22-27; 1Co 10:20; 12:2). Wicked practices of (Ro 1:18-32; Gal 2:15; Eph 5:12; 1Th 4:5; 1Pe 3:4). Moral responsibility of (Ro 2:14-15).
See Idolatry; Missions.

Prophecies of the Conversion of:
(Ge 12:3; 22:18; 49:10; Dt 32:21; Ps 2:8; 22:27-31; 46:4, 10; 65:2, 5; 66:4; 68:31-32; 72:8-11, 16,

19; 86:9; 102:15, 18-22; 145:10-11; Isa 2:2-4; 9:2, 6-7; 11:6-10; 18:7; 24:16; 35:1-2, 5-7; 40:5; 42:1-12; 45:6, 8, 22-24; 49:1, 5-6, 18-23; 54:1-3; 55:5; 56:3, 6-8; 60:1-14; 65:1; 66:12, 19, 23; Jer 3:17; 4:2; 16:19-21; Da 2:35, 44-45; 7:13-14; Hos 2:23; Joel 2:28-32; Am 9:11-12; Mic 4:3-4; Hag 2:7; Zec 2:10-11; 6:15; 8:20-23; 9:1, 10; 14:8-9, 16; Mal 1:11; Mt 3:9; 8:11; 12:17-21; 19:30; Mk 10:31; Lk 13:29-30; 21:24; Jn 10:16; Ac 9:15).
See Church, The Body of Believers, Prophecies Concerning.

Conversion of:
(Ac 10:45; 11:1-8; 13:2, 46-48; 14:27; 15:7-31; 18:4-6; 26:16-18; 28:28; Ro 1:5-7; 9:22-30; 10:19-20; 11:11-13, 17-21; 15:9-12; Gal 1:15-16; 2:2; 3:14; Eph 3:1-8; Col 3:11; 1Th 2:16; 1Ti 3:16; 2Ti 1:11; Rev 11:15; 15:4).
See Jesus the Christ, Kingdom of.

GENTILES, COURT OF THE The part of Herod's temple which the Gentiles could enter (not mentioned in the Bible). In the temple of Revelation (Rev 11:2).

GENTILES, INCLUSION OF *See Catholicity.*

GENTLENESS [351, 476, 1987, 6714, 8204, 8205, *2117, 2473, 4558, 4559, 5710*].

Of Christ: (Isa 40:11; Mt 11:29; 2Co 10:1).
See Jesus the Christ, Compassion of, Humility of, Meekness of.

Of God: (2Sa 22:36; Ps 18:35; Isa 40:11).
See God, Compassion of, Longsuffering of.

Of Paul: (1Th 2:7).

Exhortations to:
A fruit of the Spirit (Gal 5:22; Jas 3:17). Required in the Lord's servants (2Ti 2:24-26). Required in all Christians (Tit 3:1-2).
See Humility; Kindness; Meekness; Patience.

GENUBATH [1707] (*thief*). A son of Hadad the Edomite (1Ki 11:20).

GEOLOGY Origin, in God (Ge 1:9-10; 1Sa 2:8; 2Sa 22:16; Job 12:8-9; Ps 18:15; 24:1-2; 104:5; 136:6; Pr 30:4; 2Pe 3:5-7). Control, by God (Job 28:9-11; Ps 104:5-13; Pr 30:4; Hab 3:9). Infinity of (Jer 31:37). Destruction of (2Pe 3:5-7).
See Astronomy; Creation; Earth; Hot Springs; Meteorology.

GERA [1733] (perhaps *sojourner*). A name common to the tribe of Benjamin.
1. A son of Benjamin (Ge 46:21).
2. A grandson of Benjamin (1Ch 8:3, 5).
3. The father of Ehud (Jdg 3:15).
4. A son of Ehud (1Ch 8:7).
5. Father of Shimei (2Sa 16:5).

GERAH [1743]. A weight equal about 1/20 of a shekel or 1/2 gram (Ex 30:13; Lev 27:25; Nu 3:47). *See Measure.*

GERAR [1761] (*circle, region*).
1. A city of the Philistines (Ge 10:19). Abimelech, king of (Ge 20:1; 26:6). Visited by Abraham (Ge 20:1), by Isaac (Ge 26:1; 2Ch 14:13-14).
2. A valley (Ge 26:17-22).

GERASENES [*1170*]. The region around Gerasa, one of the cities of the Decapolis near the SE end of the Sea of Galilee, in which the demoniacs lived whom Jesus healed (Mt 8:28, ftn; Mk 5:1; Lk 8:26, 37). *See Gadarenes.*

GERGESENES A variant reading probably harmonizing Gadarenes and Gerasenes, the region in which Jesus exorcized demons (Mt 8:28; Mk 5:1; Lk 8:26, ftns). *See Gadarenes; Gerasenes.*

GERIZIM [1748]. Mount of blessing (Dt 11:29; 27:12; Jos 8:33). Jotham addresses the Shechemites from, against the conspiracy of Abimelech (Jdg 9:7). Samaritans worship at (Jn 4:20).

GERSHOM [1768] (*traveler there*).
1. Son of Moses (Ex 2:22; 18:3; 1Ch 23:15-16; 26:24).
2. *See Gershon.*
3. A descendant of Phinehas (Ezr 8:2).
4. A Levite (Jdg 18:30).

GERSHON, GERSHONITES [1767, 1768, 1769]. Also called Gershom. Son of Levi (Ge 46:11; Ex 6:16-17; Nu 3:17-26; 4:22-28, 38; 7:7; 26:57; Jos 21:6; 1Ch 6:1, 16-17, 20, 43, 62, 71; 15:7; 23:6).
Descendants of Gershon (Nu 3:25; 4:24, 38; 7:7).

GERUTH KIMHAM [1745] (*lodging place of Kimham*). An unidentified place near Bethlehem, at which Ishmael and his fellow assassins stopped during their flight to Egypt (Jer 41:17).

GESHAN [1642]. A descendant of Caleb (1Ch 2:47).

GESHEM [1774, 1776] (*rain shower*). An Arab who opposed the work of Nehemiah (Hebrew *Gashmu*, a variant of *Geshem*) (Ne 2:19; 6:1-2, 6, ftn).

GESHUR, GESHURITES [1770, 1771] (*bridge*).
1. District E of the sources of the Jordan. The inhabitants of, not subdued by the Israelites (Dt 3:14; Jos 12:5; 1Ch 2:23). David marries a princess of (2Sa 3:3; 1Ch 3:2). Absalom takes refuge in, after the murder of Amnon (2Sa 13:37-38; 15:8).
2. A people living S of the Philistines near Sinai. Their land was not taken at the time of the Conquest (Jos 13:2-13). Inhabitants of one of the vil-

lages of, exterminated, and the spoils taken by David (1Sa 27:8).

GETHER [1788]. The third son of Aram (Ge 10:23; 1Ch 1:17).

GETHSEMANE [*1149*] (*olive oil press*). A garden near Jerusalem. Jesus betrayed in (Mt 26:36-50; Mk 14:32-46; Lk 22:39-49; Jn 18:1-2).

GEUEL [1451] (*splendor of God [El]*). A representative from the tribe of Gad sent to spy out Canaan (Nu 13:15).

GEZER [1618] (possibly *pieces*). A Canaanite royal city perhaps also called Gob (2Sa 21:18 w 1Ch 20:4). The king of, defeated by Joshua (Jos 10:33; 12:12). Canaanites not all expelled from, but made to pay tribute (Jos 16:10; Jdg 1:29). Allotted to Ephraim (Jos 16:10; 1Ch 7:28). Assigned to Levites (Jos 21:21). Battle with Philistines at (1Ch 20:4; 2Sa 21:18). Struck by David (2Sa 5:25; 1Ch 14:16). Fortified by Solomon after Pharaoh, king of Egypt, drives out Canaanites, making Gezer a dowry for Pharaoh's daughter (1Ki 9:15-17). Pharaoh Shishak, invaded the land in Rehoboam's fifth year as king. He launched an attack from Gezer, and was able to threaten and plunder Jerusalem from there (1Ki 14:25-28; 2Ch 12:1-12). Gezer was twelfth on a list of 156 cities captured by Shishak in his twentieth year. This record is found on a huge relief in the Egyptian stele at Karnak. Shishak's raids went as far N as the Sea of Galilee.

GHOR, THE The Arabic name for the Jordan Valley, biblical Arabah. *See Arabah.*

GHOST [200+3869, *4460, 5753*]. An apparition (Isa 29:4); Jesus mistaken for (Mt 14:26; Mk 6:49; Lk 24:37-39). KJV "give up the ghost," means to breathe one's last, to die (Ge 25:8; 35:29; 49:33; Job 11:20; Mt 27:50; Jn 19:30). KJV "Holy Ghost" is NIV "Holy Spirit." *See Holy Spirit; Spirit.*

GIAH [1632] (*bubbling spring*). A place on the way to the wilderness of Gibeon (2Sa 2:24).

GIANTS People of exceptional height and strength, such as Og, king of Bashan (Jos 12:4; 13:12), and Goliath, whom David killed (1Sa 17). The Nephilim and descendants of Anak were giants to the Israelites (Dt 2:11; Nu 13:33) as were the Rephaites (Dt 2:11, 20; 3:11). *See Anakites; Nephilim; Rephaites.*

GIBBAR [1507] (*[young vigorous] man, hero*). A man whose children returned from captivity with Zerubbabel (Ezr 2:20).

GIBBETHON [1510] (*mound, hill*). A city of Dan (Jos 19:44). Allotted to the Levites (Jos 21:23). Besieged by Israel, while in possession of Philistines (1Ki 15:27; 16:15, 17).

GIBEA [1495] (*mound, hill*). A Judahite (1Ch 2:49).

GIBEAH [1497] (*mound, hill*).
1. Of Judah (Jos 15:57).
2. Of Saul. Also called Gibeah of Benjamin. The people's wickedness (Jdg 19:12-30; Hos 9:9; 10:9). Destroyed by the Israelites (Jdg 20). The city of Saul (1Sa 10:26; 15:34; 22:6). The ark of the covenant conveyed to, by the Philistines (1Sa 7:1; 2Sa 6:3). Deserted (Isa 10:29).
3. Another town in Benjamin, also called Gibeah (Jos 18:28).
4. Gibeah in the field (Jdg 20:31). Probably identical with Geba. *See Geba.*

GIBEATH HAARALOTH [1502] (*hill of foreskins*). Place where the Israelites were circumcised after the wilderness wanderings (Jos 5:3.).

GIBEATHITE [1503] (*of Gibeah*). Shemaah, two of whose sons were among David's warriors (1Ch 12:3).

GIBEON [1498, 1500] (*mound, hill*).
1. A city of the Hivites (Jos 9:3, 17; 2Sa 21:2). The people of deceive Joshua into a treaty (Jos 9). Made servants by the Israelites when their deception was discovered (Jos 9:27). The sun stands still over, during Joshua's battle with the five confederated kings (Jos 10:12-14). Allotted to Benjamin (Jos 18:25). Assigned to the Aaronites (Jos 21:17). The tabernacle located at (1Ki 3:4; 1Ch 16:39; 21:29; 2Ch 1:2-3, 13). Smitten by David (1Ch 14:16). Seven sons of Saul slain at, to avenge the inhabitants of (2Sa 21:1-9). Solomon worships at, and offers sacrifices (1Ki 3:4), God appears to him in dreams (1Ki 3:5; 9:2). Abner slays Asahel at (2Sa 2:18-32; 3:30). Ishmael, the son of Nethaniah, defeated at, by Johanan (Jer 41:11-16).
2. Pool of (2Sa 2:13; Jer 41:12).

GIBEONITE(S) [408+1500, 1498] (*people from Gibeon*). Descended from the Hivites and Amorites (Jos 9:3, 7, w 2Sa 21:2). A mighty and warlike people (Jos 10:2). Cities of (Jos 9:17).

Israel deceived by (Jos 9:4-13), made a league with (Jos 9:15). Spared on account of their oath (Jos 9:18-19). Appointed woodcutters (Jos 9:20-27). Attacked by the kings of Canaan (Jos 10:1-5). Delivered by Israel (Jos 10:6-10).

Saul sought to destroy (2Sa 21:2). Israel plagued for Saul's cruelty to (2Sa 21:1). Effected the destruction of the remnant of Saul's house (2Sa 21:4-9). The office of the temple servants probably originated in (1Ch 9:2, ftn). Part of, returned from the captivity (Ne 7:25).

GIBLITES *See Gebalites.*

GIDDALTI [1547] (*I pronounce [God as]*

Great ISBE; *I reared up* KB). A son of Heman (1Ch 25:4, 29).

GIDDEL [1543] (*big*).
1. One of the temple servants (Ezr 2:47; Ne 7:49).
2. One of Solomon's servants (Ezr 2:56; Ne 7:58).

GIDEON [1549, 1146] (*one who cuts, hacks*). Call of, by an angel (Jdg 6:11, 14). His excuses (Jdg 6:15). Promises of the Lord to (Jdg 6:16). Angel attests the call to, by miracle (Jdg 6:21-24). He destroys the altar of Baal and builds one to the Lord (Jdg 6:25-27). Tests God's word with a fleece (Jdg 6:36-40). Leads an army against and defeats the Midianites (Jdg 6:33-35; 7; 8:4-12). Ephraimites rebuke, for not inviting them to join in the campaign against the Midianites (Jdg 8:1-3). Avenges himself upon the people of Succoth (Jdg 8:14-17). Israel desires to make him king; he refuses (Jdg 8:22-23). Makes an ephod which becomes a snare to the Israelites (Jdg 8:24-27). Had seventy sons (Jdg 8:30). Death of (Jdg 8:32). Faith of (Heb 11:32).

GIDEONI [1551] (*one who cuts, hacks*). Father of Abidan (Nu 1:11; 2:22; 7:60, 65; 10:24).

GIDOM [1550] (*a cutting off, stop pursuit*). Limit of pursuit after battle of Gibeah (Jdg 20:45).

GIER EAGLE *See Birds; Osprey.*

GIFT, GIVING [*1388, 4458, 4966, 5368, 5508, 5510, 5522, 5989, 7731, 7933, 8816, 8856, 8933, 9556, 10448, *1517, 1561, 1564, 1565, 1797, 2330, 5921, 5922*]. A gift can be a blessing (1Sa 25:27), given to gain a favor (Ge 34:12), as an act of submission (Ps 68:29), an offering (Ex 28:38), a bribe (Pr 18:16). In the NT, anything given (Lk 21:1; Jas 1:17), a present (Mt 7:11), special spiritual endowment (Ro 1:11; 1Ti 4:14). *See Gifts From God.*

GIFTS FROM GOD

Himself:

In Christ, the Savior (Isa 42:6; 55:4; Jn 3:16; 4:10; 6:32-33), in the Holy Spirit, the Comforter. *See Holy Spirit.*

Temporal:

Food and clothing (Mt 6:25, 33). Rain and fruitful seasons (Ge 8:22; 27:28; Lev 26:4-5; Isa 30:23). Wisdom (2Ch 1:12). Peace (Lev 26:6; 1Ch 22:9). Gladness (Ps 4:7). Strength and power (Ps 29:11; 68:18). Wisdom and knowledge (Ecc 2:26; Da 2:21-23; 1Co 1:5-7). Talents, figurative of gifts and abilities (Mt 25:14-30).

All good things (Ps 21:2; 34:10; 84:11; Isa 42:5; Eze 11:19; Jn 16:23-24; Ro 8:32; 1Ti 6:17; Jas 1:17; 2Pe 1:3).

To be used and enjoyed (Ecc 3:13; 5:19-20; 1Ti 4:4-5). Should cause us to remember God (Dt 8:18). All creatures partake of (Ps 136:25; 145:15-16). Prayer for (Zec 10:1; Mt 6:11). *See Presents.*

Spiritual:

Of the Spirit (Ro 11:29; 12:6-8; 1Co 7:7; 12:4-11; 13:2; Eph 4:7; 1Pe 4:10). Life, eternal (Isa 42:5; Eze 11:19; Jn 3:16-17, 36; 6:27; Ro 5:16-18; 6:23). Grace (Jas 4:6). Wisdom (Pr 2:6; Jas 1:5). Repentance (Ac 11:28). Faith (Eph 2:8; Php 1:29). Rest (Mt 11:28). Glory (Jn 17:22).

See Blessings, Spiritual, From God; Charism, Charisma, Charismata; Miracles, Miraculous Gifts of the Spirit; Tongues, Gift of.

GIHON [1633] (*to gush forth*).

1. A river in Egypt (Ge 2:13).
2. Pools near Jerusalem (1Ki 1:33, 38, 45). Hezekiah brings the waters of the upper pool by an aqueduct into the city of Jerusalem (2Ch 32:4, 30; 33:14; Ne 2:13-15; 3:13-16; Isa 7:3; 22:9-11; 36:2).

GILALAI [1675]. A priest and musician (Ne 12:36).

GILBOA [1648] (*bubbling*). A hill S of Jezreel, where Saul was defeated by the Philistines and died (1Sa 28:4; 31:1-8; 1Ch 10:1-8).

GILEAD [824+1680, 1201+1682, 1201+1680, 1680, 1682] (perhaps *monument of stones*).

1. A region E of the Jordan allotted to the tribes of Reuben and Gad and the half tribe of Manasseh (Nu 32:1-30; Dt 3:13; 34:1; 2Ki 10:33). Reubenites expel the Hagrites from (1Ch 5:9-10, 18-22). Ammonites make war against, defeated by Jephthah (Jdg 11; Am 1:13). The prophet Elijah a native of (1Ki 17:1). David retreats to, at the time of Absalom's rebellion (2Sa 17:16, 22, 24). Pursued into, by Absalom (2Sa 17:26). Absalom defeated and slain in the forests of (2Sa 18:9).

Hazael, king of Syria, attacks the land of (2Ki 10:32-33; Am 1:3). Invaded by Tiglath-Pileser, king of Syria (2Ki 15:29). A grazing country (Nu 32:1; 1Ch 5:9). Exported spices, balm, and myrrh (Ge 37:25; Jer 8:22; 46:11).

Figurative of prosperity (Jer 22:6; 50:19).
2. A mountain (Jdg 7:3; SS 4:1; 6:5).
3. A city (Hos 6:8; 12:11).
4. Grandson of Manasseh (Nu 26:29-30; 27:1; 36:1; Jos 17:1, 3; 1Ch 2:21, 23; 7:14, 17).
5. Father of Jephthah (Jdg 11:1-2).
6. A chief of Gad (1Ch 5:14).

GILGAL [1652] (*circle of stones*).

1. Place of the first encampment of the Israelites W of the Jordan (Jos 4:19; 9:6; 10:6, 43; 14:6). Monument erected in, to commemorate the passage of the Jordan by the Israelites (Jos 4:19-24). Circumcision renewed at (Jos 5:2-9). Passover kept at (Jos 5:10-11). Manna ceased at, after the Passover (Jos 5:12). Quarries at (Jdg 3:19). Eglon, king of Moab, resides and is slain at (Jdg 3:14-26). A judgment seat, where Israel, in that district, came to be judged by Samuel (1Sa 7:16). Saul proclaimed king over all Israel at (1Sa 11:15; 13:4-15; 15:6-23). Agag, king of the Amalekites, slain at, by Samuel (1Sa 15:33). Tribe of Judah

assembles at, to proceed to the E side of the Jordan to conduct King David back after the defeat of Absalom (2Sa 19:14-15, 40-43). A school of the prophets at (2Ki 4:38-40).

Prophecies concerning (Hos 4:15; 9:15; 12:11; Am 4:4; 5:5).
2. A royal city in Canaan. Conquered by Joshua (Jos 12:23).

GILOH [1656]. A town near Hebron in the western foothills of Judah (Jos 15:51; 2Sa 15:12).

GILONITE [1639]. Ahithophel, one of David's counselors from the town of Giloh (2Sa 15:12; 23:34).

GIMZO [1693] (*place of sycamore trees*). A town off the Jerusalem Highway, three miles SW of Lydda (2Ch 28:18).

GIN See Snare; Trap.

GINATH [1640] (*protector*). The father of Tibni (1Ki 16:21).

GINNETHO See Ginnethon.

GINNETHON [1715]. A priest who returned to Jerusalem with Zerubbabel (Ne 10:6; 12:4).

GIRDLE See Belt; Sash.

GIRGASHITES [1739]. A Canaanite people (Ge 10:15). Land of given to Abraham and his descendants (Ge 15:21; Dt 7:1; Jos 3:10; Ne 9:8). Driven out before the Israelites (Jos 24:11).

GIRZITES [1747] (*people from Gezer*). A tribe named with the Geshurites and the Amalekites (1Sa 27:8).

GISHPA [1778] (*listener*). An overseer of the temple servants (Ne 11:21).

GITTAH-HEPHER See Gath Hepher.

GITTAIM [1786] (*two winepresses*). A town of Benjamin to which the Beerothites fled (Ne 11:31, 33; 2Sa 4:3). The site is unknown.

GITTITE(S) [1785] (*of Gath*). Natives of Gath (Jos 13:1-3; 2Sa 6:8-11; 15:18; 21:19).

GITTITH [1787]. In the titles of Psalms 8, 81, 84. It may denote a musical instrument imported from Gath or may be the title of a tune.

GIVING [*5447, 5989, 7061, 1443, 1521, 1522, 1797]. Rules for: Without ostentation (Mt 6:1-4). Regularly (1Co 16:2). Liberally (2Co 9:6-15). Cheerfully (2Co 8:11-12; 9:7).

See Alms; Beneficence; Liberality.

GIZONITE [1604]. The title of the sons of Hashem, among David's bodyguards (1Ch 11:34).

GLADIATOR One who contends with wild beasts (1Co 15:32). *See Games.*

GLADNESS [448+1637+8524, 1637, 8523, 8525, 8607]. *See Joy.*

GLASS [5612, 5613]. Was manufactured as early as 2500 B.C. by the Egyptians, and later by the Phoenicians, who promoted its commercial use, especially in jewelry. In the KJV, the glass mentioned by Paul (2Co 3:18) and by James (Jas 1:23-24) was a mirror of polished bronze. *See Mirror.* The references in Revelation to the sea of glass (Rev 4:6; 15:2) and the new Jerusalem (Rev 21:18, 21) emphasize the purity and clarity of crystal.

GLEAN, GLEANING [4377, 4378, 4380, 6618, 6622].

Laws concerning

The Hebrew custom of allowing the poor to follow the reapers, and to gather the grain or grapes that remained after the harvest (Lev 19:9-10; 23:22; Dt 24:19-20). *See Orphan; Strangers; Widow.*

Figurative:

(Jdg 8:2; Isa 17:6; Jer 49:9; Mic 7:1).

Instances of:

Ruth in the field of Boaz (Ru 2:2-3).

GLEDE *See Red Kite.*

GLORIFIED SAINTS [*1519]. Great cloud of witnesses (Heb 12:1), righteous people made perfect (Heb 12:23; Rev 6:11), 144,000 (Rev 14:1-5). Under the altar (Rev 6:9), before the throne (Rev 14:3). Sing song of redemption (Rev 14:3), of worship (Rev 15:2-4).

GLORIFYING GOD [1540, 3877, 8655, 10198, 1443+1518, 1519, 3486]. Commanded (1Ch 16:28; Ps 22:23; Isa 42:12). Due to him (1Ch 16:29) for his holiness (Ps 99:9; Rev 15:4), mercy and truth (Ps 115:1; Ro 15:9), faithfulness and truth (Isa 25:1), wondrous works (Mt 15:31; Ac 4:21), judgments (Isa 25:3; Eze 28:22; Rev 14:7), deliverances (Ps 50:15), grace to others (Ac 11:18; 2Co 9:13; Gal 1:24).

Accomplished by:

Relying on his promises (Ro 4:20), praising him (Ps 50:23), doing all to glorify him (1Co 10:31), dying for him (Jn 21:19), suffering for Christ (1Pe 4:14, 16), glorifying Christ (Ac 19:17; 2Th 1:12), bringing forth fruits of righteousness (Jn 15:8; Php 1:11), patience in affliction (Isa 24:1-3, 15), faithfulness (1Pe 4:11). Required in body and spirit (1Co 6:20). Shall be universal (Ps 86:9; Rev 5:13).

Believers:

Should resolve on (Ps 69:30; 118:28), unite in (Ps 34:3; Ro 15:6), persevere in (Ps 86:12). All the blessings of God are designed to lead to (Isa 60:21; 61:3). The holy example of the believers may lead others to (Mt 5:16; 1Pe 2:12).

All, by nature, fail in (Ro 3:23). The wicked averse to (Da 5:23; Ro 1:21). Punishment for not (Da 5:23, 30; Mal 2:2; Ac 12:23; Ro 1:21). Heavenly hosts engaged in (Rev 4:11).

Exemplified:

By David (Ps 57:5), the multitude (Mt 9:8; 15:31), the virgin Mary (Lk 1:46), the angels (Lk 2:14), the shepherds (Lk 2:20), by Jesus (Jn 17:4), the paralyzed man (Lk 5:25), the woman with infirmity (Lk 13:13), the leper whom Jesus healed (Lk 17:15), the blind man (Lk 18:43), the centurion (Lk 23:47), the church at Jerusalem (Ac 11:18), the Gentiles at Antioch (Ac 13:48), Abraham (Ro 4:20), Paul (Ro 11:36). *See Praise.*

GLORY [*1540, 2086, 2146, 3877, 3883, 7382, 8655, 9514, 10331, 1518, 1519, 1901]. Concerning God, the exhibition of his divine attributes and perfections (Ps 19:1) or the radiance of his presence (Lk 2:9). Concerning people, the manifestation of their commendable qualities, such as wisdom, righteousness, self-control, ability, etc. Glory is destiny of believers (Php 3:21; Ro 8:21; 1Co 15:43).

Spiritual:

Is given by God (Ps 84:11), is the work of the Holy Spirit (2Co 3:18).

Eternal:

Secured by the death of Christ (Heb 2:10), accompanies salvation by Christ (2Ti 2:10), inherited by believers (1Sa 2:8; Ps 73:24; Pr 3:35; Col 3:4; 1Pe 5:10), believers called to (2Th 2:14; 1Pe 5:10), enhanced by afflictions (2Co 4:17), present afflictions not worthy to be compared with (Ro 8:18), of the church shall be rich and abundant (Isa 60:11-13), the bodies of believers shall be raised in (1Co 15:43; Php 3:21), believers shall be glory of their ministers (1Th 2:19-20), afflictions of ministers are glory to believers (Eph 3:13).

Temporal:

Is given by God (Da 2:37), passes away (1Pe 1:24). The devil tries to seduce by (Mt 4:8). Of hypocrites turned to shame (Hos 4:7). Seek not, from man (Mt 6:2; 1Th 2:6). Of the wicked is in their shame (Php 3:19). Ends in destruction (Isa 5:14).

Of God:

Exhibited in Christ (Jn 1:14; 2Co 4:6; Heb 1:3). Ascribed to God (Gal 1:5).

Exhibited in his name (Dt 28:58; Ne 9:5), his majesty (Job 37:22; Ps 93:1; 104:1; 145:5, 12; Isa 2:10), his power (Ex 15:1, 6; Ro 6:4), his works (Ps 19:1; 111:3), his holiness (Ex 15:11).

Described as great (Ps 138:5), eternal (Ps 104:31), rich (Eph 3:16), highly exalted (Ps 8:1; 113:4).

Exhibited to Moses (Ex 34:5-7, w 33:18-23), Stephen (Ac 7:55), his church (Dt 5:24; Ps 102:16).

Enlightens the church (Isa 60:1-2; Rev 21:11, 23). Believers desire to behold (Ps 63:2; 90:16). God is jealous of (Isa 42:8). The earth is full of

(Isa 6:3). The knowledge of, shall fill the earth (Hab 2:14).

GLOWING METAL [3133, 4792].

1. *Glowing metal* used to describe the color of divine glory (Eze 1:4, 27; 8:2).

2. *Bronze glowing in a furnace* used in John's description of the King of Glory (Rev 1:15).

See Amber; Minerals of the Bible, 1; Stones.

GLUTTONY [1251+5883, 2361, *1143, 5741*].

General:

Impoverishes (Pr 23:21). Deadens moral sensibilities (Am 6:4-7; Lk 12:19-20, 45-46; Php 3:19). Loathsome (Pr 30:21-22).

Warnings against (Pr 30:21-22; Lk 21:34; Ro 13:13-14; 1Pe 4:2-3). Punished, by death (Dt 21:20-21), plagues (Nu 11:32-33).

Associated with drunkenness (Dt 21:20-21; Pr 23:21; Ecc 10:17; Lk 12:45-46; Ro 13:13; 1Pe 4:3). Proverb relating to (Isa 22:13; 1Co 15:32).

Instances of:

Israelites (Ex 16:20-21; Nu 11:4, 32-35; Ps 78:18). Sons of Eli (1Sa 2:12-17). Belshazzar (Da 5:1). Jesus falsely accused of (Mt 11:19; Lk 7:34).

See Pleasure, Worldly.

GNASH [3080, *1106, 1107, 5563*]. To grind the teeth together as an expression of rage (Job 16:9), hatred (Ps 37:12), frustration (Ps 112:10). In the NT it expresses anguish and failure rather than anger (Mt 8:12; 13:42, 50; 25:30).

GNASHING OF TEETH

[*1106+3848*]. Of the enemy, in maliciousness (Job 16:9; Ps 35:16; 37:12; 112:10; La 2:16). Of the lost, from anguish of spirit (Mt 8:12; 13:42; 22:13; 24:51; 25:30; Lk 13:28).

GNAT [4031, 4038, *3270*]. Plague of (Ex 8:16-19; Ps 105:31). *See Insects.*

GNOSTICISM A second-century heresy that was a mixture of Judaism, Christianity, and Greek mystery religions. Its forerunners are seen in the errors reflected in the books of Colossians, 1 and 2 Timothy, 2 Peter, and 1 John. Some of its major tenets were:

1. The human body is matter, and therefore is evil. It is to be contrasted with God, who is wholly spirit and therefore good.

2. Salvation is the escape from the body, achieved not by faith in Christ but by special knowledge (the Greek word for "knowledge" is *gnosis*, from which comes Gnosticism).

3. Christ's true humanity was denied in two ways: (1) Some said that Christ only seemed to have a body, a view called Docetism, and (2) others said that the divine Christ joined the man Jesus at baptism and left him before he died, a view called Cerinthianism, after its most prominent spokesman, Cerinthus. This view is the background of much of 1 John (see 1Jn 1:1; 2:22; 4:2-3).

4. Since the body was considered evil, it was to be treated harshly. This ascetic form of Gnosticism is the background of part Colossians (Col 2:21-23).

5. Paradoxically, this dualism also led to immorality. Since matter (and not the breaking of God's law) was considered evil, breaking his law was of no moral consequence.

GOAD [1995, 1996, *3034*]. An instrument for prodding animals (1Sa 13:21; Ac 26:14). Six hundred men slain with by Shamgar, a judge of Israel (Jdg 3:31). *See Oxgoad.*

Figurative of mental incentive (Ecc 12:11).

GOAH [1717]. A place near Jerusalem (Jer 31:39).

GOAT [735, 1531, 1537, 3604, 6436+, 7618, 8538, 8539, 10535+10615, *2252, 2253, 5543*]. Designated as one of the clean animals to be eaten (Lev 11:1-8; Dt 14:4). Used for food (Ge 27:9; 1Sa 16:20), for the passover feast (Ex 12:5; 2Ch 35:7), as a sacrifice by Abraham (Ge 15:9), by Gideon (Jdg 6:19), Manoah (Jdg 13:19).

Milk of, used for food (Pr 27:27). Hair of, used for clothing (Nu 31:20), pillows (1Sa 19:13), curtains of the tabernacle (Ex 26:7; 35:23; 36:14). Used for tents. *See Curtains; Tabernacle.* Mosaic law required that a kid should not be killed for food before it was eight days old (Lev 22:27), nor should it be boiled in its mother's milk (Ex 23:19). Numerous (Dt 32:14; SS 4:1; 6:5; 1Sa 25:2; 2Ch 17:11). Wild, in Israel (1Sa 24:2; Ps 104:18).

GOATS' HAIR [6436+, *128+1293*]. (Ex 25:4; 26:7; 35:6; 36:14; Nu 31:20).

GOB [1570] (*cistern*). Site of two of David's battles with the Philistines (2Sa 21:18-19).

GOBLET [110, 3926+7694, 3998, 10398]. *See Cup.*

GOD [446, 466, 468, 1425, 2006, 3051, 5822, 9199, 9359, 10033, *117, 356, 620, 1467, 1565, 2516, 2531, 2534, 2536, 2537, 4666, 5806*].

Access to:

Israel (Dt 4:7). The pure of heart (Ps 24:3-4). The thirsty (Isa 55:3). Gentiles (Ac 14:27). Enemies of God (Col 1:21-22). Believers (Heb 4:16; 1Pe 1:17). The cleansed (Jas 4:8).

Through hope (Ps 27:4; 43:2), fear (Ps 145:18-19; 1Pe 1:17), prayer (Mt 6:6; Heb 4:10), faith (Heb 11:6), love (1Jn 4:16), Christ (Jn 10:7, 9; 14:6; Ro 5:2; Eph 2:13, 18; 3:12; Col 1:21-22; Heb 7:19, 25; 10:19, 22; 1Pe 1:17). Satisfying (Ps 65:4).

Anger of: *See Anger of God.*

Appearance of:

To Adam (Ge 3:8-21). To Abraham (Ge 17:1; 18:2-33). To Jacob, at Peniel (Ge 32:30), at Bethel (Ge 35:7, 9). To Moses, in the burning bush (Ex 3:2; Dt 33:16; Mk 12:26; Lk 20:37; Ac 7:30), at Sinai (Ex 19:16-24; 24:10; 33:18-23). To Moses and Joshua (Dt 31:14-15). To princes of Israel, at Sinai (Ex 24:9-11). To Gideon (Jdg 6:11-24). To Solomon (1Ki 3:5; 9:2; 11:9; 2Ch 1:7-12; 7:12-22). To Isaiah (Isa 6:1-5). To Ezekiel (Eze 1:26-28).

Compassion of: *See below, Longsuffering of; Mercy of.*

Condescension of:

(Ps 113:5-6). Manifested: In reasoning, with Noah (Ge 6:11-13), with Moses (Ex 4:2-17), with sinners (Isa 1:18-20). In entering into a covenant with Abraham (Ge 15:1-21; 18:1-22). In indulging Abraham's intercession for Sodom (Ge 18:2-33). In indulging Moses' prayer to behold his glory (Ex 33:18-23). In indulging Gideon's tests (Jdg 6:36-40). In his care of man (Ps 8:4-6; 144:3). In redemption (Jn 3:16; Ro 5:8; Heb 6:17-18).

Creator:

(Ps 148:3-5; Pr 16:4; Isa 45:7; 66:2; Jer 51:19; Am 4:13; Mk 13:19; Ac 7:50; Ro 1:20; 1Co 11:12; Heb 2:10; 3:4; Rev 4:11). Of the earth (Ge 1:1-2, 9-10; 2:1-4; Ex 20:11; 1Sa 2:8; 2Ki 19:15; Ne 9:6; Job 38:4, 7-10; Ps 24:1-2; 89:11; 90:2; 95:5; 102:25; 104:2-3, 5-6, 24, 30; 119:90; 121:2; 124:8; 136:5-9; 146:5-6; Pr 3:19; 8:26-29; Isa 37:16; 40:28; 42:5; 44:24; 45:12, 18; 48:13; 51:13, 16; Jer 10:12; 27:5; 32:17; 51:15; Jnh 1:9; Ac 4:24; 14:15; 17:24-25; Rev 10:6; 14:7). Of the heavens (Ge 1:1, 6-8; 2:1-4; Ex 20:11; 2Ki 19:15; 1Ch 16:26; Ne 9:6; Job 9:8-9; 37:16, 18; Ps 8:3; 19:1, 4; 96:5; 102:25; 104:2-3, 5-6, 24, 30; 121:2; 124:8; 136:5; 146:5-6; Pr 3:19; 8:26-28; Isa 37:16; 42:5; 44:24; 45:18; Jer 32:17; Am 5:8; Ac 4:24; 14:15; Rev 10:6; 14:7). Of the sun, moon, and stars (Ge 1:14-19; Ps 136:7-9). Of the seas (Ge 1:9-10; Ex 20:11; Ne 9:6; Ps 95:5; 146:5-6; Pr 8:26-29; Jnh 1:9; Ac 4:24; 14:15; Rev 10:6; 14:7). Of vegetation (Ge 1:11-12). Of animals (Ge 1:20-25; Job 12:7-9; Jer 27:5).

Creator of mankind (Ge 1:26-28; 2:7; 5:1-2; 9:6; Ex 4:11; Dt 4:32; 32:6, 15, 18; Job 10:3, 8-9, 11-12; 31:15; 33:4; 34:19; Ps 94:9; 95:6; 100:3; 119:73; 149:2; Pr 20:12; 22:2; Ecc 7:29; 12:1; Isa 17:7; 42:5; 43:1, 7, 15; 44:2, 24; 45:12; 51:13; 64:8; Jer 27:5; Zec 12:1; Mal 2:10; Mk 10:6; Ac 17:24-29; 1Co 12:18, 24-25; Heb 12:9; 1Pe 4:19). Through Christ (Ro 11:36; 1Co 8:6; Eph 3:9; Heb 1:1-2). *See Jesus the Christ, Creator.* By his word (Ps 33:6-7, 9; 2Co 4:6; Heb 11:3; 2Pe 3:5). By his will (Rev 4:11).

Dissertations on:

His works and providence (Job 5:8-20). The administration of his government (Job 9:2-35; 10:1-22). His sovereignty (Job 12:7-20; 26:1-14). His providence and grace (Job 33:4-30; Ps 107). His righteousness (Job 34:10-30; 35:1-16; Na 1:2-9). His majesty and justice (Job 36:30-33). His majesty and works (Ps 104:10-15).

Dwells With the Righteous:

(Ex 25:8; 29:45; Lev 26:11-12; 1Ki 6:13; Eze 37:26-27; 2Co 6:16; Rev 21:3).

Eternity of:

(Ge 21:33; Ex 3:15; 15:18; Dt 32:40; 33:27; 1Ch 16:36; 29:10; Ne 9:5; Job 36:26; Ps 9:7; 41:13; 90:1-2, 4; 92:8; 93:2; 102:12, 24-27; 145:13; 146:10; Isa 40:28; 44:6; 57:15; 63:16; Jer 10:10; La 5:19; Da 4:3, 34; Hab 1:12; Ro 1:20; 16:26; Eph 3:21; 1Ti 1:17; 6:15-16; 2Pe 3:8; Rev 4:8-10; 11:17).

Faithfulness of:

(Ge 9:16; 28:15; Lev 26:44-45; Dt 4:31; Jdg 2:1; 1Sa 12:22; Isa 42:16; 44:21; 49:7, 14-16; Jer 29:10; 31:36-37; 32:40; 33:14, 20-21, 25-26; Eze 16:60; Hos 2:19-20; Ro 3:3-4; Heb 6:10, 13-19). Confidence in (Nu 23:19; Dt 32:4; 1Sa 7:28; 1Ch 28:20; Ne 1:5; Ps 36:5; 40:10; 89:1-2, 5, 8, 14, 24, 28, 33, 34; 92:1-2, 15; 94:14; 105:8, 42; 111:5, 7-9; 119:90-91; 132:11; Isa 25:1; La 3:23; Da 9:4; Mic 7:20; 1Co 1:9; 10:13; 2Co 1:18-20; 1Th 5:24; 2Th 3:3; 2Ti 2:13, 19; Tit 1:2; Heb 10:23; 11:11; 1Pe 4:19; 2Pe 3:9; 1Jn 1:9).
Exemplified (Ge 21:1; 24:27; Ex 2:24; 6:4-5; Dt 7:8-9; 9:5; Jos 21:45; 23:14; 1Ki 8:15, 20, 23-24, 56; 2Ki 8:19; 13:23; 2Ch 6:4-15; 21:7; Ne 1:5; 9:7-8; Ps 98:3; Hag 2:5; Lk 1:54-55, 68-70, 72-73; Ac 13:32-33; Heb 6:10, 13-19).

Fatherhood of:

Taught in the Old Testament (Ex 4:22; Dt 14:1; 32:5-6; 2Sa 7:14; 1Ch 28:6; 29:10; Ps 68:5; 89:26; Isa 1:2; 9:6; 63:16; 64:8; Jer 3:19; Hos 1:10; 11:1). Taught by Jesus (Mt 5:45; 6:4, 8-9; 7:11; 10:20, 29, 32-33; 11:25-27; 12:50; 13:43; 15:13; 16:17, 27; 18:10, 14, 19; 20:23; 26:29, 39; Mk 8:38; 11:25; 13:32; Lk 2:49; 10:21-22; 11:2; 11:13; 22:29; 23:46; 24:49; Jn 1:14, 18; 2:16; 4:21, 23; 5:17-23, 36-37, 43; 6:27, 32, 44-46; 8:19, 27, 38, 41-42, 49; 10:15, 29-30, 32-33, 36-38; 12:26-28, 50; 13:1, 3; 14:2, 6-13, 20-21, 23-24, 26, 31; 15:8-10, 16, 23-24, 26; 16:3, 10, 15, 23, 25-28; 17:1, 5, 11, 21, 24; 20:17, 21). Taught by the apostles (Ac 1:4; 2:33; Ro 1:3-4, 7; 8:14-16; 1Co 1:3; 8:6; 15:24; 2Co 1:3; 6:18; Gal 1:1, 3-4; 4:4-7; Eph 1:2-3, 17; 2:18; 3:14; 4:6; 5:20; 6:23; Php 1:2; Col 1:2-3, 12; 3:17; 1Th 1:1, 3; 3:11, 13; 2Th 1:1-2; 2:16; 1Ti 1:2; 2Ti 1:2; Tit 1:4; Heb 1:5-6; 12:9; Jas 1:17, 27; 3:9; 1Pe 1:2-3, 17; 1Jn 1:2; 2:1, 13, 15, 22-24; 3:1; 4:14; 2Jn 3-4, 9; Jude 1; Rev 1:5-6; 3:5; 14:1). *See Adoption, Spiritual Adoption.*

Favor of: *See below, Grace of.*

Foreknowledge of:

(Ac 15:18). Of contingencies (1Sa 23:10-12). Of future events (Isa 42:9; 44:7; 45:11; 46:9-10; 48:5-6; Jer 1:5; Da 2:28-29; Ac 2:23). Of human needs (Mt 6:8). Of the day of judgment (Mt 24:36; Mk 13:32). Of the redeemed (Ro 8:29; 11:2; 1Pe 1:2).

Glory of:

(Ps 24:8-10; 57:5, 11; 72:18-19; Isa 40:5; Php 1:11). Described (Eze 1:26-28; Hab 3:3-6). Transcendent (Ps 113:4). Shall endure forever (Ps 104:31). Ascribed by angels (Lk 2:14). To be ascribed by people (Ps 29:2; Ro 11:36).
Manifested in the burning bush (Ex 3:2). In

Mount Sinai (Ex 19:18; 20:18-19; 24:10, 17; 33:18-23; 34:5, 29-35; Dt 4:11-12, 33, 36; 5:5, 24-25; Heb 12:18-21). In the tabernacle (Ex 40:34-35). In the heavens (2Sa 22:10-15; Ps 18:9-14; 19:1). In his sovereignty (Ps 97:2-6; 145:5, 11-12; Isa 6:1-5; 24:23; Jude 24-25). In the church (Isa 35:2; 60:1-2, 19-21; 61:3; Eph 3:21). In Christ (Jn 13:31-32; 14:13; 17:1). To Ezekiel (Eze 3:12, 23; 8:4). To Stephen (Ac 7:55).

Goodness of:
(Ex 33:19; Dt 30:9; Ps 25:8-10; 31:19; 33:5; 36:7; 86:5; 100:5; 106:1; 119:68; Na 1:7; Mt 5:45; Ac 14:17; Jas 1:17). Leads to repentance (Ro 2:4). Gratefully acknowledged (1Ch 16:34; 2Ch 5:13; 7:3; Ps 68:19; 107:8-9, 43; 118:29; 135:3; 136:1; 145:7, 9; Isa 63:7).
Manifested: In gracious providence (Mt 7:11). To the righteous (Ps 31:19; La 3:25; Ro 11:22). To the wicked (Lk 6:35).

Grace of:
Unmerited favor (Dt 7:7-8; 2Ch 30:9; Eph 1:6; Tit 2:11; Heb 4:16). Divine help (Ps 84:11; 1Co 10:13; 2Co 1:12; 12:9; 1Pe 1:5). No warrant for sinful indulgence (Ro 6:1, 15). Intercessory prayer for (Jn 17:11-12, 15; 1Th 1:1; 5:28; 2Pe 1:2). Exhortation against rejecting (2Co 6:1-2). Exemplified with respect to Jacob and Esau (Ro 9:10-16).
Manifested: In drawing men to Christ (Jn 6:44-45), in redemption (Eph 1:5-9, 11-12), in justification (Ge 15:6; Ro 3:22-24; 4:4-5, 16; 5:2, 6-8, 15-21; Tit 3:7). In passing over transgression (Nu 23:20-21; Ne 9:17; Ro 3:25). In salvation (Ro 11:5-6; Eph 2:8-9; 2Ti 1:9), in calling to service (Gal 1:15-16), in spiritual growth (Eph 3:16). In spiritual gifts (1Co 1:4-8; Eph 4:7, 11).
Manifested: In character and conduct (2Co 1:12; Php 2:13), in the character and conduct of the righteous (1Co 15:10; 2Co 1:12; Php 2:13), in sustaining the righteous (1Ch 17:8; 2Co 12:9; 1Pe 1:5; Jude 24), in sustaining in temptation (1Co 10:13; Rev 3:10).
Manifestation of: To Enoch (Ge 5:24). To Noah (Ge 6:8, 17-18). To Abraham (Ge 12:2; 21:22). To Ishmael (Ge 21:20). To Isaac (Ge 26:24). To Jacob (Ge 46:3-4; 48:16). To Joseph (Ge 39:2-3, 23). To Moses (Ex 3:12; 33:12-17). To Israel (Dt 4:7). To Naphtali (Dt 33:23). To Joshua (Jos 1:5, 9). To Job (Job 10:12). To David (1Sa 25:26, 34; 2Sa 7:8-16). To Jeremiah (Jer 15:20). To the righteous (Ps 5:12; Ac 4:33).

Guidance of:
(Ge 12:1; 24:27; Ps 23:2-3; 48:14; 73:24; Pr 3:6; Jer 3:4; 32:19; Lk 1:79; Jn 10:3-4). By pillars of cloud and fire (Ex 13:21; Ne 9:19). By his presence (Ex 15:13; 33:13-15; Dt 32:10, 12; Ps 78:52; 80:1; 107:7). By the ark of the covenant (Nu 10:33). By his counsel (2Sa 22:29; Ps 5:8; 25:9; Isa 48:17). By his Spirit (Jn 16:13). Prayed for (Ps 25:5; 27:11; 31:3; 61:2). Promised (Ps 32:8; Isa 40:11; 42:16; 58:11).

Holiness of:
(Jos 24:19; 1Sa 6:20; 1Ch 16:10; Job 6:10;

15:15; 25:5; Ps 11:7; 22:3; 36:6; 47:8; 60:6; 89:35; 98:1; 105:3; 111:9; 119:142; 145:17; Pr 9:10; Isa 5:16; 6:3; 29:19, 23; 41:14; 43:14-15; 45:19; 47:4; 49:7; 52:10; 57:15; Eze 36:21-22; 39:7, 25; Da 4:8; Hos 11:9; Hab 1:12-13; Lk 1:49; Jn 17:11; Ro 1:23; 1Jn 2:20; Rev 4:8; 6:10; 15:4).
Incomparable (Ex 15:11; 1Sa 2:2; Job 4:17-19).
Without iniquity (Dt 32:4; 2Ch 19:7; Job 34:10; 36:23; Ps 92:15; Jer 2:5; La 3:38; Mt 19:17; Mk 10:18; Lk 18:19; Jas 1:13).
A reason for personal holiness (Lev 11:44; 19:2; 20:26; 21:8; 2Ch 19:7; Mt 5:48; 1Pe 1:15-16). A reason for thanksgiving (Ps 30:4; 99:3, 5, 9; Isa 12:6). A reason for reverent approach to God (Ex 3:5; Jos 5:15).
Light, figurative of. *See below, Light.*
See Sin, Separates from God; below, God, Perfections of, Righteousness of.

Human Forms and Appearances of: *See Anthropomorphisms.*

Immanence of:
(Ge 26:24; 28:15; Ex 3:12; Dt 4:7; Jos 3:7; Ac 17:27-28).

Immutable:
(Nu 23:19-20; 1Sa 15:29; Ps 102:27; Isa 40:28; Jas 1:17). In purpose (Job 23:13; Ps 33:11; Pr 19:21; Ecc 3:14; 7:13; Isa 31:2; Heb 6:17-18). In faithfulness (Ps 119:89-91). In mercy (Isa 59:1; Hos 13:14; Mal 3:6; Ro 11:29).

Impartial:
(Dt 10:17). Despises none (Job 36:5). Does not show favoritism (2Ch 19:7; Job 34:19; 37:24; Ac 10:34-35; Ro 2:6, 11; Eph 6:8-9; Col 3:25; 1Pe 1:17).

Incomparable:
(Ex 16:11; Dt 33:26; 2Sa 7:22; 1Ki 8:23; Ps 35:10; 71:19; 89:6-8; 113:5; Mic 7:18).

Incomprehensible:
(Job 15:8; 37:1-24; Isa 40:12-31; 55:8-9; Mt 11:27; 1Co 2:16).

Infinite:
(1Ki 8:27; 2Ch 2:6; 6:1, 18; Ps 147:5; Jer 23:24).

Invisible:
(Ex 20:21; 33:20; Dt 4:11-12; 4:15; 5:22; 1Ki 8:12; 2Ch 6:1; Job 9:11; 23:8-9; Ps 18:11; 97:2; Jn 1:18; 5:37; 6:46; Ro 1:20; Col 1:13-15; 1Ti 1:17; 6:16; Heb 11:27; 1Jn 4:12).

Jealous:
(Ex 20:5, 7; 34:14; Dt 4:24; 5:9, 11; 6:15; 29:20; 32:16, 21; Jos 24:19; 2Ch 16:7-9; Isa 30:1-2; Eze 23:25; 36:5; 39:25; Joel 2:18; Na 1:2; Zec 1:14; 1Co 10:22).

Judge:
(Ge 16:5; Jdg 11:27; 1Sa 2:3, 10; 24:12, 15; 1Ch 16:33; Job 21:22; Ps 11:4-5; 26:1-2; 35:24; 43:1; 50:4, 6; 58:11; 75:7; 76:8-9; 82:8; 94:1-2; 135:14; Pr 16:2; 29:26; Ecc 3:17; 11:9; 12:14; Isa 3:13-14; 28:17, 21; 30:18, 27; 33:22; Jer 32:19; Da 7:9-10; Na 1:3; Mal 3:5; Ac 17:31; 1Co 5:13; Heb 10:30-31; 12:22-23; Rev 6:16-17; 11:18; 16:5; 18:8).
Just Judge (Ge 18:21, 25; Nu 16:22; Dt 32:4; Ne

9:33; Job 4:17; 8:3; 34:10-12; Ps 7:9, 11; 9:4, 7-8; 67:4; 96:10, 13; 98:9; Isa 26:7; 45:21; Jer 32:19; Ro 2:2, 5-16; 3:4-6, 26; 11:22, 23; Eph 6:8-9; 1Pe 1:17; Rev 19:2).

Incorruptible Judge (Dt 10:17; 2Ch 19:7; Job 8:3; 34:19).

Justice of:

(Dt 32:4; 2Sa 22:25; 1Ki 8:32; Job 31:13-15; Ps 51:4; 62:12; 89:14; 97:2; 145:17; Pr 21:2-3; 24:12; Isa 61:8; Jer 9:24; 11:20; 20:12; 32:19; 50:7; Eze 14:23; 18:25, 29-30; 33:7-19; Da 9:7, 14; Na 1:3, 6; Zep 3:5; Ac 17:31; Ro 2:2, 5-16; Heb 6:10; 1Pe 1:17; 2Pe 2:9; 1Jn 1:9; Jude 6; Rev 11:18; 15:3).

Knowledge of:

(Ge 6:5; 1Sa 2:3; Job 12:13, 22; 21:22; 22:13-14; 26:6; 28:23-24; 36:4-5; 37:16; Ps 147:4-5; Pr 3:19-20; Isa 40:13-14, 26-28; 46:9-10; Mt 24:36; Mk 13:32; Ro 11:33-34; 1Co 1:25; 1Jn 1:5).

Knows the human state and condition (Ge 16:13; Ex 3:7; Dt 2:7; 2Ki 19:27; 2Ch 16:9; Job 23:10; 31:4; 34:21, 25; Ps 1:6; 11:4; 33:13-15; 37:18; 38:9; 66:7; 69:19; 103:14; 119:168; 139:1-4, 6, 12, 14-16; 142:3; Pr 5:21; 15:3, 11; Isa 29:15-16; 37:28; 66:18; Jer 23:24; 32:19; Am 9:2-4; Mt 10:29-30; 1Co 8:3).

Knows the human heart (Ge 20:6; Dt 31:21; 1Sa 16:7; 2Sa 7:20; 1Ki 8:39; 1Ch 28:9; 29:17; 2Ch 6:30; Job 11:11; Ps 7:9; 44:21; 94:9-11; Pr 15:11; 16:2; 17:3; 21:2; 24:12; Jer 11:20; 16:17; 17:10; 20:12; Eze 11:5; Am 4:13; Mt 6:4, 8, 18, 32; Lk 16:15; Ac 1:24; 15:8; 1Co 3:20; 1Th 2:4; Heb 4:13; 1Jn 3:20). *See above, Foreknowledge of; below, Wisdom of.*

Light:

(Da 2:22; Jas 1:17; 1Jn 1:5).

Longsuffering:

(Ge 6:3; 15:16; Ex 34:6; Nu 14:18; Ps 86:15; 103:8-10; Isa 5:1-4; 30:18; 48:9, 11; 57:16; Jer 7:13, 23-25; 9:24; Eze 20:17; Joel 2:13; Hab 1:2-4; Mt 21:33-41; Mk 12:1-9; Lk 20:9-16; Ac 14:16; Ro 3:25; 15:5; 1Pe 3:20).

Abused by people (Ne 9:28-31; Pr 1:24-27; 29:1; Ecc 8:11; Isa 5:1-4; Jer 7:13, 23-25; Mt 24:48-51). *See below, Mercy of.*

Manifested in deferring judgments (Mic 7:18; Lk 13:6-9; Ac 17:30; Ro 9:22-23; 2Pe 3:9, 15). In giving time for repentance (Jer 11:7; Mt 23:37; Lk 13:34; Ro 2:4).

Love of:

(Dt 4:37; 7:7-8, 13; 10:15, 18; 23:5; 33:3, 12; 2Sa 12:24; Job 7:17; Ps 42:8; 47:4; 69:16; Hos 11:1; Mal 1:2; 2Co 13:11, 14; 1Jn 3:1; 4:12, 16, 19; Jude 21). Everlasting (2Ch 20:21; Jer 31:3). Better than life (Ps 63:3).

For the wicked (Mt 18:12-14; Lk 15:4-7, 11-27; Ro 5:8; Eph 2:4-5). For the righteous (Ps 103:13; 146:8; Pr 15:9; Jn 14:21, 23; 16:27; 17:10, 23, 26; Ro 1:7; 9:13; 11:28; 2Th 2:16). For the cheerful giver (2Co 9:7).

Exemplified (Ex 19:4-6; Lev 20:24, 26; Dt 32:9-12; 2Sa 7:23-24; Ps 48:9, 14; Isa 43:1-4; 49:13-16; 54:5-6, 10; 62:4-5; 63:7-9; 66:13; Jer 3:14-15; Eze

16:8; Hos 2:19-20, 23; Zec 2:8). In forgiveness of sins (Isa 38:17; Tit 3:4-5). In the gift of his Son (Jn 3:16; 1Jn 4:8-10). In chastisements (Heb 12:6).

Mercy of:

(Ex 20:2, 6; Dt 5:10; Ex 33:19; Dt 4:31; 7:9; 1Ki 8:23; 2Ch 30:9; Ezr 9:9; Ps 18:50; 25:6, 8; 31:7; 32:10; 36:5; 57:10; 62:12; 69:16; 98:3; 108:4; 111:4; 116:5; 117:2; 119:64, 156; 138:2; 146:7-8; Isa 60:10; Jer 9:24; 31:20; 32:18; Da 9:4; Hos 2:23; Zec 10:6; Lk 6:36; Ac 17:30; Ro 9:15; 11:32; 15:9; 2Co 1:3; Heb 4:16; 1Pe 1:3; 2Pe 3:9). Everlasting (1Ch 16:34, 41; 2Ch 5:13; 7:3, 6, 14; Ezr 3:11; Ps 89:1-2, 28; 100:5; 103:17; 106:1; 107:1; 118:1-4, 29; 136:1-26).

Manifested: In withholding punishment (Ge 8:21; 18:26, 30-32; Ex 32:14; Nu 16:48; 2Sa 24:14, 16; 2Ki 13:23; Ezr 9:13; Job 11:6; Isa 12:1; 54:9; Eze 16:6, 42, 63; 20:17; Hos 11:8-9; Joel 2:13, 18; Jnh 4:2, 10-11; Mal 3:6). In rescuing from destruction (Ge 19:16; Nu 21:8; Jdg 2:18; 2Ki 14:26-27; Ne 1:10; 9:17-20, 27-31). In leading his people (Ps 15:13). In comforting the afflicted (2Co 12:9). In hearing prayer (Ex 22:27; Heb 4:16). In desire to save sinners (Dt 5:29; 32:29; Jdg 10:16; 2Ch 36:15; Isa 65:2, 8; Jer 2:9; 7:25; Eze 18:23, 31-32; 33:11; Mt 18:12-14; Lk 15:4-7; 1Ti 2:4, 6). In forbearance toward sinners (2Ch 24:18-19; Ps 145:8-9; La 3:22-23, 31-33; Da 4:22-27; Na 1:3). In granting forgiveness (Ex 34:6-7; Nu 14:18-20; 2Sa 12:13; 2Ch 7:14; Job 33:14-30; Ps 32:1-2, 5; 65:3; 78:38-39; 85:2-3; 86:5, 13, 15; 99:8; 103:3, 8-14; 130:3-4; 130:7-8; Pr 16:6; 28:13; Isa 55:7-9; Jer 3:12, 22; 31:20, 34; 33:8, 11; 36:3; 50:20; Eze 36:25; Da 9:9; Hos 14:4; Mic 7:18-19; Mt 6:14; 18:23-27; Lk 1:50, 77-78; Ac 3:19; 26:18; Ro 10:12-13; 2Co 5:19; Eph 1:6-8; 2:4-7; 1Ti 1:13; Tit 3:5; Heb 8:12; 1Jn 1:9).

Symbolized: In the atonement cover (Ex 25:17-22; 37:6-9; Lev 16:1-14; Nu 7:89; Heb 9:5).

Name of:

To be revered (Ex 20:7; Dt 5:11; 28:58; Ps 111:9; Mic 4:5; 1Ti 6:1). To be praised (Ps 34:3; 72:17). Not to be profaned (Ex 20:7; Lev 18:21; 19:12; 20:3; 21:6; 22:2, 32; Dt 5:11; Ps 139:20; Isa 52:5; Ro 2:24; Rev 16:9). Profaned (Ps 139:20).

Names of:

In the ancient world a name was not merely a label but the meaning of the name was virtually equivalent to whoever or whatever bore it (1Sa 25:25). Giving a name to anyone or anything was tantamount to owning or controlling it (Ge 1:5, 8, 10; 2:19-20; 2Sa 12:28). Changing a name could signify a promotion to a higher status (Ge 17:5; 32:28) or a demotion (2Ki 23:34-35; 24:17), and blotting out or cutting off the name of a person or thing meant that that person or thing was destroyed (2Ki 14:27; Isa 14:22; Zep 1:4; cf. Ps 83:4).

The name and being of God are often used in parallelism with each other (Ps 18:49; 68:4; 74:18; 86:12; 92:1; Isa 25:1; Mal 3:16), which stresses their essential identity. Believing in Jesus' name (Jn 3:18) is therefore the same as believing in Jesus himself. Prayer in his name would be prayer in concert with his character, mind, and purpose.

The name Jesus is the Greek form for the Hebrew Joshua or *"salvation of Yahweh."* As Yahweh's Savior his name accurately describes his work and purpose (Mt 1:21).

El and its compounds—

El [446] is the generic Semitic name for "God" or "deity." *El* is one of the oldest designations for deity in the ancient world. The word is found in several Semitic languages such as, Akkadian, Phoenician, and South Arabic. Even though the derivation of the word is uncertain, the root meaning is "power and authority" (Ge 1:1; Ps 19:1).

El Berith [451] means "god of the covenant" (Jdg 9:46) and is an alternate form of the name *Baal-Berith* (Jdg 8:33; 9:4). These are names of pagan gods and not the God of Israel. The remains of the Canaanite temple to Baal-Berith at Shechem, has been recovered.

El Bethel [450] means "God of Bethel," but is a place name, not a name of God. God directs Jacob to return to Bethel and build an altar there (Ge 35:1, 6-7).

El Elohe Israel [449] means "God [El], the God of Israel" or "mighty is the God of Israel." Though a statement about God, it is actually the name of an altar, also associated with the travels of Jacob (Ge 33:18-20).

El Elyon; See below Elyon.

El Olam [446+6409] means "God the Everlasting One" or "God of Eternity." While living among the Philistines, Abraham calls upon the name of Yahweh, the Eternal God (Ge 21:33). Isaiah quotes God as saying, "The LORD is the everlasting God, the Creator of the ends of the earth" (Isa 40:28). The Psalmist expresses that, "from everlasting to everlasting you are God" (Ps 90:1-2; cf 93:2; Isa 26:4).

El Roi [446+8011 or 8024] means "God who sees me." As Hagar wandered in the desert, the angel of the LORD appeared to her (Ge 16:7-12). After his appearance she gave Yahweh this name saying, "You are the One who sees me." The well at that place was named "Beer Lahai Roi," which means "well of the Living One who sees me" (Ge 16:14).

El Shaddai [446+8724] appears seven times (Ge 17:1; 28:3; 35:11; 43:14; 48:3; Ex 6:3; Eze 10:5). It probably means "God the Mountain," similar to "God the Rock" (Dt 32:4). Older etymology defined it as "God the Provider," understanding *Shaddai* to be derived from the word for "breast." *See below Shaddai.*

Eloah—

Eloah [468] is thought to be a singular form of "Elohim." It is used primarily in Job (42 times) as a way to refer to God, but without referring to him as the "God of Israel." In other references it is usually synonymous in meaning with *Elohim* (Ps 50:22-23), or *Yahweh* (Ps 139:19, 21), or *Adonay* (Ps 114:7). It also appears in the exilic and pos-

texilic periods (2Ch 32:15; Ne 9:17; Da 11:37-39).

Elohim (and its compounds) and Theos—

Elohim [466], the plural form of *El, Eloah* is used as a plural to refer to the many gods of the nations. But *Elohim* is used in a singular sense in the great majority of instances, and is thus referred to as "plural of majesty." In the singular sense *Elohim* is sometimes applied to the god of another people as in Chemosh, the god of the Amorites (Jdg 11:24), or Ashtoreth (Ishtar), the goddess of Sidon (1Ki 11:5), or Baal-Zebub, the god of Ekron (2Ki 1:2), but is used overwhelmingly (over 2300 times) in the OT to refer to Israel's God, meaning "the true God."

Theos [2536] is the NT counterpart of *Elohim* (Mt 22:32 w Ex 3:6). It usually refers to the true God, but can refer to pagan deities (Ac 17:18, 23; 1Co 8:5).

Yahweh, Yah, and Compounds—

Yahweh [3378] is the personal covenant name of Israel's God, the most common name for God in the OT (6829 times). *Yah* [3363] is its shortened form. The NIV consistently renders Yahweh as LORD. The name sounds like and may be derived from the Hebrew for the word "I AM" (Ex 3:14-15). The basic meaning of his name is "He who is" or "He who is truly present." or "I will be to you all that I am." For Israel, Yahweh is not merely one god among many; he is the Creator and Ruler of heaven and earth, who is worthy of and demands the exclusive homage of his people. It is important to understand that this is God's intensely personal name. The respect with which it was treated bears witness to the national feeling of Israel and also their fear of the God who is among them. This was recognized by the scribes who even avoided pronunciation of the name. They would use circumlocutions and alternate names where possible. *See below on Adonay.* In the NT, John records that Jesus made seven self-descriptions (Jn 6:35; 8:12 w 9:5; 10:7, 9; 10:11, 14; 11:25; 14:6; 15:1, 5), each one being introduced by "I am." The Greek text makes this statement solemnly emphatic and echoes God's self-revelation to Moses (Ex 3:14). In a similar fashion, Jesus expressed the eternity of his being and his oneness with the Father by saying, "I tell you the truth," Jesus answered, "before Abraham was born, I am!" (Jn 8:58). The people listening knew exactly what he meant by what he said: I AM GOD. The penalty for such blasphemy was stoning (Lev 24:16), which they fully intended to carry out (Jn 8:59).

Yahweh Nissi [3378+5812] means "Yahweh is my banner or standard." This was the name given to the altar which Moses erected to commemorate the defeat of the Amalekites at Rephidim (Ex 17:8-15).

Yahweh Rapha [3378+8324]. At Marah, on the way to Sinai, the LORD promised Israel that if they fully obeyed him, he would not bring on them the diseases he brought on Egypt. His name of assurance means "[I am] Yahweh who heals you" (Ex 15:26).

Yahweh Shalom [3378+8934] means "Yahweh is peace." The angel of the LORD appeared to Gideon to commission him to liberate Israel from the Midianites (Jdg 6:1-22). The LORD greeted him with peace, so Gideon built an altar and named it "The LORD is Peace" (Jdg 6:23-24).

Yahweh Shammah [3378+9004] means "The LORD is There." Not a name of God, this is the name given to the restored Jerusalem (Eze 48:35). The glory of God will return and Messiah will rule from New Jerusalem forever (Eze 43; cf. Rev 21). God's name is inseparably linked with Jerusalem.

Yahweh Tsabbaoth [3378+7372] means "LORD of Hosts" and is consistently translated "LORD Almighty" in the NIV (e.g., 1Sa 1:3, 11). "Hosts" can refer to, human armies (Ex 7:4; Ps 44:9), celestial bodies (Ge 2:1; Dt 4:19; Isa 40:26), or heavenly creatures such as angels (Jos 5:14; 1Ki 22:19; Ps 148:2). This title is probably best understood as a general reference to the sovereignty of God over all powers in the universe. In the NT *Tsabbaoth* is there transliterated by the Greek "Sabaoth" [4877] (Ro 9:29; Jas 5:4), but is usually *Pantokrator* [4120] (2Co 6:18; Rev 1:8; 4:8).

Yahweh Tsidkenu [3378+7406] means "Yahweh our Righteousness." This is the designation of the future king who will rise up from the line of David to rule over Israel (Jer 23:5-6). Righteousness is the divine attribute of the Messiah who imputes his righteousness to his followers and therefore is able to reconcile them to God (2Co 5:21). In a second reference, Jeremiah directs attention to Jerusalem, the capital of the King, which because of her intimate relationship to Messiah, will be given the same name and nature of the righteous monarch (Jer 33:15-16).

Yahweh Yireh [3378+8011] means "Yahweh will provide," "Yahweh will see [to it]." *Yireh* comes from the same Hebrew root as *Moriah,* the name of the region to which God sent Abraham to sacrifice Isaac (Ge 22:2; 2Ch 3:1). Both words are place names that confess Yahweh as the provider of a substitutionary sacrifice (Ge 22:14, cf. v. 8).

Adon, Adonay, and Kurios

Adon [123] or *Adonay* [151] is a title for God that emphasizes his sovereignty, that is "Lord." *Adon* is basically a title of honor. Out of respect one might address a superior with this title in the same way that we would say "sir" or "your honor." It would be used by a subject addressing a king (1Sa 24:8), a wife to her husband (Ge 18:12), a daughter or son to their father (Ge 31:35), a slave to his master (Ge 24:12; Ex 21:5), a subordinate to his leader (Nu 11:28). It therefore refers to one's position of authority and prestige (Ge 23:6; 45:8). The special spelling *Adonay* belongs preeminently to Yahweh, because he alone is the "Lord of the earth" (Jos 3:11, 13; Ps 97:5; Mic 4:13; Zec 4:14; 6:5). In the years after the Exile (after 538 B.C.), with reverence for the name of God increasing, the name *Yahweh* began to be pronounce as *Adonay* in the reading of the Scriptures. The LXX trans-

lators, out of fear of profaning the name of God, were led to translate *Yahweh* as *kurios* or "Lord." The Massoretic pronunciation of the Hebrew text continued this tradition by using the vowels of *Adonay* with the consonants of *Yahweh* as a signal that the proper name of God should be pronounced as *Adonay*. The misreading of this convention led to the misunderstanding of the name of God as *Jehovah*.

Kurios [3261] is the NT counterpart of both *Adonay* (Mt 22:44 w Ps 110:1) and *Yahweh* (Mt 4:10 w Dt 6:13). It is used as a term of respect (Mt 13:27) and submission (Jn 13:16; 15:20) as well as the title "Lord" (Mt 1:20, 22).

Shaddai—

Shaddai [8724] is used forty-eight times as a name of God, thirty-two times in Job (Job 5:17; 6:4, 14; etc.), seven times in the compound name *El Shaddai. See above El...* It probably means "[God] the Mountain," similar to "God the Rock" (Dt 32:4). Older etymology defined it as "[God] the Provider," understanding *Shaddai* to be derived from the word for "breast." The NIV consistently translates *Shaddai* as "Almighty" (Ge 17:1; Ps 91:1).

Elyon and Hupsistos—

Elyon [6610] means "the Most High" or "the exalted One" (Ge 14:17-20; Ps 18:13; Isa 14:13-14). The NT Greek uses the form *hupsistos* [5736], meaning "highest," or "most exalted." Jesus was known as, and called, the Son of the Most High God (Mk 5:7; Lk 1:32-33; 6:28). The Holy Spirit is the power of the Most High (Lk 1:35). John the Baptist would be known as a prophet of the Most High God (Lk 1:76). Jesus taught his disciples to "love your enemies, do good to them, and lend to them without expecting to get anything back," because in so doing, their reward will be great and they will prove that they are "sons of the Most High, because he is kind to the ungrateful and wicked" (Lk 6:35). The Most High God is far too great and magnificent to be limited to houses made by men (Ac 7:48-50). The early apostles were known as servants of the Most High God (Ac 16:17). Melchizedek was king of Salem and priest of the Most High God (Heb 7:1 w Ge 14:17-20).

Other descriptive titles—

The Ancient of Days (Da 7:9, 13, 22). Deliverer (2Sa 22:2; Ps 18:2). Father (Ps 89:26; Mt 16:17; Mk 14:36; Lk 22:29; Jn 5:17; 8:54; 10:29; 14:23; Ro 8:15; Gal 4:6), Everlasting Father (Isa 9:6). The First and the Last (Isa 44:6; 48:12; Rev 1:17; 2:8; 22:13). God of gods (Dt 10:17; Ps 136:2; Da 2:47; 11:36), the God of heaven and earth (Ge 24:3, 7). The Holy One (Isa 41:14; 43:14-15; 48:17), a God whose name is Holy (Isa 57:15). A Jealous God (Ex 34:14). Judge (Ge 18:25; Dt 32:36; Jdg 11:26). King of kings (1Ti 6:15; Rev 17:14; 19:16). The Living God (Jer 10:10; Da 6:26; Hos 1:10; Mt 16:16). Lord of lords (Dt 10:17; Ps 136:3; 1Ti 6:15; Rev 17:14; 19:16). Lord of kings (Da 2:47). The Mighty One (Isa 49:26; 60:16), Mighty God (Isa 9:6; 10:21; Lk

22:69). Prince (Ac 5:31), Prince of Peace (Isa 9:6). Redeemer (Job 19:25; Ps 19:14; 78:35; Isa 41:14; 43:14; 44:6; Jer 50:34). Righteous One (1Sa 45:21; Ps 4:1; 7:9). Rock appears five times in the Song of Moses (Dt 32:4, 15, 18, 30, 31), and several times in the Psalms (Ps 18:2, 31, 46; 19:14; 28:1; 78:35; 89:26), Isaiah (Isa 17:10; 26:4; 30:29; 44:8), and Habakkuk (Hab 1:12); in the NT Paul says that the Rock of Israel was Christ (1Co 10:4). The blessed and only Ruler (1Ti 6:15). Savior (Dt 32:15; 1Ch 16:35; Ps 89:26; Isa 43:3; Jn 4:42; Lk 1:47; Ac 5:31; 1Ti 1:1; 2:3; 4:10; Tit 1:3). Shield (Ps 3:3; 18:30). Strength (Ps 22:19). A Warrior (Ex 15:3). Wonderful Counselor (Isa 9:6).

Omnipotent:
(Ge 17:1; 18:14; Job 42:2; Ac 26:8; Rev 19:6; 21:22). *See below, Power of.*

Omnipresent:
(Ge 28:16; 1Ki 8:27; 2Ch 2:6; Ac 7:48-49; Ps 139:3, 5, 7-10; Jer 23:23-24; Ac 17:24, 27-28). *See below, Presence of.*

Omniscient: *See above, Knowledge of; below, Wisdom of.*

Perfection of:
(Dt 32:4; 2Sa 22:31; Ps 18:30; Mt 5:48; Ro 12:2; Jas 1:17; 1Jn 1:5; Rev 15:3). *See above, Holiness of; below, Righteousness of.*

Personality of: *See below, Unity of.*

Power of:
(Ex 9:16; 15:6-7, 11-12; Nu 11:23; Dt 7:21; 11:2; Job 37:1-23; Ps 21:13; 29:3-9; 62:11; 68:34-35; 74:13, 15; 77:14, 16, 18; 78:12-51; 79:11; 89:8, 13; 93:1, 4; 105:26-41; 106:8; 111:6; 135:6, 8-12; 147:5, 16-18; Isa 26:4; 40:12, 22, 24, 26, 28; 51:10, 15; 63:12; Jer 5:22; 27:5; 32:17, 27; Da 2:20; Mt 19:26; Mk 10:27; 14:36; Lk 1:49, 51; 18:27; 22:29; 1Co 6:14; Rev 19:1).

Supreme (Dt 32:39; Jos 4:24; 1Sa 2:6-7; 14:6; 1Ch 29:11-12; 2Ch 14:11; 25:8-9; Job 5:9; 23:13-14; 26:7-14; 36:5, 22, 27-33; 38:8, 11; 40:9; 42:2; Ps 104:7, 9, 29-30, 32; Da 4:35).

Irresistible (Dt 32:39; Job 10:7; 1Sa 2:10; 2Ch 20:6; Job 9:4-7, 10, 12-13, 19; 11:10; 12:14-16; 14:20; 41:10-11; Ps 66:3, 7; 76:7; Isa 14:24, 27; 31:3; 43:13, 16-17; 46:10-11; 50:2-3; Na 1:3-6). Incomparable (Dt 3:24; Job 40:9; Ps 89:8). Omnipotent (Ge 18:14; Jer 32:27; Mt 19:26). Everlasting (Ro 1:20).

Creation by (Jer 10:12). The resurrection of Christ by (1Co 6:14; 2Co 13:4). The resurrection of believers by (1Co 6:14).

Manifested in behalf of believers (Dt 33:26-27; 2Ch 16:9; Ezr 8:22; Ne 1:10; Jer 20:11; Da 3:17). Manifested in his works (Dt 3:24; Ps 33:9; 107:25, 29; 114:7-8; Pr 30:4; Isa 48:13; Jer 10:12-13; 51:15; Ro 1:20). *See above, Omnipotent.*

Presence of:
(Ge 16:13; 28:16; Ex 20:24; 29:42-43; 30:6; 33:14; Dt 4:34-36, 39; 1Ki 8:27; Ps 139:3, 5, 7-10; Isa 57:15; 66:1; Jer 23:23-24; 32:18-19; Jnh 1:3-4; Ac 17:24, 27-28; 1Co 12:6).

Manifested above the atonement cover. *See Shekinah.*

Preserver:
(Ne 9:6; Job 33:18; Ps 3:3; 12:7; 17:7; 68:6; 73:23; Isa 27:3; 49:8; Jer 2:6; Da 5:23; Mt 10:29-31; Lk 12:6-7; 21:18; Jn 17:11, 15; 1Pe 3:12-13; 2Pe 2:9).

Of the righteous (Ge 15:1; 28:15; 49:24-25; Ex 8:22-23; 9:26; 11:7; 12:13, 17, 23; 15:2, 13, 16-17; 19:4; 23:20-31; Dt 1:30-31; 32:10; 33:12, 25-28; Jos 23:10; 1Sa 2:9; 2Sa 22:1-51; 2Ch 16:9; Job 1:10; 5:11, 18-24; 10:12; Ps 9:9; 18:14; 23:1-6; 31:20, 23; 32:6, 8; 34:7, 15, 17, 19-22; 37:17, 23-24, 28, 32-33; 41:1-3; 46:1, 7; 50:15; 84:11; 91:1, 3-4, 7, 9-10, 14-15; 102:19-20; 103:2-5; 107:9-10, 13; 116:6; 118:13; 121:3-4, 7-8; 125:1-3; 145:14, 19-20; 146:7-8; Pr 2:7-8; 10:3, 30; Isa 25:4; 30:21, 26; 33:16; 40:11, 29, 31; 42:16; 43:2; 46:3-4; 52:12; 58:11; 63:9; Jer 31:9-10, 28; Eze 11:16; 34:11-16, 22, 31; Da 3:27-28; Joel 2:18; Zec 2:5, 8; Mt 4:6; 1Co 10:13; 2Ti 4:17-18; 2Th 3:3; Jas 4:15).

His Preserving Care Exemplified—

To Noah and his family, at the time of the flood (Ge 6:8, 13-21; 7; 8:1, 15-16). To Abraham and Sarah, in Egypt (Ge 12:17), in Gerar (Ge 20:3). To Lot, when Sodom was destroyed (Ge 19). To Hagar, when Abraham cast her out (Ge 21:17, 19). To Jacob, when he fled from home (Ge 35:3), when he fled from Laban, his father-in-law (Ge 31:24, 29), when he met Esau (Ge 33:3-10), as he journeyed in the land of Canaan (Ge 35:3). To Joseph, in Egypt (Ge 39:2, 21). To Moses, in his infancy (Ex 2:1-10).

To the Israelites: In bringing about their deliverance from bondage (Ex 1:9-12; 2:23-25; 3:7-9). In exempting the land of Goshen from the plague of flies (Ex 8:22). In preserving their cattle from the plague (Ex 9:4-7). In exempting the land of Goshen from the plague of darkness (Ex 10:21-23). In saving the firstborn, when the plague of death destroyed the firstborn of Egypt (Ex 12:13, 23). In deliverance from Egypt (Ex 13:3, 17-22; 14; 19:4; Lev 26:13). In the wilderness (Ex 40:36-38; Nu 9:17-23; 10:33; 22:12; 23:8; Dt 1:31; 23:5; 26:7-9).

In victories under Joshua, over the Canaanites (Jos 6-11; 24:11-13), under Othniel (Jdg 3:9-11), under Ehud (Jdg 3:15-30), under Shamgar (Jdg 3:31), under Deborah (Jdg 4:5), under Gideon (Jdg 7; 8:1-23), under Jephthah (Jdg 11:29-40), under David (1Sa 17:45-49), under Ahab (1Ki 20). In delivering the kingdom of Israel from Syria (2Sa 8). In delivering Israel by Jeroboam II (2Ki 14:26-27), by Abijah (2Ch 13:4-18). In delivering from the oppressions of the king of Syria (2Ki 13:2-5). To the kingdom of Judah: In delivering from Egypt (2Ch 12:2-12), from the Ethiopians (2Ch 14:11-14). In giving peace with other nations (2Ch 17). In delivering them from the army of the Assyrians (2Ki 19). To David (1Sa 17:32, 45-47; 2Sa 7; 1Ch 11:13-14). To Hezekiah (2Ki 19). To Job (Job 1:9-12; 2:6). To Jeremiah and

Baruch (Jer 36:26). To Daniel and the three Hebrew captives (Da 2:18-23; 3:27-28; 6). To Jonah (Jnh 1:17).

To the wise men of the east (Mt 2:12). To Jesus and his parents (Mt 2:13, 19-22). To Peter (Ac 12:3-17). To Paul and Silas (Ac 16:26-39). To Paul (Ac 27:24; 28:5-6, w Mk 16:18). *See below, Providence of; See Poor, God's Care.*

Providence of:

(Ge 24:7, 40-50, 56; 26:24; Lev 26:4-6, 10; Dt 8:18; 11:12-15; 15:4-6; 32:11-14; 1Sa 2:6-9; 1Ki 11:14-40; 1Ch 29:14, 16; Ps 23:1-6; 34:7; 9:10; 71:6-7, 15; Ps 107:1-43; 127:1-5; 136:5-25; 144:12-15; 147:8-9, 13-14; Pr 16:33; Ecc 2:24; 3:13; 5:19; Isa 46:4; 51:2; 55:10; Eze 36:28-38; Joel 2:18-26; Mt 5:45; Ro 8:28; Jas 4:15).

In providing for temporal necessities (Ge 1:29-30; 2:16; 8:22; 9:1-3; 28:20-21; 48:15-16; 49:24-25; Ex 16:15; Lev 25:20-22; Dt 2:7; 7:13-15; 8:4; 10:18; 28:2-13; 29:5; Ru 1:6; Ne 9:24-25; Job 5:8-11; 22:18, 25; Ps 36:6-7; 37:3, 19, 22, 25, 34; 65:9-13; 67:6; 85:12; 104:10-15; 111:5; 136:25; 145:15-16; Isa 43:20; 48:21; Jer 5:24; 27:6; Hos 2:8; Jnh 4:6; Zec 10:1; Mt 6:26, 30-33; 10:29-31; Lk 12:6-7, 24-28; 22:35; Jn 6:31; Ac 14:17; 2Co 9:10).

In sending prosperity (Ps 75:7; 127:1-2; Isa 48:14-15; 54:16-17; Eze 29:19-20). In sending adversity (1Sa 2:6-9; 2Sa 17:14; Ps 75:7; Ecc 3:10). In saving from adversity (Ge 7:1; Ex 9:26; 15:26; 23:25-26; Ps 103:3-5; 116:1-15; 118:5-6, 13-14; 146:7-9; Da 6:20-22).

In delivering from enemies (Ge 14:20; Ex 3:17; 6:7; 14:29-30; 23:22; 34:24; Dt 20:4; 23:14; 30:4, 20; 31:3, 8; 2Ki 20:6; 2Ch 20:3-30; 32:8; Ezr 8:22-23; Ps 18:17, 27; 44:1-3; 61:3; 78:52-55; 97:10; 105:14-45; Ac 7:34-36; 12:1-12; Pr 16:7). In thwarting evil purpose (Ge 37:5-20, w 45:5-7 w Ps 105:17 & Ac 7:9-10; Ex 14:4; Nu 23:7-8, 23, w 22:12-18; 24:10-13; Ezr 5:5; Ne 6:16; Est 7:10, w 6:1-12 & 9:25; Job 5:12-13, w Isa 8:9-10; Ps 33:10; Ac 5:38-39). In turning the curse into blessing (Dt 23:4, 6; Php 1:12, 19). In exalting the lowly (2Sa 7:8-9; 1Ch 17:7-8; Ps 68:6; 113:7-8).

In punishing evildoers (Dt 2:30; Jos 10:10-11, 19; Jdg 9:23-24; 1Ch 5:26; Isa 41:2, 4). In punishing rulers (Da 5:18, 22). In punishing nations (Dt 9:4-5; Job 12:23; Eze 29:19-20). In ordaining instruments of discipline (Isa 13:3-5). In using the Gentiles to execute his purpose (Ezr 6:22; Isa 44:28; 45:1-6, 13).

In fulfilling prophecy (1Ki 12:15; 2Ch 10:15; 36:22-23; Ezr 1:1; Ac 3:17-18).

In nature (Job 12:7-20; 37:6-24; 38:25-27, 41; 39:5-6; Ps 104:16-19, 24-30; 135:7; Jer 10:13; 51:16; 14:22; 31:35).

Instances of—
Saving Noah (Ge 7:1; 2Pe 2:5). The call of Abraham (Ge 12:1). Protecting Abraham, Sarah, and Abimelech (Ge 20:3-6). Deliverance of Lot (Ge 19). Care of Isaac (Ge 26:2-3), of Jacob (Ge 31:7). The mission of Joseph (Ge 37:5-10; 39:2-3,

21, 23; 45:7-8; 50:20; Ps 105:17-22). Warning Pharaoh of famine (Ge 41).

Delivering the Israelites (Ex 3:8; 11:3; 13:18; Ac 7:34-36). The pillar of cloud (Ex 13:21; 14:19-20). Dividing the Red Sea (Ex 14:21). Delaying and destroying Pharaoh (Ex 14:25-30). Purifying the waters of Marah (Ex 15:25). Supplying manna and quail (Ex 16:13-15; Nu 11:31-32). Supplying water at Meribah (Nu 20:7-11; Ne 9:10-25). Protection of homes while at feasts (Ex 34:24). In the conquest of Canaan (Ps 44:2-3). Saving David's army (2Sa 5:23-25). The revolt of the ten tribes (1Ki 12:15, 24; 2Ch 10:15). Fighting the battles of Israel (2Ch 13:12, 18; 14:9-14; 16:7-9; 20:15, 17; 22; 23; 32:21-22). Restoring Manasseh after his conversion (2Ch 33:12-13). Feeding Elijah and the widow (1Ki 17; 19:1-8). In prospering Hezekiah (2Ki 18:6-7; 2Ch 32:29), and Asa (2Ch 14:6-7), and Jehoshaphat (2Ch 17:3, 5; 20:30), and Uzziah (2Ch 26:5-15), and Jotham (2Ch 27:6), and Job (Job 1:10; 42:10, 12), and Daniel (Da 1:9).

In turning the heart of the king of Assyria to favor the Jews (Ezr 6:22). In rescuing Jeremiah (La 3:52-58; Jer 38:6-13). Restoration of the Jews (2Ch 36:22-23; Ezr 1:1). Rescuing the Jews from Haman's plot (Esther). Rebuilding the walls of Jerusalem (Ne 6:16).

Warning Joseph in dreams (Mt 1:20; 2:13, 19-20), and the wise men of the east (Mt 2:12-13). Deliverance of Paul (2Co 1:10). Restoring Epaphroditus (Php 2:27). Banishment of John to Patmos (Rev 1:9).

Mysterious and Misinterpreted—
The silence of God (Job 33:13). The adversity of the righteous (Ecc 7:15; 8:14). The prosperity of the wicked (Job 12:6; 21:7; 24:1; Ps 73:2-5, 12-17; Ecc 7:15; 8:14; Jer 12:1-2; Mal 3:14-15). Likeness in the lot of the righteous and the wicked (Ecc 9:2, 11). Permitting the violence of the wicked toward the righteous (Job 24:1-12; Hab 1:2-3, 11, 13-14).

Rejected:

By Israel (1Sa 8:7-8; Isa 65:12; 66:4). By Saul (1Sa 15:26). *See Jesus the Christ, Rejected.*

Repentance Attributed to:

(Ge 6:6-7; Ex 32:14; Jdg 2:18; 1Sa 15:35; 2Sa 24:16; 1Ch 21:15; Ps 106:45; Jer 26:19; Am 7:3; Jnh 3:10). *See Anthropomorphisms; Relent.*

Righteousness of:

(Ge 18:25; Jdg 5:11; Ps 7:9; 72:1; 88:12; 89:16; 119:40; 143:1; Isa 41:10; 56:1; Jer 4:2; 9:24; Mic 7:9; Ac 17:31).

Ascribed by people (Ex 9:27; Ezr 9:15; Job 36:3; Ps 5:8; 48:10; 71:15, 19; 89:14; 97:2; 116:5; 145:7, 17; Jer 12:1; Da 9:7, 14; 2Ti 4:8). Ascribed by Jesus (Jn 17:25). Ascribed by the angel (Rev 16:5). Revealed in the heavens (Ps 50:6). Revealed in the gospel (Ro 1:17; 3:4-6, 21-22; 10:3-4; 2Pe 1:1).

Endures forever (Ps 119:142, 144; Isa 51:8). *See above, Holiness of, Perfection of.*

Savior:

(Ex 6:6-7; Ps 3:8; 18:30; 28:8; 31:5; 33:18-19; 34:22; 37:39-40; 74:12; 76:8-9; 85:9; 96:2; 98:2-3; 111:9; 118:14; 121:7; 149:4; Isa 26:1; 33:22; 35:4; 43:3, 11-12, 14; 45:15, 17, 21-22; 46:12-13; 49:25; 50:2; 59:1; 60:16; 63:8, 16; Jer 3:23; 14:8; 33:6; Eze 37:23; Hos 1:7; 13:4; Joel 3:16; Jnh 2:9; Lk 1:68; Jn 3:16-17; Ro 8:30-32; 1Ti 2:3-4; 4:10; Tit 1:2-3; 2:10-11; 3:4-5; 1Jn 4:9-10).

Called Redeemer (Ps 19:14; Isa 41:14; 47:4; 48:17; Jer 50:34). Salvation (Ps 27:1; 62:1-2; 62:6-7; Isa 12:2). God of salvation (Ps 25:5; 65:5; 68:19-20; 88:1). Rock of salvation (Dt 32:15, 31). Shield (Dt 33:29).

Salvation from national adversity (Ex 15:2; Isa 25:4, 9; 52:3, 9-10), from sin (Job 33:24, 27-30; 44:22-24; Ro 1:16), through Christ (2Ti 1:9).

Self-Existent:

Has life in himself (Jn 5:26). Is the I am that I am (Ex 3:14). Is the first and the last (Isa 44:6). Is the living God (Jer 10:10). Lives forever (Dt 32:40). Needs nothing (Ac 17:24-25).

Sovereign:

(Ex 20:3; Job 25:2; 33:13; 41:11; Ps 44:4; 47:8; 59:13; 74:12; 82:1, 8; 83:18; 93:1-2; 95:3-5; 96:10; 97:1, 5, 9; 98:6; 103:19; 105:7; 113:4; 115:3, 16; 136:2-3; Isa 24:23; 33:22; 40:22-23; 43:15; 44:6; 52:7; 66:1; La 3:37; Mic 4:7, 13; Mal 1:14; Jn 10:29; 19:11; Ac 7:49; Ro 9:19; 11:36; Eph 4:6; 1Ti 6:15-16; Heb 1:3; Jas 4:12; Rev 4:11; 19:6).

Over heaven (2Ch 20:6). Over earth (Ex 9:29; Jos 3:11; Ps 24:1, 10; 47:2, 7-8; 50:10-12; Isa 54:5; Jer 10:10; 1Co 10:26). Over heaven and earth (Ge 14:18-20, 22; 24:3; Ex 19:5; Dt 4:39; 10:14, 17; Jos 2:11; 2Ki 19:15; 1Ch 29:11-12; Ne 9:6; Ps 89:11; 135:5-6; Mt 6:10; 11:25; Lk 10:21; Ac 17:24-26; Rev 11:4, 13, 17).

Over the spirits of all mankind (Nu 27:16; Dt 32:39; Job 12:9-10, 16-17; Ps 22:28-29; Ecc 9:1; Isa 45:23; Jer 18:1-23; Eze 18:4; Ro 14:11). In human affairs (Ps 75:6-7; Jer 27:5-7; 32:27-28; Eze 16:50; 17:24; Da 2:20-21, 47; 4:3, 17, 25, 34-35, 37; 5:18, 26-28).

Everlasting (Ex 15:18; Ps 10:16; 29:10; 66:7; 145:11-13; 146:10; La 5:19; Da 6:26).

Spirit:

(Jn 4:24; Ac 17:29). *See Holy Spirit.*

Teacher:

(Job 36:22; Ps 94:10, 12; 119:135, 171; Isa 28:26; 54:13; Jn 6:45; 1Th 4:9).

Truth:

(Ge 24:27; Ex 34:6; Nu 23:19; 1Sa 15:29; Ps 25:10; 31:5; 33:4; 43:3; 57:3, 10; 71:22; 86:11, 15; 89:14; 108:4; 132:11; 138:2; Isa 25:1; 65:16; Da 4:37; Jn 8:26; Ro 3:4, 7; Tit 1:2; Rev 6:10; 15:3).

Endures to all generations (Ps 117:2; 146:6).

Ubiquitous: *See above, Omnipresent.*

Unchangeable: *See above, Immutable.*

Unity of:

(Dt 4:35; 6:4; 2Sa 7:22; Isa 42:8). Taught by Jesus (Mk 12:29, 32; Jn 17:3). Taught by Paul (1Co 8:4, 6; Gal 3:20; Eph 4:6; 1Ti 2:5). Disbelieved in by Syrians (1Ki 20:28). Believed in by demons (Jas 2:19).

Unsearchable:

Dt 29:29; Job 5:8-9; 9:10; 11:7-9; 26:9, 14; 36:26; 37:5, 23; 77:19; 139:6; 145:3; Pr 30:4; Ecc 3:11; 11:5; Isa 40:28; 45:15; 55:8-9; Ro 11:33-34; 1Co 2:10-11, 16).

Symbolized by darkness (Ex 20:21; Dt 4:11; 5:22; 1Ki 8:12; Ps 18:11; 97:2). By the cloud upon the atonement cover (Lev 16:2).

Name of, secret (Jdg 13:18). Dwells in thick darkness (1Ki 8:12; Ps 97:2). Known only to Christ, and to those to whom Christ reveals him (Mt 11:27).

See Mysteries.

Voice of: *See Anthropomorphisms.*

Wisdom of:

(Ezr 7:25; Job 9:4; 12:13, 16; Isa 31:2; Da 2:20-22, 28; Ro 11:33; 16:27; 1Co 1:24-25). Infinite (Ps 147:5). Manifold (Eph 3:10). Ascribed by angels (Rev 7:12). Works made in (Ps 104:24; 136:5; Pr 3:19-20; Jer 10:12). *See above, Knowledge of.*

Works of:

In creation (Job 9:8-9; Ps 8:3-5; 89:11; 136:5-9; 139:13-14; 148:4-5; Ecc 3:11; Jer 10:12). Good (Ge 1:10, 18, 21, 25). Faithful (Ps 33:4). Wonderful (Ps 26:7; 40:5). Incomparable (Ps 86:8). In his overruling providence in the human affairs (Ps 26:7; 40:5; 66:3; 75:1; 111:2, 4, 6; 118:17; 145:4-17). *See Creation.*

GODLESSNESS [2866, 2868, *813, 815, 1013*].

Described as:

Destitute of the love of God (Jn 5:42, 44). Forgetting God (Job 8:11-13; Ps 9:17; 50:22; Isa 17:10; Jer 2:32). Ignoring God (Job 35:10; Ps 28:5; 52:7; 53:2-3; 54:3; 55:19; 86:14; Isa 5:12; 22:11; 30:1; 31:1; Hos 7:2-4). Forsaking God (Dt 32:15). Despising God (1Sa 2:30; Ps 36:1; Pr 14:2; Jn 15:23-25). Loving deceit (Isa 30:9-11). Devoid of understanding (Ps 14:2-3; 53:4; Isa 1:3; Ro 1:21-22; 3:11; Eph 4:18).

Rebellious (Ps 2:2; Isa 30:2; Da 5:23). Haters of God (Dt 7:10). Enemies of God (Col 1:21; Jas 4:4). Sinfulness (Ro 8:6-8). Impugning God's justice (Eze 33:17-20; Mal 2:17). Atheistic; rejecting God (Ps 10:4; 14:1; 53:1). Willfully sinning (Heb 10:26-27).

See Impenitence; Obduracy; Prayerlessness; Reprobacy; Unbelief; Wicked.

GODLINESS [466, 2883, *2327, 2354, 2356, 2357, 2536+2848, 2536, 2538*]. *See Holiness; Righteousness.*

GODLY *See Righteous.*

GODS [123, 337, 446, 466, 1425, 3942, 9214, 9572, 10033, *1228, 1483, 2536*]. *See Idol; Idolatry; Image.*

GOG [1573, *1223*] (*precious golden object*).
1. A Reubenite (1Ch 5:4).
2. A Scythian prince. Prophecy against (Eze 38; 39; Rev 20:8).

GOIIM [1582] (*nations, Gentiles*). A people who, led by King Tidal, along with three Eastern kings, Amraphel king of Shinar, Arioch king of Ellasar, and Kedorlaomer king of Elam, went to war against Bera king of Sodom, Birsha king of Gomorrah, Shinab king of Admah, Shemeber king of Zeboiim, and the king of Bela (that is, Zoar) (Ge 14:1-2, 9). This latter group of kings joined forces in the Valley of Siddim (the Salt Sea, which is the Dead Sea) (Ge 14:3).

The Goiim may have been non-Semitic tribes who lived to the N. They have been identified with the Hittites because of the resemblance of the name Tidal to the royal Hittite name Tudhaliash, and less reasonably to the Guti (in NE Mesopotamia). Goiim may be the generic Hebrew term for "nations." *See Goyim.*

GOLAN [1584]. A town in Bashan. Given to Manasseh as a city of refuge (Dt 4:43; Jos 20:8). A Levitical city (Jos 21:27; 1Ch 6:71). *See Gaulanitis.*

GOLD [234, 1309, 2298, 3021, 4188+, 6034, 7058, 10160, *5991, 5992, 5993, 5996*]. Exported from Havilah (Ge 2:11-12). From Ophir (1Ki 9:28; 10:11; 1Ch 29:4; 2Ch 8:18; Job 22:24), Tarshish (1Ki 22:48), Parvaim (2Ch 3:6), Sheba (1Ki 10:10; 2Ch 9:9; Ps 72:15), Uphaz (Jer 10:9).

Refined (Job 28:19; 31:24; Pr 8:19; 17:3; 27:21; Zec 13:9; Mal 3:3).

Used in the Arts:

Beaten work (2Ch 9:15), made into wire threads and wrought into embroidered tapestry (Ex 39:3), apparel (Ps 45:9, 13), in ornamenting the priests' garments (Ex 39), modeled into forms of fruits (Pr 25:11), into ornaments (Ge 24:22; Ex 3:22; 11:2; 28:11; Nu 31:50-51; SS 1:10; 5:14; Eze 16:17), crowns made of (Ex 25:25; 37:2-11; 39:30; Est 8:15; Ps 21:3; Zec 6:11), lampstands made of, for the tabernacle (Ex 25:31-38; 37:17-24), shields of (1Ki 10:16-17), overlaying with (Ex 25:11, 13, 24, 28; 26:27, 29; 30:5; 36:34, 36, 38; 37:2, 4, 11, 15; 1Ki 6:20-22; 28, 30, 32, 35), beds made of (Est 1:6). Wedge of (Jos 7:21; Isa 13:12).

Used as money (Ge 44:1, 8; 1Ch 21:25; Ezr 8:25-28; Isa 13:17; 60:9; Eze 7:19; 28:4; Mt 2:11; 10:9; Ac 3:6; 20:33; 1Pe 1:18). Solomon rich in (1Ki 10:2, 14, 21).

Vessels and utensils made of, for the tabernacle (Ex 25:26, 29, 38-39; 37:16), for the temple (1Ch 18:11; 22:14, 16; 29:2-7). Altar, lamps, and other articles made of (1Ki 7:49-51; 2Ki 25:15; Jer 52:19; Ezr 8:27; Da 5:3). *See above, Overlaying with.*

Belongs to God (Eze 16:17).

Figurative: (Ecc 12:6; Jer 51:7; La 4:1; 1Co 3:12).

Symbolic: (Da 2:32-45; Rev 21:18, 21). *See Goldsmith.*

GOLDEN CANDLESTICK *See Lampstand.*

GOLDEN RULE (Mt 7:12; Lk 6:31; also Lev 19:18; Ro 13:9; Gal 5:14). *See Love.*

GOLDSMITH [7671, 7672]. (2Ch 2:7, 14; Ne 3:8, 31-32; Isa 40:19; 41:7; 46:6).

GOLGOTHA [*1201*] (*skull*). The place of the crucifixion of Christ, located outside of Jerusalem (Mt 27:33; Mk 15:22) on the public road (Jn 19:20).

GOLIATH [1669] (*exile*). A giant champion of Gath. Defied the armies of Israel and is slain by David (1Sa 17; 21:9; 22:10). His sons (2Sa 21:15-22; 1Ch 20:4-8).

GOMER [1699, 1700] (*complete*).
1. Son of Japheth (Ge 10:2-3; 1Ch 1:5-6).
2. A people descended from Gomer (Eze 38:6).
3. Wife of Hosea (Hos 1:3).

GOMORRAH [6686, *1202*] (*to overwhelm with water*). One of the "cities of the plain" (Ge 10:19; 13:10). Its king defeated by Kedorlaomer (Ge 14:2, 8-11). Wickedness of (Ge 18:20). Destroyed (Ge 19:24-28; Dt 29:23; 32:32; Isa 1:9-10; 13:19; Jer 23:14; 49:18; 50:40; Am 4:11; Zep 2:9; Mt 10:14-15; Mk 6:11; Lk 9:5; Ro 9:29; 2Pe 2:6; Jude 7). *See Cities of the Plain.*

GONORRHEA Possibly among the bodily discharges of Lev 15. *See Discharge, Bodily; Disease.*

GOOD AND EVIL [*1413, 1415, 1694, 3202, 3206, 3208, 3512, 3603, 6694, 8273, 8934, 9459, *19, 16, 20, 604, 746, 2294, 2295, 2306, 2819, 2822, 3421, 4055, 5237, 5239, 5982, 6067*; See also EVIL*]. Choice between, by Adam and Eve (Ge 3). Exhortation to choose between (Jos 24:15). Conflict between (Rev 16:13-21). Subjective conflict between (Ro 7:9-25).

GOOD FOR EVIL Injunctions by Christ concerning (Mt 5:44-48; Lk 6:27-36).

Instances of: Abraham, to Abimelech (Ge 20:14-18). David, to Saul (1Sa 24:17; 26), to his enemies (Ps 35:12-14). Elisha, to the Syrians (2Ki 6:22-23). Jesus, to his crucifiers (Lk 23:34). Stephen (Ac 7:60).

See Golden Rule; Evil for Good; Nonresistance.

GOOD NEWS [1413, 1415, 2294, 2295]. (Pr 15:30; 25:25). *See Gospel.*

GOPHER WOOD *See Cypress Wood.*

GOSHEN [824+1777, 1777] (*mound of earth*).

1. A district in Egypt especially adapted to herds and flocks. Israelites dwelt in (Ge 45:10; 46:28; 47). Exempted from plagues (Ex 8:22; 9:26).

2. A town and district of Judah (Jos 10:41; 11:16; 15:51).

GOSPEL [2294, 2295, 4603] (*good news*).

From God (Jn 17:7-8, 14; 2Th 2:14). Contrasted with the law (Jn 1:16-17; Ac 12:24; 19:20; 2Co 3:6-11). Called the New Covenant (Jer 31:31-34; Heb 7:22; 8:6-13; 9:8-15; 10:9; 12:22-24).

Described as:

Dispensation of grace (Eph 3:2). Doctrine according to godliness (1Ti 6:3). Everlasting gospel or eternal good tidings (Rev 14:6). The faith (Jude 3). Glorious gospel (1Ti 1:11). Pattern of sound teaching (2Ti 1:13). Gospel of the glory of Christ (2Co 4:4). Good tidings or good news (Isa 40:9; 41:27; 52:7; 61:1; Mt 11:5; Lk 7:22; Ac 13:32-33; 1Pe 1:25). Gospel, of Christ (Ro 1:16; 1Co 9:12, 18; Gal 1:7; Php 1:27; 1Th 3:2), of God (Ro 1:1; 15:16; 1Th 2:8; 1Pe 4:17), of grace of God (Ac 20:24), of Jesus Christ (Mk 1:1), of the kingdom (Mt 4:23; 24:14), of peace (Eph 6:15), of salvation (Eph 1:13).

The kingdom of God (Lk 16:16). The law of liberty (Jas 1:25). Ministration of the Spirit (2Co 3:8). Mystery, of Christ (Eph 3:4), of the gospel (Eph 6:19). Power of God (Ro 1:16; 1Co 1:18). Preaching of Jesus Christ (Ro 16:25). Word of Christ (Col 3:16), of faith (Ro 10:8), of God (1Th 2:13; 1Pe 1:23), of life (Php 2:16), of the Lord (1Pe 1:25), of reconciliation (2Co 5:19), of salvation (Ac 13:26), of truth (Eph 1:13). Words of this life (Ac 5:20).

Likened to:

A mustard seed (Mt 13:31-32; Mk 4:30-33; Lk 13:18-19), good seed (Mt 13:24-30, 36-43), yeast (Mt 13:33), a pearl of great price (Mt 13:45-46; Lk 13:20-21), a treasure hidden in a field (Mt 13:44), a householder (Mt 20:1-16), a feast (Lk 14:16-24).

Dissemination of (Ac 14:3; 16:17; 20:24), commanded (Mt 24:14; 28:18-20; Mk 13:10; 16:15; Ac 5:20; Ro 10:15-18; 16:25-26; 1Co 1:18, 21, 24-25; 9:16-18; Eph 3:8-11). Desired by prophets, righteous, kings (Mt 13:17; Lk 23:34). Hid from the lost (2Co 4:3-4). Comes in power, word, assurance (1Th 1:5).

Proclaimed to Abraham (Gal 3:8), by angels (Lk 2:10-11; Rev 14:6). Preached by Jesus (Mt 4:23; Mk 1:14-15), by Peter (Ac 10:36), by Paul (Ac 13:32-33; 20:24; Ro 15:29; 1Co 9:16-18; Gal 2:2; Col 1:5-6, 23), to the Gentiles (Gal 2:2; Eph 3:8; Col 1:23, 26-29), to both Jews and Gentiles (Ro 1:16; 1Co 1:24), to the poor (Mt 11:4-6; Lk 7:22), to the dead (1Pe 3:19; 4:6), to every nation (Lk 2:10-11; Ro 16:26; Rev 14:6).

Life and immortality brought to light in (2Ti 1:10). Salvation through (Ro 1:16-17; 1Co 15:1-2; Eph 1:13-14; Jas 1:21; 1Pe 1:23).

Prophecies concerning:

(Isa 2:3-5; 4:2-6; 9:2, 6-7; 25:7-9; 29:18, 24; 32:3-4; 35:5-10; 40:9; 41:27; 42:6-7; 46:13; 49:13; 51:4-6; 52:7; 55:1-5; 60:1-22; 61:1-3; Jer 31:31-34; Eze 34:23-31; 47:1-12; Joel 2:28-32; Mic 4:1-7; Mt 24:14; Lk 1:67-79; 2:12-14, 34). Fulfilled by Christ (Lk 4:18-19).

See Church, The Body of Believers, Prophecies Concerning; Jesus the Christ, Kingdom of; Mission of; Kingdom of God, of Heaven; Synoptic Gospels, The.

GOSSIP [2143+8215, 8087, 5826, 5827, 6030, 6031]. Proverbs concerning (Pr 11:13; 16:28; 17:9; 26:20).

Forbidden (Lev 19:16; Ps 50:20; Pr 11:3; 20:19; Eze 22:9).

See Slander; Speaking, Evil; Talebearer.

GOURD [7225, 7226]. Carvings of decorated the temple (1Ki 6:18) and its cast metal Sea (1Ki 7:24). Elisha purifies stew made with poisonous gourds (2Ki 4:38-41).

GOUT Perhaps Asa's disease in the feet (2Ch 16:12). *See Disease.*

GOVERNMENT [5385, 6269, 10424]. Paternal functions of (Ge 41:25-57). Civil service school provided by (Da 1:3-20). Maintains a system of public instruction (2Ch 17:7-9).

Constitutional:

It was provided in the law of Moses that in the event of the establishment of a monarchy a copy of the law of Moses should be made and the king should be required to study this law all the days of his life and conform his administration to it (Dt 17:18-20). This constituted the fundamental law and had its likeness to the constitution of modern governments. When David was crowned king of all Israel he made a league in the nature of a constitution which was a basis of good understanding between himself and the people (2Sa 5:3). When Joash was enthroned a covenant was made between him and the people (2Ch 23:3, 11). This no doubt refers to the law of Moses (Dt 17:18-20), which had been preserved by Jehoiada, the priest. Zedekiah made a covenant with the people proclaiming liberty (Jer 34:8-11). That the king of the Medes and Persians was restricted by a constitution "which cannot be annulled," is evident from Da 6:12-15.

See Constitution; Israel, Israelites; Judge; Kings; Nation.

Corruption in: (1Ki 21:5-13; Pr 25:5; Mic 3:1-4, 9-11).

Instances of Corruption in: Pilate, in delivering Jesus to death to please the noisy crowd (Mt 27:24; Jn 19:12-16). Felix, who hoped for money from Paul (Ac 24:26).

See Court, Of Law, Corrupt; Church, The Body of Believers, Evil Conditions of; Corrupt; Rulers, Wicked.

Duty of Citizens to:

To pay taxes (Mt 22:17-21; Lk 20:22-25). To render obedience to civil authority (Ro 13:1-7; Tit 3:1; 1Pe 2:13-17).

God in:

(2Ch 22:7; Jer 18:6; Eze 21:25-27; 29:19-20). In appointment of Saul as king (1Sa 9:15-17; 10:1). In Saul's rejection (1Sa 15:26-28; Ac 13:22). In appointment of David (1Sa 16:1, 7, 13; 2Sa 7:13-16; Ps 89:19-37; Ac 13:22), of Solomon (1Ki 2:13-15). In counseling Solomon (1Ki 9:2-9). In magnifying Solomon (1Ch 29:25). In reproving Solomon's wickedness (1Ki 11:9-13). In raising adversaries against Solomon (1Ki 11:14, 23). In tearing the nation of Israel in two (1Ki 11:13; 12:1-24; 2Ch 10:15; 11:4). In blotting out the house of Jeroboam (1Ki 14:7-16; 15:27-30). In appointment of kings (1Ki 14:14; 16:1-2; 1Ch 28:4-5; Da 2:20-21, 37; 4:17; 5:18-23). In destruction of nations (Jer 25:12-17; Am 9:8; Hag 2:22).

Relation of God to: (Ps 22:28; Pr 8:15-16; Isa 9:6-7; Jer 1:9-10; 18:6-10; 25:12-17; Eze 21:25-27; 29:19-20; Da 2:20-21, 37; 4:17; 5:18-28; 10:13; Hos 8:4; Am 9:8; Hag 2:21-22; Jn 19:10-11).

See God, Sovereign; Jesus the Christ, Kingdom of.

Mosaic:

Administrative and judicial system (Ex 18:13-26; Nu 11:16-17, 24-25; Dt 1:9-17).

Popular Government, by a National Assembly, or Its Representatives—

Accepted the law given by Moses (Ex 19:7-8; 24:3, 7; Dt 29:10-15). Refused to make conquest of Canaan (Nu 14:1-10). Chose, or ratified, the chief ruler (1Sa 10:24; 8:4-22; 11:14-15; 2Sa 3:17-21; 5:1-3; 1Ch 29:22; 2Ch 23:3). Possessed veto power over king's purposes (1Sa 14:44-45). Constituted the court in certain capital cases (Nu 35:12, 24-25).

Delegated, Council of Elders—

Closely associated with Moses and subsequent leaders (Ex 3:16, 18; 4:29-31; 12:21; 17:5-6; 18:12; 19:7-8; 24:1, 14; Lev 4:15; 9:1; Nu 11:16-17, 30; 16:25; Dt 1:13-15; 5:23; 27:1; 29:10-15; 31:9, 28; Jos 7:6; 8:10, 32-33; 23:2-3, 6; 24:1, 24-25; Jdg 21:16-25; Ac 5:17-18, 21-41).

Miscellaneous Facts Relating to the Council—

Demands a king (1Sa 8:4-10, 19-22). Saul pleads to be honored before (1Sa 15:30). Chooses David as king (2Sa 5:3; 1Ch 11:3). Closely associated with David (2Sa 12:17; 1Ch 15:25; 21:16). Joins Absalom in his usurpation (2Sa 17:4). David rebukes (2Sa 19:11). Assists Solomon at the dedication of the temple (1Ki 8:1-3; 2Ch 5:2-4). Counsels King Rehoboam (1Ki 12:6-8, 13). Counsels King Ahab (1Ki 20:7-8). Josiah assembles, to hear the law of the Lord (2Ki 23:1; 2Ch 34:29-30).

Legislates with Ezra in reforming certain marriages with the heathen (Ezr 9:1; 10:8-14). Legislates in later times (Mt 15:2, 7-9; Mk 7:1-13). Sits as a court (Jer 26:10-24). Constitutes, with priests

and scribes, a court for the trial of both civil and ecclesiastical causes (Mt 21:23; 26:3-5, 57-68; 27:1-2; Mk 8:31; 14:43, 53-65; 15:1; Lk 22:52-54, 66-71; Ac 4:1-21; 6:9-15). Unfaithful to the city (La 1:19). Seeks counsel from prophets (Eze 8:1; 14:1; 20:1, 3). Corrupt (1Ki 21:8-14; Eze 8:11-12; Mt 26:14-15, w Mt 27:3-4).

A similar council existed among the Egyptians (Ge 50:7) and among the Midianites and Moabites (Nu 22:4, 7, and Gibeonites (Jos 9:11).

Executive officers of tribes and cities, called princes or nobles, members of the national assembly (Nu 1:4-16, 44; 7:2-3, 10-11, 18, 24, 54, 84; 10:4; 16:2; 17:2, 6; 27:2; 31:13-14; 32:2; 34:18-29; 36:1; Jos 9:15-21; 17:4; 22:13-32; 1Ki 21:11-14; Ne 3:9, 12, 16, 18-19).

The Mosaic judicial system. *See Court, Of Law; Judge; Levites; Priest; Rulers; Sanhedrin; Synagogue.*

Ecclesiastical: *See Church, The Body of Believers, Government of; Church, The Body of Believers, State; Priest.*

Imperial: (Ge 14:1; Jos 11:10; 1Ki 4:21; Est 1:1; Da 4:1; 6:1-3; Lk 2:1).

Monarchical:

Tyranny in: By Pharaoh (Ex 1:8-22; 2:23-24; 3:7; 5:1-10). By Saul (1Sa 22:6, 12-19). By David (2Sa 11:14-17). By Solomon (1Ki 2:23-25, 28-34, 36-46). By Rehoboam (1Ki 12:1-16). By Ahab and Jezebel (1Ki 21:7-16). By Jehu (2Ki 10:1-14). By Xerxes (Est 1:11-12, 19-22; 3:6-15; 8:8-13). By Nebuchadnezzar (Da 1:10; 2:5-13; 5:19). By Herod (Mk 6:27-28).

Municipal:

Based on a local council and executive officers (Dt 19:12; 21:2-8, 18-21; 22:13-21; 25:7-9; Jos 20:4; Jdg 8:14-16; 11:5-11; Ru 4:2-11; 1Sa 11:3; 16:4; 30:26; 1Ki 21:8-14; 2Ki 10:1-7; Ezr 10:8, 14; Ne 3:9, 12, 16, 18-19; La 5:14).

Patriarchal: (Ge 27:29, 37).

Provincial:

(Ezr 4:8-9; 5:3, 6; 6:6; 8:36; Ne 2:7, 9; 5:14; Da 6:1-3; Mt 27:2; 28:14; Lk 2:2; 3:1; Ac 24:1).

Representative:

(Dt 1:13-15; Jos 9:11). *See above, Delegated, Council of Elders.*

Theocratic:

(Ex 19:3-8; Dt 26:16-19; 29:1-13; Jdg 8:23; 1Sa 8:6-7; 10:19; 12:12; Isa 33:22).

See God, Sovereign; Jesus the Christ, Kingdom of.

GOVERNOR [5893, 5907, 7068, 7212, 7213, 8569, 8954, 9579, 10580, *1617, 2448, 2450*]. A provincial or city ruler (1Ki 4:7; 10:15; Ezr 2:63; Jn 18:28). Joseph (Ge 42:6), Zebul (Jdg 9:30), Gedaliah (2Ki 25:23). Tattenai (Ezr 5:3, 6). Sheshbazzar (Ezr 5:14). Nehemiah (Ne 7:65, 70; 8:9; 10:1; 12:26).

GOYIM [1582] (*nations, Gentiles*). A people, where the king of Goyim in Gilgal, was among

those defeated by Joshua (Jos 12:23). Goyim may be the generic Hebrew word for "nations." *See Goiim.*

GOZAN [1579]. A city in NE Mesopotamia on the Habor River, to which the Israelites were deported by the Assyrians (2Ki 17:6; 18:11; 19:12; 1Ch 5:26).

GRACE [2834, 2858, 2876, *5919, 5921*]. A term employed by the Biblical writers with a wide variety of meaning: charm, sweetness, loveliness (Ps 45:2), the attitude of God toward men (Tit 2:11), the method of salvation (Eph 2:5), the opposite of legalism (Gal 5:4), the impartation of spiritual power or gifts (1Co 2:6; 2Ti 2:1), the liberty which God gives to men (Jude 4).

Before meals. *See Prayer, Thanksgiving, and Before Taking Food.*

GRACE OF GOD [2834, 2858, 2876, *5919, 5921*]. Unmerited favor (Dt 7:7-8; 2Ch 30:9; Eph 1:6; Tit 2:11; Heb 4:16). Abundant (1Ti 1:14). Divine help (Ge 20:6; Job 10:12; Ps 84:11; 94:17-19; 138:3; 1Co 1:12; 12:9; 1Pe 1:5).

Growth in (Ps 84:7; Pr 4:18; Php 1:6, 9-11; 3:12-15; Col 1:10-11; 2:19; 1Th 3:10, 12-13; 2Th 1:3; Heb 6:1-3; 1Pe 2:1-3; 2Pe 3:18). Believers to be stewards of (1Pe 4:10). Intercessory prayer for (Ps 143:11; Da 9:18; Jn 17:11-12, 15; 1Th 1:1; 5:28; 2Pe 1:2). No warrant for sinful indulgence (Ro 6:1, 15). Exhortation against rejecting (2Co 6:1-2). With respect to Jacob and Esau (Ro 9:10-16).

Manifested:
In drawing people to Christ (Jn 6:44-45). In redemption (Eph 1:5-9, 11-12). In justification (Ge 15:6; Ro 3:22-24; 4:4-5, 16; 5:2, 6-8, 15-21; Tit 3:7). In passing over transgressions (Nu 23:20-21; Ne 9:17; Ro 3:25). In salvation (Ro 11:5-6; Eph 2:8-9; 2Ti 1:9). In calling to service (Gal 1:15-16). In spiritual growth (Eph 3:16). In spiritual gifts (1Co 1:4-8; Eph 4:7, 11).

In the character and conduct of the righteous (1Co 15:10; 2Co 1:12; Php 2:13). In sustaining the righteous (1Ch 17:8; Da 10:18-19; 2Co 12:9; 1Pe 1:5; 5:10; Jude 24). In sustaining temptation (Ge 20:6; 1Co 10:13; Rev 3:10).

Manifested to:
Enoch (Ge 5:24). Noah (Ge 6:8, 17-18). Abraham (Ge 12:2; 21:22). Ishmael (Ge 21:20). Isaac (Ge 26:24). Jacob (Ge 46:3-4; 48:16). Joseph (Ge 39:2-3, 23). Moses (Ex 3:12; 33:12-17). Israel (Dt 4:7). Naphtali (Dt 33:23). Joshua (Jos 1:5, 9). Job (Job 10:12). David (1Sa 25:26, 34; 2Sa 7:8-16). Daniel (Da 10:18-19). Jeremiah (Jer 15:20). The righteous (Ps 5:12; Ac 4:33).

See God, Grace of.

GRACES Christian (Mt 5:3-11; Ro 5:3-5; 1Co 13:1-8, 13; Gal 5:22-23; 1Pe 1:5-9).

See Beatitudes; Character; Charitableness; Courage; Gentleness; Hope; Kindness; Knowledge; Longsuffering; Love; Meekness; *Mercy; Patience; Peace; Perseverance; Purity; Righteousness, Fruits of; Stability; Temperance; Wisdom.*

GRAFT [*1596*]. A horticultural process by which the branches of a cultivated tree may be inserted into the trunk of a wild tree. Figurative of Gentiles partaking of Israel's covenants and blessings (Ro 11:17ff.).

GRAIN [*1339, 1841, 1889, 2446, 2567, 4152, 4966, 6658, 6894, 7833, 7850, 8195, 8672, 8690, 8692, *262, 2843, 4992, 5092*]. In valleys (Ps 65:13; Mk 4:28). A product of Egypt (Ge 41:47-49), Israel (Dt 33:28; Eze 27:17). Roasted (Ru 2:14; 1Sa 17:17; 25:18; 2Sa 17:28). Ground (2Sa 17:19). Eaten by the Israelites (Jos 5:11-12). Shocks of, burnt (Jdg 15:5). Mosaic laws concerning (Ex 22:6; Dt 23:25).

Individual heads of grain (Ge 41:5-7, 22-27; Lev 23:14; Ru 2:2; Job 24:24; Isa 17:5; Mk 4:26-29). Grain that is ripe but soft, which is roasted and eaten (Lev 2:14). The poor may pick what they can eat on the spot; refers to grain rubbed between the hands (Dt 23:25). Picked by Christ's disciples (Mt 12:1; Mk 2:23; Lk 6:1). Newly ripened heads of grain (2Ki 4:42).

Figurative: (Ps 72:16; Hos 14:7; Jn 12:24).

Symbolic: (Ge 41:5).

See Barley; Barn; Bread; Firstfruits; Glean, Gleaning; Harvest; Plants of the Bible; Reaping; Rye; Threshing; Tithes; Wheat.

GRANARY [4393, 4852, 4923]. A storehouse for grain and other dry crops (Ex 22:29; Jer 50:26; Joel 1:17).

See Barn; Storehouse.

GRANDFATHER [3]. Called Father (Ge 10:21).

GRAPE [112, 864, 1235, 1292, 1305, 3292, 4142, 6622, 6694, 7261, 8097, 9408, *306, 1084, 2843, 5091*]. Cultivated in vineyards, by Noah (Ge 9:20), Canaanites (Nu 13:24; Dt 6:11; Jos 24:13), Edomites (Nu 20:17), Amorites (Nu 21:22; Isa 16:8-9), Philistines (Jdg 15:5). Grown, at Baal Hamon (SS 8:11), Carmel (2Ch 26:10), En Gedi (SS 1:14), Jezreel (1Ki 21:1), Lebanon (Hos 14:7), Samaria (Jer 31:5), Shechem (Jdg 9:27), Shiloh (Jdg 21:20-21), Timnath (Jdg 14:5).

Culture of (Lev 25:3, 11; Dt 28:39; 2Ch 26:10; SS 6:11; Isa 5:1; Jer 31:5).

Wine made of (Jer 25:30). Wine of, forbidden to Nazirites (Nu 6:4). *See Nazirite(s).*

See Vine; Vineyards; Wine.

Figurative (Dt 32:32; Ps 128:3; Jer 2:21; Eze 15; Hos 10:1; Rev 14:18-20).

Fable of (Jdg 9:12-13). Parables of the vine (Ps 80:8-14; Eze 17:6-10; 19:10-14; Jn 15:1-5). Proverb of (Eze 18:2).

See Vine; Vineyards; Wine.

GRASS [2013+4604, 2013, 2945, 3143, 3764, 6912, 10187, 10572, *5965*]. Created on the

third creative day (Ge 1:11). Mown (Ps 72:6). God's care of (Mt 6:30; Lk 12:28). On roofs of houses (Ps 129:6).

Figurative (Ps 90:5-6; Isa 40:6; 1Pe 1:24; Jas 1:10-11).

GRASSHOPPER [2506, 2885, 3540].
(Nu 13:33; Ecc 12:5; Isa 40:22; Na 3:17).

See Locust.

GRATE [4803]. A copper network, placed under the top of the great altar, to hold the sacrifice while burning (Ex 27:4; 35:16; 38:4-5).

GRATITUDE [2373, 2374, 5921]. *See Thankfulness.*

GRAVE [3243, 7690, 7700, 8619, 8827, 87, 3646, 5439]. Prepared by Jacob (Ge 50:5). Defilement from touching (Nu 19:16, 18). Weeping at (2Sa 3:32; Jn 11:31; 20:11). Of parents, honored (2Sa 19:37). Welcomed (Job 3:20-22).

Resurrection From:

Of Lazarus (Jn 11:43-44; 12:17), of Jesus (Mt 28:5-6; 1Co 15:12-20), of believers after Jesus' resurrection (Mt 27:52-53), of all the dead foretold (Jn 5:28; 1Co 15:22-54).

See Burial; Sheol; Tomb.

GRAVE CLOTHES Preparatory to burial, the body was washed and anointed with spices, then wrapped in a winding sheet, bound with strips of cloth, and the head wrapped in a square cloth (Jn 11:44; 19:40).

GRAVEL [2953]. Figurative of food gained by fraud (Pr 20:17), of judgment (La 3:16).

GRAVEN IMAGE NIV "carved image" or "idol" of wood, stone, or metal (Dt 7:5; Isa 44:9-17; 45:20). *See Carving; Groves; High Places; Iconoclasm; Idol; Idolatry.*

GRAVING *See Engraving.*

GREAT OWL *See Birds.*

GREAT SEA *See Mediterranean Sea.*

GREATER SIDON *See Sidon.*

GREATNESS [1525, 1540, 1542, 5270, 8044, 10650, 3484, 5660]. Of God (Dt 3:24; Ps 77:13; 95:3; 104:1; 135:5; 145:3; Isa 12:6; Jer 32:18; Mal 1:11). Of Christ (Isa 53:12; 63:1; Mt 12:6; Lk 11:31; Php 2:9-10).

GREAVES [5196]. Leg armor worn below the knee (1Sa 17:6).

GREECE [3430, 1817]. Inhabitants of, called Gentiles (Mk 7:26; Jn 7:35; Ro 2:10; 3:9; 1Co 10:32; 12:13), desire to see Jesus (Jn 12:20-23), marry among the Jews (Ac 16:1), accept the Messiah (Ac 17:2-4, 12, 34), persecute the early Christians (Ac 6:9-14; 9:29; 18:17). Gentiles called Greeks (Ro 10:12; Gal 3:28; Col 3:11).

Schools of philosophy in Athens (Ac 19:9). Philosophy of (1Co 1:22-23). Poets of (Ac 17:28).

See Asceticism; Athens; Epicureans; Stoicism; Stoics.

GREED [1298, 1299, 5883, 8143, *154, 771, 4431, 4432*].

Described:

Greed is idolatry (Col 3:5). Insatiable (Pr 1:19; 21:26; Ecc 1:8; 4:8; 5:10-11; Isa 56:11). Root of evil (1Ti 6:9-11). Tends to poverty (Pr 11:24, 26; 22:16). Gains of, unstable (Job 20:15; Pr 23:4-6; Jer 17:11). Disqualifies from sacred office (Ex 18:21; 1Ti 3:3; Tit 1:7, 11; 1Pe 5:2). Disqualifies from kingdom of God (Mt 19:23-24; 22:25; Lk 18:24-25; 1Co 6:10; Eph 5:3, 5; Php 3:18-19). Denounced (Ps 10:3; Pr 1:19; Isa 5:8; Jude 11).

Forbidden:

Warnings against (Dt 15:9-10; Pr 1:19; 15:27; Hos 4:18; Hab 2:5-9; Mt 6:19-21, 24-25, 31-33; 13:22; 16:26; Mk 4:19; 7:21-23; Lk 8:14; 12:16-21; Jn 6:26-27; 1Co 5:11; 1Th 2:5; 1Ti 6:5-8; 2Ti 3:2, 5; Heb 13:5; Jas 4:2; 1Jn 2:15-17). Commandments against (Ex 20:17; Dt 5:21; Ro 13:9; Col 3:2; 1Ti 3:8). Prayer against (Ps 119:36).

Reproof for (Ne 5:7; Isa 1:23; Jer 6:13; 22:17; Eze 33:31; Hos 10:1; Mic 2:2; 3:11; 7:3; Hag 1:6; Ro 1:29). Punishment for (Ex 18:21; Job 31:24-25, 28; Isa 57:17; Jer 8:10; 51:13; Eze 22:12-13; Col 3:5-6; 2Pe 2:3, 14-17).

See Avarice; Greed; Rich, The; Riches; Worldliness.

Instances of:

Eve, in desiring the forbidden fruit (Ge 3:6). Lot, in choosing the plain of the Jordan (Ge 13:10-13). Laban, in giving Rebekah to be Isaac's wife (Ge 24:29-51), in deceiving Jacob when he served him seven years for Rachel (Ge 29:15-30), in deceiving Jacob in wages (Ge 31:7, 15, 41-42). Jacob, in defrauding Esau of his father's blessing (Ge 27:6-29), in defrauding Laban of his flocks and herds (Ge 30:35-43), in buying Esau's birthright (Ge 25:31). Balaam, in loving the wages of unrighteousness (2Pe 2:15, w Nu 22).

Achan, in hiding the treasure (Jos 7:21). Eli's sons, in taking the flesh of the sacrifice (1Sa 2:13-17). Samuel's sons, in taking bribes (1Sa 8:3). Saul, in sparing Agag and the booty (1Sa 15:8-9). David, in desiring Bathsheba (2Sa 11:2-5). Ahab, in desiring Naboth's vineyard (1Ki 21:2-16). Gehazi, in taking a gift from Naaman (2Ki 5:20-27). Israelites, in exacting usury of their brothers (Ne 5:1-11), in keeping back the portion of the Levites (Ne 13:10), in building fine houses while the house of the Lord lay waste (Hag 1:4-9), in following Jesus for the loaves and fishes (Jn 6:26).

Money changers in the temple (Mt 21:12-13; Lk 19:45-46; Jn 2:14-16). The rich young ruler (Mt 19:16-22). The rich fool (Lk 12:15-21). Judas, in betraying Jesus for thirty pieces of silver (Mt 26:15-16; Mk 14:10-11; Lk 22:3-6; Jn 12:6). The unjust steward (Lk 16:1-8). The Pharisees (Lk 16:14).

Simon Magus, in trying to buy the gift of the Holy Spirit (Ac 8:18-23). The sorcerers, in filing complaint against Paul and Silas (Ac 16:19). Demetrius, in raising a riot against Paul and Silas (Ac 19:24, 27). Felix, in hoping for a bribe from Paul (Ac 24:26). Demas, in forsaking Paul for love of the world (2Ti 4:10).

See Avarice; Bribery; Covetousness; Rich, The; Riches.

GREEK LANGUAGE Was a branch of

the Indo-European family from which most of the languages of Europe are descended. The Attic dialect spoken in Athens and its colonies on the Ionian coast was combined with other dialects in the army of Alexander the Great and was spread by his conquests through the East. A kind of "Jewish Greek," influenced by semitic thought and culture, was widely spoken in Israel and became the chief language of the early church (Ac 21:37).

GREEK VERSIONS   There   were

several early translations of the Hebrew OT into Greek. Some of the major versions were:

1. The Septuagint, originating in Alexandria in the third and second centuries B.C.. This was the Bible of the early church.

2. The version of Aquila in the early second century A.D. 125) was a word-for-word rendering of the Hebrew produced for the Jewish people when Christians took over the Septuagint.

3. The version of Theodotion, a late second-century revision of the Septuagint.

4. The version of Symmachus, an idiomatic translation probably of the second century.

GREETINGS [606, 1385, 7925, 8626, 8934, 10147, 10720, *832, 833, 5897*]. Antiquity of (Ge 18:2; 19:1).

Given:

By brothers to each other (1Sa 17:22). By inferiors to their superiors (Ge 47:7). By superiors to inferiors (1Sa 30:21). By all passersby (1Sa 10:3-4; Ps 129:8). On entering a house (Jdg 18:15; Mt 10:12; Lk 1:40-41, 44). Often sent through messengers (1Sa 25:5, 14; 2Sa 8:10). Often sent by letter (Ro 16:21-23; 1Co 16:21; Col 4:18; 2Th 3:17). Denied to persons of bad character (2Jn 10). Persons in haste excused from giving or receiving (2Ki 4:29; Lk 10:24).

Expressions Used as:

"You are welcome at my house" (Jdg 19:20).

"Long life to you! Good health to you and your household! And good health to all that is yours" (1Sa 25:6).

"Peace to this house" (Lk 10:5).

"The LORD be with you! The LORD bless you!" (Ru 2:4).

"The blessing of the LORD be upon you; we bless you in the name of the LORD" (Ps 129:8).

"The LORD bless you! I have carried out the [LORD's] instructions" (1Sa 15:13).

"God be gracious to you my son" (Ge 43:29).

"How are you, my brother?" (2Sa 20:9).

"Greetings, Rabbi!" (Mt 26:49).

"Greetings, you who are highly favored! The Lord is with you" (Lk 1:28).

"Greetings" (Mt 28:9).

Sometimes insincere (2Sa 20:9; Mt 26:49). Given to Christ in derision (Mt 27:29, w Mk 15:18).

Often Accompanied by:

Embracing and kissing (Ge 33:4; 45:14-15; Lk 15:20). Taking hold of the beard with the right hand (2Sa 20:9). Bowing frequently to the ground (Ge 33:3). Embracing and kissing the feet (Mt 28:9; Lk 7:38, 45). Touching the hem of the garment (Mt 14:36). Falling prostrate on the ground (Est 8:3; Mt 2:11; Lk 8:41). Kissing the dust (Ps 72:9; Isa 49:23). The Jews are condemned for giving only to their own countrymen (Mt 5:47). The Pharisees condemned for seeking, in public (Mt 23:7; Mk 12:38).

GREYHOUND NIV "strutting rooster" (Pr 30:31). *See Animals.*

GRIEF [*61, 63, 3324, 4088, 5352, 5714, 6772, 9342, *3382, 3383, 4291*]. Attributed to the Holy Spirit (Eph 4:30; Heb 3:10, 17).

See Affliction; Sorrow.

GRIND [1990, 3221, 3222, 4197, 8835, *241*]. To pulverize grain between two millstones (Mt 24:41; Lk 17:35). *See Mill; Millstone.*

GROUND [*141, 824, 1990, 2750, 2754, 3000, 3317, 4793, 5776, 6641, 6760, 6881, 7536, 8187, 8441, 10075, *1178, 4838, 5912*]. Man made from (Ge 2:7; 3:19, 23; Job 4:19; 33:6). Animals from (Ge 2:19). Vegetables from (Ge 2:9).

Cursed (Ge 3:17; 5:29).

GROVES [1708, 2339, 3623, *3057*].

1. Groups of fruit trees (Dt 6:11; Ecc 2:6). *See Tree.*

2. NIV "Asherah [poles]"; an image of the Canaanite goddess Asherah. *See Asherah, 2; High Places; Idolatry.*

GROWTH *See Conformity; Discipleship; Grace of God, Growth in; Holiness; Sanctification.*

GRUMBLING [4296, 8087, 9442, *1197, 1198, 1199, 5100*].

Condemned:

Forbidden (1Co 10:10; Php 2:14*; Jas 5:9*). Rebuked (Job 15:11-13*; Ecc 7:10*; La 3:39*; Ro 9:19-20*). Punishment for (Nu 14:26-37*; 17:10-11). Foolish (Pr 19:3*).

Against God:

Cain (Ge 4:13-14). Moses (Ex 5:22-23*; Nu 11:11-15). Israelites (Ex 16:8*, 12*; 17:2-3; Nu 11:1-10; 14; 16:41; 20:2-5; 21:5-6; Dt 1:26-28; Ps 44:9-26*; 106:24-26; Mal 3:14*). Korah (Nu 16:8-11). Job (Job 3; 6; 7; 9:10; 13; 16:6-14; 19:7-20; 30; 33:12-13*). David (2Sa 6:8; Ps 116:10-

11). The psalmist (Ps 73:13-22*). Elijah (1Ki 19:4, 10). Jonah (Jnh 4). Jews, against Jesus (Jn 6:41-43, 52).

Against Moses:

By the Israelites (Ex 5:21; 14:11-12; 15:24; 16:2-3; 17:2-3; Nu 14; 16:2-3, 14, 41; 20:2-5).

Against Others:

Rachel (Ge 30:1). Asaph (Ps 73:3). Solomon (Ecc 2:17-18). Hezekiah (Isa 38:10-18). Jeremiah (Jer 20:14-18; La 3). Martha (Lk 10:40*). Prodigal's brother (Lk 15:29-30).

See Doubt; Envy; Ingratitude; also Contentment; Resignation.

GUARD [*665, 1475, 2741, 3184, 4766, 4915, 5464, 5466, 5915, 6114, 7213, 7215, 8132, 9068, 9193, 1063, 1213, 3184, 4668, 5130, 5498, 5498, 5677, 5864, 5871, 5874, 5875].
Imperial guard (Ge 37:36; 2Ki 25:8; Da 2:14), runner, trusted messengers of a king (1Ki 14:27-28), bodyguard (2Sa 23:23), executioner (Mk 6:27), Roman guard (Mt 27:65).

GUDGODAH [1516] (*cleft*).
A station of the Israelites in the wilderness (Dt 10:7), probably identical with Hor Haggidgad (Nu 33:32-33).

GUEST [448+995+1074, 6639, 7924, 9369, 367, 2813, 2906, 2907, 3825, 3826, 5263, 5626].
Greetings to (Ge 18:2). Abraham's hospitality to. *See Hospitality.*

Rules for the conduct of (Pr 23:1-3, 6-8; 25:6-7, 17; Lk 10:5-7; 14:7-11; 1Co 10:27). *See Hospitality.*

GUEST ROOM [2906, 3825].
According to Jewish custom an extra or upper room was offered to those who had come to Jerusalem to celebrate the Passover (Mk 14:14; Lk 22:11).

GUIDANCE *See God, Guidance of.*

GUILE *See Conspiracy; Deceit; Hypocrisy.*

GUILELESSNESS
Truthfulness; without deceit. Commanded (Ps 34:13; 1Pe 2:1; 3:10). Of Jesus (1Pe 2:22). Of Nathanael (Jn 1:47). A grace of the righteous (Ps 32:2). *See Truthfulness.*

GUILT [870, 871, 873, 1947, 2628, 2631, 5927, 5929, 6404, 6411, 7322, 281, 1794].
The deserving of punishment because of infraction of a law. Guilt could be the result of unconscious sin (Lev 5:17) or could be incurred by the group for the sin of an individual (Jos 7:10-15). There are degrees of guilt (Lk 12:47-48; Ac 17:30), but in the sight of God all people are guilty of sin (Ro 3:19).

See Conviction, of Sin.

GUILT OFFERING [871, 873].
Sacrifice of a ram for the purpose of expiation of sins against others; in addition to the sacrifice, restitution had to be made (Lev 5:16-19; 6:5-18; 7:1-10; Nu 5:7-8). Of the Servant's self-sacrifice (Isa 53:10 w Mt 20:28; Mk 10:45). *See Offerings.*

GULL [8830].
A bird. Forbidden as food (Lev 11:16; Dt 14:15).

GUM RESIN [5753].
Fragrant ingredient used in incense (Ex 30:34). *See Aromatic Resin; Incense.*

GUNI [1586, 1587] (*spotted sand grouse*).
1. Son of Naphtali (Ge 46:24; 1Ch 7:13) and his clan (Nu 26:48).

2. Father of Abdiel (1Ch 5:15).

GUR [1595].
Place where Jehu slew Ahaziah (2Ki 9:27).

GUR BAAL [1597] (*sojourn of Baal*).
A town probably located S of Beersheba (2Ch 26:7).

GUTTER [2668].
Of the temple in Ezekiel's vision (Eze 43:13, 14, 17).

HAAHASHTARI [2028] (*the Ahashtarites*). Son of Naarah (1Ch 4:6).

HAARALOTH *See Gibeath Haaraloth.*

HABAIAH *See Hobaiah.*

HABAKKUK [2487] (*garden plant* KB). Prophet of the book which bears his name; wrote when the temple was still standing (Hab 2:20; 3:19), between c. 605-587 B.C., probably during the reign of the Judean king Jehoiakim.

HABAKKUK, BOOK OF (*garden plant* KB).

Author: Habakkuk

Date: Close to the battle of Carchemish (605 B.C.)

Outline:

I. Title (1:1).
II. Habakkuk's First Complaint: Why Does the Evil in Judah Go Unpunished? (1:2-4).
III. God's Answer: The Babylonians Will Punish Judah (1:5-11).
IV. Habakkuk's Second Complaint: How Can a Just God Use Wicked Babylon to Punish a People More Righteous Than Themselves? (1:12-2:1).
V. God's Answer: Babylon Will Be Punished, and Faith Will Be Rewarded (2:2-20).
VI. Habakkuk's Prayer: After Asking for Manifestations of God's Wrath and Mercy (as in the Past), He Closes With Confession of Trust and Joy in God (ch. 3).

See Prophets, The Minor.

HABAZZINIAH [2484] (*possibly exuberant in Yahweh*). Head of the family of Recabites (Jer 35:3).

HABERGEON NIV "(coat of) armor," "javelin." *See Armor; Breastplate; Coat of Mail.*

HABIRU A people mentioned in Mari, Nuzi, and Amarna tablets; fundamental meaning seems to be "wanderers"; of mixed racial origin, including both Semites and non-Semites. Connection with Hebrews is obscure.

HABIT [4946+8997+9453, 6122, *1621, 3443*]. (Ex 21:29, 36; Nu 22:30; Jer 13:23; 22:21; Mic 2:1; 1Ti 5:13; Heb 10:25).

HABOR [2466]. A river of Mesopotamia (2Ki 17:6; 18:11; 1Ch 5:26).

HACALIAH [2678] (*dark*). Father of Nehemiah (Ne 1:1; 10:1).

HACHILAH *See Hakilah.*

HACMONI, HACMONITE [1201+ 2685, 2685] (*wise*). Father of Jehiel and Jashobeam (2Sa 23:8, ftn; 1Ch 11:11; 27:32). *See Tahkemonite.*

HADAD [119, 2060, 2524] (*thunderer [Semitic storm god]*).

1. Grandson of Abraham (Ge 25:15).
2. A king of Edom (Ge 36:35-36; 1Ch 1:46-47).
3. Another king of Edom (Ge 36:39, ftn; 1Ch 1:50-51).
4. A member of the royal house of Edom who escaped to Egypt when David conquered Edom and then later returned to his homeland to revolt against Solomon (1Ki 11:14-25). The Hebrew actually reads "Adad" for the first "Hadad" in 1Ki 11:17, and it has been conjectured that 1Ki 11:14ff. combines two accounts, one of Hadad the Edomite and the other of Adad the Midianite. Convincing reasons have been given for identifying this Hadad with 3 above.
5. The ancient Semitic storm god who as the great Baal of the Ugaritic pantheon figured in the struggle of the religion of Israel against Canaanite religion.

HADAD RIMMON [2062]. A place in the valley of Megiddo (Zec 12:11).

HADADEZER [2061] (*[pagan god] Hadad is a help*). Son of Rehob, king of Zobah, vanquished by David (2Sa 8:3-13; 10:15-19; 1Ki 11:23; 1Ch 18:3-10; 19:6-19).

HADAR (*thunderer, Semitic storm god*).

1. Son of Ishmael (Ge 25:15 KJV). *See Hadad, 1.*
2. King of Edom (Ge 36:39, ftn.). *See Hadad, 3.*

HADAREZER *See Hadadezer.*

HADASHAH [2546] (*new*). A town in Judah (Jos 15:37).

HADASSAH [2073] (*myrtle* BDB and KB; possibly *myrtle* or *bride* IDB). The Hebrew name of Esther (Est 2:7). *See Esther.*

HADATTAH *See Hazor Hadattah.*

HADES [87] (*the underworld*). The unseen world (Mt 11:23; 16:18; Lk 10:15; 16:23; Ac 2:27, 31; Rev 1:18; 6:8; 20:13-14). The realm (or state) of the dead is usually expressed in Hebrew by *sheol* [8619] and in Greek by *hades* [87] (2Sa 22:6; Job 26:5; Ps 6:5; 17:15; 30:9; 49:15; 86:13; 88:10-12; 115:17; 116:3; Pr 15:24; 21:16; 27:20; Ecc 9:4-6; Isa 5:14; Jnh 2:2; Lk 23:42-43; Jn 8:22; 2Co 12:4).

See Grave; Hell; Immortality; Paradise;

*Righteous, Promises to; Sheol; Spirit; Wicked,
Punishment of.*

HADID [2531] (*sharp*). A city of Benjamin.
Captive of, returned from Babylon (Ezr 2:33; Ne
7:37; 11:34).

HADLAI [2536] (*resting* ISBE; *fat* IDB; *be
stout* KB). Father of Amasa (2Ch 28:12).

HADORAM [2066, 2067] (*Hadad is exalted*).
1. Descendant of Shem (Ge 10:27; 1Ch 1:21).
2. Son of Tou (1Ch 18:10). Called Joram (2Sa
8:10).
3. Hebrew *Adoram* (2Sa 20:24, ftn) or *Hadoram*
(2Ch 10:18, ftn), a variant of *Adoniram*. An officer in charge of forced labor during the reigns of
David and then Solomon. He then held the same
office under Rehoboam, Solomon's son. *See
Adoniram.*

HADRACH [2541]. A district of Syria (Zec
9:1).

HAELEPH [2030]. A town of Benjamin,
near Jerusalem (Jos 18:28).

HAGAB [2507] (*locust*). Ancestor of the
temple servants who returned with Zerubbabel
(Ezr 2:46).

HAGABA, HAGABAH [2509]
(*locust*). One of the temple servants (Ezr 2:45; Ne
7:48).

HAGAR [2057, 29] (*emigration, flight*). A
servant of Abraham and handmaid of Sarah.
Given by Sarah to Abraham to be his wife (Ge 16).
Descendants of (Ge 25:12-15; 1Ch 5:10, 19-22; Ps
83:6, ftn). Allegorically identified with slavery to
the law (Gal 4:24-25).

HAGARENES *See Hagar.*

HAGARITES, HAGERITES *See
Hagrite(s).*

HAGGAI [2516, 10247] (*festal* BDB; *born
on the feast day* KB). Haggai was a prophet who,
with Zechariah, encouraged the returned exiles to
rebuild the temple (Ezr 5:1-2; 6:14). The prophet's
name ("festal, ") may indicate he was born during
one of the three pilgrimage feasts (Unleavened
Bread, Pentecost or Weeks, and Tabernacles; cf.
Dt 16:16). Based on 2:3 Haggai may have witnessed the destruction of Solomon's temple. If so,
he must have been in his early 70s during his
ministry.

HAGGAI, BOOK OF

Author: Haggai

Date:
The messages of Haggai were given during a
four-month period in 520 B.C., the second year of
King Darius. The first message was delivered on

the first day of the sixth month (Aug. 29), the last
on the 24th day of the ninth month (Dec. 18).

Outline:
I. First Message: The Call to Rebuild the Temple
(1:1-11).
   A. The People's Lame Excuse (1:1-4).
   B. The Poverty of the People (1:5-6).
   C. The Reason God Has Cursed Them
     (1:7-11).
II. The Response of Zerubbabel and the People
(1:12-15).
   A. The Leaders and Remnant Obey (1:12).
   B. The Lord Strengthens the Workers
     (1:13-15).
III. Second Message: The Temple to Be Filled
With Glory (2:1-9).
   A. The People Encouraged (2:1-5).
   B. The Promise of Glory and Peace (2:6-9).
IV. Third Message: A Defiled People Purified
and Blessed (2:10-19).
   A. The Rapid Spread of Sin (2:10-14).
   B. Poor Harvests Because of Disobedience
     (2:15-17).
   C. Blessing to Come as the Temple Is Rebuilt
     (2:18-19).
V. Fourth Message: The Promise to Zerubbabel
(2:20-23).
   A. The Judgment of the Nations (2:20-22).
   B. The Significance of Zerubbabel (2:23).
   See Prophets, The Minor.

HAGGAN *See Beth Haggan.*

HAGGEDOLIM [2045] (*the great ones*).
The father of Zabdiel, a priest (Ne 11:14).

HAGGI, HAGGITE [2515] (*festal* BDB;
born on the feast day KB). Son of Gad (Ge 46:16)
and his clan (Nu 26:15).

HAGGIAH [2517] (*feast of Yahweh*). A
Levite (1Ch 6:30).

HAGGIDGAD *See Hor Haggidgad.*

HAGGITH [2518] (*festal* BDB; *born on the
feast day* KB). Wife of David. Mother of Adonijah
(2Sa 3:4; 1Ki 1:5, 11; 2:13; 1Ch 3:2).

HAGGOYIM *See Harosheth Haggoyim.*

HAGIOGRAPHA (*holy writings*). The
third division of the Hebrew OT: Psalms,
Proverbs, Job, Song of Solomon, Ruth, Lamentations, Ecclesiastes, Esther, Daniel, Ezra,
Nehemiah, 1 and 2 Chronicles.

HAGRI [2058] (*wanderer*). Father of Mibhar
(2Sa 23:36; 1Ch 11:38).

HAGRITE(S) [2058] (possibly *people from
Hagar*). Descendants of Hagar, mother of Ishmael
with whom Saul made war (1Ch 5:10, 19-21;
27:31; Ps 83:6, ftn).

HAHIROTH *See Pi Hahiroth.*

HAI *See Ai.*

HAIL [1351, 1352, 7943, *5897, 5898*]. (Job 38:22; Hag 2:17). Plague of, in Egypt (Ex 9:18-29; Ps 78:48; 105:32). Destroys army of the Amorites (Jos 10:11).
Figurative: (Isa 28:2; Rev 8:7; 11:19; 16:21).

HAIR [*6436, 8484, 8552, 8553, 8031, 10687, 2582]. Numbered (Mt 10:30; Lk 12:7). Worn long by women (Isa 3:24; Lk 7:38; 1Co 11:5-6, 15; 1Ti 2:9; 1Pe 3:3; Rev 9:8), by Absalom (2Sa 14:26). Worn short by men (1Co 11:14). Symbolic dividing of (Eze 5:1-2).
See Baldness; Leprosy; Mourning; Nazirite(s), Nazarite(s).

HAKILAH [2677]. A hill in Judah where David and his followers hid from Saul (1Sa 23:19; 26:3).

HAKKATAN [2214] (*the small one*). Father of Johanan (Ezr 8:12).

HAKKEREM *See Beth Hakkerem.*

HAKKORE *See En Hakkore.*

HAKKOZ [2212] (*the thorn*).
1. The eponym of a family of priests in David's time (1Ch 24:10). Members of this family were among those unable to document their claim to priestly rank after the Exile and so were suspended from office (Ezr 2:61; Ne 7:63).
2. Ancestor of Meremoth, who helped repair the wall of Jerusalem (Ne 3:4, 21).

HAKUPHA [2979] (*crooked*). One of the temple servants (Ezr 2:51; Ne 7:53).

HALAH [2712]. A place to which Israelite captives were transported (2Ki 17:6; 18:11; 1Ch 5:26).

HALAK, MOUNT OF [2748] (*bare, bald*). A mountain, the southern limit of Joshua's conquests (Jos 11:17; 12:7).

HALF-HOMER *See Homer; Measure.*

HALF-TRIBE *See Manasseh, 2.*

HALHUL [2713]. A city in Judah (Jos 15:58).

HALI [2718] (*adornment*). A border town of Asher (Jos 19:25).

HALL [395, 1074+3516, 1074, 2121, 4384, 10103, *1141, 5391*].
1. Court of the high priest's palace (Lk 22:55).
2. Official residence of a Roman governor (Mt 27:27; Mk 15:16).

HALLEL (*praise*). Two liturgical collections of Psalms read at Passover. Psalms 113-118 called the "Egyptian Hallel"; Psalm 136, "the Hallel";

Psalms 120-136 are often called the "Great Hallel." *See Passover.*

HALLELUJAH [*252*] (*praise Yahweh*). Liturgical exclamation urging all to praise Yahweh. Occurs at the beginning of Psalms 106, 111-113, 117, 135, 146-150 and at the close of 104-106, 113, 115-117, 135, 146-150. *See Praise.*

HALLOHESH [2135] (*the whisperer*). Father of Shallum (Ne 3:12). Sealed the covenant with Nehemiah (Ne 10:24).

HALLOW, HALLOWED [*39*] (*to render as holy*). To set apart for sacred use; to hold sacred; to reverence as holy (Ex 20:11; Mt 6:9).

HAM [2154, 2769].
1. Son of Noah (Ge 5:32; 9:18, 24; 1Ch 1:4). Provokes his father's wrath (Ge 9:18-27). His children (Ge 10:6-20; 1Ch 1:8-16).
2. Family name of the descendants of Ham (1Ch 4:40; Ps 78:51; 105:23, 27; 106:22).
3. Place where Kedorlaomer killed the Zuzites (Ge 14:5).

HAMAN [2172]. Prime minister of Xerxes, king of Persia (Est 3:1, 10; 7:7-10).

HAMATH, HAMATHITES [2828] (*fortress*). A city of upper Syria; the N border of the ideal limits of the Promised Land (Nu 13:21; 34:8; Jos 13:5; Eze 47:16). Solomon's kingdom extended from the Wadi of Egypt to the entrance of Hamath (1Ki 8:65), and the kingdom of Israel at the time of Jeroboam reached northward to the entrance of Hamath (2Ki 14:25; Am 6:14).
Inhabited by Canaanites (Ge 10:18). Prosperity of (Am 6:2). David receives gifts of gold and silver from Tou, king of (2Sa 8:9-10; 1Ch 18:3, 9-10). Conquest of, by Jeroboam (2Ki 14:25, 28), by the Chaldeans (2Ki 25:20-21). Israelites taken captive (Isa 11:11). Prophecy concerning (Jer 49:23). Solomon builds store cities in (2Ch 8:4).

HAMATH ZOBAH [2832] (*fortress of Zobah*). A town on the border of Israel. Subdued by Solomon (2Ch 8:3).

HAMMAHLEKOTH *See Sela Hammahlekoth.*

HAMMATH [2829, 2830] (*hot springs*).
1. Fortified city of Naphtali, c. one mile S of Tiberias (Jos 19:35).
2. Founder of Recabites (1Ch 2:55).

HAMMEDATHA [2158] (*given by the moon [god]*). Father of Haman (Est 3:1, 10; 8:5; 9:10, 24).

HAMMELECH NIV "the king" (Jer 36:26; 38:6).

HAMMER [*2153, 5216, 7079, 8392, 8822*].

A tool used for a variety of purposes: Smoothing metals (Isa 41:7), driving tent pins (Jdg 4:21), forging (Isa 44:12). Sometimes used figuratively for any crushing power (Jer 23:29; 50:23).

HAMMOLEKETH [2168] (the queen).
Daughter of Makir (1Ch 7:17-18).

HAMMON [2785] (hot springs).
1. A city of Asher (Jos 19:28).
2. A Levitical city of Naphtali (1Ch 6:76). Possibly identical with Hammath and Hammoth Dor.

HAMMOTH DOR [2831] (hot spring of Dor).
Naphtali (Jos 21:32). Possibly identical with Hammath (Jos 19:35). Called Hammon (1Ch 6:76).

HAMMUEL [2781] (God [El] of Ham KB).
A Simeonite (1Ch 4:26).

HAMMURABI
King of Babylon (c. 1704-1662 B.C.). Not the same as Amraphel (Ge 14:1-12). He was a great builder and lawgiver (Code of Hammurabi). See Texts, Ancient Near Eastern Non-Biblical Texts Relating to the Old Testament.

HAMON
See Baal Hamon; Hamon Gog.

HAMON GOG, VALLEY OF
[2163] (multitude of Gog). Prophetic name for place E of Dead Sea where the "multitude of Gog" will be buried (Eze 39:11-15).

HAMONAH [2164] (multitude).
Prophetic name of city near which Gog is defeated (Eze 39:16).

HAMOR [2791, 1846] (male donkey).
Father of Shechem. Jacob buys ground from (Ge 33:19; Jos 24:32; Jdg 9:28). Murdered by the sons of Jacob (Ge 34:26; 49:6). Called Hamor (Ac 7:16).

HAMSTRING [6828].
Disabling an animal by cutting the large tendon at the back of the knee, usually to render it useless for military service. Of horses (Jos 11:6, 9; 2Sa 8:4; 1Ch 18:4). Of oxen (Ge 49:6).

HAMUL, HAMULITE [2783, 2784] (pitied).
Son of Perez (Ge 46:12; 1Ch 2:5) and his clan (Nu 26:21).

HAMUTAL [2782] (my husband's father is like dew).
Wife of Josiah. Mother of Jehoahaz and Zedekiah (2Ki 23:31; 24:18; Jer 52:1).

HANAMEL [2856] (God [El] is gracious).
Cousin of Jeremiah, to whom he sold a field in Anathoth (Jer 32:7-12).

HANAN [2860] (gracious).
1. Son of Shashak (1Ch 8:23).
2. Son of Azel (1Ch 8:38; 9:44).
3. One of David's mighty men (1Ch 11:43).
4. One of the temple servants (Ezr 2:46; Ne 7:49).

5. A Levite (Ne 8:7; 10:10). Probably identical with the one mentioned in Ne 13:13.
6. A chief who sealed the covenant with Nehemiah (Ne 10:22, 26).
7. An officer in the temple (Jer 35:2-10).

HANANEL, TOWER OF [2861]
(God [El] is gracious). Name of a tower forming part of the wall of Jerusalem (Ne 3:1; 12:39; Jer 31:38; Zec 14:10).

HANANI [2862] (gracious).
1. Son of Heman (1Ch 25:4, 25).
2. A prophet who rebuked Asa, king of Judah (2Ch 16:7).
3. Father of Jehu the prophet (1Ki 16:1, 7; 2Ch 19:2; 20:34). Possibly identical with 2.
4. A priest (Ezr 10:20).
5. A brother of Nehemiah and keeper of the gates of Jerusalem (Ne 1:2; 7:2).
6. A priest and musician (Ne 12:36).

HANANIAH [2863, 2864, 10275] (Yahweh is gracious).
1. Son of Heman (1Ch 25:4, 23).
2. A captain of Uzziah's army (2Ch 26:11).
3. Father of Zedekiah (Jer 36:12).
4. A prophet of Gibeon who uttered false prophecies in the temple during the reign of Zedekiah (Jer 28).
5. Grandfather of Irijah (Jer 37:13).
6. Son of Shashak (1Ch 8:24).
7. Hebrew name of Shadrach. See Shadrach.
8. Son of Zerubbabel (1Ch 3:19, 21).
9. Son of Bebai (Ezr 10:28).
10. A priest (Ne 3:8).
11. Son of Shelemiah (Ne 3:30).
12. A keeper of the gates of Jerusalem (Ne 7:2).
13. One who sealed the covenant (Ne 10:23).
14. A priest in time of Jehoiakim (Ne 12:12, 41).

HAND [*2908, 3338, 4090, 10311, 1288, 942, 3638, 4140, 5931, 5935].

Ceremonial:

Laying on of hands (Heb 6:2), in consecration (Ge 48:14; Ex 29:10, 15, 19; Lev 1:4; 3:2, 8, 13; 4:15, 24, 33; 16:21), in ordaining the Levites (Nu 8:10-11), Joshua (Nu 27:18-23; Dt 34:9), Timothy (1Ti 4:14; 2Ti 1:6), in healing (Mk 6:5; 7:32; 16:18; Lk 4:40; Ac 28:8), in blessing children (Mt 19:13; Mk 10:16); in solemnizing testimony (Lev 24:14). Lifted up in benediction (Lev 9:22; Lk 24:50), in prayer. See Hands, Laying on of; Prayer, Attitudes in.

Ceremonial washing of (Mt 15:2; Mk 7:2-5). See Washings; Cleanliness.

Symbolic:

Symbolic of righteousness (Job 17:9). Washing of, a symbol of innocence (Dt 21:6; Mt 27:24).

Clasping of, in token of contract (Ezr 10:19; Pr 6:1; 17:18; Eze 17:18), of friendship (2Ki 10:15; Job 17:3). Right hand lifted up in swearing (Ge 14:22; Ps 106:26; Isa 62:8), symbol of power (Isa 23:11; 41:10), place of honor (Ps 45:9; 80:17).

Figurative:
(Mt 5:30; 18:8; Mk 9:43).

Anthropomorphic Use of:
Hand of the Lord considered limited in power (Nu 11:23), is mighty (Jos 4:24), was heavy (1Sa 5:6), against the Philistines (1Sa 7:13), on Elijah (1Ki 18:46), not limited in power (Isa 59:1), was with the early Christians (Ac 11:21). *See Anthropomorphisms.*

HANDBREADTH [3255, 3256, 3257]. A measure, about four inches (Ex 25:25; 1Ki 7:26; 2Ch 4:5; Ps 39:5; Isa 48:13; Eze 40:5, 43; Jer 52:21). *See Fingers, Fingerbreadth; Span.*

HANDKERCHIEF [5051]. Sometimes translated "cloth," used for a variety of purposes (Lk 19:20-23; Jn 11:44; 20:7; Ac 19:12).

HANDLE [296, 2005, 5896, 5951, 6885, 6913, 8990, 9530, 721]. Door knob (SS 5:5).

HANDMAID, HANDMAIDEN
Female slave or servant. *See Maid(s), Maidservant(s); Servant.*

HANDS, LAYING ON OF Ceremony having the idea of transference, identification, and devotion to God (Ex 29:10, 15, 19; Lev 16:21; Ac 8:14-17; 2Ti 1:6). *See Hand.*

HANDSTAFF NIV "war clubs" (Eze 39:9). *See Club.*

HANES [2865]. A place in Egypt (Isa 30:4).

HANGING [*2871, 9434, 551]. Not a form of capital punishment in Bible times. Where used, except 2Sa 17:23; Mt 27:5, it refers to the suspension of a body from a tree or post after the criminal had been put to death (Ge 40:19, 22; Dt 21:22).

HANGINGS [4158]. Material hung in the tabernacle so as to preserve the privacy and sacredness of that which was within (Ex 27:9-19; Mt 27:51).

HANIEL *See Hanniel, 2.*

HANNAH [2839] (*favor*). Mother of Samuel. Her trials, prayer, and promise (1Sa 1:1-18). Samuel born to, dedicates him to God, leaves him at the temple (1Sa 1:19-28). Her hymn of praise (1Sa 2:1-10). Visits Samuel at the temple(annually Sa 2:18-19). Children of (1Sa 2:20-21).

HANNATHON [2872]. A city of Zebulun (Jos 19:14).

HANNIEL [2848] (*favor of God [El]*).
1. A son of Ephod, appointed by Moses to divide the land among the several tribes (Nu 34:23).
2. A son of Ulla (1Ch 7:39).

HANOCH, HANOCHITE [2840, 2854] (*initiation*).

1. Grandson of Abraham by Keturah (Ge 25:4; 1Ch 1:33).
2. Son of Reuben (Ge 46:9; Ex 6:14; 1Ch 5:3) and his clan (Nu 26:5).

HANUKKAH [*1589*] (*dedication*). The Feast of Rededication. After Judas Maccabeus had cleansed the temple from the pollution of pagan worship (c. 165 B.C.), the twenty-fifth of Kislev (December) was kept annually in memory of this.
See Dedication; Feasts; Kislev; Maccabees; Month, 9.

HANUN [2842] (*favored*).
1. King of Ammon who provoked David to war (2Sa 10:1-5; 1Ch 19:1-5).
2. Two men who helped repair wall of Jerusalem (Ne 3:13, 30).

HAPHARAIM, HAPHRAIM [2921] (*place of two trenches*). A city of Issachar (Jos 19:19).

HAPPINESS [*245, 897, 3202, 8523, 8524, 8525, 5915*].

Of the Wicked:
Limited to this life (Ps 17:14; Lk 16:25), short (Job 20:5), uncertain (Lk 12:20), vain (Ecc 2:1; 7:6).

Is derived from their wealth (Job 21:13; Ps 52:7), their power (Job 21:7; Ps 37:35), their worldly prosperity (Ps 17:14; 73:3-4, 7), gluttony (Isa 22:13; Hab 1:16), drunkenness (Isa 5:11; 56:12), vain pleasure (Job 21:12; Isa 5:12), successful oppression (Hab 1:15). Marred by jealousy (Est 5:13), often interrupted by judgments (Nu 11:33; Job 15:21; Ps 73:18-20; Jer 25:10-11). Leads to sorrow (Pr 14:13). Leads to recklessness (Isa 22:12). Sometimes a stumbling block to saints (Ps 73:3, 16; Jer 12:1; Hab 1:13). Saints often permitted to see the end of (Ps 73:17-20), envy not (Ps 37:1). Woe against (Am 6:1; Lk 6:25).

Illustrated (Ps 37:35-36; Lk 12:16-20; 16:19-25). Exemplified: Israel (Nu 11:33). Haman (Est 5:9-11). Belshazzar (Da 5:1). Herod (Ac 12:21-23).

Of the Righteous:
In the Lord, through abundance (Ps 36:8; Ecc 2:24-26; 3:12-13, 22). In chastisement (Job 5:17-27). In fellowship (Ps 133:1). In good works (Pr 14:21; Ecc 3:12; Mt 5:3-9). In hope (Ro 5:2). In obedience (Ps 40:8; 128:1-2; 144:15; 146:5; Pr 16:20; 28:14; 29:18). In peace (Php 4:7). In persecution (Mt 3:10-11; 2Co 12:10; 1Pe 3:14; 4:12). In protection (Dt 33:29; Isa 12:2-3). In satisfaction (Ps 63:5). Trust (Pr 16:20). In wisdom (Pr 3:13-18).

Beatitudes (Mt 5:3-12).
See Joy; Peace; Praise.

HAPPIZZEZ [2204]. A governor of the temple (1Ch 24:15).

HARA [2217] (*hill, highland*). Place in Assyria to which Israelites were exiled by Assyrians (1Ch 5:26).

HARADAH [3011] (*place of fear*). One of the camps of Israel (Nu 33:24-25).

HARAM See *Beth Haram.*

HARAN [2237, 3059, 3060, 5924] (earlier *mountaineer,* but perhaps *sanctuary*).

1. Father of Lot and brother of Abraham (Ge 11:26-31).

2. Son of Caleb (1Ch 2:46).

3. A Levite (1Ch 23:9).

4. A place in Mesopotamia to which Terah and Abraham migrated (Ge 11:31; 12:4-5; Ac 7:2, 4). Death of Terah at (Ge 11:32). Abraham leaves, by divine command (Ge 12:1-5). Jacob flees to (Ge 27:43; 28:7; 29), returns from, with Rachel and Leah (Ge 31:17-21). Conquest of, by king of Assyria (2Ki 19:12). Merchants of (Eze 27:23). Idolatry in (Jos 24:2, 14; Isa 37:12).

HARARITE [2240] (*mountain dweller*). A place or family name (2Sa 23:11, 33; 1Ch 11:34).

HARASHIM See *Ge Harashim.*

HARBONA [3002, 3003] (*donkey driver*). Eunuch of Xerxes (Est 1:10; 7:9).

HARD, HARD-HEARTED See *Obduracy.*

HARDEST STONE The Lord makes Ezekiel's forehead harder than "the hardest stone" (Eze 3:9). See *Adamant; Diamond; Flint; Minerals of the Bible, 1; Stones.*

HARE See *Animals; Rabbit.*

HAREM [851, 851+1074, 2256+8721+8721]. The wives and concubines of a king (Ecc 2:8; Est 2:3, 13-14).

HAREPH [3073] (*autumn,* or *sharp* IDB; *scornful* ISBE). Son of Caleb (1Ch 2:51).

HARESETH See *Kir Hareseth.*

HARHAIAH [3015]. Father of Uzziel (Ne 3:8).

HARHAS [3030]. Grandfather of the husband of Huldah, the prophetess (2Ki 22:14). Called Hasrah (2Ch 34:22).

HARHUR [3028] (possibly *fever* BDB; possibly *raven* IDB; *one born during his mother's fever* KB). Head of a family that returned with Zerubbabel (Ezr 2:51; Ne 7:53).

HARIM [3053] (*consecrated [to Yahweh]*).

1. Priest (1Ch 24:8).

2. Family that returned with Zerubbabel (Ezr 2:39; Ne 7:35).

3. Family of priests (Ezr 2:39; 10:21; Ne 7:42; 12:15).

4. Family that married foreign wives (Ezr 10:31).

5. Father of a worker on the wall (Ne 3:11).

6. A man who sealed the covenant (Ne 10:27).

HARIPH [3040] (*one born at harvest time*).

1. One of the exiles (Ne 7:24). Probably the same as Jorah (Ezr 2:18).

2. One who sealed the covenant (Ne 10:19).

HARLOT [2390]. See *Adultery; Prostitute..*

HARLOTRY See *Adultery; Prostitute.*

HARMON [2236]. Possibly a place name (Am 4:3, ftn.).

HARNEPHER [3062] (*[pagan god] Horus is merciful*). Asherite (1Ch 7:36).

HAROD, HARODITE [3008, 3012] (*trembling*). Spring beside which Gideon encamped (Jdg 7:1). Family name of Shammah and Elika (2Sa 23:25).

HAROEH [2218] (*the seer*). Grandson of Caleb (1Ch 2:52).

HARORITE [2229]. Shammoth, one of David's mighty men (1Ch 11:27).

HAROSHETH HAGGOYIM [3099] (*Harosheth of the nations*). Town in N Israel c. sixteen miles NW of Megiddo; home of Sisera (Jdg 4:2, 13, 16).

HARP [4036, 5575, 5594, 10590, 3067, 3069]. A stringed instrument of music (Isa 38:20; Eze 33:32; Hab 3:19). With three strings (1Sa 18:6), ten strings (Ps 33:2; 92:3; 144:9; 150:4). Originated with Jubal (Ge 4:21). Made of almugwood (1Ki 10:12). David skillful in playing (1Sa 16:16, 23). Used in worship (1Sa 10:5; 1Ch 16:5; 25:1-7; 2Ch 5:12-13; 29:25; Ps 33:2; 43:4; 49:4; 57:8; 71:22; 81:2; 93:3; 98:5; 108:2; 147:7; 149:3; 150:3). Used, in national jubilees, after the triumph over Goliath (1Sa 18:6), over the armies of Ammon and Moab (2Ch 20:20-29), when the new walls of Jerusalem were dedicated (Ne 12:27, 36). Used in festivities (Ge 31:27; Job 21:11-12; Isa 5:12; 23:16; 24:8; 30:32; Eze 26:13; Rev 18:22), in mourning (Job 30:31). Hung on the willows by the captive Israelites (Ps 137:2). Heard in heaven, in John's apocalyptic vision (Rev 5:8; 14:2; 15:2). The symbol used in the Psalms to indicate when the harp was to be introduced in the music was *neginah* or *neginoth.* See *titles of Pss 4; 6; 54; 55; 61; 67; 76.*

See *Music, Instruments of, Symbols Used in.*

HARROW [8440]. Instrument for dragging or leveling off a field (Job 39:10), "breaking up the soil" (Isa 28:24; Hos 10:11). See *Picks, Iron.*

HARSHA [3095] (*deaf*). One of the temple servants (Ezr 2:52; Ne 7:54).

HART See *Deer.*

HARUM [2227] (*consecrated*). A descendant of Judah (1Ch 4:8).

HARUMAPH [3018] (*disfigured nose*). Father of Jedaiah (Ne 3:10).

HARUPHITE [3020] (*sharp* or *autumn*). Designation of Shephatiah (1Ch 12:5).

HARUZ [3027] (perhaps *gold*, or *eager*). Father-in-law of King Manasseh (2Ki 21:19).

HARVEST [658, 665, 668, 1292, 1305, 3292, 3823+3824, 7811, 7907, 7917, 8040, 9311, *1163, 2545, 2546, 2843*]. Sabbath to be observed in (Ex 34:21). Sabbath desecrated in (Ne 13:15-22).

Of wheat at Pentecost, in Israel (Ex 34:22; Lev 23:15-17), and before vintage (Lev 26:5). Of barley, before wheat (Ex 9:31-32).

Celebrated with joy (Jdg 9:27; Isa 9:3; 16:10; Jer 48:33). Promises of plentiful (Ge 8:22; Jer 5:24; Joel 2:23-24).

Figurative: (Job 24:5; Ps 10:5; Jer 8:20; Joel 3:13; Mt 9:37; 13:39; Lk 10:2; Rev 14:15).

See Pentecost, 1; Tabernacles, Feast of; Firstfruits; Reaping; Glean, Gleaning.

HASADIAH [2878] (*Yahweh is faithful*). Son of Zerubbabel (1Ch 3:20).

HASENUAH See *Hassenuah.*

HASHABIAH [3116, 3117] (*Yahweh has reckoned*).
1. Ancestor of Ethan (1Ch 6:45).
2. Ancestor of Shemaiah (1Ch 9:14; Ne 11:15).
3. Son of Jeduthun (1Ch 25:3).
4. Civil official in David's time (1Ch 26:30).
5. Overseer of tribe of Levi (1Ch 27:17).
6. Chief of Levites (2Ch 35:9).
7. Levite teacher (Ezr 8:19).
8. Chief priest (Ezr 8:24).
9. Worker on the wall (Ne 3:17).
10. Priest (Ne 12:21).
11. Ancestor of Uzzi (Ne 11:22).
12. Chief of Levites (Ne 3:17; 12:24).

HASHABNAH [3118] (probably *Yahweh has considered me*). Man who sealed covenant with Nehemiah (Ne 10:25).

HASHABNEIAH [3119] (probably *Yahweh has considered me*).
1. Father of Hattush (Ne 3:10).
2. A Levite (Ne 9:5).

HASHBADDANAH [3111] (probably *Yahweh has considered me*). A man who stood by Ezra as he read the law (Ne 8:4).

HASHEM [2244]. Father of several members of David's guard (1Ch 11:34).

HASHMONAH [3135]. A camp of the Israelites (Nu 33:29-30).

HASHUBAH [3112] (*consideration*). A descendant of King Jehoiakim (1Ch 3:20).

HASHUM [3130] (*broad-nosed*).
1. Family which returned from the Exile (Ezr 2:19; 10:33; Ne 7:22).
2. Priest who stood at side of Ezra when he read the law (Ne 8:4).
3. Chief of people who sealed the covenant (Ne 10:18). May be the same as 2.

HASHUPHA See *Hasupha.*

HASMONEANS See *Maccabees.*

HASRAH [2897]. Grandfather of Shallum (2Ch 34:22), "Harhas" (2Ki 22:14).

HASSENAAH [2189]. Father of sons who built fish gate in Jerusalem (Ne 3:3).

HASSENUAH [2190] (*the hated women*). A Benjamite and the father of Judah, a governor of Jerusalem (1Ch 9:7; Ne 11:9).

HASSHUB [3121] (*considerate*).
1. Son of Pahath-Moab (Ne 3:11).
2. One of the Captivity who assisted in repairing the wall of Jerusalem (Ne 3:23).
3. Head of a family (Ne 10:23).
4. A Levite (1Ch 9:14; Ne 11:15).

HASSOPHERETH [2191] (*the scribes*). May have once been an official title (Ezr 2:55).

HASTE [*237, 2590, 2906, 4960+5674, 5610]. In judgment, by Moses and the Israelites (Nu 32:1-19; Jos 22:10-34). See *Rashness.*

HASUPHA [3102]. Family that returned from exile with Zerubbabel (Ezr 2:43; Ne 7:46).

HAT See *Dress; Headdress; Turbans.*

HATHACH [2251] (*good*). A eunuch in the court of Xerxes (Est 4:5-6, 9-10).

HATHATH [3171] (possibly *terror* BDB and KB; possibly *weakness* IDB). A son of Othniel (1Ch 4:13).

HATIPHA [2640] (*taken captive*). One of the temple servants (Ezr 2:54; Ne 7:56).

HATITA [2638]. A gatekeeper of the temple (Ezr 2:42; Ne 7:45).

HATRED [*8533, 8534, *3631*]. Is blinding (1Jn 2:9, 11). Carnal (Gal 5:19-20). Murderous (1Jn 3:15). Unforgiving (Mt 6:15). Leads to deceit (Pr 26:24-26). Opposite of love (Pr 15:17). Prevents from loving God (1Jn 4:20). Produces strife (Pr 10:12).

Toward the righteous (Ps 25:19; 35:19; Mt 10:22; Jn 15:18-19, 23-25; 17:14).

Forbidden (Eph 4:31; Col 3:8). Toward a brother (Lev 19:17). Toward an enemy (Mt 5:43-44).

Justified against iniquity (Ps 97:10; 101:3; 119:104, 128, 163; 139:21-22). Of God (Ps 5:5; 45:7; Isa 61:8; Mal 2:16).

See Envy; Jealousy; Malice; Revenge.

HATTAAVAH *See Kibroth Hattaavah.*

HATTIL [2639] (*talkative*). A returned exile (Ezr 2:57; Ne 7:59).

HATTIN, HORNS OF (*hollows*). Hill near village of Hattin on which, tradition says, Christ delivered the Sermon on the Mount.

HATTUSH [2637].
1. Descendant of Zerubbabel (1Ch 3:22).
2. Man who returned from Babylon (Ezr 8:2).
3. Worker on the wall (Ne 3:10). May be the same as 2.
4. Man who sealed the covenant (Ne 10:4). May be the same as 2 or 3.
5. Priest who returned with Zerubbabel (Ne 12:2).

HAUGHTINESS [1467, 1468, 1469, 1470, 2294, 5294, 8123, 8124]. *See Pride.*

HAURAN [2588] (*black*). Plateau E of the Jordan and N of Gilead (Eze 47:16, 18). Called Bashan in ancient times; in the time of the Romans, Auranitis.

HAVENS *See Fair Havens.*

HAVILAH [2564] (*stretch of sand*).
1. Son of Cush (Ge 10:7; 1Ch 1:9).
2. Son of Joktan (Ge 10:29; 1Ch 1:23).
3. Land encompassed by Pishon River (Ge 2:11-12).
4. One of the boundaries of the Ishmaelites (Ge 25:18; 1Sa 15:7).

HAVVOTH JAIR [2596] (*villages of Jair*). A group of unwalled towns in the NW part of Bashan (Nu 32:41; Dt 3:14; Jos 13:30; Jdg 10:4).

HAWK [5891]. A carnivorous and unclean bird (Lev 11:16; Dt 14:15; Job 39:26).

HAY [2945, 5965]. (Pr 27:25; Isa 15:6; 1Co 3:12).

HAZAEL [2599] (*God [El] sees*). King of Syria. Anointed king by Elijah (1Ki 19:15). Conquests by (2Ki 8:28-29; 9:14; 10:32-33; 12:17-18; 13:3, 22; 2Ch 22:5-6). Conspires against, murders, and succeeds to the throne of Ben-Hadad (2Ki 8:8-15). Death of (2Ki 13:24).

HAZAIAH [2610] (*Yahweh sees*). A man of Judah (Ne 11:5).

HAZAR (*a settlement*). Often prefixed to descriptive place names. Also used for encampments of nomads.

HAZAR ADDAR [2960] (*settlement of Addar*). Also called Addar, a place on the southern boundary of Canaan (Nu 34:4; Jos 15:3).

HAZAR ENAN [2965, 2966] (*settlement of Enan*). The NE boundary point of the promised land (Nu 34:9-10; Eze 47:17; 48:1).

HAZAR GADDAH [2961] (*settlement of [pagan god] Gad*). A town in the southern district of Judah (Jos 15:27).

HAZAR HATTICON *See Hazer Hatticon.*

HAZAR SHUAL [2967] (*settlement of Shual [jackal]*). Town in S Judah (Jos 15:28; 19:3; 1Ch 4:28; Ne 11:27).

HAZAR SUSAH, HAZAR SUSIM [2963, 2964] (*settlement of Susah [horse]*). A city of Judah (Jos 19:5; 1Ch 4:31).

HAZARMAVETH [2975] (*village of [pagan god] Maveth*). Son and descendants of Joktan (Ge 10:26; 1Ch 1:20).

HAZAZON TAMAR [2954] (*Hazazon of the palm trees*). The ancient name of En Gedi, a town on W coast of Dead Sea (Ge 14:7; 2Ch 20:2).

HAZEL *See Almond.*

HAZER HATTICON [2962] (*place of Hatticon*). A place on the boundary of Hauran, probably E of Damascus (Eze 47:16).

HAZERIM (*unwalled settlements*). A district in the S of Canaan (Dt 2:23).

HAZEROTH [2972] (*settlements*). A station in the travels of the Israelites (Nu 11:35; 12:16; 33:17-18; Dt 1:1).

HAZEZON-TAMAR *See Hazazon Tamar.*

HAZIEL [2609] (*vision of God [El]*). A Levite (1Ch 23:9).

HAZO [2605]. A son of Nahor (Ge 22:22).

HAZOR [2937] (*an enclosure*).
1. City c. five miles W of waters of Merom, ruled by Jabin (Jos 11:1, 10), conquered by Joshua and, later, by Deborah and Barak (Jdg 4; 1Sa 12:9), fortified by Solomon (1Ki 9:15), its inhabitants taken into exile by Assyria (2Ki 15:29).
2. Town in S of Judah (Jos 15:23).
3. Another town in S Judah (Jos 15:25).
4. Town N of Jerusalem (Ne 11:33).
5. Region in S Arabia (Jer 49:28-33).

HAZOR HADATTAH [2939] (*new Hazor*). Probably an adjective qualifying Hazor, making it equivalent to New Hazor. A city of Judah (Jos 15:25).

HAZZELELPONI [2209]. Daughter of Etam (1Ch 4:3).

HAZZOBEBAH [2206]. Daughter of Koz (1Ch 4:8).

HAZZURIM *See Helkath Hazzurim.*

HEAD [*5265, 7721, 7949, 8031, 8484, 8553, 8569, 8672, 10646, *3051, 5092*]. Shaven when vows were taken (Ac 21:24). Diseases of (Isa 3:17). Anointed (Lev 14:18, 29).

HEAD OF THE CHURCH Christ, who gives the church life, direction, strength (Eph 1:22; 5:23; Col 1:18).

HEADBANDS [710, 4457, 8667]. Head coverings worn by priests (Ex 28:40; 29:9; Lev 8:13), by women (Isa 3:18, 20). Used in disguise (1Ki 20:38-41). *See Dress; Turban.*

HEADSTONE *See Cornerstone.*

HEALING [*776, 5340, 8324, 9499, *1407, 2542, 2543, 2611, 2615, 2617, 5392*].

In the Old Testament:
The LORD the healer (Ge 20:17; Ex 15:26; Ps 6:2; 30:2; 103:3; Ac 4:30).
In answer to prayer (Jas 5:14-16), of Miriam (Nu 12:10-15), of Jeroboam (1Ki 13:1-6), of Hezekiah (2Ki 20:1-7). By Elisha, of Naaman (2Ki 5:1-14).

By Jesus:
The nobleman's son (Jn 4:46-53). The disabled man (Mt 8:2-4; Mk 1:40-45; Lk 5:12-13). Peter's mother-in-law (Mt 8:14-15). Paralyzed man (Mt 9:2-8; Mk 2:1-12; Lk 5:17-26). The man with the withered hand (Mt 12:9-13; Mk 3:1-5; Lk 6:6-10). The centurion's servant (Mt 8:5-13; Lk 7:1-10). Demoniacs (Mt 8:28-34, w Mk 5:1-20, & Lk 8:26-36; Mt 12:22; 17:14-18; Mk 9:14-27; Lk 9:38-42; 11:14). Blind and mute (Mt 9:27-33; 12:22; 20:30-34; Mk 8:22-25; 10:46-52; Lk 18:35-43). Woman with issue of blood (Mt 9:20-22; Mk 5:25-34; Lk 8:43-48). Many sick (Mt 8:16; 9:35; 14:14, 35-36; 15:30-31; 19:2; Mk 6:5, 53-56; Lk 4:40; 9:11). Daughter of the Syrian Phoenician woman (Mt 15:22-28; Mk 7:25-30). Woman with an infirmity (Lk 13:10-13). Ten lepers (Lk 17:12-14). *See Miracles, of Jesus.*
Power of, given to the apostles (Mt 10:1, 8; Mk 3:13-15; 6:7, 13; Lk 9:1-2, 6), to the Seventy (Lk 10:9, 17), to all believers (Mk 16:18). Special gifts of (1Co 12:9, 28, 30).

By the Apostles:
The lame man, in Jerusalem (Ac 3:2-10), in Lystra (Ac 14:8-10). Sick, in Jerusalem (Ac 5:15-16), on the island of Malta (Ac 28:8-9). Aeneas (Ac 9:34).

Figurative:
Healing of disease a metaphor for forgiving of sins (Ps 103:3; Hos 7:1).
See Miracles.

HEALTH [776, 2014, 2730, 5340, 5507, 8326, 8934, *5617*]. Health was a promised blessing of the Old Covenant (Ex 15:26; Dt 7:12-16), as diseases were part of its curse (Lev 26:14-16; Dt 28:20-29, 58-63). Health can be affected by sin (Ps 38:3, 7), but not all disease is the result of sin (Jn 9:1-3).
The wish for health and wholeness (Hebrew *shalom*) was part of standard greetings (Ge 29:6; 43:27, 28; 1Sa 25:4-6; 3Jn 2). The fear of the LORD brings health (Pr 3:7-8), words of wisdom (Pr 4:20-22), good news (Pr 15:30).
See Healing.

HEAR *See Obedience.*

HEARERS [*263, 5583, 7754, 7992, 9048, 9051, 10725, *198, 201, 1653*]. Unresponsive (Eze 33:30-32; Mt 7:26-27; 13:14-15, 19-22; Lk 6:49; 8:11-14; Ro 2:13; Jas 1:22-24).
Obedient (Mt 7:24-25; 13:23; Lk 6:47-48; 8:15; Jas 1:25).

HEART [*1061, 789, 2668, 2693, 4000, 4213, 4220, 4222, 5055, 5570, 5883, 7931, 8120, 9348, 10381, *1571, 1591, 2426, 2510, 2840, 2841, 5016, 5073, 6034*]. Seat of affection and source of action (Dt 5:29; 6:5-6; 2Ch 12:14; Ps 57:7; 112:7; Pr 4:23; 14:30; 15:13-15; 16:1; Mk 9:4; 12:33, 35; 15:18-20; 23:26; Mk 7:21-23). Lives forever (Ps 22:26). Of the Gentiles, taught of God (Ro 2:14-16).

Changed:
(Ps 51:10). Instances of: Saul (1Sa 10:9), Solomon (1Ki 3:11-12), Paul (Ac 9:1-18).

Hardening of:
Forbidden (Heb 3:8, 15; 4:7). Instances of: Pharaoh (Ex 4:21; 7:3, 13, 22; 8:15, 32; 9:12, 35; 10:1; 14:8), Sihon (Dt 2:30), king of Canaan (Jos 11:20), Philistines (1Sa 6:6).

Known to God:
(Dt 31:21; 1Sa 16:7; 2Sa 7:20; 1Ki 8:39; 1Ch 28:9; 2Ch 6:30; Job 11:11; 16:19; 31:4; Ps 1:6; 44:21; 51:10; 94:11; 139:1-12; Pr 5:21; 16:2; 21:2; Isa 66:18; Jer 12:13; 17:10; Eze 11:5, 19-21; 36:25-26; Lk 16:15; Ac 1:24; 15:8; Ro 8:27; 1Co 3:20; Heb 4:12; Rev 2:23).
To Christ (Ro 8:27; Rev 2:23).

Regenerate:
Is penitent (Ps 34:18; 51:10, 17; 147:3; Pr 15:3). Renewed (Dt 30:6; Ps 51:10; Eze 11:19; 18:31; 36:26; Jn 3:3, 7; Ro 2:29; Eph 4:22-24; Col 3:9-10; Heb 10:22; Jas 4:8). Pure (Ps 24:4; 66:18; Pr 20:9; Mt 5:8; 2Ti 2:22; 1Pe 3:15). Enlightened (2Co 4:6). Established (Ps 57:7; 108:1; 112:7-8; 1Th 3:13). Refined by affliction (Pr 17:3). Tried or tested (1Ch 29:17; Ps 7:9; 26:2; Pr 17:3; Jer 11:20; 12:3; 20:12; 1Th 2:4; Heb 11:17; Rev 2:2, 10). Strengthened (Ps 27:14; 112:8; 1Th 3:13). Graciously affected of God (1Sa 10:26; 1Ch 29:18; Ezr 6:22; 7:27; Pr 16:1; 21:1; Jer 20:9; Ac 16:14).

Should Render to God:

Obedience (Dt 10:12; 11:13; 26:16; 1Ki 2:4; Ps 119:1, 12; Eph 6:6). Faith (Ps 27:3; 112:7; Ac 8:37; Ro 6:17; 10:10). Trust (Pr 3:5). Love (Dt 6:5-6; Mt 22:37). Fear (Ps 119:161; Jer 32:40). Fidelity (Ne 9:8). Zeal (2Ch 17:16; Jer 20:9). Seeking God (2Ch 19:3; 30:19; Ezr 7:10; Ps 10:17; 84:2).

Should Be:

Joyful (1Sa 2:1; Ps 4:7; 97:11; Isa 65:14; Zec 10:7). Perfect (1Ki 8:61; Ps 101:2). Upright (Ps 97:11; 125:4). Clean (Ps 51:10; 73:1). Pure (Ps 24:4; Pr 22:11; Mt 5:8; 1Ti 1:5; 2Ti 2:22; Jas 4:8; 1Pe 1:22). Sincere (Lk 8:15; Ac 2:46; Eph 6:5; Col 3:22; Heb 10:22). Repentant (Dt 30:2; Ps 34:18; 51:17). Devout (1Sa 1:13; Ps 4:4; 9:1; 27:8; 77:6; 119:10, 69, 145). Wise (1Ki 3:9, 12; 4:29; Job 9:4; Pr 8:10; 10:8; 11:29; 14:33; 23:15). Tender (1Sa 24:5; 2Ki 22:19; Job 23:16; Ps 22:14; Eph 4:32). Holy (Ps 66:18; 1Pe 3:15). Compassionate (Jer 4:19; La 3:51). Lowly (Mt 11:29).

The Unregenerate Heart:

Is full of iniquity (Ge 6:5; 8:21; 1Sa 17:28; Pr 6:14, 18; 11:20; Pr 20:9; Ecc 8:11; 9:3; Jer 4:14, 18; 17:9; Ac 8:21-23; Ro 1:21). Loves evil (Dt 19:18; Ps 95:10; Jer 17:5). A fountain of evil (Mt 12:34-35; Mk 7:21). *See Depravity.* Wayward (2Ch 12:14; Ps 101:4; Pr 6:14; 11:20; 12:8; 17:20; Jer 5:23; Heb 3:10). Blind (Ro 1:21; Eph 4:18). *See Blindness, Spiritual.* Is double (1Ch 12:33; Ps 12:2; Pr 28:14; Isa 9:9; 10:12; 46:12; Hos 10:2; Jas 1:6, 8). *See Instability.* Is hard (Ps 76:5; Eze 2:4; 3:7; 11:19; 36:26; Mk 6:52; 10:5; 16:14; Jn 12:40; Ro 1:21; 2:5). *See Impenitence; Obduracy.* Is deceitful (Jer 17:9). Proud (2Ki 14:10; 2Ch 25:19; Ps 101:5; Pr 18:12; 28:25; Jer 48:29; 49:16). *See Pride.* Is subtle (Pr 7:10). *See Hypocrisy.* Is sensual (Eze 6:9; Hos 13:6; Ro 8:7). *See Lasciviousness.* Is worldly (2Ch 26:16; Da 5:20; Ac 8:21-22). Judicially hardened (Ex 4:21; Jos 11:20; Isa 6:10; Ac 28:26-27). Malicious (Ps 28:3; 140:2; Pr 24:2; Ecc 7:26; Eze 25:15). *See Malice.* Is impenitent (Ro 2:5). *See Impenitence.* Is diabolical (Jn 13:2; Ac 5:3). Is covetous (Jer 22:17; 2Pe 2:14). *See Covetousness.* Is foolish (Pr 12:23; 22:15; Ecc 9:3). Under the wrath of God (Ro 1:18-19, 31; 2:5-6).

See Regeneration; Sanctification.

HEARTH [789, 2219, 3683, 4612]. Of an altar (Lev 6:9; Isa 30:14; Eze 43:15-16). Figurative (Isa 29:2).

HEAT [2770, 2780, 2801, 2996, 3001, 3019, 3031, 3501, 3880, 9220, 9299, 9429, *2549, 3008, 3012, 3014*]. Jonah overcome with (Jnh 4:8). *See Sunstroke.*

HEATH *See Bush.*

HEATHEN [*1620*]. Gentiles, pagans. Under this head are all who are not descendants of Abraham, Isaac and Jacob.

Described:

Cast out of Canaan (Lev 18:24-25; Ps 44:2) and their land given to Israel (Ps 78:55; 105:44; 135:12; 136:21-22; Isa 54:1-3). Excluded from the temple (La 1:10).

Wicked practices of. *See Idolatry.*

Divine Revelations Given to:

Abimelech (Ge 20:3-7), Nebuchadnezzar (Da 4:1-18), Belshazzar (Da 5:5, 24-29), Cyrus (2Ch 36:23; Ezr 1:1-4), the Magi (Mt 2:1-11), the centurion (Mt 8:5-13; Lk 7:2-9), Cornelius (Ac 10:1-7).

Pious People Among:

(Isa 65:5; Ac 10:35). Melchizedek (Ge 14:18-20). Abimelech (Ge 20). Balaam (Nu 22). Jethro (Ex 18). Cyrus (Ezr 1:1-3). Eliphaz (Job 4). Bildad (Job 8). Zophar (Job 11). Elihu (Job 32). Nebuchadnezzar, after his restoration (Da 4). The Ninevites (Jnh 3:5-10). The Magi (Mt 2:1-12). The centurion of Capernaum (Mt 8:5-13; Lk 7:2-9), of Caesarea (Ac 10). Believed in Christ (Mt 8:5-13; Lk 7:2-9).

See Gentiles.

HEAVE OFFERING *See Offerings.*

HEAVE SHOULDER *See Offerings.*

HEAVEN [5294, 9028, 10723, *1479, 2230, 4039, 4040, 4041, 5734, 5737*].

God's Dwelling Place:

(Dt 26:15; 1Ki 8:30, 39, 43, 49; 1Ch 16:31; 21:26; 2Ch 2:6; 6:21, 27, 30, 33, 35, 39; 7:14; 30:27; Ne 9:27; Job 22:12, 14; Ps 2:4; 11:4; 20:6; 33:13; 102:19; 103:19; 113:5-6; 123:1; 135:6; Ecc 5:2; Isa 57:15; 63:15; 66:1; Jer 23:24; La 3:41, 50; Da 5:23; Zec 2:13; Mt 5:34, 45; 6:9; 10:32-33; 11:25; 12:50; 16:17; 18:10, 14; Mk 11:25-26; 16:19; Ac 7:49; 55-56; Ro 1:18; Heb 8:1; Rev 8:1; 12:7-9; 21:22-27; 22:1-5).

Figurative:

Of divine government (Mt 16:19; 18:18; 23:22). Of God (Mt 21:25).

The Future Home of the Righteous:

(2Ki 2:11; Mt 5:12; 13:30, 43; Lk 16:22; Jn 12:8, 26; 13:36; 17:24; 2Co 5:1; Php 3:20; Col 1:5-6, 12; 3:9; 1Th 4:17; Heb 10:34; 11:10, 16; 12:22; 1Pe 1:4; Rev 2:7; 3:21).

Called:

A city (Heb 11:10, 16), a garden (Mt 3:12), a house (Jn 14:2-3; 2Co 5:1), a kingdom (Mt 25:34; Lk 12:32; 22:29-30), the kingdom of Christ and of God (Eph 5:5), a heavenly country (Heb 11:16), a rest (Heb 4:9; Rev 14:13), glory (Col 3:4), paradise (Lk 23:43; 2Co 12:2, 4; Rev 2:7).

Everlasting (2Co 5:1; Heb 10:34; 13:14; 1Pe 1:4; 2Pe 1:11). Allegorical representatives of (Rev 4:1-11; 5:1-14; 7:9-17; 14:1-3; 15:1-8; 21; 22:1-5). No marriage in (Mt 22:30; Lk 20:34-36). Names of the righteous written in (Lk 10:20; Heb 12:22-24). Treasures in (Mt 6:20; 19:21; Lk 12:33). Joy in (Ps 16:11; Lk 15:6-7, 10). Righteousness dwells in (2Pe 3:13). No sorrow in (Rev 7:16-17; 21:4). The wicked excluded from (Gal 5:21; Eph 5:5; Rev 22:15).

See Righteous, Promises to.

HEAVEN OPENED (Mt 3:16; Ac 7:56; 10:11; Rev 19:11).

HEAVENLY PLACES [*2230]. (Eph 1:3, 20; 2:6; 3:10).

HEAVENS, NEW To be created (Isa 65:17; 66:22; 2Pe 3:13; Rev 21:1-4).

HEAVENS, PHYSICAL (Ge 1:1; 2Ch 2:6; Job 38:31-33; Ps 19:1; 50:6; 68:33; 89:29; 103:11; 113:4; 115:16; 136:5; Jer 31:37; Eze 1:1; Mt 24:29-30; Ac 2:19-20).

Created by God (Ge 1:1; 2:1; Ex 20:11; 1Ch 16:26; 2Ch 2:12; Ne 9:6; Job 9:8; Ps 8:3; 19:1; 33:6, 9; 102:25; 148:4-6; Pr 8:27; Isa 37:16; 40:22; 42:5; 45:12, 18; Jer 10:12; 32:17; 51:15; Ac 4:24; 14:15; Heb 1:10; Rev 10:6; 14:7). *See Creation; God, Creator; Heavens, New.*

Destruction of (Job 14:12; Ps 102:25-26; Isa 51:6; Mt 5:18; 24:35; Heb 1:10-12; 2Pe 3:10-12; Rev 6:12-14; 20:11; 21:1, 4). Figurative of divine judgment (Isa 34:4).

See Sky.

HEAVING AND WAVING *See Offerings.*

HEBER, HEBERITE [2491, 2499] (*associate*).

1. An Asherite, the son of Beriah; great-grandson of Jacob (Ge 46:17; Nu 26:45; 1Ch 7:31-32).

2. Kenite whose wife Jael killed Sisera (Jdg 4:11-21; 5:24).

3. A Judahite, the father of Soco and son of Ezrah (1Ch 4:18).

4. A Benjamite and son of Elpaal (1Ch 8:17).

HEBREW [3376, 6303, *1578, 1580*]. A word supposed to be a corruption of the name of Eber, who was an ancestor of Abraham (Ge 10:24; 11:14-26). *See Genealogy.* Applied to Abraham (Ge 14:13) and his descendants (Ge 39:14; 40:15; 43:32; Ex 2:6; Dt 15:12; 1Sa 4:9; 29:3; Jnh 1:9; Ac 6:1; 2Co 11:22; Php 3:5). Used to denote the language of the Jews (Jn 5:2; 19:20; Ac 21:40; 22:2; 26:14; Rev 9:11).

See Israel, Israelites; Jews.

HEBREW LANGUAGE The NW branch of the Semitic language family; has close affinity to Ugaritic, Phoenician, Moabitic, and the Canaanite dialects; sister languages include Arabic, Akkadian, and Aramaic. Except for a few Aramaic passages in Ezra, Daniel, and Jeremiah, it is the language of the OT.

HEBREW OF THE HEBREWS A Jew of pure blood, very strict in observing the law (Php 3:4-6).

HEBREWS, EPISTLE TO THE

Author: Anonymous. Historical speculations as to authorship include Paul, Barnabas, Apollos, and Priscilla.

Date: Before the destruction of Jerusalem and the temple in A.D. 70

Outline:

I. Prologue: The Superiority of God's New Revelation (1:1-4).
II. The Superiority of Christ to Leaders of the Old Covenant (1:5-7:28).
    A. Christ Is Superior to the Angels (1:5-2:18).
        1. Scriptural proof of superiority (1:5-14).
        2. Exhortation not to ignore the revelation of God in his Son (2:1-4).
        3. Further Scriptural proof of superiority over the angels (2:5-18).
    B. Christ Is Superior to Moses (3:1-4:13).
        1. Demonstration of Christ's superiority (3:1-6).
        2. Exhortation to enter salvation-rest (3:7-4:13).
    C. Christ Is Superior to the Aaronic Priests (4:14-7:28).
        1. Exhortation to hold fast (4:14-16).
        2. Qualifications of a priest (5:1-10).
        3. Exhortation to abandon spiritual lethargy (5:11-6:12).
        4. Certainty of God's promise (6:13-20).
        5. Christ's superior priestly order (ch. 7).
III. The Superior Sacrificial Work of Our High Priest (chs. 8-10).
    A. A Better Covenant (ch. 8).
    B. A Better Sanctuary (9:1-12).
    C. A Better Sacrifice (9:13-10:18).
    D. Exhortations (10:19-39).
IV. Final Plea for Persevering Faith (chs. 11-12).
    A. Examples of Past Heroes of the Faith (ch. 11).
    B. Encouragement for Persevering Faith (12:1-11).
    C. Exhortations for Persevering Faith (12:12-17).
    D. Motivation for Persevering Faith (12:18-29).
V. Conclusion (ch. 13).
    A. Practical Rules for Christian Living (13:1-17).
    B. Request for Prayer (13:18-19).
    C. Benediction (13:20-21).
    D. Personal Remarks (13:22-23).
    E. Greetings and Final Benediction (13:24-25).

HEBRON [2496, 2497] (*association*).

1. For Jos 19:28 *See Abdon, 1.*

2. A city of Judah, S of Jerusalem. When built (Nu 13:22). Fortified (2Ch 11:10). Also called Kiriath Arba (Ge 23:2; 35:27; Jos 15:13). Abraham dwells and Sarah dies at (Ge 23:2). Hoham, king of, confederated with other kings of the Canaanites against Joshua (Jos 10:3-39). Children of Anakim dwell at (Nu 13:22; Jos 11:21). Conquest of, by Caleb (Jos 14:6-15; Jdg

1:10, 20). A city of refuge (Jos 20:7; 21:11, 13). David crowned king of Judah at (2Sa 2:1-11; 3), of Israel (2Sa 5:1-5). The burial place of Sarah (Ge 23:2), Abner (2Sa 3:32), Ish-Bosheth (2Sa 4:12). The conspirators against Ish-Bosheth hanged at (2Sa 4:12). Absalom made king at (2Sa 15:9-10). Jews of the Babylonian captivity dwell at (Ne 11:25). Pool of (2Sa 4:12).

3. Son of Kohath (Ex 6:18; Nu 3:19; 1Ch 6:2, 18; 23:12, 19).

4. The family name of Mareshah (1Ch 2:42-43; 15:9).

HEDGE [5004, 5372, 8455]. Protecting a vineyard (Isa 5:5). Of thorns (Mic 7:4; Mk 12:1). Figurative of divine protection (Job 1:10), of divine entrapment (Job 3:23). See Fence.

HEEDFULNESS [1067, 7992, 8505, 9048, 9068]. Commanded (Ex 23:13; Pr 4:25-27).

Necessary: In the care of the soul (Dt 4:9). In the house and worship of God (Ecc 5:1). In what we hear (Mk 4:24). In how we hear (Lk 3:18). In keeping God's commandments (Jos 22:5). In conduct (Eph 5:15). In speech (Pr 13:3; Jas 1:19). In worldly company (Ps 39:1; Col 4:5). In giving judgment (2Ch 19:6-7). Against sin (Heb 12:15-16). Against unbelief (Heb 3:12). Against idolatry (Dt 4:15-16). Against false Christs, and false prophets (Mt 24:4-5, 23-24). Against false teachers (Php 3:2; Col 2:8; 2Pe 3:16-17). Against presumption (1Co 10:12).

Promises to (1Ki 2:4; 1Ch 22:13).
See Obedience.

HEGAI [2043, 2051]. Eunuch in charge of Xerxes' harem (Est 2:3, 8, 15).

HEIFER [6320, 7239, 1239]. When used as sacrifice, must be without blemish and must not have come under the yoke (Nu 19:2; Dt 21:3). An atonement for murder (Dt 21:1-9). The red heifer used for the water of separation (Nu 19; Heb 9:13).

Used for plowing (Jdg 14:18), for treading out wheat (Hos 10:11). Tractable (Hos 10:11). Intractable (Hos 4:16).
See Cattle; Offerings.
Figurative: Of backsliders (Hos 4:16). Of the obedient (Hos 10:11).

HEIFER, RED See Animals.

HEIR [3769, 3772, 3101, 5169, 5626].
Literal:
Mosaic law relating to inheritance of (Nu 27:8-11; 36:1-8; Jos 17:3-6). Prescribing right of, to redeem alienated land (Lev 25:25; Ru 4:1-12). To inherit slaves (Lev 25:45-46). Firstborn son to have double portion (Dt 21:15-17). Children of wives and concubines are (Ge 15:3; 21:10; 25:5-6; Gal 4:30). All possessions left to (Ecc 2:18-19). Minor, under guardians (Gal 4:1-2).
See Birthright; Firstborn; Inheritance; Orphan; Will.

Figurative:
Of spiritual adoption (Ro 8:14-17; Gal 3:29; 4:6-7; Tit 3:7; Jas 2:5). See Adoption.

HELAH [2690] (necklace IDB; rust KB). A wife of Asher (1Ch 4:5).

HELAM [2663]. Place in Syrian desert E of Jordan where David defeated forces of Hadadezer (2Sa 10:16-17).

HELBAH [2695] (a fertile region). A town of Asher (Jdg 1:31).

HELBON [2696] (fertile). A village near Damascus, noted for fine wines (Eze 27:18).

HELDAI [2702] (mole).
1. The Netophathite. One of David's heroes (1Ch 27:15). Heled is a variant spelling (2Sa 23:29; 1Ch 11:30).
2. A leader among those returned from the Exile (Zec 6:10, 14).

HELECH [2662]. Possibly Cilicia, an area in SE (modern day) Turkey (Eze 27:11).

HELED [2699]. See Heldai, 1.

HELEK, HELEKITE [2751, 2757] (portion, lot). Son of Gilead (Jos 17:2) and his clan (Nu 26:30).

HELEM [2152] (health).
1. A descendant of Asher (1Ch 7:35).
2. Probably the same as Heldai (Zec 6:10, 14).

HELEPH [2738] (possibly sharp, cutting). A town of Naphtali (Jos 19:33).

HELEZ [2742] (vigor BDB).
1. One of David's mighty men (2Sa 23:26; 1Ch 11:27; 27:10).
2. A man of Judah (1Ch 2:39).

HELI [2459] (ascent [to God]). Father of Joseph, the husband of Mary (Lk 3:23), or perhaps the father of Mary, the mother of Jesus.

HELIOPOLIS [225] (sun [god] city). City near S end of the Nile Delta called "On" in the Bible (Ge 41:45; 46:20; Isa 19:18, ftn).
See City of Destruction.

HELKAI [2758] (Yahweh is [my] portion). A priest (Ne 12:15).

HELKATH [2762] (portion). A Levitical town (Jos 19:25; 21:31), also spelled Hukok (1Ch 6:75). See Hukok.

HELKATH HAZZURIM [2763] (possibly portion [field] of rock, or swords IDB; portion [field] of snare KB). Plain near pool of Gibeon where soldiers of Joab and Abner fought (2Sa 2:12-16).

HELL [*87, 1147, 5434*]. In the NIV, "hell" usually translates the Greek *geena* and *hades*, but is conceptually the same as the Hebrew *Sheol*, usually rendered "grave," the unseen world and abode of the dead (Ge 37:35; 42:38; 44:29, 31; Dt 32:22; 1Sa 2:6; 2Sa 22:6; 1Ki 2:6, 9; Job 7:9; 11:8; 14:13; 17:13; 21:13; 24:19; 26:6; Ps 9:17; 16:10; 18:5; 55:15; 86:13; 116:3; 139:8; Pr 5:5; 7:27; 9:18; 15:11, 24; 23:14; 27:20; Isa 5:14; 14:9, 15; 28:15, 18; 57:9; Eze 31:16-17; 32:21, 27; Am 9:2; Jnh 2:2; Hab 2:5). In the NT hell is the unseen world (Mt 11:23; 16:18; Lk 10:15; 16:23; Ac 2:27, 31; Rev 1:18; 6:8; 20:13-14), a place of torment (Mt 5:22, 29-30; 10:28; 18:9; 23:15, 33; Lk 12:5; Jas 3:6) and of captivity for fallen angels (2Pe 2:4).

Figurative:
Of divine judgments (Dt 32:22; Eze 31:15-17).

The Future State, or Abode, of the Wicked:
(Ps 9:17; Pr 5:5; 9:18; 15:24; 23:14; Isa 30:33; 33:14; Mt 3:12; 5:22, 29-30; 7:13; 8:11-12; 10:28; 13:30, 38-42, 49-50; 16:18; 18:8-9, 34-35; 22:13; 25:30, 41, 46; Mk 9:43-48; Lk 3:17; 16:23-28; Ac 1:25; 2Th 1:9; 2Pe 2:4; Jude 6, 23; Rev 2:11; 9:1-2; 11:7; 14:10-11; 19:20; 20:10, 15; 21:8).
See Grave; Hades; Sheol; Wicked, Punishment of.

HELLENISTS NIV "Grecian Jews"; Jews of the Dispersion who spoke Greek and followed some aspects of Greek culture (Ac 6:1; 9:29).

HELM *See* Rudder(s).

HELMET [3916, 5057+8031, 7746, *4330*]. A defensive headgear worn by soldiers (1Sa 17:5, 38; 2Ch 26:14; Jer 46:4; Eze 23:24).
Figurative: (Isa 59:17; Eph 6:17; 1Th 5:8).

HELON [2735] (*strength, power*). Father of Eliab (Nu 1:9; 2:7; 7:24, 29; 10:16).

HELPER [5853, 6468, 6469, 6476, *1071, 5677*]. Woman created as a helper suitable for man (Ge 2:18, 20). Yahweh is the helper of Israel (Dt 33:29; Hos 13:9), of the fatherless (Ps 10:14), of David (Ps 27:9). Eliezer means "God is my helper" (Ex 18:4, ftn.).

HELPMEET *See* Helper.

HELPS [6468, *2138, 5269*]. One of the gifts of the Spirit, probably the ability to perform helpful works in a gracious manner (1Co 12:7-11, 28-31).

HEM OF A GARMENT [4053, 4193, 7443, 8767, *5309*]. Fringes or tassels on the borders of the Israelite outer garment (Nu 15:38-39).

HEMAM *See* Homam.

HEMAN [2124] (*faithful*).
1. A man noted for wisdom, to whom Solomon is compared (1Ki 4:31; 1Ch 2:6).

2. "The Singer," a chief Levite, and musician (1Ch 6:33; 15:17, 19; 16:41). The king's seer (1Ch 25:5). His sons and daughters temple musicians (1Ch 6:33; 25:1-6). "Maskil of," title of Psalm 88. *See* Maskil.

HEMATH
1. *See* Hamath.
2. *See* Hammath, 2.

HEMDAN [2777] (*desirable*). Son of Dishon (Ge 36:26).

HEMLOCK A poisonous and bitter plant (Hos 10:4; Am 6:12). *See* Gall, 3; Plants of the Bible; Poison.

HEMORRHAGE Menstruation (Lev 15:19; Mt 9:20; Lk 8:43). A woman subject to bleeding for twelve years (Mk 5:25-29; Mk 5:24-34; Lk 8:). *See* Bleeding, Subject to; Menstruation.

HEMORRHOIDS NIV "tumors" (Dt 28:27); a disease with which the Philistines were afflicted (1Sa 5:6, 12; 6:4; 5:11). *See* Disease; Tumor.

HEN [2835, *3998*] (proper name: *gracious*).
1. Son of Zephaniah (Zec 6:14).
2. Hen protecting her chicks figurative of Jesus' desire for Jerusalem (Mt 23:37; Lk 13:34).

HENA [2184] (*[pagan god] Anath*). A city on the Euphrates (2Ki 18:34; 19:13; Isa 37:13).

HENADAD [2836] (*favor of Hadad [pagan god]*). A Levite (Ezr 3:9; Ne 3:18, 24; 10:9).

HENNA BLOSSOMS [4110]. A shrub of Israel (perhaps the cypress) with tightly clustered, aromatic blossoms (SS 1:14; 4:13).

HENOCH *See* Enoch.

HEPHER, HEPHERITE [2918, 2919, 2920] (perhaps *help*).
1. Son of Gilead, and ancestor of Zelophehad (Nu 26:32-33; 27:1; Jos 17:2-3).
2. Son of Naarah (1Ch 4:6).
3. One of David's heroes (1Ch 11:36).
4. A city W of the Jordan (Jos 12:17; 1Ki 4:10).

HEPHZIBAH [2915] (*my pleasure is in her*).
1. Wife of Hezekiah (2Ki 21:1).
2. Symbolic name given to Zion (Isa 62:4).

HERALD [7924, 10370, *3061*]. (Isa 40:3; Da 3:4). Signified by the word "preacher" (1Ti 2:7; 2Ti 1:11; 2Pe 2:5).

HERBS [246, 4865, 5353, *3303*]. Given for food (Ge 1:29-30; Pr 15:17). *See* Vegetation.

HERD [*546, 989, 1330, 6337, 6373, 8802,

36, 2576]. Herds of cattle were used in plowing, threshing, and sacrifice (Ge 18:7; Job 1:3; 42:12).

HERDSMAN [5238, 8286]. Person in charge of cattle (Ge 13:7) or pigs (Mt 8:33), despised in Egypt (Ge 46:34) but honored in Israel (Ge 47:6; 1Ch 29:29).

HEREDITY Like gives birth to like (Ge 5:3; Job 14:4; Jn 3:6-7).

Results of:

Natural, depravity (Job 21:19; Ps 51:5; 58:3; Isa 48:8; Jn 9:2; Ro 5:12; Eph 2:3).

Judicial, ordained consequences of parental conduct (Ex 20:5-6; 34:7; Nu 14:18, 33; Dt 5:9; Ps 37:28; Isa 14:20-21; 65:6-7; Jer 32:18; Ro 5:12; 1Co 15:22). Does not determine moral status (Jer 31:29-30; Eze 18:1-32; Mt 3:9).

HERES [3065] (*sun*).
1. District around Aijalon (Jdg 1:35).
2. Place E of the Jordan (Jdg 8:13).
3. Egyptian city, translated "city of destruction" (Isa 19:18), undoubtedly Heliopolis.

HERESH [3090] (*deaf, silent*). A Levite (1Ch 9:15).

HERESY [146]. Propagandism of, forbidden under severe penalties (Dt 13; Tit 3:10-11; 2Jn 10-11). Teachers of, among early Christians (Ac 15:24; 2Co 11:4; Gal 1:7; 2:4; 2Pe 2; Jude 3-16; Rev 2:2). Paul and Silas accused of (Ac 16:20-21, 23). Paul accused of (Ac 18:13). Disavowed by Paul (Ac 24:13-17). *See Teachers, False.*

HERETH [3101]. A forest in which David found refuge from Saul (1Sa 22:5).

HERMAS [2254]. Friend of Paul in the church at Rome (Ro 16:14).

HERMES [2258] (*possibly rock, cairn*).
1. Greek god (messenger), the same as Mercury in Latin. Paul mistaken for (Ac 14:12).
2. Friend of Paul in the church at Rome (Ro 16:14).

HERMOGENES [2259] (*born of Hermes*). A Christian who deserted Paul (2Ti 1:15).

HERMON, MOUNT [3056] (*consecrated place*). Mountain marking S end of Anti-Lebanon range; thirty miles SW of Damascus; 9000 ft. above sea level; marks N boundary of Israel; has three peaks. Has borne several names: the Amorites call it "Senir," (Dt 3:9), the Sidonians call it "Sirion" (Dt 3:9), "Siyon," (Dt 4:48). Probably the Mount of Transfiguration (Mt 17:1). Seat of Baal worship (Jdg 3:3). Modern Jebel es-Sheikh.

HEROD [2476]. Idumean rulers of Israel (37 B.C. to A.D. 100). Line started with Antipater, whom Julius Caesar made procurator of Judea in 47 B.C.

1. Herod the Great, first procurator of Galilee, then king of the Jews (37-4 B.C.); built Caesarea, temple at Jerusalem; slaughtered children at Bethlehem (Mt 2:1-18). At his death his kingdom was divided among his three sons: Archelaus, Herod Antipas, and Philip.

2. Archelaus ruled over Judea, Samaria, and Idumea (4 B.C. to A.D. 6), and was removed from office by the Romans (Mt 2:22).

3. Herod Antipas ruled over Galilee and Perea (4 B.C. to A.D. 39); killed John the Baptist (Mt 14:1-12); called "fox" by Jesus (Lk 13:32).

4. Philip, tetrarch of Batanaea, Trachonitis, Gaulanitis, and parts of Jamnia (4 B.C. to A.D. 34). Best of the Herods.

5. Herod Agrippa I; grandson of Herod the Great; tetrarch of Galilee; king of Israel (A.D. 37-44); killed James the apostle (Ac 12:1-23).

6. Herod Agrippa II. King of territory E of Galilee (A.D. 50-100); Paul appeared before him (Ac 25:13-26:32).

HERODIANS [2477]. They are mentioned as enemies of Jesus once in Galilee, and again at Jerusalem (Mt 22:15-22; Mk 3:6; 12:13-17; Lk 20:20-26). The Pharisees were ardent nationalists, opposed to Roman rule, while the hated Herodians, as their name indicates, supported the Roman rule of the Herods. Now, however, the Pharisees enlisted the help of the Herodians to trap Jesus in his words. After trying to put him off guard with flattery, they sprang their question: "Is it right to pay taxes to Caesar or not?" (Mt 22:17). If he said "no," the Herodians would report him to the Roman governor and he would be executed for treason. If he said "yes," the Pharisees would denounce him to the people as disloyal to his nation.

HERODIAS [2478] (*feminine form of* Herod). Granddaughter of Herod the Great who had John the Baptist put to death (Mt 14:3-6; Mk 6:17; Lk 3:19).

HERODION [2479]. A Roman Christian (Ro 16:11).

HERON [649]. Large aquatic bird Israelites could not eat (Lev 11:19; Dt 14:18).

HESED *See Ben-Hesed.*

HESHBON [3114] (*reckoning*). A city of the Amorites (Nu 21:25-35; Dt 1:4). Built by Reuben (Nu 32:37). Allotted to Gad (Jos 21:38-39). Pools at (SS 7:4). Prophecy concerning (Isa 16:8; Jer 48:2, 34-35; 49:1-3).

HESHMON [3132]. A town in the S of Judah (Jos 15:27).

HETH Son of Canaan and ancestor of the Hittites (Ge 10:15; 23:3, ftn, 5, 7, 10, 16, 18; 27:46; 49:32; 1Ch 1:13). *See Hittite(s).*

HETHLON [3158]. A place on the northern frontier of Israel (Eze 47:15; 48:1).

HEXATEUCH (*six books*). A term referring to the Pentateuch and Joshua as though it were a literary unit.

HEZEKIAH [2624, 2625, 3490, 3491, *1614*] (*Yahweh is [my] strength*).

1. King of Judah (2Ki 16:20; 18:1-2; 1Ch 3:13; 2Ch 29:1; Mt 1:9). Religious zeal of (2Ch 29; 30; 31). Purges the nation of idolatry (2Ki 18:4; 2Ch 31:1; 33:3). Restores the true forms of worship (2Ch 31:2-21). His piety (2Ki 18:2, 5-6; 2Ch 29:2; 31:20-21; 32:32; Jer 26:19). Military operations of (2Ki 18:19; 1Ch 4:39-43; 2Ch 32; Isa 36; 37). Sickness and restoration of (2Ki 20:1-11; 2Ch 32:24; Isa 38:1-8). His psalm of thanksgiving (Isa 38:9-22). His lack of wisdom in showing his resources to commissioners of Babylon (2Ki 20:12-19; 2Ch 32:25-26, 31; Isa 39). Prospered of God (2Ki 18:7; 2Ch 32:27-30). Conducts the Brook Gihon into Jerusalem (2Ki 18:17; 20:20; 2Ch 32:4, 30; 33:14; Ne 2:13-15; 3:13, 16; Isa 7:3; 22:9-11; 36:2). Scribes of (Pr 25:1). Death and burial of (2Ki 20:21; 2Ch 32:33). Prophecies concerning (2Ki 19:20-34; 20:5-6, 16-18; Isa 38:5-8; 39:5-7; Jer 26:18-19).

2. One of the exiles (Ezr 2:16; Ne 7:21; 10:17).

3. An ancestor of the prophet Zephaniah (Zep 1:1).

4. *See Hizkiah, 1.*

HEZION [2611] (*vision* BDB; *one with floppy ears* IDB). Grandfather of Ben-Hadad (1Ki 15:18).

HEZIR [2615] (*boar*).

1. A Levite (1Ch 24:15).

2. A prince of Judah (Ne 10:20).

HEZRAI *See Hezro.*

HEZRO [2968]. Also called Hezrai. A Carmelite (2Sa 23:35; 1Ch 11:37).

HEZRON, HEZRONITE [2969, 2970, 2971, *2272*] (*enclosure*).

1. A son of Perez (Ge 46:12). Ancestor of the Hezronites (Nu 26:6). An ancestor of Jesus (Mt 1:3; Lk 3:33).

2. A son of Reuben (Ge 46:9; Ex 6:14; 1Ch 4:1; 5:3). Ancestor of the Hezronites (Nu 26:21).

HIDDAI [2068]. One of David's heroes (2Sa 23:30). Called Hurai (1Ch 11:32).

HIDDEKEL *See Tigris.*

HIEL [2647] (*God [El] lives*). Rebuilder of Jericho (1Ki 16:34). In him was fulfilled the curse pronounced by Joshua (Jos 6:26).

HIERAPOLIS [*2631*] (*[pagan] sacred city*). Ancient Phrygian city near Colosse (Col 4:13).

HIEROGLYPHICS *See Writing.*

HIGGAION [2053]. A musical term probably meaning "solemn sound" or "meditation." It occurs in Ugaritic as with the meaning "to utter." According to Gesenius, it signifies the murmuring tone of a harp and therefore should be rendered in a melancholy manner (Ps 92:3). Combined with *Selah*, it may have been intended to indicate a pause in the vocal music while the instruments played an interlude (Ps 9:16, ftn). Mendelssohn translates it "meditation, thought" (Ps 19:14). Therefore, the music was to be rendered in a mode to promote devout meditation.

See Music, Symbols Used in.

HIGH PLACES [1195]. A term used to describe places of worship (Ge 12:8; 22:2, 14; 31:54; 1Sa 9:12; 2Sa 24:25; 1Ki 3:2, 4; 18:30, 38; 1Ch 16:39; 2Ch 1:3; 33:17). Signify a place of idolatrous worship (Nu 22:41; 1Ki 11:7; 12:31; 14:23; 15:14; 22:43; 2Ki 17:9, 29; Jer 7:31). Licentious practices at (Eze 16:24-43). The idolatrous, to be destroyed (Lev 26:30; Nu 33:52). Asa destroys (2Ch 14:3), Jehoshaphat (2Ch 17:6), Hezekiah (2Ki 18:4), Josiah (2Ch 23:8).

See Groves; Idolatry; Shrine.

HIGH PRIEST *See Priest.*

HIGHWAYS [2006, 5019, 5020, 6148] (*a built up road*). From, Gibeon to Beth Horon (Jos 10:10), Bethel to Shechem (Jdg 21:19), Judea to Galilee, by way of Samaria (Jn 4:3-5, 43). To Bethel (Jdg 20:31), to Gibeah (Jdg 20:31), to cities of refuge (Dt 19:3). Built by rulers (Nu 20:17; 21:22).

Figurative (Pr 16:17; Isa 11:16; 35:8-10; 40:3-4; Mt 3:3; 7:13-14).

See Roads.

HILEN [2664]. A city of Judah. Assigned to the priests (1Ch 6:58). Called Holon (Jos 15:51; 21:15).

HILKIAH [2759, 2760] (*Yahweh is [my] portion*).

1. Father of Eliakim (2Ki 18:18).

2. Merarite Levite (1Ch 6:45).

3. Merarite Levite (1Ch 26:11).

4. High priest who found book of the Law and sent it to Josiah (2Ki 22-23; 2Ch 34:14).

5. Priest who returned with Zerubbabel (Ne 12:7).

6. Father of Jeremiah (Jer 1:1).

7. Father of Gemariah who stood by Ezra at Bible reading (Ne 8:4).

HILL COUNTRY [2215, *3978*]. Any region of hills and valleys, but in Scripture generally the higher part of Judea (Lk 1:39, 65).

HILLEL [2148] (*he has praises*). Father of Abdon (Jdg 12:13, 15).

HILLS [1496, 2215, *1090, 4001*]. Perpetual (Ge 49:26; Hab 3:6).

HIN [2125]. A measure for liquids, and containing one-sixth or one-seventh of a bath. Probably equivalent to about four quarts (Ex 29:40; Lev 19:36; 23:13). *See Measure.*

HIND *See Deer.*

HINGE [6015, 7494]. A fitting enabling a door or window to swing in its place (1Ki 7:50), often used figuratively for something of great importance.

HINNOM, VALLEY OF [2183]. A valley W and SW of Jerusalem (Jos 15:8; 18:16; 2Ki 23:10; Ne 11:30). Children offered in sacrifice (2Ch 28:3; 33:6; Jer 7:31-32; 19:2, 4, 6; 32:35). Possibly valley of vision identical with (Isa 22:1, 5).

See Ben Hinnom; Topheth, Tophet.

HIP AND THIGH Hebrew idiom denoting thoroughness with which Samson slew Philistines (Jdg 15:8, KJV).

HIPPOPOTAMUS *See Behemoth.*

HIRAH [2669]. An Adullamite (Ge 38:1, 12).

HIRAM [2586, 2670, 2671] (*[my] brother is elevated*). Hiram (Hebrew *Huram*, a variant of *Hiram*), was a Phoenician king who was the first to accord the newly established King David international recognition. It was vital to him that he have good relations with the king of Israel since Israel dominated the inland trade routes to Tyre, and Tyre was dependent on Israelite agriculture for much of its food. A close relationship existed between these two realms until the Babylonian invasions. Builds a palace for David (2Sa 5:11; 1Ch 14:1; 2Ch 2:3). Aids Solomon in building the temple (1Ki 5; 2Ch 2:3-16). Dissatisfied with cities given by Solomon (1Ki 9:11-13). Makes presents of gold and seamen to Solomon (1Ki 9:14, 26-28; 10:11).

HIRE [924, 8509, 8510, *3636*]. Law concerning hired property (Ex 22:14-15).

See Employer; Master; Servant; Wages.

HIRED SERVANT [6128, 8502, 8509, *3140, 3634, 3636, 3638*]. Jacob (Ge 29:15; 30:26), re-employed (Ge 30:27-34; 31:6-7, 41). Laborers for a vineyard (Mt 20:1-15). The prodigal (Lk 15:15-19). Kindness to (Ru 2:4). Treatment of, more considerate than that accorded slaves (Lev 25:53).

Rights of:

To receive wages (Mt 10:10; Lk 10:7; Ro 4:4; 1Ti 5:18; Jas 5:4), daily (Lev 19:13; Dt 24:15). To share in spontaneous products of land in Sabbatic year (Lev 25:6). Wages of, paid in portion of flocks or products (Ge 30:31-32; 2Ch 2:10), or in money (Mt 20:2, 9-10). Oppression of, forbidden (Dt 24:14; Col 4:1). Oppressors of, punished (Mal 3:5).

Mercenary (Job 7:2). Unfaithful (Jn 10:12-13). *See Employee; Master; Servant; Wages.*

HIRELING *See Hired Servant.*

HISTORY (Job 8:8-10). *See Genesis; Joshua; Judges; Ruth; Samuel, 1 and 2; Kings, 1 and 2; Chronicles, 1 and 2; Ezra; Nehemiah; Esther; Israel, Israelites; Jesus the Christ, History of.*

HITTITE(S) [3147, 3153] (*descendants of Heth*). A tribe of Canaanites. Sons of Heth (Ge 10:15; 23:3, ftn, 5, 7, 10, 16, 18). Sell a burial site to Abraham (Ge 23). Esau intermarries with (Ge 26:34; 36:2). Dwelling place of (Ge 23:17-20; Nu 13:29; Jos 1:4; Jdg 1:26). Their land given to the Israelites (Ex 3:8; Dt 7:1; Jos 1:4). Conquered by Joshua (Jos 9:1-2; 10; 11; 12; 24:11). Intermarry with Israelites (Jdg 3:5-7; Ezr 9:1). Solomon intermarries with (1Ki 11:1; Ne 13:26). Pay tribute to Solomon (1Ki 9:20-21). Retain their own kings (1Ki 10:29; 2Ki 7:6; 2Ch 1:17). Officers from, in David's army (1Sa 26:6; 2Sa 11:3; 23:39).

HIVITE(S) [2563]. A tribe of Canaanites (Ge 10:17; 1Ch 1:15). Shechemites and Gibeonites were families of (Ge 34:2; Jos 9:7; 11:19). Esau intermarries with (Ge 26:34; 36:2). Dwelling place of (Jos 11:3; Jdg 3:3; 2Sa 24:7). Their land given to the Israelites (Ex 23:23, 28; Dt 20:17; Jdg 3:5). Conquered by Joshua (Jos 9:1; 12:8; 24:11). Pay tribute to Solomon (1Ki 9:21; 2Ch 8:8).

HIZKI [2623] (*Yahweh is [my] strength, or my strength*). A Benjamite (1Ch 8:17).

HIZKIAH [2624] (*Yahweh is [my] strength*).
1. A son of Neariah (1Ch 3:23).
2. *See Hezekiah, 3.*

HIZKIJAH *See Hezekiah, 2.*

HOBAB [2463] (*beloved, possibly deceit*). Brother-in-law of Moses (Nu 10:29; Jdg 4:11).

HOBAH [2551]. A place N of Damascus (Ge 14:15).

HOBAIAH [2469] (*Yahweh has hidden*). Priest whose descendants were excluded from priesthood (Ezr 2:61; Ne 7:63).

HOD [2087] (*grandeur*). A son of Zophah (1Ch 7:37).

HODAVIAH [2088, 2089, 2090] (*give thanks to Yahweh*).
1. Chief in Manasseh (1Ch 5:24).
2. Benjamite (1Ch 9:7).
3. Levite whose descendants returned with Zerubbabel (Ezr 2:40; 3:9; Ne 7:43).
4. Son of Elioenai (1Ch 3:24).

HODESH [2545] (*new moon*). Wife of Shaharaim (1Ch 8:9).

HODEVAH *See Hodaviah, 3.*

HODIAH [2091] (*grandeur is Yahweh*).
1. Wife of Ezra (1Ch 4:19).
2. A Levite (Ne 8:7; 9:5; 10:10, 13).
3. An Israelite chief (Ne 10:18).

HODSHI *See Tahtim Hodshi.*

HOGLAH [2519] (*partridge*). A daughter of Zelophehad (Nu 26:33; 27:1; 36:11; Jos 17:3).

HOHAM [2097]. Amorite king who entered a league against Joshua (Jos 10:3).

HOLIDAY [2182] (*a good day*). For rest. *See Sabbath.* One year in seven (Lev 25:2-7). *See Jubilee.*

HOLINESS [*7705, 7727, 7731, 10620, *39, 40, 41, 42, 43, 605, 4008, 4009, 4949*].

Defined:

Sin and holiness, sinful man and the holy Yahweh, are the dominant ideas in the Mosaic law. The supreme purpose of the system of Mosaic ordinances was to impress Israel as a separated people and through Israel to impress all people for all time that a holy God can be pleased by none but holy people. This is a central truth of the true religion. The student must, therefore, seek for this spiritual purpose through all the ordinances of the law. Defilement and uncleanness, exclusion of the unclean from the congregation atonements and atoning sacrifices, washings and purifications, whole burnt offerings, unblemished priests and unblemished offerings, typifying unblemished and uncorrupted motives in worship and service—all these were ordained as object lessons to teach that there is a difference between unholiness and holiness and thus to exalt holiness as the supreme lesson of life.

As in the books of the Mosaic law, so throughout the Holy Scriptures, the attainment of holiness is a dominant theme.

Attribute of God:

(Jos 24:19; 1Sa 6:20; Job 6:10; Ps 22:3; 47:8; 60:6; 89:35; 111:9; 145:17; Isa 5:16; 6:3; 29:19, 23; 41:14; 43:14-15; 47:4; 49:7; 57:15; Eze 36:21-22; 39:7, 25; Hos 11:9; Hab 1:12-13; Lk 1:49; Jn 17:11; Ro 1:23; Rev 4:8; 6:10; 15:4).

Described:

(Ro 14:17). As walking in uprightness (Isa 57:2). As a highway (Isa 35:8). As departing from evil (Ps 34:14; 37:27). As satisfying (Jn 6:35). As crucifying the sinful nature (Gal 5:24). As a new creature (Gal 6:15). As a new self (Eph 4:24; Col 3:10). As a rest (Heb 4:3, 9). As pure, peaceable, gentle (Jas 3:17).

Commanded:

(Ge 17:1; Ex 22:31; Lev 10:8-10; 11:44-45; 19:2; 20:7, 26; Nu 15:40; Dt 13:17; 18:13; Jos

7:13; 2Ch 20:21; Job 5:24; Ps 4:4; 97:10; Isa 52:1, 11; Mic 6:8; Zep 2:3; Mt 5:19-30, 48; 12:33; Jn 5:14; Ro 6:1-23; 1Co 3:16; 5:7; 15:34; 2Co 6:14-17; 7:1; Eph 1:4; 5:1, 3, 8-11; 1Th 4:3-4, 7; 5:22-23; 2Th 2:13; 1Ti 4:12; 5:22; 6:11-12; 2Ti 2:19, 21-22; 1Pe 1:5; 2Pe 1:5-8; 1Jn 2:1, 5, 29; 2Jn 4; Rev 18:4).

Commanded upon Israel (Ex 19:6; 22:31; Dt 7:6; 26:19; 28:9; Isa 4:3; 52:1, 11; 60:1, 21; Zec 8:3; 14:20-21).

Commanded upon the church (2Co 11:2; 1Pe 2:5, 9; Rev 19:8).

Exhortations to:

(Mt 5:30; Jn 5:14; Ro 6:13, 19; 12:1-2; 13:12-14; 1Co 6:13, 19-20; 10:31; 2Co 13:7-8; Eph 4:22-24; Col 3:5, 12-15; 1Th 2:12; 3:13; 1Ti 4:12; Tit 2:9-10, 12; 1Pe 4:1; 2Pe 3:11-12, 14; 3Jn 11).

Motives to:

God's holiness (Ge 17:1; Lev 11:44-45; 19:2; 20:26; Isa 6:1-8; Mt 5:48; 1Pe 1:15-16). God's mercies (Ro 12:1).

Taught:

By figures (Isa 61:9-11; Mt 12:33; 1Co 3:17; Eph 2:21). By inscriptions (Ex 28:36; Zec 14:20).

By disfellowship: Of the uncircumcised (Ge 17:14). Of those who violated the law, of unleavened bread (Ex 12:15), of sacrifices (Lev 17:9; 19:5-7), of purification (Nu 19:20). Of those who were defiled (Lev 7:25, 27; 13:5, 21, 26; 17:10; 18:29; 19:8; 20:3-6; Nu 5:2-3; 19:13). Of those who were guilty of blasphemy (Nu 15:31).

As a condition of fellowship: (Heb 12:14).

Typified:

In unblemished offerings (Ex 12:5; Lev 1:3, 10; 3:1, 6; 4:3, 23; 5:15; 6:6; 9:2-3; 22:19, 21; Nu 28:3, 9, 11, 19, 31; 29:2, 8, 13, 17, 20, 23, 26, 29, 32, 36). In washing of offerings (Lev 1:9, 13). In washing of priests (Ex 29:4; Lev 8:6; 1Ch 15:14). In washing of garments (Lev 11:28, 40; 13:6, 34; 14:8-9, 47; 15:5-13; Nu 19:7-8, 10, 19, 21). In purifications (Lev 12:4, 6-8; 15:16-18, 21-22, 27; 16:4, 24, 26, 28; 17:15-16). By differentiating between clean and unclean animals (Lev 11:1-47; 20:25; Dt 14:3-20).

See God, Holiness of; Sanctification.

HOLM NIV "cypress" (Isa 44:14, RSV). *See Cypress Wood.*

HOLON [2708] (perhaps *sandy*).
1. Levitical city in hill country of Judah (Jos 15:51), called Hilen (1Ch 6:58).
2. Moabite town (Jer 48:21).

HOLY *See Holiness; Sanctification.*

HOLY DAY *See Holiday.*

HOLY GHOST *See Holy Spirit.*

HOLY OF HOLIES Most holy place, in the tabernacle (Lev 4:6), in the temple (1Ki 6:16). Separated from the holy place by the veil (Ex 26:33; Heb 9:3). Contained atonement cover and ark of the testimony (Ex 26:34; 40:20-21; 1Ki 8:6), the cherubim (Ex 25:18-20; 26:34; 37:7-9; Heb 9:3-5).

Divine dwelling place (Ex 25:8, 21-22; 26:34; Lev 16:2). Entered by the high priest on the Day of Atonement (Ex 26:34; Lev 16:12-13; Heb 9:6-7). Atonement made for (Ex 26:34; Lev 16:15-17, 33).

See Holy Place; Tabernacle.

HOLY PLACE In the tabernacle and the temple. Separated from the most holy place by the veil (Ex 26:33).

Contents of: Altar of incense (Ex 30:1-6; 40:5, 26), the table of the bread of the Presence (Ex 40:4, 24; Heb 9:2), the lampstand (Ex 26:35; 40:4, 24; Heb 9:2). *See various items by name.*

Priests, ministered in (Ex 29:30; 39:1, 41; Heb 9:6), required to eat sin offering in (Lev 6:25-26; 10:17).

See Sanctuary; Tabernacle; Temple.

HOLY SPIRIT [7731+8120, 41+4460]. (Ge 1:2; Ps 51:11; Mt 1:18, 20; Gal 3:2-3, 14; 6:8; Col 1:8; Heb 6:4).

Activities:

Convinces of sin (Ge 6:3; Jn 16:8-11). Comforts (Jn 14:16-17, 26; 15:26; 16:7-14; Ac 9:31). Guides (Jn 16:13; Ac 13:2-4; 15:8, 28; 16:6-7; Ro 8:4, 14; Gal 5:16, 18, 25). Helps our infirmities (Ro 8:26). Regenerates (Jn 3:5-6; 2Co 3:3, 18; Tit 3:5-6). Sanctifies (Ro 15:16; 1Co 6:11; 2Th 2:13; 1Pe 1:2). Dwells in believers (Ro 8:11). Invites to salvation (Rev 22:17). Communion with (2Co 13:14; Php 2:1).

Given to every Christian (1Co 12:7). Given in answer to prayer (Lk 11:13; Ac 8:15), through laying on of hands (Ac 8:17-19; 19:6).

Access to the Father by (Eph 2:18). Prayer in (Eph 6:18; Jude 20). Wisdom and strength from (Ne 9:20; Zec 4:6; Eph 3:16). Liberty from (2Co 3:17). Love of God given by (Ro 5:5).

Ministers commissioned by (Ac 20:28). Christian baptism in the name of, with the name of Father and son (Mt 28:19). Gospel preached in power of (1Co 2:4, 10; 1Th 1:5; 1Pe 1:12). Word of God, sword of (Eph 6:17). Water, a symbol of (Jn 7:38-39). Demons cast out by (Mt 12:28). Power to bestow, not for sale (Ac 8:18-20).

Poured Upon: Israel (Isa 32:15; Eze 39:29). The Gentiles (Ac 10:19-20, 44-47; 11:15-16). All people (Joel 2:28-29; Ac 2:17).

Jesus and the Spirit:

Immaculate conception of Jesus by (Mt 1:20; Lk 1:35). Jesus anointed and led by (Isa 61:1; Mt 3:16; 4:1; Mk 1:10; Lk 3:22; 4:18; Jn 1:32-33; Ac 10:38; Heb 9:14). Sent in Jesus' name (Jn 14:15-17; 15:26).

Christians:

Are temples of (1Co 3:16; 6:19). Are filled with (Ac 2:4, 33; 4:8, 31; 6:5; 8:17; 11:24; 13:9, 52; Eph 5:18; 2Ti 1:14). Have fellowship with (Ro 8:9, 11; 1Co 3:16; 6:19; 2Co 13:14; Php 2:1).

Receive deposit of (2Co 1:22; 5:5; Eph 1:13-14). Are sealed with (2Co 1:22; Eph 1:13; 4:30). Have righteousness, peace, and joy in (Ro 14:17; 15:13; 1Th 1:6). Are unified by (1Co 12:13). Testifiy that Jesus is Lord by (Jn 15:26; 16:14; 1Co 12:3).

Baptism of:

(Mt 3:11; Mk 1:8; Lk 3:16; Jn 1:33; 20:22; Ac 1:5; 11:16; 19:2-6; 1Jn 2:20, 27).

Deity of: See Trinity, Holy.

Fruit of: (Ro 8:23; Gal 5:22-23).

Gifts of:

Foretold (Isa 44:3; Joel 2:28-29). Of different kinds (1Co 12:4-6, 8-10, 28). Bestowed for the confirmation of the gospel (Ro 15:19; Heb 2:4). *See Gifts From God.*

Inspiration of:

(Mt 10:20; Mk 13:11; Lk 12:12; 1Co 2:4, 10-14; 1Ti 4:1).

Instances of : Joseph (Ge 41:38). Bezalel (Ex 31:3; 35:31). The seventy elders (Nu 11:17). Balaam (Nu 24:2). Judges Othniel (Jdg 3:10), Gideon (Jdg 6:34), Jephthah (Jdg 11:29). King Saul (1Sa 11:6). King David (1Ch 28:11-12). The prophets (2Pe 1:21). Azariah (2Ch 15:1). Zechariah (2Ch 24:20).

Zechariah (Lk 1:67). Elizabeth (Lk 1:41). Simeon (Lk 2:25-26). John the Baptist (Lk 1:15). The disciples (Ac 6:3; 7:55; 8:29; 9:17; 10:45).

Intercession of: (Ro 8:26-27).

Power of:

Promised (Lk 24:49; Ac 1:8; 2:38). On Christ (Mt 12:28; Lk 4:14). On ministers (Ac 2:4; Ro 15:19). On the righteous (Ro 15:13; Eph 3:16).

Revelations from:

(Mk 12:36; Lk 2:26-27; Jn 16:13; 1Co 2:10-11; Eph 3:5; 1Ti 4:1; Heb 3:7; 2Pe 1:21; Rev 2:7, 11, 29; 14:13).

Sin Against:

(Ac 8:18-22; 1Jn 5:16). By grieving (Isa 63:10-11, 14; Eph 4:30). By resisting (Ac 5:9; 7:51; Eph 4:30; 1Th 5:19; Heb 10:29). By blaspheming (Mt 12:31-32; Mk 3:29; Lk 12:10). By lying to (Ac 5:3).

Withdrawn From Unrepentant Sinners:

(Ge 6:3; Dt 32:30; Jer 7:29; Hos 4:17-18; 9:12; Ro 1:24, 26, 28).

Instances of: Antediluvians (Ge 6:3-7). Israelites (Dt 1:42; 28:15-68; 31:17-18). Saul (1Sa 16:14; 18:12; 28:15-16; 2Sa 7:15).

Witness of:

(Ac 5:32; Ro 8:15-16; 9:1; 2Co 1:22; 5:5; Gal 4:6; Eph 1:13-14; Heb 10:15; 1Jn 3:24; 4:13; 5:6-8).

Emblems of:

Water—
(Jn 3:5; 7:38-39). Fertilizing (Ps 1:3; Isa 27:3; 44:3-4; 58:11). Refreshing (Ps 46:4; Isa 41:17-18). Freely given to those who are thirsty (Isa 55:1; Jn 4:14; Rev 22:17). Cleansing (Eze 16:9;

36:25; Eph 5:25-27; Heb 10:22). Abundant (Jn 7:37-38).

Fire—
As a guiding light as the Israelites traveled at night (Ex 13:21; Ps 78:14). Purifying (Isa 4:4; Mal 3:2-3). Searching (Zep 1:12, w 1Co 2:10).

Wind—
Powerful (1Ki 19:11, w Ac 2:2). Reviving (Eze 37:9-10, 14). Independent (Jn 3:8). The coming of the promised Holy Spirit at Pentecost (Ac 2:2).

Oil—
Consecrating (Isa 61:1). Comforting (Isa 61:3; Heb 1:9). Illuminating (Mt 25:3-4; 1Jn 2:20, 27). Healing (Lk 10:34; Jas 5:14).

Rain and Dew—
Blessing (Ps 133:3; Hos 14:5). Righteousness (Hos 10:12).

A Dove—
(Mt 3:16).

A Voice—
Guiding (Isa 30:21, w Jn 16:13). Speaking through the Twelve as they were to go out (Mt 10:20). Warning (Heb 3:7-11).

A Seal—
(Rev 7:2). Authenticating (Jn 6:27; 2Co 1:22). Securing (Eph 1:13-14; 4:30).

Tongues of Fire—
(Ac 2:3-4, 6-11).

See Titles and Names, Titles and Names of the Holy Spirit.

HOLY TRINITY *See God; Jesus the Christ; Holy Spirit; Trinity, Holy.*

HOMAGE [2556, 4200+5975+7023, *4686*].
Rendered, to Joseph (Ge 41:43), to kings (1Ki 1:16, 23, 31), to princes (Est 3:2, 5), to Mordecai (Est 6:11), to Daniel (Da 2:46). Refused, by Peter (Ac 10:25-26), by Paul and Barnabas (Ac 14:11-18), by the angel seen by John in his vision (Rev 10:10; 22:8-9).
See Worship.

HOMAM [2102, 2123]. An Edomite and a son of Lotan (Hebrew *Hemam*, a variant of *Homam*) (Ge 36:22, ftn; 1Ch 1:39).

HOME *See Family.*

HOMELESS [*841*]. (Job 24:8; La 4:5; Lk 9:58; 1Co 4:11).

HOMER [2818] (*the load a donkey can carry*). A measure. *See Measure.*

HOMESTEAD Mortgaged (Ne 5:3). When alienable, and when inalienable (Lev 25:25-34). *See Land.*

HOMICIDE
Accidental:
(Ex 21:13; Nu 35:11-15, 22-28, 32; Dt 4:41-43; 19:1-10; Jos 20:1-9). *See Cities of Refuge.*

Murder:
(Job 24:14; Ps 10:8; 38:12; 94:3, 6; Pr 12:6;

28:17; Isa 59:3; Jer 2:34; 7:9-10; 19:4; Eze 22:9; Hos 4:1-3; Hab 2:10, 12). God's abhorrence of (Ps 5:6; 9:12; Pr 6:16-17).
Forbidden (Ex 20:13; Dt 5:17; Pr 1:15-16; Jer 22:3; Mt 5:21; 19:18; Mk 10:19; Lk 18:20; Ro 13:9; 1Ti 1:9; Jas 2:11; 1Pe 4:15; 1Jn 3:12, 15).
Through conspiracy (Ps 37:32; Pr 1:11-12). In hearts of the wicked (Mt 15:19; Mk 7:21). Impenitence for (Rev 9:21). Penitence for (Ps 51:1-17). Inquest over suspected (Dt 21:1-9).

Instances of:
Cain (Ge 4:8). Lamech (Ge 4:23-24). Simeon and Levi (Ge 34:25-31). Pharaoh (Ex 1:16, 22). Moses (Ex 2:12). Ehud (Jdg 3:16-23). Abimelech (Jdg 9:5, 18, 56). Joab (2Sa 3:24-27; 20:9-10; 1Ki 2:5). Solomon (1Ki 2:23-46). Recab and Baanah (2Sa 4:5-8). David (2Sa 11:14-17; 12:9). Absalom (2Sa 13:22-29). Baasha (1Ki 15:27-29). Zimri (1Ki 16:9-11). Ahab and Jezebel (1Ki 21:1024). Hazael (2Ki 8:15). Jehu (2Ki 9:24-37). Athaliah (2Ki 11:1). Of Joash by his servants (2Ki 12:20-21). Menahem (2Ki 15:16). Of Sennacherib, by his sons (2Ki 19:37; Isa 37:38). Manasseh (2Ki 21:16; 24:4). Of Amon, by his servants (2Ki 21:23). Jehoram (2Ch 21:4). Joash (2Ch 24:21). Amaziah's soldiers (2Ch 25:12). Nebuchadnezzar (Jer 39:6). Ishmael (Jer 41:1-7).
Herod the Great (Mt 2:16). Herod the tetrarch (Mt 14:10; Mk 6:27). Barabbas (Mk 15:7; Ac 3:14).

Punishment for:
(Lev 24:17; Dt 19:11-13; Ps 55:23). By a curse (Ge 4:9-12; 49:7; Dt 27:24-25). By death (Ge 9:5-6; Ex 21:12, 14; Nu 35:16-21, 30-33; Dt 17:6; 1Ki 21:19; Eze 35:6; Hos 1:4). By everlasting punishment (Rev 21:8; 22:15).

Instances Of Punishment For—
Cain (Ge 4:11-15). The murderer of Saul (2Sa 1:15-16). David (2Sa 12:9-18). Joab (1Ki 2:31-34). Haman (Est 7:10). The murderers of Ish-Bosheth (2Sa 4:11-12), of Joash (2Ch 24:5).

HOMOSEXUAL [3879, *780, 3434*].
Sexual activity between members of the same sex is universally condemned in Scripture. Male homosexuality forbidden by law and punished by death (Lev 18:22; 20:13). Male and female homosexuality condemned (Ro 1:26). With other sexually immoral persons excluded from the kingdom of God (1Co 6:9-11). Male shrine prostitution was practiced even in the temple (1Ki 14:24; 15:12; 2Ki 23:7). Male prostitutes also translates the derogatory term "dog" (Dt 23:17-18; possibly Rev 22:15). *See Dog.*
Instances of: the men of Sodom (Ge 19:4-5; Jude 7) and Gibeah (Jdg 19:22).

HONESTY [575, 3841, 4026, 5477, 5791, 7404, 7406, *1465*].
General:
Prayer of (Ps 7:3-4). Promises for (Ps 15:5; 24:4). Pleases God (Pr 11:1; 12:22). Proceeds

from God (Pr 16:11; 20:10). Golden rule of (Mt 7:12; Lk 6:31).

Commanded:

(Lev 19:35-36; Dt 16:20; 25:13-16; Pr 4:25; Eze 45:10; Mk 10:19; Lk 3:12-13; Ro 13:13; Php 4:8; Col 3:22; 1Th 4:11-12; 1Ti 2:2; 1Pe 2:11-12).

Instances of:

Jacob, returning money placed in sacks (Ge 43:12). Samuel, incorruptible in his judicial duties (1Sa 12:3-5). Overseers of temple repairs, with whom no reckoning was kept (2Ki 12:15; 22:4-7). Treasurers of the temple (Ne 13:13).

Paul, in all his actions (Ac 24:16; 2Co 4:1-2; 7:2; 8:21). The writer of Hebrews (Heb 13:18).

See Integrity; Righteousness; Dishonesty.

HONEY [1831, 3624, 5885, *3510*]. (Ex 16:31; 2Sa 17:29; Pr 25:27; SS 4:11; Isa 7:15; Mt 3:4). Not to be offered with sacrifices (Lev 2:11). Found in rocks (Dt 32:13; Ps 81:16), upon the ground (1Sa 14:25). Samson's riddle concerning (Jdg 14:14). Sent as a present by Jacob to Egypt (Ge 43:11). Plentiful in Israel (Ex 3:8; Lev 20:24; Dt 8:8; Eze 20:6), in Assyria (2Ki 18:32). An article of merchandise from Israel (Eze 27:17).

HOOD NIV "tiaras" (Isa 3:23). *See Crown.*

HOOF [6811, 7271, 7274]. Parting of, one of the physical marks used for distinguishing clean and unclean animals (Lev 11:3-8; Dt 14:3-8).

HOOKS [2260, 2560, 2626, 2676, 4661, 7553, 9191]. For tabernacle, made of gold (Ex 26:32, 37; 36:36), silver (Ex 27:10; 38:10-12, 17, 19). In the temple, seen in Ezekiel's vision (Eze 40:43). Used for catching fish (Eze 29:4). For pruning (Isa 2:4; 18:5; Joel 3:10). *See Meat Forks.*

Figurative: (Ex 38:4).

HOOPOE [1871]. A bird forbidden as food (Lev 11:19; Dt 14:18). *See Birds.*

HOPE [344, 1059, 2675, 3498, 4438, 4440, 5223, 7595, 7747, 8432, 8433, 9214, 9347, 9536, *1623, 1639+1827, 1827, 1828, 2671, 3607, 4054, 4598*].

Godly:

In God (Ps 31:24; 33:22; 38:15; 39:7; 43:5; 71:5, 14; 78:7; 130:7; 146:5; Jer 17:7; La 3:21, 24, 26; 1Pe 1:21). A helmet (1Th 5:8). An anchor (Heb 6:18-19). Joy in (Pr 10:28; Ro 5:2; 12:12; Heb 3:6).

Of God's calling (Eph 1:18; 4:4). Of eternal life (Col 1:5-6, 23, 27; Tit 1:2; 2:13; 3:7; 1Pe 1:3, 13; 1Jn 3:3). Of the resurrection (Ac 23:6; 24:14-15; 26:6-7; 28:20). Deferred (Pr 13:12).

Of wicked shall perish (Job 8:13; 11:20; 27:8; Pr 10:28; 11:7, 23).

Grounds of:

God's Word (Ps 119:74, 81; Ro 15:4). God's mercy (Ps 33:18). Jesus Christ (1Th 1:3; 1Ti 1:1).

Instances of:

(Job 31:24, 28; Ps 9:18; 16:9; 119:116; Pr 14:32;

23:18, 22; 24:14; Hos 2:15; Zec 9:12; Ro 4:18; 5:3-5; 15:13; 1Co 13:13; 2Co 3:12; Gal 5:5; Eph 2:12; Php 1:20; 2Th 2:16; Heb 6:11; 1Pe 3:15).

See Faith.

HOPHNI [2909] (*tadpole*). Son of Eli (1Sa 1:3). Sin of (1Sa 2:12-36; 3:11-14). Death of (1Sa 4:4, 11, 17).

HOPHRA [2922]. A pharoah who ruled Egypt from 589-570 B.C. (Jer 44:30).

HOR [2216] (perhaps *mountain*). Mountain on which Aaron died (Nu 20:22-29; 21:4; 33:38-39; 34:7-8; Dt 32:50).

HOR HAGGIDGAD [2988] (*cavern of the Gidgad*). Israelite encampment (Nu 33:32-33), called Gudgodah (Dt 10:7).

HORAM [2235] (*height* ISBE). King of Gezer (Jos 10:33).

HOREB [2998] (*dry, desolate*). A range of mountains of which Sinai is chief (Ex 3:1; 17:6; 33:6; Dt 1:2, 6, 19; 4:10, 15; 5:2; 9:8; 29:1; 1Ki 8:9; 19:8; 2Ch 5:10; Ps 106:19; Mal 4:4). *See Sinai, Mount of, Desert of.*

HOREM [3054] (*consecrated*). A fortification in Naphtali (Jos 19:38).

HORESH [3092]. A stronghold in the Desert of Ziph (1Sa 23:15-19).

HORI [3036] (*cave-dweller*).
1. Son of Lotan (Ge 36:22, 30; 1Ch 1:39).
2. A Simeonite (Nu 13:5).

HORITE(S) [3037]. People conquered by Kedorlaomer (Ge 14:6), may be the same as the Hivites (Ge 34:2; Jos 9:7), thought to be Hurrians, from highlands of Media.

HORMAH [3055] (*consecration*). A city SW of the Dead Sea (Nu 14:45; 21:1-3; Dt 1:44). Taken by Judah and Simeon (Jdg 1:17; Jos 12:14). Allotted to Simeon (Jos 19:4; 1Ch 4:30). Within the territory allotted to Judah (Jos 15:30; 1Sa 30:30).

HORN [2956, 3413, 7966, 7967, 8795, 10641, *3043*]. Used to hold the anointing oil (1Sa 16:1; 1Ki 1:39). Used for a trumpet. *See Trumpet.*

Figurative:

Of divine protection (2Sa 22:3). Of power (1Ki 22:11; Ps 89:24; 92:10; 132:17).

Symbolic:

(Da 7:7-24; 8:3-9, 20; Am 6:13, ftn.; Mic 4:13; Zec 1:18-21; Rev 5:6; 12:3; 13:1, 11; 17:3-16).

HORNET [7667] (*depression, discouragement*). A hornet or wasp (Ex 23:28; Dt 7:20; Jos 24:12).

HORON *See Beth Horon.*

HORONAIM [2589] (*twin hollows, twin caves*). A town of Moab (Isa 15:5; Jer 48:3, 5, 34).

HORONITE [3061] (*citizen of Horonaim,* or more probably *of Beth Horon*). Sanballat the Horonite, who opposed Nehemiah in the restoration of Jerusalem (Ne 2:10, 19; 13:28).

HORSE [6061, 7304, 8207, 8224, *2691*].

Description of:
  Great strength (Job 39:19-25), swifter than eagles (Jer 4:13), snorting and neighing of (Isa 5:28; Jer 8:16), a vain thing for safety (Ps 33:17; Pr 21:31).
  Used by the Egyptians in war (Ex 14:9; 15:19), the Israelites (1Ki 22:4). Used for cavalry (2Ki 18:23; Jer 47:3; 51:21). Egypt famous for (Isa 31:1). Forbidden to kings of Israel (Dt 17:16). Hamstrung by Joshua (Jos 11:6, 9), David (2Sa 8:4). Israel reproved for keeping (Isa 2:7; 3:1; Eze 17:15; Hos 14:3). Exported from Egypt (1Ki 10:28-29; 2Ch 9:25, 28), from Babylon (Ezr 2:66; Ne 7:68). Bits for (Jas 3:3), bells for (Zec 14:20), harness for (Jer 46:4). Commerce in (Rev 18:13). *See above, Exported.* Dedicated to religious uses (2Ki 23:11).

Symbolic:
  (Zec 1:8; Rev 6:2-8; 9:17; 19:11-21).

HORSE GATE One of the gates of Jerusalem (Ne 3:28-32; Jer 31:38-40).

HORSE LEECH *See Leech.*

HORTICULTURE Encouraged (Lev 19:23-25; Dt 20:19-20). *See Agriculture; Graft; Pruning.*

HOSAH [2880, 2881] (*refuge*).
  1. A city of Asher (Jos 19:29).
  2. A Levite (1Ch 16:38; 26:10-11).

HOSANNA [*6057*] (*save now*). Originally a prayer, "O LORD, save us" (Ps 118:25), chanted when Jesus entered Jerusalem (Mt 21:9-15; Mk 11:9-10; Jn 12:13).

HOSEA [2107, *6060*] (*salvation*).

Author: Hosea son of Beeri

Date: About the middle of the eighth century B.C.

Outline:
I. Superscription (1:1).
II. The Unfaithful Wife and the Faithful Husband (1:2-3:5).
  A. The Children as Signs (1:2-2:1).
  B. The Unfaithful Wife (2:2-23).
    1. The Lord's judgment of Israel (2:2-13).
    2. The Lord's restoration of Israel (2:14-23).
  C. The Faithful Husband (ch. 3).
III. The Unfaithful Nation and the Faithful God (chs. 4-14).
  A. Israel's Unfaithfulness (4:1-6:3).
    1. The general charge (4:1-3).

    2. The cause declared and the results described (4:4-19).
    3. A special message to the people and leaders (ch. 5).
    4. A sorrowful plea (6:1-3).
  B. Israel's Punishment (6:4-10:15).
    1. The case stated (6:4-7:16).
    2. The judgment pronounced (chs. 8-9).
    3. Summary and appeal (ch. 10).
  C. The Lord's Faithful Love (chs. 11-14).
    1. The Lord's fatherly love (11:1-11).
    2. Israel's punishment for unfaithfulness (11:12-13:16).
    3. Israel's restoration after repentance (ch. 14).

See Prophets, The Minor.

HOSHAIAH [2108] (*Yahweh has saved*).
  1. One of the returned exiles (Ne 12:32).
  2. A distinguished Israelite captive (Jer 42:1; 43:2).

HOSHAMA [2106] (*Yahweh has heard*). Son of Jehoiachin, king of Judah (1Ch 3:18).

HOSHEA [2107] (*salvation*).
  1. The original name of Joshua (Nu 13:8, 16; Dt 32:44). *See Joshua.*
  2. A chief of Ephraim (1Ch 27:20).
  3. King of Israel. Assassinates Pekah and usurps the throne (2Ki 15:30). Evil reign of (2Ki 17:1-2). Becomes subject to Assyria (2Ki 17:3). Conspires against Assyria and is imprisoned (2Ki 17:4). Last king of Israel (2Ki 17:6; 18:9-12; Hos 10:3, 7).
  4. A Jewish exile (Ne 10:23).

HOSPITALITY [*3827, 3828, 5696, 5810, 5811, 5819*]. Unselfish (Lk 14:12-14). Deceitful guise of (Pr 9:1-5; 23:6-8). Parable of (Mt 22:2-10).

Commanded:
  (Isa 58:6-7; Mt 25:34-39; Ro 12:13; 1Ti 3:2; 5:10; Tit 1:7-8; Heb 13:2; 1Pe 4:9-11; 3Jn 5-8). Toward strangers (Ex 22:11; 23:9; Lev 19:10, 33-34; 24:22; Dt 10:18-19; 26:12-13; 27:19).

Instances of:
  Pharaoh to Abraham (Ge 12:16). Melchizedek to Abraham (Ge 14:18). Abraham to angels (Ge 18:1-8). Lot to an angel (Ge 19:1-11). Abimelech to Abraham (Ge 20:14-15). Hittites, to Abraham (Ge 23:1, ftn, 6, 11). Laban, to Abraham's servant (Ge 24:31-33), to Jacob (Ge 29:13-14). Isaac to Abimelech (Ge 26:30). Joseph to his brothers (Ge 43:31-34). Pharaoh to Jacob (Ge 45:16-20; 47:7-12). Jethro to Moses (Ex 2:20). Rahab to the spies (Jos 2:1-16). Man of Gibeah to the Levite (Jdg 19:16-21). Pharaoh to Hadad (1Ki 11:17, 22). Jeroboam to the prophet of Judah (1Ki 13:7). The widow of Zarephath to Elijah (1Ki 17:10-24). The Shunammite to Elisha (2Ki 4:8). Elisha to the Syrian spies (2Ki 6:22). Job to strangers (Job 31:32). David to Mephibosheth (2Sa 9:7-13). King of Babylon to Jehoiachin (2Ki 25:29-30). Nehemiah to rulers and Jews (Ne 5:17-19).

Martha to Jesus (Lk 10:38; Jn 12:1-2). Pharisees to Jesus (Lk 11:37-38). Zacchaeus to Jesus (Lk 19:1-10). Disciples to Jesus (Lk 24:29). The tanner to Peter (Ac 10:6, 23). Lydia to Paul and Silas (Ac 16:15). Barbarians to Paul (Ac 28:2). Publius to Paul (Ac 28:7). Phoebe to Paul (Ro 16:2). Onesiphorus to Paul (2Ti 1:16). Gaius (3Jn 5, 8).

Rewarded:

Rahab (Jos 6:17, 22-25). Widow of Zarephath (1Ki 17:10-24).

See Feasts; Guest; Inhospitableness; Strangers.

HOST [*7372, 2813, 5131*] (*army*). Army (Ge 21:22), angels (Ps 103:21; Jos 5:14). Heavenly bodies (Dt 4:19), creation (Ge 2:1). LORD of hosts (1Sa 1:3), Almighty; God, Names of, Yahweh Tsabbaoth.. One who shows hospitality (Ro 16:23; Lk 10:35). *See Hospitality.*

HOSTAGES [1201+9510]. (2Ki 14:14; 2Ch 25:24).

HOSTILITY [*368, 5286, 5378, 6584+7156, 7640, 7650, 7675, 7762, 7950, 8120, 8475, 1885, 2397*]. To the Righteous (Mic 7:6; Mt 10:21, 35-36; Mk 13:12; Lk 12:53).

HOT SPRINGS (Ge 36:24).

HOTHAM [2598] (*signet ring, seal*).
1. Son of Heber an Asherite (1Ch 7:32).
2. An Aroerite and father of two of David's mighty men (1Ch 11:44).

HOTHAN *See Hotham, 2.*

HOTHIR [2110] (*one who remains*). Son of Heman (1Ch 25:4, 28).

HOUGHING *See Hamstring.*

HOURS [6961, 2469, 4388, 6052]. A division of time. Twelve, in the day (Jn 11:9; Mt 20:3-12; 27:45-46), in the night (Ac 23:23).
Symbolic (Rev 8:1; 9:15).

HOUSE [*185, 1074, 3998, 5659, 9572, 10103, 3836, 3864, 3865, 3867, 3875*]. Built of stone (1Ki 5:17; 7:9; Ezr 6:3; Jer 51:26). Figurative (Ps 87:1; Isa 28:16; 48:13; Ro 15:20; 1Co 3:11; Eph 2:20; 1Ti 6:19; Heb 6:1; Rev 21:14). Cornerstone (Job 38:6; Ps 144:12). "A man's castle" (Dt 24:10-11).

Architecture of:

Foundations of stone (1Ki 5:17; 7:9; Ezr 6:3; Jer 51:26). Figurative (Ps 118:22; Isa 28:16; Eph 2:20; 1Pe 2:6).

Porches (Jdg 3:23; 1Ki 7:6-7), courts (Est 1:5), summer apartment (Jdg 3:20, w Am 3:15; 1Ki 17:19), inner chamber (1Ki 22:25), chambers (Ge 43:30; 2Sa 18:33; 2Ki 1:2; 4:10; Ac 1:13; 9:37;

20:8), guest chamber (Mk 14:14), pillars (Pr 9:1), with courts (Ne 8:16), lattice (Jdg 5:28), windows (Jdg 5:28; Pr 7:6), walls plastered (Da 5:5), hinges (Pr 26:14).

Roofs, flat (Jos 2:6; Jdg 16:27; 1Sa 9:25; 2Sa 11:2; 16:22; Isa 15:3; 22:1; Mt 24:17; Lk 12:3), battlements required in Mosaic law (Dt 22:8). Prayer on (Ac 10:9). Altars on (2Ki 23:12; Jer 19:13; 32:29; Zep 1:5). Booths on (Ne 8:16), used as place to sleep (Jos 2:8; Ac 10:9), as dwelling place (Pr 21:9; 25:24).

Painted (Jer 22:14; Eze 8:10, 12). Windows of (Hos 13:3). Laws regarding sale of (Lev 25:29-33; Ne 5:3). Dedicated (Dt 20:5; Ps 30 [title]).

Figurative:

(2Sa 7:18; Ps 23:6; 36:8; Jn 14:2; 2Co 5:1; 1Ti 3:15; Heb 3:2).

HOUSE OF GOD A place of prayer (Mt 21:13; Mk 11:17; Lk 19:46). Holy (Ecc 5:1; Isa 62:9; Eze 43:12; 1Co 3:17).

See Synagogue; Tabernacle; Temple.

HOUSEHOLD GODS [9572]. Used by Laban, stolen by Rachel (Ge 31:19, 30-35), by Micah, stolen by the Danites (Jdg 17:5; 18:14, 17-20). Condemned and disposed of by Jacob (Ge 35:2-4, w Ge 31:35-39). Destroyed by Josiah (2Ki 23:24). *See Idol.*

HOUSETOPS As places of resort (Jos 2:6; 1Sa 9:25; Ne 8:16; Pr 21:9; Mt 10:27; 24:17; Lk 5:19; Ac 10:9).

HUBBAH [2465] (*God has hidden [someone from danger]*). An Asherite (1Ch 7:34).

HUKKOK [2982]. A place on the boundary line of Naphtali (Jos 19:34).

HUKOK [2577]. The name of a Levitical city in Asher (1Ch 6:75), a variant spelling of Helkath (Jos 31:21). *See Helkath.*

HUL [2566]. Son of Aram (Ge 10:23; 1Ch 1:17).

HULDAH [2701] (*weasel*). A prophetess. Foretells the destruction of Jerusalem (2Ki 22:14-20; 2Ch 34:22-28).

HUMAN SACRIFICE *See Offerings, Human Sacrifices.*

HUMILIATION AND SELF-AFFLICTION [1425+7156, 3075, 4009, 2875, 5428]. Commanded (Lev 16:29-31; 23:26-32; Ezr 8:21-23; 2Ch 7:14). *See Fasting; Humility.*

HUMILITY [6708, 7560, 4246+5425, 4559, 5425]. (Ps 51:17; 69:32; 138:6; Pr 3:34; 11:2; 12:15; 16:19; Isa 57:15; 66:2; Lk 10:21; 2Co 7:6; Gal 6:14; Jas 4:6).

Commanded:

(Dt 15:15; Pr 25:6-7a; 27:2; 30:32; Ecc 5:2; Jer 45:5; Mic 6:8; Mt 18:2-4; 20:26-27; Mk 9:33-37; 10:43-44; Lk 9:46-48; 14:10; 17:10; 22:24-27; Jn 13:14-16; Ro 11:18-20, 25; 12:3, 10, 16; 1Co 3:18; 4:6; 10:12; Gal 5:26; Eph 4:1-2; 5:21; Php 2:3-11; Col 3:12; Jas 1:9-10; 4:10; 1Pe 5:3, 5-6).

Feigned, forbidden (Col 2:18-23).

Rewards of:

(Job 5:11; 22:29; Ps 138:6; Pr 15:33; 18:12; 22:4; 29:23; Mt 5:3; 23:12; Lk 1:52; 14:11; 18:13-14).

Exemplified in:

Abraham (Ge 18:27, 32). Jacob (Ge 32:10). Joseph (Ge 41:16). Moses (Ex 3:11; 4:10). David (1Sa 18:18-23; 23:14; 26:20; 2Sa 7:18-20; 1Ch 17:16-18; 29:14). The Psalmist (Ps 8:3-4; 73:22; 131:1-2; 141:5; 144:3). Solomon (1Ki 3:7; 2Ch 1:10; 2:6). Mephibosheth (2Sa 9:8). Ahab (1Ki 21:29). kings and princes of Israel (2Ch 12:6-7, 12). Josiah (2Ki 22:18-19; 2Ch 34:26, 27). Job (Job 7:17-18; 9:14-15; 40:4-5; 42:2-6). Elihu (Job 32:4-7; 33:6). Ezra (Ezr 9:13, 15). Agur (Pr 30:2-3). Isaiah (Isa 6:5). Hezekiah (Isa 38:15). Jeremiah (Jer 1:6; 10:23-24). Daniel (Da 2:30). Ezra and the Jews (Ezr 8:21, 23).

Elizabeth (Lk 1:43). John the Baptist (Mt 3:14; Mk 1:7; Lk 3:16; Jn 1:27; 3:29-30). Jesus (Mt 11:29; 13:4-16). Woman of Canaan (Mt 15:27). The righteous (Mt 25:37-40). The tax collector (Lk 18:13). Centurion (Mt 8:8; Lk 7:6-7). Peter (Ac 2:12). Paul (Ac 20:19; Ro 7:18; 1Co 2:1-3; 15:9-10; 2Co 3:5; 11:30; 12:5-12; Eph 3:8; Php 3:12-13; 4:12; 1Ti 1:15).

HUMTAH [2794] (*an [unclean] reptile*). A city of Judah (Jos 15:54).

HUNGER [1061+4848, 1991, 2652, 4103, 5883, 7023, 8279, 8280, *3350, 3763, 4277*].

General:

"Man does not live on bread alone" (Dt 8:3; Mt 4:4; Lk 4:3). Labor excites (Pr 16:26). Source of temptation (Ge 25:29-34; Ex 16:2-3; Heb 12:16). An occasion of the temptation of Jesus (Mt 4:3-4; Lk 4:2-3). Of an enemy, an opportunity for good works (Pr 25:21-22; Ro 12:20).

Experienced by Jesus (Mt 21:18; Mk 11:12). Endured, by Jesus during his temptation (Mt 4:2-4; Lk 4:2-4), by Paul for Christ's sake (1Co 4:11). Foretold as a judgment upon the Israelites (Isa 8:21; 9:20).

Figurative:

Of spiritual desire (Ps 107:9; Pr 2:3-5; Isa 55:1-2; Am 8:11-13; Mt 5:6; Lk 1:53; 6:21; Jn 6:35; 1Pe 2:2).

See Appetite; Famine; Desire, Spiritual; Thirst.

HUNTING [1944, 2924, 7399, 7421, 7473, 8103]. Authorized in the Mosaic law (Lev 17:13). By Nimrod (Ge 10:9). By Esau (Ge 27:3, 5, 30, 33). By Ishmael (Ge 21:20). Of lion (Job 10:16).

Fowling (1Sa 26:20; Ps 140:5; 141:9-10; Pr 1:17; Ecc 9:12; La 3:52; Am 3:5).

Figurative: (Jer 16:16).

HUPHAM, HUPHAMITE [2573, 2574]. Son of Benjamin and his clan (Nu 26:39).

HUPPAH [2904] (*canopy*, hence *protection*). Priest in David's time (1Ch 24:13).

HUPPIM, HUPPITES [2907] (*coast people*). Descendants of Benjamin (Ge 46:21; 1Ch 7:12, 15).

HUR [2581] (perhaps *child*).

1. An Israelite who assisted in supporting Moses' hands during battle (Ex 17:10, 12; 24:14).

2. A son of Caleb (Ex 31:2; 35:30; 38:22; 1Ch 2:19-20; 2Ch 1:5).

3. A king of Midian (Nu 31:8; Jos 13:21).

4. Called Ben-Hur, an officer of Solomon's commissary (1Ki 4:8).

5. Father of Caleb (1Ch 2:50; 4:4).

6. A son of Judah (1Ch 4:1).

7. A ruler (Ne 3:9).

HURAI [2584]. One of David's heroes (1Ch 11:32). Also called Hiddai (2Sa 23:30).

HURAM, HURAM-ABI [2586, 2587, 2671] (*brother of the exalted one*).

1. Benjamite (1Ch 8:5).

2. King of Tyre (2Ch 2:3, ftn, 11-12). Usually called Hiram (Hebrew *Huram*, a variant of *Hiram*). *See Hiram.*

3. Tyrian craftsman whose full name is Huram-Abi, is sent by King Hiram to execute the artistic work of the interior of the temple (1Ki 7:13-45; 2Ch 2:13; 4:11-16).

HURI [2585] (*linen weaver* ISBE). Father of Abihail (1Ch 5:14).

HURRIANS *See Horite(s), Horim.*

HUSBAND [408, 1249, 1251, 8276, *467, 476*].

Relation to His Wife:

In general (Ge 2:23-24; Mt 19:5-6; Mk 10:7; 1Co 7:3-5). Love for (Eph 5:22-33; Col 3:19). Headship of (1Co 11:3). Chastity of (Pr 5:15-20; Mal 2:14-16). Rights of (1Co 7:3, 5). Sanctified in the wife (1Co 7:14, 16).

May give wife certificate of divorce (Dt 24:1-4). Law relating to, in cases where wife's virtue is questioned (Nu 5:11-31; Dt 22:13-21). Exemptions for (Dt 24:5).

Duties of (Ecc 9:9; Col 3:19; 1Pe 3:7). Family provider (Ge 30:30; 1Ti 5:8).

Examples:

Faithful: Isaac (Ge 24:67), Joseph (Mt 1:19-20). Unreasonable and oppressive (Est 1:10-22).

Figurative:

(Isa 54:5-6; Jer 3:14; 31:32; Hos 2:19-20). *See Family; Marriage.*

HUSBANDMAN *See Agriculture; Farmer.*

HUSBANDRY *See Agriculture; Animals; Farmer.*

HUSHAH [2592] (perhaps *haste*). Son of Ezer (1Ch 4:4). Probably called Shuah (1Ch 4:11).

HUSHAI [2593]. An Arkite. A counselor of David who overthrew counsels of Ahithophel (2Sa 15:32, 37; 16:16-18; 17:5-15; 1Ch 27:33).

HUSHAM [2595]. A Temanite (Ge 36:34-35; 1Ch 1:45-46).

HUSHATHITE [3144]. Family name of Sibbecai, one of David's heroes (2Sa 21:18; 1Ch 11:29; 20:4; 27:11).

HUSHIM [2594, 3123].
1. Son of Dan (Ge 46:23). Also called Shuham (Nu 26:42). *See Shuham, Shuhamite.*
2. Wife of Shaharaim (1Ch 8:8, 11).

HUSHITES [3131]. Benjamites; descendants of Aher (1Ch 7:12).

HUSK The skin or heads of grain (Nu 6:4; 2Ki 4:42). *See Pods.*

HUZ Son of Nahor (Ge 22:21). *See Uz.*

HUZOTH *See Kiriath Huzoth.*

HYACINTH *See Colors, Figurative and Symbolic.*

HYBRIDIZING Forbidden (Lev 19:19).

HYENA [363]. A scavenging wild dog that roams the desert (Isa 13:22; 34:14; Jer 50:39). *See Animals.*

HYGIENE (1Co 6:18; 9:25). *See Sanitation and Hygiene.*

HYKSOS A W Semitic people who ruled an Egyptian empire embracing Syria and Palestine; the core of their rule over Egypt was from 1648-1540.

HYMENAEUS [5628] (*of [pagan god] Hymen*). Apostate Christian excommunicated by Paul (1Ti 1:19-20; 2Ti 2:16-18).

HYMN [9335, 5630, 5631, 6010, 6011]. *See Psalms; Song.*

HYPOCRISY [6623, 5347, 5694, 5695] (*pretender, pretentious*).
Described:
(Job 31:33-34; Ps 5:6, 9; 52:4; 78:34-37; Isa 29:13; 32:5-6; 48:1-2; 58:2-5; Jer 12:2; 17:9; Eze 33:30-32; Hos 6:4; 10:1, 4; Zec 7:5-6; Mt 15:3-9; 21:28-32; Mk 7:5-13; 9:50; 14:34-35; Lk 18:11-

12; Ro 9:6-7; 1Co 5:8; 13:1; 2Co 4:2; 1Jn 1:6, 10; 2:4, 9, 19; 4:20; Rev 3:1).

Betrays friends (Ps 55:12-14, 20-23; Pr 11:9; 25:19; Ob 7; Zec 13:6).

Hypocrisy of prostitutes (Pr 7:10-21), of false teachers (Mic 3:11; Ro 16:17-18; 2Pe 2:1-3, 17, 19), of dishonest buyers (Pr 20:14).

Condemned:
Abhorred by God (Job 13:16; Ps 50:16-17; Pr 15:8; 21:27; Isa 1:9-15; 9:17; 10:6; 58:2-5; 61:8; 65:2-5; 66:3-5; Jer 5:2; 6:20; 7:4, 8-10; Eze 5:11; 20:39; Hos 8:13; 9:4; 11:12; Am 5:21-27; Zec 7:5-6; Mal 1:6-14; 2:13).

Rebuked by Jesus (Mt 3:7-8; 7:7-8; 9:13; 15:7-9; 16:3; 23:2-33; Lk 6:46; 11:39, 42, 44; 12:54-56; 13:13-17; Jn 6:26, 70; 7:19; 15:2, 6; Rev 2:9; 3:9).

Exposed by Paul (Ro 2:1, 3, 17-29; 2Co 5:12; Gal 6:3; Php 3:2, 18-19; 1Ti 4:2; 2Ti 3:5, 13; Tit 1:16).

Warning to (Job 15:31, 33-34; 17:8; 20:4-5; 27:8-10; 34:30). Warning against (Pr 23:6-8; 26:18-19, 23-26; Jer 9:8; Mic 7:5; Mt 6:1-2, 5, 16, 24; 7:5, 15, 21-23; 16:6; 23:14; Mk 8:15; 12:38-40; Lk 12:1-2; 13:26-27; 16:13, 15; 20:46-47; Jas 1:8, 22-24, 26; 3:17; 4:8; 1Pe 2:1, 16; Jude 12-13).

Punishment for (Job 8:13-15; 36:13-14; Ps 55:23; 101:7; Isa 29:15-16; 33:14; 42:21-22; Eze 5:11; 14:3-4, 7-8; Hos 8:13; 9:4; Mt 22:12-13; 24:50-51; 25:41-45; Ro 1:18).

See Deceit; Deception.

Instances of:
Jacob, in impersonating Esau and deceiving his father (Ge 27). Jacob's sons, in deception of their father concerning Joseph (Ge 37:29-35). Joseph's deception of his brothers (Ge 42-44). Pharaoh (Ex 8:15, 28-29, 32; 9:27-35; 10:8-29). Balaam (Jude 11, w Nu 22-24). Delilah, the wife of Samson (Jdg 16). Jael (Jdg 4:8-21). Ehud (Jdg 3:15-25). The Assyrian field commander (2Ki 18:17-37). Ahaz (Isa 7:12, w 17-25). Johanan (Jer 42:1-12, 20, 22). Ishmael (Jer 41:6-7). The false prophets (Eze 13:1-23).

Herod (Mt 2:8). Judas (Mt 26:25, 48; Jn 12:5-6). Pilate (Mt 27:24). Pharisees (Mt 15:1-9; 22:18; Mk 12:13-14; Jn 8:4-9; 9:24; 19:15). The ruler (Lk 13:14-17). Spies sent to entrap Jesus (Lk 20:21). Priests and Levites (Lk 10:31-32). Chief priests (Jn 18:28). Ananias and Sapphira (Ac 5:1-10). Simon (Ac 8:18-23). Peter and others at Antioch (Gal 2:11-14). Judaizing Christians in Galatia (Gal 6:13). False teachers at Ephesus (Rev 2:2).

See Conspiracy; Treachery.

HYSSOP [257, 5727]. A plant indigenous to western Asia and northern Africa (1Ki 4:33).
Ceremonial Use:
The Israelites used, in sprinkling the blood of the Passover lamb upon the frames of their doors (Ex 12:22), in sprinkling blood in purifications (Lev 14:4, 6, 51-52; Heb 9:19). Used in the sacrifices of separation (Nu 19:6). Used in giving Jesus vinegar on the cross (Jn 19:29).

Figurative of spiritual cleansing (Ps 51:7).

I AM WHO I AM A name of God (Ex 3:14; Rev 1:4, 11, 17). *See God, Names of, Yahweh; Yahweh.*

IBEX [1913]. Probably a species of antelope (Dt 14:5).

IBHAR [3295] (*he chooses*). Son of David (2Sa 5:15; 1Ch 3:6; 14:5).

IBLEAM [3300]. A town given to the tribe of Manasseh (Jos 17:11). Ahaziah slain there (2Ki 9:27). Generally identified with Bileam (1Ch 6:70).

IBNEIAH [3307, 3308] (*Yahweh built*). A Benjamite (1Ch 9:8).

IBRI [6304] (*Hebrew*). A Levite (1Ch 24:27).

IBSAM [3311] (*fragrance*). Son of Tola (1Ch 7:2).

IBZAN [83] (*swift*). The tenth judge of Israel (Jdg 12:8-10), had thirty sons and thirty daughters.

ICE [7938, 7943]. (Job 6:16; 37:10; 38:29; Ps 147:17; Eze 1:22).

ICHABOD [376] (*where is the glory?*). Son of Phinehas, Eli's son (1Sa 4:18-22).

ICONIUM [2658]. A city of Asia Minor. Paul preaches in (Ac 13:51; 14:21). Is persecuted by the people of (Ac 14:1-6; 2Ti 3:11).

ICONOCLASM Idols to be destroyed (Ex 23:24; 34:13; Nu 33:52; Dt 7:5, 25-26; 12:1-4; Jdg 2:2; Jer 50:2). Destroyed by, Jacob (Ge 35:2-4), Moses (Ex 32:19-20), Gideon (Jdg 6:28-32), David (2Sa 5:21; 1Ch 14:12), Jehu (2Ki 10:26-28), Jehoiada (2Ki 11:18), Hezekiah (2Ki 18:3-6), Josiah (2Ki 23:4-20), Asa (2Ch 14:3-5; 15:8-16), Jehoshaphat (2Ch 17:6; 19:3), Jews (2Ch 30:14), Manasseh (2Ch 33:15).

See Idolatry.

IDALAH [3339]. A town of Zebulun (Jos 19:15).

IDBASH [3340] (*honey*). A descendant of Judah (1Ch 4:3).

IDDO [120, 3346, 3587, 6333, 6341, 6342, 10529] (probably *Yahweh has adorned*).
1. Father of Ahinadab (1Ki 4:14).
2. A descendant of Gershom (1Ch 6:21).
3. A son of Zechariah (1Ch 27:21).
4. A prophet (2Ch 9:29; 12:15; 13:22).
5. Ancestor of Zechariah (Ezr 5:1; 6:14; Zec 1:1, 7).
6. A priest (Ne 12:4, 16).
7. The chief of the Jews established at Casiphia (Ezr 8:17).

IDENTIFICATION With Jesus, price of (Mt 4:19; 8:22; 9:9; 16:24; 19:21; Mk 2:14; 8:34; 10:21; Lk 5:27; 9:23; 18:22; Jn 15:14, 18-19; 16:2). Indication of (Jn 10:27; 12:26; Ac 11:26). *See Discipleship.*

IDLENESS [966, 5663, 6791, 8199, 9170, 734, 863, 864, 865, 1632]. Comparisons regarding (Pr 15:19; 18:9; 22:13; 26:13-16; Ecc 4:5). Poverty from (Pr 6:6-11; 10:4-5; 12:9, 24, 27; 13:4; 14:23; 19:15; 20:4, 13; 23:21; 24:30-34; Ecc 10:18). Denounced (Pr 21:25-26; Isa 56:10; Lk 19:20-24; 2Th 3:10-11; 1Ti 5:13).

A sin of Sodom (Eze 16:49). Other instances of (Mt 20:6-7; Ac 17:21).

See Laziness; Slothfulness; Industry.

IDOL [224, 1425, 5011, 5381, 6166, 6770, 7181, 8736, 9572, 1628, 1631] (*image*).

Manufacture of (Ex 20:4; 32:4, 20; Dt 4:23; Isa 40:19-20; 44:9-12, 17; Hab 2:18; Ac 19:24-25). Manufacture of forbidden (Ex 20:4; 34:17). Made of gold (Ex 32:3-4; Ps 115:4-7; 135:15-17; Isa 2:20; 30:22; 31:7; Hos 8:4), silver (Isa 2:20; 30:22; 31:7; Hos 8:4), wood and stone (Lev 26:1; Dt 4:28; 2Ki 19:18; Isa 37:19; 41:6; 44:13-19; Eze 20:32). Coverings of (Isa 30:22).

Prayer to, unanswered (1Ki 18:25-29). Falls down before the ark of Yahweh (1Sa 5:1-5). Used by Michal to save the life of David (1Sa 19:13-17). Derided (Ps 115:4-8; 135:15-18; Isa 44:9-17). To be abandoned (Isa 2:20). To be destroyed (Dt 12:3). Things offered to, not to be eaten (Ex 34:15). Paul's instructions concerning eating things offered to (1Co 8; 10:25-33).

See Iconoclasm; Idolatry.

IDOLATRY [496, 1658, 2393, 3913, 4024, 9572, 1629, 1630] (*image*).

Wicked Practices of:

Human sacrifices (Lev 18:21; 20:2-5; Dt 12:31; 18:10; 2Ki 3:26-27; 16:3; 17:17-18; 21:6; 23:10; 2Ch 28:3; 33:6; Ps 106:37-38; Isa 57:5; Jer 7:31; 19:4-7; 32:35; Eze 16:20-21; 20:26, 31; 23:37, 39; Mic 6:7), practices of, relating to the dead (Dt 14:1), licentiousness (Ex 32:6, 25; Nu 25:1-3; 1Ki 14:24; 15:12; 2Ki 17:30; 23:7; Eze 16:17; 23:1-44; Hos 4:12-14; Am 2:8; Mic 1:7; Ro 1:24, 26-27; 1Co 10:7-8; 1Pe 4:3-4; Rev 2:14, 20-22; 9:20-21; 14:8; 17:1-6).

Other Customs of:

Offered burnt offerings (Ex 32:6; 1Ki 18:26; Ac 14:13), libations (Isa 57:6; 65:11; Jer 7:18; 19:13; 32:29; 44:17, 19, 25; Eze 20:28), of wine (Dt 32:38), of blood (Ps 16:4; Zec 9:7), meat offerings

(Isa 57:6; Jer 7:18; 44:17; Eze 16:19), peace offerings (Ex 32:6).

Incense burned on altars (1Ki 12:33; 2Ch 30:14; 34:25; Isa 65:3; Jer 1:16; 11:12, 17; 44:3; 48:35; Eze 16:18; 23:41; Hos 11:2). Prayers to idols (Jdg 10:14; Isa 44:17; 45:20; 46:7; Jnh 1:5). Praise (Jdg 16:24; Da 5:4).

Singing and dancing (Ex 32:18-19). Music (Da 3:5-7). Cutting the flesh (1Ki 18:28; Jer 41:5). Kissing (1Ki 19:18; Hos 13:2; Job 31:27). Bowing (1Ki 19:18; 2Ki 5:18). Tithes and gifts (2Ki 23:11; Da 11:38; Am 4:4-5).

Annual Feasts:

(1Ki 12:32; Eze 18:6, 11-12, 15; 22:9; Da 3:2-3).

Objects of:

Sun, moon, and stars (Dt 4:19; 2Ki 17:16; 21:3, 5; 2Ch 33:3, 5; Job 31:26-28; Jer 7:17-20; 8:2; Eze 8:15-16; Zep 1:4-5; Ac 7:42). Images of angels (Col 2:18), animals (Ro 1:23). Gods of Egypt (Ex 12:12). Golden calf (Ex 32:4). Bronze serpent (2Ki 18:4). Net and dragnet (Hab 1:16). Pictures (Nu 33:52; Isa 2:16). Pictures on walls (Eze 8:10). Earrings (Ge 35:4).

See Artemis; Shrine.

Folly of:

(Dt 4:28; 32:37-38; Jdg 6:31; 10:14; 1Sa 5:3-4; 12:21; 1Ki 18:25-29; 19:18; 2Ch 25:15; Ps 106:19-20; 115:4-5, 8; 135:15-18; Isa 37:19; 44:9-20; 45:20; 46:1-2, 6-7; Jer 2:28; 11:12; 16:19-20; 48:13; 51:17; Hos 8:5-6; Zec 10:2; Ac 14:13, 15; 17:22-23, 29; Ro 1:22-23; 1Co 8:4; 10:5; 12:2; Gal 4:8; Rev 9:20).

Illustrated by contrast of idols with the true God (Ps 96:5; Isa 40:12-26; 41:23-29; Jer 10:5; 14:22; Da 5:23; Hab 2:18-20). Exemplified in the ruin of Israel (2Ch 28:22-23).

Denounced:

(Dt 12:31; 27:15; Job 31:26-28; Ps 44:20-21; 97:7; Isa 42:17; 45:16; Jer 3:1-11; 32:34-35; Eze 16:16-63; 43:7-9; Hos 1:2; 2:2-5; 4:12-19; 5:1-3; 9:10; 13:2-3; Jnh 2:8; Am 4:4-5; Hab 1:16; Ac 17:16-29; Ro 1:25; 1Co 6:9-10).

Forbidden:

(Ge 35:2; Ex 20:3-6, 23; 23:13, 24, 32-33; 34:14, 17; Lev 19:4; 26:1, 30; Dt 4:15-28; 5:7-9; 7:2-5, 16; 11:16-17; 16:21-22; Ps 81:9; Eze 8:8-18; 14:1-8; 16:15-63; 20:7-8, 16, 18, 24, 27-32, 39; 23:7-49; Ac 15:20-29; 19:26, 14-20, 22-22; 1Jn 5:21).

Prophecies Relating to:

(Isa 46:1-2). Its punishments (Nu 33:4; Dt 31:16-21, 29; Isa 21:9; Jer 51:44, 47, 52). Its end (Isa 2:8, 18, 20; 17:7-8; 27:9; Jer 10:11, 15; Hos 10:2; 14:8; Mic 5:13-14; Zep 2:11; Zec 13:2).

Punishment of:

(Dt 8:19; 11:28; 13:6-9; 17:2-5; 28:14-18; 30:17-18; 32:15-26; Jdg 2:3; Ne 9:27-37; Ps 16:4; 59:8; 78:58-64; 106:34-42; Isa 1:29-31; 2:6-22; 30:22; 65:3-7; Jer 1:15-16; 5:1-17; 7; 8:1-2, 19; 13:9-27; 16:11-6; 18:13-17; 19; 22:5-9; 44; Eze 6; 8:8-18; 9; 14:1-8; 16:15-63; 20:7-8, 24-39; 22:4; 23:9-10, 22-49; 44:10-12; Hos 8:5-14; 10;

13:14; 5:5; Mic 1:1-9; 5:12-14; 6:16; Zep 1; Mal 2:11-13; Rev 21:8; 22:15).

See Groves; High Places; Iconoclasm; Idol; Prostitute.

IDUMEA [2628] (*[land of] Edom*). Greek and Roman name for Edom (Mk 3:8).

IEZER, IEZERITE [404, 405] (*my [father] is help*). Chief in the tribe of Manasseh (Nu 26:30). Also called Abiezer (Jos 17:2). *See Abiezer, 1.*

IFS OF THE BIBLE *See Blessings, Spiritual, Contingent Upon Obedience.*

IGAL [3319] (*he redeems*).
1. Spy of Issachar (Nu 13:7).
2. One of David's heroes (2Sa 23:36).
3. Descendant of Jehoiachin (1Ch 3:22).

IGDALIAH [3323] (*Yahweh is great*). Father of Hanan (Jer 35:4).

IGEAL (*he redeems*). Son of Shemaiah (1Ch 3:22).

IGNORANCE [7344, 51, 52, 53].
Characteristic of Mankind:

(Job 8:9; 28:12-13, 20-21; Pr 8:5; 19:2; Ecc 7:23-24; Jer 10:23; Hos 4:14; Jn 13:7).

Concerning God (1Sa 3:7; Job 11:7-8, 12; 36:26, 29; 37:5, 15-16, 19, 23; Ps 139:6; Pr 30:3-4; Ac 17:23, 30), his works (Ecc 3:11; 8:17; 11:5), his wisdom (1Co 2:7-10).

Concerning the Holy Spirit (Ac 19:2).

Concerning the Scripture (Mt 22:29; Mk 12:24; Jn 20:9; 1Ti 1:7).

Concerning the future (Pr 27:1; Ecc 8:6-7; Ac 1:7; 1Co 13:9, 12).

Concerning snares of the wicked (Pr 7:6-23; 9:14-18; 22:3; 27:12).

Remedy for (Jas 1:5-6).

Sins of:

Sacrifices for: Unintentional sin by the anointed priest (Lev 4:1-12), by the whole community of Israel (Lev 4:13-21; Nu 15:22-26), by a leader (Lev 4:22-26), by a member of the community (Lev 4:27-35; 5:1-19; Nu 15:27-29; Eze 45:20). Forgiven (1Ti 1:12-13; Heb 5:2). Forgiven on account of reparation (Ge 20:1-7).

Evil consequences of:

(Isa 5:13; Hos 4:6). Alienates from God (Eph 4:18-19). Darkens understanding (Lk 23:34; Jn 16:2-3; 1Co 2:8).

Punishment of:

(Eze 3:18; 33:6, 8; Lk 12:48). By fines (Lev 22:14).

Instances of: Pharaoh (Ge 12:11-17). Abimelech (Ge 20:1-18).

See Knowledge; Wisdom.

IIM [6517] (*heaps, ruins*).
1. For KJV Nu 33:45, *See Iyim.*

2. A town in the extreme S of Judah (Jos 15:29).

IJE-ABARIM See *Iye Abarim*.

IJON [6510] (*place of heaps [of stone]*). A town of Naphtali (1Ki 15:20; 2Ki 15:29; 2Ch 16:4).

IKKESH [6837] (*crooked, perverted*). Father of Iri (2Sa 23:26; 1Ch 11:28; 27:9).

ILAI [6519]. One of David's heroes (1Ch 11:29), called Zalmon (2Sa 23:28).

ILLEGITIMATE [2424, 3785]. Excluded from the assembly of the Lord to the tenth generation (Dt 23:2). Had no claim to paternal care or the usual privileges and discipline of legitimate children.

Instances of:
Ishmael (Ge 16:3, 15; Gal 4:22), Moab and Ammon (Ge 19:36-37), Jephthah (Jdg 11:1), David's child by Bathsheba (2Sa 11:2-5). Jesus slanderously accused of being (Jn 8:41).

Figurative: (Heb 12:8).

ILLYRICUM [2665]. Also called Dalmatia. Visited, by Paul (Ro 15:19), by Titus (2Ti 4:10). Now part of Yugoslavia.

IMAGE [1952, 5011, 6166, 6771, 7181, 7512, 9322, 9454, 10614, *1479*, *1635*, *5916*].

Manufactured Images: *See Idol; Idolatry.*

Figurative:
Mankind created in, of God (Ge 1:26-27; 5:1; 9:6; Jas 3:9). Regenerated into (Ps 17:15; Ro 8:29; 2Co 3:18; Eph 4:24; Col 3:10; 1Jn 3:1-3). Christ, of God (Col 1:15; Heb 1:3). *See Image of God.*

IMAGE, NEBUCHADNEZZAR'S Symbolic figure seen by Nebuchadnezzar in a dream, the meaning of which Daniel interpreted (Da 2).

IMAGE OF GOD [7512, *1635*]. Mankind is created in God's image (Ge 1:26-27; 5:1, 3; 9:6; 1Co 11:7; Eph 4:24; Col 3:10; Jas 3:9). The image is not corporeal but rational, spiritual, and social. The fall of man destroyed, but did not obliterate the image. Restoration of the image begins with regeneration.

IMAGE WORSHIP See *Idol.*

IMAGINATION [4213, 4742]. Of mankind: Evil (Ge 6:5; 8:21; Dt 29:19-20; Pr 6:16-18). Vain (Ro 1:21). An abomination to God (Pr 6:16-18). Condemned, as equal to act (Mt 5:28).
Known by God (1Ch 28:9). To be subjected (2Co 10:3-5).

IMLAH [3550, 3551] (*fullness*). Father of Micaiah the prophet (1Ki 22:8-9; 2Ch 18:7-8).

IMMANENCE OF GOD See *Condescension of God.*

IMMANUEL [6672, *1842*] (*God with us*). Isaiah foretold the birth of this child, a sign to Ahaz that God would come near in judgment (Isa 7:14-25). Isaiah's son is called Immanuel (Isa 8:8, 10) and might be the immediate fulfillment. The prophecy is applied to Jesus, whose name means "Yahweh is salvation." He is God come near to save (Mt 1:22-23). *See Jesus the Christ, Prophecies Concerning; Messianic Hope.*

IMMER [612, 613] (*lamb* KB).
1. A family of priests (1Ch 9:12; Ezr 2:37; 10:20; Ne 7:40; 11:13).
2. Head of a division of priests (1Ch 24:14).
3. Name of a man or town (Ezr 2:59; Ne 7:61).
4. Father of Zadok (Ne 3:29).
5. Father of Pashhur (Jer 20:1-2).

IMMORTALITY [440+4638, *114*, *914*, *915*]. The biblical concept of immortality is not simply the survival of the soul after bodily death, but the self-conscious continuance of the whole person, body and soul together, in a state of blessedness, due to the redemption of Christ and the possession of "eternal life." The Bible nowhere attempts to prove this doctrine but everywhere assumes it as an undisputed postulate. The condition of believers in their state of immortality is not a bare endless existence but a communion with God in eternal satisfaction and blessedness.
Exemption from death and annihilation. *See Annihilation.*

Apparently Understood:
By David (2Sa 12:23; Ps 21:4; 22:26; 23:6; 37:18, 27; 86:12; 133:3; 145:1-2). By Nehemiah (Ne 9:5). By Job (Job 14:13). By the psalmists (Ps 49:7-9; 73:26; 121:8). By Moses (Ex 3:6; Mt 22:32; Mk 12:26-27; Lk 20:36-38; Ac 7:32). By Abraham (Heb 11:10).

Implied:
In the translation of Enoch (Ge 5:24; Heb 11:5). In the translation of Elijah (2Ki 2:11). In redemption from Sheol (Ps 16:10-11). In the spirit returning to God (Ecc 3:21; 12:7). In the soul surviving the death of the body (Mt 10:28). In the appearance of Moses and Elijah at the transfiguration of Jesus (Mt 17:2-9; Mk 9:2-10; Lk 9:29-36). In the abolition of death (Isa 25:8). In the Savior's promise to his disciples (Jn 14:2-3). In the resurrection (Isa 26:19; Da 12:2-3; Jn 6:40; 1Co 15:12-25; 1Th 4:13-18; 5:10). In eternal inheritance (Ac 20:32; 26:18; Heb 9:15; 1Pe 1:3-5). In the everlasting punishment of the wicked (2Th 1:7-9). In the Judgment (2Pe 3:7).

Taught:
By Christ (Mt 16:26; 19:16-17; 25:46; Mk 10:30; Lk 9:25; 10:25-28; Jn 3:14-16, 36; 5:39-40; 6:39-40, 44, 47, 50-58; 10:28; 11:25-26; 14:19; 17:2-3; Rev 3:4). By Paul (Ro 2:7; 6:22-23; 1Co 15:12-25; 2Co 5:1; Gal 6:8; Col 1:5-6; 2Th 2:16; 1Ti 4:8;

6:12, 19; 2Ti 1:9-10; Tit 1:2; 3:7). By John (1Jn 2:17, 25; 5:13; Rev 1:7; 22:5). By Jude (Jude 21). In Hebrews (Heb 9:15; 10:34; 11:5, 10, 13-16; 13:14).

See Eternal Life; Resurrection; Righteous, Promises to; Judgment; Wicked, Punishment of.

IMMUTABILITY *(not changeable).* The perfection of God by which he is devoid of all change in essence, attributes, consciousness, will, and promises (Mal 3:6; Ps 33:11; 102:26).

IMNA [3557] *(possibly he is withheld* BDB; *luck, fortune* IDB). Son of Helem (1Ch 7:35).

IMNAH, IMNITE [3555] *(good fortune).*
1. Firstborn of Asher (Ge 46:17; Nu 26:44; 1Ch 7:30).
2. A Levite (2Ch 31:14).

IMPENITENCE Leads to destruction (Mt 24:38-39, 48-51; Lk 13:3; 13:5; Rev 16:9-21).

Admonitions Against:
(Ps 95:8; Jer 6:16-19; 2Co 12:21; Heb 3:8; Rev 2:5, 16, 21-22; 3:3).

Judgments:
Denounced against (Lev 23:29; 26:22-43; Dt 29:19-21; 1Sa 15:23; Ps 50:17, 21; 68:21; 81:11-12; 107:11-12; Pr 1:24-31; 11:3; 15:10, 32; 19:16; 28:13-14; 29:1; Eze 3:19, 26; 33:4-5, 9; Hos 7:13-14; Mt 11:16-21; 12:41-42; 13:15; 23:37-38; Lk 7:35; 10:13; 13:34; Ro 2:4-5).

Denounced against Israel's (Isa 65:12, 15; 66:4; Jer 12:11; 13:17, 27; 14:10; 15:6-7; 19:15; 26:4-6; Eze 3:19, 26; 20:8, 13, 21; Da 9:13; Zec 7:11-13; Mal 2:2).

Reason Given for Impenitence:
Evil company (Jer 2:25). Hypocrisy (Jer 3:10). Idolatry (Isa 46:12-13; Jer 44:17; Eze 20:8; Hos 4:17; 11:2, 7; Rev 9:20-21). Lack of understanding or spiritual blindness (Job 33:14; Ps 32:9; 82:5; Pr 26:11; Hos 5:4). Leniency (Ecc 8:11; Isa 26:10). Material abundance (Ps 52:1; Isa 32:9-11). Obstinacy (Isa 48:4, 8; Jer 8:5-7; Eze 2:4; Ac 7:51). Rebellion (Job 9:2, 4; 24:13; Ps 10:3; 50:7; 78:8; Pr 21:29; Isa 57:11; Jer 5:21-24; 6:10, 16-19; 44:10; Eze 2:4-5; 12:2; 22:8, 13, 21). Refusal to listen (Ps 58:3-5; 106:24-25; Isa 28:12; 42:22-25; Jer 6:16-19; 7:13-14, 24, 28; 11:8; 16:12; 17:23; 22:21; 25:4; 26:4-6; 29:19; 32:33; 35:14-17; 44:16-17; Eze 3:5-7; 20:8; Zec 1:4; 7:11-13; Mt 13:15; Lk 16:31). Seeming lack of hope (Jer 2:25; 18:12).

Instances of:
Pharaoh (Ex 9:30, 34; 10:27; 14:5-9). Israelites (Nu 14:22-23; 2Ki 17:14; 2Ch 24:19; 36:16-17; Ne 9:16-17, 29-30; Jer 36:31). Eli's sons (1Sa 2:25). Amaziah (2Ch 25:16). Manasseh (2Ch 33:10). Amon (2Ch 33:23). Zedekiah (2Ch 36:12-13; Jer 37:2). Jehoiakim and his servants (Jer 36:22-24). Belshazzar (Da 5:22-23). The rich young man (Mt 19:22). Jews who opposed Jesus (Mt 27:4, 25; Mk 3:5).

See Affliction, Of the Wicked; Backsliders; Blindness, Spiritual; Infidelity; Obduracy; Unbelief; Reprobates.

IMPORTS [995, 2256+3655+6590, 2424, 3655, 4604].

Of Israel:
From Egypt: Horses, chariots, and linen (1Ki 10:28-29; 2Ch 1:16).

From Gilead: Spices, balm, and myrrh (Ge 37:25).

From Ophir: Gold (1Ki 10:11; 22:48; 1Ch 29:4).

From Tarshish: Gold, silver, ivory, apes, and baboons (1Ki 10:22; 2Ch 9:21), silver, iron, tin, lead, bronze, and slaves (Eze 27:12-13).

From Arabia: Sheep and goats (Eze 27:21).

Of Egypt:
From Gilead: Spices, balm, and myrrh (Ge 37:25).

Of Tyre:
All commodities from and of the trade world (Eze 27:12-25).

IMPORTUNITY *See Prayer.*

IMPOSTORS [1200, 4418]. Deceivers who lead others astray (2Co 6:8); a general word for evil men, cheaters, who also lead others astray (2Ti 3:13).

IMPRECATION Instances of: Ruth (Ru 1:17). Samuel (1Sa 3:17). David (2Sa 1:21; 3:28-29). Shimei (2Sa 16:5, 13).

IMPRECATORY PSALMS 35, 58, 69, 70, 83, 109, 137, 140, among others. These contain expressions of an apparent vengeful attitude towards enemies. For some people these psalms constitute one of the "moral difficulties" of the OT. In his covenant with Abraham, God promises to curse those who curse his people (Ge 12:3). *See Curse; Psalms.*

IMPRISONMENT [*5464+, 3973, 6037, 10054, *1301, 5871, 5872].
Of Joseph (Ge 39:20). Jeremiah (Jer 38:6). John the Baptist (Mt 11:2; 14:3). Apostles (Ac 5:18). Paul and Silas (Ac 16:24). Peter (Ac 12:4).

Debtors (Mt 5:26; 18:30).

See Prison; Prisoners; Punishment.

IMPUTATION *See Impute.*

IMPUTE To attribute something to a person, or reckon something to the account of another.

Aspects of the Doctrine Found in the NT:
1. The imputation of Adam's sin to his posterity.
2. The imputation of the sin of man to Christ.
3. The imputation of Christ's righteousness to the believer (Ge 2:3; Ro 3:24; 5:15; Gal 5:4; Tit 3:7; 1Pe 2:24).

IMRAH [3559] *(he rebels).* A chief of the tribe of Asher (1Ch 7:36).

IMRI [617] (*Yahweh spoke*).
1. A man of Judah (1Ch 9:4).
2. Father of Zaccur (Ne 3:2).

INCARNATION (*taking on flesh*). The
doctrine that the eternal son of God became
human, and that he did so without in any manner
or degree diminishing his divine nature (Jn 1:4;
Ro 8:3; 1Ti 3:16). *See Jesus the Christ, Incarnation of.*

INCENDIARISM *See Arson.*

INCENSE [2802, 4247, 5231, 5232,
5767+8194, 7777, 7787, 7789, 7792, 10478,
2592, 2593, 2594, 3337].

General:
Formula for compounding (Ex 30:34-35). Uses
of (Ex 30:36-38; Lev 16:12; Nu 16:17, 40, 46; Dt
33:10). Compounded by Bezalel (Ex 37:29), by
priests (1Ch 9:30). Offered, morning and evening
(Ex 30:7-8; 2Ch 13:11), on the golden altar (Ex
30:1-7; 40:5, 27; 2Ch 2:4; 32:12), in making
atonement (Lev 16:12-13; Nu 16:46-47; Lk 1:10).
Unlawfully offered by Nadab and Abihu (Lev
10:1-2), Korah, Dathan, and Abiram (Nu 16:16-
35), by Uzziah (2Ch 26:16-21). Offered in idolatrous worship (1Ki 12:33; Jer 41:5; Eze 8:11).
Presented by the wise men to Jesus (Mt 2:11).
See Altar of Incense.

Figurative:
Of prayer (Ps 141:2). Of praise (Mal 1:11). Of an
acceptable sacrifice (Eph 5:2).

Symbolic:
Of the prayers of saints (Rev 5:8; 8:3-4).

INCEST

Defined and Forbidden:
(Lev 18:6-18; 20:11-12, 17-21; Dt 22:30; 27:20-
23; Eze 22:11; 1Co 5:1).

Instances of:
Lot with his daughters (Ge 19:31-36). Abraham
(Ge 20:12-13). Nahor (Ge 11:29). Reuben (Ge
35:22; 49:4). Amram (Ex 6:20). Judah (Ge 38:16-
18; 1Ch 2:4). Amnon (2Sa 13:14). Absalom (2Sa
16:21-22). Israel (Am 2:7). Herod (Mt 14:3-4; Mk
6:17-18; Lk 3:19).

Instances of Marriage of Near Relatives:
Abraham with Sarah (Ge 20:11-13). Isaac with
Rebekah (Ge 24:15, 67). Jacob with Leah and
Rachel (Ge 29:23, 30). Rehoboam (2Ch 11:18).

INCINERATION *See Cremation.*

INCOMPARABILITY OF GOD
See God, Incomparable; None Like God.

INCONSISTENCY Hypocritical (Mt
7:3-5; 23:3-4). Inexcusable (Ro 2:1, 21-23).
Instances of: Jehu (2Ki 10:16-31). The Jews, in
oppressing the poor (Ne 5:8-9), in accusing Jesus
of violating the Sabbath (Jn 7:22-23). Peter and
the other disciples, in requiring of the Gentiles that

which they did not require of themselves (Gal
2:11-14).
See Deceit; Deception; Hypocrisy.

INDECISION About God (1Ki 18:21; Hos
10:2; Mt 6:24). About ethics (Mt 26:41; Jas 1:8;
4:17; Rev 3:15).
See Decision; Instability; Lukewarmness.
Instances of: Moses at the Red Sea (Ex 14:15).
Joshua at Ai (Jos 7:10). Esther (Est 5:8). Rulers,
who believed in Jesus (Jn 12:42). Felix (Ac
24:25).

INDIA [2064]. Probably the eastern limit of
the kingdom of Xerxes (Est 1:1; 8:9).

INDICTMENTS [6219].

Instances of:
Naboth on charge of blasphemy (1Ki 21:13, w
21:1-16). Jeremiah of treasonable prophecy, but
of which he was acquitted (Jer 26:1-24), a second
indictment (Jer 37:13-15). Three Hebrew captives
on the charge of resistance to authority (Da 3:12,
w 3:1-28; 6:13, w 6:1-24).
Jesus, under two charges, first, of blasphemy (Mt
26:61, w Mk 14:58; Mt 26:63-65, w Mk 14:61-64;
Lk 22:67-71; Jn 19:7), second, of treason (Mt
27:11, 37; Mk 15:2, 26; Lk 23:2-3, 38; Jn 18:30,
33; 19:12, 19-22).
Stephen for blasphemy (Ac 6:11, 13). Paul (Ac
17:7; 18:13; 24:5; 25:18-19, 26-27). Paul and
Silas (Ac 16:20-21).
Indictment rejected (Ac 18:14-16).

INDIGESTION Of Timothy (1Ti 5:23). *See
Disease.*

INDUSTRY Brings prosperity (Pr 10:4-5;
12:11, 24, 27; 13:4, 11; 21:5; 22:29; 28:19). Commanded (Ge 2:15; Ex 23:12; 35:2; Dt 5:13; Pr
20:13; 27:23-27; Ecc 9:10; 11:4, 6; Ro 12:11; Eph
4:28; 1Th 4:11-12; 2Th 3:10-12; 1Ti 5:8). Instigated (Pr 16:26). Profitable (Pr 14:4, 23).
Reflections concerning (Ecc 1:3; 2:10-11, 17-22).

Exemplified:
By ants and conies (Pr 30:25-26). By prudent
wife (Pr 31:13-27).

Instances of:
Jeroboam (1Ki 11:28). Paul (Ac 18:3; 20:33-34;
1Co 4:12; 1Th 2:9; 2Th 3:8).
*See Frugality; Idleness; Labor; Slothfulness;
Work.*

INFANTICIDE The killing of children.
Commanded by Pharaoh (Ex 1:15-16; Ac 7:19);
by God concerning Midianite boys (Nu 31:17); by
Herod (Mt 2:16-18).

INFANTS *See Children.*

INFERTILITY *See Barrenness.*

INFIDELITY

Relating to God:
Disbelief in God (Nu 15:30-31; 2Ch 32:14-19;

Isa 29:16). Prosperity tempts to (Dt 32:15). Arguments against (Job 12:7-25; Ps 94:8-9; Isa 10:15; 19:16; 45:9, 18; Ro 1:20; 9:20-21).

Exemplified—

In mocking God (Ps 14:1, 6; 50:21; Isa 57:4-11; Eze 36:2; Da 3:15; Ac 17:18; 2Pe 3:3-4; Jude 18-19). In mocking God's servants (1Ki 22:24; 2Ki 2:23; 2Ch 30:6, 10; 36:16; Jer 17:15; 43:2; Eze 20:49; Ac 2:13).

In rejecting God (Ex 5:2; Job 15:25-26; 21:14-15; Ps 14:1; 53:1; 106:24-25; Jer 2:31). In rejecting Christ (Mt 12:24; 27:39-44; Mk 3:22; Lk 11:15; 19:14, 27). By Antichrist (Da 7:25; 8:25; 11:36-37).

In doubting God's help (Ex 17:7; Ps 3:2; 78:19-20, 22; 107:11-12). In impugning God's holiness (Job 35:3; Ps 10:11, 13; Eze 18:2, 29; Mal 1:7; 3:14), God's knowledge (Job 22:13-14, 17; Ps 59:7; 64:5; 73:11; Isa 29:15; Eze 8:12), God's mercy (Ps 42:3), God's righteousness (Eze 18:2, 29).

Punishment for—

(Nu 15:30-31; Dt 29:19-21; Ps 12:3-4; Pr 3:34; 9:12; 19:29; 24:9; Isa 3:8; 5:18-19, 24-25; 28:9-10, 14-22; 47:10-11; Jer 5:12, 14; 48:42; 50:24, 29; Eze 9:9-10; 32:20; Hos 7:5, 13, 15; Am 5:18; 7:16-17; Mic 7:10; Zep 1:12; Lk 19:14, 27; Heb 10:28-29; 2Pe 2:1).

Relating to Friends:

(Ps 41:9; Mt 26:14-16, 47-50; Mk 14:10-11, 43-46; Lk 22:3-6, 47-48; Jn 13:18; 18:2-5).

See Presumption; Skepticism; Unbelief.

INFINITY *See God, Infinite.*

INFIRMITY [2716, *819*]. Physical (Ecc 12:3). Of Isaac (Ge 27:1). Of Jacob (Ge 48:10). Moses exempt from (Dt 34:7). Caleb exempt from (Jos 14:11). Of Eli (1Sa 3:2). Of Barzillai (2Sa 19:32).

See Affliction; Blindness; Deafness; Lameness; Old Age; Taste.

INFLAMMATION [1945]. Disease brought as a curse for unfaithfulness to Yahweh (Dt 28:22). *See Disease.*

INFLUENCE [6476, *72*, *1543*].

Intercession in Behalf of Friends:

Of Jonathan for David (1Sa 19:1-6; 20:4-9). Solicited, Bathsheba for Adonijah (1Ki 2:13-18). Offered, Elisha for Shunammite woman (2Ki 4:12-13). Of nobles of Judah in behalf of Tobiah (Ne 6:17-19). Of mother of Zebedee's children for sons (Mt 20:20-24). Of Blastus for Tyre and Sidon (Ac 12:20).

Good Influences:

Injunctions concerning (Mt 5:13-16; Mk 4:21-22; Lk 8:16; 11:33-36; Jn 7:38; 1Co 7:14, 16; Php 2:15; 1Th 1:7-8; 1Ti 6:1; Heb 11:4; 1Pe 2:11-12; 3:1-2, 15-16).

Instances of—

David over his successors (1Ki 3:3; 2Ki 18:3; 22:2; 2Ch 29:2; 34:2). Asa over Jehoshaphat (1Ki

22:42-43). Joash over Amaziah (2Ki 14:3). Amaziah over Azariah (2Ki 15:1-3). Uzziah over Jotham (2Ki 15:34). Josiah, in religious zeal (2Ki 22; 23:1-25; 2Ch 34:33). Hezekiah, for religious reform (2Ch 29-31). Ezra, against marriage with idolaters (Ezr 10:1, 9). Nehemiah, during the rebuilding of the walls of Jerusalem (Ne 4:7-23; 5).

Evil Influences:

Of ruler over servants (Pr 22:12). Of wicked parents over children (Jer 17:1-2). Of wicked priest and people (Hos 4:9). Warnings against (Pr 22:24-25; Lk 12:1; 1Co 5:6-8; Gal 5:7-9; 2Ti 2:14, 17-18; Heb 12:15). Parable of (Mt 13:24-25).

Instances of—

Eve over Adam (Ge 3:6). Solomon's wives (1Ki 11:3-4). The young men over Rehoboam (1Ki 12:8-14; 2Ch 10:8-14). Rehoboam over Abijah (1Ki 15:3). Jeroboam over Nadab (1Ki 15:25-26). Jezebel over Ahab (1Ki 21:4-16, 25). Ahab over Ahaziah (1Ki 22:52-53; 2Ki 8:25-27). Ahab over Jehoram (2Ki 8:16, 18; 2Ch 21:5-6; 22:3-5). Jeroboam over Israel (2Ki 17:21-22). Manasseh over Judah (2Ki 21:9; 2Ch 33:9). Manasseh over Amon (2Ki 21:20-21). Jehoiakim over Jehoiachin (2Ki 24:9).

Political Influence:

(1Ki 2:13-18; 2Ki 4:12-13; Ne 6:17-19; Pr 19:6; 29:26; Da 5:10-12; Mt 20:20-24; Ac 12:20).

See Example; Politics.

INGATHERING, FEAST OF [658].
See Tabernacles, Feast of.

INGRAFTING *See Graft.*

INGRATITUDE

To God:

(Ro 1:21; 2Ti 3:2). Prosperity tempts (Dt 6:10-12; 8:12-14; 32:6, 13, 15, 18; 2Ch 26:15-16; Jer 5:7-9, 24; Hos 13:6). Punishment for (Dt 28:47-48; 1Ki 16:1-3; 2Ch 32:25; Ps 78:16-17, 27-32, 42-68; Da 5:18, 20-21).

Instances of—

(Nu 16:9-10). Israel (Dt 31:16; Jdg 2:10-12; 8:34-35; 10:11, 13-14; 1Sa 8:7-8; 10:19; Ne 9:25-26, 35; Ps 106:7, 21; Isa 1:2; Jer 2:6-9, 17, 31; 4:7; 7:13, 19; 11:1, 3; Am 3:1-2; Mic 6:3-4). Saul (1Sa 15:17, 19). David (2Sa 12:7-9). Baasha (1Ki 16:1-2). Jerusalem (Eze 16:17). Humanity (Ro 1:21; 2Ti 3:2).

Ingratitude to Jesus:

The nine lepers (Lk 17:12-18). His own people (Jn 1:11).

Ingratitude of Person to Person:

(Pr 17:13; 2Ti 3:2).

Instances of—

Laban to Jacob (Ge 31). Pharaoh's cupbearer to Joseph (Ge 40:23). Israelites to Moses (Ex 16:3; 17:2-4; Nu 16:12-14), to Gideon (Jdg 8:35). Shechemites (Jdg 9:17-18). Men of Keilah to David (1Sa 23:5-12). Saul to David (1Sa 24). Nabal (1Sa 25:21). David to Joab (1Ki 2:5-6), with the history of Joab's services to David. *See*

Joab. David to Uriah (2Sa 11:6-17). David's companions to David (Ps 35:11-16; 38:20; 41:9; 109:4-5). Citizens (Ecc 9:14-16). Joash (2Ch 24:22). Jeremiah's enemies (Jer 18:20).

INHERITANCE [1598, 2750, 3769, 3772, 4625, 5706, 5709, *2883*, *3099*, *3100*, *3101*, *3102*, *4757*]. Of children (Ge 24:36; 25:5; 2Ch 21:3). Of children of concubines (Ge 15:3; 21:9-11; 25:6). Of children of polygamous marriages (Dt 21:15). Of daughters (Nu 27:8; Job 42:15). Of all mankind (Ecc 2:18-19). Of servants (Pr 17:2). Of real estate inalienable (1Ki 21:3; Jer 32:6-8; Eze 46:16-18).

Law concerning (Nu 27:6-11). Lesson concerning, of prodigal (Lk 15:12, 25-31). Proverbs concerning (Pr 17:2; 20:21).

Instance of Israel to Joseph (Ge 48:21-22).

Figurative: Spiritual (Mt 25:34; Ac 20:32; 26:18; Ro 8:16-17; Gal 4:7; Eph 1:11-14; Col 3:24; Tit 3:7; Heb 1:14; 9:15-17).

See Firstborn; Heir; Testament; Will.

INHOSPITABLENESS Instances of: Toward the Israelites: Edom (Nu 20:1, 18-21), Sihon (Nu 21:22-23), Ammonites and Moabites (Dt 23:3-6). Men of Gibeah toward a Levite (Jdg 19:15). Nabal toward David (1Sa 25:10-17). Samaritans toward Jesus (Lk 9:53). *See Hospitality.*

INIQUITIES, OUR [2633, 6411]. (Job 14:17; Ps 40:12; 90:8; 130:3; Isa 59:2; 64:6; Jer 2:22; Mic 7:10). *See Sin.*

INIQUITY [224, 6406, 6411]. General references to (Job 15:16; Ps 41:6; 53:1; Isa 5:18; Jer 30:14; Eze 9:9; Hos 14:1; Mic 2:1; Mt 23:28; 24:12; Ro 6:19). *See Sin.*

INJUSTICE [224, 4202+5477, 4754, 6406, 6637, 8400]. An abomination to God (Pr 17:15). To the righteous (Pr 29:27).

In civil administration (Ps 82:2; Ecc 5:8; La 3:34-36). In gains, unstable (Pr 28:8; Am 5:11-12). Judged (Pr 11:7; Ecc 3:16; Lk 16:10; 1Th 4:7; Rev 22:11). Practiced by the wicked (Isa 26:10), without shame (Zep 3:5). Protection from, given (Ps 12:5), interceded (Ps 43:1).

God innocent of (2Ch 19:7; Eze 18:25-29; Ro 3:5-8; 9:14-18; Heb 6:10). Job innocent of (Job 16:16-17; 31:13-15).

INK [1902, *3506*]. Any liquid used with pen or brush to form written characters (Jer 36:18; 2Co 3:3; 2Jn 12; 3Jn 13).

INKHORN *See Writing Kit.*

INN [*2906*, *4106*]. A lodging place for travelers. Inns in the modern sense were not very necessary in ancient times, since travelers found hospitality the rule (Ex 2:20; Jdg 19:15-21; 2Ki 4:8; Ac 28:7; Heb 13:2). Ancient inns were usually mere shelters for man and beast, although often strongly fortified.

INNOCENCE [5931, 7405, 7407]. Signified by washing the hands (Dt 21:6; Ps 26:6; Mt 27:24). Found in Daniel (Da 6:22), Jeremiah (Jer 2:35). Professed by Pilate (Mt 27:24). Contrasted with guilt (Ge 2:25; 3:7-11).

INNOCENT [870, 2341, 2855, 3838, 5927, 5929, 7404, 7405, 9447, 10229, *54*, *127*, *193*, *360*, *1465*, *1467*, *2754*]. Not to suffer for guilty (Dt 24:16; 2Ki 14:6; 2Ch 25:4; Jer 31:29-30; Eze 18:20).

INNOCENTS, SLAUGHTER OF The slaughter, by Herod the Great, of children in Bethlehem (Mt 2:16-18). *See Infanticide; Murder.*

INNUENDO (Ps 35:19; Pr 6:13; 10:10). *See Accusation, False.*

INQUEST Into an unsolved murder (Dt 21:1-9).

I.N.R.I The initials of the Latin superscription on the cross of Jesus, standing for IESUS NAZARENUS, REX IUDAEORUM, "Jesus of Nazareth, King of the Jews" (Mt 27:37; Mk 15:26; Lk 23:38; Jn 19:19).

INSANITY [3248+9801, 8713, *3419*, *3444*]. (Pr 26:18). Sent as a judgment from God (Dt 28:28; Zec 12:4).

Feigned by David (1Sa 21:13-15). Nebuchadnezzar's (Da 4:32-34). Jesus accused of (Mk 3:21; Jn 10:20). Paul (Ac 26:24-25). Cured by Jesus (Mt 4:24; 17:15).

Demonic:
Saul (1Sa 16:14; 18:10).

False accusation of:
Against Jesus (Mk 3:21; Jn 10:20), against Paul (Ac 26:24-25; 2Co 5:13).

See Demons, Possession by.

INSCRIPTIONS On gravestones (2Ki 23:17). On the turban of the high priest (Ex 28:36). On the sacred diadem (Ex 39:30). On the bells of horses (Zec 14:20).

Over Jesus at the Crucifixion (Mt 27:37; Mk 15:26; Lk 23:38; Jn 19:19). Precepts written on the doorframes and gates and worn on the hand and forehead (Dt 6:6-9; 11:18-20; Isa 57:8).

INSECTS [9238]. Created by God (Ge 1:24-25). Fed by God (Ps 104:25, 27; Ps 145:9, 15).

Divided Into:
Clean and fit for food (Lev 11:21-22). Unclean and abominable (Lev 11:23-24).

Mentioned in Scripture:
Ant (Pr 6:6; 30:25). Bee (Jdg 14:8; Ps 118:12; Isa 7:18). Cricket (Lev 11:22). Flea (1Sa 24:14). Fly (Ex 8:22; Ecc 10:1; Isa 7:18). Gnat (Ex 8:16; Ps 105:31; Mt 23:24). Grasshopper (Lev 11:22; Jdg 6:5; Job 39:20; Ps 78:46; Isa 33:4; Na 3:15-16). Hornet (Dt 7:20). Katydid (Lev 11:22). Locust (Ex 10:12-13; Joel 1:4; 2:25). Maggot (Ex 16:20).

Moth (Job 4:19; 27:18; Isa 50:9). Spider (Job 8:14; Isa 59:5). Worm (Job 25:6; Mic 7:17).

INSINCERITY See Hypocrisy.

INSINUATION See Innuendo.

INSOMNIA Instances of: Xerxes (Est 6:1). Nebuchadnezzar (Da 6:18).

INSPECTION GATE [5152]. One of the gates of Jerusalem (Ne 3:31). See Miphkad.

INSPIRATION [8120] (breathed into).

Claims that the Scriptures are Inspired:

(2Ti 3:16; 1Ki 13:20; 2Ch 33:18; 36:15; Ne 9:30; Job 33:14-16; Isa 51:16; Jer 7:25; 17:16; Da 9:6, 10; Hos 12:10; Joel 2:28; Am 3:7-8; Zec 7:12; Lk 1:70; Ac 3:18; Ro 1:1-2; 1Co 12:7-11; Heb 1:1; 2Pe 1:21; Rev 10:7; 22:6, 8).

Instances of People Inspired by God:

Enoch (Jude 14). Joseph (Ge 40:8; 41:16, 38-39). Moses (Ex 3:14-15; 4:12, 15, 27; 6:13, 29; 7:2; 19:9-19; 24:16; 25:22; 33:9, 11; Lev 1:1; Nu 1:1; 7:8-9; 9:8-10; 11:17, 25; 12:6-8; 16:28-29; Dt 1:5-6; 5:4-5, 31; 34:10-11; Ps 103:7). Aaron (Ex 6:13; 12:1). The tabernacle workers (Ex 28:3; 31:3, 6; 35:31; 36:1). The seventy elders (Nu 11:16-17, 24-25). Eldad and Medad (Nu 11:26-29). Balaam (Nu 23:5, 16, 20, 26; 24:2-4, 15-16). Joshua (Dt 34:9; Jos 4:15).

Samuel (1Sa 3:1, 4-10, 19-21; 9:6, 15-20; 15:16). Saul (1Sa 10:6-7, 10-13; 19:23-24). Messengers of Saul (1Sa 19:20, 23). David (2Sa 23:2-3; 1Ch 28:19; Mk 12:36). Nathan (1Ki 14:5). Elijah (1Ki 17:1, 24; 19:15; 2Ki 10:10). Micaiah (1Ki 22:14, 28; 2Ch 18:27). Elisha (2Ki 2:9; 3:11-12, 15; 6:8-12, 32; 15:8). Jahaziel (2Ch 20:14). Azariah (2Ch 15:1-2). Zechariah, the son of Jehoiada (2Ch 24:20; 26:5). Isaiah (2Ki 20:4; Isa 6:1-9; 8:11; 44:26; Ac 28:25). Jeremiah (2Ch 26:12; Jer 1:9; 2:1; 7:1; 11:1, 18; 13:1-3; 16:1; 18:1; 20:9; 23:9; 24:4; 25:3; 26:1-2, 12; 27:1-2; 29:30; 33:1; 34:1; 42:4, 7; Da 9:2). Ezekiel (Eze 1:1, 3; 2:1-2, 4-5; 3:10-12, 14, 16-17, 22, 24, 27; 8:1; 11:1, 4-5, 24; 33:22; 37:1; 40:1; 43:5-6). Daniel (Da 2:19; 7:16; 8:16; 9:22; 10:7-9). Hosea (Hos 1:1-2). Joel (Joel 1:1). Amos (Am 3:7-8; 7:14-15). Obadiah (Ob 1). Jonah (Jnh 1:1; 3:1-2). Micah (Mic 1:1; 3:8). Habakkuk (Hab 1:1). Haggai (Hag 1:13). Zechariah (Zec 2:9; 7:8).

Elizabeth (Lk 1:41). Zechariah (Lk 1:67). Simeon (Lk 2:26-27). Disciples (Mt 10:19; Mk 13:11; Lk 12:11; Lk 12:12; 21:14-15; Ac 21:4). The apostles (Ac 2:4). Philip (Ac 8:29). Agabus (Ac 11:28; 21:10-11). John the apostle (Rev 1:10-11).

See Genius; Prophecy; Prophets; Revelation; Word of God, Inspiration of.

INSTABILITY

Warnings Against:

(Pr 24:21-22; 27:8; Mt 6:24; 8:19-22; 12:25; 13:20-21; Mk 4:16-17; Lk 8:13; 9:57-62; Eph 4:14; Heb 13:9; Jas 1:6-8; 4:8; 2Pe 2:14; Rev 2:4; 3:2).

Instances of:

Reuben (Ge 49:4). Pharaoh (Ex 8:15, 32; 9:34; 10:8-11, 16-20; 14:5). Israel (Ex 19:8; 24:3, 7; 32:8-10; Jdg 2:17; 1Ki 18:21; Ps 106:12-13; Jer 2:36). Saul in his feelings toward David (1Sa 18:19). David, in yielding to lust (2Sa 11:2-4). Solomon, in yielding to his idolatrous wives (1Ki 11:1-8). Ephraim and Judah (Hos 6:4). Jews (Hos 6:4-5; Jn 5:35). Lot's wife (Lk 17:32). Disciples (Jn 6:66). Mark (Ac 15:38). Galatians (Gal 1:6; 4:9-11).

See Backsliding; Hypocrisy; Indecision.

INSTINCT [5879, 5880, 6035]. Of animals (Pr 1:17; Isa 1:3). Of birds (Jer 8:7). See Animals; Birds.

INSTRUCTION [*1067, 1819, 1821, 3579, 3723, 4375, 4592, 5184, 7422, 8505, 9368, 1439, 1948, 1953, 2994, 3364, 4132, 4133, 5204]. Provision for, made by the state (2Ch 17:7-9; Da 1:3-5, 17-20). Sought (Ps 90:12; 119:12; 143:8, 10). Paying attention to, commanded (Pr 4:1-2, 10, 13, 20; 5:1-2; 22:17; 23:12, 23). Lack of (2Ch 15:3; Pr 24:30-34). Hatred (Ps 50:17; Pr 1:29-30; 5:12-13; Jer 32:33; Lk 20:1-2). From nature (Pr 24:30-34; Ecc 1:13-18; 3; 4:1; Mt 6:25-30). From the study of human nature (Ecc 3-12).

In religion:

(Ex 24:12; Lev 10:11; Dt 24:8; 27:14-26; 31:9-13; 33:10; 2Ch 17:8-9; 35:3; Ne 8:7-13; Mal 2:6-7). By means of the law (Dt 27:1-26; Ro 2:18; Gal 3:24-25). By means of proverbs (Pr 1:1-6, 20-30). By means of the song of Moses (Dt 31:19; 32:1-44). By priests (Ezr 7:10; Mal 2:7). By Jesus (Mt 5:1-2; Mk 6:2; 12:35; Lk 4:16-21; 19:47; 20:1-8; 21:37-38; 24:27; Jn 7:14; 8:2). By preachers (Ro 10:14; 1Co 12:28-29; Eph 4:11; Col 1:2, 8). By teachers (2Ki 23:2; Ne 8:7-8; 1Co 12:28-29; Eph 4:11).

By symbols. See Symbols and Similitudes. By parables. See Parable. Inscriptions on doors and gates (Dt 11:20-21), on monuments (Jos 8:30-35). The public reading of the law (Dt 31:9-13; Jos 8:34-35; Ne 8:2-3).

By Object Lessons:

Passover feast (Ex 12:26-27). Dedication of firstlings (Ex 13:14-16). Phylacteries (Ex 13:9, 16). Inscriptions (Ex 28:36; 39:30; Dt 6:6-9; 11:18-20; Zec 14:20; Mt 37:37). The pot of manna, a reminder of God's care (Ex 16:32). The sacred oil, a symbol of holiness (Ex 30:31). The pillar of twelve stones at the fords of the Jordan (Jos 4:7, 19-24). Tassels on the borders of garments (Nu 15:38-39). The garment torn in pieces (1Ki 11:30-32). The symbolic wearing of sackcloth and going barefoot (Isa 20:2-3). The linen belt (Jer 13:1-11). Potter's vessel (Jer 19:1-12). Basket of figs (Jer 24). Bonds and yokes (Jer 27:2-11; 28). By stones being put in a brick pavement (Jer 43:8-13). Illustrations on a tile (Eze 4:1-3). Lying on one side in public view for a long period (Eze 4:4-8). Eating bread baked with dung (Eze 4:9-17). Shaving the head (Eze 5). Moving household goods (Eze 12:3-16). Sighing (Eze 21:6-7). The boiling pot (Eze 24:1-14). Widowhood (Eze 24:16-27). Two sticks joined together (Eze 37:16-22).

Of Children:

By parents, commanded (Ex 10:2; 12:26-27; 13:8-10, 14-16; Dt 4:9-10; 6:6-9; 11:18-19; Ps 78:5-8; Pr 22:6; Isa 38:19; Eph 6:4). Law concerning (Dt 31:9-13; Jos 8:35). Exemplified (Ps 34:11; Pr 20:7; Ac 22:3; 2Ti 3:15).

See Children.

By Types:

See Washings; Blemish; Defilement; Disfellowship; Types.

See Firstborn; Holiness; Passover; Pillar; Purification.

INSTRUMENTALITY *See Agency.*

INSTRUMENTS, MUSICAL *See Music.*

INSURGENTS Army of, David's (1Sa 22:1-2).

INSURRECTION [5086, 5087]. (Ps 64:2). Described by David (Ps 55). Led by Bicri (2Sa 20), Absalom. *See Absalom.* Barabbas (Mk 15:7).

INTEGRITY [575, 622, 3841, 4797, 7406, 7407, 9447, 9448, 9450, 239, 917].

General:

Essential (Ex 18:21; Lk 16:10; 2Co 8:21). Commanded (Dt 16:19-20; Pr 4:25-27; Isa 56:1; Mic 6:8; Zec 7:9; Lk 3:13-14; 6:31; 11:42; Ro 13:5; 14:5, 14, 22; Eph 6:6; Php 4:8; Col 3:22-23; 1Ti 1:5; 3:9; Tit 1:7-8; 1Pe 2:12; 3:16).

Rewards of (2Sa 22:21; Ps 15:1-5; 18:20; 24:3-5; Pr 10:9; 20:7; 28:20; Isa 26:7; 33:15-16; Jer 7:5, 7; Eze 18:5, 7-9).

Proverbs concerning (Pr 2:2, 5, 9; 3:3-4; 4:25-27; 10:9; 11:3, 5; 12:22; 14:30; 15:21; 16:11; 19:1; 20:7; 21:3, 15; 22:11; 28:6, 20).

Instances of:

Pharaoh, when he learned that Sarah was Abraham's wife (Ge 12:18-20). Abraham, in instructing his family (Ge 18:19). Abimelech, when warned of God that the woman he had taken into his household was Isaac's wife (Ge 26:9-11). Jacob, in the care of Laban's property (Ge 31:39). Joseph, in resisting Potiphar's wife (Ge 39:8-12), in his innocence of the charge on which he was cast into the dungeon (Ge 40:15). Moses, in taking nothing from the Israelites in consideration of his services (Nu 16:15). Samuel, in exacting nothing from the people on account of services (1Sa 12:4-5). Workmen, who repaired the temple (1Ki 12:15; 22:7).

Priests who received the offerings of gold and other gifts for the renewing of the temple under Ezra (Ezr 2:24-30, 33-34). Nehemiah, in his reforms and in receiving no compensation for his own services (Ne 5:14-19). Job (Job 1:8; 10:7; 13:15; 16:17; 27:4-6; 29:14; 31:1-40). The psalmist (Ps 7:3-5, 8; 17:3; 26:1-3; 69:4; 73:15; 119:121). The Recabites, in keeping the Nazirite vows (Jer 35:12-19). Daniel, in maintaining uprightness of character (Da 6:4). The three Hebrews, who refused to worship Nebuchadnezzar's idol (Da 3:16-21, 28). Levi, in his life and service (Mal 2:6).

Joseph, the husband of Mary, in not jealously accusing her of immorality (Mt 1:19). Zacchaeus, in the administration of his wealth (Lk 19:8). Nathanael, in whom was no guile (Jn 1:47). Joseph, a counselor (Lk 23:50-51). Peter, when offered money by Simon (Ac 8:18-23). Paul and Barnabas (Ac 14:12-15). Paul (Ac 23:1; 24:16; Ro 9:1; 2Co 4:2; 5:11; 7:2; 1Th 2:4). The author of Hebrews (Heb 13:18).

See Character; Dishonesty; Honesty; Justice; Righteousness.

INTEMPERANCE *See Abstinence; Drunkard; Drunkenness; Temperance; Wine.*

INTERCESSION [4885, 7003, 7137, 1950, 1961, 5659].

Of People With God:

(Jer 27:18). Priestly (Ex 28:12, 29-30, 38; Lev 10:17). For spiritual blessing (Nu 6:23-26; 1Sa 12:23; Job 1:5; 42:8-10). To avert judgment (Ge 20:7; Ex 32:9-14; Nu 14:11-21; 16:45-50; Dt 9:18-29; Isa 65:8). For deliverance from enemies (1Sa 7:5-9; Isa 37:4). For healing of disease (Jas 5:14-16). For stubborn sinners, unavailing (Jer 7:16; 11:14; 14:11).

Commanded—

(Jer 29:7; Joel 2:17; Mt 5:44; Eph 6:18; 1Ti 2:1-2; 1Jn 5:16).

Examples of—

(Ge 48:16; Ex 32:31-32; 34:9; Nu 10:35-36; 27:16-17; Jos 7:8-9; Jdg 5:31; Ru 2:12; 1Sa 1:17; 12:23; 2Sa 24:17; 1Ki 8:29, 38-39, 44-45; 1Ch 29:18-19; 2Ch 6:40-41; 30:18-19; Ps 7:9; 12:1; 20:1-4; 25:22; 28:9; 36:10; 51:18; 80:1-2, 14-19; 122:7-8; 125:4; 132:9-10; 134:3; 141:5; Isa 62:1; 63:17-19; 64:8-12; Jer 18:20; Eze 9:8; 11:13; Da 9:3-19; Joel 2:17; Mic 7:14; Mt 5:44; 6:10; Ac 7:60; 8:15; Ro 1:9; 10:1; 1Co 1:3; 2Co 9:10, 14; 13:7; Gal 1:3; 6:16; Eph 1:15-19; 3:14-19; Php 1:3-5, 9; Col 1:3-4, 9; 2:1-2; 4:12; 1Th 1:2; 3:10, 12-13; 5:23; 2Th 1:11; 2:16-17; 3:5, 16; 2Ti 1:3; 4:16; Phm 4, 6; Heb 13:20-21; 1Pe 5:10).

Instances of—

Abraham, in behalf of Sodom (Ge 18:23-32), in behalf of Abimelech (Ge 20:17-18). Abraham's servant, in behalf of his master (Ge 24:12). Jacob, in behalf of his children (Ge 49). Moses, in behalf of Pharaoh (Ex 8:12-13, 30-31; 9:33; 10:18-19). Moses for Israel (Nu 16:20-22; 21:7; Dt 33:6-17; Ps 106:23), for Miriam (Nu 12:13-15). David, for Israel (2Sa 24:17). Solomon, for Israel (1Ki 8:29-53). Ezra, for Israel (Ezr 9:5-15). Nehemiah, in behalf of Judah and Jerusalem (Ne 1:4-9). Asaph, for the church (Ps 80-83). The "Sons of Korah," for the church (Ps 85:1-7). Jeremiah, for Israel (Am 7:2-6). Syrian Phoenician woman, for her daughter (Mt 15:22). Disciples, in behalf of Peter's wife's mother (Lk 4:38-39). Parents, for demon-possessed son (Mt 17:15; Mk 9:17-27). Others, who sought Jesus in behalf of the afflicted (Mt 12:22; 15:22, 30; 17:14-18; Mk 1:32; 2:3; Lk 5:18-20; Jn 4:47, 49). Paul for the church (Ac 20:32). Onesiphorus (2Ti 1:16, 18). For Paul, by the churches (Ac 14:26; 15:40).

Requested—

By Pharaoh, of Moses (Ex 8:8, 28; 9:28; 10:17; 12:32), and by the Israelites (Nu 21:7). By Israel, of Samuel (1Sa 12:19). By Jeroboam, of a prophet (1Ki 13:6). By Hezekiah, of Isaiah (2Ki 19:1-4). By Zedekiah, of Jeremiah (Jer 37:3), and by Johanan (Jer 42:1-6). By Daniel, of Shadrach, Meshach, and Abednego (Da 2:17-18). By Darius, of the Jews (Ezr 6:10). By Simon the sorcerer, of Peter (Ac 8:24). By Paul, of the churches (Ro 15:30-32; 2Co 1:11; Eph 6:19-20; 1Th 5:25; 2Th 3:1; Heb 13:18).

Answered—

Of Moses in behalf of Pharaoh, for the plague of frogs to be ended (Ex 8:12, 15), the plague of flies (Ex 8:30-32), the plague of rain, thunder, and hail (Ex 9:27-35), plague of locusts (Ex 10:16-20), plague of darkness (Ex 10:21-23); for the Israelites, during the battle with the Amalekites (Ex 17:11-14), after the Israelites had made the golden calf (Ex 32:11-14, 31-34; Dt 9:18-29; 10:10; Ps 106:23), after the murmuring of the people (Ex 33:15-17), when the fire of the Lord consumed the people (Nu 11:1-2), when the people murmured on account of the report of the spies (Nu 14:11-20), that the poisonous snakes might be taken away (Nu 21:4-9); that Miriam's leprosy might be healed (Nu 12:13); in behalf of Aaron, on account of his sin in making the golden calf (Dt 9:20). Of Samuel, for deliverance from the oppressions of the Philistines (1Sa 7:5-14). The prophet of Israel, for the restoration of Jeroboam's shriveled hand (1Ki 13:1-6). Of Elijah, for the raising from the dead the son of the hospitable widow (1Ki 17:20-23). Of Elisha, for the raising from the dead the son of the Shunammite woman (2Ki 4:33-36). Of Isaiah, in behalf of Hezekiah and the people, to be delivered from Sennacherib (2Ki 19).

Intercessional Influence of the Righteous—

(Ge 18:26-32; 19:22; 26:4-5, 24; 1Ki 11:12-13, 34; 15:4; 2Ki 8:19; 2Ch 21:7; Ps 103:17-18; Isa 37:35; Jer 5:1; Eze 14:14, 16, 18, 20; Mt 24:22; Ro 11:27-28; Rev 5:8; 8:3-4).

Intercession of People With Jesus: *See Mediation.*

Intercession of People with People:

Instances of: Reuben for Joseph (Ge 37:21-22). Judah for Joseph (Ge 37:26-27). Judah with Joseph (Ge 44:18-34). Pharaoh's chief baker for Joseph (Ge 41:9-14). Rahab for her people (Jos 2:12-13). Aaron for Miriam (Nu 12:12). Jonathan

for David (1Sa 19:1-7). Abigail for Nabal (1Sa 25:23-35). Joab for Absalom (2Sa 14:1-24). Bathsheba, for Solomon (1Ki 1:11-22, 28-31), for Adonijah (1Ki 2:13-25). Esther for her people (Est 7:2-6). Ebed-Melech for Jeremiah (Jer 38:7-13). Elisha offers to see the king for the Shunammite (2Ki 4:13). The king of Syria for Naaman (2Ki 5:6-8). Paul for Onesimus (Phm 10-21).

Intercession of Jesus:

(Lk 22:31-32; 23:33-34; Jn 14:16; 17:9, 11, 15-17, 20-22; Ro 8:34; Heb 7:25; 9:24; 1Jn 2:1-2).
See Jesus the Christ, Mediation of.

See Children, Of the Righteous, Blessed of God; Prayer, Intercessory.

INTEREST [5967, 5968, 8750, 9552, *3534, 4309, 5527*]. Income from lending money.

Charging Interest:

From a poor Israelite, forbidden (Ex 22:25; Lev 25:36-37; Dt 23:19). From a stranger, authorized (Dt 23:20). Unprofitable (Pr 28:8). Rebuked (Ne 5:1-13; Eze 22:12).

Charging No Interest:

Rewarded (Ps 15:5; Eze 18:8-9, 17). Lender and borrower equal before God (Isa 24:2).

See Borrowing; Debt; Debtor; Lending; Money; Usury.

INTERMARRY [995, 3161]. The patriarchs did not allow marriage outside their clan: Abraham (Ge 24:3), Jacob (Ge 28:1). Exceptions: Esau (Ge 26:34-35), Judah and his sons (Ge 38), Joseph (Ge 41:45, 50), Moses (Nu 12:1). Aaron and Miriam judged for criticizing Moses' intermarriage (Nu 12:1-15).

Israel was forbidden to intermarry with the Canaanites for religious reasons, not racial (Dt 7:1-6; Jos 23:12-13). Negative results of (Jdg 3:6-7), Solomon (1Ki 11:1-6), returned exiles (Ezr 9:14-15).

There are no racial barriers in the church (Col 3:11). Even marriage between believers and unbelievers does not have to end in divorce (1Co 7:12-16), though is not recommended (2Co 6:14-18). *See Marriage.*

INTERMEDIATE STATE Period of time which elapses between death and the resurrection. For the righteous it is one of blessedness (2Co 5:8); for the wicked it is one of conscious suffering (Lk 16:19-31).

INTERPRETATION [7354, 7355, 8694, 10599, 10600+, *1359, 1450, 1507, 2146, 2255*]. Of dreams. *See Dream.* Of foreign tongues (1Co 14:9-19). *See Tongues, Gift of.*

INTERPRETER [2706, 4885, *1449*]. Of dreams (Ge 40:8; 41:16; Da 2:18-30). Of languages (Ge 42:23; 2Ch 32:31; Ne 8:8; Job 33:23). In Christian churches (1Co 12:10, 30; 14:5, 13, 26-28).

Figurative (Job 33:23).

INTOLERANCE

Religious:
Exemplified by Cain (Ge 4:8), Joshua (Nu 11:24-28), James and John (Mk 9:38-39; Lk 9:49), the Jews, in persecuting Jesus. *See Jesus the Christ, Rejected.*

History of:
In persecuting the disciples (Ac 4:1-3, 15-21; 17:13), Stephen (Ac 6:9-15; 7:57-59; 8:1-3), Paul (Ac 13:50; 17:5; 18:13; 21:28-31; 22:22-23; 23:2).

Of Idolatrous Religions:
Taught by Moses (Ex 22:20; Dt 13; 17:1-7). Exemplified by: Elijah (1Ki 18:40), Jehu (2Ki 10:18-31), by the Jews, at the time of the religious revival under the leadership of Azariah (2Ch 15:12-13).
See Persecution.

INTOXICANTS *See Beer; Fermented Drink; Wine.*

INTOXICATION [*3499*]. *See Abstinence; Drunkenness.*

INTRIGUE [744, 2648, 2761, 4600, 8222]. *See Conspiracy.*

INVECTIVE *See Satire.*

INVENTION [*2388, 5054*]. Of musical instruments: By Jubal (Ge 4:21), by David (1Ch 23:5; 2Ch 7:6; 29:26; Am 6:5).
The use of metals (Ge 4:22). Machines of war (2Ch 26:15).

INVESTIGATION [1335, 2011, 8626, 9365, *374, 2428, 4158*]. By Solomon, into nature and design of things (Ecc 1:13-18; 2:1-12; 7:25; 8:17; 12:9-14).

INVITATIONS [*7924, 2813, 2263, 4151, 5251*]. The "Comes" of God's Word (Ge 7:1; Nu 10:29; Isa 18; 55:1; Mt 11:28; 22:4; Lk 14:17; Rev 22:17). Divine pleading (Pr 1:24; Isa 1:18; 55:1; Eze 18:31; Mic 6:3; Mt 23:37; Ro 10:21; 2Co 5:20).
Divine call: To repentance (Jer 35:15; Eze 33:11; Hos 6:1; Mt 22:3; 2Co 5:20; Rev 3:20). To leadership (Ge 12:1; Ex 3:10; Jdg 6:14; 1Ki 19:19; Isa 6:8; Ac 26:16). Universality of (Isa 45:22; 55:1; Mt 22:9; Jn 7:37; Ro 10:12; 1Ti 2:4; Rev 22:17).
Refused by people (Ps 81:11; Isa 65:12; Jer 7:13; Hos 9:17; Mt 22:3; Jn 5:40; Ro 10:21). Warnings (Ge 19:17; Dt 29:20; Jos 24:20; 1Sa 12:15; Isa 28:14; Jer 13:16; Jnh 3:4; Heb 12:25; 2Pe 3:17).

IPHDEIAH [3635] (*Yahweh redeems*). A Benjamite (1Ch 8:25).

IPHTAH [3652] (*he opens*). A city of Judah (Jos 15:43).

IPHTAH EL [3654] (*God [El] opens*). A valley in Zebulun (Jos 19:14, 27).

IR [6553] (possibly *stallion donkey*). A Benjamite (1Ch 7:12).

IR NAHASH [6560] (*city of Nahash*). Whether a man or a town is not clear (1Ch 4:12, ftn). *See Nahash.*

IR SHEMESH [6561] (*city of Shemesh*). A city of Dan (Jos 19:41).

IRA [6562] (possibly *stallion donkey*).
1. The Jairite, David's priest (2Sa 20:26).
2. The Ithrite, one of David's heroes (2Sa 23:38; 1Ch 11:40).
3. From Tekoa, one of David's heroes (2Sa 23:26; 1Ch 11:28; 27:9).

IRAD [6563]. Son of Enoch (Ge 4:18).

IRAM [6566]. A chief of Edom (Ge 36:43; 1Ch 1:54).

IRI [6565] (perhaps *donkey's colt*). A son of Bela (1Ch 7:7).

IRIJAH [3713] (*Yahweh sees*). A captain of the guard who imprisoned the prophet Jeremiah (Jer 37:13-14).

IRON [1366, 3712, 10591, *3013, 4969, 4970*].
1. First recorded use of (Ge 4:22). Ore of (Dt 8:9; Job 28:2). Melted (Eze 22:20). Used in the temple (1Ch 22:3; 29:2, 7).
Articles Made of—
Ax (2Ki 6:6; 2Ch 18:10; Ecc 10:10; Isa 10:34), bed (Dt 3:11), breastplate (Rev 9:9), chariot (Jos 17:16, 18; Jdg 1:19; 4:3), fetters (Ps 105:18; 107:10, 16; 149:8), file (Pr 27:17), furnace (Dt 4:20; 1Ki 8:51; Jer 11:4), gate (Ac 12:10), harrow (2Sa 12:31), horn (1Ki 22:11; 2Ch 18:10; Mic 4:13), idols (Da 2:33; 5:4, 23), pans (Eze 4:3; 27:19), pen (Job 19:24; Jer 17:1), pillars (Jer 1:18), rods (Ps 2:9; Rev 2:27; 12:5; 19:15), threshing instruments (Am 1:3), tools (1Ki 6:7), vessels (Jos 6:24), weapons (Nu 35:16; 1Sa 17:7; Job 20:24; 41:7), yokes (Dt 28:48; Jer 28:13-14).
See Steel.
Figurative (2Sa 23:7; Jer 15:12; 1Ti 4:2).
2. A city of Naphtali (Jos 19:38).

IRONY Instances of: Michal to David (2Sa 6:20). Elijah to the priests of Baal (1Ki 18:27). Job to his accusers (Job 12:2). Ezekiel to the prince of Tyre (Eze 28:3-5). Micaiah (1Ki 22:15). Amos to the Samaritans (Am 4:4). Jesus to Pharisees (Mk 2:17). Pharisees and Herodians to Jesus (Mt 22:16). Roman soldiers to Jesus (Mt 27:29; Mk 15:17-19; Lk 23:11; Jn 19:2-3). Pilate, calling Jesus king (Mk 15:19; Jn 19:15). Superscription of Pilate over Jesus (Mt 27:37; Mk 15:26; Lk 23:38; Jn 19:19). Agrippa to Paul (Ac 26:28).
See Sarcasm; Satire.

IRPEEL [3761] (*God [El] heals*). A city of Benjamin (Jos 18:27).

IRRIGATION [9197]. Of gardens (Dt 11:10; Pr 21:1; Ecc 2:6; Isa 58:11).
Figurative (1Co 3:6, 8).

IRU [6564]. Eldest son of Caleb (1Ch 4:15).

ISAAC [3663, 3773, 2693] (*he laughs, he will laugh,* some contexts *mock;* other contexts *El [God] laughs*).

1. Miraculous son of Abraham (Ge 17:15-19; 18:1-15; 21:1-8; Jos 24:3; 1Ch 1:28; Gal 4:28; Heb 11:11). Ancestor of Jesus (Mt 1:2). Offered in sacrifice by his father (Ge 22:1-19; Heb 11:17; Jas 2:21). Is provided a wife from among his kindred (Ge 24; 25:20). Abrahamic covenant confirmed in (Ge 26:2-5; 1Ch 16:15-19). Dwells in the south country at the well Beer Lahai Roi (Ge 24:62; 25:11). With Ishmael, buries his father in the cave of Machpelah (Ge 25:9). Esau and Jacob born to (Ge 25:19-26; 1Ch 1:34; Jos 24:4). Dwells in Gerar (Ge 26:7-11). Prospers (Ge 26:12-14). Possesses large flocks and herds (Ge 26:14). Digs wells, and is defrauded of them by the herdsmen of Abimelech (Ge 26:15, 21). Removes to the valley of Gerar, afterward called Beersheba (Ge 26:22-33). His old age, last blessing upon his sons (Ge 27:18-40). Death and burial of (Ge 35:27-29; 49:31). His filial obedience (Ge 22:9). His peaceableness (Ge 26:14-22). Was a prophet (Ge 27:28-29, 39-40; Heb 11:20). Has devoutness (Ge 24:63; 25:21; 26:25; Mt 8:11; Lk 13:28). Prophecies concerning (Ge 17:16-21; 18:10-14; 21:12; 26:2-5, 24; Ex 32:13; 1Ch 16:16; Ro 9:7).

2. A designation of the ten tribes (Am 7:9).

ISAIAH, BOOK OF

Author: Isaiah son of Amoz

Date: Between c. 701 and 681 B.C.

Outline:

Part 1: The Book of Judgment (chs. 1-39):

I. Messages of Rebuke and Promise (chs. 1-6).
  A. Introduction: Charges Against Judah for Breaking the Covenant (ch. 1).
  B. The Future Discipline and Glory of Judah and Jerusalem (chs. 2-4).
    1. Jerusalem's future blessings (2:1-5).
    2. The discipline of Judah (2:6-4:11).
    3. The restoration of Zion (4:2-6).
  C. The Nation's Judgment and Exile (ch. 5).
  D. Isaiah's Unique Commission (ch. 6).
II. Prophecies Occasioned by the Aramean and Israelite Threat Against Judah (chs. 7-12).
  A. Ahaz Warned Not to Fear the Aramean and Israelite Threat (ch. 7).
  B. Isaiah's Son and David's Son (8:1-9:7).
  C. Judgment Against Israel (9:8-10:4).
  D. The Assyrian Empire and the Davidic Kingdom (10:5-12:6).
    1. The destruction of Assyria (10:5-34).
    2. The establishment of the Davidic king and his kingdom (ch. 11).
    3. Songs of joy for deliverance (ch. 12).
III. Judgment Against the Nations (chs. 13-23).

  A. Against Assyria and Its Ruler (13:1-14:27).
  B. Against Philistia (14:28-32).
  C. Against Moab (chs. 15-16).
  D. Against Aram and Israel (ch. 17).
  E. Against Cush (ch. 18).
  F. Against Egypt and Cush (chs. 19-20).
  G. Against Babylon (21:1-10).
  H. Against Dumah (Edom) (21:11-12).
  I. Against Arabia (21:13-17).
  J. Against the Valley of Vision (Jerusalem) (ch. 22).
  K. Against Tyre (ch. 23).
IV. Judgment and Promise (the Lord's Kingdom) (chs. 24-27).
  A. Universal Judgments for Universal Sin (ch. 24).
  B. Deliverance and Blessing (ch. 25).
  C. Praise for the Lord's Sovereign Care (ch. 26).
  D. Israel's Enemies: Punished but Israel's Remnant Restored (ch. 27).
V. Six Woes: Five on the Unfaithful in Israel and One on Assyria (chs. 28-33).
  A. Woe to Ephraim (Samaria)—and to Judah (ch. 28).
  B. Woe to David's City, Jerusalem (29:1-14).
  C. Woe to Those Who Rely on Foreign Alliances (29:15-24).
  D. Woe to the Obstinate Nation (ch. 30).
  E. Woe to Those Who Rely on Egypt (chs. 31-32).
  F. Woe to Assyria—but Blessing for God's People (ch. 33).
VI. More Prophecies of Judgment and Promise (chs. 34-35).
  A. The Destruction of the Nations and the Avenging of God's People (ch. 34).
  B. The Future Blessings of Restored Zion (ch. 35).
VII. A Historical Transition From the Assyrian Threat to the Babylonian Exile (chs. 36-39).
  A. Jerusalem Preserved From the Assyrian Threat (chs. 36-37).
    1. The siege of Jerusalem by Sennacherib and the Assyrian army (ch. 36).
    2. The Lord's deliverance of Jerusalem (ch. 37).
  B. The Lord's Extension of Hezekiah's Life (ch. 38).
  C. The Babylonian Exile Predicted (ch. 39).

Part 2: The Book of Comfort (chs. 40-66):

VIII. The Deliverance and Restoration of Israel (chs. 40-48).
  A. The Coming of the Victorious God (40:1-26).
  B. Unfailing Strength for the Weary Exiles (40:27-31).
  C. The Lord of History (41:1-42:9).
  D. Praise and Exhortation (42:10-25).
  E. The Regathering and Renewal of Israel (43:1-44:5).
  F. The Only God (44:6-45:25).

G. The Lord's Superiority over Babylon's Gods (ch. 46).

H. The Fall of Babylon (ch. 47).

I. The Lord's Exhortations to His People (ch. 48).

IX. The Servant's Ministry and Israel's Restoration (chs. 49-57).

A. The Call and Mission of the Servant (49:1-13).

B. The Repopulation of Zion (49:14-26).

C. Israel's Sin and the Servant's Obedience (ch. 50).

D. The Remnant Comforted Because of Their Glorious Prospect (51:1-52:12).

E. The Sufferings and Glories of the Lord's Righteous Servant (52:13-53:12).

F. The Future Glory of Zion (ch. 54).

G. The Lord's Call to Salvation and Covenant Blessings (55:1-56:8).

H. The Condemnation of the Wicked in Israel (56:9-57:21).

X. Everlasting Deliverance and Everlasting Judgment (chs. 58-66).

A. False and True Worship (ch. 58).

B. Zion's Confession and Redemption (ch. 59).

C. Zion's Peace and Prosperity (ch. 60).

D. The Lord's Favor (ch. 61).

E. Zion's Restoration and Glory (62:1-63:6).

F. Prayer for Divine Deliverance (63:7-64:12).

G. The Lord's Answer: Mercy and Judgment (ch. 65).

H. Judgment for False Worshipers and Blessing for True Worshipers (ch. 66).

ISAIAH [3833, 2480] (*Yahweh saves*).

The Prophet:

Son of Amos (Isa 1:1). Prophecies in the days of Uzziah, Jotham, Ahaz, and Hezekiah, kings of Judah (Isa 1:1; 6:1; 7:1, 3; 14:27; 20:1; 36:1; 38:1; 39:1), at the time of the invasion by the Assyrian supreme commander (Isa 20:1). Symbolically wears sackcloth, and walks barefoot, as a sign to Israel (Isa 20:2-3). Comforts and encourages Hezekiah and the people in the siege of Jerusalem by Sennacherib, king of Assyria (2Ki 18; 19; Isa 37:6-7). Comforts Hezekiah in his affliction (2Ki 20:1-11; Isa 38). Performs the miracle of the returning shadow to confirm Hezekiah's faith (2Ki 20:8-11). Reproves Hezekiah's folly in exhibiting his resources to the commissioners from Babylon (2Ki 20:12-19; Isa 39). Is chronicler of the times of Uzziah and Hezekiah (2Ch 26:22; 32:32).

The Prophecies:

Foretells punishment of the Jews for idolatry, and reproves self-confidence and distrust of God (Isa 2:6-20). Foretells the destruction of the Jews (Isa 3). Promises to the remnant restoration of divine favor (Isa 4:2-6; 6). Delineates in the parable of the vineyard the ingratitude of the Jews, and reproves it (Isa 5:1-10). Denounces existing corruption (Isa 5:8-30).

Foretells the ill success of the plot of the Is-

raelites and Syrians against Judah (Isa 7:1-6). Pronounces calamities against Israel and Judah (Isa 7:16-25; 9:2-6). Foretells prosperity under Hezekiah, and the manifestation of the Messiah (Isa 9:1-7). Pronounces vengeance upon the enemies of Israel (Isa 9:8-12). Denounces the wickedness of Israel, and foretells the judgments of God (Isa 9:13-21). Pronounces judgments against false prophets (Isa 10:1-4). Foretells the destruction of Sennacherib's armies (Isa 10:5-34), the restoration of Israel and the triumph of the Messiah's kingdom (Isa 11).

The burden of Babylon (Isa 13; 14:1-28). Denunciation against the Philistines (Isa 14:9-32). Burden of Moab (Isa 15-16). Burden of Damascus (Isa 17). Obscure prophecy, supposed by some authorities to be directed against the Assyrians, by others against the Egyptians, and by others against the Ethiopians (Isa 18). The burden of Egypt (Isa 19-20). Denunciations against Babylon (Isa 21:1-10). Prophecy concerning Seir (Isa 21:11-12), Arabia (Isa 21:13-17), concerning the conquest of Jerusalem, the captivity of Shebna, and the promotion of Eliakim (Isa 22:1-22), the overthrow of Tyre (Isa 23), the judgments upon the land, but that a remnant of the Jews would be saved (Isa 25-27).

Reproves Ephraim for his wickedness, and foretells the destruction by Shalmaneser (Isa 28:1-5). Declares the glory of God upon the remnant who are saved (Isa 28:5-6). Exposes the corruption in Jerusalem and exhorts to repentance (Isa 28:7-29). Foretells the invasion of Sennacherib, the distress of the Jews and the destruction of the Assyrian army (Isa 29:1-8). Denounces the hypocrisy of the Jews (Isa 29:9-17). Promises a reformation (Isa 29:18-24). Reproves the people for their confidence in Egypt, and their contempt of God (Isa 30:1-17; 31:1-6). Declares the goodness and patience of God toward them (Isa 30:18-26; 32-35).

Reproves the Jews for their spiritual blindness and infidelity (Isa 42:18-25). Promises ultimate restoration of the Jews (Isa 43:1-13). Foretells the ultimate destruction of Babylon (Isa 43:14-17; 47). Exhorts the people to repent (Isa 43:22-28). Comforts the church with promises, exposes the folly of idolatry, and their future deliverance from captivity by Cyrus (Isa 44; 45:1-5; 48:20). Foretells the conversion of the Gentiles, and triumph of the gospel (Isa 45:5-25). Denounces the evils of idolatry (Isa 46). Reproves the Jews for their idolatries and other wickedness (Isa 48). Exhorts to sanctification (Isa 56:1-8). Foretells calamities to Judah (Isa 57-58; 59:9-12).

Foreshadows the person and the kingdom of the Messiah (Isa 32-35; 42; 45; 49-56; 59:15-21; 60-66).

ISCAH [3576]. Daughter of Haran and sister of Lot (Ge 11:29).

ISCARIOT [2697] (*man of Kerioth* or *of the assassins*). *See Judas.*

ISHBAH [3786] (*he boasts, congratulates*). Father of Eshtemoa (1Ch 4:17).

ISHBAK [3791]. Son of Abraham and Keturah (Ge 25:2; 1Ch 1:32).

ISHBI-BENOB [3787]. A giant warrior slain by Abishai (2Sa 21:16).

ISH-BOSHETH [410] (*man of shame*). Son of Saul. Called Esh-Baal (1Ch 8:33; 9:39). Made king by Abner (2Sa 2:8-10). Deserted by Abner (2Sa 3:6-12). Restores Michal, David's wife, to David (2Sa 3:14-16). Assassinated (2Sa 4:5-8). Avenged by David (2Sa 4:9-12).

ISHHOD [412] (*man of grandeur*). One of the tribe of Manasseh (1Ch 7:18).

ISHI [3831] (*God has saved*).
1. A play on the two Hebrew words for husband. In this verse the first is "husband"; the second is "master" which is identical with the name of the god Baal. There will be such a vigorous reaction against Baal worship that this Hebrew word for "master" will no longer be used of the Lord (Hos 2:16, ftn).
2. A son of Appaim (1Ch 2:31).
3. A descendant of Judah (1Ch 4:20).
4. A Simeonite (1Ch 4:42).
5. One of the heads of Manasseh (1Ch 5:24).

ISHIAH See Isshiah.

ISHIJAH [3807] (*Yahweh forget*). One of the sons of Harim (Ezr 10:31).

ISHMA [3816] (*desolate* ISBE; *God [El] he heard* KB). A descendant of Judah (1Ch 4:3).

ISHMACHIAH See Ismakiah.

ISHMAEL [3817] (*God [El] he heard*).
1. Son of Abraham (Ge 16:11, 15-16; 1Ch 1:28). Prayer of Abraham for (Ge 17:18, 20). Circumcised (Ge 17:23-26). Promised to be the father of a nation (Ge 16:11-12; 17:20; 21:12-13, 18). Sent away by Abraham (Ge 21:6-21). With Isaac buries his father (Ge 25:9). Children of (Ge 25:12-18; 1Ch 1:29-31). Daughter of, marries Esau (Ge 28:9; 36:2-3). Death of (Ge 25:17-18).
2. Father of Zebadiah (2Ch 19:11).
3. A son of Azel (1Ch 8:38; 9:44).
4. One of the captains of hundreds (2Ch 23:1).
5. A priest of the Exile (Ezr 10:22).
6. A son of Nethaniah. Assassinated Gedaliah, governor of Judah under king of Babylon, and takes captive many Jews (Jer 40:8-16; 41:1-11; 2Ki 25:23-25). Defeated by Johanan and put to flight (Jer 41:12-15).

ISHMAELITE(S) [3818] (*one from Ishmael*). Descended from Abraham's son, Ishmael (Ge 16:15-16; 1Ch 1:28). Divided into twelve tribes (Ge 25:16). Heads of tribes (Ge 25:13-15; 1Ch 1:29-31).

Original possessions of (Ge 25:18). Governed by kings (Jer 25:24). Dwelt in tents (Isa 13:20). Rich in cattle (1Ch 5:21). Wore ornaments of gold (Jdg 8:24). Were the merchants of the east (Ge 37:25; Eze 27:20-21). Traveled in large companies or caravans (Ge 37:25; Job 6:19). Waylaid and plundered travelers (Jer 3:2). Often confederate against Israel (Ps 83:6).

Called:
Hagrites, either Ishmaelites (descendants of Hagar; Ge 16) or a group mentioned in Assyrian inscriptions as an Aramean confederacy (1Ch 5:10, 19-22; 27:31), are named among the enemies of Israel (Ps 83:6). Arabs (Isa 13:20).

Overcome by:
Gideon (Jdg 8:10-24). Reubenites and Gadites (1Ch 5:10, 18-20). Uzziah (2Ch 26:7). Sent presents to Solomon (1Ki 10:15; 2Ch 9:14). Sent flocks to Jehoshaphat (2Ch 17:11).

Prophecies Concerning:
To be numerous (Ge 16:10; 17:20). To be wild and savage (Ge 16:12). To be warlike and predatory (Ge 16:12). To be divided into twelve tribes (Ge 17:20). To continue independent (Ge 16:12). To be a great nation (Ge 21:13, 18). To be judged with the nations (Ge 25:23-25). Their glory to be diminished (Isa 21:13-17). Their submission to Christ (Ps 72:10, 15). Probably preached to by Paul (Gal 1:17).

ISHMAIAH [3819, 3820] (*Yahweh heard*).
1. Gibeonite (1Ch 12:4).
2. Chief of Zebulunites (1Ch 27:19).

ISHMEELITE See Ishmaelite(s).

ISHMERAI [3821] (*Yahweh guards*). A chief Benjamite (1Ch 8:18).

ISHOD See Ishhod.

ISHPAH [3834] (*he judged*). A Benjamite (1Ch 8:16).

ISHPAN [3836] (possibly *may God judge*). Son of Shashak (1Ch 8:22).

ISHTAR Semitic goddess worshiped in Phoenicia, Canaan, Assyria, and Babylonia, and sometimes even by the Israelites. Some identify her with Ashtoreth or Ashtaroth (Jdg 2:13; 10:6; 1Ki 11:5; 2Ki 23:13).

ISHTOB (*man of Tob*). See Tob, 2.

ISHUAH See Ishvah.

ISHUAI See Ishvi, Ishvite.

ISHVAH [3796] (*he will level*). Son of Asher (Ge 46:17; 1Ch 7:30).

ISHVI, ISHVITE [3798, 3799].
1. Son of Asher (Ge 46:17; 1Ch 7:30) and his clan (Nu 26:44).
2. Son of Saul (1Sa 14:49).

ISLAND, ISLE [362, 3761, 3762].

1. Dry land, as opposed to water (Isa 42:15).
2. Body of land surrounded by water (Jer 2:10).
3. Coastland (Ge 10:5; Isa 20:6).
4. The farthest regions of the earth (Isa 41:5; Zep 2:11).

ISMAIAH See Ishmaiah.

ISMAKIAH [3577] (Yahweh sustains).
Overseer of the temple (2Ch 31:13).

ISPAH See Ishpah.

ISRAEL, ISRAELITES [278, 3776+, 10335, 2702+, 2703+] (he struggles with God [El]).

1. A name given to Jacob (Ge 32:24-32; 2Ki 17:34; Hos 12:3-4).
2. A name of the Christ in prophecy (Isa 49:3).
3. A name given to the descendants of Jacob, a nation. Also called Israelites and Hebrews (Ge 43:32; Ex 1:15; 9:7; 10:3; 21:2; Lev 23:42; Jos 13:6; 1Sa 4:6; 13:3, 19; 14:11, 21; Php 3:5).

Tribes of:

Tribes of Israel were named after the sons of Jacob. In lists usually the names Levi and Joseph, two sons of Jacob, do not appear. The descendants of Levi were consecrated to the rites of religion, and the two sons of Joseph, Ephraim and Manasseh, were adopted by Jacob in Joseph's stead (Ge 48:5; Jos 14:4), and their names appear in the lists of tribes instead of those of Levi and Joseph, as follows: Asher, Benjamin, Dan, Ephraim, Gad, Issachar, Judah, Manasseh, Naphtali, Reuben, Simeon, Zebulun.

Names of, seen in John's vision, on the gates of the New Jerusalem (Rev 21:12).

Prophecies, concerning (Ge 15:5, 13; 25:23; 26:4; 27:28-29, 40; 48:19; 49; Dt 33), of the multitude of (Ge 13:16; 15:5; 22:17; 26:4; 28:14), of their captivity in Egypt (Ge 15:13-14; Ac 7:6-7).

Divided into families, each of which had a chief (Nu 25:14; 26; 36:1; Jos 7:14; 1Ch 4-8).

Number of, who went into Egypt (Ge 46:8-27; Ex 1:5; Dt 10:22; Ac 7:14). Number of, at the time of the Exodus (Ex 12:37-38, w Ge 47:27; Ex 1:7-20; Ps 105:24; Ac 7:17). Number of, fit for military service when they left Egypt (Ex 12:37), at Sinai, by tribes (Nu 1:1-50), after the plague (Nu 26), when David numbered (2Sa 24:1-9; 1Ch 21:5-6; 27:23-24), after the Captivity (Ezr 2:64; Ne 7:66-67), in John's apocalyptic vision (Rev 7:1-8).

Early History:

Dwelt in Goshen (Ge 46:28-34; 47:4-10, 27-28).
Dwelt in Egypt 430 years (Ge 15:13; Ex 12:40-41; Ac 7:6; Gal 3:17). Were enslaved and oppressed by the Egyptians (Ex 1-2; 5; Ac 7:18-36). Their groaning heard by God (Ex 2:23-25). Moses commissioned as deliverer (Ex 3:2-22; 4:1-17). The land of Egypt plagued on their account. See Egypt. Exempt from the plagues (Ex 8:22-23; 9:4-6, 26; 10:23; 11:7; 12:13). Children were spared when

the firstborn of Egypt were slain (Ex 12:13, 23). Instituted the Passover (Ex 12:1-28). Borrowed jewels from the Egyptians (Ex 11:2-3; 12:35-36; Ps 105:37). Urged by the Egyptians to depart (Ex 12:31-39). Journey from Rameses to Succoth (Ex 12:37-39). Made the journey by night (Ex 12:42). The day of their deliverance to be a memorial (Ex 12:42; 13:3-16). Led of God (Ex 13:18, 21-22). Providentially cared for (Dt 8:3-4; 29:5-6; 34:7; Ne 9:21; Ps 105:37). See Manna; Cloud, Pillar of.

Journey from Succoth, to Etham (Ex 13:20), to Pi Hahiroth (Ex 14:2; Nu 33:5-7). Pursued by the Egyptians (Ex 14:5-31). Pass through the Red Sea (Ex 14:19-22; Ps 78; 105-107; 136). Order of march (Nu 2). Journey to Marah (Ex 15:23; Nu 33:8). Murmur on account of the bitter water (Ex 15:23-25); water of sweetened (Ex 15:25). Journey to Elim (Ex 15:27; Nu 33:9). The itinerary (Nu 33).

Murmured for food (Ex 16:2-3). Provided with manna and quails (Ex 16:4-36). Murmured for want of water at Rephidim (Ex 17:2-7), water miraculously supplied from the rock at Meribah (Ex 17:5-7). Defeat the Amalekites (Ex 17:13; Dt 25:17-18). Arrive at Sinai (Ex 19:1; Nu 33:15). At the suggestion of Jethro, Moses' father-in-law, they organize a system of government (Ex 18:25; Dt 1:9-18). The message of God to them, requiring that they shall be obedient to his commandments, and as a reward they would be to him a holy nation, and their reply (Ex 19:3-8). Sanctify themselves for receiving the law (Ex 19:10-15). The law delivered to (Ex 20-23; 24:1-4; 25-31; Lev 1-25; 27; Dt 5; 15:16). The people receive it and covenant obedience to it (Ex 24:3, 7). Idolatry of (Ex 32; Dt 9:17-21). The anger of the Lord in consequence (Ex 32:9-14). Moses' indignation; breaks the tables of stone; enters the camp; commands the Levites; three thousand slain (Ex 32:19-35). Visited by a plague (Ex 32:35). Obduracy of (Ex 33:3; 34:9; Dt 9:12-29). God withdraws his presence (Ex 33:1-3). The mourning of, when God refused to lead them (Ex 33:4-10). Tablets renewed (Ex 34). Pattern for the tabernacle and its furnishings, and forms of worship to be observed (Ex 25-31). Gifts consecrated for the creation of the tabernacle (Ex 35; 36:1-7; Nu 7). The building of the tabernacle; the manufacture of its furnishings, including the garments of the priests; and their sanctification (Ex 36:8-38; 37-40). First sacrifice offered by under the law (Lev 8:14-36; 9:8-24). Second Passover observed (Nu 9:1-5).

March out of the wilderness (Nu 10:11-36). Itinerary (Nu 33). Order of camp and march (Nu 2). Arrive at the border of Canaan (Nu 12:16). Send twelve spies to view the land (Nu 13; 32:8; Dt 1:22, 25; Jos 14:7). Return with a majority and minority report (Nu 13:26-33; 14:6-10). Murmuring over the report (Nu 14:1-5). The judgment of God upon them in consequence of their unbelief and murmuring (Nu 14:13-39). Reaction, and their purpose to enter the land; are defeated by the Amalekites (Nu 14:40-45; Dt 1:41-45). Stay at

Kadesh (Dt 1:46). Return to the wilderness, where they remain thirty-eight years, and all die except Joshua and Caleb (Nu 14:20-39). Rebellion of Korah, Dathan, and Abiram (Nu 16:1-40; Dt 11:6). Murmur against Moses and Aaron; are plagued; 14, 700 die; plague stayed (Nu 16:41-50). Murmur for want of water in Meribah; the rock is struck (Nu 20:1-13). Are refused passage through the country of Edom (Nu 20:14-21). The death of Aaron (Nu 20:22, 29; 33:38-39; Dt 10:6).

Defeat the Canaanites (Nu 21:1-3). Are scourged with serpents (Nu 21:4-9). Defeat Sihon, king of the Amorites (Nu 21:21-32; Dt 2:24-35), and Og, the king of Bashan (Nu 21:33-35; Dt 3:1-17). Arrive in the plains of Moab, at the fords of the Jordan (Nu 22:1; 33:48-49). Commit idolatry with the people of Moab (Nu 25:1-5). Visited by a plague in consequence; 24,000 die (Nu 25:6-15; 26:1). The people numbered for the allotment of the land (Nu 26). The daughters of Zelophehad sue for an inheritance (Nu 27:1-11; Jos 17:3-6). Conquest of the Midianites (Nu 31). Nations dread (Dt 2:25). Renew the covenant (Dt 29). Moses dies, and people mourn (Dt 34). Joshua appointed leader (Nu 27:18-23; Dt 31:23). *See Joshua, 1.*

All who were numbered at Sinai perished in the wilderness except Caleb and Joshua (Nu 26:63, 65; Dt 2:14-16). Piety of those who entered Canaan (Jos 23:8; Jdg 2:7-10; Jer 2:2-3). Men chosen to allot the lands of Canaan among the tribes and families (Nu 34:17-29). Remove from Shittim to Jordan (Jos 3:1). Cross Jordan (Jos 4). Circumcision observed and Passover celebrated (Jos 5). Jericho taken (Jos 6). Ai taken (Jos 7-8). Make a covenant with the Gibeonites (Jos 9). Defeat the five Amorite kings (Jos 10). Conquest of the land (Jos 21:43-45, w Jdg 1). The land allotted (Jos 15-21).

Two-and-a-half tribes return from west side of the Jordan; erect a memorial to signify the unity of the tribes; the memorial misunderstood; the controversy which followed; its amicable adjustment (Jos 22). Joshua's exhortation immediately before his death (Jos 23). Covenant renewed, death of Joshua (Jos 24; Jdg 2:8-9). Religious fidelity during the life of Joshua (Jos 24:31; Jdg 2:7).

Under the Judges:

Public affairs administered 450 years by the judges (Jdg 2:16-19; Ac 13:20). The original inhabitants not fully expelled (Jdg 1:27-36; 3:1-7). Reproved by an angel for not casting out the original inhabitants (Jdg 2:1-5). People turn to idolatry (Jdg 2:10-23). Delivered for their idolatry to the king of Mesopotamia during eight years; their repentance and deliverance (Jdg 3:8-11). Renew their idolatry, and are put under tribute to the king of Moab during eighteen years; repent and are delivered by Ehud; eighty years of peace follow (Jdg 3:12-30). Shamgar resists a foray of the Philistines and delivers Israel (Jdg 3:31). People again do evil and are put under bonds for twenty years to the king of Syria (Jdg 4:1-3).

Delivered by Deborah, a prophetess, and judged (Jdg 4-5). Seven years of bondage to the Midianites; delivered by Gideon (Jdg 6-7; 8:1-28). *See Gideon.* Return to idolatry (Jdg 8:33-34).

Abimelech foments an intertribal war (Jdg 9). Judged, by Tola twenty-three years (Jdg 10:1-2), by Jair twenty-two years (Jdg 10:3-4). People backslide, and are given over to the Philistines for discipline eighteen years; repent and turn to the Lord; delivered by Jephthah (Jdg 10:6-18; 11). Ephraimites go to war against other tribes; defeated by Jephthah (Jdg 12:1-7). Judged, by Ibzan seven years (Jdg 12:8-10), by Elon ten years (Jdg 12:11-12), by Abdon eight years (Jdg 12:13-15). Backslide again and are disciplined by the Philistines forty years (Jdg 13:1). Judged by Samson twenty years (Jdg 15:20, w Jdg 13-16). Scandal of the Bethlehemite's concubine, and the consequent war between the Benjamites and the other tribes (Jdg 19-21). Judged by Eli forty years (1Sa 4:18, w 1Sa 1-4). Smitten by the Philistines at Ebenezer (1Sa 4:1-2, 10-11). Demand a king (1Sa 8:5-20; Hos 13:10).

The United Kingdom:

Saul anointed king (1Sa 10; 11:12-15; 12:13). Ammonites invade Israel, are defeated (1Sa 11). Philistines smitten (1Sa 14). Amalekites defeated (1Sa 15). David anointed king (1Sa 16:11-13). Goliath slain (1Sa 17). Israel defeated by the Philistines, and Saul and his sons killed (1Sa 31). *See Saul.* David defeats the Amalekites (1Sa 30; 2Sa 1:1), made king (2Sa 2:4, 11). Ish-Bosheth made king (2Sa 2:8-10).

The conflict between the two political factions (2Sa 2:12-32; 3:1).

David made king over all Israel (2Sa 5:1-5). Conquests of David (2Sa 8), Absalom's rebellion (2Sa 15-18). *See David.*

Solomon anointed king (1Ki 1:32-40). Temple built (1Ki 6). Solomon's palace built (1Ki 7). Solomon's death (1Ki 11:41-43). *See Solomon.*

The Revolt of the Ten Tribes:

Foreshadowing circumstances indicating the separation: Disagreement after Saul's death (2Sa 2; 1Ch 12:23-40; 13). Lukewarmness of the ten tribes, and zeal of Judah for David in Absalom's rebellion (2Sa 19:41-43). The rebellion of Sheba (2Sa 20). The two factions are distinguished as Israel and Judah during David's reign (2Sa 21:2). Providential (Zec 11:14).

Revolt consummated under Rehoboam, son and successor of Solomon (1Ki 12). The ten tribes that revolted from the house of David also called Ephraim (Hos 7:8, 11), Jacob (Hos 12:2).

Israel (The Ten Tribes):

War continued between the two kingdoms all the days of Rehoboam and Jeroboam (1Ki 14:30), and between Jeroboam and Abijah (1Ki 15:7), and between Baasha and Asa (1Ki 15:16, 32). Famine prevails in the reign of Ahab (1Ki 18:1-6). Israel, also called Samaria, invaded by, but defeats, Ben-Hadad, king of Syria (1Ki 20). Moab rebels (2Ki 1:1; 3). Army of Syria invades Israel, but peacefully withdraws through the tact of the prophet Elisha (2Ki 6:8-23). Samaria besieged (2Ki 6:24-33; 7), city of, taken, and the people carried to Assyria (2Ki 17). The land repopulated (2Ki 17:24).

The remnant that remained after the able-bodied were carried into captivity associated with the kingdom of Judah (2Ch 30:18-26; 34:6; 35:18).

The Kings of Israel			
	Names	Ruled	Dates B.C.
1.	Jeroboam I	22 years	930-909
2.	Nadab	2 years	909-908
3.	Baasha	24 years	908-886
4.	Elah	2 years	886-885
5.	Zimri	7 days	885
6.	Omri	12 years	885-874
7.	Ahab	22 years	874-853
8.	Ahaziah	2 years	853-852
9.	Joram	12 years	852-841
10.	Jehu	28 years	841-814
11.	Jehoahaz	17 years	814-798
12.	Jehoash	16 years	798-782
13.	Jeroboam II	41 years	793-753
14.	Zechariah	6 months	753
15.	Shallum	1 month	752
16.	Menahem	10 years	752-742
17.	Pekahiah	2 years	742-740
18.	Pekah	20 years	752-732
19.	Hoshea	9 years	732-722

Note: Some kings, such as Jehoash and Jeroboam II, had overlapping reigns.

See also the chart at Kings; each king by name.
Prophecies Concerning—
Of captivity, famine, and judgments (1Ki 14:15-16; 17:1; 20:13-28; 2Ki 7:1-2, 17; 8:1; Isa 7:8; 8:4-7; 9:8-21; 17:3-11; 28:1-8; Hos 1:1-9; 2:1-13; 4-10; 11:5-6; 12:7-14; 13; Am 2:6-16; 3-9).

Of restoration (Hos 2:14-23; 11:9-11; 13:13-14; 14:8). Of the reunion of the ten tribes and Judah (Jer 3:18; Eze 37:16-22).

Judah:

The nation composed of the tribes of Judah and Benjamin, called Judah (Isa 11:12-13; Jer 4:3), and Jews ruled by the descendants of David. *See Jews.*

In the historical books of the Kings and the Chronicles the nation is called Judah, but in the prophecies it is frequently referred to as Israel (Isa 8:14; 49:7).

Rehoboam succeeds Solomon. In consequence of his arbitrary policy ten tribes rebel (1Ki 12). Other circumstances of his reign (1Ki 14:21-31; 2Ch 10-12). Death of Rehoboam (1Ki 14:31). Abijah's wicked reign (1Ki 15:1-8; 2Ch 13),

Asa's good reign (1Ki 15:9-24; 2Ch 14-16). Asa makes a league with Ben-Hadad, king of Syria , to make war against Israel (1Ki 15:16-24). Jehoshaphat succeeds Asa (1Ki 15:24; 2Ch 17:20; 21:1), joins Ahab against the king of Syria (1Ki 22). *See Jehoshaphat.* Jehoram, also called Joram, reigns in the place of his father, Jehoshaphat (2Ki 8:16-24; 2Ch 21). Edom revolts (2Ki 8:20-22). Ahaziah also called Azariah (2Ch 22:6) and Jehoahaz (2Ch 21:17; 25:23), succeeds Jehoram (2Ki 8:24-29; 2Ch 22); slain by Jehu (2Ki 9:27-29; 2Ch 22:8-9); Athaliah, his mother, succeeds him (2Ki 11:1-16; 2Ch 22:10-12; 23:1-15).

The Kings (and Queen) of Judah			
	Name	Ruled	Dates B.C.
1.	Rehoboam	17 years	930-913
2.	Abijah	3 years	913-910
3.	Asa	41 years	910-869
4.	Jehoshaphat	25 years	872-848
5.	Jehoram	8 years	848-841
6.	Ahaziah	1 year	841
7.	Queen Athaliah	6 years	841-835
8.	Joash	40 years	835-796
9.	Amaziah	29 years	796-767
10.	Uzziah / Azariah	52 years	792-740
11.	Jotham	16 years	750-735
12.	Ahaz	16 years	732-715
13.	Hezekiah	29 years	715-686
14.	Manasseh	55 years	697-642
15.	Amon	2 years	642-640
16.	Josiah	31 years	640-609
17.	Jehoahaz	3 months	609
18.	Jehoiakim	11 years	609-598
19.	Jehoiachin	3 months	598-597
20.	Zedekiah / Mattaniah	11 years	597-586

Note: Some kings, such as Uzziah and Jotham, had overlapping reigns.

See also the chart at Kings; each king by name.

Jehoash, also called Joash, succeeds Athaliah (2Ki 11:21; 12:1-21; 2Ch 24). The temple repaired (2Ki 12). Amaziah reigns, and Judah is invaded by the king of Israel; Jerusalem is taken and the sacred things of the temple carried away (2Ki 14:1-20; 2Ch 25). Azariah, also called Uzziah, succeeds him (2Ki 14:21-22; 15:1-7; 2Ch 26). Jotham succeeds Uzziah (2Ki 15:7, 32-38; 2Ch 27). Rezin, king of Syria, invades Judah (2Ki 15:37). Jotham is succeeded by Ahaz (2Ki 16:1; 2Ch 28). Judah is invaded by kings of Samaria and Syria; Ahaz hires the king of Assyria to make war on the king of Syria (2Ki 16:5-9). Ahaz changes the fashion of the altar in the temple (2Ki 16:10-18). Hezekiah succeeds Ahaz (2Ki 16:19-20; 2Ch 29-32). His good reign (2Ki 18:1-8). He revolts from the sovereignty of the king of Assyria (2Ki 18:7). King of Assyria invades Judah and blasphemes the God of Judah; his army overthrown (2Ki 18:9-37; 19). Hezekiah's sickness and miraculous restoration (2Ki 20). Succeeded by Manasseh (2Ki 20:21; 2Ch 33:1-20). Manasseh's wicked reign (2Ki 21:1-18). Amon succeeds Manasseh on the throne (2Ki 21:18-26; 2Ch 33:20-25).

Josiah succeeds Amon; the temple is repaired; the Book of the Law recovered; religious revival follows; and the king dies (2Ki 22; 23:1-30; 2Ch 34-35). Josiah is succeeded by Jehoahaz, who reigns three months, is dethroned by the king of Egypt, and the land put under tribute (2Ki 23:30-35; 2Ch 36:1-3). Jehoiakim is elevated to the throne; becomes tributary to Nebuchadnezzar for three years; rebels; is conquered and carried to Babylon (2Ki 24:1-6; 2Ch 36:4-8). Jehoiachin is made king, suffers invasion, and is carried to Babylon (2Ki 24:8-16; 2Ch 36:9-10). Zedekiah is made king by Nebuchadnezzar; rebels; Nebuchadnezzar invades Judah, takes Jerusalem, and carries the people to Babylon, despoiling the temple (2Ki 24:17-20; 25; 2Ch 36:11-21). The poorest of the people are left to occupy the country and are joined by fragments of the army of Judah, the dispersed Israelites in other lands, and the king's daughters (2Ki 25:12, 22-23; Jer 39:10; 40:7-12; 52:16). Gedaliah appointed governor over (2Ki 25:22). His administration favorable to the people (2Ki 25:23-24; Jer 40:7-12). Conspired against and slain by Ishmael (2Ki 25:25; Jer 40:13-16; 41:1-3). Ishmael seeks to betray the people to the Ammonites (Jer 41:1-18). The people take refuge in Egypt (2Ki 25:26; Jer 41:14-18; 42:13-18).

Captivity of Judah—

Great wickedness the cause of their adversity (Eze 5-7; 16; 23:22-44). Dwell in Babylon (Da 5:13; 6:13; Jer 52:28-30) by the Kebar River (Eze 1:1; 10:15). Patriotism of (Ps 137). Plotted against, by Haman (Est 3). Are saved by Esther (Est 4-9). Cyrus decrees their restoration (2Ch 36:22-23; Ezr 1:1-4). Cyrus directs the rebuilding of the temple and the restoration of the vessels that had been carried to Babylon (2Ch 36:23; Ezr 1:3-11). Proclamation renewed by Darius and Artaxerxes (Ezr 6:1-14). Ezra returns with 1, 754 of the captives to Jerusalem (Ezr 2). Temple rebuilt and dedicated (Ezr 3-6). Artaxerxes issues proclamation to restore the temple service (Ezr 7). Priests and Levites authorized to return (Ezr 8). Corruption among the returned captives; reform (Ezr 9-10).

Nehemiah leads 49, 942 captives back to the land (Ne 7; 7:5-67; Ps 85; 87; 107; 126). Wall of Jerusalem rebuilt and dedicated (Ne 2-6; 12). The law read and expounded (Ne 8). Solemn feast is kept, priests are purified; and the covenant sealed (Ne 8-10). One-tenth of the people, to be determined by lot, volunteer to dwell in Jerusalem, and the remaining nine parts dwell in other cities (Ne 11). Catalog of the priests and Levites who came up with Zerubbabel (Ne 12). Nehemiah reforms

various abuses (Ne 13). Expect a Messiah (Lk 3:15). Many accept Jesus as the Christ (Messiah) (Jn 2:23; 10:42; 11:45; 12:11; Ac 21:20). Reject Jesus. *See Jesus the Christ, Rejected.*

Rejected by God (Mt 21:43; Lk 20:16).

Prophecies Concerning Israel and Judah:

Of their rejection of the Messiah (Isa 8:14-15; 49:5, 7; 52:14; 53:1-3; Zec 11; 13; Mt 21:33; 22:1).

Of war and other judgments (Dt 28:49-57; 2Ki 20:17-18; 21:12-15; 22:16-17; 23:26-27; Isa 1:1-24; 3; 4:1; 5; 6:9-13; 7:17-25; 8:14-22; 9; 10:12; 22:1-14; 28:14-22; 29:1-10; 30:1-17; 31:1-3; 32:9-14; Jer 1:11-16; 4:5-31; 6; 7:8-34; 8; 9:9-26; 10:17-22; 11:9-23; 13:9-27; 14:14-18; 15:1-14; 16; 17:1-4; 18:15-17; 19; 20:5; 21:4-7; 22:24-30; 25:8-38; 28; 34; 37; 38:1-3; 42:13-22; 43-45; La 5:6; Eze 4-5; 11:7-12; 12; 15-17; 19; 22:13-22; 23:22-35; 24; 33:21-29; Da 9:26-27; Joel 2:1-17; Am 2:4-5; Mic 2:10; 3; 4:8-10; Hab 1:6-11; Zep 1; Zec 11; 14:1-3; Mal 4:1; Mt 21:33-34; 23:35-38; 24:2, 14-42; Mk 13:1-13; Lk 13:34-35; 19:43-44; 21:5-25; 23:28-31; Rev 1:7).

Dispersion of (Isa 24:1; Jer 9:16; Hos 9:17; Joel 3:6, 20; Am 9:9; Eze 4:13; 5:10, 12; 20:23; 36:19; Da 9:7; Jn 7:35; Ac 2:5).

Of blessing and restoration (Isa 1:25-27; 2:1-5; 4:2-6; 11:11-13; 25; 26:1-2, 12-19; 27:13; 29:18-24; 30:18-26; 32:15-20; 33:13-24; 35; 37:31-32; 40:2, 9; 41:27; 44; 49:13-23; 51; 52:1-12; 60; 61:4-9; 62; 66:5-22; Jer 3:14-18; 4:3-18; 12:14-16; 23:3; 24:1-7; 29:1-14; 30:3-22; 32:36-44; 33; 44:28; Eze 14:22-23; 16:60-63; 20:40-41; 36:1-38; 37:12, 21; Da 11:30-45; 12:1; Joel 3; Am 9:9-15; Ob 17-21; Mic 2:12-13; 5:3; Zep 2:7; Zec 1:14-21; 2:8; 10:5-12; 12:1-14; 13; 14:3-21; Mal 3:4; Ro 11; 2Co 3:16; Rev 7:15).

ISRAELITES *See Israel, Israelites.*

ISSACHAR [1201+3779, 3779, 2704] *(there is reward, Ge. 30:18; may [God] show mercy IDB; hired hand KB).*

1. Fifth son of Jacob (Ge 30:18; Ex 1:3; 1Ch 2:1). Jacob's prophetic benedictions upon (Ge 49:14-15). In the time of David (1Ch 7:1-5).

2. Tribe of. Descended from Jacob's son (Ge 30:17-18). Prophecies concerning (Ge 49:14-15; Dt 33:18-19).

Persons selected from to number the people (Nu 1:8), to spy out the land (Nu 13:7). To divide the land (Nu 34:26). Strength of, on leaving Egypt (Nu 1:28-29; 2:6). Encamped under the standard of Judah east of the tabernacle (Nu 2:5). Next to and under the standard of Judah in the journeys of Israel (Nu 10:14-15). Offering of, at the dedication (Nu 7:18-23). Families of (Nu 26:23-24). Strength of, on entering Canaan (Nu 26:25). On Gerizim said amen to the blessings (Dt 27:12). Bounds of their inheritance (Jos 19:17-23). Assisted Deborah against Sisera (Jdg 5:15). Officers of, appointed by David (1Ch 27:18), appointed by Solomon (1Ki 4:17). Some of, at David's coronation (1Ch 12:32). Number of warriors belonging to, in David's time (1Ch 7:2, 5). Many of, at Hezekiah's Passover (2Ch 30:18). Remarkable persons of (Jdg 10:1; 1Ki 15:27).

ISSHIAH [3807, 3808] (*Yahweh forgets*).
1. Man of Issachar (1Ch 7:3).
2. A disaffected Israelite who joined David at Ziklag; one of David's heroes (1Ch 12:6).
3. A Kohathite Levite (1Ch 23:20).
4. A Levite (1Ch 24:21).

ISSUE OF BLOOD *See Bleeding, Subject to; Hemorrhage.*

ISUAH *See Ishvah.*

ISUI *See Ishvi.*

ITALIAN REGIMENT [2713]. Cohort of Italian soldiers stationed in Caesarea when Peter preached to Cornelius (Ac 10:1).

ITALY [2712]. (Ac 27:1; Heb 13:24). Aquila and Priscilla expelled from (Ac 18:2).

ITCH [3063, 5999, *3117*]. A skin disease (Lev 13:30-37; 14:54; Dt 28:27). *See Disease; Scall.*

ITHAI [416, 915]. One of David's valiant men (2Sa 23:29; 1Ch 11:31).

ITHAMAR [418] (possibly *[is]land of palms* BDB; *[father] of Tamar* KB). Son of Aaron (Ex 6:23; 28:1; 1Ch 6:3). Entrusted with money of the tabernacle (Ex 38:21). Charged with duties of the tabernacle (Nu 4:28; 7:8). Forbidden to lament the death of his brothers, Nadab and Abihu (Lev 10:6-7). Descendants of (1Ch 24:1-19).

ITHIEL [417] (*God [El] is with me*).
1. A Benjamite (Ne 11:7).
2. An unidentified person (Pr 30:1).

ITHLAH [3849] (*hanging, lofty place*). A city of Dan (Jos 19:42).

ITHMAH [3850] (*fatherless* KB; *purity* ISBE). A Moabite (1Ch 11:46).

ITHNAN [3854]. A town in the extreme S of Judah (Jos 15:23).

ITHRA (*abundance* BDB; *what remained* KB). Hebrew Ithra is a variant of Jether (2Sa 17:25, ftn). Father of Amasa (2Sa 17:25; 1Ch 2:17). *See Jether, 3.*

ITHRAN [3864] (*what is over, profit* KB; *excellent* ISBE).
1. Son of Dishon (Ge 36:26; 1Ch 1:41).
2. Son of Zophah (1Ch 7:37).

ITHREAM [3865] (*remainder of the people*). Son of David (2Sa 3:5; 1Ch 3:3).

ITHRITE(S) [3863] (*excellence,* or

preeminence ISBE; *remainder* KB). Family of two of David's heroes (2Sa 23:38; 1Ch 11:40).

ITINERARY Of the Israelites (Nu 33; Dt 10:6-7). *See Israel, Israelites.*

ITTAH-KAZIN *See Eth Kazin.*

ITTAI [915] (possibly *with me* BDB).
1. Gittite who became a loyal follower of David (2Sa 15:18-22; 18:2, 5).
2. *See Ithai.*

ITUREA [2714] (*pertaining to Jetur*). Region NE of Israel; its people descended from Jetur, son of Ishmael, and from whom the name Iturea is derived (Ge 25:15), ruled by Philip (Lk 3:1).

IVAH *See Ivvah.*

IVORY [9094, 9105, *1804*]. (SS 5:1, 4; 7:4; Eze 27:15). Exported from, Tarshish (1Ki 10:22; 2Ch 9:21), the coasts of Cyprus, the Hebrew is Kittim (Eze 27:6).

Ahab's palace made of (1Ki 22:39). Other houses made of (Ps 45:8; Am 3:15). Other articles made of: Stringed instruments (Ps 45:8), thrones (1Ki 10:18; 2Ch 9:17), benches (Eze 27:6), beds (Am 6:4), vessels (Rev 18:12).

IVVAH [6394]. District in Babylon conquered by the Assyrians (2Ki 18:34; 19:13; Isa 37:13).

IYE ABARIM [6516] (*heaps of Abarim [regions beyond]*). One of the places where Israel camped in the desert (Nu 21:11; 33:44). Also called Iyim (Nu 33:45, ftn).

IYIM [6517]. (Nu 33:45). *See Iye Abarim.*

IYYAR *See Month, 2; Ziv.*

IZHAR, IZHARITES [3659, 3660] (*the shining one*). Son of Kohath (Ex 6:18, 21; 1Ch 6:2, 18, 38; 23:12, 18) and his descendants (Nu 3:27; 1Ch 24:22; 26:23, 29).

IZLIAH [3468] (*long living, eternal* IDB; *Yahweh delivers* ISBE). A Benjamite son of Elpaal (1Ch 8:18).

IZRAHIAH [3474] (*Yahweh, he shines*). Grandson of Tola (1Ch 7:3).

IZRAHITE [3473] (*shining*). Family name of Shamhuth (1Ch 27:8).

IZRI [3673] (*Yahweh designs*). Perhaps the same as Zeri. Leader of the fourth division of Levitical singers (1Ch 25:11).

IZZIAH [3466] (*may Yahweh sprinkle [in atonement]* BDB; *Yahweh unites* ISBE). An Israelite of the Parosh family who marries an idolatrous wife (Ezr 10:25).

J

JAAKAN, JAAKANITES [1201+ 3622]. Son of Ezer (Ge 36:20-21, 27; Dt 10:6; 1Ch 1:42). A Horite (1Ch 1:42), and the same as Akan (Ge 36:27). *See Akan; Bene Jaakan.*

JAAKOBAH [3621] (*may [deity] protect* IDB). Descendant of Simeon (1Ch 4:36).

JAALA [3606, 3608]. One of the servants of Solomon returned from exile (Ezr 2:56; Ne 7:58).

JAALAM *See Jalam.*

JAAN *See Dan Jaan.*

JAANAI *See Janai.*

JAAR [3625]. An alternate name for Kiriath Jearim (Ps 132:6, ftn). *See Kiriath Jearim.*

JAARE-OREGIM [3629]. Father of El-hanan, who slew the giant brother of Goliath (2Sa 21:19). Spelled Jair (1Ch 20:5).

JAARESHIAH [3631] (*Yahweh plants*). Son of Jeroham (1Ch 8:27).

JAASAU *See Jaasu.*

JAASIEL [3634] (*God [El] does*). One of David's warriors (1Ch 11:47). Son of Abner (1Ch 27:21).

JAASU [3632]. Of the family of Bani (Ezr 10:37).

JAAZANIAH [3279, 3280, 3471] (*Yahweh listens*).
1. Also called Jezaniah (Jer 40:8, ftn). A Maacathite captain who joined Gedaliah at Mizpah (2Ki 25:23; Jer 42:1).
2. A Recabite (Jer 35:3).
3. An idolatrous zealot (Eze 8:11).
4. A wicked prince of Judah (Eze 11:1-13).

JAAZER *See Jazer.*

JAAZIAH [3596] (*may Yahweh nourish* IDB). A descendant of Merari (1Ch 24:26-27).

JAAZIEL [3595] (*God [El] strengthens* ISBE). A Levite musician (1Ch 15:18).

JABAL [3299]. Son of Lamech. A shepherd (Ge 4:20).

JABBOK [3309] (*flowing*). A stream on the E of the Jordan, the northern boundary of the possessions of the Ammonites (Nu 21:24; Jdg 11:13), of the Reubenites and the Gadites (Jos 12:2; Dt 3:16). The northern boundary of the Amorites (Jdg 11:22).

JABESH [3314, 3315] (*dry*).
1. Father of King Shallum (2Ki 15:8-13).
2. Short term for Jabesh-Gilead (1Ch 10:12).

JABESH GILEAD [3316] (*dry Gilead*). A city E of the Jordan (Jdg 21:8-15). Besieged by the Ammonites (1Sa 11:1-11). Saul and his sons buried at (1Sa 31:11-13; 2Sa 2:4; 1Ch 10:11-12). Bones of Saul and his son removed from, by David, and buried at Zela (2Sa 21:12-14).

JABEZ [3583, 3584] (*to grieve*).
1. A city of Judah (1Ch 2:55).
2. The head of a family (1Ch 4:9-10).

JABIN [3296] (*perceptive*).
1. King of Hazor, defeated and slain by Joshua (Jos 11).
2. Another king of Hazor, defeated by Barak (Jdg 4; 1Sa 12:9; Ps 83:9).

JABNEEL [3305] (*God [El] will build*).
1. A town in N border of Judah, just S of Joppa (Jos 15:11), modern Yebna. Called Jabneh (2Ch 26:6). Later called Jamnia.
2. Frontier town of Naphtali (Jos 19:33), modern Tell en-Naam.

JABNEH [3306]. A Philistine city (2Ch 26:6). *See Jabneel, 1.*

JACAN [3602]. A Gadite (1Ch 5:13).

JACHIN, JACHINITES *See Jakin.*

JACINTH [4385, 5611] (*hyacinth*). A precious stone in the high priest's breastpiece (Ex 28:19; 39:12), in the foundation of New Jerusalem (Rev 21:20). *See Minerals of the Bible, 1; Stones.*

JACKAL [280, 8785, 9478, 9490]. A carnivorous scavenger, inhabiting the desert. Often translated "dragon" in the KJV (Job 30:29; Ps 44:19; Isa 13:21, 22; Jer 9:11; Mal 1:3).

JACKAL WELL Named only in Ne 2:13; possibly En Rogel or the Pool or Siloam. *See En Rogel; Siloam, Pool of.*

JACOB [3620, 2609] (*follower, replacer, one who follows the heel*). Son of Isaac and twin brother of Esau (Ge 25:24-26; Jos 24:4; 1Ch 1:34; Ac 7:8). Ancestor of Jesus (Mt 1:2). Given in answer to prayer (Ge 25:21). Obtains Esau's birthright for a bowl of stew (Ge 25:29-34; Heb 12:16). Fraudulently obtains his father's blessing (Ge 27:1-29; Heb 11:20). Esau seeks to kill, escapes to Paddan Aram (Ge 27:41-46; 28:1-5; Hos 12:12). His vision of the stairway (Ge 28:10-22). God confirms the covenant of Abraham to (Ge 28:13-22; 35:9-15; 1Ch 16:13-18).

Lives in Haran with his uncle, Laban (Ge 29; 30; Hos 12:12). Serves fourteen years for Leah and Rachel (Ge 29:15-30; Hos 12:12). Sharp practice of, with the flocks and herds of Laban (Ge 30:32-43). Dissatisfied with Laban's treatment and returns to the land of Canaan (Ge 31). Meets angels of God on the journey and calls the place Mahanaim (Ge 32:1-2). Dreads to meet Esau; sends him presents; wrestles with an angel (Ge 32). Name of, changed to Israel (Ge 32:28; 35:10). *See Israel*. Reconciliation of, with Esau (Ge 33:4). Journeys to Succoth (Ge 33:17), to Shechem where he purchases a parcel of ground from Hamor, and erects an altar (Ge 33:18-20). His daughter, Dinah, raped and avenged (Ge 34).

Returns to Bethel, where he builds an altar and dedicates a pillar (Ge 35:1-7). Deborah, Rebekah's nurse, dies, and is buried at Bethel (Ge 35:8). Journeys to Ephrath; Benjamin is born to; Rachel dies, and is "buried on the way to Ephrath (that is, Bethlehem)" (Ge 35:16-19; 48:7). Erects a monument at Rachel's grave (Ge 35:20). The incest of his son, Reuben, and his concubine, Bilhah (Ge 35:22). List of the names of his twelve sons (Ge 35:23-26). Returns to Kiriath Arba, the city of his father (Ge 35:27). Lives in the land of Canaan (Ge 37:1).

His partiality for his son, Joseph, and the consequent jealousy of his other sons (Ge 37:3-4). Joseph's prophetic dream concerning (Ge 37:9-11). His grief over the loss of Joseph (Ge 37:34-35). Sends into Egypt to buy grain (Ge 42:1-2; 43:1-14). His grief over the detention of Simeon and the demand for Benjamin to be taken into Egypt (Ge 42:36). His love for Benjamin (Ge 43:14; 44:29). Hears that Joseph still lives (Ge 45:26-28).

Moves to Egypt (Ge 46:1-7; 1Sa 12:8; Ps 105:23; Ac 7:14-15). List of his children and grandchildren who went down into Egypt (Ge 46:8-27). Meets Joseph (Ge 46:28-34). Pharaoh receives him and is blessed by Jacob (Ge 47:1-10). The land of Goshen assigned to (Ge 47:11-12, 27). Lives in Egypt seventeen years (Ge 47:28). Exacts promise from Joseph to bury him with his fathers (Ge 47:29-31). His benediction upon Joseph and his two sons (Ge 48:15-22). Gives the land of the two Amorites to Joseph (Ge 48:22; Jn 4:5).

His final prophetic benedictions upon his sons: Reuben (Ge 49:3-4), Simeon and Levi (Ge 49:5-7), Judah (Ge 49:8-12), Zebulun (Ge 49:13), Issachar (Ge 49:14-15), Dan (Ge 49:16-18), Gad (Ge 49:19), Asher (Ge 49:20), Naphtali (Ge 49:21), Joseph (Ge 49:22-26), Benjamin (Ge 49:27). Charges his sons to bury him in the field of Machpelah (Ge 49:29-30). Death of (Ge 49:33). Body of, embalmed (Ge 50:2). Forty days mourning for (Ge 50:3). Burial of (Ge 50:4-13). Descendants of (Ge 29:31-35; 30:1-24; 35:18, 22-26; 46:8-27; Ex 1:1-5; 1Ch 2-9).

Prophecies concerning himself and descendants (Ge 25:23; 27:28-29; 28:10-15; Ge 31:3; 35:9-13; 46:3; Dt 1:8; Ps 105:10-11). His wealth (Ge 36:6-7). Well of (Jn 4:5-30).

JACOB'S WELL Well near base of Mt. Gerizim where Jesus talked with a Samaritan woman (Jn 4).

JADA [3360] (*shrewd one* BDB; *[God] has cared* IDB). A Judahite, son of Onam (1Ch 2:26, 28).

JADAH [3586] (*honeycomb*). Most Hebrew manuscripts have Jarah. Descendant of Gibeon (1Ch 9:42, ftn), Jehoaddah (1Ch 8:36).

JADAU *See Jaddai*.

JADDAI [3350]. An Israelite who married a foreign woman during the Captivity (Ezr 10:43).

JADDUA [3348] (*one known*).
1. Prince who sealed covenant (Ne 10:21).
2. Son of Jonathan; priest who returned from Babylon (Ne 12:11).

JADON [3347] (*frail one* or *Yahweh rules* IDB). One who helped in rebuilding of Jerusalem wall (Ne 3:7).

JAEL [3605] (*mountain goat*). Wife of Heber and killer of Sisera (Jdg 4:17-22; 5:6, 24).

JAGUR [3327]. A town of Judah (Jos 15:21).

JAHATH [3511] (*snatch up*).
1. Grandson of Judah (1Ch 4:1-2).
2. Great-grandson of Levi (1Ch 6:16-20).
3. Levite (1Ch 23:10-11).
4. Levite (1Ch 24:22).
5. Merarite Levite (2Ch 34:8-12). *See Merari*.

JAHAZ [3403] (perhaps *a trodden* or *open place*). Also called Jahzah. A Levitical city in Reuben, taken from the Moabites (Jos 13:18; 21:36; Isa 15:4; Jer 48:21). Sihon defeated at (Nu 21:23; Dt 2:32; Jdg 11:20).

JAHAZIAH *See Jahzeiah*.

JAHAZIEL [3487] (*God [El] will see*).
1. A disaffected Israelite who joined David at Ziklag (1Ch 12:4).
2. A priest (1Ch 16:6).
3. Son of Hebron (1Ch 23:19; 24:23).
4. A Levite, and prophet (2Ch 20:14).
5. A chief, or the father of a chief, among the exiles, who returned from Babylon (Ezr 8:5).

JAHDAI [3367] (*Yahweh lead*). A descendant of Caleb (1Ch 2:47).

JAHDIEL [3484] (*God [El] gives joy*). Head of a family of Manasseh (1Ch 5:24).

JAHDO [3482] (*[God] gives joy*). Son of Buz (1Ch 5:14).

JAHLEEL, JAHLEELITE [3499, 3500] (*wait for God [El]* BDB; possibly *may God*

[El] show himself friendly IDB). Son of Zebulun (Ge 46:14; Nu 26:26).

JAHMAI [3503] (*protect*). Son of Tola (1Ch 7:2).

JAHZAH [3404]. A city of Reuben (1Ch 6:78). *See Jahaz.*

JAHZEEL, JAHZEELITE [3505] (*God [El] apportions*). A son of Naphtali and his clan (Nu 26:48). Also spelled Jahziel (Ge 46:24; 1Ch 7:13).

JAHZEIAH [3488] (*Yahweh sees*). Israelite who opposed Ezra in the matter of divorcing wives (Ezr 10:15).

JAHZERAH [3492] (possibly *prudent*). A priest (1Ch 9:12).

JAHZIEL [3505, 3507]. *See Jahzeel.*

JAILER [991, 1302]. Of Philippi, converted (Ac 16:27-34).

JAIR, JAIRITE [3281, 3285, 3600] (*he gives light*).
1. Son of Manasseh. Founder of twenty-three cities in Gilead (Nu 32:41; Dt 3:14; Jos 13:30; 1Ki 4:13; 1Ch 2:22-23).
2. A judge of Israel (Jdg 10:3-5).
3. A Benjamite (Est 2:5).
4. Father of Elhanan (1Ch 20:5).

JAIRUS [2608] (*he gives light*). A ruler of the synagogue in Capernaum (Mt 9:18). Daughter of, restored to life (Mt 9:18, 23-26; Mk 5:22-43; Lk 8:41-56).

JAKAN *See Akan; Jaakan, Jaakanites.*

JAKEH [3681] (*prudent*). Father of Agur, a writer of proverbs (Pr 30:1).

JAKIM [3691] (*he will establish*).
1. A Benjamite (1Ch 8:19).
2. Head of a priestly division in the tabernacle service (1Ch 24:12).

JAKIN, JAKINITE [3520, 3521, 3522] (*he establishes*).
1. Son of Simeon (Ge 46:10; Ex 6:15; Nu 26:12). Called Jarib (1Ch 4:24).
2. One of Solomon's bronze pillars erected at the temple. It stood on the right (south) side of the porch (1Ki 7:21; 2Ch 3:17). *See Boaz, 2.*
3. A priest who returned from exile to Jerusalem (1Ch 9:10; Ne 11:10).
4. A priest, head of one of the courses (1Ch 24:17).

JALAM [3609]. Son of Esau (Ge 36:5, 14, 18; 1Ch 1:35).

JALON [3534]. Son of Ezra (1Ch 4:17).

JAMBRES [2612]. An Egyptian magician (Ex 7:11; 2Ti 3:8).

JAMES [2610] (*follower, replacer, one who follows the heel*; same as Jacob).
1. An apostle. Son of Zebedee and Salome (Mt 4:21; 27:56). *See Salome.* Brother of John, and a fisherman (Lk 5:10). Called to be an apostle (Mt 4:21-22; 10:2; Mk 1:19-20; Lk 6:14; Ac 1:13). Surnamed Boanerges by Jesus (Mk 3:17).
A close companion of Jesus, and present at the large catch of fish (Lk 5:10), the healing of Peter's mother-in-law (Mk 1:29), the raising of Jairus' daughter (Mk 5:37; Lk 8:51), the transfiguration of Jesus (Mt 17:1; Mk 9:2; Lk 9:28), in Gethsemane (Mt 26:37; Mk 14:33), at the sea of Tiberias when Jesus revealed himself to the disciples after his resurrection (Jn 21:2; 1Co 15:7). Asks Jesus concerning his second coming (Mk 13:3). Bigotry of (Lk 9:54). Civil ambitions of (Mt 20:20-23; Mk 10:35-41). Martyred (Ac 12:2).
2. The younger, an apostle. Son of Alphaeus (Mt 10:3; Mk 3:18; 15:45; Lk 6:15).
3. Brother of Jesus (Mt 13:55; Mk 6:3; Gal 1:19; 2:9, 12). The brother of Judas (Jude) and Joseph (Mt 13:55; Mk 6:3; Jude 1). A witness of Christ's resurrection (1Co 15:7). Addresses the council at Jerusalem in favor of liberty for the Gentile converts (Ac 15:13-21). Disciples sent by, to Antioch (Gal 2:12). Hears of the success attending Paul's ministry (Ac 21:18-19). Epistle of (Jas 1:1).
4. Father of apostle Judas (not Iscariot) (Lk 6:16; Ac 1:13).

JAMES, EPISTLE OF

Author: James, brother of Jesus. *See James, 3.*

Date: In the early 60s, possibly before A.D. 50

Outline:
I. Greetings (1:1).
II. Trials and Temptations (1:2-18).
  A. The Testing of Faith (1:2-12).
  B. The Source of Temptation (1:13-18).
III. Listening and Doing (1:19-27).
IV. Favoritism Forbidden (2:1-13).
V. Faith and Deeds (2:14-26).
VI. Taming the Tongue (3:1-12).
VII. Two Kinds of Wisdom (3:13-18).
VIII. Warning Against Worldliness (ch. 4).
  A. Quarrelsomeness (4:1-3).
  B. Spiritual Unfaithfulness (4:4).
  C. Pride (4:5-10).
  D. Slander (4:11-12).
  E. Boasting (4:13-17).
IX. Warning to Rich Oppressors (5:1-6).
X. Miscellaneous Exhortations (5:7-20).
  A. Concerning Patience in Suffering (5:7-11).
  B. Concerning Oaths (5:12).
  C. Concerning the Prayer of Faith (5:13-18).
  D. Concerning Those Who Wander from the Truth (5:19-20).
See General Letters.

JAMES THE YOUNGER, THE LESS *See James, 2.*

JAMIN, JAMINITE [3546, 3547] (possibly *right hand* BDB; *south, an indication of [good] fortune* KB).
1. Son of Simeon (Ge 46:10; Ex 6:15; Nu 26:12; 1Ch 4:24).
2. Descendants of Hezron (1Ch 2:27).
3. A priest who expounded the law to the exiles who returned to Jerusalem (Ne 8:7).

JAMLECH [3552] (*he will reign*). Descendant of Simeon (1Ch 4:34).

JANAI [3614] (*he will answer*). A Gadite chief (1Ch 5:12).

JANIM [3565]. A city of Judah (Jos 15:53).

JANNAI [*2613*] (*he will answer?*). Ancestor of Joseph (Lk 3:24).

JANNES [*2614*]. An Egyptian magician (Ex 7:11; 2Ti 3:8).

JANOAH [3562] (*resting place*).
1. Town of Naphtali (2Ki 15:29).
2. Town on boundary of Ephraim (Jos 16:6-7).

JANUM *See Janim.*

JAPHETH [3651] (*enlarge*). Son of Noah (Ge 5:32; 6:10; 7:13; 10:21); had seven sons (Ge 10:2); descendants were maritime peoples (Ge 10:5); blessed by Noah (Ge 9:20-27).

JAPHIA [3643, 3644] (perhaps *may the deity shine*).
1. King of Lachish killed by Joshua (Jos 10:3).
2. Son David (2Sa 5:15; 1Ch 3:7).
3. City in E border of Zebulun (Jos 19:12).

JAPHLET [3646] (*he delivers* IDB; possibly *he escapes* ISBE). Grandson of Beriah (1Ch 7:33).

JAPHLETITES [3647] (*of Japhlet*). Clan on W border of Ephraim (Jos 16:1-3).

JAPHO *See Joppa.*

JAR(S) [1318, 3902, 3998, 5532, 5574, *223*, *3040*, *5007*, *5620*]. For holding water (Ge 24:14-26; Ru 2:9; Jn 2:6-7), flour (1Ki 17:10-16). Containing manna, kept in the ark (Ex 16:33; Heb 9:4). Figurative of fragile human body in which believers minister the New Covenant (2Co 4:7).

JARAH (*honeycomb*). *See Jadah.*

JAREB NIV "great king" of Assyria (Hos 5:13; 10:6).

JARED [3719, *2616*] (*servant* KB).
1. A descendant of Seth (Ge 5:15-16, 18-20; 1Ch 1:2).
2. An ancestor of Jesus (Lk 3:37).
3. Son of Mahalalel (1Ch 1:2).

JARESIAH *See Jaareshiah.*

JARHA [3739]. Egyptian slave of Sheshan (1Ch 2:34-35).

JARIB [3743] (*Yahweh contends*).
1. Son of Simeon (1Ch 4:24).
2. A chief among the Captivity (Ezr 8:16).
3. A priest who married an idolatrous wife (Ezr 10:18).

JARKON *See Me Jarkon.*

JARMUTH [3754] (*height*).
1. City of Judah sixteen miles W by S of Jerusalem (Jos 15:35), modern Tell Yarmuk.
2. Levite city of Issachar (Jos 21:28-29). Ramoth (1Ch 6:73), Remeth (Jos 19:21).

JAROAH [3726] (*soft, delicate*). A descendant of Gad (1Ch 5:14).

JASHAR, BOOK OF [3839] (*upright, straight*). Author of book quoted (Jos 10:13; 2Sa 1:18), in LXX version (1Ki 8:53).

JASHEN [3826] (possibly *asleep*). Father of some of David's heroes (2Sa 23:32), Hashem (1Ch 11:34).

JASHER, BOOK OF *See Jashar, Book of.*

JASHOBEAM [3790] (*the people return*).
1. Hero who joined David at Ziklag (1Ch 12:6).
2. One of David's leaders (1Ch 11:11), Adino the Eznite in Hebrew and Septuagint (2Sa 23:8, ftn).
3. Hacmoni (1Ch 27:2-3). *See above, 2.* May be the same.

JASHUB, JASHUBITE [3793, 3795] (*he returns*).
1. Son of Issachar (Ge 46:13; Nu 26:24).
2. Shear-Jashub, a son of Isaiah (Isa 7:3).
3. Man who married foreign wife (Ezr 10:29).

JASHUBI LEHEM [3788] (*[they] returned to Lehem*). A descendant of Shelah (1Ch 4:22).

JASIEL *See Jaasiel.*

JASON [*2619*] (*to heal*). A Christian at Thessalonica (Ac 17:5-7, 9) and possibly Paul's relative (Ro 16:21).

JASPER [1486, 3835, *2618*]. A precious stone set in the high priest's breastplate (Ex 28:20; 39:13; Job 28:18; Eze 28:13; Rev 4:3; 21:11, 18-19). *See Minerals of the Bible, 1; Stones.*

JATHNIEL [3853] (*God [El] hires* BDB; *God [El] is forever* KB). Son of Meshelemiah (1Ch 26:2).

JATTIR [3848] (possibly *preeminence* IDB). A Levitical city (Jos 15:48; 21:14; 1Sa 30:27; 1Ch 6:57).

JAVAN [3430].

1. A son of Japheth. Father of Elishah, Tarshish, Kittim, and Rodanim (Ge 10:4; 1Ch 1:7). Javan is same as Greek Ionia, with whom the Hebrews traded (Isa 66:19; Joel 3:4-6).

2. A city in Arabia in which the Phoenicians traded (Eze 27:13, 19).

JAVELIN [3959, 6038, 8657, 9233]. A heavy lance (Eze 39:9), used by Goliath (1Sa 17:6), by Saul (1Sa 18:11; 19:9-10).

JAZER [3597] (*he helps*).

1. Taken from the Amorites (Nu 21:32; 32:1, 3, 35). Ammonite stronghold E of the Jordan, probably c. fourteen miles N of Heshbon; assigned to Gad (Jos 13:24-25), later given to Levites; a city of refuge E of the Jordan (Jos 21:39).

2. Sea of (Jer 48:32).

JAZIZ [3467]. Overseer of David's flocks (1Ch 27:31).

JEALOUSY [6523, 7861, 7862, 7863+, 7868, *2419, 2420, 4143*].] (Pr 6:34; 27:4; Ecc 4:4; SS 8:6). Law concerning, when husband is jealous of his wife (Nu 5:12-31). Image of (Eze 8:3-4). Forbidden (Ro 13:13).

Attributed to God (Ex 20:5; 34:13-14; Nu 25:11; Dt 29:20; 32:16, 21; 1Ki 14:22; Ps 78:58; 79:5; Isa 30:1-2; 31:1, 3; Eze 16:42; 23:25; 36:5-6; 38:19; Zep 1:18; 3:8; Zec 1:14; 8:2; 1Co 10:22).

See Anthropomorphisms.

A desire to emulate (Ro 10:19; 11:11).

See Emulation; Envy.

Figurative: (2Co 11:2).

Instances of:

Cain, of Abel (Ge 4:5-6, 8). Sarah, of Hagar (Ge 16:5). Joseph's brothers, of Joseph (Ge 37:4-11, 18-28). Saul, of David (1Sa 18:8-30; 19:8-24; 20:24-34). Joab, of Abner (2Sa 3:24-27). Nathan, of Adonijah (1Ki 1:24-26). Ephraimites, of Gideon (Jdg 8:1), of Jephthah (Jdg 12:1). The brother of the prodigal son (Lk 15:25-32). Sectional, between Israel and the tribe of Judah (2Sa 19:41-43).

JEALOUSY, WATER OF *See Water of Bitterness.*

JEARIM [3630] (*timberlands*). Hill on N border of Judah (Jos 15:10).

JEATHERAI [3290]. Descendant of Gershom (1Ch 6:21).

JEBERECHIAH [3310] (*Yahweh blesses*). Father of Zechariah (Isa 8:2).

JEBUS [3293]. Name of Jerusalem when in possession of Jebusites (Jos 15:63; Jdg 19:10),

taken by Israelites (Jdg 1:8), but stronghold not captured until David's time (2Sa 5:7-8).

JEBUSITE(S) [3294] (*of Jebus*). One of the tribes of Canaan (Dt 7:1). Land of, given to Abraham and his descendants (Ge 15:21; Ex 3:8, 17; 23:23-24; Dt 20:17; Ex 33:2; 34:10-11). Conquered by Joshua (Jos 10-12; 24:11), by David (2Sa 5:6-9). Jerusalem within the territory of (Jos 18:28). Not exterminated, but intermarry with the Israelites (Jdg 3:5-6; Ezr 9:1-2; 10:18-44). Pay tribute to Solomon (1Ki 9:20-21).

JECAMIAH *See Jekamiah.*

JECOLIAH [3524, 3525] (*Yahweh is able*). Mother of King Uzziah (2Ch 26:3; 2Ki 15:2).

JECONIAH [2651]. Variant of Jehoiachin (Jer 22:24, 28; 37:1). *See Jehoiachin.* King of Judah, captured by Nebuchadnezzar (2Ki 24:1-12).

JEDAIAH [3355, 3361] (*Yahweh has favored* IDB, or *Yahweh knows*).

1. Descendant of Simeon (1Ch 4:37).

2. A returned exile (Ne 3:10).

3. A priest of the Captivity (1Ch 9:10; 24:7; Ezr 2:36; Ne 7:39).

4. A priest who lived at Jerusalem after the return of the Captivity (Ne 11:10; 12:6, 19; Zec 6:10, 14).

5. Another priest, who returned from Babylon with Nehemiah (Ne 12:7, 21).

JEDIAEL [3356] (*known of God [El]*).

1. Son of Benjamin (1Ch 7:6, 10-11).

2. Son of Shimri (1Ch 11:45).

3. A Manassite chief who joined David at Ziklag (1Ch 12:20).

4. Son of Meshelemiah (1Ch 26:2).

JEDIDAH [3352] (*beloved* BDB; *lovely, beloved* KB). Mother of King Josiah (2Ki 22:1).

JEDIDIAH [3354] (*beloved of Yahweh*). Name that Nathan gave to Solomon (2Sa 12:24-25).

JEDUTHUN [3349, 3357]. A musician of the temple (1Ch 16:41; 25:1). Called Ethan (1Ch 6:44; 15:17). *See titles of Psalms 39, 62, 77.*

JEEZER, JEEZERITES *See Abiezer, 1; Iezer.*

JEGAR SAHADUTHA [3337] (*witness heap*). Name given by Laban to heap of stones set up as memorial of covenant between him and Jacob; called Galeed by Jacob (Ge 31:47-48).

JEHALLELEL [3401] (*he shall praise God [El]* BDB; *God [El] shines forth* IDB).

1. Descendant of Judah (1Ch 4:16).

2. Merarite Levite (2Ch 29:12).

JEHATH [3511]. Son of Gershon (1Ch. 6:20).

JEHDEIAH [3485] (*Yahweh rejoices [in his works]*).
1. Descendant of Moses (1Ch 24:20).
2. Man in charge of David's donkeys (1Ch 27:30).

JEHEZKEL [3489] (*God [El] gives strength*). Priest in David's time (1Ch 24:16).

JEHIAH [3496] (*Yahweh lives*). A Levite, and doorkeeper of the ark (1Ch 15:24).

JEHIEL [3493] (*God [El] lives*).
1. A Levite gatekeeper (1Ch 15:18). Probably identical with Jehiah. *See Jehiah.*
2. A Gershonite Levite (1Ch 23:8; 29:8).
3. A companion of David's sons (1Ch 27:32).
4. Son of Jehoshaphat (2Ch 21:2).
5. Son of Heman (2Ch 29:14).
6. A Levite overseer in the temple (2Ch 31:13).
7. A priest who gave extraordinary offerings for the Passover (2Ch 35:8).
8. Father of Obadiah (Ezr 8:9).
9. Father of Shecaniah (Ezr 10:2).
10. Name of two priests who married idolatrous wives (Ezr 10:21, 26).

JEHIELI [3494] (*of Jehiel*). Son of Ladan (1Ch 26:21-22).

JEHIZKIAH [3491] (*Yahweh gives strength*). Israelite chief in days of Ahaz, king of Judah (2Ch 28:12).

JEHOADDAH [3389]. Descendant of King Saul (1Ch 8:36), Jadah (1Ch 9:42).

JEHOADDIN [3390, 3391] (probably *Yahweh is delight*). Wife of King Joash of Judah (2Ch 25:1), Jehoaddin (2Ki 14:2).

JEHOAHAZ [3370, 3407] (*Yahweh holds*).
1. Son of Jehu and king of Israel (2Ki 10:35; 13:1-9).
2. Son of Jehoram, king of Judah (2Ch 21:17). *See Ahaziah.*
3. Also called Shallum. King of Judah and successor of Josiah (2Ki 23:30-31; 1Ch 3:15; 2Ch 36:1; Jer 22:11). Wicked reign of (2Ki 23:32). Pharaoh Neco, king of Egypt, invades the kingdom of Judah, defeats him, and takes him captive to Egypt (2Ki 23:33-35; 2Ch 36:3-4). Prophecies concerning (Jer 22:10-12).

JEHOASH, JOASH [3371, 3409] (*Yahweh bestows* ISBE; *man of Yahweh* KB).
1. Grandson of Benjamin (1Ch 7:8).
2. Descendant of Judah (4:22).
3. Father of Gideon (Jdg 6:12).
4. Keeper of David's supply of oil (1Ch 27:28).
5. Israelite who joined David at Ziklag (1Ch 12:3).
6. Son of King Ahab (1Ki 22:26).
7. King of Judah (2Ki 11-13; 2Ch 24-25).

8. King of Israel (2Ki 13:10-13; 14:8-16; 2Ch 25:17-24).

JEHOHANAN [3380] (*Yahweh has been gracious*).
1. A gatekeeper of the tabernacle (1Ch 26:3).
2. A military chief under Jehoshaphat, whose corps consisted of 280,000 men (2Ch 17:15). Probably identical with a captain of a hundred (2Ch 23:1).
3. Son of Bebai (Ezr 10:28).
4. A priest among the exiles who returned from Babylon (Ne 12:13).
5. A choir member in the temple (Ne 12:42).

JEHOIACHIN [3382, 3422, 3526, 3527, 4037] (*Yahweh supports*). (Jer 22:24; 37:1). King of Judah and successor to Jehoiakim (2Ki 24:6-8; 1Ch 3:16; 2Ch 36:8-9; Jer 24:1). Wicked reign of (2Ki 24:9; 2Ch 36:9). Nebuchadnezzar invades his kingdom, takes him captive to Babylon (2Ki 24:10-16; 2Ch 36:10; Est 2:6; Jer 27:20; 29:1-2; Eze 1:2). Confined in prison thirty-seven years (2Ki 25:27). Released from prison by Evil-Merodach and promoted above other kings, and honored until death (2Ki 25:27-30; Jer 52:31-34). Prophecies concerning (Jer 22:24-30; 28:4). Sons of (1Ch 3:17-18). Ancestor of Jesus, called Jeconiah (Mt 1:11, 12).

JEHOIADA [3381] (*Yahweh has known*).
1. Father of Benaiah, one of David's officers (2Sa 8:18).
2. A high priest. Overthrows Athaliah, the usurping queen of Judah, and establishes Jehoash upon the throne (2Ki 11; 2Ch 23). Salutary influence of, over Joash (Hebrew *Jehoash*, a variant of *Joash*) (2Ki 12:2, ftn; 2Ch 24:2, 22). Directs the repairs of the temple (2Ki 12:4-16; 2Ch 24:4-14). Death of (2Ch 24:15-16).
3. A priest who led 3, 700 priests armed for war (1Ch 12:27).
4. Son of Benaiah (1Ch 27:34).
5. A returned exile (Ne 3:6).
6. A priest mentioned in Jeremiah's letter to the captive Israelites (Jer 29:26).

JEHOIAKIM [3383] (*Yahweh lifts up, establishes*). Also called Eliakim. King of Judah (1Ch 3:15). Wicked reign and final overthrow of (2Ki 23:24-37; 24:1-6; 2Ch 36:4-8; Jer 22:13-19; 26:22-23; 36; Da 1:1-2). Dies and is succeeded by his son, Jehoiachin (2Ki 24:6).

JEHOIARIB [3384] (*Yahweh argues [for me]*).
1. Priest in days of David (1Ch 24:7).
2. Priest who returned from exile (1Ch 9:10). *See Joiarib.*

JEHONADAB [3386]. *See Jonadab, 2.*

JEHONATHAN [3387] (*Yahweh has given*).
1. Overseer of David's property (1Ch 27:25).

2. Levite (2Ch 17:8).

3. Priest (Ne 12:18).

JEHORAM [3393, 3456, *2732*] (*Yahweh exalts*).

1. King of Judah (1Ki 22:50; 2Ki 8:16; 1Ch 3:11; 2Ch 21:5). Ancestor of Jesus (Mt 1:8). Marries Athaliah, whose wicked counsels influence his reign for evil (2Ki 8:18-19; 2Ch 21:6-13).

Slays his brothers to strengthen himself in his sovereignty (2Ch 21:4, 13). Edom revolts from (2Ki 8:20-22; 2Ch 21:8-10). Philistines and Arabs invade his territory (2Ch 21:16-17). Death of (2Ch 21:18-20; 2Ki 8:24). Prophecy concerning (2Ch 21:12-15).

2. A son of Ahab. *See Joram.*

3. A priest commissioned to go through Israel and instruct the people in the law (2Ch 17:8).

JEHOSHABEATH *See Jehosheba.*

JEHOSHAPHAT [3398, 3399, *2734*] (*Yahweh has judged*).

1. David's recorder (2Sa 8:16; 20:24; 1Ki 4:3; 1Ch 18:15).

2. One of Solomon's district officers (1Ki 4:17).

3. King of Judah. Succeeds Asa (1Ki 15:24; 22:41; 1Ch 3:10; 2Ch 17:1; Mt 1:8). Strengthens himself against Israel (2Ch 17:2). Inaugurates a system of public instruction in the law (2Ch 17:7-9). His wise reign (1Ki 22:43; 2Ch 17:7-9; 19:3-11). His system of tribute (2Ch 17:11). His military forces and armament (2Ch 17:12-19). Joins Ahab in an invasion of Ramoth Gilead (1Ki 22; 2Ch 18). Rebuked by the prophet Jehu (2Ch 19:2). The allied forces of the Amorites, Moabites, and other tribes invade his territory and are defeated by (2Ch 20). Builds ships for commerce with Tarshish; ships are destroyed (1Ki 22:48-49; 2Ch 20:35-37). Joins Jehoram, king of Israel, in an invasion of the land of Moab, and defeats the Moabites (2Ki 3). Makes valuable gifts to the temple (2Ki 12:18). Death of (1Ki 22:50; 2Ch 21:1). Religious zeal of (1Ki 22:43, 46; 2Ch 17:1-9; 19; 20:1-32; 22:9). Prosperity of (1Ki 22:45, 48; 2Ch 17-20). Bequests of, to his children (2Ch 21:2-3).

4. Father of Jehu (2Ki 9:2, 14).

5. A priest who assisted in bringing the ark from Obed-Edom (1Ch 15:24).

JEHOSHAPHAT, VALLEY OF

(*valley of Yahweh's judgment*). Symbolic name for a valley where all nations will be gathered by Yahweh for judgment (Joel 3:2, 12), also called "the valley of decision" (Joel 3:14).

JEHOSHEBA [3394, 3395] (*Yahweh is an oath* ISBE; *Yahweh gives plenty, satisfies* KB). Daughter of King Jehoram; wife of high priest Jehoiada; hid Joash from Athaliah (2Ki 11:2). Also spelled Jehoshabeath (1Ch 22:11, ftn).

JEHOSHUA, JEHOSHUAH *See Joshua, 1.*

JEHOVAH A misreading of the name of God, Yahweh. Hebrew was originally written using only consonants. The pronunciation (and vowels) of the Hebrew Bible was handed down orally. When the vowels were eventually added to the Hebrew text, the name Yahweh was no longer pronounced. Instead, out of reverence, the title *Adonay* (Lord) was substituted. In keeping with this oral tradition, the Jewish scribes inserted into Yahweh the vowels for Adonay, resulting in the spelling Yehowah, though the name was still pronounced Adonay in oral reading. In c. 1520 the Christian scholar Petrus Galatinus introduced the hybrid spelling Jehovah, which became widely used in English versions, literature, and hymns. In the NIV, Yahweh is represented by LORD.

See God, Names of; Yahweh.

JEHOVAH-JIREH *See God, Names of, Yahweh Yireh.*

JEHOVAH-NISSI *See God, Names of, Yahweh Nissi.*

JEHOVAH-RAPAH *See God, Names of, Yahweh Raphah.*

JEHOVAH-SHALOM *See God, Names of, Yahweh Shalom.*

JEHOVAH-SHAMMAH *See God, Names of, Yahweh Shammah.*

JEHOVAH-TSIDKENU *See God, Names of, Yahweh Tsidkenu.*

JEHOZABAD [3379] (*Yahweh endows*).

1. Son of Shomer, and one of the assassins of King Jehoash (2Ki 12:21; 2Ch 24:26).

2. Son of Obed-Edom (1Ch 26:4).

3. A Benjamite chief who commanded 180,000 men (2Ch 17:18).

JEHOZADAK [3392] (*Yahweh is just*). Also called Jozadak. A priest of the Exile (1Ch 6:14-15; Hag 1:1, 12, 14; 2:2, 4; Zec 6:11).

JEHU [3369] (*Yahweh is he*).

1. The prophet who announced the wrath of Yahweh against Baasha, king of Israel (1Ki 16:1, 7, 12; 2Ch 19:2; 20:34).

2. Son of Nimshi, king of Israel (1Ki 19:16; 2Ki 9:1-4). Religious zeal of, in killing idolaters (2Ki 9:14-37; 10:1-28; 2Ch 22:8-9). His territory invaded by Hazael, king of Syria (2Ki 10:32-33). Prophecies concerning (1Ki 19:17; 2Ki 10:30; 15:12; Hos 1:4). Death of (2Ki 10:35).

3. Son of Obed (1Ch 2:38).

4. Son of Joshibiah (1Ch 4:35).

5. A Benjamite (1Ch 12:3).

JEHUBBAH *See Hubbah.*

JEHUCAL [3385, 3426] (*Yahweh is capable*). Man sent by King Zedekiah to Jeremiah for prayers (Jer 37:3). Prince who put Jeremiah in

prison (Hebrew *Jucal*, a variant of *Jehucal*) (Jer 38:1, ftn).

JEHUD [3372] (*declare*). Town in Dan, c. seven miles E of Joppa (Jos 19:45).

JEHUDI [3375] (*Jew*). Prince in Jehoiakim's court (Jer 36:14, 21).

JEHUDIJAH NIV "Judean" wife of Mered (1Ch 4:18).

JEHUSH See Jeush, 4.

JEIEL [3599] (*God [El] has preserved* IDB; possibly *God [El] sweeps up* KB).
1. Also called Jehiel. A Reubenite (1Ch 5:7).
2. A Benjamite (1Ch 9:35).
3. One of David's heroes (1Ch 11:44).
4. A Levite and singer in the tabernacle service (1Ch 15:18, 21; 16:5).
5. A Levite, ancestor of Jahaziel, who encouraged Judah against their enemies (2Ch 20:14).
6. A scribe during the reign of Uzziah (2Ch 26:11).
7. A Levite who cleansed the temple (2Ch 29:13).
8. A chief of the Levites who gave, with other chiefs, "five thousand Passover offerings and five hundred head of cattle for the Levites" for sacrifice (2Ch 35:9).
9. A son of Adonikam, an exile who returned to Jerusalem with Ezra (Ezr 8:13).
10. A priest who was defiled by marriage to an idolatrous woman (Ezr 10:43).

JEKABZEEL [3677] (*God [El] gathers*). A city in the S of Judah (Ne 11:25).

JEKAMEAM [3694] (*[my] kinsman establishes*). Son of Hebron (1Ch 23:19; 24:23).

JEKAMIAH [3693] (*Yahweh will establish*).
1. Judahite (1Ch 2:41).
2. Son of King Jehoiachin (Jehoiachin) (1Ch 3:18).

JEKUTHIEL [3688] (*God [El] will nourish*). Son of Ezra (1Ch 4:18).

JEMIMAH [3544] (*dove*). Daughter of Job born after restoration from affliction (Job 42:14).

JEMUEL [3543]. Son of Simeon (Ge 46:10; Ex 6:15). Also called Nemuel (Nu 26:9, 12; 1Ch 4:24). See Nemuel, 1.

JEPHTHAH [3653, 2650] (*Yahweh opens, frees*). A judge of Israel. Illegitimate and therefore not entitled to inherit his father's property (Jdg 11:1-2). Escapes the violence of his half-brothers, lives in the land of Tob (Jdg 11:3). Recalled from the land of Tob by the elders of Gilead (Jdg 11:5). Made captain of the host (Jdg 11:5-11) and made head of the land of Gilead (Jdg 11:7-11). His mes-sage to the king of the Ammonites (Jdg 11:12-28). Leads the host of Israel against the Ammonites (Jdg 11:29-33). His rash vow concerning his daughter (Jdg 11:31, 34-40). Falsely accused by the Ephraimites (Jdg 12:1). Leads the army of the Gileadites against the Ephraimites (Jdg 12:4). Judges Israel six years, dies, and is buried in Gilead (Jdg 12:7). Faith of (Heb 11:32).

JEPHUNNEH [3648] (*perhaps may he [God] turn* or *turned*).
1. Father of Caleb (Nu 13:6).
2. Son of Jether (1Ch 7:38).

JERAH [3733] (*moon [god?]*). Son of Joktan (Ge 10:26; 1Ch 1:20).

JERAHMEEL, JERAHMEELITE [3737, 3738] (*God [El] will have compassion*).
1. Son of Hezron (1Ch 2:9).
2. Son of Kish (1Ch 24:29).
3. An officer of Jehoiakim, king of Judah (Jer 36:26).

JERASH See Gerasenes.

JERED [3719] (*rose* IDB; *servant* KB). A Judahite (1Ch 4:18).

JEREMAI [3757] (possibly *fat*). Of the family of Hashum (Ezr 10:33).

JEREMIAH, BOOK OF
Author: Jeremiah, son of Berekiah
Date: Between 626 and 586 B.C.

Outline:
I. Call of the Prophet (ch. 1).
II. Warnings and Exhortations to Judah (chs. 2-35).
  A. Earliest Discourses (chs. 2-6).
  B. Temple Message (chs. 7-10).
  C. Covenant and Conspiracy (chs. 11-13).
  D. Messages Concerning the Drought (chs. 14-15).
  E. Disaster and Comfort (16:1-17:18).
  F. Command to Keep the Sabbath Holy (17:19-27).
  G. Lessons from the Potter (chs. 18-20).
  H. Condemnation of Kings, Prophets and People (chs. 21-24).
  I. Foretelling the Babylonian Exile (chs. 25-29).
  J. Promises of Restoration (chs. 30-33).
  K. Historical Appendix (chs. 34-35).
III. Suffering and Persecutions of the Prophet (chs. 36-38).
  A. Burning Jeremiah's Scroll (ch. 36).
  B. Imprisoning Jeremiah (chs. 37-38).
IV. The Fall of Jerusalem and Its Aftermath (chs. 39-45).
  A. The Fall Itself (ch. 39).
  B. Accession and Assassination of Gedaliah (40:1-41:15).
  C. Migration to Egypt (41:16-43:13).
  D. Prophecy Against Those in Egypt (ch. 44).

E. Historical Appendix: Promise to Baruch (ch. 45).

V. Judgment Against the Nations (chs. 46-51).
  A. Against Egypt (ch. 46).
  B. Against Philistia (ch. 47).
  C. Against Moab (ch. 48).
  D. Against Ammon (49:1-6).
  E. Against Edom (49:7-22).
  F. Against Damascus (49:23-27).
  G. Against Kedar and Hazor (Arabia) (49:28-33).
  H. Against Elam (49:34-39).
  I. Against Babylon (chs. 50-51).

VI. Historical Appendix (ch. 52).

JEREMIAH [3758, 3759, *2635*] (*Yahweh loosens [the womb]* BDB; *Yahweh lifts up* IDB; possibly *Yahweh shoots, establishes* KB). One of the greatest Hebrew prophets (c. 640-587 B.C.); born into priestly family of Anathoth, two-and-a-half miles NE of Jerusalem; called to prophetic office by a vision (Jer 1:4-10), and prophesied during last five kings of Judah (Josiah, Jehoahaz II, Jehoiakim, Jehoiachin, Zedekiah), probably helped Josiah in his reforms (2Ki 23), warned Jehoiakim against Egyptian alliance, prophetic roll destroyed by king (Jer 36), persecuted by nobility in days of the last king (Jer 36-37), Nebuchadnezzar kind to him after the destruction of Jerusalem (Jer 39:11-12), compelled to go to Egypt with Israelites who slew Gedaliah, and there he died (Jer 43:6-7).

Six other Jeremiahs are briefly mentioned in the OT:
1. Benjamite who came to David at Ziklag (1Ch 12:4).
2. A Gadite (1Ch 12:10).
3. A Gadite (1Ch 12:13).
4. A Manassite (1Ch 5:24).
5. Father of the wife of King Josiah (2Ki 23:30-31).
6. A Recabite (Jer 35:3).

JEREMOTH [3756] (*swollen* or *obese*).
1. A Benjamite (1Ch 7:8).
2. A Benjamite (1Ch 8:14).
3. Descendant of Elam who put away foreign wife (Ezr 10:26).
4. Descendant of Zattu who put away foreign wife (Ezr 10:27).
5. Descendant of Bani who put away foreign wife (Ezr 10:29).

JERIAH [3745, 3746] (*Yahweh founds*). A descendant of Hebron (1Ch 23:19; 24:23; 26:31).

JERIBAI [3744] (*Yahweh pleads*). A valiant man of David's guard (1Ch 11:46).

JERICHO [3735, *2637*] (*moon city*).
1. A city E of Jerusalem and near the Jordan (Nu 22:1; 26:3; Dt 34:1). Called the City of Palm Trees (Dt 34:3). Situation of, pleasant (2Ki 2:19). Rahab the harlot lived in (Jos 2; Heb 11:31). Joshua sees the "captain of the host" of the Lord near (Jos 5:13-15). Besieged by Joshua seven days; fall and destruction of (Jos 6; 24:11). Situated within the territory allotted to Benjamin (Jos 18:12, 21). The Kenites lived at (Jdg 1:16). King of Moab makes conquest of, and establishes his capital at (Jdg 3:13). Rebuilt by Hiel (1Ki 16:34). Company of "the sons of the prophets," lived at (2Ki 2:4-5, 15, 18). Captives of Judah, taken by the king of Israel, released at, on account of the denunciation of the prophet Obed (2Ch 28:7-15). Inhabitants of, taken captive to Babylon, return to, with Ezra and Nehemiah (Ezr 2:34; Ne 7:36), assist in repairing the walls of Jerusalem (Ne 3:2). Blind men healed at, by Jesus (Mt 20:29-34; Mk 10:46; Lk 18:35). Zacchaeus lived at (Lk 19:1-10).
2. Plain of (2Ki 25:5; Jer 52:8).
3. Waters of (Jos 16:1). Purified by Elisha (2Ki 2:18-22).

JERIEL [3741] (*founded of God [El]* BDB; *God [El] will see* IDB). Son of Tola (1Ch 7:2).

JERIJAH *See Jeriah.*

JERIMOTH [3748, 3756] (*swollen* or *obese*). *See also Jeremoth.*
1. Son of Bela (1Ch 7:7).
2. A disaffected Israelite, who denounced Saul and joined David at Ziklag (1Ch 12:5).
3. Son of Mushi (1Ch 23:23; 24:30).
4. Son of Heman (1Ch 25:4, 22).
5. A ruler of the tribe of Naphtali (1Ch 27:19).
6. A son of David (2Ch 11:18).
7. A Levite (2Ch 31:13).

JERIOTH [3750] (*tents*). Wife of Caleb. Probably identical with Azubah (1Ch 2:18).

JEROBOAM [3716] (*the people increase* BDB).
1. First king of Israel after the revolt. Promoted by Solomon (1Ki 11:28). Ahijah's prophecy concerning (1Ki 11:29-39; 14:5-16). Flees to Egypt to escape from Solomon (1Ki 11:26-40). Recalled from Egypt by the ten tribes on account of disaffection toward Rehoboam, and made king (1Ki 12:1-20; 2Ch 10:12-19). Subverts the religion of Moses (1Ki 12:25-33; 13:33-34; 14:9, 16; 16:2, 26, 31; 2Ch 11:14; 13:8-9). Hand of, paralyzed (1Ki 13:1-10). His wife sent to consult the prophet Ahijah concerning her child (1Ki 14:1-18). His wars with Rehoboam (1Ki 14:19, 30; 15:6; 2Ch 11:1-4). His war with Abijah (1Ki 15:7; 2Ch 13). Death of (1Ki 14:20; 2Ch 13:20).
2. King of Israel. Successor to Jehoash (2Ki 14:16, 23). Makes conquest of Hamath and Damascus (2Ki 14:25-28). Wicked reign of (2Ki 14:24). Prophecies concerning (Am 7:7-13). Death of (2Ki 14:29). Genealogies written during his reign (1Ch 5:17).

JEROHAM [3736] (*he will be compassionate*).
1. A Levite, and grandfather of Samuel (1Sa 1:1; 1Ch 6:27, 34).

2. A chief of the tribe of Benjamin (1Ch 8:27).

3. A descendant of Benjamin (1Ch 9:8).

4. A priest, and father of Adaiah, who lived in Jerusalem after the Exile (1Ch 9:12; Ne 11:12).

5. Father of two Israelites who joined David at Ziklag (1Ch 12:7).

6. The father of Azarel (1Ch 27:22).

7. Father of Azariah (2Ch 23:1).

JERUB-BAAL [3715] (*Baal contends*). See Gideon.

JERUB-BESHETH [3717] (*Shame [Baal] contends*). See Gideon.

JERUEL [3725] (*God [El] is a foundation*). A wilderness in the S of Judah (2Ch 20:16).

JERUSALEM [3731, 10332, 2643, 2647] (*foundation of Shalem [peace]*).

Called:

Jebus (Jos 18:28; Jdg 19:10), Zion (1Ki 8:1; Zec 9:13), City of David (2Sa 5:7; Isa 22:9), Salem (Ge 14:18; Ps 76:2), Ariel (Isa 29:1), City of God (Ps 46:4), City of the Great King (Ps 48:2), City of Judah (2Ch 25:28), The Perfection of Beauty, The Joy of the Whole Earth (La 2:15), The Throne of the Lord (Jer 3:17), Holy Mountain (Da 9:16, 20), Holy City (Ne 11:1, 18; Mt 4:5), City of our festivals (Isa 33:20), City of Truth (Zec 8:3), to be called "The LORD Our Righteousness" (Jer 33:16), Yahweh Shammah (Eze 48:35), *See God, Names of: Yahweh Shammah*. New Jerusalem (Rev 21:2, 10-27).

Situation and appearance of (Ps 122:3; 125:2; SS 6:4; Mic 4:8). Walls of (Jer 39:4).

Gates of:

Benjamin Gate (Jer 37:13; 38:7; Zec 14:10). Corner Gate (2Ki 14:13; 2Ch 25:23; 26:9; Jer 31:38; Zec 14:10). Dung Gate (Ne 2:13; 3:13, 14; 12:31). East Gate (1Ch 26:14; 2Ch 31:14; Ne 3:29). Ephraim Gate (2Ki 14:13; 2Ch 25:23; Ne 8:16; 12:39). First Gate (Zec 14:10). Fish Gate (2Ch 33:14; Ne 3:3; 12:39; Zep 1:10). Fountain Gate (Ne 2:14; 3:15; 12:37). Foundation Gate (2Ch 23:5). Gate of Joshua (2Ki 23:8). Gate of the guards (2Ki 11:19). Horse Gate (2Ch 23:15; Ne 3:28; Jer 31:40). Inspection Gate (Ne 3:31). Jeshanah [Old] Gate (Ne 3:6; 12:39). King's Gate (1Ch 9:18). Middle Gate (Jer 39:3). New Gate (Jer 26:10; 36:10). North Gate (1Ch 26:14). Potsherd Gate (Jer 19:2). Shalleketh Gate (1Ch 26:16). Sheep Gate (Ne 3:1, 32; 12:39; Jn 5:2). South Gate (1Ch 26:15). Sur Gate (2Ki 11:6). Upper Gate (2Ki 15:35; 2Ch 23:20; 27:3). Upper Gate of Benjamin (Jer 20:2). Valley Gate (2Ch 26:9; Ne 2:13, 15; 3:13). Water Gate (Ne 3:26; 8:1, 3, 16; 12:37). West Gate (1Ch 26:16).

Gates of the twelve tribes in Ezekiel's vision (Eze 48:31-34). Measurement of (Eze 45:6).

Buildings:

High priest's palace (Jn 18:15). Barracks (Ac 21:34). Stairway of Ahaz (2Ki 20:11). Stairs (Ne 9:4).

Squares and Streets:

Square on the east side (2Ch 29:4). Square before the house of God (Ezr 10:9). Square before the Water Gate (Ne 8:1, 3, 16), by the Gate of Ephraim (Ne 8:16). Street of the bakers (Jer 37:21). Streets of Jerusalem (Jer 5:1; 7:17, 34; 11:6, 13; 14:16; 33:10; 44:6, 9, 17, 21; Zec 8:4).

Towers:

See Beth Millo; Hananel, Tower of; Meah; Ophel; Siloam, Tower of.

Places in and Around:

Moriah (2Ch 3:1). The tomb of Jesus (Jn 19:41). *See Gethsemane; Golgotha; Jehoshaphat, Valley of; Olives, Mount of; Topheth, Topheth.*

History of:

Melchizedek ancient king and priest of (Ge 14:18). King of, confederated with the four other kings of the Amorites, against Joshua and the hosts of Israel (Jos 10:1-5). Confederated kings defeated, and the king of Jerusalem slain by Joshua (Jos 10:15-26). Fell to Benjamin in the allotment of the land of Canaan (Jos 18:28). Conquest of, made by David (2Sa 5:7). The inhabitants of, not expelled (Jos 15:63; Jdg 1:21). Conquest of Mount Zion, made by David (1Ch 11:4-6). The citadel of Mount Zion, occupied by David, and called the City of David (2Sa 5:5-9; 1Ch 11:7). Ark brought to, by David (2Sa 6:12-19). The threshing floor of Araunah within the citadel of (2Sa 24:16). David purchased and built an altar upon it (2Sa 24:16-25). The city built around the citadel (1Ch 11:8). The capital of David's kingdom by divine appointment (1Ki 15:4; 2Ki 19:34; 2Ch 6:6; 12:13).

Fortified by Solomon (1Ki 3:1; 9:15). The temple built within the citadel. *See Temple.*

The chief Levites lived in (1Ch 9:34). The high priest lived at (Jn 18:15). Annual feasts kept at (Eze 36:38, w Dt 16:16, & Ps 122:3-5; Lk 2:41; Jn 4:20; 5:1; 7:1-14; 12:20; Ac 18:21). Prayers of the Israelites made toward (1Ki 8:38; Da 6:10). Beloved (Ps 122:6; 137:1-7; Isa 62:1-7). *See Country, Love of; Patriotism*. Oaths taken in the name of (Mt 5:35).

Captured and pillaged by: Shishak, king of Egypt (1Ki 14:25-26; 2Ch 12:9), Jehoash, king of Israel (2Ki 14:13-14; 2Ch 25:23-24), Nebuchadnezzar, king of Babylon (2Ki 24:8-16; 25:1-17; 2Ch 36:17-21; Jer 1:3; 32:2; 39; 52:4-7, 12-24; La 1:5-8). Walls of, restored and fortified by: Uzziah (2Ch 26:9-10), Jotham (2Ch 27:3), Manasseh (2Ch 33:14). Water supply brought in from the Gihon by Hezekiah (2Ki 18:17; 20:20; 2Ch 32:3-4, 30; Ne 2:13-15; Isa 7:3; 22:9-11; 36:2). Besieged by: Pekah (2Ki 16:5), the Philistines (2Ch 21:16-17), Sennacherib (2Ki 18:13-37; 19:20-37; 2Ch 32). Rebuilding of ordered by proclamation of Cyrus (2Ch 36:23; Ezr 1:1-4). Rebuilt by Nehemiah under the direction of Artaxerxes (Ne 2-6). Wall of, dedicated (Ne 12:27-43). Temple restored. *See Temple.*

Roman rulers resided at: Herod I (Mt 2:3),

Pontius Pilate (Mt 27:2; Mk 15:1; Lk 23:1-7; Jn 18:28-29), Herod III (Ac 12:1-23).

Life and miracles of Jesus connected with: *See Jesus the Christ, History of.*

Gospel preached first preached at (Mic 4:2; Lk 24:47; Ac 1:4; 2:14). Day of Pentecost at (Ac 2). Stephen martyred at (Ac 6:8-7:60). Disciples persecuted and dispersed from (Ac 8:1-4; 11:19-21).

For personal incidents occurring there: *See biographies of individuals; Israel, Israelites.*

Prophecies Concerning:

Prophecies against (Isa 3:1-8; Jer 9:11; 19:6, 15; 21:10; 26:9, 11; Da 9:2, 27; Mic 1:1; 3:12); of pestilence, famine, and war in (Jer 34:2; Eze 5:12; Joel 3:2-3; Am 2:5); of the destruction of (Jer 7:32-34; 26:18; 32:29, 31-32; Da 9:24-27). Destruction of, foretold by Jesus (Mt 23:37-38; 24:15; Mk 13:14-23; Lk 13:35; 17:26-37; 19:41-44; 21:20-24).

Prophecies of the rebuilding of (Isa 44:28; Jer 31:38-40; Eze 48:15-22; Da 9:25; Zec 14:8-11). Of final restoration (Joel 3:20-21; Zec 2:2-5; 8).

Sins of:

Wickedness (Lk 13:33-34). Catalog of abominations in (Eze 22:3-12, 25-30; 23; 33:25-26). Led Judah to sin (Mic 1:5).

JERUSALEM, NEW City of God referred to as coming down out of heaven from God (Rev 3:12; 21:2). Described as the mother of believers (Gal 4:26).

JERUSHA [3729, 3730] (*possession*). Wife of King Uzziah and mother of King Jotham (2Ki 15:33; 2Ch 27:1).

JESARELAH [3777]. Ancestral head of a course of musicians (1Ch 25:14, ftn). Also called Asarelah (1Ch 25:2).

JESHAIAH [3832, 3833] (*Yahweh saves*).
1. Grandson of Zerubbabel (1Ch 3:21).
2. Son of Jeduthun (1Ch 25:3, 15).
3. Grandson of Eliezer (1Ch 26:25).
4. A Jew of the family of Elam, who returned from exile (Ezr 8:7).
5. A Levite who joined Ezra to return to Jerusalem (Ezr 8:19).
6. A Benjamite, detailed by lot to live in Jerusalem after the Exile (Ne 11:7).

JESHANAH [3827] (*old*).
1. A city on the N of Benjamin (2Ch 13:19).
2. Gate in NW corner of Jerusalem in Nehemiah's time (Ne 3:6).

JESHEBEAB [3784] (*father lives*). Priest, and head of the fourteenth course (1Ch 24:13).

JESHER [3840] (perhaps *the deity shows himself just*). Son of Caleb (1Ch 2:18).

JESHIMON [3810] (*a waste, a desert*).
1. A place in the Sinai peninsula, E of the Jordan (Nu 21:20; 23:28).

2. A place in the desert of Judah (1Sa 23:24; 26:1).

JESHIMOTH See Beth Jeshimoth.

JESHISHAI [3814] (*aged*). A Gadite (1Ch 5:14).

JESHOHAIAH [3797] (possibly *Yahweh humbles*). A descendant of Simeon (1Ch 4:36).

JESHUA [3800, 3801, 10336] (*Yahweh saves*).
1. A priest, head of the ninth course (1Ch 24:11). Nine hundred and seventy-three of his descendants returned from Babylon (Ezr 2:36; Ne 7:39).
2. A Levite, had charge of the tithes (2Ch 31:15). His descendants returned with Ezra from Babylon (Ezr 2:40; Ne 7:43).
3. Also called Joshua. A priest who accompanied Zerubbabel from Babylon (Ezr 2:2; Ne 7:7; 12:1). Descendants of (Ne 12:10). He rebuilt the altar (Ezr 3:2). Assisted Zerubbabel in restoring the temple (Ezr 3; 4:1-6; 5; Hag 1:1, 12-14; 2:2). Contended with those who sought to defeat the rebuilding (Ezr 4:1-3; 5:1-2). Symbolic of the restoration of Israel (Zec 3; 6:9-15).
4. Father of Jozabad (Ezr 8:33).
5. Son of Pahath-Moab (Ezr 2:6; Ne 7:11).
6. Father of Ezer (Ne 3:19).
7. A Levite who explained the law to the people when Ezra read it (Ne 8:7; 12:8).
8. A Levite who sealed Nehemiah's covenant (Ne 10:9).
9. A city of Judah (Ne 11:26).

JESHURUN [3843] (*upright*). A name used poetically for Israel (Dt 32:15; 33:5, 26; Isa 44:2).

JESIAH See Isshiah, 2 & 3.

JESIMIEL [3774] (*God [El] will establish*). A descendant of Simeon (1Ch 4:36).

JESSE [414, 3805, 2649]. Father of David (Ru 4:17; 1Sa 17:12). Ancestor of Jesus (Mt 1:5-6). Samuel visits, under divine command, to select from his sons a successor to Saul (1Sa 16:1-13). Saul asks, to send David to become a member of his court (1Sa 16:19-23). Sons in Saul's army (1Sa 17:13-28). Lives with David in Moab (1Sa 22:3-4). Descendants of (1Ch 2:13-17).

JESTING Foolish, forbidden (Eph 5:4; Mt 12:36).

JESUI, JESUITES See Ishvi, 1; Ishvites.

JESUS THE CHRIST [2652] (*Yahweh Saves, Anointed One*).

History of:

Birth and Childhood—
Genealogy of (Mt 1:1-17; Lk 3:23-38).
The angel Gabriel appears to Mary (Lk 1:26-38). Mary visits Elizabeth (Lk 1:39-56). Mary's

magnificat (Lk 1:46-55). An angel appears to Joseph concerning Mary (Mt 1:18-25).

Birth of (Lk 2:1-7). Angels appear to the shepherds (Lk 2:8-20). Magi visit (Mt 2:1-12). Circumcision of (Lk 2:21). Is presented in temple (Lk 2:21-38). Flight into, and return from, Egypt (Mt 2:13-23). Disputes with the doctors in the temple (Lk 2:41-52).

Ministry—

Is baptized by John (Mt 3:13-17; Mk 1:9-11; Lk 3:21-23). Temptation of (Mt 4:1-11; Mk 1:12-13; Lk 4:1-13). John's testimony concerning him (Jn 1:1-18). Testimony of John the Baptist concerning (Jn 1:19-34). Disciples adhere to (Jn 1:35-51).

Miracles at Cana of Galilee (Jn 2:1-12). Drives the money changers from the temple (Jn 2:13-25). Nicodemus comes to (Jn 3:1-21). Baptizes (Jn 3:22; 4:2). Returns to Galilee (Mt 4:12; Mk 1:14; Lk 4:14; Jn 4:1-3). Visits Sychar, and teaches the Samaritan woman (Jn 4:4-42). Teaches in Galilee (Mt 4:17; Mk 1:14-15; Lk 4:14-15; Jn 4:43-45). Heals a nobleman's son of Capernaum (Jn 4:46-54). Is rejected by the people of Nazareth, lives at Capernaum (Mt 4:13-16; Lk 4:16-31). Chooses Peter, Andrew, James, and John as disciples, miracle of the catch of fishes (Mt 4:18-22; Mk 1:16-20; Lk 5:1-11).

Preaches throughout Galilee (Mt 4:23-25; Mk 1:35-39; Lk 4:42-44). Heals a demoniac (Mk 1:21-28; Lk 4:31-37). Heals Peter's mother-in-law (Mt 8:14-17; Mk 1:29-34; Lk 4:38-41). Heals a leper in Galilee (Mt 8:2-4; Mk 1:40-45; Lk 5:12-16). Heals a paralytic (Mt 9:2-8; Mk 2:1-12; Lk 5:17-26). Calls Matthew (Mt 9:9; Mk 2:13-14; Lk 5:27-28). Heals an invalid at the pool of Bethesda on the Sabbath day, is persecuted, and makes his defense (Jn 5:1-47). Defines the law of the Sabbath on the occasion of his disciples picking the heads of grain (Mt 12:1-14; Mk 3:1-6; Lk 6:6-11). Withdraws from Capernaum to the Sea of Galilee, where he heals many (Mt 12:15-21; Mk 3:7-12).

Goes up onto a mountain, and calls and ordains twelve disciples (Mt 10:2-4; Mk 3:13-19; Lk 6:12-19). Delivers the "Sermon on the Mount" (Mt 5-7; Lk 6:20-49). Heals the centurion's servant (Mt 8:5-13; Lk 7:1-10). Raises from the dead the son of the widow of Nain (Lk 7:11-17). Receives the message from John the Baptist (Mt 11:2-19; Lk 7:18-35). Rebukes the unbelieving cities about Capernaum (Mt 11:20-30). Anointed by a sinful woman (Lk 7:36-50). Preaches in the cities of Galilee (Lk 8:1-3).

Heals a demoniac, and denounces the scribes and Pharisees (Mt 12:22-37; Mk 3:19-30; Lk 11:14-20). Replies to the scribes and Pharisees who seek a sign from him (Mt 12:38-45; Lk 11:16-36). Denounces the Pharisees and other hypocrites (Lk 11:37-54). Discourses to his disciples (Lk 12:1-59). Parable of the barren fig tree (Lk 13:6-9). Parable of the sower (Mt 13:1-23; Mk 4:1-25; Lk 8:4-18). Parable of the weeds, and other teachings (Mt 13:24-53; Mk 4:26-34).

Crosses the Sea of Galilee, and stills the tempest (Mt 8:18-27; Mk 4:35-41; Lk 8:22-25). Casts out

the legion of demons (Mt 8:28-33; Mk 5:1-21; Lk 8:26-40). Returns to Capernaum (Mt 9:1; Mk 5:21; Lk 8:40). Eats with tax collectors and sinners, and speaks on fasting (Mt 9:10-17; Mk 2:15-22; Lk 5:29-39). Raises to life the daughter of Jairus, and heals the woman who has the issue of blood (Mt 9:18-26; Mk 5:22-43; Lk 8:41-56). Heals two blind men and casts out a mute spirit (Mt 9:27-34). Returns to Nazareth (Mt 13:53-58; Mk 6:1-6). Teaches in various cities in Galilee (Mt 9:35-38).

Instructs his disciples and empowers them to heal diseases and cast out unclean spirits (Mt 10; Mk 6:6-13; Lk 9:1-6). Herod falsely supposes him to be John, whom he had beheaded (Mt 14:1-2, 6-12; Mk 6:14-16, 21-29; Lk 9:7-9). The Twelve return; he goes to the desert; multitudes follow him; he feeds five thousand (Mt 14:13-21; Mk 6:30-44; Lk 9:10-17; Jn 6:1-14). Walks on the water (Mt 14:22-36; Mk 6:45-56; Jn 6:15-21). Teaches in the synagogue in Capernaum (Jn 6:22-65). Disciples forsake him (Jn 6:66-71).

He justifies his disciples in eating without washing their hands (Mt 15:1-20; Mk 7:1-23). Heals the daughter of the Syrian Phoenician woman (Mt 15:21-28; Mk 7:24-30). Heals a mute man (Mt 15:29-31; Mk 7:31-37). Feeds four thousand (Mt 15:32-39; Mk 8:1-9). Refuses to give a sign to the Pharisees (Mt 16:1-4; Mk 8:10-12). Cautions his disciples against the yeast of hypocrisy (Mt 16:4-12; Mk 8:13-21). Heals a blind man (Mk 8:22-26). Foretells his death and resurrection (Mt 16:21-28; Mk 8:31-38; 9:1; Lk 9:21-27).

Is transfigured (Mt 17:1-13; Mk 9:2-13; Lk 9:28-36). Heals a demoniac (Mt 17:14-21; Mk 9:14-29; Lk 9:37-43). Foretells his death and resurrection (Mt 17:22-23; Mk 9:30-32; Lk 9:43-45). Miracle of tribute money in the fish's mouth (Mt 17:24-27). Reproves the ambition of his disciples (Mt 18:1-35; Mk 9:33-50; Lk 9:46-50). Reproves the intolerance of his disciples (Mk 9:38-39; Lk 9:49-50).

Journeys to Jerusalem to attend the Feast of Tabernacles, passing through Samaria (Lk 9:51-62; Jn 7:2-11). Commissions the Seventy (Lk 10:11-19). Heals ten lepers (Lk 17:11-19). Teaches in Jerusalem at the Feast of Tabernacles (Jn 7:14-53; 8). Answers a lawyer, who tests his wisdom with the question, "What must I do to inherit eternal life?" by the parable of the good Samaritan (Lk 10:25-37). Hears the report of the Seventy (Lk 10:17-24). Teaches in the house of Mary, Martha, and Lazarus, in Bethany (Lk 10:38-42).

Teaches his disciples to pray (Lk 11:1-13). Heals a blind man, who, because of his faith in Jesus, was excommunicated (Jn 9). Teaches in Jerusalem (Jn 9:39-41; 10:1-21). Teaches in the temple at Jerusalem, at the Feast of Dedication (Jn 10:22-39). Goes across the Jordan to escape violence from the rulers (Jn 10:40-42; 11:3-16).

Returns to Bethany and raises Lazarus from the dead (Jn 11:1-46). Escapes to the city of Ephraim from the conspiracy led by Caiaphas, the high priest (Jn 11:47-54). Journeys toward Jerusalem to attend the Passover; heals many who are diseased and teaches the people (Mt 19:1-2; Mk 10:1; Lk 13:10-35). Dines with a Pharisee on the Sabbath (Lk 14:1-24). Teaches the multitude the conditions of discipleship (Lk 14:25-35).

Tells the parables of the lost sheep, the lost piece of silver, prodigal son, unjust steward (Lk 15:1-32; 16:1-13). Reproves the hypocrisy of the Pharisees (Lk 16). Tells the parable of the rich man and Lazarus (Lk 16:19-31). Teaches his disciples concerning offenses, meekness, and humility (Lk 17:1-10). Teaches the Pharisees concerning the coming of his kingdom (Lk 17:20-37). Tells the parables of the unjust judge, and the Pharisee and tax collector praying in the temple (Lk 18:1-14).

Interprets the law concerning marriage and divorce (Mt 19:3-12; Mk 10:2-12). Blesses little children (Mt 19:13-15; Mk 10:13-16; Lk 18:15-17). Receives the rich young ruler, who asks what he must do to inherit eternal life (Mt 19:16-22; Mk 10:17-22; Lk 18:18-24). Tells the parable of the vineyard (Mt 20:1-16). Foretells his death and resurrection (Mt 20:17-19; Mk 10:32-34; Lk 18:31-34). Listens to the mother of James and John in behalf of her sons (Mt 20:20-28; Mk 10:35-45). Heals two blind men at Jericho (Mt 20:29-34; Mk 10:46-50; Lk 18:35-43). Visits Zacchaeus (Lk 19:1-10). Tells the parable of the pounds (Lk 19:11-28).

Final Week in Jerusalem—

Goes to Bethany six days before the Passover (Jn 12:1-9). Triumphal entry into Jerusalem, while the people throw palm branches in the way (Mt 21:1-11; Mk 11:1-11; Lk 19:29-44; Jn 12:12-19). Enters the temple (Mt 21:12; Mk 11:11; Lk 19:45). Drives the money changers out of the temple (Mt 21:12-13; Lk 19:45-46). Heals the sick in the temple (Mt 21:14). Teaches daily in the temple (Lk 19:47-48).

Performs the miracle of causing the barren fig tree to wither (Mt 21:17-22; Mk 11:12-14, 20-22). Tells the parable of the two sons (Mt 21:28-31), the parable of the wicked farmers (Mt 21:33-46; Mk 12:1-12; Lk 20:9-19), of the marriage (Mt 22:1-14; Lk 14:16-24). Tested by the Pharisees and Herodians and enunciates the duty of the citizen to his government (Mt 22:15-22; Mk 12:13-17; Lk 20:20-26). Tried by the Sadducees concerning the resurrection of the dead (Mt 22:23-33; Mk 12:18-27; Lk 20:27-40) and by a lawyer (Mt 22:34-40; Mk 12:28-34). Exposes the hypocrisies of the scribes and Pharisees (Mt 23; Mk 12:38-40; Lk 20:45-47).

Extols the widow who casts two small copper coins into the treasury (Mk 12:41-44; Lk 21:1-4). Verifies the prophecy of Isaiah concerning the unbelieving Jews (Jn 12:37-50). Foretells the destruction of the temple and of Jerusalem (Mt 24; Mk 13; Lk 21:5-36). Laments over Jerusalem (Mt 23:37; Lk 19:41-44). Tells the parables of the ten virgins and of the talents (Mt 25:1-30). Foretells the scenes of the Day of Judgment (Mt 25:31-46).

Anointed with precious ointment (Mt 26:6-13; Mk 14:3-9; Jn 12:1-8). Last Passover, and institution of the Lord's Supper (Mt 26:17-30; Mk 14:12-25; Lk 22:7-20). Washes the disciples' feet (Jn 13:1-17). Foretells his betrayal (Mt 26:23; Mk 14:18-21; Lk 22:21; Jn 13:18). Accuses Judas of his betrayal (Mt 26:21-25; Mk 14:18-21; Lk 22:21-23; Jn 13:21-30). Teaches his disciples, and comforts them with promises, including the gift of the Holy Spirit (Jn 14-16). Last prayer (Jn 17).

Arrest, Crucifixion, Resurrection—

Moves to Gethsemane (Mt 26:30, 36-46; Mk 14:26, 32-42; Lk 22:39-46; Jn 18:1). Is betrayed and apprehended (Mt 26:47-56; Mk 14:43-54, 66-72; Lk 22:47-53; Jn 18:2-12).

Trial of, before Caiaphas (Mt 26:57-58, 69-75; Mk 14:53-54, 66-72; Lk 22:54-62; Jn 18:13-18, 25-27). Led by the council to Pilate (Mt 27:1-2, 11-14; Mk 15:1-5; Lk 23:1-5; Jn 18:28-38). Arraigned before Herod (Lk 23:6-12). Tried before Pilate (Mt 27:15-26; Mk 15:6-15; Lk 23:13-25; Jn 18:39-40; 19:1-16). Mocked by the soldiers (Mt 27:27-31; Mk 15:16-20). Is led away to be crucified (Mt 27:31-34; Mk 15:20-23; Lk 23:26-32; Jn 19:16-17).

Crucified (Mt 27:35-56; Mk 15:24-41; Lk 23:33-49; Jn 19:18-30). Taken from the cross and buried (Mt 27:57-66; Mk 15:42-47; Lk 23:50-56; Jn 19:31-42).

Arises from the dead (Mt 28:2-15; Mk 16:1-11; Lk 24:1-12; Jn 20:1-18). Is seen by Mary Magdalene (Mt 28:1-10; Mk 16:9; Jn 20:11-17), by Peter (Lk 24:34; 1Co 15:5). Appears to two disciples who journey to Emmaus (Mk 16:12-13; Lk 24:13-35). Appears in the midst of the disciples, when Thomas is absent (Mk 16:14-18; Lk 24:36-49; Jn 20:19-23), when Thomas was present (Jn 20:26-29), at the Sea of Galilee (Mt 28:16; Jn 21:1-14), to the apostles and five hundred believers on a mountain in Galilee (Mt 28:16-20, w Ac 10:40-42; 13:31; 1Co 15:6-7). Appears to James, and also to all the apostles (Ac 1:3-8; 1Co 15:7).

Ascension and Additional Appearances—

Ascends to heaven (Mk 16:19-20; Lk 24:50-53; Ac 1:9-12). Appears to Paul (Ac 9:3-17; 18:9; 22:14, 18; 23:11; 26:16; 1Co 9:1; 15:8). Stephen's vision of (Ac 7:55-56). Appears to John on Patmos (Rev 1:10-18).

Miscellaneous Facts Concerning:

Was with the Israelites in the wilderness (1Co 10:4, 9; Heb 11:26; Jude 5).

Brothers of (Mt 13:55; Mk 6:3; 1Co 9:5; Gal 1:19). Sisters of (Mt 13:56; Mk 6:3).

Appearances of, After His Resurrection:

To Mary Magdalene and other women (Mt 28:1-10; Mk 16:9; Lk 24:1-10; Jn 20:11-17). To Peter (Lk 24:34; 1Co 15:5). To two disciples who journey to Emmaus (Mk 16:12-13; Lk 24:13-31). In the midst of the disciples, when Thomas is absent, in Jerusalem (Jn 20:19-23), when Thomas is present (Mk 16:14-18; Lk 24:36-49; Jn 20:26-29; 1Co 15:5). To certain disciples, Sea of Galilee (Jn

21:1-14). To the eleven disciples, mountain in Galilee (Mt 28:16). To upwards of five hundred, Galilee (1Co 15:6). To James, and also all the apostles, Jerusalem (Ac 1:3-8; 1Co 15:7). To Paul (Ac 9:3-6; 23:11; 26:13-18; 1Co 9:1; 15:8).

In Stephen's vision (Ac 7:55-56). To John, in a vision, on Patmos (Rev 1:10-18).

Ascension of:

(Mk 16:19; Lk 24:50-51; Jn 14:2-4; Ac 1:9; 3:21; Eph 1:20; 4:8-10; 1Ti 3:16; Heb 1:3; 4:14; 9:24). Foretold (Ps 47:5; 68:18; Lk 24:26, 50; Jn 1:51; 6:62; 7:33; 14:2-3, 12, 28; 16:5, 7, 10, 16, 28; 17:13; 20:17).

Atonement by:

(Ro 3:24-26; 5:11, 15; 1Th 1:10; Heb 13:12; 1Jn 2:2; 3:5; 4:10; Rev 5:6, 9; 13:8).

Made once for all (Heb 7:27; 9:24-28; 10:10, 12, 14; 1Pe 3:18). Vicarious (Isa 53:4-12; Mt 20:28; Jn 6:51; 11:49-51; Gal 1:4; 3:13; Eph 5:2; 1Th 5:9-10; Heb 2:9; 1Pe 2:24).

Through his blood (Lk 22:20; 1Co 1:23; Eph 2:13-15; Heb 9:12-15, 25-26; 12:24; 13:12, 19-21; 1Jn 5:6; Rev 1:5; 5:9; 7:14; 12:11).

For reconciliation (Ro 5:1-21; 2Co 5:18-19, 21; Eph 2:6-17; Col 1:20-22; Heb 2:17).

For remission of sins (Zec 13:1; Mt 26:28; Lk 24:46-47; Jn 1:29; Ro 4:25; 1Co 15:3; Gal 1:3-4; Eph 1:7; Col 1:14; Heb 1:3; 10:1-20; 1Jn 1:7; 3:5).

Atonement Typified—
(Ex 29:36-37; 30:10, 15-16; Lev 1:4; 5:6, 16, 18; 6:7; 8:34; 9:2-3, 7; 10:17; 12:7-8; 14:18-20, 31, 53; 15:14-15, 29-30; 16:6, 10-11, 16-18, 24, 27, 30, 32-34; 17:11; 23:27-28; 25:9; Nu 8:19, 21; 16:46; 25:13; 28:22, 30; 29:5; 31:50).

Atoning blood (Mt 26:28; Mk 14:24; Lk 22:20; Eph 1:7; 2:13; Heb 9:14; 10:19; 1Jn 1:7). Atoning blood of, typified (Ex 12:7, 13, 22-23; 24:6, 8; 29:12, 15, 20-21; 30:10; Lev 1:5, 10-11; 3:2, 8, 13; 4:5-7, 17-18, 25, 30, 34; 5:8-9; 6:30; 7:2; 8:2, 15, 19, 23-24, 30; 9:9, 18; 14:6, 14-15, 25; 16:14-15, 18-19, 27; 17:6, 11; Nu 18:17; 19:2-4; Dt 12:27; 2Ki 16:13, 15; 2Ch 29:22; 30:16; 35:11; Eze 43:20; 45:19-20; 1Pe 1:19).

Benevolence of:

Manifested in his companionship with sinners (Mt 9:10-12; Mk 2:14-17; Lk 5:30; 15:2; 19:10-12). *See below, Compassion of; Love of.*

Compassion of:

For those who were in spiritual distress (Isa 42:3; Mt 9:36; 12:20; 18:12-13; 23:37; Mk 1:41; 6:34; Lk 7:13; 13:34; 15:4-9, 20-24; 19:41-42; Jn 11:33-38; 18:8-9; 2Co 8:9; Heb 4:15; 5:2). For those who were in temporal adversity (Isa 53:4; 63:9; Mt 8:3, 16-17; 14:14; 15:32; 20:34; Mk 8:2-3). For his sheep (Isa 40:11; Mk 6:34).

Condescension of:

(Lk 22:27; Jn 13:5, 14; 2Co 8:9; Php 2:7-8; Heb 2:11).

Confessing: *See Confession, of Christ; Testimony, Religious.*

Creator:

(Jn 1:3, 10; 1Co 8:6; Eph 3:9; Col 1:16-17; Heb 1:2, 10; Rev 3:14).

Death of:

(Jn 12:32-33; Ac 5:30; 7:52; Heb 2:14; 12:2, 24; Rev 5:12; 13:8).

Death foretold by God (Ge 3:15; Heb 2:14). By the psalmist (Ps 22:1, 17-18; Mt 27:46; Mk 15:34; Ps 22:17; Mt 27:36; Lk 23:35; Ps 22:18; Mt 27:35; Mk 15:24; Lk 23:34; Jn 19:23-24; Ps 34:20; Jn 19:36; Ps 69:21; Mt 27:34, 48; Mk 15:36; Lk 23:36; Jn 19:28-30). By Isaiah (Isa 52:14; 53:7-12). By Zechariah (Zec 13:7; Mt 26:31). By Jesus himself (Mt 12:40; 16:4, 21; 17:12-13, 22-23; 20:17-19; 21:33-39; 26:2, 12, 18; Mk 8:31; 9:31; 10:32-34; 14:8-9; Lk 9:22, 44; 12:50; 17:25; 18:31-33; 22:15, 21, 37; Jn 2:19, 21; 10:11, 15, 17-18; 12:7, 24, 32-34; 14:19; 18:11).

Paul's testimony concerning Jesus' death (Ac 17:3; 26:22-23; 1Co 1:17-18, 23-24; 2:2; 15:3-4; 2Co 4:10-11; 13:4; Gal 3:1; 1Th 2:15; 4:14).

See above, History of, for Circumstances of the Death of.

Purpose of His Death—
To make reconciliation (Ro 5:6-11; Eph 2:13-16).

To redeem (Isa 53:4-6, 8, 10-12; Mt 20:28; 26:28; Mk 10:45; 14:24; Jn 6:51; 10:11, 17; 11:49-52; Ac 20:28; 26:23; Ro 3:24-25; 8:3, 32; 1Co 5:7; 6:20; 8:11; 15:3; Gal 1:4; 3:13; 4:4-5; Eph 1:6-7; 5:2, 25-27; Col 1:14, 20, 22; 2:14-15; 1Th 1:10; 2:6; Tit 2:14; Heb 2:9-10, 14-15, 18; 7:27; 9:12-17, 25-26, 28; 10:10, 12, 14, 17-20; 1Pe 1:18-19; 2:21, 24; 3:18; 1Jn 2:2; 3:16; 4:10; Rev 1:5-6; 5:9-10; 13:8).

To purge sins (Zec 13:1; Lk 24:46-47; Jn 1:29; Heb 1:3; 13:11-12; 1Jn 1:7; Rev 7:14-15).

To secure forgiveness (Ac 5:30-31; Ro 4:25).

To save (Jn 3:14-17; Ro 6:3-5, 9-10; 14:9, 15; 2Co 5:14-15, 19, 21; 8:9; Gal 2:20; 1Th 5:9-10).

Vicarious Death of—
(Isa 53:4-12; Mt 20:28; Jn 6:51; 11:49, 51; Gal 3:13; Eph 5:2; 1Th 5:9-10; Heb 2:9; 1Pe 2:24).

Vicarious death of, typified (Ex 29:11, 15-16, 20; 29:38-42; Lev 1:5, 11, 15; 3:2, 8, 13; 4:4, 15, 24, 29; 6:25; 7:2; 8:15, 19; 9:8, 15, 18-19, 23-24; 14:13, 19, 25; 2Ch 29:22, 24; 30:15; 35:1).

See Atonement; Redemption.

Voluntary Death of—
(Isa 50:6; 53:12; Lk 9:51; 12:50; 22:15, 42; Jn 10:17-18; 18:5, 8, 11; Php 2:8; Heb 7:27; 9:26; 1Jn 3:16).

Divine Sonship of:

Testified to—
By God, at his baptism (Mt 3:17; Mk 1:11; Lk 3:22), at the transfiguration (Mt 17:5; Mk 9:7; Lk 9:35; 2Pe 1:17), in his commandment to believe in (1Jn 3:23).

By Jesus himself (Mt 11:27; Mt 26:63-64; 27:43; Mk 14:61-62; Lk 10:22; 22:70; Jn 3:16-18, 34-36; 6:27, 40, 46, 57; 9:35-37; 11:4; 19:7).

By the disciples (Mt 14:33; 1Jn 4:14), unclean spirits (Mt 8:29; Mk 3:11; 5:7, w Lk 8:28; Lk

4:41), Mark (Mk 1:1), John the Baptist (Jn 1:34), John the apostle (Jn 1:14, 18; 1Jn 1:7; 2:22-24; 3:8, 23; 4:9, 10, 14; 5:5, 9-13, 20; 2Jn 3; Rev 2:18), Nathanael (Jn 1:49), Martha (Jn 11:27), the centurion (Mt 27:54; Mk 15:39), Peter (Ac 3:13; 13:33), Paul (Ro 1:3-4, 9; 8:3, 29, 32; 1Co 1:9; 15:24, 27-28; 2Co 1:3, 19; Gal 1:16; 4:4; Eph 1:3; Col 1:3; 1Th 1:10), the author of Hebrews (Heb 1:1-3, 5; 4:14; 5:5, 8; 6:6; 7:3; 10:29).

Other Evidences—

Declared God to be his Father (Mt 15:13; 18:10, 19; 20:23; 26:53, 63-64; Lk 10:22; 22:29; Jn 5:19-21, 23, 26-27, 30, 36-37; 8:16, 19, 26-29, 38, 49, 54; 10:15, 17-18, 29-30, 36-38; 11:41; 12:49-50; 13:3; 14:7, 9-11, 13, 16, 20-21, 23-24, 28, 31; 15:1, 8-10, 15, 23-24; 16:15, 27-28, 32; 17:1-26; 20:17, 21).

Peter's confession of (Mt 16:15-17).

Prophecies concerning (Ps 2:7; Lk 1:32, 35).

Worshiped by the disciples as the Son of God (Mt 14:33).

See below, Deity of; Relation of, to the Father; Son of God; Son of Man.

Deity of:

Indicated by the Titles Ascribed to Him—

Immanuel (Isa 7:14, w Mt 1:23). First and Last (Rev 1:17; 22:13). God (Ps 102:24-27, w Heb 1:10-13; Jn 1:1; 20:28; Ro 9:5; 1Jn 5:20-21), God and Savior Jesus Christ (2Pe 1:1). God our Savior (Tit 2:13). Holy One (Ac 3:14). Lord of lords and King of kings (Rev 17:14). Lord (Ps 110:1 w Mt 22:42-45; Isa 40:3 w Mt 3:3; Ac 20:28). Lord Almighty (Isa 8:13-14; 1Pe 2:8). My Lord and My God (Jn 20:28). Lord of all (Ac 10:36; Ro 10:12). Mighty God (Isa 9:6). Only born of the Father (Jn 1:14, 18; 3:16, 18; 1Jn 4:9), Son of God (Mt 26:63-67; Mk 1:1; 15:39; 1Co 1:9; 2Co 1:19; Gal 2:20; Eph 4:13; Heb 1:2; 2Pe 1:17; 1Jn 1:2-3; 3:23; 5:10, 12-13, 20), Son of Man (Da 7:13-14; Mt 11:19; 12:8). *See above, Divine Sonship of; below, Son of God; Son of Man.*

Addressed as Yahweh (LORD)—

(Isa 40:3 w Mt 3:3). King or LORD of glory (Ps 24:7, 10; 1Co 2:8; Jas 2:1). The LORD our righteousness (Jer 23:5-6; 1Co 1:30), The LORD all (Ps 97:9; Jn 3:31), The First and the last, the Alpha and the Omega (Isa 44:6, w Rev 1:17; Isa 48:12-16, w Rev 22:13). Yahweh's fellow and equal (Zec 13:7; Php 2:6). LORD Almighty (Isa 6:1-3 w Jn 12:41; Isa 8:13-14 w 1Pe 2:8). LORD (Ps 110:1; Mt 22:42-45). Yahweh the Shepherd (Isa 40:10-11; Heb 13:20). LORD, for whose glory all things were created (Pr 16:4; Col 1:16). Lord the messenger of the covenant (Mal 3:1; Lk 7:27). Invoked as LORD (Joel 2:32; 1Co 1:2).

Equality With God—

As the eternal God and Creator (Ps 102:24-27; Heb 1:8, 10-12). The Mighty God (Isa 9:6), the great God and Savior (Hos 1:7, w Tit 2:13), God over all (Ro 9:5), God the Judge (Ecc 12:14, w 1Co 4:5; 2Co 5:10; 2Ti 4:1), Immanuel (Isa 7:14, w Mt 1:23), Lord of lords and King of kings (Da 10:17, w Rev 1:5; 17:14), the Holy and Righteous One (1Sa 2:2, w Ac 3:14).

The Lord from heaven (1Co 15:47). Lord of the Sabbath (Ge 2:3, w Mt 12:8), Lord of all (Ac 10:36; Ro 10:11-13). Son of God (Mt 26:63-67), the only born Son of the Father (Jn 1:14, 18; 3:16, 18; 1Jn 4:9). His blood is called the blood of God (Ac 20:28). One with the Father (Jn 10:30, 38; 12:45; 14:7-10; 17:10). As sending the Spirit equally with the Father (Jn 14:16, w Jn 15:26). As unsearchable equally with the Father (Jn 14:16). As Creator of all things (Isa 40:28; Jn 1:3; Col 1:16), supporter and preserver of all things (Ne 9:6, w Col 1:17; Heb 1:3). Acknowledged by Old Testament saints (Ge 17:1, w 48:15-16; 32:24-30, w Hos 12:3-5; Jdg 6:22-24; 13:21-22; Job 19:25-27).

Is one with the Father (Jn 5:17-18, 23; 10:30, 33, 38; 12:45; 14:7-11; 17:11, 21-22). Sends the Holy Spirit equally with the Father (Jn 14:16). Identical with the Adonay (Lord) of the Old Testament (Jn 12:40-41, w Isa 6:8-11), and the Yahweh (LORD) of the Old Testament (Jn 19:37, w Zec 12:10).

Has power to forgive sins (Mt 1:21; 9:6; Mk 2:5; Lk 5:20; Col 3:13). Paul's apostleship from (Gal 1:1). Invoked with the Father and the Spirit in benedictions (Ro 1:7; 1Co 1:3; 2Co 1:2; Gal 1:3; Eph 1:2; 6:23-24; 1Th 1:1; 3:11; 2Th 1:1-2; 2:16-17; 2Ti 1:2). All power given to (Mt 28:17-18). Eternity ascribed to (Jn 1:1-2; 1Jn 1:1). *See below, Eternity of.* Is judge (2Co 5:10). *See below, Judge.*

Testimony Concerning His Deity—

By the Father (Jn 5:32, 34, 37; 6:27; 8:18; Ac 13:33; 1Jn 5:9), at his baptism (Mt 3:16-17; Mk 1:11; Lk 3:22), at his transfiguration (Mt 17:5; Mk 9:7; Lk 9:35; 2Pe 1:17).

By Jesus concerning himself (Jn 5:18, 31, 36; 8:18, 42; 10:33, 36, 38; 12:45; 14:11-13; 16:27-28; 17:5, 8, 24-25; 19:7), to Peter and other disciples (Mt 16:16-17; Mk 8:29-30; Lk 9:20-21), to the Jews (Mt 22:43-44; Jn 5:23; 10:30, 33, 36, 38; 12:45), to his disciples (Jn 16:27-28), to the restored blind man (Jn 9:35-37), to Philip (Jn 14:7-11, 20), to Caiaphas (Mt 26:63-64; Mk 14:61-62; Lk 22:67-70), to Pilate (Jn 18:36-37; 1Ti 6:13).

By the angel, to Joseph (Mt 1:23), to Mary (Lk 1:32, 35). John the Baptist (Jn 1:29-34; 5:33). John, the apostle (Jn 1:14, 18; 13:3; 1Jn 2:22-24). The disciples (Jn 16:30). Paul (Ac 9:20). The author of the epistle to the Hebrews (Heb 11:26). The Scriptures (Jn 5:39). Thomas (Jn 20:28). Demons (Mt 8:29; Mk 1:23-24; 3:11; 5:6-7; Mk 4:34, 41).

Eternity of:

Called everlasting Father (Isa 9:6). Was before creation (Jn 1:1-2, 15; 17:5, 24; Col 1:17; 2Ti 1:9). Was from the beginning (1Jn 2:13). Was from everlasting (Mic 5:2). Continues forever (Ps 102:24-27 w Heb 1:10-13; Ps 110:4; Eph 3:21; Heb 7:16, 24-25; Rev 5:13-14). The same yesterday and today and forever (Heb 13:8).

Exaltation of:

(Ps 2:8-9; 68:18; Eph 4:8). In glory (Mt 26:64;

Mk 16:19; Lk 22:69; 24:26; Jn 7:39; Ac 2:33-34; 3:20-21; 7:55-56; Ro 8:17, 34; Eph 1:20-22; 4:10; Col 3:1; 1Ti 3:16; Heb 1:3; 10:12-13; 12:2; 1Pe 3:22; Rev 3:21). As Lord of heaven and earth (Php 2:9-11; Col 2:15). As Savior (Ac 5:31). As priestly mediator (Heb 4:10, 14; 6:20; 7:26; 8:1; 9:24).

An Example:

Claimed himself (Mt 11:29; 20:28; Mk 10:43-45; Lk 22:26-27; Jn 10:4; 13:13-15, 34; 17:14, 18, 21-22; Rev 3:21). Referred to by Paul (Ro 8:29; 13:14; 15:2-7; 2Co 4:10; 8:9; 10:1; Gal 3:27; 6:2; Eph 4:13, 15, 24; 5:2; 6:9; Php 2:5-8; Col 3:10-11, 13; 1Th 1:6). Referred to by other apostles (Heb 3:1; 12:2-4; 1Pe 1:15; 2:21-24; 3:17-18; 1Jn 2:6; 3:1-3, 16; 4:17).

Faith in: *See Faith in Christ; Salvation, Conditions of.*

Faithfulness of:

(Isa 11:5; Lk 4:43; Jn 7:18; 8:29; 9:4; 14:3; 17:8; Heb 3:2; Rev 1:5; 3:14). In mediation (Heb 2:17).

Genealogy of: *See above, History of.*

Glorification of:

(Jn 7:39; 12:16; 17:1; Ac 7:55-56; Heb 8:1).

Head of the Church:

(Ps 118:22-23, w Mt 21:42-43, & Mk 12:10; Isa 28:16, w Eph 2:2-22, & 1Pe 2:6; Lk 20:17-18, w 1Pe 2:7; Jn 15:1-8; 1Co 3:11; Eph 1:22-23; 4:15; 5:23-32; Col 1:18; 2:10, 19; 3:11; Rev 2:2-28; 3:1, 7; 22:16).

Holiness of:

Foretold (Ps 45:7; Isa 11:4-5; Jer 23:5; Zec 9:9). Professed by himself (Jn 5:30; 7:18; 8:46; 14:30; Rev 3:7).

Testified to: By the angel to his mother (Lk 1:35). By demons (Mk 1:24; Lk 4:34). By the centurion at the Crucifixion (Lk 23:47). By Stephen (Ac 7:52). By Peter (Jn 6:69; Ac 3:14; 4:27-30; 1Pe 1:19; 2:22). By John (1Jn 2:1, 29; 3:5). By Paul (Ac 13:35; 2Co 5:21). By the author of Hebrews (Heb 1:9; 4:15; 7:26-28; 9:14).

Humanity of:

(Ps 22:22; Jn 1:14). Took on himself human nature (Php 2:7-8; Heb 2:9-10, 14-18). Was born of flesh (Isa 9:6; Mt 1:18-25; Lk 2:11-14; 1Jn 4:2; 2Jn 7).

Called: Seed of the woman (Ge 3:15; Gal 4:4), son of David (Mt 20:30-31; 21:9; 22:42; Mk 12:35; Lk 18:38), a prophet like Moses (Dt 18:15-19; Ac 3:22-23; 7:37).

Humility of:

(2Co 8:9; Php 2:7-8). Became a servant (Lk 22:27; Jn 13:5, 14). *See below, Meekness of.*

Impeccability of: *See above, Holiness of; below, Temptation of.*

Incarnation of:

(Jn 16:28; 1Ti 3:16). Foretold (Ge 3:15; Dt 18:15-18; Ps 2:7; Isa 7:14-16; 9:6; 11:1; Jn 7:42; Ac 13:33; Heb 1:5). Accomplished through the generation of the Holy Spirit (Mt 1:1, 16-18, 23; Lk 1:26-56). Was made a little lower than the angels (Heb 2:9, 14). Was made flesh (Lk 24:39;

Jn 1:14; 20:27; Ro 8:3; 1Co 15:47; 2Co 5:16; Gal 4:4; Php 2:7-8; Heb 1:3, 6; 2:9-18; 10:5; 1Jn 1:1-3; 4:2; 2Jn 7). Came in the lineage of Judah (Heb 7:14). Was of the seed of David (Mt 22:45; Ro 1:3; 9:5; Rev 22:16). Was the son of Mary (Mt 13:55; Lk 2:1-21).

See above, Humanity of; below, Relation of, to the Father.

Intercession of: *See below, Mediation of.*

Judge:

(Mt 3:12 w Lk 3:17; Mt 25:31-34; Ac 10:42; Ro 2:16; 1Co 4:4-5; 2Co 5:10; 2Ti 4:1, 8; Rev 2:23). Prophecy concerning (Isa 2:4 w Mic 4:3; Isa 11:3-4; Mic 5:1). Ordained of God (Jn 5:22; Ac 17:31). Righteous (2Ti 4:8).

Justice of:

(2Sa 23:3; Zec 9:9; Mt 27:19; Jn 5:30; Ac 3:14; 22:14).

King:

Prophecies concerning (Ge 49:10; 1Sa 2:10; 2Sa 7:12 w Ac 2:30; Ps 2:6; 18:43-44; 45:3-7; 72:5, 8, 11; 89:3-4, 19-21, 23, 27, 29, 36-37; 110:1-2; 132:11, 17-18; Isa 9:6-7; 22:22; 32:1; 52:7, 13; Jer 23:5; 30:9; 33:17; Eze 37:24-25; Da 2:35, 44; 7:13-14; Hos 3:5; Mic 5:2, 4; Zec 6:12-13; 9:9-10; Mt 2:2, 6; 21:5; 22:42-45; Lk 1:32-33; Ac 2:30). Appointed by the Father as King (Lk 22:29-30; Ac 2:30, 36 w 2Sa 7:12; Ac 5:31; Eph 1:20-22; Heb 2:7-8).

Authority of Jesus as King (Mk 2:28; Jn 5:27). Universal kingdom (Mt 11:27 w Lk 10:22; Mt 28:18; Lk 19:27; Jn 3:31, 33; 13:3; 17:2; Ro 9:5; 10:12; 14:9; Col 2:10; Heb 1:2-13; 2:7-8; 1Pe 3:22; Rev 3:7, 14, 21).

Dominion of Jesus, universal (Ac 10:36; 1Co 15:23-28; Eph 1:20-22; Php 2:9-11; Rev 1:5-7, 18; 11:15). Future glory of Jesus as King (Mt 19:28; 25:31-34; 26:64; Mk 14:62; Lk 22:69; Heb 10:12-13; Rev 5:13).

Kingship of: Avowed by himself (Mt 21:5; 27:11; Lk 23:2; Jn 18:36-37). Ascribed, by disciples (Lk 19:38; Jn 1:49; 12:13, 15; Ac 17:7). In superscription on the cross (Jn 19:12, 19). Symbolic statements concerning (Rev 5:5, 12; 6:2, 15-17; 14:14; 17:14; 19:11-12, 15-16).

See below, Lordship of.

Kingdom of:

Brings joy and gladness (Ps 46:4; Isa 25:6; 35; 52:9; 55:12). Brings peace (Ps 46:9; Isa 11:6-9). Is within us (Lk 17:21). Truth (Jn 18:37). Is not of this world (Jn 18:36).

Keys of (Mt 16:19). Glad tidings of (Lk 8:1). Mysteries of (Lk 8:10). Is not meat and drink (Ro 14:17).

Likened to—

A man who sowed good seed (Mt 13:24-30, 38-43; Mk 4:26-29). A mustard seed (Mt 13:31-32; Mk 4:30-31; Lk 13:18-19). Yeast (Mt 13:33; Lk 13:21). A treasure (Mt 13:44). A pearl (Mt 13:45). A net (Mt 13:47-50). A king who called his servants to account (Mt 18:23-35). A landowner (Mt 20:1-16). A king who made a marriage feast for his son (Mt 22:2-14; Lk 14:16-24). Ten virgins (Mt 25:1-13). A man who entrusted property to his servants (Mt 25:14-30; Lk 19:12-27).

Prophecies Concerning—

Its character: To enlighten (Jer 31:34; Heb 8:11). To bring peace (Ps 46:9; Isa 65:25; Mic 4:3-7). To bring salvation (Isa 62:11). To bring joy (Isa 25:6; 35:1-10; 42:1-7, 18-21; Lk 2:10). Shall be a river of salvation (Eze 47:1-12; Zec 14:8-9, 16, 20-21).

Will be forever (Isa 51:6, 8; Lk 1:33; Heb 1:8; 2Pe 1:11). Transforms (Isa 35:1-10; 55:12-13; 65:17-25). Future glory and greatness (Isa 49:22-23; Hag 2:7-9; Rev 21:9-27).

Universality of the kingdom (Ge 12:3; 22:18; 49:10; Ps 72:5, 8-11, 16-17, 19; 89:1-37; 113:3; Isa 9:6-7; 40:4-11; 42:1-7; 49:1-26; 52:10; 54:1-3; 59:19-21; Jer 3:14-19; Da 2:35, 44; 7:13-14, 18, 22, 27; Hab 2:14; Zec 9:1, 10; Mt 8:11; Lk 13:29-30; Rev 14:6). Unity of the kingdom (Jn 10:16).

Growth of the kingdom (Mt 13:31-33; Lk 13:21). Ends of earth shall turn to him (Ps 66:4; 86:9; Isa 2:2-4; 45:14; 60:1-9; Jer 3:17; 16:19-21; 33:16; Eze 17:22-23; Mic 4:1-4; Zep 2:11; Zec 2:10-11; 6:15; 8:20-23). Shall include all nations (Ps 2:8; 68:31-32; 110:4-6; Hos 2:23; Am 9:11-12; Mal 1:11).

Final triumph of the kingdom (Ge 3:15; Ps 2:9; Isa 11:1-13; Da 2:44; 7:9-14, 27; Mt 16:18; Ac 2:34-35; 1Co 15:24-28; Eph 1:10; Php 2:10-11; Heb 10:13; 12:23-24, 27-28; Rev 5:9-10, 13-14; 6:2; 11:15; 12:10; 19:11-21; 20:1-3).

Secular notions concerning: To restore the kingdom of Israel (Mk 11:9-10; Jn 6:14-15; Ac 1:6-7). Rank of princes in the kingdom of (Mt 20:20-23; Mk 10:35-40; Lk 9:46-48).

Love of:

(Ps 69:9; Rev 3:9, 19). Jesus' love compels us (2Co 5:13-14), surpasses knowledge (Eph 3:17-19).

Jesus' love for his disciples (Jn 10:3-4, 11, 14-16; 13:1, 23; 14:1-3, 18, 21, 27; 15:9-13, 15; 17:6-26; Ro 8:35, 37-39; 2Th 2:13). For children (Mt 19:13-15; Mk 10:13-14, 16; Lk 18:15-16). For his mother (Jn 19:26-27). For the lost (Isa 40:11; Mt 18:12-13; Mk 8:12; Lk 13:34).

Jesus' love exemplified: In renunciation (2Co 8:9; Php 2:6-8). In compassion (Isa 42:3; Mt 9:36; 14:14; 15:32; Lk 7:13; 22:31-32; Jn 11:5, 33-36; Ac 10:38; Heb 4:15). In his heart for others (Mt 23:37; Lk 23:28, 34; Jn 18:8-9). In his sacrifice (Gal 2:20; Eph 5:2, 25, 29-30; 1Jn 3:16; Rev 1:5). In his vicarious suffering (Isa 53:4; Mt 8:17; Ro 15:3). In redemption (Ps 72:14; Isa 63:9).

Lordship of:

The sovereignty of the Messiah, as conceived by Old Testament writers, seems best described by the word "King," but New Testament writers use the word "Lord." *See above, King.* Jesus said of himself, the Son of Man is Lord even of the Sabbath (Mt 12:8; Mk 2:28).

The student will find suggestions for profitable reflection in a study of the various forms of expression used by the authors of the epistles in

which they attribute Lordship to our Savior (Mt 12:8; Ac 2:36; Ro 1:7; 5:1, 11, 21; 6:23; 7:25; 8:39; 10:9; 13:14; 14:14; 15:6, 30; 16:20; 1Co 1:2-3, 7-10; 5:4; 6:11; 8:6; 9:1; 11:25; 12:3; 15:31, 57; 16:23; 2Co 1:2-3, 14; 4:5, 14; 8:9; 11:31; 13:14; Gal 1:3; 6:14, 18; Eph 1:2-3, 17; 3:11; 5:20; 6:23-24; Php 1:2, 11; 2:19; 3:20; 4:23; Col 1:3; 2:6; 3:17, 24; 1Th 1:1, 3; 4:1; 5:10, 24, 28; 2Th 1:1-2, 7, 12; 2:1, 8, 15-16; 3:6, 12, 18; 1Ti 1:2, 12; 6:3, 14; 2Ti 1:2; Phm 1, 3, 5, 25; Jas 1:1; 2:1; 1Pe 1:3; 3:15; 2Pe 1:2, 8, 14, 16; 2:20; 3:18; Jude 4, 18, 21, 25).

Mediation of:

(Jn 14:6, 14; 16:23-24, 26; 20:31; Ro 1:8; 5:1-2; 6:23; 1Co 6:11; 15:57; 2Co 1:20; Eph 3:12; 4:32; 5:20; Col 3:17; 1Ti 2:1, 3, 5; Heb 9:11-28; 13:15; 1Pe 2:5; 1Jn 2:1-2, 12).

As a priest (Ps 110:4; Zec 6:13; Heb 2:17; 3:1-2; 4:14-15; 5:5-6, 10; 6:19-20; 7:1, 3, 19, 21, 24-28; 8:1-2, 6; 9:11; 10:19-21). Through his sacrifice (Eph 2:13-18; Heb 10:11-12; 12:24).

Exemplified in his intercession (Isa 53:12; Lk 13:8-9; 22:31-32; 23:33-34; Jn 14:16; 17:9, 11, 15-17, 19-22; Ro 8:34).

See below, Priesthood of.

Meekness of:

(Mt 11:29; Mk 14:60-61; 15:3-5; 2Co 10:1; Php 2:8). Prophecies concerning (Ps 45:4; Isa 42:1-3; 50:5-6; 52:1, 14; 53:7; Mt 12:19-20; 21:5; Ac 8:32).

Exemplified in not resenting false accusation (Mk 2:6-11). In submitting to enemies (Mt 26:47-63; 27:12-14; Jn 8:48-50; Heb 12:2-3; 1Pe 2:23). In praying for enemies (Lk 23:34). In becoming a servant (Php 2:7).

See above, Humility of; Meekness.

Messiah:

Messianic Psalms (Ps 2:1-12; 67:1-7; 68:1-35; 69:1-36; 72:1-20; 96:1-13; 98:1-9; 110:1-7). Prophecies concerning the Messiah (Da 9:25-26; Ac 3:18-20).

Simeon's testimony to the Messiah (Lk 2:28-32). Andrew's belief in the Messiah (Jn 1:41, 45). Peter's confession of the Messiah (Mt 16:15-16; Mk 8:29; Lk 9:20; Jn 6:69). Was proclaimed as Messiah by apostles (Ac 9:22; 13:27; 17:2-3; 26:6-7, 22-23; 28:23; Ro 1:1-3; 1Co 15:3; 1Pe 1:10-11; 2Pe 1:16-18; 1Jn 5:6-9).

Jesus' own testimony to his messiahship (Mt 11:3-6; 26:63-64; Lk 24:27; Jn 4:25-26, 29, 42; 5:33, 36-37, 39, 46; 6:27; 8:14, 17-18, 25, 28, 56; 13:19).

Was called David's son (Mt 22:42-45; Mk 12:35-37; Lk 20:41-44). Is the anointed of God (Ps 2:2; Ac 4:26-27).

See also, King; Lordship of; below, Son of Man. See also, Messianic Hope.

Miracles of:

Water made wine (Jn 2:1-11).

First miraculous catch of fishes (Lk 5:1-11).

Demoniac in the synagogue healed (Mk 1:23-26; Lk 4:33-36).

Heals Simon's wife's mother (Mt 8:14-15; Mk 1:29-31; Lk 4:38-39).

Heals diseases in Galilee (Mt 4:23-24; Mk 1:34).

Miracles at Jerusalem (Jn 2:23).

Cleanses the leper (Mt 8:1-4; Mk 1:40-45; Lk 5:12-16).

Heals the paralytic (Mt 9:1-8; Mk 2:1-12; Lk 5:17-26).

Heals the crippled man (Jn 5:1-16).

Restores the withered hand (Mt 12:9-13; Mk 3:1-5; Lk 6:6-11).

Heals multitudes from Judah, Jerusalem, and coasts of Tyre and Sidon (Lk 6:17-19).

Heals the centurion's servant (Mt 8:5-13; Lk 7:1-10).

Heals demoniacs (Mt 8:16-17; Lk 4:40-41).

Raises the widow's son (Lk 7:11-16).

Heals in Galilee (Lk 7:21-22).

Heals a demoniac (Mt 12:22-37; Mk 3:20-30; Lk 11:14-15, 17-23).

Stills the tempest (Mt 8:23-27; Mk 4:35-41; Lk 8:22-25; Mt 14:32).

Healing of the diseased in the land of Gennesaret (Mt 14:34-36).

The demoniacs in Gadarenes healed (Mt 8:28-34; Mk 5:1-20; Lk 8:26-39).

Raises Jairus' daughter (Mt 9:18-19, 23-26; Mk 5:22-24, 35-43; Lk 8:41-42, 49-56).

Heals the woman with the issue of blood (Mt 9:20-22; Mk 5:25-34; Lk 8:43-48).

Opens the eyes of two blind men in the house (Mt 9:27-31).

A demon cast out and a mute man cured (Mt 9:32-33).

Five thousand fed (Mt 14:15-21; Mk 6:35-44; Lk 9:12-17; Jn 6:5-14).

Heals sick in Galilee (Mt 14:14).

Walking on the sea (Mt 14:22-33; Mk 6:45-52; Jn 6:14-21).

The daughter of the Syrian Phoenician healed (Mt 15:21-28; Mk 7:24-30).

Healing of the lame, blind, mute, and maimed, near the Sea of Galilee (Mt 15:30).

Four thousand fed (Mt 15:32-39; Mk 8:1-9).

One deaf and mute cured (Mk 7:31-37).

One blind cured (Mk 8:22-36).

Child healed (Mt 17:14-21; Mk 9:14-29; Lk 9:37-43).

Piece of money in the fish's mouth (Mt 17:24-27).

The ten lepers cured (Lk 17:11-19).

Opening the eyes of one born blind (Jn 9).

Raising of Lazarus (Jn 11:1-54).

Woman with the spirit of infirmity cured (Lk 13:10-17).

The dropsy cured (Lk 14:1-6).

Two blind men cured near Jericho (Mt 20:29-34; Mk 10:46-52; Lk 18:35-43).

The fig tree blighted (Mt 21:17-22; Mk 11:12-14, 20-24).

Healing of Malchus's ear (Lk 22:49-51).

Second catch of fishes (Jn 21:6).

Not particularly described (Mt 4:23-24; 14:14; 15:30; Mk 1:34; Lk 6:17-19; 7:21-22; Jn 2:23;

3:2). Resurrection (Mt 28:6; Mk 16:6; Lk 24:6; Jn 20:1-18). Holds the vision of his disciples, that they should not recognize him (Lk 24:16, 31, 35). His appearances and disappearances (Lk 24:15, 31, 36-45; Jn 20:19, 26). Opening the understanding of his disciples (Lk 24:45). His Ascension (Lk 24:51; Ac 1:9).

See Miracles.

Mission of:

(Isa 42:7; Mt 18:12-14; Lk 12:49-53; Jn 4:25, 34; 18:37). To fulfill the Law and the Prophets (Mic 5:2; Mt 5:17; Ro 10:4). To be Lord of all (Ro 14:9; 15:8-9; 2Co 5:15; Eph 4:10). To glorify the Father (Jn 17:4).

To preach the gospel (Isa 61:1; Mt 4:23; 9:13; Mk 1:38; Lk 4:18-19, 43; 5:31-32; 8:1). To preach repentance (Lk 5:30-32; 24:47; Ac 3:26; 5:31). To bring life (Jn 6:51; 10:10; 2Co 5:14, 21). To give light (Isa 9:2; 42:6; Lk 1:78-79; 2:30-32, 34; Jn 1:1-9; 9:39; 12:46-47).

To condemn sin (Ro 8:3-4). To die for sinners (Ro 5:6-8). To be propitiation for sin (Mt 20:28; Mk 10:45; Lk 24:26, 46; Jn 6:51; Ac 26:23; Ro 4:24-25; 5:6-8; 2Co 5:18; Gal 1:3-4; 4:4-5; Heb 2:9, 14; 9:26; 1Jn 3:5, 8; 4:8, 10). To purge sins (Zec 13:1; Mal 3:2-3). To give remission of sins (Ac 10:43; Ro 4:25). To destroy the works of the devil (Ge 3:15; Jn 3:8).

To bring salvation (Mt 1:21; 15:24; 18:12-14; Lk 19:10; Jn 3:13-17; Ro 14:15; 1Ti 1:15). To deliver from fear of death (Heb 2:15). To deliver from temptation (Heb 2:18). To comfort the contrite (Isa 61:1-3). To baptize with the Holy Spirit and with fire (Mt 3:11-12; Lk 3:16). To preach to spirits in prison (1Pe 3:19; 4:6, cf. Eph 4:9).

Names, Appellations, and Titles of:

Adam (1Co 15:45). Advocate (1Jn 2:1). Almighty (Rev 1:8). Alpha and Omega (Rev 22:13). Amen (Rev 3:14). Angel (Ge 48:16; Ex 23:20). Angel of his presence (Isa 63:9). Anointed (Ps 2:2). Apostle (Heb 3:1). Arm of the Lord (Isa 51:9-10). Atoning sacrifice (1Jn 2:2). Author of life (Ac 3:15). Author of salvation (Heb 2:10). Author and perfecter of our faith (Heb 12:2).

Banner for the peoples (Isa 11:10). Beginning and End (Rev 22:13). Blessed and only Ruler (1Ti 6:15). Branch (Jer 23:5; Zec 3:8). Bread of life (Jn 6:48). Bridegroom (Mt 9:15). Bright Morning Star (Rev 22:16).

Capstone (Mt 21:42). Carpenter (Mk 6:3). Carpenter's son (Mt 13:55). Chief Shepherd (1Pe 5:4). Child (Isa 9:6; Lk 2:27). Chosen one (Isa 42:1). Chosen by God (1Pe 2:4). Chosen and precious cornerstone (1Pe 2:6). Christ (Mt 1:16). The Christ (Mt 16:20; Mk 14:61, 62; Lk 9:20). Christ, a king (Lk 23:2). Christ Jesus (Ro 3:24; 8:1; 1Co 1:2, 30). Christ Jesus our Lord (1Ti 1:12; Ro 8:39). Christ of God (Lk 9:20). Christ of God, the Chosen One (Lk 23:35). Christ the Lord (Lk 2:11). Christ the power of God and the wisdom of God (1Co 1:24). Christ, the Son of God (Jn 11:27). Christ, the Son of the Blessed One (Mk 14:61). Commander (Isa 55:4). Commander of the

Lord's army (Jos 5:14). Consolation of Israel (Lk 2:25). Cornerstone (Eph 2:20). Counselor (Isa 9:6). Covenant for the people (Isa 42:6).

David (Jer 30:9). Deliverer (Ro 11:26). Desired of all nations (Hag 2:7). Doctor (Mt 9:12). Eternal life (1Jn 5:20). Everlasting Father (Isa 9:6). Exact representation of God's being (Heb 1:3).

Faithful and True (Rev 19:11). Faithful witness (Rev 1:5). Faithful and true witness (Rev 3:14). The First and the Last (Rev 1:17; 2:8; 22:13). Firstborn (Heb 1:6). Firstborn from the dead (Rev 1:5). Foundation (Isa 28:16). Fountain (Zec 13:1). Friend of tax collectors and sinners (Mt 11:19).

Gate (Jn 10:7). Gift of God (Jn 4:10). Glorious Lord Jesus Christ (Jas 2:1). Glory of Israel (Lk 2:32). God (Jn 20:28). God and Savior of Israel (Isa 45:15). God of all the earth (Isa 54:5). God over all, forever praised (Ro 9:5). God the One and Only (Jn 1:18). God with us (Mt 1:23). Good Shepherd (Jn 10:11, 14). Good Teacher (Mk 10:17). Great God and Savior (Tit 2:13). Great high priest (Heb 4:14). Great Shepherd of the sheep (Heb 13:20). Guarantee (Heb 7:22).

Head of every man (1Co 11:3). Head of the body, the church (Col 1:18). Head of the church (Eph 5:23). Heir of all things (Heb 1:2). High priest (Heb 4:15). Holiness (1Co 1:30). Holy One (Ps 16:10). Holy One of God (Mk 1:24). Holy One of Israel (Isa 41:14; 54:5). Holy and Righteous One (Ac 3:14). Holy servant Jesus (Ac 4:30). Our Hope (1Ti 1:1). Horn of salvation (Lk 1:69).

I am (Jn 8:58). Immanuel (Isa 7:14; Mt 1:23). Indescribable gift (2Co 9:15). Innocent man (Mt 27:19). Israel (Isa 49:3).

Jesus (Mt 1:21). Jesus Christ (Mt 1:1; Jn 1:17; 17:3; Ac 2:38; 4:10; 9:34; 10:36; 16:18; Ro 1:6; 2:16; 5:15, 17; 1Co 2:2; 2Co 1:19; 4:5; Gal 2:16; Php 1:11; 2:11; 2Ti 2:8; Heb 13:8; 1Jn 1:3; 2:1). Jesus Christ our Lord (Ro 5:21; 7:25; 1Co 1:9; Jude 25). Jesus Christ our Savior (Tit 3:6). Jesus of Nazareth (Mk 1:24; Lk 24:19). Jesus of Nazareth, King of the Jews (Jn 19:19). Jesus, the King of the Jews (Mt 27:37). Jesus the Son of God (Heb 4:14). Jesus, the Son of Joseph (Jn 6:42). Judge (Ac 10:42).

King (Mt 21:5). King of Israel (Jn 1:49). King of kings (1Ti 6:15; Rev 17:14). King of glory (Ps 24:7-10). King of the ages (Rev 15:3). King of the Jews (Mt 2:2). King over the whole earth (Zec 14:9).

Lamb (Rev 5:6, 8; 6:16; 7:9-10, 17; 12:11; 13:8; 14:1, 4; 15:3; 17:14; 19:7, 9; 21:9, 14, 22-23, 27). Lamb of God (Jn 1:29). Lawgiver (Isa 33:22). Leader (Isa 55:4). Life (Jn 14:6). Light, everlasting (Isa 60:20). Light of the world (Jn 8:12). Light for the Gentiles (Isa 42:6). Light, true (Jn 1:9). Living bread (Jn 6:51). Living Stone (1Pe 2:4). Lion of the tribe of Judah (Rev 5:5). Lord (Jn 20:28). Lord Almighty (Jas 5:4). Lord of all (Ac 10:36; Ro 10:12). Lord of lords (Rev 17:14; 19:16). Lord Our Righteousness (Jer 23:6). Lord God Almighty (Rev 15:3). Lord and Savior Jesus Christ (2Pe 1:11; 3:18). Lord Christ (Col 3:24). Lord Jesus (Ac 7:59; Col 3:17; 1Th 4:2). Lord

Jesus Christ (Ac 11:17; 15:26; 28:31; Ro 5:1, 11; 13:14). Lord mighty in battle (Ps 24:8). Lord of the dead and the living (Ro 14:9). Lord of the Sabbath (Mk 2:28). Lord's Christ (Lk 2:26). Lord, your holy one (Isa 43:15). Lord, your redeemer (Isa 43:14).

Man Christ Jesus (1Ti 2:5). Man of sorrows (Isa 53:3). Man who is close to me [the Lord] (Zec 13:7). Master (Mt 23:8). Mediator (1Ti 2:5). Messenger of the covenant (Mal 3:1). Messiah (Jn 1:41). Mighty God (Isa 9:6). Mighty One of Israel (Isa 1:24). Mighty one of Jacob (Isa 49:26). Mighty to save (Isa 63:1). Morning star (2Pe 1:19; Rev 22:16).

Nazarene (Mt 2:23).

Offspring of David (Rev 22:16). Offspring of the woman (Ge 3:15). The One and Only (Jn 1:14). One and only Son (Jn 3:16, 18). One he [the Father] loves (Eph 1:6). Only God our Savior (Jude 25). Overseer (1Pe 2:25).

Passover lamb (1Co 5:7). Perfecter of faith (Heb 12:2). Power of God (1Co 1:24). Physician (Lk 4:23). Precious cornerstone (Isa 28:16). Priest (Heb 7:17). Prince (Ac 5:31). Prince of Peace (Isa 9:6). Prophet (Dt 18:15, 18; Mt 21:11; Lk 24:19).

Rabbi (Jn 1:49). Rabboni (Jn 20:16). Radiance of God's glory (Heb 1:3). Ransom (1Ti 2:6). Redeemer (Isa 59:20). Resurrection and life (Jn 11:25). Redemption (1Co 1:30). Righteous Branch (Jer 23:5). Righteous Judge (2Ti 4:8). Righteous One (Ac 7:52; 22:14). Righteous servant (Isa 53:11). Righteousness (1Co 1:30). Rising sun (Lk 1:78). Rock (1Co 10:4). Rock that makes them fall (1Pe 2:8). Root of David (Rev 5:5; 22:16). Root of Jesse (Isa 11:10). Rose of Sharon (SS 2:1). Ruler (Mt 2:6; 1Ti 6:15). Ruler of God's creation (Rev 3:14). Ruler of the kings of the earth (Rev 1:5). Ruler over Israel (Mic 5:2).

Sacrifice (1Jn 2:2). Salvation (Lk 2:30). Sanctuary (Isa 8:14). Savior (Lk 2:11). Savior, Christ Jesus (2Ti 1:10). Savior Jesus Christ (Tit 2:13; 2Pe 1:1). Savior of the body (Eph 5:23). Savior of the world (1Jn 4:14). Scepter (Nu 24:17). Second man from heaven (1Co 15:47). Seed of Abraham (Gal 3:16). Servant (Isa 42:1). Servant of rulers (Isa 49:7). Serves in the sanctuary (Heb 8:2). Shepherd (Mk 14:27). Shepherd and Overseer of souls (1Pe 2:25). Shepherd, Chief (1Pe 5:4). Shepherd, good (Jn 10:11). Shepherd, great (Heb 13:20). Shepherd of Israel (Ps 80:1). Shiloh (Ge 49:10, ftn). Son he [God] loves (Col 1:13). Son of Abraham (Mt 1:1). Son of David (Mt 9:27). Son of the Father (2Jn 3). Son of God. *See Jesus the Christ, Son of God.* Son of Man. *See Jesus the Christ, Son of Man.* Son of the Blessed One (Mk 14:61). Son of the Most High (Lk 1:32). Star (Nu 24:17). Stone (Mt 21:42). Stone that causes men to stumble (1Pe 2:8). Sun of righteousness (Mal 4:2). Sure foundation (Isa 28:16).

Teacher (Jn 3:2). Tested stone (Isa 28:16). True God (1Jn 5:20). True vine (Jn 15:1). Truth (Jn 14:6).

Vine (Jn 15:1).

Way (Jn 14:6). Who is, who was, and who is to

come (Rev 1:4). Wisdom (Pr 8:12). Wisdom of God (1Co 1:24). Witness (Isa 55:4; Rev 1:5). Wonderful Counselor (Isa 9:6). Word (Jn 1:1). Word of God (Rev 19:13). Word of life (1Jn 1:1).

Yahweh. *See in list above: I am, Lord, and* LORD.

In His Name—

(1Co 6:11; Php 2:9; Col 3:17; Rev 19:16). Baptism (Mt 28:19; Ac 2:38). Life (Jn 20:31). Miracles performed (Ac 3:6; 4:10; 19:13). Prayer (Jn 14:13; 16:23-24, 26; Eph 5:20; Col 3:17; Heb 13:15). Preaching (Lk 24:47). Faith (Mt 12:21; Jn 1:12; 2:23). Remission of sins (Lk 24:47; Ac 10:43; 1Jn 2:12). Salvation (Ac 4:12; 10:43). Those who use his name must turn away from wickedness (2Ti 2:19).

See above, Intercession of; below, Priesthood of.

Obedience of:

Foretold (Ps 40:8; Isa 11:5-6; Heb 10:7-9). To his parents (Lk 2:51). To God (Lk 2:49; Jn 4:34; 5:30, 36; 6:38; 8:29, 46, 55; 9:4; 14:31; 15:10; 17:4).

Exemplified: In his baptism (Mt 3:15). Sufferings (Mt 26:39, 42; Mk 14:36; Lk 22:42; Heb 5:8). Death (Jn 19:30; Php 2:8).

Omnipotence of:

(Ps 45:3-5; 110:3; Isa 9:6; 40:10; 50:2-3; 63:1; Mt 6:7; 12:13, 28-29; 28:18; Mk 3:27; Lk 5:17; 9:1; 11:20-22; Jn 2:10; 5:21, 28-29; 10:17-18, 28; Php 3:20-21; Col 1:17; 2Th 1:9; 1Ti 6:16; Heb 1:3; 7:25; 2Pe 1:16; Rev 1:8; 3:7; 5:12).

Omnipresence of:

(Mt 18:20; 28:20; Jn 3:13; Eph 1:23).

Omniscience of:

(Col 2:3; Rev 2:18, 23; 5:5, 12). Manifested in his knowledge, of the Father (Mt 11:27; Jn 7:29). Knowledge of human hearts (Mt 9:4; 12:25; 17:27; 22:18; Mk 2:8; Lk 5:22; 6:8; 9:46-48; 11:17; 22:10-12 w Mk 14:13-15; Jn 1:48; 2:24-25; 4:16-19, 28-29; 5:42; 6:64; 13:11; 21:17). Knowledge of future events (Mt 24:25; Jn 13:1, 3, 10; 16:30, 32; 18:4; 21:6). The coin in the fish's mouth (Mt 17:27), the presence of schools of fish (Lk 5:4-7; Jn 21:6).

Our example:

(Jn 10:4; Heb 3:1-2; 1Jn 2:6; Rev 14:4). In meekness (Mt 11:29; Heb 12:2-4; 1Pe 2:21-24). Humility (Lk 22:26-27; Jn 13:13-15, 34; 2Co 10:1; Php 2:5-8). Ministering (Mt 20:28; Mk 10:43-45; 2Co 8:9, w 8:5-11; Gal 6:2). Loving others (Jn 13:34; Eph 5:2). Character (Ro 8:29; 15:2-3, 5, 7; 1Pe 1:15-16; 1Jn 3:1-3, 16; 4:17). Enduring suffering (1Pe 3:17-18).

Parables of:

The wise and foolish builders (Mt 7:24-27; Lk 6:47, 49).

The two debtors (Lk 7:41-47).

The rich fool (Lk 12:16-21).

The servants waiting for their lord (Lk 12:35-40).

Barren fig tree (Lk 13:6-9).

The sower (Mt 13:3-9, 18-23; Mk 4:1-9, 14-20; Lk 8:5-8, 11-15).

The weeds (Mt 13:24-30, 36-43).

Seed growing secretly (Mk 4:26-29).

Mustard seed (Mt 13:31-32; Mk 4:30-32; Lk 13:18-19).

Yeast (Mt 13:33; Lk 13:20-21).

Hid treasure (Mt 13:44).

Pearl of great price (Mt 13:45-46).

Fishing net (Mt 13:47-50).

Unmerciful servant (Mt 18:23-35).

Good Samaritan (Lk 10:30-37).

Friend at midnight (Lk 11:5-8).

Good shepherd (Jn 10:1-16).

Great supper (Lk 14:15-24).

Lost sheep (Mt 18:12-14; Lk 15:3-7).

Lost piece of money (Lk 15:8-10).

The prodigal and his brother (Lk 15:11-32).

The unjust steward (Lk 16:1-9).

Rich man and Lazarus (Lk 16:19-31).

Importunate widow (Lk 18:1-8).

Pharisee and tax collector (Lk 18:9-14).

Laborers in the vineyard (Mt 20:1-16).

The pounds (Lk 19:11-27).

The two sons (Mt 21:28-32).

Wicked farmers (Mt 21:33-44; Mk 12:1-12; Lk 20:9-18).

Marriage of the king's son (Mt 22:1-14).

Fig tree in leaf (Mt 24:32; Mk 13:28-29).

Man taking a far journey (Mk 13:34-37).

Ten virgins (Mt 25:1-13).

Talents (Mt 25:14-30).

The vine (Jn 15:1-5).

Passion of: *See below, Sufferings of.*

Possibility of Sinning: *See below, Temptation of.*

Perfections of:

(Col 2:3). Is the image of God (2Co 4:4; Col 1:15). All the fullness of the Father lived in him (Col 1:19; 2:9). Righteous (Isa 11:5; Jn 7:18; 2Co 1:19). Without deceit (Isa 53:9). Sinless (Mt 27:3-4; Ac 13:28; 2Co 5:21). Faithful (2Th 3:3; 2Ti 2:13; Heb 3:2). Full of grace and truth (Jn 1:14, 18; Col 2:3). Just in judgment (Jn 5:30).

Perfected through sufferings (Heb 2:10).

Perfections of typified (Lev 21:17-21).

Persecutions of: *See Persecution.*

Popularity of:

(Mt 4:24; 8:1; 13:2; 14:13, 35; 19:1-2; 21:8-11; Mk 1:33; 2:2; 3:7, 20; 5:21; 6:33, 55-56; 10:1; 11:8-10; 12:37; Lk 4:14-15, 42; 5:1; 9:11; 12:1; 19:35-38; Jn 6:15; 12:12-13, 19).

Power of:

(Ps 110:3; 1Co 1:24). Called Mighty God (Isa 9:6). Has all power (Mt 28:18; Jn 10:17-18, 28; 17:2; Php 3:20-21; 2Th 1:9; 1Ti 6:16; 2Pe 1:16; Rev 3:7; 5:12).

Manifested: In creation (Jn 1:3, 10; Col 1:16). Salvation of men (Heb 7:25). Upholding all things (Col 1:17; Heb 1:3). In forgiving sins (Mt 9:2, 6; Mk 2:5, 10; Lk 5:20, 24; Col 3:13). In healing diseases (Mt 8:3, 16; 9:6-7; 12:13; Mk 5:27-34; Lk 5:17; 6:19; Ac 10:38). Casting out demons (Mt 8:16; 12:28-29; Mk 3:27; Lk 11:20-22). Stilling the tempest (Mt 8:27). Giving the apostles power to heal (Mt 10:1; Mk 6:7; Lk 9:11). Resurrection (Jn 2:19; 10:17-18).

Prayers of:

(Mt 11:25-26; Lk 3:21; 11:1). In secret (Mt 14:23; Mk 1:35; 6:46; Lk 5:16; 6:12; 9:18, 28-29). At the grave of Lazarus (Jn 11:41-42). For Peter (Lk 22:32). For believers (Jn 17:1-26). In Gethsemane (Mt 26:36-39; Mk 14:32-35; Lk 22:42-44; Heb 5:7). On the cross (Mt 27:46; Lk 23:34, 46).

Preexistence of:

Was in the beginning (Jn 1:1-3; 1Jn 2:13-14; Rev 3:14). Came from heaven (Jn 3:13; 6:62; Php 2:5-7). Came from the Father (Jn 13:3; 16:28). Was before creation (Jn 17:5, 24; 2Ti 1:9; 1Jn 1:1-2; 1Pe 1:20). Maker of all things (Jn 1:3; 1Co 8:6; Col 1:15-17; Heb 1:1-2, 8-12; Rev 4:11). Was before Abraham (Jn 8:56-58). With the Israelites in the wilderness (1Co 10:4, 9; Jude 5).

Prescience of: *See above, Omniscience of.*

Priesthood of:

Appointed and called by God (Heb 3:1-2; 5:4-5), after the order of Melchizedek (Ps 110:4; Heb 5:6; 6:20; 7:15-17), superior to Aaron and the Levitical priests (Heb 7:11, 16, 22; 8:1-2, 6). Consecrated with an oath (Heb 7:20-21). Has an unchangeable priesthood (Heb 7:23, 28). Is of unblemished purity (Heb 7:26, 28), faithful (Heb 3:2). Needed no sacrifice for himself (Heb 7:27).

Offered himself as a sacrifice (Heb 9:14, 26). His sacrifice superior to all others (Heb 9:13-14, 23). Offered sacrifice but once (Heb 7:27). Made reconciliation (Heb 2:17). Obtained redemption for us (Heb 9:12). Entered into heaven (Heb 4:14; 10:12). Sympathizes with saints (Heb 2:18; 4:15). Intercedes (Heb 7:25; 9:24). Blesses (Nu 6:23-26; Ac 3:26). On his throne (Zec 6:13). Appointment of, an encouragement to steadfastness (Heb 4:14).

Typified: Melchizedek (Ge 14:18-20). Aaron and his sons (Ex 40:12-15).

Promises of, to his disciples:

Of everlasting life (Mt 19:28; Mk 10:29-30; Lk 18:29-30; 23:43; Jn 5:25-29; 6:54, 57-58; 12:25-26). Of power (Lk 24:49; Jn 7:38-39; Ac 1:4-8). Of the Counselor (Jn 14:16, 26; 15:26-27; 16:7-14). Of his mediatorship (Jn 16:23-24, 26).

Prophecies Concerning:

(Ge 3:15; 22:18; 26:4; 28:14; Isa 53:2-12; Mt 8:17; Gal 3:8, 16).

Described in Prophecy as—

The branch (Isa 11:1; Jer 23:5-6; 33:15; Zec 3:8; Ro 15:12). Capstone and Cornerstone (Ps 118:22; Isa 28:16). Banner for the peoples (Isa 11:10). Fountain for sin (Zec 13:1). King (Zec 9:9). Leader and commander (Isa 55:4-5). Light to the Gentiles (Isa 42:6-7; 49:6; 52:10, 15; Lk 2:31-32). Lord (Isa 40:3, 5; 35:2; Jer 31:34; Mal 3:1-3; Lk 3:4). God's chosen one (Isa 42:1). Priest (Ps 110:4). Prophet (Dt 18:15, 18; Ac 3:22-24). Redeemer (Isa 59:20). Ruler over Israel (Mic 5:2). Savior (Isa 62:10-11; Mt 1:21; Lk 1:31). Seed of

woman (Ge 3:15). Shepherd (Isa 40:11; Eze 34:23). Son of man (Da 7:13-14).

Future Glory and Power—

(Rev 19:11-12, 15). To have universal dominion (Ps 72:5, 8-11, 17, 19; Isa 2:2-4; 9:6-7; 60:1-9; Da 2:35, 44; 7:18, 22, 27; Mic 4:1-4). To be King of kings (Ps 72:5, 8-11, 17, 19; Rev 1:5-7; 11:15; 12:10; 17:14; 19:16; 20:4, 6). To sit at right hand of God (Mk 14:62; 1Pe 3:22). To be judge (Jude 14-15; Rev 2:23; 6:16-17; 14:14-16).

Prophet:

(Dt 18:15, 18; Mt 21:11, 46; Lk 7:16; 13:33; 24:19; Jn 4:19; 6:14; 7:40; 9:17; Ac 3:22-23; 7:37). Foretold (Isa 52:7; Na 1:15).

Anointed with the Holy Spirit (Isa 42:1; 61:1, w Lk 4:18; Jn 3:34). Reveals God (Mt 11:27; Jn 3:2, 13, 34; 17:6, 14, 26; Heb 1:1-2). Declared his doctrine to be that of the Father (Jn 8:26, 28; 12:49-50; 14:10, 24; 15:15; 17:8, 26). Foretold things to come (Mt 24:3-35; Lk 19:41-44). Faithful (Lk 4:43; Jn 17:8; Heb 3:2; Rev 1:5; 3:14). Abounded in wisdom (Lk 2:40, 47, 52; Col 2:3). Mighty in deed and word (Mt 13:54; Mk 1:27; Lk 4:32; Jn 7:46). Humble in his teaching (Isa 42:2; Mt 12:17-20). God commands us to hear (Dt 18:15; Ac 3:22). God will severely visit neglect of (Dt 18:15, 18-19; Ac 3:23; Heb 2:3).

Received:

Crowds attend his ministry (Mt 8:1; 13:2; 14:13, 35; 19:1-2; Mk 1:37, 45; 2:2, 15; 3:7, 20-21; 4:1; 5:21; 10:1; 11:18; 12:37; Lk 9:11; 12:1; 19:48; 21:38; Jn 6:2; 8:2).

Many believe on him (Mt 4:24; 21:8-11, 15; Mk 2:12; 6:55-56; 11:8-10; Lk 6:17-19; 7:16-17; 19:36-38, 47-48; 23:27; Jn 2:11, 23; 4:45; 8:30; 10:41-42; 11:45-48; 12:9, 11-13, 18-21, 42).

Authority of his teaching confessed (Mk 1:22; Lk 4:32; Jn 3:2; 7:46).

With astonishment and gladness (Mt 9:8, 27-28, 33; 13:54; 15:31; Mk 1:27; 2:12; 5:42; 7:37; Lk 4:36-37, 42; 5:26; 13:17; 18:43; Jn 7:31, 40-44; 9:17, 24-25, 29-30, 33; 11:37).

Instances of his being received: By Matthew (Mt 9:9), by Peter and other fishermen (Mk 1:16-20; Lk 5:3-11), by Philip (Jn 1:43, 45), by Nathanael (Jn 1:45-50), by Zacchaeus (Lk 19:1-10), by thief on the cross (Lk 23:40-42), by three thousand at Pentecost (Ac 2:41; 4:4).

Redeemer: *See below, Savior. See Redemption.*

Rejected:

(Lk 9:26; 10:16; 11:23; Heb 6:4-6; 1Pe 2:4, 7-8; 1Jn 2:22-23; 4:3; 2Jn 7).

Rejected by the Jews (Mt 13:54-58 w Isa 6:9-10; Mt 23:37; Mk 6:3-6; Lk 7:34; 13:34; 19:27, 42; 22:67; Jn 1:11; 5:38, 40, 43; 7:3-5, 12-13, 15, 25-27; 8:13, 21-22, 24, 45-47, 53; 9:16-17, 24; 10:20-21, 24, 33; 11:46-48; 12:37, 48; Ac 13:46; 18:5-6; 22:18; 28:24-25, 27; Ro 3:3; 9:31-32; 10:16, 21; 1Co 1:8). By Gadarenes or Gerasenes (Mt 8:34; Mk 5:17; Lk 8:37). By Gentiles (1Co 1:23). By followers (Jn 6:36, 60-66).

Prophecies concerning his rejection (Ps 2:1-3; 118:22; Isa 53:1-4; Lk 9:44). Foretold by himself

(Mt 11:16-19; Mk 9:12; Lk 4:23-29; 7:31-35; 17:25; Jn 15:18, 20, 24). In the parable of the feast (Lk 14:16-24 w Mt 22:2-14). In the parable of the house built on the sand (Mt 7:26; Lk 6:46-49).

Punishment for rejection of, foretold (Mt 8:12; 10:14-15, 33; 12:38-45; Mk 12:1-12; 16:16; Lk 20:9-18; 2Ti 2:12; Heb 6:6; 10:29; 2Pe 2:1).

Relation of, to the Father:

(Ps 110:1; Mt 11:27; 1Th 5:18; Heb 2:9).

Called God his Father (Mt 20:23; 26:39; Mk 13:32; Rev 2:27).

With God in the beginning (Jn 1:1-2, 14). Was sent by God (Jn 3:34-35; 4:34; 6:27, 32-33, 38-40, 44-46; 7:16, 28-29, 33; 8:16, 19, 28-29, 38, 40, 42, 49, 54-55; 9:4; 11:41-42; 12:44, 49-50; 17:1-10, 24-26; 1Co 1:30; Heb 3:2; 1Pe 2:4, 23; 1Jn 4:9-10, 14). Endued with the Holy Spirit (Isa 42:1; 61:1; Mic 5:4; Ac 10:38).

Is the Son of God (Jn 5:19-26, 37, 45; Ro 8:32; 15:6; Heb 1:2-3; 5:5-10; 2Pe 1:17). Is one with the Father (Jn 10:18, 25, 30, 32-33, 36-38; 14:7, 9-14, 20, 24; 15:23-26). Is subject to the Father (Ps 110:1; Mk 10:40; Jn 20:17; Ac 2:22, 33, 36; 3:13, 26; 4:27; 1Co 15:24, 27-28). Is the image of God (2Co 4:4, 6; Php 2:6; Col 1:15, 19).

God raised him from the dead (Ac 13:37; Ro 1:4; Eph 1:17, 20-22; 1Pe 1:21). Ascended to the Father (Lk 24:51; Jn 16:5, 10, 28; Ac 1:9-11; Rev 3:12, 21).

See above, Deity of; Humanity of; Divine Sonship of.

Resurrection of:

Prophecies concerning (Ps 2:7; 16:9-10; Isa 55:3; Ac 13:13-34). Foretold by himself (Mt 12:40; 16:4, 21; 17:23; 20:19; 26:32; 27:52-53, 63; Mk 8:31; 9:9-10; 10:34; 14:58; Lk 9:22; 18:33; 24:7, 46; Jn 2:19, 21-22).

Certified by angels (Mt 28:6-7; Mk 16:6-7; Lk 24:5-7). Mary Magdalene (Mt 28:1-8; Mk 16:10; Lk 24:10; Jn 20:18). Clopas and his fellow disciple on the road to Emmaus (Mk 16:12-13; Lk 24:13-35). Luke (Ac 1:3, 22). Peter (Ac 2:24, 31-32 w Ps 16:9-10; Ac 3:15; 4:10, 33; 5:30-32; 10:40-41; 1Pe 1:3, 21; 3:18, 21). Paul (Ac 13:30-34 w Ps 2:7; Ac 17:2-3, 31; 26:23; 26:26; Ro 1:4; 4:24-25; 5:10; 6:4-5, 9-10; 8:11, 34; 1Co 6:14; 15:3-8, 12-19; 15:20-23; 2Co 4:10-11, 14; 5:15; 13:4; Gal 1:1; Eph 1:20; Php 3:10; Col 1:18; 2:12; 1Th 1:10; 4:14; 2Ti 2:8). The author of Hebrews (Heb 13:20). John (Rev 1:5, 18). Appeared to the eleven apostles after his resurrection (Mk 16:14; Lk 24:36-51; Jn 20:19-29).

Rose for our justification (Ro 4:25). Rose for our salvation (Ro 5:10; 10:9). An earnest of the general resurrection (Ro 6:5; 1Co 6:14; 15:21-23; 2Co 4:14; 1Th 4:14; 1Pe 1:3). The theme of apostolic preaching (Ac 2:24, 31-32; 3:15; 4:10, 33; 5:30-32; 10:40-41; 17:2-3).

See Resurrection.

Reticence of:

(Isa 53:7; Mt 26:63; 27:12, 14; Mk 14:61; 15:4-5; Jn 19:9; 1Pe 2:23).

Revelation by:

Concerning his kingdom (Mt 8:11-12; 10:23, 34; 13:24-50; 16:18, 28; 21:43-44; 24:14; Mk 9:1; 16:17-18; Lk 9:27; 12:40-53; 13:24-35; 17:20-37; Jn 4:21, 23; 5:25-29; 6:39, 54; 12:35; 13:19; 14:29; 16:4). His rejection by the Jews (Mt 21:33-44; Lk 17:25). His betrayal (Mt 26:21, 23-25). His crucifixion (Jn 3:14; 8:28; 12:32, w Lk 24:6-7). Judgments upon the Jews (Mt 23:37-39). The destruction of the temple, and Jerusalem (Mt 24; Mk 13; Lk 19:41-44). The destruction of Capernaum (Mt 11:23; Lk 10:15).

Concerning persecutions of Christians (Mt 23:34-36). His being forsaken by his disciples (Jn 16:32). Lazarus (Jn 11:4, 11, 23, 40). Peter (Jn 21:18-23). Fame of the woman who anointed his head (Mt 26:13; Mk 14:8-9). False Christs (Mt 24:4-5, 23-26; Mk 13:5-6, 21-23; Lk 17:23-24; 21:8). Things to come (Rev 1:1).

Concerning his death and resurrection (Mt 12:39-40; 16:21; 17:12, 22-23; 20:18-19; 21:33-39; 26:2, 18, 21, 23-24, 45-46; 27:63; Mk 8:31; 9:31; 10:32-34; Lk 9:22-24; 17:25; 18:31-33; 22:15, 37; Jn 2:19; 10:15, 17; 12:7, 23, 32; 13:18-27; 14:19; 16:20, 32). His ascension (Jn 7:33-34; 8:21; 13:33; 16:10, 16).

Righteousness of: *See above, Holiness of.*

Salvation by: *See Salvation.*

Savior:

(Mt 1:21; Ac 5:31; 13:23, 38-39, 47; 15:11; 16:31; 1Co 1:30; 15:57; Eph 5:23; Php 3:20; 1Ti 1:1, 15; 2Ti 1:9-10, 12; 2:10; 3:15; Tit 1:4; Heb 2:3; 5:9; 2Pe 1:11; 2:20; 1Jn 3:5; 4:9, 14; 5:11-13).

Savior through his death (Ro 3:25; 4:25; 5:1, 6, 8-10; Gal 1:4; 2:20; Eph 2:13-18, 20; 5:2, 25-26; Col 1:12-14; 1Th 1:10; 5:9-10; Tit 2:13-14; 1Pe 1:18-19; 3:18; 1Jn 4:10). Through his resurrection (Ac 3:26; Ro 10:9; 1Co 15:17; 1Pe 3:21).

Savior by his intercession (Heb 7:22, 25). By redemption (Ro 3:24). By reconciliation (Ro 5:15, 17-19, 21; 2Co 5:18-19, 21; Eph 2:7, 13-18, 20; Heb 2:17).

The only Savior (Ac 4:12; 1Co 3:11).

Prophecies concerning him as Savior (Ps 72:4, 12-14, 17; Isa 42:6-7; 49:6, 8-9, 16-17; 59:20; 61:1-3; Zec 9:9; Mal 4:2; Lk 1:68-77; 4:18-19).

Illustrated: By parables of lost sheep and lost coin (Mt 18:12-13; Lk 15:1-10).

Testified to by angels (Lk 2:11). By Simeon (Lk 2:30-32). By himself (Mt 9:12-13; Lk 5:31-32; 19:10; Jn 5:33-34, 40; 6:27, 32-33, 35, 37, 39, 51, 53-58; 7:37-39; 8:12; 9:5, 39; 10:7, 9-11, 14-16, 27-28; 11:25-26; 12:47; 14:6; 17:2-3, 12). By John (Jn 1:29). By the people of Sychar (Jn 4:42). By the heavenly host (Rev 5:5-14).

See above, Death of; Purpose of His Death.

Second Coming:

(Mt 26:64; Jn 14:28-29; 21:22; Ac 1:11; 3:20-21; 1Co 11:26; Php 3:20-21; 1Th 1:10; 2:19; 3:13; 4:15-17; 2Th 2:1-5; 2:8; 1Ti 6:14-15; Tit 2:13; 2Pe 3:3-4).

At an unexpected time (Mt 24:3, 27, 30-31, 36-39, 42-44; 25:6, 10, 13, 19; Mk 13:1-37; Lk 12:37-40; 17:22-30; 21:5-35; 1Th 5:2-3, 23; 2Pe 3:8-14; Rev 16:15; 22:20).

Coming in heavenly glory (Mt 16:27; 25:31; Mk 8:38; 13:26-27; 14:62; Lk 9:26; 21:27).

Coming to judge the world (Mt 16:27; 25:31-46; Lk 19:12-13, 15; 1Co 1:7-8; 4:5; 2Th 1:7-10; 2Ti 4:1; Rev 22:12).

Coming to receive his saints (Jn 14:3, 18; 1Co 15:23; Col 3:4; 2Th 1:10; 2Ti 4:8; Heb 9:28; 1Pe 5:4; 1Jn 3:2).

Exhortations in view of his coming (Jas 5:7-9; 1Pe 1:7, 13; 4:13; 1Jn 2:28; Rev 3:11).

Shepherd:

Jesus the true shepherd: Foretold (Ge 49:24; Isa 40:11; Eze 34:23; 37:24). The chief (1Pe 5:4). The good (Jn 10:11, 14). The great (Mic 5:4; Heb 13:20).

His sheep he knows (Jn 10:14, 27). He calls (Jn 10:3). He gathers (Isa 40:11; Jn 10:16). He guides (Ps 23:3; Jn 10:3-4). He feeds (Ps 23:1-2; Jn 10:9). He cherishes tenderly (Isa 40:11). He protects and preserves (Jer 31:10; Eze 34:10; Zec 9:16; Jn 10:28). He laid down his life for (Zec 13:7; Mt 26:31; Jn 10:11, 15; Ac 20:28). He gives eternal life to (Jn 10:28).

Typified: David (1Sa 16:11).

Son of God:

Acclaimed by God (Ps 2:4 w Ac 13:13; Ps 89:26-27; Mt 3:17; 17:5; Mk 1:11; 9:7; Lk 3:22; 9:35; 2Pe 1:17).

Proclaimed by angels (Lk 1:32, 35; Rev 2:18).

Claimed by Christ (Mt 10:40; 11:27; 15:13; 18:10, 19; 20:23; 21:37; 26:53, 63-64; 27:43; Mk 14:61-62; Lk 10:22; 20:13; 22:29, 70; Jn 5:17-37; 6:27, 38, 40, 46, 57, 69; 7:17, 28-29; 8:16, 19, 26-29, 38-42, 49, 54; 9:35-37; 10:15-18, 29-30, 36-38; 11:4, 27, 41; 12:49-50; 14:7-13, 16, 20, 24, 28, 31; 15:1, 8-10, 23-24; 16:5, 15, 27-28, 32; 17:1; 20:17, 21, 31). As equality with the Father (Mt 10:40; 11:27; Lk 10:22; Jn 1:1-2; 8:16, 19; 10:15-18, 29-30, 36-38; 14:7-13, 16, 20, 24, 28, 31; 15:23-24; 16:15).

Sonship recognized by the disciples (Mt 14:33; 16:15-17). By Peter (Mt 16:15-17). By the centurion (Mt 27:54; Mk 15:39). By Nathanael (Jn 1:49-50). By Martha (Jn 11:27). By Satan, who tempted him (Mt 4:3, 6; Lk 4:3, 9). By demons (Mk 3:11; 5:7; Lk 4:41; 8:28).

Claim to sonship recognized by the Jews (Mt 27:43; Jn 19:7). By the high priest (Mk 14:61-62).

Testified to by Mark (Mk 1:1). By Luke (Ac 3:13). By John (Jn 1:1-2, 14, 18, 34; 3:16-18, 34-36; 13:3; 1Jn 1:7; 2:22-24; 3:8, 23; 4:9-10, 14; 5:5, 9-10, 13, 20; 2Jn 3). By Paul (Ro 1:3-4, 9; 8:3, 29, 32; 1Co 1:9; 15:24, 27-28; 2Co 1:3, 19; Gal 1:16; 4:4; Eph 1:3; 3:14; Col 1:3, 15, 19; 3:17; 1Th 1:10). In Hebrews (Heb 1:1-3, 5; 4:14; 5:5, 8; 6:6; 7:3; 10:29).

Belief in, basis of eternal life (Jn 1:1-2, 12; 3:16-18, 34-36; 6:40; 20:31; 1Jn 2:22-24; 3:23; 5:5,

9-10, 13, 20), for growth and purity (Jn 15:1, 8-10; 1Jn 1:7).

Denial of, basis of antichrist (1Jn 2:22-24).

See above, Deity of; Relation of, to the Father. See Son of God.

Son of Man:

Used in a messianic sense (Da 7:13-14).

Used by Jesus: Of himself (Mt 11:19, 27; 16:13; Mk 14:21, 41; Lk 6:22; 7:34; 18:31; Jn 1:51; 3:13). In a messianic sense, of his coming (Mt 10:23; 16:27-28; 24:27, 30, 37, 44; 25:13, 31; Mk 13:26; Lk 9:26; 12:40; 17:22, 24, 26, 30; 18:8; 21:27), his kingdom (Mt 16:28; 19:28; Mk 8:38; 14:62), his judgment (Mt 24:29-30; Mk 8:38; Lk 9:26; 12:8, 10; 21:36), his lordship or deity (Mt 12:8; 13:37, 41; 16:13, w 16:16, 27-28; 19:28; 24:27; Mk 2:28; Lk 6:5; 12:8, 10; 17:22, 24; 21:36; 22:69; Jn 12:23; 13:31), his suffering and death (Mt 12:40; 17:9, 12, 22; 20:18, 28; 26:2, 24-25; Mk 8:31; 9:9, 12, 31; 10:33-34, 45; 14:21, 41; Lk 9:22, 44; 11:30; 17:22-26; 18:31; 22:22, 48; 24:7; Jn 3:14; 8:28; 12:23; 13:31), his resurrection (Mt 12:40; 17:9, 22-23; 20:18-19; Mk 8:31; 9:9, 31; 10:33-34; Jn 6:62; 12:23; 13:31).

Of himself, as the supreme human (Mt 8:20; 12:32), a servant of mankind (Mt 20:28; Mk 10:45; Lk 9:56, 58), the forgiver of sins (Mt 9:6; Mk 2:10; Lk 5:24; 12:10), the Redeemer (Mt 18:11; 20:28; Lk 12:8; 19:10; 6:27, 53).

Used by the angel at the empty tomb, in quoting Christ (Lk 24:7); Stephen, in his vision of Jesus (Ac 7:56); John, in his vision of Jesus (Rev 1:13; 14:14).

Synonymous with *Christ*, as used by, Caiaphas the high priest (Mk 26:63, w 26:65; Mt 14:61-62), the religious leaders (Lk 22:70, w 22:66-71, w 23:35), the people in questioning him (Jn 12:34).

The title is a reference to the human nature of Jesus, designating him as the God-Man (Mt 8:20; 12:32).

See Son of Man.

Sovereignty of: *See above, King; Lordship of.*

Sufferings of:

Foretold: By the psalmist (Ps 22:6-8, 11-13, 17-21, w Mt 27:35 & Mk 15:24 & Lk 23:34 & Jn 19:23-24; Ps 69:7-9, 20), by prophets (Isa 50:6; 52:13-14; 53:1-12, w Mt 26:67 & 27:26 & Lk 22:37 & Jn 12:38; Mic 5:1; Zec 11:12-13; Lk 24:26, 46; 1Pe 1:11), by himself (Mt 16:21; 17:12, 22-23; 20:17-19; Mk 8:31; 9:12; 10:32-34; Lk 9:22; 18:31-33; Jn 3:14; 13:21).

In Gethsemane (Mt 26:38-45; Mk 14:34-39; Lk 22:42-44; Jn 18:11). In Pilate's judgment hall (Mt 27:24-30; Mk 15:15-20; Jn 19:16-18). At his crucifixion (Mt 27:31-50; Mk 15:34, 36; Lk 23:33-46; Jn 19:28).

Apostolic teaching concerning his suffering (Ac 3:18; 17:3; 2Co 1:5; Php 2:8; 3:10; Heb 2:9; 4:15; 5:7-8; 12:2-3; 1Pe 1:11; 2:21-23; 3:18; 4:1, 13; Rev 5:6; 19:13).

See above, Death of.

Sympathy of: *See above, Compassion of, Love of.*

Teacher:
(Mt 5:1-2; Jn 7:46; Ac 1:1). From God (Jn 3:2).
Taught with authority (Mt 7:29; 23:8; Mk 1:22).
Without respect of persons (Mt 22:16; Mk 12:14;
Lk 20:21). By the lake shore (Mk 4:1). In cities
and villages (Mt 11:1; Mk 6:6; Lk 23:5). In synagogues (Mt 4:23; Mk 1:21; Lk 4:15; 6:6). In the
temple (Mt 21:23; 26:55; Mk 12:35; Lk 21:37; Jn
8:2). In the wilderness (Mk 6:34).

Temptation of:
(Lk 22:28). By the devil (Mt 4:1-11; Mk 1:12-13;
Lk 4:1-13).
In all points as we are (Heb 4:15).

Typified:
In offerings (Ge 4:4; 8:20; 22:13; Ex 12:5-7;
24:5; 29:36-37; Lev 1:4, 10-12; 3:6, 12; 4:3-7,
14-18, 20, 23-25, 28-30, 32-34; 5:6-11, 16, 18;
6:6-7; 7:2; 8:14-15, 18-19, 22-24; 9:2, 7-9, 18;
12:6-8; 14:12-14, 25, 30-31; 15:15, 29-30; 16:3, 5,
9, 11, 14-16, 21-22; 19:21-22; 22:18-19; 23:12,
18-19, 27-28; Nu 6:10-11, 14, 16-17; 8:8, 12;
15:24-25, 27; 28:3-4, 9, 11, 15, 19, 22-23, 27, 30;
29:5, 8, 11, 13, 16-34, 38; 1Ch 29:21; 2Ch 7:5;
29:21-24; Ezr 6:17, 20; 8:35; Eze 43:18-27; 45:15,
18-23).
In the Passover (Ex 12:3, 5; Nu 28:16). In the
cornerstone (Isa 28:16; Mt 12:10-11).
In David (Eze 34:23-24; 37:24-25; Hos 3:5).
Solomon (Ps 72). Hezekiah (Isa 32:1).

Unchangeable: (Heb 13:8).

Union of, With the Righteous: See Righteous,
Union of, with Christ.

Wisdom of:
(Mk 6:2; Lk 2:40, 46-47, 52; Jn 7:15). See above,
Omniscience.

Worship of:
(1Co 1:2; 2Co 12:8-9; Php 2:10-11). John's
vision of (Rev 5:8-9, 12-14; 7:10).
Worship commanded (Jn 5:23; Heb 1:6).
Instances of: By the wise men (Mt 2:2). By a
certain ruler (Mt 9:18). By the disciples (Mt
14:33). By the Canaanite woman (Mt 15:25). By a
leper (Mt 8:2). By women after his resurrection
(Mt 28:9). By the eleven disciples after his resurrection (Mt 28:17; Lk 24:52). By the multitudes
(Mk 11:9-10 w Mt 21:9). By Simon Peter (Lk
5:8). By the blind man whom Jesus healed (Jn
9:38). By evil spirits (Mk 3:11). By a demon-possessed man (Mk 5:6-7). By Stephen (Ac 7:59-60).
By Paul (1Ti 1:12; 2Pe 3:18).

Zeal of:
For God's house (Lk 2:49; Jn 2:17; Ps 69:9). In
obedience to God (Jn 4:32, 34; 9:4; Ro 15:3). In
doing good (Ac 10:38). In preaching the gospel
(Mt 4:23; 9:35; Mk 6:6; Lk 4:43 w Mk 1:38; 8:1).
In giving himself as a sacrifice (Lk 9:51; 12:50;
13:32-33; 1Ti 6:13).

JESUS, JUSTUS See Justus, 3.

JETHER [3858, 3859] (abundance).
1. Jethro is the father-in-law of Moses (Ex 4:18).

2. Gideon's eldest son (Jdg 8:20-21).
3. Father of Amasa (2Sa 17:25; 1Ch 2:17).
4. Judahite (1Ch 2:32).
5. Judahite (1Ch 4:17).
6. Asherite, same as Ithran (1Ch 7:37, w 7:38).

JETHETH [3867]. Edomite chieftain (Ge
36:40; 1Ch 1:51).

JETHLAH See Ithlah.

JETHRO [3858, 3861] (remainder KB). A
priest of Midian and father-in-law of Moses (Ex
3:1), personal name probably Reuel (Ex 2:18;
3:1), father of Zipporah, whom Moses married
(Ex 3:1-2), advised Moses (Ex 18:14-24).

JETUR [3515]. Son of Ishmael and descend-
ants (Ge 25:15; 1Ch 1:31), Itureans of NT times.

JEUEL [3590] (God [El] has preserved).
1. Judahite (1Ch 9:6).
2. Levite (2Ch 29:13).
3. Leader in Ezra's company (Ezr 8:13).

JEUSH [3593] (perhaps may God aid).
1. Son of Esau (Ge 36:5).
2. Benjamite (1Ch 7:10).
3. Gershonite Levite (1Ch 23:10-11).
4. Descendant of Jonathan (1Ch 8:39).
5. Son of Rehoboam (2Ch 11:19).

JEUZ [3591] (he comes to help BDB; possibly
encouraged IDB). Head of a Benjamite family
(1Ch 8:10).

JEWEL, JEWELRY [74, 2717, 2719,
3016, 3998, 6344+, 6736, 7382, 3345, 5992]. Articles of jewelry in OT times: diadems, bracelets,
necklaces, anklets, rings for fingers, gold nets for
hair, pendants, amulets and pendants with magical
meanings, jeweled perfume and ointment boxes,
crescents for camels; used for personal adornment
and utility and for religious festivals. Not much
said about jewelry in NT; most condemnatory (1Ti
2:9; Jas 2:2). The New Jerusalem is adorned with
jewels (Rev 21:19).
See Minerals of the Bible, 1; Stones.

JEWS [*3373, 3374, 10316, 2678, 2679, 2680,
2681+, 4364] (from Judah). A corrupted form of
Judah, and applied to the people of the kingdom of
Judah and Benjamin (2Ki 16:6; 25:25; 2Ch
32:18). After the dissolution of the kingdom of
Israel, the name was applied to all Israelites as
well as to those of the two tribes (Mt 27:11; Ac
2:5).
Sins that led to the Captivity of (Isa 1:4-25; 2:6-
10; 3:9; 59:2-15; 65:2-7; Jer 5:1; 6:21-28; 44:1-3;
Eze 5:6; 12:2; 16:2, 15-47, 57-63). See the book of
Jeremiah, which deals chiefly with the sins of and
the corrective judgments of God to be inflicted
upon.
Captive in Babylon (2Ki 24:1-20; 25:1, 21).
Haman's plot against (Est 3:6-15). Feast of Purim

instituted to commemorate their deliverance from Haman's plot (Est 9:26-32).

The proclamation of Cyrus authorizing their return to the land of Canaan (2Ch 36:22-23; Ezr 1:2-4), and of Artaxerxes (Ezr 7:11-26).

After the Captivity:

Return from Babylon (Ezr 7:1-9; 8:31-32). Lists of those who returned from Babylon (Ezr 2:1-67; 8:1-20; Ne 7:6-69; 12:1-21). Rebuild the temple (Ezr 3:8-13). Rebuilding suspended during the reign of Artaxerxes (Ezr 4:1-24). Resumption of the rebuilding interfered with by Tattenai, governor of the province, by protest followed by a letter to Darius (Ezr 5). Darius' reply to Tattenai authorizing the rebuilding of the temple; temple completed (Ezr 6:1-15).

Vessels of the temple, that were taken to Babylon by Nebuchadnezzar, returned by command of Cyrus (Ezr 1:7-11; 6:5). Liberality of Artaxerxes toward the temple (Ezr 7:14-23).

Made marriages among the Canaanites: Ezra instituted reforms (Ezr 10). Rebuilt the walls of Jerusalem under proclamation of Artaxerxes (Ne 2; 3; 4; 5; 6). Walls dedicated (Ne 12:27-43).

Mission of Jesus to (Mt 10:5-6; 15:24; Mk 7:27). Some accept Jesus (Jn 2:23; 10:42; 11:45; 12:11; Ac 21:20). Others disbelieve in Jesus (Mt 13:5-8; Jn 5:38, 40, 43; 6:36; 12:37). Reject Jesus (Lk 13:34; 17:25; Jn 1:11). Crucify Jesus. *See Crucifixion.* Devout, among them (Ac 2:5). Spurned Paul's preaching (Ac 13:46; 18:5-6; 28:24-27). Persecuted Paul (Ac 9:22-23; 13:50; 20:3, 19; 23:12-30; 2Co 11:24). Entrusted with the oracles of God (Ac 7:38; Ro 3:1-2).

Prophecies Concerning:

Their rejection of the Messiah (Isa 49:5, 7; 52:14; 53:1-3; Zec 13; Mt 21:33-39; 22:1-5).

War and other judgments (Isa 3; 4:1; 5; 6:9-13; 7:17-25; 8:14-22; 10:12; 22:1-14; 28:14-22; 29:1-10; 30:1-17; 31:1-3; 32:9-14; Jer 1:11-16; 4:5-31; 6; 7:8-34; 8; 9:9-26; 10:17-22; 11:9-23; 13:9-27; 14:14-18; 15:1-14; 16; 17:1-4; 18:15-17; 19; 20:5; 21:4-7; 22:24-30; 25:8-38; 28; 34; 37; 38:1-3; 42:13-22; 43-45; La 5:6; Eze 4; 5; 11:7-12; 12; 15-17; 19; 22:13-22; 23:22-35; 24; 33:21-29; Da 9:26-27; Joel 2:1-17; Am 2:4-5; Mic 3; 4:8-10; Hab 1:6-11; Zep 1; Zec 14:1-3; Mal 4:1; Mt 21:33-45; 23:35-38; 24:2, 14-42; Mk 13:1-13; Lk 13:34-35; 19:43-44; 21:5-25; 23:28-31; Rev 1:7).

Dispersion of (Isa 24:1; Jer 9:16; Hos 9:17; Joel 3:6, 20; Am 9:9; Eze 4:13; 5:10, 12; 20:23; 36:19; Da 9:7).

Blessing and restoration of (Isa 1:25-27; 2:1-5; 4:2-6; 11:11-13; 25; 26:1-2, 12-19; 27:13; 29:18-24; 30:18-26; 32:15-20; 33:13-24; 35; 37:31-32; 40:2, 9; 41:27; 44; 49:13-23; 51; 52:1-12; 60; 61:4-9; 62; 66:5-22; Jer 3:14-18; 4:3-18; 12:14-16; 23:3; 24:1-7; 30:3-22; 32:36-44; 33; 44:28; Eze 14:22-23; 16:60-63; 20:40-41; 36:1-38; 37:12, 21; Da 11:30-45; 12:1; Joel 3; Am 9:9-15; Ob 17-21; Mic 2:12-13; 5:3; Zep 2:7; Zec 1:14-21; 2; 8; 10:5-12; 12:1-14; 13; 14:3-21; Mal 3:4; Ro 11).

See Israel, Israelites; Judah.

JEZANIAH [3470] (*Yahweh gives ear*). Also known as Azariah (Jer 42:1, ftn), as was King Uzziah (2Ki 14:21, ftn; 2Ch 26:1, ftn). *See also, Jaazaniah, 1.*

JEZEBEL [374, 2630] (possibly *unexalted, unhusbanded* BDB). Daughter of Ethbaal, a Sidonian, and wife of Ahab (1Ki 16:31). Worshiped idols and persecuted the prophets of God (1Ki 18:4, 13, 19; 2Ki 3:2, 13; 9:7, 22). Vowed to kill Elijah (1Ki 19:1-3). Wickedly accomplishes the death of Naboth (1Ki 21:5-16). Death of, foretold (1Ki 21:23; 2Ki 9:10). Death of, at the hand of Jehu (2Ki 9:30-37).

Figurative (Rev 2:20).

JEZER, JEZERITE [3672, 3673] (*formed, fashioned*). Son of Naphtali (Ge 46:24; Nu 26:49; 1Ch 7:13).

JEZIAH See Izziah.

JEZIEL [3465]. A disaffected Israelite who joined David at Ziklag (1Ch 12:3).

JEZLIAH See Izliah.

JEZOAR See Zohar, 3.

JEZRAHIAH [3474] (*Yahweh will arise or shine*).
1. Descendant of Issachar called Izrahiah (1Ch 7:3).
2. Musician (Ne 12:42).

JEZREEL, JEZREELITE [3475, 3476, 3477] (*God [El] will sow or scatter*).
1. A city in the S of Judah (Jos 15:56; 1Sa 25:43; 27:3; 29:1, 11).
2. A city of Issachar (Jos 19:18; 2Sa 2:9). Ahab's residence in (1Ki 18:45-46; 21:1). Naboth's vineyard in (1Ki 21:1). Joram's residence in (2Ki 8:29). Jehu kills King Ahab, his wife, and friends at (2Ki 9:15-37; 10:11). Prophecies concerning (Hos 1:4-5, 11).
3. A valley (Jos 17:16). Place of Gideon's battle with the Midianites (Jdg 6:33). Place of the defeat of the Israelites under Saul and Jonathan (1Sa 29:1, 11; 31:1-6; 2Sa 4:4).
4. A descendant of Etam (1Ch 4:3).
5. Figurative of Israel (Hos 1:4-5, 11).

JIBSAM See Ibsam.

JIDLAPH [3358] (*he weeps*). Son of Nahor (Ge 22:22).

JIMNA, JIMNAH See Imnah.

JIPHTAH See Iphtah.

JIPHTHAH-EL See Iphtah El.

JOAB [3405] (*Yahweh is father*).
1. Son of David's sister (1Ch 2:16). Commander

of David's army (2Sa 8:16; 20:23; 1Ch 11:6; 18:15; 27:34). Dedicated spoils of his battles (1Ch 26:28). Defeated the Jebusites (1Ch 11:6). Defeats and slays Abner (2Sa 2:13-32; 3:27; 1Ki 2:5). Destroys all the males in Edom (1Ki 11:16). See *Psalm 60, title*. Defeats the Ammonites (2Sa 10:7-14; 1Ch 19:6-15). Captures Rabbah (2Sa 11:1, 15-25; 12:26-29; 1Ch 20:1-2).

Secures the return of Absalom to Jerusalem (2Sa 14:1-24). Barley field of, burned by Absalom (2Sa 18). Rebukes David for lamenting the death of Absalom (2Sa 19:1-8). Replaced by Amasa as commander of David's army (2Sa 17:25; 19:13). Kills Amasa (2Sa 20:8-13; 1Ki 2:5). Causes Sheba to be put to death (2Sa 20:16-22). Opposes the numbering of the people (2Sa 24:3; 1Ch 21:3). Numbers the people (2Sa 24:4-9; 1Ch 21:4-5; 27:23-24). Supports Adonijah as successor to David (1Ki 1:7; 2:28). Slain by Benaiah, under Solomon's order (1Ki 2:29-34).

2. A grandson of Kenaz (1Ch 4:14).

3. An Israelite (or the name of two Israelites) whose descendants returned from Babylon to Jerusalem (Ezr 2:6; 8:9; Ne 7:11).

4. "House of Joab" (1Ch 2:54). Probably identical with 1. See *Atroth Beth Joab*.

JOAH [3406] (*Yahweh is brother*).

1. Son of Asaph (2Ki 18:18, 26; Isa 36:3, 11, 22).

2. A descendant of Gershom (1Ch 6:21; 2Ch 29:12).

3. A son of Obed-Edom (1Ch 26:4).

4. A Levite, who repaired the temple (2Ch 34:8).

JOAHAZ [3407] (*Yahweh grips*). Father of Joah, recorder of King Josiah (2Ch 34:8).

JOANAN [2720]. An ancestor of Jesus (Lk 3:27).

JOANNA [2721] (probably feminine form of *John*). Wife of Cuza, the steward of Herod Agrippa, and a disciple of Jesus (Lk 8:3; 24:10).

JOASH [3371, 3409, 3447] (*Yahweh has bestowed*).

1. Son of Beker (1Ch 7:8).

2. Keeper of the stores of oil (1Ch 27:28).

3. Father of Gideon (Jdg 6:11, 29, 31; 7:14; 8:13, 29-32).

4. Son of Ahab, king of Israel (1Ki 22:26; 2Ch 18:25).

5. Also called Jehoash. See *Jehoash, Joash*. Son of Ahaziah and king of Judah. Saved from his grandmother by Jehosheba, his aunt, and hidden for six years (2Ki 11:1-3; 2Ch 22:11-12). Anointed king by the priest, Jehoiada (2Ki 11:12-21; 2Ch 23). Righteousness of, under influence of Jehoiada (2Ki 12:2; 2Ch 24:2). Repaired the temple (2Ki 12:4-16; 2Ch 24:4-14, 27). Wickedness of, after Jehoiada's death (2Ch 24:17-22). Secured peace from Hazael, king of Syria, by gift of dedicated treasures from the temple (2Ki 12:17-18; 2Ch 24:23-24). Prophecy against (2Ch 24:19-20). Put Jehoiada's son to death (2Ch 24:20-22;

Mt 23:35). Diseases of (2Ch 24:25). Conspired against and slain (2Ki 12:20-21; 2Ch 24:25-26).

6. A king of Israel. See *Jehoash, Joash*.

7. A descendant of Shelah (1Ch 4:22).

8. One of David's officers (1Ch 12:3).

JOATHAM See *Jotham, 3*.

JOB [373, 6275, 3873] (*where is my father*, or perhaps *where is my father, O God?*).

1. A man who lived in Uz (Job 1:1). Righteousness of (Job 1:1, 5, 8; 2:3; Eze 14:14, 20). Riches of (Job 1:3). Trial of, by affliction of Satan (Job 1:13-19; 2:7-10). Fortitude of (Job 1:20-22; 2:10; Jas 5:11). Visited by Eliphaz, Bildad, and Zophar as comforters (Job 2:11-13). Complaints of, and replies by his three friends (Job 3-37). Replied to by God (Job 38-41). Submission of, to God (Job 40:3-5; 42:1-6). Later blessings and riches of (Job 42:10-16). Death of (Job 42:16-17).

2. See *Jashub*.

JOB, BOOK OF

Author: Anonymous

Date: Anytime from the reign of Solomon to the Exile.

Outline:

I. Prologue (chs. 1-2).
  A. Job's Happiness (1:1-5).
  B. Job's Testing (1:6-2:13).
    1. Satan's first accusation (1:6-12).
    2. Job's faith despite loss of family and property (1:13-22).
    3. Satan's second accusation (2:1-6).
    4. Job's faith during personal sufferings (2:7-10).
    5. The coming of the three friends (2:11-13).

II. Dialogue-Dispute (chs. 3-27).
  A. Job's Opening Lament (ch. 3).
  B. First Cycle of Speeches (chs. 4-14).
    1. Eliphaz (chs. 4-5).
    2. Job's reply (chs. 6-7).
    3. Bildad (ch. 8).
    4. Job's reply (chs. 9-10).
    5. Zophar (ch. 11).
    6. Job's reply (chs. 12-14).
  C. Second Cycle of Speeches (chs. 15-21).
    1. Eliphaz (ch. 15).
    2. Job's reply (chs. 16-17).
    3. Bildad (ch. 18).
    4. Job's reply (ch. 19).
    5. Zophar (ch. 20).
    6. Job's reply (ch. 21).
  D. Third Cycle of Speeches (chs. 22-26).
    1. Eliphaz (ch. 22).
    2. Job's reply (chs. 23-24).
    3. Bildad (ch. 25).
    4. Job's reply (ch. 26).
  E. Job's Closing Discourse (ch. 27).

III. Interlude on Wisdom (ch. 28).

IV. Monologues (29:1-42:6).
  A. Job's Call for Vindication (chs. 29-31).
    1. His past honor and blessing (ch. 29).

2. His present dishonor and suffering (ch. 30).

3. His protestations of innocence and final oath (ch. 31).

B. Elihu's Speeches (chs. 32-37).
1. Introduction (32:1-5).
2. The speeches themselves (32:6-37:24).
a. First speech (32:6-33:33).
b. Second speech (ch. 34).
c. Third speech (ch. 35).
d. Fourth speech (chs. 36-37).

C. Divine Discourses (38:1-42:6).
1. God's first discourse (38:1-40:2).
2. Job's response (40:3-5).
3. God's second discourse (40:6-41:34).
4. Job's repentance (42:1-6).

V. Epilogue (42:7-17).
A. God's Verdict (42:7-9).
B. Job's Restoration (42:10-17).

JOBAB [3411, 3412] (*howl*).
1. Son of Joktan (Ge 10:29; 1Ch 1:23).
2. Second king of Edom (Ge 36:33; 1Ch 1:44-45).
3. King of Madon (Jos 11:1; 12:19).
4. Benjamite (1Ch 8:9).
5. Benjamite (1Ch 9:18).

JOCHEBED [3425] (*Yahweh is glorious*).
Mother of Miriam, Aaron, and Moses (Ex 6:20; Nu 26:59). Nurses Moses when he is adopted by Pharaoh's daughter (Ex 2:1-9).

JODA [3511]. An ancestor of Joseph, the father (so it was thought) of Jesus (Lk 3:26).

JOED [3444] (*Yahweh is witness*). A Benjamite (Ne 11:7).

JOEL [3408, 2727] (*Yahweh is God [El]*).
1. Son of Samuel (1Sa 8:2; 1Ch 6:33; 15:17).
2. A Simeonite (1Ch 4:35).
3. A Reubenite (1Ch 5:4, 8).
4. A Gadite (1Ch 5:12).
5. A Kohathite Levite (1Ch 6:36).
6. Descendant of Issachar (1Ch 7:3).
7. One of David's valiant men (1Ch 11:38). Called "Igal son of Nathan" (2Sa 23:36).
8. Name of two Gershonites (1Ch 15:7, 11; 23:8; 26:22).
9. Prince of Manasseh (1Ch 27:20).
10. A Kohathite who assisted in the cleansing of the temple (2Ch 29:12).
11. One of Nebo's family (Ezr 10:43).
12. Son of Zicri (Ne 11:9).
13. One of the twelve minor prophets, probably lived in the days of Uzziah (Joel 1:1; Ac 2:16).

JOEL, BOOK OF

Author: Joel

Date: As early as the ninth century B.C. to as late as the postexilic period (sixth century), after Haggai and Zechariah. In either case, its message is not significantly affected by its dating.

Outline:
I. Title (1:1).
II. Judah Experiences a Foretaste of the Day of the Lord (1:2-2:17).
A. A Call to Mourning and Prayer (1:2-14).
B. The Announcement of the Day of the Lord (1:15-2:11).
C. A Call to Repentance and Prayer (2:12-17).
III. Judah Is Assured of Salvation in the Day of the Lord (2:18-3:21).
A. The Lord's Restoration of Judah (2:18-27).
B. The Lord's Renewal of His People (2:28-32).
C. The Coming of the Day of the Lord (ch. 3).
1. The nations judged (3:1-16).
2. God's people blessed (3:17-21).
See Prophets, The Minor.

JOELAH [3443] (*let him help*). One of David's recruits at Ziklag (1Ch 12:7).

JOEZER [3445] (*Yahweh is help*). A Korahite, who joined David at Ziklag (1Ch 12:6).

JOGBEHAH [3322] (*height*). City in Gilead assigned to Gad (Nu 32:35; Jdg 8:11).

JOGLI [3332] (perhaps *may God reveal*). A prince of Dan (Nu 34:22).

JOHA [3418].
1. A Benjamite (1Ch 8:16).
2. One of David's valiant men (1Ch 11:45).

JOHANAN [3419] (*Yahweh is gracious*).
1. Jewish leader who tried to save Gedaliah from plot to murder him (Jer 40:13-14), took Jews, including Jeremiah, to Egypt (Jer 40-43).
2. Son of King Josiah (1Ch 3:15).
3. Son of Elioenai (1Ch 3:24).
4. Father of Azariah, high priest in Solomon's time (1Ch 6:9-10).
5. Benjamite; joined David at Ziklag (1Ch 12:4).
6. Gadite; warrior in David's army (1Ch 28:12).
7. Ephraimite chief (2Ch 28:12).
8. Exile who left Babylon with Ezra (Ezr 8:12).
9. Son of Tobiah, who married a Jewess in days of Nehemiah (Ne 6:18).
10. Son of Eliashib (Ezr 10:6).
11. High priest, grandson of Eliashib (Ne 12:22).

JOHN [2722] (*Yahweh is gracious*).
1. John the Baptist. *See John the Baptist.*
2. The apostle, the son of Zebedee, and brother of James. *See John, the Apostle.*
3. John Mark. *See Mark.*
4. Father of Simon Peter (Jn 1:42; 21:15, 17).
5. Jewish religious dignitary who called Peter and John to account for their preaching about Jesus (Ac 4:6).
6. Father of Mattathias (1Mc 2:1).
7. Eldest son of Mattathias (1Mc 9:36).
8. Father of Eupolemus (2Mc 4:11).
9. John Hyrcanus, son of Simon (1Mc 13:53; 16:1).

10. Jewish envoy (2Mc 11:17).

JOHN, 1, 2 and 3

Author: The apostle John, son of Zebedee

Date: Between A.D. 85 and 95

Outline of 1 John:

I. Introduction: The Reality of the Incarnation (1:1-4).

II. The Christian Life as Fellowship With the Father and the Son (1:5-2:28).
   A. Ethical Tests of Fellowship (1:5-2:11).
      1. Moral likeness (1:5-7).
      2. Confession of sin (1:8-2:2).
      3. Obedience (2:3-6).
      4. Love for fellow believers (2:7-11).
   B. Two Digressions (2:12-17).
   C. Christological Test of Fellowship (2:18-28).
      1. Contrast: apostates versus believers (2:18-21).
      2. Person of Christ: the crux of the test (2:22-23).
      3. Persistent belief: key to continuing fellowship (2:24-28).

III. The Christian Life as Divine Sonship (2:29-4:6).
   A. Ethical Tests of Sonship (2:29-3:24).
      1. Righteousness (2:29-3:10a).
      2. Love (3:10b-24).
   B. Christological Tests of Sonship (4:1-6).

IV. The Christian Life as an Integration of the Ethical and the Christological (4:7-5:12).
   A. The Ethical Test: Love (4:7-5:5).
      1. The source of love (4:7-16).
      2. The fruit of love (4:17-19).
      3. The relationship of love for God and love for one's spiritual brother (4:20-5:1).
      4. Obedience: the evidence of love for God's children (5:2-5).
   B. The Christological Test (5:6-12).

V. Conclusion: Great Christian Certainties (5:13-21).
   See General Letters.

Outline of 2 John:

I. Salutation (1-3).

II. Commendation (4).

III. Exhortation and Warning (5-11).

IV. Conclusion (12-13).
   See General Letters.

Outline of 3 John:

I. Salutation (1-2).

II. Commendation of Gaius (3-8).

III. Condemnation of Diotrephes (9-10).

IV. Exhortation to Gaius (11).

V. Example of Demetrius (12).

VI. Conclusion (13-14).
   See General Letters.

JOHN MARK *See Mark, John.*

JOHN, THE APOSTLE Son of Zebedee and Salome, and brother of James (Mt 4:21; 27:56; Mk 15:40; Ac 12:1-2), lived in Galilee, probably in Bethsaida (Lk 5:10; Jn 1:44), fisher-man (Mk 1:19-20), became disciple of Jesus through John the Baptist (Jn 1:35), called as an apostle (Mk 1:19-20; Lk 5:10), one of three apostles closest to Jesus (the others are Peter and James), at raising of Jairus' daughter (Mk 5:37; Lk 8:51), transfiguration (Mt 17:1; Mk 9:2; Lk 9:28), Gethsemane (Mt 26:37; Mk 14:33), asked Jesus to call fire down on Samaritans, and given name Boanerges (sons of thunder) (Mk 3:17; Lk 9:54), mother requested that John and James be given places of special honor in coming kingdom (Mk 10:35), helped Peter prepare Passover (Lk 22:8), lay close to Jesus' breast at Last Supper (Jn 13:25), present at trial of Jesus (Jn 18:15-16), witnessed crucifixion of Jesus (Jn 19:26-27), recognized Jesus at Sea of Galilee (Jn 21:1-7), active with Peter in apostolic church (Ac 3:1-4:22; 8:14-17). Lived to an old age; fourth Gospel, three letters and Revelation attributed to him. *See John, 1, 2 and 3; John, the Gospel of; Revelation.*

JOHN THE BAPTIST Forerunner of Jesus; son of Zechariah and Elizabeth, both of priestly descent (Lk 1:5-25, 56-58), lived as Nazirite in desert (Lk 1:15; Mt 11:12-14, 18), began ministry beyond Jordan in the fifteenth year of Tiberias Caesar (Lk 3:1-3), preached baptism of repentance in preparation of coming of Messiah (Lk 3:4-14), baptized Jesus (Mt 3:13-17; Mk 1:9-10; Lk 3:21; Jn 1:32), bore witness to Jesus as Messiah (Jn 1:24-42), imprisoned and put to death by Herod Antipas (Mt 14:6-12; Mk 6:17-28), praised by Jesus (Mt 11:7-14; Lk 7:24-28), disciples loyal to him long after his death (Ac 18:25).

JOHN, THE GOSPEL OF

Author: The apostle John, son of Zebedee

Date: Traditionally toward the end of the first century, c. A.D. 85 or later. More recently, some scholars have suggested a date as early as the 50s and no later than 70.

Outline:

I. Prologue (1:1-18).

II. Beginnings of Jesus' Ministry (1:19-51).
   A. The Ministry of His Forerunner (1:19-34).
   B. Jesus' Introduction to Some Future Disciples (1:35-51).

III. Jesus' Public Ministry: Signs and Discourses (chs. 2-11).
   A. Changing Water to Wine (2:1-11).
   B. Cleansing the Temple (2:12-25).
   C. Interview with Nicodemus (3:1-21).
   D. Parallel Ministry With John the Baptist (3:22-4:3).
   E. Journey Through Samaria: The Woman at the Well (4:4-42).
   F. Healing of the Official's Son (4:43-54).
   G. To Jerusalem for an Annual Feast (ch. 5).
   H. The Feeding of the 5000 and the Sermon on the Bread of Life (ch. 6).
   I. Jesus at the Feast of Tabernacles (chs. 7-8).
   J. Healing of the Man Born Blind (ch. 9).
   K. Parable of the Good Shepherd (10:1-21).

L. Debating at the Feast of Dedication (10:22-39).
M. Ministry in Perea (10:40-42).
N. The Raising of Lazarus (ch. 11).
IV. The Passion Week (chs. 12-19).
  A. The Anointing of Jesus' Feet (12:1-11).
  B. The Triumphal Entry (12:12-19).
  C. The Coming of the Greeks (12:20-36).
  D. Continued Jewish Unbelief (12:37-50).
  E. Farewell Discourses (chs. 13-17).
    1. Discourse at the Last Supper (chs. 13-14).
    2. Discourse on the way to Gethsemane (chs. 15-16).
    3. Jesus' prayer of intercession (ch. 17).
  F. Jesus' Betrayal and Arrest (18:1-12).
  G. The Trials of Jesus (18:13-19:15).
  H. The Crucifixion and Burial (19:16-42).
V. The Resurrection (20:1-29).
VI. The Statement of Purpose (20:30-31).
VII. Epilogue (ch. 21).
See Synoptic Gospels, The.

JOIADA [3421] (*Yahweh knows*).
1. Repaired walls of Jerusalem (Ne 3:6).
2. Son of Eliashib (Ne 12:10; 13:28).

JOIAKIM [3423] (*Yahweh lifts up*). Father of Eliashib (Ne 12:10, 12, 26).

JOIARIB [3424] (*Yahweh contends, pleads [your case]*).
1. A returned exile (Ezr 8:16).
2. A descendant of Judah (Ne 11:5).
3. A priest who returned from Babylon (Ne 12:6, 19).
See Jehoiarib.

JOKDEAM [3680]. A city in Judah (Jos 15:56).

JOKIM [3451] (*Yahweh lifts up*). A descendant of Shelah (1Ch 4:22).

JOKMEAM [3695] (*let the people arise*). A Levitical city of Ephraim (1Ch 6:68).

JOKNEAM [3696]. A Levitical city of Zebulun (Jos 12:22; 19:11; 21:34). *See Jokmeam.*

JOKSHAN [3705]. Son of Abraham, by Keturah (Ge 25:2-3, 6; 1Ch 1:32).

JOKTAN [3690] (*smaller*). Son of Eber (Ge 10:25-26, 29; 1Ch 1:19-20, 23).

JOKTHEEL [3706].
1. A city of Judah (Jos 15:38).
2. A name given by Amaziah to Sela, stronghold of Edom (2Ki 14:7; 2Ch 25:11-12). *See Sela.*

JONA *See Jonah.*

JONADAB [3386, 3432] (*Yahweh is generous, noble*).
1. The son of Shimeah, David's brother (2Sa 13:3). His complicity with Amnon in his rape of

Tamar (2Sa 13:3-5). Comforts David on death of Amnon (2Sa 13:32-35).
2. A Kenite who helped Jehu abolish Baal worship (temporarily) in Samaria (2Ki 10:15-27). *Jonadab* is spelled "Jehonadab" in this passage (2Ki 10:15-23). He was also a leader of a conservative movement that was characterized by various practices of a settled agricultural society, including the building of houses, the sowing of crops, and the use of wine. *See Nazirite(s).*
His followers still adhered to these principles nearly 250 years later and were known as Recabites (Jer 35:5-10, 16-19). *See Recabite(s).*

JONAH [3434, *980*, *2731*] (*dove*). Prophet of Israel; son of Amittai; predicted victory over Syria through Jeroboam II, who reigned c. 793-753 B.C.; author of book of Jonah (2Ki 14:25; Jnh 1:1).

JONAH, BOOK OF

Author: Traditionally the prophet Jonah

Date: Before the fall of Samaria in B.C. 722-721

Outline:
I. Jonah Flees His Mission (chs. 1-2).
  A. Jonah's Commission and Flight (1:1-3).
  B. The Endangered Sailors' Cry to Their Gods (1:4-6).
  C. Jonah's Disobedience Exposed (1:7-10).
  D. Jonah's Punishment and Deliverance (1:11-2:1; 2:10).
  E. Jonah's Prayer of Thanksgiving (2:2-9).
II. Jonah Reluctantly Fulfills His Mission (chs. 3-4).
  A. Jonah's Renewed Commission and Obedience (3:1-4).
  B. The Endangered Ninevites' Repentant Appeal to the Lord (3:5-9).
  C. The Ninevites' Repentance Acknowledged (3:10-4:4).
  D. Jonah's Deliverance and Rebuke (4:5-11).
See Prophets, The Minor.

JONAM [*2729*] (*Yahweh is gracious*). An ancestor of Christ (Lk 3:30).

JONAN *See Jonam.*

JONAS *See Jonah; John, 4.*

JONATH-ELEM-RECHOKIM

NIV "To [the tune of] A Dove on Distant Oaks" (Ps 56:T). Probably the melody to which Ps 56 was sung. *See Music, Symbols Used in.*

JONATHAN [3387, 3440] (*gift of Yahweh*).
1. A Levite of Bethlehem, who becomes a priest for Micah, accepts idolatry, joins the Danites (Jdg 17:7-13; 18:1-30).
2. Son of Saul (1Sa 14:49). Victory of, over the Philistine garrison of Geba (1Sa 13:3-4, 16), over Philistines at Micmash (1Sa 14:1-18). Under Saul's curse pronounced against any who might take food before he was avenged of his enemies (1Sa 14:24-30, 43). Rescued by the people (1Sa

14:43-45). Love of, for David (1Sa 18:1-4; 19:1-7; 20; 23:16-18). Killed in battle with Philistines (1Sa 31:2, 6; 2Sa 21:12-14; 1Ch 10:2). Buried by inhabitants of Jabesh Gilead (1Sa 31:11-13). Mourned by David (2Sa 1:12, 17-27). Son of, cared for by David (2Sa 4:4; 9; 1Ch 8:34).

3. Son of Abiathar (2Sa 15:27). Acts as spy for David (2Sa 15:27-28; 17:17-22). Informs Adonijah of Solomon's succession to David (1Ki 1:42-48).

4. Nephew of David, slays a giant and becomes one of David's chief warriors (2Sa 21:21; 1Ch 20:7).

5. One of David's heroes (2Sa 23:32; 1Ch 11:34).

6. A son of Jada (1Ch 2:32-33).

7. Secretary of the cabinet of David (1Ch 27:32).

8. Father of Ebed (Ezr 8:6).

9. Son of Asahel (Ezr 10:15).

10. Also called Johanan. A descendant of Jeshua (Ne 12:11-12).

11. Name of two priests (Ne 12:14, 35).

12. A scribe (Jer 37:15, 20; 38:26).

13. Son of Kareah (Jer 40:8).

JOPPA [3639, 2673] (*beautiful*). An ancient walled town on coast of Israel, c. thirty-five miles NW of Jerusalem; assigned to Dan; mentioned in Amarna letters; seaport for Jerusalem. In NT times Peter raised Dorcas to life there (Ac 9:36ff) and received the vision of a sheet filled with animals (Ac 10:1ff; 11:5ff). Modern Jaffa.

JORAH [3454] (*one born during harvest*). Family which returned with Zerubbabel (Ezr 2:18). Also called Hariph (Ne 7:24).

JORAI [3455] (possibly *Yahweh sees* IDB; *whom Yahweh teaches* ISBE). A Gadite (1Ch 5:13).

JORAM [3393, 3456] (*Yahweh is exalted*). Short form of Jehoram. *See Jehoram.*

1. Son of king of Hamath (2Sa 8:10).

2. Levite (1Ch 26:25).

3. Son of Ahab, king of Israel (2Ki 8:29).

4. King of Judah (2Ki 8:21-24; 11:2; 1Ch 3:11; Mt 1:8).

5. Priest (2Ch 17:8).

JORDAN [3720, 2674] (*descent*).

River of:

A river in Israel. Empties into the Dead Sea (Jos 15:5). Fords of (Ge 32:10; Jos 2:7; Jdg 3:28; 7:24; 8:4; 10:9; 12:5-6; 2Sa 2:29; 17:22, 24; 19:15, 31; 1Ch 19:17). Swelling of, at harvest time (Jos 3:15; Jer 12:5), and in the early spring (1Ch 12:15). The waters of, miraculously parted for the passage of the Israelites (Jos 3; 4; 5:1; Ps 114:3), of Elijah (2Ki 2:6-8), of Elisha (2Ki 2:14). Crossed at a ford (2Sa 19:18). Naaman washes in, for the healing of his leprosy (2Ki 5:10-14). John the Baptist baptizes in (Mt 3:6; Mk 1:5), baptizes Jesus in (Mt 3:13; Mk 1:19).

Plain of:

(Ge 13:10-12). Israelites camped in (Nu 22:1; 26:3, 63). Solomon's foundry in (1Ki 7:46; 2Ch 4:17).

JORIM [2733]. Ancestor of Jesus (Lk 3:29).

JORKEAM [3767]. Descendant of Caleb (1Ch 2:44).

JOSABAD *See Jozabad, 1.*

JOSAPHAT *See Jehoshaphat.*

JOSE *See Joshua, 5.*

JOSECH [2738]. Father of Semein; ancestor of Jesus (Lk 3:26).

JOSEDECH *See Jozadak.*

JOSEPH [3388, 3441, 2736, 2737] (*he will add*).

1. Son of Jacob (Ge 30:24). Personal appearance of (Ge 39:6). His favorite child (Ge 33:2; 37:3-4, 35; 48:22; 1Ch 5:2; Jn 4:5). His father's partiality for, excites the jealousy of his brothers (Ge 37:4, 11, 18-28; Ps 105:17; Ac 7:9). His prophetic dreams of his fortunes in Egypt (Ge 37:5-11). Sold into Egypt (Ge 37:27-28). Is falsely reported to his father as killed by wild beasts (Ge 37:29-35). Is bought by Potiphar, an officer of Pharaoh (Ge 37:36). Is prospered of God (Ge 39:2-5, 21, 23). Is falsely accused, and cast into prison; is delivered by the friendship of another prisoner (Ge 39; 40; Ps 105:18). Is an interpreter of dreams: of the two prisoners (Ge 40:5-23); of Pharaoh (Ge 41:1-37). His name is changed to Zaphenath-Paneah (Ge 41:45). Is promoted to authority next to Pharaoh at thirty years of age (Ge 41:37-46; Ps 105:19-22). Takes as his wife the daughter of the priest of On (Ge 41:45). Provides against the years of famine (Ge 41:46-57). Exports the produce of Egypt to other countries (Ge 41:57). Sells the stores of food to the people of Egypt, exacting of them all their money, flocks and herds, lands and lives (Ge 47:13-26). Exempts the priests from the exactions (Ge 47:22, 26).

His father sends down into Egypt to buy grain (Ge 42-44). Reveals himself to his brothers, sends for his father, provides the land of Goshen for his people, and sustains them during the famine (Ge 45; 46; 47:1-12). His two sons (Ge 41:50, 52; Dt 33:13-17). *See Ephraim; Manasseh, 1.* Mourns the death of his father (Ge 50:1-14). Exacts a pledge from his brothers to convey his remains to Canaan (Ge 50:24-25; Heb 11:22, w Ex 13:19; Jos 24:32; Ac 7:16). Death of (Ge 50:22-26).

Kindness of heart (Ge 40:7-8). His integrity (Ge 39:7-12), humility (Ge 41:16; 45:7-9), wisdom (Ge 41:33-57), piety (Ge 41:51-52), faith (Ge 45:5-8). Was a prophet (Ge 41:38-39; 50:25). God's providence with (Ge 39:2-5; Ps 105:17-22). Descendants of (Ge 46:20; Nu 26:28-37).

2. Father of Igal the spy (Nu 13:7).

3. Of the sons of Asaph (1Ch 25:2, 9).

4. A returned exile (Ezr 10:42).

5. A priest (Ne 12:14).

6. Husband of Mary (Mt 13:55; Mk 6:3; Mt 1:18-25; Lk 1:27). His genealogy (Mt 1:1-16; Lk 3:23-38). An angel appears and testifies to the innocency of his betrothed (Mt 1:19-24). Lives at Nazareth (Lk 2:4). Belongs to the city of Bethlehem (Lk 2:4). Goes to Bethlehem to be enrolled (Lk 2:1-4). Jesus born to (Mt 1:25; Lk 2:7). Presents Jesus in the temple (Lk 2:22-39). Returns to Nazareth (Lk 2:39). Warned in a dream to escape to Egypt in order to save the child's life (Mt 2:13-15). Warned in a dream to return to Nazareth (Mt 2:19-23). Attends the annual feast at Jerusalem with his family (Lk 2:42-51).

7. Of Arimathea. Requests the body of Jesus for burial in his own tomb (Mt 27:57-60; Mk 15:42-47; Lk 23:50-56; Jn 19:38-42).

8. Three ancestors of Joseph, 6 (Lk 3:24, 26, 30).

9. One of the brothers of Jesus (Mt 13:55; Mk 6:3).

10. Also called Barsabbas and Justus. One of the two persons nominated in place of Judas (Ac 1:21-23).

11. A Levite, called Barnabas by the apostles (Ac 4:36). *See Barnabas.*

12. A designation of the ten tribes of Israel (Am 5:6).

JOSES [2736].

1. Son of Mary, 2; brother of the younger James (Mt 27:56; Mk 15:40, 47).

2. *See Joseph, 9.*

3. *See Joseph, 11.*

JOSHAH [3459] (*gift of Yahweh*). A descendant of Simeon (1Ch 4:34).

JOSHAPHAT [3461] (*Yahweh judges*).

1. One of David's mighty men (1Ch 11:43).

2. Priest (1Ch 15:24).

JOSHAVIAH [3460] (*Yahweh places*). One of David's bodyguards (1Ch 11:46).

JOSHBEKASHAH [3792] (*one sitting in request [prayer?]*). Leader of the seventeenth course of musicians (1Ch 25:4, 24).

JOSHEB-BASSHEBETH [3783] (*one sitting in the seat*). A Tahkemonite, who was the chief of the Three; one of David's mighty men (2Sa 23:8). This is probably a corruption of Jashobeam, a Hacmonite (1Ch 11:11).

JOSHIBIAH [3458] (*Yahweh places*). A Simeonite (1Ch 4:35).

JOSHUA [2107, 3397, 3800, 2652] (*Yahweh saves*).

1. Also called Hoshea (Nu 13:8). Son of Nun (1Ch 7:27). Intimately associated with Moses (Ex 24:13; 32:17; 33:11). A religious zealot (Nu 11:28). Sent with others to view the promised land

(Nu 13:8). Makes favorable report (Nu 14:6-10). Rewarded for his courage and fidelity (Nu 14:30, 38; 32:12). Commissioned, ordained, and charged with the responsibilities of Moses' office (Nu 27:18-23; Dt 1:38; 3:28; 31:3, 7, 23; 34:9). Divinely inspired (Nu 27:18; Dt 34:9; Jos 1:5, 9; 3:7; 8:8). His life miraculously preserved when he made a favorable report of the land (Nu 14:10). Promises to (Jos 1:5-9). Leads the people into the land of Canaan (Jos 1-4; Ac 7:45; Heb 4:8). Renews circumcision of the Israelites; reestablishes the Passover; has a vision of the angel of God (Jos 5). Besieges and takes Jericho (Jos 6). Takes Ai (Jos 7-8). Makes a league with the Gibeonites (Jos 9:3-27). The kings of the six nations of the Canaanites confederate against him (Jos 9:1-2), make war upon the Gibeonites, are defeated and slain (Jos 10). Defeats seven other kings (Jos 10:28-43). Makes conquest of Hazor (Jos 11). Completes the conquest of the whole land (Jos 11:23). List of the kings whom Joshua killed (Jos 12). Allots the land (Jos 13-19). Sets the tabernacle up in Shiloh (Jos 18:1). Sets apart cities of refuge (Jos 20), forty-eight cities for the Levites (Jos 21). Exhortation of the Israelites, before his death (Jos 23-24). Survives the Israelites who refused to enter Canaan (Nu 26:63-65). His portion of the land (Jos 19:49-50). Death and burial of (Jos 24:29-30). Esteem in which he was held (Jos 1:16-18). Faith of (Jos 6:16). Military genius of, as exhibited at the defeat of the Amalekites (Ex 17:13), at Ai (Jos 8), in Gibeon (Jos 10), at Hazor (Jos 11). Age of, at death (Jdg 2:8).

2. An Israelite (1Sa 6:14, 18).

3. A governor of Jerusalem (2Ki 23:8).

4. The postexilic high priest. *See Jeshua, 3.*

5. An ancestor of Jesus (Lk 3:29).

JOSHUA, BOOK OF

Author: Traditionally Joshua the son of Nun

Date: Traditionally before 1375 B.C.

Outline:

I. The Entrance into the Land (1:1-5:12).
    A. The Exhortations to Conquer (ch. 1).
    B. The Reconnaissance of Jericho (ch. 2).
    C. The Crossing of the Jordan (chs. 3-4).
    D. The Consecration at Gilgal (5:1-12).
II. The Conquest of the Land (5:13-12:24).
    A. The Initial Battles (5:13-8:35).
        1. The victory at Jericho (5:13-6:27).
        2. The failure at Ai because of Achan's sin (ch. 7).
        3. The victory at Ai (8:1-29).
        4. The covenant renewed at Shechem (8:30-35).
    B. The Campaign in the South (chs. 9-10).
        1. The treaty with the Gibeonites (ch. 9).
        2. The long day of Joshua (10:1-15).
        3. The southern cities conquered (10:16-43).
    C. The Campaign in the North (ch. 11).
    D. The Defeated Kings of Canaan (ch. 12).
III. The Distribution of the Land (chs. 13-21).
    A. Areas Yet to Be Conquered (13:1-7).

B. The Land East of the Jordan for Reuben, Gad and Half of Manasseh (13:8-33).

C. The Lands Given to Judah and "Joseph" at Gilgal (chs. 14-17).

D. The Lands Given to the Remaining Tribes at Shiloh (chs. 18-19).

1. The tabernacle at Shiloh (18:1-10).

2. The allotments for Benjamin, Simeon, Zebulun, Issachar, Asher, Naphtali, and Dan (18:1-10).

3. The town given to Joshua (19:49-51).

E. The Cities Assigned to the Levites (chs. 20-21).

1. The six cities of refuge (ch. 20).

2. The forty-eight cities of the priests (ch. 21).

IV. Epilogue: Tribal Unity and Loyalty to the Lord (chs. 22-24).

A. The Altar of Witness by the Jordan (ch. 22).

B. Joshua's Farewell Exhortation (ch. 23).

C. The Renewal of the Covenant at Shechem (24:1-28).

D. The Death and Burial of Joshua and Eleazar (24:29-33).

JOSIAH [3287, 3288, *2739*] (*let or may Yahweh give*).

1. King of Judah (2Ki 21:24-26; 22:1; 1Ch 3:14; 2Ch 33:25). Ancestor of Jesus (Mt 1:10-11). Slain in battle with Pharaoh Neco (2Ki 23:29-30; 2Ch 35:20-24). Lamentations for (2Ch 35:25). Piety of, exemplified in his repairing the temple (2Ki 22:3-7; 2Ch 34:1-4). Anxiety, when the copy of the law was discovered and read to him (2Ki 22:8-20; 2Ch 34:14-33), in keeping a solemn Passover (2Ki 23:21-23; 2Ch 35:1-19). Prophecies concerning (1Ki 13:1-3). Destroys the altar and high places of idolatry (2Ki 23:3-20, 24-25).

2. Son of Zephaniah (Zec 6:10).

JOSIAS *See Josiah.*

JOSIPHIAH [3442] (*Yahweh will add*). Ancestor of family which returned with Ezra (Ezr 8:10).

JOT NIV "the smallest letter" of the Hebrew alphabet (Mt 5:17-18). Used figuratively to emphasize the importance of the smallest details of the law.

JOTBAH [3513] (*good, pleasant*). A place in Judah (2Ki 21:19). Possibly the same as Jotbathah (Dt 10:7).

JOTBATHAH [3514] (*good, pleasant*). The twentieth encampment of Israel (Nu 33:33-34; Dt 10:7). Possibly the same as Jotbah (2Ki 21:19).

JOTHAM [3462, *2718*] (*Yahweh completes*).

1. Son of Gideon; speaker of the first biblical parable (Jdg 9:5-57).

2. Judahite (1Ch 2:47).

3. Eleventh king of Judah; son of Uzziah, whose regent he was for a time; successful, righteous king (2Ki 15:5-38; 2Ch 27); contemporary of Isaiah (Isa 1:1), Hosea (Hos 1:1), Micah (Mic 1:1), ancestor of Jesus (Mt 1:9).

JOURNEY, SABBATH DAY'S

[*2006, 5023, 6296, *623*, *3847*, *4636*]. Three thousand feet (Ac 1:12).

JOY [*5375, 8131, 8523, 8525, 8262, 8264, 8607, 9558, *5897*, *5915*]. (Ps 30:5; Ps 30:11; Ps 33:21; Ps 97:11; Ps 132:16; Pr 29:6).

General:

From God (Ecc 2:26; Ro 15:13). In the Lord (Ps 9:2; 104:34; Isa 9:3; 29:19; 41:16; 61:10; Lk 1:47; Ro 5:11). In Christ (Php 3:3; 4:4; 1Pe 1:8). In the word of God (Ps 19:8; 119:14, 16, 111, 162; Jer 15:16). In worship (Dt 7:10; Ezr 6:22; Ne 12:43; Ps 42:4; 43:4; 71:23; Isa 56:7; Zep 3:14; Zec 2:10; 9:9).

A fruit of the Spirit (Gal 5:22; Eph 5:18-19). For salvation (Ps 13:5; 20:5; 21:1, 6; 35:9; Isa 12:2-3; 25:9; 35:1-2, 10; 55:12; Ro 5:2; 14:17). On account of a good conscience (2Co 1:12). Over a sinner's repentance (Lk 15:6-10, 22-32).

Under adversity (Ps 126:5-6; Isa 61:3; Mt 5:12; Ac 5:41; 2Co 6:10; 7:4; 8:2; 12:10; Col 1:11; 1Th 1:6; Heb 10:34; Jas 1:2; 1Pe 4:13). Fullness of (Ps 16:11; 36:8; 63:5; Jn 15:11; 16:24; Ac 2:28; 1Jn 1:4). Everlasting (Isa 51:11; 61:7). In heaven (Mt 25:21; Lk 15:7, 10).

Attributed to God (Dt 28:63; 30:9; Jer 32:41).

Commanded:

(Dt 12:18; Ne 8:10; Ps 2:11; 5:11; 32:11; 68:3; 97:12; 100:1-2; 105:3, 43; 149:2, 5; Joel 2:23; Lk 2:10; 6:23; 10:20; Ro 12:12; 1Th 5:16).

Instances of:

Moses and the Israelites, when Pharaoh and his army were destroyed (Ex 15:1-22). Deborah and the Israelites, when Sisera was overthrown (Jdg 5). Jephthah's daughter, when he returned from his victory over the Ammonites (Jdg 11:34). Hannah, when Samuel was born (1Sa 2:1-11). Naomi, when Boaz showed kindness to Ruth (Ru 2:20; 4:14). David, over the offerings of the princes and people for the house of God (1Ch 29:10-19). Jews, over the hanging of Haman (Est 8:15-16, w Est 7:10).

The Israelites: When Saul was presented as their king (1Sa 10:24), when David killed Goliath (1Sa 18:6-7), when they repaired to David to Hebron to make him king (1Ch 12:40), when they took the ark from Kiriath Jearim (1Ch 13:8), when they brought the ark from the house of Obed-Edom to Jerusalem (1Ch 15:16, 25, 28), when they made gifts to the house of God (1Ch 29:9), when they turned away from idolatry (2Ch 15:14-15; 23:18, 21; 29:30, 36; 30:21, 23, 26), when the foundation of the second temple was laid (Ezr 3:11-13), when they kept the dedication of the temple, and the feast of tabernacles under Ezra (Ezr 6:16, 22), after hearing again the word of God (Ne 8:9-18).

when the Wall of Jerusalem was dedicated (Ne 12:43).

Elizabeth, when Mary visited her (Lk 1:5-44). Mary, when she visited Elizabeth (Lk 1:46-56). Zechariah, when John was born (Lk 1:67-79). The angels, when Jesus was born (Lk 2:13-14). The shepherds when they saw the infant Jesus (Lk 2:20). The Magi (Mt 2:10). Simeon, when Jesus was presented in the temple (Lk 2:28-32).

The disciples, because the demons were subject to them (Lk 10:17). The father, when his prodigal son returns (Lk 15:20-32). The angels, when sinners repent (Lk 15:7, 10). The disciples, when Jesus triumphantly entered Jerusalem (Mt 21:8-9; Mk 11:8-9; Mk 11:8-10). The women who returned from the Lord's tomb (Mt 28:8). The disciples, after the resurrection of Jesus (Lk 24:41), in the temple after the Ascension of Jesus (Lk 24:53), in the temple because they had received the gift of the Holy Spirit (Ac 2:46-47).

The crippled man, healed by Peter (Ac 3:8). Paul, when he went up to Jerusalem (Ac 20:22-24). Paul and Silas, in the jail at Philippi (Ac 16:25). Rhoda, when she heard Peter at the gate (Ac 12:14). The disciples at Jerusalem, when Peter told them about the conversion of Cornelius and other Gentiles (Ac 11:18). Barnabas, when he saw the success of the gospel at Antioch (Ac 11:22-23).

Paul and the Corinthians, because the excommunicated member repented (2Co 1:24; 2:3). Paul and Titus, because of the hospitality of the Corinthians (Ro 15:32; 1Co 16:18 2Co 7:13, w 2Co 8:6). The Macedonians, when he prayed for the Philippians (Php 1:4). The Thessalonians, when they believed Paul's gospel (1Th 1:6). Paul, rejoicing over his converts (1Th 2:19-20; 3:9; Phm 7). Early Christians, when they believed in Jesus (1Pe 1:8-9).

See Happiness; Praise; Thanksgiving.

Of the Wicked:

Short (Job 20:5). Meaningless (Ecc 2:10; 7:6; 11:8-9). Shallow (Pr 14:13; 15:21). Overshadowed by impending judgment and sorrow (Pr 14:13; Ecc 11:8-9; Isa 16:10; Jas 4:10).

JOZABAD [3416] (*Yahweh bestowed*).

1. One of the two servants of Joash, who killed him in Millo (2Ki 12:21).

2. Gederathite; joined David at Ziklag (1Ch 12:4).

3. Two Manassites who also joined David (1Ch 12:20).

4. Levites (2Ch 31:13).

5. Chief Levite (2Ch 35:9).

6. Levite who assisted Ezra (Ezr 8:33).

7. Man who put foreign wife away (Ezr 10:22).

8. Another such man (Ezr 10:23).

9. Levite who helped Nehemiah (Ne 8:7).

10. Chief Levite in Nehemiah's time (Ne 11:16).

JOZACHAR (*Yahweh remembered*). *See Jehozabad, 1; Jozabad, 1; Zabad, 4.*

JOZADAK [3449, 10318] (*Yahweh is*

righteous). Father of Jeshua the high priest who returned with Zerubbabel (Ezr 3:2, 8; 5:2; 10:18; Ne 12:26). Called Jehozadak in Haggai and Zechariah. *See Jehozadak.*

JUBAL [3415]. Son of Lamech. Inventor of harp and flute (Ge 4:21).

JUBILEE [3413]. Called: Year of the Lord's favor (Isa 61:2). The year of freedom (Eze 46:17).

Laws concerning: (Lev 25:8-55; 27:17-24; Nu 36:4).

See Emancipation; Sabbatic Year.

JUBILEES, BOOK OF Jewish apocalyptic book written in intertestamental period.

JUCAL *See Jehucal.*

JUDA *See Judah.*

JUDAEA *See Judea.*

JUDAH [3373+, 3374, 3376, 10315, *2683*] (*praised*).

1. Son of Jacob (Ge 35:23). Intercedes for Joseph's life when his brothers were about to slay him, and proposes that they sell him to the Ishmaelites (Ge 37:26-27). Takes two wives (Ge 38:1-6). Lives at Kezib (Ge 38:5). His incest with his daughter-in-law (Ge 38:12-26). Goes down into Egypt for grain (Ge 43:1-10; 44:14-34; 46:28). Prophetic benediction of his father upon (Ge 49:8-12). The ancestor of Jesus (Mt 1:2-3; Rev 5:5).

2. Tribe of: Prophecies concerning (Ge 49:10). Enrollment of the military forces of, at Sinai (Nu 1:26-27; 2:4), at Bezek (1Sa 11:8; 2Sa 24:9), in the plain of Moab (Nu 26:22). Place of, in camp and march (Nu 2:3, 9; 10:14). By whom commanded (Nu 2:3). Moses' benediction upon (Dt 33:7). Commissioned of God to lead in the conquest of the promised land (Jdg 1:1-3, w Jdg 1:4-21). Make David king (2Sa 2:1-11; 5:4-5). Rebuked by David for lukewarmness toward him after Absalom's defeat (2Sa 19:11-15). Accused by the other tribes of stealing the heart of David (2Sa 19:41-43). Loyal to David at the at the time of the insurrection led by Sheba (2Sa 20:1-2). Is accorded the birthright forfeited by Reuben (1Ch 5:1-2; 28:4; Ps 60:7). Loyal to the house of David at the time of the revolt of the ten tribes (1Ki 12:20). Inheritance of (Jos 15; 18:5; 19:1, 9).

3. Name of two exiled priests (Ezr 10:23; Ne 12:8).

4. A Benjamite (Ne 11:9).

5. A prince or priest who assisted in the dedication of the walls of Jerusalem (Ne 12:34, 36).

JUDAISM [2682, 4670].

1. The religion of the Jews in NT times (Gal 1:13-14).

2. "Converts to Judaism" (Ac 2:11; 6:5; 13:43). Gentiles who adopted the religious beliefs and customs of the Jews.

JUDAS [2683] (Greek for *Judah*).

1. Surnamed Iscariot. Chosen as an apostle (Mt 10:4; Mk 3:19; Lk 6:16; Ac 1:17). Treasurer of the disciples (Jn 12:6; 13:29). His greed exemplified by his protest against the breaking of the box of ointment (Jn 12:4-6), by his bargain to betray Jesus for a sum of money (Mt 26:14-16; Mk 14:10-11; Lk 22:3-6; Jn 13:2). His apostasy (Jn 17:12). Betrays the Lord (Mt 26:47-50; Mk 14:43-45; Lk 22:47-49; Jn 18:2-5; Ac 1:16-25). Returns the money to the rulers of the Jews (Mt 27:3-10). Hangs himself (Mt 27:5; Ac 1:18). Prophecies concerning (Mt 26:21-25; Mk 14:18-21; Lk 22:21-23; Jn 13:18-26; 17:12; Ac 1:16, 20, w Ps 41:9; 109:8; Zec 11:12-13).

2. One of the brothers of Jesus (Mt 13:55; Mk 6:3) and writer of the epistle of Jude (Jude 1).

3. Brother of James (Lk 6:16; Ac 1:13).

4. An apostle, probably identical with Lebbaeus, or Thaddaeus (Jn 14:22).

5. Of Galilee, who stirred up a sedition among the Jews soon after the birth of Jesus (Ac 5:37).

6. A disciple who entertained Paul (Ac 9:11).

7. Surnamed Barsabbas. A Christian sent to Antioch with Paul and Barnabas (Ac 15:22-32).

JUDE [2683] (*Judah*). The writer of the last of the NT epistles. The brother of James (Jude 1:1), probably brother of Jesus (Mk 6:3).

JUDE, EPISTLE OF

Author: Jude the brother of Jesus and James

Date: Probably c. A.D. 65

Outline:

I. Salutation (1-2).
II. Occasion for the Letter (3-4).
  A. The Change of Subject (3).
  B. The Reason for the Change: The Presence of Godless Apostates (4).
III. Warning Against the False Teachers (5-16).
  A. Historical Examples of the Judgment of Apostates (5-7).
    1. Unbelieving Israel (5).
    2. Angels who fell (6).
    3. Sodom and Gomorrah (7).
  B. Description of the Apostates of Jude's Day (8-16).
    1. Their slanderous speech deplored (8-10).
    2. Their character graphically portrayed (11-13).
    3. Their destruction prophesied (14-16).
IV. Exhortation to Believers (17-23).
V. Concluding Doxology (24-25).
  See General Letters.

JUDEA [3373, 3374, 2677, 2681, 2683] (*land of the Judahites, Jews*).

1. Greek spelling of Judah. The southern division of Israel. It extended from the Jordan and Dead Sea to the Mediterranean, and from Shiloh on the N to the wilderness on the S (Mt 4:25; Lk 5:17; Jn 4:47, 54). The term is applied to all of Israel (Lk 1:5). The term is applied to the territory E of Jordan (Mt 19:1; Mk 10:1; Lk 23:5).

2. Wilderness of. Called Beth Arabah (Jos 18:22). John the Baptist preaches in (Mt 3:1; Lk 3:3).

JUDGE [*466, 1906, 1907, 3248, 3519, 4213, 5477, 6885, 7132, 7213, 9149, 9150, 9370, 10170, 10171, 10188, 373, 1037, 1191, 1359, 1471, 3210, 3212, 3213, 3216].

Character of and Precepts Relating to:

Must be righteous (Ex 18:21-22; Lev 19:15; Dt 16:18-20; 1Ki 3:9; Ps 58:1-2; 72:1-4, 4), intelligent (Dt 1:12-13; Isa 28:6). Must judge righteously (Dt 1:16-17).

Jurisdiction of as judge (1Sa 2:25). Inferior and superior judges (Dt 17:8-11). Held circuit courts (1Sa 7:16). Rules for guidance of (Ex 18:22; Dt 19:16-19; 25:1-3; 2Ch 19:5-10; Pr 24:23; Eze 44:24; Jn 7:24).

Kings and other rulers as (2Sa 8:15; 15:2; 1Ki 3:16-28; 10:9; 2Ki 8:1-6; Ps 72:1-4; Mt 27:11-26; Ac 23:34-35; 24; 25:11-12). Priests and Levites as (Dt 17:9; 1Ch 23:4; 2Ch 19:8; Eze 44:23-24; Mt 26:57-62). Women as: Deborah (Jdg 4:4).

Persian government provided (Ezr 7:25).

Corrupt:

(1Sa 8:3; Ps 82:2-4; Isa 5:22-23; Da 9:12; Mic 7:3; Zep 3:3).

Instances of: Eli's sons (1Sa 2:12-17, 22-25). Samuel's sons (1Sa 8:1-5). The judges of Jezreel (1Ki 21:8-13). Pilate (Mt 27:24, 26; Mk 15:15, 19-24). Felix (Ac 24:26-27).

Of Israel:

Executives and leaders of the nation. During the time when the land was ruled by judges (Jdg 2:16-19; Ac 13:20).

Othniel (Jdg 3:9-11). Ehud (Jdg 3:15, 30). Shamgar (Jdg 3:31). Deborah (Jdg 4:4-5). Gideon (Jdg 6:11-40; 7:8). Abimelech (Jdg 9:1-54). Tola (Jdg 10:1-2). Jair (Jdg 10:3-5). Jephthah (Jdg 12:7). Ibzan (Jdg 12:8-10). Elon (Jdg 12:11-12). Abdon (Jdg 12:13-14). Samson (Jdg 15:20; 16:31). Eli (1Sa 4:18). Samuel (1Sa 7:6, 15-17). The sons of Samuel (1Sa 8:1-5).

See Court, Of Law;   God, Judge; Justice; Witness.

JUDGES, BOOK OF

Author: Anonymous; traditionally Samuel

Date: Possibly between 1040 and 1000 B.C.

Outline:

I. Prologue: Incomplete Conquest and Apostasy (1:1-3:6).
  A. First Episode: Israel's Failure to Purge the Land (1:1-2:5).
  B. Second Episode: God's Dealings with Israel's Rebellion (2:6-3:6).
II. Oppression and Deliverance (3:7-16:31).
  Major Judges (A-F)   *Minor Judges* (1-6)
  A. Othniel Defeats Aram Naharaim (3:7-11).
  B. Ehud Defeats Moab (3:12-30).
    1. Shamgar (3:31).

C. Deborah Defeats Canaan (chs. 4-5).
D. Gideon Defeats Midian (chs. 6-8).
(Abimelech, the anti-judge, ch. 9).
  2. Tola (10:1-2).
  3. Jair (10:3-5).
E. Jephthah Defeats Ammon (10:6-12:7).
  4. Ibzan (12:8-10).
  5. Elon (12:11-12).
  6. Abdon (12:13-15).
F. Samson Checks Philistia (chs. 17-21).
III. Epilogue: Religious and Moral Disorder (chs. 17-21).
A. First Episode (chs. 17-18; see 17:6; 18:1).
  1. Micah's corruption of religion (ch 17).
  2. The Danites' departure from their tribal territory (ch. 18).
B. Second Episode (chs. 19-21; see 19:1; 21:25).
  1. Gibeah's corruption of morals (ch. 19).
  2. The Benjamites' removal from their tribal territory (chs. 20-21).

JUDGING See Uncharitableness.

JUDGMENT [*466, 1906, 1907, 3248, 3519, 4213, 5477, 6885, 7132, 7213, 9149, 9150, 9370, 10170, 10171, 10188, *373, 1037, 1191, 1359, 1471, 3210, 3212, 3213, 3216].

General:

Forewarned (Ecc 11:9; 12:14; Mt 8:29 w 2Pe 2:4 & Jude 6; Mt 13:30, 40-43, 49-50; Mt 25:31-46; Mk 8:38; Ac 24:25; 2Th 1:7-8; Heb 6:2).

Fierce and fiery (Mt 3:12; 10:15; 11:22; 12:36-42; Lk 3:17; 10:10-14; 11:31-32; 13:24-29; Ac 2:19-20).

According to opportunity and works (Ge 4:7; 1Sa 26:23; Job 34:11-12; Ps 62:12; Pr 12:14; 24:11-12; Isa 3:10-11; 59:18; Jer 17:10; 32:19; Eze 7:3-4, 27; 18:4-9; 18:19-32; 33:18-20; Hos 4:9; 12:2; Zec 1:6; Mt 25:1-30; Lk 12:47-48; 13:6-9; 19:12-27; Jn 3:19-20; Ro 2:5-12; 1Co 3:8, 12-15; 2Co 11:15; Gal 6:7-8; Eph 6:7-8; Col 3:25; Heb 10:26-30; 12:25; Jas 2:13; 1Pe 1:17; 2Pe 2:20-21; Rev 2:23; 20:12-13).

Design of:

To exhibit a basis for rewards and punishments (2Co 5:10; 2Ti 4:8; Rev 11:18; 22:12). To reveal secrets (Ecc 12:14; Lk 12:2-3; Ro 2:16; 1Co 3:13).

Who Will Be the Judge:

God as Judge (1Ch 16:33; Ps 9:7; 50:4, 6; 96:13; 98:9; Ecc 12:14; Da 7:9-10; Ro 2:5, 16; 3:6; 2Ti 4:8; Heb 10:30; 12:23; 13:4; 1Pe 4:5; Rev 20:11-15).

Jesus Christ as Judge (Mt 7:22-23; 13:30, 40-43, 49-50; 16:25, 27; 25:31-46; Mk 8:38; Jn 5:22; 12:48; Ac 10:42; 17:31; Ro 2:16; 14:10; 1Co 4:5; 2Co 5:10; 2Th 1:7-8; 2Ti 4:1; 2Pe 2:9; 3:10; Rev 1:7; 6:15-17).

The saints as judges (Mt 19:28; 1Co 6:2; Jude 14).

Time of:

Appointed (Mt 13:30; Ac 17:31; Heb 9:27; 2Pe 3:7, 10-12). Known to God only (Mk 13:32).

Who Will Be Judged:

The righteous and wicked (Ecc 3:17; Mt 25:31-46; Jude 14-15; Rev 11:18). The wicked (Job 21:30; Eze 18:20-28; 2Pe 2:9; 3:7). The living and the dead (Ac 10:42; 2Ti 4:1; 1Pe 4:5). All must be made manifest (Mk 4:22; Ac 17:31; 2Co 5:10). Kings and princes, slaves and freemen (Rev 6:15-16). Fallen angels (2Pe 2:4; Jude 6).

See God, Judge; Jesus the Christ, Judge; Punishment, According to Deeds.

JUDGMENT, HALL OF See Praetorium.

JUDGMENT SEAT (Mt 27:19; Ac 18:12; 25:10). Of Christ (Ro 14:10).

JUDGMENTS [5477, 8652, 9150, *373, 3210, 3213]. Denounced against Solomon (1Ki 11:9-14, 23), Jeroboam (1Ki 14:7-15), Ahab and Jezebel (1Ki 21:19-24), Ahaziah (2Ch 22:7-9), Manasseh (2Ch 33:11). Against disobedience (Lev 26:14-39; Dt 28:15-68; 29:1-29; 32:19-43).

Design of:

To correct (Dt 30:1-2; 1Ki 8:33-34; 2Ch 7:13; Job 5:17; 23:10; 34:31-32; Ps 94:12-13; 107:10-14, 17; Pr 3:11; Isa 9:13-14; 26:9; Jer 24:5; 30:11; La 1:5, 12; Eze 20:37, 43; Hos 2:6-7; 5:15; 1Co 11:32; Heb 12:5-11). To humble (2Co 12:7).

Misunderstood:

(Jer 16:10; Joel 2:17). No escape from (Ex 20:7; 34:7; Isa 2:10, 12-19, 21; Eze 14:13-14; Am 5:16-20; 9:1-4; Mt 23:33; Heb 2:1-3; 10:28-29; 12:25; Rev 6:16-17). *See Escape.* Executed by human instrumentality (Jer 51:2). Delayed (Ps 10:6; 50:21; 55:19). *See Punishment, Delayed.*

Instances of:

On the serpent (Ge 3:14-15), Eve (Ge 3:16), Adam (Ge 3:17-19), Cain (Ge 4:11-15), the Antediluvians (Ge 6-7), Sodomites (Ge 19:23-25).

Egyptians, the plagues and overthrow (Ex 7-13; 14:1-31). Nadab and Abihu (Lev 10:1-3). Miriam (Nu 12:1-15).

Upon the Israelites: For worshiping Aaron's calf (Ex 32:35), for murmuring (Nu 11:1, 33-34; 14:22-23, 32, 35-37; 21:6; 25:4-5, 9). The forty years wandering, a judgment (Nu 14:26-39; 26:63-65; Dt 2:14-17), delivered into the hands of the Assyrians (2Ki 17:6-41), Chaldeans (2Ch 36:14-21).

Upon the Canaanites: (Lev 18:25; Dt 7; 12:29-32), with the conquest of, by Joshua. *See Canaanite(s).*

Upon Abimelech (Jdg 9:52-57), Uzzah (2Sa 6:7), Eli's house (1Sa 2:27-36, w 1Sa 4:10-22), the prophet of Judah, for disobedience (1Ki 13:1-24), Zimri (1Ki 16:18-19), Gehazi (2Ki 5:27), Sennacherib (2Ki 19:35-37), Hananiah, the false prophet (Jer 28:15, 17).

See Chastisement, From God; Punishment; Sin, Punishment of.

JUDITH [3377] (*Jewess* or *Judahite*).
1. Wife of Esau (Ge 26:34).

2. Heroine of the apocryphal book of Judith.

JULIA [2684] (*of Julian [the family of Julius Caesar]*). A Christian woman in Rome (Ro 16:15).

JULIUS [2685] (*of Julian [the family of Julius Caesar]*). Roman centurion to whom Paul was entrusted (Ac 27:1, 3).

JUNIAS [2687]. A relative or countryman of Paul (Ro 16:7). Possibly a feminine name and an apostle.

JUNIPER *See Broom Tree.*

JUPITER Latin for the god Zeus. *See Zeus.*

JURISDICTION *See Church, The Body of Believers, State.*

JURY Of ten elders (Ru 4:2). Of seventy elders (Nu 11:16-17, 24-25).

JUSHAB-HESED [3457] (*loyal love will be returned*). Son of Zerubbabel (1Ch 3:20).

JUST, THE *See Righteous.*

JUST SHALL LIVE BY FAITH
(Hab 2:4; Ro 1:17; Gal 3:11; Heb 10:38).

JUSTICE [1906, 1907, 2006, 4793, 4797, 5477, 5742, 7405, 7406, 7407, 8190, 9149, 10169, *1466, 1472, 1688, 1689, 3213*]. From God (Ps 72:1-2; Pr 29:26).

Commanded (Ex 23:1-3, 6-8; Lev 19:13-15; Dt 16:18-20; 25:1-4; Ps 82:3-4; 106:3; Pr 18:5; Isa 1:17; Jer 7:5, 7; La 3:35-36; Mic 6:8; Zec 7:9; 8:16; Jn 7:24, 51).

Must be impartial (Pr 24:23; 28:21). Can be perverted (Ecc 3:16; 5:8; Isa 59:14-15; Jer 22:3; Am

5:7, 11-12; Mic 7:3; Hab 1:4; Mt 12:7). Will be rewarded (Jer 22:4, 15-16; Eze 18:5-9).

Of God: *See God, Justice of.*

See Court, Of Law; Injustice; Judge.

JUSTIFICATION [*2342, 7136, 7405, 8750, *1466+ 1650, 1467, 1468, 1470*]. The act of divine grace which restores the sinner to the relationship with God that he would have had if he had not sinned; pardon of sin. The word is used also to denote the state of the sinner after he is restored to divine favor.

Not imputing guilt to the sinner (Ps 32:2; Isa 53:11; Zec 3:4; Jn 5:24; Ro 4:6; 8:1).

Comes from God (Isa 45:24-25; 50:8; 54:17; 61:10; Ro 3:25; 8:30, 33; 2Co 5:19, 21; Tit 3:7). Achieved through Christ (Isa 53:11; Jer 23:6; Ac 13:39; Ro 3:20-25; 5:9, 11, 16-18, 21; 1Co 1:30; 6:11; Col 2:13-14). Is based on his righteousness (Ps 71:16; 89:16; Isa 42:21; 46:12-13; 51:5-6; 56:1; Ro 1:16-17; Gal 5:4-6).

Is not by the law (Ro 3:20; Gal 2:16; 3:11; 5:4-6). Is by faith (Ge 15:6; Hab 2:4; Ro 1:16-17; 3:20-22, 24, 28, 30; 4:2-25; 5:1; 9:30-32; 10:4, 6, 8-11; Gal 2:14-21; 3:6, 8-9, 21-22, 24; 5:4-6; Php 3:8-9; Heb 11:4, 7; Jas 2:20-23, 26).

Fruits of: Peace (Ro 5:1). Holiness (Ro 6:22).

Example of: Abraham (Ge 15:6; Ro 4:3).

See Adoption; Forgiveness; Regeneration; Sanctification; Sin, Confession of, Forgiveness of.

JUSTUS [2688] (*just*).

1. A disciple nominated with Matthias to succeed Judas Iscariot (Ac 1:23).

2. A believer in Corinth (Ac 18:7).

3. Also called Jesus. A disciple in Rome (Col 4:11).

JUTTAH [3420] (*extended, inclined*). A Levitical city in Judah (Jos 15:55; 21:16).

KAB *See Cab; Measure.*

KABZEEL [7696] (*God [El] collects*). A city of Judah (Jos 15:21; 2Sa 23:20; 1Ch 11:22).

KADESH [7729] (*sacred place*). Also known as En Mishpat (Ge 14:7). A place c. seventy miles S of Hebron, in the vicinity of which Israel wandered for thirty-seven years (Dt 1:46; Nu 33:37-38; Dt 2:14). Miriam died there (Nu 20:1), Moses sent spies to Israel from there (Nu 13:21-26; Dt 1:19-25), Moses displeased God there by striking the rock instead of speaking to it (Nu 20:2-13). Often called Kadesh Barnea (Nu 32:8; Dt 2:14).

KADESH BARNEA [7732] (*sacred place of Barnea*). *See Kadesh.*

KADMIEL [7718] (*[stand] before God [El]*).
1. A Levite (Ezr 2:40; 3:9; Ne 7:43; 12:8, 24).
2. A Levite who assisted in leading the worship of the people (Ne 9:4-5; 10:9).

KADMONITES [7720] (*easterners*). Ancient Arab tribe between Egypt and Euphrates (Ge 15:18-21).

KAIN [7805] (*smith*).
1. Town in Judah (Jos 15:57).
2. Tribal name (Nu 24:22; Jdg 4:11). *See Kenite(s).*

KALLAI [7834] (*swift*). A priest (Ne 12:20).

KAMAI *See Leb Kamai.*

KAMON [7852]. Place where Jair was buried (Jdg 10:5).

KANAH [7867] (*reed*).
1. Brook flowing between Ephraim and Manasseh into the Mediterranean (Jos 16:8; 17:9).
2. City c. eight miles SE of Tyre, near boundary of Manasseh (Jos 19:28).

KAREAH [7945] (*bald head*). Father of Johanan, governor of Judah in the time of Gedaliah (2Ki 25:23; Jer 40:8, 13; 41:11, 13-14, 16).

KARKA [7978] (*floor, ground*). A city of Judah (Jos 15:3).

KARKOR [7980]. Place E of Jordan where Gideon defeated Midianites (Jdg 8:10). Exact location unknown.

KARNAIM [7969]. (*horns*). A city conquered by Israel (Am 6:13).

KARTAH [7985] (*city*). A city of Zebulun (Jos 21:34).

KARTAN [7986]. A Levitical city in Naphtali (Jos 21:32).

KATTATH [7793]. A city in Zebulun (Jos 19:15).

KATYDID [6155]. An insect permitted as food (Lev 11:22). *See Insects.*

KAZIN *See Eth Kazin.*

KEBAR [3894]. A river of Mesopotamia (Eze 1:1, 3; 3:15, 23; 10:15, 22; 43:3).

KEDAR [7723] (*mighty*).
1. Son of Ishmael (Ge 25:13; 1Ch 1:29).
2. A nomadic clan of the Ishmaelites (Ps 120:5; SS 1:5; Isa 21:16; 42:11; 60:7; Jer 49:28). Flocks of (Isa 60:7; Jer 49:28). Princes and commerce of (Eze 27:21).

KEDEMAH [7715] (*east*). Son of Ishmael (Ge 25:15; 1Ch 1:31).

KEDEMOTH [7717] (*east*). A city of Moab, allotted to Reuben and the Merarite Levites (Jos 13:18; 1Ch 6:79). Encircled by a wilderness of same name (Dt 2:26).

KEDESH [7730] (*sacred place*).
1. A city of Judah (Jos 15:23). Possibly identical with Kadesh Barnea.
2. Called also Kishion and Kishon. A Canaanite city taken by Joshua (Jos 12:22; 19:20; 21:28; 1Ch 6:72).
3. Called also Kedesh in Naphtali. A city of refuge (Jos 20:7; 21:32). Home of Barak and Heber (Jdg 4:6, 9, 11). Captured by Tiglath-Pileser (2Ki 15:29).

KEDESH NAPHTALI (*sacred place of Naphtali*). *See Kedesh, 3.*

KEDORLAOMER [3906] (*servant of [the deity] Lagamar*). King of Elam (Ge 14:1-16).

KEDRON *See Kidron.*

KEEPERS Of the prison (Ge 39:22; Ac 5:23; 12:6; 16:27, 36).

KEHELATHAH [7739] (*assembly*). An encampment of Israel (Nu 33:22-23).

KEILAH [7881].
1. One of a group of nine cities in the southern part of Israel allotted to Judah (Jos 15:44). Philistines make a predatory excursion against, after harvest (1Sa 23:1). David rescues (1Sa 23:2-13).

Rulers of, aid in restoring the wall of Jerusalem after the Captivity (Ne 3:17-18).

2. A descendant of Caleb (1Ch 4:19).

KELAIAH [7835] (perhaps *Yahweh has dishonored*). Called also Kelita. A Levite who divorced his Gentile wife after the Captivity and assisted Ezra in expounding the law (Ezr 10:23; Ne 8:7; 10:10).

KELAL [4006] (*perfection, completeness*). Son of Pahath-Moab (Ezr 10:30).

KELITA See *Kelaiah*.

KELUB [3991] (*basket*).
1. A descendant of Caleb (1Ch 4:11).
2. Father of Ezri (1Ch 27:26).

KELUBAI See *Caleb, 1*.

KELUHI [3988]. Son of Bani (Ezr 10:35).

KEMUEL [7851] (*God's [El's] mound* ISBE).
1. Son of Nahor; uncle of Laban and Rebekah (Ge 22:21).
2. Prince of Ephraim (Nu 34:24).
3. Father of Hashabiah, leading Levite (1Ch 27:17).

KENAANAH [4049] (*toward Canaan*).
1. Father of the false prophet Zedekiah (1Ki 22:11, 24; 2Ch 18:10, 23).
2. Brother of Ehud (1Ch 7:10).

KENAN [7809, 2783]. Great-grandson of Adam (1Ch 1:2). Enosh is the father of Kenan (Ge 5:9-14).

KENANI [4039] (*Yahweh strengthens*). A Levite (Ne 9:4).

KENANIAH [4040, 4041] (*Yahweh strengthens*).
1. A Levite (1Ch 15:22, 27).
2. An Izharite (1Ch 26:29).

KENATH [7875] (*possession*). Amorite city in region of Bashan in kingdom of Og (Nu 32:42; 1Ch 2:22-23).

KENAZ [7869] (*hunting*).
1. Grandson of Esau (Ge 36:11, 15; 1Ch 1:36).
2. A chief of Edom (Ge 36:42; 1Ch 1:53).
3. Brother of Caleb (Jos 15:17; Jdg 1:13; 3:9, 11; 1Ch 4:13).
4. Grandson of Caleb (1Ch 4:15).

KENITE(S) [7804, 7808] (*of the [copper] smiths*).
1. A Canaanite tribe whose country was given to Abraham (Ge 15:19; Nu 24:21-23).
2. The descendants of Jethro, a Midianite, father-in-law of Moses. Joined the Israelites and lived at Jericho (Jdg 1:16; 4:11; 1Ch 2:55), later in the wilderness of Judah (Jdg 1:16-17). Jael, one of the, betrayed and killed Sisera (Jdg 4:17-21).

KENIZZITE(S) [7870]. Descendants of Kenaz (Ge 15:19). Caleb (Nu 32:12) and Othniel (Jos 15:17) were Kenizzites.

KENOSIS (*emptying*). A term applied to Christ's taking the form of a servant in the Incarnation (Php 2:7).

KEPHAR AMMONI [4112] (*village of Ammonites*). A town of Benjamin (Jos 18:24).

KEPHIRAH [4098] (*village*). A city of the Hivites (Jos 9:17; 18:26; Ezr 2:25; Ne 7:29).

KERAMIM See *Abel Keramim*.

KERAN [4154]. A Horite (Ge 36:26; 1Ch 1:41).

KERCHIEF See *Handkerchief*.

KEREN-HAPPUCH [7968] (*horn of [cosmetic] eyeshadow;* i.e., *cosmetic case*). Youngest daughter of Job (Job 42:14).

KERETHITE(S) [4165] (possibly *Cretans* BDB KB; *executioners* ISBE). A Philistine tribe, which allied with David and, with the Pelethites, formed his bodyguard (1Sa 30:14, 16; 2Sa 8:18; 15:18; 20:7, 23; 1Ki 1:38, 44; 1Ch 18:17; Eze 25:16; Zep 2:5). Solomon's escort at his coronation (1Ki 1:38).

KERIOTH, KERIOTH HEZRON [7954, 7955] (*town of Hezron*).
1. A city of Judah (Jos 15:25).
2. A city of Moab (Jer 48:24, 41; Am 2:2).

KERITH [4134] (*cut off, perish*). A brook near Jericho (1Ki 17:3-7).

KEROS [7820]. Ancestor of the temple servants who returned with Zerubbabel (Ezr 2:44; Ne 7:47).

KERUB [4132]. Name of a place or person (Ezr 2:59; Ne 7:61).

KESALON [4076]. A landmark in the N boundary of Judah (Jos 15:10).

KESED [4168] (*Chaldean [Babylonian]*). Son of Nahor (Ge 22:22).

KESIL [4069]. A town in the S of Israel (Jos 15:30). Probably identical with Bethul (Jos 19:4), and Bethuel (1Ch 4:30).

KESULLOTH [4063] (*loins or flanks [of Mt. Tabor]* BDB). A city of Issachar (Jos 19:18). Probably identical with Kisloth Tabor (Jos 19:12) and Tabor (1Ch 6:77).

KETTLE [1857, 5908]. Cooking vessel or basket (1Sa 2:14).

KETURAH [7778] (*incense, scented one*).

Abraham's second wife. Mother of six sons, ancestors of Arabian tribes (Ge 25:1-6; 1Ch 1:33).

KEY [5158, 3090]. (Jdg 3:25). A symbol of authority (Isa 22:22; Mt 16:19; Rev 1:18; 3:7; 9:1; 20:1). *See Binding and Loosing.*

Figurative: key of knowledge (Lk 11:52).

KEZIAH [7905] (*cassia [cinnamon]*). Second daughter of Job (Job 42:14).

KEZIB [3945] (*deceit*). Birthplace of Shelah (Ge 38:5), probably identical with Cozeba (1Ch 4:22), and Aczib (Jos 15:44).

KEZIZ *See Emek Keziz.*

KIBROTH HATTAAVAH [7701]
(*graves of lust, greed*). A station where the Israelites were miraculously fed with quail (Nu 11:31-35; 33:16-17; Dt 9:22).

KIBZAIM [7698]. A Levitical city in Ephraim (Jos 21:22).

KID *See Animals; Goats.*

KIDNAPPING [1704+, 1705]. Forbidden (Ex 21:16; Dt 24:7).

Instance of (Jdg 21:20-23).

KIDNEY [4000]. Used with surrounding fat as a burnt offering (Ex 29:13, 22; Lev 3:4, 10, 15; 4:9). Regarded as the seat of the emotions; usually translated "heart" (Ps 7:9; 16:7).

KIDON [3961]. Place where Uzzah was stricken to death because he had put his hand on the ark (1Ch 13:9-11). Called Nacon's threshing floor (2Sa 6:6).

KIDRON [7724, 3022]. Brook of, running S under the eastern wall of Jerusalem between Jerusalem and the Mount of Olives (1Ki 2:37; Ne 2:15; Jer 31:40). David flees from Absalom across (2Sa 15:23). Destruction of idols at, by Asa, Josiah, and the Levites (1Ki 15:13; 2Ki 23:6, 12; 2Ch 29:16). Source of, closed by Hezekiah (2Ch 32:1-4). Jesus crossed, on the night of his agony (Jn 18:1).

KILEAB [3976]. A son of David (2Sa 3:3). Also called Daniel (1Ch 3:1).

KILION [4002] (*annihilation*). Son of Elimelech and Naomi, married Orpah (Ru 1:2-5; 4:9-10).

KILLING *See Homicide.*

KILMAD [4008]. Merchants of (Eze 27:23).

KIMHAM [4016]. A Gileadite (2Sa 19:37-38, 40; Jer 41:17).

KINAH [7807] (*lament, dirge*). A city of Judah (Jos 15:22).

KINDNESS [1691, 2858, 2876, 3512, *14, 2307, 5789, 5792, 5982, 5983*].

Commanded: (Zec 7:9-10; Mt 5:42; Lk 6:30; 6:34-35; Ac 20:35; Ro 12:15; 15:1-2; Gal 6:1-2, 10; Eph 4:32; Col 3:12; 1Pe 3:8-9; 1Jn 3:17-18). To enemies (Ex 23:4-5; Lk 6:34-35). To strangers (Lev 19:34). To a brother (Dt 22:1).

Inspired by love (1Co 13:4-7). Commends ministers (2Co 6:6). Rewards of (Pr 14:21; Mt 5:7; 25:34-35).

Of God (Lk 6:35). Of good women (Pr 31:26; 1Ti 5:9-10). Of good men (Ps 112:5; Heb 5:2). Of Jesus. *See Jesus the Christ, Compassion of.*

Instances of:

Hittites to Abraham (Ge 23:6, 11). Keeper of the prison to Joseph (Ge 39:21-23). Pharaoh to Jacob (Ge 45:16-20; 47:5-6). Pharaoh's daughter to Moses (Ex 2:6-10). Moses to Jethro's daughters (Ex 2:17, 19). Jethro to Moses (Ex 2:20). Rahab to the spies (Jos 2:4-16). Boaz to Ruth (Ru 2:8-16; 3:15). David to Nabal (1Sa 25:15-16). Abigail to David (1Sa 25:14-35). David to Mephibosheth (2Sa 9:1-13). Joab to Absalom (2Sa 14:1-24). Obadiah to the prophets of the Lord (1Ki 18:4). Ahab to Ben-Hadad (1Ki 20:32-34). The Shunammite woman to Elisha (2Ki 4:8-10). Elisha to the Shunammite woman (2Ki 4:13-17, 28-37; 8:1). Evil-Merodach to Jehoiachin (2Ki 25:28-30). Jehosheba to Joash (2Ch 22:11). Nehemiah and the nobles to the people (Ne 5:8-19). Mordecai to Esther (Est 2:7). Ebed-Melech to Jeremiah (Jer 38:7-13). Nebuchadnezzar to Jeremiah (Jer 39:11-12).

Joseph to Mary (Mt 1:19, 24). Centurion to his servant (Lk 7:2-6). Jews to Mary and Martha (Jn 11:19, 33). John to Mary (Jn 19:27). Felix to Paul (Ac 24:23). Julius to Paul (Ac 27:3, 43). Barbarians to Paul (Ac 28:2, 7). Onesiphorus to Paul (2Ti 1:16-18).

KINE *See Cattle.*

KINGDOM OF GOD, OF HEAVEN
[806, 4867, 4889, 4895, 4930, 4931, 4939, 10424, *993, 2026*]. The sovereign rule of God manifested in Christ to defeat His enemies, creating a people over whom He reigns, and issuing in a realm or realms in which the power of His reign is experienced. All they are members of the kingdom of God who voluntarily submit to the rule of God in their lives. Entrance into the kingdom is by the new birth (Jn 3:3-5); two stages in the kingdom of God; present and future in an eschatological sense; Jesus said that his ability to cast out demons was evidence that the kingdom of God had come among men (Mt 12:28). "Kingdom of heaven" is used exclusively in Matthew (33 times). Likened to, a man who sowed good seed (Mt 13:24-30, 38-43; Mk 4:26-29), a grain of mustard seed (Mt 13:31-32; Mk 4:30-31; Lk 13:18-19), leaven (Mt 13:33; Lk 13:21), a treasure (Mt 13:44), a pearl (Mt 13:45), a net (Mt 13:47-50), a king who called his servants

to a reckoning (Mt 18:23-35), a house owner (Mt 20:1-16), a king who made a marriage feast for his son (Mt 22:2-14; Lk 14:16-24), ten virgins (Mt 25:1-13), a man traveling into a far country, who called his servants, and delivered to them his goods (Mt 25:14-30; Lk 19:12-27).

"My kingdom is not of this world" (Jn 18:36).

Children of the (Mt 18:3; 19:14; Mk 10:14; Lk 18:16). Rich cannot enter (Mt 19:23-24; Mk 10:23-25; Lk 18:24-25, 29-30). Keys of (Mt 16:19). Glad tidings of (Lk 8:1). Mysteries of (Lk 8:10). Is not eating and drinking (Ro 14:17).

See Church, The Body of Believers; Jesus, Kingdom of.

KINGDOM OF ISRAEL See Israel.

KINGDOM OF JUDAH See Judah.

KINGDOM OF SATAN The realm of Satan's influence (Mt 12:26; Lk 11:18).

KINGS [3782, 4482, 4887, 4889, 4930, 10421, 995, 996, 5203].

In Israel:

Israel warned against seeking (1Sa 8:9-18). Sin of Israel in seeking (1Sa 12:17-20). Israel in seeking, rejected God as their king (1Sa 8:7; 10:19). Israel asked for, that they might be like the nations (1Sa 8:5, 19-20). First given to Israel in anger (Hos 13:11). God reserved to himself the choice of (Dt 17:14-15; 1Sa 9:16-17; 16:12). When first established in Israel, not hereditary (Dt 17:20, w 1Sa 13:13-14; 15:28-29). Rendered hereditary in the family of David (2Sa 7:12-16; Ps 89:35-37). Of Israel not to be foreigners (Dt 17:15). Laws for the government of the kingdom by, written by Samuel (1Sa 10:25).

Forbidden to accumulate: Horses (Dt 17:16). Wives (Dt 17:17). Treasure (Dt 17:17).

Required to write and keep a copy of the divine law (Dt 17:18-20). Had power to make war and peace (1Sa 11:5-7). Often exercised power arbitrarily (1Sa 22:17-18; 2Sa 1:15; 4:9-12; 1Ki 2:23, 25, 31). Sometimes nominated their successors (1Ki 1:33-34; 2Ch 11:22-23). Punished for transgressing the divine law (2Sa 12:7-12; 1Ki 21:18-24).

Called the Lord's anointed (1Sa 16:6; 24:6; 2Sa 19:21).

Ceremonies at Inauguration of:

Anointing (1Sa 10:1; 16:13; Ps 89:20). Crowning (2Ki 11:12; 2Ch 23:11; Ps 21:3). Proclaiming with trumpets (2Sa 15:10; 1Ki 1:34; 2Ki 9:13; 11:14). Enthroning (1Ki 1:35, 46; 2Ki 11:19). Strapping on the sword (Ps 45:3). Putting into their hands the books of the law (2Ki 11:12; 2Ch 23:11). Covenanting to govern lawfully (2Sa 5:3). Receiving homage (1Sa 10:1; 1Ch 29:24). Shouting "Long live the King!" (1Sa 10:24; 2Sa 16:16; 2Ki 11:12). Feasting (1Ch 12:38-39; 29:22). Attended by a bodyguard (1Sa 13:2; 2Sa 8:18; 1Ch 11:25; 2Ch 12:10). Dwelt in royal palaces (2Ch 9:11; Ps

45:15). Arrayed in royal apparel (1Ki 22:30; Mt 6:29). Names of, often changed at their accession (2Ki 23:34; 24:17).

Officers of:

Prime minister (2Ch 19:11, w 2Ch 28:7). First Counselor (1Ch 27:33). Confident or king's special friend (1Ch 27:33). Comptroller of the household (1Ki 4:6; 2Ch 28:7). Scribe or secretary (2Sa 8:17; 1Ki 4:3). Captain of the host (2Sa 8:16; 1Ki 4:4). Captain of the guard (2Sa 8:18; 20:23). Recorder (2Sa 8:16; 1Ki 4:3). Providers for the king's table (1Ki 4:7-19). Master of the wardrobe (2Ki 22:14; 2Ch 34:22). Treasurer (1Ch 27:25). Storekeeper (1Ch 27:25). Overseer of, the tribute (1Ki 4:6; 12:18), royal farms (1Ch 27:26), royal vineyards (1Ch 27:27), royal plantations (1Ch 27:28), royal herds (1Sa 21:7; 1Ch 27:29), royal camels (1Ch 27:30), royal flocks (1Ch 27:31). Armor-bearer (1Sa 16:21). Cupbearer (1Ki 10:5; 2Ch 9:4). Approached with greatest reverence (1Sa 24:8; 2Sa 9:8; 14:22; 1Ki 1:23). Presented with gifts by strangers (1Ki 10:2, 10, 25; 2Ki 5:5; Mt 2:11). Right hand of, the place of honor (1Ki 2:19; Ps 45:9; 110:1). Attendants of, stood in their presence (1Ki 10:8; 2Ki 25:19). Exercised great hospitality (1Sa 20:25-27; 2Sa 9:7-13; 19:33; 1Ki 4:22-23, 28).

Their Revenues Derived From:

Voluntary contributions (1Sa 10:27, w 1Sa 16:20; 1Ch 12:39-40). Tribute from foreign nations (1Ki 4:21, 24-25; 2Ch 8:8; 17:11). Tax on produce of the land (1Ki 4:7-19). Tax on foreign merchandise (1Ki 10:15). Their own flocks and herds (2Ch 32:29). Produce of their own lands (2Ch 26:10).

Conspiracies Against:

Absalom against David (2Sa 15:10). Adonijah against Solomon (1Ki 1:5-7). Jeroboam against Rehoboam (1Ki 12:12, 16). Baasha against Nadab (1Ki 15:27). Zimri against Elah (1Ki 16:9-10). Omri against Zimri (1Ki 16:17). Jehu against Joram (2Ki 9:14). Shallum against Zechariah (2Ki 15:10). Menahem against Shallum (2Ki 15:14). Pekah against Menahem (2Ki 15:25).

The Kings of Israel and Judah:

See chart on the following page. See also each king by name and the outlines of the books of Kings and Chronicles.

Relation to God:

God chooses (Dt 17:15; 1Ch 28:4-6). God ordains (Ro 13:1). God anoints (1Sa 16:12; 2Sa 12:7). Set up by God (1Sa 12:13; Da 2:21). Removed by God (1Ki 11:11; Da 2:21). Christ is the Prince of (Rev 1:5). Christ is the King of (Rev 17:14). Reign by direction of Christ (Pr 8:15). Resistance to, is resistance to the ordinance of God (Ro 13:2). Supreme judges of nations (1Sa 8:5). Resistance to, is resistance to the ordinance of God (Ro 13:2). Able to enforce their commands (Ecc 8:4). Numerous subjects the honor of (Pr 14:28). Not saved by their armies (Ps 33:16). Dependent on the earth (Ecc 5:9). Throne of, established by righteousness and justice (Pr 16:12; 29:14).

The Kings of the United Kingdom				
	Name	Ruled	Dates B.C.	Biblical References
1.	Saul	40 years	1050-1010	1Sa 11:15,31; 1Ch 10
2.	David	40 years	1010-970	2Sa 2:4; 1Ki 2:11; 1Ch 11-29
3.	Solomon	40 years	970-930	1Ki 1:39; 11:43; 2Ch 1-9
The Kings (and Queen) of Judah				
1.	Rehoboam	17 years	930-913	1Ki 12:1-24; 14:21-31; 2Ch 10:1-17; 12
2.	Abijah	3 years	913-910	1Ki 15:1-8; 2Ch 13
3.	Asa	41 years	910-869	1Ki 15:9-24; 2Ch 14; 16:14
4.	Jehoshaphat	25 years	872-848	1Ki 22:41-50; 2Ch 17; 21:1
5.	Jehoram	8 years	848-841	2Ki 8:16-24; 21
6.	Ahaziah	1 year	841	2Ki 8:25-29; 9:16-29; 2Ch 22:1-9
7.	Queen Athaliah	6 years	841-835	2Ki 11:1-3; 2Ch 22:10-12
8.	Joash	40 years	835-796	2Ki 11:4; 12; 2Ch 23-24
9.	Amaziah	29 years	796-767	2Ki 14:1-20; 2Ch 25
10.	Uzziah / Azariah	52 years	792-740	2Ki 14:21-22; 15:1-7; 2Ch 26
11.	Jotham	16 years	750-735	2Ki 15:32-38; 2Ch 27
12.	Ahaz	16 years	732-715	2Ki 16; 2Ch 28
13.	Hezekiah	29 years	715-686	2Ki 18-20; 2Ch 29-32
14.	Manasseh	55 years	697-642	2Ki 21:1-18; 2Ch 33:1-20
15.	Amon	2 years	642-640	2Ki 21:19-26; 2Ch 33:21-25
16.	Josiah	31 years	640-609	2Ki 22; 23:1-30; 2Ch 34-35
17.	Jehoahaz	3 months	609	2Ki 23:31-33; 2Ch 36:1-4
18.	Jehoiakim	11 years	609-598	2Ki 23:34-37; 24:1-6; 2Ch 36:5-8
19.	Jehoiachin	3 months	598-597	2Ki 24:8-16; 2Ch 36:9-10
20.	Zedekiah / Mattaniah	11 years	597-586	2Ki 24:17-20; 25:1-7; 2Ch 36:11-21
The Kings of Israel				
1.	Jeroboam I	22 years	930-909	1Ki 12:20,25; 14:20
2.	Nadab	2 years	909-908	1Ki 15:25-27,31
3.	Baasha	24 years	908-886	1Ki 15:28-34; 16:1-7
4.	Elah	2 years	886-885	1Ki 16:8-14
5.	Zimri	7 days	885	1Ki 16:11-12,15-20
6.	Omri	12 years	885-874	1Ki 16:23-28
7.	Ahab	22 years	874-853	1Ki 16:29-22:40
8.	Ahaziah	2 years	853-852	1Ki 22:51-53; 2Ki 1
9.	Joram	12 years	852-841	2Ki 3-9:26
10.	Jehu	28 years	841-814	2Ki 9:3-10; 36
11.	Jehoahaz	17 years	814-798	2Ki 13:1-9
12.	Jehoash	16 years	798-782	2Ki 13:10-25; 14:8-16
13.	Jeroboam II	41 years	793-753	2Ki 14:23-29
14.	Zechariah	6 months	753	2Ki 15:8-12
15.	Shallum	1 month	752	2Ki 15:13-15
16.	Menahem	10 years	752-742	2Ki 15:16-22
17.	Pekahiah	2 years	742-740	2Ki 15:23-26
18.	Pekah	20 years	752-732	2Ki 15:27-31; 16:5
19.	Hoshea	9 years	732-722	2Ki 17:1-6

Should:

Fear God (Dt 17:19). Serve Christ (Ps 2:10-12). Keep the law of God (1Ki 2:3). Study the Scriptures (Dt 17:19). Promote the interests of the Church (Ezr 1:2-4; 6:1-12). Nourish the Church (Isa 49:23). Rule in the fear of God (2Sa 23:3). Maintain the cause of the poor and oppressed (Pr 31:8-9). Investigate all matters (Pr 25:2). Not pervert judgment (Pr 31:5). Prolong their reign by hating greed (Pr 28:16).

Specially Warned Against:

Impurity (Pr 31:3). Lying (Pr 17:7). Listening to lies (Pr 29:12). Intemperance (Pr 31:4-5). The gospel to be preached to (Ac 9:15; 26:27-28). Without understanding, are oppressors (Pr 28:16). Often reproved by God (1Ch 16:21). Judgments upon, when opposed to Christ (Ps 2:2, 5, 9).

When Good:

Regard God as their strength (Ps 99:4). Speak righteously (Pr 16:10). Love righteous lips (Pr 16:13). Abhor wickedness (Pr 16:12). Reject evil (Pr 20:8). Punish the wicked (Pr 20:26). Favor the wise (Pr 14:35). Honor the diligent (Pr 22:29). Befriend the good (Pr 22:14). Are pacified by submission (Pr 16:14; 25:15). Evil counselors should be removed from (2Ch 22:3-4; Pr 25:5).

Good exemplified: David (2Sa 8:15). Asa (1Ki 15:11). Jehoshaphat (1Ki 22:43). Amaziah (2Ki 15:3). Uzziah (2Ki 15:34). Hezekiah (2Ki 18:3). Josiah (2Ki 22:2).

Should Be:

Honored (Ro 13:7; 1Pe 2:17). Feared (Pr 24:21). Revered (1Sa 24:8; 1Ki 1:23, 31). Obeyed (Ro 13:1, 5; 1Pe 2:13). Prayed for (1Ti 2:1-2). Folly of resisting (Pr 19:12; 20:2). Punishment for resisting the lawful authority of (Ro 13:2). Guilt and danger of stretching out the hand against (1Sa 26:9; 2Sa 1:14). Curse not, even in thought (Ex 22:28; Ecc 10:20). Speak no evil of (Job 34:18; 2Pe 2:10). Pay tribute to (Mt 22:21; Ro 13:6-7). Be not presumptuous before (Pr 25:6). Wicked despise (2Pe 2:10; Jude 8).

KING'S GARDEN Near the Pool of Siloam (2Ki 25:4; Jer 39:4; 52:7; Ne 3:15).

KING'S HIGHWAY Ancient N and S route E of the Jordan through Edom and Moab (Nu 20:17; 21:22). The road is still in use.

KING'S VALLEY Valley of Shaveh E of Jerusalem (Ge 14:17; 2Sa 18:18).

KINGS, 1 and 2

Author: Anonymous; Jewish tradition credits Jeremiah

Date: Between 562 B.C. and 538

Outline:

I. The Solomonic Era (1:1-12:24).
  A. Solomon's Succession to the Throne (1:1-2:12).
  B. Solomon's Throne Consolidated (2:13-46).
  C. Solomon's Wisdom (ch. 3).

  D. Solomon's Reign Characterized (ch. 4).
  E. Solomon's Building Projects (5:1-9:9).
    1. Preparation for building the temple (ch. 5).
    2. Building the temple (ch. 6).
    3. Building the palace (7:1-12).
    4. The temple furnishings (7:13-51).
    5. Dedication of the temple (ch. 8).
    6. The Lord's response and warning (9:1-9).
  F. Solomon's Reign Characterized (9:10-10:29).
  G. Solomon's Folly (11:1-13).
  H. Solomon's Throne Threatened (11:14-43).
  I. Rehoboam's Succession to the Throne (12:1-24).
II. Israel and Judah From Jeroboam I/Rehoboam to Ahab/Asa (12:25-16:34).
  A. Jeroboam I of Israel (12:25-14:20).
  B. Rehoboam of Judah (14:21-31).
  C. Abijah of Judah (15:1-8).
  D. Asa of Judah (15:9-24).
  E. Nadab of Israel (15:25-32).
  F. Baasha of Israel (15:33-16:7).
  G. Elah of Israel (16:8-14).
  H. Zimri of Israel (16:15-20).
  I. Omri of Israel (16:21-28).
  J. Ahab of Israel (16:29-34).
III. The Ministries of Elijah and Elisha and Other Prophets From Ahab/Asa to Joram/Jehoshaphat (17:1-2Ki 8:15).
  A. Elijah (and Other Prophets) in the Reign of Ahab (17:1-22:40).
    1. Elijah and the drought (ch. 17).
    2. Elijah on Mount Carmel (ch. 18).
    3. Elijah's flight to Horeb (ch. 19).
    4. A prophet condemns Ahab for sparing Ben-Hadad (ch. 20).
    5. Elijah condemns Ahab for seizing Naboth's vineyard (ch. 21).
    6. Micaiah prophesies Ahab's death; its fulfillment (22:1-40).
  B. Jehoshaphat of Judah (22:41-50).
  C. Ahaziah of Israel; Elijah's Last Prophecy (22:51-2Ki 1:18).
  D. Elijah's Translation; Elisha's Inauguration (2Ki 2:1-18).
  E. Elisha in the Reign of Joram (2:19-8:15).
    1. Elisha's initial miraculous signs (2:19-25).
    2. Elisha during the campaign against Moab (ch. 3).
    3. Elisha's ministry to needy ones in Israel (ch. 4).
    4. Elisha heals Naaman (ch. 5).
    5. Elisha's deliverance of one of the prophets (6:1-7).
    6. Elisha's deliverance of Joram from Aramean raiders (6:8-23).
    7. Aramean siege of Samaria lifted, as Elisha prophesied (6:24-7:20).
    8. The Shunammite's land restored (8:1-6).
    9. Elisha prophesies Hazael's oppression of Israel (8:7-15).

IV. Israel and Judah From Joram/Jehoram to the Exile of Israel (2Ki 8:16-17:41).
  A. Jehoram of Judah (8:16-24).
  B. Ahaziah of Judah (8:25-29).
  C. Jehu's Revolt and Reign (chs. 9-10).
    1. Elisha orders Jehu's anointing (9:1-13).
    2. Jehu's assassination of Joram and Ahaziah (9:14-29).
    3. Jehu's execution of Jezebel (9:30-37).
    4. Jehu's slaughter of Ahab's family (10:1-17).
    5. Jehu's eradication of Baal worship (10:18-36).
  D. Athaliah and Joash of Judah; Repair of the Temple (chs. 11-12).
  E. Jehoahaz of Israel (13:1-9).
  F. Jehoash of Israel; Elisha's Last Prophecy (13:10-25).
  G. Amaziah of Judah (14:1-22).
  H. Jeroboam II of Israel (14:23-29).
  I. Azariah of Judah (15:1-7).
  J. Zechariah of Israel (15:8-12).
  K. Shallum of Israel (15:13-16).
  L. Menahem of Israel (15:17-22).
  M. Pekahiah of Israel (15:23-26).
  N. Pekah of Israel (15:27-31).
  O. Jotham of Judah (15:32-38).
  P. Ahaz of Judah (ch. 16).
  Q. Hoshea of Israel (17:1-6).
  R. Exile of Israel; Resettlement of the Land (17:7-41).
V. Judah From Hezekiah to the Babylonian Exile (2Ki 18-25).
  A. Hezekiah (chs. 18-20).
    1. Hezekiah's good reign (18:1-8).
    2. The Assyrian threat and deliverance (18:9-19:37).
    3. Hezekiah's illness; alliance with Babylon (ch. 20).
  B. Manasseh (21:1-18).
  C. Amon (21:19-26).
  D. Josiah (22:1-23:30).
    1. Repair of the temple; discovery of the Book of the Law (ch. 22).
    2. Renewal of the covenant; end of Josiah's reign (23:1-30).
  E. Jehoahaz Exiled to Egypt (23:31-35).
  F. Jehoiakim: First Babylonian Invasion (23:36-24:7).
  G. Jehoiachin: Second Babylonian Invasion (24:8-17).
  H. Zedekiah (24:18-20).
  I. Babylonian Exile of Judah (25:1-21).
  J. Removal of the Remnant to Egypt (25:22-26).
  K. Elevation of Jehoiachin in Babylon (25:27-30).

KINNERETH [4054, 4055] (*zithers, lyres*).
1. A district in the N of Israel (Jos 11:2; 1Ki 15:20).
2. A city in Naphtali (Jos 19:35).
3. The sea of (Nu 34:11; Jos 12:3; 13:27). *See Galilee, Sea of.*

KINSMAN [278, 1457, 4530, 4531, 7940]. Family or friends (Job 19:14), of same tribe (1Ch 12:2, 29; 2Ch 29:34; Ezr 8:17), fellow Israelites (2Ch 28:8). Figurative of wisdom (Pr 7:4). *See Kinsman-Redeemer.*

KINSMAN-REDEEMER [1457]. A close relative responsible for protecting the interests of needy members of the extended family. To provide an heir for a brother who had died (Ge 38:6-11; Dt 25:5-10; Ru 3-4). *See Levirite Marriage.* To redeem land that a poor relative had sold outside the family (Lev 25:25-28). To redeem a relative who had been sold into slavery (Lev 25:47-49). To avenge the killing of a relative (Nu 35:19-21). *See Avenger of Blood.*

KIOS [5944]. An island W of Smyrna (Ac 20:15).

KIR [7816, 7817] (*walled enclosure*). The inhabitants of Damascus carried into captivity to, by the king of Assyria (2Ki 16:9). Prophecies concerning (Isa 22:6; Am 1:5; 9:7).

KIR HARESETH [7818, 7819] (*walled [city] of pottery fragments*). A city of Moab (2Ki 3:25; Isa 16:7, 11; Jer 48:31, 36). Called Kir of Moab (Isa 15:1).

KIR OF MOAB *See Kir.*

KIRIATH [7956] (*city of*). City of Benjamin (Jos 18:28).

KIRIATH ARBA [7957, 7959] (*city of four*). Ancient name for Hebron (Ge 23:2; Jos 14:15; 15:54; 20:7).

KIRIATH BAAL *See Kiriath Jearim.*

KIRIATH HUZOTH [7960] (*city of Huzoth [outside spaces]*). A residence of Balak (Nu 22:39).

KIRIATH JEARIM [7961] (*city of timberlands*). Called also Baalah, one of the four cities of the Gibeonites. Inhabitants of, not destroyed, on account of the covenant made by the Israelites with the Gibeonites, but put under servitude (Jos 9:17, w Jos 9:3-27).
  In the territory allotted to Judah (Jos 15:9, 60; 18:14). The Philistines bring the ark to (1Sa 6:21, w 1Sa 6:1-21), ark remains twenty years at (1Sa 7:1-2; 1Ch 13:5-6). David brings the ark from (2Sa 6:1-11; 1Ch 13:5-8; 2Ch 1:4). Inhabitants of, who were taken into captivity to Babylon, returned (Ezr 2:25; Ne 7:29). Uriah, the prophet, an inhabitant of (Jer 26:20).

KIRIATH SANNAH [7962] (*city of Sannah*). A city of Judah (Jos 15:49); also called Kiriath Sepher and Debir. *See Debir; Kiriath Sepher.*

KIRIATH SEPHER [7963] (*city of*

scribe). A city of Judah (Jos 15:15-16); also called Kiriath Sannah; Debir. *See Debir; Kiriath Sannah.*

KIRIATHAIM [7964] (*two cities*).
1. Town in Moab N of Arnon. Assigned to Reuben (Nu 32:37; Jos 13:19).
2. City of Gershonite Levites in Naphtali (1Ch 6:76). Called Kartan (Jos 21:32).

KIRIOTH *See Kerioth, Kerioth Hezron.*

KIRJATH-ARIM *See Kiriath Jearim.*

KISH [7821, *3078*] (*bow, power*).
1. Father of Saul (1Sa 9:1-3; 10:21; 2Sa 21:14). Called Kish (Ac 13:21).
2. A Benjamite (1Ch 8:30; 9:36).
3. A Levite (1Ch 23:21-22; 24:29).
4. A Levite (2Ch 29:12).
5. Great-grandfather of Mordecai (Est 2:5).

KISHI [7823] (possibly *gift* IDB; *snarer* ISBE). Also called Kushaiah. Father of Ethan, a chief assistant in the temple music (1Ch 6:44; 15:17).

KISHION [8002]. City of Issachar (Jos 19:20). Also called Kedesh (1Ch 6:72).

KISHON [7822] (*cunning*). A river of Israel emptying into the Mediterranean near the northern base of Mount Carmel. Sisera defeated here, and his army destroyed (Jdg 4:7, 13; 5:21; Ps 83:9). Prophets of Baal destroyed by Elijah at (1Ki 18:40).

KISLEV [4075]. Month nine in sacred sequence, month three in civil sequence (Ezr 10:9; Jer 36:9, 22; Zec 7:1). The rainy season (November-December); the season for planting. The Feast of Dedication (Jn 10:22).
See Dedication; Feasts; Hanukkah; Maccabees; Month, 9.

KISLON [4077] (*slow* IDB; *strength* ISBE). Father of Eldad (Nu 34:21).

KISLOTH TABOR [4079]. A place on the border of Zebulun (Jos 19:12). Called Tabor (1Ch 6:77). Probably the same as Kesulloth (Jos 19:18).

KISS [5965, 5975, *2968*, *5797*, *5799*]. Of affection (Ge 27:26-27; 31:55; 33:4; 48:10; 50:1; Ex 18:7; Ru 1:14; 2Sa 14:33; 19:39; Lk 15:20; Ac 20:37). The feet of Jesus kissed by the penitent woman (Lk 7:38).
Deceitful (Pr 27:6), of Joab, when he killed Amasa (2Sa 20:9-10), of Judas, when he betrayed Jesus (Mt 26:48; Lk 22:48).
Holy (Ro 16:16; 2Co 13:12; 1Th 5:26; 1Pe 5:14).

KITE [370, 1798, 8012]. A bird forbidden as food (Lev 11:14; Dt 14:13).

KITLISH [4186]. Town in lowlands of Judah (Jos 15:40), site unknown.

KITRON [7790] (*incense,* [*sacrificial*] *smoke*). A city of Zebulun (Jdg 1:30).

KITTIM [4183].
1. Descendants of Javan (Ge 10:4; 1Ch 1:7).
2. The Hebrew name for Cyprus; probably inhabited islands of the Mediterranean (Isa 23:1, 12; Jer 2:10; Eze 27:6).
3. Prophecies concerning (Nu 24:24; Da 11:30).

KNEADING TROUGH [4297, 5400]. Shallow vessel for kneading dough with hands (Ex 8:3; 12:34).

KNEE [1386, 4156, 10072, 10123, *1205*, *1206*, *4686*].] Bowing the knee or kneeling as an act of reverence (Ge 41:43; 2Ki 1:13), and subjection (Isa 45:23; Php 2:10).

KNIFE [2995, 4408, 4661, 7644, 8501, 9509]. An edged tool used by Abraham in offering Isaac (Ge 22:6, 10). Of flint, used in circumcision (Ex 4:25; Jos 5:2, 3). Used for pruning (Isa 18:5), by scribes (Jer 36:23).

KNOB *See Capital.*

KNOWLEDGE [*1978, 1981, 3359, 4529, 5795, 7924, 8011, 10313, 10430, *1182*, *1192*, *1194*, *1196*, *2105*, *2106*, *2179*, *2813*, *3857*]. Of good and evil (Ge 2:9, 17; 3:22). Is power (Pr 3:20; 24:5). Desire for (1Ki 3:9; Ps 119:66; Pr 2; 3; 12:1; 15:14; 18:15). Rejected (Hos 4:6). Those who reject are destroyed (Hos 4:6). Fools hate (Pr 1:22, 29). A divine gift (1Co 12:8). Is pleasant (Pr 2:10). Shall be increased (Da 12:4).
The earth shall be full of (Isa 11:9). Fear of the Lord is the beginning of (Pr 1:7). Of more value than gold (Pr 8:10). The priest's lips should keep (Mal 2:7).
Of salvation (Lk 1:77). Key of (Lk 11:52). Now we know in part (1Co 13:9-12). Of God more than burnt offering (Hos 6:6). Of Christ (Php 3:8).
See God, Knowledge of; Jesus the Christ, Omniscience of; Wisdom.

KOA [7760]. People E of Tigris, between Elam and Media (Eze 23:23).

KOHATH [7740, 7741]. Second son of Levi (Ge 46:11; Ex 6:16). Grandfather of Moses, Aaron, and Miriam (Nu 26:58-59). Father of the Kohathites, one of the divisions of the Levites (Ex 6:18; Nu 3:19, 27).
See Levites.

KOLAIAH [7755] (*Yahweh's voice*).
1. A Benjamite and ancestor of Sallu (Ne 11:7).
2. Father of the false prophet Ahab (Jer 29:21).

KORAH, KORAHITE(S) [7946, 7948, *3169*] (*shaven, bald*).
1. Son of Esau (Ge 36:5, 14, 18; 1Ch 1:35).
2. Grandson of Esau (Ge 36:16).
3. Descendant of Caleb (1Ch 2:43).

4. Levite from whom the Korahites were descended (Ex 6:24; 1Ch 6:22).

KORAZIN [*5960*]. Denunciation against (Mt 11:21; Lk 10:13).

KORE [7927] (*proclaimer*).

1. A Korahite (1Ch 9:19; 26:1).

2. A Levite, keeper of the East Gate (2Ch 31:14).

KORHITE(S) *See Korah, Korahite(s), 4; Levites.*

KOZ [7766] (*thorn*). The father of Anub and Hazzobebah (1Ch 4:8).

KUE [7745, 7750]. Probably Cilicia in SE Asia Minor (1Ki 10:28; 2Ch 1:16).

KUSHAIAH [7773]. Merarite Levite (1Ch 15:17). Also called Kishi (1Ch 6:44).

LAADAH [4355] (perhaps *having a fat neck or throat*). Son of Shelah (1Ch 4:21).

LAADAN *See Ladan.*

LABAN [4238, 4239] (*white*).
1. Son of Bethuel (Ge 28:5). Brother of Rebekah (Ge 22:23; 24:15, 29). Receives the servant of Abraham (Ge 24:29-33). Receives Jacob and gives him his daughters in marriage (Ge 29:12-30). Jacob becomes his servant (Ge 29:15-20, 27; 30:27-43). Outwitted by Jacob (Ge 30:37-43; 31:1-21). Pursues Jacob, overtakes him in hill country of Gilead, and covenants with him (Ge 31:22-55).
2. Place in Plains of Moab (Dt 1:1).

LABOR [*2655, 3330, 3333, 4989, 5126, 6025, 6026, 6268, 6275, 6661, 6662, 7189, 7674, 8492, *3159, 3160*]. Honorable (Ps 128:2; Pr 21:25; 1Th 4:11). Laborers protected by laws (Dt 24:14). Creative work of God described as labor (Ge 2:2). Difficult labor the result of the curse (Ge 3:17-19). Sleep of labor sweet (Ecc 5:12).
Labor commanded (Ge 3:19; Ex 20:9-11; 23:12; 34:21; Lev 23:3; Lk 13:14; Ac 20:35; Eph 4:28; 1Th 4:11; 2Th 3:10-12).
Compensation for (Lev 19:13; Dt 25:4; 1Co 9:9; 1Ti 5:18; Jer 22:13; Mal 3:5; Mt 20:1-15; Lk 10:7; Jas 5:4). Of servants must not be oppressive (Dt 24:14-15).
Paul, an example (2Th 3:8-13).
See Capital and Labor; Employee; Employer; Idleness; Industry; Master; Servant.

LACE Cord used to bind high priest's breastplate to the ephod (Ex 28:28, 37; 39:21, 31).

LACHISH [4337]. Canaanite royal city and Judean border fortress, occupying a strategic valley twenty-five miles SW of Jerusalem. It is identified with Tell ed-Duweir (Tell Lakhish). Joshua captured it (Jos 10:31-33); destroyed by Nebuchadnezzar along with Jerusalem (2Ki 24-25; Jer 34:7), resettled after the Exile (Ne 11:30). Lachish Letters (ostraca) from the time of Jeremiah reveal much about the city.

LACHRYMATORY A container for holding the tears of mourners (Ps 56:8, ftn).

LADAN [4356].
1. A descendant of Ephraim (1Ch 7:26).
2. A Levite, called also Libni (1Ch 6:17; 23:7-9; 26:21).

LADDER (Ge 28:12, ftn). *See Stairs.*

LAEL [4210] (*[belonging] to God [El]*). Father of Eliasaph (Nu 3:24).

LAHAD [4262] (perhaps *slow, indolent*). A descendant of Judah (1Ch 4:2).

LAHAI-ROI *See Beer Lahai Roi.*

LAHMAS [4314]. Town in Judean Shephelah (Jos 15:40). Probably modern Khirbet el-Lahm.

LAHMI [4313]. Brother of Goliath. Slain by Elhanan (2Sa 21:19; 1Ch 20:5).

LAISH [4331, 4332] (*lion*).
1. A Sidonian city at the N. extremity of Israel (Jdg 18:7, 14, 27, 29). Called also Leshem (Jos 19:47), and afterwards Dan. *See Dan, 3; Leshem.*
2. A native of Gallim; a Benjamite, whose son became the husband of Michal, David's wife (1Sa 25:44; 2Sa 3:15).
3. *See Laishah.*

LAISHAH [4333] (*lion*). A town near Jerusalem (Isa 10:30).

LAKE OF FIRE [*3349*]. Place of final judgment (Rev 19:20; 20:10, 14-15; 21:8).

LAKKUM [4373]. Town of Naphtali (Jos 19:33), location unknown.

LAMA SABACHTHANI *See Eloi, Eloi, Lama Sabachthani.*

LAMB [3231, 3897, 3898, 4166, 4167, 7175, 8445+, *303, 768, 4247*]. Used, for food (Dt 32:14; Am 6:4), for sacrifices (Ge 4:4; 22:7), especially at Passover (Ex 12:3-5). Sacrificial lambs typical of Christ (Jn 1:29; Rev 5:6, 8).
Offering of (Lev 3:7; 5:6; 22:23; 23:12; Nu 7:15, 21; 28:3-8), at the daily morning and evening sacrifices (Ex 29:38-42). Offering of, at the Feast of Passover (Ex 12:15), Pentecost (Lev 23:18-20), Tabernacles (Nu 29:13-40), the New Moon (Nu 28:11), trumpets (Nu 29:2). Offering of, on the Sabbath day (Nu 28:9), at purifications (Lev 12:6; 14:10-25), by the Nazirite (Nu 6:12), for sin of ignorance (Lev 4:32).

Figurative:
The wolf living with, a figure of Messiah's reign (Isa 11:6; 65:25). A type of young believers (Jn 21:15).
A name given to Christ (Jn 1:29, 36; Rev 5:6, 8, 12-13; 6:1, 16; 7:9-10, 14; 12:11; 13:8; 14:4, 10; 17:14; 19:7, 9; 21:9, 14, 22-23, 27; 22:1, 3). Jesus compared to (Isa 53:7; Ac 8:32; 1Pe 1:19).

LAMB OF GOD A title of Jesus (Jn 1:29; Rev 6:16; 7:9-10, 14, 17; 12:11; 13:8; 14:1, 4; 15:3; 17:14; 19:7; 21:9, 14, 22-23, 27; 22:1, 3).

LAME *See Disease.*

LAMECH [4347, *3285*].
1. Father of Jabal, Jubal, and Tubal-Cain (Ge 4:18-24).
2. Son of Methuselah, and father of Noah, lived 777 years (Ge 5:25-31; 1Ch 1:3). Ancestor of Jesus (Lk 3:36).

LAMENESS [5048, 5783, 7177, 7519, 6000]. Disqualified priest from exercising the priestly office (Lev 21:18). Disqualified animals for sacrificial uses (Dt 15:21). Hated by David (2Sa 5:8). Healed by Jesus (Mt 11:5; 15:31; 21:14; Lk 7:22), by Peter (Ac 3:2-11).

LAMENTATIONS [61, 627, 640, 650, 2047, 3538, 2411, 5654, 6199, 7801, 7806, 8490]. Of David (Ps 60:1-3). Of Jeremiah (La 1-5). Of Ezekiel (Eze 19; 28:12-19). *See Elegy.*

LAMENTATIONS, BOOK OF
Author: Anonymous, traditionally Jeremiah

Date: Shortly after the fall of Jerusalem in 586 B.C.

Outline:
I. Jerusalem's Misery and Desolation (ch. 1).
II. The Lord's Anger Against His People (ch. 2).
III. Judah's Complaint—and Basis of Consolation (ch. 3).
IV. The Contrast Between Zion's Past and Present (ch. 4).
V. Judah's Appeal for God's Forgiveness (ch. 5).

LAMP [240, 4963, 5775, 5944, *3286, 3394*].
Figurative: Of joy (Jer 25:10). Life (Job 18:5-6; 21:17; Pr 13:9; 20:20). The word of God (Ps 119:105; Pr 6:23; 2Pe 1:19). Spiritual illumination (Mt 6:22). Religious influence (Mt 5:15; Mk 4:21; Lk 8:16; 11:33). Jesus is the lamp of the New Jerusalem (Rev 21:23).
Symbolic (Rev 4:5; 8:10).
See Lampstand.

LAMPSTAND [4963, 10456, *3393*].
Of the Tabernacle:
Made of gold after divine pattern (Ex 25:31-40; 37:17-24; Nu 8:4), burned olive oil (Ex 27:20). Place of (Ex 26:35; 40:24-25; Heb 9:2). Furniture of (Ex 25:38; 37:23; Nu 4:9-10). Burned every night (Ex 27:20-21). Trimmed every morning (Ex 30:7). Carried by Kohathites (Nu 4:4, 15). Called the lamp of God (1Sa 3:3).
Of the Temple:
Ten branches of (1Ki 7:49-50). Of gold (1Ch 28:15; 2Ch 4:20). Taken with other spoils to Babylon (Jer 52:19).
Symbolic (Zec 4:2, 11; Rev 1:12-13, 20; 2:5; 11:4).

LANCE [3959]. *See Javelin; Spear.*

LAND [*141, 824, 1074, 1473, 2475, 3000, 3317, 5226, 5659, 5709, 8441, 10075, *1178, 2982, 6001, 6005*]. Appeared on third creative day (Ge 1:9). Original title to, from God (Ge 13:14-17;

15:7; Ex 23:31; Lev 25:33). Bought and sold (Ge 23:3-18; 33:19; Ac 4:34; 5:1-8).
Sale and redemption, laws concerning (Lev 25:15-16, 23-33; 27:17-24; Nu 36:4; Jer 32:7-16, 25, 44; Eze 46:18). Conveyance of, by written deeds and other forms (Ge 23:3-20; Ru 4:3-8, 11; Jer 32:9-14), witnessed (Ge 23:10-11; Ru 4:9-11; Jer 32:9-14).
Sold for debt (Ne 5:3-5). Rights in, alienated (2Ki 8:1-6). Leased (Lk 20:9-16; Mt 21:33-41).
Priest's part in (Ge 47:22; Eze 48:10). King's part in (Eze 48:21). Widow's share in (Ru 4:3-9). Unmarried woman's rights in (Nu 27:1-11; 36:1-11).
To rest every seventh year for the benefit of the poor (Ex 23:11). Products of, for all (Ecc 5:9). Monopoly of (Ge 47:20-26; Isa 5:8; Mic 2:1-2). *See Mortgage.*
Rules for apportioning Canaan among the tribes (Eze 47:22). *See Canaan.*

LANDMARKS (*border*). Protected from fraudulent removal (Dt 19:14; 27:17; Job 24:2; Pr 22:28; 23:10; Hos 5:10). *See Boundary Stones.*

LANES [5850]. Country lanes (Lk 14:21). *See Streets.*

LANGUAGE [848, 1821, 3376, 4383, 8557, 9553, 10392, *155, 1185, 1365, 3281, 3282, 3378, 5889*]. Unity of (Ge 11:1, 6). Confusion of (Ge 11:1-9; 10:5, 20, 31). Dialects of the Jews (Jdg 12:6; Mt 26:73). Many spoken at Jerusalem (Jn 19:20; Ac 2:8-11).
Gift of (Mk 16:17; Ac 2:7-8; 10:46; 19:6; 1Co 12:10; 14). *See Tongues, Gift of.*
Mentioned in Scripture:
Aramaic (2Ki 18:26; Ezr 4:7; Da 2:4). Of Ashdod (Ne 13:24). Babylonian [or Chaldean] (Da 1:4). Canaanite (Isa 19:18). Egyptian (Ac 2:10; Ps 81:5). Greek (Jn 19:20; Ac 21:37). Hebrew (Ne 9:11; 16:16). Of Judah (Ne 13:24). Latin (Jn 19:20). Lycaonia (Ac 14:11). Parthia and other lands (Ac 2:9-11).

LANTERN [3286]. (Jn 18:3).

LAODICEA [3293]. A Phrygian city. Paul's concern for (Col 2:1). Epaphras' zeal for (Col 4:13). Epistle to the Colossians to be read in (Col 4:15-16). Message to, through John (Rev 1:11; 3:14-22).

LAODICEA, CHURCH AT See Laodicea.

LAODICEANS, EPISTLE TO
Letter mentioned by Paul (Col 4:16). This is probably a letter of Paul that was not preserved for the canon. Some theorize it may be the letter to the Ephesians as a circular letter. An apocryphal epistle to the Laodiceans exists in Latin.

LAPIDARY One who cuts precious stones (Ex 31:5; 35:33).

LAPPED [4379]. A Hebrew verb used to indicate alertness (Jdg 7:5-7) and disgust (1Ki 21:19; 22:38).

LAPPIDOTH [4366] (*flames*). Husband of Deborah (Jdg 4:4).

LAPWING See Hoopoe.

LARCENY See Theft.

LASCIVIOUSNESS Unbridled lust, licentiousness, wantonness.

Condemned:

Forbidden (Col 3:5; 1Th 4:3-6). Warnings against (Pr 2:16-18; 5:3-5, 8-13; 7:6-27; 9:13-18; 30:18-20; 31:3; Ro 13:13; 1Co 6:13, 15-18; 1Pe 4:2-3; Jude 4, 7).

Sinful practices in (Joel 3:3; Ro 1:22-29). Proceeds from unregenerate heart (Mk 7:21-23; Gal 5:19; Eph 4:17-19). Impenitence in (2Co 12:21). Excludes from the kingdom of God (1Co 6:9-10, 13, 15-18; 9:27; Gal 5:19, 21; Eph 5:5).

Lascivious practices in idolatrous worship. See Idolatry, Wicked practices of.

See Adultery; Homosexual; Incest; Lust; Prostitute; Rape; Sensuality.

Figurative: (Eze 16:15-59). See Prostitute.

Instances of:

Sodomites (Ge 19:5). Lot's daughters (Ge 19:30-38). Judah (Ge 38:15-16). The Gibeahites (Jdg 19:22-25). Eli's sons (1Sa 2:22). David (2Sa 5:13; 11:2-27). Amnon (2Sa 13:1-14). Solomon (1Ki 11:1-3). Rehoboam (2Ch 11:21-23). Persian kings (Est 2:3, 13-14, 19).

LASEA [3297]. Seaport on S coast of Crete. Visited by Paul (Ac 27:8).

LASHA [4388]. Place near Sodom and Gomorrah (Ge 10:19). Site not identified.

LASHARON [4389] (*[belonging to] Sharon*). King of, killed by Joshua (Jos 12:18).

LASHES [5782, 6424, 8765].

1. Beating could subject the culprit to abuse, so the law kept the punishment from becoming inhumane (Dt 25:2-3). Solomon uses hyperbole to illustrate that a rebuke has greater influence on a wise man than a hundred lashes will have on a fool (Pr 17:10). Compare Paul's experience (2Co 11:24). See Stripes.

2. A figurative description of Jerusalem experiencing the wrath of God finally being rebuilt into the Holy City, the New Jerusalem (Isa 54:11-12, w Rev 21:10, 18-21).

See Assault and Battery; Bruise(s); Flog, Flogging; Scourging; Stoning.

LAST [*340, 2274]. First and last: a title of Yahweh (Isa 44:6; 48:12), of Jesus (Rev 1:17; 2:8; 22:13). See Titles and Names.

The first will be last and the last first (Nu 24:20; Mt 19:30; 20:16; Mk 9:35; 10:31; Lk 13:30).

LAST DAYS [344, 2274]. The days before the final judgment (Jn 12:48), when God's kingdom is established on earth (Isa 2:2-4; Mic 4:1-8), and Israel is restored to her God (Hos 3:5). Began with the coming of Jesus and of the Spirit (Ac 2:16-21; Heb 1:2; 1Pe 1:20). The time of the resurrection (Jn 6:39-44, 54; 11:24). A time of great trouble and deception (1Ti 3:1-17; 2Pe 3:3-17; Jude 18-19), culminating in the Second Coming of Christ (1Pe 1:5). See Day of the Lord; Eschatology.

LATCHET See Thong.

LATIN [4872]. The language of the Roman Empire, used in Israel in NT times (Jn 19:20).

LATRINE [4738]. Temple of Baal used as (2Ki 10:27).

LATTICE [876, 3048, 8422]. Latticework used for privacy, ventilation, decoration (Jdg 5:28; 2Ki 1:2; Pr 7:6).

LAUGHTER [6600, 7464, 7465, 8468, 8471, 1151, 1152, 2860]. Used to express joy (Ge 21:6; Lk 6:21), derision (Ps 2:4), disbelief (Ge 18:13).

LAUNDERER [3891]. See Fuller.

LAVER See Bronze Basin; Bronze Sea.

LAW [*2017, 2976, 2978, 5477, 9368, 10186, 492, 491, 1208, 2003, 3788, 3791, 3795].

1. Ten Commandments given to Moses (Ex 20:3-17; Dt 5:6-21), summarizing God's requirements of mankind.

2. The Torah, first five books of OT (Mt 5:17; Lk 16:16).

3. The whole OT (Jn 10:34; 12:34).

4. God's will in words, acts, precepts (Ex 20:1-17; Ps 19:1-14).

The Purpose of the Law—

Under the old covenant, believers manifested their faith in Yahweh by observing the law for their own good (Dt 6:4-9; 10:12-13; 30:1-16). Christ fulfilled the law; respected, loved it, and showed its deeper significance (Mt 5:17-48). The law prepared the way for the coming of Christ (Gal 3:24). The law could not bring victory over sin (Ro 3-8; Gal).

Jesus' summary of the law: It demands perfect love for God, and love for one's neighbor comparable to that which one has for oneself (Mt 22:35-40).

Made for the lawless (1Ti 1:8-10). Must be obeyed (Mt 22:21; Lk 20:22-25).

Law of God:

(Ps 119:1-8; Jas 1:25). Spiritual (Ro 7:14). Must be obeyed (1Jn 5:3). Love, the fulfilling of (Ro 13:10; 1Ti 1:5).

See Litigation; Commandments and Statutes, Of God; Duty, Of People to God.

Law of Moses:

Contained in the books of Exodus, Leviticus, Numbers, and Deuteronomy. Divine authority for (Ex 19:16-24; 20:1-2; 24:12-18; 32:15-16; 34:1-4, 27-28; Lev 26:46; Dt 4:10-13, 36; 5:1-22; 9:10; 10:1-5; 33:2-4; 1Ki 8:9; Ezr 7:6; Ne 1:7; 8:1; 9:14; Ps 78:5; 103:7; Isa 33:22; Mal 4:4; Ac 7:38, 53; Gal 3:19; Heb 9:18-21).

Given at Sinai (Ex 19; Dt 1:1; 4:10-13, 44-46; 32:2; Hab 3:3). Received by the disposition of angels (Dt 32:2; Ps 68:17; Ac 7:53; Gal 3:19; Heb 2:2). Was given because of transgression until the Messiah came (Gal 3:19). Engraved on stone (Ex 20:3-17; 24:12; 31:18; 32:16; 34:29; 40:20; Dt 4:13; 5:4-22; 9:10), on monuments (Dt 27:2-8; Jos 8:30-35),

See Tablets of the Law; Commandments and Statutes, Of God.

Preserved in the ark of the covenant (Ex 25:16; Dt 31:9, 26). To be written on doorframes (Dt 6:9; 11:20) and as a symbol on the forehead and a sign on the hand (Ex 13:9, 16; Dt 6:4-9; 11:18-21), meaning the law was to govern society, home, personal thoughts and actions. Children instructed in. See Children; Instruction.

Expounded by priests and Levites (Lev 10:11; Dt 33:10; 2Ch 35:3), by princes, priests, and Levites (Ezr 7:10; Ne 8:1-18), from city to city (2Ch 17:7-10), in synagogues (Lk 4:16; Ac 13:14-52; 15:21, w Ac 9:20, & 14:1; 17:1-3; 18:4, 26). Expounded to the assembled nation at the feast of tabernacles in the sabbatic year (Dt 31:10-13). Rehearsed by Moses, with many admonitions (Dt 4:44-46; 5-34).

Obedience to, commanded (Dt 4:40; 5:32; 6:17; 7:11; 8:1, 6; 10:12-13; 11:1, 8, 32; 13:4; 16:12; 27:1; 30:16; 32:46; Jos 1:7; 22:5; 1Ki 2:3; 8:61; 2Ki 17:37). Found by Hilkiah in the house of the Lord (2Ki 22:8; 2Ch 34:14).

Blessings and curses of, responsively read by Levites and people at Ebal and Gerizim (Dt 27:12-26; Jos 8:33-35).

Formed a constitution on which the civil government of the Israelites was founded, and according to which rulers were required to rule (Dt 17:18-20; 2Ki 11:12; 2Ch 23:11). See Constitution; Government.

Was given because of transgressions until the coming of the Messiah (Gal 3:19). Was committed to the Jews (Ro 3:1-2). Brings the knowledge of sin (Ro 3:20; 7:7).

Prophecies in, of the Messiah (Lk 24:44; Jn 1:45; 5:46; 12:34; Ac 26:22-23; 28:23; Ro 3:21-22). See Jesus the Christ, Prophecies Concerning.

Epitomized by Jesus (Mt 22:40; Mk 12:29-33; Lk 10:27).

Temporary (Jer 3:16; Da 9:27; Heb 10:1-18). Weakness of the law (Ro 8:3, 6).

Fulfilled by Christ (Mt 5:17-45; Ac 6:14; 13:39; Ro 10:3-4; Eph 2:15; Heb 8:4-13; 9:8-24; 10:3-9). Superseded by the gospel (Lk 16:16-17; Jn 1:17; 4:20-24; 8:35; Gal 4:30-31; Ac 10:28; 15:1-20; 21:20-25; Ro 7:1-6; 2Co 3:7-14; Gal 2:3-9, 19; 4:4-31; 5:1-18; Col 2:14-23; Heb 7:5-9).

LAW OF MOSES See Law.

LAWGIVER [2980, 3794]. God is the only absolute lawgiver (Jas 4:12), instrumentally, Moses bears this description (Jn 1:17; 7:19).

LAWSUITS [1907+1907+4200, 5477, 8190, 3210]. To be avoided (Pr 25:8-10; Mt 5:25-26; 1Co 6:1-8).

See Actions at Law; Adjudication at Law; Arbitration; Compromise; Court, Of Law; Justice.

LAWYER [3788, 4842]. One versed in the law of Moses. Test Jesus with questions (Mt 22:35; Lk 10:25-37). Jesus' satire against (Lk 11:45-52). Tertullus presents case against Paul (Ac 24:1-2). Zenas (Tit 3:13). See Litigation.

LAYING ON OF HANDS Symbolic act signifying impartation of inheritance rights (Ge 48:14-20), gifts and rights of an office (Nu 27:18, 23), dedication of animals (Lev 1:4), priests (Nu 8:10), people for special service (Ac 6:6; 13:3).

LAZARUS [3276] (one whom God helps).
1. Brother of Martha and Mary; raised from the dead by Jesus (Jn 11:1-12:19).
2. Beggar who died and went to Abraham's side (Lk 16:19-31). See Abraham's Side.

LAZINESS [4206, 6790, 6792, 8244, 8332, 734, 3821, 3891]. (Pr 12:27; 18:9; 19:24; 21:25; 22:13; 26:13-16).

Brings adversity (Pr 12:24; Ecc 10:18), destruction (Pr 13:4; 19:15; 20:4; 23:21; 24:30-34).

Admonitions against (Pr 6:6-11; 10:4-5, 26; 15:19). Denounced (Mt 25:26-27). Of ministers, denounced (Isa 56:10). Forbidden (Ro 12:11; Heb 6:12).

See Idleness; Slothfulness.

LEAD [6769]. A mineral (Ex 15:10). Purified by fire (Nu 31:22; Jer 6:29; Eze 22:18, 20). Used in making inscriptions on stone (Job 19:24). Refining (Jer 6:29; Eze 22:18, 20). Trade in (Eze 27:12). Used for weighing (Zec 5:7-8).

LEADERSHIP [3338, 7213, 2175, 4613]. Instances of: Abraham, Moses, Joshua, Gideon, Deborah. See each under its own entry.

LEAF [6290, 6591, 6997, 2400+5877]. Leaf of a tree, page of a book, leaf of a door. Metaphorically, green leaves symbolize prosperity, and dry leaves ruin and decay (Ps 1:3; Pr 11:28; Job 13:25; Isa 1:30).

LEAGUE See Alliances; Treaty.

LEAH [4207] (possibly wild cow BDB; wild cow, gazelle IDB; cow KB [cf. Rachel = ewe]). Daughter of Laban (Ge 29:16). Married to Jacob (Ge 29:23-26). Children of (Ge 29:31-35; 30:9-13, 17-21). Flees with Jacob (Ge 31:4, 14, 17; 33:2-7). "Built up the house of Israel" (Ru 4:11).

LEANNOTH [4361] (*the suffering of affliction*, NIV; *sickness or suffering poem*, JB). See *Music, Symbols Used in*.

LEARNING [1067, 1981, 2683, 3359, 4375, *1207, 3443, 4785*]. See *Instruction; Knowledge*.

LEASE See *Land; Renting*.

LEASING An obsolete word for falsehood (Ps 4:2; 5:6).

LEATHER [6425, 9391, *1294*] (*skin*). Designates the tanned hide of animals. Skins were used for rough clothing as well as for armor, bags, sandals, and writing materials (Lev 13:48; Eze 16:10; Mt 3:4; Heb 11:37).

LEAVEN [2809] (*piece of fermented dough*). For bread (Ex 12:34, 39; Hos 7:4; Mt 13:33). Leavened bread used with peace offering (Lev 7:13; Am 4:5), with wave offering (Lev 23:15-17). Leavened bread forbidden with meat offerings (Lev 2:11; 6:17; 10:12; Ex 23:18; 34:25), at the Passover (Ex 12:19-20; 13:3-4, 7; 23:18), with blood (Ex 23:18; 34:25).

A type of sin (1Co 5:6-8).

Figurative:

Of the hypocrisy of the Pharisees (Mt 16:6-12; Mk 8:15; Lk 12:1). Of other evils (1Co 5:6-8; Gal 5:9). Parable of (Mt 13:33; Lk 13:21).

LEB KAMAI [4214] (*the heart of my attackers*). A cryptogram (hidden code) for Babylon (Jer 51:1 ftn). See *Babylon*.

LEBANA, LEBANAH [4245] (*white*). Ancestor of a family which returned from the Exile (Ezr 2:45; Ne 7:48).

LEBANON [4248] (*white, snow*). A mountain range. Northern boundary of the land of Canaan (Dt 1:7; 3:25; 11:24; Jos 1:4; 9:1). Early inhabitants of (Jdg 3:3). Snow of (Jer 18:14). Streams of (SS 4:15). Cedars of (Jdg 9:15; 2Ki 19:23; 2Ch 2:8; Ps 29:5; 104:16; Isa 2:13; 14:8; Eze 27:5). Other trees (2Ki 19:23; 2Ch 2:8). Flower of (Na 1:4). Beasts of (Isa 40:16). Fertility and productiveness of (Hos 14:5-7). "Palace of the Forest of," (1Ki 7:2-5). Valley of (Jos 11:17; 12:7). Tower of (SS 7:4). Solomon had store cities (1Ki 9:19). Figurative: (Isa 29:17; Jer 22:6).

LEBAOTH [4219] (*lionesses*). Town in S Judah (Jos 15:32), also called Beth Lebaoth (Jos 19:6), and probably Beth Biri (1Ch 4:31).

LEBBAEUS [*one near to*] *my heart*). An alternate reading in some mss for Thaddaeus, one of Christ's apostles (Mt 10:3). See *Thaddaeus*.

LEBO HAMATH [4217] (*the entrance to Hamath*). A city located on the Orontes River of Northern Syria, though it might be "the entrance to Hamath" rather than a named city (Nu 13:21; 34:8 and ftns). See *Hamath*.

LEBONAH [4228] (*frankincense*). A city on the highway from Bethel to Shechem (Jdg 21:19).

LECAH [4336] (*to you*). A town or person in Judah (1Ch 4:21).

LEECH [6598]. Bloodsucking parasite, personifying greed (Pr 30:15). See *Animals*.

LEEK [2946]. A herb of the lily family, similar in flavor to the onion (Nu 11:5).

LEES (*something preserved*). Sediment of wine (Isa 25:6). Also used figuratively to describe blessings of messianic times, spiritual lethargy, inevitability of God's judgment (Jer 48:11; Ps 75:8).

LEFT [*8520, 8521]. Used with a variety of meanings. Simple direction; North (Ge 14:15). Lesser blessing (Ge 48:13-19). Characteristic of Benjamites (Jdg 3:15, 21; 20:16).

LEFT-HANDED [360+3338+3545, 8521]. Characteristic of Benjamites (Jdg 3:15; 20:16; 1Ch 12:2).

LEGALISTIC [*1877+3795*]. Seeking God's favor by keeping the letter of the law without keeping its spirit (Mt 23:23-24). Legalists in the early church required circumcision for salvation (Ac 15:1-29). Paul's first letter, Galatians, was written to combat legalistic teaching about the Christian life (Gal 3:2, 10-14; 4:9-11).

The Christian lives a life of grace, not works (Eph 2:8-9) and is not judged by ritual observance of special diet or holy days (Ro 14:1-18; Col 2:16-19; Heb 13:9). See *Commandments and Statutes, Of Men; Grace*.

LEGENDS See *Inscriptions*.

LEGION [3305] (*military company*).
1. Largest unit in the Roman army, including infantry and cavalry.
2. Vast number (Mt 26:53; Mk 5:9).

LEGISLATION Class, forbidden (Ex 12:49; Lev 24:22; Nu 9:14; 15:15, 29; Gal 3:28). Supplemental, concerning Sabbath-breaking (Nu 15:32-35), inheritance (Nu 27:1-11). See *Government; Law*.

LEGS [3751, 4157, 5274, 8079, 8797, 9393, 10284+10626, 10741, *4546, 5003*]. Of the crucified broken (Jn 19:31-32).

LEHABITES [4260]. Descendants of Mizraim (Ge 10:13; 1Ch 1:11).

LEHEM See *Jashubi Lehem*.

LEHI [4306] (*jawbone*). Place where Samson killed a thousand Philistines with a jawbone of a donkey (Jdg 15:9, 14).

LEMUEL [4345] (*[belonging] to God [El]*).

A king, otherwise unknown, to whom his mother taught the maxims in Pr 31:1-9.

LENDING [2118, 4278, 5957, 5989, 6292, *1247*, *3079*].

To the Poor, Commanded:
(Lev 25:35; Dt 15:7, 11). Commanded by Christ (Mt 5:42; Lk 6:34-35). Encouraged (Ps 112:5; Pr 19:17). God, the merciful Lender (Ps 37:25-26). Borrower to be released in the year of release (Dt 15:1-6).

Things Forbidden as Security of Loans:
Millstones (Dt 24:6). Widow's cloak (Dt 24:17).

Lender:
Forbidden to take interest from poor Hebrews (Ex 22:25-27; Lev 25:36-37; Dt 23:19-20). Forbidden to enter debtor's house for security (Dt 24:10-11). Forbidden to keep overnight clothing left in pledge (Dt 24:12-13).

Oppression of borrower (Ne 5:1-13). Is master of borrower (Pr 22:7). Lender and borrower will be equal (Isa 24:1-2). Wicked, punished (Pr 28:8; Eze 18:13).

See Borrowing; Interest; Money.

LENTIL(S) [6378]. (Ge 25:34; 2Sa 17:28; 23:11; Eze 4:9).

LEOPARD [5807, 10480, *4203*]. A carnivorous animal (SS 4:8). Fierceness of (Jer 5:6; 13:23; Hos 13:7; Hab 1:8).
Figurative: Taming of, the triumph of the gospel (Isa 11:6).

LEPROSY [7665, 7669, *3319*, *3320*]. The word is used for various diseases affecting the skin—not necessarily leprosy (Hansen's disease).

General:
Law concerning (Lev 13-14; 22:4; Nu 5:1-3; 12:14; Dt 24:8; Mt 8:4; Lk 5:14; 17:14). Entailed (2Ki 5:27). Isolation of lepers (Lev 13:46; Nu 5:2; 12:14; 2Ki 15:5; 2Ch 26:21). Separate burial (2Ch 26:23).

Sent as a judgment. On Miriam (Nu 12:1-10), Gehazi (2Ki 5:27), Azariah/Uzziah (2Ki 15:5; 2Ch 26:20-21). Other instances: Four lepers outside Samaria (2Ki 7:3), Simon (Mk 14:3).

Healed:
Miriam (Nu 12:13-14), Naaman (2Ki 5:8-14), by Jesus (Mt 8:3; Mk 1:40-42; Lk 5:13; 17:12-14). Disciples empowered to heal (Mt 10:8).

LESBIAN Sexual activity between females is condemned (Ro 1:26). *See Homosexual.*

LESHEM [4386] (*lion*). City renamed Dan, at extreme N of Israel (Jos 19:47), variant of Laish. *See Dan, 3; Laish.*

LETHEK [4390]. About 10 bushels (330 liters) (Hos 3:2). *See Measure.*

LETTER [115, 4181, 4844, 6219, 10007, 10496, *1207*, *1211*, *2186*, *2740*]. Designates an alphabetical symbol, rudimentary education (Jn 7:15), written communication, the external (Ro 2:27, 29), Jewish legalism (Ro 7:6; 2Co 3:6). In ancient times correspondence was privately delivered. Archaeology has uncovered many different kinds of letters. *See Writing.*

LETTERS [115, 6219, *1207*, *2186*]. Written by David to Joab (2Sa 11:14), king of Syria to king of Israel (2Ki 5:5-6), the field commander to Hezekiah (Isa 37:9-14), king of Babylon to Hezekiah (Isa 39:1), Sennacherib to Hezekiah (2Ki 19:14). Of Artaxerxes to Nehemiah (Ne 2:7-9). Open letter from Sanballat to Nehemiah (Ne 6:5). Luke to Theophilus, the books of Luke and Acts (Ac 1:1). Claudius Lysias to Felix (Ac 23:25-30). Letter of intercession by Paul to Philemon in behalf of Onesimus (Phm 1), of recommendation (2Co 3:1). In the NT, the books of Romans through Jude and Rev 1-3. *See Writing.*

LETUSHITES [4322] (*sharpened*). Descendants of Dedan, grandson of Abraham (Ge 25:3).

LEUMMITES [4212] (perhaps *peoples* or *hordes*). Descendants of Dedan (Ge 25:3).

LEVI [4290, 4291, *3322*] (perhaps *wild cow* or *person pledged for a debt or vow*). Son of Jacob (Ge 29:34; 35:23; 1Ch 2:1). Avenges the seduction of Dinah (Ge 34; 49:5-7). Jacob's prophecy regarding (Ge 49:5-7). His age at death (Ex 6:16). Descendants of, made ministers of religion. *See Levites.*

LEVIATHAN [4293] (*coiled one [like a serpent]*). Possibly a crocodile (Job 41; Ps 104:26). A sea monster figurative of forces of chaos opposed to Yahweh (Job 3:8; Ps 74:14; Isa 27:1). *See Dragon; Serpent.*

LEVIRATE MARRIAGE Jewish custom according to which when an Israelite died without male heirs, his nearest relative married the widow, and their firstborn son became the heir of the first husband (Dt 25:5-10; Ru 3-4). *See Kinsman-Redeemer.*

LEVITES [278, 4290+, 4291+, 10387, *3324*, *3325*] (*of Levi*). The descendants of Levi. Set apart as ministers of religion (Nu 1:47-54; 3:6-16; 16:9; 26:57-62; Dt 10:8; 1Ch 15:2). Substituted in the place of the firstborn (Nu 3:12, 41-45; 8:14, 16-18; 18:6). Religious zeal of (Ex 32:23-28; Dt 33:9-10; Mal 2:4-5). Consecration of (Nu 8:6-21). Sedition among, led by Korah, Dathan, Abiram, and On, on account of jealousy toward Moses and Aaron (Nu 16, w 4:19-20).

Three Divisions of:
Each having the name of one of its progenitors. Gershon, Kohath, and Merari (Nu 3:17). Gershonites and their duties (Nu 3:18-26; 4:23-26; 10:17). Ruling chief over the Gershonites was the second son of the ruling high priest (Nu 4:28).

Kohathites, consisting of the families of the Amramites, Izharites, Hebronites, Uzzielites (Nu 3:27; 4:18-20). Of the Amramites, Aaron, and his family were set apart as priests (Ex 28:1; Nu 3:38; 8:1-14; 17; 18:1), the remaining families appointed to take charge of the ark, table, lampstand, altars and vessels of the sanctuary, the hangings, and all the service (Nu 3:27-32; 4:2-15). The chief over the Kohathite was the oldest son of the ruling high priest (Nu 3:32; 1Ch 9:20). Merarites (Nu 3:20, 33-37; 4:31-33; 7:8; 10:17; 1Ch 6:19, 29-30; 23:21-23). The chief over the Merarites was the second son of the ruling high priest (Nu 4:33).

Place of, in camp and march (Nu 1:50-53; 2:17; 3:23-35). Cities assigned to, in the land of Canaan (Jos 21). Lodged in the chambers of the temple (1Ch 9:27, 33; Eze 40:44). Resided also in villages outside of Jerusalem (Ne 12:29).

Age of, when inducted into office (Nu 4:3, 30, 47; 8:23-26; 1Ch 23:3, 24, 27; Ezr 3:8), when retired from office (Nu 4:3, 47; 8:25-26).

Functions of:

Had charge of the tabernacle in camp and on the march (Nu 1:50-53; 3:6-9, 21-37; 4:1-15, 17-49; 8:19, 22; 18:3-6), and of the temple (1Ch 9:27-29; 23:2-32; Ezr 8:24-34).

Bore the ark of the covenant (Dt 10:8; 1Ch 15:2, 26-27). Ministered before the ark (1Ch 16:4). Custodians and administrators of the tithes and other offerings (1Ch 9:26-29; 26:28; 29:8; 2Ch 24:5, 11; 31:11-19; 34:9; Ezr 8:29-30, 33; Ne 12:44). Prepared the bread of the Presence (1Ch 23:28-29). Assisted the priests in preparing the sacrifice (2Ch 29:12-36; 2Ch 35:1-18). Killed the Passover for the children of the Captivity (Ezr 6:20-21). Teachers of the law (Dt 33:10; 2Ch 17:8-9; 30:22; 35:3; Ne 8:7-13; Mal 2:6-7). Were judges (Dt 17:9; 1Ch 23:4; 26:29; 2Ch 19:8-11; Ne 11:16). *See Judge.*

Were scribes of the sacred books. *See Scribe.* Pronounced the blessings of the law in the responsive service at Mount Gerizim (Dt 27:12; Jos 8:33). Were gatekeepers of the temple. *See Gatekeepers.* Were overseers in building and the repairs of the temple (1Ch 23:2-4; Ezr 3:8-9). Were musicians of the temple service. *See Music.* Supervised weights and measures (1Ch 23:29).

List of those who returned from the Captivity (Ezr 2:40-63; 7:7; 8:16-20; Ne 7:43-73; 12). Sealed the covenant with Nehemiah (Ne 10:9-28).

Privileges of:

In lieu of landed inheritance, forty-eight cities with suburbs were assigned to them (Nu 35:2-8, w 18:24 & 26:62; Dt 10:9; 12:12, 18-19; 14:27-29; 18:1-8; Jos 13:14; 14:3; 18:7; 1Ch 6:54-81; 13:2; 2Ch 23:2; Eze 34:1-5). Assigned to, by families (Jos 21:4-40). Suburbs of their cities were inalienable for debt (Lev 25:32-34). Tithes and other offerings (Nu 18:24, 26-32; Dt 18:1-8; 26:11-13; Jos 13:14; Ne 10:38-39; 12:44, 47). Firstfruits (Ne 12:44, 47). Spoils of war, including captives (Nu 31:30, 42-47). *See Tithes.* Tithes withheld from

(Ne 13:10-13; Mal 3:10). Pensioned (2Ch 31:16-18). Owned lands (Dt 18:8, w 1Ki 2:26). Land allotted to, by Ezekiel (Eze 48:13-14).

Enrollment of, at Sinai (Nu 1:47-49; 2:33; 3:14-39; 4:2-3; 26:57-62; 1Ch 23:3-5). Degraded from the Levitical office by Jeroboam (2Ch 11:13-17; 13:9-11). Loyal to the ruler (2Ki 11:7-11; 2Ch 23:7).

Intermarry with Canaanites (Ezr 9:1-2; 10:23-24). Exempt from enrollment for military duty (Nu 1:47-54, w 1Ch 12:26). Subordinate to the sons of Aaron (Nu 3:9; 8:19; 18:6).

Prophecies Concerning:

(Jer 33:18; Eze 44:10-14; Mal 3:3), of their repentance of the crucifixion of the Messiah (Zec 12:10-13). John's vision concerning (Rev 7:7).

LEVITICUS *(relating to the Levites).*

Author: Moses

Date: Between 1445 and 1406 B.C.

Outline:

I. The Five Main Offerings (chs. 1-7).
  A. Their Content, Purpose and Manner of Offering (1:1-6:7).
  B. Additional Regulations (6:8-7:38).
II. The Ordination, Installation and Work of Aaron and His Sons (chs. 8-10).
III. Laws of Cleanness—Food, Childbirth, Infections, etc. (chs. 11-15).
IV. The Day of Atonement and the Centrality of Worship at the Tabernacle (chs. 18-20).
V. Moral Laws Covering Incest, Honesty, Thievery, Idolatry, etc. (chs. 18-20).
VI. Regulations for the Priests, the Offerings and the Annual Feasts (21:1-24:9).
VII. Punishment for Blasphemy, Murder, etc. (24:10-23).
VIII. The Sabbath Year, Jubilee, Land Tenure and Reform of Slavery (ch. 25).
IX. Blessings and Curses for Covenant Obedience and Disobedience (ch. 26).
X. Regulations for Offerings Vowed to the Lord (ch. 27).

LEVY [6740, 6741] A tribute imposed by a conquering king (2Ki 23:33; 2Ch 36:3).

LEX TALIONIS *See Retaliation.*

LIARS [*3941, 3942, 3950, 3951, 5327, 8736, 9214, 6014, 6016, 6017, 6022, 6026]. All people are liars (Ps 116:11). Satan the father of lies (Jn 8:44, 55). Ungodly (1Ti 1:10). Characterisitc of Cretans (Tit 1:12). Eternally punished (Rev 21:8).

God cannot lie (Nu 23:19; Tit 1:2; Heb 6:18).

See Deceit; Deception; False Witness; Falsehood; Hypocrisy.

LIBATION [5821] *(pour [as an offering]).* Pouring out of wine or some other liquid as an offering to a deity as an act of worship (Ex 29:40-41; Jer 44:17-25). *See Offerings, Drink.*

LIBERALITY [3338].

Commanded:

(Ex 22:29-30; 23:15; 34:20; Lev 23:22; 25:35-43; Dt 12:11-12, 17-19; Pr 3:27-28; Mt 5:42; Ac 20:35; Ro 12:8; 2Co 8:7, 9, 11-14, 24; 1Ti 6:18; Heb 13:16).

In offerings, for tabernacle (Ex 25:1-8; 35:4-29; 36:3-6; 38:8). For the temple (Hag 1:8). With the Levites (Dt 12:11-12, 17-19; 18:1-8). For the temple commanded by Cyrus (Ezr 1:2-4). In offerings for sacrifice (2Sa 24:24).

In paying tithes (Dt 14:27-29). In gifts to God (Ps 76:11).

In gifts to the poor (Dt 15:7-11; 24:19-22; Ne 8:10; Ps 41:1-3; Isa 58:6-7; Mt 19:21-22; Mk 10:21; Lk 3:10-11; Ro 12:13; 15:27; 2Co 9:6-15; Gal 2:10; Eph 4:28; 1Ti 5:16; 6:17-19; Jas 2:15-16; 1Jn 3:17-18). By the noble woman (Pr 31:20). In gifts to liberated Hebrew slaves (Dt 15:12-18).

Giving according to ability (Nu 35:8; Dt 16:10, 17; 1Co 16:1-3; 2Co 8:12). Giving without a show (Mt 6:1-4). Giving of freewill (Lev 19:5; 22:9; 1Ch 29:5; Pr 21:26; 2Co 8:12; 9:1-6; Phm 14). Giving with love (1Co 13:3).

Rewards for giving (Ps 112:5, 9; Pr 3:9-10; 11:24-25; 13:7; 14:21; 19:6, 17; 22:9; 28:27; Ecc 11:1-2; Isa 32:8; 58:10-12; Eze 18:7-16; Mal 3:10-12; Mt 5:42; 25:34-40, 46; Lk 6:30-38; 12:33-34; Heb 6:10).

See Alms; Beneficence; Charitableness; Giving; Minister; Poor, Duty to; Rich, The; Riches; Tithes.

Instances of:

King of Sodom to Abraham (Ge 14:21). Jacob, consecrating the tenth of his income (Ge 28:22). Pharaoh to Joseph's people (Ge 45:18-20). Israelites at the building of the tabernacle (Ex 35:21-29; 36:3-7; 38:8; Nu 7; 31:48-54; Jos 18:1). Reubenites (2Sa 22:24-29). David (Ps 132:1-5; 2Sa 7:2; 1Ch 17:1; 1Sa 8:11; 1Ki 7:51; 8:17-18; 1Ch 21:24; 22; 26:26; 28:2; 29:2-5, 17). Barzillai and others to David (2Sa 17:27-29; 19:32). Araunah for sacrifice (2Sa 24:22-23). Joab to David (2Sa 12:26-28).

Israelites' offerings for the temple 1Ch 29:6-9, 16-17). Samuel (1Ch 26:27-28). Solomon (1Ki 4:29; 5:4-5; 2Ch 2:1-6; 1Ki 6; 7:51; 8:13). Queen of Sheba to Solomon (1Ki 10:10). Asa and Abijah (1Ki 15:15). Elisha toward Elijah (1Ki 19:21). Jehoshaphat (2Ki 12:18). Joash and his people (2Ki 12:4-14; 2Ch 24:4-14). David (1Ch 16:3). Hezekiah (2Ch 29; 30:1-12; 31:1-10, 21). Manasseh (2Ch 33:16). Josiah (2Ki 22:3-6; 2Ch 34:8-13; 35:1-19).

Jews after the Captivity (Ezr 1:5-6; 2:68-69; 3:2-9; 5:2-6; 6:14-22; 8:25-35; Ne 3; 4:6; 6:3; 7:70-72; 10:32-39; 13:12, 31; Hag 1:12-19). Cyrus (Ezr 1:2-4, 7-11; 3:7; 5:13-15; 6:3). Darius (Ezr 6:7-12). Artaxerxes (Ezr 7:13-27; 8:24-36).

The Magi (Mt 2:11). Centurion (Lk 7:4-5). Mary Magdalene (Lk 8:2-3). The good Samaritan (Lk 10:33-35). Poor widow (Lk 21:2-4). Christians in Jerusalem (Ac 2:44-45; 4:32-37), in Antioch (Ac 11:29), at Philippi (Php 4:18), Corinth (2Co 8:19; 9:1-13), Macedonia (2Co 8:1-4). People of Malta to Paul (Ac 28:10).

LIBERTINES *See Freedman.*

LIBERTY [2002]. Freedom, whether physical, moral, or spiritual. Israelites who had become slaves were freed in the Year of Jubilee (Lev 25:8-17). Through Christ's death and resurrection the believer is free from sin's dominion (Jn 1:29; 8:36; Ro 6-7), Satan's control (Ac 26:18), the law (Gal 3), fear, the second death, future judgment.

Of Hebrew Servants:

In the seventh year (Ex 21:2; Dt 15:12; Jer 34:14), in year of Jubilee (Lev 25:10, 40).

Political: (Ac 22:28).

Religious: In Rome (Ac 28:31).

Spiritual: (Ps 119:45; Isa 61:1; Lk 4:18; Jn 8:32-33, 36; Ro 6:6, 22; 8:1-2; 1Co 7:22; 2Co 3:17; Gal 2:4; 1Pe 2:16).

Figurative: Of the gospel (Jas 1:25; 2:12).

LIBNAH [4243] (*white*).

1. A station of the Israelites in the desert (Nu 33:20).

2. A city of Judah, captured by Joshua (Jos 10:29-32, 39; 12:15). Allotted to the priests (Jos 21:13; 1Ch 6:57). Sennacherib besieged; his army defeated near (Ki 19:8, 35; Isa 37:8-36).

LIBNATH *See Shihor Libnath.*

LIBNI, LIBNITE(S) [4249, 4250] (*[descendant of] Libni* or *white*).

1. Son of Gershon (Ex 6:17; Nu 3:18; 1Ch 6:17, 20). Descendants called Libnites (Nu 3:21; 26:58).

2. Grandson of Merari (1Ch 6:29).

LIBRARIES Libraries, both public and private, were not uncommon in ancient times in the Oriental, Greek, and Roman worlds. The Dead Sea Scrolls are one example of an ancient library that has survived to modern times.

LIBYA, LIBYANS [4275, 3340]. A people of N Africa, W of Egypt, who were allies of Egypt (2Ch 12:3; 16:8; Eze 30:5; 38:5; Da 11:43; Ac 2:10). Also called Put. *See Put, 2.*

LICE *See Gnat.*

LICENTIOUSNESS *See Adultery; Lasciviousness.*

LIEUTENANTS *See Satrap; Secretary.*

LIFE [*344, 1414, 2006, 2644, 2649, 2652, 3427, 5883, 6409, 419, 482, 1053, 1586, 2409, 2437, 2443, 2461, 4344, 6034]. Breath of (Ge 2:7). Called breath of God (Job 27:3). Tree of (Ge 2:9; 3:22, 24; Pr 3:18; 13:12; Rev 2:7). Sacredness of, an inference from what is taught in the law

concerning murder. *See Homicide.* Meaninglessness of (Ecc 1-7).

Length of:

Long life promised (Ge 6:3; Ps 91:16), to Solomon (1Ki 3:11-14), to the wise (Pr 3:16; 9:11), to the obedient (Dt 4:40; 22:7; Pr 3:1-2), to those who honor parents (Ex 20:12; Dt 5:16), to those who show kindness to animals (Dt 22:7), given to those who fear God (Pr 10:27; Isa 65:20).

See Longevity.

Brevity of (Job 47:9; Job 10:9, 20-21; 13:12, 25, 28; Ps 89:47-48; 90:10; 146:4; Isa 2:22). Compared, to a shadow (1Ch 29:15; Job 8:9; 14:1-2; Ps 102:11; 144:3; 144:4; Ecc 6:12). To a weaver's shuttle (Job 7:6-10). To a courier (Job 9:25-26). To a handbreadth (Ps 39:4-5, 11). To a wind (Ps 78:39). To grass (Ps 90:3, 5-6, 9-10; 102:11; 103:14-16; Isa 40:6-8, 24; 51:12; Jas 1:10-11; 1Pe 1:24). To a leaf (Isa 64:6). To a vapor (Jas 4:14).

Weary of: Job (Job 3; 7:1-3; 10:18-19). Jeremiah (Jer 20:14-18), Elijah (1Ki 19:1-4), Jonah (Jnh 4:8), Paul (Php 1:21-24).

See Suicide.

Hated (Ecc 2:17). To be hated for Christ's sake (Lk 14:26). What shall a man give in exchange for (Mt 16:26; Mk 8:37). He that loses it for Christ's sake shall save it (Mt 10:39; 16:25-26; Lk 9:24; Jn 12:25).

Uncertainty of (1Sa 20:3; Job 4:19-21; 17:1; Pr 27:1; Lk 12:20). End of, certain (2Sa 14:14; Ps 22:29; Ecc 1:4; Isa 38:12).

See Death, Physical.

Comes From God:

(Ge 2:7; Dt 8:3; 30:20; 32:39; 1Sa 2:6; Job 27:3; Ps 30:3; 104:30; Ecc 12:7; Isa 38:16; Ac 17:25, 28; Ro 4:17; 1Ti 6:13; Jas 4:15).

Spiritual Life:

(Dt 8:3). From Christ (Jn 1:4; 6:27, 33, 35; 10:10; 17:2-3; Ro 6:11; 8:10; Col 3:4). Through faith (Jn 1:12; 5:24-26, 40; 6:40, 47; 11:25-26; 20:31; Gal 2:19-20). Signified, in figure of new birth (Jn 3:3-8; Tit 3:5). In figure of death, burial, and resurrection (Ro 6:4-8).

Everlasting Life:

(Ps 21:4; 121:8; 133:3; Isa 25:8; Da 12:2; Mt 19:16-21, 29; 25:46; Mk 10:17-21, 29-30; Lk 18:18-22, 29-30; 20:36; Jn 3:14-16, 36; 4:14; 5:24-25, 29, 39; 6:27, 40, 47, 50-58, 68; 10:10, 27-28; 12:25, 50; 17:2-3; Ac 13:46, 48; Ro 2:7; 5:21; 6:22-23; 1Co 15:53-54; 2Co 5:1; Gal 6:8; 1Ti 1:16; 4:8; 6:12, 19; 2Ti 1:10; Tit 1:2; 3:7; 1Jn 2:25; 3:15; 5:11-13, 20; Jude 21; Rev 1:18).

See Immortality.

LIFE, THE BOOK OF Figurative expression denoting God's record of those who inherit eternal life (Php 4:3; Rev 3:5; 21:27).

LIGHT [*239, 240, 4401, 5585, 5586, 5944, *847, *3290, *5766, *5890, *5894, *5895].

Physical:

Created (Ge 1:3-5; Ps 74:16; Isa 45:7; 2Co 4:6).

Miraculous (Ex 13:21; Dt 1:33; Mt 17:2; Mk 9:3; Lk 9:29; Ac 9:3; 12:7; 26:13).

Figurative:

(1Ki 11:36). Of the Lord (Ps 27:1; Isa 60:19-20; Jas 1:17; 1Jn 1:5, 7; 2:8-10). Of the Lord's word (Ps 119:105; Pr 6:23). Of personal influence for righteousness (Mt 5:14-16; Mk 4:21; Lk 8:16). Of the righteous (Lk 16:8; Eph 5:8, 14; Php 2:15; 1Th 5:5). Of John the Baptist (Jn 5:35). Of spiritual understanding (Isa 8:20; Lk 1:33-36; 2Co 4:6). Of the gospel (2Co 4:4, 6). Of spiritual wisdom (Ps 119:130; Isa 2:5; 2Pe 1:19). Of righteousness (Mt 5:16; Ac 26:18; 1Pe 2:9). Of heavenly glory (Rev 21:23).

Of Christ's heavenly glory (1Ti 6:16). Of Christ's kingdom (Isa 58:8). Of the Savior (Isa 49:6; Mal 4:2; Mt 4:16; Lk 2:32; Jn 1:4-5, 7-9; 3:19-21; 8:12; 9:5; 12:35-36, 46; Rev 21:23).

LIGHTNING [240, 836, 1027, 1397+1398, 1398, 4365, 8404, *847, *848, *1993]. (Job 28:26; 37:3; 38:25, 35; Ps 18:14; 77:18; 78:48; 97:4; 135:7; 144:6; Jer 10:13; 51:16; Eze 1:13-14; Da 10:6; Na 2:4; Zec 9:14; 10:1; Mt 24:27; 28:3; Lk 10:18; Rev 4:5; 8:5; 11:19; 16:18). Plague of, sent upon Egypt (Ex 9:23; Ps 77:18; 78:48; 105:32).

LIGN ALOES *See Aloes.*

LIGURE *See Jacinth.*

LIKHI [4376] (*take, marry*). Manassite (1Ch 7:19).

LILY [8808, *3211]. The principal capitals of the temple ornamented with carvings of (1Ki 7:19, 22, 26). Molded on the rim of the bronze Sea in the temple (1Ki 7:26; 2Ch 4:5). Lessons of trust gathered from (Mt 6:28-30; Lk 12:27).

Figurative of the lips of the beloved (SS 5:13).

LIME [8487]. (Isa 33:12; Am 2:1).

LINE [74, 204, 339, 448+4578+7156, 643, 1074, 1201, 1858, 2006, 2446, 2475, 2562, 5055, 5120, 5487, 5916+9247, 6885, 7742, 9292, 9352, *45, *3980, *4255]. Usually a measuring line (2Sa 8:2; Ps 78:55), a portion (Ps 16:6), sound made by a musical chord (Ps 19:4).

LINE OF JUDGMENT The divine (2Ki 21:13; Isa 28:17; 34:11; La 2:8; Am 7:8).

LINEN [355, 965, 1009, 2583, 4158, 6041, 7324, 9254, *1115, *1116, *3024, *3351, *3856, *4984]. Exported from Egypt (1Ki 10:38; Eze 27:7), from Syria (Eze 27:16). Curtains of the tabernacle made of (Ex 26:1; 27:9). Robes of priests made of (Ex 28:5-8, 15, 39-42), of royal households made of (Ge 41:42; Est 8:15). Garments for men made of (Ge 41:42; Eze 9:2; Lk 16:19), for women (Isa 3:23; Eze 16:10-13). Bedding made of (Pr 7:16). Mosaic law forbade its being mingled with wool (Lev 19:19; Dt 22:11). The body of Jesus wrapped in (Mk 15:46; Jn 20:5).

Figurative:

Pure and white, of righteousness (Rev 15:6; 19:8, 14).

LINTEL Horizontal beam forming the upper part of the doorway (Ex 12:22-23).

LINUS [3352]. A Christian at Rome (2Ti 4:21).

LION [787, 793, 4097, 4216, 4233, 4234, 4330, 8828, 10069, *3329*].

General:

King of beasts (Mic 5:8). Fierceness of (Job 4:10; 28:8; Ps 7:2; Pr 22:13; Jer 2:15; 49:19; 50:44; Hos 13:8). The roaring of (Ps 22:13; Pr 20:2). Strength of (Pr 30:30; Isa 38:13; Joel 1:6). Instincts of, in taking prey (Ps 10:9; 17:12; La 3:10; Am 3:4; Na 2:12). Lair of, in the jungles (Jer 4:7; 25:38).

Kept in captivity (Da 6). Sent as judgment upon the Samaritans (2Ki 17:25-26). Slain by Samson (Jdg 14:5-9), David (1Sa 17:34, 36), Benaiah (2Sa 23:20), saints (Heb 11:33). Disobedient prophet slain by (1Ki 13:24-28), an unnamed person slain by (1Ki 20:36). Used for the torture of criminals (Da 6:16-24; 7:12; 2Ti 4:17).

The bases in the temple ornamented by moldings of (1Ki 7:29, 36). Twelve statues of, on the stairs leading to Solomon's throne (1Ki 10:19-20). Samson's riddle concerning (Jdg 14:14, 18). Proverb of (Ecc 9:4). Parable of (Eze 19:1-9).

Figurative:

Of a ruler's wrath (Pr 19:12; Jer 5:6; 50:17; Hos 5:14), of Satan (1Pe 5:8), of divine judgments (Isa 15:9).

Symbolic:

(Ge 49:9; Isa 29:1; Eze 1:10; 10:14; Da 7:4; Rev 4:7; 5:5; 9:8, 17; 13:2).

LITIGATION To be avoided (Mt 5:25; Lk 12:58; 1Co 6:1-8). *See Actions at Law; Adjudication at Law; Arbitration; Compromise.*

LITTER *See Wagon.*

LITTLE EVILS So called (Pr 6:10; Ecc 10:1; SS 2:15; 1Co 5:6).

LITTLE OWL *See Birds.*

LIVER [3879, 5355]. Considered center of life and feeling (Pr 7:23), used especially for sacrifice (Ex 29:13) and divination (Eze 21:21).

LIVERY *See Dress; Land, Conveyance of.*

LIVING CREATURES [2651, *2442*]. Possibly identical with cherubim (Eze 1:5-22; 3:13; Rev 4:6-9).

LIVING GOD [2645, 10261, *2409*]. Title emphasizing the reality and existence of the true God (Dt 5:26; Jos 3:10; 1Sa 17:26; Ps 42:2; 84:2;

Isa 37:17; Jer 23:36; Da 6:26; Mt 26:63; Ac 14:15; 1Th 1:9; Heb 10:31; Rev 7:2).

LIZARD [3947, 4321, 7370, 8532]. Unclean; not permitted as food (Lev 11:29-30; Pr 30:28).

LO-AMMI [4204] (*not my people*). Symbolic naming for Hosea's third child to represent a break in the covenant relationship between the Lord and Israel (Ex 6:7; Jer 7:23). This break would later be restored (Hos 1:9-10, ftn; 2:1, 23). The warnings became more severe in moving from the first to the third child. *See Lo-Ruhamah; Ruhamah.*

LO DEBAR [4203, 4274] (*no pasture*). A city in Manasseh (2Sa 9:4-5; 17:27). Home of Mephibosheth, the lame son of Jonathan (2Sa 9:3-5).

LOAVES [2705, 3971, 4312, *788*]. Miracle of the five (Mt 14:15-21; 16:9; Mk 6:37-44; Lk 9:12-17; Jn 6:5-13), of the seven (Mt 15:34-38; 16:10; Mk 8:1-10). *See Bread.*

LOBBYING To frustrate rebuilding the temple (Ezr 4:4-5).

LOCK [4980, 5835, 6037, *2881*, *3091*, *5168*]. Beams of wood or iron used for fastening gates or doors (SS 5:5; Lk 11:7).

LOCUST [746, 1466, 1479, 1612, 2506, 2885, 3540, 7526, *210*]. Authorized as food (Lev 11:22), used as (Mt 3:4; Mk 1:6). Plague of (Ex 10:1-19; Ps 105:34-35). Devastation by (Dt 28:38; 1Ki 8:37; 2Ch 7:13; Isa 33:4; Joel 1:4-7; Rev 9:7-10). Sun obscured by (Joel 2:2, 10). Instincts of (Pr 30:27).

See Grasshopper.

Figurative (Jer 46:23).

Symbolic (Rev 9:3-10).

LOD [4254]. A city in Benjamin (1Ch 8:12; Ezr 2:33; Ne 7:37; 11:35). Called Lydda (Ac 9:38).

LODGE [3519, 4180, 4472, 4869, *2907*, *5685*]. Temporary shelter built in a garden for a watchman guarding ripening fruit (Isa 1:8).

LOFT *See Upper Chamber, Upper Room.*

LOG [4253]. A measure for liquids, holding about a pint (Lev 14:10, 12, 15, 24).

LOGIA Greek word for the nonbiblical sayings of Christ, such as those in the so-called Gospel of Thomas discovered in 1945.

LOGOS Usually rendered "word," in the Johannine writings it also appears as a title of Jesus: "The Word" (Jn 1:1ff; 1Jn 1:1; Rev 19:13). In the OT God creates by the word (Ge 1:3; Ps 33:9). In the Judaism of NT times, "word" was used as a way of referring to God himself. In Greek philosophy, "word" refers to the dynamic principle of reason operating in the world and forming a medium of communion between God and man. *See Jesus the Christ, Names, Appellations, and Titles of; Logos.*

LOIN [4072, 5516]. Part of the body between the ribs and thighs (Lev 3:4, 10, 15), vulnerable (Dt 33:11), a seat of strength (Job 40:16).

LOIS [3396] (perhaps *more desirable, better*). Grandmother of Timothy, commended by Paul for her faith (2Ti 1:5).

LONGEVITY (Ge 6:3; Ps 90:10).

Promised:
To the obedient under the old covenant (Ex 20:12; Dt 4:40; 22:7). To the righteous (Job 5:26; Ps 21:4; 34:11-13; 91:16; Pr 3:2, 16; 9:11; 10:27; Isa 65:20; 1Pe 3:10-11). To Solomon (1Ki 3:11-14).

Instances of:
Adam, 930 years (Ge 5:5). Seth, 912 years (Ge 5:8). Enos, 905 years (Ge 5:11). Kenan, 910 years (Ge 5:14). Mahalalel, 895 years (Ge 5:17). Jared, 962 years (Ge 5:20). Enoch, 365 years (Ge 5:23). Methuselah, 969 years (Ge 5:27). Lamech, 777 years (Ge 5:31). Noah, 950 years (Ge 9:29). Shem (Ge 11:11). Arphaxad (Ge 11:13). Shelah (Ge 11:15). Eber (Ge 11:17). Peleg (Ge 11:19). Reu (Ge 11:21). Serug (Ge 11:23). Nahor (Ge 11:25). Terah, 205 years (Ge 11:32). Sarah, 127 years (Ge 23:1). Abraham, 175 years (Ge 25:7). Isaac, 180 years (Ge 35:28). Jacob, 147 years (Ge 47:28). Joseph, 110 years (Ge 50:26). Amram, 173 years (Ex 6:20). Aaron, 123 years (Nu 33:39). Moses, 120 years (Dt 31:2; 34:7). Joshua, 110 years (Jos 24:29). Eli, 98 years (1Sa 4:15). Barzillai, 80 years (2Sa 19:32). Job, 140 years (Job 42:16). Jehoiada, 130 years (2Ch 24:15). Anna, 84 years (Lk 2:36-37). Paul (Phm 9).
See Life; Old Age.

LONGSUFFERING [678+800]. (1Ti 1:16). A Christian grace (1Co 13:4, 7; 2Co 6:4-6; Gal 5:22; Col 1:11; 2Ti 3:10; 4:2). Commanded (Eph 4:2; Col 3:12-13).
See Charitableness; God, Longsuffering of; Patience.

LOOKING BACKWARD Toward the old life (Ge 19:17, 26; Nu 11:5; 14:4; Lk 9:62).

LOOKING GLASS *See Mirror.*

LORD [(Yahweh: 3051, 3363, 3378) 123, 151, 1484, 8606, 10437, *1305, 2894, 3258, 3259, 3261, 3448*]. A term applied to both men and God, expressing varied degrees of honor, dignity, and majesty; applied also to idols (Ex 22:8; Jdg 2:11, 13), used of Jesus as Messiah (Ac 2:36; Php 2:9-11; Ro 1:4; 14:8). *See God, Names of; Titles and Names; Yahweh.*

LORD'S DAY The day especially associated with the Lord Jesus Christ; a day consecrated to the Lord; the first day of the week, commemorating the resurrection of Jesus (Jn 20:1-25;

Rev 1:10) and the pouring out of the Spirit (Ac 2:1-41), set aside for worship (Ac 20:7).

LORD'S PRAYER Prayer taught by Jesus as a model of how his disciples should pray (Mt 6:9-13; Lk 11:2-4).

LORD'S SUPPER Instituted by Christ on the night of his betrayal immediately after the Passover Feast to be a memorial of his death and a visible sign of the blessings of the new covenant.
Variously called: Body and blood of Christ (Mt 26:26, 28), communion of the body and blood of Christ (1Co 10:16), bread and cup of the Lord (1Co 11:27), breaking of bread (Ac 2:42; 20:7), Lord's Supper (1Co 11:20).
Not to be observed unworthily (1Co 11:27-32).
See Eucharist.

LO-RUHAMAH [4205] (*no compassion*). Symbolic name given to Hosea's daughter (Hos 1:6, 8; 2:4, 23). The naming represents a reversal of the love (compassion) that God had earlier shown to Israel (Ex 33:19; Dt 7:6-8) but was later promised again (Hos 2:23). *See Lo-Ammi; Ruhamah.*

LOST SHEEP Parable of (Mt 18:12-13; Lk 15:4-7).

LOST, THE *See Wicked, Punishment of.*

LOT [4288, *3397*]. The son of Haran. Accompanies Terah from Ur of the Chaldeans to Haran (Ge 11:31). Migrates with Abraham to the land of Canaan (Ge 12:4). Accompanies Abraham to Egypt; returns with him to Bethel (Ge 13:1-3). Rich in flocks, herds, and servants; separates from Abraham and locates in Sodom (Ge 13:5-14). Taken captive by Kedorlaomer; rescued by Abraham (Ge 14:1-16). Providentially saved from destruction in Sodom (Ge 19; Lk 17:28-29). Righteous (2Pe 2:7-8). Disobediently protests against going to the mountains, and chooses Zoar (Ge 19:17-22). His wife disobediently longs after Sodom, and becomes a pillar of salt (Ge 19:26; Lk 17:32). Commits incest with his daughters (Ge 19:30-38). Descendants of. *See Ammonite(s); Moabite(s).*

LOT, THE [1598, 2750, 3926+4987, 5162, 7877, *3102, 3275*]. (Pr 16:33; 18:18; Isa 34:17; Joel 3:3). The scapegoat chosen by (Lev 16:8-10).
The land of Canaan divided among the tribes by (Nu 26:55; Jos 15; 18:10; 19:51; 21; 1Ch 6:61, 65; Eze 45:1; 47:22; 48:29; Mic 2:5; Ac 13:19). Saul chosen king by (1Sa 10:20-21). Priests and Levites designated by, for sanctuary service (1Ch 24:5-31; 26:13; Ne 10:34; Lk 1:9). Used after the Captivity (Ne 11:1). An apostle chosen by (Ac 1:26). Achan's guilt discovered by (Jos 7:14-18), Jonathan's (1Sa 14:41-42), Jonah's (Jnh 1:7). Used to fix the time for the execution of condemned persons (Est 3:7; 9:24). The garments of

Jesus divided by (Ps 22:18; Mt 27:35; Mk 15:24; Jn 19:23-24).

For Feast of, *See Casting Lots; Purim.*

LOTAN [4289] (*of Lot*). Son of Seir (Ge 36:20, 22, 29).

LOTS, CASTING *See Casting Lots; Lot, The.*

LOTUS [7365]. A water plant (Job 40:21-22). *See Plants of the Bible.*

LOVE [*170, 171, 172, 173, 1856, 2668, 2876, 2883, 3137, 3351, 8163, 8533, 26, 27, 28, 921, 5789, 5797]. (1Co 13; 14:1; Col 1:8; 2:2; 1Th 1:3; 5:8; 1Ti 6:11; 2Ti 1:7; Phm 5; Heb 10:24; 1Jn 4:7, 16-18).

The theme of the Song of Songs, and often allegorized representing the love of God for Israel, of the Messiah for the church and of his church for the Messiah (SS 1-8). *See Church, Loved.*

Love of Person for Person:
(Ro 5:7; Jas 1:27). Defined (1Co 13:1-13). In the parable of the good Samaritan (Lk 10:25-37). Is edifying (1Co 8:1). Is precious (Pr 15:17). Is unquenchable (Pr 17:17; SS 8:6-7). Is a fruit of the Spirit (Gal 5:22). Promotes peace (Pr 10:12; 17:9). A proof, of discipleship of Jesus (Jn 13:34-35), of regeneration (1Jn 3:14, 19).

Commanded—
(Lev 19:18; Mt 5:40-42; 7:12; 19:19; 22:39-40; Mk 12:30-33; Lk 6:30-38; Ro 12:9, 15; 13:8-10; 1Co 10:24; 16:14; Gal 6:1-2, 10; Eph 4:2, 32; 5:2; Php 1:9; Col 3:14; 1Th 3:12; 1Ti 1:5; 4:12; 6:11; 2Ti 2:22; Jas 2:8; 2Pe 1:7; 1Jn 4:20-21). Toward strangers (Lev 19:34; Dt 10:19). Toward enemies (Pr 24:17; Mt 5:43-48; Lk 6:35; Ro 12:14, 20). Toward fellow Christians (Jn 13:14-15, 34-35; 15:12-13, 17; Ro 12:9-10, 15-16; 14:19, 21; 15:1-2, 5, 7; 16:1-2; 1Co 14:1; 2Co 8:7-8; Gal 5:13-14; 6:1-2, 10; Eph 4:2, 32; Php 2:2; Col 2:2; 3:12-14; 1Th 3:12; 5:8, 11, 14; 1Pe 1:22; Phm 16; Heb 10:24; 13:13; 1Pe 1:22; 2:17; 3:8-9; 4:8; 2Pe 1:7; 1Jn 3:11, 14, 16-18, 19, 23; 4:7, 11-12, 20-21; 2Jn 5). Demonstrated by obedience (1Jn 5:1-2).

Rewards of (Mt 10:41-42; 25:34-40, 46; Mk 9:41; 1Jn 2:10).

Instances of—
Abraham for Lot (Ge 14:14-16). Moses for Israel (Ex 32:31-32). David and Jonathan (1Sa 18:1; 20:17). Israel for David (1Sa 18:16). David's subjects for David (2Sa 15:30; 17:27-29). Hiram for David (1Ki 5:1). Obadiah for the prophets (1Ki 18:4). Nehemiah for Israelites (Ne 5:10-18). Job's friends (Job 42:11). Centurion for his servant (Lk 7:2-6). Good Samaritan (Lk 10:29-37). Stephen (Ac 7:60). Roman Christians for Paul (Ac 28:15). Priscilla and Aquila for Paul (Ro 16:3-4).

Exemplified by Paul (Ac 26:29; Ro 1:11-12; 9:1-3; 1Co 4:9-16; 8:13; 2Co 1:3-6, 14, 23-24; 2:4; 3:2; 4:5; 6:4-6, 11-13; 7:1-4; 11:2; 12:14-16, 19-21; 13:9; Gal 4:19-20; Eph 3:13; Php 1:3-5, 7-8, 23-26; 2:19; 4:1; Col 1:3-4, 24, 28-29; 2:1, 5; 4:7;

1Th 2:7-8, 11-12, 17-20; 3:5, 7-10, 12; 2Th 1:4; 2Ti 1:3-4, 8; 2:10; Tit 3:15; Phm 9, 12, 16).

See Brother; Fraternity; Friendship; Golden Rule.

Love of Man for Woman:
Isaac for Rebekah (Ge 24:67). Jacob for Rachel (Ge 29:20, 30). Shechem for Dinah (Ge 34:3, 12). Boaz for Ruth (Ru 2-4).

Love of People for God:
Defined (1Jn 5:3; 2Jn 6). Incompatible with love of the world (1Jn 2:15), with hatred of brother (1Jn 4:20-21), with guilty fear (2Ti 1:7; 1Jn 4:18). Reasons for (Ps 116:1; 1Jn 4:19).

The gift of God (Dt 30:6; 2Ti 1:7). Through the Holy Spirit (Ro 5:5).

Commanded (Dt 6:5; 10:12; 11:1, 13, 22; 19:9; 30:16, 19-20; Jos 22:5; 23:11; Ps 31:23; Pr 23:26; Mt 22:37-38; Mk 12:29-30, 32-33; Lk 11:42; 2Th 3:5; Jude 21). Tested (Dt 13:3). Obedience proof of (1Jn 2:5; 5:1-2; 2Jn 6).

Leads to generosity (1Jn 3:17-18), hate of evil (Ps 97:10), love from God (Ps 8:1-8). Rewards of (Ex 20:6; Dt 5:10; 7:9; Ps 37:4; 69:35-36; 91:14; 145:20; Isa 56:6-7; Jer 2:2-3; Ro 8:28; 1Co 8:3). Exemplified (Ps 18:1; 63:5-6; 73:25-26; 103).

Love of People for Jesus:
Commanded (Mt 10:37-38; Jn 15:9; 1Co 16:22). Love of God produces (Jn 8:42). Obedience results from (Jn 14:15, 21, 23; 2Co 5:6, 8, 14-15). Rewards of (Mt 25:34-40, 46; Mk 9:41; Lk 7:37-50; Jn 16:27; Eph 6:24; 2Ti 4:8; Heb 6:10; Jas 1:12; 2:5).

Instances of—
Mary (Mt 26:6-13; Lk 10:39; Jn 12:3-8). Peter (Mt 17:4; Jn 13:37; 18:10; 20:3-6; 21:15-17). The healed demoniac (Mk 5:18; Lk 8:38). Thomas (Jn 11:16). The disciples (Mk 16:10; Lk 24:17-41; Jn 16:27; 20:20). Mary Magdalene and other disciples (Mt 27:55-56, 61; 28:1-9; Lk 8:2-3; 23:27, 55-56; 24:1-10; Jn 20:1-2, 11-18). Joseph of Arimathea (Mt 27:57-60). Nicodemus (Jn 19:39-40). Women of Jerusalem (Lk 23:27). Paul (Ac 21:13; Php 1:20-21, 23; 3:7-8; 2Ti 4:8). Philemon (Phm 5). Early Christians (1Pe 1:8; 2:7), lost that love (Rev 2:4).

Of Children for Parents: *See Children.*

Of God: *See God, Love of.*

Of Jesus: *See Jesus the Christ, Love of.*

Of Money:
A root of all kinds of evil (1Ti 6:10). *See Avarice; Riches.*

Of Parents for Children: *See Parents.*

LOVE FEAST [27] (*agape feast*). A common meal eaten by early Christians in connection with the Lord's Supper to express and deepen brotherly love (1Co 11:18-22, 33-34; Jude 12).

LOVERS [170, 172, 1856, 6311, 7108, 8276, 920, 921, 5795, 5796, 5798, 5806].

Instances Within or Resulting in Marriage:
Isaac and Rebekah (Ge 24:67). Jacob and Rachel

(Ge 29:20, 30). Boaz and Ruth (Ru 2-4). The beloved and her lover (SS 1-8).

Instances Outside of Marriage:

Shechem and Dinah (Ge 34:3, 12). Gomer and her lovers (Hos 1-3).

Figurative of Disloyalty to Yahweh:

Israel and pagan gods (Jer 3:1-2; Hos 2). Jerusalem and political allies (La 1:2; Eze 16:33-42; 23).

LOVING-KINDNESS [2876]. The kindness and mercy of God toward people (Ps 17:7; 26:3).

LOYALTY [339, 586, 2876, 3922, 5466+ 9068, *1188*]. Commanded (Ex 22:28; Nu 27:20; Ezr 6:10; 7:26; Job 34:18; Pr 24:21; Ecc 8:2; 10:4; Ro 13:1; Tit 3:1). Enforced (Ezr 10:8; Pr 17:11). Disloyalty (2Pe 2:10). *See Patriotism.*

Instances of:

Israelites (Jos 1:16-18; 2Sa 3:36-37; 15:23, 30; 18:3; 21:17; 1Ch 12:38). David (1Sa 24:6-10; 26:6-16; 2Sa 1:14). Uriah (2Sa 11:9). Ittai (2Sa 15:21). Hushai (2Sa 17:15-16). David's soldiers (2Sa 18:12-13; 23:15-16). Joab (2Sa 19:5-6). Barzillai (2Sa 19:32). Jehoiada (2Ki 11:4-12). Mordecai (Est 2:21-23).

LUBIM(S) *See Libya, Libyans; Put, 2.*

LUCAS *See Luke.*

LUCIFER Latin for "morning star" (Isa 14:12); a title of the king of Babylon, often understood as a reference to the devil. *See Devil; Satan.*

LUCIUS [*3372*].
1. A Christian at Antioch (Ac 13:1).
2. A relative of Paul (Ro 16:21).

LUD [4276]. A son of Shem (Ge 10:22; 1Ch 1:17).

LUDITES [4276]. Descendants of Mizraim (Ge 10:13; 1Ch 1:11). Perhaps the same as the Lydians. *See Lydia, Lydians.*

LUHITH [4284]. A city of Moab (Isa 15:5; Jer 48:5).

LUKE [*3371*]. A disciple. A physician (Col 4:14). Wrote to Theophilus (Lk 1:1-4; Ac 1:1-2). Accompanies Paul in his tour of Asia and Macedonia (Ac 16:10-13; 20:5-6), to Jerusalem (Ac 21:1-18), to Rome (Ac 27:28; 2Ti 4:1; Phm 24).

LUKE, GOSPEL OF

Author: Traditionally Luke, the companion of Paul

Date: The two most commonly suggested periods for dating the Gospel of Luke are: (1) A.D. 59-63, and (2) the 70s or the 80s.

Outline:

I. The Preface (1:1-4).
II. The Coming of Jesus (1:5-2:52).
   A. The Annunciations (1:5-56).
   B. The Birth of John the Baptist (1:57-80).
   C. The Birth and Childhood of Jesus (ch. 2).
III. The Preparation of Jesus for His Public Ministry (3:1-4:13).
   A. His Forerunner (3:1-20).
   B. His Baptism (3:21-22).
   C. His Genealogy (3:23-38).
   D. His Temptation (4:1-13).
IV. His Ministry in Galilee (4:14-9:9).
   A. The Beginning of the Ministry in Galilee (4:14-41).
   B. The First Tour of Galilee (4:42-5:39).
   C. A Sabbath Controversy (6:1-11).
   D. The Choice of the Twelve Apostles (6:12-16).
   E. The Sermon on the Plain (6:17-49).
   F. Miracles in Capernaum and Nain (7:1-18).
   G. The Inquiry of John the Baptist (7:19-29).
   H. Jesus and the Pharisees (7:30-50).
   I. The Second Tour of Galilee (8:1-3).
   J. The Parables of the Kingdom (8:4-21).
   K. The Trip Across the Sea of Galilee (8:22-39).
   L. The Third Tour of Galilee (8:40-9:9).
V. His Withdrawal to Regions Around Galilee (9:10-50).
   A. To the Eastern Shore of the Sea of Galilee (9:10-17).
   B. To Caesarea Philippi (9:18-50).
VI. His Ministry in Judea (9:51-13:21).
   A. Journey Through Samaria to Judea (9:51-62).
   B. The Mission to the Seventy (10:1-24).
   C. The Lawyer and the Parable of the Good Samaritan (10:25-37).
   D. Jesus at Bethany With Mary and Martha (10:38-42).
   E. Teachings in Judea (11:1-13:21).
VII. His Ministry in and Around Perea (13:22-19:27).
   A. The Narrow Door (13:22-30).
   B. Warning Concerning Herod (13:31-35).
   C. At a Pharisee's House (14:1-23).
   D. The Cost of Discipleship (14:24-35).
   E. The Parables of the Lost Sheep, the Lost Coin and the Prodigal Son (ch. 15).
   F. The Parable of the Shrewd Manager (16:1-18).
   G. The Rich Man and Lazarus (16:19-31).
   H. Miscellaneous Teachings (17:1-10).
   I. Ten Healed of Leprosy (17:11-19).
   J. The Coming of the Kingdom (17:20-37).
   K. The Persistent Widow (18:1-8).
   L. The Pharisee and the Tax Collector (18:9-14).
   M. Jesus and the Children (18:15-17).
   N. The Rich Young Ruler (18:18-30).
   O. Christ Foretells His Death (18:31-34).
   P. A Blind Beggar Given His Sight (18:35-43).
   Q. Jesus and Zacchaeus (19:1-10).
   R. The Parable of the Ten Minas (19:11-27).
VIII. His Last Days: Sacrifice and Triumph (19:28-24:53).
   A. The Triumph Entry (19:28-44).

B. The Cleansing of the Temple (19:45-48).
C. The Last Controversies With the Jewish Leaders (ch. 20).
D. The Olivet Discourse (ch. 21).
E. The Last Supper (22:1-38).
F. Jesus Praying in Gethsemane (22:39-46).
G. Jesus' Arrest (22:47-65).
H. Jesus on Trial (22:66-23:25).
I. The Crucifixion (23:26-56).
J. The Resurrection (24:1-12).
K. The Post-Resurrection Ministry (24:13-49).
L. The Ascension (24:50-53).
See Acts of the Apostles; Synoptic Gospels, The.

LUKEWARMNESS [*5950*]. Instances of: The Reubenites and other tribes, when Deborah called on them to assist Sisera (Jdg 5:16-17). Israel (Hos 10:2). The Jews (Ne 3:5; 13:11; Hag 1:2-11). The church, at Pergamum (Rev 2:14-16), Thyatira (Rev 2:20-24), Sardis (Rev 3:1-3), Laodicea (Rev 3:14-16).
See Backsliding; Blindness, Spiritual; Complacency.

LUNACY *See Insanity; Demons.*

LUST [2388+, 2393, 2773, 2801, 6311, 6312, 9373, *2123, 3979, 4079, 4432*] (*evil desires*). Sinful (Job 31:9-12; Mt 5:28). Worldly (1Jn 2:16-17). Chokes the word (Mk 4:19). Tempts to sin (Ge 3:6; Jas 1:14-15; 2Pe 2:18).
Forbidden (Ex 20:17; Pr 6:24-25; Ro 13:14; Eph 4:22; Col 3:5; 1Th 4:5; Tit 2:12; 1Pe 2:11). Warnings against (1Co 10:6-7; 2Ti 2:22).Wicked under power of (Jn 8:44; Ro 1:24, 26-27; 1Ti 6:9; Jas 4:1-3; 1Pe 4:3; 2Pe 3:3; Jude 16, 18). Of Israelites (Ps 106:13-14).
The righteous restrain (1Co 9:27).
See Adultery; Covetousness; Homosexual; Incest; Lasciviousness; Sensuality.

LUTE [4036, 8956]. Stringed instrument used to accompany songs of praise (1Sa 18:6; 2Ch 20:28). *See Music, Instruments of.*

LUZ [4281] (*almond tree*).
1. Town on N boundary of Benjamin (Jos 16:2; 18:13).

2. Hittite town (Jdg 1:26).

LYCAONIA [*3377, 3378*]. A province of Asia Minor. Paul visits towns of (Ac 14:6-21; 16:1-2).

LYCIA [*3379*]. A province of Asia Minor. Paul visits (Ac 27:5).

LYDDA [*3375*]. Called also Lod. A city of Benjamin (1Ch 8:12; Ezr 2:33; Ne 11:35). Peter heals Aeneas in (Ac 9:32-35).

LYDIA, LYDIANS [4276, *3376*].
1. A woman of Thyatira, who with her household, was converted through the preaching of Paul (Ac 16:14-15). Entertains Paul and Silas (Ac 16:15, 40).
2. A country and people in the N Africa or Asia Minor; mercenary warriors (Isa 66:19; Jer 46:9; Eze 27:10; 30:5). Perhaps the same as the Ludites. *See Ludites.*

LYING [*3941, 3942, 3950, 3951, 5327, 8736, 9214, *6014, 6016, 6017, 6022, 6026*]. Lying spirit from God (1Ki 22:21-23; 2Ch 18:20-22). *See Falsehood; Hypocrisy; Liars.*

LYRE [4036, 5575, 10676]. Used in religious services (2Sa 6:5; 1Ch 13:8; 16:5; 25:1, 5-6; 2Ch 29:25; Ps 33:2; 57:8; 71:22; 81:2; 92:3; 108:2; 144:9; 150:3). At the dedication of the new wall when the captives returned (Ne 12:27). Used in idolatrous worship (Da 3:5, 7, 10, 15).
See Music, Instruments of.

LYSANIAS [*3384*]. A tetrarch (Lk 3:1).

LYSIAS [*3385*]. Chief captain of Roman troops in Jerusalem (Ac 24:7, ftn; 24:22). *See Claudius Lysias.*

LYSTRA [*3388*]. A city of Lycaonia to which Paul and Barnabas fled from persecutions in Iconium (Ac 14:6-23; 2Ti 3:11). Church of, elders ordained for, by Paul and Barnabas (Ac 14:23). Timothy a resident of (Ac 16:1-4).

M

MAACAH [5081, 5082, 5084] (perhaps *dull, stupid*).

1. Son of Nahor (Ge 22:24).
2. Mother of Absalom (2Sa 3:3; 1Ch 3:2).
3. Father of Achish, king of Gath (1Sa 27:2). Possibly the same as Maoch. (1Ki 2:39).
4. Mother of Abijah and grandmother of Asa (1Ki 15:2, 10-13; 2Ch 11:20-23; 15:16). Also called Micaiah (2Ch 13:2, ftn).
5. Wife of Makir (1Ch 7:15-16).
6. Concubine of Caleb (1Ch 2:48).
7. Wife of Jeiel (1Ch 8:29; 9:35).
8. Father of Hanan (1Ch 11:43).
9. Father of Shephatiah (1Ch 27:16).
10. A small kingdom E of Bashan. *See Maacathite(s).*

MAACATHITE(S) [5084]. People of the nation of Maacah, in the region of Bashan (Dt 3:14; Jos 12:5; 13:11; 2Sa 10:6, 8; 23:34; 1Ch 4:19; 19:6-7).

MAADAI [5049] (*ornaments*). Israelite who married a foreign woman (Ezr 10:34).

MAADIAH *See Moadiah.*

MAAI [5076] (*to be compassionate*). Priest who blew trumpet at dedication of wall (Ne 12:36).

MAALEH-ACRABBIM *See Scorpion Pass.*

MAARATH [5125] (*barren*). A city of Judah (Jos 15:59).

MAASAI [5127] (*work of Yahweh*). Priestly family after the Exile (1Ch 9:12).

MAASEIAH, MAHSEIAH [5128, 5129] (*Yahweh is a refuge*).

1. Levite musician (1Ch 15:18, 20).
2. Army captain who assisted Jehoiada in overthrowing Athaliah (2Ch 23:1).
3. Officer of Uzziah (2Ch 26:11).
4. Son Ahaz, king of Judah (2Ch 28:7).
5. Governor of Jerusalem in Josiah's reign (2Ch 34:8).
6. A priest who married a foreigner (Ezr 10:18).
7. A priest who married a foreigner (Ezr 10:21).
8. A priest who married a foreigner (Ezr 10:22).
9. Israelite who married a foreigner (Ezr 10:30).
10. Father of Azariah (Ne 3:23).
11. Priest; assistant of Ezra (Ne 8:4).
12. Man who explained law to people (Ne 8:7).
13. Chief who sealed covenant with Nehemiah (Ne 10:25).
14. Descendant of son of Baruch (Ne 11:5).
15. Benjamite (Ne 11:7).
16. Priest who blew trumpet at dedication of temple (Ne 12:41).

MAATH [*3399*] (*to be small*). An ancestor of Jesus (Lk 3:26).

MAAZ [5106] (perhaps *angry* or *wrath*). A son of Ram (1Ch 2:27).

MAAZIAH [5068, 5069] (*Yahweh is a refuge*).

1. A priest (1Ch 24:18).
2. A priest who sealed the covenant with Nehemiah (Ne 10:8).

MACBANNAI [4801] (*clad with a cloak*). A Gadite warrior (1Ch 12:13).

MACBENAH [4800] (*bond*). A descendant of Caleb (1Ch 2:49). "Father of" may mean "founder of" or "leader of" a city.

MACCABEES (*hammer*). Hasmonean Jewish family of Modein (or Modin) that led revolt against Antiochus Epiphanes, king of Syria, and won freedom for the Jews. The family consisted of the father, Mattathias, an aged priest, and his five sons: Johanan, Simon, Judas, Eleazar, and Jonathan. The name Maccabee was first given to Judas, perhaps because he inflicted sledgehammer blows against the Syrian armies, and later was also used for his brothers. The revolt began in 168 B.C. The temple was recaptured and sacrifices were resumed in 165 B.C. The cleansing of the temple and resumption of sacrifices have been celebrated annually ever since in the Feast of Dedication. The Maccabees served as both high priests and kings. The story of Maccabees is told in two books of the Apocrypha, I and II Maccabees.

The following were the most prominent of the Maccabees: Judas (166-160 B.C.), Jonathan (160-142 B.C.), Simon (142-134 B.C.), John Hyrcanus (134-104 B.C.), Aristobulus (104-103 B.C.), Alexander Jannaeus (103-76 B.C.), Alexandra (76-67 B.C.), Aristobulus II (66-63 B.C.). In 63 B.C. the Romans took over when Pompey conquered the Israelites.

See Dedication; Feasts; Hanukkah; Kislev; Month, 9; Testaments, Time Between.

MACEDONIA [*3423, 3424*]. A province in N Greece. Paul has a vision concerning (Ac 16:9), preaches in, at Philippi (Ac 16:12), revisits (Ac 20:1-6; 2Co 2:13; 7:5). Church at, sends contributions to the poor in Jerusalem (Ro 15:26; 2Co 8:1-5). Timothy visits (Ac 19:22). Disciples in (Ac 19:22; 27:2).

MACEDONIAN EMPIRE, THE Called the kingdom of Greece (Da 11:2).

Illustrated by the:

Bronze part of the image in Nebuchadnezzar's dream (Da 2:32, 39). Leopard with four wings and four heads (Da 7:6, 17). Shaggy goat with notable horn (Da 8:5-8, 21). Philippi the chief city of (Ac 16:12).

Predictions Respecting:

Conquest of the Medo-Persian kingdom (Da 8:6-7; 11:2-3). Power and greatness of Alexander its last king (Da 8:8; 11:3). Division of it into four kingdoms (Da 8:8, 22). Divisions of it ruled by strangers (Da 11:4). History of its four divisions (Da 11:4-29). The little horn to arise out of one of its divisions (Da 8:8-12). Gospel preached in, by God's desire (Ac 16:9-10). Liberality of the churches of (2Co 8:1-5).

MACHAERUS Fortress stronghold built by Alexander Janneus (c. 90 B.C.) and used as a citadel by Herod Antipas; located on E of Dead Sea; John the Baptist was put to death there (Mt 14:3ff).

MACHI *See Maki.*

MACHIR *See Makir.*

MACHPELAH [4834] (*double [cave]*). The burying place of Sarah, Abraham, Isaac, Rebekah, Leah, and Jacob (Ge 23:9, 17-20; 25:9; 49:30-31; 50:13; Ac 7:16).

MACNADEBAI [4827] (possibly *possession of Nebo*). Israelite who divorced foreign wife (Ezr 10:40).

MADAI [4512] (*Medes*). People descended from Japheth (Ge 10:2; 1Ch 1:5).

MADMANNAH [4525, 4526] (*dung place*).
1. Town in S Judah eight miles S of Kiriath Sepher (Jos 15:31).
2. Grandson of Caleb (1Ch 2:48-49).

MADMEN [2099, 2100, 2147, 4522, 8713, 8714, 3419, 4197] (sounds like *be silenced*).
1. A place (Jer 48:2).
2. A maniac, of insane persons (1Sa 21:15). *See Insanity.*

MADMENAH [4524] (*dunghill*). City of Benjamin (Isa 10:31).

MADNESS *See Insanity; Madmen.*

MADON [4507] (*contention*). Canaanite city near modern Qarn Hattin (Jos 11:1; 12:19).

MAGADAN [3400]. Town on the NW shore of Sea of Galilee, three miles N of Tiberias. Also called Magdala, the home of Mary Magdalene (Mt 15:39). Mark (8:10) has "Dalmanutha." *See Dalmanutha.*

MAGBISH [4455] (perhaps *thick*). Name of man or place (Ezr 2:30).

MAGDALA *See Dalmanutha; Magadan.*

MAGDALENE [3402] (*of Magdala*). *See Mary, 3.*

MAGDIEL [4462] (*choice gift of God [El]*). Chief of Edom (Ge 36:43; 1Ch 1:54).

MAGGOT [8231, 9357] Infested leftover manna (Ex 16:20, 24). Synonymous with "worm" (Job 25:6). *See Animals.*

MAGI [3407]. Originally a religious caste among the Persians; devoted to astrology, divination, and interpretation of dreams. Later the word came to be applied generally to fortune-tellers and exponents of esoteric religious cults throughout the Mediterranean world (Ac 8:9; 13:6, 8). Nothing is known of the Magi of the Nativity story (Mt 2); they may have come from S Arabia.

MAGIC [2490, 3033, 4086, 10282, 3404, 5758, 5760, 5761]. The art or science of influencing or controlling the course of nature, events, and supernatural powers through occult science of mysterious arts (Ge 41:8; Ex 7:11, 22; 8:7, 18; Ac 19:19). Includes necromancy, exorcism, dreams, shaking arrows, inspecting entrails of animals, divination, sorcery, astrology, soothsaying, divining by rods, witchcraft (1Sa 28:8; Eze 21:21; Ac 16:16).

MAGICIAN [3033, 10282]. A person who claims to understand and explain mysteries by magic (Da 1:20). Failed to interpret Pharaoh's dreams (Ge 41:8, 24), Nebuchadnezzar's (Da 2:2-13; 4:7). Worked apparent miracles (Ex 7:11-12, 22; 8:7, 18).

MAGISTRATE(S) [10735, 10767, 807, 5130]. An officer of civil law (Jdg 18:7; Ezr 7:25; Lk 12:11, 58; Ac 16:20, 22, 35, 38). Obedience to, commanded (Tit 3:1).
See Government; Rulers.

MAGNA CARTA *See Constitution.*

MAGNANIMITY Instances of: Joshua and the elders of Israel to the Gibeonites who had deceived the Israelites (Jos 9:3-27). Of Moses. *See Moses.* David to Saul (1Sa 24:3-11). Ahab to Ben-Hadad (1Ki 20:32-34).
See Charitableness.

MAGNIFICAT Song of praise by Mary (Lk 1:46-55).

MAGOG [4470, 3408] (perhaps *land of Gog*).
1. Son of Japheth (Ge 10:2; 1Ch 1:5).
2. Land of God.
Various identifications: Scythians, Lydians, Tartars of Russia. Used symbolically for forces of evil (Rev 20:7-9).

MAGOR-MISSABIB [4474] (*terror on every side*). A symbolic name given by Jeremiah to Pashhur (Jer 20:3-6).

MAGPIASH [4488] (*moth killer*). Israelite who sealed covenant with Nehemiah (Ne 10:20).

MAGUS, SIMON *See Simon, 8.*

MAHALAH *See Mahlah, 2.*

MAHALALEL [4546, *3435*] (*praise of God [El]*).
1. Son of Kenan (Ge 5:12-17; 1Ch 1:2; Lk 3:37).
2. A man of Judah (Ne 11:4).

MAHALATH [4714, 4715] (*the suffering of affliction* NIV; *sickness or suffering poem*, JB).
1. Daughter of Ishmael (Ge 28:9).
2. Wife of Rehoboam (2Ch 11:18).
3. Musical term in the titles of Pss 53 and 88. Possibly the name of a tune. The Hebrew appears to be the word for "suffering" or "sickness." Perhaps the Hebrew phrase indicates here that the psalm is to be used in a time of affliction, when the godless mock. *See Music, Symbols Used in.*

MAHALI *See Mahli, 1.*

MAHANAIM [4724] (*double camp*). The place where Jacob had the vision of angels (Ge 32:2). The town of, allotted to Gad (Jos 13:26, 30). One of the Levitical cities (Jos 21:38). Ish-Bosheth establishes himself at, when made king over Israel (2Sa 2:8-12). David lodges at, during Absalom's rebellion (2Sa 17:27-29; 1Ki 2:8).

MAHANEH DAN [4723] (*camp of Dan*).
1. Place between Zorah and Eshtaol (Jdg 13:25).
2. Place W of Kiriath Jearim (Jdg 18:12).

MAHARAI [4560] (*impetuous* ISBE). One of David's warriors (2Sa 23:28; 1Ch 11:30; 27:13).

MAHATH [4744] (perhaps *tough*).
1. Kohathite; ancestor of Heman (1Ch 6:35).
2. Levite who helped Hezekiah (2Ch 29:12; 31:13).

MAHAVITE [4687] (*villagers*). Family name of Eliel, one of David's warriors (1Ch 11:46).

MAHAZIOTH [4692] (*visions*). Son of Heman (1Ch 25:4, 30).

MAHER-SHALAL-HASH-BAZ [4561] (*quick to the plunder, swift to the spoil*). Symbolic name Isaiah gave his son (Isa 8:1, 3).

MAHLAH [4702] (perhaps *weak one*).
1. Daughter of Zelophehad (Nu 26:33; 27:1ff; 36; Jos 17:3ff).
2. Grandson of Manasseh (1Ch 7:18).

MAHLI [4706] (perhaps *shrewd, cunning*).
1. Son of Merari (Ex 6:19; 1Ch 6:19; Ezr 8:18).

2. Son of Mushi (1Ch 6:47; 23:23; 24:30).

MAHLITE(S) [4707]. Descendant of Mahli, son of Merari (Nu 3:33; 26:58; 1Ch 23:22).

MAHLON [4705] (*sick*). Son of Naomi and first husband of Ruth (Ru 1:2, 5; 4:9-10).

MAHOL [4689] (*place of round-dancing*). Father of Heman, Calcol, and Darda (1Ki 4:31).

MAID(S), MAIDSERVANT(S) [563, 5855, 9148, *4087*]
1. Female slave or servant (Ge 12:16; 16:1; Lk 12:45).
2. Female personal servant or attendant (Ge 24:61; 1Sa 25:42; Est 2:9).
See Servant.

MAIDEN(S) [1426, 1435, 6625].
1. Young woman (Ps 68:25; 148:12).
2. Young woman of marriageable age, probably a virgin (Ge 24:43; Ps 78:63; Isa 62:5; Jer 2:32).

MAIL
1. Sending of letters (2Sa 11:14-15; 1Ki 21:8-11; 2Ki 5:5-7; Est 3:13; 8:10; 2Pe 3:16). *See Letter; Letters.*
2. Armor (1Sa 17:5). *See Armor.*

MAIMED [3024, *3245*]. Not acceptable as sacrifices (Lev 22:22). *See Disease.*

MAJESTY [129, 158, 398, 466, 1452, 1454, 1455, 1525, 1542, 2077, 2086, 3636, 4889, 5905, 10199, *1518*, *3261*, *3484*, *3485*, *3488*]. Name of God (Heb 1:3; 8:1). *See God.*

MAJORITY AND MINORITY REPORTS Of the spies (Nu 13:26-33; 14:6-10).

MAKAZ [5242]. A place in Judah (1Ki 4:9).

MAKHELOTH [5221] (*assemblies*). An encampment of Israel (Nu 33:25-26).

MAKI [4809] (perhaps *reduced* or *bought*). Gadite; father of Geuel, one of 12 spies (Nu 13:15).

MAKIR, MAKIRITE [4810, 4811] (*bought*).
1. One of the sons of Manasseh (Ge 50:23). Father of the Makirites (Nu 26:29; 36:1). The land of Gilead allotted to (Nu 32:39-40; Dt 3:15; Jos 13:31). Certain cities of Bashan given to (Jos 13:31; 17:1).
2. A man of Lo Debar who took care of Jonathan's lame son, Mephibosheth (2Sa 9:4-5; 17:27).

MAKKEDAH [5218] (*locality of shepherds*). A city in Judah, conquered by Joshua (Jos 10:28; 12:16). Five kings of the Amorites hide in a cave of, and are slain by Joshua (Jos 10:5, 16-27).

MAKTESH (*mortar*). A district where merchants traded (Zep 1:11, ftn). *See Agora; Market.*

MALACHI [4858] (*my messenger* or *messenger of Yahweh*). Prophet of Judah who lived c. 450-400 B.C.; author of OT book which bears his name; nothing known of him beyond what is said in his book; contemporary of Nehemiah (Mal 2:11-17; Ne 13:23-31).

MALACHI, BOOK OF

Author: The prophet Malachi

Date: c. 433 to 400 B.C.

Outline:

I. Title (1:1).
II. Introduction: God's Covenant Love for Israel Affirmed (1:2-5).
III. Israel's Unfaithfulness Rebuked (1:6-2:16).
   A. The Unfaithfulness of the Priests (1:6-2:9).
      1. They dishonor God in their sacrifices (1:6-14).
      2. They do not faithfully teach the law (2:1-9).
   B. The Unfaithfulness of the People (2:10-16).
IV. The Lord's Coming Announced (2:17-4:6).
   A. The Lord Will Come to Purify the Priests and Judge the People (2:17-3:5).
   B. A Call to Repentance in View of the Lord's Coming (3:6-18).
      1. An exhortation to faithful giving (3:6-12).
      2. An exhortation to faithful service (3:13-18).
   C. The Day of the Lord Announced (ch. 4).
See Prophets, The Minor.

MALCAM [4903] (*their king* ISBE KB; or *[servant of] Malk [pagan god]*).
1. A Benjamite (1Ch 8:9).
2. Either Molech, a god of the Moabites and Ammonites (Jer 49:1, 3; Am 1:15; Zep 1:5, ftns) or their king; maybe both. *See Molech.*

MALCHIAH, MALCHIJAH *See Malkijah.*

MALCHIEL *See Malkiel.*

MALCHIJAH *See Malkijah, 2, 3, 4, 7, 11, 12.*

MALCHIRAM *See Malkiram.*

MALCHI-SHUA *See Malki-Shua.*

MALCHUS [3438] (*king*). Servant of the high priest; Peter assaults in Gethsemane; healed by Jesus (Mt 26:51; Mk 14:47; Lk 22:50-51; Jn 18:10).

MALEFACTOR *See Criminals.*

MALELEEL *See Mahalalel, 1.*

MALFEASANCE IN OFFICE

Illustrated in the Parables of Jesus: The tenants of the vineyard (Mk 12:1-8; Lk 20:9-15). The rich man's manager (Lk 16:1-7).

MALICE [224, 2095, 8273, 8288, 8534, 8624, 2798, 2799, 4504].

Characteristics:

Outgrowth of original sin (Ge 3:15). Is hated by God (Pr 6:16-19). Reacts (Job 15:35; Ps 7:15-16; 10:7, 14; Jer 20:10). Blinds those possessed of (1Jn 2:9-11; 4:20). Is murderous (1Jn 3:13-15). Preludes divine forgiveness (Mt 6:15; 18:28-35).

Is forbidden (Lev 19:14, 17-18; 2Ki 6:21-22; Pr 20:22; 24:17-18, 29; Zec 7:10; 8:17; Mt 5:38-41; Lk 6:29; Ro 12:19; 1Co 5:8; 14:20; Eph 4:31; Col 3:8; 1Th 5:15; 1Pe 2:1; 3:9). The wicked filled with (Dt 32:32-33; Ps 10:7-10, 14; Pr 4:16-17; 6:14; 21:10; 30:14; Isa 59:4-6; Mt 13:25, 28; Jn 8:44; Ro 1:29-32; Gal 5:19-21; Tit 3:3; 3Jn 10). Punishment for (Dt 27:17-18; Pr 6:14-15; 17:5; 28:10; Isa 29:20-21; 32:6; Eze 18:18; 26:2-3; 28:3, 6-7, 12-17; Am 1:11; Mic 2:1; Mt 26:52; Jas 2:13).

Proverbs concerning (Pr 4:16-17; 6:14-16, 18-19; 10:6, 12; 11:17; 12:10; 14:17, 22; 15:17; 16:30; 17:5; 20:22; 21:10; 24:8, 17-18, 29; 26:2, 27; 28:10; 30:14).

Instances of:

Cain toward Abel (Ge 4:8; 1Jn 3:12). Ishmael toward Sarah (Ge 21:9). Sarah toward Hagar (Ge 21:10). Philistines toward Isaac (Ge 26:12-15, 18-21). Esau toward Jacob (Ge 27:41-42). Joseph's brothers toward Joseph (Ge 37:2-28; 42:21; Ac 7:9-10). Potiphar's wife toward Joseph (Ge 39:14-20). Ammonites toward the Israelites (Dt 23:3-4). Saul toward David (1Sa 18:8-29; 19; 20:30-33; 22:6-23; 23:7-28; 26:1-2, 18). David toward Michal (2Sa 6:21-23), toward Joab (1Ki 2:5-6), toward Shimei (1Ki 2:8-9). Shimei toward David (2Sa 16:5-8). Ahithophel toward David (2Sa 17:1-3). Jezebel toward Elijah (1Ki 19:1-2). Ahaziah toward Elijah (2Ki 1:7-15). Jehoram toward Elisha (2Ki 6:31). Samaritans toward the Jews (Ezr 4; Ne 2:10; 4:6). Haman toward Mordecai (Est 3:5-15; 5:9-14). Not practiced by Job (Job 31:29-30). The psalmist's enemies (Ps 22:7-8; 35:15-16, 19-21; 38:16, 19; 41:5-8; 55:3; 56:5-6; 57:4, 6; 59:3-4, 7; 62:3-4; 64:2-6; 69:4, 10-12, 26; 86:14; 102:8; 109:2-5, 16-18; 140:1-4); the psalmist demands retribution (Ps 10:7-10, 14; 70:2-3; 71:10-13, 24). Jeremiah's enemies (Jer 26:8-11; 38:1-6). Nebuchadnezzar toward Zedekiah (Jer 52:10-11). Daniel's enemies (Da 6:4-15).

Herodias toward John (Mt 14:3-11; Mk 6:24-28). James and John toward the Samaritans (Lk 9:54). Enemies of Jesus (Ps 22:11; Mt 27:18, 27-30, 39-43; Mk 12:13; 15:10-11, 16-19, 29-32; Lk 11:53-54; 23:10-11, 39; Jn 18:22-23). Paul's enemies (Ac 14:5, 19; 16:19-24; 17:5; 19:24-35; 21:27-31, 36; 22:22-23; 23:12-15; 25:3; Php 1:15-17).

See Conspiracy; Hatred; Homicide; Jealousy; Persecution; Retaliation; Revenge.

MALINGERING Instances of: David

feigning madness (1Sa 21:13-15), the sluggard (Pr 6:9-11).

MALKIEL, MALKIELITE [4896, 4897] (*God [El] is [my] king*). An Asherite; son of Beriah (Ge 46:17; Nu 26:45; 1Ch 7:31).

MALKIJAH [4898, 4899] (*Yahweh is [my] king*).
1. Gershonite (1Ch 6:40).
2. Ancestor of Adaiah (1Ch 9:12; Ne 11:12).
3. Priest (1Ch 24:9).
4. Israelite who married a foreigner (Ezr 10:25).
5. Another who married a foreigner (Ezr 10:25).
6. Another who married a foreigner (Ezr 10:31).
7. Son of Harim (Ne 3:11).
8. Son of Recab (Ne 3:14).
9. Goldsmith (Ne 3:31).
10. Man who assisted Ezra (Ne 8:4).
11. Israelite who sealed covenant with Nehemiah (Ne 10:3).
12. Priest (Ne 12:42). May be same as 11.
13. Father of Pashhur who helped arrest Jeremiah (Jer 21:1; 38:1).

MALKIRAM [4901] (*[my] king is exalted*). Son of Jehoiachin (1Ch 3:18).

MALKI-SHUA [4902] (*[my] king saves*). Son of King Saul (1Sa 14:49; 31:2; 1Ch 8:33; 9:39; 10:2).

MALLOTHI [4871] (*my expression*). Son of Heman, a singer (1Ch 25:4, 26).

MALLOWS *See Salt Herbs.*

MALLUCH [4866] (*counselor* ISBE; *king* KB).
1. Levite; ancestor of Ethan (1Ch 6:44).
2. Man who married foreign woman (Ezr 10:29).
3. Another such man (Ezr 10:32).
4. Priest who returned with Zerubbabel (Ne 10:4; 12:2).
5. Chief of people who sealed covenant (Ne 10:27).
6. Head of a priestly family (Ne 12:14).

MALTA [3514]. An island in the Mediterranean. Paul shipwrecked there (Ac 28:1-10).

MAMMON (*wealth*). Aramaic word for riches (Mt 6:24; Lk 16:11, 13).

MAMRE [4934, 4935] (*strength*).
1. A plain near Hebron. Abraham resides in (Ge 13:18; 14:13), entertains three angels and is promised a son (Ge 18:1-15). Isaac lives in (Ge 35:27).
2. An Amorite and confederate of Abraham (Ge 14:13, 24).

MAN *See Mankind.*

MAN OF SIN *See Antichrist(s).*

MAN, SON OF A phrase used by God in addressing Daniel (Da 8:17) and Ezekiel (over eighty times), by Daniel in describing a person he saw in a night vision (Da 7:13-14), and many times by Jesus when referring to himself, undoubtedly identifying himself with the Son of Man of Daniel's prophecy and emphasizing his union with mankind (Lk 9:26; 19:10; 22:48; Jn 6:62).
See Jesus the Christ, Son of Man; Son of Man.

MANAEN [3441] (*comforter*). An associate of Herod in his youth, and a Christian teacher (Ac 13:1).

MANAHATH [4969, 4970] (*resting place*).
1. Son of Shobal (Ge 36:23; 1Ch 1:40).
2. A city in Benjamin (1Ch 8:6).

MANAHATHITES [4971] (*of Manahath*).
1. Descendants of Shobal, son of Caleb (1Ch 2:52).
2. Descendants of Salma, son of Caleb (1Ch 2:54).

MANASSEH [4985, 4986, 3442] (*one that makes to forget*).
1. Son of Joseph and Asenath (Ge 41:50-51; 46:20), adopted by Jacob on his deathbed (Ge 48:1, 5-20).
2. Tribe of. Descendants of Joseph. The two sons of Joseph, Ephraim and Manasseh, were reckoned among the primogenitors of the twelve tribes, taking the places of Joseph and Levi.
   Adopted by Jacob (Ge 48:5). Prophecy concerning (Ge 49:25-26). Enumeration of (Nu 1:34-35; 26:29-34). Place of in camp and march (Nu 2:18, 20; 10:22-23). Blessing of Moses on (Dt 33:13-17). Inheritance of one-half of the tribe E of the Jordan (Nu 32:33, 39-42). One-half of the tribe W of the Jordan (Jos 16:9; 17:5-11). The eastern half assist in the conquest of the country W of the Jordan (Dt 3:18-20; Jos 1:12-15; 4:12-13). Join the other eastern tribes in erecting a monument to testify to the unity of all Israel; misunderstood; makes satisfactory explanation (Jos 22). Join Gideon in war with the Midianites (Jdg 6-7). Malcontents of, join David (1Ch 12:19, 31). Smitten by Hazael (2Ki 10:33). Return from the Captivity (1Ch 9:3). Reallotment of territory to, by Ezekiel (Eze 48:4). Affiliate with the Israelites in the reign of Hezekiah (2Ch 30). Incorporated into kingdom of Judah (2Ch 15:9; 34:6-7). 144,000 from (Rev 7:6).
   See Israel, Tribes of.
3. The father of Gershom (Jdg 18:30).
4. King of Judah. History of (2Ki 21:1-18; 2Ch 33:1-20; Mt 1:10).
5. Two Jews who put away their Gentile wives after the Captivity (Ezr 10:30, 33).

MANASSES *See Manasseh.*

MANASSITES [1201+4985, 4986] (*forgetting*). Descendants of Joseph's son Manasseh (Ge 41:51).

MANDRAKE [1859]. (Ge 30:14-16; SS 7:13).

MANEH See Mina.

MANGER [17, 5764]. Stall or trough for feeding livestock (Job 39:9; Pr 14:4; Isa 1:3; Lk 2:7-16).

MANKIND [*132, 408, 632, 1033, 1201, 1414, 1475, 1505, 2344, 2351, 3529, 3782, 3813, 4855, 5493, 5883, 6269, 6639, 8502, 10050, 10131, 10392, 81, 467, 474, 476, 1651, 3734, 4922].

Created:
Male and Female (Ge 1:26-27; 2:7; 5:1-2; Dt 4:32; Job 4:17; 10:2-3, 8-9; 31:15; 33:4; 34:19; 35:10; 36:3; Ps 8:5; 100:3; 119:73; 138:8; 139:14-15; Ecc 7:29; Isa 17:7; 42:5; 43:7; 45:12; 64:8; Jer 27:5; Zec 12:1; Mal 2:10; Mt 19:4; Mk 10:6; Heb 2:7).

A little lower than the angels (Job 4:18-21; Ps 8:5; Heb 2:7-8), than God (Ps 8:5). Above other creatures (Mt 10:31; 12:12).

Design of:
To have dominion over all creation (Ge 1:26, 28; 2:19-20; 9:2-3; Ps 8:6-8; Jer 27:6; 28:14; Da 2:38; Heb 2:7-8; Jas 3:7). For the glory and pleasure of God (Pr 16:4; Isa 43:7).

Equality of all people (Job 21:26; 31:13-15; Ps 33:13-15; Pr 22:2; Mt 20:25-28; 23:8-10; 23:11; Mk 10:42-44; Ac 10:28, 34-35; 17:26). Equality under the gospel (Gal 3:28). See Race, 1.

Mortal (Job 4:17; Ecc 2:14-15; 3:20; 1Co 15:21-22; Heb 9:27). See Immortality. Insignificance of (Ge 6:3; 18:27; Job 4:18-19; 7:17; 15:14; 22:2-5; 25:2-6; 35:2-8; 38:4, 12-13; Ps 8:3-4; 78:39; 144:3-4).

A spirit (Job 4:19; 14:10; 32:8; Ps 31:5; Pr 20:27; Ecc 1:8; 3:21; 12:7; Isa 26:9; Zec 12:1; Mt 4:4; 10:28; 26:41; Mk 14:38; Lk 22:40; 23:46; 24:39; Jn 3:3-8; 4:24; Ac 7:59; Ro 1:9; 2:29; 7:14-25; 1Co 2:11; 6:20; 7:34; 14:14; 2Co 4:6-7, 16; 5:1-9; Eph 3:16; 4:4; 1Th 5:23; Heb 4:12; Jas 2:26).

See Duty; Ignorance; Neighbor; Women; Young Men.

MANNA [4942, 3445] (What is it?; possibly food). Miraculously given to Israel for food in the wilderness (Ex 16:4, 15; Ne 9:15).

Called:
God's manna (Ne 9:20). Bread of heaven (Ps 105:40). Bread from heaven (Ps 78:24). Angel's food (Ps 78:25). Spiritual food (1Co 10:3). Previously unknown (Dt 8:3, 16).

Described as:
Like coriander seed (Ex 16:31; Nu 11:7). White (Ex 16:31). Like in color to resin (Nu 11:7), taste to wafers made with honey (Ex 16:31), taste to oil (Nu 11:8). Like frost (Ex 16:14). Fell after the evening dew (Nu 11:9). None fell on the Sabbath (Ex 16:26-27). Gathered every morning (Ex 16:21). An omer of, gathered for each person (Ex

16:16). Two portions of, gathered the sixth day on account of the Sabbath (Ex 16:5, 22-26). He that gathered much or little had sufficient and nothing left over (Ex 16:18). Melted away by the sun (Ex 16:21).

Given:
When Israel murmured for bread (Ex 16:2-3). In answer to prayer (Ps 105:40). Through Moses (Jn 6:31-32). To exhibit God's glory (Ex 16:7). As a sign of Moses' divine mission (Jn 6:30-31). For forty years (Ne 9:21). As a test of obedience (Ex 16:4). To teach that man does not live by bread only (Dt 8:3, w Mt 4:4). To humble and prove Israel (Dt 8:16). If kept longer than a day (except on the Sabbath) began to spoil (Ex 16:19-20).

The Israelites:
At first covetous of (Ex 16:17). Ground, made into cakes and baked in pans (Nu 11:8). Counted, inferior to food of Egypt (Nu 11:4-6). Loathed (Nu 21:5). Punished for despising (Nu 11:10-20). Punished for loathing (Nu 21:6). Ceased when Israel entered Canaan (Ex 16:35; Jos 5:12).

Illustrative of:
Christ (Jn 6:32-35). Blessedness given to saints (Rev 2:17). A golden pot of, laid up in the holiest for a memorial (Ex 16:32-34; Heb 9:4).

MANNERS Polite social customs. Obeisance to strangers (Ge 18:2; 19:1). Standing while guests eat (Ge 18:8), in presence of superiors (Ge 31:35; Job 29:8), of the aged (Lev 19:32). Courteousness commanded (1Pe 3:8). Rule for guests (Pr 23:1-2; 1Co 10:27). See Salutations.

MANOAH [4956] (rest). A Danite of Zorah and father of Samson (Jdg 13:2-24).

MANSERVANT [6269]. See Servant.

MANSIONS [1074, 2292]. Spacious homes of the rich that offer no protection from God's judgment (Ps 49:14; Isa 5:9; Am 3:15; 5:11).

MANSLAUGHTER See Fratricide; Homicide; Infanticide; Regicide.

MANSLAYER A person who has killed another human being accidentally; the manslayer could find asylum in cities of refuge (Nu 35; Dt 4:42; 19:3-10; Jos 20:3). See Cities of Refuge.

MANTLE [6486]. Torn in token of grief (Ezr 9:3; Job 1:20; 2:12). Of Elijah (1Ki 19:19; 2Ki 2:8, 13-14). See Dress.

MANURE [4523, 7616, 3161]. Used as fertilizer (Isa 25:10; Lk 13:8; 14:34-35).

MANUSCRIPTS, DEAD SEA See Dead Sea Scrolls.

MAOCH [5059] (a poor one). The father of Achish, king of Gath, who protected David (1Sa

27:2; 29:1-11). Possibly the same as Maacah, 2. *See Maacah, 2.*

MAON [5062, 5063] (*dwelling*).
1. Descendant of Caleb (1Ch 2:42-45).
2. Town S of Hebron (1Sa 23:24-28; 25:1-3).

MAONITES [5062]. Enemies of Israel (Jdg 10:11-12), possibly from Maon 2, also called Meunim or Maûns. *See Meunim, Meunites.*

MARA [5259] (*bitter*). Name Naomi called herself (Ru 1:20).

MARAH [5288] (*bitter*). The first station of the Israelites, where Moses made the bitter waters sweet (Ex 15:22-25; Nu 33:8-9).

MARALAH [5339]. A landmark on the boundary of Zebulun (Jos 19:11).

MARANATHA (*our Lord has come* or *our Lord, come!*). An expression of greeting and encouragement, marking the desire of Christians for the Lord's return (1Co 16:22).

MARBLE [74+8880, 9253, 3454] (*marble* or *alabaster*). In the temple (1Ch 29:2). Pillars of (Est 1:6; SS 5:15). Merchandise of (Rev 18:12). Mosaics of (Est 1:6).

MARCABOTH *See Beth Marcaboth.*

MARCHESHVAN *See Bul; Month, 8.*

MARCUS *See Mark, John.*

MARDUK [5281]. Marduk, the chief god of the Babylonians (Jer 50:2).

MARESHAH [5358, 5359] (perhaps *head place*).
1. A city of Judah (Jos 15:44; 2Ch 11:8; 14:9-10). Birthplace of Eliezer the prophet (2Ch 20:37). Prophecy concerning (Mic 1:15).
2. Father of Hebron (1Ch 2:42).
3. A son of, or possibly a city founded by, Laadah (1Ch 4:21).

MARI Ancient city of Euphrates Valley, discovered in 1933 and subsequently excavated. Twenty thousand cuneiform tablets have been found, throwing much light upon ancient Syrian civilization. Mari kingdom was contemporary with Hammurabi of Babylon and the Amorite tribes of Canaan, ancestors of the Hebrews.

MARINER [362, 4876]. (1Ki 9:27; 2Ch 8:18; Isa 42:10; Eze 27:27). Perils of (Ps 107:23-30; Jnh 1:5; Ac 27:17-44). Cowardice of (Ac 27:30). *See Commerce; Ship.*

MARK [*2980, 4182, 7483, 8574, 9306, 9338, 9344, 9419, *4956, *5116, *5596, *5916]. A word with various meanings: a special sign of ownership (Eze 9:4, 6; Rev 7:2-8), signature (Job 31:35), a target (1Sa 20:20), a form of tattooing banned by

the Lord (Lev 19:28), a goal to be attained (Php 3:14), a particular brand denoting the nature or rank of men (Rev 13:16).
See Mark, John.

MARK, GOSPEL OF

Author: Anonymous, traditionally John Mark

Date : Possibly in the 50s or early 60s A.D.

Outline:

I. The Beginnings of Jesus' Ministry (1:1-13).
   A. His Forerunner (1:1-8).
   B. His Baptism (1:9-11).
   C. His Temptation (1:12-13).
II. Jesus' Ministry in Galilee (1:14-6:29).
   A. Early Galilean Ministry (1:14-3:12).
      1. Call of the first disciples (1:14-20).
      2. Miracles in Capernaum (1:21-34).
      3. A tour of Galilee (1:21-34).
      4. Ministry in Capernaum (2:1-22).
      5. Sabbath controversy (2:23-3:12).
   B. Later Galilean Ministry (3:13-6:29).
      1. Selection of the twelve apostles (3:13-19).
      2. Teachings in Capernaum (3:20-35).
      3. Parables of the kingdom (4:1-34).
      4. Trip across the Sea of Galilee (4:35-5:20).
      5. More Galilee miracles (5:21-43).
      6. Unbelief in Jesus' hometown (6:1-6).
      7. Six apostolic teams tour Galilee (6:7-13).
      8. King Herod's reaction to Jesus' ministry (6:14-29).
III. Withdrawals From Galilee (6:30-9:32).
   A. To the Eastern Shore of the Sea of Galilee (6:30-52).
   B. To the Western Shore of the Sea of Galilee (6:53-7:23).
   C. To Phoenicia (7:24-30).
   D. To the Region of the Decapolis (7:31-8:10).
   E. To the Vicinity of Caesarea Philippi (8:11-9:32).
IV. Final Ministry in Galilee (9:33-50).
V. Jesus' Ministry in Judea and Perea (ch. 10).
   A. Teaching Concerning Divorce (10:1-12).
   B. Teaching Concerning Divorce (10:13-16).
   C. The Rich Young Man (10:17-31).
   D. Prediction of Jesus' Death (10:32-34).
   E. A Request of Two Brothers (10:35-45).
   F. Restoration of Bartimaeus's Sight (10:46-52).
VI. The Passion of Jesus (chs. 11-15).
   A. The Triumphal Entry (11:12-19).
   B. The Cleansing of the Temple (11:12-19).
   C. Concluding Controversies With Jewish Leaders (11:20-12:44).
   D. The Olivet Discourse Concerning the End of the Age (ch. 13).
   E. The Anointing of Jesus (14:1-11).
   F. The Arrest, Trial and Death of Jesus (14:12-15:47).
VII. The Resurrection of Jesus (ch. 16).
See Synoptic Gospels, The.

MARK, JOHN [3453] (Mark [Latin] *large hammer*; John [Hebrew] *Yahweh is gracious*).

Author of the second Gospel. John was his Jewish name, Mark (Marcus) his Roman; called John (Ac 13:5, 13), Mark (Ac 15:39), "John, also called Mark" (Ac 12:12), relative of Barnabas (Col 4:10), accompanied and then deserted Paul on first missionary journey (Ac 12:25; 13:13), went with Barnabas to Cyprus after Paul refused to take him on his second missionary journey (Ac 15:36-39), fellow-worker with Paul (Phm 24), recommended by Paul to church at Colosse (Col 4:10), may have been the young man of Mark 14:51-52. Early tradition makes him the "interpreter" of Peter in Rome and founder of the church in Alexandria.

MARKET [2575, 4847, 5326, 6087, 7337, *59, 61, 1866+3875, 3425*]. A place for general merchandise. Held at gates. *See Gates.* Judgment seat at (Ac 16:19). Trade of, in Tyre, consisted of horses, horsemen, mules, horns, ivory, and ebony, emeralds, purple, embroidered wares, linen, coral, agate, honey, balm, wine, wool, oil, cassia, calamus, charioteers' clothing, lambs, rams, goats, precious stones, and gold, spices, and costly apparel (Eze 27:13-25). *See Agora.*

MAROTH [5300] (*bitterness*). A city of Judah (Mic 1:12).

MARRIAGE [*829, 851+, 1249+, 1436, 2118+4200, 3782, 4374, 4374, 5951, 5989, 9393, 1138, 1139, 1140, 1141, 1181, 1222+, 2400, 3284, 3650*].

General:
Divine institution of (Ge 2:18, 20-24; Mt 19:4-6; Mk 10:7-8; 1Co 6:16; Eph 5:31). Based on principle of creation (1Co 11:11-12; Ge 2:18).

Unity of husband and wife in (Ge 2:23-24; Mt 19:5-6; Mk 10:2-10; 1Co 6:16; Eph 5:31, 33). Obligations greater, inferior in duty to God (Dt 13:6-10; Mt 19:29; Lk 14:26). Indissoluble except for adultery (Mal 2:13-16; Mt 5:31-32; Mk 10:11-12; Lk 16:18; Ro 7:1-3; 1Co 7:39-40). Dissolved by death (Mt 22:29-30; Mk 12:24-25; Ro 7:1-3).

Commended (Pr 18:22; Heb 13:4). Commanded of exiled Israelites (Jer 29:6). Commanded because of immorality (1Co 7:1-7).

None in the resurrection state (Mt 22:29-30; Mk 12:24-25). Levirate (the brother required to marry a brother's widow) (Ge 38:8, 11; Dt 25:5-10; Ru 4:5; Mt 22:24-27; Mk 12:19-23; Lk 20:28-33).

Mosaic Laws Concerning:
Of priests (Lev 21:1, 7, 13-15). Captives (Dt 21:10-14). Divorced persons (Dt 24:1-5). A virgin, not pledged to be married, who has been seduced (Ex 22:16-17). Within tribes (Nu 36:8). Incestuous, forbidden (Lev 18:6-18 w Dt 22:30; Lev 20:14, 17, 19-21; Mk 6:17-18).

Among antediluvians (Ge 6:2). Among relatives, Abraham and Sarah (Ge 11:29; 12:13; 20:2, 9-16), Isaac and Rebekah (Ge 24:3-4, 67), Jacob and his wives (Ge 28:2; 29:15-30). Levirate (the brother required to marry a brother's widow) (Ge 38:8, 11; Dt 25:5-10; Ru 4:5; Mt 22:24-27; Mk 12:19-23; Lk 20:28-33).

Intermarriage. *See Intermarry.*

Various Principles:
Parents contract for their children: Hagar selects a wife for Ishmael (Ge 21:21). Abraham for Isaac (Ge 24). Laban arranges for his daughters' marriage (Ge 29). Samson asks his parents to procure him a wife (Jdg 14:2). Parents' consent required in the Mosaic law (Ex 22:17). Presents given to parents to secure their favor (Ge 24:53; 34:12; 1Sa 18:25). Nuptial feasts (Ge 29:22; Jdg 14:12; Est 2:18; Mt 22:11-12). Jesus present at (Jn 2:1-5). Ceremony attested by witnesses (Ru 4:1-11; Isa 8:1-3). Bridegroom exempt one year from military duty (Dt 24:5). Bridal ornaments (Isa 49:18; Jer 2:32). Bridal presents (Ge 24:53). Herald preceded the bridegroom (Mt 25:6). Wedding robes adorned with jewels (Isa 61:10). Festivities attending (Jer 7:34; 16:9; 25:10; Rev 18:23).

Wives obtained by purchase (Ge 29:20, 27-29; 31:41; Ru 4:10; 2Sa 3:14; Hos 3:2; 12:12), by kidnapping (Jdg 21:21-23). Given by kings (1Sa 17:25; 18:17, 27). Daughters given in, as rewards of valor (Jdg 1:12; 1Sa 17:25; 18:27).

Wives taken by edict (Est 2:2-4, 8-14). David gave 100 foreskins for a wife (2Sa 3:14).

Wives among the Israelites must be Israelites (Ex 34:16; Dt 7:3-4; Ezr 9:1-2, 12; Ne 10:30; 13:26-27; Mal 2:11). Betrothal a quasi-marriage (Mt 1:18; Lk 1:27).

Discouraged among the Corinthians (1Co 7:1, 8-9, 25-40). Celibacy deplored (Jdg 11:38; Isa 4:1). Unhappiness in (Pr 21:9, 19).

Marriage of widows (Ro 7:1-3; 1Co 7:39-40; 1Ti 5:14). Marriage of ministers (Lev 21:7-8, 13-14; Eze 44:22; 1Co 9:5; 1Ti 3:2, 12).

Prophecies concerning the forbidding of (1Ti 4:1, 3).

Figurative:
(Isa 54:5; 62:4-5; Jer 3:14; 31:32; Eze 16:8; Hos 2:19-20; Eph 5:23-32; Rev 19:7-9) Parables of (Mt 22:2-10; 25:1-10; Mk 2:19-20; Jn 3:29; 2Co 11:2).

See Bride; Bridegroom; Divorce; Husband; Intermarry; Wife.

MARROW [4672, 3678]. Heart of the bone (Job 21:24), used figuratively of good things (Ps 63:5; Isa 25:6).

MARS HILL *See Areopagus.*

MARSENA [5333]. Counselor of King Xerxes (Est 1:10-14).

MARSH [106, 1289, 1465]. Swamp lands (Eze 47:11).

MARTHA [*3450*] (*a lady, [female] lord*). Sister of Mary and Lazarus (Jn 11:1). Ministers to Jesus (Lk 10:38-42; Jn 12:2). Beloved by Jesus (Jn 11:5).

See Lazarus; Mary, 4.

MARTYR [*3459*] (*witness*). One who dies to bear witness to a cause (Ac 22:20; Rev 17:6).

MARTYRDOM Of prophets (Mt 23:34; Lk 11:50; Rev 16:6). Followers of Jesus exposed to (Mt 10:21-22, 39; 23:34; 24:9; Mk 13:12; Lk 21:16-17). Spirit of, required by Jesus (Mt 16:25; Lk 9:24; Jn 12:25). Possessed by the righteous (Ps 44:22; Ro 8:36; Rev 12:11). Must be based on love (1Co 13:3).

Prophetic reference to (Rev 6:9-11; 11:7-12; 17:6).

See Persecution.

Instances of:

Abel (Ge 4:3-8). Prophets slain by Jezebel (1Ki 18:4, 13). Zechariah (2Ch 24:21-22). John the Baptist (Mt 6:18-28). Jesus. *See Jesus the Christ, Death of.* Stephen (Ac 7:58-60). James the apostle (Ac 12:2). The prophets (Mt 22:6; 23:35; Ro 11:3; 1Th 2:15; Heb 11:32-37).

MARY [*3451*] (perhaps *fat one; See Miriam*).

1. *See Mary, The Virgin.*

2. Mother of James and Joses (Mt 27:56; Mk 15:40; Lk 24:10), probably the wife of Clopas (Jn 19:25), witnessed Crucifixion and visited grave on resurrection morning (Mt 27:56; 28:1).

3. Mary Magdalene; Jesus cast seven demons out of her (Mk 16:9; Lk 8:2), appears at Jesus' crucifixion (Mt 27:55-56; Mk 15:40-41; Jn 19:25), followed body of Jesus to grave (Mt 27:61) and was first to learn of the Resurrection (Mt 28:1-8; Mk 16:9; Lk 24:1-12; Jn 20:1-9, 18). *See Dalmanutha; Magadan.*

4. Mary of Bethany; sister of Lazarus and Martha; lived in Bethany (Jn 11:1), commended by Jesus (Lk 10:42), anointed feet of Jesus (Jn 12:3).

5. Mother of John Mark; sister of Barnabas (Col 4:10), home in Jerusalem meeting place of Christians (Ac 12:12).

6. Christian at Rome (Ro 16:6).

MARY, THE VIRGIN [*3451*] (perhaps *fat one; See Miriam*). Wife of Joseph (Mt 1:18-25), relative of Elizabeth, the mother of John the Baptist (Lk 1:36), of the seed of David (Ac 2:30; Ro 1:3; 2Ti 2:8), mother of Jesus (Mt 1:18, 20; Lk 2:1-20), attended to ceremonial purification (Lk 2:22-38), fled to Egypt with Joseph and Jesus (Mt 2:13-15), lived in Nazareth (Mt 2:19-23), took twelve-year-old Jesus to temple (Lk 2:41-50), at wedding in Cana of Galilee (Jn 2:1-11), concerned for Jesus' safety (Mt 12:46; Mk 3:21, 31ff; Lk 8:19-21), at the cross of Jesus (Jn 19:25ff) where she was entrusted by Jesus to the care of John (Jn 19:25-27), in the Upper Room (Ac 1:14).

Distinctive Roman Catholic doctrines about Mary: Perpetual Virginity, Intercession, Immaculate Conception (1854), and Assumption of Mary (1950).

MASCHIL *See Maskil.*

MASH Variant spelling of Meshech, son of Aram (Ge 10:22-23, ftn). *See Meshech.*

MASHAL [*5443*]. Also called Mishal (Jos 19:26; 21:30). *See Mishal.* A Levitical city in Asher (1Ch 6:74).

MASKIL [*5380*]. Occurs in the titles of several psalms (Pss 32; 42; 44-45; 52-55; 74; 78; 88-89; 142). The Hebrew word perhaps indicates that these psalms contain instruction in godliness (14:2; 53:2, "any who understand"; 41:1, "he who has regard"; 47:7, ftn).

See Music, Symbols Used in.

MASKING *See Disguises.*

MASON [74+3093, 1553, 2935]. A trade in the time of David (2Sa 5:11), of later times (2Ki 12:12; 22:6; 1Ch 14:1; Ezr 3:7).

MASREKAH [*5388*] (perhaps *yineyard*). Royal city of King Samlah, in Edom (Ge 36:31, 36-37; 1Ch 1:47-48).

MASSA [*5364*] (*burden, oracle*). Tribe descended from Ishmael near Persian Gulf (Ge 25:14; 1Ch 1:30).

MASSACRE [1947]. Authorized by Moses (Dt 20:13, 16). Decree to destroy the Jews (Est 3).

Instances of: Inhabitants of Heshbon (Dt 2:34), of Bashan (Dt 3:6), of Ai (Jos 8:24-26), of Hazor (Jos 11:11-12), of the cities of the seven kings (Jos 10:28-40). Midianites (Nu 31:7-8). Prophets of Baal (1Ki 18:40). Worshipers of Baal (2Ki 10:18-28). Sons of Ahab (2Ki 10:1-8). Royal family of Athaliah (2Ki 11:1). Inhabitants of Tiphsah (2Ki 15:16). Edomites (2Ki 14:7).

See Captive.

MASSAH [*5001*] (*test, try*). Site of rock in Horeb from which Moses drew water (Ex 17:1-7; Dt 6:16; 9:22), connected with Meribah (Dt 33:8).

MASTER [123, 1067, 1251, 4856+6913, 5440, 7864, *804, 1305, 1437, 2181, 3259, 3261*]. Yahweh called (Jer 31:32, ftn; Hos 2:16). *See Baali.* Jesus called (Mt 8:19; 10:25; 23:8; 26:18, 25, 49; Mk 14:45; Lk 8:24; Jn 13:13-14). Jesus spoke against abuse of the title (Mt 23:8). *See Lord.*

MASTER, OF SERVANTS

Duties to Servants:

Must allow Sabbath rest (Dt 5:14). Compensate (Jer 22:13; Ro 4:4; Col 4:1; 1Ti 5:18). Pay promptly (Lev 19:13; Dt 24:15; Jas 5:4). Forbidden to oppress (Lev 19:13; 25:43; Dt 24:14; Job 31:13-14; Pr 22:16; Mal 3:5). Forbidden to threaten (Eph 6:9). Exhorted to show kindness (Phm 10-16). Exhorted to show wisdom (Pr 29:12, 21).

See Employer; Employee; Hired Servant; Servant.

Good Masters:

Abraham (Ge 18:19). Job (Job 31:13-15). The centurion (Lk 7:2).

Unjust Masters:

Instances of: Sarah to Hagar (Ge 16:6). Laban to Jacob (Ge 31:7). Potiphar's wife to Joseph (Ge 39:7-20). Violent, to be punished (Ex 21:20-21, 26-27).

MASTER CRAFTSMAN
Instances of: Tubal-Cain (Ge 4:22), Bezalel (Ex 31:2-11; 35:30-35), Huram or Huram-Abi (1Ki 7:13-50; 2Ch 2:13-14; 4:11-18), Wisdom (Pr 8:30), Paul (1Co 3:10). *See Art.*

MATERIALISM
Love of possessions.

Love of money:

A root of all kinds of evil (1Ti 6:10). Insatiable (Ecc 4:7-8; 5:10-11). Forbidden in overseer (1Ti 3:2-3; Tit 1:7). Materialists do not love God (Mt 6:24; 1Jn 2:15-17; 3:17).

Treasures in Heaven Versus Materialism:

(Mt 6:19-21; 1Ti 6:17-19).

See Avarice; Greed; Love, Of Money; Rich, The; Riches.

MATHUSALA
See Methuselah.

MATRED
[4765] (perhaps *spear*). Mother of Mehetabel, wife of Hadad (Ge 36:39), who is called "Hadad" (1Ch 1:50).

MATRI
[4767] (*rainy*). Head of Benjamite family (1Sa 10:21).

MATTAN
[5509] (*gift*).
1. A priest of Baal slain in the idol temple at Jerusalem (2Ki 11:18; 2Ch 23:17).
2. Father of Shephatiah (Jer 38:1).

MATTANAH
[5511] (*gift*). Encampment of Israel in wilderness (Nu 21:18-19).

MATTANIAH
[5514, 5515] (*gift of Yahweh*).
1. Original name of King Zedekiah (2Ki 24:17).
2. Chief choir leader and watchman (Ne 11:17; 12:8, 25).
3. Levite (2Ch 20:14).
4. Son of Elam (Ezr 10:26).
5. Son of Zattu (Ezr 10:27).
6. Son of Pahath-Moab (Ezr 10:30).
7. Son of Bani (Ezr 10:37).
8. Grandfather of Hanan (Ne 13:13).
9. Son of Heman; head musician (1Ch 25:4-5, 7, 16).
10. Levite who assisted Hezekiah (2Ch 29:13).

MATTATHA
[3477]. An ancestor of Jesus (Lk 3:31).

MATTATHAH
See Mattattah.

MATTATHIAS
[3478] (*gift of Yahweh*).
1. Assistant of Ezra, spelled Mattithiah (Ne 8:4).
2. Name borne by two ancestors of Christ (Lk 3:25-26).
3. Priest; founder of Maccabee family (1Mc 2). *See also, 1Mc 11:70; 16:14-16; 2Mc 14:19.*

MATTATTAH
[5523] (*gift*). One of the family of Hashum (Ezr 10:33).

MATTENAI
[5513] (*gift*).
1. Two Israelites who put away their Gentile wives after the Captivity (Ezr 10:33, 37).
2. A priest in the time of Joiakim (Ne 12:19).

MATTHAN
[3474] (*gift*). Grandfather of Joseph, Mary's husband (Mt 1:15).

MATTHAT
[3415] (*gift of God*).
1. Father of Heli, ancestor of Joseph (Lk 3:23).
2. Father of Jorim, and ancestor of Joseph (Lk 3:29).

MATTHEW
[3414] (*gift of Yahweh*). Son of Alphaeus (Mk 2:14), tax collector, also called Levi (Mk 2:14; Lk 5:27), called by Jesus to become disciple (Mt 9:9; Mk 2:14; Lk 5:27) and gave feast for Jesus; appointed apostle (Mt 10:3; Mk 3:18; Lk 6:15; Ac 1:13).

MATTHEW, GOSPEL OF

Author: Anonymous, traditionally the apostle Matthew

Date: Probably in the late 60s A.D.

Outline:

I. The Birth and Early Years of Jesus (chs. 1-2).
   A. His Genealogy (1:1-17).
   B. His Birth (1:18-2:12).
   C. His Sojourn in Egypt (2:13-23).
II. The Beginnings of Jesus' Ministry (3:1-4:11).
   A. His Forerunner (3:1-12).
   B. His Baptism (3:13-17).
   C. His Temptation (4:1-11).
III. Jesus' Ministry in Galilee (4:12-14:12).
   A. The Beginning of the Galilean Campaign (4:12-25).
   B. The Sermon on the Mount (chs. 5-7).
   C. A Collection of Miracles (chs. 8-9).
   D. The Commissioning of the Twelve Apostles (ch. 10).
   E. Ministry Throughout Galilee (chs. 11-12).
   F. The Parables of the Kingdom (ch. 13).
   G. Herod's Reaction to Jesus' Ministry (14:1-12).
IV. Jesus' Withdrawals From Galilee (14:13-17:20).
   A. To the Eastern Shore of the Sea of Galilee (14:13-15:20).
   B. To Phoenicia (15:21-28).
   C. To the Decapolis (15:29-16:12).
   D. To Caesarea Philippi (16:13-17:20).
V. Jesus' Last Ministry in Galilee (17:22-18:35).
   A. Prediction of Jesus' Death (17:22-23).
   B. Temple Tax (17:24-27).
   C. Discourse on Life in the Kingdom (ch. 18).
VI. Jesus' Ministry in Judea and Perea (chs. 19-20).
   A. Teaching Concerning Divorce (19:1-12).
   B. Teaching Concerning Little Children (19:13-15).
   C. The Rich Young Man (19:16-30).

D. The Parable of the Workers in the Vineyard (20:1-16).

E. Prediction of Jesus' Death (20:17-19).

F. A Mother's Request (20:20-28).

G. Restoration of Sight at Jericho (20:29-34).

VII. Passion Week (chs. 21-27).

A. The Triumphal Entry (21:1-11).

B. The Cleansing of the Temple (21:12-17).

C. The Last Controversies With the Jewish Leaders (21:18-23:39).

D. The Olivet Discourse Concerning the End of the Age (chs. 24-25).

E. The Anointing of Jesus' Feet (26:1-13).

F. The Arrest, Trials and Death of Jesus (26:14-27:66).

VIII. The Resurrection (ch. 28).

See Synoptic Gospels, The.

MATTHIAS [3416] (*gift of Yahweh*). Apostle chosen by lot to take place of Judas (Ac 1:15-26), had been follower of Christ (Ac 1:21-22).

MATTITHIAH [5524, 5525] (*gift of Yahweh*).

1. A Levite who had charge of the baked offerings (1Ch 9:31).

2. A Levite musician (1Ch 15:18, 21; 16:5).

3. A chief of the fourteenth division of temple musicians (1Ch 25:3, 21).

4. An Israelite who divorced his Gentile wife after the Captivity (Ezr 10:43).

5. A prince who stood by Ezra when he read the law to the people (Ne 8:4).

MATTOCK [908] (*cut in, plow*). Single-headed farming tool with point on one side and broad edge on other side (1Sa 13:20-21; Isa 7:25).

MAUL *See Club.*

MAW One of the stomachs of a ruminating animal (Dt 18:3).

MAZZAROTH *See Constellations.*

Biblical Weights and Measures and Approximate Equivalents						
Dry Capacity:					
1.	Cor or homer	10 ephahs	6 bushels	220 liters	1Ki 4:22; 5:11; 2Ch 2:10; 27:5; Ezr 7:22
2.	Lethek	5 ephahs	3 bushels	110 liters	Hos 3:2
3.	Ephah	10 omers	3/5 bushel	22 liters	Ex 16:36; Lev 5:11; Nu 5:15; Jdg 6:19; Ru 2:17; 1Sa 1:24; Isa 5:10; Eze 45:10-11,13,24; Am 8:5
4.	Seah	1/3 ephah	7 quarts	7.3 liters	Ge 18:6; 1Sa 25:18; 1Ki 18:32; 2Ki 7:1,16,18
5.	Omer	1/10 ephah	2 quarts	2 liters	Ex 16:16,18,22,32-33,36
6.	Cab	1/18 ephah	1 quart	1 liter	2Ki 6:25
Liquid Capacity:					
1.	Bath	1 ephah	6 gallons	22 liters	1Ki 7:26,38; 2Ch 2:10; 4:5; Ezr 7:22; Isa 5:10; Eze 45:10-11,14; Lk 16:6
2.	Hin	1/6 bath	4 quarts	4 liters	Ex 29:40; 30:24; Lev 19:36; 23:13; Nu 15:4-10; 28:5,7,14; Eze 4:11; 45:24; 46:5,7,11,14
3.	Log	1/72 bath	1/3 quart	0.3 liter	Lev 14:10,12,14,21,24
Weight:					
1.	Talent	60 minas	75 pounds	34 kilograms	Ex 25:39; 38:27
2.	Mina	50 shekels	1.25 pounds	0.6 kilogram	1Ki 10:17; Ezr 2:69; Da 5:26-28
3.	Shekel	2 bekas	2/5 ounce	11.5 grams	Ge 20:16; Eze 45:12
4.	Pim	2/3 shekel	1/3 ounce	7.6 grams	1Sa 13:21, ftn
5.	Beka	10 gerahs	1/5 ounce	5.5 grams	Ge 24:22; Ex 38:26
6.	Gerah	1/20 shekel	1/50 ounce	0.6 gram	Ex 30:13; Lev 27:25
Length:					
1.	Cubit		18 inches	0.5 meter	Ge 6:15-16; Rev 21:17
2.	Span		9 inches	23 cm.	Ex 28:16; 1Sa 17:4; Isa 40:12; La 2:20; Eze 43:13
3.	Handbreadth		3 inches	8 centimeters	Ex 25:25; 1Ki 7:26; 2Ch 4:5; Ps 39:5; Eze 43:13
4.	Finger		0.75 inch	1.85 cm.	Jer 52:21

ME JARKON (*waters of Jarkon [greenish?]*). A city in Dan (Jos 19:46).

MEADOW [4120, 5303, 5661].
1. Place where reeds grow (Ge 41:2, 18).
2. Pastureland (Jdg 20:33).

MEAH NIV "Hundred" (Ne 3:1; 12:38). See *Tower, Of the Hundred.*

MEAL See *Grain.*

MEAL OFFERING See *Offerings.*

MEANINGLESS See *Vanity, 1.*

MEARAH (*cave*). See *Arah, 4.*

MEASURE [*406, 4394+6330, 4499, 4500, 5374, 6015+6017, 7742, *3582, 3586*].

False and Just:
Just (Lev 19:35-36; Dt 25:13-16; Pr 16:11).
False (Hos 12:7-9). An abomination (Pr 11:1; 20:10, 23; Mic 6:10-12). See *Dishonesty; Integrity.*

Table of Measures:
See chart on the facing page.

MEAT [1414, 3181, 3186, 4657, 4950, 5984, 7002, 7507, 8638, *3200, 3425, 4465*]. See *Food.*

MEAT FORKS Used in the tabernacle (Ex 27:3; 38:3; Nu 4:14; 1Sa 2:13-14). Made of gold (1Ch 28:17), of bronze (2Ch 4:16).

MEAT OFFERING See *Offerings, Meat.*

MEBUNNAI [4446] (*well built*). One of David's bodyguards (2Sa 23:27), called Sibbecai (2Sa 21:18).

MECHANIC See *Art; Master Craftsman.*

MECHERATHITE See *Mekerathite.*

MECONAH [4828] (*foundation*). A city in Judah (Ne 11:28).

MEDAD [4773] (*beloved*). One of the seventy elders who did not go to the tabernacle with Moses, but prophesied in the camp (Nu 11:26-29).

MEDAN [4527] (*dissension*). Son of Abraham and Keturah (Ge 25:2; 1Ch 1:32).

MEDDLING [6297, *258*]. See *Busybody; Talebearer.*

MEDEBA [4772]. A city of Moab (Nu 21:30). An idolatrous high place (Isa 15:2). Allotted to Reuben (Jos 13:9, 16). David defeats army and the Ammonites at (1Ch 19:7-15).

MEDES [4512, 4513, 10404, *3597*]. Inhabitants of Media. Israelites distributed among, when carried to Assyria (2Ki 17:6; 18:11). Palace in the Babylonian province of (Ezr 6:2). An essential part of the Medo-Persian Empire (Est 1:1-19). Supremacy over the Babylonian Empire (Da 5:28, 31; 9:1; 11:1).

MEDIA [4512, 10404]. See *Medes.*

MEDIATION [4885, 7136, *3542*].

Between People and God:
(Ex 18:19; Job 9:33; Gal 3:19). Solicited by Israel (Ex 20:19-20; Dt 5:27).
Instances of: By Moses (Ex 32:11-13; 34:9; Nu 14:13-19; 27:5; Dt 5:5; 9:18-20, 25-29). Aaron (Nu 16:47-48). Joshua (Jos 7:6-9). Samuel (1Sa 8:10, 21). David (2Sa 24:17).

Between People and Jesus:
In behalf of the afflicted (Mt 12:22; 15:30; Mk 1:32). The four friends for the paralytic (Mt 2:3-12; 9:2-8; Lk 5:18-20). Jairus (Mt 9:18; Mk 5:23; Lk 8:41). The nobleman for his son (Jn 4:47, 49). The father of the demoniac for his son (Mt 17:15; Mk 9:17-18). The Syrian Phoenician woman for her daughter (Mt 15:22; Mk 7:24-26). The disciples for Peter's mother-in-law (Mk 1:30; Lk 4:38-39).

Between Persons:
Reuben for Joseph (Ge 37:21-22). Judah for Joseph (Ge 37:26-27). Pharaoh's chief baker for Joseph (Ge 41:9-13, w 40:14). Jonathan for David (1Sa 19:1-7). Abigail for Nabal (1Sa 25:23-35). Joab for Absalom (2Sa 14:1-24). Bathsheba for Solomon (1Ki 1:15-31), for Adonijah (1Ki 2:13-25). Ebed-Melech for Jeremiah (Jer 38:7-13). Elisha offers to see the king for the Shunammite (2Ki 4:13). The king of Syria for Naaman (2Ki 5:6-8). Paul for Onesimus (Phm 10-21).
See Intercession; Jesus, Mediation of.

MEDICINE [1565]. Used (Isa 38:21; Lk 10:34; 1Ti 5:23). See *Disease; Physician.*
Figurative (Pr 17:22; Isa 1:6; Jer 8:22; 30:13; 46:11; 51:8-9; Eze 47:12; Rev 22:2).

MEDITATION [1948, 2047, 2052, 2053, 8452, 8488, 8490, 8491]. On the Lord (Ps 63:5-6; 104:34; 139:17-18). On the law of the Lord (Ps 1:2; 19:14; 49:3; 119:11, 15-16, 23, 48, 55, 59, 78, 97-99; 119:148). Commanded (Jos 1:8). On the works of the Lord (Ps 77:10-12; 143:5).
Instances of: Isaac (Ge 24:63). David (Ps 4:4; 39:3).

MEDITERRANEAN SEA Mentioned in Scripture as: The Sea (Nu 34:5; Ps 80:11). The Great Sea (Nu 34:6-7; Jos 1:4; 9:1; 15:12, 47; 23:4; Eze 47:10, 15, 20; 48:28). Sea of the Philistines (Ex 23:31). The western sea (Dt 11:24; Joel 2:20; Zec 14:8).

MEDIUM [200+, 6726]. A spiritist; one who consults the dead (Lev 19:31; 20:6; Dt 18:9-13; Isa 8:19-22). Punished by death in the law (Lev 20:27). Saul and the medium at Endor (1Sa 28:3-25; 1Ch 10:13-14). See *Necromancer, Necromancy; Sorcery; Spiritists.*

MEEKNESS [6705, 6714, *4558*, *4559*].

Described:

Advantageous (Ps 25:9; Pr 14:29; 17:1; 19:11; Ecc 7:8; 10:4; Am 3:3; 1Co 13:4-5, 7). Honorable (Pr 20:3). Potent (Pr 15:1, 18; 16:32; 25:15; 29:8). A fruit of the Spirit (Gal 5:22-23, 26).

Commanded (Zep 2:3; Mt 5:38-41 w Lk 6:29; Mt 11:29; Mk 9:50; Ro 12:14, 18; 14:19; 1Co 6:7; 7:15; 10:32; 2Co 13:11; Gal 6:1; Eph 4:1-2; Php 2:14-15; Col 3:12-13; 1Th 5:14-15; 1Ti 3:3; 6:11; 2Ti 2:24-25; Tit 2:2, 9; 3:2; Heb 10:36; 12:14; Jas 1:4, 19, 21; 3:13; 1Pe 2:18-23; 3:4, 11, 15; 2Pe 1:5-7).

Rewards of (Ps 22:26; 37:11; 76:8-9; 147:6; 149:4; Isa 29:19; Mt 5:5; 11:29).

Instances of:

God (La 3:22, 28-30).

Abraham (Ge 13:8-9). Isaac (Ge 26:20-22). Moses (Ex 16:7-8; 17:2-7; Nu 12:3; 16:4-11). Gideon (Jdg 8:2-3). Hannah (1Sa 1:13-16). Saul (1Sa 10:27). David (1Sa 17:29; 2Sa 16:9-14; Ps 38:13-14). Psalmist (Ps 120:5-7).

Jesus (Isa 11:4; 42:1-4; 53:7; La 3:28-30; Mt 11:29; 12:19-20; 26:47-54; 27:13-14; Mk 15:4-5; Lk 23:34; 2Co 10:1; 1Pe 2:21-23). *See Jesus the Christ, Humility of; Meekness of.* Stephen (Ac 7:60). Paul (Ac 21:20-26; 1Co 4:12-13; 2Co 12:10; 1Th 2:7; 2Ti 4:16). The Thessalonians (2Th 1:4). Job (Jas 5:11). The archangel (Jude 9).

See Humility; Kindness; Patience.

MEGIDDO [4459, 4461] (*place of troops*). City on the Great Road linking Gaza and Damascus, connecting the coastal plain and the Plain of Esdraelon or Megiddo (Jos 12:21; 17:11; Jdg 1:27; 5:19), fortified by Solomon (1Ki 9:15), wounded Ahaziah died there (2Ki 9:27), Josiah lost life there in battle with Pharaoh Neco (2Ki 23:29-30; 2Ch 35:20-27). Large-scale excavations have revealed a great deal of material of great archaeological value.

MEGIDDON *See Megiddo.*

MEHETABEEL *See Mehetabel, 2.*

MEHETABEL [4541] (*God [El] does good*).

1. Wife of Hadad (Ge 36:39; 1Ch 1:50).

2. A person whose grandson tried to intimidate Nehemiah (Ne 6:10).

MEHIDA [4694] (possibly *bought as slave*). A person whose descendants returned from Babylon (Ezr 2:52; Ne 7:54).

MEHIR [4698] (*hired hand*). Son of Kelub (1Ch 4:11).

MEHOLAH, MEHOLATHITE [4716]. A city in Issachar, probably the same as Abel Meholah. Barzillai and his son Adriel lived there (1Sa 18:19; 2Sa 21:8). *See Abel Meholah.*

MEHUJAEL [4686]. Descendant of Cain; father of Methushael (Ge 4:18).

MEHUMAN [4540]. Eunuch of Xerxes, king of Persia (Est 1:10).

MEHUNIM *See Maonites; Meunim, Meunites, 2.*

MEKERATHITE [4841] (*one of Mekerath*). Description of Hepher (1Ch 11:36).

MEKONAH *See Meconah.*

MELAH *See Tel Melah.*

MELATIAH [4882] (*Yahweh sets free*). A Gibeonite who assisted in repairing the wall of Jerusalem (Ne 3:7).

MELCHESEDEC *See Melchizedek.*

MELCHI *See Melki.*

MELCHIAH *See Malkijah.*

MELCHISHUA, MELCHI-SHUA *See Malki-Shua.*

MELCHIZEDEK [4900, *3519*] (*[my] king is Zedek [just]*). Priest and king of Salem (Jerusalem); blessed Abram in the name of Most High God and received tithes from him (Ge 14:18-20), type of Christ, the Priest-King (Ps 110:4; Heb 5:6-10; 6:20; 7).

MELEA [*3507*]. Ancestor of Jesus (Lk 3:31).

MELECH [4890] (*king*). Son of Micah (1Ch 8:35; 9:41).

MELICU *See Malluch, 6.*

MELITA *See Malta.*

MELKI [*3518*] (*my king*).

1. Ancestor of Jesus (Lk 3:24).

2. Remote ancestor of Jesus (Lk 3:28).

MELODY [2053, 5834]. *See Music.*

MELON [19, 5252]. (Nu 11:5).

MELZAR NIV "guard" (Da 1:11, 16). *See Guard.*

MEMBER [408, 1201, 4632, 4946, 5883, 6830, *741*, *1085*, *2363*, *3517*, *3858*, *3865*, *3875*, *5362*]. Any feature or part of the body (Job 17:7; Jas 3:5).

MEMORIAL [260, 2349, 2355, 3338, *3649*]. Passover (Ex 12:14). *See Passover.*

Firstborn set apart as a (Ex 13:12-16). Pot of manna (Ex 16:32-34). Feast of Tabernacles (Lev 23:43). Shoulder stones of the ephod (Ex 28:12). Atonement money (Ex 30:16). The twelve stones of Jordan (Jos 4:1-9).

The Lord's Supper (Lk 22:19; 1Co 11:24-26).
See Pillar.

MEMPHIS [5132, 5862]. Capital city of
Egypt, on W bank of Nile, c. twenty miles S of
modern Cairo; its destruction foretold (Isa 19:13;
Jer 2:16; 44:1; 46:14, 19; Eze 30:13, 16).

MEMUCAN [4925]. One of the seven nobles
of Xerxes who counseled the king to divorce
Queen Vashti (Est 1:14-21).

MENAHEM [4968] (*comforter*). Sixteenth
king of Israel; evil; slew his predecessor, Shallum
(2Ki 15:13-22).

MENAN *See Menna.*

MENE, MENE, TEKEL, PARSIN
[10428+10593+10770]. Four Aramaic words,
probably meaning "numbered, numbered,
weighed, and divided," which suddenly appeared
on the walls of Belshazzar's banquet hall (Da
5:25-28).

MENI *See Destiny, 2.*

MENNA [3527]. An ancestor of Jesus (Lk
3:31).

MENSES *See Menstruation.*

MENSTRUATION [1865]. Law relating
to (Lev 15:19-30; 20:18; Eze 18:6). Cessation of,
in old age (Ge 18:11). Immunities of women
during (Ge 31:35). Uncleanness of (Isa 30:22).
Figurative (Isa 30:22; La 1:17; Eze 36:17).
See Bleeding, Subject to.

MEON *See Baal Meon; Beth Baal Meon; Beth
Meon.*

MEONENIM *See Soothsayers' Tree.*

MEONOTHAI [5065] (*my dwellings*).
Father of Ophrah (1Ch 4:14).

MEPHAATH [4789] (*splendor*). A Levitical city in Reuben (Jos 13:18; 21:37; 1Ch 6:79; Jer
48:21).

MEPHIBOSHETH [5136] (*from the
mouth of shame* [a derogatory term for Baal]).
1. Son of Saul, whom David surrendered to the
Gibeonites to be slain (2Sa 21:8-9).
2. Son of Jonathan (2Sa 4:4). Also called Merib-
Baal (1Ch 8:34; 9:40). Was lame (2Sa 4:4). David
entertains him at his table (2Sa 9:1-7; 21:7).
Property restored to (2Sa 9:9-10). His ingratitude
to David at the time of Absalom's usurpation (2Sa
16:1-4; 19:24-30). Property of, confiscated (2Sa
16:4; 19:29-30).

MERAB [5266] (*abundant*). Daughter of
King Saul (1Sa 14:49). Betrothed to David by
Saul (1Sa 18:17-18), but given to Adriel as his
wife (1Sa 18:19).

MERAIAH [5316] (*loved by Yahweh*). A
priest (Ne 12:12).

MERAIOTH [5318] (*rebellious*).
1. High priest (1Ch 6:6-7).
2. Priest; ancestor of Hilkiah (1Ch 9:11).
3. Another priestly ancestor of Helkai (Ne
12:15). May be same as "Meremoth" (Ne 12:3).

MERARI, MERARITE(S) [5356,
5357] (*bitter*). Youngest son of Levi; progenitor of
Merarites (Nu 3:17, 33-37; Jos 21:7, 34-40).

MERATHAIM [5361] (*double rebellion*).
Symbolic name for Babylon (Jer 50:21).

MERCENARIES [8502]. *See Soldiers.*

MERCHANDISE [4836, 5229, 6087,
6442, 8219, *5007*]. *See Commerce.*

MERCHANT [*2142, 4047, 4051, 6086,
8217, *1867*]. (Ge 23:16; 37:28; 1Ki 10:15, 28;
2Ch 9:14; Ne 3:32; 13:20; Job 41:6; SS 3:6; Isa
23:2; 47:15; Eze 17:4; 27:13, 17, 21-36; 38:13;
Hos 12:7; Na 3:16; Mt 13:45; Rev 18:3, 11, 23).
See Commerce.

MERCURIUS, MERCURY *See
Hermes, 1.*

MERCY [2571, 2798, 2799, 2858, 2876,
8163, 8171, 9382, 9384, 10664, *447, 1796, 1799,
1799+5073, 2661, 3880, 3881*]. (Ps 85:10; Pr
20:28; Hos 4:1; Jas 2:13).
A grace of the godly (Ps 37:25-26; Pr 11:17;
12:10; 14:22, 31; Ro 12:8). Iniquity atoned by (Pr
16:6). Of the wicked, cruel (Pr 12:10).
Commanded (Pr 3:3; Hos 12:6; Mic 6:8; Mt
9:13; 12:7; 23:23; Lk 6:36; Col 3:12-13). To be
shown with cheerfulness (Ro 12:8).
Rewards of (2Sa 22:26; Ps 18:25; 37:25-26; Pr
14:21; 21:21; Mt 5:7).
See God, Mercy of; Kindness.
Instances of: The prison keeper, to Joseph (Ge
39:21-23). Joshua to Rahab (Jos 6:25). The Israelites to the man of Bethel (Jdg 1:23-26). David
to Saul (1Sa 24:10-13, 17).

MERCY SEAT *See Atonement Cover;
Tabernacle.*

MERED [5279] (*rebel*). Son of Ezra (1Ch
4:17-18).

MEREMOTH [5329] (*elevations*).
1. Priest who returned from the Exile (Ne 12:3).
2. Another priest who returned from the Exile
(Ezr 8:33; Ne 3:4, 21).
3. Man who divorced foreign wife (Ezr 10:36).
4. Priest who signed covenant with Nehemiah
(Ne 10:5).

MERES [5332] (*worthy*). One of the princes
of Persia (Est 1:14).

MERIBAH [5313] (*to strive, contend*).
1. Place NW of Sinai where God gave Israelites water from a rock (Ex 17:1-7).
2. Place near Kadesh Barnea where God also gave Israelites water from a rock. Because of Moses' loss of temper God did not permit him to enter the Promised Land (Nu 20:1-13). Also called Meribah Kadesh (Nu 27:14; Dt 32:51).

MERIBAH KADESH [5315]. *See Meribah, 2.*

MERIB-BAAL [5311] (*Baal contends*). Son of Jonathan (1Ch 8:34; 9:40). *See Mephibosheth, 2.*

MERIT Personal. *See Grace.*

MERODACH *See Marduk.*

MERODACH-BALADAN [5282] (*Marduk has given a son*). Twice king of Babylon (722-710; 703-702 B.C.), invited Hezekiah to join conspiracy against Assyria (2Ki 20:12-19; Isa 39:1-8).

MEROM [5295] (*high place*). Place near headwaters of Jordan river where Joshua defeated N coalition (Jos 11:5, 7). Possibly identified with Tell el-Khirba.

MERON *See Shimron Meron.*

MERONOTH, MERONOTHITE [5331]. A place near Gibeon (Ne 3:7) and its inhabitants (1Ch 27:30).

MEROZ [5292]. A place N of Mount Tabor. Deborah and Barak curse the inhabitants of, in their song of triumph (Jdg 5:23).

MESECH *See Meshech.*

MESHA [4791, 4795, 4796, 5392].
1. Place in S Arabia (Ge 10:30).
2. Benjamite (1Ch 8:9).
3. Descendant of Judah (1Ch 2:42).
4. King of Moab in days of Ahab, Ahaziah, and Jehoram (2Ki 3:4).

MESHACH [4794, 10415] (perhaps *I have become weak*). His Hebrew name was Mishael. He was taken as a captive to Babylon with Daniel, Hananiah, and Azariah, where each one was given a Babylonian name (Da 1:6-20; 2:17, 49; 3:12-30). Mishael was given the Akkadian name Meshach.

Shadrach, Meshach, and Abednego were chosen to learn the language and the ways of the Babylonians so that they could enter the king's service (Da 1:3-5, 17-20), c. 605 B.C. These three were eventually thrown into Nebuchadnezzar's furnace because they refused to bow down and worship the huge golden image that he had made (Da 3:1, 4-6, 8-30).

MESHECH [5434].
1. Son of Japheth (Ge 10:2; 1Ch 1:5).
2. Son of Shem (Ge 10:23; 1Ch 1:17).
3. A tribe (Ps 120:5; Eze 27:13; 32:26; 38:2-3); descendants of.

MESHELEMIAH [5452, 5453] (*Yahweh repays*). Father of Zechariah (1Ch 9:21; 26:1-2, 9), "Shelemiah" (1Ch 26:14).

MESHEZABEL [5430] (*God delivers*).
1. Ancestor of Meshullam (Ne 3:4).
2. Covenanter with Nehemiah (Ne 10:21).
3. Judahite (Ne 11:24).

MESHILLEMITH [5454] (*restitution*). A priest (1Ch 9:12).

MESHILLEMOTH [5451] (*restitution*).
1. Father of an Ephraimite who protested against the attempt of the Israelites to enslave their captive brothers (2Ch 28:12-13).
2. A priest (Ne 11:13).

MESHOBAB [5411]. A Simeonite (1Ch 4:34).

MESHULLAM [5450] (*restitution* KB).
1. Grandfather of Shaphan (2Ki 22:3).
2. Son of Zerubbabel (1Ch 3:19).
3. Leading Gadite (1Ch 5:13).
4. Chief Benjamite (1Ch 8:17).
5. Father of Sallu (1Ch 9:7).
6. Benjamite of Jerusalem (1Ch 9:8).
7. Priest (1Ch 9:11; Ne 11:11).
8. Ancestor of priest (1Ch 9:12).
9. Kohathite (2Ch 34:12).
10. Israelite who returned with Ezra (Ezr 8:16).
11. Opposed divorcing foreign wives (Ezr 10:15).
12. Divorced foreign wife (Ezr 10:29).
13. Son of Berekiah; helped rebuild Jerusalem wall (Ne 3:4, 30; 6:18).
14. Another repairer of wall (Ne 3:6).
15. Helper of Ezra (Ne 8:4).
16. Priest (Ne 10:7).
17. Priest who sealed covenant (Ne 10:20).
18. Benjamite (Ne 11:7).
19. Priest (Ne 12:13).
20. Possibly the same man (Ne 12:33).
21. Another priest (Ne 12:16).
22. Levite (Ne 12:25).

MESHULLEMETH [5455] (*restitution*). Wife of Manasseh and mother of Amon (2Ki 21:19).

MESOBAITE *See Mezobaite.*

MESOPOTAMIA [3544] (*[land] between rivers*). The country between the Tigris and the Euphrates. Abraham a native of (Ac 7:2). Nahor lived in (Ge 24:10). People who lived in, called Syrians (Ge 25:20). Balaam from (Dt 23:4). The Israelites subjected to, eight years under the judgments of God (Jdg 3:8), delivered from, by Othniel (Jdg 3:9-10). Chariots hired from, by the Ammonites (1Ch 19:6-7). People of, present at Pentecost (Ac 2:9).

See Babylon; Chaldea.

MESS
Any dish of food sent to the table (Ge 43:34; 2Sa 11:8; Heb 12:16).

MESSENGER
[1413, 2296, 4637, 4855, 5583, 7495, 6269, 8078, 8938, 10541, *34*, *693*] (*send*). Figurative (Hag 1:13; Mal 2:7; 3:1; 4:5-6; Mt 11:10; Mk 1:2; Lk 7:27). Of Satan (2Co 12:7).

MESSIAH
[5431, *3549*] (*anointed*). The basic meaning of the Hebrew *mashiah* and the Greek *christos* is "anointed one."

In the OT the word is used of prophets, priests, and kings who were consecrated to their office with oil. The expression "the Lord's anointed" and its equivalent is not used as a technical designation of the Messiah, but refers to the king of the line of David ruling in Jerusalem and anointed by the Lord through the priest. With the possible exception of Da 9:25-26, the title "Messiah" as a reference to Israel's eschatological king does not occur in the OT. It appears in this sense later in the NT, where he is almost always called "the Christ." The OT pictures the Messiah as one who will put an end to sin and war and usher in universal righteousness and through his death will make vicarious atonement for the salvation of sinful people.

The NT concept of the Messiah is developed directly from the teaching of the OT. Jesus of Nazareth is the Messiah; he claimed to be the Messiah (Mt 23:63-64; Mk 14:61-62; Lk 22:67-70; Jn 4:25-26) and the claim was acknowledged by his disciples (Mt 16:16; Mk 8:29; Lk 9:20; Ac 4:27; 10:38).

See Jesus the Christ, Messiah.

MESSIANIC HOPE
(Mt 13:17; Jn 8:56; Ac 9:22; Heb 11:13; 1Pe 1:10-12). Created by prophecy (Ge 49:10; Nu 24:17; 1Sa 1:10; 2Sa 7:12-13; Isa 9:6-7; 11:1-9; 33:17; 40:3-5; 55:3-5; 62:10-11; Jer 23:5-6; 33:15-17; Da 2:44; 7:13-14; 9:24-27; Mic 5:2; Zec 9:9; Mal 3:1-3; Ac 13:27), by the covenant with David to establish his throne forever (2Sa 7:12-16; 1Ch 17:11-14; 22:10; 28:7), by the messianic psalms (Pss 2; 16; 21; 45; 72; 87; 89; 96; 110; 132:11, 17-18).

Confirmed in the vision of Mary (Lk 1:30-33). Exemplified, by the priest Zechariah (Lk 1:68-79), by the prophet Simeon (Lk 2:25, 29-32), by the prophetess Anna (Lk 2:36-38), by the wise men of the East (Mt 2:1-12), by John the Baptist (Mt 11:3), by the people (Jn 7:31, 40-42; 12:34), by Caiaphas (Mt 26:63; Mk 14:61), by Joseph of Arimathea (Mk 15:43; Lk 23:51), by the disciples on the way to Emmaus (Lk 24:21), by Paul (Ac 26:6-7).

See Jesus the Christ, Prophecies Concerning.

MESSIAS
See Messiah.

METAL
[1031, 3133, 4607, 5011, 5816, 5822, 7110]. *See Bronze; Copper; Gold; Iron; Lead; Silver; Tin.*

METAPHOR
A figure of speech that describes by comparison without using the word "like" or "as." Used extensively in the Song of Songs, for example "How beautiful you are, my darling! Oh, how beautiful! Your eyes are doves" (SS 1:15). Jesus spoke in metaphors (Mt 5:13-16). *See Parable.*

METEOROLOGY

Weather Described:

Controlled by God (Ge 2:5-6; 27:39; Job 9:7; 26:7-8, 11; Ps 19:2-6; 104:2-3, 7, 13, 19-20; 107:25; Ecc 11:3; Isa 13:13; 24:18; 50:3; Jer 4:11-12; 10:13; 51:16; Da 2:21; Hos 8:7; Joel 2:30-31; Am 9:6; Na 1:3; Mt 24:27; 24:29; 21:25; Jn 3:8; Ac 2:19-20; 2Pe 2:17; Jude 12). Tempest stilled by Jesus (Mt 8:24-27; Lk 8:22-25).

Weather, affected by godly prayers (1Sa 12:16-18; 1Ki 18:41-45; Isa 5:5-6; Jas 5:17-18). Forecast of weather (Mt 16:2-3; Lk 12:54-56).

Weather in the land of Uz (Job 27:20-21; 28:24-27; 29:19; 36:27-33; 37:6-22; 38:8-11, 22, 24-37). Weather in Israel (Ps 18:10-15; 29:3-10; 48:7; 65:8-12; 133:3; 135:6-7; 147:7-8; 148:7-8; Pr 25:23; 26:1; 30:4; Ecc 1:6-7; Hos 6:4; 13:15). The autumnal storms of the Mediterranean (Ac 27:9-20, 27).

Phenomena of:

The deluge (Ge 7:8). Fire from heaven on the cities of the plain (Ge 19:24-25). Plagues of hail, thunder, and lightning in Egypt (Ex 9:22-29; Ps 78:17-23), of darkness (Ex 10:22-23). East wind that divided the Red Sea (Ex 14:21), that brought the quails (Nu 11:31-32; Ps 78:26-28). Pillar of cloud and fire. *See Pillar.* Sun stood still (Jos 10:12-13). Dew on Gideon's fleece (Jdg 6:36-40). Stars in their courses fought against Sisera (Jdg 5:20). Stones from heaven (Jos 10:11). Fire from heaven at Elijah's command (2Ki 1:10-14). The whirlwind which carried Elijah to heaven (2Ki 2:1, 11).

Wind under God's control (Ps 107:25). East wind (Ps 48:7). Rain, formation of (Ps 135:6-7). Dew, copious (Ps 133:3). Rain in answer to Samuel's prayer (1Sa 12:16-18), Elijah's prayer (1Ki 18:41-45). Rain discomfits the Philistine army (1Sa 7:10). Wind destroyed Job's children (Job 1:18-19). Darkness at the Crucifixion (Mt 27:45; Lk 23:44-45).

See Astronomy; Celestial Phenomena; Dew; Hail; Rain; Weather.

Symbolic:

Used in the Revelation (Rev 6:12-14; 7:1; 8:3-12; 9:1-2, 17-19; 10:1-6; 11:6; 12:1-4, 7-9; 14; 15:1-4; 16:8, 17-21; 19:11-18; 20:11; 21:1).

METEYARD
Archaic word for "measures of length" (Lev 19:35).

METHEG AMMAH [5497] (*the bridle of the metropolis*). A town David took from the Philistines (2Sa 8:1).

METHUSAEL *See Methushael.*

METHUSELAH [5500, 3417] (*man of the javelin*). Son of Enoch and grandfather of Noah (Ge 5:21-27; 1Ch 1:3).

METHUSHAEL [5499] (perhaps *man of God*). Father of Lamech (Ge 4:18).

MEUNIM, MEUNITES [5064] (*the people of Maon*).
1. People conquered by the Simeonites (1Ch 4:41); fought against Jehoshaphat (2Ch 20:1) and Uzziah (2Ch 26:7).
2. Counted among the temple servants (Ezr 2:50; Ne 7:52). May be the descendants of 1.
See Maonites.

ME-ZAHAB [4771] (*waters of gold*). Grandfather of Mehetabel (Ge 36:39; 1Ch 1:50).

MEZOBAITE [5168]. Name of place otherwise unknown (1Ch 11:47).

MIAMIN *See Mijamin.*

MIBHAR [4437] (*choice*). One of David's valiant men (1Ch 11:38).

MIBSAM [4452] (*sweet odor*).
1. Son of Ishmael (Ge 25:13; 1Ch 1:29).
2. Son of Shallum (1Ch 4:25).

MIBZAR [4449] (*bastion*). Chief of Edom (Ge 36:42; 1Ch 1:53).

MICA [4775, 4777] (*who is like Yahweh?*).
1. Grandson of Jonathan (2Sa 9:12). See Micah, 3.
2. A Levite; descendant of Asaph (1Ch 9:15; Ne 11:17, 22).
3. A Levite covenanter (Ne 10:11), possibly the same as 2.

MICAH [4777, 4781] (*who is like Yahweh?*).
1. Ephraimite whose mother made an image for which he secured a priest; both image and priest were later stolen by the tribe of Dan (Jdg 17-18).
2. Reubenite (1Ch 5:5).
3. Grandson of Jonathan (1Ch 8:34; 9:40). See Mica, 1.
4. Levite (1Ch 23:20).
5. Father of Abdon, one of Josiah's officers (2Ch 34:20). See Micaiah, 2.
6. Prophet Micah, the Moreshethite; prophesied in the reigns of Jotham, Ahaz, and Hezekiah (Mic 1:1; Jer 26:18).

MICAH, BOOK OF

Author: The prophet Micah of Moresheth
Date: Sometime between 750 and 686 B.C.

Outline:
I. Superscription (1:1).
II. Judgment Against Israel and Judah (1:2-3:12).
  A. Introduction (1:2).
  B. The Predicted Destruction (1:3-7).
  C. Lamentation for the Destruction (1:8-16).
  D. Corruption in Micah's Society (2:1-11).
  E. Hope in the Midst of Gloom (2:12-13).
  F. The Leaders Condemned (ch. 3).
III. Hope for Israel and Judah (chs. 4-5).
  A. The Coming Kingdom (ch. 4).
  B. The Coming King (5:1-5a).
  C. Victory for the People of God (5:5b-15).
IV. The Lord's Case Against Israel (ch. 6).
  A. The Lord's Accusation (6:1-8).
  B. The Coming Judgment (6:9-16).
V. Gloom Turns to Triumph (ch. 7).
  A. Micah Laments the Corruption of His Society (7:1-6).
  B. Micah's Assurance of Hope (7:7).
  C. A Bright Future for God's People (7:8-13).
  D. Victory for God's Kingdom (7:14-20).
See Prophets, The Minor.

MICAIAH [4777, 4779, 4780, 4781] (*who is like Yahweh?*).
1. A prophet living in Samaria who predicted the death of King Ahab (1Ki 22; 2Ch 18).
2. Father of Acbor, one of Josiah's officers (2Ki 22:12-14). See Micah, 5.
3. Daughter of Uriel of Gibeah (2Ch 13:2).
4. Offical of Jehoshaphat; a teacher (2Ch 17:7).
5. Ancestor of priest in Nehemiah's time (Ne 12:35).
6. Priest (Ne 12:41).
7. Grandson of Shaphan (Jer 36:11-13).
8. See Maacah, 4.

MICE *See Rat(s).*

MICHA *See Mica.*

MICHAEL [4776, 3640] (*who is like God [El]?*).
1. An Asherite (Nu 13:13).
2. Two Gadites (1Ch 5:13-14).
3. A Gershonite Levite (1Ch 6:40).
4. A descendant of Issachar (1Ch 7:3).
5. A Benjamite (1Ch 8:16).
6. A captain of the thousands of Manasseh who joined David at Ziklag (1Ch 12:20).
7. Father of Omri (1Ch 27:18).
8. Son of Jehoshaphat. Slain by his brother, Jehoram (2Ch 21:2-4).
9. Father of Zebadiah (Ezr 8:8).
10. The archangel. His message to Daniel (Da 10:13, 21; 12:1). Contention with the devil (Jude 9). Fights with the dragon (Rev 12:7).

MICHAH *See Micah.*

MICHAIAH *See Micaiah.*

MICHAL [4783] (*who is like God [El]?*). Daughter of Saul. Given to David as a reward for slaying Goliath (1Sa 18:22-28). Rescues David from death (1Sa 19:9-17). Saul forcibly separates them, and she is given in marriage to Paltiel (1Sa 25:44). David recovers her to himself (2Sa 3:13-16). Ridicules David on account of his religious zeal (2Sa 6:16, 20-23).

MICHMASH See Micmash.

MICHRI See Micri.

MICHTAM See Miktam.

MICMASH [4820, 4825] (perhaps hidden place). A place in Benjamin eight miles NE of Jerusalem; Jonathan led Israelites to victory over Philistines there (1Sa 14:31; Ne 11:31).

MICMETHATH [4826] A city between Ephraim and Manasseh (Jos 16:6; 17:7).

MICRI [4840]. A Benjamite (1Ch 9:8).

MIDDIN [4516]. A city in Judah in the wilderness just W of the Dead Sea (Jos 15:61).

MIDDLE WALL See Dividing Wall.

MIDIAN [824+4518, 4518, 1178+3409]. Son of Abraham by Keturah (Ge 25:2, 4; 1Ch 1:32-33).

MIDIANITE(S) [4518, 4520]. Descendants of Midian, son of Abraham by Keturah (Ge 25:1-2, 4; 1Ch 1:32-33). Called Ishmaelites (Ge 37:25, 28; Jdg 8:24). Were merchants (Ge 37:28). Buy Joseph and sell him to Potiphar (Ge 37:28, 36). Defeated by the Israelites under Phinehas; five of their kings slain, the women taken captives, their cities burned, and rich spoils taken (Nu 31). Defeated by Gideon (Jdg 6-8). Owned multitudes of camels and large quantities of gold (Isa 60:6). A snare to the Israelites (Nu 25:16-18). Prophecies concerning (Isa 60:6; Hab 3:7).

MIDNIGHT [2021+2942+4326, 2940+4326, 3543, 3545+3816]. Scenes at (Ex 11:4; Mt 25:6; Ac 16:25; 20:7).

MIDWIVES [3528]. Assist in childbirth (Ge 35:17; 38:28). Save Israelite boys in Egypt (Ex 1:15-21).

MIGDAL EDER [4468]. See Eder, 1.

MIGDAL EL [4466] (tower of God [El]). A city of Naphtali (Jos 19:38).

MIGDAL GAD [4467] (tower of Gad). A city of Judah (Jos 15:37).

MIGDOL [4465] (tower).
1. A place near the Red Sea where the Israelites encamped (Ex 14:2; Nu 33:7-8).
2. A city on the NE border of lower Egypt (Jer 44:1; 46:14).

MIGRON [4491] (precipice). A city in Ben-

jamin. Saul encamps near, under a pomegranate tree (1Sa 14:2). Prophesy concerning (Isa 10:28).

MIJAMIN [4785] (from the right hand).
1. Priest in David's time (1Ch 24:9).
2. A man who divorced his foreign wife (Ezr 10:25).
3. Covenanter priest (Ne 10:7).
4. Priest who returned from the Exile (Ne 12:5).

MIKLOTH [5235] (rods).
1. A Benjamite of Jerusalem (1Ch 8:32; 9:37-38).
2. A ruler in the reign of David (1Ch 27:4).

MIKNEIAH [5240] (Yahweh acquires). A doorkeeper of the temple and musician (1Ch 15:18, 21).

MIKTAM [4846]. The term always stands in the superscription of Davidic prayers occasioned by great danger (Ps 16, 56-60). Variously related to words for "golden," "inscription," and "atonement." See Music, Symbols Used in.

MILALAI [4912]. A priest who took part in the dedication of the walls of Jerusalem (Ne 12:36).

MILCAH [4894] (queen).
1. Wife of Nahor and mother of Bethuel (Ge 11:29; 22:20-23; 24:15, 24, 47).
2. Daughter of Zelophehad. Special legislation in regard to the inheritance of (Nu 26:33; 27:1-7; 36:1-12; Jos 17:3-4).

MILCOM See Molech.

MILDEW [3766, 5596, 7076, 7669] (yellow, pale). Fungus growth destructive of grains and fruits (Dt 28:22; 1Ki 8:37; Am 4:9; Hag 2:17).

MILE [3627, 5084]. Equal to about 3, 500 cubits or 8.6 stadia (Eze 45:3; Mt 5:41; Lk 24:13).

MILETUS [3626]. A seaport in Asia Minor. Paul visits (Ac 20:15), and sends to Ephesus for the elders of the church, and addresses them here (Ac 20:17-38). Trophimus left sick at (2Ti 4:20).

MILITARY INSTRUCTION Of children (2Sa 1:18). See Armies.

MILK [2692, 2772, 1128]. Used for food (Ge 18:8; Jdg 4:19; SS 5:1; Eze 25:4; 1Co 9:7). Of goats (Pr 27:27), sheep (Dt 32:14; Isa 7:21-22), camels (Ge 32:15), cows (Dt 32:14; 1Sa 6:7, 10). Churned (Pr 30:33). Kid not to be cooked in its mother's milk (Ex 23:19; Dt 14:21).
Figurative (Ex 3:8, 17; 13:5; 33:3; Nu 13:27; Dt 26:9, 15; Isa 55:1; 60:16; Jer 11:5; 32:22; Eze 20:6; Joel 3:18; 1Co 3:2; Heb 5:12-13; 1Pe 2:2).

MILL [1003, 8160, 3685]. (Jer 25:10). Upper and lower stones of (Dt 24:6; Job 41:24; Isa 47:2). Used in Egypt (Ex 11:5). Operated by women (Mt 24:41), and captives (Jdg 16:21; La 5:13). Manna

ground in (Nu 11:8). Sound of, to cease (Rev 18:22). *See Grind; Millstone.*

MILLENNIUM The Latin for a thousand years, from (Rev 20:1-15).

It refers to a period when Christ rules and Satan is bound; when Jesus shall have triumphed over all forms of evil (1Co 15:24-28; 2Th 2:8; Rev 14:6-18; 19:11-16). At the restoration of all things (Ac 3:21). When the creation shall be delivered from the corruption of evil (Ro 8:19-21). When the Son of Man shall sit on the throne of his glory (Mt 19:28; Lk 22:28-30), and the righteous shall be clothed with authority (Da 7:22; Mt 19:28; Lk 22:28-30; 1Co 6:2; Rev 2:5), and possess the kingdom (Mt 25:34; Lk 12:32; 22:29).

Christ rules from his throne in Zion or Jerusalem (Isa 65:17-25; Zep 3:11-13; Zec 9:9-10; 14:16-21). Christ fulfills the promise of the kingdom of God on earth (Mt 16:18-19; 26:29; Mk 14:25; Heb 8:11).

Amillennialists believe Jesus is reigning now. *Premillennialists* believe Jesus will literally reign on earth for a thousand years after his second coming. *Postmillennialists* believe the Church will Christianize the world for a long period of time after which Christ will return.

See Church, The Body of Believers, Prophecies Concerning; Jesus the Christ, Kingdom of; Second Coming of.

MILLET [1893]. (Eze 4:9).

MILLO *See Beth Millo.*

MILLSTONE [3218, 7115, 8160, *3684+, 3685+*]. Not to be taken in pledge (Dt 24:6). Probably used in executions by drowning (Mt 18:6; Mk 9:42; Lk 17:2). Abimelech killed by one being hurled upon him (Jdg 9:53). Figurative of the hard heart (Job 41:24). *See Grind; Mill.*

MINA [4949, *3641*]. In the sexagesimal system (based on the number 60) that originated in Mesopotamia, there were 60 shekels in a mina and 60 minas in a talent. A shekel, which was about two-fifths of an ounce of silver, was the average wage for a month's work. Thus a mina would be the equivalent of five years' wages, and a talent would be 300 years' wages (1Ki 10:17, ftn, w 2Ch 9:16, ftn; Ezr 2:69; Ne 7:71-72, ftn). *See Measure.*

MINCING [2143+2256+3262] (*to go like a little child, i.e., to trip along*). To speak, walk, or behave in an affectedly elegant, dainty, or nice manner. Used of the haughty women of Zion (Isa 3:16).

MIND [*2349, 4000, 4213, 4222, 5714, 5883, 8120, 10381, 10646, *1379, 2014, 2840, 3212, 3419, 3564, 3784, 3808, 5404, 5858, 5859, 6034*]. In Scripture it often means "heart" or "soul." In the NT it is often used in an ethical sense (Ro 7:25; Col 2:18).

MINERALS OF THE BIBLE The science of mineralogy is a recent one, and did not exist in ancient times. It is often impossible to be certain that when a mineral name is used in the Bible, it is used with the same meaning as that attached to modern mineralogy. The following minerals are mentioned in the Bible:

Precious Stones:

Agate (Ex 28:19; 39:12), amethyst (Ex 28:19; 39:12; Rev 21:20), aromatic resin or resin (Ge 2:12; Nu 11:7), beryl (Ex 28:17; 39:10; Eze 28:13; Rev 21:20), carnelian (Rev 4:3; 21:20), chalcedony (Rev 21:19), chrysolite (Da 10:6; Rev 21:20), chrysoprase (Rev 21:20), coral (Job 28:18; Eze 27:16), crystal (Job 28:17; Rev 4:6; 21:11; 22:1), emerald (Ex 28:18; 39:11), glowing metal (Eze 1:4, 27; 8:2; Rev 1:15), hardest stone (Eze 3:9; Zec 7:12), jacinth (Ex 28:19; 39:12; Rev 9:17), jasper (Ex 28:20; 39:13; Job 28:18; Eze 28:13; Rev 4:3; 21:11, 18, 19), onyx (Ge 2:12; Ex 25:7; 28:9, 20; 35:9, 27; 39:6, 13; 1Ch 29:2; Job 28:16; Eze 28:13), pearl (Rev 21:21), ruby (Ex 28:17; 39:10; Job 28:18; Eze 28:13, 16), sapphire (Ex 24:10; 28:18; 39:11; Eze 1:26; 10:1; 28:13; Rev 21:19), sardonyx (Rev 21:20), sparkling jewels (Isa 54:12), topaz (Ex 28:17; 39:10; Job 28:19; Eze 28:13; Rev 21:20), turquoise (Ex 28:18; Eze 27:16).

Metals:

Gold (Ge 2:11-12), silver (Mt 10:9), iron (Nu 31:22), bronze (Ge 4:22; Ezr 8:27), lead (Ex 15:10), tin (Nu 31:22), glowing metal (Eze 1:4, 27; 8:2), dross (Ps 119:119; Pr 25:4; Isa 1:22, 25; Eze 22:18-19).

Common Minerals:

Alabaster (Mt 26:7; Mk 14:3; Lk 7:37), flint (Isa 5:28; 50:7; Jer 17:1; Eze 3:9; Zec 7:12), marble (1Ch 29:2; Est 1:6; SS 5:15; Rev 18:12), soda (Pr 25:20; Jer 2:22), sulfur (Ge 19:24; Dt 29:23; Job 18:15; Ps 11:6; Isa 30:33; 34:9; Eze 38:22; Lk 17:29; Rev 9:17-18; 14:10; 19:20; 20:10; 21:8), water.

See Stones.

MINES, MINING [4604]. An ancient occupation; described in (Job 28:1-11; Dt 8:9; 1Ki 7:13-50).

MINGLED PEOPLE Non-Israelite people who left Egypt with the Israelites (Ex 12:38). The term is also used for the mixed blood of certain of Israel's enemies (Jer 25:20; 50:37).

MINIAMIN [4975] (*from the right, good fortune*).

1. Levite (2Ch 31:15).

2. Head of a family of priests (Ne 12:17).

3. A priest in Nehemiah's time (Ne 12:41).

MINISTER [2143, 6268, 6275, 6641, 9250, *692, 1354, 1355, 1356, 3302, 3311, 3313, 3364*] (*servant*).

1. An officer in civil government. Joseph (Ge 41:40-44), Iri (2Sa 20:26), Zabud (1Ki 4:5), Ahithophel (1Ch 27:33), Zebadiah (2Ch 19:11),

Elkanah (2Ch 28:7), Haman (Est 3:1), Mordecai (Est 10:3, w Est 8; 9), Daniel (Da 2:48; 6:1-3).

See Cabinet.

2. A sacred teacher.

Good Ministers:

Likened to sowers (Ps 126:6; Mt 13:3-8; Mk 4:3-8; Lk 8:5-8). Teachers of schools (1Sa 19:20; 2Ki 2:3, 5, 15; 4:38; 2Ch 15:3; 17:7-9; Ac 13:1).

Hired (Jdg 17:10; 18:4). Exempt from taxation (Ezr 7:24). In politics (2Sa 15:24-27). In war (2Ch 13:12-14).

Influential in public affairs (1Sa 12:6-10), designate kings (1Sa 9:15-16; 10:1; 16:1-13), recommend civil and military appointments (2Ki 4:13).

In vigorous opposition with rulers: Samuel with Saul (1Sa 13:11-14; 15:10-31), Nathan with David (2Sa 12:1-4), Elijah with Ahab (1Ki 18:17-18).

Recreation for (Mk 6:31-32). Take leave of congregations (Ac 20:17-38). Personal bearing of (Tit 2:7-8). Fraud with ecclesiastical authority (Gal 1:15-24; 2:1-9). Work of, will be tried (1Co 3:12-15). Responsibility of (Eze 3:17-21; 33:8; Mt 10:14-40; Ac 18:6; 20:26-27; 1Co 1:23; 2Co 2:15-17; 5:11, 18-19; 1Ti 6:20). Speaking evil of, forbidden (Jude 8, 10). Clothed with authority (1Th 5:12; Tit 1:13-14; 2:15; 3:1-2, 8-9; Heb 13:6-7, 17). *See the epistles to Timothy and Titus in their entirety.* Clothed with salvation (2Ch 6:41). Exhorted to grow in grace (1Ti 6:11; 2Ti 2:22).

Marriage of (Lev 21:7-15; Mt 8:14; Mk 1:30; 1Co 9:5; 1Ti 3:2, 12; Tit 1:5-7).

Incorruptible: Balaam (Nu 22:18, 37-38; 23:8, 12; 24:12-14, w 2Pe 2:15-16), Micaiah (1Ki 22:13-14), Peter (Ac 8:18-23). Patience of (Jas 5:10). Inconsistent (Mt 23:7-3).

Love of, for the church, exemplified by Paul (Php 1:7; 1Th 1:2-4; 2:8, 11). Kindness to, Ebed-Melech to Jeremiah (Jer 38:7-13). Fear of (1Sa 16:4). Example to the flock (Php 3:17; 2Th 3:9; 1Ti 4:12; Tit 2:1, 7-8; 1Pe 5:3). Intolerance of (Mt 15:23; 19:13; Mk 10:13; Lk 18:15). Message of, rejected (Jer 7:27; Eze 33:30-33). God's care of (1Ki 17:1-16; 19:1-8; Mt 10:29-31; Lk 12:6-7). Their calling, glorious (2Co 3:7-11). Discouragements of (Isa 30:10-11; 53:1; Eze 3:8-9, 14; Hab 1:2-3; Mt 13:57; Mk 6:3-4; Lk 4:24; Jn 4:44).

Defended (Jer 26:16-24; Ac 23:9). Beloved (Ac 20:37-38; 21:5-6).

Sent out in teams of two: Disciples (Mk 6:7), Paul and Barnabas (Ac 13:2-3), Judas and Silas (Ac 15:27), Barnabas and Mark (Ac 15:37, 39), Paul and Silas (Ac 15:40), Paul and Titus (2Co 8:19, 23), Timothy and Erastus (Ac 19:22), Titus and a companion (2Co 12:18).

Call of—

(Am 2:11; Mt 9:38; Ro 10:14-15; Eph 4:11-12; Heb 5:4). Aaron and his sons (Ex 28:1; 1Ch 23:13; Heb 5:4). Levites (Nu 3:5-13; 16:5, 9). Samuel (1Sa 3:4-10). Elisha (1Ki 19:16, 19). Isaiah (Isa 6:8-10). Jeremiah (Jer 1:5). Jonah (Jnh 1:1-2; 3:1-2).

The twelve apostles (Mt 4:18-22 w Mk 1:17-20;

Mt 9:9; Mk 2:14; Lk 5:27 w Mt 10:1-5; Jn 1:43). The seventy-two disciples (Lk 10:1-2). Paul (Ac 13:2-3; 20:24; 22:12-15; 26:14-18; Ro 1:1; 1Co 1:1, 27-28 w 2Co 1:1 & Col 1:1; 1Co 9:16-19; 2Co 5:18-20; Gal 1:15-16; Eph 3:7-8; Col 1:25-29; 1Ti 1:11; Tit 1:5). Barnabas (Ac 13:2-3). Archippus (Col 4:17).

See Call, Personal; Excuses.

Character and Qualifications of—

(Lev 10:3-11). Blameless (1Ti 3:2-4, 7-13; Tit 1:5-9). Compassionate (Heb 5:2). Consecrated (Nu 16:9-10). Consistent (Ro 2:21-23). Courageous (Jer 1:7-8, 17-19; Ac 20:22, 24; 2Ti 1:7). Diligent (2Ch 29:11; 1Co 15:10). Eager to serve (Isa 6:8). Endued with power (Lk 24:49; Ac 1:8; 4:8, 31; Gal 2:8). Gentle (2Ti 2:24-25). A good example (Tit 2:1, 7-8, 15; Jas 3:1, 13, 16-18). Holy (Lev 21:6; Isa 6:7; 52:11; Mal 2:6; Jn 17:17; 1Co 9:27; 2Ti 2:21; Tit 1:5-9). Humble (Mt 20:25-28; 23:8, 10-11; Lk 22:27; Jn 13:13-17; 15:20; 2Co 4:5). Meek (1Co 4:12-13; 2Co 10:1). Patient (Jas 5:10). Persevering (Mt 10:22-24; 2Co 4:1, 8-10). Prepared (Ezr 7:10). Responsible (1Pe 4:10-11). Saved (2Ch 6:41). Sincere (2Co 4:1-2). Strong (2Ti 2:1). Tactful (1Co 9:18-23; 10:23, 28-33; 2Co 6:3; 12:16). Willing to suffer hardship (2Ti 2:3; 4:5). Wise (Mal 2:7; Pr 11:30; Mt 10:16; Lk 6:39; 2Co 4:6; 2Ti 2:7; 3:14, 16-17).

Not quarrelsome (2Ti 2:14, 23-24; Tit 3:9). Not of the world (Jn 15:19; 17:16). Not entangled with the world (2Ti 2:4-5).

Zealous (Jer 20:9; Eze 34:1-31; 2Ti 1:6-8; 4:2). *See Zeal.* Instances of: Titus (2Co 8:16-17), Epaphroditus (Php 2:25-30), Epaphras (Col 4:12-13), John, in his vision (Rev 5:4-5).

Faithful (1Sa 2:35; Mt 24:45; Lk 12:42-44; Ac 20:22, 24; 1Co 2:2; 2Co 6:4-7). Instances of: Moses (Dt 4:26; 30:19; Heb 3:2, 5), Micaiah (2Ch 18:12-13), Azariah (2Ch 26:16-20), Balaam (Nu 22:18, 38; 23:8, 12; 24:12-14), Nathan (2Sa 12:1-14), Isaiah (Isa 22:4-5; 39:3-7), Jeremiah (Jer 17:16; 26:1-15; 28; 37:9-10, 16-18), John the Baptist (Mt 3:2-12; Mk 6:18; Lk 3:7-19), the apostles (Ac 4:19-20, 31; 5:21, 29-32), Peter (Ac 2:14-40; 3:12-26; 4:8-12; 8:18-23), Paul (Ac 15:25-26; 17:16-17; 19:8; 20:26-27), Tychicus (Col 4:7).

See the epistles to Timothy and Titus in their entirety.

Described as—

Administering God's grace (1Pe 4:10). Ambassadors for Christ (2Co 5:20; Eph 6:20). Angels of the church (Rev 1:20; 2:1, 8, 12, 18; 3:1, 7, 14). Apostles (Lk 6:13; Rev 18:20). Apostles of Jesus Christ (Tit 1:1). Defenders of the gospel (Php 1:7). Elders (1Ti 5:17; 1Pe 5:1). Entrusted with God's work (Tit 1:7), with the secret things of God (1Co 4:1). Evangelists (Eph 4:11; 2Ti 4:5). Fishers of men (Mt 4:19; Mk 1:17). God's fellow workers (1Th 3:2). Lights (Jn 5:35). Men of God (Dt 33:1; 1Ti 6:11). Messengers of the Church (2Co 8:23), of the LORD Almighty (Mal 2:7). Ministers of God (Isa 61:6), before the LORD (Joel 2:17), of Christ (Ro 15:16; 1Ti 4:6), of a new covenant (2Co 3:6), in the Sanctuary (Eze 45:4).

Overseers (Ac 20:28). Pastors (Eph 4:11). Preachers (Ro 10:14; 1Ti 2:7), of righteousness (2Pe 2:5). Servants of the Church (2Co 4:5), of God (Tit 1:1; Jas 1:1), of the gospel (Eph 3:7; Col 1:23), of Jesus Christ (Php 1:1; Jude 1), of the Lord (2Ti 2:24), of the Word (Lk 1:2). Shepherds (Jer 23:4). Soldiers of Christ (Php 2:25; 2Ti 2:3-4). Stars (Rev 1:20; 2:1). Teachers (Isa 30:20; Eph 4:11). Watchmen (Isa 62:6; Eze 33:7). Witnesses (Ac 1:8; 5:32; 26:16). Workers (Mt 9:38; Phm 1), together with God (2Co 6:1).

Duties of—
(Eph 4:11-12). To preach (Mt 10:7; Ro 1:14-15). To preach the unsearchable riches of Christ (Eph 3:8-12). To admonish (Isa 58:1; 62:6-7). To exhort (2Co 5:20; 1Ti 4:13; 6:17-18; 2Pe 1:12-16). To warn (Jer 7:25; Eze 33:1-9). To reprove (Eze 6:11; 34; Jnh 1:2; 2Co 7:8). *See Reproof.* To teach (Lev 10:11; 2Ki 17:27-28; 2Ch 15:3; Ezr 7:10; Jer 26:2; Eze 44:23; Mt 10:7, 27; 28:19-20; Mk 10:43-45; Ac 5:20; 6:4; 16:4; 18:9-10; 26:16-18; Ro 1:15; 12:6-7; 2Co 10:8; Eph 3:8-10; 4:11-12; 1Ti 2:7; 4:13-16; 2Ti 2:2, 14-15, 24-25; 4:1-2, 5). To teach the lordship of Jesus (2Co 4:5). To serve (Mt 20:25-28; Mk 10:43-45; 2Co 4:5). To make disciples of Christ (Mt 28:19-20). To win souls (Pr 11:30; Jn 4:35-38; 2Co 5:18, 20). To witness for Christ (Lk 24:48; Jn 15:27; Ac 1:22; 10:42; 22:15). To do the work of an evangelist (2Ti 4:5). To give himself continually to prayer (Ac 6:4). To lament over the worldliness and sins of the church (Joel 1:13-15; 2:17). To speak boldly (Eph 6:20). To minister to all without respect of persons or races (Ro 1:14-15). To exercise authority in the church (Mt 16:19; 18:18; 1Co 4:19-21; 2Co 7:8-9, 12, 15; 13:2-3; 13:10; 2Th 3:4; 1Ti 1:3-4, 11, 18; 5:19-22; 1Pe 5:1-3). To feed the flock (Jer 3:15; 23:4, 22, 28; Jn 21:15-17; Ac 20:28; 1Co 14:1-33; 1Pe 5:2-4). To strengthen the discouraged (Lk 22:32). To comfort the people (Isa 40:1-2, 9, 11; 1Th 3:2).

Charges delivered to: (Nu 18:1-7; 27:18-23; Dt 31:7-8, 14-23; Jos 1:1-9; Jer 1:18-19; Eze 3:4). Jesus to the twelve (Mt 10:5-42), to the seventy-two (Lk 10:1-16). Paul charges Timothy (1Ti 1:18-20; 2; 3; 4; 5; 6; 2Ti 1:6-13; 2; 3; 4).

Duty of the Church to—
To esteem (1Th 5:12-13). To pray for (Heb 13:18; 2Ch 6:41; Ps 132:9; Mt 9:37-38; Ac 4:29; 12:5; Ro 15:30-32; 2Co 1:11; Eph 6:18-20; Php 1:9; Col 4:2-4; 1Th 5:25; 2Th 3:1-2; Phm 22; Heb 13:19). To imitate the example of (1Co 11:1; Php 3:17; 2Th 3:7; Heb 13:7). To submit to the authority of (1Co 11:2; 16:16; 1Th 5:12-13; 2Th 3:4; Heb 13:7, 17). To provide for the support, of priest and Levite (Nu 18:20-21; Dt 10:9; 14:27; 18:1-4; Jos 13:14; 18:7; Jer 31:14; Eze 44:28), of the twelve apostles (Mt 10:9-10; Mk 6:8; Lk 22:35), of the seventy-two disciples (Lk 10:7-8), of Christian preachers (1Co 9:3-4, 7-14; Gal 6:6; Php 4:10-18; 1Ti 5:18). Right of support, waived by Paul (Ac 20:33-35; 1Co 9:15-18; 2Co 11:7-10; 12:13-18; 1Th 2:5-6, 9; 2Th 3:7-9).

See Church, The Body of Believers, Responsibilities and Duties.

Hospitality to—
Woman of Zarephath to Elijah (1Ki 17:10-16). The Shunammite to Elisha (2Ki 4:8-10). The barbarians to Paul (Ac 28:1-10). Simon the tanner to Peter (Ac 9:43). The Philippian jailer (Ac 16:33-34). Aquila and Priscilla to Paul (Ac 18:3), to Apollos (Ac 18:26). Justus to Paul (Ac 18:7). Philip the evangelist to Paul (Ac 21:8-10).

Joys of—
(Jn 4:36-38; 2Co 2:14; 7:6-7; Php 2:16; 1Th 2:13, 19-20; 3:8-9; 2Jn 4; 3Jn 4).

Ordination of—
Matthias (Ac 1:26), seven deacons (Ac 6:5-6), Paul and Barnabas (Ac 13:3), Timothy (1Ti 4:14). *See Levites; Priest.*

Prayer for—
Commanded (Mt 9:37-38; Lk 10:2; Ro 15:30-32; 2Co 1:11; Eph 6:18-20; Php 1:19; Col 4:2-4; 1Th 5:25; 2Th 3:1-2; Phm 22; Heb 13:18-19). Exemplified (2Ch 6:41; Ps 132:9; Ac 1:24-25; 4:29; 6:6; 12:5; 14:23).

Precepts for Guidance of—
(Jer 1:7-8, 17-19; Eze 2:6-8; Mt 7:6; 10:7-8, 11-13, 16, 25-28; Lk 10:1-11; Col 4:17; 1Ti 1:3-4, 11, 18-19; 4:6-7, 12-16; 5:1-3, 7-11, 19-22; 6:3-4, 10-14, 17-21; 2Ti 1:6-8; 2:2-7, 14-16, 23-25; 4:1-2, 5; 1Pe 5:1-4; 2Pe 1:12-16).

Promises to—
(2Sa 23:6-7; Ps 126:5-6; Jer 1:7-10, 17-19; 15:20-21; 20:11; Da 12:3; Mt 10:28-31; 28:20; Lk 10:19; 12:11-12; 24:49; Jn 4:36-38; Ac 1:4-5, 8; 18:9-10; 1Co 3:8; 9:9-10; 2Co 2:14-16; 7:6-7; Php 2:16; 1Th 2:13, 19-20; 3:8-9; 1Pe 5:4; 3Jn 4). *See Righteous, Promises to.*

Success Attending—
Jonah (Jnh 1:5-6, 9, 14, 16; 3:4-9). Apostles (Ac 2:1-4, 41). Philip (Ac 8:6, 8, 12). Peter (Ac 9:32-35). Paul (Ac 13:16-43; 1Co 4:15; 9:2; 15:11; 2Co 3:2-3; 12:12; 13:4; Php 2:16; 1Th 1:5). Apollos (Ac 18:24-28). *See Revivals.*

Trials and Persecutions of—
Foretold (Mt 10:16-27 w Jn 13:16; Mt 23:34). Rehearsed (Mt 23:34). Instances of: Elijah (1Ki 22:24-27; 2Ch 18:23-26). Hanani (2Ch 16:10). Zechariah (2Ch 24:20-22, 25; Mt 23:35; Lk 11:51). Isaiah (Isa 20:2-3). Jeremiah (Jer 11:19-21; 15:10, 15; 17:15-18; 18:18-23; 20:1-3, 7-18; 32:2-3; 33:1; 37:15-21; 38:6-13; 39:15; 43:1-7; La 3:53-55). Ezekiel (Eze 3:24-25; 24:15-18). Hosea (Hos 1:2). Amos (Am 5:10; 7:10-17). The apostles (Ac 5:17-42). Peter (Ac 12:3-19). Paul (Ac 9:23-25, 29-30; 14:4-6, 11-20; 16:16-24; 17:5-10, 13-14; 18:12-13; 20:3; 21:27-40; 22:22-30; 23:10-35; 24:26-27; 27:9-44; 1Co 2:1-4; 4:9-13; 2Co 6:4-10; 7:5; 11:23-33; 12:7-10; Eph 3:1, 13; 2Ti 1:8, 16; 2:9; 4:16-17). *See Paul, Persecutions of; also, Accusation, False; Persecution.*

Zealous—
Titus (2Co 8:16-17). Epaphroditus (Php 2:25-30). Epaphras (Col 4:12-13). Tychicus (Col 4:7). John, in his vision (Rev 5:4-5). *See Zeal.*

False and Corrupt:

(1Ki 12:31; Ne 13:29; Jer 2:8; 6:13-14; 8:10-11; 12:10; La 2:14; Eze 22:25, 28; 44:8, 10; Hos 9:7-8; Zep 3:4; Mal 1:6-10; 2Ti 4:3). Mercenary (1Sa 8:3; Isa 56:11; Mic 3:11). Presumptuous (Dt 18:20-22; Jn 5:43). Insincere (Php 1:15-16). Senseless (Jer 10:21). Adulterous (1Sa 2:22; Jer 23:14; Hos 6:9). Murderous (Hos 6:9). Pervert the truth (2Co 2:17; 11:3-4, 13-15; Gal 1:6-8; 1Ti 4:1-3, 7). Lead the people astray (Isa 3:12; Jer 50:6). Addicted to alcohol (Isa 28:7; 56:12). Indifferent to good and evil (Isa 56:10; Eze 22:26). Desired by the wicked (Isa 30:10-11; Jer 5:13-14, 30-31; Am 2:11-12; Mic 2:11).

Condemned—

Denunciations against false ministers (Isa 5:20; Jer 23:11-40; La 4:13-14; Eze 13:1-23; 34:1-10, 16-22; Mt 23:4-7, 13-14, 36; 2Pe 2:1-22).

Warnings against false ministers (Dt 13:1-4; Isa 8:19-20; Jer 14:13-16; 27:9-18; Mt 5:19; 7:15-23; 15:9, 13-14 w Lk 6:39; Mt 23:3-4, 13; 24:4-5, 11, 24, 26, 48-51; Mk 13:21-22; Lk 21:8; Jn 10:1, 5, 8, 10, 12-13; Ac 20:20, 30; Eph 4:14; Php 3:2; Col 2:4, 8, 18-19; 1Ti 1:3-7; 6:3-5; 2Ti 2:17-18; Tit 1:10-14; 1Jn 2:18-19, 22-23, 26; 4:1-3, 5; 2Jn 7, 10-11; Rev 2:12, 14-15, 18, 20-23).

Judgments upon false ministers (Isa 29:10-11; Hos 5:1; Gal 5:10).

Punishment of false ministers (Dt 13:1, 5; 18:20; Isa 43:27-28; Jer 14:15; 23:1-2, 11, 15, 21; 27:9-18; La 4:13-14; Eze 14:9-10; Hos 4:5-6, 8-13; Mic 3:5-7; Zec 10:3; 13:2-5; Mal 2:1-3, 8-9; Lk 12:45-46; 2Pe 2:3; Jude 4, 11).

Instances of—

Nadab and Abihu (Lev 10:1-2). Korah, Dathan, and Abiram (Nu 16:1-40). Eli's sons (1Sa 2:12-17, 22, 25, 29, 34; 3:13; 4:11). Samuel's sons (1Sa 8:1-3). The old prophet of Bethel (1Ki 13:11-32). Jonathan (Jdg 17:7-13; 18). Noadiah (Ne 6:14). Priests under, Jehoash (2Ki 12:7; 2Ch 24:5-6). Hezekiah (2Ch 30:3, 5). Priests and Levites (Ezr 2:61-62; Ne 7:63-64; 12; 10:18-24; Ne 13:4-9, 28-29; Zec 7:5-6). Hananiah (Jer 28). Jonah (Jnh 1:1-6). Scribes and Pharisees (Mt 23:15-16), Caiaphas (Mt 26:2-3, 57, 63-65; Jn 11:49-51; 18:14). Judas (Mt 26:14-16, 21-25, 47-50; 27:3-5; Jn 12:4-6; Ac 1:18). Judaizing Christians (Gal 3:1-2; 4:17; 6:12-13). Hymenaeus (1Ti 1:20; 2Ti 2:17-18). Alexander (1Ti 1:20). Philetus (2Ti 2:17-18).

MINNI [4973]. A district of Armenia (Jer 51:27).

MINNITH [4976]. A place E of the Jordan (Jdg 11:33; Eze 27:17).

MINOR PROPHETS, THE See
Prophets, The Minor.

MINORITY REPORT *See Reports.*

MINORS Legal status of (Gal 4:1-2). *See Orphan; Young Men.*

MINSTREL NIV "harpist" (1Sa 16:23); "flute players" (Mt 9:23). *See Flute; Harp.*

MINT [2455] (*sweet odor*). (Mt 23:23; Lk 11:42).

MIPHKAD *See Gate, Inspection.*

MIRACLES [4603, 7098, 7099, *1539, 2240, 4956, 5469*].

General:

Called: Marvelous things (Ps 78:12), marvelous works (Ps 105:5; Isa 29:14), signs and wonders (Jer 32:21; Jn 4:48; 2Co 12:12).

Performed through the power of God (Jn 3:2; Ac 14:3; 15:12; 19:11), of the Holy Spirit (Mt 12:28; Ro 15:19; 1Co 12:9-10, 28-30), in the name of Christ (Mk 16:17; Ac 3:16; 4:30). Faith required in those who perform (Mt 17:20; 21:21; Jn 14:12; Ac 3:16; 6:8). Faith required in those for whom they were performed (Mt 9:28; Mk 9:22-24; Ac 14:9). Power to work, given the disciples (Mk 3:14-15; 16:17-18, 20). Demanded by unbelievers (Mt 12:38-39; 16:1; Lk 11:16, 29; 23:8).

Alleged miracles performed by magicians (Ex 7:10-12, 22; 8:7), by other impostors (Mt 7:22). Performed through the powers of evil (2Th 2:9; Rev 16:14). Done in support of false religions (Dt 13:1-2), by false Christs (Mt 24:24), by false prophets (Mt 24:24; Rev 19:20), by the medium of Endor (1Sa 28:7-14), by Simon (Ac 8:9-11). Not to be regarded (Dt 13:3). Deceive the ungodly (2Th 2:10-12; Rev 13:14; 19:20). A mark of apostasy (2Th 2:3, 9; Rev 13:13).

List of Miracles and Supernatural Events:

In the Old Testament—

Creation (Ge 1). Flood (Ge 7-8). Confusion of tongues (Ge 11:1-9). Fire on Abraham's sacrifice (Ge 15:17). Conception of Isaac (Ge 17:17; 18:12; 21:2). Destruction of Sodom (Ge 19). Lot's wife turned to salt (Ge 19:26). Closing of the wombs of Abimelech's household (Ge 20:17-18). Opening of Hagar's eyes (Ge 21:19). Conception of Jacob and Esau (Ge 25:21). Opening of Rachel's womb (Ge 30:22).

Burning bush (Ex 3:2). Transformation of Moses' rod into a serpent (Ex 4:3-4, 30; 7:10, 12). Moses' leprosy (Ex 4:6-7, 30). Plagues in Egypt. *See Plague.* Pillar of cloud and fire (Ex 13:21-22; 14:19-20). Passage of the Red Sea (Ex 14:22). Destruction of Pharaoh and his army (Ex 4:23-30). Sweetening the waters of Marah (Ex 15:25). Manna (Ex 16:4-31). Quail (Ex 16:13). Defeat of Amalek (Ex 17:9-13). Transfiguration of the face of Moses (Ex 34:29-35). Water from the rock (Ex 17:5, 7). Thundering and lightning on Sinai (Ex 19:16-20; 24:10, 15-17; Dt 4:33). Miriam's leprosy (Nu 12:10-15). Judgments by fire (Nu 11:1-3). Destruction of Korah (Nu 16:31-35; Dt 11:6-7). Plague (Nu 16:46-50). Aaron's rod buds (Nu 17:1-9). Waters from the rock in Kadesh (Nu 20:8-11). Plague of serpents (Nu 21:6-9). Destruction of Nadab and Abihu (Lev 10:1-2). Balaam's donkey speaks (Nu 22:23-30). Preservation of Moses (Dt 34:7).

Jordan divided (Jos 3:14-17; 4:16-18). Fall of Jericho (Jos 6:20). Midianites destroyed (Jdg 7:16-22). Hail on the confederated kings (Jos 10:11). Sun and moon stand still (Jos 10:12-14).

Dew on Gideon's fleece (Jdg 6:37-40). Samson's strength (Jdg 14:6; 16:3, 29-30). Samson supplied with water (Jdg 15:19).

Fall of Dagon (1Sa 6:7-14). Tumors (1Sa 5:9-12; 6:1-18). Destruction of the people of Beth Shemesh (1Sa 6:19-20). Thunder (1Sa 12:16-18). Destruction of Uzzah (2Sa 6:1-8). Plague in Israel (1Ch 21:14-26).

Fire on the sacrifices of Aaron (Lev 9:24), of Gideon (Jdg 6:21), of Manoah (Jdg 13:19-20), of Solomon (2Ch 7:1), of Elijah (1Ki 18:38).

Jeroboam's hand withered (1Ki 13:3-6). Appearance of blood (2Ki 3:20-22). Panic of the Syrians (2Ki 7:6-7). Elijah is fed by ravens (1Ki 17:6), by an angel (1Ki 19:1-8), increases the widow's meal and oil (1Ki 17:9-16; Lk 4:26), raises the widow's son (1Ki 17:17-24). Rain in answer to Elijah's prayer (1Ki 18:41-45). Elijah brings fire on Ahaziah's army (2Ki 1:10-12), divides Jordan (2Ki 2:8). Elijah's translation (2Ki 2:11).

Elisha divides Jordan (2Ki 2:14), sweetens the waters of Jericho (2Ki 2:19-22), increases a widow's oil (2Ki 4:1-7), raises the Shunammite's child (2Ki 4:18-37), renders the poisoned stew harmless (2Ki 4:38-41), feeds one hundred men (2Ki 4:42-44), cures Naaman (2Ki 5:1-19), strikes Gehazi with leprosy (2Ki 5:26-27), causes the ax to float (2Ki 6:6), reveals the counsel of the king of Syria (2Ki 6:12), causes the eyes of his servant to be opened (2Ki 6:17), strikes with blindness the army of the king of Syria (2Ki 6:18), the dead man restored to life (2Ki 13:21).

Destruction of Sennacherib's army (2Ki 19:35; Isa 37:36), return of the shadow on the stairway (2Ki 20:9-11), Hezekiah's cure (Isa 38:21), deliverance of Shadrach, Meshach, and Abednego (Da 3:23-27), of Daniel (Da 6:22), the sea calmed on Jonah being cast into it (Jnh 1:15), Jonah in the fish's belly (Jnh 1:17; 2:10), his plant (Jnh 4:6-7).

Surrounding the Birth of Jesus—
Conception by Elizabeth (Lk 1:18, 24-25). The incarnation of Jesus (Mt 1:18-25; Lk 1:26-80). The appearance of the star of Bethlehem (Mt 2:1-9). The deliverance of Jesus (Mt 2:13-23).

Of Jesus—
Water changed into wine (Jn 2:1-11). Heals the nobleman's son (Jn 4:46-54). Catch of fish (Lk 5:1-11). Heals the demoniac (Mk 1:23-26; Lk 4:33-36). Heals Peter's mother-in-law (Mt 8:14-17; Mk 1:29-31; Lk 4:38-39). Cleanses the leper (Mt 8:1-4; Mk 1:40-45; Lk 5:12-16). Heals the paralytic (Mt 9:1-8; Mk 2:1-12; Lk 5:17-26). Heals the crippled man (Jn 5:1-16). Restores the withered hand (Mt 12:9-13; Mk 3:1-5; Lk 6:6-11). Restores the centurion's servant (Mt 8:5-13; Lk 7:1-10). Raises the widow's son to life (Lk 7:11-16). Heals a demoniac (Mt 12:22-37; Mk 3:11; Lk

11:14-15). Stills the tempest (Mt 8:23-27; 14:32; Mk 4:35-41; Lk 8:22-25). Casts demons out of two men of Gadara (Mt 8:28-34; Mk 5:1-20; Lk 8:26-39). Raises from the dead the daughter of Jairus (Mt 9:18-19, 23-26; Mk 5:22-24, 35-43; Lk 8:41-42, 49-56). Cures the woman with the issue of blood (Mt 9:20-22; Mk 5:25-34; Lk 8:43-48). Restores two blind men to sight (Mt 9:27-31). Heals a demoniac (Mt 9:32-33). Feeds five thousand people (Mt 14:15-21; Mk 6:35-44; Lk 9:12-17; Jn 6:5-14). Walks on the sea (Mt 14:22-33; Mk 6:45-52; Jn 6:16-21). Heals the daughter of the Syrian Phoenician woman (Mt 15:21-28; Mk 7:24-30). Feeds four thousand people (Mt 15:32-39; Mk 8:1-9). Restores one deaf and mute (Mk 7:31-37). Restores a blind man (Mk 8:22-26). Restores a possessed child (Mt 17:14-21; Mk 9:14-29; Lk 9:37-43). Tribute money obtained from a fish's mouth (Mt 17:24-27). Restores ten lepers (Lk 17:11-19). Opens the eyes of a man born blind (Jn 9). Raises Lazarus from the dead (Jn 11:1-46). Heals the woman with the spirit of infirmity (Lk 13:10-17). Cures a man with dropsy (Lk 14:1-6). Restores two blind men near Jericho (Mt 20:29-34; Mk 10:46-52; Lk 18:35-43). Curses a fig tree (Mt 21:17-22; Mk 11:12-14, 20-24). Heals the ear of Malchus (Lk 22:49-51). Second catch of fish (Jn 21:6).

Of the Disciples of Jesus—
By the seventy-two (Lk 10:17-20), by other disciples (Mk 9:39; Jn 14:12), by the apostles (Ac 3:6, 12-13, 16; 4:10, 30; 9:34-35; 16:18). Peter cures the sick (Ac 5:15-16), Aeneas (Ac 9:34), raises Dorcas (Ac 9:40), announces the death of Ananias and Sapphira (Ac 5:5, 10). Peter and John cure a lame man (Ac 3:2-11). Peter and other apostles delivered from prison (Ac 5:19-23; 12:6-11; 16:26). Philip carried away by the Spirit (Ac 8:39). Paul strikes Elymas with blindness (Ac 13:11), heals a cripple (Ac 14:10), casts out evil spirits and cures sick (Ac 16:18; 19:11-12; 28:8-9), raises Eutychus to life (Ac 20:9-12), shakes a viper off his hand (Ac 28:5). Paul cured of blindness (Ac 9:3-6, 17-18).

Convincing Effect of, on:

The Israelites (Ex 4:28-31; 14:31; Nu 17:1-13). Pharaoh's servants (Ex 10:7). Pharaoh (Ex 10:16-17; 12:31-32). Egyptians (Ex 12:33; 1Sa 6:6). The Canaanites (Jos 2:9-11; 5:1). Gideon (Jdg 6:17-22, 36-40; 7:1). People who witnessed Elijah's (1Ki 18:24, 37-39). Naaman (2Ki 5:14-15). Nebuchadnezzar (Da 2:47; 3:28-29; 4:2-3). Darius (Da 6:20-27).

Simon Peter (Lk 5:4-11). Disciples of Jesus (Jn 2:11, 22-23; 20:30-31). The nobleman whose child Jesus healed (Jn 4:48-53). People who witnessed Christ's (Jn 7:31; 11:43-45; 12:10-11). People who witnessed Philip's (Ac 8:6). People who witnessed Peter's (Ac 9:32-42). Sergius Paulus, the deputy (Ac 13:8-12). Gentiles (Ro 15:18-19).

Resisted by the hard-hearted (Ne 9:17; Ps 78:10-32; Jn 9:24-28; 15:24-25).

Design of:

To reveal God (Ex 7:5, 17; 8:8-10, 22; 9:4-16, 29; 10:1-2; 14:4, 18; Dt 4:33-39; Jos 4:23-24; 1Ki 18:24, 37-39; Jer 32:20). Produce faith in God (Ex 14:31; Nu 14:11; Jos 3:7-17; 2Ch 7:1-3; Ps 106:9-12). Produce the fear of God (1Sa 12:17-18; Da 6:20-27; Jnh 1:14-16). Encourage obedience (Ex 16:4-6; 19:4-5; Dt 11:1-8; 29:1-9; Jdg 2:7; Ps 78:10-32). Glorify God (Lk 5:26; Jn 11:4; Ac 4:21-22). Testify to the messiahship of Jesus (Mt 11:2-5 w Lk 7:19-22; Mk 2:9-12; Lk 5:24-26; 18:42-43; Jn 2:11; 4:48; 5:36; 11:4, 40-42; 14:11; 15:24). Glorify Jesus (Ac 3:1-10, 12-13). Testify to God's servants (Ex 4:2-9; 19:9; Nu 16:28-35; 1Sa 12:17-18; Zec 2:9; Ac 2:22; Heb 2:4). Preserve the righteous (Da 3:28-29; 6:20-27). Change wicked purposes (Ex 3:19-20; 9:16-17; 10:16-17; 11:1-10; 12:29-33; 14:24-25).

Miraculous Gifts of the Spirit:

Foretold (Isa 35:4-6; Joel 2:28-29). Of different kinds (1Co 12:4-6). Enumerated (1Co 12:8-10, 28). Christ was endued with (Mt 12:28). Poured out on Pentecost (Ac 2:1-4). Communicated on preaching the gospel (Ac 10:44-46), by laying on of the apostles' hands (Ac 8:17-18; 19:6), for the confirmation of the gospel (Mk 16:20; Ac 14:3; Ro 15:19; Heb 2:4), for the edification of the church (1Co 12:7; 14:12-13). To be sought after (1Co 12:31; 14:1). Temporary nature of (1Co 13:8). Not to be neglected (1Ti 4:14; 2Ti 1:6), or despised (1Th 5:20), or purchased (Ac 8:20).

See Gifts From God, Spiritual.

MIRE [3226, 3431, 8347]. Figurative of distress (Ps 40:2; 69:2).

MIRIAM [5319] (variously *bitterness, plump one, the wished-for child, one who loves* or *is loved*).

1. Sister of Aaron and Moses; saved life of the baby Moses (Ex 2:4, 7-8), prophetess (Ex 15:20), criticized Moses for his marriage (Nu 12), buried at Kadesh (Nu 20:1).

2. Judahite (1Ch 4:17).

MIRMAH [5328] (*deceit*). A Benjamite (1Ch 8:10).

MIRROR [1663, 5262, 8023, 2269]. Ancient mirrors were made of polished metal (Ex 38:8; Job 37:18; 1Co 13:12; 2Co 3:18; Jas 1:23). *See Glass.*

MISCARRY [8897]. Of people, a judgment of God (Hos 9:14). Lack of in people and in animals, a sign of God's blessing (Ge 31:38; Ex 23:25-26; Job 21:10). *See Abortion.*

MISCEGENATION *See Intermarry.*

MISER (Ecc 4:7-8).

MISGAB NIV "stronghold"; a place otherwise unknown (Jer 48:1).

MISHAEL [4792, 10414] (*who belongs to God [El]?*).

1. A son of Uzziel, helps carry the bodies of Nadab and Abihu out of the camp (Ex 6:22; Lev 10:4).

2. A Jew who stood by Ezra when he read the law to the people (Ne 8:4).

3. Also called Meshach. *See Meshach.*

MISHAL [5398]. Levitical city in Asher (Jos 19:26; 21:30), also called Mashal (1Ch 6:74). *See Mashal.*

MISHAM [5471]. Son of Elpaal (1Ch 8:12).

MISHMA [5462] (*rumor*).

1. Son of Ishmael (Ge 25:14; 1Ch 1:30).

2. Of the tribe of Simeon (1Ch 4:25-26).

MISHMANNAH [5459] (*fatness*). A Gadite who joined David at Ziklag (1Ch 12:10).

MISHPAT *See En Mishpat.*

MISHRAITES [5490]. Clan of Kiriath Jearim in Judah (1Ch 2:53).

MISJUDGMENT Instances of: Of the Reubenites and Gadites (Nu 32:1-33; Jos 22:11-31). Of Hannah (1Sa 1:14-17).

See Accusation, False; Uncharitableness.

MISPAR [5032] (*number*). Coworker of Zerubbabel (Ezr 2:2). "Mispereth" (Ne 7:7).

MISPERETH [5033]. Also called Mizpar. A Jew who returned with Zerubbabel from Babylon (Ezr 2:2; Ne 7:7).

MISREPHOTH MAIM [5387] (*waters of Misrephoth [lime burning]*). Place near Sidon and Tyre (Jos 11:8; 13:6).

MISSIONARY JOURNEYS OF PAUL [1355].

I. The First Missionary Journey, c. A.D. 46-48 (Ac 13:1-14:28).
   A. Barnabas and Saul are Sent From Antioch (13:1-3).
   B. Ministry at Cyprus (13:4-13).
      1. Preaching in the synagogues (13:4-5).
      2. Controversy with Bar-Jesus (13:6-13).
   C. Ministry at Antioch (13:14-50).
      1. Paul preaches on first Sabbath (13:14-43).
      2. Paul preaches on second Sabbath (13:44-50).
   D. Ministry at Iconium (13:51-14:5).
   E. Ministry at Lystra (14:6-20).
      1. A lame man is healed (14:6-10).
      2. Paul and Barnabas are deified (14:11-18).
      3. Paul is stoned (14:19-20).
   F. Ministry on the Return Trip (14:21-25).
   G. Report on the First Missionary Journey (14:26-28).
II. The Jerusalem Council (15:1-35).

A. Debate Over Gentiles Keeping the Law
(15:1-5).
B. Peter Preaches Salvation Through Grace
(15:6-11).
C. Paul and Barnabas Testify (15:12).
D. James Proves Gentiles are Free From the
Law (15:13-21).
E. The Council Sends an Official Letter
(15:22-29).
F. Report to Antioch (15:30-35).
III. The Second Missionary Journey, c. A.D.
49-52 (Ac 15:36-18:22).
A. Contention Over John Mark (15:36-41).
B. Derbe and Lystra: Timothy is Circumcised
(16:1-5).
C. Troas: Macedonian Call (16:6-10).
D. Philippi: Extensive Ministry (16:11-40).
1. Lydia is converted (16:11-15).
2. Spirit of divination is cast out (16:16-24).
3. Philippian jailer is converted (16:25-34).
4. Paul is released from prison (16:35-40).
E. Thessalonica: "Turn the World Upside
Down" (17:1-9).
F. Berea: Many Receive the Word (17:10-15).
G. Athens: Paul's Sermon on Mars' Hill
(17:16-34).
H. Corinth: One-and-a-Half Years of Ministry
(18:1-17).
1. Paul works with Aquila and Priscilla
(18:1-3).
2. Jews reject Paul (18:4-6).
3. Crispus, the Gentile, is converted
(18:7-11).
4. Gallio will not try Paul (18:12-17).
I. Return Trip to Antioch (18:18-22).
IV. The Third Missionary Journey, c. A.D. 53-57
(Ac 18:23-21:16).
A. Galatia and Phrygia: Strengthening the
Disciples (18:23).
B. Ephesus: Three Years of Ministry
(18:24-19:41).
1. Apollos teaches effectively (18:24-28).
2. Disciples of John receive the Holy Spirit
(19:1-7).
3. Paul teaches in Tyrannus' school
(19:8-10).
4. Miracles are performed at Ephesus
(19:11-20).
5. Timothy and Erastus are sent to
Macedonia (19:21-22).
6. Demetrius causes uproar at Ephesus
(19:23-41).
C. Macedonia: Three Months of Ministry
(20:1-5).
D. Troas: Eutychus Falls From Loft (20:6-12).
E. Miletus: Paul Bids Farewell to Ephesian
Elders (20:13-38).
F. Tyre: Paul is Warned About Jerusalem
(21:1-6).
G. Caesarea: Agabus's Prediction (21:7-16).
V. The Trip to Rome, c. A.D. 57-59 (Ac
21:17-28:31).
A. Paul Witnesses in Jerusalem (21:17-23:33).
1. Paul conforms to Jewish customs
(21:17-26).
2. Paul's arrest (21:27-39).
3. Paul's defense before the crowd
(21:40-22:23).
4. Paul's defense before the centurion
(22:24-29).
5. Paul's defense before the Sanhedrin
(22:30-23:11).
6. Jews' plan to kill Paul (23:12-22).
7. Paul's rescue (23:23-33).
B. Paul's Witnesses in Caesarea (23:34-28:31).
1. Paul is tried before Felix (23:34-24:27).
2. Paul is tried before Festus (25:1-22).
3. Paul is tried before Agrippa
(25:23-26:32).
C. Paul Witnesses in Rome (27:1-28:31).
1. Paul's witness during the shipwreck
(27:1-44).
2. Paul's witness on Malta (28:1-15).
3. Paul's witness in Rome (28:16-31).
VI. The Fourth Missionary Journey, c. A.D. 62-68.

It is clear from Ac 13:1-21:17 that Paul went on
three missionary journeys. There is also reason to
believe that he made a fourth journey after his
release from the Roman imprisonment recorded in
Ac 28. The conclusion that such a journey did
indeed take place is based on: (1) Paul's declared
intention to go to Spain (Ro 15:24, 28), (2)
Eusebius's implication that Paul was released following his first Roman imprisonment (*Ecclesiastical History*, 2.22.2-3) and (3) statements in early
Christian literature that he took the gospel as far as
Spain (Clement of Rome, *Epistle to the Corinthians*, ch. 5; *Actus Petri Vercellenses*, chs. 1-3;
Muratorian Canon, lines 34-39).

The places Paul may have visited after his
release from prison are indicated by statements of
intention in his earlier writings and by subsequent
mention in the Pastoral Letters. The order of his
travel cannot be determined with certainty, but the
itinerary that follows seems likely.

1. Rome: released from prison in c. A.D. 62.
2. Spain: c. A.D. 62-64 (Ro 15:24, 28).
3. Crete: c. A.D. 64-65 (Tit 1:5).
4. Miletus: c. A.D. 65 (2Ti 4:20).
5. Colosse: c. A.D. 66 (Phm 22).
6. Ephesus: c. A.D. 66 (1Ti 1:3).
7. Philippi: c. A.D. 66 (Php 2:23-24; 1Ti 1:3).
8. Nicopolis: c. A.D. 66-67 (Tit 3:12).
9. Rome: c. A.D. 67.
10. Martyrdom: c. A.D. 67/68.
See Paul; Pastoral Epistles.

MISSIONS [*1355*]. Spreading the good
news throughout the world.

General:
Religious propagandism (2Ki 17:27-28; 1Ch
16:23-24). Commanded (Ps 96:3, 10; Mt 28:19;
Mk 16:15; Lk 24:47-48). Prophecy concerning
(Mt 24:14; Mk 13:10). Peter's vision concerning
(Ac 10:9-20).

Ordained by Jesus (Mt 24:14; 28:19; Mt 16:15-
16; Lk 24:47-49). Saul and Barnabas ordained for

(Ac 13:2-4, 47). Paul appointed to (Ac 26:14-18; 1Co 16:9). Practiced by the psalmist (Ps 18:49). Practiced by Jonah (Jnh 3:1-9). Symbolized by the flying angel (Rev 14:6-7).

Missionary hymn (Ps 96).

The first to do homage to the Messiah were Gentiles (Mt 2:11).

See Gentiles, Conversion of; Heathen; Jesus the Christ, King; Jesus the Christ, Kingdom of.

Missionaries, All Christians Should Be:

After the example of Christ (Ac 10:38). Women and children as well as men (Ps 8:2; Pr 31:26; Mt 21:15-16; Php 4:3; 1Ti 5:10; Tit 2:3-5; 1Pe 3:1). The zeal of idolaters should provoke to (Jer 7:18). The zeal of hypocrites should provoke to (Mt 23:15). An imperative duty (Jdg 5:23; Lk 19:40). The principle on which (2Co 5:14-15). However weak they may be (1Co 1:27). From their calling as saints (Ex 19:6; 1Pe 2:9). As faithful stewards (1Pe 4:10-11).

In youth (Ps 71:17; 148:12-13). In old age (Dt 32:7; Ps 71:18). In the family (Dt 6:7; Ps 78:5-8; Isa 38:19; 1Co 7:16; 1Pe 2:12). In first giving their own selves to the Lord (2Co 8:5). In declaring what God has done for them (Ps 66:16; 116:16-19). In hating one's life for Christ (Lk 14:26). In openly confessing Christ (Mt 10:32). In following Christ (Lk 14:27; 18:22). In preferring Christ above all relations (Lk 14:26; 1Co 2:2). In joyfully suffering for Christ (Heb 10:34). In forsaking all for Christ (Heb 10:34). In a holy example (Mt 5:16; Php 2:15; 1Th 1:7). In holy conduct (1Pe 2:12). In holy boldness (Ps 119:46). In dedicating themselves to the service of God (Jos 24:15; Ps 27:4). In devoting all property to God (1Ch 29:2-3, 14, 16; Ecc 11:1; Mt 6:19-20; Mk 12:44; Lk 12:33; 18:22, 28; Ac 2:45; 4:32-34).

In holy conversation (Ps 37:30, w Pr 10:31; Pr 15:7; Eph 4:29; Col 4:6). In talking of God and his works (Ps 71:24; 77:12; 119:27; 145:11-12). In showing forth God's praises (Isa 43:21).

In inviting others to embrace the gospel (Ps 34:8; Isa 2:3; Jn 1:46; 4:29). In seeking the edification of others (Ro 14:19; 15:2; 1Th 5:11). In admonishing others (1Th 5:14; 2Th 3:15). In reproving others (Lev 19:17; Eph 5:11). In teaching and exhorting (Ps 34:11; 51:13; Col 3:16; Heb 3:13; 10:25). In interceding for others (Col 4:3; Heb 13:18; Jas 5:16). In aiding ministers in their labors (Ro 16:3, 9; 2Co 11:9; Php 4:14-16; 3Jn 6). In giving a reason for their faith (Ex 12:26-27; Dt 6:20-21; 1Pe 3:15). In encouraging the weak (Isa 35:3-4; Ro 14:1; 15:1; 1Th 5:14). In visiting and relieving the poor and sick (Lev 25:35; Ps 112:9, w 2Co 9:9; Mt 25:36; Ac 20:35; Jas 1:27). With a willing heart (Ex 35:29; 1Ch 29:9, 14). With great generosity (Ex 36:5-7; 2Co 8:3).

Encouragement to (Pr 11:25, 30; 1Co 1:27; Jas 5:19-20). Blessedness of (Da 12:3). Illustrated (Mt 25:14; Lk 19:13).

See Minister.

MIST [6727, 874, 944, 3920].

1. Steamy vapor rising from the ground (Ge 2:6).

2. Dimness of vision (Ac 13:11).

3. Description of false teachers (2Pe 2:17).

MITE(S) *See Money; Penny.*

MITHCAH [5520] (*sweetness*). An encampment of the Israelites (Nu 33:28-29).

MITHNITE [5512]. Family name of Joshaphat (1Ch 11:43).

MITHRAISM Cult of Mithras, Persian sun-god, widely disseminated in the Roman Empire in the first century A.D.

MITHREDATH [5521] (*gift to [pagan deity] Mithra*).

1. Treasurer of Cyrus (Ezr 1:8).

2. A Persian officer who joined in writing a letter hostile to the Jews (Ezr 4:7).

MITRE *See Turban.*

MITYLENE [3639]. Capital of Lesbos. Paul visits (Ac 20:14-15).

MIXED MARRIAGE *See Intermarry.*

MIXED MULTITUDE Non-Israelites who traveled and associated with the Israelites (Nu 11:4-6; Ne 13:3).

MIZAR [5204] (*small*). A hill near Mt. Hermon (Ps 42:6).

MIZPAH [5206, 5207] (*lookout point*).

1. A city allotted to Benjamin (Jos 18:26). The Israelites assemble at (Jdg 20:1-3), and decree the penalty to be executed upon the Benjamites for their mistreatment of the Levite's concubine (Jdg 20:10). Assembled by Samuel that he might reprove them for their idolatry (1Sa 7:5). Crown Saul king of Israel at (1Sa 10:17-25). A judgment seat of Samuel (1Sa 7:16). Walled by Asa (1Ki 15:22; 2Ch 16:6). Temporarily the capital of the country after the Israelites had been carried away captive (2Ki 25:23, 25; Jer 40:6-15; 41:1-14). Captivity returned to (Ne 3:7, 15, 19).

2. A valley near Lebanon (Jos 11:3, 8).

3. A city in Moab. David gives his parents to the care of the king of (1Sa 22:3-4).

4. A city in the lowland of Judah (Jos 15:38).

5. A town in Gilead (Jos 10:17; Jdg 11:34). May be the location of a treaty between Jacob and Laban (Ge 31:48-49).

MIZPAR *See Mispar.*

MIZPEH *See Mizpah.*

MIZRAIM [5213] (Hebrew word for *Egypt*). Son of Ham (Ge 10:6, 13; 1Ch 1:8, 11), progenitor of the Egyptians, a people of N Africa, Hamitic people of Canaan.

MIZZAH [4645] (*terror*). Son of Reuel (Ge 36:13, 17; 1Ch 1:37).

MNASON [*3643*]. A native and Christian of Cyprus who entertained Paul (Ac 21:16).

MOAB [824+4566, 4565, 4566, 4566+8441, 4567] (*seed*).
1. Son of Lot (Ge 19:37).
2. Plains of. Israelites come in (Dt 2:17-18). Military forces numbered in (Nu 26:3, 63). The law rehearsed in, by Moses (Nu 35-36; Dt 29-33). The Israelites renew their covenant in (Dt 29:1). The land of promise allotted in (Jos 13:32).

MOABITE STONE Black basalt stele, two by four feet, inscribed by Mesha king of Moab, with thirty-four lines in the Moabite language (practically a dialect of Hebrew), giving his side of the story (2Ki 3).

MOABITE(S) [408+4566, 1201+4566, 4566, 4567]. Descendants of Lot through his son Moab (Ge 19:37). Called the people of Chemosh (Nu 21:29). The territory E of Jordan, bounded on the N by the Arnon River (Nu 21:13; Jdg 11:18). Israelites commanded not to distress the Moabites (Dt 2:9). Refuse passage of Jephthah's army through their territory (Jdg 11:17-18). Balak was king of (Nu 22:4), calls for Balaam to curse Israel (Nu 22-24; Jos 24:9; Mic 6:5). Are a snare to the Israelites (Nu 25:1-3; Ru 1:4; 1Ki 11:1; 1Ch 8:8; Ezr 9:1-2; Ne 13:23). Land of, not given to the Israelites as a possession (Dt 2:9, 29). David takes refuge among, from Saul (1Sa 22:3-4). David conquers (2Sa 8:2; 23:20; 1Ch 11:22; 18:2-11). Israelites had war with (2Ki 3:5-27; 13:20; 24:2; 2Ch 20). Prophecies concerning judgments upon (Jer 48).

MOADIAH [4598, 5050] (perhaps *Yahweh assembles* or *Yahweh promises*). A chief priest who returned from the Exile with Zerubbabel at the time of Joiakim (Ne 12:5, 17).

MOB [7736, *4062*, *4063*]. At Thessalonica (Ac 17:5), Jerusalem (Ac 21:28, 30), Ephesus (Ac 19:29-40).

MOCKING [*3070, 3075, 4329, 4352, 4370, 5593, 9511, 1850*]. Ishmael mocks Sarah (Ge 21:9). Elijah mocks the priests of Baal (1Ki 18:27). Zedekiah mocks Micaiah (1Ki 22:24). Children mock Elisha (2Ki 2:23). The tormentors of Job mock (Job 15:12; 30:1). The persecutors of Jesus mock him (Mt 26:67-68; 27:28-31, 39-44; Mk 10:34; 14:65; 15:17-20, 29-32; Lk 23:11; Jn 19:2-3, 5; 1Pe 2:23). The Ammonites mock God (Eze 25:3). Tyre mocks Jerusalem (Eze 26:2). The wicked mock (Isa 28:15, 22; 2Pe 3:3).
   See *Scoffing*.
   Figurative (Ecc 7:16; 1Co 7:31).

MODESTY [*2362*]. Of women (1Ti 2:9).
   Instances of: Moses (Nu 12:3). Saul (1Sa 9:21). Vashti (Est 1:11-12). Elihu (Job 32:4-7).
   See *Humility*.

MOLADAH [4579] (*generation*). Town c. ten miles E of Beersheba (Ne 11:26).

MOLDING [2425] (*wreath* or *border*). (Job 28:2; Eze 24:11). The decorative ledge of gold around the ark of the covenant (Ex 25:11; 37:2), the table (Ex 25:24-25; 37:11-12), and the incense altar (Ex 30:3-4; 37:26-27). Of images (Ex 32:4, 8; 34:17; Lev 19:4; Dt 9:12), pillars (1Ki 7:15), bronze Sea (1Ki 7:23), done in the plain of Jordan (1Ki 7:46; 2Ch 4:17), mirrors (Job 37:18).

MOLECH [4891, 4903, 4904, *3661*] (*"shameful" king*) Molech is the deliberate mis-vocalization of the name of a pagan god. The consonants for the word king, *melek*, are combined with the vowels for shame, *bosheth*.
   An idol of the Ammonites (Ac 7:43). Worshiped by the wives of Solomon, and by Solomon (1Ki 11:1-8). Children sacrificed to (2Ki 23:10, w Jer 32:35; 2Ki 16:3; 21:6; 2Ch 28:3; Isa 57:5; Jer 7:31; Eze 16:20-21; 20:26, 31; 23:37, 39, w Lev 18:21; 20:2-5). See *Malcam, 2*.

MOLE(S) NIV "chameleon" (Lev 11:30), "rodent" (Isa 2:20). See *Animals; Chameleon*.

MOLID [4582] (*descendant*). A descendant of Judah, the son of Abishur and his wife Abihail (1Ch 2:29).

MOLTEN IMAGE See *Tabernacle*.

MONARCHY Described by Samuel (1Sa 8:11-18). See *Government; Kings*.

MONEY [*4084, 10362, 736, 921, 2238, 3142, 3440, 5507, 5910, 5975*]. Silver used as (Ge 17:12-13, 23, 27; 20:16; 23:9, 13; 31:15; 37:28; 42:25-35; 43:12-23; 44:1-8; 47:14-18; Ex 12:44; 21:11, 21, 34-35; 22:7, 17, 25; 30:16; Lev 22:11; 25:37, 51; 27:15, 18; Nu 3:48-51; 18:16; Dt 2:6, 28; 14:25-26; 21:14; 23:19; Jdg 5:19; 16:18; 17:4; 1Ki 21:2, 6, 15; 2Ki 5:26; 12:4, 7-16; 15:20; 22:7, 9; 23:35; 2Ch 24:5, 11, 14; 34:9, 14, 17; Ezr 3:7; 7:7; Ne 5:4, 10-11; Est 4:7; Job 31:39; Ps 15:5; Pr 7:20; Ecc 7:12; 10:19; Isa 43:24; 52:3; 55:1-2; Jer 32:9-10, 25, 44; La 5:4; Mic 3:11; Mt 25:18, 27; 28:12, 15; Mk 14:11; Lk 9:3; 19:15, 23; 22:5; Ac 7:16; 8:20).
   Gold used as (Ge 13:2; 24:35; 44:8, w 44:1; 1Ch 21:25; Ezr 8:25-27; Isa 13:17; 46:6; 60:9; Eze 7:19; 28:4; Mt 2:11; 10:9; Ac 3:6; 20:33; 1Pe 1:18).
   Copper used as (Mt 10:9; Mk 6:8; 12:42; Lk 21:2).
   Weighed (Ge 23:16; 43:21; Job 28:15; Jer 32:9-10; Zec 11:12). Image on (Mt 22:20-21). Conscience (Jdg 17:2; Mt 27:3, 5). Ransom atonement (Ex 30:12-16; Lev 5:15-16). Sin offering (2Ki 12:16). Value of, varied corruptly (Am 8:5). Love of, the root of evil (1Ti 6:10). See *Materialism*.
   See *Daric; Drachma; Gerah; Penny; Pound; Shekel; Silver; Talent*.

MONEY CHANGERS [3142]. Those
who changed foreign currency into sanctuary
money at a profit (Mt 21:12; Mk 11:15; Jn 2:14-
15).

MONITOR LIZARD [3947]. Unclean for
food (Lev 11:30). See Animals.

MONOPOLY Of lands (Isa 5:8; Mic 2:2),
by Pharaoh (Ge 47:19-26), of food (Pr 11:26).

MONOTHEISM (one God). Belief that
there is but one God.

MONSTERS [9490]. See Animals; Behemoth; Leviathan; Serpent.

MONTH [2544, 3732, 10333, 3604, 5485,
5564]. Sun and moon for signs and seasons (Ge
1:14). The beginning and ending of the Flood (Ge
7:11; 8:4).

Twelve months reckoned to a year (1Ki 4:7; 1Ch
27:1-15; Est 2:12). Time computed by months (Ge
29:14; Nu 10:10; Jdg 11:37; 1Sa 6:1; Ps 81:3; Rev
22:2). Months in prophecy (Rev 11:2).

1. Abib (Post-Exilic name: **Nisan**)
March-April
Month 7 in civil sequence. The Jewish calendar
began with (Ex 12:2; 13:4; Dt 16:1). Passover
instituted and celebrated in (Ex 12:1-28; 23:15).
Israelites left Egypt in (Ex 13:4). Tabernacle set
up in (Ex 40:2, 17). Israelites arrive at Zin in (Nu
20:1). Cross Jordan in (Jos 4:19). Jordan overflows
in (1Ch 12:15). After the Captivity called
Nisan (Ne 2:1; Est 3:7). Decree to put the Jews to
death in (Est 3:12). The death of Jesus in (Mt
26:27).

Season: Spring; Later rains.

Agriculture: Barley and flax harvest begin.

Feasts: 14th, Passover (Ex 12:18; Lev 23:5);
15-21st, Unleavened Bread (Lev 23:6); 16th,
Firstfruits (Lev 23:10f).

2. Ziv (Post-Exilic name: **Iyyar**) **April-May**
Month 8 in civil sequence. Israel numbered in
(Nu 1:1, 18). Passover to be observed in, by the
unclean and others who could not observe it in the
first month (Nu 9:10-11). Israel departed from the
wilderness of Zin in (Nu 10:11). Temple begun in
(1Ki 6:1; 2Ch 3:2). An irregular Passover
celebrated in (2Ch 30:1-27). Rebuilding of the
temple begun in (Ezr 3:8).

Season: Dry season begins.

Agriculture: Barley harvest.

Feasts: 14th, Later Passover (Nu 9:10-11).

3. Sivan (Post-Exilic name) **May-June**
Month 9 in civil sequence. Asa renews the covenant
of himself and people in (2Ch 15:10).

Agriculture: Early figs ripen; Wheat harvest.

Feasts: 6th, Pentecost or Feast of Weeks (Lev
23:15ff); Harvest.

4. Tammuz (Post-Exilic name) **June-July**
Month 10 in civil sequence. The number only

appears in the Bible. Jerusalem taken by Nebuchadnezzar
in (Jer 39:2; 52:6-7).

Agriculture: Tending vines.

Feasts: None.

5. Ab (Post-Exilic name) **July-August**
Month 11 in civil sequence. Number only mentioned.
Aaron died on the first day of (Nu 33:38).
Temple destroyed in (2Ki 25:8-10; Jer 1:3; 52:12-
30). Ezra arrived at Jerusalem in (Ezr 7:8-9).

Agriculture: Ripening of grapes, figs, and olives.

Feasts: None.

6. Elul (Post-Exilic name)
August-September
Month 12 in civil sequence. Wall of Jerusalem
finished in (Ne 6:15). Temple built in (Hag 1:14-
15).

Agriculture: Processing grapes, dates, summer
figs, and olives.

Feasts: None.

7. Ethanim (Post-Exilic name: **Tishri**)
September-October
Month 1 in civil sequence. Feasts held in (Lev
23:24, 27; Ne 8:13-15). Jubilee proclaimed in
(Lev 25:9). Solomon's temple dedicated in (1Ki
8:2). Altar rebuilt and offerings renewed in (Ezr
3:1, 6).

Season: Autumn (early) rains begin.

Agriculture: Plowing.

Feasts: 1st, Trumpets (Nu 29:1; Lev 23:24);
10th, Atonement (Le 16:29ff; 23:27ff); 15-21st,
Tabernacles or Booths (Lev 23:34ff); 22nd,
Solemn assembly (Lev 23:36).

8. Bul (Post-Exilic name: **Marcheshvan**)
October-November
Month 2 in civil sequence. The temple finished
in (1Ki 6:38). Jeroboam's idolatrous feast in (1Ki
12:32-33; 1Ch 27:11).

Season: Plowing.

Agriculture: Winter figs; sowing of wheat and
barley.

Feasts: None.

9. Kislev (Post-Exilic name)
November-December
Month 3 in civil sequence.

Agriculture: Sowing.

Feasts: 25th, Hanukkah or Dedication (1Mc
4:52f; Jn 10:22).

10. Tebeth (Post-Exilic name)
December-January
Month 4 in civil sequence. Nebuchadnezzar besieges
Jerusalem in (2Ki 25:1; Jer 52:4). Esther
chosen queen (Est 2:16).

Season: Winter rains begin (snow on high
ground).

Agriculture: None.

Feasts: None.

11. Shebat (Post-Exilic name)
January-February
Month 5 in civil sequence. Moses probably died
in (Dt 1:3).

Agriculture: None.

Feasts: None.

12. Adar (Post-Exilic name)
February-March
Month 6 in civil sequence. Second temple finished in (Ezr 6:15). Feast of Purim (Est 9:1-26).
Agriculture: Almond trees bloom; citrus fruit harvest.
Feasts: Purim.

13. Adar Sheni (not in Bible)
Second Adar is an intercalary month added about every three years so the lunar calendar would correspond to the solar year.
See Calendar; Time. See also each month by name.

MONUMENT [3338, 5167, 5893]. *See Pillar.*

MOON [2544, 3732, 3734, 4057, 4244, 4401, *3741, 4943*]. Created by God (Ge 1:16; Ps 8:3; 136:7-9). Its light (Job 31:26; Ecc 12:2; SS 6:10; Jer 31:35; 1Co 15:41). Its influences (Dt 33:14; Ps 121:6). Seasons of (months) (Ps 104:19). Joseph's dream concerning (Ge 37:9). Stand still (Jos 10:12-13; Hab 3:11). Worship of, forbidden (Dt 4:19; 17:3). Worshiped (2Ki 23:5; Job 31:26-27; Jer 7:18; 8:2; 44:17-19, 25). No light of, in eternity (Rev 21:23).

Figurative:
Shining of (Isa 30:26; 60:19; Rev 21:23). Darkening of (Job 25:5; Isa 13:10; 24:23; Eze 32:7; Joel 2:10, 31; 3:15; Mt 24:29; Mk 13:24; Lk 21:25; Ac 2:20; Rev 6:12; 8:12).

Symbolic: (Rev 12:1).

Feast of the New Moon:
(Nu 10:10; 28:11-15; 1Ch 23:31; 2Ch 31:3; Ezr 3:5). Trade at time of, prohibited (Am 8:5).

MORAL AGENCY *See Contingencies.*

MORAL LAW *See Law.*

MORALITY *See Duty of People to People; Integrity; Neighbor.*

MORASTHITE *See Moresheth.*

MORDECAI [5283] (*pagan Babylonian god Marduk*). A Jewish captive in Persia (Est 2:5-6). Foster father of Esther (Est 2:7). Informs Xerxes of a conspiracy against his life, and is rewarded (Est 2:21-23; 6:1-11). Promoted in Haman's place (Est 8:1-2, 15; 10:1-3). Intercedes with Xerxes for the Jews; establishes the festival of Purim in commemoration of their deliverance (Est 8-9).

MOREH [4622] (*[place of] instructor*).
1. A plain near Shechem and Gilgal (Ge 12:6; Dt 11:30).
2. A hill in the plain of Jezreel where the Midianites encamped (Jdg 7:1, 12).

MORESHETH [4629] (*possession of*

Gath). Hometown of Micah; probably Moresheth Gath (Jer 26:18; Mic 1:1).

MORESHETH GATH [4628] (*possession of Gath*). Town c. five miles W of Gath in the Shephelah (Mic 1:14). *See Moresheth.*

MORIAH [5317]. Place to which Abraham to offer up Isaac (Ge 22:2). Solomon built temple on Mt. Moriah (2Ch 3:1), but it is not certain whether it is the same place.

MORNING [*1332, 5974, 6727, 8840, 8899, 4745, 4746, 4748, 5892*]. The second part of the day at the Creation (Ge 1:5, 8, 13, 19, 23, 31). The first part of the natural day (Mk 16:2). Ordained by God (Job 38:12). Began with first dawn (Jos 6:15; Ps 119:147). Continued until noon (1Ki 18:26; Ne 8:3). Dawning of calls for rejoicing (Ps 65:8).

The Jews:
Generally rose early in (Ge 28:18; Jdg 6:28). Eat but little in (Ecc 10:16). Went to the temple in (Lk 21:38; Jn 8:2). Offered a part of the daily sacrifice in (Ex 29:38-39; Nu 28:4-7). Devoted a part of to prayer and praise (Ps 5:3; 59:16; 88:13). Gathered the manna in (Ex 16:21). Began their journeys in (Ge 22:3). Held courts of justice in (Jer 21:12; Mt 27:1). Contracted covenants in (Ge 26:31). Transacted business in (Ecc 11:6; Mt 20:1). Was frequently cloudless (2Sa 23:4). A red sky in, a sign of bad weather (Mt 16:3). Ushered in by the morning stars (Job 38:7).

Illustrative:
Of the resurrection day (Ps 49:14). Breaking forth, of the glory of the church (SS 6:10; Isa 58:8). Star of, of the glory of Christ (Rev 22:16). Star of, of reward of saints (Rev 2:28). Clouds in, of the short-lived profession of hypocrites (Hos 6:4). Wings of, of rapid movements (Ps 139:9). Spread upon the mountains, of heavy calamities (Joel 2:2).

MORNING SACRIFICE *See Offerings.*

MORNING STAR [2122, *843, 5892*]. Figurative of the glory of the king of Babylon (Isa 14:12). Of Jesus (2Pe 1:19; Rev 2:26; 22:16).

MORSEL [4269]. A choice bit of food (Pr 18:8; 26:22).

MORTAL, MORTALITY [132, 632, 928+5883, 1414, 4637, 8358, *2570, 5778*]. A mortal is a being subject to death (Ro 8:11; 1Co 15:53-54).

MORTAR [2817, 4521, 4847].
1. An instrument for crushing grain (Nu 11:8; Pr 27:22). *See Grinding; Mill.*
2. A cement (Ex 1:14). Tar used as, in building tower of Babel (Ge 11:3). Used to plaster houses (Lev 14:42-45). Untempered, not enduring (Eze

13:10-15; 22:28). To be trodden to make firm (Na 3:14).

Figurative (Isa 41:25).

MORTGAGE (*take on pledge, give in pledge, exchange*). On land (Ne 5:3). *See Land.*

MORTIFICATION (*self-denial*). Instances of: David's ambassadors, sent to Hanun (2Sa 10:1-5). Judas (Mt 27:3-5). *See Humility.*

MOSAIC [8367]. Picture or design made by setting tiny squares or cones of varicolored marble, limestone, or semiprecious stones in some medium such as plaster to tell a story or to form a decoration (Est 1:6).

MOSERAH [4594] (*possession*). An encampment of the Israelites where Aaron died (Dt 10:6). Probably identical with Moseroth, below.

MOSEROTH [5035] (*possession*). An encampment of the Israelites (Nu 33:30-31).

MOSES [5407, 10441, *3707*] (*drawn out* Ex 2:10; Egyptian for *son*).

Personal History:

A Levite and son of Amram (Ex 2:1-4; 6:20; Ac 7:20; Heb 11:23). Hidden in an basket (Ex 2:3). Discovered and adopted by the daughter of Pharaoh (Ex 2:5-10). Learned in all the wisdom of Egypt (Ac 7:22). His loyalty to his race (Heb 11:24-26). Takes the life of an Egyptian; flees from Egypt; finds refuge among the Midianites (Ex 2:11-22; Ac 7:24-29). Joins himself to Jethro, priest of Midian; marries Jethro's daughter Zipporah; has two sons (Ex 2:15-22; 18:3-4). Is herdsman for Jethro in the desert of Horeb (Ex 3:1). Has the vision of the burning bush (Ex 3:2-6). God reveals to him his purpose to deliver the Israelites and bring them into the land of Canaan (Ex 3:7-10). Commissioned as a leader of the Israelites (Ex 3:10-22; 6:13). His rod miraculously turned into a serpent, his hand made leprous, and each restored (Ex 4:1-9, 28). With his wife and sons leaves Jethro to perform his mission (Ex 4:18-20). His controversy with his wife on account of circumcision (Ex 4:20-26). Meets Aaron in the wilderness (Ex 4:27-28).

With Aaron assembles the leaders of Israel (Ex 4:29-31). With Aaron goes before Pharaoh, in the name of Yahweh demands the liberties of his people (Ex 5:1). Rejected by Pharaoh; hardships of the Israelites increased (Ex 5). People murmur against Moses and Aaron (Ex 5:20-21; 15:24; 16:2-3; 17:2-3; Nu 14:2-4; 16:41; 20:2-5; 21:4-6; Dt 1:12, 26-28). *See Israel.* Receives comfort and assurance from the land (Ex 6:1-8). Unbelief of the people (Ex 6:9). Renews his appeal to Pharaoh (Ex 6:11). Under divine direction brings plagues upon the land of Egypt (Ex 7-12). Secures the deliverance of the people and leads them out of Egypt (Ex 13). Crosses the Red Sea; Pharaoh and his army are destroyed (Ex 14). Composes a song for the Israelites on their deliverance from Pha-

raoh (Ex 15). Joined by his family in the wilderness (Ex 18:1-12).

Institutes a system of government (Ex 18:13-26; Nu 11:16-30; Dt 1:9-18). Receives the law and ordains various statutes. *See Law of Moses.* Face of, transfigured (Ex 34:29-35; 2Co 3:13). Sets up the tabernacle. *See Tabernacle.* Reproves Aaron for making the golden calf (Ex 32:22-23), for irregularity in the offerings (Lev 10:16-20). Jealousy of Aaron and Miriam toward (Nu 12). Rebellion of Korah, Dathan, and Abiram against (Nu 16). Appoints Joshua as his successor (Nu 27:22-23; Dt 31:7-8, 14, 23; 34:9).

Not permitted to enter Canaan, but views the land from the top of Pisgah (Nu 27:12-14; Dt 3:17; 3:23-29; 32:48-52; 34:1-8). Death and burial of (Nu 31:2; Dt 32:50; 34:1-6). Body of, disputed over (Jude 9). 120 years old at death (Dt 31:2). Mourning for, thirty days in the plains of Moab (Dt 34:8). His virility (Dt 31:2; 34:7).

Present with Jesus on the Mount of Transfiguration (Mt 17:3-4; Mk 9:4; Lk 9:30).

Type of Christ (Dt 18:15-18; Ac 3:22; 7:37).

Benedictions of:

Upon the people (Lev 9:23; Nu 10:35-36; Dt 1:11). Last benediction upon the tribes (Dt 33).

Character of:

Murmurings of (Ex 5:22-23; Nu 11:10-15). Impatience of (Ex 5:22-23; 6:12; 32:19; Nu 11:10-15; 16:15; 20:10; 31:14). Respected and feared (Ex 33:8). Faith of (Nu 10:29; Dt 9:1-3; Heb 11:23-28). Called the man of God (Dt 33:1). God spoke to, as a man to his friend (Ex 33:11). Magnified of (Ex 19:9; Nu 14:12-20; Dt 9:13-29, w Ex 32:30). Magnanimity of, toward Eldad and Medad (Nu 11:29). Meekness of (Ex 14:13-14; 15:24-25; 16:2-3, 7-8; Nu 12:3; 16:4-11). Obedience of (Ex 7:6; 40:16, 19, 21). Unaspiring (Nu 14:12-20; Dt 9:13-29, w Ex 32:30).

Intercessory Prayers of: *See Intercession, Instances of; Intercession, Solicited; Intercession, Answered, .*

Miracles of: *See Miracles.*

Prophecies of:

(Ex 3:10; 4:5, 11-12; 6:13; 7:2; 17:16; 19:3-9; 33:11; Nu 11:17; 12:7-8; 36:13; Dt 1:3; 5:31; 18:15, 18; 34:10, 12; Hos 12:13; Mk 7:9-10; Ac 7:37-38).

MOSES, ASSUMPTION OF

Pseudonymous Jewish apocalyptic book, probably written early in the early first century A.D.; gives prophecy of future of Israel. Possibly quoted in Jude 9.

MOSES, LAW OF *See Law.*

MOST HIGH [6583, 6604, 6610, 10546, 10548, *5736*]. Title of God (Ge 14:18-19, 20, 22; Ps 7:17). *See God, Names of, Elyon.*

MOST HOLY PLACE *See Holy of Holies.*

MOTE *See Speck.*

MOTH [6931, *1181+4963, 4962*]. An insect (Job 4:19; 27:18; Ps 39:11). Destructive of garments (Job 13:28; Isa 50:9; 51:8; Hos 5:12). Figurative (Mt 6:19-20; Jas 5:2).

MOTHER [562, 851, 1485, 3528, *298, 1222, 1666, 3120, 3613, 3836, 5577*].

Relationship With:

Reverence for, commanded (Ex 20:12; Lev 19:3; Dt 5:16; Pr 23:22; Mt 15:4; 19:19; Mk 7:10; 10:19; Lk 18:20; Eph 6:2). To be obeyed (Dt 21:18; Pr 1:8; 6:20). Love for (1Ki 19:20). Must be subordinate to love for Christ (Mt 10:37).—Dishonoring of, to be punished (Ex 21:15; Lev 20:9; Pr 20:20; 28:24; 30:11, 17; Mt 15:4-6; Mk 7:10-12). Incest with, forbidden (Lev 18:7).

Sanctifying influence of (1Co 7:14; 2Ti 1:5). Wicked (Ge 27:6-17; 2Ki 11:1-3).

Love of:

(Isa 49:15; 66:13). Exemplified by: Hagar (Ge 21:14-16). The mother of Moses (Ex 2:1-3). Hannah (1Sa 1:20-28). Rizpah (2Sa 21:8-11). Bathsheba (1Ki 1:16-21). The mother whose child was brought to Solomon (1Ki 3:16-26). The woman whose sons were to be taken for debt (2Ki 4:1-7). The Shunammite (2Ki 4:18-37). Mary the mother of Jesus (Lk 2:41-50). The bereaved mothers of Bethlehem (Mt 2:16-18). The Syrian Phoenician woman (Mt 15:21-28; Mk 7:24-30).

Grieves over wayward children (Pr 10:1; 19:26; 29:15). Rejoices over good children (Pr 23:23-25).

MOTHER-IN-LAW [2792, 3165, *4289*]. Not to be defiled (Lev 18:17; 20:14; Dt 27:23). Conflict with (Mic 7:6; Mt 10:35). Beloved by Ruth (Ru 1:14-17). Peter's, healed by Jesus (Mk 1:30-31).

MOTIVE [3671, 8120, *1087, 4733*]. Ascribed to God (Ps 106:8; Eze 36:21-22, 32). Right, required (Mt 6:1-18). Sinful, illustrated by Cain (Ge 4:7; 1Jn 3:12).

Misunderstood: The tribes of Reuben and Gad, in asking inheritance E of Jordan (Nu 32:1-33), when they built the memorial (Jos 22:9-34). David's, by King Hanun (2Sa 10:2-3; 1Ch 19:3-4). The king of Syria, in sending presents to the king of Israel by Naaman (2Ki 5:5-7). Job in his righteousness (Job 1:9-11; 2:4-5).

MOTTO *See Inscriptions.*

MOUNT EPHRAIM *See Ephraim.*

MOUNT OF BEATITUDES Site of the Sermon on the Mount (Mt 5-7), exact location unknown. *See Beatitudes; Hattin, Horns of; Sermon on the Mount.*

MOUNTAIN [844, 850, 2065, 2215, 2378, 6152, 7600, 10296, *4001*]. Melted (Ps 97:5; Dt 4:11; 5:23; Jdg 5:5; Isa 64:1-3; Mic 1:4; Na 1:5).

Overturning and removing of (Job 9:5; 14:18; 28:9; Eze 38:20), by faith (Mt 17:20; 21:21; Mk 11:23). Abraham offers Isaac upon Mount Zion, the site of the temple (Ge 22:2). *See Zion.* Horeb appointed as a place for the Israelites to worship (Ex 3:12). Signals from (Isa 13:2; 18:3; 30:17). Used for idolatrous worship (Dt 12:2; 1Sa 10:5; 1Ki 14:23; Jer 3:6; Hos 4:13).

Jesus tempted upon (Mt 4:8; Lk 4:5). Jesus preaches from (Mt 5:1). Jesus goes up into, for prayer (Mt 14:23; Lk 6:12; 9:28), is transfigured upon (Mt 17:1-9; Mk 9:2-10; Lk 9:28-36), meets his disciples on, after his resurrection (Mt 28:16-17).

Burning mountains. *See Volcanoes.*

MOURNING [*61, 63, 65, 1134, 5027, 5631, 5653, 6199, 7722, 9302, *4292, 4291, 3081, 3164*].

For the Dead:

Head uncovered (Lev 10:6; 21:10), lying on the ground (2Sa 12:16), personal appearance neglected (2Sa 14:2), cutting the flesh (Lev 19:28; 21:1-5; Dt 14:1; Jer 16:6-7; 41:5), lamentations (Ge 50:10; Ex 12:30; 1Sa 30:4; Jer 22:18; Mt 2:17-18), fasting (1Sa 31:13; 2Sa 1:12; 3:35). Priests prohibited, except for nearest of kin (Lev 21:1-11). For Nadab and Abihu forbidden (Lev 10:6). Sexes separated in (Zec 12:12, 14).

Hired mourners (2Ch 35:25; Ecc 12:5; Jer 9:17; Mt 9:23).

Abraham mourned for Sarah (Ge 23:2), Egyptians, for Jacob seventy days (Ge 50:1-3), Israelites, for Aaron thirty days (Nu 20:29).

David's lamentations over the death of Saul and his sons (2Sa 1:17-27), the death of Abner (2Sa 3:33-34), the death of Absalom (2Sa 18:33).

Jeremiah and the singing men and singing women lament for Josiah (2Ch 35:25).

For Calamities and Other Sorrows:

Tearing the garments (Ge 37:29, 34; 44:13; Nu 14:6; Jdg 11:35; 2Sa 1:2, 11; 3:31; 13:19, 31; 15:32; 2Ki 2:12; 5:8; 6:30; 11:14; 19:1; 22:11, 19; Ezr 9:3, 5; Job 1:20; 2:12; Isa 37:1; Jer 41:5; Mt 26:65; Ac 14:14). Wearing mourning dress (Ge 38:14; 2Sa 14:2). *See Sackcloth.* Cutting or plucking off the hair and beard (Ezr 9:3; Jer 7:29). *See Baldness.* Covering the head and face (2Sa 15:30; 19:4; Est 6:12; Jer 14:3-4), and the upper lip (Lev 13:45; Eze 24:17, 22; Mic 3:7). Laying aside ornaments (Ex 33:4, 6). Walking barefoot (2Sa 15:30; Isa 20:2). Laying the hand on the head (2Sa 13:19; Jer 2:37). Ashes put on the head (Eze 27:30). Dust on the head (Jos 7:6). Dressing in black (Jer 14:2). Sitting on the ground (Isa 3:26).

Caused ceremonial defilement (Nu 19:11-16; 31:19; Lev 21:1). Prevented offerings from being accepted (Dt 26:14; Hos 9:4).

See Elegy.

MOUSE *See Rat(s).*

MOUTH [1744, 2674, 4498, 4918, 7023, 7156, 7339, 7895, 8557, 10588, *930, 931, 3364,*

5125, 5779]. Has various connotations: literal mouth, language, opening; sometimes personified (Ps 119:108; Pr 15:14; Rev 19:15).

MOWING [1600, 286]. This was done by hand with a short sickle—originally of flint, later of metal (Ps 72:6; Jas 5:4). The king's share were the portion of the harvest taken as taxes (Am 7:1).

MOZA [4605] (sunrise).
1. A son of Caleb (1Ch 2:46).
2. A Benjamite (1Ch 8:36-37; 9:42-43).

MOZAH [5173]. A Benjamite city (Jos 18:26).

MUFFLER See Veil.

MULBERRY TREE [5189]. (Lk 17:6).

MULE [7234, 7235]. Uses of: For royal riders (2Sa 13:29; 18:9; 1Ki 1:33, 38), by saints in Isaiah's prophetic vision of the kingdom of Christ (Isa 66:20), as pack animals (2Ki 5:17; 1Ch 12:40). Tribute paid in (1Ki 10:25). Used in barter (Eze 27:14), by the exiles returning from Babylon (Ezr 2:66; Ne 7:68), in war (Zec 14:15).

MULTITUDE FED Miraculously (Ex 16:13; Nu 11:31; 2Ki 4:43; Mt 14:21; 15:38).

MUMMIFICATION See Embalming.

MUNITIONS Fortifications (Na 2:1).

MUPPIM [5137]. Son or descendant of Benjamin (Ge 46:21). Called Shupham (Nu 26:39) and Shuppim (1Ch 7:12, 15). Shephuphan may be the same person (1Ch 8:5).

MURDER [1947, 2222, 4637, 5782, 8357, 5377, 5838, 5839, 5840]. Forbidden on penalty of death (Ge 9:4-6; Ex 21:14; Lev 24:17; Dt 19:11-13), a murdered man's nearest relative had the duty to pursue the slayer and kill him (Nu 35:19), but the slayer could flee to a city of refuge, where he would be tried and then either turned over to the avenger or be protected (Nu 35:9-34; Dt 19:1-10). See Homicide; Infanticide; Regicide.

MURMURING See Grumbling.

MURRAIN A plague of Egypt (Ex 9:3, 6; Ps 78:50).

MUSHI, MUSHITE(S) [4633, 4634]. Merarite Levite; progenitor of Mushites (Ex 6:19; Nu 3:20; 26:58; 1Ch 6:19, 47; 23:21, 23).

MUSIC [2369, 2376, 2379, 2727, 4944, 5593, 5904, 7754, 8877, 9512, 10233, 5246, 5889, 6010].
Used:
At the crowning of kings (1Ki 1:39-40; 2Ch 23:13, 18). In national triumphs (Ex 15:1-21; Nu 21:17-18; Jdg 5:1-31; Jdg 11:34; 1Sa 18:6-7). In worship (1Ch 6:31-32; 15:16-22, 24, 27-28; 16:4-42; 23:5; 25:1-7; 2Ch 5:12-13; 20:19, 21-22, 28;

29:25-30; 35:15; Ezr 2:64-65; 3:10-11; Ne 12:27-47; Ps 33:1-3; 68:4, 25-26, 32; 81:1-3; 87:7; 92:1-3; 95:1-2; 98:1-8; 104:33; 105:2; 135:1-3; 144:9; 149:1-3, 6; 150:1-6; Mk 14:26; 1Co 14:15; Eph 5:19; Col 3:16; Heb 2:12). At the offering of sacrifices (2Ch 29:27-28). In idolatrous worship (Da 3:4-7, 10, 15). For dancing (Mt 11:17). In joy (Ge 31:27; 2Sa 19:35; Job 21:12; Ecc 2:8; Isa 5:12). In revelry (Am 5:12; 6:5). In mourning (2Ch 35:25). In preparing for funerals (Mt 9:23).

Refrained from in sorrow (Job 30:31; Pr 25:20; Isa 16:10; 24:8-9; Eze 26:13; Rev 18:22). Captive Jews refrained from (Ps 137:1-4).

Teachers of (1Ch 15:22; 25:7-8; 2Ch 23:13). Physical effect of, on people (1Sa 16:15-16, 23; Eze 33:32). Choir director (Ne 12:42). Chief musician (Ne 12:42; Hab 3:19). Chambers for musicians in the temple (Eze 40:44). In heaven (Rev 5:8-9; 14:2-3; 15:2-3).

Allegorical (Rev 5:8-9; 14:2-3; 15:2-3; 18:22). Symbolic of judgment (Isa 23:16). Of God's emotions (Isa 30:29, 32; Jer 31:4).

Instruments of:
Invented by Jubal (Ge 4:21), David (1Ch 23:5; 2Ch 7:6; 29:26; Am 6:5). Made by Solomon (1Ki 10:12; 2Ch 9:11; Ecc 2:8), Tyrians (Eze 28:13).

Kinds—
Horn (Da 3:5, 7, 10). See Trumpet. Cymbal (1Ch 15:19, 28; 1Co 13:1). See Cymbal. Flute (Ge 4:21; Da 3:5, 7, 10, 15). Gittith, possibly a stringed instrument (Ps 8; 81; 84, T). Harp (1Sa 10:5; 16:16, 23; 1Ch 16:5). See Harp. Lyre (1Ch 16:5). See Lyre. Pipe (1Sa 10:5; Isa 30:20; Da 3:5, 10, 15). See Pipe. Sistrum (2Sa 6:5). Tambourine (Ex 15:20). See Tambourine. Trumpet (Jos 6:4). See Trumpet. Zither (Da 3:5, 7, 10, 15).

Symbols Used in:
Many of psalm titles contain terms that may indicate the tunes of songs popular at the time of the psalmists. This practice of setting new words to an old tune is common to the hymnology of every age.

Aijeleth Shahar, NIV "To [the tune of] The Doe of the Morning" (Ps 22:T). This is probably a tune designation.

Alamoth (1Ch 15:20; Ps 46:T). The Hebrew word means "maidens." It may refer to "maidens playing tambourines" to accompany the music.

Al-taschith, NIV "[To the tune of] Do Not Destroy" (Titles of Ps 57-59; 75). The phrase also occurs in Isa 65:8, leading some to deduce it is the name of a vintage or wine-making song.

Gittith (Titles of Pss 8; 81; 84). This may mean a Gittite lyre or the name of a tune.

Higgaion (Ps 9:16). The word is also translated "meditation" (Ps 19:14), "melody" (Ps 92:3), and "mutter" (La 3:62). Combined with "Selah," it may have been intended to indicate a pause in the vocal music while the instruments played an interlude, a time for devout meditation.

Jonath-elem-rechokim, NIV "To [the tune of] A Dove on Distant Oaks" (Ps 56:T). This is probably a tune designation.

Mahalath (Ps 53:T), *Mahalath Leannoth* (Ps 88:T). The Hebrew appears to be the word for "suffering" or "sickness." Perhaps it indicates that the psalms are to be used in a time of affliction, such as when the godless mock.

Maskil (Titles of Pss 32; 42; 44; 45; 52; 53; 54; 55; 74; 79; 88; 89; 142). Related to a word meaning "to instruct" or "to become wise by instruction," it may indicate a psalm that instructs or that is skillfully made.

Miktam (Titles of Pss 16; 56-60). Variously related to words for "golden," "inscription," and "atonement."

Muth-Labben, NIV "To [the tune of] The Death of the Son" (Ps 9:T). This may be a variant of *alamoth* or a funeral song.

Neginah and *Neginoth*, NIV "stringed instruments" (Titles of Pss 4; 54-55; 61; 67; Hab 3:19). This seems to indicate that the song should be accompanied by stringed instruments.

Nehiloth, NIV "flutes" (Ps 5:T). This seems to indicate accompaniment (perhaps exclusively) by wind instruments (Ps 5).

Selah. This term appears seventy-one times in the Psalms and in Hab 3:3, 9, 13. Its meaning is not clear. Possibly it signified a pause in the vocal music while an instrumental interlude played.

Sheminith. (1Ch 15:21; Ps 6:T; 12:T). Related to the word for "eighth," this may have indicated an octave or accompaniment by a eight-stringed instrument.

Shiggaion (Ps 7:T) and *Shigionoth* (Hab 3:1). These could be tune designations or literary categories.

Shoshannim NIV "To [the tune of] Lilies" (Ps 45; 69:T) and *Shushan-eduth,* NIV "To [the tune of] The Lily of the Covenant" (Ps 60:T; 80:T). Again, these are probably tune designations.

MUSTARD SEED [*4983*]. Kingdom of heaven compared to (Mt 13:31-32; Mk 4:31-32; Lk 13:19). Faith compared to (Mt 17:20).

MUSTER [*599, 665, 6641, 7212, 7213, 7695, 7735*]. Of troops (1Sa 14:17; 2Sa 20:4; 1Ki 20:26; 2Ki 25:29; Isa 13:4). *See Armies.*

MUTE [*522, 228, 936, 3273*]. Stricken of God (Ex 4:11; Lk 1:20, 64), miraculous healing of, by Jesus (Mt 9:32-33; 12:22; 15:30-31; Mk 7:37; 9:17, 25-26). *See Deafness.*

MUTH-LABBEN NIV "To [the tune of] The Death of the Son" (Ps 9:T). Probably name of the tune to which the psalm was sung. *See Music, Symbols Used in.*

MUTILATORS [*2961*]. Sarcastic term for

Judaizers who required circumcision for salvation (Php 3:2). *See Circumcision.*

MUTINY Israelites against Moses (Nu 14:4). *See Conspiracy; Rebellion.*

MUZZLE [*2888, 4727, 3055, 5821*]. Mosaic law forbade muzzling of oxen while they were treading out the grain (Dt 25:4).

MYRA [*3688*]. A city of Lycia. Paul visits (Ac 27:5-6).

MYRRH [*4320, 5255, 3693, 5043, 5046*]. A fragrant gum. A product of the land of Canaan (SS 4:6, 14; 5:1). One of the compounds in the sacred anointing oil (Ex 30:23). Used as a perfume (Est 2:12; Ps 45:8; Pr 7:17; SS 3:6; 5:13). Brought by wise men as a present to Jesus (Mt 2:11). Offered to Jesus on the cross (Mk 15:23). Used for embalming (Jn 19:39). Trade in (Ge 37:25; 43:11).

MYRTLE [*2072*]. (Ne 8:15; Isa 41:19; 55:13; Zec 1:8). *See Plants of the Bible; Tree.*

MYSIA [*3695*]. District occupying NW end of Asia Minor bounded by the Aegean, the Hellespont, the Propontis, Bithynia, Phrygia, and Lydia. In 133 B.C. it fell to the Romans and they made it a part of the province of Asia. Traversed by Paul (Ac 16:7-8).

MYSTERIES [*2984, 10661, 3696*].
Of God (Dt 29:29; Job 15:8; Ps 25:14; Pr 3:32; Am 3:5; Heb 5:11).

Of redemption (Mt 11:25; 13:11, 35; Mk 4:11; Lk 8:10; Ro 16:25-26; 1Co 2:7-10; 2Co 3:12-18; Eph 1:9-10; 3:3-5, 9, 18-19; 6:19; Col 1:25-27; 2:2; 4:3; 1Ti 3:9, 16; 1Pe 1:10-12; Rev 10:7).

Of regeneration (Jn 3:8-12).

Of iniquity (2Th 2:7).

MYSTERY RELIGIONS   Greco-Roman religious movement that thrived from c. 700 B.C. to A.D. 400. To gain access to the divine mysteries, specially appointed priests carefully prepared individuals through stages of initiation, instruction, and secret revelation. The enlighted were then joined with the divine and could receive healing, success, and immortality. Though the word "mystery" is used in the NT (Ro 11:25; 16:25; 1Co 15:51; Eph 3:3-9), the openness of the preaching of the gospel makes it clear that Christianity is not a mystery religion. *See Mysteries.*

MYTHS [*3680*]. Untrue stories or speculations about religion that are contrary to sound doctrine and godliness (1Ti 1:4; 4:7; 2Ti 4:4; Tit 1:14).

NAAM [5839] (*pleasant*). Son of Caleb (1Ch 4:15).

NAAMAH [5841, 5842] (*pleasant*).
1. Daughter of Lamech and Zillah (Ge 4:22).
2. Wife of Solomon; mother of Rehoboam (1Ki 14:21, 31).
3. Town in Judah (Jos 15:41), site unknown.

NAAMAN, NAAMITE [5844, 5845, 3722] (*pleasantness*).
1. Son of Benjamin (Ge 46:21).
2. Son of Bela and his clan (Nu 26:40; 1Ch 8:4).
3. Son of Ehud (1Ch 8:7).
4. A Syrian general healed of leprosy by Elisha (2Ki 5:1-23; Lk 4:27).

NAAMATHITE [5847] (*of Naamath*). Designation of Zophar (Job 2:11; 11:1; 20:1; 42:9).

NAARAH [5856, 5857] (*[young] woman*).
1. Wife of Ashhur (1Ch 4:5f).
2. Place on border of Ephraim (Jos 16:7).

NAARAI [5858] (*young man of Yahweh*). Also called Paarai. One of David's heroes (1Ch 11:37).

NAARAN [5860]. A city in the eastern limits of Ephraim (1Ch 7:28).

NAARATH *See Naarah, 2.*

NAASHON, NAASSON *See Nahshon.*

NABAL [5573] (*fool*). Rich shepherd of Maon in Judah who insulted David and was saved from vengeance by his wife Abigail, who after Nabal's death became David's wife (1Sa 25:1-42).

NABATEA, NABATEANS Arabian tribe named in the Apocrypha but not in Bible. Their king, Aretas IV, controlled Damascus when Paul was there (2Co 11:32). Capital was Petra. *See Petra; Sela.*

NABONIDAS, NABONIDUS (*[pagan god] Nabu is wonderful*). Last ruler of Neo-Babylonian Empire (556-539 B.C.), his son Belshazzar (Da 5; 7:1; 8:1) was coregent with him from the third year of his reign.

NABOPOLASSAR (*[pagan god] Nabu protect the son!*). First ruler of the Neo-Babylonian Empire (626-605 B.C.). Allied with Medes and Scythians, he overthrew the Assyrian Empire, destroying Nineveh in 612 B.C., as prophesied (Zep 2:13-15).

NABOTH [5559] (*a sprout*). A Jezreelite. His vineyard forcibly taken by Ahab; stoned at the instigation of Jezebel (1Ki 21:1-19). His murder avenged (2Ki 9:21-36).

NACHOR *See Nahor, 1.*

NACON [5789] (*established*). Benjamite at whose threshing floor Uzzah was killed for touching the ark (2Sa 6:6). Also called Kidon (1Ch 13:9, ftn). The place was subsequently called Perez Uzzah. *See Perez Uzzah.*

NADAB [5606] (*volunteer, free will offering*).
1. Son of Aaron (Ex 6:23). Called to Mount Sinai with Moses and Aaron to worship (Ex 24:1, 9-10). Set apart to priesthood (Ex 28:1, 4, 40-43). Offers unauthorized fire to God and is destroyed (Lev 10:1-2; Nu 3:4; 26:61). Buried (Lev 10:4-5). His family forbidden to mourn (Lev 10:6-7).
2. Son and successor of Jeroboam (1Ki 14:20). His wicked reign; murdered by Baasha (1Ki 15:25-31).
3. Great-grandson of Jerahmeel (1Ch 2:28, 30).
4. A Benjamite (1Ch 8:30; 9:36).

NAGGAI [3710]. An ancestor of Jesus (Lk 3:25).

NAGGING [7439]. Proverbs concerning (Pr 19:13; 21:9, 19; 25:24; 26:21; 27:15). Jezebel's destroys Samson (Jdg 16:16).

NAHALAL [5634] (*watering place*). Also spelled Nahalol (Jdg 1:30). A Levitical city within Zebulun's territory (Jos 19:15; 21:35; Jdg 1:30).

NAHALIEL [5712] (*wadi of God [El]*). A station of the Israelites (Nu 21:19).

NAHALOL, NAHALLAL [5636]. *See Nahalal.*

NAHAM [5715] (*repent, console*). Descendant of Judah through Caleb (1Ch 4:19).

NAHAMANI [5720] (*Yahweh has consoled*). A Jewish exile (Ne 7:7).

NAHARAI [5726]. Beerothite, Joab's armor-bearer (2Sa 23:37).

NAHARAIM *See Aram Naharaim.*

NAHASH [5731] (*viper* or *copper*).
1. Ammonite king defeated by Saul (1Sa 11:1-2; 12:12).
2. Ammonite king whose son insulted David's messengers, and David avenged the insult (2Sa 10; 1Ch 19).
3. Father of Abigail and Zeruiah (2Sa 17:25).

See also Ir Nahash.

NAHATH [5740] (*descent; possibly rest*).
1. Son of Reuel (Ge 36:13, 17; 1Ch 1:37).
2. A Levite, grandson of the Kohathite Elkanah (1Ch 6:26); probably the same as Tohu (1Sa 1:1), and Toah (1Ch 6:34).
3. A Levite and overseer of the sacred offerings in the time of Hezekiah (2Ch 31:13).

NAHBI [5696] (perhaps *hidden* or *timid*). A leader of Naphtali and one of the twelve spies (Nu 13:14).

NAHOR [5701, 3732] (apparently from Assyrian place name Til-Nahiri, *the mound of Nahuru*).
1. Grandfather of Abraham (Ge 11:22-26; 1Ch 1:26). In the lineage of Christ (Lk 3:34).
2. Brother of Abraham (Ge 11:26; Jos 24:2). Marriage and descendants of (Ge 11:27, 29; 22:20-24; 24:15, 24).

NAHSHON [5732, 3709] (*small viper*). A captain of Judah's host (Ex 6:23; Nu 1:7; 2:3; 7:12, 17; 10:14). In the lineage of Christ (Mt 1:4; Lk 3:32).

NAHUM [5699, 3725] (*comfort*).
1. Author of book of Nahum; native of Elkosh; prophesied 663-612 B.C. (Na 1:1; 3:8-11).
2. An ancestor of Jesus (Lk 3:25).

NAHUM, BOOK OF

Author: The prophet Nahum

Date: Between 663 and 612 B.C.

Outline:

I. Title (1:1).
II. Nineveh's Judge (1:2-15).
   A. The Lord's Kindness and Sternness (1:2-8).
   B. Nineveh's Overthrow and Judah's Joy (1:9-15).
III. Nineveh's Judgment (ch. 2).
   A. Nineveh Besieged (2:1-10).
   B. Nineveh's Desolation Contrasted With Her Former Glory (2:11-13).
IV. Nineveh's Total Destruction (ch. 3).
   A. Nineveh's Sins (3:1-4).
   B. Nineveh's Doom (3:5-19).
See Prophets, The Minor.

NAIL [5021, 5383, 7632, 10303, 2464, 4669, 4699].
1. Fingernail (Dt 21:12; Da 4:33; 7:19).
2. Tent peg (Jdg 4:21-22; 5:26), peg driven into wall to hang things on (Ezr 9:8; Isa 22:23-25).
3. Nails of metal: iron, bronze, gold (1Ch 22:3; 2Ch 3:9).

NAIN [3723] (*pleasant, delightful*). A city in Galilee. Jesus restores to life a widow's son in (Lk 7:11).

NAIOTH [5766] (*dwellings*). Place in or near

Ramah of Benjamin where Samuel lived with a band of prophets (1Sa 19:18-20:1).

NAKED [3338, 5067, 5113, 5122, 6567, 6867, 6872, 6873, 6880, *1218*, *1219*].]
1. Without any clothing (Ge 2:25; 3:7-11).
2. Poorly clad (Job 22:6).
3. Without an outer garment (Jn 21:7). Often used figuratively for spiritual poverty (Rev 3:17) and a lack of power (Ge 42:9).

NAME [*606, 2352, 9005, 10721, *3306*, *3950*, *3951*]. Value of a good (Pr 22:1; Ecc 7:1). A new name given, to persons who have spiritual adoption (Isa 62:2), to Abraham (Ge 17:5), Sarah (Ge 17:15), Jacob (Ge 32:28), Peter (Mt 16:18), Paul (Ac 13:9). Intercessional influence of the name of Jesus. *See Jesus the Christ, In His Name.*
Symbolic (Hos 1:3-4, 6, 9; 2:1), of prestige (1Ki 1:47).

NAMES OF GOD *See God, Names of; Titles and Names.*

NAMES OF JESUS *See Jesus the Christ, Names, Appellations, and Titles of; Titles and Names.*

NANNAR (*lightgiver*). Name given at Ur to Babylonian moon-god Sin.

NAOMI [5843] (*my joy*). Wife of Elimelech; mother-in-law of Ruth; lived in Moab; returns to Bethlehem; kinswoman of Boaz (Ru 1-4).

NAPHISH [5874] (*refreshed*). The eleventh son of Ishmael; progenitor of a tribe, probably the Nephussim (Ge 25:15; 1Ch 1:31; 5:19).

NAPHOTH [5868] (*heights*). A town assigned to Manasseh, also called Dor and Naphoth Dor (Jos 17:11, ftn). Conquered by Joshua (Jos 11:2; 12:23). *See Dor; Naphoth Dor.*

NAPHOTH DOR [5869] (*heights of Dor*). A town assigned to Manasseh, also called Dor and Naphoth (Jos 17:11, ftn). *See Dor; Naphoth.*

NAPHTALI, NAPHTALITES

[824+5889, 1201+ 5889, 5889, *3750*] (*wrestling*).
1. Son of Jacob and Bilhah (Ge 30:7-8; 35:25). Jacob blesses (Ge 49:21). Sons of (Ge 46:24; 1Ch 7:13).
2. Tribe of. Census of (Nu 1:42-43; 26:48-50). Position assigned to, in camp and march (Nu 2:25-31; 10:25-27). Moses' benediction on (Dt 33:23). Inheritance of (Jos 19:32-39; Jdg 1:33; Eze 48:3).
Defeat Sisera (Jdg 4:6, 10; 5:18). Follow Gideon (Jdg 6:35; 7:23). Aid in conveying the ark to Jerusalem (Ps 68:27). Military operations of (1Ch 12:34, 40), against (1Ki 15:20; 2Ki 15:29; 2Ch 16:4).
Prophecies concerning (Isa 9:1-2; Rev 7:6).

NAPHTUHITES [5888]. The inhabitants of central Egypt (Ge 10:13; 1Ch 1:11).

NAPKIN Cloth for wiping perspiration off (Lk 19:20; Jn 11:44; 20:7).

NARCISSUS [3727]. A believer at Rome (Ro 16:11).

NARD [5948, 3726]. An aromatic plant (SS 4:13-14). *See Perfume; Plants of the Bible.*

NATHAN [5990, 3718] (*gift*).
1. Prophet during reigns of David and Solomon; told David that not he but Solomon was to build the temple (2Sa 7; 1Ch 17), rebuked David for sin with Bathsheba (2Sa 12:1-25), helped get throne for Solomon (1Ki 1:8-53), wrote chronicles of reign of David (1Ch 29:29) and Solomon (2Ch 9:29), associated with David in arranging musical services for house of God (2Ch 29:25).
2. Son of David (2Sa 5:14; 1Ch 14:4).
3. Father of Igal (2Sa 23:36).
4. Judahite (1Ch 2:36).
5. Israelite who returned from the Exile (Ezr 8:16).
6. Man who put away his foreign wife (Ezr 10:39).

NATHANAEL [3720] (*gift of God [El]*). Disciple of Jesus (Jn 1:45-51), identified commonly with Bartholomew. Church Fathers use the two names interchangeably.

NATHAN-MELECH [5994] (*gift of king* or *gift of Melek, Molech, Malk [pagan god]*). Officer of Josiah (2Ki 23:11).

NATION [824, 1580, 4211, 5476, 6639, 10040, *1620, 5876*]. People divided into nations after the Flood (Ge 10:1-32). Ordained of God (Ac 17:26). Righteousness exalts (Pr 14:34).

Peace of:
(Job 34:29; Ps 33:12; 89:15-18). Promises of peace to (Lev 26:6; 1Ki 2:33; 2Ki 20:19; 1Ch 22:9; Ps 29:11; 46:9; 72:3, 7; 128:6; Isa 2:4; 14:4-7; 60:17-18; 65:25; Jer 30:10; 50:34; Eze 34:25-28; Hos 2:18; Mic 4:3-4; Zec 1:11; 3:10; 8:4-5; 9:10; 14:11). Prayer for peace (Jer 29:7; 1Ti 2:1-2). Peace given by God (Jos 21:44; 1Ch 22:18; 23:25; Ps 147:13-14; Ecc 3:8; Isa 45:7). Instances of national peace (Jos 14:15; Jdg 3:11, 30; 1Ki 4:24-25). *See War.*

Sins of:
Involved in sins, of rulers (Ge 20:4, 9; 2Sa 24:10-17; 1Ki 15:26, 30, 34; 2Ki 24:3; 1Ch 21:7-17; Jer 15:4), of other individuals, as Achan (Jos 7:1, 11-26).
Atonement made for (2Ch 29:21). Penitent, promises to (Lev 26:40-42; Dt 4:29-31; 5:29; 30:1-10; 2Ch 7:13-14; Jer 3:22).
In adversity, prayer of (Jdg 6:7; 10:10; 21:2-4; 2Ch 7:13-14; Ps 74; Jer 3:21; 31:18; Joel 2:12), prayer for (Ezr 9:6-15; Ne 1:4-11; Ps 74; 84:1-7; Isa 63:7-19; Jer 6:14; 8:11, 20-21; 9:1-2; 14:7, 20; La 2:20-22; Da 9:3-21). *See Sin, National.*

Judgments Against:
Chastisement of (Lev 18:24-30; 26:28; Dt 11:2; 2Ch 6:24, 26, 28; 7:13-14; Ps 106:43; Isa 14:26-27; Jer 2:30; 5:29; 18:6-10; 25:12-33; 30:14; 31:18-20; 46:28; Eze 2:3-5; 39:23-24; Da 7:9-12; 9:3-16; La 1:5; Hos 7:12; 10:10; Joel 1:1-20; Am 9:9; Zep 3:6, 8; Hag 2:17). Perish (Ps 9:17; Isa 60:12).
Judgments denounced against, on account of its unrighteousness (Dt 9:5; Ps 9:17; Isa 3:4-8; 14:24-27; 19:4; 59:1-15; 60:12; Jer 2:19, 35-37; 5:6-29; 6; 9:7-26; 12:14, 17; 18:6-10; 25:12-33; 50:45-46; 51; Eze 2:9-10; 7; 22:12-31; 24:6-24; 33:25-29; Hos 4:1-10; 7:12-13, 16; 13; Am 2; 3; 5; 9:8-10; Mic 6:13-16; Zep 3:8).
Instances of punishment of: The Canaanites (Dt 9:5). The Sodomites (Ge 19:24-25, 28-29; La 4:6). The Egyptians (Ex 7-11; 12:1-36; 14). The Israelites (2Sa 21:1; 24:14-16; 2Ki 24:2-4, 20; 2Ch 28:1, 5-8, 16-19; 29:8-9; 30:7; 36:16-20; Ezr 9:7; Ne 9:36-37; Jer 2:15-16; 30:11-15; La 1:3, 8, 14; Eze 36:16-20; 39:17-24; Joel 1:1-20; Am 4:6-11).
See Government; Kings; Rulers.

NATIONAL RELIGION Supported by taxes (Ex 30:11-16; 38:26). Ministers of, supported by state (1Ki 18:19; 2Ch 11:13-15). Subverted by Jeroboam (1Ki 12:26-33; 2Ch 11:13-15). Idolatrous, established by Jeroboam (1Ki 12:26-33).

NATIONS BLESSED BY ABRAHAM (Ge 12:2; 18:18; 22:18; 26:4; Ac 3:25; Gal 3:8).

NATURAL Natural death (Nu 16:29; 19:16, 18), sleep (Jn 11:13), physical relations (Ro 1:26-27), body (1Co 15:44, 46), instincts (Jude 1:19).

NATURAL RELIGION *See Religion, Natural.*

NATURALIZATION Giving rights of citizenship to aliens (Ac 22:28).
Figurative (Eph 2:12-13, 19).

NATURE [2522, 3517, 3671, 4922, 5882]. The entire compass of one's life (Jas 3:6). The inherent character of a person or thing (Ro 1:26; 2:14; 11:21-24). Disposition (2Pe 1:4). Sinful nature (Ro 7:18, 25; 1Co 5:5; Gal 5:13).
Laws of, uniform in operation: In the vegetable kingdom (Ge 1:11, 12; Mt 7:16-18; Lk 6:43-44; 1Co 15:36-38; Gal 6:7; Jas 3:12), animal kingdom (Ge 1:21, 24-25; Jer 13:23), succession of seasons (Ge 8:22), succession of day and night (Ge 8:22; Jer 33:20).

NAUGHTINESS *See Sin.*

NAUM *See Nahum.*

NAVE *See Rim.*

NAVEL [9219]. "Belly button" (SS 7:2).

NAVIGATION Sounding in (Ac 27:28). *See Commerce; Mariner; Navy.*

NAVY Solomon's (1Ki 9:26), Hiram's (1Ki 10:11), of Kittim (Da 11:30, ftn, 40).
See Commerce; Mariner.

NAZARENE [*3716, 3717*] (possibly *sprout, branch*).
1. Inhabitant of Nazareth (Mt 2:23); possibly a wordplay on the Hebrew *nezer,* "branch," a messianic title (cf. Isa 11:1). *See Branch.*
2. A Christian (Ac 24:5).

NAZARETH [*3714, 3716, 3717*] (possibly *sprout, branch* or *watchtower*). A village in Galilee. Joseph and Mary live at (Mt 2:23; Lk 1:26-27, 56; 2:4, 39, 51). Jesus from (Mt 21:11; Mk 1:24; 10:47; Lk 4:34; 18:37; 24:19). People of, reject Jesus (Lk 4:16-30). Its name infamous (Jn 1:46).

NAZARETH DECREE An inscription on a slab of white marble, dating c. A.D. 40-50, by Claudius Caesar, found in Nazareth, decreeing capital punishment for anyone disturbing graves and tombs.

NAZIRITE(S) [*5687, 5693, 5694*] (*one under sacred vow*). An Israelite who consecrated himself or herself and took a vow of separation and self-imposed abstinence for the purpose of some special service. The Nazirite vow included a renunciation of wine, prohibition of the use of the razor, and avoidance of contact with a dead body. The period of time for the vow was anywhere from 30 days to a lifetime (Nu 6:1-21; Jdg 13:5-7; Am 2:11, 12).
Instances of: Samson (Jdg 13:5, 7; 16:17). Samuel (1Sa 1:11). Recabites (Jer 35). John the Baptist (Mt 11:18; Lk 1:15; 7:33).
See Abstinence; Wine.

NEAH [*5828*]. A border town in Zebulun (Jos 19:13). The site is unknown.

NEAPOLIS [*3735*] (*new city*). A seaport of Macedonia. Paul visits (Ac 16:11).

NEARIAH [*5859*] (*[young] man of Yahweh*).
1. Son of Shemaiah (1Ch 3:22-23).
2. A Simeonite leader (1Ch 4:42).

NEBAI [*5763*] (*thrive*). Signer of the covenant with Nehemiah (Ne 10:19).

NEBAIOTH [*5568*]. Son of Ishmael (Ge 25:13; 28:9; 36:3; 1Ch 1:29). Prophecies concerning (Isa 60:7).

NEBALLAT [*5579*]. A town occupied by the Benjamites after the Captivity (Ne 11:34).

NEBAT [*5565*] (*look to, regard [approvingly]*). Father of Jeroboam (1Ki 11:26; 12:2).

NEBO [*5549, 5550, 5551*] (*height* or *Mount of Nabu [Nebo]*).
1. A city allotted to Reuben (Nu 32:3, 38; 1Ch 5:8). Prophecies concerning (Isa 15:2; Jer 48:1, 22).
2. A mountain range E of the Jordan. Moses views Canaan from (Dt 32:49-50), dies on (Dt 34:1).
3. A city in Judah (Ezr 2:29; Ne 7:33).
4. The ancestor of certain Jews (Ezr 10:43).
5. A Babylonian idol (Isa 46:1).

NEBO-SARSEKIM [*5552*]. A prince of Nebuchadnezzar who entered Jerusalem when it fell (Jer 39:3, ftn).

NEBUCHADNEZZAR [*5556, 5557, 10453*] (*Nebo protect my boundary stone* BDB and IDB; *Nebo protect my son!* KB).
1. The fourth Dynasty ruler of the Old Babylonian Empire (c. 1140 B.C.).
2. Ruler of the Neo-Babylonian Empire (605-562 B.C.); son of Nabopolassar; conquered Pharaoh Neco at Carchemish (605 B.C.); destroyed Jerusalem and carried Israelites into captivity (587 B.C.) (2Ki 25:1-21); succeeded by son Evil-Merodach. Often mentioned in OT (1Ch 6:15; 2Ch 36; Ezr 1:7; 2:1; 5:12, 14; 6:5; Ne 7:6; Est 2:6; Jer 21:2; 52:4; Da 1-5).

NEBUSHAZBAN [*5558*] (*Nebo [Nabu] save me!*). Chief officer of Nebuchadnezzar (Jer 39:11-14).

NEBUZARADAN [*5555*] (*Nebo [Nabu] has given seed [offspring]*). Nebuchadnezzar's general when the Babylonians besieged Jerusalem (2Ki 25:1, 11-12, 20; Jer 52:12ff), conducted captives to Babylon.

NECK [*1738, 1744, 4305, 5154, 5883, 6902, 6904, 7023, 7418, 10611, 5549*]. Term often used in Bible with literal and figurative meanings (Ex 32:9; Dt 9:13; Ps 75:5; Ac 7:51).

NECKLACE [*3921, 6735, 7454, 8054, 8448*]. Ornamental chain worn around the neck (Isa 3:19).

NECO [*5785, 5786*]. Pharaoh of Egypt (609-595 B.C.); defeated Josiah at battle of Megiddo (2Ki 23:29; 2Ch 35:20ff); defeated by Nebuchadnezzar at battle of Carchemish (2Ki 24:7; Isa 10:9; Jer 46:2).

NECROMANCER, NECROMANCY Consulting with the dead; forbidden by Mosaic law (Dt 18:10-11), King Saul consulted with the medium of Endor (1Sa 28:7-25). Judgment upon (Isa 8:19; 29:4).
See Medium; Sorcery; Witchcraft.

NEDABIAH [*5608*] (*Yahweh volunteers*). A son of Jehoiachin (1Ch 3:18).

NEEDLE'S EYE [1017, 4827]. Figure used by Jesus (Mt 19:24; Mk 10:25; Lk 18:25). Jesus does not say that salvation is threatened by possessing riches but that those who are wealthy will have great difficulty subordinating their riches to the will of God; in addition, a wealthy man will not enter the kingdom of God based on his riches, but only on the saving grace of God and the finished work of Jesus Christ (Mt 19:25-26).

NEEDLEWORK Art of working in with the needle various kinds of colored threads in cloth (Jdg 5:30; Ps 45:14).

NEESING NIV "snorting" (Job 41:18).

NEGEV [824+5582, 5582] (dry [land], hence south country). The desert region lying to the S of Judea, sometimes translated "the south" (Ge 12:9; 13:1; 20:1; Nu 13:29; 1Sa 27:5-6).

NEGINAH See Music, Symbols Used in.

NEGINOTH See Music, Symbols Used in.

NEHELAMITE [5713] (perhaps of Nehelam or a play on the word for dream). Designation of Shemaiah, a false prophet (Jer 29:24, 31-32).

NEHEMIAH [5718] (Yahweh has comforted).
1. Leader of Jews who returned with Zerubbabel (Ezr 2:2; Ne 7:7).
2. Son of Azbuk; helped rebuild walls of Jerusalem (Ne 3:16).
3. Son of Hacaliah; governor of Persian province of Judah after 444 B.C.; cupbearer to King Artaxerxes of Persia (Ne 1:11; 2:1); rebuilt walls of Jerusalem (Ne 1:4-6); cooperated with Ezra in numerous reforms (Ne 8); nothing known of the end of his life.

NEHEMIAH, BOOK OF
Author: Nehemiah

Date: c. 430 B.C.

Outline:

I. Nehemiah's First Administration (chs. 1-12).
  A. Nehemiah's Response to the Situation in Jerusalem (ch. 1).
    1. News of the plight of Jerusalem (1:1-4).
    2. Nehemiah's prayer (1:5-11).
  B. Nehemiah's Journey to Jerusalem (ch. 2).
    1. The king response (2:1-8).
    2. The journey itself (2:9-10).
    3. Nehemiah's nocturnal inspection of the walls (2:11-16).
    4. His exhortation to rebuild (2:17-18).
    5. The opposition of Sanballat, Tobiah and Geshem (2:19-20).
  C. List of the Builders of the Wall (ch. 3).
    1. The northern section (3:1-7).
    2. The western section (3:8-13).
    3. The southern section (3:14).

4. The eastern section (3:15-32).
  D. Opposition to Rebuilding the Wall (ch. 4).
    1. The derision of Sanballat and Tobiah (4:1-5).
    2. The threat of attack (4:6-15).
    3. Rebuilding the wall (4:16-23).
  E. Social and Economic Problems (ch. 5).
    1. The complaints of the poor (5:1-5).
    2. The cancellation of debts (5:6-13).
    3. Nehemiah's unselfish example (5:14-19).
  F. The Wall Rebuilt Despite Opposition (ch. 6).
    1. Attempts to snare Nehemiah (6:1-9).
    2. The hiring of false prophets (6:10-14).
    3. The completion of the wall (6:15-19).
  G. List of Exiles (7:1-73a).
    1. Provisions for the protection of Jerusalem (7:1-3).
    2. Nehemiah's discovery of the list of returnees (7:4-5).
    3. The returnees delineated (7:6-72).
    4. Settlement of the exiles (7:73a).
  H. Ezra's Preaching and the Outbreak of Revival (7:73b-10:39).
    1. The public exposition of the Scriptures (7:73b-8:12).
    2. The Feast of Tabernacles (8:13-18).
    3. A day of fasting, confession and prayer (9:1-5a).
    4. A recital of God's dealings with Israel (9:5b-31).
    5. Confession of sins (9:32-37).
    6. A binding agreement (9:38).
    7. A list of those who sealed it (10:1-29).
    8. Provisions of the agreement (10:30-39).
  I. New Residents of Judah and Jerusalem (ch. 11).
    1. New residents for Jerusalem (11:1-24).
      a. Introductory remarks (11:1-4a).
      b. Residents from Judah (11:4b-6).
      c. From Benjamin (11:7-9).
      d. From the priests (11:10-14).
      e. From the Levites (11:15-18).
      f. From the temple staff (11:25-36).
    2. New residents for Judah (11:25-36).
      a. Places settled by those from Judah (11:25-30).
      b. Places settled by those from Benjamin (11:31-35).
      c. Transfer of Levites from Judah to Benjamin (11:36).
  J. Lists of Priests and the Dedication of the Wall (ch. 12).
    1. Priests and Levites from the first return (12:1-9).
    2. High priests and Levites since Joiakim (12:10-26).
    3. Dedication of the wall of Jerusalem (12:27-43).
    4. Regulation of the temple offerings and services (12:44-47).
II. Nehemiah's Second Administration (ch. 13).
  A. Abuses During His Absence (13:1-5).
    1. Mixed marriages (13:1-3).

2. Tobiah's occupation of the temple quarters (13:4-5).

B. Nehemiah's Return (13:6-9).
 1. His arrival (13:6-7).
 2. His expulsion of Tobiah (13:8-9).

C. Reorganization and Reforms (13:10-31).
 1. Offerings for the temple staff (13:10-14).
 2. The abuse of the Sabbath (13:15-22).
 3. Mixed marriages (13:23-29).
 4. Provisions of wood and firstfruits (13:30-31).

NEHILOTH *See Music, Symbols Used in.*

NEHUM [5700] (*comfort*). Chief of Judah who returned with Zerubbabel; also called "Rehum" (Ezr 2:2; Ne 7:7).

NEHUSHTA [5735] (*[strong as or color of] bronze*). Wife of Jehoiakim, king of Judah, and mother of Jehoiachin (2Ki 24:6, 8).

NEHUSHTAN [5736] (combination of *bronze* and *viper*). The bronze serpent (2Ki 18:4).

NEIEL [5832]. A landmark on the boundary of Asher (Jos 19:27).

NEIGHBOR [408, 824, 6017, 6660, 7940, 8276, 8907, *1150, 4340, 4341, 4446, 4489*]. Defined (Lk 10:25-37). Duty to, defined in the Golden Rule (Mt 7:12).

Love does no harm to (Ro 13:10). Love for, commanded (Lev 19:18; Mt 19:19; 22:39; Mk 12:31-33; Lk 10:25-37; Ro 13:9-10; Gal 5:14; Jas 2:8-9). Kindness to, commanded (Ex 23:4-5; Dt 22:1-4; Isa 58:6-7; Gal 6:10). Charitableness toward, commanded (Ro 15:2). Benevolence toward, commanded (Pr 3:28-29). Righteous treatment of, commanded (Zec 8:16-17). Honesty toward, commanded (Lev 19:13). Kindness to, rewarded (Isa 58:8-14; Mt 25:34-46). Righteous treatment of, rewarded (Ps 15:1-3).

False witness against, forbidden (Ex 20:16; Lev 19:16). Hatred of, forbidden (Lev 19:17). Oppression of, denounced (Jer 22:13). Penalty for violation of the rights of (Lev 6:2-5).

See Duty; Mankind.

NEKEB *See Adami Nekeb.*

NEKODA [5928]. Head of a family of temple servants who could not prove Israelite descent (Ne 7:50, 62; Ezr 2:60).

NEMUEL, NEMUELITE [5803, 5804].
 1. Brother of Dathan and Abiram (Nu 26:9).
 2. Son of Simeon (Nu 26:12; 1Ch 4:24). Also called Jemuel (Ge 46:10; Ex 6:15). *See Jemuel.*

NEPHEG [5863] (*sprout, shoot*).
 1. Brother of Korah, Dathan, and Abiram (Ex 6:21).
 2. Son of David (2Sa 5:15; 1Ch 3:7; 14:6).

NEPHEW [278+1201,   1201+2157]. Grandson (Jdg 12:14), descendant (Job 18:19; Isa 14:22), grandchild (1Ti 5:4).

NEPHILIM [5872] (*ones falling [upon], hence violent ones, possibly giants*). Antediluvians (Ge 6:4), aboriginal dwellers in Canaan (Nu 13:32-33), not angelic fallen beings (Dt 1:28).

NEPHISH *See Naphish.*

NEPHISHESIM *See Nephussim.*

NEPHTHALIM, NEPTHALIM *See Naphtali.*

NEPHTOAH [5886] (*an opening*). Spring and town on the border of Judah and Benjamin (Jos 15:9; 18:15), two miles NW of Jerusalem; modern Lifta.

NEPHUSSIM [5866, 5867]. A family of the temple servants (Ezr 2:50; Ne 7:52).

NEPOTISM Of Joseph (Ge 47:11-12). Of Saul (1Sa 14:50). Of David (2Sa 8:16; 19:13). Of Nehemiah (Ne 7:2).

NER [5945] (*lamp*).
 1. Father of Abner (1Sa 14:50; 26:14).
 2. Grandfather of King Saul (1Ch 8:33).

NEREUS [*3759*] (*pagan Greek deity*). A Christian at Rome (Ro 16:15).

NERGAL [5946] (*pagan deity*). Babylonian deity of destruction (2Ki 17:30).

NERGAL-SHAREZER [5947] (*Nergal protect the prince!*). The name of princes of Babylon (Jer 39:3, 13).

NERI [*3760*] (*lamp of Yahweh*). An ancestor of Jesus (Lk 3:27).

NERIAH [5949, 5950] (*lamp of Yahweh*). Father of Baruch (Jer 32:12).

NERIGLISSAR *See Nergal-Sharezer.*

NERO (*family name*). The fifth Roman emperor (A.D. 54-68); killed many Christians when Rome burned in A.D. 64; called "Caesar" (Ac 25:11; Php 4:22).

NEST [748, 4402, 7860, 7873, 8905, 10709, *2943*]. Bird's (Nu 24:21; Mt 8:20). Birds stir up (Dt 32:11).

NET [3052, 4821, 5178, 5182, 8407, *311, 312, 1473, 4880*]. Of interwoven chains (1Ki 7:17). Hidden in a pit (Ps 35:7-8). Set for birds (Pr 1:17), wild animals (Isa 51:20). Fish caught in (Mt 4:18-21; 13:47; Lk 5:4; Jn 21:6-11).

See Snare.

Figurative: (Job 18:8; 19:6; Ps 9:15; 10:9; 25:15; 31:4; 35:7-8; 57:6; 66:11; 140:5; 141:10; Pr

12:12; 29:5; Ecc 7:26; 9:12; Isa 19:8; Eze 26:5,
14; 47:10; Hos 7:12).

NETAIM [5751]. Residence of Judahite pot-
ters (1Ch 4:23).

NETHANEL [5991] (*God [El] has given*).
1. The prince of Issachar. Numbers the tribe (Nu
1:8). Captain of the host of Issachar (Nu 2:5;
10:15). Liberality of, for the tabernacle (Nu 7:18-
23).
2. A priest and doorkeeper for the ark (1Ch
15:24).
3. A Levite (1Ch 24:6).
4. Son of Obed-Edom and gatekeeper of the
temple (1Ch 26:4).
5. A prince sent by Jehoshaphat to teach the law
in the cities of Judah (2Ch 17:7).
6. A Levite (2Ch 35:9).
7. A priest who divorced his Gentile wife (Ezr
10:22).
8. A priest (Ne 12:21).
9. A Levite and musician (Ne 12:36).

NETHANIAH [5992, 5993] (*Yahweh has
given*).
1. Father of Ishmael (2Ki 25:23, 25; Jer 40:8,
14-15; 41:1-2, 6-7, 9-12).
2. A singer and chief of the temple musicians
(1Ch 25:2, 12).
3. A Levite appointed by Jehoshaphat to accompany the princes who were to teach the law in
Judah (2Ch 17:8).
4. Father of Jehudi (Jer 36:14).

NETHINIM *See Temple Servants.*

**NETOPHAH,
NETOPHATHITE(S)** [5743, 5756]
(*trickle, drip*). Village of Judah and its inhabitants;
c. three miles S of Jerusalem (2Sa 23:28-29; 1Ch
2:54; 9:16; Ne 12:28).

NETTLES [7853]. A stinging plant (Pr
24:31; Isa 34:13).
Figurative (Job 30:7; Hos 9:6; Zep 2:9).

NETWORK [8407, 8422]. White cloth (Isa
19:9), ornamental carving upon pillars of
Solomon's temple (1Ki 7:18, 42), a grate for the
great altar of burnt offerings at the tabernacle (Ex
27:4; 38:4).

NEW BIRTH The corruption of human nature requires (Jn 3:6; Ro 8:7-8). None can enter
heaven without (Jn 3:3). Is of the will of God (Jas
1:18). Is of the mercy of God (Tit 3:5). Is for the
glory of God (Isa 43:7).
Effected by:
God (Jn 1:13; 1Pe 1:3). Christ (1Jn 2:29). The
Holy Spirit (Jn 3:6; Tit 3:5). By means of: The
word of God (Jas 1:18; 1Pe 1:23). The resurrection of Christ (1Pe 1:3). The ministry of the gospel
(1Co 4:15).

Described as:
A new creation (2Co 5:17; Gal 6:15; Eph 2:10).
Newness of life (Ro 6:4). A spiritual resurrection
(Ro 6:4-6; Eph 2:1, 5; Col 2:12; 3:1). A new heart
(Eze 36:26). A new spirit (Eze 11:19; Ro 7:6).
Putting on the new man (Eph 4:24). The inward
man (Ro 7:22; 2Co 4:16). Circumcision of the
heart (Dt 30:6, w Ro 2:29; Col 2:11). Partaking of
the divine nature (2Pe 1:4). The washing of
regeneration (Tit 3:5). All saints partake of (Ro
8:16-17; 1Pe 2:2; 1Jn 5:1).
Produces:
Likeness to God (Eph 4:24; Col 3:10). Likeness
to Christ (Ro 8:29; 2Co 3:18; 1Jn 3:2). Knowledge
of God (Jer 24:7; Col 3:10). Hatred of sin (1Jn 3:9;
5:18). Victory over the world (1Jn 5:4). Delight in
God's law (Ro 7:22).
Evidenced by:
Faith in Christ (1Jn 5:1). Righteousness (1Jn
2:29). Brotherly love (1Jn 4:7). Connected with
adoption (Isa 43:6-7; Jn 1:12-13). Literalistic ob-
jection to (Jn 3:4). Manner of effecting illustrated
(Jn 3:8). Preserves from Satan's devices (1Jn
5:18).

NEW COVENANT *See Covenants,
Major in the Old Testament.*

NEW CREATION *See Regeneration.*

NEW MOON Feast of (Nu 10:10; 28:11-
15; 1Ch 23:31; 2Ch 31:3). Commerce at time of,
suspended (Am 8:5).

NEW TESTAMENT A collection of
twenty-seven documents regarded by the church
as inspired and authoritative, consisting of four
Gospels, the Acts of the Apostles, twenty-one letters, and the book of Revelation. All were written
during the apostolic period, either by apostles or
by men closely associated with the apostles. The
Gospels tell the story of the coming of the Messiah, God in the flesh, to become the Savior of the
world. Acts describes the beginnings and growth
of the church. The letters set forth the significance
of the person and work of Christ and rules for the
Church. Revelation tells of the consummation of
all things in Jesus Christ. The formation of the NT
canon was a gradual process, the Holy Spirit
working in the church and guiding it to recognize
and choose those Christian books God wanted
brought together to form the Christian counterpart
of the Jewish OT. By the end of the fourth century,
the NT canon was basically settled.

NEW THINGS (Isa 42:9; 43:19; 48:6;
65:17; 2Co 5:17; Rev 21:5).

NEW YEAR *See Feasts; Trumpets, Feast
of.*

NEZIAH [5909] (*director [of worship]*). One
of the temple servants (Ezr 2:54; Ne 7:56).

NEZIB [5908] (*pillar, garrison*). A city in Judah (Jos 15:43).

NIBHAZ [5563]. An idol (2Ki 17:31).

NIBSHAN [5581]. A city of Judah (Jos 15:62).

NICANOR [3770] (*victor*). A deacon of the church at Jerusalem (Ac 6:5).

NICODEMUS [3773] (*victor over people*). Pharisee; member of the Sanhedrin; came to Jesus at night for conversation (Jn 3); spoke up for Jesus before the Sanhedrin (Jn 7:25-44); brought spices for burial of Jesus (Jn 19:39-42).

NICOLAITANS [3774] (*follower of Nicolas*). A heretical sect with immoral practices (Rev 2:6, 15).

NICOLAS [3775] (*victor over people*). A proselyte of Antioch and deacon of the church at Jerusalem (Ac 6:5-6).

NICOPOLIS [3776] (*victory city*). City in Epirus in NW Greece, founded by Augustus Caesar (Tit 3:12).

NIGER [3769] (*black*). Surname of Simeon, leader of the church at Antioch (Ac 13:1-3).

NIGHT [*621, 874, 4325, 4326, 4328, 4869, 6847, 10391, *887, *3816, *5871*]. (Ge 1:5, 16, 18). Meditations in (Ps 19:2; 77:6; 119:148; 139:11). Worship in (Ps 134:1). Jesus prays all night (Lk 6:12). No night in heaven (Rev 21:25; 22:5). Divided into hours (Ac 23:23). Used figuratively (Isa 15:1; 21:11-12; Jn 9:4; Ro 13:12; 1Th 5:5).

NIGHT HAWK See Screech Owl.

NILE [3284]. The main river of Egypt and of Africa, 4,050 miles long; it begins at Lake Victoria and flows northward to the Mediterranean; the annual overflow deposits sediment which makes N Egypt one of the most fertile regions in the world. Moses was placed on the Nile in a basket of papyrus (Ex 2:3); the turning of the Nile into blood was one of the ten plagues (Ex 7:20-21); on its bank grows the reed from which the famous papyrus writing material is made. See River of Egypt.

NIMRAH [5809] (*spotted leopard* BDB; *basin of limpid [clear] water* KB). A city of Gad (Nu 32:3).

NIMRIM, WATERS OF [5810] (*limpid [clear] waters* KB; *wholesome waters* BDB; possibly *waters of leopards* IDB). Waters on the borders of Gad and Moab (Isa 15:6; Jer 48:34).

NIMROD [5808] (perhaps *to rebel,* or *the Arrow, the mighty hero*). Son of Cush. "A mighty hunter before the LORD" (Ge 10:8-9; 1Ch 1:10). Founder of Babylon. See Babylon.

NIMRUD Ancient Calah in Assyria, founded by Nimrod (Ge 10:11, 12).

NIMSHI [5811]. Father of Jehu (2Ki 9:2, 20).

NINEVEH [5770, 3780]. A capital of the Assyrian Empire (Ge 10:11-12). Nineveh and its surrounding region had a population of upwards of 120,000 when Jonah preached (Jnh 4:11). Extent of (Jnh 3:4). Sennacherib in (2Ki 19:36-37; Isa 37:37-38). Jonah preaches in (Jnh 1:1-2; 3). Nahum prophesies against (Na 1-3). Zephaniah foretells the desolation of (Zep 2:13-15).

NISAN [5772]. Babylonian name for Abib (Ne 2:1; Est 3:7). See Abib; Month, 1.

NISROCH [5827]. An idol (2Ki 19:36-37; Isa 37:37-38).

NITRE See Soda.

NO See Thebes.

NOADIAH [5676] (*meet with Yahweh*).
1. Levite who returned to Jerusalem after the Exile (Ezr 8:33).
2. False prophetess who tried to terrorize Nehemiah (Ne 6:14).

NOAH [5695, 5829, 3820] (*rest, comfort*).
1. Son of Lamech (Ge 5:28-29), righteous in a corrupt age (Ge 6:8-9; 7:1; Eze 14:14), warned people of the Flood 120 years (Ge 6:3), built an ark (Ge 6:12-22), saved from the Flood with wife and family, together with beasts and fowl of every kind (Ge 7:8), repopulated earth (Ge 9:10), lived 950 years.
God establishes a covenant with (Ge 9:8-17). See Covenants, Major in the Old Testament.
2. Daughter of Zelophehad (Nu 26:33; 27:1; 36:11; Jos 17:3).

NOB [5546]. A city of Benjamin (Ne 11:31-32). Called "the town of the priests" (1Sa 22:19). Home of Ahimelech the priest (1Sa 21:1; 22:11). Probable seat of the tabernacle in Saul's time (1Sa 21:4, 6, 9). David flees to, and is aided by Ahimelech (1Sa 21:1-9; 22:9-10). Destroyed by Saul (2Sa 22:19). Prophecy concerning (Isa 10:32).

NOBAH [5561, 5562] (*barking*).
1. Manassite; took Kenath from Amorites (Nu 32:42).
2. Town near which Gideon defeated the Midianites (Jdg 8:11).

NOBAI See Nebai.

NOBLE [2657, 2985, 3202, 5618, 5619, 7312, 2302, 2819, 4948, 5507]. A word which is used to describe people who were renowned for deeds performed or in some other way were distinguished for skills or genius; people of high rank, position, title, or one well born (Jdg 5:13; Ezr

4:10; Est 6:9; Pr 17:26; Lk 19:12-27; 1Co 1:26), persons who possess high moral qualities or ideals (Ps 16:3; Isa 32:5; Ac 17:11), anything having qualities of a very high order (Eze 17:8, 23; 1Ti 3:1; Lk 21:5).

A nobleman supports and defends his community. He has a generous heart (Ex 35:5, 22; 2Ch 29:31; Nu 21:18; 1Ch 28:21). He is one belonging to a king (Jn 4:46-53). The noble wife is praised in Pr 31:10-31.

NOD [5655] (*wandering*). Region E of Eden to which Cain went (Ge 4:16).

NODAB [5656]. Tribe of Arabs, probably Ishmaelites E of the Jordan (1Ch 5:19).

NOE *See Noah.*

NOGAH [5587] (*joy, splendor*). Son of David (1Ch 3:7; 14:6).

NOHAH [5666] (*rest*). Son of Benjamin (1Ch 8:2).

NOLLE PROSEQUI The complaint against Paul (Ac 18:12-17).

NON *See Nun.*

NONCONFORMITY *See Church, The Body of Believers; State; Form; Formalism.*

NONE LIKE GOD (Ex 8:10; 15:11; Dt 33:26; 2Sa 7:22; 1Ki 8:23; 1Ch 17:20; Ps 89:6; Isa 40:18; Mk 12:32).

NONRESISTANCE Commanded (Mt 5:38-41; Ro 12:17-21; 1Th 5:15; 1Pe 2:19-23). Forgive those who wrong you (Mt 18:15, 21-35; Lk 6:36-37; Eph 4:32; Jas 2:13; 1Pe 3:9). Love your enemies (Ex 23:4-5; Job 31:29-30; Pr 25:21-22; Mt 5:43-48; 6:14-15; Lk 6:27-36; 10:30-37; Ro 12:17-21; 13:10; 1Jn 3:10-11). Return good for evil (Pr 15:1; 25:21-22; Mt 5:38-41; 6:14-15; Ro 12:17-21; 1Th 5:15; 1Pe 3:9). Seek peace (Ps 34:14; 133:1-3; Mt 5:9; 18:15; 2Co 13:11; Gal 5:22; Col 3:12-13; Heb 12:14; Jas 3:17-18; 1Pe 3:11). Suffer gladly for Christ (Mt 5:10-12; Lk 6:22-23; Jn 15:20; Ac 5:41; Ro 12:14; 1Co 4:12-13; 13:7; Gal 5:22; Col 3:12-13; 1Pe 2:19-23; 3:14). Christ, our example (Lk 23:34; 1Pe 2:19-23; 1Jn 2:6). Exemplified by Stephen (Ac 7:60).

See Revenge; Good for Evil; Evil for Good.

NOON [2021+3427+4734, 7416, *1761+6052, 2465+ 3545, 3540*]. (Dt 28:29; Job 11:17; Ps 55:17; 91:6; Isa 58:10; Ac 22:6).

NOPH *See Memphis.*

NOPHAH [5871]. A city of Sihon (Nu 21:30).

NORTH [7600+, 8520, 8522, *1080*]. Often merely as a point of the compass; but sometimes a particular country, usually Assyria or Babylonia (Jer 3:18; 46:6; Eze 26:7; Zep 2:13).

NORTHEASTER [*2350*]. A hurricane-force E wind the Mediterranean; shipwrecked Paul (Ac 27:14).

NOSE [678, 5690, 5705]. Jewels for (Pr 11:22; Isa 3:21; Eze 16:12). Mutilated (Eze 23:25).

NUBIANS [3934]. An African people (Da 11:43).

NUCLEAR WAR Some see a reference to nuclear war in predictions of the fiery destruction of the earth (Zep 1:18; 2Pe 3:7, 10) and in the seven trumpets of Revelation (Rev 8:5-9:19).

NUMBERS [*2118*, 4848, 4948, 5031, 5070, 6369, 7023, 7212, 8041, 8044, 8049, *749, 750, 2653, 4436, 4498*]. Hebrews did not use figures to denote numbers. They spelled numbers out in full; from second century B.C. they used Hebrew letters of the alphabet for numbers. Numbers were often used symbolically; some had special religious significance (Ge 2:2; Ex 20:3-17; Dt 6:4), especially 1, 3, 7, 10, 12, 40, 70, 666, 1000.

NUMBERS, BOOK OF

Author: Traditionally ascribed to Moses

Date: 1445 to 1406 B.C.

Outline:

I. Israel at Sinai, Preparing to Depart for the Promised Land (1:1-10:10).
  A. The Commands for the Census of the People (chs. 1-4).
    1. The numbers of men from each tribe mustered for war (ch. 1).
    2. The placement of the tribes around the tabernacle and their order for march (ch. 2).
    3. The placement of the Levites around the tabernacle, and the numbers of the Levites and the firstborn of Israel (ch. 3).
    4. The numbers of the Levites in their tabernacle service for the Lord (ch. 4).
  B. The Commands for Purity of the People (5:1-10:10).
    1. The test for purity in the law of jealousy (ch. 5).
    2. The Nazirite vow and the Aaronic benediction (ch. 6).
    3. The offerings of the twelve leaders at the dedication of the tabernacle (ch. 7).
    4. The setting up of the lamps and the separation of the Levites (ch. 8).
    5. The observance of the Passover (9:1-14).
    6. The covering cloud and the silver trumpets (9:15-10:10).
II. The Journey From Sinai to Kadesh (10:11-12:16).
  A. The Beginning of the Journey (10:11-36).
  B. The Beginning of the Sorrows: Fire and Quail (ch. 11).

C. The Opposition of Miriam and Aaron (ch. 12).

III. Israel at Kadesh, the Delay Resulting From Rebellion (14:1-20:13).
A. The Twelve Spies and Their Mixed Report of the Good Land (ch. 13).
B. The People's Rebellion Against God's Commission, and Their Defeat (ch. 14).
C. A Collection of Laws on Offerings, the Sabbath and Tassels on Garments (ch. 15).
D. The Rebellion of Korah and His Allies (ch. 16).
E. The Budding of Aaron's Staff: A Sign for Rebels (ch. 17).
F. Concerning Priests, Their Duties and Their Support (ch. 18).
G. The Red Heifer and the Cleansing Water (ch. 19).
H. The Sin of Moses (20:1-13).

IV. The Journey From Kadesh to the Plains of Moab (20:14-22:1).
A. The Resistance of Edom (20:14-21).
B. The Death of Aaron (20:22-29).
C. The Destruction of Arad (21:1-3).
D. The Bronze Snake (21:4-9).
E. The Song of the Well (21:10-20).
F. The Defeat of Sihon and Og (21:21-30).
G. Israel Enters Moab (21:31-22:1).

V. Israel on the Plains of Moab, in Anticipation of Taking the Promised Land (22:2-32:42).
A. Balak of Moab Hires Balaam to Curse Israel (22:2-41).
B. Balaam Blesses Israel in Seven Oracles (chs. 23-24).
C. The Baal of Peor and Israel's Apostasy (ch. 25).
D. The Second Census (ch. 26).
E. Instructions for the New Generation (chs. 27-30).
1. The inheritance for women (27:1-11).
2. The successor to Moses (27:12-23).
3. Commands regarding offerings (28:1-15).
4. Commands regarding festivals (28:16-29:40).
5. Commands regarding vows (ch. 30).
F. The War Against Midian (ch. 31).
G. The Settlement of the Transjordan Tribes (ch. 32).

VI. Appendixes Dealing With Various Matters (chs. 33-36).
A. The Stages of the Journey (ch. 33).
B. The Land of Inheritance (chs. 34-35).
C. The Inheritance for Women (ch. 36).

NUN [5673] (*fish* hence *fertile, productive*). Father of Joshua (Ex 33:11).

NURSE [587, 3437, 3567, 4787, 6402, *1923, 2558, 5555*]. (Ge 24:59; 35:8; Ex 2:7; Ru 4:16; 2Ki 11:2; Isa 60:4; 1Th 2:7). Careless (2Sa 4:4).

NUT [100, 1063]. Pistachio and almond (Ge 43:11), perhaps walnut (SS 6:11).

NYMPHA [*3809*]. A Christian of Laodicea. House of, used as a place of worship (Col 4:15).

OAK [381, 461, 464, 473]. A tree. Grew in Israel (Ge 35:4). Absalom hung in the boughs of (2Sa 18:9, 14). Deborah buried under (Ge 35:8). Oars made of (Eze 27:6).

Figurative (Am 2:9).

OAR [5414, 5415, 8868, *1785*]. For propelling boats (Isa 33:21; Eze 27:6, 29).

OATH [457, 460, 8123, 8652+, 8678, *354, 2019, 2155, 3923, 3992, 3993, 4053*]. A solemn and binding promise.

Used In Solemnizing Covenants:

Between Abraham and the king of Sodom (Ge 14:22-23), and Abimelech (Ge 21:22-23), between Isaac and Abimelech (Ge 26:26-29, 31). Abraham requires oath of his servant Eliezer (Ge 24:2-3, 9). Esau confirms the sale of his birthright by (Ge 25:33). Jacob confirms the covenant between him and Laban by (Ge 31:53), requires Joseph to swear that he would bury Jacob with his fathers (Ge 47:28-31). Joseph requires a like oath (Ge 50:25). Rahab requires an oath from the spies (Jos 2:12-14; 6:14). The Israelites confirm the covenant with the Hivites (Jos 9:3-20). Moses covenants with Caleb by (Jos 14:9). The elders of Gilead confirm their pledge to Jephthah by (Jdg 11:10). The Israelites swear in Mizpah (Jdg 21:5). Ruth swears to Naomi (Ru 1:17). Boaz swears to Ruth (Ru 3:13). Saul swears to Jonathan (1Sa 19:6). Jonathan and David confirm a covenant by (1Sa 20:3, 13-17). David swears to Saul (1Sa 24:21-22; 2Sa 21:7). Saul swears to the medium of Endor (1Sa 28:10). David swears not to eat until the sun goes down (2Sa 3:35). Joab confirms his word to David (2Sa 19:7). David swears to Bathsheba that Solomon confirms his word by (1Ki 2:23), so also does Shimei (1Ki 2:42). Elisha seals his vow to follow Elijah by (2Ki 2:2). King of Samaria confirms his word with an (2Ki 6:31). Gehazi confirms his lie by (2Ki 5:20). Jehoiada requires an oath from the rulers (2Ki 11:4). Zedekiah violates (2Ch 36:13). Ezra requires, of the priests and Levites (Ezr 10:5, 19), so also does Nehemiah (Ne 5:12-13). Zedekiah swears to Jeremiah (Jer 38:16). Gedaliah confirms his word by (Jer 40:9).

Peter confirms his denial of Jesus by (Mk 14:71). Used to cast out demons (Ac 19:13); used by Gadarene demoniac in an attempt to keep Jesus from casting out the legion (Mk 5:7).

Used in solemnizing testimony (Ex 22:10-11; Nu 5:19-24; Dt 6:13; 10:20; 1Ki 8:31-32; Ps 15:1-4; Heb 6:16). Used in confirming allegiance to sovereigns (Ecc 8:2). Used as a result of returning to God (Jer 4:2).

Attributed to God (Ge 22:16; Ps 89:35; 95:11; 105:9; 132:11; Isa 14:24; 45:23; Jer 11:5; 22:5; 49:13; 51:14; Lk 1:73; Heb 3:11, 18; 4:3; 6:13-14, 17; 7:21, 28; Rev 10:6).

Christ's teachings concerning (Mt 23:18-22). Required of Christ (Mt 26:63).

Paul confirms certain statements by (2Co 1:23; Gal 1:20).

Written in the law of Moses (Da 9:11). Mosaic law concerning (Ex 23:1). Samuel affirms his honesty of administration by (1Sa 12:5).

Heard, in Daniel's vision (Da 12:7). In John's vision (Rev 10:5-6).

Profane and Wicked:

Forbidden (Ex 20:7; Lev 19:12; Dt 5:11; Mt 5:33-37; Jas 5:12). Unrighteous, forbidden (Lev 19:12; Hos 4:15). Punishment for (Lev 6:2-5).

Made by Israelites (Isa 48:1; Jer 5:2, 7; 7:8-9). By Herod (Mt 14:7, 9; Mk 6:23, 26). By enemies of Paul (Ac 23:12-14).

Idolatrous: (Jer 12:16).

See Covenant; False Witness; God, Name of; Perjury.

OBADIAH [6281, 6282] (*servant [worshiper] of Yahweh*).

1. Governor of Ahab's household (1Ki 18:3-16).
2. Judahite (1Ch 3:21).
3. Chief of Issachar (1Ch 7:3).
4. Son of Azel (1Ch 8:38).
5. Levite who returned from captivity (1Ch 9:16). Also called Abda (Ne 11:17).
6. Gadite soldier (1Ch 12:9).
7. Father of Ishmaiah, prince of Zebulun (1Ch 27:19).
8. Prince of Judah (2Ch 17:7).
9. Merarite Levite (2Ch 34:12).
10. Jew who returned from captivity (Ezr 8:9).
11. Priestly covenanter with Nehemiah (Ne 10:5).
12. Gatekeeper in Jerusalem (Ne 12:25).
13. A prophet who wrote the book of Obadiah.

OBADIAH, BOOK OF

Author: The prophet Obadiah

Date:

If Obadiah relates to the invasion of Jerusalem by Philistines and Arabs during the reign of Jehoram (853-841 B.C.) (2Ki 8:20-22; 2Ch 21:8-20), the prophet would be a contemporary of Elisha.

If Obadiah relates to the Babylonian attacks on Jerusalem (605-586), the prophet would be a contemporary of Jeremiah. This alternative seems more likely.

Outline:

I. Title and Introduction (1).
II. Judgment on Edom (2-14).
    A. Edom's Destruction Announced (2-7).
        1. The humbling of her pride (2-4).
        2. The completeness of her destruction (5-7).
    B. Edom's Destruction Reaffirmed (8-14).

1. Her shame and destruction (8-10).
2. Her crimes against Israel (11-14).
III. The Day of the Lord (15-21).
  A. Judgment on the Nations but Deliverance for Zion (15-18).
  B. The Lord's Kingdom Established (19-21).
See Prophets, The Minor.

OBAL [6382]. Called also Ebal. A son of Joktan (Ge 10:28; 1Ch 1:22).

OBDURACY Callousness, hardness. Angers God (Ps 78:31; Isa 57:17). Warnings against (Ps 95:8-11; Heb 3:8, 15; 4:7). Punishment for (Lev 26:23-25; Ps 78:31-32; Pr 1:24-31; 29:1; Jer 3:2; Am 4:6-11).

  Instances of: The antediluvians (Ge 6:3, 5, 7). Sodomites (Ge 19:14). Pharaoh (Ex 7:14, 22-23; 8:15, 19, 32; 9:7, 12, 35; 10:20, 28; 11:10; 14:5-8). Israelites (Nu 14:22; Ne 9:28-29; Ps 78:32; Isa 9:13-14; Jer 2:20; 5:3; Am 4:6-12; Zec 7:11-12). Sons of Eli (1Sa 2:22-25). Brothers of a rich man (Lk 16:31). Mankind in the last days (Rev 9:20-21).

  See Afflictions, Of the Wicked; Impenitence; Reprobacy.

OBED [6381, *2725*] (*servant [worshiper]*).
1. Son of Boaz and grandfather of David (Ru 4:17-22; 1Ch 2:12; Mt 1:5; Lk 3:32).
2. Son of Ephlal and grandson of Zabad (1Ch 2:37-38).
3. One of David's heroes (1Ch 11:47).
4. Son of Shemaiah. A gatekeeper of the temple (1Ch 26:7).
5. Father of Azariah (2Ch 23:1).

OBED-EDOM [6273] (*servant [worshiper] of Edom*).
1. A Korahite Levite. Doorkeeper of the ark (1Ch 15:18, 24; 26:4-8). David leaves the ark with (2Sa 6:10; 1Ch 13:13-14). Ark removed from (2Sa 6:12; 1Ch 15:25). Appointed to sound with harps (1Ch 15:21). Appointed to minister before the ark (1Ch 16:4-5, 37-38).
2. A doorkeeper of the temple (1Ch 16:38).
3. A caretaker of the vessels of the temple in time of Amaziah (2Ch 25:24).

OBEDIENCE [*3682, 5915, 6913, 9048, 9068, *2848, 4272, 4275, 5498, 5633, 5634, 5675, 5875*].

General:
  Better than sacrifice (1Sa 15:22; Ps 40:6-9; Pr 21:3; Jer 7:22-23; Hos 6:6; Mic 6:6-8; Mt 9:13; 12:7; Mk 12:33; Heb 10:8-9).
  Commanded (Ge 17:9; Ex 23:22; Lev 19:19, 36-37; 20:8, 22; 22:31; Nu 15:38-40; 30:2; Dt 4:1-40; 5:1-33; 6:1-25; 8:1-6, 11-20; 10:12-13; 11:1-3, 8-9, 13-28, 32; 13:4; 26:16-18; 27:1-10; 32:46; Jos 22:5; 23:6-7; 24:14-15; 1Sa 12:14, 20, 24; 15:22; 2Ki 17:37-38; 1Ch 16:15; 28:9-10, 20; Ezr 7:23; Ps 76:11; Pr 7:1; Ecc 12:13; Jer 26:13; 38:20; Da 7:27; Mal 4:4; Eph 6:6-8; Php 2:12; 1Ti 6:14, 18; Jas 1:22-25; 2:10-12; 1Pe 1:2, 14).

Proof of love (Jn 14:15, 21; 1Jn 2:5-6; 5:2-3; 2Jn 6, 9), under Mosaic law (Lev 18:5; Eze 20:11, 13, 21; Lk 10:28; Ro 10:5; Gal 3:10, 12). Proof that we know God (1Jn 2:3-4).
  Vows of (Ex 24:7; Jos 24:24; Ps 119:15, 106, 109). Prayer for guidance in (Ps 143:10).
  Cannot be rendered to two masters (Mt 6:24).

Rewards:
  (Ge 18:19; Lev 26:3-13; Nu 14:24; Dt 7:12-15; 28:1-15; Jos 14:6-14; 2Ki 21:8; Isa 1:19).
  Rewarded by: Prosperity (Dt 7:9, 12-15; 15:4; Jos 1:8; 1Ki 2:3-4; 9:3-5; 1Ch 22:13; 28:7-8; 2Ch 26:5; 27:6; Job 36:11; Pr 28:7; Jer 7:3-7; 11:1-5; 22:16; Mal 3:10-12; 1Jn 3:22). Long life (Dt 4:1, 40; 32:47; 1Ki 3:14; Pr 3:1-2; 19:16). Victory over enemies (Ex 23:22; Pr 16:7). Triumph over adversities (Mt 7:24-25; Lk 6:46-48). Divine favor (Ex 19:5; 20:6; Dt 5:10; 11:26-27; 12:28; 1Ki 8:23; Ne 1:5; Ps 25:10; 103:17-18, 20; 112:1; 119:2; Pr 1:33; Jer 7:23; 11:4; Mt 5:19; 25:20-23; Lk 11:28; 12:37-38; Jn 12:26; 13:17; Jas 1:25; Rev 22:7). Fellowship with Christ (Mt 12:50; Mk 3:35; Lk 8:21; Jn 14:23; 15:10, 14; 1Jn 3:24). Everlasting life (Mt 19:17, 29; Jn 8:51; 1Jn 2:17; Rev 2:10).

Exemplified:
  (Dt 33:9; Ps 1:2; 103:1-22; 1Th 1:9; Rev 2:19). Noah (Ge 6:9, 22; 7:5; Heb 11:7). Abraham (Ge 12:1-4; 17:23; 18:19; 21:4; 22:12, 18; 26:3-5; Ne 9:8; Ac 7:3-8; Heb 11:8-17; Jas 2:21). Bethuel and Laban (Ge 24:50). Jacob (Ge 35:1, 7). Laban (Ge 31:29). Moses (Nu 27:12-22; Heb 3:2-3). Moses and Aaron (Ex 7:6; 40:16, 21, 23, 32). Israelites (Ex 12:28; 32:25-29; 39:42-43; Nu 9:20-21, 23; Dt 33:9; Jos 22:2; Jdg 2:7; Ps 99:7). Israelites under the preaching of Haggai (Hag 1:12). Caleb (Nu 14:24; Dt 1:36; Jos 14:6-14). Joshua (Jos 10:40; 11:15). Reubenites (Jos 22:2-3). Gibeon (Jdg 6:25-28). David (1Ki 11:6, 34; 15:5; 2Ch 29:2; Ac 13:22). Elijah (1Ki 17:5).
  The psalmist (Ps 17:3; 26:3-6; 119:30-31, 40, 44, 47-48, 51, 55-56, 59-60, 67, 69, 100, 102, 105-106, 110, 112, 119, 166-168). Elisha (1Ki 19:19-21). Hezekiah (2Ki 18:6; 20:3; 2Ch 31:20-21; Isa 38:3). Josiah (2Ki 22:2; 23:24-25). Asa (2Ch 14:2). Jehoshaphat (2Ch 17:3-6; 20:32; 22:9). Uzziah (2Ch 26:4-5). Jotham (2Ch 27:2). Levites (2Ch 29:34). Cyrus (Ezr 1:1-4). Ezra (Ezr 7:10). Hanani (Ne 7:2). Job (Job 1:8). The three Hebrews (Da 3). Jonah (Jnh 3:3). Ninevites (Jnh 3:5-10).
  Zechariah (Lk 1:6). Simeon (Lk 2:25). Joseph (Mt 1:24; 2:14). Mary (Lk 1:38). Jesus (Mt 3:15; 26:39, 42; Lk 22:42; Jn 4:32, 34; 5:30; 6:38; 8:28-29; 9:4; 12:49-50; 14:31; 17:4; Php 2:8; Heb 3:2). By, John the Baptist (Mt 3:15). John and James (Mk 1:19-20). Matthew (Mt 9:9). Simon and Andrew (Mk 1:16-18). Levi (Mk 2:14). The rich young man (Mt 19:20; Mk 10:20; Lk 18:21). The disciples (Jn 17:6; Ac 4:19-20; 5:29). Cornelius (Ac 10:2). Paul (Ac 23:1; 24:17; 26:4-5; Php 3:7-14; 2Ti 1:3). Paul and Timothy (2Co 1:12; 6:3). Paul, Timothy, and Silas (1Th 2:1). The Christians at Rome (Ro 6:17).
  To Civil Law. *See Citizens.*

Filial. *See Children.*

See Blessings, Spiritual, Contingent Upon Obedience; Commandments and Statutes, Of God; Duty; Faithfulness; Law.

OBEISANCE
The act of bowing low or of prostrating oneself in token of respect or submission (Ge 43:28; Ex 18:7; 2Sa 1:2). *See Worship, Attitudes in.*

OBIL
[201] (*camel driver*). An Ishmaelite. Camel-keeper for David (1Ch 27:30).

OBJECT TEACHING
See Instruction.

OBLATION
See Offerings.

OBLIGATION
[673, 5466, 5929, 8966, 10419+10420, *4050, 4052*]. A motive of obedience (Dt 4:32-40; 6-11; 26:16; 32:6; 1Sa 12:24; 1Ch 16:12; Ro 2:4; 2Co 5:15). Acknowledgment of (Ps 116:12-14, 17). *See Duty.*

OBLIQUITY
See Depravity.

OBOTH
[95] (*fathers*). A camping place of Israel in the forty years' wandering (Nu 21:10-11; 33:43-44).

OBSEQUIOUSNESS
See Tact.

OBSTETRICS
(Eze 16:4). *See Midwives.*

OCCULTISM
See Sorcery.

OCCUPATIONS AND PROFESSIONS
Artisan—a worker with any materials, as carpenter, smith, engraver, etc.— author; baker; barber; beggar; carpenter; clerk; coppersmith; counselor; cupbearer; doctor; diviner; dyer; farmer; fisherman; gatekeeper; herdsman; hunter; judge; launderer; lawyer; magician; mason; medium; musician; nurse; perfumer; physician; plowman; potter; preacher; priest; prophet; rabbi; recorder; robber; ruler; sailor; scribe; seer; servant; sheepshearer; shepherd; silversmith; singer; slave; smith; soldier; sorcerer; spinner; steward; tanner; taskmaster; tax collector; teacher; tentmaker; tiller; town clerk; treasurer; watchman; weaver; witch; writer.

See each occupation by name.

OCRAN
[6581] (*trouble*). An Asherite and the father of Pagiel who numbered Israel (Nu 1:13; 2:27; 10:26).

ODED
[6389] (*restorer*).
1. A prophet in Samaria (2Ch 28:9).
2. Father of the prophet Azariah (2Ch 15:1).

ODOR
[3853]. Pleasant or unpleasant smell (Ge 8:21; Lev 1:9-17; Jn 11:39). Also used figuratively (Ro 5:8).

OFFENSE
[*6411, 7321, 7322, *4997, 4998*].
Used in a variety of ways: Injury, hurt, damage, occasion of sin, stumbling block, infraction of the law, sin, transgression, state of being offended.

OFFERINGS
[*852, 871, 2284, 2285, 2627, 2633, 2853, 4003, 4854, 4966, 5605, 5607, 5818, 5821, 6590, 6592, 7175, 7731, 7787, 7928, 7933, 8968, 9343, 9485, 9556, 10432, *1126, 3906, 4712, 4714, 5064*]. Holy (Lev 2:3; 6:17, 25, 27, 29; 7:1, 6; 10:12; Nu 18:9-10). Offered at door of the tabernacle (Lev 1:3; 3:2; 17:4, 8-9) of the temple (1Ki 8:62; 12:27; 2Ch 7:12).

All animal sacrifices, must be eight days old or over (Lev 22:27), must be without blemish (Ex 12:5; 29:1; Lev 1:3, 10; 22:18-25; Dt 15:21; 17:1; Eze 43:23; Mal 1:8, 14; Heb 9:14; 1Pe 1:19). *See Bruise(s), 2,* must be salted (Lev 2:13; Eze 43:24; Mk 9:49), accompanied with leaven (Lev 7:13; Am 4:5), without leaven (Ex 23:18; 34:25), eaten (1Sa 9:13). Ordinance relating to scapegoat (Lev 16:7-26). Atonement for sin made by. *See Atonement.*

Figurative:
(Ps 51:17; Jer 33:11; Ro 12:1; Php 4:18; Heb 13:15).

Animal Sacrifices:
A type of Christ (Ps 40:6-8, w Heb 10:1-14; Isa 53:11-12, w Lev 16:21; Jn 1:29; 1Co 5:7; 2Co 5:21; Eph 5:2; Heb 9:19-28; 10:1, 11-12; 13:11-13; Rev 5:6).

Burnt:
(Lev 9:2). Its purpose was to make an atonement for sin (Lev 1:4; 7). Ordinances concerning (Ex 29:15-18; Lev 1; 5:7-13; 6:9-13; 17:8-9; 23:18, 26-37; Nu 15:24-25; 19:9; 28:26-31; 29). Accompanied by other offerings (Nu 15:3-16). Skins of, belonged to priests (Lev 7:8). Offered daily, morning and evening (Ge 15:17; Ex 29:38-42; Lev 6:20; Nu 28; 29:6; Nu 16:40; 2Ch 2:4; 13:11; Ezr 3:3; Eze 46:13-15). Music with (Nu 10:10).

Offered, by Noah (Ge 8:20), in idolatrous worship (Ex 32:6; 1Ki 18:26; 2Ki 10:25; Ac 14:13). For cleansing leprosy (Lev 14).

Daily:
Sacrificial (Ex 29:38-42; Lev 6:20; Nu 28:3-8; 29:6; 1Ki 18:29; 1Ch 16:40; 2Ch 2:4; 13:11; Ezr 3:3-6; 9:4-5; Ps 141:2; Eze 46:13-15; Da 9:21, 27; 11:31).

Drink:
Libations of wine offered with the sacrifices (Ge 35:14; Ex 29:40-41; 30:9; Lev 23:13, 18; Nu 6:17; 15:24; 28:5-15, 24-31; 29:6-11, 18-40; 2Ki 16:13; 1Ch 29:21; 2Ch 29:35; Ezr 7:17).

Fellowship:
Laws concerning (Ex 20:24; 24:5; Lev 3:6; 7:11-18; 9:3-4, 18-22; 19:5; 23:10; Nu 6:14; 10:10). Offered, by the tribal leaders (Nu 7:17, 23, 29, 35, 41, 47, 53, 59, 65, 71, 77, 83, 88), by Joshua (Jos 8:31), by David (2Sa 6:17; 24:25).

Offered in idolatrous worship (Ex 32:6). Offered by harlots (Pr 7:14).

Free Will:

(Lev 23:38; Nu 29:39; Dt 12:6; 2Ch 31:14; Ezr 3:5). Must be perfect (Lev 22:17-25). To be eaten, at tabernacle (Lev 7:16-17). With meat and drink offerings (Nu 15:1-16). Obligatory (Dt 16:10), when signified in a vow (Dt 23:23).

Guilt:

Ordinances concerning (Lev 5; 6:1-7; 7:1-7; 14:10-22; 15:15, 29-30; 19:21-22; Nu 6:12; Ezr 10:19). To be eaten by the priests (Lev 7:6-7; 14:13; Nu 18:9-10). Offered by idolaters (1Sa 6:3, 8, 17-18). *See below, Sin.*

Heave: *See below, Presentation or Wave.*

Human Sacrifices:

Forbidden (Lev 18:21; 20:2-5; Dt 12:31). Offered by Abraham (Ge 22:1-19; Heb 11:17-19), by Canaanites (Dt 12:31), Moabites (2Ki 3:27), Israelites (2Ki 16:3; 2Ch 28:3; 2Ki 23:10; Isa 57:5; Jer 7:31; 19:5; 32:35; Eze 16:20-21; 20:26, 31; 23:37, 39), by the Sepharvites to idols (2Ki 17:31). To demons (Ps 106:37-38), to Baal (Jer 19:5-6).

Meat:

Ordinances concerning (Ex 29:40-41; 30:9; 40:29; Lev 2; 5:11-12; 6:14-23; 7:9-13, 37; 9:17; 23:13, 16-17; Nu 4:16; 5:15, 18, 25-26; 8:8; 15:3-16, 24; 18:9; 28:5, 9, 12-13, 20-21, 26-31; 29:3-4, 14). To be eaten in the Holy Place (Lev 10:13; Nu 18:9-10). Offered with animal sacrifices (Nu 15:3-16). Not mixed with leaven (Lev 2:4, 11; 6:14-18; 10:12-13; Nu 6:15, 17). Storerooms for, in the temple (Ne 12:44; 13:5-6), provided for in the vision of Ezekiel (Eze 42:12).

Peace: *See above, Fellowship.*

Presentation or Wave:

Given to the priests' families as part of their share (Lev 10:14; Nu 5:9; 18:10-19, 24). Consecrated by being elevated by the priest (Ex 29:27). Consisted of the right thigh or hindquarter (Ex 29:27-28; Lev 7:12-14, 32, 34; 10:15), spoils, including captives and other articles of war (Nu 31:29, 41). When offered (Lev 7:12-14; Nu 6:20; 15:19-21). In certain instances this offering was brought to the tabernacle, or temple (Dt 12:6, 11, 17-18). To be offered on taking possession of the land of Canaan (Nu 15:18-21).

Sin:

Ordinances concerning (Ex 29:10-14, w Heb 13:11-13; Lev 4; 5; 6:1-7, 26-30; 9:1-21; 12:6-8; 14:19, 22, 31; 15:30; 23:19; Nu 6:10-11, 14, 16; 8:8, 12; 15:27; 28:15, 22-24, 30; 29:5-6, 11, 16-38). Temporary (Da 11:31; Heb 9-10).

Special Sacrifices:

In consecration of the altar. *See Altar.* Of priests. *See Priest.* Of the temple. *See Temple, Solomon's.* For leprosy. *See Leprosy.* For defilement. *See Defilement.*

Thank:

Ordinances concerning (Lev 7:11-15; 22:29; Dt 12:11-12).

Trespass: *See above, Guilt.*

Vow:

(Lev 7:16-17; 22:17-25; Dt 23:21-23).

Wave:

Ordinances concerning (Ex 29:22, 26-28; Lev 7:29-34; 8:25-29; 9:19-21; 10:14-15; 23:10-11, 17, 20; Nu 5:25; 6:19-20). Belonged to the priests (Ex 29:26-28; Lev 7:31, 34; 8:29; 9:21; 23:20; Nu 18:11, 18). To be eaten (Lev 10:14-15; Nu 18:11, 18-19, 31).

Wood:

Fuel for the temple (Ne 10:34; 13:31).

Insufficiency of:

(Heb 8:7-13; 9:1-15; 10:1-12, 18-20). Unavailing, when not accompanied by piety (1Sa 15:22; Ps 40:6; 50:8-14; 51:16-17; Pr 21:3, 27; Isa 1:11-14; 66:3; Jer 6:20; 7:21-23; 14:12; Hos 6:6; 8:13; Am 5:21-24; Mic 6:6-8; Mt 9:13; 12:7; Mk 12:33).

OFFICER [*5592, 5853, 5893, 6036, 6247, 6269, 7068, 7212, 7224, 8042, 8097, 8569, 8853, 8957, 10061, 10716, *1672, 3489, 4485, 4551, 4812, 5130, 5677*].

Civil:

Chosen by the people (Dt 1:13-16), appointed by kings (2Sa 8:16-18; 20:23-26; 1Ki 4:1-19; 9:22; Ezr 7:25). *See Government; Judge; Rulers.*

Ecclesiastical: *See Priest; Levites; Apostle; Elders; Deacon; Minister.*

OFFSCOURING Term of contempt; NIV "scum" (La 3:45; 1Co 4:13).

OG [6384]. King of Bashan. A man of gigantic stature (Nu 21:33; Dt 3:11; Jos 12:4; 13:12). Defeated and slain by Moses (Nu 21:33-35; Dt 1:4; 3:1-7; 29:7; 31:4; Jos 2:10; 9:10; Ps 135:10-11; 136:18-20). Land of, given to Gad, Reuben, and Manasseh (Nu 32:33; Dt 3:8-17; 4:47-49; 29:7-8; Jos 12:4-6; 13:12, 30-31; 1Ki 4:19; Ne 9:22; Ps 136:20-21).

OHAD [176]. Son of Simeon (Ge 46:10; Ex 6:15).

OHEL [186] (*[skin] tent*). Son of Zerubbabel (1Ch 3:20).

OHOLAH [188] (*she who has a tent*). In God's parable to Ezekiel (ch. 23), Oholah is a woman representing Samaria, who with her sister Oholibah (Jerusalem) was accused of being unfaithful to Yahweh. Imaginary characters, figurative of idolatry (Eze 23:4-5, 36, 44).

OHOLIAB [190] (*tent of [my] Father*). A craftsman of the tabernacle (Ex 31:6; 35:34; 36:1-2; 38:23).

OHOLIBAH [191] (*my tent is in her*). See *Oholah.*

OHOLIBAMAH [192] ([*my*] *tent is a high place*).

1. One of Esau's three wives (Ge 36:2, 18, 25). Also called Judith the daughter of Beeri (Ge 26:34).

2. An Edomite chief (Ge 36:41; 1Ch 1:52), probably so named from the district of his possession.

OIL [2016, 3658, 5417, 9043, 10442, *230*, *1778*]. Sacred (Ex 30:23-25; 31:11; 35:8, 15, 28; 37:29; 39:38; Nu 4:16; 1Ch 9:30). Compounded by Bezalel (Ex 37:1, 29). Punishment for profaning (Ex 30:31-33). Used for idols (Eze 23:41). Illuminating, for tabernacle (Ex 25:6; 27:20; Lev 24:2-4). Of olives (Ex 25:6).

For domestic use (Mt 25:3). Used for food (Lev 2:4-5; 14:10, 21; Dt 12:17; 1Ki 17:12-16; Job 29:6; Pr 21:17; Eze 16:13; Hos 2:5). For the head (Ps 23:5; 105:15; Lk 7:46). For anointing kings (1Sa 10:1; 16:1, 13; 1Ki 1:39).

Tribute paid in (Hos 12:1). Commerce in (2Ki 4:1-7).

See Anointing; Ointment.

OIL TREE See Plants of the Bible.

OINTMENT [5350, 9043]. (Job 41:31). Used in care of newborns (Eze 16:9).

OLD AGE [*1201, 2416, 2418, 2419, 2420, 2421, 3427, 3813, 6409, 8484, *1179*]. Wise (1Ki 12:6-8; 2Ch 10:6-8; Job 12:12). Devout (Lk 2:37). Exemplary, commanded (Tit 2:2-3). Deference toward (Lev 19:32; Job 32:4-9). Righteous, is glorious (Pr 16:31). Wasted, is bitter (Ge 47:9; Ecc 6:3, 6; 12:1-7).

Promised to the righteous (Ge 15:15; Job 5:26; Ps 34:12-14; 91:14, 16; Pr 3:1-2). God's care in (Isa 46:4). Psalmist prays not to be forsaken in (Ps 71:9, 18). David enjoys (1Ch 29:28). Paul, the aged (Phm 9).

Infirmities in (2Sa 19:34-37; Ps 90:10). Vigor in (Dt 34:7; Ps 92:12-14). Join in praise to the Lord (Ps 148:12-13).

See Longevity; Infirmity.

OLD GATE See Jeshanah, 2.

OLD TESTAMENT In Protestant Bibles, thirty-nine books from Genesis to Malachi: Five of law, twelve of history, five of poetry, five of major prophets, and twelve of minor prophets. In the Hebrew Bible, the same contents are organized into twenty-four books from Genesis to Chronicles: Five of law, eight of the prophets, and eleven of miscellaneous writings. All of these books were regarded by Israelites as Scripture, inspired and authoritative, before the first century A.D. (Mt 5:17-20; Lk 24:44; Jn 17:17; 2Ti 3:16). They appeared over a period of c. 1000 years. The authors of many of them are unknown.

OLIVE [1737, 2339, 3658, 4184, 7414, 9043, 10442, *66*, *1777*, *1778*, *2814*]. A fruit tree. Branch

of, brought by the dove to Noah's ark (Ge 8:11). Common to the land of Canaan (Ex 23:11; Dt 6:11; 8:8), Israelites commanded to cultivate in the land of promise (Dt 28:40). Branches of, used for booths (Ne 8:15). Produces blooms (Job 15:33). Precepts concerning gleaning the fruit of (Dt 24:20; Isa 17:6). Cherubim made of the wood of (1Ki 6:23, 31-33). Fable of (Jdg 9:8).

Figurative:

Of prosperity (Ps 128:3). The wild, a figure of the Gentiles; the cultivated, of the Jews (Ro 11:17-21, 24).

Symbolic: (Zec 4:2-12; Rev 11:4).

Fruit of:

Oil extracted from, used as illuminating oil in the tabernacle (Ex 39:37; Lev 24:2; Zec 4:12).

See Oil.

OLIVES, MOUNT OF [2339, *1777*, *1779*]. A ridge, c. one mile long, with four identifiable summits, E of Jerusalem, beyond the Valley of Jehoshaphat, through which flows the Kidron stream. Gethsemane, Bethphage, and Bethany are on its slopes (2Sa 15:30; Zec 14:4; Mt 21:1; 24:3; 26:30; Mk 11:1; 13:3; 14:26; Lk 19:29, 37; 22:39; Jn 8:1; Ac 1:12).

OLIVET See Olives, Mount of.

OLYMPAS [3912]. A believer at Rome (Ro 16:15).

OMAR [223] (*speaker*). Son of Eliphaz, grandson of Esau (Ge 36:11, 15; 1Ch 1:36).

OMEGA [6042]. Alpha and Omega, a title of Christ, meaning he is the beginning and end of all things (Rev 1:8, 11; 21:6; 22:13). *See Jesus the Christ, Names of; Titles and Names.*

OMER [6685]. One-tenth part of an ephah. A dry measure containing, according to the Rabbis, two quarts, but according to Josephus, three and one-half quarts (Ex 16:16-18, 36).

OMNIPOTENCE (*all power*). The attribute of God which describes his ability to do whatever he wills. He cannot do anything contrary to his nature as God, such as to ignore sin, to sin, or to do something absurd or self-contradictory. God is not controlled by his power, but has complete control over it; otherwise he would not be a free being. Although the word "omnipotence" is not found in the Bible, the Scriptures clearly teach the omnipotence of God (Job 42:2; Jer 32:17; Mt 19:26; Lk 1:37; Rev 19:6).

See God, Omnipotent; Jesus the Christ, Power of.

OMNIPRESENCE (*all presence*). The attribute of God by virtue of which he fills the universe in all its parts and is present everywhere at once. Not a part, but the whole of God is present in every place. The Bible teaches the omnipresence of God (Ps 139:7-12; Jer 23:23-24; Ac

17:27-28). This is true of all three members of the Trinity.

See God, Omnipresent.

OMNISCIENCE *(all knowing)*. The attribute by which God perfectly and eternally knows all things which can be known, past, present, and future. God's omniscience is clearly taught in Scripture (Ps 147:5; Pr 15:11; Isa 46:1).

See God, Knowledge of; Jesus the Christ, Omniscience of.

OMRI [6687] *(thrive, live long* ISBE).

1. King of Israel. Was commander of the army of Israel, and was proclaimed king by the army upon news of the assassination of King Elah (1Ki 16:16). Defeats his rival, Tibni, and establishes himself (1Ki 16:17-22). Surrendered cities to the king of Syria (1Ki 20:34). Wicked reign and death of (1Ki 16:23-28). Denounced by Micah (Mic 6:16).

2. Son of Beker, grandson of Benjamin (1Ch 7:8).

3. A descendant of Perez (1Ch 9:4).

4. Son of Michael, and ruler of tribe of Issachar in time of David (1Ch 27:18).

ON [227, 228] *(sun [god] city)*.

1. Capital of lower Egypt (Ge 41:45; 46:20).

2. A leader of the Reubenites who rebelled against Moses (Nu 16:1).

ONAM [231] *(intense, strong)*. A son of Shobal (Ge 36:23; 1Ch 1:40).

ONAN [232] *(powerful, intense)*. Son of Judah. Slain for his refusal to raise seed to his brother (Ge 38:4, 8-10; 46:12; Nu 26:19; 1Ch 2:3).

ONE AND ONLY [3666]. A title applied to Jesus by John (Jn 1:14, 18; 3:16, 18; 1Jn 4:9), and once in Hebrews (Heb 11:17). It emphasizes the unique relationship of Jesus to God the Father. In ancient mss of Jn 1:18, Jesus is called God the One and Only, a clear reference to his deity.

ONE ANOTHER Responsibilities of fellow believers to (1Pe 4:7-10). All believers members of (Ro 12:5; Eph 4:25).

Commanded to:

Admonish (Ro 15:14; Col 3:16, w 2Th 3:15). Assemble together with (Heb 10:24). Bear burdens of (Gal 6:2). Comfort (1Th 4:18; 5:11, w 14). Confess faults to (Jas 5:16). Consider above self (Heb 10:24). Be courteous (1Pe 3:8). Edify (Ro 14:18; 1Th 5:11). Encourage (Heb 10:24). Equality with (Ro 12:16; 15:5, 7; 1Co 11:33; 12:25; Php 2:3). Exhort daily (Heb 3:13). Have fellowship with (1Jn 1:7). Forgive (Eph 4:32; Col 3:13). Do good to (1Th 5:15). Be hospitable to (1Pe 4:9), in greeting (Ro 16:16; 1Co 16:20; 2Co 13:12; 1Pe 5:5). Be kind to (Eph 4:32). Love (Jn 13:34-35; 15:12, 17; Ro 12:10; 13:8; 1Co 12:25; Gal 5:13; Eph 4:2, 32; 1Th 3:12; 4:9; 1Pe 1:22; 2:17; 3:8; 1Jn 3:11, 23; 4:7, 11-12; 2Jn 5). Minis-

ter to (1Pe 4:10). Be patient with (Eph 4:2; Col 3:13). Be at peace with (Mk 9:50; 1Th 5:13). Pray for (Jas 5:16). Prefer (Ro 12:10; Php 2:3; 1Ti 5:21). Provoke to love and good works (Heb 10:24). Serve (Gal 5:13; 1Pe 4:10), by washing feet of (Jn 13:14). Be subject to (1Pe 5:5), husband and wife, each to be subject to (Eph 5:21). Teach (Col 3:16). Wait for (1Co 11:33).

Love of, exemplified (2Th 1:3).

Commanded Not to:

Deceive (1Co 7:5), devour and consume (Gal 5:15), do evil to (1Th 5:5), envy (Gal 5:26), grudge (Jas 5:9), judge (Ro 14:13), lie to (Lev 19:11; Col 3:9), owe anything to (Ro 13:8), provoke (Gal 5:26), speak evil of (Jas 4:11).

ONE GOD (Dt 4:35; 6:4; 32:39; 2Sa 7:22; 1Ch 17:20; Ps 83:18; 86:10; Isa 43:10; 44:6; 45:18; Mk 12:29; 1Co 8:4; Eph 4:6; 1Ti 2:5; 1Jn 5:7). That God is one (Dt 6:4) does not deny the doctrine of the Trinity, for the same word is used of husband and wife as "one flesh" (Ge 2:24).

ONESIMUS [3946] *(useful)*. Runaway slave of Philemon of Colosse; converted through Paul, who wrote the letter to Philemon in his behalf (Col 4:9; Phm).

See Philemon, Epistle to.

ONESIPHORUS [3947] *(one bringing usefulness)*. A Christian of Ephesus (2Ti 1:16-17; 4:19).

ONION [1294]. Enjoyed by Israel in Egypt (Nu 11:5).

ONLY-BEGOTTEN *See One and Only.*

ONO [229] *(strong)*. Town in Benjamin, c. six miles SE of Joppa (1Ch 8:12; Ne 6:2; 11:35).

ONYCHA [8829]. A component of the sacred perfume, made from the shells of a species of mussel, possessing an odor (Ex 30:34).

ONYX [8732]. Exported from Havilah (Ge 2:12). Contributed by Israelites for the priests' garments (Ex 25:7; 35:9). Used in the breastplate (Ex 28:9-12, 20; 39:6, 13). Used in building the temple (1Ch 29:2). Precious stone (Job 28:16; Eze 28:13). Seen in the foundations of the city of the New Jerusalem in John's apocalyptic vision (Rev 21:20).

See Minerals of the Bible, 1; Stones.

OPHEL [6755] *(mound, hill)*. A gate in the wall of the city and the temple (2Ch 27:3; 33:14; Ne 3:26-27).

OPHIR [234].

1. Son of Joktan (Ge 10:29; 1Ch 1:23).

2. A country celebrated for its gold and other valuable merchandise. Products of, used by Solomon and Hiram (1Ki 9:28; 10:11; 2Ch 8:18; 9:10). Jehoshaphat sends ships to, which are wrecked (1Ki 22:48). Gold of, proverbial for its

fineness (1Ch 29:4; Job 22:24; 28:16; Ps 45:9; Isa 13:12).

OPHNI [6756]. A town of the Benjamites (Jos 18:24).

OPHRAH [6763, 6764] (*young gazelle*).

1. A city in Benjamin (Jos 18:23; 1Sa 13:17). Possibly identical with Ephron (2Ch 13:19) and Ephraim (Jn 11:54).

2. A city in Manasseh, home of Gideon (Jdg 6:11, 24; 8:27, 32; 9:5).

3. Son of Meonothai and descendant of Judah through Kenaz and Othniel (1Ch 4:14).

OPINION [1819, 4213, 6191, *1506*].

Public:

Kings influenced by. *See Kings.* Jesus inquires about (Mt 16:13; Lk 9:18). Feared by Nicodemus (Jn 3:2), Joseph of Arimathea (Jn 19:38), the parents of the man who was born blind (Jn 9:21-22), rulers who believed in Jesus but feared the Pharisees (Jn 12:42-43), chief priests who feared to answer the questions of Jesus (Mt 21:26; Mk 11:18, 32; 12:12), and to further persecute the disciples (Ac 4:21; 5:26).

Concessions to:

By Paul in circumcising Timothy (Ac 16:3). James and the Christian elders who required Paul to observe certain rites (Ac 21:18-26). Disciples who urged circumcision (Gal 6:12). Peter and Barnabas with others (Gal 2:11-14).

See Prudence.

Corrupt Yielding to:

By Herod, in the case of John the Baptist (Mk 6:26), of Peter (Ac 12:3), by Peter, concerning Jesus (Mt 26:69-75), by Pilate (Mt 27:23-27; Mk 15:15; Lk 23:13-25; Jn 18:38-39; 19:4-16), by Felix and Festus, concerning Paul (Ac 24:27; 25:9).

OPPORTUNITY [4595, *177, 929, 2320, 2321, 2323, 2789, 5536*]. Providential (1Co 16:9; 2Co 2:12). Neglected (Lk 12:47). Spurned (Pr 1:24-25; Mt 23:34-38; Lk 14:16-24). Lost (Nu 14:40-43; Pr 1:28; Jer 8:20; Hos 5:6; Mt 24:50-51; 25:1-10, 24-28; Lk 19:20-24; 13:25-28). Terrible consequences of neglecting (Eze 3:19; Mt 25:3-13, 24-30, 41-46).

Terrible consequences of spurning (Pr 1:24-32; Mt 10:14-15; 11:20-24).

The measure of responsibility (Pr 1:24-30; Jer 8:20; Eze 3:19; 33:1-17; Hos 5:6; Mt 10:14-15; 11:20-24; Mt 23:34-38; 25:1-46 w Lk 19:20-24; Lk 12:47; 13:25-28; 14:16-24).

See Judgment, According to Opportunity and Works; Responsibility.

OPPRESSION [*1916, 3561, 4315, 4316, 5601, 6662, 6700, 6705, 6714, 6808, 6935, 6943, 6945, 7439, 7674, 7675, 8368, 8719*]. Seeming hopelessness under (Ecc 4:1). Proverbs concerning (Pr 3:31; 14:31; 22:16, 22; 28:3; 30:14; Ecc 4:1; 5:8; 7:7).

God:

A refuge from (Ps 9:9; 12:5). Promises aid against (Ps 12:5; 72:4, 14; Isa 58:6; Jer 50:34). God will judge (Ps 10:17-18; 103:6; Ecc 5:8; Isa 10; Jer 21:12; 22:17; Eze 22:7; Am 4:1; Mic 2:2; Hab 2:5-11; Mal 3:5; Jas 5:4). God will reward those who fight against (Isa 33:15-16).

National:

God judges (Ac 7:7), relieved (Ex 3:9; 12:30-39; Dt 26:7-8; Jdg 2:14; 6-8; 10-11; 2Ki 13; Isa 52:4). Prayer for deliverance from (Ps 17:8-9; 44:24; 74:21; 119:121, 134; Isa 38:14).

Oppressors:

Punished (Job 27:13-23; Ps 72:4; 103:6; Isa 10). Oppression forbidden (Ex 22:21-24; Dt 23:15-16; 24:14-15; Pr 22:22; Zec 7:10). Oppression warned against (Ps 62:10; Eze 45:9; Jas 2:6). Command to relieve the oppressed (Isa 1:17).

Instances of:

Hagar, by Sarah (Ge 16:6). Jacob, by Laban (Ge 31:39). Israelites, by Egyptians (Ex 1:10-22; 5), by Assyrians (Isa 52:4). Rehoboam resolves to oppress the Israelites (1Ki 12:14). Strangers and the poor and needy, by Israelites (Eze 22:29; Am 5:11-12; 8:4-6). Of people, by the scribes and Pharisees (Mt 23:2-4).

ORACLE [5363, 5442, 5536, 7877] (*speak*). Utterance of prophecy. KJV "burden," (Isa 14:28; 15:1; Eze 12:10; Na 1:1) or "parable" (Nu 23:7, 18; 24:3, 4, 15, 16, 20, 21, 23) or "prophecy" (Pr 30:1; 31:1).

ORACLES [5363]. NIV "words" of God. Scriptures called (Ac 7:38; Ro 3:2; Heb 5:12; 1Pe 4:11).

ORATOR A public speaker. Instances of: Judah (Ge 44:18-34). Aaron (Ex 4:14-16). Moses (Dt 1-4:40). Jonah (Jnh 3:4-10). Peter (Ac 2:14-40; 3:12-26; 4:8-12; 10:34-48; 11:4-17). Stephen (Ac 7:2-60). Paul and Barnabas (Ac 14:14-17). Paul (Ac 13:16-41; 17:22-31; 22:1-21; 24:10-21; 26:1-29; 27:21-25). James (Ac 15:13-21). Apollos (Ac 18:24-28). Herod (Ac 12:21). The city clerk (Ac 19:35-41). Tertullus (Ac 24:1).

ORDAIN, ORDINATION

[3338+4848, 3569, 3670, 3922, 4854, 5989, 6913, 7422, *2936*]. An act of conferring a sacred office upon someone, as: Deacons (Ac 6:6), missionaries (Ac 13:3), elders (Ac 14:23). OT priests were ordained to office (Ex 28:41; 29:9).

Instances of: Priests (Ex 29:1-9, 19-35; 40:12-16; Lev 8:6-35; Heb 7:21). Apostles (Mk 3:14). Ministers: the seven (Ac 6:5-6), Paul and Barnabas (Ac 13:2-3), Timothy (1Ti 4:14).

ORDINANCE [2976, 2978, 5477]. A decree of the Law (Ex 12:14, 24, 43; 13:10; 15:25; Nu 9:14; 10:8; 15:15; 18:8; Isa 24:5; Mal 4:4; Ro 13:2; 1Pe 2:13).

Insufficiency, in salvation (Isa 1:10-17; Gal 5:6; 6:15; Eph 2:15; Col 2:14, 20-23; Heb 9:1, 8-10).

See Form; Formalism.

OREB [6855] (*raven*).
1. A prince of Midian, overcome by Gideon and killed by the Ephraimites (Jdg 7:25; 8:3; Ps 83:11).
2. A rock E of the Jordan, where Oreb was slain (Jdg 7:25; Isa 10:26).

OREN [816] (*fir or cedar BDB IDB; laurel* KB). Son of Jerahmeel (1Ch 2:25).

ORGAN *See Flute; Music, Instruments of.*

ORION [4068]. The constellation of (Job 9:9; 38:31; Isa 13:10; Am 5:8).

ORNAN *See Araunah.*

ORONTES The chief river of Syria, c. 400 miles long, rises in Anti-Lebanon range and flows N for most of its course.

ORPAH [6905] (*neck, the girl with a full mane[?], or rain cloud*). Daughter-in-law of Naomi (Ru 1:4, 14).

ORPHAN [3846, *4003*]. To be visited (Jas 1:27). Beneficent provision for (Dt 14:28-29; 16:10-11, 14; 24:19-22; 26:12-13). Kindness toward (Job 29:12-13; 31:16-18, 21). God the friend of (Ex 22:22-24; Dt 10:18; Ps 10:14; 10:17-18; 27:10; 68:5; 146:9; Pr 23:10-11; Jer 49:11; Hos 14:3; Mal 3:5). Justice to, required (Dt 24:17-22; 27:19; Ps 82:3; Isa 1:17, 23; Jer 7:6-7; 22:3). Oppressed (Job 6:27; 22:9; 24:3, 9; Isa 10:1-2; Jer 5:28).
See Adoption; Children; Widow.
Instances of: Lot (Ge 11:27-28). Daughters of Zelophehad (Nu 27:1-5). Jotham (Jdg 9:16-21). Mephibosheth (2Sa 9:3). Joash (2Ki 11:1-12). Esther (Est 2:7). A type of Zion in affliction (La 5:3).

OSEE *See Hosea.*

OSHEA *See Joshua.*

OSNAPPAR *See Ashurbanipal.*

OSPRAY *See Vulture.*

OSPREY [8164, 8168]. A carnivorous bird. Forbidden as food (Lev 11:13; Dt 14:12).

OSSIFRAGE *See Vulture.*

OSTENTATION In prayer and almsgiving (Mt 6:1; Pr 25:14; 27:2). *See Boasting.*

OSTIA The port of Rome on the Tiber, some sixteen miles from the city.

OSTRACA Inscribed fragments of pottery, or potsherds. Some important ancient documents have come down to us in this form, i.e., the Lachish Letters.

OSTRICH [3612, 8266]. A large, flightless bird that does not take care of its young well (Job 39:13-18; La 4:3).

OTHNI [6978]. Son of Shemaiah (1Ch 26:7).

OTHNIEL [6979]. Son of Kenaz and nephew of Caleb. Conquers Kiriath Sepher, and as reward secures Caleb's daughter as his wife (Jos 15:16-20; Jdg 1:12-13). Becomes deliverer and judge of Israel (Jdg 3:8-11). Death of (Jdg 3:11). Descendants of (1Ch 4:13-14).

OUCHES *See Filigree.*

OUTCASTS [5615]. General references to (Isa 11:12; 16:3; 27:13; Jer 30:17).

OVEN [9486]. Ancient ovens were primitive, often a hole in the ground coated with clay and in which a fire was made. The dough was spread on the inside and baked. Sometimes ovens were made of stone, from which the fire was raked when the oven was very hot and into which the unbaked loaves were placed (Ex 8:3; Lev 2:4; 7:9; 11:35; 26:26; Hos 7:4-7).
Figurative (Ps 21:9; Mal 4:1; Mt 6:30; Lk 12:28).

OVERCOMING [2200, 3523, 3899, 3983, 5162, 6296, *2093, 2487, 2952, 2996, 3771, 5309*]. *See Perseverance.*

OVERSEER [8853, *2175, 2176*]. Ruler (Pr 6:7). Office of church leadership, traditionally "bishop," (Ac 20:28; Php 1:1; 1Ti 3:1-7) same as an elder (Tit 1:5-9; 1Pe 5:1-4). A title of Christ (1Pe 2:25). *See Elders.*

OVERWEIGHT *See Corpulency.*

OWL [1426+3613, 3568, 3927, 7684, 7887, 7889, 9379, 9492]. Several kinds of carnivorous birds (Isa 14:23; 34:11; Zep 2:14). Unclean for food (Lev 11:16-18; Dt 14:15-17). Lives in the desert (Job 30:29; Ps 102:6; Isa 13:21; 34:11-15; 43:20; Jer 50:39; Mic 1:8).

OWNER OF A SHIP Usually captained his ship or contracted to state service (Ac 27:11).

OX [476, 546, 1330, 7228, 7538, 8028, 8802, *1091, 3675, 5436*]. *See Bull; Cattle; Wild Ox.*

OXGOAD [1330+4913]. A pointed stick used to prod the ox on to further effort. Used by Shamgar to kill six hundred Philistines (Jdg 3:31).

OZEM [730].
1. Son of Jesse (1Ch 2:15).
2. Son of Jerahmeel (1Ch 2:25).

OZIAS *See Uzziah, 1.*

OZNI, OZNITE [269, 270] (*my ear, my hearing*). Son of Gad and his clan (Nu 26:16).

PAARAI [7197] (*devotee of Peor*). One of David's valiant men (2Sa 23:35). Called Naarai (1Ch 11:37).

PACK ANIMALS Used for transporting army supplies (1Ch 12:40).

PADDAN ARAM [7019, 7020] (*plain of Aram*).

1. Region near the head of the fertile crescent; sometimes called simply "Paddan," (Ge 48:7, ftn). Another name for Aram Naharaim (Ge 24:10). Literally "Aram of the two rivers"—the Euphrates and the Tigris. Naharaim was the northern part of the area called later by the Greeks "Mesopotamia"—literally "between the rivers." It was located NE of Canaan, the area known today as Syria.

2. A town near Shechem (Ge 33:18, ftn).

PADON [7013] (*ransom*). One of the temple servants (Ezr 2:44; Ne 7:47).

PAGIEL [7005] (perhaps *fortune of God* or *God is entreated,* less probably *God has met his worshiper*). Son of Ocran and leader of the tribe of Asher at the time of the Exodus (Nu 1:13; 2:27; 7:72, 77; 10:26).

PAHATH-MOAB [7075] (*supervisor of Moab*). The ancestor of an influential family of Judah, which returned to Jerusalem from the Captivity (Ezr 2:6; 10:30; Ne 3:11; 7:11).

PAI See Pau.

PAIN [2477, 2655, 2659, 2660, 2714, 3872, 3873, 4799, 6772, 6776, 6778, 7496, 7828, 9377, *989, 992, 3383, 4506*]. Experienced on earth (Job 14:22; 30:17-18; La 3:5; Rev 16:10). Chastens (Job 33:19). None in Heaven (Rev 21:4).

See *Afflictions.*

PAINTING [3949, 7037]. Around the eyes, to enhance their appearance (2Ki 9:30; Jer 4:30; Eze 23:40). Of rooms (Jer 22:14). Of portraits (Eze 23:14).

PALACE [810, 1074, 1131, 2121, 5092, 5249, 6247, 10206, *885, 994, 3875, 4550*]. For kings (1Ki 21:1; 2Ki 15:25; Jer 49:27; Am 1:12; Na 2:6). Of David (2Sa 7:2). Of Solomon (1Ki 7:1-12). At Babylon (Da 4:29; 5:5; 6:18). At Susa (Ne 1:1; Est 1:2; 7:7; Da 8:2).

Archives kept in (Ezr 6:2). Proclamations issued from (Am 3:9).

Figurative of a government (Am 1:12; 2:2; Na 2:6).

PALAL [7138] (*he has judged*). Son of Uzai.

One of the workmen in rebuilding the walls of Jerusalem (Ne 3:25).

PALE HORSE Symbol of death (Rev 6:8).

PALESTINE The name is derived from Philistia, an area along the S seacoast occupied by the Philistines (Ps 60:8). The original name was Canaan (Ge 12:5); after the Conquest it came to be known as Israel (1Sa 13:19), and in the Greco-Roman period, Judea, Samaria, and Galilee. The land was c. seventy miles wide and 150 miles long, from the Lebanon mountains in the N to Beersheba in the S. The area W of the Jordan was 6000 miles; E of the Jordan, 4000 miles. In the N, from Acco to the Sea of Galilee was twenty-eight miles. From Gaza to the Dead Sea in the S, fifty-four miles.

Physically, the land is divided into five parts: the Plain of Sharon and the Philistine Plain along the coast; adjoining it, the Shephelah, or foothills region; then the central mountain range; after that the Jordan valley; and E of the Jordan the Transjordan plateau.

The varied configuration of Palestine produces a great variety of climate. The Maritime Plain has an annual average temperature of 57 degrees at Joppa; Jerusalem averages 63 degrees; while Jericho and the Dead Sea area have a tropical climate. As a result, plants and animals of varied latitudes may be found.

Before the Conquest the land was inhabited by Canaanites, Amorites, Hittites, Horites, and Amalekites. These were conquered by Joshua, the judges, and the kings. The kingdom was split in 931 B.C.; the N kingdom was taken into captivity by the Assyrians in 722 B.C.; the S kingdom by the Babylonians in 587 B.C. From 587 B.C. to the time of the Maccabees the land was under foreign rule by the Babylonians, Persians, Alexander the Great, Egyptians, and Syrians. In 63 B.C. the Maccabees lost control of the land to the Romans, who held it until the time of Mohammed.

In NT times Palestine W of the Jordan was divided into Galilee, Samaria, and Judea; and E of the Jordan into the Decapolis and Perea.

See *Philistia; Philistines.*

PALLU, PALLUITE [7101, 7112] (*wonderful*). Son of Reuben (Ge 46:9; Ex 6:14; Nu 26:5, 8; 1Ch 5:3).

PALM SUNDAY See *Triumphal Entry of Jesus.*

PALM TREE [4093, 9469, 9472, 9474, *5836*]. Deborah judged Israel under (Jdg 4:5). Wood of, used in the temple (1Ki 6:29, 32, 35; 2Ch 3:5). In the temple seen in the vision of Ezekiel (Eze 40:16; 41:18). Branches of, thrown in the way when Jesus made his triumphal entry into Jerusalem (Jn 12:13). Jericho was called the City of Palm Trees (Dt 34:3).

Figurative: Of the prosperity of the righteous (Ps 92:12). Used as a symbol of victory (Rev 7:9).

PALMER WORM *See Locust.*

PALMS, CITY OF *See Jericho.*

PALSY *See Paralysis.*

PALTI [7120] (*[God (El)] is [my] deliverance*).
1. Spy from Benjamin (Nu 13:9),
2. *See Paltiel, 2.*

PALTIEL [7120, 7123] (*God [El] is [my] deliverance*).
1. Prince of Issachar (Nu 34:26).
2. Son-in-law of Saul (1Sa 25:44; 2Sa 3:15).

PALTITE [7121] (*delivered*). One of David's mighty men (2Sa 23:26), "Pelonite" (1Ch 11:27; 27:10).

PAMPHYLIA [4103]. A province in Asia Minor. Men of, in Jerusalem (Ac 2:10). Paul goes to (Ac 13:13-14; 14:24). John, surnamed Mark, in (Ac 13:13; 15:38). Sea of (Ac 27:5).

PAN(S) [3963, 4679, 4709, 5306, 5389, 6105, 7505]. Clay pan for cooking the grain offering (Lev 2:7; 7:9). For baking bread (2Sa 13:9). Silver pans of the temple (Ezr 1:9). Iron (Eze 4:3).

PANIC [2169, 3010, 3169, 4539, 6907, 8185, 9451]. In armies (Lev 26:17; Dt 32:30; Jos 23:10; Ps 35:5). From God (Ge 35:5; Ex 15:14-16; Jdg 7:22; 1Sa 14:15-20; 2Ki 7:6-7; 2Ch 20:22-23).
See Armies.

PANNAG *See Confection.*

PANTOMIME By Isaiah (Isa 20:2-3). By Ezekiel (Eze 4:1-8; 12:18). Agabus (Ac 21:11).

PAPER [5925]. (2Jn 12). *See Parchment.*

PAPHOS [4265]. A city of Cyprus. Paul blinds a sorcerer in (Ac 13:6-13).

PAPS NIV "breasts" (Lk 23:28) or "chest" (Rev 1:13). *See Breast.*

PAPYRUS [15, 1687] (*reed plant*). A reed which grows in swamps and along rivers or lakes, especially along the Nile; from eight to twelve feet tall; used to make baskets, sandals, boats, and especially paper, the most common writing material of antiquity (Job 8:11; Isa 18:2). The NT books were undoubtedly all written on papyrus. Moses' basket of (Ex 2:3).

PARABLE [1948, 4886, 5442, 4130] (*to be similar, to be comparable*).

Defined:
1. Proverbial saying used in wisdom and prophetic discourse (Ps 78:2; Pr 1:6).
2. A story in which things in the spiritual realm are compared with events that could happen in the temporal realm; or, an earthly story with a heavenly meaning (Eze 17; 24; Mt 13; Lk 15). Differs from a fable, myth, allegory, or proverb. A characteristic teaching method of Jesus.

Listing of:
Of the trees (Jdg 9:8-15). Of the lamb (2Sa 12:1-6). Of the woman of Tekoa (2Sa 14:5-12). Of the garment torn to pieces (1Ki 11:30-32). Of the prisoner of war (1Ki 20:39-42). Of the thistle and cedar (2Ki 14:9). Of a vine of Egypt (Ps 80:8-16). Of the vineyard (Isa 5:1-7; 27:2-3). Of the farmer (Isa 28:23-29). Of the skins filled with wine (Jer 13:12-14). Of the two eagles (Eze 17). Of lions' cubs (Eze 19:1-9). Of Oholah and Oholibah (Eze 23). The boiling pot (Eze 24:3-5). The plant (Jnh 4:10-11).

The sheet let down from heaven in Peter's vision (Ac 10:10-16). The two covenants (Gal 4:22-31). The mercenary soldier (2Ti 2:3-4). Husbandman (2Ti 2:6). Furnished house (2Ti 2:20-21). The athlete (2Ti 2:5). Mirror (Jas 1:23-25).

See Jesus the Christ, Parables of; Symbols and Similitudes; Types.

PARACLETE (*comforter, exhorter*). One who pleads another's cause. Used by Christ of the Holy Spirit in John's Gospel (Jn 14:16, 26; 15:26; 16:7), and of Christ (1Jn 2:1).

PARADISE [4137] (*park or garden*). Park (Ecc 2:5), forest (Ne 2:8), orchard (SS 4:13), home of those who die in Christ (Lk 23:43).

PARADOX Of wealth (Pr 13:7). Wisdom (1Co 3:18). Life (Mt 10:39; 16:25; Mk 8:35; Lk 17:33; Jn 12:25). Christian life (2Co 6:4, 8-10; 12:4, 10-11; Eph 3:17-19; Php 3:7). New Jerusalem (Rev 21:18, 21).

PARAH [7240] (*cow*). A Benjamin city (Jos 18:23).

PARALLELISM A characteristic of OT Hebrew poetry. Rather than rhyming words as in English poetry, Hebrew poetry rhymes thoughts by comparison and contrast of two or three lines. Two major categories of parallelism are "synonymous," in which the parallel lines echo similar ideas, and "antithetical," in which the parallel lines contrast. In the NIV, parallelism is shown by indentation: the indented line is parallel to the preceding line.

Examples of Synonymous Parallelism—
¹Why do the nations conspire
  and the peoples plot in vain?
²The kings of the earth take their stand
  and the rulers gather together
against the LORD
  and against his Anointed One.

³"Let us break their chains," they say,
   "and throw off their fetters."
⁴The One enthroned in heaven laughs;
   the Lord scoffs at them. (Ps 2:1-4)

Examples of Antithetical Parallelism—
For the LORD watches over the way of
      the righteous,
   but the way of the wicked will perish. (Ps 1:6)
The fear of the LORD is the beginning of
      knowledge,
   but fools despise wisdom and discipline.
      (Pr 1:7)

See Poetry; Psalms.

PARALYSIS [7028, *3831, 4166, 4168*] *(lame)*. Cured by Jesus (Mt 4:24; 8:6, 13; 9:2, 6), by Philip (Ac 8:7), by Peter (Ac 9:33-34).

PARAMOUR *See Lovers.*

PARAN, MOUNT PARAN, DESERT OF PARAN [7000] *(plain)*. Desert or wilderness of (Ge 21:21; Nu 10:12; 12:16; 13:3, 26; Dt 1:1). Mountains of (Dt 33:2; Hab 3:3). Israelites encamp in (Nu 12:16). David takes refuge in (1Sa 25:1). Hadad flees to (1Ki 11:17-18).

PARBAR NIV "the court to the west" of the temple (1Ch 26:18).

PARCHED LAND [62, 2990, 3081, 3083, 3312, 5980, 6546, 7457, 7480, 7533]. Symbolic of loss of strength or blessing (Job 30:1; Ps 143:6). Changed to flowing springs, symbolic of blessing (Ps 107:35; Isa 35:1).

PARCHMENT [*3521*]. Writing material made of animal skins, probably copies of books of the OT in 2Ti 4:13.

PARDON [4105, 5927, 5951, 6142]. Forgiveness. God demands a righteous ground for pardoning the sinner—the atoning work of Christ (Ex 34:9; 1Sa 15:25-26; Isa 55:7). *See Atonement; Forgiveness.*

PARENTAL BLESSINGS Very important in OT times; often prophetic of a child's future (Ge 27:4, 12, 27-29).

PARENTS [3, 3+562+2256, *1204, 4252, 4591*].

General:
   To be revered (Ex 20:12; Lev 19:3; Dt 5:16; Mt 15:4; 19:19; Mk 7:10; 10:19; Lk 18:20). Obeyed (Pr 1:8; 6:20; 23:22; Eph 6:1; Col 3:20).
   Covenant blessings of, entailed upon children (Ge 6:18; Ex 20:6; Ps 103:17). Curses upon, entailed upon children (Ex 20:5; Lev 20:5; Isa 14:20; Jer 9:14; La 5:7). Involved in children's wickedness (1Sa 2:27-36; 4:10-18). Cursing of, to be punished (Ex 21:17; Lev 20:9).

Beloved:
   By Joseph (Ge 46:29). Rahab (Jos 2:12-13). Ruth (Ru 1:16-17). Elisha (1Ki 19:20).
   Mother, beloved (Pr 31:28).

Duties of:
   Fathers to direct household (Ge 18:19; Lev 20:9; Pr 3:12; 13:24; 19:18; 1Ti 3:4-5, 12; Tit 1:6; Heb 12:7). To govern with kindness (Eph 6:4; Col 3:21). A prerequisite to church leadership (1Ti 3:4-5, 12). To provide for children (2Co 12:14; 1Ti 5:8). To instruct children in righteousness (Ex 10:2; 12:27; 13:8, 14; Dt 4:9-10; 6:7, 20-25; 11:18-21; 32:46; Ps 78:5-6; Pr 22:6, 15; 27:11; Isa 38:19; Joel 1:3; Eph 6:4; 1Th 2:11). To discipline children (Pr 19:8; 22:6, 15; 23:13-14; 29:15, 17).

Indulgent:
   Eli (1Sa 2:27-36; 3:13-14), David (1Ki 1:6).

Influence of:
   Evil (1Ki 15:26; 22:52-53; 2Ki 8:27; 21:20; 2Ch 21:6; 22:3). Good (1Ki 22:43; 2Ki 15:3, 34). *See Influence.*

Love of:
   Reflection of God's love (Ps 103:13; Pr 3:12; Isa 49:15; 66:13; Mt 7:9-11; Lk 11:11-13). Must be exceeded by love for Christ (Mt 10:37). To be taught (Tit 2:4).
   Love Exemplified—
   By Hagar (Ge 21:15-16), Rebekah's mother (Ge 24:55), Isaac and Rebekah (Ge 25:28), Isaac (Ge 27:26-27), Laban (Ge 31:26-28), Jacob (Ge 37:3-4; 42:4, 38; 43:13-14; 45:26-28; 48:10-11), Moses' mother (Ex 2), Naomi (Ru 1:8-9), Hannah (1Sa 2:19), David (2Sa 12:18-23; 13:38-39; 14:1, 33; 18:5, 12-13, 33; 19:1-6), Rizpah (2Sa 21:10), the mother of the infant brought to Solomon by the harlots (1Ki 3:22-28), Mary (Mt 12:46; Lk 2:48; Jn 2:5; 19:25), Jairus (Mk 5:23), father of the demoniac (Mk 9:24), nobleman (Jn 4:49).

Paternal Blessings:
   Of Noah (Ge 9:24-27), Abraham (Ge 17:18), Isaac (Ge 27:10-40; 28:3-4), Laban (Ge 31:55), Jacob (Ge 48:15-20; 49:1-28), reproaches (Ge 9:24-25; 49:3-7).

Partiality of:
   Isaac for Esau (Ge 25:28), Rebekah for Jacob (Ge 25:28; 27:6-17), Jacob for Joseph (Ge 33:2; 37:3; 48:22), for Benjamin (Ge 42:4). *See Partiality.*

Prayers in Behalf of Children:
   Of Hannah (1Sa 1:27), David (2Sa 7:25-29; 1Ch 17:16-27; 2Sa 12:16; 1Ch 22:12; 29:19), Job (Job 1:5).
   See Children, Instruction of.

PARLOR *See Upper Room.*

PARMASHTA [7269] *(the very first)*. Son of Haman (Est 9:9).

PARMENAS [4226] *(steady, reliable)*. One of seven men chosen for daily ministration to the poor (Ac 6:5).

PARNACH [7270]. Father of Elizaphan (Nu 34:25).

PAROSH [7283] (*flea*). The ancestor of one of the families which returned to Jerusalem from captivity in Babylon (Ezr 2:3; 8:3; Ne 7:8; 10:14).

PAROUSIA (*presence, coming*). A Greek word frequently used in NT of our Lord's return (Mt 24:3; 1Co 15:23; 1Th 3:13; 4:15; 2Pe 1:16).

PARRICIDE One who murders his father, mother, or a close relative (2Ki 19:37; 2Ch 32:21; Isa 37:38).

PARSHANDATHA [7309]. One of the ten sons of Haman (Est 9:7).

PARSIMONY Stinginess with money or resources. Of the Jews toward the temple (Hag 1:2, 4, 6, 9), toward God (Mal 3:8-9). Punishment of (Hag 1:9-11). *See Liberality.*

PARSIN [10593]. Aramaic for "divided," symbolic of the division of Babylon between the Medes and Persians (Da 5:24-28).

PARTHIANS [4222]. The inhabitants of Parthia, a country NW of Persia (Ac 2:9).

PARTIALITY [5365+7156, 5795+7156, 5951+7156, 3284+4725, 4622]. Forbidden, among Christians (1Ti 5:21), by parents (Dt 21:15-17). Effects upon children (Ge 37:4). *See Parents.*

Instances of:
Of Brothers: Joseph for Benjamin (Ge 43:30, 34).

Of parents: Isaac for Esau (Ge 25:25), Rebekah for Jacob (Ge 25:28; 27:6-17), Jacob, for Joseph (Ge 33:2; 37:3-4; 48:22), for Benjamin (Ge 42:4).

Of husbands: Jacob for Rachel (Ge 29:30), Elkanah for Hannah (1Sa 1:4-5).

See Respect of Persons.

PARTICEPS CRIMINIS

Participating in evil (2Jn 11). *See Collusion.*

PARTITION, MIDDLE WALL OF

See Dividing Wall.

PARTNERSHIP [476, 2492, 2500, 3126, 3128, 3581, 5007, 5212]. With God (1Co 3:7, 9; 2Co 6:1; Php 2:13).

PARTRIDGE [7926]. (1Sa 26:20; Jer 17:11).

PARUAH [7245] (*blooming* ISBE; *cheerful* KB). Father of Jehoshaphat (1Ki 4:17).

PARVAIM [7246]. An unknown gold region (2Ch 3:6).

PAS DAMMIM [7169] (*place of blood*). A battle between David and the Philistines, fought at (1Ch 11:13). Called Ephes Dammim (1Sa 17:1).

PASACH [7179] (*to divide*). Son of Japhlet (1Ch 7:33).

PASCHAL LAMB *See Passover.*

PASEAH [7176] (*hobbling one*).
1. A son of Eshton (1Ch 4:12).
2. Ancestor of a family which returned to Jerusalem from captivity in Babylon (Ezr 2:49; Ne 7:51).
3. Father of Jehoiada, probably identical with preceding (Ne 3:6).

PASHHUR [7319] (perhaps *be quiet,* and *round about*).
1. A priest, son of Malkijah (1Ch 9:12). An influential man and ancestor of an influential family (Jer 21:1; 38:1; Ezr 2:38; 10:22; Ne 7:41; 10:3; 11:12).
2. Son of Immer and governor of the temple. Beats and imprisons Jeremiah (Jer 20:1-6).
3. Father of Gedaliah, who persecuted Jeremiah (Jer 38:1).

PASSAGE [2006, 4544, 4047, 4343]. Ford of a river (Ge 32:23), mountain pass (1Sa 13:23), a crossing (Jos 22:11).

PASSENGERS *See Commerce.*

PASSION [678, 2123, 4077, 4792].
1. Lust or desire (Hos 7:6; 1Co 7:9).
2. Often used as a technical term of the suffering of Jesus. *See Jesus the Christ, Sufferings of.*

PASSIVITY *See Nonresistance.*

PASSOVER [7175, 2038, 4247] (*pass over, spare*). Institution of (Ex 12:3-49; 23:15-18; 34:18; Lev 23:4-8; Nu 9:2-5, 13-14; 28:16-25; Dt 16:1-8, 16; Ps 81:3, 5). Design of (Ex 12:21-28). Special Passover, for those who were unclean, or on a journey, to be held in the second month (Nu 9:6-12; 2Ch 30:2-4). Lamb killed by Levites, for those who were ceremonially unclean (2Ch 30:17; 35:3-11; Ezr 6:20). Strangers authorized to celebrate (Ex 12:48-49; Nu 9:14).

Observed at place designated by God (Dt 16:5-7), with unleavened bread (Ex 12:8, 15-20; 13:3, 6; 23:15; Lev 23:6; Nu 9:11; 29:17; Dt 16:3-4; Mk 14:12; Lk 22:7; Ac 12:3; 1Co 5:8). Penalty for neglecting to observe (Nu 9:13).

Reinstituted by Ezekiel (Eze 45:21-24).

Observation of, renewed by the Israelites on entering Canaan (Jos 5:10-11), by Hezekiah (2Ch 30:1), by Josiah (2Ki 23:22-23; 2Ch 35:1, 18), after return from captivity (Ezr 6:19-20). Observed by Jesus (Mt 26:17-20; Lk 22:15; Jn 2:13, 23; 13). Jesus in the temple at the time of (Lk 2:41-50). Jesus crucified at the time of (Mt 26:2; Mk 14:1-2; Jn 18:28). The lamb of, a type of Christ (1Co 5:7). Lord's supper ordained at (Mt 26:26-28; Mk 14:12-25; Lk 22:7-20).

Prisoner released at, by the Romans (Mt 27:15;

Mk 15:6; Lk 23:16-17; Jn 18:39). Peter imprisoned at the time of (Ac 12:3).

Christ called our Passover (1Co 5:7).

See Feasts; Hallel.

PASSPORTS *See Safe-Conduct.*

PASTOR [4478] A leader of the church (Eph 4:11), possibly the same as elder and overseer. *See Elders; Overseer.*

PASTORAL EPISTLES A common title for 1 and 2 Timothy and Titus, which were written by the apostle Paul to his special envoys sent on specific missions in accordance with the needs of the hour. They give instruction to Timothy and Titus concerning the pastoral care of churches. Though some date the Pastorals within the framework of Acts, most scholars believe all three were written not long after the events of Ac 28. After his imprisonment in Rome (c. A.D. 60-62), Paul most likely began his fourth missionary journey. *See Missionary Journeys of Paul.*

First Timothy was written to Timothy at Ephesus while Paul was still traveling in the coastal regions of the Aegean Sea. Titus was written to Titus in Crete (c. A.D. 63-65), probably from Nicopolis or some other city in Macedonia. Second Timothy was written from Rome toward the end of Paul's second imprisonment shortly before he was executed (A.D. 67 or 68).

The epistles concern church organization and discipline, including such matters as the appointment of bishops and deacons, the opposition of heretical or rebellious members, and the provision for maintenance of doctrinal purity.

Certain themes and phrases recur throughout the Pastoral Letters: (1) *God the Savior.* Three times in 1 Timothy and three times in Titus God the Father is called Savior (1Ti 1:1; 2:3; 4:10; Tit 1:3; 2:10; 3:4). Once in 2 Timothy and three times in Titus Jesus is also called Savior (2Ti 1:10; Tit 1:4; 2:13; 3:6). (2) *Sound doctrine, faith, and teaching.* Correct teaching, in keeping with that of the apostles (1Ti 1:10; 6:3; 2Ti 1:13; 4:3; Tit 1:9). The teaching is called "sound" not only because it builds up in the faith, but because it protects against the corrupting influence of false teachers. (3) *Godliness.* A key word (along with "godly") in the Pastorals, occurring eight times in 1 Timothy (2:2; 3:16; 4:7-8; 6:3, 5-6, 11), once in 2 Timothy (3:5) and once in Titus (1:1), but nowhere else in the writings of Paul. (4) *Controversies.* Appearing in (1Ti 1:4; 6:4; 2Ti 2:23; Tit 3:9); (5) *Trustworthy sayings.* A clause found nowhere else in the NT but used five times in the Pastorals (1Ti 1:15; 3:1; 4:9; 2Ti 2:11; Tit 3:8).

The authorship of these letters has been disputed because of differences in vocabulary and style from the other epistles ascribed to Paul, and because their references to his travels do not accord with the itineraries described in Acts. The differences though real, have been exaggerated, and

can be explained on the basis of a change of time, subject matter, scribes, and destination.

See also Church, New Testament Church, Qualifications for Elders/Overseers and Deacons; Timothy, 1 and 2; Titus.

PASTURE [*1824, 4494, 5337, 5338, 5659, 5661, 8286, 3786]. A place to graze sheep (Jn 10:9; Ge 29:7); essential for survival of flocks (Ge 47:4; 1Ch 4:39-41; Job 39:8; Isa 14:30; Jer 14:6); where David worked (2Sa 7:8; 1Ch 17:7); for cattle (1Ki 4:23); a figure of peace (Ps 23:2; Ps 37:3); a figure of God's flock (Ps 74:1; 79:13; 83:12; 95:7; 100:3; Jer 23:1-3; 50:7, 19; Eze 34:14); for camels (Eze 25:5). Pasturelands were the environs around towns and villages (Nu 35).

PATARA [4249]. A Lycian city in Asia Minor. Visited by Paul (Ac 21:1-2).

PATHROS *See Upper Egypt.*

PATHRUSITES [7357] (*of Pathros*). A descendant of Mizraim and ancestor of the Philistines (Ge 10:14; 1Ch 1:12).

PATHS, RIGHT (Ps 16:11; 23:3; 25:10; 119:35; Pr 2:9; 4:11, 18; Isa 2:3; 26:7; Heb 12:13).

PATHWAY OF SIN General references to (Pr 2:15; 12:15; 13:15; 14:12; 15:9; Isa 49:8; Mt 7:13). Walking in (Dt 29:19; Jer 7:24; Eph 2:2; Php 3:18; 1Pe 4:3; 2Pe 2:10; 3:3; Jude 18).

PATIENCE [*4206, 3428, 3429, 5705]. Commended (Ecc 7:8-9; La 3:26-27). Commanded (Ps 37:7-9; Eph 4:2; Col 3:12-13; 1Th 5:14; 1Ti 6:11; 2Ti 2:24-25; Tit 2:2; Heb 12:1; Jas 5:7-8; 2Pe 1:5-6). A fruit of tribulation (Ro 5:3-4; Rev 1:9). A grace of the righteous (Lk 8:15; 21:19; Ro 2:7; 8:25; 12:12; 15:4-5; 1Co 13:4-5; 2Co 6:4-6; 12:12; Col 1:10-11; 1Th 1:3; 2Th 3:5; Heb 6:12; 10:36; Jas 1:3-4, 19; 1Pe 2:19-23; Rev 14:12). Prerequisite of a overseer (1Ti 3:2). Propagates peace (Pr 15:18). Possible because of God's righteousness (Rev 13:10).

Instances of: Isaac toward the people of Gerar (Ge 26:15-22). Moses (Ex 16:7-8). Job (Job 1:21; Jas 5:11). David (Ps 40:1). Simeon (Lk 2:25). Paul (2Ti 3:10). Prophets (Jas 5:10). The Thessalonians (2Th 1:4). The church at Ephesus (Rev 2:2-3) and Thyatira (Rev 2:19). John (Rev 1:9).

Of Jesus (1Pe 2:21-23; Rev 1:9). *See Jesus the Christ.*

See Longsuffering; Meekness.

PATMOS [4253]. An island in the Aegean Sea. John an exile on (Rev 1:9).

PATRIARCHAL GOVERNMENT *See Government.*

PATRIARCHS, PATRIARCHAL AGE [4252, 4256] (*first father [of a nation, tribe]*). Name given in NT to those who founded

the Hebrew race and nation: Abraham (Heb 7:4), sons of Jacob (Ac 7:8-9), David (Ac 2:29). The term is now commonly used to refer to the persons whose names appear in the genealogies and covenant-histories before the time of Moses (Ge 5, 11).

PATRICIDE Killing one's father. Of Sennacherib (2Ki 19:37; Isa 37:38; 1Ti 1:9).

PATRIOTISM Commanded (Ps 51:18; 122:6-7). Exhortation concerning (2Sa 10:12). Religious ceremony for the fostering of, commanded (Dt 26:1-11). Appealed to in battle (2Sa 10:12). Songs of: Deborah (Jdg 5:1-31), Israel (Ps 85:1-13; 137:1-6). Lack of, lamented (La 5:1-22).

Instances of:
Moses (Heb 11:24-26). Deborah and Barak (Jdg 4:5). The tribes of Zebulun and Naphtali (Jdg 5:18-20). Eli (1Sa 4:17-18). Phinehas' wife (1Sa 4:19-22). Joab (2Sa 10:12). Uriah (2Sa 11:11). The Psalmist (Ps 51:18; 85:1-13). Hadad (1Ki 11:21-22). The lepers of Samaria (2Ki 7:9). Israelite exiles (Ne 1:1-11; 2:1-20; Ps 137:1-6). Nehemiah (Ne 1:2, 4-11; 2:3). The Jews in public defense (Ne 2:3; 4:1-23). Isaiah (Isa 62:1). Jeremiah (Jer 8:11, 21-22; 9:1-2; La 5:1-22).

Lacking in:
The tribes of Reuben, Asher, and Dan (Jdg 5:15-17). Inhabitants, of Meroz (Jdg 5:23), of Succoth and Peniel (Jdg 8:4-17).
See Country, Love of.

PATROBAS [4259] (*father of existence*). A believer at Rome (Ro 16:14).

PATTERN Of the tabernacle (Heb 8:5-9:23). *See Tabernacle.*

PAU [7185] (*groaning, bleating*). A city of Edom (Ge 36:39; 1Ch 1:50).

PAUL [4263] (*little*).
Background and conversion:
Also called Saul (Ac 8:1; 9:1; 13:9). Of the tribe of Benjamin (Ro 11:1; Php 3:5). Personal appearance of (2Co 10:1, 10; 11:6). Born in Tarsus (Ac 9:11; 21:39; 22:3). Educated at Jerusalem in the school of Gamaliel (Ac 22:3; 26:4). A zealous Pharisee (Ac 22:3; 23:6; 26:5; 2Co 11:22; Gal 1:14; Php 3:5). A Roman (Ac 16:37; 22:25-28). Persecutes the Christians; present at and gives consent to the stoning of Stephen (Ac 7:58; 8:1, 3; 9:1; 22:4). Sent to Damascus with letters for the arrest and return to Jerusalem of Christians (Ac 9:1-2).

His vision and conversion (Ac 9:3-22; 22:4-19; 26:9-15; 1Co 9:11; 15:8; Gal 1:13; 1Ti 1:12-13). Is baptized (Ac 9:18; 22:16). Called to be an apostle (Ac 22:14-21; 26:14-21; 26:16-18; Ro 1:1; 1Co 1:1; 9:1-2; 15:9; Gal 1:1, 15-16; Eph 1:1; Col 1:1; 1Ti 1:1; 2:7; 2Ti 1:1, 11; Tit 1:1, 3). Preaches in Damascus (Ac 9:20, 22). Is persecuted by the Jews (Ac 9:23-24). Escapes by being let down from the wall in a basket; goes to Arabia (Gal

1:17), Jerusalem (Ac 9:25-26; Gal 1:18-19). Received by the disciples in Jerusalem (Ac 9:26-29). Goes to Caesarea and returns to Tarsus (Ac 9:30; 18:22).

Brought to Antioch by Barnabas (Ac 11:25-26). Teaches at Antioch one year (Ac 11:26). Brings the contributions of the Christians in Antioch to the Christians in Jerusalem (Ac 11:27-30). Returns with John to Antioch (Ac 12:25).

First Missionary Journey:
See Missionary Journeys of Paul. Sent to the Gentiles (Ac 13:2-3, 47-48; 22:17:21; Ro 11:13; 15:16; Gal 1:15-24). Visits Seleucia (Ac 13:4), Cyprus (Ac 13:4). Preaches at Salamis (Ac 13:5), at Paphos (Ac 13:6). Sergius Paulus the proconsul is converted (Ac 13:7-12). Contends with Elymas the sorcerer (Ac 13:6-12). Visits Perga in Pamphylia (Ac 13:13). John, a companion of, departs for Jerusalem (Ac 13:13). Visits Antioch in Pisidia and preaches in the synagogue (Ac 13:14-41). His message received gladly by the Gentiles (Ac 13:42, 49). Persecuted and expelled (Ac 13:50-51). Visits Iconium and preaches to the Jews and Greeks; is persecuted; escapes to Lystra; goes to Derbe (Ac 14:1-6). Heals a crippled man (Ac 14:8-10). The people attempt to worship him (Ac 14:11-18). Is persecuted by Jews from Antioch and Iconium and is stoned (Ac 14:19; 2Co 11:25; 2Ti 3:11). Escapes to Derbe, where he preaches the gospel, and returns to Lystra, Iconium, and to Antioch, encourages the disciples, and ordains elders (Ac 14:19-23). Revisits Pisidia, Pamphylia, Perga, Attalia, and returns to Antioch (Ac 14:24-28).

Contends with the Judaizing Christians against circumcision (Ac 15:1-2). Refers the question of circumcision to the apostles and elders at Jerusalem (Ac 15:2, 4). He declares to the apostles at Jerusalem the miracles and wonders God had done among the Gentiles by them (Ac 15:12). Returns to Antioch, accompanied by Barnabas, Judas, and Silas, with letters to the Gentiles (Ac 15:22, 25).

Second Missionary Journey:
See Missionary Journeys of Paul. Makes his second tour of the churches (Ac 15:36). Chooses Silas as his companion, and passes through Syria and Cilicia, confirming the churches (Ac 15:36-41). Visits Lystra; circumcises Timothy (Ac 16:1-5). Goes through Phrygia and Galatia; is forbidden by the Holy Spirit to preach in Asia; visits Mysia; desires to go to Bithynia, but is restrained by the Spirit; goes to Troas, where he has a vision of a man saying, "Come over into Macedonia, and help us"; he immediately proceeds to Macedonia (Ac 16:6-10). Visits Samothrace and Neapolis; comes to Philippi, the chief city of Macedonia; visits a place of prayer at the riverside; preaches the Word; the merchant, Lydia of Thyatira, is converted and baptized (Ac 16:11-15). Exorcizes a demon from a fortune-teller (Ac 16:16-18). Persecuted, beaten, and cast into prison with Silas; sings songs of praise in the prison; an earthquake shakes the prison; he preaches to the alarmed

jailer, who believes and is baptized with his household (Ac 16:19-34). Is released by the civil authorities on the ground of his being a Roman citizen (Ac 16:35-39; 2Co 6:5; 11:25; 1Th 2:2). Is received at the house of Lydia (Ac 16:40). Visits Amphipolis, Apollonia, and Thessalonica; preaches in the synagogue (Ac 17:1-4). Is persecuted (Ac 17:5-9; 2Th 1:1-4). Escapes to Berea by night; preaches in the synagogue; many honorable women and men believe (Ac 17:10-12). Persecuted by the Jews who come from Thessalonica; is conducted by the brothers to Athens (Ac 17:13-15). Disputes on Mars' Hill with philosophers (Ac 17:16-34).

Visits Corinth; lives with Aquila and his wife, Priscilla, who were tentmakers; joins in their trade; reasons in the synagogue every Sabbath; is rejected by the Jews; turns to the Gentiles; stays there one year and six months, teaching the word of God (Ac 18:1-11). Persecuted by Jews, taken before the proconsul; accusation dismissed; takes his leave after many days, and sails to Syria, accompanied by Aquila and Priscilla (Ac 18:12-18). Visits Ephesus, where he leaves Aquila and Priscilla; enters a synagogue, where he reasons with the Jews; starts on his return journey to Jerusalem; visits Caesarea, and returns to Antioch (Ac 18:19-22).

Third Missionary Journey:

See Missionary Journeys of Paul. Returning to Ephesus, passes through Galatia and Phrygia, strengthening the disciples (Ac 18:18-23). Baptizes disciples of John in the name of the Lord Jesus; preaches in the synagogue, remains in Ephesus for two years; heals the sick (Ac 19:1-12). Jewish exorcists are beaten by a demon and many Ephesians believe, bringing their books of sorcery to be burned (Ac 19:13-20; 1Co 16:8-9). Sends Timothy and Erastus into Macedonia, but he himself remains in Asia for a period of time (Ac 19:21-22). The spread of the gospel through his preaching interferes with the idol-makers; he is persecuted, and a great uproar of the city is created; the city clerk appeases the people; dismisses the accusation against Paul, and disperses the people (Ac 19:23-41; 2Co 1:8; 2Ti 4:14).

Proceeds to Macedonia after encouraging the churches in those parts; comes into Greece and stays three months; returns through Macedonia, accompanied by Sopater, Aristarchus, Secundus, Gaius, Timothy, Tychicus, and Trophimus (Ac 20:1-6). Visits Troas; preaches until the break of day; restores to life Eutychus, who fell from the window (Ac 20:6-12). Visits Assos, Mitylene, Kios, Samos, and Miletus, hurrying to Jerusalem, to be there at Pentecost (Ac 20:13-16). Sends for the elders of the church of Ephesus; tells them of how he had preached in Asia, and of his tests and afflictions testifying repentance toward God; declares he was compelled by the Spirit to go to Jerusalem; exhorts them to watch over themselves and their flock; kneels down, prays, and departs (Ac 20:17-38). Visits Cos, Rhodes, Patara; takes a ship for Tyre; stays seven days; is brought on his way by the disciples to the outskirts of the city; kneels, prays, and leaves; comes to Ptolemais; greets the brothers and stays one day (Ac 21:1-7). Departs for Caesarea; enters the house of Philip the evangelist; is warned by Agabus not to go to Jerusalem; proceeds to Jerusalem (Ac 21:8-16).

Arrest and Trials:

See Missionary Journeys of Paul. Is received warmly by the brothers; talks of the things that had been done among the Gentiles by his ministry; enters the temple; the people are stirred against him by the Jews from Asia; an uproar is created; he is thrown out of the temple; the commander of the troops interposes and arrests him (Ac 21:17-33). His defense (Ac 21:33-40; 22:1-21). Is confined in the barracks (Ac 22:24-30). Is brought before the Sanhedrin; his defense (Ac 22:30; 23:1-5). Is returned to the barracks (Ac 23:10). Is encouraged by a vision, promising him that he must testify in Rome (Ac 23:11). Jews conspire against his life (Ac 23:12-15). Thwarted by his nephew (Ac 23:16-22). Is escorted to Caesarea by a military guard (Ac 23:23-33). Is confined in Herod's palace in Caesarea (Ac 23:35). His trial before Felix (Ac 24). Remains in custody for two years (Ac 24:27). His trial before Festus (Ac 25:1-12). Appeals to Caesar (Ac 25:10-12). His examination before Agrippa (Ac 25:13-27; 26).

Is taken to Rome in custody of Julius, a centurion, and guard of soldiers; boards the ship, accompanied by other prisoners, and sails along the coast of Asia; stops at Sidon and Myra (Ac 27:1-5). Transferred to a ship of Alexandria; sails past Cnidus, Crete, and Salmone to Fair Havens (Ac 27:6-8). Predicts loss of the ship; his advice not heeded, and the voyage resumed (Ac 27:9-13). The ship encounters a hurricane; Paul encourages and comforts the officers and crew; the soldiers advise putting the prisoners to death; the centurion interferes, and all 276 on board are saved (Ac 27:14-44). The ship is wrecked, and all on board take refuge on the island of Malta (Ac 27:14-44). Kind treatment by the inhabitants of the island (Ac 28:1-2). Is bitten by a viper and miraculously preserved (Ac 28:3-6). Heals the chief official's father and others (Ac 28:7-10). Is delayed in Malta three months; proceeds on the voyage; delays at Syracuse; sails by Rhegium and Puteoli; meets brothers who accompany him to Rome from the Forum of Appius; arrives at Rome and is permitted to live by himself in custody of a soldier (Ac 28:11-16). Calls the chief Jews together; states his situation; is kindly received; expounds the gospel; testifies to the kingdom of heaven (Ac 28:17-29). Lives two years in his own hired house, preaching and teaching (Ac 28:30-31).

Sickness of in Asia (2Co 1:8-11). Caught up to the third heavens (2Co 12:1-4). Has "a thorn in the flesh" (2Co 12:7-9; Gal 4:13-14). His independence of character (1Th 2:9; 2Th 3:8).

Persecutions of:

(Ac 9:16, 23-25, 29; 14:19; 16:19-25; 20:22-24;

21:13, 27-33; 22:22-24; 23:10, 12-15; Ro 8:35-37; 1Co 4:9, 11-13; 2Co 1:8-10; 4:8-9; 6:4-5, 8-10; 11:23-27, 32-33; 12:10; Gal 5:11; 6:17; Php 1:30; Col 1:24; 1Th 2:2, 14-15; 3:4; 2Ti 1:12; 2:9-10; 3:11-12; 4:16-17).

Character of:
(2Co 10:1, 10; 11:6; Gal 4:13). Cheerful in adversity (Ac 10:25; Ro 8:35-37; 2Co 4:8-10; 12:10; 2Ti 2:10; 3:11-12; 4:16-17). Courageous (Ac 9:29; 20:22-24; 21:13; Eph 6:20; 1Th 2:2). Purposeful, even when the Holy Spirit warns him not to go to Jerusalem (Ac 20:22-23; 21:4, 10-14). Indomitable (Ro 8:35-37; 1Co 4:9-13; 2Co 4:8-12; 6:4-10; 11:23-33; 12:10; 1Th 2:2; 2Ti 1:12; 3:11; 4:17). Joyous in suffering (Ac 16:25; Php 2:17; Col 1:24; 2Ti 2:9). Meek (1Co 4:12-13; 2Ti 4:16). Self-forgetful (1Co 4:9, 11-13). Self-supporting (Ac 18:3; 20:33-35; 2Co 11:7, 9; 1Th 2:9; 2Th 3:8). Tactful (1Co 9:19-22; 10:33; Phm 8-21). Zealous (Ro 9:3; 2Co 5:11-14; 6:4-10; 11:22-33; 12:10, 14-15; Php 3:6-16; Col 1:29). Ready for death (2Ti 4:6-8).

PAULUS, SERGIUS [4263]. Roman proconsul of Cyprus; became a Christian through Paul (Ac 13:6-12).

PAVEMENT, STONE [4246, 4861, 8367, 3346]. The courtyard outside the palace in Jerusalem where Pilate passed public sentence on Jesus (Jn 19:13).

PAVILION [2903, 6109] (booth, tent). Movable tent or canopy (1Ki 20:12; Jer 43:10). Figuratively of God's protection (Ps 27:5) or majesty (Job 36:29).

PAWN See Surety.

PAZZEZ See Beth Pazzez.

PEACE [1388, 4957, 5341, 5663, 5739, 8092, 8922, 8932, 8934, 8966, 9200, 457, 1644, 1645, 1646, 1647].

From God:
(Nu 6:26; Ps 29:11; 85:8; Isa 26:12; 57:19; 1Co 14:33).

Social:
Beneficence of (Ps 133:1; Pr 15:17; 17:1, 14; Ecc 4:6). Honorable (Pr 20:3).
Commanded (Ge 45:24; Ps 34:14; Jer 29:7; Mk 9:50; Ro 12:18; 14:19; 2Co 13:11; Eph 4:3, 31-32; 1Th 5:13; 1Ti 2:2; 2Ti 2:22; Heb 12:14; 1Pe 3:10-11). Love of, commanded (Zec 8:19). Promised (Lev 26:6; Job 5:23-24; Isa 2:4; 11:6-9, 13; 60:17-18; Hos 2:18). The righteous assured of (Pr 16:7). Broken by the gospel (Mt 10:21-22, 34-36; Lk 12:51-53). Moses' efforts in behalf of, resented (Ex 2:13-14; Ac 7:26-29).
Promoters of peace promised: Joy (Pr 12:20). Adoption (Mt 5:9). Fruit of righteousness (Jas 3:17-18). God's favor (Lk 2:14).
Instances of promoters of peace: Abraham (Ge

13:8-9), Abimelech (Ge 26:29), Mordecai (Est 10:3). David (Ps 120:6-7).
See Charitableness; Nation, Peace of.

Spiritual:
Through Christ (Isa 2:4; 9:6-7; 11:6, 13; Mic 4:3, 5; Lk 1:79; Jn 7:38; 14:27; Ac 10:36; Ro 5:1; 10:15). To the world (Isa 2:4; 11:6-9; Lk 2:14). To God's children (Isa 54:10, 13).
From God (Job 34:29; Ps 29:11; 72:3, 7; 85:8; Jer 33:6; Eze 34:25; Hag 2:9; Mal 2:5; Ro 15:13, 33; 16:20; 1Co 1:3; 14:33; 2Co 1:2; Gal 1:3; Php 4:7, 9; 1Th 1:1; 5:23; 2Th 3:16; 1Ti 1:2; 2Ti 1:2; Tit 1:4; Phm ; Heb 13:20; Rev 1:4). From Christ (Mt 11:29; Jn 14:27; 16:33; 20:19; Eph 2:14-17; Col 3:15; Rev 1:4-5).
A fruit of the Spirit (Ro 14:17; Gal 5:22). A fruit of righteousness (Ro 2:10). Assured to the righteous (Ps 37:4, 11, 37; 125:1, 5; Pr 3:17, 24; Isa 26:3, 12; 32:2, 17-18; 55:2, 12; 57:1-2, 19; Ro 8:6).
Through the reconciliation of Christ (Isa 53:5; Jn 7:38; Ro 5:1; Col 1:20), acquaintance with God (Job 22:21, 26; Ps 4:8; 17:15; 73:25-26; Isa 12:1-2; 25:7-8; 28:12; Lk 2:29), loving God's law (Ps 1:1-2; 119:165), obedience (Ps 25:12-13; Isa 48:18; Jer 6:16).
No peace to the wicked (Isa 48:22; 57:21). To be made with God (Isa 27:5).
See Charitableness; Joy; Praise.

PEACE OFFERINGS See Fellowship Offerings; Offerings.

PEACOCK See Baboons; Ostrich.

PEARL [3449]. (Rev 17:4; 18:12, 16). "Pearl of great price" (Mt 13:45-46). Ornaments made of (1Ti 2:9).

Figurative:
Teaching should be given in accordance with the spiritual capacity of the learners (Mt 7:6).

Symbolic:
The twelve gates of the Holy City, the New Jerusalem, are each made of a single pearl (Rev 21:21).
See Minerals of the Bible, 1; Stones.

PECULIAR PEOPLE See Saints.

PEDAHEL [7010] (God [El] ransoms). Chief of Naphtali (Nu 34:28).

PEDAHZUR [7011] (the Rock ransoms). Father of Gamaliel (Nu 1:10; 2:20; 7:54, 59; 10:23).

PEDAIAH [7015, 7016] (Yahweh ransoms).
1. Grandfather of Jehoiakim (2Ki 23:36).
2. Father of Zerubbabel (1Ch 3:18).
3. Father of Joel, chief of Manasseh (1Ch 27:20).
4. Man who helped build the wall of Jerusalem (Ne 3:25).
5. A Benjamite, the father of Joed (Ne 11:7).
6. Levite; temple treasurer (Ne 13:13).

PEEP NIV "chirp" of a bird (Isa 10:14); "whisper" of a medium supposed to come from the dead (Isa 8:19).

PEKAH [7220] (*he has opened*). The son of Remaliah the eighteenth king of Israel; murdered Pekahiah; reigned from 752-732 B.C. (2Ki 15:27); made a league with Damascus against Judah (2Ki 15:37-38); became subject to Assyria (2Ki 15:29); murdered by Hoshea (2Ki 15:25-31; 2Ch 28:5-15).

PEKAHIAH [7222] (*Yahweh opens*). Israel's seventeenth king; son of Menahem; wicked and idolatrous (2Ki 15:24); murdered by Pekah (2Ki 15:22-25).

PEKOD [7216] (*visitation*). Aramean tribe living to the E and near the mouth of the Tigris (Jer 50:21; Eze 23:23).

PELAIAH [7102, 7126] (*Yahweh is spectacular*).
1. Son of Elioenai (1Ch 3:24).
2. A Levite who assisted Ezra in instructing the people in the law (Ne 8:7; 10:10).

PELALIAH [7139] (*Yahweh intercedes in arbitration*). A priest; the father of Jeroham and Amzi (Ne 11:12).

PELATIAH [7124, 7125] (*Yahweh rescues*).
1. Grandson of Zerubbabel (1Ch 3:21).
2. A Simeonite military leader (1Ch 4:42).
3. A man who sealed a covenant with Nehemiah (Ne 10:22).
4. A prince of Israel; Ezekiel prophesied against him (Eze 11:2, 13).

PELEG [7105, 5744] (*water canal*). The son of Eber (Ge 10:25; 11:16-19; 1Ch 1:19, 25; Lk 3:35).

PELET [7118] (*rescue*).
1. Son of Jahdai (1Ch 2:47).
2. Son of Azmaveth (1Ch 12:3).

PELETH [7150] (perhaps *swift*, or *swiftness*).
1. A Reubenite (Nu 16:1).
2. Son of Jonathan (1Ch 2:33).

PELETHITES [7152] (*courier*). A part of David's bodyguard (1Ki 1:38; 2Sa 8:18; 20:7, 23; 1Ch 18:17). Absalom's escort (2Sa 15:18).

PELICAN See *Owl*.

PELLA A city E of the Sea of Galilee; one of the cities forming the Decapolis.

PELONITE(S) [7113] (*separates*). Designation of two of David's mighty men: Helez (1Ch 11:27; 27:10) and Ahijah (1Ch 11:36).

PELUSIUM [6096]. An Egyptian city on the E arm of the Nile, KJV "Sin" (Eze 30:15-16).

PEN [1074+2025, 1312, 3032, 4813, 6485, *885, 2812, 3037*]. (Jdg 5:14; Ps 45:1; Isa 8:1; Jer 8:8; 3Jn 13). Made of iron (Job 19:24; Jer 17:1).

PENALTY [871, 2365, 6741, 7322, 9150, 10186, *165+2505, 521, 3210*].
Vicariously assumed:
By Rebekah (Ge 27:13), Abigail (1Sa 25:24), the woman of Tekoa (2Sa 14:9), the persecutors of the Jews (Mt 27:25), Jesus for the human race (Gal 3:13). Paul desires to assume for Israel (Ro 9:3). *See Suffering, Vicarious.*
See Fine; Judgments; Punishment; Sin, Punishment of; Wicked, Punishment of. See also penalties under various crimes, such as Murder.

PENCE See *Money; Penny.*

PENDANTS [5755]. Articles of jewelry (Jdg 8:26). *See Dress.*

PENIEL [7159, 7161] (*face of God [El]*). The place where Jacob wrestled with the angel of Yahweh (Ge 32:24-32), not far from Succoth (Jdg 8:8-9, 17). Also spelled Penuel (Ge 32:31; Jdg 8:8; 1Ki 12:25, ftns).

PENINNAH [7166] (possibly *pearls, coral branches* BDB; *woman with rich hair* KB). One of the wives of Elkanah (1Sa 1:2).

PENITENCE See *Repentance; Sin, Confession of.*

PENITENT [8740].
Promises to:
Of mercy (Lev 26:40-42; Dt 4:29-31; 30:1-10; 2Ki 22:19; 1Ch 28:9; Job 22:23-29; 33:26-28; Ps 6:8-9; 9:10; 22:26; 90:14-15; 145:18-19; 147:3; Isa 27:5; Mt 5:4; 7:7-11 w Lk 11:9-13; Mt 12:20, 31; Lk 12:10).
Of forgiveness (Ps 32:5-6; 34:18; 51:17; 86:5; Isa 55:7; Eze 18:21-23; 33:10-16; Mt 6:14-15; 11:28-30; Lk 6:37; 15:4-32 w Mt 18:12-14; Lk 18:10-14; Jn 6:37; Ac 13:38-39; 1Jn 1:9).
Of salvation (Ps 145:18-19; Lk 4:18; 19:10; Ro 10:9-13; Heb 7:25).
Of divine favor (Nu 5:6-7; Isa 66:2).
See Forgiveness; Repentance; Sin, Confession of. See also, Obduracy; Reprobacy.

PENKNIFE See *Knife.*

PENNY [837, 3119, 3321]. The smallest Roman copper coin (Mt 5:26; Mk 12:42; Lk 12:6, 59). *See Money.*

PENS [774, 1556, 1556+7366, 4813].
1. Walled enclosure for livestock (Nu 32:16, 24, 36; Jn 10:1, 16).
2. Instrument for writing (Ps 45:1; Isa 8:1; Jer 8:8; 3Jn 13).

PENSION Of Levites (2Ch 31:16-18).

PENTATEUCH, THE (*five books,* i.e.,

the *torah* or law). The first five books of the Bible; covers the period of time from the creation to the end of the Mosaic era; authorship is attributed to Moses in Scripture.

Outline:

1. Era of beginnings (Ge 1:1-11:32).
2. Patriarchal period (Ge 12:1-50:26).
3. Emancipation of Israel (Ex 1:1-19:2).
4. Religion of Israel (Ex 19:3-Lev 27:34).
5. Organization of Israel (Nu 1:1-10:10).
6. Wilderness wanderings (Nu 10:11-22:1).
7. Preparations for entering Canaan (Nu 22:2-36:13).
8. Retrospect and prospect (Dt 1-34).

PENTECOST [4300] (*fiftieth [day]*).

1. The Israelite Feast of Weeks (Ex 34:22; Dt 16:9-11), also called the Feast of Harvest (Ex 23:16) and the day of firstfruits (Nu 28:26), which fell on the fiftieth day after Passover. The feast originally celebrated the dedication of the firstfruits of the wheat harvest, the last crop to ripen. The ritual of the feast is described (Lev 23:15-21). Institution of (Ex 23:16; 34:22; Lev 23:15-21; Nu 28:26-31; Dt 16:9-12, 16). Called in the NT the Day of Pentecost (Ac 2:1; 20:16; 1Co 16:8). *See Annual Feasts; Feasts.*

2. The Christian Pentecost fell on the same day as the Israelite Feast of Weeks. The coming of the Holy Spirit (Ac 2) transformed the Israelite festival into a Christian anniversary, marking the beginning of the Christian church.

PENUEL [7158] (*face of God [El]*).

1. Son of Hur and chief of Gedor (1Ch 4:4).
2. Son of Shashak (1Ch 8:25).
3. Variant spelling of Peniel. *See Peniel.*

PENURIOUSNESS *See Parsimony.*

PEOPLE [*132, 278, 408, 1074, 1201, 1414, 1580, 2446, 3782, 4211, 5476, 5883, 6337, 6638, 6639, 10050, 10553, 41, 81, 476, 1620, 3295, 3836, 4063, 5626].* Common. Heard Jesus gladly (Mt 7:28; 9:8, 33; 13:54; Mk 6:2).

PEOR [7186] (*opening*).

1. A mountain in Moab near the town of Beth Peor (Dt 3:29).
2. Contraction for Baal Peor (Nu 25:18; 31:16; Jos 22:17). *See Baal Peor.*

PERAEA *See Perea.*

PERATH [7310]. In Hebrew it has the same spelling as Euphrates (Jer 13:4-7, ftn). Some identify it with Wadi Farah (Parah, Jos 18:23) near Anathoth.

PERAZIM, MOUNT [7292] (*breaking out*). Usually identified with Baal Perazim, where David obtained a victory over the Philistines (2Sa 5:20; 1Ch 14:11).

PERDITION (*ruin, destruction*). In the NT

the word refers to the final state of the wicked, one of loss or destruction (Jn 17:12; Php 1:28; 2Th 2:3; 1Ti 6:9).

PERDITION, SON OF A phrase used to designate Judas Iscariot (Jn 17:12) and the "man of lawlessness" who is the Antichrist (2Th 2:3).

PEREA (*beyond the Jordan*). The name given by Josephus to the region E of the Jordan; known in the Gospels as "across the Jordan" (Mt 4:15, 25; Mk 3:7-8).

PERES [10593] (*divided*). One of the words written on a wall for Belshazzar and interpreted by Daniel (Da 5:1-29).

PERESH [7303] (*offal eviscerated* BDB; *dung* ISBE; *contents of stomach [not intestine]* KB). Son of Makir (1Ch 7:16).

PEREZ, PEREZITE [7289, 7291, 5756] (*breaking out*). A son of Judah by Tamar (Ge 38:29; 1Ch 2:4), descendants of (Ge 46:12; Nu 26:20-23; 1Ch 2:5; 9:4), return from the Captivity (Ne 11:4, 6). In the lineage of David and Jesus (Ru 4:12; Mt 1:3; Lk 3:33).

PEREZ UZZAH [7290] (*breaking out of Uzzah*). The name of the place where Uzzah was struck dead for touching the ark of God (2Sa 6:8, ftn). Perez Uzzah means *outbreak against Uzzah;* the place name memorialized a divine warning that was not soon forgotten.

See Nacon.

PERFECTION [*4003, 4005, 9459, 5455, 5457].* Major idea: complete or whole, rather than without fault or shortcoming. None without sin (1Ki 8:46; 2Ch 6:36; Ecc 7:20).

From God (Ps 18:32; 1Pe 5:10). Through Christ (Col 1:21-22, 28; 2:9-11; Heb 10:14; 13:20-21; 1Pe 5:10; 1Jn 3:6-10). Through God's love (1Jn 4:12).

Ascribed to:

Noah (Ge 6:8-9), Jacob (Nu 23:21), David (1Ki 11:4, 6), Asa (1Ki 15:14), Job (Job 1:1), Zechariah and Elizabeth (Lk 1:6), Nathanael (Jn 1:47). The peaceful (Ps 37:31, 37). The wise (1Co 2:6). Man of God (2Ti 3:17). The self-controlled (Jas 3:2). Those who obey God's word (1Jn 2:5).

Blessings of:

(Ps 106:3; 119:1-3, 6; Mt 5:6). Reward of (Ps 37:31, 37; Pr 2:21; Lk 6:40; 1Jn 5:18).

Commanded:

(Ge 17:1; Dt 5:32; 18:13; Jos 23:6; 1Ki 8:61; 1Ch 28:9; Mt 5:48; 2Co 7:1; 13:11; Php 1:10; 2:15; Col 3:14; Jas 1:4). Requirements for (Dt 5:32; Jos 23:6; 1Ki 8:61; 1Ch 29:19; Mt 19:21; 2Co 7:1). Program for (Eph 4:11-13; Heb 6:1; 1Jn 2:5).

Desire for:

(Mt 5:6; 2Ti 3:17). In Job (Job 9:20-21). In David (Ps 101:2). In Paul (Php 3:12-15).

Prayer for:

(1Ch 29:19; 2Co 13:9; Col 4:12; 1Th 3:10, 13; Heb 13:20-21).

God is Perfect:

(Dt 32:4; 2Sa 22:31; Ps 18:30; 19:7; 50:2). *See God, Perfection of; Holiness; Sanctification.*

PERFIDY *See Conspiracy; Hypocrisy; Treachery.*

PERFUME, PERFUMER [1411, 5349, 5678, 5883, 5948, 6057, 7787, 8379, 8384, 9043, *3690*, *3693*].

1. For personal use (Pr 7:17; 27:9; SS 1:12; 3:6; Isa 3:20, 24), burial (2Ch 16:14).

2. For sacred incense (Ex 30:34-38; 37:29). *See Nard.*

PERGA [*4308*]. The capital of Pamphylia. Paul preaches in (Ac 13:13-14; 14:25).

PERGAMUM [*4307*]. A city of Mysia. One of the "seven churches" (Rev 1:11; 2:12-17).

PERIDA [7263] (*single, unique*). One of the servants of Solomon. Descendants of, returned to Jerusalem, from captivity in Babylon (Ne 7:57). Called Peruda (Ezr 2:55).

PERIZZITES [7254] (*villager*). One of the seven nations in the land of Canaan (Ge 13:7). Territory of, given to Abraham (Ge 15:20; Ex 3:8; 23:23). Doomed to destruction (Dt 20:17). Not all destroyed; Israelites marry among (Jdg 3:5-7; Ezr 9:1-2).

See Canaanite(s).

PERJURY [2021+4200+8678+9214, *2156*]. (Isa 48:1; Jer 5:2; 7:9; 1Ti 1:9-10).

Condemned:

Forbidden (Lev 19:12; Zec 8:17; Mt 5:33). Penalty for (Lev 6:2-7). Judgments upon perjurers (Hos 10:4; Zec 5:3-4; Mal 3:5).

Instances of:

Zedekiah (2Ch 36:13). Witnesses against Naboth (1Ki 21:8-13), against David (Ps 35:11), against Jesus (Mt 26:59-61; Mk 14:56-59), against Stephen (Ac 6:11, 13-14). Peter, when he denied Jesus with an oath (Mt 26:74; Mk 14:71).

See Falsehood; False Witness; Oath.

PERSECUTION [6715, 8103, *1502*, *1503*, *2567*, *2568*, *2808*].

Of Jesus:

(Ac 4:27; Heb 12:2-3; 1Pe 4:1). Meekly endured (Isa 50:6).

Foretold (Ge 3:15; Isa 49:7; 50:6; 52:14; 53:2-10; Mic 5:1; Zec 12:10; Mt 2:13). Typified, in the persecutions of Israel's kings (Ps 2:1-5; 22:1-2, 6-8, 11-21; 69:1-21; 109:25; Ro 15:3).

Persecution by the Jews (Mt 12:14; 22:15; 26:3-

4; Mk 12:13; 15:14; Lk 6:11; 11:53-54; 20:20; 22:2-5, 52-53; 23:23; Jn 5:16; 7:1, 7, 19; 11:57; 15:18, 20-21; 18:22-23; 19:6, 15; Ac 2:23). In making false imputation (Mt 12:24; Mk 3:22; Lk 11:15; Jn 10:20). In bringing false accusation (Mt 11:19; Lk 7:34; Jn 8:29-30). In acts of violence (Lk 4:28-29; 22:63-65 w Mt 26:67; Mk 14:65). In seeking false testimony (Mt 26:59). In seeking his death (Mt 26:14-16; Mk 3:6, 21; 14:1, 48; 11:18; Lk 19:47; Jn 7:20, 30, 32; 8:37, 40, 48, 52, 59; 10:31). In crucifying him (Ac 3:13-15; 7:52; 13:27-29; 1Co 2:8).

Persecution by Herod (Lk 13:31; 23:11). Persecution by the Roman soldiers (Mt 27:25-30; Mk 15:15-20; Jn 19:2-3).

Forsaken by God (Mk 15:34).

Of the Righteous:

(Ge 49:23; Ps 11:2; 37:32; 38:20; 74:7-8; 119:51, 61, 69, 78, 85-87, 95, 110, 157, 161; Pr 29:10, 27; Isa 26:20; 29:20-21; 59:15; Jer 11:19; 15:10; 18:18; Am 5:10; Ro 8:35; 2Co 12:10; Gal 4:29; 6:17).

By mocking (Ps 42:3, 10; 69:9-12; 119:51; Jer 20:7-8). By violence (Ps 94:5; Jer 2:30; 50:7; Ac 5:29, 40-42; 7:52; Gal 6:12, 17; 1Th 2:2, 14-15; Jas 2:6). By ecclesiastical censure (Jn 9:22, 34; 12:42; 2Ti 4:16-17).

Divine permissions of, mysterious (Hab 1:13). The mode of divine chastisement (La 1:3). Done to church members (Ac 8:1, 4; 11:19-21; Php 1:12-14, 18). Powerless to separate from the love of Christ (Ro 8:17, 35-39).

Exhortations to courage under (Isa 51:12, 16; Heb 12:3-4; 13:13; 1Pe 3:14, 16-17; 4:12-14, 16, 19). Courageously endured (Jer 26:11-14; 1Co 4:9-13; 2Co 4:8-12; 6:4-5, 8-10; 11:23-27; 12:10; 2Th 1:4; 2Ti 1:8, 12; 2:9-10; Heb 11:25-27; 11:33-38; Jas 5:6, 10). Rejoicing under (Ro 5:3; Col 1:24; 1Th 1:6; Heb 10:32-34). Perseverance under (Ps 44:15-18, 22).

Prayer for deliverance from (Ps 70:1-5; 83:1; 140:1, 4; 142:6). Deliverance from (Ps 124; 129:1-2). John's vision concerning (Rev 2:3, 10, 13; 6:9-11; 7:13-17; 12:10-11; 17:6; 20:4).

Of Christians, foretold (Mt 20:22; 23:34-35; 24:8-10; Mk 13:9-13; Lk 21:12-19; Jn 15:18-21; 16:1-2; 2Ti 3:2-3, 12-13; 1Jn 3:1, 13). Christ offers consolation (Mk 8:38; 9:42; Lk 6:22-23; 17:33; Jn 14:27). Promises to those who endure (Mt 5:10-12; 10:16-18, 21-23, 28-31; Lk 6:22-23). Should provoke love (1Co 13:3).

Instances of:

Abel (Ge 4:8; Mt 23:35; 1Jn 3:12). Lot (Ge 19:9). Moses (Ex 2:15; 17:4). David (Ps 31:13; 56:5; 59:1-2). Prophets martyred by Jezebel (1Ki 18:4). Gideon (Jdg 6:28-32). Elijah (1Ki 18:10; 19; 2Ki 1:9; 2:23). Micaiah (1Ki 22:26; 2Ch 18:26). Elisha (2Ki 6:31). Hanani (2Ch 16:10). Zechariah (2Ch 24:21; Mt 23:35). Job (Job 1:9; 2:4-5; 12:4-5; 13:4-13; 16:4-21; 17:2; 19:1-5; 30:1-10). Jeremiah (Jer 11:19; 15:10, 15; 17:15-18; 18:18-23; 26; 32:2; 33:1; 36:26; 37; 38:1-6). Uriah (Jer 26:23). The prophets (2Ch 36:16; Mt

21:35-36; 1Th 2:15). The three Hebrews of the Captivity (Da 3:8-23). Daniel (Da 6). The Jews (Ezr 4; Ne 4).

John the Baptist (Mt 14:3-12). James (Ac 12:2). Simon (Mk 15:21). The disciples (Jn 9:22, 34; 20:19). Lazarus (Jn 9:22, 34; 12:10; 20:19). The apostles (Ac 4:3-16, 18; 5:18-42; 12:1-19; Rev 1:9). Stephen (Ac 6:9-15; 7:1-60). The church (Ac 8:1; 9:1-14; Gal 1:13). Timothy (Heb 13:23). John (Rev 1:9). Antipas (Rev 2:13). The church of Smyrna (Rev 2:8-10).

Paul (2Ti 2:9-10; 4:16-17; Ac 9:16, 23-25, 29; 16:19-25; 21:2-33; 22:22-24; 23:10, 12-15; 1Co 4:9, 11-13; 2Co 1:8-10; 4:8-12; 6:4-5, 8-10; 11:23-27, 32-33; Col 1:24; 1Th 2:2, 14-15; 2Ti 1:8, 12; 3:11-12). *See Paul.*

PERSEPOLIS Capital of Persia, thirty miles NE of modern Shiraz; founded by Darius I (521-486 B.C.); destroyed by Alexander the Great in 331 B.C.

PERSEVERANCE [2846, 2152, 5702, 5705].

From the Lord:
(Ps 37:24, 28; Ro 8:30, 33-35; 1Co 1:8-9; 2Co 1:21-22). Acknowledged (Ps 73:24; 138:8; Ro 8:37-39; Col 2:7; 2Ti 4:18). Promised (Jer 32:40; Jn 6:34-40; 10:28-29).

Commanded:
(1Ch 16:11; Hos 12:6; 1Th 5:21; 2Th 2:15-17; 2Ti 2:1, 3, 12; 3:14; Tit 1:9; Jas 1:4, 25; 1Pe 4:16; 5:8-9; Rev 22:11). Exhortations to (Ac 11:23; 13:43; 14:21-22; 1Co 15:58; 16:13; Gal 5:1, 10; Eph 4:14-15; 6:13, 18; Php 1:27; 3:16; 4:1; Col 1:10, 22-23; 1Th 3:8; 2Th 3:15; 2Ti 1:13; Heb 2:1; 6:1, 11-12, 15; 10:23, 35-36; 12:5-15; 13:9, 13; 2Pe 3:17-18; Rev 16:15).

A proof of discipleship (Jn 8:31-32). A condition of fruitfulness (Jn 15:4-5, 7, 9). Intercessory prayer for (Lk 22:31-32).

Motives to:
The example, of Moses (Heb 3:5). Of the prophets (Jas 5:10-11). Of Christ (Heb 3:6, 14; 12:2-4). The intercession of Christ (Heb 4:14). The heavenly witnesses (Heb 12:1). Acceptance by Christ (2Co 5:9, 15; 1Pe 1:4-7).

Rewards contingent upon (Gal 6:9; Jas 1:12; Rev 2:7, 10-11, 17, 25-28; 3:5, 11, 21; 14:12; 21:7). Eternal life contingent upon (Mt 10:22; 24:13; Mk 13:13; Ro 2:6-7; 2Pe 1:10-11).

Lacking in:
The wayside and other hearers (Mk 4:3-8). Churches of Asia (Rev 2:5; 3:1-3, 14-18).

Instances of:
Caleb and Joshua, in representing the land of promise (Nu 14:24, 38). The righteous (Job 17:9; Pr 4:18).

In prayer, Abraham in interceding for Sodom (Ge 18:23-32), Jacob (Ge 32:24-26), Elijah for rain (1Ki 18:42-45), Paul for the removal of the thorn in his flesh (2Co 12:7-9).

See Character; Instability; Stability.

PERSIA [7273, 7275, 10060, 10594, 10595].

In Biblical History:
An empire which extended from India to Ethiopia, comprising 127 provinces (Est 1:1; Da 6:1). Government of, restricted by constitutional limitations (Est 8:8; Da 6:8-12). Municipal governments in, provided with dual governors (Ne 3:9, 12, 16-18). The princes advisory in matters of administration (Da 6:1-7). Status of women in, queen sat on the throne with the king (Ne 2:6). Vashti divorced for refusing to appear before the king's courtiers (Est 1:10-22; 2:4).

Israel captive in (2Ch 36:20), captivity foretold (Hos 13:16). Men of in the Syrian army (Eze 27:10).

Rulers of:
Xerxes (Est 1:3). Darius (Da 5:31; 6; 9:1). Artaxerxes I (Ezr 4:7-24). Artaxerxes II (Ezr 7; Ne 2; 5:1). Cyrus (2Ch 36:22-23; Ezr 1; 3:7; 4:3; 5:13-14, 17; 6:3; Isa 41:2-3; 44:28; 45:1-4, 13; 46:11; 48:14-15). Princes of (Est 1:14).

System of justice (Ezr 7:25). Prophecies concerning (Isa 13:17; 21:1-10; Jer 49:34-39; 51:11-64; Eze 32:24-25; 38:5; Da 2:31-45; 5:28; 7; 8; 11:1-4).

See Babylon; Chaldea.

PERSIS [4372] (*female Persian*). A Christian woman in Rome (Ro 16:12).

PERSONAL CALL *See Call, Personal; Minister, Call of.*

PERSONIFICATION Of wisdom (Pr 1; 2:1-19; 8-9). Of the Israel and/or the Church, in allegorical interpretation (SS 1-8). *See Pantomime.*

PERUDA [7243] (*single, unique*). One of the servants of Solomon. Descendants of, return to Jerusalem from captivity in Babylon (Ezr 2:55). Called Perida (Ne 7:57).

PERVERSENESS [4279, 6390, 6835, 6836, 6838, 9316, 9337, 1406, 4415]. (Pr 11:3; 12:8; 15:4; 28:6; Eze 9:9; Mt 17:17; 1Ti 6:5).

PESHITTA (*simple*, i.e., no marginal notes). Ancient Syriac translation of the Bible.

PESTILENCE [1822, 8404, 3369]. Sent as a judgment (Lev 26:16, 25). Sent upon the Egyptians. *See Egypt; Plague.*

PESTLE [6605]. An instrument used to grind in a mortar (Pr 27:22).

PETER, 1 and 2
1 Peter:
Author: The apostle Peter
Date: In the early 60s A.D.
Outline:
I. Salutation (1:1-2).

II. Praise to God for His Grace and Salvation (1:3-12).
III. Exhortations to Holiness of Life (1:13-5:11).
  A. The Requirement of Holiness (2:4-12).
  B. The Position of Believers (2:4-12).
    1. A spiritual house (2:4-8).
    2. A chosen people (2:9-10).
    3. Aliens and strangers (2:11-12).
  C. Submission to Authority (2:13-3:7).
    1. Submission to rulers (2:13-17).
    2. Submission to masters (2:18-20).
    3. Christ's example of submission (2:21-25).
    4. Submission of wives to husbands (3:1-6).
    5. The corresponding duty of husbands (3:7).
  D. Duties of All (3:8-17).
  E. Christ's Example (3:18-4:6).
  F. Conduct in View of the End of All Things (4:7-11).
  G. Conduct of Those Who Suffer for Christ (4:12-19).
  H. Conduct of Elders (5:1-4).
  I. Conduct of Young Men (5:5-11).
IV. The Purpose of the Letter (5:12).
V. Closing Greetings (5:13-14).
  See General Letters.

2 Peter:

Author: The apostle (Simon) Peter

Date: Probably between 65 and 68.

Outline:

I. Introduction (1:1-2).
II. Exhortation to Growth in Christian Virtues (1:3-11).
  A. The Divine Enablement (1:3-4).
  B. The Call for Growth (1:5-7).
  C. The Value of Such Growth (1:8-11).
III. The Purpose and Authentication of Peter's Message (1:12-21).
  A. His Aim in Writing (1:12-15).
  B. The Basis of His Authority (1:16-21).
IV. Warning Against False Teachers (ch. 2).
  A. Their Coming Predicted (2:1-3a).
  B. Their Judgment Assured (2:3b-9).
  C. Their Characteristics Set Forth (2:10-22).
V. The Fact of Christ's Return (3:1-16).
  A. Peter's Purpose in Writing Restated (3:1-2).
  B. The Coming of Scoffers (3:3-7).
  C. The Certainty of Christ's Return (3:8-10).
  D. Exhortations Based on the Fact of Christ's Return (3:11-16).
VI. Concluding Remarks (3:17-18).
  See General Letters.

PETER, SIMON [3064, 4377] (*rock, stone*).

Also called Simon and Cephas (Mt 16:16-19; Mk 3:16; Jn 1:42). Simeon (Ac 15:14, ftn). A fisherman (Mt 4:18; Lk 5:1-7; Jn 21:3). Call of (Mt 4:18-20; Mk 1:16-18; Lk 5:1-11). His wife's mother healed (Mt 8:14; Mk 1:29-30; Lk 4:38). An apostle (Mt 10:2; 16:18-19; Mk 3:16; Lk 6:14; Ac 1:13). An evangelist (Mk 1:36-37). Confesses Jesus as Christ (Mt 16:16-19; Mk 8:29; Lk 9:20; Jn 6:68-69). His presumption in rebuking Jesus (Mt 16:22-23; Mk 8:32-33), when the throng was pressing Jesus and the woman touched him (Lk 8:45), when Jesus foretold his persecution and death (Mt 16:21-23; Mk 8:31-33), in refusing to let Jesus wash his feet (Jn 13:6-11). Present at the healing of Jairus's daughter (Mk 5:37; Lk 8:51), at the transfiguration (Mt 17:1-4; Mk 9:2-6; Lk 9:28-33; 2Pe 1:16-18), in Gethsemane (Mt 26:36-46; Mk 14:33-42; Lk 22:40-46). Seeks the interpretation of the parable of the manager (Lk 12:41), of the law of forgiveness (Mt 18:21), of the law of defilement (Mt 15:15), of the prophecy of Jesus concerning his second coming (Mk 13:34). Walks upon the water of the Sea of Galilee (Mt 14:28-31). Sent with John to prepare the Passover (Lk 22:8). Calls attention to the withered fig tree (Mk 11:21). His failure foretold by Jesus, and his profession of fidelity (Mt 26:33-35; Mk 14:29-31; Lk 22:31-34; Jn 13:36-38). Cuts off the ear of Malchus (Mt 26:51; Mk 14:47; Lk 22:50). Follows Jesus to the high priest's palace (Mt 26:58; Mk 14:54; Lk 22:54; Jn 18:15). His denial of Jesus and his repentance (Mt 26:69-75; Mk 14:66-72; Lk 22:55-62; Jn 18:17-18, 25-27). Visits the tomb (Lk 24:12; Jn 20:2-6). Jesus sends message to, after the Resurrection (Mk 16:7). Jesus appears to (Lk 24:34; 1Co 15:4-5). Present at the Sea of Tiberias when Jesus appeared to his disciples; leaps into the sea, and comes to land when Jesus is recognized, is commissioned to feed the flock of Christ (Jn 21:1-23).

Remains in Jerusalem (Ac 1:13). His statement before the disciples concerning the death of Judas, and his recommendation that the vacancy in the apostleship be filled (Ac 1:15-22). Preaches at Pentecost (Ac 2:14-40). Heals the crippled man in the portico of the temple (Ac 3). Accused by the council; his defense (Ac 4:1-23). Foretells the death of Ananias and Sapphira (Ac 5:1-11). Imprisoned and scourged; his defense before the council (Ac 5:17-42). Goes to Samaria (Ac 8:14). Prays for the baptism of the Holy Spirit (Ac 8:15-18). Rebukes Simon, the sorcerer, who desires to purchase like power (Ac 8:18-24). Returns to Jerusalem (Ac 8:25). Receives Paul (Gal 1:18; 2:9). Visits Lydda; heals Aeneas (Ac 9:32-34). Visits Joppa; stays with Simon the tanner; raises Dorcas from the dead (Ac 9:36-43). Has a vision of a sheet containing clean and unclean animals (Ac 10:9-16). Receives the servant of the centurion; goes to Caesarea; preaches and baptizes the centurion and his household (Ac 10). Advocates, in the council of the apostles and elders, the preaching of the gospel to the Gentiles (Ac 11:1-18; 15:7-11). Imprisoned and delivered by an angel (Ac 12:3-19). Writes two letters (1Pe 1:1; 2Pe 1:1).

Miracles of. *See Miracles, Of the Disciples of Jesus.*

PETHAHIAH [7342] (*Yahweh opens*).

1. A priest in the reign of David (1Ch 24:16).

2. A Levite who divorced his Gentile wife (Ezr 10:23).

3. A Levite, probably identical with 2 (Ne 9:5).

4. A counselor of Artaxerxes (Ne 11:24).

PETHOR [7335]. A city in Mesopotamia. Home of the prophet Balaam (Nu 22:5; Dt 23:4).

PETHUEL [7333] (*God's opening*). Father of the prophet Joel (Joel 1:1).

PETITION [1335, 2349, 8629, 9382, 9384, 9525, *1255, 1872, 1961, 2656*]. Right of, recognized by Pharaoh (Ex 5:15-18), Israel (Nu 27:1-5; 32:1-5; 36:1-5; Jos 17:4, 14, 16; 21:1-2), David (1Ki 1:15-21), Rehoboam (1Ki 12:1-17; 2Ch 10), Jehoram (2Ki 8:3, 6).

PETRA (*rock, cliff, rock grotto*). OT Sela (Jdg 1:36; 2Ki 14:7; Isa 16:1). Capital city of the Nabateans. *See Nabatea, Nabateans; Sela.*

PEULLETHAI [7191] (*worker, wage earner*). A gatekeeper of the tabernacle (1Ch 26:5).

PHALEC *See Peleg.*

PHALLU *See Pallu.*

PHALTI *See Palti.*

PHALTIEL *See Paltiel.*

PHANUEL [5750] (*face of God [El]*). Father of Anna the prophetess (Lk 2:36).

PHARAOH [7281, 5755] (*the great house*).

1. King of Egypt at the time of Abraham (Ge 12:14-20; Ps 105:14).

2. Ruler of Egypt at the time of the famine. *See Egypt; Israel, Israelites.*

3. Ruler of Egypt at the time of the deliverance and exodus of the Israelites. *See Israel, Israelites.*

4. Father-in-law of Mered (1Ch 4:18).

5. Ruler of Egypt at the time of David (1Ki 11:17-22).

6. Father-in-law of Solomon (1Ki 3:1; 9:16).

7. At the time of Hezekiah (2Ki 18:21).

8. Pharaoh Neco. His invasion of Assyria, Josiah's death (2Ki 23:29-35; 24:7; 2Ch 35:20-24; 36:3-4; Jer 46:2; 47:1).

9. Pharaoh. (Jer 37:4-7; 44; Eze 17:15-17). Prophecies concerning (Jer 44:30; 46:25-26; Eze 29; 30:21-26).

PHARES, PHAREZ *See Perez.*

PHARISEES [5757] (*separate ones*). A sect of the Jews (Ac 15:5). Doctrines of (Mt 15:9), concerning the Resurrection (Ac 23:6, 8), association with tax collectors and sinners (Mt 9:11-13).

Traditions of, in regard to fasting (Mt 9:14; Lk 18:12), the washing of hands (Mt 15:1-3; Mk 7:1-15), the duties of children to parents (Mt 15:4-9), the Sabbath (Mt 12:2-8). Denounced by Jesus (Mt 23:2-36; Lk 11:39-44). Hypocrisy of, reproved by John (Mt 3:7-10), by Jesus (Mt 6:2-8, 16-18; 15:1-9; 16:1-12; 21:33-46; 23:2-33; Lk 11:14-54; 12:1;

15:1-9). Reject John (Lk 7:30), Christ (Mt 12:38-39; 15:12; Jn 7:48). Come to Jesus with questions (Mt 19:3; 22:15-22).

Minister to Jesus (Lk 7:36; 11:37; 14:1). Become disciples of Jesus (Jn 3:1; Ac 15:5; 22:5).

Paul a Pharisee (Ac 23:6; 26:5).

See Herodians; Sadducees; Testaments, Time Between.

PHAROSH *See Parosh.*

PHARPAR [7286]. A river of Damascus. Referred to by Naaman (2Ki 5:12).

PHARZITES *See Perez, Perezite.*

PHASEAH *See Paseah.*

PHASELIS Rhodian colony in Lycia (1Mc 15:23).

PHASELUS Latinization of Phasael, the son of Antipater the Idumean, and brother of Herod the Great.

PHEBE *See Phoebe.*

PHENICE *See Phoenicia; Phoenix.*

PHENICIA *See Phoenicia.*

PHICOL [7087]. Chief captain of the Philistines (Ge 21:22, 32; 26:26).

PHILADELPHIA [5788] (*love of brother, sister*). A city of Lydia. One of the seven churches (Rev 1:11; 3:7-13).

PHILANTHROPY *See Alms; Beneficence; Charitableness; Giving; Liberality; Neighbor; Poor.*

PHILEMON [5800] (*beloved*). Convert of Paul at Colosse; Epistle to Philemon written to him.

PHILEMON, EPISTLE TO

Author: The apostle Paul

Date: c. A.D. 60

Outline:

I. Greetings (1-3).

II. Thanksgiving and Prayer (4-7).

III. Paul's Plea for Onesimus (8-21).

IV. Final Request, Greetings and Benedictions (22-25).

PHILETUS [5801] (*beloved*). False teacher in the church at Ephesus (2Ti 2:17).

PHILIP [5805] (*horse lover*).

1. King of Macedonia; father of Alexander the Great; founder of city of Philippi in Macedonia (1Mc 1:1).

2. Philip V, king of Macedonia (1Mc 8:5).

3. Governor of Jerusalem under Antiochus, regent of Syria (2Mc 5:22).

4. Herod Philip. Married Herodias (Mt 14:3; Mk 6:17; Lk 3:19).

5. Herod Philip II, tetrarch of Batanaea, Trachonitis, Gaulanitis, and parts of Jamnia. Best of Herods (Lk 3:1).

PHILIP THE APOSTLE
Native of Bethsaida, the same town as Andrew and Peter (Jn 1:44), undoubtedly first a disciple of John the Baptist (Jn 1:43), brought his friend Nathanael to Jesus (Jn 1:45), called to apostleship (Mt 10:3; Mk 3:18; Lk 6:14), faith tested by Jesus before feeding of the 5000 (Jn 6:5-6), brought Greeks to Jesus (Jn 12:20-23), asked to see the Father (Jn 14:8-12), in the Upper Room with 120 (Ac 1:13).

PHILIP THE EVANGELIST
Chosen one of the seven (Ac 6:5). A Hellenist, or Greek-speaking Jew, preached in Samaria (Ac 8). Ethiopian eunuch converted through him (Ac 8:26-40). Paul stayed at his home in Caesarea, where he lived with his four unmarried daughters who were prophetesses (Ac 21:8-9).

PHILIPPI
[5803, 5804, 5805]. A city of Macedonia. Paul preaches in (Ac 16:12-40; 20:1-6; 1Th 2:1-2). Contributes to the maintenance of Paul (Php 4:10-18). Paul sends Epaphroditus to (Php 2:25). Paul writes a letter to the Christians of (Php 1:1).

PHILIPPIANS, EPISTLE TO

Author: The apostle Paul

Date: c. A.D. 61

Outline:

I. Salutation (1:1-2).
II. Thanksgiving and Prayer for the Philippians (1:3-11).
III. Paul's Personal Circumstances (1:12-26).
IV. Exhortations (1:27-2:18).
　A. Living a Life Worthy of the Gospel (1:27-30).
　B. Following the Servant Attitude of Christ (2:1-18).
V. Paul's Associates in the Gospel (2:19-30).
　A. Timothy (2:19-24).
　B. Epaphroditus (2:25-30).
VI. Warnings Against Judaizers and Antinomians (3:1-4:1).
　A. Against Judaizers or Legalists (3:1-16).
　B. Against Antinomians or Libertines (3:17-4:1).
VII. Final Exhortations, Thanks and Conclusion (4:2-23).
　A. Exhortations Concerning Various Aspects of the Christian Life (4:2-9).
　B. Concluding Testimony and Repeated Thanks (4:10-20).
　C. Greetings and Benediction (4:21-23).

PHILISTIA
[7148, 7149]. The seacoast in the W of Dan and Simeon (Ps 60:8; 87:4; 108:9).

PHILISTINES
[7148, 7149]. Descendants of Mizraim (Ge 10:14; 1Ch 1:12; Jer 47:4; Am 9:7). Called Kerethites (1Sa 30:14-16; Eze 25:16; Zep 2:5), Casluhites (Ge 10:14; 1Ch 1:12; Caphtor (Jer 47:4; Am 9:7). Territory of (Ex 13:17; 23:31; Dt 3:13; Jos 13:3; 15:47).

Rulers of (Jos 13:3; Jdg 3:3; 16:5, 30; 1Sa 5:8, 11; 6:4, 12; 7:7; 29:2, 6-7). Kings of: Abimelech I (Ge 20), Abimelech II (Ge 26), Achish (1Sa 21:10-15; 27:2-12; 28:1-2; 29).

Allowed to remain in Canaan (Jdg 3:3-4). Shamgar slays six hundred with an oxgoad (Jdg 3:31). For their history during the leadership of Samson (Jdg 13-16). Defeat the Israelites; take the ark; suffer plagues, and return the ark (1Sa 4-6). Army of (1Sa 13:5). Defeated by Samuel (1Sa 7), by Saul and Jonathan (1Sa 14; 13-14). Their champion, Goliath, slain by David (1Sa 17). David slays two hundred (1Sa 18:22-30). David finds refuge among (1Sa 27). Defeat the Israelites and slay Saul and his sons (1Sa 31; 1Ch 10:1). Defeated by David (2Sa 5:17-25; 23:9-16; 1Ch 14:8-16). Pay tribute to Jehoshaphat (2Ch 17:11). Defeated by Hezekiah (2Ki 18:8).

Prophecies against (Isa 9:11-12; 14:29-31; Jer 25:17-20; 47; Eze 25:15-17; Am 1:6-8; Zep 2:4-7; Zec 9:5-7).

PHILOLOGUS
[5807] (*lover of words* [*education*]). Christian in Rome to whom Paul sent a salutation (Ro 16:15).

PHILOSOPHY
[5814, 5815, 5186] (*lover of discernment, lover of wisdom*). The nature of things (Ecc 1-7). A philosophical discourse on wisdom (Job 28). Philosophical inductions and deductions relating to God and his providence (Job 5:8-20; 9; 10:2-21; 12:6-24; 33:12-30; 37). Reveals the mysteries of providence (Pr 25:2; Ro 1:19-20). Is not sufficient for an adequate knowledge of God (1Co 1:21-22), or of salvation through the atonement of Jesus Christ (1Co 2:6-10). Employment of, was not Paul's method of preaching the gospel (1Co 1:17, 19, 21; 2:1-5, 13). Greek schools of (Ac 17:18). Rabbinical (Col 2:8, 16-19; 1Ti 6:20).

See Aratus; Asceticism; Epicureans; Gnosticism; Stoicism; Stoics; Reasoning; Wisdom.

PHINEHAS
[7090] (*the Negro*).
1. Son of Eleazar and grandson of Aaron (Ex 6:25; 1Ch 6:4, 50; 9:20; Ezr 7:5; 8:2), who slew Zimri and Cozbi at God's command (Nu 25:6-15; Ps 106:30).

God establishes a covenant with (Nu 25:10-13). *See Covenants, Major in the Old Testament.*

2. Son of Eli; sinful priest (1Sa 1:3; 2:12-17, 22-25, 27-36; 3:11-13). He and his brother were killed by Philistines (1Sa 4).

3. Father of Eleazar who returned from exile (Ezr 8:33).

PHLEGON
[5823] (*burning*). A disciple in Rome (Ro 16:14).

PHOEBE [5833] (*radiant*). A deaconess of the church at Cenchrea (Ro 16:1).

PHOENICIA [4046, 5834] (*land of purple [dye for trading]*, possibly *land of date palms*). Country along Mediterranean coast, c. 120 miles long, extending from Arvad (Arados, 1Mc 15:23) to Dor, just S of Carmel. The Semitic name for the land was Canaan. The term Phoenicia is from a Greek word meaning "purple-red," perhaps because the Phoenicians were the discoverers of the crimson-purple dye derived form the murex shellfish. The people were Semites who came in a migration from the Mesopotamian region during the second millennium B.C. They became great seafarers, establishing colonies at Carthage and Spain, and perhaps even reached England. Inhabitants of, descended from Canaan (Ge 10:15, 18-19). Called Sidonians (Jdg 18:7; Eze 32:30). They were famous shipbuilders (Eze 27:9) and carpenters (1Ki 16:31; 18:19). Hiram, one of their kings was friendly with David and Solomon (2Sa 5:11; 1Ki 5:1-12; 2Ch 2:3-16), and another Hiram helped Solomon in the building of the temple in Jerusalem (1Ki 7:13-47; 2Ch 2:13-14). Jews from, hear Jesus (Mk 3:8). Jesus healed a Syrian Phoenician woman's daughter in its regions (Mk 7:24-30). Paul visited Christians there (Ac 15:3; 21:2-7; 27:3).

PHOENIX [5837]. Town on the S coast of Crete (Ac 27:12).

PHRYGIA [5867]. An inland province of Asia Minor. People from, in Jerusalem (Ac 2:10). Paul in (Ac 16:6; 18:23).

PHURAH See *Purah*.

PHUT See *Put*.

PHUVAH See *Puah*.

PHYGELUS [5869] (*fugitive*). A Christian in Asia. Turns from Paul (2Ti 1:15).

PHYLACTERY [5873] (*safeguard, means of protection*). A small box containing slips of parchment on which were written portions of the law (Ex 13:9, 16; Dt 6:4-9; 11:18). Worn ostentatiously on the forehead and left arm (Mt 23:5).

PHYSICIAN [8324, 2620]. (2Ch 16:12; Mt 9:12; Mk 5:26; Lk 8:43). Proverbs about (Mk 2:17; Lk 4:23). Luke a physician (Col 4:14).
Figurative (Job 13:4; Jer 8:22; Lk 5:31).

PHYSIOGNOMY The art of discovering temperament and character from outward appearance. Character revealed in (Isa 3:9). See *Countenance; Face*.

PHYSIOLOGY The human body (Job 10:11; Ps 139:14-16; Pr 14:30). See *Hygiene*. Figurative of the Church (Eph 4:16; Col 2:19).

PI-BESETH (*temple [house] of Bastet [pagan goddess]*). See *Bubastis*.

PI HAHIROTH [7084] (*temple [house] of Hathor [pagan goddess]*; possibly *mouth of canals*). The place on the W shore of the Red Sea where Pharaoh overtook the Israelites (Ex 14:2, 9; Nu 33:7-8).

PICKS, IRON [3044]. An instrument of iron used by prisoners of war (2Sa 12:31; 1Ch 20:3), who were used by victorious kings as menial laborers in royal building projects (1Ki 9:20-21; cf. also Ex 1:11).

PICTURES See *Idol; Idolatry*.

PIECE OF SILVER See *Silver*.

PIERCING THE EAR [4125, 8361]. A token of servitude for life (Ex 21:6; Dt 15:17; Ps 40:6).

PIETY [3711]. Religious duty.

PIG [2614, 5956]. An unclean animal (Lev 11:7; Dt 14:8; Isa 65:4; 66:3, 17). Possessed by demons (Mt 8:30-33). See *Animals*.

PIGEON [1578, 3433, 4361] (*young bird*). Used as sacrifice (Ge 15:9; Lev 1:14; 5:7; 12:8; 14:22; Lk 2:24). See *Dove*.

PILATE, PONTIUS [4397] (*family name*). Roman governor of Judea (Mt 27:2; Lk 3:1). Causes slaughter of certain Galileans (Lk 13:1). Tries Jesus and orders his crucifixion (Mt 27; Mk 15; Lk 23; Jn 18:28-40; 19; Ac 3:13; 4:27; 13:28; 1Ti 6:13). Allows Joseph of Arimathea to take Jesus' body (Mt 27:57-58; Mk 15:43-45; Lk 23:52; Jn 19:38).

PILDASH [7109] (*steely* ISBE; *spider* KB). Son of Nahor (Ge 22:22).

PILEHA See *Pilha*.

PILGRIM See *Sojourners*.

PILGRIMAGE [4472, 5019].
1. Jews were expected to make pilgrimages to the temple in Jerusalem for the great feasts (Ps 120-134; Ac 2:5-11).
2. The NT describes Christians as pilgrims or aliens (Heb 11:13; 1Pe 2:11).

PILHA [7116] (*millstone* IDB; *plowman* ISBE; *harelip* KB). One of those who sealed the covenant with Nehemiah (Ne 10:24).

PILLAR [2312, 4117, 5164, 5167, 5170, 5907, 6641, 6647, 5146]. Of Solomon's temple (1Ki 7:13-22; 2Ki 25:17). Broken and carried to Babylon (2Ki 25:13; Jer 52:17, 20-21). Of Solomon's palaces (1Ki 7:6). Pillar of salt, Lot's wife turned to (Ge 19:26; Lk 17:32).
Used to mark roads (Jer 31:21).

Monuments erected to commemorate events: By Jacob, his vision of angels (Ge 28:18, w 31:13; 35:14), his covenant with Laban (Ge 31:45); by Moses, the covenant between Yahweh and Israel (Ex 24:4); by Joshua, the passing over Jordan (Jos 4:1-9, w Dt 27:2-6; Jos 8:30), at Shechem (Jos 24:25-27, w Jdg 9:6); by Samuel, the discomfiture of the Philistines (1Sa 7:12); by Absalom, to keep his name in remembrance (2Sa 18:18). As a boundary (Jos 15:6, w 18:17), a marker (1Sa 20:19), a landmark (2Sa 20:8; 1Ki 1:9). Prophecy of one in Egypt (Isa 19:19). Monuments of idolatry, to be destroyed (Dt 12:3).

Figurative (Rev 3:12).

PILLAR OF CLOUD AND FIRE

God guided Israel out of Egypt and through the wilderness by a pillar of cloud by day and fire by night (Ex 13:21-22). The pillar of cloud rested over the tent of meeting outside the camp whenever the Lord met Moses there (Ex 33:7-11). The cloud and fire were divine manifestations. *See Celestial Phenomena.*

PILLOW

1. A support for the head (Ge 28:11, 18; 1Sa 26:7, 11, 16).
2. NIV "magic charms" (Eze 13:18, 20).

PILOT [*3237, 3995*] Captain or operator of a ship (Ac 27:11; Jas 3:4).

PILTAI [7122] (*Yahweh rescues*). A priest who returned to Jerusalem from captivity in Babylon (Ne 12:17).

PIM *See Measure.*

PIN [3845, 5782]. Tent peg (Jdg 4:21; 5:26), stick for beating wool in the loom (Jdg 16:13-14). KJV "crisping pins" (Isa 3:22) are NIV "purses."

PINE [581, 815, 1360]. A tree (Ne 8:15; Isa 41:19; 60:13).

PINING AWAY (Lev 26:39; La 4:9; Eze 4:17; 24:23; 33:10).

PINNACLE (*sun,* or *a little wing*). On a building, a turret, battlement, pointed roof or peak. Satan tried to get Jesus to throw himself down from the pinnacle of the temple (Mt 4:5-6; Lk 4:9).

PINON [89, 7091] (*darkness* ISBE; name related to *famous copper mines* KB). Chief of Edom of the family of Esau (Ge 36:40-41; 1Ch 1:52).

PIPE [7574, 10507]. A wind instrument of music. Used in religious services (1Sa 10:5; Isa 30:29). *See Music, Instruments of.*

PIRAM [7231] (possibly *wild donkey* IDB; *indomitable* ISBE; possibly *zebra* KB). A king of the Amorites. Overcome and slain by Joshua (Jos 10:3, 16-18, 24-27).

PIRATHON, PIRATHONITE [7284, 7285]. A place in the land of Ephraim (Jdg 12:15). Men of (Jdg 12:13; 2Sa 23:30; 1Ch 11:31; 27:14).

PISGAH [7171]. A ridge or mountain E of the Jordan, opposite to Jericho. The Israelites come to (Nu 21:20). The water courses flowing from Mount Pisgah were a boundary of the country assigned to the Reubenites and Gadites (Dt 3:17; 4:49; Jos 12:3). Balaam prophesies on (Nu 23:14-24). Moses views Israel from (Dt 3:27; 34:1-4).

PISHON [7093]. One of the rivers of Eden (Ge 2:11).

PISIDIA [*4407, 4408*]. A province in Asia Minor. Paul visits (Ac 13:14; 14:24).

PISIDIAN ANTIOCH *See Antioch, 2; Pisidia.*

PISON *See Pishon.*

PISPAH [7183]. An Asherite (1Ch 7:38).

PISTACHIO [1063]. Nuts, in a gift sent by Jacob to Joseph (Ge 43:11). *See Plants of the Bible; Tree.*

PIT [931, 1014, 1585, 4509, 7074, 8757, 8846, 8864, *1073, 5700*]. Bitumen deposit "tar pits" (Ge 14:10), deep place (Ge 37:20-29; Mt 12:11), well or cistern (Jer 14:3; Lk 14:5), earthen vessel (Lev 11:33), death, grave, or Sheol (Job 33:18; Isa 14:15; Nu 16:30, 33).

PITCH [182, 854+3125, 2413, 4109, 5742, 5749, 5989, 9546].

1. Pitch or tar (Ge 14:10; Ex 2:3). *See Caulkers; Tar.*
2. To encamp (Ge 12:8; 31:25; Ex 17:1; Nu 1:51; Jos 8:11).

PITCHER [3902, 7987, *3829*]. Jars for temple service and personal use (Ex 25:29; 37:16; 1Ch 28:17; Ecc 12:6; Mk 7:4).

PITHOM [7351] (*temple [house] of [pagan god] Atum*). Egyptian store city in a valley between the Nile and Lake Timsah; dedicated to the sun god Atum (Ex 1:11).

PITHON [7094]. Son of Micah (1Ch 8:35; 9:41).

PITY [365, 2571, 2798, 2858, 5714, 8163, 8171, *1796, 3091+3836+5073, 5072*]. Tender, considerate, compassionate feeling for others.

Commanded (Job 6:14; 1Pe 3:8). For the poor (Pr 19:17; 28:8). Forbidden: to Canaanites (Dt 7:16), to idolatrous proselytizers (Dt 13:8), to murderers (Dt 19:13), to false witnesses (Dt 19:21), to wife in certain situations (Dt 25:12).

Withholding of, from Jesus, prefigured in David (Ps 69:20). Of God (Ps 103:13; Isa 63:9; Joel 2:18;

Jnh 4:11; Jas 5:11), withheld from reprobates (Jer 13:14; 21:7; Eze 5:11; 7:4; 8:18; 9:5, 10; Zec 11:6).

Required of believers (Isa 1:17; Mt 18:28-35).

See God, Mercy of; Jesus the Christ, Compassion of; Mercy.

PLACE OF ATONEMENT *See Atonement Cover.*

PLAGUE [1815, 1822, 4487, 4638, 4804, 5595, 5596, 5597, 5598, 7776, 8103, *2505*, *4435*].
As a judgment on the Egyptians (Ps 105; 135:8-9; Ac 7:36). The plague of blood (Ex 7:14-25), frogs (Ex 8:1, 15), lice (Ex 8:16-19), flies (Ex 8:20). On cattle (Ex 9:1-7). Of boils and blains (Ex 9:8-12), hail (Ex 9:18-34), locusts (Ex 10:1-20), darkness (Ex 10:21-23). Death of the firstborn (Ex 11:4-7; 12:17, 29-30).

On the Israelites: On account of idolatry (Ex 32:35), after eating quail (Nu 11:33), after refusing to enter the promised land (Nu 14:37), after murmuring on account of the destruction of Korah (Nu 16:41-50), of serpents (Nu 21:6), for the sin of Peor (Jos 22:17), on account of David's sin (2Sa 24:10-25).

On the Philistines (1Sa 6:4-5).

Denounced as a judgment (Lev 26:21; Dt 28:59). Foretold (Rev 11:6; 15:1, 6-8; 16; 22:18-19).

See Judgments; Pestilence.

PLAIN [930, 1326, 3971, 4793, 6677, 10117, *5745*, *5746*, *5894*]. Broad stretch of level land (Ge 11:2; Eze 3:22).

PLAN OF SALVATION *See Jesus the Christ, Mission of; Redemption; Salvation.*

PLANE [6895]. A tool (Isa 44:13). *See Tools.*

PLANE TREE Possibly a chestnut tree (Ge 30:37; Eze 31:8).

PLANET *See Astronomy; Stars.*

PLANTS OF THE BIBLE [*2445, 4760, 5749, 6912, 9278, *3303*, *5062*, *5885*]. The following plants are mentioned in the Bible. Some of them are not identifiable with certainty.

Acacia tree (Ex 25:10ff), algum tree (2Ch 2:8; 9:11), almond (tree) (Ge 30:37; Ex 25:33-36; Ecc 12:5; Jer 1:11), almugwood (1Ki 10:11, 12; 2Ch. 2:8, 9:10 ftn.), aloes (Nu 24:6; Ps 45:8; Pr 7:17; SS 4:14; Jn 19:39), apple tree (SS 2:3; 8:5; Joel 1:12).

Balm (Ge 37:25; 43:11; 2Ch 28:15; Jer 8:22; 46:11; Eze 27:17), barley (Hos 3:2), beans (2Sa 17:28; Eze 4:9), brambles (Isa 34:13; Jdg 9:14-15), briers (Jdg 8:7, 16; Job 31:40; Isa 5:6, 7:23; Eze 28:24), broom tree (1Ki 19:3-4; Job 30:4; Ps 120:4), bush (burning bush) (Ex 3:2-3).

Calamus (SS 4:14; Isa 43:24; Jer 6:20; Eze 27:19), caraway (Isa 28:25-27), cassia (Ex 30:22-25; Ps 45:8; Eze 27:19), cedar (Lev 14:4, 6, 49; Nu 19:6; 2Sa 5:11; 1Ki 5:8), cedars of Lebanon (1Ki 4:33; Eze 31:3, 5), cinnamon (Ex 30:23; Pr

7:17; SS 4:14; Rev 18:13), citron wood (Rev 18:12), coriander (Ex 16:31; Nu 11:7), crocus (Isa 35:1), cucumber (Nu 11:5), cummin (Isa 28:26-27; Mt 23:23), cypress (Ge 6:14; Isa 41:19, 44:14, 60:13; Eze 27:6).

Date (Nu 33:9), dill (Mt 23:23), ebony (Eze 27:15), fig (Ge 3:6-7; Dt 8:8; Jdg 9:10-11; 1Ki 4:25), fir (Isa 41:19; 60:13), flax (Ex 9:31; Jos 2:6; Jdg 15:14), frankincense (Ex 30:34; Rev 18:13), galbanum (Ex 30:34-36), garlic (Nu 11:5), gourd (1Ki 6:18; 7:24; 2Ki 4:39), grain (Lev 23:14), grape (Ge 40:10-11), green tree (Ps 37:35), gum resin (Ex 30:34).

Henna blossoms (SS 1:14; 4:13), herbs, bitter herbs (Ex 12:8), hyssop (Ex 12:22; Lev 14:4; Ps 51:7; 1Ki 4:33), leeks (Nu 11:5), lentils (Ge 25:29-30, 34; 2Sa 17:28), lilies (1Ki 7:19, 22, 26; SS 5:13; Mt 6:28; Lk 12:27), linen (Est 1:5-6).

Mandrakes (Ge 30:14-16; SS 7:13), melon (Nu 11:5; Isa 1:8; Jer 10:5), millet (Eze 4:9; 27:17), mint (Mt 23:23; Lk 11:42), mulberry tree (Lk 17:6), mustard (Mt 13:31-32; 17:20; Mk 4:31; Lk 13:19), myrrh (Ge 37:25-27; 43:11; Est 2:12; Pr 7:17; SS 1:13; Mt 2:11), myrtle (Isa 41:19, 55:13; Zec 1:7-10), nettles (Isa 34:13), nut trees (SS 6:11), nuts [pistachio] (Ge 43:11).

Oak (Ge 35:4; Zec 11:2), olive tree (Jdg 9:8; Job 15:33; Ps 52:8; Isa 17:6; Isa 41:19), onion (Nu 11:5), onycha (Ex 30:34-35), palm (Nu 33:9), pine tree (1Ki 5:10; Isa 60:13), plane tree (Ge 30:37; Eze 31:8), poisonous weeds (Hos 10:4), pomegranate (Dt 8:8; 1Sa 14:2), poplars (Ge 30:37; Lev 23:40; Job 40:22; Ps 137:2; Isa 15:7, 44:4), reed (Job 40:15, 20-22), reeds (Ex 2:3; Job 8:11), resin (Ge 2:12; Nu 11:6-7), rose of Sharon (SS 2:1-2), rue (Lk 11:42), rush (Isa 9:6).

Saffron (SS 4:14), salt herbs (Job 30:1, 3-4), seaweed (Jnh 2:5), seed pods (2Ki 6:25, ftn.), spelt (Ex 9:32; Isa 28:5; Ezr 4:9), spices (Ge 37:25; 43:11; Ex 25:6; Mt 23:23), sycamore (1Ki 10:27; 1Ch 27:28; 2Ch 1:15; Am 7:14; Lk 19:4), terebinth (Isa 6:13; Hos 4:13), thistles (Ge 3:18; 2Ki 14:9; Heb 6:8), thorns (Isa 7:19; Mt 27:29; Mk 15:17; Jn 19:5), tumbleweed (Ps 83:13; Isa 17:13), vine (Ge 9:20, 40:9-11; Jnh 4:5-7), weeds (Job 31:40; Pr 24:31; Mt 13:25), wheat (Ge 30:14; Dt 8:8), wild vine (2Ki 4:39; Jer 2:21), willow (Eze 17:5), wormwood (Rev 8:11).

See Tree.

PLASTER [3212, 3220, 6760, 8487, 10142].
In Egypt stone buildings, even the finest granite, were plastered, inside and out, to make a smooth surface for decoration (Dt 27:2, 4). The poor used a mixture of clay and straw. In Israel an outside clay coating would have to be renewed after the rainy season.

PLASTER, MEDICINAL A cake of figs applied to a boil (Isa 38:21).

PLATE, PLATTER [7488, 7883, *4402*].
Dedicated to the tabernacle (Nu 7:13, 19, 25, 31,

37, 43, 49, 55, 61, 67, 73, 79, 84-85). John the Baptist's head carried on (Mt 14:8, 11).

PLEADING [*1335, 1819, 1906, 2858, 7003, 7754, 8189, 8262, 9382, *1289,*3306,*4151*]. (Dt 17:8). Of the guilty (Jos 7:19-21). Jesus declined to plead (Mt 26:62; Mk 15:2; Lk 23:3; Jn 18:33-34). Prisoners required to plead (Ac 7:1). *See Defense.*

PLEASANT LAND [2275]. The land of Israel (Ps 106:24; Zec 7:14; cf. Jer 3:19; 12:10; Dt 8:7-9). *See Israel.*

PLEASING AROMA [5767, *2298, 2380*]. Of sacrifices (Ge 8:21; Ex 29:18, 25, 41; Lev 1:9, 13, 17; 2:2, 9, 12; 3:5, 16; 4:31; 6:15, 21; 8:21, 28; 17:6; 23:13, 18; 26:31; Nu 15:3, 7, 10, 13, 14, 24; 18:17; 28:2, 6, 8, 13, 24, 27; 29:2, 6, 8, 13, 36; Eze 6:13; 16:19; 20:28, 41). Of Christian service (2Co 2:15; Eph 5:2; Php 4:18). *See Offerings.*

PLEASURE, WORLDLY Unfulfilling (Job 21:12-13; Ecc 1:17; 2:1-13; 1Ti 5:6). Proverbs and parables concerning (Pr 9:17; 15:21; 21:17; Lk 8:14).

Rejected and judged by God (Job 20:12-16; Isa 5:11-12; 22:12-13; 47:8-9; Am 6:1; Ro 1:32; 2Th 2:12). Rejected by Moses (Heb 11:25-26), by Paul (2Ti 3:4; Tit 3:3), by Peter (2Pe 2:13).

See Gluttony; Happiness; Joy; Worldliness.

PLEDGE [674, 829, 2471, 2478, 2481, 5989, 6287, 6641, 6842, 6860, 9364, 9546, *2090,*4411*].
1. Personal property of a debtor held to secure a payment (Ge 38:17-18). Law of Moses was concerned with protection of the poor. A pledged outer garment had to be restored at sunset for a bed covering (Ex 22:26-27), a widow's clothing could not be taken (Dt 24:17), a handmill or its upper millstone could not be taken (Dt 24:6).

2. In marriage *See Betrothal.*

PLEIADES [3966] (*heap, group [of stars]*). Stars in the constellation Taurus (Job 9:9; 38:31).

PLINY Gaius Plinius Caecilius Secundus, called "the Younger," Roman governmental official, famous as the author of literary letters covering all types of subjects, one of which contains a description of the Christian church in Bithynia, a province which Pliny governed in A.D. 112. The letter, together with the reply of the emperor Trajan are important evidence for the official attitude towards the Christians.

PLOTTING [*2047, 2372, 2750, 2754, 3086, 3108, 3619, 4742, 6783, 6870, 8003, *2101*]. General references to (Est 3:9; Ps 36:4; 37:12; Pr 6:14; Isa 32:7; Mic 2:1). Against Christ (Mt 12:14; 26:4; 27:1; Lk 6:11; 19:47; 22:4; Jn 5:16; 11:47, 53).

General examples of (Ge 37:18; Nu 16:3; Jdg 9:1; 2Ki 12:20; 14:19; Da 6:4; Mt 12:14; Ac 23:13).

PLOW [1330, 3045, 3086, 6268, 7114, 9439, *769, 770*]. The ancient plow consisted of a forked stick, the trunk hitched to the animals which drew it, the branch braced and terminating in the share, which was at first the sharpened end of the branch, later a metal point. It was ordinarily drawn by a yoke of oxen (Job 1:14; Am 6:12). Such a plow did not turn over the soil; it did little more than scratch the surface.

Figurative of afflictions (Ps 129:3).

PLOWSHARE [908, 4739] (*the blade of a plow*). To beat swords into plowshares was symbolic of an age of peace (Isa 2:4), to beat plowshares into swords portended coming war (Joel 3:10).

PLUMB LINE [74, 74+974, 643, 5487]. A cord with a weight, the plummet, tied to one end; used in testing whether a wall is perpendicular (Am 7:7-9; 2Ki 21:13; Isa 28:17).

PLUMMET *See Plumb Line.*

POCHERETH *See Pokereth-Hazzebaim.*

PODS [1807, *3044*]. Seed pods eaten in famine (2Ki 6:24). Perhaps carob, eaten by the prodigal son and the pigs (Lk 15:16). *See Plants of the Bible.*

POET [5439, *4475*] (*doer,* or *a maker*). Paul quotes from pagan poets (Ac 17:28; 1Co 15:32; Tit 1:12). A great deal of the OT is written in the form of poetry.

POETRY
Acrostic:
(Ps 25; 34; 37; 111; 112; 119; 145; Pr 31:10-31; La 1-5).
Didactic:
Moses' song (Dt 32). The book of Job, the Proverbs, the Song of Songs, much of the books of prophecy. *See Psalms, Topically Arranged.*
Elegy:
On the death of Saul (2Sa 1:19-27). Of Abner (2Sa 3:33-34). *See Elegy.*
Epic:
Moses' song (Ex 15:1-19). Miriam's song (Ex 15:21). Deborah's song (Jdg 5) David's song of praise (2Sa 22).
Lyrics, Sacred:
Moses' and Miriam's songs (Ex 15). Hannah's song (1Sa 2:1-10). The song of Elizabeth (Lk 1:42-45). Of Mary (Lk 1:46-55). Of Zechariah (Lk 1:68-79). The Psalms. *See Psalms.*
See Parallelism

POETS, PAGAN, QUOTATIONS FROM Paul quotes pagan poets in arguments. Examples include: Cleanthes (Ac 17:28), Epimenides (Tit 1:12), Menander (1Co 15:33).

POISON [2779, 7301, 8032, 2503+5516, 2675, 2808]. A substance producing a deadly effect, like the venom of reptiles (Dt 32:24, 33; Job 20:16; Ps 58:4). Vegetable poisons were known in antiquity: poisonous weeds (Hos 10:4), wild gourd (2Ki 4:39-40). A poisoned drink is referred to in Mark (Mk 16:18).

POKERETH-HAZZEBAIM [7097] (*pitfall of gazelles*, i.e., *gazelle hunter*). The ancestor of a family which returned to Jerusalem from captivity in Babylon (Ezr 2:57; Ne 7:59).

POLE [895, 964, 4573, 4574, 5812, 7771]. Used to carry the ark (Ex 24:13-15), the table of the bread of the Presence (Ex 25:27-28), the bronze altar (Ex 27:6-7), the incense altar (Ex 30:4-5). Standard on which the bronze serpent was displayed (Nu 21:8-9).

POLICY *See Diplomacy.*

POLITARCH City magistrate of Thessalonica (Ac 17:6, 8). Sixteen epigraphical inscriptions with the word have been discovered.

POLITICS Statecraft.
Corruption in:
(Ps 12:8), in the court of Xerxes (Est 3), of Darius (Da 6:4-15).
Instances of:
Absalom, electioneering for the throne (2Sa 15:2-6). Pilate, condemning Jesus to gratify popular clamor (Mt 27:23-27; Mk 15:15; Lk 23:13-25; Jn 18:38-39; 19:4-13).
Ministers:
Zadok the priest, a partisan of David (2Sa 15:24-29). Nathan the prophet influences the selection of David's successor (1Ki 1:11-40).
Women in:
The wise woman of Abel, who saved the city through diplomacy (2Sa 20:16-22). Bathsheba, in securing the crown for Solomon (1Ki 1:15-21). Herodias, in influencing the administration of Herod (Mt 14:3-11; Mk 6:17-28). Mother of Zebedee's children, in seeking favor for her sons (Mt 20:20-23).
Influence in. *See Influence, Political.*
See Diplomacy; Government.

POLL TAX *See Tax.*

POLLUTION [2866, 5614, 8845, 246, 834, 3620]. Ceremonial or moral defilement, profanation, and uncleanness (Ex 20:25; 2Pe 2:20). *See Corruption; Defilement; Unclean, Uncleanness; Sanitation and Hygiene.*

POLLUX [1483]. With Castor, one of the twin gods, sons of Zeus and patrons of sailors (Ac 28:11).

POLYGAMY (*many marriages*). Forbidden (Dt 17:17; Lev 18:18; Mal 2:14-15; Mt 19:4-5;

Mk 10:2-8; 1Ti 3:2, 12; Tit 1:6). Authorized (2Sa 12:8).
Examples of:
Tolerated (Ex 21:10; 1Sa 1:2; 2Ch 24:3). Practiced by, (Job 27:15), Lamech (Ge 4:19), Abraham (Ge 16), Esau (Ge 26:34; 28:9), Jacob (Ge 29:30), Ashhur (1Ch 4:5), Gideon (Jdg 8:30), Elkanah (1Sa 1:2), David (1Sa 25:39-44; 2Sa 3:2-5; 5:13; 1Ch 14:3), Solomon (1Ki 11:1-8), Rehoboam (2Ch 11:18-23), Abijah (2Ch 13:21), Jehoram (2Ch 21:14), Joash (2Ch 24:3), Ahab (2Ki 10:1), Jehoiachin (2Ki 24:15), Belshazzar (Da 5:2, w 1Ch 2-8), Hosea (Hos 3:1-2). Mosaic law respecting the firstborn in (Dt 21:15-17).
Sought by women [polyandry] (Isa 4:1).
The Evil Effects of:
Husband's favoritism in (Dt 21:15-17), Jacob's (Ge 29:30; 30:15), Elkanah's (1Sa 1:5), Rehoboam's (2Ch 11:21). Domestic infelicity, in Abraham's family (Ge 16; 21:9-16), Jacob's (Ge 29:30-34; 30:1-23), Elkanah's (1Sa 1:4-7). Upon Solomon (1Ki 11:4-8).
See Concubinage; Marriage.

POLYTHEISM (Ge 31:19; 35:2, 4; Jos 24:2, 23; Jdg 2:13; 3:7; 10:16; 17:5; Jer 2:28; 11:13; Da 4:8; 1Co 8:5).

POMEGRANATE [8232]. A fruit. Abounded in the land of Canaan (1Sa 14:2). Brought by the spies to show the fruitfulness of the land of Canaan (Nu 13:23). Figures of the fruits of, were embroidered on the ephod (Ex 28:33-34; 39:24), carved on the pillars of the temple (1Ki 7:18, 20, 42; Jer 52:22-23). Wine made of (SS 8:2).

POMMEL *See Capital.*

PONTIUS PILATE [4508]. *See Pilate, Pontius.*

PONTUS [4507, 4509] (*sea*). A province of Asia Minor (Ac 2:9; 1Pe 1:1). Aquila lived in (Ac 18:2).

POOL [106, 1391, 4784, 6524, 3148]. Of Gibeon (2Sa 2:13; Jer 41:12). Of Hebron (2Sa 4:12). Of Samaria (1Ki 22:38). Of Heshbon (SS 7:4).
Of Jerusalem: Upper pool (2Ki 18:17; Isa 36:2), lower pool (Isa 22:9), Siloam (Jn 9:7, 11), called Siloam (Ne 3:15, ftn), and probably identical with the king's pool (Ne 2:14).

POOR [*36, 1924, 1930, 3769, 4575, 4728, 5014, 6705, 8133, 8203, 8273, 1797, 4775, 4777].
Proverbs Concerning:
(Ps 37:16 w Isa 29:19; Pr 10:15; 13:7-8, 23; 18:23; 19:1, 4, 7, 17, 22; 20:13; 21:13; 22:2, 9; 23:21; 24:20-21, 31; 28:6, 8, 11, 19; 29:14; Ecc 4:6, 13; 6:8; 9:15-16). Always part of the society (Mt 26:11; Mk 14:7; Jn 12:8).

Attitudes toward:

Job (Job 30:25). Jesus and the poor widow (Mk 12:43-44). Lazarus (Lk 16:20-21). Judas (Jn 12:6). James (Jas 1:9-10).

Duty to:

(Ex 22:25-27; 23:11; Lev 19:9-10; 25:25-28, 35-43; Dt 14:28-29; 15:2-14; 24:12-21; 26:12-13; Ne 8:10; Ps 37:21, 26; 41:1-3; 112:4-5, 9; Pr 28:27; 29:7; 31:9, 20; Isa 1:7; 16:3-4; 58:7, 10; Eze 18:7; Da 4:27; Zec 7:10; Mt 5:42; 19:21; 25:35-36; Mk 14:7; Lk 3:11; 6:30; 11:41; 12:33; 14:12-14; 18:22; 19:8; Ac 20:35; Ro 12:8, 13, 20; 1Co 13:3; 16:1-2; 2Co 6:10; 8:9; 9:5-7; Gal 2:10; 6:10; Eph 4:28; 1Ti 5:9-10, 16; Heb 13:3; Jas 1:27; 2:2-9, 15-16; 5:4; 1Jn 3:17-19).

God's care of:

(1Sa 2:7-8; Job 5:15-16; 31:15; 34:18-19, 28; 36:6, 15; Ps 9:18; 10:14; 12:5; 14:6; 34:6; 35:10; 68:10; 69:33; 72:2, 4, 12-14; 74:21; 102:17; 107:9, 36, 41; 109:31; 113:7-8; 132:15; 140:12; 146:5, 7; Pr 22:2, 22-23; 29:13; Ecc 5:8; Isa 11:4; 14:30, 32; 25:4; 29:19; 41:17; Jer 20:13; Zep 3:12; Zec 11:7; Mt 11:5; Lk 4:18; 7:22; 16:22; Jas 2:5).

See God, Goodness of, Providence of.

The Poor, Without Friends:

(Pr 14:20; 19:4, 7). Wisdom of, despised (Ecc 9:15-16).

Warning against neglect of (Pr 20:13; 21:13; 22:16; Eze 16:49). Neglect of, by the disciples (Ac 6:1-6). Neglect of, denounced (Mt 25:42, 45).

Kindness to:

Commanded (Ne 8:10, 12). Rewarded (Ps 41:1-3; Isa 58:10; Lk 14:12-14).

Righteous treatment of, required (Ps 82:3-4; Pr 22:22; 31:9; Isa 1:17). Rewarded (Pr 29:14; Jer 22:16; Eze 18:7, 16-17; Da 4:27). Compassion toward (Job 30:25; Pr 14:21; 29:7; Heb 13:3; Jas 1:27).

Liberality to (Pr 31:20; Isa 58:7; Mt 5:42, w Lk 6:30; Lk 3:11; 19:8; Ro 12:8, 13, 20; 1Co 13:3; 16:1-2; 2Co 9:1-15; Gal 2:10; Eph 4:28; 1Ti 5:9-10, 16; Jas 2:15-16; 1Jn 3:17). Liberality to, rewarded (Pr 19:17; 22:9; 28:27; Ps 112:9; Mt 19:21; 25:34-36; Lk 6:35; 12:33; 18:22; Ac 20:35).

Instances of Kindness—

Ruth, to Naomi (Ru 2:2, 11). Boaz, to Ruth (Ru 2:8-16; 3:15). Elijah, to the widow of Zarephath (1Ki 17:12-24). Elisha, to the prophet's widow (2Ki 4:1-7). The Jews (Est 9:22). Job (Job 29:11-17; 31:16-22, 38-40). The Temanites (Isa 21:14). Nebuzaradan (Jer 39:10).

The good Samaritan (Lk 10:33-35). Zacchaeus (Lk 19:8). Dorcas (Ac 9:36). Cornelius (Ac 10:2, 4). Christian church, at Jerusalem (Ac 6:1), at Antioch (Ac 11:29-30). Churches of Macedonia and Achaia (Ro 15:25-26; 2Co 8:1-5). By Paul (Ro 15:25).

Oppression of:

(Ne 5:1-13; Job 20:19-21; 22:6-7, 9-11; 24:4, 7-12; Ps 10:2, 8-10; 37:14; 109:16; Pr 14:31; 17:5; 19:7; 22:7, 16; 28:3, 15; 30:14; Ecc 5:8; Isa 3:14-15; 10:1-2; 32:6-7; Eze 18:12; 22:29; Am 2:6; 4:1; 5:11-12; 8:4-6; Hab 3:14; Jas 2:6; 5:4). Oppression forbidden (Dt 24:14; Zec 7:10).

Instances of oppression of (2Ki 4:1; Ne 5:1-5).

Mosaic laws concerning:

Atonement money of, must be uniform with that of the rich (Ex 30:15). Inexpensive offerings authorized for (Lev 5:7; 12:8; 14:21-22).

Discrimination, in favor of, forbidden (Ex 23:3; Lev 19:15); against, forbidden (Ex 23:6; Jas 2:2-9).

Exactions of interest from, forbidden (Ex 22:25; Lev 25:35-37). Garments of, taken in pledge, to be restored (Ex 22:26; Dt 24:12-13). To participate triennially in the tithes (Dt 14:28-29; 26:12-13). Gleanings reserved for (Lev 19:9-10; 23:22; Dt 24:19-21). To share the products of the land in the seventh year (Ex 23:11). To be released from servitude, in seventh year (Dt 15:12), in Jubilee (Lev 25:39-43). Alienated lands of, to be restored in Jubilee (Lev 25:25-28).

Figurative:

Poor in spirit (Isa 66:2; Mt 5:3; Lk 6:20).

See Alms; Beneficence; Creditor; Debtor; Employee; Employer; Liberality; Orphans; Poverty; Rich, The; Riches; Servants; Wages; Widow.

POPLAR [4242, 6857] (white). A tree (Ge 30:37; Hos 4:13).

POPLARS, RAVINE OF A brook, probably on the boundary between Moab and Edom (Isa 15:7).

POPULARITY Instances of: David (2Sa 3:36). Absalom (2Sa 15:2-6, 13). Job (Job 29).

POPULARITY OF JESUS

(Mt 4:24; 8:1; 13:2; 14:13, 35; 19:1-2; 21:8-9; Mk 1:33; 2:2; 3:7, 20; 5:21; 6:33, 55-56; 10:1; 11:8-10; 12:37; Lk 4:14-15, 42; 5:1; 9:11; 12:1; 19:35-38; Jn 6:2, 15; 12:12-13, 19).

PORATHA [7054]. Son of Haman (Est 9:8).

PORCH [395, 4997]. An area with a roof supported by columns: colonnade (1Ki 7:6ff), porch (Jdg 3:23, ftn), place before a court (Mk 14:68), gateway (Mt 26:71).

PORCIUS [4517]. See Festus, Porcius.

PORPHYRY [985]. A purple stone used in mosaics (Est 1:6).

PORPOISE See Sea Cow.

PORTERS See Gatekeepers.

PORTION [260, 2475, 2745, 2750, 2754, 2976, 3338, 4595, 4950, 4987, 5368, 5419, 5467, 7023, 7731, 8123, 9556]. A part; less than the whole of anything; share (Nu 31:30, 47; Ne 8:10, 12).

POST [4647, 5226, 5466, 6641, 7212, 8492, *2653*].

1. Of the tabernacle (Ex 26:32, 37; 27:1-17). Of a city gate (Jdg 16:3).

2. Of a watchman (Ne 7:3; 13:11; Ecc 10:4; Isa 62:6).

POSTERITY PROMISED [2446].
(Ge 15:5, 18; 17:20; 22:17; 26:14; Lev 26:9; Dt 7:13; Ro 4:18).

POT [1857, 3671, 3968, 3998, 5350, 5574, 6105, 6775, 7248, 7831]. Utensil of metal of clay for holding liquids or other substances (2Ki 4:38).

POTENTATE See *Rulers.*

POTIPHAR [7035] (*he whom [pagan god] Ra gives*). An officer of Pharaoh. Joseph's master (Ge 37:36; 39:1).

POTIPHERA [7036] (*he whom [pagan god] Ra gives*). A priest of On. Joseph's father-in-law (Ge 41:45, 50; 46:20).

POTSHERD [3068, 3084]. A fragment of earthenware (Job 2:8; Isa 45:9).

POTTAGE See *Stew.*

POTTER [3450, *3038*]. See *Occupations and Professions.*

POTTER'S FIELD Piece of ground which the priests bought with the money Judas received for betraying our Lord (Mt 27:7).

POTTER'S GATE Of Jerusalem (Jer 19:2).

POTTERY [3084, 3450+, 3998, *5007*]. One of the oldest crafts in the Bible lands. The place where potter's clay was dug was called "potter's field" (Mt 27:7). Pottery was shaped by hand on a potter's wheel, powered by foot or by an apprentice (Jer 18:3-6), then dried and baked in a kiln.

Many different items were made: basins, bowls, cups, dishes, flasks, jars, lamps, ovens, pots. Thousands of objects have been found by the archaeologists. Careful study has been made of the historical development of pottery styles, so that experts can date and place pottery with considerable accuracy.

POUND [*1669*+3354, *5418*]. A talent equaled about seventy-five pounds (Ex 25:39, ftn), a mina about 1.25 pounds (1Ki 10:17, ftn), forty shekels about one pound (Ge 3:15, ftn). See *Measure.*

POVERTY [2895, 2896, 3769, 4728, 8133, 8203, *4775, 5729, 5730*]. (1Sa 2:7). Destructive (Pr 10:15). A source of temptation (Pr 30:8-9). To be preferred over wealth, with trouble (Pr 15:16), without right (Pr 16:8; Ecc 4:6). See *Poor.*

Caused, by laziness (Pr 6:11; 20:13; 24:33-34),

by drunkenness (Pr 23:21), by evil associations (Pr 28:19).

POWER [*226, 600, 1475, 1476, 1524, 2432, 2616, 2617, 3338, 3946, 6434, 6437, 6786, 6793, 7502, 7756, 10130, 10717, 10768, *794, 1539, 1543, 1918, 2026, 2708, 3197*].

Of Christ:

As the Son of God, is the power of God (Jn 5:17-19; 10:28-30), as man, is from the Father (Ac 10:38).

Described as supreme (Eph 1:20-21; 1Pe 3:22), unlimited (Mt 28:18), over all flesh (Jn 17:2), over all things (Jn 3:35; Eph 1:22), glorious (2Ti 1:9), everlasting (1Ti 6:16). Is able to subdue all things (Php 3:21).

Exemplified in, creation (Jn 1:3, 10; Col 1:16), upholding all things (Col 1:17; Heb 1:3), salvation (Isa 63:1; Heb 7:25), His teaching (Mt 7:28-29; Lk 4:32), working miracles (Mt 8:27; Lk 5:17), enabling others to work miracles (Mt 10:1; Ac 5:31), giving spiritual life (Jn 5:21, 25-26), giving eternal life (Jn 17:2), raising the dead (Jn 5:28-29), rising from the dead (Jn 2:19; 10:18), overcoming the world (Jn 16:33), overcoming Satan (Col 2:15; Heb 2:14), destroying the works of Satan (1Jn 3:8), ministers should make known (2Pe 1:16).

Saints made willing by (Ps 110:3), aided by (Heb 2:18), strengthened by (Php 4:13; 2Ti 4:17), preserved by (2Ti 1:12; 4:18), bodies of, shall be changed by (Php 3:21), rests upon saints (2Co 12:9). Present in the assembly of saints (1Co 5:4). Shall be specially manifested at his second coming (Mk 13:26; 2Pe 1:16). Shall subdue all power (1Co 15:24). The wicked shall be destroyed by (Ps 2:9; Isa 11:4; 63:3; 2Th 1:9).

See Jesus the Christ, Omnipotence of; Power of.

Of God:

One of his attributes (Ps 62:11).

Expressed by the voice of God (Ps 29:3, 5; 68:33), finger of God (Ex 9:3, 15; Isa 48:13), arm of God (Job 40:9; Isa 52:10), thunder of his power (Job 26:14).

Described as, great (Ps 79:11; Na 1:3), strong (Ps 89:13; 136:12), glorious (Ex 15:6; Isa 63:12), mighty (Job 9:4; Ps 89:13), everlasting (Isa 26:4; Ro 1:20), sovereign (Ro 9:21), effectual (Isa 43:13; Eph 3:7), irresistible (Dt 32:39; Da 4:35), incomparable (Ex 15:11-12; Dt 3:24; Job 40:9; Ps 89:8), unsearchable (Job 5:9; 9:10), incomprehensible (Job 26:14; Ecc 3:11).

All things possible to (Mt 19:26). Nothing too hard for (Ge 18:14; Jer 32:27). Can save by many or by few (1Sa 14:6). Is the source of all strength (1Ch 29:12; Ps 68:35).

Exemplified, in the creation (Ps 102:25; Jer 10:12), in establishing and governing all things (Ps 65:6; 66:7), in the miracles of Christ (Lk 11:20), in the resurrection of Christ (2Co 13:4; Col 2:12), in the resurrection of saints (1Co 6:14), in making the gospel effectual (Ro 1:16; 1Co 1:18, 24), in delivering his people (Ps 106:8), in the destruction of the wicked (Ex 9:16; Ro 9:22).

Saints, long for exhibitions of (Ps 63:1-2), have confidence in (Jer 20:11), receive increase of grace by (2Co 9:8), strengthened by (Eph 6:10; Col 1:11), upheld by (Ps 37:17; Isa 41:10), supported in affliction by (2Co 6:7; 2Ti 1:8), delivered by (Nu 1:10; Da 3:17), exalted by (Job 36:22), kept by, for salvation (1Pe 1:5). Exerted in behalf of saints (1Ch 16:9). Works in and for saints (2Co 13:4; Eph 1:19; 3:20). The faith of saints stands in (1Co 2:5).

Should be acknowledged (1Ch 29:11; Isa 33:13), pleaded in prayer (Ps 79:11; Mt 6:13), feared (Jer 5:22; Mt 10:28), magnified (Ps 21:13; Jude 25). Efficiency of ministers is through (1Co 3:6-8; Gal 2:8; Eph 3:7). Is a ground of trust (Isa 26:4; Ro 4:21).

The wicked do not know (Mt 22:29), have it against them (Ezr 8:22), shall be destroyed by it (Lk 12:5).

The heavenly host magnified (Rev 4:11; 5:13; 11:17).

See God, Omnipotent, Power of.

Of the Holy Spirit:
Is the power of God (Mt 12:28, w Lk 11:20). Christ worked his miracles (Mt 12:28).

Exemplified in creation (Ge 1:2; Job 26:13; Ps 104:30), the conception of Christ (Lk 1:35), raising Christ from the dead (1Pe 3:18), giving spiritual life (Eze 37:11-14, w Ro 8:11), working miracles (Ro 15:19), making the gospel efficacious (1Co 2:4; 1Th 1:5), overcoming all difficulties (Zec 4:6-7). Promised by the Father (Lk 24:49). Promised by Christ (Ac 1:8).

Saints upheld by (Ps 51:12), strengthened by (Eph 3:16), enabled to speak the truth boldly by (Mic 3:8; Ac 6:5, 10; 2Ti 1:7-8), helped in prayer by (Ro 8:26), abound in hope by (Ro 15:13). Qualifies ministers (Lk 24:49; Ac 1:8-9). God's word the instrument of (Eph 6:17).

See Holy Spirit.

Spiritual:
From God (Isa 40:29-31; Lk 24:49; 1Co 1:24-28; Php 2:13; 2Ti 1:7). From Christ (2Co 12:9; Eph 1:19-20). From the Holy Spirit (Jn 7:38-39; Ac 1:8; 2:2-4). On believers (Ac 6:8, 10; 1Co 4:19-20; Heb 6:5). In the spirit of Elijah (Lk 1:17).

In preaching (Ac 4:33; 6:10; 1Th 1:5), of Christ (Lk 4:32). Through prayer (Job 32:28; Mk 9:29; Lk 24:49; Ac 1:14; 2:1; 2:2-4).

PRAETOR Originally the highest Roman magistrate; later, officials elected to administer justice; under the principate the office declined in prestige, power, and functions.

PRAETORIAN GUARD (*residence of the Praetor [leader]*). Guard of imperial palace or provincial governor; NIV "palace guard" (Php 1:13) and "Caesar's household" (Php 4:22).

PRAETORIUM [4550] (*residence of the Praetor [leader]*). In the Gospels it refers to the temporary palace or headquarters of the Roman governor while in Jerusalem (Mt 27:27; Mk 15:16), the palace of Herod at Caesarea (Ac 23:35).

PRAISE [*1385, 2146, 2376, 3344, 9335, 10122, 10693, *140, *1518, *1519, *2018, *2046, *2047, *2328, *2329, *2330*].

Examples of:
(Ps 7:17; 22:22-23; 28:6-7; 32:11; 34:1-3; 41:13; 42:4; 51:15; 65:1; 71:8, 14-15; 75:1; 79:13; 81:1; 84:4; 86:12; 89:95; 104:33-34; 109:30; 113:1-2; 115:18; 118:15; 140:13; 145:1-21; 146:1-10; 148:1-14; 149:1-9; 150; Isa 24:15-16; 25:1; 35:10; 38:19; 43:21; 49:13; 51:3; 52:7-10; Jer 31:7; Ro 11:36; 16:27; 1Co 15:57; Eph 3:20-21; Heb 2:12; Jude 25; Rev 1:6; 14:7).

With music (Ps 33:2-3; 43:3-4; 47:1, 6-7; 57:7-9 w 108:1-3; 66:1-2, 4; 67:4; 68:4, 32-34; 69:30; 71:22; 81:1; 92:1-3; 95:1-2; 98:4-6; 104:33; 144:9; 149:2-3; 150:3-5; Jas 5:13).

Daily (1Ch 23:30; Ps 92:1-2; 145:2). In the night (Ps 42:8; 63:5-6; 77:6; 92:1-3; 119:62; 134:1; 149:5; Ac 16:25). Seven times a day (Ps 119:164).

Congregational (Ps 22:22; 26:12; 68:26; 111:1; 116:18-19; 134:1-2; 135:2; 149:1).

For God's goodness and mercy (Ps 13:6; 63:3-6; 100:5; 101:1; 106:1, 48; 107:8-9, 15, 21, 31; 117:2; 118:29; 136; 138:2; 144:1-2; 145:7-9, 14-21; 146:7-9; Isa 12:1-6; Jer 33:11). For God's greatness (Ps 48:1; 145:3, 10-12; 147:1-20; Isa 24:14). For God's holiness (Ps 99:2, 5, 9). For God's works (Ps 9:1-2; 107:8-9, 15, 21, 31-32; 145:4-6, 10-13; 147:12-18; 150:2). For deliverance from enemies (Ge 14:20; Ps 44:7-8; 54:6-7; 69:16). For salvation (Isa 61:3).

Commanded:
(Dt 8:10; Ps 9:11; 30:4; 32:11; 33:1-3; 69:34; 70:4; 95:1-2, 6-7a; 96:1-4, 7-9; 97:12; 100:1-5; 105:1-5; 117:1; 134:1-2; 135:1-3, 19-21; Isa 42:10-12; Eph 5:19; Heb 13:15; 1Pe 4:11; 5:11). All nations to praise God (Ps 69:34; 103:22; 148:1-14).

Angels exhorted to (Ps 103:20-21; 148:2). In heaven (Ne 9:6; Job 38:7; Ps 103:20-21; 148:2-4; Isa 6:3; Eze 3:12; Lk 2:13-14; 15:7, 10; Rev 1:6; 4:8-11; 5:9-14; 7:9-12; 11:16-17; 14:2-3; 15:3-4; 19:1-6).

Instances of:
Song of Moses, after the passage of the Red Sea (Ex 15:1-19). Miriam (Ex 15:21). Deborah, after defeating the Canaanites (Jdg 5:1-31). Hannah (1Sa 2:1-10). David, celebrating his deliverance from the hand of Saul (2Sa 22 w Ps 18). On bringing the ark to Zion (1Ch 16:8-36). At the close of his reign (1Ch 29:10-19). The choir when Solomon brought the ark into the temple (2Ch 5:13). Israelites (2Ch 7:2-3; Ne 9:5-6). Daniel (Da 2:20, 23). Nebuchadnezzar (Da 4:37). Jonah (Jnh 2:9).

Mary (Lk 1:46-55). Shepherds (Lk 2:20). The leper (Lk 17:15). Jesus and his disciples (Mt 26:30; Mk 14:26). Disciples (Ac 2:46-47; 4:24). Paul and Silas, in prison (Ac 16:25).

Psalms of:

For God's goodness to Israel (Pss 46; 48; 65:66; 68; 76; 81; 85; 98; 105; 124; 126; 129; 135; 136). For God's goodness to the righteous (Pss 23; 34; 36; 91; 100; 103; 107; 117; 121). For God's goodness to individuals (Pss 9; 18; 22; 30; 40; 75; 103; 108; 116; 118; 138; 144). For God's attributes (Pss 8; 19; 22; 24; 29; 33; 47; 50; 65-66; 76-77; 92-93; 95-99; 104; 111; 113-115; 134; 139; 147-148; 150).

See Glorifying God; Hallelujah; Prayer; Thankfulness.

PRAYER [*606, 1819, 6983, 7137, 9525, 10114, 10612, *1255, 1289, 2263, 2377, 4666, 4667*]. (Ps 17:1, 6; 22:1-2, 19; 28:1-2; 35:22; 55:1-2, 16-17; 57:2; 61:1-2; 70:5; 102:1-2; 130:1-2; 141:1-2; 142:1-2).

General:

Attitudes in: *See Worship.*

Boldness in: Commanded (Heb 4:16). Exemplified by Abraham in his inquiry concerning Sodom (Ge 18:23-32), by Moses, supplicating for assistance in delivering Israel (Ex 33:12, 18). Secret (Mt 24:63; Mt 6:6). Silent (Ps 5:1). Weeping in (Ezr 10:1). In a loud voice, satirized by Elijah (1Ki 18:27).

Long: Of Pharisees (Mt 23:14), scribes (Mk 12:40; Lk 20:47). Profuse, to be avoided (Ecc 5:2; Mt 6:7). Vain repetitions of, to be avoided (Mt 6:7).

Daily: In the morning (Ps 5:3; 88:13; 143:8; Isa 32:2). Morning and evening (Ps 92:2). Twice daily (Ps 88:1). Three times a day (Ps 55:17; Da 6:10). In the night (Ps 119:55, 62). All night (Lk 6:12). Without ceasing (1Th 5:17).

Disbelief in: (Job 21:15).

Family: By Abraham (Ge 12:7-8; 13:4, 8). By Jacob (Ge 35:3, 7). Cornelius (Ac 10:2).

Hypocritical, forbidden (Mt 6:5). Discreet (Ecc 5:2; Mt 6:6).

"Lord's prayer": A model taught to the disciples (Mt 6:9-12; Lk 11:2-4). *See below, Of Jesus.*

Of the righteous, acceptable: (Pr 15:8, 29). Spirit of, from God (Zec 12:10). Divine help in (Ro 8:26).

Postures in: Bowing (Ge 24:26, 48, 52; Ex 4:31; 34:8-9; 2Ch 29:29). Kneeling (1Ki 8:54; 2Ch 6:13; Ezr 9:5; Ps 95:6; Da 6:10; Lk 22:41; Ac 20:36; 21:5). Hands uplifted (1Ki 8:22; 2Ch 6:12-13; Ezr 9:5; Isa 1:15; La 3:41; 1Ti 2:8). Standing (Lk 18:11, 13).

Power of (Mk 9:28-29; Jas 5:16-18). Accompanied by works (Ne 4:9). Kept in divine remembrance (Rev 5:8; 8:3-4).

Prayer contest: Proposed by Elijah (1Ki 18:24-39).

Public, should edify (1Co 14:14-15). Social (Mt 18:19; Ac 1:13-14; 16:16, 25; 20:36; 21:5). Held in private houses (Ac 1:13-14; 12:12), in the temple (Ac 2:46; 3:1). Perseverance in (Ro 12:12; Eph 6:18). Evils averted by (Jer 26:19).

Private commanded (Mt 6:6). Exemplified by Lot (Ge 19:20), Eliezer (Ge 24:12), Jacob (Ge

32:9-12), Gideon (Jdg 6:22, 36, 39), Hannah (1Sa 1:10), David (2Sa 7:18-29), Hezekiah (2Ki 20:2), Isaiah (2Ki 20:11), Manasseh (2Ch 33:18-19), Ezra (Ezr 9:5-6), Nehemiah (Ne 2:4), Jeremiah (Jer 32:16-25), Daniel (Da 9:3, 19), Jonah (Jnh 2:1), Habakkuk (Hab 1:2), Anna (Lk 2:37), Jesus (Mt 14:23; 26:36, 39; Mk 1:35; Lk 9:18, 29), Paul (Ac 9:11), Peter (Ac 9:40; 10:9), Cornelius (Ac 10:30).

Rebuked: Of Moses, at the Red Sea (Ex 14:15), when he prayed to see Canaan (Dt 3:23-27). Of Joshua (Jos 7:10).

Submissiveness in: Exemplified by Jesus (Mt 26:39; Mk 14:36; Lk 22:42), David (2Sa 12:22-23), Job (Job 1:20-21).

Signs asked for, as assurance of answer: By Abraham's servant (Ge 24:14, 42-44). By Gideon (Jdg 6:36-40).

Answer to:

Promised—

(Ex 33:17-20; 1Ki 8:22-53; 1Ch 28:9; 2Ch 6; Job 8:5-6; 12:4; 22:27; 33:26; Ps 10:17; 81:10; Pr 10:24; 15:8, 29; 16:1; Isa 58:9; 65:24; Eze 36:37; Mt 6:5-8; 18:19-20; 21:22; Mk 11:24-25; Lk 11:9-13; 18:6-8; 21:36; 4:10, 23-24; Jn 16:23-27; Ro 8:26; 10:12-13; Eph 2:18; 3:20; Heb 4:16; 10:22-23; Jas 1:5-7; 1Jn 3:22; 5:14-15).

Promised to those in adversity (Ex 6:5-6 w Ac 7:34; Ex 22:23, 27; Ps 9:10, 12; 18:3; 32:6; 34:15, 17; 37:4-5; 38:15; 50:15; 55:16-17; 56:9; 65:2, 5; 69:32-33; 86:7; 91:15; 102:17-20; Isa 19:20; 30:19; 31:9; Joel 2:18-19, 32; Zec 10:1, 6; 13:9). Promised to those who diligently seek God (2Ch 7:14; Ps 145:18-19; Pr 2:3, 5-6; Isa 55:6; Jer 29:12-13; 33:3; La 3:25; Am 5:4-6; Zep 2:3; Zec 13:9; Mt 7:7-11; Jn 9:31; 15:7, 16; Heb 11:6; Jas 4:8, 10; 5:16). Promised to the meek (Mk 11:25). Promised to the penitent (Dt 4:30-31; 2Ch 7:13-15).

Delayed—

(Ps 22:1-2; 40:1; 80:4; 88:14; Jer 42:2-7; Hab 1:2; Lk 18:7).

Withheld: Of Balaam (Dt 23:5; Jos 24:10). Of Job (Job 30:20, w 42:12). Of the Israelites, when attacked by the Amorites (Dt 1:45). The prayer of Jesus, "Let this cup pass" (Mt 26:39, 42, 44, w 45-75 & Mt 27).

Differs From Request—

Exceeds petition (Eph 3:20). Solomon asked wisdom; the answer included wisdom, riches, honor and long life (1Ki 3:7-14; 2Ch 1:7-12). Disciples prayed for Peter, the answer included Peter's deliverance (Ac 12:15, w v.5).

Moses asked to see God's face; God revealed his goodness (Ex 33:18-20). Moses asked to be permitted to cross the Jordan; the answer was permission to view the land of promise (Dt 3:23-27). Martha and Mary asked Jesus to come and heal their brother Lazarus; Jesus delayed, but raised Lazarus from the dead (Jn 11). Paul asked that the thorn in the flesh be removed; the answer was a promise of grace to endure it (2Co 12:8-9).

Answered—

(Job 34:28; Ps 3:4; 4:1; 6:8-9; 18:6; 21:2, 4; 22:4-5, 24; 28:6; 30:2-3; 31:22; 34:4-6; 40:1; 66:19-20; 77:1-2; 81:7; 99:6-8; 106:44; 107:6, 13; 116:1-8; 118:5, 21; 119:26; 120:1; 138:3; La 3:57-58; Hos 12:4; Jnh 2:1-2, 7; Lk 23:42-43; Ac 4:31; 2Co 12:8-9; Jas 5:17-18).

Instances of—

Cain (Ge 4:13-15). Abraham, for a son (Ge 15), entreating for Sodom (Ge 18:23-33), for Ishmael (Ge 17:20), for Abimelech (Ge 20:17). Hagar, for deliverance (Ge 16:7-13). Abraham's servant, for guidance (Ge 24:12-52). Rebekah, concerning her pains in pregnancy (Ge 25:22-23). Jacob, for deliverance from Esau (Ge 32:9-32; 33:1-17).

Moses, for help at the Red Sea (Ex 14:15-16), at the waters of Marah (Ex 15:25), at Horeb (Ex 17:4-6), in the battle with the Amalekites (Ex 17:8-14), concerning the murmuring of the Israelites for flesh (Nu 11:11-35), in behalf of Miriam's leprosy (Nu 12:13-15). Moses, Aaron, and Samuel (Ps 99:6).

Israelites: For deliverance from bondage (Ex 2:23-25; 3:7-10; Ac 7:34), from Pharaoh's army (Ex 14:10-30), from the king of Mesopotamia (Jdg 3:9, 15), Sisera (Jdg 4:3, 23-24; 1Sa 12:9-11), Ammon (Jdg 10:6-18; 11:1-33), for God's favor under the reproofs of Azariah (2Ch 15:1-15), from Babylonian bondage (Ne 9:27).

Gideon, asking the token of dew (Jdg 6:36-40). Manoah, asking about Samson (Jdg 13:8-9). Samson, asking for strength (Jdg 16:28-30). Hannah, asking for a child (1Sa 1:10-17, 19-20). David, asking whether Keilah would be delivered into his hands (1Sa 23:10-12), and Ziklag (1Sa 30:8), whether he should go into Judah after Saul's death (2Sa 2:1), whether he should go against the Philistines (2Sa 5:19-25). David, in adversity (Ps 118:5; 138:3). Solomon, asking wisdom (1Ki 3:1-13; 9:2-3).

Elijah, raising the widow's son (1Ki 17:22), asking fire on his sacrifice (1Ki 18:36-38), rain (1Ki 17:1; 18:1, 42-45; Jas 5:17). Elisha, leading the Syrian army (2Ki 6:17-20). Jabez, asking for prosperity (1Ch 4:10). Abijah, for victory over Jeroboam (2Ch 13:14-18). Asa, for victory over Zerah (2Ch 14:11-15). The people of Judah (2Ch 15:15). Jehoshaphat, for victory over the Canaanites (2Ch 18:31; 20:6-7). Jehoahaz, for victory over Hazael (2Ki 13:4). Priests and Levites, when blessing the people (2Ch 30:27). Hezekiah and Isaiah, for deliverance from Sennacherib (2Ki 19:14-20; 2Ch 32:20-23), to save Hezekiah's life (2Ki 20:1-7, 11; 2Ch 32:24). Manasseh, for deliverance from the king of Babylon (2Ch 33:13, 19). Reubenites, for deliverance from the Hagrites (1Ch 5:20). The Jews, returning from the Captivity (Ezr 8:21, 23). Ezekiel, to have the baking of his bread of affliction changed (Eze 4:12-15). Daniel, for the interpretation of Nebuchadnezzar's dream (Da 2:19-23), interceding for the people (Da 9:20-23), in a vision (Da 10:12).

Zechariah, for a son (Lk 1:13). The leper, for healing (Mt 8:2-3; Mk 1:40-43; Lk 5:12-13). Cen-

turion, for his servant (Mt 8:5-13; Lk 7:3-10; Jn 4:50-51). Peter, asking that Tabitha be restored (Ac 9:40). The disciples, for Peter (Ac 12:5-17). Paul, to be restored to health (2Co 1:9-11).

Confession in:

(Lev 26:40; Ezr 10:1; Lk 15:21; 16:13). Commanded (Lev 5:5; Nu 5:6-7; Jer 3:13, 25). A condition of forgiveness (1Ki 8:47, 49-50; Pr 28:13; 1Jn 1:9).

Instances of—

(Jdg 10:10, 15; 1Sa 12:10; Ne 9:2-3, 33-35; Ps 31:10; 32:5; 38:4, 18; 40:11-12; 41:4; 51:2-5; 69:5; 106:6; 119:176; 130:3). Moses for Israel (Ex 32:31-32; 34:9). Ezra confesses for Judah (Ezr 9:6-15). Nehemiah confesses for Judah (Ne 1:4-11). Isaiah confesses for Judah (Isa 14:20-21; 59:12-15; 64:5-7). Jeremiah confesses for Judah (Jer 14:7, 20; La 1:18, 20; 3:42). Daniel confesses for Judah (Da 9:5-15).

Commanded:

(1Ch 16:11, 35; Ps 105:3-4; Isa 55:6; La 3:1; Lk 18:1; Eph 1:18; Php 4:6; Col 4:2; 1Th 5:17-18; 1Ti 2:8; Heb 4:16).

Exemplified:

By Eliezer (Ge 24:12). Jacob (Ge 32:9-12). Gideon (Jdg 6:22, 36, 39). Hannah (1Sa 1:10, 13). David (2Sa 7:18-29). Solomon at the dedication of the temple (1Ki 8:23-53; 2Ch 6:14-42). Hezekiah (2Ki 20:2). Isaiah (2Ki 20:11). Manasseh (2Ch 33:18-19). Ezra (Ezr 9:5-15). Nehemiah (Ne 2:4). Jeremiah (Jer 32:16-25). Daniel (Da 9:3-19). Jonah (Jnh 2:1-9). Habakkuk (Hab 1:2). Anna (Lk 2:37). Jesus (Mt 14:23; 26:36, 39; Mk 1:35; 6:46; Lk 5:16; 6:12; 9:18, 28-29). Paul (Ac 9:11). Peter (Ac 9:40; 10:9). Cornelius (Ac 10:30).

Persistence in:

(Ps 17:1-6; 22:1-2, 19; 28:1-2; 35:22-23; 55:1-2, 16-17; 57:2; 61:1-2; 70:5; 86:3, 6; 88:1-2, 9, 13; 102:1-28; 119:145-147; 130:1-2; 141:1-2; 142:1-2; Isa 62:7; Hos 12:4; Lk 11:5-8; 18:1-7).

Instances of—

Abraham (Ge 18:23-32). Jacob (Ge 32:24-30). Moses (Ex 32:32; 33:12-16; 34:9; Dt 9:18, 25). Gideon (Jdg 6:36-40). Samson (Jdg 16:28). Hannah (1Sa 1:10-11). Elijah (1Ki 18:24-44; Jas 5:17-18). Hezekiah (2Ki 19:15-19; Isa 38:2-3). Asa (2Ch 14:11). Ezra (Ezr 9:5). Nehemiah (Ne 1:4-11; 9:32). Isaiah (Isa 64:12). Daniel (Da 9:3, 17-19). Sailors (Jnh 1:14). Habakkuk (Hab 1:2).

Two blind men of Jericho (Mt 20:30-31; Mk 10:48; Lk 18:39). The Syrian Phoenician woman (Mt 15:22-28; Mk 7:25-30). The centurion (Mt 8:5; Lk 7:3-4). Jesus (Mt 26:39, 42; Mk 14:36, 39; Lk 22:42-44; Heb 5:7). Paul (2Co 12:8). Believers (Ro 8:26; Eph 6:18).

Imprecatory:

Asking for vengeance against enemies (Nu 16:15; 22:6-11; 23:7-8; 24:9-10; Dt 11:29-30; 27:11-13; 33:11; Jos 8:33-34; Jdg 16:28; 2Sa 16:10-12; Ne 4:4-5; 5:13; Job 3:1-10; 27:7; Ps 5:10; 6:10; 9:20; 10:2, 15; 25:3; 28:4; 31:17-18; 35:4, 8, 26; 40:14-15; 54:5; 55:9, 15; 56:7; 58:7;

59:5, 11, 15; 68:1-2; 69:23-24, 27-28; 70:2-3; 71:13; 79:10, 12; 83:13-17; 94:2; 109:7, 9-20, 28-29; 119:78, 84; 129:5; 140:9-10; 143:12; 144:6; Jer 11:20; 12:3; 15:15; 17:18; 18:21-23; 20:12; La 1:22; 3:64-66; Gal 1:8-9; 2Ti 4:14-15). *See Imprecation.*

In Adversity:

By Jacob (Ge 43:14). Moses (Ex 32:32). The Israelites (Nu 20:16; Dt 26:7; Jdg 3:9). David (2Sa 22:7). Hezekiah (2Ki 19:16, 19). Jehoshaphat (2Ch 20:4-13). Manasseh (2Ch 33:12-13). The Psalmist (Ps 5:1-12; 7:1-2, 6-7; 13:1-4; 22:1-21; 25:2, 16-19, 22; 27:11-12; 28:1; 31:1-4, 9, 14-18; 35:1-28; 38:1-22; 43:1-5; 44:4, 23-26; 54:1-3; 55:1-17; 56:1-13; 57:1-2; 59:1-17; 64:1-2; 69:1-36; 70:1-5; 71:1-24; 74:1-23; 79:1-13; 94:1-23; 102; 108:6, 12; 109:1-2, 21, 26-28; 120:2; 140:1-13; 142:1-2, 5-7; 143:1-12). Jeremiah (Jer 15:15). Jonah (Jnh 2:1-9). Stephen (Ac 7:59-60). Paul and Silas (Ac 16:25).

In Behalf of the Nations: *See Nation, Sin of.*

Intercessory:

(Ge 20:7; Jer 27:18; 29:7; Mt 5:44; Eph 6:18-19; 1Ti 2:1; Heb 13:20-21; Jas 5:14-16).

Priestly (Ex 28:12, 29-30, 38; Lev 10:17). For spiritual blessing (Nu 6:23-26; 1Sa 12:23; Job 1:5; 42:8-10). To avert judgments (Ge 20:7; Ex 32:9-14; Nu 14:11-21; 16:45-50; Dt 9:18-20, 25-29; Isa 65:8). For deliverance from enemies (1Sa 7:5-9; Isa 37:4). For healing disease (Jas 5:14-16).

For the unrepentant, unavailing (Jer 7:16; 11:14; 14:11).

Of Moses for Israel (Ex 32:11-14, 31-32; 34:9; Nu 14:19; 21:7; Dt 9:18, 20, 24-29). Of Joshua for Israel (Jos 7:6-7). Of Boaz for Ruth (Ru 2:12). Of Eli for Hannah (1Sa 1:17). Of Samuel for Israel (1Sa 7:9; 12:23). Of David, for Israel (2Sa 24:17; 1Ch 29:18), for Solomon (1Ch 29:19). Of Solomon (1Ki 8:31-53; 2Ch 6:22-42). Of Hezekiah for transgressors (2Ch 30:18-19). Of Job for his three friends (Job 42:8-10). Of the Psalmist for the righteous (Ps 7:9; 28:9; 36:10; 80:14-15). Of Daniel for Israel (Da 9:3-19). Of Jesus for his murderers (Lk 23:34). Of Stephen for his murderers (Ac 7:60). Of Peter and John for Samaritan believers (Ac 8:15). Of the recipients of bounty for Corinthian donors (2Co 9:14).

Of Paul, for unbelieving Jews (Ro 10:1), for Roman Christians (Ro 1:9), for Ephesian Christians (Eph 1:15-19; 3:14-19), for Philippian Christians (Php 1:3-5, 9), for Colossian Christians (Col 1:3, 9), for Thessalonian Christians (1Th 1:2; 3:10, 12-13; 5:23; 2Th 1:11-12; 2:16-17; 3:5, 16), for Onesiphorus (2Ti 1:16, 18), for Philemon (Phm 4). Of Philemon for Paul (Phm 22).

See Intercession; Jesus the Christ, Mediation of; Mediation.

Requested (Nu 21:7; Ro 15:30-32; 2Co 1:11; Eph 6:19; Col 4:3; 1Th 5:25; 2Th 3:1; Heb 13:18). *See Intercession, Solicited.*

Of Jesus:

(Mt 6:9-13; 11:25-26; Lk 3:21; Lk 11:1-4; Jn 12:27-28). Before day (Mk 1:35). In secret (Mt

14:23; Mk 1:35; 6:46; Lk 5:16; 6:12; 9:18, 28-29). In a mountain (Mt 14:23; Mk 6:46; Lk 6:12; 9:28). In the wilderness (Lk 5:16). Thanksgiving before eating (Mt 14:19; 15:36; 26:26-27; Mk 6:41; 8:6; 1Co 11:24). In distress (Jn 12:27; Heb 5:7). In blessing children (Mt 19:13, 15; Mk 10:16). At the grave of Lazarus (Jn 11:41-42). For Peter (Lk 22:31-32). For believers (Jn 17:1-26). For the Comforter, the Holy Spirit (Jn 14:16). In Gethsemane (Mt 26:36-44; Mk 14:32-35; Lk 22:41-44; Heb 5:7). On the cross (Mt 27:46; Lk 23:34, 46). Present ministry, at the right hand of the Father (Heb 7:25), Of his apostles (Ac 1:24-25).

See Jesus the Christ, Prayers of.

Of the Wicked, Not Heard:

(Dt 1:45; 2Sa 22:42; Job 35:12-13; Ps 18:41; 66:18; Pr 1:24-28; 15:8, 29; 21:13, 27; 28:9; Isa 1:15; 45:19; 59:2; Jer 11:11; 14:12; 15:1; 18:17; La 3:8, 44; Eze 8:18; 20:8, 31; Hos 5:6; Mic 3:4; Zec 7:12-13; Mal 2:11-13; Jn 9:31; Jas 1:6-7; 4:3). *See Wicked, Prayers of.*

To idols (1Ki 18:26-29). *See Idolatry.*

Penitential:

Of David (Ps 51:1-17), the tax collector (Lk 18:13). *See above, Confession in; See Sin, Confession of.*

Pleas Offered in:

(Ex 33:13; Nu 14:13-19; 16:22; Dt 3:24-25; 9:26-29; Jos 7:7-9; 2Sa 7:25-29; 2Ki 19:15-19; 2Ch 14:11; Ne 9:32; Ps 9:19-20; 38:16; 71:18; 74:10-11, 18, 20-23; 79:10-12; 83:1-2, 18; 119:42, 73, 146, 149, 153; 143:11-12; Isa 37:15-20; 63:17-19; La 3:56-63; Joel 2:17).

Pleas based on God's mercy (Ps 69:13, 16; 109:21, 26-27; 115:1; 119:124). God's providence (Ps 4:1; 27:8). God's promises (Ge 32:9-12; Ex 32:13; 1Ki 8:25-26, 59-60; Ne 1:8-9; Ps 89:49-51; 119:43, 49, 116; Jer 14:21). Personal consecration (Ps 119:94). Personal righteousness (Ps 86:1-2, 4-5, 17; 119:38, 145, 173-176; Jer 18:20).

Thanksgiving, and Before Taking Food:

(Jos 9:14; 1Sa 9:13; Ro 14:6; 1Co 10:30-31; 1Ti 4:3-5).

See Praise; Thankfulness.

Exemplified—

By Jesus (Mt 14:19; 15:36; 26:26-27; Mk 6:41; 8:6-7; 14:22-23; Lk 9:16; 22:19; Jn 6:11, 23; 1Co 11:24). By Paul (Ac 27:35).

PRAYERFULNESS Commanded (Ro 12:12; Col 4:2; 1Th 5:17). Spirit of, from God (Zec 12:10).

Exemplified by: The psalmist (Ps 5:1-3; 42:8; 109:4; 116:2). Daniel (Da 6:10). Anna (Lk 2:37). The apostles (Ac 6:4). Cornelius (Ac 10:2). Peter (Ac 10:9). Paul (Ro 1:9; Eph 1:15-16; Col 1:9; 1Th 3:10; 2Ti 1:3). Widows (1Ti 5:5).

See Prayer; Prayerlessness.

PRAYERLESSNESS (Jos 9:14; Job 15:4; 21:14-15; Ps 14:4; 53:4; 79:6; Isa 43:22; 64:7; Jer 10:21, 25; Da 9:13; Hos 7:7; Jnh 1:6; Zep 1:6). *See Prayer.*

PREACHING [5752, 10452, *1877+3364*, *2294*, *2294+ 2295*, *2295*, *2859*, *3060*, *3062*, *3281*, *3364+3836*, *4155*]. The act of exhorting, prophesying, reproving, teaching.

General:

Noah called preacher (2Pe 2:5). Solomon called preacher (Ecc 1:1, 12). Sitting while (Mt 5:1; Lk 4:20; 5:3). Moses slow to (Ex 4:10-12).

Appointed and practiced by Jesus as the method of promulgating the gospel (Mt 4:17; 11:1; Mk 16:15, 20; Lk 4:18-19, 43). Attested to by Paul (Tit 1:3). Grave responsibility of (2Co 2:14-17).

Repentance, the subject, of John the Baptist's (Mt 3:2; Mk 1:4, 15; Lk 3:3), of Christ's (Mt 4:17; Mk 1:15), the apostles' (Mk 6:12). The gospel of the kingdom of God, the subject of Christ's (Mk 1:14-15; 2:2; Lk 8:1). Christ crucified and risen, the burden of Paul's (Ac 17:3).

Jesus preaches to the spirits in prison (1Pe 3:19; 4:9, w Eph 4:9).

Preaching Should:

Edify (1Co 14:1-25). Be skillful (2Ti 2:15-16). Be in power (1Th 1:5). Be with boldness (Ac 13:46; 2Co 3:12-13). Not be, with mere human strategy (Mt 26) with deceit or flattery (1Th 2:3-6).

Effective Preaching:

By Azariah (2Ch 15:1-15), Jonah (Jnh 3), Haggai (Hag 1:7-12), Peter (Ac 2:14-41), Philip (Ac 8:5-12, 27-38), Paul (Ac 9:20-22; 13:16-43). *See Revivals.*

Impenitence Under:

Asa (2Ch 16:7-10), Ahab (2Ch 18:7-26), the Jews (Ac 13:46). *See Obduracy.*

See Minister; Call, Personal.

PRECEPTS [2976, 5477, 7218]. *See Commandments and Statutes, Of God; Law.*

PRECIOUS STONES In the breastpiece of the high priest the stones were set, probably, in the order of the tribes of the Israelites. The first stone, ruby, was probably the tribal stone for Reuben; topaz for Simeon; beryl for Levi; turquoise for Judah; sapphire for Issachar; emerald for Zebulun; jacinth for Dan; agate for Naphtali; amethyst for Asher; chrysolite for Gad; onyx for Joseph; jasper for Benjamin (Ex 28:9-21; 39:6-14). Voluntary offerings of, by the Israelites for the breastpiece and ephod (Ex 35:27). Exported, from Sheba (1Ki 10:2, 10; 2Ch 9:1, 9; Eze 27:22), from Ophir (1Ki 10:11; 2Ch 9:10).

Partial catalog of (Eze 28:13). Seen in the foundation of the New Jerusalem in John's apocalyptic vision (Rev 21:19-21). In kings' crowns (2Sa 12:30; 1Ch 20:2).

Figurative (Isa 54:11-12).

See Stones; Agate; Amethyst; Beryl, 1; Carbuncle; Crystal; Diamond; Emerald; Jasper; Ruby; Sapphire; Sardis; Topaz.

PREDESTINATION [*4633*]. According to the purpose of grace (Ex 33:19; Isa 44:1-2, 7;

Mal 1:2-3; Ac 13:48; Ro 8:28-30, 33; 9:11-29; 11:5, 7-8; 1Co 1:26-29; Eph 1:4-5, 9-11; 3:11; 2Th 2:13; 2Ti 1:9; Tit 1:1-2; 1Pe 1:2, 20).

Of prosperity to Abraham (Ge 21:12; Ne 9:7-8). Of Joseph's mission to Egypt (Ge 45:5-7; Ps 105:17-22). Of Israel as a nation (Ge 21:12; Dt 4:37; 7:7-8; 10:15; 32:8; 1Sa 12:22; Ps 33:12; 135:4). Of Ishmael as a nation (Ge 21:12-13; 25:12-18). Of famine in Egypt (Ge 41:30-32). Of judgment to Pharaoh (Ex 9:16). Of David as king (2Ch 6:6; Ps 78:67-68, 70-72). Of Jehu's dynasty (2Ki 10:30; 15:12). Of the dividing of Solomon's kingdom (1Ki 11:11-12, 31-39; 12:15). Of mercy to the widow at Sidon (Lk 4:25-27).

Of the destruction of the Canaanites (Jos 11:20), of Ben-Hadad (1Ki 20:42), of Ahaziah (2Ch 22:7), of Amaziah and the idolatrous Israelites (2Ch 25:20).

Acknowledged by Job (Job 23:13-14). Of agent to execute divine judgments (2Ki 19:25; 2Ch 22:7; Hab 1:12). Of Jeremiah as prophet (Jer 1:4-5). Of revelation to a chosen people (Mt 11:25-26; Lk 8:10; 1Co 2:7).

Of the death of Jesus (Mt 26:24; Mk 14:21; Lk 22:22; 24:26-27; Ac 2:23; 3:18; 4:28; Rev 13:8).

Of Paul to the ministry (Ac 9:15; Gal 1:15-16; 1Ti 2:7).

Of the times and bounds of nations (Ac 17:26). Of times and seasons (Ac 1:7).

Of the standard of righteousness (Eph 2:10). Of the kingdom prepared for the righteous (Mt 25:34).

Of salvation and election (Mt 20:16; 20:23; 24:22, 40; Mk 13:20, 22; Lk 10:20; 17:34-36; 18:7; Jn 6:37, 39, 44-45; 15:16, 19; 17:2, 6, 9; Ac 2:39, 47; 13:48; 22:14; Ro 1:6; 8:28-30, 33; 11:5, 7-8; 1Co 1:26-29; Eph 1:9-11; Col 3:12; 1Th 1:4; 2:12-13; 2Ti 1:9; Tit 1:1-2; Jas 1:18; 1Pe 1:2, 20; 2Pe 1:10).

Of the wicked, to the day of evil (Pr 16:4), to condemnation (Jude 4). Of the day of judgment (Ac 17:31).

See Election.

PREJUDICE *See Respect of Persons.*

PREPAREDNESS [*273*, 430, 2284, 3670, 3922, 6885, 6913, 7155, 7727, 7756, 8492, 2286, 2936, 2941, 4187, 4472, 4602]. (Mt 24:44; 25:1-13; Mk 13:32-37; Lk 12:35-48; 19:41-44). *See Faithfulness.*

PRESBYTERY *See Elders.*

PRESCIENCE *See God, Foreknowledge of.*

PRESENTS [*1388*, 4950, 5989, 9556; See also Gifts]. To Abraham, by Pharaoh (Ge 12:16), by Abimelech (Ge 20:14). To Rebekah (Ge 24:22). To Esau (Ge 32:13-15). To prophets (1Ki 14:3; 2Ki 4:42). To those in adversity (Job 42:10-11).

Betrothal (Ge 24:53). Marriage (Est 2:18). Propitiatory (Ge 32:20; 33:8-11; 1Sa 25:27-35; Pr

21:14). To confirm covenants (Ge 21:28-30; 1Sa 18:3-4). Rewards of service (Da 5:7). Kings to kings (2Sa 8:10; 1Ki 10:10, 13; 15:18-19).

To corrupt courts, forbidden (Ex 23:8; Dt 16:19; 27:25; Isa 5:23). *See Bribery; Liberality.*

PRESIDENTS *See Administrators.*

PRESS [2005, 2616, 4315, 7439, 8103, 8104, 8492, *1503, 1592, 2989, 3332*]. Crowd (Mk 2:4; Lk 8:19).

PRESSVAT NIV "wine vat" (Hag 2:16). *See Wine.*

PRESUMPTION [928+2295, 2326, 6753]. (Dt 29:19-20; Ps 10:6; 19:13; 73:8-9).

Admonitions Against:
(Pr 25:6-7; Lk 14:7-11). Warning against (1Co 10:9-12). Excommunication for (Nu 15:30). Proverbs concerning (Pr 18:12-13; 25:6-7a). Punishment for (Jer 23:34).

Sins of:
The self-righteous (Isa 65:5; Lk 18:11-12). The selfish rich, in forgetting God (Lk 12:18-20). Temptation to (Dt 6:16; Mt 4:5-7; Lk 4:9-11).

In ignoring God (Isa 10:15; 29:16; 37:23-25; Ro 9:23-25, 20-21; Jas 4:13-15). Questioning God's righteousness (Isa 58:3; Ro 9:20-21). Defying God (Job 15:25; Ps 94:7; Isa 5:18-25; 14:13-14; 28:14-18, 22; 29:15-16, 20; 40:27; 45:9-10; Ro 1:32; 9:20-21; 2Th 2:3). Reviling God's prophet (1Ki 22:24). Despising the lordship of Christ, and the authority of the Church (2Pe 2:10-11).

Instances of:
Satan, when he said to Eve, "You will not surely die" (Ge 3:1-5). Builders of Babel (Ge 11:4). Abraham, in questioning about Sodom (Ge 18:23-32). Pharaoh (Ex 5:2). Moses, in scolding Yahweh (Nu 11:11-15, 22). Nadab and Abihu (Lev 10:1-2). Israelites, in ascending to the top of the hill against the Amalekites (Nu 14:44-45, w Dt 1:43). Murmuring (Ex 14:11-12; 17:2, 7; Nu 16:41; 21:5; 1Co 10:9-12). In reviling God (Mal 1:6-7, 12; 3:7-8, 13). Korah, Dathan, and Abiram (Nu 16:3).

Saul, in sacrificing (1Sa 13:8-14), sparing the Amalekites (1Sa 15:3, 9-23). Men of Beth Shemesh (1Sa 6:19). Uzzah, in steadying the ark (2Sa 6:6-7). David's anger at Uzzah's death (2Sa 6:8). David, in numbering Israel (2Sa 24:1-17). Jeroboam (1Ki 13:4). Ben-Hadad (1Ki 20:10). The Syrians, in limiting the sovereignty of God (1Ki 20:23, 28). Zedekiah (1Ki 22:24-25; 2Ch 18:23-24). Uzziah (2Ch 26:16). Sennacherib (2Ki 19:22; 2Ch 32:13-14; Isa 37:23-25). Job, in cursing the day of his birth (Job 3), reproved by Eliphaz (Job 4:5). Jonah (Jnh 4:1-8).

Peter, in objecting to Jesus' statement that he must be killed (Mt 16:21-23; Mk 8:32), in reflecting on his knowledge when he asked, amid a throng, who touched him (Lk 8:45), in objecting to Jesus washing his feet (Jn 13:8), in asking Jesus, "What shall this man do?" (Jn 21:20-22).

The disciples, in rebuking those who brought little children to Jesus (Mt 19:13; Mk 10:13-14; Lk 18:15), in their indignation at the anointing of Jesus (Mt 26:8-9; Mk 14:4-5; Jn 12:5), reproving Jesus (Jn 7:3-5). The brothers of Jesus (Jn 7:3-5). James and John, in desiring to call down fire on the Samaritans (Lk 9:54). Those who reviled Jesus (Mt 27:42-43; Mk 15:29-32). Theudas (Ac 5:36). Sons of Sceva (Ac 19:13-14). Diotrephes (3Jn 9).
See Blasphemy; Mocking; Pride.

PRETORIUM *See Praetorium.*

PRICK *See Goad; Thorn.*

PRIDE [*1450, 1452, 1454, 1455, 1467, 1469, 1575, 2086, 2295, 5294, 8123, 8124, 8146, *3016, 3017, 3018, 5662, 5881*].

Condemned:
Admonitions against (Dt 8:11-14, 17-20; Ps 49:11; 75:4-6; Jer 9:23; Mt 23:5-7; Lk 14:8-9; 20:46-47; Ro 11:17-21, 25; 12:3, 16; 1Co 4:6-8, 10; 5:2, 6; 8:1-2; 10:12; 13:4; 14:38; 2Co 10:5, 12, 18; Gal 6:3; Eph 4:17; Php 2:3; 1Ti 2:9; 6:3-4, 17; 2Ti 3:2, 4; 1Pe 5:3; Rev 3:17-18).

Prayer regarding (Ps 9:20; 10:2-6, 11). Prevented by divine discipline (2Co 12:7). Proceeds from the carnal mind (Mk 7:21-22; 1Jn 2:16). Leads, to strife (Pr 13:10; 28:25), to destruction (Pr 15:25; 16:18; 17:19; 18:11-12; Isa 14:12-16; 26:5; 28:3; Da 11:45; Zep 3:11; Mal 4:1; 1Ti 3:6; Rev 18:7-8).

Rebuked (1Sa 2:3-5; 2Ki 14:9-10; 2Ch 25:18-19; Job 12:2; Jer 13:9, 15, 17; Hab 2:4-5, 9). Repugnant to God (Job 37:24; Ps 12:3; 18:27; 31:23; 101:5; 138:6; Pr 6:16-17; 8:13; 16:5; Jer 50:31-32; Jas 4:6).

The proud shall be humbled (Lev 26:19; Ps 52:6-7; Pr 11:2; Isa 2:11-17; 3:16-26; 5:13; 13:11; 22:16, 19; 23:7, 9; 24:4, 21; Jer 49:4, 16; Da 4:37; Ob 3-4; Mt 23:12; Mk 10:43; Lk 1:52; 9:46; 18:14; Rev 18:7-8).

Pride discussed with Job (Job 11:12; 12:2-3; 13:2, 5; 15:1-13; 18:3-4; 21:31-32; 32:9-13; 37:24). Proverbs concerning (Pr 3:34; 6:16-17; 8:13; 10:17; 11:2; 12:9, 15; 13:10; 14:21; 15:5, 10, 12, 25, 32; 16:5, 18-19; 17:19; 18:11-12; 21:4, 24; 25:14, 27; 26:5, 12, 16; 27:2; 28:11, 25; 29:8, 23; 30:12-13). Cited by the psalmists (Ps 10:2-6, 11; 49:11; 52:7; 73:6, 8-9; 119:21, 69-70, 78).
See Rich, The.

Instances of:
Pharaoh (Ex 7-11; 12:29-36; 14). Ahithophel (2Sa 17:23). Naaman (2Ki 5:11-13). Hezekiah (2Ki 20:13; 2Ch 32:25-26, 31; Isa 39:2). Uzziah (2Ch 26:16-19). Haman (Est 3:5; 5:11, 13; 6:6; 7:10).

Moab (Isa 16:6-7; Jer 48:7, 14-29; Zep 2:9). Israel (Isa 9:9-10; Hos 5:5; 7:10). Assyria (Isa 10:5-16; Eze 31:10-11). Jerusalem (Eze 16:56). Tyre (Eze 28:2-9, 17). Egypt (Eze 30:6). Nebuchadnezzar (Da 4:30-34; 5:20). Moab and Ammon (Zep 2:9). Nineveh (Zep 2:15).

The Scribes and Pharisees (Mt 20:6; 23:6-8, 11-

12; Mk 10:43; 12:38-39; Lk 9:46; 11:43; 18:14; 20:45-47). Herod (Ac 12:21-23).

See Ambition.

PRIEST [2424, 3912, 3913, 3914, 10347, 797, 2634, 2632, 2633, 2636].

Before the Mosaic Covenant:

Melchizedek (Ge 14:18; Heb 5:6, 10-11; 6:20; 7:1-21). Jethro (Ex 2:16). Priests in Israel before the giving of the law (Ex 19:22, 24).

Mosaic:

(Ex 28:1-4; 29:9, 44; Nu 3:10; 18:7; 1Ch 23:13). Hereditary descent of office (Ex 27:21; 28:43; 29:9). Consecration of (Ex 29:1-9, 19-35; 40:12-16; Lev 6:20-23; 8:6-35; Heb 7:21). Is holy (Lev 21:6-7; 22:9, 16). Washings of (Ex 40:30-32; Lev 16:24). Must be without blemish (Lev 21:17-23). Vestments of (Ex 28:2-43; 39:1-29; Lev 6:10-11; 8:13; Eze 44:17-19). Put on vestments in the temple (Eze 42:14; 44:19). Atonement for (Lev 16:6, 24; Eze 44:27). Defilement and purification of (Lev 21:1-15; Eze 44:22). Chambers for, in the temple (Eze 40:45-46). Exempt from tax (Ezr 7:24). Armed and organized for war at the time of the disaffection toward Saul (1Ch 12:27-28). Beard and hair of (Eze 44:20).

Twenty-four courses of (1Ch 24:1-19; 28:13, 21; 2Ch 8:14; 31:2; 35:4-5; Ezr 2:36-39; Ne 13:30).

Chosen by lot (Lk 1:8-9, 23),

Usurpations of the office of (Nu 3:10; 16; 18:7; 2Ch 26:18). Jeroboam appointed priests who were not of the sons of Levi (1Ki 12:31; 13:33).

See Levites; Minister.

Compensation for—

No part of the land of Canaan allowed to (Nu 18:20; Dt 10:9; 14:27; 18:1-2; Jos 13:14, 33; 14:3; 18:7; Eze 44:28). Provided with cities and suburbs (Lev 25:32-34; Nu 35:2-8; Jos 21:1-4, 13-19, 41-42; 1Ch 6:57-60; Ne 11:3, 20; Eze 45:1-6; 48:8-20). Own lands sanctified to the Lord (Lev 27:21). Tithes of the tithes (Nu 18:8-18, 26-32; Ne 10:38). Part of the spoils of war, including captives (Nu 31:25-29). Firstfruits (Lev 23:20; 24:9; Nu 18:12-13, 17-18; Dt 18:3-5; Ne 10:36). Redemption money (Lev 27:23), of the firstborn (Nu 3:46-51; 18:15-16). Things devoted (Lev 27:21; Nu 5:9-10; 18:14). Fines (Lev 5:16; 22:14; Nu 5:8). Trespass money and other trespass offerings (Lev 5:15, 18; Nu 5:5-10; 18:9; 2Ki 12:16). The bread of the Presence (Ex 25:30; Lev 24:5-9; 2Ch 2:4; 13:11; Ne 10:33; Mt 12:4; Heb 9:2). *See Bread, Consecrated.* Portions of sacrifices and offerings (Ex 29:27-34; Lev 2:2-3, 9-10; 5:12-13, 16; 6:15-18, 26; 7:6-10, 31-34; 10:12-14; 14:12-13; Nu 6:19-20; 18:8-19; Dt 18:3-5; 1Sa 2:13-14; Eze 44:28-31; 45:1-4; 1Co 9:13; 10:18).

Regulations by Hezekiah concerning compensation (2Ch 31:4-19). Portion of the land allotted to, in redistribution in Ezekiel's vision (Eze 48:8-14). For sustenance of their families (Lev 22:11-13; Nu 18:11, 19).

Duties of—

To offer sacrifices (Lev 1:4-17; 2:2, 16; 3:5, 11, 13, 16; 4:5-12, 17, 25-26, 30-35; 1Ch 16:40; 2Ch 13:11; 29:34; 35:11-14; Ezr 6:20; Heb 10:11). *See Offerings.* To offer the first fruits (Lev 23:10-11; Dt 26:3-4). To pronounce benedictions (Nu 6:22-27; Dt 21:5; 2Ch 30:27). Teach the law (Lev 10:11; Dt 24:8; 27:14; 31:9-13; 33:10; Jer 2:8; Mal 2:7). Light the lamps in the tabernacle (Ex 27:20-21; 2Ch 13:11; Lev 24:3-4). Keep the sacred fire always burning (Lev 6:12-13). To furnish a quota of wood for the sanctuary (Ne 10:34). Responsible for the sanctuary (Nu 4:5-15; 18:1, 5, 7). To act as scribes (Ezr 7:1-6; Ne 8:9). Be present at and supervise the tithing (Ne 10:38). Sound the trumpet in calling assemblies and in battle (Nu 10:2-10; 31:6; Jos 6; 2Ch 13:12). Examine lepers. *See Leprosy.* Purify the unclean (Lev 15:31). *See Defilement.* Value things devoted (Lev 27:8, 12). Officiated in the holy place (Heb 9:6). Chiefs of Levites (Nu 3:9, 32; 4:19, 28, 33; 1Ch 9:20). To act as magistrates (Nu 5:14-31; Dt 17:8-13; 19:17; 21:5; 2Ch 19:8; Eze 44:23-24). To encourage the army on the eve of battle (Dt 20:2-4). Bear the ark through the Jordan (Jos 3; 4:15-18), in battle (1Sa 4:3-5).

Figurative (Ex 19:6; Isa 61:6; 1Pe 2:9; Rev 1:6; 5:10; 20:6).

High Priest:

Moses did not designate Aaron chief or high priest. The function he served was superior to that of other priests. The title appears after the institution of the office (Lev 21:10-15; Nu 3:32). Qualifications of, consecration of, etc. *See above, Mosaic.*

Clothing of (Ex 28:2-43; 39:1-31; Lev 8:7-9). Respect due to (Ac 23:5).

Duties of—

Had charge of the sanctuary and altar (Nu 18:2, 5, 7). To offer sacrifices (Heb 5:1; 8:3). To designate subordinate priests for duty (Nu 4:19; 1Sa 2:36). To officiate in consecrations of the Levites (Nu 8:11-21). To have charge of the treasury (2Ki 12:10; 22:4; 2Ch 24:6-14; 34:9). To light the lamps of the tabernacle (Ex 27:20-21; 30:8; Lev 24:3-4; Nu 8:3). To burn incense (Ex 30:7-8; 1Sa 2:28; 1Ch 23:13). To place bread of the Presence on the table every Sabbath (Lev 24:8). To offer for his own sins of ignorance (Lev 4:3-12).

On the Day of Atonement (Ex 30:10; Lev 16; Heb 5:3; 9:7, 22-23).

Judicial (Nu 5:15; Dt 17:8-13; 1Sa 4:18; Hos 4:4; Mt 26:3, 50, 57, 62; Ac 5:21-28; 23:1-5). To number the people (Nu 1:3). Officiate at the choice of the ruler (Nu 27:18-19, 21). To distribute the spoils of war (Nu 31:26-29).

Compensation of. *See above, Compensation for.*

A second priest, under the high priest (Nu 3:32; 4:16; 31:6; 1Ch 9:20; 2Sa 15:24; 2Ki 25:18; Lk 3:2).

Miscellaneous Facts Concerning:

Priestly office performed by prophets (1Sa 16:5). Loyal to Rehoboam at the time of the revolt of the ten tribes (2Ch 11:13). Zeal of (1Ch 9:10-13), in purging the temple (2Ch 29:4-17). Wickedness of (2Ch 36:14). Taken with the captives to Babylon (Jer 29:1). Return from the Captivity (Ezr 1:5; 2:36-39, 61, 70; 3:8; 7:7; 8:24-30; Ne 7:39-42, 63-73; 10:1-8; 12:1-7). Polluted by marrying idolatrous wives (Ezr 9:1-2; 10:5, 18-19; Ne 10:28). Restore the altar and offer sacrifices (Ezr 3:1-7). Supervise the building of the temple (Ezr 3:8-13). Inquire of John the Baptist whether he was the Christ (Jn 1:19). Conspire to destroy Jesus (Mt 26:3-5, 14-15, 47, 51; Mk 14:10-11, 43-47, 53-66; 15:1; Lk 22:1-6, 50, 54, 66-71; 23:1-2; Jn 11:47; 19:15-16, 18). Try and condemn Jesus (Mt 26:57-68; 27:1-2; Mk 14:53-65; Lk 22:54-71; 23:13-24; Jn 18:15-32). Incite the people to ask that Barabbas be released and Jesus destroyed (Mt 27:20; Mk 15:11; Lk 23:18). Persecute the disciples (Ac 22:5). Reprove and threaten Peter and John (Ac 4:6-21; 5:17-41). Try, condemn, and stone Stephen (Ac 6:12-15; 7). Paul brought before (Ac 22:30; 23:1-5). Many converts among (Ac 6:7).

Corrupt:

(Jer 23:11-12; Eze 22:26; Lk 10:31). Instances of: Eli's sons (1Sa 2:12-17, 22), of the returned exiles (Ezr 9:1-2; 10:18-22; Ne 13:4-9, 13, 28-29). Idolatrous (1Ki 12:32; 2Ki 10:19; 11:18; 23:5; 2Ch 23:17; 34:4-5; Jer 48:35; Hos 10:5; Zep 1:4).

PRIMOGENITURE *See Birthright; Firstborn.*

PRINCE OF PEACE *See Jesus.*

PRINCE, PRINCESS [1201+, 2980, 5592, 5618, 5687, 5954, 7278, 7312, 8138, 8569, *795, 807*]. A prince is a leader, an exalted person clothed with authority. A princess is the daughter or wife of a chief or king. The prince may be the head of a family or tribe, a ruler, governor, magistrate, satrap, or royal descendant (Nu 22:8; 1Sa 18:30). He may also be a spiritual ruler (Isa 9:6) or the ruler of demons (Mt 9:34).

PRINCIPALITIES

1. Rule; ruler (Eph 1:21; Tit 3:1).
2. Order of powerful angels and demons (Ro 8:38; Eph 3:10; 6:12). *See Demons.*

PRINT A mark made by pressure (Lev 19:28; Jn 20:25).

PRISCILLA, PRISCA [*4571*]. Priscilla (diminutive of Prisca) was the wife of the Jewish Christian Aquila, with whom she is always mentioned in the NT; tentmakers; had a church in their house; taught Apollos; assisted Paul (Ac 18:2, 26; Ro 16:3; 1Co 16:19; 2Ti 4:19).

PRISON [*1074+, 3975, 4993, 1300, 1303, 1313, 4140, 5871*]. Prisoners were often put in dry wells or cisterns (Ge 37:24; Jer 38:6-13), or dungeons which were part of a palace (1Ki 22:27). The Herods and the Romans had royal prisons (Lk 3:20; Ac 12:4; 23:10, 35). Jesus foretells imprisonment for his disciples (Lk 21:12). Disobedient spirits are now in prison (1Pe 3:19). Satan will be imprisoned (Rev 20:7).

PRISONERS [*659, 673, 4374, 8660, 8664, 170, 1300, 1304, 1313, 5257*].

General:

Required to labor (Jdg 16:21). Kept on bread and water of affliction (1Ki 22:27; 2Ch 18:26; Isa 30:20), in chains (Ac 12:6), in stocks (Pr 7:22; Jer 29:26; Ac 16:24).

Confined in the court of the palace (Jer 32:2), house of the scribe (Jer 37:15), house of captain of the guard (Ge 40:3). Visited by friends (Mt 11:2; Ac 24:23). Bound to soldiers (Ac 12:6-7).

Severe hardships of, mitigated (Jer 37:20-21). Cruelty to (Jer 38:6; La 3:53-54). *See Captive.* Keepers responsible for (Ac 12:18-19). Tortured to extort self-incriminating testimony (Ac 22:24). Flogged (Mt 27:26; Mk 15:15; Ac 16:23, 33; 2Co 6:5; 11:23-24). *See Flog, Flogging; Scourging.* Permitted to make defense (Ac 24:10; 25:8, 16; 26:1; 2Ti 4:16).

Kindness to: By the prison keeper to Jeremiah (Jer 38:7-28), by Philippian jailer to Paul (Ac 16:33), by Felix (Ac 24:23), by Julius, the centurion (Ac 27:1, 3; 28:16, 31). To be visited and ministered to (Mt 25:35-46). Released at feasts (Mt 27:15-17; Mk 15:6; Lk 23:17; Jn 18:39).

Of War:

Put to death (Jos 10:16-27; 1Sa 15:33; 27:11; 2Sa 12:31; 2Ki 25:7; 1Ch 20:3; Hos 13:16; Am 1:13; La 3:34), by divine command (Nu 31:9, 17). Thumbs and toes cut off (Jdg 1:6-7). Blinded (2Ki 25:7). *See Captive.*

Consolations for (Ps 69:33; 79:11; 102:19-20; 146:7).

See Captive; Imprisonment.

Examples of:

Joseph (Ge 39:20-23; 40; 41:44). Jeremiah (Jer 38:6-28; 39:14). John the Baptist (Mt 11:2; 14:3-12; Mk 6:17; Lk 3:20). Jesus (Mt 26:47-75; 27; Mk 14:43-72; 15; Lk 22:47-71; 23; Jn 18:3-40; 19). Apostles (Ac 5:17-42). Peter (Ac 12:3-19). Paul (Ac 16:19-40; 21:27-40; 22-28). Silas (Ac 16:19-40).

Figurative: (Isa 61:1; Lk 4:18).

PRIVILEGE *See Judgment, According to Opportunity and Works; Responsibility.*

PRIZE [*3701, 1092, 2857, 2898*]. A reward of competition according to the rules (1Co 9:24-27), figurative of living the Christian life by faith (Php 3:14; Col 2:18).

PROBATION A period of critical examination and evaluation (Ro 5:3-4).

Adam on (Ge 2:15-17; 3:3). Amorites (Ge 15:16). Solomon (1Ki 3:14; 9:4-9, w 11:9-12). Taught in parables of the talents and minas (Mt 25:14-30; Lk 19:12-27), the fig tree (Lk 13:6-9), embezzling steward (Lk 16:1-12). Taught by the author of Hebrews (Heb 6).

None after death (Mt 12:32; 25:10-13; 26:4).

See Perseverance.

PROCHORUS *See Procorus.*

PROCLAMATION [*1413, 1819, 2349, 4887, 5583, 5989, 6218, 7754, 7924, 9048, *550, 1334, 2294, 2859, 3062, 3281*]. Imperial (2Ch 30:1-10; Est 1:22; 6:9; 8:10-14; Isa 40:3, 9; Da 3:4-7; 4:1; 5:29). Emancipation (2Ch 36:23; Ezr 1:1-4).

PROCONSUL [*478*] *(for the consul).* Roman official who served as deputy consul in a Roman province; term of the office was usually one year; Sergius Paulus and Gallio were proconsuls (Ac 13:7; 18:12).

PROCORUS [*4743*]. An early Christian deacon (Ac 6:5).

PROCRASTINATION (Eze 11:2-3; 12:22, 27-28). Rebuked (Mt 8:21-22; Lk 9:59, 61). Admonition against (1Th 5:2-3). Forbidden (Ex 22:29). Warning against (Heb 3:7-19).

Parables of: Evil servant (Mt 24:48-51). The five foolish virgins (Mt 25:2-13).

See Excuses.

Instances of: Pharaoh (Ex 8:10). Elisha (1Ki 19:20-21). Esther (Est 5:8). Disciple of Christ whose father died (Mt 8:21; Lk 9:59, 61). Felix (Ac 24:25).

PROCURATOR The governor of a Roman province appointed by the emperor; often subject to the imperial legate of a larger political area. Pilate, Felix, and Festus were procurators (Mt 27:2; Ac 23:24; 26:30).

PRODIGAL SON Parable of (Lk 15:11-32).

PRODIGALITY *See Extravagance; Frugality; Industry.*

PROFANATION Of God's name (Lev 20:3; Pr 30:9), forbidden (Ex 20:7; 18:21; 19:12; 21:6; 22:2-3; Dt 5:11).

Instances of: (Ps 139:20; Isa 52:5; Ro 2:24). Of the Sabbath (Ne 13:15-22; Eze 20:12-13, 16; 22:8; 23:38). Of the house of God (2Ch 33:7; Ne 13:7; Jer 7:11; Mt 21:13; Mk 11:17; Lk 19:46). Of holy things: Forbidden (Lev 22:15).

See Profane; Profanity.

PROFANE [*2725, 2729*] *(unloose, set free).* To desecrate or defile (Ex 31:14; Lev 19:8, 12; Eze 22:26; Mt 12:5), common as opposed to holy (Eze 28:16; 42:20), godless, unholy (Heb 12:16).

See Sacrilege.

PROFANITY Of the name of God. *See God, Name of.* Of the Sabbath. *See Sabbath.*

See Blasphemy; Oath.

PROFESSION [*2040, 3934*]. False (Pr 20:6; Hos 8:2). Of faith in Jesus. *See Confession; Testimony, Religious.*

PROGNOSTICATION By astrologers (Isa 47:13). *See Prophecy; Prophets.*

PROHIBITION Of the use of intoxicating beverages. To priests on duty (Lev 10:9). To Nazirites (Nu 6:3-4).

See Abstinence; Commandments and Statutes, Of God; Drunkenness.

PROMISCUITY [*2388, 9373*]. Punished by death under the law (Dt 22:20-21).

Figurative of Israel's alliances with the nations and their gods (Eze 16; 23).

See Adultery; Bestiality; Fornication; Homosexual; Prostitute.

PROMISE [*606, 614, 1819, 1821, 4439, 8678, *2039, 2040, 3923, 4600*]. First promise of the Redeemer (Ge 3:15), promise repeated to Abraham (Ge 12:2, 7), promise made to David that his house would continue forever (2Sa 7:12-13, 28). Jesus' promise of the Spirit fulfilled at Pentecost. There are hundreds of promises made to believers (Jas 2:5; 1Ti 4:8; 2Pe 3:9).

PROMISES [*606, 614, 1819, 1821, 4439, 8678, *2039, 2040, 3923, 4600*]. To the afflicted. *See Afflictions, Consolation Under.* To backsliders. *See Backsliders.* To children. *See Children.* To orphans. *See Orphans.* To the righteous. *See Righteous.* To seekers. *See Seekers.*

PROMISES, OR GROUND OF ASSURANCE

General:

(Heb 6:12; Jas 2:5; 2Pe 1:4; 3:13). Against the recurrence of universal flood (Ge 9:11). Of answer to prayer (Job 22:27; Ps 2:8; 145:19; Isa 58:9; 65:24; Jer 29:12; 33:3; Mt 6:6; 7:7-8, 11; 17:20; 18:19; 21:22; Mk 11:24; Lk 11:13; Jn 14:13-14; 15:7, 16; 16:23-24; Jas 1:5; 5:15-16; 1Jn 5:14-15). Of blessings upon worshipers (Ex 20:24; Isa 40:31). Of comfort in sorrow (Ps 46:1; 50:15; 146:8; 147:3; Isa 43:2; Lk 6:21; 2Co 1:3-4; 7:6). Of spiritual enlightenment (Isa 29:18, 24; 35:5-6; 42:16; Mt 10:19; Lk 21:14-15; Jn 7:17; 8:12, 32; Heb 8:10). Of God's presence (Ex 3:12; Dt 31:8; 1Sa 10:7). Of Christ's presence with believers (Mt 18:20; 28:20). Of forgiveness (Ps 130:4; Isa 1:18; 43:25; 55:7; Jer 31:34; 33:8; Mt 6:14; 12:31-32; Mk 3:28; Lk 12:10; Ac 10:43; 13:38-39; Jas 5:15-16; 1Jn 1:9). Of healing (Jas 5:15). Of the Holy Spirit (Joel 2:28; Lk 11:13; 24:49; Jn 7:38-39; 14:16-17, 26; 15:26; 16:7; Ac 2:38). Of spiritual adoption (Lev 26:12; 2Co 6:17-18; Heb 8:10). Of victory of the Messiah over Satan (Ge 3:15).

Given:

To believers (Jer 17:7-8; Mk 16:16-18; Jn 3:15-16; 5:24; 6:35, 40, 47; 7:38; 11:25; 14:12-14; Ro

9:33; 10:9, 11). Backsliders (Lev 26:40-42; Dt 30:1-3; 2Ch 30:9; Jer 3:12-15; Hos 14:4; Mal 3:7). Children (Ex 20:12; Dt 5:16; Mt 19:14; Mk 10:14; Lk 18:15-16; Eph 6:3).

To the burdened (Mt 11:28-29). The afflicted (Job 33:24-28; 36:15; Ps 9:9; 12:5; 18:27; 41:3; La 3:31). Orphans and widows (Dt 10:18; Ps 68:5; 146:9; Pr 15:25; Jer 49:11).

To seekers (Dt 4:29; 1Ch 28:9; 2Ch 15:2; Ezr 8:22; Ps 34:10; 145:18; Jer 29:13; Mt 5:6; 6:33; Lk 6:21; Jn 6:37; Ro 10:13; Heb 11:6).

To the faithful (Mt 25:21, 23; Lk 12:42-44; 19:16-19; Ro 2:7, 10; Rev 2:10). The forgiving, of divine forgiveness (Mt 6:14; Mk 11:25; Lk 6:37). The humble (Isa 57:15; Mt 5:3; 18:4; 23:12; Lk 6:20; 14:11; 18:14; Jas 4:6; 1Pe 5:5-6). The compassionate giver (Ps 41:1-3; 112:9; Pr 3:9-10; 11:25; 22:9; 28:27; Ecc 11:1; Isa 58:10-11; Mt 6:4; Lk 6:38; 2Co 9:6, 8). The meek (Ps 10:17; 22:26; 25:9; 37:11; 147:6; 149:4; Pr 29:23; Isa 29:19; Mt 5:5). The merciful (2Sa 22:26; Ps 18:25; 41:1-3; Mt 5:7). Ministers (Ps 126:5-6; Jer 1:8; 20:11; Da 12:3; Mt 28:20; Jn 4:36-37; 1Pe 5:4).

To the obedient (Ex 15:26; 19:5-6; 20:6, w Dt 5:11; Ex 23:22, 25-26; Dt 4:40; 6:2-3; 12:28; 28:1-6; 30:2-10; 1Ki 3:14; Ne 1:5; Ps 1:1, 3; 25:10; 103:17-18; 119:1-2; Pr 1:33; Isa 1:19; Jer 7:23; Eze 18:19; Mal 3:10-11; Mt 5:19; 12:50; Mk 3:35; Lk 8:21; 11:28; Jn 8:51; 12:26; 14:21, 23; 15:10; 1Jn 2:5, 17; 3:24).

To those who fear the Lord (Ps 34:7; 103:11-13, 17; 112:1; 115:13; 128:1-6; 145:19; Pr 10:27; 19:23; Ecc 7:18; 8:12). Those who have spiritual desire (Isa 55:1; Mt 5:6; Lk 6:21). Those who endure to the end (Mt 10:22; 24:13; Mk 13:13; Rev 2:7, 11, 17, 26-28; 3:5, 12, 21; 21:7). Those who love their enemies (Mt 5:44-45). Those who rebuke the wicked (Pr 24:25). Those who confess Christ (Mt 10:32; Ro 10:9; 1Jn 2:23; 4:15). Peacemakers, of sonship (Mt 5:9). Penitents (Lev 26:40-42; Dt 4:20-31; 2Ch 7:14; 30:9; Ps 34:18; 147:3; Isa 1:18; 55:7; Mt 5:4). The poor (Ex 22:27; Job 36:15; Ps 12:5; 35:10; 69:33; 72:2, 4, 12-14; 109:31; 132:15; Pr 22:22-23; Jas 41:17). The pure in heart (Mt 5:8). Persecuted saints (Mt 5:10-11; Lk 6:22-23; 21:12-18; 1Pe 4:14).

To the righteous (Job 17:9; 36:11; Ps 1:1-3; 34:7, 22; 37:4-5; 55:22; 119:1, 105; 138:8; 145:20; 146:8; Pr 25:22; Isa 58:8; Jer 17:7; Mt 6:30, 33; 10:22, 42; 24:13; Lk 6:35; 18:6-8; Ro 5:9; 8:30-31; 1Co 2:9; 3:21-22; Gal 6:9; Php 4:7; 2Th 3:3; Rev 2:17, 26, 28; 3:5; 14:13). The wise of heart (Pr 2:10-21).

Concerning:

Answer to prayer (Pr 15:29; Mk 11:23-24; Jn 14:13-14; Ac 10:4; 1Pe 3:12; 1Jn 3:22). Blessings upon their children (Ps 103:17; 112:2-3; Isa 59:21). Comfort (Isa 25:8; 66:13-14; Mt 5:4; Jn 14:16-18; Rev 21:4).

Deliverance, from temptation (1Co 10:13; Jas 4:7; 2Pe 2:9), from trouble (Job 5:19-24; Ps 33:18-19; 34:15, 17; 50:15; 97:10-11; Pr 3:25-26; Isa

41:10-13; 43:2). Divine help (Ps 55:22; Isa 41:10-11, 13; 2Co 12:9; Php 4:19; Heb 13:5-6). Divine guidance (Ps 25:12; 32:8; 37:23-24; 48:14; 73:24; Pr 3:5-6; 58:11). Divine mercy (Ps 32:10; 103:17-18; Mal 3:17). Divine presence (Ge 26:3, 24; 28:15; 31:3; Ex 33:14; Dt 31:6, 8; Jos 1:5; 1Ki 6:13; Hag 1:13; 2:4-5; Mt 18:20; 28:20; Jn 14:17, 23; 2Co 6:16; 13:11; Php 4:9; Heb 13:5; Jas 4:8; Rev 21:3). Divine likeness (1Jn 3:2). The ministry of angels (Heb 1:14).

Peace (Isa 26:3; Jn 16:33; Ro 2:10). Providential care (Ge 15:1; Ex 23:22; Lev 26:5-6, 10; Dt 33:27; 1Sa 2:9; 2Ch 16:9; Ezr 8:22; Job 5:15; Ps 34:9-10; 37:23-26; 121:2-8; 125:1-3; 145:19-20; Pr 1:33; 2:7; 3:6; 10:3; 16:7; Isa 49:9-11; 65:13-14; Eze 34:11-17, 22-31; Lk 12:7; 21:18; 1Pe 5:7). Overruling providence (Ro 8:28; 2Co 4:17). Spiritual enlightenment (Isa 2:3; Jn 8:12). Seeing God (Mt 5:8). Spiritual blessings (Isa 64:4; 1Co 2:9).

Refuge in adversity (Ps 33:18-19; 62:8; 91:1, 3-7, 9-12; Pr 14:26; Na 1:7). Strength in adversity (Ps 29:11). Security (Ps 32:6-7; 84:11; 121:3-8; Isa 33:16). Temporal blessings (Lev 25:18-19; 26:5; Dt 28:1-13; Ps 37:9; 128:1-6; Pr 2:21; 3:1-4, 7-10; Mt 6:26-33; Mk 10:30; Lk 18:29-30). Wisdom (Jas 1:5).

The gift of faith (Heb 4:9). Heavenly rest (Heb 4:9). Eternal life (Da 12:2-3; Mt 19:29; 25:46; Mk 10:29-30; Lk 18:29-30; Jn 3:15-16, 36; 4:14; 5:24, 29; 6:40; 10:28; 12:25; 17:2; Ro 2:7; 6:22-23; Gal 6:8; 1Th 4:15-17; 1Ti 1:16; 4:8; Tit 1:2; 1Jn 2:25; 5:13; Rev 22:5). Living with Christ (Jn 14:2-3; 17:24; Col 3:4; 1Th 4:17; 5:10). Everlasting remembrance (Ps 112:6). Names written in heaven (Lk 10:20).

Resurrection (Jn 5:29; 1Co 15:48-57; 2Co 4:14; 1Th 4:16). Future glory (Mt 13:43; Ro 8:18; Col 3:4; 2Ti 2:10; 1Pe 1:5; 5:4; Rev 7:14-17). Treasure in heaven (Mt 10:21; Lk 18:22). Inheritance (Mt 25:34; Ac 20:32; 26:18; Col 1:12; 3:24; Tit 3:7; Heb 9:15; Jas 2:5; 1Pe 1:4). Heavenly reward (Mt 5:12; 13:43; 2Ti 4:8; Heb 11:16; Jas 1:12; 2Pe 1:11; Rev 2:7, 10; 22:5, 12, 14). Reigning forever (Rev 22:5, w 1Co 4:8; Rev 5:10; 11:15).

See Blessings, Spiritual; God, Goodness of; Jesus the Christ, Compassion of, Love of.

PROMOTION (Ps 75:6-7; 78:70-71; 113:7-8). As a reward of merit (1Ch 11:6).

Instances of: Abraham (Ge 12:2). Joseph, from imprisoned slave to prince (Ge 41:1-45). Moses, from exile to lawgiver. *See Moses.* Aaron, from slave to high priest. *See Aaron.* Saul, from obscurity to a scepter. *See Saul.* David, from shepherd to throne. *See David.* Jeroboam, from slave to the throne (1Ki 11:26-35). Baasha, "out of dust" to the throne (1Ki 16:1-2). Daniel, from captive to premier (Da 2:48). *See Daniel.* Shadrach, Meshach, and Abednego (Da 3:30).

PROPAGATION Of species, commanded (Ge 1:11-12, 21-25, 28; 9:1, 7). *See Barrenness.*

PROPERTY [8, 296, 299, 1821+3972+ 9455, 2745, 3769, 4084, 4856, 5126, 5239, 5659, 5709, 7871, 8214, 8965, 10479, *1050, 3228, 5639*].

In Real Estate:
(Ge 23:17-18; 26:20). Rights in, violated (Ge 21:25-32; 26:18-22). Dedicated (Lev 27:16-25). *See Land.*

Dwellings:
Alienated for debt (Lev 25:14-15). Confiscation of Naboth's vineyard (1Ki 21:15-16). Priests exempt from taxes (Ge 47:22). Restriction of to lineal descendants (Nu 27:1-11; 36:1-9). Inherited (Ecc 2:21). Landmarks of, not to be removed (Dt 19:14; 27:17).

Personal:
Rights in, sacred (Ex 20:17; Dt 5:21). Laws concerning trespass of, and violence to (Ex 21:28-36; 22:9; Dt 23:25). Strayed, to be returned to owner (Lev 6:3-4; Dt 22:1-3). Hired (Ex 22:14-15), or loaned (Ex 22:10-15). Sold for debt (Pr 22:26-27), rights of redemption of (Jer 32:7). Dedicated to God, redemption of (Lev 27:9-13, 26-33). In slaves (Ex 21:4).

PROPHECY [1821, 5547, 5363, 5553, 5566, 5752, 10451, *4460, 4735, 4736*] (*speak before*). Concerning the Church. *See Church, The Body of Believers, Prophecies Concerning.* Relating to various countries, nations, and cities. *See under their respective names.* Respecting individuals. *See individuals by name.*

Concerning Jesus the Messiah:
The first messianic prophecy (Ge 3:15), concerns the announcement of the victor over Satan, the victor described as "the seed of the woman."

Messianic Prophecies and Fulfillments	
Ge 12:3; 18:18; 22:18	Ac 3:25; Gal 3:8
Ge 17:7, 19; 22:16-17	Lk 1:55, 72-74
Dt 18:15, 18	Ac 3:22-23
Ps 2:1-2	Ac 4:25-26
Ps 2:7	Ac 13:33; Heb 1:5; 5:5
Ps 8:2	Mt 21:16
Ps 8:4-6	Heb 2:6-8
Ps 16:8-11	Ac 2:25-28, 31
Ps 16:10	Ac 13:35
Ps 22:1	Mt 27:46; Mk 15:34
Ps 22:18	Mt 27:35; Mk 15:24; Lk 23:34; Jn 19:24
Ps 22:22	Heb 2:12
Ps 31:5	Lk 23:46
Ps 41:9	Jn 13:18; Ac 1:16
Ps 45:6-7	Heb 1:8-9
Ps 68:18	Eph 4:8-13
Ps 69:21	Mt 27:34, 48; Mk 15:23, 36; Lk 23:36; Jn 19:28-29
Ps 69:25; 109:8	Ac 1:20
Ps 78:2	Mt 13:35
Ps 95:7-11	Heb 3:7-11; 4:3, 5-7
Ps 102:25-27	Heb 1:10-12
Ps 110:1	Mt 22:43-44; Mk 12:36-37; Lk 20:42-44; Ac 2:34-36; Heb 1:13
Ps 110:4	Heb 5:6; 7:15-17, 21
Ps 118:22-23	Mt 21:42; Mk 12:10-11; Lk 20:17; Ac 4:11; Eph 2:20; 1Pe 2:7
Ps 118:25-26	Mt 21:9; Mk 11:9; Lk 13:35; Jn 12:13
Ps 132:11, 17	Lk 1:69; Ac 2:30
Isa 7:14	Mt 1:23
Isa 9:1-2	Mt 4:15-16
Isa 9:7; Da 7:14, 27	Lk 1:32-33
Isa 11:10	Ro 15:12
Isa 25:8	1Co 15:54-55
Isa 28:16	Ro 9:33; 10:11; 1Pe 2:6
Isa 40:3-5	Mt 3:3; Mk 1:3; Lk 3:4-6; Jn 1:23
Isa 42:1-4	Mt 12:17-21
Isa 49:6	Lk 2:32; Ac 13:47-48; 26:23
Isa 53:1	Jn 12:38; Ro 10:16
Isa 53:3-6	Ac 26:22-23
Isa 53:4-6, 11	1Pe 2:24-25
Isa 53:4	Mt 8:17
Isa 53:9	1Pe 2:22
Isa 53:12	Mk 15:27-28; Lk 22:37
Isa 54:13	Jn 6:45
Isa 55:3	Ac 13:34
Isa 59:20-21	Ro 11:26-27
Jer 31:31-34	Heb 8:8-12; 10:16-17
Hos 1:10	Ro 9:26
Hos 2:23	Ro 9:25; 1Pe 2:10
Joel 2:28-32	Ac 2:16-21; Ro 10:13
Am 9:11-12	Ac 15:16-17
Mic 5:2	Mt 2:5-6; Jn 7:42
Hab 1:5	Ac 13:40-41
Hag 2:6	Heb 12:26
Zec 9:9	Mt 21:4-5; Jn 12:14-15
Zec 11:13	Mt 27:9-10
Zec 12:10	Jn 19:34
Zec 13:7	Mt 26:31, 56; Mk 14:27, 50
Mal 3:1	Mt 11:10; Mk 1:2; Lk 7:27
Mal 4:5-6	Mt 11:13-14; 17:10-13; Mk 9:11-13; Lk 1:16-17

See Jesus the Christ, Prophecies Concerning; Jesus the Christ, King, Prophecies Concerning.

General:

Inspired (Isa 28:22; Lk 1:70; 2Ti 3:16; 2Pe 1:21). "The word of the Lord came to," Elijah (1Ki 17:8; 21:17, 28), Isaiah (Isa 2:1; 8:5; 13:1; 14:28; 38:4), Jeremiah (Jer 1:4; 7:1; 11:1; 13:8; 16:1; 18:1; 25:1-2; 26:1; 27:1; 29:30; 30:1, 4; 32:1, 6, 26; 33:1, 19, 23; 34:12; 35:12; 36:1; 37:6; 40:1; 43:8; 44:1; 46:1; 49:34; 50:1), Ezekiel (Eze 3:16; 6:1; 7:1; 11:14; 12:1, 8, 17, 21; 13:1; 14:12; 15:1; 16:1; 17:1, 11; 18:1; 20:45; 21:1, 8, 18; 22:1, 17, 23; 23:1; 24:1, 5, 20; 25:1; 26:1; 27:1; 28:1, 11, 20; 29:1, 17; 30:1, 20; 31:1; 32:1, 17; 33:1, 23; 34:1; 35:1; 36:16; 37:15; 38:1), Amos (Am 7:14-15), Jonah (Jnh 3:1), Haggai (Hag 2:1, 10, 20), Zechariah (Zec 1:7; 4:8; 6:9; 7:1, 4, 8; 8:1, 18).

Publicly proclaimed (Jer 11:6). Exemplified in pantomime (Eze 4; 5:1-4; Ac 21:11). Written, by an amanuensis (Jer 45:1), in books (Jer 45:1; 51:60).

Proof of God's foreknowledge (Isa 43:9). Sure fulfillment of (Eze 12:22-25, 28; Hab 2:3; Mt 5:18; 24:35; Ac 13:27, 29). Cessation of (La 2:9).

Of apostasy (1Jn 2:18; Jude 17-18), false teachers (2Pe 2:3). Tribulations of the righteous (Rev 2:10).

Miscellaneous, Fulfilled:

The birth and zeal of Josiah (1Ki 13:2; 2Ki 23:1-20). Death of the prophet of Judah (1Ki 13:21-22, 24-30). Extinction of Jeroboam's house (1Ki 14:5-17), of Baasha's house (1Ki 16:2-3, 9-13). Concerning the rebuilding of Jericho (Jos 6:26; 1Ki 16:34). The drought, foretold by Elijah (1Ki 17:14). Destruction of Ben-Hadad's army (1Ki 20:13-30). The death of a man who refused to kill a prophet (1Ki 20:35-36). The death of Ahab (1Ki 20:42; 21:18-24; 22:31-38). The death of Ahaziah (2Ki 1:3-17). Elijah's translation (2Ki 2:3-11). Cannibalism among the Israelites (Lev 26:29; Dt 28:53; 2Ki 6:28-29; Jer 19:9; La 4:10). The death of the Samaritan lord (2Ki 7:2, 19-20). The end of the famine in Samaria (2Ki 7:1-18). Jezebel's tragic death (1Ki 21:23; 2Ki 9:10, 33-37). The killing of Syria by Joash (2Ki 13:16-25). Conquests of Jeroboam (2Ki 14:25-28). Four generations of Jehu to sit upon the throne of Israel (2Ki 10:30, w 15:12). Destruction of Sennacherib's army, and his death (2Ki 19:6-7, 20-37). The captivity of Judah (2Ki 20:17-18; 24:10-16; 25:11-21).

Concerning Christ. *See Jesus the Christ, Prophecies Concerning. See above, Concerning Jesus the Messiah.*

Concerning John (Mt 3:3). Rachel weeping for her children (Jer 31:15; Mt 2:17-18). Deliverance of Jeremiah (Jer 39:15-18). Invasion of Judah by the Chaldeans (Hab 1:6-11), fulfilled (Jer 25; 2Ch 36:17-21), betrayal of Jesus by Judas, prophecy (Ps 41:9), fulfillment (Jn 13:18; 18:1-9), Judas' self-destruction (Ps 69:25; Ac 1:16, 20), fulfilled (Mt 27:5; Ac 1:16-20). Outpouring of the Holy Spirit (Joel 2:28-29), fulfilled (Ac 2:16-21).

Spiritual blindness of the Israelites (Isa 6:9; 29:13), fulfilled (Mk 7:6-7; Ac 28:25-27). Mission of Jesus (Ps 68:18), fulfilled (Eph 4:8, 10). *See Jesus the Christ, Mission of.* Captivity of the Israelites (Jer 25:11-12; 29:10, 14; 32:3-5; Da 9:2, w 2Ki 25:1-8; Ezr 1). Of the destruction of the ship in which Paul sailed (Ac 27:10, 18-44). *See Prophetesses; Prophets.*

PROPHETESSES [5567, 4739] (*speak before*). Miriam (Ex 15:20). Deborah (Jdg 4:4). Huldah (2Ki 22:14). False (Eze 13:17-19). Isaiah's wife (Isa 8:3). All the daughters of Israel (Joel 2:28-29). Noadiah (Ne 6:14). Elizabeth (Lk 1:41-45). Anna (Lk 2:36-38). Daughters of Philip (Ac 21:9). Jezebel (Rev 2:20).

See Women.

PROPHETS [967, 2602, 5547, 5566, 5567, 5752, 10455, 4737, 4739, 6021] (*speak before*).

General:

Called seers (1Sa 9:19; 2Sa 15:27; 24:11; 2Ki 17:13; 1Ch 9:22; 29:29; 2Ch 9:29; 12:15; 29:30; Isa 30:10; Mic 3:7). Schools of (1Ki 20:35; 2Ki 2:3-15; 4:1, 38; 9:1). Kept the chronicles or records (1Ch 29:29; 2Ch 9:29; 12:15). Not honored in their own country (Mt 13:57; Lk 4:24-27; Jn 4:44). Officiate at installation of kings (1Ki 1:32-35). Counselors to kings (1Ki 22:6-28; 2Ki 6:9-12; Isa 37:2-3; Jer 27:12-15).

Inspired by angels (Zec 1:9, 13-14, 19; Ac 7:53; Gal 3:19; Heb 2:2). Persecutions of (2Ch 36:16; Am 2:12). Martyrs (Jer 2:30; Mt 23:37; Mk 12:5; Lk 13:34; 1Th 2:15; Heb 11:37; Rev 16:6).

Compensation of: Presents (1Sa 9:7-8; 1Ki 14:3; 2Ki 4:42; 8:8-9; Eze 13:19). Presents refused by (Nu 22:18; 1Ki 13:7-8; 2Ki 5:5, 16).

Inspiration of: (1Ki 13:20; 2Ch 33:18; 36:15; Ne 9:30; Job 33:14-16; Jer 7:25; Da 9:6, 10; Hos 12:10; Joel 2:28; Am 3:7-8; Zec 7:12; Lk 1:70; Ac 3:18; Ro 1:1-2; 1Co 12:7-11; Heb 1:1; 2Pe 1:21; Rev 10:7; 22:6, 8).

Examples of Prophets:

Enoch (Jude 14). Joseph (Ge 40:8; 41:16, 38-39). Moses (Ex 3:14-15; 4:12, 15, 27; 6:13, 29; 7:2; 19:9-19; 24:16; 25:22; 33:9, 11; Lev 1:1; Nu 1:1; 7:89; 9:8-10; 11:17, 25; 12:6-8; 16:28-29; Dt 1:5-6; 5:4-5, 31; 34:10-11; Ps 103:7). Aaron (Ex 6:13; 12:1). Eleazar (Nu 26:1). Balaam (Nu 23:5, 16, 20, 26; 24:2-4, 15-16). Joshua (Jos 4:15).

Samuel (1Sa 3:1, 4-10, 19-21; 9:6, 15-20; 15:16). Saul (1Sa 10:6-7, 10-13; 19:23). Saul's men (1Sa 19:20). David (2Sa 23:2-3; Mk 12:36). Nathan (2Sa 7:3-4; 2Sa 7:8). Gad (2Sa 24:11). Ahijah (1Ki 14:5). Elijah (1Ki 17:1, 24; 19:15; 2Ki 10:10). Micaiah (1Ki 22:14, 28; 2Ch 18:27). Elisha (2Ki 2:9; 3:11-12, 15; 5:8; 6:8-12, 32). Jahaziel (2Ch 20:14). Azariah (2Ch 15:1-2). Zechariah, the son of Jehoiada (2Ch 24:20; 26:5).

Isaiah (2Ki 20:4; Isa 6:1-9; 8:11; 44:26; Ac 28:25). Jeremiah (2Ch 36:12; Jer 1:1-19; 2:1; 7:1; 11:1, 18; 13:1-3; 16:1; 18:1; 20:9; 23:9; 24:4; 25:3; 26:1-2, 12; 27:1-2; 29:30; 33:1; 34:1; 42:4, 7; Da 9:2). Ezekiel (Eze 1:1, 3; 2:1-2, 4-5; 3:10-

12, 14, 16-17, 22, 24, 27; 8:1; 11:1, 4-5, 24; 33:22; 37:1; 40:1; 43:5-6). Daniel (Da 2:19; 7:16; 8:16; 9:22; 10:7-9). Hosea (Hos 1:1-2). Joel (Joel 1:1). Amos (Am 3:7-8; 7:14-15). Obadiah (Ob 1). Jonah (Jnh 1:1; 3:1-2). Micah (Mic 1:1; 3:8). Habakkuk (Hab 1:1). Haggai (Hag 1:13). Zechariah, the son of Berekiah (Zec 2:9; 7:8).

Elizabeth (Lk 1:41). Zechariah (Lk 1:67). Simeon (Lk 2:26-27). John the Baptist (Lk 3:2). The apostles (Ac 2:4). Philip (Ac 8:29). Agabus (Ac 11:28; 21:10-11). Disciple at Tyre (Ac 21:4), John the apostle (Rev 1:10-11).

See Revelation; Word of God, Inspiration of.

False:

(Dt 18:21-22; 1Ki 13:18; Ne 6:12; Jer 23:16-27, 30-32; La 2:14). Warnings against (Dt 13:1-3; Mt 24:5, 23-24, 26; Mk 13:6, 21-22; Lk 21:8). Denunciations against (Dt 18:20; Jer 14:15). Punishment of (Dt 18:20; Jer 14:13-16; 20:6; 28:16-17; 29:32; Zec 13:3). Drunken (Isa 28:7).

Instances of—
Noadiah (Ne 6:14), four hundred in Samaria (1Ki 22:6-12; 2Ch 18:5), Pashhur (Jer 20:6), Hanani (Jer 28; Ro 15:16).

Idolatrous—
(1Ki 18:19, 22, 25-28, 40).

See Minister, False and Corrupt.

PROPHETS, THE MINOR

Also known as "The Book of the Twelve." In Ecclesiasticus (an Apocryphal book written c. 190 B.C.), Jesus ben Sirach spoke of "the twelve prophets" (Sir 49:10) as a unit parallel to Isaiah, Jeremiah and Ezekiel. He thus indicated that these twelve prophecies were at that time thought of as a unit and were probably already written together on one scroll, as is the case in later times. Josephus (*Against Apion*, 1.8.3) also was aware of this grouping. Augustine (*The City of God*, 18.25) called them the "Minor Prophets," referring to the small size of these books by comparison with the major prophetic books and not at all suggesting that they are of minor importance.

In the tradition of Jewish canon these works are arranged in what was thought to be their chronological order:

(1) the books that came from the period of Assyrian power (Hosea, Joel, Amos, Obadiah, Jonah, Micah),

(2) those written about the time of the decline of Assyria (Nahum, Habakkuk, Zephaniah) and

(3) those dating from the postexilic era (Haggai, Zechariah, Malachi).

On the other hand, their order in the Septuagint (the earliest Greek translation of the OT) is: Hosea, Amos, Micah, Joel, Obadiah, Jonah, Nahum, Habakkuk, Zephaniah, Haggai, Zechariah, Malachi (the order of the first six was probably determined by length, except for Jonah, which is placed last among them because of its different character).

In any event, it appears that within a century after the composition of Malachi the Jews had brought together the twelve shorter prophecies to form a book (scroll) of prophetic writings, which was received as canonical and paralleled the three major prophetic books of Isaiah, Jeremiah and Ezekiel. The great Greek manuscripts Alexandrinus and Vaticanus place the minor prophets before the major prophets, but in the traditional Jewish canon and in all modern versions they appear after them.

PROPITIATION *(to cover)*. To appease the wrath of God so that his justice and holiness will be satisfied and he can forgive sin. Propitiation does not make God merciful; it makes divine forgiveness possible. An atonement must be provided; in OT times, animal sacrifices; now, the death of Christ for man's sin. Through Christ's death propitiation is made for man's sin (Ro 3:25; 5:1, 10-11; 2Co 5:18-19; Col 1:20-22; 1Jn 2:2; 4:10; Heb 9:5).

See Atonement.

PROSELYTE A person of Gentile origin who had accepted the Jewish religion, whether living in Israel or elsewhere (Mt 23:15; Ac 2:10; 6:5; 13:43). A distinction was apparently made between uncircumcised proselytes, i.e., those who had not fully identified themselves with the Jewish nation and religion; and circumcised proselytes, those who identified themselves fully with Judaism. *See Converts.*

PROSPERITY [*2014, 3201, 3202, 3206, 3208, 3512, 7407, 7503, 8505, 8934, 10613, 10713, 10720]. From God (Ge 33:11; 49:24-26; Ps 127:1; 128:1-2). Design of (Ecc 7:14). Promised to the righteous (Job 22:23-27).

Evil effects of: Pride in (2Ch 32:25). Forgetfulness of God in (2Ch 12:1; 26:16; Hos 4:7). The prosperous despise the unfortunate (Job 12:5). Dangers of (Dt 8:10-18; 31:20; 32:15; Jer 5:7; Hos 13:6).

Instances of wisdom in: Joseph and Daniel as deduced from their general conduct. *See Joseph, 1; Daniel.*

See Blessings, Temporal; Rich, The; Riches.

PROSTITUTE [924, 2388, 2390, 3978, 7728, 9373, *3434, 4520*]. Forbidden (Lev 19:29; Dt 23:17). Punishment of (Lev 21:9). Shamelessness of (Pr 2:16; 7:11-27; 9:13-18). Schemes of (Pr 7:10; 9:14-17; Isa 23:15-16; Hos 2:13). To be shunned (Pr 5:3-20; 7:25-27).

In ancient heathen worship a special class of prostitutes was connected with shrines and temples (Ge 38:15, 21, 22), male (1Ki 14:24; 15:12). *See Shrine.* Their earnings were not to be received at the temple (Dt 23:17-18). The term is often used in the OT to refer to religious unfaithfulness (Ex 34:15-16; Isa 1:21; Jer 2:20; Eze 23).

Rahab (Jos 2:3-6; 6:17, 23, 25; Heb 11:31). Jephthah, the son of (Jdg 11:1). Gomer (Hos 1:2-3; 3:3). Babylon (Rev 17).

PROSTRATION *See Obeisance; Worship, Attitude in.*

PROTRACTED MEETINGS (1Ki
8:65; 2Ch 7:8-10; 30:23). *See Revivals.*

PROUD [*1450, 1452, 1454, 1455, 1467,
1469, 1575, 2086, 2295, 5294, 8123, 8124, 8146,
3016, 3017, 3018, 5662, 5881]. *See Pride.*

PROVENDER *See Fodder.*

PROVERB [5439, 5442, *4130, 4231*]. Pithy
saying, comparison or question expressing a
familiar or useful truth (Ge 10:9; 1Sa 10:12;
Proverbs). Design of (Pr 1:1-4). Written and compiled by Solomon (Pr 1:1; 25:1).

Miscellany of:
(1Sa 10:12; 24:13-14; 2Sa 3:8; 20:18; 1Ki 20:11;
Pr 1:17; Eze 12:22-23; 16:44; 18:2-4, w Jer 31:29;
Hos 4:9; Mt 12:33, w Lk 6:44; Lk 4:23; 14:34; Jn
1:46; 1Co 15:33; Gal 6:7).
*See Proverbs, The Book of Proverbs Arranged
Topically.*

PROVERBS, BOOK OF

Authors: Although the book begins with a title
ascribing the proverbs to Solomon, it is clear from
later chapters that he was not the only author of
the book. Pr 22:17 and 24:23 refer to the "sayings
of the wise." Ch. 30 is attributed to Agur son of
Jakeh and 31:1-9 to King Lemuel.

Date: If Solomon is granted a prominent role in
the book, most of Proverbs would stem from the
tenth century B.C. The role of Hezekiah's men
(25:1) indicates that important sections of
Proverbs were compiled and edited from 715 to
686 B.C. Perhaps it was also at this time that the
sayings of Agur (ch. 30) and Lemuel (31:1-9) and
the other "sayings of the wise" (22:17-24:22;
24:23-34) were added to the Solomonic collections.

Outline:
I. Prologue: Purpose and Theme (1:1-7).
II. The Superiority of the Way of Wisdom
   (1:8-9:18).
   A. Appeals and Warnings Confronting Youth
      (1:8-33).
      1. Enticements to secure happiness by
         violence (1:8-19).
      2. Warnings against rejecting wisdom
         (1:20-33).
   B. Commendation of Wisdom (chs. 2-4).
      1. Benefits of accepting wisdom's
         instructions (ch. 2).
      2. Wisdom's instructions and benefits
         (3:1-20).
      3. Wisdom's instructions and benefits
         (3:21-35).
      4. Challenge to hold on to wisdom (ch. 4).
   C. Warnings Against Folly (chs. 5-7).
      1. Warning against adultery (ch. 5).
      2. Warning against perverse ways (6:1-19).
      3. Cost of committing adultery (6:20-35).
      4. Warning against the enticements of an
         adulteress (ch. 7).

   D. Appeals Addressed to Youth (chs. 8-9).
      1. Wisdom's appeal (ch. 8).
      2. Invitations of wisdom and folly (ch. 9).
III. The Main Collection of Solomon's Proverbs
   (10:1-22:16).
IV. The Thirty Sayings of the Wise
   (22:17-24:22).
V. Additional Sayings of the Wise (24:23-34).
VI. Hezekiah's Collection of Solomon's
   Proverbs (chs. 25-29).
VII. The Words of Agur (ch. 30).
VIII. The Words of King Lemuel (31:1-9).
IX. Epilogue: The Ideal Wife (31:10-31).

The Book of Proverbs Arranged Topically:
Introduction to Wisdom—
The call of Wisdom (8:1-36; 9:1-6). Benefits of
following Wisdom (2:1-22; 3:13-24). Dangers of
rejecting Wisdom (1:20-33; 9:13-18). Solomon'
personal plea (4:1-27).

Proverbs of Solomon and Sayings of the Wise—
Value of wise sayings (22:17-21). Purpose of the
Proverbs (1:1-7).

Preeminence of God: Fear of the Lord (9:10-12;
10:27; 14:2, 26-27; 15:33; 19:23; 28:14). Trust in
God or self (3:5-8; 14:12, & 16:25; 16:3, 20; 18:2,
4, 10; 19:3; 20:24; 21:22; 26:12; 28:26; 29:25).
Divine providence (15:3; 16:1, 4, 9, 33; 19:21;
21:30-31; 22:12; 27:1).

Insight and Ignorance: Wisdom and folly
(13:14; 14:24; 15:24; 16:22; 17:12; 24:7, 13-14).
Dealing with fools (26:4-11; 27:22; 29:9). Discernment and understanding (10:13, 23; 13:15;
14:6, 8, 15, 33; 15:21; 16:16; 17:24; 19:8; 20:5;
20:12). Knowledge (10:14; 13:16; 14:18; 15:14;
18:15; 19:2; 20:15; 21:11-12; 23:3-4).

Sharing and Responding to Wisdom: Advice and
rebuke (3:1-2; 9:7-9; 10:8; 12:15; 13:1; 13:13;
15:31; 17:10; 19:16, 20, 25, 27; 23:9; 25:12; 27:5-
6; 27:17; 29:1). Value of Advisors (11:14; 15:22;
20:18; 24:5-6). Discipline (3:11-12; 10:17; 12:1;
13:18, 24; 15:5, 10, 12, 32; 19:18; 20:30; 22:6, 15;
23:13-14; 29:15, 17, 19, 21). Lawkeeping (28:4, 7,
9; 29:18). Repentance (14:9; 28:13).

Good and Evil: Righteousness and wickedness
(10:6-7, 16, 28-30; 11:5-10, 18-20, 23; 12:2-3,
5-8, 12, 21, 28; 13:9, 21, 25; 14:11, 19, 23; 15:6,
9; 20:7; 21:18; 24:15-16; 28:12, 28; 29:2, 16, 27).
Integrity and perversion (10:9; 13:6; 15:26; 21:8;
24:8-9; 28:18; 29:10). Appropriate consequences
(3:33-35; 10:3, 22; 10:24-25; 11:21, 27, 30-31;
14:14, 22; 16:7; 17:13; 18:3; 19:29; 21:12, 16, 21;
22:8; 26:1, 3, 27).

Sincere Motivation: Motive and the heart (15:11;
16:2; 17:3; 20:11, 27; 21:2; 27:19). False worship
(15:8, 29; 21:3, 27). Duplicity (6:12-15; 10:10-11;
11:3; 16:30; 20:14; 23:6-8; 26:23-26).

Concern for others: Love and faithfulness (3:3-
4; 16:6; 20:6; 25:19). Love, hatred, and compassion (10:12; 15:17; 17:5; 24:17-18; 25:21-22).
Kindness and mercy (11:16-17; 12:10, 25; 21:10).
Overstaying welcome (25:16-17).

Concern for Self: Pride and humility (11:2; 12:9;
13:7, 10; 15:25; 16:5, 18-19; 18:12; 19:10; 20:9;

21:4, 24; 22:4; 25:27; 26:16; 27:2; 27:21; 29:23). Selfishness (18:1). Jealousy (27:4). Envy (14:30; 24:19-20). Greed (28:25).

Control of Self: Self-control (25:28; 29:11). Rashness (20:25; 21:5; 25:8; 29:20). Temper and patience (12:16; 14:16-17, 29; 15:18; 16:32; 19:11, 19; 22:24-25; 29:8, 22). Drunkenness and gluttony (20:1; 23:19-21; 23:29-35). Adultery (5:1-23; 6:20-35; 7:1-27; 22:14). Prostitution (23:26-28; 29:3).

Control of the Tongue: Wise and foolish talk (14:3; 15:2, 7; 16:23; 18:6-7; 19:1; 23:15-16). Righteous and wicked talk (10:20-21, 31-32; 11:11; 12:13-14; 13:2; 15:28; 17:4). Appropriate speech (15:23; 16:21, 24; 25:11; 27:14). Maintaining silence (10:19; 12:23; 13:3; 17:28; 18:13; 21:23). Controlled speech (15:1; 17:27; 25:15). Flattery (26:28; 28:23; 29:5). Slander and gossip (10:18; 11:13; 16:28; 17:9; 18:8, & 26:22; 20:19; 26:20). Hurtful talk (11:12; 12:18; 15:4; 16:27; 25:23; 26:2). Quarreling (17:14, 19; 20:3; 22:10; 26:21). Lying (12:19, 22; 17:20; 19:5, 22; 21:6). Power of tongue (18:20-21).

Disharmony and Strife: Solicitation to evil (1:10-19; 16:29; 25:26; 27:3; 28:10). Violence (3:31-32; 21:7; 21:29). Murderers (28:17). Causing others harm (3:29-30). Revenge (20:22; 24:28-29). Dissension and strife (6:16-19; 17:1; 18:18-19). Meddling (26:17).

Honesty: Truthfulness (12:20; 13:5; 24:26; 26:18-19). Accurate weights (11:1; 16:11; 20:10, 23). Boundary stones (22:28; 23:10-11). Wrongfully obtained gains (10:2; 13:11; 20:17, 21). Bribery (15:27; 17:8, 23; 21:14).

Justice: False witnesses (12:17; 14:5, 25; 19:9, 28; 21:28; 25:18). Open-mindedness (18:17). Judicial justice (17:15, 26; 18:5; 21:15; 24:11-12, 23-25; 28:5; 29:26).

Economic Well-Being: Wealth and poverty (3:9-10; 10:15; 11:4, 28; 13:8; 14:20; 15:16; 17:16; 18:11, 23; 19:4, 6-7; 22:2, 7; 23:4-5; 27:7; 28:6, 8, 11, 20-22). Benevolence and generosity (3:27-28; 11:24-26; 13:22; 14:21; 18:16; 19:17; 21:13; 22:9; 25:14; 28:27). Oppression of the poor (13:23; 14:31; 15:15; 16:8; 22:16, 22-23; 29:7, 13). Industriousness (6:6-11; 10:4-5, 26; 12:11, 24, 27; 13:4; 14:4, 23; 15:19; 16:26; 18:9; 19:15; 19:24, & 26:15; 20:4, 13, 17; 21:25-26; 22:29; 24:27, 30-34; 26:14; 27:18, 23-27; 28:19). Conservation (21:20). Surety for another (6:1-5; 11:15; 17:18; 20:16, & 27:13; 22:26-27).

Persons and Attributes: Parents and children (1:8-9; 10:1; 11:29; 15:20; 17:2, 6, 21, 25; 19:26; 20:20; 23:22-25; 28:24). The elderly (16:31; 20:29). Women and wives (11:22; 12:4; 14:1; 18:22; 19:13-14; 21:9, & 25:24; 21:19; 27:15-16). Kings and rulers (14:28, 35; 16:10, 12-15; 17:7, 11; 19:12; 20:2, 8, 26, 28; 21:1; 22:11; 23:1-3; 24:21-22; 25:2-7; 28:2-3; 28:15-16; 29:4, 12, 14). Messengers (13:17; 25:13). Companions (12:26; 13:20; 14:7; 17:17; 18:24; 24:1-2; 27:8-10; 29:24).

Various Concerns: Caution (16:17; 22:3, & 27:12; 22:5). Reputation (22:1; 25:9-10). Courage

(3:25-26; 14:32; 22:13; 24:10; 26:13; 28:1). Hope (13:12; 13:19; 23:17-18).

Various Observations: Joy and grief (14:10, 13; 15:13; 17:22; 18:14; 25:20; 27:11; 29:6). Good news (15:30; 25:25). Curiosity (27:20).

The sayings of Agur son of Jakeh (30:1-33).

The sayings of King Lemuel (31:1-9).

A wife of noble character (31:10-31).

PROVIDENCE [7213]. The universal sovereign reign of God; God's preserving and governing all his creatures, and all their actions (Job 9:5-6; 28:25; Ps 104:10-25; 145:15; 147:9; Mt 4:4; 6:26-28; Lk 12:6-7; Ac 17:25-28). General providence includes the government of the entire universe, especially the affairs of men. Special providence is God's particular care over the life and activity of the believer (Ro 8:28).

See God, Providence of.

PROVINCE [4519, 10406, *823, 824, 825, 2065, 3070*]. Unit of an empire, like those of the Roman Empire. In Persia they were called satrapies. Rome's provinces were divided into two categories: imperial, those requiring a frontier army, and ruled by a legate appointed by the emperor; senatorial, those presenting no major problems and ruled by someone appointed by the Senate—a proconsul (Ac 13:7).

PROVOCATION [1741, 4087, 4088+, 7861, 7911, 8074, *4614*]. Any cause of God's anger at sin (1Ki 15:30; 21:22; Eze 20:28; Ne 9:18, 26).

PROXY In priest's service (2Ch 30:17). *See Substitution; Suffering, Vicarious.*

PRUDENCE [1067, 6874, 6891, 6893, 8505].

General:

(Job 34:3-4; Ps 112:5; Hos 14:9; Mt 7:6).

In restraining speech (Ps 39:1; Pr 12:8; 21:23; 23:9; 26:4; 29:11; Am 5:13). In heeding counsel (Pr 15:5; 20:18). In restraining appetite (Pr 23:1-2). In avoiding strife (Pr 25:8-10; 29:8). In refraining from making a guarantee (Pr 6:1-2).

Proverbs concerning (Pr 8:12; 11:13, 15, 29; 12:8, 16, 23; 13:16; 14:8, 15-16, 18; 15:5, 22; 16:20-21; 17:2, 18; 18:15-16; 19:2; 20:5, 16, 18; 21:5, 20, 23; 22:3, 7, 26-27; 23:1-3, 9; 24:6, 27; 25:8-10; 26:4-5; 27:12; 29:8, 11; Ecc 7:16-17; 8:2-3; 10:1, 10). Illustration of (Lk 14:28-32). Injunctions concerning (Ro 14:16; 1Co 6:12; 8:8-13; 10:25-33; Col 4:5; Jas 1:19).

See Diplomacy; Gentleness; Wisdom.

Instances of:

Jacob, in his conduct toward Esau (Ge 32:3-21), toward his sons, after Dinah's defilement (Ge 34:5, 30). Joseph, in the affairs of Egypt (Ge 41:33-57). Jethro's advice to Moses (Ex 18:17-23). The Israelites, in the threatened war with the two-a-one-half tribes (Jos 22:10-34). Saul, in not slaying the Jabesh Gileadites (1Sa 11:13). David, in his overthrowing Ahithophel's counsel (2Sa 15:33-37). Abigail, in averting David's wrath (1Sa 25:18-31). Achish, in dismissing David (1Sa 29). Elijah, in his flight from Jezebel (1Ki 19:3-4). Rehoboam's counselors (1Ki 12:7). Jehoram, in suspecting a Syrian stratagem (2Ki 7:12-13). Nehemiah, in conduct of affairs at Jerusalem (Ne 2:12-16; 4:13-23). Daniel (Da 1:8-14). Certain elders of Israel (Jer 26:17-23).

Jesus, in charging those who were healed not to advertise his miracles (Mt 9:30; 16:20; Mk 3:12; 5:43; 7:36; 8:30; 9:9), going to the feast secretly (Jn 7:10), in restricting his public appearances (Jn 11:54; 12:36), in avoiding his enemies (Mt 12:14-16; Mk 3:7; Jn 11:47-54). Joseph, in his conduct toward Mary (Mt 1:19). Peter, in escaping Herod (Ac 12:17). Paul, in circumcising Timothy (Ac 16:3), in performing temple rites (Ac 21:20-26), in setting the Jewish sects on each other (Ac 23:6), avoiding suspicion in administering the gifts of the churches (2Co 8:20), his lack of, in his persistence in going to Jerusalem despite the warnings of the Spirit and his friends (Ac 20:22-25, 37-38; 21:10-14), Paul and Barnabas, in escaping persecution (Ac 14:6), Paul and Silas, in escaping from Berea (Ac 17:10-15). The town clerk of Ephesus, in averting a riot (Ac 19:29-41).

See Diplomacy; Tact.

PRUNING [2377, 4661, 2748]. To care for and increase productivity of vines (Lev 25:3-4; Isa 5:6; 18:5). Pruning hook (Isa 2:4; 18:5; Joel 3:10; Mic 4:3). Figurative of discipline (Jn 15:2-6).

PSALMODY *See Music.*

PSALMS [3344, 4660, 5380, 9335, 6011].

Psalms Outside the Book of:

Of Moses celebrating the deliverance at the Red Sea (Ex 15:1-19). Didactic songs composed by Moses, celebrating the providence, righteousness, and judgments of God (Dt 32:1-43; Ps 90). Song of Deborah, celebrating Israel's victory over Sisera (Jdg 5). Of Hannah, in thankfulness for a son (1Sa 2:1-10). Of David, celebrating his deliverance (2Sa 22), on the occasion of removing the ark (1Ch 16:7-36), at the close of his reign (2Sa 23:2-7; 1Ch 29:10-19). Of Isaiah (Isa 12; 25-26). Of Hezekiah, celebrating deliverance from death (Isa 38:9-20). Of Mary (Lk 1:46-55). Elizabeth (Lk 1:42-45). Zechariah (Lk 1:68-79).

Book of Psalms:

Collection and Structure—
The Hebrew Psalter is divided into five books:
1. Psalms 1-41.
2. Psalms 42-72.
3. Psalms 73-89.
4. Psalms 90-106.
5. Psalms 107-150.

The formation of psalters probably goes back to the early days of the first (Solomon's) temple or even to the time of David. The Psalter was put into its final form by postexilic temple personnel, who completed it probably in the third century B.C.

Topically Arranged—
Psalms of affliction (Ps 3-5; 11; 13; 16-17; 22; 26-28; 31; 35; 41-42; 44; 54-57; 59-64; 69-71; 74; 77; 79-80; 83-84; 86; 88-89; 102; 109; 120; 123; 129; 137; 140-143). Didactic psalms (Ps 1; 5; 7; 9-12; 14-15; 17; 24-25; 32; 34; 36-37; 39; 49; 50; 52-53; 58; 73; 75; 82; 84; 90-92; 94; 101; 112; 119; 121; 125; 127-128; 131; 133). Historical psalms (Ps 78; 105-106). Imprecatory psalms. *See Prayer, Imprecatory.* Intercessional psalms (Ps 20; 67; 122; 132; 144). Messianic Psalms. *See Jesus the Christ, Messiah, Messianic Psalms.* Penitential psalms (Ps 6; 25; 32; 38; 51; 102; 130; 143). Psalms of praise (Ps 8; 19; 24; 29; 33; 47; 50; 65-66; 76-77; 93; 95-97; 99; 104; 111; 113-115; 134; 139; 147-148; 150). Prophetic psalms (Ps 2; 16; 22; 40; 68-69; 72; 87; 97; 110; 118).

Psalms of thanksgiving: For God's goodness to Israel (Ps 21; 46; 48; 65-66; 76; 81; 85; 98; 105; 124; 126; 129; 135-136; 149). For God's goodness to good people (Ps 23; 34; 36; 91; 100; 103; 107; 117; 121; 145-146). For God's mercies to individuals (Ps 9; 18; 30; 34; 40; 75; 103; 108; 118; 138; 144).

Superscriptions and authorship—
Of the 150 psalms, only 34 lack superscriptions of any kind (only 17 in the Septuagint). If the superscriptions refer to authorship, authors include Moses (Ps 90), David (Ps 3-9; 11-32; 34-41; 51-65; 68-70; 86; 101; 103; 108-110; 122; 124; 131; 133; 138-145), Solomon (Ps 72; 127), Asaph (Ps 50; 73-83), sons of Korah (Ps 42; 44-49; 84-85; 87-88), Heman (Ps 88), Ethan (Ps 89). Many of the psalm titles include musical terms in Hebrew, some designating ancient melodies, others preserving musical instructions. The meaning of some of these terms is uncertain or unknown. *See Music, Symbols Used in.*

PSALMS OF SOLOMON One of the pseudepigrapha, consisting of 18 psalms in imitation of the canonical psalms, probably written between 64 and 46 B.C.

PSALTERY *See Harp; Lyre.*

PSEUDEPIGRAPHA *(writing under a false name).* Books not in the Hebrew canon or the Apocrypha, ascribed to earlier biblical authors. They were written chiefly during the intertestamental, apostolic, and post-apostolic periods.

PTOLEMAIS [4767]. A seaport in Asher, formerly called Acco. Paul visits (Ac 21:7).
See Acco.

PTOLEMY Common name of the fifteen Macedonian kings of Egypt whose dynasty extended from the death of Alexander the Great in 323 B.C. to the murder of Ptolemy XV, son of Julius Caesar and Cleopatra in 30 B.C.; Ptolemy I, Soter (323-285 B.C.); Ptolemy II, Philadelphus (285-246 B.C.); LXX translated, Golden Age of Ptolemaic Egypt; Ptolemy III (c. 246-221 B.C.); Ptolemy IV, Philopator (221-203 B.C.); Ptolemy V,

Epiphanes (203-181 B.C.); Ptolemy VI, Philometor (181-146 B.C.); Ptolemy VII, Neos Philopator (146-117 B.C.); Ptolemy XI was not the last of the male line of Ptolemy I, killed by Alexandrians; Ptolemy XII (51-47 B.C.) fled to Rome; Ptolemy XIII had Cleopatra as his wife.

See Testaments, Time Between.

PUAH [7025, 7026, 7045] (perhaps from the Ugaritic meaning *girl*).
1. Son of Issachar (Ge 46:13; Nu 26:23, ftn; 1Ch 7:1).
2. A Hebrew midwife (Ex 1:15).
3. Father of Tola (Jdg 10:1).

PUBLIC OPINION Jesus inquires about (Mt 16:13; Mk 8:27; Lk 9:18).

Feared By:
Nicodemus (Jn 3:2), by Joseph of Arimathea (Jn 19:38), by the parents of the man who was born blind (Jn 9:21-22), by rulers who believed in Jesus but feared the Pharisees (Jn 12:42-43), by Herod (Mt 14:5), by chief priests (Mt 21:26; Mk 11:18, 32; Lk 12:12; 20:6), by those who feared to further persecute the disciples (Ac 4:21; 5:26).

Kings Influenced By:
Saul (1Sa 14:45; 15:24), David (2Ch 20:21), Hezekiah (2Ch 30:2), Zedekiah (Jer 38:19, 24-27), Herod (Mt 14:5; Ac 12:2-3), Pilate (Jn 19:6-13).

Concessions by:
By Paul in circumcising Timothy (Ac 16:3). By James and the Christian elders who required Paul to observe certain rites (Ac 21:18-26). By disciples who urged circumcision (Gal 6:12). By Peter and Barnabas with others (Gal 2:11-14).

Corrupt Yielding to:
By Herod in the case of John the Baptist (Mk 6:26), Peter (Ac 12:3). By Peter concerning Jesus (Mt 26:69-75; Mk 14:66-72; Lk 22:54-62). By Pilate (Mt 27:23-27; Mk 15:15; Lk 23:13-25; Jn 18:38-39; 19:4-16). By Felix and Festus concerning Paul (Ac 24:27; 25:9).

PUBLICANS *See Tax Collectors.*

PUBLIUS [4511] (*first*). Chief man in the island of Malta. Father of, healed by Paul (Ac 28:7-8).

PUDENS [4545] (*modest*). A Christian in Rome (2Ti 4:21).

PUHITES *See Puthites.*

PUITE [7027]. The descendants of Puah, of the tribe of Issachar (Nu 26:23, ftn; 1Ch 7:1). *See Puah.* The Masoretic Text has "through Puvah, the Punite."

PUL [7040].
1. King of Assyria. Forced tribute from Menahem, king of Israel (2Ki 15:19; 1Ch 5:26).
2. A place or tribe in Africa (Isa 66:19).

PULPIT NIV "platform" used primarily as a position from which to speak (Ne 8:4).

PULSE NIV "lentils" (2Sa 17:28) and "vegetables" (Da 1:12, 16). *See Vegetarians; Vegetation.*

PUNISHMENT [*2633, 3519, 3579, 4592, 5477, 5782, 5933, 6411, 6740, 7212, 7213, 9150, 9350, 1472, 1689, 1690, 3136, 4584, 5512]. Assumed for others (Ge 27:13; 1Sa 25:24; 2Sa 14:9; Mt 27:25).

See Affliction; Afflictions; Chastisement, From God; Fine; Judgments; Penalty; Retaliation; Wicked, Punishment of.

Death Penalty:
Shall not be remitted (Nu 35:31). In the Mosaic law the death penalty was inflicted for murder (Ge 9:5-6; Nu 35:16-21, 30-33; Dt 17:6), adultery (Lev 20:10; Dt 22:24), incest (Lev 20:11-12, 14), bestiality (Ex 22:19; Lev 20:15-16), sodomy (Lev 18:22; 20:13), promiscuity (Dt 22:21-24), rape of an engaged virgin (Dt 22:25), perjury (Zec 5:4), kidnapping (Ex 21:16; Dt 24:7), a priest's daughter who became a prostitute (Lev 21:9), witchcraft (Ex 22:18), offering human sacrifice (Lev 20:2-5), striking or cursing father or mother (Ex 21:15, 17; Lev 20:9), disobedience to parents (Dt 21:18-21), theft (Zec 5:3-4), blasphemy (Lev 24:11-14, 16, 23), Sabbath desecration (Ex 35:2; Nu 15:32-36), prophesying falsely or propagating false doctrines (Dt 13:1-10), sacrificing to false gods (Ex 22:20), refusing to abide by the decision of a court (Dt 17:12), treason (1Ki 2:25; Est 2:23), sedition (Ac 5:36-37).

Modes of execution of Death Penalty—
Burning (Ge 38:24; Lev 20:14; 21:9; Jer 29:22; Eze 23:25; Da 3:19-23), stoning (Lev 20:2, 27; 24:14; Nu 14:10; 15:33-36; Dt 13:10; 17:5; 22:21, 24; Jos 7:25; 1Ki 21:10; Eze 16:40), hanging (Ge 40:22; Dt 21:22-23; Jos 8:29), beheading (Mt 14:10; Mk 6:16, 27-28), crucifixion (Mt 27:35, 38; Mk 15:24, 27; Lk 23:33), the sword (Ex 32:27-28; 1Ki 2:25, 34, 46; Ac 12:2). Executed by the witnesses (Dt 13:9; 17:7; Ac 7:58), by the congregation (Nu 15:35-36; Dt 13:9).

Not inflicted on testimony of less than two witnesses (Nu 35:30; Dt 17:6; 19:15).

Minor Offenses:
Punishable by scourging (Lev 19:20; Dt 22:18; 25:2-3; Pr 17:10; 19:29; 20:30; Mt 27:26; Mk 15:15; Lk 23:16; Jn 19:1; Ac 22:24, 29), imprisonment (Ge 39:20; 40). *See Prison.* Confinement within limits (1Ki 2:26, 36-38).

By God:
According to deeds (Job 34:11; Ps 62:12; Pr 12:14; 24:12; Isa 59:13; Jer 17:10; Eze 7:3, 27; 16:59; 39:24; Zec 1:6; Mt 5:22; 16:27; 25:14-30; Mk 12:40; Lk 12:47-48; 2Pe 3:7).

See Judgment, According to Opportunity and Works.

See parables of the vineyard (Isa 5:1-7), landowner (Mt 21:33-41), talents (Mt 25:14-30), servants (Lk 12:47-48).

Imposed on children (Ex 34:7; Jer 31:29; La 5:7). Not imposed on children (Dt 24:16; 2Ch 25:4).

Delayed (Ps 50:21; 55:19; Pr 1:24-31; Ecc 8:11-13; Hab 1:2-4).

Design of, to secure obedience (Ge 2:17; Ex 20:3-5; Lev 26:14-39; Dt 13:10-11; 17:13; 19:19-20; 21:21-22; Pr 19:25; 21:11; 26:3). *See Judgments, Design of.*

No escape from (Ge 3:7-19; 4:9-11; Job 11:20; 34:21-22; Pr 1:24-31; 11:21; 16:5; 29:1; Isa 10:3; Jer 11:11; 15:1; 25:28-29; Eze 7:19; Am 2:14-16; 9:1-4; Zep 1:18; Mt 10:28; 23:33; Ro 2:3; 1Th 5:2-3; Col 3:25; Heb 2:3; 12:25-26; Rev 6:15-17).

Eternal (Isa 34:8-10; Da 12:2; Mt 3:12; 10:28; 18:8; 25:41, 46; Mk 3:29; Lk 3:17; Jn 5:29; Heb 6:2; 10:28-31; Rev 14:10-11; 19:3; 20:10).

See Wicked, Punishment of.

PUNISHMENT, EVERLASTING

Is taught in Scripture for those who reject God's love revealed in Christ (Mt 25:46; Da 12:2). The final place of everlasting punishment is called the "lake of fire" (Rev 19:20; 20:10, 14-15), also called "the second death" (Rev 14:9-11; 20:6). "Hell" in Scripture translates the word *Hades,* the unseen realm where the souls of all the dead are. *Gehenna* is the place of punishment of *Hades; paradise* is the place of blessing of *Hades* (Lk 16:19-31). The reason for eternal punishment is man's rejection of God's provision for the forgiveness of sin through the life and work of Jesus Christ, God's Son (Jn 3:16-18).

See Hades; Hell.

PUNITE *See Puite.*

PUNON [7044]. A city of Edom. A camping ground of the Israelites, in their forty years' wandering (Nu 33:42-43).

PUR [7052] (*lots*). Lot cast to destroy Jews in the time of Esther (Est 3:7; 9:24, 26). Feast of Purim is a Jewish festival commemorating the deliverance of the Jews from mass murder by Haman. *See Lot, The; Purim.*

PURAH [7242] (*branch* ISBE; *imposing* KB). A servant of Gideon (Jdg 7:10-11).

PURIFICATION [2633, 3198, 3200, 49, 50, 2752]. In studying the Mosaic law relating to purifications, it must be kept in mind that sin defiles. To keep this great truth constantly before the mind of the Israelites, specific ordinances concerning purifications were given to Moses; the purpose being, by this object lesson, to teach that sin defiles and only the pure in heart can see God. Therefore, certain incidents, such as eating that which had died of itself, touching the dead, etc., were signified as defiling, and definite ceremonies were prescribed for persons who were defiled. During the period of defilement, and when performing the ceremonies required of them, the defiled were expected to contemplate the defilement of sin and the need of purification of the heart.

Required:

Sanitary and symbolic (Ex 19:10, 14; Heb 9:10). For women after childbirth (Lev 12:6-8; Lk 2:22). After menstruation (Lev 15:19-33; 2Sa 11:4). After intercourse (Lev 15:16-18). For a discharge (Lev 15:4-18). For those cleansed of leprosy (Lev 14:8-9). For eating that which died of itself (Lev 17:15). For those who had slain in battle (Nu 31:19-24).

Of priests (Ex 29:4; 30:18-21; 40:12, 30-32; Lev 8:6; 16:4, 24, 26, 28; 22:3; Nu 19:7-8; 2Ch 4:6). Of Levites (Nu 8:6-7, 21). Of lepers. *See Leprosy.* Of the Jews before the Passover (Jn 11:55).

By fire, for things that resist fire (Nu 31:23). By blood (Ex 24:5-8; Lev 14:6-7; Heb 9:12-14, 19-22). By abstaining from sexual intercourse (Ex 19:15). By washing in water, parts of animal sacrifices (Lev 1:9, 13; 9:14; 2Ch 4:6).

Penalty to be imposed upon those who do not observe the ordinances concerning (Lev 7:20-21; 22:3; Nu 19:13, 20).

Water of (Nu 19:17-21; 31:23). Washing hands in water, symbolic of innocence (Dt 21:6; Ps 26:6). Traditions of the elders concerning (Mt 15:2; Mk 7:2-5, 8-9; Lk 11:38).

See Washing; Defilement; Sanitation and Hygiene; Spiritual Purification.

Practiced by:

Jacob (Ge 35:2). Moses (Ex 19:10, 14). Aaron (Ex 29:4; 30:18-21; 40:12, 30-32; Lev 8:6). Paul, to show his fidelity to the law (Ac 21:24, 26).

Figurative:

(Ps 26:6; 51:7; Eze 36:25). *See Spiritual Purification.*

PURIM [7052] (*lots*). A feast instituted to commemorate the deliverance of the Jews from the plot of Haman (Est 9:20-32). *See Annual Feasts; Lot, The; Pur.*

PURITY [*1338, 1405, 2341, 2342, 2348, 2627, 2633, 3196, 3197, 3198, 3200, 6034, 7058, 7727, 48, 49, 54, 55, 299, 2751, 2751, 2752, 2754, 4410]. A Christian virtue (1Ti 4:12; 5:22; Tit 1:15). Word of God pure (Ps 12:6; 19:8; 119:140).

Of the human heart (Ps 24:3-5; 65:3; Pr 15:26; 20:9; 21:8; 30:12; Isa 1:18, 25; 6:7; Mic 6:11; 1Ti 1:5; 2Ti 2:21-22; Heb 10:2).

Blessedness of (Mt 5:8). Prayer for (Ps 51:7; Da 12:10; Heb 9:13-14). Through divine discipline (Mal 3:2-3; Jn 15:2), the blood of Christ (Heb 9:13-14).

Commanded (1Ti 3:9; 5:22; 2Ti 1:3; 2:21-22; Jas 4:8; 1Pe 1:22). Meditation upon, commanded (Php 4:8).

Jesus our pattern in (1Jn 3:3). Exemplified by Paul (2Ti 1:3).

See Holiness; Sanitation and Hygiene; Spiritual Purification.

For symbolisms of purity, *See Colors, Figurative*

and Symbolic, White; Defilement; Purification; Washings.

PURPLE [760, 763, 9355, 10066, *4525, 4526, 4527*]. A color highly esteemed in ancient times; because of its costliness, it became a mark of distinction to wear robes of purple. Royalty was so dressed. The color included various shades between crimson and violet (Ex 25:4; 26:36; 28:15; 35:6; Jdg 8:26; 2Ch 2:14).

  See Colors, Figurative and Symbolic.

PURSE [3038, 3967, 7655, 7975, *964*]. A bag for holding money (Pr 1:14; 7:20; Hag 1:6; Lk 10:4).

PURTENANCE Entrails (Lev 1:9).

PURVEYOR Those providing supplies to Solomon (1Ki 4:7-19, 27).

PUT [*7033].
  1. Son of Ham (Ge 10:6; 1Ch 1:8).
  2. The descendants of Put, or the country inhabited by them; Put has also been taken to signify Egypt and is often associated with the Libyans (Isa 66:19, ftn; Eze 27:10; 30:5; 38:5; Jer 46:9; Na 3:9). See Libya.

PUTEOLI [*4541*] (Latin *rotten [sulfur] smell* or *well, spring*). Seaport of Italy, eight miles W of Naples; nearest harbor to Rome (Ac 28:13-14).

PUTHITES [7057] (*simple*). Family descended from Caleb (1Ch 2:50, 53).

PUTIEL [7034] (*he whom God [El] gives*). The father-in-law of Eleazar the priest (Ex 6:25).

PUVAH See Puah.

PYGARG See Ibex.

PYRAMIDS (possibly *pointed* [like a flame tongue, or a wheat tip]). Tombs with superstructures of triangular form made for the interment of royalty in Egypt. About eighty survive. See Ziggurat.

PYRRHUS [*4795*] (*fiery red*). Father of Sopater (Ac 20:4).

QUAIL [8513]. Miracle of, in the wilderness of Sin (Ex 16:13), Kibroth Hattaavah (Nu 11:31-32; Ps 105:40).

QUARANTANIA The mountain where according to tradition Satan tempted Jesus to worship him (Mt 4:8-10), Tell el-Sultan, a short distance W of OT Jericho.

QUARANTINE For prevention of the spread of disease. *See Sanitation and Hygiene.*

QUARRIES [1014+5217, 5024, 5825, 8696]. A place to remove building stone (Jos 7:5; 1Ki 5:17, 6:7; Ecc 10:9; Isa 51:1).

QUARTUS [*3181*] (*fourth [born]*). A Christian in Corinth (Ro 16:23).

QUATERNION (*four*). A squad of four soldiers (Ac 12:4).

QUEEN [1485, 1509, 4867, 4887, 4893, 4906, 8576, 8712, 10423, *999*]. The wife of a king (1Ki 11:19). Crowned (Est 1:11; 2:17). Divorced (Est 1:10-22). Sits on the throne with the king (Ne 2:6). Makes feasts for the women of the royal household (Est 1:9). Exerts an evil influence in public affairs. *See Jezebel.* Counsels the king (Da 5:10-12). Queen of Sheba visits Solomon (1Ki 10:1-13). Candace, of Ethiopia (Ac 8:27).

Queen Athaliah was the only independent female ruler of Israel or Judah. *See Athaliah.*

Queen of Heaven (Jer 7:18; 44:7-19, 25). *See Idolatry; Queen of Heaven.*

QUEEN OF HEAVEN Probably Ishtar, Babylonian female deity (Jer 7:18; 44:17-25). *See Idolatry.*

QUICKENING Coming to life. Of the church: By the Father (Ps 71:20; 80:18; Ro 4:17; 8:11; Eph 2:1; 1Ti 6:13), by the Holy Spirit (Jn 6:63; Ro 8:11; 2Co 3:6; 1Pe 3:18). *See Life; Regeneration; Resurrection.*

QUICKSANDS NIV "sandbars" (Ac 27:17). *See Sandbars.*

QUIRINIUS [*3256*]. Governor of Syria A.D. 6-9. His census of A.D. 6 at the request of the emperor Augustus is referred to in Ac 5:37. Another census, in which Joseph and Mary were registered, is mentioned in Lk 2:2. This may indicate Quirinius served an earlier term as governor of Syria and Luke mentions his "first" (NIV) and otherwise unknown census. Or the verse may be translated "This was *before* the census that took place while Quirinius was governor of Syria."

QUIVER [880, 9437] (from a root meaning *to hang, suspend*). For arrows (Ge 27:3; Isa 22:6).

RA Egyptian sun-god. Joseph married a daughter of the priest of On, center of the cult of Ra (Ge 41:45, 50). The plague of darkness was an insult against Ra (Ex 10:21-23).

RAAMAH [8309, 8311].
1. Son of Cush (Ge 10:7; 1Ch 1:9).
2. A place in Arabia (Eze 27:22).

RAAMIAH [8313] (*Yahweh has thundered*). An Israelite who returned from captivity with Zerubbabel (Ne 7:7).

RAAMSES *See Rameses.*

RABBAH [8051] (*chief, capital [city]*).
1. A town in Judah (Jos 15:60), not now identifiable.
2. Capital of Ammon, represented today by Amman, the capital of Jordan, twenty-two miles E of Jordan (Jos 13:25; 2Sa 11:1; 12:27-29; 1Ch 20:1; Jer 49:2-3). Subsequently captured by Ptolemy Philadelphus (285-247 B.C.), who changed its name to Philadelphia; became one of the cities of the Decapolis. Twice spelled "Rabbath" (Dt 3:11; Eze 21:20).

RABBATH-AMMON (*chief city of Ammon*). *See Rabbah.*

RABBI, RABBONI [4806, 4808] (*[my] great one, [my] master*). The title of a teacher (Mt 23:7-8; Jn 3:2). Ostentatiously used by the Pharisees (Mt 23:7). Used in addressing John the Baptist (Jn 3:26), in addressing Jesus (Mt 26:25, 49; Mk 9:5; 10:51; 11:21; 14:45; Jn 4:31; 9:2; 11:8 Jn 1:38, 49; 3:2; 6:25). Jesus called "Rabboni" (Jn 20:16). Forbidden by Jesus as a title to his disciples (Mt 23:8).

RABBIM *See Bath Rabbim.*

RABBIT [817]. Forbidden as food (Lev 11:6; Dt 14:7). *See Animals.*

RABBITH [8056] (*great*). A city in Issachar (Jos 19:20).

RABBLE [132+8044, 671]. (Ex 12:38; Nu 11:4; Mt 26:47; Ac 16:22; 17:5).

RABBONI [4808] (*[my] great one, [my] master*). Variant of Rabbi, the Aramaic word for Teacher (Jn 20:16).

RABMAG NIV "high official"; the Babylonian title of Nergal-Sharezer (Jer 39:3, 13).

RABSARIS NIV "chief officer"; a title used of Assyrian (2Ki 18:17) and Babylonian officials (Jer 39:3, 13).

RABSHAKEH NIV "field commander"; a title of a Assyrian officer sent by Sennacherib against Jerusalem. He speaks publicly in Hebrew to cause disloyalty to Hezekiah and a surrender of the city (2Ki 18:17-37; 19:4, 8; Isa 36; 37:4, 8).

RACA [4819] (*empty [headed]*). A term of contempt and scorn (Mt 5:22).

RACAL [8218] (*trade*). A city in Judah (1Sa 30:29).

RACE
1. Human. Unity of (Ge 3:20; Mal 2:10; Ac 17:26). *See Mankind.*
2. Foot race. Figurative: (Ps 19:5; Ecc 9:11; 1Co 9:24; Gal 5:7; Php 2:16; Heb 12:1-2).

RACHAB *See Rahab.*

RACHAL *See Racal.*

RACHEL [8162, 4830] (*ewe*). Daughter of Laban and wife of Jacob. Meets Jacob at the well (Ge 29:9-12). Jacob serves Laban fourteen years to secure her for his wife (Ge 29:15-30). Sterility of (Ge 29:31). Her grief in consequence of her sterility; gives her maid to Jacob in order to secure children in her own name (Ge 30:1-8, 15, 22-34). Later fertility of; becomes the mother of Joseph (Ge 30:22-25), of Benjamin (Ge 35:16-18, 24). Steals the household images of her father (Ge 31:4, 14-19, 33-35). Her death and burial (Ge 35:18-20; 48:7; 1Sa 10:2).

RADDAI [8099] (possibly *beating down* ISBE; *Yahweh rules* KB). Son of Jesse (1Ch 2:14).

RAGAU *See Reu.*

RAGUEL *See Jethro; Reuel, 2.*

RAHAB [8105, 8147, 4805, 4829] (*spacious, broad*).
1. A prostitute of Jericho who hid Israelites spies (Jos 2:1), mother of Boaz; great-grandmother of King David (Mt 1:5; Ru 4:18-21), shining example of faith (Heb 11:31).
2. Mythical monster of the deep; enemy of Yahweh (Job 9:13; Ps 89:10), applied to Egypt (Ps 87:4; Isa 30:7; 51:9).

RAHAM [8165] (*compassion*). Son of Shema (1Ch 2:44).

RAHEL *See Rachel.*

RAIL [2147]. Taunts of the enemy (Ps 102:6). *See Slander; Speaking or Speech, Evil.*

RAIMENT *See Cloth; Clothing; Dress; Garment; Robe.*

RAIN [1772, 1773, 4763, 4764, 4784, 4919, 5752, 8053, 8319, 8852, *536*, *1101*, *1104*, *2262*+ *3915*, *5624*]. Forty days of, at the time of the Flood (Ge 7:4, 10-12, 17-24). The plague of, upon Egypt (Ex 9:22-26, 33-34). Miraculously caused by Samuel (1Sa 12:16-19), by Elijah (1Ki 18:41-45). David delivered by (2Sa 5:17-21; Isa 28:21). North wind unfavorable to (Pr 25:23). Withheld as judgment (Dt 11:17; 28:24; 1Ki 8:35; 2Ch 7:13; Jer 3:3; Am 4:7; Zec 14:17). The earth shall no more be destroyed by (Ge 9:8-17). Sent by God (Dt 11:13-14; Job 37:6; Isa 30:23; Jer 5:24; 14:22). Contingent upon obedience (Lev 26:3-4; Dt 11:13-14). Prayer for (1Ki 8:35-36; 2Ch 6:26-27). Answer to prayer for, promised (2Ch 7:13-14; Zec 10:1). Withheld, in answer to prayer (Jas 5:17-18).

In Israel the rainy season extends from October to April; the dry season, from May to September. The early rain occurs in October and November (Ps 84:6; Isa 30:23; Jer 5:24), the latter rain in March and April (Dt 29:23; Pr 16:15; Jer 3:3; 5:24; Zec 10:1). Crops are therefore planted so that they will grow during the rainy season.

"Rain" is often used in the OT in a figurative sense. An abundance of rain denotes the rich blessing of Yahweh upon his people (Dt 28:12), lack of rain is a sign of God's displeasure (Dt 28:23-24). In Canaanite religion, Baal was conceived of as the god of rain, and was therefore ardently worshiped.

RAINBOW [8008, 2692]. A token that the earth shall never again be destroyed by flooding (Ge 9:8-16; Eze 1:28). *See Meteorology.*

Symbolic (Rev 4:3; 10:1).

RAISIN [862, 6694, 7540]. Preserved grapes. Given by Abigail to David (1Sa 25:18). Given to the famished Egyptian to revive him (1Sa 30:12). Given by Ziba to David (2Sa 16:1). Given to David at Ziklag (1Ch 12:40).

RAISING From the dead. *See Dead; Resurrection.*

RAKEM [8388] (*weaver, embroider*). A descendant of Makir, son of Manasseh (1Ch 7:16).

RAKKATH [8395] (*narrow place*). A fortified city in Naphtali (Jos 19:35), probably near the Sea of Galilee on the site of Tiberias.

RAKKON [8378] (*narrow place*). A city in Dan (Jos 19:46).

RAM [380, 4854, 8226, *730*] (As a proper name *high, exalted*).

1. The son of Hezron and an ancestor of Jesus (Ru 4:19; 1Ch 2:9-10). Called Aram (Mt 1:3-4; Lk 3:33).

2. The son of Jerahmeel (1Ch 2:25, 27).

3. An ancestor, probably of Elihu (Job 32:2).

4. A sheep. Skins of, used for the roof of the tabernacle (Ex 26:14; 39:34). Seen in Daniel's

vision (Da 8:3, 20). Used in sacrifice. *See Offerings.*

Trumpets made of the horns of. *See Horn; Trumpet.*

5. A weapon used to break down doors and gates. *See Battering Ram.*

RAMAH [8230, *4821*] (*elevated spot*).

1. A city allotted to Benjamin (Jos 18:25; Jdg 19:13). Attempted fortification of, by King Baasha; destruction of, by Asa (1Ki 15:17-22; 2Ch 16:1-6). People of, return from the Babylonian Captivity (Ezr 2:26; Ne 7:30; 11:33). Jeremiah imprisoned in (Jer 40:1). Prophecies concerning (Isa 10:29; Jer 31:15; Hos 5:8; Mt 2:18).

2. A city of S Judah allotted to the tribe of Simeon (Jos 19:8).

3. A city of Asher (Jos 19:29).

4. A city of Naphtali (Jos 19:36).

5. Also called Ramathaim. A city in the hill country of Ephraim (Jdg 4:5; 1Sa 1:1). Home of Elkanah (1Sa 1:1, 19; 2:11), and of Samuel (1Sa 1:19-20; 7:17; 8:4; 15:34; 16:13). David flees to (1Sa 19:18). Samuel dies and is buried in (1Sa 25:1; 28:3).

See Ramoth Gilead.

RAMATH *See Ramah, 2.*

RAMATH LEHI [8257] (*height [hill] of Lehi*). The place where Samson killed a thousand Philistines with the jawbone of a donkey (Jdg 15:17).

RAMATH MIZPAH [8256] (*height [hill] of Mizpah [watch tower]*). Northern boundary line of Gad (Jos 13:26). Also called Mizpah, Galeed, and Jegar Sahadutha (Ge 31:47-49).

RAMATHAIM-ZOPHIM, RAMATHAIM ZUPHIM (*two heights of Zophim*). *See Ramah, 5.*

RAMATHITE [8258] (*of Ramah*). Designation of Shimei, King David's overseer in charge of the vineyards (1Ch 27:27).

RAMESES [8314] (*Ra [pagan sun god] created him*).

1. Egyptian store city built by Israelites (Ex 1:11), possibly the modern San el-Habar in the NE part of the Delta.

2. The name of eleven Egyptian pharaohs, of whom Rameses II (c. 1301-1234 B.C.) was the most famous, many scholars holding that he was the pharaoh of the Exodus. Some of these pharaohs must have had at least an indirect influence on Israelite life, but none of them is mentioned in the OT.

RAMIAH [8243] (*Yahweh is exalted*). An Israelite in the time of Ezra who married a foreign wife (Ezr 10:25).

RAMOTH [8030, 8230] (height).

1. Ramoth in Gilead. See Ramoth Gilead.

2. Ramoth Negev. A place probably in the south of Simeon (Jos 19:8; 1Sa 30:27). See Ramah, 2.

3. A city of Issachar, allotted to the Levites (1Ch 6:73).

4. See Jeremoth, 6.

RAMOTH GILEAD [8240] (heights in Gilead). A city of Gad, and a city of refuge (Dt 4:43; Jos 20:8; 1Ch 6:80). One of Solomon's district governors at (1Ki 4:13). In the possession of the Syrians (1Ki 22:3). Besieged by Israel and Judah; Ahab slain at (1Ki 22:29-36; 2Ch 18). Recovered by Joram; Joram wounded at (2Ki 8:28-29; 9:14-15; 2Ch 22:5-6). Elisha anoints Jehu king at (2Ki 9:1-6).

RAMS' HORNS [3413, 8795]. See Shofar; Trumpet.

RAMS' SKINS Skins of sheep; used for clothing of shepherds and covering for the tabernacle (Ex 25:5).

RANSOM [4105, 4111, 7009, 7014, 7018, 8815, 519, 667, 3389]. Of a human life (Ex 21:30; 30:12; Job 36:18; Ps 49:7-8; Pr 6:35; 13:8; Hos 13:14).

Jesus as (Mt 20:28; Mk 10:45; 1Ti 2:5-6; Heb 9:15).

Figurative (Job 33:24; Isa 35:10; 51:10).

See Jesus the Christ, Redeemer; Savior, Saviour; Redemption.

RAPACITY Of the wicked (Lk 11:39; 20:14, 47; Jn 10:12; Ac 20:29; Gal 5:15; Jas 4:2; 1Pe 5:8). See Greed; Wicked.

RAPE [2256+6700+8886, 3359, 6700, 8711]. Law imposes death penalty for (Dt 22:25-27). Captives afflicted with (Isa 13:16; La 5:11; Zec 14:2).

Instances of: Dinah by Shechem (Ge 34:1-2). The servant of a Levite by Benjamites; tribe of Benjamin nearly exterminated by the army of the other tribes as punishment for (Jdg 19:22-30; 20:35). Tamar by Amnon; avenged in the death of Amnon at the hand of Absalom, Tamar's brother (2Sa 13:6-29, 32-33).

RAPHA, RAPHAH [8325, 8334, 8335] (possibly one healed).

1. Son of Benjamin (1Ch 8:2).

2. A descendant of Jonathan also called Rephaiah (1Ch 9:43) and Raphah (1Ch 8:37). See Rephaiah, 4.

3. An ancestor of certain Philistine warriors (2Sa 21:16, 20, 22; 1Ch 20:4, 6, 8). See Rephaites.

RAPHU [8336] (healed). The father of Palti, who was sent from the tribe of Benjamin to spy out the land of Canaan (Nu 13:9).

RAPTURE Theological term not used in the Bible. The imminent translation or removal from earth of the Church at the second coming of Christ (Mt 24:36-42; Mk 13:32; Ac 1:7, 11; 1Co 15:50-52; 1Th 4:14-18; Tit 2:13; 1Pe 3:12; Rev 1:7). Includes both living and dead (1Co 15:50-52; Php 3:20-21; 1Th 4:13-17; 1Jn 3:2). Followed by the marriage of the Church to Christ (Mt 25:1-10; 2Co 11:2; Eph 5:23, 32; Rev 19:6-9), believers being rewarded (Mt 25:19; 1Co 3:12-15; 2Co 5:10; 2Ti 4:8; 1Pe 5:2).

See Second Coming of Christ, The.

RAS SHAMRA (fennel mound). The modern name of the mound marking the site of the ancient city of Ugarit, located on the Syrian coast opposite the island of Cyprus; an important commercial center; destroyed by Sea Peoples who overran the area c. 1200 B.C.; reached the peak of prosperity in 1500-1200 B.C. Several hundred clay tablets, forming part of a scribal library, were found from 1929 through 1936; personal and diplomatic correspondence; business, legal, and governmental records; veterinary texts, and most importantly, religious literature. These throw a great deal of light upon Canaanite religion and culture, and Hebrew literary style; they show striking similarities between Canaanite and Hebrew systems of worship. They clarify our knowledge of the world in which Israel developed. See Texts, Ancient Near Eastern Non-Biblical Texts Relating to the Old Testament.

RASH [993, 5030, 6204]. Regulations for determining whether clean or unclean (Lev 13-14). See Disease.

RASHNESS [1051, 4362, 4439, 4554, 4637].(Ps 116:11; Pr 19:2). Admonitions against (Pr 25:8; Ecc 5:2; 7:9). Folly of (Pr 14:29; 29:20). Leads to poverty (Pr 21:5).

Instances of:

Moses, in slaying the Egyptian (Ex 2:11-12; Ac 7:24-25), when he struck the rock (Nu 20:10-12). Jephthah's vow (Jdg 11:31-39). Israel's vow to destroy the Benjamites (Jdg 21:1-23). Uzzah, in steadying the ark (2Sa 6:6-7). David, in his generosity to Ziba (2Sa 16:4, w 19:26-29). Rehoboam, in forsaking the counsel of the old men (1Ki 12:8-15). Josiah, in fighting against Neco (2Ch 35:20-24). Naaman, in refusing to wash in the Jordan (2Ki 5:11-12).

Peter, in cutting off the ear of Malchus (Mt 26:51; Mk 14:47; Lk 22:50). James and John, in desiring to call down fire on the Samaritans (Lk 9:54). Paul, in persisting to go to Jerusalem against the repeated admonitions of the Holy Spirit (Ac 21:4, 10-15). The centurion, in rejecting Paul's counsel (Ac 27:11).

RAT(S) [6572]. Forbidden as food (Lev 11:29), used as food (Isa 66:17). Images of (1Sa 6:4-5, 11, 18).

RAVEN [6854, 3165] (crow, raven). A black carnivorous bird (Pr 30:17; SS 5:11). Forbidden as

food (Lev 11:15; Dt 14:14). Preserved by Noah in the ark (Ge 8:7). Fed Elijah (1Ki 17:4-6). Cared for by divine providence (Lk 12:24).

RAVISHMENT *See Rape.*

RAZOR [4623, 9509] (*any instrument of iron*). Priests of Israel were not permitted to cut their beard (Lev 21:5). Nazirites could not use the razor as long as they were under vows (Nu 6:5).

READING [*606, 7924, 10637, *336, 342*]. Taught (Dt 6:9; 11:20).

READINGS, SELECT

Judah's Defense (Ge 44:18-34). Joseph Revealing His Identity (Ge 45:1-15). The Deliverance of the Israelites From Pharaoh (Ex 14:5-30). Song of Moses When Pharaoh and His Army Were Overthrown (Ex 15:1-19). David's Lament Over Absalom (2Sa 18:19-33). Lights and Shadows (Ru 1:1-22). Elijah's Miraculous Preservation (1Ki 17:1-16). Elisha and the Widow's Oil (2Ki 4:1-7). Naaman the Leper (2Ki 5:1-14). Esther's Triumph (Est 4:1-17; 7:1-10).

The Brevity of Life (Job 14:1-10). Nature's Testimony (Job 28:1-28). God's Challenge to Job (Job 38). The Beasts of the Field (Job 39).

The Righteous and the Wicked in Contrast (Ps 1). The Triumphant King (Ps 2). Mankind in Nature (Ps 8). Mankind in Extremity (Ps 18:1-19). Confidence in God (Ps 23). The King of Glory (Ps 24). The Glory of God (Ps 29). Our Refuge (Ps 46). The Majesty of God (Ps 77:13-20). The Joy of the Righteous (Ps 84). The State of the Glory (Ps 91). The New Song (Ps 98). The Majesty and Providence of God (Ps 104). In Captivity (Ps 137). The Omnipresence of God (Ps 139). Old Age (Ecc 12:1-7).

Christ's Kingdom Foreshadowed (Isa 35:1-10). The Omnipotence and Incomparableness of God (Isa 40:1-30). The Wrath of God (Am 9:1-6). The Majesty of God (Hab 3:3-13).

Mary's Magnificat (Lk 1:46-56). The Prophetic Blessing of Zechariah (Lk 1:67-80). The Beatitudes (Mt 5:1-16). God's Providence (Mt 6:26-34). Wise and Foolish Builders (Mt 7:21-27). The Good Samaritan (Lk 10:25-37). The Prodigal Son (Lk 15:11-32). The Raising of Lazarus (Jn 11:1-45). The Betrayal (Lk 22:47-62). The Resurrection (Lk 24:1-12).

Peter at Pentecost (Ac 2:1-36). Stephen's Defense (Ac 7). Paul and Silas in Prison (Ac 16:16-40). Paul on Mars' Hill (Ac 17:22-31). Paul Before Felix (Ac 24:1-27). Paul Before Agrippa (Ac 26:1-32). Love (1Co 13). The New Heaven and the New Earth (Rev 21:1-7). The River of Life (Rev 22:1-21).

REAIA *See Reaiah, 2.*

REAIAH [8025] (*Yahweh has seen*).
1. A man of Judah, son of Shobal (1Ch 4:2). Apparently called Haroeh (1Ch 2:52).
2. Son of Micah, a Reubenite (1Ch 5:5).

3. Ancestor of a family that returned to Jerusalem from captivity in Babylon (Ezr 2:47; Ne 7:50).

REAPING [5162, 7907, 7917, 9530, *2400, 2545*]. In ancient times done either by pulling up grain by roots or cutting with a sickle. The stalks are then bound into bundles and taken to threshing floor (Ps 129:7).

Laws concerning gleaning at the time of reaping (Lev 19:9-10; 23:22; Dt 24:19-20).

Figurative (Ps 126:6; Hos 10:12-13; Jn 4:35-38), of deeds that produce own harvest (Pr 22:8; Hos 8:7; 1Co 9:11; Gal 6:7-8).

REASONING [*9312, *1363, 3357*]. With God (Job 13:3, 17-28). God reasons with people (Ex 4:11; 20:5, 11; Isa 1:18; 5:3-4; 43:26; Hos 4:1; Mic 6:2).

Natural understanding (Da 4:36). To be applied to religion (1Co 10:15; 1Pe 3:15). Not a sufficient guide in human affairs (Dt 12:8; Pr 3:5; 14:12). Of the Pharisees (Lk 5:21-22; 20:5). Of Paul from the Scriptures (Ac 17:2; 18:4, 19; 24:25). The gospel cannot be explained by human wisdom (1Co 1:18-2:14).

See Investigation; Philosophy; Wisdom.

REBA [8064] (*fourth part*). A king of Midian. Slain by the Israelites (Nu 31:8; Jos 13:21).

REBECCA *See Rebekah.*

REBEKAH [8071, *4831*] (possibly *choice calf*). Daughter of Bethuel, grand-niece of Abraham (Ge 22:20-23). Becomes Isaac's wife (Ge 24:15-67; 25:20). Mother of Esau and Jacob (Ge 25:21-28; Ro 9:10). Passes as Isaac's sister (Ge 26:6-11). Displeased with Esau's wives (Ge 26:34-35). Prompts Jacob to deceive Isaac (Ge 27:5-29). Sends Jacob to Laban (Ge 27:42-46). Burial place of (Ge 49:31).

REBELLION [*5277, 5286, 5308, 5897, 6240, 6253, 7321, 7322, 10439, *538, 2060, 3334, 4177*]. Treasonable (Pr 17:11).

Instances of: Absalom (2Sa 15-18). Sheba (2Sa 20). Revolt of the ten tribes (1Ki 12:16-20; 2Ch 10; 13:5-12).

See Sin.

REBUKE [*1721, 1722, 3519, 8189, 9349, 9350, *1791, 1794, 2203*]. Cain rebukes God (Ge 4:13-14). Pharaoh rebukes Abraham for calling his wife his sister (Ge 12:18-19). Abimelech rebukes Abraham for a like offense (Ge 20:9-10). Abimelech rebukes Isaac for similar conduct (Ge 26:9-10). Isaac and Laban rebuke each other (Ge 31:26-42). Jacob rebukes Simeon and Levi for killing Hamor and Shechem (Ge 34:30). Reuben rebukes his brothers for their treatment of Joseph (Ge 42:22). Israelites rebuke Moses and tempt God (Ex 17:7). Deborah rebukes Israel in her poem (Jdg 5:16-23). David rebukes Joab for killing Abner (2Sa 3:28-31). Joab rebukes David for lamenting the death of Absalom (2Sa 19:5-7).

Jesus rebukes his disciples because of their unbelief (Mt 8:26; 14:31; 16:8-11; 17:17; Mk 4:40; Lk 8:25), for slowness of heart (Mt 15:16; 16:8-9, 11; Mk 7:18; Lk 24:25; Jn 14:9), for sleeping in Gethsemane (Mt 26:40; Mk 14:27), for forbidding children to be brought to him (Mt 19:14; Mk 10:14; Lk 18:16).

David prays to escape Yahweh's rebuke (Ps 6:1; 38:1). Do not rebuke a mocker (Pr 9:8), an older man (1Ti 5:1).

RECAB [8209] (probably *rider* or *horseman*, from *to mount, ride*).

1. Son of Rimmon. Murders Ish-Bosheth, son of Saul; put to death by David (2Sa 4:5-12).

2. Father of Jehonadab (2Ki 10:15, 23; 1Ch 2:55; Jer 35:6, 8, 16, 19). Ancestor of the Recabites (Jer 35).

3. Father of Malkijah (Ne 3:14).

RECABITE(S) [8211]. A family of Kenites descended from Recab, through Jonadab (1Ch 2:55; Jer 35:6). Commanded by Jonadab to drink no wine (Jer 35:6); perpetuation of the family promised as a reward (Jer 35).

See Abstinence; Nazirite(s).

RECAH [8212]. Unknown place in tribe of Judah (1Ch 4:12).

RECHAB *See Recab.*

RECHABITE(S) *See Recabite(s).*

RECHAH *See Recah.*

RECIPROCITY Returning good for good (Ro 15:27; 1Co 9:11; Gal 6:6). *See One Another.*

RECONCILIATION [557, 639, 1367, 2903, 2904].

Between People:

(Mt 5:23-26). Between Esau and Jacob (Ge 33:4, 11). Between Saul and David (1Sa 19:7). Between Pilate and Herod (Lk 23:12).

Between God and People:

Through atonement of animal sacrifices (Lev 8:15; Eze 45:15). After the seventy weeks of Daniel's vision (Da 9:24).

Through Christ (Ro 5:1, 10; 11:15; 2Co 5:18-21; Eph 2:15-18; Col 1:20-22; Heb 2:17).

See Atonement; Jesus the Christ, Mission of; Propitiation; Redemption.

RECONNAISSANCE Of Jericho (Jos 2:1-24), Bethel (Jdg 1:23), Laish (Jdg 18:2-10). *See Spies.*

RECORDER [4654]. *See Occupations and Professions.*

RECREATION *See Rest.*

RED [131, 137, 145, 1798, 2813, 6068, 8012, 9266, 135+6055, 2261, 4791, 4793, 4794]. Blood-like or blood-red color (Ex 25:5; 26:14; 35:7; Zec 1:8; Rev 6:4).

RED HEIFER Ashes of red heifer were used for removal of certain types of ceremonial uncleanness (Nu 19:9).

RED KITE A carnivorous bird, unclean for food (Dt 14:13).

RED SEA [3542+6068, 2261+2498]. "Sea of Reeds" in NIV ftns. The locusts that devastated Egypt destroyed in (Ex 10:19). Israelites cross; Pharaoh and his army drowned in (Ex 14; 15:1, 4, 11, 19; Nu 33:8; Dt 11:4; Jos 2:10; 4:23; 24:6-7; Jdg 11:16; 2Sa 22:16; Ne 9:9-11; Ps 66:6; 78:13, 53; 106:7-11, 22; 136:13-15; Isa 43:16-17; Ac 7:36; 1Co 10:1-2; Heb 11:29). Israelites camp by (Ex 14:2, 9; Nu 14:25; 21:4; 33:10-11; Dt 1:40; 2:1-3). Boundary of the promised land (Ex 23:31). Solomon builds ships on (1Ki 9:26).

REDEEMED, THE [1457, 1460, 7009, 60, 1973, 3390, 3391+4472]. (Isa 35:9; 51:11; Mt 8:11; Rev 5:9; 7:9; 14:4; 19:6).

REDEEMER [1457]. *See Jesus the Christ, Savior; Redemption.*

REDEMPTION [1453, 1460, 7009, 7012, 7014, 7017, 667, 3391] (*to tear loose; a ransom*). Deliverance from the enslavement of sin and release to a new freedom by the sacrifice of the Redeemer, Jesus Christ. The death of Christ is the redemptive price. The word contains both the ideas of deliverance and the price of that deliverance, or ransom (Ro 3:24; Gal 3:13; Eph 1:7; 1Pe 1:18-19).

Of Person or Property:

(Ex 13:13; Lev 25:25-34; 27:2-33; Ro 4:3-10). Redemption money paid to priests (Nu 3:46-51). Of the firstborn (Ex 13:13; 34:20; Lev 27:27; Nu 3:40-51; 18:15-17).

Of Land:

(Lev 27:19-20; Jer 32:7). In Hebrew society, any land that was forfeited through economic distress could be redeemed by the nearest of kin. If not so redeemed, it returned to its original owner in the Year of Jubilee (Lev 25:24-34).

Of Our Souls:

(Ps 111:9; 130:7). Through Christ (Mt 20:28; Mk 10:45; Lk 2:38; Ac 20:28; Ro 3:24-26; 1Co 1:30; 6:20; 7:23; Gal 1:4; 2:20; 4:4-5; Eph 1:7; 5:2; Col 1:14, 20-22; 1Ti 2:6; Tit 2:14; Heb 9:12, 15; 1Pe 1:18-19; Rev 5:9-10).

See Atonement; Ransom; Redeemer.

REED [109, 286, 6068, 7866, 2812]. A water plant (Isa 19:6-7; 35:7; Jer 51:32). Used as a measuring device of six cubits (Eze 40:3-8; 41:8; 42:16-19; 45:1; Rev 11:1; 21:15-16). Mockingly given to Jesus as a symbol of royalty (Mt 27:29). Jesus struck with (Mt 27:30; Mk 15:19).

Figurative of weakness (1Ki 14:15; 2Ki 18:21; Isa 36:6; 42:3; Eze 29:6; Mt 11:7; 12:20).

REEDS, SEA OF *See Red Sea.*

REELAIAH [8305]. A returned captive from Babylon (Ezr 2:2).

REFINING [2423, 7671, *1507*, *4792*]. The process of eliminating by fire the dross of metals. Of gold (1Ch 28:18). Of silver (1Ch 29:4). Of wine (Isa 25:6).

Figurative: Of the corrective judgments of God (Isa 1:25; 48:10; Jer 9:7; Zec 13:9; Mal 3:2-3). Of the purity of the word of God (Ps 18:30; 119:140).

REFUGE, CITIES OF [*5236]. *See Cities of Refuge.*

REFUGEE SLAVES Laws concerning (Dt 23:15-16). Onesimus (Phm 1). *See Servant.*

REGEM [8084] (*friend*). Son of Jahdai (1Ch 2:47).

REGEM-MELECH [8085] (*friend of king,* possibly *chief of troops of the king*). A captive sent as a messenger from the Jews in Babylon to Jerusalem (Zec 7:2).

REGENCY *See Deputy.*

REGENERATION The new birth, the inner recreating of fallen human nature by the gracious working of the Holy Spirit. It changes human disposition from godlessness, lawlessness, rebellion, self-seeking, and unbelief to a desire to love and serve God.

Necessity of (Jer 13:23; Mt 12:33-35; 18:3; Mk 10:15; Lk 18:17; Jn 3:3, 5; Tit 3:5-6).

Parables of (Mt 13:23, 33; Mk 4:20, 26-29; Lk 13:21).

Also Called:

Born again or born from above (Jn 3:3-8; 1Pe 1:2-3, 22-23). Born of God (Jn 1:12-13, 16; Jas 1:18; 1Jn 2:27, 29; 3:9, 14; 4:7; 5:1, 4-5, 11-12, 18). Born by the Spirit (Jn 3:5-6; Gal 4:29), through the Holy Spirit (Eze 12:10; Jn 3:5-8; 1Co 12:13; 2Th 2:13; 1Pe 1:2-3, 22-23). Circumcision of the heart (Dt 29:4; 30:6; Eze 44:7, 9; Ro 2:28; Col 2:11-13). Change of heart (Ps 51:2, 7, 10; Jer 24:7; 31:33-34 w Heb 8:10-11; Jer 32:28-40; Eze 11:19-20; 18:31; 36:26-27, 29; Ro 12:2). New creature (2Co 5:17; Gal 6:15; Eph 4:22-24; Col 3:9-10). Spiritual cleansing (Jn 15:3; Ac 15:9; 1Co 6:11). Spiritual illumination (Jn 6:44-45; 8:12; Ac 26:18; 1Co 2:11-16; 2Co 4:6; Eph 5:14; Heb 10:16). To make spiritually alive (Heb 6:21). Spiritual resurrection (Jn 5:24; Ro 6:3-23; 8:2-4; Gal 2:20).

Other Scriptures Related to:

(1Ki 8:58; Ps 36:9; 65:3; 68:18; 110:3; Pr 4:23; 12:28; 14:27; Isa 1:16-17, 25; 4:4; 12:3; 26:12; 32:3-4, 15, 17; 35:5-6; 42:16; 43:7; 44:3-5; 55:1-3; Jer 17:13-14; 24:7; 31:3; 33:6; Eze 16:9; Lk 1:16-17; Jn 4:10, 14; 10:9-10; 13:8; 17:2; Ac 2:38, 47; 3:26; 11:17, 21; 16:14; Ro 7:6, 24; 15:16; 1Co 1:9, 24, 30; 3:6-7, 9; 15:10; 2Co 1:21-22; 3:3, 18;

Php 1:6; Heb 4:12; Jas 5:19-20; 1Pe 2:3, 9; 2Pe 1:3-4).

See Atonement; Conversion; Reconciliation; Redemption; Righteous; Salvation; Sanctification; Sin, Forgiveness of.

REGICIDE (*murder of a king.*) Of Ehud (Jdg 3:16-23). Of Saul (2Sa 1:16). Of Ish-Bosheth (2Sa 4:5-8). Of Nadab (1Ki 15:27-29). Of Elah (1Ki 16:9-11). Of Joram (2Ki 9:24). Of Ahaziah (2Ki 9:27). Of Joash (2Ki 12:20-21). Of Amaziah (2Ki 14:19-20). Of Zechariah (2Ki 15:10). Of Shallum (2Ki 15:14). Of Pekahiah (2Ki 15:25). Of Pekah (2Ki 15:30). Of Sennacherib (2Ki 19:36-37; Isa 37:37-38).

See Homicide.

REGISTRATION [3509, 4180, 5918, 7212, *616*]. Of citizens (Isa 4:3). *See Census.*

REHABIAH [8152, 8153] (*Yahweh has enlarged*). Son of Eliezer (1Ch 23:17; 24:21; 26:25).

REHOB [8149, 8150] (*broad, wide [place, market]*).
1. Father of Hadadezer, king of Zobah (2Sa 8:3, 12).
2. A Levite who sealed the covenant with Nehemiah (Ne 10:11).
3. A town in northern Israel. The limit of the investigation made by the twelve spies (Nu 13:21). Possessed by the Syrians (2Sa 10:6, 8). Called Beth Rehob (2Sa 10:6).
4. A town of Asher (Jos 19:28).
5. A Levitical city of Asher (Jos 19:30; 21:31; 1Ch 6:75). Canaanites not driven from (Jdg 1:31).

REHOBOAM [8154, *4850*] (*[my] people will enlarge, expand*). Successor to Solomon as king (1Ki 11:43; 2Ch 9:31). Refuses to reform abuses (1Ki 12:1-15; 2Ch 10:1-15). Ten tribes, under the leadership of Jeroboam, who successfully revolt from (1Ki 12:16-24; 2Ch 10:16-19; 11:1-4). Builds fortified cities; is temporarily prosperous (2Ch 11:5-23). Invaded by the king of Egypt and despoiled (1Ki 14:25-28; 2Ch 12:1-12). Death of (1Ki 14:31; 2Ch 12:16). Genealogy and descendants of (1Ch 3; Mt 1:7).

REHOBOTH [8151] (*broad, wide [places, markets]*).
1. A city built by Asshur (Ge 10:11).
2. A city of the Edomites (Ge 36:37; 1Ch 1:48).
3. The name given to a well dug by Isaac (Ge 26:22).

REHUM [8156, 10662] (*[he] is compassionate*).
1. A captive who returned to Jerusalem from Babylon (Ezr 2:2). Called Nehum (Ne 7:7).
2. An official who wrote a letter to Artaxerxes, influencing him against the Jews (Ezr 4:8-9, 17, 23).
3. A Levite who repaired part of the wall of Jerusalem (Ne 3:17).

4. A Jew of the Exile who signed the covenant with Nehemiah (Ne 10:25).

5. A priest who returned to Jerusalem from the Captivity in Babylon (Ne 12:3).

REI [8298] *(friendly or [my] friend)*. An Israelite loyal to David at the time of the usurpation of Adonijah (1Ki 1:8).

REINS KJV word for internal parts; kidneys as the seat of the emotions (Ps 7:9; 26:2; Jer 17:10; Job 19:27). *See Heart; Kidney.*

REJECTION [*2396, 4415, 5540, 5759, 6073, 6136, 6440, *119*, *578*, *627*, *723*]. Of God (1Sa 8:7; 10:19; 2Ki 17:15; Lk 7:30). *See God, Rejected.*

Of Israel by God (Nu 14:12, 26-37; 2Ki 17:20; Jer 6:30; 7:29; 14:19; La 5:22). Of Saul by God (1Sa 15:23, 26).

Of Jesus. *See Jesus the Christ, Rejected.*

REKEM [8389, 8390] *(friendship)*.

1. A king of the Midianites, slain by the Israelites (Nu 31:8; Jos 13:21).

2. A son of Hebron (1Ch 2:43-44).

3. A city in Benjamin (Jos 18:27).

RELEASE [*3655, 5927, 5929, 6142, 7337, 8938, *668*, *2934*, *3395*]. Year of: *See Jubilee; Sabbatic Year.*

RELENT [5714, 8740]. God relents, or changes his mind, in response to change in his people (Jer 18:5-10; 26:1-6, 12-13, 17-19). In response to the intercession of Moses, when Israel sinned with the golden calf (Ex 32:11-14); of Amos (Am 7:1-6). Because of his covenant love (Ps 106:44-45; Joel 2:13-14; Jnh 3:8-4:2).

Requests for God to relent (Job 6:29; Ps 90:13-16).

God will not relent when his people deserve his judgment (Jer 4:27-28; Eze 24:14).

See Repentance.

RELIGION [*1272*, *2355*, *2579*].

False: (Dt 32:31-33).

See Idolatry; Intolerance; Teachers, False.

Family: *See Family.*

National:

Supported by taxes (Ex 30:11-16; 38:26). Priests supported by the state (1Ki 18:19; 2Ch 11:13-15). Subverted by Jeroboam (1Ki 12:26-33; 2Ch 11:13-15). Idolatrous established by Jeroboam (1Ki 12:26-33).

Natural:

(Job 12:7-16; 37:1-24; Ps 8:1-9; 19:1-6; Ac 14:17; 17:23-28; Ro 1:18-20; 10:16-18). *See Revivals.*

True, As Presented By:

Jesus (Mt 22:36-40). In the "Sermon on the Mount": True blessedness (Mt 5:2-16), fulfillment of the law (Mt 5:17-48), "acts of righteousness" (Mt 6:1-18), service and treasure (Mt 6:19-21),

judgment (Mt 7:1-6), asking (Mt 7:7-11), the "golden rule" (Mt 7:12), wholehearted commitment to God (Mt 7:13-29; Mt 22:26-35).

Paul (Ro 8:18; 10:1-13; 12:1-21; Gal 5:22-25; 1Th 5:15-23). James (Jas 1:27; 2:8-26). Peter (1Pe 2:5-9). Jude (Jude 20-21).

See Blessings, Spiritual; Commandments and Statutes, Of God; Duty; Graces; Regeneration; Repentance; Sanctification; Sin, Forgiveness of.

Instances of Properly Religious Persons:

Abel (Ge 4:4-8; Heb 11:4). Noah (Ge 6-9). Abraham (Ge 12:1-8; 15; 17; 18:22-33). Jacob (Ge 28:10-22; 32:24-32). Moses (Ex 3:2-22; Dt 32-32). Jethro (Ex 18:12). Joshua (Jos 1). Gideon (Jdg 6-7). Samuel (1Sa 3). David. *See Psalms.* Solomon (1Ki 5:3-5; 2Ch 6). Jehu (2Ki 10:16-30). Hezekiah (2Ki 18:3-7; 19:14-19). Jehoshaphat (2Ch 17:3-9; 19-20). Jabez (1Ch 4:9-10). Asa (2Ch 14-15). Josiah (2Ki 22-23). Daniel (Da 6:4-22). The three Hebrews (Da 3). Zechariah (Lk 1:13, 67-79). Simeon (Lk 2:25-35). Anna the prophetess (Lk 2:36-37). The centurion (Lk 7:1-10). Cornelius (Ac 10). Eunice and Lois (2Ti 1:5).

See for additional instances John, Paul, Peter, Simon, Stephen, and other apostles and disciples, also each of the prophets.

RELIGIOUS [2504, *1273*, *2038*, *2580*, *3310*].

Coercion:

(Ex 22:20; 2Ch 15:12-15; Da 3:2-6; 6:26-27). *See Intolerance.*

Revivals:

(Zec 8:20-23). Prayer for (Hab 3:2). Prophecies concerning (Isa 32:15; Joel 2:28; Mic 4:1-8). *See Revivals.*

Testimony:

(Ps 18:49; 22:22; 26:12; 34:8-9; Isa 45:24; 1Co 13:1; Rev 12:11). *See Testimony, Religious.*

REMALIAH [8248] *(Yahweh has adorned)*. Father of Pekah, king of Israel (2Ki 15:25, 27, 30; 16:1, 5; 2Ch 28:6; Isa 7:1, 4; 8:6).

REMETH [8255] *(heights)*. A city in Issachar (Jos 19:17-21), probably, Ramoth (1Ch 6:73), and Jarmuth (Jos 21:29).

REMMON *See Rimmon, 2.*

REMMON-METHOAR *See Rimmon, 3.*

REMNANT [3856, 7129, 8636, 8637, 8642, *2905*, *3307*, *5698*].

1. People who survived political or military crises (Jos 12:4; 13:12).

2. Spiritual core of Israel who would survive God's judgment and become the seed of the new people of God (Isa 10:20-23; 11:11-12; Jer 32:38-39; Zep 3:13; Zec 8:12).

REMORSE [*3564*]. (Pr 1:25-27). Of the promiscuous (Pr 5:7-13). Of the lost (Lk 13:28).

Of the wicked (Pr 28:1; Isa 2:19; 57:20-21; Eze 7:16-18, 25-26). Of Israelites (Eze 33:10). Of believers (1Jn 3:20).

Instances of: David (Ps 31:10; 38:2-6; 51:1-19). Isaiah (Isa 6:5). Jeremiah (La 1:20). Peter (Mt 26:75). Judas (Mt 27:3-5). The Jews (Ac 2:37). Paul (Ac 9:6).

See Conviction, of Sin; Penitent; Repentance; Sin, Confession of.

REMPHAN *See Rephan.*

RENDING [7973]. Of garments, a token of affliction (Ge 37:29, 34; 44:13; Nu 14:6; Jdg 11:35; 2Sa 1:2, 11; 3:31; 13:19, 31; 15:32; 2Ki 2:12; 5:8; 6:30; 11:14; 19:1; 22:11, 19; Ezr 9:3, 5; Job 1:20; 2:12; Isa 36:22; 37:1; Jer 41:5; Mt 26:65; Ac 14:14).

Figurative (Joel 2:13). Symbol of dividing of a kingdom (1Sa 15:27-28).

RENTING [*1686, 3637*]. Land (Mt 21:33-41; Lk 20:9-16). Houses (Ac 28:30).

RENUNCIATION (Php 3:7-8). Of self for others, exemplified, by Moses (Ex 32:32), Jesus (Php 2:7), Paul (Ro 9:3; 2Co 13:7). Of self for Christ (Mt 16:25; Lk 14:26-33; 17:33; Jn 12:25). Of business for Christ (Mt 4:20; 9:9; Mk 1:18-20; 2:14; Lk 5:27-28).

Of possessions for Christ (Mt 19:21-29; Mk 10:21-30; Lk 18:22-30). Of one's all for Christ, illustrated by parable (Mt 13:44-46).

Of the will, to the Father, exemplified by Jesus (Mk 14:36; Lk 22:42; Jn 5:30; 6:38).

See Self-Denial.

REPENTANCE [4044, 5714, 8740, 8746, *3564, 3566, 3567*]. (Ps 34:14, 18; Isa 22:12).

Exhortations to:
(Pr 1:22-23; Jer 6:16-18; 7:3; 26:3; Hos 6:1; 14:1-3; Am 5:4-6; Mt 3:2).

Commanded (Dt 32:29; 2Ch 30:6-9; Job 36:10; Isa 22:12; 31:6; 44:22; 55:6-7; Jer 3:4, 12-14, 19, 22; 18:11; 25:5-6; 26:13; 35:15; Eze 12:1-5; 14:6; 18:30-32; 33:10-12, 14-16, 19; Da 4:27; Hos 10:12; 14:1-2; Joel 1:14; 2:12-13, 15-17; Am 4:12; Jnh 3:8-9; Hag 1:7; Zec 1:3; Mt 4:17; Mk 1:4, 15; 6:12; Lk 3:3; Ac 2:38; 3:19; 8:22; 17:30; Rev 2:5, 16; 3:2-3, 19).

Source:
Gift of God (2Ti 2:25). Gift of Christ (Ac 5:31). Goodness of God leads to (Ro 2:4). Tribulation leads to (Dt 4:30; 30:1-3; 1Ki 8:33-50; 2Ch 6:36-39; Job 34:31-32).

Condition:
Of forgiveness (Lev 26:40-42; Dt 4:29-31; 30:1-3, 8; 1Ki 8:33-50; 2Ch 6:36-39; 7:14; Ne 1:9; Job 11:13-15; 22:23; Ps 34:18; Pr 28:13; Isa 55:7; Jer 3:4, 12-14, 19; 7:5-7; 18:7-8; 36:3; Eze 18:21-23, 27-28, 30-31; Am 5:6; Mal 3:7; Mt 5:4; Lk 13:1-5; 1Jn 1:9). Of divine favor (Lev 26:40-42; 2Ch 7:14; Isa 57:15).

Foretold:
Of Israel (Jer 50:4-5; Eze 11:18-20; Hos 3:5; Zec 12:10). Universal (Ps 22:27; Ro 14:11).

Rewards of:
(Isa 59:20; Pr 1:23; Jer 7:3, 5, 7; 24:7; Eze 18:21-23, 27-28).

Preached by:
John the Baptist (Mt 3:2, 7-8; Mk 1:4, 15; Lk 3:3). Jesus (Mt 4:17; Mk 1:15; Lk 5:32). Peter (Ac 2:38, 40; 3:19; 8:22). Paul (Ac 17:30; 20:21; 26:20). The apostles (Mk 6:12).

To be preached to all nations (Lk 24:47). Joy in heaven over (Lk 15:1-10).

Unavailing, to Israel (Nu 14:39-45), to Esau (Heb 12:16-17).

Attributed to God:
God relents, or changes his mind, in response to change in his people (Ge 6:6-7; Ex 32:14; Dt 32:36; Jdg 2:18; 1Sa 15:11, 35; 2Sa 24:16; 1Ch 21:15; Ps 106:45; 110:4; 135:14; Jer 15:6; 18:1-10; 26:3; 42:10; Joel 2:13; Am 7:3, 6; Jnh 3:9-10). *See Relent.*

God will not repent (Nu 23:19; 1Sa 15:29; Ps 110:4; Ro 11:29).

Exemplified:
By Job (Job 7:20-21; 9:20; 13:23; 40:4; 42:5-6), David (Ps 32:5; 38:3-4, 18; 40:12; 41:4; 51:1-4, 7-17), the Israelites (Nu 21:7; 2Ch 29:6; Jer 3:21-22, 25; 14:7-9, 20; 31:18-19; La 3:40-41), Daniel for the Jews (Da 9:5-7; 10:12), the prodigal son (Lk 15:17-20).

Instances of:
Joseph's brothers, for their ill treatment of Joseph (Ge 42:21; 50:17-18). Pharaoh, for his hardness of heart (Ex 9:27; 10:16-17). Balaam, for his spiritual blindness (Nu 22:34, w 22:24-35). Israelites, for worshiping the golden calf (Ex 33:3-4), for their murmuring on account of the lack of bread and water, when the plague of fiery serpents came upon them (Nu 21:4-7), when rebuked by an angel for not expelling the Canaanites (Jdg 2:1-5), for their idolatry, when afflicted by the Philistines (Jdg 10:6-16; 1Sa 7:3-6), for asking for a king (1Sa 12:16-20), in the time of Asa, under the preaching of Azariah (2Ch 15:1-15), under the preaching of Oded (2Ch 28:9-15), under the influence of Hezekiah (2Ch 30:11). Achan, for his theft (Jos 7:19-21). Saul, at the reproof of Samuel for not destroying the Amalekites (1Sa 15:24, w 15:6-11). Job (Job 42:6).

David, at the rebuke of Nathan, the prophet (2Sa 12:11, 13, w 12:7-14; Ps 32:5; 38:3-4, 18; 40:12; 41:4; 51:1-4, 7-17), for numbering Israel (2Sa 24:10, 17). The psalmist (Ps 106:6; 119:59-60, 176; 130:1-3). *See Psalms, Topically Arranged.*

Rehoboam, when his kingdom was invaded, and Jerusalem besieged (2Ch 12:1-12). Isaiah (Isa 6:5). Hezekiah, for his pride (Isa 38:15), at the time of his sickness (2Ch 32:26), when reproved by the prophet Micah (Jer 26:18-19). Ahab, when reproved by Elijah for his idolatry (1Ki 21:27). Jehoahaz (2Ki 13:4). Josiah, when he heard the law which had been discovered in the temple (2Ki 22:11-20). Manasseh, when he was carried captive to Babylon by the king of Assyria (2Ch 33:12-13). Jonah, after his punishment (Jnh 2:2-9). The Ninevites, at the preaching of Jonah (Jnh 3:5, 9-10).

The Jews of the Exile, at the dedication of the temple (Ezr 6:21; 9:4, 6, 10, 13-14), for their idolatrous marriages (Ezr 10), for their oppressive usury (Ne 5:1-13), after hearing the law expounded by Ezra (Ne 9:1-3), under the preaching of Haggai (Hag 1).

The Jews under the preaching of John the Baptist (Mt 3:6). The woman who anointed Jesus with oil (Lk 7:37-48). The disobedient son (Mt 21:29). The prodigal son (Lk 15:17-21). The tax collector (Lk 18:13). Peter, of his denial of Jesus (Mt 26:75; Mk 14:72; Lk 22:62). The Ephesians, under the preaching of Paul (Ac 19:18).

See Conviction, of Sin; Penitence; Remorse; Sin, Confession of; Sin, Forgiveness of.

REPETITION [*606, 1819, 6218, 8049, 9101, *4625*]. In Prayers: *See Babbling; Prayer, Persistence in.*

REPHAEL [8330] (*God [El] heals*). A gatekeeper of the temple in the time of David (1Ch 26:7).

REPHAH [8338] (possibly *rich* IDB; *easy [life]* KB). A grandson of Ephraim (1Ch 7:25).

REPHAIAH [8341] (*Yahweh heals*).
1. A descendant of David (1Ch 3:21).
2. A Simeonite captain (1Ch 4:42).
3. Son of Tola, of the tribe of Issachar (1Ch 7:2).
4. A descendant of Jonathan (1Ch 9:43). Also called Raphah (1Ch 8:37).
5. Governor over half of Jerusalem in the time of Nehemiah (Ne 3:9).

REPHAIM *See Rephaites.*

REPHAIM, VALLEY OF [8329]
(*sunken, powerless ones [giants]* BDB; possibly *shades, ghosts of the dead [giants]* KB). Fertile plain S of Jerusalem, three miles from Bethlehem (Jos 15:8; 18:16; 2Sa 5:18, 22; 23:13; 1Ch 11:15; 14:9; Isa 17:4-5).

REPHAITES [8328] (*mighty*). Giant people who lived in Canaan even before Abraham's time (Ge 14:5; 15:20; Dt 2:11, 20; 3:11, 13; Jos 12:4; 13:12; 17:15; 1Ch 20:4). *See Giants.*

REPHAN [*4818*]. A pagan god noted in Ac 7:43 quoting the LXX (Am 5:26, ftn). In Am 5:26, the NIV translates the Hebrew word "pedestal," though the ftn offers the proper name "Kaiwan." The Egyptian *repa* and the Assyrian "Kaiwan" both refer to the planet Saturn, which may harmonize the two texts. *See Chiun.*

REPHIDIM [8340] (possibly *supports, rests* BDB; *resting place* KB). Encampment of Is-

raelites in the wilderness; there Moses struck a rock to secure water (Ex 17:1-7; 19:2), battle with Amalekites took place there (Ex 17:8-16).

REPORTS [*606, 995, 1804, 1819, 1821, 5583, 5989, 9019, 9048, 9051, 9053, *334, 550, 3364*]. Majority and minority, of spies (Nu 13:26-33; 14:6-10).

REPROBACY Admonitions against (2Co 13:5-7; Heb 3:10-12, 17-19; 6:4-9; 12:15-17). Curses denounced against (Dt 28:15-68; 31:17-18; Isa 65:12; Hos 9:12; Mk 3:29; Heb 10:26-31). *See Reprobates.*

REPROBATE Moral corruption, unfitness, disqualification, disapproved (Ro 1:28; 1Co 9:27). *See Reprobacy; Reprobates.*

REPROBATES (Jer 6:30; Ro 1:21-32; 2Ti 3:8; 1Jn 5:16; Jude 4-13; Rev 22:4).
Described as:
Men of corrupt minds (2Ti 3:8), vessels of wrath (Ro 9:22). Moral insensibility (Isa 22:12-14; 28:13; 29:9-12; Mt 13:14-15; 15:14; Ro 11:7-8). Rejected of God (Ps 81:11-12; Pr 1:24-28; Jer 6:30; 7:16; 15:1; Hos 5:6; Mt 15:14; 25:8-13; Lk 13:24-28; 14:24; Jn 10:26; Ro 1:21-26, 28; 2Th 2:10-11; Heb 3:10-12, 17-19; 6:4-8; 10:26-31). Admonitions against (Heb 12:15-17).

Instances of:
Antediluvians (Ge 6:5-7). Sodomites (Ge 13:13; 19:13; Jude 7). Jannes and Jambres (2Ti 3:8). Eli's house (1Sa 3:14). Saul (1Sa 15:23; 16:14; 18:12; 28:15). Judas (Jn 17:12). Angels (Jude 6). Antichrist (2Th 2:7-12).
In Israel (Nu 14:26-48; Dt 1:42; Isa 6:9-10; Heb 3:10-12, 17-19; Jude 5). In the Church (2Co 13:5-7; Heb 3:10-12, 17-19; 6:4-9; Jude 4-13).
See Obduracy; Reprobacy.

REPRODUCTION *See Propagation.*

REPROOF, REPROVE [3519].
Commanded:
(Lev 19:17; Ps 141:5; Pr 9:7-8; 10:17; 26:5; Mt 18:15-17; Lk 17:3-4; Eph 5:11; 1Th 5:14, 20; 2Ti 4:2; Tit 1:13; Heb 3:13).
Of elders, forbidden (1Ti 5:1-2).

Profitable:
(Pr 13:18; 15:5, 31-32; 27:5-6; 28:23; Ecc 7:5).
Wise profit by (Pr 17:10; 19:25; 21:11; 25:12).

Needed in the Church:
(Eph 4:15; Php 3:1; 1Th 5:14; 1Ti 5:1-2, 20; 2Ti 4:2; Tit 1:13; Heb 3:13).

Hated:
(Pr 10:17; 12:1; 15:10, 12; Am 5:10; Jn 7:7; Gal 4:16). By the Israelites (Nu 14:9-10; Jer 26:11). By Ahab (1Ki 18:17; 21:20; 22:8). By Asa (2Ch 16:10). By Herodias (Mk 6:18-19). By people of Nazareth (Lk 4:28-29). Jews (Ac 5:33; 7:54).

Faithfulness in:
Instances of: Moses, of Pharaoh (Ex 10:29;

11:8), of the Israelites (Ex 16:6-7; 32:19-30; Nu 14:41; 20:10; 32:14; Dt 1:12, 26-43; 9:16-24; 29:2-4; 31:27-29; 32:15-18), of Eleazar (Lev 10:16-18), of Korah (Nu 16:9-11). Israelites, of the two-a-one-half tribes (Jos 22:15-20), of the tribe of Benjamin (Jdg 20:12-13).

Samuel, of Saul (1Sa 15:14-35). Jonathan, of Saul (1Sa 19:4-5). Nathan, of David (2Sa 12:1-9). Joab, of David (2Sa 19:1-7; 24:3; 1Ch 21:3). The prophet Gad, of David (2Sa 24:13). Shemaiah, of Rehoboam (2Ch 12:5). A prophet of Judah, of Jeroboam (1Ki 13:1-10; 2Ch 13:8-11). Elijah, of Ahab (1Ki 18:18-21; 21:20-24), of Ahaziah (2Ki 1). Micaiah, of Ahab (1Ki 22:14-28). Elisha, of Jehoram (2Ki 3:13-14), of Gehazi (2Ki 5:26), of Hazael (2Ki 8:11-13), of Jeroboam (2Ki 13:19).

Amos, of the Israelites (Am 7:12-17). Isaiah, of Hezekiah (2Ki 20:17). Jehoash, of Jehoiada (2Ki 12:7). Azariah, of Asa (2Ch 15:2), of Uzziah (2Ch 26:17-18). Hanani, of Asa (2Ch 16:7-9). Jehu, of Jehoshaphat (2Ch 19:2). Zechariah, of the princes of Judah (2Ch 24:20). Oded, of the people of Samaria (2Ch 28:9-11). Jeremiah, of the cities of Judah (Jer 26:8-11). Ezra, of the men of Judah and Benjamin (Ezr 10:10). Nehemiah, of the Jews (Ne 5:6-13), of the corruptions in the temple, and of the violation of the Sabbath (Ne 13). Daniel, of Nebuchadnezzar (Da 4:27), of Belshazzar (Da 5:17-24).

Jesus, of the Jews: When Pharisees and Sadducees came to him desiring a sign (Mt 16:1-4; Mk 8:11-12), of the scribes and Pharisees (Mt 23; Lk 11:37-54), of the Pharisees (Lk 16), when they brought the woman who was taken in adultery (Jn 8:7).

Jesus, in his parables: Of the king's feast (Lk 14:16-24), of the two sons (Mt 21:28-32), of the vineyard (Mt 21:33-46; Mk 12:1-12; Lk 20:9-20), of the barren fig tree (Lk 13:6-9), the withering of the fig tree (Mt 21:17-20; Mk 11:12-14).

John the Baptist, of the Jews (Mt 3:7-12; Lk 3:7-9), of Herod (Mt 14:3; Mk 6:17; Lk 3:19-20). Peter, of Simon, the sorcerer (Ac 8:20-23). Stephen, of the high priest (Ac 7:51-53). Paul, of Elymas, the sorcerer (Ac 13:9-11), of Ananias, the high priest (Ac 23:3). Paul and Silas, of the magistrates of Philippi (Ac 16:37-40).

See One Another; Reprobacy.

REPTILES [8254, 2260]. (1Ki 4:33; Ac 10:12; 11:6; Ro 1:23). Adder (Job 20:16). Cobra (Isa 11:8). Chameleon (Lev 11:30). Frog (Ex 8:2). Gecko (Lev 11:30). Lizards (Lev 11:29-30). Serpent (Job 20:14, 16). Skink (Lev 11:30). Snake (Ex 7:9-12). Viper (Ge 49:17; Isa 59:5). *See Animals.*

REPUTATION, GOOD [1804, 9053, 3456, 3950]. (Pr 3:4; 22:1; Ecc 7:1). Of Mordecai (Est 9:4). Of overseers (1Ti 3:7). *See Character; Name.*

RESEN [8271]. A town founded by Nimrod (Ge 10:8-12), between Nineveh and Calah.

RESERVOIR [1391+4784, 4784+5224, 5225]. A place where water is collected and kept for use when wanted, chiefly in large quantities. Because most of W Asia was subject to periodic droughts, and because of frequent sieges, reservoirs and cisterns were a necessity (2Ch 26:10; 18:31; Ecc 2:6).

RESHEPH [8405] (*flame, flash of fire*). Grandson of Ephraim (1Ch 7:25).

RESIGNATION

Commanded:

(Ps 4:4; 46:10; Lk 21:19; Ro 12:12; Php 2:14; Col 1:10-11; Jas 1:9-10; 4:7; 1Pe 4:12-13, 19). Under chastisement and afflictions (Job 5:17; Pr 3:11; 18:14; Jer 51:50; La 3:39; Mic 6:9; 1Th 3:3; 2Ti 2:3; 4:5; Heb 2:6-12; 12:5, 9; Jas 5:11, 13; 1Pe 1:6). Under bereavement (1Th 4:13-18).

Exemplified by:

Aaron (Lev 10:1-3). The Israelites (Jdg 10:15). Eli (1Sa 3:18). David (2Sa 12:23; 15:26; 16:10-11; 24:14). The Shunammite (2Ki 4:26). Hezekiah (2Ki 20:19; Isa 39:8). Nehemiah (Ne 9:33). By Esther (Est 4:16). Job (Job 1:13-22; 2:9-10; 34:31; Jas 5:11). The psalmists (Ps 39:9; 103:10; 119:75). Jeremiah (Jer 10:19; La 1:18). Daniel (Da 9:14). Micah (Mic 7:9).

Jesus (Mt 26:39; Mk 14:36; Lk 22:42; Jn 18:11). The thief on the cross (Lk 23:40-41). Stephen (Ac 7:59-60). Agabus, Luke, and others when Paul insisted on going to Jerusalem (Ac 21:14). Paul (Ro 5:3-5; 2Co 6:4-10; 7:4; Php 1:20-24; 4:11-12; 2Ti 4:6). Paul and Silas (Ac 16:25). Thessalonian believers (2Th 1:4). Hebrew believers (Heb 10:34).

See Afflicted Believers; Affliction; Afflictions, Made Beneficial.

RESIN [978, 5753]. *See Aromatic Resin; Gum Resin.*

RESPECT [*3359, 3707, 3877, 1956, 3455, 4948, 5507, 5832]. To the aged (Lev 19:32). To rulers (Pr 25:6). To a host (Lk 14:10). To one another (Ro 12:10; Php 2:3; 1Pe 2:17).

RESPECT OF PERSONS Favoritism (Pr 24:23; 28:21; Jas 2:1-9). God does not have (Dt 10:17; 2Ch 19:7; Job 31:13-15; 34:19; Ac 10:34; 15:9; Ro 2:11-12; 10:12; Eph 6:8-9; Col 3:25; 1Pe 1:17). *See God, Justice of; Justice.*

RESPONSIBILITY [5466, 6411, 6584, 3972+5148, 5970]. Attempts to shift: Adam (Ge 3:12-13), Eve (Ge 3:13), Sarah (Ge 16:5, w 16:2), Esau (Ge 27:36, w Ge 25:29-34), Aaron (Ex 32:22-24), Saul (1Sa 15:20-21), Pilate (Mt 27:24). Assumed by the Jews for the death of Jesus (Mt 27:25).

Personal (Eze 14:14-20; 18:20, 30; Mt 12:37; Jn 9:41; 15:22-24; Ro 14:12; 1Co 3:8, 13-15; Gal 6:5; 1Pe 4:5; Rev 2:23).

According to privilege (Eze 18:1-30; 33:1-19;

Mt 10:11-15; 11:20-24; 12:41-42; 23:31-35; 25:14-30; Mk 6:11; Lk 9:5; 10:10-15; 11:31-32, 49-51; 13:6-9; 19:12-27; 21:1-4; Jn 3:18-19; 12:48; 15:22, 24; Ac 17:30-31; Ro 12:3, 6-8; Eph 4:7; 1Ti 6:20).

See Judgment, According to Opportunity and Works.

RESPONSIVE RELIGIOUS SERVICE

Reciting the curses of the covenant (Dt 27:14-26). In worship (Ps 48; 118:2-4; 124:1; 129:1). At the dedication of the wall of Jerusalem (Ne 12).

REST

[*1954, 1957, 3782, 4328, 4955, 4957, 5663, 8069, 8070, 8089, 8697, 8702, 8886, 8905, 9200, *398, 399, 2923, 2924*]. Divine institution for. *See Sabbath.* Commanded (Ex 16:23; 20:10; 23:12; 31:15; 34:21; 35:2; Dt 5:12, 14).

The annual feasts added rest days: First and last days of feasts of Passover and Tabernacles (Ex 12:16; Lev 23:5-8, 39-40; Nu 28:18, 25; 29:12, 35), Pentecost (Nu 28:26), Trumpets (Lev 23:24-25; Nu 29:1), Atonement (Lev 16:29-31; 23:27-28; Nu 29:7). In seventh year (Ex 23:11; Lev 25:1-4). In the Year of Jubilee (Lev 25:11-12).

Recommended by Jesus (Mk 6:31-32; 7:24, w Mt 8:18, 24). Heavenly (2Th 1:7). Spiritual (Mt 11:29; Heb 4:1-11).

See Peace, Spiritual; Resignation.

RESTITUTION

[5989, 8740, 8966]. To be made for injury to life, limb, or property (Ex 21:30-36; Lev 24:18), for theft (Ex 22:1-4; Pr 6:30-31; Eze 33:15), for dishonesty (Lev 6:2-5; Nu 5:7; Job 20:18; Eze 33:15; Lk 19:8).

RESTORATION

[*1215, 2542, 2616, 2649, 6441, 7756, 8740, 8966, 10354, 10754, *635, 2936*]. Of the Jews. *See Israel; Israelites.* Of all things (Ac 3:21; Rev 21:1-5).

RESURRECTION

[*414, 1587, 1983*].

In the Old Testament:

As understood by Job (Job 14:12-15; 19:25-27). By the psalmists (Ps 16:9-10; 17:15; 49:15). By the prophets (Isa 25:8; 26:19; Da 12:2-3, 13; Hos 13:14).

In the New Testament:

Debated by the Pharisees and Sadducees (Ac 23:6, 8; 24:14-15; 26:6-8; Mt 22:23-32).

Taught by Jesus (Mt 22:30-32; 24:31; Mk 12:25-27; Lk 14:14; 20:27-38; Jn 5:21, 25, 28-29; 6:39-40, 44, 54; 11:23-25). By the apostles (Ac 4:1-2; 17:18, 31-32; 23:6-8; 24:14-15; 26:6-8; Ro 4:16-21; 8:10-11, 19, 21-23; 1Co 6:14; 15:12-57; 2Co 4:14; 5:1-5; Php 3:10-11, 21; Rev 20:5-6; Heb 6:2; 11:35).

Error in the early church (2Ti 2:18; 1Co 15:12-58).

Of Jesus:

Typified by Isaac (Ge 22:13; Heb 11:19), by Jonah (Jnh 2:10, w Mt 12:40). Foretold (Ps 16:9-10), by himself (Mt 16:21; 17:9, 23; 20:19; 26:61;

27:63; Mk 8:31; 9:9-10, 31; 10:34; Lk 9:22; 18:33; 24:7, 46; Jn 2:19-21; 10:17-18; 14:19).

Appearances after the resurrection (Mt 27:53; 28:2-15; Mk 16:1-11; Lk 24:1-12; Jn 20:1-18; Rev 1:18). Denied by the Jews (Mt 28:12-15).

Raised by the power of God (Ac 2:24, 32; 3:15, 26; 4:10; 5:30; 10:40; 15:20, 30, 33-34, 37; 17:31; Ro 4:24; 8:11; 10:9; 1Co 6:14; 15:15; 2Co 4:14; Gal 1:4; Eph 1:20; Col 2:12; 2Ti 1:10; 1Pe 1:21), for our justification (Ro 4:25; 1Pe 3:21). Guarantee of general resurrection (1Co 15:12-15; 1Pe 1:3).

The theme of apostolic preaching (Ac 2:24, 31-32; 3:15; 4:10, 33; 5:30-32; 10:40-41; 17:2-3, 18).

See Grave; Jesus the Christ, Resurrection of.

Special Resurrections:

Of saints after Christ's resurrection (Mt 27:52-53). The two witnesses (Rev 11:11).

See Dead, Raised to Life.

At Christ's Second Coming:

(1Th 4:14, 16). The first resurrection (Rev 20:4-6). Of all the dead (Jn 5:28-29; Ac 24:15; 1Co 15:20-21; Rev 20:13).

Figurative:

Of the restoration of Israel (Eze 37:1-14). Of regeneration (Ro 6:4; Eph 2:1, 5-6; Col 2:12; 3:1).

RETALIATION

[*518*]. (Ps 10:2). Judicial, ordained in Mosaic law (Ex 21:23-25; Lev 24:17-22; Dt 19:19-21). Malicious, forbidden (Lev 19:18; Pr 20:22; 24:29; Mt 5:38-44; 7:1-2; Lk 9:54; Ro 12:17, 19; 1Co 6:7-8; 1Th 5:15; 1Pe 3:9). Warning against (Pr 26:27; Isa 33:1; Mt 7:1-2).

See Avenger of Blood; Hatred; Malice; Revenge. Instances of: Israelites on the Amalekites (Dt 25:17-19, w 1Sa 15:1-9). Gideon on the princes of Succoth (Jdg 8:7, 13-16), kings of Midian (Jdg 8:18-21), Peniel (Jdg 8:8, 17). Joab on Abner (2Sa 3:27, 30). David upon Michal (2Sa 6:21-23), on Joab (1Ki 2:5-6), Shimei (1Ki 2:8-9). Jews on their enemies (Est 9).

RETICENCE OF JESUS

[Isa 53:7; Mt 26:63; 27:12, 14; Mk 14:61; 15:4-5; Jn 19:9, 1Pe 2:23). *See Jesus the Christ, Reticence of.*

RETRIBUTION

[1691, 1692, 8936, *501*]. *See Sin, Punishment of.*

REU

[8293, *4814*] (*friend [of God]*). Son of Peleg and ancestor of Abraham and of Jesus (Ge 11:18-21; 1Ch 1:25; Lk 3:35).

REUBEN

[1201+8017, 1201+8018, 8017, 8018, *4857*] (*see, a son!* [Ge. 29:32]; *substitute a son* IDB). Son of Jacob (Ge 29:32; 1Ch 2:1). Brings mandrakes to his mother (Ge 30:14). Commits incest with one of his father's concubines, and, in consequence, forfeits the birthright (Ge 35:22; 49:4; 1Ch 5:1). Tactfully seeks to save Joseph from the conspiracy of his brothers (Ge 37:21-30; 42:22). Offers to become surety for Benjamin (Ge 42:37). Jacob's prophetic benediction upon (Ge 49:3-4). His children (Ge 46:9; Ex 6:14; 1Ch 5:3-6; Nu 16:1).

REUBENITE(S) [1201+8017, 8018] (*of Reuben*). The descendants of Reuben. Military enrollment of, at Sinai (Nu 1:20-21), in Moab (Nu 26:7). Place of, in camp and march (Nu 2:10). Standard of (Nu 10:18). Have their inheritance east of the Jordan (Nu 32; Dt 3:1-20; Jos 13:15-23; 18:7). Assist the other tribes in conquest of the region west of the Jordan (Jos 1:12-18; 22:1-6). Unite with the other tribes in building a monument to signify the unity of the tribes on the east of the Jordan with the tribes on the west of the river; monument misunderstood; the explanation and reconciliation (Jos 22:10-34). Reproached by Deborah (Jdg 5:15-16). Taken captive into Assyria (2Ki 15:29; 1Ch 5:26).

See Israel.

REUEL [8294] (*friend of God [El]*).

1. Son of Esau (Ge 36:4, 10).

2. Father-in-law of Moses (Ex 2:16-22), probably the same as Jethro (Ex 3:1). *See Jethro.*

3. The father of Eliasaph (Nu 2:14). Called Deuel (Nu 1:14).

4. Benjamite (1Ch 9:8).

REUMAH [8020]. A concubine of Nahor (Ge 22:24).

REVELATION [1821, 2606, 2612, *636, 637*]. The doctrine of God's making himself and relevant truths known to mankind. Revelation is of two kinds: general and special. General revelation is available to all people, and is communicated through nature, conscience, and history. Special revelation is revelation given to particular people at particular times (although it may be intended for others as well), and comes chiefly through the Bible and Jesus Christ.

God reveals himself to Moses (Ex 3:1-6, 14; 6:1-3). The law is revealed (Ex 20-35; Lev 1-7). The pattern of the temple (1Ch 28:11-19). The sonship of Jesus (Mt 3:17; 16:17; 17:5). The nature of the Father through the Son (Jn 1:18; 14:8).

See Inspiration; Prophecy; Prophets; Word of God, Inspiration of.

REVELATION, BOOK OF THE

Author: The apostle John

Date: Probably in the latter part of Nero's reign (A.D. 54-68) or the latter part of Domitian's reign (81-96).

Outline:

I. Introduction (1:1-8).
  A. Prologue (1:1-3).
  B. Greetings and Doxology (1:4-8).
II. Jesus Among the Seven Churches (1:9-20).
III. The Letters to the Seven Churches (chs. 2-3).
  A. Ephesus (2:1-7).
  B. Smyrna (2:8-11).
  C. Pergamum (2:12-17).
  D. Thyatira (2:18-29).
  E. Sardis (3:1-6).
  F. Philadelphia (3:7-13).
  G. Laodicea (3:14-22).
IV. The Throne, the Scroll and the Lamb (chs. 4-5).
  A. The Throne in Heaven (ch. 4).
  B. The Seven-Sealed Scroll (5:1-5).
  C. The Lamb Slain (5:6-14).
V. The Seven Seals (6:1-8:1).
  A. First Seal: The White Horse (6:1-2).
  B. Second Seal: The Red Horse (6:3-4).
  C. Third Seal: The Black Horse (6:5-6).
  D. Fourth Seal: The Pale Horse (6:7-8).
  E. Fifth Seal: The Souls Under the Altar (6:9-11).
  F. Sixth Seal: The Great Earthquake (6:12-17).
  G. The Sealing of the 144,000 (7:1-8).
  H. The Great Multitude (7:9-17).
  I. Seventh Seal: Silence in Heaven (8:1).
VI. The Seven Trumpets (8:2-11:19).
  A. Introduction (8:2-5).
  B. First Trumpet: Hail and Fire Mixed With Blood (8:6-7).
  C. Second Trumpet: A Mountain Thrown in the Sea (8:8-9).
  D. Third Trumpet: The Star Wormwood (8:10-11).
  E. Fourth Trumpet: A Third of the Sun, Moon and Stars Struck (8:12-13).
  F. Fifth Trumpet: The Plague of Locusts (9:1-12).
  G. Sixth Trumpet: Release of the Four Angels (9:13-21).
  H. The Angel and the Little Scroll (ch. 10).
  I. The Two Witnesses (11:1-14).
  J. Seventh Trumpet: Judgments and Rewards (11:15-19).
VII. Various Personages and Events (chs. 12-14).
  A. The Woman and the Dragon (ch. 12).
  B. The Two Beasts (ch. 13).
  C. The Lamb and the 144,000 (14:1-5).
  D. The Harvest of the Earth (14:6-20).
VIII. The Seven Bowls (chs. 15-16).
  A. Introduction: The Song of Moses and the Seven Angels With the Seven Plagues (ch. 15).
  B. First Bowl: Ugly and Painful Sores (16:1-2).
  C. Second Bowl: Sea Turns to Blood (16:3).
  D. Third Bowl: Rivers and Springs of Water Become Blood (16:4-7).
  E. Fourth Bowl: Sun Scorches People With Fire (16:8-9).
  F. Fifth Bowl: Darkness (16:10-11).
  G. Sixth Bowl: Euphrates River Dries Up (16:12-16).
  H. Seventh Bowl: Tremendous Earthquake (16:17-21).
IX. Babylon: The Great Prostitute (17:1-19:5).
  A. Babylon Described (ch. 17).
  B. The Fall of Babylon (ch. 18).
  C. Praise for Babylon's Fall (19:1-5).
X. Praise for the Wedding of the Lamb (19:6-10).
XI. The Return of Christ (19:11-21).

XII. The Thousand Years (20:1-6).
XIII. Satan's Doom (20:7-10).
XIV. Great White Throne Judgment (20:11-15).
XV. New Heaven, New Earth, New Jerusalem (21:1-22:5).
XVI. Conclusion (22:6-21).

REVELING
[2510, 6357, 6600, 6601, 6611, 7464, 8471, 8525, *1960, 4089*]. Any extreme intemperance and lustful indulgence, usually accompanying pagan worship (Gal 5:21; 1Pe 4:3).

REVENGE
[5933, 5934, 5935, *1688+4932*]. Forbidden (Lev 19:18; Pr 24:29; Ro 12:17, 19; 1Th 5:15; 1Pe 3:9). Jesus an example of forbearing (1Pe 2:23). Rebuked by Jesus (Lk 9:54-55). Inconsistent with a Christian spirit (Lk 9:55). Proceeds from a spiteful heart (Eze 25:15). Punishment for (Eze 25:15-17; Am 1:11-12).

Exemplified:

By Simeon and Levi (Ge 34:25). By Samson (Jdg 15:7-8; 16:28-30). By Joab (2Sa 3:27). By Absalom (2Sa 13:23-29). By Jezebel (1Ki 19:2). By Ahab (1Ki 22:27). By Haman (Est 3:8-15). By the Edomites (Eze 25:12). By the Philistines (Eze 25:15). By Herodias (Mk 6:19-24). By James and John (Lk 9:54). By the chief priests (Ac 5:33). By the Jews (Ac 7:54-59; 23:12).

See Retaliation; Vengeance.

REVENUE
[5006, 9202, 9311, 10063, 10402, *5465*]. Solomon's (2Ch 9:13-14).

See Tax.

REVERENCE
[*1593, 3707, 3711, 10167, 2325, 5828, 5832*]. For God (Ge 17:3; Ex 3:5; 19:16-24; 34:29-35; Isa 45:9). *See Fear of God.* For God's house (Lev 19:30; 26:2). For ministers (1Sa 16:4; Ac 28:10; 1Co 16:18; Php 2:29; 1Th 5:12-13; 1Ti 5:17; Heb 13:7, 17). *See Minister.* For Kings (1Sa 24:6; 26:9, 11; 2Sa 1:14; 16:21; Ecc 10:20; 1Pe 2:17). *See Rulers.* For magistrates (Ex 22:28; 2Pe 2:10; Jude 8). *See Rulers.* For parents (Ex 20:12; Lev 19:3; Isa 45:10). *See Parents.* For the aged (Lev 19:32; Job 32:4-7).

REVILE, REVILING
[1552, 5540, 7837, 8475]. To revile is to address or speak of someone abusively; to reproach (Ex 21:17; Zep 2:8; Mk 15:32; 1Co 6:10).

REVIVALS

Religious:

(Zec 8:20-23). Prayer for (Hab 3:2). Prophecies concerning (Isa 32:15; Joel 2:28; Mic 4:1-8; Hab 3:2).

Instances of:

Under Joshua (Jos 5:2-9), Samuel (1Sa 7:1-6), Elijah (1Ki 18:17-40), Jehoash and Jehoiada (2Ki 11-12; 2Ch 23-24), Hezekiah (2Ki 18:1-7; 2Ch 29-31), Josiah (2Ki 22-23; 2Ch 34-35), Asa (2Ch 14:2-5; 15:1-14), Manasseh (2Ch 33:12-19). In Nineveh (Jnh 3:4-10). At Pentecost and post-Pen-

tecostal times (Ac 2:1-42, 46-47; 4:4; 5:14; 6:7; 9:35; 11:20-21; 12:24; 14:1; 19:17-20).

See Religion.

REVOLT
[5277, 6240, 7321, 7756, 10492, *189, 415, 923*]. Of the ten tribes (1Ki 12:1-24).

REWARD
[*2750, 3877, 5989, 7190, 8510, 8740, 8966, 10454, 625, 3632, 3635*]. (Isa 40:10-11). In Moses' choice (Heb 11:26). For bravery (1Sa 17:25; Jdg 1:13).

A Motive:

To repentance (Lev 26:40-45; Isa 1:16-20; Ac 26:18). To obedience (Ex 20:6; Lev 25:18-19; 26:3-13; Dt 4:40; 6:3, 18; 11:13-16, 18-21, 26-29; 27:12-26; Jos 8:33; Isa 1:16-20; 3:10; Eph 6:1-3; Heb 12:28). To faithfulness (Mt 24:45-47; 25:14-33; Lk 12:42-44; 19:12-27; 1Co 3:8; Rev 2:10; 22:12). To righteous conduct (Ro 2:10; 1Pe 3:9-12). To patience (Heb 10:36). To perseverance (Mt 10:22; 24:13; Mk 13:13; Ro 2:6-7; Gal 6:9; Rev 2:17, 25-27; 3:5, 11-12, 21; 21:7). To honesty (Dt 25:15).

To follow Christ (Mt 10:32; 16:24-27; 20:1-16; 25:34-46; Mk 10:21; Lk 12:8; 2Pe 1:10-11). To endure persecution (Lk 6:22-23; Heb 10:34). To endure tribulation (Rev 2:7, 10; 7:17). To love enemies (Lk 6:35). To deliver the oppressed (Jer 17:24-26; 22:3-4). To honor parents (Ex 20:12; Eph 6:1-3). To honor the Sabbath (Jer 17:24-26). To give generously (Dt 15:9-11; 24:19). To show kindness to animals (Dt 22:6-7).

See Blessings, Spiritual, Contingent Upon Obedience; Punishment; Righteous, Promises to; Sin, Separates From God; Wicked, Punishment of.

REZEPH
[8364] (*heated stones, live coals*). A city destroyed by the Assyrians (2Ki 19:12; Isa 37:12).

REZIA
See Rizia.

REZIN
[8360].

1. A king of Syria who harassed the kingdom of Judah (2Ki 15:37; 16:5-9). Prophecy against (Isa 7:1-9; 8:4-8; 9:11).

2. A returned Babylonian captive (Ezr 2:48; Ne 7:50).

REZON
[8139] (*prince* IDB; *high official* KB). King of Damascus. An adversary of Solomon (1Ki 11:23-25).

RHEGIUM
[4836]. A city of Italy. Touched by Paul on the way to Rome (Ac 28:13).

RHESA
[4840]. An ancestor of Jesus (Lk 3:27).

RHODA
[4851] (*rose*). A servant or slave girl in the home of Mary, John Mark's mother (Ac 12:13).

RHODES
[8102, *4852*] (*rose*). An island on the SW tip of Asia Minor; commercial center until crippled by Rome is 166 B.C.; famous for Colos-

sus, a statue of Helios; Paul stopped off there (Ac 21:1).

RIBAI [8192] (*opponent*). A Benjamite. The father of Ittai (2Sa 23:29; 1Ch 11:31).

RIBBON [2562]. Ribbon used in poetic imagery (SS 4:3). Tassels of thread on the corners of garments; NIV "cord" (Nu 15:38).

RIBLAH [8058].

1. A city on the boundary of Canaan and Israel, N of the Sea of Galilee (Nu 34:11).

2. An important town on the E bank of the Orontes River fifty miles S of Hamath. There Pharaoh Neco (609 B.C.) put King Jehoahaz II of Judah in chains. Also in this place, Nebuchadnezzar killed the sons of King Zedekiah of Judah (587 B.C.) and put out his eyes. Following this, Zedekiah was carried off in chains to Babylon (2Ki 25:6f; Jer 39:5-7). It is possible that the two Riblahs may be the same.

RICH, THE [*238, 419, 2016, 2104, 2657, 2890, 3202, 3702, 3883, 5794, 6938, 6947, 6948, 9045, *4454, *4456, *4457, *4458*].

Admonitions to:

(Jer 9:23; 1Ti 6:17-19; Jas 1:9-11). Not to trust riches for divine favor (Ps 49:16-18; Ecc 7:19; Zep 1:18).

Characteristics of:

Wicked (Job 21:7-15; Ps 73:3-9; Pr 28:8, 20, 22; Jer 5:27-28; Lk 12:15-21; 16:19-31; Jas 2:6-7). Immoral (Jer 5:7-8). Deluded (Pr 11:28; 13:7; 18:11). Conceited (Pr 28:11). Proud (Ps 73:3, 6, 8-9; Eze 28:5). Arrogant (Ps 73:8). Oppressive (Ne 5:1-13; Mic 6:10-13; Jas 5:4). Cruel to the poor (Pr 18:23). Envied (Ps 73:3-22). Hated (Job 27:19, 23). Denounced (Isa 5:8; Jer 17:11; 22:13-15; Am 6:1-6; Lk 6:24-25; Jas 5:1-4).

Have many friends (Pr 14:20; 19:9). Made so by God (Ecc 5:19-20). Difficult to enter the kingdom (Mt 19:24; Mk 10:17-27; Lk 18:24-25). Unscrupulous methods of (Jer 5:26-28). Discrimination in favor of, in the church, forbidden (Jas 2:1-9). Divine judgments against (Job 27:13-23; Ps 52:1-7; 73:18-20).

Instances of Righteous Rich:

Abraham (Ge 13:2; 24:35). Isaac (Ge 26:12-14). Solomon (1Ki 10:23; 2Ch 9:22). Jehoshaphat (2Ch 18:1). Hezekiah (2Ki 20:12-13). Job (Job 1:3; 31:24-25, 28). Joseph of Arimathea (Mt 27:57). Zacchaeus (Lk 19:2).

See Riches.

RICHES [238, 2104, 2657, 2776, 2890, 3702, 3883, 4759, 5794, 6217, 6948, 8214, *3353, *4458*].

(1Sa 2:7; Ps 37:16; 52:7; Pr 11:4; 14:24; 15:6, 16-17; 16:8; 19:4; Ecc 4:8; 5:11-14; 6:1-2; 7:11-12; 10:19; Isa 5:8; Jer 48:36). Delusive (Pr 11:28; Lk 12:16-21). Unstable (Pr 23:5; 27:24).

Unsatisfying to the covetous (Ecc 5:10-12). A snare (Dt 6:10-12; 8:7-17; 31:20; 32:15; Pr 30:8-9; Jer 5:7-8; Hos 12:8; Mt 13:22; 19:16-24; Mk

4:19; 10:17-25; Lk 16:19-26; 18:18-25; 1Ti 6:9-11, 17).

Worthless in the day of calamity (Eze 7:17, 19; Zep 1:18). Fraudulently gotten, unprofitable (Pr 10:2; 21:6; 28:8; Jer 17:11). Admonitions against the desire for (Pr 23:4; 28:20, 22; 1Ti 6:9-11, 17). The heart not to be set upon (Ps 62:10; Mt 6:19-21).

Liberality with (Pr 13:7-8). Benevolent use of, required (1Jn 3:17).

Figurative (Rev 3:17-18).

See Covetousness; Rich, The.

RIDDLE [2648, 10019] (*hidden saying, proverb*). Any "dark saying" of which the meaning is not immediately clear and may be found by shrewd thought (Nu 12:8; Pr 1:6). It may be a parable (Ps 49:4), or something for men to guess (Jdg 14:12-19), or just a hard question (1Ki 10:1; 2Ch 9:1).

RIGHTEOUS [3838, 7404, 7405, 7406, 7407, 9448, *1464, *1465, *1466, *1467, *1468, *1469*].

Compared with:

The sun (Jdg 5:31; Mt 13:43), stars (Da 12:3), lights (Mt 5:14; Php 2:15). Mount Zion (Ps 125:1-2), Lebanon (Hos 14:5-7). Treasure (Ex 19:5; Ps 135:4), treasured possession (Mal 3:17). Gold (Job 23:10; La 4:2), vessels of gold and silver (2Ti 2:20), stones of a crown (Zec 9:16), living stones (1Pe 2:5).

Babies (Mt 11:25; 1Pe 2:2), little children (Mt 18:3; 1Co 14:20), obedient children (1Pe 1:14), members of the body (1Co 12:20, 27), soldiers (2Ti 2:3-4), runners in a race (1Co 9:24; Heb 12:1), wrestlers (2Ti 2:5), good servants (Mt 25:21), strangers and pilgrims (1Pe 2:11).

Sheep (Ps 78:52; Mt 25:33; Jn 10), lambs (Isa 40:11; Jn 21:15), calves of the stall (Mal 4:2), lions (Pr 28:1; Mic 5:8), eagles (Ps 103:5; Isa 40:31), doves (Ps 68:13; Isa 60:8), thirsty deer (Ps 42:1), good fish (Mt 13:48).

Dew and showers (Mic 5:7), watered gardens (Isa 58:11), unfailing springs (Isa 58:11), vines (SS 6:11; Hos 14:7), branches of a vine (Jn 15:2, 4-5), pomegranates (SS 4:13), good figs (Jer 24:2-7), lilies (SS 2:2; Hos 14:5), poplars by flowing streams (Isa 44:4), trees planted by rivers (Ps 1:3), cedars in Lebanon (Ps 92:12), palm trees (Ps 92:12), green olive trees (Ps 52:8; Hos 14:6), fruitful trees (Ps 1:3; Jer 17:8), grain (Hos 14:7), wheat (Mt 3:12; 13:29-30), salt (Mt 5:13).

Relation to God:

(Lev 20:24-26). Access to God (Ps 31:19-20; Isa 12:6). Few (Mt 7:14; 22:14). Righteous and wicked, circumstances of, contrasted (Job 8; Ps 17:14-15). *See below, Contrasted With the Wicked.*

At the judgment. *See Judgment.*

Fellowship of. *See Fellowship.*

Hatred toward. *See Persecution.*

Joy of. *See Joy.*

Perseverance of. *See Perseverance.*

Contrasted With the Wicked:

(Ps 1:1-6; 11:5; 17:14-15; 32:10; 37:17-22, 37-38; 73:1-28; 75:10; 91:7-8; Pr 2:21-22; 3:32-33; 4:16-19; 10:3, 6, 9, 11, 16, 20-21, 23-25, 28-32; 11:3, 5-6, 8-14, 18-21, 23, 31; 12:3, 5-7, 10, 12-13, 21, 26; 13:5-6, 9, 17, 21-22, 25; 14:2, 11, 19, 22-32; 15:6, 8-9, 28-29; 22:5, 8-9; 24:16; 28:1, 4-5, 13-14, 18; 29:2, 6-7, 27; Isa 32:1-8; 65:13-14; Ro 2:7-10; Eph 2:12-14; Php 2:15; 1Th 5:5-8; Tit 1:15; 1Pe 4:17-18; 1Jn 3:3-17).

See Wicked, Contrasted With the Righteous; Described as.

Described:

(Ps 1:1-3; 15:1-5; 24:3-5; 37:26, 30-31; 84:7; 112:1-10; 119:1-3; Isa 33:15-16; 51:1; 62:12; 63:8; Jer 17:7-8; 31:12-14, 33-34; Eze 18:5-9; Zec 3:2, 7-8). As dead to sin (Ro 6:2, 11; Col 3:3). Freed from sin (Ro 6:7, 18, 22; 1Jn 3:6, 9).

Good (Lk 6:45). Pure (Mt 5:8; 1Jn 3:3; 2Ti 2:21-22). Holy (Dt 7:6; Eph 1:4; 4:24; Col 1:22; 3:12; 1Pe 1:15; 2Ti 2:19; Heb 3:1). Sanctified (1Co 1:2; 6:11). Godly (Ps 4:3; 2Pe 2:9). Wise (Ps 37:30; Pr 2:9-12). Faithful (Mt 24:45; 25:21, 23; Lk 19:17; Eph 1:1; Col 1:2; Rev 17:14). Merciful (Mt 5:7). Meek (Mt 5:5; 2Ti 2:25). Industrious (Eph 4:28; 2Jn 9). Stable (Mt 7:24-27; Eph 4:14). Saved (Ac 2:47). Saints (Ro 1:7; 1Co 1:2; Eph 1:1). Chosen (1Pe 2:9; Rev 17:14). Spotless (Jas 1:27). Separate (Ex 33:16). Obedient (Mt 12:50; Jn 15:14; 1Jn 2:3, 5). New creature (2Co 5:17; Eph 2:10; 4:23-24; Col 3:9-10). Spiritually minded (Ro 8:4, 6). Patient, long-suffering, joyful (Col 1:11; 1Th 1:3). Peaceful, meek, gentle, patient (2Ti 2:21-25). Blameless, harmless, and without blemish (Eph 1:4; Php 2:15). Kind, tenderhearted, forgiving (Eph 4:32).

Servants of Christ (Eph 6:6). Servants of righteousness (Ro 6:19). Children of light (1Th 5:5). Children of God (Ro 8:14, 16; 1Jn 3:2). A temple of God (2Co 6:16). Beloved of God (Ro 1:7). Poor in spirit (Mt 5:3). Hungering and thirsting after righteousness (Mt 5:6). Growing in grace (Ps 84:7; Eph 4:13). Imitators of Christ (1Pe 4:1-2; 1Jn 2:6). Salt of the earth (Mt 5:13). City set on a hill (Mt 5:14). Led by the spirit (Ro 8:14; Gal 5:18). Filled with goodness and knowledge (Ro 15:14; Col 1:9-13). Grounded in love (Eph 3:17). Following Christ (Mt 10:38; 16:24; Mk 8:34; Lk 9:23). Rooted in Christ (Col 2:7).

Hating falsehood (Pr 13:5), abhorring wickedness (Ps 101:3-4), having renounced dishonesty (2Co 4:2). Without bitterness, wrath, anger, clamor, evil speaking, malice (Eph 4:31). Grieved by the wickedness of the wicked (Ps 119:158; Ac 17:16; 2Pe 2:7-8).

Happiness of:

(Job 5:17-27; Pr 3:13-18; 16:20; Mt 4:3-12). Satisfying (Ps 36:8; 63:5). Under fiery trials (1Pe 4:12-13). Under persecution (Mt 5:10-12).

Promises to and Comfort of:

Deliverance from temptation (1Co 10:13; 2Pe 2:9). Deliverance from trouble (Job 5:19-24; Ps 34:15, 17; 50:15; 91:15; 97:10-11; Pr 3:25-26; Isa 41:10-13; 43:2). Refuge in adversity (Ps 33:18-19; 62:8; 91:1-15; Pr 14:26; Na 1:7). Strength in adversity (Ps 29:11). Security (Ps 32:6-7; 84:11; 121:3-8; Isa 33:16). Providential care (Ge 15:1; Ex 23:22; Lev 26:5-6, 10; Dt 33:27; 1Sa 2:9; 2Ch 16:9; Ezr 8:22; Job 5:15; Ps 34:9-10; 125:1-3; 145:19-20; Pr 1:33; 2:7; 3:6; 10:3; 16:7; Isa 49:9-11; 65:13-14; Eze 34:11-17, 22-31; Lk 12:7, 32; 21:18; 1Pe 5:7). Overruling providence (Ro 8:28; 2Co 4:17).

Answer to prayer (Pr 15:29; Mk 11:23-24; Jn 14:13-14; Ac 10:4; 1Pe 3:12; 1Jn 3:22). Temporal blessings (Lev 25:18-19; 26:5; Dt 28:1-13; Ps 37:9; 128:1-6; Pr 2:21; 3:1-4, 7-10; Mt 6:26-33; Mk 10:30; Lk 18:29-30). Blessings upon their children (Ps 103:17; 112:2-3).

Righteous Receive—

Comfort in tribulation (Isa 25:8; 66:13-14; Mt 5:4; Jn 14:16-18; Rev 21:4). Joy (Isa 35:10; 51:11). Spiritual enlightenment (Isa 2:3; Jn 8:12). Peace (Isa 26:3; Ro 2:10). Seeing God (Mt 5:8). Inconceivable spiritual blessings (Isa 64:4; 1Co 2:9). The rest of faith (Heb 4:9). Wisdom (Jas 1:5). Divine help (Ps 55:22; Isa 41:10-13; Heb 13:5-6). Divine guidance (Ps 25:12; 32:8; 37:23-24; 48:14; 73:24; Pr 3:5-6). Divine mercy (Ps 32:10; 103:17-18; Mal 3:17). The divine presence (Ge 26:3, 24; 28:15; 31:3; Ex 33:14; Dt 31:6, 8; Jos 1:5; 1Ki 6:13; Hag 1:13; 2:4-5; Mt 28:20; Jn 14:17, 23; 2Co 6:16; 13:11; Php 4:9; Heb 13:5; Rev 21:3). The divine likeness (1Jn 3:2). The ministry of angels (Heb 1:14). Dwelling with Christ (Jn 14:2-3; Col 3:4; 1Th 4:17; 5:10). Everlasting remembrance (Ps 112:6). Having names written in heaven (Lk 10:20).

Resurrection (Jn 5:29; 1Co 15:48-57; 2Co 4:14; 1Th 4:16). Future glory (Ro 8:18; Col 3:4; 2Ti 2:10; 1Pe 5:4). Inheritance (Mt 5:12; 13:43; 2Ti 4:8; Heb 11:16; Jas 1:12; 2Pe 1:11; Rev 2:7, 10; 22:5, 12, 14). Eternal life (Da 12:2-3; Mt 19:29; 25:46; Mk 10:29-30; Lk 18:29-30; Jn 3:15-18, 36; 4:14; 5:24, 29; 6:39-40; 10:28; 12:25-26; Ro 2:7; 6:22-23; Gal 6:8; 1Th 4:15-17; 1Ti 1:16; 4:8; Tit 1:2; 1Jn 2:25; 5:13; Rev 7:14-17).

Contingent upon perseverance (Heb 10:36; Rev 2:7, 10-11, 17, 26-28; 3:4-5, 10, 12, 21; 21:7).

See Adoption; Affliction, Comfort in; God, Preserver, Providence of.

Promises in specific areas. *See the specific topic.*

Union of:

With God (1Jn 3:24; 4:13, 15-16; 2Jn 9).

With Christ (Jn 6:51-58; 14:20; 15:1-11; 17:21-23, 26; Ro 8:1; 12:5; 1Co 6:13-20; 10:16; 2Co 13:5; Gal 2:20; Col 1:27; 2:6-7; 1Jn 2:6, 24, 28; 3:6, 24; 5:12, 20; 2Jn 9).

See Adoption; Communion; Fellowship, with Christ.

RIGHTEOUSNESS [7404, 7405, 7406, 7407, *1465, 1466, 1468, 2319*]. (Ps 15:1-5; 24:3-5; 106:3; Pr 11:5-6, 18, 30; Hos 10:12; Mt 5:20;

Lk 1:75; Jn 16:8, 10; Ro 6:19-22; 8:4; Eph 4:24; Jas 1:27).

Required:

(Isa 28:17; Hos 10:12; Mic 6:8; Zec 7:9-10; 8:16-17; Mal 3:3; Mt 5:20; 23:23; Lk 3:10-14; 13:6-9; Ro 6:19-22; 7:4-6; 8:4; 14:17-19; 2Ti 2:22; 1Jn 3:10). Commanded in official administration (Jer 22:3, 6).

Imputed:

On account of obedience (Rev 6:25; Ps 106:31; Eze 18:9), on account of faith (Ge 15:6; Ro 4:3, 5, 9, 11, 13, 20, 22, 24; Gal 3:6; Jas 2:23). Proof of regeneration (1Jn 2:29). Exalts a nation (Pr 14:34). Safeguards life (Pr 10:2, 16; 11:19; 12:28; 13:6). Winning others to, rewarded (Da 12:3).

Fruits of:

(Ps 1:3; Mt 7:16-18; 12:35; Lk 6:43; Jn 15:4-8; 2Co 9:10; Gal 5:22-23; Php 1:11; Col 3:12-15; 1Th 1:3; Tit 2:2-6, 11-12; 1Pe 3:8-14; 2Pe 1:5-8; 1Jn 3:7). Generosity (Ac 11:29). Peace (Isa 32:17; Jas 3:8).

Symbolized:

(Eze 47:12; Rev 22:2). Figuratively described as a garment (Job 29:14; Isa 61:10; Zec 3:4; Mt 22:11-14; Rev 6:11; 7:9; 19:8).

Of God: *See God, Righteousness of.*

Of Jesus: *See Jesus the Christ, Holiness of; Righteousness of.*

See also, Sin, Fruits of; Works, Good.

RIM [1473, 4995, 8557]. The rim of a wheel (1Ki 7:33; Eze 1:18).

RIMMON [8233, 8234, 8235] (*pomegranate,* or *Rimmon [pagan thunder, storm god]*).

1. Father of the murderers of Ish-Bosheth (2Sa 4:2, 5, 9).

2. A city S of Jerusalem (Zec 14:10). Allotted to Judah (Jos 15:32; Ne 11:29), afterward to Simeon (Jos 19:7; 1Ch 4:32). Also called En Rimmon (Ne 11:29).

3. A city of Zebulun (Jos 19:13). Also called Rimmono (1Ch 6:77).

4. A rock in Benjamin (Jdg 20:45, 47; 21:13).

5. A Syrian idol (2Ki 5:18).

RIMMON-METHOAR *See Rimmon, 3.*

RIMMON PEREZ [8236] (*pomegranate pass [breach]*). A camping place of the Israelites (Nu 33:19-20).

RIMMON, ROCK OF (*pomegranate rock*). The fortress to which 600 Benjamites fled after escaping slaughter (Jdg 20:45, 47; 21:13), near Gibeah.

RIMMONO [8237]. *See Rimmon, 3.*

RING [2597, 3192, 5690, 6584, 10536, *1234, 5993*]. Of gold (Nu 31:50). Worn as a sign of office (Ge 41:42). Given as a token (Est 3:10, 12; 8:2-10). Worn in the nose (Pr 11:22; Isa 3:21).

Offerings of, to the tabernacle (Ex 35:22; Nu 31:50).

RINGSTRAKED *See Streaked.*

RINNAH [8263] (*ringing cry [of joy] to Yahweh*). A son of Shimon (1Ch 4:20).

RIOT [*189, 2572, 2573, 5087*]. To squander in evil ways (Pr 23:20; 28:7), waste (Tit 1:6; 1Pe 4:4), revelry (Ro 13:13), luxury (2Pe 2:13).

RIPHATH [8196]. A son of Gomer (Ge 10:3; 1Ch 1:6).

RISING [*2436, 3655, 4667, 5951, 6590, 6590, 6641, 7756, 8123, 10624, 414, 422, 424, 482, 1586*].

Early:

(Pr 31:15). For devotions (Ps 5:3; 59:16; 63:1; 88:13; SS 7:12; Isa 26:9). Practiced by the wicked (Pr 27:14; Mic 2:1; Zep 3:7), by drunkards (Isa 5:11). Illustrates spiritual diligence (Ro 13:11-12).

Instances of:

Lot (Ge 19:23). Abraham (Ge 19:27; 21:14; 22:3). Isaac (Ge 26:31). Abimelech (Ge 20:8). Jacob (Ge 28:18; 32:31). Laban (Ge 31:55). Moses (Ex 8:20; 9:13). Joshua (Jos 3:1; 6:12, 15; 7:16). Gideon (Jdg 6:38). Elkanah (1Sa 1:19). Samuel (1Sa 15:12). David (1Sa 17:20). Mary (Mk 16:2; Lk 24:1). Apostles (Ac 5:21).

See Industry.

Late:

Consequences of (Pr 6:9-11; 24:33-34).

See Idleness; Slothfulness.

RISSAH [8267] (*dew* ISBE). Encampment of Israelites in the wilderness (Nu 33:21-22), site unknown.

RITHMAH [8414] (*[place of] broom plants*). A camping place of the Israelites (Nu 33:18-19).

RIVER [3284, 3542, 3720, 4784, 5045, 5643, 5707, 10468, *4532*]. May refer to large streams (Ge 2:10-14), the Nile (Ge 41:1; 2Ki 19:24), a winter torrent, the bed of which is dry during summer (Am 6:14); fountain stream (Ps 119:136).

Figurative: Of salvation (Ps 36:8; 46:4; Isa 32:2; Eze 47:1-12; Rev 22:1-2). Of grief (Ps 119:136; La 3:48).

RIVER OF EGYPT [3284, 5643, 5707].

1. The Brook or Wadi of Egypt on the SW border of Israel, flowing into the Mediterranean Sea (Ge 15:18; Nu 34:5; 2Ki 24:7; Isa 27:12), probably modern Wadi el-Arish, though some identify it with the Nile.

2. The Nile (Am 8:8; 9:5).

See Egypt; Nile.

RIVERS [3284, 5643, 5707, *4532*]. Names of: Abana (2Ki 5:12). Arnon (Dt 2:36). Kebar (Eze 1:1). Euphrates (Ge 2:14). Gozan (2Ki 17:6; 1Ch 5:26). Jordan. *See Jordan.* Kanah (Jos 16:8).

Kishon (Jdg 5:21). Of Egypt (Ex 1:22). Pharpar (2Ki 5:12). Pishon (Ge 2:11). Tigris (Ge 2:14). Ulai (Da 8:16).

RIZIA [8359] (possibly *pleasant one* KB). An Asherite (1Ch 7:39).

RIZPAH [8366] (*heated stones, live coals*). Concubine of Saul (2Sa 3:7). Guards the bodies of her sons hanged by command of David (2Sa 21:8-11).

ROADS [784, 2006, 3718, 4618, 5019, 5986, 7483, *1451, 2853, 3847*]. May refer to paths or highways; hundreds of allusions to roads in the Bible; road robbers quite common (Mt 11:10; Lk 10:30); Romans built highways throughout the empire, some of which are still in use; used by traders, travelers, and armies; Paul used Roman roads on his missionary journeys; the statement "All roads lead to Rome" shows how well provided the Roman empire was with roads. *See Highways.*

ROBBERS [7265, 8720, 774, *3334*]. (Pr 1:11-16). Dens of (Jer 7:11). Bands of (Hos 6:9; 7:1).

ROBBERY [1024, 1608+1611, 1608+1610, 1610, 7693].

Illegal seizure of another's property; forbidden by law (Lev 19:13); highways unsafe (Jdg 5:6; Lk 10:30; 2Co 11:26); houses built to resist robbers; even priests sometimes turned to pillage (Hos 6:9); denounced by prophets (Isa 61:8; Eze 22:29); withholding tithes and offerings from God's storehouse regarded as robbery (Mal 3:8). *See Theft.*

ROBE [*168, 955, 4189, 4230, 4252, 4860, 5077, 8515, 10517, 2264, 2668, 4525, 5124, 5948*]. Of righteousness (2Ch 6:41; Isa 61:10; Rev 6:11; 7:9, 13). Parable of the man who was not dressed in a wedding garment (Mt 22:11).
See Dress.

ROBINSON'S ARCH The remains of ancient Jerusalem masonry, named for the American archaeologist Edward Robinson, who discovered it in 1838. Giant stones, projecting from the SW wall of the temple enclosure are evidently part of an arch that in Herod's time supported a monumental stairway.

ROBOAM *See Rehoboam, 2.*

ROCK [74, 1643, 2734, 4091, 6152, 7446, 10006, *3292, 4376, 5536+5550*]. Struck by Moses for water (Dt 8:15; Ps 78:15-16, 20). Houses in (Jer 49:16; Ob 3; Mt 7:24-25). Oil from (Job 29:6; Dt 32:13). Name of deity (Dt 32:4). *See God, Names of.*

Figurative (2Sa 22:32, 47; 23:3; Ps 18:2; 31:2; 40:2; Isa 17:10; 32:2; Mt 16:18; 1Co 10:4).

ROD [2643, 4751, 4962, 7866, 8657, *2812*,

4811]. Branch, stick, staff; symbol of authority (Ex 4:2, 17, 20; 9:23; 14:16), discipline symbolized by rod (Mic 5:1), messianic ruler (Isa 11:1), affliction (Job 9:34).

ROD OF AARON (Ex 7:9-10, 12, 15, 19-20; 8:5, 16-17; Nu 17:6, 8, 10; Heb 9:4).

ROD OF CORRECTION (Ps 89:32; Pr 10:13; 13:24; 22:15; 23:14; 26:3; 29:15; La 3:1).

ROD OF MOSES (Ex 4:2, 17, 20; 7:19; 8:16; 9:23; 10:13; 14:16; 17:5, 9).

RODANIM [8102] (*people of Rhodes*). The son of Javan; most manuscripts of the Masoretic Text have *Dodanim* (Ge 10:4, ftn). Tribe descended from Javan, son of Japheth (1Ch 1:7).

RODENTS [2923]. (Isa 2:20). *See Animals; Rat(s).*

ROE DEER [3502]. Permitted as food (Dt 14:5). *See Deer.*

ROGELIM [8082] (*[place of] treaders, fullers [one who cleans clothes by kneading with no soap]*). A town near Mahanaim whose citizens assisted David (2Sa 17:27, 29; 19:31).

ROHGAH [8108]. Son of Shomer (1Ch 7:34).

ROI *See Beer Lahai Roi.*

ROLL [1670, 1676, 1723, 6015, 7147, 7571+7572, 7886, 8740, *653, 1813, 3244, 4685, 4771*]. Sheets of papyrus or parchment (made of skin) sewn together to make a long sheet of writing material which was wound around a stick to make a scroll (Isa 34:4; Jer 36; Eze 3:1-3; Rev 5; 10:1-10).

ROLLER NIV "splint" (Eze 30:21).

ROMAMTI-EZER [8251] (*[he is my] highest help*). Son of Heman (1Ch 25:4, 31).

ROMAN EMPIRE City of Rome founded in 753 B.C.; a monarchy until 509 B.C.; a republic from 509 to 31 B.C.; the empire began in 31 B.C., fell in the fifth century A.D. Rome extended its hold over all Italy and eventually over the whole Mediterranean world, Gaul, half of Britain, the Rhine-Danube rivers, and as far as Parthia.

Augustus, the first Roman emperor, divided the Roman provinces into senatorial districts, which were ruled by proconsuls (Ac 13:7; 18:12; 19:38), and imperial districts ruled by governors (Mt 27:2; Lk 2:2; Ac 23:24). Moral corruption was among the causes of the decline and fall of the Roman Empire. Roman reservoirs, aqueducts, roads, public buildings, statues survive.

Many Roman officials are referred to in the NT, including the emperors Augustus (Lk 2:1),

Tiberius (Lk 3:1), Claudius (Ac 11:28), and Nero (Ac 25:11-12).

ROMANS, EPISTLE TO THE

Author: The apostle Paul

Date: Probably written in the early spring of A.D. 57

Outline:

I. Introduction (1:1-15).
II. Theme: Righteousness From God (1:16-17).
III. The Unrighteousness of All Mankind (1:18-3:20).
  A. Gentiles (1:18-32).
  B. Jews (2:1-3:8).
  C. Summary: All People (3:9-20).
IV. Righteousness Imputed: Justification (3:21-5:21).
  A. Through Christ (3:21-26).
  B. Received by Faith (3:27-4:25).
    1. The principle established (3:27-31).
    2. The principle illustrated (ch. 4).
  C. The Fruits of Righteousness (5:1-11).
  D. Summary: Man's Unrighteousness Contrasted With God's Gift of Righteousness (5:12-21).
V. Righteousness Imparted: Sanctification (chs. 6-8).
  A. Freedom From Sin's Tyranny (ch. 6).
  B. Freedom From the Law's Condemnation (ch. 7).
  C. Life in the Power of the Holy Spirit (ch. 8).
VI. God's Righteousness Vindicated: The Problem of the Rejection of Israel (chs. 9-11).
  A. The Justice of the Rejection (9:1-29).
  B. The Cause of the Rejection (9:30-10:21).
  C. Facts That Lessen the Difficulty (ch. 11).
    1. The rejection is not total (11:1-10).
    2. The rejection is not final (11:11-24).
    3. God's ultimate purpose is mercy (11:25-36).
VII. Righteousness Practiced (12:1-15:13).
  A. In the Body—the Church (ch. 12).
  B. In the World (ch. 13).
  C. Among Weak and Strong Christians (14:1-15:13).
VIII. Conclusion (15:14-33).
IX. Commendation and Greetings (ch. 16).

ROME [4871, 4873]. The capital of the Roman Empire. The Jews were excluded from Rome by Claudius (Ac 18:2). Paul's visit to Rome. *See Paul.* Visited by Onesiphorus (2Ti 1:16-17). Paul desires to preach in (Ro 1:15). Abominations in (Ro 1:18-32). Christians in (Ro 16:5-17; Php 1:12-18; 4:22; 2Ti 4:21).

ROOF [1511, 2674, 4918, 6264, 7415, 7771, 7815, *1560, 5094*].
See House, Architecture of.

ROOM [*1074, 2540, 4384, 5226, 6608, 7521, 333, 2906, 5008, 5421, 5536, 5673, 6003*].
  1. Chamber in a house (Ac 1:13). Used as a place for private prayer (Mt 6:6).

2. Place or position in society (Mt 23:6; Lk 14:7-8; 20:46).

ROOSTER [2435+5516, *232*]. Stately in its stride (Pr 30:31). Its crowing a sign of Peter's denial of Jesus (Mt 26:34, 74-75; Mk 13:35; 14:30, 68, 72).

ROOT [4035, 9245+, 9247, 10743, *1748, 4844, 4845*]. Usually used in a figurative sense.
  1. Essential cause of something (1Ti 6:10).
  2. Foundation or support of something (2Ki 19:20; Job 5:3).
  3. Injured roots means loss of life or vitality (Job 31:12; Isa 5:24).
  4. Root of Jesse and Root of David, messianic titles (Isa 11:10; Ro 15:12; Rev 5:5; 22:16). *See Titles and Names, Of Jesus.*

ROPE [2475, 4593, 4798, 5940, 6310, *1069, 2415, 5389*]. Threefold (Ecc 4:12). Worn on the head as an emblem of servitude (1Ki 20:31-32). Used in casting lots (Mic 2:5).
  Figurative: Of love (Hos 11:4). Of affliction (Job 36:8). Of temptations (Ps 140:5; Pr 5:22).

ROSE [*2483*]. Or "crocus" (SS 2:1; Isa 35:1).

ROSETTA STONE   Inscribed basalt slab, found on Rosetta branch of the Nile in 1799, with text in hieroglyphics, demotic (a cursive Egyptian language), and Greek. It furnished the key for the decipherment of hieroglyphics.

ROSH [8033] (*head, leader*).
  1. Son of Benjamin (Ge 46:21).
  2. Chief of three nations that are to invade Israel during the latter days (Eze 38:2; 39:1).

ROW, ROWERS *See Ship.*

RUBY [138, 3905, 7165]. A precious stone (Job 28:18; Pr 20:15; 31:10; La 4:7; Eze 27:16). In the priestly breastplate (Ex 28:17; 39:10). In the Garden of Eden (Eze 28:13).
  See Minerals of the Bible, 1; Sardius; Stones.

RUDDER(S) [*4382*]. Used to steer a ship (Ac 27:40; Jas 3:4).

RUDDY [131, 137, 145]. Red or fair complexion (1Sa 16:12).

RUDE [858] (*untrained, ignorant of rules*). Technically not trained (2Co 11:6).

RUDIMENTS (*first principles or elements of anything*). Elements (Gal 4:3, 9; 2Pe 3:10, 12), first principles (Heb 5:12), physical elements of the world (2Pe 3:10, 12).

RUE [*4379*]. (Lk 11:42).

RUFUS [*4859*] (*red haired*).
  1. Brother of Alexander and son of Simon of Cyrene who bore the cross (Mk 15:21).
  2. Friend of Paul (Ro 16:13).

RUHAMAH (*pitied*). A symbolic name of Israel used to indicate the return of God's mercy (Hos 2:1; cf Ro 9:25-26; 1Pe 2:10). A play on words is involved, for the second child of Gomer, wife of Hosea, was called Lo-Ruhamah, denoting a time when God had turned his back on Israel because of her apostasy. The NT references apply to Gentiles coming into the Church (Ro 9:25-26; 1Pe 2:10).

See Lo-Ammi; Lo-Ruhamah.

RULERS [*380, 5440, 5592, 5601, 5618, 5954, 6249, 7903, 8142, 8569, 8954, 9149, 10715, 794, 801, 807, 1541, 2451*].

General:

Appointed and removed by God. *See Government, God in.*

Chastised (Da 4). *See Nation.*

Monarchical. *See Kings.*

Patriarchal (Ge 27:29, 37). Instances of: Nimrod (Ge 10:8-10). Abraham (Ge 14:13-24; 17:6; 21:21-32). Melchizedek (Ge 14:18). Isaac (Ge 26:26-31). Judah (Ge 38:24). Heads of families (Ex 6:14). Ishmael (Ge 17:20). Esau and the chiefs of Edom (Ge 36).

Theocratic. *See Government.*

Ordained of God (2Ch 9:8; Ro 13:1-2, 4; 1Pe 2:14). Appointed by God (1Sa 9:15-17; 10:1; 15:17; 16:1, 7, 13; 2Sa 7:13-16; 1Ki 14:14; 16:1-4; 1Ch 28:4-5; 29:25; Ps 89:19-37; Da 2:21, 37; 5:21; Ac 13:22). Accountable to God (2Ch 19:6-7).

Servants of the people (1Ki 12:7; 2Ch 10:7; Eze 34:2-4). Loyalty to, commanded (Eze 7:26). Must not be reviled (Ex 22:28; 2Sa 16:9; 19:21; Ecc 10:20; Ac 23:5; 2Pe 2:10-11; Jude 8).

Righteous, beloved (Pr 29:2, 14). A terror to evildoers (Pr 14:35; Ro 13:3). Incompetent, oppress (Pr 28:16). Corrupted, by evil counselors (Pr 25:5), by gifts (Pr 29:4; Isa 1:23; Am 5:11-12; Mic 7:3).

Mosaic law concerning atonement for sins of (Lev 4:22-26).

Character and Qualifications of:

(Nu 27:16-17; 2Sa 23:4; Pr 20:8, 26, 28). Diligent (Ro 12:8). Wise (Ge 41:33; Dt 1:13; Ps 2:10; Pr 20:26; 28:2). Merciful (Isa 16:5; Zec 7:9).

Required to know the law (Jos 1:8; Ezr 7:25), to fear the Lord (Ps 2:11), to be truthful (Pr 17:7), to be righteous (Ex 18:21; Dt 16:19; 27:19; 2Sa 23:3-4; Pr 16:10, 12), to judge justly (Ex 18:16, 20-21; 23:3, 6-7, 9; Lev 19:15; 24:22; Dt 1:16-17; 25:1; 2Ch 9:8; Ps 82:2-4; Pr 31:9; Isa 16:5; 58:6; Jer 22:2-3; Zec 7:9-10; 8:16).

Should not drink wine (Pr 31:4-5). Forbidden to take bribes (Ex 23:8; Dt 16:19), to show partiality (Lev 19:15; Dt 1:17; 16:19; Pr 24:23).

Duties of:

To rule in righteousness (Isa 58:6; Jer 22:1-3). To be judges (2Ch 9:8). To judge according to law (Dt 17:18-19; Jos 1:7-8). In judicial functions to make thorough investigations (Dt 19:18-19).

Righteous, Instances of:

Pharaoh, in his treatment of Abraham (Ge 12:15-20). Abimelech, in his treatment of Abraham (Ge 20), of Isaac (Ge 26:6-11). Joseph, in his conduct of the affairs of Egypt (Ge 41:37-57). Pharaoh, in his treatment of Jacob and his family (Ge 47:5-10; 50:1-6). Moses, in his administration of the affairs of the Israelites (Nu 16:15). *See Government, Mosaic.* Samuel, in not taking reward for judgment (1Sa 12:3-4). Saul, after the defeat of the Ammonites (1Sa 11:12-13).

Solomon, in his judgment between the two women who claimed the same child (1Ki 3:16-28), according to the testimony of the queen of Sheba (1Ki 10:6-9). Asa, in abolishing sodomy and other abominations of idolatry (1Ki 15:11-15; 2Ch 14:2-5). Jehoshaphat, in walking in the ways of the Lord (1Ki 22:41-46; 2Ch 17:3-10; 19; 20:3-30). Hezekiah, in his fear of the Lord (2Ki 18:3; 20:1-11; 2Ch 30; 31). Josiah, in repairing the temple and in other good works (2Ki 22; 23; 2Ch 34; 35). Cyrus, in emancipating the Jews (Ezr 1). Darius, in advancing the rebuilding of the temple (Ezr 6:1-12). Artaxerxes, in commissioning Ezra to restore the forms of worship at Jerusalem (Ezr 7; Ne 2; 5:14). Nehemiah (Ne 4; 5). Daniel. *See Daniel.* King of Nineveh, in repenting and proclaiming a fast (Jnh 3:6-9).

Wicked:

(Ne 9:34-37; Ps 58:1-2; 82:2; 94:20-21; Ecc 3:16-17; 5:8; Isa 5:7; 28:14-15; Hos 7:3). Oppress the people (Ex 3:9; 1Sa 8:10-18; Job 35:9; Pr 28:15-16; Am 4:1; 5:11-12). Pervert justice (Dt 27:19). Cause people to mourn (Pr 29:2; Ecc 4:1). A public calamity (Ecc 10:16; Isa 5:22-23). An abomination to God (Pr 17:15). Abhorred by men (Pr 21:24; 29:2).

Admonitions to (Eze 34:2-4, 7-10; 45:9). Denounced (Eze 34:2-4, 7-10; Am 4:1-2; Mic 3:1, 9-11; Zep 3:3). Divine judgment upon (Isa 3:14-15; 10:1-3; 30:33; 40:23; Jer 5:28-29; Eze 21:25-26; Hos 5:10; Am 5:11-12; Zep 1:8).

Instances of—

Potiphar, putting Joseph into prison (Ge 39:20, w 40:15). Pharaoh, oppressing the Israelites (Ex 1-11). Adoni-Bezek, torturing seventy kings (Jdg 1:7). Abimelech, slaying his seventy brothers (Jdg 9:1-5). Eli's sons, desecrating the sacrifices (1Sa 2:12-17), debauching themselves and the worshipers (1Sa 2:22). Samuel's sons, taking bribes (1Sa 8:1-5).

Saul, sparing Agag and the best of the booty (1Sa 15:8-35), in jealousy plotting against David (1Sa 18:8-29), seeking to slay David (1Sa 19), slaying Ahimelech and the priests (1Sa 22:7-19), Hanun, mistreating David's servants (2Sa 10:4; 1Ch 19:2-5). David, numbering Israel and Judah (2Sa 24:1-9; 1Ch 21:1-7; 27:23-24). Solomon, luxurious and idolatrous (1Ki 11:1-13), oppressing the people (1Ki 12:4; 4:7-23). Rehoboam, making the yoke heavy (1Ki 12:8-11; 2Ch 10:1-15).

Jeroboam, perverting the true worship (1Ki 12:26-33; 13:1-5; 14:16), exalting wicked persons to the priesthood (1Ki 12:31; 13:33; 2Ki 17:32; 2Ch 11:14-15; Eze 44:7, w Nu 3:10). Abijah, walking in the sins of Rehoboam (1Ki 15:3). Nadab, walking in the ways of Jeroboam (1Ki 15:26). Baasha, walking in the ways of Jeroboam (1Ki 15:33-34). Asa, imprisoning the seer and oppressing the people (2Ch 16:10). Zimri, walking in the ways of Jeroboam (1Ki 16:19). Omri, walking in the ways of Jeroboam (1Ki 16:25-29). Ahab, serving Baal (1Ki 16:30-33; 21:21-26), confiscating Naboth's vineyard (1Ki 21, w 1Sa 8:14; 1Ki 22:38; 2Ki 9:26). Jehoram, following the sins of Jeroboam (2Ki 3:2-3). Hazael, committing atrocities (2Ki 8:12; 10:32; 12:17; 13:3-7). Jehoram, walking in the ways of the kings of Israel (2Ki 8:18; 2Ch 21:13). Jehu, did not depart from the sins of Jeroboam (2Ki 10:29). Jehoahaz, in following the sins of Jeroboam (2Ki 13:1-2). Jehoash, in following the wicked example of Jeroboam (2Ki 13:10-11). Jeroboam II, not departing from the sins of Jeroboam (2Ki 14:23-24). Zechariah, Menahem, Pekahiah, and Pekah, following the sins of Jeroboam (2Ki 15:9, 18, 24, 28), conspiring against and slaying Pekahiah (2Ki 15:25). Hoshea, who conspired against Pekah (2Ki 15:30), in permitting Baal worship (2Ki 17:1-2, 7-18). Ahaz, burning his children in idolatrous sacrifice (2Ki 16:3; 2Ch 28:2-4). Manasseh, who committed the abominations of the heathen (2Ki 21:1-17; 2Ch 33:2-7). Amon, who followed the evil example of Manasseh (2Ki 21:19-22). Jehoahaz, who followed in the ways of his fathers (2Ki 23:32). Jehoiakim, in walking in the ways of his fathers (2Ki 23:37), and Jehoiachin (2Ki 24:9). Zedekiah, following the evil example of Jehoiakim (2Ki 24:19; 2Ch 36:12-13) and persecuting Jeremiah (Jer 38:5-6). Joash, killing Zechariah (2Ch 24:2, 17-25). Ahaziah, doing evil like the house of Ahab (2Ch 22:1-9). Amaziah, worshiping the gods of Seir (2Ch 25:14). Uzziah, invading the priest's office (2Ch 26:16).

Xerxes and Haman, decreeing the death of the Jews (Est 3). Nebuchadnezzar, commanding to destroy the wise men (Da 2:1-13), and committing the three Hebrews to the furnace (Da 3:1-23). Belshazzar, in drunkenness and committing sacrilege (Da 5:22-23). Darius, in deifying himself (Da 6:7, 9). The princes, conspiring against Daniel (Da 6:1-9).

Herod the Great, slaying the children in Bethlehem (Mt 2:16-18). Herod Antipas, in beheading John the Baptist (Mt 14:1-11), in craftiness and tyranny (Lk 13:31-32; 23:6-15). Herod Agrippa, persecuting the church (Ac 12:1-19). Pilate, delivering Jesus for crucifixion (Mt 27:11-26; Mk

15:15). Chief priests, elders, and all the council, seeking false witness against Jesus (Mt 26:59). Ananias, commanding that Paul be struck (Ac 23:2).

See Government; Judge; Kings.

RUMAH [8126] (*height*). Home of Pedaiah, whose daughter Zebidah bore Jehoiakim to Josiah, king of Judah (2Ki 23:36), perhaps Arumah near Shechem, or Rumah in Galilee.

RUNNER [*5938, 8132, *5556*]. A bodyguard running before kings and princes (1Sa 8:11; 2Sa 15:1; 1Ki 1:5). An athlete (Job 9:25; 1Co 9:24). *See Army; Games.*

RUSH [*6068]. A water plant (Isa 19:6). *See Plants of the Bible; Reed.*

RUTH [8134, *4858*] (*friendship* BDB; *refreshed [as with water]* IDB; possibly *comrade, companion* ISBE). A Moabitess who married a son of Elimelech and Naomi of Bethlehem (Ru 1:1-4), ancestor of Christ (Mt 1:5), the Book of Ruth is about her.

RUTH, BOOK OF

Author: Anonymous, Jewish tradition points to Samuel

Date: During the period of the monarchy

Outline:
I. Introduction: Naomi Emptied (1:1-5).
II. Naomi Returns From Moab (1:6-22).
  A. Ruth Clings to Naomi (1:6-18).
  B. Ruth and Naomi Return to Bethlehem (1:19-22).
III. Ruth and Boaz Meet in the Harvest Fields (ch. 2).
  A. Ruth Begins Work (2:1-7).
  B. Boaz Shows Kindness to Ruth (2:8-16).
  C. Ruth Returns to Naomi (2:17-23).
IV. Ruth Goes to Boaz at the Threshing Floor (ch. 3).
  A. Naomi Instructs Ruth (3:1-5).
  B. Boaz Pledges to Secure Redemption (3:6-15).
  C. Ruth Returns to Naomi (3:16-18).
V. Boaz Arranges to Marry Ruth (4:1-12).
  A. Boaz Confronts the Unnamed Kinsman (4:1-8).
  B. Boaz Buys Naomi's Property and Announces His Marriage to Ruth (4:9-12).
VI. Conclusion: Naomi Filled (4:13-17).
VII. Epilogue: Genealogy of David (4:18-22).

RYE *See Spelt.*

S

SABACHTHANI [4876]. *See Eloi, Eloi, Lama Sabachthani.*

SABAEANS *See Sabeans; Seba.*

SABAOTH, LORD OF [7372, 4877] (*Yahweh of [angelic] armies*). Regularly translated "LORD Almighty" in the NIV. *See Almighty; God, Names of; Yahweh Tsabbaoth.*

SABBATH [*8701, 4640, 4878, 4879] (*cease, rest*).

A Time of Rest:

(Ge 2:2-3; Lev 23:25; 26:34-35). Holy (Ex 16:23; Ex 20:8, 11; 31:14; 35:2; Dt 5:12; Ne 9:14; Isa 58:13-14; Eze 44:24). A sign (Ex 31:13, 16-17; Eze 20:12-13, 16, 20-21, 24). The Lord is represented as resting on (Ge 2:2-3; Ex 31:17; Heb 4:4).

Rest on, commanded (Ex 16:28-30; 23:12; 31:15; 34:21; 35:2-3; Lev 6:29-31; 19:3, 30; 23:1-3, 27-32; 26:2; Dt 5:12-15; 2Ch 36:21; Jer 17:21-22, 24-25, 27; Lk 23:56), of servants and animals (Ex 16:5, 23-30; 20:10; Mk 16:1; Lk 23:56).

Observation of:

Offerings prescribed for (Lev 24:8; Nu 28:9-10; 1Ch 9:32; 23:31; 2Ch 2:4; Eze 46:4-5). Song for (Ps 92:1-15; 118:24). Preparation for (Ex 16:5, 22; Mt 27:62; Mk 15:42; Lk 23:54; Jn 19:31). Religious usages on (Ge 2:3; Mk 6:2; Lk 4:16, 31; 6:6; 13:10; Ac 13:14). Worship on (Eze 46:1, 3; Ac 15:21; 16:13). Commanded (Eze 46:1, 3). Religious instruction on (Mk 6:2; Lk 4:16, 31; 6:6; 13:10; Ac 13:14, 27, 42, 44; 15:21; 17:2; 18:4). Apostles taught on (Ac 13:14-43, 44-48; 17:2; 18:4). Hypocritical observance, provokes divine displeasure (Isa 1:13; La 2:6; Eze 20:12-13, 16, 21, 24; Am 8:5). Rewards for observance of (Isa 56:2, 4-7; 58:13-14; Jer 17:21-22, 24-25).

Observed by: Moses (Nu 15:32-34). Nehemiah (Ne 13:15, 21). The women preparing to embalm the body of Jesus (Lk 23:56). Paul (Ac 13:14). The disciples (Ac 16:13). John (Rev 1:10).

Violations of:

Punished, by death (Ex 35:2; Nu 15:32-36), by judgments (Jer 17:27). Instances of: Gathering manna (Ex 16:27). Gathering sticks (Nu 15:32). By men from Tyre (Ne 13:16). Inhabitants of Jerusalem (Jer 17:21-23). Profanation of (Ex 16:27-28; Nu 15:32-36; Ne 10:31; 13:15, 21; Jer 17:21-23; Eze 22:8; 23:38).

Christ's Interpretation of:

(Mt 12:1-8, 10-13; Lk 6:1-10; Mk 2:23-28; 13:10-17; 14:1-5; Jn 7:21-24; 9:14). Christ is Lord of (Mt 12:8; Mk 2:28; Lk 6:5). Christ performed miracles on (Mt 12:10-13; Mk 3:1-5; Lk 6:1-10; Lk 13:10-17; Jn 5:5-14; 7:21-24). Christ taught on (Mk 1:21-22; 6:2; Lk 4:16, 31; 6:6; 13:10-17).

The Christian and the Sabbath:

Christian not to be judged regarding (Col 2:16; Ro 1:1-12).

The first day of the week is called the Lord's day (Mt 28:1, 5-7; Mk 16:9; Jn 20:1, 11-16, 19, 26; Ac 20:7; 1Co 16:2; Rev 1:10).

SABBATH, COVERT FOR THE

NIV "Sabbath canopy" (2Ki 16:18).

SABBATH, DAY AFTER THE

The waving of the sheaf in Lev 23:11 may be on the day after the ordinary weekly Sabbath or after the first day of the Passover.

SABBATH DAY'S JOURNEY

A limited journey (c. 3000 feet) which Rabbinic scholars thought a Jew might travel on the Sabbath without breaking the law (Ac 1:12; cf. Ex 16:29; Nu 35:5; Jos 3:4).

SABBATIC YEAR

A rest recurring every seventh year. Called the Year of Release (Dt 15:9; 31:10). Ordinances concerning (Ex 23:9-11; Lev 25). Israelite servants set free in (Ex 21:2; Dt 15:12; Jer 34:14). Creditors required to release debtors in (Dt 15:1-6, 12-18; Ne 10:31). Ordinances concerning instruction in the law during (Dt 31:10-13; Ne 8:18). Punishment to follow a violation of the ordinances concerning (Lev 26:34-35, w 32-41; Jer 34:12-22). *See Jubilee.*

SABBEUS

See Shemaiah, 17.

SABEANS

[6014, 8644, 8645]. One of the Sabean monarchs was the famous Queen of Sheba (1Ki 10:1, 4, 10, 13; 2Ch 9:1, 3, 9, 12). *See Sheba, 7.* The Sabeans were a merchant people from Sheba who in early times lived in SW Arabia (modern Yemen) in a region bordering Ophir and Havilah (Isa 45:14; Eze 23:42 cf. Eze 27:20-22). Romans called it *Arabia Felix.* Sabean raiders invaded the land of Uz and killed Job's flocks and servants (Job 1:15; Isa 43:3). Prophecies concerning (Isa 43:3; Joel 3:8). Giants among (Isa 45:14). Proverbial drunkards (Eze 23:42, ftn). They were slave traders (Joel 3:8). *See Seba.*

SABTA, SABTAH

[6029, 6030]. A son of Cush (Ge 10:7; 1Ch 1:9), perhaps also a place in S Arabia.

SABTECA

[6031]. A son of Cush (Ge 10:7; 1Ch 1:9).

SACAR

[8511] (*reward [given by God]*, possibly *hired hand*).

1. Father of Ahiam (1Ch 11:35), "Sharar" (2Sa 23:33, ftn). *See Sharar.*

2. Son of Obed-Edom (1Ch 26:4).

SACKBUT See Lyre.

SACKCLOTH [2520, 8566, 4884]. A symbol of mourning (1Ki 20:31-32; Job 16:15; Isa 15:3; Jer 4:8; 6:26; 49:3; La 2:10; Eze 7:18; Da 9:3; Joel 1:8). Worn by Jacob when it was reported to him that Joseph had been devoured by wild beasts (Ge 37:34). Animals covered with, at the time of national mourning (Jnh 3:8).

See Mourning.

SACRAMENT (*something obligated [to do]*). A symbolic rite instituted by Christ setting forth the central truths of the Christian faith: death and resurrection with Christ and participation in the redemptive benefits of Christ's mediatorial death. The Roman Catholic Church has seven sacraments; the Protestant Church has two, often called ordinances: baptism and the Lord's Supper.

SACRED PLACES (Dt 12:5, 11; 14:23; 15:20; 16:2; 17:8; Jos 9:27; 18:1; 1Ch 22:1; 2Ch 7:15; Ps 78:68). *See Tabernacle; Temple.*

SACRIFICES [*852, 2284, 2285, 4966, 6296, 6590, 6592, 6592, 6913, 7787, 7928, 8596, 8821, 9458, 10638, 1628, 2602, 2604, 2662, 4712, 4714].

Figurative:

(Isa 34:6; Eze 39:17; Zep 1:7-8; Ro 12:1; Php 2:17; 4:18). Of self-denial (Php 3:7-8). Of praise (Ps 116:17; Jer 33:11; Hos 14:2; Heb 13:15). "Fruit of the lips" signifies praise (Hos 14:2).

See Bruise(s), 2; Offerings.

SACRILEGE (*stealing,* hence, *profaning something sacred*). Profaning holy things. Forbidden (Lev 19:8; 1Co 3:17; Tit 1:11; 1Pe 5:2).

Instances of:

Esau sells his birthright (Ge 25:33). Nadab and Abihu offer unauthorized fire (Lev 10:1-7; Nu 3:4). Of Uzzah (2Sa 6:6-7). Of Uzziah (2Ch 26:16-21). Of Korah and his company (Nu 16:40). Of the people of Beth Shemesh (1Sa 6:19). Of Ahaz (2Ch 28:24). Of money changers in the temple (Mt 21:12-13; Lk 19:45; Jn 2:14-16). Of those who profaned the Lord's Supper (1Co 11:29).

SADDLE [2502, 4121, 4496, 8210] (*to ride, riding seat*). Getting a beast ready for riding (Ge 22:3; Nu 22:21; Jdg 19:10; 2Sa 16:1; 17:23). Donkeys were not ridden with saddles; when carrying heavy burdens they had a thick cushion on their backs.

SADDUCEES [4881] (*followers of Zadok;* possibly *righteous*). A Jewish religious sect in the time of Christ. Beliefs: Acceptance only of the Law and rejection of oral tradition; denial of the Resurrection, immortality of the soul, and the spirit world (Mk 12:18; Lk 20:27; Ac 23:8); they supported the Maccabeans; a relatively small group, but generally held the high priesthood; they were denounced by John the Baptist (Mt 3:7-8) and Jesus (Mt 16:6, 11-12); they opposed Christ (Mt 21:12f; Mk 11:15f; Lk 19:47) and the apostles (Ac 5:17, 33). *See Testaments, Time Between.*

SADOC See Zadok.

SAFE-CONDUCT [6296]. Letters or passports provided to Nehemiah (Ne 2:7).

SAFFRON [4137]. *See Plants of the Bible.*

SAHADUTHA See Jegar Sahadutha.

SAIL See Ship.

SAILORS [408+641, 4876, 3731]. *See Mariner; Occupations and Professions.*

SAINTS [2883, 7705, 10620, 41] (*unique, consecrated, holy ones*).

1. A member of God's covenant people Israel, whether a layman (Ps 34:9; 79:1; 85:8), or a leader (2Ch 6:41; Ps 16:3).

2. A NT believer (Ac 9:13; 2Co 1:1). The saints are the Church (2Co 1:1), people called out of the world to be God's own people. Throughout the Bible the saints are urged to live lives befitting their position (Eph 4:1; Col 1:10), for even saints can sin (1Jn 1:10-2:2). *See Sanctification; Holiness.*

SAKIA [8499] (possibly *one who looks to Yahweh* KB). Son of Shaharaim (1Ch 8:10).

SALAH, SALA (*missile* or *petition* ISBE; possibly *javelin* KB). *See Shelah, 1.*

SALAMIS [4887] (*peace*). A city of Cyprus. Paul and Barnabas preach in (Ac 13:4-5).

SALATHIEL See Shealtiel, 2.

SALECAH [6146] A city on the NE boundary of Bashan (Dt 3:10; Jos 12:5; 13:11; 1Ch 5:11); possibly identified with Salkhad.

SALEM [8970, 4889] (*peace*). Name of a city of which Melchizedek was king (Ge 14:18; Ps 76:2; Heb 7:1-2), probably Jerusalem.

SALIM [4890]. A place near Aenon W of Jordan (Jn 1:28; 3:23, 26; 10:40).

SALLAI [6144] (possibly *God had restored*).

1. A Benjamite dwelling in Jerusalem (Ne 11:8).

2. *See Sallu.*

SALLU [6132, 6139] (possibly *he restores*).

1. A Benjamite dwelling in Jerusalem (1Ch 9:7; Ne 11:7).

2. A priest who returned to Jerusalem with Zerubbabel (Ne 12:20).

SALMA [8514] (*little spark* KB).

1. A son of Caleb (1Ch 2:51, 54).

2. *See Salmon.*

SALMON [8517, 4885, 4891] (*little spark* KB). The father of Boaz, the husband of Ruth (Ru 4:20-21; 1Ch 2:11). In the lineage of Joseph (Mt 1:4-5; Lk 3:32). Also spelled Salma (Ru 4:20, ftn).

SALMONE [4892]. A promontory of Crete (Ac 27:7).

SALOME [4897] (*peaceful, prosperous one*).
1. The wife of Zebedee and the mother of James and John (Mt 27:56; Mk 15:40; 16:1), ministered to Jesus (Mk 15:40-41), present at the crucifixion of Jesus (Mt 27:56), came to the tomb to anoint the body of Jesus (Mk 16:1).
2. The daughter of Herodias; as a reward for her dancing she obtained the head of John the Baptist (Mt 14:3-11; Mk 6:17-28). Her name is not given in the Gospels, but in Josephus.

SALT [4865, 4873, 4875, 4877, 7490, 10420, *229, 266, 4395*]. Lot's wife turned into a pillar of (Ge 19:26). The city of Salt (Jos 15:62). The valley of salt (2Sa 8:13; 2Ki 14:7). Salt sea (Ge 14:3; Nu 34:12; Dt 3:17; Jos 3:16; 12:3; 15:2). Salt pits (Zep 2:9). All animal sacrifices were required to be seasoned with (Lev 2:13; Ezr 6:9; Eze 43:24; Mk 9:49). Used in ratifying covenants (Nu 18:19; 2Ch 13:5). Elisha casts, into the pool of Jericho, to purify it (2Ki 2:20-21).
Symbolic: Of fidelity (Nu 18:19; 2Ch 13:5), of barrenness and desolation (Dt 29:23; Jdg 9:45; Jer 17:6; Zep 2:7).
Figurative: Of the saving efficacy of the church (Mt 5:13; Mk 9:49-50; Lk 14:34). Of wise conversation (Col 4:6).

SALT, CITY OF A city in the wilderness of Judah, between Nibshan and En Gedi (Jos 15:62), the site of which is uncertain; possibly Qumran.

SALT, COVENANT OF A covenant confirmed with sacrificial meals at which salt was used (Lev 2:13; Nu 18:19).

SALT HERBS [4865]. A plant that grows in harsh terrain (Job 30:4).

SALT SEA See *Dead Sea.*

SALT, VALLEY OF A valley between Jerusalem and Edom in which great victories were won over the Edomites (2Sa 8:13; 2Ki 14:7; 2Ch 25:11).

SALU [6140] (*restored* IDB). Father of Zimri (Nu 25:14).

SALUTATIONS See *Greetings.*

SALVATION [3802, 3828, 3829, 7407, 9591, *5401, 5403*].
Call to:
(Dt 30:19-20; Isa 55:1-3, 6-7; Lk 3:6; Ac 16:31; Heb 2:3).

Signifying:
Gracious providence (Dt 32:15; Ps 68:19-20; 91:16; 95:1; 116:13; 149:4; Isa 12:2-3). Personal deliverance from enemies (2Sa 22:36; Ps 3:8; 18:2; 37:39; Isa 1:18; 32:1-4). National deliverance from enemies (Ex 15:2; 1Ch 16:35; Ps 98:2-3; 106:8; Isa 46:12-13; Jer 3:23). A divine standard of righteousness (Isa 56:1), the saving power of divine truth (Isa 45:17), the light and glory of Zion (Isa 62:1). The promised Messiah (Jn 4:22). Personal righteousness (2Ch 6:41; Ps 132:16). Eternal life (1Th 5:8-9; 1Pe 1:5, 9; 1Jn 5:11). Everlasting (Isa 45:17; 52:10). Liberty (Isa 61:1-3; Mt 11:28-30).
To be developed (Php 2:12; 1Th 5:8-10; Jude 3).

From God:
(Ps 3:8; 36:8-9; 37:39; 68:18-20; 91:16; 98:2-3; 106:8; 121:1-8; Isa 46:12-13; 51:4-5; 63:9; Jer 3:23; 21:8; Eze 18:32; Joel 2:32; 1Pe 1:5; 1Jn 2:25).

Through Christ—
(Isa 61:10; Mt 1:21; Lk 19:10; 24:46-47; Jn 3:14-17; 11:51-52; Ac 4:12; 13:26, 38-39, 47; 16:30-31; Ro 5:15-21; 7:24-25; 9:30-33; 1Co 6:11; Gal 1:4; 3:13-14; Eph 1:9-10, 13; 2Ti 1:9-10; 2:10; Tit 3:5-7; Heb 2:3, 10; 5:9; 7:25; 1Jn 4:9-10; 5:11; Jude 3; Rev 3:20; 5:9).

By—
The atonement (1Co 1:18, 21, 24-25; Gal 1:4; 3:8, 13-14, 21, 26-28; Col 1:20-23, 26-27; 1Ti 2:6; Rev 5:9), the Resurrection (Ro 5:10), the gospel (Ro 1:16; Jas 1:21), the grace of God (Eph 2:8-9; Tit 2:11; 2Pe 3:15), the word of God (Jas 1:21), the power of God (1Co 1:18).

Message of:
Foretold by the prophets (Isa 29:18-19, 24; 35:8; Lk 2:31-32; 1Pe 1:10). By angels (Lk 2:9-14). From the seed of Abraham (Ge 12:13). Proclaimed by Christ (Lk 19:10; Jn 12:32). Preached by the apostles (Ac 11:17-18; 16:17). Wisdom for, derived from the Scriptures (2Ti 3:15). Praise for, ascribed to God and the Lamb (Rev 7:9-10).

For:
Israel (Isa 45:17; 46:12-13; Ac 13:26, 38-39, 47; Ro 1:16).
The Gentiles (1Ki 8:41-43; Isa 52:10, 15; 56:1, 6-8; Mt 21:31; 24:14; Jn 10:16; Ac 11:17-18; 15:7-9, 11; 28:28; Ro 11:11-12; 15:9, 16; Gal 3:8, 14; Eph 3:6, 9).
All people (Mt 18:14; 22:9-10; 22:14; Lk 2:10, 31-32; 3:6; 13:29; Gal 3:28; Eph 2:14, 17; Col 3:11; 1Ti 2:3-4; 4:10; 2Pe 3:9; Rev 5:9; 7:9-10; 14:6; 22:17).
Experienced by Moses (Ex 15:2). Priests clothed with (2Ch 6:41; Ps 132:16).

From:
From sin (Mt 1:21; Mk 2:17; Lk 5:31-32). From spiritual hunger and thirst (Jn 4:14; 6:35; 7:37-38).

See Adoption; Redemption; Regeneration; Sanctification.

Conditions of:

Repentance (Mt 3:2; Mk 1:4; Lk 3:8; Ac 2:38; 3:19; 2Co 7:10). Faith in Christ (Mk 16:15-16; Jn 3:14-18; 5:24; 6:47; 9:35; 11:25-26; 12:36; 20:31; Ac 2:21; 16:30-31; 20:21; Ro 1:16-17; 3:21-30; 4:1-25; 5:1-2; 10:4, 8-13; Gal 2:16; 3:8, 26-28; Eph 2:8; Php 3:9; 2Th 2:13; 1Ti 1:15-16; Heb 4:1-2; 1Pe 1:9). Supreme love to Christ (Lk 14:25-27). Renunciation of the world (Mt 19:16-21; Lk 14:33; 18:18-26). Choice (Dt 30:19-20; Ps 65:4; Eph 1:4-5). Seeking God (Am 5:4). Fear of God (Pr 14:27; 15:23; 16:6; Mal 4:2).

Not by works (Ro 3:28; 4:1-25; 9:30-33; Ro 11:6; Gal 2:16; Eph 2:8-9; 2Ti 1:9-10; Tit 3:5-7).

See Blessings, Spiritual, Contingent Upon Obedience; Faith; Obedience; Perseverance; Repentance.

Plan of:

(Jn 17:4; Heb 6:17-20). Foreordained (Eph 1:4-6; 3:11). Described as a mystery (Mt 13:11; Mk 4:11; Lk 8:10; Ro 16:25-26; 1Co 2:7-9; Eph 1:9-10, 13; 3:9-10; 6:19; Col 1:26-27; 1Ti 3:16; Rev 10:7).

Includes—

The incarnation of Christ (Gal 4:4-5). The atonement by Christ (Jn 18:11; 19:28-30; Ac 3:18; 17:3; Ro 16:25-26; 1Co 1:21-25; 2:7-9; Eph 1:7-11; 3:18; 6:19; Col 1:26-27; Heb 2:9-18; 10:10). Initial grace (Jn 6:37, 44-45, 65; Eph 2:5; Tit 2:11). The election of grace (2Th 2:13-14; 2Ti 1:9-10). Inheritance (Heb 1:14). Regeneration (Jn 3:3-12).

Sets Forth—

Reconciliation to God through Christ (2Co 5:18-19; Col 1:9, 19-23; Heb 2:14-18). Righteousness by faith in the atonement of Christ, as opposed to righteousness by works (Ro 10:3-9; 16:25-26; Eph 2:6-10).

Offered and Rejected—

(Dt 32:15; Mt 22:3-13; 23:37; Lk 14:16-24; Jn 5:40).

Parables of: (Lk 15:2-32).

Illustrated by:

A horn (Ps 18:2; Lk 1:69), a tower (2Sa 22:51), a helmet (Isa 59:17; Eph 6:17), a shield (2Sa 22:36), a lamp (Isa 62:1), a cup (Ps 116:13), clothing (2Ch 6:41; Ps 132:16; 149:4; Isa 61:10), wells (Isa 12:3), walls and bulwarks (Isa 26:1; 60:18), chariots (Hab 3:8), a victory (1Co 15:57).

Typified by the bronze snake (Nu 21:4-9, w Jn 3:14-15).

See Atonement; Jesus the Christ, Mission of; Redemption; Regeneration; Sanctification; Sin, Forgiveness of.

SAMARIA [9076, 9085, 10726, 4899] (*belonging to clan of Shemer, 1Ki. 16:24, BDB*).

1. City of, built by Omri (1Ki 16:24). Capital of the kingdom of the ten tribes (1Ki 16:29; 22:51; 2Ki 13:1, 10; 15:8). Besieged by Ben-Hadad (1Ki 20; 2Ki 6:24-33; 7). The king of Syria is led into, by Elisha, who miraculously blinds him and his army (2Ki 6:8-23). Ahab ruled in. *See Ahab;*

Jezebel. Besieged by Shalmaneser, king of Assyria, three years; taken; the people carried away to Halah and Habor, cities of the Medes (2Ki 17:5-6; 18:9-11). Idolatry of (1Ki 16:32; 2Ki 13:6). Temple of, destroyed (2Ki 10:17-28; 23:19). Paul and Barnabas preach in (Ac 15:3). Visited by Philip, Peter, and John (Ac 8:5-25).

2. Country of (Isa 7:9). Foreign colonies distributed among the cities of, by the king of Assyria (2Ki 17:24-41; Ezr 4:9-10). Roads through, from Judea into Galilee (Lk 17:11; Jn 4:3-8). Jesus journeys through (Jn 4:1-42), heals lepers in (Lk 17:11-19). The good Samaritan from (Lk 10:33-35). No dealings between the Jews and the inhabitants of (Jn 4:9). Expect the Messiah (Jn 4:25). Disciples made from the inhabitants of (Jn 4:39-42; Ac 8:5-8, 4-17, 25). Jesus forbids the apostles to preach in the cities of (Mt 10:5).

SAMARITAN PENTATEUCH *See Samaritan(s), 2.*

SAMARITAN(S) [4899, 4901, 4902] (*of Samaria*).

1. The inhabitants of the region of Samaria (2Ki 17:26; Mt 10:5; Lk 9:52; 10:33; Jn 4:9, 30, 40; Ac 8:25). After the captivity of the N kingdom colonists from Babylonia, Syria, Elam, and other Assyrian territories (2Ki 17:24-34), intermarried with remnants of Jews in Samaria; held in contempt by the Jews (Ne 4:1-3; Mt 10:5; Jn 4:9-26).

2. The sect which derived its name from Samaria, a term of contempt with the Jews (Jn 8:48). Religion of the Samaritans was based on the Pentateuch alone.

SAMGAR, SAMGAR-NEBO

[6161]. Depending on word division, Samgar is the city of Nergal-Sharezer, a Babylonian official at the siege of Jerusalem, or Samgar-Nebo is himself an official (Jer 39:3 and ftn).

See Nebo-Sarsekim.

SAMLAH [8528] (*a garment*). One of the ancient kings of Edom (Ge 36:36-37; 1Ch 1:47-48).

SAMOS [4904] (*heights, lofty place*). An island in the Aegean Sea. Visited by Paul (Ac 20:15).

SAMOTHRACE [4903] (*Thracian Samos*). An island in the Aegean Sea. Visited by Paul (Ac 16:11).

SAMSON [9088, 4907] (*little one of Shemesh [pagan sun god]* or *sunny* IDB KB; *strong,* Josephus *Antiq.* 5.8.4). A judge of Israel (Jdg 16:31). A Danite, son of Manoah; miraculous birth of; a Nazirite from his mother's womb; the mother forbidden to drink wine or strong drink, or to eat any unclean thing during gestation (Jdg 13:2-7, 24-25). Desires a Philistine woman for his wife; slays a lion (Jdg 14:1-7). His marriage feast and the riddle propounded (Jdg 14:8-19). Wife of, estranged (Jdg 14:20; 15:1-2). Is avenged for the estrangement of his wife (Jdg 15:3-8). His great strength (Jdg 15:7-14; Heb 11:32). Slays a thousand Philistines with the jawbone of a donkey (Jdg 15:13-17). Miraculously supplied with water (Jdg 15:18-19). Consorts with Delilah, a harlot; her plots with the Philistines to overcome him (Jdg 16:4-20). Is blinded by the Philistines and confined to hard labor in prison; pulls down the pillars of the temple, killing himself and many Philistines (Jdg 16:21-31; Heb 11:32).

SAMUEL [9017, 4905] (his name is God [El] BDB IDB ISBE; heard of God, KD; the unnamed god is El KB).

1. Last of the judges (1Sa 7:15), and first of the prophets after Moses (2Ch 25:18; Jer 15:1). A seer (1Sa 9:9) and priest (1Sa 2:18, 27, 35). The son of Elkanah and Hannah (1Sa 1:19-20), birth the result of special providence. Brought up by Eli (1Sa 3), anointed Saul (1Sa 10) and David (1Sa 16:13). Traditional author of biblical books which bear his name, died at Ramah (1Sa 25:1).

2. Descendant of Issachar (1Ch 7:2).

SAMUEL, 1 and 2

Author: Anonymous, some have suggested Zabud, son of Nathan the prophet, who is referred to in 1Ki 4:5 as the "personal adviser" to King Solomon.

Date: Probably shortly after Solomon's death (930 B.C.)

Chronology of the Books of Samuel (all dates B.C.):

1105: Birth of Samuel (1Sa 1:20).
1080: Birth of Saul.
1050: Saul anointed to be king (1Sa 10:1).
1040: Birth of David.
1025: David anointed to be Saul's successor (1Sa 16:1-13).
1010: Death of Saul and beginning of David's reign over Judah in Hebron (2Sa 1:1; 2:1, 4, 11).
1003: Beginning of David's reign over all Israel and capture of Jerusalem (2Sa 5).
997-992: David's wars (2Sa 8:1-14).
991: Birth of Solomon (2Sa 12:24; 1Ki 3:7; 11:42).
980: David's census (2Sa 24:1).
970: End of David's reign (2Sa 5:4-5; 1Ki 2:10-11).

Outline:

I. Historical Setting for the Establishment of Kingship in Israel (1Sa 1-7).
   A. Samuel's Birth, Youth and Calling to Be a Prophet; Judgment on the House of Eli (1Sa 1-3).
   B. Israel Defeated by the Philistines, the Ark of God Taken and the Ark Restored; Samuel's Role as Judge and Deliverer (1Sa 4-7).
II. The Establishment of Kingship in Israel

Under the Guidance of Samuel the Prophet (1Sa 8-12).
   A. The People's Sinful Request for a King and God's Intent to Give Them a King (1Sa 8).
   B. Samuel Anoints Saul Privately to Be King (1Sa 9:1-10:16).
   C. Saul Chosen to Be King Publicly by Lot at Mizpah (1Sa 10:17-27).
   D. The Choice of Saul as King Confirmed by Victory Over the Ammonites (1Sa 11:1-13).
   E. Saul's Reign Inaugurated at a Covenant Renewal Ceremony Convened by Samuel at Gilgal (1Sa 11:14-12:25).
III. Saul's Kingship is a Failure (1Sa 13-15).
IV. David's Rise to the Throne; Progressive Deterioration and End of Saul's Reign (1Sa 16:1-2Sa 5:5).
   A. David Is Anointed Privately, Enters the Service of King Saul and Flees for His Life (1Sa 16-26).
   B. David Seeks Refuge in Philistia, and Saul and His Sons Are Killed in Battle (1Sa 27-31).
   C. David Becomes King Over Judah (2Sa 1-4).
   D. David Becomes King Over All Israel (2Sa 5:1-5).
V. David's Kingship in Its Accomplishments and Glory (2Sa 5:6-9:12).
   A. David Conquers Jerusalem and Defeats the Philistines (2Sa 5:6-25).
   B. David Brings the Ark to Jerusalem (2Sa 6).
   C. God Promises David and Everlasting Dynasty (2Sa 7).
   D. The Extension of David's Kingdom Externally and the Justice of His Rule Internally (2Sa 8).
   E. David's Faithfulness to His Covenant With Jonathan (2Sa 9).
VI. David's Kingship in Its Weaknesses and Failures (2Sa 10-20).
   A. David Commits Adultery and Murder (2Sa 10-12).
   B. David Loses His Sons Amnon and Absalom (2Sa 13-20).
VII. Final Reflections on David's Reign (2Sa 21-24).

SANBALLAT [6172] (Sin [pagan moon god] has given life). A very influential Samaritan who tried unsuccessfully to defeat Nehemiah's plans for rebuilding the walls of Jerusalem (Ne 4:1ff; 6:1-14; 13:28).

SANCTIFICATION [39, 40]. Separated, set apart, made holy: For God (Ex 33:16; Dt 7:6). From iniquity (2Ti 2:21).

By:

God (Ex 29:44; 31:13; Lev 20:8; 21:8, 15, 23; 22:9, 16; Jer 1:5; Eze 20:12; 37:28). In Christ (1Co 1:2, 30; 6:11; Eph 5:25-27; Heb 2:11; 10:10, 14; 13:12). By the Holy Spirit (Ro 15:16; 2Th 2:13-14; 1Pe 1:2).

By the blood of Christ (Heb 9:14; 13:12). By faith in Christ (Ac 26:17-18). By the truth (Jn

17:17, 19). By confession of sin (1Jn 1:9). By intercessory prayer for (1Th 5:23). Sanctification is the will of God (1Th 4:3-4).

Instances of:

The altar sanctifies the gift (Ex 29:37; 30:29; Mt 23:19).

The Sabbath (Ge 2:3; Dt 5:12; Ne 13:22). Mount Sinai (Ex 19:23). The tabernacle (Ex 29:43-44; 30:26, 29; 40:34-35; Lev 8:10; Nu 7:1). The furniture of the tabernacle (Ex 30:26-29; Nu 7:1). The altar of burnt offerings (Ex 29:36-37; 40:10-11; Lev 8:11, 15; Nu 7:1). The basin (Ex 30:23; Lev 8:11). The temple (2Ch 29:5, 17, 19).

Houses (Lev 27:14-15). Land (Lev 27:16-19, 22). Offerings (Ex 29:27). Material things by anointing (Ex 40:9-11).

The firstborn of Israelites (Ex 13:2; Lev 27:26; Nu 8:17; Dt 15:19). Eleazar to get the ark (1Sa 7:1). Jesse to offer a sacrifice (1Sa 16:5). Job's children, by Job (Job 1:5).

Of Levites (1Ch 15:12, 14; 2Ch 29:34; 30:15), commanded (1Ch 15:12; 2Ch 29:5). Of priests (1Ch 15:14; 2Ch 5:11; 30:24), commanded (Ex 19:22). Of Aaron and his sons (Ex 28:41; 29:33, 44; 40:13; Lev 8:12, 30). Of Israel (Ex 29:10, 14)l, commanded (Ex 19:10; Lev 11:44; 20:7; Nu 11:18; Jos 3:5; 7:13; Joel 2:16).

Of the Corinthian Christians (1Co 1:2; 6:11; 7:14). Of the church (Eph 5:26; 1Th 5:23; Jude 24).

See Holiness; Purity; Sin, Forgiveness; Spiritual Purification.

SANCTUARY [185, 1074, 1808, 2121, 5219, 7163, 7164, 7731, *41, 3302, 3875*] (*sacredness, apartness, place apart, sacred place, holy place*).

1. The tabernacle or temple, where God established his earthly abode.

2. Judah (Ps 114:2).

3. Place of asylum (1Ki 2:28f).

4. In plural, idolatrous shrines (Am 7:9).

5. Earthly sanctuary a type of the heavenly sanctuary, in which Christ is high priest and sacrifice (Heb 10:1-18).

SAND [2567, 6760, 9220, *302*]. Found in the desert and on the shores of large bodies of water; symbolic of numberlessness, vastness (Ge 22:17; Jer 33:22; 1Ki 4:29), weight (Job 6:3), and instability (Mt 7:26).

SANDAL [5836, 5837, *4908, 5687*]. Taken off on holy ground (Ex 3:5; Jos 5:15; Ac 7:33), in mourning (Eze 24:17), in token of refusal to observe the Levirate marriage (Dt 25:9; Ru 4:7-8). Of the Israelites did not wear out (Dt 29:5). Poor sold for a pair of (Am 2:6; 8:6). Made of leather (Eze 16:10), thong of (Ge 14:23; Isa 5:27; Mk 1:7), untying of, a humble service (Lk 3:16).

See Dress.

SANDBARS [*1458+5536, 5358*]. Off the

shores of N Africa S of Crete; site of Paul's shipwreck (Ac 27:17, 41).

SANHEDRIN [*5284*] (*sit together*). Highest Jewish tribunal during Greek and Roman periods; its origin is unknown; when Jerusalem fell to the Romans in A.D. 70; in the time of Jesus it had authority only in Judea, but its influence was recognized even in the Diaspora (Ac 9:2; 22:5; 26:12). Composed of seventy members, plus the president, who was the high priest; members drawn from chief priests, scribes, and elders (Mt 16:21; 27:41; Mk 8:31; 11:27; 14:43, 53; Lk 9:22); the secular nobility of Jerusalem; final court of appeal for all questions connected with the Mosaic law; could order arrests by its own officers of justice (Mt 26:47; Mk 14:43; Ac 4:3; 5:17f; 9:2); did not have the right of capital punishment in the time of Christ (Jn 18:31-32). *See Elders, Council of.*

SANITATION AND HYGIENE

Relating to:

Carcasses (Lev 5:2; 10:4-5; 11:24-40; 22:4, 6; Nu 9:6, 10; 19:11-16; 31:19; Dt 21:22-23). Childbirth (Lev 12:3; Eze 16:4). Circumcision. *See Circumcision.* Contagion (Lev 5:2-3; 7:19, 21; 11:24-40; Nu 9:6, 10; 19:11-16, 22; 31:19-20). Infectious skin diseases (Lev 13-14; Nu 5:2-4; Dt 24:8). Bodily discharges (Lev 15:2-33; 22:4-8).

For Prevention of the Spread of Disease:

By washing (Lev 13:6, 34, 53-54, 58-59; 14:8-9, 46, 48, 54-57; 15:2-28; Nu 31:19-20, 22-24; Dt 23:10-11). By burning (Lev 7:19; 13:51-52, 55-57; Nu 31:19-20, 22-23). By isolation, *i.e.,* quarantine (Lev 13:2-5, 31-33, 45-50; 14:34-38; 15:19; Nu 5:2-3; 12:10, 14-15; 2Ki 7:3; 15:5; 2Ch 26:21; Lk 17:12). By demolishing infected houses (Lev 14:39-45).

Food:

Acceptable: Animals with split hoof that chew cud (Lev 11:2-3; Dt 14:6). Aquatic animals having fins and scales (Lev 11:9; Dt 14:9). Certain insects (Lev 11:22).

Forbidden: Fat (Lev 3:17; 7:23-25). Blood (Lev 3:17; 7:26-27; 17:10-14; 19:26; Dt 12:16, 20-25; 15:22-23). Meat that touched anything unclean (Lev 7:19). Meat of fellowship and thank offerings remaining until the second day (Lev 7:15; 22:30). Meat of vow or voluntary offerings left until the third day (Lev 7:16, 18; 19:5-8). Animals that only chew cud or only have a split hoof (Lev 11:4, 8, 26; Dt 14:7-8). Aquatic animals without fins and scales (Lev 11:10-12; Dt 14:10). Animals dying of themselves or torn by beasts (Ex 22:31; Lev 17:15; 22:8; Dt 14:21). Certain insects (Lev 11:23). Certain creatures that move on the ground (Lev 11:20-21, 28-31, 41). Certain birds (Lev 11:13-18).

Waste Products:

Disposition (Ex 29:14, 34; Lev 4:11-12, 21; 6:30; 7:17, 19; 8:17, 32; 9:11; 16:27-28; 19:6; Dt 23:12-13; Heb 13:11).

Women in Childbirth: (Lev 12:2, 4-5).

Penalties Concerning:
(Dt 28:15, 21-22, 27, 35, 45, 59-62).
See Defilement; Leprosy; Purification; Unclean, Uncleanness; Washings.

SANNAH *See Kiriath Sannah.*

SANSANNAH [6179] (*a palm branch*). A city of Judah (Jos 15:31).

SAPH [6198] (*a basin, threshold*). A Philistine giant, slain by one of David's heroes (2Sa 21:18; 1Ch 20:4).

SAPHIR *See Shaphir.*

SAPPHIRA [4912] (*beautiful*). The wife of Ananias; struck dead at Peter's feet because she lied (Ac 5:1-10).

SAPPHIRE [6209, 4913].
1. A precious stone (Ex 24:10; Eze 28:13).
2. Set in the priestly breastplate (Ex 28:18; 39:11).

Symbolic:
Throne of God (Ex 24:10; Eze 1:26; 10:1). Seen in the foundation of the Holy City, the New Jerusalem in John's apocalyptic vision (Rev 21:19).

Figurative:
Ezekiel uses imagery of the Creation and the Fall to picture the career of the king of Tyre; unlike Adam, who was naked, the king is pictured as a fully clothed priest, ordained to guard God's holy place; the nine stones listed are among the twelve worn by the priest (Eze 28:13).
See Minerals of the Bible, 1; Stones.

SARAH, SARAI [8577, 8584, 4925] (*princess*).
1. .The wife of Abraham (Ge 11:29-31; 12:5). Near of kin to Abraham (Ge 12:10-20; 20:12). Abraham represents her as his sister, and Abimelech, king of Gerar, takes her; she is restored to Abraham by means of a dream (Ge 20:1-14). Is sterile; gives her maid, Hagar, to Abraham as a wife to bear his child (Ge 16:1-3). Her jealousy of Hagar (Ge 16:4-6; 21:9-14). Her miraculous conception of Isaac (Ge 17:15-21; 18:9-15). Name changed from Sarai to Sarah (Ge 17:15). Gives birth to Isaac (Ge 21:3, 6-8). Death and burial of (Ge 23; 25:10). Character of (Heb 11:11; 1Pe 3:5-6).
2. The daughter of Asher (Ge 46:17; Nu 26:46; 1Ch 7:30).

SARAPH [8598] (*burning one, serpent*). A descendant of Shelah (1Ch 4:22).

SARCASM

Instances of:
Cain's self-justifying argument when God asked him where Abel was (Ge 4:9). Israelites reproaching Israel (Nu 11:20; Jdg 10:14). Balak reproach-
ing Balaam (Nu 24:11). Joshua to descendants of Joseph (Jos 17:15). By Jotham (Jdg 9:7-19), Samson (Jdg 14:18). The men of Jabesh to Nahash (1Sa 11:10). Eliab to David (1Sa 17:28). Elijah to the priests of Baal (1Ki 18:27). David's reply to Michal's irony (2Sa 6:21). Ahab's reply to Ben-Hadad (1Ki 20:11). Jehoash to Amaziah (2Ki 14:9-10; 2Ch 25:18-19). The field commander to Hezekiah (2Ki 18:23-24). Sanballat's address to the army of Samaria (Ne 4:2-3). Zophar to Job (Job 11:12). Job to Zophar (Job 12:2-3). Of Solomon (Pr 26:16). The persecutors of Jesus (Mt 27:28-29; Lk 23:11; Jn 19:2-3, 5, 15). Paul (1Ti 4:7). Agrippa to Paul (Ac 26:28).
See Irony; Satire.

SARDINE *See Carnelian; Minerals of the Bible.*

SARDIS [4915]. Chief city of Lydia; famous for arts and crafts; patron of mystery cults (Rev 1:11; 3:1-6).

SARDITE *See Sered, Seredite.*

SARDIUS *See Carnelian; Minerals of the Bible, 1; Ruby; Stones.*

SARDONYX [4918]. A precious stone seen in the foundation of the Holy City, the New Jerusalem (Rev 21:20). *See Minerals of the Bible, 1; Stones.*

SAREPTA *See Zarephath.*

SARGON [6236] (*firm, faithful king* BDB; *the king is legitimate* IDB).
1. Sargon I, king and founder of early Babylonian Empire (2400 B.C.). Not referred to in the Bible.
2. Sargon II (722-705 B.C.), an Assyrian king (Isa 20:1), successor of Shalmaneser who captured Samaria (2Ki 17:1-6), defeated Egyptian ruler So (2Ki 17:4), destroyed the Hittite Empire; succeeded by his son Sennacherib.

SARID [8587] (*survivor*). A village on the boundary of Zebulun (Jos 19:10, 12); modern Tel Shadud, N of Megiddo.

SARON *See Sharon.*

SARSECHIM *See Nebo-Sarsekim.*

SARUCH *See Serug.*

SASH [77, 258, 2512, 2514, 8005, 2438]. A belt or waistband. Worn by the high priest (Ex 28:4, 39; 39:29; Lev 8:7; 16:4), by other priests (Ex 28:40; 29:9; Lev 8:13), by women (Isa 3:18-24), by Jesus in John's vision (Rev 1:13). Commerce in (Pr 31:24). *See Belt; Dress.*

SATAN [8477, 4928] (*hostile opponent*).
1. As a common noun; enemy or adversary (1Sa 29:4; 1Ki 5:4; 11:14; Ps 38:20; 109:6).
2. As a proper noun; the chief of the fallen spirits,

the grand adversary of God and man (Jn 1:6, 12; 2:1; Zec 3:1), hostile to everything good. Not an independent rival of God, but is able to go only as far as God permits (Job 1:12; 2:6; Lk 22:31). Basically evil; story of his origin not told, but he was originally good; fell as a star out of heaven because of pride (possibly Isa 14:12; Eze 29:12-19; Lk 10:18; 1Ti 3:6). Ruler of a powerful kingdom standing in opposition to God (Mt 12:26; Lk 11:18); continually seeks to defeat the divine plans of grace toward mankind (1Pe 5:8); defeated by Christ at Calvary (Ge 3:15; Jn 3:8).

Sterilizes the heart (Mt 13:19, 38-39; Mk 4:15; Lk 8:12). Causes spiritual blindness (2Co 4:4), physical infirmities (Lk 13:16).

Devices of (2Co 2:11; 12:7; Eph 6:11-12, 16; 1Th 2:18; 1Ti 3:6-7).

Hymenaeus and Alexander delivered to (1Ti 1:20). Contends with Michael (Jude 9). Ministers of, masquerade as apostles of Christ (2Co 11:15).

To be resisted (Eph 4:27; Jas 4:7; 1Pe 5:8-9). Resistance of, effectual (1Jn 2:13; 5:18). Gracious deliverance from the power of (Ac 27:18; Col 1:13). Persecutes the church (Rev 2:10, 13-14).

Christ accused of being (Mt 9:34; Mk 2:22-26; Lk 11:15, 18). Paul accuses Elymas the sorcerer of being (Ac 13:10).

Called:
Beelzebub (Mt 12:24; Mk 3:22; Lk 11:15). Belial (2Co 6:15). The devil (Mt 4:1; 13:39; Lk 4:2-6; Rev 20:2). Satan (1Ch 21:1; Job 1:6; Zec 3:1; Lk 22:31; Jn 13:27; Jn 13:27; 26:18; Ro 16:20). Possibly Apollyon (Rev 9:11) and Lucifer (Isa 14:12, KJV). *See Titles and Names, Of the Devil.*

Character of:
Accuser (Job 1:6-7, 9-12; 2:3-7). Adversary (Lk 22:31, 53; 1Pe 5:8). Deceiver of the whole world (Rev 12:9). Murderer and liar (Jn 8:44; Ac 5:3). Sinned from the beginning (1Jn 3:8). Subtle (Ge 3:1; 2Co 11:3). Tempter (Mt 4:3; 1Co 7:5; 1Th 3:5; 1Ti 5:15). Transforms himself into an angel of light (2Co 11:14).

Described as:
Accuser of our brothers (Rev 12:10). Ancient serpent (Rev 12:9; 20:2). Angel of the bottomless pit (Rev 9:11). Enemy (Mt 13:29). Father of lies (Jn 8:44). Great dragon (Rev 12:9). Evil one (Mt 13:19, 38). Power of darkness (Col 1:13). Prince of this world (Jn 12:31; 14:30; 16:11), of demons (Mt 12:24), of the power of the air (Eph 2:2). Ruler of the darkness of this world (Eph 6:12). Spirit that works in the children of disobedience (Eph 2:2). The god of this world (2Co 4:4).

Instances of Temptations of:
Eve (Ge 3:1, 4-5, 14-15; 2Co 11:3). Job (Job 1:13-22; 2:7-10). David (1Ch 21:1). Jesus (Mt 4:1-11; Mk 1:13; Lk 4:1-13; Jn 14:30). Judas (Jn 13:2, 27).

Kingdom of:
Called gates of hell (Mt 16:18). To be destroyed (Ge 3:15; Mt 13:30; Ro 16:20; 1Jn 3:8).

Symbolized:
By the serpent (Ge 3:13; 2Co 11:3). By the dragon (Rev 12:3-4).

Synagogue of: (Rev 2:9; 3:9).
See Demons.

Destiny of:
A conquered enemy of believers (Jn 12:31; 16:9-10; 1Jn 3:8; Col 2:15). Judged already (Jn 16:11). Under perpetual curse (Ge 3:14; Isa 65:25). To be cast out of this world (Jn 12:31), bound (Rev 20:1-3), cast into the lake of fire (Mt 25:41; Rev 20:10).

SATIRE Hannah's song of exultation over Peninnah (1Sa 2:1-10, w 1:5-10). Of Jesus against hypocrites (Mt 23:2-33; Mk 12:13-40; Lk 11:39-54). *See Irony; Sarcasm.*

SATRAP [346, 10026] (*protector of the land*). An official in the Persian Empire who ruled several small provinces (satraps), each having its own governor. (Ezr 8:36; Est 3:12; 8:9; 9:3; Da 3:2-3, 27; 6:1-7).

SATYR NIV "goat idols" (Lev 17:7; 2Ch 11:15); "wild goats" (Isa 34:14).

SAUL [8620, 4910, 4930] (*asked,* possibly *dedicated to God*).
1. Also called Shaul. King of Edom (Ge 36:37-38; 1Ch 1:48-49).
2. King of Israel. A Benjamite, son of Kish (1Sa 9:1-2). Sons of (1Ch 8:33). His personal appearance (1Sa 9:2; 10:23). Made king of Israel (1Sa 9; 10; 11:12-15; Hos 13:11). Dwells at Gibeah of Saul (1Sa 14:2; 15:34; Isa 10:29). Defeats the Philistines (1Sa 13; 14:46, 52). Kills the Amalekites (1Sa 15). Is reproved by Samuel for usurping the priestly functions (1Sa 13:11-14), for disobedience in not slaying the Amalekites; the loss of his kingdom foretold (1Sa 15). Dedicates the spoils of war (1Sa 15:21-25; 1Ch 26:28). Sends messengers to Jesse, asking that David be sent to him as musician and armor-bearer (1Sa 16:17-23). Defeats the Philistines after Goliath is slain by David (1Sa 17). His jealousy of David; gives his daughter, Michal, to David to be his wife; becomes David's enemy (1Sa 18). Tries to slay David; Jonathan intercedes and incurs his father's displeasure; David's loyalty to him; Saul's repentance; prophesies (1Sa 19). Hears Doeg against Ahimelech and slays the priest and his family (1Sa 22:9-19). Pursues David to the wilderness of Ziph; the Ziphites betray David to (1Sa 23). Pursues David to En Gedi (1Sa 24:1-6). His life saved by David (1Sa 24:5-8). Saul's contribution for his bad faith (1Sa 24:16-22). David is again betrayed to, by the Ziphites; Saul pursues him to the hill of Hakilah; his life spared again by David; his confession and his blessing upon David (1Sa 26). Slays the Gibeonites; crime avenged by the death of seven of his sons (2Sa 21:1-9). His kingdom invaded by Philistines; seeks counsel of the medium of Endor, who foretells his death (1Sa

28:3-25; 29:1). Is defeated and with his sons is slain (1Sa 31), their bodies exposed in Beth Shan; rescued by the people of Jabesh and burned; bones of, buried under a tree at Jabesh (1Sa 31, w 2Sa 1; 2; 1Ch 10). His death a judgment on account of his sins (1Ch 10:13).

3. Of Tarsus. *See Paul.*

SAVIOR [3802, 3829, 4635, 9591, *5400*]

(*deliverer*). One who saves, delivers, or preserves from any evil or danger, whether physical or spiritual, temporal or eternal; term applied both to people (Jdg 3:9, 15; 2Ki 13:5; Ne 9:27; Ob 21) and to God (Ps 44:3, 7; Isa 43:11; 45:21; 60:16; Jer 14:8; Hos 13:4). In NT it is never applied to people, but only to God and Christ (Lk 1:47; 1Ti 1:1; 2:3; 4:10; Tit 1:3). Savior is preeminently the title of the Son (2Ti 1:10; Tit 1:4; 2:13; 3:6; 2Pe 1:1; 1Jn 4:10).

See God, Savior; Jesus the Christ, Savior.

SAVOR Taste (Mt 5:13; Lk 14:34), smell (Joel 2:20). Also used metaphorically (2Co 2:14; Eph 5:2; Php 4:18).

SAVORY MEAT NIV "tasty food." Meals made by Jacob and Esau for their father Isaac prior to receiving his blessings (Ge 27:4, 9, 14, 17, 31).

SAW [4490, *4569*]. Used as an instrument of torture (Heb 11:37), for cutting stone (2Sa 12:31; 1Ki 7:9).

Figurative (Isa 10:15).

SCAB [1599+6760]. Disease of the skin (Lev 13:2, 6-8; 14:56; 21:20; 22:22; Dt 28:27; Isa 3:17).

See Disease; Sanitation and Hygiene.

SCAFFOLD NIV "platform" (2Ch 6:13).

SCALE [1925, 4404, 6590, 7144, 7866, 7989, 10396, *2433, 3318*].

1. Only fish having fins and scales were permitted as food for Hebrews (Lev 11:9-12).

2. Instrument for weighing (Isa 40:12; Pr 16:11; 20:23).

SCALL NIV "itch," an infectious skin disease (Lev 13:30-37; 14:54; Dt 28:27). *See Disease; Leprosy; Sore.*

SCAPEBIRD (Lev 14:4-7, 53).

SCAPEGOAT [6439]. The second of two goats for which lots were cast on the Day of Atonement (Lev 16:8, 10, 26). The first was sacrificed as a sin offering, but the second had the people's sins transferred to it by prayer and was then taken into the wilderness and released.

See Azazel.

SCARLET [9106, 9443, *3132*]. Probably a bright rich crimson. Scarlet cloth was used for the hangings of the tabernacle (Ex 25:4), high priest's

vestments (Ex 39:1), royal or expensive apparel (2Sa 1:24). Sins are "as scarlet" (Isa 1:18).

See Colors, Figurative and Symbolic.

SCEPTER [2980, 4751, 8657, 9222, *4811*]

(*royal staff*). A staff used by kings to signify favor or disfavor to those who desired audience (Est 5:2; 8:4). A symbol of authority (Nu 24:17; Isa 14:5). Made of gold (Est 4:11), of iron (Ps 2:9; Rev 2:27; 12:5).

Figurative (Ge 49:10; Nu 24:17; Isa 9:4).

SCEVA [*5005*]. Chief priest living in Ephesus whose seven sons were exorcists (Ac 19:14-17).

SCHISM (*division*). A formal division inside a religious group (1Co 12:25). *See Divisions.*

SCHOOL Company of the prophets at Naioth (1Sa 19:20), Bethel (2Ki 2:3), Jericho (2Ki 2:5, 15), Gilgal (2Ki 4:38), Jerusalem, probably (2Ki 22:14; 2Ch 34:22). Crowded attendance at (2Ki 6:1). In the home (Dt 4:9-10; 6:7, 9; 11:19-20; Ps 78:5-8). Assembly to hear public reading of the law (Dt 31:10-13).

State (2Ch 17:7-9; Da 1:3-21). Of Gamaliel (Ac 5:34; 22:3). Of Tyrannus (Ac 19:9).

See Instruction; Psalms, Topically Arranged; Sons of the Prophets.

SCIENCE Observations of, and deductions from, facts (Job 26:7-14; 28; Ecc 1:13-17). The key of knowledge (Lk 11:52; Ro 2:20). *See Astronomy; Geology; Philosophy.*

SCOFFER [408+4371, *1851, 2970*]. One who derides, mocks (2Pe 3:3).

SCOFFING [4352, 4610, 5377, 8471, 9239, 9506, *1848*].

By:

The people of Israel (2Ch 30:6-10; 36:16; Ps 78:19-20; 107:11-12; Hos 7:5). Unbelievers (Ps 42:3, 10; 73:8-9, 11-12; Pr 1:22, 25; Jer 17:15; 43:2; La 1:7; Eze 8:12; 9:9; 12:22; 2Pe 3:3-4). The Wicked, at God's requirements (Job 21:14-15; Isa 10:15; 57:4; Eze 11:2-3; 33:20).

Against:

Christ (Mt 12:24; Mk 3:22; Lk 4:23; 11:15; 16:14). The first Christians (Ac 2:13). Paul (Ac 13:45; 17:18, 32).

Proverbs Concerning:

(Pr 1:22, 25; 3:34; 9:12; 13:1; 14:6, 9; 19:29; 21:11, 24; 22:10; 24:9).

Punishment for:

(Pr 3:24; 9:12; 19:29; Isa 5:18-19, 24-25; 29:20; Heb 10:29).

See Hatred; Malice; Unbelief.

Instances of:

Ishmael (Ge 21:9). Children at Bethel (2Ki 2:23). Ephraim and Manasseh (2Ch 30:10). Chiefs of Judah (2Ch 36:16). Sanballat (Ne 4:1). Enemies of Job (Job 30:1, 9). Enemies of David (Ps 35:15-16). Rulers of Israel (Isa 28:14). Ammonites (Eze

25:3). Tyrians (Eze 26:2). Heathen (Eze 36:2-3). Soldiers (Mt 27:28-30; Lk 23:36). Chief priests (Mt 27:41). Pharisees (Lk 16:14). The men who held Jesus (Lk 22:63-64). Herod (Lk 23:11). People and rulers (Lk 23:35). Some of the multitude (Ac 2:13). Athenians (Ac 17:32).

SCORNERS [*996, 3075, 4009, 4353, 5653, 9240]. (Ps 1:1; Pr 9:12; 21:11, 24). An abomination (Pr 24:9). Admonitions to (Pr 1:22-23). Punishment of (Pr 19:29; Isa 29:20). Warnings against (Pr 3:34; 13:1; 14:6; 19:29; 22:10; 29:8).

See Mocking; Scoffing.

SCORPION [6832, 5026]. A venomous insect common in the wilderness through which the Israelites journeyed (Dt 8:15). Power over, given to the seventy-two (Lk 10:19). Unfit for food (Lk 11:12). Sting of in the tail (Rev 9:10).

Symbolic (Rev 9:3, 5, 10).

Figurative: Of enemies (Eze 2:6). Of cruelty (1Ki 12:11, 14).

SCORPION PASS A chain of hills in the south of Israel (Nu 34:4; Jdg 1:36). Area assigned to tribe of Judah (Jos 15:3).

SCOURGING [3579, 5596, 8765]. Corporal punishment by stripes. Prescribed in the Mosaic law for fornication (Lev 19:20; Dt 22:18), for other offenses (Dt 25:2). Forty stripes the maximum limit (Dt 25:3). Fatal (Job 9:23), of servants avenged (Ex 21:20). Foretold by Jesus as a persecution of the Christians (Mt 10:17).

Of children. See Children, Correction and Punishment; Punishment.

Instances of:

Of Jesus (Mt 20:19; 27:26; Mk 15:15; Jn 19:1). Of Paul and Silas (Ac 16:23). Of Paul (Ac 21:32; 22:24; 2Co 11:24-25). Of Sosthenes (Ac 18:17).

Figurative:

Of the oppressions of rulers (1Ki 12:11). Of the evil tongue (Job 5:21).

See Assault and Battery; Bruise(s); Lashes; Stoning; Stripes.

SCREECH OWL [7887, 9379]. Forbidden as food (Lev 11:16; Dt 14:15). See Birds.

SCRIBE [6221, 8853] (write, copy). A writer and transcriber of the law (2Sa 8:17; 20:25; 1Ki 4:3; 2Ki 12:10; 18:37; 19:2; 1Ch 24:6; 27:32; Ne 13:13; Jer 36:12). King's secretary (2Ki 12:10-12; 22:1-14; Est 3:12; 8:9). Mustering officer of the army (2Ki 25:19; 2Ch 26:11). Instructors in the law (Mt 7:29; 13:52; 17:10; 23:2-3). See Levites. Test Jesus with questions, bringing to Jesus a woman taken in adultery (Jn 8:3). Members of the council (Mt 2:4). Conspire against Jesus (Mt 26:3, 57; 27:41; Mk 14:1; Lk 22:66). Hypocrisy of, reproved by Jesus (Mt 15:20; 9:3; 12:38; 15:1; 16:21; 20:18; 21:15).

SCRIPTURES [6219, 1207, 1210] (writ-

ing). The Word of God (Jer 30:2). Interpreted by doctors (Jn 3:10; 7:52). Inspired (2Ti 3:16).

See Word of God.

SCROLL [1663, 4479, 5532, 6219, 10399, 1044, 1046, 1047]. A document made of papyrus or smoothed skins of animals sewn together to make a long strip which was wound around sticks at both ends (Isa 34:4; Jer 36; Eze 2:1-3; Rev 5; 10:1-10). They varied in length from a few feet to thirty-five feet. The codex form of a book was not used until the second century A.D.

SCROLLS, DEAD SEA See Dead Sea Scrolls.

SCULPTURE See Art.

SCURVY See Disease; Scab; Sore.

SCYTHIAN [5033]. A nomadic people, savage and uncivilized, living N and E of the Black Sea (Col 3:11).

SEA [3542, 4784, 8254, 9391, 9490, 10322, 102, 343, 1113, 1879, 2498, 3237, 4283, 5007]. Creation of (Ge 1:9-10; Ps 95:5; 148:4-5). Limits of established by God (Ge 1:9-10; Ps 33:7; Jer 5:22). Calmed by Jesus (Mt 8:24-26; Mk 4:37-39). Jesus walked on (Mt 14:25-31). Dead, to be given up by, at the Resurrection (Rev 20:13).

Symbolic:

In Daniel's vision (Da 7:2-3). In John's apocalyptic vision (Rev 4:6; 8:8-9; 10:2, 5-6, 8; 13:1; 15:2; 16:3; 21:1).

Waves of:

Reuben is as turbulent as (Ge 49:3-4). God walks on (Job 9:8). God controls (Job 38:8, 11; Ps 65:7; 89:9; 93:3-4; Jer 5:22). The wicked are like (Isa 57:20-21; Jude 13). Jesus controls (Mt 8:23-26; 14:32; Mk 4:35-41). Jesus walks through on the surface of the sea of Galilee (Mt 14:22-33). When God's people are built up and become mature, attaining to the whole measure of the fullness of Christ, they will no longer be tossed back and forth by every deceitful doctrine and scheme like the waves of the sea (Eph 4:14). Doubters are like (Jas 1:6).

SEA, BRONZE The great basin in Solomon's temple where the priests washed their hands and feet preparatory to temple ministry (1Ki 7:23-26; 2Ch 4:2-6).

SEA COW [9391]. Native to the Red Sea. Skins of, used for covering of tabernacle (Ex 25:5; 26:14; 35:7, 23; 36:19; 39:34; Nu 4:6, 8, 10-12, 14, 25). For sandals (Eze 16:10).

SEA MEW See Birds.

SEA MONSTER [9490]. Figurative of forces of chaos opposed to God (Job 7:12; Ps 74:13; Isa 27:1; Eze 32:2). See Dragon; Leviathan.

SEA OF GALILEE
Called Sea of Kinnereth (Nu 34:11; Dt 3:17; Jos 12:3; 13:27). Lake of Gennesaret (Lk 5:1). Sea of Tiberias (Jn 21:1). Jesus calls disciples on the shore of (Mt 4:18-22; Lk 5:1-11). Jesus teaches from a boat on (Mt 13:13). Miracles of Jesus on (Mt 8:24-32; 14:22-33; 17:27; Mk 4:37-39; Lk 5:1-9; 8:22-24; Jn 12:1-11).

SEA OF GLASS
A crystalline pavement or basin before the throne of God (Rev 4:6; 15:2).

SEA OF JAZER
Perhaps the Dead Sea (Jer 48:32).

SEAL
[2597, 3159, 3160, 3973, 6258, *5381*, *5382*].

1. A stamp used for signifying documents. Given as a pledge (Ge 38:18). Engraved (Ex 28:11, 21, 36; 39:6, 14, 30; 2Ti 2:19). Decrees signified by (1Ki 21:8; Est 8:8).

Documents sealed with: Ahab's letter, under false pretenses (1Ki 21:8), covenants (Ne 9:38; 10:1; Isa 8:16), decrees (Est 8:8; Da 6:9), deeds (Jer 32:10). Treasures secured by (Dt 32:34). Lion's den made sure by (Da 6:17), tomb of Jesus (Mt 27:66).

Circumcision a seal of righteousness (Ro 4:11).

Figurative: Of secrecy (Da 12:9; Rev 5:1). Of certainty of divine approval (Jn 6:27; 2Co 1:22; Eph 1:13; 4:30; Rev 7:3-4). In John's vision (Rev 6; 8:1; 10:4).

2. An amphibious animal. Skins of were used as a covering of the tabernacle (Ex 25:5; 26:14; 35:7, 23; 36:19; 39:34; Nu 4:25).

SEAMEN
[2480]. *See Mariner.*

SEASONS
[3045, 3074, 3427, 4595, 4873, 6961, 10232, *178*, *2323*, *2789*]. (Ge 1:14; 8:22; Ps 104:19; Jer 33:20; Da 2:21; Mt 21:41; 24:32; Mk 12:2; Ac 1:7; 1Th 5:1).

SEAT
[*3782*, 4058, 4632, 10338, *1037*, *2757*, *2764*, *2767*, *4751*]. Chair, stool, throne (1Sa 20:18; Lk 1:52).

SEBA
[6013].

1. Son of Cush (Ge 10:7; 1Ch 1:9).
2. A region in Ethiopia (Ps 72:10; Isa 43:3). *See Sabeans; Sheba.*

SEBAM
[8423] (*sweet smell*). A town in Reuben (Nu 32:3), also called Sibmah (Nu 32:38), E of the Dead Sea, but the exact location is unknown.

SEBAT
See Shebat.

SECACAH
[6117] (*thicket, cover*). A village in the wilderness of Judah (Jos 15:61), location unknown.

SECHU
See Secu.

SECOND ADAR
This intercalary month (not in the Bible) was added about every three years so the lunar calendar would correspond to the solar year.

See Adar Sheni; Month, 13.

SECOND COMING OF CHRIST
Called the:
Times of refreshing from the presence of the Lord (Ac 3:19). Times of restitution of all things (Ac 3:21, w Ro 8:21). Last time (1Pe 1:5). Appearing of Jesus Christ (1Pe 1:7). Revelation of Jesus Christ (1Pe 1:13). Glorious appearing of the great God and our Savior (Tit 2:13). Coming of the day of God (2Pe 3:12). Day of our Lord Jesus Christ (1Co 1:8).

Foretold by:
Prophets (Da 7:13; Jude 14). Jesus (Mt 25:31; Jn 14:3). Apostles (Ac 3:20; 1Ti 6:14). Angels (Ac 1:10-11). Signs preceding (Mt 24:3). The time of, unknown (Mt 24:36; Mk 13:32).

The Manner of:
In clouds (Mt 24:30; 26:64; Rev 1:7). In the glory of his Father (Mt 16:27). In his own glory (Mt 25:31). In flaming fire (2Th 1:8). With power and great glory (Mt 24:30). As he ascended (Ac 1:9, 11). With a shout and the voice of the archangel (1Th 4:16). Accompanied by angels (Mt 16:27; 25:31; Mk 8:38; 2Th 1:7). With his saints (1Th 3:13; Jude 14). Suddenly (Mk 13:36). Unexpectedly (Mt 24:44; Lk 12:40). As a thief in the night (1Th 5:2; 2Pe 3:10; Rev 16:15). As the lightning (Mt 24:27). The heavens and earth shall be dissolved (2Pe 3:10, 12). They who shall have died in Christ shall rise first at (1Th 4:16). The saints alive at, shall be caught up to meet him (1Th 4:17). Is not to make atonement (Heb 9:28, w Ro 6:9-10; Heb 10:14).

The Purposes of:
To complete the salvation of saints (Heb 9:28; 1Pe 1:5). Be glorified in his saints (2Th 1:10). Be marveled at among those who believe (2Th 1:10). Bring to light the hidden things of darkness (1Co 4:5). Judge (Ps 50:3-4, w Jn 5:22; 2Ti 4:1; Jude 15; Rev 20:11-13). Reign (Isa 24:23; Da 7:14; Rev 11:15). Destroy death (1Co 15:25-26). Every eye shall see him at (Rev 1:7). Should be always considered as at hand (Ro 13:12; Php 4:5; 1Pe 4:7). Blessedness of being prepared for (Mt 24:46; Lk 12:37-38).

The Saints:
Assured of (Job 19:25-26). Love (2Ti 4:8). Look for (Php 3:20; Tit 2:13). Wait for (1Co 1:7; 1Th 1:10). Speed its coming (2Pe 3:12). Pray for (Rev 22:20). Should be ready for (Mt 24:44; Lk 12:40). Should watch for (Mt 24:42; Mk 13:35-37; Lk 21:36). Should be patient unto (2Th 3:5; Jas 5:7-8). Shall be preserved unto (Php 1:6; 2Ti 4:18; 1Pe 1:5; Jude 24). Shall not be ashamed at (1Jn 2:28; 1Jn 4:17). Shall be blameless at (1Co 1:8; 1Th 3:13; 5:23; Jude 24). Shall be like him at (Php 3:21; 1Jn 3:2). Shall see him as he is (1Jn 3:2). Shall appear with him in glory at (Col 3:4). Shall receive a crown of glory at (2Ti 4:8; 1Pe 5:4).

Shall reign with him at (Da 7:27; 2Ti 2:12; Rev 5:10; 20:6; 22:5). Faith of, will be praised at (1Pe 1:7).

The Wicked:

Scoff at (2Pe 3:3-4). Presume upon the delay of (Mt 24:48). Shall be surprised by (Mt 24:37-39; 1Th 5:3; 2Pe 3:10). Shall be punished at (2Th 1:8-9). The man of sin to be destroyed at (2Th 2:8). Illustrated (Mt 25:6; Lk 12:36, 39; 19:12, 15).

See Jesus the Christ, Second Coming.

SECOND DEATH (Rev 19:20; 20:14; 21:8). Righteous exempt from (Rev 2:11). *See Punishment, Eternal; Wicked, Punishment of.*

SECRET [401+5583, 928+4537, 1821, 2668, 4268, 4319, 5041, 5915, 6259, 6260, 6623, 7621, 8078, 9502, 3220, 3224, 3225, 3291, 3679, 3696]. Alms to be given in (Mt 6:4). Prayer to be offered in (Mt 6:6). Of others not to be divulged (Pr 25:9; Mt 18:15).

Belong to God (Dt 29:29; Ps 25:14). God knows secrets of the heart (Dt 31:21; 1Sa 16:7; 2Sa 7:20; 2Ki 19:27; Ps 44:21; 90:8; Heb 4:12-13).

Shall be revealed and judged (Ecc 12:14; Da 2:28, 47; Am 3:7; Mk 4:22; Lk 8:16-17; Ro 2:16; 1Co 4:5).

See Mysteries.

SECRETARY [6221, 10516]. (2Sa 8:17; 20:24; 1Ki 4:3; 2Ki 12:10-12; 18:18, 37; 22:1-14; 1Ch 27:32; Est 3:12; 8:9). Military (2Ki 25:19; 2Ch 26:11). *See Amanuensis; Scribe.*

SECT [146, 899] (sect, party, school). Religious group with distinctive doctrine: Sadducees (Ac 5:17); Pharisees (Ac 15:5; 26:5), Christians (Ac 24:5; 28:22).

SECU [8497] (lookout point). Village near Ramah (1Sa 19:22).

SECUNDUS [4941] (second). A Thessalonian Christian. Accompanies Paul from Corinth (Ac 20:4-6).

SECURITY [*622, 1053, 1055, 2471, 3782, 3922, 4440, 6184, 6842, 8631, 8932, 856].

In Salvation:

The theological teaching which maintains the certain continuation of the salvation of those who are saved; also known as the perseverance of the saints (Jn 10:28; Ro 8:38-39; Php 1:6; 2Th 3:3; 1Pe 1:5).

False:

From the evils of sin. Promises peace and long life (Job 29:18). Is ignorant of God and truth (Ps 10:4; 50:21). Trusts in lies (Isa 28:15; Rev 3:17). Is inconsiderate and forgetful (Isa 47:7). Relies on earthly treasures (Jer 49:4, 16). Is deceived by pride (Ob 3; Rev 18:7). Puts off the evil day (Am 6:3). Leads to increased guilt (Ecc 8:11). Its refuge will be swept away (Isa 28:17). Ruin shall

overtake it (Isa 47:9; Am 9:10). God is against it (Jer 21:13; Eze 39:6; Am 6:1).

See Confidence, False; Self-Deception; Self-Delusion.

For Debt:

A guarantee to pay: not to be taken if essential to life (garments) or livelihood (millstones) (Ex 22:26; Dt 24:6, 6, 17); not to be used as unreasonable leverage upon the disadvantaged (Job 22:6; 24:3, 9; Eze 18:16; Am 2:8).

Instances of: Judah (Ge 43:9; 44:32); fields and vineyards (Ne 5:3).

Warnings against: (Pr 6:1; 11:15; 17:18; 20:16). *See Debt.*

SEDITION [10083]. Charged against Paul (Ac 24:5). How punished (Ac 5:36-37).

SEDUCER *See Impostors.*

SEDUCTION [2744, 5615, 7331, 1284]. (2Ti 3:6, 13). Laws concerning (Ex 22:16-17; Dt 22:23-29). *See Rape.*

Instances of: Of Dinah (Ge 34:2). Tamar (2Sa 13:1-14).

SEED [1807, 2433, 2445, 2446, 3079, 7237, 1399, 2843, 3133, 5062, 5065, 5076, 5078]. Every herb, tree, and grass, yields its own (Ge 1:11-12, 29). Each kind has its own body (Lev 19:19; Dt 22:9). Not to be mingled in sowing (Lev 19:19; Dt 22:9).

Parables concerning (Mt 13; Lk 8).

Illustrative (Ecc 11:6; Hos 10:12; 2Co 9:6; Gal 6:7-8).

Sowing of, type of burial of the body (1Co 15:36-38).

SEEDTIME [2446]. *See Agriculture.*

SEEKERS [*1329, 1335, 2011, 2704+, 8838, 1699, 2426].

Must:

Have faith (Heb 11:6). Remember God's mercies (Isa 51:1). Count the cost (Lk 14:26-33).

Seeking God:

Commanded (1Ch 16:11; 22:19; Ps 105:4; Isa 26:8-9; Hos 10:12; Joel 2:12-13; Am 5:4-6, 8, 14; Zep 2:3; Mt 6:33; Jas 4:8; Rev 22:17). For salvation (Ge 49:18). To sacrifice (2Ch 11:16). The result of adversity (Ps 78:34; 83:16; Hos 5:15). Prophesied (Jer 50:4; Hos 3:5; Zec 8:20-23). Punishment for not seeking (2Ch 15:13; Isa 8:19). Not of self (Ro 3:11). By unrepentant sinners, vain (Am 8:12; Lk 13:24).

See Seeking God.

Promises:

(Jn 6:37). Of finding God (Dt 4:29; 1Ch 28:9; 2Ch 15:2, 12; Pr 8:17, 34-35; Isa 45:19, 22; Jer 29:13; Ac 17:27). Of pardon (2Ch 30:18-19; Ps 69:32; Isa 55:6-7; Eze 18:21-23; Ac 2:21). Of salvation (Heb 9:28). Of providential care (1Ch 26:5; Ezr 8:22; Ps 34:4; 81:10; 145:19; Isa 49:9-12, 23; Mt 6:33). Of spiritual blessings (Job 8:5-6; Ps 9:10; 22:26; 24:3-6; 40:1-4; 63:1-8; 70:4-5;

119:2; 145:18-19; Pr 2:3-5; 28:5; Isa 44:3-4; 45:19, 22; 55:6-7; 61:1-3; La 3:25-26, 41; Mt 5:6; 6:33; 7:7-11; Lk 6:21; 11:9-13; Ac 2:21; Ro 10:12-13; Heb 7:25; Rev 3:20; 21:6).

Instances of:

Asa (2Ch 14:7). Jehoshaphat (2Ch 17:3-4). Uzziah (2Ch 26:5). Hezekiah (2Ch 31:21). Josiah (2Ch 34:4). Ezra (Ezr 7:10). Job (Job 5:8). David (Ps 17:1-2; 25:5, 15; 27:4, 8; 34:4; 40:1-2; 63:1-8; 143:6). The psalmists (Ps 33:20; 42:1-4; 77:1-9; 84:2; 119:10; 130:5-6). The beloved for her lover (SS 3:1-4). Daniel (Da 9:3-4). The Magi (Mt 2:1-2). Cornelius, the Centurion (Ac 10:7, 30-33).

See Backsliders; Penitent; Sin, Confession of; Sin, Forgiveness of; Zeal.

SEEKING GOD [*1329, 1335, 2011, 2704+, 8838, *1699, *2426*]. Commanded (Isa 55:6; Mt 7:7).

Includes Seeking:

His name (Ps 83:16). His Word (Isa 34:16). His strength (1Ch 16:11; Ps 105:4). His commandments (1Ch 28:8; Mal 2:7). His precepts (Ps 119:45, 94). His kingdom (Mt 6:33; Lk 12:31). His righteousness (Mt 6:33). Christ (Mal 3:1; Lk 2:15-16). Honor which comes from him (Jn 5:44). Justification by Christ (Gal 2:16-17). The city which God has prepared (Heb 11:10, 16; 13:14). By prayer (Job 8:5; Da 9:3). In his house (Dt 12:5; Ps 27:4).

Should Be:

Immediate (Hos 10:12). Evermore (Ps 105:4). While he may be found (Isa 55:6). With the heart (Dt 4:29; 1Ch 22:19). In the day of trouble (Ps 77:2).

Ensures:

His being found (Dt 4:29; 1Ch 28:9; Pr 8:17; Jer 29:13). His favor (La 3:25). His protection (Ezr 8:22). His not forsaking us (Ps 9:10). Life (Ps 69:32; Am 5:4, 6). Prosperity (Job 8:5-6; Ps 34:10). Being heard by him (Ps 34:4). Understanding all things (Pr 28:5). Gifts of righteousness (Hos 10:12). Imperative upon all (Isa 8:19). Afflictions designed to lead to (Ps 78:33-34; Hos 5:15). None, by nature, are found to be engaged in (Jas 4:2, w Ro 3:11; Lk 12:23, 30).

The Saints:

Specially exhorted to (Zep 2:3). Desirous of (Job 5:8). Purpose, in heart (Ps 27:8). Prepare their hearts for (2Ch 30:19). Set their hearts to (2Ch 11:16). Engage in, with the whole heart (2Ch 15:12; Ps 119:10). Early in (Job 8:5; Ps 63:1; Isa 26:9). Earnest in (SS 3:2, 4). Characterized by (Ps 24:6). Is never in vain (Isa 45:19). Blessedness of (Ps 119:2). Leads to joy (Ps 70:4; 105:3). Ends in praise (Ps 22:26). Promise connected with (Ps 69:32). Shall be rewarded (Heb 11:6).

The Wicked:

Are gone out of the way of (Ps 14:2-3, w Ro 3:11-12). Do not prepare their hearts for (2Ch 12:14). Refuse, through pride (Ps 10:4). Not led to, by affliction (Isa 9:13). Sometimes pretend to

(Ezr 4:2; Isa 58:2). Rejected, when too late in (Pr 1:28). They who neglect are denounced (Isa 31:1). Punishment of those who neglect (Zep 1:4-6).

Exemplified:

Asa (2Ch 14:7). Jehoshaphat (2Ch 17:3-4). Uzziah (2Ch 26:5). Hezekiah (2Ch 31:21). Josiah (2Ch 34:3). Ezra (Ezr 7:10). David (Ps 34:4). Daniel (Da 9:3-4).

SEER [2602, 8014]. An older term for prophet (1Sa 9:9). *See Prophets.*

SEGUB [8437] *(exalted).*

1. Son of Hiel, the rebuilder of Jericho (1Ki 16:34).

2. Grandson of Judah (1Ch 2:4-5, 21-22).

SEIR [8541, 8542, 8543] *(hairy, shaggy, covered with trees* BDB IDB; possibly *the place of the goats* or *the place of Esau* [Ge 25:25, BDB]; *small forest, rich forest* KB). A Horite; an ancestor of the inhabitants of the land of Seir (Ge 26:20; 1Ch 1:38).

SEIR, LAND OF and MOUNT

1. Alternate names for the region occupied by the descendants of Edom or Esau. Originally called the land of Seir (Ge 32:3), later called Edom (Ge 36:8-9), extends S from Moab on both sides of the Arabah c. one hundred miles; mountainous; in the Greek period it was called Idumea. Mt. Seir c. 3, 500 feet high. "Seir" also used for people who lived in Mt. Seir (Eze 25:8).

2. Region on the border of Judah W of Kiriath Jearim (Jos 15:10).

SEIRAH [8545] *(place of the goats* BDB possibly *woody hills* IDB KB; *shaggy forest* ISBE). A town in Ephraim, probably in the SE part (Jdg 3:26).

SEIZING [*296, 1608, 2616, 3769, 4374, 5162, 8964, 9530, *2138, *3195, *3284, *4389, *5197, *5275]. Of property. *See Land.*

SEIZURES [4944]. An affliction resulting from demon possession (Mt. 4:24; 17:5). Some feel this is a reference to epilepsy. *See Disease.*

SELA [6153] *(rocky crags, cliffs).* An Edomite city (Isa 16:1; 42:11), also called Joktheel (2Ki 14:7). *See Joktheel.* Later the capital of the Nabateans, called Petra by the Greeks. *See Nabatea, Nabateans; Petra.*

SELA HAMMAHLEKOTH [6154] *(slippery rock* BDB). A cliff in the wilderness of Maon (1Sa 23:28).

SELAH [6138] This term appears seventy-one times in the Psalms and in Hab 3:3, 9, 13. Its meaning is not clear. Possibly it signified a pause in the vocal music while an instrumental interlude played.

See Music, Symbols Used in.

SELED [6135] (*jump for joy*). A descendant of Jerahmeel (1Ch 2:30).

SELEUCIA [4942]. A seaport of Syrian Antioch, founded by Seleucus I in 300 B.C. (Ac 13:4).

SELEUCIDS A dynasty of rulers of the kingdom of Syria (it included Babylonia, Bactria, Persia, Syria, and part of Asia Minor), descended from Seleucus I, a general of Alexander the Great. It lasted from 312 to 64 B.C., when the Romans took it over. One of them, Antiochus Epiphanes, precipitated the Maccabean War by trying forcibly to Hellenize the Jews. *See Testaments, Time Between.*

SELF-CONDEMNATION [896]. (1Ki 8:31-32; Job 9:20; Pr 5:12-13; Mt 23:31; Ro 2:1; 1Jn 3:20; Rev 1:7).

Parables of (Mt 21:33-41; 25:24-27; Mk 12:1-12; Lk 19:21-22).

Instances of: Achan (Jos 7:19-25). David (1Sa 24:1-15; 26:1-20; 2Sa 12:5-7; 24:17). Ahab (1Ki 20:39-42). Jonah (Jnh 1:12). Those who condemned the woman (Jn 8:9).

See Self-Incrimination; Remorse; Repentance.

SELF-CONFIDENCE *See Confidence, False.*

SELF-CONTROL [4200+5110+8120, 202, 203, 1602, 3768, 5404, 5407, 5409].

A Virtue:

Without self-control temptation and evil may freely assault a person (Pr 25:28). Of Saul (1Sa 10:27). Of David (1Sa 24:1-15; 26:1-20). Of Jesus (Mt 26:62-63; 27:12-14).

Paul instructed concerning self-control in relation to righteousness (Ac 24:25), the marriage bed (1Co 7:5); as a fruit of the Spirit (Gal 5:23); in contrast to the godlessness of the last days (1Th 5:8; 2Ti 3:3; 2Th 1:6). Overseers and deacons must have a life that is characterized by self-control (1Ti 3:2; Tit 1:8). Taught by leaders and exemplified by older believers (Tit 2:2, 5-6); taught by the grace of God (Tit 2:12).

Peter lists self-control as one of the qualities of a godly life (2Pe 1:6). A believer should continually be prepared for Christ's return, exhibiting a self-controlled life (1Pe 1:13; 4:7). Be self-controlled and prepared for the devil, who prowls about looking for those who have a false sense of security which therefore make them prime candidates for his trap in the world's system (1Pe 4:7).

Sexual Self-control:

Vow of (Job 31:1). Commanded (Mt 5:27-28; Ro 13:13; 1Co 7:1-9, 25-29, 36-38; Col 3:5; 1Ti 4:12; 5:1-2).

Instances of—

Joseph (Ge 39:7-12). Uriah (2Sa 11:8-13). Boaz (Ru 3:6-13). Joseph, husband of Mary (Mt 1:24-25). Eunuchs (Mt 19:12). Paul (1Co 7:8; 9:27). Believers (Rev 14:1, 4-5).

See Abstinence; Chastity; Discipline; Graces, *Christian; Patience; Rashness; Self-Discipline; Tact.*

SELF-DECEPTION (Jas 1:26). *See Confidence, False; Security, False.*

SELF-DEFENSE Accused heard in (Mt 27:11-14; Mk 15:2-5; Lk 23:3; Jn 7:51; Ac 2:37-40; 22; 23; 24:10-21; 26). *See Defense.*

SELF-DELUSION A characteristic of the wicked (Ps 49:18). Prosperity frequently leads to (Ps 30:6; Hos 12:8; Lk 12:17-19). Obstinate sinners often given up to (Ps 81:11-12; Hos 4:17; 2Th 2:10-11).

Exhibited In Thinking That:

Our own ways are right (Pr 14:12), we should adhere to established wicked practices (Jer 44:17), we are pure (Pr 30:12), we are better than others (Lk 18:11), we are rich in spiritual things (Rev 3:17), we may have peace while in sin (Dt 29:19), we are above adversity (Ps 10:6), gifts entitle us to heaven (Mt 7:21-22), privileges entitle us to heaven (Mt 3:9; Lk 13:25-26), God will not punish our sins (Jer 5:12), Christ will not come to judge (2Pe 3:4), our lives will be prolonged (Isa 56:12; Lk 12:19; Jas 4:13).

Frequently persevered in to the last (Mt 7:22; 25:11-12; Lk 13:24-25). Fatal consequences of (Mt 7:23; 24:48-51; Lk 12:20; 1Th 5:3).

Exemplified:

Ahab (1Ki 20:27, 34). Israelites (Hos 12:8). Jews (Jn 8:33, 41). Church of Laodicea (Rev 3:17).

See Confidence, False; Security, False.

SELF-DENIAL (Lk 21:2-4; 1Co 6:12; 9:12, 15, 18-19, 23, 25-27; 10:23-24; 2Co 6:3; Php 2:4-8; 3:7-9; 2Ti 2:4; Tit 2:12; Heb 13:13; Rev 12:11).

In Respect to:

Appetite (Pr 23:2; Da 10:3). Sinful pleasures (Mt 5:29-30; 18:8-9; Mk 9:43). Carnality (Ro 6:6; 8:12-13, 35-36; 13:14; 1Co 9:27; Gal 5:16-17, 24; Col 3:5; Tit 2:12; 1Pe 2:11-12, 14-16).

Required of Christ's Disciples:

(Mt 8:19-22; 10:37-39; 16:24-25; 19:12, 21; Mk 2:14; 8:34-35; 10:29; Lk 5:11; 9:23-24, 57-58; 12:33; 14:26-27, 33; 18:27-30; Jn 12:25; 2Ti 2:4; Heb 13:13; 1Pe 4:1; 3Jn 7). For a brother's sake (Ro 14:1-22; 15:1-5; 1Co 8:10-13; 10:23-24; Php 2:4). For the sake of the ministry (2Co 6:3). Christ's teachings concerning (Mk 12:43-44; Lk 21:2-4).

Parables of:

(Mt 13:44-46; 18:8-9; Mk 9:43).

Instances of:

Abraham, when he accorded to Lot his preference for the grazing lands of Canaan (Ge 13:9; 17:8), in offering Isaac (Ge 22:12). Moses, in choosing suffering over pleasure (Heb 11:25), in taking no compensation from the Israelites (Nu 16:15). Samuel, in his administration of justice (1Sa 12:3-4). The widow of Zarephath, in sharing with Elijah the last of her sustenance (1Ki 17:12-15).

David, in paying for the threshing floor (2Sa 24:24). The psalmist (Ps 132:3-5). Daniel, in refusing royal food (Da 1:8), in refusing rewards from Belshazzar (Da 5:16-17). Esther, in risking her life for her people (Est 4:16). The Recabites, in refusing wine or fermented drink, or even to plant vineyards (Jer 35:6-7).

Peter and other apostles, in abandoning their vocations to follow Jesus (Mt 4:20; 9:9; Mk 1:16-20; 2:14; Lk 5:11, 27-28), in forsaking all (Mt 19:27; Mk 10:28; Lk 5:28). The widow, who cast all into the treasury (Lk 21:4). The early Christians, in having everything in common (Ac 2:44-45; 4:34). Joseph, in selling his possessions and giving all to the apostles (Ac 4:36-37).

Paul (1Co 10:23-24; Gal 2:20; 6:14), in not counting even his life valuable to himself (Ac 20:24; 21:13; Php 3:7-8), in laboring for his own support while he taught (Ac 20:34-35; 1Co 4:12; 10:33), in not exercising his authority (1Co 6:12; 9:12, 15, 18-19, 23-27).

See Cross; Humility.

SELF-DISCIPLINE [5406]. Needed: Not to give in to sin (Ro 6:12-14); to "run the race" of life according to the rules (1Co 9:24-27; 2Ti 2:1-7). Contrasted to timidity (2Ti 1:7). *See Self-Control.*

SELF-EXALTATION Christian attitude toward (2Co 10:5, 17-18). Christ's teaching concerning (Mk 12:38). Parables of (Lk 14:7-11).

Self-deception of (Isa 5:21; 1Co 3:18; 8:2; Gal 6:3). Punishment for (Eze 31:10-14; Ob 3-4).

Instances of: Job (Job 12:3). Pharaoh (Ex 9:17). Korah, Dathan, and Abiram (Nu 16:1-11). Sennacherib (2Ch 32:9-19). Prince of Tyre, making himself God (Eze 28:2, 9-10). Nebuchadnezzar (Da 4:30; 5:20). Belshazzar (Da 5:22-23). Simon the sorcerer (Ac 8:9-11). Herod, when deified by the people (Ac 12:20-23). The man of lawlessness (2Th 2:4).

See Pride; Self-Righteousness.

SELF-EXAMINATION
Commanded:
(Ps 4:4; Hag 1:7; 1Co 11:28, 31; 2Co 13:5; Gal 6:4). By inference (Jer 17:9).

Conversion as a result of (Ps 119:59; La 3:40).

Exemplified by:
Job (Job 13:23). David (Ps 19:2; 26:2; 139:23-24). The psalmist (Ps 77:6; 119:59). The disciples (Mt 26:22; Mk 14:19).

See Meditation; Repentance; Sin, Confession of.

SELF-INCRIMINATION Under ancient customs, accused persons were required to give self-incriminating testimonies of guilt of the offense charged and were, on occasions, scourged to force self-incriminating testimony whether guilty or innocent (Nu 5:11-27; 2Sa 1:10, 16; 1Ki

8:31-32; 2Ch 6:22; Ac 22:24). Instances of: Achan (Jos 8:19-25). *See Self-Condemnation.*

SELF-INDULGENCE [202, 5059]. Instances of: Solomon (Ecc 2:10). The rich fool (Lk 12:16-20). The rich man as contrasted to Lazarus (Lk 16:19). *See Gluttony; Idleness; Slothfulness; also, Self-Denial.*

SELFISHNESS [1299, 9294, 2249].
Denounced:
Admonitions against (Lk 6:32-34; Ro 14:15; 15:1-3; 1Co 10:24; Gal 6:2; Php 2:4). Christ's example against (Ro 15:3; 2Co 5:15; Php 2:5-8). Judged (Pr 18:17; 24:11-12; Hag 1:4, 9-10).

Exemplified by:
Corrupt officials (Mic 3:11). Corrupt priests and prophets (Eze 34:18; Zec 7:6). Those who accumulate too much (Pr 11:26; Isa 5:8; Mt 19:21-22). The self-indulgent (Ro 14:15; 2Ti 3:2-4). Those unsympathetic with the unfortunate (Pr 28:27; Jas 2:15-16; 1Jn 3:17). Cain (Ge 4:9). The Gadites and Reubenites (Nu 32:6). David's friends (Ps 38:11). The Israelites (Hag 1:4; Mal 1:10). Early Christians (Php 2:20-21).

See Liberality; Poor; Unselfishness.

SELF-RIGHTEOUSNESS
Described as:
Assertive (Pr 20:6; Mt 7:22-23). Delusive (Pr 12:15; 16:2; 21:2; 28:26; Isa 28:20; 50:11; 64:6; Hos 12:8; Mt 7:22-23; 22:12-13; Gal 6:3).

Denounced:
(Job 12:2; Pr 25:14, 27; 26:12; 30:12-13; Isa 5:21; 65:3-5; Jer 2:13, 22-23, 34-35; 8:8; Eze 33:24-26; Am 6:13; Mt 9:10-13; Mk 2:16; 8:15; Lk 5:30; 16:14-15; 18:9-14; 22:12-13; 23:29-31; Ro 11:19-21).

Admonitions against (Dt 9:4-6; 1Sa 2:9; Pr 27:2, 21; Jer 7:4; Hab 2:4; 2Co 1:9; 10:17-18).

Judgments against (Pr 14:12; Isa 28:17; 50:11; Jer 8:8; 49:4, 16; Zep 3:11).

Proverbs concerning (Pr 12:15; 14:12; 16:2; 20:6; 21:2; 25:14, 27; 26:12; 27:2, 21; 28:13, 26; 30:12-13).

Parables concerning (Lk 7:36-50; 10:25-37; 15:25-32; 18:9-14).

Paul's instruction regarding (Ro 2:17-20; 3:27; 10:3; 11:19-21; 2Co 1:9; 10:17-18; Gal 6:3).

Instances of:
Job accused of (Job 11:4; 32:1-2; 33:8-9; 35:2, 7-8). Israelites (Nu 16:3; Ro 2:17-20; 10:3). Saul (1Sa 15:13-21). The wicked (Ps 10:5-6).

Pharisees (Mt 9:10-13; Mk 2:16-17; Lk 5:30; 7:39; 15:2; 16:14-15; 18:9-14; Jn 9:28-41). The rich young ruler (Mt 19:16-22; Mk 10:17-22; Lk 18:18-23). The lawyer (Lk 10:25-29). Church of Laodicea (Rev 3:17-18).

See Hypocrisy; Self-Exaltation.

SELF-WILL Stubbornness.
Forbidden:
(2Ch 30:8; Ps 75:5). Ministers should be without

(Tit 1:7), warn their people against (Heb 3:7-12), pray that their people may be forgiven for (Ex 34:9; Dt 9:27). Characteristic of the wicked (Pr 7:11; 2Pe 2:10). The wicked will not cease from (Jdg 2:19). Punishment for (Dt 21:21; Pr 29:1).

Proceeds From—
Unbelief (2Ki 17:14), pride (Ne 9:16, 29), an evil heart (Jer 7:24). God knows (Isa 48:4). Exhibited in refusing to listen to God (Pr 1:24), refusing to listen to the messengers of God (1Sa 8:19; Jer 44:16; Zec 7:11), refusing to walk in the ways of God (Ne 9:17; Isa 42:24; Ps 78:10), refusing to listen to parents (Dt 21:18; Jer 5:3; 7:28), rebelling against God (Dt 31:27; Ps 78:8), resisting the Holy Spirit (Ac 7:51), walking in the counsels of an evil heart (Jer 7:24, w Jer 23:17), hardening the neck (Ne 9:16), hardening the heart (2Ch 36:13), going backward and not forward (Jer 7:24), heinousness of (1Sa 15:23).

Illustrated: (Ps 32:9; Jer 31:18).

Exemplified:
Simeon and Levi (Ge 49:6). Israelites (Ex 32:9; Dt 9:6, 13). Saul (1Sa 15:19-23). David (2Sa 24:1). Josiah (2Ch 35:22). Zedekiah (2Ch 36:13).
See Obduracy.

SELVEDGE NIV the "edge" of each of the two curtains which covered the boards of the tabernacle (Ex 26:4; 36:11).

SEM *See Shem.*

SEMAKIAH [6165] (*Yahweh sustains, consecrates*). The son of Shemaiah (1Ch 26:7).

SEMEI *See Shimei, 18.*

SEMEIN [4946] (*Yahweh has heard*). An ancestor of Christ (Lk 3:26).

SEMITES (*of Shem*). A diverse group of ancient peoples whose languages are related, belonging to the Semitic family of languages; their world was the Fertile Crescent. The principal Semitic peoples of ancient times: Akkadians—including Babylonians and Assyrians; Arameans; Canaanites—including Edomites, Ammonites, and Moabites; Hebrews; Arabs; Ethiopians (Ge 10:22-31).

SENAAH [6171]. Descendants of Senaah (sometimes spelled Hassenaah), returned with Zerubbabel (Ezr 2:35; Ne 7:38).

SENATE *See Elders, Council of.*

SENATOR *See Elders; Occupations and Professions.*

SENEH [6175] (*thorny BDB; possibly [cliff shaped like] a tooth IDB*). A rock protecting the garrison of the Philistines at Micmash (1Sa 14:5).

SENIR [8536]. The Amorite name of Mt. Hermon (Dt 3:9; 1Ch 5:23; SS 4:8; Eze 27:5).

SENNACHERIB [6178] (*[pagan moon god] Sin has increased the brothers BDB ISBE; Sin replace the [lost] brothers! IDB*). The king of Assyria (705-681 B.C.), the son and successor of Sargon II; a great builder and conqueror; invaded Judah in the time of Hezekiah, but his army was miraculously destroyed (2Ki 18; 19; Isa 36; 37). Accounts of his campaigns recorded on clay prisms survive.

SENSUALITY [816, 2952, 4922]. (Ecc 2:24; 8:15; 11:9).
Of the glutton (Isa 22:13). Of the drunkard (Isa 56:12). Of the selfish rich (Lk 12:19-20; 16:25). Epicurean Philosophy Justifies (Isa 22:13; 1Co 15:32).
Admonition against (Jas 5:5). Warning against (Jude 18-19).
See Adultery; Drunkenness; Fornication; Gluttony; Homosexual; Lasciviousness; Self-Indulgence; also, Abstinence; Continence; Self-Denial; Temperance.

SENTRY [5874]. *See Watchman.*

SENUAH (*sons of the hated [rejected] woman, i.e., the poor class BDB*). *See Hassenuah.*

SEORIM [8556] (*one born at the time of the barley [harvest]*). A descendant of Aaron; head of the fourth course of priests (1Ch 24:1-8).

SEPHAR [6223]. A mountain in Arabia (Ge 10:30).

SEPHARAD [6224]. A place to which the inhabitants of Jerusalem were exiled (Ob 20); possibly Sardis or Sparta.

SEPHARVAIM [6226]. An Assyrian city, from which the king of Assyria colonized Samaria (2Ki 17:24, 31; 18:34; 19:13; Isa 36:19; 37:13).

SEPHARVITES [6227]. The people of Sepharvaim (2Ki 17:31).

SEPHER *See Kiriath Sepher.*

SEPTUAGINT (*seventy*). A translation of the OT into Greek, prepared in Alexandria in the second and third centuries B.C. *See Testaments, Time Between; Texts and Versions.*

SEPULCHRE *See Burial.*

SEPULCHRE, CHURCH OF THE HOLY One of two main sites identified as the tomb of Jesus; built by Constantine in A.D. 325.

SERAH [8580] (*one who explains, opens, extends IDB; abundance ISBE KB*). *See Sarah, 2.*

SERAIAH [8588, 8589] (*Yahweh persists BDB ISBE; Yahweh is prince IDB; Yahweh contends KB*).

1. David's secretary. Probably the same as Sheva, Shisha, and Shavsha. (2Sa 8:17; 20:25; 1Ki 4:3; 1Ch 18:16).

2. Chief priest at the time of the taking of Jerusalem (2Ki 25:18). Father of Ezra (Ezr 7:1). Slain by Nebuchadnezzar (2Ki 25:18-21; Jer 52:24-27).

3. An Israelite captain who surrendered to Gedaliah (2Ki 25:23; Jer 40:8).

4. The son of Kenaz (1Ch 4:13-14).

5. A Simeonite (1Ch 4:35).

6. A priest who returned from the Babylonian captivity (Ezr 2:2; Ne 12:1, 12). Called Azariah (Ne 7:7).

7. One who sealed the covenant with Nehemiah (Ne 10:2). Possibly identical with 6, above.

8. A ruler of the temple after the Captivity (Ne 11:11).

9. The son of Azriel. Commanded by King Jehoiakim to seize Jeremiah (Jer 36:26).

10. A servant of Zedekiah (Jer 51:59, 61).

SERAPHS [8597] (*burning ones, [winged] serpents*). Celestial beings whom Isaiah saw standing before the enthroned Lord (Isa 6:2-3, 6-7). Possibly the same as the "living creatures" (Rev 4:6-9).

SERED, SEREDITE [6237, 6238]. The son of Zebulun and his descendants (Ge 46:14; Nu 26:26).

SERGEANTS NIV "officers." *See Occupations and Professions.*

SERGIUS PAULUS [4950]. A Roman deputy and convert of Paul (Ac 13:7-12).

SERMON ON THE MOUNT

The Sermon on the Mount is the first of five great discourses in Matthew (chs. 5-7; 10; 13; 18; 24-25). It contains three types of material: (1) beatitudes, or declarations of blessedness (5:1-12), (2) ethical admonitions (5:13-20; 6:1-7:23) and (3) contrasts between Jesus' ethical teaching and Jewish legalistic traditions (5:21-48). The sermon ends with a short parable stressing the importance of practicing what has just been taught (7:24-27) and an expression of amazement by the crowds at the authority with which Jesus spoke (7:28-29).

Opinion differs as to whether the sermon is a summary of what Jesus taught on one occasion or a compilation of teachings presented on numerous occasions. Matthew possibly took a single sermon and expanded it with other relevant teachings of Jesus. Thirty-four of the verses in Matthew's account of the sermon occur in different contexts in Luke than the so-called "Sermon on the Plain" (Lk 6:17-49).

The Sermon on the Mount's call to moral and ethical living is so high that some have dismissed it as being completely unrealistic or have projected its fulfillment to the future kingdom. There is no doubt, however, that Jesus (and Matthew) gave the sermon as a standard for all Christians, realizing that its demands cannot be met in our own power. It is also true that Jesus occasionally used hyperbole to make his point. For example, Jesus is not teaching self-mutilation (Mt 5:29-30), for even a blind man can lust. The point is that we should deal as drastically with sin as necessary.

SERPENT [5729, 7352, 8597, 9490, *4058*]. Satan appears in the form of, to Eve (Ge 3:1-15; 2Co 11:3). Subtlety of (Ge 3:1; Ecc 10:8; Mt 10:16). Curse upon (Ge 3:14-15; 49:17). Metaphorically feeds on the dust (Ge 3:14; Isa 65:25; Mic 7:17). Unfit for food (Mt 7:10). Venom of (Dt 32:24, 33; Job 20:16; Ps 58:4; 140:3; Pr 23:31-32; Ac 28:5-6). The staff of Moses transformed into (Ex 4:3; 7:15). Poisonous, sent as a plague upon the Israelites (Nu 21:6-7; Dt 8:15; 1Co 10:9); the wound of miraculously healed by looking upon the bronze image set up by Moses (Nu 21:8-9). Charming of (Ps 58:4-5; Ecc 10:11; Jer 8:17). Mentioned in Solomon's riddle (Pr 30:19). Constriction of (Rev 9:19). Sea serpent (Am 9:3). The seventy-two given power over (Lk 10:19). The apostles given power over (Mk 16:18; Ac 28:5).

Figurative (Pr 23:32; Isa 14:29).

See Adder; Cobra; Dragon; Viper.

SERUG [8578, *4952*] (*descendant* i.e., *younger branch* BDB). An ancestor of Abraham (Ge 11:20-23; 1Ch 1:26). Called Serug (Lk 3:35).

SERVANT [*408, 563, 5853, 5855, 5987, 6269, 9148, 9250, 10523, *1356, 1527, 1528, 3313, 3860, 4087, 4090, 5281, 5677*]. Distinguished as a bond servant (who was a slave) and hired servant.

Bond Servant:

Laws of Moses concerning (Ex 20:10; 21:1-11, 20-21, 26-27, 32; Lev 19:20-22; 25:6, 10, 35-55; Dt 15:14; 15:12, 14, 18; 24:7). Kidnapping and slave trading forbidden (Dt 21:10-14; 24:7; 1Ti 1:10; Rev 18:13).

Fugitive, not to be returned to master (Dt 23:15-16). David erroneously supposed to be a fugitive slave (1Sa 25:10). Instances of fugitive: Hagar, commanded by an angel to return to her mistress (Ge 16:9). Sought by Shimei (1Ki 2:39-41). Interceded for, by Paul (Phm 10-21).

Bought and sold (Ge 17:13, 27; 37:28, 36; 39:17; Lev 22:11; Dt 28:68; Est 7:4; Eze 27:13; Joel 3:6; Am 8:6; Rev 18:13). Captives of war made (Dt 20:14; 21:10-14; 2Ki 5:2; 2Ch 28:8, 10; La 5:13), captive bondservants shared by priests and Levites (Nu 31:28-47). Thieves punished by being made (Ex 43:18; Ex 22:3). Defaulting debtors made (Lev 25:39; Mt 18:25). Children of defaulting debtors sold for (2Ki 4:1-7).

Voluntary servitude of (Lev 25:47; Dt 15:16-17; Jos 9:11-21). Given as dowry (Ge 29:24, 29). Owned by priests (Lev 22:11; Mk 14:66). Slaves owned slaves (2Sa 9:10). The master might marry or give in marriage (Ex 21:7-10; Dt 21:10-14; 1Ch 2:34-35). Taken in concubinage (Ge 16:1-2, 6;

30:3, 9). Used as soldiers by Abraham (Ge 14:14). Rights of those born to a master (Ge 14:14; 17:13, 27; Ex 21:4; Pr 29:21; Ecc 2:7; Jer 2:14).

Must be circumcised (Ge 17:13, 27; Ex 12:44).

Must enjoy religious privileges with the master's household (Dt 12:12, 18; 16:11, 14; 29:10-11).

Must have rest on the Sabbath (Ex 20:10; 23:12; Dt 5:14).

Servitude threatened, as a national punishment, for disobedience of Israel (Dt 28:68; Joel 3:7-8). Degrading influences of bondage exemplified by cowardice (Ex 14:11-12; 16:3; Jdg 5:16-18, 23).

Social status of (Mt 10:24-25; Lk 17:7-9; 22:27; Jn 13:16). Equal status of, with other disciples of Jesus (1Co 7:21-22; 12:13; Gal 3:28; Eph 6:8).

Proverbs concerning (Pr 12:9; 13:17; 17:2; 19:10; 25:13; 26:6; 27:18, 27; 29:19, 21; 30:10, 21-23).

Parables of (Mt 24:45-51; Lk 12:35-48; 16:1-13).

Conspiracy by. *See Conspiracy.*

Cruelty to—
Hagar (Ge 16:1-21; Gal 4:22-31). Joseph (Ge 37:26-28, 36). The Israelites (Ex 1:8-22; 2:1-4; 5:7-9; Dt 6:12, 21; Ac 7:19, 34). Sick, abandoned (1Sa 30:13). Gibeonites (Jos 9:22-27). Canaanites (1Ki 9:21). Jews in Babylon (2Ch 36:20; Est 1:1-10), freeing of (2Ch 36:23; Ezr 1:1-4).

Admonitions against cruelty to (Jer 22:13).

Kindness to—
(Ps 123:2; Pr 29:21). Commanded (Lev 25:43; Eph 6:9). Exemplified by Job (Job 19:15-16; 31:13-14), by Boaz (Ru 2:4), by the centurion (Mt 8:8-13; Lk 7:2-10), by Paul (Phm 1-21).

Duties of—
To be faithful (1Co 4:2). Obedient (Mt 8:9; Eph 6:5-9; Col 3:22-25; Tit 2:9-10; 1Pe 2:18-20). To honor masters (Mal 1:6; 1Ti 6:1-2).

Warning to (Zep 1:9).

Figurative (Lev 25:42, 55; Ps 116:16; Isa 52:3; Mt 24:45, 51; Lk 12:35-48; 16:1-13; 17:7-9; Jn 8:32-35; Ro 6:16-22; 1Co 4:1-2; 7:21-23; Gal 5:13; 1Pe 2:16; 2Pe 2:19; Rev 7:3).

Good, Instances of—
Joseph (Ge 39:2-20; 41:9-57; Ac 7:10), Elisha (2Ki 2:1-6). Servants of Abraham (Ge 24), of Boaz (Ru 2:4), of Jonathan (1Sa 14:7), of Abigail (1Sa 25:14-17), of David (2Sa 12:18; 15:15, 21), of Ziba (2Sa 9), of Naaman (2Ki 5:2-3, 13), of Nehemiah (Ne 4:16, 23), of centurion (Mt 8:9), of Cornelius (Ac 10:7), Onesimus (Phm 11). Servants in the parable of the pounds and talents (Mt 25:14-23; Lk 19:12-19).

Redeemed (Ne 5:8). Freed (2Ch 36:23; Ezr 1:1-4; Jer 34:8-22; Ac 6:9; 1Co 7:21). Called Freedmen (Ac 6:9). Tact in management of (Ecc 7:21).

Wicked and Unfaithful, Instances of—
Jeroboam (1Ki 11:26), Gehazi (2Ki 5:20-27), Zimri (1Ki 16:9-10; 2Ki 9:31), Onesimus (Phm 11).

Servants of Abraham and Lot (Ge 3:7), of Abimelech (Ge 21:25), of Ziba (2Sa 16:1-4, w 2Sa 19:26-27), of Absalom (2Sa 13:28-29; 14:30), of Shimei (1Ki 2:39), of Joash (2Ki 12:19-21), of

Amon (2Ki 21:23), of Job (Job 19:15-16). In the parable of the talents and pounds (Mt 25:24-30; Lk 19:20-26). In the parable of the vineyard (Mt 21:33-41; Mk 12:1-9).

See Employee; Employer; Master.

Hired Workers:
Jacob (Ge 29:15; 30:26), reemployed (Ge 30:27-34; 31:6-7, 41). Parable of laborers for a vineyard (Mt 20:1-15). Of the father of the prodigal son (Lk 15:17, 19), of the prodigal son (Lk 15:5-19).

Kindness to (Ru 2:4). Treatment of, more considerable than that accorded slaves (Lev 25:53). Await employment in the marketplace (Mt 20:1-3).

Mercenary (Job 7:2). Unfaithful (Jn 10:12-13).

Rights of—
Receive wages (Mt 10:10; Lk 10:7; Ro 4:4; 1Ti 5:18; Jas 5:4). Daily payment of wages (Lev 19:13; Dt 24:15). Share in spontaneous products of land in the seventh year (Lev 25:6). Wages of, paid in a portion of the flocks or products (Ge 30:31-32; 2Ch 2:10), or in money (Mt 20:2, 9-10).

Oppression of, forbidden (Dt 24:14; Col 4:1), punished (Mal 3:5).

See Master, of Servants; Wages.

SERVANT OF THE LORD
Agent of the LORD such as the patriarchs (Ex 32:13), Moses (Nu 12:7f), and the prophets (Zec 1:6).

Used as a title for the Messiah in Isaiah 40-66. The NT applies Isaiah's Servant passages to Jesus (Isa 42:1-4; Mt 12:16-21).

See Jesus the Christ, Messiah; Obedience of.

SERVICE
[*2118, 3655, 3656, 3912, 4200+, 5466, 6268, 6269, 6275, 6641, 7372, 8492, 9068, 9149, 9250, 10586, *1354*, *1355*, *1526*, *3302*, *3311*]. Refers to all sorts of work from the most inferior and menial to the most honored and exalted (Lev 23:7f; Nu 3:6ff).

SERVITOR
See Occupations and Professions; Servant.

SETH
[9269, *4953*] (*determined, granted*, Ge 4:25; *restitution* KB).

1. The third son of Adam and Eve, born after the murder of Abel. Name is a play on "granted," Eve said, "God has granted me another child in place of Abel, since Cain killed him" (Ge 4:25). It was through Seth that the genealogy of Noah passed (Ge 4:25-26; 5:3, 8; 1Ch 1:1; Lk 3:38).

2. *See Sheth..*

SETHUR
[6256] (*concealed [by deity]* IDB). One of the twelve spies (Nu 13:13).

SEVEN
[8651, 8679, 8685, 10696, *2231*, *2232*, *2233*]. Interesting facts concerning the number.

Days:
Week consists of (Ge 2:3; Ex 20:11; Dt 5:13-14). Noah in the ark before the Flood (Ge 7:4, 10), remains in the ark after sending out the dove (Ge 8:10-12). Mourning for Jacob lasted (Ge 50:10),

of Job (Job 2:13). The plague of bloody waters in Egypt lasted (Ex 7:25). The Israelites circled Jericho (Jos 6:4). The Passover lasted (Ex 12:15). Saul directed by Samuel to wait at Gilgal for the prophet's command (1Sa 10:8; 13:8). The elders of Jabesh Gilead ask for a truce of (1Sa 10:8; 13:8). Dedication of the temple lasted double (1Ki 8:65). Ezekiel sits by the Kebar River in astonishment (Eze 3:15). The Feast of Tabernacles lasted (Lev 23:34, 42). Consecration of priests and altars lasted (Ex 29:30, 35; Eze 43:25-26). Defilements lasted (Lev 12:2; 13:4). Fasts of (1Sa 31:13; 2Sa 12:16, 18, 22). The firstborn of flocks and sheep shall remain with the mother before being offered (Ex 22:30). The feast of Xerxes continued (Est 1:5). Paul stayed at Tyre (Ac 21:4), at Puteoli (Ac 28:14).

Weeks:

In Daniel's vision concerning the coming of the Messiah (Da 9:25). Ten times (Da 9:24-27). The period between the Passover and Pentecost (Lev 23:15).

Months:

Holy convocations in the seventh month (Lev 23:24-44; Nu 29; Eze 45:25).

Years:

Jacob serves for each of his wives (Ge 29:15-30). Of plenty (Ge 41:1-32, 53). Famine lasted in Egypt (Ge 41:1-32, 54-56), in Canaan (2Sa 24:13; 2Ki 8:1). Insanity of Nebuchadnezzar (Da 4:32). Seven times, the period between the Jubilees (Lev 25:8).

Miscellaneous Sevens:

Of clean beasts taken into the ark (Ge 7:2). Abraham gives Abimelech seven lambs (Ge 21:28). Rams and bulls required in sacrifices (Lev 23:18; Nu 23:1; 29:32; 1Ch 15:26; Eze 45:23). Blood sprinkling seven times (Lev 4:6; 14:7), oil (Lev 14:16). Seven cows and seven heads of grain in Pharaoh's vision (Ge 41:2-7). Israelites marched around Jericho seven times, on the seventh day sounding seven trumpets (Jos 6:4). Elisha's servant looked seven times for the appearance of rain (1Ki 18:43). Naaman was required to wash in the Jordan seven times (2Ki 5:10).

Seven steps in the temple seen in Ezekiel's vision (Eze 40:22, 26). The heat of Nebuchadnezzar's furnace intensified sevenfold (Da 3:19). The light of the sun intensified sevenfold (Isa 30:26). The threatened sevenfold punishment of Israel (Lev 26:18-21). Silver purified seven times (Ps 12:6). Worshiping seven times a day (Ps 119:164). Seven eunuchs at the court of Xerxes (Est 1:10), seven princes (Est 1:14). Seven counselors at the court of Artaxerxes (Ezr 7:14). Seven maidens given to Esther (Est 2:9). Symbolic of many sons (Ru 4:15; 1Sa 2:5; Jer 15:9), of liberality (Ecc 11:1-2). Seven wise men (Pr 26:16). Seven women shall seek polyandrous marriage (Isa 4:1). Seven shepherds to be sent forth against Assyria (Mic 5:5-6). Seven lamps and pipes (Zec 4:2).

See Seven Words From the Cross.

Seven ministers in the apostolic church (Ac 6:3). Seven churches in Asia (Rev 1:4, 20). Seven seals (Rev 5:1). Seven thunders (Rev 10:3). Seven heads and seven crowns (Rev 12:3; 13:1; 17:9). Seven kings (Rev 17:10). Seven stars (Rev 1:16, 20; 3:1; Am 5:8). Seven spirits (Rev 1:4; 3:1; 4:5; 5:6). Seven eyes of the Lord (Zec 3:9; 4:10; Rev 5:6). Seven golden lampstands (Rev 1:12). Seven angels with seven trumpets (Rev 8:2). Seven plagues (Rev 15:1). Seven horns and seven eyes (Rev 5:6). Seven angels with seven plagues (Rev 15:6). Seven golden bowls (Rev 15:7). Scarlet colored beast having seven heads (Rev 17:3, 7).

SEVEN WORDS FROM THE CROSS
The seven statements Jesus made from the cross. No single Gospel account recounts them all:

"Father, forgive them, for they do not know what they are doing." (Lk 23:34).

"I tell you the truth, today you will be with me in paradise." (Lk 23:43).

"Dear woman, here is your son," and to the disciple "Here is your mother." (Jn 19:26-27).

"My God, my God, why have you forsaken me?" (Mt 27:46-47; Mk 15:34-36).

"I am thirsty." (Jn 19:28).

"It is finished." (Jn 19:30).

"Father, into your hands I commit my spirit." (Lk 23:46; cf.Mt 27:50; Mk 15:37).

SEVENTY
[8679, *1573*]. Seventy descendants of Jacob in Egypt (Ex 1:5; Dt 10:22). The council of the Israelites composed of seventy elders (Ex 24:1, 9; Nu 11:16, 24-25). Seventy-two (KJV seventy) disciples sent forth by Jesus (Lk 10:1-17). The Jews in captivity in Babylon seventy years (Jer 25:11-12; 29:10; Da 9:2; Zec 1:12; 7:5). *See Israel.*

SEVENTY WEEKS, THE
The name applied to a period of time (probably 490 years) referred to in Daniel (Da 9:24-27).

SEVENTY-TWO, THE
Seventy-two (KJV seventy) disciples were sent on a preaching mission by Jesus (Lk 10:1-17).

SEXUAL PURITY
See *Chastity; Self-Control.*

SEXUAL RELATIONS
See *Adultery; Bestiality; Fornication; Homosexual; Incest; Prostitute; Rape.*

SHAALABBIN
[9125] (*site of foxes*). Town between Ir Shemesh and Aijalon (Jos 19:42).

SHAALBIM
[9124] (site of foxes). A town, probably in central Israel, won by Danites from Amorites (Jdg 1:35).

SHAALBONITE
[9126]. Designation of

Eliahba, one of David's mighty men (2Sa 23:32; 1Ch 11:33).

SHAALIM, LAND OF [9127] (possibly *[land of] hollow depth* KB). A region probably near the N boundary of Benjamin's territory (1Sa 9:4).

SHAAPH [9131].
1. Son of Jahdai (1Ch 2:47).
2. Son of Caleb (1Ch 2:49).

SHAARAIM [9139] (*double gates*).
1. A town in Judah (Jos 15:36; 1Sa 17:52).
2. A town in Simeon (1Ch 4:31), "Sharuhen" (Jos 19:6), and "Shilhim" (Jos 15:32).

SHAASHGAZ [9140]. A eunuch of Xerxes' court (Est 2:14).

SHABBETHAI [8703] (*one born at Sabbath* ISBE KB).
1. A Levite, assistant to Ezra (Ezr 10:15).
2. An expounder of the Law (Ne 8:7).
3. A chief Levite, attendant of the temple (Ne 11:16).

SHACHIA *See Sakia.*

SHACKLES [3890, 4591, 4593, 5733, 6040]. Made of bronze (Jdg 16:21; 2Ki 25:7; 2Ch 33:11; 36:6; Jer 39:7; 52:11). Used for securing prisoners (2Ch 33:11; 36:6; Mk 5:4). *See Chains; Fetters.*

SHADDAI [8724] (*the Mountain One* IDB; other suggestions: 1. *mountain* 2. *maternal goddess of many breasts* 3. *self-sufficient* 4. *an Akkadian spirit, Shad* 5. *almighty, omnipotent* KB). *Shaddai* is used forty-eight times as a name of God, thirty-two times in Job (Job 5:17; 6:4, 14; etc.), seven times in the compound name *El Shaddai*. The NIV consistently translates *Shaddai* as "Almighty" (Ge 17:1; Ps 91:1).
See God, Names of, Shaddai.

SHADOW [694, 696, 7498, 7511, 7516, 5014, 5572]. Used literally, figuratively (1Ch 29:15; Ps 17:8; Isa 30:3), theologically (Col 2:17; Heb 8:5; 10:1).

SHADOW OF DEATH *See Darkness.*

SHADRACH [8731, 10701] (*servant of [pagan moon god] Aku*). His Hebrew name was Hananiah. He was taken as a captive to Babylon with Daniel, Mishael, and Azariah, where each one was given a Babylonian name (Da 1:6-20; 2:17, 49; 3:12-30). Hananiah was renamed Shadrach.

Shadrach, Meshach, and Abednego were chosen to learn the language and the ways of the Chaldeans (Babylonians) so that they could enter the king's service (Da 1:3-5, 17-20), c. 605 B.C. These three were eventually thrown into Nebuchadnezzar's furnace because they refused to bow

down and worship the huge golden image that he had made (Da 3:1, 4-6, 8-30).

SHAFT [5707, 6770, 7562, 7866, *5853*].
1. Stem of the gold lampstand (Ex 25:31; 37:17).
2. Shaft of a spear (1Sa 17:7).
3. Water (2Sa 5:8) or mine shaft (Job 28:4).

SHAGEE [8707] (*wanderer, meanderer [like feeding sheep]*). The father of Jonathan, one of David's guard (1Ch 11:34).

SHAHAR *See Zereth Shahar.*

SHAHARAIM [8844] (*one born at early [reddish] dawn* KB). A Benjamite (1Ch 8:8).

SHAHAZUMAH [8833] (*elevated place*). A city in Issachar (Jos 19:22).

SHALEM (*peace* or *safe*). *See Paddan Aram, 2.*

SHALIM, LAND OF *See Shaalim, Land of.*

SHALISHA [8995] (*a third part*). A district bordering on the Mount Ephraim (1Sa 9:4).

SHALISHAH *See Baal Shalishah.*

SHALLEKETH [8962] (possibly *[gate of] sending forth* BDB). One of the gates of the temple (1Ch 26:16).

SHALLUM [8935] (*peace, well being, prosperity*).
1. The son of Naphtali (1Ch 7:13), "Shillem" (Ge 46:24; Nu 26:48-49). *See Shillem, Shillemite.*
2. The son of Shaul (1Ch 4:25).
3. The son of Sismai (1Ch 2:40-41).
4. The son of Korah chief of the gatekeepers (1Ch 9:17, 19, 31; Ne 7:45), "Meshelemiah" (1Ch 26:1), "Shelemiah" (1Ch 26:14).
5. The son of Zadok (1Ch 6:12f), "Meshullam" (1Ch 9:11; Ne 11:11).
6. A king of Israel (2Ki 15:10-15).
7. The father of Jehizkiah (2Ch 28:12).
8. Husband of the prophetess Huldah (2Ki 22:14).
9. The king of Judah (1Ch 3:15), better known as Jehoahaz II.
10. The uncle of Jeremiah (Jer 32:7).
11. The father of Maaseiah (Jer 35:4).
12. A Levite who divorced his foreign wife (Ezr 10:24).
13. A man who divorced his foreign wife (Ezr 10:42).
14. A ruler who helped build Jerusalem's walls (Ne 3:12).

SHALLUN [8937] (*recompense*). A Jew who repaired a gate of Jerusalem (Ne 3:15).

SHALMAI [8978] (perhaps *Yahweh is well-being*). An ancestor of the temple servants that returned with Zerubbabel (Ezr 2:46; Ne 7:48).

SHALMAN [8986] (abbreviation of *Shalmaneser* IDB ISBE). Either a contraction of Shalmaneser or the Moabite king Salamanu (Hos 10:14).

SHALMANESER [8987] (*the god Shulman is chief*, or *Sulmanu is leader*). The title of five Assyrian kings, of whom one is mentioned in the OT, another refers to an Israelite king.
1. Shalmaneser III (859-824 B.C.), the son of Ashurnasirpal; inscription left by him says that he opposed Ben-Hadad of Damascus and Ahab of Israel, and made Israel tributary.
2. Shalmaneser V (726-722 B.C.), the son of Tiglath-Pileser; received tribute from Hoshea; besieged Samaria and carried the N tribes of Israel into captivity (2Ki 17:3; 18:9), "Shalman" (Hos 10:14).

SHAMA [9052] (*one obedient [to Yahweh]*). One of David's heroes (1Ch 11:44).

SHAMARIAH See *Shemariah, 2*.

SHAMBLES NIV "meat market" (1Co 10:25).

SHAME [*1017, 1019, 1425, 2365, 3075, 4007, 4009, 4583, 6872, 7830, *158, 1959, 2875*]. Of Adam and Eve: no shame before the Fall (Ge 2:25), but after (Ge 3:10). Jesus is ashamed of those who deny him (Mk 8:38; Lk 9:26). Of believers who do not continue in Christ (1Jn 2:28). Of the cross (Heb 12:2).
Destitute of, the Israelites when they worshiped the golden calf (Ex 32:25), the unjust (Zep 3:5).

SHAMED See *Shemed*.

SHAMELESSNESS [1017+4202, 2365]. Of the wicked (Jer 6:15; 8:12; Zep 3:5).

SHAMER
1. See *Shemer*.
2. See *Shemer; Shomer, 2*.

SHAMGAR [9011] (*[the pagan Hurrian god] Shimke gave [a son]* IDB). The son of Anath; judge; killed 600 Philistines with an oxgoad (Jdg 3:31; 5:6).

SHAMHUTH [9016] (possibly *one born at a time of a horrible event* KB). David's fifth divisional army commander (1Ch 27:8). See *Shammah, 4*.

SHAMIR [9033, 9034] (possibly *thorny* or *emery [flint]*).
1. A town in Judah c. thirteen miles SW of Hebron (Jos 15:48).
2. A town in Ephraim; the home of Tola (Jdg 10:1f).
3. A temple attendant (1Ch 24:24).

SHAMMA [9007] (*astonishment*). The son of Zophah, an Asherite (1Ch 7:37).

SHAMMAH [9007, 9015] (*waste*).
1. The grandson of Esau (Ge 36:13, 17; 1Ch 1:37).
2. The brother of David (1Sa 16:9; 17:13), also called Shimea (1Ch 20:7) and Shimeah (2Sa 13:3, 32).
3. One of David's mighty men (2Sa 23:11), also called Shagee (1Ch 11:34).
4. Another of David's mighty men (2Sa 23:33), also called Shammoth (1Ch 11:27) and Shamhuth (1Ch 27:8). May be the same as 3.

SHAMMAI [9025] (*Yahweh has heard*).
1. The son of Onam (1Ch 2:28, 32).
2. The father of Maon (1Ch 2:44-45).
3. The son of Ezra (1Ch 4:17).

SHAMMOTH [9021] (*desolation*). One of David's mighty men (1Ch 11:27), apparently the same as Shammah, 4 (2Sa 23:25) and Shamhuth (1Ch 27:8).

SHAMMUA [9018, 9055] (possibly *[Yahweh] hears* KB; *rumor*, ZPEB).
1. The son of Zaccur; Reubenite spy (Nu 13:4).
2. The son of David and Bathsheba (2Sa 5:14; 1Ch 14:4).
3. A Levite; the father of Abda (Ne 11:17), also called Shemaiah (1Ch 9:16).
4. A priest (1Ch 24:14; Ne 12:6, 18).

SHAMMUAH See *Shammua, 2*.

SHAMSHERAI [9091] (a combination of *Shemesh [pagan sun god]* and *Shamar [guard]*). The son of Jeroham (1Ch 8:26).

SHAN See *Beth Shan*.

SHAPHAM [9171]. A chief of Gad (1Ch 5:12).

SHAPHAN [9177] (*rock badger*).
1. A secretary of King Josiah (2Ki 22:3-14; 2Ch 34:8-20). The father of Gemariah (Jer 36:10-12).
2. The father of Ahikam and the grandfather of Gedaliah (2Ki 22:12; 25:22; 2Ch 34:20; Jer 26:24; 39:14; 40:5, 9, 11; 41:2; 43:6).
3. The father of Elasah (Jer 29:3).
4. The father of Jaazaniah (Eze 8:11).

SHAPHAT [9151] (*he judges*).
1. A Simeonite spy (Nu 13:5).
2. The father of Elisha the prophet (1Ki 19:16, 19).
3. A Gadite chief in Bashan (1Ch 5:12).
4. A herdsman of David (1Ch 27:29).
5. The son of Shemaiah (1Ch 3:22).

SHAPHER See *Shepher, Mount*.

SHAPHIR [9160] (*lovely*). A town probably in SW Israel (Mic 1:10-15).

SHARAI [9232]. A descendant of Bani who divorced his Gentile wife (Ezr 10:40).

SHARAIM *See Shaaraim, 1.*

SHARAR [9243] (*firm*). The father of one of David's mighty men (2Sa 23:33), "Sacar" (1Ch 11:35). *See Sacar, 1.*

SHARE [*430, 2475, 2490, 2745, 2750, 2976, 4950, 5989, *3123, 3125, 3126, 3556, 3561, 3576, 3581, 5170*]. Plowshare (1Sa 13:20).

SHAREZER [8570] (*[pagan god] protect the king!*).

1. The son of the Assyrian king Sennacherib (2Ki 19:37; Isa 37:38).

2. Contemporary of Zechariah the prophet (Zec 7:2).

SHARON [9227, *4926*] (*plain, level country*).

1. Israel coastal plain between Joppa and Mount Carmel (1Ch 27:29; Isa 35:2; Ac 9:35).

2. Suburbs of Sharon possessed by the tribe of Gad (1Ch 5:16).

3. *See Lasharon.*

4. Figurative of fruitfulness, glory, peace (Isa 35:2; 65:10).

SHARONITE [9228] (*of Sharon*). Shitrai, in charge of David's herds in Sharon (1Ch 27:29).

SHARUHEN [9226]. A Simeonite town in Judah's territory (Jos 19:6). Apparently the same as Shilhim (Jos 15:32), and Shaaraim (1Ch 4:31); possibly identified with Tell el-Farah.

SHASHAI [9258] (*noble*). A descendant of Bani, who put away his Gentile wife (Ezr 10:40).

SHASHAK [9265]. A Benjamite (1Ch 8:14, 25).

SHAUL, SHAULITE [8620, 8621] (*asked,* possibly *dedicated to God*).

1. The son of Simeon and his descendants (Ge 46:10; Ex 6:15; Nu 26:13; 1Ch 4:24).

2. An ancient king of Edom (Ge 36:37; 1Ch 1:48-49).

3. Son of Uzziah (1Ch 6:24).

SHAVEH KIRIATHAIM [8754] (*level plain of two towns*). The plain where Kedorlaomer defeated the Emites (Ge 14:5), probably on the E of the Dead Sea (Nu 32:37).

SHAVEH, VALLEY OF [8753] (*level valley*). The valley where, after rescuing his nephew Lot, Abraham met the king of Sodom (Ge 14:17).

SHAVING [*1605, 1662, 6296, 7942, 7947, 3834*]. The priests and Nazirites were prohibited from shaving (Lev 21:5; Nu 6:5), Hebrews generally wore beards. Shaving was often done for religious reasons, as an act of contrition (Job 1:20), consecration for Levites (Nu 6:9; 8:7),

cleansing for lepers (Lev 14:8f; 13:32ff), also as an act of contempt (2Sa 10:4).

SHAVSHA [8807]. David's secretary (1Ch 18:16), also called Shisha (1Ki 4:3), Seraiah (2Sa 8:17), and Sheva (2Sa 20:25).

SHEAF [524, 1538, 6658, 6684]. A handful of grain left behind by the reaper, gathered and bound by women and children, and later taken to the threshing-floor (Jer 9:22; Ru 2:7, 15). Some sheaves were left behind for the poor (Dt 24:19).

SHEAL [8627] (*May God grant!, asking*). A descendant of Bani, who put away his Gentile wife (Ezr 10:29).

SHEALTIEL [8630, 9003, 10691, *4886*] (*I have asked [him] of God [El]* BDB ISBE KB; possibly *God [El] is a shield, God [El] is a victor* IDB).

1. Father of Zerubbabel and an ancestor of Jesus (1Ch 3:17; Ezr 3:2, 8; 5:2; Ne 12:1; Hag 1:1, 12, 14; 2:2, 23).

2. A son of Jehoiachin, king of Judah (Mt 1:12), or of Neri (Lk 3:27). He may have been the real son of Neri, but only the legal heir of Jehoiachin.

SHEARIAH [9138] (possibly *Yahweh breaks*). The son of Azel; descendant of Jonathan (1Ch 8:38; 9:44).

SHEARING HOUSE *See Beth Eked.*

SHEAR-JASHUB [8639] (*a remnant will return*). The symbolic name of Isaiah's oldest son (Isa 7:3; 8:18).

SHEBA [8644, 8680, 8681] (*seven* or *oath*).

1. The son of Raamah (Ge 10:7; 1Ch 1:9).

2. The son of Joktan (Ge 10:28; 1Ch 1:22).

3. The son of Jokshan (Ge 25:3; 1Ch 1:32).

4. A Benjamite who led an insurrection against David (2Sa 20).

5. A Gadite (1Ch 5:13).

6. A city of Simeon (Jos 19:2).

7. Queen of, visits Solomon (1Ki 10:1-13; 2Ch 9:1-12). Kings of, bring gifts to Solomon (Ps 72:10). Rich in gold (Ps 72:15), incense (Jer 6:20). Merchandise of (Eze 27:22-23; 38:13). Prophecies concerning the people of, coming into the kingdom of Messiah (Isa 60:6).

See Sabeans; Seba.

SHEBAH *See Shibah.*

SHEBAM *See Sebam.*

SHEBANIAH [8676, 8677].

1. Trumpeter priest (1Ch 15:24).

2. Levite who signed covenant with Nehemiah (Ne 9:4-5; 10:10).

3. Another Levite who signed a covenant (Ne 10:12).

4. A priest who signed a covenant (Ne 10:4).

5. Priest (Ne 12:14).

SHEBARIM (*quarry*). A place, called the "stone quarries" in the NIV, near Ai to which Israelite soldiers were chased (Jos 7:5, ftn).
See Quarries; Stones.

SHEBAT [8658] (*[the month of] destroying [rain]*). Month eleven in sacred sequence (Zec 1:7); month five in civil sequence. Winter (January-February). *See Month, 11.*

SHEBER [8693] (possibly *lion* IDB; possibly *breaking* or *crushing* or *roughly broken grain* KB). The son of Caleb (not the Israelite spy of the land of Canaan) (1Ch 2:48).

SHEBNA [8674, 8675] (*[Yahweh] return now* IDB).
1. A scribe of Hezekiah (2Ki 18:18, 26, 37; 19:2; Isa 36:3, 11, 22; 37:2).
2. An official of the king (Isa 22:15-19).

SHEBUEL (possibly *captive of God [El]* or *God [El] restores*). *See Shubael.*

SHECANIAH [8908, 8909] (*Yahweh has taken up his abode*).
1. The head of the tenth course of priests in the days of David (1Ch 24:11).
2. Levite (2Ch 31:15).
3. Descendant of David (1Ch 3:21-22).
4. Man who returned with Ezra (Ezr 8:3).
5. Another man who returned with Ezra (Ezr 8:5).
6. Man who proposed to Ezra that foreign wives be put away (Ezr 10:2-4).
7. Keeper of E gate of Jerusalem in the time of Nehemiah (Ne 3:29).
8. The father-in-law of Tobiah the foe of Nehemiah (Ne 6:18).
9. The chief priest who returned with Zerubbabel (Ne 12:3).

SHECHEM, SHECHEMITE [8901, 8902, 8903, 8904, 5374] (possibly *shoulder [saddle of a hill]* BDB; *shoulders [and upper part of the back]* KB).
1. A district in the central part of the land of Canaan. Abraham dwells in (Ge 12:6). Jacob buys a piece of ground in, and builds an altar (Ge 33:18-20). The flocks and herds of Jacob kept in (Ge 37:12-14). Joseph buried in (Jos 24:32). Jacob buried in (Ac 7:16, w Ge 50:13).
2. Also called Sychar, a city of refuge in Mount Ephraim (Jos 20:7; 21:21; Jdg 21:19). Joshua assembled the tribes of Israel at, with all their elders, chiefs, and judges, and presented them before the Lord (Jos 24:1-28). Joshua buried at (Jos 24:30-32). Abimelech made king at (Jdg 8:31; 9). Rehoboam crowned at (1Ki 12:1). Destroyed by Abimelech (Jdg 9:45), rebuilt by Jeroboam (1Ki 12:25). Men of, slain by Ishmael (Jer 41:5). Jesus visits; disciples made in (Jn 4:1-42).
3. Son of Hamor; seduces Jacob's daughter; slain by Jacob's sons (Ge 33:19; 34; Jos 24:32; Jdg 9:28).

4. Descendant of Manasseh and his clan (Nu 26:31; Jos 17:2).
5. Son of Shemida (1Ch 7:19).

SHECHINAH *See Shekinah.*

SHEDEUR [8725] (*Shaddai is light*, or *Shaddai is fire*). Reubenite; father of Elizur (Nu 1:5; 2:10; 7:30; 10:18).

SHEEP [1374, 2378, 3897, 4166, 5924, 6373, 6402, 7366, 7892, 8161, 8445, 9068, 885, 4477, 4583, 4585]. Offered in sacrifice, by Abel (Ge 4:4), by Noah (Ge 8:20), by Abraham (Ge 22:13). *See Offerings.* Required in the Mosaic offerings. *See Offerings.*
The land of Bashan adapted to the raising of (Dt 32:14), Bozrah (Mic 2:12), Kedar (Eze 27:21), Nebaioth (Isa 60:7), Sharon (Isa 65:10). Jacob's management of (Ge 30:32-40). Milk of, used for food (Dt 32:14). Shearing of (Ge 31:19; 38:12-17; Isa 53:7), feasting at the time of shearing (1Sa 25:11, 36; 2Sa 13:23). First fleece of, belonged to priests and Levites (Dt 18:4). Tribute paid in (2Ki 3:4; 1Ch 5:21; 2Ch 17:11).

Figurative:
(1Ch 21:17; Ps 74:1; Jer 13:20). Of backsliders (Jer 50:6). Of lost sinners (Mt 9:36; 10:6). Of the righteous (Jer 50:17; Eze 34; Mt 26:31; Mk 14:27; Jn 10:1-16). Of the defenselessness of ministers (Mt 10:16).
Parable of the lost (Mt 18:11-13; Lk 15:4-7).

SHEEP GATE An ancient gate of Jerusalem (Ne 3:1, 32; 12:39; Jn 5:2).

SHEEP MARKET NIV "Sheep Gate" (Jn 5:2).

SHEEP PEN [1312, 4813, 885]. Enclosure for protection of sheep (Nu 32:16; Jdg 5:16; 1Sa 24:3; Jn 10:1, 16).

SHEEPMASTER *See Occupations and Professions; Shepherd.*

SHEEP-SHEARER [1605]. *See Occupations and Professions.*

SHEERAH [8641] (*blood relationship* or *female relative* IDB; *remainder* KB). The daughter of Ephraim; the descendants built three villages (1Ch 7:24).

SHEET [5012, 7063, 3855, 5007]. A large piece of linen (Ac 10:11; 11:5).

SHEHARIAH [8843] (*he seeks Yahweh*). The son of Jeroham; Benjamite (1Ch 8:26).

SHEKEL [4084, 7088, 9203] (*weight*). A weight, equal to twenty gerahs (Ex 30:13; Nu 3:47; Eze 45:12). Used to weigh silver (Jos 7:21; Jdg 8:26; 17:2-3). Fractions of, used in currency (Ex 30:13; 1Sa 9:8; Ne 10:32). Used to weigh gold (Ge 24:22; Nu 7:14, 20-86; Jos 7:21; 1Ki 10:16), cinnamon (Ex 30:23), hair (2Sa 14:26), iron (1Sa 17:7), myrrh (Ex 30:23), rations (Eze 4:10). Fines paid in (Dt 22:19, 29). Fees paid in (1Sa 9:8). Sanctuary revenues paid in (Ex 30:13; Ne 10:32).

Of different standards: Of the sanctuary (Ex 30:13), of the king's weight (2Sa 14:26). Corrupted (Am 8:5).

SHEKINAH
Jewish term for the dwelling presence of God's glory (Ex 25:22; Lev 16:2; 2Sa 6:2; 2Ki 19:14-15; Ps 80:1; Isa 37:16; Eze 9:3; 10:18; Heb 9:5). Not used in the Bible.

SHELAH
[8925, 8941, 8989, 4885] (*missile [a weapon], sprout* ISBE).

1. Son of Arphaxad and ancestor of Joseph (Ge 10:24; 11:12-15; 1Ch 1:18, 24; Lk 3:35).

2. Son of Judah (Ge 38:5, 11, 14, 26; 46:12; Nu 26:20; 1Ch 2:3; 4:21).

3. The father of Zechariah (Ne 11:5).

SHELANITE
[8989] (*missile [a weapon], sprout* ISBE). Descendants of Shelah (Nu 26:20). *See Shelah, 2.* Apparently called Shilonites (1Ch 9:5). *See Shilonite(s), 2.*

SHELEMIAH
[8982, 8983] (*Yahweh pays back,* possibly *restores peace offering of Yahweh*).

1. Doorkeeper of tabernacle (1Ch 26:14), in previous verses of this chapter he is called "Meshelemiah."

2. Son of Cushi (Jer 36:14).

3. Man sent to arrest Jeremiah (Jer 36:26).

4. Father of a man whom Zedekiah sent to Jeremiah to ask his prayers (Jer 37:3).

5. The son of Hananiah (Jer 37:13).

6. Two men who divorced foreign wives (Ezr 10:39, 41).

7. Father of Hananiah (Ne 3:30).

8. Priest; treasurer (Ne 13:13).

SHELEPH
[8991] (*one plucked out, drawn out*). The son of Joktan (Ge 10:26; 1Ch 1:20).

SHELESH
[8994] (*triplet* KB; possibly *obedient* or *gentle* IDB). The son of Helem (1Ch 7:35).

SHELISHIYAH
See Eglath Shelishiyah.

SHELOMI
[8979] (*at peace*). The father of Ahihud, Asherite prince (Nu 34:27).

SHELOMITH
[8984, 8985] (*at peace*).

1. Daughter of Dibri; her son was killed for blasphemy (Lev 24:10-12, 23).

2. The daughter of Zerubbabel (1Ch 3:19).

3. Cousin of Moses (1Ch 23:18).

4. A descendant of Moses (1Ch 26:25).

5. Child of Rehoboam (2Ch 11:20).

6. An ancestor of a family that returned with Ezra (Ezr 8:10).

SHELOMOTH
[8977] (*at peace*).

1. Gershonite Levite (1Ch 23:9).

2. Izharite Levite (1Ch 24:22).

SHELUMIEL
[8981] (*God [El] is [my] peace*). The son of Zurishaddai and leader of Simeon in the time of Moses (Nu 1:6; 2:12; 7:36, 41; 10:19).

SHEM
[9006, 4954] (*name, fame*). The son of Noah. Preserved in the ark (Ge 5:32; 6:10; 7:13; 9:18; 1Ch 1:4). His filial conduct (Ge 9:23-27). The descendants of (Ge 10:1, 21-31; 11:10-29; 1Ch 1:17-54). In genealogy of Jesus (Lk 3:36).

SHEMA
[9050, 9054] (*he hears*).

1. A town in S Judah (Jos 15:26).

2. The son of Hebron (1Ch 2:43-44).

3. The son of Joel (1Ch 5:8).

4. A Benjamite (1Ch 8:13).

5. An assistant of Ezra (Ne 8:4).

6. The Hebrew name for, "Hear, O Israel: The LORD our God, the LORD is one" (Dt 6:4, ftn).

SHEMAAH
[9057] (possibly *Yahweh hears*). The father of Ahiezer and Joash, soldiers of David (1Ch 12:3).

SHEMAIAH
[9061, 9062] (*Yahweh hears*).

1. Simeonite prince (1Ch 4:37).

2. Reubenite (1Ch 5:4), possibly the same as Shema of (1Ch 5:8).

3. The chief Levite (1Ch 15:8, 11).

4. A Levite scribe (1Ch 24:6).

5. The son of Obed-Edom (1Ch 26:4, 6-7).

6. A prophet who forbade Rehoboam to war against Israel (1Ki 12:22-24).

7. A descendant of David (1Ch 3:22).

8. A Merarite Levite (1Ch 9:14; Ne 12:18).

9. A Levite who returned from exile (1Ch 9:16). Also called Shammua (Ne 11:17).

10. A Levite (2Ch 17:8).

11. A Levite who cleansed the temple (2Ch 29:14).

12. A Levite who assisted in the distribution of food (2Ch 31:15).

13. A Levite in the days of Josiah (2Ch 35:9).

14. A Levite who returned with Ezra (Ezr 8:13).

15. One whom Ezra sent back for ministers (Ezr 8:16), possibly the same as (Ezr 8:13).

16. A priest who divorced his foreign wife (Ezr 10:21).

17. Another priest who divorced his foreign wife (Ezr 10:31).

18-23. Men who played various roles in Nehemiah's rebuilding and in the dedication of the Jerusalem wall (Ne 3:29; 6:10ff; 10:8; 12:6, 18, 34, 35, 36, 42).

24. The father of Uriah the prophet (Jer 26:20).

25. A false prophet who fought against Jeremiah (Jer 29:24-32).

26. The father of Delaiah, a prince in the days of Jehoiakim (Jer 36:12).

SHEMARIAH
[9079, 9080] (*Yahweh guards, preserves*).

1. One of David's mighty men (1Ch 12:5).

2. The son of Rehoboam, king of Judah (2Ch 11:19).

3. A man who put away his foreign wife (Ezr 10:32).

4. Another man who put away his foreign wife (Ezr 10:41).

SHEMEBER [9008]. The king of Zeboiim, a city near the Dead Sea (Ge 14:2).

SHEMED [9013] (*destruction*). The son of Elpaal (1Ch 8:12).

SHEMER [9070] (possibly *watch* IDB; possibly *sediment of wine from which clear wine is made* KB). *See Shomer, 1, 3, 4.*

SHEMESH *See Beth Shemesh; En Shemesh; Ir Shemesh.*

SHEMIDA, SHEMIDAITE [9026, 9027] (possibly *the name knows* BDB KB; possibly *[pagan god] Eshmun has known* IDB). The son of Gilead; a family descended from Shemida (Nu 26:32; Jos 17:2; 1Ch 7:19).

SHEMINITH [9030] (*eight [strings]*). A musical term of uncertain meaning, possibly "octave" (1Ch 15:21; Ps 6; 12, titles).
See Music, Symbols Used in.

SHEMIRAMOTH [9035] (*heights, heavens* BDB; possibly *proper name of a pagan goddess* KB).

1. A Levite musician (1Ch 15:18, 20; 16:5).

2. A Levite sent by Jehoshaphat to instruct the people in the law (2Ch 17:8).

SHEMUEL [9017] (possibly *his name is God [El]* BDB IDB ISBE; *the unnamed god is El* KB; *heard of God [El]* KD).

1. A Simeonite leader (Nu 34:20).

2. *See Samuel, 2.*

SHEN [9095] (*tooth, crag [of rock]*). An unidentified site near which Samuel erected the stone "Ebenezer" (1Sa 7:12).

SHENAZZAR [9100] (*may [the moon god] Sin protect*). The son of Jehoiachin (1Ch 3:18).

SHENIR *See Senir.*

SHEOL (possibly *place of inquiry [of the dead]* BDB; *desolate place, no-country underworld* KB). The OT name for the place of departed souls, corresponding to the NT word "Hades." When translated "hell" it refers to the place of punishment, but when translated "grave" the reference is to the place of the dead in general. It often means the state or state of the soul between death and resurrection. The clearest indication of different conditions in Sheol is in Christ's parable of the rich man and Lazarus (Lk 16:19-31).
See Grave; Hades; Hell.

SHEPHAM [9172] (*nakedness*). A place in NE of Canaan, near Sea of Galilee (Nu 34:10-11).

SHEPHATIAH [9152, 9153] (*Yahweh has judged*).

1. The son of David (2Sa 3:4).

2. The son of Reuel (1Ch 9:8).

3. One of David's mighty men (1Ch 12:5).

4. A Simeonite prince (1Ch 27:16).

5. The son of King Jehoshaphat (2Ch 21:2).

6. The founder of a family which returned with Zerubbabel (Ezr 2:4).

7. One of the children of Solomon's servants whose descendants returned with Zerubbabel (Ezr 2:57).

8. One whose descendants returned with Ezra (Ezr 8:8). May be the same as Ezr 2:57.

9. The son of Mahalalel (Ne 11:4).

10. The prince who wanted Jeremiah to be put to death for prophesying (Jer 38:1).

SHEPHELAH, THE (*lowland*). Hilly country between the mountains of Judah and the maritime plain S of the plain of Sharon, extending through the country of Philistia along the Mediterranean (Jos 12:8).

SHEPHER, MOUNT [9184]. A mountain, camping place of the Israelites in the desert (Nu 33:23-24).

SHEPHERD [1012, 5924, 7695, 8286, 8657, 9068, *799, 4477, 4478*].

General:

One who cares for flocks (Ge 31:38-40; Ps 78:52-53; Jer 31:10; Am 3:12; Lk 2:8). David defends his flock against a lion and a bear (1Sa 17:34-35). Causes the flock to rest (Ps 23:2; SS 1:7; Jer 33:12). Numbers the flock (Lev 27:32; Jer 33:13). Knows his flock by name (Jos 10:3-5). Keeps the sheep and goats apart (Mt 25:32). Waters the flocks (Ge 29:2-10). Keeps the flocks in folds (Nu 32:16; 1Sa 24:3; 2Sa 7:8; Jn 10:1). Watch towers of (2Ch 26:10; Mic 4:8). Dogs of (Job 30:1). Was an abomination to the Egyptians (Ge 46:34). Angels appeared to (Lk 2:8-20).

Instances of:

Abel (Ge 4:2). Rachel (Ge 29:9). Daughters of Jethro (Ex 2:16). Moses (Ex 3:1). David (1Sa 16:11; 2Sa 7:8; Ps 78:70).

Figurative:

(Ge 49:24). Of prophets, priests, Levites, and civil authorities (Eze 34). Of Cyrus (Isa 44:28). Of Yahweh (Ps 23; Isa 40:11). Of Christ (Zec 13:7; Mt 26:31; Mk 14:27; Jn 10:1-16; Heb 13:20; 1Pe 2:25).

SHEPHI *See Shepho.*

SHEPHO [9143] (possibly *track, bare ways formed without human work by the traffic caravans* KB). Early descendant of Seir (Ge 36:23; 1Ch 1:40). Lesser known brother of Groucho, Harpo, and Chico.

SHEPHUPHAN [9146] (perhaps *serpent*). The son of Bela (1Ch 8:5).

SHERAH *See Sheerah.*

SHERD *See Potsherd*

SHEREBIAH [9221] (possibly *Yahweh has sent burning heat* BDB).

1. A prominent Levite in Ezra's time (Ezr 8:18, 24).
2. Covenanter with Nehemiah (Ne 10:12).
3. Levite who returned with Zerubbabel (Ne 12:8).
4. The chief Levite (Ne 12:24).

SHERESH [9246] (*root, rootstock, sucker [of a plant]*). The son of Makir (1Ch 7:16).

SHEREZER *See Sharezer.*

SHERIFF (Da 3:2-3). *See Magistrates.*

SHESHACH [9263] (cryptogram for *Babel [Babylon]*). Perhaps a cryptogram for "Babel" or "Babylon" (Jer 25:26, ftn; 51:41, ftn).

SHESHAI [9259] (possibly *sixth [child]*). The son of Anak (Nu 13:22; Jos 15:14; Jdg 1:10).

SHESHAN [9264]. A descendant of Jerahmeel (1Ch 2:31, 34-35).

SHESHBAZZAR [9256, 10746] (*may [the pagan moon god named] Sin protect [the father]*). A Jewish official whom Cyrus made deputy governor of Judah and who helped lay the foundation of the temple (Ezr 1:8, 11; 5:14, 16). Some believe that Sheshbazzar and Zerubbabel were the same person for the following reasons:

1. Both were governors (Ezr 5:14; Hag 1:1; 2:2).
2. Both are said to have laid the foundation of the temple (Ezr 3:2-8; 5:16; Hag 1:14-15; Zec 4:6-10).
3. Jews in Babylon were often given "official" Babylonian names (cf. Da 1:7).
4. Josephus (*Antiq.*, 11.1.3) seems to identify Sheshbazzar with Zerubbabel.

Others point out, however:

1. The Apocrypha distinguishes between the two men (1Es 6:18).
2. Sheshbazzar was likely an elderly man at the time of the return, while Zerubbabel was probably a younger contemporary.
3. Sheshbazzar may have been viewed as the official governor, while Zerubbabel served as the popular leader (Ezr 3:8-11).
4. Whereas the high priest Jeshua is associated with Zerubbabel, no priest is associated with Sheshbazzar.
5. Although Sheshbazzar presided over the foundation of the temple in 536 B.C., so little was accomplished that Zerubbabel had to preside over a second foundation sixteen years later (Hag 1:14-15; Zec 4:6-10).

Others identify Sheshbazzar with Shenazzar (1Ch 3:18), the fourth son of King Jehoiachin. Zerubbabel would then have been Sheshbazzar's

nephew (compare 3:2 with 1Ch 3:18). *See Zerubbabel.*

SHETH [9269] (*sons of tumult,* or *sons of pride, compensation*). A designation for Moab (Nu 24:17).

SHETHAR [9285]. A prince of Persia (Est 1:14).

SHETHAR-BOZENAI [10750] (*delivering the kingdom*). Persian official who tried to hinder Jews (Ezr 5:3, 6).

SHEVA [8737] (*vanity, emptiness* IDB; *one who will emulate* IDB KB).

1. David's scribe (2Sa 20:25), perhaps the same as "Seraiah" (1Ch 2:49). *See Seraiah, 1.*
2. The son of Caleb (1Ch 2:49).

SHEWBREAD *See Bread, Consecrated.*

SHIBAH [8683] (possibly *seven* BDB ISBE; possibly *oath* BDB IDB; *plenty* KB). The name of the well dug by Isaac's servants. A town of Beersheba named from this well (Ge 26:31-33, ftn). Called Beersheba in NIV.

SHIBBOLETH [8672] (*flowing stream* BDB KB; or *ear of grain* IDB). A word differently pronounced on the two sides of the Jordan, and was used by the men of Gilead to determine whether the speaker was of Ephraim or not. Those who said "Sibboleth" instead of "Shibboleth" were killed. Forty-two thousand Ephraimites were killed at the fords of the Jordan at that time (Jdg 12:5-6).

SHIBMAH *See Sibmah.*

SHICRON *See Shikkeron.*

SHIELD [1713, 2910, 4059, 4482, 6114, 6116, 6317, 7558, 8949, 2599].

Defensive Armor:
Different kinds of (Ps 35:2; Eze 38:4). Used by Saul (2Sa 1:21), by the Benjamites (2Ch 14:8; 17:17). Uzziah equipped the Israelites with (2Ch 26:14). Made of bronze (1Ki 14:27), of gold (2Sa 8:7; 1Ki 10:16-17; 2Ch 9:15-16), of wood (Eze 39:9-10). Stored in armories (1Ki 10:17; 2Ch 11:12; 32:5, 27), in the tabernacle (2Ki 11:10; 2Ch 23:9). Covered when not in use (Isa 22:6). Painted red (Na 2:3). *See Armor.*

Figurative:
Of God's protection (Ge 15:1; Dt 33:29; 2Sa 22:3, 36; Ps 5:12; 18:2, 35; 59:11; 84:9, 11; 89:18; Pr 30:5). Of God's truth (Ps 91:4). Of kings (Ps 47:9). Of an entire army (Jer 46:3).

SHIGGAION [8710] (*go astray, wander [i.e., a wild, passionate song, with rapid changes in rhythm]* BDB; possibly Akkadian for *dirge* KB). A musical term of unknown meaning found in the heading of (Ps 7).
See Music, Symbols Used in.

SHIGIONOTH [8710] (*go astray, wander [i.e., a wild, passionate song, with rapid changes in rhythm]* BDB; possibly Akkadian for *dirge* KB). The plural of *shiggaion*. The heading of Habakkuk's psalm (Hab 3:1).

See Music, Symbols Used in.

SHIHON *See Shion.*

SHIHOR [8865] (possibly *black water* BDB; Egyptian *Canal of [pagan god] Horus* KB). May refer to the Nile, a stream which separated Egypt from Israel, or a branch of the Nile (Jos 13:3; 1Ch 13:5; Isa 23:3; Jer 2:18).

SHIHOR LIBNATH [8866]. A small stream on the S border of Asher (Jos 19:26).

SHIKKERON [8914] (possibly *drunkenness* IDB; *hog bean plant* IDB). A town on the N boundary of Judah (Jos 15:11).

SHILHI [8944] (possibly *[my] javelin [thrower?]* IDB KB). Father-in-law of Jehoshaphat, king of Judah (1Ki 22:42; 2Ch 20:31).

SHILHIM [8946]. A city of Judah (Jos 15:32).

SHILLEM, SHILLEMITE [8973, 8980] (*recompense* BDB IDB; possibly *whole, healthy, complete* KB). The son of Naphtali (Ge 46:24; 1Ch 7:13), and his descendants (Nu 26:49).

SHILOAH [8942]. A stream or pool (Isa 8:6). Probably identical with Siloah and Siloam. *See Siloam, Pool of.*

SHILOH [8870, 8872, 8926, 8931].
1. A city in Ephraim, c. twelve miles N and E of Bethel where the tabernacle remained from the time of Joshua to the days of Samuel (Jdg 21:19; 1Sa 4:3), Benjamites kidnapped wives (Jdg 21:15-24), residence of Eli and Samuel (1Sa 3:21), home of the prophet Ahijah (1Ki 14:3), a ruin in Jeremiah's time (Jer 7:12, 14).
2. A word of uncertain meaning regarded by many Jews and Christians as a reference to the Messiah, the NIV has "until he comes to whom it belongs" (Ge 49:10, ftn).

SHILONI *See Shelah, 3.*

SHILONITE(S) [8872] (*of Shiloh*).
1. A man of Shiloh (1Ki 12:15; 15:29; 2Ch 9:29; 10:15).
2. Apparently denotes a descendant of Shelah (1Ch 9:5). *See Shelanite.*

SHILSHAH [8996] (possibly *obedient* or *gentle* IDB; *third [part, child?], triplet* KB). An Asherite; the son of Zophah (1Ch 7:37).

SHIMEA [9055] (*he has heard* or *he is obedient*).
1. Brother of David (1Ch 20:7). Perhaps the same as "Shammah" (1Sa 16:9), "Shimeah" (2Sa 21:21).
2. The son of David and Bathsheba (1Ch 3:5).
3. A Merarite Levite (1Ch 6:30).
4. A Gershonite Levite (1Ch 6:39).

SHIMEAH [9009, 9056] (*he has heard* or *he is obedient*).
1. The brother of David (2Sa 13:3, 32; 21:21).
2. A Benjamite (1Ch 8:32), "Shimeam" (1Ch 9:38).

SHIMEAM [9010]. *See Shimeah, 2.*

SHIMEATH [9064] (*guardian, watcher*). The mother of an assassin of King Joash (2Ki 12:21; 2Ch 24:26).

SHIMEATHITES [9065]. A family of scribes (1Ch 2:55).

SHIMEI, SHIMEITES [9059, 9060] (*Yahweh has heard*, or *famous*).
1. Son of Gershon (Ex 6:17; Nu 3:18; 1Ch 6:17; 23:7, 10) and his descendants (Nu 3:21).
2. A Benjamite. Curses David; David's magnanimity toward (2Sa 16:5-13; 19:16-23, w 1Ki 2:36-46).
3. An officer of David (1Ki 1:8).
4. One of Solomon's district governors (1Ki 4:18).
5. A son of Jesse (1Ch 2:13).
6. The grandson of Jehoiachin (1Ch 3:19).
7. The son of Zaccur (1Ch 4:26-27).
8. A Reubenite. The son of Gog (1Ch 5:4).
9. A Merarite. The son of Libni (1Ch 6:29).
10. A Gershonite. The son of Jahath (1Ch 6:42).
11. The father of a family in Benjamin (1Ch 8:21).
12. A Levite (1Ch 23:9).
13. A leader of singers in the time of David (1Ch 25:17).
14. David's overseer of vineyards (1Ch 27:27).
15. A son of Heman (2Ch 29:14).
16. A Levite. The treasurer of tithes and offerings in the time of Hezekiah (2Ch 31:12-13).
17. A Levite who put away his Gentile wife (Ezr 10:23).
18. The name of two Israelites who put away Gentile wives (Ezr 10:33, 38).
19. A Benjamite. The grandfather of Mordecai (Est 2:5).
20. The ancestor of a family (Zec 12:13). Possibly identical with 1.

SHIMEON [9058] (possibly *offspring of hyena and wolf* BDB KB). An Israelite who divorced his Gentile wife (Ezr 10:31).

SHIMHI *See Shimei, 11.*

SHIMI *See Shimei, 1.*

SHIMMA *See Shimea, 1.*

SHIMON [8873]. A man of Judah (1Ch 4:20).

SHIMRATH [9086] (*guardian, watchman*). The son of Shimei (1Ch 8:21).

SHIMRI [9078] (*Yahweh guards, preserves*).
1. The son of Shemaiah; a Simeonite (1Ch 4:37).
2. The father of Jediael and Joha, two of David's mighty men (1Ch 11:45).
3. A Merarite Levite doorkeeper (1Ch 26:10).
4. A Levite who assisted in cleansing the temple (2Ch 29:13).

SHIMRITH [9083] (*guardianess, watch woman*). A Moabitess; the mother of Jehozabad who helped kill Joash, king of Judah (2Ch 24:26), "Shomer" (2Ki 12:21).

SHIMROM *See Shimron, 1.*

SHIMRON, SHIMRONITE [9074, 9075, 9084] (*guardian, watchman*).
1. The son of Issachar (Ge 46:13; 1Ch 7:1) and his descendants (Nu 26:24).
2. A town in N Canaan whose king fought Joshua (Jos 11:1ff; probably Shimron Meron. *See Shimron Meron.*

SHIMRON MERON [9077]. A city conquered by Joshua (Jos 12:20). Probably identical with Shimron, 2. *See Shimron, 2.*

SHIMSHAI [10729] (*one given to [pagan sun god] Shemesh*). A scribe who tried to hinder the Jews in rebuilding the temple (Ezr 4:8-9, 17, 23).

SHINAB [9098] (*[pagan god] Sin is his father*). The king of Admah. A Canaanite city, later destroyed (Ge 14:2).

SHINAR [824+9114, 9114]. An alluvial plain of Babylonia in which lay the cities of Babel, Erech, Akkad, and Calneh (Ge 10:10), the Tower of Babel was built there (Ge 11:1-9), Amraphel, king of Shinar, invaded Canaan (Ge 14:1, 9). Elsewhere rendered Babylon(ia): Nebuchadnezzar transported the temple treasures to (Da 1:2, ftn), Jews exiled to (Zec 5:11, ftn).

SHION [8858]. A town in Issachar near Nazareth (Jos 19:19).

SHIP [641+9576, 641, 7469, *3729, 3730, 4434, 4450*]. Built, by Noah (Ge 6:13-22), by Solomon (1Ki 9:26; 2Ch 8:17), by Jehoshaphat (1Ki 22:48; 2Ch 20:35-36), of cypress wood (Ge 6:14), of fir wood (Eze 27:5), of papyrus (Isa 18:2), sealed with pitch (Ge 6:15).
Equipped with, rudder (Ac 27:40; Jas 3:4), rigging (Isa 33:23; Ac 27:19), sails (Isa 33:23; Ac 27:1, 9, 17, 40), embroidered sails (Eze 27:7), masts (Isa 33:23; Eze 27:5), oars (Jnh 1:13; Mk 6:48), figurehead (Ac 28:11), anchor (Ac 27:29-30, 40; Heb 6:19), lifeboats (Ac 27:30, 32).
Used, in commerce (Ac 21:3; 27:10), in commerce with Tarshish (1Ki 22:48; Isa 60:9; Jnh 1:3), with Ophir (1Ki 10:11; 2Ch 8:18), with

Adramyttium (Ac 27:2), for passenger traffic (Isa 60:9; Jnh 1:3; Ac 20:13; 27:2, 37; 28:11).
Repaired by caulking (Eze 27:9).
Wrecked, at Ezion Geber (1Ki 22:48; 2Ch 20:35-37), at Malta (Ac 27:14-44).
Warships used by Kittim (Nu 24:24; Da 11:30).
See Mariner.

SHIPHI [9181] (*flowing abundance*). The father of Ziza (1Ch 4:37).

SHIPHMITE [9175] (*family name of Zabdi*). Vineyard overseer (1Ch 27:27).

SHIPHRAH [9186] (*beautiful, fair*). A Hebrew midwife who saved Hebrew boy babies (Ex 1:15-21).

SHIPHTAN [9154] (*he has judged*). The father of the representative of Ephraim on the committee which divided the promised land among the Israelites (Nu 34:24).

SHISHA [8881]. The father of two of Solomon's secretaries (1Ki 4:3), may be identical with Seraiah (2Sa 8:17), Sheva (2Sa 20:25), and Shavsha (1Ch 18:16).

SHISHAK [8882]. The first Egyptian Pharaoh mentioned by name in the Bible; the founder of the twenty-second dynasty (945-924 B.C.), gave refuge to Jeroboam (1Ki 11:40), invaded Jerusalem in the reign of Rehoboam (1Ki 14:25f).

SHITRAI [8855] (*scribe, officer*). A chief shepherd of David (1Ch 27:29).

SHITTAH *See Beth Shittah.*

SHITTAH TREE NIV "acacia." *See Acacia Wood; Plants of the Bible; Tree.*

SHITTIM [8850] (*acacia trees*).
1. Also called Abel Shittim (Nu 33:49). A camping place of Israel (Nu 25:1; 33:49). Joshua sends spies from (Jos 2:1). Valley of (Joel 3:18). Balaam prophesies in (Mic 6:5). *See Abel Shittim.*
2. Hebrew for acacia (Joel 3:18).
See Acacia Wood.

SHIZA [8862]. A Reubenite. The father of one of David's mighty men (1Ch 11:42).

SHOA [8778] (*rich*). People mentioned in association with the Babylonians, Chaldeans, and Assyrians (Eze 23:23). May be Sutu of Amarna letters.

SHOBAB [8744] (*one who turns back, repents*).
1. The grandson for Hezron (1Ch 2:18).
2. The son of David (2Sa 5:14; 1Ch 3:5; 14:4).

SHOBACH [8747]. The captain of the host of Hadadezer. Slain by David's army (2Sa 10:16, 18). Also called Shophach (1Ch 19:16, 18).

SHOBAI [8662] (possibly *captive* or *Yahweh returns*). A gatekeeper, whose descendants returned to Jerusalem with Zerubbabel (Ezr 2:42; Ne 7:45).

SHOBAL [8748] (perhaps a nickname *basket*).
1. Chief of the Horites (Ge 36:20, 23, 29).
2. Ephrathite; founder of Kiriath Jearim (1Ch 2:50, 52).
3. Grandson of Judah (1Ch 4:1-2).

SHOBEK [8749] (*victor* IDB). A Jew who sealed the covenant with Nehemiah (Ne 10:24).

SHOBI [8661] (possibly *captive* or *Yahweh returns*). The son of Nahash. Brought supplies to David in his flight from Absalom (2Sa 17:27).

SHOCHO *See Soco, 2.*

SHOE *See Sandal.*

SHOFAR (*ram horn*). A trumpet of ram's horn (Jos 6:4-6, 8, 13). *See Trumpet.*

SHOHAM [8733] (*carnelian [precious stone]*). A Merarite (1Ch 24:27).

SHOMER [9071] (*guardian, watchman*).
1. A man who sold the hill of Samaria to Omri, king of Israel (1Ki 16:24).
2. The father of Jehozabad, conspirator of Joash of Judah (2Ki 12:20-21).
3. A Merarite Levite (1Ch 6:46).
4. The great-grandson of Asher (1Ch 7:32, 34).

SHOPHACH [8791]. A Syrian general slain by David (1Ch 19:16, 18), "Shobach" (2Sa 10:16).

SHOPHAN *See Atroth Shophan.*

SHORE [362, 824, 3338, 8557, *129, 302, 839, 1178, 4305*]. Coast line or beach (Jos 15:2; Jdg 5:17; Mt 13:2).

SHOSHANNIM NIV "Lilies." *See Music, Symbols Used in.*

SHOULDER [2432, 4190, 7418, 8900, *6049*]. The shoulder of a sacrificed ox or sheep went to the priest as his portion (Dt 18:8), the sacred furniture of the tabernacle had to be carried upon the shoulders (Nu 7:6-9).

SHOULDER PIECE
1. Part of the ephod in which the front and the back were joined together (Ex 28:7-8).
2. A piece of meat taken from the shoulder of an animal (Eze 24:4).

SHOUTING [*606, 2116, 6699, 7412, 7754, 7924, 8131, 8262, 8264, 9558, 1066, 2215, 3189, 3198, 3306*]. In joy and praise (1Ch 15:28; 2Ch 15:12-14; Ezr 3:11-13; Ps 47:1; Isa 12:6; Lk 17:15; 19:37-41; Ac 3:8-9; Rev 5:12-14).

See Clap; Praise; Worship.
In battle (Jos 6:20; Jdg 7:18; 1Sa 17:20, 52; 2Ch 13:15).

SHOVEL [3582, 4665]. A utensil in the tabernacle (Ex 27:3; 38:3; Nu 4:14), temple (1Ki 7:40; Jer 52:18).

SHOWBREAD *See Bread, Consecrated.*

SHRINE [1074, 1195, 2215, 2540, 5219, 6109, 6551, 7728, 8229, *3724, 5008*]. Places of idolatrous worship, often a high place (Eze 16:24-25, 31, 39). Frequented by temple prostitutes (Ge 38:21-22; Dt 23:17; Hos 4:14), including male prostitutes (1Ki 14:24; 15:12; 22:46; 2Ki 23:7; Job 36:14). A shrine also refers to an idolatrous symbol, certain small idol houses, made by the silversmith, Demetrius, and sold to the worshipers of the Temple of Diana (Ac 19:24).

See Artemis; Groves; High Places; Idolatry; Prostitute.

SHRIVELED HAND [3312, *3830, 3831*]. As a judgment (1Ki 13:4). Jesus heals on the Sabbath (Mt 12:10-13 w Mk 3:1-6; Lk 6:6-11). *See Disease.*

SHROUD [2502, 4059, 4287, 8492]. A sheet to cover the dead (Isa 25:7).

SHRUB *See Plants of the Bible.*

SHUA [8781, 8783] (*prosperity* ISBE).
1. A Canaanite whose daughter became Judah's wife (Ge 38:2, 12).
2. Heber's daughter (1Ch 7:32).

SHUAH [8756] (*depression, lowland [an Aramean land on the Euphrates River]*).
1. The son of Abraham by Keturah (Ge 25:2; 1Ch 1:32).
2. *See Shua, 1.*
3. *See Shuhah.*

SHUAL [8786, 8787] (*fox* or *jackal*).
1. District near Micmash (1Sa 13:17).
2. The son of Zophah (1Ch 7:36).

SHUBAEL [8649, 8742] (possibly *captive of God [El]*, or *God [El] restores*).
1. The son of Gershom son of Moses (1Ch 23:16; 26:24).
2. The son of Amram (1Ch 24:20).
3. A singer, the son of Heman (1Ch 25:4, 20).

SHUHAH [8758] (*pit, depression*). Kelub's brother (1Ch 4:11).

SHUHAM, SHUHAMITE [8761, 8762]. The son of Dan and his clan (Nu 26:42-43); also called Hushim (Ge 46:23). *See Hushim, 1.*

SHUHITE [8760] (*of Shuah*). Bildad, one of Job's friends (Job 2:11; 8:1; 18:1; 25:1); possibly a descendant of Shuah, 1.

SHULAMMITE [8769] (*peaceful*). A designation of the beloved in the Song of Songs (SS 6:13); possibly the same as Shunammite.

SHUMATHITES [9092] (*garlic*). Family of Kiriath Jearim (1Ch 2:53).

SHUNAMMITE [8774].
1. A person from Shunem. Abishag, the woman who nourished David (1Ki 1:3), desired by Adonijah as wife (1Ki 2:13-25).
2. A woman who gave hospitality to Elisha and whose son he raised to life (2Ki 4:8-37).

SHUNEM [8773]. A city of Issachar (Job 19:18), three-and-a-half miles N of Jezreel; the site of a Philistine encampment before battle (1Sa 28:4), the home of Abishag, David's nurse (1Ki 1:3), home of a woman who befriended Elisha (2Ki 4:8-37).

SHUNI, SHUNITE [8771, 8772]. The son of Gad (Ge 46:16) and his clan (Nu 26:15).

SHUPHAM, SHUPHAMITE [8792, 8793]. The son of Benjamin and progenitor of Shuphamites (Nu 26:39). May be the same as Shephuphan (1Ch 8:5).

SHUPPIM [9157].
1. A Levite (1Ch 26:16).
2. See Shuppites.

SHUPPITES [9158]. Descendants of Ir (1Ch 7:12, 15).

SHUR [8804] (*wall*). A wilderness southwest of Israel (Ge 16:7; 20:1; 25:18; Ex 15:22; 1Sa 15:7; 27:8).

SHUSHAN See Susa.

SHUSHAN-EDUTH (*lily of testimony*). See Music, Symbols Used in.

SHUTHELAH, SHUTHALHITE [8811, 9279].
1. The son of Ephraim and his clan (Nu 26:35-36).
2. The son of Zabad; father of Ezer and Elead (1Ch 7:21).

SHUTTLE [756]. Part of a weaving loom; used as a figure of the shortness of life (Job 7:6).

SIA [6103] (*assembly*). Progenitor of the temple servants that returned with Zerubbabel (Ne 7:47), "Siaha" (Ezr 2:44).

SIAHA [6104]. See Sia.

SIBBECAI [6021]. One of David's mighty men, designated "Hushathite" (2Sa 21:18; 1Ch 11:29; 20:4; 27:11), killed the Philistine "Saph" (2Sa 21:18).

SIBBOLETH [6027]. See Shibboleth.

SIBMAH [8424]. A city of Reuben (Nu 32:38; Jos 13:19; Isa 16:8-9; Jer 48:32). Apparently also called Sebam (Nu 32:3).

SIBRAIM [6028]. A place on the N boundary of Israel (Eze 47:16).

SICHEM See Shechem, 1.

SICILY An island lying off the "toe" of Italy, visited by Paul (Ac 28:12). See Syracuse.

SICK, THE [108, 2703, 5823, 779, 819+2400, 820, 822, 2400+2809, 2827, 2879]. Visiting (Ps 41:6). Visiting, a duty (Mt 25:36, 43; Jas 1:27). See Afflicted; Affliction; Disease.

SICKLE [3058, 4478, 1535] (*reaping hook*). A tool used for cutting grain, sometimes also for pruning (Dt 16:9; Joel 3:13; Mk 4:29). Used figuratively for God's judgment (Joel 3:13; Rev 14:14).

SICKNESS [2716, 4700, 4701, 819, 820+3798, 3433]. Figurative of sin and judgment (Isa 1:5-6; Hos 5:13). See Affliction; Disease; Sick, The.

SIDDIM, VALLEY OF [8443] (possibly *valley of furrows, valley of demons* BDB; *valley of bordering furrows* KB). Vale of, a valley of uncertain location. Scene of the king of Sodom (Ge 14:3, 8, 10).

SIDON [7477, 7479, 4972, 4973] (*fishery*).
1. The son of Canaan (Ge 10:15; 1Ch 1:13).
2. A city on the northern boundary of the Canaanites, twenty-two miles N of Tyre (Ge 10:19). Designated by Jacob as the border of Zebulun (Ge 49:13). Was on the northern boundary of Asher (Jos 19:28; 2Sa 24:6). Belonged to the land of Israel according to the promise (Jos 13:6). Inhabitants of lived in security (Jdg 18:7). Israelites failed to make the conquest of (Jdg 1:31; 3:3). The inhabitants of, contributed cedar for the first and second temple (1Ki 5:6; 1Ch 22:4; Ezr 3:7). Solomon marries a woman of (1Ki 11:1). Chief gods were Baal and Ashtoreth (1Ki 11:5, 33; 2Ki 23:13). Jezebel, wife of King Ahab, was a daughter of a king of Sidon (1Ki 16:31). People of, come to hear Jesus (Mk 3:8; Lk 6:17). Inhabitants of, offend Herod (Ac 12:20-23).
Commerce of (Isa 23:2, 4, 12). Seamen of (Eze 27:8). Prophecies concerning (Jer 25:15-22; 27:3-11; 47:4; Eze 28:21-23; 32:30; Joel 3:4-8). Jesus visits the region of, and heals the daughter of the Syrian Phoenician woman (Mt 15:21-28; Mk 7:24-31). Visited by Paul (Ac 27:3).

SIEGE [369+784, 1032, 1911, 2006, 2837+6584, 5189, 5193, 6149, 6164, 7443, 7674, 9068]. An offer of peace must be made to the city before beginning (Dt 20:10-12). Conducted by erecting embankments parallel to the walls of the besieged city (Dt 20:19-20; Isa 29:3; 37:33). Battering rams used in. See Battering Ram. Distress of the inhabitants during (2Ki 6:24-29; 25:3; Isa 9:20; 36:12; Jer 19:9). Cannibalism in (2Ki 6:28-29).

Instances of:

Of Jericho (Jos 6). Rabbah (2Sa 11:1), Abel (2Sa 20:15), Gibbethon (1Ki 15:27), Tirzah (1Ki 16:17). Jerusalem, by the children of Judah (Jdg 1:8), by David (2Sa 5:6, 9), by Rezin, king of Syria, and Pekah, son of Remaliah, king of Israel (2Ki 16:5), by Nebuchadnezzar (2Ki 24:10-11; Da 1:1; 2Ki 25:1-3; Jer 52), by Sennacherib (2Ch 32:1-23). Samaria (1Ki 20:1; 2Ki 6:24; 17:5; 18:9-11).

SIEVE [3895, 5864]. A sifting device for grain; made of reeds, horsehair, or strings (Isa 30:28; Am 9:9). Also used figuratively (Lk 22:31).

SIGN [226, 253, 4603, 5727, 5812, 7483, 9338, *1893*, *4956*, *5518*]. A miracle to confirm faith (Mt 12:38; 16:4; 24:30; Mk 8:11-12; 13:4; Jn 2:11; 3:2; 4:48). Asked for by, and given to Abraham (Ge 15:8-17), Moses (Ex 4:1-9), Gideon (Jdg 6:17, 36-40), Hezekiah (2Ki 20:8), Zechariah (Lk 1:18). Given to Jeroboam (1Ki 13:3-5).

A token of coming events (Mt 16:3-4; 24:3).

See Miracles.

SIGNAL [4911, 5368, 5812, 8131, 9239, 9546, 10084, *1935*, *4956*, *5361*]. Used in war (Isa 18:3).

See Armies; Ensign; Trumpet.

SIGNET [2597, 3192, 10536]. *See Seal.*

SIHON [6095]. King of the Amorites. His seat of government at Heshbon (Nu 21:26). The proverbial chant celebrating the victory of Sihon over the Moabites (Nu 21:26-30). Conquest of his kingdom by the Israelites (Nu 21:21-25; Dt 2:24-37; 3:2, 6, 8).

SIHOR *See Shihor.*

SILAS [4976, 4977] (*asked, possibly dedicated to God*). Also called Silvanus (1Th 1:1, ftn). Sent to Paul, in Antioch, from Jerusalem (Ac 15:22-34). Becomes Paul's companion (Ac 15:40-41; 2Co 1:19; 1Th 1:1; 2Th 1:1). Imprisoned with Paul in Philippi (Ac 16:19-40). Driven, with Paul, from Thessalonica (Ac 17:4-10). Left by Paul at Berea (Ac 17:14). Rejoins Paul at Corinth (Ac 17:15; 18:5). Carries Peter's epistle to Asia Minor (1Pe 5:12).

SILENT YEARS, FOUR
HUNDRED *See Testaments, Time Between.*

SILK [4986]. Wearing apparel made of (Pr 31:22; Eze 16:10, 13). Merchandise of (Rev 18:22). *See Linen.*

SILLA [6133] (*embankment*). A place of uncertain location (2Ki 12:20).

SILOAH *See Siloam.*

SILOAM, POOL OF [8940, *4978*] (*sent*). A reservoir located within the city walls of Jerusalem at the S end of the Tyropean Valley; receives water through a 1, 780-foot tunnel from En Rogel (Ne 3:15; Lk 13:4; Jn 9:7, 11), constructed by Hezekiah in the late eighth century B.C. "Shiloah" (Isa 8:6). The pool today is called Birket Silwan and a nearby village is Silwan. *See Siloam, Village of.*

SILOAM, TOWER OF Probably part of the fortification system of the Jerusalem wall, near the pool of Siloam (Lk 13:4).

SILOAM, VILLAGE OF Not mentioned in the Bible; the modern village (Silwan) situated across the valley E of the Gihon Spring.

SILVANUS *See Silas.*

SILVER [4084, 7988, 10362, *735*, *736*, *738*, *1324*, *1534*] (*pale, white*). From Tarshish (Eze 27:12). Refining of (Pr 17:3; 25:4; 26:23; Eze 22:18-22; Jer 6:29-30; Zec 13:9; Mal 3:3). *See Refining.*

Used for money (Ge 13:2; 17:12; 20:16; 23:13-16; Am 8:6; Mt 10:9; 26:15; Mk 14:11; Ac 19:19). *See Money.* For ornamentation of, and in the manufacture of, the utensils for the tabernacle (Ex 26:19; 27:17; 35:24; 36:24; 38:25; Nu 7:13, 19, 25, 31, 37, 43, 49, 55, 61, 67, 73, 79, 85), of the temple (1Ch 28:14; 29:2-5; Ezr 5:14; 6:5; 8:26; Da 5:2). Cups made of (Ge 44:2), trumpets (Nu 10:2), cords (Ecc 12:6), chains (Isa 40:19), shrines (Ac 19:24), idols (Ex 20:23; Isa 30:22; Hos 13:2), baskets, or filigree (Pr 25:11), jewels (SS 1:11). *See Jewel, Jewelry.* Towers, figurative (SS 8:9). Vessels of (Nu 7:85; 1Ki 10:25; 2Sa 8:10; 2Ki 12:13; 1Ch 18:10; 2Ch 24:14; Ezr 1:6; 5:14; 6:5; 8:26; Da 5:2; 11:8).

Abundance of (1Ki 10:27; 1Ch 22:14; 29:2-7; 2Ch 1:15; Ecc 2:8; Isa 2:7). Dross from (Pr 25:4; 26:23). Rejected (Jer 6:30). Workers in (2Ch 2:14; Ac 19:24). *See Smith.*

Symbolic (Da 2:32, 35).

SILVERSMITH [7671, *737*]. (Ac 19:24). *See Smith.*

SIMEON [1201+9058, 9058, 9063, *5208*] (*he has heard* or *obedient one*).

1. The son of Jacob (Ge 29:33; 35:23; Ex 1:1-2; 1Ch 2:1). With Levi avenges upon the Shechemites the seduction of Dinah (Ge 34; 49:5-7). Goes down to Egypt to buy grain; is bound by Joseph and detained (Ge 42:24, 36; 43:23). His sons (Ge 46:10; Ex 6:15; 1Ch 4:24-37). Descendants of (Nu 26:12-14).

See below, Tribe of.

2. Tribe of: Military enrollment of, at Sinai (Nu 1:22-23; 2:13), in the plains of Moab (Nu 26:14). Place of, in camp and march (Nu 2:12; 10:18-19). Inheritance allotted to (Jos 19:1-9; Jdg 1:3-17; 1Ch 4:24-43). Stood on Mount Gerizim to bless at the time of the rehearsal of the law (Dt 27:12).

Joined with the people of Judah and Benjamin in the renewal of the Passover (2Ch 15:9, w 15:1-15). Idolatry of (2Ch 34:6, w 34:1-7).

See Israel.

3. A devout man in Jerusalem. Blesses Jesus in the temple (Lk 2:25-35).

4. An ancestor of Jesus (Lk 3:30).

5. A disciple. Also called Niger (Ac 13:1).

6. Hebrew name of Peter (Ac 15:14, ftn). *See Peter, Simon.*

SIMEONITE(S) [1201+9058, 9058, 9063] (*of Simeon*). A member of the tribe of Simeon.

SIMILITUDE (*likeness*). Pattern, resemblance, similarity (Nu 12:8; 2Ch 4:3; Ps 106:20; Heb 7:15).

SIMON [*1639+4981, 4981, 5208*] (*he has heard* or *obedient one*).

1. *See Peter, Simon.*

2. One of the twelve apostles. Called the Zealot (Mt 10:4; Mk 3:18; Lk 6:15; Ac 1:13). *See Zealot.*

3. A brother of Jesus (Mt 13:55; Mk 6:3).

4. A leper. Jesus dines with (Mt 26:6; Mk 14:3).

5. A man of Cyrene. Compelled to carry Jesus' cross (Mt 27:32; Mk 15:21; Lk 23:26).

6. A Pharisee. Jesus dines with (Lk 7:36-44).

7. The father of Judas Iscariot (Jn 6:71; 12:4; 13:2, 26).

8. A sorcerer. Converted by Philip; rebuked by Peter (Ac 8:9-13, 18-24).

9. A tanner. Peter lodges with (Ac 9:43; 10:6, 17, 32).

SIMON MACCABEUS Hasmonean ruler in Israel (143-134 B.C.).

SIMONY Ecclesiastical corruption, named after Simon the sorceror (Ac 8:9-19).

SIMPLE [7331, 7343, 7344, 7785, 7837]. Naive; easily led into wrong-doing (Ps 19:7; 119:130; Pr 7:7).

SIMRI *See Shimri, 3.*

SIN [*2627, 2628, 2629, 2631, 2633, 6097, 6404, 6411, 7321, 7322, 8273, 279, 280, 281, 283, 4183, 4579, 4922, 4997, 4998*].

Adamic:

Original, of Adam (Ge 3:6; Hos 6:7; Ro 5:12, 15-19).

Sin Nature:

The inherited tendencies to evil (Mt 7:17-18; 12:33-35; Mk 7:20-23; Lk 6:45; Ro 6:6; 7:17, 20, 23, 25; 8:3, 5-7; Gal 5:16-17; Eph 2:3; Jas 1:14; 4:17).

Defined:

Transgressing the law (Hos 6:8; Mt 5:28; 1Co 8:12; Heb 12:15; Jas 2:10-11; 4:17; 1Jn 3:4; 5:17). Turning away from God (Dt 29:18; Ps 95:10). Not seeking God (2Ch 12:14). Foolish thoughts (Pr 24:8-9). Self-deception (Isa 42:20). That which is not of faith (Ro 14:23).

See Atonement; Conviction, of Sin; Depravity; Regeneration; Repentance; Reprobacy; Salvation; Sanctification; Wicked, Punishment of.

Against the body (Ecc 5:6). Against conscience (Ro 14:23). Against knowledge (Pr 26:11; Lk 12:47-48; Jn 9:41; 15:22; Ro 1:21, 32; 2:17-23; Heb 10:26; Jas 4:17; 2Pe 2:21-22). *See Ignorance, Sins of.* Attempts to cover, vain (Ge 3:10; Job 31:33; Isa 29:15; 59:6).

Christ's description of (Mt 5:2-20; Jn 8:34, 44).

Deceitful (Heb 3:13). Defiles (Ps 51:2, 7; Isa 1:18; Heb 12:15; 1Jn 1:7). *See Defilement.* Degrees in (Job 7:41-47; 12:47-48). Dominion of (Ro 3:9). Enslaves (Jn 8:34; Ro 6:16; 2Pe 2:19).

From the heart (Isa 44:20; Jer 7:24; 17:9; Eze 20:16; Mt 5:28; 7:17-18; 12:33-35; 15:8, 11, 16-19; Lk 6:45). Of the tongue (Ecc 5:6). In thought (Pr 24:9). Fools mock at (Pr 14:9). Little sins (SS 2:15). Magnitude of (Job 22:5; Ps 25:11).

None in heaven (Rev 22:3-4).

Parable of (Mt 13:24-25, 33, 39). Paul's discussion of the responsibility for (Ro 2-9). Pleasures of (Jn 20:12-16; 21:12-13; Lk 8:14; Heb 11:25). *See Pleasure, Worldly.*

Reproach to God (2Sa 12:14).

Secret sins (Ps 19:12; 44:22; 64:2; 90:8; Ecc 12:14; Eze 8:12; 11:5; Mt 10:26; Lk 8:17; 12:2-3; Jn 3:20; Ro 2:16; Eph 5:12). Sinfulness of (Job 22:5; Ps 25:11; Isa 1:18; Ro 7:13).

To be hated (Dt 7:26; Ps 119:113).

Confession of:

(1Ki 8:47; Pr 28:13). Signified by placing hands on the head of the offering (Lev 3:2, 13; 4:4, 15, 24, 29, 33; 16:21; Nu 8:12). Illustrated in parables, of the prodigal son (Lk 15:17-21). Of the Pharisee and the tax collector (Lk 18:13).

To God, commanded (Lev 5:5-10; 16:21). Exemplified by Israel (Nu 14:40; Jdg 10:10; 1Sa 7:6), by Saul (1Sa 15:2, 4), by David (2Sa 12:13; 24:10, 17; 1Ch 21:17), by the psalmist (Ps 32:5; 38:3-4, 18; 40:11-12; 41:4; 51:2-5; 69:5; 73:21-22; 119:59-60, 176), by the Jews (2Ch 29:6; Ezr 9:4-7, 10-15; Ne 9:2-38; Ps 106:6; Isa 26:13; 59:12-15; 64:5-7; Jer 3:21-22, 25; 8:14-15; 14:7, 20; 31:18-19; La 3:40-42; Da 9:5-6, 8-11, 15), by Job (Job 7:20; 9:20; 13:23; 40:4; 42:5-6), by Isaiah (Isa 6:5), by Jeremiah (La 1:18-20), by Paul (1Co 15:9).

To believers, commanded (Jas 5:16; 1Jn 1:8-10).

Consequences of:

Look on the face (Isa 3:9). Guilty fear (Ge 3:7-10; Pr 10:24; 25:1). Depraved conscience (Pr 30:20). Judgment (Jer 5:25). Trouble (Isa 57:20-21; Jer 4:18).

Effects upon children (Ex 20:5; 34:7; Lev 26:39-40; Nu 14:33; Dt 5:9; Ps 21:10; 37:28; 109:9-10; Pr 14:11; Isa 14:20-22; 65:7; Jer 32:18; La 5:7; Ro 5:12-21). Attributed to Job's children because of Job's alleged wickedness (Job 5:4; 18:19; 21:19). Punishment for, not brought upon children (Dt 24:16; 2Ki 14:6; 2Ch 25:4; Jer 31:29-30; Eze 18:2-4, 20).

No escape from (Ge 3:8-19; Isa 28:18-22; Am

9:2-4; Mt 23:33; Heb 2:3). *See Punishment, No Escape From; Wicked.*

Conviction of:

Produced by dreams (Job 33:14-17), by visions (Ac 9:3-9), by afflictions (Job 33:18-20; La 1:20; Lk 15:17-21), by adversity (Ps 107:4-6, 10-14, 17-20, 23-30), by the gospel (Ac 2:37), by religious testimony (1Co 14:24-25), by the conscience (Jn 8:9; Ro 2:15), by the Holy Spirit (Jn 16:7-11). *See Conviction, of Sin; Repentance, Instances of.*

Forgiveness of:

(Ac 26:18; Eph 1:7). Promised (Ex 34:6-7; Lev 4:20, 26, 31, 35; 5:4-13; Nu 14:18; 15:25; Dt 4; Ps 130:4; Isa 1:6-18; 43:25-26; 44:21-22; 55:6-7; Jer 31:34; 33:8; Eze 18:21-22; 33:14-16; Mt 12:31; Mk 3:28; Heb 8:12; 10:17; Jas 5:15; 1Jn 1:7, 9). Blessedness of (Ps 32:1-2; Ro 4:7-8).

Instances of Forgiveness—

Israelites (Nu 14:20; Ps 85:2-3; 99:8; 103:12). David (2Sa 12:13; Ps 32:5). Isaiah (Isa 6:7). Paralytic (Mt 9:2, 6; Mk 2:5; Lk 5:20, 24). The prostitute (Lk 7:48; Jn 8:11). Believers (Col 2:13).

Conditions of Forgiveness—

Repentance (Mt 3:6; Lk 3:3; 13:3, 5; Ac 2:38; 3:19). Faith (Ac 10:36, 43; 13:38-39; 26:16-18). Confession of sins (1Jn 1:7, 9). Parable of (Mt 18:23-27).

Through the shedding of blood (Heb 9:22). The mission of Christ to secure (Mt 1:21; 26:28; Lk 24:47; 1Jn 2:1-2, 12; Rev 1:5).

Prayer for (Ps 19:12; 25:7, 11; 51:9; 79:9). Spirit of (Mt 6:12, 14-15; 18:35; Mk 11:25). Intercessory prayer for (1Ki 8:22-50). Apostolic (Jn 20:23).

See Atonement; Conviction, of Sin; Offerings; Repentance.

Fruits of:

(Dt 29:18; Mk 7:21-23; 1Co 3:3; 6:9-11; Gal 5:19-21; 1Pe 4:3; Jas 5:11). Fruits of original sin (Ge 3:7-24; 4:9-13; Ro 5:12-21). God's anger (Jer 7:19). Moral insensibility (Pr 30:20). No peace (Isa 57:20-21). Shame (Pr 3:35). Withholding of God's goodness (Jer 7:19).

Destruction and death (Ge 6:5-7; 1Ki 13:33-34; Job 5:2; Ps 5:10; 94:23; Pr 5:22-23; 10:24, 29-31; 11:18-19, 27, 29; Isa 3:9, 11; 9:18; 14:21; Jer 14:16; 21:14; Eze 11:21; 22:31; 23:31-35; Hos 12:14; 13:9; Ro 6:23).

The same as sown (Job 4:8; 13:26; 20:11; Ps 9:15-16; 10:2; 141:10; Pr 1:31; 11:5-7; 12:13, 14-21, 26; 22:8; Isa 50:11; Jer 4:18; 21:14; Eze 11:21; Hos 8:7; 10:13; Mic 7:13; Ro 7:5; Gal 6:7-8).

Proverbs concerning (Pr 1:31; 3:35; 5:22-23; 8:36; 10:24, 29-31; 11:5-7, 18-19, 27, 29; 12:13-14, 21, 26; 13:5-6, 15; 22:8; 28:1; 29:6; 30:20).

Known:

To God (Ge 3:11; 4:10; 18:13; Ex 16:8-9, 12; Nu 12:2; 14:26-27; Dt 1:34; 31:21; 32:34; Jos 7:10-15; 10:14; 11:11; 13:27; 14:16-17; 20:27; 24:23; 34:21-22, 25; Ps 44:20-21; 69:5; 90:8; 94:11; Ecc 5:8; Isa 29:15; Jer 2:22; 16:17; 29:23; Eze 21:24;

Hos 5:3; 7:2; Am 5:12; 9:1-4, 8; Hab 2:11; Mal 2:14; Mt 10:26).

To Jesus (Mt 26:46; Lk 6:8; Jn 4:17-19; 5:42; 6:64; 13:11; Rev 2:23).

To the Holy Spirit (Ac 5:3-11).

See God, Omniscient; Jesus the Christ, Omniscience of.

Love of:

(Job 15:16; 20:12-13; Pr 2:14; 4:16-17; 10:23; 16:30; 26:11; Jer 14:10; Eze 20:16; Hos 4:8; 9:10; Mic 7:3; Jn 3:19-20; 12:43; 1Pe 3:19-20; 2Pe 2:22).

See Reprobacy; Wicked, Described As.

Moved to:

By the devil (Mt 13:24-25, 38-39; Jn 8:34, 44; Eph 2:1-2; 1Jn 3:6, 8-10, 15). By the fallen nature (Gal 5:16-17; Eph 2:3; Jas 1:14-15; 4:1-3).

National, Punishment of:

(Ge 6:5-7; 7:21-22; Lev 26:14-38; Dt 32:30; 2Sa 24:29-30; Isa 19:4; Jer 12:17; 25:31-33; 46:28; Eze 16:49-50; Jnh 1:2).

See Government; Nation.

Instances of—

The Sodomites (Ge 18:20). Egyptians (Ex 7-14). *See Egypt.* Israelites (Lev 26:14-39; Dt 32:30; 2Sa 21:1; 24:1; 2Ki 24:3-4, 20; 2Ch 36:21; Ezr 9; Ne 9:36-37; Isa 1:21-23; 3:4, 8, 5; 59:1-15; Jer 2; 5; 6; 9; 23; 30:11-15; La 1:3, 8, 14; 4:6; Eze 2; 7; 22; 24:6-14; 28:18; 33:25-26; 36:16-20; 39:23-24; 44:4-14; Hos 4:1-11; 6:8-10; 7:1-7; 13; Am 2; 5; Mic 6; 7:2-6). Babylon (Jer 50:45-46; 51). *See Babylon; See also prophecies cited under Assyria; Damascus; Edom; Elam; Ethiopia; Philistines; Syria.*

Not imputed:

To righteous (Ps 32:2; Ro 4:6-8), to ignorant (Ro 4:15; 5:13), to redeemed (2Co 5:19).

Progressive:

(Dt 29:19; 1Ki 16:31; Ps 1:1; Isa 5:18; 30:1; Jer 9:3; 16:11-12; Hos 13:2; 2Ti 3:13; Jas 1:14-15). Progressiveness exemplified in Joseph's brothers, from jealousy (Ge 37:4), to conspiracy (Ge 37:18), to murder (Ge 37:20). *See also, Cain; Abel.* Retroactive (Ps 7:15-16; 9:15-16; 10:2; 94:23; Pr 1:31; 5:22-23; 8:36; 11:5-6, 27, 29; Isa 3:9, 11; Jer 2:19; 4:8; 7:19). A root of bitterness (Dt 29:18; Heb 12:15).

Punishment of:

(Ge 2:17; 3:16-19; 4:10-14; 6:5-7; 18:20; 19:13; Ex 32:33-34; 34:7; Lev 19:8; 26:14-21; Nu 15:30-31; 32:23; Dt 28:15-68; 1Ki 13:33-34; 1Ch 21:7-27; Job 21:17; Ps 95:10-11; Pr 1:24-32; Jer 44:2-6; Eze 18:4; Mt 25:41, 46; Ro 6:23).

See Punishment; Wicked, Punishment of.

Pollution of:

Typified, by the defilement caused by touching any unclean thing (Lev 5:2-3; 11:24-28, 31; 22:5), by eating any unclean thing (Lev 11:41-47), by touching a dead body (Lev 21:1; Nu 5:2; 9:6, 10; 19:11, 13, 16; 31:19), by skin diseases (Lev 13:3, 8, 11, 20, 25, 27, 30, 36, 44-46, 51, 55; 14:44; Nu

5:2-3), by sexual impurities (Lev 15:1-33; 22:4; Dt 23:10-11).

Repentance for:

Commanded (2Ch 30:7-9; Job 36:10; Ps 34:14; Pr 1:22-23; Isa 22:12; 31:6; 44:22; 55:6-7; Jer 3:4, 12-14, 19; 6:8, 16; 18:11; 25:5; 26:13; 35:15; Eze 14:6; 18:30-32; 33:10-12; Da 4:27; Hos 6:1; 10:12; 14:1-2; Joel 1:14; 2:12-13, 15-18; Am 4:12; Jnh 3:8-9; Zec 1:3; Mt 4:17; Mk 1:15; 6:12; Ac 2:38, 40; 3:19; 8:22; 17:30; 20:21; Jas 4:8-10; Rev 2:5, 16; 3:2-3, 19).

Gift, of God (2Ti 2:25), of Christ (Ac 5:31). Tribulation leads to (Dt 4:30; 1Ki 8:33-50; 2Ch 6:36-39; Ps 107:4-6, 10-14, 17-20, 23-30). Goodness of God leads to (Ro 2:4).

A condition of pardon (Lev 26:40-42; Dt 4:29-31; 30:1-3; 2Ch 7:14; Ne 1:9; Pr 28:13; Jer 7:5-7; 36:3; Eze 18:21-23, 27-28, 30-31; Mal 3:7; 1Jn 1:9).

Repugnant:

To God (Ge 6:6-7; Lev 18:24-30; Nu 22:32; Dt 25:16; 32:19; 2Sa 11:27; 1Ki 14:22; Ps 5:4-6; 10:3; 11:5; 78:59; 95:10; 106:40; Pr 3:32; 6:16-19; 11:20; 15:8-9, 26; 21:27; Isa 43:24; Jer 25:7; 44:4, 21-22; Hab 1:13; Zec 8:17; Lk 16:15). *See God, Holiness of.*

To Christ (Rev 2:6, 15).

To the righteous (Ge 39:7-9; Dt 7:26; Job 1:1; 21:16; 22:18; Ps 26:5, 9; 84:10; 101:3-4, 7; 119:104, 113, 128, 163; 120:2, 5-7; 139:19-22; Pr 8:13; 29:27; Jer 9:2; Ro 7:15, 19, 23-24; 2Pe 2:7-8; Jude 23; Rev 2:2). *See Holiness.*

Separates From God:

(Dt 31:17-18; Jos 7:12; 2Ch 24:20; Ps 78:59-61; Isa 59:1-2; 64:7; Eze 23:18; Hos 9:12; Am 3:2-3; Mic 3:4; Mt 7:23; 25:41; Lk 13:27; Ro 8:7; Heb 12:14). *See God, Holiness of; Wicked, Punishment of.*

Works spiritual death (Ro 5:12, 21; 6:21, 23; 7:13; Eph 2:1; Jas 1:15).

By the righteous, dishonors God (2Sa 12:14), a reproach (2Sa 12:14).

Against the Holy Spirit, unpardonable (Mt 12:31; Mk 3:29; Lk 12:10; 1Jn 5:16-17).

Typified:

The design of the Mosaic ordinances was to impress the Israelites, and through them the consciences of all people for all time, with the offensiveness of sin. To produce this effect the Mosaic law contained numerous types of sin, the design of which was to teach that sin is repugnant to God, and that it separates from God and from the righteous. Hence, we find many object lessons about uncleanness and defilement, blemishes, separation from the congregation, atonements and atoning sacrifices, washings and purifications; all of which were designed to typify the corruption of sin and the necessity, in order to please a holy Yahweh, that sin must be purged and the heart purified.

By blemishes that disqualified animals for sacrifices (Ex 12:5; Lev 1:10; 3:1, 6; 4:3, 23; 5:15; 6:6; 9:2-3; 22:19-22; Nu 28:3, 9, 11, 19, 31; 29:2, 8, 13, 17, 20, 23, 26, 29, 32, 36). By blemishes of priests, disqualifying them from performing sacred offices (Lev 21:17-23). By unclean animals (Lev 11:1-47; 20:25; Dt 14:3-20).

Its effect, in separating the wicked from God and from the righteous, by excluding the defiled and unclean from the congregation (Lev 7:20, 25, 27; 13:5, 26, 33; 15:19; 17:9-10, 15; 18:29; 19:8; 20:3-6; Nu 5:2-3; 19:20; Dt 23:10-11).

Words for:

Missing the mark (Ro 5:12). Overstepping the boundary, or trespassing (Ro 4:15). Blunder, or offense (Ro 5:15). Disobedience, or disregard (Ro 5:19). Unrighteousness (Ro 1:18). Ungodliness (Ro 1:18). Lawlessness (Tit 2:14).

SIN, CITY OF *See Pelusium.*

SIN, DESERT OF *(desert of clay* or possibly *desert of Sin [pagan moon god]).* The wilderness through which the Israelites passed; between Elim and Mount Sinai (Ex 16:1; 17:1; Nu 33:11-12).

SIN MONEY NIV "money from ... sin offerings" (2Ki 12:16). *See Blood Money.*

SINA *See Sinai.*

SINAI, MOUNT OF; DESERT OF [6099, 4982] *(Sin [pagan moon god]; glare [from white chalk]* ISBE).

1. A mountain in the peninsula E of the Red Sea. Israelites arrive in their wanderings in the wilderness (Ex 19:2; Dt 1:2). The law delivered to Moses upon (Ex 19:3-25; 20; 24:12-18; 32:15-16; 34:2-4; Lev 7:38; 25:1; 26:46; 27:34; Nu 3:1; Dt 4:15; 5:26; 29:1; 33:2; Ne 9:13; Ps 68:8, 17; Mal 4:4; Ac 7:30, 38).

God establishes a covenant (Ex 19-24). *See Covenants, Major in the Old Testament.*

Figurative of the law (Gal 4:24-25).

See Horeb; Israel, Israelites.

2. Desert of. Israelites journeyed in (Nu 10:12), kept the Passover in (Nu 9:1-5), numbered in (Nu 26:64).

SINCERITY [*537, 605, 1636]. Does not exempt from guilt (Ge 20). *See Ignorance, Sins of.* Forgiveness of enemies must be sincere (Mt 18:35). Servants must render honest service (Eph 6:5-7). Whatever is done must be in (1Co 10:31). Jesus was an example of (1Pe 2:22). Ministers should be examples of (Tit 2:7). Opposed to human wisdom (2Co 1:12).

Should characterize our love to God (2Co 8:8, 24), our love to Jesus (Eph 6:24), our service to God (Jos 24:14), our faith (1Ti 1:5), our love to one another (Ro 12:9; 1Pe 1:22; 1Jn 3:18), our whole conduct (2Co 1:12), the preaching of the gospel (2Co 2:17; 1Th 2:3-5).

A characteristic of the doctrines of the gospel (1Pe 2:2). The gospel sometimes preached without (Php 1:16). The wicked devoid of (Ps 5:9; 55:21). Exhortations to (1Co 5:8; 1Pe 2:1). Blessedness of (Ps 32:2).

Exemplified:
By men of Zebulun (1Ch 12:33). By Hezekiah (Isa 38:3). By Nathanael (Jn 1:47). By Paul (2Co 1:12). By Timothy (2Ti 1:5). By Lois and Eunice (2Ti 1:5).

SINEW [1630, 5278]. Tendon, in contrast to bone structure (Ge 32:32; Job 40:17; Eze 37:6-8).

SINFULNESS [222, 2627, 2628, 2629, 2633, 3202+4202, 6411, 7322, 8278, *279*, *281*, *283*, *2123*, *4505*, *4920*, *4922*]. Universal (1Ki 8:46; 2Ch 6:36; Ps 14:3; Ecc 7:20; Ro 3:23; 11:32; 1Jn 1:8, 10). *See Depravity; Sin.*

SINGERS [2952, 5834, 8876, 8877, 10234]. *See Music.*

SINGLE EYE NIV "good eye"; connotes generosity (Mt 6:22). *See Eye.*

SINIM *See Aswan.*

SINITES [6098]. A tribe of Canaanites (Ge 10:17; 1Ch 1:15).

SINLESSNESS (Ps 119:3). The believer's goal (Php 1:9-11; 1Th 3:13; 5:23; 1Pe 4:1-2; 1Jn 3:6, 9; 5:18). Impossible to attain (1Jn 1:8, 10).

SINNER [2627, 2629, 2633, 7321, *283*, *283+467*, *283+476*, *1794*, *4126*]. *See Wicked.*

SIN OFFERING [2627, 2631, 2633, 10260, *281*].

Offered:
For sins of ignorance (Lev 4:2, 13, 22, 27). At the consecration of priests (Ex 29:10, 14; Lev 8:14). At the consecration of Levites (Nu 8:8). At the expiration of a Nazirite's vow (Nu 6:14). On the Day of Atonement (Lev 16:3, 9). Was a most holy sacrifice (Lev 6:25, 29). Probable origin of (Ge 4:4, 7).

Consisted of:
A young bull for priests (Lev 4:3; 9:2, 8; 16:3, 6). A young bull or he-goat for the congregation (Lev 4:14; 16:9; 2Ch 29:23). A male goat for a ruler (Lev 4:23). A female goat or female lamb for a private person (Lev 4:28, 32). Sins of the offerer transferred to, by laying on of hands (Lev 4:4, 15, 24, 29; 2Ch 29:23). Was killed in the same place as the burnt offering (Lev 4:24; 6:25).

The blood of:
For a priest or for the congregation, brought by the priest into the tabernacle (Lev 4:5, 16). For the priest or for the congregation, sprinkled seven times before the Lord, outside the veil, by the priest with his finger (Lev 4:6, 17). For a priest or for the congregation, put upon the horns of the altar of incense (Lev 4:7, 18). For a ruler or for a private person put upon the horns of the altar of

burnt offering by the priest with his finger (Lev 4:25, 30). In every case poured at the foot of the altar of burnt offering (Lev 4:7, 18, 30; 9:9). Fat, kidneys, etc. burned on the altar of burnt offering (Lev 4:8-10, 19, 26, 31; 9:10).

When a priest or the congregation, the skin, carcass, burned without the camp (Lev 4:11-12, 21; 6:30; 9:11). Was eaten by the priests in a holy place when its blood had not been brought into the tabernacle (Lev 6:26, 29, w 30). Aaron rebuked for burning and not eating that of the congregation, its blood not having been brought into the tabernacle (Lev 10:16-18, w 9:9, 15). Whatever touched the flesh of, was rendered holy (Lev 6:27). Garments sprinkled with the blood of, to be washed (Lev 6:27). Laws respecting the vessels used for boiling the flesh of (Lev 6:28). Was typical of Christ's sacrifice (2Co 5:21; Heb 13:11-13).

SION *See Siyon, Mount; Zion.*

SIPHMOTH [8560]. A city of Judah (1Sa 30:28).

SIPPAI [6205]. A Philistine giant (1Ch 20:4). Called Saph (2Sa 21:18).

SIRACH, SON OF The author of Ecclesiasticus also known as the Wisdom of Jesus ben Sirach; wrote c. 190-170 B.C. *See Apocrypha.*

SIRAH [6241]. A well, c. one mile N of Hebron (2Sa 3:26).

SIRION [8590] (*coat of mail*). A Sidonian name of Mount Hermon (Dt 3:9; Ps 29:6). *See Hermon, Mount; Siyon, Mount.*

SISAMAI *See Sismai.*

SISERA [6102].
1. Captain of the army of Jabin, king of Hazor; defeated in battle by Barak; slain by Deborah (Jdg 4:5; 1Sa 12:9; Ps 83:9).
2. Ancestor of the temple servants who returned with Zerubbabel (Ezr 2:53; Ne 7:55).

SISMAI [6183] (possibly *belonging to Sisam* [*pagan god*]). The son of Eleasah (1Ch 2:40).

SISTER [295, 1426, 1860, 3304, *80*].
1. A full or half-sister (Ge 20:12; Dt 27:22).
2. Wife (SS 4:9).
3. A woman of the same country or tribe (Nu 25:18).
4. Blood relatives (Mt 13:56; Mk 6:3).
5. Female fellow Christian (Ro 16:1; 2Jn 15).

SISTRUMS [4983]. Percussion instruments (2Sa 6:5). *See Music, Instruments of.*

SITHRI [6262] (possibly *Yahweh is my hiding place*). Kohathite Levite; cousin of Aaron and Moses (Ex 6:22).

SITNAH [8479] (*hostility*). A well dug by Isaac between Gerar and Rehoboth (Ge 26:21).

SIVAN [6094]. Month three in sacred sequence (Est 8:9), month nine in civil sequence. Time of the wheat harvest (May-June) and the Feast of Weeks or Pentecost (Dt 16:9-12). *See Month, 3.*

SIYON, MOUNT [8481]. A name of Mount Hermon (Dt 4:48, ftn w 3:9). *See Hermon, Mount; Sirion.*

SKEPTICISM (Job 21:15; 22:17; Ps 14:1; 53:1; Zep 1:12; Mal 3:14). Of Pharaoh (Ex 5:2). Of Thomas (Jn 20:25-28). *See Unbelief.*

SKILL [*682, 1067, 2681, 2682, 2683, 3110, 3359, 4542, *5492*]. Examples of (Ex 28:3; 31:3; 35:35; 38:23; 1Ki 7:14; 1Ch 22:15; 2Ch 2:13; 26:15).

SKIN [1414, 1654, 2293, 2827, 5532, 5574, 6425+, 7320, 7665, 7669, *829*]. Clothes of (Ge 3:21). For covering the tabernacle (Ex 25:5; Nu 4:8-14). Diseases of (Lev 13:38-39; Dt 28:27, 35; Job 7:5). *See Boil; Leprosy.*

SKINK [2793]. Unclean for food (Lev 11:30). *See Animals.*

SKIRT [8670, 8767]. *See Dress.*

SKULL [1653, 7721, *3191*]. *See Golgotha.*

SKY [8836, 9028, 10723, *113, 4041*]. Clouds, firmament; also used figuratively (Dt 33:26).

SLANDER [224, 1804, 1819, 1984+5989, 4387, 8078, 8215, 8476, 8806, *1059, 1060, 2895, 2896, 3367*].

Characteristics of:
Comes from the evil heart (Lk 6:45). Often arises from hatred (Ps 109:3). Idleness leads to (1Ti 5:13).

The wicked addicted to (Ps 50:20). Hypocrites addicted to (Pr 11:9). A characteristic of the devil (Rev 12:10). The wicked love (Ps 52:4). They who indulge in, are fools (Pr 10:18).

Women warned against (Tit 2:3). Ministers' wives should avoid (1Ti 3:11).

Christ was exposed to (Ps 35:11; Mt 26:60). Rulers exposed to (Jude 8). Ministers exposed to (Ro 3:8; 2Co 6:8). The nearest relations exposed to (Ps 50:20). Saints exposed to (Ps 38:12; 109:2; 1Pe 4:4).

Saints should, keep their tongues from (Ps 34:13, w 1Pe 3:10), lay aside (Eph 4:31), be warned against (Tit 3:1-2), give no occasion for (1Pe 2:12; 3:16), return good for (1Co 4:13), blessed in enduring (Mt 5:11), characterized as avoiding (Ps 15:1,3).

Should not be listened to (1Sa 24:9). Causes anger (Pr 25:23). A fruit of wickedness (Ro 1:29-30; 2Co 12:20; 2Pe 2:10).

Forbidden (Ex 23:1; 1Ti 3:11; Tit 2:3; 3:2; Jas 4:11; 1Pe 2:1). Punishment for (Dt 19:16-21; 22:13-19; Ps 101:5; 1Co 6:10).

Instances of:
Joseph, by Potiphar's wife (Ge 39:14-18). Land of Canaan misrepresented by the spies (Nu 14:36). Of Mephibosheth, by Ziba (2Sa 16:3; 19:24-30). Of David, by his enemies (Ps 31:13; 35:21; 41:5-9; 64:3; 140:3). Of Naboth, by Jezebel (1Ki 21:9-14). Of Jeremiah, by the Jews (Jer 6:28; 18:18). Of the Jews, of one another (Jer 9:4).

Of Jesus, by the Jews falsely charging that he was a drunkard (Mt 11:19), that he blasphemed (Mk 14:64; Jn 5:18), that he had a demon (Jn 8:48, 52; 10:20), that he was seditious (Lk 22:65; 23:5), that he was a king (Lk 23:2; Jn 18:37, w 19:1-5). Of Paul. *See Paul.*

Effects of:
Separating friends (Pr 16:28; 17:9), deadly wounds (Pr 18:8; 26:22), strife (Pr 26:20), discord among brothers (Pr 6:19), murder (Ps 31:13; Eze 22:9). End of, is wicked madness (Ecc 10:13). People shall give account for (Mt 12:36).

The Tongue:
(Job 5:21). Is venomous (Ps 140:3; Ecc 10:11), is destructive (Pr 11:9).

See Accusation, False; Backbiting; False Witness; Falsehood; Speaking or Speech, Evil.

SLAVE, SLAVERY [*563, 4989, 5601, 6268, 6269, 6275, 6683, 6806, 9148, *1525, 1526, 1528, 1529, 1530, 4087*]. Both the OT and the NT included regulations for societal situations such as slavery and divorce (Dt 24:1-4), which were the results of the hardness of hearts (Mt 19:8). Such regulations did not encourage or condone such situations but were divinely given, practical ways of dealing with the realities of the day.

See Servant.

SLAYER, THE [2222]. NIV "one accused of murder" (Nu 35:11-28; Dt 4:42; 19:3-6; Jos 20:3). *See Cities of Refuge.*

SLEEP [*448+995, 3359, 3822, 3825, 5670, 8101, 8886, 9104, 9554, 10733, *2761, 3121*]. From God (Ps 127:2). Of the sluggard (Pr 6:9-10). Of Jesus (Mt 8:24; Mk 4:38; Lk 8:23). A symbol of death (Job 14:12; Mt 9:24; Mk 5:39; Lk 8:52; Jn 11:11-12; 1Th 4:14). *See Death, Physical.*

SLIME [1014+8622, 8846]. Slime pit (Job 9:31; Ps 40:2). *See Caulkers; Pitch; Tar.*

SLING [74+928+2021, 5275, 7843, 7845, 7847]. Used for throwing stones (Pr 26:8). David slays Goliath with (1Sa 17:40-50). Dexterous use of (Jdg 20:16; 2Ki 3:25; 2Ch 26:14).

SLIP [3655, 4572, 4880, 5048, 5742, 6073, 7520, *1728, 1767, 4208*]. A cutting from a plant (Isa 17:10).

SLOTHFULNESS Characteristic of the sluggard (Pr 10:4-5, 26; 13:4; 15:19; 18:9; 19:15, 24; 20:4; 21:25; 22:13; 23:21; 24:30-34; 26:13-16; Isa 56:10).

Results in: poverty (Pr 10:4-5; 12:24, 27; 13:4;

15:19; 18:9; 19:15, 24; 20:4; 21:25; 23:21; 24:30-34; 26:13-16; Ecc 10:18), condemnation (Mt 25:26-27).

Condemned: The ant, an example against (Pr 6:6-11). Christians are not to be lazy (Ro 12:11; 2Th 3:10-12; Heb 6:12).

See Idleness; Industry.

SLOW TO ANGER [*336, 800, *1096].
(Ne 9:17; Ps 103:8; 145:8). *See God, Longsuffering; Longsuffering.*

SLUG [8671]. Melting away (Ps 58:8). *See Animals.*

SLUGGARD [6789]. *See Idleness; Laziness; Slothfulness.*

SMITH A worker in metals. Tubal-Cain (Ge 4:22). Bezalel (Ex 31:1-11). The Philistines (1Sa 13:19). Jewish, carried captive to Babylon (2Ki 24:14; Jer 24:1). The manufacturers of idols (Isa 41:7; 44:12). Genius of, from God (Ex 31:3-5; 35:30-35; Isa 54:16).

SMITING *See Assault and Battery.*

SMITING AND SCOURGING OF JESUS *See Flog, Flogging.*

SMOKE [5366, 5368, 6727, 6939, 6940, 6942, 7798, 2837]. Rising from destruction (Ge 19:28; Jos 8:20; Rev 19:3).

Figurative of God's presence (Ex 19:18; Isa 6:4; Rev 15:8), of short-lived humanity (Ps 37:20; 68:2; 102:3; Hos 13:3).

SMYRNA [5044]. An ancient seaport on the W coast of Asia Minor forty miles N of Ephesus; the seat of an important Christian church (Rev 1:11; 2:8-11).

SNAIL NIV "skink" (Lev 11:30), "slug" (Ps 58:8). *See Animals.*

SNAKE *See Serpent.*

SNARE [1335, 3338, 3687, 4613, 5178, 5180, 7062, 7545, 8407, 8938, 4075]. A device for catching birds and animals (Ps 124:7), also used figuratively (Ps 91:3).

SNIFF [5870, 8634]. Smelling the wind (Jer 2:24). Showing contempt for God's sacrifices (Mal 1:13).

SNOUT [678]. Long projecting nose of a beast, as of a pig (Pr 11:22).

SNOW [8919, 8920, 10758, 5946]. Falls in elevated areas of Israel in January and February, but soon melts; Mt. Hermon covered with snow even in summer; used for cooling purposes. Used figuratively for righteousness and purity (Isa 1:18; Ps 51:7; Mt 28:3; Rev 1:14).

SNUFF [1980, 3882, 4931]. *See Sniff.*

SNUFFDISHES NIV "trays" for the lamps of the tabernacle and temple. *See Wick Trimmers.*

SNUFFERS *See Wick Trimmers.*

SO [6046]. A king of Egypt with whom Hoshea, king of Israel, made an alliance, so bringing down the wrath of Assyria upon Israel (2Ki 17:4), possibly Oskoron.

SOAP [1383, 9921]. In a modern sense was unknown in OT times, but launderers made a cleansing material compounded from vegetable alkali (Jer 2:22; Mal 3:2). *See Soda.*

SOBERMINDEDNESS [5404].
Commanded (Ro 12:3; 1Pe 1:13; 4:7; 5:8), to women (1Ti 3:11; Tit 2:4-5), to men (Tit 2:2, 6), to ministers (1Ti 3:2; Tit 1:8).

SOBRIETY [3516+3655, 5404]. Commanded (1Pe 1:13; 5:8). The gospel designed to teach (Tit 2:12). With watchfulness (1Th 5:6). With prayer (1Pe 4:7). Required in ministers (1Ti 3:2-3; Tit 1:8), wives of ministers (1Ti 3:11), aged men (Tit 2:2), young men (Tit 2:6), young women (Tit 2:4), all saints (1Th 5:6, 8). Women should exhibit in dress (1Ti 2:9). We should estimate our character and talents with (Ro 12:3). We should live in (Tit 2:12). Motive for (1Pe 4:7; 5:8).

See Temperance; Drunkenness; Self-Control.

SOCO [8459] (perhaps *thorny place*).
1. Son of Heber (1Ch 4:18).
2. A city in Judah, built by Rehoboam (2Ch 11:7; 28:18).

SOCOH [8458] (possibly *thorny place* IDB).
1. A town in Judah (Jos 15:35; 1Sa 17:1; 1Ki 4:10); NW of Adullam; identified with Khirbet Shuweikeh.
2. Another city by this name ten miles SW of Hebron (Jos 15:48).

SODA [1342, 6003]. A mixture of washing and baking sodas found in deposits around alkali lakes of Egypt. Used to make soap (Job 9:30; Pr 25:20; Jer 2:22). *See Soap.*

SODI [6052] (*Yahweh confides*). The father of a Zebulun spy (Nu 13:10).

SODOM [6042, 1178+5047, 5047]. Situated in the plain of the Jordan (Ge 13:10). The southeastern limit of the Canaanites (Ge 10:19). Lot dwells at (Ge 13:12). The king of, joins other kings of the nations resisting the invasion of Kedorlaomer (Ge 14:1-12). Wickedness of the inhabitants of (Ge 13:13; 19:4-13; Dt 32:32; Isa 3:9; Jer 23:14; Eze 16:46, 48-49; Jude 7). Abraham's intercession for (Ge 18:16-33). Destroyed on account of the wickedness of the people (Ge 19:1-29; Dt 29:23; Isa 13:19; Jer 49:18; 50:40; La 4:6; Am 4:11; Zep 2:9; Mt 10:15; Lk 17:29; Ro 9:29; 2Pe 2:6).

Figurative of wickedness (Dt 23:17; 32:32; Isa 1:10; Eze 16:46-56).

SODOMITES *(of Sodom).* Inhabitants of Sodom. Wickedness of (Ge 19:4-14). Destroyed by fire as a judgment (Ge 19:24-25). To be judged according to opportunity (Mt 11:24; Lk 10:12). *See Homosexual.*

SODOMY *See Homosexual.*

SOJOURNERS Temporary residents (Ge 12:10; 20:1; 21:34; 47:4; Lev 18:26; 20:2; 25:40; Nu 15:15; Dt 26:5; Jdg 17:7; Ru 1:1; Heb 11:9).

SOLDER *See Welding.*

SOLDIERS [*408+4878, 408+7372, 1201+ 2657, 1475, 2657, 6639, 8081, *5061*, *5129*, *5132*, *5369*]. Military enrollment of Israel in the wilderness of Sinai (Nu 1; 2), in the plains of Moab (Nu 26). Levies of, in the ration of one man to ten subject to duty (Jdg 20:10). Dressed in scarlet (Na 2:3). Cowards, excused from duty as (Dt 20:8; Jdg 7:3). Others exempt from service (Dt 20:5-9; 24:5). Come to John (Lk 3:14). Mock Jesus (Mt 27:27-31; Mk 15:16-20; Lk 23:11, 36-37). Officers concerned in the betrayal of Jesus (Lk 22:4). Crucified Jesus (Mt 27:27, 31-37; Mk 15:16-24; Jn 19:23-24). Guard the tomb (Mt 27:65; 28:11-15). Guard prisoners (Ac 12:4-6; 28:16). Maintain the peace (Ac 21:31-35). Their duty as sentinels (Ac 12:19). Perform escort duty (Ac 21:31-33, 35; 22:24-28; 23:23, 31-33; 27:1, 31, 42-43; 28:16).

Figurative: Of the divine protection (Isa 59:16-17). Of the Christian (Eph 6:11-17; 2Ti 2:3). *See Armies.*

SOLOMON [8976, *5048*] *(peace, well being).* Son of David by Bathsheba (2Sa 12:24; 1Ki 1:13, 17, 21). Named Jedidiah, by Nathan the prophet (2Sa 12:24-25). Ancestor of Joseph (Mt 1:6). Succeeds David to the throne of Israel (1Ki 1:11-48; 2:12; 1Ch 23:1; 28; Ecc 1:12). Anointed king a second time (1Ch 29:22). His prayer for wisdom and his vision (1Ki 3:5-14; 2Ch 1:7-12). Covenant renewed in a vision after the dedication of the temple (1Ki 9:1-9; 2Ch 7:12-22). His rigorous reign (1Ki 2).

Builds the temple (1Ki 5; 6; 9:10; 1Ch 6:10; 2Ch 2; 3; 4; 7:11; Jer 52:20; Ac 7:45-47). Dedicates the temple (1Ki 8; 2Ch 6). Renews the courses of the priests and Levites and the forms of service according to the regulations of David (2Ch 8:12-16; 35:4; Ne 12:45).

Builds his palace (1Ki 3:1; 7:1, 8; 9:10; 2Ch 7:11; 8:1; Ecc 2:4), his house of the forest of Lebanon (1Ki 7:2-7), for Pharaoh's daughter (1Ki 7:8-12; 9:24; 2Ch 8:11; Ecc 2:4). Ivory throne of (1Ki 7:7; 10:18-20). Porches of judgment (1Ki 7:7). Builds Millo, the wall of Jerusalem; the cities of Hazor, Megiddo, Gezer, Beth Horon, Baalath, Tadmor; store cities and cities for chariots and for cavalry (1Ki 9:15-19; 2Ch 9:25). Provides an armory (1Ki 10:16-17). Plants vineyards and or-

chards of all kinds of fruit trees; makes pools (Ecc 2:4-6), imports apes and baboons (1Ki 10:22). Drinking vessels of his houses (1Ki 10:21; 2Ch 9:20). Musicians and musical instruments of his court (1Ki 10:12; 2Ch 9:11; Ecc 2:8). The splendor of his court (1Ki 10:5-9, 12; 2Ch 9:3-8; Ecc 2:9; Mt 6:29; Lk 12:27).

Commerce of (1Ki 9:28; 10:11-12, 22, 28-29; 2Ch 1:16-17; 8:17-18; 9:13-22, 28). Presents received by (1Ki 10:10; 2Ch 9:9, 23-24). Is visited by the queen of Sheba (1Ki 10:1-13; 2Ch 9:1-12). Wealth of (1Ki 9; 10:10, 14-15, 23, 27; 2Ch 1:15; 9:1, 9, 13, 24, 27; Ecc 1:16). Has seven hundred wives and three hundred concubines (1Ki 11:3, w Dt 17:17); their influence over him (1Ki 11:3). Marries one of Pharaoh's daughters (1Ki 3:1). Builds idolatrous temples (1Ki 11:1-8; 2Ki 23:13). His idolatry (1Ki 3:3-4; 2Ki 23:13; Ne 13:26).

Extent of his dominions (1Ki 4:21, 24; 8:65; 2Ch 7:8; 9:26). Receives tribute (1Ki 4:21; 9:21; 2Ch 8:8). Officers of (1Ki 2:35; 4:1-19; 2Ch 8:9-10). His suppliers (1Ki 4:7-19). Divides his kingdom into subsistence departments; the daily subsistence rate for his court (1Ki 4:7-23, 27-28).

Military equipment of (1Ki 4:26, 28; 10:16-17, 26, 28; 2Ch 1:14; 9:25, w Dt 17:15-16). Cedes certain cities to Hiram (1Ki 9:10-13; 2Ch 8:2). Wisdom and fame of (1Ki 4:29-34; 10:3-4, 8, 23-24; 1Ch 29:24-25; 2Ch 9:2-7, 22-23; Ecc 1:16; Mt 12:42). Piety of (1Ki 3:5-15; 4:29; 8). Beloved of God (2Sa 12:24). Justice of, illustrated in his judgment of the two harlots (1Ki 3:16-28). Oppressions of (1Ki 12:4; 2Ch 10:4).

Reigns forty years (2Ch 9:30). Death of (2Ch 9:29-31).

Prophecies concerning (2Sa 7:12-16; 1Ki 11:9-13; 1Ch 17:11-14; 28:6-7; Ps 132:11).

A type of Christ (Ps 45:2-17; 72).

SOLOMON, SONG OF *See Song of Solomon, Song of Songs.*

SOLOMON'S POOLS Three pools near Jerusalem from which water was brought by means of aqueducts to Jerusalem (Ecc 2:6). They are still in use.

SOLOMON'S PORCH Colonnade built by Solomon on the E side of the temple area (Jn 10:23; Ac 3:11; 5:12).

SOLOMON'S SERVANTS Slaves used by Solomon in his temple for menial tasks; their descendants returning from Babylon under Zerubbabel (Ezr 2:55, 58; Ne 7:57, 60; 11:3).

SOLOMON'S TEMPLE *See Temple.*

SON [132, 408, 1201, 1337, 2351, 3495, 3528, 3529, 10120, *271*, *980*, *3666*, *3836*, *4757*, *5451*, *5626*].

1. A direct male offspring (Ge 4:25, 26).
2. A male descendant generations removed (Mt 1:1).

3. The member of a guild or profession (1Ki 20:35).

4. Spiritual son (1Ti 1:18).

5. Address to a younger man (1Sa 3:6).

6. Adopted son (Ex 2:10).

7. Native (La 4:2).

8. Possessor of a quality (Jn 12:36).

9. Used of Jesus in a unique sense. *See One and Only; Son of God; Son of Man.*

SON OF GOD
A title of Jesus referring to his equality, eternity, and consubstantiality with the Father and the Spirit in the eternal Triune Godhead (Jn 5:18, 23, 36). Christ claimed to be eternal, equal and of the same substance as the Father. He is uniquely God's son. *See Jesus the Christ, Son of God; One and Only.*

SON OF MAN
1. A human being (Eze 2:1, 3, 8ff; Ps 8:4).

2. Used in a messianic sense (Da 7:13-14). Jesus applies the term to himself many times in the Gospels (Mt 8:20; 9:6; 10:23; 11:19; 12:8, etc). Sometimes he uses it in connection with his earthly mission, but he also uses it when describing his final triumph as Redeemer and Judge (Mt 16:27f; 19:28; 24:30; 25:31). The phrase identifies him with humanity (cf. Heb 2:14-18) and with the heavenly Son of Man (Da 7:13-14). *See Jesus the Christ, Son of Man.*

SONG
[2369, 2379, 5593, 5631, 7754, 8262, 8264, 8876, 8877, 8878, *6046*]. Sung at the Passover (Mt 26:30; Mk 14:26). Didactic (Dt 32). *See Psalms, Topically Arranged.* Personification of the church (SS 1-8). Of Moses (Ex 15:1-19). Of Deborah and Barak (Jdg 5). Of Hannah (1Sa 2:1-10). Of David (2Sa 22:2-51; 23:1-7). Of Mary (Lk 1:46-55). Of Moses and the Lamb (Rev 15:3-4). New (Ps 33:3; 40:3). Prophetic. *See Psalms, Topically Arranged.* Spiritual, singing of, commanded (Eph 5:19; Col 3:16). Of praise. *See Poetry; Praise; Psalms, Topically Arranged; Thankfulness.* Of redemption (Rev 5:9-10). Of the redeemed (Rev 14:2-5). Of thanksgiving. *See Psalms, Topically Arranged; Thankfulness.* War (Ex 15:1-21; Nu 21:27-30; Jdg 5; 2Sa 1:19-27; 22). Solomon wrote one thousand and five (1Ki 4:32).

See Poetry; Praise; Psalms, Topically Arranged.

SONG OF DEGREES
See Ascents, Songs of; Music.

SONG OF SOLOMON, SONG OF SONGS
Author: Verse 1 appears to ascribe authorship to Solomon

Date: In the tenth century B.C. during Solomon's reign

Outline:

I. Title (1:1).

II. First Meeting (1:2-2:7).

III. Second Meeting (2:8-3:5).

IV. Third Meeting (3:6-5:1).

V. Fourth Meeting (5:2-6:3).

VI. Fifth Meeting (6:4-8:4).

VII. Literary Climax (8:5-7).

VIII. Conclusion (8:8-14).

SONG OF THE THREE HEBREW CHILDREN
An addition to the book of Daniel found in the OT Apocrypha. Anonymous; written before 100 B.C.

SON-IN-LAW
[3161, 3163]. Unjust, Jacob (Ge 30:37-42). Faithful, Peter (Mk 1:29-30; Lk 4:38).

SONS OF GOD, CHILDREN OF GOD
Any personal creatures of God: angelic beings (Job 1:6; 2:1; 38:7), the entire human race (Ac 17:28), the regenerate as distinguished from the unregenerate (1Jn 3:10). The "sons of God" (Ge 6:1-4).

SONS OF THE PROPHETS
NIV usually "company of the prophets." Members of prophetic guilds or schools; gathered around great prophets like Samuel and Elijah for common worship, united prayer, religious fellowship, and instruction of the people (1Sa 10:5, 10; 2Ki 4:38, 40). In the times of Elijah and Elisha they lived together at Bethel, Jericho, and Gilgal (2Ki 2:3, 5; 4:38). *See School.*

SOOTHSAYER, SOOTHSAYING
[6726, 7876]. One claiming power to foretell future events (Jos 13:22; Jer 27:9), interpret dreams (Da 4:7), and reveal secrets (Da 2:27).

SOOTHSAYERS' TREE
[6726]. A pagan shrine near Shechem (Jdg 9:37), possibly the great tree of Moreh (Ge 12:6).

SOP
NIV "piece of bread" used to dip food from a common platter (Jn 13:26-27).

SOPATER
[5396] (*saving one's father*). Berean Christian; companion of Paul (Ac 20:4).

SOPHERETH
[6072] (*scribe*). A servant of Solomon, whose descendants returned from captivity to Jerusalem (Ne 7:57).

See Hassophereth.

SORCERY
[4175, 4176, 4177, 5727, 5728, 6726, *3405, 3407, 4319*]. Divination by an alleged assistance of evil spirits. Forbidden (Lev 19:26-28, 31; 20:6; Dt 18:9-14). Denounced (Isa 8:19; Mal 3:5).

Practiced: By, the Egyptians (Isa 19:3, 11-12), the magicians (Ex 7:11, 22; 8:7, 18), Balaam (Nu 22:6; 23:23, w 22; 23), Jezebel (2Ki 9:22), the Ninevites (Na 3:4-5), the Babylonians (Isa 47:9-13; Eze 21:21-22; Da 2:2, 10, 27), Belshazzar (Da 5:7, 15), Simon the sorceror (Ac 8:9, 11), Elymas (Ac 13:8), the young woman at Philippi (Ac

16:16), vagabond Jews (Ac 19:13), sons of Sceva (Ac 19:14-15), astrologers (Jer 10:2; Mic 3:6-7), false prophets (Jer 14:14; 27:9; 29:8-9; Eze 13:6-9; 22:28; Mt 24:24).

To cease (Eze 12:23-24; 13:23; Mic 5:12).

Messages of, false (Eze 21:29; Zec 10:2; 2Th 2:9). Diviners shall be confounded (Mic 3:7). Belongs to the works of the flesh (Gal 5:20). Wickedness of (1Sa 15:23). Vainness of (Isa 44:25). Punishment for (Ex 22:18; Lev 20:27; Dt 13:5). Divining by familiar spirits (Lev 20:27; 1Ch 10:13; 2Ch 33:6; Isa 8:19; 19:3; 29:4), by entrails (Eze 21:21), by images (2Ki 23:24; Eze 21:21), by rods (Hos 4:12).

Saul consulted the medium of Endor (1Sa 28:7-25).

Books of, destroyed (Ac 19:19).

SORE [1734, 2307, 3539, 4649, 4804, 5596, 8558, 8825, *1814*, *1815*]. Laws to determine whether clean or unclean (Lev 13). Festering sores disqualified from priesthood (Lev 21:20) or acceptable offering (Lev 22:22). Figurative of judgment for sin (Jer 30:13). *See Disease.*

SOREK, VALLEY OF [8604] (*[blood red grapes]; hence, choice vines*). A valley in the Philistine territory c. eight-and-a-half miles S of Joppa (Jdg 16:4).

SORROW [16, 65, 224, 1790, 3326, 4088, 9342, *3382, 3383, 3851, 4337*]. God takes notice of Hagar's (Ge 21:17-20), Israelites (Ge 3:7-10).

For sin (2Co 7:10-11). *See Repentance; Sin, Confession of.*

No sorrow in heaven (Rev 21:4). "Sorrow and sighing will flee away" (Isa 35:10).

Of Hannah (1Sa 1:15). Of David for Absalom (2Sa 18:33; 19:1-8). Of Mary and Martha (Jn 11:19-40). Jeremiah (La 1:12). Jesus (Isa 53:11; Mt 26:37-44; Mk 14:34-42; Lk 22:42-44).

From bereavement: Of Jacob for Joseph (Ge 37:34-35), for Benjamin (Ge 43:14).

Of the lost (Mt 8:12; 13:42, 50; 22:13; 24:51; 25:30; Lk 13:28; 16:23). *See Wicked, Punishment of.*

See Affliction, Consolation Under; Suffering.

SOSIPATER [5399] (*saving ones father*). Kinsman of Paul (Ro 16:21).

SOSTHENES [5398].
1. Chief ruler of the synagogue in Corinth (Ac 18:17).
2. A Christian with whom Paul wrote the first letter to the Corinthians (1Co 1:1).

SOTAI [6055]. A servant of Solomon whose descendants returned from captivity to Jerusalem (Ezr 2:55; Ne 7:57).

SOUL [2855+5929, 3869+4222, 3883, 5883, *6034*]. The immortal, nonmaterial part of a human being (Mt 10:28; Rev 6:9; 20:4). Can represent the whole person (Jdg 5:21) or one's life (Job 33:18;

Ps 26:9). Used with heart to represent the will and emotions (Dt 4:29; 6:4). *See Immortality; Mankind, A Spirit; Spirit.*

SOUNDING [*1075*]. In navigation (Ac 27:28).

SOUTH [1999, 3542, 3545, 3556, 5582+, 9402+, *2381, 3540, 3803*].
1. A direction of the compass (Ge 13:14).
2. The Negev, an indefinite area lying between Israel and Egypt (Ge 12:9; 13:1; 1Sa 27:8-12; 2Ch 28:18).

SOVEREIGNTY OF GOD [123, 151, 10424, 10718, *1305*]. The supreme authority of God. He is not subject to any power or law which could be conceived as superior to or other than himself (Isa 45:9; Ro 9:20-21).

See God, Sovereign; Jesus the Christ, King.

SOWER [2445, 2446+5433, 3655, 4669, 7046, *2178, 5062, 5725*]. Parable of the (Mt 13:3-8; Mk 4:3-20; Lk 8:5-8). Sowing (Ecc 11:4; Isa 28:25).

Figurative (Ps 126:5; Pr 11:18; Isa 32:20; Hos 8:7; 10:12; Gal 6:7-8).

SPAIN [*5056*]. The westernmost peninsula of Europe. Paul hoped to visit this Roman province (Ro 15:24, 28).

SPAN [2455, 2698, 3427, 8145]. About nine or ten inches (Ex 28:16; 39:9).

SPARROW [7606, *5141*]. Nests of (Ps 84:3). Two sold for a penny (Mt 10:29; Lk 12:6).

SPEAKING OR SPEECH [*522, 606, 608, 614, 1819, 1821, 2047, 3120, 4863, 5583, 7023, 7754, 8488, 8557, 10425, *238, 2895, 3281, 3306, 3364, 3455, 4231, 4245*].

Evil:

(Ps 10:8; 52:2-4; Isa 32:6-7; Jer 20:10; Jude 8, 10). Causes strife (Pr 15:1; 16:27-28; 17:9; 25:23). Excludes from kingdom of heaven (1Co 6:10). Hated by God (Pr 6:16-19; 8:13).

Characteristic of mankind (Ro 1:29-30; 3:13-14). Not characteristic of a Christian (Eph 4:25, 29, 31; 5:4; Tit 3:2; Jas 1:26; 3:5-6, 8-10; 4:11; 1Pe 2:1; 3:9-10).

Forbidden (Ex 22:28; Ps 34:13; Pr 4:24; 6:16-19; Mt 5:22, 37; 12:34-37; Ac 23:5; Eph 4:25, 29, 31; Tit 3:2; Jas 1:26; 3:5-6, 8-10; 4:11; 1Pe 2:1; 3:9-10). Punishment for (Ps 12:3-4; 52:1-4).

Proverbs concerning (Pr 4:24; 6:16-19; 8:13; 10:11, 19, 31-32; 11:11; 12:5-6, 13, 17-19; 13:3; 14:25; 15:1, 4, 28; 16:27-28; 17:4, 9, 20; 18:8, 21, 23; 19:1, 22-23; 24:2; 25:23; 26:20-23, 28; Ecc 10:11, 20).

Prayers for deliverance from curse of (Ps 64:2-5; 70:3; 120:1-7).

Self-accusation: Solomon (Ecc 7:22). Isaiah (Isa 6:5). Paul (Ac 23:5).

Instances of—
Against Job (Job 19:18). Against Lot, those of Sodom (2Pe 2:7-8, 10). Against Moses (Ps 106:33). Against the psalmists (Ps 35:21; 41:5-9; 69:12, 26; 102:8; 119:23). Against the church, those of the circumcision (Tit 1:10-11). False teachers (Jude 8, 10).

See Accusation, False; Blasphemy; Busybody; Falsehood; Flattery; Slander; Talebearer; Uncharitableness.

Foolish:
(Job 13:5; 16:3-4; 38:2). Accountable to God (Mt 12:36-37). Forbidden (Pr 30:18). Not characteristic of a Christian (Eph 5:4).

Proverbs concerning (Pr 10:14; 12:23; 13:3; 14:3; 15:2, 7, 14; 18:6-7, 13; 26:4, 7, 9; 29:11, 20; 30:10; Ecc 5:3, 5; 10:13-14).

See Fool.

Wise:
(Job 16:5; 27:4; Am 5:13; Zep 3:13; Zec 8:16; Rev 14:17). As good as nails (Ecc 12:11). Precious as jewels (Pr 20:16).

Edifying (Eph 4:29). Rewards of (Ps 15:1-3; 50:23; Pr 14:3; 22:11).

Of the noble woman (Pr 31:26).

Admonitions concerning, to believers (Eph 4:22, 25, 29; Php 1:27; Col 4:6; Jas 1:19, 26; 3:2, 13; 1Pe 2:12; 3:15-16). Christ's words concerning (Mt 12:35, 37; Lk 6:45).

Of psalmists (Ps 37:30; 39:1; 77:12; 119:13, 27, 46, 54, 172; 141:3; 145:5-7, 11-12).

Proverbs concerning (Pr 10:11, 13, 19-21, 31-32; 11:12-14; 12:6, 14, 16-20, 23; 13:2-3; 14:3; 15:1-2, 4, 7, 23, 26, 28; 16:21, 23-24; 17:7, 27-28; 18:4, 20; 19:1; 20:15; 21:23; 22:11; 24:6; 25:11, 15; 26:5; 29:11; 31:26; Ecc 3:7; 9:17; 10:12; 12:9-11).

Prayer concerning (Ps 141:3).

See Wisdom.

SPEAR [1360, 2851, 3959, 4751, 7528, 8242, *3365*]. Spears and javelins differed in weight and size but had similar uses.

An implement of war (2Ki 11:10; Ne 4:13). Goliath's (1Sa 17:7). Saul's (1Sa 18:10-11). Stored in the temple (2Ch 23:9). To be changed into pruning hooks (Isa 2:4; Mic 4:3). Pruning hooks to be beaten into (Joel 3:10). Thrust into Jesus' side (Zec 12:10; Jn 19:34; 20:27; Rev 1:7). For catching fish (Job 41:7, 26). *See Armory.*

SPECK [*2847*]. Particle of dust or splinter of wood in one's eye, figurative of improper judgment (Mt 7:3-5; Lk 6:41-42). *See Judgment.*

SPECKLED [5923, 7380]. Mottled in color (Ge 30:25-43). *See Streaked.*

SPELT [4081]. A small grain grown in Egypt (Ex 9:32). Cultivated in Canaan (Isa 28:25). Used in bread (Eze 4:9).

SPERMATORRHEA A disease of the genitals (possibly Lev 15:16).

SPICES [86, 1411, 5008, 5350, 5780, 6160,

8380, *319*, *808*, *2455*]. In the formula for the sacred oil (Ex 25:6; 35:8). Stores of (2Ki 20:13). Used in the temple (1Ch 9:29). Exported from Gilead (Ge 37:25). Sent as a present by Jacob to Joseph (Ge 43:11). Presented by the queen of Sheba to Solomon (1Ki 10:2, 10). Sold in the markets of Tyre (Eze 27:22). Used in the embalming of Asa (2Ch 16:14). Prepared for embalming the body of Jesus (Mk 16:1; Lk 23:56; 24:1; Jn 19:39-40).

SPIDER [6571]. Web of, figurative of the hope of the hypocrite (Job 8:14; Isa 59:5).

SPIES [4855, 8078, 9068, *34*, *1588*, *2946*]. (Ge 42:9). Sent to investigate Canaan (Nu 13), Jazer (Nu 21:32), Jericho (Jos 2:1). Used by David (1Sa 26:4), at the court of Absalom (2Sa 15:10; 17:1-17). Pharisees acted as (Lk 20:20). In the church of Galatia (Gal 2:4). *See Reconnaissance.*

SPIKENARD *See Nard; Perfume, 2.*

SPINDLE [7134]. Implement used in spinning (Ex 35:24; Pr 31:19).

SPINNING [755, 3211, 4757, *3756*]. By hand (Ex 35:25; Pr 31:19).

SPIRIT [200, 466, 4000, 4213, 5883, 5972, 8120, 10658, *899+3836+5858*, *4460*, *5249*, *6035*] (*breath, wind, spirit*). The immortal, nonmaterial part of a human being, similar to the soul (Job 7:11). Represents one's lifeforce or strength (Ge 45:27; Jas 2:26), character (Nu 14:24; Dt 2:30; 1Pe 3:4), desire (2Sa 13:39), heart or emotions (Ps 73:21; 77:6). The self is often called "spirit" when the direct relationship of the individual to God is the point of emphasis (2Ti 4:22; Phm 25). *See Ghost; Immortality; Mankind, A Spirit; Soul.*

SPIRIT, HOLY *See Holy Spirit.*

SPIRITISTS [3362]. Divination by means of communication with the spirit of the dead (necromancy) was known and practiced in the ancient Near East.

Consulting of:
Forbidden (Lev 19:31; 20:6, 27; Dt 18:10-11), vain (Isa 8:19; 19:3). Those who consulted, to be cut off (Lev 20:6, 27).

Instances of Consulting of:
Saul (1Sa 28:3-25; 1Ch 10:13-14). Manasseh (2Ki 21:6; 2Ch 33:6). A slave girl (Ac 16:16-18).

See Demons; Medium; Necromancer; Necromancy; Sorcery; Witchcraft.

SPIRITS IN PRISON Those who in the days of Noah refused his message (1Pe 3:18-20; 4:6). The exact interpretation of this passage is strongly debated.

SPIRITS [356, 8120, 8327, *4460*]. *See Demons.*

SPIRITUAL ADOPTION *See*
Adoption, Spiritual.

SPIRITUAL BLESSINGS *See*
Blessings, Spiritual; Holy Spirit; Sanctification.

SPIRITUAL BLINDNESS
Blindness, Spiritual.

SPIRITUAL BOASTING (Ro 11:18-21). Incompatible, with faith (Ro 3:27; Eph 2:8-10), with humility (1Co 1:29, w 1:17-31; 4:6-7; 2Co 10:12-16). In the Lord, approved (Jer 9:24; 2Co 10:17-18; Gal 6:14).
See Boasting, Spiritual.

SPIRITUAL DEATH Alienation from the life of God; a state of condemnation (Ro 7:9, 11; 8:5-6, 13; Eph 4:18). Making alive from (Jn 5:24-26; Ro 5:12, 15; Eph 2:1, 5-6; 5:14; Col 2:13).
See Death, Physical; Second Death.

SPIRITUAL DESIRE *See Desire, Spiritual.*

SPIRITUAL DILIGENCE *See Zeal.*

SPIRITUAL GIFTS Extraordinary gifts of the Spirit given to Christians to equip them for the service of the Church (Ro 11:29; 12:6-8; 1Co 12:4-11, 28-30; Eph 4:7-11; 1Pe 4:10-11).
See Charism, Charisma, Charismata; Holy Spirit; Tongues, Gift of.

SPIRITUAL HUNGER *See Hunger, Figurative.*

SPIRITUAL PEACE (Isa 27:5; 54:1, 10, 13; 55:2, 12; 57:19; Eze 34:25; Lk 2:14, 29; Ro 5:1; 1Co 14:33). Christ's kingdom, a kingdom of (Isa 9:6; 11:6-9, 13; Mic 5:5; Lk 1:79; Ac 10:36).
See Peace, Spiritual.

SPIRITUAL PURIFICATION (Ps 65:3; 73:1; Pr 20:9; Jn 13:8-9). By corrective judgments (Isa 4:3-4). By mercy and truth (Pr 16:6). By the Holy Spirit (1Co 6:11; Tit 3:5-6). By the blood of Christ (Heb 1:3; 9:14; 2Pe 1:9; 1Jn 1:7; Rev 1:5; 7:14).
Of the Church (Eph 5:26).
Commanded (Isa 1:16; Mt 23:26; Ac 22:16; 1Co 5:7; 2Co 7:1; Heb 10:22; Jas 4:8).
Promised (Isa 1:18; Jer 33:8; Eze 36:25; Da 12:10; Zec 13:1; 1Jn 1:9). Prayer for (Ps 51:2, 7; 79:9).
See Purification; Sanctification.

SPIRITUAL UNDERSTANDING (Mt 13:23; Lk 10:21-22; Jn 7:17). Of apostles (Mt 13:16-17; Lk 8:10; 10:23-24). Of Peter (Mt 16:16-17). Of Mary (Lk 10:39, 42).
Lacking, in disciples (Mt 15:15-16; Lk 24:25), in Jews (Mt 13:11-16; Jn 6:26, 41, 52; 9:28-29, 39-41; 12:27-40; Ac 28:24-27).

Commanded:
Concerning, the importance of preaching (Mt 11:13-15), the importance of parables (Mt 13:9, 43; Lk 8:8), the character of the disciples of Jesus (Lk 14:33-35), the Holy Spirit's message to the churches (Rev 2:7).
See Wisdom, Spiritual.

SPIRITUALISM *See Necomancer; Sorcery.*

SPIRITUALITY Described as the great and enduring good (Lk 10:42), as love and devotion to God (Dt 6:5; Jos 22:5; 1Ki 8:23; Ps 1:2; 51:6).
Brings peace (Isa 26:3; Jer 33:6; Ro 8:6; 14:17), indifference to worldly good (1Co 7:29-31; Col 3:1-3), thirst for heavenly blessings (Mt 5:6; Jn 6:27).
Is produced by the indwelling of the Holy Spirit (Jn 14:16-17; Ro 8:4).

SPITTING [3762, 7794, 8371, 8394, 9531, *1840, 1870, 4772*]. In the face, as an indignity (Nu 12:14; Dt 25:9; Job 30:10; Mt 26:67; 27:30). Jesus used spittle in healing (Mk 7:33; 8:23).

SPOILS [4917, 8965, *660, 5036*]. Of war (Ge 14:11-12; Nu 31:9-10; Dt 2:35). Divided between the combatants and noncombatants of the Israelites, including priests and Levites (Nu 31:25-54; 1Sa 30:24). Dedicated to the Lord (1Sa 15:15; 1Ch 26:27; 2Ch 15:11).

SPOKES [3140]. Rods connecting the rim of a wheel with the hub. Basins for washing of sacrifices were set on bases moving upon wheels. The spokes were part of these wheels (1Ki 7:27-33).

SPONGE [*5074*]. (Mt 27:48; Mk 15:36; Jn 19:29).

SPOONS Of the tabernacle (Ex 25:29; Nu 4:7; 7). Of the temple (1Ki 7:50; 2Ch 4:22).

SPOT [994, 1353, 2494, 3229, 5226, 9393, *834, 5536*]. Blemish, blot (SS 4:7; Job 11:15; Lev 24:19ff; Pr 9:7; Jude 23).

SPOUSE *See Bride; Marriage.*

SPREAD [*1819, 2118, 2143, 2430, 3655, 5417, 5427, 5742, 5759, 5951, 5989, 6296, 6885, 7233, 7287, 7298, 7313, 8316, 8392, 889, 1424, 2002, 5143*]. Scatter, disperse (Mt 21:8; Mk 1:28).

SPRING [*1657, 3655, 4432, 4784, 4919, 5078, 5227, 6524, 6590, 7255, 7541, 9102+9588, 9333, 4380*].
1. Of water. Hot (Ge 36:24).
Figurative: muddied or salty (Pr 25:26; Jas 3:11).
See Wells.
2. Season of, promised annual return of (Ge 8:22). Described (Pr 25:25; SS 2:11-13).

SPRINKLING [*2450, 4670, 5684, 6590, *4822, 4823]. Of blood (Lev 14:7, 51; 16:14; Heb 9:13, 19, 21; 11:28; 1Pe 1:2). *See Blood.* Of water (Nu 8:7; Eze 36:25; Heb 9:19; 10:22).

STABILITY [6641]. Of character (Ps 57:7; 108:1; 112:7).

Commanded (1Co 7:20; 15:58; 2Th 2:15; Heb 10:23; 13:9; Jas 1:23-25; Rev 22:11). Rewarded (Mt 10:22; 24:13; Mk 4:20; 2Th 3:3).

See Character; Decision; Perseverance.

STABLE *See Pasture.*

STACHYS [5093] (*head of grain*). A Christian in Rome (Ro 16:9).

STACTE *See Gum Resin.*

STADIA [5084]. Plural of *stadion*, about 202 yards (Rev 14:20; 21:16).

STAFF [1475, 2980, 4751, 4957, 5234, 5475, 6469, 8657, *2812, 4811]. Used as weapons (Mt 27:30; Mk 15:19).

Symbolic (Zec 11:7-14).

See Rod.

STAIRS [4294, 5090, 5092, 6150]. Steps leading to an upper chamber (1Ki 6:8; Ac 21:40), or some other elevated place (Ne 9:4; Eze 40:6; 43:17). Jacob's vision of a stairway from earth to heaven (Ge 28:10-22). The sign to Hezekiah on the stairway of Ahaz (1Ki 20:1-12).

STAKE [928, 3845]. Tent pin or tent pole (Ex 27:19; Isa 33:20).

STALL [774, 1074, 5272, 8348, *5764]. A place for care of livestock or compartment in a stable for one animal (2Ch 32:28). Solomon's barns provided stalls for 4000 horses (2Ch 9:25).

STAMMERING [6589]. (Isa 32:4; 33:19). Of Moses (Ex 4:10).

STANDARD [74, 253, 1840, 4500, 5477, 5504, 5812, *2848, 3836+4922]. An ensign used by each of the tribes of Israel in camp and march (Nu 1:52; 2:2). Banners used as (Ps 20:5; SS 6:4, 10). Used in war (Jer 4:21). Used to signal the route to defended cities (Jer 4:6); to call attention to news (Jer 50:2; 51:12).

See Armies; Banner; Ensign.

Figurative (Isa 49:22; 62:10; Jer 4:6).

STARS [2122, 3919, 7372, 9028, *843, 849, 5891, 5892]. Created by God (Ge 1:16; Job 26:13; Ps 8:3; 33:6; 136:7, 9; Am 5:8). Differ in splendor (1Co 15:41). Worship of, forbidden (Dt 4:19). Worshiped (2Ki 17:16; 21:3; 23:5; Jer 19:13; Am 5:26; Zep 1:5; Ac 7:42-43). Constellations of (Isa 13:10), Orion (Job 9:9; Am 5:8), serpent (Job 26:13), Planets (2Ki 23:5), the morning star (Job 38:7; Rev 2:28; 22:16). Darkening of (Job 9:7; Ecc 12:2; Isa 13:10; 34:4; Joel 2:10; 3:15; Rev

8:11-12). Comets (Jude 13). Falling of (Da 8:10; 9:1; 12:4). Guides the wise men (Mt 2:2, 7, 9-10).

Figurative:

Of the deliverer (Nu 24:17). Seven stars of the seven churches (Rev 1:16, 20). Crown of twelve stars (Rev 12:1). Of Jesus (Rev 22:16).

STATE *See Church, The Body of Believers, State; Government.*

STATECRAFT Wisdom in (Pr 28:2). School in (Da 1:3-5). Skilled in.

Instances of: Joseph (Ge 47:15-26), Samuel (1Sa 11:12-15), Nathan (1Ki 1:11-14), Jeroboam (1Ki 12:26-33), Daniel. *See Daniel.*

See Government; Kings; Rulers.

STATURE [1541, 7757, *2461]. Natural height of an animal body (2Sa 21:20; Isa 45:14; Lk 19:3).

STAVES *See Staff.*

STEADFASTNESS [3922, 6164, *2530]. (Ps 57:7; 108:1; 112:7; Ro 14:4; 1Th 3:8; Col 1:23; Jas 1:25).

Commanded (1Co 7:20; 15:58; 16:13; Gal 6:1; Eph 6:11, 13-14; Php 1:27; 4:1; 1Th 5:21; 2Th 2:15; 3:13; Heb 10:23; 13:9; Jas 1:25; 1Pe 5:9).

Rewards of (Mt 10:22; 24:13; Mk 13:13; Rev 2:7, 10-11, 17, 25-28; 3:5, 11-12, 21; 21:17).

See Decision; Perseverance; Stability.

STEALING [665, 1608, 1704, 2118, 8845, *3096, 3802]. *See Theft.*

STEEL Steel is not mentioned in the Bible. *See Bronze.*

STELE (*erect block* or *shaft*). Narrow, upright slab of stone with an inscription cut on it to commemorate an event, mark a grave, or give a votive likeness of a deity. Prevalent especially in Egypt and Greece.

STEPHANAS [5107] (*victor's wreath*). A Christian in Corinth, whose household Paul baptized (1Co 1:16; 16:15, 17).

STEPHEN [5108] (*victor's wreath*). A Christian martyr. Appointed one of the committee of seven to oversee power of (Ac 6:5, 8-10). False charges against (Ac 6:11-15). Defense of (Ac 7). Stoned (Ac 7:54-60; 8:1; 22:20). Burial of (Ac 8:2). Gentle and forgiving spirit of (Ac 7:59-60).

STERILITY [6829]. Of women. *See Barrenness.*

STEW [5686]. Soup of vegetables and meat (Ge 25:29-30, 34; 2Ki 4:38-39).

STEWARD [1074+8042, 5853, 6125]. (Ge 15:2; 43:19; 1Ch 28:1; Lk 8:3). Must be faithful (1Co 4:1-2; Tit 1:7; 1Pe 4:10).

Figurative: The faithful steward described (Lk

12:35-38, 42). The unfaithful, described (Lk 16:1-8). The parable of the pounds (Lk 19:12-27), of the talents (Mt 25:14-30).

STEWARDSHIP Of the gospel (1Co 9:17; Gal 2:7; Col 1:25; 1Th 2:4; 1Ti 1:11; Tit 1:3).

STICKS [*202, 5234, 6770, 8657, *2812*]. Used as cymbals (Eze 37:16).

STIFF-NECKED [6902+7996, 6902+7997, *5019*]. See Impenitence; Obduracy.

STOCK [2446, 4551, 7212, *3833*].
1. Wooden idol worshiped by apostate Israel (Isa 44:19; Jer 2:27).
2. Family (Lev 25:47; Isa 40:24; Ac 13:26; Php 3:5).
3. Instrument of punishment in which head, hands, and feet were fastened (2Ch 16:10; Jer 20:2; Job 13:27).

STOICISM [*5121*]. A Grecian philosophy, inculcating doctrines of severe morality, self-denial, and inconvenient services.
Scripture analogies to: John the Baptist, wears camel's hair and subsists on locusts and wild honey (Mt 3:4), comes "neither eating nor drinking" (Mt 11:18; Lk 7:33). Jesus requires self-denial and crosses (Mt 10:38-39; 16:24; Mk 8:34-35; Lk 9:23-26; 14:27), the subordination of natural affection (Mt 10:37; Lk 14:26). Paul teaches that the "law of my mind" is at war with the "law of sin at work within my members" (Ro 7:23, w 7:14-24), that the body must be kept under (1Co 9:27), advises celibacy (1Co 7:1-9, 25-26, 32-33, 39-40).
School of, at Athens (Ac 17:18).
See Aratus; Asceticism; Cleanthes.

STOICS ([*learners on the painted] porch*]).
See Aratus; Asceticism; Cleanthes; Stoicism.

STOMACHER NIV "fine clothing" (Isa 3:24).

STONES [*74, 1473, 1607, 5167, 6232, 8083, 10006, *3342, 3343, 3344, 3345*]. Commandments engraved upon (Ex 24:12; 31:18; 34:1-4; Dt 4:13; 5:22; 9:9-11; 10:1-3). The law of Moses written upon (Jos 8:32). Houses built of (Isa 9:10; Am 5:11). Temple built of (1Ki 5:17-18; 7:9-12; Mt 24:2; Lk 19:44; 21:5-6). Prepared in the quarries (1Ki 6:7). Hewn (Ex 34:1; Dt 10:1; 1Ki 5:17; 6:36; 7:9; 2Ki 12:12; 22:6; 1Ch 22:2; 2Ch 34:11; La 3:9). Sawn (1Ki 7:9). Stonemasons (1Ki 5:18; 2Ki 12:12; 1Ch 22:15).
City walls built of (Ne 4:3). Memorial pillars of (Ge 28:18-22; 31:45-52; Jos 4:2-9, 20-24; 24:25; 1Sa 7:12). Great, as landmarks, Abel (1Sa 6:18), Ezel (1Sa 20:19), Zoheleth (1Ki 1:9).
Cast upon accursed ground (2Ki 3:19, 25). Used in building altars (Jos 8:31), for weighing (Lev 19:36), for closing tombs (Mt 27:60; Mk 15:46; 16:3). Tombs cut in (Mt 27:60; Mk 15:46; 16:3).

Idols made of (Dt 4:28; 28:36, 64; 29:17; 2Ki 19:18; Isa 37:19; Eze 20:32).
Great, in Solomon's temple (1Ki 5:17-18; 7:9-12). Magnificent, in Herod's (Mk 13:1). Skill in throwing (Jdg 20:16; 1Ch 12:2). See Sling.
See Adamant; Chalcedony; Marble; Onyx; Pillar. See below, Precious.
Figurative—
(Ge 49:24; Zec 3:9). Of temptation, "a stone that causes men to stumble" (Isa 8:14; Ro 9:33; 1Pe 2:8). Of Christ, "a tested stone, a precious cornerstone for a sure foundation" (Isa 28:16), of Christ's rejection, the rejected corner stone (Ps 118:22; Mt 21:42-44; Mk 12:10; Lk 20:17-18; Ac 4:11; 1Pe 2:4), the true foundation (Isa 28:16; Mt 16:18; 1Co 3:11; Eph 2:20; Rev 21:14). Of Christ, the source of spiritual water (1Co 10:4). Of the impenitent heart (Eze 36:26). Of the witness of the Spirit, the white stone (Rev 2:17).
Symbolic—
Of the kingdom of Christ (Da 2:34, 45).
Precious:
In the breastplate and ephod (Ex 28:9-21; 39:6-14). Voluntary offerings of, by the Israelites for the breastplate and ephod (Ex 35:27). Exported from Sheba (1Ki 10:2, 10; 2Ch 9:9-10; Eze 27:22), Ophir (1Ki 10:11). Partial catalog of (Eze 28:13). Seen in the foundation of the New Jerusalem in John's apocalyptic vision (Rev 21:19-20).
In kings' crowns (2Sa 12:30; 1Ch 20:2).
Figurative: (Isa 54:11-12).
See Adamant; Agate; Amber; Amethyst; Bdellium; Beryl; Carbuncle; Carnelian; Chalcedony; Chrysolite; Chrysoprase; Coral; Crystal; Diamond; Emerald; Flint; Glowing Metal; Hardest Stone; Jacinth; Jasper; Minerals of the Bible, 1; Onyx; Pearl; Ruby; Sapphire; Sardius; Sardonyx; Topaz; Turquoise.

STONING [*6232, 8083+, *3342, 3344*]. The ordinary form of capital punishment prescribed by Hebrew law (Lev 20:2) for blasphemy (Lev 24:16), idolatry (Dt 13:6-10), desecration of the Sabbath day (Ex 31:15; 35:2; Nu 15:32-36), human sacrifice (Lev 20:2), occultism (Lev 20:27).
Unlike unintentional sins, for which there are provisions of God's mercy, one who sets his hand defiantly to despise the word of God and to blaspheme his name must be punished. The one who sins defiantly (literally "with a high hand"), whether in the case of the willful blasphemer (Ex 20:7; 22:28; Lev 24:11-16), or the Sabbath-breaker (Ex 31:12-15; 35:2), was guilty of high-handed rebellion and was judged with death (Nu 15:30-31, 32-36).
Execution took place outside city (Lev 24:14; 1Ki 21:10, 13; Ac 7:58).
See Assault and Battery; Bruise(s); Flog, Flogging; Lashes; Scourging; Stripes.

STOOL [78].
1. Delivery stool (Ex 1:16).
2. Footstool. Figurative: Of the earth (Isa 66:1;

Mt 5:35; Ac 7:49); temple (1Ch 28:2; La 2:1); sanctuary (Ps 99:5; 132:7), enemies of Jesus (Ps 110:1; Mt 22:44; Mk 12:36; Lk 20:43; Ac 2:35; Heb 1:13). *See Footstool.*

STORE CITIES [*5016]. Supply depots for provisions and arms (1Ki 9:15-19; 2Ch 8:4-6; 16:4).

STOREHOUSE [238, 238, 667, 1074+]. Place for keeping treasures, supplies, and equipment (Dt 28:8; 1Ch 29:16; 2Ch 31:10; Mal 3:10). *See Barn; Granary.*

STORK [2884] (*kindly, loyal one*). Forbidden as food (Lev 11:19). Nest of, in fir trees (Ps 104:17). Migratory (Jer 8:7).
Figurative (Zec 5:9).

STOVE Household stoves usually made of clay; were small and portable, burning charcoal; the well-to-do had metal stoves or braziers (Jer 36:22ff).

STRAIGHT [448+6298+7156, 3837, 3838, 3841, 4200+5790, 4200, 4793, 4797, 5019, 5584, 6590, 9461, *867, 1838, 2312, 2316, 2318*]. Name of a street in Damascus (Ac 9:11).
Figurative of righteousness, "straight paths" (Isa 40:3-4; Mt 3:3; Heb 12:13).

STRAIT GATE *See Gates, Figurative.*

STRAKES Archaic word for:
1. "White stripes" (Ge 30:37). *See Stripes, 4.*
2. "Greenish or reddish depressions" (Lev 14:37).

STRANGERS [1591, 1731, 2319, 2424, 3359+4202, 5796, 5799, 9369, *259, 3828, 4215, 4229, 4230, 5810*]. Mosaic law relating to: Authorized bondservice of (Lev 25:44-45), usury of (Dt 15:3; 23:20), sale to, of flesh of animals that had died (Dt 14:21), forbid their being made kings over Israel (Dt 17:15), their eating the Passover (Ex 12:43, 48), their eating things offered in sacrifice (Ex 29:33; Lev 22:10, 12, 25), their blaspheming (Lev 24:16), their approaching the tabernacle (Nu 1:51), their eating blood (Lev 17:10), injustice to (Ex 12:49; Lev 24:22; Nu 9:14; Dt 1:16; Jer 22:3), oppression of, forbidden (Ex 22:21; Lev 23:9; Dt 24:14, 17; 27:19; Jer 22:3). Instances of oppression of (Eze 22:29; Mal 3:5).
Required to observe the Sabbath (Ex 20:10; 23:12). Might offer sacrifices (Lev 17:8; 22:18-19). Were buried in separate burial places (Mt 27:7).
Kindness to, required (Lev 19:33-34). Love of, commanded (Dt 10:18-19). Abhorrence of, forbidden (Dt 23:7). Marriage with, forbidden (Dt 25:5). Hospitality to. *See Hospitality.*
See Alms; Foreigner; Heathen; Proselyte.

STRANGLE [2871, 4725, *4465*]. To deprive of life by choking. Israelites were forbidden to eat flesh from strangled animals (Lev

17:12). At the Jerusalem council even Jewish Christians were forbidden to eat such meat (Ac 15:20).

STRATEGY [6783]. In war (Ge 14:14-15; 32:7-8; Jos 8:3-25; Jdg 7:16-23; 20:29-43; 2Sa 15:32-34, w 17:7-14; Ne 6; Isa 15:1; Jer 6:5).
See Ambush; Armies.

STRAW [5495, 7990, 9320, *2811*]. Used for feed (Ge 24:32; Isa 65:25), for brick (Ex 5:7).

STRAY [5610, 5615, 5742, 6073, 8178, 8706, 8740, 8938, 9494]. Animals straying to be returned (Ex 23:4; Dt 22:1-3). Instances of animals straying, Kish's (1Sa 9).

STREAKED [6819]. Mottled or blotchy of color, characterizing Laban's sheep (Ge 30:35; 31:8, 12). *See Speckled.*

STREAM OF EGYPT *See River of Egypt.*

STREETS [*2006, 2575, 8148, 8798, *3847, 4423, 4860*]. (Pr 1:20; Na 2:4; Mk 6:56; Lk 14:21; Ac 9:11).

STRENGTH [*226, 579, 599, 1475, 1476, 1504, 1524, 2006, 2432, 2616, 2616, 2617, 2621, 2657, 3338, 3946, 4097, 4394, 6434, 6437, 6786, 8435, 9361, 10768, 10772, *1011, 1540, 1543, 1904, 1932, 2185, 2708, 2709, 2710, 3194, 3489, 3869, 5105, 5114*]. A title given Yahweh (1Sa 15:29). Spiritual. *See Power, Spiritual.*

STRIFE [4506, 5175, 8190, *2251*].

General:
(Ps 55:9; 80:6). Domestic (Pr 19:13; 21:19; 25:24). Hated by God (Isa 58:4; Hab 1:3).
Christ brings (Mt 10:34-36; Lk 12:51-53, 58-59).
Caused by: Busybodies (Pr 26:20). Perversity (Pr 16:28). Hatred (Pr 10:12). Lusts (Jas 4:1-2). Pride (Pr 13:10). Scornfulness (Pr 22:10). Wrath (Pr 15:18; 29:22; 30:33). Excessive indulgence in intoxicating drinks (Pr 23:29-30).
Destructive (Mt 12:25; Mk 3:24-25; Lk 11:17).

Exhortations against:
(Ge 13:8; 45:24; Ps 31:20; Pr 3:30; 17:14; 25:8; Mt 5:25, 39-41; Ro 12:18; 13:13; 14:1, 19, 21; 16:17-18; 1Co 4:6-7; 2Co 12:20; Gal 5:15, 20; Php 2:3, 14-15; 1Ti 3:2-3; 6:3-5, 20-21; 2Ti 2:14, 23-25; Tit 3:1-3, 9; Jas 3:14-16).
Punishment for (Isa 41:11-12; Ro 2:8-9). Correction of (Mt 18:15-17).
Abstinence from, honorable (Pr 20:3).
Prayers concerning (Ps 55:9; 1Ti 2:8).
Proverbs concerning (Pr 3:30; 6:12-14, 16-19; 10:12; 13:10; 15:18; 17:1, 14, 19; 18:6, 19; 19:13; 20:3; 21:19; 22:10; 23:29-30; 25:8, 24; 26:17, 20-21; 27:15; 28:25; 29:22; 30:33).
See Anger; Envy; Jealousy; Malice.

Instances of:
Between Abraham and Lot's herdsmen (Ge 13:6-7), Abimelech's (Ge 21:25), Isaac's and

those of Gerar (Ge 26:20-22). Laban and Jacob (Ge 31:36). Israelites (Dt 1:12). Jephthah and his brothers (Jdg 11:2), and Ephraimites (Jdg 12:1-6). Israel and Judah, about David (2Sa 19:41-43).

Disciples, over who might be the greatest (Mk 9:34; Lk 22:24). Jews, concerning Jesus (Jn 10:19). Christians at Antioch, about circumcision (Ac 15:2). Paul and Barnabas, about Mark (Ac 15:38-39). Pharisees and Sadducees, concerning the Resurrection (Ac 23:7-10). Christians, at Corinth (1Co 1:10-12; 3:3-4; 6:1-7; 11:16-21). At Philippi (Php 1:15-17).

STRIKER [*2118, 2150, 4804, 5595, 5597, 5782, 7003, 9546, 10411, *3139*, *4091*, *4250*, *4684*, *4703*, *5597*].

See Violence.

STRINGED INSTRUMENTS
[5593]. *See Music.*

STRIPES [7203].
1. Wounds inflicted by scourges for punishment (Ex 21:25). *See Bruise(s), 1.*
2. Authorized by Jewish law for certain offenses (Dt 25:2-3). *See Lashes, 1.*
3. Practiced also by Romans (Mt 27:26 & Jn 19:1, w Isa 53:5). Roman floggings were so brutal that sometimes the victim died before crucifixion. *See Flog, Flogging.*
4. The Hebrew terms for the words "poplar" and "white stripes" are puns on the name Laban. As Jacob had gotten the best of Esau (whose other name, Edom, means "red") by means of red stew (Ge 25:30), so he now tries to get the best of Laban (whose name means "white") by means of white branches (Ge 30:37). *See Strakes, 1.*

See also, Assault and Battery; Scourging; Stoning.

STRIVING WITH GOD Folly of (Job
9:3; 33:13; 40:2; Isa 45:9; Ro 9:20).

STRONG DRINK *See Beer; Fermented Drink; Wine.*

STUBBLE [7990]. Figurative of the wick-
ed (Ex 15:7; Job 21:18; Ps 83:13; Isa 5:24; 40:24; 41:2; 47:14; Jer 13:24; Joel 2:5; Na 1:10; Mal 4:1).

STUBBORNNESS [4213+, 6253, 6437,
7996, 7997, 8001, 9244, *4801*, *5016*, *5018*]. *See Obduracy.*

STUDENTS [9441, *3412*]. Poverty of (2Ki
4:1). In state school (Da 1). In schools of the prophets (1Sa 19:20; 1Ki 20:35; 2Ki 2:2-3, 5, 7, 15; 4:1). *See Instruction; School.*

STUMBLING [*1892, 4173, 4842, 5597,
9023, *4682*, *4684*, *4760*, *4998*]. Causes of (Ps 69:6). Stone of (Isa 8:14; Ro 9:32-33; 1Pe 2:8). Stumbling block (Lev 19:14; Ps 119:165; Isa 57:14; Jer 6:21; Eze 3:20; 7:19; 14:3-4, 7; Zep 1:3;

Lk 11:52; Ro 11:9; 14:13; 1Co 1:23; 8:9-13; Rev 2:14).

See Temptation.

SUAH [6053] (possibly *offal, dung, viscera*). An Asherite. The son of Zophah (1Ch 7:36).

SUBJECTS [*3899, 4044, 5989, 6268, 6269, *1944*, *5679*, *5718*]. *See Citizens; Government; Patriotism; Rulers.*

SUBMISSION [*14, 3338+5989, 5202, 5976, 6122, 6268, 6700, 9393, *1505*, *2340*, *5640*, *5717*, *5718*]. To authority: Jesus an example of (Mt 26:39, 42; Mk 14:36; Lk 22:42; Heb 5:8).
Of Paul (1Co 16:7).

See Obedience.

SUBSTITUTION [4614, 9455]. (Ge 22:13; Ex 28:38). The offering for the offerer (Lev 1:4; 16:21-22). The Levites for the firstborn of the Israelites (Nu 3:12, 41, 45; 8:18). The life of Ahab for that of Ben-Hadad (1Ki 20:42).
Of Christ for us (Isa 53:4-6; 1Co 5:7; 2Co 5:21; Gal 3:13; 1Pe 2:24).

See Suffering, Vicarious.

SUBURB *See Pasture.*

SUCATHITES [8460]. One of three clans of scribes who lived at Jabez (1Ch 2:55).

SUCCESSION Of priests, irregularity in (Heb 7:1-28). *See Priest.* Of kings. *See Kings.*

SUCCOTH [6111] (*booths*).
1. A city probably east of the Jordan. Jacob builds a house in (Ge 33:17). Allotted to Gad (Jos 13:27). People of, punished by Gideon (Jdg 8:5-8, 14-16). Located near the Jordan (1Ki 7:46; 2Ch 4:17; Ps 60:6; 108:7).
2. First camping place of the Israelites on leaving Rameses (Ex 12:37; 13:20; Nu 33:5-6).

SUCCOTH BENOTH [6112]. A pagan idol brought into Samaria after Assyria had captured it (2Ki 17:24-30).

SUCHATHITES *See Sucathites.*

SUDDEN EVENTS (Ecc 9:12; Mal 3:1; Mt 24:27; Mk 13:36; Lk 2:13; Ac 2:2; 9:3; 16:26).

SUETONIUS A Roman writer (c. A.D. 69-140), famous for his *Lives of the Caesars.*

SUFFERING [*2118, 2703, 4799, 5186, 5253, 5951, 6700, 6713, 6714, 6715, 6740, 8317, 10472, *1181*, *2568*, *3465*, *4077*, *4248*, *5224*, *5309*].

For Christ:
Promised by Christ (Mt 10:34-36; Lk 12:51-53, 58-59; Ac 9:16). Fellowship with Christ on account of (Php 3:10). Conditions of joint heirship with Christ (Ro 8:17-22, 26). A privilege (Php 1:29). Rejoicing in (Ac 5:41; Col 1:24).

Motives for patient enduring of: Future glory (Ro 8:17-18; 2Co 4:8-10; 2Co 4:11-12, 17-18; 1Pe 4:13-14). Reigning with Christ (2Ti 2:12; Rev 22:5).

Consolations in (2Co 1:7; Php 2:27-30; 2Ti 2:12; 1Pe 5:10). Patience in (1Co 4:11-13; 2Th 1:4-5; Jas 5:10; 1Pe 4:14).

See Affliction; Persecution.

Of Christ:

Purpose of his coming (Lk 24:46-47; Jn 6:51; 10:11, 15; 11:50-52). Reason for his coming (Ro 4:25; 5:6-8; 14:15; 1Co 1:17-18, 23-24; 15:3; 2Co 5:14-15; Gal 1:4; 2:20-21; Eph 5:2, 25; 1Th 5:9-10; Heb 2:9-10, 14, 18; 5:8-9; 9:15-16, 28; 10:10, 18-20; 1Pe 2:21, 24; 3:18; 4:1; 1Jn 3:16).

See Atonement; Jesus the Christ, Death of; Purpose of His Death; Sufferings of.

Vicarious:

(Ex 9:13-16; Jn 15:13; Ro 9:3; 1Pe 2:21-24; 1Jn 3:16).

See Jesus the Christ, Sufferings of; Penalty, Vicariously Assumed; above, Suffering, Of Christ. Instance of: Goliath, for the Philistines (1Sa 17).

SUICIDE (Am 9:2; Rev 9:6). Temptation to, of Jesus (Mt 4:5-6; Lk 4:9-11). Of the Philippian jailer (Ac 16:27). *See Death, Physical, Desired.* Instances of: Samson (Jdg 16:29-30). Saul and his armor-bearer (1Sa 31:4-5; 1Ch 10:4-5). Ahithophel (2Sa 17:23). Zimri (1Ki 16:18). Judas (Mt 27:5; Ac 1:18).

SUING [*5477, 8189, 8190, 8191, *3210, 3212*]. (Mt 5:40). *See Creditor; Debtor.*

SUKKITES [6113]. Mercenary soldiers, possibly Libyan, who joined Shishak in his invasion of Judah (2Ch 12:3).

SUKKOTH *See Succoth.*

SULFUR [1730, *2520, 2523*]. Fire and, rained upon Sodom (Ge 19:24; Lk 17:29). In Israel (Dt 29:23). Figurative of God's judgment (Job 18:15; Ps 11:6; Isa 30:33; Eze 38:22; Rev 9:17-18; 14:10; 19:20; 21:8). *See Minerals of the Bible.*

SUMER One of two political divisions, Sumer and Akkad, originally comprising Babylonia.

SUMMER [5249, 7810, 7811, 10627, *2550*]. Season of, promised while the earth remains (Ge 8:22). Cool rooms for (Jdg 3:20, 24; Am 3:15). Fruits of (2Sa 16:1-2; Isa 16:9; 28:4; Jer 40:10, 12; 48:32; Am 8:1-2; Mic 7:1). Drought of (Ps 32:4). Given by God (Ps 74:17). The time for labor and harvest (Pr 6:6-8; 10:5; 30:25; Jer 8:20). Snow in (Pr 26:1). Threshing in (Da 2:35). Approach of (Mt 24:32; Mk 13:28; Lk 21:30).

Figurative (Jer 8:20).

SUMMER HOUSE, SUMMER PALACE The wealthy had separate residences for hot and cold seasons. Called a "summer house" (Am 3:15), a "summer palace" (Jdg 3:20, ftn). *See Winter Apartment, Winter House.*

SUN [240, 2780, 3064, 3427, 7416, 8840, 9087, *424, 2463*]. Created (Ge 1:14-18; Ps 74:16; 136:7; Jer 31:35). Rising and setting of (Ecc 1:5). Diurnal motion of (Ps 19:4, 6). Worship of, forbidden (Dt 4:19; 17:3). Worshiped (Job 31:26-28; Jer 8:2; Eze 6:4, 6; 8:16). Kings of Judah dedicate horses to (2Ki 23:11).

Miracles concerning: Darkening of (Ex 10:21-23; Isa 5:30; 24:23; Eze 32:7; Joel 2:10, 31; 3:15; Am 8:9; Mic 3:6; Mt 24:29; 27:45; Mk 13:24; 15:33; Lk 21:25; 23:44-45; Ac 2:20; Rev 6:12; 8:12; 9:2; 16:8). Stands still (Jos 10:12-13; Hab 3:11). Shadow of, goes back on Ahaz's stairway (2Ki 20:11; Isa 38:8).

Light of, not needed in eternity (Rev 21:23).

Figurative (Ps 84:11; Mal 4:2; Jdg 5:31; Isa 30:26; 60:19-20; Jer 15:9; Rev 1:16; 12:1; 19:17).

SUN, WORSHIP OF Worship of the sun found varied forms in the ancient world. Even the Israelites at times worshiped sun images (Lev 26:30; Isa 17:8). Shamash was a great sun god of the ancient Middle East. Phoenicia worshiped a sun Baal, Baal Hamon. In Egypt the center of sun worship was On, or Heliopolis, where the sun was called Re.

SUNDAY The first day of the week, commemorating the resurrection of Jesus (Jn 20:1-25), and the Day of Pentecost (Ac 2:1-41). For a time after the Ascension of Jesus the Christians met on the seventh and the first days of the week, but as the Hebrew Christian churches declined in influence, the tendency to observe the Hebrew Sabbath slowly passed. The disciples at Troas worshiped on the first day (Ac 20:7). Paul admonished the Corinthians to lay by in store as God had prospered them, doing it week by week on the first day (1Co 16:2). The term "Lord's Day" occurs (Rev 1:10).

SUN-DIAL NIV "stairway" (2Ki 20:11; Isa 38:8). *See Stairs.*

SUNSTROKE (2Ki 4:19).

SUPER-APOSTLES [*693+5663*]. Paul's critics (2Co 11:5; 12:11).

SUPEREROGATION The doctrine of excessive and meritorious righteousness (Eze 33:12-13; Lk 17:10).

SUPERSCRIPTION (*inscription*).

1. The wording on coins (Mt 22:20).

2. Words written on a board attached to the cross naming the crime of which the condemned was accused (Mk 15:26; Lk 23:38; Jn 19:19-20).

3. Titles of the Psalms. *See Music, Symbols Used in; Psalms.*

SUPERSTITION (Ac 25:19).

Instances of:

Israelites in supposing that their defeat in battle with the Philistines was due to their not having brought the ark of the covenant with them (1Sa 4:3, w 4:10-11), attributing their calamities to having stopped offering sacrifices to the Queen of Heaven (Jer 44:17-19). Philistines in refusing to step on the threshold where the image of Dagon had repeatedly fallen (1Sa 5:5).

The belief of the Syrians concerning the help of the gods (1Ki 20:23). Nebuchadnezzar in supposing that the spirit of the gods was upon Daniel (Da 4:8-9). The sailors who threw Jonah into the sea (Jnh 1:4-16). The disciples in supposing they saw a spirit when Jesus came walking upon the sea (Mt 14:26; Mk 6:49-50). Herod in imagining that John the Baptist had risen from the dead (Mk 6:14, 16).

The Gadarenes on account of Jesus casting demons out of the demoniac (Mt 8:34). The disciples who were frightened at the appearance of Peter (Ac 12:14-15). The Ephesians in their sorceries (Ac 19:13-19). The people of the island of Malta in imagining Paul to be a god (Ac 28:6).

See Idolatry; Sorcery.

SUPERSTITIOUS NIV "very religious" (Ac 17:22), could either commend or criticize the Athenians.

SUPH, SUPHAH [6069, 6071] (*reeds, rushes*). Used for these words (Nu 21:14; Dt 1:1). Suph is an unidentified region E of the Jordan; Suphah, is probably the region of the Red Sea.

SUPPER [1268, 1270]. *See Feasts; Eucharist.*

SUPPER, LORD'S *See Lord's Supper.*

SUPPLICATION [2858, 9382, 9384]. *See Prayer.*

SUPREME COMMANDER [9580]. Commander-in-chief of the Assyrian army (Isa 20:1; 2Ki 18:17).

SUR [6075]. The gate of the temple (2Ki 11:6).

SURETY *See Security, For Debt; Debt.*

SURFEITING Overindulgence of food or drink; dissipation (Lk 21:34).

SUSA [8809, 10704].

1. Capital of the Medo-Persian Empire (Est 1:2-3; 8:15).

2. King's palace at (Ne 1:1; Est 1:2, 5; 2:5, 8; 4:8, 16; 8:14-15; 9:11, 15).

SUSAH *See Hazar Susah.*

SUSANCHITES NIV "of Susa" (Ezr 4:9). *See Susa.*

SUSANNA [5052] (*lily*).

1. Woman who ministered to Christ (Lk 8:1-3).

2. Heroine of *The History of Susanna,* in the OT Apocrypha.

SUSI [6064] (*[my] horse*). A Manassite (Nu 13:11).

SUSIM *See Hazar Susah.*

SUSPICION [*7861, 5707*]. *See Accusation, False.*

SWADDLING BAND Bands of cloth in which a newborn baby was wrapped (Lk 2:7, 12). Used figuratively (Job 38:9).

SWALLOW [2000]. Builds its nest in the sanctuary (Ps 84:3). Chattering of, figurative of the mourning of the afflicted (Isa 38:14). Migration of (Jer 8:7).

SWAN *See White Owl.*

SWEARING [457, 606, 5951, 8652, 8678, *3923, 3991*]. *See Blasphemy; God, Name of; Oath.*

SWEAT [2399, *2629*]. (Ge 3:19). An offense in the sanctuary (Eze 44:18). Of blood (Lk 22:44).

SWEAT, BLOODY Physical manifestation of the agony of Jesus in Gethsemane (Lk 22:44). Christ's sweat most likely did not become bloody, but "his sweat was like great drops of blood falling to the ground" as if from an open wound.

SWEET INCENSE Made of spices (Ex 25:6). *See Incense.*

SWEET SAVOR *See Pleasing Aroma.*

SWELLING [1301, 7377, 7379, 8143, 8421, *4399*]. Usually "pride"; or means the flooding of the Jordan in the spring (Jer 12:5; 49:19; 50:44). It refers to the tumult of a stormy sea (Ps 46:3).

SWIFT [2590, 3616+3618, 4554, 4559, 6101, 7824, 7837, *3955, 5442*]. An amphibious bird (Isa 38:14; Jer 8:7).

SWINE *See Animals; Pig.*

SWORD, THE [2995, 4839, 7347, 8939, *3479, 4855*]. Probable origin of (Ge 3:24). Was pointed (Eze 21:15). Frequently had two edges (Ps 149:6).

Described as:

Sharp (Ps 57:4). Bright (Na 3:3). Glittering (Dt 32:41; Job 20:25). Oppressive (Jer 46:16). Hurtful (Ps 144:10). Carried in a sheath or scabbard (1Ch 21:27; Jer 47:6; Eze 21:3-5). Suspended from the belt (1Sa 17:39; 2Sa 20:8; Ne 4:18; Ps 45:3).

Was Used:

By the patriarchs (Ge 34:25; 48:22). By the Jews (Jdg 7:22; 2Sa 24:9). By heathen nations (Jdg 7:22; 1Sa 15:33). For self-defense (Lk 22:36). For destruction of enemies (Nu 21:24; Jos 6:21). For punishing criminals (1Sa 15:33; Ac 12:2). Sometimes for self-destruction (1Sa 31:4-5; Ac 16:27). Hebrews early acquainted with making of (1Sa 13:19). In time of war, plowshares made into (Joel 3:10). In time of peace, made into plowshares (Isa 2:4; Mic 4:3). Sharpened and furbished before going to war (Ps 7:12; Eze 21:9). Was brandished over the head (Eze 32:10). Was thrust through enemies (Eze 16:40). Often threatened as a punishment (Lev 26:25, 33; Dt 32:25). Often sent as a punishment (Ezr 9:7; Ps 78:62). Was one of God's four sore judgments (Eze 14:21). Those slain by, communicated ceremonial uncleanness (Nu 19:16).

Illustrative:

Of the Word of God (Eph 6:17, w Heb 4:12). Of the word of Christ (Isa 49:2, w Rev 1:16). Of the justice of God (Dt 32:41; Zec 13:7). Of the protection of God (Dt 33:29). Of war and contention (Mt 10:34). Of severe and heavy calamities (Eze 5:2, 17; 14:17; 21:9). Of deep mental affliction (Lk 2:35). Of the wicked (Ps 17:13). Of the tongue of the wicked (Ps 57:4; 64:3; Pr 12:18). Of persecuting spirit of the wicked (Ps 37:14). Of the end of the wicked (Pr 5:4). Of false witnesses (Pr 25:18). Of judicial authority (Ro 13:4). Drawing of illustrative of war and destruction (Lev 26:33; Eze 21:3-5). Putting into its sheath illustrative of peace and friendship (Jer 47:6). Living by illustrative of violence (Ge 27:40). Not departing from one's house illustrative of perpetual calamity (2Sa 12:10).

SYCAMINE NIV "mulberry tree" (Lk 17:6).

SYCAMORE-FIG [9204, 5191]. A tree. Abundant in the land of Canaan (1Ki 10:27; 2Ch 1:15; 9:27; Isa 9:10). Groves of, cared for (1Ch 27:28). Destroyed by frost (Ps 78:47). Care of (Am 7:14). Zacchaeus climbs into (Lk 19:4).

SYCHAR [5373]. A village one half mile N of Jacob's well, on the E slope of Mt. Ebal (Jn 4:5).

SYCHEM *See Shechem, 1.*

SYENE *See Aswan.*

SYMBOLS, AND SIMILITUDES [253, 2355, 3213, 4603, 5694, 531].

General

Almond tree branch (Jer 1:11). Altar split apart (1Ki 13:3, 5). Basket for measuring (Zec 5:6-11). Belt (Jer 13:1-7; Ac 21:11). Blood sprinkled (Ex 24:8). Book cast into Euphrates (Jer 51:63). Bow shot (2Ki 13:15-19). Bread (Mt 26:26; Mk 14:22; Lk 22:19). Breaking of clay jar (Jer 19). Change of residence (Eze 12:3-11). Childlike (Mt 18:3; Mk 10:14-15; Lk 18:16-17). Circumcision, of the covenant of Abraham (Ge 17:11; Ro 4:11). Cooking (Jer 1:13; Eze 4:9-15; 24:3-5). Curtain of the temple torn in two (Mt 27:51; Mk 15:38; Lk 23:45). Darkness (Ex 20:21; Lev 16:2; 1Ki 8:12; Ps 18:11; 97:2; Heb 12:18-

19). Death [without mourning] (Eze 24:16-19). Deeds of land (Jer 32:1-16). Eating food with anxiety (Eze 12:17-20). Figs [basket of good and bad] (Jer 24). Fish [Jonah in the] (Mt 16:4; Lk 11:29-30). Food (2Ki 19:29; Isa 37:30). Fruit [basket of] (Jer 24:1-3; Am 8:1-2).

Handwriting on the wall (Da 5:5-6, 16-28). Harvest (2Ki 19:29). Invitation by enemy to approach (1Sa 14:8-12). Isaiah's children (Isa 8:18). Manna [in the desert] (Jn 6:31-58). Marrying a prostitute (Hos 1:2-9; 3:1-4). Men meeting Saul (1Sa 10:2-7). Mosaic rites [system of] (Heb 9:9-10, 18-23). Mute (Eze 3:26-27; 24:27; 29:21; 33:22; Lk 1:20-22, 62-64). Nakedness (Isa 20:2-4). Passover [of the sparing of the firstborn] (Ex 12:3-28). Passover [atonement made by Christ] (1Co 5:7). Pillar of cloud (Ex 13:21-22; 14:19-20; 19:9, 16). Plumb line (Am 7:7-8). Posture [lie on side] (Eze 4:4-8). Pot for cooking (Eze 24:1-5). Praying toward the temple (1Ki 8:29; Da 6:10). Rainbow (Ge 9:12-13).

Sacrificial animals (Ge 15:8-11; Jn 1:29, 36). Salt [gracious words] (Col 4:6). Salt, Covenant of (Nu 18:19). Scroll flying (Zec 5:2-4). Shadow on Ahaz's stairway (2Ki 20:8-11; Isa 38:7-8). Shaving head and beard (Eze 5:1-4). Siege (Eze 4:1-3). Snake of bronze [lifted up, of Christ] (Nu 21:8-9; Jn 3:14). Spiritual rest [Canaan] (Heb 3:11-12; 4:5). Star in the east (Mt 2:2). Sticks and staffs (Eze 37:16-17; Zec 11:7, 10-11, 14). Striken rock [of Christ] (Ex 17:6; 1Co 10:4). Tabernacle and sanctuary (Ps 15:1; Eze 37:27; Heb 8:2, 5; 9:1-12, 23-24). Thunder and lightning on Mount Sinai (Ex 19:9, 16). Thunder and rain (1Sa 12:16-18). Trees of life and knowledge (Ge 2:9, 17; 3:3, 24; Rev 22:2). Unclean food [preparing of] (Eze 4:9-17). Vine (Eze 15:2; 19:10-14). Water [lapping of] (Jdg 7:4-8). Water to drink [drawing of in hospitality] (Ge 24:13-15, 42-44). Waving and ritual offering (Ex 29:24-28; Lev 8:27-29; 9:21). Wine (Jer 25:15-17; Mt 26:27; Mk 14:23; Lk 22:17). Wine [of the atoning blood] (Mt 26:27-29; Mk 14:23-25; Lk 22:17-18, 20). Wineskins (Jer 13:12; 19:1-2, 10). Wounding (1Ki 20:35-40). Yokes (Jer 27:2-3; 28:10).

Of the Holy Spirit:

Water (Jn 3:5; 7:38-39): cleansing by (Eze 16:9; 36:25; Eph 5:26; Heb 10:22), making prosperous (Ps 1:3; Isa 27:3, 6; 44:3-4; 58:11).

Fire (Mt 3:11): refining (Isa 4:4; Mal 3:2-3), guiding (Ex 13:21; Ps 78:14), searching (Zep 1:12, w 1Co 2:10). Flame shaped like tongues (Ac 2:3, 6, 11).

Wind (SS 4:16): incomprehensible (Jn 3:8; 1Co 2:11), powerful (1Ki 19:11, w Ac 2:2), quiet but present (Jn 3:8), reviving, life giving (Eze 37:9-10, 14).

Oil (Ps 45:7): healing (Isa 1:6; Lk 10:34; Rev 18:13), joy causing (Isa 61:3; Heb 1:9), illuminating (Zec 4:2-3, 11-13; Mt 25:3-4; 1Jn 2:20, 27), consecrating (Ex 29:7; 30:30; Isa 61:1).

Rain and dew (Ps 72:6): enriching and fertilizing (Eze 34:26-27; Hos 6:3; 10:12; 14:5), refreshing

(Ps 68:9; Isa 18:4), abundant (Ps 133:3), imperceptible (2Sa 17:12, w Mk 4:26-28).

Dove (Mt 3:16).

Voice (Isa 6:8): speaking (Mt 10:20), guiding (Isa 30:21, w Jn 16:13), warning (Heb 3:7-11).

Seal (Rev 7:2): impressing (Job 38:14, w 2Co 3:18), guarantee (Eph 1:13-14; 4:30; 2Co 1:22).

See Holy Spirit, Emblems of.

Washings, a symbol of purity. *See Washings; Purification.* For symbolisms of color, *See Colors, Figurative and Symbolic.*

See also, Allegory; Instruction, By Object Lessons; By Types; In Religion.

SYMEON *See Simeon.*

SYMPATHY [5653, 5714, 8171, *5217, 5218*]. (Ecc 7:2). Commanded (Ro 12:15; Jas 1:27; 1Pe 3:8). In Christ (Php 2:1-2).

Instances of:

David with Hanun (2Sa 10:2). The Jewish maid with Naaman (2Ki 5:1-4). Job's friends (Job 2:11-13), turned against Job (Job 6:14; 22:29). Ebed-Melech with Jeremiah (Jer 38:7-13). Nebuchadnezzar with Daniel (Da 6:18-23).

The four friends with the crippled man whom they took to Jesus (Mk 2:3-4). Others with the helpless whom they brought to Jesus (Mt 4:24). The good Samaritan with the man who fell among robbers (Lk 10:33-35). The Jews with Martha and Mary (Jn 11:19, 31, 33). The people of Malta with the shipwrecked mariners (Ac 28:1-2).

See Afflicted; Afflictions; Jesus the Christ, Compassion of; Kindness; Pity; Poor.

SYNAGOGUE [697, *801*, 5252] (*place of gathering*).

1. Primarily an assembly (Ac 13:43; Jas 2:2). Constitutes a court of justice (Lk 12:11; Ac 9:2). Had powers of criminal courts (Mt 10:17; Mt 23:34; Ac 22:19; 26:11), of ecclesiastical courts (Jn 9:22, 34; 12:42; 16:2).

2. Place of assembly. Scriptures read and expounded in (Ne 8:1-8; 9:3, 5; Mt 4:23; 9:35; 13:54; Mk 1:39; Lk 4:15-33; 13:10; Jn 18:20; Ac 9:20; 13:5-44; 14:1; 15:21; 17:2, 10; 18:4, 19, 26). In Jerusalem (Ac 6:9), Damascus (Ac 9:2, 20), other cities (Ac 14:1; 17:1, 10; 18:4). Built by Jairus (Lk 7:5), Jesus performed healing in (Mt 12:9-13; Lk 13:11-14). Alms given in (Mt 6:2).

Of Satan (Rev 2:9; 3:9).

See Church, Place of Worship; Testaments, Time Between.

SYNAGOGUE, MEN OF THE GREAT Or of the Great Assembly, a college of learned men supposedly organized by Nehemiah after the return from exile (Ne 8-10), to which Jewish tradition attributed the origination and authoritative promulgation of many ordinances and regulations.

SYNOPTIC GOSPELS, THE

A careful comparison of the four Gospels reveals that Matthew, Mark, and Luke are noticeably similar, while John is quite different. The first three Gospels agree extensively in language, in the material they include, and in the order in which events and sayings from the life of Christ are recorded. (Chronological order does not appear to have been rigidly followed in any of the Gospels, however.) Because of this agreement, these three books are called the Synoptic Gospels (*syn,* "together with"; *optic,* "seeing"; thus "seeing together"). For an example of agreement in content see Mt 9:2-8; Mk 2:3-12; Lk 5:18-26. An instance of verbatim agreement is found in Mt 10:22a; Mk 13:13a; Lk 21:17. A mathematical comparison shows that 91 percent of Mark's Gospel is contained in Matthew, while 53 percent of Mark is found in Luke. Such agreement raises questions as to the origin of the Synoptic Gospels. Did the authors rely on a common source? Were they interdependent? Questions such as these constitute what is known as the Synoptic Problem. Several suggested solutions have been advanced:

1. *The use of oral tradition.* Some have thought that tradition had become so stereotyped that it provided a common source from which all the Gospel writers drew.

2. *The use of an early Gospel.* Some have postulated that the Synoptic authors all had access to an earlier Gospel, now lost.

3. *The use of written fragments.* Some have assumed that written fragments had been composed concerning various events from the life of Christ and that these were used by the Synoptic authors.

4. *Mutual dependence.* Some have suggested that the Synoptic writers drew from each other with the result that what they wrote was often very similar.

5. *The use of two major sources.* The most common view currently is that the Gospel of Mark and a hypothetical document, called *Quelle* (German for "source") or *Q,* were used by Matthew and Luke as sources for most of the materials included in their Gospels.

6. *The priority and use of Matthew.* Another view suggests that the other two Synoptics drew from Matthew as their main source.

7. *A combination of most of the above.* This theory assumes that the authors of the Synoptic Gospels made use of oral tradition, written fragments, mutual dependence on other Synoptic writers or on their Gospels, and the testimony of eyewitnesses.

SYNTYCHE [*5345*] (*coincidence, success*). Christian woman at Philippi (Php 4:2).

SYRACUSE [*5352*]. A city of Sicily. Paul visits (Ac 28:12).

SYRIA [*5353*]. Highlands lying between the Euphrates river and the Mediterranean Sea. Called Aram, from the son of Shem (Ge 10:22-23; Nu 23:7; 1Ch 1:17; 2:23). In the time of Abraham it seems to have embraced the region between the

rivers Tigris and Euphrates (Ge 24:10, w 25:20), including Paddan Aram (Ge 25:20, ftn; 28:5).

Minor kingdoms within the region: Aram Zobah, also called Zobah (1Sa 14:47; 2Sa 8:3; 10:6, 8; 1Ki 11:23; 1Ch 18:5, 9; 19:6; Ps 60, title), Geshur (2Sa 15:8), Aram Rehob, also called Beth Rehob (2Sa 10:6, 8), Damascus (2Sa 8:5-6; 1Ch 18:5-6), Hamath (2Sa 8:9-10).

Conquest of: By David (2Sa 8:3-13), by Jeroboam (2Ki 14:25, 28), by Tiglath-Pileser, king of Assyria (2Ki 16:7-9; 18:33-34). People of, colonized in Samaria by the king of Assyria (2Ki 17:24). Confederate with Nebuchadnezzar (2Ki 24:2; Jer 39:5).

The Roman province of, included the land of Canaan (Lk 2:2-3), and Phoenicia (Mk 7:26; Ac 21:3). The fame of Jesus extended over (Mt 4:24).

Paul goes to, with letters to apprehend the Christians; is converted and begins his evangelistic ministry (Ac 9:1-31). *See Paul.*

Paul preaches in (Ac 15:41; 18:18; 21:3; Gal 1:21). Damascus, the capital of. *See Damascus.*

Wars between, and the kingdoms of Judah and Israel. *See Israel.* Prophecies concerning (Isa 7:8-16; 8:4-7; 17:1-3; Jer 1:15; 49:23-27; Am 1:3-5; Zec 9:1).

SYRIAC *See Aramaic.*

SYRIAC VERSIONS *See Texts and Versions.*

SYRIA-MAACHAH *See Aram Maacah.*

SYRIAN [5354]. The people of Syria (Lk 4:27). *See Aram, 6; Aramaic; Syria.*

SYRIAN PHOENICIAN [5355]. The nationality of a woman whose daughter was cured by Jesus (Mt 15:21-28; Mk 7:24-30).

SYRTIS [5358]. Banks of quicksand off the coast of Libya (Ac 27:17).

TAANACH [9505]. A city conquered by Joshua (Jos 12:21). Allotted to Manasseh (Jos 17:11; 1Ch 7:29). Canaanites not driven from (Jos 17:12; Jdg 1:27). Assigned to the Levites (Jos 21:25). The scene of Barak's victory (Jdg 5:19). One of Solomon's district governors at (1Ki 4:12).

TAANATH SHILOH [9304] (possibly *approach to Shiloh* IDB). Town on the NE border of Ephraim (Jos 16:6), c. ten miles E of Shechem.

TABALIAH [3189] (*Yahweh has dipped*). The son of Hosah (1Ch 26:11).

TABBAOTH [3191] (*[ornamental or signet] ring*). A family of temple servants who returned with Zerubbabel (Ezr 2:43; Ne 7:46).

TABBATH [3195] (possibly *good*). A place probably E of the Jordan between Jabesh Gilead and Succoth (Jdg 7:22).

TABEAL *See Tabeel, 2.*

TABEEL [3174, 3175] (*God [El] is good*).
1. A Persian official in Samaria (Ezr 4:7).
2. The father of one whom the kings of Syria and Israel sought to make king in Judah instead of Ahaz (Isa 7:6).

TABERAH [9323] (*burning*). An encampment of Israel in the wilderness where fire of the Lord consumed some complainers (Nu 11:1-3; Dt 9:22), the site is unidentified.

TABERNACLE [185, 5438, 6109, *5008, 5009*]. One existed before Moses received the pattern authorized on Mount Sinai (Ex 33:7-11). The one instituted by Moses was called Sanctuary (Ex 25:8), Tent of Meeting (Ex 27:21; 33:7; 2Ch 5:5), Tabernacle of the Testimony (Ex 38:21; Nu 1:50), Tent of the Testimony (Nu 17:7-8; 2Ch 24:6), Temple of the Lord (1Sa 1:9; 3:3), House of the Lord (Jos 6:24).

The pattern of, revealed to Moses (Ex 25:9; 26:30; 39:32, 42-43; Ac 7:44; Heb 8:5). Materials for, voluntarily offered (Ex 25:1-8; 35:4-29; 36:3-7). Value of the substance contributed for (Ex 38:24-31). Workmen who constructed it were inspired (Ex 31:1-11; 35:30-35).

Description of: Frame (Ex 26:15-37; 36:20-38). Outer covering (Ex 25:5; 26:7-14; 36:14-19). Second covering (Ex 25:5; 26:14; 35:7, 23; 36:19; 39:34). Curtains of (Ex 26:1-14, 31-37; 27:9-16; 35:15, 17; 36:8-19, 35, 37). Court of (Ex 27:9-17; 38:9-16, 18; 40:8, 33).

Holy Place (Ex 26:31-37; 40:22-26; Heb 9:2-6, 8). The Most Holy Place (Ex 26:33-35; 40:20-21; Heb 9:3-5, 7-8).

Furniture of (Ex 25:10-40; 27:1-8, 19; 37; 38:1-

8). *See Altar; Ark; Atonement Cover; Bread, Consecrated; Lampstand; Cherubim.*

Completed (Ex 39:32). Dedicated (Nu 7). Sanctified (Ex 29:43; 40:9-16; Nu 7:1). Anointed with holy oil (Ex 30:25-26; Lev 8:10; Nu 7:1). Sprinkled with blood (Lev 16:15-20; Heb 9:21, 23). Filled with the cloud of glory (Ex 40:34-38).

How prepared for removal during the travels of the Israelites (Nu 1:51; 4:5-15). How and by whom carried (Nu 4:5-33; 7:6-9). Strangers forbidden to enter (Nu 1:51). Duties of the Levites concerning. *See Levites.* Defilement of, punished (Lev 15:31; Nu 19:13, 20; Eze 5:11; 23:38). Duties of the priests in relation to. *See Priest.* Israelites worship at (Nu 10:3; 16:19, 42-43; 20:6; 25:6; 1Sa 2:22; Ps 27:4). Offerings brought to (Lev 17:4; Nu 31:54; Dt 12:5-6, 11-14).

Tribes encamped around, while in the wilderness (Nu 2). All males required to appear before, three times each year (Ex 23:17). Tabernacle tax (Ex 20:11-16).

Carried in front of the Israelites in the line of march (Nu 10:33-36; Jos 3:3-6). The Lord reveals himself at (Lev 1:1; Nu 1:1; 7:89; 12:4-10; Dt 31:14-15).

Pitched at Gilgal (Jos 4:18-19), at Shiloh (Jos 18:1; 19:51; Jdg 18:31; 20:18, 26-27; 21:19; 1Sa 2:14; 4:3-4; Jer 7:12, 14), at Nob (1Sa 21:1-6), at Gibeon (1Ch 21:29). Renewed by David and pitched on Mount Zion (1Ch 15:1; 16:1-2; 2Ch 1:4). Solomon offers sacrifice (2Ch 1:3-6). Brought to the temple by Solomon (2Ch 5:5, w 1Ki 8:1, 4-5).

Symbol of spiritual things (Ps 15:1; Heb 8:2, 5; 9:1-12, 24).

See Levites; Priest; Temple.

TABERNACLES, FEAST OF

[6109, *5009*]. Also called the Feast of Ingathering. Instituted (Ex 23:16; 34:22; Lev 23:34-43; Nu 29:12-40; Dt 16:13-16). Design of (Lev 23:42-43). The law read in connection with, every seventh year (Dt 31:10-12; Ne 8:18). Observance of, after the captivity (Ezr 3:4; Ne 8:14-18), by Jesus (Jn 7:2, 14). Observance of, omitted (Ne 8:17). Penalty for not observing (Zec 14:16-19).

Jeroboam institutes an idolatrous feast to correspond to, in the eighth month (1Ki 12:32-33; 1Ch 27:11).

TABITHA [*5412*] (*gazelle*). A Christian woman in Joppa; befriended poor widows; raised from dead by Peter (Ac 9:36-43).

TABLE [2200, 4990, 5121, 5492, 8947, *367, 369, 404, 2879, 2884, 4752, 5263, 5544*].
1. Table for food (Jdg 1:7; 1Ki 2:7).
2. Lord's table = Lord's Supper (1Co 10:21).

3. "Wait on tables" (Ac 6:2) refers to distribution of food, etc., to the Christian poor.

4. Tabernacle and temple were provided with various tables (Ex 25:23-30).

TABLE OF CONSECRATED BREAD
Twelve loaves of consecrated, unleavened bread were placed on a table in the Holy Place in the tabernacle and temple (Ex 25:30; Lev 24:5-9).

TABLET [4246, 4283, *4400, 4419*]
1. Stone or clay tablets for writing (Ex 24:12; Eze 4:1; Lk 1:63). Metaphorical (2Co 3:3). *See Tablets of the Law.*
2. *See Dress.*

TABLETS OF THE LAW
Stone tablets on which Moses wrote the Ten Commandments (Ex 31:18; 32:15-16; Dt 4:13; 5:22). *See Commandments and Statutes, Of God.*

TABOR [9314].
1. A mountain on the border of Issachar (Jos 19:22; Jdg 8:18; Ps 89:12; Jer 46:18; Hos 5:1). Assembling place of Barak's army (Jdg 4:6, 12, 14).
2. A plain located by the great tree of Tabor (1Sa 10:3).
3. A Levitical city in Zebulun (1Ch 6:77). *See Kisloth Tabor.*

TABRET *See Tambourine.*

TABRIMMON [3193] (*[pagan god] Rimmon is good*).
The father of Ben-Hadad, king of Syria (1Ki 15:18).

TACHE *See Clasp.*

TACHMONITE *See Tahkemonite.*

TACKLE [*5006*].
The masts and rigging of a ship (Isa 33:23; Ac 27:19).

TACT [10302].
(Pr 15:1; 25:15). In preaching (1Co 9:19-22; 2Co 12:6). Of Gideon (Jdg 8:1-3). Of Saul, in managing malcontents (1Sa 10:27; 11:7, 12-15). Nabal's wife (1Sa 25:18-37). In David's popular methods: In mourning for Abner (2Sa 3:28-37), in organizing the temple music (1Ch 15:16-24), in securing popular consent to bringing the ark to Jerusalem (1Ch 13:1-4). Mephibosheth (2Sa 9:8). Joab's trick in obtaining David's consent to the return of Absalom (2Sa 14:1-22). The woman of Tekoa (2Sa 14:4-20). The wise woman of Abel (2Sa 20:16-22). Solomon, in arbitrating between the harlots (1Ki 3:24-28), Mordecai, in concealing Esther's nationality (Est 2:10). Esther, in placating the king (Est 5-7). Paul, in circumcising Timothy (Ac 16:3), in turning the preaching of adversaries to account (Php 1:10-22), in stimulating benevolent giving (2Co 8:1-8; 9:1-5), in arraying the two religious factions of the Jews against each other when he was in trouble (Ac 23:6-10). The town clerk of Ephesus (Ac 19:35-41). The church council at Jerusalem (Ac 21:20-25).
See Wisdom.

TACTICS *See Armies; Strategy.*

TADMOR [9330] (*palm tree*).
A city in the desert NE of Damascus (1Ki 9:18; 2Ch 8:4), a fabulously rich trade metropolis later called Palmyra. Magnificent ruins have been excavated.

TAHAN, TAHANITE [9380, 9385] (*possibly grace, favor*).
1. The son of Ephraim and his clan (Nu 26:35).
2. A descendant of Ephraim (1Ch 7:25).

TAHAPANES *See Tahpanhes.*

TAHASH [9392] (*a species of dolphin*).
The son of Nahor and Reumah (Ge 22:24).

TAHATH [9394, 9395] (*compensation*).
1. Camping place of the Israelites (Nu 33:26-27).
2. A Kohathite (1Ch 6:24, 37).
3. The name of two Ephraimites (1Ch 7:20).

TAHKEMONITE [9376].
The family of David's chief captain (2Sa 23:8); also spelled Hacmonite (1Ch 11:11).

TAHPANHES [9387] (*the fortress of Penhase [the Black Man]*).
A fortress city at the E edge of the Nile Delta to which Israelites fled after the fall of Jerusalem (Jer 2:16; 43:7-9; 44:1; 46:14; Eze 30:18).

TAHPENES [9388] (title *wife of the king*).
A queen of Egypt (1Ki 11:19-20).

TAHREA [9390] (possibly *clever one* BDB).
The grandson of Mephibosheth (1Ch 9:41), also spelled Tarea (1Ch 8:35).

TAHTIM HODSHI [9398].
A place E of Jordan in the land of the Hittites (2Sa 24:6).

TAILORING (Ex 31:2-3, 6, 10; 39:1).

TALEBEARER (*The vice of repeating damaging reports, either true or false*). (Ps 15:1-3; Pr 11:13; 20:19).
Separates friends (Pr 16:28; 17:9). Causes strife (Pr 26:20), tension (Pr 18:8).
Is forbidden (Lev 19:16; 1Ti 5:11, 13).
See Busybody; Gossip; Slander; Speaking, Evil.
Instances of: Joseph (Ge 37:2). Israelites (2Sa 3:23). Tobiah (Ne 6).
See Backbiting; Slander.

TALENT [3971, 10352, *5419*].
A weight equal to sixty minas or about seventy-five pounds (1Ki 9:14, 28; 10:10, 14; Ex 25:39; 38:27). Parables of the (Mt 18:23-34; 25:15-30). *See Measure.*

TALES [*1212*].
Avoid myths and old wives' tales (1Ti 4:7). *See Myths.*

TALITHA KOUM [*3182+5420*]. Aramaic for "Little girl, get up!" (Mk 5:41).

TALKING [*606, 1819, 6218, 7023, 8557, 515, 1368, 3281, 3306, 3364, 3917, 5196*]. With God. *See Communion.*

TALMAI [9440] (possibly *[my] furrow maker*).
   1. A son of Anak (Nu 13:22; Jos 15:14; Jdg 1:10).
   2. King of Geshur (2Sa 3:3; 13:37; 1Ch 3:2).

TALMON [3236] (perhaps *brightness*). A gatekeeper of the temple (1Ch 9:17). Family of, returned from captivity with Zerubbabel (Ezr 2:42; Ne 7:45; 11:19; 12:25).

TALMUD (*education, instruction*). A collection of Jewish tradition of the early Christian centuries; The two forms: Palestinian and Babylonian.

TAMAH *See Temah.*

TAMAR [9470, 9471, 2500] (*date palm*).
   1. The wife of Er, then of Onan; mother of Perez and Zerah (Ge 38; Mt 1:3).
   2. Daughter of David; abused by his half brother Amon (2Sa 13:1-33).
   3. The daughter of Absalom (2Sa 14:27).
   4. Unidentified borderland site in restored Israel (Eze 47:19; 48:28).
   5. A city in Syria, more commonly known as Tadmor, later Palmyra.

TAMARISK [869]. A tree (1Sa 22:6; 31:13), planted by Abraham (Ge 21:33). *See Tree.*

TAMBOURINE [9512, 9528]. Used by Miriam (Ex 15:20), by Jephthah's daughter (Jdg 11:34). Used in religious service (2Sa 6:5; 1Ch 13:8; Ps 68:25; 81:2; 149:3; 150:4). Used in dances (Job 21:12). *See Music, Instruments of.*

TAMIR *See Tadmor.*

TAMMUZ [9452].
   1. Month four in sacred sequence, month ten in civil sequence. Not mentioned by name in the Bible. Ezekiel called in the fourth month (Eze 1:1); Nebuchadnezzar breaks through the wall of Jerusalem (Jer 39:1). The time for tending vines (June-July). *See Month, 4.*
   2. The fertility god worshiped in Mesopotamia, Syria, and Israel; corresponded to Osiris in Egypt and Adonis of the Greeks (Eze 8:14).

TANACH *See Taanach.*

TANHUMETH [9489] (*comfort*). The father of Seraiah (2Ki 25:23; Jer 40:8).

TANIS *See Zoar.*

TANNER, TANNING [*1114*]. Tanning is the conversion of skin into leather by removing the hair and soaking it in tanning solution (Ex 25:5; 26:14; Ac 10:6).

TANTALIZING NIV "provoking" (1Sa 1:6-7); "taunt" (1Ki 18:27).

TAPESTRY [763]. (Pr 7:16; 31:22). Of the tabernacle (Ex 26:1-14, 31-37; 27:9-17; 36:8-18). Gold thread woven in (Ex 39:3). In palaces (Est 1:6; SS 1:5). In groves (2Ki 23:7). *See Curtains; Embroidery; Veil.*

TAPHATH [3264] (possibly *little child*). The daughter of Solomon (1Ki 4:11).

TAPPUAH [9516, 9517] (*apple*).
   1. A city of Judah (Jos 12:17; 15:34).
   2. A city in Ephraim (Jos 16:8; 17:8).
   3. A city near Tirzah in Samaria (2Ki 15:16); a variant reading for Tiphsah. *See Tiphsah, 2.*
   4. The son of Hebron (1Ch 2:43).

TAR [2819]. A flammable substance, asphalt (Ge 14:10). Lumps of asphalt are often seen even today floating in the southern end of the Dead Sea. Used as mortar in building the Tower of Babel (Ge 11:3), and in setting the burnt brick which formed the outer layers of the ziggurat of Ur. It was used by Moses' mother to caulk the papyrus basket (Ex 2:3), as for the rafts and reed boats on the Euphrates.
   See Caulkers; Pitch.

TARAH *See Terah, 2.*

TARALAH [9550]. A city of Benjamin between Irpeel and Zelah (Jos 18:28).

TAREA [9308]. A son of Micah (1Ch 8:35). Called Tahrea (1Ch 9:41).

TARES *See Weeds, 2.*

TARGET [4766, 5133]. A defensive article of armor. Made of bronze (1Sa 17:6), of gold (1Ki 10:16; 2Ch 9:15). Used by spearmen (2Ch 14:8). *See Shield.*

TARIFF *See Duty, 1.*

TARPELITES *See Tripolis.*

TARSHISH [9576, 9578] (possibly *[precious stone] yellow jasper* BDB; possibly *greedy one* IDB; *foundry, refinery* KB).
   1. The son of Javan (Ge 10:4).
   2. A place in the W Mediterranean, perhaps in Spain or Tunisia (2Ch 9:21; 20:36-37; Ps 72:10; Jn 1:3).
   3. "Ships of Tarshish"; large, seagoing trade ships (1Ki 9:26; 10:22; 22:48; 2Ch 9:21).
   4. Great-grandson of Benjamin (1Ch 7:10).
   5. Persian prince (Est 1:14).

TARSUS [5432, 5433]. Capital of Cilicia, in Asia Minor. Paul's birthplace (Ac 9:11; 21:39; 22:3). Paul sent to, from Jerusalem, to avoid assassination (Ac 9:30). Paul brought from, by Barnabas (Ac 11:25-26).

TARTAK [9581]. A god worshiped by Avvites, colonists in Samaria (2Ki 17:31).

TARTAN *See Supreme Commander.*

TASKMASTER One who burdens another with labor: overseer (Ex 1:11; 3:7; 5:6, 10, 13).

TASSEL(S) [1544, 7492, *3192*]. Prescribed for garments worn by the Israelites, to remember God's commands (Nu 15:38-41; Dt 22:12). Made long by the Pharisees (Mt 23:5).

TASTE [430, 2118, 2674, 3247, 3248, 5352, 6853, 7023, *1174*]. The sense of, lost (2Sa 19:35). Figurative (Job 27:2; Ps 34:8; 119:103; Heb 6:4-5; 1Pe 2:3); taste death (Mt 16:28; Mk 9:1; Lk 9:27; Jn 8:52; Heb 2:9). *See Savor; Savory Meat.*

TATTENAI [10779]. The Persian governor ordered to assist the Jews in rebuilding the temple (Ezr 5:3, 6; 6:6, 13).

TATTLER *See Gossip; Talebearer.*

TATTOO [7882]. Pagan custom; forbidden (Lev 19:28). *See Mark.*

TAVERNS, THREE A place, c. thirty-three miles SE of Rome where Paul met Roman Christians (Ac 28:15).

TAX [4501, 5368, 5601, 6885, 10402, *803, 3056, 3284, 5467, 5468*]. Census (Ex 30:11-16; 38:26; Ne 10:32; Lk 2:1). Jesus pays (Mt 17:24-27).

Land (Ge 41:34, 48; 2Ki 23:35). Land mortgaged for (Ne 5:3-4). Priests exempted from (Ge 47:26; Ezr 7:24). Paid in grain (Am 5:11; 7:1), in provisions (1Ki 4:7-28).

Personal (1Ki 9:15; 2Ki 15:19-20; 23:35). Resisted by Israelites (1Ki 12:18; 2Ch 10:18). Worldwide, levied by Caesar.

Collectors of *See Tax Collectors.*

TAX COLLECTORS [5601, *803, 3284, 5467*]. Disreputable (Isa 33:18; Da 11:20; Mt 5:46-47; 9:11; 11:19; 18:17; 21:31; Lk 18:11). Repent under the preaching of John the Baptist (Mt 21:32; Lk 3:12; 7:29). Matthew, the collector of Capernaum, becomes an apostle (Mt 9:9; 10:3; Mk 2:14; Lk 5:27). Parable concerning (Lk 18:9-14). Zacchaeus, chief among, receives Jesus into his house (Lk 19:2-10).

TEACHERS [1067, 4340, 4621, 6221, 7738, 10516, *1208, 1437, 2762, 3791, 6015*]. Samuel, head of school of the prophets (1Sa 19:20). Elisha, head of, at Gilgal (2Ki 4:38).

Itinerant (2Ch 17:7-9). Of public assemblies (Ne 8:1-8, 13, 18). Should receive compensation (Gal 6:6).

See Instruction; Jesus, Teacher; Minister, Duties of.

False:
Admonition against (Dt 13:1-3; Mt 5:19; 7:15; 15:2-20; 23:2-33; Lk 11:38-52).
See Heresy; Minister, False and Corrupt.

TEACHING *See Instruction; Minister, Duties of.*

TEAR *See Rending.*

TEARS [1140, 1940, 1965, 4784, *1232, 3081*]. (Ps 6:6; 39:12; 42:3). Wash Jesus' feet (Lk 7:38, 44). Observed by God (Ps 56:8; Isa 38:3-5). Wiped away (Rev 7:17). None in heaven (Rev 21:4). Figurative (Ps 80:5).

TEBAH [3182, 3183, 3187] (possibly *one born at the time or place of slaughtering* KB IDB).
1. The son of Nahor (Ge 22:24).
2. A city of Zobah, E of Anti-Lebanon Mountains (1Ch 18:7-9, ftn); a city belonging to Hadadezer, Hebrew Betah (2Sa 8:8, ftn).

TEBALIAH *See Tabaliah.*

TEBETH [3194]. Month ten in sacred sequence, month four in civil sequence (December-January). Esther taken to King Xerxes (Est 2:16). *See Month, 10.*

TECHNICALITIES Legal (Mt 12:2, 10; Lk 6:2, 7).

TEETH [7092, 9094, 10730, *3848*]. (Pr 10:26). Gnashing of (Ps 112:10; La 2:16; Mt 8:12; 13:42, 50; 22:13; 24:51; 25:30; Mk 9:18; Lk 13:28).

TEHAPHNEHES *See Tahpanhes.*

TEHINNAH [9383] (*supplication for favor*). The son of Eshton (1Ch 4:12).

TEIL TREE *See Terebinth.*

TEKEL [10770]. Weighed (Da 5:25, 27).

TEKOA, TEKOITE [9541, 9542].
1. The son of Ashhur (1Ch 2:24; 4:5). Some authorities interpret these passages to mean that Ashhur colonized the town of Tekoa.
2. A city in Judah (2Ch 11:6). Home of the woman who interceded for Absalom (2Sa 14:2, 4, 9). Rebuilt by Rehoboam (2Ch 11:6). Desert of (2Ch 20:20). People of, work on the new wall of Jerusalem (Ne 3:5, 27). Prophecy concerning (Jer 6:1). Home of Amos (Am 1:1).

TEKOAH *See Tekoa, 2.*

TEL A mound or hill that marks the site of an ancient city. Composed of accumulated debris, usually covering a number of archaeological or historical periods and showing numerous building levels or strata (Dt 13:16; Jer 30:18). In the following four place names.

TEL ABIB [9425] (*mound of barley* ISBE; Akkadian *mound of storm tide* KB; *mound of flood* IDB). A place on the Kebar River where Ezekiel lived (Eze 3:15).

TEL ASSAR [9431] (*ruined city mound of Assar*). A city or district conquered by the Assyrians (2Ki 19:12; Isa 37:12).

TEL HARSHA [9426] (*the ruined city mound of the deaf mute*). A place in Babylonia (Ezr 2:59; Ne 7:61).

TEL MELAH [9427] (*ruined city and mound of salt*). Babylonian town, probably not far N of Persian Gulf (Ezr 2:59; Ne 7:61).

TELAH [9436] (*fissure, split, fracture*). The son of Rephah (1Ch 7:25).

TELAIM [3230] (*lambs*). The place where Saul mustered an army against Amalek (1Sa 15:4), may be the same as Telem in Judah (Jos 15:24).

TELEM [3234, 3235] (*brightness*).
1. A city of Judah (Jos 15:24).
2. A gatekeeper who put away his Gentile wife (Ezr 10:24).

TELL EL AMARNA *See Amarna, Tell El; Ras Shamra.*

TEMA [824+9401, 9401] (*on the right side, hence south country*).
1. The son of Ishmael (Ge 25:15; 1Ch 1:30).
2. A people of Arabia, probably descended from Tema, Ishmael's son (Job 6:19; Isa 21:14; Jer 25:23).

TEMAH [9457]. One of the temple servants (Ezr 2:53; Ne 7:55).

TEMAN [9403] (*on the right side*, hence *south country*).
1. The grandson of Esau (Ge 36:11).
2. Edomite chief (Ge 36:42).
3. A city in NE Edom (Jer 49:7).

TEMANI, TEMANITE(S) [9404] (*on the right side, southern*). Inhabitant of Teman (Ge 36:34). Of Eliphaz, one of Job's friends (Job 2:11; 4:1).

TEMENI [9405] (*one from the right*, hence *southerner*). The son of Ashhur (1Ch 4:6).

TEMPER [3013, 8120]. *See Anger; Malice; Self-Control.*

TEMPERANCE (Php 4:5; Tit 1:8; 2Pe 1:6). In eating (Pr 23:1-3; 25:16). In the use of wine (1Ti 3:8; Tit 2:3).

Commanded (Ro 13:14; 1Th 5:6-8; 1Ti 3:2; Tit 2:2-3, 12; 2Pe 1:5-6).

Practiced: By athletes (1Co 9:25, 27). By Daniel (Da 1:8, 12-16).

See Abstinence; Drunkenness; Self-Control; Wine.

TEMPLE [395, 924, 1074, 2121, 5219, 5987, 7731, 8377, 10103, 10206, 10497, *1126*, *1627*, *2639*, *2641*, *2644*, *2645*, *3301*, *3724*, *3753*, *5130*, *5677*].

Solomon's:

Described—
Also called Father's House (Jn 2:16). Glorious Temple (Isa 60:7). Holy Mountain (Isa 27:13). Holy and Glorious Temple (Isa 64:11). Holy Temple (Ps 79:1; 1Ch 29:3). House of Prayer (Isa 56:7; Mt 21:13). House of God (1Ch 29:2). House of the God of Jacob (Isa 2:3). House of the Lord (Jer 28:5). Mountain of the Lord's Temple (Isa 2:2). Palatial structure (1Ch 29:1, 19). Sanctuary (2Ch 20:8; 2Ch 36:17). Temple of the Lord (2Ki 11:10; 2Ch 23:9). Temple for Sacrifice (2Ch 7:12). Tent of the Testimony (2Ch 24:6). Zion (Ps 20:2; 48:12; 74:2; 87:2; Isa 2:3).

Greatness of (2Ch 2:5-6). Beauty of (Isa 64:11). Holiness of (1Ki 8:10; 9:3; La 1:10; Mt 23:17; Jn 2:14-16).

History—
David undertakes the building of (2Sa 7:2-3; 1Ch 22:7; 28:2; Ps 132:2-5; Ac 7:46), forbidden of God because he was a warrior (2Sa 7:4-12; 1Ki 5:3; 1Ch 22:8; 28:3). Not asked for by God (2Sa 7:7). The building of, committed to Solomon (2Sa 7:13). David makes preparations of (1Ch 22; 28:14-18; 29:1-5; 2Ch 3:1; 5:1).

Solomon builds (Ac 7:47; 2Sa 7:13). Solomon conscripts laborers for the building of (1Ki 5:13-16; 2Ch 2:2, 17-18). Materials for, furnished by Hiram (1Ki 5:8-18). Pattern and building of (1Ki 6; 7:13-51; 1Ch 28:11-19; 2Ch 3; 4; Ac 7:47). Time when begun (1Ki 6:1, 37; 2Ch 3:2), finished (1Ki 6:38). Site of (1Ch 21:28-30; 22:1; 2Ch 3:1), where Abraham offered Isaac (Ge 22:2, 4).

Materials prepared for (1Ki 5:17-18). No tools used on temple site (1Ki 6:7). Foundations of (1Ki 5:17-18; Lk 21:5).

Destroyed by Nebuchadnezzar, and the valuable contents carried to Babylon (Jer 24:13; 25:9-17; 2Ch 36:7, 19; Ps 79:1; Isa 64:11; Jer 27:16, 19-22; 28:3; 52:13, 17-23; La 2:7; 4:1; Ezr 1:7). Vessels of, used by Belshazzar (Da 5:2-3). Destruction of, foretold (Isa 66:6; Jer 27:18-22; Eze 7:22, 25; Mt 24:2; Mk 13:2).

Restoration of, ordered by Cyrus (Ezr 1:7-11).

Areas and Furnishings of—
Inner Sanctuary (1Ki 6:19-20; 8:6). Called the Most Holy Place (2Ch 3:8), innermost room (1Ki 6:27).

Most Holy Place: Description of (1Ki 6:16, 19-35; 2Ch 3:8-14; 4:22). Contents of the Most Holy Place: Ark (1Ki 6:19; 8:6; 2Ch 5:2-10), cherubim (1Ki 6:23-28; 2Ch 3:10-13; 5:7-8). Called Holy Place (1Ki 8:8, 10), the main hall (2Ch 3:5).

Description of (1Ki 6:15-18; 2Ch 3:3, 5-7, 14-17). *See Ark; Atonement Cover; Cherubim; Curtains; Veil.*

Holy Place (1Ki 8:8, 10). Contents of the holy place: The Golden table of the Bread of Presence (1Ki 7:48; 2Ch 29:18). *See Bread, Consecrated.* Other tables of gold and silver (1Ch 28:16; 2Ch 4:18-19). Lampstands and their utensils (1Ki 7:49-50; 1Ch 28:15; 2Ch 4:7, 20-22). *See Lampstand.* Altar of incense and its furniture (1Ki 6:20; 7:48, 50; 1Ch 28:17-18; 2Ch 4:19, 22). *See Altar of Incense.*

Porch of, called Porch of the Lord (2Ch 15:8). Dimensions of (1Ki 6:3; 2Ch 3:4). Doors of (2Ch 29:7). Overlaid with gold (2Ch 3:4). Pillars of (1Ki 7:15-22; 2Ki 11:14; 23:3; 25:17; 2Ch 3:15-17; 4:12-13).

Structure around (1Ki 6:5-10; 2Ki 11:2-3). Offerings brought to (Ne 10:37-39). Treasuries in. *See Treasure.*

Courts of: Of the priests (2Ch 4:9), inner (1Ki 6:36), surrounded by rows of stones and cedar beams (1Ki 6:36; 7:12). Contents of the courts: Altar of burnt offering (2Ch 15:8). *See Altar.* The Sea of cast metal (1Ki 7:23-37, 44, 46; 2Ch 4:2-5, 10), ten basins (1Ki 7:38-46; 2Ch 4:6). Large court of (2Ch 4:9; Jer 19:14; 26:2).

Sabbath canopy and royal entryway (2Ki 16:18).

Gates of: Upper Gate (2Ki 15:35). New Gate (Jer 26:10; 36:10). Gate facing east (Eze 46:1, 12).

Gifts received at (2Ch 24:8-11).

Uses of—

A dwelling place of the Lord (1Ki 8:10-11, 13; 9:3; 2Ki 21:7; 1Ch 29:1; 2Ch 5:13-14; 7:1-3, 16; Eze 10:3-4; Mic 1:2), to contain the ark of the covenant (1Ki 8:21), for the offering of fragrant incense (2Ch 2:4), for the regular offering of consecrated bread and the burnt offerings (2Ch 2:4), for prayer and worship (1Ki 8; 2Ki 19:14-15; 2Ch 30:27; Isa 27:13; 56:7; Jer 7:2; 26:2; Eze 46:2-3, 9; Zec 7:2-3; 8:21-22; Mk 11:17; Lk 1:10; 2:37; 18:10; Ac 3:1; 22:17), prayer made toward (1Ki 8:38; Da 6:10; Jnh 2:4), for weapon storage (2Ki 11:10; 2Ch 23:9-10), for refuge (2Ki 11:15; Ne 6:10-11).

Facts About—

Dedication of (1Ki 8; 2Ch 5-7), services in, organized by David (1Ch 15:16; 23:24). Sacking and pillaging by Shishak (1Ki 14:25-26), by Jehoash, king of Israel (2Ki 14:14). Repaired by Jehoash, king of Judah (2Ki 12:4-14; 2Ch 24:7-14), by Josiah (2Ki 22:3-7; 2Ch 34:8-13). Ahaz changes the detailed plans (2Ki 16:10-17). Purified by Hezekiah (2Ch 29:15-19). Converted into an idolatrous shrine by Manasseh (2Ki 21:4-7; 2Ch 33:4-7).

Treasures of, used in the purchase of peace: By Asa, from Ben-Hadad (1Ki 15:18), by Jehoash, king of Judah, from Hazael (2Ki 12:18), by Hezekiah, from the king of Assyria (2Ki 18:15-16). Jews swore by (Mt 23:16-22).

Ezekiel's Vision: (Eze 37:26, 28; 40-48).

The Second:

Rebuilt by Zerubbabel (Ezr 1; 2:68-69; 3:2-13; 4; 5:2-17; 6:3-5; Ne 7:70-72; Isa 44:28; Hag 2:3). Building of, suspended (Ezr 4), resumed (Ezr 4:24; 5; 6; Hag 1:2-9; 2:15; Zec 8:9), finished (Ezr 6:14-15), dedicated (Ezr 6:15-18). Artaxerxes' favorable action toward (Ezr 7:11-28; 8:25-34).

Prophecies of its restoration (Isa 44:28; Da 8:13-14; Hag 1; 2; Zec 1:16; 4:8-10; 6:12-15; 8:9-15; Mal 3:1).

Herod's—

Forty-six years in building (Jn 2:20). Massive and beautiful stones of (Mk 13:1; Lk 21:5). Magnificence of (Mt 24:1). Beautiful gate of (Ac 3:10). Solomon's Colonnade (Jn 10:23; Ac 3:11; 5:12). Treasury of (Mk 12:41-44). Zechariah receives promise of a son (Lk 1:5-23, w 1:57-64). Jesus the infant brought to, according to the law and custom (Lk 2:21-39), Simeon blesses Jesus in (Lk 2:25-35), Anna the prophetess never left (Lk 2:36-37).

Jesus in, when a youth (Lk 2:46), taken to the highest point of, in his temptation (Mt 4:5-7; Lk 4:9-12), teaches in (Mk 11:27-33; 12:35-44; 14:49; Jn 5:14-47; 7:14-28; 8; 10:23-38; 18:20), performs miracles in (Mt 21:14-15), drives money changers from (Mt 21:12-13; Mk 11:15-17; Lk 19:45-46; Jn 2:15-16).

Officer of temple guard (Lk 22:52; Ac 4:1; 5:24, 26). Judas threw the money into (Mt 27:5). Veil of, torn at the time of the crucifixion (Mt 27:51).

The disciples worship in, after the resurrection (Lk 24:53; Ac 2:46; 3:1). Peter heals the crippled man at the gate of (Ac 3:1-16). Disciples preach in (Ac 5:20-21, 42). Paul's vision in (Ac 22:17-21). Paul observes the rights of (Ac 21:26-30), is arrested in (Ac 21:33).

Prophecies concerning its destruction, by Daniel (Da 8:11-15; 11:30-31). Jesus predicts the destruction of (Mt 24; Mk 13:2; Lk 21:6).

Figurative:

Of the body of Jesus (Mt 26:61; 27:40; Jn 2:19). Of the indwelling of God (1Co 3:16-17; 2Co 6:16). Of the church (Eph 2:21; 2Th 2:4; Rev 3:12). Of the kingdom of Christ (Rev 11; 14:15, 17). Of Christ, the head of the church, sending forth the forces of righteousness against the powers of evil (Rev 15:5-8; 16:1-17).

Idolatrous:

Of Dagon, at Ashdod (1Sa 5:2), of the calves, at Bethel (1Ki 12:31, 33), of Rimmon, at Damascus (2Ki 5:18), of Baal, at Samaria (2Ki 10:21, 27), at Babylon (2Ch 36:7; Da 1:2), of Diana, at Ephesus (Ac 19:27).

Trophies stored in (1Sa 31:10; 1Ch 10:9-10; Da 1:2).

See Tabernacle.

TEMPLE SERVANTS [5987, 10497].

Large group of servants who performed menial tasks in the temple (1Ch 9:2; Ezr 2:43-58; 8:17-20; Ne 7:46-56), probably descended from Midianites (Nu 31:47), Gibeonites (Jos 9:23), and other captives. Usually listed with the priests, Levites, singers, and gatekeepers (Ezr 2:70).

TEMPORAL BLESSINGS *See Blessings.*

TEMPTATION [585, 4279, 4280] (*trial, proof*). Has two meanings: Any attempt to entice or tempt into evil; a testing which aims at an ultimate spiritual good.

Temptation to Evil:
(Pr 12:26; Ro 8:35-39). Called snares of death (Pr 13:14; 14:27).

The way of escape from (1Co 10:13). Christ gives help in (Heb 2:18; 4:15; Rev 3:10). The Lord delivers from (2Pe 2:9).

Benefits of: (Jas 1:2-4, 12; 1Pe 1:6-7).

Leading into:
To be avoided (Mt 5:29-30; 6:9; Mk 9:42-48; Lk 17:1; Ro 14:13, 15, 21; 1Co 7:5; 8:9-13; 10:28-32). Prayer against being led into (Mt 6:13; 26:41; Mk 14:38; Lk 11:4; 22:40, 46). Not to lead others into (Ro 14:13-15, 21; 1Co 7:5; 8:9-13; 10:28-32).

Instances of—
Abraham, of Pharaoh (Ge 12:18-19), of Abimelech (Ge 20:9). Rebekah, of Jacob (Ge 27:6-14). Balak, of Balaam (Nu 22:5-7, 16-17; 23:11-13, 25-27). Eli's sons, of Israel (1Sa 2:24-25). Gideon, of Israel (Jdg 8:27). The old prophet of Bethel, of the prophet of Judah (1Ki 13:15-19). Jeroboam, of Israel (1Ki 15:30, 34).

Resistance to:
Commanded (Dt 7:25-26; Pr 1:10-19; 4:14-15; 5:3, 8; 19:27; Mt 24:42-44; 25:13; 26:41; Mk 13:21-22; 13:33-37; 14:37-38; Ro 6:12-14; 12:21; Eph 6:11, 13-17; Jas 4:7; 1Pe 5:8-9; 1Jn 4:4). Source of resistance (Ps 17:4; 73:2-25; 94:17-18). Rewards to those who resist (Isa 33:15-16; Jas 1:12; Rev 3:10).

Instances of—
Joseph (Ge 39:7-12). Balaam (Nu 22:7-18, 38; 23:7-12, 18-24). David (1Sa 26:5-25). The prophet of Judah (1Ki 13:7-9). Micaiah (1Ki 22:13-28). The people of Jerusalem (2Ki 18:30-36). Job (Job 1:6-21; 2:4-10; 31:1, 5-17, 19-34, 38-40). Recabites (Jer 35:5-9). Nehemiah (Ne 4:9).

Jesus (Mt 4:1-11; 26:38-42; Lk 4:1-3; Heb 4:15; 12:3-4).

Sources of:
Cherished pleasures (Mt 5:29-30; 18:7-9; Mk 9:43-45). Evil company (Ex 34:13-16; Pr 2:10-16). Adultery and sexual desires (Pr 5:1-20; 6:24-29; 7:1-27; 9:15-18; Ecc 7:26). Sinful desires (Ro 7:5; Gal 5:17; Jas 1:13-15; 2Pe 2:18; 1Jn 2:16-17). False teachers (Mt 18:6-7; Lk 17:1; 1Jn 2:26; 4:1-3; Rev 2:20). Persecutions (Jn 16:1-2). Prosperity (Dt 8:10-17; Lk 12:16-21). Riches (Mt 19:16-24; Mk 10:17-30; 1Ti 6:9-10). Cares, riches and pleasures (Mt 13:22; Lk 8:13-14; 21:34-38).

Satan (Ge 3:1-5; 1Ch 21:1; Mk 4:15, 17; Lk 22:3, 31-32; 2Co 2:11; 11:3, 14-15; 12:7; Gal 4:14; Eph 4:27; 6:11, 13-17; 1Th 3:5; 1Ti 5:15; Jas 4:7; 1Pe 5:8-9; Rev 12:10-11, 17).

Wicked people (Pr 16:29; 28:10; Hos 7:5; Am 2:12; Mt 5:19; 2Ti 3:13).

See Demons; Faith, Trial of; Satan.

Warnings Against Yielding to:
(Ex 34:12-16; Dt 8:11-20; Pr 2:10-16; 5:1-21; 6:27-28; 7:1-27; 9:15-18; Ecc 7:26; Jer 2:25; Mt 26:31, 41; Mk 14:37-38; Lk 21:34-36; 22:40; 1Co 16:13; Eph 6:11, 13-17; Heb 12:3-4; 1Pe 4:7; 5:8-9; 2Pe 3:17; Rev 3:2-3).

Instances of—
Adam and Eve (Ge 3:1-19). Sarah, to lie (Ge 12:13; 18:13-15; 20:13). Isaac, to lie (Ge 26:7). Jacob to defraud Esau (Ge 27:6-13). Achan (Jos 7:21). David, to commit adultery (2Sa 11:2-5), to number Israel (1Ch 21). Solomon, to become an idolater through the influences of his wives (1Ki 11:4; Ne 13:26). The prophet of Judah (1Ki 13:11-19). Hezekiah (2Ki 20:12-20; Isa 39:1-4, 6-7). Peter (Mt 26:69-74; Mk 14:67-71; Lk 22:55-60).

Of Jesus:
(Lk 22:28). In all points as we are (Heb 4:15). By the devil (Mt 4:1-11; Mk 1:12-13; Lk 4:1-13). Before his crucifixion (Mt 26:38-42).

Test of God:
Design of, a test (Ps 66:10-13; 119:101, 110; Da 12:10; Zec 13:9; 1Pe 1:6-7; 4:12). Of fidelity (Dt 13:1-3; 2Ch 32:31; Job 1:8-22; 2:3-10). Of obedience (Ge 22:1-14; Dt 8:2, 5; Heb 11:17).

Benefits of (Jas 1:2-4, 12; 1Pe 1:6-7). Rewards of (Isa 33:15-16; Lk 12:35-38; Jas 1:12; 1Jn 4:4).

See Affliction; Afflictions; Faith, Trial of.

TEN [6917, 6924, 6927, 6930, 8047, 8052, 10573, 10649, *1274, 3689, 3691, 3692*]. Used for an indefinite number (Ge 31:7; Lev 26:26; Nu 14:22; Zec 8:23).

TEN COMMANDMENTS *See Commandments and Statutes, Of God; Decalogue.*

TENANTS [1251, 5757, 9369, *1177*]. Evicted (Mt 21:41; Mk 12:9; Lk 20:16).

TENONS NIV "projections" on tabernacle boards to hold the boards in place (Ex 26:17).

TENSION *See Anxiety.*

TENT [182, 185, 2837, 3749, 3845, 3857, 5438, 6108, 6109, 7688, *5008, 5011, 5012, 5013*]. Used for dwelling (Ge 4:20), by Noah (Ge 9:21), by Abraham (Ge 12:8; 13:18; 18:1), by Lot (Ge 13:5), by Moses (Ex 18:7), by Israelites (Nu 24:5-6; 2Sa 20:1; 1Ki 12:16), by the Midianites (Jdg 6:5), by Cushites (Hab 3:7), by Arabs (Isa 13:20), by shepherds (Isa 38:12; Jer 6:3). Women had tents apart from men (Ge 24:67; 31:33). Used for cattle (2Ch 14:15). Manufacture of (Ac 18:3). Used as a place of worship. *See Tabernacle.*

TERAH [9561, 9562, *2508*].
1. The son of Nahor (Ge 11:24-25), father of Abraham, Nahor, Haran (Ge 11:26), idolater (Jos

24:2), went as far as Haran with Abraham (Ge 11:24-32).

2. The encampment of the Israelites in wilderness (Nu 33:27-28).

TERAPHIM *See Household Gods; Idolatry.*

TEREBINTH [461]. A small tree (Isa 6:13; Hos 4:13).

TERESH [9575] (perhaps *desire*). A Persian eunuch. Plotted against Xerxes (Est 2:21-23; 6:2).

TERRACE [4864, 8727, 8805]. Steps leading up to the temple (2Ch 9:11).

TERROR [*399, 987, 988, 1166, 1243, 1286, 1287, 1593, 3006, 3010, 3154, 3169, 3707+, 4471, 4616, 4745, 6907, 7064, 7065, 10097, 10167, *5429, 5832*]. Extreme fear or dread; or sometimes the one who causes such agitation (Ge 35:5; Ps 55:4; 2Co 5:11).

TERTIUS [5470] (*third*). Paul's amanuensis in writing the book of Romans (Ro 16:22).

TERTULLUS [5472] (*third*). Diminutive of Tertius; lawyer employed by the Jews to state their case against Paul before Felix (Ac 24:1).

TESTAMENT
1. A covenant. *See Covenant.*
2. Testamentary disposition or will. *See Will, A Testament.*
3. Divisions of the English Bible. *See New Testament, Old Testament.*

TESTAMENTS OF THE TWELVE PROPHETS
A pseudepigraphal document that claims to report the last words of the twelve sons of Jacob; probably written c. second century A.D.

TESTAMENTS, TIME BETWEEN
A time of the realignment of traditional power blocs and the passing of a Near Eastern cultural tradition that had been dominant for almost 3000 years.

In biblical history, the approximately 400 years that separate the time of Nehemiah from the birth of Christ are known as the intertestamental period (c. 432-5 B.C.). Sometimes called the "silent" years, they were anything but silent. The events, literature and social forces of these years would shape the world of the NT.

History:
With the Babylonian captivity, Israel ceased to be an independent nation and became a minor territory in a succession of larger empires. Very little is known about the latter years of Persian domination because the Jewish historian Josephus, our primary source for the intertestamental period, all but ignores them.

With Alexander the Great's acquisition of Israel (332 B.C.), a new and more insidious threat to

Israel emerged. Alexander was committed to the creation of a world united by Greek language and culture, a policy followed by his successors. This policy, called Hellenization, had a dramatic impact on the Jews.

At Alexander's death (323 B.C.) the empire he won was divided among his generals. Two of them founded dynasties—the Ptolemies in Egypt and the Seleucids in Syria and Mesopotamia— that would contend for control of Israel for over a century.

The rule of the Ptolemies was considerate of Jewish religious sensitivities, but in 198 B.C. the Seleucids took control and paved the way for one of the most heroic periods in Jewish history.

The early Seleucid years were largely a continuation of the tolerant rule of the Ptolemies, but Antiochus IV Epiphanes (whose title means "God made manifest" and who ruled 175-164 B.C.) changed that when he attempted to consolidate his fading empire through a policy of radical Hellenization. While a segment of the Jewish aristocracy had already adopted Greek ways, the majority of Jews were outraged.

Antiochus's atrocities were aimed at the eradication of Jewish religion. He prohibited some of the central elements of Jewish practice, attempted to destroy all copies of the Torah (the Pentateuch), and required offerings to the Greek god Zeus. His crowning outrage was the erection of a statue of Zeus and the sacrificing of a pig in the Jerusalem temple itself.

Opposition to Antiochus was led by Mattathias, an elderly villager from a priestly family, and his five sons: Judas (Maccabeus), Jonathan, Simon, John, and Eleazar. Mattathias destroyed a Greek altar established in his village, Modein, and killed Antiochus's emissary. This triggered the Maccabean revolt, a 24-year war (166-142 B.C.) that resulted in the independence of Judah until the Romans took control in 63 B.C.

The victory of Mattathias's family was Pyrrhic, however. With the death of his last son, Simon, the Hasmonean dynasty that they founded soon evolved into an aristocratic, Hellenistic regime sometimes hard to distinguish from that of the Seleucids. During the reign of Simon's son, John Hyrcanus, the orthodox Jews who had supported the Maccabees fell out of favor. With only a few exceptions, the rest of the Hasmoneans supported the Jewish Hellenizers. The Pharisees were actually persecuted by Alexander Janneus (103-76 B.C.).

The Hasmonean dynasty ended when, in 63 B.C., an expanding Roman empire intervened in a dynastic clash between the two sons of Janneus, Aristobulus II and Hyrcanus II. Pompey, the general who subdued the East for Rome, took Jerusalem after a three-month siege of the temple area, massacring priests in the performance of their duties and entering the Most Holy Place. This sacrilege began Roman rule in a way that Jews could neither forgive nor forget.

Literature:

During these unhappy years of oppression and internal strife, the Jewish people produced a sizable body of literature that both recorded and addressed their era. Three of the more significant works are the Septuagint, the Apocrypha and the Dead Sea Scrolls.

Septuagint—

Jewish legend says that seventy-two scholars, under the sponsorship of Ptolemy Philadelphus (c. 250 B.C.), were brought together on the island of Pharos, near Alexandria, where they produced a Greek translation of the OT in seventy-two days. From this tradition the Latin word for seventy, "Septuagint," became the name attached to the translation. The Roman numeral for seventy, LXX, is used as an abbreviation for it.

Behind the legend lies the probability that at least the Torah (the five books of Moses) was translated into Greek c. 250 B.C. for the use of the Greek-speaking Jews of Alexandria. The rest of the OT and some noncanonical books were also included in the LXX before the dawning of the Christian era, though it is difficult to be certain when.

The Septuagint quickly became the Bible of the Jews outside Israel who, like the Alexandrians, no longer spoke Hebrew. It would be difficult to overestimate its influence. It made the Scriptures available both to the Jews who no longer spoke their ancestral language and to the entire Greek-speaking world. It later became the Bible of the early church. Also, its widespread popularity and use contributed to the retention of the Apocrypha by some branches of Christendom.

Apocrypha—

Derived from a Greek word that means "hidden," Apocrypha has acquired the meaning "false," but in a technical sense it describes a specific body of writings. This collection consists of a variety of books and additions to canonical books that, with the exception of 2 Esdras (c. A.D. 90), were written during the intertestamental period. Their recognition as authoritative in Roman and Eastern Christianity is the result of a complex historical process.

The canon of the OT accepted by Protestants today was very likely established by the dawn of the second century A.D., though after the fall of Jerusalem and the destruction of the temple in 70. The precise scope of the OT was discussed among the Jews until the Council of Jamnia (c. 90). This Hebrew canon was not accepted by the early church, which used the Septuagint. In spite of disagreements among some of the church fathers as to which books were canonical and which were not, the Apocryphal books continued in common use by most Christians until the Reformation. During this period most Protestants decided to follow the original Hebrew canon while Rome, at the Council of Trent (1546) and more recently at the First Vatican Council (1869-70), affirmed the larger "Alexandrian" canon that includes the Apocrypha.

The Apocryphal books have retained their place primarily through the weight of ecclesiastical authority, without which they would not commend themselves as canonical literature. There is no clear evidence that Jesus or the apostles ever quoted any Apocryphal works as Scripture (Jude 14). The Jewish community that produced them repudiated them, and the historical surveys in the apostolic sermons recorded in Acts completely ignore the period they cover. Even the sober, historical account of 1 Maccabees is tarnished by numerous errors and anachronisms.

There is nothing of theological value in the Apocryphal books that cannot be duplicated in canonical Scripture, and they contain much that runs counter to its teachings. Nonetheless, this body of literature does provide a valuable source of information for the study of the intertestamental period.

Dead Sea Scrolls—

In the spring of 1947 an Arab shepherd chanced upon a cave in the hills overlooking the southwestern shore of the Dead Sea that contained what has been called "the greatest manuscript discovery of modern times."

The documents and fragments of documents found in those caves, dubbed the "Dead Sea Scrolls," included OT books, a few books of the Apocrypha, apocalyptic works, pseudepigrapha (books that purport to be the work of ancient heroes of the faith), and a number of books peculiar to the sect that produced them.

Approximately a third of the documents are Biblical, with Psalms, Deuteronomy and Isaiah—the books quoted most often in the NT—occurring most frequently. One of the most remarkable finds was a complete 24-foot-long scroll of Isaiah.

The Scrolls have made a significant contribution to the quest for a form of the OT texts most accurately reflecting the original manuscripts; they provide copies a thousand years closer to the originals than were previously known. The understanding of Biblical Hebrew and Aramaic and knowledge of the development of Judaism between the Testaments have been increased significantly. Of great importance to readers of the Bible is the demonstration of the care with which OT texts were copied, thus providing objective evidence for the general reliability of those texts.

Social Developments:

The Judaism of Jesus' day is, to a large extent, the result of changes that came about in response to the pressures of the intertestamental period.

Diaspora—

The Diaspora (dispersion) of Israel begun in the Exile accelerated during these years until a writer of the day could say that Jews filled "every land and sea."

Jews outside Israel, cut off from the temple, concentrated their religious life in the study of the Torah and the life of the synagogue (see below). The missionaries of the early church began their Gentile ministries among the Diaspora, using their Greek translation of the OT.

Sadducees—

In Israel, the Greek world made its greatest impact through the party of the Sadducees. Made up of aristocrats, it became the temple party. Because of their position, the Sadducees had a vested interest in the status quo.

Relatively few in number, they wielded disproportionate political power and controlled the high priesthood. They rejected all religious writings except the Torah, as well as any doctrine (such as the Resurrection) not found in those five books.

Synagogue—

During the Exile, Israel was cut off from the temple, divested of nationhood and surrounded by pagan religious practices. Her faith was threatened with extinction. Under these circumstances, the exiles turned their religious focus from what they had lost to what they retained—the Torah and the belief that they were God's people. They concentrated on the law rather than nationhood, on personal piety rather than sacramental rectitude, and on prayer as an acceptable replacement for the sacrifices denied to them.

When they returned from the Exile, they brought with them this new form of religious expression, as well as the synagogue (its center), and Judaism became a faith that could be practiced wherever the Torah could be carried.

The emphases on personal piety and a relationship with God, which characterized synagogue worship, not only helped preserve Judaism but also prepared the way for the Christian gospel.

Pharisees—

As the party of the synagogue, the Pharisees strove to reinterpret the law. They built a "hedge" around it to enable Jews to live righteously before God in a world that had changed drastically since the days of Moses. Although they were comparatively few in number, the Pharisees enjoyed the support of the people and influenced popular opinion if not national policy. They were the only party to survive the destruction of the temple in A.D. 70 and were the spiritual progenitors of modern Judaism.

Essenes—

An almost forgotten Jewish sect until the discovery of the Dead Sea Scrolls, the Essenes were a small, separatist group that grew out of the conflicts of the Maccabean age. Like the Pharisees, they stressed strict legal observance, but they considered the temple priesthood corrupt and rejected much of the temple ritual and sacrificial system. Mentioned by several ancient writers, the precise nature of the Essenes is still not certain, though it is generally agreed that the Qumran community that produced the Dead Sea Scrolls was an Essene group.

Because they were convinced that they were the true remnant, these Qumran Essenes had separated themselves from Judaism at large and devoted themselves to personal purity and preparation for the final war between the "Sons of Light and the Sons of Darkness." They practiced an apocalyptic faith, looking back to the contributions of their "Teacher of Righteousness" and forward to the coming of two, and possibly three, Messiahs. The destruction of the temple in A.D. 70, however, seems to have delivered a death blow to their apocalyptic expectations.

Attempts have been made to equate aspects of the beliefs of the Qumran community with the origins of Christianity. Some have seen a prototype of Jesus in their "Teacher of Righteousness," and both John the Baptist and Jesus have been assigned membership in the sect. There is, however, only a superficial, speculative base for these conjectures.

TESTIMONY [5583, 6332, 6343, 6699, 7023, 9496, 282, 2909, 3455+3456+4005, 3455, 3456, 3457, 3459, 5125, 6018, 6019].

Commandments:

Those revealed to Moses (Ex 25:16; Dt 4:44-45; 1Ki 2:3). Kept in the ark (Ex 25:16, 21). Engraved on tablets (Ex 31:18; 32:15; 38:21). Atonement cover was over (Ex 26:34; 30:6; 40:20).

Ark, called ark of (Ex 25:22; 26:34; 40:3, 5, 20-21). Tabernacle called tabernacle of (Nu 1:50, 53; 9:19; 10:11). *See Ark; Tabernacle.*

See Commandments and Statutes, Of God; Decalogue.

Legal: *See Evidence; Witness.*

Religious:

(Ps 18:49; 22:22; 26:12; 34:1-4, 8-9; 77:12; 119:13, 26-27, 46, 67, 71; Isa 43:10; 44:8; 45:24; 1Co 1:5-6; 12:3; 15:15).

Required of the righteous (1Ch 16:8-9; Ps 9:11; Isa 12:4-6; 43:10; 44:8; Jer 51:10; Mt 4:21; 5:15-16, 19-20; Mk 4:21; 5:19-20; Lk 8:16, 39; 24:48; Jn 15:27; Ac 1:8, 22; 3:15; 5:32; 13:31; Ro 10:9-10; Eph 5:19; 2Ti 1:8; 1Pe 3:15; 5:12).

Concerning God's, faithfulness (Ps 73:23-26, 28; 89:1), glory (Ps 145:11-12), merciful providence (Ps 40:1-3; 54:7; 91:2-13; Da 4:2-3; Ac 14:15-17), righteousness (Ps 35:28; 71:16), salvation (Ps 30:1-6; 40:1-3; 62:1-2; 66:16-20; 71:15, 18; Gal 2:20; Php 3:4-14; Tit 3:3-7; Heb 2:3, 12), words (Ps 119:172), works (Ps 71:17, 24; 145:4-7, 10-12; Jer 51:10; Ac 2:11).

Concerning confidence in God (Ps 16:5-9; 18:2-3, 35-36; 23:1-6; 26:6-7; 27:1-6, 13; 28:6-8; 30:1-6). Rewards of (Mt 10:32; Lk 12:8). Victory by (Rev 12:11).

Exemplified by:

Job (Job 19:25-27). The psalmist (Ps 35:28; 40:1-3, 9; 57:7-9; 116:1-19). Nebuchadnezzar (Da 4:34-37). The woman of Sychar (Jn 4:28-30, 39, 41-42). The blind man whom Jesus healed (Jn 9:17, 30-33). The apostles to the resurrection of Jesus (Ac 4:33; 1Jn 1:1-4). The disciples at Pentecost (Ac 2:4-11). Peter (Ac 4:18-20; 1Pe 5:1, 12; 2Pe 1:16). John (Ac 4:18-20; 1Jn 1:1-4).

Paul's conversion (Ac 22:1-16; 26:12-23), devotion to Christ (1Co 13:1; Php 3:4-14), confidence in Christ (2Co 4:13-14; 5:1; 2Ti 1:12), hope of the crown of righteousness (2Ti 4:7-8), hope of eternal life (Tit 1:1-2).

TETRARCH [5489, 5490]. Ruler of a fourth part of a region (Mt 14:1; Lk 3:1; 9:7; Ac 13:1).

TEXTS, ANCIENT NEAR EASTERN NON-BIBLICAL TEXTS RELATING TO THE OLD TESTAMENT

Major representative examples of ancient Near Eastern non-biblical documents that provide parallels to or shed light on various OT passages.

Amarna Letters: [Canaanite Akkadian]—*fourteenth century* B.C. Hundreds of letters, written primarily by Canaanite scribes, illuminate social, political and religious relationships between Canaan and Egypt during the reigns of Amenhotep III and Akhenaten.

Amenemope's Wisdom: [Egyptian]—*early first millennium* B.C. Thirty chapters of wisdom instruction are similar to Pr 22:17-24:22 and provide the closest external parallels to OT wisdom literature.

Atrahasis Epic: [Akkadian]—*early second millennium* B.C. A cosmological epic depicts Creation and early human history, including the Flood (cf. Ge 1-9).

Babylonian Theodicy: [Akkadian]—*early first millennium* B.C. A sufferer and his friend dialogue with each other (cf. Job).

Cyrus Cylinder: [Akkadian]—*sixth century* B.C. King Cyrus of Persia records the conquest of Babylon (cf. Da 5:30; 6:28) and boasts of his generous policies toward his new subjects and their gods.

Dead Sea Scrolls: [Hebrew, Aramaic, Greek]—*third century* B.C. to *first century* A.D. Several hundred scrolls and fragments include the oldest copies of OT books and passages.

Ebal Tablets: [Sumerian, Eblaite]—*mid-third millennium* B.C. Thousands of commercial, legal, literary, and epistolary texts describe the cultural vitality and political power of a prepatriarchal civilization in northern Syria.

Elephantine Papyri: [Aramaic]—*late fifth century* B.C. Contracts and letters document life among Israelites who fled to southern Egypt after Jerusalem was destroyed in 586 B.C.

Enuma Elish: [Akkadian]—*early second millennium* B.C. Marduk, the Babylonian god of cosmic order, is elevated to the supreme position in the pantheon. The seven-tablet epic contains an account of creation (cf. Ge 1-2).

Gezer Calendar: [Hebrew]—*tenth century* B.C. A schoolboy from west-central Israel describes the seasons, crops and farming activity of the agricultural year.

Gilgamesh Epic: [Akkadian]—*early second millennium* B.C. Gilgamesh, ruler of Uruk, experiences numerous adventures, including a meeting with Utnapishtim, the only survivor of a great deluge (cf. Ge 6-9).

Hammurapi's Code: [Akkadian]—*eighteenth century* B.C. Together with similar law codes that preceded and followed it, the Code of Hammurapi exhibits close parallels to numerous passages in the Mosaic laws of the OT.

Hymn to the Aten: [Egyptian]—*fourteenth century* B.C. The poem praises the beneficence and universality of the sun in language somewhat similar to that used in Ps 104.

Ishtar's Descent: [Akkadian]—*first millennium* B.C. The goddess Ishtar temporarily descends to the netherworld, which is pictured in terms reminiscent of OT descriptions of Sheol.

Jehoiachin's Ration Dockets: [Akkadian]—*early sixth century* B.C. Brief texts from the reign of Nebuchadnezzar II refer to rations allotted to Judah's exiled king Jehoiachin and his sons (cf. 2Ki 25:27-30).

King Lists: [Sumerian]—*late third millennium* B.C. The reigns of Sumerian kings before the Flood are described as lasting for thousands of years, reminding us of the longevity of the pre-Flood patriarchs in Ge 5.

Lachish Letters: [Hebrew]—*early sixth century* B.C. Inscriptions on pottery fragments vividly portray the desperate days preceding the Babylonian siege of Jerusalem in 588-586 B.C. (cf. Jer 34:7).

Lamentation Over the Destruction of Ur: [Sumerian]—*early second millennium* B.C. The poem mourns the destruction of the city of Ur at the hands of the Elamites (cf. the OT book of Lamentations).

Ludlul Bel Nemeqi: [Akkadian]—*late second millennium* B.C. A suffering Babylonian nobleman describes his distress in terms faintly reminiscent of the experience of Job.

Mari Tablets: [Akkadian]—*eighteenth century* B.C. Letters and administration texts provide detailed information regarding customs, language, and personal names that reflect the culture of the OT patriarchs.

Merneptah Stele: [Egyptian]—*thirteenth century* B.C. Pharaoh Merneptah figuratively describes his victory over various peoples in western Asia, including "Israel."

Mesha Stele (Moabite Stone): [Moabite]—*ninth century* B.C. Mesha, king of Moab (see 2Ki 3:4), rebels against a successor of Israel's king Omri.

Murashu Tablets: [Akkadian]—*fifth century* B.C. Commercial documents describe financial transactions engaged in by Murashu and Sons, a Babylonian firm that did business with Jews and other exiles.

Mursilis's Treaty with Duppi-Tessub: [Hittite]—*mid-second millennium* B.C. King Mursilis imposes a suzerainty treaty on King Duppi-Tessub. The literary outline of this and other Hittite treaties is strikingly paralleled in OT covenants established by God with his people.

Nabonidus Chronicle: [Akkadian]—*mid-sixth century* B.C. The account describes the absence of King Nabonidus from Babylon. His son Belshazzar is therefore the regent in charge of the kingdom (cf. Da 5:29-30).

Nebuchadnezzar Chronicle: [Akkadian]—*early sixth century* B.C. A chronicle from the reign of Nebuchadnezzar II includes the Babylonian account of the siege of Jerusalem in 597 B.C. (2Ki 24:10-17).

Nuzi Tablets: [Akkadian]—*mid-second millennium* B.C. Adoption, birthright sale and other legal documents graphically illustrate OT patriarchal customs current centuries earlier.

Pessimistic Dialogue: [Akkadian]—*early first millennium* B.C. A master and his servant discuss the pros and cons of various activities (cf. Ecc 1-2).

Ras Shamra Tablets: [Ugaritic]—*fifteenth century* B.C. Canaanite deities and rulers experience adventures in epics that enrich our understanding of Canaanite mythology and religion and of OT poetry.

Sargon Legend: [Akkadian]—*first millennium* B.C. Sargon I (the Great), ruler of Akkad in the late third millennium B.C. claims to have been rescued as an infant from a reed basket found floating in a river (cf. Ex 2).

Sargon's Display Inscription: [Akkadian]—*eighth century* B.C. Sargon II takes credit for the conquest of Samaria in 722/721 B.C. and states that he captured and exiled 27, 290 Israelites.

Sennacherib's Prism: [Akkadian]—*early seventh century* B.C. Sennacherib vividly describes his siege of Jerusalem in 701 B.C., making Hezekiah a prisoner in his own royal city (but cf. 2Ki 19:35-37).

Seven Lean Years Tradition: [Egyptian]—*second century* B.C. Egypt experiences seven years of low Nile levels and famine, which, by a contractual agreement between Pharaoh Djoser (twenty-eighth century B.C.) and a god, will be followed by prosperity (cf. Ge 41).

Shalmaneser's Black Obelisk: [Akkadian]—*ninth century* B.C. Israel's king Jehu (or his servant) presents tribute to Assyria's king Shalmaneser III. Additional Assyrian and Babylonian texts refer to other kings of Israel and Judah.

Shishak's Geographical List: [Egyptian]—*tenth century* B.C. Pharaoh Shishak lists the cities that he captured or made tributary during his campaign in Judah and Israel (cf. 1Ki 14:25-26).

Siloam Inscription: [Hebrew]—*late eighth century* B.C. A Judahite workman describes the construction of an underground conduit to guarantee Jerusalem's water supply during Hezekiah's reign (cf. 2Ki 20:20; 2Ch 32:30).

Sinuhe's Story: [Egyptian]—*twentieth to nineteenth centuries* B.C. An Egyptian official of the twelfth dynasty goes into voluntary exile in Syria and Canaan during the OT patriarchal period.

Tale of Two Brothers: [Egyptian]—*thirteenth century* B.C. A young man rejects the amorous advances of his older brother's wife (cf. Ge 39).

Wenamun's Journey: [Egyptian]—*eleventh century* B.C. An official of the Temple of Amun at Thebes in Egypt is sent to Byblos in Canaan to buy lumber for the ceremonial barge of his god.

TEXTS AND VERSIONS

Old Testament

Major Hebrew texts—

1. The oldest copies of the Hebrew OT are the famous Dead Sea Scrolls, dating from 250 B.C. to c. A.D. 70. *See Dead Sea Scrolls; Testaments, Time Between.*

2. Portions of the OT text include the Nash Papyrus (second century B.C.) and the Cairo Genizah fragments (sixth to ninth centuries A.D.).

3. The Masoretes preserved and standardized the Hebrew text between the sixth and tenth centuries A.D.. The oldest examples of this text type include the Cairo Codex of the Prophets (895), the Aleppo Codex (c. 900-925) and the Leningrad Codex (1008).

4. The Samaritan Pentateuch (eleventh century A.D.).

Major versions—

1. Greek: Septuagint (250-100 B.C.); second century A.D. versions by Aquila, Theodotion, and Symmachus; by Origen c. A.D. 240.

2. Aramaic (first to fifth century A.D.).

3. Syriac (second or third century A.D.).

4. Latin: Old Latin (second century A.D.), Jerome's Vulgate (383-405 A.D.).

New Testament

Major Greek texts—

Greek manuscripts of portions or of the whole of the NT total nearly 5000. Of these, c. 70 are papyri, 250 uncials, 2, 500 minuscules, and 1800 lectionaries.

1. Fragments and books on papyrus date back to the second century A.D., such as Bodmer Papyrus p^{66} of John.

2. Codex Sinaiticus (fourth century) contains the entire NT.

3. Codices Alexandrinus (fifth century) and Vaticanus are nearly complete.

4. Quotations from the early church fathers also provide an ancient witness to the NT.

Major versions—

1. Latin (second to fourth centuries).

2. Syriac (second to sixth centuries).

3. Coptic (second and third centuries).

THADDAEUS [*2497*] (possibly *breast nipple*). One of the twelve apostles (Mt 10:3; Mk 3:18). This name does not appear in (Lk 6:16; Ac 1:13), the name "Judas son of James" occurs instead. Little is known about him.

See Lebbaeus.

THAHASH *See Tahash.*

THAMAH *See Temah.*

THAMAR *See Tamar, 1.*

THANK OFFERINGS *See Offerings.*

THANKFULNESS   [*3344,   9343,
10312, 2328, 2373, 2374, 5921].

To God:

Commanded or required (Ge 35:1; Ex 12:14, 17,
42; 13:3, 8-10, 14-16; 16:32; 34:26; Lev 19:24;
23:14; Dt 12:18; 16:9-15; 26:10; Jdg 5:11; Ps
50:14-15). Commanded (Ps 48:11; 106:1; Pr 3:9-
10; Ecc 7:14; Isa 48:20; Joel 2:26; Ro 2:4; 15:27;
Eph 1:16; 5:4, 19-20; Php 4:6; Col 1:12; 2:7;
3:15-17; 4:2; 1Th 5:18; Heb 13:15; Jas 1:9). Exhorted (Ps 98:1; 105:1, 5, 42-45; 107:1-2, 15, 22,
42-43; 118:1, 4; Col 3:15; 1Ti 2:1; 4:3-5).

Jesus set an example of (Mt 11:25; 15:36; 26:27;
Mk 8:6-7; 14:23; Lk 22:17, 19; Jn 6:11, 23;
11:41).

Should Be Offered—

To God (Ps 30:4; 50:14; 75:1; 92:1; 97:12;
106:1; 118:1; 2Co 9:11; Eph 5:4, 19-20; Php 4:6;
Col 1:12; 2:7; 3:15-17; 4:2; 1Th 5:18; 1Ti 2:1;
Heb 13:15), through Christ (Ro 1:8; Col 3:17; Heb
13:15), in the name of Christ (Eph 5:20), in behalf
of ministers (2Co 1:11), in private worship (Da
6:10), in public (1Ch 23:30; 25:3; Ne 11:17; Ps
35:18), in everything (1Th 5:18), upon the completion of great undertakings (Ne 12:31, 40),
before taking food (Mt 14:19; Mk 8:9; Lk 24:30;
Jn 6:11; Ac 27:35), always (Eph 1:16; 5:20; 1Th
1:2), as the remembrance of God's holiness (Ps
30:4; 97:12).

For—

The goodness and mercy of God (Ps 68:19;
79:13; 89:1; 100:4; 106:1; 107:1; 116:12-14, 17;
136:1-3; Isa 63:7), the gift of Christ (2Co 9:15),
Christ's power and reign (Rev 11:17), the reception and effectual working of the word of God in
others (1Th 2:13), deliverance, from adversity (Ps
31:7, 21; 35:9-10; 44:7-8; 54:6-7; 66:8-9, 12-16,
20; 98:1), through Christ, from indwelling sin (Ro
7:23-25), providential deliverance (Ex 12:14, 17,
42; 13:3, 8-10, 14-16; Jdg 5:11; Ps 105:1-45;
107:1-2, 15, 22, 42-43; 136:1-26; Joel 2:26), victory over death and the grave (1Co 15:57), wisdom and might (Da 2:23), the triumph of the
gospel (2Co 2:14), the conversion of others (Ro
6:17), faith exhibited by others (Ro 1:8; 2Th 1:3),
love exhibited by others (2Th 1:3), the grace bestowed on others (1Co 1:4; Php 1:3-5; Col 1:3-6),
the zeal exhibited by others (2Co 8:16), nearness
of God's presence (Ps 75:1), appointment to the
ministry (1Ti 1:12), willingness to offer our
property for God's service (1Ch 29:6-14), the
supply of our bodily wants (Ro 14:6-7; 1Ti 4:3-4),
all men (1Ti 2:1), all things (2Co 9:11; Eph 5:20),
temporal blessings (Ro 14:6-7; 1Ti 4:3-5).

By—

Ministers appointed to offer, in public (1Ch 16:4,
7; 23:30; 2Ch 31:2).

Saints, exhorted to (Ps 105:1; Col 3:15), resolve
to offer (Ps 18:49; 30:12), habitually offer (Da
6:10), offer sacrifices of (Ps 116:17), abound in
the faith with (Col 2:7), magnify God by (Ps
95:2), come before God with (Ps 95:2), should
enter God's gates with (Ps 100:4). Of hypocrites,
full of boasting (Lk 18:11). The wicked averse to
(Ro 1:21).

The heavenly host (Rev 4:9; 7:11-12; 11:16-17).

Accompanied By—

Should be accompanied by intercession for
others (1Ti 2:1; 2Ti 1:3; Phm 4). Should always
accompany prayer (Ne 11:17; Php 4:6; Col 4:2).
Should always accompany praise (Ps 92:1; Heb
13:15). Expressed in psalms (1Ch 16:7).

Cultivated, by the Feast of Tabernacles (Dt 16:9-
15), by thank offerings (Ex 34:26; Lev 19:24;
23:14; Dt 12:18; 26:10; Pr 3:9-10), by songs (1Ch
16:7-36; Ps 95:2; 100).

Instances of—

Eve (Ge 4:1, 25). Noah (Ge 8:20). Melchizedek
(Ge 14:20). Lot (Ge 19:19). Abraham (Ge 12:7).
Sarah (Ge 21:6-7). Abraham's servant (Ge 24:27).
Isaac (Ge 26:22). Leah (Ge 29:32-35). Rachel (Ge
30:6). Jacob (Ge 32:10; 35:3, 7; 48:11, 15-16).
Joseph (Ge 41:51-52).

Moses (Ex 15:1-18). Miriam (Ex 15:19-21).
Jethro (Ex 18:10). Israel (Ex 4:31; 15:1-18; Nu
21:17; 31:49-54; 1Ch 29:22). Deborah (Jdg 5).
Hannah (1Sa 1:27-28; 2:1-10). Samuel (1Sa 7:12).

David (2Sa 6:21; 1Ch 29:13). Solomon (1Ki
8:15, 56; 2Ch 6:4). Queen of Sheba (1Ki 10:9).
Hiram (2Ch 2:12). Jehoshaphat's army (2Ch
20:27-28). The psalmist (Ps 9:1-2, 4; 13:6; 22:23-
25; 26:7; 28:7; 30:1, 3, 11-12; 31:7, 21; 35:9-10,
18; 40:2-3, 5; 41:11-12; 44:7-8; 54:6-7; 56:12-13;
59:16-17; 66:8-9, 12-16, 20; 68:19; 71:15, 23-24;
79:13; 89:1; 92:1-2, 4; 98:1; 100:4; 102:18-20;
104:1; 116:12-14, 17; 119:65, 108; 136).

Isaiah (Isa 63:7). Daniel (Da 2:23; 6:22). Nebuchadnezzar (Da 4:2, 34). The mariners (Jnh 1:16).
Jonah (Jnh 2:9). Ezra (Ezr 7:27). The Levites (2Ch
5:12-13; Ne 9:4-38). The Jews (Ne 12:31, 40, 43).

The shepherds (Lk 2:20). Simeon (Lk 2:28).
Anna (Lk 2:38).

Those whom Jesus healed: The paralyzed man
(Lk 5:25), the demoniac (Lk 8:39), the woman
bent with infirmity (Lk 13:13), one of the ten
lepers (Lk 17:15-16), blind Bartimaeus (Lk
18:43), the centurion for his son (Jn 4:53).

The lame man healed by Peter (Ac 3:8). Early
Christians (Ac 2:46-47). Paul (Ac 27:35; 28:15;
Ro 1:8; 6:17; 1Co 1:4; 2Co 2:14; Php 1:3-5; Col
1:3-6; 2Th 1:3; 1Ti 1:12).

See Joy; Praise; Psalms; Worship.

Of Person to Person:

The Israelites, to Joshua (Jos 19:49-50). The
spies, to Rahab (Jos 6:22-25). Saul, to the Kenites
(1Sa 15:6). Naomi, to Boaz (Ru 2:19-20). David,
to the men of Jabesh Gilead (2Sa 2:5-7), to Hanun

(2Sa 10:2), to Barzillai (1Ki 2:7). Paul, to Phoebe (Ro 16:1-4), to Onesiphorus (2Ti 1:16-18). The people of Malta, to Paul (Ac 28:10).

THANKSGIVING [2117, 3344, 9343, 2330, 2374]. By Jesus (Mt 11:25; 15:36; 26:27; Mk 8:6-7; 14:23; Lk 22:17, 19; Jn 6:11, 23; 11:41).

For food, commonly called "grace" (1Sa 9:13; Mt 14:19; 15:36; Mk 6:41; 8:6-7; Lk 9:16; 24:30; Jn 6:11, 23; Ac 27:35; Ro 14:6; 1Co 10:30-31; 1Ti 4:3-5).

Instances of: Jesus (Mt 14:19; Mk 8:6-7). Paul (Ac 27:35).

See Praise; Prayer, Thanksgiving; Thankfulness.

THARA *See Terah, 2.*

THARSHISH *See Trade and Travel; Tarshish, 2, 4.*

THEATER [2519]. A place for dramatic and musical performances (Ac 19:29, 31).

THEBES [5530, 5531] *(town, village).* Capital of Egypt during the eighteenth dynasty (KJV "No"); on the E bank of the Nile; famous for temples; cult center of the god Amon (Jer 46:25), denounced by prophets (Jer 46:25; Eze 30:14-16).

THEBEZ [9324]. A city in Ephraim about halfway from Beth Shan to Shechem; Abimelech, the son of Gideon, slain there (Jdg 9:50; 2Sa 11:21).

THEFT [1706, 3092, 3113]. (Na 3:1; Mt 6:19-20; 15:19; Mk 7:21-22; Ro 2:21; Rev 9:21).

Forbidden:
(Ex 20:15; Lev 19:11, 13; Dt 5:19; 23:24-25; Ps 62:10; Mt 19:18; Lk 18:20; Ro 13:9; Eph 4:28; Tit 2:10; 1Pe 4:15). Penalty for (Ex 21:16; 22:1-4, 10-15; Lev 6:2-5; Pr 6:30-31; Zec 5:3; Mt 27:38, 44; Mk 15:27). Restitution for things stolen required of the penitent (Eze 33:15).

Instances of:
Rachel, of the household gods (Ge 31:19, 34-35). Achan (Jos 7:11). Micah (Jdg 17:2). The spies of Laish (Jdg 18:14-27). Israelites (Eze 22:29; Hos 4:1-2). Judas (Jn 12:6).

See Dishonesty; Robbery; Thief, Thieves.

THELASAR *See Tel Assar.*

THEOCRACY *(rule of God).* Established (Ex 19:8; 24:3, 7; Dt 5:25-29; 33:2-5; Jdg 8:23; 1Sa 12:12). Rejected by Israel (1Sa 8:7, 19; 10:19; 2Ch 13:8).

See God, Sovereign; Government.

THEOLOGY *See God.*

THEOPHANY *(appearance of God).* Visible appearance of God, generally in human form (Ge 3:8; 4; 28:10-17).

THEOPHILUS [2541] *(friend of God).* A

man to whom the Gospel of Luke and Acts of the Apostles are addressed (Lk 1:3; Ac 1:1). Nothing is known of him.

THESSALONIANS, 1 and 2

1 Thessalonians:

Author: the apostle Paul

Date: c. A.D. 51

Outline:
I. The Thanksgiving for the Thessalonians (ch 1).
   A. The Grounds for the Thanksgiving (1:1-4).
   B. The Genuineness of the Grounds (1:5-10).
II. The Defense of the Apostolic Actions and Absence (chs. 2-3).
   A. The Defense of the Apostolic Actions (2:1-16).
   B. The Defense of the Apostolic Absence (2:17-3:10).
   C. The Prayer (3:11-13).
III. The Exhortations to the Thessalonians (4:1-5:22).
   A. Primarily Concerning Personal Life (4:1-12).
   B. Concerning the Coming of Christ (4:13-5:11).
   C. Primarily Concerning Church Life (5:12-22).
IV. The Concluding Prayer, Greetings and Benediction (5:23-28).

2 Thessalonians:

Author: the apostle Paul

Date: c. A.D. 51 or 52

Outline:
I. Introduction (ch. 1).
   A. Salutation (1:1-2).
   B. Thanksgiving for Their Faith, Love and Perseverance (1:3-10).
   C. Intercession for Their Spiritual Progress (1:11-12).
II. Instruction (ch. 2).
   A. Prophecy Regarding the Day of the Lord (2:1-12).
   B. Thanksgiving for Their Election and Calling (Their Position) (2:13-15).
   C. Prayer for Their Service and Testimony (Their Practice) (2:16-17).
III. Injunctions (ch. 3).
   A. Call to Prayer (3:1-3).
   B. Charge to Discipline for the Disorderly and Lazy (3:4-15).
   C. Conclusion, Greeting and Benediction (3:16-18).

THESSALONICA [2552, 2553]. A city of Macedonia. Paul visits (Ac 17:1; Php 4:16). People of, accompany Paul (Ac 20:4; 27:2). Paul writes to Christians in (1Th 1:1; 2Th 1:1). Demas goes to (2Ti 4:10).

THEUDAS [2554] *(gift of God).* A Jew who led a rebellion against Rome (Ac 5:36-37).

THICKET [1454, 2560, 3091, 3623, 6019, 6020, 6109, 6266]. (1Sa 13:6; Jer 4:7).

THIEF, THIEVES [1704, 1705, *3095*]. In Mosaic law, punishment of thieves was very severe (Ex 22:1-4).

Penalty for (Dt 24:7; Pr 6:30-31; Eze 18:10, 13; Zec 5:3; Mt 27:38, 44; Mk 15:27).

Collusion with (Ps 50:18). Excluded from the kingdom of God (1Co 6:10). Desecrated the temple (Mt 21:13; Mk 11:17; Lk 19:45-46). Disgraceful (Jer 2:26). Worship of, offensive to God (Jer 7:9-10).

Christ's coming again as unexpected as (Rev 3:3).

Figurative (Ob 5; Jn 10:1).

See Theft.

THIGH [3751, 7066, 8797, 10334, *3611*]. To put one's hand under the thigh of another was to enhance the sacredness of an oath (Ge 24:2, 9; 47:29).

THIMNATHAH *See Timnah.*

THIRST [5883, 6546, 7532, 7533, 7534, 7536, 8115, *1498*, *1499*]. Figurative of the ardent desire of the devout mind (Ps 42:1-4; 63:1; 143:6; Isa 55:1; Am 8:11-13; Mt 5:6; Jn 4:14-15; 7:37; Rev 21:6; 22:17).

See Desire, Spiritual; Diligence; Hunger, Figurative; Zeal.

THISTLE [1998, 2560, *5560*]. Exists in many varieties in Israel. Used figuratively for trouble, desolation, judgment, wickedness (Nu 33:55; Pr 24:31; 15:19; Isa 5:6; 2Co 12:7).

THOMAS [*2605*] (*twin*). Called Didymus. One of the twelve apostles (Mt 10:3; Mk 3:18; Lk 6:15). Present at the raising of Lazarus (Jn 11:16). Asks Jesus the way to the Father's house (Jn 14:5). Absent when Jesus first appeared to the disciples after the Resurrection (Jn 20:24). Skepticism of (Jn 20:25). Sees Jesus after the Resurrection (Jn 20:26-29; 21:1-2). Lives with the other apostles in Jerusalem (Ac 1:13-14). Loyalty of, to Jesus (Jn 11:16; 20:28).

THOMAS, GOSPEL OF A Gnostic gospel consisting entirely of sayings attributed to Jesus; dated c. A.D. 140; found at Nag Hammadi in Egypt in 1945.

THONG [3857, 8579, *2666*]. Strap to fasten a sandal to the foot. Used figuratively of something small and insignificant (Ge 14:23; Isa 5:27). Untying of, an act of humble service (Mk 1:7; Lk 3:16).

THORN [353, 2537, 2560, 5004, 6106, 6141, 7553, 7564, 7764, 7853, 8885, *180*, *181*, *5022*]. The ground cursed with (Ge 3:18). Used as an awl (Job 41:2), for fuel (Ps 58:9; 118:12; Ecc 7:6). Hedges formed of (Hos 2:6; Mic 7:4). Crown of,

mockingly put on Jesus' head (Mt 27:29; Mk 15:17; Jn 19:2, 5).

Figurative:

Of afflictions (Nu 33:55; 2Co 12:7). Of the adversities of the wicked (Pr 22:5). Of the evils that spring from the heart to choke the truth (Mt 13:7, 22).

THORN IN THE FLESH [*5022*]. Paul's description of a physical ailment from which he prayed to be relieved (2Co 12:7). What it was is not known.

THOUGHTS, GOD'S (Ps 40:5, 17; 139:17; Isa 55:9; Jer 29:11).

THOUSAND [*547, 8047, 8052, 10038, 10649, 3689, 3692, 4295, 5483, 5942, 5943*]. Often used symbolically in the Bible. In the OT sometimes means "many" (1Sa 21:11; 2Ch 15:11), "family" (Nu 10:4).

THOUSAND YEARS As a day to the Lord (Ps 90:4; 2Pe 3:8). Satan bound (Rev 20:1-3). The reign of Christ (Rev 20:4-6). *See Millennium.*

THRACE Kingdom and later a Roman province, in SE Europe, E of Macedonia (2Mc 12:35).

THREAD [2562, 9106]. (Ge 14:23; Jdg 16:21; SS 4:3).

THREATENINGS [*1722, 1819, 1821, 9412, 581*]. Of God against the wicked (Lev 26:16; Jos 23:15; 1Sa 12:25; 1Ki 9:7; Ps 7:12; Isa 14:23; 66:4; Mal 3:5).

THREE HOLY CHILDREN, SONG OF Apocryphal additions to the OT book of Daniel; probably written in the first century B.C.

THREE TAVERNS [*5553*]. A town in Italy. Roman Christians meet Paul in (Ac 28:15).

THRESHING [1755, 1889, 1912, 2468, 3023, 4617, 6322, 10010, *272*]. By beating (Ru 2:17), by treading (Dt 25:4; Isa 25:10; Hos 10:11; 1Co 9:9; 1Ti 5:18). With instruments of wood (2Sa 24:22), of iron (Am 1:3), with a cart wheel (Isa 28:27-28). Floors for (Ge 50:10-11; Jdg 6:37; Ru 3:2-14; 1Sa 23:1; 2Sa 6:6; Hos 9:2; Joel 2:24). Floor of Araunah bought by David for a place of sacrifice (2Sa 24:16-25). Floor for, in barns (2Ki 6:27).

THRESHING FLOOR [1755, *272*]. A place where grain was threshed, usually clay soil packed to a hard, smooth surface (Dt 25:4; Isa 28:27; 1Co 9:9).

THRESHOLD [5159, 6197]. A piece of wood or stone at the bottom of a door, which has to be crossed on entering a house.

THRONE [2292, 3782, 4058, 4632, 4887, 10372, 10424, *1037*, *2585*] (*judgment seat*). Of Pharaoh (Ge 41:40; Ex 11:5). Of David (1Ki 2:12, 24; Ps 132:11-12; Isa 9:7; Jer 13:13; 17:25; Lk 1:32). Of Solomon (1Ki 2:19; 2Ch 9:17-19). Of ivory (1Ki 10:18-20). Of Solomon, called the throne of the LORD (1Ch 29:23). Of Herod (Ac 12:21). Of Israel (1Ki 8:20; 10:9; 2Ch 6:10).

Abdicated by David (1Ki 1:32-40).

Figurative:

Anthropomorphic use of: Of God (2Ch 18:18; Ps 9:4, 7; 11:4; 47:8; 89:14; 97:2; 103:19; Isa 6:1; 66:1; Mt 5:34; 23:22; Heb 8:1; 12:2; Rev 14:3, 5), of Christ (Mt 19:28; 25:31; Ac 2:30; Rev 1:4; 3:21; 4:2-10; 7:9-17; 19:4; 21:5; 22:3).

THRUSH A bird (Isa 38:14; Jer 8:7). *See Birds.*

THUMB [984+3338, 991]. Blood put on, in consecration (Ex 29:20; Lev 8:23), in purification (Lev 14:14, 25). Oil put on (Lev 14:17, 28). Of prisoners cut off (Jdg 1:6-7). *See Hand.*

THUMMIM [9460]. *See Urim and Thummim.*

THUNDER [2150, 2162, 7754, 8275, 8306, 8308, 9583, *1103*, *5889*]. Sent as a plague upon the Egyptians (Ex 9:3-24), the Philistines, in battle with the Israelites (1Sa 7:10). Sent as a judgment (Isa 29:6). On Sinai (Ex 19:16; Ps 77:18; Heb 12:18-19). A token of divine anger (1Sa 12:17-18). A manifestation of divine power (Job 26:14; Ps 77:18). Sons of Zebedee called sons of (Mk 3:17).

THUNDER, SONS OF A title given James and John by Jesus (Mk 3:17).

THUTMOSE (*[Egyptian god] Thoth is born*). The name of four kings of Egypt of the eighteenth dynasty, centering in Thebes. Under their rule, Egypt attained her greatest power. Thutmose III may have been the Pharaoh who enslaved the Hebrews (Ex 1:8).

THYATIRA [2587]. A city in the Roman province of Asia; on the boundary of Lydia and Mysia; noted for weaving and dyeing (Ac 16:14; Rev 2:18-29).

THYINE *See Citron Wood.*

TIARAS [7566]. (Isa 3:23). *See Crown; Jewel, Jewelry.*

TIBERIAS [5500]. A city on the W shore of the Sea of Galilee; built by Herod Antipas and named for the emperor Tiberius; a famous health resort; after A.D. 70 it became a center of rabbinic learning. Modern Tabariya.

TIBERIAS, SEA OF *See Sea of Galilee.*

TIBERIUS [5501]. The second Roman

emperor (A.D. 14-37); reigning emperor at the time of Christ's death (Lk 3:1).

TIBHATH *See Tebah, 2.*

TIBNI [9321]. The son of Ginath; unsuccessful competitor for the throne of Israel (1Ki 16:21).

TIDAL [9331]. King of Goiim; confederate of Kedorlaomer (Ge 14:1-17).

TIGLATH-PILESER [9325, 9433] (*my trust is in the son of [the temple] Esharra*). A famous Assyrian king (745-727 B.C.); great conqueror; received tribute from King Azariah of Judah and King Menahem of Samaria (2Ki 15:19-20), Ahaz secured his help against Pekah of Israel and Rezin of Syria; deported Trans-Jordanian Israelites (1Ch 5:6, 26), Ahaz gave tribute to him (2Ch 28:20-21).

TIGRIS [2538] (*arrow*). One of the two great rivers of the Mesopotamian area; 1, 150 miles long (Ge 2:14; Da 10:4).

TIKVAH [9537] (*hope*).
1. Father-in-law of the prophetess Huldah (2Ki 22:14). *See Tokhath.*
2. Father of Jahzeiah (Ezr 10:15).

TILE [*3041*]. Ceiling tiles (Lk 5:19).

TILGATH-PILNESER *See Tiglath-Pileser.*

TILON [9400]. The son of Shimon (1Ch 4:20).

TIMAEUS [5505] (*precious, valuable*). The father of Bartimaeus (Mk 10:46).

TIMBREL *See Tambourine.*

TIME [*255, 339+, 801, 928, 1887+, 2256, 2375, 2725, 2976, 3338, 3427, 4595, 4951, 6388, 6409, 6961, 7193, 8049, 8079, 9108, 9378, 10232, 10317, 10530, 10530, 275, 1309, 1671, 2093, 2232, 2453, 2465, 2789, 4121, 4490, 4537, 4625, 4672, 5538, 5565, 5568, 5988, 5989, 6052*]. In the early biblical period, time was marked by sunrise and sunset, phases of the moon, seasons, and years (Ge 1:14). *See Calendar.*

Ancient people had no method of reckoning long periods of time. They dated from great and well-known events, like the Exodus, the Babylonian Exile, the earthquake (Am 1:1), and especially the reigns of kings (1Ki 15:1; Hag 1:1). The year was lunar (354 days, 8 hours, 38 seconds), divided into twelve lunar months, with seven intercalary months added over nineteen years. The Hebrew month began with the new moon. Early Hebrews gave the months names; later they used numbers; and after the Exile they used Babylonian names. *See Month.*

Months were divided by the Jews into weeks of seven days, ending with the Sabbath (Ex 20:11; Dt 5:14-15). Days were divided into twenty-four hours of sixty minutes of sixty seconds. The Roman day began at midnight and had twelve hours (Jn 11:9), the Hebrew day was reckoned from sunset. Night was divided into watches. At first the Hebrews had three watches; in the time of Christ there were four. *See Day; Watches of the Night.*

TIMES, OBSERVER OF A person who has a superstitious regard for days regarded as lucky or unlucky, as decided by astrology (Dt 18:8-14).

TIMNA [9465] (*lot, portion*).
1. Concubine of Eliphaz (Ge 36:12).
2. Sister of Lotan (Ge 36:22).
3. Chieftain of Edom (Ge 36:40).
4. Son of Eliphaz (1Ch 1:36).

TIMNAH [9463] (*lot, portion*).
1. A town about two-and-a-half miles west of Beth Shemesh (Ge 38:12-14; 2Ch 28:18).
2. A town on the border of Judah approximately three miles SW of Beth Shemesh (Jos 15:10), possibly modern Tell Batash.
3. A town in the hill country of Judah (Jos 15:57), possibly the same as 1.
4. A Philistine town (Jdg 14:1-5), possibly the same as 1.

TIMNATH *See Timnah.*

TIMNATH HERES [9466] (*place of the sun [worship]*). A city in the hill country of Ephraim (Jdg 2:9).

TIMNATH SERAH [9467] (*place of the sun [worship]*). Given to Joshua (Jos 19:50). Joshua buried in (Jos 24:30). Modern Khirbet Tibnah.

TIMNITE [9464]. A native of Timnah (Jdg 15:3-6).

TIMON [5511] (*precious, valuable*). One of seven ministers (Ac 6:5).

TIMOTHEUS *See Timothy.*

TIMOTHY [5510] (*precious one of God*). Parentage of (Ac 16:1). Reputation and Christian faith of (Ac 16:2; 1Co 4:17; 16:10; 2Ti 1:5; 3:15). Circumcised; becomes Paul's companion (Ac 16:3; 1Th 3:2). Left by Paul at Berea (Ac 17:14). Rejoins Paul at Corinth (Ac 17:15; 18:5). Sent into Macedonia (Ac 19:22). Rejoined by Paul; accompanies Paul to Asia (Ac 20:1-4). Sent to the Corinthians (1Co 4:17; 16:10-11). Preaches to the Corinthians (2Co 1:19). Sent to the Philippians (Php 2:19, 23). Sent to the Thessalonians (1Th 3:2, 6). Sent by Paul in Ephesus (1Ti 1:3). Joins Paul in the Epistle to the Philippians (Php 1:1), to the Colossians (Col 1:1-2), to the Thessalonians (1Th 1:1; 2Th 1:1), to Philemon (Phm 1).

Zeal of (Php 2:19-22; 1Ti 6:12). Power of (1Ti 4:14; 2Ti 1:6). Paul's love for (1Co 4:17; Php

2:22; 1Ti 1:2, 18; 2Ti 1:2-4). Paul writes to (1Ti 1:1-2; 2Ti 1:1-2).

TIMOTHY, 1 and 2

1 Timothy:

Author: the apostle Paul

Date: c. A.D 63-65

Outline:

I. Salutation (1:1-2).
II. Warning Against False Teachers (1:3-11).
  A. The Nature of the Heresy (1:3-7).
  B. The Purpose of the Law (1:8-11).
III. The Lord's Grace to Paul (1:12-17).
IV. The Purpose of Paul's Instructions to Timothy (1:18-20).
V. Instructions Concerning the Administration of the Church (chs. 2-3).
  A. Public Worship (ch. 2).
    1. Prayer in public worship (2:1-8).
    2. Women in public worship (2:9-15).
  B. Qualifications for Church Officers (3:1-13).
    1. Overseers (3:1-7).
    2. Deacons (3:8-13).
  C. Purpose of These Instructions (3:14-16).
VI. Methods of Dealing With False Teaching (ch. 4).
  A. False Teaching Described (4:1-5).
  B. Methods of Dealing With It Explained (4:6-16).
VII. Methods of Dealing With Different Groups in the Church (5:1-6:2).
  A. The Older and Younger (5:1-2).
  B. Widows (5:3-16).
  C. Elders (5:17-25).
  D. Slaves (6:1-2).
VIII. Miscellaneous Matters (6:3-19).
  A. False Teachers (6:3-5).
  B. Love of Money (6:6-10).
  C. Charge to Timothy (6:11-16).
  D. The Rich (6:17-19).
IX. Concluding Appeal (6:20-21).

2 Timothy:

Author: the apostle Paul

Date: c. A.D. 66-67

Outline:

I. Introduction (1:1-4).
II. Paul's Concern for Timothy (1:5-14).
III. Paul's Situation (1:15-18).
IV. Special Instructions to Timothy (ch. 2).
  A. Call for Endurance (2:1-13).
  B. Warning About Foolish Controversies (2:14-26).
V. Warning About the Last Days (ch. 3).
  A. Terrible Times (3:1-9).
  B. Means of Combating Them (3:10-17).
VI. Paul's Departing Remarks (4:1-8).
  A. Charge to Preach the Word (4:1-5).
  B. Paul's Victorious Prospect (4:6-8).
VII. Final Requests and Greetings (4:9-22).
See Church, The Body of Believers, Qualifications for Elders/Overseers and Deacons; Missionary Journeys of Paul; Pastoral Epistles.

TIN [974]. (Nu 31:22; Eze 22:18, 20; 27:12).

TINKLING The sound of small bells worn by women on chain fastened to anklets (Isa 3:16).

TIPHSAH [9527].
1. City on Euphrates (1Ki 4:24).
2. A town, apparently not far from Tirzah in Samaria (2Ki 15:16); some versions have Tappuah. *See Tappuah, 3.*

TIRAS [9410]. The son of Japheth (Ge 10:2; 1Ch 1:5).

TIRATHITES [9571]. A family of scribes in Jabez (1Ch 2:55).

TIRE [3333, 3615, 3878, 6546, 7918, *1591, 3159*] (*headdress*). Ornamental headdress (Eze 24:17, 23; Isa 3:20; 61:10).

TIRHAKAH [9555]. An Egyptian king, third of the twenty-fifth dynasty; defeated by Sennacherib (2Ki 19:9; Isa 37:9), and later by Esarhaddon and Ashurbanipal.

TIRHANAH [9563]. The son of Caleb and Maacah (1Ch 2:48).

TIRIA [9409]. The son of Jehallelel (1Ch 4:16).

TIRSHATHA *See Governor.*

TIRZAH [9573, 9574] (*pleasant one* or *compensation*).
1. A daughter of Zelophehad (Nu 26:33; 36:11; Jos 17:3). Special legislation in regard to the inheritance of (Nu 27:1-11; 36; Jos 17:3-4).
2. A city of Canaan. Captured by Joshua (Jos 12:24). Becomes the residence of the kings of Israel (1Ki 14:17; 15:21, 33; 16:6, 8-9, 15, 17, 23). Royal residence moved from (1Ki 16:23-24). Base of military operations of Menahem (2Ki 15:14, 16). Beauty of (SS 6:4).

TISHBE, TISHBITE [9585, 9586]. The designation of Elijah (1Ki 17:1), probably to be identified with modern el-Istib, little W of Mahanaim.

TISHRI *See Ethanim; Month, 7.*

TITHES [5130, 6923] (*a tenth*). Paid by Abraham to Melchizedek (Ge 14:20; Heb 7:2-6). Jacob vows a tenth of all his property to God (Ge 28:22).
Mosaic laws instituting (Lev 27:30-33; Nu 18:21-24; Dt 12:6-7, 17, 19; 14:22-29; 26:12-15). Customs relating to (Ne 10:37-38; Am 4:4; Heb 7:5-9). Tithe of tithes for priests (Nu 18:26; Ne 10:38). Stored in the temple (Ne 10:38-39; 12:44; 13:5, 12; 2Ch 31:11-12; Mal 3:10).
Payment of, resumed in Hezekiah's reign (2Ch 31:5-10). Under Nehemiah (Ne 13:12). Withheld (Ne 13:10; Mal 3:8).

Customary in later times (Mt 23:23; Lk 11:42; 18:12). Observed by idolaters (Am 4:4-5).
See Alms; Beneficence; Giving; Liberality; Tax.

TITLE [4033, *3950*]. To real estate. *See Land.*

TITLES AND NAMES

Of God: *See God, Names of.*

Titles and Names of Christ:
Adam, Last (1Co 15:45). Almighty (Rev 1:8). Alpha and Omega (Rev 1:8; 22:13). Amen (Rev 3:14). Angel of his presence (Isa 63:9). Angel of the Lord (Ex 3:2; Jdg 13:15-18). Angel (Ge 48:16; Ex 23:20-21). Apostle (Heb 3:1). Arm of the Lord (Isa 51:9; 53:1). Author of life (Ac 3:15). Author and Perfecter of our faith (Heb 2:10; 12:2).
Blessed and only Ruler (1Ti 6:15). Branch (Jer 23:5; Zec 3:8; 6:12). Bread of Life (Jn 6:35, 48).
Chief Shepherd (1Pe 5:4). Chief Cornerstone (Eph 2:20; 1Pe 2:6). Chosen One of God (Isa 42:1). Christ of God (Lk 9:20). Commander of the Lord's army (Jos 5:14-15). Commander (Isa 55:4). Consolation of Israel (Lk 2:25). Counselor (Isa 9:6).
David (Jer 30:9; Eze 34:23). Defender (1Jn 2:1). Deliverer (Ro 11:26). Door (Jn 10:7).
Eternal life (1Jn 1:2; 5:20). Everlasting Father (Isa 9:6).
Faithful witness (Rev 1:5; 3:14). First and Last (Rev 1:17; 2:8). Firstborn of the dead (Rev 1:5). Firstborn of all creation (Col 1:15).
Glory of the Lord (Isa 40:5). God over all (Ro 9:5). God (Isa 40:9; Jn 20:28). Good Shepherd (Jn 10:14). Great High Priest (Heb 4:14). Guarantee (Heb 7:22).
Head of the Church (Eph 5:23; Col 1:18). Heir of all things (Heb 1:2). Holy One of God (Mk 1:24). Holy One (Ps 16:10, w Ac 2:27, 31). Holy One of Israel (Isa 41:14). Horn of salvation (Lk 1:69).
I Am (Ex 3:14, w Jn 8:58; 22:13). Immanuel (Isa 7:14, w Mt 1:23). Israel's Ruler (Mic 5:1).
Jesus (Mt 1:21; 1Th 1:10).
King of the Jews (Mt 2:2). King of Israel (Jn 1:49). King of Kings (1Ti 6:15; Rev 17:14). King of the ages (Rev 15:3). King (Zec 9:9, w Mt 21:5). Lamb of God (Jn 1:29, 36). Lamb (Rev 5:6, 12; 13:8; 21:22; 22:3). Lawgiver (Isa 33:22). Leader (Isa 55:4). Life (Jn 14:6; Col 3:4; 1Jn 1:2). Light of the world (Jn 8:12). Lion of the tribe of Judah (Rev 5:5). Lord of all (Ac 10:36). Lord of glory (1Co 2:8). Lord our righteousness (Jer 23:6). Lord God Almighty (Rev 15:3). Lord God of the prophets (Rev 22:6).
Mediator (1Ti 2:5). Mighty One of Jacob (Isa 60:16). Mighty God (Isa 9:6). Morning Star (Rev 22:16).
Nazarene (Mt 2:23).
One and Only (Jn 1:14). One Before Us (Heb 6:20). Our Passover (1Co 5:7).
Prince of peace (Isa 9:6). Prophet (Lk 24:19; Jn 7:40).
Ransom (1Ti 2:6). Redeemer (Job 19:25; Isa 59:20; 60:16). Resurrection and life (Jn 11:25).

Righteous One (Ac 7:52). Rock (1Co 10:4). Root of Jesse (Isa 11:10). Root of David (Rev 22:16). Root and Offspring of David (Rev 22:16). Ruler of the kings of the earth (Rev 1:5). Ruler of the creation of God (Rev 3:14). Ruler over Israel (Mic 5:2). Ruler (Mt 2:6).

Savior (2Pe 2:20; 3:18). Servant (Isa 42:1; 52:13). Shepherd and Overseer of Souls (1Pe 2:25). Son of the Most High (Lk 1:32). Son of man (Jn 5:27; 6:37). Son of David (Mt 9:27). Son of God (Lk 1:35; Jn 1:49). Son of the Blessed One (Mk 14:61). Star (Nu 24:17). Sun of righteousness (Mal 4:2).

The desired of all nations (Hag 2:7). True Light (Jn 1:9). True Vine (Jn 15:1). True God (1Jn 5:20). Truth (Jn 14:6).

Way (Jn 14:6). Wisdom (Pr 8:12). Witness (Isa 55:4). Wonderful (Isa 9:6). Word of Life (1Jn 1:1). Word (Jn 1:1; 1Jn 5:7). Word of God (Rev 19:13).

Titles and Names of the Church:

Assembly of the saints (Ps 89:7). Assembly of the saints (Ps 149:1). Body of Christ (Eph 1:22-23; Col 1:24). Bride of Christ (Rev 21:9). Church of the Firstborn (Heb 12:23). Church of the first-born (Heb 12:23). Church of the Living God (1Ti 3:15). Church of God (Ac 20:28). City of the Living God (Heb 12:22). Council of the upright (Ps 111:1). Dwelling of God (Eph 2:22).

Family in heaven and on earth (Eph 3:15). Flock of God (Eze 34:15; 1Pe 5:2). Flock of Christ (Jn 10:16). God's field (1Co 3:9). God's inheritance (Joel 3:2; 1Pe 5:3). God's building (1Co 3:9). Golden lampstand (Rev 1:20). Holy City (Rev 21:2). House of the God of Jacob (Isa 2:3). House of Christ (Heb 3:6). House(hold) of God (1Ti 3:15; Heb 10:21; Eph 2:19). Inheritance (Ps 28:9; Isa 19:25). Israel of God (Gal 6:16). Lamb's bride (Rev 19:7; 21). Mount Zion (Ps 2:6; Heb 12:22). Mountain of the Lord's house (Isa 2:2).

New Jerusalem (Rev 21:2). Pillar and foundation of the truth (1Ti 3:15). Portion of the Lord (Dt 32:9). Princess (Ps 45:13). Sanctuary of God (Ps 114:2). Shoot of God's Planting (Isa 60:21). Sought After, the City no longer Deserted (Isa 62:12). Spiritual house (1Pe 2:5). Temple of the Living God (2Co 6:16). Temple of God (1Co 3:16-17). Vineyard (Jer 12:10; Mt 21:41).

Titles and Names of the Devil:

Abaddon (Rev 9:11). Accuser of our brothers (Rev 12:10). Ancient serpent (Rev 12:9; 20:2). Angel of the Abyss (Rev 9:11). Apollyon (Rev 9:11). Beelzebub (Mt 12:24). Belial (2Co 6:15). Coiling serpent (Isa 27:1). Dominion of darkness (Col 1:13). Dragon (Isa 27:1; Rev 20:2). Enemy (Mt 13:39; 1Pe 5:8). Evil one (Mt 13:19, 38). Evil spirit (1Sa 16:14; Mt 12:43).

Father of lies (Jn 8:44). Gliding serpent (Isa 27:1). God of this age (2Co 4:4). Leviathan (Isa 27:1). Liar (Jn 8:44). Lying spirit (1Ki 22:22). Murderer (Jn 8:44). Powers of this dark world (Eph 6:12). Prince of demons (Mt 12:24). Prince of this world (Jn 14:30). Red dragon (Rev 12:3).

Ruler of the kingdom of the air (Eph 2:2). Satan (1Ch 21:1; Job 1:6). Serpent (Ge 3:4, 14; 2Co 11:3). Spirit that works in those disobedient (Eph 2:2). Tempter (Mt 4:3; 1Th 3:5).

Titles and Names of the Holy Spirit:

Breath of the Almighty (Job 33:4). Counselor (Jn 14:16, 26; 15:26). Eternal Spirit (Heb 9:14). God (Ac 5:3-4). Good Spirit (Ne 9:20; Ps 143:10). Holy Spirit (Ps 51:11; Lk 11:13; Eph 1:13; 4:30). Power of the Most High (Lk 1:35).

Sevenfold Spirit (Rev 1:4 ftn). Spirit of fear of the Lord (Isa 11:2). Spirit of knowledge (Isa 11:2). Spirit of understanding (Isa 11:2). Spirit of power (Isa 11:2). Spirit of truth (Jn 14:17; 15:26). Spirit of holiness (Ro 1:4). Spirit of glory (1Pe 4:14). Spirit of fire (Isa 4:4). Spirit of judgment (Isa 4:4; 28:6). Spirit of revelation (Eph 1:17). Spirit, The (Mt 4:1; Jn 3:6; 1Ti 4:1). Spirit of counsel (Isa 11:2). Spirit of Christ (Ro 8:9; 1Pe 1:11). Spirit of the Father (Mt 10:20). Spirit of God (Ge 1:2; 1Co 2:11; Job 33:4). Spirit of the Lord (Isa 11:2; Ac 5:9). Spirit of wisdom (Isa 11:2; Eph 1:17). Spirit of his Son (Gal 4:6). Spirit of sonship (Ro 8:15). Spirit of life (Ro 8:2; Rev 11:11). Spirit of prophecy (Rev 19:10). Spirit of grace (Zec 12:10; Heb 10:29). Willing Spirit (Ps 51:12).

Titles and Names of Ministers:

Administers of the grace of God (1Pe 4:10). Ambassadors for Christ (2Co 5:20). Apostles of Jesus Christ (Tit 1:1). Apostles (Lk 6:13; Eph 4:11; Rev 18:20). Deacons (Ac 6:1ff; 1Ti 3:8; Php 1:1). Elders (1Ti 5:17; 1Pe 5:1). Entrusted with the secrets of God (1Co 4:1). Entrusted with God's work (Tit 1:7). Evangelists (Eph 4:11; 2Ti 4:5). Fellow workers with God (2Co 6:1). Fishers of men (Mt 4:19; Mk 1:17). Messengers of the Church (Rev 1:20; 2:1 ftn). Messenger of the Lord Almighty (Mal 2:7).

Ministers of the New Covenant (2Co 3:6). Ministers in the sanctuary (Eze 45:4). Ministers of the Lord (Joel 2:17). Ministers of Christ (Ro 15:16; 1Co 4:1). Overseers (Ac 20:28; Php 1:1; 1Ti 3:1; Tit 1:7). Pastors (Jer 3:15; Eph 4:11). Preachers (Ro 10:14; 1Ti 2:7). Representatives of the Church (2Co 8:23).

Servant of the Church (Col 1:24-25). Servant of this gospel (Eph 3:7; Col 1:23). Servants of the word (Lk 1:2). Servants of the Church (2Co 4:5). Servants of righteousness (2Co 11:15). Servants of God (2Co 6:4). Servants of God (Tit 1:1; Jas 1:1). Servants of the Lord (2Ti 2:24). Servants of Jesus Christ (Php 1:1; Jude 1). Shepherds (Jer 23:4). Soldiers of Christ (Php 2:25; 2Ti 2:3). Stars (Rev 1:20; 2:1). Teachers (Isa 30:20; Eph 4:11). Watchmen (Isa 62:6; Eze 33:7). Witnesses (Ac 1:8; 5:32; 26:16). Workers (Mt 9:38, w Phm 1; 1Th 2:2).

Titles and Names of Saints:

Believers (Ac 5:14; 1Ti 4:12). Blessed by the Father (Mt 25:34). Blessed by the Lord (Ge 24:31; 26:29). Brothers (Mt 23:8; Ac 12:17). Brothers of Christ (Lk 8:21; Jn 20:17). Called to belong to Jesus Christ (Ro 1:6).

Children of Abraham (Gal 3:7). Children (Jn 13:33; 1Jn 2:1). Children of the free woman (Gal 4:31). Children of promise (Ro 9:8; Gal 4:28). Children of the Lord (Dt 14:1). Children of the resurrection (Lk 20:36). Children of God (Jn 1:12; Php 2:15; 1Jn 3:1-2). Children of God (Jn 11:52; 1Jn 3:10). Chosen instrument (Ac 9:15). Chosen ones (1Ch 16:13). Chosen people (1Pe 2:9). Chosen of God (Col 3:12; Tit 1:1). Christians (Ac 11:26; 26:28). co-heirs with Christ (Ro 8:17). Dear brothers (1Co 15:58; Jas 2:5). Dearly loved children (Eph 5:1). Disciples of Christ (Jn 8:31; 15:8).

Faithful brothers in Christ (Col 1:2). Faithful in the land, The (Ps 101:6). Faithful, The (Ps 12:1). Fellow citizens with God's people (Eph 2:19). Fellow servants (Rev 6:11). Freedman (1Co 7:22). Friends of God (2Ch 20:7; Jas 2:23). Friends of Christ (Jn 15:15). Glorious ones (Ps 16:3). Godly, The (Ps 4:3; 2Pe 2:9). Guests of the bridegroom (Mt 9:15). Heirs with you of the gracious gift of life (1Pe 3:7). Heirs of God (Ro 8:17; Gal 4:7). Heirs together with Israel (Eph 3:6). Heirs of promise (Heb 6:17; Gal 3:29). Holy brothers (Heb 3:1). Holy people (Dt 26:19; Isa 62:12). Holy nation (Ex 19:6; 1Pe 2:9). Holy priesthood (1Pe 2:5). Inheritors of salvation (Heb 1:14). Inheritors of the kingdom (Jas 2:5). Instrument for noble purposes (2Ti 2:21).

Kingdom of priests (Ex 19:6). Kings and priests to serve God (Rev 1:6). Lambs (Isa 40:11; Jn 21:15). Letter from Christ (2Co 3:3). Light of the world (Mt 5:14). Living stones (1Pe 2:5). Loved of God (Ro 1:7). Man of God (1Ti 6:11; 2Ti 3:17). Members of Christ (1Co 6:15; Eph 5:30). Oaks of righteousness (Isa 61:3). Obedient children (1Pe 1:14). Objects of mercy (Ro 9:23).

People close to God's heart (Ps 148:14). People of God (Heb 4:9; 1Pe 2:10). People saved by the Lord (Dt 33:29). People of Zion (Ps 149:2; Joel 2:23). Pillars in the temple of God (Rev 3:12). Ransomed of the Lord (Isa 35:10; Isa 51:11). Righteous, The (Hab 2:4). Royal priesthood (1Pe 2:9). Salt of the earth (Mt 5:13). Sheep of Christ (Jn 10:1-16; 21:16). Slaves of Christ (1Co 7:22; Eph 6:6). Slaves to Righteousness (Ro 6:18).

Sons of the Living God (Ro 9:26). Sons of Jacob (Ps 105:6). Sons of the Most High (Lk 6:35). Sons of light (Lk 16:8; Eph 5:8; 1Th 5:5). Sons of the day (1Th 5:5). Sons of the Father (Mt 5:45). Sons of the kingdom (Mt 13:38). Treasured possession (Ex 19:5; Dt 14:2; Tit 2:14; 1Pe 2:9). Witnesses for God (Isa 44:8).

Titles and Names of the Wicked:

Accursed brood (2Pe 2:14). Base and nameless brood (Job 30:8). Brood of rebels (Isa 57:4). Brood of evildoers (Isa 1:4; 14:20). Brood of vipers (Mt 3:7; 12:34). Child of the devil (Ac 13:10; 1Jn 3:10). Children unwilling to hear the Lord's instruction (Isa 30:9). Children unfaithful (Dt 32:20). Children given to corruption (Isa 1:4). Clasp hands with Pagans (Isa 2:6). Corrupt

generation (Ac 2:40). Crooked and depraved generation (Php 2:15).

Deceitful children (Isa 30:9). Disobedient ones (Eph 2:2; Col 3:6). Enemies of God (Php 3:18). Enemies of the cross of Christ (Php 3:18). Enemies of everything right (Ac 13:10). Evil men (Ps 37:1; Pr 4:14; 2Ti 3:13). Evil generation (Dt 1:35). Evildoer (Ps 101:8; Pr 17:4; Ps 28:3; 36:12). Evildoers (Hos 10:9). Failers of a test (2Co 13:5-7). Fools (Pr 1:7; Ro 1:22). Foreigners (Ps 144:7). God-haters (Ps 81:15; Ro 1:30). Hardened rebels (Jer 6:28). Invent ways of doing evil (Ro 1:30). Men of this world (Ps 17:14). Mockers (Ps 1:1). Natural children (Ro 9:8).

Objects of wrath (Ro 9:22; Eph 2:3). Obstinate children (Eze 2:4; Isa 30:1; 65:2). Offspring of liars (Isa 57:4). Offspring of the wicked (Ps 37:28; Isa 14:20). Opposers of the Lord (1Sa 2:10). People loaded with guilt (Isa 1:4). People of this world (Lk 16:8). Perverse generation (Dt 32:20; Mt 17:17). Proud, The (Job 41:34). Rebellious people (Isa 30:9). Rebellious house (Eze 2:5, 8; 12:2). Senseless children (Jer 4:22). Sinful generation (Mk 8:38). Sinners (Ps 26:9; Pr 1:10; Ps 37:38). Slaves to sin (Jn 8:34; Ro 6:20). Slaves of Depravity (2Pe 2:19). Snakes (Mt 23:33). Son of hell (Mt 23:15). Sons of the evil one (Mt 13:38). Stubborn and rebellious generation (Ps 78:8). Transgressors (Ps 51:13).

Warped and crooked generation (Dt 32:5). Wicked men (Dt 13:13; 2Ch 13:7). Wicked traitors (Ps 59:5). Wicked generation (Mt 12:45; 16:4). Wicked servants (Mt 25:26). Wicked and adulterous generation (Mt 12:39). Wicked of the earth (Ps 75:8). Wicked people (2Sa 7:10). Worthless servants (Mt 25:30). Wrongdoers (1Pe 2:14). *See also Wicked, Compared With.*

TITTLE NIV "the least stroke of a pen"; figurative of the smallest details of the law (Mt 5:18; Lk 16:17).

TITUS [5519]. A Greek companion of Paul. Paul's love for (2Co 2:13; 7:6-7, 13-14; 8:23; Tit 1:4). With Paul in Macedonia (2Co 7:5-6). Affection of, for the Corinthians (2Co 7:15). Sent to Corinth (2Co 8:6, 16-22; 12:17-18). Character of (2Co 12:18). Accompanies Paul to Jerusalem (Gal 2:1-3, w Ac 15:1-29). Left by Paul in Crete (Tit 1:5), to rejoin him in Nicopolis (Tit 3:12). Paul writes to (Tit 1:1-4). With Paul in Rome; goes to Dalmatia (2Ti 4:10).

TITUS, EPISTLE TO

Author: the apostle Paul

Date: Probably between A.D. 63 and 65

Outline:

I. Salutation (1:1-4).
II. Concerning Elders (1:5-9).
   A. Reasons for Leaving Titus in Crete (1:5).
   B. Qualifications of Elders (1:6-9).
III. Concerning False Teachers (1:10-16).
IV. Concerning Various Groups in the
   Congregations (ch. 2).

A. The Instructions to Different Groups (2:1-10).

B. The Foundation for Christian Living (2:11-14).

C. The Duty of Titus (2:15).

V. Concerning Believers in General (3:1-8).

  A. Obligations as Citizens (3:1-2).

  B. Motives for Godly Conduct (3:3-8).

VI. Concerning Response to Spiritual Error (3:9-11).

VII. Conclusion (3:12-15).

See Church, The Body of Believers; Qualifications for Elders/Overseers and Deacons; Missionary Journeys of Paul; Pastoral Epistles.

TITUS, FLAVIUS VESPASIANUS

A Roman emperor (A.D. 79-81); captured and destroyed Jerusalem in A.D. 70.

TITUS JUSTUS *See Justus.*

TIZITE

[9407]. The designation of Joha, one of David's soldiers (1Ch 11:45).

TOAH

[9346]. An ancestor of Samuel (1Ch 6:34), probably the same as "Nahath" (1Ch 6:26), and perhaps "Tohu" (1Sa 1:1). *See Nahath, 2; Tohu.*

TOB

[3204] (*good*).

1. A district in Syria, extending NE from Gilead, to which Jephthah fled (Jdg 11:3, 5).

2. Place in Israel which supplied Ammonites with soldiers against David (2Sa 10:6, 8).

TOB-ADONIJAH

[3207] (*good is [my] lord Yahweh*). A Levite sent by Jehoshaphat to instruct the people in the law (2Ch 17:8).

TOBIAH

[3209] (*Yahweh is good*).

1. An ancestor of a family of Babylonian captives (Ezr 2:60; Ne 7:62).

2. An enemy of the Jews in the time of Nehemiah. Opposes the rebuilding of the wall of Jerusalem (Ne 2:10, 19; 4:3, 7-8). Conspires to injure and intimidate Nehemiah (Ne 6:1-14, 19). Subverts nobles of Judah (Ne 6:17-18). Allies himself with Eliashib, the priest (Ne 13:4-9).

TOBIJAH

[3209, 3210] (*Yahweh is good*).

1. A Levite chosen by Jehoshaphat to instruct the people in the law (2Ch 17:8).

2. A captive in Babylon (Zec 6:10, 14).

TOBIT, BOOK OF *See Apocrypha.*

TOCHEN *See Token, 2.*

TOE

[720, 991, 8079, 10064]. Anointed in consecration (Ex 29:20; Lev 8:23-24), in purification (Lev 14:14, 17, 25, 28). Of prisoners of war cut off (Jdg 1:6-7). Six, on each foot (2Sa 21:20; 1Ch 20:6).

TOGARMAH

[9328]. Son of Gomer (Ge 10:3; 1Ch 1:6). Descendants of (Eze 27:14; 38:6).

TOHU

[9375]. An ancestor of Samuel (1Sa 1:1), probably the same as "Nahath" (1Ch 6:26), and perhaps "Toah" (1Ch 6:34). *See Nahath, 2; Toah.*

TOI *See Tou.*

TOKEN

[9421] (*measure*).

1. A sign (Ex 3:12). Sun and moon for time and seasons (Ge 1:14). The mark of Cain (Ge 4:15). Rainbow, that the world might no more be destroyed by a flood (Ge 9:12-17). Circumcision, of the covenant of Abraham (Ge 17:11). Presents (Ge 21:27, 30). Miracles of Moses, of the divine authority of his missions (Ex 4:1-9). Blood of the Passover lamb (Ex 12:13). The Passover (Ex 13:9). Consecration of the firstborn (Ex 13:14-16). The Sabbath (Ex 31:13, 17), a fringe (Nu 15:38-40). Scarlet thread (Jos 2:18, 21). Cover of the altar (Nu 16:38-40). Aaron's rod (Nu 17:10). Memorial stones (Jos 4:2-9). Dew on Gideon's fleece (Jdg 6:36-40). Prayer for tokens of mercy (Ps 86:17).

See Miracles.

2. A city in Simeon (1Ch 4:32).

TOKHATH

[9534]. Father-in-law of Huldah the prophetess; also called Tokhath (2Ch 34:22, ftn). *See Tikvah.*

TOLA, TOLAITE

[9356, 9358] (*worm of scarlet*).

1. The son of Issachar (Ge 46:13).

2. Judged Israel twenty-three years (Jdg 10:1-2).

TOLAD

[9351]. City of Simeon (1Ch 4:29).

TOLERANCE

[5564, 5663, 6641, *496*, *918*, *1002*]. Religious (Mic 4:4-5; Mk 9:38-40; Lk 9:49-50; Ac 17:11; 28:31; Ro 14; 1Co 10:28-32). *See Intolerance.*

TOLL *See Tribute; Tax.*

TOMB

[1074, 1539, 7690, 7700, *3645*, *3646*, *5439*]. A burial place. Most Hebrew burying sites were unmarked; some kings were buried in a vault in Jerusalem (2Sa 2:32; Ne 2:3). Tombs of NT times were natural or man-made caves, sealed with circular stones weighing from one to three tons (Lk 24:2; Jn 20:1). *See Grave; Pillar; Tombstone.*

TOMBSTONE

[7483]. At the tomb of the man of God from Judah (2Ki 23:17). A pillar at Rachel's grave (Ge 35:20). *See Pillar.*

TONGS

[4920]. Used to tend the lamps in the temple (1Ki 7:49). In Isaiah's vision (Isa 6:6). *See Wick Trimmers.*

TONGUE

[2674, 3087, 3883, 4357, 4383, 8557, *1185*, *2280*]. Language (Ge 10:5, 20; Isa

66:18; Rev 7:9). Confusion of (Ge 11:1-9). Gift of (Ac 2:1-18, 33; 10:46; 19:6; 1Co 12:10, 28, 30; 14).

Chattering (Pr 10:8, 19). Restrained by wisdom (Pr 17:27; 21:23; Ecc 3:7). Hasty (Pr 29:20).

An evil. *See Speaking, Evil; Slander.*

TONGUES, CONFUSION OF

Punishment by God for arrogant attempt to build tower reaching to heaven (Ge 11:1-9).

TONGUES, GIFT OF

A spiritual gift (Mk 16:17; Ac 2:1-13; 10:44-46; 19:6; 1Co 12; 14). The gift appeared on the day of Pentecost with the outpouring of the Holy Spirit on the assembled believers (Ac 2:1-13). The phenomenon appeared again in the home of Cornelius (Ac 10:44-11:17), at Ephesus (Ac 19:6), and in the church at Corinth (1Co 12; 14). Instruction regarding the use of tongues in worship (1Co 12-14).

TONGUES OF FIRE

One of the phenomena that occurred at the outpouring of the Holy Spirit on the Day of Pentecost. Symbolic of the Holy Spirit who came in power on the church (Ac 2:3).

TOOLS

[1366, 2995, 3032, 3086, 3998, 5108, 6485]. The following kinds are mentioned in the Bible: cutting, boring, forks and shovels, carpentry, drawing, measuring, tilling, metalworking, stoneworking.

TOOTH

[9094, 3848]. Both human and animal teeth are mentioned (Nu 11:33; Dt 32:24), figurative use is common: cleanness of teeth, famine (Am 4:6), gnashing of teeth, rage and despair (Job 16:9), oppression (Pr 30:14), plenty (Ge 49:12).

TOPAZ

[7077, 5535].

1. A precious stone (Eze 28:13; Rev 21:20).
2. In the priestly breastplate (Ex 28:17; 39:10).

Figurative:
Topaz cannot compare to the price of wisdom (Job 28:19):

Symbolic:
Seen in the foundation of the Holy City, the New Jerusalem (Rev 21:20).

See Minerals of the Bible, 1; Stones.

TOPHEL

[9523] (*cement*). A place in the wilderness where Moses addressed the Israelites (Dt 1:1), possibly modern el-Tafila, fifteen miles SE of the Dead Sea.

TOPHETH

[9532, 9533]. A place in the valley of the sons of Hinnom or Ben Hinnom (2Ki 23:10). Israelite children burned in sacrifice to Molech there (2Ki 23:10; Jer 7:31-32; 19:6, 11-14; 32:35; cf. 2Ch 28:3; 33:6). Destroyed by Josiah (2Ki 23:10). Horror of (Isa 30:33).

See Ben Hinnom; Hinnom, Valley of.

TOPOGRAPHY

Of Canaan (Jos 13:15-33; 15; 18:9).

TORAH

[9368; NT *nomos: 3795*]. Divine law (Ex 13:9); instruction (Ex 16:4, 28); the Law of Moses (1Ki 2:3); the Book of the Law (Dt 28:61); the entire Jewish Scriptures (Jn 10:34). *See Law.*

TORCHES

[2338, 4365, 3286, 5749]. (Jdg 7:16; 15:4; Na 2:3; Jn 18:3).

TORMENTOR

[3324, 9354]. Conquerors of Israel (Ps 137:3; Isa 51:23). Abusive jailers (Mt 18:34).

TORMENTS

[*1286, 2813, 3324, 989, 990, 992]. Of the wicked (Lk 16:23-28; Rev 14:10-11).

See Wicked, Punishment of.

TORTOISE

See Lizard.

TOTAL ABSTINENCE

See Abstinence.

TOU

[9495, 9497]. King of Hamath who congratulated David for victory over Hadadezer (2Sa 8:9-11; 1Ch 18:9-10).

TOW

NIV "thong, tinder, wick." Short fibers of flax or hemp (Jdg 16:9; Isa 1:31; 43:17).

TOWEL

[3317]. A cloth for wiping and drying (Jn 13:4-5).

TOWER

[859, 1032, 1467, 1468, 1469, 3227, 4463, 5164, 7610, 8123, 4788]. Of Babel (Ge 11:1-9). Of Eder (Ge 35:21). Peniel (Jdg 8:8-9, 17). Of Shechem (Jdg 9:46, 49). Of the Hundred (Ne 3:1; 12:39). Of Hananel (Ne 3:1; 12:39; Jer 31:38; Zec 14:10). Of David (SS 4:4). Of Aswan (Eze 29:10). Of Siloam (Lk 13:4). In the walls of Jerusalem (2Ch 26:9; 32:5; Ne 12:38-39). Of other cities (2Ch 14:7).

In the desert (2Ch 26:10). For watchmen or sentinels (2Ki 9:17; 18:8). As fortress (Mt 21:33).

Parable (Lk 14:28-29).

See Fortification; Ziggurat.

Figurative of divine protection (2Sa 22:3, 51; Ps 18:2; 61:3; 144:2; Pr 18:10).

TOWN

[*6551, 7953, 9133, 4484]. In ancient times, large cities had towns or villages surrounding them for protection (Nu 21:25, 32; Jos 15:45-47), sometimes it means an unwalled town (Dt 3:5; 1Sa 16:4).

TOWNCLERK

See City Clerk.

TRACONITIS

[5551] (*rough, stony district*). An area of c. 370 sq. miles S of Damascus; tetrarchy of Philip (Lk 3:1).

TRADE AND TRAVEL

Trade in the OT:

Ur of the Chaldeans a trading port; Egypt, from earliest times, a great trading nation (Ge 37:25).

First organized commerce of Hebrew people was under Solomon, who formed a partnership with the great mercantile cities of Tyre and Sidon (1Ki 9:27-28; 10:11); after the death of Solomon, Israel again became an agricultural nation.

Trade in the NT:

Jewish trade and commerce have small place in the Gospels. Through the NT times, trade, in the wider sense of the word, was in the hands of Rome and of Italy.

Travel:

Motives for travel: Trade, colonization, exploration, migration, pilgrimage, preaching, courier service, exile. Travel had serious hazards (Ac 27-28; 2Co 11:25-27); was facilitated by wonderful Roman roads, some of which still are used. Regular passenger service by land or sea was unknown.

TRADE GUILDS Societies of tradesmen organized chiefly for the purpose of social interaction (Ac 19), not trade unions in the modern sense.

TRADERS [2493, 4048, 6086, 8217, *435*]. *See Commerce; Merchant.*

TRADITION [2976, 4600, *4142, 4161*]. The decisions and minor precepts taught by Paul (1Co 11:2; 2Th 2:15; 3:6).

Commandments of men (Mt 12:1-8; 15:2-6; Mk 7:3-9; Lk 6:1-11; Col 2:8; 1Pe 1:18). Not authoritative (Mt 15:3-20; 1Ti 1:4; 4:7). *See Commandments and Statutes, of Men.*

TRAFFIC [6086]. Commerce suspended on the Sabbath (Ne 13:15-22).

TRAIN [*2852, 4340, 8647, 8767, *168, 169, 1214, 4082*].

1. Retinue of a monarch (Ps 68:18).
2. Skirt of a robe (Isa 6:1).
3. To educate or discipline (2Sa 22:35; Pr 22:6).

TRAITOR [953, 8004, 8745, *4140, 4595*]. Judas (Mt 26:14-16, 46-50; Mk 14:10-11, 43-45; Lk 22:3-6, 21-23, 47-48; Jn 13:2, 27-30; 18:2-8, 13).

See Treason.

TRAMP NIV "bandit" (Pr 6:11).

TRANCE [*1749*] (*a throwing of the mind out of its normal state*). A mental state in which the senses are partially or wholly suspended and the person is unconscious of his environment while he contemplates some extraordinary object (Ac 10:9-16; 22:17-21).

TRANS-EUPHRATES [2021+5643+6298, 10002+10468+10526, 10191+10468+10526]. The region beyond the Euphrates; from the Persian perpective it included Israel and its neighbors (Ezr 4:10-20; 5:6; 6:6).

TRANSFIGURATION [*3565*]. Of

Moses (Ex 34:29-35). Of Jesus (Mt 17:2-9; Mk 9:2-10; Lk 9:29-36; 2Pe 1:16-18). Of Stephen (Ac 6:15). *See Translation.*

TRANSGRESSION [6296, 7321, 7322, *490, 491, 4126, 4183*]. Breaking of a law (Pr 17:19; Ro 4:15). *See Sin.*

TRANSJORDAN (*beyond [East of] the Jordan*). A large plateau E of Jordan, comprised in modern Hashemite Kingdom of Jordan; in the NT times, the Perea and the Decapolis; in OT times, Moab, Ammon, Gilead, and Bashan. Associated with Moses; Joshua; the tribes of Reuben, Gad, and Manasseh; David; Nabateans.

TRANSLATION [10597, *1450, 2257*]. Removal from earth to heaven. Of Enoch (Ge 5:24; Heb 11:5). Of Elijah (2Ki 2:1-12). Of Jesus (Mk 16:19; Lk 24:51; Ac 1:9-11). Desired by Paul (2Co 5:4).

TRANSLATIONS OF THE BIBLE Ancient: *See Texts and Versions.*

TRANSPORTATION In ancient times done chiefly by camels, donkeys, horses, and boats.

TRAP [744, 3052, 3704, 4334, 4613, 4650, 4892, 5422, 5943, 7062, 7072, 8407, 8819, 8827, 9530, *2138, 2560, 4074, 4075, 4279*]. (Jos 23:13; Job 18:10; Jer 5:26).

TRAVAIL Pangs of childbirth (Ge 35:16; 38:27; 1Sa 4:19), trouble (Isa 23:4; 54:1), to be weak or sick (Jer 4:31), weariness (Ex 18:8).

TRAVEL [*782, 2006, 2143, 5023, 6296, *1451, 2262, 5321*]. *See Trade and Travel.*

TREACHERY [954, 956, 3950, 5085+5086, 5327, *2947, 4595*]. (Jer 9:8). Of Rahab to her people (Jos 2). Of the man of Bethel (Jdg 1:24-25). Of Jael (Jdg 4:18-21). Of the Shechemites (Jdg 9:23). Of Joab (2Sa 3:26-27). Of Baanah and Recab (2Sa 4:6). Of David to Uriah (2Sa 11). Of Joab to Amasa (2Sa 20:9-10). Of Jehu (2Ki 10:18-28). Of the enemies of Nehemiah (Ne 6).

See Conspiracy; Treason.

TREASON [8004].

Instances of:

Of Aaron and Miriam against Moses (Nu 12:1-11). Of Korah, Dathan, and Abiram against Moses and Aaron (Nu 16:1-33). Of Rahab against Jericho (Jos 2). Of the betrayer of Bethel (Jdg 1:24-25). Of the Shechemites against Abimelech (Jdg 9:22-25). Of the Ephraimites against Jephthah (Jdg 12:1-4). Of the Israelites against Saul (1Sa 10:27), against Rehoboam (1Ki 12:16-19). Of the Egyptian servant against the Amalekites (1Sa 30:15-16). Of Abner against Ish-Bosheth (2Sa 3:6-21). Of Jehoiada against Athaliah (2Ki 11:14-16). Of Absalom against his father. *See Absalom.*

Death penalty for (Est 2:23).

Jesus falsely accused of (Mt 27:11, 29-30; Lk 23:2-3, 38; Jn 19:12, 14-15, 19). Paul falsely accused of (Ac 17:7).

David's amnesty of the traitors (2Sa 19:16-23), to Amasa (2Sa 19:13).

See Conspiracy; Treachery.

TREASURE [*238, 1709, 2773, 2890, 4718, 4759, 4837, 6035, 7621, 10133, *1126, 2565*]. A thing of highly estimated value. Money (Ge 42:25, 27-28, 35; 43:23, w 43:18, 21-22). Valuables of the temple and royal residence (1Ki 14:26; 2Ki 20:13).

Cannot save life (Job 20:20). Jesus forbids the hoarding of (Mt 6:19; 19:21; Lk 12:33). Hidden (Mt 13:44).

Figurative:

Of God's people (Ex 19:5; Dt 7:6). Of wisdom (Pr 2:4; 24:4; Col 2:3). Of spiritual understanding (Mt 13:52; Col 2:3), spiritual calling (2Co 4:6-7). Treasures in heaven (Mt 6:19-21; 19:21; Lk 12:33-34). Gospel called (2Co 4:7). Parables of (Mt 13:44, 52).

TREASURE CITIES NIV "store cities" for Pharaoh (Ex 1:11).

TREASURE HOUSE *See Treasury.*

TREASURER [1601, 4837, 10133, 10139]. One trusted with charge of the treasury. *See Treasury.* Of the temple (2Ki 12:5, 7). Of Persia (Ezr 1:8; 7:21). Of Babylon (Da 3:2, 3).

TREASURY [238, 1709, 10103, 10148, 10479, *1125, 1126, 3168*]. Of kings (2Ki 14:14; 2Ch 32:27-28; Ezr 1:7-8; Est 3:9). Records preserved in (Ezr 6:1). *See Archives.* Treasurer in charge of (Ezr 7:20-21). *See Treasurer.*

Tabernacle used for (Jos 6:19, 24). Solomon's temple used for (1Ki 7:51; 2Ki 12:4-14, 18; 22:4-5; 1Ch 28:11-12; Mt 27:6; Mk 12:41, 43; Lk 21:1; Jn 8:20). Under the charge of the Levites (1Ch 26:20). Storerooms provided in the temple for various kinds of offerings (Ne 10:38-39; 13:5, 9, 12; Mal 3:10). Priests and Levites in charge of (1Ch 9:26; 26:20-28; Ne 12:44; 13:13). Pagan temples used for (Da 1:2).

TREATY [1382, 2256+3208+8934, 4162, 8966]. Between nations: Israelites and Gibeonites (Jos 9:3-15), Judah and Syria (1Ki 15:19). Cession of territory by (1Ki 9:10-14; 20:34). Sacredness of (Jos 9:16-21, w 2:8-21).

Reciprocity (1Ki 5:1-12). With idolatrous nations forbidden (Ex 34:12, 15).

See Covenant.

TREE [100, 461, 471, 869, 1360, 2339, 6770, 7771, 8232, 8316, 8413, 9196, 9300, 9469, 9474, 9515, 10027, *66, 1285, 1777, 2814, 3833, 5189, 5190, 5191*]. Israel in ancient times was far more wooded than today. Over 25 different kinds of trees have been identified as having grown in the Holy Land. Trees were venerated by heathen people; Hebrews forbidden to plant a tree near a sacred altar (Dt 16:21). Known by its fruit (Mt 7:17-19; Lk 6:43-44).

Specific Trees:

Acacia tree (Ex 25:10ff). Algum tree (2Ch 2:8; 9:11). Almond tree (Ge 30:37; Ex 25:33-36; Ecc 12:5; Jer 1:11). Almug tree (1Ki 10:11, 12; 2Ch. 2:8, 9:10 ftn). Apple tree (SS 2:3; 8:5; Joel 1:12). Balsam trees (2Sa 5:23-24). Broom tree (1Ki 19:3-4; Job 30:4; Ps 120:4). Cedar Wood (Lev 14:4, 6, 49, 51, 52; 2Sa 5:11; 2Sa 7:2; 1Ki 4:33). Citron Wood (Rev 18:12). Cypress Wood (Ge 6:14; Isa 44:14, 60:13; Eze 27:6). Fig tree (Dt 8:7). Fir (Isa 41:19; 60:13; SS 1:17. Fruit trees (Ge 1:29; Lev 19:23). Incense tree (SS 4:14). Mulberry tree (Lk 17:6). Mustard tree (Mt 13:32; Lk 13:18). Myrtle tree (Ne 8:15). Nut trees (SS 6:11). Oak (Ge 35:4; Zec 11:2; Eze 6:13). Olive tree (Jdg 9:8; Job 15:33; Ps 52:8; Isa 17:6; Isa 41:19). Palm trees (Ex 15:27). Pine tree (1Ki 5:10; Ps 104:17 ;Isa 60:13). Pistachio (Ge 43:11). Plane tree (Ge 30:37; Eze 31:8). Pomegranate (Dt 8:8; 1Sa 14:2). Poplars (Ge 30:37; Lev 23:40; Job 40:22; Ps 137:2; Isa 15:7, 44:4). Sycamore-fig tree (1Ki 10:27; 1Ch 27:28; 2Ch 1:15; Am 7:14; Lk 19:4). Tamarisk tree (Ge 21:33; 1Sa 22:6; 31:13). Terebinth (Isa 6:13; Hos 4:13).

Generic and Symbolic Trees:

Bad tree (Mt 7:18; 12:33; Lk 6:43). Eden trees (Eze 31:9, 18). Execution tree (Dt 21:23; Ac 5:30; 10:39; 13:29). Field trees (Isa 55:12). Forest trees (1Ch 16:33; Ps 96:12). Good tree (2Ki 3:19, 25; Mt 7:17, 12:33; Lk 6:43). Great trees (Ge 13:18; 14:13; Jos 19:33). Great tree (Ge 12:6). Green tree (Ps 37:35; Lk 23:30). Tree of Knowledge (Ge 2:9). Leafy tree (Eze 20:28). Tree of Life (Ge 3:22-24; Pr 3:18, 11:30, 13:12; 15:4; Rev 2:7; 22:2, 19). Lofty tree (Isa 10:33). Shade tree (Ne 8:15). Spreading tree (Dt 12:2; 1Ki 14:23; 2Ki 16:4, 17:10). Wild olive tree (Ro 11:24). Of Nebuchadnezzar (Da 4:1-27).

See Plants of the Bible; Tree of Knowledge; Tree of Life.

TREE OF KNOWLEDGE A special tree in the garden of Eden, set apart by the Lord as an instrument to test the obedience of Adam and Eve (Ge 2:9, 17; 3:3-6, 11-12, 17).

TREE OF LIFE Another special tree in the Garden of Eden; its fruit conferred immortality on persons eating it (Ge 2:9; 3:22, 24; Rev 22:2).

TRENCH [3022, 9498]. Rampart, entrenchment (2Sa 20:15; 1Sa 17:20; 26:5).

TRES TABERNAE *See Three Taverns.*

TRESPASS [*4183*]. (Ex 22:9). Of an ox (Ex 21:28-36). Of a brother (Mt 18:15-18; Lk 17:3-4). Creditor shall not enter a debtor's house to take a pledge (Dt 24:10). *See Sin.*

TRESPASS OFFERING *See Guilt Offering; Offerings.*

TRIAL [4999, 5477, 6641, 9149, 72, 185, 2568+, 3212, 4225, 4280]. Before court (Lev 24:10-14). Right of (Jn 7:51; Ac 16:37-39; 22:25-30). *See Court, Of Law; Justice; Prisoners.*

TRIAL OF JESUS Betrayed by Judas into the hands of the Jewish religious leaders, Jesus was first brought before Annas, former high priest, and father-in-law of the current high priest Caiaphas, for a brief examination (Jn 18:13); then before dawn he appeared before the Sanhedrin in the palace of Caiaphas, where he was questioned and insulted (Mk 14:60-65; Lk 22:63-64); at dawn he appeared before the Sanhedrin again and was condemned to death (Lk 22:66-70); next he was brought by the Sanhedrin before Pilate, who after an examination pronounced him innocent (Jn 18:33-38), but the Jews would not hear of his being released.

Pilate therefore sent him to Herod Antipas, who was also present for the Passover, on the plea that he belonged to Herod's jurisdiction. Herod, however, merely mocked Jesus and returned him to Pilate uncondemned (Lk 23:2-12); Pilate then gave the Jews the opportunity of choosing for release either Barabbas or Jesus, and the Jews chose Barabbas; another attempt by Pilate to have Jesus released met with failure, for the Jews threatened him if he did not carry out their wishes; after the Roman soldiers flogged and mocked Jesus, he was crucified (Mk 15:16-20).

See Jesus, History of.

TRIBE, TRIBES [1074, 1201, 1228, 4722, 4751, 4985, 7259, 7470, 8657, 10694, 1559, 5876]. The tribes of Israel were descended from the twelve sons of Jacob, with Joseph's sons, Ephraim and Manasseh forming two, while no tribal territory was allotted to Levi (Ge 48:5; Nu 26:5-51; Jos 13:7-33; 15-19). The leaders of the tribes are called by various names: princes, rulers, heads, chiefs (Ex 34:31; Nu 1:16; Ge 36:1ff); before the Israelites entered the promised land two tribes, Reuben and Gad, and half of Manasseh chose to settle on the E side of the Jordan (Nu 32:33). During the period of the Judges in Israel, the tribes were each one a law to themselves. When David became king over the whole land the 12 tribes were unified. He appointed a captain over each tribe (1Ch 27:16-22). The captivities wiped out tribal distinctions.

TRIBULATION, GREAT [2568]. A period of suffering sent from God upon the earth at the end time because of its awful wickedness (Da 12:1; Mt 24:21).

TRIBUTE [4830, 4966, 4989, 5362, 5957, 10107]. From conquered nations (Jos 16:10; Jdg 1:30-33; 2Ki 15:19; 23:35; Mt 17:24-27; 22:15-22; Lk 2:1-5). By Arabs to Solomon (2Ch 9:14), to Jehoshaphat (2Ch 17:11). *See Duty; Levy; Tax.*

TRIMMERS, WICK [4662, 4920]. *See Wick Trimmers.*

TRINITY, HOLY (*triad, union of three*). The word "trinity" is not used in the Bible. Plurality in the unity of God is implied in the OT; Father, Son, and Spirit are all called "God" in the NT.

Implied in the Old Testament:
God speaks of self in the plural (Ge 1:26; 3:22; Isa 6:3, 8). LORD, Servant, and Spirit (Isa 11:2-3; 42:1 w Mt 12:48; Isa 48:16). Tri-holiness of God suggests (Isa 6:3; Rev 4:8).

Implied in the NT:
Father, Son, and Spirit (Mt 28:19; Lk 3:22 w Mt 3:16; Jn 3:34-35; 14:16-17, 26; 15:26; 16:7, 13-15; Ac 1:2, 4-5; 2:33; 10:36-38; Ro 1:3-4; 8:9-11, 26-27; 1Co 12:3-6; 2Co 1:21-22; 5:5; 13:14; Gal 4:4, 6; 2Th 2:13-14, 16; 1Ti 3:16; Tit 3:4-6; Heb 9:14; 1Pe 1:2; 3:18; 1Jn 5:6-7). Tri-holiness of God suggests (Isa 6:3; Rev 4:8).

Relationships Within the Godhead:
The Father and the Son (Mt 11:27; Lk 9:26; Jn 3:35; 5:19-27; 6:27; 10:36; 17:1; Ac 13:33; Heb 1:5; 5:5; 2Pe 1:17; 1Jn 1:3; 2:22-24).

The Father and the Holy Spirit (Isa 42:1; 48:16; 63:9-10; 1Co 2:10-11; 6:19).

Jesus and the Holy Spirit (Isa 61:1-3; Lk 4:18; Mt 1:18, 20; 12:28; 28:19; Lk 1:35; 4:1, 14; Jn 1:32-33; 7:39; 20:22; 1Co 8:6; 2Co 3:17; Php 1:19; Col 2:2).

See Angel [of the Lord]; God; Holy Spirit; Jesus the Christ, Deity of.

TRIPOLIS [10305]. People sent as colonists to Samaria by the Assyrians (Ezr 4:9-10).

TRIUMPH [1452, 1504, 2116+6702, 2616, 3523, 5627, 6451, 6600, 6636, 8123, 8131, 8934, 2581, 3771] (*to lead in triumph*). In Roman times a magnificent procession in honor of a victorious general (2Co 2:14; Col 2:15).

TRIUMPHAL ENTRY OF JESUS Into Jerusalem (Ps 118:26; Zec 9:9; Mt 21:5, 8-10; Mk 11:7-11; Lk 19:35-38; Jn 12:12-13).

TROAS [5590]. A chief city and port of the Roman Province of Asia, on the Aegean coast, c. ten miles from the ruins of ancient Troy; known as Alexandria Troas (Ac 16:8; 20:5; 2Co 2:12).

TROGYLLIUM A promontory thrusting SW from the Asian mainland N of Miletus, opposite the island of Samos (Ac 20:15, KJV).

TROPHIES Goliath's head and armor (1Sa 17:54; 21:9), Saul's (1Sa 31:8-10). Placed in temples. *See Temple.*

TROPHIMUS [5576] (*nourished [child]*). An Ephesian companion of Paul. Accompanies Paul from Greece to Asia (Ac 20:4). With Paul in

Jerusalem; made the occasion of an attack on Paul (Ac 21:27-30). Left ill at Miletus (2Ti 4:20).

TROUBLE [*1314, 6579, 6662, 7192, 7639, 7650, 7674, 8273, 8288, 8288, 8317, 86, 1943, 2567, 2568, 5429]. Being anxious, forbidden (Mt 6:25-34; Php 4:6). Remedy for anxiety (Jn 16:6-7; 1Pe 5:7).

See Affliction; Anxiety; Suffering.

Instances of:

Israelites at the Red Sea (Ex 14:10-12), about water (Ex 15:23-25; 17:2-3; Nu 20:1-13), food (Ex 16:2-3; Nu 11:4-33). When Moses remained on Mount Sinai (Ex 32:1). When the spies brought their adverse report (Nu 13:28-29, 31-33; 14:1-4, w 14:4-12). Elijah, under the broom tree and in the cave (1Ki 19:4-15). The disciples, as to how the multitude could be fed (Mt 14:15; Mk 6:37), in the tempest, when Jesus was asleep in the ship (Mt 8:23-26; Mk 4:36-39; Lk 8:22-24), when Jesus was crucified (Lk 24:4-9, 24-31, 36-40). Mary at the tomb (Jn 20:11-17). The people in the shipwreck (Ac 27:22-25, 30-36).

TRUCE In battle (2Sa 2:26-31).

TRUMPET [2955, 2956, 8795, 9540, 9546, 9558, 4894, 4895]. Made of ram's horn (Jos 6:4-6, 8, 13), of silver (Nu 10:2).

Uses of:

Prescribed by Moses (Nu 10:1-10). Used in war (Job 39:24-25; Jer 4:19; 6:1, 17; 42:14; 51:27; Eze 7:14; Am 2:2; 3:6; Zep 1:16; 1Co 14:8). To summon soldiers, by Phinehas (Nu 31:6), by Ehud (Jdg 3:27), by Gideon (Jdg 6:34), by Saul (1Sa 13:3), by Joab (2Sa 2:28; 18:16; 20:22), by Absalom (2Sa 15:10), by Sheba (2Sa 20:1), by Nehemiah (Ne 4:18, 20). Gideon's soldiers (Jdg 7:8-22). In war, of Abijah (2Ch 13:12, 14). In the siege of Jericho (Jos 6:4-20).

Sounded in time of danger (Eze 33:3-6; Joel 2:1). Used at Sinai (Ex 19:13-19; 20:18; Heb 12:19), on the Day of Atonement (Isa 27:13), at the Jubilee (Lev 25:9), at the bringing up of the ark (2Sa 6:5, 15; 1Ch 13:8; 15:28), the anointing of kings (1Ki 1:34, 39; 2Ki 9:13; 11:14), dedication of Solomon's temple (2Ch 5:12-13; 7:6), in worship (1Ch 15:24; 16:42; 25:5; Ps 81:3-4), at Jehoshaphat's triumph (2Ch 20:28), at the foundation of the second temple (Ezr 3:10-11), at the dedication of the wall (Ne 12:35, 41).

Figurative:

(Isa 27:13; Eze 33:3; Joel 2:1; Zec 9:14; Mt 6:2).

Symbolic:

(Mt 24:31; 1Co 15:52; 1Th 4:16; Rev 1:10; 4:1; 8; 9:1-14; 10:7; 11:15).

See Horn; Music, Instruments of.

TRUMPETS, FEAST OF When and how observed (Lev 23:24-25; Nu 29:1-6). Celebrated after the captivity with joy (Ne 8:2, 9-12).

See Feasts.

TRUST [*575, 586, 1053, 2879, 4073, 4440, 7747, 10041, 3874, 4275, 4409, 4412]. *See Faith.*

TRUSTEE [3874]. Mosaic law concerning (Ex 22:7-13; Lev 6:2-7). The parable of the pounds (Mt 25:14-28; Lk 19:12-27).

See Steward.

TRUTH [*575, 586, 589, 597, 622, 995, 4027, 7406, 7999, 9214, 10327, 237, 238, 239, 240, 242, 297, 1188, 4048]. Truth and faithful(ness) are translated from the same Hebrew and Greek words. *See Faithfulness.*

Characteristics of:

(Ps 85:10-11). Precious (Pr 23:23). Preserves (Ps 46:11; 61:7; 91:4; Pr 20:28). Purifies (Pr 16:6; 1Pe 1:22). Sanctifies (Jn 17:17, 19; 2Th 2:13). Brings freedom (Jn 8:32).

Reaches to the clouds (Ps 57:10; 108:4). Endures forever (Ps 100:5; 117:2). Ways of the Lord in (Ps 25:10).

The foundation of which Christ is the cornerstone (Eph 2:20). Came by Jesus Christ (Jn 1:17; 8:45; 14:6; 18:37-38; Eph 2:20). Revealed to the righteous (Ps 57:3; 86:11).

Word of God called the word of (Jn 17:17; Eph 1:13; Col 1:5; 2Ti 2:15; Jas 1:18). Scripture of (Da 10:21).

Acceptance of, necessary to salvation (2Th 2:12-13; 1Ti 2:4; 2Ti 2:25; 3:7; Heb 10:26). Rejection of, brings condemnation (2Th 2:10-12; Tit 1:14). To be taught by parents to children (Isa 38:19). Church is the pillar of (1Ti 3:15).

Believers should worship God in (Jn 4:24, w Ps 145:18), serve God in (Jos 24:14; 1Sa 12:24), walk before God in (1Ki 2:4; 2Ki 20:3), keep religious feasts with (1Co 5:8), value as inestimable (Pr 23:23), love (Zec 8:19), rejoice in (1Co 13:6), speak to one another (Eph 4:25), execute judgment with (Zec 8:16), meditate upon (Php 4:8), bind about the neck (Pr 3:3), write upon the tables of the heart (Pr 3:3).

The fruit of the light (Eph 5:9). They who speak, show righteousness (Pr 12:17), are the delight of God (Pr 12:22), will be established forever (Pr 2:1).

The wicked are destitute of truth (Isa 59:14-15; Da 9:13; Hos 4:1; 1Ti 6:5). The wicked resist (2Ti 3:8; 4:4), turn away from (2Ti 4:4), speak not (Jer 9:5), plead not for (Isa 59:4), are not valiant for (Jer 9:3), punished for lack of (Jer 9:5, 9; Hos 4:1, 3). *See Wicked.*

The Gospel As:

Came by Christ (Jn 1:17). Is in Christ (1Ti 2:7). John bore witness to (Jn 5:33). Is according to godliness (Tit 1:1). Is sanctifying (Jn 17:17, 19). Is purifying (1Pe 1:22). Is part of the Christian armor (Eph 6:14). Revealed abundantly to saints (Jer 33:6). Abides continually with saints (2Jn 2).

Should be acknowledged (2Ti 2:25). Should be believed (2Th 2:12-13; 1Ti 4:3). Should be obeyed (Ro 2:8; Gal 3:1). Should be loved (2Th 2:10). Should be manifested (2Co 4:2). Should be rightly divided (2Ti 2:15). The church is the pillar and ground of (1Ti 3:15).

The devil is devoid of (Jn 8:44).

Of the Gospel:

(2Ti 4:3-4; Tit 1:1, 14; 2:1; Jas 1:18, 21, 23, 25; 2:13; 5:19; 1Pe 1:22-25; 2:2, 8; 3:1; 5:12; 2Pe 1:12). *See God, Truth.*

Of God:

Is one of his attributes (Dt 32:4; Isa 65:16). Often linked with his mercy (Ps 85:10-11; 93:3; 100:5).

He keeps, forever (Ps 146:6), abundant (Ex 34:6), inviable (Nu 23:19; Tit 1:2), enduring to all generations (Ps 100:5). Exhibited in his ways (Rev 15:3), works (Ps 33:4; 111:7; Da 4:37), judicial statutes (Ps 19:9), word (Ps 119:160; Jn 17:17), fulfillment of promises in Christ (2Co 1:20), fulfillment of His covenant (Mic 7:20), dealings with saints (Ps 25:10), deliverance of saints (Ps 57:3), punishment of the wicked (Rev 16:7). Is a shield and buckler to saints (Ps 91:4).

Believers should confide in (Ps 31:5; Tit 1:2). Plead in prayer (Ps 89:49). Pray for its manifestation to ourselves (2Ch 6:17). Pray for its exhibition to others (2Sa 2:6). Make known, to others (Isa 38:19). Magnify (Ps 71:22; 138:2).

Is denied by the devil (Ge 3:4-5), the self-righteous (1Jn 1:10), unbelievers (1Jn 5:10).

Attribute:

Of God (Ex 34:6; Dt 32:4; Ps 31:5; 40:10-11; 71:22; 86:15; 89:14; 115:1; 117:2; 138:2; 146:6; Isa 25:1; 65:16; Jer 4:2; 5:3). Exhibited in His government (Ps 119:151), in His judgments (Ps 96:13; Ro 2:2), in His word (Jn 17:19), in His works (Ps 111:7-8; Da 4:37).

Of Christ (Jn 1:14; 14:6).

Of the Holy Spirit (Jn 14:17; 16:13; 1Jn 5:7-8).

Of the Righteous (Ps 51:6; Pr 3:3; Jn 3:21; 3Jn 3).

Righteous, should be prepared with (Eph 6:14), should know (1Ti 4:3; 1Jn 2:21; 3:19; 4:6), should love (Zec 8:19; 2Th 2:10), should rejoice in (1Co 13:6), should meditate upon (Php 4:8).

TRUTHFULNESS [574, 575, 622, *237, 239*]. Commended (Pr 12:17, 19). Commanded (Zec 8:16; Eph 4:25; Col 3:9). Magistrates should be men of (Ex 18:21). Fearlessness in (2Co 12:6; Gal 4:16). Of Job (Job 27:4; 36:4).

Wicked, lack (Jer 9:5). Satan, devoid of (Jn 8:44). *See Satan; Wicked.*

TRYPHENA [*5586*] (*dainty*). A Christian woman friend of Paul's in Rome (Ro 16:12).

TRYPHOSA [*5589*] (*delicate*). A Christian woman friend of Paul's in Rome (Ro 16:12).

TUBAL [9317]. The son of Japheth (Ge 10:2; 1Ch 1:5). Descendants of, become a nation (Isa 66:19; Eze 27:13; 32:26; 38:2-3; 39:1).

TUBAL-CAIN [9340]. The son of Lamech and Zillah; worker in bronze and iron (Ge 4:22).

TUMBLEWEED [1650]. Symbolic of wicked blown away in judgment (Ps 83:13; Isa 17:13). *See Plants of the Bible.*

TUMOR [3224, 6754]. A disease with which the Philistines were afflicted (1Sa 5:6, 9, 12; 6:4-5, 11, 17). *See Disease; Hemorrhoids.*

TUNIC [955, 4189, 4230+4496, 4496, *5945*]. A shirtlike garment worn by men and women under other clothes in Bible times. Worn by priests (Ex 28:4, 39-40). Saul offers his to David (1Sa 17:38-39), as does Jonathan (1Sa 18:4). *See Dress.*

TURBAN [3178, 5200, 6996, 7565, 10368]. Headcovering. Worn by the high priest (Ex 28:3, 37-39), by other priests (Eze 44:18), by royalty (Eze 21:26). *See Headbands.*

TURQUOISE [5876, 7037]. In the high priest's breastpiece (Ex 28:18; 39:11), in the temple (1Ch 29:2). Commerce in (Eze 27:16). *See Minerals of the Bible; Stones.*

TURTLE, TURTLEDOVE See *Dove, Turtle.*

TUTOR (2Ki 10:1; Ac 22:3; Gal 4:1-2).

TWELVE, THE See *Apostles.*

TWILIGHT [1068+2021+6847, 5974]. (1Sa 30:17; 2Ki 7:5; Job 3:9; Eze 12:6).

TWINS [9298, 9339, *1483*]. Jacob and Esau (Ge 25:24-26). Perez and Zerah (Ge 38:27-30). *See Castor and Pollux.*

TWO-AND-A-HALF TRIBES [2256+2942+9109] Reuben, Gad, and half of Manasseh settled in the Trans-Jordan (Jos 14:3).

TYCHICUS [*5608*] (*good fortune*). An Asian companion of Paul. Accompanies Paul from Greece to Asia (Ac 20:4). With Paul in Nicopolis (Tit 3:12), in Rome (Eph 6:21-22; Col 4:7-8). Sent to Ephesus (Eph 6:21-22; 2Ti 4:12), to Colosse (Col 4:7-8).

TYPES

Miscellaneous:

Bride, a type of the church (Rev 21:2, 9; 22:17). The sanctuary a type of the heavenly sanctuary (Ex 40:2, 24; Heb 8:2, 5; 9:1-12). The saving of Noah and his family, of the salvation through the gospel (1Pe 3:20-21).

Defilement a type of sin. *See Defilement; Purification.* Leaven a type of sin. *See Leaven.* Washings a type of purification. *See Washings.*

See Allegory; Parable; Symbols and Similitudes.

Of Sin: *See Blemish; Defilement; Leaven.*

Of the Savior:

(Col 2:17; Heb 9:7-15, 18-28; 10:1-10). High priest, typical of the mediatorship (Ex 28:1, 12, 29-30, 38; Lev 16:15; Zec 6:12-13, w Heb 5; 8:2;

10:21). The institutions ordained by Moses (Mt 26:54; Lk 24:25-27, 44-47; Col 2:14-17; Heb 10:1-14). The sacrifices (Lev 4:2-3, 12; Heb 9:7-15, 18-25; 10:1-22, 29; 13:11-13; 1Pe 1:19; Rev 5:6). The morning and evening sacrifice (Jn 1:29, 36). The red heifer (Nu 19:2-6, w Heb 9:13-14). The Passover lamb (1Co 5:7). The bronze altar (Ex 27:1-2, w Heb 13:10). The bronze basin (Ex 30:18-20, w Zec 13:1; Eph 5:26-27). Atonement cover (Ex 25:17-22, w Heb 4:16). The veil (Ex 40:21; 2Ch 3:14, w Heb 10:20). Manna (Jn 6:32-35; 1Co 10:3). Cities of refuge (Nu 35:6, w Heb 6:18). Bronze snake (Nu 21:9; Jn 3:14-15). Tree of life (Ge 2:9, w Jn 1:4; Rev 22:2).

Adam (Ro 5:14; 1Co 15:45). Abel (Ge 4:8, 10, w Heb 12:24). Noah (Ge 5:29, w 2Co 1:5). Melchizedek (Heb 7:1-17). Moses (Dt 18:15, 18; Ac 3:20, 22; 7:37; Heb 3:2-6). David (2Sa 8:15; Ps 89:19-20; Eze 37:24; Php 2:9). Eliakim (Isa 22:20-22; Rev 3:7). Jonah (Jnh 1:17, w Mt 12:40).

TYRANNUS [5598] (*ruler*). A Greek teacher in whose school Paul preached after he was expelled from the synagogue (Ac 19:9).

TYRANNY [6945]. (Pr 28:16; Isa 54:11-14). *See Government.*

TYRE, TYRIANS [7450, 7660, *5601, 5602*] (*rocky place*).

1. Kingdom of; Hiram, king of (1Ki 5:1-2; 2Ch 2:3). Sends material to David for his palace (2Ch 2:3). Men and materials sent from, to Solomon, for the building of the temple and palaces (1Ki 5:1-11; 9:10-11; 2Ch 2:3-16).

See Hiram.

2. City of. Situated on the shore of the Mediterranean. On the northern boundary of Asher (Jos 19:29). Pleasant site of (Hos 9:13). Fortified (Jos 19:29; 2Sa 24:7). Commerce of (1Ki 9:26-28; 10:11; Isa 23; Eze 27; 28:1-19; Zec 9:2; Ac 21:3). Merchants of (Isa 23:8). Antiquity of (Isa 23:7). Riches of (Isa 23:8; Zec 9:3). Besieged by Nebuchadnezzar (Eze 26:7; 29:18).

Jesus goes to the coasts of (Mt 15:21). Heals the daughter of the Syrian Phoenician woman near (Mt 15:21-28; Mk 7:24-31). Multitudes from, come to hear Jesus and to be healed of their diseases (Mk 3:8; Lk 6:17). Herod's hostility toward (Ac 12:20-23). Paul visits (Ac 21:3-7).

To be judged according to its opportunity and privileges (Mt 11:21-22; Lk 10:13-14).

Prophecies relating to (Ps 45:12; 87:4; Isa 23; Jer 25:22; 27:1-11; 47:4; Eze 26-28; Joel 3:4-8; Am 1:9-10; Zec 9:2-4).

TYROPEON VALLEY (*valley of the cheese makers*). A valley in Jerusalem separating W and E hills and joining Kidron and Hinnom valleys on the S.

U

UCAL [432] (possibly *I am consumed*, or *I cease*). An obscure word; usually taken as son or pupil of Agur (Pr 30:1).

UEL [198] (possibly *will of El [God]* BDB KB). An Israelite who divorced his Gentile wife (Ezr 10:34).

UGARIT *See Amarna, Tell El; Ras Shamra; Texts, Ancient Near Eastern Non-Biblical Texts Relating to the Old Testament.*

ULAI [217]. A river in Elam near Susa on whose bank Daniel saw a vision (Da 8:2, 16).

ULAM [220] (*first, leader*).
  1. The son of Sheresh (1Ch 7:16-17).
  2. The son of Eshek (1Ch 8:39-40).

ULLA [6587]. An Asherite (1Ch 7:39).

UMMAH [6646]. A city of Asher (Jos 19:30).

UNBELIEF [602].

Characteristics of:
  Caused by spiritual blindness (Isa 6:9-10; Mt 13:13-15, 58; Lk 13:34; 19:41-42; Jn 12:37, 39-40, 47). Hardens the heart (Ps 95:8-11; Heb 3:12; 3:16-19; Ac 19:9). Rejects Christ (Isa 53:1-3; Jn 12:38; Mk 6:3, 6; Jn 1:11; 5:38, 40, 44, 46-47; 10:25-26). Displeases God (Ps 78:19-22; Heb 11:6). Makes God a liar (1Jn 5:10). Does not nullify God's faithfulness (Ro 3:3-4). Allows God to extend his mercy (Ro 11:20, 30-32). Characteristic of all mankind (Ro 11:20, 30-32; 2Th 3:2).
  Illustrated (Ro 10:6-7, 16; 2Pe 3:4). Parable of (Mk 4:24-25; Lk 8:12, 18; 14:16-24).
  At Christ's second coming (Lk 18:8). The spirit of the antichrist (1Jn 2:22-23; 4:3).
  Used as an excuse by Moses (Ex 4:1).

Condemned:
  Leads to: Defeat (Isa 7:9). Destruction (Ro 11:20; 2Th 2:12). Reproof (Jn 16:8-9). Condemnation (Ro 14:23). Rejection (1Pe 2:7-8). Instability (Jas 1:6-7).
  Admonitions against (Ac 13:40-41; 2Co 6:14-16; Heb 3:12, 16-19; 4:1-3, 6, 11; 12:25).

UNBELIEVERS [578, 602, 603]. Are spiritually blind (Jn 14:17; 1Co 2:14; 2Pe 3:4-7). Are impure (Tit 1:15). Make God a liar (1Jn 5:10). Will not be convinced (Lk 16:31; 22:67; Jn 4:48; 12:37-40). God's forbearance toward (Ro 10:16, 21). Shall be destroyed (Jer 5:12-14; Mt 10:14-15; Lk 12:46; Jn 8:24; 12:48; Ac 13:41; 1Co 1:18; 2Th 2:11-12; Jude 5-7; Rev 21:8). Tongues a sign to (1Co 14:22).

Instances of:
  Eve (Ge 3:4-6). Moses (Nu 11:21-23) and Aaron (Nu 20:12). Israelites (Dt 9:23; 2Ki 17:14; Ps 78; 106:7, 24; Isa 58:3; Mal 1:2, 7). Naaman (2Ki 5:12). Samaritan lord (2Ki 7:2).
  Disciples (Mt 17:17; Lk 24:11, 25). Zechariah (Lk 1:20). Chief priests (Mt 21:32; Lk 22:67). The Jews (Mt 11:16-19; Mk 1:45; 2:6-11; 8:11-12; 15:29-32; Lk 7:31-35; Jn 5:38, 40, 43, 46-47; Ac 22:18; 28:24). Disciples (Mt 17:20; Mk 4:38, 40; 16:14, 16; Lk 24:11, 21, 25-26, 36-45; Jn 6:36, 60-62, 64, 66, 70-71). The father of a child possessed with a spirit confesses (Mk 9:24). Brothers of Christ (Jn 7:5). Thomas (Jn 20:25). Jews of Iconium (Ac 14:2). Thessalonian Jews (Ac 17:5). Jews in Jerusalem (Ro 15:31). Ephesians (Ac 19:9). Saul (1Ti 1:13). People of Jericho (Heb 11:31).

UNBELIEVING ISRAELITES

Destroyed (Nu 14:11, 13-39; 32:11; Dt 1:34-35; Ps 95:11; 106:26; 1Co 10:5, 10; Heb 3:17; Jude 5).

UNBLEMISHED [320]. Offerings must be (Ex 12:5; Lev 22:21; Eph 5:27; 1Pe 1:19).

UNCHARITABLENESS (Isa 29:21).

Admonitions Against:
  (Mt 7:1-5; Lk 6:37-42; 12:57; Jn 7:24; 8:7; Ro 2:1; 14:1-15; 1Co 4:3-5, 7; 13:1-6). Forbidden (Jas 4:11-12).
  See Accusation, False; Charitableness; Judgment; Slander; Speaking, Evil; Talebearer.

Instances of:
  The Israelites toward Moses, charging him with having made them abhorred by the Egyptians (Ex 5:21), charging him with bringing them out of Egypt to die (Ex 14:11-12), in murmuring against Moses. *See Murmuring, Instances of.*
  The tribes west of Jordan toward the two and a half tribes (Nu 32:1-33; Jos 22:11-31). Of Eli toward Hannah (1Sa 1:14-17).
  Eliab toward David, charging him with presumption, when he offered to fight Goliath (1Sa 17:28). Princes of Ammon toward David, when he sent commissioners to convey his sympathy to Hanun (2Sa 10:3). Bildad toward Job (Job 8). Eliphaz toward Job (Job 15; 22; 42:7-8). Zophar toward Job (Job 11:1-6; 20). Nathanael, when he said, "Can any good thing come out of Nazareth" (Jn 1:46). The Jews, charging Paul with teaching contrary to the law and against the temple (Ac 21:28).

UNCIAL LETTERS A style of handwriting that uses capitals for most letters. Early Greek manuscripts of the NT were written in uncials.

UNCIRCUMCISED [6888, 213+, 598, 2177].
  1. One who has not submitted to the Jewish rite of circumcision.

2. Gentiles (Ge 34:14; Jdg 14:3; Ro 4:9).

3. One whose heart is not open to God (Jer 4:4; 6:10; Ac 7:51).

UNCLE [278, 1856].
1. Brother of one's father or mother (2Ki 24:17).
2. Any kinsman on father's side (Lev 10:4; Am 6:10).

UNCLEAN, UNCLEANNESS
[*1458, 3237, 3238, 3240, 5614, 7002, *176*, *3123*, *3124*].
1. Two kinds of uncleanness: Moral and ceremonial.
2. Foods regarded as unclean in the OT: Animals that did not chew the cud and have a split hoof; animals and birds that eat blood or carrion; anything strangled or that died of itself (Lev 11:1-8, 26-28); water creatures without scales and fins (Lev 11:9-12); insects without hind legs for jumping (Lev 11).
3. Other forms of ceremonial uncleanness; contact with the dead (Lev 11:24-40; 17:15; Nu 19:16-22), leprosy (Lev 13; 14; Nu 5:2), sexual discharge (Lev 15:16-33), childbirth (Lev 12:6-8). In Christianity uncleanness is moral, not ceremonial.
See Purification.

UNCLOTHED [1694]. Figurative (Mt 22:11; 2Co 5:3; Rev 3:17; 16:15).

UNCTION *See Anointing.*

UNDEFILED Any person or thing not tainted with moral evil (Ps 119:1; Heb 7:26; 13:4; 1Pe 1:4).

UNDERGARMENTS [4829, *5945*].
For the priests (Ex 28:42; 39:28; Lev 6:10; 16:4; Eze 44:18). Of Jesus (Jn 19:23). *See Dress.*

UNDERSETTERS NIV "supports" for the movable stands in Solomon's temple (1Ki 7:30, 34).

UNFAITHFULNESS [574+4202, 953, 957, 2388, 2393, 2394, 3950, 5085, 5086, 5538, 8745, *4518*].
Characteristics of:
Unfaithful in little, unfaithful in much (Lk 16:10). Brings spiritual bankruptcy (Mt 13:12; 25:29). Brings destruction (Jn 15:2). Brings condemnation (Lk 19:12-27; Mt 25:41-46). God deals with accordingly (Pr 24:11-12; Mt 25:8-13, 24-30, 41-46).
Denounced:
In the parables of the vineyard (Isa 5:1-7; Mt 21:33-43; Mk 12:1-9). In the parable of the empty vine (Hos 10:1-2). In the parable of the slothful servant (Mt 25:24-30; Lk 19:20-27).
Illustrated:
By the unfruitful tree (Mt 3:10; Mk 11:13-14). By the unfruitful branch (Jn 15:2, 4, 6). By blindness (2Pe 1:8-9).

See Sin, Fruits of; Unfruitfulness; also, Righteousness, Fruits of.
Of friends: *See Friends, False.*

UNFRUITFULNESS [*182*]. Punished (Isa 5:1-10; Mt 3:10 w Lk 3:9; Mt 7:19; 13:3-7 w Mk 4:3-7, 14-19 & Lk 8:4-14; Mt 21:19-20; Mk 11:13; Lk 3:9; 13:6-9; Jn 15:2, 4; 15:6).
See Sin, Fruits of; Unfaithfulness; also, Righteousness, Fruits of.

UNGODLY [2868, 2869, 2870, 2883+4202, 8401, *96*, *813*, *814*, *815*]. To be avoided (Ps 1:1). Seem to materially prosper (Ps 73:11). Judged (Ps 1:6; 3:7; 2Pe 3:7). Christ died for (Ro 5:6), therefore God justifies (Ro 4:5). Law made for (1Ti 1:9).
See Wicked.

UNICORN *See Wild Ox.*

UNION [2482, *1182*]. Advantages of (Pr 15:22; Ecc 4:9-12).
Of the righteous: *See Unity, Of the Righteous; Righteous, Union of, with Christ.*

UNITY [285, 3480, *1651*, *1942*].
Of the Godhead: *See God, Unity of.*
Of the Righteous:
(Ps 133:1; Isa 52:8; Ac 4:32). Advantages of (Pr 15:22; Ecc 4:9-12). Fraternal (Mt 23:8).
Commanded among Christians (Ro 12:16; 14:19; 15:5-6; 1Co 1:10; 2Co 13:11; Eph 4:3; Php 1:27; 2:2; 3:16-17; 1Pe 3:8). Christ's prayer for, of the church (Jn 17:11, 21-23).
See Communion; Fellowship; One Another.

UNKNOWN GOD Inscription on an altar at Athens dedicated to an unknown god that worshipers did not want to overlook (Ac 17:23).

UNKNOWN TONGUE KJV "unknown" is a translator's insertion (in italics) for the term normally rendered simply "tongues" (1Co 14:2, 4, 13-14, 19, 27). *See Tongues, Gift of.*

UNLEARNED Illiterate (Ac 4:13; 2Pe 3:16), nonprofessional (1Co 14:16, 23f).

UNLEAVENED [5174, *109*]. Unmixed with yeast (1Co 5:7-8).

UNLEAVENED BREAD [5174, *109*]. Bread made without yeast (Ex 12:8).

UNLEAVENED BREAD, FEAST OF *See Feasts.*

UNNI [6716] (*Yahweh has answered*).
1. A Levite; musician (1Ch 15:18, 20).
2. A Levite; musician (Ne 12:9).

UNPARDONABLE SIN Blasphemy against the Holy Spirit (Mt 12:31-32; Mk 3:28-29; Lk 12:10); either attributing to Satan the work of the Holy Spirit through Jesus, or rejecting the

testimony of the Holy Spirit regarding the person and work of Jesus Christ. Possibly the same as the sin that leads to death (1Jn 5:16-17).

Instances of unpardoned sin: Israel (Nu 14:26-45), Eli's house (1Sa 3:14).

UNSELFISHNESS

Commanded:

In the royal law (Jas 2:8). In the church (Ro 12:10; 15:1; 1Co 10:24; Gal 6:2; Php 2:3-4).

Inspired by:

Love (1Co 13:4-5). Jesus' love (2Co 5:14-15).

Instances of:

Abraham (Ge 13:9; 14:23-24). King of Sodom (Ge 14:21). Hittites (Ge 23:6, 11). Judah (Ge 44:33-34). Moses (Nu 11:29; 14:12-19). Gideon (Jdg 8:22-23). Saul (1Sa 11:12-13). Jonathan (1Sa 23:17-18). David (1Sa 24:17; 2Sa 15:19-20; 23:16-17; 1Ch 21:17; Ps 69:6). Araunah (2Sa 24:22-24). Nehemiah (Ne 5:14-18). Jews (Est 9:15). Daniel (Da 5:17). Jonah (Jnh 1:12-13).

Joseph (Mt 1:19). Jesus (Ro 15:3; 2Co 8:9). The disciples (Ac 4:34-35). Priscilla and Aquila (Ro 16:3-4). Paul (1Co 10:33; Php 1:18; 4:17; 2Th 3:8). Philemon (Phm 13-14). Onesiphorus (2Ti 1:16-18).

See Charitableness; Fellowship; Fraternity; Selfishness.

UNTEMPERED MORTAR *See Whitewash.*

UNWORTHINESS [7781, 7837, *397, 945*]. (Mt 10:37; 22:8; Ac 13:46).

UPHARSIN *See Parsin.*

UPHAZ [233]. A place where gold was obtained (Jer 10:9; Da 10:5), location unknown. Perhaps "Ophir" should be read. *See Ophir, 2.*

UPPER CHAMBER, UPPER ROOM [6608, *333*]. A room built on the wall or roof of a house (1Ki 17:19; Ac 20:9); scene of the Lord's Last Supper (Mk 14:15; Lk 22:12).

UPPER EGYPT [7356]. Pathros; southern Egypt. Israelite captives in (Isa 11:11, ftn; Jer 44:1, 15; Eze 29:14). Prophecy against (Eze 30:14). *See Egypt.*

UPRIGHTNESS [2341, 3837, 3838, 3841, 3842, 4793, 4797, 5791, 5893, 6641, 7404, *1465, 1469*]. *See Righteousness.*

UR [243, 244] (*flame, light*). Father of Eliphal (1Ch 11:35). Possibly the same as Ahasbai (2Sa 23:34). *See Ahasbai.*

UR OF THE CHALDEANS A city in S Mesopotamia, c. 140 miles SE of old Babylon; the early home of Abraham (Ge 11:28, 31; 15:7; Ne 9:7).

URBANUS [4042] (*refined, elegant*). A Roman Christian (Ro 16:9).

URI [247, 788] (*Yahweh is [my] flame, light*).

1. The father of Bezalel (Ex 31:2; 35:20; 38:22; 1Ch 2:20; 2Ch 1:5).

2. The father of Geber (1Ki 4:19).

3. The temple gatekeeper who divorced his foreign wife (Ezr 10:24).

URIAH [249, 250, *4043*] (*Yahweh is [my] flame, light*).

1. A Hittite; the husband of Bathsheba (2Sa 11:3).

2. High priest during the reign of Ahaz of Judah, for whom he built a pagan altar in the temple (2Ki 16:10-16).

3. A priest who aided Ezra (Ne 8:4).

4. The father of Meremoth (Ezr 8:33; Ne 3:4).

5. The son of Shemaiah, a prophet of Kiriath Jearim, in the time of Jehoiakim. Prophesies against Judah (Jer 26:20). Fled to Egypt; taken; slain by Jehoiakim (Jer 26:21-23).

URIEL [248] (*God [El] is [my] flame, light*).

1. A Kohathite Levite (1Ch 6:24).

2. A chief of the Kohathites who assisted in bringing the ark from the house of Obed-Edom (1Ch 15:5, 11).

3. The father of Maacah, wife of Rehoboam (2Ch 13:2, ftn).

URIJAH *See Uriah.*

URIM AND THUMMIM [242] (*lights and perfections*). Signifying light and perfection. In the breastplate (Ex 28:30; Lev 8:8). Eleazar to ask counsel for Joshua, after the judgment of (Nu 27:21). Priests only might interpret (Dt 33:8; Ezr 2:63; Ne 7:65). Israelites consult (Jdg 1:1; 20:18, 23). Withheld answer from King Saul (1Sa 28:6).

USURPATION

Of Political Functions:

By Absalom (2Sa 15:1-12). By Adonijah (1Ki 1:5-9). By Baasha (1Ki 15:27-28). By Zimri (1Ki 16:9-10). By Jehu (2Ki 9:11-37). By Athaliah (2Ki 11:1-16). By Shallum (2Ki 15:10). *See Rebellion.*

In Ecclesiastical Affairs:

By Saul, in assuming priestly functions (1Sa 13:8-14). By Solomon, in thrusting Abiathar out of the priesthood (1Ki 2:26-27). By Uzziah, in assuming priestly offices (2Ch 26:16-21). By Ahaz (2Ki 16:12-13).

See Church, The Body of Believers; State; Government, Ecclesiastical.

Of Executive Power:

In ordering Naboth's death and confiscation of his vineyard (1Ki 21:7-19). In the scheme of Joseph to dispossess the Egyptians of their real and personal property (Ge 47:13-26). Of Pharaoh, making bondservants of the Israelites (Ex 1:9-22). Moses accused of (Nu 16:3).

USURY [5391, 5957, 5968]. Interest, not necessarily unreasonable exaction, but all income from loans. Forbidden (Ex 22:25; Lev 25:35-37; Dt 23:19; Ps 15:5; Pr 28:8; Jer 15:10; Eze 18:8, 13, 17; 22:12). Exaction of, rebuked (Ne 5:1-13). Authorized, of strangers (Dt 23:20). Exacted by the Jews (Eze 22:12). Just men innocent of the vice of requiring (Eze 18:8).

See Interest; Money.

UTHAI [6433] (possibly *superiority of Yahweh* IDB; possibly *[my] restoration* KB).
1. The son of Ammihud (1Ch 9:4).
2. A man who returned with Ezra (Ezr 8:14).

UZ [824+6420, 6419, 6420].
1. The son of Nahor (Ge 22:21).
2. The son of Aram (Ge 10:23; 1Ch 1:17).
3. The son of Dishan (Ge 36:28).
4. The country in which Job lived (Job 1:1); the site is uncertain.

UZAI [206] (*Yahweh has given ear, listened*). Father of Palal (Ne 3:25).

UZAL [207].
1. The son of Joktan (Ge 10:27; 1Ch 1:21).
2. A region, perhaps Yemen or the area between Haran and the Tigris (Eze 27:19).

UZZA [6438] (*strength*).
1. The son of Shimei (1Ch 6:29).
2. The son of Ehud (1Ch 8:7).
3. The owner or caretaker of a garden in which Manasseh and Amon were buried (2Ki 21:18, 26).
4. One whose children returned under Zerubbabel (Ezr 2:49; Ne 7:51).

UZZA, GARDEN OF [6438]. A garden in which Manasseh and his son were buried (2Ki 21:18, 26).

UZZAH [6438, 6446] (*strong, fierce one*). The son of Abinadab; slain for touching the ark to steady it when the oxen carrying it stumbled (2Sa 6:3-8; 1Ch 13:6-11).

UZZEN SHEERAH [267] (perhaps *ear of Sheerah*). A town built by Ephraim's daughter Sheerah (1Ch 7:24).

UZZI [6454] (*Yahweh is [my] strength*).
1. Descendant of Aaron (1Ch 6:5, 51; Ezr 7:4).
2. The grandson of Issachar (1Ch 7:2-3).
3. A Benjamite (1Ch 7:7).
4. The father of Elah (1Ch 9:8).
5. An overseer of the Levites (Ne 11:22).
6. A priest in the family of Jedaiah (Ne 12:19).

UZZIA [6455] (*[my] strength* or *Yahweh is [my] strength*). One of David's mighty men (1Ch 11:44).

UZZIAH [6459, 6460, 3852] (*Yahweh is [my] strength*).
1. Also called Azariah. The king of Judah (2Ki 14:21; 15:1-2; 2Ch 26:1, 3). Rebuilds Elath (2Ki 14:22; 2Ch 26:2). Reigns righteously (2Ki 15:3; 2Ch 26:4-5). Defeats the Philistines (2Ch 26:6-7). Takes tribute from the Ammonites; strengthens the kingdom (2Ch 26:8). Strengthens the fortifications of Jerusalem (2Ch 26:9). Promotes cattle raising and agriculture (2Ch 26:10). Military establishment of (2Ch 26:11-15). Is presumptuous in burning incense; stricken with leprosy; quarantined (2Ch 26:16-21; 2Ki 15:5). Jotham regent during quarantine of (2Ki 15:5; 2Ch 26:21). Death of (2Ki 15:7; 2Ch 26:23). History of, written by Isaiah (2Ch 26:22; Isa 1:1). Earthquake in the reign of (Am 1:1; Zec 14:5). An ancestor of Jesus and listed in Matthew's record of Jesus' genealogy (Mt 1:8-9).
2. The son of Uriel (1Ch 6:24).
3. The father of Jonathan (1Ch 27:25).
4. A priest who divorced his Gentile wife (Ezr 10:21).
5. The father of Athaiah (Ne 11:4).

UZZIEL, UZZIELITES [6457, 6458] (*God [El] is [my] strength*).
1. A Kohathite Levite (Ex 6:18, 22; Lev 10:4).
2. The son of Ishi; Simeonite (1Ch 4:42).
3. Head of Benjamite family (1Ch 7:7).
4. The son of Heman (1Ch 25:4), also known as Azarel (1Ch 25:18). *See Azarel, 2.*
5. A Levite who helped in cleansing the temple (2Ch 29:14-19).
6. The son of Harhaiah (Ne 3:8). Anyone descended from Uzziel, the Levite, was known as an Uzzielite (Nu 3:27; 1Ch 15:10; 26:23).

VAGABOND NIV "wanderer, wandering." A word used in a curse pronounced upon Cain (Ge 4:12, 14), in an imprecatory prayer of David (Ps 109:10), and of professional exorcists (Ac 19:13).

VAIL See Curtains; Veil.

VAIN REPETITIONS See Babbling.

VAIZATHA [2262] (possibly given of the best one BDB). The son of Haman (Est 9:9).

VALLEY [692, 1326, 1628, 5707, 6677, 5754, 5929]. Low-lying ground; plain, ravine, gorge, a wadi (Dt 34:6; Jos 10:40; Lk 3:5).

Mentioned in Scripture:

Achor (Jos 7:24; Isa 65:10; Hos 2:15). Aijalon (Jos 10:12). Baca (Ps 84:6). Beracah (2Ch 20:26). Bokim (Jdg 2:5). Craftsmen (1Ch 4:14, ftn). Elah (1Sa 17:2; 21:9). Emek Keziz (Jos 18:21). Eshcol (Nu 32:9; Dt 1:24). Gad (2Sa 24:5). Gerar (Ge 26:17). Gibeon (Isa 28:21). Hebron (Ge 37:14). Ben Hinnom or Tophet (Jos 18:16; 2Ki 23:10; 2Ch 28:3; Jer 7:32). Hamon Gog (Eze 39:11). Iphtah El (Jos 19:14, 27). Jehoshaphat or decision (Joel 3:2, 14). Jericho (Dt 34:3). Jezreel (Hos 1:5). King's Valley (Ge 14:17; 2Sa 18:18). Lebanon (Jos 11:17). Megiddo (2Ch 35:22; Zec 12:11). Moab, where Moses was buried (Dt 34:6). Rephaim (Jos 15:8; 18:16; 2Sa 5:18; Isa 17:5). Salt (2Sa 18:13; 2Ki 14:17). Shaveh (Ge 14:17; 2Sa 18:18). Shittim (Joel 3:18). Siddim (Ge 14:3, 8, 10). Sorek (Jdg 16:4). Succoth (Ps 60:6). Zeboim (1Sa 13:18; Ne 11:34). Zephathah (2Ch 14:10). Zered (Nu 21:12).

VALLEY GATE A gate in the Jerusalem walls (Ne 2:13; 3:13; 12:31, 38), location uncertain.

VALOR [52+4213, 2657]. See Courage.

VANIAH [2264] (possibly worthy of love IDB). A man who divorced his foreign wife (Ezr 10:36).

VANITY [401, 448+2855, 2039, 4200+8198, 4202, 8198, 8736, 9214, 9332, 1632, 3029, 3031, 3472].

1. Archaic word meaning "temporary" or "meaningless":

"Temporary, a breath." Every human is but a breath (Ps 39:5, 11; 62:9; 144:4). Beauty is fleeting (Ps 39:11; Pr 31:30). Wealth acquired by lies (Pr 21:6).

"Futile, meaningless, in vain, worthless." A consequence of the Fall (Ro 8:20). Human life (Job 7:16; Ecc 6:12), youth and vigor (Ecc 11:10), thoughts (Ps 94:11), help (Ps 60:11; La 4:17). Worldly wisdom (Ecc 2:15, 21; 1Co 3:20),

pleasure (Ecc 2:1-3, 10-11; Ps 39:6; 127:2), activity (Ps 39:6; Ecc 2:4-11). Accumulating wealth (Ecc 2:26; 4:8), love of wealth (Ecc 5:10; 6:2). Everything (Ecc 1:2). Foolish controversies (1Ti 1:6-7; 6:20; 2Ti 2:14, 16; Tit 3:9). The conduct of the ungodly (1Pe 1:18). The religion of hypocrites (Isa 1:13; Jas 1:26), pagans (Mt 6:7). Faith without works is (Jas 2:14).

The wicked, especially characterized by (Job 11:11). Fools follow those given to (Pr 12:11), leading to poverty (Pr 28:19). Saints hate the thoughts of (Ps 119:113), pray to be kept from (Ps 119:37; Pr 30:8), avoid (Ps 24:4), avoid those given to (Ps 26:4).

2. See Pride.

VASHNI KJV Samuel's firstborn (1Ch 6:28). NIV follows the LXX and supplies "Joel" as the firstborn (cf. 1Sa 6:33; 8:2; 15:17), rendering vashni as "the second." See Joel, 1.

VASHTI [2267] (one beautiful, desired). The wife of Xerxes; queen of Persia; divorced (Est 1:19).

VEDAN A place whose merchants traded with Tyre (Eze 27:19, NRSV). Translated as the Hebrew conjunction vav and the proper name Danites/Dan in the NIV and KJV. See Dan, 2.

VEGETARIANS Persons who eat no meat. Daniel chooses to eat only vegetables (Da 1:11-16). Christians are not to judge or be judged by diet (Ro 14).

VEGETATION [2013, 6912, 7542]. Created the third day (Ge 1:11; 2:5). For food (Ge 1:29-30).

VEIL [4485, 5003, 5029, 6260, 6486, 7539, 7581, 8304, 2820, 2821].

1. Scarf used for concealment or for protection against the elements (Ge 24:65; 1Co 11:4-16). Worn by Rebekah (Ge 24:65), by Tamar (Ge 38:14, 19), by Moses, to screen his face when he descended from Mount Sinai (Ex 34:33, 35). Metaphoric of failing to understand the gospel (2Co 3:14-18; 4:3-4).

2. See Curtains.

VEIN NIV "mine" for silver (Job 28:1). See Mines, Mining.

VENERATION For parents (Ge 48:15-16). See Old Age; Parents; Reverence.

VENGEANCE [1947, 5933, 5934, 5935]. Any punishment meted out in the sense of retribution (Jdg 15:7; Jer 11:20; 20:12). It belongs to God

(Dt 32:35-36; Ps 94:1; Lk 18:7-8; Ro 12:19; 2Th 1:6; Heb 10:30; Rev 6:10).

Instance of: Sons of Jacob on Hamor and Shechem (Ge 34:20-31).

See Judgments; Revenge; Retaliation.

VENISON NIV "(wild) game," taken in hunting (Ge 25:28; 27:5-33).

VENTRILOQUISM Possibly a trick of mediums and spiritists (Isa 29:4).

VERDICT [1821+5477, 5477, 6783, 10690, *3213*]. Against Jesus (Mt 26:66; 27:24-26; Mk 15:15; Lk 23:24; Jn 19:16). *See Court, Of Law.*

VERMILION *See Red.*

VERSIONS OF THE BIBLE
Ancient: *See Texts and Versions.*

VESSEL [3998, 8500]. Any material thing which may be used for any purpose, whether a tool, implement, weapon, or receptacle (Isa 22:24; 52:11; 66:20). A ship (Isa 2:16).

KJV "earthen vessels" is NIV "jars of clay" (2Co 4:7). *See Jar(s).* KJV "weaker vessel" is NIV "weaker partner" (1Pe 3:7). *See Women.*

VESTMENTS [4252]. Of priests. *See Priest.*

VESTRY *See Wardrobe.*

VESTURE An archaic word for garments (Ge 41:42; Dt 22:12; Ps 22:18). Sometimes used metaphorically (Ps 102:26; Heb 1:12).
See Cloak; Clothing; Dress; Robe.

VIA DOLOROSA The traditional route which our Lord traveled on the day of his crucifixion from the judgment seat of Pilate to the place of his crucifixion (Mt 27:26, 31, 33).

VIAL *See Bowl.*

VICARIOUS DEATH The ram for Isaac (Ge 22:13). Jesus for sinners. *See Jesus the Christ, Death of; Mission of; Savior; Sufferings of; also, Atonement; Suffering, Vicarious.*

VICEGERENCY Imputed authority. Of Elisha, in miraculously rewarding the Shunammite (2Ki 4:16-17), in cursing Gehazi (2Ki 5:27). Of the apostles (Mt 16:19; 18:18; Jn 20:23).

VICTORIES [928+3338+5989, 1476, 2657, 3523, 3802, 3828, 3829, 4804, 5782, 9370, 9591, *3772*, *3777*]. In battle, from God (Ps 55:18; 76:5-6). Celebrated in song (Jdg 5; 2Sa 22), by women (1Sa 18:6-7; 2Sa 1:20).
See Armies; War.

VICTUAL Food.

VIGILANCE [5915, 9081]. Instances of:

The LORD in the Exodus (Ex 12:42). King of Jericho (Jos 2:1-3).
See Watchman.

VILLAGE [1426, 2958, 4099, 4107, 4108, 6551, 7253, *3267, 3268, 4484*]. Villages were usually grouped around a fortified town to which the people could flee in a time of war (2Ch 8:18).

VINE [339+6618, 1201+7238, 1728, 2367, 4144, 5687, 7813, 8602, 8603, *306*]. Degeneracy of (Jer 2:21). Fable of (Jdg 9:12-13). Pruned (Isa 5:6; Jn 15:1-5). Parables of (Ps 80:8-14; Eze 17:6-10; 19:10-14). *See Vineyards.*

Symbolic (Jn 15:1-5).

VINEGAR [2810, *3954*]. A sour wine. Forbidden to the Nazirites (Nu 6:3). Used with food (Ru 2:14; Ps 69:21; Pr 10:26; 25:20). Offered to Christ on the cross (Mt 27:34, 48; Jn 19:29, w Mk 15:23).

VINEYARDS [1292, 4142, 4144, 9224, *307, 308*]. Origin and antiquity of (Ge 9:20). The design of planting (Ps 107:37; 1Co 9:7). Frequently walled or fenced with hedges (Nu 22:24; Pr 24:31; Isa 5:2, 5). Cottages built in, for the keepers (Isa 1:8). Provided with the apparatus for making wine (Isa 5:2; Mt 21:33). The stones carefully gathered out of (Isa 5:2).

Laws Respecting:
Not to be planted with different kinds of seed (Dt 22:9). Not to be cultivated during the sabbatical year (Ex 23:11; Lev 25:4). The spontaneous fruit of, not to be gathered the sabbatical or jubilee year (Lev 25:5, 11). Compensation in kind to be made for injury done to (Ex 22:5). Strangers entering, allowed to eat the fruit of, but not to take any away (Dt 23:24).

The gleaning of, to be left for the poor (Lev 19:10; Dt 24:21). The fruit of new, not to be eaten for three years (Lev 19:23), to be holy to the Lord in the fourth year (Lev 19:24), to be eaten by the owners from the fifth year (Lev 19:25).

Planters of, not liable to military service till they had eaten of the fruit (Dt 20:6). Frequently rented out to tenant farmers (SS 8:11; Mt 21:33). Rent of, frequently paid by part of the fruit (Mt 21:34). Were often mortgaged (Ne 5:3-4). Estimated rent of (SS 8:11; Isa 7:23). Estimated profit arising from, to the cultivators (SS 8:12). The poor engaged in the culture of (2Ki 25:12; Isa 61:5). Members of the family often wrought in (SS 1:6; Mt 21:28-30). Mode of hiring and paying laborers for working in (Mt 20:1-2). Of the kings of Israel superintended by officers of state (1Ch 27:27).

The Vintage or Ingathering of:
Was a time of great rejoicing (Isa 16:10). Sometimes continued to the time of sowing seed (Lev 26:5). Failure in, occasioned great grief (Isa 16:9-10). Of red grapes particularly esteemed (Isa 27:2). The produce of, was frequently destroyed by enemies (Jer 48:32). The whole produce of, often destroyed by insects (Dt 28:39; Am 4:9). In

unfavorable seasons produced but little wine (Isa 5:10; Hag 1:9, 11). The wicked judicially deprived of the enjoyment of (Am 5:11; Zep 1:13). The Recabites forbidden to plant (Jer 35:7-9). Of the slothful man neglected and laid waste (Pr 24:30-31).

Illustrative:

Of Israel (Isa 5:7; 27:2; Jer 12:10; Mt 21:23).

VINEYARDS, PLAIN OF THE See
Abel Keramim.

VINTAGE [4142]. (Lev 26:5; Jdg 8:2; Isa 16:10; 24:13; 32:10; Jer 48:32; Mic 7:1). *See Vine; Vineyards.*

VIOL See *Lyre; Music, Instruments of.*

VIOLENCE [*2803, 2805, 6449, 7265, 8719, 1040, 1042, 44385616]. A cause of the Flood (Ge 6:11-13). Prayer for deliverance from (2Sa 22:49; Ps 7:9; Hab 1:2-3). Divorce (Mal 2:16). An overseer must not be (1Ti 3:3; Tit 1:7).

VIPER [6582, 7625, 7626, 9159, 835, 2399]. A poisonous snake (Dt 32:24; Isa 59:5). Fastens on Paul's hand (Ac 28:3).

Figurative (Ge 49:17; Ps 140:3; Pr 23:32; Mt 3:7; 23:33; Lk 3:7).

See Adder; Cobra; Serpent.

VIRGIN [408+3359+4202, 1435, 1436, 2351+3359+5435, 6625, 4221].

General:

Proofs of (Dt 22:13-21). Dowry of (Ex 22:17). Character of, to be protected (Dt 22:17-21, 23-24). Betrothal of, a quasi-marriage (Dt 22:23-24). Distinguishing apparel of (2Sa 13:18). Priests might marry none but (Lev 21:14). Mourn in the temple (La 1:4; 2:10). Virginity, bewailed (Jdg 11:37-39).

Parable of the wise and foolish (Mt 25:1-13). Advised by Paul not to marry (1Co 7).

Mother of Jesus (Isa 7:14; Mt 1:23; Lk 1:27). *See Virgin Birth.*

Figurative:

Of the Church (Isa 62:5; Jer 14:17; 31:4, 13; 2Co 11:2). Of personal purity (1Co 7:25, 37; Rev 14:4).

VIRGIN BIRTH The NT teaching that Jesus Christ became a human being without the mediation of an earthly father, not born by means of sexual intercourse, but as a result of the supernatural overshadowing of the Holy Spirit (Mt 1:18-25; Lk 1:26-2:7).

VIRGINITY See *Virgin.*

VIRTUE Positive character traits (Col 3:12-14). See *Character.*

VISION [2600, 2606, 2607, 2608, 2612, 4690, 5260, 5261, 8011, 8015, 10255, 10256, 3965, 3969+3972, 3969, 3970]. A mode of revelation

(Nu 12:6; 1Sa 3:1; 2Ch 26:5; Ps 89:19; Pr 29:18; Jer 14:14; 23:16; Da 1:17; Hos 12:10; Joel 2:28; Ob 1; Hab 2:2; Ac 2:17).

Examples of:

Of Abraham, concerning his descendants (Ge 15:1-17). Of Jacob, of the stairway with ascending and descending angels (Ge 28:12), at Beersheba (Ge 46:2). Of Job, of a spirit (Job 4:12-16). Of Moses, of the burning bush (Ex 3:2), of the glory of God (Ex 24:9-11; 33:18-23). Of the Israelites, of the manifestation of the glory of God (Ex 24:10, 17; Heb 12:18-21). Of Balaam, in a trance. *See Balaam.* Of Joshua, of the captain of the Lord's host (Jos 5:13-15).

Of David, of the angel of the Lord by the threshing floor of Araunah (1Ch 21:15-18, ftn v.15). *See Araunah.* Of Elisha, at the translation of Elijah (2Ki 2:11). Of Elisha's servant, of the chariots of the Lord (2Ki 6:17). Of Micaiah, of the defeat of the Israelites; of the Lord on his throne; and of a lying spirit (1Ki 22:17-23; 2Ch 18:16-22).

Of Isaiah, of the Lord and his glory in the temple (Isa 6), of the valley of vision (Isa 22). Of Jeremiah, of an almond rod (Jer 1:11), of the boiling pot (Jer 1:13). Of Ezekiel, of the glory of God (Eze 1:3, 12-14; 3:12-14; 3:23), of the scroll (Eze 2:9), of the man of fire (Eze 8-9), of the coals of fire (Eze 10:1-7), of the dry bones (Eze 37:1-14), of the city and temple (Eze 40-48), of the waters (Eze 47:1-12). Of Daniel, of the four beasts (Da 7), of the Ancient of Days (Da 7:9-27), of the ram and the goat (Da 8), of the angel (Da 10).

Of Amos, of grasshoppers (Am 7:1-2), of fire (Am 7:4), of a plumb line (Am 7:7-8), of summer fruit (Am 8:1-2), of the temple (Am 9:1). Of Zechariah, of horses (Zec 1:8-11), of horns and carpenters (Zec 1:18-21), of the high priest (Zec 3:1-5), of the golden lampstand (Zec 4), of the flying scroll (Zec 5:1-4), of the mountains and chariots (Zec 6:1-8).

Of Zechariah, in the temple (Lk 1:13-22). Of John the Baptist, at the baptism of Jesus (Mt 3:16; Mk 1:10; Lk 3:22; Jn 1:32-34). Peter, James, and John, of the transfiguration of Jesus and the appearance of Moses and Elijah (Mt 17:1-9; Lk 9:28-36). Of the people, of the tongues of fire at Pentecost (Ac 2:2-3). Of Stephen, of Christ (Ac 7:55-56).

Of Paul, of Christ, on the way to Damascus (Ac 9:3-6; 1Co 9:1), of Ananias (Ac 9:12), of a man of Macedonia, saying, "Come over to Macedonia and help us" (Ac 16:9), in Corinth (Ac 18:9-10), in a trance (Ac 22:17-21), of paradise (2Co 12:1-4). Of Ananias, of Christ (Ac 9:10-12). Of Cornelius, the centurion, of an angel (Ac 10:3). Of Peter, of the sheet let down from heaven (Ac 10:9-18).

Of John on the Isle of Patmos—

Of Christ and the golden lampstands (Rev 1:10-20), the open door (Rev 4:1), a rainbow and throne (Rev 4:2-3), twenty-four elders (Rev 4:4), seven lamps (Rev 4:5), sea of glass (Rev 4:6), four living creatures (Rev 4:6-8), book with seven seals (Rev

5:1-5), golden bowls (Rev 5:8), of the six seals (Rev 6), four horses (Rev 6:2-8), earthquake and celestial phenomena (Rev 6:12-14).

Four angels (Rev 7:1), sealing of the 144, 00 (Rev 7:2-8), of the seventh seal and seven angels (Rev 8-11), of the censer (Rev 8:5), hail and fire (Rev 8:7), mountain cast into the sea (Rev 8:8-9), falling star (Rev 8:10-11; 9:1), the third part of sun and moon and stars darkened (Rev 8:12), bottomless pit (Rev 9:2), locusts (Rev 9:3-11), four angels loosed from the Euphrates (Rev 9:14), army of horsemen (Rev 9:16-19), angel having a book (Rev 10:1-10), seven thunders (Rev 10:3-4), measurement of the temple (Rev 11:1-2), two witnesses (Rev 11:3-12), court of the Gentiles (Rev 11:2), two olive trees and two lampstands (Rev 11:4), the beast out of the bottomless pit (Rev 11:7), fall of the city (Rev 11:13), second and third woes (Rev 11:14), a woman clothed with the sun and the birth of the male child (Rev 12), a red dragon (Rev 12:4-17), war in heaven (Rev 12:7-9), the beast rising out of the sea (Rev 13:1-10), the beast coming out of the earth (Rev 13:11-18).

The Lamb on Mount Zion (Rev 14:1-5), the angel having the everlasting gospel (Rev 14:6-7), the angel proclaiming the fall of Babylon (Rev 14:8-13), the Son of man with a sickle (Rev 14:14-16), an angel reaping the harvest (Rev 14:14-20), angel coming out of the temple (Rev 14:17-19), an angel having power over fire (Rev 14:18), the vine and the winepress (Rev 14:18-20), angel having the seven last plagues (Rev 15), sea of glass (Rev 15:2), temple opened (Rev 15:5), the plague upon the people who had the mark of the beast (Rev 16:2), sea turned into blood (Rev 16:3), the seven angels with the seven bowls of the wrath of God (Rev 16-17), destruction of Babylon (Rev 18), of the multitude praising (Rev 19:1-9), of him who is faithful and true riding a white horse (Rev 19:11-16), an angel in the sun (Rev 19:17-21).

Satan bound a thousand years (Rev 20:1-3), thrones of judgment, and the resurrection, and the freeing of Satan (Rev 20:1-10), the great white throne (Rev 20:11), opening of the Book of Life (Rev 20:12), death and hell (Rev 20:14), New Jerusalem (Rev 21), river of life (Rev 22:1), Tree of Life (Rev 22:2). *See Revelation, Book of.*

VISITATION A divine visit for purpose of rewarding or punishing people for their deeds (Jer 10:15; Lk 19:44; 1Pe 2:12).

VISITORS [2111, 4228]. *See Guest.*

VOICE, OF GOD (Eze 1:24, 28; 10:5; Jn 5:37; 12:28-30; Ac 7:31; 9:4, 7; 26:14-15). *See Anthropomorphisms.*

VOLCANOES Smoking or flaming mountains symbolic of God's presence (Dt 4:11; 5:23; Jdg 5:5; Ps 97:5; 104:32; 144:5; Isa 34:9-10; 64:1-3; Jer 51:25; Mic 1:4; Na 1:5-6).

See Earthquakes; Mountain.

VOLUPTUOUSNESS *See Lasciviousness; Sensuality.*

VOPHSI [2265]. The father of Nahbi (Nu 13:14).

VOWS [5623, 5624, 5883+6886, 7023+7198, 2376]. A part of Israel's worship (Ps 22:25; 61:8; 65:1). Heard by God (Ps 61:5). Obligatory (Nu 30:2; Dt 23:21-23; Job 22:27; Ps 50:14; 56:12; 66:13-14; 76:11; Ecc 5:4-5; Na 1:15). In affliction (Ps 116:14-19).

Mosaic Laws Concerning:

Must be voluntary (Lev 22:18-25; 23:37-38; Nu 15:2-16; 29:39).

Must be performed (Lev 5:4-13; Nu 30:2-16). *See above, Obligatory.* Estimation of the redemption price of things offered in vows, to be made by the priest, according to age and gender of the person making the offering (Lev 27:1-13). The redemptive price of the offering of real estate, to be valued by the priest (Lev 27:14-15), of a field (Lev 27:16-25).

Of women (Nu 30:3-16). Of Nazirites (Nu 6:1-21). Unintentional (Lev 5:4-5). Offerings devoted under (Lev 5:6-13; 7:16-18; 27:1-25; Nu 15:2-16). Things offered in, must be perfect (Lev 22:18-25).

Edible things offered in, to be eaten the same day they were offered (Lev 7:16-18). Things offered in, to be brought to the tabernacle or temple (Dt 12:6, 11, 17-18, 26), belonged to the priests (Nu 18:14).

Things forbidden to pay a vow (Dt 23:18).

Traditions that invalidate vows (Mk 7:11-13).

See Contract; Covenant.

Rash Vows:

(Pr 20:25; Ecc 5:6). By Jephthah (Jdg 11:29-40), by Israelites (Jdg 20:7-11).

Instances of:

Of Jacob (Ge 28:20-22). Of the mother of Micah, in the dedication of silver for the making of an idol (Jdg 17:2-3). Of Hannah, to consecrate to the Lord the child for which she prayed (1Sa 1:11, w 1:27-28). Of Elkanah (1Sa 1:21). Of Absalom (2Sa 15:7-8). Of Job, not to entertain thoughts of fornication (Job 31:1). Of David (Ps 132:2).

Of Jephthah, and of the Israelites. *See above, Rash Vows.*

Of Ananias and Sapphira, in the dedication of the proceeds of the sale of their land (Ac 5:1-11). Of the Jews, to kill Paul (Ac 23:12-15).

See Nazirite(s).

VULTURE [370, 5979, 6465, 7272, 108]. The name given to several kinds of large birds of prey, usually feeding on carrion; unclean for food (Lev 11:13; Dt 14:12; Mic 1:16; Hab 1:8).

WADI [5707, 5711] (*ravine, valley*). A valley which forms the bed of a stream during the winter, but which dries up in the summer (Ge 26:19).

WADI OF EGYPT *See River of Egypt.*

WAFERS [7613, 8386]. Thin cakes (Ex 16:31; 1Ch 23:29).

WAGES [924, 5382, 7189, 7190, 8509, 8510, *1324*, *3635*, *4072*]. Of Jacob (Ge 29:15-30; 30:28-34; 31:7, 41).

Laborer entitled to (Dt 25:4; Mt 10:10; Lk 10:7; Ro 4:4). Must be paid (Col 4:1). Must be paid promptly (Lev 19:13; Dt 24:15). Withholding of, denounced (Jer 22:13; Mal 3:5; Jas 5:4). Wasting of, denounced (Hag 1:6). Contentment with, commanded (Lk 3:14).

Parable concerning (Mt 20:1-15).

Figurative of (Ro 6:23).

WAGON [1649, 7369]. Used to carry supplies (Isa 66:20; Eze 23:24; 26:10). *See Cart(s).*

WAHEB [2259]. If this is a proper noun then it is an unknown place in Moab. Its meaning is uncertain (Nu 21:14).

WAIL [*1134*, 3536, 3538, 5027, 5631, 7591, *3081*]. In ancient funeral processions wailing relatives and hired mourners and musicians preceded body to grave (Jer 9:17-21; Am 5:16; Mt 9:23). Of the wicked (Mt 13:42).

WAITING [*741*, 2565, 2675, 3498, 3782, 4538, 5893, 6218, 6641, 7595, 7747, 8432, 9068, *587*, *1354*, *1683*, *1910*, *2705*, *4657*, *4659*].

Upon God:

As the God of providence (Jer 14:22), as the God of salvation (Ps 25:5), as the giver of all temporal blessings (Ps 104:27-28; 145:15-16).

Is good (Ps 52:9). God calls us to (Zep 3:8). Exhortations and encouragements to (Ps 27:14; 37:7; Hos 12:6).

For—

Mercy (Ps 123:2), pardon (Ps 39:7-8), the consolation of Israel (Lk 2:25), salvation (Ge 49:18; Ps 62:1-2), guidance and teaching (Ps 25:5), protection (Ps 33:20; 59:9-10), the fulfillment of his word (Hab 2:3), the fulfillment of his promises (Ac 1:4), hope of righteousness by faith (Gal 5:5), coming of Christ (1Co 1:7; 1Th 1:10).

Attitudes in Waiting—

Should be with the soul (Ps 62:1, 5), with earnest desire (Ps 130:6), with patience (Ps 37:7; 40:1), with resignation (La 3:26), with hope in his word (Ps 130:5), with full confidence (Mic 7:7), continually (Hos 12:6), all the day (Ps 25:5), specially in adversity (Ps 59:1-9; Isa 8:17), in the way of his judgments (Isa 26:8).

Those Who Wait Upon God—

They who engage in, wait upon him only (Ps 62:5), are heard (Ps 40:1), are blessed (Isa 30:18; Da 12:12), experience his goodness (La 3:24-26), shall not be ashamed (Ps 25:3; Isa 49:23), shall renew their strength (Isa 40:31), shall inherit the earth (Ps 37:9), shall be saved (Pr 20:22; Isa 25:9), shall rejoice in salvation (Isa 25:9), shall receive the glorious things prepared by God for them (Isa 64:4).

Saints resolve on (Ps 52:9; 59:9). Saints have expectation from (Ps 62:5). Saints plead, in prayer (Ps 25:21; Isa 33:2). The patience of saints often tried in (Ps 69:3).

Predicted of the Gentiles (Isa 42:4; 60:9). Illustrated (Ps 123:2; Lk 12:36; Jas 5:7).

Exemplified:

Jacob (Ge 49:18), David (Ps 39:7), Isaiah (Isa 8:17), Micah (Mic 7:7), Joseph (Mk 15:43).

Faith; Hope.

WALKING [*886, 2006, 2143, 6015, 6296, 7575, 10207, *1451*, *4135*, *4344*, *4513*].

With God—a Godly Lifestyle:

According to his commands (Dt 5:33; Ps 1; Jer 7:23); in his ways (Dt 28:9; Jos 22:5); in the old paths (Jer 6:16); as taught by him (1Ki 8:36; Isa 2:3; 30:21); uprightly (Pr 2:7); in his statutes and judgments (Eze 37:24); in newness of life (Ro 6:4); not after the flesh, but after the Spirit (Ro 8:1; Gal 5:16); honestly, as in the day (Ro 13:13); by faith, not by sight (2Co 5:7); in love, following Christ (Eph 5:2); worthy of the Lord (Col 1:10); in Christ (Col 2:6); by the gospel rule (Php 3:16); in the light, as God is (1Jn 1:7); in white clothing (Rev 3:4); in the light of heaven (Rev 21:24).

Instances of: Enoch (Ge 5:24), Noah (Ge 6:9).

WALLED CITIES Settlements were enclosed with walls for protection against invasion (Lev 25:29-31; 1Ki 4:13). *See Walls.*

WALLS [382, 1074, 1230, 1290, 1473, 1553, 1555, 1556, 2570, 2658, 2666, 4185, 4190, 4321, 5243, 5603, 6017, 7252, 7288, 7815, 10376, 10703, *3546*, *5446*, *5526*, *5850*]. Of the cities: Of Bashan, destroyed by the Israelites (Dt 3:5-6). Of Jericho (Jos 2:15; 6). Of Jerusalem. *See Jerusalem.* Of Babylon (Jer 51:44), broad (Jer 51:58). Of Beth Shan (1Sa 31:10). Of Rabbah (2Sa 11:20). Of Abel (2Sa 20:15, 21).

Houses built upon (Jos 2:15). Double (2Ki 25:4; Isa 22:11). Sentinels on. *See Watchman.*

Figurative of the New Jerusalem (Rev 21:12, 14, 17-21).

WAR [*1741*, 2995, 4309, 4878, 7304, 7372, 7930, 8131, 8569, 9558, *4482*, *4483*, *5129*]. Divine approval of (2Sa 22:35). Civil (Jdg 12:1-6;

20; 2Sa 2:12-31; 3:1; 20; 1Ki 14:30; 16:21; Isa 19:2), forbidden (2Ch 11:4), averted (Jos 22:11-34). Enemy harangued by general of opposing side (2Ki 18:19-36; 2Ch 13:4-12). Of extermination (Nu 31:7-17; Dt 2:33-34; 3:6; 20:13-18; Jos 6:21, 24; 8:24-25; 10:2-40; 11:11-23; 1Sa 15:3-9; 27:8-11).

Tumult of (Am 2:2). Slain in, neglected (Isa 14:19; 18:6). Evils of (2Sa 2:26; Ps 46:8; 79:1-3; 137:9; Isa 3:5, 25-26; 5:29-30; 6:11-12; 9:5, 19-21; 13:15-16; 15; 16:9-10; 18:6; 19:2-16; 32:13-14; 33:8-9; 34:7-15; Jer 4:19-31; 5:16-17; 6:24-26; 7:33-34; 8:16-17; 9:10-21; 10:20; 13:14; 14:18; 15:8-9; 19:7-9; 25:33; 46:3-12; 47:3; 48:28, 33; 51:30-58; La 1-5; Eze 33:27; 39:17-19; Hos 10:14; 13:16; Joel 2:2-10; Am 1:13; 6:9-10; 8:3; Na 2:10; 3:3, 10; Zec 14:2; Lk 21:20-26; Rev 19:17-18).

To cease (Ps 46:9; Isa 2:4; Mic 4:3).

Wars and rumors of (Mt 24:6; Mk 13:7; Lk 21:9).

God and War—

God in (Ex 14:13-14; Dt 1:30; 3:21-22; 7:17-24; 20:1, 4; 31:6-8, 23; 32:29-30; Jos 1:1, 5-7, 9; Jdg 1:2; 6:16; 7:9; 11:29; 1Sa 17:45-47; 19:5; 30:7-8; 2Sa 5:22-24; 22:18; 1Ki 20:28; Ps 18:34; 76:3; Jer 46:15; Am 5:8-9; Zec 10:5). God uses, as a judgment (Ex 23:24; Lev 26:17, 31-39; Dt 28:25-68; 32:30; Jdg 2:14; 2Ki 15:37; 1Ch 5:22, 26; 21:12; 2Ch 12:1-12; 15:6; 24:23-24; 33:11; 36; Job 19:29; Ps 44:9-16; 60:1-3; 105:25; Isa 5:1-8, 25-30; 9:8-12; 13:3-4, 9; 19:2; 34:2-6; 43:28; 45:7; Jer 12:7, 12; 46:15-17, 21; 47:6-7; 48:10; 49:5; 50:25; Eze 23:22-25; Am 3:6; 4:11; Zep 1:7-18; Zec 8:10; 14:2).

Repugnant to God (1Ch 22:8-9; Ps 68:30; 120:6-7; Rev 13:10). God sends panic in (Ex 15:14-16), threatens defeat in (Dt 32:25; 1Sa 2:10; 2Ch 18:12-16; Isa 30:15-17; Eze 15:6-8; 21:9-17), inflicts defeat in (Jos 7:12-13; 2Ch 12:5-8; 24:23-24; Ps 48:4-7; Pr 11:14; 20:18). Wisdom required in (Pr 21:22; 24:6; Ecc 9:14-18; Lk 14:31-32).

See Armies; Armor; Fort; Soldiers; Strategy; Tower; Watchman.

Figurative:

Warfare of Saints—

Is not after the flesh (2Co 10:3). Is a good warfare (1Ti 1:18-19). Called the good fight of faith (1Ti 6:12).

Is against the devil (Ge 3:15; 2Co 2:11; Eph 6:12; Jas 4:7; 1Pe 5:8; Rev 12:17), the flesh (Ro 7:23; 1Co 9:25-27; 2Co 12:7; Gal 5:17; 1Pe 2:11), enemies (Ps 38:19; 56:2; 59:3), the world (Jn 16:33; 1Jn 5:4-5), death (1Co 15:26, w Heb 2:14-15).

Often arises from the opposition of friends or relatives (Mic 7:6; Mt 10:35-36). To be carried on under Christ, as our Captain (Heb 2:10), under the Lord's banner (Ps 60:4), with faith (1Ti 1:18-19), with a good conscience (1Ti 1:18-19), with steadfastness in the faith (1Co 16:13; 1Pe 5:9, w Heb 10:23), with earnestness (Jude 3), with watchfulness (1Co 16:13; 1Pe 5:8), with sobriety (1Th 5:6;

1Pe 5:8), with endurance of hardness (2Ti 2:3, 10), with self-denial (1Co 9:25-27), with confidence in God (Ps 27:1-3), with prayer (Ps 35:1-3; Eph 6:18), without earthly entanglements (2Ti 2:4). Mere professors do not maintain (Jer 9:3).

Saints are all engaged in (Php 1:30), must stand firm in (Eph 6:13-14), exhorted to diligence in (1Ti 6:12; Jude 3). Encouraged in (Isa 41:11-12; 51:12; Mic 7:8; 1Jn 4:4), helped by God in (Ps 118:13; Isa 41:13-14), protected by God in (Ps 140:7), comforted by God in (2Co 7:5-6), strengthened by God in (Ps 20:2; 27:14; Isa 41:10), strengthened by Christ in (2Co 12:9; 2Ti 4:17), delivered by Christ in (2Ti 4:18), thank God for victory in (Ro 7:25; 1Co 15:57).

Armor for—

A belt of truth (Eph 6:14), the breastplate of righteousness (Eph 6:14), readiness from the gospel (Eph 6:15), shield of faith (Eph 6:16), helmet of salvation (Eph 6:17; 1Th 5:8), sword of the Spirit (Eph 6:17). Called armor of God (Eph 6:11), weapons of righteousness (2Co 6:7), armor of light (Ro 13:12), not weapons of the world (2Co 10:4). Mighty through God (2Co 10:4-5), the whole is required (Eph 6:13), must be put on (Ro 13:12; Eph 6:11), to be on the right hand and the left (2Co 6:7).

Victory in—

Is from God (1Co 15:57; 2Co 2:14), through Christ (Ro 7:25; 1Co 15:57; 2Co 12:9; Rev 12:11), by faith (Heb 11:33-37; 1Jn 5:4-5), over the devil (Ro 16:20; 1Jn 2:14), over the flesh (Ro 7:24-25; Gal 5:24), over the world (1Jn 5:4-5), over all that exalts itself (2Co 10:5), over death and the grave (Isa 25:8; 26:19; Hos 13:14; 1Co 15:54-55), triumphant (Ro 8:37; 2Co 10:5).

They who overcome in, shall eat of the hidden manna (Rev 2:17), eat of the tree of life (Rev 2:7), be clothed in white garments (Rev 3:5), be pillars in the temple of God (Rev 3:12), sit with Christ in his throne (Rev 3:21), have a white stone and on it a new name written (Rev 2:17), have power over the nations (Rev 2:26), have the name of God written upon them by Christ (Rev 3:12), have God as their God (Rev 21:7), have the morning star (Rev 2:28), inherit all things (Rev 21:7), be confessed by Christ before God the Father (Rev 3:5), be sons of God (Rev 21:7), not be hurt by the second death (Rev 2:11), not have their names blotted out of the book of life (Rev 3:5).

Symbolized by a red horse (Rev 6:4).

In Heaven:

Symbolic (Rev 12:7).

WAR SONGS Celebrating the destruction of Pharaoh's army (Ex 15:1-21); victory over Sihon, king of the Amorites (Nu 21:24-30); victory over Sisera (Jdg 5); David's victories over his enemies and his deliverance from Saul (2Sa 22). David's lament over the defeat of Saul (2Sa 1:19-27).

WARDROBE [955, 4921]. Place where

royal or ceremonial garments were kept (2Ki 10:22; 22:14; 34:22). *See Dress.*

WARFARE [4878, 6009]. *See War, Figurative; In Heaven.*

WARNING [*606, 1819, 2302, 3579, 4592, 5583, 6386, *1371, 1839, 2203, 3805, 4625, 5683, 5976*]. *See Wicked, Warned.*

WARRIORS [52, 408+2657, 1201+2657, 1475, 1476, 2514, 6008, 6883, 7250, 7251, 7940]. (Nu 32:17; Jos 4:13; 1Ch 8:40; 12:2, 8, 21; 2Ch 14:8; 17:18; 25:5; 26:13).

WARTS [3301]. Unacceptable on a sacrificial animal (Lev 22:22).

WASHERMAN'S FIELD [3891]. A field outside Jerusalem where fullers or launderers washed the cloth that they were processing (2Ki 18:17; Isa 7:3; 36:2).

WASHINGS [1342, 8175, 8177, *968, 2752, 3373, 3782, 4459*]. (Ex 19:10, 14; Mt 15:2; Mk 7:2-5, 8-9; Lk 11:38; Heb 9:10).

General:
Of priests (Ex 29:4; 30:18-21; 40:12, 31-32; Lev 8:6; 16:4, 24, 26, 28; Nu 19:7-10, 19; 2Ch 4:6). Of burnt offerings (Lev 1:9, 13; 9:14; 2Ch 4:6). Of the dead (Ac 9:37). Of infants (Eze 16:4). Of the face (Mt 6:17). Of feet (Ge 18:4; 19:2; 24:32; 43:24; Ex 30:19, 21; 40:31; Jdg 19:21; 2Sa 11:8; SS 5:3; Lk 7:38, 44; Jn 13:5; 1Ti 5:10). Of hands (Ex 30:18-21; 40:30-32), as a token of innocency (Dt 21:6; Ps 26:6; Mt 27:24).

For defilement of, lepers (Lev 14:8-9), those having bloody issue (Lev 15:5-13), those having eaten that which died (Lev 17:15-16).

Traditions of, not observed by Jesus (Lk 11:38-39).

Figurative:
Of baptism (Ac 22:16). Of believers (1Co 6:11; Tit 3:5; Heb 1:3; 9:14; 2Pe 1:9; 1Jn 1:7, 9). Of bodies (Heb 10:22). Of the Church (Eph 5:26). Of conscience (Heb 9:14; 10:22). Of hands (Ps 73:13; Jas 4:8). Of leaven (1Co 5:7). Of robes (Rev 7:14; 22:14).

Of regeneration (Ps 51:7; Pr 30:12; Isa 1:16; 4:4; Zec 13:1; 1Co 6:11; Eph 5:26; Tit 3:5).

Of sin: Corporate (Ps 79:9; Isa 1:16, 18; 4:3-4; Da 12:10; Zec 13:1; Jn 13:8; 2Co 7:1; Rev 1:5). General (Pr 16:6). Personal (Ps 51:2; 65:3; Pr 20:9; Jn 13:8; 2Pe 1:9; 1Jn 1:7, 9).

By Christ, work and blood of (Eph 5:26; Tit 3:5-6; Heb 1:3; 9:14; 1Jn 1:7; Rev 1:5; 7:14).

See Defilement; Fuller; Purification; Regeneration; Soap.

WASTE PLACES [1429, 2999, 3810, 4497, 5118, 5409, 6858, 9014, 9039, 9332]. Restored (Isa 35:1; 41:19; 44:26; 49:19; 51:3; 52:9; 58:12; 61:4; Eze 36:10).

WATCH [*874, 3359, 5564, 5915, 6524, 7595, 7595, 8011, 9068, 9193, 9207, 10255, *70, 1063, 1213, 2426, 2555, 3972, 4190, 4668, 5023, 5871*]. A man or group of men set to guard a city, crops, etc. (Ne 4:9; Mt 27:62-66).

WATCHES OF THE NIGHT

Divisions into which hours of the night were divided. Jews had a threefold division; Romans, fourfold (Jdg 7:19; Mk 6:48). *See Time.*

WATCHFULNESS [7219, *1213*]. (Ps 102:7; Hab 2:1; 1Co 9:27).

In Prayer:
(Ne 4:9; Mt 26:41; Mk 13:33; Eph 6:18; Col 4:2; 1Pe 4:7).

Commanded:
(Dt 4:15; 6:17; Jos 22:5; 23:11; 1Ki 2:3-4; 8:25; 2Ch 19:7; Job 36:18-21; Pr 8:34; 16:17; Na 2:1; Mt 18:10; 24:42-51; 25:13; Mk 4:24; 13:32-37; Lk 8:18; 11:35; 12:35-40; 17:3; 21:34-36; Ro 11:20; 1Co 10:12; 11:28; 16:13; Gal 6:1; Eph 5:15; Col 2:8; 1Th 5:4, 6, 21; Heb 2:1; 1Pe 5:8; 2Pe 1:19; 1Jn 5:18).

Upon: Israel (Dt 27:9). Young men (Ps 119:9; Pr 4:23-27). Married men (Mal 2:15). Ministers (Ac 20:28-31; 1Co 3:10; Col 4:2; 1Ti 4:16; 2Ti 4:5).

Over: Motives (Mt 6:1-5). Conscience (Lk 11:35). The heart (Pr 4:23; 28:26). The tongue (Ps 39:1; 141:3; Jas 3:5-8).

Against: Hypocrisy (Mt 16:6). Apostasy (2Jn 8). Lethargy (Ro 13:11; 1Pe 1:13, 17). Backsliding (Dt 4:9, 23; Heb 3:12; 12:15; Jude 20-21; Rev 3:2-3, 11). Worldliness (1Co 7:29-31). Covetousness (Mt 24:42-47; Mk 13:33-37; Lk 12:15, 35-40). Idolatry (Ex 23:13; Dt 4:23; 11:16; 12:13). Evil associations (Ex 34:12; Php 3:2; 2Pe 3:17). False teachers (Mt 7:15; Mk 13:22-23; Ac 20:28-31; 1Jn 4:1). Deceivers (Mt 24:4).

See Temptation.

WATCHMAN [5915, 7595, 9068, *2601*]. A sentinel. On the walls of cities (SS 3:3; 5:7), of Jerusalem (2Sa 13:34; 18:24-25; Ne 4:9; 7:3; Isa 52:8; 62:6), of Babylon (Jer 51:12). On towers (2Ki 9:17; 2Ch 20:24; Isa 21:5-12; Jer 31:6). At the gates of the temple (2Ki 11:6-7). Alarm of, given by trumpets (Eze 33:3-6). Unfaithfulness in the discharge of duty, punished by death (Eze 33:6; Mt 28:14; Ac 12:19). *See Guard.*

WATER [1926, 3722, 4763, 4784, 5482, 5574, 5635, 5689, 7562, 8612, 8796, 9197, *533, 536, 1184, 2498, 4395, 4540, 5620, 5621, 5623*].

General:
Creation of (Ps 148:4-5). Covered the whole earth (Ge 1:9). Daily allowance of (Eze 4:11). City waterworks (2Ki 20:20). Vision of by Ezekiel (Eze 47:1-5). Of separation (Nu 19:2-22). Libation of (1Sa 7:6). Irrigation with. *See Irrigation.*

Miraculously supplied to the Israelites (Ex 17:1, 6; Nu 20:11), to Samson (Jdg 15:19), to Jehoshaphat's army (2Ki 3:16-20). Purified by Elisha (2Ki 2:19-22). Red Sea divided (Ex 14:21-22), the

Jordan River (Jos 3:14-17; 2Ki 2:6-8, 14). Jesus walks on (Mt 14:25). Changed to wine (Jn 2:1-11), to blood (Rev 16:3-5).

Figurative:
  Water of life (Jn 4:14; 7:37-39; Rev 21:6; 22:17). Of affliction (2Sa 22:17; Ps 69:1; Isa 30:20; 43:2). Of salvation (Isa 12:3; 49:10; 55:1; Eze 36:25; Jn 4:10; 7:38). Domestic love (Pr 5:15).

Symbolic:
  (Isa 8:7; Rev 8:11; 12:15; 16:4; 17:1, 15).

WATER JAR
Clay or stone jars for carrying or holding water (Ru 2:9; Jn 2:6-7; 4:28). *See Jar(s)*.

WATER OF BITTERNESS
Water mingled with dust which a woman suspected of unfaithfulness was expected to drink to prove her innocence (Nu 5:12-31).

WATER OF SEPARATION
Water for removal of impurity (Nu 19:9, 13, 20-21; 31:23).

WATERSPOUT
NIV "waterfalls" (Ps 42:7).

WATERWAY
See Aqueduct.

WAVE OFFERING
Sacrificial portion waved before the Lord (Ex 29:24-27; Lev 7:30; 8:27-29). *See Offerings.*

WAVES
[1195, 1644, 1922, 3338, 4784, 5403, *2498, 3115, 3246*]. *See Sea, Waves of.*

WAX
[1880]. (Ps 22:14; 68:2; 97:5; Mic 1:4).

WAY
[*448, 784, 1821, 2006, 2143, 2256, 3869, 3970, 4027, 5477, 6330, 8938, 10068, *419, 2262, 2426, 3847, 3931, 4048, 4513, 4636, 6058*].

Figurative:
  Of holiness (Ps 16:11; Isa 35:8-9; Jer 6:16; Hos 14:9). Of righteousness, narrow (Mt 7:14). Of sin, broad (Mt 7:13). Jesus the (Jn 14:6; Heb 9:8). Doctrines taught by Christ (Ac 9:2; 19:23; 22:4; 24:14, 22).

WAYFARING MAN
Traveler (Jdg 19:17; 2Sa 12:4; Isa 33:8; 35:8).

WAYS OF GOD
Perfect (Ps 18:30), righteous or just (Ps 145:17; Da 4:37; Hos 14:9; Rev 15:3), higher than human ways (Isa 55:9), eternal (Hab 3:6).

WEAK
[*1924, 2143, 2703, 3908, 6714, 6949, 8205, *819, 820, 822*]. Duty of the strong to (Job 4:3-4; Isa 35:3-7; Mt 25:35, 40; Ro 14:1-23; 15:1-3; 1Co 8:7-13; 9:22; 2Co 11:29; Gal 6:1-2; Jas 5:19-20). *See Kindness.*

WEALTH
[*226, 1524, 1540, 2104, 2162, 2657, 3856, 3860, 3877, 3883, 3946, 6938, 6947, 6948, 8214, *3228, 3440, 4355, 4454, 4456, 4458*]. Abundance of possessions, whether material, so-

cial, or spiritual. In early history of Israel, wealth consisted largely of flocks and herds, silver and gold, bronze, iron, and clothing (Jos 22:8). God taught Israel that he was the giver of their wealth (Dt 8:18), taught them to be generous (Pr 11:24). Jesus did not condemn wealth but stressed the difficulty of the rich in entering the kingdom of God (Mt 19:24; Lk 16:19-31).

WEANING
[1694]. To wean is to accustom a child to depend upon other food than its mother's milk; celebrated by a feast (Ge 21:8), and with an offering (1Sa 1:24).

WEAPONS
[2210, 2723, 2995, 3998, 5977, 8939, *3960*]. *See Armor.*

WEASEL
[2700]. A small, carnivorous animal, allied to the ferret; for Israelites, unclean (Lev 11:29).

WEATHER
[*2304*]. There is no Hebrew word corresponding to "weather, " but the Israelites were keenly aware of weather phenomena. The great topographical diversity of Israel assures a variety of weather on a given day: on the top of Mt. Hermon (9, 232 feet above sea level) there is snow on the ground the year round; while at Jericho (800 feet below sea level) the heat is oppressive in summer, and the region around the Dead Sea (1, 290 feet below sea level) is intolerable in summer. On the coast even the hottest summer day is made bearable by refreshing breezes from the Mediterranean. Signs of (Mt 16:2-3). Sayings concerning (Job 37:9, 17, 22). *See Meteorology.*

WEAVING
[755, 756, 8687]. (Isa 19:9; 38:12). Bezalel skilled in (Ex 35:35). Wrought by women (2Ki 23:7). Of the ephod (Ex 28:32; 39:22). Of coats (Ex 39:27).
  Weaver's shuttle (Job 7:6), beam (Jdg 16:14; 2Sa 21:19; 1Ch 11:23).

WEDDING
[2146, 3164, 3353, 8005, 8287, 8933, *1141*]. A joyous occasion, celebrated with music, feasting, drinking of wine, joking; after the Exile written contracts were drawn up and sealed; bridegroom went to the bride's home with friends and escorted her to his own house (Mt 25:7); festive apparel expected of guests; festivities lasted one or two weeks (Ge 29:27; Jdg 14:12).

WEDGE
[4383]. A bar of gold (Jos 7:21, 24).

WEEDING
(Mt 13:28).

WEEDS
[947, 3017, 8032, *2429, 5198*].
  1. A general term for obnoxious plants (Job 31:40).
  2. Probably bearded darnel, a poisonous plant resembling wheat (Mt 13:25-30).

WEEK
[*8651, 4879, 4879*]. *See Calendar; Time.*

WEEKS, FEAST OF [8651]. Pentecost, celebrated fifty days after the sheaf waving on the sixteenth of Nisan (Ex 34:18-26).
See Annual Feasts; Feasts; Pentecost.

WEEPING [*1134, 1140, 5027, *3081, 3088*].
(Ro 12:15; 1Co 7:30). In perdition, the outer darkness (Mt 8:12; 22:13; 24:51; 25:30). None in heaven (Rev 7:17). Penitential (Jer 50:4; Joel 2:12).

Instances of Penitential:
The Israelites (Jdg 2:4-5). Peter (Mt 26:75; Mk 14:72; Lk 22:62). While doing good (Ps 126:5-6). For others (Jer 9:1). On account of tribulation (Jer 22:10; Am 5:16-17).

Instances of:
Of Abraham for Sarah (Ge 23:2). Of Esau (Ge 27:38). Of Jacob and Esau (Ge 33:4). Of Jacob (Ge 37:35). Of Joseph (Ge 42:24; 43:30; 45:2, 14; 46:29; 50:1, 17). Of Hannah (1Sa 1:7). Of Jonathan and David (1Sa 20:41). Of David (2Sa 1:17; 3:32; 13:36; 15:23, 30; 18:33). Of Hezekiah (2Ki 20:3; Isa 38:3). Of Jesus, over Jerusalem (Lk 19:41), at the grave of Lazarus (Jn 11:35). Of Mary, when she washed the feet of Jesus (Lk 7:38; Jn 11:2, 33). Of Mary Magdalene (Jn 20:11). Of Paul (Ac 20:19; Php 3:18).

WEIGHTS AND MEASURES
Balances were used for scales (Lev 19:36; Pr 16:11), and stones for weights (Lev 19:36). For biblical weights and measures, *See Measure.*

WELDING [1817]. A process used to join metals together (Isa 41:7).

WELLS [931, 1014, 5078, 7769, *4380, 5853*].
The occasion of feuds: between Abraham and Abimelech (Ge 21:25-30), between Isaac and Abimelech (Ge 26:15-22, 32-33). Of Jacob (Jn 4:6). Of Solomon (Ecc 2:6). Of Uzziah (2Ch 26:10). Of Hezekiah. *See Gihon.* At Haran (Ge 24:16).
Figurative: Of salvation (Isa 12:3; Jn 4:14). Without water (Jer 15:18; 2Pe 2:17).
See Spring.

WEN *See Warts.*

WEST [294, 339, 340, 2025+5115, 3542+, 4427+9087, 5115, 6298+, *1553*]. Used figuratively with "east" to denote great distance (Ps 103:12).

WHALE *See Fish; Sea Monster.*

WHEAT [1339, 2636, 10272, *4992, 5965*].
(Rev 6:6). Grown in Israel (1Ki 5:11; Ps 81:16; 147:14). Offerings of (Nu 18:12). Prophecy of the sale of a measure of, for a penny (Rev 6:6). Parables of (Mt 13:25; Lk 16:7). Winnowing of (Mt 3:12; Lk 3:17). Ground in a mortar (Pr 27:22). Chaff of (Jer 23:28; Mt 3:12; Lk 3:17). Growth of, figurative of vicarious death (Jn 12:24).
Figurative: Of God's mercy (Ps 81:16; 147:14). Of self-righteousness (Jer 12:13).

WHEEL [78, 236, 1649, 1651, 10143, 2200+3338]. Potter's (Jer 18:3).
Figurative (Pr 20:26; Ecc 12:6).
Symbolic (Eze 1:15-21; 3:13; 10:9-19; 11:22).

WHELP *See Cub.*

WHIP [8765, 8849, *4811, 5848*]. (1Ki 12:11; Pr 26:3; Na 3:2).

WHIRLWIND [1649, 6070, 6192, 6193, 6194, 8120]. Destructive (Pr 1:27). From the south in the land of Uz (Job 37:9), in the valley of the Euphrates (Isa 21:1), in the land of Canaan (Zec 9:14). From the north (Eze 1:4). Elijah translated in (2Ki 2:1, 11). God answered Job in (Job 38:1).
See Meteorology.

Figurative:
Of the judgment of God (Jer 23:19; 30:23). Of the fruits of unrighteousness (Hos 8:7). Of divine judgments (Eze 1:4).

WHISPER [1804, 1821, 1960+7754, 1960, 4317, 4318+7440, 7627, 8557, 9066, *1197, 1198, 3281*]. *See Busybody; Slander; Talebearer.*

WHISPERER A slanderer (Ro 1:29; 2Co 12:20). *See Slander; Speaking, Evil.*

WHITE [1009, 2580, 4235, 4237, 7467, 8202, 8484, 9492, 10254, 10490, *3326, 3328*]. *See Colors, Figurative and Symbolic.*

WHITE OWL Forbidden as food (Lev 11:18; Dt 14:16). *See Owl.*

WHITEWASH [3212, 3225, 9521, *3154*].
Used to "repair" a flimsy wall (Eze 13:10-16). Whitewashed tomb or wall a picture of hypocrisy (Mt 23:27-28; Ac 23:3).

WHOEVER Of condemnation (Ex 32:33; Dt 18:19; Mt 5:22; Jn 8:34; Ro 2:1; 1Jn 2:23; 3:4, 10, 15; 2Jn 9).
Of salvation (Lk 12:8; Jn 4:14; Ac 10:43; 1Jn 5:1; Rev 22:17).

WHORE, WHOREDOM *See Adultery; Idolatry; Fornication; Prostitute.*

WHOREMONGER *See Adultery; Sensuality.*

WICK TRIMMERS [4662, 4920]. Used to trim and adjust the wicks of the lamps in the temple and the tabernacle (Ex 37:23; Nu 4:9; 1Ki 7:50; 2Ki 12:13; 25:14; 2Ch 4:22; Jer 52:18).

WICKED [*1175, 2365, 4659, 6405, 6406, 6411, 8273, 8278, 8288, 8317, 8399, 8400, 8401, 8402, 94, 96, 490, 2805, 4505*].

General:
God is angry with (Ps 5:5-6; 7:11; Ro 9:13; 1Co 10:5). Spirit of God withdrawn from (Ge 6:3; Hos 4:17-19; Ro 1:24, 26, 28). Hate the righteous (Mt

5:11-12; Lk 6:22-23). Worship of, offensive to God (Ps 50:16-17; Isa 1:10-15).

God's mercy to (Job 33:14-30), love for (Dt 5:29; 32:29; Mt 18:11-14; Jn 3:16-17; Ro 5:8; 1Jn 3:16; 4:9-10). Gospel invitation to, illustrated by the parables of the householder (Mt 20:1-16), and marriage supper (Mt 22:1-14).

Prosperity of (Job 5:3-5; 12:6; 15:21-23, 27, 29; 20:5, 22; 21:7-13; Ps 37:1, 35-36; 49:10-15; 73:3-22; 92:6-7; Ecc 8:12-13; Jer 12:1-2; Hab 1:3-4, 13-17; Mal 3:15). Hate reproof (1Ki 22:8; 2Ch 18:7). Dread God (Job 18:11).Temporal punishment of (Job 15:20-35; 18:5-21; 20:5-29; 21:7-33; 24:2-24; 27:13-23; Jer 5:25; Eze 11:10; 12:19-20; Zec 14:17-19). False hope to (Job 8:13-18).

Warned (Jer 7:13-15, 23-25; 25:4-6; 26:2-7, 12-13; 29:17-19; Eze 33:8; Da 4:4-27; 5:4-29; Zep 2:1-2; Lk 3:7-9; 1Co 10:11; Jude 4-7; Rev 3:1-3, 16-19). Terrors of, at the judgment (Rev 1:7). Death of (Ps 49:14; 73:4).

Compared With:

Ashes under the feet (Mal 4:3), bad fish (Mt 13:48), bad trees (Lk 6:43), beasts (Ps 49:12; 2Pe 2:12), the blind (Zep 1:17; Mt 15:14), bronze and iron (Jer 6:28; Eze 22:18), briers and thorns (Isa 55:13; Eze 2:6), bulls of Bashan (Ps 22:12), burning thorns (Ps 118:12), bushes in the wastelands (Jer 17:6), chaff (Job 21:18; Ps 1:4; Mt 3:12).

Clouds without rain (Jude 12), corpses trampled underfoot (Isa 14:19), deaf cobras (Ps 58:4), dogs (Pr 26:11; Mt 7:6; 2Pe 2:22), dross (Ps 119:119; Eze 22:18-19), early dew that passes away (Hos 13:3), earthenware coated with glaze (Pr 26:23), fading leaves (Isa 1:30), fiery furnace (Ps 21:9; Hos 7:4), fools building upon sand (Mt 7:26), fuel for the fire (Isa 9:19).

Garden without water (Isa 1:30), goats (Mt 25:32), grass that withers (2Ki 19:26; Ps 37:2; 92:7), green plants that die away (Ps 37:2), horses charging into the battle (Jer 8:6), idols (Ps 115:8), lions hungry for prey (Ps 17:12), melting wax (Ps 68:2), morning mist (Hos 13:3), moth-eaten garments (Isa 50:9; 51:8), pigs (Mt 7:6), poor figs (Jer 24:8), rejected branches (Isa 14:19), rejected silver (Jer 6:30), rocky places (Mt 13:5).

Scorpions (Eze 2:6), serpents (Ps 58:4; Mt 23:33), smoke through a window (Hos 13:3), sows (2Pe 2:22), springs without water (2Pe 2:17), storms sweeping by (Pr 10:25), straw before the wind (Job 21:18), stubble (Mal 4:1), tossing sea (Isa 57:20), tumbleweeds (Ps 83:13), visions of the night (Job 20:8), wandering stars (Jude 13), wayward children (Mt 11:16), weeds (Mt 13:38), whitewashed tombs (Mt 23:27), wild waves of the sea (Jude 13), wild donkey's colts (Job 11:12).

See Base Fellows; Impenitence; Obduracy; Penitence; Reprobate; Reprobacy; Seekers; Sin, Confession of.

Contrasted With the Righteous:

(Ps 1:1-6; 11:5; 17:14-15; 32:10; 37:17-22, 37-38; 73:1-28; 75:10; 91:7-8; 107:33-38; 125:5; Pr 2:21-22; 3:32-33; 4:16-19; 10:3, 6, 9, 11, 16, 20-21, 23-25, 28-32; 11:3, 5-6, 8-11, 18-21, 23, 31;

12:2-3, 5-7, 10, 12-13, 21, 26; 13:5-6, 9, 17, 21-22, 25; 14:2, 11, 19, 22, 32; 15:6, 8-9, 28-29; 21:15, 18, 26, 29; 22:5, 8-9; 24:16; 28:1, 4-5, 13-14, 18; 29:2, 6-7, 27; Isa 32:1-8; 65:13-14; Mal 3:18; Ro 2:7-10; Eph 2:12-14; Php 2:15; 1Th 5:5-8; Tit 1:15; 1Pe 4:17-18; 1Jn 1:6-7; 3:3-17).

Present and future state of the wicked and righteous contrasted (Job 8; Ps 49). *See below.*

Described as:

(Job 8:13-17; 15:16, 20-35; Ps 10:4-11; 36:1-4; 73:4-12; Isa 59:2-8; Jer 2:22-25). Abomination (Pr 13:9; 15:9; Hos 9:10). Alienated (Col 1:21). Beasts (Ps 49:20). Dogs (Ps 59:6; 2Pe 2:22; Rev 22:15). Horse rushing into battle (Jer 8:6).

Blind (Eze 12:2). Carnal (Ro 8:5, 7-8; 9:8). Children of the devil (Jn 8:44; Ac 13:10; 1Jn 3:10). Perverse (Jer 9:6; Ro 1:21; 2:4-5; Php 2:15). Despising God (Job 21:14; Ro 11:28). Contentious (Ro 2:8). Corrupt (Ps 53:1; 73:8; Isa 59:3; Jer 2:22; Eze 16:47; 20:16; Mic 7:2-4; Tit 1:15). Loving darkness (Jn 3:19-20). Dead in sin (Eph 2:1-3; 1Jn 3:14). Delighting in lies (Ps 62:4), in perversity (Pr 2:13-19).

Defiled (Tit 1:15-16). Depraved (Isa 1:4-6; Jer 17:9; 30:12-15; Ro 1:20-32; 3:10-18; 1Ti 1:9-10; 2Ti 3:2-9, 13; Tit 3:2; 2Pe 2:10, 12-19; Jude 12-13). Destitute of faithfulness (Ps 5:9). Destitute of the love of God (Jn 5:42). Devilish (1Jn 3:8). Devisers of evil (Ps 52:1-4; 64:3-6; Pr 4:16; 6:12-15; 10:23; Isa 32:6-7; Jer 4:22). Enemies (Ro 5:10; Col 1:21). Filthy (Ezr 9:11). Full of bitterness (Ac 8:23).

Uncircumcised (Isa 52:1; Jer 6:10; Eze 28:10; 31:18; 32:19-32). Uncircumcised of heart (Lev 26:41; Eze 44:7; Ac 7:51), of lips (Ex 6:12). Disobedient (Jer 11:8; Tit 1:16). Alienated from God (Col 1:21). Full of bitterness and venom (Dt 32:32-33; Ps 58:3-5). Grievous sinners (Ge 13:13; 18:20; Job 22:5; Isa 1:4-6).

Hating: Correction (Pr 15:10; Am 5:10). Instruction (Ps 50:17; Pr 1:29-30). The light (Jn 3:20).

Being in moral darkness (Mt 4:16; 6:23; Lk 1:79; Eph 4:17-18). Not knowing the way of the Lord (Jer 5:4). Lewd (Jer 11:15). Lost (Lk 19:10). Loving wickedness (Ps 7:14; Jer 14:10; Hos 4:8; Mic 3:2). Malicious toward the righteous (Ps 37:12; 94:3-8; 140:9). Mocking sin (Pr 14:9). Obdurate (Ps 10:4, 11; Pr 1:29-30; Isa 26:10-11; Eze 3:7). Outsiders (Mk 4:11). Past feeling (Eph 4:19). Progressing in wickedness (Isa 30:1, 10-11; Jer 9:3; 2Ti 3:13). Rebellious (Dt 9:24).

Sensual (Php 3:19; Jude 19). Servants of sin (Jn 8:34). Shameful (Eph 5:11-12). Shameless (Jer 6:15; 8:12; Zep 3:5). Unscrupulous (Job 24:2-24; Ps 10:4-10; Isa 5:18-23; Jer 5:26-28; 9:2-6). Sold to work iniquity (1Ki 21:20). Stiff-necked (Dt 9:13; Ac 7:51). Under condemnation (Jn 3:18-19). Unclean (Ezr 9:11; Job 14:4; Hag 2:14). Ungodly (Ro 5:6), without strength (Ro 5:6). Vomit (Lev 18:25). Wretched, miserable, poor, blind, naked (Rev 3:17-18).

Happiness of:

Sensual (Isa 22:13; 56:12). Limited to this life

(Lk 16:25). Ends suddenly (Job 21:12-13; Lk 12:19-20).

Hope of:

Shall perish (Job 8:13; 11:20; 27:8; Pr 10:28).

Prayers of:

Abominable to God (Pr 15:8, 29; 21:27; 28:9).

Not answered (Dt 1:45; 1Sa 28:6; 2Sa 22:42; Job 27:9; 35:12-13; Ps 18:41; 66:18; Pr 1:24-28; 21:13, 27; Isa 1:15; 59:2; Jer 11:11; 14:12; 18:17; La 3:8, 44; Eze 8:18; 20:3, 31; Hos 5:6; Mic 3:4; Zec 7:13; Mal 1:9; 2:11-13; Jn 9:31; Jas 1:6-7; 4:3; 1Pe 3:7).

On behalf of, not answered (Dt 3:26; Jer 15:11).

Prosperity of:

(Job 12:6; 21:7-13; Ps 73:3-12; Jer 12:1-2; Mal 3:15). Brief (Job 5:3-5; 15:21, 23, 27, 29; 20:5, 22-23; 21:17-18; 24:24; Ps 37:35-36; 49:10-14; 73:18-19; 92:7; Ecc 8:12-13).

Punishment of:

(Ge 4:7; Ex 20:5; 34:7; Nu 32:23; 1Sa 3:11-14; 2Sa 3:39; 7:14; 22:27-28; 23:6-7; 1Ki 21:20-21; Job 8:20, 22; 11:20; 18:5-21; 19:29; 21:7-33; 27:13-23; 36:12, 17; Ps 3:7; 5:5; 18:14, 26-27; 36:12; 37:1-2, 9-10, 17, 20, 22, 34-38; 64:7-8; 73:18-20, 27; 91:8; 97:3; 107:17, 33-34; 119:21, 118-119, 155; 129:4; 146:9; 147:6; Pr 3:33; 10:3, 6-8, 14, 24-25, 27-31; 11:3, 5-8, 19, 21, 23, 31; 13:2, 5-6, 9, 21, 25; 14:12, 19, 32; 16:4-5; 22:5, 23; Ecc 8:12-13; Isa 3:11; 26:21; Jer 21:14; 36:31; La 3:39; Eze 3:18-20; 18:1-32; 33:7-20; Hos 14:9; Am 3:2; Mic 2:3; 6:13; Mt 15:13; Ro 1:18; 2:5, 8-9; Col 3:25; 1Th 1:10; 1Pe 3:12; 2Pe 2:3-9, 12-17; Jude 5-7; Rev 14:10-11).

By—

Chastisements (Ps 89:32; 1Co 5:5; 1Ti 1:20). Judgments (Ex 32:35; Lev 26:14-39; Dt 11:26-28; 28:15-68; 30:15, 18-19; Job 20:5-29; Ps 11:6; 21:9-10; 39:11; 75:8; 78:49-51; Isa 5:11-14, 24; 9:18; 10:3; 13:9, 11, 14-22; 24:17-18; 28:18-22; 65:12-15; Jer 5:25; 8:12-14, 20-22; 14:10, 12; 25:31; 44:2-14, 23-29; 49:10; La 3:39; 4:22; 5:16-17; Eze 5:4, 8-17; 9:5-7, 10; 20:8; 22:14, 20-21, 31; 24:13-14; Hos 2:9-13; 5:4-6, 9; 9:7, 9, 15; Joel 2:1-2; 3:13-16; Am 5:18-20; Lk 12:46; 1Co 10:5-11; 1Ti 5:24; Heb 10:26-31; 1Pe 4:17-18).

Sorrow (Ge 3:16-19; Job 15:20-24; Ps 32:10; Ecc 2:26; Isa 50:11). Trouble (Isa 48:22; 57:20-21). Being rejected of the Lord (1Ch 28:9; 2Ch 15:2; Mt 10:33; Mk 8:38; Lk 9:26; 13:27-28; Mt 7:23; Jn 8:21; 2Ti 2:12-13; Heb 6:8). Being excluded from the kingdom of heaven (1Co 6:9-10; Gal 5:19-21; Eph 5:5; Rev 21:27; 22:19). Being blotted from God's book (Ex 32:33).

Destruction (Ge 6:3, 7, 12-13; Nu 15:31; Dt 7:9-10; 1Sa 12:25; 1Ch 10:13-14; Job 4:8-9; 31:3; Ps 2:9; 7:11-13; 9:5, 17; 34:16, 21; 52:5; 55:19, 23; 92:7, 9; 94:13, 23; 101:8; 104:35; 106:18, 43; 145:20; Pr 2:22; 12:7; 21:12, 15-16; 24:20; Isa 11:4; 13:8; 64:5-7; Jer 13:14, 16, 22; Eze 25:7; Hos 7:12-13; Am 8:14; Na 1:2, 8-10; Zep 1:12-18; Zec 5:2-4; Mal 4:1; Mt 3:10, 12 w Lk 3:17; Mt 7:13, 19; 10:28 w Lk 12:4-5; Mt 21:41, 44 w Mk 12:1-9 & Lk 20:16, 18; Mt 24:50-51; Lk 9:24-25

w Mt 16:26 & Mk 8:36; Lk 19:27; Jn 5:29; Ac 3:23; Ro 2:12; 9:22; 1Co 3:17; Php 3:19; 1Th 5:3; 2Th 2:8-10). Sudden destruction (Pr 6:15; 24:22; 28:18; 29:1). Everlasting destruction (2Th 1:9). Everlasting contempt (Da 12:2). Everlasting fire (Isa 28:18-22; Mt 18:8-9; 25:41; Mk 9:43; Rev 20:15; 21:8).

Death (Ge 2:17; Ps 1:4-6; Pr 16:25; 19:16; Hos 13:1, 3; Am 9:1-5, 10; Ro 5:12, 21; 6:16, 21; 8:2, 6, 13; 1Co 15:21-22; 2Co 7:10; Gal 6:8; 1Jn 3:14-15; Jas 1:15; 5:20; Rev 2:22-23). The second death (Rev 21:8).

Condemnation to hell (Mt 23:33; Mk 16:16; Jn 3:15-16, 18, 36). Being cast into outer darkness (Mt 8:12; 22:13; 25:30). The last judgments (Rev 6:15-17; 9:4-6, 15, 18; 11:18; 16:2-21; 18:5; 19:15, 17-21; 20:10, 15; 21:8, 27; 22:19). Everlasting (Mt 25:46; Rev 14:10-11; 20:10). Degrees in (Mt 10:15; 11:22, 24; Mk 12:40). No escape from (Job 34:22; 1Th 5:3; Heb 2:3).

God has no pleasure in the death of (Eze 18:23; 33:11).

Punishment Illustrated in Parables—

The weeds (Mt 13:24-30, 38-42, 49-50). The talents (Mt 25:14-30). The barren fig tree (Lk 13:6-9). The man who built his house on the sand (Mt 7:26-27; Lk 6:49). Lazarus and the rich man (Lk 16:22-28).

Woes Against the Wicked:

(Isa 5:8, 11, 18-23; Mt 26:24; Mk 14:21; Lk 11:52; 17:1-2; 22:22; Jude 11).

Warned:

(Jer 7:13-15, 23-25; 25:4-6; 26:2-7, 12-13; 29:17-19; Eze 33:8; Da 4:4-27; 5:4-29; Zep 2:1-2; Lk 3:7-9; 1Co 10:11; Rev 3:1-3, 16-19).

See Hell; Judgments; Punishment.

WIDOW [530, 531, 851+4637, 851, 3304, 1222, 5939].

Mosaic Laws Concerning:

High priest forbidden to marry (Lev 21:14). Supported by father, when daughter of priest (Lev 22:13). Vows of, binding (Nu 30:9). Entitled to glean in the orchards and harvest fields (Dt 24:19-21). Levirate marriage of (Dt 25:5-10).

Care of commanded (Dt 14:28-29; 16:11, 14; Isa 1:17; Jer 7:6-7).

Widow's dowry. *See Dowry.*

In the Church:

Remarriage of, authorized (Ro 7:3; 1Co 7:39; 1Ti 5:14). Remarriage of, discouraged (1Co 7:8-9).

Qualifications for widows in 1Ti 5:3-16 may indicate a church office.

Kindness to:

Exemplified by Job (Job 29:13; 31:16, 22). God, the friend of (Dt 10:18; Ps 68:5; 146:9; Pr 15:25; Jer 49:11). Care of in the church (Ac 6:1; 1Ti 5:3-6, 9-12, 16; Jas 1:27).

Oppression of:

(Job 22:9; 24:3, 21; Ps 94:6; Isa 1:23; Eze 22:7; Mk 12:40; Lk 20:47).

Oppression of, forbidden (Ex 22:22-24; Dt 24:17; 27:19; Isa 10:2; Jer 22:3; Zec 7:10; Mal 3:5).

Instances of:

Naomi (Ru 1:3). Ruth (Ru 1-4). The widow of Zarephath, who sustained Elijah during a famine (1Ki 17). The woman whose sons Elisha saved from being sold for debt (2Ki 4:1-7). Anna (Lk 2:36-37). The woman who gave two mites in the temple (Mk 12:41-44; Lk 21:2), of Nain, whose only son Jesus raised from the dead (Lk 7:11-15).

See Levirate Marriage; Marriage; Women.

WIFE [851+, 3304, 7675, *1222+*, *3836*].

Described:

Called a helper (Ge 2:18, 20), desire of the eyes (Eze 24:10). Compared to a fruitful vine (Ps 128:3).

Beloved, by Isaac (Ge 24:67), by Jacob (Ge 29:30). Hated (Ge 29:31-33).

Contentious (Pr 19:13; 21:9, 19; 25:24). Instances of: Zipporah (Ex 4:25), Peninnah (1Sa 1:6-7).

Loyal, Jacob's (Ge 31:14-16).

Unfaithful (Nu 5:12-31). Instances of: Potiphar's (Ge 39:7), Bathsheba (2Sa 11:2-5).

Prudent (Pr 19:14). Tactful: Abigail (1Sa 25:3, 14-34), Esther (Est 5:5-8; 7:1-4). Virtuous (Pr 12:4; 31:10-12). Incorruptible or strong-willed: Vashti (Est 1:10-12). Wise (Pr 14:1).

Marrying of:

Commended (Pr 18:22; 1Co 7:2; 1Ti 5:14).

Bought (Ge 29:18-30; 31:41; Ex 21:7-11; Ru 4:10). Obtained by kidnapping (Jdg 21:21). Procured (Ge 24; 34:4-10; 38:6).

Duty:

Husband to wife (1Co 7:2-5, 27; Eph 5:25, 28, 31, 33; Col 3:19; 1Pe 3:7).

Wife to husband: To be obedient (1Co 14:34-35; Eph 5:22, 24; Col 3:18; Tit 2:5; 1Pe 3:1, 6). To be affectionate (Tit 2:4). To be faithful (Tit 3:11).

Relation of, to the husband (Ge 2:18, 23-24; 1Co 7:2-5, 10-11, 13, 39; 11:3, 8-9, 11-12).

Domestic duties of (Ge 18:6; Pr 31:13-27).

Vows of (Nu 30:6-16). *See Vow.*

Instances of Evil Influence of:

Eve (Ge 3:6, 12). Solomon's wives (1Ki 11:1-8; Ne 13:26). Jezebel (1Ki 21:25; 2Ki 9:30-37). Haman's (Est 5:14). Herodias (Mt 14:3, 6-11; Mk 6:17, 24-28).

See Husband; Marriage; Parents; Widow; Women.

WILD OX [8028]. A powerful animal (Nu 23:22; 24:8; Ps 92:9); two-horned (Dt 33:17); wild and difficult to catch (Job 39:9-12; Ps 29:6); KJV "unicorn." *See Animals.*

WILDERNESS [4497, 6858]. Wandering of the Israelites in. *See Israel.* Typical of the sinner's state (Dt 32:10). Jesus' temptation in (Mt 4:1; Mk 1:12-13; Lk 4:1).

See Deserts.

WILL [*2911, 2914, 4213, 8356, 10668, *1087*, *1088, 1089, 2525, 2526, 2527*].

The Mental Faculty:

Freedom of, recognized by God (Ge 4:6-10; Dt 5:29; 1Ki 20:42; Isa 1:18-20; 43:26; Jer 36:3, 7; Jn 7:17).

See Blessings, Spiritual, Contingent Upon Obedience; Choice; Contingencies.

Of God:

Defined: God's purpose (2Ti 1:9, w Eph 1:9), God's plan (1Co 12:11; 2Co 1:15; Jas 3:4), God's will (Ac 27:12; Eph 1:11).

The supreme rule of duty (Mt 6:10; 12:50 w Mk 3:35; Mt 26:39, 42; Mk 14:36; Lk 22:42; Jn 4:34; 5:30; 6:38-40; Ro 12:2; Eph 5:17). Plans of the righteous subject to (Ac 18:21; Ro 1:10; 15:32; 1Co 4:19; 16:7; Heb 6:3; Jas 4:15).

"Lord's prayer" concerns (Mt 6:10; Lk 11:2). *See Agency.*

Reasons for Wanting to Know—

Love for God (Jn 14:15, 21, 23-24), desire to please God (1Jn 3:22). Blessings in this life (1Pe 3:10-12), rewards in the future life (1Co 3:10-15; 2Ti 4:8; Heb 10:35). Avoid discipline (1Co 3:16-17; 11:31-32; 1Pe 4:17). Good example to other believers (1Co 4:16; 1Th 1:7; 2Th 3:9; Heb 13:7). Will not be ashamed at the Second Coming (1Jn 2:28). Glorify God (1Co 10:31; Col 3:17, 23; Heb 12:10; 2Pe 1:4). Obligation to know (Eph 5:15-17).

How God Reveals—

Through his Word (Ps 119:105; 2Ti 3:16-17). Through control of thoughts, indirectly (2Co 7:8-11; 12:7; 1Pe 1:6-7; 4:12-13; Jas 1:2-4), directly (Pr 16:1, 9; 21:1; Eph 2:13), through Satan (Job 1:12; 2:6). Through the control of circumstances (Pr 16:9; 20:24; Ac 2:23; 4:28; Eph 1:11). Until revelation is complete, through dreams (Ge 20:3, 6; 31:11, 24; 1Ki 3:5; Mt 2:12-13) and visions (Ge 15:1; Zec 1:7-8; Ac 10:10-11).

Prerequisites: Spiritual maturity (Isa 55:8-9; 1Co 2:7; Eph 4:14; Col 1:9; 1Ti 3:6; Heb 5:13-14; 13:21), through the teaching ministry of the Holy Spirit (Jn 16:13-14; 1Co 2:12-14; 1Jn 2:27), through application in testings (Php 3:15; Heb 5:14; 12:7, 11; Jas 1:2-5). Yieldedness or self-denial (Ro 6:13, 19; 12:1; 1Pe 2:9; Rev 1:6), discipleship (Mt 16:24; Mk 8:34; Lk 9:23). Desire to know God's will (Jn 7:17), to do it (Mk 4:24-25; Ac 10:22, 35, 44, 47; 1Jn 2:11). Willingness to obey daily (Mt 16:24; Mk 8:34; Lk 9:23; Ro 6:16; Php 2:13; 2Pe 2:19). Faith (Pr 37:5; Pr 3:5-6; Ro 14:23; 2Co 5:7; Php 2:13; Heb 11:17, 27). Patience (Ps 37:7; Jas 1:5-6). Common sense (Tit 2:12). Peace of God (Col 3:15). A clear conscience (Ro 14:23).

A Testament:

Of Abraham (Ge 25:5-6). Jacob (Ge 48:49). David (1Ki 2:1-9). Jehoshaphat (2Ch 21:3). May not be annulled (Gal 3:15). In force after death only (Heb 9:16-17). *See Testament; Wills.*

WILLFULNESS *See Obduracy; Self-Will.*

WILLOW [7628]. A type of tree growing along the brook or near water; several species in Israel; symbol of joy (Lev 23:40; Job 40:22), sorrow (Ps 137:2).

WILLOWS, BROOK OF THE *See Poplars, Ravine of.*

WILLS

Statements, oral or written in a form, to which law courts give effect, by which property may be disposed of after death (Heb 9:16-17). *See Covenant; Will, A Testament.*

WIMPLE *See Cloak.*

WIND [1999, 6193, 7600, 7708, 8120, 8551, 9402, 10658, *448, 449, 3803, 4460, 4463, 4466*].

Characterized:
Blasting (2Ki 19:7, 35).
East: Hot and blasting in Egypt (Ge 41:6), in the valley of the Euphrates (Eze 19:12), in Canaan (Hos 13:15; Lk 12:55), at Nineveh (Jnh 4:8), tempestuous in Uz (Job 27:21).
West: Took away the plague of locusts from the land of Egypt (Ex 10:19).
North: Free from humidity in Canaan (Pr 25:23).
South: Soothing (Job 37:17), tempestuous (Job 37:9), purifying (Job 37:21).

Figurative:
(Hos 4:19). Of the judgments of God (Jer 22:22; Hos 13:15; Mt 7:25). Of the Spirit (Jn 3:8). Of heresy (Eph 4:14).

WINDOW [748, 2707, 9209, 10348, *2600*]. An opening in a wall (Ge 6:16; 26:8; Jos 2:15, 21; 1Ki 6:4; Eze 40:16-36; Ac 20:9).

WINE [1074+8042, 2810, 3516, 3676, 4641, 4932, 6011, 6747, 9069, 9197, 9408, 10271, *1183, 3885, 3954*].

General
Made from grapes (Ge 49:11; Jer 40:10, 12), from pomegranates (SS 8:2). Kept in wineskins (Jos 9:4, 13; Job 32:19; Jer 13:12; Mt 9:17; Lk 5:37-38), in jars (Jer 48:12), in vats (1Ch 27:27), in buildings (2Ch 32:28). Commerce in (Rev 18:13). Banquets of (Est 5:6). Plentiful in Canaan (Dt 33:28; 2Ki 18:32).
Fermented (Lev 10:9; Nu 6:3; Dt 14:26; 29:6). New wine, a staple (Hos 2:8, 22; 7:14; Joel 2:24; Hag 1:11; Mk 2:22; Lk 5:37-39). Aged wine, a delicacy (Isa 25:6; Jer 48:11). Old wine (Lk 5:39).

Positive Use of:
Offered with sacrifices (Ex 29:40; Lev 23:13; Nu 15:5, 10; 18:12; 28:7, 14; Dt 14:23; Ne 10:39).
For enjoyment (Ps 4:7; 104:15; Pr 31:6-7; Ecc 2:3; Isa 25:6; Zec 9:17; 10:7).
Recommended by Paul to Timothy (1Ti 5:23).
Given by Melchizedek to Abraham (Ge 14:18). Used at meals (Mt 26:27-29; Mk 14:23). Made by Jesus at the marriage feast in Cana (Jn 2:9-10). Used in the Lord's Supper (Mt 26:27-29; Lk 22:17-20). Given to Jesus at the Crucifixion, possibly as a pain killer (Mt 27:48; Mk 15:23; Lk 23:36; Jn 19:29).

Negative Use of:
Drunkenness condemned (Pr 20:1; Isa 5:11, 22; 24:9; 28:1, 3, 7; 56:12; Jer 23:9; Hos 4:11; Joel 1:5; Am 6:6; Hab 2:5; Eph 5:18; 1Ti 3:8; Tit 2:3). Addiction and craving condemned (Pr 21:17; 23:29-32; Joel 1:5). Children sold for (Joel 3:3).
Instances of drunkenness—
Noah (Ge 9:21), Lot (Ge 19:32), Joseph and his brothers (Ge 43:34), Nabal (1Sa 25:36), Amnon (2Sa 13:28-29), Xerxes (Est 1:10), kings of Israel (Hos 7:5). Falsely charged against Jesus (Mt 11:19; Lk 7:34) and the disciples (Ac 2:13).

Abstinence From:
Required—
Of Levites while on duty (Lev 10:9; Eze 44:21). Of Nazirites during their vow (Nu 6:3). Of Samson's mother during her pregnancy (Jdg 13:4-5). *See Nazirite(s).* Required of kings and rulers (Pr 31:4-5). Of John the Baptist (Lk 1:15).
Chosen—
By Daniel to avoid defilement (Da 1:8-20), in mouring (Da 10:3). By the Recabites to honor a vow (Jer 35:6, 8, 14, 16). With bread, denied to the Israelites in the desert (Dt 29:6). Temperance allowed the guests at Xerxes' banquet (Est 1:8).
For the sake of the weaker brother (Ro 14:21). Possibly abstained from by Timothy (1Ti 5:23).

Figurative:
Of, the divine judgments (Ps 60:3; 75:8; Jer 51:7; Rev 14:10; 16:19), the joy of wisdom (Pr 9:2, 5), the joys of religion (Isa 55:6; 55:1; Joel 2:19), abominations (Rev 14:9; 17:2; 18:3).

Symbolic:
Of the blood of Jesus (Mt 26:28; Mk 14:23-24; Lk 22:20; Jn 6:53-56).
See Abstinence; Drunkenness; Vine; Vineyards.

WINEBIBBER *See Drunkard; Drunkenness; Wine.*

WINEPRESS [1780, 3676, 7053, *3332, 5700*]. (Nu 18:27, 30; Dt 15:14; Jdg 6:11). In vineyards (Isa 5:2; Mt 21:33; Mk 12:1).
Figurative: Treading the winepress of the judgments of God (Isa 63:2-3; La 1:15; Rev 14:19-20).

WINESKIN [199, 2827, 5532, 5574, *829*]. Made of tanned whole skins of animals (Mt 9:17). *See Wine.*

WING [88, 4053, 6416, 10149, *4763*]. Often used figuratively (Ps 18:10; 55:6; 68:13; Pr 23:5; Mt 23:37).

WINNOWING [2430, 4665, *4768*]. Separating kernels of threshed grain from chaff; done by shaking bunches of grain into air so that the kernels fall to the ground, while the chaff is blown away by the wind (Ru 3:2).

Figurative:

Of Israel in destroying its enemies (Isa 41:15-16). God's judgment separating evil people from good (Jer 15:7; 51:2; Mt 3:12; Lk 3:17). The character of a good king, not all kings (Pr 20:8; 20:26).

WINTER [1773, 3069, 3074, 6255, *4199, 4200, 5930*]. Annual return of, shall never cease (Ge 8:22). Plowing in, in Canaan (Pr 20:4). Rainy season in, in Canaan (SS 2:11). Shipping suspended in, on the Mediterranean Sea (Ac 27:12; 28:11). Paul remains for one, at Nicopolis (Tit 3:12). Summer and winter houses (Jer 36:22; Am 3:15).

See Meteorology.

WINTER APARTMENT,
WINTER HOUSE The wealthy had separate residences for hot and cold seasons. Called a "winter apartment" (Jer 36:22), a "winter house" (Am 3:15).

See Summer House, Summer Palace.

WISDOM [1069, 2681, 2682, 2683, 2684, 4213, 4220, 8505, 8507, 9312, 9370, 10265, 10266, 10539, *5053, 5054, 5055, 5317, 5860, 5861*]. (Job 32:9; Ps 2:10; 90:12; Pr 2:1-20; 4:18-20; 7:4; 9:1-6; 10:13, 21, 23; 12:1, 8, 15; 13:14-16; 14:6-8, 16, 18, 33; 15:2, 7, 14, 33; 16:16, 20-24; 17:10, 24; 18:15; 19:8, 20; 21:11; Ecc 8:1, 5; 9:13-18; 10:12; 12:11; Isa 11:9; 29:24; Mt 11:19; Lk 1:17; 7:35; 21:15; Jas 1:5).

Spiritual:

(Dt 32:29; Job 5:27; 8:8, 10; 12:2-3, 7-13, 16-17, 22).

The fear of the Lord is the beginning of (Ps 111:10; Pr 1:7; 9:10; Isa 33:6). Is revealed to the obedient (Ps 107:43; Pr 28:5, 7; 29:3; Ecc 8:5; Da 12:3-4, 10; Hos 6:3, 6; 14:9; Mt 6:22-23; Lk 11:34-36; Jn 7:17; 10:4, 14; 1Co 2:6-10; 8:3; 1Jn 4:6). Exemplified (Ps 9:10; 76:1; Pr 1:5; 11:12; Mt 7:24-25; 25:1-13; Mk 12:32-34; Ac 6:10; Ro 15:14; 1Co 13:11; Php 3:7-8, 10; 1Th 5:4-5; Jas 3:13).

Commended—

(Pr 3:13-26; 24:3-7; Ecc 7:11-12, 19; 10:1, 12). Is above value (Job 28:12-19; Pr 3:13-15; 16:16). Exhortations to attain to (Pr 2:1-20; 4:4-13, 18-20; 22:17-21; 23:12, 19; 23:23; 24:13-14; Ro 16:19; 1Co 8:3; 14:20; 2Co 8:7; Eph 5:15-17; Col 3:10, 16; 2Pe 3:18).

Parable of (Mt 25:1-13).

Personified (Pr 1:20-33; 8; 9:1-18).

See Knowledge; Speaking or Speech, Wise.

From God—

(Ex 4:12; 8:4, 10; Dt 4:5-6, 35-36; 29:4; 1Ch 22:12; Ne 9:20; Job 4:3; 11:5-6; 22:21-22; 28:20-28; 32:7-8; 33:16; 35:10-11; 36:22; 38:36-37; Ps 16:7; 19:1-2; 25:8-9, 12, 14; 32:8; 36:9; 51:6; 71:17; 94:12; 112:4; 119:130; Pr 1:23; 2:6-7; 3:5-6; Ecc 2:26; Isa 2:3; 11:1-3; 30:21; 42:6-7, 16; 48:17; 54:13; Jer 9:23-24; 24:7; Da 1:17; 2:21-23; 11:32-33; Mt 11:25-27; 13:11; 16:16-17; Lk 1:76-79; 12:11-12; 21:15; 24:32, 45; Jn 1:1, 4-5, 7-9,

17; 6:45; 8:12, 31-32; 9:5, 39; 12:46; 14:7; 16:13-14; 17:3, 6-8, 25-26; 18:37; Ro 1:19-20; 1Co 1:30; 2:9, 11-14; 12:8; 2Co 3:15; 4:6; Gal 4:9; Eph 4:11-13; Php 3:15; Col 1:26-28; 1Ti 2:4; 2Ti 1:7; 3:15; Jas 3:17; 2Pe 1:2-5, 8, 12; 3:18; 1Jn 2:20, 27; 5:20). *See God, Wisdom of.*

Exemplified—

Of Joseph (Ge 41:16, 25-39; Ac 7:10). Of Moses (Ac 7:22). Of Bezalel (Ex 31:3-5; 35:31-35; 36:1). Of Oholiab (Ex 31:6; 35:34-35; 36:1), of other skilled artisans (Ex 36:2), of women (Ex 35:26). Of Hiram (1Ki 7:14; 2Ch 2:14). Of Solomon (1Ki 3:12, 16-28; 4:29-34; 5:12; 10:24). Of Ethan, Heman, Calcol, and Darda (1Ki 4:31). Of the princes of Issachar (1Ch 12:32). Of Ezra (Ezr 7:25). Of Daniel (Da 1:17; 5:14). Of Paul (2Pe 3:15). Of the Magi (Mt 2:1-12).

Prayer for (Nu 27:21; Jdg 20:18, 23, 26-28; 1Ki 3:7, 9; 8:36; 2Ch 1:10; Job 34:32; Ps 5:8; 25:4-5; 27:11; 31:3; 39:4; 43:3; 86:11; 90:12; 119:12, 18-19, 26-27, 33-34, 66, 68, 73, 80, 124-125, 135, 144, 169, 171; 139:24; Eph 1:16-19; 3:14-19; 6:18-20; Php 1:9; Col 1:9-10; 2:1-3; 4:2-4; 2Ti 2:7; Jas 1:5).

To be possessed in humility (Jer 9:23-24; Jas 3:13). *See Desire, Spiritual.* Solomon's prayer for. *See Solomon.*

Promised (Jn 8:22). Opportunity to obtain, forfeited (Pr 1:24-31). Shall become universal.

Worldly:

Condemned—

(Job 4:18-21; 5:13; 11:2, 12; 37:24). Desired by Eve (Ge 3:6-7). Misleading (Pr 21:30; Isa 47:10; 1Co 8:1-2). Ending in death (Pr 16:25). Folly of (Ecc 2:1-26; 7:11-13, 16-25; 8:1, 16-17; Jer 8:7-9; 49:7; Mt 6:23; Ro 1:21-23). Increases sorrow (Ecc 1:18; Isa 47:10-11).

Denounced (2Co 1:12). Woe denounced against (Isa 5:21). Shall perish (Isa 29:14-16). Illustration of (Mt 7:24-27; Lk 16:8).

Admonitions against (Pr 3:7; Col 2:8; 1Ti 6:20-21). Admonitions against glorying in (Jer 9:23-24).

Heavenly things not discerned by (Mt 11:25; Lk 10:21). Gospel not to be preached with (1Co 1:17-26; 2:1-14). To be renounced in order to attain spiritual wisdom (1Co 3:18-20).

Commended—

Council of others commanded (Pr 15:22; 20:18; 24:3-7). Wise application of, profitable (Ecc 10:10; Isa 28:24-29).

Of God: *See God, Wisdom of.*

Of Jesus: *See Jesus the Christ, Wisdom of.*

WISDOM OF JESUS, SON OF
SIRACH *See Apocrypha.*

WISDOM OF SOLOMON *See*
Apocrypha.

WISE MEN

1. Men of understanding and skill in ordinary affairs (Pr 1:5; Job 15:2; Ps 49:10), came to be

recognized as a distinct class, listed with priests and prophets (Jer 18:18), and also found outside Israel (Ge 41:8; Ex 7:11; Da 2:12-5:15).

2. The Magi (Mt 2:1-12), astrologers who came from the East. Their number and names are not given in Scripture. *See Magi.*

WITCH One (usually a woman) in league with evil spirits who practices witchcraft, sorcery, and divination; condemned by law (Ex 22:18; Dt 18:9-14; 1Sa 28:3, 9; 2Ki 23:24; Isa 8:19; Ac 19:18-19). *See Divination; Medium; Sorcery; Spiritists; Witchcraft.*

WITCHCRAFT [4175, 4176, *5758*]. Detestable to God (Dt 18:9-13; 2Ki 17:17; 2Ch 33:6; Na 3:4; Gal 5:19). To be destroyed (Mic 5:12).
See Divination; Sorcery; Spiritists; Witch.

WITHE NIV "thong" (Jdg 16:7-9).

WITHERED HAND Hand wasted away through some form of atrophy (Mk 3:1-6).

WITNESS [1068+9048, 6332, 6338, 6386, 7032, *3455, 3456, 3457, 3459, 5210, 6019, 6020*]. (Lev 5:1; Pr 18:17). Qualified by oath (Ex 22:11; Nu 5:19, 21; 1Ki 8:31-32), by laying hands on the accused (Lev 24:14). Two necessary to establish a fact (Nu 35:30; Dt 17:6; 19:15; Mt 18:16; Jn 8:17; 2Co 13:1; 1Ti 5:19; Heb 10:28). Required to cast the first stone in executing sentence (Dt 13:9; 17:5-7; Ac 7:58).

To the transfer of land (Ge 21:25-30; 23:11, 16-18; Ru 4:1-9; Jer 32:9-12, 25, 44). To marriage (Ru 4:10-11; Isa 8:2-3). Incorruptible (Ps 15:4). Corrupted by money (Mt 28:11-15; Ac 6:11, 13).

Figurative of instruction in righteousness (Rev 11:3).
See Court, Of Law; Evidence; Falsehood; False Witness; Holy Spirit; Testimony, Religious.

WITNESS OF THE SPIRIT Direct, personal communication by the Holy Spirit that we are children of God (Ro 8:15-16), or some other truth (Ac 20:23; 1Ti 4:1).

WITNESSING FOR CHRIST (Lk 2:17, 38; 24:48; Ac 1:8; 10:39; 22:15; 23:11; 26:22). Of John the Baptist (Jn 1:15; 3:26). Of the apostles (Jn 15:27; 19:35; Ac 10:39-43; 1Jn 1:1-5), to his resurrection (Ac 1:22; 2:32; 3:15; 4:33; 5:32; 1Co 15:3-8).

WIZARD *See Spiritists.*

WOLF [2269, *3380*]. Ravenous (Ge 49:27; Jer 5:6; Eze 22:27; Zep 3:3; Jn 10:12).

Figurative: Of the enemies of the righteous (Mt 7:15; 10:16; Jn 10:12; Ac 20:29). Of the reconciling power of the gospel (Isa 11:6).

WOMEN [*851, 1426, 1435, 3251, 5922, 9148, *1222, 4087*].
General:
Creation of (Ge 1:27; 2:21-22). Named (Ge

2:23). Fall of and curse upon (Ge 3:1-16; 2Co 11:3; 1Ti 2:14). Promise to (Ge 3:15).

Took part in ancient worship (Ex 15:20-21; 38:8; 1Sa 2:22), in choir (1Ch 25:5-6; Ezr 2:65; Ne 7:67). Served at the entrance to the Tent of Meeting (Ex 38:8; 1Sa 2:22). Consecrated jewels to tabernacle (Ex 35:22), mirrors (Ex 38:8). Required to attend the reading of the law (Dt 31:12; Jos 8:35). Ministered in the tabernacle (Ex 38:8; 1Sa 2:22). Religious privileges of, among early Christians (Ac 1:14; 12:12-13; 1Co 11:5; 14:34; 1Ti 2:11).

Purifications of after menstruation (Lev 15:19-33; 2Sa 11:4), childbirth (Lev 12; Lk 2:22). Difference in ceremonies made between male and female children (Lev 12). Vows of (Nu 30:3-16).

Had their own tents (Ge 24:67; 31:33). Domestic duties of (Ge 18:6; Pr 31:15-19; Mt 24:41). Cooked (Ge 18:6). Spun (Ex 35:25-26; 1Sa 2:19; Pr 31:19-24). Embroidered (Pr 31:22). Made garments (1Sa 2:19; Ac 9:39). Gleaned (Ru 2:7-8, 15-23). Kept vineyards (SS 1:6). Tended flocks and herds (Ge 24:11, 13-14, 19-20; 29:9; Ex 2:16). Worked in fields (Isa 27:11; Eze 26:6, 8). Doorkeeper (Mt 26:69; Jn 18:16-17; Ac 12:13-14). Did not serve in army (Isa 19:16; Jer 50:37; 51:30; Na 3:13).

Veiled the face (Ge 24:65), *See Veil.* Forbidden to wear men's clothing (Dt 22:5). Ornaments of (Isa 3:16-23; Jer 3:32). Wore hair long (1Co 11:5-15). Commended for modesty in dress (1Ti 2:9-10; 1Pe 3:3-6).

Compassionate to her children (Isa 49:15), rejoice with dancing (Jdg 11:34; 21:21; Jer 31:13), courteous to strangers (Ge 24:17-20), wise (1Sa 25:3; 2Sa 20:16-22), weaker partner but co-heir (1Pe 3:7).

Property rights of: In inheritance (Nu 27:1-11; 36; Jos 17:3-6; Job 42:15), to sell real estate (Ru 4:3-9).

First to sin (Ge 3:6). Last at the cross (Mt 27:55-56; Mk 15:40-41). First at the tomb (Mk 15:46-47; 16:1-6; Lk 23:27-28, 49, 55-56; 24:1-10). First to whom the risen Lord appeared (Mk 16:9; Jn 20:14-18). Converted by preaching of Paul (Ac 16:14-15; 17:4, 12, 34).

Virtuous, held in high esteem (Ru 3:11; Pr 11:16, 22; 12:4; 14:1; 31:10-30). *See below, Good.*

Zealous in promoting superstition and idolatry (Jer 7:18; Eze 13:17, 23). Active in instigating iniquity (Nu 31:15-16; 1Ki 21:25; Ne 13:26). Guilty of lesbianism (Ro 1:26). *See below, Wicked.*

Could not marry without consent of parents, father (Ge 24:3-4; 34:6; Ex 22:17; Jos 3:16-17; 1Sa 17:25; 18:17-27). Not to be given in marriage considered a calamity (Jdg 11:37; Ps 78:63; Isa 4:1). When charged with infidelity, guilt or innocence was determined by trial (Nu 5:12-31). Sold for husband's debts (Mt 18:25). Taken captive (Nu 31:9, 15, 17-18, 35; La 1:18; Eze 30:17-18).

Punishment to be inflicted on men for seducing, when betrothed (Dt 22:23-27). Punishment for seducing, when not betrothed (Ex 22:16-17; Dt 22:28-29). Protected during menstruation (Lev 18:19; 20:18). Treated with cruelty in war (Dt 32:25; La 2:21; 5:11).

In Leadership:

Rulers of nations—
Deborah, judge and prophetess (Jdg 4:4); Athaliah, queen of Judah (2Ki 11:1-16; 2Ch 22:2-3, 10-12; 23:1-15); Jezebel, queen of Israel (1Ki 16:31); as rulers in Israel (Isa 3:12); Queen of Sheba (1Ki 10:1-13; 2Ch 9:1-9, 12); Esther, queen of Persia (Est 2:17); Candace, queen of Ethiopia (Ac 8:27).

Patriots—
Miriam (Ex 15:20), Deborah (Jdg 4:4-16; 5), women of Israel (1Sa 18:6), of Thebez (Jdg 9:50), of Abel (2Sa 20:16-22), Esther (Est 4:4-17; 5:1-8; 7:1-6; 8:1-8), of the Philistines (2Sa 1:20). Aid in defensive operations (Jdg 9:53).

Influential in public affairs—
The wise woman from Tekoa (2Sa 14:1-21), Bathsheba (1Ki 1:15-21), Jezebel (1Ki 21:7-15, 25), Athaliah (2Ki 11:1, 3; 2Ch 21:6; 22:3), Huldah (2Ki 22:14-20; 2Ch 34:22-28), the queen of Babylon (Da 5:9-13), Pilate's wife (Mt 27:19).
In business (1Ch 7:24; Pr 31:14-18, 24).

Poets—
Miriam (Ex 15:21), Deborah (Jdg 5), Hannah (1Sa 2:1-10), Elizabeth (Lk 1:42-45), Mary (Lk 1:46-55).

Prophets—
Miriam (Ex 15:20-21; Mic 6:4), Deborah (Jdg 4:4-5), Huldah (2Ki 22:14-20; 2Ch 34:22-28), Anna (Lk 2:36-38), Philip's daughters (Ac 21:9).

False prophets and mediums—
The medium at Endor (1Sa 28:7-25), false prophets (Eze 13:17-23), Noadiah the prophetess (Ne 6:14).

In the church—
Present at the selection of Matthias (Ac 1:13-26), present at Pentecost (Ac 2:1-18), churches met in women's homes (Ac 12:12; 16:40; Ro 16:3-5; 1Co 1:11; 16:19; Col 4:15; 2Jn), teachers (Ac 18:26; Tit 2:3-5), deaconesses or wives of deacons (Ro 16:1-2; 1Ti 3:11), and if Junias was a woman, apostles (Ro 16:7). Widow may have been a church officer (1Ti 5:1-16).

Social Status of:

In Persia (Est 1:10-22; Da 5:1-12). In Roman empire (Ac 24:24; 25:13, 23; 26:30).
Paul's precepts concerning women in the church (Gal 3:28; 1Co 11:5-15; 14:34-35; Eph 5:22-24; Col 3:18; 1Ti 2:9-12; 3:11; 5:1-16; Tit 2:3-5).
See Widow; Wife. See also, Husbands; Parents.

Good:

Good wife, from the Lord (Pr 12:4; 18:22; 19:13-14; 31:10-31; 1Ti 2:9-10; 3:11; 5:3-16; Tit 2:3-5). Virtuous (Ru 3:11; Pr 11:16, 22; 12:4; 14:1). Affectionate (2Sa 1:26), to offspring (Isa 49:15). Illustrated by the five wise virgins (Mt 25:1-10).

Instances of—
Deborah, a judge, prophetess, and military leader (Jdg 4:5). Mother of Samson (Jdg 13:23). Naomi

(Ru 1:2; 3:1; 4:14-17). Ruth (Ru 1:4, 14-22, & Ru 2-4). Hannah, the mother of Samuel (1Sa 1:9-18, 24-28). Widow of Zarephath, who fed Elijah during the famine (1Ki 17:8-24). The Shunammite, who gave hospitality to Elisha (2Ki 4:8-38). Vashti (Est 1:11-12). Esther (Est 4:15-17; 5:1-8; 7:1-6; 8:1-8).

Mary (Lk 1:26-38). Elizabeth (Lk 1:6, 41-45). Anna (Lk 2:37). The widow who cast her mite into the treasury (Mk 12:41-44; Lk 21:2-4). Mary and Martha (Mk 14:3-9; Lk 10:42; Jn 11:5). Mary Magdalene (Mk 16:1; Lk 8:2; Jn 20:1-2, 11-16). Pilate's wife (Mt 27:19). Dorcas (Ac 9:36). Lydia (Ac 19:14). Priscilla (Ac 18:26). Phoebe (Ro 16:1-2). Julia (Ro 16:15). Mary (Ro 16:6). Lois and Eunice (2Ti 1:5). Philippians (Php 4:3). The chosen lady (2Jn).

Figurative—
Of the church of Christ (Ps 45:2-15; Gal 4:26; Rev 12:1). Of saints (Mt 25:1-4; 2Co 11:2; Rev 14:4).

Wicked:

(2Ki 9:30-37; 23:7; Jer 44:15-19, 25; Eze 8:14; Ro 1:26). Zeal of, in licentious practices of idolatry (2Ki 23:7; Hos 4:13-14), in promoting superstition and idolatry (Jer 7:18; Eze 13:17, 23). Careless (Isa 32:9-11). Contentious (Pr 27:15-16). Fond of self-indulgence (Isa 32:9-11), of ornaments (Jer 2:32). Guilty of lesbianism (Ro 1:26). Subtle and deceitful (Pr 6:24-29, 32-35; 7:6-27; Ecc 7:26). Weak-willed (2Ti 3:6).

Active in instigating iniquity (Nu 31:15-16; 1Ki 21:25; Ne 13:26). Idolatrous (Nu 31:15-16; 2Ki 23:7; Ne 13:26; Jer 7:18). Gossips (1Ti 5:11-13). Haughty and vain (Isa 3:16). Odious (Pr 30:23). Guileful and licentious (Pr 2:16-19; 5:3-20; 6:24-29, 32-35; 7:6-27; Ecc 7:26; Eze 16:32; Ro 1:26). Commits forgery (1Ki 21:8). Subtle and deceitful (Pr 6:24-29, 32-35; 7:6-27; Ecc 7:26). Illustrated by the five foolish virgins (Mt 25:1-12).

Instances of Wicked—
Eve, in yielding to temptation and seducing her husband (Ge 3:6; 1Ti 2:14). Sarah, in her jealousy and malice toward Hagar (Ge 21:9-11, w 21:12-21). Lot's wife, in her rebellion against her situation, and against the destruction of Sodom (Ge 19:26; Lk 17:32). The daughters of Lot, in their incestuous lust (Ge 19:31-38). Rebekah, in her partiality for Jacob and her actions to secure for him Isaac's blessing (Ge 27:11-17). Rachel, in her jealousy of Leah (Ge 30:1), in stealing images (Ge 31:19, 34). Leah in her imitation of Rachel in the matter of children (Ge 30:9-18). Tamar, in her adultery (Ge 38:14-24). Potiphar's wife, in her lust and slander against Joseph (Ge 39:7-20).

Miriam, in her sedition with Aaron against Moses (Nu 12). Rahab, in her harlotry (Jos 2:1). Delilah, in her conspiracy against Samson (Jdg 16:4-20). Peninnah, the wife of Elkanah, in her jealous taunting of Hannah (1Sa 1:4-8). The Midianite woman in the camp of Israel, taken in adultery (Nu 25:6-8).

Michal, in her derision of David's religious zeal

(2Sa 6:16, 20-23). Bathsheba, in her adultery and in becoming the wife of her husband's murderer (2Sa 11:4-5, 27; 12:9-10). Solomon's wives, in their idolatrous and wicked influence over Solomon (1Ki 11:1-11; Ne 13:26). Jezebel, in her persecution and destruction of the prophets of the Lord (1Ki 18:4, 13); in her persecution of Elijah (1Ki 19:2), ;in her conspiracy against Naboth to despoil him of his vineyard (1Ki 21:1-16); in her evil influence over Ahab (1Ki 21:25, w 21:17-27, & 2Ki 9:30-37). The cannibal mothers of Samaria (2Ki 6:28-29). Athaliah, in destroying the royal household and usurping the throne (2Ki 11:1-16; 2Ch 22:10, 12; 23:12-15).

Noadiah, a false prophetess, in troubling the Jews when they were restoring Jerusalem (Ne 6:14). Haman's wife, in counseling him to hang Mordecai (Est 5:14; 6:13). Job's wife, in counseling him to curse God (Job 2:9; 19:17). The idolatrous wife of Hosea (Hos 1:2-3; 3:1).

Herodias, in her incestuous marriage with Herod (Mt 14:3-4; Mk 6:17-19; Lk 3:19) and causing the death of John the Baptist (Mt 14:6-11; Mk 6:24-28). The daughter of Herodias, in her complicity with her mother in causing the death of John the Baptist (Mt 14:8; Mk 6:18-28). Sapphira, in her blasphemous falsehood (Ac 5:2-10).

Figurative—

Of backsliding (Jer 6:2; Rev 17:4, 18). Of the wicked (Isa 32:9, 11; Mt 25:1-13).

Symbolic—

Of wickedness (Zec 5:7-8; Rev 17; 19:2).

See Widow; Wife.

WONDERFUL [7098, 7099, 7100, *1902, 2514, 2515*]. The acts of God (1Ch 16:9; Ps 26:7; 107:8, 15, 21, 24, 31). The name of God is (Jdg 13:18, ftn). A name of the Messiah (Isa 9:6).

See Jesus the Christ, Names of; Titles and Names.

WOOL [1600, 7547, 9106+9357, 10556, 2250]. Used for clothing (Lev 13:47-52, 59; Pr 31:13; Eze 34:3; 44:17). Prohibited in the priest's temple dress (Eze 44:17). Mixing of, with other fabrics forbidden (Lev 19:19; Dt 22:11). Fleece of (Jdg 6:37). First fleece of, belonged to the priests (Dt 18:4).

WORD [*3364*]. A title of Jesus (Jn 1:1, 14; 1Jn 5:7; Rev 19:13). *See Jesus the Christ, Names of; Logos.*

WORD OF GOD

Written Word; the Bible:

Psalms of (Ps 19; 119).

Called—

Book (Ps 40:7; Rev 22:19). Book of the Lord (Isa 34:16). Book of the Law (Ne 8:3; Gal 3:10). Holy Scriptures (Ro 1:2; 2Ti 3:15). Law of the Lord (Ps 1:2; Isa 30:9). Oracles (Zec 9:1; 12:1; Mal 1:1). Scriptures (1Co 15:3). Scriptures of Truth (Da 10:21). Sword of the Spirit (Eph 6:17).

The Word (Jas 1:21-23; 1Pe 2:2). Word of God

(Lk 11:28; Heb 4:12). Good Word of God (Heb 6:5). Word of Christ (Col 3:16). Word of Life (Php 2:16). Word of Truth (Pr 22:21; Eph 1:13; 2Ti 2:15; Jas 1:18).

Compared to—

A lamp (Ps 119:105; Pr 6:23). Fire (Jer 23:29). Seed (Mt 13:38, 18-23, 37-38; Mk 4:3-20, 26-32; Lk 8:5-15). To a two-edged sword (Heb 4:12).

To Be—

Publicly read (Ex 24:7; Dt 31:11-13; Jos 8:33-35; 2Ki 23:2; 2Ch 17:7-9; Ne 8:1-8, 13, 18; Isa 2:3; Jer 36:6; Ac 13:15, 27; Col 4:16; 1Th 5:27). Instruction of, to be desired (Ps 119:18-19). The people stood and responded saying "Amen" (Ex 24:7; Dt 27:12-26; Ne 8:5-6).

Publicly expounded (Ne 8:8), by Jesus (Lk 4:16-27; 24:27, 45; Jn 2:22), by the apostles (Ac 2:16-47; 8:32, 35; 17:2; 28:23).

Searched (Ac 17:11). Searching of, commanded (Isa 34:16; Jn 5:39; 7:52). To be studied (2Ti 2:15; 1Pe 2:2-3). Various portions to be compared (2Pe 2:20). Studied by rulers (Dt 17:18-19; Jos 1:8). Taught to children (Dt 6:7; 11:19; 21:12-13; Ps 78:5).

Obeyed (Dt 4:5-6; 29:29; Ps 78:1, 7; Isa 34:16; Eze 44:5; Hab 2:2; Mt 7:24-25; Lk 6:47-48; 11:28; Ro 16:26; 1Co 11:2; 1Th 4:1-2; 2Th 2:14-15; Heb 2:1-3; Jas 1:25; 2Pe 3:1-2; Jude 3, 17; Rev 1:3). Believed (Mk 1:15; 1Jn 5:11, 13). Longed for (Ps 119:20, 131; Am 8:11-13). Walked after (Ps 119:30).

In the heart (Dt 30:11-14; Job 22:22; Ps 37:31; 40:8; 119:11; Pr 6:20-21; Isa 51:7; Eze 3:10; Ro 10:6-8). Meditated upon (Jos 1:8; Ps 1:2; 119:15, 23, 48, 78, 97, 99, 148). Worn on the hand and forehead (Ex 13:9; Dt 6:8; 11:18). Written on the doorframes (Dt 6:9; 11:20). In public places (Dt 27:2-3, 8; Jos 8:32). Placed inside of the ark of the covenant (Ex 40:20), beside the ark (Dt 31:26), read in public assemblies (Dt 31:11), *See above, In Public Places.* Taught in the Psalms (Dt 31:19, 21; Ps 119:54). Used for teaching and admonishing one another (1Co 10:11; Col 3:16). Instruction (2Ti 3:16-17).

Not To Be—

Added to nor taken from (Dt 4:2; 12:32; Pr 30:6; Rev 22:18-19). Handled deceitfully (2Co 4:2). Broken (Jn 10:35).

Nature of—

Comforting (Ps 119:28, 50, 52, 76, 83, 92). Delight of the righteous (Job 23:12; Ps 1:2; 119:16, 24, 35, 77, 103, 143, 162, 174). Desired more than gold (Ps 119:72, 127). Edifying (Ps 119:98, 99, 104, 130; Ac 20:32; Ro 4:23-24; 15:4; 1Ti 4:6; 1Jn 2:7-8, 12, 14, 21). Effective (Isa 55:11). Enduring forever (Ps 119:89, 138, 152; Isa 40:8; Mk 13:31; Lk 16:17; 1Pe 1:23-25). Full of hope (Ps 119:81; Col 1:5). Full of joy (Jer 15:16; 1Jn 1:4).

Inspired (Ex 19:7; 20:1; 24:3-4, 12; 31:18; 32:16; 34:27, 32; Lev 26:46; Dt 4:5, 10, 14; 2Ki 17:13; 2Ch 33:18; Ps 99:7; 147:19; Isa 34:16; 59:21; Jer 30:2; 36:1-2, 27-28, 32, 59-64; Eze 11:25; Da 10:21; Hos 8:12; Zec 7:12; Ac 1:16;

28:25; Ro 3:1-2; 1Co 2:12-13; 14:37; Eph 6:17; 1Th 2:13; 2Ti 3:16-17; Heb 1:1-2; 3:7-8; 4:12; 2Pe 1:21; 3:2, 15; Rev 1:1-2, 11, 17-19; 2:7; 22:6-8).

Life giving (Ps 119:25, 93; Jas 1:18; 1Pe 1:23). Living (Heb 4:12). Loved (Ps 119:47-48, 70, 97, 111, 113, 119, 159, 163, 167). Part of the Christian armor (Eph 6:17). Perfect (Ps 19:7; Jas 1:24). Powerful (Lk 1:37; Heb 4:12). Praiseworthy (Ps 56:4). Pure (Ps 12:6; 19:8; 119:140; Pr 30:5). Restraining (Ps 17:4; 119:11). Revered (Ps 119:161; 138:2).

Sanctifying (Jn 15:3; 17:17, 19; Eph 5:26; 1Ti 4:5). Spirit and life (Jn 6:63). Spiritual food, bread (Dt 8:3; Mt 4:4). Standard of righteous (Ps 119:138, 144, 172; Isa 8:20). Truth (Ps 19:7, 9; 33:4, 6; 93:5; 111:7-8; 119:86). Truth (Ps 119:142, 151, 160; 1Th 2:13; Jas 1:18). Wonderful (Ps 119:129).

Bears the test of criticism and experience (2Sa 22:31; Ps 18:30). Cleanses life of youth (Ps 119:9). Convicts of sin (2Ki 22:9-13; 2Ch 17:7-10; 34:14-33). Gives peace (Ps 119:165). Inspires faith (Ro 10:17; Heb 11:3). Makes free (Ps 119:45; Jn 8:32). Makes wise (Ps 119:99; 2Ti 3:15). Rejoices the heart (Ps 119:111; Jer 15:16). Spirit of, gives life (2Co 3:6). Standard of judgment, the world to be judged by (Jn 12:48; Ro 2:16). Works salvation (1Th 2:13; 1Pe 1:23).

Fulfilled by Jesus (Mt 5:17; Lk 24:27; Jn 19:24). Testify of Jesus (Jn 5:39; 20:31; Ac 10:43; 18:28; 1Co 15:3; Heb 10:7). *See Jesus the Christ, Prophecies Concerning.*

Ignorance of—

(Mt 22:29; Mk 12:24).

Disbelief in (Lk 16:31; 24:25; Jn 5:46-47; 8:37; 2Ti 4:3-4; 1Pe 2:8; 2Pe 3:15-16).

Rejected by the wicked (Ps 50:16-17; Pr 1:29; 13:13; Isa 5:24; 28:9-14; 30:9-11; 53:1; Jer 6:10; 8:9; Hos 8:12; Am 2:12; Mic 2:6; Mk 7:9, 13; Lk 16:31; 24:25; Jn 3:20; 5:46-47; 8:37, 45; Ac 13:46; 1Co 1:18, 22-23; 2Ti 4:3-4; 1Pe 2:8; 2Pe 3:15-16; Rev 22:19).

See Commandments and Statutes, Of God.

Jesus, the Living Word:

(Jn 1:1, 14; 1Jn 5:7; Rev 19:13). *See Jesus the Christ, Names of; Logos.*

WORDS [*606, 609, 614, 1819, 1821, 4383, 4863, 7023, 7754, 8938, 9048, 10418, *3364, 3306, 3359, 4048, 4839, 5125, 5889*].

Of Jesus:

Gracious (Lk 4:22), spirit and life (Jn 6:63), eternal life (Jn 6:68), shall judge (Jn 12:47-48).

Of the Wise:

As goads, and as nails well fastened (Ecc 12:11), gracious (Ecc 10:12). Spoken in season (Pr 15:23; Isa 50:4). Fitly spoken, like apples of gold in settings of silver (Pr 25:11). Of the perfect man, gentle (Jas 3:2). Of the teacher, should be plain (1Co 14:9, 19).

Should be acceptable to God (Ps 19:14).

Unwise:

Unprofitable, to be avoided (2Ti 2:14). Unspeakable, heard by Paul in paradise (2Co 12:4). Vain, not to be regarded (Ex 5:9; Eph 5:6), like a tempest (Job 8:2). Without knowledge, darken counsel (Job 38:2). Idle, account must be given for in the day of judgment (Mt 12:36-37).

Hasty, folly of (Pr 29:20). In a multitude of, is sin (Pr 10:19). Fool known by the multitude of (Ecc 5:3), will swallow himself (Ecc 10:12-14). Seditious, deceive the simple (Ro 16:18). Deceitful, are a snare to him who utters them (Pr 6:2). Of the hypocrite, softer than oil (Ps 55:21). Of the talebearer, wounds to the soul (Pr 18:8).

See Busybody; Slander; Speaking, Evil; Talebearer.

WORK [*1215, 1911, 2006, 3098, 3330, 3828, 4144, 4856, 5126, 6268, 6275, 6662, 6913, 6913, 7188, 7189, 7190, 7258, 7756, 8391, 8502, 8697, 10525, *1918, 1919, 2237, 2239, 2240, 2435, 3159, 3160, 4472, 5300, 5301*]. *See Industry; Labor.*

WORKS, GOOD [*1911, 2006, 5126, 6268, 6913, 7188, 7189, *1919, 2240, 2435*].

General:

(2Co 9:8; Eph 2:10; Php 2:13; Col 1:10; 1Th 1:3, 7-8; 2Th 2:17, 21; Jas 1:22-27; 3:17-18).

Under the Law (Lev 18:5; Eze 20:11, 13, 20; Lk 10:28; Ro 10:5; Gal 3:12). In humanitarian service (Eze 18:7-8; Mt 10:42; 25:35-46; Jas 1:27). Hypocritical (Mt 6:1-4).

Jesus an example of (Jn 10:32; Ac 10:38). Ministers should be patterns of (Tit 2:7). Ministers should exhort to (1Ti 6:17-18; Tit 3:1, 8, 14). Holy women should manifest (1Ti 2:10; 5:10). Manifest faith (Ps 37:3; Mt 19:16-21; Ro 2:13; Gal 6:4; Jas 2:14-26). Scriptures given for (Tit 2:14).

God is glorified by (Mt 25:34-46; Jn 15:2-8, 14; 1Co 3:6-9; Php 1:11; Heb 13:21). Designed to lead others to glorify God (Mt 5:16; 1Pe 2:12). A blessing attends (Jas 1:25). God remembers (Dt 6:25; 24:13; Ps 106:30-31; Jer 22:15-16; Eze 18:5-9; Mt 6:1-4; 18:5; 25:34-36; Lk 6:35, 14; Ac 10:14, 38; Heb 6:9-10; Rev 14:13; 22:14).

Of the righteous, are manifest (1Ti 5:25). God remembers (Ne 13:14; Heb 6:9-10). Shall be brought into judgment (Ecc 12:14, w 2Co 5:10). In the judgment, will be an evidence of faith (Mt 25:34-40, w Jas 2:14-20).

Parables relating to: The talents and pounds (Mt 25:14-29; Lk 19:12-27), the laborers in the vineyard (Mt 20:11-15), the two sons (Mt 21:28-31), the barren fig tree (Lk 13:6-9).

Commanded:

(Ps 37:3; Mt 3:8; Jn 14:2-8, 14) To ministers (Tit 2:7), women professing godliness (1Ti 2:10), widows (1Ti 5:10). To Christians (Mt 5:16; Col 3:13; Tit 3:1-2, 8, 14; Heb 10:24; Jas 1:22-27; 3:13; 1Pe 2:12). To the rich (1Ti 6:18). To be done without a show (Mt 6:1-4). Following the example of the faithful (Heb 10-14). Zeal in (Tit 2:14).

Insufficient for Salvation:

(Ps 49:7-8; 127:1-2; Ecc 1:14; Isa 13:14; 57:12; 64:6; Eze 7:19; 33:12-19; Da 9:18; Mt 5:20; Lk 17:7-10; 18:9-14; Ac 13:39; Ro 3:20-21; 4:1-25; 8:3; 9:16, 31-32; 11:6; 1Co 13:1-3; Gal 2:16, 21; 3:10-12, 21; 4:9-11; 5:2, 4, 6, 18; 6:15; Eph 2:8-9; Php 3:3-9; Col 2:20-23; 2Ti 1:9; Tit 3:4-5; Heb 4:3-10; 6:1-2; 9:1-14; Jas 2:10-11).

WORKS OF GOD
In creation (Job 9:8-9; Ps 8:3-5; 89:11; 136:5-9; 139:13-14; 148:4-5; Ecc 3:11; Jer 10:12), good (Ge 1:10, 18, 21, 25). Faithful (Ps 33:4). Wonderful (Ps 26:7; 40:5). Incomparable (Ps 86:8). In his overruling providence in human affairs (Ps 26:7; 40:5; 66:3; 75:1; 111:2, 4, 6; 118:17; 145:4-17).

See also, God, Works of.

WORLD
[824, 2535, 2698, 9315, 10075, *172, 1178, 3179, 3180, 3232, 3876, 4246, 4920, 4922*].

1. Universe (Jn 1:10).
2. Human race (Ps 9:8; 96:13; Ac 17:31).
3. Unregenerate humanity (Jn 15:18; 1Jn 2:15).
4. Roman Empire (Lk 2:1).

WORLDLINESS
[*94, 96, 3176, 3180+ 3836, 4920, 4921, 4922*].

Described:

(Ecc 1:8; 8:15; Isa 56:12; Jn 15:19; Tit 3:3; 2Pe 2:12-15, 18-19). Proverbial theme (Isa 22:13; Lk 12:19; 1Co 15:32). Tends to poverty (Pr 21:17; Hag 1:6). Fatal to spirituality (Gal 6:8; Php 3:19; 1Ti 5:6). Chokes the Word (Mt 13:22; Mk 4:19; Lk 8:14).

Leads to: The rejection of the gospel (Mt 22:2-6; Lk 14:17-24). The rejection of Christ (Jn 5:44; 12:43). Moral insensibility (Isa 22:13; 32:9-11; 47:7-9). Death (Pr 14:12-13).

Prosperity of is short-lived (Job 20:4-29; 21:11-15; Ps 49:16-18; Isa 24:7-11; 28:4).

Prayer regarding (Ps 73:2-22). Parables of (Lk 16:1-13, 19-25). Vanity of (Ecc 2:1-12; 6:11-12).

Admonitions Against:

(Pr 23:20-21; 27:1, 7; Ecc 7:2-4; 11:9-10; Hos 9:1, 11, 13; Am 6:3-7; 8:10; Mic 2:10; 6:14, 19, 24; Mt 6:25-34; 16:26; 24:28; Mk 8:36-37; Lk 17:26-29, 33; 21:34; Jn 12:25; Ro 12:2; 1Co 7:29-31; 10:6; Col 3:2, 5; 2Ti 2:4, 22; 3:2-9; Tit 2:12; Jas 2:1-4; 4:4, 9; 5:5; 1Pe 1:14, 24; 2:11; 4:1-4; 1Jn 2:15-17). Denounced (Isa 5:11-12; 47:8-9; Jude 11-13, 16, 19).

Moses' choice against (Heb 11:24-26).

Instances of:

Antediluvians (Mt 24:38-39; Lk 17:26-27). Sodomites (Lk 17:28-29). Esau (Ge 25:31-34; Heb 12:16). Jacob (Ge 25:31-34; 27:36; 30:37-43). Judah (Ge 37:26-27). Israelites (1Sa 8:19-20). Balaam (2Pe 2:15; Jude 11, w Nu 22; 23; 24). Eli's sons (1Sa 2:12-17). Gehazi (2Ki 5:20-27).

Herod (Mt 14:6-7). The disciples (Mt 18:1-4; Mk 9:34; Lk 9:46-48). The rich fool (Lk 12:16-21). Dives (Lk 16:19-25). The worldly steward (Lk 16:1-13). Cretans (Tit 1:12).

See Worldly Pleasure.

WORLDLY CARE
See Anxiety.

WORLDLY PLEASURE
(Job 20:12; Ecc 7:4; Isa 22:13; 2Ti 3:4; Tit 3:3). Rejected by Moses (Heb 11:25). To be rejected by the righteous (1Pe 4:3-4). Brings poverty (Pr 21:17). Chokes righteousness (Lk 8:14). Leads to suffering (Isa 47:8-9; 2Pe 3:13), spiritual death (1Ti 5:6). Denounced (Isa 5:11-12; Jas 5:5). Folly of (Ecc 1:17; 2:1-13).

See Worldliness.

WORLDLY WISDOM
Desired by Eve (Ge 3:6-7). Misleading (Isa 47:10). Increases sorrow (Ecc 1:18). Shall perish (Isa 29:14). Heavenly things not discerned by (Mt 11:25; Lk 10:21). Gospel not to be preached with (1Co 1:17-26; 2:1-14). To be renounced in order to attain spiritual wisdom (1Co 3:18-20). Admonitions against (Col 2:8; 1Ti 6:20-21). Admonitions against glorying in (Jer 9:23-24).

See Wisdom.

WORM
[6182, 8231, 9357, *1905, 5037, 5038*]. Low form of life (Ex 16:24; Isa 51:8; Ac 12:23), used metaphorically of mankind's insignificance (Job 25:6; Isa 41:14).

WORMWOOD
[*952*]. Bitter plant that grows in wastelands; name of a star that turns water bitter (Rev 8:11).

WORSHIP
[*1251, 2556, 3707, 3710, 6268, 6913, 7537, 10504, 10586, 3301, 3302, 4686, 4934, 4936*].

General:

To be rendered to God only (Ex 20:3; Dt 5:7; 6:13; Mt 4:10; Lk 4:8; Ac 10:26; 14:15; Col 2:18; Rev 19:10; 22:8). Not needed by God (Ac 17:24-25).

Divine presence in (Ex 29:42-43; 40:34-35; Lev 19:30; Nu 17:4; 1Ki 8:3-11; 2Ch 5:13-14; Ps 77:13; 84:4; Isa 56:7; Mt 18:20; Ac 2:1-4; Heb 10:25).

Origin of (Ge 4:26). Of Jesus. *See Jesus the Christ, Worship of.*

Acceptable to God (Ge 4:4; 8:21). Of the wicked, rejected (Ge 4:5, 7). *See Prayer, of the Wicked.* "Iniquity of the holy things" (Ex 28:38).

Sanctuary instituted for (Ex 25:8, 22; 29:43; 40:34-35; Nu 17:4).

Attitudes in: Bowing (Ex 34:8; 2Ch 20:18). Prostration (Ge 17:3; Mk 3:11).

Prayer in. *See Prayer.*

Benedictions pronounced. *See Benedictions.*

With music (2Ch 5:13-14; Ezr 3:10-11; Ps 100:1-2; 126:1-3; Isa 30:29; 38:20). Rendering praise (Ps 22:22; 138:2; 149:1). Thanksgiving (Ps 35:18; 100:4; 116:17).

In spirit and truth (Jn 4:23-24; 1Co 14:15; Php 3:3). Renews strength (Isa 40:31). Loved by God's people (Ps 27:4; 84:1-4; 84:10; Zec 8:21). Reward of (Ps 65:4; 92:13-14; 122:1).

Preparation for (Ex 19:10-13, 21-24; 20:24-25; 30:19, 21; Lev 10:3; Ps 26:6; Isa 56:6-7; Zep 3:18; Mal 3:3-4). Requirements of (Ps 24:3-6; 51:18-19).

Proprieties in (Ecc 5:1-2; 1Co 11:13, 20-22; 14:2-19). Reverence in (Ex 3:5; 19:10-12, 21-24; 24:1-2; Ecc 5:1; Hab 2:20). Private (Mt 6:6; 14:23; Lk 6:12).

At night (Isa 30:29; Ac 16:25). Jesus prays at night (Lk 6:12). In the temple (Jer 26:2; Lk 18:10; 24:53; Ac 3:1). In the heavenly temple (Rev 11:1). In private homes (Ac 1:13-14; 5:42; 12:12; 20:7-9; Ro 16:5; 1Co 16:19; Col 4:15; Phm 2). Anywhere (Jn 4:21-24). To become universal (Isa 45:23; Ro 14:11; Php 2:10).

Of hypocrites, despised by God (Isa 1:11-15; 29:13-16; Hos 6:6; Am 5:21-24). Of the wicked, rejected (Ge 4:5, 7).

Of angels, forbidden (Rev 19:10; 22:8-9).

Commanded:

(Ge 35:1; Ex 15:1; 23:17-18; 34:23; Dt 12:5-7, 11-12; 16:6-8; 31:11-13; 33:19; 2Ki 17:36; 1Ch 16:29; Ne 10:39; Ps 29:2; 45:11; 76:11; 96:8-9; 97:7; 99:5; Isa 12:5-6; 49:13; 52:9; Jer 31:11-12; Joel 1:14-15; 2:15-17; Na 1:15; Hag 1:8; Zec 14:16-18; Mt 8:4; Mk 1:44; Lk 4:8; 5:14; 1Ti 2:8; Heb 10:25; 12:28; Rev 14:7; 19:10).

Summons to (Ps 95:6; Isa 2:3; Mic 4:2).

Family:

(Dt 16:11, 14). Of Abraham (Ge 12:7-8; 13:4, 18). Of Jacob (Ge 35:2-3). Of Job (Job 1:5). Of the Philippian jailer (Ac 16:34).

National:

(Rev 15:4). The whole nation required to assemble for, including men, women, children, servants, and strangers (Dt 16:11; 31:11-13), in Mount Gerizim and Mount Ebal (Jos 8:32-35). The word of God read in public assemblies (Ex 24:7; Dt 27:12-26; 31:11-13; Jos 8:33-35; 2Ki 23:1-3; Ne 8:1-8, 13-18; Mt 21:23; Lk 4:16-17).

See Affliction; Prayer Under; Blasphemy; Children; Church; The Body of Believers; Consecration; Dedication; Idolatry; Instruction, in Religion; Levites; Minister; Music; Offerings; Praise; Prayer; Preaching; Priest; Psalms; Religion; Sacrilege; Servant; Strangers; Tabernacle; Temple; Thanksgiving; Women; Word of God; Young Men.

Instances of:

Israel (Ex 15:1-2; Ps 107:6-8, 32). Moses (Ex 34:8). Solomon (2Ch 7:1). Priests and Levites (2Ch 30:27). Psalmists (Ps 5:7; 42:4; 48:9; 55:14; 63:1-2; 66:4, 13-14; 89:7; 93:5; 103:1-4; 116:12-14, 17; 119:108; 132:7, 13-14). Isaiah (Isa 49:13; 52:9).

WORSHIPERS [*6985, *3302, *4686, *4687, *4936]. Examples of (Ge 22:5; 24:26; Ex

34:8; Jos 5:14; Jdg 7:15; 1Sa 1:28; 2Sa 12:20; 2Ch 7:3; Ne 8:6; Job 1:20; Rev 4:10; 7:11; 11:16).

WOUNDS [928+995, 2467, 2726, 3872, 4731, 4804, 5596, 5782, 6780, 7206, *3698, *4435, *5546*]. Treatment of (Pr 20:30; Isa 1:6; Lk 10:34). By Jesus' wounds we are healed (Isa 53:5; 1Pe 2:24).

WRATH [399, 678, 2404, 2405, 2408, 2779, 3019, 5757, 6301, 6552, 7288, 7911, 7912, 8075, 10634, *2596, *3973*].

1. Anger of people (Ge 30:2; 1Sa 17:28), may be evil (2Co 12:20), or a reaction to evil (1Sa 20:34), or a work of the flesh (Gal 5:20). *See Anger.*

2. Anger of God—reaction of a righteous God against sinful people and evil in all forms (Dt 9:7; Isa 13:9; Ro 1:18; Eph 5:6; Rev 14:10, 19). *See Anger of God.*

WREATHS [4324, 6498, *5098*]. Decorating the tabernacle and temple (Ex 28:14; 1Ki 7:17; 2Ch 4:12).

WRESTLE [84, 8883, *76*]. To contend by grappling with an opponent (Ge 32:24-25), used figuratively (Ge 30:8; Eph 6:12).

WRITING [*1821, 4180, 4181, 4844, 6219, 6221, 10375, 10673, *1207, *1210, *1211, *1582, *2107, *2108, *2182, *4592*]. Discovered to be in use in Mesopotamia as early as 3200 B.C., its development credited to the Sumerians. They had a primitive, nonalphabetic linear writing, not phonetic but pictographic, ideas being recorded by means of pictures of sense-symbols, rather than by sounds-symbols. The next stage in the history of writing was the introduction of the phonogram, or the type of sign which indicates a sound, and afterward came alphabetic scripts. The Egyptians first developed an alphabetic system of writing. Hebrews derived their alphabet from Phoenicians. Semitic writing dating between 1900 and 1500 B.C. has been found at Serabit el-Khadim in Sinai. Greeks received their alphabet from Phoenicians and Arameans.

Writing mentioned in Bible (Ex 17:14). Ten Commandments written with the finger of God (Ex 31:18; 32:15-16). Ancient writing materials: clay, wax, wood, metal, plaster (Dt 27:2-3; Jos 8:32; Lk 1:63), later, parchment (2Ti 4:13), and papyrus (2Jn 12). Instruments of writing: reed on papyrus and parchment; stylus on hard material (Ex 32:4).

See Book; Engraving; Ink; Letters; Pen; Tablet, 1.

WRITING KIT In Ezekiel's vision (Eze 9:2-3, 11).

XERXES [347].

1. Xerxes is a transliteration of the Greek form of the Persian name Khshayarshan; KJV Ahasuerus. The king of Persia mentioned in the book of Esther and Ezr 4:6. Xerxes succeeded his father Darius the Great and reigned from 486 to 465 B.C.

2. Father of Darius the Mede (Da 9:1).

YAHWEH [3363, 3378] (*He who is [I am]* or *He who causes to be*). The Hebrew personal name for God, Yahweh, is translated in the NIV as LORD. God revealed his name as "I AM WHO I AM," his eternal covenant name implying self-existence and saving presence (Ex 3:14-17).

YHWH is often called the "tetragrammaton," referring to the "four letters" or consonants of Yahweh.

See God, Names of, Yahweh; Jehovah.

YARMUK, WADI EL Stream six miles SE of Sea of Galilee flowing into Jordan, marked S boundary of Bashan.

YARN [9106+9357, 9418].

1. Blue, purple, and scarlet yarn used to embroider the tabernacle and priestly garments (Ex 25:4; 26:1; 28:5), in the temple (1Ch 2:7, 14; 3:14). Used in cleansing sacrifices (Lev 14:4, 6, 49, 51-52).

2. *See Kue.*

YAUDI [3373]. A place in N Aram or the same as Judah (2Ki 14:28, ftn).

YEAR [*2645, 3427, 9102, 10732, *1454*, *1929*, *2291*, *2465*, *4373*, *5478*]. (Ge 1:14). Divided into months (Ex 12:2; Nu 10:10; 28:11). *See Month.*

Annual feasts (Lev 25:5). *See Feasts.*

Redemption of houses sold, limited to one (Lev 25:29-30). Land to rest one, in seven (Lev 25:5). Of release (Dt 15:9).

Age computed by: of Abraham (Ge 25:7), of Jacob (Ge 47:9). *See Longevity.*

A thousand, with the Lord as one day (Ps 90:4; 2Pe 3:8). Satan to be bound a thousand (Rev 20:2-4, 7).

See Jubilee; Millennium; Time.

YEAST [2806, 2809, 4721, 5174, 8419, *109*, *2434*]. *See Leaven.*

YHWH *See Lord; Yahweh.*

YOKE [3998, 4573, 4574, 4593, 6026, 6296, 6585, 7537, 7538, *2282*, *2414*, *2433*]. Wooden frame for joining two draft animals; a wooden bar held on neck by thongs around neck (Nu 19:2; Dt 21:3). Yoke of oxen is a pair (1Sa 14:14; Lk 14:19).

Figurative of:

Oppression (Lev 26:13; 1Ki 12:4; 2Ch 10:4, 9-11; Isa 9:4; 10:27; Jer 28:2, 4, 10; 30:8), the bondage of sin (La 1:14), burdensome ordinances (Ac 15:10; Gal 5:1), discipleship to Christ (Mt 11:29-30), discipline (La 3:27).

Removal, of figurative of deliverance (Ge 27:40; Jer 2:20; Mt 11:29-30).

YOKEFELLOW [5187] (*yoked together*). Person united to another by close bonds, as in marriage or labor (Php 4:3, ftn).

YOM KIPPUR Hebrew for "Day of Atonement." *See Feasts.*

YOUNG MEN, WOMEN [*711, 1033, 1201, 1426, 1435, 1531, 3528, 3529, 4097, 5830, 5853, 5855, 6402, 7228, 7262, 7582, 7582, 7783, 7785, *3733*, *3734*, *3742*]. *Note:* In the proverbs throughout this entry, "son" can be read as an inclusive term for both male and female children.

Wise and Foolish:

Wise, exemplified in Moses' wise choice (Ex 24:3-5; Heb 11:24-26). A comfort to parents (Pr 10:1; 15:20; 29:3). Glory of (Pr 20:29).

Foolish, a sorrow to parents (Pr 10:1; 17:25; 19:13, 26; 28:7).

Wise and foolish, contrasted (Pr 10:1; 13:1; 15:20). *See below, Folly of.*

Admonitions to:

(Pr 3:1-5; 4:20-27; 6:1-5, 20-25; 19:27; 23:15-26; 24:1-12, 15-34; 27:11). Against lust (2Ti 2:22-23). Against drunkenness (Pr 23:20-21; 23:29-35). Against loving the world (1Jn 2:13-17). Against the snares of the adulteress (Pr 5:3-14; 6:24-35; 7:1-27; 23:27-28; 31:1-3). Against the enticements of sinners (Pr 1:10-16). Against evil companions (Pr 2:12-15; 4:14-15; 24:1-2).

Exhortations to:

Be sober-minded (Tit 2:6). Be an example of piety (1Ti 4:12). Keep the heart with all diligence (Pr 4:23). Paying attention to God's word (Ps 119:9). Seek wisdom (Pr 2:1-8; 3:13-23; 4:5-13; 24:13-14). Obey parents (Pr 6:20-23; 23:22-26). Obey the Lord (Pr 3:5-12). Praise the Lord (Ps 148:12-13).

Instances of Religious: *See Joseph, 1; Joshua; Samuel; David; Solomon; Uriah.*

Foolish, Exemplified:

Esau (Ge 25:31-34; Heb 12:16-17), Rehoboam's counselors (1Ki 12:8-11). Rehoboam (1Ki 12:13-14). The rich young ruler (Mt 19:16-22; Mk 10:17-22; Lk 18:18-23). The prodigal son (Lk 15:11-32).

See also, Children; Parents.

ZAANAIM *See Zaanannim.*

ZAANAN [7367]. A place of uncertain location (Mic 1:11).

ZAANANNIM [7588]. A plain near Kedesh (Jos 19:33; Jdg 4:11).

ZAAVAN [2401] (possibly *trembling, terror*). A son of Ezer (Ge 36:27; 1Ch 1:42).

ZABAD [2274] (*he bestows*).
1. Son of Nathan (1Ch 2:36-37).
2. An Ephraimite (1Ch 7:21).
3. One of David's valiant men (1Ch 11:41).
4. An assassin of King Joash (2Ch 24:26). Also called Jozabad (2Ki 12:21). *See Jozabad, 1.*
5. Three Israelites who divorced their Gentile wives (Ezr 10:27, 33, 43).

ZABBAI [2287] (perhaps *God has given*).
1. Son of Bebai (1Ch 10:28).
2. Father of Baruch (Ne 3:20).

ZABBUD *See Zaccur, 5.*

ZABDI [2275] (*Yahweh bestows*).
1. Father of Carmi (Jos 7:1, 17-18, ftn). *See Zimri, 3.*
2. A Benjamite (1Ch 8:19).
3. A Shiphmite in charge of David's wine vats (1Ch 27:27).
4. Son of Asaph (Ne 11:17).

ZABDIEL [2276] (*God [El] bestows*).
1. Father of Jashobeam (1Ch 27:2).
2. An chief officer of 128 able men who lived in Jerusalem (Ne 11:14).

ZABUD [2280] (*[he has] bestowed upon*). A chief officer of Solomon (1Ki 4:5).

ZABULON *See Zebulun.*

ZACCAI [2347] (*Yahweh has remembered*, or perhaps *Yahweh remember*). A Jew whose descendants returned from the Exile (Ezr 2:9; Ne 7:14).

ZACCHAEUS [2405] (*righteous, pure one*). Chief tax collector; climbed sycamore tree to see Jesus and became his disciple (Lk 19:8).

ZACCUR [2346] (*remembering*).
1. Father of Reubenite spy, Shammua (Nu 13:4).
2. Simeonite (1Ch 4:26).
3. Son of Merari (1Ch 24:27).
4. Son of Asaph; musician (1Ch 25:1-2; Ne 12:35).
5. A returned exile (Ezr 8:14).

6. Son of Imri who helped rebuild walls of Jerusalem (Ne 3:2).
7. Man who sealed covenant with Nehemiah (Ne 10:12).
8. Father of Hanan (Ne 13:13).

ZACHARIAH *See Zechariah, 1 & 15.*

ZACHARIAS *See Zechariah, 30 & 31.*

ZACHER *See Zeker.*

ZADOC *See Zadok, 10.*

ZADOK [7401, 4882] (*righteous one*).
1. High priest in time of David's reign (2Sa 19:11; 20:25; 1Ch 15:11; 16:39). Removes the ark from Jerusalem at the time of Absalom's usurpation; returns with it at David's command (2Sa 15:24-36; 17:15, 17-21). Stands aloof from Adonijah at the time of his attempted usurpation (1Ki 1:8, 26). Summoned by David to anoint Solomon (1Ki 1:32-40, 44-45). Performs the function of high priest after Abiathar was deposed by Solomon (1Ki 2:35; 1Ch 29:22).
2. Father of Jerusha (2Ki 15:33; 2Ch 27:1).
3. Son of Ahitub (1Ch 6:12).
4. A man of valor (1Ch 12:28).
5. Son of Baana (Ne 3:4).
6. A priest (Ne 3:29).
7. A returned exile (Ne 10:21).
8. Son of Meraioth (Ne 11:11).
9. A treasurer of the temple (Ne 13:13).
10. Descendant of Zerubbabel and an ancestor of Jesus (Mt 1:14).

ZAHAM [2300] (*putrid, loathsome*). Grandson of Solomon (2Ch 11:19).

ZAHAR [7466]. An area NW of Damascus (Eze 27:18); modern Sahra.

ZAIR [7583] (*small, insignificant*, hence *narrow pass*). Village E of Dead Sea where Jehoram NIV, broke through the lines of the Edomites (2Ki 8:21).

ZALAPH [7523] (*low, prickly shrub [caper plant]*). Father of man who helped Nehemiah repair walls (Ne 3:30).

ZALMON [7514, 7515] (*in his image, a copy; black hill*).
1. Forest near Shechem (Jdg 9:48).
2. One of David's mighty men (2Sa 23:28), called "Ilai the Ahohite" (1Ch 11:29).

ZALMONAH [7517] (*dark, gloomy, shaded place*). Encampment of Israelites in wilderness, SE of Edom (Nu 33:41-42).

ZALMUNNA [7518] (*protection refused*). King of Midian (Jdg 8:5-21; Ps 83:11).

ZAMZUMMITES [2368] (*babblers*). Ammonite name for Rephaites (Dt 2:20), lived E of Jordan. May be same as Zuzites (Ge 14:5). *See Rephaites; Zuzites.*

ZANOAH [2391, 2392] (*rejected*).
1. A city of W Judah (Jos 15:34; Ne 3:13; 11:30).
2. A city of E Judah (Jos 15:56).
3. A descendant of Caleb (1Ch 4:18).

ZAPHENATH-PANEAH [7624] (*the [pagan] god speaks and he [the newborn] lives*). Name given to Joseph by Pharaoh (Ge 41:45).

ZAPHON [7601] (possibly *North* or *[proper name of a god]*, *Zephon*). Territory E of Jordan assigned to Gad (Jos 13:27); possibly modern *Amateh.*

ZARA, ZARAH *See Zerah.*

ZAREAH A city of Judah (Ne 11:29). *See Zorah.*

ZAREATHITES *See Zorathites.*

ZARED *See Zered.*

ZAREDA *See Zeredah.*

ZAREPHATH [7673, 4919] (possibly *smelting place* BDB; *place of pigmenting, staining* KB). A city between Tyre and Sidon. Elijah performs two miracles in (1Ki 17:8-24; Lk 4:26).

ZARETHAN [7681]. Place in Ephraim or Manasseh near Beth Shan and Adam (Jos 3:16; 1Ki 4:12), and near Succoth (1Ki 7:46; 2Ch 4:17). Exact site not known.

ZARETH-SHAHAR *See Zereth Shahar.*

ZARHITES *See Zerahite(s).*

ZARTANAH, ZARTHAN *See Zarethan.*

ZATTU [2456].
1. One whose descendants returned with Zerubbabel (Ezr 2:8; 10:27; Ne 7:13).
2. One who sealed the covenant with Nehemiah (Ne 10:14). Probably the same as 1.

ZAVAN *See Zaavan.*

ZAZA [2321] (*a form of a shortened nickname; term of endearment*). Son of Jonathan (1Ch 2:33).

ZEAL [3013, 5883, 7861, 7863, 2419, 2420, 2421, 5080, 5082] (*zeal, jealousy*).

General:
Without love, unprofitable (1Co 13:3). Without knowledge (Nu 11:27-28; Jdg 11:30-31, 34-35;

Ecc 7:16; Mt 8:19-20; Lk 9:57-58; Jn 16:2; Ac 21:20; Ro 10:2-3; Gal 1:13-14).
Wisdom of (Pr 11:30).

Required (Isa 62:6-7; Mt 5:13-16; Mk 4:21-22; Lk 8:16-17; Ac 10:42; 1Co 15:58; Tit 2:14; 3:1). Commanded (Jos 24:15-16; Ezr 7:23; Ps 60:4; 96:2; Ecc 9:10; Isa 60:1; Hag 2:4; Ro 12:11; 1Co 7:29-35; Gal 6:9; Eph 5:15-16; 6:10-20; Php 1:27-28; Col 4:5; 2Th 3:13; Heb 12:1-2; 13:13-15; 1Pe 2:2; 2Pe 1:10-11; 3:14; Jude 3, 22-23; Rev 3:19).
Expected (Hab 2:2; Zec 14:20-21; 2Co 4:8-10, 13, 16-18; Gal 4:18; Php 2:15).
Rewards of (Da 12:3; Mt 25:21, 23; Lk 19:17-19; Jas 5:20).

Exemplified in:
Moses (Ex 2:12; 11:8; 32:19-20, 31-32; Nu 10:29; 11:29; Dt 9:18-19). Phinehas (Nu 25:7-13; Ps 106:30). Joshua (Nu 11:27-29; Jos 7:6; 24:14-16). Gideon (Jdg 6:11-32). Jephthah (Jdg 11:30-31, 34-39). Samuel (1Sa 12:23; 15:11, 35; 16:1).
David (1Sa 17:26; 2Sa 6; 7:2; 8:11-12; 24:24; 1Ch 29:17; Ps 40:8-10; 42:1-2; 51:13; 69:7-9; 71:17-18). Solomon (1Ki 8:31-53; 2Ch 6:22-42). Elijah (1Ki 19:10). Obadiah (1Ki 18:3-4). Micaiah (1Ki 22:14). Jehu (2Ki 9:10). Jehoiada (2Ki 11:4-17; 2Ch 23:1-17). Asa (1Ki 15:11-15; 2Ch 14:1-5, 15). Israelites (2Ch 15:15; Eze 9:4). Jehoshaphat (2Ch 17:3-10, 19).
Isaiah (Isa 6:8; 62:1). Hezekiah (Isa 37:1). Josiah (2Ki 22:11-13; 2Ch 34:3-7, 29-33). Priests (Eze 44:15). Ezra (Ezr 7:10; 9:10; Ne 8:1-6, 13, 18). Nehemiah (Ne 4; 5; 13:7-9, 15-28). Job (Job 16:19). Psalmist (Ps 119:53, 126, 136, 139, 158). Jeremiah (Jer 9:1-3; 13:17; 18:20; 20:9; 25:3-4; 26:12-15). Three Hebrews (Da 3:17-18). Habakkuk (Hab 1:2-4). Old Testament faithful (Heb 11).
Jesus (Mt 23:27; Lk 19:41; Jn 4:34-35; 9:4). Anna (Lk 2:38). Andrew and Philip (Jn 1:41-46). Apostles (Mk 16:20; Ac 4:31, 33; 5:21, 25, 29-32, 41-42; 8:4, 25, 30, 35, 40; 11:19-20, 24, 26). Two blind men proclaiming the miracle of healing, contrary to the injunction of Jesus (Mt 9:30-31). The restored leper (Mk 1:44-45). Man delivered of demons (Mk 5:19-20).
Peter (Mt 16:22; Mk 14:29-31; Lk 22:33; Ac 2:14-40; 3:12-26; 4:2, 8-12, 18-20; 5:29-32; 2Pe 1:12-15). Samaritan woman (Jn 4:28-30, 39).
Paul and Barnabas (Ac 14:14-15).
Timothy (Php 2:22). Phoebe (Ro 16:1-2). Epaphroditus (Php 2:26, 30). Corinthians (1Co 14:12; 2Co 7:11; 9:2). Thessalonians (1Th 1:2-8). Ephesians (Rev 2:2-3, 6). Christian Jews (Heb 10:34). John (Ac 4:8-13, 18-20; 3Jn 4; Rev 5:4).

Paul—
For the evangelization of the Jews (Ro 9:1-3; 10:1; 11:14).
In his ministry (Ac 9:21-29; 14:1-28; 15:25-26; 17:16-17, 22-31; 19:8-10; 20:18-24, 26-27, 31, 33-34; 21:13; 24:14-25; 26:1-18; Ac 26:19-29; 28:23, 30-31; Ro 1:1, 8-9, 14-32; 1Co 4:1-21; 9:12-27; 2Co 1:12, 17-19; 5:9, 11, 13-14, 20; 6:3-11; 11:16-33; 12:10-21; Gal 1:15-16; 2:2; 4:19; Eph 6:20; Php 1:18, 20, 24-25, 27; 2:16-17; 3:4-

16; Col 1:28-29; 2:1, 5; 1Th 1:5-6; 2:2-11; 2Th 3:7-9; 2Ti 1:3, 7, 11-13).

In his piety (1Co 4:12; 10:33; 15:31; 2Co 4:8-18; 11:22-33; 12:10; Php 3:4-16; 4:11-12, 17; 2Ti 3:10-11).

In providing self-support (Ac 20:33-34; 1Co 4:12; 2Co 11:7-12; 2Th 3:7-9).

In suffering for Christ (Ac 21:13; 2Co 6:4-5, 8-10; 11:22-33; 12:10, 14-15, 21; 2Ti 2:9-10; 3:10-11).

In Punishing the Wicked:

Moses and Levites (Ex 32:20, 26-29). Phinehas (Nu 25:11-13; Ps 106:30-31). Israelites (Jos 22:11-20; Jdg 20). Samuel (1Sa 15:33). David (2Sa 1:14; 4:9-12). Elijah (1Ki 18:40). Jehu (2Ki 10:15-28). Jehoiada (2Ki 11:18). Josiah (2Ki 23:20).

In Reproving Iniquity: See Reproof, Faithfulness in.

ZEALOT [2421, 2831]. Member of Jewish patriotic party started to resist Roman rule over Israel; violent; fanatical.

ZEALOT, SIMON THE [2421, 2831]. An apostle (Mt 10:4; Mk 3:18; Lk 6:15; Ac 1:13), was known either for religious zeal or for membership in the party of the Zealots. See Simon, 2; Zealot.

ZEBADIAH [2277, 2278] (Yahweh bestows).

1. Benjamite (1Ch 8:15).
2. Another Benjamite (1Ch 8:17).
3. Ambidextrous Benjamite soldier of David (1Ch 12:1-2, 7).
4. Korahite gatekeeper (1Ch 26:2).
5. Son of Asahel (1Ch 27:7).
6. Levite sent by Jehoshaphat to teach law to residents of Judah (2Ch 17:8).
7. Son of Ishmael; head of Jehoshaphat's affairs (2Ch 19:11).
8. Son of Michael; returned with Ezra (Ezr 8:8).
9. Son of Immer; priest who divorced foreign wife (Ezr 10:20).

ZEBAH [2286] (sacrifice). King of Midian defeated and slain by Gideon (Jdg 8:10, 12, 18, 21; Ps 83:11).

ZEBAIM See Pokereth-Hazzebaim.

ZEBEDEE [2411] (Yahweh bestows). Father of James and John (Mt 4:21; 20:20; 27:56; Mk 1:20).

ZEBIDAH [2288] (given). Wife of Josiah, king of Judah (2Ki 23:36).

ZEBINA [2289] (one bought, purchased). Son of Nebo (Ezr 10:43).

ZEBOIIM, ZEBOIM [7375, 7391] (hyenas).

1. Called Zeboiim: One of the cities in the valley of Siddim (Ge 10:19; 14:2, 8; Dt 29:23; Hos 11:8).
2. Called Zeboim: A city and valley in Benjamin (1Sa 13:18; Ne 11:34).

ZEBUDAH See Zebidah.

ZEBUL [2291] (elevation, height, lofty [temple]). An officer of Abimelech (Jdg 9:28-41).

ZEBULONITES See Zebulun.

ZEBULUN, ZEBULUNITE [1201+2282, 2282, 2283, 2404] (honor Ge. 30:20 ISBE).

1. Son of Jacob and Leah (Ge 30:20; 35:23; 46:14; 49:13; Ex 1:3; 1Ch 2:1). Descendants of (Ge 46:14; Nu 26:26-27).
2. Tribe of. Place of, in march and camp (Nu 2:3, 7; 10:14, 16). Territory awarded to (Ge 49:13; Jos 19:10-16; Mt 4:13). Aboriginal inhabitants of the territory of, not expelled (Jdg 1:30). Levitical cities of (Jos 21:34-35; 1Ch 6:77). Moses' benediction upon (Dt 33:18-19).

Loyalty of, in resisting the enemies of Israel: With Barak against Sisera (Jdg 4:6, 10; 5:14, 18), with Gideon against the Midianites (Jdg 6:35), with David when made king over Israel (1Ch 12:33, 38-40). Joins with Hezekiah in renewing the Passover (2Ch 30:11, 18). Conquest of, by Tiglath-Pileser; carried to Assyria into captivity (2Ki 15:29; Isa 9:1). Jesus lived in the land of (Mt 4:15). Twelve thousand sealed (Rev 7:8).

See Israel.

ZECHARIAH [2357, 2358, 10230, 2408] (Yahweh remembers).

1. Son of Jeroboam II, and last of the house of Jehu, whose reign lasted six months (2Ki 10:30; 14:29; 15:8-12).
2. Reubenite chief (1Ch 5:7).
3. Korahite, son of Meshelemiah (1Ch 9:21; 26:2, 14).
4. Benjamite (1Ch 9:37).
5. Levite; musician (1Ch 15:20; 16:5).
6. Priest; trumpeter (1Ch 15:24).
7. Levite (1Ch 24:25).
8. Merarite Levite (1Ch 26:11).
9. Manassite chief; father of Iddo (1Ch 27:21).
10. Prince who taught in cities of Judah (2Ch 17:7).
11. Father of prophet Jahaziel (2Ch 20:14).
12. Son of Jehoshaphat; killed by Jehoram (2Ch 21:2-4).
13. Son of Jehoiada, the high priest; stoned (2Ch 24:20-22).
14. Prophet in reign of Uzziah (2Ch 26:5).
15. Grandfather of Hezekiah and father of Abijah, wife of Ahaz (2Ki 18:2; 2Ch 29:1).
16. Levite; son of Asaph (2Ch 29:13).
17. Kohathite who assisted in repair of temple in days of Josiah (2Ch 34:12).
18. Temple ruler (2Ch 35:8).
19. Man who returned with Ezra (Ezr 8:3).

20. Another man who returned with Ezra (Ezr 8:11).

21. Adviser of Ezra (Ne 8:4; Ezr 8:15-16).

22. Man who divorced foreign wife (Ezr 10:26).

23. Judahite (Ne 11:4).

24. Another Judahite (Ne 11:5).

25. Son of Pashhur; aided rebuilding of walls (Ne 11:12).

26. Son of Iddo; priest (Ne 12:16).

27. Priest; son of Jonathan; trumpeter (Ne 12:35, 41).

28. Son of Jeberekiah (Isa 8:2).

29. Prophet; son of Berekiah and grandson of Iddo (Zec 1:1), returned with Zerubbabel; contemporary with Haggai.

30. Father of John the Baptist (Lk 1:5), righteous priest; angel announced to him he would have a son (Lk 1:5-80).

31. Son of Berekiah; slain between altar and temple (Mt 23:35; Lk 11:51).

ZECHARIAH, BOOK OF

Author: Zechariah son of Berekiah

Dates (correlated with Haggai and Ezra):

1. Haggai's first message (Hag 1:1-11; Ezr 5:1): Aug. 29, 520 B.C.

2. Resumption of the building of the temple (Hag 1:12-15; Ezr 5:2): Sept. 21, 520

3. Haggai's second message (Hag 2:1-9): Oct. 17, 520

4. Beginning of Zechariah's preaching (1:1-6): Oct./Nov., 520

5. Haggai's third message (Hag 2:10-19): Dec. 18, 520

6. Haggai's fourth message (Hag 2:20-23): Dec. 18, 520

7. Tattenai's letter to Darius concerning the rebuilding of the temple (Ezr 5:3-6:14).: 519-518

8. Zechariah's eight night visions (1:7-6:8): Feb 15, 519

9. Joshua crowned (6:9-15): Feb 16 (?), 519

10. Repentance urged, blessings promised (chs. 7-8).: Dec. 7, 518

11. Dedication of the temple (Ezr 6:15-18): Mar. 12, 516

12. Zechariah's final prophecy (chs. 9-14): After 480 (?)

Outline:

Part I (chs. 1-8):

I. Introduction (1:1-6).
   A. The Date and the Author's Name (1:1).
   B. A Call to Repentance (1:2-6).

II. A Series of Eight Night Visions (1:7-6:8).
   A. The Horseman among the Myrtle Trees (1:7-17).
   B. The Four Horns and the Four Craftsmen (1:18-21).
   C. A Man with a Measuring Line (ch. 2).
   D. Clean Garments for the High Priest (ch. 3).
   E. The Gold Lampstand and the Two Olive Trees (ch. 4).
   F. The Flying Scroll (5:1-4).

G. The Woman in a Basket (5:5-11).
   H. The Four Chariots (6:1-8).

III. The Symbolic Crowning of Joshua the High Priest (6:9-15).

IV. The Problem of Fasting and the Promise of the Future (chs. 7-8).
   A. The Question by the Delegation from Bethel (7:1-3).
   B. The Rebuke by the Lord (7:4-7).
   C. The Command to Repent (7:8-14).
   D. The Restoration of Israel to God's Favor (8:1-17).
   E. Kingdom Joy and Jewish Favor (8:18-23).

Part II (chs. 9-14):

V. Two Prophetic Oracles: The Great Messianic Future and the Full Realization of God's Kingdom (chs. 9-14).
   A. The First Oracle: The Advent and Rejection of the Messiah (chs. 9-11).
      1. The advent of the Messianic King (chs. 9-10).
      2. The rejection of the Messianic Shepherd-King (ch. 11).
   B. The Second Oracle: The Advent and Reception of the Messiah (chs. 12-14).
      1. The deliverance and conversion of Israel (chs. 12-13).
      2. The Messiah's coming and his kingdom (ch. 14).

See Prophets, The Minor.

ZEDAD [7398] (*a siding*). A place near Hamath (Nu 34:8; Eze 47:15).

ZEDEKIAH [7408, 7409] (*Yahweh is [my] righteousness*).

1. Made king of Judah by Nebuchadnezzar (2Ki 24:17-18; 1Ch 3:15; 2Ch 36:10; Jer 37:1). Breaks his allegiance to Nebuchadnezzar (2Ki 24:20; 2Ch 36:13; Jer 52:3; Eze 17:12-21). Forms an alliance with the king of Egypt (Eze 17:11-18). The allegiance denounced by Jeremiah (2Ch 36:12; Jer 21; 24:8-10; 27:12-22; 32:3-5; 34; 37:7-10, 17; 38:14-28), by Ezekiel (Eze 12:10-16; 17:12-21). Imprisons Jeremiah on account of his denunciations (Jer 32:2-3; 37:15-21; 38:5-28). Seeks the intercession of Jeremiah with God in his behalf (Jer 21:1-3; 37:3; 28:14-27). Wicked reign of (2Ki 24:19-20; 2Ch 36:12-13; Jer 37:2; 38:5, 19, 24-26; 52:2). Nebuchadnezzar destroys the city and temple, takes him captive to Babylon, blinds his eyes, slays his sons (2Ki 25:1-10; 2Ch 36:17-20; Jer 1:3; 32:1-2; 39:1-10; 51:59; 52:4-30).

2. Grandson of Jehoiakim (1Ch 3:16).

3. A chief prince of the exiles who returned to Jerusalem (Ne 10:1).

4. A false prophet (Jer 29:21-23).

5. A prince of Judah (Jer 36:12).

6. A false prophet. Prophesies to Ahab victory over the Syrians, instead of defeat (1Ki 22:11; 2Ch 18:10). Smites Micaiah, the true prophet (1Ki 22:24; 2Ch 18:23).

ZEEB [2270] (*wolf*). A prince of Midian (Jdg 7:25; 8:3; Ps 83:11).

ZEKER [2353] (*memorial*). Son of Jeiel (1Ch 8:31), called Zechariah (1Ch 9:37). *See Zechariah, 4.*

ZELA [7521] (*side, slope*). Saul buried in (2Sa 21:14).

ZELAH [7522] (*side, slope*). A city in Benjamin (Jos 18:28).

ZELEK [7530] (*cry aloud* KB). An Ammonite (2Sa 23:37; 1Ch 11:39).

ZELOPHEHAD [7524] (*shadow of dread, terror* [i.e., *protection from dread and terror*]). Grandson of Gilead. His daughters petition for his inheritance (Nu 27:1-11; 36; Jos 17:3-6; 1Ch 7:15).

ZELOTES *See Zealot.*

ZELZAH [7525]. A city of Benjamin (1Sa 10:2).

ZEMARAIM [7549] (possibly *double peak* KB).
1. Town c. four miles N of Jericho assigned to tribe of Benjamin (Jos 18:22).
2. Mountain in Ephraim upon which King Abijah rebuked King Jeroboam (2Ch 13:4).

ZEMARITES [7548] (*[snow, wool] white*; possibly *peak, height*). A tribe descended from Canaan (Ge 10:18; 1Ch 1:16).

ZEMIRAH [2371] (possibly *song [with instrumental accompaniment]* KB; possibly *Yahweh has helped* IDB). Grandson of Benjamin (1Ch 7:8).

ZENAN [7569] (*place of flocks*). A city of Judah (Jos 15:37).

ZENAS [2424] (*gift of Zeus*). A Christian believer and lawyer (Tit 3:13).

ZEPHANIAH [7622, 7623] (*Yahweh has hidden [to shelter]* or *Yahweh has hidden [as a treasure]*).
1. Ancestor of prophet Samuel (1Ch 6:36).
2. Author of book of Zephaniah (Zep 1:1), of royal descent; principal work done in Josiah's reign; contemporaries were Nahum and Habakkuk.
3. Priest, son of Maaseiah (2Ki 25:18-21; Jer 21:1).
4. Father of a Josiah to whom God sent the prophet Zechariah (Zec 6:10).

ZEPHANIAH, BOOK OF

Author: The prophet Zephaniah

Date: Probably between 640 and 627 B.C.

Outline:
I. Introduction (1:1-3).
   A. Title: The Prophet Identified (1:1).
   B. Prologue: Double Announcement of Total Judgment (1:2-3).
II. The Day of the Lord Coming on Judah and the Nations (1:4-18).
   A. Judgment on the Idolaters in Judah (1:4-9).
   B. Wailing throughout Jerusalem (1:10-13).
   C. The Inescapable Day of the Lord's Wrath (1:14-18).
III. God's Judgment on the Nations (2:1-3:8).
   A. Call to Repentance (2:1-3).
   B. Judgment on Philistia (2:4-7).
   C. Judgment on Moab and Ammon (2:8-11).
   D. Judgment on Cush (2:12).
   E. Judgment on Assyria (2:13-15).
   F. Judgment on Jerusalem (3:1-5).
   G. Jerusalem's Refusal to Repent (3:6-8).
IV. Redemption of the Remnant (3:9-20).
   A. The Nations Purified, the Remnant Restored, Jerusalem Purged (3:9-13).
   B. Rejoicing in the City (3:14-17).
   C. The Nation Restored (3:18-20).
   See Prophets, The Minor.

ZEPHATH [7634] (*watchtower* IDB). A Canaanite city c. twenty-two miles SW of S end of Dead Sea; destroyed by tribes of Judah and Simeon and renamed "Hormah" (Jdg 1:17, ftn).

ZEPHATHAH [7635] (*watchtower* IDB). Valley near Mareshah in W part of Judah (2Ch 14:10).

ZEPHI *See Zepho.*

ZEPHO [7598] (possibly *gaze* BDB ISBE). The grandson of Esau (Ge 36:11, 15; 1Ch 1:36).

ZEPHON, ZEPHONITE [7602, 7604] (possibly *gaze* BDB; possibly *look out [tower]*, *watch* KB). A son of Gad and his descendants (Ge 46:16; Nu 26:15).

ZER [7643]. A city in Naphtali (Jos 19:35).

ZERAH [2438, 2439, 2406] (*dawning, shining, or flashing [red or scarlet] light* KB).
1. Son of Reuel (Ge 36:13, 17; 1Ch 1:37).
2. Father of Jobab (Ge 36:33; 1Ch 1:44).
3. Son of Judah and Tamar (Ge 38:30; 46:12; Nu 26:20; 1Ch 2:4, 6).
4. Son of Simeon (Nu 26:13; 1Ch 4:24).
5. A Gershonite (1Ch 6:21).
6. A Levite (1Ch 6:41).
7. King of Ethiopia, possibly Pharaoh Osorkon I (2Ch 14:9-15).

ZERAHIAH [2440] (*Yahweh shines brightly [red or scarlet]; Yahweh has risen [like the sun]* BDB).
1. Levite in ancestry of Ezra (1Ch 6:6, 51).
2. Leader of 200 who returned with Ezra (Ezr 8:4).

ZERAHITE(S) [1201+2438, 2439] (*those who shine*).
1. Descendants of Zerah, son of Judah (Nu 26:20; Jos 7:17; 1Ch 27:11, 13).
2. Descendants of Zerah, son of Simeon (Nu 26:13).

ZERED, VALLEY OF, BROOK OF
[2429] (*valley of [some kind of] plant*). Valley between Moab and Edom; encampment of Israel in wilderness wanderings (Nu 21:12; Dt 2:13-14).

ZEREDAH [7649]. A city or district on the N of Mount Ephraim, but in Manasseh, and the birthplace of Jeroboam (1Ki 11:26).

ZEREDATHAH *See Zarethan.*

ZERERAH [7678]. Part of Valley of Jezreel to which Midianites fled from Gideon (Jdg 7:22).

ZERESH [2454] (possibly *[pagan goddess] Kirisha* BDB IDB; *gold* ISBE; *mop-head* KB). Wife of Haman the Agagite (Est 5:10, 14; 6:13).

ZERETH [7679] (*splendor*). Son of Ashhur (1Ch 4:7).

ZERETH SHAHAR [7680] (*the glory of dawn*). A city in Reuben (Jos 13:19).

ZERI [7662] (*balsam* IDB). The son of Jeduthun (1Ch 25:3).

ZEROR [7657] (*money bag, pouch,* or possibly *pebbles* KB). Benjamite; great-grandfather of King Saul (1Sa 9:1).

ZERQA *See Jabbok.*

ZERUAH [7654] (*one with skin disease*). Mother of Jeroboam (1Ki 11:26).

ZERUBBABEL [2428, 10239, 2431] (*offspring [seed] of Babylon* BDB ISBE KB; *scion* i.e., *one grafted into the [plant] of Babylon* IDB). Directs the rebuilding of the altar and temple after his return from captivity in Babylon (Ezr 3:2-8; 4:2-3; 5:2; Hag 1:12-14). Leads the freed Jews back from Babylon (Ezr 2; Ne 12). Appoints the Levites to inaugurate the rebuilding of the temple (Ezr 3:2-8). Prophecies relating to (Hag 2:2; Zec 4:6-10). In the genealogy of Joseph (Mt 1:12; Lk 3:27).
Possibly the same as Sheshbazzar (Ezr 1:8, 11; 5:14, 16). *See Sheshbazzar.*

ZERUIAH [7653] (*perfumed resin* IDB KB). Sister of David (1Ch 2:16). Mother of three of David's great soldiers (1Ch 2:16; 2Sa 2:18; 3:39; 16:9-11; 17:25).

ZETHAM [2457] (possibly *olive tree*). A son of Ladan (1Ch 23:8; 26:22).

ZETHAN [2340] (*olive tree* or *one who deals in olives*). Son of Bilhan (1Ch 7:10).

ZETHAR [2458] (possibly *conqueror* BDB; *slayer* KB). Chamberlain of Xerxes (Est 1:10).

ZEUS [2416] (*shine, bright*). Chief of Greek gods, corresponding to Roman Jupiter (Ac 14:12-13).

ZIA [2333] (possibly *trembler* IDB). A Gadite (1Ch 5:13).

ZIBA [7471] (*gazelle*). Member of Saul's household staff (2Sa 9:2), appointed by David to work for Mephibosheth; slandered Mephibosheth (2Sa 19:24-30).

ZIBEON [7390] (*hyena*).
1. A Hivite (Ge 36:2, 14).
2. Son of Seir (Ge 36:20, 24, 29; 1Ch 1:38, 40).

ZIBIA [7384] (*gazelle*). Early descendant of Benjamin (1Ch 8:9).

ZIBIAH [7385] (*gazelle*). Woman of Beersheba who married King Ahaziah; mother of King Joash (2Ki 12:1; 2Ch 24:1).

ZICRI [2356] (*Yahweh remembers* IDB).
1. A Levite; son of Izhar, cousin of Aaron and Moses (Ex 6:21).
2. Three Benjamites (1Ch 8:19, 23, 27).
3. A Levite; ancestor of Mattaniah who returned from captivity (1Ch 9:15), "Zabdi" (Ne 11:17).
4. Two chiefs in the days of David; a descendant of Eliezer (1Ch 26:25), father of Eliezer, a Reubenite (1Ch 27:16).
5. Father of Amasiah; a soldier (2Ch 17:16).
6. Father of Elishaphat (2Ch 23:1).
7. An Ephraimite; killed the son of Ahaz (2Ch 28:7).
8. Father of Joel, the overseer of the Benjamites (Ne 11:9).
9. A descendant of Abijah; a priest (Ne 12:17).

ZIDDIM [7403] (*place on the sides or flanks [of the hill]*). A city in Naphtali (Jos 19:35).

ZIDKIJAH *See Zedekiah, 3.*

ZIDON *See Sidon.*

ZIDONIANS *See Sidon.*

ZIF *See Ziv.*

ZIGGURAT (*pinnacle*). Temple tower of the Babylonians, consisting of a lofty structure in the form of a pyramid, built in successive stages, with staircases on the outside and a shrine at the top. The tower of Babel may have been a ziggurat (Ge 11:1-9). *See Pyramids; Tower.*

ZIHA [7484].
1. Head of family of temple servants that returned with Zerubbabel (Ezr 2:43; Ne 7:46).

2. Leader of the temple servants (Ne 11:21).

ZIKLAG [7637]. A city within the territory allotted to the tribe of Judah (Jos 15:31). Reallotted to the tribe of Simeon (Jos 19:5). David lives at (1Sa 27:5-6; 2Sa 1:1; 1Ch 12:1). Amalekites destroy (1Sa 30). Inhabited by the returned exiles of Judah (Ne 11:28).

ZIKRI See Zicri.

ZILLAH [7500] (*[God is my] shadow [i.e., protection]*). Wife of Lamech (Ge 4:19, 22-23).

ZILLETHAI [7531] (*shadow of Yahweh*).
1. A Benjamite (1Ch 8:20).
2. A captain of Manasseh (1Ch 12:20).

ZILPAH [2364] (*short-nosed person* KB). Leah's handmaid (Ge 29:24). Mother of Gad and Asher by Jacob (Ge 30:9-13; 35:26; 37:2; 46:18).

ZIMMAH [2366] (*consider, plan* ISBE).
1. A son of Jahath (1Ch 6:20).
2. Two Gershonites (1Ch 6:42; 2Ch 29:12).

ZIMRAN [2383] (*wild goats, sheep* ISBE). Son of Abraham (Ge 25:2; 1Ch 1:32).

ZIMRI [2381, 2382] (*wild goats, sheep* ISBE; possibly *awe of Yahweh* IDB).
1. Prince of Simeon; slain by Phinehas, grandson of Aaron, for committing adultery with Midianite woman (Nu 25:14).
2. The fifth king of N kingdom; murdered King Elah; ruled seven days (c. 885 B.C.); overthrown by Omri (1Ki 16:8-20).
3. Son of Zerah; grandson of Judah (1Ch 2:6). See Zabdi, 1.
4. Benjamite; father of Moza (1Ch 8:36; 9:42).
5. Unknown tribe in East (Jer 25:25).

ZIN [7554]. A desert S of Judah (Nu 13:21; 20:1; 27:14; 33:36; 34:3-4; Dt 32:51; Jos 15:1, 3).

ZINA (possibly *dry place*). See Ziza.

ZION [7482, 4994] (*citadel*). Taken from the Jebusites by David (2Sa 5:6-9; 1Ch 11:5-7). Called thereafter "the city of David" (2Sa 5:7, 9; 6:12, 16; 1Ki 8:1; 1Ch 11:5, 7; 15:1, 29; 2Ch 5:2). Ark of the covenant placed in (2Sa 6:12, 16; 1Ki 8:1; 1Ch 15:1, 29; 2Ch 5:2). Removed from to Solomon's temple on Mount Moriah (1Ki 8:1; 2Ch 5:2, w 2Ch 3:1).

Collectively, the place, the forms, and the assemblies of Israelite worship (2Ki 19:21, 31; Ps 9:11; 48:2, 11-12; 74:2; 132:13; 137:1; Isa 35:10; 40:9; 49:14; 51:16; 52:1-2, 7-8; 60:14; 62:1, 11; Jer 31:6; 50:5; La 1:4; Joel 2:1, 15; Mt 21:5; Jn 12:15; Ro 9:33; 11:26; 1Pe 2:6). Name of, applied to Jerusalem (Ps 87:2, 5; 149:2; SS 3:11; Isa 33:14, 20; Jer 9:19; 30:17; Zec 9:13). Called the city of God (Ps 87:2-3; Isa 60:14). Restoration of, promised (Isa 51:3, 11, 16; 52:1-2, 7-8; 59:20; 60:14; Ob 17, 21; Zep 3:14, 16; Zec 1:14, 17; 2:7,

10; 8:2-3; 9:9, 13). Name of, applied to the city of the redeemed (Heb 12:22; Rev 14:1).
See Church, Place of Worship; Jerusalem.

ZIOR [7486] (*small, insignificant*). Town in S Judah probably near Hebron (Jos 15:54).

ZIPH [2334, 2335].
1. City in Negev, probably c. four miles S by E from Hebron (Jos 15:55).
2. Wilderness named from above city where David hid (1Sa 23:14-24; 26:1-2).
3. City in W Judah (2Ch 11:8).
4. Calebite family name (1Ch 2:42).
5. Judahite (1Ch 4:16).

ZIPHAH [2336]. A son of Jehallelel (1Ch 4:16).

ZIPHIMS See Ziphites.

ZIPHION (possibly *gaze* BDB ISBE; possibly *place of the lookout, tower* KB). See Zephon.

ZIPHITES [2337]. Inhabitants of Ziph (1Sa 23:19; 26:1-5; Ps 54:T).

ZIPHRON [2412]. A place in the N of Israel (Nu 34:9).

ZIPPOR [7607] (*bird, swallow*). Father of Balak (Nu 22:2, 4, 10, 16; 23:18; Jos 24:9).

ZIPPORAH [7631] (*bird, swallow*). Wife of Moses (Ex 2:16-22). Reproaches Moses (Ex 4:25-26). Separates from Moses, is brought again to him by her father (Ex 18:2-6). May have been a Cushite (Nu 12:1).

ZITHER [10630]. A stringed instrument (Da 3:5, 7, 10, 15). *See Music, Instruments of.*

ZITHRI See Sithri.

ZIV [2304] (*bright [as in colorful flowers]*). Month two in sacred sequence, month eight in civil sequence. Also called Iyyar (not in the Bible). Time of the barley harvest (April-May); the dry season begins. Solomon begins building the temple (1Ki 6:1, 37). The later Passover is celebrated (Nu 9:10-11). *See Month, 2.*

ZIZ [7489] (possibly *ascent where the flowers grow*). Cliff near W side of Red Sea on way from En Gedi to Tekoa (2Ch 20:16).

ZIZA [2330, 2331] (a childish duplicated abbreviation, like "mama," as a name of endearment, IDB ISBE).
1. Simeonite; son of Shiphi (1Ch 4:37-41).
2. Son of Rehoboam and brother of Abijah, kings of Judah (2Ch 11:20).
3. A son of Shimei (1Ch 23:10-11, ftn).

ZIZAH See Ziza, 3.

ZOAN [7586]. A city in Egypt. Built seven

years after Hebron in the land of Canaan (Nu 13:22). Prophecies concerning (Eze 30:14). Wise men from, were counselors of Pharaoh (Isa 19:11, 13). Princes of (Isa 30:4).

ZOAR [7593] (*small, insignificant*). A city of the Moabites near the Jordan (Ge 13:10). Territory of (Dt 34:3; Isa 15:5; Jer 48:34). King of, fought against Kedorlaomer (Ge 14:2, 8). Not destroyed with Sodom and Gomorrah (Ge 19:20-23, 30).

ZOBAH [7419, 7420]. Also called Aram Zobah; Hamath Zobah. A kingdom in the N of Israel (1Sa 14:47). Conquest of, by David (2Sa 8:3-8, 12; 1Ki 11:23-24; 1Ch 18:2-9). Its inhabitants mercenaries of the Ammonites against David (2Sa 10:6-19; 1Ch 19:6-19). David writes a psalm after the conquest of (Ps 60, title). Invaded by Solomon (2Ch 8:3).

See Aram Maacah; Aram Naharaim.

ZOBEBAH (*one who slithers [like a lizard] or one born in a covered wagon*). See Hazzobebah.

ZODIAC *See Constellations; Mazzaroth.*

ZOHAR [7468] (*one yellowish red, tawny*).
1. Hittite; father of Ephron from whom Abraham purchased field of Machpelah (Ge 23:8; 25:9).
2. Son of Simeon, second son of Jacob (Ge 46:10; Ex 6:15); "Zerah" (Nu 26:13; 1Ch 4:24).
3. A son of Helah, wife of Ashhur (1Ch 4:7).

ZOHELETH [2325] (*serpent*). Stone or ledge by En Rogel (1Ki 1:9).

ZOHETH [2311] (*proud*). Son of Ishi (1Ch 4:20).

ZOPHAH [7432] (*bellied jug*). Son of Helem (1Ch 7:35-36).

ZOPHAI [7433] (*[dripping, full] honeycomb*). Ancestor of Samuel the prophet (1Ch 6:26), also called Zuph (1Ch 6:35).

ZOPHAR [7436] (possibly *peep, twitter [as a bird]* KB). One of Job's three friends (Job 2:11; 11; 20; 42:7-9).

ZOPHIM [7614] (*watchers, lookouts*).
1. A place on the top of Pisgah (Nu 23:14).
2. A city on Mount Ephraim (1Sa 1:1).

ZORAH [7666]. A city of Dan or Judah (Jos 15:33; 19:41). The city of Samson (Jdg 13:2, 24-25; 16:31). Representatives of the tribe of Dan sent from, to spy out the land with a view to its conquest (Jdg 18). Fortified by Rehoboam (2Ch 11:10). Repopulated after the Captivity (Ne 11:29).

ZORATHITES [7670]. Inhabitants of Zorah (1Ch 2:53).

ZOREAH *See Zorah.*

ZORITES [7668]. Judahite family, descendants of Salma (1Ch 2:54).

ZOROBABEL *See Zerubbabel.*

ZUAR [7428] (*little one*). Father of Nethanel (Nu 1:8; 2:5; 7:18, 23; 10:15).

ZUPH, ZUPHITE [7431, 7434] (*honeycomb*).
1. Ancestor of the prophet Samuel (1Sa 1:1; 1Ch 6:35), also called Zophai (1Ch 6:26).
2. District in Benjamin, near N border (1Sa 9:5), Location unknown.

ZUR [7448] (*rock*).
1. King of Midian slain by Israel (Nu 25:15; 31:8).
2. Son of Jeiel (1Ch 8:29, ftn; 8:30).

ZURIEL [7452] (*God [El] is [my] rock*). Son of Abihail, prince of Merarite Levites in wilderness (Nu 3:35).

ZURISHADDAI [7453] (*Shaddai is [my] rock*). Father of Shelumiel (Nu 1:6; 2:12; 7:36, 41; 10:19).

ZUZITES [2309] (*strong nations* ISBE; *babblers* KB). A people defeated by Kedorlaomer and his allies (Ge 14:5). May be the same as Zamzummites. *See Rephaites; Zamzummites.*

Index of
G/K → Strong's
Numbers

How to Use This Index

This index shows the relation between the Goodrick-Kohlenberger (G/K) numbering system, introduced in *The NIV Exhaustive Concordance* (Zondervan, 1990), and the classic numbering system of James Strong.

G/K numbers follow the entry heads and are in square brackets:

FATHER [3, 408, 587, 3528, 10003, *574, 1164, 4252, 4257*].

1. If the G/K number is in roman (non-italic) type, from one to four digits (e.g., 3, 408, 3528), it is a Hebrew word that is found in the Old Testament. Match that number to Strong's numbers in the "Hebrew Old Testament" section, pages 525-49.

2. If the G/K number is in roman type and is five digits long (e.g., 10003), it is an Aramaic word that is found in the Old Testament. Match that number to Strong's numbers in the "Aramaic Old Testament" section, pages 550-51.

3. If the number is in *italics* (e.g., *574, 1164*), it is a Greek word that is found in the New Testament. Match that number to Strong's numbers in the "Greek New Testament" section, pages 551-61.

In the Index, the numbers usually correspond one-to-one:

```
145.............................................132
"...................................................726
146....................................129+5346
```

1. If a G/K number matches more than one Strong's number, the ditto sign (") is used for the additional occurrences.

2. If a G/K number matches a combination of Strong's numbers, the plus sign (+) shows this relationship.

3. If there is no Strong's number following a G/K number, that means there is no word in Strong's vocabulary to relate to (e.g., *928, 319*).

For a complete index of Strong's to G/K numbers, please consult *The NIV Exhaustive Concordance*.

**HEBREW
OLD
TESTAMENT**

G/K	STRONG	G/K	STRONG	G/K	STRONG
3	1	76	71	160	143	246	219
5	5	78	70	161	146	247	221
6	6	79	74	162	146	248	222
8	9	80	75	163	150	249	223
14	14	82	77	165	152	250	223
15	16	83	78	166	152	253	226
16	17	84	79	167	154	255	227
17	18	85	80	168	155	256	229
19	20	86	81	170	157	257	231
23	21	88	83	171	159	260	234
24	22	89	84	172	158	263	238
25	23	90	85	173	160	265	241
26	24	92	87	176	161	267	242
28	26	93	52	177	162	268	243
29	27	94	53	178	163	269	244
30	28	95	88	179	164	270	244
31	29	96	89	182	167	271	245
32	29	97	90	185	168	272	246
33	30	98	91	186	169	273	247
34	31	99	92	188	170	274	248
35	32	100	93	189	174	275	249
36	34	101	94	190	171	276	250
38	32	104	97	191	172	278	251
39	36	106	98	192	173	279	254
40	37	108	99	193	174	280	255
42	39	109	100	195	175	281	256
43	40	110	101	198	177	282	256
44	41	112	103	199	178	283	257
45	42	113	105	200	178	285	259
46	74	115	107	201	179	286	260
47	43	118	110	202	181	287	261
48	44	119	111	203	183	288	264
49	33	120	112	204	184	291	265
50	45	121	123	206	186	292	266
52	47	122	130	207	187	293	267
53	48	123	113	208	188	294	268
54	49	124	114	209	189	295	269
55	50	126	115	211	191	296	270
56	51	129	117	213	192	298	271
57	52	130	118	217	195	299	272
58	53	131	119	220	198	300	273
59	54	132	120	222	200	301	274
61	56	134	121	223	201	302	274
62	56	136	121	224	205	303	275
63	57	137	122	225	206	304	276
"	59	138	124	226	202	305	278
64	58	141	127	227	203	306	277
"	59	142	128	228	204	307	279
65	60	144	126	229	207	308	281
68	62	145	132	231	208	309	281
69	63	"	726	232	209	310	282
70	64	146	129+5346	233	210	311	283
71	65	147	131	234	211	312	284
72	66	148	133	236	212	313	285
73	67	150	135	237	213	314	286
74	68	151	136	238	214	315	287
75	72	152	137	239	215	316	288
		153	138	240	216	317	289
		154	138	241	217	318	290
		155	139	242	224	319	291
		156	140	243	218	320	292
		157	141	244	218	321	293
		158	142	245	219	322	294

G/K	STRONG	G/K	STRONG	G/K	STRONG	G/K	STRONG
323	295	412	379	494	455	573	529
324	296	413	380	495	456	574	529
325	297	414	3448	496	457	575	530
326	298	416	863	497	458	576	531
327	299	417	384	498	460	577	532
328	300	418	385	499	461	578	550
329	301	419	386	500	463	579	533
330	302	420	387	501	462	581	535
331	303	422	390	502	464	585	538
333	304	423	391	503	465	586	539
334	306	424	392	504	466	587	539
335	308	426	394	505	467	"	541
336	309	427	395	506	468	588	542
337	312	429	397	507	469	589	543
338	313	430	398	508	470	592	549
339	310	431	400	509	471	596	550
340	314	432	401	510	472	597	551
341	315	433	402	511	473	599	553
342	316	438	406	512	474	600	554
344	319	439	407	513	475	603	557
346	323	440	408	514	476	604	558
347	325	446	410	515	477	605	558
351	328	448	413	516	478	606	559
353	329	449	415	517	448	607	559
354	329	450	416	522	483	608	562
355	330	451	1286	523	484	609	561
359	333	452	414	524	485	612	564
360	334	454	418	525	486	613	564
362	339	455	419	526	487	614	565
363	338	456	420	530	490	616	567
365	337	457	422	531	491	617	566
367	341	460	423	533	440	618	568
368	342	461	424	534	493	619	568
369	343	462	425	535	494	620	569
370	344	463	425	536	495	621	570
371	345	464	427	537	496	622	571
373	347	466	430	538	497	624	573
374	348	468	433	539	498	627	578
376	350	469	435	540	499	631	605
380	352	471	436	541	500	632	582
381	352	472	356	542	500	633	583
382	352	473	437	543	501	637	588
385	354	474	438	546	504	639	590
386	364	475	439	547	505	640	592
387	355	476	441	550	467	641	591
"	365	477	441	551	508	642	593
389	357	478	442	554	510	643	594
390	356	479	443	555	511	645	596
391	356	480	444	556	512	649	601
392	358	481	445	557	513	650	602
393	359	482	446	558	514	652	604
395	361	483	447	559	514	654	609
396	362	484	448	560	515	658	614
397	359	485	419	562	517	659	615
398	366	"	449	563	519	660	616
399	367	486	450	564	520	661	617
400	368	487	451	565	522	662	618
401	369	488	452	570	525	663	619
404	372	489	452	"	527	664	621
405	373	490	453	"	539	665	622
406	374	491	453	571	526	666	623
408	376	492	454	572	527	667	624
410	378	493	454	"	528	668	625

G/K	STRONG	G/K	STRONG	G/K	STRONG	G/K	STRONG
671	628	770	719	847	796	937	884
672	630	771	722	848	797	938	878
673	631	772	722	850	799	939	880
674	632	773	721	851	802	940	881
675	634	774	220	852	801	941	882
676	635	"	723	854	380	943	886
678	639	776	724	855	804	947	890
680	646	777	725	856	805	949	892
681	641	778	727	857	805	950	893
682	642	779	728	858	806	951	894
685	644	780	730	859	803	953	898
688	647	781	731	860	807	954	899
691	649	782	732	862	809	955	899
692	650	783	733	864	811	956	900
694	652	784	734	865	812	957	901
696	653	785	736	866	812	958	902
697	654	787	738	867	813	960	903
702	658	788	221	869	815	961	904
704	660	789	741	870	816	962	904
706	662	790	740	871	817	964	905
707	663	791	740	872	818	965	906
708	664	792	743	873	819	966	907
709	665	793	744	874	821	967	907
710	666	794	745	876	822	971	911
711	667	796	746	877	823	973	912
712	668	798	747	878	824	974	913
713	669	800	750	879	825	978	916
714	672	801	752	880	827	979	917
715	672	804	751	881	828	982	920
716	672	805	757	882	829	984	931
717	672	806	758	883	830	987	926
718	673	807	758+4601	884	831	988	928
719	675	808	763	885	832	989	929
720	676	809	760	886	833	990	930
727	682	810	759	887	833	991	931
728	682	811	762	888	836	992	932
729	683	"	7421	892	838	993	933
730	684	813	764	895	842	994	934
731	685	814	765	896	843	995	935
733	687	815	766	897	835	996	936
735	689	816	767	900	847	997	937
736	690	818	769	901	848	998	938
739	692	820	770	902	850	1001	941
741	693	821	771	903	851	1003	943
742	694	822	774	904	851	1004	945
744	696	823	775	907	854	1007	946
746	697	824	776	908	855	1009	948
748	699	825	777	909	856	1010	949
749	700	826	779	912	860	1012	951
750	701	827	780	915	863	1014	953
752	702	829	781	916	862	1016	953+6228
"	706	831	783	918	864	1017	954
755	707	832	840	922	867	1019	955
756	708	833	841	923	388	1022	959
758	709	835	844	924	869	"	960
759	709	836	784	925	868	"	5240
760	710	"	800	926	871	1023	961
761	712	839	788	928		1024	962
763	713	840	789	930	874	1026	964
764	714	841	790	931	875	1027	965
765	715	843	792	932	876	1028	966
766	716	844	794	935	879	1030	968
767	742	846	795	936	883	1031	969

G/K	STRONG	G/K	STRONG	G/K	STRONG	G/K	STRONG
1032	971	1128	1030	1221	1138	1296	1213
1033	970	1130	1054	1222	1139	1298	1214
1038	980	1131	1055	1223	1142	1299	1215
1040	972	1133	1056	1224	1140	1301	1216
1047	977	1134	1058	1225	1141	1302	1217
1049	978	1136	1063	1226	1141	1304	1218
1051	981	"	1073	1227	1143	1305	1219
1053	982	1137	1061	1228	1144	1309	1220
1055	983	1138	1064	1229	1145	"	1222
1059	986	1140	1065	1230	1146	1310	1221
1061	990	1141	1066	1231	1148	1311	1221
1062	991	1144	1069	1232	1150	1312	1223
1063	992	1145	1070	1233	1152	1313	1224
1064	993	1146	1071	1234	1153	1314	1226
1067	995	1147	1060	1235	1154	1315	1225
1068	996	1148	1062	"	1155	1316	1226
1069	998	1150	1074	1240	1158	1317	1227
1070	1000	1151	1076	1241	1166	1319	1229
1072	1002	1155	1078	1242	1160	1320	1230
1074	1004	1157	1112	1243	1161	1321	1231
1077	1007	1159	1083	1244	1162	1322	1232
1078	1008	1160	1084	1245	1162	1323	1233
1079	1009	1161	1085	1248	1165	1325	1235
1080	1004+791	1163	1088	1249	1166	1326	1237
1081	1010	1166	1091	1251	1167	1329	1239
1082	1011	1167	1090	1252	1168	1330	1241
1083	1012	1168	1090	1253	1170	1332	1242
1084	1013	1169	1092	1254	1171	1335	1245
1085	1014	1171	1095	1255	1174	1337	1248
1086	1015	1173	1098	1256	1176	1338	1249
1087	1016	1175	1100	1257	1177	1339	1250
1088	1017	1176	1101	1258	1178	1342	1253
1089	1018	1182	1104	1259	1179	1343	1254
1091	1004+1588	1185	1106	1260	1186	1349	1256
1093	1020	1186	1106	1261	1187	1351	1258
1094	1021	1188	1108	1262	1188	1352	1259
1095	1022	1189	1109	1263	1189	1353	1261
1096	1024	1190	1109	1264	1190	1354	1260
1097	1025	1192	1111	1265	1193	1355	1260
1098	1026	1193	1114	1267	1173	1356	1262
1099	1027	1195	1116	1268	1175	"	1274
1100	1028	1196	1117	1269	1182	1358	1263
1101	1029	1197	1118	1270	1183	1360	1265
1102	1031	1198	1119	"	1184	1361	1266
1103	1032	1199	1120	1271	1185	1363	1268
1105	1033	1200	1120	1272	1191	1365	1269
1106	1034	1201	1121	1273	1192	1366	1270
1107	1035	1203	1125	1274	1194	1367	1271
1108	1036	1204	1126	1275	1195	1371	1281
1109	1037	1205	1127	1276	1196	1373	1275
1110	1010	1206	1128	1277	1197	1374	1277
1112	1024	1207	1130	1281	1199	1376	1279
1113	1039	1208	2011	1283	1202	1377	1282
1115	1041	1209	1132	1284	1201	1378	1280
1116	1042	1210	1133	1285	1203	1379	1276
1117	1043	1211	1134	1286	1204	1380	1283
1120	1046	1212	1135	1287	1205	1381	1284
1121	1047	1213	1136	1289	1207	1382	1285
1123	1049	1214	1151	1290	1208	1383	1287
1124	1050	1215	1129	1291	1209	1385	1288
1125	1051	1217	1121	1292	1210	1386	1290
1126	1052	1218	1131	1294	1211	1387	1292
1127	1053	1220	1137	1295	1212	1388	1293

G/K	STRONG	G/K	STRONG	G/K	STRONG	G/K	STRONG
1389	1294	1477	1371	1556	1448	1655	1540
1390	1294	1478	1372	1557	1449	1656	1542
1391	1295	1479	1462	1558	1450	1657	1543
1392	1296	1480	1373	1562	1453	1658	1544
1393	1296	1481	1374	1565	1456	1661	1546
1396	1298	1482	1385	1570	1359	1662	1548
1397	1299	1483	1375	1573	1463	1663	1549
1398	1300	1484	1376	1575	1467	1665	1551
1399	1301	1485	1377	1578	1469	1667	1553
1401	1302	1486	1378	1579	1470	1668	1554
1402	1303	1488	1380	1580	1471	1669	1555
1403	1304	1489	1381	1581	1472	1670	1556
1404	1304	1490	1382	1582	1471	1672	1557
1405	1305	1494	1387	1583	1473	1674	1559
1407	1306	1495	1388	1584	1474	1675	1562
1408	1268	1496	1389	1585	1475	1676	1563
1410	1308	1497	1390	1586	1476	1678	1565
1411	1313	1498	1393	1587	1477	1680	1568
"	1314	1500	1391	1588	1478	1681	1567
1412	1315	1504	1396	1591	1481	1682	1569
1413	1319	"	1399	1593	1481	1687	1573
1414	1320	1505	1397	1595	1483	1690	1577
1415	1309	1506	1398	1597	1485	1691	1576
1418	1310	1507	1402	1598	1486	1692	1578
1419	1311	1508	1403	1599	1487	1693	1579
1420	1312	1509	1404	1600	1488	1694	1580
1421	1316	1510	1405	1601	1489	1695	1581
1425	1322	1511	1406	1603	1492	1696	1582
1426	1323	1512	1407	1604	1493	1697	1583
1427	1324	1513	1408	1605	1494	1699	1586
1429	1326	"	1409	1606	1495	1700	1586
1432	1328	1514	1410	1607	1496	1701	1587
1433	1328	1516	1412	1608	1497	1702	1587
1434	1329	1522	1416	1610	1498	1703	1588
1435	1330	1524	1419	1611	1500	1704	1589
1436	1331	1525	1420	1612	1501	1705	1590
1437	1332	1529	1446	1613	1502	1706	1591
1442	1337	1530	1446	1618	1507	1707	1592
1443	1338	1531	1423	1623	1512	1708	1593
1444	1339	1532	1425	1624	1513	"	1594
1450	1343	1533	1424	1625	1513	1709	1595
1451	1345	1534	1426	1626	1514	1713	1598
1452	1346	1535	1427	1627	1515	1715	1599
1453	1350	1536	1428	1628	1516	1717	1601
1454	1347	1537	1429	1629	2798	1718	1602
1455	1348	1538	1430	1630	1517	1720	1603
1457	1350	1539	1430	1631	1518	1722	1606
1458	1351	1540	1431	1632	1520	1723	1607
1460	1353	1541	1432	1633	1521	1724	1608
1462	1354	1542	1433	1634	1522	1725	1609
1463	1356	1543	1435	1637	1524	1728	1612
1464	1356	1545	1436	1640	1527	1729	1613
1465	1360	1546	1436	1642	1529	1730	1614
1466	1357	1547	1437	1643	1530	1731	1616
1467	1361	1548	1438	1644	1530	1732	1615
1468	1362	1549	1439	1645	1561	1733	1617
"	1364	1550	1440	1647	1532	1734	1618
1469	1364	1551	1441	1648	1533	1735	1619
1470	1363	1552	1442	1649	1534	1736	1619
1473	1366	1553	1443	1651	1536	1737	1620
1474	1367	1554	1445	1652	1537	1738	1621
1475	1368	1555	1444	1653	1538	1739	1622
1476	1369	"	1447	1654	1539	1741	1624

G/K	STRONG	G/K	STRONG	G/K	STRONG	G/K	STRONG
1742	1625	1843	1717	1944	1814	2060	1908
1743	1626	1845	1735	1946	1817	2061	1909
1744	1627	1847	1719	1947	1818	2062	1910
1745	1628+3643	1848	1719	1948	1819	2064	1912
1747	1511	"	1720	1952	1823	2065	1921
1748	1630	1854	1728	1954	1824	2066	1913
1749	1631	1855	1729	1957	1826	2067	1913
1752	1634	1856	1730	1960	1827	2068	1914
1753	1636	1857	1731	1962	1829	2071	1916
1755	1637	1858	1732	1968	1835	2072	1918
1761	1642	1859	1736	1969	1835	2073	1919
1763	1644	1860	1733	1970	1842	2075	1921
1767	1648	1861	1734	1972	1837	2077	1926
1768	1647	1862	1737	1973	1838	2086	1935
1769	1649	1865	1739	1974	1839	2087	1936
1770	1650	1868	1742	1975	1840	2088	1937
1771	1651	1871	1744	1978	1844	2089	1938
1772	1652	1873	1746	1979	1845	2090	1939
1773	1653	1874	1746	1980	1846	2091	1940
1774	1654	1880	1749	1981	1847	"	1941
1776	1654	1885	1754	1984	1848	2094	1942
1777	1657	1887	1755	1986	1850	2095	1942
1778	1658	1888	1756	1987	1851	2097	1944
1780	1660	1889	1758	1989	1853	2098	1945
1781	1661	1892	1762	1990	1854	2099	1947
1783	1662	1893	1764	1991	1856	2100	1948
1784	1667	1895	1766	1994	1860	2102	1950
1785	1663	1896	1767	1995	1861	2104	1952
1786	1664	1897	1769	1996	1861	2106	1953
1787	1665	1900	1771	1997	1862	2107	1954
1788	1666	1901	1772	1998	1863	2108	1955
1790	1669	1902	1773	1999	1864	2110	1956
1794	1709	1903	1774	2000	1866	2111	1957
1795	1673	1904	1775	2002	1865	2116	1959
1796	1674	1905	1776	2003	1867	2117	1960
1798	1676	1906	1777	2005	1869	2118	1961
1799	1756	1907	1779	2006	1870	2121	1964
1800	1677	1909	1783	2007	1871	2122	1966
1804	1681	1911	1785	2010	1874	2123	1967
1805	1682	1912	1786	2011	1875	2124	1968
1806	1683	1913	1788	2013	1877	2125	1969
1807	1686	1914	1787	2014	1878	2135	3873
1808	1687	1915	1789	2016	1880	2136	1974
1809	1688	1916	1790	2017	1881	2142	1979
1810	1688	1917	1792	2018	1885	2143	1980
1811	1690	1918	1793	2019	1886	"	3212
1812	1689	1919	1793	2021		2146	1984
1813	1691	1920	1794	2025		2147	1984
1815	1692	1922	1796	2027	1889	2148	1985
1819	1696	1923	1817	2028	326	2150	1986
1821	1697	1924	1800	2030	507	2152	1987
1822	1698	1925	1801	2039	1892	2153	1989
1828	1704	1926	1802	2040	1893	2154	1990
1829	1705	1930	1803	2041	1894	2157	
1831	1706	1931	1804	2042	1895	2158	4099
1833	1708	1932	1805	2043	1896	2162	1995
1834	1709	1933	1806	2045	1419	2163	1996
1836	1710	1934	1806	2047	1897	2164	1997
1837	1712	1935	1807	2051	1896	2168	4447
1839	1713	1936	1808	2052	1901	2169	2000
1840	1714	1939	1810	2053	1902	2172	2001
1841	1715	1942	1812	2057	1904	2180	2009
1842	1716	1943	1813	2058	1905	2182	2010

G/K	STRONG	G/K	STRONG	G/K	STRONG	G/K	STRONG
2183	2011	2304	2099	2405	2195	2500	2278
2184	2012	2307	2100	2408	2197	2502	2280
2189	5570	2309	2104	2410	2199	2504	2282
2190	5570	2311	2105	2411	2201	2506	2284
2191	5618	2312	2106	2412	2202	2507	2285
2200	2015	2319	2114	2413	2203	2509	2286
2204	6483	2321	2117	2414	2131	2510	2287
2206	6637	2325	2120	2415	2131	2514	2290
2208	2020	2326	2102	2416	2204	2515	2291
2209	6753	2330	2124	2417	2206	2516	2292
2210	2021	2331	2125	2418	2205	2517	2293
2212	6976	2333	2127	2419	2207	2518	2294
2214	6997	2334	2128	2420	2209	2519	2295
2215	2022	2335	2128	2421	2208	2520	2296
"	2042	2336	2129	2423	2212	2524	2301
2216	2023	2337	2130	2424	2214	2531	2307
2217	2024	2338	2131	2425	2213	2535	2309
2218	7204	2339	2132	2427	2215	2536	2311
2219	2025	2340	2133	2428	2216	2537	2312
2222	2026	2341	2134	2429	2218	2538	2313
2225	2029	2342	2135	2430	2219	2540	2315
2227	2037	2343	2137	2432	2220	"	2316
2228	2032	2344	2138	2433	2221	2541	2317
2231	2032	2346	2139	2436	2224	2542	2318
2235	2036	2347	2140	2438	2226	2544	2320
2237	2039	2348	2141	2439	2227	2545	2321
2240	2043	2349	2142	2440	2228	2546	2322
2244	2044	2351	2145	2445	2232	2551	2327
2247	2046	2352	2143	2446	2233	2555	2331
2251	2047	2353	2144	2450	2236	2556	2331
2256		2355	2146	2454	2238	2558	2332
2260	2053	2356	2147	2455	2239	2560	2336
2262	2055	2357	2148	2456	2240	2562	2339
2264	2057	2358	2148	2457	2241	2563	2340
2265	2058	2361	2151	2458	2242	2564	2341
2267	2060	2363	2152	2463	2246	2565	2342
2269	2061	2364	2153	2465	3160	2566	2343
2270	2062	2365	2154	2466	2249	2567	2344
2274	2066	2366	2155	2467	2250	2570	2346
2275	2067	2367	2156	2468	2251	2571	2347
2276	2068	2368	2157	2469	2252	2573	2349
2277	2069	2369	2158	2471	2254	2574	2350
2278	2069	2371	2160	2473	2254	2575	2351
2279	2070	2372	2161	2475	2256	2577	2712
2280	2071	2375	2165	2477	2256	2580	2353
2282	2074	2376	2167	2478	2258	2581	2354
2283	2075	2377	2168	2480	2259	2583	2355
2284	2076	2378	2169	2481	2258	2584	2360
2285	2077	2379	2172	2482	2256	2585	2359
2286	2078	2381	2174	2483	2261	2586	2361
2287	2079	2382	2174	2484	2262	2587	2361
2288	2080	2383	2175	2487	2265	2588	2362
2289	2081	2388	2181	2489	2266	2589	2773
2291	2073	2390	2181	2490	2267	2590	2363
"	2083	"	2185	2491	2268	"	2439
2292	2073	2391	2182	2492	2270	2592	2364
2293	2085	2392	2182	2493	2271	2593	2365
2294	2086	2393	2183	2494	2272	2594	2366
2295	2087	2394	2184	2495	2274	2595	2367
2296	2088	2396	2186	2496	2275	2596	2334
2298	2091	2399	2188	"	5683	2597	2368
2300	2093	2401	2190	2497	2275	2598	2369
2302	2094	2404	2194	2499	2277	2599	2371

G/K	STRONG	G/K	STRONG	G/K	STRONG	G/K	STRONG
2600	2372	2688	2456	2779	2534	2876	2617
2602	2374	2690	2458	2780	2535	2878	2619
2605	2375	2692	2461	2781	2536	2879	2620
2606	2377	2693	2459	2782	2537	2880	2621
2607	2380	2695	2462	2783	2538	2881	2621
2608	2378	2696	2463	2784	2539	2883	2623
2609	2381	2697	2464	2785	2540	2884	2624
2610	2382	2698	2465	2789	2543	2885	2625
2611	2383	2699	2466	2791	2544	2888	2629
2612	2384	2700	2467	2792	2545	2890	2633
2613	2385	2701	2468	2794	2547	2893	2637
2614	2386	2702	2469	2796	2548	2895	2639
2615	2387	2703	2470	2798	2550	2896	2640
2616	2388	2704	2470	"	2565	2897	2641
2617	2389	2705	2471	2799	2551	2899	2643
2623	2395	2706	2472	2801	2552	2903	2646
2624	2396	2707	2474	2802	2553	2904	2647
2625	2396	2708	2473	2805	2555	2906	2649
2626	2397	2712	2477	2807	2556	2907	2650
2627	2398	2713	2478	2808	2556	2908	2651
2628	2399	2714	2479	2809	2557	2909	2652
2629	2400	2716	2483	2810	2558	2910	2653
2631	2401	2717	2481	2813	2560	2911	2654
2633	2403	2718	2482	2816	2563	2913	2655
2634	2404	2719	2484	2817	2563	2914	2656
2635	2405	2720	2485	2818	2563	2915	2657
2636	2406	2723	2488	2819	2564	2917	2659
2637	2407	2725	2490	2824	2570	2918	2660
2638	2410	2726	2490	2827	2573	2919	2660
2639	2411	2727	2490	2828	2574	2921	2663
2640	2412	2728	2491	2829	2575	2924	2664
2643	2415	2729	2491	2830	2575	2928	2668
2644	2416	2731	2492	2831	2576	2932	2671
2645	2416	2733	2495	2832	2578	2933	2672
2647	2419	2734	2496	2834	2580	2935	2672
2648	2420	2735	2497	2835	2581	2937	2674
2649	2421	2738	2501	2836	2582	2939	2675
"	2425	2741	2502	2837	2583	2940	2676
2651	2416	2742	2503	2839	2584	2942	2677
2652	2416	2743	2504	2840	2585	2943	2678
2655	2342	2744	2505	2842	2586	2945	2682
2657	2428	2745	2505	2843	2587	2946	2682
2658	2426	2747	2509	2846	2590	2952	2686
"	2430	"	2511	2847	2590	2953	2687
2659	2427	2748	2510	2848	2592	2954	2688
2660	2427	2750	2506	2851	2595	2955	2690
2663	2431	2751	2507	2853	2598	2956	2689
2664	2432	2754	2513	2855	2600	2958	2691
2666	2434	2757	2516	2856	2601	"	2699
2668	2436	2758	2517	2858	2603	2960	2692
2669	2437	2759	2518	2860	2605	2961	2693
2670	2438	2760	2518	2861	2606	2962	2694
2671	2438	2761	2519	2862	2607	2963	2701
2674	2441	2762	2520	2863	2608	2965	2703
2675	2442	2763	2521	2864	2608	2966	2704
2676	2443	2767	2524	2865	2609	2967	2705
2677	2444	2769	2526	2866	2610	2968	2695
2678	2446	2770	2527	2868	2611	2969	2696
2681	2449	2772	2529	2869	2612	2970	2696
2682	2450	2773	2530	2870	2613	2971	2697
2683	2451	2775	2532	2871	2614	2972	2698
2684	2454	2776	2530	2872	2615	2975	2700
2685	2453	2777	2533	2874	2616	2976	2706

G/K	STRONG	G/K	STRONG	G/K	STRONG	G/K	STRONG
2977	2707	3063	2775	3163	2860	3257	2947
2978	2708	3064	2775	3164	2861	3262	2952
2979	2709	3065	2776	3165	2859	3264	2955
2980	2710	3068	2777	3169	2865	3265	2956
2982	2712	3069	2778	3171	2867	3272	2964
2984	2714	3070	2778	3174	2870	3274	2966
2985	2715	3073	2780	3175	2870	3279	2970
2988	2735	3074	2779	3178	2871	3280	2970
2990	2717	3075	2781	3181	2874	3281	2971
2992	2720	3076	2782	3182	2875	3283	2974
2995	2719	3079	2785	3183	2874	3284	2975
2996	2721	3080	2786	3184	2876	3285	2972
2998	2722	3081	2787	3185	2879	3286	2976
2999	2723	3083	2788	3186	2878	3287	2977
3000	2724	3084	2789	3187	2880	3288	2977
3001	2725	3086	2790	3189	2882	3290	2979
3002	2726	"	2794	3191	2884	3292	2981
3003	2726	3087	2790	3192	2885	3293	2982
3006	2729	3090	2792	3193	2886	3295	2984
3008	5878	3091	2793	3194	2887	3296	2985
3010	2731	3093	2796	3195	2888	3299	2989
3011	2732	3094	2795	3196	2889	3300	2991
3012	2733	3095	2797	"	2890	3302	2992
3013	2734	3098	2799	3197	2891	3303	2993
"	8474	3099	2800+1471	3198	2892	3304	2994
3015	2736	3100	2801	3200	2893	3305	2995
3016	2737	3101	2802	3201	2896	3306	2996
3017	2738	3102	2817	3202	2896	3307	2997
3018	2739	3105	2835	3204	2897	3308	2998
3019	2740	3108	2803	3206	2898	3309	2999
3020	2741	3110	2803	3207	2899	3310	3000
3021	2742	3111	2806	3208	2896	3311	3005
3022	2742	3112	2807	3209	2900	3312	3001
3023	2742	3114	2809	3210	2900	3313	3002
3024	2782	3116	2811	3211	2901	3314	3003
3025	2742	3117	2811	3212	2902	3315	3003
3026	2742	3118	2812	3213	2903	3316	3003
3027	2743	3119	2813	3214	2904	3317	3004
3028	2744	3120	2814	3218	2911	3318	3006
3030	2745	3121	2815	3220	2902	3319	3008
3031	2746	3123	2366	3221	2912	3320	3009
3032	2747	3124	2821	3222	2913	3322	3011
3033	2748	3125	2822	3224	2914	3323	3012
3036	2752	3127	2821	3226	2916	3324	3013
3037	2753	3128	2824	3227	2918	3326	3015
3038	2754	"	2825	3228	2919	3327	3017
3040	2756	3130	2828	3229	2921	3328	3016
3043	2757	3132	2829	3230	2923	3330	3018
3044	2757	3133	2830	3231	2922	3332	3020
3045	2758	3135	2832	"	2924	3333	3021
3048	2762	3136	2833	3234	2928	3337	3026
3049	2763	3137	2836	3235	2928	3338	3027
3051	2764	3140	2839	3236	2929	3339	3030
3052	2764	3143	2842	3237	2930	3340	3031
3053	2766	3144	2843	3238	2931	3344	3034
3054	2765	3147	2845	3240	2932	3346	3035
3055	2767	3153	2850	3243	2934	3347	3036
3056	2768	3156	2853	3244	2935	3348	3037
3058	2770	3158	2855	3247	2938	3349	3038
3059	2771	3159	2856	3248	2940	3350	3035
3060	2771	3160	2858	3251	2945	3351	3039
3061	2772	3161	2859	3255	2947	3352	3040
3062	2774	3162	2859	3256	2948	3353	3038

G/K	STRONG	G/K	STRONG	G/K	STRONG	G/K	STRONG
3354	3041	3425	3115	3501	3179	3587	3260
3355	3042	3426	3116	3502	3180	3590	3262
3356	3043	3427	3117	3503	3181	3591	3263
3357	3038	3429	3119	3505	3183	3593	3266
3358	3044	3430	3120	3507	3185	3595	3268
3359	3045	3431	3121	3509	3187	3596	3269
3360	3047	3432	3122	3510	3188	3597	3270
3361	3048	3433	3123	3511	3189	3599	3273
3363	3050	3434	3124	3512	2895	3600	3265
3367	3056	3437	3126	"	3190	3602	3275
3369	3058	3440	3129	3513	3192	3603	3276
3370	3059	3441	3130	3514	3193	3604	3277
3371	3060	3442	3131	3515	3195	3605	3278
3372	3055	3443	3132	3516	3196	3606	3279
3373	3063	3444	3133	3519	3198	3607	3280
3374	3064	3445	3134	3520	3199	3608	3279
3375	3065	3446	3289	3521	3199	3609	3281
3376	3066	3447	3135	3522	3200	3612	3283
3377	3067	3448	3318	3523	3201	3613	3284
3378	3068	3449	3136	3524	3203	3614	3285
"	3069	3450	3335	3525	3203	3615	3286
3379	3075	3451	3079	3526	3204	3616	3288
3380	3076	"	3137	3527	3204	3618	3288
3381	3077	3452	3384	3528	3205	3619	3289
3382	3078	3454	3088	3529	3206	3620	3290
3383	3079	"	3139	3533	3209	3621	3291
3384	3080	3455	3140	3534	3210	3622	3292
3385	3081	3456	3141	3535	3211	3623	3264
3386	3082	3457	3142	3536	3213	"	3293
3387	3083	3458	3143	3538	3215	3624	3293
3388	3084	3459	3144	3539	3217	3629	3296
3389	3085	3460	3145	3540	3218	3630	3297
3390	3086	3461	3146	3542	3220	3631	3298
3391	3086	3462	3147	3543	3223	3632	3299
3392	3087	3465	3149	3544	3224	3634	3300
3393	3088	3466	3150	3545	3225	3635	3301
3394	3089	3467	3151	3546	3226	3636	3302
3395	3090	3468	3152	3547	3228	3637	3303
3397	3091	3470	3153	3549	3227	3639	3305
3398	3092	3471	3153	3550	3229	3640	3306
3399	3092	3473	3155	3551	3229	3642	3308
3400	3093	3474	3156	3552	3230	3643	3309
3401	3094	3475	3157	3555	3232	3644	3309
3402	3095	3476	3157	3556	3233	3646	3310
3403	3096	3477	3158	3557	3234	3647	3311
3404	3096	"	3159	3559	3236	3648	3312
3405	3097	3480	3162	3561	3238	3651	3315
3406	3098	3482	3163	3562	3239	3652	3316
3407	3099	3484	3164	3565	3241	3653	3316
3408	3100	3485	3165	3567	3243	3654	3317
3409	3101	3487	3166	"	5134	3655	3318
3411	3103	3488	3167	3568	3244	3656	3320
3412	3103	3489	3168	3569	3245	3658	3323
3413	3104	3490	3169	3572	3247	3659	3324
3415	3106	3491	3169	3573	3248	3661	3326
3416	3107	3492	3170	3574	3250	3663	3327
3418	3109	3493	3171	3576	3252	3667	3331
3419	3110	3494	3172	3577	3253	3670	3335
3420	3194	3495	3173	3579	3256	3671	3336
3421	3111	3496	3174	3582	3257	3672	3337
3422	3112	3498	3176	3583	3258	"	3340
3423	3113	3499	3177	3584	3258	3673	3339
3424	3114	3500	3178	3586	3294	3675	3341

G/K	STRONG	G/K	STRONG	G/K	STRONG	G/K	STRONG
3676	3342	3764	3418	3846	3490	3937	3573
3677	3343	3766	3420	3848	3492	3939	3575
3678	3344	3767	3421	3849	3494	3940	3575
3680	3347	3769	3423	3850	3495	3941	3576
3681	3348	3771	3424	3853	3496	3942	3577
3682	3349	3772	3425	3854	3497	3943	3578
3683	3344	3773	3446	3856	3499	3944	3579
3687	3353	3774	3450	3857	3499	3945	3580
3688	3354	3776	3478	3858	3500	3946	3581
3690	3355	3777	3480	3859	3501	3947	3581
3691	3356	3779	3485	3860	3502	3949	3583
3693	3359	3782	3427	3861	3503	3950	3584
3694	3360	3783	3429	3863	3505	3951	3585
3695	3361	3784	3428	3864	3506	3959	3591
3696	3362	3786	3431	3865	3507	3961	3592
3701	3368	3787	3430	3867	3509	3963	3595
3702	3366	3788	3433	3869		3966	3598
3704	3369	3790	3434	3870		3967	3599
3705	3370	3791	3435	3872	3510	3968	3600
3706	3371	3792	3436	3873	3511	3969	3601
3707	3372	3793	3437	3877	3513	3970	3602
3710	3373	3795	3432	3878	3515	3971	3603
3711	3374	3796	3438	3879	3516	3972	3605
3712	3375	3797	3439	3880	3514	3973	3607
3713	3376	3798	3440	3882	3518	3975	3608
3715	3378	3799	3441	3883	3519	3976	3609
3716	3379	3800	3442	3886	3521	3978	3611
3717	3380	3801	3442	3887	3522	3979	3612
3718	3381	3802	3444	3888	3524	3980	3613
3719	3382	3805	3448	3890	3525	3983	3615
3720	3383	3807	3449	3891	3526	3987	3618
3721	3384	3808	3449	3894	3529	3988	3622
3722	3384	3810	3452	3895	3531	3990	3619
3723	3384	3813	3453	3897	3532	3991	3620
3725	3385	3814	3454	3898	3535	3992	3621
3726	3386	3816	3457	3899	3533	3994	3623
3729	3388	3817	3458	3900	3534	3996	3625
3730	3388	3818	3459	3901	3536	3997	3626
3731	3389	3819	3460	3905	3539	3998	3627
3732	3391	3820	3460	3906	3540	4000	3629
3733	3392	3821	3461	3908	3543	4002	3630
3734	3394	3822	3462	3910	3544	4003	3632
3735	3405	"	8153	3912	3547	4004	3633
3736	3395	3823	3462	3913	3548	4005	3634
3737	3396	3824	3465	3914	3550	4006	3636
3738	3397	3825	3463	3916	3553	4007	3637
3739	3398	3826	3464	3918	3555	4008	3638
3741	3400	3827	3466	3919	3556	4009	3639
3743	3402	3828	3467	3920	3557	4011	3641
3744	3403	3829	3468	3921	3558	4012	3641
3745	3404	3831	3469	3922	3559	4016	3643
3746	3404	3833	3470	3923	3560	4019	3645
3748	3406	3834	3472	3924	3561	4021	3646
3749	3407	3835	3471	3926	3563	4024	3649
3750	3408	3836	3473	3927	3563	4025	3650
3751	3409	3837	3474	3929	3564	4026	3651
3754	3412	3838	3477	3931	3566	4027	3651
3756	3406	3839	3477	3932	3568	4031	3654
3757	3413	3840	3475	3933	3568	4033	3655
3758	3414	3841	3476	3934	3569	4034	3656
3759	3414	3842	3483	"	3571	4035	3657
3761	3416	3843	3484	3935	3570	4036	3658
3762	3417	3845	3489	3936	3572	4037	3659

G/K	STRONG	G/K	STRONG	G/K	STRONG	G/K	STRONG
4038	3654	4120	3733	4210	3815	4315	3905
4039	3662	4121	3733	4211	3816	4316	3906
4040	3663	4123	3734	4212	3817	4317	3907
4041	3663	4126	3739	4213	3820	4318	3908
4042	3663	4131	3742	4216	3833	4319	3814
4044	3665	4132	3743	4219	3822	"	3909
4046	3667	4134	3747	4220	3823	4320	3910
4047	3667	4135	3748	4222	3824	4321	3911
4048	3669	4137	3750	4228	3829	4322	3912
4049	3668	4138	3751	4229	3830	4324	3914
4050	3669	4139	3752	4230	3830	4325	3915
4051	3669	4140	3753	4233	3833	4326	3915
4053	3671	4142	3754	4234	3833	4328	3885
4054	3672	4144	3755	4235	3835	4329	3887
4055	3672	4145	3756	4236	3835	4330	3918
4057	3677	4146	3757	4237	3836	4331	3919
4058	3676	4147	3758	4238	3837	4332	3919
"	3678	4149	3759	4239	3837	4333	3919
4059	3680	4150	3760	4242	3839	4334	3920
4063	3694	4151	3760	4243	3841	4336	3922
4064	3682	4152	3759	4244	3842	4337	3923
4067	3684	4153	3761	4245	3838	4340	3925
4068	3685	"	3762	4246	3840	4341	3928
4069	3686	4154	3763	"	3843	4345	3927
4072	3689	4156	3766	4247	3828	4347	3929
4073	3689	4157	3767	4248	3844	4352	3932
4074	3690	4158	3768	4249	3845	4353	3933
4075	3691	4159	3769	4250	3846	4355	3935
4076	3693	4161	3771	4252	3847	4356	3936
4077	3692	4162	3772	4253	3849	4357	3937
4078	3695	4164	3773	4254	3850	4360	3939
4079	3696	4165	3774	4260	3853	4361	6030
4081	3698	4166	3775	4262	3855	4362	3886
4084	3701	4167	3776	4268	3858	4365	3940
4085	3703	4168	3777	4269	3859	4366	3941
4086	3704	4169	3778	4274	3810	4370	3887
4087	3707	4172	3781	4275	3864	4371	3944
4088	3708	4173	3782	4276	3865	4373	3946
4089	3708	4175	3784	"	3866	4374	3947
4090	3709	4176	3785	4278	3867	4375	3948
4091	3710	4177	3786	4279	3868	4376	3949
4093	3712	4180	3789	4280	3869	4377	3950
4094	3713	4181	3791	4281	3870	4378	3951
4095	3713	4182	3793	4284	3872	4379	3952
4096	3714	4183	3794	4287	3875	4380	3953
4097	3715	4184	3795	4288	3876	4383	3956
4098	3716	4185	3796	4289	3877	4384	3957
4099	3715	4186	3798	4290	3878	4385	3958
4103	3720	4188	3800	4291	3878	4386	3959
4104	3721	4189	3801	"	3881	4387	3960
4105	3722	4190	3802	4292	3880	4388	3962
4107	3723	4193	3803	4293	3882	4389	8289
4108	3724	4194	3803	4294	3883	4393	3965
4109	3724	4195	3804	4296	3885	4394	3966
4110	3724	4196	3805	4297	3888	4401	3974
4111	3724	4197	3806	4299	3891	4402	3975
4112	3726	4200		4305	3895	4404	3976
4113	3725	4202	3808	4306	3896	4407	3978
4114	3727	4203	3810	4309	3898	4408	3979
4116	3731	4204	3818	4310	3898	4409	3980
4117	3730	4205	3819	4312	3899	4415	3988
4118	3732	4206	3811	4313	3902	4419	3990
4119	3733	4207	3812	4314	3903	4420	3991

G/K	STRONG	G/K	STRONG	G/K	STRONG	G/K	STRONG
4422	3993	4523	4087	4622	4176	4734	4276
4423	3994	4524	4088	4623	4177	4737	4279
4427	3996	4525	4089	4625	4180	4739	4281
"	3997	4526	4089	4628	4182	"	4282
4428	3998	4527	4091	4629	4183	4740	4283
4429	3999	4529	4093	4632	4186	4742	4284
4432	4002	4530	4129	4633	4187	4743	4285
4436	4005	4531	4130	4634	4188	4744	4287
4437	4006	4537	4100	4635	3467	4746	4289
4438	4007	4538	4102	4637	4191	4751	4294
4439	4008	4539	4103	"	4192	4753	4296
4440	4009	4540	4104	4638	4194	4754	4297
4445	4011	4541	4105	4640	4196	4757	4299
4446	4012	4542	4106	4641	4197	4759	4301
4448	4013	4544	4108	4645	4199	4760	4302
4449	4014	"	4109	4647	4201	4761	4303
4452	4017	4546	4111	4649	4205	4762	4304
4455	4019	4547	4112	4650	4204	4763	4305
4457	4021	4551	4115	4654	2142	4764	4306
4458	4022	4554	4116	4655	4208	4765	4308
"	4030	4558	4119	4657	4207	4766	4307
4459	4023	4559	4120	4659	4209	4767	4309
4461	4023	4560	4121	4660	4210	4771	4314
4462	4025	4561	4122	4661	4211	4772	4311
4463	4026	4565	4124	4662	4212	4773	4312
4465	4024	4566	4124	4665	4214	4775	4316
4466	4027	4567	4125	4666	4216	4776	4317
4467	4028	4570	4127	4667	4217	4777	4318
4470	4031	4572	4131	4669	4218	4779	4320
4472	4033	4573	4132	4670	4219	4780	4322
4474	4036	4574	4133	4671	4220	4781	4321
4476	4035	4575	4134	4672	4221	4782	4323
4477	4037	4576	4135	4684	4230	4783	4324
4478	4038	4578	4136	4686	4232	4784	4325
4479	4039	4579	4137	4687	4233	4785	4326
4482	4043	4580	4138	4688	4234	4787	3243
4485	4044	4582	4140	4689	4235	4789	4158
4487	4046	4583	3971	4690	4236	4790	4330
4488	4047	4586	4143	4692	4238	4791	4331
4490	4050	4587	4144	4694	4240	4792	4332
4491	4051	4588	4145	4695	4241	4793	4334
4494	4054	"	4328	4698	4243	4794	4335
4496	4055	4589	4146	4700	4245	4795	4338
4497	4057	4591	4147	4701	4245	4796	4337
4498	4057	4592	4148	4702	4244	4797	4339
4499	4058	4593	4147	4703	4246	4798	4340
"	4059	4594	4149	4705	4248	4799	4341
4500	4060	4595	4150	4706	4249	4800	4343
4501	4060	4598	4153	4707	4250	4801	4344
4503	4063	4600	4156	4713	4256	4802	4346
4506	4066	4603	4159	4714	4257	4803	4345
"	4079	4604	4161	4715	4258	4804	4347
"	4090	4605	4162	4716	4259	4805	4348
4507	4068	4607	4164	4717	4260	4806	4349
4509	4071	4610	4167	4718	4261	4807	4350
4512	4074	4612	4169	4722	4264	"	4369
4513	4075	4613	4170	4723	4265	4809	4352
4516	4081	4614	4171	4724	4266	4810	4353
4518	4080	4616	4172	4725	4267	4811	4354
4519	4082	4617	4173	4727	4269	4813	4356
4520	4084	4618	4174	4728	4270	4820	4363
"	4092	4619	4175	4731	4273	4821	4364
4521	4085	4621	4175	4732	4274	4825	4363

G/K	STRONG	G/K	STRONG	G/K	STRONG	G/K	STRONG
4826	4366	4912	4450	5020	4547	5121	4635
4827	4367	4915	4453	5021	4548	5122	4636
4828	4368	4917	4455	5022	4549	5125	4638
4830	4371	4918	4455	5023	4550	5126	4639
4833	4374	4919	4456	5024	4551	5127	4640
4834	4375	4920	4457	5025	4551	5128	4641
4836	4377	4923	4460	5027	4553	5129	4641
4837	4378	4925	4462	5028	4554	5130	4643
4839	4380	4927	4464	5029	4555	5131	4642
4840	4381	4930	4467	5030	4556	5132	4644
4841	4382	4931	4468	5031	4557	5133	4645
4842	4383	4932	4469	5032	4558	5135	4647
4844	4385	4933	4470	5033	4559	5136	4648
4846	4387	4934	4471	5035	4149	5137	4649
4847	4388	4935	4471	5037	4562	5147	4658
"	4389	4939	4475	5041	4565	5148	4659
4848	4390	4942	4478	5042	4566	5152	4662
4852	4395	4944	4482	5044	4569	"	4663
4854	4394	4946	4480	5045	4569	5154	4665
4855	4397	4948	4487	5046	4570	5158	4668
4856	4399	4949	4488	5047	4570	5159	4670
4858	4401	4950	4490	5048	4154	5161	4671
4860	4403	4955	4494	"	4571	5162	4672
4861	4404	4956	4495	"	5976	5163	4673
4863	4405	4957	4496	5049	4572	5164	4674
4864	4407	4960	4498	5050	4573	5167	4676
4865	4408	4962	4500	5055	4578	5168	4677
4866	4409	4963	4501	5057	4581	5170	4678
4867	4410	4966	4503	5058	4581	5171	4679
4869	4411	4968	4505	5059	4582	5172	4680
4871	4413	4969	4506	5062	4584	5173	4681
4873	4414	4970	4506	5063	4584	5174	4682
4875	4417	4971	2679	5064	4586	5175	4683
4876	4419	"	2680	5065	4587	5178	4685
4877	4420	4973	4508	5067	4589	5180	4686
4878	4421	4975	4509	5068	4590	5181	4686
4879	4423	4976	4511	5069	4590	5182	4685
4880	4422	4980	4514	5070	4591	5183	4685
4882	4424	4981	4515	5076	4597	5184	4687
4885	3887	4984	4518	5077	4598	5185	4688
"	3945	4985	4519	5078	4599	"	4699
4886	4426	4986	4520	5080	4600	5186	4689
4887	4427	4987	4521	5081	4601	5189	4692
4889	4428	4989	4522	5082	4601	5190	4692
"	4429	4990	4524	5084	4602	5191	4693
4890	4428	4993	4525	5085	4603	5193	4694
4891	4432	4994	4525	5086	4604	5195	4696
4892	4434	4995	4526	5090	4608	5196	4697
4893	4436	4996	4527	5092	4609	5199	4700
4894	4435	4997	4528	5095	4611	5200	4701
4895	4438	4999	4531	5096	4612	5201	4702
4896	4439	5000	4531	5099	4615	5202	4703
4897	4440	5001	4532	5103	4618	5204	4706
4898	4441	5003	4533	5104	4585	5206	4708
4899	4441	5004	4534	5106	4619	5207	4709
4900	4442	5006	4536	5108	4621	5212	4713
4901	4443	5008	4538	5110	4623	5213	4714
4902	4444	5009	4539	5113	4626	5214	4715
4903	4445	5011	4541	5115	4628	5216	4717
4904	4445	5012	4541	5117	4631	"	4718
4906	4446	5014	4542	5118	4632	5217	4718
4908	5243	5016	4543	5120	4630	5218	4719
4911	4448	5019	4546	"	4634	5219	4720

G/K	STRONG	G/K	STRONG	G/K	STRONG	G/K	STRONG
5220	4721	5317	4179	5418	4888	5537	5003
5221	4722	5318	4812	5422	4889	5538	5005
5223	4723	5319	4813	5426	4893	5540	5006
5224	4723	5323	4817	5427	4894	5542	5007
5225	4724	5324	4818	5428	4896	5546	5011
5226	4725	5326	4819	5430	4898	5547	5012
5227	4726	5327	4820	5431	4899	5549	5015
5229	4728	5328	4821	5433	4901	5550	5015
5231	6999	5329	4822	5434	4902	5551	5015
5232	6999	5331	4824	5435	4904	5552	5562
5233	4730	5332	4825	5436	4189	5553	5016
5234	4731	5333	4826	5438	4908	5555	5018
5235	4732	5335	4828	5439	4911	5556	5019
5236	4733	5338	4830	5440	4910	5557	5019
5237	4734	5339	4831	5442	4912	5558	5021
5238	4735	5340	4832	5443	4913	5559	5022
5240	4737	5341	4832	5447	4916	5561	5025
5241	4738	5345	4836	5450	4918	5562	5025
5242	4739	5348	4839	5451	4919	5563	5026
5243	4740	5349	4840	5452	4920	5564	5027
5246	4744	5350	4841	5453	4920	5565	5028
5249	4747	5352	4843	5454	4921	5566	5030
5252	4750	5353	4844	5455	4922	5567	5031
5253	4751	5354	4845	5458	4924	5568	5032
5255	4753	5355	4846	5459	4925	5570	5034
5259	4755	5356	4847	5462	4927	5571	5034
5260	4758	5357	4848	5464	4929	5572	5036
5261	4759	5358	4762	5466	4931	5573	5037
5262	4759	5359	4762	5470	4935	5574	5035
5263	4760	5361	4850	5471	4936	5575	5035
5265	4761	5362	4853	5475	4938	5577	5038
"	4763	5363	4853	5476	4940	5579	5041
5266	4764	5364	4854	5477	4941	5581	5044
5267	4765	5365	4856	5481	8246	5582	5045
5270	4768	5366	4858	5482	4945	5583	5046
5272	4770	5368	4864	5487	4949	5584	5048
5274	4772	5369	4869	5490	4954	5585	5050
5275	4773	5372	4881	5492	4960	5586	5051
5277	4775	5374	4884	5495	4963	5587	5052
5279	4778	5375	4885	5496	4964	5592	5057
5281	4781	5377	4890	5497	4965	5593	5058
5282	4757	5378	4895	5499	4967	5594	5059
5283	4782	5380	4905	5500	4968	5595	5060
5286	4784	5381	4906	5504	4971	5596	5061
5288	4785	5382	4909	5508	4976	5597	5062
5289	4786	5383	4930	5509	4977	5598	5063
5292	4789	5385	4951	5510	4979	5601	5065
5294	4791	5386	4955	5511	4980	5603	5067
5295	4792	5387	4956	5512	4981	5605	5068
5298	4835	5388	4957	5513	4982	5606	5070
5300	4796	5391	4855	5514	4983	5607	5071
5301	4797	5392	4852	5515	4983	5608	5072
"	4798	5398	4861	5516	4975	5610	5074
5303	4800	5400	4863	5520	4989	5614	5079
5307	4178	5403	4867	5521	4990	5615	5080
"	4803	5407	4872	5522	4991	5618	5081
5308	4805	5409	4875	5523	4992	5619	5082
5309	4806	5411	4877	5524	4993	5623	5087
5311	4807	5412	4878	5525	4993	5624	5088
"	4810	5413	4879	5530	4996	5627	5090
5313	4809	5414	4880	5531	527+4996	5631	5092
5315	4809+6946	5415	4880	5532	4997	5634	5096
5316	4811	5417	4886	5536	5002	5635	5097

G/K	STRONG	G/K	STRONG	G/K	STRONG	G/K	STRONG
5636	5096	5752	5197	5853	5288	"	7721
5640	5101	5753	5198	5855	5291	5954	5387
5643	5104	5755	5188	5856	5292	5955	5387
5648	5106	5756	5199	5857	5292	5957	5378
5653	5110	5757	5201	5858	5293	"	5383
5654	5112	5759	5203	5859	5294	5958	5377
5655	5113	5763	5109	5860	5295	5960	5382
5656	5114	5764	5205	5862	5297	5963	5386
5659	5116	5766	5121	5863	5298	5965	5390
5661	4999	5767	5207	5864	5299	5967	5391
5663	5117	5770	5210	5866	5300	5968	5392
5666	5119	5772	5212	5867	5300	5972	5397
5670	5123	5775	5216	5870	5301	5974	5399
5673	5126	5776	5215	5871	5302	5975	5401
5674	5127	5780	5219	5872	5303	5976	5401
5676	5129	5782	5221	5874	5305	5977	5402
5678	5130	5783	5223	5877	5307	5979	5404
5684	5137	5785	5224	5883	5315	5980	5405
5687	5139	"	6549	5885	5317	5984	5409
5689	5140	5786	5224	5886	5318	5986	5410
5690	5141	5789	5225	5888	5320	5987	5411
5692	5144	5790	5226	5889	5321	5989	5414
5693	5144	"	5227	5890	5322	5990	5416
5694	5145	5791	5228	5891	5322	5991	5417
5695	5146	"	5229	5893	5324	5992	5418
5696	5147	5792	5230	5896	5325	5993	5418
5699	5151	5794	5233	5897	5327	5994	5419
5700	5149	5795	5234	5900	5328	5999	5424
5701	5152	5796	5234	5904	5329	6008	5431
5702	5153	5797	5236	5905	5331	6009	5432
5703	5154	5799	5237	5906	5332	6010	5433
5704	5155	5803	5241	5907	5333	6011	5435
5705	5156	5804	5242	5908	5334	6013	5434
5706	5157	5805	5244	5909	5335	6014	5436
5707	5158	5807	5246	5911	5337	6015	4141
5709	5159	5808	5248	5915	5341	"	4142
5710		5809	5247	5916	5342	"	5437
5711	5158	5810	5249	5918	5344	6017	5439
5712	5160	5811	5250	5919	5344	6019	5442
5713	5161	5812	5251	5922	5347	6020	5441
5714	5162	5816	5257	5923	5348	6021	5444
5715	5163	5821	5262	5924	5349	6024	5448
5716	5164	5822	5262	5926	5350	6025	5449
5717	5165	5823	5263	5927	5352	6026	5450
5718	5166	5825	5265	5928	5353	6027	5451
5719	5150	5827	5268	5929	5355	6028	5453
5720	5167	5828	5269	5931	5356	6029	5454
5726	5171	5829	5270	5933	5358	6030	5454
5727	5172	5830	5271	5934	5359	6031	5455
5728	5173	5832	5272	5935	5360	6032	5456
5729	5175	5833	5273	5940	5364	6034	5462
5731	5176	5834	5273	5942	5366	6035	5459
5732	5177	5835	5274	5943	5367	6036	5461
5733	5178	5836	5274	5944	5216	6037	5462
5735	5179	5837	5275	5945	5369	6038	5462
5736	5180	5839	5277	5946	5370	6040	5465
5739	5183	5840	5278	5947	5371	6041	5466
5740	5184	5841	5279	5948	5373	6042	5467
5742	5186	5842	5279	5949	5374	6046	5471
5743	5200	5843	5281	5950	5374	6050	5474
5746	5189	5844	5280	5951	4984	6051	5475
5749	5193	5845	5283	"	5375	6052	5476
5750	5194	5847	5284	"	5379	6053	5477

G/K	STRONG	G/K	STRONG	G/K	STRONG	G/K	STRONG
6055	5479	6161	5562	6274	5655	6361	5729
6057	5480	6164	5564	6275	5656	6363	5733
6059	5482	6165	5565	6277	5658	6365	5734
6061	5483	6166	5566	6278	5658	6367	5734
6064	5485	6171	5570	6279	5660	6368	5735
6068	5488	6172	5571	6280	5661	6369	5736
6069	5489	6174	5572	6281	5662	6373	5739
6070	5492	6175	5573	6282	5662	6374	5740
6071	5492	6177	5575	6283	5663	6375	5740
6072	5618	6178	5576	6284	5664	6376	5738
6073	3249	6179	5578	6285	5659	6377	5741
"	5493	6182	5580	6287	5667	6378	5742
6074	5494	6183	5581	6290	5687	6379	5755
6075	5495	6184	5582	6292	5670	6380	5743
6086	5503	6186	5585	6294	5671	6381	5744
"	5505	6191	5587	6296	5674	6382	5745
6087	5504	6192	5590	6297	5674	6384	5747
6092	5509	6193	5591	6298	5676	6385	5748
6094	5510	6194	5591	6299	5677	6386	5749
6095	5511	6195	5592	6301	5678	6389	5752
6097	5512	6197	5592	6302	5679	6390	5753
6098	5513	6198	5593	6303	5680	6394	5755
6099	5514	6199	5594	6304	5681	6398	5757
6101	5483	6204	5597	6305	5682	"	5761
6102	5516	6205	5598	6307	5684	6399	5761
6103	5517	6209	5601	6310	5688	6400	5762
6104	5517	6212	5604	6311	5689	6401	5765
6105	5518	6214	5605	6312	5691	6402	5763
6106	5518	6217	5607	6313	5690	6403	5764
6108	5520	6218	5608	6314	5692	6404	5766
6109	5521	6219	5612	6316	5694	6405	5767
6111	5523	6221	5608	6317	5699	6406	5766
6112	5524	6223	5611	6319	5695	6407	5768
6113	5525	6224	5614	6320	5697	6408	5768
6114	5526	6226	5617	6321	5698	6409	5769
6116	5526	6227	5616	6322	5699	6411	5771
6117	5527	6232	5619	6323	5700	6414	5774
6118	5528	6233	5493	6324	5700	6416	5775
6119	5530	6235	5621	6326	5697+7992	6419	5780
6122	5532	6236	5623	6329	5703	6420	5780
6125	5532	6237	5624	6330	5704	6422	5786
6128	7936	6238	5625	6332	5707	6424	5782
6130	5536	6240	5627	6333	5714	6425	5785
6132	5543	6241	5626	6335	5710	6426	5787
6133	5538	6246	5630	6336	5711	6427	5788
6135	5540	6247	5631	6337	5712	6430	5791
6136	5541	6249	5633	6338	5713	6433	5793
6138	5542	6252	5636	6341	5714	6434	5794
6139	5543	6253	5637	6342	5714	6436	5795
6140	5543	6255	5638	6343	5715	6437	5797
6141	5544	6256	5639	6344	5716	6438	5798
6142	5545	6258	5640	6346	5717	6439	5799
6144	5543	6259	5641	6347	5718	6440	5800
6145	5547	6260	5643	6348	5718	6441	5800
6146	5548	6262	5644	6350	5720	6442	5801
6148	5549	6264	5646	6351	5721	6443	5802
6149	5550	6265	5645	6353	5723	6444	5803
6150	5551	6266	5645	6354	5724	6445	5804
6152	5553	6268	5647	6355	5725	6446	5798
6153	5554	6269	5650	6356	5726	6448	5806
6154	5555	6270	5651	6357	5727	6451	5810
6159	5560	6272	5653	6359	5731	6452	5811
6160	5561	6273	5654	6360	5731	6453	5812

G/K	STRONG	G/K	STRONG	G/K	STRONG	G/K	STRONG
6454	5813	6538	5884	6627	5963	6717	6043
6455	5814	6539	5885	6628	5961	6719	6044
6456	5815	6540	5887	6630	5964	6721	6045
6457	5816	6542	5879	6631	5964	6722	6046
6458	5817	6544	5881	6634	5968	6723	6047
6459	5818	6546	5889	6636	5970	6724	6048
6460	5818	6547	5890	6637	5766	6726	6049
6461	5819	6548	5891	6639	5971	6727	6051
6462	5820	6549	5891	6640	5973	6728	6052
6463	5820	6550	5778	6641	5975	6729	6053
6464	5821	6551	5892	6646	5981	6730	6054
6465	5822	6552	5892	6647	5982	6731	6055
6467	5825	6553	5893	6648	5983	6732	6055
6468	5826	6554	5895	6649	5984	6733	6057
6469	5828	6555	5895	"	5985	6735	6059
6470	5827	6560	5904	6650	5986	6736	6060
"	5829	6561	5905	6651	5987	6737	6062
6472	5829	6562	5896	6653	5988	6738	6063
6473	5809	6563	5897	6654	5989	6739	6063
6474	5830	6564	5900	6655	5990	6740	6064
6475	5832	6565	5901	6657	5992	6741	6066
6476	5833	6566	5902	6658	5995	6742	6067
6478	5835	6567	5903	6659	5996	6743	6068
6479	5836	6569	5857	6660	5997	6744	6068
6480	5837	6570	5907	6661	5998	6745	6069
6481	5838	6571	5908	6662	5999	6746	6070
6482	5838	6573	5910	6663	6000	6747	6071
6483	5840	6574	5911	6667	6002	6753	6075
6484	5841	6575	5912	6668	6003	6754	6076
6485	5842	6578	5915	6672	6005	6755	6077
6486	5844	6579	5916	6673	6006	6756	6078
6491	5847	6580	5917	6674	6007	6760	6083
6497	5849	6581	5918	6675	6008	6761	6081
6498	5850	6582	5919	6676	6009	6763	6084
6499	5851	6583	5920	6677	6010	6764	6084
6500	5852	6584	5921	6678	6013	6766	6085
6501	5853	6585	5923	6681	7104	6767	6085
6502	5854	6587	5925	6683	6014	6769	5777
6503	5855	6589	5926	6684	6016	6770	6086
6504	5857	6590	5927	6685	6016	6771	6087
6506	5858	6591	5929	6686	6017	6772	6087
6507	5858	6592	5930	6687	6018	6775	6089
6509	5857	6594	5932	6688	6019	6776	6089
6510	5859	6595	5933	6689	6020	6780	6094
6514	5861	6597	5935	6690	6021	6783	6098
6515	5862	6599	1175	6691	6022	6787	6100
6516	5863	6600	5937	6692	6023	6789	6102
6517	5864	6601	5938	6693	6024	6790	6103
6519	5866	6602	5939	6694	6025	6791	6104
6520	5867	6603	5941	6695	6026	6792	6103
6521	5867	6604	5942	6699	6030	6793	6105
6523	5770	6605	5940	6700	6031	6795	6106
6524	5869	6608	5944	6701	6031	6796	6107
6526	5871	6610	5945	6702	6030	6801	6111
6527	5872	6611	5947	6704	6034	6806	6113
6528	5873	6612	5948	6705	6035	6808	6115
6529	5874	6613	5949	6707	6036	6810	6117
6530	5875	6614	5950	6708	6038	6811	6119
6532	5876	6618	5953	6710	6061	6822	6126
6533	5877	6622	5955	6713	6039	6826	6130
6535	5880	6623	5956	6714	6041	6829	6135
6536	5882	6625	5959	6715	6040	6830	6133
6537	5883	6626	5960	6716	6042	6831	6134

G/K	STRONG	G/K	STRONG	G/K	STRONG	G/K	STRONG
6832	6137	6915	6214	7025	6312	7118	6404
6833	6138	6916	6215	7026	6312	7119	6405
6834	6139	6917	6218	7027	6324	7120	6406
6835	6140	6918	6221	7028	6313	7121	6407
6836	6141	6919	6222	7032	6315	7122	6408
6837	6142	6922	6230	7033	6316	7123	6409
6838	6143	6923	6237	7034	6317	7124	6410
6840	6144	6924	6235	7035	6318	7125	6410
6841	6147	6927	6235	7036	6319	7126	6411
6842	6148	6930	6240	7037	6320	7127	6412
6845	6150	6931	6211	7038	6321	7128	6412
6847	6153	6937	6220	7040	6322	7129	6413
6850	6154	6938	6223	7041	6323	7132	6416
6851	6152	6939	6225	7044	6325	7134	6418
6853	6156	6940	6227	7045	6326	7136	6419
6854	6158	6941	6228	7046	6327	7137	6419
6855	6159	6942	6226	7052	6332	7138	6420
6856	6157	6943	6231	7053	6333	7139	6421
6857	6155	6944	6232	7054	6334	7144	6425
6858	6160	6945	6233	7057	6336	7147	6428
6859	6161	6947	6238	7058	6337	7148	6429
6860	6162	6948	6239	7061	6340	7149	6430
6861	6163	6949	6244	7062	6341	7150	6431
6862	6163	6956	6253	7063	6341	7152	6432
6863	6164	6958	6252	7064	6342	7154	6436
6865	6166	6959	6255	7065	6343	7155	6437
6866	6166	6961	6256	7066	6344	7156	3942
6867	6168	6962	6278	7068	6346	"	6440
6869	4632	6968	6262	7073	6352	7157	6434
6870	6170	6970	6265	7074	6354	"	6438
6872	6172	6973	6269	7075	6355	7158	6439
6873	6174	6974	6270	7076	6356	7159	6439
6874	6175	6975	6271	7077	6357	7161	6439
6876	6177	6976	6271	7079	6360	7163	6441
6877	6178	6978	6273	7081	6363	7164	6442
6878	6179	6979	6274	7082	6363	7165	6443
6879	6180	6983	6279	7083	6364	7166	6444
6880	6181	6985	6282	7084	6367	7169	6450
6881	6182	6987	6281	7087	6369	7171	6449
6882	6183	6991	6285	7088		7174	6452
6883	6184	6995	6286	7089	6371	7175	6453
6884	6185	6996	6287	7090	6372	7176	6454
6885	6186	6997	6288	7091	6373	7177	6455
6886	6187	7000	6290	7092	6374	7178	6456
6888	6189	7002	6292	7093	6376	7179	6457
6889	6190	7003	6293	7094	6377	7180	6458
6891	6191	7005	6295	7097	6380	7181	6459
6893	6195	7007	6297	7098	6381	7183	6462
6894	6194	7009	6299	7099	6382	7185	6464
6895	6196	7010	6300	7100	6383	7186	6465
6896	6197	7011	6301	7101	6384	7188	6466
6897	6198	7012	6302	7102	6411	7189	6467
6899	6199	7013	6303	7103	6385	7190	6468
6901	6200	7014	6304	7105	6389	7191	6469
6902	6203	7015	6305	7108	6370	7192	6470
6904	6202	7016	6305	7109	6394	7193	6471
6905	6204	7017	6306	7110	6393	7197	6474
6906	6205	7018	6306	7112	6396	7198	6475
6907	6206	7019	6307	7113	6397	7203	6479
6909	6208	7020	6307	7114	6398	7205	6481
6911	6210	7022	6309	7115	6400	7206	6482
6912	6212	7023	6310	7116	6401	7212	6485
6913	6213	"	6366	7117	6403	7213	6486

G/K	STRONG	G/K	STRONG	G/K	STRONG	G/K	STRONG
7215	6488	7301	6567	7409	6667	7512	6754
7216	6489	7303	6570	7412	6670	7514	6756
7218	6490	7304	6571	7414	6671	7515	6756
7219	6491	7305	6571	7415	6672	7516	6757
7220	6492	7309	6577	7416	6672	7517	6758
7222	6494	7310	6578	7418	6677	7518	6759
7223	6495	7312	6579	7419	6678	7519	6760
7224	6496	7319	6583	7420	6678	7520	6761
7225	6497	7320	6584	7421	6679	7521	6763
7226	6498	7321	6586	7422	6680	7522	6762
7228	6499	7322	6588	7426	6684	7523	6764
7230	6501	7324	6593	7427	6685	7524	6765
7231	6502	7325	6594	7428	6686	7525	6766
7232	6503	7329	6598	7431	6689	7526	6767
7233	6504	7330	6599	7432	6690	7528	6767
7234	6505	7331	6601	7433	6689	7529	6767
7235	6506	7333	6602	7434	6689	7530	6768
7236	6508	7334	6603	7436	6691	7531	6769
7237	6507	7335	6604	7439	6693	7532	6770
7238	6509	7337	6605	7440	6694	7533	6772
7239	6510	7338	6605	7443	6696	7534	6771
7240	6511	7339	6607	7446	6697	7535	6773
7241	6501	7342	6611	7448	6698	7536	6774
7242	6513	7343	6612	7450	6865	7537	6775
7243	6514	7344	6612	7451	6699	7538	6776
7245	6515	7347	6609	7452	6700	7539	6777
7246	6516	7348	6616	7453	6701	7540	6778
7248	6517	7351	6619	7454	6677	7542	6780
7250	6518	7352	6620	7457	6704	7543	6781
7251	6520	7354	6622	7464	6711	7545	6782
7252	6519	7355	6623	7465	6712	7546	6784
7253	6521	7356	6624	7467	6715	7547	6785
7254	6522	7357	6625	7468	6714	7548	6786
7255	6524	7366	6629	7469	6716	7549	6787
7256	6524	7367	6630	7470	6728	7553	6791
7258	6525	7369	6632	7471	6717	7554	6790
7259	6526	7370	6632	7473	6718	7558	6793
7261	6528	7371	6633	7474	6718	7560	6800
7262	6529	7372	6635	7476	6720	7562	6794
7263	6514	7373	6643	7477	6721	7564	6796
7265	6530	7374	6643	7479	6722	7565	6797
7267	6532	7375	6636	7480	6723	7569	6799
7269	6534	7377	6638	7481	6724	7571	6801
7270	6535	7379	6639	7482	6726	7572	6802
7271	6536	7380	6641	7483	6725	7574	6804
7272	6538	7382	6643	7484	6727	7575	6805
7273	6539	7383	6643	7486	6730	7579	6808
7274	6541	7384	6644	7488	6731	7581	6809
7275	6542	7385	6645	7489	6732	7582	4704
7278	6546	7386	6646	7490	6731	"	6810
7281	6547	7389	6648	7491	6733	7583	6811
7282	6550	7390	6649	7494	6735	7586	6814
7283	6551	7391	6650	"	6737	7588	6815
7284	6552	7396	6654	7495	6735	7590	6817
7285	6553	7398	6657	"	6737	7591	6818
7286	6554	7399	6658	7498	6738	7593	6820
7287	6555	7401	6659	"	6752	7595	6822
7288	6556	7403	6661	7500	6741	7598	6825
7289	6557	7404	6662	7503	6743	7600	6828
7290	6560	7405	6663	7505	6745	7601	6829
7291	6558	7406	6664	"	6747	7602	6827
7292	6559	7407	6666	7507	6748	7604	6831
7298	6566	7408	6667	7511	6751	7606	6833

G/K	STRONG	G/K	STRONG	G/K	STRONG	G/K	STRONG
7607	6834	7696	6909	7794	6958	7886	7088
7610	6836	7698	6911	"	7006	7887	7090
7613	6838	7699	6912	7798	7008	7889	7091
7614	6839	7700	6913	7801	6969	7892	7094
7616	6832	7701	6914	7803	7014	7894	7096
7618	6842	7703	6916	7804	7014	7895	7097
7619	6843	7705	6918	7805	7014	7902	7100
7621	6845	7707	6920	7806	7015	7903	7101
7622	6846	7708	6921	7807	7016	7904	7102
7623	6846	7710	6924	7808	7017	7905	7103
7624	6847	7711	6924	7809	7018	7907	7105
7625	6848	7713	6926	7810	6974	7908	7105
7626	6848	7715	6929	7811	7019	7911	7107
7627	6850	7717	6932	7813	7021	7912	7110
7628	6851	7718	6934	7815	7023	7917	7114
7630	6854	7719	6931	7816	7024	7918	7114
7631	6855	7720	6935	7817	7024	7919	7115
7632	6856	7721	6936	7818	7025	7924	7121
7633	6858	7722	6937	7819	7025	7926	7124
7634	6857	7723	6938	7820	7026	7927	6981
7635	6859	7724	6939	7821	7027	7930	7128
7637	6860	7725	6940	7822	7028	7933	7133
7639	6862	7727	6942	7823	7029	7935	7134
7640	6862	7728	6945	7824	7031	7936	7136
7641	6862	"	6948	7829	7034	7938	7135
7643	6863	7729	6946	7830	7036	7940	7138
7644	6864	7730	6943	7831	7037	7942	7139
7649	6868	7731	6944	7833	7039	"	7144
7650	6869	7732	6947	7834	7040	7943	7140
7653	6870	7735	6950	7835	7041	7944	7142
7654	6871	7736	6951	7837	7043	7945	7143
7655	6872	7738	6953	7839	7045	7946	7141
7657	6872	7739	6954	7840	7046	7947	7146
7660	6876	7740	6955	7841	7047	7948	7145
7661	6875	7741	6956	7843	7049	7949	7146
7662	6874	7742	6957	7844	7049	7950	7147
7665	6879	7746	6959	7845	7050	7953	7151
7666	6881	7747	6960	7847	7051	7954	7152
7667	6880	7754	6963	7850	7054	7955	2696+7152
7668	6882	7755	6964	7851	7055	7957	7153
7669	6883	7756	6965	7852	7056	7959	7153
7670	6882	7757	6967	7853	7057	7960	7155
7671	6884	7760	6970	"	7063	7961	7157
7672	6885	7761	6971	7854	7058	7962	7158
7673	6886	7762	6973	7860	7064	7963	7158
7674	3334	7764	6975	7861	7065	7964	7156
"	6887	7766	6976	7862	7067	7966	7160
7675	6887	7769	6979	7863	7068	7967	7161
7678	6888	7771	6982	7864	7069	7968	7163
7679	6889	7773	6984	7865	7069	7971	7165
7680	6890	7776	6986	7866	7070	7973	7167
7681	6891	"	6987	7867	7071	7975	7169
7684	6893	7777	6988	7868	7072	7978	7173
7685	6894	7778	6989	7869	7073	7980	7174
7686	6895	7781	6994	7870	7074	7985	7177
7688	6898	7782	6995	7872	7076	7986	7178
7689	6899	7783	6996	7873	7077	7988	7192
7690	6900	7785	6996	7875	7079	7989	7193
7692	6904	7787	6999	7876	7080	7990	7179
"	6905	7789	7002	7877	7081	7991	7180
7693	6906	7790	7003	7881	7084	7992	7181
7694	6907	7792	7004	7882	7085	7996	7185
7695	6908	7793	7005	7885	7087	7997	7186

G/K	STRONG	G/K	STRONG	G/K	STRONG	G/K	STRONG
7999	7189	8099	7288	8205	7390	8306	7481
8000	7189	8100	7289	8206	7392	8308	7482
8001	7190	8101	7290	8207	7393	8309	7483
8002	7191	8102	1721	8208	7395	8311	7484
8003	7194	8103	7291	8209	7394	8313	7485
8004	7195	8104	7292	8210	7396	8314	7486
8005	7196	8105	7293	8211	7394	8316	7488
8008	7198	"	7294	8212	7397	8317	7489
8011	7200	8108	7303	8213	7398	8319	7491
"	7202	8115	7301	8214	7399	8323	7494
8012	7201	8120	7307	8215	7400	8324	7495
8014	7203	8123	7311	8217	7402	8325	7498
8015	7203	8124	7312	8218	7403	8327	7496
8017	7205	8126	7316	8219	7404	8328	7497
8018	7206	8131	7321	8222	7407	8329	7497
8020	7208	8132	7323	8224	7409	8330	7501
8023	7209	8133	7326	8226	7410	8332	7503
8025	7211	8134	7327	8228	7411	8334	7498
8028	7214	8137	7332	8229	7413	8335	7510
8029	7215	8138	7333	8230	7414	8336	7505
8030	7216	8139	7331	8231	7415	8338	7506
8031	7218	8142	7336	8232	7416	8340	7508
"	7226	8143	7337	8233	7417	8341	7509
8032	7219	8145	7341	8234	7417	8347	7516
8033	7220	8146	7342	8235	7417	8348	7517
8037	7223	8147	7343	8236	7428	8353	7520
8040	7225	8148	7339	8240	7433	8354	7521
8041	7227	8149	7340	8242	7420	8356	7522
8042	7227	8150	7340	8243	7422	8357	7523
8043	7228	8151	7344	8244	7423	8358	7524
8044	7230	8152	7345	8245	7423	8359	7525
8047	7233	8153	7345	8248	7425	8360	7526
8049	7235	8154	7346	8251	7320	8363	7529
8051	7237	8156	7348	8254	7431	8364	7530
8052	7239	8158	7350	8255	7432	8366	7532
8053	7241	8160	7347	8256	7434	8367	7531
8054	7242	8161	7353	8257	7437	8368	7533
8055	7243	8162	7354	8258	7435	8371	7536
8056	7245	8163	7355	8262	7440	8376	7540
8058	7247	8164	7360	8263	7441	8377	7541
8064	7254	8165	7357	8264	7442	8378	7542
8067	7256	8167	7358	"	7444	8379	7543
8069	7257	8168	7360	8266	7443	8380	7544
8070	7258	8171	7356	8267	7446	8384	7548
8071	7259	8175	7364	8270	7448	8385	7549
8072	7262	8177	7367	8271	7449	8386	7550
8073	7263	8178	7368	8273	7451	8387	7551
8074	7264	8185	7374	8275	7452	8388	7552
8075	7267	8187	7376	8276	7453	8389	7552
8078	7270	8189	7378	8278	7455	8390	7552
"	8637	8190	7379	8279	7456	8391	7553
8079	7272	8191	7379	8280	7457	8392	7554
8081	7273	8192	7380	"	7458	8394	7556
8082	7274	8193	7306	8282	7459	8395	7557
8083	7275	8194	7381	8286	7473	8399	7561
8084	7276	8195	7383	8287	7462	8400	7562
8085	7278	8196	7384	8288	7465	8401	7563
8087	5372	8198	7385	8291	7463	8402	7564
"	7279	8199	7386	8293	7466	8404	7565
8088	7280	8200	7387	8294	7467	8405	7566
8089	7280	8202	7388	8298	7472	8407	7568
8092	7281	8203	7389	8304	7479	8409	7570
8097	7287	8204	7391	8305	7480	8410	7571

G/K	STRONG	G/K	STRONG	G/K	STRONG	G/K	STRONG
8413	7574	8528	8072	8638	7607	8732	7718
8414	7575	8529	8071	8639	7610	8733	7719
8421	7613	8532	8079	8641	7609	8736	7723
8422	7638	8533	8130	8642	7611	8737	7724
"	7639	8534	8135	8644	7614	8740	7725
8423	7643	8536	8149	8645	7615	8742	7619
8424	7643	8538	8163	8647	7617	8744	7727
8425	7646	8539	8163	8648	7618	8745	7728
8432	7663	8541	8165	8649	7619	8746	7729
8435	7682	8542	8165	8651	7620	8747	7731
8437	7687	8543	8165	8652	7621	8748	7732
8440	7702	8545	8167	8654	7622	8749	7733
8441	7704	8551	8178	8655	7623	8750	7737
8442	7704	8552	8181	8657	7626	8753	7740
8443	7708	8553	8185	8658	7627	8754	7741
8445	2089	8555	8184	8660	7628	8756	7744
"	7716	8556	8188	8661	7629	8757	7745
8446	7717	8557	8193	8662	7630	8758	7746
8448	7720	8558	5596	8664	7633	8760	7747
8452	7742	8559	8222	8667	7636	8761	7748
8455	7753	8560	8224	8668	7637	8762	7749
8458	7755	8562	5606	8669	7622	8765	7752
8459	7755	8566	8242	8670	7640	8767	7757
8460	7756	8569	8269	8672	7641	8769	7759
8464	7797	8570	8272	8674	7644	8770	7762
8466	7811	8574	8279	8675	7644	8771	7764
8468	7814	8576	8282	8676	7645	8772	7765
8471	7832	8577	8283	8677	7645	8773	7766
8475	7852	8578	8286	8678	7650	8774	7767
8476	7853	8580	8294	8679	7651	8775	7768
8477	7854	8584	8297	8680	7652	8778	7772
8479	7856	8585	8299	8681	7652	8781	7770
8481	7865	8587	8301	8683	7656	8783	7774
8484	7872	8588	8304	8685	7658	8785	7776
8487	7875	8589	8304	8687	7660	8786	7777
8488	7878	8590	8303	8690	7666	8787	7777
8489	7880	8594	8311	8691	7667	8788	7778
8490	7879	8595	8312	8692	7668	8791	7780
8491	7881	8596	8313	8693	7669	8792	8197
8492	7760	8597	8314	8694	7667	8793	7781
"	7787	8598	8315	8696	7671	8795	7782
8497	7906	8599	8316	8697	7673	8796	7783
8499	7634	8602	8291	8701	7676	8797	7785
8500	7914	8603	8321	8702	7677	8798	7784
8501	7915	8604	7796	8703	7678	8802	7794
8502	7916	"	8291	8704	7683	8804	7793
"	7917	8606	7786	8705	7684	8805	7791
8505	7919	"	8323	8706	7686	8806	8324
8507	7922	8607	8342	8707	7681	8807	7798
8509	7937	8611	7945	8709	7691	8808	7799
8510	7939	8612	7579	8710	7692	8809	7800
8511	7940	8619	7585	8711	7693	8811	7803
8513	7958	8620	7586	8712	7694	8815	7809
8514	8007	8621	7587	8713	7696	8816	7810
8515	8008	8622	7588	8714	7697	8820	7817
8517	8012	8624	7589	8717	7700	8822	7819
8520	8040	8626	7592	8720	7703	"	7820
"	8041	8627	7594	"	7736	8825	7822
8521	8041	8629	7596	8721	7705	8827	7825
8522	8042	8630	7597	8724	7706	8828	7826
8523	8055	8631	7599	8725	7707	8829	7827
8524	8056	8636	7604	8727	7709	8830	7828
8525	8057	8637	7605	8731	7714	8831	7829

G/K	STRONG	G/K	STRONG	G/K	STRONG	G/K	STRONG
8833	7831	8920	7950	9012	8045	9094	8127
8835	7833	8921	7950	9013	8106	9095	8129
8836	7834	8922	7951	9014	8047	9098	8134
8837	7835	8925	7956	9015	8048	9100	8137
8838	7836	8926	7887	9016	8049	9101	8132
8839	7838	8931	7887	9017	8050	"	8138
8840	7837	8932	7962	9018	8051	9102	8141
8843	7841	8933	7964	9019	8052	9104	8142
8844	7842	8934	7965	9021	8054	9105	8143
8845	516	8935	7967	9023	8058	9106	8144
"	7843	8936	7966	9024	8059	9114	8152
8846	7845	8937	7968	9025	8060	9120	8159
8847	7848	8938	7971	9026	8061	9124	8169
8849	7850	8939	7973	9027	8062	9125	8169
8850	7851	8940	7975	9028	8064	9126	8170
8851	7857	8941	7974	9030	8067	9127	8171
8852	7858	8942	7975	9031	8068	9130	8173
8853	7860	8944	7977	9032	8068	9131	8174
8855	7861	8946	7978	9033	8069	9133	8179
8856	7862	8947	7979	9034	8069	9138	8187
8858	7866	8949	7982	9035	8070	9139	8189
8862	7877	8955	7991	9037	8074	9140	8190
8864	7882	8956	7991	9039	8077	9141	8191
8865	7883	8957	7991	9041	8078	9143	8195
8866	7884	8959	7993	9042	8080	9146	8197
8868	7885	8960	7994	9043	8081	9147	8194
8870	7887	8962	7996	9048	8085	9148	8198
8872	7888	8964	7997	9050	8087	9149	8199
8873	7889	8965	7998	9051	8088	9150	8201
8876	7891	8966	7999	9052	8091	9151	8202
8877	7892	8968	8002	9053	8089	9152	8203
8878	7892	8969	8003	9054	8090	9153	8203
8880	7893	8970	8004	9055	8092	9154	8204
8881	7894	8973	8006	9056	8093	9155	8205
8882	7895	8976	8010	9057	8094	9157	8206
8883	7896	8977	8013	9058	8095	9159	8207
8886	7901	8978	8073	9059	8096	9160	8208
8890	7908	8979	8015	9060	8097	9165	8216
8891	7909	8980	8016	9061	8098	9166	8217
8892	7909	8981	8017	9062	8098	9170	8220
8893	7910	8982	8018	9063	8099	9171	8223
8894	7911	8983	8018	9064	8100	9172	8221
8895	7913	8984	8019	9065	8101	9175	8225
8897	7921	8985	8019	9066	8102	9176	8227
8898	7923	8986	8020	9068	8104	9177	8227
8899	7925	8987	8022	9069	8105	9180	8229
8900	7926	8989	8023	9070	8106	9181	8230
"	7929	"	8024	9071	7763	9184	8234
8901	7927	8990	8025	9074	8110	9185	8235
8902	7927	8991	8026	9075	8110	9186	8236
8903	7928	8994	8028	9076	8111	9191	8240
8904	7930	8995	8031	9077	8112	9193	8245
8905	7931	8996	8030	9078	8113	9196	8247
"	7933	8997	8032	9079	8114	9197	8248
8907	7934	9000	8029	9080	8114	9198	8249
8908	7935	9003	7597	9083	8116	"	8250
8909	7935	9005	8034	9084	8117	9199	8251
8910	7937	9006	8035	9085	8118	9202	8254
8911	7941	9007	8037	9086	8119	9203	8255
8912	7937	9008	8038	9087	8121	9204	8256
8913	7943	9009	8039	9088	8123	9207	8259
8914	7942	9010	8043	9091	8125	9209	8261
8919	7949	9011	8044	9092	8126	9210	8262

G/K	STRONG	G/K	STRONG	G/K	STRONG	G/K	STRONG
9213	8266	9322	8403	9404	8489	9495	8583
9214	8267	9323	8404	9405	8488	9496	8584
9217	8285	9324	8405	9407	8491	9497	8583
9219	8270	9325	8407	9408	8492	9498	8585
9220	8273	9328	8425	9409	8493	9499	8585
9221	8274	9329	8410	9410	8494	9503	8588
9222	8275	9330	8412	9412	8496	9505	8590
9224	8281	9331	8413	"	8501	9506	8591
"	8284	9332	8414	9413	8497	9507	5774
9226	8287	9333	8415	9418	8504	9509	8593
9227	8289	9334	8417	9419	8505	9510	8594
9228	8290	9335	8416	9421	8507	9511	8595
9232	8298	9337	8419	9425	8512	9512	8596
9233	8302	9338	8420	9426	8521	9514	8597
9234	8302	9339	8380	9427	8528	9515	8598
9238	8318	9340	8423	9431	8515	9516	8599
9239	8319	9342	8424	9433	8407	9517	8599
9240	8322	9343	8426	9434	8518	9523	8603
9243	8325	9344	8427	9436	8520	9525	8605
9244	8307	9346	8430	9437	8522	9527	8607
9245	8327	9350	8433	9438	2048	9528	8608
9246	8329	9351	8434	9439	8525	9530	8610
9247	8326	9352	8435	9440	8526	9531	8611
"	8328	9354	8437	9441	8527	9532	8612
9249	8333	9355	8438	9442	8519	9533	8613
9250	8334	9356	8439	9443	8529	9535	8615
9253	8336	9357	8438	9447	8535	9536	8615
9254	8336	9358	8440	9448	8537	9537	8616
9256	8339	9359	8441	9449	8539	9540	8619
9258	8343	9360	8442	9450	8538	9541	8620
9259	8344	9365	8446	9451	8541	9542	8621
9263	8347	9366	8447	9452	8542	9546	8628
9264	8348	"	8448	9453	8543	9550	8634
9265	8349	9367	8449	9454	8544	9552	8636
9266	8350	9368	8451	9455	8545	9553	8638
9269	8352	"	8452	9457	8547	9554	8639
9271	8356	9369	8453	9458	8548	9555	8640
9272	8354	9370	8454	9459	8549	9556	8641
9275	8358	9373	8457	9460	8550	9558	8643
9276	8360	9375	8459	9462	8552	9560	8645
9278	8362	9376	8461	9463	8553	9561	8646
9279	8364	9379	8464	9464	8554	9562	8646
9285	8369	9380	8465	9465	8555	9563	8647
9293	8377	9381	8466	9466	8556	9567	8649
9294	8378	9382	8467	9467	8556	9571	8654
9298	8382	9383	8468	9469	8558	9572	8655
9300	8384	9384	8469	9470	8559	9573	8656
9302	8386	9385	8466	9471	8559	9574	8656
9304	8387	"	8470	9472	8560	9575	8657
9306	8388	9387	8471	9474	8561	9576	8659
9307	8389	9388	8472	9475	8562	9577	8658
9308	8390	9389	8473	9478	8565	9578	8659
9309	839	9390	8475	"	8568	9581	8662
"	8391	9391	8476	9482	8570	9583	8663
9310	8392	9392	8477	9486	8574	9585	8664
9311	8393	9393	8478	9487	8575	9586	8664
9312	8394	9394	8480	9488	8575	9591	8668
9314	8396	9395	8480	9489	8576	9592	8669
9315	8398	9398	8483	9490	8577		
9316	8397	9400	8436	9491	8580		
9317	8422	9401	8485	9492	8580		
9320	8401	9402	8486	9493	8581		
9321	8402	9403	8487	9494	8582		

ARAMAIC OLD TESTAMENT

G/K	STRONG
10002	
10003	2
10004	4
10006	69
10007	104
10009	144
10010	147
10012	149
10017	252
10019	280
10020	307
10021	311
10026	324
10030	399
10033	426
10038	506
10039	521
10040	524
10041	540
10054	613
10055	620
10056	629
10057	633
10058	636
10060	670
10063	674
10064	677
10066	711
10068	735
10069	738
10070	746
10072	755
10074	756
10075	772
10077	778
10078	783
10079	787
10081	826
10083	849
10084	852
10086	861
10093	895
10094	896
10103	1005
10105	1113
10107	1093
10108	1096
10109	1113
10111	1124
10112	1147
10114	1156
10117	1236
10119	1251
10120	1247
10122	1289
10123	1291
10125	1321

G/K	STRONG
10126	1325
10129	1358
10133	1411
10137	1519
10139	1490
10140	1505
10142	1528
10143	1535
10145	1547
10149	1611
10150	1635
10151	1655
10155	1678
10160	1722
10164	1757
10166	1761
10167	1763
10170	1780
10180	1836
10181	1841
10183	1859
10184	1868
10186	1882
10187	1883
10191	
10198	1922
10206	1965
10207	1981
10208	1983
10212	2002
10228	2122
10229	2136
10230	2148
10232	2166
10234	2171
10239	2217
10245	2269
10247	2292
10249	2306
10254	2358
10255	2370
10263	2423
10264	2429
10265	2445
10266	2452
10267	2493
10271	2562
10272	2591
10273	2597
10275	2608
10279	2635
10282	2749
10284	2783
10286	2816
10296	2906
10299	2920
10301	2939
10302	2942
10303	2953
10305	2967
10309	3007
10311	3028
10312	3029

G/K	STRONG
10313	3046
10315	3061
10316	3062
10317	3118
10318	3136
10322	3221
10327	3330
10331	3367
10332	3390
10333	3393
10334	3410
10335	3479
10336	3443
10338	3488
10347	3549
10348	3551
10350	3567
10352	3604
10353	3606
10354	3635
10362	3702
10367	3734
10368	3737
10370	3744
10372	3764
10373	3779
10375	3792
10376	3797
10381	3825
10382	3831
10383	3848
10387	3879
10389	3900
10390	3904
10391	3916
10392	3961
10396	3977
10398	3984
10399	4040
10401	4056
10402	4061
10404	4076
"	4077
10406	4083
10410	4203
10411	4223
10414	4333
10415	4336
10417	4398
10418	4406
10419	4415
10420	4416
10421	4430
10423	4433
10424	4437
10428	4484
10430	4486
10435	4577
10437	4756
10439	4779
10441	4873
10442	4887
10444	4903

G/K	STRONG
10446	4953
10447	4961
10448	4978
10451	5013
10452	5017
10453	5020
10454	5023
10455	5029
10461	5069
10468	5103
10471	5135
10473	5174
10480	5245
10483	5261
10490	5343
10492	5376
10495	5403
10496	5407
10504	5457
10507	5481
10515	5609
10516	5613
10517	5622
10518	5632
10523	5649
10524	5665
10525	5673
10526	5675
10529	5714
10533	5776
10534	5784
10535	5796
10536	5824
10537	5831
10538	5839
10539	5843
10540	5870
10541	5894
10546	5943
10548	5946
10550	5957
10551	5962
10556	6015
10560	6050
10561	6056
10562	6065
10572	6211
10573	6236
10585	6392
10586	6399
10588	6433
10590	6460
10591	6523
10593	6537
10594	6540
10595	6543
10597	6568
10599	6590
10600	6591
10601	6600
10611	6676
10612	6739
10614	6755

G/K	STRONG	G/K	STRONG	G/K	STRONG	G/K	STRONG
10615	6841			*110*	*107*	*243*	*231*
10616	6853	**GREEK**		*111*	*108*	*244*	*232*
10620	6922	**NEW**		*113*	*109*	*246*	*234*
10624	6966	**TESTAMENT**		*114*	*110*	*252*	*239*
10625	6992			*117*	*112*	*253*	*240*
10626	7001			*119*	*114*	*254*	*241*
10627	7007	*2*	*2*	*121*	*116*	*258*	*244*
10628	7010	*3*	*3*	*122*	*117*	*259*	*245*
10634	7109	*5*	*5*	*123*	*118*	*260*	*246*
10637	7123	*6*	*6*	*126*	*120*	*262*	*248*
10641	7162	*7*	*7*	*128*	*122*	*264*	*250*
10646	7217	*8*	*8*	*129*	*123*	*266*	*252*
10647	7229	*9*	*9*	*130*	*124*	*267*	*253*
"	7260	*10*	*10*	*131*	*125*	*268*	*254*
10649	7240	*11*	*11*	*132*	*126*	*270*	*1*
10650	7238	*12*	*12*	*134*	*128*	*271*	*256*
10655	7271	*13*	*13*	*135*	*129*	*272*	*257*
10658	7308	*14*	*14*	*136*	*130*	*273*	*258*
10661	7328	*16*	*15*	*138*	*132*	*281*	*266*
10662	7348	*19*	*18*	*140*	*134*	*282*	*267*
10664	7359	*20*	*19*	*143*	*137*	*283*	*268*
10668	7470	*26*	*25*	*145*	*138*	*286*	*270*
10673	7560	*27*	*26*	*146*	*139*	*287*	*271*
10675	7868	*28*	*27*	*149*	*142*	*297*	*281*
10676	5443	*29*	*28*	*153*	*146*	*298*	*282*
10678	7690	*34*	*32*	*154*	*147*	*300*	*284*
10687	8177	*36*	*34*	*155*	*148*	*302*	*285*
10690	7595	*37*	*35*	*156*	*149*	*303*	*286*
10691	7598	*39*	*37*	"	*150*	*306*	*288*
10693	7624	*40*	*38*	*162*	*156*	*307*	*289*
10694	7625	*41*	*39*	*165*	*158*	*308*	*290*
10696	7655	"	*40*	"	*159*	*309*	*291*
10701	7715	*46*	*45*	*168*	*161*	*311*	*906+293*
10703	7792	*49*	*48*	*170*	*163*	*312*	*293*
10704	7801	*50*	*49*	*172*	*165*	*314*	*294*
10705	7844	*51*	*50*	*173*	*166*	*315*	*295*
10709	7932	*52*	*51*	*176*	*169*	*319*	
10710	7954	*53*	*52*	*177*	*170*	*320*	*299*
10717	7985	*59*	*58*	*178*	*171*	*321*	*300*
10718	7990	*60*	*59*	*182*	*175*	*322*	*301*
10721	8036	*61*	*60*	*185*	*178*	*326*	*305*
10723	8065	*66*	*65*	*189*	*181*	*333*	*508*
10725	8086	*68*	*67*	*192*	*184*	*336*	*314*
10726	8115	*69*	*68*	*198*	*189*	*337*	*315*
10729	8124	*70*	*69*	*201*	*191*	*340*	*318*
10730	8128	*72*	*33*	*202*	*192*	*342*	*320*
10732	8140	"	*71*	*203*	*193*	*343*	*321*
10735	8200	*76*	*75*	*210*	*200*	*353*	*331*
10741	8243	*77*	*76*	*213*	*203*	*354*	*332*
10743	8330	*79*	*78*	*214*	*204*	*356*	*334*
10746	8340	*80*	*79*	*217*	*207*	*367*	*345*
10748	8355	*81*	*80*	*223*	*211*	*369*	*347*
10750	8370	*82*	*81*	*225*	*213*	*373*	*350*
10754	8421	*87*	*86*	*229*	*217*	*374*	*351*
10756	8450	*93*	*92*	*230*	*218*	*393*	*367*
10758	8517	*94*	*93*	*231*	*219*	*397*	*371*
10767	8614	*96*	*94*	*233*	*221*	*404*	*377*
10770	8625	*99*	*96*	*235*	*223*	*406*	*379*
10777	8652	*101*	*98*	*236*	*224*	*414*	*386*
10779	8674	*102*	*99*	*237*	*225*	*415*	*387*
		108	*105*	*239*	*227*	*416*	*388*
		109	*106*	*241*	*229*	*418*	*390*
				242	*230*	*419*	*391*

G/K	STRONG	G/K	STRONG	G/K	STRONG	G/K	STRONG
424	395	605	572	779	732	914	861
431	401	608	575	782	734	915	862
435	405	615	582	783	735	918	863
436	406	616	583	785	737	920	865
437	407	617	584	788	740	921	866
438	408	620	586	790	742	923	868
448	416	623	589	791	743	925	870
449	417	625	591	793	745	929	874
457	425	630	596	794	746	932	877
467	435	633	599	797	749	933	878
470	438	636	601	799	750	937	881
471	439	637	602	800	751	938	882
472	440	638	603	801	752	939	883
473	441	639	604	802	753	942	886
476	444	642	607	803	754	943	885
478	446	644	609	804	755	944	887
483	451	650	615	807	758	945	888
484	452	653	617	808	759	949	892
490	458	660	622	809	760	952	894
491	459	661	623	813	763	955	896
492	460	662	624	814	764	956	897
496	463	663	625	815	765	958	899
501	468	664	626	816	766	960	901
504	472	665	627	818	768	962	903
508	476	667	629	819	769	963	904
515	471	668	630	820	770	964	905
"	483	687	647	822	772	965	906
517	485	691	650	823	773	966	907
518	486	692	651	824	774	967	908
519	487	693	652	825	775	968	909
522	490	697	656	829	779	972	912
523	491	709	668	834	784	973	913
525	493	714	673	835	785	974	914
526	494	716	675	837	787	975	915
531	499	721	680	839	788	976	916
532	500	"	681	840	789	978	918
533	501	722	682	841	790	979	919
536	504	725	685	843	792	980	920
537	505	728	688	847	796	982	921
538	506	730	689	849	798	983	922
544	513	732	690	850	799	984	923
551	519	734	692	858	807	985	924
557	525	735	693	861	810	989	928
565	533	736	694	863	812	990	929
569	536	737	695	864	813	991	930
570	537	738	696	866	815	992	931
572	538	740	697	869	818	993	932
573	539	741	698	874	822	995	935
574	540	745	702	877	825	996	936
577	543	746	703	880	828	999	938
578	544	751	707	884	832	1002	941
579	545	752	708	885	833	1003	942
581	547	753	709	886	834	1005	944
585	551	755	711	887	835	1006	945
587	553	756	712	888	836	1007	946
592	558	761	716	892	839	1013	952
593	559	762	717	894	841	1015	954
598	564	766	720	896	843	1016	955
599	565	768	721	899	846	1017	4476
601	569	769	722	"	847	1018	956
602	570	770	723	"	848	1021	958
603	571	771	724	904	851	1022	959
604	573	774	727	912	859	1023	960

G/K	STRONG	G/K	STRONG	G/K	STRONG	G/K	STRONG
1024	961	1150	1069	1283	1184	1496	1370
1027	1007	1151	1070	1284	1185	1498	1372
1029	963	1152	1071	1288	1188	1499	1373
1031	964	1155	1074	1289	1189	1502	1376
1033	965	1157	1076	1291	1190	1503	1377
1034	966	1160	1077	1292	1191	1504	1378
1036	967	1161	1078	1293	1192	1505	1379
1037	968	1163	1081	1294	1193	1506	1380
1039	969	1164	1080	1296	1194	1507	1381
1044	974	1166	1082	1300	1198	1509	1382
1046	975	1169	1085	1301	1199	1515	1388
1047	976	1170	1086	1302	1200	1517	1390
1049	978	1172	1087	1303	1201	1518	1391
1058	986	1174	1089	1304	1202	1519	1392
1059	987	1175	1090	1305	1203	1520	1393
1060	988	1177	1092	1313	1210	1521	1394
1061	989	1178	1093	1318	1214	1522	1395
1063	991	1181	1096	1320	1216	1525	1397
1065	993	1182	1097	1321	1217	1531	1403
1066	994	1183	1098	1324	1220	1532	1404
1067	1003	1184	1099	1328	1223	1534	1406
1069	996	1185	1100	1333	1228	1535	1407
1073	999	1186	1101	1347	1242	1537	1409
1075	1001	1188	1103	1354	1247	1539	1411
1078	1003	1190	1105	1355	1248	1543	1415
1080	1005	1197	1111	1356	1249	1548	1420
1084	1009	1198	1112	1359	1252	1553	1424
1085	1010	1201	1115	1363	1256	1560	1430
1087	1012	1202	1116	1365	1258	1561	1431
1088	1013	1204	1118	1367	1259	1564	1434
1089	1014	1205	1119	1368	1260	1565	1435
1090	1015	1206	1120	1369	1261	1573	1440
1091	1016	1207	1121	1371	1263	1575	1442
1092	1017	1208	1122	1375	1267	1576	1443
1096	1021	1210	1124	1380	1272	1578	1445
1098	1023	1211	1125	1384	3859	1579	1446
1100	1025	1212	1126	1385	1276	1580	1447
1103	1027	1213	1127	1398	1286	1582	1449
1106	1030	1218	1131	1399	1287	1586	1453
1107	1031	1222	1135	1406	1294	1587	1454
1109	1033	1223	1136	1407	1295	1588	1455
1111	1035	1227	1139	1409	1297	1589	1456
1114	1038	1228	1140	1425	1311	1591	1573
1115	1039	1229	1141	1436	1319	1592	1458
1117	1041	1230	1142	1437	1320	1593	1459
1119	1042	1234	1146	1441	1324	1596	1461
1120	1043	1235	1147	1443	1325	1602	1466
1122	1045	1236	1148	1449	1328	1613	1477
1123	1046	1237	1149	1450	1329	1614	1478
1124	1048	1239	1151	1451	1330	1619	1483
1127	1050	1240	1152	1454	1333	1620	1484
1128	1051	1245	1156	1464	1341	1621	1485
1130	1053	1247	1155	1465	1342	1626	1491
1131	1054	1248	1158	1466	1343	1628	1494
1133	1056	1253	1138	1467	1344	1629	1496
1134	1057	1255	1162	1468	1345	1630	1495
1136	1058	1264	1169	1469	1346	1635	1504
1137	1059	1268	1172	1473	1350	1636	1505
1141	1062	1270	1173	1477	1354	1639	1488
1143	1064	1272	1175	1479	1356	"	1498
1146	1066	1273	1174	1483	1359	"	1510
1147	1067	1274	1176	1485	1361	"	1511
1149	1068	1279	1179	1491	1365	"	1526

G/K	STRONG	G/K	STRONG	G/K	STRONG	G/K	STRONG
"	2070	1848		2095	1911	2272	2074
"	2071	1850	1702	2096	1912	2279	2083
"	2252	1851	1703	2103	1919	2280	2084
"	2258	1855	1705	2107	1923	2281	2085
"	2277	1866	1712	2108	1924	2282	2086
"	2468	1867	1713	2111	1927	2283	2087
"	5600	1870	1716	2117	1933	2291	2094
"	5607	1872	1718	2118	1934	2293	2096
1650	1519	1877	1722	2121	1937	2294	2097
1651	1520	1891	1730	2123	1939	2295	2098
"	3391	1892	1731	2126	1941	2296	2099
1665	1486	1893	1732	2129	1944	2300	2103
1666	1537	1894	1733	2130	1945	2302	2104
1669	1540	1901	1740	2134	1946	2304	2105
1672	1543	1902	1741	2138	1949	2305	2106
1683	1551	1903	1742	2140	1950	2306	2107
1686	1554	1905	1744	2144	1953	2307	2108
1688	1556	1907	1746	2150	1959	2309	2110
1693	1561	1909	1747	2152	1961	2313	2114
1694	1562	1910	1748	2155	1964	2320	2119
1699	1567	1918	1753	2156	1965	2321	2120
1711	1577	1919	1754	2175	1984	2323	2122
1720	1585	1922	1757	2176	1985	2325	2124
1721	1586	1923	1758	2177	1986	2327	2126
1723	1588	1926	1760	2178	4687	2328	2127
1724	1589	1927	1761	2182	1989	2330	2129
1728	1593	1929	1763	2186	1992	2331	2130
1742	1605	1935	1770	2189	1995	2332	2131
1748	1610	1942	1775	2203	2008	2336	2135
1749	1611	1944	1777	2208	2012	2337	2136
1755	1616	1946	1779	2210	2014	2339	2145
1757	1617	1947	1780	2211	2015	2350	2148
"	1619	1950	1783	2224	2026	2354	2150
1761	1623	1953	1785	2230	2032	2355	2151
1767	1628	1956	1788	2231	2033	2356	2152
1775	1634	1960	1792	2232	2034	2357	2153
1777	1636	1961	1793	2233	2035	2359	2155
1778	1637	1963	1795	2235	2037	2362	2157
1779	1638	1965	1797	2237	2038	2366	2161
1780	1639	1966	1798	2238	2039	2371	2166
1785	1643	1968	1800	2239	2040	2373	2168
1789	1648	1970	1802	2240	2041	2374	2169
1794	1651	1973	1805	2244	2047	2376	2171
1796	1653	1983	1815	2245	2048	2381	2176
1797	1654	1987	1818	2247	2050	2386	2180
1800	1657	1989	1820	2249	2052	2387	2181
1801	1658	2014	1839	2250	2053	2388	2182
1804	1661	2016	1841	2251	2054	2394	2187
1806	1662	2018	1843	2252	2055	2395	2188
1808	1663	2019	1844	2253	2056	2398	2190
1809	1664	2024	1848	2254	2057	2399	2191
1811	1666	2026	1849	2257	2059	2400	2192
1814	1668	2037	1858	2258	2060	2404	2194
1817	1671	2038	1859	2259	2061	2405	2195
1818	1672	2039	1860	2260	2062	2406	2196
1825	1678	2040	1861	2262	2064	2408	2197
1829	1681	2045	1866	2263	2065	2411	2199
1830	1682	2061	1882	2264	2066	2414	2201
1839	1690	2065	1885	2266	2068	2415	2202
1840	1692	2069	1887	"	5315	2416	2203
1842	1694	2071	1889	2268	2069	2418	2206
1843	1695	2073	1891	2269	2072	2419	2205
1846	1697	2093	1909	2270	2073	2420	2206

G/K	STRONG	G/K	STRONG	G/K	STRONG	G/K	STRONG
2421	2207	2543	2323	2661	2433	2779	2532
"	2208	2545	2325	2662	2434	2780	2533
2424	2211	2546	2326	2663	2435	2782	2535
2426	2212	2550	2330	2665	2437	2783	2536
2427	2213	2552	2331	2666	2438	2789	2540
2428	2214	2553	2332	2667	2439	2790	2541
2429	2215	2554	2333	2668	2440	2791	2542
2431	2216	2555	2334	2669	2441	2794	2545
2432	2217	2558	2337	2673	2445	2798	2549
2433	2218	2563	2342	2674	2446	2799	2550
2435	2220	2567	2346	2675	2447	2800	2551
2439	2224	2568	2347	2677	2449	2803	2554
2442	2226	2569	2348	2678	2450	2804	2555
2455	2238	2570	2349	2679	2451	2805	2556
2456	2239	2572	2350	2680	2452	2806	2557
2459	2242	2573	2351	2681	2453	2808	2559
2460	2243	2576	2353	2682	2454	2811	2562
2461	2244	2579	2356	2683	2455	2812	2563
2463	2246	2580	2357	2684	2456	2813	2564
2464	2247	2582	2359	2685	2457	2816	2568
2465	2250	2587	2363	2687	2458	2819	2566
2469	2256	2588	2364	2688	2459	"	2570
2473	2261	2589	2365	2689	2460	2820	2571
2474	2262	2591	2367	2691	2462	2822	2573
2476	2264	2593	2369	2692	2463	2823	2574
2477	2265	2596	2372	2693	2464	2825	2575
2478	2266	2598	2374	2694	2465	2828	2578
2479	2267	2599	2375	2697	2469	2830	2580
2480	2268	2600	2376	2699	2471	2831	2581
2481	2269	2601	2377	2702	2474	2833	2582
2487	2274	2603	2379	2703	2475	2837	2586
2497	2280	2605	2381	2704	2466	2838	2587
2498	2281	2606	2382	2705	2476	2842	2591
2499	2282	2608	2383	2710	2480	2843	2590
2500	2283	2609	2384	2712	2482	2844	2592
2503	2286	2610	2385	2713	2483	2846	2594
2505	2288	2612	2387	2714	2484	2848	2596
2506	2289	2613	2388	2715	2485	2853	2600
2507	2290	2614	2389	2716	2486	2856	2602
2508	2291	2616	2391	2718	2488	2857	2603
2509	2292	2618	2393	2720	2489	2858	2604
2510	2293	2619	2394	2721	2489	2859	2605
2513	2296	2620	2395	"	2490	2860	2606
2514	2297	2628	2401	2722	2491	2875	2617
2515	2298	2629	2402	2725	5601	2876	2618
2516	2299	2630	2403	2727	2493	2878	2620
2519	2302	2631	2404	2729	2494	2879	2621
2520	2303	2632	2405	2731	2495	2881	2623
2522	2305	2634	2407	2732	2496	2883	2624
2523	2306	2635	2408	2733	2497	2886	2627
2525	2307	2637	2410	2734	2498	2898	2638
2526	2308	2639	2411	2736	2500	2903	2643
2527	2309	2643	2415	2737	2501	2904	2644
2528	2310	2646	2418	2738	2501	2905	2645
2529	2310	2647	2419	2739	2502	2906	2646
2530	2311	2649	2421	2748	2508	2907	2647
2531	2312	2650	2422	2751	2511	2909	2649
2534	2314	2651	2423	2752	2512	2915	2655
2536	2316	2652	2424	2754	2513	2925	2665
2537	2317	2653	2425	2755	2514	2932	2671
2538	2318	2658	2430	2756	2515	2933	2672
2541	2321	2659	2431	2757	2516	2934	2673
2542	2322	2660	2432	2764	2521	2936	2675

G/K	STRONG	G/K	STRONG	G/K	STRONG	G/K	STRONG
2941	2680	*3106*	2823	*3232*	2937	*3343*	3035
2943	2682	*3109*	2825	*3233*	2938	*3344*	3036
2946	2685	*3113*	2829	*3234*	2939	*3345*	3037
2947	2686	*3115*	2831	*3237*	2942	*3346*	3038
2952	2691	*3116*	2832	*3245*	2948	*3349*	3041
2967	2704	*3117*	2833	*3246*	2949	*3350*	3042
2968	2705	*3118*	2834	*3247*	2950	*3352*	3044
2969	2706	*3119*	2835	*3248*	2951	*3356*	3048
2970	2707	*3120*	2836	*3249*	2952	*3357*	3049
2973	2709	*3121*	2837	*3250*	2953	*3359*	3051
2983	2719	*3123*	2839	*3251*	2954	*3364*	3056
2989	2723	*3124*	2840	*3254*	2956	*3365*	3057
2991	2725	*3126*	2842	*3255*	2957	*3369*	3061
3007	2802	*3128*	2844	*3256*	2958	*3371*	3065
3013	2743	*3130*	2845	*3262*	2963	*3372*	3066
3016	2744	*3132*	2847	*3264*	2965	*3373*	3067
3017	2745	*3135*	2850	*3267*	2968	*3374*	3068
3018	2746	*3139*	2852	*3268*	2969	*3375*	3069
3019	2584	*3140*	2853	*3270*	2971	*3376*	3070
3020	2747	*3142*	2855	*3271*	2972	*3377*	3071
3022	2748	*3145*	2857	*3272*	2973	*3378*	3072
3025	2751	*3148*	2861	*3273*	2974	*3379*	3073
3029	2754	*3155*	2868	*3275*	2975	*3380*	3074
3030	2755	*3156*	2869	*3276*	2976	*3382*	3076
3034	2759	*3159*	2872	*3281*	2980	*3383*	3077
3035	2760	*3160*	2873	*3284*	2983	*3384*	3078
3038	2763	*3161*	2874	*3285*	2984	*3385*	3079
3041	2766	*3165*	2876	*3286*	2985	*3386*	3080
3043	2768	*3167*	2878	*3290*	2989	*3388*	3082
3047	2772	*3169*	2879	*3291*	2990	*3390*	3084
3051	5776	*3172*	2882	*3292*	2991	*3391*	3085
3055	5392	*3173*	2883	*3293*	2993	*3392*	3086
3056	2778	*3174*	2884	*3297*	2996	*3394*	3088
3057	2779	*3175*	2885	*3301*	2999	*3395*	3089
3058	2780	*3176*	2886	*3302*	3000	*3396*	3090
3061	2783	*3179*	2888	*3303*	3001	*3397*	3091
3063	2785	*3180*	2889	*3305*	3003	*3399*	3092
3064	2786	*3181*	2890	*3306*	2036	*3400*	3093
3066	2787	*3182*	2891	"	2046	*3402*	3094
3067	2788	*3184*	2892	"	3004	*3404*	3095
3069	2790	*3189*	2896	"	4483	*3405*	3096
3070	2791	*3190*	2897	*3307*	3005	*3407*	3097
3077	2792	*3191*	2898	*3310*	3008	*3408*	3098
3078	2797	*3195*	2902	*3316*	2982	*3409*	3099
3079	5531	*3197*	2904	*3317*	3012	*3411*	3100
3080	2798	*3200*	2907	*3318*	3013	*3412*	3101
3081	2799	*3204*	2911	*3319*	3014	*3413*	3102
3086	2803	*3205*	2912	*3320*	3015	*3414*	3156
3087	2804	*3206*	2913	*3321*	3016	*3415*	3158
3088	2805	*3207*	2914	*3322*	3017	*3416*	3159
3090	2807	*3208*	2915	*3324*	3019	*3417*	3103
3091	2808	*3209*	2916	*3325*	3020	*3419*	3105
3092	2809	*3210*	2917	*3326*	3021	*3421*	3107
3093	2810	*3211*	2918	*3328*	3022	*3423*	3109
3095	2812	*3212*	2919	*3329*	3023	*3424*	3110
3096	2813	*3213*	2920	*3330*	3024	*3428*	3114
3097	2814	*3214*	2921	*3332*	3025	*3429*	3115
3098	2815	*3215*	2922	*3334*	3027	*3433*	3119
3099	2816	*3222*	2929	*3337*	3030	*3434*	3120
3101	2818	*3223*	2930	*3338*	3031	*3435*	3121
3102	2819	*3228*	2933	*3339*	3032	*3438*	3124
3104	2821	*3229*	2934	*3340*	3033	*3440*	3126
3105	2822	*3231*	2936	*3342*	3034	*3441*	3127

G/K	STRONG	G/K	STRONG	G/K	STRONG	G/K	STRONG
3442	3128	3604	3375	3727	3488	3855	3607
3443	3129	3611	3382	3729	3490	3858	3609
3444	3130	3613	3384	3730	3491	3864	3614
3445	3131	3616	3388	3731	3492	3868	3618
3446	3132	3620	3392	3732	3493	3869	3619
3449	3135	3621	3393	3733	3494	3871	3618
3450	3136	3622	3394	3734	3495	3873	3622
3451	3137	3626	3399	3735	3496	3874	3623
3453	3138	3627	3400	3738	3498	3875	3624
3454	3139	3631	3404	3741	3561	3876	3625
3455	3140	3634	3407	3742	3501	3880	3628
3456	3141	3635	3408	3745	3504	3882	3627
3457	3142	3636	3409	3749	3507	3884	3630
3459	3144	3637	3410	3750	3508	3885	3631
3463	3146	3638	3411	3751	3509	3886	3632
3464	3147	3639	3412	3756	3514	3891	3636
3465	3148	3640	3413	3758	3516	3898	570
3466	3149	3641	3414	3759	3517	3899	3640
3474	3157	3643	3416	3760	3518	3906	3646
3477	3160	3645	3418	3761	3519	3910	3650
3478	3161	3646	3419	3762	3520	3912	3652
3479	3162	3648	3421	3763	3521	3918	3657
3484	3168	3649	3422	3764	3522	3920	
3486	3170	3654	3426	3768	3525	3923	3660
3494	3178	3655	3428	3769	3526	3929	3666
3499	3182	3656	3429	3770	3527	3931	3668
3500	3183	3657	3430	3771	3528	3933	3670
3501	3184	3658	3431	3773	3530	3934	3671
3506	3188	3659	3432	3774	3531	3941	3677
"	3189	3661	3434	3775	3532	3942	3678
3507	3190	3662	3435	3776	3533	3946	3682
3508	3199	3666	3439	3780	3536	3947	3683
3510	3192	3669	3442	3781	3537	3950	3686
3514	3194	3671	3444	3782	3538	3951	3687
3516	3195	3673	3446	3788	3544	3952	3688
3517	3196	3674	3447	3790	3546	3954	3690
3518	3197	3675	3448	3794	3550	3955	3691
3519	3198	3678	3452	3798	3554	3958	3694
3521	3200	3684	3458	3802	3557	3959	3695
3523	3202	3685	3458	3803	3558	3960	3696
3527		3688	3460	3805	3560	3972	3708
3531	3306	3689	3461	3809	3564	3973	3709
3533	3308	3692	3463	3811	3565	3974	3710
3534	3309	3693	3464	3812	3566	3978	3714
3537	3312	3695	3465	3813	3567	3979	3715
3540	3314	3696	3466	3816	3571	3991	3726
3542	3316	3698	3468	3820	3575	3995	3730
3543	3317	3699	3469	3821	3576	3997	3732
3544	3318	3700	3470	3825	3578	3998	3733
3545	3319	3704	3474	3826	3579	4001	3735
3546	3320	3707	3475	3827	3580	4003	3737
3549	3323	3709	3476	3828	3581	4004	3738
3552	3326	3710	3477	3830	3383	4014	3747
3564	3338	3714	3478	3831	3584	4017	3749
3565	3339	3716	3479	3833	3586	4029	3762
3566	3340	3717	3480	3834	3587	4033	3765
3567	3341	3718	3481	3836	3588	4039	3770
3578	3350	3720	3482	"	5120	4041	3772
3579	3351	3722	3497	3847	3598	4042	3773
3581	3353	3723	3484	3848	3599	4043	3774
3582	3354	3724	3485	3849	3600	4044	3775
3587	3359	3725	3486	3852	3604	4045	3776
3597	3370	3726	3487	3853	3605	4047	3778

G/K	STRONG	G/K	STRONG	G/K	STRONG	G/K	STRONG
"	5023	4197	3913	4379	4076	4513	4198
"	5025	4199	3914	4380	4077	4517	4201
"	5026	4200	3915	4385	4082	4518	4202
"	5123	4203	3917	4388	4083	4519	4203
"	5124	4213	3925	4389	4084	4520	4204
"	5125	4219	3931	4394	4088	4521	4205
"	5126	4221	3933	4395	4089	4525	4209
"	5127	4222	3934	4397	4091	4526	4210
"	5128	4226	3937	4399	4092	4527	4211
"	5129	4228	3939	4402	4094	4530	4213
"	5130	4230	3941	4403	4095	4532	4215
4048	3779	4231	3942	4406	4098	4539	4221
4050	3781	4232	3943	4407	4099	4540	4222
4051	3782	4243	3953	4408	4099	4541	4223
4052	3783	4244	3954	4409	4100	4545	4227
4053	3784	4245	3955	4411	4102	4546	4228
4055	3786	4246	3956	4412	4103	4547	4229
4056	3787	4247	3957	4414	4105	4550	4232
4057	3788	4249	3959	4415	4106	4552	4234
4058	3789	4252	3962	4418	4108	4556	4238
4062	3792	4253	3963	4423	4113	4558	4239
4063	3793	4256	3966	4431	4123	4559	4240
4066	3795	4257	3967	4432	4124	4563	4243
4067	3796	4258	3968	4434	4126	4564	4244
4070	3798	4259	3969	4435	4127	4565	4245
4072	3800	4260	3964	4436	4128	4569	4249
4077	3804	4262	3971	4439	4132	4571	4251
4082	3809	4263	3972	4443	4136	4589	4267
4084	3811	4265	3974	4449	4142	4590	4268
4086	3813	4267	3976	4450	4143	4591	4269
4087	3814	4270	3979	4454	4145	4592	4270
4103	3828	4272	3980	4456	4147	4595	4273
4106	3829	4275	3982	4458	4149	4603	4283
4110	3833	4279	3985	4459	4150	4606	4286
4111	3834	4280	3986	4460	4151	4613	4291
4112	3835	4284	3990	4463	4154	4614	4292
4120	3841	4289	3994	4465	4156	4625	4302
4126	3847	4290	3995	4466	4157	"	4277
4130	3850	4291	3996	4472	4160	"	4280
4133	3853	4292	3997	4475	4163	4633	4309
4134	3854	4300	4005	4477	4165	4636	4311
4135	3855	4301	4006	4478	4166	4637	4312
4137	3857	4307	4010	4479	4167	4640	4315
4138	3858	4308	4011	4480	4168	4657	4327
4140	3860	4309	4012	4482	4170	4659	4328
4142	3862	4311	4014	4483	4171	4666	4335
4143	3863	4314	4016	4484	4172	4667	4336
4148	3868	4318	4020	4486	4174	4668	4337
4151	3870	4319	4021	4487	4175	4669	4338
4155	3874	4330	4030	4488	4176	4670	4339
4156	3875	4340	4039	4498	4118	4673	4341
4157	3876	4343	4042	"	4119	4674	4342
4158	3877	4344	4043	"	4183	4680	4346
4161	3880	4355	4052	4499	4184	4682	4348
4165	3884	4361	4058	4503	4188	4684	4350
4166	3885	4362	4059	4504	4189	4686	4352
4168	3886	4364	4061	4505	4190	4687	4353
4170	3888	4369	4066	"	4191	4689	4355
4171	3889	4372	4069	4506	4192	4694	4358
4172	3890	4373	4070	4507	4193	4699	4362
4183	3900	4374	4071	4508	4194	4709	4371
4187	3904	4376	4073	4509	5117	4719	4380
4190	3906	4377	4074	4511	4196	4720	4381

G/K	STRONG	G/K	STRONG	G/K	STRONG	G/K	STRONG
4721	4382	4860	4505	4962	4597	5068	4693
4725	4383	4861	4506	4963	4598	5069	4694
4733	4392	4871	4514	4969	4603	5072	4697
4735	4394	4872	4515	4970	4604	5073	4698
4737	4396	4873	4516	4972	4605	5074	4699
4739	4398	4876	4518	4973	4606	5075	4700
4743	4402	4877	4519	4975	4608	5080	4705
4745	4404	4878	4520	4976	4609	"	4706
4746	4405	4879	4521	4977	4610	"	4707
4749	4408	4881	4523	4978	4611	5081	4708
4758	4416	4882	4524	4981	4613	"	4709
4763	4420	4884	4526	4982	4614	5082	4710
4764	4421	4885	4527	4983	4615	5083	4711
4767	4424	4886	4528	4984	4616	5084	4712
4768	4425	4887	4529	4986	4596	5086	4955
4772	4429	4889	4532	4987	4577	5087	4714
4773	4430	4890	4530	4988	4618	5088	4715
4775	4432	4891	4533	4990	4619	5089	4716
4777	4434	4892	4534	4992	4621	5090	4717
4778	4435	4894	4536	4994	4622	5091	4718
4780	4436	4895	4537	4997	4624	5092	4719
4783	4439	4897	4539	4998	4625	5093	4720
4784	4440	4899	4540	5005	4630	5094	4721
4785	4441	4901	4541	5007	4632	5096	4723
4786	4442	4902	4542	5008	4633	5098	4725
4787	4443	4903	4543	5009	4634	5107	4734
4789	4445	4904	4544	5014	4639	5108	4736
4790	4446	4905	4545	5016	4641	5109	4735
4792	4448	4907	4546	5019	4644	5110	4737
4795		4908	4547	5021	4646	5111	4738
4796	4451	4910	4549	5022	4647	5121	4770
4798	4454	4912	4551	5023	4648	5122	4747
4801	4457	4913	4552	5026	4651	5125	4750
4805	4460	4914	4553	5027	4652	5128	4753
4806	4461	4915	4554	5028	4653	5129	4754
4808	4462	4917	4556	5030	4655	5130	4755
4811	4464	4918	4557	5031	4656	5131	4756
4814	4466	4919	4558	5033	4658	5136	4760
4815	4467	4920	4559	5036	4661	5141	4765
4819	4469	4921	4560	5037	4662	5146	4769
4820	4470	4922	4561	5038	4663	5148	4571
4821	4471	4924	4563	5039	4664	"	4671
4822	4472	4925	4564	5040	4665	"	4675
4823	4473	4926	4565	5043	4666	"	4771
4827	4476	4928	4567	5044	4667	"	5209
4829	4477	4930	4569	5046	4669	"	5210
4830	4478	4931	4570	5047	4670	"	5213
4831	4479	4932	4572	5048	4672	"	5216
4832	4480	4934	4574	5049	4673	5157	4779
4836	4484	4936	4576	5051	4676	5168	4788
4838	4486	4939	4578	5052	4677	5169	4789
4839	4487	4941	4580	5053	4678	5177	4797
4840	4488	4942	4581	5054	4679	5186	4804
4842	4489	4943	4582	5055	4680	5187	4805
4844	4491	4946	4584	5056	4681	5189	4807
4845	4492	4947	4585	5058	4683	5190	4808
4850	4497	4948	4586	5059	4684	5191	4809
4851	4498	4950	4588	5061	4686	5192	4810
4852	4499	4952	4562	5062	4687	5193	4811
4855	4501	4953	4589	5063	4688	5197	4815
4857	4502	4954	4590	5064	4689	5198	4816
4858	4503	4956	4592	5065	4690	5202	4820
4859	4504	4958	4594	5066	4691	5205	4823

G/K	STRONG	G/K	STRONG	G/K	STRONG	G/K	STRONG
5206	4824	5406	4995	5585	5169	5753	5326
5207	4825	5412	5000	5586	5170	5754	5327
5208	4826	5419	5007	5589	5173	5755	5328
5209	4827	5420	5008	5590	5174	5756	5329
5210	4828	5425	5012	5592	5176	5757	5330
5217	4834	5428	5014	5596	5179	5758	5331
5218	4835	5429	5015	5597	5180	5760	5331
5228	4844	5432	5018	5598	5181	5764	5336
5232	4847	5433	5019	5601	5183	5770	5337
5236	4850	5434	5020	5602	5184	5771	5342
5237	4851	5435	5021	5603	5185	5772	5343
5239	4851	5436	5022	5604	5186	5776	5344
5251	4863	5439	5028	5605	5187	5778	5347
5252	4864	5446	5038	5608	5190	5780	5349
5257	4869	5448	5040	5610	5191	5784	5351
5263	4873	5450	5042	5611	5192	5785	5355
5269	4878	5451	5043	5612	5193	5786	5356
5271	4880	5454	5045	5613	5194	5788	5357
5278	4886	5455	5046	5618	5199	5789	5359
5281	4889	5457	5048	5620	5201	5790	5360
5284	4892	5462	5053	5621	5202	5797	5361
5287	4893	5465	5056	5622	5203	5799	5368
5300	4903	5468	5058	5623	5204	5800	5370
5301	4904	5470	5060	5625	5206	5801	5371
5303	4906	5472	5061	5626	5207	5802	5372
5309	4912	5477	5062	5627	5208	5803	5373
5313	4916	5478	5063	5628	5211	5804	5374
5317	4920	5485	5072	5630	5214	5805	5375
5321	4922	5488	5074	5631	5215	5806	5376
5322	4923	5489	5075	5643	5229	5807	5377
5323	4894	5490	5076	5655	5240	5808	5378
5327	4927	5491	5077	5659	5241	5809	5379
5341	4937	5492	5078	5660	5242	5810	5380
5345	4941	5493	5079	5677	5257	5811	5381
5347	4942	5498	5083	5679	5259	5813	5382
5349	4944	5500	5085	5682	5262	5814	5384
5352	4946	5501	5086	5683	5263	5815	5385
5353	4947	5503	5088	5685	5264	5816	5386
5354	4948	5505	5090	5687	5266	5818	5387
5355	4949	5510	5095	5689	5268	5821	5389
5358	4950	5511	5096	5694	5272	5823	5392
5365	4957	5516	5100	5695	5273	5824	5393
5369	4961	5519	5103	5696	5274	5826	5394
5371	4963	5526	5109	5698	2640	5827	5396
5373	4965	5527	5110	5700	5276	5828	5397
5374	4966	5534	5115	5702	5278	5832	5399
5377	4969	5535	5116	5705	5281	5833	5401
5381	4972	5536	5117	5707	5283	5834	5402
5382	4973	5543	5131	5710	5285	5836	5403
5386	4976	5546	5134	5711	5286	5837	5404
5388	4978	5551	5139	5712	5287	5838	5405
5389	4979	5553	5140+4999	5727	5301	5839	5406
5391	4981	5555	5142	5729	5303	5842	5407
5392	4982	5557	5169	5736	5310	5845	5410
5393	4983	5560	5146	5738	5312	5847	5413
5395	4985	5563	5149	5741	5314	5848	5415
5396	4986	5564	5150	5742	5341	5850	5416
5398	4988	5572	5157	5743	5316	5853	5418
5399	4989	5575	5160	5744	5317	5854	5421
5400	4990	5576	5161	5745	5318	5855	5422
5401	4991	5581	5165	5746	5319	5858	5423
5403	4992	5583	5167	5749	5322	5860	5426
5404	4993	5584	5168	5750	5323		5428

G/K	STRONG	G/K	STRONG	G/K	STRONG	G/K	STRONG
5861	5429	5910	5475	5966	5529	6018	5576
5864	5432	5912	5476	5967	5522	6019	5577
5867	5435	5913	5477	5970	5532	6020	5575
5869	5436	5914	5478	5971	5533	6021	5578
5871	5438	5915	5479	5975	5536	6022	5579
5872	5439	5919	5483	5976	5537	6023	5580
5873	5440	5921	5485	5982	5543	6025	5582
5874	5441	5922	5486	5984	5545	6030	5587
5875	5442	5924	5488	5985	5546	6031	5588
5876	5443	5925	5489	5986	5547	6034	5590
5877	5444	5929	5493	5987	5548	6035	5591
5878	5445	5930	5494	5991	5552	6040	5596
5879	5446	5931	5495	5992	5553	6042	5598
5880	5447	5938	5502	5993	5554	6047	5604
5881	5448	5939	5503	5994	5555	6048	5605
5882	5449	5941	5506	5995	5556	6049	5606
5888	5455	5944	5508	5996	5557	6051	5609
5889	5456	5945	5509	6000	5560	6052	5610
5891	5458	5946	5510	6001	5561	6053	5611
5897	5463	5950	5513	6005	5564	6055	5613
5898	5464	5951	5514	6010	5567	6057	5614
5900	5466	5954	5517	6011	5568	6058	5615
5903	5469	5958	5521	6012	5569	6060	5617
5905	5470	5960	5523	6013	5570	6064	5621
5907	5472	5962	5525	6014	5571	6065	5621
5908	5473	5963	5526	6016	5573	6067	5623
5909	5474	5965	5528	6017	5574		